# THE LIBRARY ATLAS

FOURTEENTH EDITION

Edited by

**Harold Fullard, M.Sc.,**
DIRECTOR OF CARTOGRAPHY

**& H. C. Darby, C.B.E., Litt. D., F.B.A.**
EMERITUS PROFESSOR OF GEOGRAPHY
UNIVERSITY OF CAMBRIDGE

GEORGE PHILIP
LONDON · MELBOURNE · MILWAUKEE

First Edition  November 1938
Fourteenth Edition  Spring 1980

British Library Cataloguing
in Publication Data
The library atlas. — 14th ed
  1. Atlases, British
  912    G1019

ISBN 0 540 05367 8

© 1980 George Philip & Son
Printed in Great Britain by
George Philip Printers Ltd., London

# Preface

THE LIBRARY ATLAS is in two parts – one general, the other economic – the same arrangement as in previous editions, except that for this edition the economic part has been redesigned and revised.

The first part has already appeared under the title of The University Atlas, which since its original publication more than thirty years ago has been through eighteen editions, each of which has in its turn been revised and improved.

For the eighth edition in 1958, the atlas was completely redesigned because it was considered that only an entirely new version would meet the needs of the post-war years. In that edition we made two significant changes: a substantial increase in the scale of the sectional maps, and a re-arrangement of the atlas into an easily portable size, convenient for frequent use and able to stand on a bookshelf.

For the twelfth edition in 1967, the style of colouring of the maps was completely changed to provide lighter and clearer layer colours. This in turn made possible the inclusion of hill-shading to complement the layer colouring and bring out clearly relief features without impairing the detail of names, settlements and communications.

For the nineteenth edition, 1978, the content of the atlas was completely re-examined, and the lay-out of a large number of maps were redesigned – in particular those covering Asia, Australasia and Latin America. This enabled larger scales to be provided for (a) China, south-east Asia, Japan, the Tashkent area and the southern Urals; (b) south-east Australia and New Guinea; and (c) Mexico, the West Indies and eastern Brazil. Other new maps covered the Indian Ocean, the North Sea, the French départments, the Benelux countries, Switzerland, Alaska and California. The design of yet other maps was altered to secure a more effective presentation, e.g., the world maps of climate.

As in previous editions, international boundaries have been drawn to show the *de facto* situation where there are rival claims to territory. The preliminary matter includes a summary of the projections used, and also climatic graphs for over 200 stations.

Spellings of names are in the forms given in the latest official lists, and generally agree with the rules of the Permanent Committee on Geographical Names and the United States Board on Geographic Names. A list of changed place names and names for which alternatives are often used appears with the index which contains over 60,000 entries.

We have used the information provided by various United Nations departments, especially that of Economic and Social Affairs and that of Food and Agriculture. Statistics for some countries are incomplete and the latest official estimates have been accepted.

We gratefully acknowledge the help of many official organisations and individuals, and especially thank the Meteorological Office for extracting data for the climate graphs.

H. FULLARD
H.C. DARBY

# Contents

# Principal Countries of the World

| Country | Area in thousands of square km | Population in thousands | Density of population per sq. km | Capital Population in thousands |
|---|---|---|---|---|
| Afghanistan | 647 | 20 339 | 31 | Kabul (588) |
| Albania | 29 | 2 616 | 91 | Tiranë (192) |
| Algeria | 2 382 | 17 910 | 8 | Algiers (1 503) |
| Angola | 1 247 | 6 761 | 5 | Luanda (475) |
| Argentina | 2 767 | 26 056 | 9 | Buenos Aires (8 436) |
| Australia | 7 687 | 14 074 | 2 | Canberra (215) |
| Austria | 84 | 7 518 | 90 | Vienna (1 593) |
| Bangladesh | 144 | 80 558 | 559 | Dacca (1 730) |
| Belgium | 31 | 9 931 | 325 | Brussels (1 075) |
| Belize | 23 | 149 | 6 | Belmopan (5) |
| Benin | 113 | 3 286 | 29 | Porto-Novo (104) |
| Bhutan | 47 | 1 232 | 26 | Thimphu (60) |
| Bolivia | 1 099 | 5 950 | 5 | Sucre (237) La Paz (655) |
| Botswana | 600 | 710 | 1 | Gaborone (37) |
| Brazil | 8 512 | 112 239 | 13 | Brasilia (763) |
| Brunei | 6 | 190 | 33 | Bandar Seri Begawan (37) |
| Bulgaria | 111 | 8 804 | 79 | Sofia (965) |
| Burma | 677 | 31 512 | 47 | Rangoon (1 586) |
| Burundi | 78 | 3 966 | 142 | Bujumbura (157) |
| Cambodia | 181 | 8 606 | 48 | Phnom Penh (2 000) |
| Cameroon | 475 | 6 666 | 14 | Yaoundé (314) |
| Canada | 9 976 | 23 316 | 2 | Ottawa (693) |
| Central African Emp. | 623 | 2 370 | 4 | Bangui (187) |
| Chad | 1 284 | 4 197 | 3 | Ndjamena (193) |
| Chile | 757 | 10 656 | 14 | Santiago (3 595) |
| China | 9 597 | 958 030 | 90 | Peking (7 570) |
| Colombia | 1 139 | 25 048 | 22 | Bogota (2 855) |
| Congo | 342 | 1 440 | 4 | Brazzaville (290) |
| Costa Rica | 51 | 2 071 | 41 | San José (234) |
| Cuba | 115 | 9 474 | 82 | Havana (1 861) |
| Cyprus | 9 | 640 | 69 | Nicosia (147) |
| Czechoslovakia | 128 | 15 031 | 118 | Prague (1 173) |
| Denmark | 43 | 5 088 | 118 | Copenhagen (1 251) |
| Djibouti | 22 | 111 | 5 | Djibouti (62) |
| Dominican Republic | 49 | 4 978 | 102 | Santo Domingo (818) |
| Ecuador | 284 | 7 556 | 27 | Quito (600) |
| Egypt | 1 001 | 38 741 | 39 | Cairo (5 921) |
| El Salvador | 21 | 4 123 | 196 | San Salvador (380) |
| Equatorial Guinea | 28 | 322 | 11 | Rey Malabo (37) |
| Ethiopia | 1 222 | 28 925 | 24 | Addis Abeba (1 133) |
| Fiji | 18 | 600 | 33 | Suva (118) |
| Finland | 337 | 4 737 | 14 | Helsinki (825) |
| France | 547 | 53 105 | 97 | Paris (9 863) |
| French Guiana | 91 | 64 | 1 | Cayenne (25) |
| Gabon | 268 | 534 | 2 | Libréville (251) |
| Gambia | 11 | 553 | 49 | Banjul (48) |
| Germany, East | 108 | 16 765 | 155 | East Berlin (1 101) |
| Germany, West | 249 | 61 396 | 247 | Bonn (285) |
| Ghana | 239 | 10 475 | 44 | Accra (738) |
| Greece | 132 | 9 284 | 70 | Athens (2 101) |
| Greenland | 2 176 | 56 | 0.02 | Godthåb (4) |
| Guatemala | 109 | 6 436 | 59 | Guatemala (717) |
| Guinea | 246 | 4 646 | 19 | Conakry (526) |
| Guinea-Bissau | 36 | 544 | 15 | Bissau (65) |
| Guyana | 215 | 827 | 4 | Georgetown (182) |
| Haiti | 28 | 4 749 | 171 | Port-au-Prince (703) |
| Honduras | 112 | 2 831 | 25 | Tegucigalpa (274) |
| Hong Kong | 1 | 4 514 | 4 320 | Victoria (849) |
| Hungary | 93 | 10 648 | 114 | Budapest (2 076) |
| Iceland | 103 | 222 | 2 | Reykjavik (118) |
| India | 3 288 | 625 018 | 190 | Delhi (3 647) |
| Indonesia | 2 027 | 143 282 | 71 | Jakarta (4 576) |
| Iran | 1 648 | 34 274 | 21 | Tehran (4 496) |
| Iraq | 435 | 11 907 | 27 | Baghdad (2 969) |
| Irish Republic | 70 | 3 197 | 45 | Dublin (815) |
| Israel | 21 | 3 611 | 174 | Jerusalem (336) |
| Italy | 301 | 56 446 | 187 | Rome (2 884) |
| Ivory Coast | 322 | 5 152 | 16 | Abidjan (850) |
| Jamaica | 11 | 2 085 | 190 | Kingston (573) |
| Japan | 372 | 113 863 | 306 | Tokyo (11 684) |
| Jordan | 98 | 2 779 | 28 | Amman (672) |
| Kenya | 583 | 14 337 | 25 | Nairobi (776) |
| Korea, North | 121 | 16 651 | 138 | Pyongyang (1 500) |
| Korea, South | 98 | 36 436 | 370 | Seoul (6 879) |
| Kuwait | 18 | 1 129 | 63 | Kuwait (775) |
| Laos | 237 | 3 464 | 15 | Vientiane (177) |
| Lebanon | 10 | 3 056 | 294 | Beirut (702) |
| Lesotho | 30 | 1 214 | 40 | Maseru (29) |
| Liberia | 111 | 1 796 | 16 | Monrovia (172) |
| Libya | 1 760 | 2 444 | 1 | Tripoli (551) |
| Luxembourg | 3 | 356 | 138 | Luxembourg (78) |
| Madagascar | 587 | 8 520 | 15 | Antananarivo (378) |
| Malawi | 118 | 5 526 | 47 | Lilongwe (103) |
| Malaysia | 330 | 12 600 | 38 | Kuala Lumpur (452) |
| Mali | 1 240 | 5 994 | 5 | Bamako (400) |
| Malta | 0.3 | 332 | 1 051 | Valletta (14) |
| Mauritania | 1 031 | 1 481 | 1 | Nouakchott (135) |
| Mauritius | 2 | 909 | 444 | Port Louis (141) |
| Mexico | 1 973 | 64 594 | 33 | Mexico (11 943) |
| Mongolia | 1 565 | 1 531 | 1 | Ulan Bator (400) |
| Morocco | 447 | 18 245 | 41 | Rabat (596) |
| Mozambique | 783 | 9 678 | 12 | Maputo (384) |
| Namibia | 824 | 852 | 1 | Windhoek (61) |
| Nepal | 141 | 13 136 | 93 | Katmandu (210) |
| Netherlands | 41 | 13 853 | 339 | Amsterdam (989) |
| New Zealand | 269 | 3 105 | 12 | Wellington (329) |
| Nicaragua | 130 | 2 312 | 18 | Managua (500) |
| Niger | 1 267 | 4 859 | 4 | Niamey (130) |
| Nigeria | 924 | 66 628 | 72 | Lagos (1 477) |
| Norway | 324 | 4 042 | 12 | Oslo (645) |
| Oman | 212 | 817 | 4 | Muscat (25) |
| Pakistan | 804 | 75 278 | 94 | Islamabad (77) |
| Panama | 76 | 1 771 | 23 | Panama (428) |
| Papua New Guinea | 462 | 2 905 | 6 | Port Moresby (113) |
| Paraguay | 407 | 2 805 | 7 | Asunción (565) |
| Peru | 1 285 | 16 520 | 13 | Lima (3 303) |
| Philippines | 300 | 45 028 | 150 | Manila (1 438) |
| Poland | 313 | 34 698 | 111 | Warsaw (2 080) |
| Portugal | 92 | 9 733 | 106 | Lisbon (1 612) |
| Puerto Rico | 9 | 3 303 | 371 | San Juan (515) |
| Rumania | 238 | 21 658 | 91 | Bucharest (1 934) |
| Rwanda | 26 | 4 455 | 169 | Kigali (90) |
| Saudi Arabia | 2 150 | 9 522 | 4 | Riyadh (667) |
| Senegal | 196 | 5 115 | 26 | Dakar (799) |
| Sierra Leone | 72 | 3 470 | 48 | Freetown (214) |
| Singapore | 0.6 | 2 308 | 3 973 | Singapore (2 308) |
| Somali Republic | 638 | 3 354 | 5 | Mogadishu (230) |
| South Africa | 1 221 | 26 129 | 21 | Pretoria (562) Cape Town (1 097) |
| Spain | 505 | 36 351 | 72 | Madrid (3 520) |
| Sri Lanka | 66 | 13 971 | 213 | Colombo (592) |
| Sudan | 2 506 | 16 953 | 7 | Khartoum (334) |
| Surinam | 163 | 448 | 3 | Paramaribo (151) |
| Swaziland | 17 | 497 | 29 | Mbabane (21) |
| Sweden | 450 | 8 255 | 18 | Stockholm (1 355) |
| Switzerland | 41 | 6 327 | 153 | Berne (286) |
| Syria | 185 | 7 845 | 42 | Damascus (1 097) |
| Taiwan | 36 | 15 500 | 431 | Taipei (3 050) |
| Tanzania | 945 | 17 500 | 19 | Dar-es-Salaam (752) |
| Thailand | 514 | 44 039 | 86 | Bangkok (4 702) |
| Togo | 56 | 2 348 | 42 | Lomé (135) |
| Trinidad and Tobago | 5 | 1 098 | 215 | Port of Spain (63) |
| Tunisia | 164 | 6 065 | 37 | Tunis (944) |
| Turkey | 781 | 42 134 | 54 | Ankara (1 701) |
| Uganda | 236 | 12 353 | 52 | Kampala (331) |
| United Arab Emirates | 84 | 236 | 3 | Abu Dubai (236) |
| U.S.S.R. | 22 402 | 262 442 | 12 | Moscow (7 819) |
| United Kingdom | 244 | 55 852 | 229 | London (6 970) |
| United States | 9 363 | 216 817 | 23 | Washington (3 022) |
| Upper Volta | 274 | 6 319 | 23 | Ouagadougou (169) |
| Uruguay | 178 | 2 814 | 16 | Montevideo (1 230) |
| Venezuela | 912 | 12 737 | 14 | Caracas (2 576) |
| Vietnam | 330 | 47 872 | 145 | Hanoi (1 444) |
| Western Samoa | 3 | 151 | 53 | Apia (33) |
| Yemen (Sana) | 195 | 7 078 | 35 | Sana (135) |
| Yemen (South) | 333 | 1 797 | 5 | Aden (285) |
| Yugoslavia | 256 | 21 718 | 84 | Belgrade (775) |
| Zaïre | 2 345 | 26 376 | 11 | Kinshasa (2 008) |
| Zambia | 753 | 5 347 | 7 | Lusaka (401) |
| Zimbabwe-Rhodesia | 391 | 6 740 | 17 | Salisbury (568) |

# Principal Cities of the World

*The population figures used are from censuses or more recent estimates and are given in thousands for towns and cities over 500 000. Where possible the population of the metropolitan areas is given e.g. Greater London, Greater New York, etc.*

## AFRICA

**ALGERIA (1974)**
Algiers ... 1 503

**EGYPT (1974)**
Cairo ... 5 921
Alexandria ... 2 320
El Giza ... 893

**ETHIOPIA (1977)**
Addis Abeba ... 1 133

**GHANA (1970)**
Accra ... 738

**GUINEA (1972)**
Conakry ... 526

**IVORY COAST (1976)**
Abidjan ... 850

**KENYA (1977)**
Nairobi ... 776

**LIBYA (1973)**
Tripoli ... 551

**MOROCCO (1973)**
Casablanca ... 1 753
Rabat-Salé ... 596

**NIGERIA (1975)**
Lagos ... 1 477
Ibadan ... 847

**SENEGAL (1976)**
Dakar ... 799

**SOUTH AFRICA (1970)**
Johannesburg ... 1 433
Cape Town ... 1 097
Durban ... 843
Pretoria ... 562

**TANZANIA (1978)**
Dar-es-Salaam ... 752

**TUNISIA (1976)**
Tunis ... 944

**ZAIRE (1972-4)**
Kinshasa ... 2 008
Kananga ... 601

**ZIMBABWE-RHODESIA (1976)**
Salisbury ... 568

## ASIA

**AFGHANISTAN (1976)**
Kabul ... 588

**BANGLADESH (1974)**
Dacca ... 1 730
Chittagong ... 890

**BURMA (1973)**
Rangoon ... 1 586

**CAMBODIA (1973)**
Phnom Penh ... 2 000

**CHINA (1970)**
Shanghai ... 10 820
Peking ... 7 570
Tientsin ... 4 280
Shenyang ... 2 800
Wuhan ... 2 560
Canton ... 2 500
Chungking ... 2 400
Nanking ... 1 750
Harbin ... 1 670
Luta ... 1 650
Sian ... 1 600
Lanchow ... 1 450
Taiyuan ... 1 350
Tsingtao ... 1 300
Chengtu ... 1 250
Changchun ... 1 200
Kunming ... 1 100
Tsinan ... 1 100
Fushun ... 1 080
Anshan ... 1 050
Chengchow ... 1 050
Hangchow ... 960
Tangshan ... 950
Paotow ... 920
Tzepo ... 850
Changsha ... 825
Shihkiachwang ... 800
Tsitsihar ... 760
Soochow ... 730
Kirin ... 720
Suchow ... 700
Foochow ... 680
Nanchang ... 675
Kweiyang ... 660
Wusih ... 650
Hofei ... 630
Hwainan ... 600
Penki ... 600
Loyang ... 580
Nanning ... 550
Huhehot ... 530
Sining ... 500
Wulumuchi ... 500

**HONG KONG (1971)**
Kowloon ... 2 195
Victoria ... 849

**INDIA (1971)**
Calcutta ... 7 031
Bombay ... 5 971
Delhi ... 3 647
Madras ... 3 170
Hyderabad ... 1 796
Ahmedabad ... 1 742
Bangalore ... 1 654
Kanpur ... 1 275
Pune ... 1 135
Nagpur ... 930
Lucknow ... 749
Jaipur ... 615
Agra ... 592
Varanasi ... 584
Madurai ... 549
Indore ... 543

**INDONESIA (1971)**
Jakarta ... 4 576
Surabaya ... 1 556
Bandung ... 1 202
Semarang ... 647
Medan ... 636
Palembang ... 583

**IRAN (1976)**
Tehran ... 4 496
Esfahan ... 672
Mashhad ... 670
Tabriz ... 599

**IRAQ (1970)**
Baghdad ... 2 969

**ISRAEL (1975)**
Tel Aviv-Jaffa ... 1 181

**JAPAN (1975)**
Tokyo ... 11 684
Osaka ... 2 750
Yokohama ... 2 659
Nagoya ... 2 080
Kyoto ... 1 462
Kobe ... 1 364
Sapporo ... 1 277
Kitakyushu ... 1 064
Kawasaki ... 1 025
Fukuoka ... 1 022
Hiroshima ... 842
Sakai ... 758
Chiba ... 675
Sendai ... 597
Amagasaki ... 536
Okayama ... 523
Higashiosaka ... 501

**JORDAN (1976)**
Amman ... 672

**KOREA, NORTH (1967-70)**
Pyongyang ... 1 500

**KOREA, SOUTH (1975)**
Seoul ... 6 879
Pusan ... 2 450
Taegu ... 1 309
Inchon ... 797
Kwangju ... 606
Taejon ... 506

**KUWAIT (1975)**
Kuwait ... 775

**LEBANON (1971)**
Beirut ... 702

**PAKISTAN (1972)**
Karachi ... 3 499
Lahore ... 2 165
Lyallpur ... 822
Hyderabad ... 628
Rawalpindi ... 615
Multan ... 542

**PHILIPPINES (1975)**
Manila ... 1 438
Quezon City ... 995
Davao ... 516

**SAUDI ARABIA (1974)**
Riyadh ... 667
Jedda ... 561

**SINGAPORE (1977)**
Singapore ... 2 308

**SRI LANKA (1974)**
Colombo ... 592

**SYRIA (1977)**
Damascus ... 1 097
Aleppo ... 843

**TAIWAN (1973)**
Taipei ... 3 050
Kaohsiung ... 1 115
Tainan ... 513

**THAILAND (1977)**
Bangkok ... 4 702

**TURKEY (1975)**
Istanbul ... 2 547
Ankara ... 1 701
Izmir ... 637

**VIETNAM (1973-76)**
Ho Chi Minh City ... 3 461
Hanoi ... 1 444
Haiphong ... 1 191

## AUSTRALASIA

**AUSTRALIA (1976)**
Sydney ... 3 021
Melbourne ... 2 604
Brisbane ... 958
Adelaide ... 900
Perth ... 805

**NEW ZEALAND (1977)**
Auckland ... 746

## EUROPE

**AUSTRIA (1976)**
Vienna ... 1 593

**BELGIUM (1971)**
Brussels ... 1 075
Antwerp ... 673

**BULGARIA (1975)**
Sofia ... 965

**CZECHOSLOVAKIA (1976)**
Prague ... 1 173

**DENMARK (1977)**
Copenhagen ... 1 251

**FINLAND (1976)**
Helsinki ... 825

**FRANCE (1975)**
Paris ... 9 863
Lyon ... 1 152
Marseille ... 1 004
Lille ... 929
Bordeaux ... 591

**GERMANY, EAST (1976)**
East Berlin ... 1 101
Leipzig ... 565
Dresden ... 509

**GERMANY, WEST (1976)**
West Berlin ... 1 951
Hamburg ... 1 699
München ... 1 315
Cologne ... 981
Essen ... 670
Frankfurt am Main ... 626
Dortmund ... 624
Düsseldorf ... 615
Stuttgart ... 590
Duisburg ... 582
Bremen ... 568
Hannover ... 547

**GREECE (1971)**
Athens ... 2 101
Thessaloniki ... 557

**HUNGARY (1975)**
Budapest ... 2 076

**IRISH REPUBLIC (1971)**
Dublin ... 815

**ITALY (1976)**
Rome ... 2 884
Milano ... 1 705
Napoli ... 1 224
Torino ... 1 191
Genova ... 801
Palermo ... 673

**NETHERLANDS (1975-77)**
Rotterdam ... 1 032
Amsterdam ... 989
s'Gravenhage ... 681

**NORWAY (1976)**
Oslo ... 645

**POLAND (1976)**
Warsaw ... 2 080
Lódz ... 1 087
Kraków ... 883
Wroclaw ... 580
Poznań ... 522

**PORTUGAL (1975)**
Lisbon ... 1 612
Oporto ... 1 315

**RUMANIA (1977)**
Bucharest ... 1 934

**SPAIN (1974)**
Madrid ... 3 520
Barcelona ... 1 810
Valencia ... 713
Sevilla ... 569
Zaragoza ... 547

**SWEDEN (1975)**
Stockholm ... 1 357
Göteborg ... 691

**SWITZERLAND (1976)**
Zürich ... 714

**U.S.S.R. (1977)**
Moscow ... 7 819
Leningrad ... 4 425
Kiyev ... 2 079
Tashkent ... 1 689
Baku ... 1 435
Kharkov ... 1 405
Gorkiy ... 1 319
Novosibirsk ... 1 304
Minsk ... 1 231
Kuybyshev ... 1 204
Sverdlovsk ... 1 187
Tbilisi ... 1 042
Odessa ... 1 039
Omsk ... 1 026
Chelyabinsk ... 1 007
Dnepropetrovsk ... 995
Donetsk ... 984
Perm ... 972
Kazan ... 970
Erevan ... 956
Ufa ... 942
Rostov ... 921
Volgograd ... 918
Alma-Ata ... 871
Saratov ... 856
Riga ... 816
Krasnoyarsk ... 769
Voronezh ... 764
Zaporozhye ... 760
Lvov ... 642
Krivoy Rog ... 641
Yaroslavl ... 577
Karaganda ... 576
Krasnodar ... 552
Novokuznetsk ... 537
Izhevsk ... 534
Irkutsk ... 532
Vladivostok ... 526
Khabarovsk ... 524
Barnaul ... 522
Frunze ... 511
Tula ... 510

**UNITED KINGDOM (1974-77)**
London ... 6 970
Birmingham ... 1 003
Glasgow ... 881
Liverpool ... 561
Manchester ... 516
Sheffield ... 507

**YUGOSLAVIA (1971)**
Belgrade ... 775
Zagreb ... 602

## NORTH AMERICA

**CANADA (1976)**
Toronto ... 2 803
Montréal ... 2 802
Vancouver ... 1 166
Ottawa ... 693
Winnipeg ... 578
Edmonton ... 554
Québec ... 542
Hamilton ... 529

**CUBA (1975)**
Havana ... 1 861

**DOMINICAN REPUBLIC (1970)**
Santo Domingo ... 818

**GUATEMALA (1973)**
Guatemala City ... 717

**HAITI (1977)**
Port-au-Prince ... 703

**JAMAICA (1971**
Kingston ... 573

**MEXICO (1976)**
Mexico City ... 11 943
Guadalajara ... 2 076
Monterrey ... 1 725
Ciudad Juárez ... 545
Tijuana ... 536
León de los Aldamas ... 526

**NICARAGUA (1974)**
Managua ... 500

**PUERTO RICO (1976)**
San Juan ... 515

**UNITED STATES (1975)**
New York ... 16 679
Los Angeles ... 10 350
Chicago ... 7 658
Philadelphia ... 5 643
Detroit ... 4 669
San Francisco ... 4 592
Boston ... 3 553
Washington ... 3 022
Cleveland ... 2 902
Dallas ... 2 544
Houston ... 2 482
St. Louis ... 2 367
Pittsburgh ... 2 322
Miami ... 2 288
Baltimore ... 2 148
Minneapolis-St Paul ... 2 011
Seattle ... 1 822
Atlanta ... 1 790
Cincinnati ... 1 626
Milwaukee ... 1 585
San Diego ... 1 585
Denver ... 1 417
Tampa ... 1 348
Buffalo ... 1 327
Kansas City ... 1 290
Phoenix ... 1 221
Indianapolis ... 1 139
New Orleans ... 1 094
Portland ... 1 083
Columbus ... 1 069
San Antonio ... 982
Rochester ... 971
Providence ... 904
Louisville ... 888
Sacramento ... 880
Memphis ... 867
Dayton ... 836
Albany ... 798
Birmingham ... 791
Salt Lake City ... 783
Toledo ... 779
Norfolk ... 773
Greensboro ... 764
Nashville ... 748
Oklahoma City ... 746
Hartford ... 731
Honolulu ... 705
Jacksonville ... 693
Syracuse ... 648
Scranton ... 635
Allentown ... 624
Charlotte ... 593
Tulsa ... 586
Richmond ... 585
Orlando ... 583
Omaha ... 573
Grand Rapids ... 564
Springfield ... 549
Youngstown ... 549
Greenville ... 525
Flint ... 519

## SOUTH AMERICA

**ARGENTINA (1975)**
Buenos Aires ... 8 436
Rosario ... 807
Córdoba ... 791

**BOLIVIA (1976)**
La Paz ... 655

**BRAZIL (1975)**
São Paulo ... 7 199
Rio de Janeiro ... 4 858
Belo Horizonte ... 1 557
Recife ... 1 250
Salvador ... 1 237
Fortaleza ... 1 110
Pôrto Alegre ... 1 044
Nova Iguaçu ... 932
Belém ... 772
Curitiba ... 765
Brasilia ... 763
Duque de Caxias ... 537
São Gançalo ... 534
Goiania ... 518
Santo André ... 515

**CHILE (1976)**
Santiago ... 3 595
Valparaiso ... 611
Concepción ... 513

**COLOMBIA (1973)**
Bogotá ... 2 855
Medellin ... 1 159
Cali ... 990
Barranquilla ... 692

**ECUADOR (1974)**
Guayaquil ... 823
Quito ... 600

**PARAGUAY (1974)**
Asunción ... 565

**PERU (1972)**
Lima ... 3 303

**URUGUAY (1975)**
Montevideo ... 1 230

**VENEZUELA (1976)**
Caracas ... 2 576
Maracaibo ... 792

# Climate Graphs

The climate graphs should be used in conjunction with the maps illustrating the climate of the World, and also the more detailed maps of the climates of the Continents and the British Isles. For each of the Continents and the British Isles about thirty different stations have been selected so that practically every type of climate throughout the world is covered by the graphs. Complete temperature, pressure and rainfall statistics have been obtained for all except a few stations where pressure statistics were not available. Wherever possible the graphs show average observations based upon long period means, and in all other cases over as long a period as possible. The latest available statistics have been consulted throughout.

Small maps are given on each sheet of graphs showing the location of every station. The figure after the name of the station gives the height in metres of the station above sea-level, so that comparisons between stations can be made after allowing for elevation. For temperature, measurements are given in degrees Centigrade; for pressure, millibars; and for rainfall, in millimetres. The temperature graphs show the monthly means of daily maximum and minimum actual temperatures: from these the mean monthly actual temperatures can easily be determined. The mean annual range of temperature is given above the temperature graphs.
The pressure graphs show the mean monthly pressure at sea-level, except in cases of high-level stations, where the height to which the pressure has been reduced is noted.

The rainfall graphs show the average monthly rainfall, and above them is given the average total annual rainfall. These graphs have been drawn to show the rainfall on the same scale for all stations to facilitate true comparisons between them. Where the rainfall graph extends over to the temperature graph the rainfall scale has been continued at the side of the graph.

On the temperature maps the actual temperatures and sea-level isotherms for the two extreme months of the year, January and July, are given. This information is supplemented by the graphs so that a far more complete picture of temperature changes can now be visualized. A comparison of stations in high latitudes with those in low latitudes renders apparent the importance of the seasonal changes due to insolation. In high latitudes the annual range of temperature is considerable. It decreases gradually as the equator is approached where there is scarcely any variation throughout the year. Another important factor in determining the range is the position of a station in relation to the sea, which exercises a strong moderating influence. The graphs for Africa illustrate the differences in seasons in the northern and southern hemispheres. The influence of the sea also shows itself in the small differences between the mean daily maxima and minima of seaside stations as compared with inland stations. Those most remote from the sea experience a large diurnal range.

The graphs reveal very clearly the intimate connection existing between temperature and pressure. This is perhaps nowhere more clearly indicated than in Asia, where the intense winter cold of the interior coincides with a high pressure system, and the warmth of summer with a low pressure system. As the graphs deal only with land stations all the great pressure systems of the world cannot be demonstrated. Their influence is discernible however in the pressure graphs for many of the stations, e.g., the permanent low pressure system centred on Iceland and the permanent high pressure system based on the Azores, seen in the graphs for Reykjavík and Lisboa respectively, and the permanent equatorial low pressures. One further factor having an important bearing on local climate in high mountain regions deserves mention, namely, the influence of height in reducing pressure. Reduced to sea-level, the pressures for Quito and Guayaquil would appear to be the same, but the graphs reveal the differences which actually exist.

The rainfall maps in the atlas show broadly seasonal rainfall for summer and winter. These are now supplemented by the rainfall graphs, a study of which enables greater distinctions to be drawn between the various rainfall regions, by showing both the amount of precipitation and the months in which it occurs—factors of prime significance for vegetation. In classifying the different rainfall regimes attention should be paid to the factor of relief and the connection noted between the low pressures and convectional rains of equatorial regions.

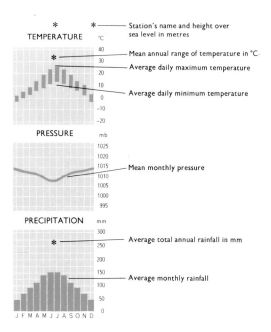

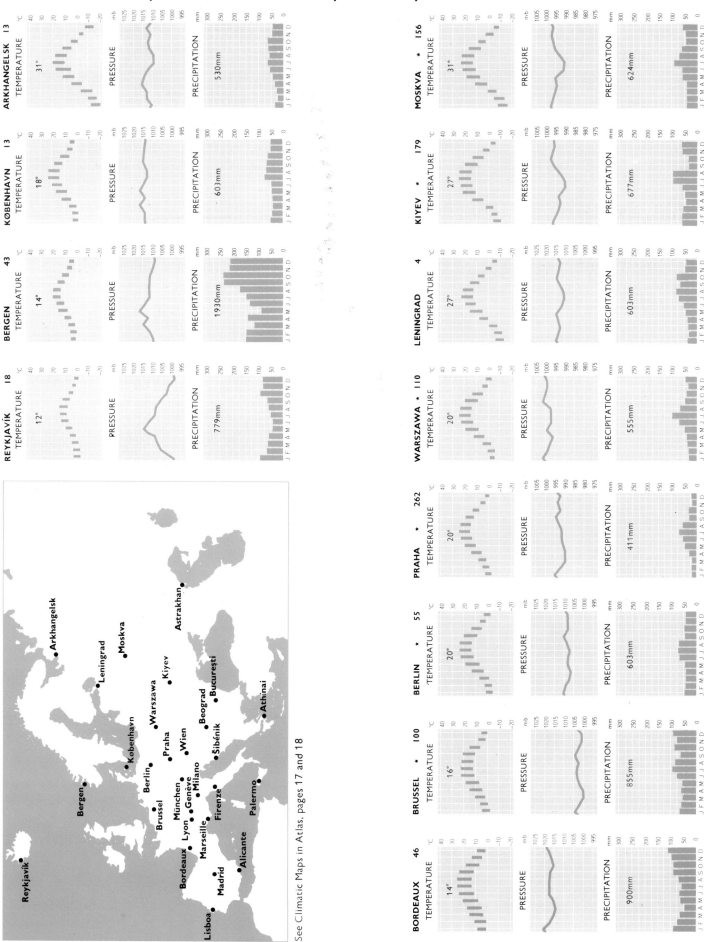

See Climatic Maps in Atlas, pages 17 and 18

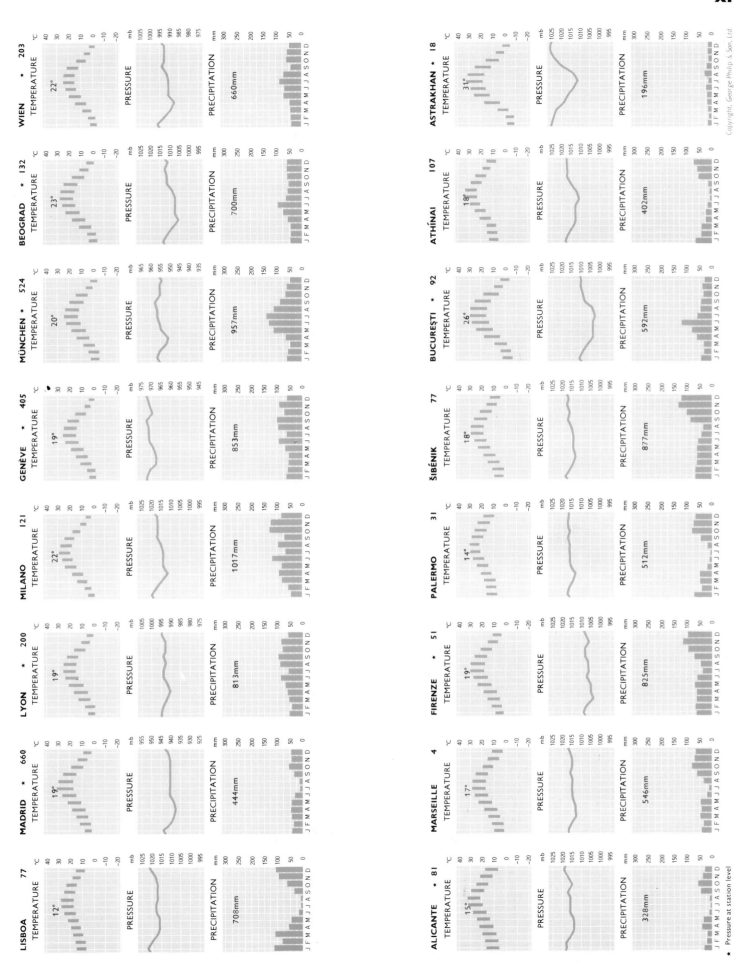

★ Pressure at station level

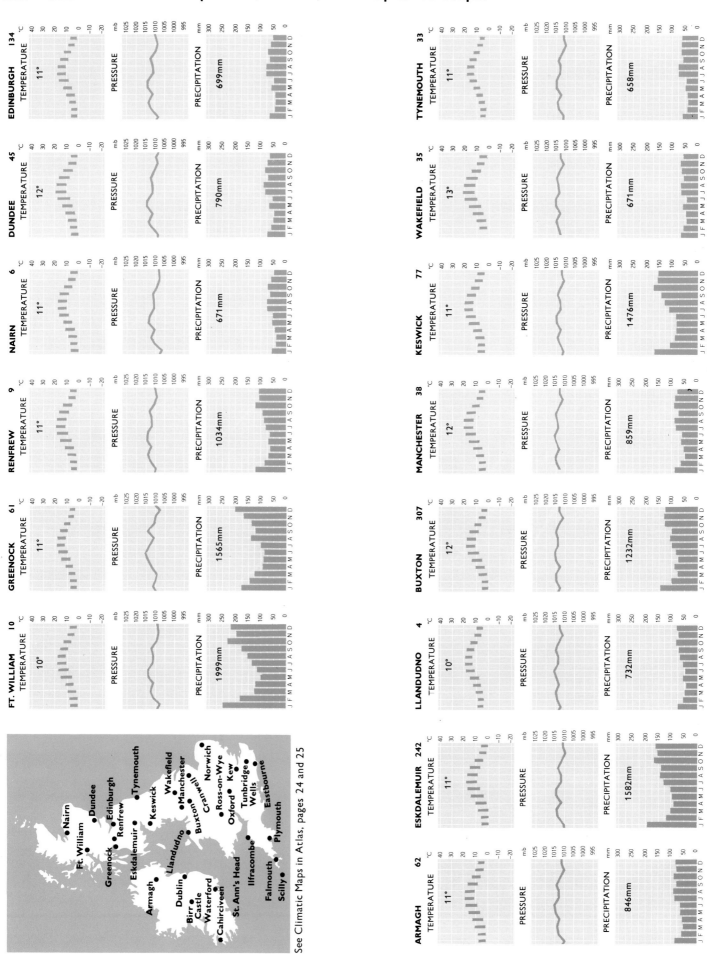

See Climatic Maps in Atlas, pages 24 and 25

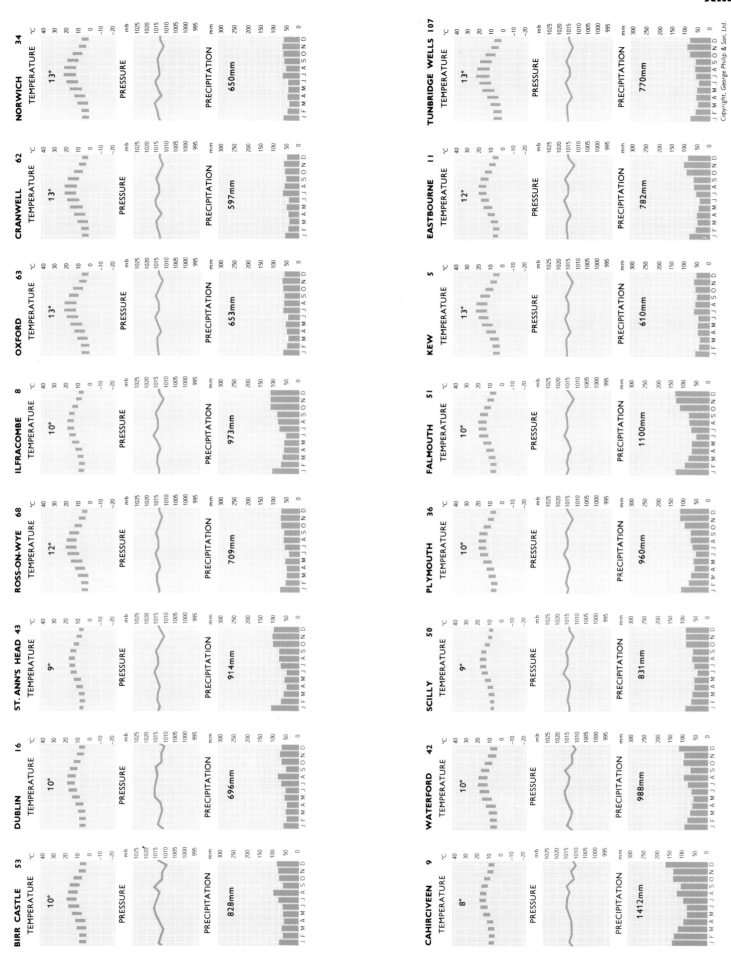

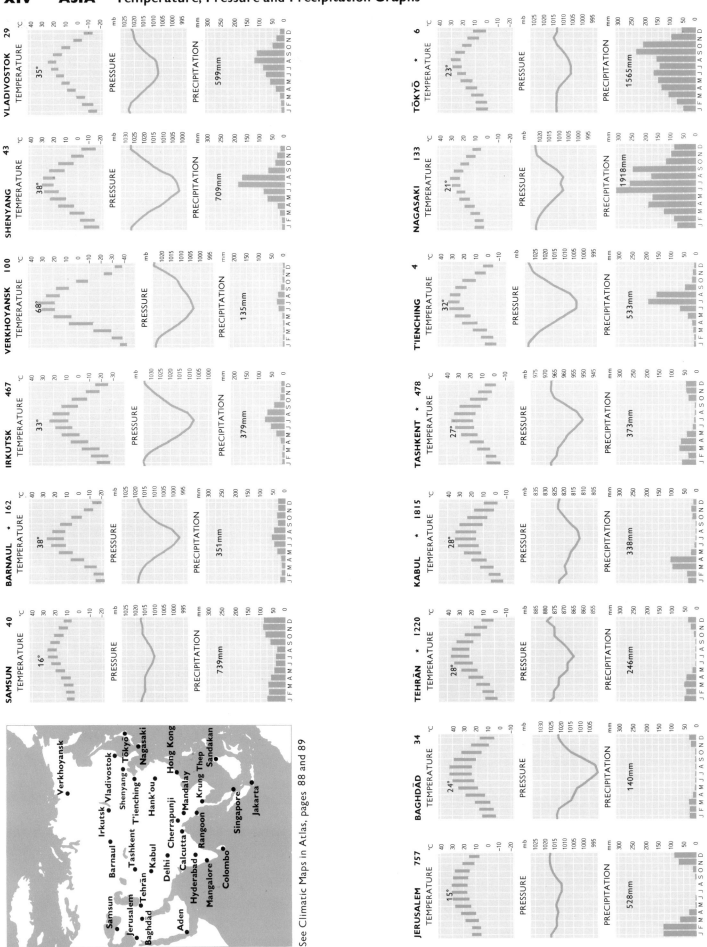

See Climatic Maps in Atlas, pages 88 and 89

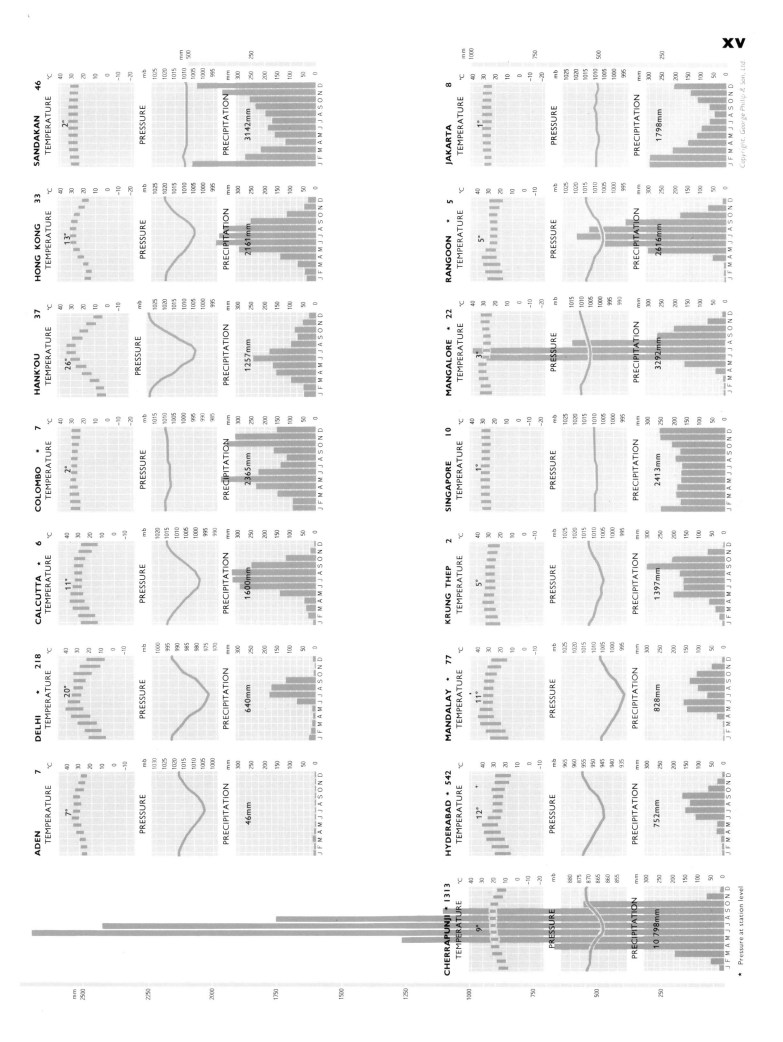

**XV**

* Pressure at station level

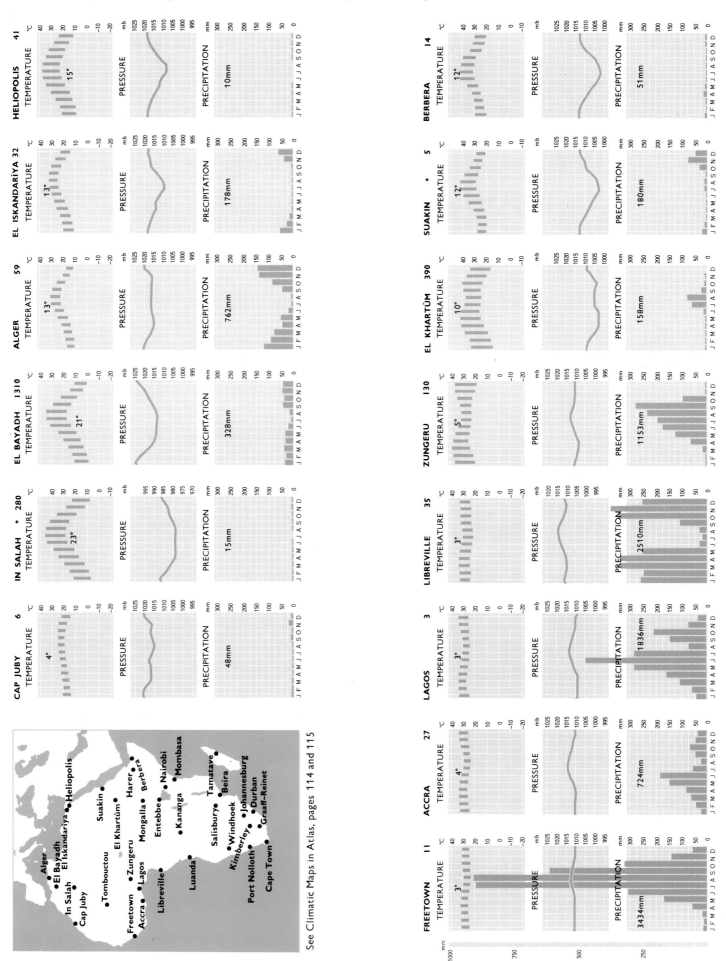

See Climatic Maps in Atlas, pages 114 and 115

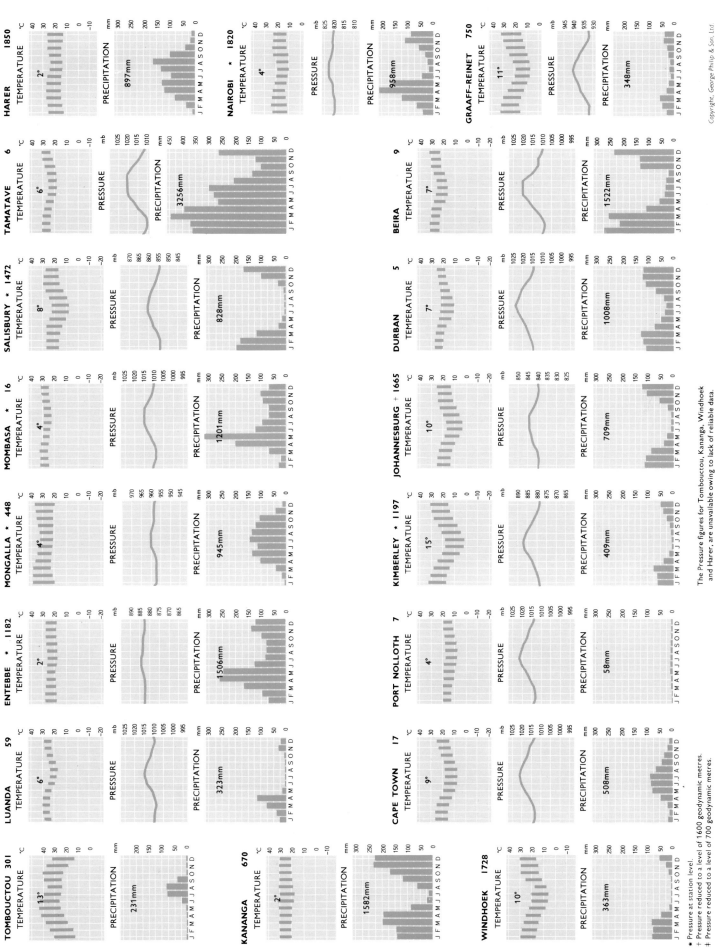

HARER 1850
TEMPERATURE °C
PRECIPITATION
2°
897mm

NAIROBI ★ 1820
TEMPERATURE °C
PRESSURE mb
PRECIPITATION
4°
958mm

GRAAFF-REINET 750
TEMPERATURE °C
PRESSURE mb
PRECIPITATION
11°
348mm

TAMATAVE 6
TEMPERATURE °C
PRESSURE mb
PRECIPITATION
6°
3256mm

BEIRA 9
TEMPERATURE °C
PRESSURE mb
PRECIPITATION
7°
1522mm

SALISBURY ★ 1472
TEMPERATURE °C
PRESSURE mb
PRECIPITATION
8°
828mm

DURBAN 5
TEMPERATURE °C
PRESSURE mb
PRECIPITATION
7°
1008mm

MOMBASA ★ 16
TEMPERATURE °C
PRESSURE mb
PRECIPITATION
4°
1201mm

JOHANNESBURG + 1665
TEMPERATURE °C
PRESSURE mb
PRECIPITATION
10°
709mm

MONGALLA ★ 448
TEMPERATURE °C
PRESSURE mb
PRECIPITATION
4°
945mm

KIMBERLEY ★ 1197
TEMPERATURE °C
PRESSURE mb
PRECIPITATION
15°
409mm

ENTEBBE ★ 1182
TEMPERATURE °C
PRESSURE mb
PRECIPITATION
2°
1506mm

PORT NOLLOTH 7
TEMPERATURE °C
PRESSURE mb
PRECIPITATION
4°
58mm

LUANDA 59
TEMPERATURE °C
PRESSURE mb
PRECIPITATION
6°
323mm

CAPE TOWN 17
TEMPERATURE °C
PRESSURE mb
PRECIPITATION
9°
508mm

TOMBOUCTOU 301
TEMPERATURE °C
PRECIPITATION
13°
231mm

KANANGA 670
TEMPERATURE °C
PRECIPITATION
2°
1582mm

WINDHOEK 1728
TEMPERATURE °C
PRESSURE mb
PRECIPITATION
10°
363mm

The Pressure figures for Tombouctou, Kananga, Windhoek and Harer, are unavailable owing to lack of reliable data.

★ Pressure at station level.
+ Pressure reduced to a level of 1600 geodynamic metres.
‡ Pressure reduced to a level of 700 geodynamic metres.

Copyright, George Philip & Son, Ltd.

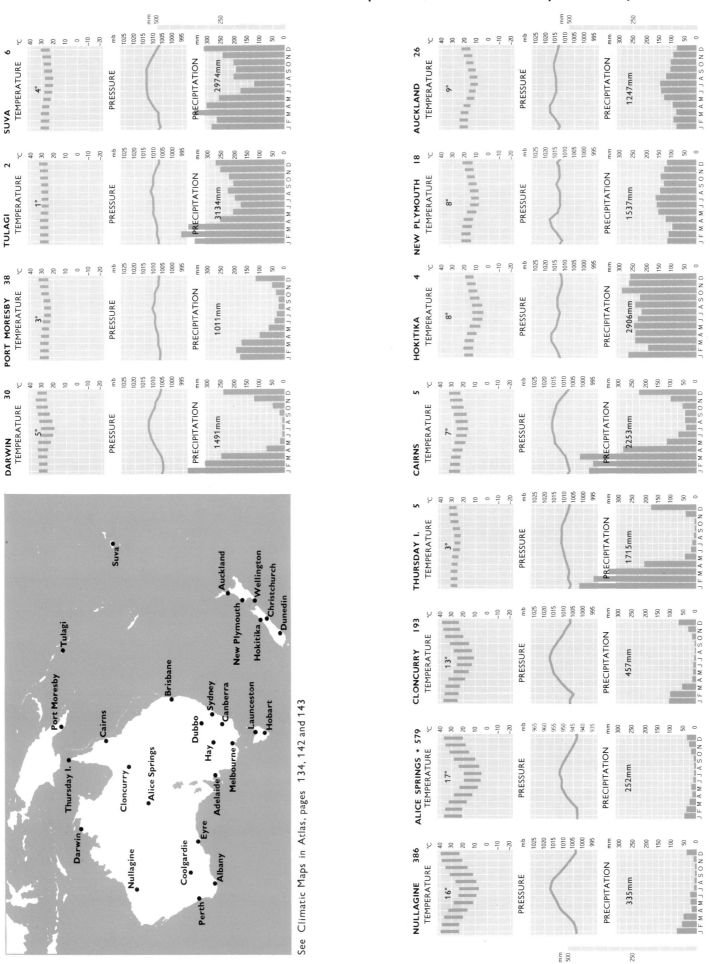

See Climatic Maps in Atlas, pages 134, 142 and 143

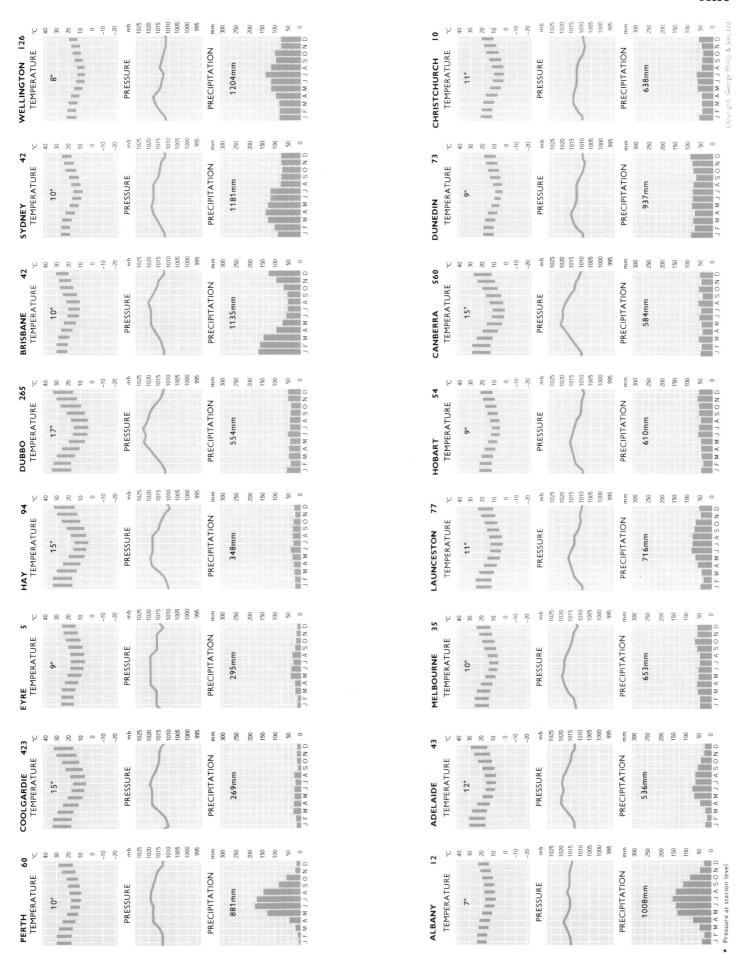

XIX

* Pressure at station level

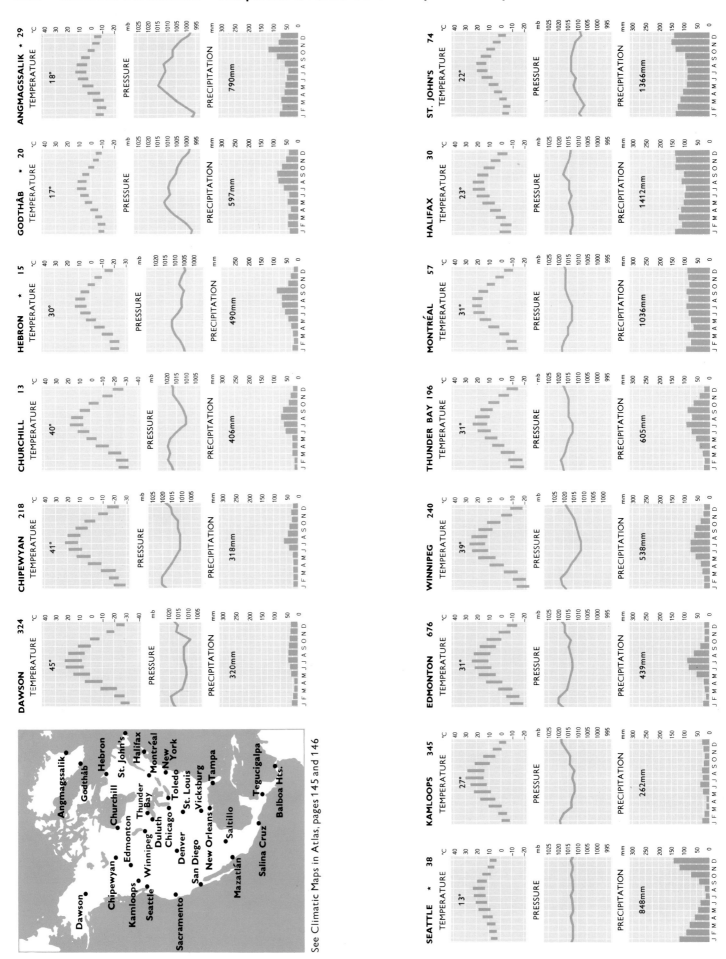

See Climatic Maps in Atlas, pages 145 and 146

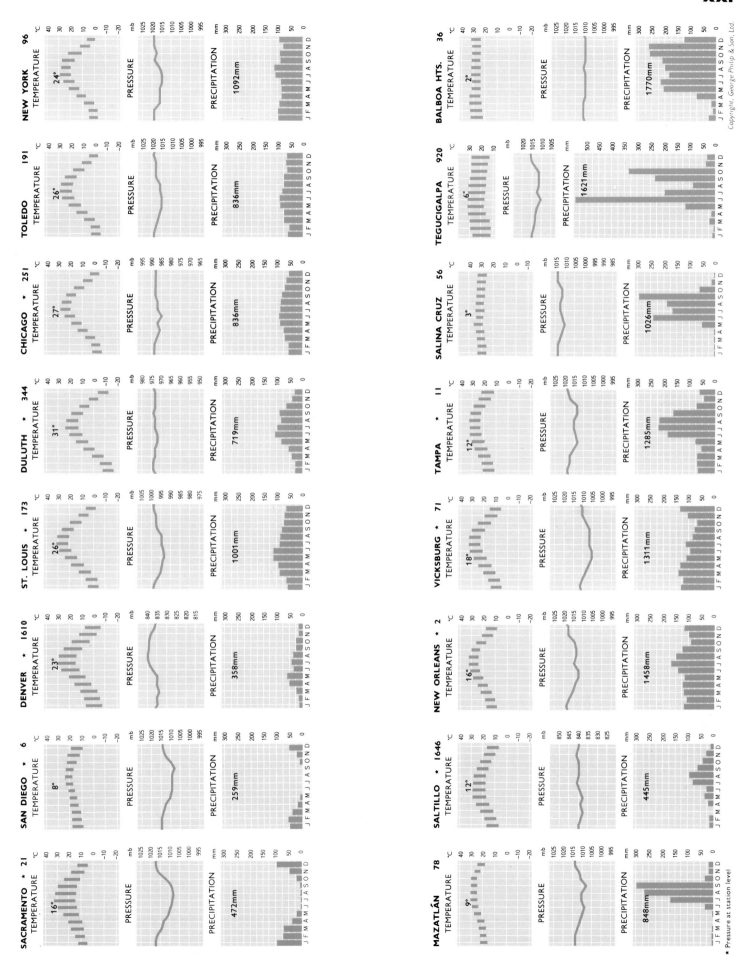

★ Pressure at station level

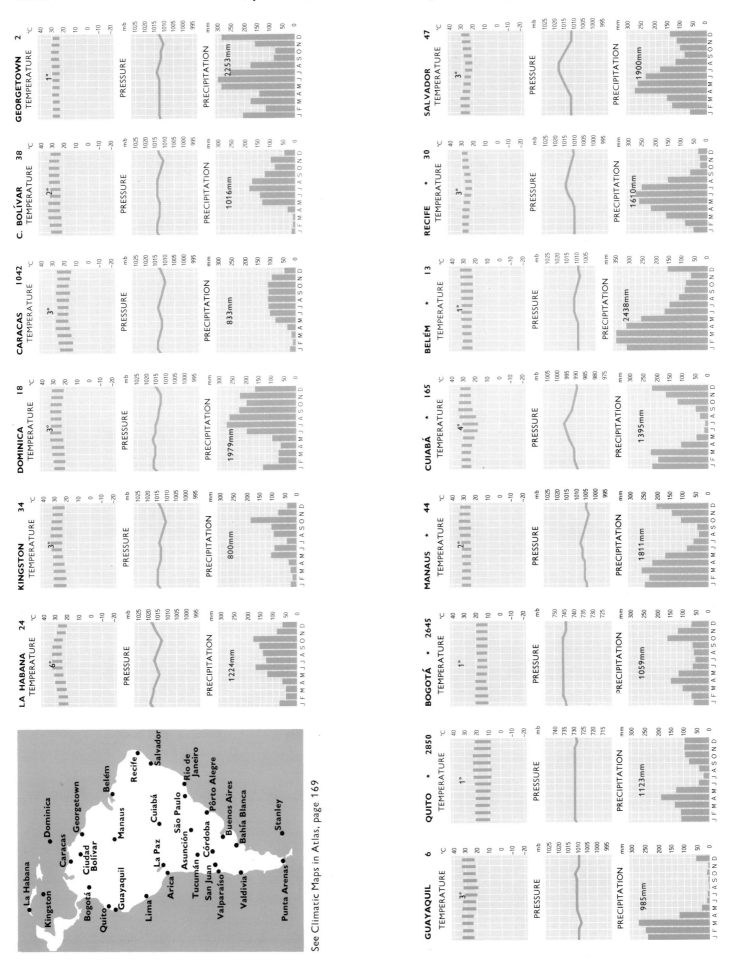

See Climatic Maps in Atlas, page 169

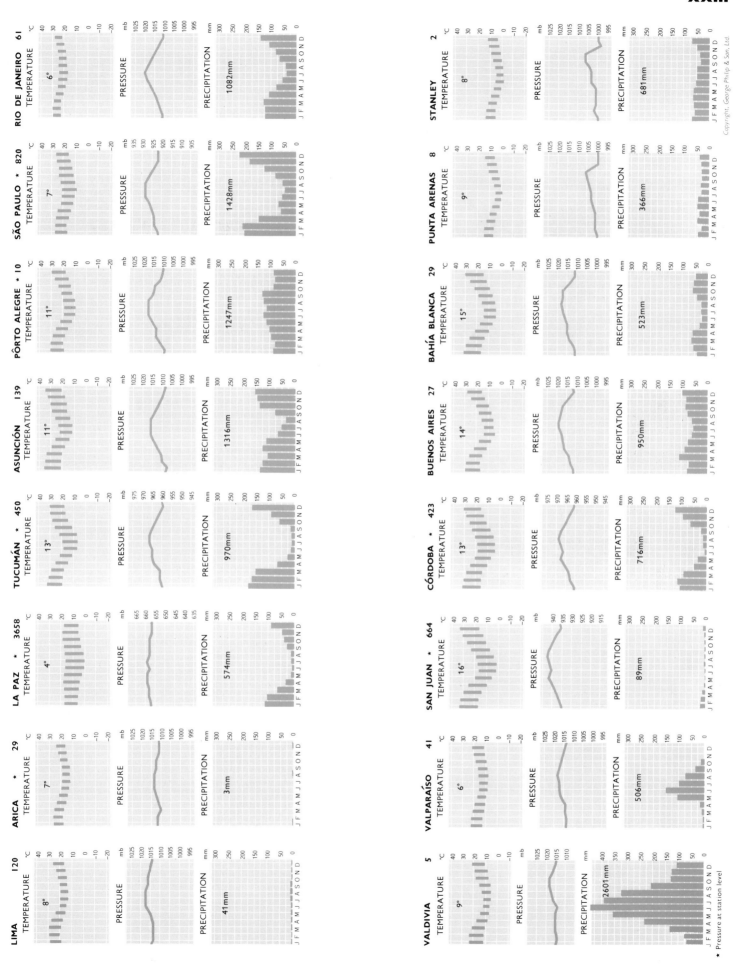

* Pressure at station level

# Projections Used

# GENERAL REFERENCE

Abbreviations of measures used — ft Feet; mm {Millimetres / Millimeters}; cm {Centimetres / Centimeters}; m {Metres / Meters}; km {Kilometres / Kilometers}; mb Millibars

City and Town symbols in order of size

∴ Sites of Archæological or Historical Importance

International Boundaries

International Boundaries (Undemarcated or Undefined)

Internal Boundaries

Principal Roads

Tracks, Seasonal and other Roads

Road Tunnels

Principal Railways

Other Railways

Railways under construction

Railway Tunnels

Principal Canals

Principal Oil Pipelines

Principal Air Routes

☼ Principal Airports

Principal Shipping Routes (Distances in Nautical Miles)

Perennial Streams

Seasonal Streams

Seasonal Lakes, Salt Flats

Swamps, Marshes

Wells in Desert

Permanent Ice

≍ Passes

▲ 8848 Height above sea-level ⎫
▼ 8050 Depth below sea-level ⎬ in metres
1134 Height of lake-level ⎭

CONVERSION SCALE

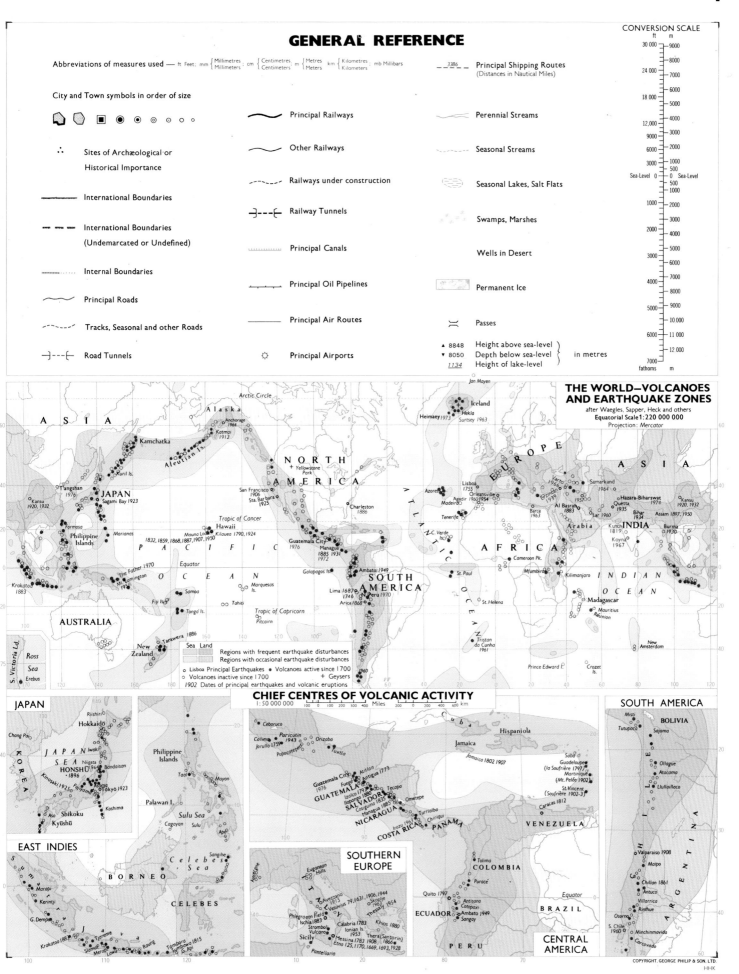

THE WORLD—VOLCANOES AND EARTHQUAKE ZONES
after Waegles, Sapper, Heck and others
Equatorial Scale 1:220 000 000
Projection: Mercator

Sea Land
Regions with frequent earthquake disturbances
Regions with occasional earthquake disturbances
○ Lisboa Principal Earthquakes ● Volcanoes active since 1700
○ Volcanoes inactive since 1700 + Geysers
1902 Dates of principal earthquakes and volcanic eruptions

CHIEF CENTRES OF VOLCANIC ACTIVITY
1:50 000 000

JAPAN

EAST INDIES

SOUTHERN EUROPE

CENTRAL AMERICA

SOUTH AMERICA

COPYRIGHT. GEORGE PHILIP & SON. LTD.
HHK

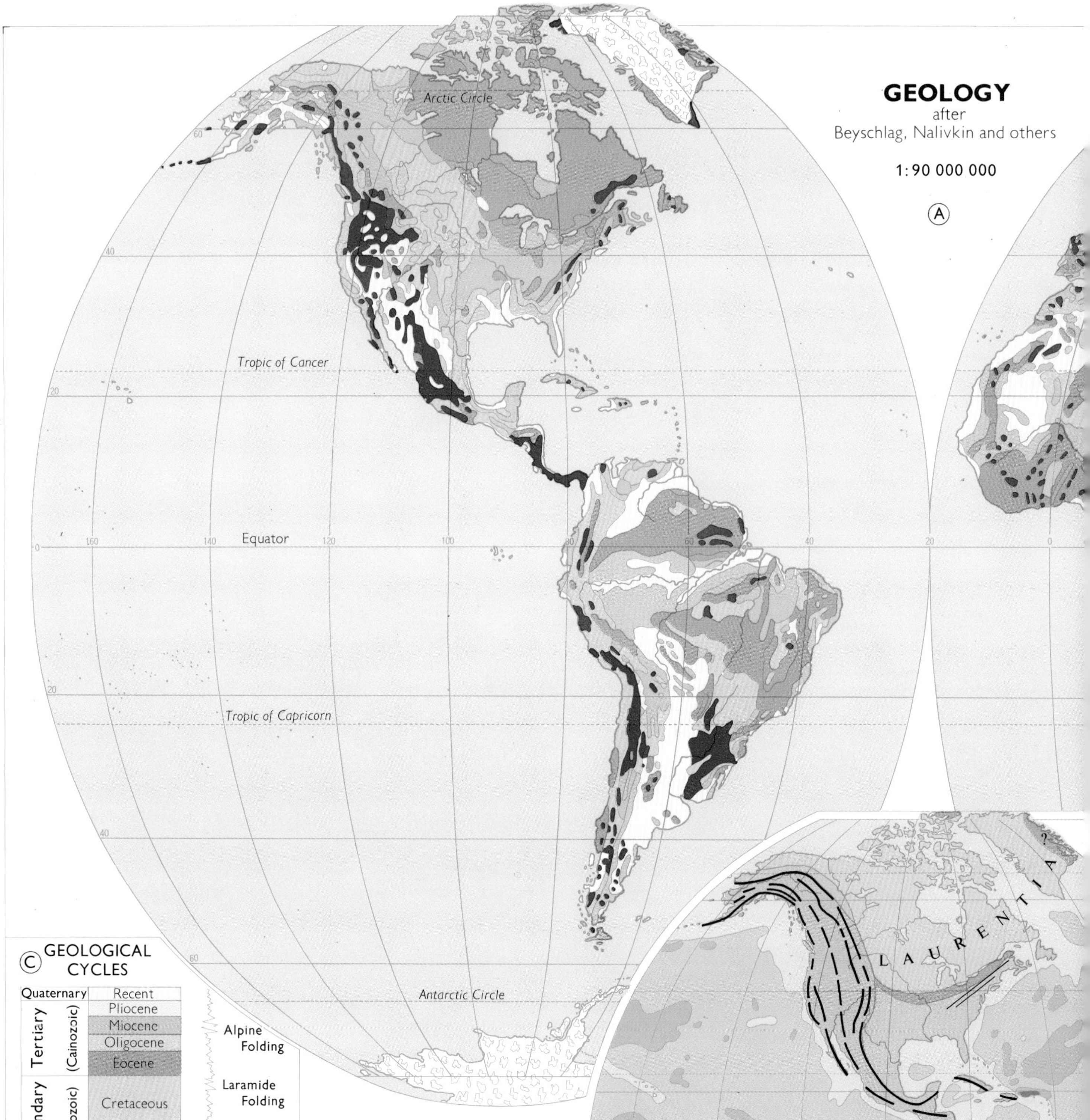

**GEOLOGY**
after
Beyschlag, Nalivkin and others

1:90 000 000

Ⓐ

**Ⓒ GEOLOGICAL CYCLES**

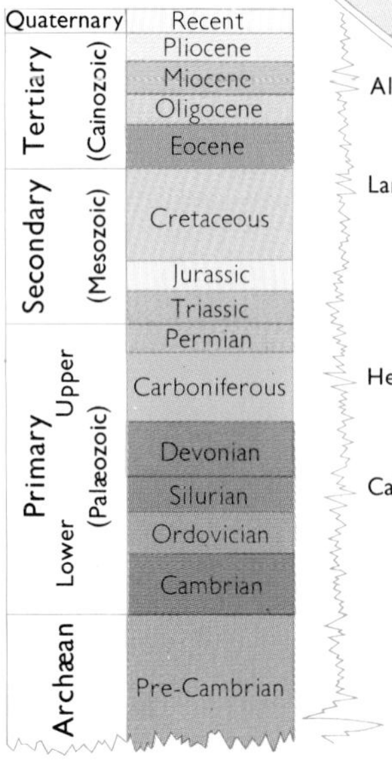

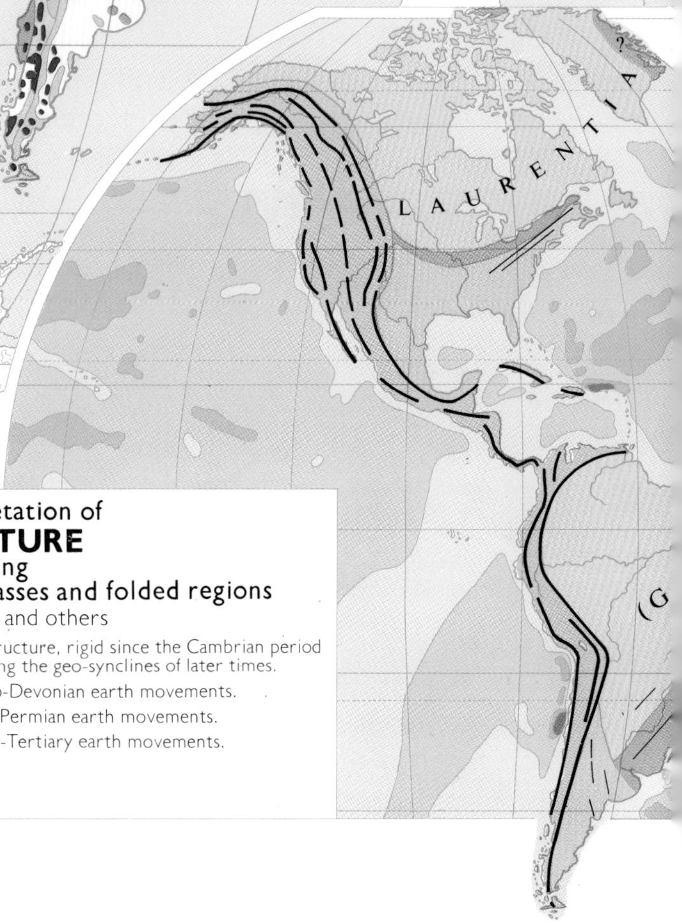

| | | |
|---|---|---|
| Quaternary | Recent | |
| Tertiary (Cainozoic) | Pliocene | |
| | Miocene | Alpine Folding |
| | Oligocene | |
| | Eocene | |
| Secondary (Mesozoic) | Cretaceous | Laramide Folding |
| | Jurassic | |
| | Triassic | |
| Primary Upper (Palæozoic) | Permian | |
| | Carboniferous | Hercynian Folding |
| | Devonian | |
| Lower | Silurian | Caledonian Folding |
| | Ordovician | |
| | Cambrian | |
| Archæan | Pre-Cambrian | |

Ⓑ     An Interpretation of
**STRUCTURE**
showing
the distribution of rigid masses and folded regions
after L. Kober and others

Pre-Cambrian tables composite in structure, rigid since the Cambrian period and forming stable elements separating the geo-synclines of later times.

Regions of Caledonian folding; Siluro-Devonian earth movements.

Regions of Hercynian folding; Carbo-Permian earth movements.

Regions of Tertiary folding; Cretaceo-Tertiary earth movements.

The Great Rift Valley

Main Trend lines

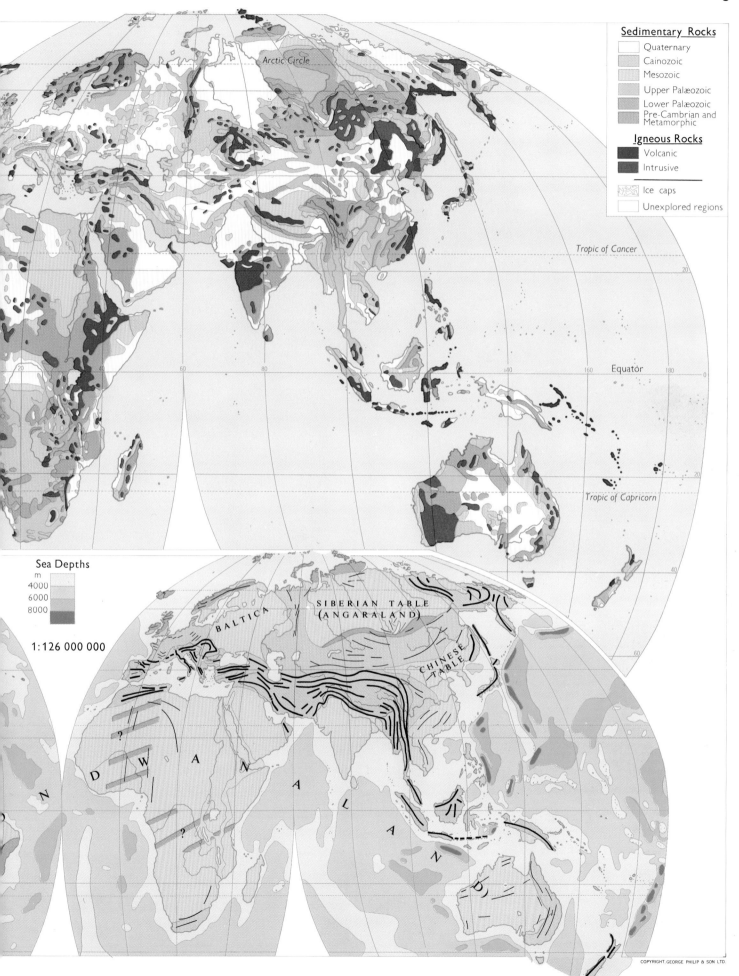

Sedimentary Rocks
Quaternary
Cainozoic
Mesozoic
Upper Palæozoic
Lower Palæozoic
Pre-Cambrian and Metamorphic

Igneous Rocks
Volcanic
Intrusive

Ice caps
Unexplored regions

Arctic Circle

Tropic of Cancer

20

Equator

Tropic of Capricorn

40

60

Sea Depths
m
4000
6000
8000

1:126 000 000

BALTICA

SIBERIAN TABLE
(ANGARALAND)

CHINESE TABLE

G O N D W A N A L A N D

?

?

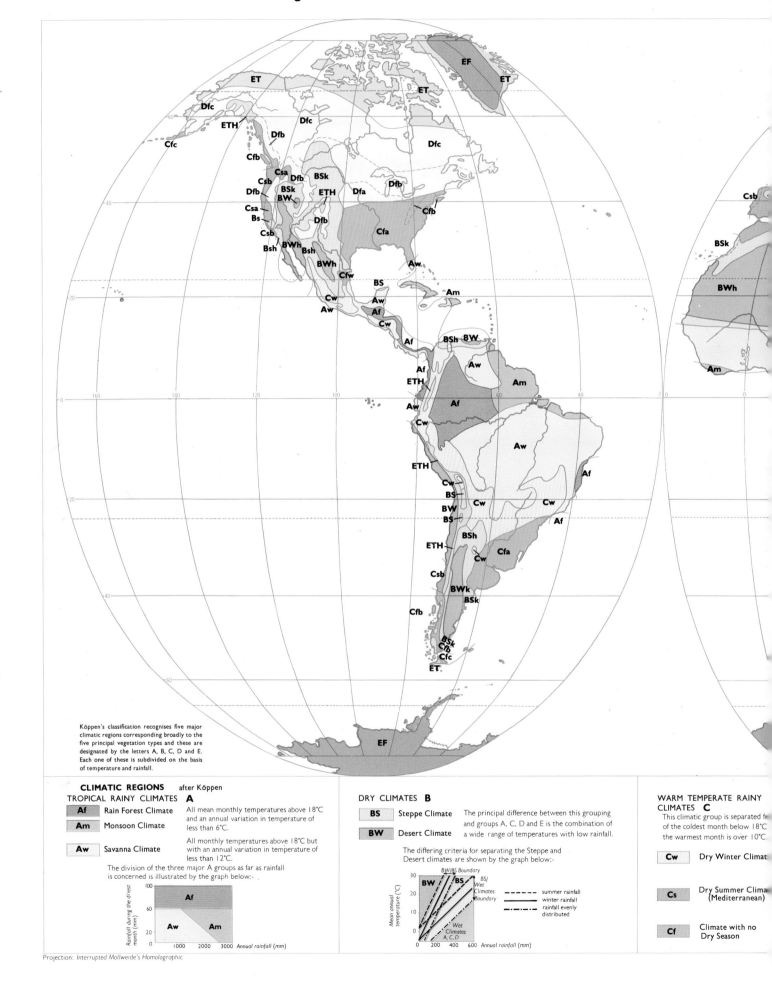

Köppen's classification recognises five major
climatic regions corresponding broadly to the
five principal vegetation types and these are
designated by the letters A, B, C, D and E.
Each one of these is subdivided on the basis
of temperature and rainfall.

**CLIMATIC REGIONS**   after Köppen
**TROPICAL RAINY CLIMATES** **A**

| | | |
|---|---|---|
| **Af** | Rain Forest Climate | All mean monthly temperatures above 18°C and an annual variation in temperature of less than 6°C. |
| **Am** | Monsoon Climate | |
| **Aw** | Savanna Climate | All monthly temperatures above 18°C but with an annual variation in temperature of less than 12°C. |

The division of the three major A groups as far as rainfall
is concerned is illustrated by the graph below:-

**DRY CLIMATES** **B**

| | | |
|---|---|---|
| **BS** | Steppe Climate | The principal difference between this grouping and groups A, C, D and E is the combination of a wide range of temperatures with low rainfall. |
| **BW** | Desert Climate | |

The differing criteria for separating the Steppe and
Desert climates are shown by the graph below:-

**WARM TEMPERATE RAINY
CLIMATES** **C**
This climatic group is separated f
of the coldest month below 18°C
the warmest month is over 10°C

| | |
|---|---|
| **Cw** | Dry Winter Climat |
| **Cs** | Dry Summer Clima (Mediterranean) |
| **Cf** | Climate with no Dry Season |

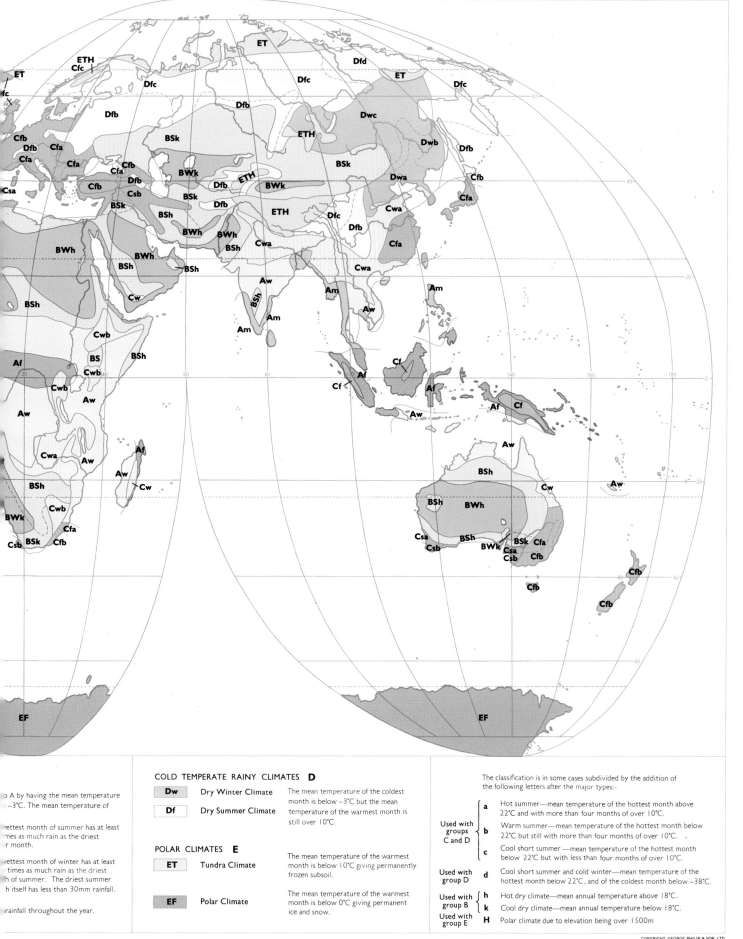

ET
ETH
Cfc
fc

Dfc
Dfb
Dfc
Dfd
ET
Dfc
Dfb
Dfb
Dwc
ETH
Dwb
Dfb
Cfb

Cfb
Dfb
Cfa
Cfa
Cfa
Cfb
BSk
BWk
Dwa
Cfa
Csa
Cfb
Csa
ETH
BWk
Dfb
Cfa
BSk
Dfb
Cwa
Csa
BSk
BSh
ETH
Cfa
BSb
BSh
BWh
BWh
BWh
Cwa
BSh
BWh
BSh
BWh
BSh
Cwa
BSh
Cw
Aw
Am
Am
BWh
BSh
Aw
Aw
Cwb
Af
BS
BSh
Am
Af
Cf
Cwb
Cf
Cf
Aw
Cwb
Af
Af
Aw
Aw
Af
Af
Cf
Aw
Cwa
Aw
Af
Aw
Aw
Aw
Cw
BSh
BSh
BSh
Cw
Aw
Cwb
BWk
Cfa
BWh
Csa
Csb
Cfb
BSh
BSk
Cfa
Csa
BWk
Cfb
BSk
Cfb
Csb
BSk
Cfb
Cfb
EF
EF

## COLD TEMPERATE RAINY CLIMATES  D

| Dw | Dry Winter Climate | The mean temperature of the coldest month is below −3°C but the mean temperature of the warmest month is still over 10°C. |
| Df | Dry Summer Climate | |

## POLAR CLIMATES  E

| ET | Tundra Climate | The mean temperature of the warmest month is below 10°C giving permanently frozen subsoil. |
| EF | Polar Climate | The mean temperature of the warmest month is below 0°C giving permanent ice and snow. |

The classification is in some cases subdivided by the addition of the following letters after the major types:-

Used with groups C and D
- **a** Hot summer—mean temperature of the hottest month above 22°C and with more than four months of over 10°C.
- **b** Warm summer—mean temperature of the hottest month below 22°C but still with more than four months of over 10°C. .
- **c** Cool short summer —mean temperature of the hottest month below 22°C but with less than four months of over 10°C.

Used with group D
- **d** Cool short summer and cold winter—mean temperature of the hottest month below 22°C, and of the coldest month below −38°C.

Used with group B
- **h** Hot dry climate—mean annual temperature above 18°C.
- **k** Cool dry climate—mean annual temperature below 18°C.

Used with group E
- **H** Polar climate due to elevation being over 1500m

o A by having the mean temperature
−3°C. The mean temperature of

ettest month of summer has at least
mes as much rain as the driest
r month.

ettest month of winter has at least
times as much rain as the driest
h of summer. The driest summer
h itself has less than 30mm rainfall.

rainfall throughout the year.

1:190 000 000

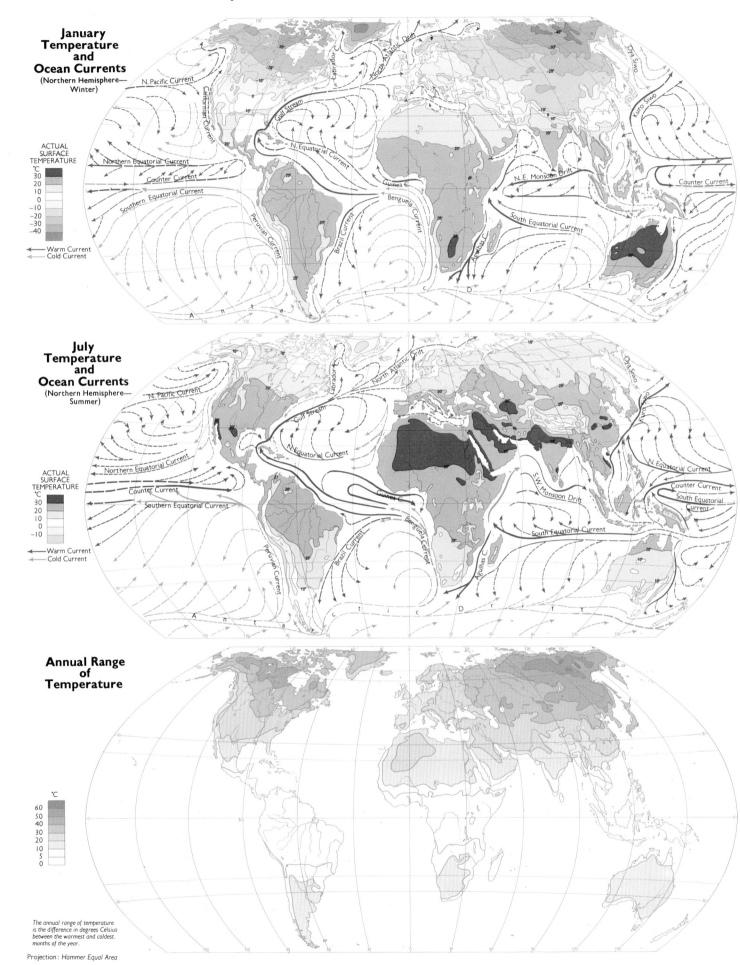

**January
Temperature
and
Ocean Currents**
(Northern Hemisphere—
Winter)

ACTUAL
SURFACE
TEMPERATURE
°C
30
20
10
0
-10
-20
-30
-40

→ Warm Current
→ Cold Current

N. Pacific Current
Californian Current
Northern Equatorial Current
Counter Current
Southern Equatorial Current
Peruvian Current
Gulf Stream
N. Equatorial Current
Guinea C.
Benguela Current
Brazil Current
Labrador C.
North Atlantic Drift
Agulhas C.
N.E. Monsoon Drift
South Equatorial Current
Counter Current
Oya Siwo
Kuro Siwo
A    n    t    a    r    c    t    i    c    D    r    i    f    t

**July
Temperature
and
Ocean Currents**
(Northern Hemisphere—
Summer)

ACTUAL
SURFACE
TEMPERATURE
°C
30
20
10
0
-10

→ Warm Current
→ Cold Current

N. Pacific Current
Northern Equatorial Current
Counter Current
Southern Equatorial Current
Peruvian Current
Gulf Stream
N. Equatorial Current
Guinea C.
Benguela Current
Brazil Current
Labrador C.
North Atlantic Drift
Agulhas C.
S.W. Monsoon Drift
South Equatorial Current
Counter Current
South Equatorial Current
N. Equatorial Current
Oya Siwo
Kuro Siwo
A    n    t    a    r    c    t    i    c    D    r    i    f    t

**Annual Range
of
Temperature**

°C
60
50
40
30
20
10
5
0

The annual range of temperature
is the difference in degrees Celsius
between the warmest and coldest
months of the year.

Projection: Hammer Equal Area

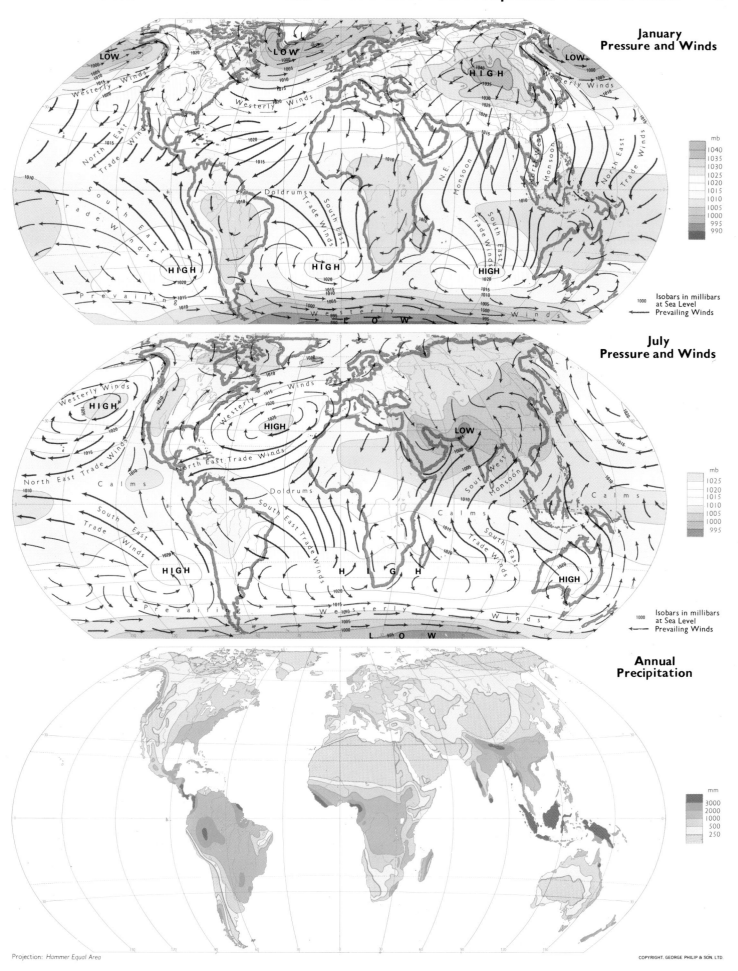

January
Pressure and Winds

July
Pressure and Winds

Annual
Precipitation

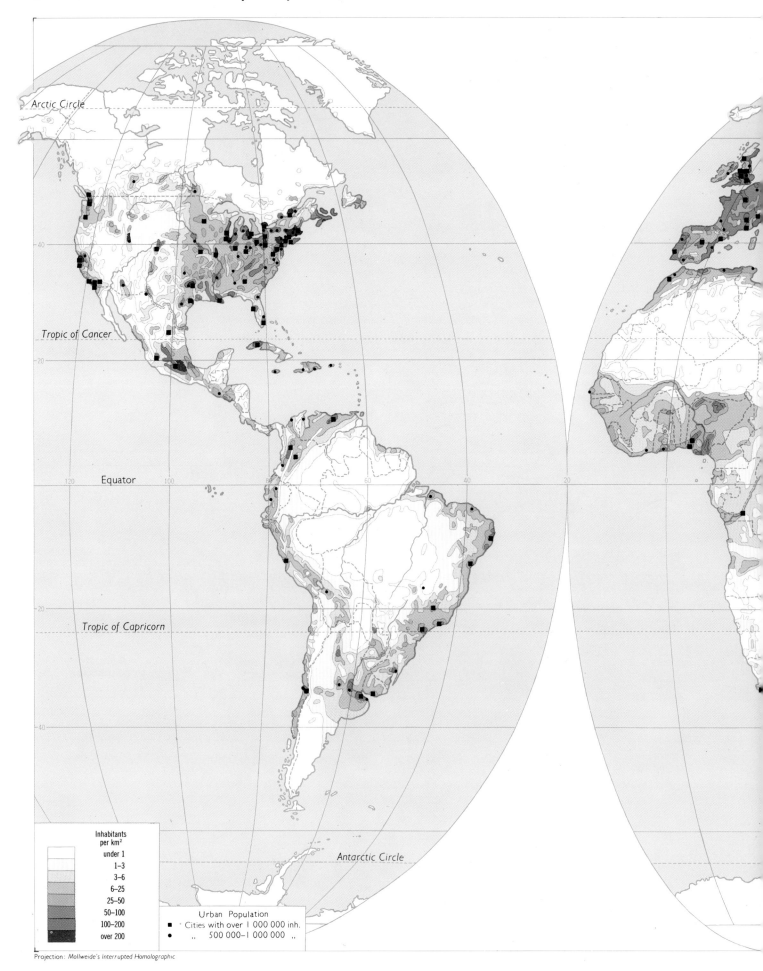

Arctic Circle

Tropic of Cancer

Equator

Tropic of Capricorn

Antarctic Circle

| Inhabitants per km² |
|---|
| under 1 |
| 1–3 |
| 3–6 |
| 6–25 |
| 25–50 |
| 50–100 |
| 100–200 |
| over 200 |

Urban Population
■    Cities with over 1 000 000 inh.
●    „    500 000– 1 000 000   „

Projection: Mollweide's interrupted Homolographic

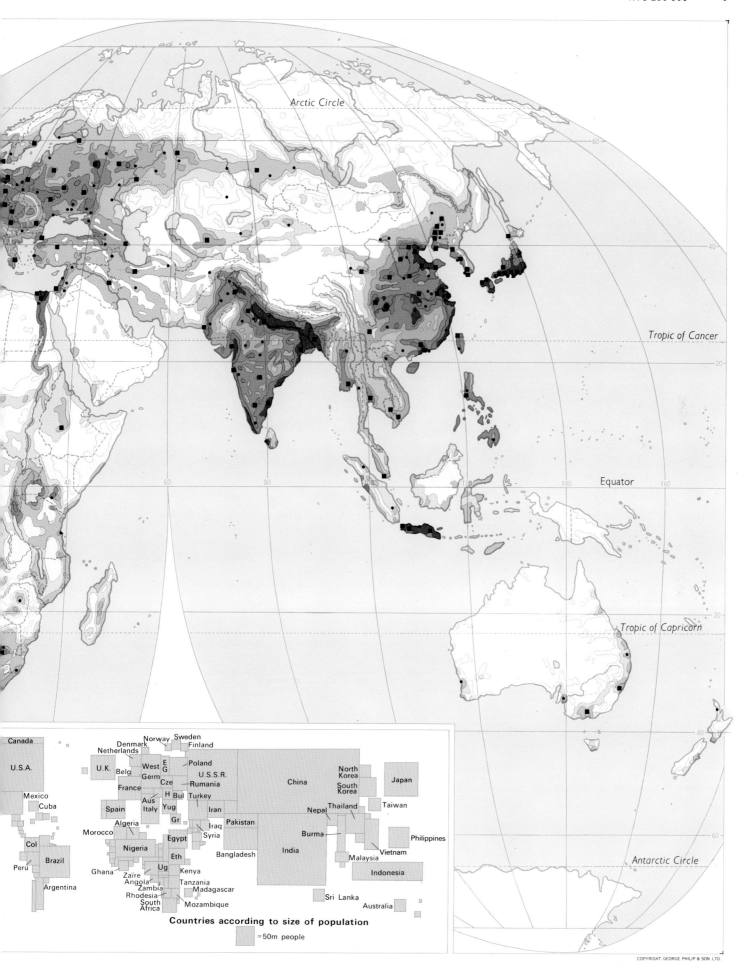

1:73 200 000

**9**

Arctic Circle

Tropic of Cancer

Equator

Tropic of Capricorn

Antarctic Circle

Canada

U.S.A.

Mexico

Cuba

Col

Peru

Brazil

Argentina

Norway  Sweden

Denmark  Finland

Netherlands

Poland

U.K.  West  E
         Germ  G
Belg         Cze

France  H Bul
U.S.S.R.
Rumania

Spain  Aus  Yug
       Italy

Morocco  Algeria  Gr

Nigeria  Egypt  Iraq
              Syria

Ghana  Zaïre  Ug  Kenya
Angola
Zambia  Tanzania  Madagascar
Rhodesia
South  Mozambique
Africa

Turkey

Iran

Pakistan

Nepal  Thailand

Burma

Bangladesh  India

Eth

China

North
Korea

South
Korea

Japan

Taiwan

Philippines

Vietnam

Malaysia

Indonesia

Sri Lanka

Australia

**Countries according to size of population**

▢ =50m people

COPYRIGHT GEORGE PHILIP & SON. LTD.

Projection: Hammer Equal Area

ARCTIC REGIONS

EUREKA
TEMPERATURE
Range 51.7°C
°C
10
0
-10
-20
-30
-40
Eureka
80°00N
85°56W

PRESSURE
M.S.L.
mb
1025
1020
1015
1010
1005
1000

ANNUAL
PRECIPITATION
Total 58.2mm.
mm
50

J F M A M J J A S O N D

m
4000
3000
2000
1000
400
200
0

Arctic Explorers
Cook 1778
Franklin 1826–47
McClure 1850–53
Nordenskiöld ("Vega") 1878–79
De Long 1881
Nansen ("Fram") 1893–96
Abruzzi & Cagni 1899–1900
Sverdrup 1902
Peary 1892–1906
Amundsen 1903–6 & 1926
Peary 1908–9
Knud Rasmussen 1912
Koch 1913
Stefánsson 1914–15
Byrd 1926 (by air)
Wilkins 1928 (by air)
Lindsay 1934
Papanin (Drift of Soviet
  Expedition) 1937–38
"Sedov" 1937–40
Knuth (Danish Pearyland
  Expedition) 1948–49

Projection: Zenithal Equidistant

Seas open all year
Extreme limits of
drift-ice
Seas covered by
pack-ice in Spring
Seas permanently
covered by pack-ice
Ice-caps and
permanent ice shelf

Progress of Exploration
Coasts explored before    1800
     "      "      between 1800 & 1850
     "      "      between 1850 & 1900
     "      "      since   1900
+ Byrd   Highest latitudes reached by explorers
  1926   with date

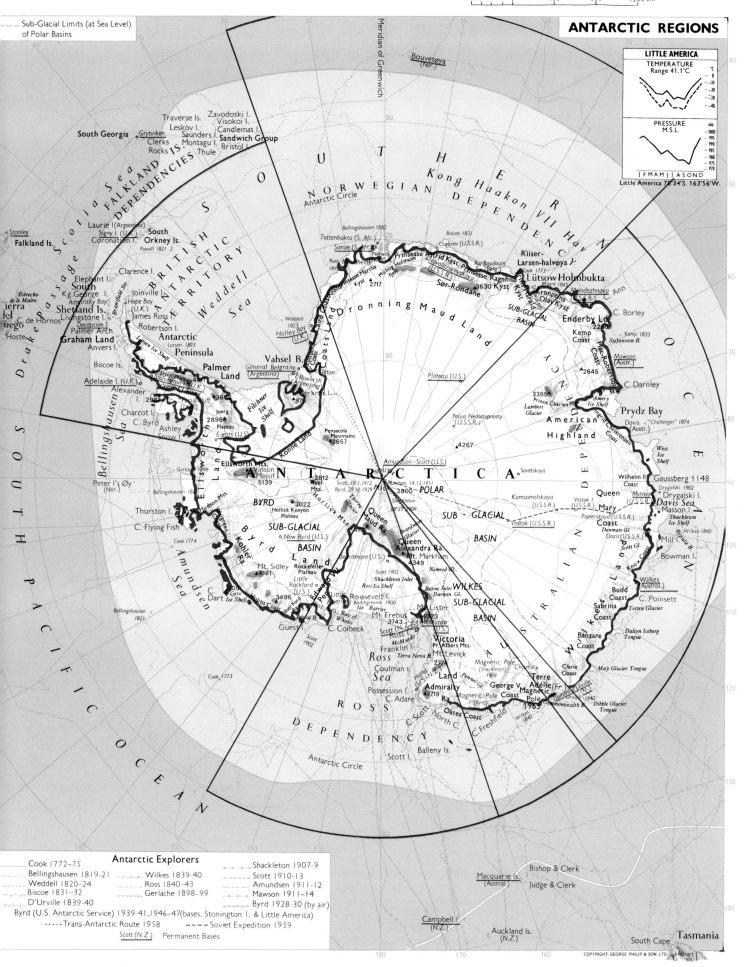

1 : 35 000 000

400    0    400    800    1200 km

ANTARCTIC REGIONS

LITTLE AMERICA
TEMPERATURE
Range 41.1°C
°C
0
–10
–20
–30
–40

PRESSURE
M.S.L.
mb
1000
995
990
985
980
975
970
J F M A M J J A S O N D
Little America 78°34'S. 163°56'W.

Sub-Glacial Limits (at Sea Level)
of Polar Basins

Bouvetøya
(Nor.)

SOUTHERN

S    O    U    T    H    E    R    N

Kong Haakon VII Hav

NORWEGIAN DEPENDENCY

Antarctic Circle

Traverse Is.    Zavodoski I.
Leskov I.    Visokoi I.
Candlemas I.
South Georgia    Grytviken    Saunders I.    Sandwich Group
Clerks    Montagu I.
Rocks    Is    Thule    Bristol I.

Scotia    Sea    FALKLAND

Falkland Is.    Laurie I.(Argentina)
Signy I. (U.K.)    South
Coronation I.    Orkney Is.
Powell 1821 2

Stanley

Clarence I.

Elephant I.
South
Kg.George I.
Shetland Is.    Joinville
Livingstone I.    Hope Bay
Deception I.    (U.K.)
Palmer Arch.    James Ross I.
Graham Land    Robertson I.
Anvers I.    Antarctic
Peninsula
Biscoe Is.    Palmer
Adelaide I. (U.K.)    Land
Alexander    General Belgrano
I.    (Argentina)
Charcot I.    Ellsworth
C. Byrd    (Argentina)
Ashley    Berkner I.
Snow I.

Weddell
Sea

Vahsel B.

Filchner
Ice
Shelf

Ronne Land

Pensacola
Mountains

Dronning    Maud    Land

Plateau (U.S.)

SUB-GLACIAL
BASIN

Sør-Rondane

Prinsesse Astrid Kyst
Prinsesse Ragnhild
Kyst

Enderby Ld

Kemp
Coast

Mawson
(Austr.)

C. Borley

C. Darnley

Prydz Bay

Davis    "Challenger" 1874
(Austr.)

American
Highland

West
Ice
Shelf

ANTARCTICA

POLAR

SUB-GLACIAL

BASIN

Sovetskaya

Komsomolskaya
(U.S.S.R.)

Vostok 1
(U.S.S.R.)

Vostok (U.S.S.R.)

Wilhelm II
Coast

Queen
Mary
Coast

Gaussberg 1148

Drygalski 1902

Davis Sea
Masson I.
Shackleton
Ice Shelf

Bowman I.

Amundsen-Scott (U.S.)

2800

Queen    Maud    Ra.

Byrd
Land

SUB-GLACIAL
BASIN

New Byrd (U.S.)

Mt. Sidley
Rockefeller
Plateau    Little
Rockford
(U.S.)

Queen
Alexandra Ra.    Mt. Markham

Shackleton Inlet

Ross Ice Shelf

WILKES

SUB-GLACIAL

BASIN

Budd
Coast

Sabrina
Coast

C. Poinsett

Totten Glacier

Banzare
Coast

Dalton Iceberg
Tongue

Little
America    Roosevelt I.

Bay of
Whales

C. Colbeck

Ross
Sea

Coulman I.

Possession I.
C. Adare

M. Lister

Mt. Erebus
McMurdo
Ross I.

Franklin I.
Terra Nova B.

Victoria
Pr. Albert Mts.

Mt. Levick

Land

Admiralty
Ra.

Oates Coast

George V    Coast

Magnetic Pole
1909

Magnetic
Pole
1965

Terre
Adélie (Fr.)

Clarie
Coast

May Glacier Tongue

Dibble Glacier
Tongue

ROSS
DEPENDENCY

Antarctic Circle

Scott I.

Balleny Is.

SOUTH    PACIFIC    OCEAN

Drake    Passage

Amundsen
Sea

Bellingshausen
Sea

Thurston I.

C. Flying Fish

Peter I's Øy
(Nor.)

Macquarie Is.
(Austral.)

Campbell I.
(N.Z.)

Auckland Is.
(N.Z.)

Bishop & Clerk

Judge & Clerk

South Cape    Tasmania

Antarctic Explorers

Cook 1772–75
Bellingshausen 1819–21
Weddell 1820–24
Biscoe 1831–32
D'Urville 1839–40
Byrd (U.S. Antarctic Service) 1939–41,1946–47(bases, Stonington I. & Little America)
Trans-Antarctic Route 1958

Wilkes 1839–40
Ross 1840–43
Gerlache 1898–99

Shackleton 1907–9
Scott 1910–13
Amundsen 1911–12
Mawson 1911–14
Byrd 1928–30 (by air)

Soviet Expedition 1959

Scott (N.Z.)    Permanent Bases

COPYRIGHT. GEORGE PHILIP & SON LTD

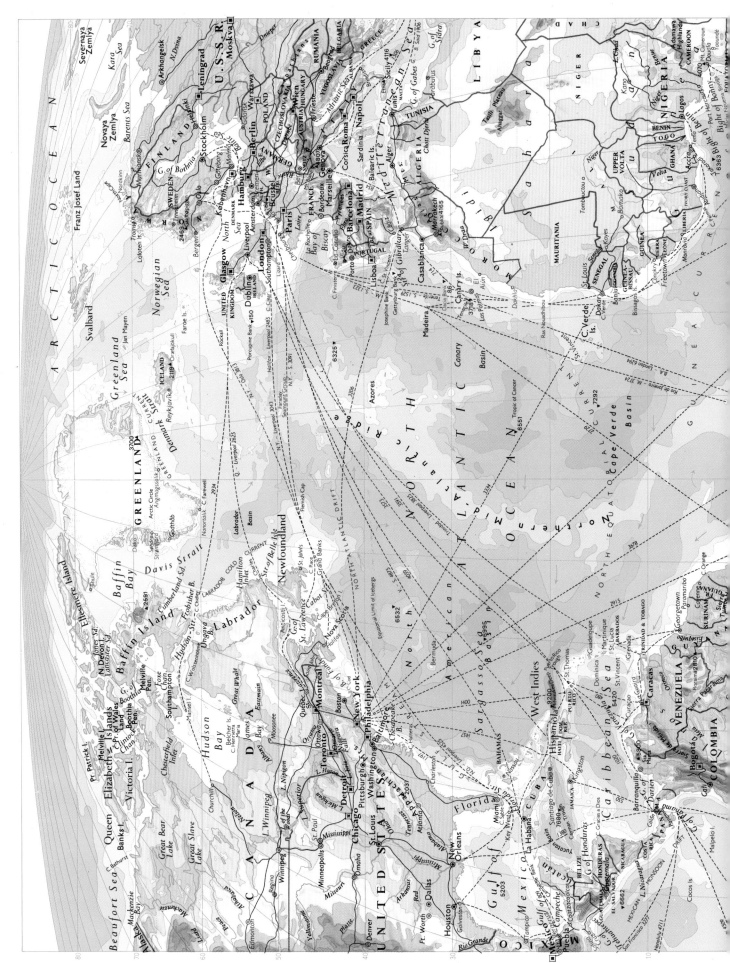

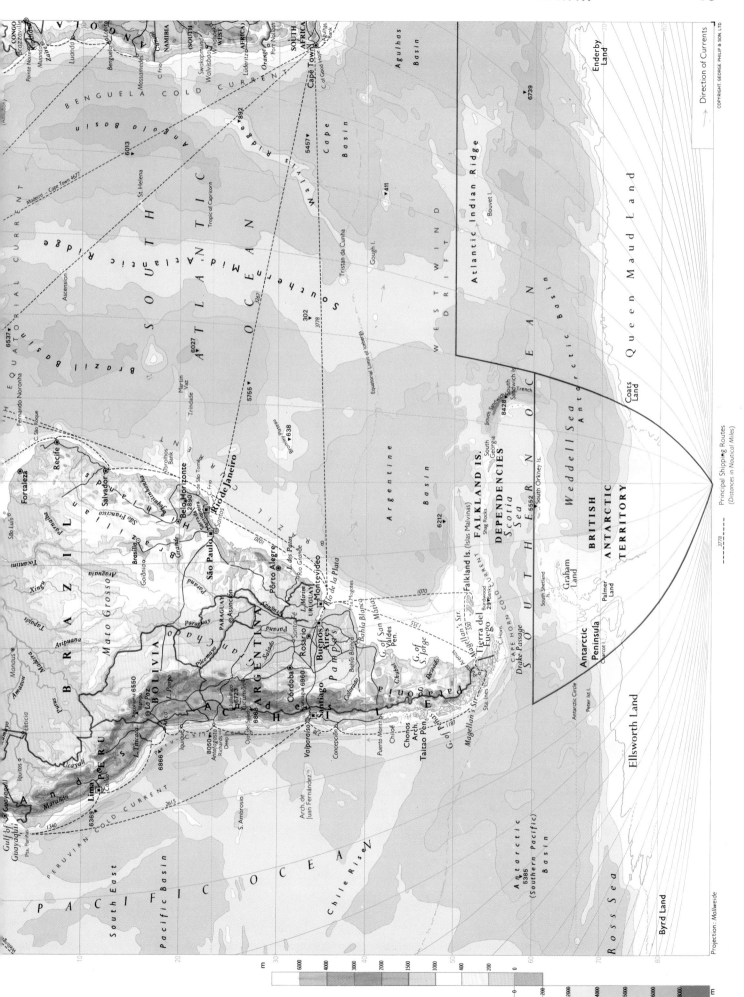

Direction of Currents

COPYRIGHT GEORGE PHILIP & SON LTD

Principal Shipping Routes
(Distances in Nautical Miles)

3778

Projection: Mollweide

1:20 000 000

200    0    200    400    600    800 km

Projection: Bonne    West from Greenwich   0   East from Greenwich

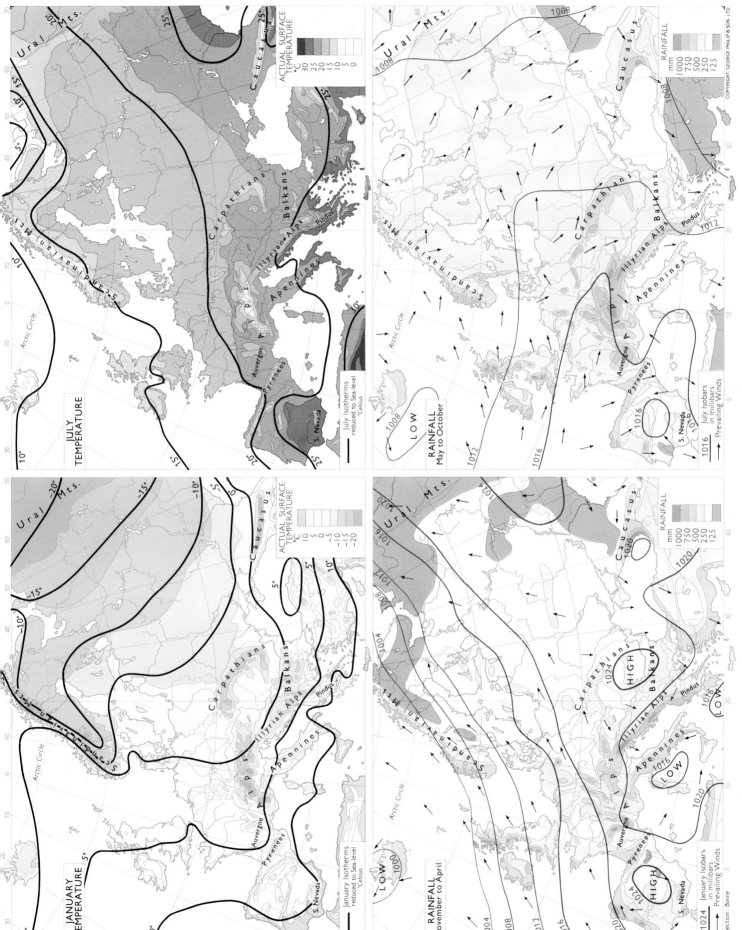

1 : 40 000 000

400   0   400   800   1200   1600 km

ACTUAL SURFACE
TEMPERATURE
°C
30
25
20
15
5
0

JULY
TEMPERATURE

July Isotherms
reduced to Sea-level
°Celsius

RAINFALL
mm
1000
750
500
250
125

LOW

RAINFALL
May to October

July Isobars
in millibars
Prevailing Winds

COPYRIGHT GEORGE PHILIP & SON LTD.

ACTUAL SURFACE
TEMPERATURE
°C
10
5
0
-5
-10
-15
-20

JANUARY
TEMPERATURE

January Isotherms
reduced to Sea-level
°Celsius

RAINFALL
mm
1000
750
500
250
125

HIGH

LOW

LOW

HIGH

RAINFALL
November to April

January Isobars
in millibars
Prevailing Winds

Projection: Bonne

HHK

1 : 35 000 000

400    0    400    800    1200 km

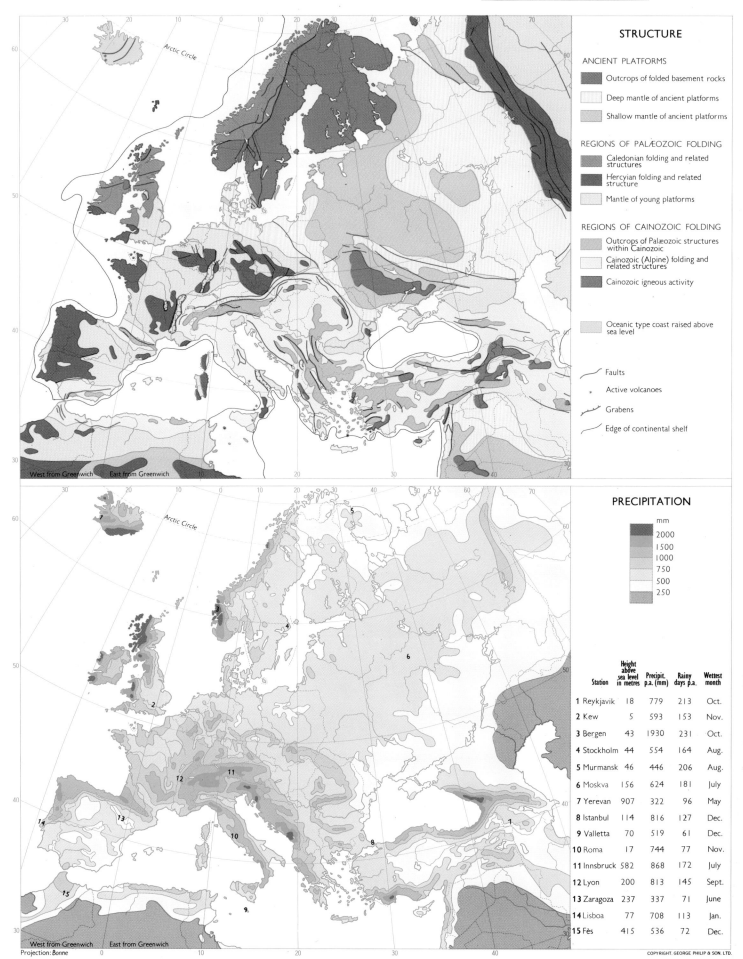

## STRUCTURE

ANCIENT PLATFORMS

- Outcrops of folded basement rocks
- Deep mantle of ancient platforms
- Shallow mantle of ancient platforms

REGIONS OF PALÆOZOIC FOLDING

- Caledonian folding and related structures
- Hercyian folding and related structure
- Mantle of young platforms

REGIONS OF CAINOZOIC FOLDING

- Outcrops of Palæozoic structures within Cainozoic
- Cainozoic (Alpine) folding and related structures
- Cainozoic igneous activity

- Oceanic type coast raised above sea level

- Faults
- Active volcanoes
- Grabens
- Edge of continental shelf

## PRECIPITATION

mm
2000
1500
1000
750
500
250

| Station | Height above sea level in metres | Precipit. p.a. (mm) | Rainy days p.a. | Wettest month |
|---|---|---|---|---|
| 1 Reykjavik | 18 | 779 | 213 | Oct. |
| 2 Kew | 5 | 593 | 153 | Nov. |
| 3 Bergen | 43 | 1930 | 231 | Oct. |
| 4 Stockholm | 44 | 554 | 164 | Aug. |
| 5 Murmansk | 46 | 446 | 206 | Aug. |
| 6 Moskva | 156 | 624 | 181 | July |
| 7 Yerevan | 907 | 322 | 96 | May |
| 8 Istanbul | 114 | 816 | 127 | Dec. |
| 9 Valletta | 70 | 519 | 61 | Dec. |
| 10 Roma | 17 | 744 | 77 | Nov. |
| 11 Innsbruck | 582 | 868 | 172 | July |
| 12 Lyon | 200 | 813 | 145 | Sept. |
| 13 Zaragoza | 237 | 337 | 71 | June |
| 14 Lisboa | 77 | 708 | 113 | Jan. |
| 15 Fès | 415 | 536 | 72 | Dec. |

Projection: Bonne

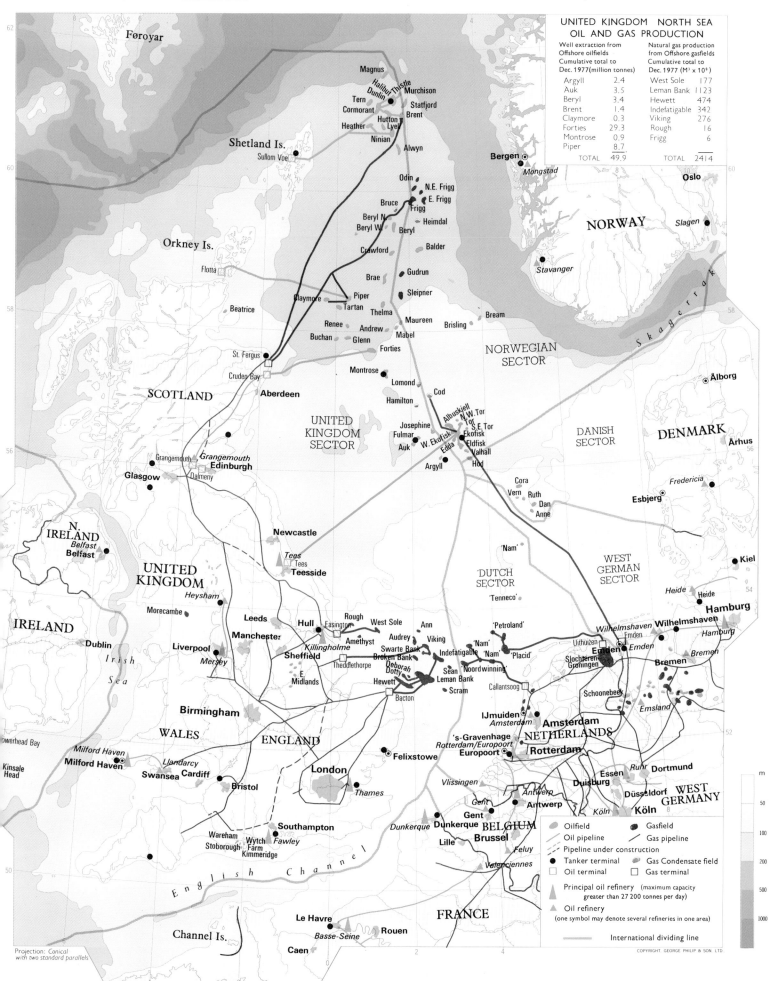

1 : 6 000 000

| UNITED KINGDOM NORTH SEA OIL AND GAS PRODUCTION | | | |
|---|---|---|---|
| Well extraction from Offshore oilfields Cumulative total to Dec. 1977(million tonnes) | | Natural gas production from Offshore gasfields Cumulative total to Dec. 1977 (M³ x 10⁸) | |
| Argyll | 2.4 | West Sole | 177 |
| Auk | 3.5 | Leman Bank | 1123 |
| Beryl | 3.4 | Hewett | 474 |
| Brent | 1.4 | Indefatigable | 342 |
| Claymore | 0.3 | Viking | 276 |
| Forties | 29.3 | Rough | 16 |
| Montrose | 0.9 | Frigg | 6 |
| Piper | 8.7 | | |
| TOTAL | 49.9 | TOTAL | 2414 |

Legend:

- Oilfield
- Gasfield
- Oil pipeline
- Gas pipeline
- Pipeline under construction
- Tanker terminal
- Gas Condensate field
- Oil terminal
- Gas terminal
- Principal oil refinery (maximum capacity greater than 27 200 tonnes per day)
- Oil refinery (one symbol may denote several refineries in one area)
- International dividing line

Projection: Conical with two standard parallels

COPYRIGHT GEORGE PHILIP & SON. LTD.

m
50
100
200
500
1000

# EUROPE : Density of Population

1: 20 000 000

200 0 200 400 600 800 km

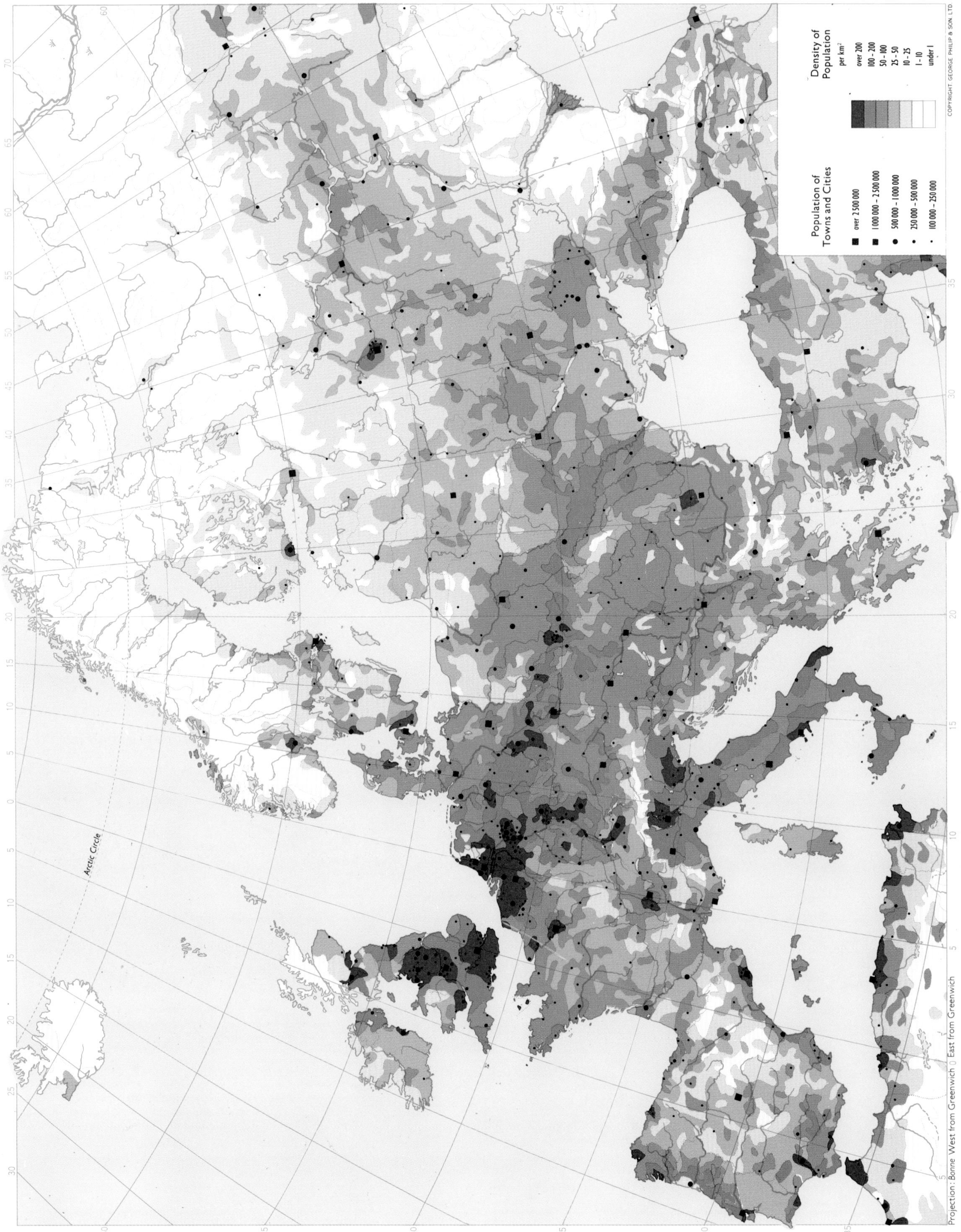
Density of Population
per km²
over 200
100 - 200
50 - 100
25 - 50
10 - 25
1 - 10
under 1
Population of Towns and Cities
over 2 500 000
1 000 000 - 2 500 000
500 000 - 1 000 000
250 000 - 500 000
100 000 - 250 000
Arctic Circle
Projection: Bonne West from Greenwich 0 East from Greenwich

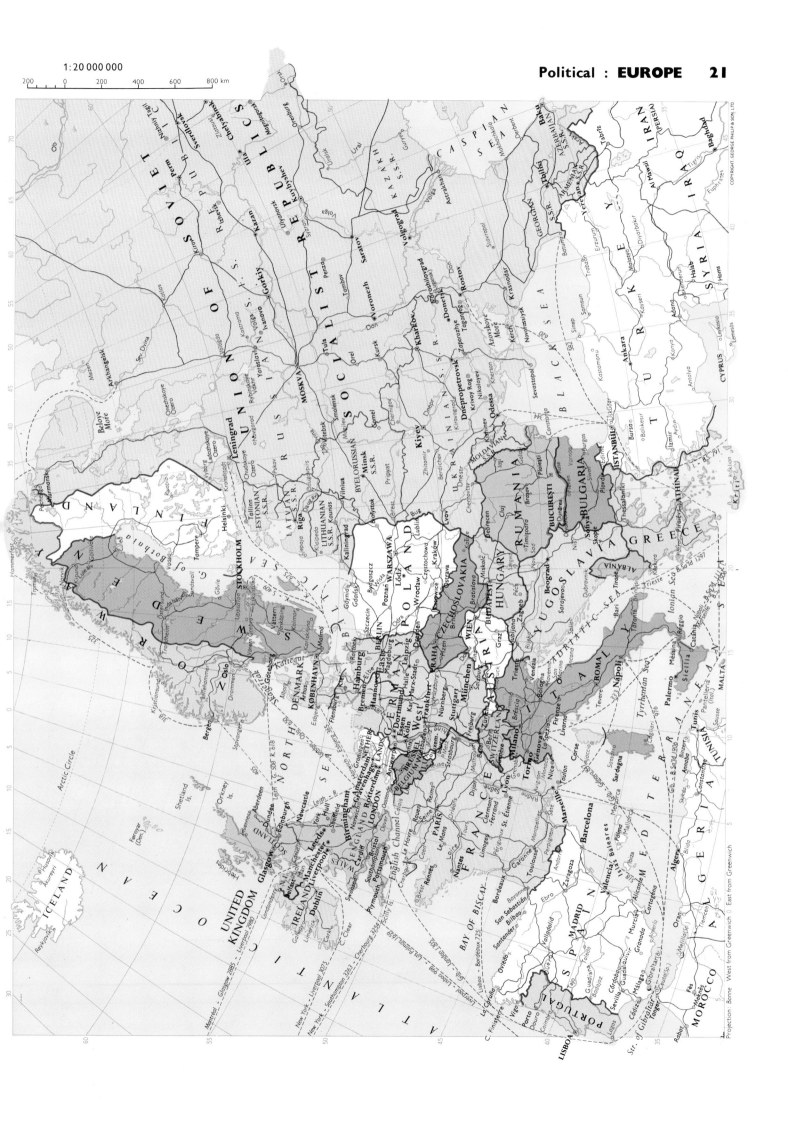

1:20 000 000

1 : 4 000 000

50    0    50    100    150 km

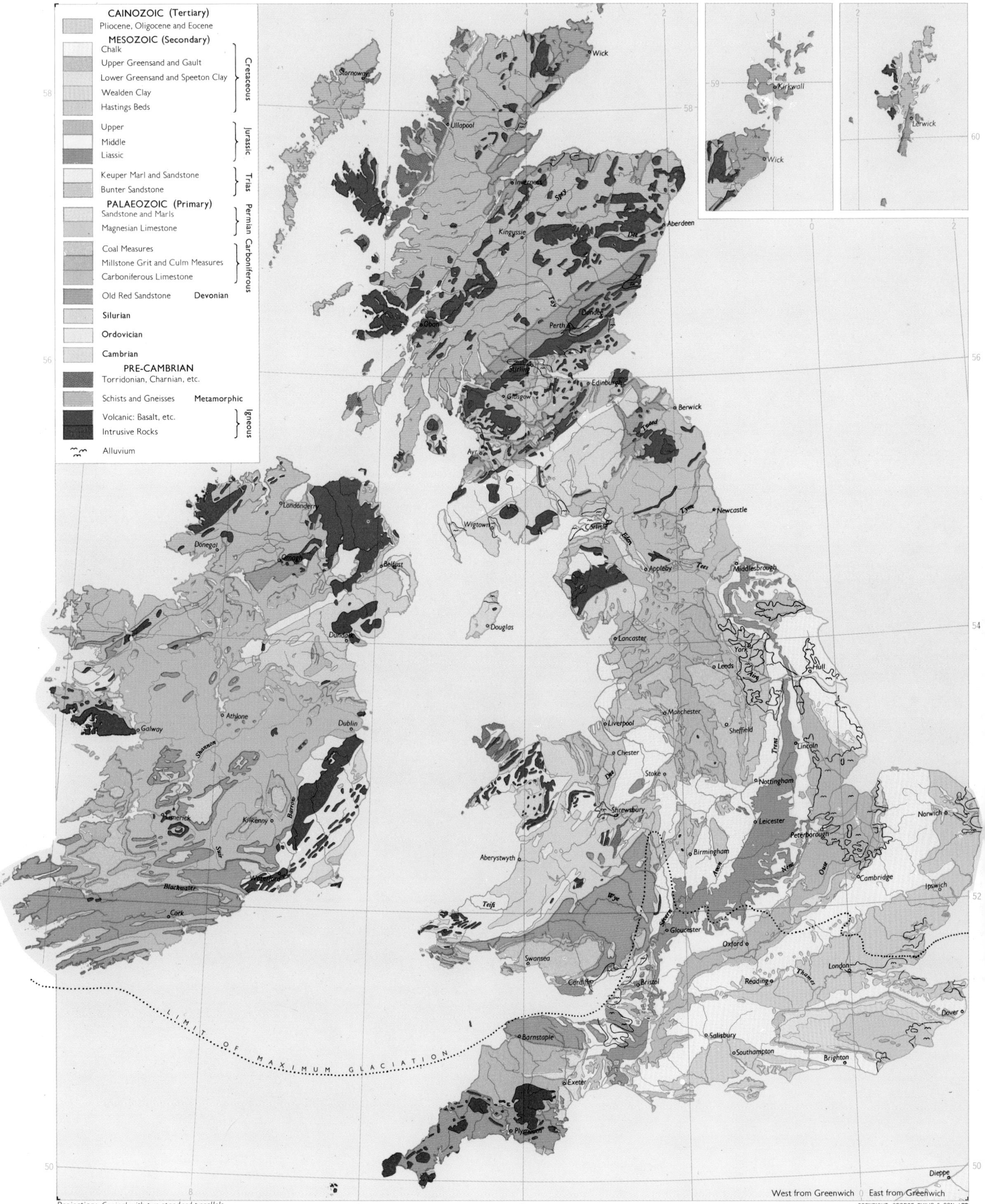

## Legend

**CAINOZOIC (Tertiary)**
Pliocene, Oligocene and Eocene

**MESOZOIC (Secondary)**
Chalk
Upper Greensand and Gault
Lower Greensand and Speeton Clay
Wealden Clay
Hastings Beds
— Cretaceous

Upper
Middle
Liassic
— Jurassic

Keuper Marl and Sandstone
Bunter Sandstone
— Trias

**PALAEOZOIC (Primary)**
Sandstone and Marls
Magnesian Limestone
— Permian

Coal Measures
Millstone Grit and Culm Measures
Carboniferous Limestone
— Carboniferous

Old Red Sandstone    Devonian

Silurian

Ordovician

Cambrian

**PRE-CAMBRIAN**
Torridonian, Charnian, etc.

Schists and Gneisses    Metamorphic

Volcanic: Basalt, etc.
Intrusive Rocks
— Igneous

Alluvium

LIMIT OF MAXIMUM GLACIATION

West from Greenwich | East from Greenwich

Projection: *Conical with two standard parallels*

COPYRIGHT. GEORGE PHILIP & SON. LTD.

Place names: Stornoway, Wick, Kirkwall, Lerwick, Ullapool, Inverness, Stary, Kingussie, Aberdeen, Oban, Dee, Tay, Dundee, Perth, Stirling, Edinburgh, Glasgow, Ayr, Berwick, Tweed, Carlisle, Eden, Newcastle, Tyne, Appleby, Teers, Middlesbrough, Londonderry, Wigtown, Donegal, Omagh, Belfast, Douglas, Lancaster, York, Ouse, Hull, Leeds, Dundalk, Athlone, Dublin, Liverpool, Manchester, Sheffield, Chester, Stoke, Lincoln, Galway, Shannon, Trent, Nottingham, Limerick, Kilkenny, Barrow, Leicester, Peterborough, Norwich, Shrewsbury, Birmingham, Dee, Cork, Blackwater, Suir, Aberystwyth, Teifi, Cambridge, Ipswich, Gloucester, Wye, Oxford, Nene, Ouse, Swansea, Cardiff, Bristol, Reading, Thames, London, Barnstaple, Salisbury, Southampton, Brighton, Dover, Exeter, Plymouth, Dieppe

1 : 4 000 000

50      0       50        100        150 km

Projection: Conical with two standard parallels

COPYRIGHT. GEORGE. PHILIP & SON. LTD.

West from Greenwich  0  East from Greenwich

m
1000
400
200
100
0
50
100
200
m

1:4 000 000

50   0   50   100   150 km

ANNUAL PRECIPITATION
AND
ISOBARS

ANNUAL PRECIPITATION

mm

2500
2000
1500
1250
1000
750
625
500

ANNUAL ISOBARS

1011 mb   (in Millibars)

WIND ROSES

Frequency of wind
from each direction
is indicated by the
length of each arrow

Based partly on information supplied by the Meteorological Office
and on the Climatological Atlas of the British Isles.

Projection: Conical with two standard parallels

West from Greenwich   East from Greenwich

COPYRIGHT. GEORGE PHILIP & SON. LTD.

1:8 500 000

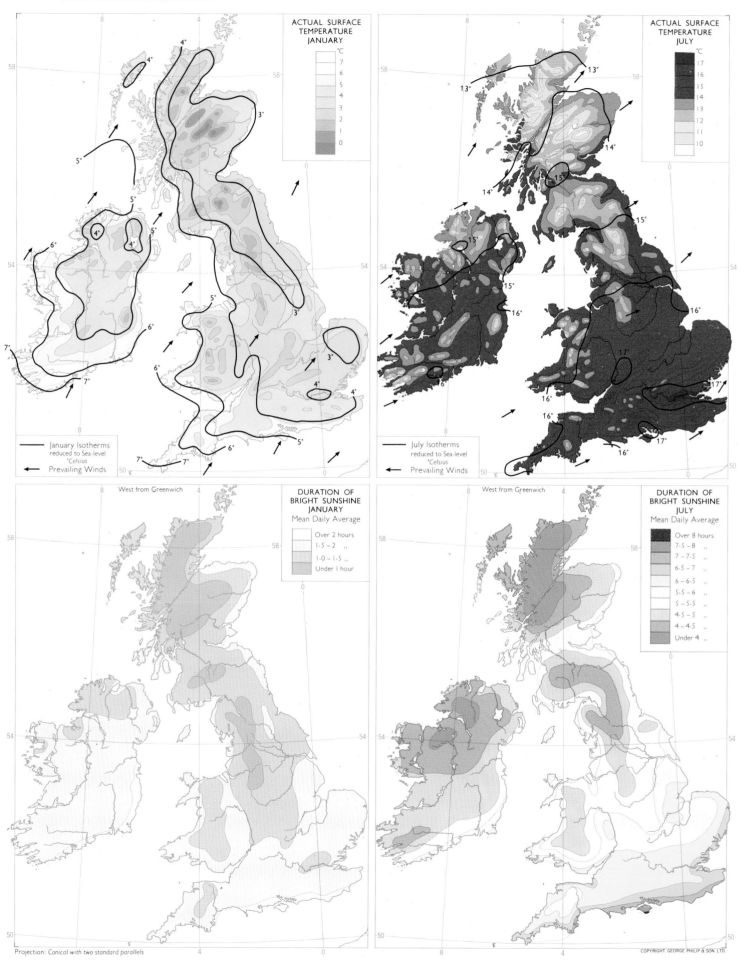

ACTUAL SURFACE
TEMPERATURE
JANUARY
°C
7
6
5
4
3
2
1
0

January Isotherms
reduced to Sea-level
°Celsius
Prevailing Winds

ACTUAL SURFACE
TEMPERATURE
JULY
°C
17
16
15
14
13
12
11
10

July Isotherms
reduced to Sea-level
°Celsius
Prevailing Winds

West from Greenwich

DURATION OF
BRIGHT SUNSHINE
JANUARY
Mean Daily Average

Over 2 hours
1·5 – 2 ,,
1·0 – 1·5 ,,
Under 1 hour

West from Greenwich

DURATION OF
BRIGHT SUNSHINE
JULY
Mean Daily Average

Over 8 hours
7·5 – 8 ,,
7 – 7·5 ,,
6·5 – 7 ,,
6 – 6·5 ,,
5·5 – 6 ,,
5 – 5·5 ,,
4·5 – 5 ,,
4 – 4·5 ,,
Under 4 ,,

Projection: Conical with two standard parallels

COPYRIGHT. GEORGE PHILIP & SON. LTD.

1 : 4 000 000

50   0   50   100   150 km

ATLANTIC OCEAN

NORTH SEA

IRISH SEA

St. George's Channel

ENGLISH CHANNEL

Bristol Channel

Cardigan Bay

**SCOTLAND**

CAITHNESS
SUTHERLAND
ROSS AND CROMARTY
INVERNESS
MORAY
NAIRN
BANFF
ABERDEEN
KINCARDINE
ANGUS
PERTH
ARGYLL
FIFE
STIRLING
CL.—Clackmannan
KIN.—Kinross
W. Loth.—West Lothian
MIDLOTHIAN
E. LOTHIAN
BERWICK
ROXBURGH
SELKIRK
PEEBLES
LANARK
RENFREW
BUTE
AYR
DUMFRIES
KIRKCUDBRIGHT
WIGTOWN

Outer Hebrides
Inner Hebrides
Lewis
Harris
North Uist
Benbecula
South Uist
Barra
Skye
Rhum
Eigg
Coll
Tiree
Mull
Islay
Jura
Arran
Kintyre

Stornoway
Thurso
Wick
Golspie
Lairg
Ullapool
Dingwall
Inverness
Fort William
Elgin
Banff
Fraserburgh
Peterhead
Aberdeen
Stonehaven
Montrose
Arbroath
Forfar
Dundee
Perth
St. Andrews
Stirling
Dunfermline
Kirkcaldy
Falkirk
Edinburgh
Glasgow
Paisley
Greenock
Helensburgh
Kilmarnock
Ayr
Prestwick
Saltcoats
Irvine
Dumfries
Stranraer
Kirkcudbright
Wigtown
Carlisle
Newcastle
Berwick-on-Tweed
Alnwick
Galashiels
Hawick
Jedburgh
Moffat
Sanquhar
Peebles
Motherwell
Hamilton
Dumbarton

Orkney Is.
ORKNEY
Westray
N. Ronaldsay
Sanday
Stronsay
Mainland
Kirkwall
Hoy
South Ronaldsay
Thurso
Wick
CAITHNESS

Shetland Is.
ZETLAND
Unst
Yell
Mainland
Lerwick
Foula
Fair I.

NORTHERN IRELAND
ULSTER
LONDONDERRY
ANTRIM
TYRONE
FERMANAGH
ARMAGH
DOWN
DONEGAL
MONAGHAN
CAVAN
LEITRIM
SLIGO
MAYO
ROSCOMMON
CONNACHT
GALWAY
CLARE
LONGFORD
WESTMEATH
MEATH
OFFALY
LAOIS
KILDARE
DUBLIN
WICKLOW
CARLOW
KILKENNY
WEXFORD
TIPPERARY
LIMERICK
KERRY
CORK
WATERFORD
MUNSTER
LEINSTER
**IRELAND**

Belfast
Londonderry
Coleraine
Larne
Bangor
Lisburn
Armagh
Newry
Downpatrick
Dundalk
Drogheda
Dublin
Dún Laoghaire
Bray
Wicklow
Arklow
Wexford
Waterford
Cork
Limerick
Tralee
Killarney
Galway
Sligo

ENGLAND
WALES

NORTHUMBERLAND
DURHAM
CUMBERLAND
WESTMORLAND
NORTH RIDING
WEST RIDING
EAST RIDING
YORKSHIRE
LANCASHIRE
CHESHIRE
DERBY
NOTTS
LINCOLN
LINDSEY
KESTEVEN
HOLLAND
NORFOLK
SUFFOLK
STAFFORD
SHROPSHIRE
LEICESTER
RUTLAND
NORTHAMPTON
HUNTS
CAMBS
ISLE OF ELY
WARWICK
WORCESTER
HEREFORD
GLOUCESTER
OXFORD
BUCKS
BEDFORD
HERTFORD
ESSEX
MONMOUTH
WILTS
BERKS
SURREY
KENT
SUSSEX
HANTS
DORSET
SOMERSET
DEVON
CORNWALL
MIDDLESEX
LONDON

CAERNARVON
DENBIGH
FLINT
ANGLESEY
MERIONETH
MONTGOMERY
CARDIGAN
RADNOR
BRECKNOCK
PEMBROKE
CARMARTHEN
GLAMORGAN

ISLE OF MAN
Douglas
Barrow

Newcastle
Tynemouth
South Shields
Sunderland
Gateshead
Durham
Hartlepool
Stockton
TEESSIDE
Middlesbrough
Darlington
Whitby
Scarborough
Northallerton
Ripon
York
Beverley
Hull
Grimsby
Lincoln
Boston
Kings Lynn
Norwich
Gt. Yarmouth
Lowestoft
The Wash
Peterborough
Cambridge
Bury St. Edmunds
Ipswich
Colchester
Harwich
Chelmsford
St. Albans
Watford
Luton
Bedford
Northampton
Leicester
Oakham
Nottingham
Derby
Mansfield
Chesterfield
Sheffield
Rotherham
Barnsley
Doncaster
Scunthorpe
Wakefield
Leeds
Bradford
Halifax
Huddersfield
Keighley
Burnley
Blackburn
Bolton
Preston
Blackpool
Liverpool
Birkenhead
Manchester
Salford
Stockport
Oldham
Macclesfield
St. Helens
Warrington
Crewe
Stoke-on-Trent
Wrexham
Shrewsbury
Stafford
Wolverhampton
Walsall
Birmingham
Coventry
Rugby
Kidderminster
Worcester
Leamington
Stratford-upon-Avon
Hereford
Gloucester
Cheltenham
Oxford
Aylesbury
Buckingham
Swindon
Reading
Windsor
Slough
Kingston
LONDON
Gillingham
Margate
Canterbury
Chatham
Maidstone
Ashford
Dover
Folkestone
Hastings
Eastbourne
Brighton
Worthing
Newhaven
Lewes
Chichester
Portsmouth
Southampton
Isle of Wight
Newport
Bournemouth
Poole
Weymouth
Dorchester
Exeter
Torquay
Plymouth
Devonport
Truro
St. Austell
Camborne
Penzance
Falmouth
Land's End
Lizard
Start Pt.
Isles of Scilly
Lundy
Bude
Barnstaple
Ilfracombe
Bristol
Bath
Weston-super-Mare
Wells
Taunton
Yeovil
Salisbury
Winchester
Guildford
Aldershot
Reigate
Southend
Monmouth
Newport
Cardiff
Swansea
Llanelli
Merthyr Tydfil
Rhondda
Port Talbot
Brecon
Llandovery
Llandrindod Wells
Aberystwyth
Cardigan
Fishguard
Milford Haven
Haverfordwest
Pembroke
Llanidloes
Welshpool
Montgomery
Dolgelley
Barmouth
Denbigh
Rhyl
Caernarvon
Holyhead
Llandudno

Projection: Conical with two standard parallels

West from Greenwich    East from Greenwich

1:4 000 000

50    0    50    100    150 km

The DISTRICTS of Northern Ireland have been numbered and can be identified by reference to this table.

| | | | |
|---|---|---|---|
| 1 | Londonderry | 14 | Craigavon |
| 2 | Limavady | 15 | Armagh |
| 3 | Coleraine | 16 | Newry & Mourne |
| 4 | Ballymoney | 17 | Banbridge |
| 5 | Moyle | 18 | Down |
| 6 | Larne | 19 | Lisburn |
| 7 | Ballymena | 20 | Antrim |
| 8 | Magherafelt | 21 | Newtownabbey |
| 9 | Cookstown | 22 | Carrickfergus |
| 10 | Strabane | 23 | North Down |
| 11 | Omagh | 24 | Ards |
| 12 | Fermanagh | 25 | Castlereagh |
| 13 | Dungannon | 26 | Belfast |

1 Merseyside
2 Greater Manchester
3 West Yorkshire
4 South Yorkshire
5 West Glamorgan
6 Mid Glamorgan
7 South Glamorgan

Orkney Is.
Westray    N. Ronaldsay
ORKNEY    Sanday
Stronsay
Hoy    Kirkwall
South Ronaldsay
Thurso
HIGHLAND
Wick

Shetland Is.
Unst
Yell
Mainland    SHETLAND
Foula    Lerwick
Fair I.

ATLANTIC

OCEAN

WESTERN ISLES

Outer Hebrides

Inner Hebrides

SCOTLAND

HIGHLAND

GRAMPIAN

Thurso    Wick
Lairg    Golspie
Ullapool    Invergordon
Dingwall    Elgin    Lossiemouth
**Inverness**    Nairn    Banff    Fraserburgh
Moray Firth    Peterhead
Kingussie    Ballater    Balmoral    **Aberdeen**
Fort William    Stonehaven
Blair Atholl
Forfar    Montrose
TAYSIDE    Arbroath
Grieff    **Perth**    **Dundee**
St. Andrews
CENTRAL    FIFE
Stirling    Kirkcaldy
**Falkirk**    Dunfermline    Dunbar
Helensburgh    **Edinburgh**
Greenock    Dumbarton    LOTHIAN    Berwick-on-Tweed
Paisley    **Glasgow**    Leith
STRATHCLYDE    Hamilton Motherwell    Galashiels
Kilmarnock    Peebles
BORDERS    Alnwick
Ayr    Hawick
Jedburgh    NORTHUMBERLAND
DUMFRIES
AND    Dumfries    **Newcastle**
GALLOWAY    South Shields
Wigtown    Carlisle    Gateshead    TYNE & WEAR    **Sunderland**
Kirkcudbright    Durham
Solway Firth    DURHAM    Hartlepool
CUMBRIA    Stockton    CLEVELAND
Whitehaven    Appleby    Darlington    Middlesbrough    Whitby
St. Bee's Hd.    Kendal    Northallerton    Scarborough
ISLE OF MAN
Douglas    NORTH    Flamborough Hd.
Barrow    YORKSHIRE
Ripon    York
Morecambe Bay    Lancaster    HUMBER-SIDE
Blackpool    LANCASHIRE    Keighley    Leeds    Hull
Preston    Burnley    Bradford    Spurn Hd.
Blackburn    Halifax    Wakefield    Scunthorpe    Grimsby
Liverpool    Bolton    Huddersfield    Barnsley    Doncaster
Bay    St. Helens    Salford    Oldham    Rotherham    LINCOLN
**Liverpool**    Manchester    Stockport    Sheffield    Lincoln
Birkenhead    Macclesfield    DERBY    Chesterfield    Boston    The Wash
Chester    Crewe    Matlock    NOTTS    Kings Lynn
CHESHIRE    Stoke-on-Trent    **Derby**    Nottingham    NORFOLK    Norwich
CLWYD    Wrexham    STAFFORD    Burton-upon-Trent    Gt. Yarmouth
GWYNEDD    Stafford    LEICESTER    Peterborough    Lowestoft
Dolgellau    Shrewsbury    Wolverhampton    **Leicester**
Welshpool    SALOP    Walsall    Huntingdon    CAMBRIDGE    SUFFOLK
**Birmingham**    Coventry    Rugby    Wellingborough    Cambridge    Bury St. Edmunds
POWYS    Kidderminster    WARWICK    Leamington    NORTHAMPTON    Ipswich
Llandrindod Wells    Worcester    Stratford-upon-Avon    Bedford    Colchester
HEREFORD    Warwick    Northampton    BEDFORD    ESSEX    Harwich    The Naze
Hereford    WORCESTER    Buckingham
DYFED    Cheltenham    GLOUCESTER    Luton    HERTFORD
Gloucester    Monmouth    OXFORD    BUCKS    Hertford    St. Albans    Chelmsford
Brecon    **Oxford**    Aylesbury    Watford    Southend
WALES    GWENT    Rhondda    Slough    **LONDON**    Chatham
Merthyr Tydfil    Newport    Swindon    Windsor    Gillingham    Margate
Llanelli    Reading    Kingston    Maidstone    Canterbury
Swansea    Port Talbot    **Cardiff**    **Bristol**    BERKS    SURREY    KENT    Dover
Weston-super-Mare    AVON    Bath    Aldershot    Reigate    Ashford    Folkestone
Bristol Channel    WILTS    Guildford
Lundy    Wells    Salisbury    Winchester    WEST    EAST    Hastings
Ilfracombe    SOMERSET    Southampton    SUSSEX    SUSSEX    Eastbourne
Barnstaple    HANTS    Chichester    Brighton    Lewes    Worthing
Hartland Point    Taunton    Yeovil    Newhaven
DEVON    DORSET    Portsmouth    Newport
Bude    Exeter    Axminster    Poole    ISLE OF WIGHT
Dorchester    Bournemouth
Weymouth
CORNWALL    Devonport    Torquay
St. Austell    **Plymouth**    Start Pt.
Truro    Camborne
Penzance    Falmouth
Land's End    **ENGLISH CHANNEL**
Lizard    Dieppe
Isles of Scilly

IRELAND

DONEGAL    Letterkenny    Lifford    NORTHERN IRELAND
Donegal    Coleraine    **Londonderry**    Larne
Donegal Bay    Ballymena
Erris Hd.    Killala Bay    Enniskillen    Bangor
Sligo    **Belfast**    Lisburn
SLIGO    LEITRIM    Armagh    Downpatrick    Dundrum
Ballina    MONAGHAN    Newry
MAYO    Castlebar    Clones    Dundalk
Westport    ROSCOMMON    CAVAN    Cavan    Drogheda
CONNACHT    Longford    Ceanannus Mor    An Uaimh
Roscommon    Longford    MEATH    Balbriggan
Connemara    Athlone    Mullingar
GALWAY    Corrib    WESTMEATH    **Dublin**
Galway    DUBLIN (Baile Atha Cliath)
Galway Bay    Athenry    OFFALY    Tullamore    Naas    Bray    **Dún Laoghaire**
Port Laoise    KILDARE    Wicklow
CLARE    Birr    LEINSTER    LAOIS    Carlow
Ennis    Nenagh    Kilkenny    Arklow
Kilrush    Thurles    CARLOW    Enniscorthy
Limerick    TIPPERARY    KILKENNY    WEXFORD
MUNSTER    Tipperary    New Ross    Wexford
LIMERICK    Clonmel    Carrick-on-Suir    Rosslare
Listowel    Rath Luirc    Carnsore Pt.
KERRY    Tralee    Mallow    WATERFORD    **Waterford**
Killarney    Fermoy    Dungarvan
Cahirciveen    CORK    Youghal
**Cork**    Cobh
Bantry    Bandon    Kinsale    Cork Harbour
C. Clear

ATLANTIC

IRISH SEA

St. George's Channel

Cardigan Bay

Caernarfon Bay

Projection: Conical with two
standard parallels

1:1 000 000

10    0    10    20    30    40 km

West from Greenwich    0    East from Greenwich    1

Motorways
Motorways under construction

**FRANCE**

Calais

Boulogne

Strait of Dover

1:1 000 000

10    0    10    20    30    40 km

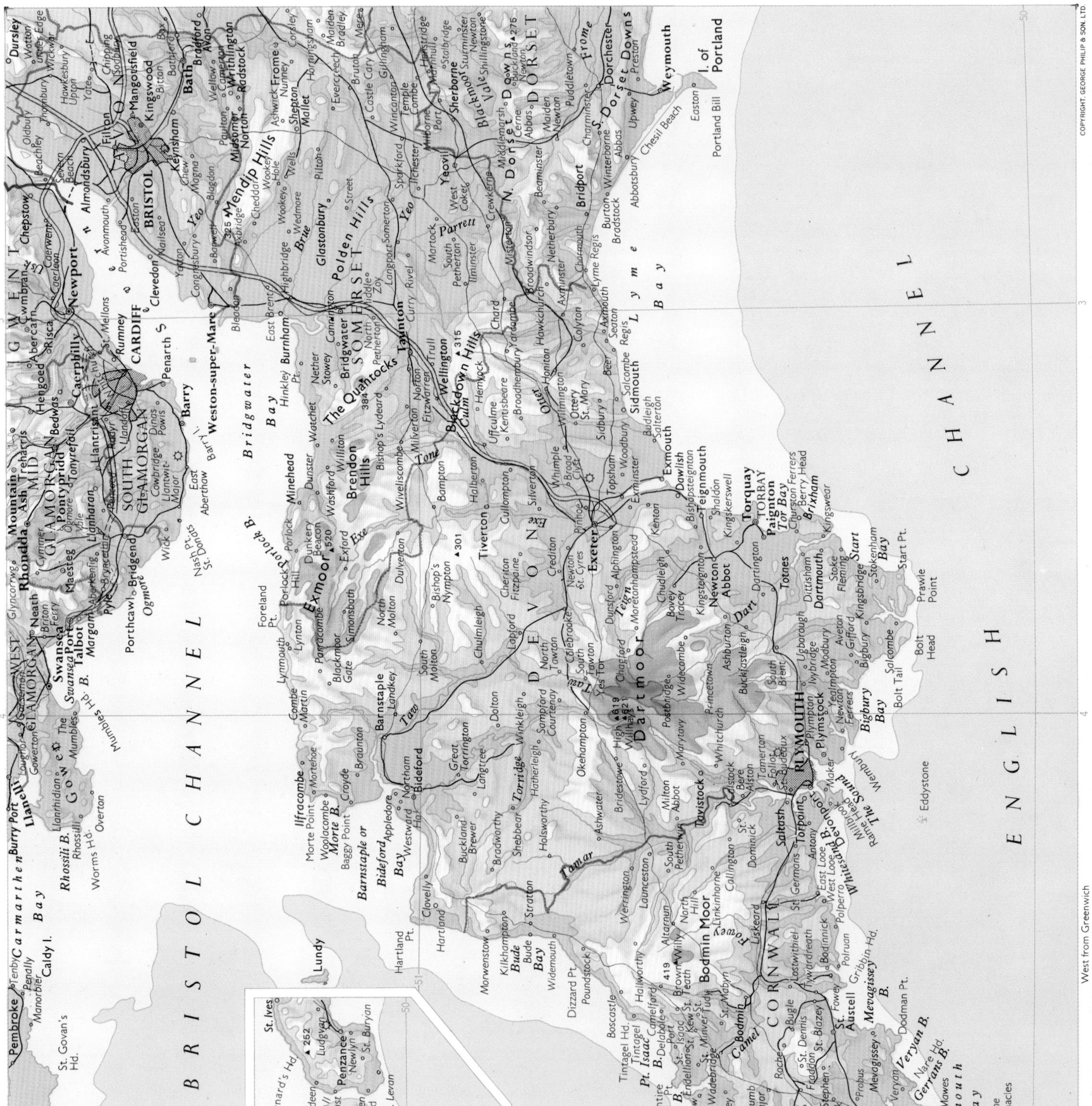

GWENT

GLAMORGAN

SOUTH GLAMORGAN

MID GLAMORGAN

WEST GLAMORGAN

Bristol
CARDIFF
Newport
Caerphilly
Barry
Weston-super-Mare
Bath
Swansea
Llanelli
Pembroke
Tenby

SOMERSET

DORSET

DEVON

CORNWALL

Exeter
Taunton
Glastonbury
Bridgwater
Yeovil
Sherborne
Dorchester
Weymouth
I. of Portland
Portland Bill

Torquay
TORBAY
Paignton
Brixham
PLYMOUTH
Totnes
Start Pt.
Bolt Head
Bolt Tail
Prawle Point

Exmoor
Dartmoor
High Willhays
Bodmin Moor
The Quantocks
Brendon Hills
Mendip Hills
Polden Hills
Blackdown Hills
Culm Hills
Quantock Hills
Dorset Downs
S. Dorset Downs
N. Dorset Downs

Barnstaple
Bideford
Ilfracombe
Morte Pt.
Baggy Point
Hartland Pt.
Clovelly
Bude
Bude Bay
Boscastle
Tintagel Hd.
Padstow
Wadebridge
Newquay
Watergate B.
Truro
Falmouth
Falmouth Bay
Helston
Redruth
Camborne
St. Ives
St. Ives B.
Penzance
Mount's Bay
St. Michael's Mount
Land's End
C. Cornwall
Lizard Pt.
The Manacles
Black Hd.

Lundy

BRISTOL CHANNEL

ENGLISH CHANNEL

Eddystone
Wolf Rk.

West from Greenwich

COPYRIGHT GEORGE PHILIP & SON LTD.

Projection: Conical with two standard parallels

**SCILLY ISLES**
on same scale

Isles of Scilly
Tresco
Bryher
St. Martin's
St. Mary's
Hugh Town
Crow Sound
St. Mary's Sound
Broad Sound
St. Agnes

Gurnard's Hd.
Pendeen
C. Cornwall
St. Just
Sennen
Land's End
Ludgvan
Penzance
Newlyn
St. Buryan
St. Levan

Based upon the Ordnance Survey Map with the permission
of the Controller of Her Majesty's Stationery Office.
Crown Copyright Reserved.

m   600   400   200   100   0

m   50

50

1:1 000 000

10   0   10   20   30   40 km

The Skerries
Wylfa Head
Cemaes Bay
Amlwch
Carmel Head
Parys Mt.
128
Dulas B.
Moelfre
Llanfechell
Llanerchymedd
Red Wharf B.
Holyhead
Holyhead B.
Bodedern
Pentraeth
Puffin I.
Conwy B.
Gt. Ormes Hd.
Lit. Ormes Hd.
Rhos on Sea
Colwyn Bay
Rhyl
Prestatyn
Newton le Willows
LIVERPOOL
Booth
St.Helens
Prescot
Whiston
Huyton
Warrington
New Brighton
Wallasey
MERSEYSIDE
Hoylake
West Kirby
Birkenhead
Bebington
Garston
Widnes
Runcorn
Mersey
Weaverham
Holy I.
Valley
Gwalchmai
Anglesey
Beaumaris
Llangefni
Menai Bridge
Bangor
Deganwy
Conwy
Penmaenmawr
Llandudno
Abergele
Colwyn
Rhuddlan
Mostyn
Holywell
Flint
Port Sunlight
Bromborough
Neston
Connah's Quay
Upton
Ellesmere Port
Helsby
Frodsham
Stanlow
Northwich
Aberffraw
Newborough
Port Dinorwic
Caernarfon
Llanberis
Bethesda
Carnedd Llewelyn
1062
Rhaeadr
Ogwen
Dolgarrog
Betws-y-coed
Trefriw
Llanrwst
Llanfairfechan
St. Asaph
Llanfair Talhaiarn
Henllan
Denbigh
Northop
Mold
Buckley
Hawarden
Hope
Chester
Tarporley
Kelsall
Winsford
CHESHIRE
Nantwich
Malltraeth B.
Waenfawr
Pen-y-groes
Tal-y-sarn
Llanllyfni
Snowdon
1085
Dolwyddelan
Penmachno
Llangernyw
Llansannan
Bylchau
Llandyrnog
Ruthin
Llanarmon
Treuddyn
Caergwrle
Brymbo
Minera
Holt
Wardle
Whitchurch
Audlem
Caernarfon Bay
Clynnog-fawr
Beddgelert
GWYNEDD
Blaenau Ffestiniog
Ffestiniog
Conwy
CLWYD
Cerrigydrudion
Gwyddelwern
Rhosllanerchrugog
Ruabon
Wrexham
Overton
Malpas
Llanaelhaiarn
564
Tremadog
Maentwrog
Arenig Fawr
853
Bala
Llandderfel
Glyn Ceiriog
Oswestry
Market Drayton
Nefyn
Tudweiliog
Llanor
Criccieth
Porthmadog
Trawsfynydd
Llanuwchllyn
L. Tegid
(Bala L.)
Berwyn Mts
827
Llanrhaeadr-ym-Mochnant
Llanfyllin
Whittington
Wem
Llannor
Pwllheli
Llanbedrog
Llanystumdwy
Harlech
Talsarnau
Llanbedr
Llethr
754
Llanuwchllyn
Aran Fawddwy
905
L. Vyrnwy
Llanfihangel
Llanymynech
Llanymynech
Ellesmere
Prees
Whittington
Myddle
Shawbury
Crudgington
Lleyn Peninsula
Aberdaron
Rhiw
Abersoch
St. Tudwal's Is.
Llanbedr
Llanenddwyn
Llanaber
Barmouth
Llanelltyd
Dolgellau
(Dolgelley)
892
Cader Idris
Dinas Mawddwy
Mallwyd
Llangynog
Llanfair Caereinion
Guilsfield
Welshpool
Shrewsbury
Westbury
Minsterley
Bicton
Ercall
Condover
Wellington
The Wrekin
407
Coalbrookdale
Braich-y-pwll
Bardsey Sd.
Bardsey I.
Porth Neigwl
Trwyn Cilan
Tremadog Bay
Llwyngwril
Llangelynin
Tal-y-llyn
Corris
Cemmaes Road
Abergynolwyn
Tywyn
Cwrt
Llanbrynmair
Wynnstay
Tregynon
Berriew
Vyrnwy
Severn
Montgomery
Chirbury
Lydham
Acton Burnell
Stiper Stones
528
Church Stretton
Ironbridge
Brosely
Much Wenlock
Wenlock Edge
Ditton Priors
Clee Hills
Cardigan Bay
Aberdovey
Dovey
Borth
Machynlleth
Carno
Trefeglwys
Caersws
Newtown
Kerry
Llanidloes
Clun Forest
Long Mtn
Forden
The Long Mynd
Corve
113
Aberystwyth
Rheidol
Devil's Bridge
Ystwyth
Plynlimon
(Pumlumon)
752
Llangurig
Severn
Wye
Ithon
St. Harman
Llanbister
Beguildy
Clun
Clunbury
Craven Arms
Bromfield
Ludlow
Llanrhystyd
Llanilar
Ystrad
Ystrad Meurig
Ystbyty Ystwyth
Reservoirs
POWYS
Rhayader
Radnor Forest
Knighton
Wigmore
Brimfield
Mortimers Cross
Kingsland
Tenbury
Llanon
Mynydd Bach
361
Pontrhydfendigaid
Elan
Drygarn Fawr
645
Elan Village
Newbridge on Wye
660
Radnor
Penybont
New Radnor
Old Radnor
Hundred House
Presteigne
Eardisland
Pembridge
Leominster
Aberaeron
New Quay
Aberarth
Tregaron
Llanddewi-Brefi
Llanafan-fawr
Llandrindod Wells
Newchurch
Weobley
Bodenham
Llangranog
Llanarth
Bettws Bledrws
Llanwrtyd Wells
Builth Wells
Eardisley
Clifford
Dorstone
Credenhill
HEREFORD AND WORCESTER
Cemaes Hd.
Aberporth
Lampeter
Llanwenog
Llanybyther
Teifi
Tywi
Mynydd Eppynt
Upper Chapel
Hay
Hereford
Marden
Lugwardine
St. Dogmaels
Cardigan
Cilgerran
Newcastle Emlyn
Llandyfriog
Llandysul
Pumpsaint
Llandovery
Llanwrda
Llandovery
Llanwrda
Llangadog
Senny Bridge
Brecon
Talgarth
811
Peterchurch
Madley
Fownhope
Ross on Wye
Strumble Hd.
Goodwick
Fishguard B.
Dinas Hd.
Nevern
Crymmych
DYFED
Pencader
Llansawel
Myddfai
Cray
Tretower
Black Mountains
Crucorney
Llanvihangel
Goodrich
St. David's Hd.
David's
Fishguard
Newport
Prescelly
Mynydd Prescelly
536
Greenway
Letterston
Trelech
Cynwyl Elfed
Abergwili
Llanarthney
Llandeilo
Mynydd Du
(Black Mt.)
Fforest Fawr
886
Brecon Beacons
Crickhowell
Abergavenny
Monmouth
Mitchel Troy
Forest of Dean
St. Briavels
Ramsey I.
St. Brides Bay
Haverfordwest
Narberth
Templeton
Whitland
St. Clears
Carmarthen
Meidrim
Llandissilio
Wolf's Castle
Llanpumsaint
Llandybie
Peny-groes
Brynaman
Abercrave
Ystradgynlais
Glyn Neath
Resolven
Hirwaun
Merthyr Tydfil
Tredegar
Rhymney
Bargoed
Brynmawr
Blaenavon
Ebbw Vale
Abertillery
Blaina
Abersychan
Raglan
Llandogo
Tintern
Broad Haven
Johnston
Milford Haven
Neyland
Pembroke Dock
Laugharne
Pendine
Kidwelly
Ammanford
Gwaun-Cae-Gurwen
Seven Sisters
Glyn-neath
Aberdare
Aberdulais
Clydach
Aberdare
Aberdare Mountain
Rhondda
Treharris
Hengoed
Abercarn
Risca
Pontypool
Cwmbran
Skomer I.
Dale
Sageston
Saundersfoot
Tenby
Penally
Llanstephan
Ferryside
Burry Port
Pembrey
Llanelli
Loughor
Gowerton
Pontardulais
Llangennech
Pontardawe
Garnswllt
Neath
Port Talbot
WEST GLAMORGAN
Cymmer
MID GLAMORGAN
Pontypridd
Tonyrefail
Bedwas
Caerphilly
Abercarn
Caerleon
Newport
GWENT
Usk
Chepstow
Beachley
Oldbury
Skokholm
St. Ann's Head
Angle
Pembroke
Manorbier
Caldy I.
Carmarthen Bay
Swansea
Swansea B.
The Mumbles
Rhossili
Porteynon
Worms Hd.
Mumbles Hd.
Margam
Aberkenfig
Maesteg
Bridgend
Porthcawl
Ogmore
Llanharan
Llantrisant
Pencoed
Pontyclun
Llanharry
St. Mellons
Rumney
CARDIFF
Penarth
Clevedon
Portishead
Avonmouth
BRISTOL
AVON
Filton
David's Hd.
Linney Hd.
Milford Haven
Gower
Rhossili B.
Llanrhidian
SOUTH GLAMORGAN
Cowbridge
Llantwit Major
Dinas Powis
Barry
Weston-super-Mare
Congresbury
Yatton
Yeo
Chew Magna
Banwell
Nash Pt.
St. Donats
East Aberthaw
Barry I.
Bleadon
Axbridge
825
Mendip Hills
Cheddar
Blagdon
BRISTOL CHANNEL
Bridgwater Bay
Nailsea
East Brent

**m**
1000
800
600
400
200
100
0
50
100
**m**

Projection: Conical with two standard parallels

COPYRIGHT. GEORGE PHILIP & SON. LTD.

Based upon the Ordnance Survey Map with the permission of the Controller of Her Majesty's Stationery Office. Crown Copyright Reserved.

West from Greenwich

══════  Motorways
= = = =  Motorways under construction

Projection : Conical with two standard parallels

Motorways
Motorways under construction

Projection: Conical with two standard parallels

West from Greenwich

**1 : 1 000 000**

10        0        10        20        30        40 km

Tummel
L. Tummel
Schichallion
1081

Pass of Killiecrankie
Kirkmichael
Pitlochry

Fearnan        Aberfeldy        Dalguise
Kenmore        Dalguise
Lawers
ch Tay        Kirriemuir

Brechin
Dykehead
Montrose

Forfar
Friockheim
Inverkeilor
Lunan B.
Glamis
Marywell

Blairgowrie
Rattray
Carmyllie

Dunkeld        Coupar Angus        455        Muirdrum        Arbroath
B. Chonzie        Glen        Almond        Carnoustie
930        Almond        Burrelton        Barry        Buddon Ness
Longforgan        Monifieth        Buddon Ness
Fillans        Comrie        Stanley        Invergowrie        Dundee        Broughty Ferry

N O R T H

Crieff        Methven        New Scone        Balbeggie        Tayport
Strath        Earn        Inchture        Newport on Tay
Muthill        Dunning        Bridge        Wormit
Braco        Br.        Errol of        Leuchars
Doune        Earn
Gleneagles        Auchterarder        Newburgh        Guard Bridge
Dunblane        Abernethy        Cupar        St.Andrews
Sheriff        Blackford        Kingsbarns
720        Dollar        Ochil        Hills        Ladybank        Ceres
Dunblane        Alva        Kinross        Falkland        Freuchie        Crail
Tillicoultry        Leslie        Markinch        Windygates        Anstruther E. & W.
Stirling        Clackmannan        L.        Glenrothes        Leven        Pittenweem
Alloa        Leven        Auchterderran        Elie        St. Monans
Bannockburn        Kincardine        Lochgelly        Methil        Earlsferry        I. of May
Cowdenbeath        Buckhaven
Denny        Larbert        Dunfermline        Kirkcaldy        East Wemyss
Grangemouth        Kinghorn        Dysart
Falkirk        Bo'ness        Inverkeithing        Burntisland        Bass Rock
Bannock        Forth Bridge        Aberdour        North Berwick
Queensferry        North Queensferry        Whitekirk
Linlithgow        Leith        Gullane
Cumbernauld        Musselburgh        Cockenzie        Aberlady        Dunbar
Kirkintilloch        EDINBURGH        Prestonpans

S E A

Coatbridge        Bathgate        Mid        Tranent        Haddington        E. Linton
Airdrie        Calder        Tyne        Garvald        Cockburnspath        St. Abb's Hd.
Uddingston        Currie        Dalkeith        Gifford        St. Abb's
Fauldhouse        West        Loanhead        Newtongrange        Whiteadder        Grantshouses        Caldingham
Motherwell        Calder        Penicuik        Bonnyrigg        Gorebridge        535        Cranshaws        Reston        Eyemouth
Wishaw        Carluke        Pentland Hills        562        Lammermuir Hills        Preston        Chirnside
Kilbride        Carlops        West Linton        Fountainhall        Duns        Burnmouth
Larkhall        Shotts        Lauder        Greenlaw        Berwick on Tweed
Stonehouse        Forth        Carnwath        Newbigging        Dolphinton        851        Tweedmouth
Blackwood        Carstairs        Blyth Bridge        Stow        Gordon        Scremerston
Lesmahagow        Lanark        Moffoot Hills        Peebles        Earlston        Kelso        Norham        Holy I.
Dungavel        Biggar        Innerleithen        Leitholm        Lowick        Budle Bay
Douglas        748        Stobo        Coldstream        Barmoor        Farne Is.
Coalburn        Broughton        Galashiels        Kelso        Castle        Bamburgh
irkirk        Symington        Melrose        Flodden        Belford        N. Sunderland        Seahouses
593        Crawford        830        Yarrow        Selkirk        St.        Till        Doddington        Beadnell
Cairn Table        Broad Law        Newtown        Boswells        Maxwellheugh        Woller
Abington        Ettrick Forest        Roxburgh        Chatton
Leadhills        622        Tweedsmuir        Ancrum        Embleton
Kirkconnel        Green        733        B O R D E R S        Jedburgh        Morebattle        The Cheviot        Longhoughton
Lowther        Hawick        816        Breamish        Lesbury
Sanquhar        Res.        Bonchester        Glanton        Alnwick
Leodhills        Moffat        Bridge        Alnmouth
Carronbridge        Beattock        Teviothead        Aln        Shilbottle
Thornhill        Peel Fell        Alnwint        Coquet        Warkworth        Coquet I.
Moniaive        Closeburn        602        Catcleugh        Rothbury         Amble        Houxley
St. Ann's        Kielder        Rochester        Longframlington        Felton        Druridge B.
432        Boreland        N.Tyne        Elishaw        Simonside        Widdrington
Dunscore        Lochmaben        Newcastleton        Falstone        Otterburn        441        Longhorsley        Ellington
Torthorwald        Langholm        N O R T H U M B E R L A N D        Hepscott        Lynemouth
Lincluden        Kirkwhelpington        Cambo        Ashington
Dumfries        Hightae        Sighty Crag        Bellingham        Ridsdale        Newbiggin by the Sea
D GALLOWAY        Dalton        Canonbie        519        Redesmouth        Wansbeck        Morpeth        Bedlington
Collin        Ecclefechan        Rowanburn        Wark        Birtley        Blyth
Galloway        Crocketford        Eaglesfield        Roadhead        Stannington        Cowpen        Blyth
L.        Haugh of        New        Annan        Gretna        Humshaugh        Chollerton        Cramlington        Seaton Delaval
Ken        Urr        Abbey        Ruthwell        Green        Longtown        Belsay        Hartley
Penpont        Bankend        Smithfield        Gilsland        Chesters        Ponteland        Earsdon        Whitley Bay
Carronbridge        Cummertrees        Brampton        Greenhead        Stamfordham        Brunton        NEWCASTLE        Tynemouth
Balmaclellan        Crockerford        Bowness        Rockcliffe        HADRIAN'S        WALL        Heddon        UPON TYNE        Wallsend
Corsock        P. Carlisle        Stanwix        Haydon        Prudhoe        Ryton        South Shields
Crossmichael        Dalbeattie        589        Kirkbean        Hayton        Bridge        Gorbridge        Newburn        Blaydon        Jarrow        TYNE AND
Crossford        Carlisle        Haltwhistle        Hexham        Gateshead        WEAR
Castle        Caulkerbush        Lambley        Allen        Catton        Slaley        Birtley        Sunderland
Douglas        Kirkbride        Newton        Cumwhinton        Allendale        Stanley        Wear        Washington
Auchencairn        Arlosh        Croglin        Town        Derwent        Consett        Chester le        Ryhope
Kirkcudbright        Beckfoot        Wigton        Thursby        Alston        Edmundbyers        Leadgate        Street        Houghton le Spring
Dundrennan        Allonby        Abbey        Red Dial        Annfield Plain        Seaham
Kirkcudbright        Aspatria        Town        High Hesket        Castleside        Lanchester        Hetton le Hole        Murton
B.        Crosby        Mealsgate        Collier Law        Brandon        Easington        Easington Colliery
Maryport        Bothel        Kirkoswald        516        Durham        Peterlee        Horden
Fothergill        Caldbeck        Lazonby        Weardale        Wolsingham        Willington        Castle Eden
Flimby        High Pike        Cross Fell        St. Johns        Brancepeth        Wheatley
Seaton        658        Melmerby        893        Chapel        D U R H A M        Trimdon        Hartlepool &
Workington        Dearham        C U M B R I A        Stanhope        Tow Law        West Hartlepool
Harrington        Bassenthwaite        Greystoke        Penrith        Crook        Spennymoor        Ferryhill        Greatham
Distington        Cockermouth        L.        Skelton        Temple        Sowerby        Teesdale        Bishop Auckland        Sedgefield
Parton        Great        Thornthwaite        Greta        Pooley        Kirkby Thore        Middleton in        West Auckland        Shildon        Wolviston        Tees
Clifton        931        Keswick        Bridge        Teesdale        Newton        Billingham        B.
Whitehaven        Lowes        Threlkeld        Kirkby        Appleby        Mickleton        Aycliffe        Thornaby-
Rowrah        Water        Derwent Water        Ullswater        Stephen        790        Cothersone        Staindrop        Stockton        on-Tees
Buttermere        Thirlmere        Hoff        Mickle Fell        Winston        Gainford        on Tees        Middlesbrough
Crummock        Shap        Brough        Bowes        Barnard        Yarm        CLEVELAND
Water        Castle        Darlington

Inchcape or
Bell Rock

_Firth of Forth_

_Strath        Earn_

F I F E
Fife Ness

_Firth of Tay_

_Tweed_
_Till_

_Eden_

Motorways
Motorways under construction

Based upon the Ordnance Survey Map with the permission
of the Controller of Her Majesty's Stationery Office.
Crown Copyright Reserved.

COPYRIGHT. GEORGE PHILIP & SON. LTD.

**SHETLAND ISLANDS** on same scale

Herma Ness
Haroldswick
Bluemull Sd.
Baltasound
Balta
Unst
Ramna Stacks
Cullivoe
Uyeasound
Mu Ness
Point of Fethaland
Whale Firth
Colgrave Sd.
Fetlar
The Faither
North Roe
Mid Yell
The Snap
Yell
Ronas Hill 450
Burravoe
Esha Ness
Hillswick
Lunna Ness
St. Magnus Bay
SHETLAND
Skaw Taing
Out Skerries
Brae
Muckle Roe
Voe
Whalsay
Papa Stour
The Haa
Sandness
Sd. of Papa
Walls
S Nesting Bay
Vaila
Easter Skeld
Score Hd.
Gruting Voe
Lerwick
I. of Noss
Scalloway
Bressay
West Burra
Hamnavoe
Bard Hd.
293
Bressay Sd.
Kettla Ness
Noss Ness
Hoswick
Mousa
St. Ninian's I.
Scousburgh
Boddam
Fitful Hd.
B. of Quendale
Sumburgh Hd.

Kyle
C. Wrath
L. Inchard
L. Laxford
Handa I.
Kinlochbervie
Scourie
B. St
Butt of Lewis
Port of Ness
Pt. of Stoer
Drumbeg
Quinag
South Dell
Ness
Cellar Hd.
Assynt
809
Borve
Eddrachillis Bay
Barvas
North Tolsta
Tolsta Hd.
Stoer
Canisp
814
Shawbost
Carloway
291
Newmarket
Broad Bay
Tiumpan Hd.
Rhu Coigach
Enard Bay
Lochinver
Ledm
Gallan Hd.
Great Bernera
Stornoway
Portaguiran
Eye Peninsula
Elphin
Uig
Melbost
Bayble
Summer Isles
L. Lurgainn
Croma Hills
L. Roag
Lewis
Lochs
Chicken Hd.
Coigach
575
Gisla
Callanish
Cromore
Ullapool
Aird Brenish
Balallan
L. Erisort
Park
Crossbost
Strathkan
Loch Langavat
Kintaravay
Gravir
Kebock Hd.
L. Broom
Scarp
Greenstone Pt.
Gruinard B.
Husinish
N. Harris
Ardvourlie Castle
571
L. Shell
Mellon Charles
Ardchar
Husinish Pt.
799
Beinn Mhor
Mellon Charles
Aultbea
An Teallach
1062
W. L. Tarbert
Sd. of Shiant
Melvaig
L. Ewe
Taransay
Ardhasig
L. Seaforth
Shiant Is.
Poolewe
Sd. of Taransay
Tarbert
WESTERN
Scalpay
Fionn Loch
L. na Sealga
Toe Hd.
E. L. Tarbert
Kerrysdale
L. Maree
981
Slioch
Fannich
Scarastavore
S. Harris
Leverburgh
Henderson
Talladale
W
Pabbay
Rodel
Longa I.
Gairloch
1053
Sd. of Pabbay
Renish Pt.
L. Gairloch
Torridon
Kinlochewe
Berneray
Rubha Hunish
ISLES
L. Torridon
Fasag
Kilmaluag
Shieldaig
Achnasheen
Haskeir Is.
Kilmaluag
Little Minch
North Minch
Griminish Pt.
Vaternish Pt.
Loch Snizort
Uig
Rona
Achnashellach
Soflas
Dunvegan Head
Waternish
Trotternish
Coulags
Monar Forest
North Uist
Lochmaddy
Stein
The Storr 719
Sound of Raasay
Applecross Forest
1052
L. Monar
Paible
L. Maddy
Milovaig
Lephin
Applecross
Lochcarron
Mullardoch
Clachan
Dunvegan
Roskhill
Raasay
Monach Is.
Carinish
347
Eaval
488
Portree
Toscaig
Kishorn
Sgurr na Lap
Sound of Monach
Baleshare
Gramisdale
Ronay
Bracadale
Stromemore
1150
Grimsay
L. Bracadale
Coillore
Crowlin Is.
Plockton
Carn Eige
Mullardoch
Benbecula
Wiay
L. Harport
Scalpay
L. Carron
1182
Glen A
Ardivachar Pt.
Bagh nam Faoileann
Fermed
Carron
Stromeferry
L. Af
L. Bee
Carbost
Drynach
Kyle of Lochalsh
Auchtertyre
Dornie
Howmore
South Uist
605 Hecla
Minginish
Sligachan
Kyleakin
L. Alsh
Inverinate
A Chralaig
Rubha Ardvule
620 B. Mhor
Cuillin Hills
Bla Bheinn
Glenelg
1120
L. Eynort
1009
928
Broadford
The Saddle
Glen Shiel
Glen
Daliburgh
Gleabrittle
1010
Cluanie
Lochboisdale
Rubh'an Dunain
L. Hourn
L. Quoich
L. Boisdale
Soay Sd.
L. Eishort
Isle Ornsay
Toldoun
Glen Garry
Soay
L. Scavaig
Elgol
Teangue
Knoydart
Sound of Barra
Cuillin Sound
Inverie
Greian Hd.
Eriskay
Canna
Sanday
Armadale
Sound of Sleat
1040
Sgurr na
Barra
Kinloch
Ardvasar
L. Arkaig
384
Rhum
Pt. of Sleat
L. Nevis
983
Castlebay
Bruernish Pt.
Rhum
810
Mallaig
Culvain
Gairlochy
Vatersay
Eigg
Morar
Loch Morar
Caledonian Canal
Sandray
Sd. of Eigg
Arisaig
Glenfinnan
Corpach
Pabbay
394
Lechailort
Kinlocheil
Mingulay
Muck
Sd. of Arisaig
882
L. Eil
Berneray
Barra Head
Shona
Moidart
S
Kinlochmoidart
L. Moidart
Loch Shiel
1347
Ben Ne
241
Ardgour
888
Pt. of Ardnamurchan
Ardnamurchan
Salen
Corran
North
Kilchoan
527
Sunart
Strontian
Ballachulish
Coll
Mingo
L. Sunart
Clabhach
Morvern
Arinagour
Caliach Pt.
1148
Tobermory
Calgary
Drimnin
Tiree
Dervaig
Portnacroish
Scarinish
Treshnish Isles
Sd. of Mull
STRATH
Caoles
L. Frisa
Lochaline
Loch Linnhe
Lismore I.
Hynish B.
Passage of Tiree
L. Tuath
Salen
Glen
Hynish

m
1000
800
600
400
200
100
0
0
50
100
m

1:1 000 000

10    10    20    30    40 km

**ORKNEY ISLANDS**
on same scale

Mull Hd.    Papa    Hollandstoun    Dennis
Noup    Papa    Westray    N. Ronaldsay    Hd.
Hd.    Pierowall    Westray    N. Ronaldsay Firth
Westray    The North    Start Pt.
Berst Ness    Rapness    Sound    Overbister    Sanday
Sacquoy Hd.    Eday    Sanday Sound
Eynhallow Sd.    Wasbister    Papa Stronsay
Brough Hd.    Rousay    Egilsay    Whitehall
Twatt    Brinyan    Wyre    Stronsay
Redland    Dounby    Gairsay    Aith    Stronsay
L. of Harray    Finstown    Wyde    Shapinsay    Lamb Hd.
Voy    Firth    Auskerry
L. of Stenness    O  R  K    Shapinsay Sd.
Stromness    Kirkwall    Deer Sd.    Mull Hd.
Graemsay Sd.    Mainland    Deerness
Hoy    Orphir    Gritley
Old Man    Ward Hill    St. Mary's    Pt. of Ayre    Copinsay
of Hoy    477    Scapa Flow    Rose Ness
Rora Hd.    Burray
Rackwick    Hoy    Flotta    St. Margaret's
Lyness    Hope    South Ronaldsay
Hurliness    S. Walls    Burray
Tor Ness    Swona    Cleat
*Pentland    Firth*
Dunnet    Stroma    Pentland Skerries
Hd.    John o'
Mey    Groats    Duncansby Hd.
Canisbay

**NORTH**

**SEA**

COPYRIGHT. GEORGE PHILIP & SON. LTD.

Based upon the Ordnance Survey Map with the permission
of the Controller of Her Majesty's Stationery Office.
Crown Copyright Reserved.

DISTRICTS IN
NORTHERN IRELAND

1 Londonderry
2 Limavady
3 Coleraine
4 Ballymoney
5 Moyle
6 Larne
7 Ballymena
8 Magherafelt
9 Cookstown
10 Strabane
11 Omagh
12 Fermanagh
13 Dungannon
14 Craigavon
15 Armagh
16 Newry and Mourne
17 Banbridge
18 Down
19 Lisburn
20 Antrim
21 Newtownabbey
22 Carrickfergus
23 North Down
24 Ards
25 Castlereagh
26 Belfast

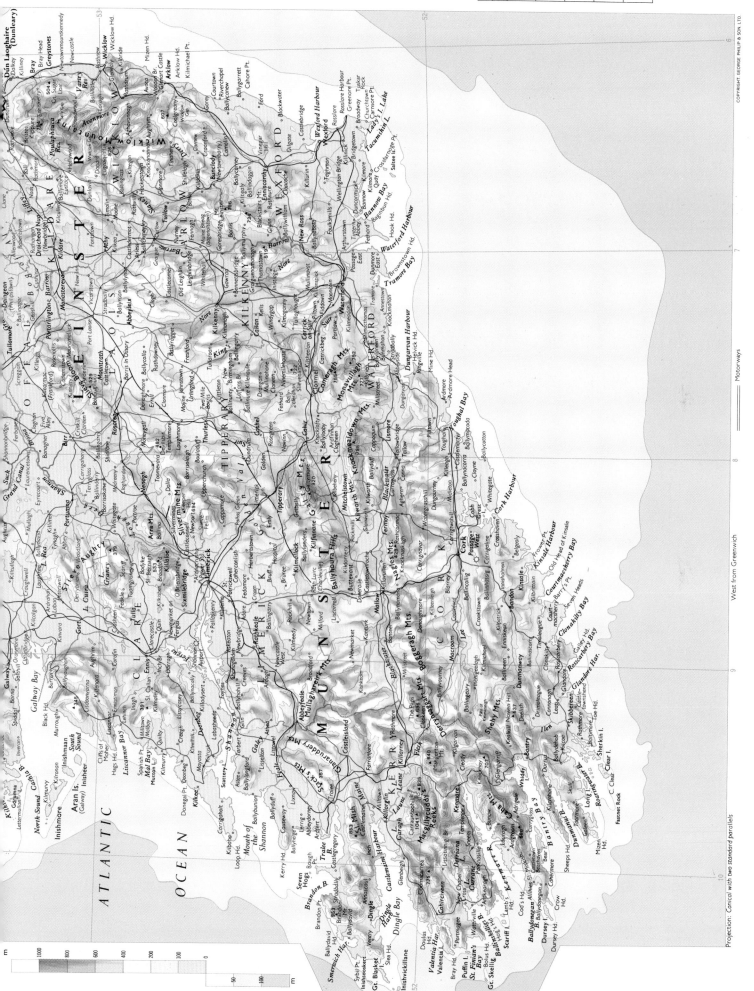

**39**

1:1 250 000

10   0   10   20   30   40   50 km

COPYRIGHT GEORGE PHILIP & SON LTD.

Projection: Conical with two standard parallels

West from Greenwich

Motorways

ATLANTIC OCEAN

LEINSTER

WICKLOW

WEXFORD

KILKENNY

WATERFORD

MUNSTER

TIPPERARY

LIMERICK

CLARE

KERRY

CORK

Galway Bay

Aran Is. (Galway) Inisheer

North Sound
South Sound

Dingle Bay
Bantry Bay

m
1000
800
600
400
200
100
0

m
50
100

1 : 4 000 000

50    0    50    100    150 km

Inhabitants

per km²
under 6
6–12
12–25
25–50
50–100
100–200
over 200

■ Cities with over
500 000 inhabitants

● Cities with 100 000
– 500 000 inhabitants

West from Greenwich    East from Greenwich

Projection: Conical with two standard parallels

COPYRIGHT. GEORGE PHILIP & SON. LTD.

1:5 000 000

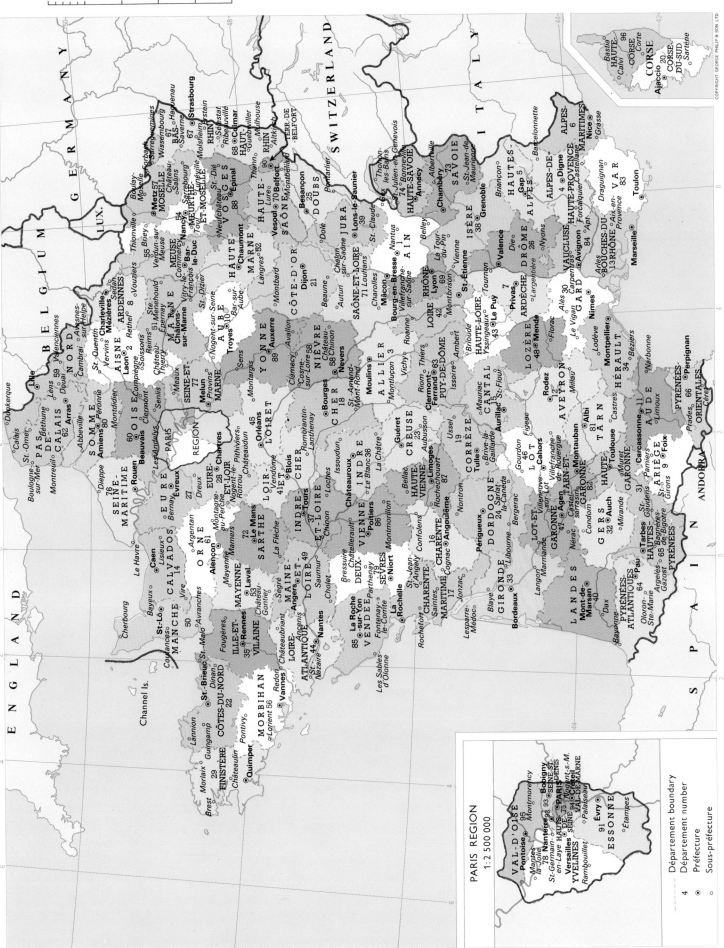

PARIS REGION
1:2 500 000

— — — Département boundary
4 Département number
⦿ Préfecture
○ Sous-préfecture

ENGLAND

English Channel

CHANNEL
ISLANDS

Guernsey
St. Peter Port
Jersey
St. Helier

Baie de la Seine

Cherbourg
Le Havre
Rouen
Caen

CALVADOS

NORMANDIE
Collines de Normandie

Brest
Morlaix
St-Brieuc
BRETAGNE
CÔTES-DU-NORD
Rennes
Laval
Le Mans

Mer d'Iroise
Quimper
MORBIHAN
Lorient
Vannes

Belle-Ile

St-Nazaire
Nantes
LOIRE-ATLANTIQUE
ANJOU
Angers
Tours

Baie de Bourgneuf
Ile de Noirmoutier

MAINE
TOURAINE

Ile d'Yeu

La Roche-sur-Yon
VENDÉE
DEUX-SÈVRES
VIENNE
Poitiers

Les Sables-d'Olonne

PLAINES ET SEUIL DU POITOU

Pertuis Breton
Ile de Ré
La Rochelle
AUNIS
Niort
Pertuis d'Antioche
Rochefort
CHARENTE-MARITIME
Ile d'Oléron
ANGOUMOIS
CHARENTE
Cognac
Angoulême
LIMOUSIN

Mer d'Iroise

West from Greenwich     East from Greenwich

1:2 500 000

10 0 10 20 30 40 50 60 70 80 90 100 km

COPYRIGHT GEORGE PHILIP & SON LTD.

1:2 500 000

10  0  10  20  30  40  50  60  70  80  90  100 km

SWITZERLAND

FRANCE

ITALY

PROVENCE

ALPES-DE-HAUTE-PROVENCE

ALPES MARITIMES

LYON

Grenoble

MARSEILLE

Toulon

TORINO

MILANO

GENOVA

Golfo di Génova

LIGURIAN SEA

MEDITERRANEAN SEA

CORSICA

HAUTE CORSE

CORSE DU SUD

Ajaccio

Bastia

Elba

Livorno

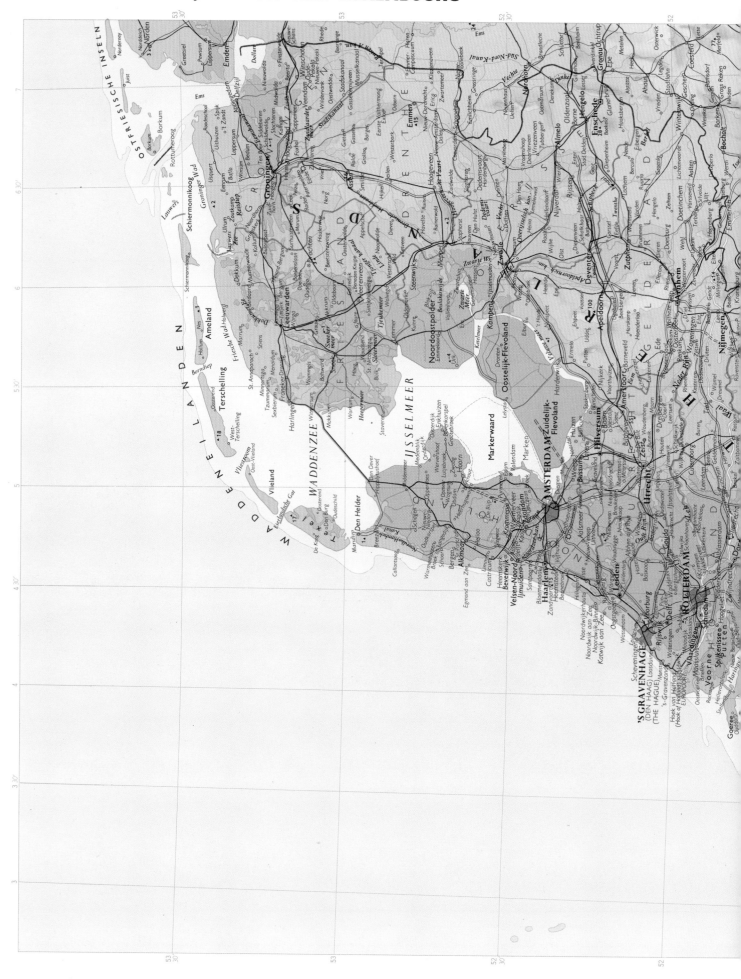

1:1 250 000

10 5 0 10 20 30 40 50 km



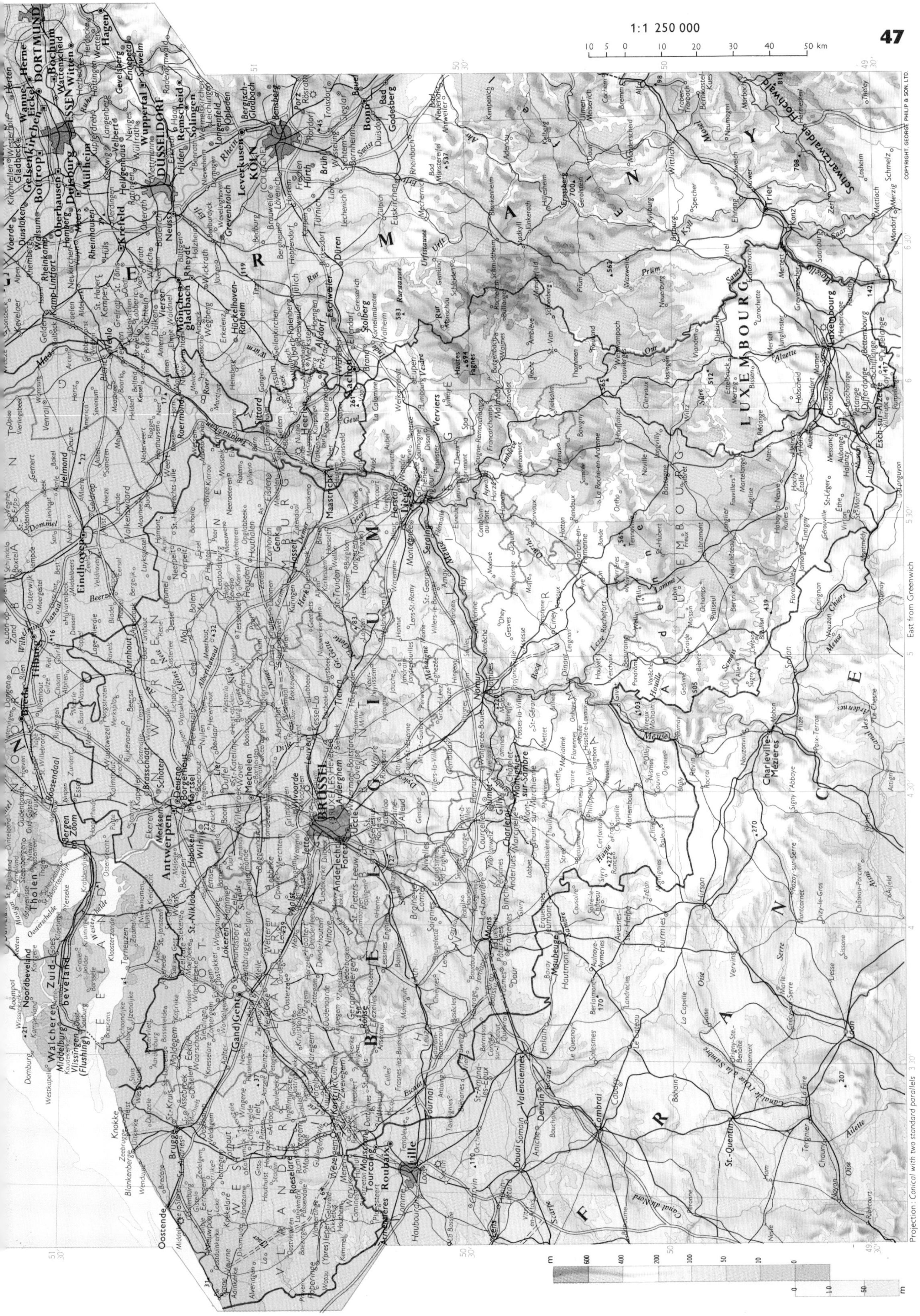
BRUSSEL (BRUXELLES)
Antwerpen
Gent
Liège
Luxembourg
LUXEMBOURG
Köln (Cologne)
Düsseldorf
Essen
Dortmund
Lille
Namur
Maastricht
Aachen
Oostende
Charleville-Mézières
East from Greenwich
Projection: Conical with two standard parallels

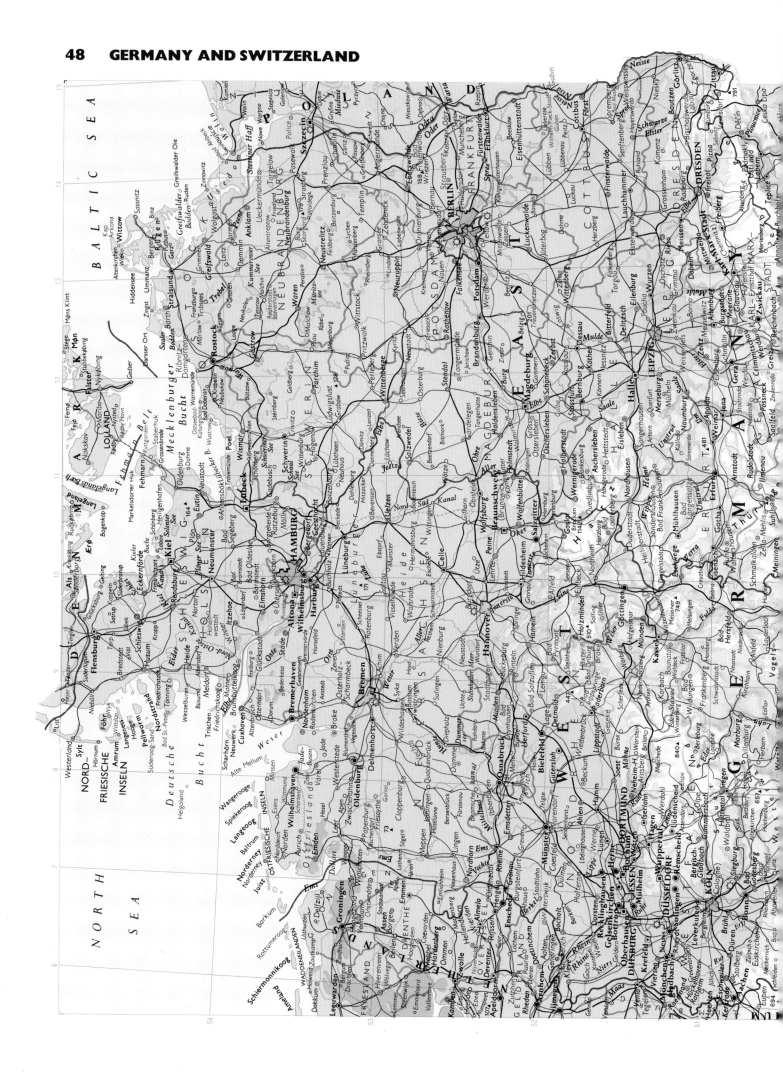

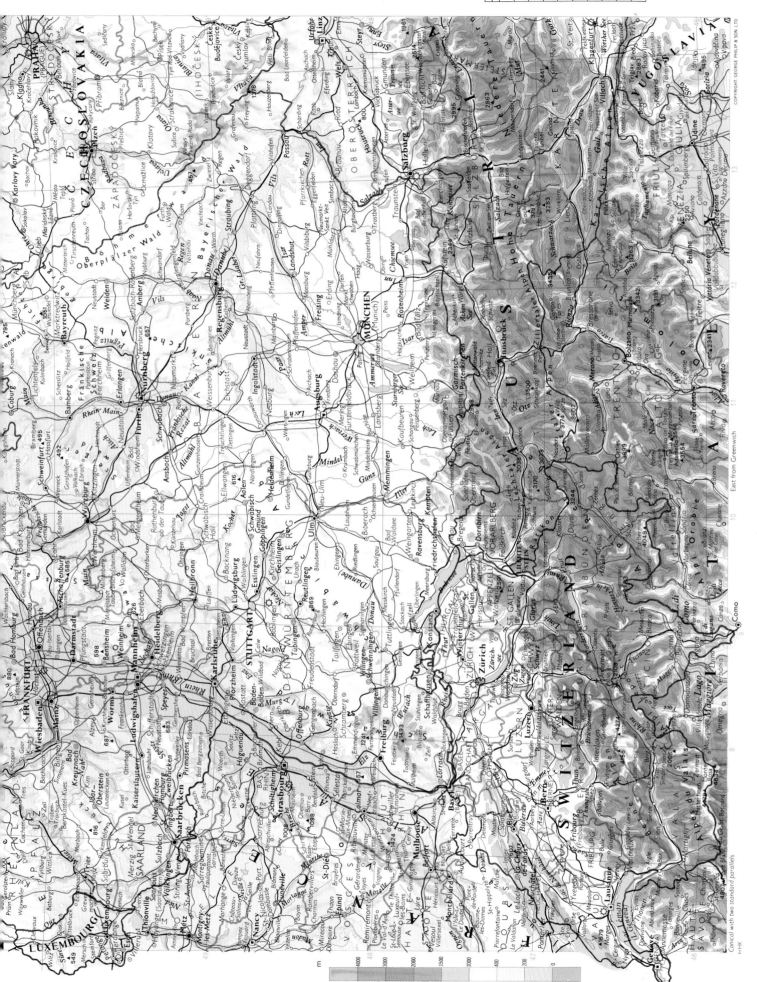

1:2 500 000

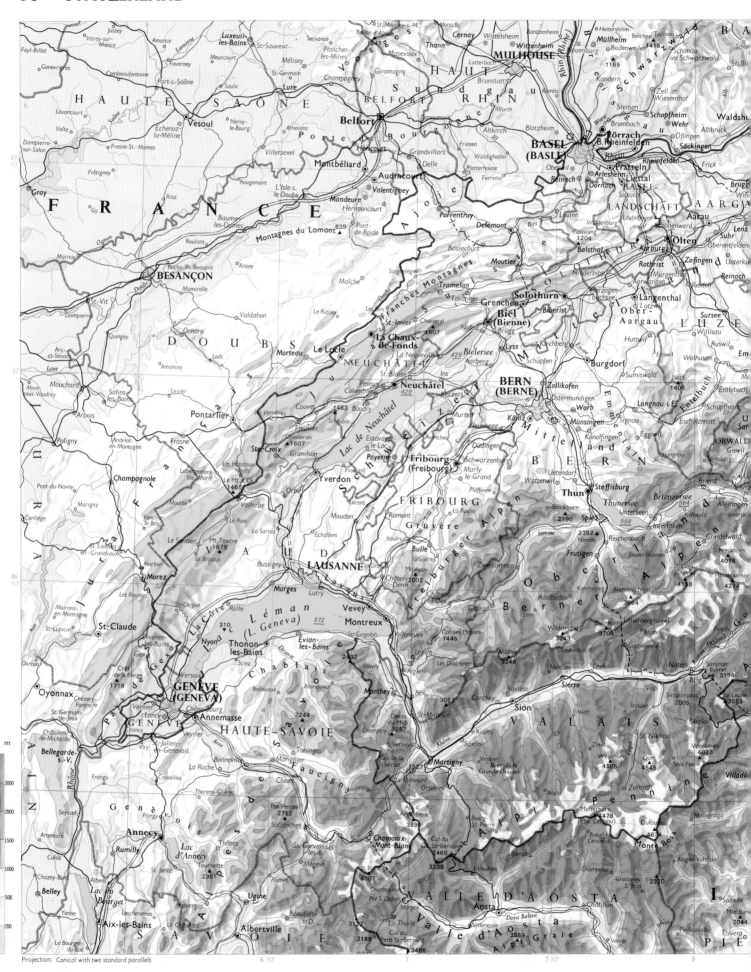

1 : 1 000 000

10          0          10          20          30          40 km

**51**

Projection: Conical with two standard parallels

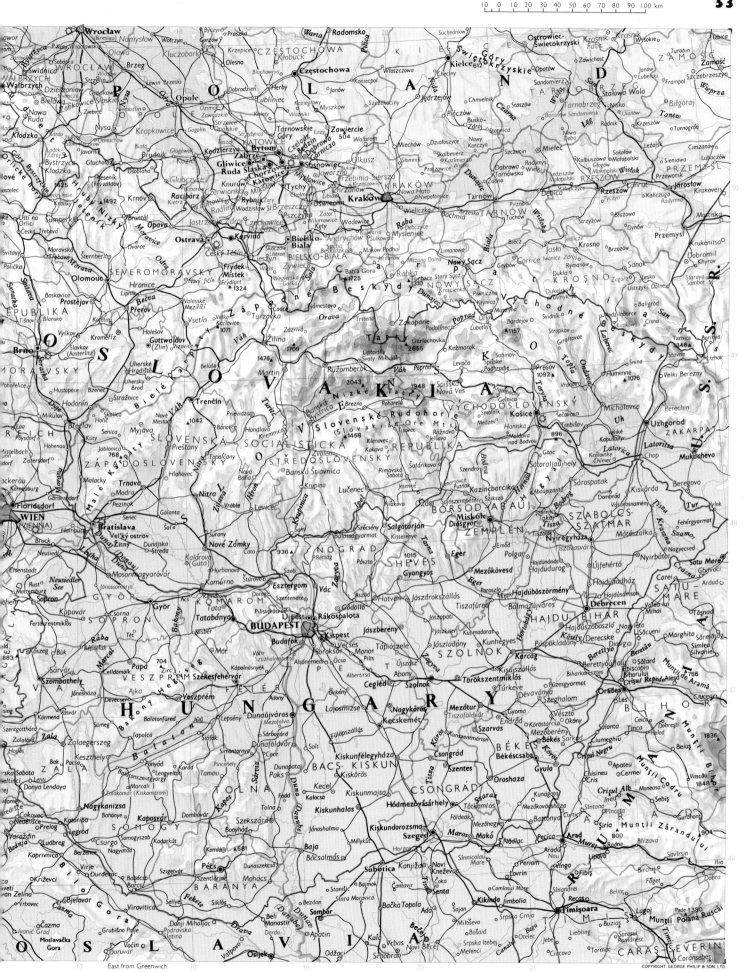

1 : 3 000 000

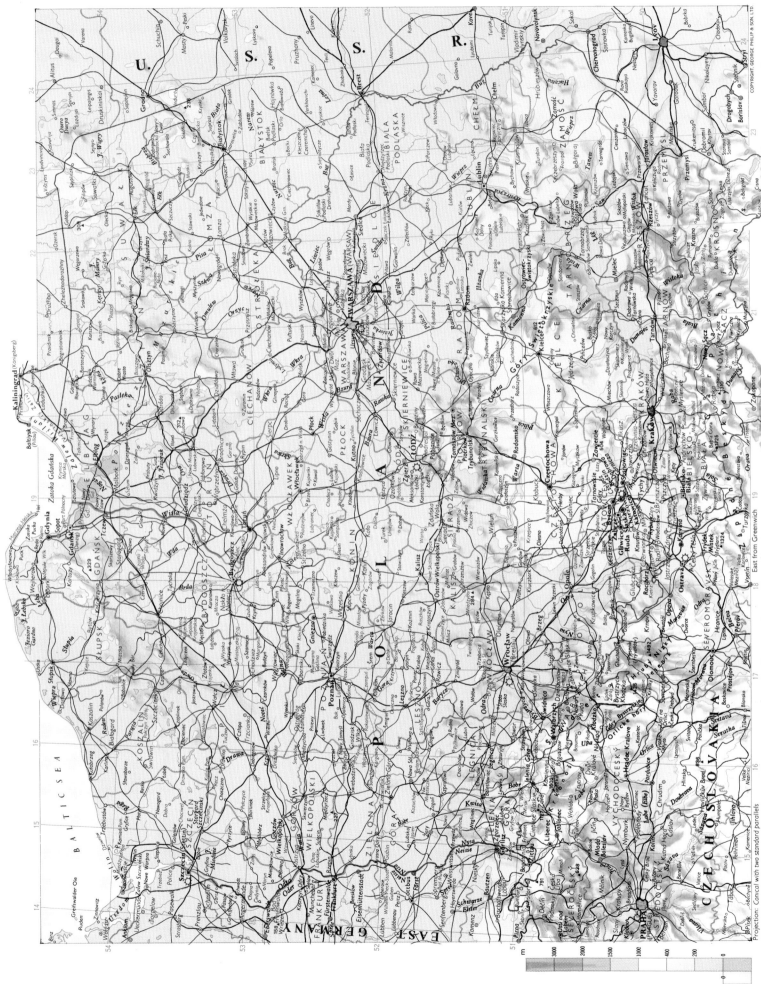

1:5 000 000

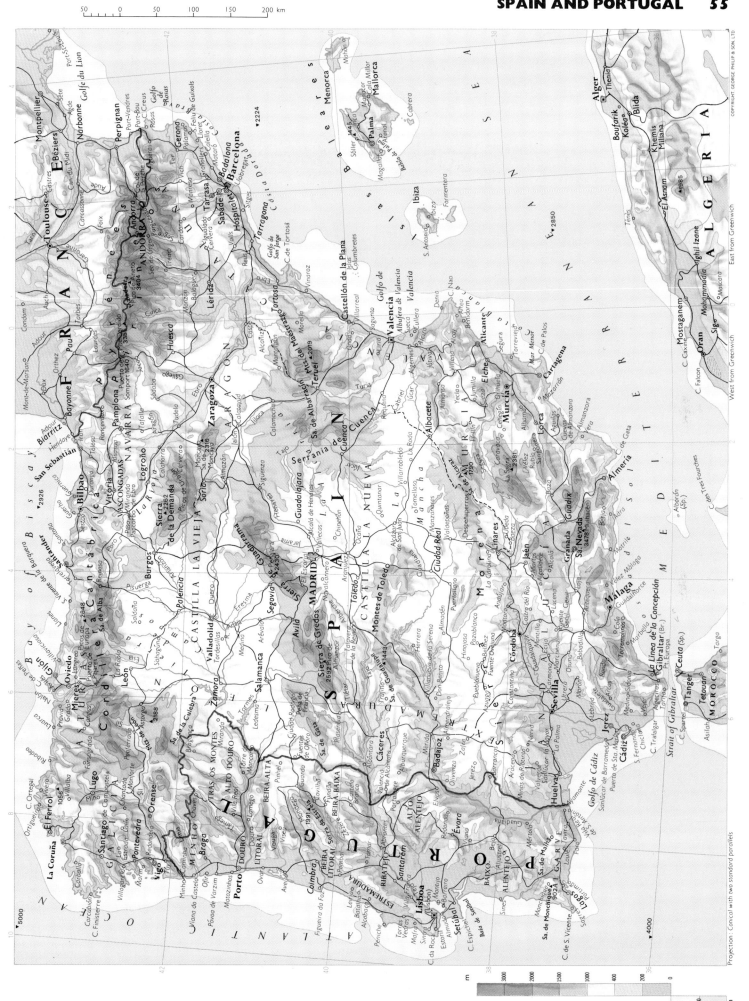

Projection: Conical with two standard parallels

1 : 2 500 000

10  0  10  20  30  40  50  60  70  80  90  100 km

MEDITERRANEAN  SEA

MOROCCO

Projection: Conical with two standard parallels

COPYRIGHT GEORGE PHILIP & SON LTD

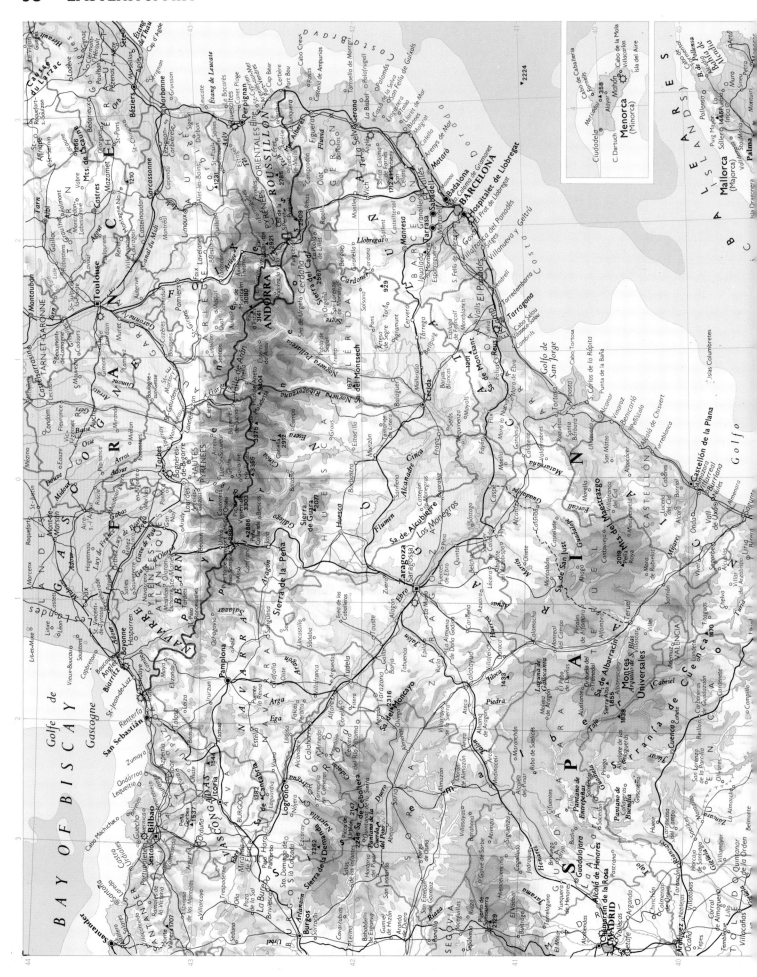

1:2 500 000

Projection: Conical with two standard parallels

COPYRIGHT GEORGE PHILIP & SON, LTD

1:10 000 000

100    0    100    200    300    400 km

**61**

POLAND
Poznan
Łódź
Warszawa
Brest
Pinsk
Polesye
Pripyat
Chernigov
Desna
Konotop
Nezhin
Sumy
Belgorod
Kazanskaya
Kharkov
Volgograd
Legnica
Wrocław
Radom
Lublin
Lutsko
Rovno
Zhitomir
Kiyev
Pereyaslav-Khmelnitskiy
Poltava
S.      R.
Voroshilovgrad
(Lugansk)
Kamensk-Shakhtinskiy
Tsimlyanskoye
Vdkhr.
Chorzów
Kraków
Tarnów
Przemyśl
Lvov
Vinnitsa
U.
Belaya Tserkov
Cherkassy
(Dnieper)
Pavlograd
Kremenchug
Artemovsk
Slavyansk
Ostrava
Jablunkovsky Pr.
Kielce
Kamenets-Podol'skiy
Uman
Kirovograd
Dneprodzerzhinsk
Dnepropetrovsk
Donetsk
Gorlovka
Makeyevka
Shakhty
Novocherkassk
550
2655
Tatry
Slavkov
Banská Štiavnica
Miskolc
Košice
Kolomyya
Prut
Chernovtsy
Beltsy
MOLDAVIAN
M.S.S.R.
Tiraspol
Bendery
Krivoy Rog
Pervomaysk
Voznesensk
Zaporozhye
Zhdanov
(Mariupol)
Taganrog
Rostov
Don
Manych
Oz. Manych Gudilo
Stavropol
Bratislava
Budapest
Debrecen
Oradea
Cluj
Iasi
Botosani
Siret
Kishinev
Odessa
Nikolayev
Kherson
Perekop
Melitopol
Berdyansk
Sea of Azov
Kerch
Yeisk
Tikhoretsk
Armavir
Maykop
Kubaň
HUNGARY
Kecskemét
Körös
Pietrosul
2305
Pietrosul
2102
Dnestrovskiy
Belgorod
Dnestrovskiy
Karkinitskiy Zaliv
M. Tarkhankut
Yevpatoriya
Krymskaya
(Crimea)
Simferopol
1545
Feodosiya
Novorossiysk
Tuapse
Hódmezővásárhely
Szeged
Arad
RUMANIA
Sibiu
Negoiu
2535
Brasov
(Orasul Stalin)
Galati
Braila
Ismail
Sulina
Sevastopol
Balaklava
Yalta
Batumi
Pécs
Balaton
Timişoara
Mures
Carpaţii Meridionali
Poarta de Fier
Turnu-Severin
Pitesti
Ploiesti
Bucuresti
Constanta
BLACK   SEA
2211
Ince Burnu
Sinop
Poti
Sukhumi
Zagreb
Novi Sad
Petrovaradin
Beograd
Craiova
Dunarea (Danube)
Ruse
Silistra
Tolbukhin
Inebolu
Samsun
Giresun
Tirebolu
Trabzon
Rize
Brod
Sava
Smederevo
Kragujevac
Morava
Vidin
Pleven
Turnovo
Varna
Kuzey Anadolu Daglari
BOSNA
Banja Luka
Sarajevo
Niš
Stara Planina
Sipchenski pr.
Sliven
Burgas
Samsun
Zonguldak
Kastamonu
2565
Çankırı
Amasya
Çorum
Tokat
Sivas
Erzincan
Unac
Mostar
Durmitor
2522
Novi Pazar
Morava
SRBIJA
Sofiya
Iskür
Maritsa
Edirne
Ereğli
Bolu
Yozgat
Kızıl Irmak
Sebin Karahisar
Erzincan
Split
Lastovo
Dubrovnik
(Ragusa)
CRNA GORA
2764
Skopje
Vardar
Strumica
BULGARIA
Musala
2925
Plovdiv
Rhodopi Planina
Tekirdağ
Istanbul
Karadeniz Boğazı
(Bosporus)
Üsküdar
Izmit
Sakarya
Ankara
Kırşehir
Keban
Gürün
Malatya
Kotor
Cetinje
Shkodër
Tirana
Durrës
Elbasan
Bitola
Sérrai
Kavalla
Alexandroúpolis
Enez
Marmara Denizi
Iznik Gölü
Bilecik
Bursa
Eskişehir
Kütahya
Sivrihisar
Tuz Gölü
Kayseri
Erciyas Dağı
3770
Bari
Barletta
Brindisi
ALBANIA
Vlora
GREECE
Thessaloniki
Gelibolu
(Gallipoli)
Gökçeada
Çanakkale
Troy
Bandirma
Balikesir
Ayvalik
Manisa
Afyon-Karahisar
Bolvadin
Büyük Menderes
Egridir Gölü
Beyşehir
Gölü
Konya
Karaman
Aksaray
Niğde
Maraş
Gaziantep
Táranto
Golfo di Táranto
C. Sta. Maria di Leuca
Oros Olimbos
2917
Límnos
Athos
2033
Lésvos
Vorial Sporadhes
Évvoia
Khios
Ikaría
Sámos
Aydın
Denizli
Isparta
Egridir
Burdur
Toros Daglari
Antalya
Mersin
Tarsus
Adana
Osmaniye
Iskenderun Körfezi
Halab
La Sila
1929
Kérkira
Nótia Píndhos
Vóial Píndhos
Lárisa
Vólos
Aegean Sea
Mersin
Silifke
Antakya
SYRIA
Al Ladhiqiyah
Hama'
Reggio
di Messina
Levkás
Ithaki Nisos
Návpaktos
Thívai
Andros
Khioni
Kefallinía
Korinthiakós Kólpos
Korinthos
Patrai
Athínai
Piraiévs
Síros
Kikládhes
Náxos
Ios
Dhodhekánisos
Eğmeli
3086
Antalya
Antalya Körfezi
Rhodos
Ródhos
4486
Megiste
(Kastellórizon)
Levkosia
(Nicosia)
Morfou
Ammókhostos
(Famagusta)
Tarabulus
Baniyas
Homs
Ionian
Sea
Zákinthos
Olympia
Pelopónnisos
Návplion
Spárti
Kalamata
Pílos
Milos
Thíra
Kárpathos
CYPRUS
Troódhos
1951
Lárnax
Lemesos
Tarabulus
Bayrut
(Beirut)
Sayda
LEBANON
Dimashq
(Damascus)
ash Sheikh
2814
5121
Ákra Taínaron
Kíthira
Andikíthira
Khaniá
Kriti
Ídhi Oros
2456
Iráklion
Jabal ad
Durúz
Bosra
Haifa
Akka
Jordan
ISRAEL
Tel Aviv-Yafo
Jerusalem
Ammán
JORDAN
Bahr el
Miyet
395
4135
M   E   D   I   T   E   R   R   A   N   E   A   N       S   E   A
Gaza
Karak
Petra
Ma'án
3174
Al Marj
(Barce)
Cyrene
Derna
Khalij Bómba
Tobruq
Rashid
Bahra el Burullus
Dumyat
Bur Saîd
El 'Arish
Banghazi
Khalij el Salúm
Salúm
Matrûh
El 'Alamein
El Iskandarîya
El Mahalla
el Kubra
Tanta
El Qantara
Isma 'iliya
Buheirat Murrat-el-Kubra
Gebel
el Tíh
El Suweis
Es Sina
2637
Al 'Aqabah
Khalîj Surt
Barqa
L   I   B   Y   A
EGYPT
El Faiyûm
EL
QÁHIRA
Nile
Beni Suêf
Suez
Canal
Khalîj es Suweis
Khalîj al 'Aqaba

------ Division between Greeks
and Turks in Cyprus;
Turks to the north.

East from Greenwich

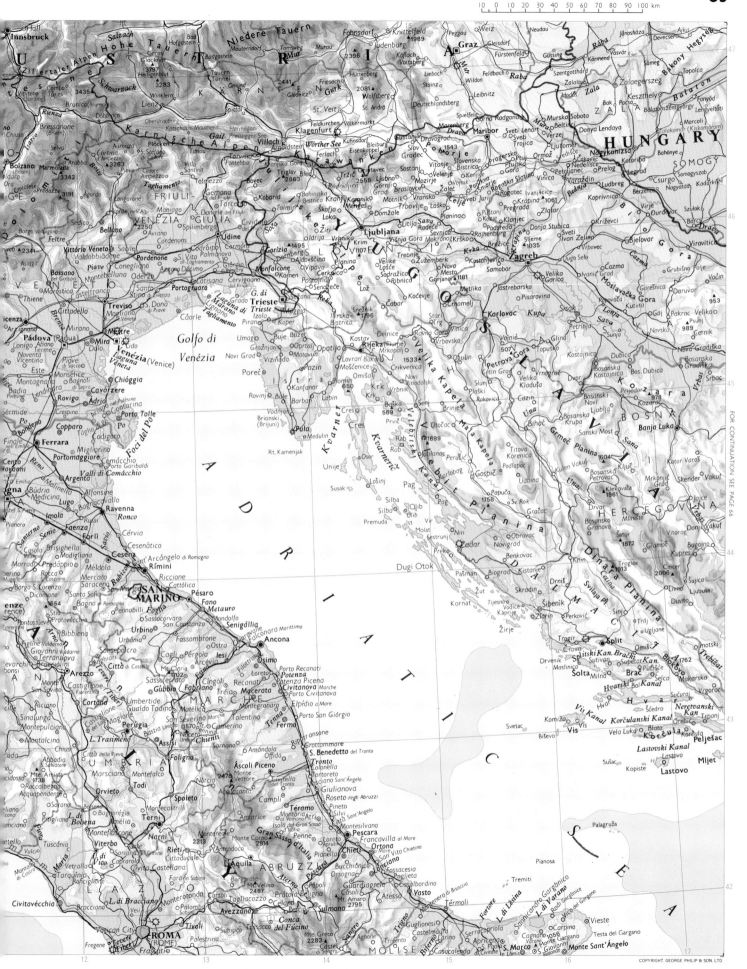

10  0  0  10  20  30  40  50  60  70  80  90  100 km

FOR CONTINUATION SEE PAGE 66

1 : 2 500 000

10 0 10 20 30 40 50 60 70 80 90 100 km

**65**

ADRIATIC

SEA

IONIAN

SEA

MEDITERRANEAN SEA

ALBANIA

Strait of Otranto

Drini

Durrësi (Durazzo)

Tirana (Tiranë)

BERATI

Vlorg (Valona)

Kérkira (Corfu)

G. di Manfredónia

G. di Salerno

G. di Policastro

Golfo di Táranto

BASILICATA

CALABRIA

Golfo di Sant'Eufémia

Golfo di Squillace

Isole Eólie o Lípari (Æolian Is.)

Str. di Messina

Messina

Réggio di Calábria

Fóggia

Bari

Brindisi

Lecce

Táranto

Matera

Potenza

Cosenza

Catanzaro

Crotone

Catánia

Siracusa

COPYRIGHT. GEORGE PHILIP & SON LTD.

HHK

Projection: Conical with two standard parallels

East from Greenwich

m
3000
2000
1500
1000
400
200
0
200
2000
m

1 : 2 500 000

10 0 10 20 30 40 50 60 70 80 90 100 km

1:2 500 000

10 0 10 20 30 40 50 60 70 80 90 100 km

COPYRIGHT GEORGE PHILIP & SON LTD

A E G E A N   S E A

Kólpos Kallonís
Plomárion
Ayiássos
Kar Burun
1212
Onoúsa
Çeşme
Alaçatı
1297
Kardhámila
Vrondádhos
Khíos (Chios)
Kolokíndi
Psará
Psará
Áyios Minás
Ákra Mastikho
Ikaría
Foúrnoi
Kírikos
Foúrnoi
Kínaros
Levítha
Ofidhoúsa
Astipálaia
Astipálion
Amorgós
822
957
1262
Khamilonísion

Skópelos
Skiáthos
Skíros
792
Skántzoúra
Skiropoúla
Kími
Oxílithos
Andípsara
Píperi
Andros
Andros
994
Tínos
Mikonos
Dhragonisi
Náxos
Náxos
1001
Íos
Thíra
Thíra
Thirasía
Khristianá
Anáfi
Makrá
Avgó
Dhenoúsa
Koufonísia

Ákra Kaféreús
Okhthoniá
Kárystos
Kími
Gávrion
Síros
Ermoúpolis
Síros
Rínia
Dhílos
Páros
Páros
706
Andíparos
Dhespotikó
Irákleia
Skinoúsa
Skhoinoúsa

Dhía
Iráklion (Candia)
Khersónisos
Akrotíri
Kólpos Soúdhas
Khaniá (Canea)
2456
Ídhi Óros
2453
Timbákion
Melámbes
1231
Kólpos Mesará
Paximádhia
Ákra Líthinon
Gávdhopoúla
Gávdhos

S E A   O F   C R E T E
(Sea of Candia)

K I K L A D H E S (C Y C L A D E S)
A R K H I P É L A G O S

Kéa
560
Kíthnos
Sérifos
Sífnos
Sérifos
Apollonía
Kímolos
Mílos
751
Mílos
Folégandros
Síkinos
Anáfi
Andímilos
Ananes
Falkonéra
Karávi
Parapóla
Poúni
Andikíthira
Ákra Vódsa
Kíthira (Cerigo)
Kíthira
Ákra Kapéllo
Ákra Spáthi
Ákra Vódsa

Megálo Petalí

ATHÍNAI (ATHENS)
Kifisiá
Kallithéa
Peiraiévs (Piraeus)
Salamís
Saronikós Kólpos
Aíyina
Méthana
Póros
Galatás
Ídhra
Spétsai
Ídhra
Ermióni
Spétsai

Érétria
Khalkís (Chalcis)
1743
1413
A T T I K I
Marathón
Pendélikon
Rhamnoús
Eleusís
Mégara
Perakhóra

Korinthiakós Kólpos
Kórinthos
Loutráki
Corinth Canal
Xilókastron
Argolikós Kólpos
Náfplion
Árgos
Mikínai (Mycenae)
Pórdión
Ástros
Leonídhion

P R O T I K I   E L L A S
DHITIKI
KALÓ

Párnon Óros
1935
Spárti (Sparta)
Evrótas
Taíyeto Óros
2404
Kalámata
Messiniakós Kólpos
Lakonikós Kólpos
Yíthion
Ákra Maléa
Monemvasía
Neápolis
712
Epídhauros Limera
Eláfonisos
Kótronas
Ákra Tainaron

Pátrai
Pátraïkós Kólpos
Áyion
Aíyion
Dhíakoptón
Kalávrita
2341
2376
L. Stimfalías
2355
Dhervéni
Trípolis
A R K A D H I A
1421
Megalópolis
1214
Kalamáta
Andrítsaina
Isári
Óros
Pírgos
Longá
M E S S I N I A
Khóra
Pílos
Methóni
Sapiéntza

A K H A Ï A
G R E
Tripótama
Kalávrita
Dháfni L.
2224
Olimbía
Alféos
Nédha
Lángadhia
Kiparissiakós Kólpos
Filiatrá
Gargaliánoi
Próti
Kalonerón
Kiparissía

Pátras
Kilíni
Gastoúni
Amalιás
Pírgos
Eliá
Manolás
Kaïáfas
Epitálion
Zákharo
Katákolon
Strófadhes

P E L O P Ó N N I S O S
Ákra Pápas
Mesolóngion
Ayiolóngon
Etolikón
Agrínion
Trikhonís
Limni Trikhomis
Limni Krêmastón
1589
A K A R N A N I A
Astakós
Ákra Skinári
1628
Sámi
Argostólion
Póros
756
Zákinthos (Zante)
Zákinthos
Kefallinía (Cephalonia)
Itháki (Ithaca)
Kióni
Vathí
Astakós
Mítikas

Levkás (Santa Maura)
Levkás
1158
Préveza
Vónitsa
Nicópolis
Amvrakikós Kólpos
Árta
Ákra Doúkaton
Fiskárdon
Asos
Lixoúrion

I O N I A N   I S L A N D S

I O N I A N   S E A

Skópelos
Ópsara
Glóssa
Mandoúdhion
Istiaía
Limni
Aidhipsoú
Óros
Dhírfis
1743
Chalkís

Lamía
Limni Xiniás
Stilís
1726
Óthris
Lárisa
Farsala
Almirós
Stilída
Vólos
Pelion

Karpenísion
2315
2510
Ágrafa
Gjóna
2457
Amfíssa
Delfoí (Delphi)
Levádhia (Thebes)
Thívai
Atalándi
Kifisós
Martínon

V Á R D O U S I A
Parnassós
2457
Véloukhi
Evinos
Timfristós
2315
Karpenísion
M O R N O S
Návpaktos
Aíyion
Dhomvrainí

O T Í A
T H É S S A L Y

V A R D O U S I A
P I N D U S
Prévezon
Préledh

Continuation Eastwards on same scale

M U G L A
Y D I N
Büyük
Samsun Dağı
1367 Beşparmak Dağı
1412
Vatárion
Marmarís
Bozburun
Kerme Körfezi
1175
Datça (Resadiye)
Cumbali
Sími
Kara
Yalí
846
Tílos (Piscopi)
Nísiros
Kos
Kálimnos
Léros
Kílimnos
Pátmos
Lípsoi
Foúrnoi
Kálimnos
Marathókambos
1153
Vathí
Karlóvasi
Sámos
Kuşada Körfezi
Efes (Ephesus)
Kuşadası
Söke
Koçarli
Miletus
Farnakonisi
Ayathonísi
Arkoí
Ákra Parasspós
Astakídha
Ávia Marina
Kísos
Stenón Kasos

R Ó D H O S (Rhodes)
Ródhos
Alándou
Arkhángelos
1215
Ákra Líndhos
Tríanda
Emboná
Mónolithos
Stenón Karpáthos
Kárpathos
1215
Pegádhia
Posídion
Ákra Kastéllou
Ólimbos
Kálathos

D O D H E K Á N I S O S (DODECANESE)

East from Greenwich

Projection: Conical with two standard parallels

m
3000
2000
1500
1000
400
200
0
200
2000
m

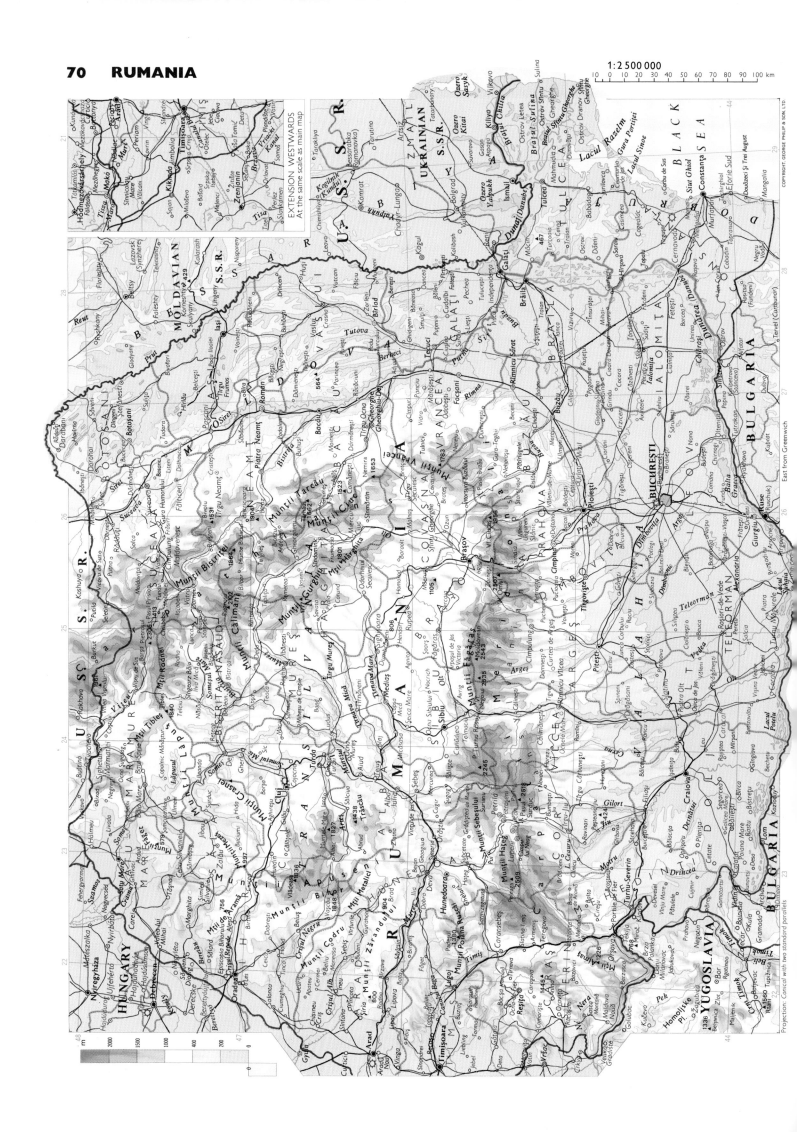

1:2 500 000

10 0 10 20 30 40 50 60 70 80 90 100 km

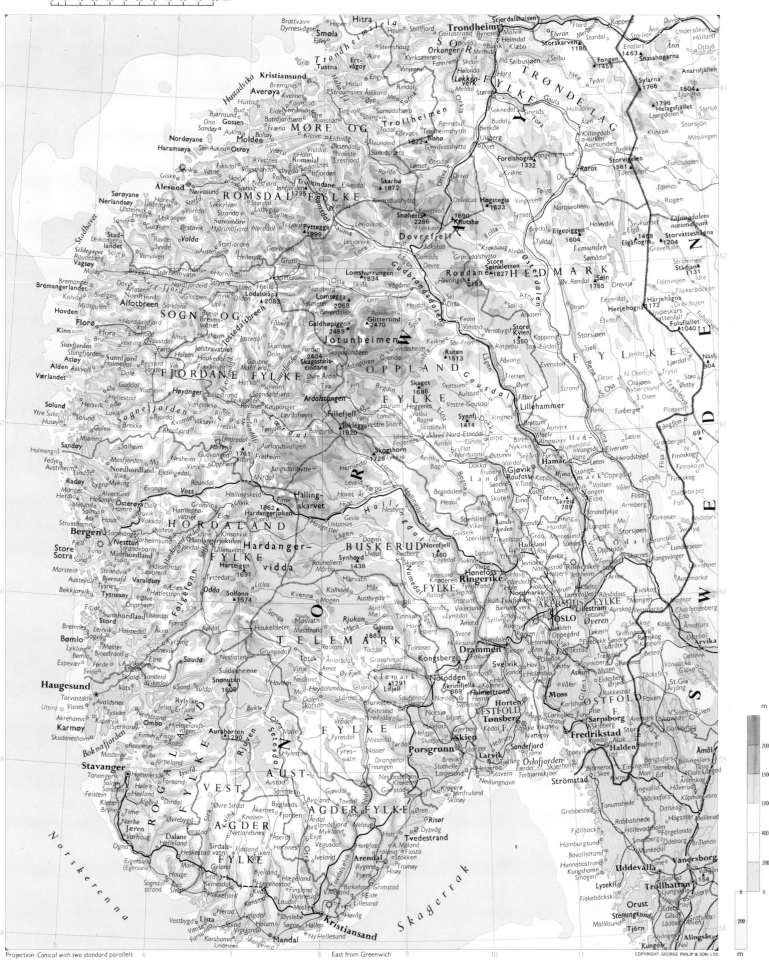

Projection: Conical with two standard parallels

East from Greenwich

COPYRIGHT. GEORGE PHILIP & SON. LTD.

1 : 2 500 000

10 0 10 20 30 40 50 60 70 80 90 100 km

BALTIC SEA

POLAND

GERMANY

Projection : Conical with two standard parallels

East from Greenwich

COPYRIGHT GEORGE PHILIP & SON LTD.

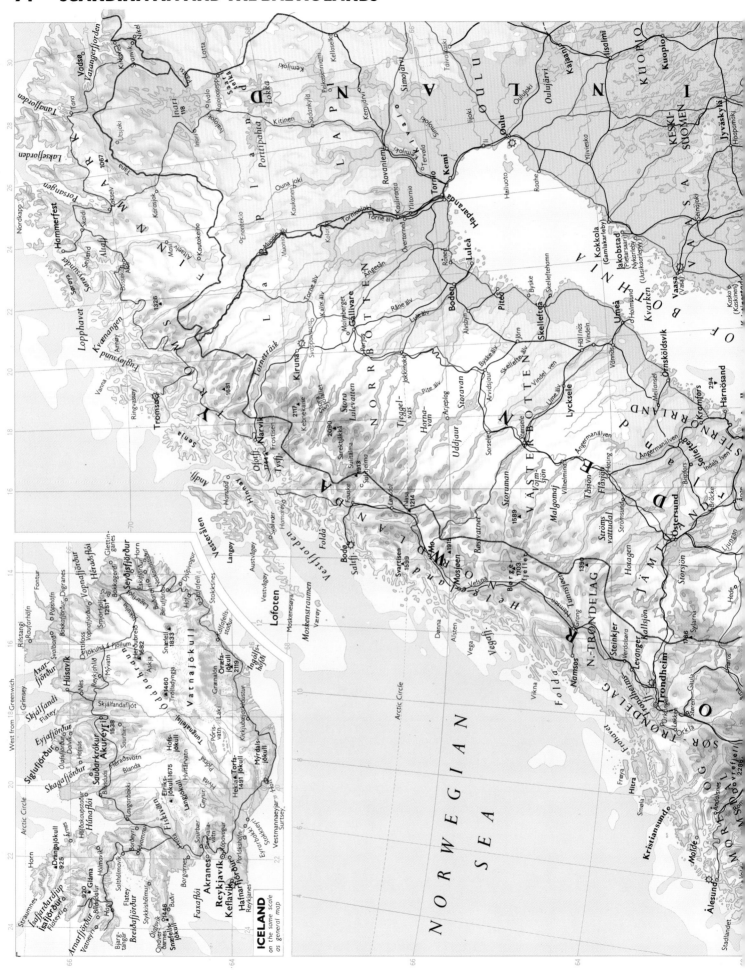

NORWEGIAN SEA

ICELAND
on the same scale
as general map

1 : 5 000 000

50    100    150    200 km

**R.S.F.S.R.**

**FINLAND**

Heinola · Loviisa · Kotka · Kouvola · Porvoo
HELSINKI (Helsingfors)
Hämeenlinna · Hyvinkää · Riihimäki
Lahti · Kerava
TAMPERE · HÄME · Turku (Åbo) · Hangö (Hanko)
Pori · Rauma · Uusikaupunki · TURUN JA PORI
Kokemäenjoki · Salo · Kemiö

**ESTONIAN S.S.R.**
Tallinn · Rakvere · Kunda · Valga
Viljandi · Haapsalu · Pärnu · Valmiera · Cēsis
Hiiumaa (Dagö) · Saaremaa (Ösel) · Kingisepp
Paldiski · Möisaküla · Ruhnu

**LATVIAN S.S.R.**
Riga · Jelgava · Daugava · Bauska
Rīgas Jūras Līcis (Gulf of Riga)
Ventspils · Kuldīga · Tukums · Šiauliai
Liepāja · Telšiai · Jonava

**LITHUANIAN S.S.R.**
Klaipėda · Kaunas · Vilnius · Grodno
Sovetsk · Taurage · Nemunas
Kaliningrad · Chernyakhovsk · Augustów
Białystok · Suwałki · Łomża · Ostrołęka
Narew · Ostrów

**POLAND**
Gdynia · Gdańsk · Zatoka Gdańska
Elbląg · Malbork · Grudziądz · Toruń
Bydgoszcz · Chojnice · Szczecinek
Słupsk · Koszalin · Szczecin (Stettin)

**BALTIC SEA**
Gotland · Visby · Fårö · Gotska Sandön
Öland · Bornholm · Rønne · Rügen

**SWEDEN**
STOCKHOLM · Uppsala · Enköping · Eskilstuna
Södertälje · Nynäshamn · Oxelösund · Nyköping
Norrköping · Linköping · Motala · Mjölby
Västerås · Köping · Örebro · Karlskoga
Gävle · Söderhamn · Hudiksvall · Sundsvall
Bollnäs · Ljusdal · Mora · Falun · Borlänge
Hedemora · Avesta · Fagersta · Hagfors
KOPPARBERG · VÄSTMANLAND · SÖDERMANLAND
ÖSTERGÖTLAND · ÖREBRO · VÄRMLAND
Vänern · Vättern · Karlstad · Arvika · Kristinehamn
Mariestad · Lidköping · Skövde · Falköping
Trollhättan · Vänersborg · Uddevalla · Alingsås
GÖTEBORG OCH BOHUS · ÄLVSBORG
Göteborg · Mölndal · Borås · Ulricehamn
Jönköping · Nässjö · Huskvarna · Tranås
Eksjö · Vetlanda · Västervik · Oskarshamn
Kalmar · Nybro · Växjö · Ljungby · Värnamo
KRONOBERG · KALMAR · JÖNKÖPING
BLEKINGE · Karlskrona · Karlshamn · Ronneby
Sölvesborg · Kristianstad · HALLAND
Halmstad · Falkenberg · Varberg
Ängelholm · Helsingborg · Landskrona
Malmö · Lund · Trelleborg · Ystad · Simrishamn

**NORWAY**
Bergen · Voss · Hardanger fjorden · Sognefjorden
Stavanger · Sandnes · Haugesund · Egersund
Flekkefjord · Farsund · Mandal · Kristiansand
Arendal · Grimstad · Lillesand · Risør · Kragerø
ROGALAND · VEST-AGDER · AUST-AGDER
TELEMARK · BUSKERUD · OPPLAND · HEDMARK
Skien · Larvik · Sandefjord · Tønsberg · Horten
Drammen · OSLO · Kongsberg · Notodden
Hamar · Gjøvik · Lillehammer · Elverum
Kongsvinger · Moss · Halden · Sarpsborg
Fredrikstad · ØSTFOLD · AKERSHUS
Jotunheimen · Galdhøpiggen 2469 · Gausta 1883

**DENMARK**
Frederikshavn · Hjørring · Aalborg · Thisted
Limfjorden · Randers · Århus · Viborg · Herning
Silkeborg · Horsens · Vejle · Fredericia · Kolding
Esbjerg · Varde · Ribe · Åbenrå · Haderslev
SJÆLLAND · FYN · Odense · Svendborg · Nyborg
København (Copenhagen) · Roskilde · Korsør
Store Bælt · Lille Bælt · Kattegat · Skagerrak
Helsingør · The Sound · Nykøbing · Falster

**WEST GERMANY**
Rostock · Wismar · Schwerin · Lübeck · Hamburg
Kiel · Kieler Bucht · Flensburg · Neumünster
Bremen · Bremerhaven · Wilhelmshaven · Oldenburg
Emden · Cuxhaven · Elbe · Weser · Lüneburg

**NETHERLANDS**
Groningen

Projection: Conical with two standard parallels

East from Greenwich

COPYRIGHT GEORGE PHILIP & SON, LTD.

m   2000   1500   1000   400   200   0

m   200   0

R.S.F.S.R.
1. Daghestan A.S.S.R.
2. Kabardino–Balkar A.S.S.R.
3. Mari A.S.S.R.
4. Mordovian A.S.S.R.
5. North Ossetian A.S.S.R.
6. Tatar A.S.S.R.
7. Udmurt A.S.S.R.
8. Chuvash A.S.S.R.
9. Checheno–Ingush A.S.S.R.
   AZERBAIJAN
10. Nakhichevan A.S.S.R.
    GEORGIA
11. Abkhaz A.S.S.R.
12. Adzhar A.S.S.R.

Projection: Conical Orthomorphic with two standard parallels

East from Greenwich

1:20 000 000

200   0   200   400   600   800 km

Mys Dezhneva
(East C.)

St. Lawrence I.
(U.S.A.)

ARCTIC OCEAN

Mys Arkticheskiy

Ostrov
Shmidt

Ostrov
Komsomolets

Ostrov
Pioner

Ostrov Oktyabrskoy
Revolyutsii

965

Ostrov Bolshevik

Severnaya
Zemlya

Proliv Vilskutskogo

Mys Dezhneva

Chukotskoye
More

Chukotskiy Khrebet

2562

Koryakskiy Khrebet

Ostrov Vrangelya

Ostrova Delong

Ostrova Delong

Ostrov
Bennett

Ostrov
Henrietta

Ostrov
Jeanette

Novosibirskiye Ostrova

Ostrova Delong

Ostrov Faddeyevskiy

Ostrov
Novaya Sibir

3800

East Siberian Sea

Ostrova
Medvezhii

1853

1732

Bolshoy Anyuy

Sredinnyy Khrebet

Bering
Sea

374

Ostrov Malyy
Lyakhovskiy

Ostrov Bolshoy
Lyakhovskiy

Lyakhovskiye Ostrova

Proliv Dmitriya Lapteva

Laptev
Sea

Polu Ostrov
Kamchatka

4750

Mt. Klyuchevskaya 4850

Poluostrov Taymyr

Gory Byrranga

1146

Ostrov Bolshoy
Begichev

Oz. Taymyr

Nordvik

Ust Olenek

Olenek

Tiksi

Tit-Ary

962

Arctic Circle

VERKHOYANSKIY

Verkhoyansk

2389

YAKUT

KHREBET

Srednekolymsk

3147

Pobeda

KHREBET CHERSKOGO

Gora Chen
2682

2359

Magadan

Petropavlovsk-
Kamchatskiy

3456

Gory
Putorana

1701

1104

Vilyuysk

Vilyuy

YAKUT A. S. S. R.

Yakutsk

Aldan

Okhotsk

Sea of Okhotsk

1780

SOCIALIST REPUBLIC

Olekminsk

2246

Ostrov Bolshoy
Shantar

Tatarskiy Proliv

Sakhalin

Kirensk

2999

3482

Nikolayevsk-
na-Am.

2028

Yuzhno-Sakhalinsk

Bratsk

Krasnoyarsk

STANOVOY KHREBET

Komsomolsk

26404

Sovetskaya Gavan

Kurilskiye Ostrova

Chita

1530

Blagoveshchensk

Birobidzhan

Khabarovsk

SIKHOTE ALIN

Cheremkhovo

Angarsk

Irkutsk

Ulan Ude

BURYAT A.S.S.R.

YABLONOVYY KHREBET

Amur

3669

Hokkaidō

2290

Sapporo

Hakodate

3491

Ulaanbaatar
(Ulan Bator)

2800

MONGOLIA

Ch'ich'ihaerh

Haerhpin
Pei

Ussuriysk

Vladivostok

Nakhodka

Sea of JAPAN

Honshū

1949

Ch'angch'un

Chilin

Chongjin

GOBI

3957

4925

MONGOLIA

Ch'ihfeng

Shenyang
(Mukden)

Fushun

Anshan

North

Wŏnsan

Kanazawa

INNER

MONGOLIA

Paot'ou

Changchiak'ou
(Kalgan)

2400

Peip'ing

Yingk'ou

Antung

Lüta

P'yongyang

Sŏul

Inch'ŏn

South

Taejŏn

Pusan

1:10 000 000

100  0  100  200  300  400 km

COPYRIGHT. GEORGE PHILIP & SON, LTD.

**Legend (inset box):**
1 Kabardino-Balkar A.S.S.R.
2 North Ossetian A.S.S.R.
3 Nakhichevan A.S.S.R. (Azer.)
4 Checheno-Ingush A.S.S.R.
Karagiye Depression

**Seas and water:**
CASPIAN SEA
BLACK SEA
Azovskoye More (Sea of Azov)
MEDITERRANEAN SEA
Levant
Marmara Denizi
Kara Bogaz Gol.

**Regions / Republics:**
K I R G I Z   S T E P P E
K A Z A K H S K A Y A   Nizmennost
Privolzhsk.
KALMYK A.S.S.R.
Ergeni Vozvyshennost
U K R A I N E
MOLDAVIAN S.S.R.
RUMANIA
BULGARIA
TURKEY
Anadolu
SYRIA
Badiyat ash Sham
IRAQ
I R A N ( P E R S I A )
Alborz
GEORGIAN S.S.R.
ABKHAZ A.S.S.R.
ADZHAR
ARMENIAN S.S.R.
AZERBAIJAN
DAGESTAN A.S.S.R.
Kavkaz (Caucasus Mountains)
Bol. Kavkaz
Zakavkazye
Kuzey Anadolu Dağları
Toros Dağları
Anadolu Dağları
LEBANON
CYPRUS
Dhodhekanisos

**Cities and towns:**
Tehrān  Qom  Semnān  Āmul  Bābol  Rasht  Bandar-e Pahlavī  Astara  Ardabīl  Zenjān  Qazvīn  Hamadān  Kermānshāh  Saveh  Qom  Kāshān  Ardestān  Khorramābād  Borūjerd  Kum
Baku  Alyat Pristan  Alyat  Stepanakert  Agdam  Shemakha  Kuba  Derbent  Kizlyar  Makhachkala
Tabriz  Maragheh  Rezā'īyeh  Reza'iyeh  Miandoab  Urmia  Maku  Khoi  Van  Bitlis  Mush  Erzurum  Erzincan  Kars  Artvin  Trabzon  Rize  Giresun  Ordu  Samsun  Sinop  Amasya  Tokat  Sivas  Kayseri  Yozgat  Çorum  Çankırı  Ankara  Kırşehir  Nevşehir  Kırıkkale  Kastamonu  Zonguldak  Ereğli  Bolu  Adapazarı  İzmit  İstanbul  Üsküdar  Bursa  Bilecik  Eskişehir  Afyon  Kütahya  Uşak  Manisa  İzmir (Smyrna)  Aydın  Denizli  Muğla  Isparta  Burdur  Konya  Karaman  Ereğli  Niğde  Adana  Mersin  Tarsus  İskenderun  Antakya  Gaziantep  Urfa  Diyarbakır  Mardin  Malatya  Elazığ  Maraş  Antalya  Alanya  Silifke
Halab (Aleppo)  Hamā'  Homs  Dimashq (Damascus)  Tarabulus  Bayrūt (Beirut)  Sayda  El Ladhiqiya (Latakia)  Baniyas  Tadmur (Palmyra)
Al Mawṣil  Kirkūk  Arbīl  Baghdad  Tikrīt  Sāmarrā'  Ramadi  Hīt  Āna  Dayr az Zawr  Raqqa  Harran
Tbilisi  Kutaisi  Poti  Batumi  Sukhumi  Sochi  Ordzhonikidze  Grozny  Nalchik  Kislovodsk  Pyatigorsk  Georgiyevsk  Mineralnye Vody  Stavropol  Armavir  Maykop  Tikhoretsk  Kropotkin  Krasnodar  Novorossiysk  Tuapse
Yerevan  Leninakan  Kirovakan  Echmiadzin  Nakhichevan
Rostov  Taganrog  Azov  Zhdanov  Berdyansk  Melitopol  Kerch  Feodosiya  Yalta  Simferopol  Sevastopol  Yevpatoriya  Dzhankoy  Kherson  Nikolayev  Odessa  Kishinev  Tiraspol  Bendery
Volgograd (Stalingrad)  Astrakhan  Guryev  Makat  Volzhskiy  Dubovka  Kamyshin  Kalach  Urda
Kharkov  Belgorod  Sumy  Poltava  Kremenchug  Dnepropetrovsk  Dneprodzerzhinsk  Zaporozhye  Donetsk  Makeyevka  Gorlovka  Kramatorsk  Slavyansk  Lugansk (Voroshilovgrad)  Shakhty  Kamensk  Novocherkassk  Novoshakhtinsk
Kiyev (Kiev)  Zhitomir  Vinnitsa  Berdichev  Cherkassy  Uman  Kirovograd  Krivoy Rog  Nikopol  Kakhovka
Bucureşti (Bucharest)  Braşov  Piteşti  Ploieşti  Galaţi  Brăila  Constanţa  Sulina  Iaşi  Bacău  Chernovtsy  Ivano-Frankovsk  Kolomyya  Kamenets Podolskiy  Khmelnitskiy  Belaya Tserkov
Varna  Burgas  Sliven  Ruse  Silistra  Edirne  Tekirdağ  Çanakkale  Gelibolu (Gallipoli)  Balıkesir  Bandırma  Çanakkale
Ródhos  Kárpathos  Sámos

**Rivers and physical features:**
Volga  Ural  Don  Kuban  Terek  Kura  Araks  Dnepr  Dnestr (Dnister)  Prut  Siret  Danube  Tisa  Dijlah (Tigris)  Nahr al Furāt (Euphrates)  Firat  Kızıl Irmak  Sakarya

**Elevations:**
Demavend 5604  Elbrus 5633  Ararat 5165  4824  5047  4168  3957  Erciyas Dağı 3770  2565  3086  4486  2305  2707  2635  2217

m  4000  2000  1000  400  200  0
m  0  200  1000  2000  4000

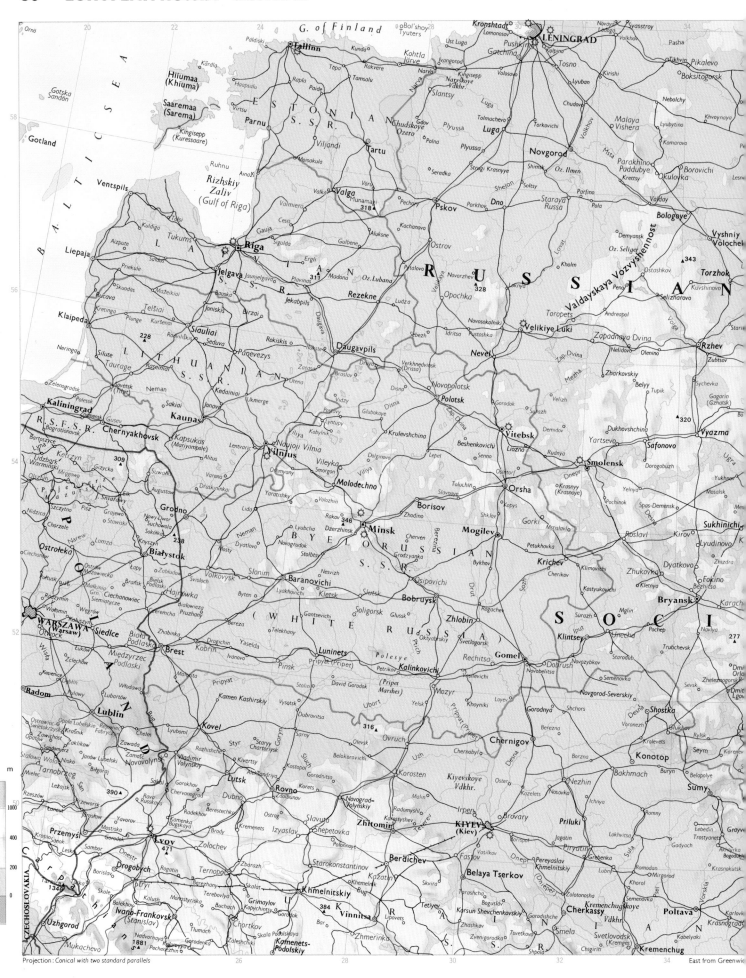

G. of Finland

BALTIC SEA

Gotska Sandön

Hiiumaa (Khiuma)

Saaremaa (Sarema)

Gotland

Kingisepp (Kuressaare)

Ruhnu

Rizhskiy Zaliv (Gulf of Riga)

ESTONIAN S.S.R.

LATVIAN S.S.R.

LITHUANIAN S.S.R.

R.S.F.S.R.

Kaliningrad

Kaunas

BYELORUSSIAN S.S.R. (WHITE RUSSIA)

POLAND

CZECHOSLOVAKIA

RUSSIAN S.F.S.R.

Leningrad

Novgorod

Pskov

Minsk

Vitebsk

Smolensk

WARSZAWA (Warsaw)

Brest

Lublin

Lvov

KIYEV (Kiev)

Valdayskaya Vozvyshennost

Polesye (Pripet Marshes)

UKRAINIAN S.S.R.

Projection: Conical with two standard parallels

East from Greenwich

m
1000
400
200
0
200
m

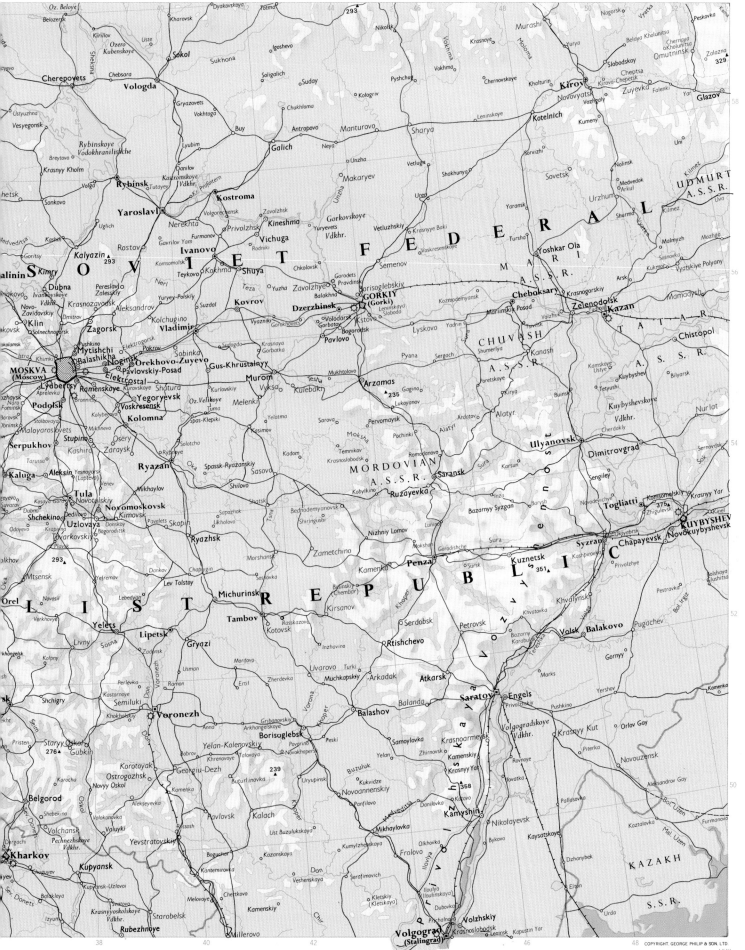

1:5 000 000

50    0    50    100    150    200 km

Oz. Beloye
Belozersk
Kirillov
Ozero
Uste    Kubenskoye
Dyakovskaya    Totma
293
Nikolsk
Murashi
Nagorsk    Oz. Vyatka
Peskovka
Slobodskoy    Omutninsk
Chernaya    329

Kharovsk    Igoshevo
Krasnoye    Belaya Kholunitsa    oKholunitsa
Zalazna

Sokol    Sukhona    Pyshchug    Vokhma    Krasnoye
Vokhma    Vozhgaly    Kirovo-Chepetsk    Falenki    Yar
Cherepovets    Chebsara    Soligalich    Suday    Chernovskoye    Khalturin    Zuyevka    Glazov

Vologda    Vokhtoga    Kologriv    Yurya    KIROV    Novovyatsk
Gryazovets    Chukhloma    Sharya    Kotelnich    Kumeny    Uni    58

Vesyegonsk    Breytovo
Rybinskoye    Vodokhranilishche    Buy    Antropovo    Manturovo    Leninskoye    Sovetsk    Urzhum    Nolinsk
Krasnyy Kholm    Lyubim    Galich    Neya    Medvedok    UDMURT
Ustyuzhna    Volga    Danilov    Makaryev    Unzha    Vetluga    Shakhunya    Yaransk    Arkul    A.S.S.R.
etsk    Sonkovo    Rybinsk    Tutayev    Vologrechensk    Ured    Shurma    Kilmez    Uva

Yaroslavl    Nerekhta    Kostroma    Zavolzhsk    Gorkovskoye    Vetluzhskiy    Krasnyye Baki    Tursha    Kilmez    56
alinin    Uglich    Rostov    Gavrilov Yam    Privolzhsk    Vdkhr.    Voskresenskoye    YOSHKAR OLA    Malmyzh    Mazhga
S    O    V    I    E    T        F    E    D    E    R    A    L        Sosnovka
Kimry    Kalyazin    293    Furmanov    Ivanovo    Yuryevets    Semenov    M A R I    Kukmor    Vyatskiye Polyany
Pereslavl    Komsomolsk    Shuya    Chkalovsk    A.S.S.R.    Arsk
novo    Dubna    Zalesskiy    Yuryev-Polskiy    Kokhma    Gorodets    Kozmodemyansk    Shumerlya
Ivankovskoye    Krasnozavodsk    Suzdal    Vyazniki    Pravdinsk    CHEBOKSARY    Krasnogorskiy    Mamadysh
Novo-    Vdkhr.    Aleksandrov    Kolchugino    Borisoglebskiy    Mariinskiy Posad    Zelenodolsk    KAZAN
Zavidovskiy    Dmitrov    GORKIY    CHUVASH    Volzhs    T    A    T    A    R
Klin    Zagorsk    Vladimir    Kovrov    Dzerzhinsk    (Gorki)    Leninskaya    A.    S.    S.    R.
Solnechnogorsk    Pokrov    Volodarsk    Kstovo    Sloboda    Kanash    Chistopol
kovsk    Pushkino    Elektrogorsk    Sudogda    Bogorodsk    Lyskovo    Yadrin    A.    S.    S.    R.
Mytishchi    Elektrostal    Krasnaya    Pavlovo    Shumerlya    Kamskoye    Kuybyshev
Balashikha    Noginsk    Orekhovo-Zuyevo    Gorbatov    Pyana    Sergach    Ustye    Bilyarsk
MOSKVA    Lyubertsy    Pavlovskiy-Posad    Gus-Khrustalnyy    Murom    Tesha    Mukhtolovo    Poretskoye    Kuybyshevskoye
(Moscow)    Ramenskoye    Shatura    Vyksa    Kulebaki    Arzamas    Kirya    Tetyushi    Vdkhr.    Nurlat
Nara-    Podolsk    Kurovskoye    Oz.Velikoye    Kasimov    Melenki    235    Gagino    Alatyr    Buinsk    Cherdakly
Fominsk    Yegoryevsk    Tuma    Spas-Klepiki    Lukoyanov    Ulyanovsk    Dimitrovgrad    54
Maloyaroslavets    Voskresensk    Kolomna    Yelatma    Sarova    Pervomaysk    Pochinki    Alatyr
brovsk    Stupino    Mikhnevo    Solotcha    Kadom    Moksha    Ardatov    Alatyr    Sengiley
Kashira    Rybnoye    Temnikov    Romodanovo    Sura    Karsun
Serpukhov    Osery    Zaraysk    Krasnoslobodsk    MORDOVIAN    Saransk    Inza    Baryah    Togliatti    375
Tarussa    Ryazan    Spassk-Ryazanskiy    Sasovo    A.S.S.R.    Ruzayevka    Novodevichye    Zhigulevsk    Komsomolskiy    Krasnyy Yar
Kaluga    Aleksin    Yesnogorsk    Mikhaylov    Shilovo    Kobylkino    Bazarnyy Syzgan    Syzran    KUYBYSHEV
eyevo    (Laptevo)    Venev    Shatsk    Nizhniy Lomov    Inza    Oktyabrsk    Chapayevsk    Novokuybyshevsk
Tula    Novotulskiy    Bednodemyanovsk    Tsna    Shiringushi    Privolzhye    Kashpirovka
Shchekino    Pedilovo    Novomoskovsk    Sapozhok    Likholovo    Sursk    Kuznetsk    351
Odoyevo    Kimovsk    Dankov    Pavelets    Skopin    Zametchino    Morshansk    Mokshan    Penza    L    I    C
Uzlovaya    Donskoy    Chaplygin    Gorodishche    Sura
Krapivna    Bogoroditsk    Ryazhsk    Lebedyan    Kamenka    Bazarny
Tovarkovskiy    Plavsk    Lev Tolstoy    Kirsanov    Karabulak
293    Kaly    Michurinsk    Bolshaya
khov    Mtsensk    Novosil    L    I    S    T        R    E    P    U    B    Kuznetsk    358    Khvalynsk    Pestravka
Yefremov    Verkhovye    Tambov    Kotovsk    Rasskazovo    Serdobsk    Petrovsk    Khvatovka    Volsk    Balakovo    Pugachev
Orel    Yelets    Livny    Sosna    Lipetsk    Gryazi    Mordovo    Inzhavino    Rtishchevo    Bazarny    Khvalynsk    Gornyy
Kolpny    Zadonsk    Usman    Uvarovo    Turki    Arkadak    Atkarsk    Marks    Yershov
Novosil    Perlevka    Ramon    Zherdevka    Ertil    Muchkapskiy    Balanda    Saratov    Engels    Pushkino    Kamenka
sk    Shchigry    Semiluki    Khokholskiy    Anna    Gribanovskiy    Peski    Samoylovka    Volgogradskoye    Krasnyy Kut    Orlov Gay
Voronezh    Arkhangelskoye    Balashov    Krasnoarmeysk    Vdkhr.
Pristen    Staryy Oskol    Gubkin    276    Yelan-Kolenovskiy    Povarino    Novokhopersk    Yelan    Zhirnovsk    Kamenskiy    Piterka    Novouzensk
Korotoyak    Bobrov    Talovaya    239    Buzuluk    Uryupinsk    Krasnyy Yar    Novatka
Belgorod    Ostrogozhsk    Georgiu-Dezh    Kukvidze    Novoannenskiy    358    50
Novyy Oskol    Kamenka    Pavlovsk    Kalach    Panfilovo    Danilovka    Pallasovka    Aleksandrov Gay
Shebekina    Volokonovka    Alekseyevka    Ust Buzulukskaya    Novoannenskiy    Kovo    Kamyshin    Bol Uzen
Volchansk    Oskol    Valuyki    Rossosh    Mikhaylovka    Nikolayevsk    Kaztalovka    Mal Uzen    Furmanovo
Pechnezhskoye    Kumylzhenskaya    Frolovo    Olkhovka    Bykovo    Kaysatskoye    KAZAKH
Kharkov    Kupyansk    Boguchar    Kazanskaya    Don    Serafimovich    Ilovlya    Urda    S.    S.    R.
vy    Kupyansk-Uzlovoi    Kantemirovka    Veshenskaya    Ilovlinskaya    Dzhanybek    Elton
Sev Donets    Balakleya    Melovoye    Chir    Prichalok    Kapustin Yar
Krasnyyoskolskoye    Chertkovo    Kletskiy    Dubovka    Kapustin Yar
Izyum    Vdkhr.    Starobelsk    Kamenskiy    (Kletskaya)    Krasnoslobodsk    Leninsk    Kapustin Yar
Rubezhnoye    Millerovo    VOLGOGRAD    Volzhskiy
(Stalingrad)    COPYRIGHT. GEORGE PHILIP & SON. LTD.
HHK

38    40    42    44    46    48

Projection: Conical with two standard parallels

1:5 000 000

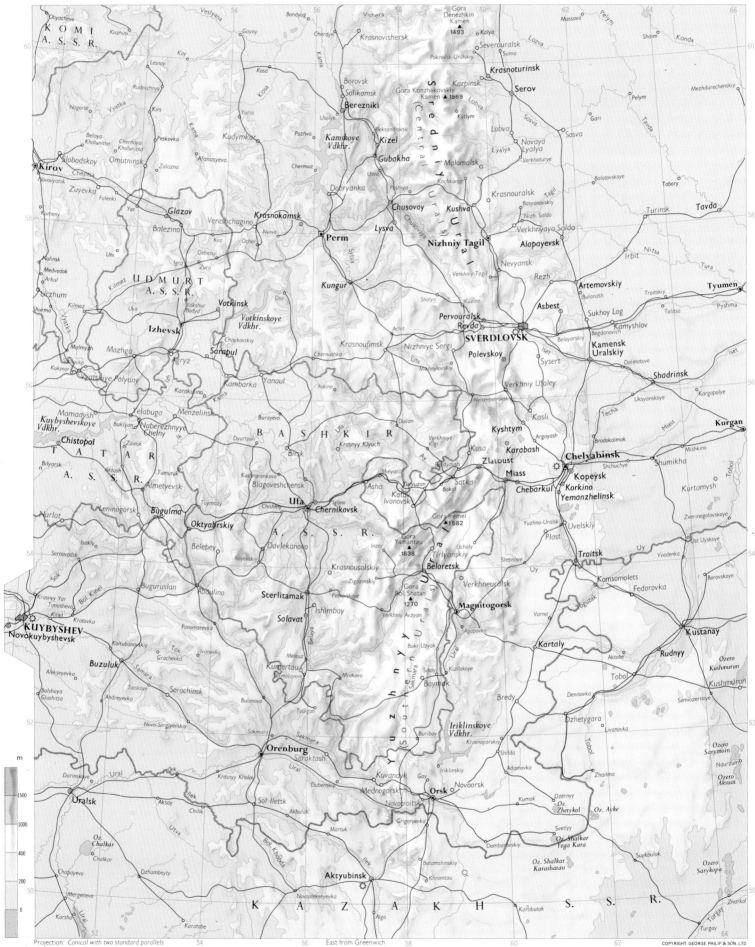

Projection: Conical with two standard parallels          East from Greenwich

1:5 000 000

50    0    50    100    150    200 km

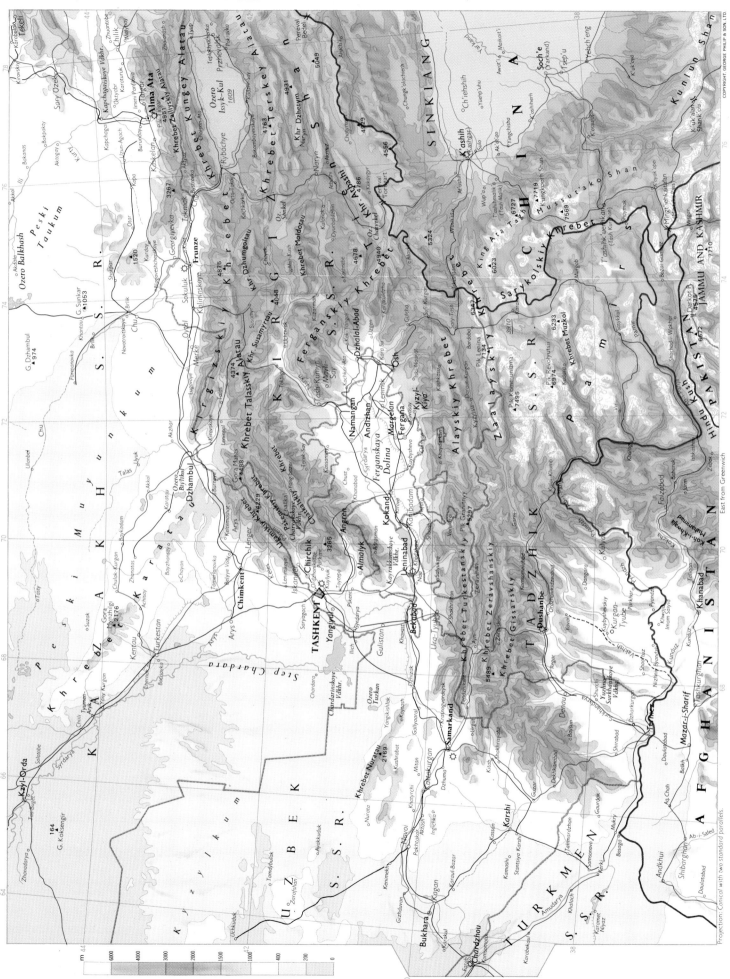

Projection: Conical with two standard parallels.

East from Greenwich

COPYRIGHT GEORGE PHILIP & SON LTD

m   6000  4000  3000  2000  1500  1000  400  200  0

1:50 000 000

500   0   500   1000   1500   2000 km

COPYRIGHT GEORGE PHILIP & SON, LTD.

PACIFIC OCEAN

ARCTIC OCEAN

INDIAN OCEAN

Aleutian Is.
7822
Bering Str.
C. Dezhnitsa
Bering Sea
Kamchatka Peninsula
4750
Sredinny Ra.
Sea of Okhotsk
Sakhalin
Kuril Is.
Hokkaido
5442
Honshu
Japan
Sea of Japan
Shikoku
Kyushu
Ryukyu Is.
Korea Str.
Bonin Is.
Iwo Jima
Volcano Is.
Tropic of Cancer
Guam Is.
Cape Johnson Deep 10 497
Caroline Is.
Pelew Is.
Mindanao
Philippine Is.
Luzon
Formosa
Hainan
G. of Tonkin
Halmahera
Moluccas
Celebes
Celebes Sea
Ceram
Banda Sea
Arafura Sea
New Guinea
Australia
Timor
Flores
Bali
Java Sea
Java
Sunda Is.
Sumatra
Str. of Sunda
Borneo
Kinabalu 4101
Palawan
Sulu Sea
South China Sea
Makasar Strait
East China Sea
Yellow Sea
Hwang-ho
Hai-ho
Great Plain of China
Plain of China
Si-kiang
Song-koi (Red) R.
Mekong
Menam
G. of Siam
Malay Peninsula
Str. of Malacca
Andaman Is.
Nicobar Is.
Bay of Bengal
Irrawaddy
Salween
Brahmaputra
Ganges
Ceylon
Palk Strait
Laccadive Is.
Maldive Is.
Chagos Arch.
Equator
Eastern Ghats
Western Ghats
Deccan
Godavari
Krishna
C. Comorin
Gulf of Mannar
India
Narmada
Tapti
Jumna
Indus
Sutlej
Thar Desert
Sulaiman Ra.
Kunlun Shan
Plateau of Tibet
Everest 8848
Tsangpo
Lop Nor
Takla Makan
Tarim Basin
Tarim
Turfan Basin
Tien Shan
L. Balkhash
Ili
Chu
Pamirs
Communism Pk. 7495
Hindu Kush
Karakoram Ra. 8611
Amu Darya
Syr Darya
Aral Sea
Turanian Plain
Caspian Sea
Plateau of Iran
Elburz Mts.
Demavend
Great Salt Desert
Zagros Mts.
Persian Gulf
G. of Oman
Tigris
Euphrates
Mesopotamia
Arabia
Ar Rub al Khali
G. of Aden
Socotra
Ras Asir (C. Guardafui)
Somali Peninsula
Red Sea
Suez Canal
Sinai Pen.
Dead Sea
Syrian Desert
Cyprus
Taurus Mts.
Anatolia
Ararat 5165
Elbruz 5633
Caucasus
Black Sea
Bosporus
Danube
Carpathians
Adriatic Sea
Mediterranean Sea
Libyan Desert
Nile
Lake Victoria
Arabian Sea
Seychelles
Amirantes

Kamchatka Peninsula
Wrangel I.
New Siberian Is.
Chelyuskin
Taimyr Peninsula
Severnaya Zemlya
Laptev Sea
Kara Sea
Novaya Zemlya
Barents Sea
Svalbard
Greenland
Iceland
British Isles
North Cape
Kola Pen.
White Sea
Finland
Scandinavia
Baltic Sea
North Sea
Rhine
Elbe
Oder
Vistula
N. Dvina
Kolguyev
Kanin
North European Plain
Russian Central Uplands
Dnepr
Don
Volga
Ural
Ural Mountains
1640
West Siberian Plain
Ob
Irtysh
Tobol
Narodnaya 1894
Steppe of Kazakhstan
Kolyma
Gydan Ra. (Kolyma)
Verkhoyansk Range
Stanovoy Ra.
Indigirka
Yana
Lena
Aldan
Central Siberian Plateau
Olenek
Yenisei
Lower Tunguska
Angara
Sayan Mts.
Altai
Belukha 4506
Plateau of Mongolia
Selenga
L. Baikal
Yablonovy Ra.
Amur
Sikhote Alin Ra.
Shingari
Manchurian Plain
Great Khingan Mts.
Koko Nor
Himalaya
Jaxartes

East from Greenwich
Projection

1:50 000 000

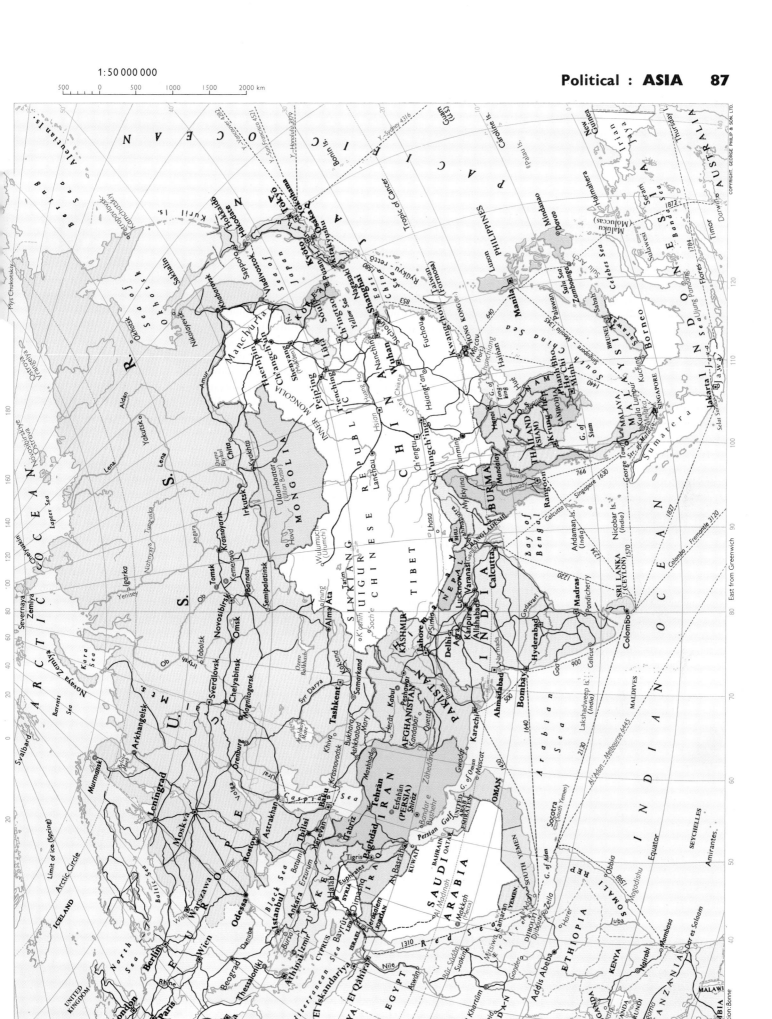

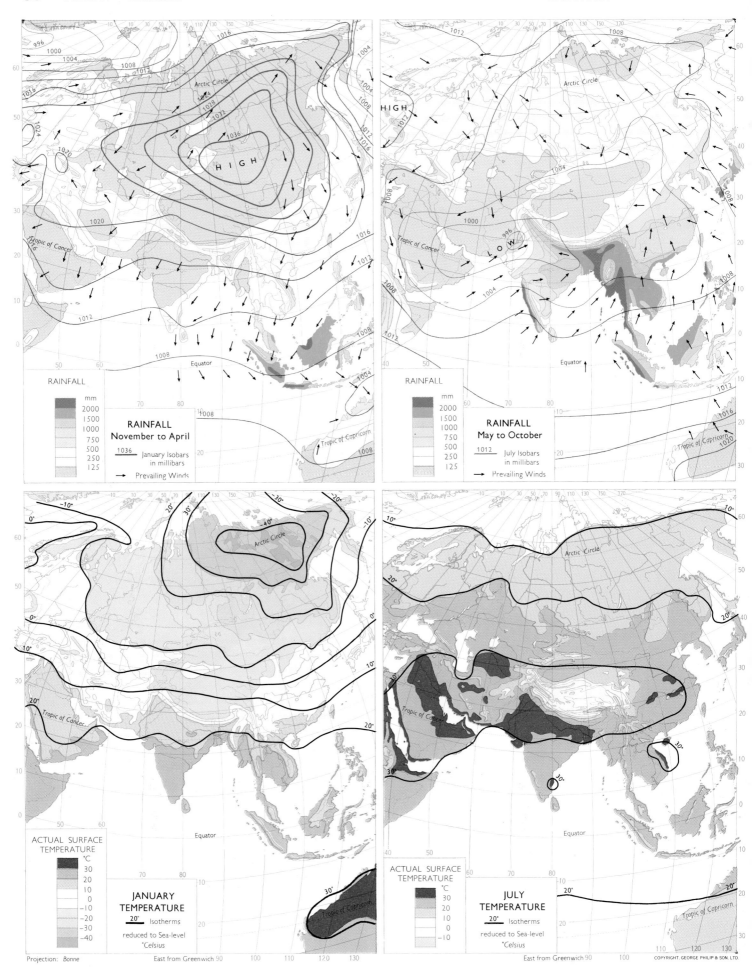

RAINFALL

mm
2000
1500
1000
750
500
250
125

**RAINFALL**
**November to April**

1036 ⎯ January Isobars
in millibars

→ Prevailing Winds

RAINFALL

mm
2000
1500
1000
750
500
250
125

**RAINFALL**
**May to October**

1012 ⎯ July Isobars
in millibars

→ Prevailing Winds

ACTUAL SURFACE
TEMPERATURE

°C
30
20
10
0
-10
-20
-30
-40

**JANUARY**
**TEMPERATURE**

20° ⎯ Isotherms
reduced to Sea-level
°Celsius

ACTUAL SURFACE
TEMPERATURE

°C
30
20
10
0
-10

**JULY**
**TEMPERATURE**

20° ⎯ Isotherms
reduced to Sea-level
°Celsius

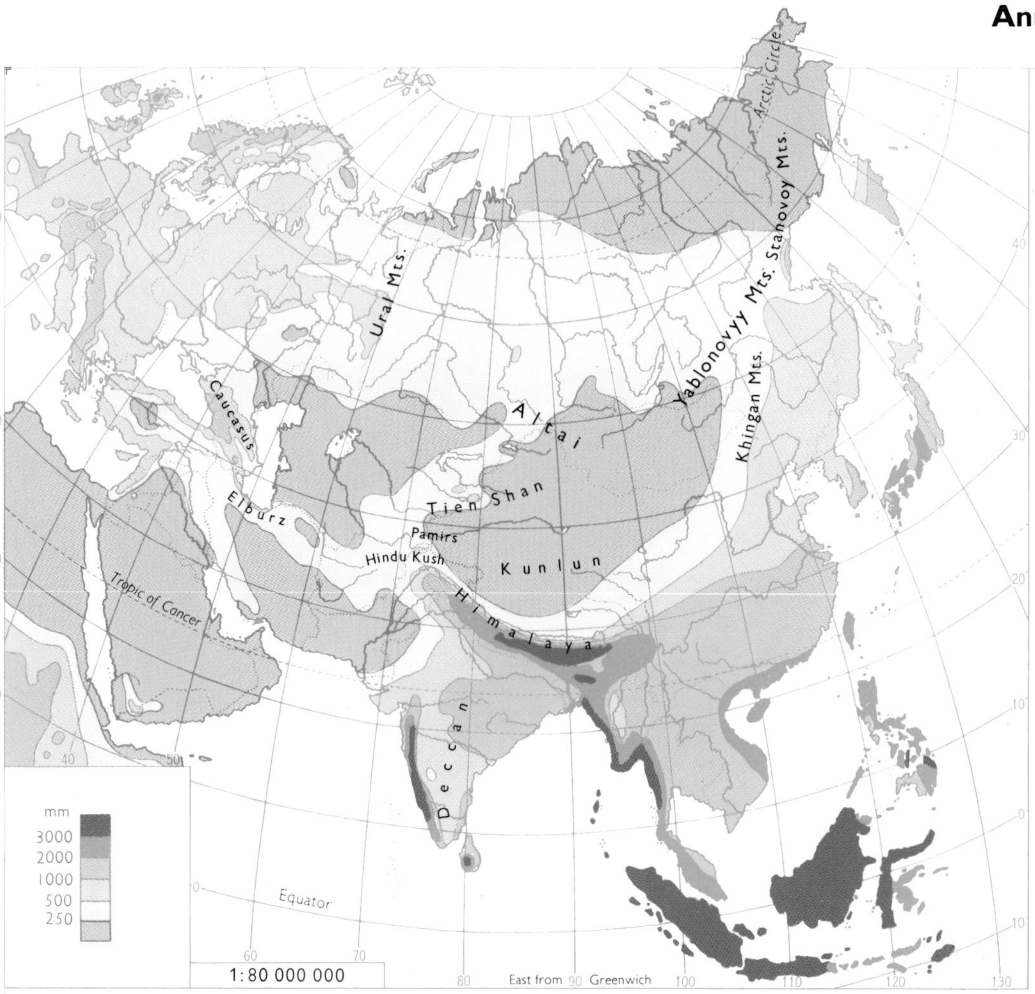

Ural Mts.
Caucasus
Elburz
Tropic of Cancer
Altai
Tien Shan
Pamirs
Hindu Kush
Kunlun
Himalaya
Yablonovyy Mts.
Khingan Mts.
Stanovoy Mts.
Arctic Circle
Deccan
Equator
East from Greenwich

mm
3000
2000
1000
500
250

1 : 80 000 000

# INDIA: MONSOONS

THEIR EVOLUTION

IS SHOWN BY

MONTHLY

CLIMATE

MAPS

RAINFALL
mm per month

mm
25
50
100
200
400

—— ISOTHERMS
*Temperature in degrees Celsius*

—— ISOBARS
*(Pressure in millibars)*

⟵ WINDS

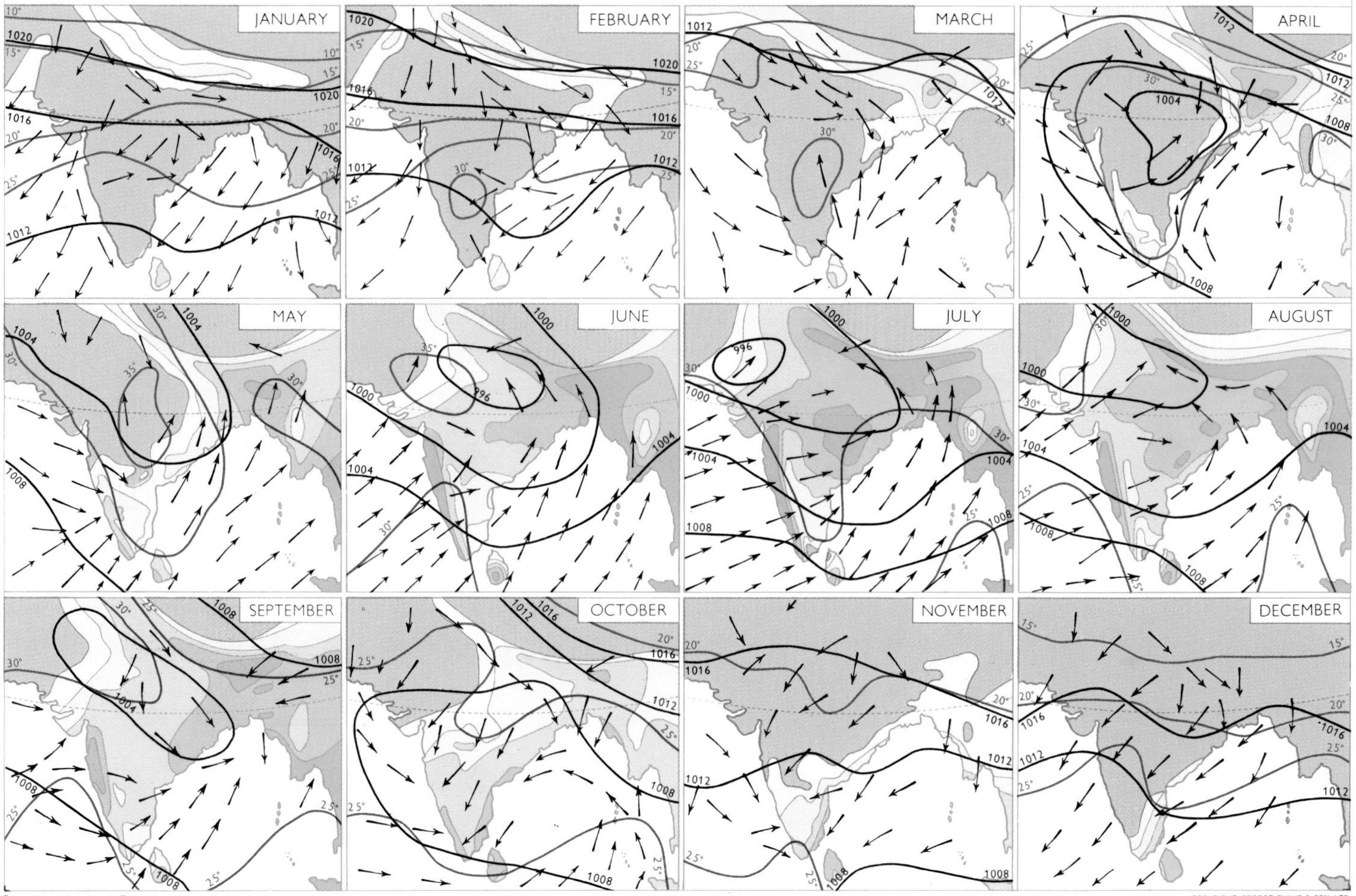

JANUARY FEBRUARY MARCH APRIL

MAY JUNE JULY AUGUST

SEPTEMBER OCTOBER NOVEMBER DECEMBER

Projection: Lambert's Equivalent Azimuthal

1:1 000 000

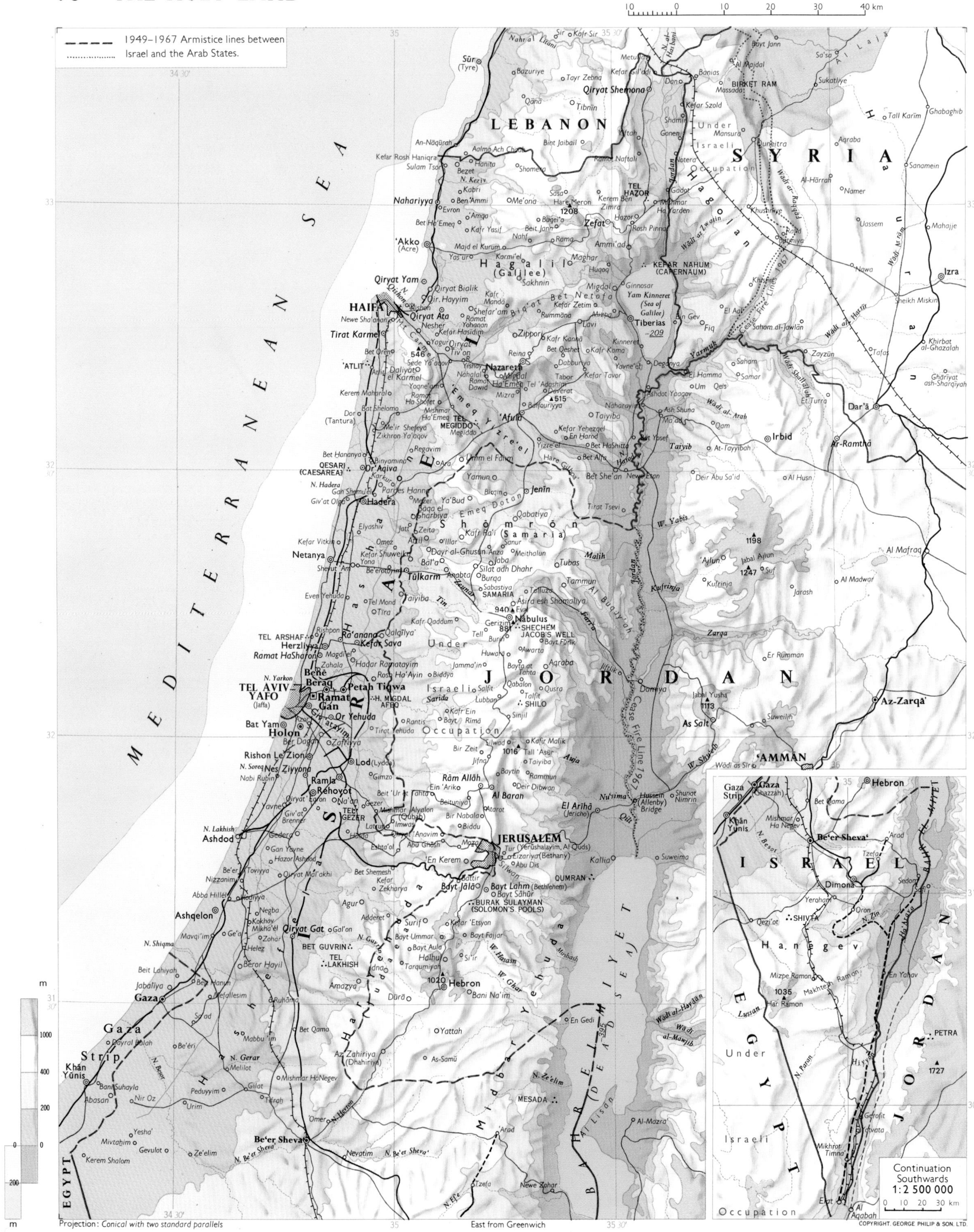

10   0   10   20   30   40 km

1949–1967 Armistice lines between
Israel and the Arab States.

MEDITERRANEAN SEA

LEBANON

SYRIA

Sūr (Tyre)
Nahr el Lītāni
Bazūriye
Tayr Zebna
Kefar Gil'adi
Metulla
Banias
BIRKET RAM
Massada
Bayt Jann
Sa'sa'
Al Lajā
Sukaltīye
Ghabaghib
Qiryat Shemona
Qāna
Tibnin
Kefar Szold
Aqraba
Namer
Tall Karim
An-Nāqūrah
Aalma Ach Cha'b
Bint Jbail
Shamir
Under
Israeli
Occupation
Qunaitra
Khushnīye
Uassem
Mahajje
Kefar Rosh Haniqra
Honita
Ramot Naftali
Notera
Wādī ar Ruqqād
Al-Ḥārrah
Nahariyya
Bezet
Shomera
Gonen
Jordan
Ha Yarden
Izra
Sulam Tsor
Ben 'Ammi
Sasa
Kerem Ben
Zimra
El Al
Sheikh Miskin
Akko (Acre)
Evron
'Amqa
Me'ona
Hare Meron
1208
Mishmar
Ha Yarden
Nawa
Majd el Kurum
Yas'ur
Kafr Yasif
Bet Jann
Rosh Pinna
Zefat
TEL HAZOR
Gadot
Khisfin
Karmi'el
Maghar
Ammi'ad
Qiryat Yam
Qiryat Bialik
Qir. Hayyim
Sakhnin
Migdal
Ginnosar
KEFAR NAHUM
(CAPERNAUM)
En Gev
Fiq
Hagalil (Galilee)
Qana
Bet Netofa
Yam Kinneret (Sea of Galilee)
Soham al-Jawlān
HAIFA
Nesher
Kefar Hasidim
Shefar'am
Ramat
Yohanan
Zippori
Kafr Kanna
Kinneret
Khirbat al-Ghazalah
Qiryat Ata
Tiberias
-209
Tirat Karmel
Bet Oren
546
Yagur
Qiryat Tiv'on
Reina
Bet Qeshet
Kafr Kama
Degania
Ash Shuna
Zayzūn
'ATLIT
Sede Ya'aqov
Nahalal
Nazaret
Tabor
Kefar Tavor
Um Qēs
Samar
Daliyat el Karmel
Yishay
Ramat David
Tel 'Adashim
Naharayim
Al Ḥamma
Tafas
Abu Daliya
Ramat
Ho'Shofet
Mizra
Ha'Emeq
Ashdot Ya'aqov
Dar'ā
Kerem Mahoral
Yoqne'am
Emeq Yizre'el
515
Deverat
Wādī al-'Arab
Ghāriyat ash-Sharqīyah
Dor (Tantura)
Mishmar
Ho'Emeq
TEL MEGIDDO
Afula
Kefar Yehezgel
En Harod
At-Turra
Irbid
Bet Shemesh
Megiddo
Yizre'el
Bet HaShitta
Taiyib
At-Tayyiba
Ar-Ramthā
QESARI (CAESAREA)
Or 'Aqiva
Binyamina
Umm el Fahm
Hare Gilboa
Bet Alfa
Newe Eitan
Bet She'an
Deir Abu Sa'id
Al Husn
Taiyib
Hadera
Pardes Hanna
Ya'Bud
Emeq Dotan
Shōmrôn (Samaria)
Qabatiya
Tirat Tsevi
W. Yabis
Al Mafraq
Gan Shomron
Baqa el Gharbiya
Jenin
Meser
Zeita
Kafr Ra'i
Sanur
Tubas
Malik
1198
Netanya
Kefar Vitkin
Elyashiv
Omez
Atil
Dayr al-Ghusun
Anza
Meithalun
Tammun
Al Bu'ayjah
1247
Ajlun
Jabal Ajlun
Al Madwar
Kefar Shuweika
Yona
Jaba
Silat adh Dhahr
Sabastiya
Tubas
Kufrinja
Jarash
Be'erotayim
Tülkarm
Anabta
Taffuza
Jerash
Tel Mond
Tira
Taiyiba
Tın
Asira esh Shamaliya
SAMARIA
Kafr Qaddum
940
Fv'a
Zarqa
Er Rümman
Even Yehuda
Ra'anana
Qalqilya
Nabulus
Zarqa
Kfar Sava
Tell
Burin
SHECHEM
JACOB'S WELL
Bayt Fürik
TEL ARSHAF
Herzliyya
Ramat HaSharon
Hadar Ramatayim
Jamma'in
Bayta
Aqraba
Awarta
Benē
Beraq
Rosh Ha'Ayin
Biddya
Huwara
JORDAN
Tel Aviv Yafo (Jaffa)
Petah Tiqwa
Israeli
Sarida
Lubban
Bayt Dajan
Ramat Gan
H. MIGDAL AFEQ
Salfit
Qabalan
Talfit
Qusra
As Salt
Az-Zarqā'
Or Yehuda
Rantis
Kafr Ein
Bayt Rima
Sinjil
Jabal Yusha
1113
Bat Yam
'Azaryim
SHILO
Holon
Tirat Yehuda
Occupation
Bir Zeit
1016
Tall 'Asur
Kafir Malik
Suweilih
Rishon Le'Zion
Zafriyya
Jifna
Baytin
Taiyiba
Rammun
'AMMAN
Nes Ziyyona
Lod (Lydda)
Râm Allâh
Rammun
Wādī as Sir
Ramla
Gimzo
'En 'Arïha
Deir Dibwan
Nabi Rubin
Rehovot
Beit 'Ur it-Tahta
Atarot
Nu'eima
Shunat Nimrin
Na'an
Al Baran
Yavne
Gezer
Mishmar Ayyalon
Beituniya
El Arïha (Jericho)
Hussein (Allenby) Bridge
Giv'at Brenner
Latrun
Abu Ghosh
JERUSALEM
(Yerushalayim, Al-Quds)
Qili
N. Lakhish
TEL GEZER
Imwas (Qubab)
Bir Nabala
Biddu
El'Azariya (Bethany)
Kallia
Ashdod
Gedera
Mevo Hazor
Na'an
Abu Dis
Suweima
En Kerem
Batir
Gan Yavne
Hazor Ashdod
Bayt Jālā
Bayt Lahm (Bethlehem)
QUMRAN
Nizzanim
Tovjya
Kefar Zekharya
Bayt Sāhūr
Be'er Toviyya
Agur
BURAK SULAYMAN (SOLOMON'S POOLS)
Abba Hillel
Hodiyya
Adderet
Surif
Kefar 'Etsyon
Ashqelon
Negba
Mikha'el
Gal'on
Bayt Ummar
Bayt Fajjar
Kokhav
Qiryat Gat
Halhul
Tarqumiyah
Si'ir
Mavqi'im
Helez
Zohar
BET GUVRIN
Idna
W. Hasan
N. Shiqma
Ruhama
TEL LAKHISH
Amazya
1020
Hebron
Bani Na'im
Beit Lahiya
Jabaliya
Bet Hanun
Bet Qama
Dūrā
Gaza
Sa'ad
Be'eri
N. Gerar
Gilat
Az Zahiriya (Dhahiriya)
As-Samū
En Gedi
Gaza Strip
Payral Balah
Mabbu'a
Peduyyim
Mishmar HaNegev
Yattah
Khān Yūnis
Bani Suhayla
Nir Oz
Urim
Omer
MESADA
Al-Mazra'
Abasan
Yesha'
Mivtahim
Gevulot
Ze'elim
N. Be'er Sheva
'Arad
N. Ze'elim
Kerem Shalom
Be'er Sheva
Nevatim
Newe Zohar
EGYPT
Tzela
N. Efe

— Inset map (Continuation Southwards) —

Gaza
Ghazzah
Hebron
Bet Qama
Khān Yūnis
Mishmar HaNegev
Be'er Sheva'
'Arad
ISRAEL
Dimona
Qezi'ot
SHIVTA
Oron
Sedom
HaNegev
1035
Yeroham
Mizpe Ramon
Makhtesh Ramon
En Yahav
JORDAN
Har Ramon
PETRA
Under
Israeli
Occupation
Lussan
N. Paran
Ovta
1727
EGYPT
Mikhrot Timna
Gerofit
Yotvata
Elat
Al Aqabah

Continuation Southwards
1:2 500 000
0  10  20  30 km

m
1000
400
200
0
0
200
m

Projection: Conical with two standard parallels          East from Greenwich          COPYRIGHT GEORGE PHILIP & SON. LTD.

1:15 000 000

100   0   100   200   300   400   500   600 km

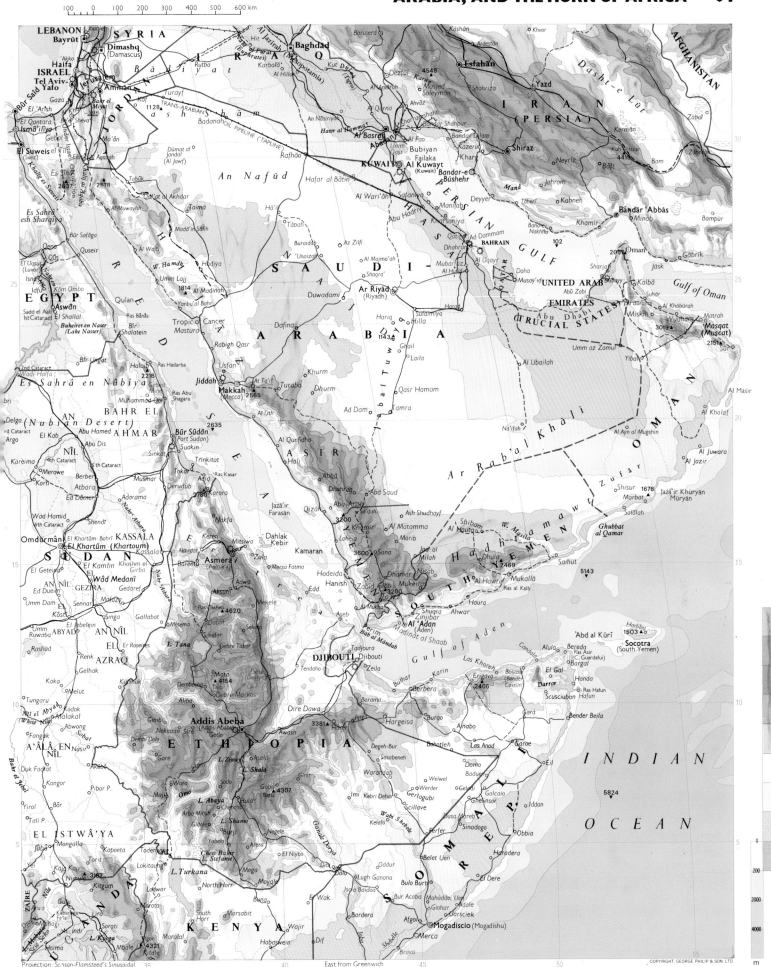

LEBANON
Bayrût
Jounieh
SYRIA
Dimashq
(Damascus)
ISRAEL
Haifa
'Akko
Tel Aviv-
Yafo
Jerusalem
Amman
JORDAN
Gaza
Bûr Sa'îd
El 'Arîsh
El Qantara
Isma'îliya
El Suweis
(Suez)
Es Sahrâ
esh Sharqîya
Gebel
Katherina

IRAQ
Al Jazîra
Hît
Rutba
Furât
(Euphrates)
Baghdad
Karbala
Al Hilla
An Nâsiriyah
Al Qurna
Hawr al Hammâr
Al Basra
Abâdân
Umm Qasr
Bubiyan
Failaka
Al Fao
Bandar Dilam
KUWAIT   Al Kuwayt
(Kuwait)

IRAN
(PERSIA)

Esfahân
4548
Yazd
Dezfûl
Karûn
Masjed
Soleymân
Shahriza
Ahvâz
Bandar-e
Bûshehr
Shiraz
Neyrîz
Kermân
Bâft
Bam
Zâbol
AFGHANISTAN
Dasht-e Lût

EGYPT
Aswân
1st Cataract
El Shallal
Buheiret en Naser
(Lake Nasser)
Qena
Quseir
Isna
Idfu
Kôm Ombo
Edfu
'Aqaba
Tabûk
Al Muwaylih
Al Wajh
Umm Lajj
Yanbu' al Bahr
Al Madînah
1814
Hodiya
Ha'il
Buraidah
Az Zilfi
Al Majma'ah
Shaqra
Ar Riyad
(Riyadh)
Duwadami
Sulaiyil
Hariq
Hilla

SAUDI-
ARABIA

An Nafûd
Hafar al Bâtin
Al Wari'ah
Safaniya
Al Qatif
Dhahran
BAHRAIN
Al Uqayr
Doha
QATAR
UNITED ARAB
EMIRATES
(TRUCIAL STATES)
Abu Dhabi
Abû Zabi
Sharjah
OMAN

RED SEA

Jiddah
Makkah
(Mecca) 2565
At Ta'if
Turaba
Rabigh Qasr
Mastura
Tropic of Cancer
Dafina
Khurm
Dhurm
Laila
Qasr Hamam
Ad Dam
Tamra

Ar Rab' al Khâli

OMAN
Masqat
(Muscat)
2151
Gulf of Oman

PERSIAN GULF

EL
AHMAR
BAHR
(Nubian Desert)
AN
Es Sahrâ en Nûbiya
2216
Bûr Sûdân
(Port Sudan)
2635
Suakin
Sinkat
Tokar
Trinkitat
Ras Kasar

ASIR
Al Qunfidha
Hali
Abhâ
Dhahran
Abâ Saud
3200
Jîzân
Qizân
Sa'dah
Khamir
Al Matamma
Najran
Marib
Shabwa
HADHRAMAUT
Shibam
Al Hauta
W. Masila
Ghubbat
al Qamar
Mukalla
5143

SUDAN
KHARTOUM
Omdurman
El Khartûm
El Khartûm Bahrî
KASSALA
Kassala
Keren
Mitsiwa
Asmera
(Asmara)
Aksum
Mekele
4620
Ras Dashen

YEMEN
Sana
3600
Dhamar
Hodeida
Zabid
Mukeiras
3200
Ta'iz
Al Mukha
SOUTH YEMEN
Al 'Adan
('Aden)
Madînat al Shaab
Haura
Ahwar
Zinjibar
Shuqra
5143

ETHIOPIA
L. Tana
4154
Gondar
Debre Tabor
Debre Markos
4620
Addis Abeba
(Addis Ababa)
3381
Harer

DJIBOUTI
Djibouti
Zeila
Bulhar
Berbera
Hargeisa
Burao
Las Khoreh
Bosaso
Alula
Bereda
Ras Asir
(C. Guardafui)
Socotra
(South Yemen)
1503
'Abd al Kûrî

Gulf of Aden

INDIAN
OCEAN

SOMALI
REP.
5824
Eil
Garoe
Obbia
Mogadiscio
(Mogadishu)
Merca
Brava

KENYA
L. Turkana
3187
Marsabit
Wajir
Moyale
Dif
El Wak
Habaswein

ZAIRE
UGANDA
L. Kyoga
4321
Soroti
Lira

Projection: Sanson-Flamsteed's Sinusoidal

East from Greenwich

COPYRIGHT GEORGE PHILIP & SON, LTD.

m
4000
3000
2000
1500
1000
400
200
0
200
2000
4000
m

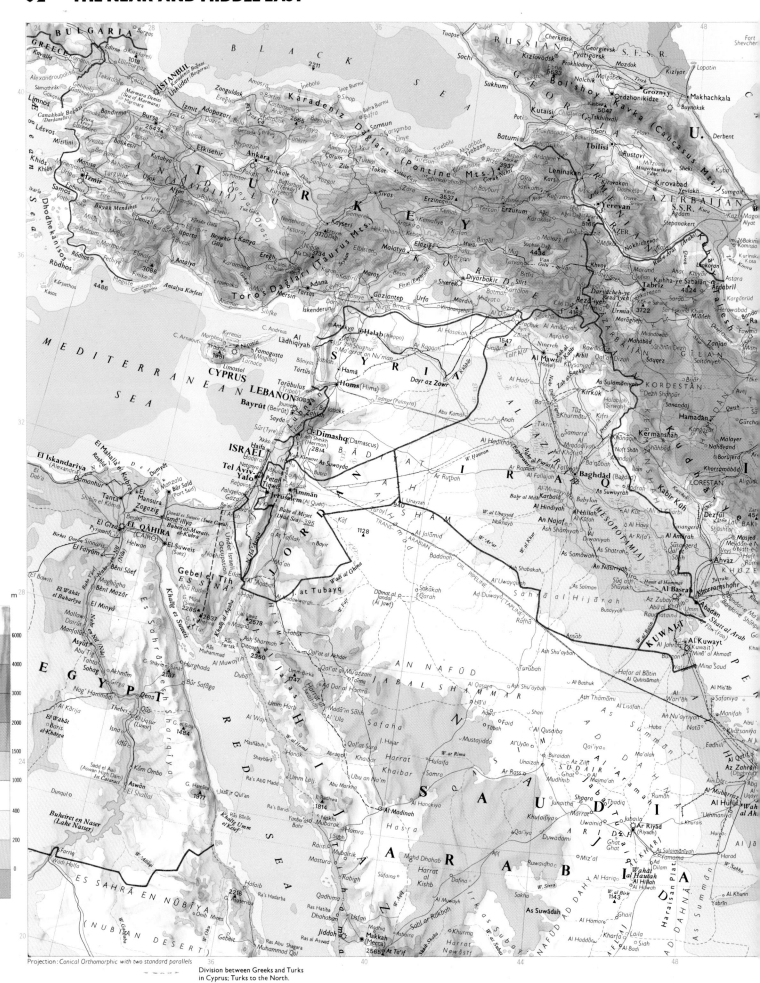

Division between Greeks and Turks
in Cyprus; Turks to the North.

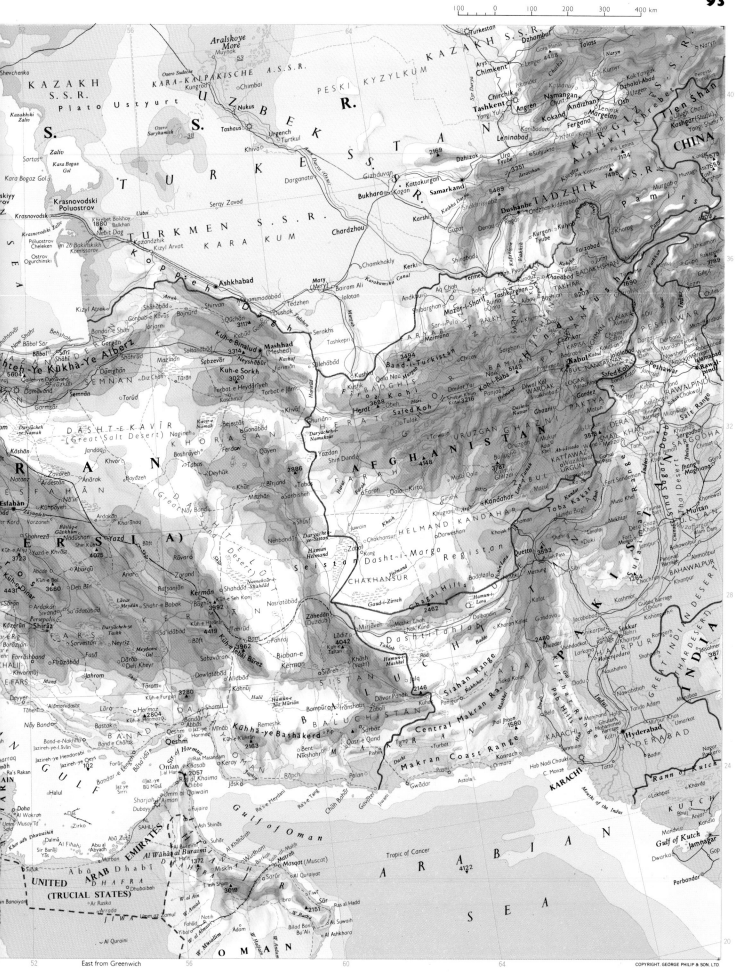

1 : 10 000 000

100    0    100    200    300    400 km

KAZAKH S.S.R.

Aralskoye More

Muynak

Osero Sudoche

KARA-KALPAKISCHE A.S.S.R.

Chimbai

Kungrod

PESKI KYZYLKUM

KAZAKH S.S.R.

Turkestan

Dzhambul

Gora Manas

Taloss

Chimkent

Arys

Lenger 4488

Naryn

Shevchenko

KAZAKH S.S.R.

Plato Ustyurt

Nukus

Tashaus

Urgench

Turtkul

Khiva

UZBEK

S.S.R.

Chirchik

Angren

Tashkent

Yangi Yul

Kokand

Namangan

Chust

Andizhan

Fergana

Osh

Leninsk

Margelan

Kok Yangak

Uzgen

KIRGIZ

Kyzyl

Dzhalal-Abad

Tien Shan

Ulugh Chat

Kashgar (Shufu)

Yangi Shehr

CHINA

7579

Kazakhiki Zaliv

S.

S.

R.

Osero Saryykamish

Darganata

Gizhduvan

Dzhizak

Suyukta

2169

Zeravshan

3351

Pik Lenina

7134

Alayskiy

Pik Kommunizma 7495

Khrebet

7655

Mustagh

7719

7789

Sartass

Kara Bogaz Gol

Kara Bogaz Gol

Krasnovodski Poluostrov

Krasnovodsk

Uzboi

Seray Zavod

Bukhara

Kogan

Karshi

Guzar

Samarkand

Shakhrisyabz

Kulab

Kattakurgan

5489

Dushanbe

TADZHIK

Ordzhonikidzeabad

Regar

Kurgan-Tyube

Khorog

S.S.R.

Pamirs

4409

Shevchenko

Krasnovodski Zaliv

Kara Kum

Ostrov Ogurchinski

Cheleken

Nebit Dag

Balkhan

1880

Bolshoy

Kazandzhik

Kizyl Arvat

Bairam Ali

Ioloton

Kerki

Shirabad

Denau

Termez

Kundu

Kurgan-Tyube

Khanabad

Faizabad

Jurm

BADAKHSHAN

7890

Ishkuan

Gilgit

TURKMEN S.S.R.

Ashkhabad

Atrak

Mary (Mary)

Karakumskiy Canal

Andkhui

Aq Cha

Balkh

Mazar-i-Sharif

Tashkurghan

Buina

Baghlan

TAKHAR

Koksha

8203

Shirvan

Dushak

Tedzhen

Serakhs

Shibarghan

Sar-i-Pul

Samangan

BAGHLAN

Charikar

Darya-ye Panj

Jalalabad

PESHAWAR

Peshawar

Islamabad

Rawalpindi

RAWALPINDI

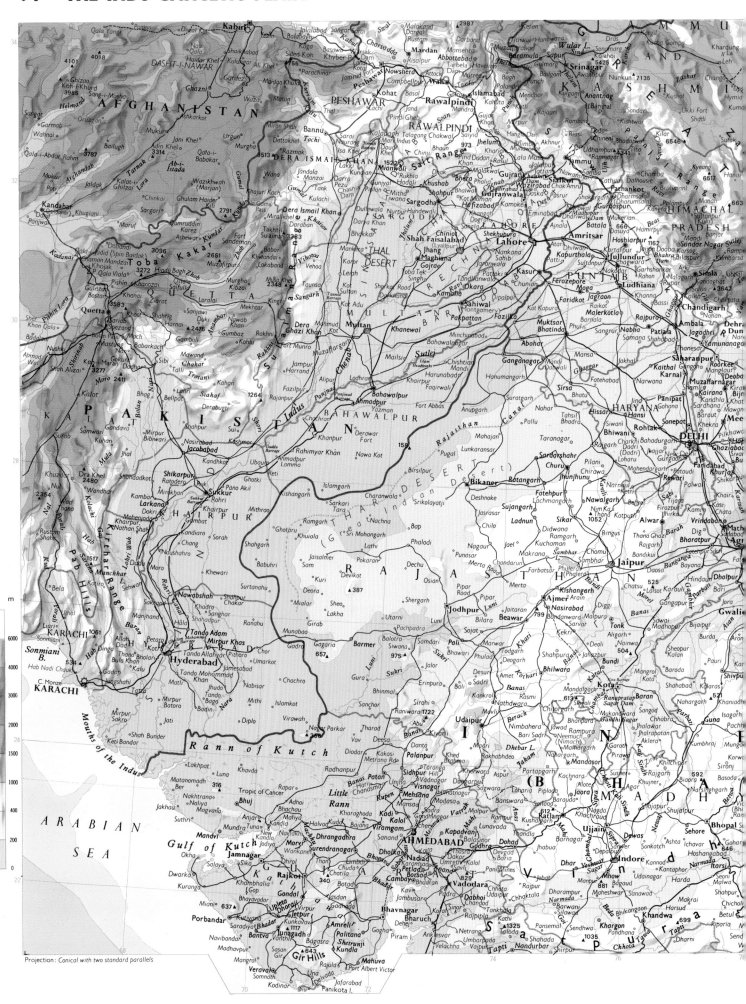

Projection: Conical with two standard parallels

1:6 000 000

50  0  50  100  150  200  250 km

## JAMMU AND KASHMIR
On same scale as Main Map

U.S.S.R.

Karakoram Mountains

Kunlun Shan

SODA PLAINS

Aksai Chin

PESHAWAR

Nanga Parbat

Deosai Mountains

JAMMU

Zaskar Mountains

KASHMIR

Srinagar

Anantnag

Banihal

RawaIpindi

Islamabad

Jammu

HIMACHAL PRADESH

Sialkot

CHINESE

REPUBLIC

Kangtissu Shan

Aling Shan

Ch'alolo Hu

K'otzu Hu

Ch'ienmo Shan

Ch'angchenmo Shan

Pangong Tso

Leh

Tso Morari

TIBET

Mt. Everest

Kanchenjunga

SIKKIM

Gangtok

BHUTAN

Kathmandu

Lalitapur

Pokhara

Annapurna

Dhaulagiri

Manaslu

N  E  P  A  L

Darjeeling

Kalimpong

Siliguri

Jalpaiguri

ASSAM

Garo Hills

Brahmaputra

Cooch Behar

Goalpara

Dhubri

Rangpur

Dinajpur

Mymensingh

Rampur

Moradabad

Bareilly

Pilibhit

Shahjahanpur

Lucknow

KANPUR

U  T  T  A  R   P  R  A  D  E  S  H

Faizabad

Gorakhpur

Ayodhya

Basti

Deoria

Azamgarh

Jaunpur

Allahabad

Varanasi

Mirzapur-cum-Vindhyachal

Ghazipur

Ballia

Chapra

Dinapur

Patna

Arrah

Muzaffarpur

Darbhanga

Motihari

Bettiah

Madhubani

Purnea

Katihar

Bhagalpur

Monghyr

Gaya

BIHAR

Ranchi

Jamshedpur

Hazaribagh

Dhanbad

Asansol

Durgapur

Burdwan

Purulia

Bankura

Bishnupur

Midnapore

Kharagpur

CALCUTTA

Howrah

BANGLADESH

DACCA

Narayanganj

Khulna

Barisal

Jessore

Krishnagar

Nabadwip

Berhampore

Murshidabad

Pabna

Rajshahi

Bogra

W  E  S  T   B  E  N  G  A  L

Malda

English Bazar

Jabalpur

M  A  D  H  Y  A   P  R  A  D  E  S  H

Maikala Range

Bilaspur

Raigarh

Sambalpur

Raurkela

Hirakud Dam

O  R  I  S  S  A

Balasore

Mouths of the Ganga

The Sandheads

Sunderbans

East from Greenwich

1:6 000 000

50  0  50  100  150  200  250 km

B A Y   O F   B E N G A L

Coromandel Coast

MADRAS

TAMIL NADU

KARNATAKA

MYSORE

BANGALORE

GOA

ARABIAN SEA

Malabar Coast

SRI LANKA
(CEYLON)

Gulf of Mannar

Palk Strait

Little Basses
Great Basses

East from 80 Greenwich

Projection: Conical with two standard parallels

m   3000   2000   1500   1000   400   200   0

m   0   200   2000   4000

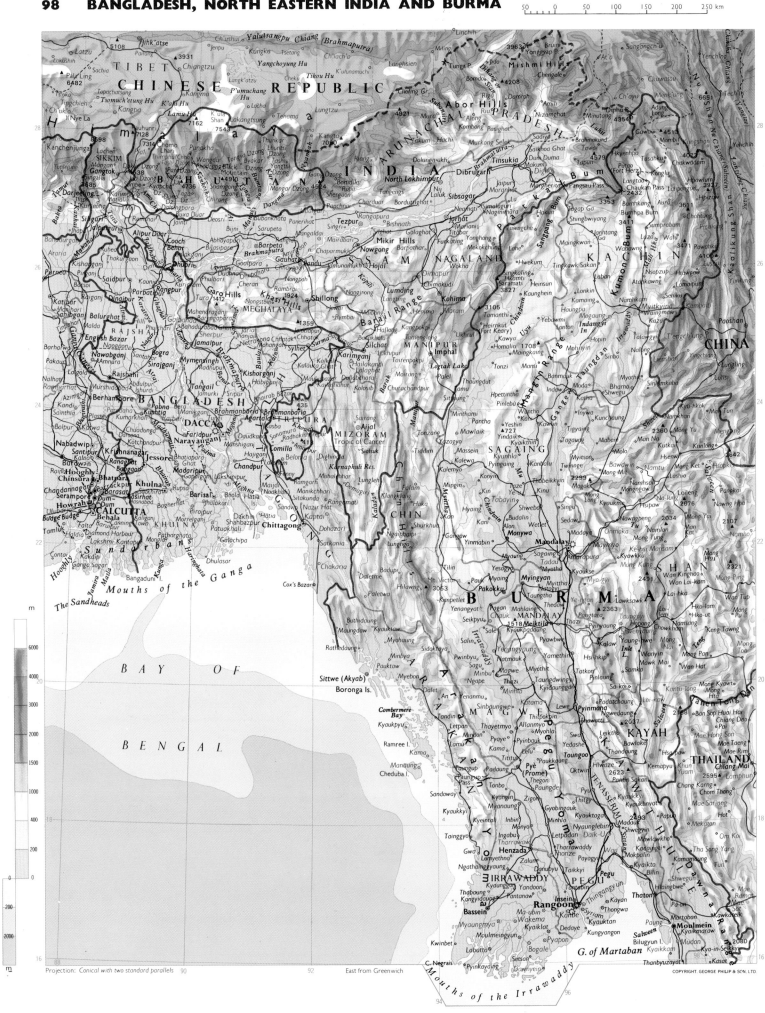

1:6 000 000

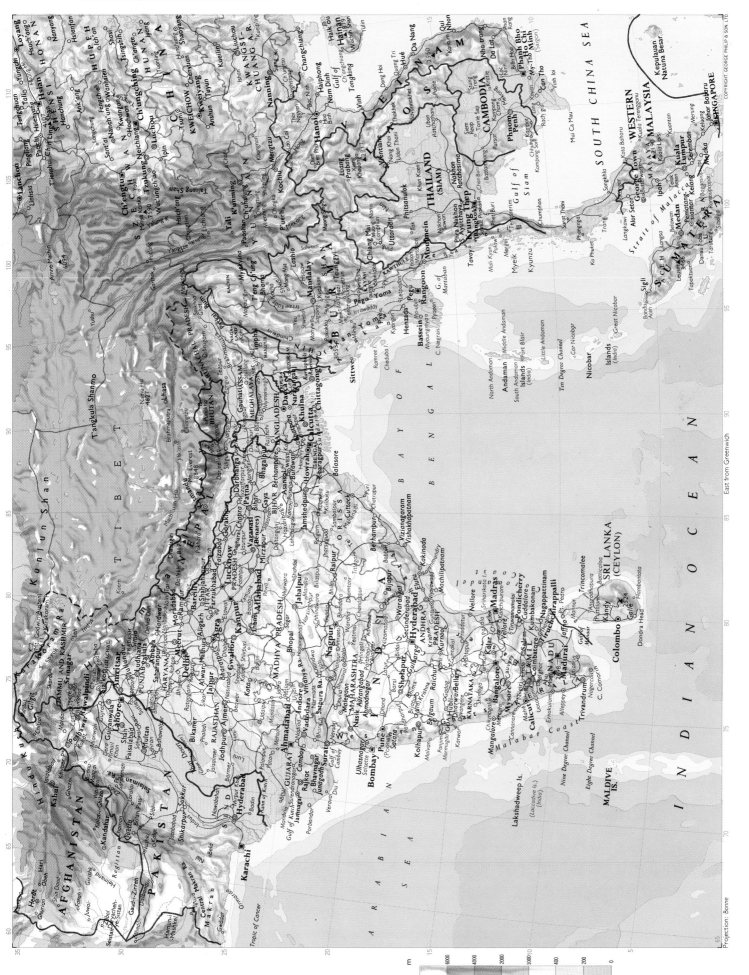

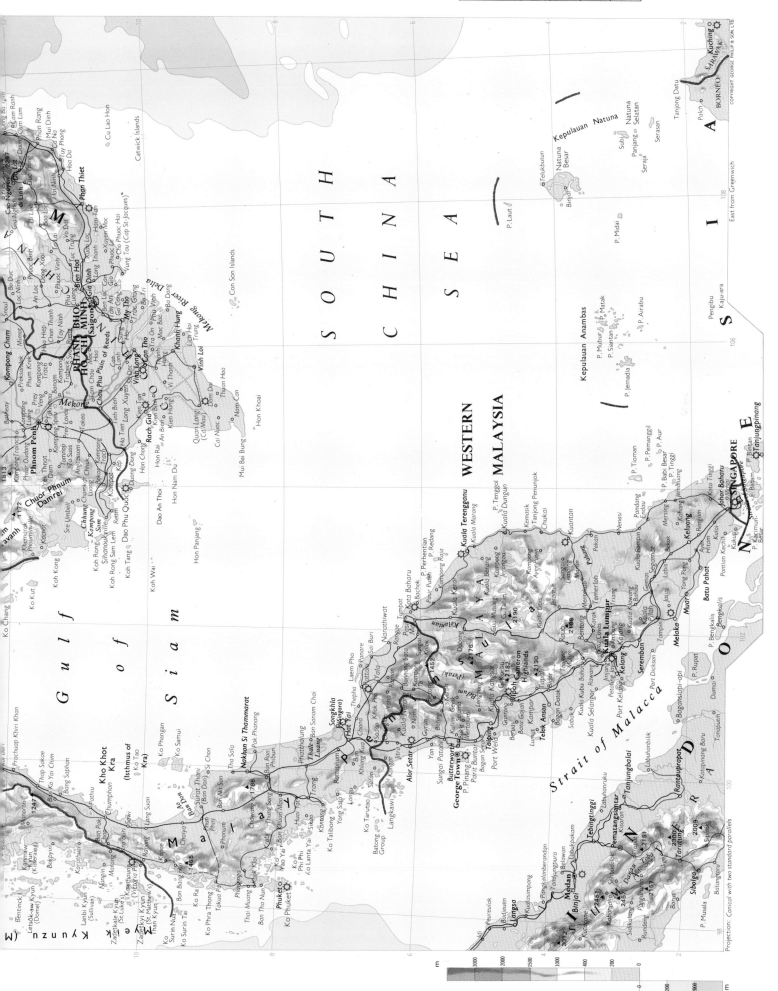

1:6 000 000

50  0  50  100  150  200  250 km

East from Greenwich

SOUTH

CHINA

SEA

Gulf

of

Siam

Strait of Malacca

WESTERN

MALAYSIA

BORNEO

SARAWAK

Kuching

Kepulauan Natuna

Natuna
Besar

Kepulauan Anambas

SINGAPORE

Johor Baharu

Kuala Lumpur

Kuala Terengganu

Kota Baharu

George Town
P. Pinang

Ipoh

Taiping

Butterworth

Alor Setar

Hat Yai
Songkhla
(Singora)

Nakhon Si Thammarat

Phuket
Ko Phuket

Phnom Penh

HO CHI MINH
(Saigon)

Phan Thiet

Kho Khot
Kra

Isthmus of
Kra

Medan

Pematangsiantar

Tebingtinggi

Sibolga

Kyunzu
Kyun

Con Son Islands

Catwick Islands

Projection: Conical with two standard parallels

COPYRIGHT GEORGE PHILIP & SON LTD

m  3000  2000  1500  1000  400  200  0

m  0  200  2000

East from Greenwich

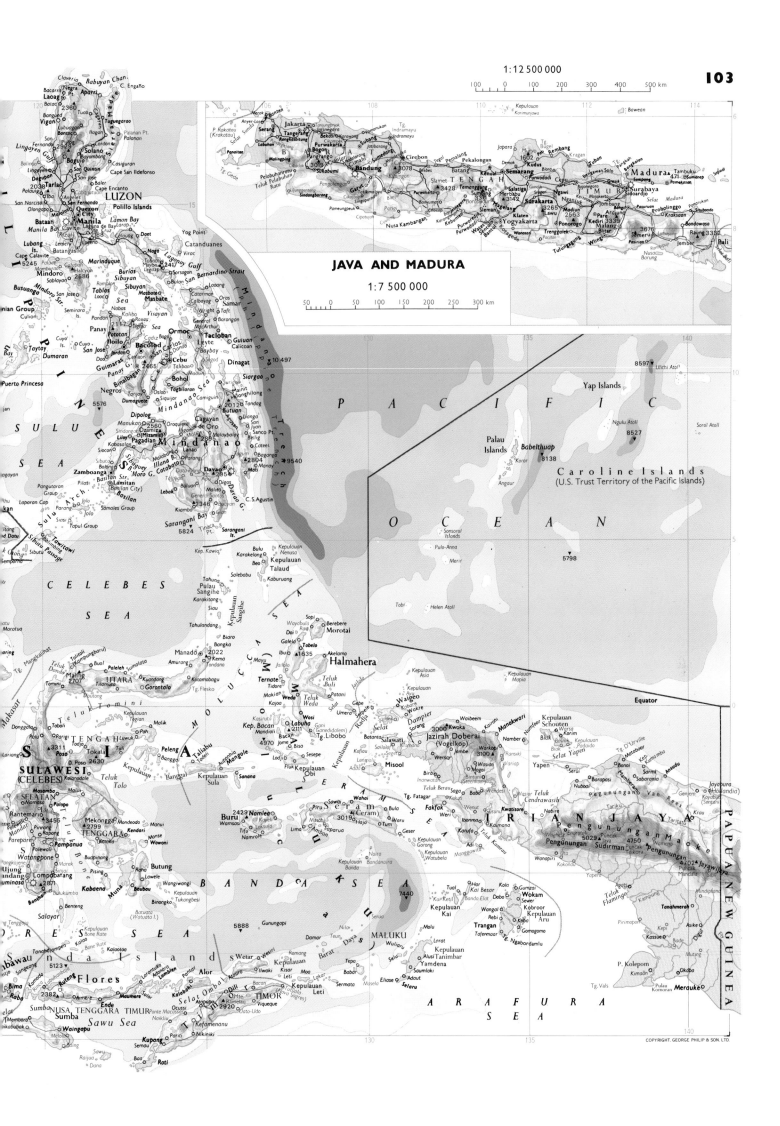

1 : 30 000 000

200   0   200   400   600   800   1000 km

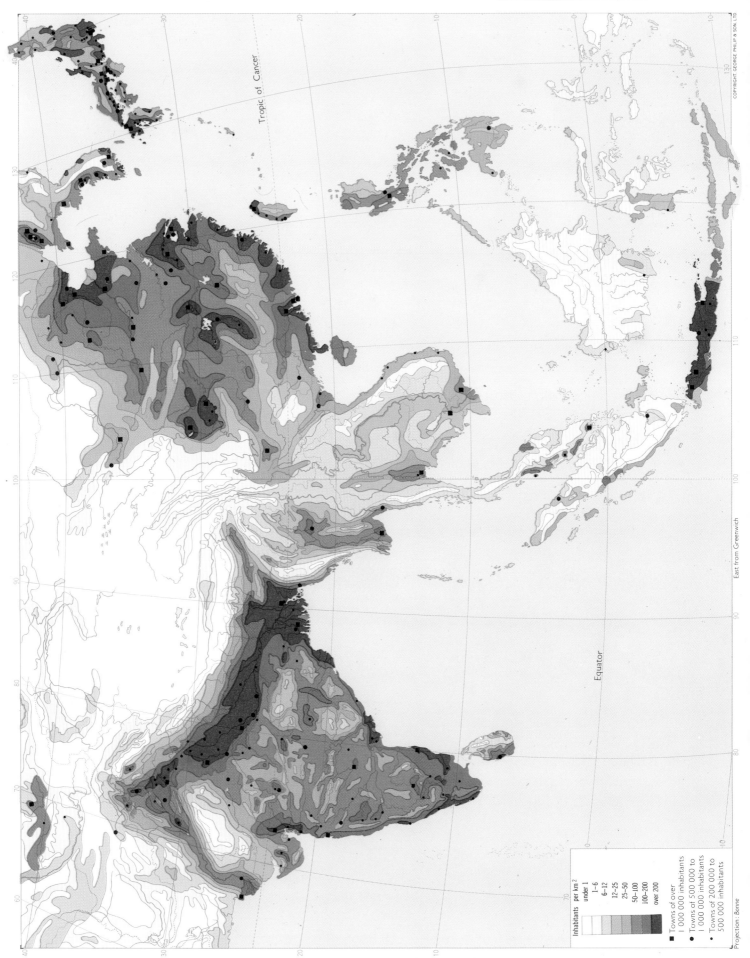

Tropic of Cancer

East from Greenwich

Equator

COPYRIGHT GEORGE PHILIP & SON. LTD

| Inhabitants  per km² | |
| --- | --- |
| | under 1 |
| | 1–6 |
| | 6–12 |
| | 12–25 |
| | 25–50 |
| | 50–100 |
| | 100–200 |
| | over 200 |

■ Towns of over 1 000 000 inhabitants
● Towns of 500 000 to 1 000 000 inhabitants
● Towns of 200 000 to 500 000 inhabitants

Projection: Bonne

1:20 000 000

200    0    200    400    600    800 km

U. S. S. R.

UNION OF SOVIET SOCIALIST REPUBLICS

KAZAKH S.S.R.

KIRGIZ S.S.R.

M O N G O L I A

Ulan Ude

Irkutsk

Ulaanbaatar

S I N K I A N G

(Autonomous Region)

U I G H U R

Takla Makan

Ala Shan

Nan Shan

K'un lun Shan

K'un lun Shan

Kunlun Shan

T I B E T

K'un lun Shan

N E P A L

KASHMIR

JAMMU

BHUTAN

ASSAM

BANGLA DESH

I N D I A

CALCUTTA

BAY OF BENGAL

BURMA

THAILAND (SIAM)

LAOS

VIETNAM

C H I N A

PEIPING

Tientsin

Shanghai

SHANGHAI

Nanking

Wuhan

Hong Kong

Macao

Kowloon

Victoria

SOUTH CHINA SEA

PHILIPPINES

Luzon

TAIWAN (Formosa)

Taipei

Kaohsiung

EAST CHINA SEA

RYUKYU-rettō

Tropic of Cancer

YELLOW SEA

NORTH KOREA

P'yongyang

SOUTH KOREA

Taegu

Pusan

JAPAN

Fukuoka

Nagasaki

Vladivostok

Harbin

Shenyang

GREAT WALL

Lanchou

Chungking

Ch'ungch'ing

Kunming

Chengtu

Sian

Huang Ho

Chang Chiang

Projection: Bonne

East from Greenwich

COPYRIGHT GEORGE PHILIP & SON LTD

m    6000    4000    3000    2000    1500    1000    600    400    200    0

m    200    2000    4000    6000

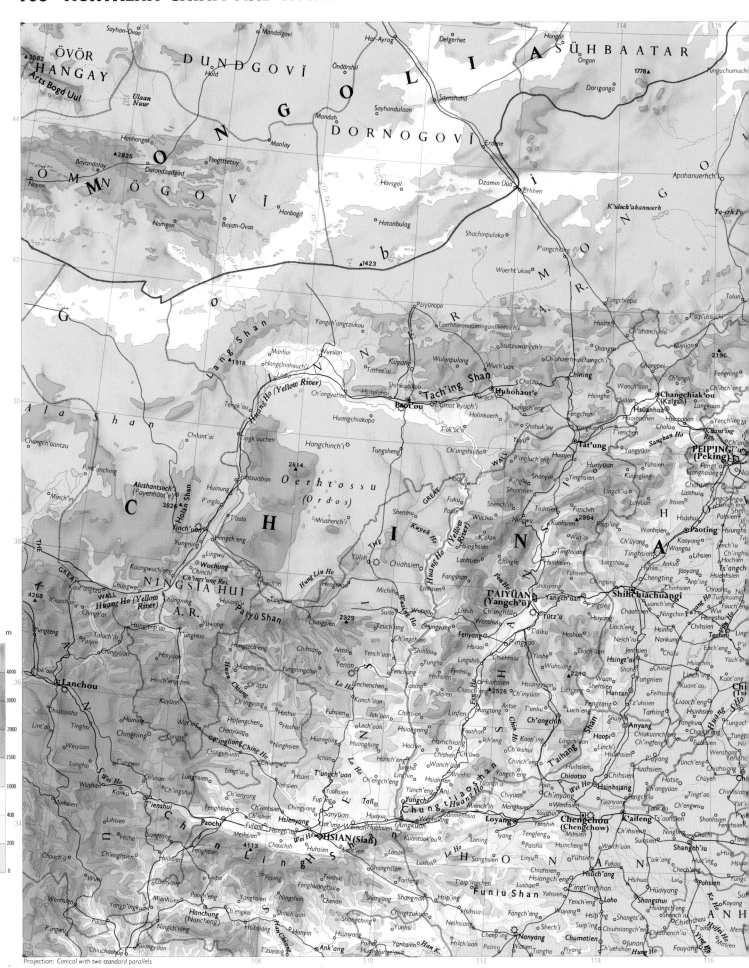

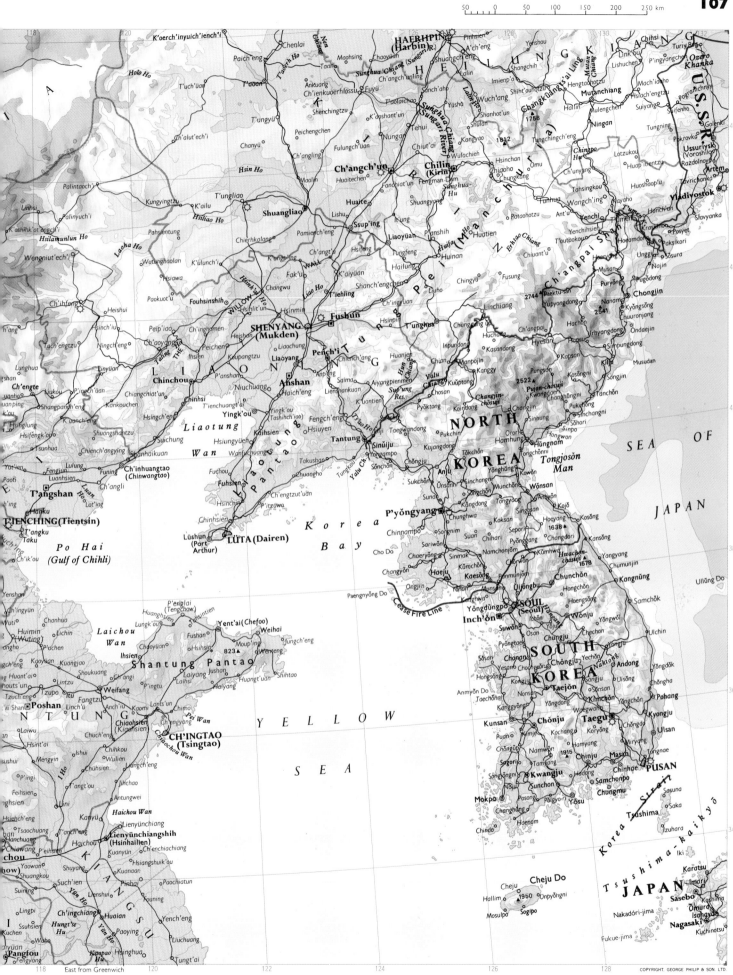

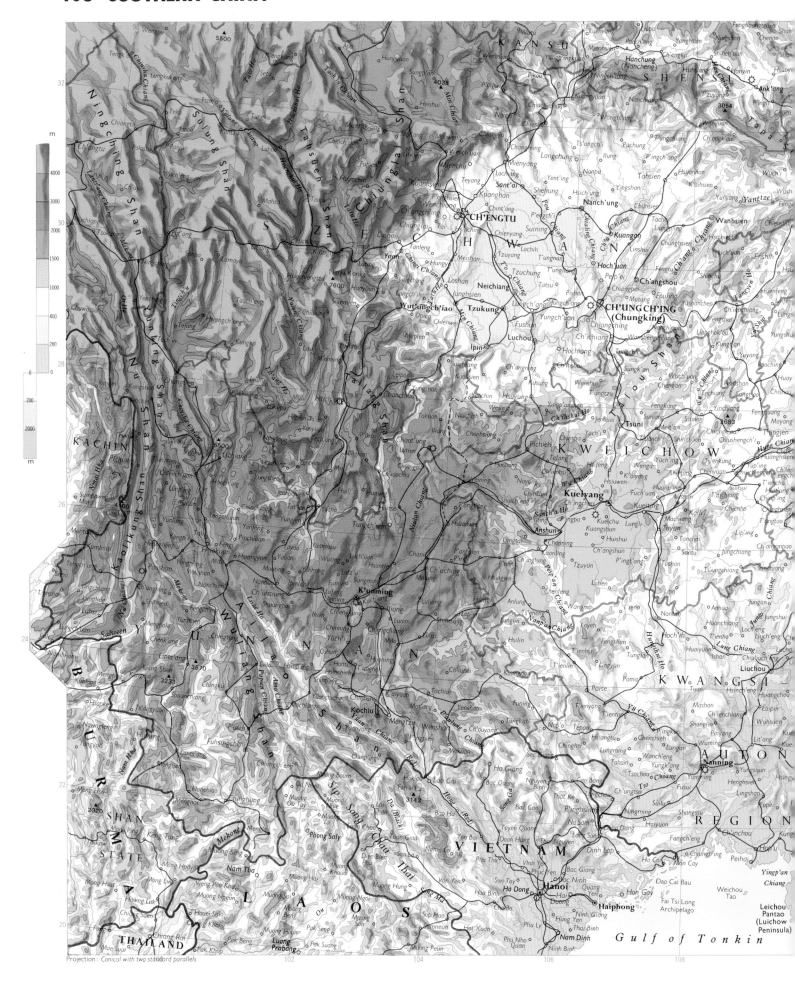

SHANGHAI

KIANGSU

Nant'ung
Haimen
Ch'ungming Tao

Nanking (NANCHING)

Chenchiang
Ch'angchou
Wuhsi
Suchow (Soochow)

HONAN

Nanyang
Chumatien

Hofei

Huainan
Pangfou

ANHWEI

Wuhu

Hangchou

Ningpo

HUPEH

Ich'ang
WUHAN
Hanyang
Wuch'ang

Huangshih

CHEKIANG

Wenchou

Shashih

Ch'angsha

Nanch'ang

KIANGSI

HUNAN

Shaoyang

Hengyang

Fuchou (Foochow)

FUKIEN

TAIWAN

(FORMOSA)

T'AIPEI

Chilung

Hsinchu

T'aichung

Changhua

Chiai

Hsiamen (Amoy)

Ch'uanchou

Shant'ou (Swatow)

HUANG

KWANGTUNG

KWANGCHOU (Canton)

Foshan

Wuchou

Kaohsiung

T'ainan

Tropic of Cancer

HONG KONG (U.K.)
Kowloon
VICTORIA
Macau (Port.)

Chanchiang (Tsamkong)

Luzon
Strait

SOUTH CHINA SEA

Tungsha Tao

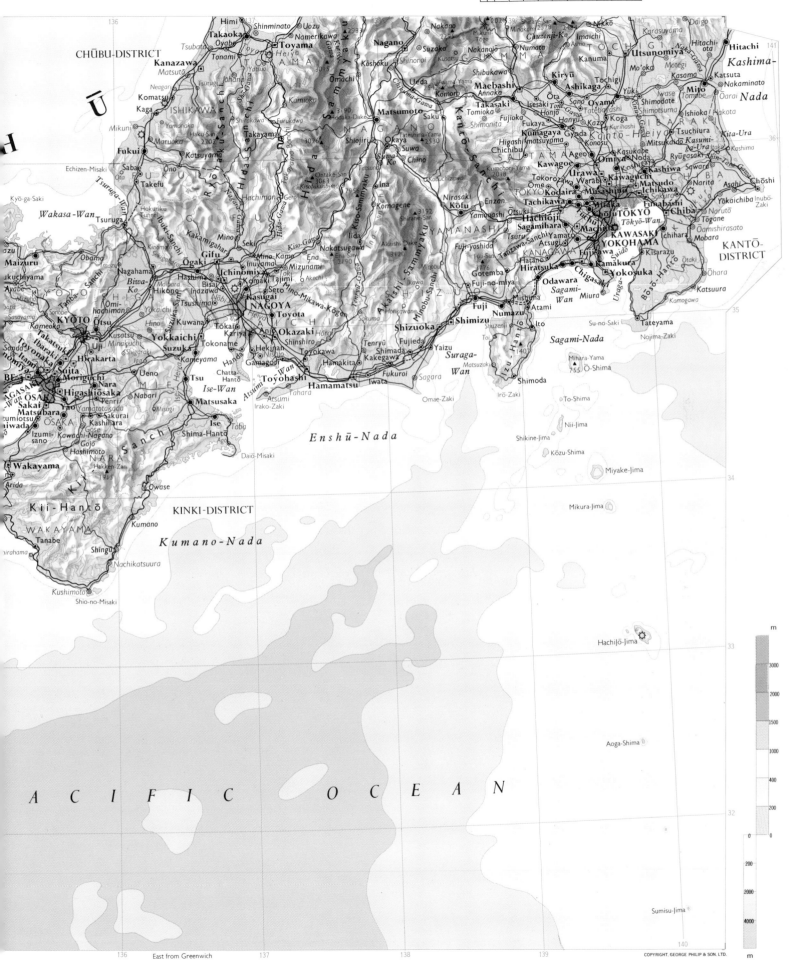

1:2 500 000

10 0 10 20 30 40 50 60 70 80 90 100 km

**III**

CHŪBU-DISTRICT

Himi
Takaoka
Shinminato  Uozu  Namerikawa
Oyabe
Tsubata  Toyama
Tonami  Heiya
Kanazawa
Matsutō
ISHIKAWA
Komatsu
Neagari
Kaga
Mikuni
Maruoka
Fukui
Katsuyama
Echizen-Misaki
Sabae  Ōno
Takefu
Tsuruga
Kyō-ga-Saki  Wakasa-Wan
Tsuruga
Obama
Maizuru
Ayabe
Takayama
Furukawa
Kamioka
Hodaka-Dake 3190
Matsumoto

Nakano
Nagano
Suzaka
Nakagomi
Kōshoku  Shinonoi
Ueda  Asama-Yama
Komoro
Saku

Takasaki
Maebashi
Annaka
Tomioka
Shimonita
Fujioka
Chichibu

Nikkō
Imaichi
Ashio
TOCHIGI
Utsunomiya
Mo'oka  Motegi
Tochigi
Kanuma
Sano  Oyama
Ōta  Tatebayashi
Kiryū
Ashikaga
Honjo
Fukaya  Hanyū  Gyōda
Kumagaya
Higashi-matsuyama
SAITAMA
Ōme

Hitachi
Hitachi-ōta
Kashima-Nada
Nakaminato
Ōarai
Katsuta
Kasama
Mito
Ishioka  Hakota
IBARAKI
Mitsukaido  Kasumi-ga-Ura
Tsuchiura
Ryūgasaki  Kita-Ura
Kashima
CHIBA
Narita  Asahi
Chōshi
Inubō-Zaki

FUKUI
Ono  Hachiman
Gifu
Seki
Takayama

GIFU
Mino
Ōgaki  Hashima
Inuyama
Ichinomiya  Komaki  Tajimi
Bisai  Inazawa  Kasugai  Seto
Tsushima
NAGOYA
Kuwana  Toyota
Tōkai  Kariya  Anjo
Yokkaichi  To.koname  Okazaki
Suzuka  Kameyama
Handa
Tsu  Gamagori
Matsusaka  Toyohashi
Ise-Wan  Hamamatsu
Atsumi-Hantō
Irako-Zaki  Tahara

NAGANO
Shiojiri
Okaya
Suwa
Chino
Ina
Komagane
Iida

YAMANASHI
Nirasaki
Kōfu
Yamanashi
Ōtsuki
Tsuru
Fuji-yoshida

Kōfu
Komae

Kōchi-Heiya
Urawa
Kawagoe
Warabi
Kawaguchi
Ageo
Kasukabe
Matsudo
TOKYO
Kodaira
Tachikawa
Hachiōji
Machida
Sagamihara
Yamato
KANAGAWA
Atsugi
Hiratsuka
Fujisawa
Kamakura
Yokosuka

TOKYO
Tōkyō-Wan
Chiba
Ichikawa
Funabashi
Narita
Sakura
Mobara
Kisarazu
Ōtaki
Katsuura
Kamogawa
BŌSŌ-Hantō

KAWASAKI
YOKOHAMA

Odawara
Atami
Mishima
Numazu
Ito

Sagami-Wan
Miura
Uraga
Tateyama
Nojima-Zaki

Sagami-Nada

Shizuoka  Shimizu
Fuji
Fujieda
Yaizu
Shimada
Kakegawa
Fukuroi
Iwata
Sagara
Omae-Zaki
Daio-Misaki

Suruga-Wan
Matsuzaki
Shimoda
Irō-Zaki

Su-no-Saki

Enshū-Nada

Mihara-Yama 755  Ō-Shima

To-Shima
Nii-Jima
Shikine-Jima
Kōzu-Shima
Miyake-Jima

Mikura-Jima

Kumano-Nada

KINKI-DISTRICT

KYŌTO
Ōtsu
Kusatsu
Uji
Kameoka
Ibaraki
Takatsuki
Toyonaka
Suita
Moriguchi
OSAKA
Sakai
Matsubara
Higashiosaka
Yao
Izumi-sano
Iwakata
Kashihara
Nara
Tenri
Sakurai
Ueno
Nabari
Gose
Gojo
Hashimoto
Wakayama
Arida
WAKAYAMA
Tanabe
Shirahama
Kushimoto
Shio-no-Misaki
Shingū
Nachikatsuura
Kumano
Owase
Kii-Hantō
Ise
Shima-Hantō
Ago

Hachijō-Jima

Aoga-Shima

P A C I F I C   O C E A N

Sumisu-Jima

KANTŌ-DISTRICT

East from Greenwich

COPYRIGHT. GEORGE PHILIP & SON. LTD.

m
3000
2000
1500
1000
400
200
0

200
2000
4000

m

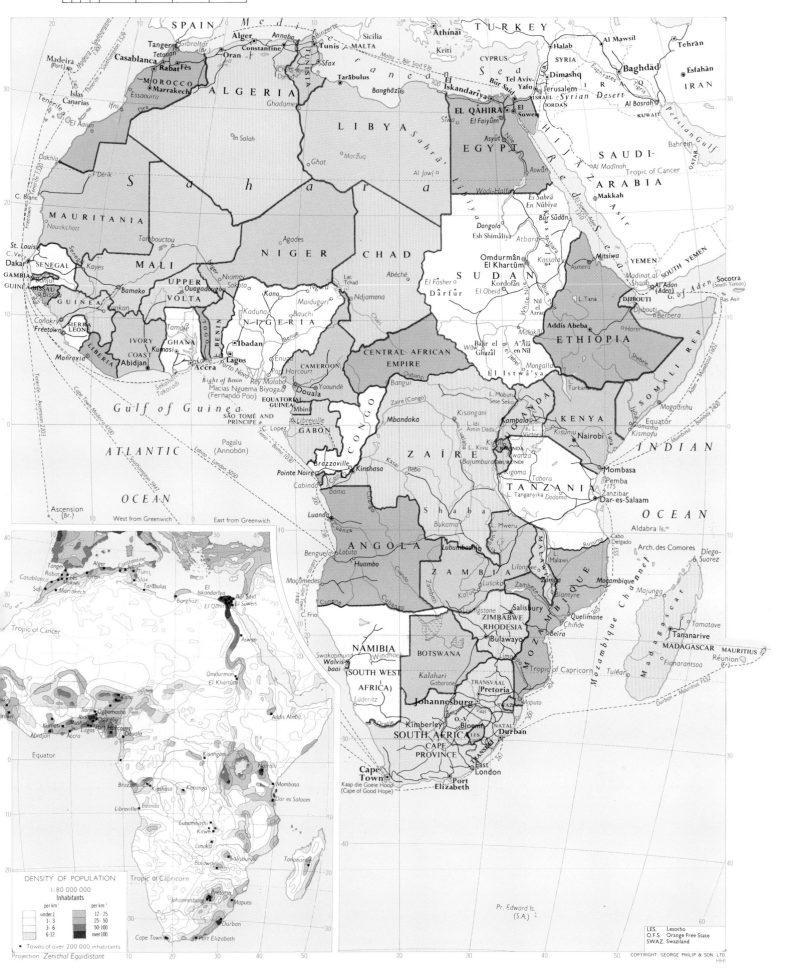

1:40 000 000

400    0    400    800    1200    1600 km

DENSITY OF POPULATION
1:80 000 000
Inhabitants

| per km² | per km² |
|---|---|
| under 1 | 12- 25 |
| 1- 3 | 25- 50 |
| 3- 6 | 50-100 |
| 6-12 | over 100 |

• Towns of over 200 000 inhabitants

Projection : Zenithal Equidistant

LES.   Lesotho
O.F.S.  Orange Free State
SWAZ.  Swaziland

COPYRIGHT. GEORGE PHILIP & SON. LTD.
HHI

1 : 40 000 000

400    0    400    800    1200    1600 km

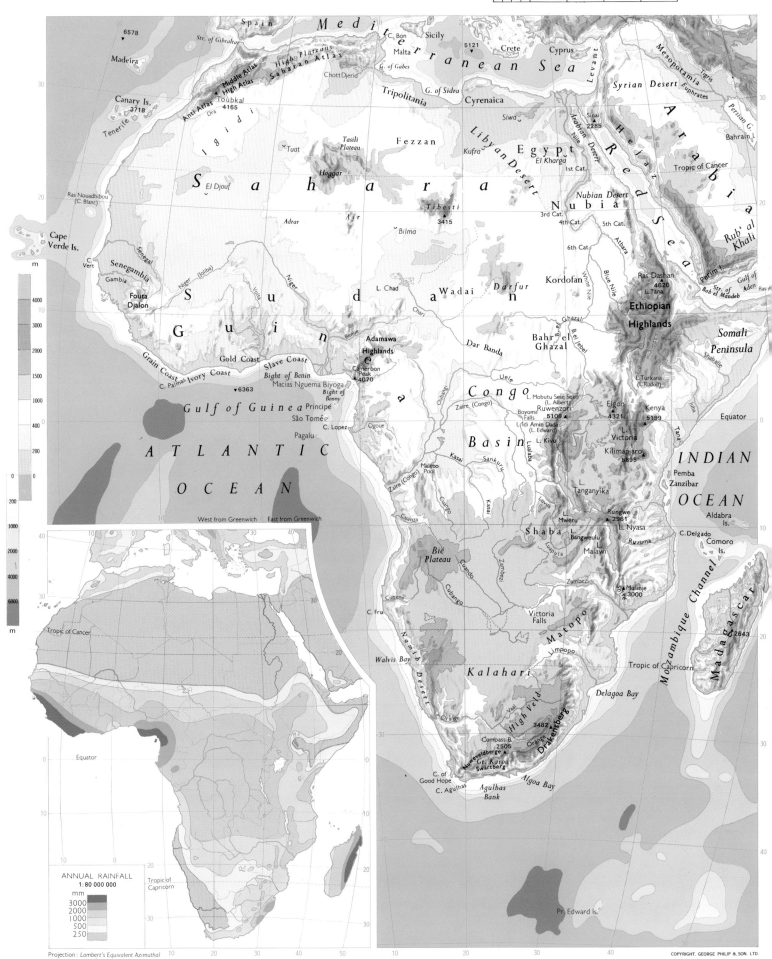

m
4000
3000
2000
1500
1000
400
200
0
200
1000
2000
4000
6000
m

ANNUAL RAINFALL
1 : 80 000 000
mm
3000
2000
1000
500
250

Projection : *Lambert's Equivalent Azimuthal*

COPYRIGHT. GEORGE. PHILIP & SON. LTD.

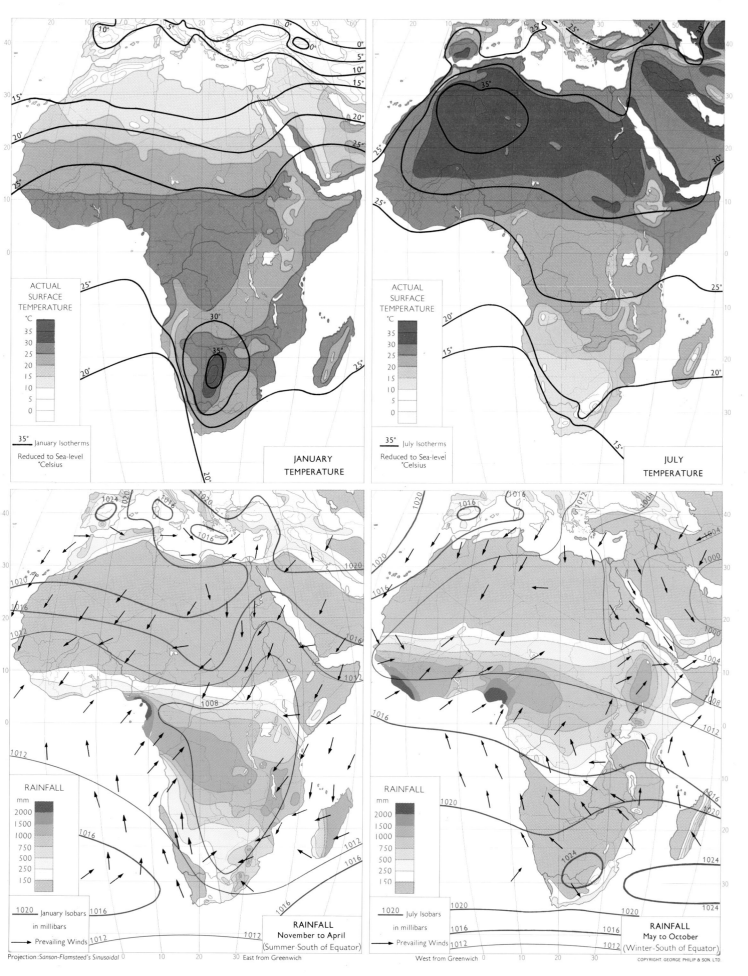

ACTUAL
SURFACE
TEMPERATURE
°C
35
30
25
20
15
10
5
0

35° January Isotherms
Reduced to Sea-level
°Celsius

JANUARY
TEMPERATURE

ACTUAL
SURFACE
TEMPERATURE
°C
35
30
25
20
15
10
5
0

35° July Isotherms
Reduced to Sea-level
°Celsius

JULY
TEMPERATURE

RAINFALL
mm
2000
1500
1000
750
500
250
150

1020 January Isobars
in millibars
Prevailing Winds

RAINFALL
November to April
(Summer-South of Equator)

RAINFALL
mm
2000
1500
1000
750
500
250
150

1020 July Isobars
in millibars
Prevailing Winds

RAINFALL
May to October
(Winter-South of Equator)

Projection: *Sanson-Flamsteed's Sinusoidal*    East from Greenwich

West from Greenwich    COPYRIGHT. GEORGE PHILIP & SON. LTD.

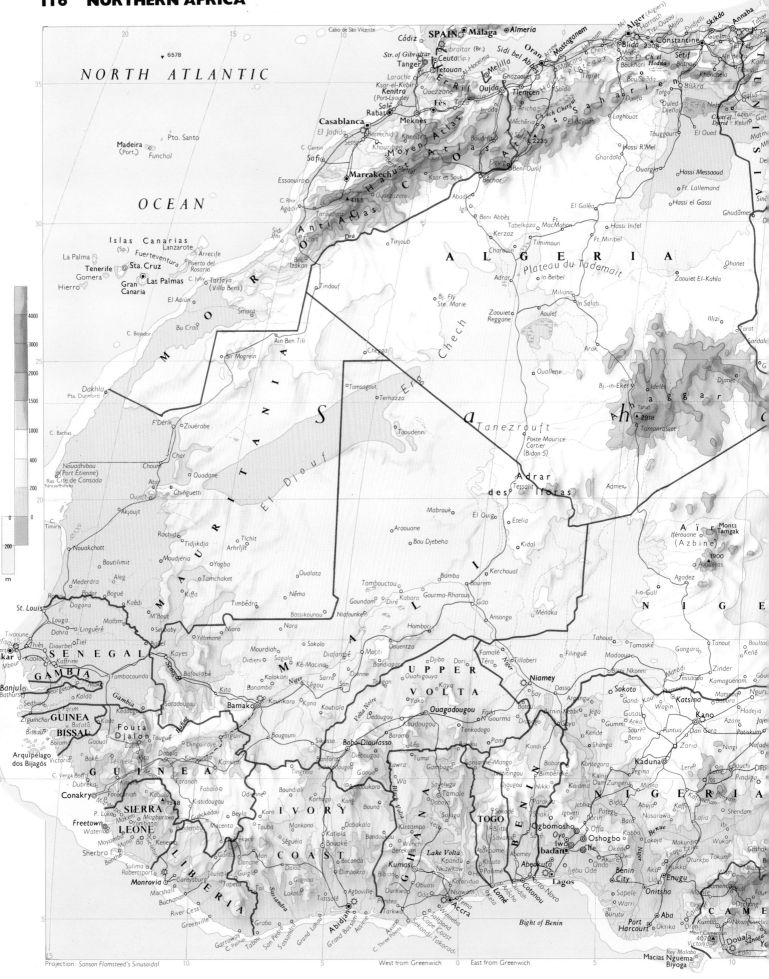

NORTH ATLANTIC

OCEAN

SPAIN

Cabo de São Vicente
Cádiz •Málaga •Almería
Gibraltar (Br.)
Str. of Gibraltar Ceuta (Sp.)
Tanger Sidi bel Abbès
Tetouan Melilla
Larache Al-Hoceima
Kenitra Oujda
(Port-Lyautey)
Salé Fès Taza
Rabat
Meknes
Casablanca Berrechid
El Jadida Settat Khenifra
Khouribga
Safi Moyen Atlas
Béni Mellal
Essaouira
C. Cantin Marrakech
C. Rhir
Agadir Taroudant
Anti Atlas
Sidi Ifni
Tiznit Dra

Alger (Algers)
Harrach
Blida 2308 Constantine
Sétif
Tlemcen
Saïda
El Bayadh Laghouat
Béchar
Ghardaïa
Hassi R'Mel
Hassi Messaoud
Ft. Lallemand
Hassi el Gassi
Ghudamès

ALGERIA

Madeira
(Port.)
Pto. Santo
Funchal

Islas Canarias
(Sp.)
Lanzarote
La Palma Fuerteventura
Tenerife Arrecife
Sta. Cruz Puerto del
Gomera Rosario
Hierro Gran
Canaria Las Palmas
El Aáiun

Plateau du Tademaít

MOROCCO

Smara

Bu Craa

C. Bojador

Dakhla
Pta. Durnford

Bir Mogrein

MAURITANIA

Ain Ben Tili

Tindouf

Adrar

In Belbel

Chech

Erg

Taoudenni

Araouane

Bj. Fly
Ste. Marie
Zaouiet
Reggane
Aoulef
In Salah
Tanezrouft
Poste Maurice
Cortier
(Bidon 5)

Bj.-in-Eker
Idelès
Arak
Djanet
Illizi
Ahaggar
Tahat
2918
Tamanrasset

C. Barbas
F'Dérik
Zouérate
Chinguetti
Choum
Ouadane

Nouadhibou
(Port Étienne)
Cité de Cansada
Ras Nouadhibou
Atar
Oujeft

Rachid
Tichít
Arhrîjît
Tidjikdja
Kiffa
Tamchaket
Oualata
Néma
Bou Djebeha

Mabrouk

El Ouig Etelia

Kidal

Monts
Tamgak
Iférouane
(Azbine)
1900

Akjoujt

Moudjéria
Yogba

Timbédra
Nioro

Nouakchott
Boutilimit
Aleg
Mederdra

Podor
Bogué
Kaédi
M'Bout
Sélibaby

St. Louis
Dagana
Louga Linguère
Tivaouane
Rufisque Thiès
Dakar
Mbour Kaolack
GAMBIA
Banjul
(Bathurst)

SENEGAL

Yélimane
Nara
Nioro

MALI

Tombouctou
Goundam
Diré
Bamba
Bourem
Gao
Ansongo
Ménaka

Kerchoual

Tahoua
Tamaské
Tanout
Gangara
Madaoua
Birni Nkonni

In-Gall
Agadez

NIGER

Zinder
Tessaoua
Gouré
Kaduna

Niafounké
Hombori

Diourbel
Tiel
Bakel
Matam
Sokolo
Mourdiah
Didiéni
Ségou
Banamba
Koulikoro
Kati
Bamako
Bafoulabé
Kayes
Kolokani
Ké-Macina
Diafarabé
Mopti
Bandiagara
Douentza
Djibo Dori
Famalé
Téra
Tillaberi
Niamey
Say
Dosso
Birni-Kebbi
Gusau
Sokoto
Gummi
Katsina
Kano

Tambacounda
Kédougou
Satadougou
Kita
Kangaba
Sikasso
Koutiala
Bobo-Dioulasso
Ouahigouya
Kaya
Ouagadougou
Fada
N'Gourma

UPPER
VOLTA

Kandi

BENIN

Tiébélé
Boromo
Diébougou
Tenkodogo

Koudougou

GUINEA
BISSAU
Bissau
Bolama
Arquipélago
dos Bijagós

Fouta
Djalon
Tougué
Labé
Gaoual
Boké

Dabola
Siguiri
Bougouni
Banfora
Bouna

Kankan

Faranah
Dinguiraye
Kouroussa

GUINEA
Conakry

Kissidougou
Beyla
Korhogo

IVORY

Dabakala
Katiola

GHANA

Tamale

TOGO

Sokodé
Atakpamé

NIGERIA

Kaduna
Zaria
Abuja
Minna
Ilorin
Oshogbo
Ogbomosho
Oyo
Ibadan
Ife
Lagos
Benin
City
Onitsha
Enugu
Aba
Port
Harcourt

SIERRA
LEONE
Freetown

Kenema
Bo

LIBERIA
Monrovia

Man
Danané

COAST

Daloa
Gagnoa

Bouaké

Kumasi
Obuasi

Abidjan
Grand Bassam

Lake Volta

Accra

Lomé
Cotonou
Porto-Novo

Bight of Benin

CAMEROON
Douala
Mont Cameroun
4070

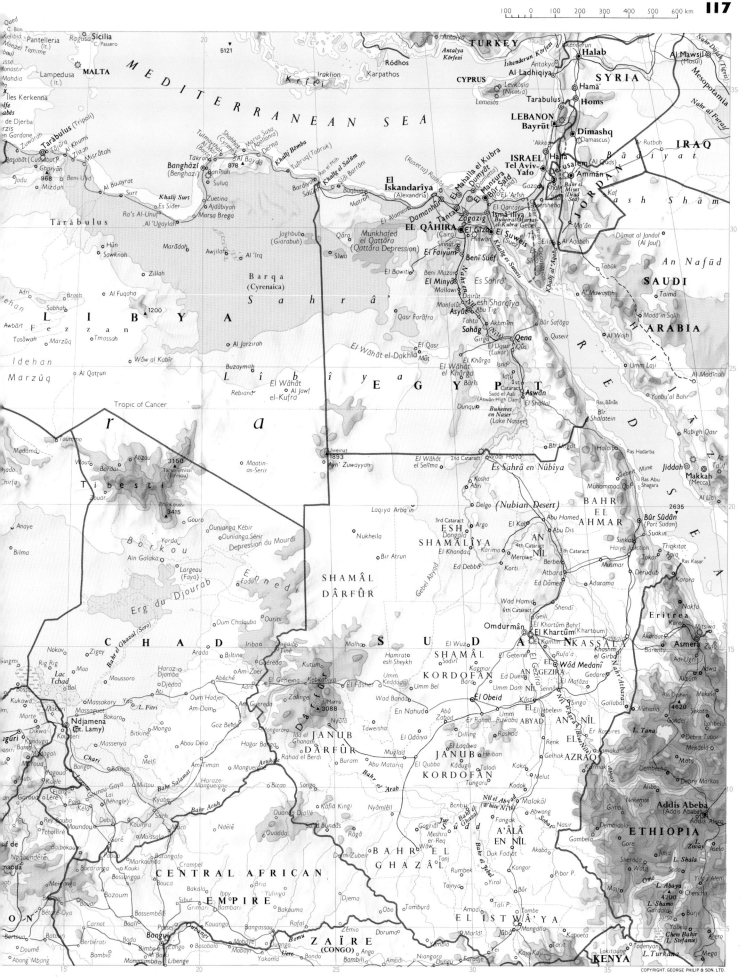

1:15 000 000

100   0   100   200   300   400   500   600 km

**MEDITERRANEAN SEA**

TURKEY
CYPRUS
SYRIA
LEBANON
Bayrût
Dimashq (Damascus)
IRAQ
ISRAEL
Tel Aviv-Yafo
Amman
JORDAN

**MALTA**
Sicilia

Tarābulus (Tripoli)

Banghāzī (Benghazi)

El Iskandarîya (Alexandria)
EL QÂHIRA (Cairo)
El Gîza
El Suweis

**L I B Y A**

Tarâbulus
Barqa (Cyrenaica)

Sahrâ'

**E G Y P T**

Tropic of Cancer

Aswân

SAUDI
ARABIA

Makkah (Mecca)

RED SEA

Es Sahrâ en Nûbiya
(Nubian Desert)

BAHR
EL AHMAR

Bûr Sûdân (Port Sudan)

**T i b e s t i**

ESH SHAMÂLIYA

AN NÎL

Eritrea
Asmera

**C H A D**

SHAMÂL DÂRFÛR

Omdurmân
El Khartûm (Khartoum)

**S U D A N**

SHAMÂL KORDOFAN

EL GEZIRA

Wâd Medanî

Ndjamena (Ft. Lamy)

JANUB DÂRFÛR

El Obeid

AN NÎL EL ABYAD

JANUB KORDOFAN

AN NÎL EL AZRAQ

L. Tana

Addis Abeba (Addis Ababa)

**ETHIOPIA**

**CENTRAL AFRICAN EMPIRE**

BAHR EL GHAZÂL

A'ÂLÂ EN NÎL

EL ISTWÂ'YA

**ZAÏRE (CONGO)**

KENYA

L. Turkana

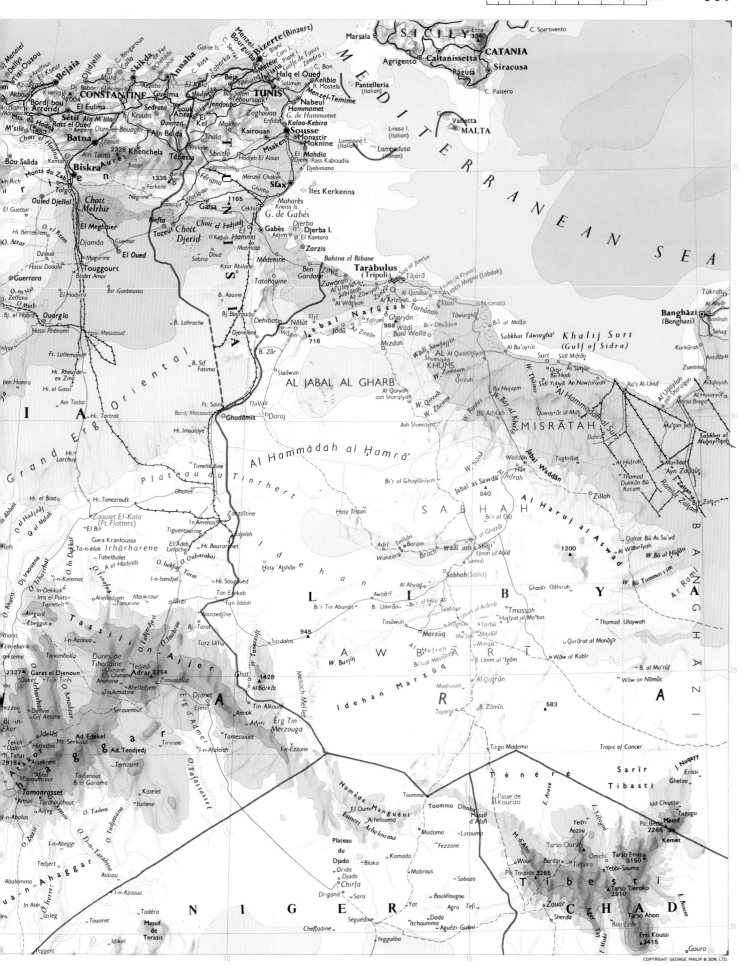

1 : 8 000 000

50   0   50   100   150   200   250   300 km

**119**

MEDITERRANEAN SEA

SICILY

C. Spartivento

Marsala · Etna 3340
Agrigento · Caltanissetta · CATANIA
Ragusa · Siracusa
C. Passero

Gela
Pantelleria (Italian)

Linosa I. (Italian)
Lampione I. (Italian)
Lampedusa (Italian)

Valletta
MALTA

El Menaiel · Dellys
Tizi-Ouzou
Azazga
Bejaia · Djidjelli · Collo · Skikda
El Kseur · Bougaroun
Dr. Babor
Bordj bou · Arreridj
CONSTANTINE · Guelma
Sétif · Aïn M'lila
Rass el Oued
M'sila · 1863
Batna · 2328 Khenchela · Tébessa
Biskra
Bou-Saâda
Monts du Zab
Ouled Djellal
El Meghaier
Djamâa
El Oued
Touggourt

Annaba
Bizerte (Binzert)
Béja · TUNIS
Nabeul
Hammamet
Kairouan · Sousse · Monastir · Moknine
Sfax
G. de Gabès
Gabès · Djerba I.
Médenine
Tarâbulus (Tripoli)
Zuwārah

Banghāzī (Benghazi)

Grand Erg Oriental

T U N I S I A

L I B Y A

AL JABAL AL GHARB

Al Hammādah al Hamrā'

Khalij Surt (Gulf of Sidra)

MISRĀTAH

SABHAH

Al Harūj al Aswad

Ghudāmis

Plateau du Tinrhert

Idehan Murzūq

N I G E R

Tassili n'Ajjer

A h a g g a r

Tamanrasset

Massif de Terazit

Plateau du Djado

Tropic of Cancer

T C H A D

Tibesti

Emi Koussi 3415

COPYRIGHT. GEORGE PHILIP & SON. LTD.

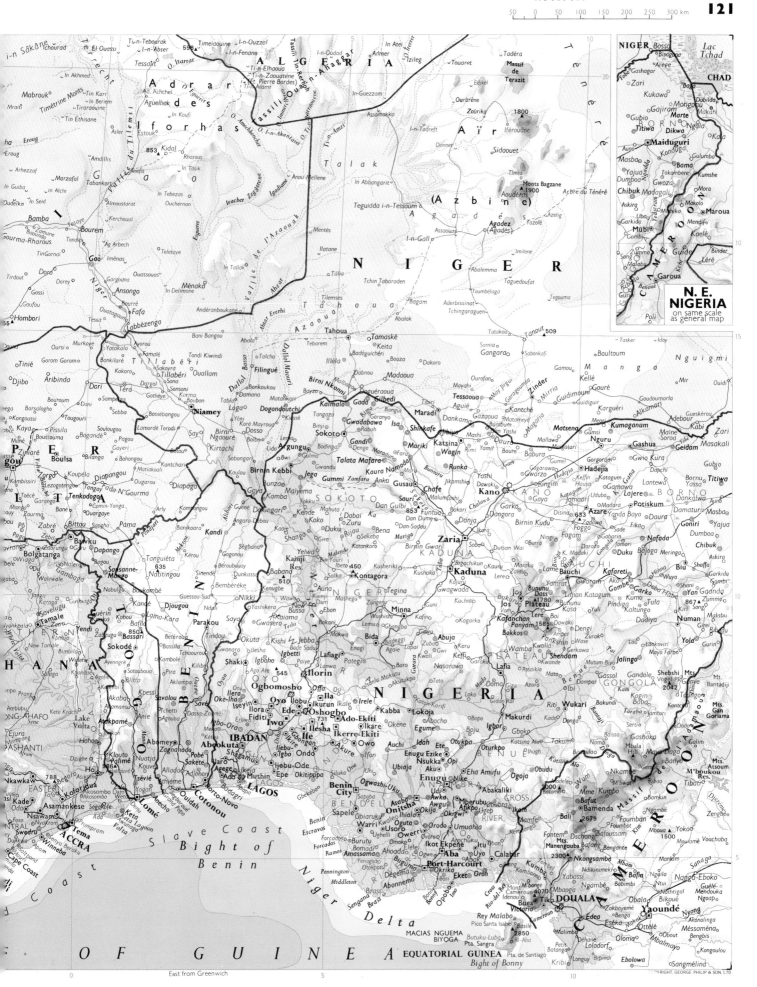

1 : 8 000 000

50    0    50    100   150   200   250   300 km

ALGERIA

Adrar des Iforhas

A ï r

(Azbine)

N I G E R

NIGER

CHAD

N. E.
NIGERIA
on same scale
as general map

I

G

A

O

Niamey

NIGERIA

SOKOTO

Kano

KANO

BORNO

Kaduna

KADUNA

BAUCHI

Sokoto

Katsina

Zaria

PLATEAU

Jos

Plateau

GONGOLA

B E N I N

P E R

V

O

L

T

A

H A N A

EASTERN

Tamale

Bolgatanga

ACCRA

Tema

Winneba

Cape Coast

Slave Coast

Bight of
Benin

Niger Delta

MACIAS NGUEMA
BIYOGA

EQUATORIAL GUINEA

OF GUINEA

Bight of Bonny

East from Greenwich

LAGOS

IBADAN

Abeokuta

Ife

Oshogbo

Ilorin

Ogbomosho

Oyo

Benin
City

Warri

Port-Harcourt

Aba

Enugu

Onitsha

Calabar

ANAMBRA

IMO

CROSS
RIVER

BENDEL

OYO

ONDO

OGUN

KWARA

NIGER

Abuja

Minna

Bida

Makurdi

BENUE

Lafia

Yola

Numan

CAMEROUN

DOUALA

Yaoundé

Maiduguri

Maroua

Garoua

Lac
Tchad

COPYRIGHT GEORGE PHILIP & SON, LTD

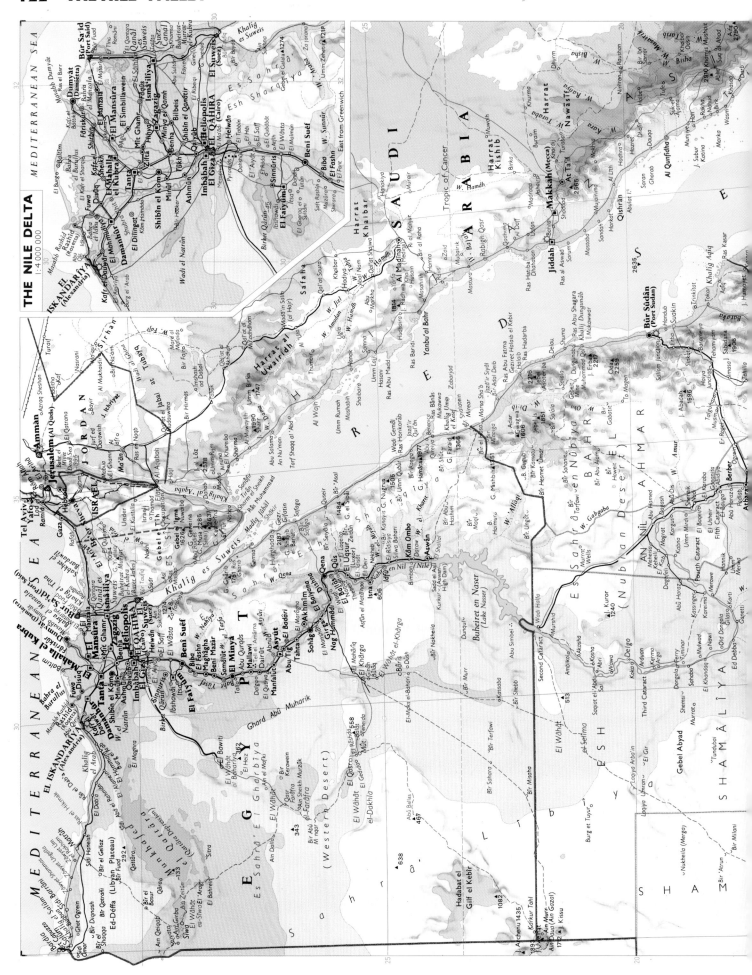

**THE NILE DELTA**
1:4 000 000

MEDITERRANEAN SEA

1:8 000 000

50  0  50  100  150  200  250  300 km

ETHIOPIA

ADDIS ABEBA (Addis Ababa)

SUDAN

KORDOFÂN

DARFUR

BAHR EL ARAB

UGANDA

KENYA

ZAÏRE (CONGO)

CENTRAL AFRICAN EMPIRE

SOMALI REP.

YEMEN

DJIBOUTI

Khartûm (Khartoum)
El Khartûm
Omdurmân

Wad Medani

El Obeid
En Nahud

Kassala
Gedaref

Asmera (Asmara)
Keren
Mitsiwa

Aksum
Gonder
L. Tana
Dese
Mekele

Dire Dawa

Jima

Gore

L. Turkana (L. Rudolf)

Juba

Malakal

Hodeida

Projection: Lambert's Equivalent Azimuthal

East from Greenwich

COPYRIGHT GEORGE PHILIP & SON LTD

m  4000  3000  2000  1500  1000  400  200  0  200  m

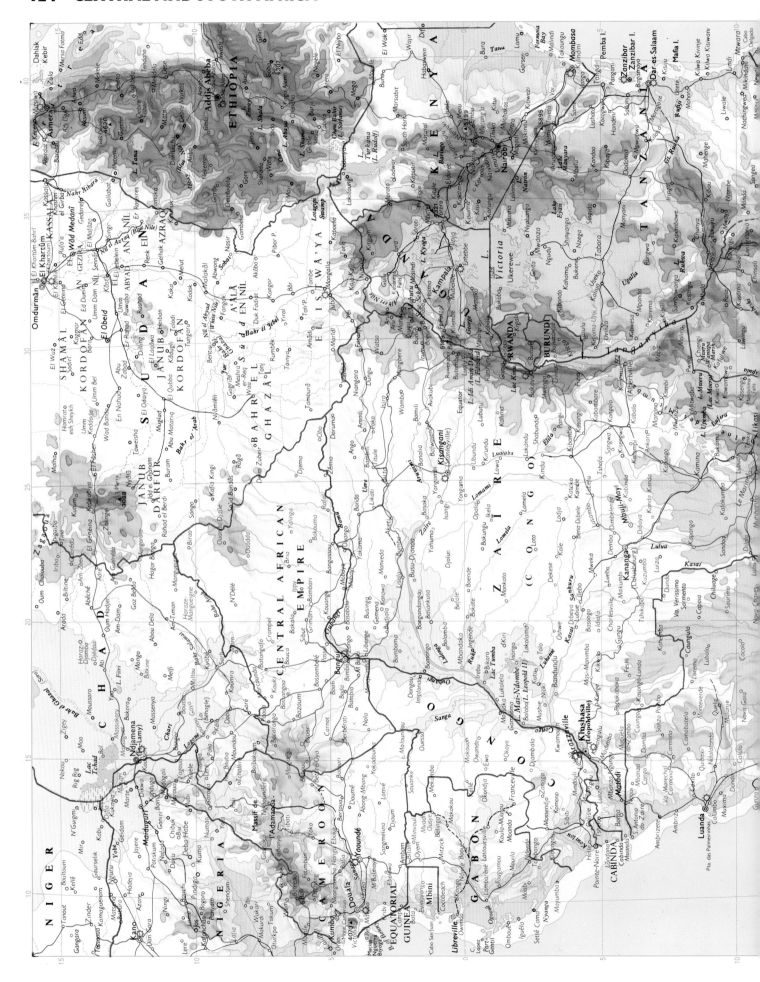

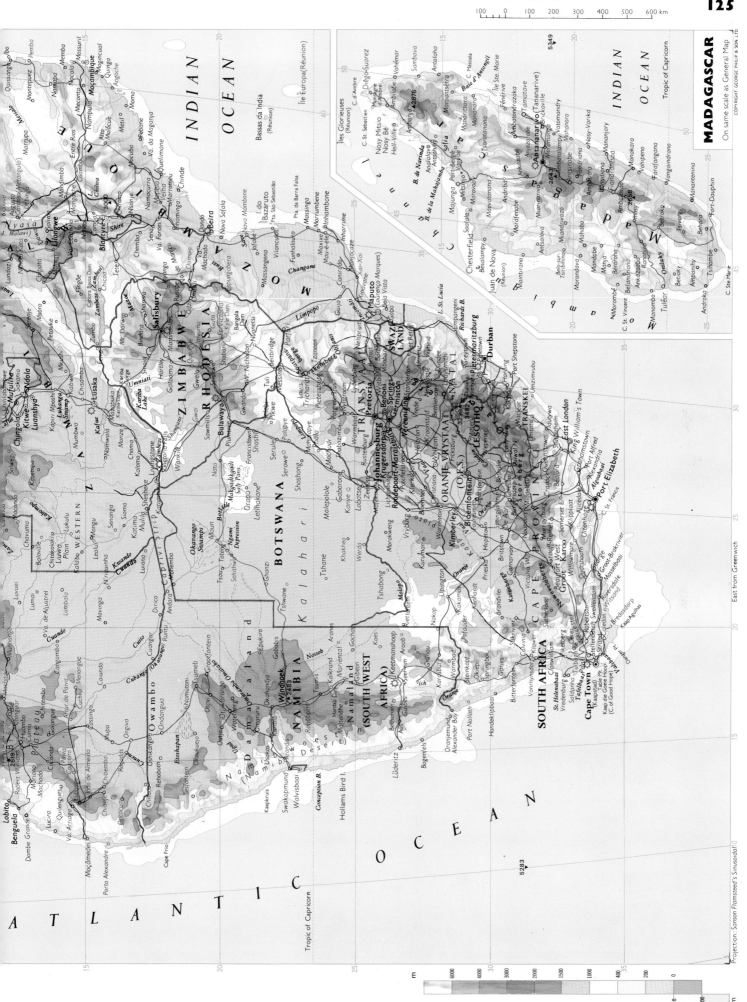

1 : 15 000 000

100    0    100    200    300    400    500    600 km

INDIAN OCEAN

INDIAN OCEAN

ATLANTIC OCEAN

Tropic of Capricorn

East from Greenwich

Projection: Samson Flamsteed's Sinusoidal

ZIMBABWE

RHODESIA

BOTSWANA

Kalahari

NAMIBIA (SOUTH WEST AFRICA)

Namib Desert

SOUTH AFRICA

CAPE PROVINCE

TRANSVAAL

ORANGE FREE STATE (O.F.S.)

NATAL

TRANSKEI

LESOTHO

SWAZILAND

Cape Town

Durban

East London

Port Elizabeth

Johannesburg

Pretoria

Bloemfontein

Kimberley

Windhoek

Salisbury

Bulawayo

Lusaka

Groot Karroo

m    6000    4000    3000    2000    1500    1000    400    200    0

m    200    0

5283

5349

2876

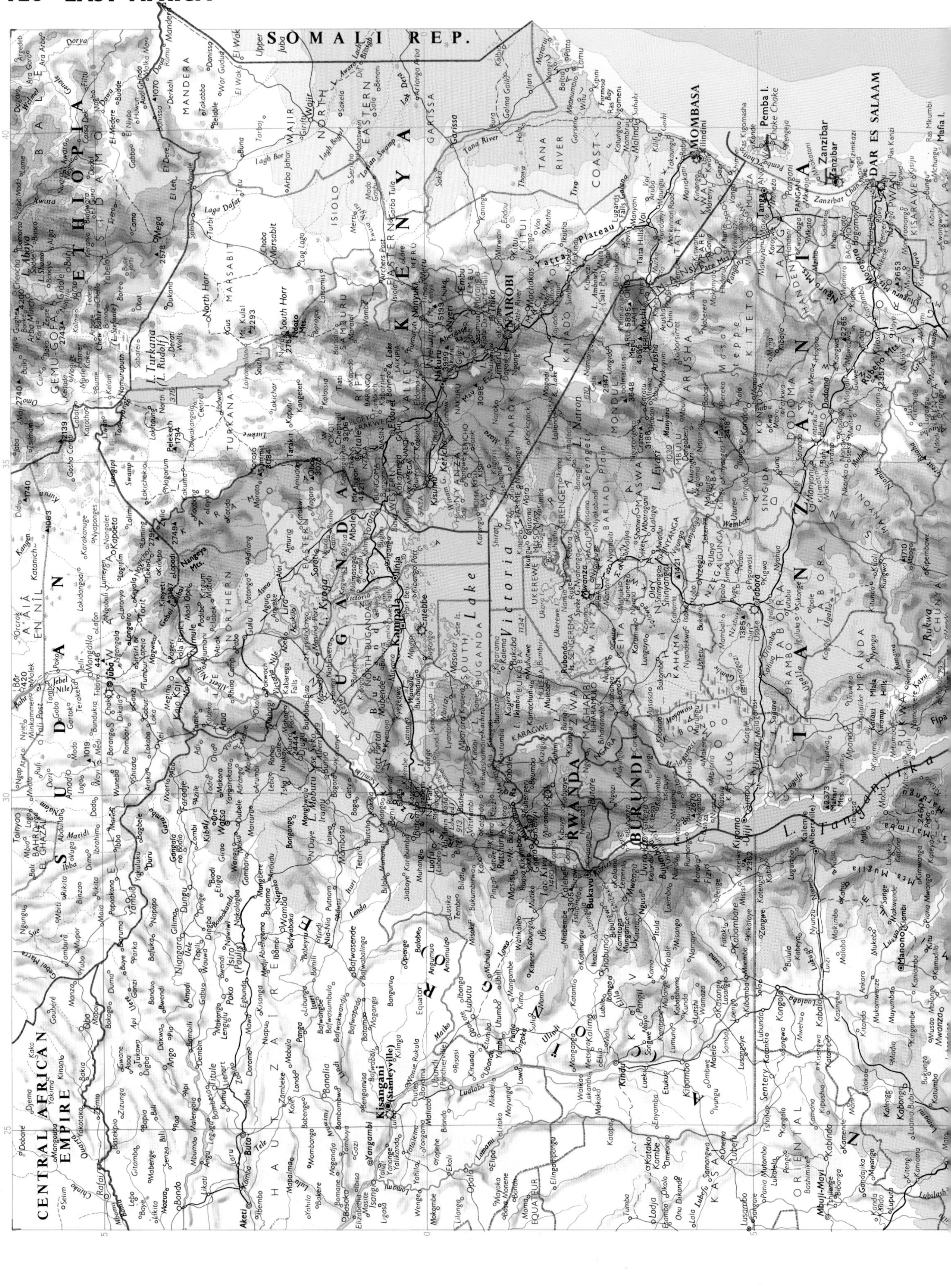

**Countries:** SOMALI REP., ETHIOPIA, KENYA, UGANDA, SUDAN, CENTRAL AFRICAN EMPIRE, ZAIRE, RWANDA, BURUNDI, TANZANIA

**Major cities and locations:** NAIROBI, MOMBASA, DAR ES SALAAM, Zanzibar, Kampala, Entebbe, Jinja, Kisumu, Nakuru, Tabora, Dodoma, Arusha, Bukavu, Kigoma, Kisangani (Stanleyville), Mwanza, Juba

**Water bodies:** Victoria Lake, L. Tanganyika, L. Turkana (L. Rudolf), L. Mobutu, L. Kyoga, L. Rukwa, Pemba I., Mafia I.

**Provinces/regions:** NORTH EASTERN, EASTERN, COAST, NYANZA, WESTERN, RIFT VALLEY, CENTRAL, TANGA, ARUSHA, KITETO, DODOMA, TABORA, KIGOMA, ORIENTAL

1 : 8 000 000

50    0    50   100   150   200   250   300 km

I N D I A N

O C E A N

COPYRIGHT GEORGE PHILIP & SON, LTD.

East from Greenwich

Projection: Lambert's Equivalent Azimuthal

m   6000  4000  3000  2000  1500  1000  400  200   0   200  2000  m

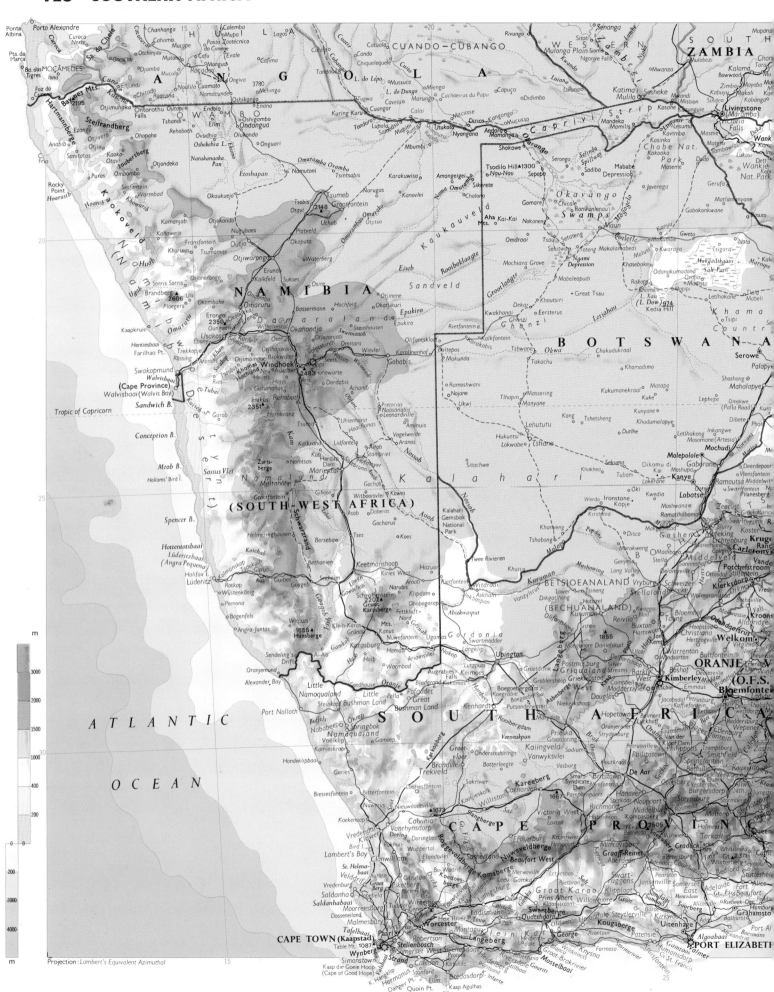

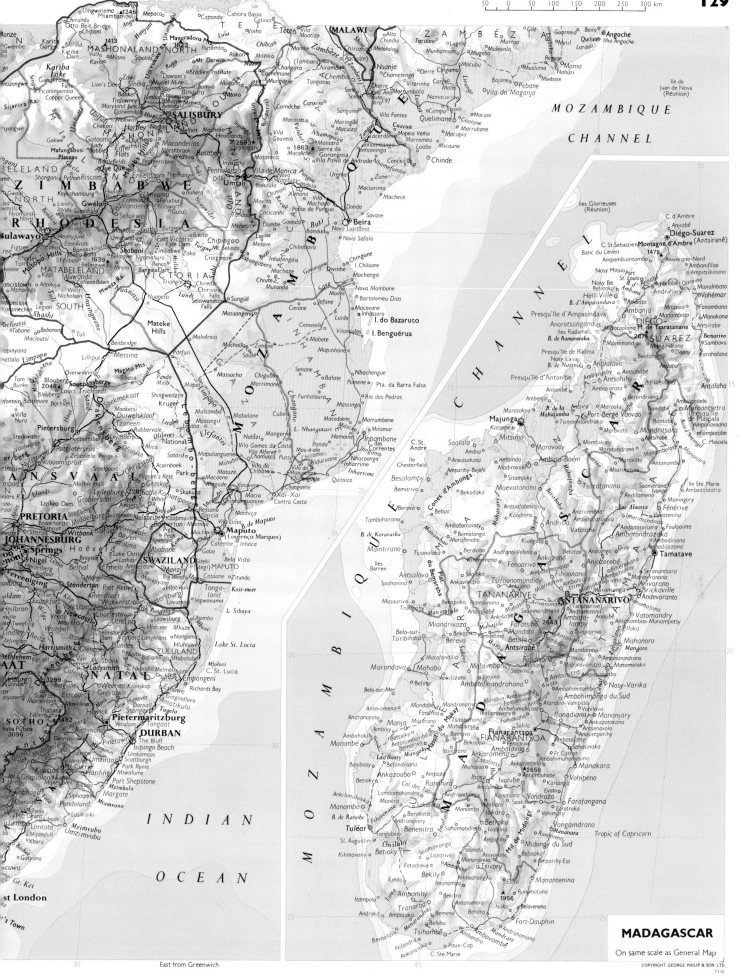

MOZAMBIQUE

CHANNEL

MOZAMBIQUE CHANNEL

INDIAN

OCEAN

**MADAGASCAR**

On same scale as General Map

COPYRIGHT. GEORGE. PHILIP & SON. LTD.

FHK

East from Greenwich

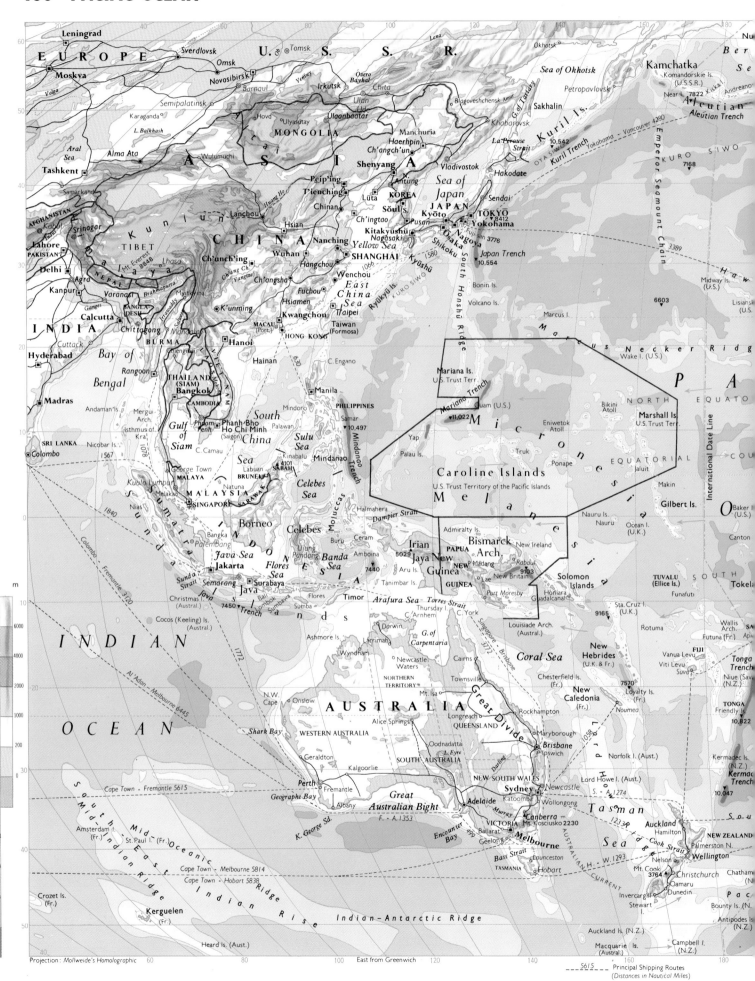

## EUROPE

Leningrad
Moskva
Sverdlovsk
Omsk
Tomsk

## U. S. S. R.

Novosibirsk
Barnaul
Semipalatinsk
Karaganda
L. Balkhash
Alma Ata
Tashkent
Samarkand
Aral Sea
Volga
Yenisei
Irkutsk
Ozero Baykal
Chita
Ulan
Ulaanbaatar

## MONGOLIA

Hovd
Ulyasutay
Lena
Blagoveshchensk
Amur
Khabarovsk

Okhotsk
Sea of Okhotsk
Kamchatka
Komandorskie Is. (U.S.S.R.)
Petropavlovsk
Near I. 7822
Aleutian
Aleutian Trench
Andreanof

Sakhalin
Gulf of Tartary
La Perouse Strait
Kuril Is.
10,542
Kuril Trench
Yokohama
Vancouver 4280
Emperor Seamount Chain
KURO SIWO
7168
3389
Hawaii

## ASIA

AFGHANISTAN
Kabul
Wulumuchi
Kun lun
TIBET
Lanchou
Hsian
Peiping
T'ienching
Shenyang
Ch'angch'un
Manchuria
Haerhpin
CHINA
Chinan
Ch'ingtao
Antung
KOREA
Soul S.
Pusan
Vladivostok
Hakodate
Sendai
Sea of Japan
JAPAN
Kyoto
Osaka
Nagoya
TOKYO
Yokohama
8412
Fujisan 3776

Lahore
PAKISTAN
Srinagar
Delhi
Agra
Kanpur
Varanasi
Mt. Everest 8848
Lhasa
NEPAL
Himalaya
Brahmaputra
Ganges
BANGLADESH
Calcutta
Cuttack
Chittagong
BURMA
Mandalay
Myitkyina
Irrawaddy
Salween
Hsian
Wuhan
Hangchou
Ch'angsha
Wenchou
K'unming
Hsiamen
Fuchow
Kwangchou
MACAU (Port.)
HONG KONG
Taipei
Taiwan (Formosa)
Hainan
Nanching
SHANGHAI
Chang Ch.
Yangtze
Hwang Ho
Hsin
Kweiyang
1066
East China Sea
1580
Kyūshū
KURO SIWO
Ryūkyū Is.
South Honshū Ridge
Shikoku
Japan Trench
10,554
Bonin Is.
Volcano Is.
Marcus I.
6603
Midway Is. (U.S.)
Lisianski (U.S.)

INDIA
Hyderabad
Madras
Bay of Bengal
Rangoon
Andaman Is.
Mergui Arch.
THAILAND (SIAM)
Bangkok
Gulf of Siam
CAMBODIA
Phnom Penh
Phanh Bho Ho Chi Minh (Saigon)
C. Camau
VIET NAM
Hanoi
Mindoro
Manila
PHILIPPINES
Samar
10,497
Palawan
Sulu Sea
C. Engano
Mindanao
Kinabalu
Mindanao Trench
4101
SABAH
BRUNEI
Labuan
Celebes Sea
Halmahera
Dampier Strait
Marianas Trench
11,022
Guam (U.S.)
Mariana Is. U.S. Trust Terr.
Yap
Palau Is.
Eniwetok Atoll
Bikini Atoll
Truk
Ponape
Marshall Is. U.S. Trust Terr.
Wake I. (U.S.)
NORTH
Necker Ridge
EQUATOR
PA
P A
Marcus Necker Ridge
Micronesia
Jaluit

SRI LANKA
Colombo
1567
Nicobar Is.
Isthmus of Kra
1078
George Town
MALAYA
Kuala Lumpur
Natuna
Melaka
SINGAPORE
MALAYSIA
SARAWAK
1840
Nias
Sumatra
Bangka
Palembang
INDONESIA
Borneo
Celebes
Buru
Ceram
Amboina
Aru Is.
Irian Jaya
5029
New Guinea
PAPUA NEW GUINEA
Madang
Lae
New Britain
New Ireland
Rabaul
9103
Bismarck Arch.
Admiralty Is.
Caroline Islands
U.S. Trust Territory of the Pacific Islands
Melanesia
Nauru I. Nauru
Ocean I. (U.K.)
Makin
Gilbert Is.
EQUATORIAL
Baker I. (U.S.)
Canton
O
International Date Line

INDIAN
OCEAN
Colombo - Fremantle 3120
Christmas I. (Austral.)
Cocos (Keeling) Is. (Austral.)
Java Sea
Jakarta
Semarang
Surabaya
Java
Sunda Strait
Sunda Islands
7450
Java Trench
1772
Bali
Lombok
Sumbawa
Flores
Sumba
Flores Sea
Banda Sea
7440
Moluccas
Ujung Pandang
Timor
Tanimbar Is.
Arafura Sea
Torres Strait
Thursday I.
C. York
C. Arnhem
G. of Carpentaria
Port Moresby
SOLOMON Islands
Honiara
Guadalcanal
9165
Sta. Cruz I. (U.K.)
Rotuma
TUVALU (Ellice Is.)
Funafuti
SOUTH
Tokelau
WALLIS
Futuna (Fr.)

Al 'Adan - Melbourne 6445
Cape Town - Fremantle 5615
Geographe Bay
Amsterdam I. (Fr.)
St. Paul I. (Fr.)
South
Mid Indian Ridge
Crozet Is. (Fr.)
Kerguelen (Fr.)
Heard Is. (Aust.)
Mid Oceanic Ridge
East Indian Rise
Indian - Antarctic Ridge
Ashmore Is.
Darwin
N.W. Cape
Onslow
Shark Bay
WESTERN AUSTRALIA
Geraldton
Kalgoorlie
Perth
Fremantle
Albany
K. George Sd.
Great Australian Bight
F. - A. 1353
Lacrima
Wyndham
Newcastle Waters
NORTHERN TERRITORY
Mt. Isa
Alice Springs
Oodnadatta
L. Eyre
SOUTH AUSTRALIA
AUSTRALIA
Longreach
QUEENSLAND
Cairns
Townsville
Brisbane
Rockhampton
Maryborough
Ipswich
Great Divide
Coral Sea
New Hebrides (U.K. & Fr.)
Chesterfield Is. (Fr.)
New Caledonia (Fr.)
Noumea
7570
Loyalty Is. (Fr.)
Norfolk I. (Aust.)
FIJI
Vanua Levu
Viti Levu
Suva
Niue (Sav.) (N.Z.)
TONGA Trench
TONGA Friendly Is.
10,822
Lord Howe I. (Aust.)
S - A 1274
Darling
Murray
NEW SOUTH WALES
Sydney
Newcastle
Wollongong
Katoomba
Canberra
VICTORIA Mt. Kosciusko 2230
Ballarat
Geelong
Melbourne
Encounter Bay
Bass Strait
TASMANIA
Launceston
Hobart
Tasman Sea
1233
W. 1293
Auckland
Hamilton
NEW ZEALAND
Cook Strait
Palmerston N.
Nelson
Wellington
Mt. Cook 3764
Christchurch
Oamaru
Dunedin
Invercargill
Stewart
Chatham
Auckland Is. (N.Z.)
Macquarie Is. (Austral.)
Campbell I. (N.Z.)
Bounty Is. (N.Z.)
Antipodes Is. (N.Z.)
AUSTRALIAN CURRENT
Singapore 3721
Brisbane
Lord Howe Rise
Kermadec Is. (N.Z.)
Kermadec Trench
10,047
9165

Projection: Mollweide's Homolographic    East from Greenwich

m
6000
4000
2000
1000
200
0
0
200
2000
4000
6000
8000
m

5615   Principal Shipping Routes (Distances in Nautical Miles)

ALASKA

Bristol Bay
Gulf of Alaska
Prince of Wales I.
Queen Charlotte Is.

GREENLAND
C. Farewell

BRITISH
ISLES

C A N A D A

NORTH AMERICA

NORTH

Juneau
Sitka
6050
Kitimat
Prince Rupert
Dawson Creek
L. Athabaska
Churchill
Lynn Lake
Hudson Bay
Belcher Is.
James Bay
Scheffervlle
Hamilton Inlet
Labrador
Strait of Belle Isle
Newfoundland

Vancouver I.
Vancouver
Victoria
Seattle
Tacoma
Portland

Edmonton
Prince Albert
Saskatoon
L. Winnipeg
Winnipeg
Medicine Hat
Regina
Calgary
Spokane
Helena
Bismarck
Missouri

Duluth
L. Superior
Sault Ste Marie
St. Paul
L. Huron
Minneapolis
Milwaukee
CHICAGO
Michigan
Detroit

St. Lawrence
Montréal
Québec
Ottawa
Toronto
L. Ontario
Buffalo
Pittsburgh
Fredericton
Saint John
Anticosti
G. of St Lawrence
Pr. Edward I.
C. Breton I.
C. Race
Sable I.
New York
Southampton 3091

C. Blanco
Mendocino Séascarp
C. Mendocino
6741
Sacramento
Oakland
San Francisco
4418

Boise
Snake
Butte
Cheyenne
Des Moines
Salt Lake City
Colorado
Denver
Kansas City
St. Louis

UNITED STATES

Indianapolis
Cincinnati

Boston
C. Sable
NEW YORK
Philadelphia
Baltimore
Washington
Richmond
Norfolk

ATLANTIC

OCEAN

Murray Seascarp
2419
2091

Los Angeles
San Diego

Santa Fé
Oklahoma
El Paso
Ciudad Juárez
Austin

Little Rock
Dallas
Memphis
Atlanta
Mississippi

C. Hatteras
Savannah
Jacksonville

New York - Recife 3678
Bermuda (U.K.)
N.Y. - C. 1972

Ridge
Hawaiian Is.
(U.S.A.)
Honolulu
Oahu
Hawaii

Tropic of Cancer

Clarion Fracture Zone

Guadalupe
6225
Pto. Eugenia
C. S. Lucas

Sierra Madre
Gulf of California
Torreón
Monterrey

Guadalajara
Revilla Gigedo Is.
(Mexico)
Aguascalientes
México
Puebla
5700
Veracruz
6226

San Antonio
Houston
Galveston
New Orleans
Mobile
Tampa
Gulf of Mexico
Miami

Tampico
San Luis Potosí
Mérida
Yucatan Channel
La Habana
CUBA
Florida Strait
BAHAMAS

West Indies
Hispaniola
HAITI
DOM. REP.
JAMAICA
Kingston
Santo Domingo
PUERTO RICO
St. Thomas
Virgin Is.
Leeward Is.
9200
7680

Ston I. (U.S.)

I F I C

CURRENT

471 I
Equator

Clipperton Fracture Zone
Clipperton I. (Fr.)

Acapulco
BELIZE
GUATEMALA
Guatemala
EL SALVADOR
HONDURAS
Tegucigalpa
NICARAGUA
Managua
CENTRAL AMERICA
San José
COSTA RICA
PANAMA
Panamá
Colón
3277
S. E. MONSOON DRIFT

Caribbean Sea
Barranquilla
Curaçao (Ne.)
Maracaibo
Caracas
Orinoco
VENEZUELA
Guadeloupe (Fr.)
Martinique (Fr.)
BARBADOS
Windward Is.
TRINIDAD & TOBAGO

E A N

CURRENT

CURRENT

Palmyra Is. (U.S.)
Washington I. (U.K.)
Fanning I. (U.K.)
Christmas I.

Christmas Island Ridge

Jarvis I. (U.S.)

Galápagos
(Ecuador)

Cocos I.
835
Medellín
Bogotá
Cali
COLOMBIA

Guayaquil
ECUADOR
Quito
Chimborazo 6267
Cuenca
Iquitos
Manaus
Amazon

BRAZIL

nix Is.
& U.S.)
QUATORIAL
Malden I.
Starbuck I.

Tahiti - Panamá 4570

C. S. Francisco
C. Pariñas
Lobos I.
Chiclayo
Trujillo

SOUTH

Tongareva
Penrhyn Is.
Manihiki
Suwarrow Is.
(Suvorov)
(U.S.)

Vostok
Flint I.
Caroline I.

Marquesas Is.
(Fr.)

AMERICA

6369
Callao
PERU
Lima

3666

PERUVIAN CURRENT
706

Cook Islands
Society Is. (Fr.)
Windward
Hervey Is.
Tahiti (Fr.)
Leeward Is.

Tuamotu Archipelago
(Fr.)

Auckland - Panamá 6510

Cuzco
Arequipa
Illampu & Ancohuma 6550
Titicaca
La Paz
6866
BOLIVIA
Peru

Austral
Seamount Chain

Rarotonga

Tubuai Is.
(Austral Is.)
(Fr.)

Rapa Iti
(Fr.)

Pitcairn I. (U.K.)
Ducie I. (U.K.)

Southeast
Pacific Basin

Tropic of Capricorn

Iquique
Chile
8050
Antofagasta
Trench
Salta
Tucumán

PARAGUAY
Asunción
Corrientes
Pto. Alegre

stern

East Pacific Ridge

Sala-y-Gomez
(Chile)

Easter Is.
(Chile)

San Félix (Chile)
San Ambrosio (Chile)

Arch. de Juan Fernández
(Chile)
Alejandro Selkirk
Robinson Crusoe

Aconcagua 6960
Valparaíso
Santiago
Concepción
Neuquen

Córdoba
Rosario
Buenos Aires
La Plata
Río de la Plata
Santa Fé
Paraná
URUGUAY
Paysandú
Montevideo
Mar del Plata

ARGENTINA

Chile Rise

Pacific-
Antarctic
Basin

Basin

Pacific - Antarctic Ridge

WEST WIND DRIFT

CAPE HORN CURRENT

Chonos Arch.

G. of Penas

Wellington

Patagonia

P.A. - Valparaíso 1414
G. of San Matias
G. of San Jorge
P. Deseado
Buenos Aires - Montevideo
P.A. 1335 1295
Sta. Cruz
Punto
Punta Arenas
Str. of Magellan
Tierra del Fuego
C. Horn

Falkland Is. (U.K.)
Stanley

SOUTH

ATLANTIC
Argentine
Basin
6212
OCEAN

South Georgia

160    140    120    100    West from Greenwich    80    60    40

COPYRIGHT GEORGE PHILIP & SON. LTD.

Projection: Bonne

East from Greenwich

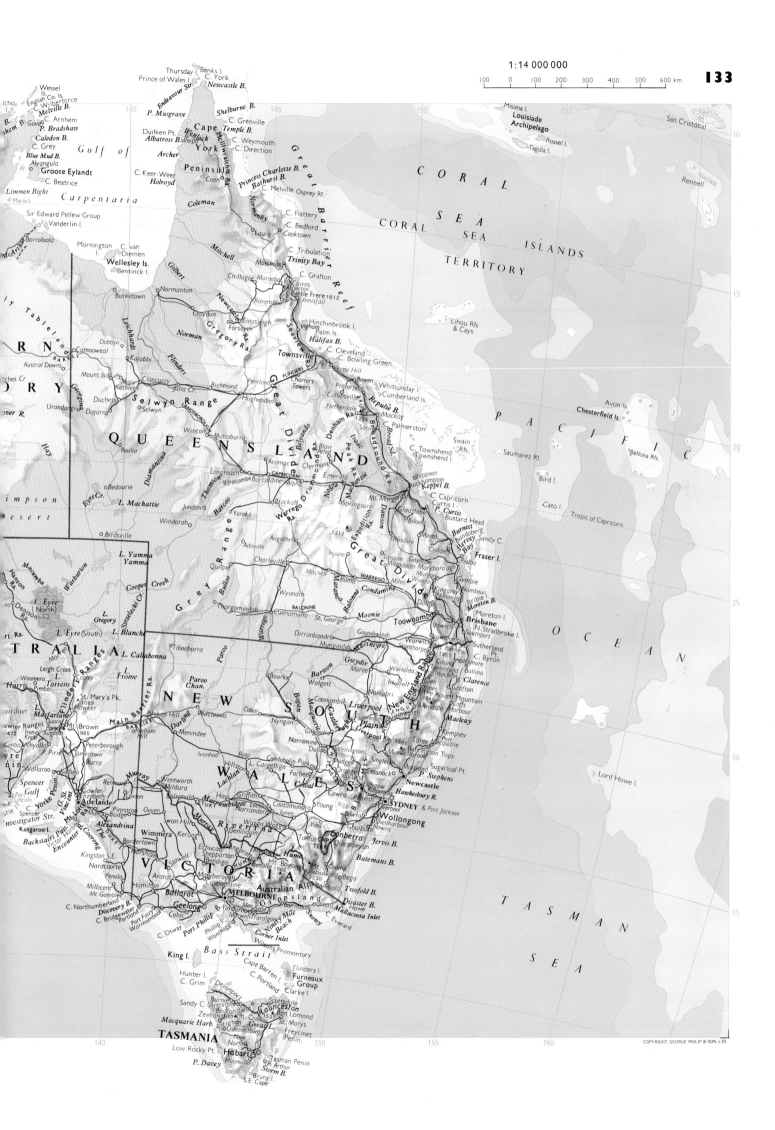

1:14 000 000

100   0   100   200   300   400   500   600 km

Wessel
Is.
Icho
Co. Is.
C. Wilberforce
B.
Melville B.
hem B.
Gove
C. Arnhem
P. Bradshaw
Caledon B.
C. Grey
Blue Mud B.
Alyangula
Groote Eylandt
C. Beatrice
Limmen Bight
Maria I.

Gulf of

Carpentaria

Sir Edward Pellew Group
Vanderlin I.

McArthur
Borroloola

Mornington
I.
C. van
Diemen

Wellesley Is.
Bentinck I.

RN Tableland
BARKLY
Camooweal
Austral Downs
ches Cr
Dobbyn
Burketown

ORY

Mount Isa
Kajabbi
Cloncurry
Duchess
Dajarra
Selwyn
Selwyn Range

QUEENSLAND

Thursday I.  Banks I.
Prince of Wales I.  C. York
Newcastle B.
Endeavour Str.
Shelburne B.
P. Musgrave
C. Grenville
Temple B.
Cape
Wenlock
York
Duifken Pt.
Albatross B.
C. Weymouth
C. Direction
Archer
Holroyd
Peninsula
Coen
Princess Charlotte B.
Bathurst B.
C. Melville  Osprey Rf.

Coleman

C. Flattery
C. Bedford
Cooktown
C. Tribulation
Mossman
Trinity Bay
Cairns
Atherton
Innisfail
Battle Frere 1612
Hinchinbrook I.
Ingham
Palm Is.
Halifax B.
C. Cleveland
C. Bowling Green

Mitchell

Gilbert
Croydon
Normanton
Einasleigh
Forsayth

Norman

Gregory Ra.

Chillagoe Mareeba
Ravenshoe

Townsville
Ayr
Home Hill

Flinders
Georgina
Leichhardt

Mary Kathleen
Julia Cr.
Richmond
Hughenden
Pentland
Charters Towers
Bowen
Proserpine
Collinsville
Netherdale

Whitsunday I.
Cumberland Is.

Urandangi
Winton
Muttaburra
Aramac

LANDSBOROUGH
Longreach
Ilfracombe Barcaldine
Alpha
Clermont
Emerald
Mackay
Palmerston

Boulia
Bedourie

Diamantina

Jundah
Barcoo
Blackall
Yaraka

Isaac

Broad Sd.
C. Townshend
Townshend I.

Springsure
1312
Expedition Ra.

St. Lawrence

Swain
Rfs.

Birdsville

Windorah

Augathella
Charleville
Tambo
Adavale

Dawson

Theodore

Gladstone
Biloela
P. Curtis
Curtis I.
Bustard Head

Burnett
Bundaberg
Childers
Hervey Bay
Sandy C.
Fraser I.

Injune
Roma
Mitchell
WARREGO
Miles

Taroom
Wandoan
Goomeri
Murgon
Wondai
Kingaroy

Gympie
Nanango
Yambou

Simpson Desert
Bedourie

Eyre Cr.
L. Machattie

QUEENSLAND

Cooper Creek

Grey Range

Quilpie
Bulloo
Wyandra

Warrego
Cunnamulla

Thargomindah

St. George
BALONNE
Maranoa
Balonne
Condamine

Moonie
Dalby
Toowoomba
Ipswich
Brisbane
N. Stradbroke I.

Bribie I.
Moreton B.
Moreton I.

Dirranbandi
Mungindi
Goondiwindi
Warwick
Stanthorpe
Southport

Tibooburra

Paroo
Chan.

L. Yamma
Yamma
L. Gregory
L. Blanche

L. Eyre
(North)
S2
L. Eyre
(South)
L. Callabonna

Denison
Ra.
Macumba
Warburton
Hanson

TRALIA

Leigh Creek
L. Frome

Flinders Ranges

St. Mary's Pk.
1089
Hawker

NEW

Bourke

Darling

Menindee

Barwon
Walgett

Macintyre
Warialda
Moree

Gwydir

Tenterfield
Casino
Lismore
Mt. Lindesay
1361
Glen Innes
Inverell

New England Ra.

SOUTH

Ballina
Clarence
Grafton

Narrabri

Coffs Harbour
The Round Mountain

Woomera
L. Torrens
Pimba

Iron Knob
Kimba
472
Whyalla
Cowell
Cleve

Iron
Baron
Port Pirie
Jamestown
Burra

Broken Hill
Wilcannia

Cobar

Nyngan

Bogan
Gilgandra

Narromine
Dubbo
Wellington

Liverpool
Liverpool Ra.
1585

Tamworth
Barrington Tops
Gloucester

Gunnedah

Taree
Port Macquarie
Kempsey
Macleay

Hillston

Roto
Ivanhoe

Condobolin
Parkes

Orange
Bathurst
Mudgee

Singleton
Maitland
Cessnock
Newcastle
P. Stephens
Sugarloaf Pt.

Peterborough

Wallaroo
Kadina
Spencer
Gulf
Port Lincoln

Murray

Renmark
Wentworth
Mildura
Balranald

Hay

LACHLAN
Lachlan
Cootamundra
Carrathool
Griffith
Narrandera

WALES

Forbes
Cowra
Young
Grenfell

Temora
Junee
Wagga Wagga

Goulburn

Yass

SYDNEY & Port Jackson
Liverpool
Penrith
Katoomba
Wollongong
Shellharbour

Jervis B.

Adelaide
Elizabeth
Gawler
Pinnaroo
Loxton

Murray Bridge
Tailem Bend
Ouyen

Swan Hill
Kerong

Murrumbidgee
Deniliquin
Riverina

Narrandera

Tumut
Canberra
Queanbeyan

Batemans B.

Kangaroo I.
Victor Harbor
Cape Jervis
Backstairs Pass.

Kingston S.E.

Encounter B.
Coorong

Bordertown

VICTORIA

Wimmera
Horsham

Warracknabeal
Stawell

Echuca
Shepparton
Nagambie
Benalla
Wangaratta

HUME

Mt. Bogong
1986

Mt. Kosciusko
2230
Mt. Bogong
Bombala
Cooma
Snowy

Delegate
Bega

Twofold B.
Disaster B.

Mt. Gambier
Millicent
Penola
Naracoorte

Hamilton
Ararat
Ballarat

Castlemaine
Maryborough

Bendigo

MELBOURNE

Australian Alps
Gippsland

Bairnsdale
Sale
Maffra

Mallacoota Inlet
C. Everard

C. Northumberland
Discovery B.
Portland
C. Bridgewater

Colac
Geelong
Queenscliff
Port Phillip
Warrnambool
Port Fairy
C. Otway

Traralgon
Moe
Maxwell
Ninety Mile
Beach

Corner Inlet
Wilsons Promontory

King I.

Bass Strait

Hunter I.
C. Grim
Devonport
Burnie
Sandy C.
Ulverstone
Zeehan
Macquarie Harb.

Cape Barren I.
C. Portland
Flinders I.
Furneaux
Group

Scottsdale
Beaconsfield
Launceston
Ben Lomond
1572
St. Marys
Great L.

Freycinet
Penin.

TASMANIA

Low Rocky Pt.
P. Davey
Storm B.
Hobart
Tasman Penin.
S.E. Cape
Bruny I.
New Norfolk
Huonville
C. Arthur

CORAL

SEA

CORAL

SEA

SEA  ISLANDS

TERRITORY

Misima I.
Louisiade
Archipelago
Rossel I.
Tagula I.

San Cristóbal

Rennell

Lihou Rfs
& Cays

Chesterfield Is.

Avon Is.

PACIFIC

Saumarez Rf.

Bird I.

Bellona Rfs.

Cato I.

Tropic of Capricorn

OCEAN

Lord Howe I.

TASMAN

SEA

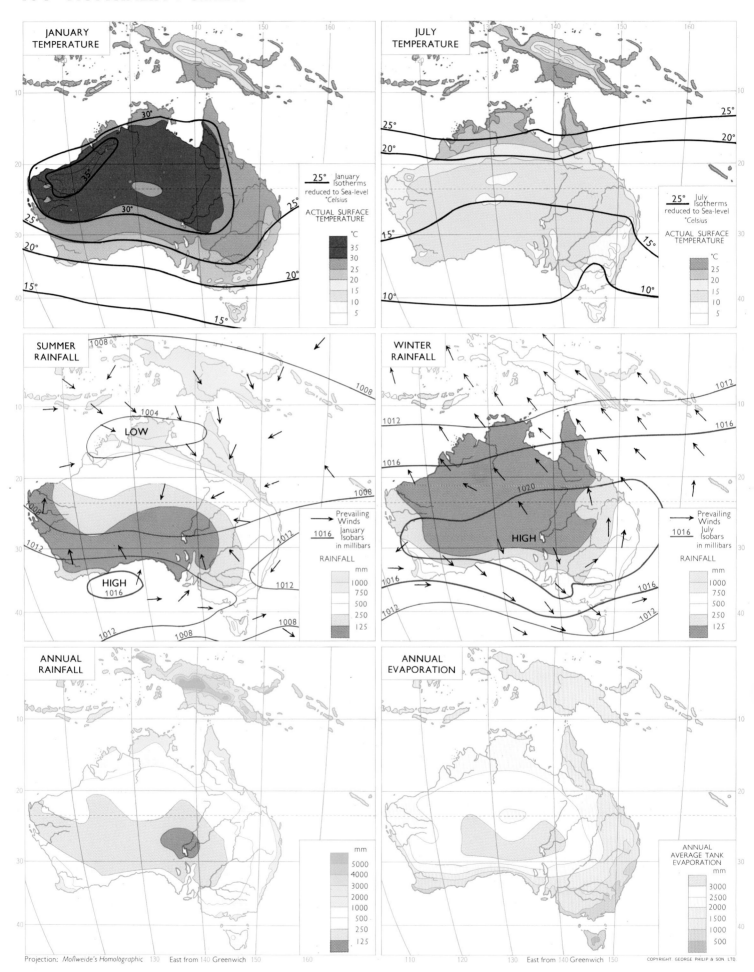

JANUARY TEMPERATURE

25° January Isotherms reduced to Sea-level °Celsius

ACTUAL SURFACE TEMPERATURE

°C
35
30
25
20
15
10
5

JULY TEMPERATURE

25° July Isotherms reduced to Sea-level °Celsius

ACTUAL SURFACE TEMPERATURE

°C
25
20
15
10
5

SUMMER RAINFALL

LOW

HIGH
1016

→ Prevailing Winds January
1016 Isobars in millibars

RAINFALL
mm
1000
750
500
250
125

WINTER RAINFALL

HIGH

→ Prevailing Winds July
1016 Isobars in millibars

RAINFALL
mm
1000
750
500
250
125

ANNUAL RAINFALL

mm
5000
4000
3000
2000
1000
500
250
125

ANNUAL EVAPORATION

ANNUAL AVERAGE TANK EVAPORATION
mm
3000
2500
2000
1500
1000
500

Projection: *Mollweide's Homolographic*   East from 140 Greenwich

East from 140 Greenwich

COPYRIGHT GEORGE PHILIP & SON LTD.

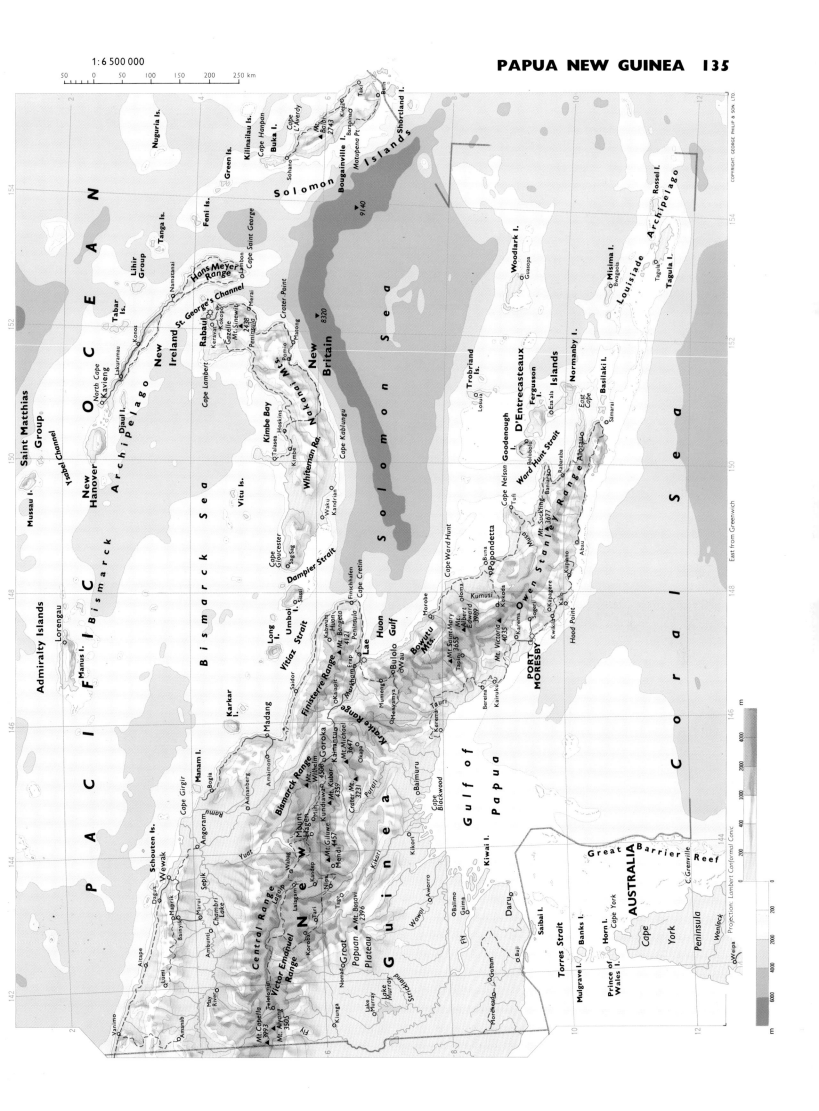

1 : 6 500 000

50    0    50    100    150    200    250 km

COPYRIGHT. GEORGE PHILIP & SON LTD

East from Greenwich

Projection: Lambert Conformal Conic

**P A C I F I C    O C E A N**

Nuguria Is.

Kilinailau Is.

Cape Hanpan
Buka I.
Mt. Balbi ▲ 2743
Cape L'Averdy

Green Is.

Feni Is.

Tanga Is.

Sohano

Bougainville I.
Motupena Pt.
Shortland I.
Taki
Beni
Kieta
Barapinao

Lihir Group

**S o l o m o n    I s l a n d s**

Saint Matthias Group

Mussau I.

Hans Meyer Range

St. George's Channel

Namatanai

Tabar Is.

Cape Saint George
Lambom
Merai

New Hanover

North Cape
Kavieng
Lakuramau

Djaul I.

Konos

Ysabel Channel

**N e w    I r e l a n d**

**A r c h i p e l a g o**

9140 ▼

**S o l o m o n    S e a**

8320 ▼

Rabaul
Keravat
Kokopo
Gazelle Peninsula
Mt. Sinewit ▲ 2438
Pomio
Matong

Crater Point

**N e w    B r i t a i n**

Cape Lambert

Kimbe Bay
Talasea
Kimbe
Hoskins

**N a k a n a i    M t s.**

**Whiteman Ra.**

Cape Kablungu

**B i s m a r c k    S e a**

Vitu Is.

Waku
Kandrian

Cape Gloucester
Sag Sag

Dampier Strait

Cape Cretin

Siassi

Long I.
Umboi I.

**V i t i a z    S t r a i t**

Saidor

Finschhafen

**Admiralty Islands**

Lorengau

Manus I.

**B i s m a r c k**

Karkar I.

Madang

Manam I.

Bogia

Cape Girgir

Schouten Is.

Wewak

Dagua

Aitape

Angoram

Ramu

Annanberg

Amaimon

Bainyik
Maprik
Marui
Ambunti

**Sepik**

Chambri Lake

Lumi
May River

Yanimo

Amanab

**C e n t r a l    R a n g e**

Telefomin

Mt. Capella ▲ 3993
Mt. Aiyang ▲ 3505

Oksapmin

Nomad

**G r e a t    P a p u a n    P l a t e a u**

Kopiago

Lake Murray

Kiunga

Tari

Koroba

**Victor Emanuel Range**

Lagaip
Wabag

Laiagam
Mendi
Nipa

Tage

**F l y**

Kikori

Lake Murray

**Bismarck Range**

Mount Hagen
Mt. Wilhelm ▲ 4508
Mt. Giluwe ▲ 4457
Kundiawa
Kandep

Mt. Michael ▲ 3647
Goroka

Kamanua
Okapa
Mt. Kubor ▲ 4359
Crater Mt. ▲ 3231

**Kratke Range**

Okapa

Mt. Bosavi ▲ 2296

Mijili

Purari

**F i n i s t e r r e    R a n g e**

Kabwum
Mt. Bangeta ▲ 4121
Huon Peninsula

Markham

Okapiti

Mt. Sarawaget ▲ 4121

**L a e**

Lae

Bulolo
Wau

Mumeng

Kikori

Kaiari

Baimuru

Cape Blackwood

**H u o n    G u l f**

Huon
Morobe

**B o w u t u    M t s.**

Okenkwamya

Tauri
Kerema

**G u l f    o f    P a p u a**

Baimuru

Cape Blackwood

Kiwai I.

Balimo
Gaima

Wawoi
Aworro

Daru

Wowoi

Buji

Aramia

Morehead
Gobam

Torres Strait

Saibai I.

Mulgrave I.

Banks I.

Prince of Wales I.
Horn I.
Cape York

Daru

**AUSTRALIA**

**Great    Barrier    Reef**

C. Grenville

Weipa

**C a p e    Y o r k    P e n i n s u l a**

**C o r a l    S e a**

Cape Ward Hunt

Cape Nelson
Tufi

Popondetta
Buna

Kumusi
Kokoda
Oloma
Oro Bay
Karema

Sogeri
Kwikila
Kapagere
Kalo
Kairuku
Bereina

Mt. Saint Mary ▲ 3655
Mt. Albert Edward ▲ 3989
Mt. Victoria ▲ 4035
Tapini

**Owen Stanley Range** 3677

Mt. Suckling ▲

Ward Hunt Strait

**PORT MORESBY**

Hood Point
Abau
Kupiano

Kairuku

**P a p u a**

Trobriand Is.

Losuia

Woodlark I.

Guasopa

**D'Entrecasteaux Islands**

Goodenough I.
Bolubolu
Esa'ala
Fergusson I.
Normanby I.
East Cape
Alotau
Baniara
Kabababa

Samarai

Basilaki I.

Misima I.
Bwagaoia

Rossell I.

Tagula I.
Tagula

**L o u i s i a d e    A r c h i p e l a g o**

**C o r a l    S e a**

m

6000
4000
2000
1000
400
200
0

m

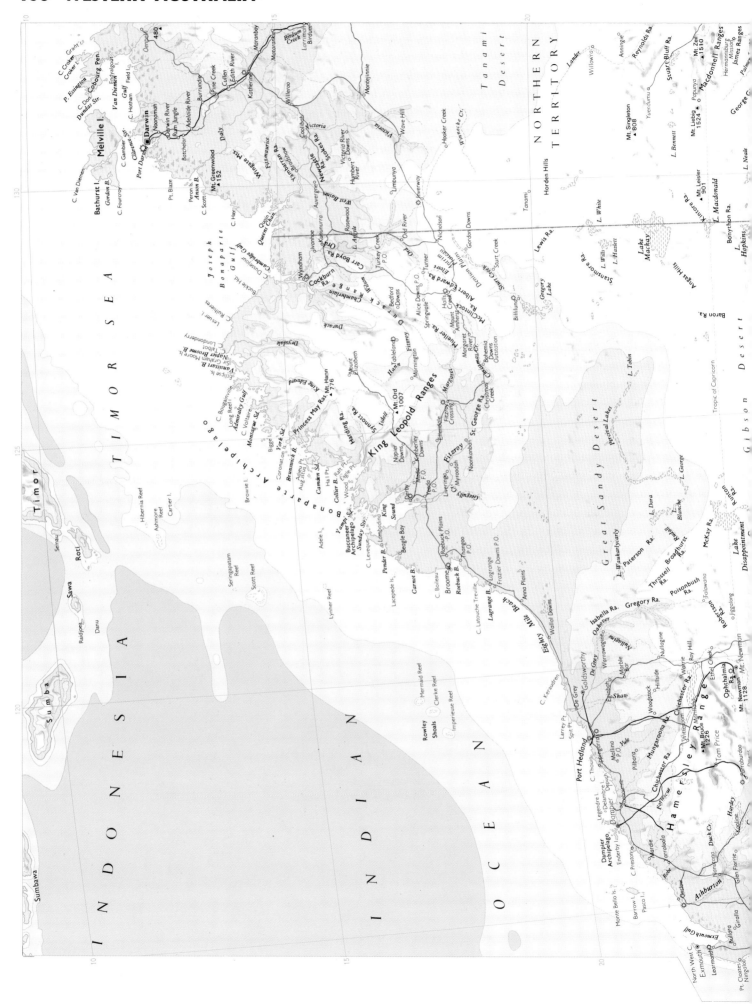

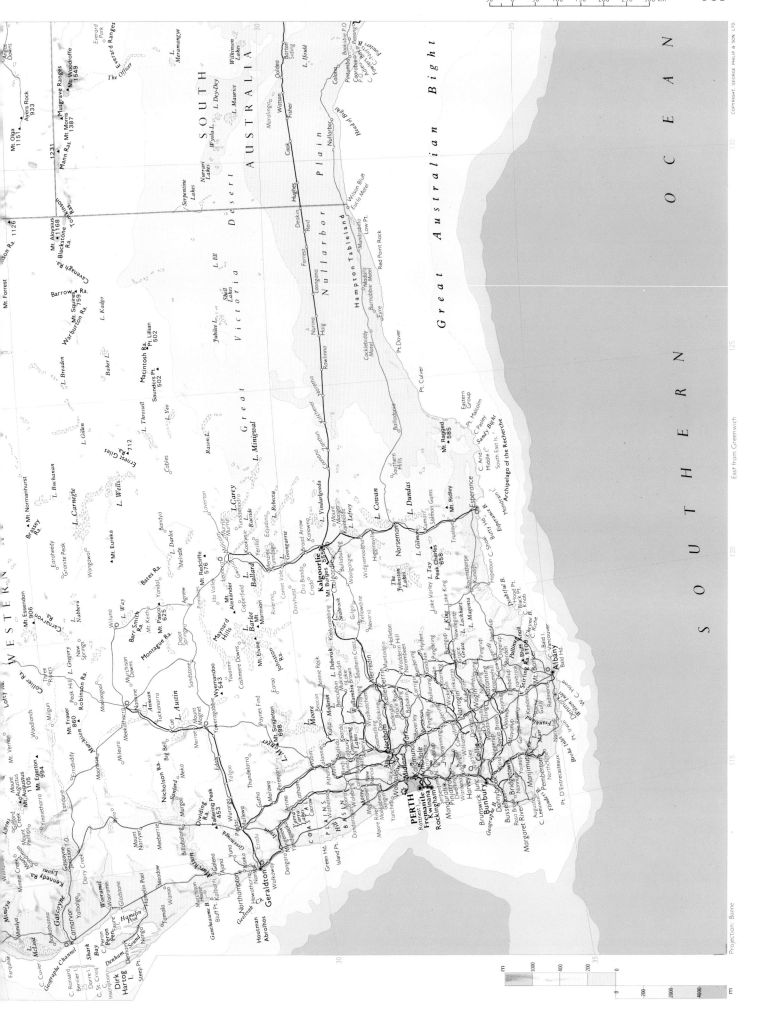

1:8 000 000

50   0   50   100   150   200   250   300 km

East from Greenwich

Projection: Bonne

S O U T H   A U S T R A L I A

W E S T E R N

Great Victoria Desert

Nullarbor Plain

Hampton Tableland

Great   Australian   Bight

O C E A N

S O U T H E R N

Mt. Olga
1151
Ayers Rock
933
Musgrave Ranges
Mt. Woodroffe
1549
Mann Ra. Mt. Morris
1387
1231
The Officer
Everard Ranges
Everard Park
Angas Downs

Mt. Normanhurst
Brassey Ra.
Mt. Eureka
Mt. Aloysius
1168
Blackstone Ra.
Cavenagh Ra.
Mon Ra. 1126
Mt. Forrest
Mt. Squires Ra. 759
Warburton Ra.
Barrow Ra.

L. Meramangye
L. Wilkinson Lakes
L. Dey-Dey
L. Maurice
Serpentine Lakes
Narrari Lakes
Wynda L.

Barton Siding
L. Hould
Ooldea
Cook
Fisher
Watson
Moralinga
Fowlers Bay
Penong
Coorabie P.O.
Coorabie
Pimbinna
Bookabie P.O.
Nullarbor
Head of Bight
Yalata

Colona
Hughes
Deakin
Forrest
Reid
Loongana
Nurina
Haig
Rawlinna
Naretha
Kitchener
Zanthus
Karonie

Cocklebiddy Motel
Madura Motel
Mundrabilla
Eucla Motel
Wilson Bluff
Low Pt.
Eyre
Burnabbie Motel
Red Point Rock
Pt. Culver
Pt. Dover

L. Carnegie
L. Breaden
L. Buchanan
L. Gillen
L. Kadgo
Baker L.
L. Wells

Mt. Redcliffe
576
Ernest Giles Ra.
712
L. Throssell
L. Yeo
Cables
Rason L.
Jubilee L.
L. Ell
L. Rebecca
Shell Lakes
L. Minigwal
L. Carey
L. Cowan
L. Dundas

Saunders Pt.
502
Macintosh Ra.
Pt. Lillian
502

Loverton
Balladonia
Mt. Ragged
585
Eastern Group
C. Arid
Middle I.
Sandy Bight
South East Is.
Archipelago of the Recherche
Montague I.
Southern Hills
Cape Le Grand

Esperance
Esperance B.
Mt. Ridley
Salmon Gums
Norseman
Dundas
Widgiemooltha
Higginsville
Mt. Monger
Coolgardie
KALGOORLIE
Mt. Burges
Boulder

Eyre
Peak Charles 658
L. King
L. Varley L. Tay
Ravensthorpe
Hopetoun
Bremer B.
Doubtful B.
Hood Pt.
Point Ann
Black Pt.
Pt. Henry
C. Knob
Bald I.
Two Peoples B.
C. Riche
C. Vancouver
Bald Hd.

W E S T E R N   A U S T R A L I A

Mt. Forrest
Three Rivers
Collier Ra.
Robinson Ra.
Peak Hill
L. Gregory
Mt. Fraser 860
New Springs
Murchison Downs
Cosmore Downs

Mt. Vernon
Mt. Augustus
1105
Mt. Egerton 994
Mt. Essendon 906
Carnarvon Ra.
Bates Ra.
Barr Smith Ra.
Mt. Way
L. Way
Nabberu
L. Nabberu
Yandal
Depot Springs
Mt. Keith
Mt. Pasco 625
Montague Ra.
Wyemandoo 543
Mt. Elvire
Barlee Ra.
Mt. Alexander
Maynard Hills
Johnston Ra.

Wiluna
Agnew
Lawlers
Leonora
Leinster
Mt. Margaret
Murrin
Morgans
Malcolm
Menzies
Broad Arrow

The Granites
Gwalia
Kookynie
Niagara
Yerilla
Edjudina
Yundamindra
Laverton
Mt. Celia
Burtville
Banjawarn
Yundamindra

L. Moore
Mt. Singleton 698
Mt. Gibson
Wogarno
Lake Austin
Cue
Big Bell
Mount Magnet
Sandstone
Youanmi

Mingenew
Mullewa
Murchison House
Meekatharra
Nannine
Meka
Tuckanarra
Mileura
Murgoo
Errabiddy
Landor
Cobra
Mt. Gould
Woodlands
Milgun
Daggar Hills

Dairy Creek
Gascoyne Jc.
Williambury
Minnie Creek
Kennedy Ra.
Lyons R.
Mt. Phillips
Phillips
Mt. Sandiman
Towera
Gifford Creek
Lyons
Lyndon

Mardathuna
Boolathana
Brick House
Carnarvon
Wooramel
Yalbalgo
Yaringa
Byro
Murchison
L. Austin
Mt. Narryer
Muggon
Yuin
Yalgoo
Morawa
Perenjori
Latham
Coorow
Carnamah
Three Springs
Eneabba
Watheroo
Moora

Shark Bay
Denham
Dirk Hartog I.
Dorre I.
Bernier I.
Inscription Pt.
C. Ronsard
C. Cuvier
C. St. Cricq
Useless Inlet
Hamelin Pool
Peron Peninsula
Nanga
Tamala
Wooramel
Gladstone
Overlander

Geographe Channel
C. Farquhar
Quobba
Point Quobba
Babbage I.
Pelican Pt.
Maud Landing
Minilya R.
Woorabinda
Peron Pt.
Steep Pt.
Useless Loop

Hamelin Pool
Galena
Kalbarri
Northampton
Howatharra
Geraldton
Greenough
Walkaway
Dongara
Irwin R.
Mingenew
Arrowsmith R.
Green Hd.
Island Pt.
Leeman
Coolimba
Houtman Abrolhos
Port Gregory
Horrocks
Bluff Pt.

L. Grace
Nungarin
Bodallin
Southern Cross
Yellowdine
Boorabbin
Coolgardie
Bullabulling
Bonnie Rock
Beacon
Bencubbin
Mukinbudin
Westonia
Marvel Loch
Bullfinch
Koorda
Wyalkatchem
Mukinbudin
Nungarin
Merredin
Kellerberrin
Bruce Rock
Corrigin
Quairading
Bullaring
Kondinin
Hyden
Lake King
Newdegate
Lake Grace
Pingrup
Ongerup
Gnowangerup
Jerramungup
Borden
Cranbrook
Tambellup
Broomehill
Katanning
Wagin
Dumbleyung
Kukerin
Kulin
Narembeen
Bruce Rock
Shackleton
Doodlakine
Baandee
Tammin

PERTH
Fremantle
Rottnest I.
Kwinana
Rockingham
Armadale
Mundaring
Midland
Kalamunda
Mandurah
Pinjarra
Waroona
Harvey
Yarloop
Brunswick Junction
Bunbury
Busselton
Dunsborough
Capel
Boyanup
Donnybrook
Bridgetown
Boyup Brook
Nannup
Augusta
C. Leeuwin
Margaret River
Cowaramup
Vasse
Geographe B.
Pt. D'Entrecasteaux

Northam
York
Beverley
Brookton
Pingelly
Cuballing
Narrogin
Wickepin
Williams
Collie
Darkan
Boddington
Wandering
Pingelly
Wagin
Collie R.
Donnelly R.
Manjimup
Pemberton
Northcliffe
Walpole
Nornalup
C. Beaufort
Broke Inlet
Windy Harbour
Pt. Nuyts
Denmark
Wilson Inlet
ALBANY
Stirling Ra. 1106
Bluff Knoll
Kendenup
Mt. Barker
Porongurup
Gull Rock
Frankland

Lake King
L. Magenta
L. Cronin
Mt. Holland
Marvel Loch

COASTAL PLAIN
Mortlock R.
Avon R.
Swan R.
Moore R.
Canning R.
Blackwood R.
Frankland R.

L. MacLeod
Mt. Murchison Ra.
Nicholson Ra.
Tallering Peak 453
Dividing Ra.
Greenhills
Badgingarra
Dandaragan
Gingin
Toodyay
Goomalling
Wongan Hills
Dalwallinu
Wubin
Mt. Marshall
Paynes Find
Sandstone
Yalgoo

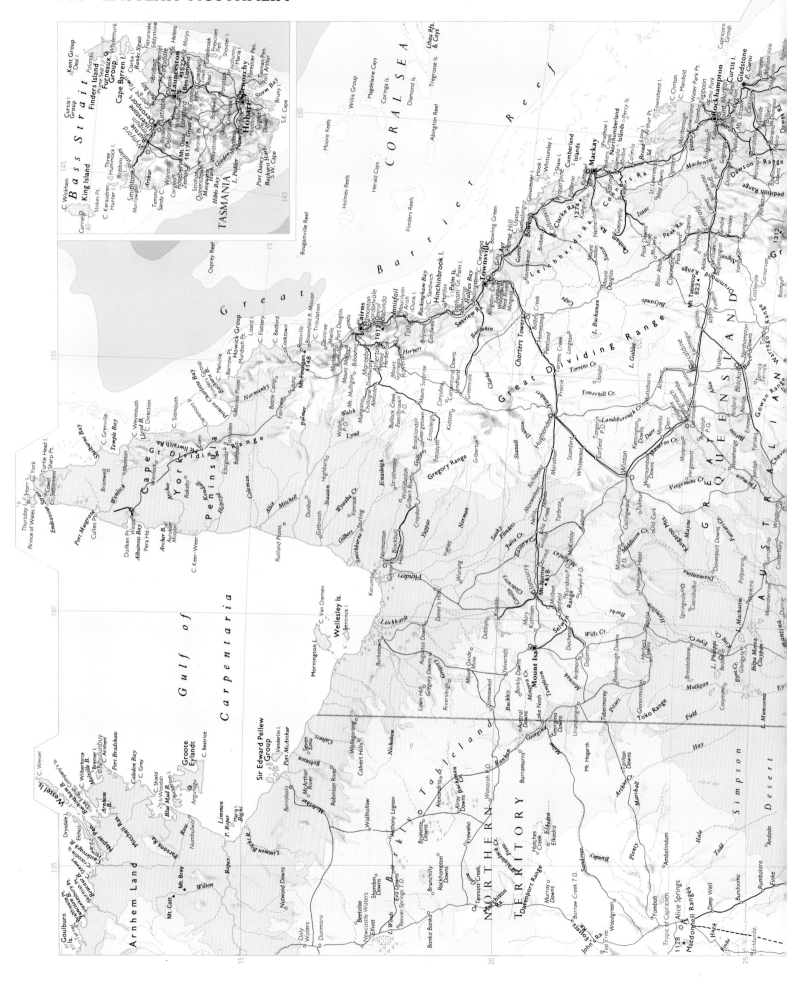

50   0   50   100   150   200   250   300 km

TASMAN

SEA

QUEENSLAND

Maryborough
Gympie
Nambour
Caloundra
Redcliffe
Sandgate
BRISBANE
Ipswich
Southport
Surfers Paradise
Coolangatta
Murwillumbah
Tweed Heads
Lismore
Byron Bay
Ballina

Toowoomba
Warwick
Stanthorpe

Grafton
Coffs Harbour
Dorrigo
Bellingen
Nambucca Heads
Macksville
Kempsey
Port Macquarie
Taree
Forster
Gloucester

NEW SOUTH WALES

Tamworth
Armidale
Inverell
Moree

Gunnedah
Narrabri
Walgett
Bourke

Dubbo
Bathurst
Orange
SYDNEY
Newcastle
Maitland
Cessnock
Gosford
Wollongong
Port Kembla

CANBERRA
COMMONWEALTH TERR.

Wagga Wagga
Albury

BASIN

Charleville

Darling

Cobar

Broken Hill

Wilcannia

Griffith
Narrandera
Leeton

Hay

Deniliquin

Wentworth
Mildura

MELBOURNE
Geelong
Ballarat
Bendigo
Shepparton
Wangaratta
Wodonga

VICTORIA

Warrnambool
Portland
Mount Gambier

SOUTH AUSTRALIA

Lake Eyre North
Lake Eyre South

Lake Torrens

Lake Gairdner

Port Augusta
Whyalla
Port Pirie

ADELAIDE
Gawler
Glenelg
Brighton

Kangaroo I.

Spencer Gulf

Eyre Peninsula

Port Lincoln

King Island

Flinders Island
Furneaux Group
Cape Barren I.

Bass Strait

East from Greenwich

m   1500   1000   400   200

0   200   2000   4000   m

Parakylia
Leigh Creek
Copley
Benbonyathe 1058
Lake Frome
Broughams Gate
Packsaddle
Caradoc
Peri Lake
L. Younghusband
Mt. Deception 682
Beltana
Nilpena
McDougalls Well
White Cliffs
Koonawarra
Momba
Tilpa
L. Hanson
Koolymilka P.O.
Arcoona
Parachilna
Frome Downs
Benagerie
Mulga Valley
Glen Gowrie
L. Hart
Woomera
Wirraminna Pimba
Wilpena Cr.
Mooleulooloo
Wilangee
Grassmere
Menamurtee
Wilcannia
Wongala
Poopello L.
Island Lagoon
Pernatty Lagoon
St. Mary Pk. 1165
Langidoon
Sturts Meadows
Lake Gairdner
Woocalla
Hawker
Siccus
Silverton
Stephens Creek
Cawkers Well
Volo
Goonalga
L. Macfarlane
Cotabena
Gordon
Mount Victor
Mingary
Cockburn
Broken Hill
Wahratta
Slamannon
Baden Park
Hesso
Quorn
Carrieton
Olary
Mutooroo
Menindee L.
Menindee
Teryaweyna L.
Mt. Ive
Mt. Brown 965
Eurelia
Mannahill
Leonora Downs
Mount Manara
Port Augusta West
Wilmington
Paratoo
Yunta
Cawndilla L.
Boolaboolka L.
Gypsum L.
Port Augusta
Orroroo
Netley Gap
Tandou L.
Iron Knob
Nectar Brook
969 Mt. Remarkable
Black Rock
Kimberley
Popio L.
Gum Lake
Darnick
Beilpajah
Iva
Siam
Booleroo Centre
Peterborough
Quondong
Oakbank
L. Popilta
Tartna Point
Mossg
Buckleboo
Whyalla
Laura
Jamestown
Terowie
Morganville
Traveller's Lake
Pooncarie
Manfred
Clare
Lake Gilles
Port Pirie
Gladstone
Braemar
Canopus
Belmore
Lethero
Culpara
Darke Peak
Crystal Brook
Gulnare
Mt. Bryan 934
Morgan
Bulpunga
Burtundy
Arumpo
Magenta
Pondooma
Hallett
Hatfield P.O.
Cowell
Port Broughton
Spalding
Gluepot
L. Victoria
Bidura
Oxley
Rudall
Snowtown
Brinkworth
Burra
Wentworth
Lachla
Wallaroo
Blyth
Clare
Farrell Flat
Murray
Renmark
Merbein
Mildura
Wyalong
Willamulka
Bute
Hoyleton
Robertstown
Berri
Yamba
Red Cliffs
Pitarpunga L.
Maude
Arno Bay
Kadina
Bowmans
Riverton
Point Pass
Waikerie
Barmera
Morkalla
Werrimull
Nangiloc
Benanee
Murrumbidgee
Moonta
Balaklava
Owen
Truro
Eudunda
Holder
Loxton
Taplan
Robinvale
Balranald
Ungarra
Maitland
Owen
Kapunda
Angaston
Maggea
Mantung
Veitch
Nowingi
Hattah
Bannerton
Koolounong
Perekerten
Tumby Bay
Port Victoria
Ardrossan
Mallala
Nuriootpa
Tanunda
Sedan Swan Reach
Wanbi
Annuello
Kulwin
Natya
Moulamein
Koppio
Minlaton
Sanderson
Copeville
Kunlara
Alawoona
Meribah
Ouyen
Piangil
Poonindie
Port Adelaide
Gawler
Salisbury Elizabeth
Mannum
Kalyan
Sandalwood
Peebinga
Walpeup
Pier Millan
Nyah West
Niemur
Edwa
Port Lincoln
C. Donington
Corny Pt.
ADELAIDE
Glenelg
Woodside
Karoonda
Marama
Cowangie
Tutye
Underbool
Patchewollock
L. Tyrrell
Waitchie
Swan Hill
Wakool
THISTLE I.
Carribee
Brighton
McLaren Vale
Mt. Barker
Monteith
Tailem Bend
Peake
Pinnaroo
Lameroo
Yarto
Speed
Ultima
Meatian
West Pt.
GAMBIER IS.
Marion Bay
Willunga
Strathalbyn
Cooke Plains
Geranium
Hopetown
Berriwillock
Curyo
Quambatook
Tragowel
Mincha
Investigator
C. Spencer
Normanville
Finniss
Milang
L. Alexandrina
Yumali
Coonalpyn
L. Albacutya
Yaapeet
Rainbow
Birchip
Avoca
Kerang
Cohuna
Western River
Kingscote
Penneshaw
Victor Harbour
Cape Jervis
Goolwa
Meningie
L. Albert
Culburra
Tintinara
Keith
Yanac
Lake Hindmarsh
Brim
Warracknabeal
Litchfield
Charlton
Mitiamo
Lockington
Roche
KANGAROO I.
Vivonne
D'Estrees Bay
Backstairs Passage
Encounter Bay
The Coorong
Salt Creek
Bordertown
Diapur
Nhill
Jeparit
Antwerp
Donald
Minyip
Wedderburn
Cope Cope
Korong Vale
C. du Couedic
C. Gantheaume
Vivonne Bay
Wolseley
Kaniva
Dimboola
Murtoa
St. Arnaud
Inglewood
Bridgewater
Lacepede Bay
Kingston S.E.
C. Jaffa
Frances
Goroke
Natimuk
Gorae (Carpolac)
Glenorchy
Deep Lead
Bolangum
Emu
Dunolly
Maldon
Eaglehawk
Ben
Reedy Creek
Kybybolite
Jallumba
Toolondo
Wimmera
Maryborough
Castlemaine
VIC
Naracoorte
Stawell
Talbot
Clunes
Kyneton
Woode
Beachport
George
Kalangadoo
Penola
Glenelg
Balmoral
Mt. William 1167
Maroona
Ararat
Beaufort
Waubra
Daylesford
Rivoli B.
Millicent
Englefield
Cavendish
Willaura
Creswick
BALLARAT
L. Bonney
Nangwarry
Casterton
Coleraine
Hamilton
Dunkeld
Mininera
Scarsdale
Elaine
Bac
Ma
Mount Gambier
Dartmoor
Branxholme
Penshurst
Skipton
Derrinallum
Werri
C. Northumberland
Port MacDonnell
Heywood
Condah
Macarthur
Mortlake
Cressy
Inverleigh
Lara
Discovery Bay
Portland
Portland Bay
Port Fairy
Koroit
Camperdown
Alvie
Winchelsea
Queenscli
C. Bridgewater
C. Nelson
Warrnambool
Allansford
Cobden
Colac
Aireys Inlet
Lorne
Port Campbell
Lavers Hill
Forrest
Apollo Bay
C. Otway

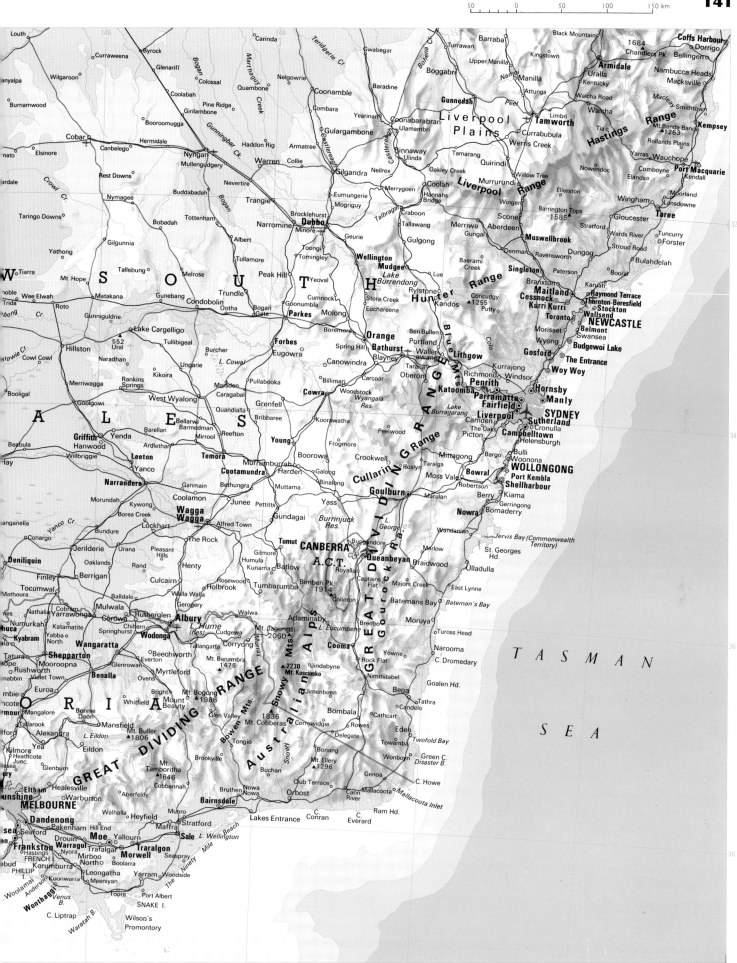

1 : 4 000 000

50    0    50    100    150 km

Louth
anyalpa
Wilgaroon
Curraweena
Byrock
Carinda
Gwabegar
Barraba
Turrawan
Black Mountain
1684
Chandlers Pk.
Coffs Harbour
Dorrigo
Bellingen

Wilgaroon
Glenariff
Bogan
Colossal
Coolabah
Pine Ridge
Girilambone
Creek
Coonamble
Combara
Baradine
Yearinan
Coonabarabran
Ulamambri
Gunnedah
Upper Manilla
Namoi
Manilla
Attunga
Armidale
Uralla
Kentucky
Walcha Road
Macksville

Burnamwood
Booroomugga
Hermidale
Nelgowrie
Quambone
Gulargambone
Peel
Liverpool
Plains
Tamworth
Currabubula
Werris Creek
Limbri
Walcha
Tia
Walcha
Comboyne
Macleay
Smithtown
Kempsey

Cobar
Canbelego
Haddon Rig
Warren
Collie
Nyngan
Mullengudgery
Gilgandra
Neilrex
Oakley Ck.
Quirindi
Willow Tree
Murrurundi
Wingen
Nowendoc
Elandso
Rollands Plains
Port Macquarie
Kendall

Elsinore
nato
rdale
Crowl Cr.
Rest Downs
Nymagee
Nevertire
Trangie
Brocklehurst
Dubbo
Minore
Merrygoen
Mogriguy
Coolah
Hannahs Bridge
Scone
1585
Barrington Tops
Gloucester
Stratford
Wards River
Tuncurry
Forster

Taringo Downs
Buddabadah
Bobadah
Tottenham
Narromine
Geurie
Talbragar
Craboon
Tallawang
Gulgong
Merriwa
Gungal
Aberdeen
Denman
Muswellbrook
Ravensworth
Dungog
Stroud Road
Bulahdelah

Yathong
Gilgunnia
Nymagee
Tullamore
Toongi
Tomingley
Wellington
Mudgee
Lake
Burrendong
Baerami Creek
Singleton
Paterson
Boorat

W
Tiarra
Mt. Hope
Tallebung
Melrose
Peak Hill
Yeoval
Lue
Rylstone
Kandos
Putty
Branxton
Maitland
Cessnock
Kurri Kurri
Raymond Terrace
Thornton-Beresfield
Stockton
Wallsend
NEWCASTLE

Wee Elwah
noble
Trida
Matakana
Gunebang
Condobolin
Ootha
Bogan Gate
Parkes
Molong
Store Creek
Eucharena
Hunter
Range
Coricudgy
1255
Ben Bullen
Colo
Toronto
Belmont
Swansea

Roto
Lake Cargelligo
552
Ural
Tullibigeal
Burcher
Forbes
Orange
Spring Hill
Bathurst
Blayney
Portland
Wallerawang
Lithgow
Morisset
Wyong
Budgewoi Lake

Hillston
Naradhan
Kikoira
Ungarie
L. Cowal
Eugowra
Canowindra
Carcoar
Oberon
Richmond
Windsor
Gosford
Woy Woy
The Entrance

Cowl Cowl
owie Cr
Merriwagga
Rankins Springs
Marsden
Caragabal
Pullabooka
Grenfell
Koorawatha
Woodstock
Wyangala Res.
Lake Burragorang
Katoomba
Penrith
Parramatta
Hornsby
Manly

Booligal
Goolgowi
West Wyalong
Bribbaree
Young
Cowra
Peelwood
The Oaks
Fairfield
Liverpool
SYDNEY
Sutherland

Beabula
Griffith
Yenda
Hanwood
Barellan
Barmedman
Mirrool
Reefton
Frogmore
Crookwell
Mittagong
Camden
Picton
Campbelltown
Helensburgh
Cronulla

Hay
Willbriggie
Leeton
Yanco
Ardlethan
Temora
Boorowa
Taralga
Roslyn
Bargo
Bulli
Woonona
WOLLONGONG

anganella
Merriwagga
Narrandera
Ganmain
Bethungra
Harden
Galong
Binalong
Marulan
Moss Vale
Robertson
Bowral
Berry
Port Kembla
Shellharbour

Yanco Cr.
Morundah
Kywong
Coolamon
Junee
Pettitts
Yass
Gundagai
Burrinjuck Res.
L. George
Wandanian
Kiama
Gerringong
Bomaderry
Nowra

Conargo
Deniliquin
Jerilderie
Urana
The Rock
Lockhart
Alfred Town
Wagga Wagga
Tumut
CANBERRA
A.C.T.
Bungendore
Queanbeyan
Braidwood
Jervis Bay (Commonwealth Territory)
St. Georges Hd.

Finley
Tocumwal
Berrigan
Oaklands
Pleasant Hills
Rand
Henty
Culcairn
Rosewood
Humula
Kunama
Batlow
Royalla
Captains Flat
Majors Creek
Ulladulla
East Lynne

Mathoura
Cobram
Yarrawonga
Mulwala
Walla Walla
Geropery
Holbrook
Tumbarumba
Bimberi Pk.
1914
Colinton
Bredbo
Bateman's Bay
Batemans Bay
Moruya

Nathalia
Numurkah
Kyabram
Katamatite
Springhurst
Chiltern
Corowa
Rutherglen
Albury
Wodonga
L. Hume (Res.)
Cudgewa
Walwa
Mt. Jagungal
2060
Adaminaby
L. Eucumbene
Cooma
Rock Flat
Numeralla
Tuross Head
C. Dromedary
Narooma

huca
Tatura
Shepparton
Mooroopna
Rushworth
Wangaratta
Beechworth
Everton
Myrtleford
Corryong
Tallangatta
Murray
Mt. Benambra
1475
Jindabyne
Nimmitabel
Bega
Goalen Hd.

ope
nabbin
ncote
Euroa
Violet Town
Benalla
Glenrowan
Ovens
Bright
Mount Beauty
Whitfield
Mt. Bogong
1986
Mt. Kosciusko
2230
Jimenbuen
Bombala
Tathra
Cathcart
Candelo

mour
mbie
Mangalore
Bonnie Doon
Mansfield
L. Eildon
Mt. Buller
1806
Glen Valley
Mt. Cobberas
1836
Corrowidgie
Delegate
Rowes
Eden
Twofold Bay

Tallarook
Alexandra
Eildon
Bowen Mts.
Snowy Mts.
Tongio
Bonang
Towamba
Wonboyn
Green C.
Disaster B.

ury
Yea
Glenburn
Mt. Tamboritha
1646
Cobbannah
Buchan
Mt. Ellery
1296
Genoa
C. Howe

eses
Kilmore
Heathcote Junc.
Healesville
Aberfeldy
Brookville
Bruthen
Nowa Nowa
Club Terrace
Orbost
Mallacoota
Mallacoota Inlet

unshine
MELBOURNE
Dandenong
Warburton
Walhalla
Heyfield
Munro
Stratford
Lakes Entrance
C. Conran
C. Everard
Ram Hd.

sea
Seaford
Pakenham
Hill End
Maffra
L. Wellington
Beach
Ninety Mile

Frankston
Hastings
FRENCH
PHILLIP
Drouin
Nyora
Moe
Yallourn
Trafalgar
Sale
Seaspray

Korumburra
Warragul
Mirboo North
Morwell
Traralgon
Yarram
Woodside

Woolamai
Anderson
Wonthaggi
Leongatha
Meeniyan
Toora
Port Albert
The

C. Liptrap
Venus B.
Koonwarra
SNAKE I.
Waratah B.
Wilson's Promontory

LIVERPOOL Plains

Liverpool Range

Hastings Range

Hunter Range

Blue Mts.

GREAT DIVIDING RANGE

Cullarin Range

Gourock Ra.

Australian Alps

Snowy Mts.

GREAT DIVIDING RANGE

S O U T H   W A L E S

V I C T O R I A

T A S M A N

S E A

COPYRIGHT. GEORGE PHILIP & SON LTD

146        148        150        152

1:3 500 000

20  0  20  40  60  80  100 km

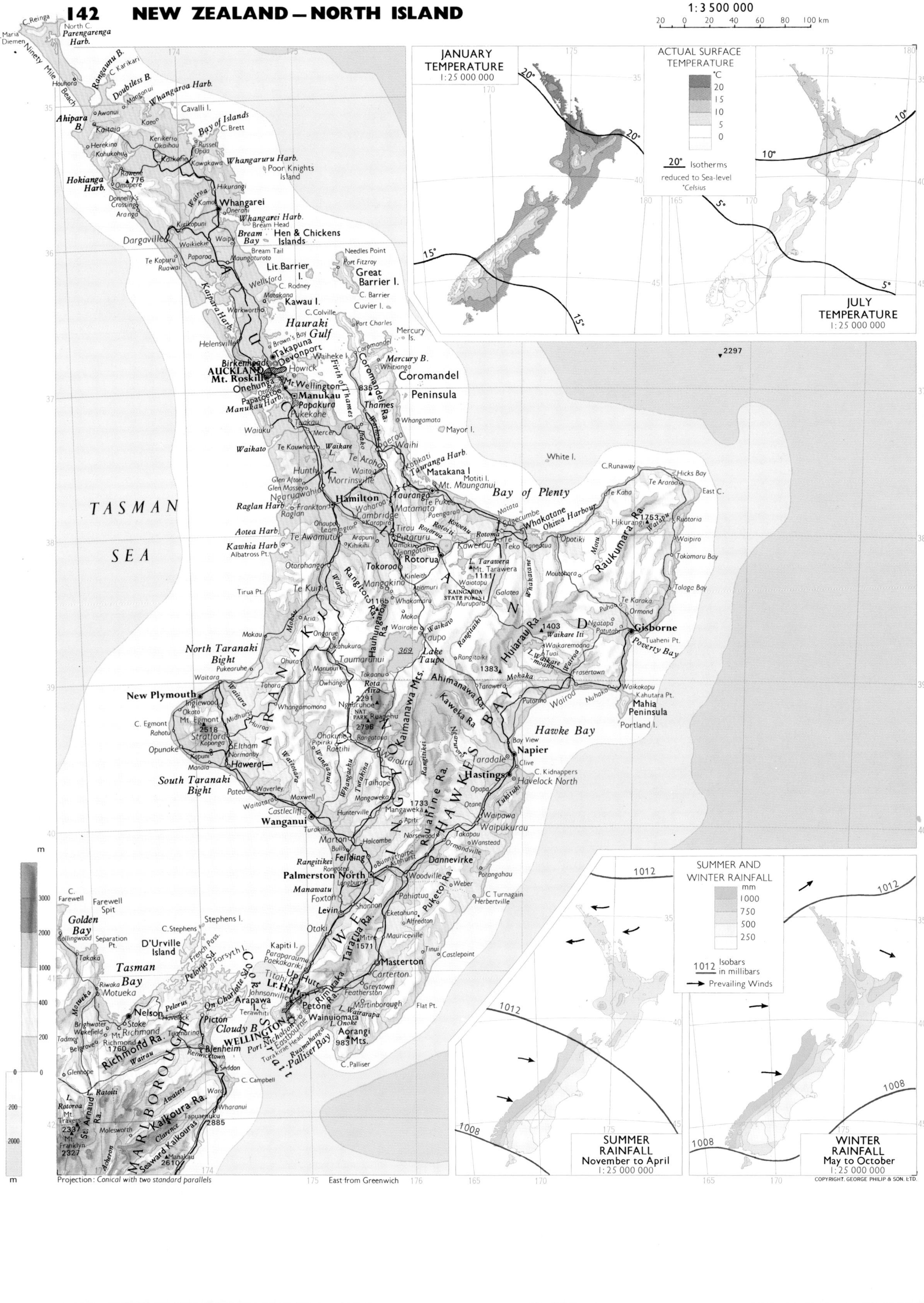

JANUARY
TEMPERATURE
1:25 000 000

ACTUAL SURFACE
TEMPERATURE
°C
20
15
10
5
0

20° Isotherms
reduced to Sea-level
°Celsius

JULY
TEMPERATURE
1:25 000 000

TASMAN

SEA

C. Maria van Diemen
C. Reinga
North C.
*Parengarenga Harb.*
Ninety Mile Beach
Houhora
*Ahipara B.*
Awanui
Kaitaia
Herekino
Kohukohu
*Hokianga Harb.*
Donnelly's Crossing
Rawene
Omapere
776
Aranga
Dargaville
Te Kopuru
Ruawai
Paparoa
Maungaturoto
Wellsford
Helensville

Rangaunu B.
C. Karikari
Doubtless B.
Mangonui
Kaeo
Kerikeri
Okaihau
Kaikohe
Kawakawa
Kamo
Onerahi
**Whangarei**
Kaikohe
*Whangaroa Harb.*
Cavalli I.
C. Brett
Russell
Opua
*Bay of Islands*
Poor Knights Island
*Whangaruru Harb.*
Hikurangi
Waiotira
Waipu
*Bream Bay*
Bream Tail
Bream Head
*Whangarei Harb.*
**Hen & Chickens Islands**
Needles Point
Port Fitzroy
C. Barrier
**Great Barrier I.**
Cuvier I.
Port Charles
C. Colville
Mercury Is.
Mercury B.
Whitianga

*Kaipara Harb.*
Werkworth
Matakana
C. Rodney
Kawau I.
**Lit. Barrier I.**
*Hauraki Gulf*
Brown's Bay
Waiheke I.
Howick
**AUCKLAND**
Birkenhead
Takapuna
Devonport
**Mt. Roskill**
Onehunga
Mt. Wellington
*Manukau Harb.*
**Manukau**
Papatoetoe
Otahuhu
**Papakura**
Pukekohe
Tuakau
Waiuku
Mercer
Te Kauwhata
Waikare
*Firth of Thames*
Coromandel
**Coromandel Peninsula**
Thames
Paeroa
Te Aroha
Waihi
Waitoa
Waihou
Whangamata
Mayor I.
Matakana I.
White I.
Motiti I.
C. Runaway
Hicks Bay
Te Araroa
East C.

Waikato
Huntly
Glen Afton
Glen Massey
Ngaruawahia
Frankton
**Hamilton**
Raglan Harb.
Raglan
Whatawhata
Morrinsville
Cambridge
Karapiro
Tirau
Putaruru
Matamata
**Tauranga**
Mt. Maunganui
Te Puke
Paengaroa
*Tauranga Harb.*
Rotoehu
Te Puke
Matata
Kawerau
Whakatane
*Bay of Plenty*
Te Kaha
Ohiwa Harbour
Opotiki
Waipiro
Tokomaru Bay
Tolaga Bay

*Aotea Harb.*
Te Awamutu
Arapuni
Kihikihi
Leamington
Ohaupo
**Rotorua**
Kaingaroa
*Kawhia Harb.*
Albatross Pt.
Otorohanga
Te Kuiti
Mangakino
Tokoroa
Mt. Tarawera 1111
L. Tarawera
Waiotapu
KAINGAROA STATE FOREST
Murupara
Galatea
Te Karaka
Ormond
Puha
**Gisborne**
1403 Waikare Iti
Ngatapa
Patutahi
*Poverty Bay*
Tuaheni Pt.

Tirua Pt.
Mokau
Aria
Ongarue
Kaimai
Whakamaru
Mokai
Atiamuri
1165
369
**Lake Taupo**
Taupo
Taumarunui
Tokaanu
Owhango
Manunui
Rangitaiki
1383
Mohaka
Waikaremoana
L. Waikaremoana
Tuai
Frasertown
Waikokopu
Kahutara Pt.
*Mahia Peninsula*
Portland I.

*North Taranaki Bight*
Waitara
Pukearuhe
**New Plymouth**
Inglewood
Okato
Mt. Egmont 2518
*Stratford*
Kaponga
Opunake
Rahotu
Midhirst
Whangamomona
Rota Aira
Ohakune 2291
Ngauruhoe
NAT. PARK
Ruapehu 2796
Raetihi
Pipiriki
Rangataua
Waiouru
*Kaimanawa Mts.*
Kaweka Ra.
Tarawera
Putorino
Wairoa
Nuhaka
Bay View
Taradale
**Napier**
Clive
C. Kidnappers
*Hawke Bay*

Mokau
Mandla
Normanby
Kapuni
**Hawera**
*South Taranaki Bight*
Patea
Waverley
Maxwell
Castlecliff
1733
**Wanganui**
Turakina
Marton
Bulls
Hunterville
Mangaweka
Apiti
Taihape
Mangaweka
Ormondville
Waipawa
Norsewood
**Hastings**
Havelock North
Otane
Waipawa
Waipukurau
Danevirke
Woodville
Porangahau
Weber
C. Turnagain
Herbertville

*Rangitikei*
Rongotea
Halcombe
**Feilding**
Bunnythorpe
Ashhurst
**Palmerston North**
*Manawatu*
Foxton
Shannon
Levin
Otaki
Pahiatua
Eketahuna
Alfredton
Mauriceville
Tinui
Castlepoint

C. Farewell
*Farewell Spit*
*Golden Bay*
Collingwood
Separation Pt.
**D'Urville Island**
C. Stephens
Stephens I.
French Pass
Forsyth I.
Kapiti I.
Paraparaumu
Paekakariki
1571
Mitre
**Masterton**
Carterton
Tinui

*Tasman Bay*
Takaka
Riwaka
Motueka
Pelorus
Pelorus Sd.
Havelock
**Nelson**
Brightwater
Stoke
Wakefield
Tadmor
Belgrove
Mt. Richmond 1760
*Richmond Ra.*
Okiwi Bay
*Queen Charlotte Sd.*
**Picton**
*Arapawa*
*Cloudy B.*
Port Nicholson
**WELLINGTON**
Johnsonville
Terawhiti
Eastbourne
Petone
Wainuiomata
*Up. Hutt*
*Lr. Hutt*
Titahi B.
Greytown
Featherston
Martinborough
Carterton
*Wairarapa*
L. Wairarapa
L. Onoke
Flat Pt.
**Aorangi 983 Mts.**
Palliser Bay
C. Palliser

**MARLBOROUGH**
L. Rotoroa
Mt. Travers 2338
*St. Arnaud Ra.*
Franklyn 2327
Glenhope
L. Rotoiti
Murchison
Owen
Tophouse
Wairau
**Blenheim**
Renwicktown
Seddon
Ward
Wharanui
Molesworth
Clarence
*Kaikoura Ra.*
Tapuaenuku 2885
*Seaward Kaikouras*
Manakau 2610
Kekerengu
C. Campbell

*East from Greenwich*

Projection: Conical with two standard parallels

m
3000
2000
400
200
0
0
200
2000
m

SUMMER AND
WINTER RAINFALL
mm
1000
750
500
250

1012 Isobars
in millibars
Prevailing Winds

1012

1008

SUMMER
RAINFALL
November to April
1:25 000 000

WINTER
RAINFALL
May to October
1:25 000 000

COPYRIGHT. GEORGE PHILIP & SON. LTD.

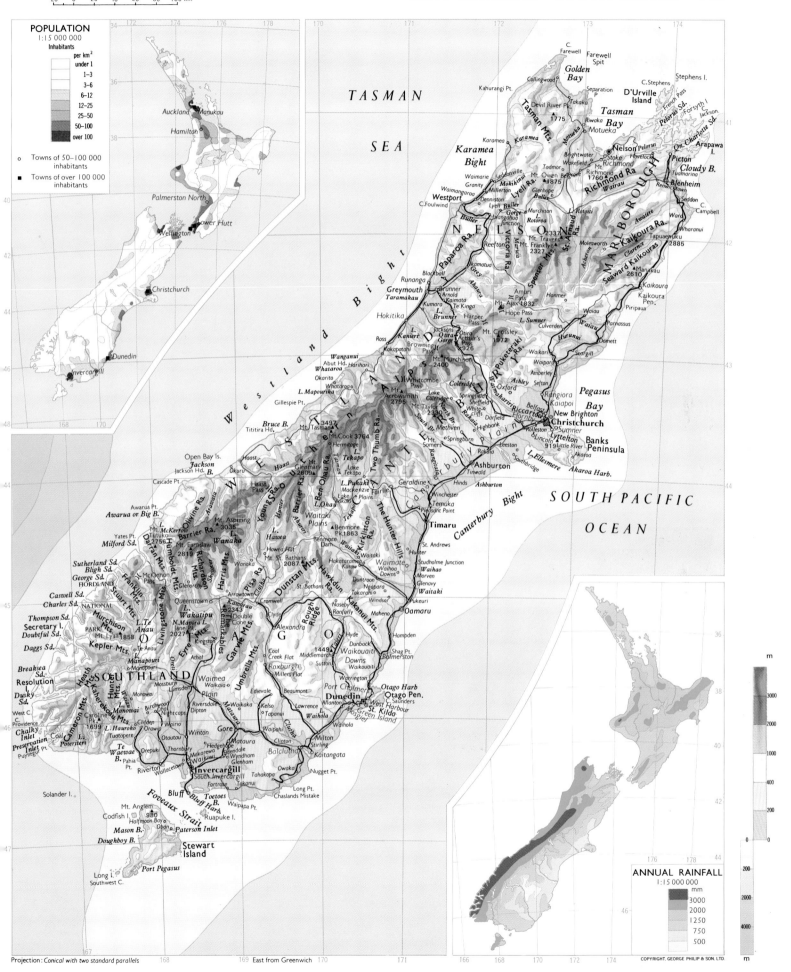

1 : 3 500 000
20  0   20  40  60  80  100 km

POPULATION
1:15 000 000
Inhabitants

per km²
under 1
1–3
3–6
6–12
12–25
25–50
50–100
over 100

○ Towns of 50–100 000
inhabitants
■ Towns of over 100 000
inhabitants

Auckland  Manukau
Hamilton

Palmerston North

Lower Hutt
Wellington

Christchurch

Dunedin

Invercargill

TASMAN

SEA

C. Farewell
Farewell Spit
Golden Bay
Stephens I.
Collingwood
Kahurangi Pt.
Devil River Pt.
Takaka
Separation P
D'Urville Island
C. Stephens
French Pass
Forsyth I.
Jackson
Tasman Mts.
1775
Riwaka
Motueka
Pelorus Sd.
Arapawa I.
Karamea
Karamea Mts.
Brightwater
Stoke
Nelson
Pelorus
Havelock
On. Charlotte Sd.
Picton
Cloudy B.
Karamea Bight
Wakefield
Wairau
Tuamarina
Wairau
Seddonville
Granity
Waimarie
Millerton
Mt. Owen
1760
Richmond Ra.
Mt. Richmond
Blenheim
Renwicktown
Mokihinui
Westport
C. Foulwind
Denniston
Lyell
Glenhope
Murchison
L. Rotoiti
Seddon
C. Campbell
Ward
Wharanui
Buller
Gorge
Wangahua Junction
L. Rotoroa
St. Arnaud Ra.
Mt. Travers
Mt. Franklyn
2327
Spenser Mts.
Molesworth
Awatere
Tapuaenuku
2885
NELSON
Blackball
Grey
Reefton
Victoria Ra.
Kaikoura Ra.
Seaward Kaikouras
Manakau
2610
Kaikoura
MARLBOROUGH
Runanga
Greymouth
Brunner
Kumara
Arnold
Ahaura
Inangahua
Matakitaki
Hanmer
Clarence
Kaikoura Pen.
Piripaua
Taramakau
Te Kinga
L. Brunner
Amuri Pass
Mt. Ajax 1832
Hope Pass
Waiau
Parnassus
Hokitika
Kaniere
Jacksons
Otira
Harper Pass
L. Sumner
Culverden
Waiau
Waikari
Waipara
Ross
Kakapotahi
Otira Gorge
Arthur's Pass 926
Mt. Crossley 1972
Ashley
Sefton
Scargill
Domett
WESTLAND
Wanganui
Abut Hd.
Harihari
Okarito
L. Mapourika
Browning Pass
Mt. Murchison 2400
Whitcombe Pass
Lake Coleridge
Springfield
Sheffield
Oxford
White cliffs
Darfield
Rangiora
Kaiapoi
Belfast
Pegasus Bay
Whataroa
Mt. Taylor 2330
North Br.
Rakaia
Riccarton
New Brighton
Gillespie Pt.
Bruce B.
Tititira Hd.
Mt. Tasman
3497
Mt. Cook 3764
Hermitage
L. Tekapo
Lake Tekapo
South Br.
Methven
Highbank
Rolleston
Lincoln
Christchurch
Sumner
Lyttelton
Little River
919
Banks Peninsula
Akaroa Harb.
L. Ellesmere
Leeston
Southbridge
Rakaia
Springburn
Mt. Somers
Ashburton
Tinwald
Akaroa
Open Bay Is.
Jackson
Jackson Hd. B.
Cascade Pt.
Glenmary
Mt. Sefton
2609
Two Thumb Ra.
L. Pukaki
Lake Pukaki
Mackenzie Plains
Fairlie
Geraldine
Winchester
Hinds
Ashburton
SOUTH PACIFIC
OCEAN
CANTERBURY
Haast
Haast Pass
Ben Ohau Ra.
L. Ohau
Waitaki Plains
Temuka
Pleasant Point
Canterbury Bight
Awarua Pt.
Awarua or Big B.
Yates Pt.
Milford Sd.
Mt. Aspiring 3035
Mt. McKerrow
Tutoko 2756
Mt. Earnslaw 2819
Olivine Ra.
Dart Mts.
Barrier Ra.
Youngs Ra.
Hunter
L. Hawea
Howea Flat
Benmore
Dam
Mt. St. Bathans 2087
Benmore Pk. 1863
The Hunter Hills
Hunter
St. Andrews
Studholme Junction
Timaru
Sutherland Sd.
Bligh Sd.
George Sd.
FIORDLAND
Caswell Sd.
Charles Sd.
Franklin Mts.
Stuart Mts.
McKinnon Pass
L. Te Anau
Glenorchy
Harris Mts.
Richardson Mts.
Pisa Ra.
Wanaka
L. Wanaka
Lindis Pass
Waitaki
Hakataramea
Kurow
Waimate
Waihao
Downs
Waihao
Morven
Glenavy
Thompson Sd.
Secretary Is.
Doubtful Sd.
Murchison Mts.
Mt. Lyall 1858
Kepler Mts.
Manapouri
Mavora L.
Jane Pk. 2027
The Remarkables
Kingston
Cromwell
Clyde
St. Bathans
Garvie Mts.
Hawkdun Ra.
Kakanui Mts.
Naseby
Ranfurly
Duntroon
Ngapara
Tokarahi
Windsor
Pukeuri
Oamaru
Daggs Sd.
OTAGO
Eyre Mts.
Athol
Alexandra
Rough Ridge
Hampden
Breaksea Sd.
Resolution Is.
Dusky Sd.
Heath Mts.
Kaherekoau Mts.
Hunt Mts.
Caroline Pk. 1699
Manowai
Livingstone Mts.
Mossburn
Lumsden
Waimea Plain
Nightcaps
Edievale
Coal Creek Flat
Roxburgh
Millers Flat
Middlemarch
Sutton
Hyde
Dunback
Waikouaiti Downs
Shag Pt.
Palmerston
Waikouaiti
Warrington
Port Chalmers
Otago Harb.
Otago Pen.
Saunders
West Harbour
Dunedin
St. Kilda
Mosgiel
Green Island
Chalky Inlet
Preservation Inlet
Puysegur Pt.
Cameron Mts.
Coal I.
L. Poteriteri
Clifden
Tuatapere
L. Hauroko
Orawia
Birchwood
Dipton
Riversdale
Waikaia
Kelso
Tapanui
Lawrence
Clinton
Beaumont
Balclutha
Milton
Stirling
Kaitangata
Waihola
Waihola
Solander I.
Te Waewae B.
Pahia Pt.
Orepuki
Riverton
Wallacetown
Otautau
Thornbury
Winton
Makarewa
Waikiwi
Gore
Mataura
Hedgehope
Edendale
Wyndham
Glenham
Waikaka
Waipahi
Waimahaka
Invercargill
South Invercargill
Fortrose
Bluff
Bluff Harb.
Toetoes B.
Waipapa Pt.
Tahakopa
Takanui
Long Pt.
Chaslands Mistake
Nugget Pt.
Mt. Anglem
Foveaux Strait
Codfish I.
980
Halfmoon Bay
Oban
Paterson Inlet
Mason B.
Doughboy B.
Stewart Island
Long I.
Southwest C.
Port Pegasus
SOUTHLAND
Westland Bight
Tasman Bay

ANNUAL RAINFALL
1:15 000 000
mm
3000
2000
1250
750
500

m
3000
2000
1000
400
200
0
200

Projection: Conical with two standard parallels

East from Greenwich

COPYRIGHT. GEORGE PHILIP & SON. LTD.

ATLANTIC

OCEAN

Iceland

Greenland Sea

Denmark Strait

Gunnbjorns Field 3700

Petermanns Peak 2940

Greenland

Godhavn

Julianehåb

Thule

Kane Basin

Nares Str.

Ellesmere I.

Axel Heiberg

Sverdrup Land

Parry Is.

Queen Elizabeth Islands

Devon I.

Melville I.

N. Magnetic 1965

Viscount Melville Sound

Bathurst I.

Lancaster Sound

Prince of Wales I.

Somerset I.

M'Clure Strait

Banks I.

Victoria I.

Boothia Pen.

Gulf of Boothia

Baffin Island

Baffin Bay

Davis Strait

Cumberland Sound

Frobisher Bay

Resolution I.

Foxe Basin

Foxe Channel

Southampton I.

Melville Pen.

Chesterfield Inlet

Arctic Circle

Hudson Strait

Ungava Peninsula

Payne L.

Belcher Is.

C. Henrietta Maria

James Bay

Eastmain

Labrador

Laurentian Plateau

Hamilton Inlet

Belle Isle Strait

Newfoundland

St. John's

C. Breton

Gulf of St. Lawrence

Nova Scotia

Bay of Fundy

Halifax

C. Sable

C. Cod

Nantucket I.

Bermuda

C. Hatteras

Chesapeake Bay

New York

Philadelphia

Washington

Allegheny Mts.

Appalachian Mts.

Blue Ridge

Cumberland Plateau

Atlanta

Memphis

St. Louis

Chicago

L. Michigan

L. Huron

Toronto

Detroit

L. Ontario

Niagara Falls

Hamilton

Ottawa

Montreal

Quebec

L. Erie

Ohio

Tennessee

Mississippi

Missouri

Minneapolis

Kansas City

Dallas

Red R.

Arkansas

Ozark Plateau

Llano Estacado

Colorado

Gila

Los Angeles

Wasatch Mountains

Great Basin

Grand Canyon Plateau

Colorado Plateau

Sierra Nevada

Mt. Whitney 4418

Death Valley

Mt. Shasta 4317

Sacramento

Cascade Range

San Francisco

C. Mendocino

Portland

Columbia

Seattle

Mt. Rainier 4392

Coast Range

Vancouver I.

Juan de Fuca Strait

Queen Charlotte Strait

Queen Charlotte Islands

Alexander Archipelago

C. Flattery

Coast Mountains

Mt. Waddington 4042

Mt. Robson 3954

Kicking Horse Pass

Yellowhead Pass

Crowsnest Pass

Calgary

Edmonton

Selkirk Mts.

Finlay

Peace

N. Saskatchewan

S. Saskatchewan

Regina

Winnipeg

Lake Winnipeg

Nelson

Churchill

Reindeer L.

Athabasca

Athabasca L.

Great Slave L.

Great Bear L.

Mackenzie

Back

Dubawnt

Denver

Mt. Elbert 4399

Pikes Pk. 4364

N. Platte

S. Platte

Rocky Mountains

Peace

Fraser

Skeena

Mackenzie Mts.

Porcupine

Brooks Range

Yukon

Alaska Range

Mt. McKinley 6194

Mt. Logan 6050

Mt. St. Elias 5489

Kodiak I.

Gulf of Alaska

C. St. James

Great Plains

Mt. Washington 1917

Hudson

7391

ARCTIC

OCEAN

3800

Beaufort Sea

C. Bathurst

C. Barrow

Alaska

Wrangel I.

C. Barrow

Pr. of Wales

Bering Strait

C. Dezhnev

Asia

St. Lawrence I.

Nunivak I.

Bering Sea

Aleutian Islands

Alaska Pen.

PACIFIC

Mendocino Seascarp

Murray Seascarp

Tropic of

OCEAN

P A C I F I C

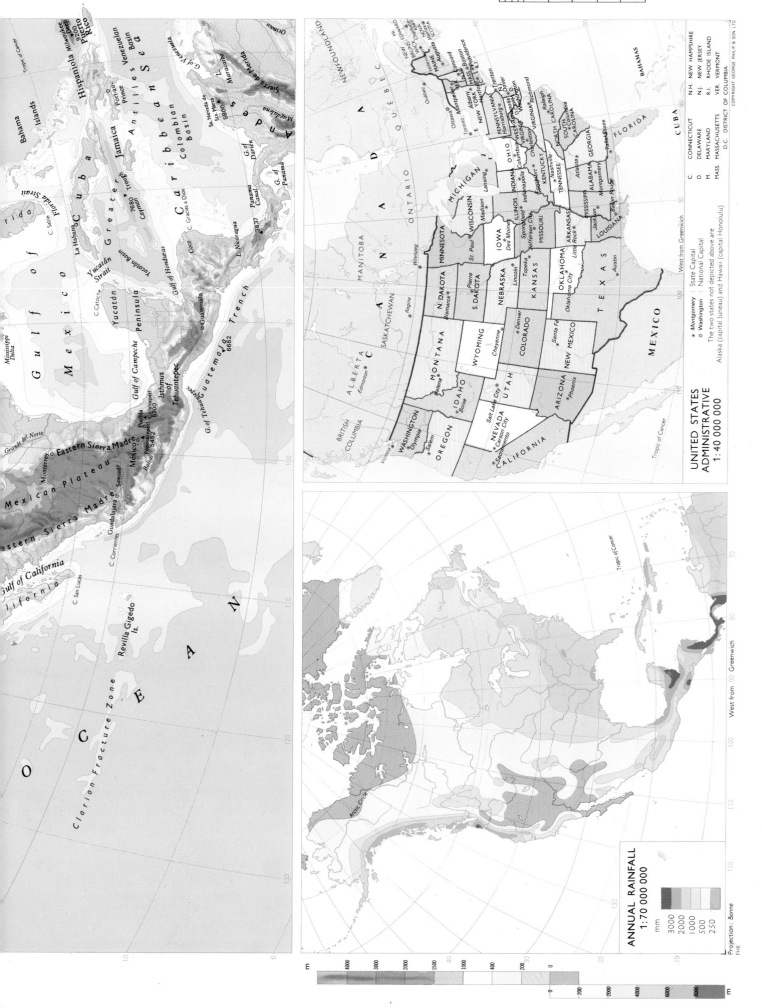

**145**

1 : 30 000 000

200  0  200  400  600  800  1000 km

Tropic of Cancer

Bahama
Islands

*La Habana*

Florida Strait

Bahama

C. Sable

**Gulf of
Mexico**

Mississippi
Delta

Yucatán Basin

C. Catoche

Yucatán
Strait

**Cuba**

Jamaica

*Guatemala*

Gulf of Honduras

7680 Cayman
Trough

C. Gracias a Dios

Coco

L. Nicaragua

3837

**Hispaniola**

**Milwaukee
Deep
9200 Puerto
Rico**

Port-au-
Prince

St. María
5800

Venezuelan
Basin

Prince

**Greater**

**Antilles**

**Sea**

**Caribbean**

Colombian
Basin

Maracaibo

Sierra de Mérida

Magdalena

G. of Venezuela

G. of
Darién

G. of
Panama

Panama
Canal

**C A R I B B E A N**

G. of Campeche

Yucatán Peninsula

Isthmus
of
Tehuantepec

Guatemala Trench

6662

G. of Tehuantepec

*México*
Popocatépetl
5452

Orizaba
5700
Puebla

Eastern Sierra Madre

Monterrey

**Mexican Plateau**

Seazín

Balsas

Guadalajara

Western Sierra Madre

C. Corrientes

Grande del Norte

Gulf of California

C. San Lucas

California

Revilla Gigedo
Is.

Clarion Fracture Zone

**P A C I F I C   O C E A N**

**UNITED STATES
ADMINISTRATIVE**
1 : 40 000 000

NEWFOUNDLAND

QUÉBEC

ONTARIO

MANITOBA

SASKATCHEWAN

ALBERTA

BRITISH
COLUMBIA

**C A N A D A**

NEW
BRUNSWICK

PR.
EDWARD

NOVA
SCOTIA

MAINE
Augusta

N.H.
VERMONT
Montpelier
Concord

Québec

Montreal

Ottawa

Toronto

Albany
NEW YORK

MASS. Boston
Providence R.I.
Hartford CONN.

Trenton N.J.

PENNSYLVANIA
Harrisburg

Dover DEL.

MICHIGAN

Lansing

OHIO

Columbus

WEST
VIRGINIA

MARYLAND
Washington D.C.

VIRGINIA Richmond

Raleigh

WISCONSIN
Madison

Winnipeg

MINNESOTA
St. Paul

IOWA
Des Moines

ILLINOIS
Springfield

INDIANA
Indianapolis

Frankfort
KENTUCKY

Nashville

TENNESSEE

NORTH
CAROLINA

SOUTH
CAROLINA
Columbia

Charleston

ATLANTIC

Regina

N. DAKOTA
Bismarck

S. DAKOTA
Pierre

NEBRASKA
Lincoln

Topeka
KANSAS

MISSOURI
Jefferson City

ARKANSAS
Little Rock

MISSISSIPPI
Jackson

ALABAMA
Montgomery

GEORGIA
Atlanta

Tallahassee

FLORIDA

MONTANA
Helena

Edmonton

IDAHO
Boise

WYOMING
Cheyenne

COLORADO
Denver

OKLAHOMA
Oklahoma City

LOUISIANA
Baton Rouge

WASHINGTON
Olympia

Salem
OREGON

NEVADA
Carson City

Salt Lake City
UTAH

Sacramento

CALIFORNIA

ARIZONA
Phoenix

NEW MEXICO
Santa Fe

**T E X A S**

Austin

M E X I C O

Victoria

80

West from Greenwich

90

100

Tropic of Cancer

CUBA

BAHAMAS

* Montgomery : State Capital
⊛ Washington : National Capital

The two states not depicted above are

Alaska (capital Juneau) and Hawaii (capital Honolulu)

C. CONNECTICUT
D. DELAWARE
M. MARYLAND
MASS. MASSACHUSETTS
D.C. DISTRICT OF COLUMBIA

N.H. NEW HAMPSHIRE
N.J. NEW JERSEY
R.I. RHODE ISLAND
VER. VERMONT

COPYRIGHT GEORGE PHILIP & SON LTD

**ANNUAL RAINFALL**
1 : 70 000 000

mm
3000
2000
1000
500
250

Arctic Circle

Tropic of Cancer

70

80

West from 90 Greenwich

100

110

120

130

Projection: Bonne
FHK

m
4000
3000
2000
1500
1000
400
200
0

m
0
200
2000
4000
6000
8000

40

30

20

10

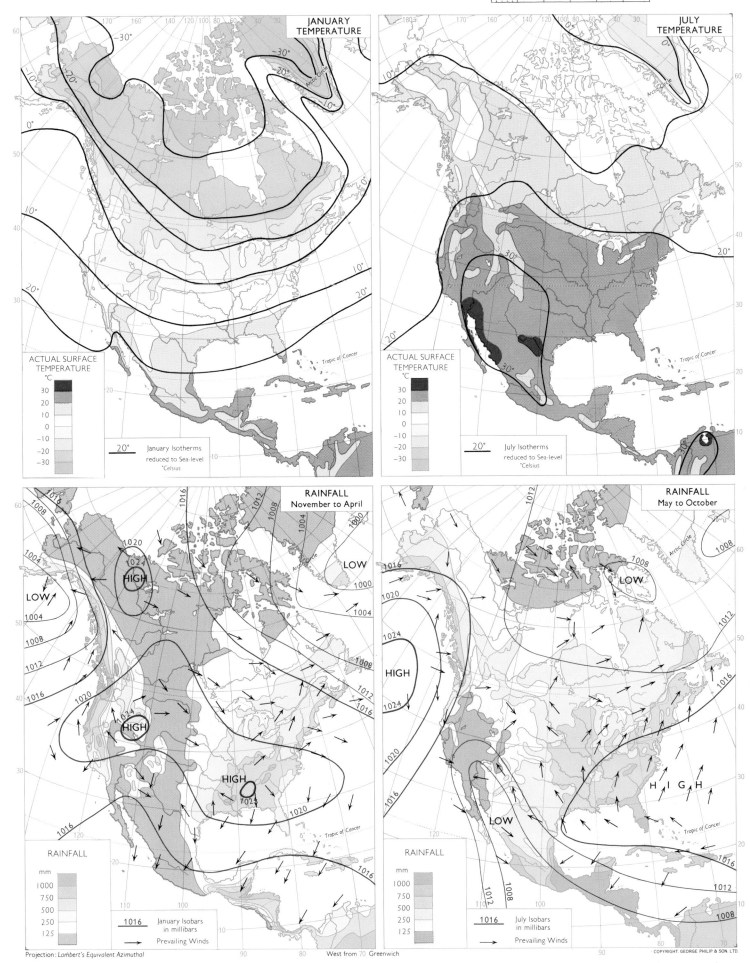

1 : 70 000 000

500   0   500   1000   1500   2000   2500 km

JANUARY
TEMPERATURE

JULY
TEMPERATURE

ACTUAL SURFACE
TEMPERATURE
°C

30
20
10
0
-10
-20
-30

20°   January Isotherms
reduced to Sea-level
°Celsius

ACTUAL SURFACE
TEMPERATURE
°C

30
20
10
0
-10
-20
-30

20°   July Isotherms
reduced to Sea-level
°Celsius

RAINFALL
November to April

RAINFALL
May to October

HIGH
LOW
LOW
HIGH
HIGH

LOW

HIGH

LOW

H I G H

RAINFALL

mm
1000
750
500
250
125

1016   January Isobars
in millibars
→   Prevailing Winds

RAINFALL

mm
1000
750
500
250
125

1016   July Isobars
in millibars
→   Prevailing Winds

Projection: Lambert's Equivalent Azimuthal

West from 70 Greenwich

COPYRIGHT GEORGE PHILIP & SON, LTD.

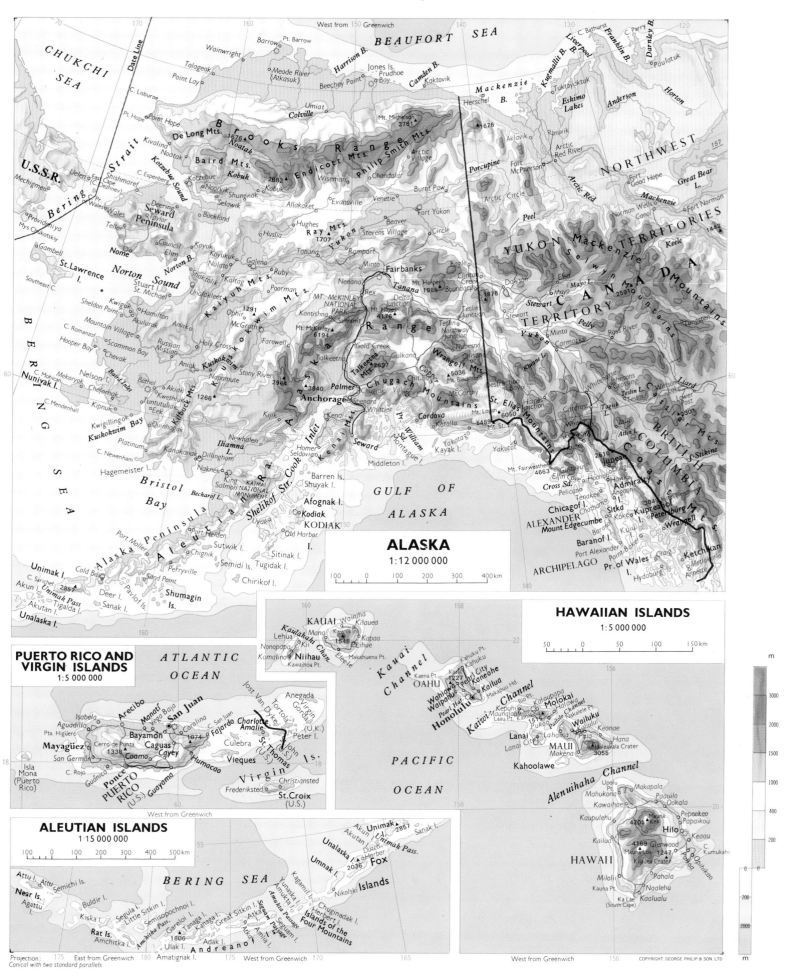

## ALASKA
### 1:12 000 000
100  0  100  200  300  400km

CHUKCHI SEA

BEAUFORT SEA

U.S.S.R.

Bering Strait

Date Line

West from 150 Greenwich

Pt. Barrow
Barrow
Wainwright
Tolageak
Point Lay
Meade River (Atkasuk)
Beechey Point
Prudhoe Bay
Camden B.
Kaktovik
Mt. Michelson 2781
C. Lisburne
Pt. Hope
Point Hope
Umiat
Colville

Mackenzie
Herschel B.
Kugmallit B. B.
C. Bathurst
Franklin B.
Liverpool
C. Parry
Darnley B.
Paulatuk

De Long Mts. 1676
Noatak
Brooks Range
Endicott Mts.
Philip Smith Mts.
4676
Aklavik
Inuvik
Arctic Red River
Fort McPherson
Fort Good Hope

NORTHWEST
157

Baird Mts.
2682
Wiseman
Chandalar
Arctic Village
Porcupine
Fort
Arctic Red
Mackenzie
Norman Wells
Fort Norman
1443
Keele
Great Bear L.

Kivalina
Kotzebue Sound
Kobuk
Kobuk
Selawik
Allakaket
Hughes
Evansville
Venetie
Burnt Paw
Arctic Circle
Peel
Canol

C. Espenberg
Kotzebue
Noorvik
Shungnak
Huslia
Fort Yukon
Beaver

Shishmaref
Deering
Taylor
Buckland
Koyukuk
Yukon
Rampart
Circle
Dawson
Elsa
Mayo
25910
Selwyn Mountains
Tungsten

Mechigmen
Uelen (C. Dezhnev)
East Cape
Wales
Wales
Teller
Seward Peninsula
Council
Koyuk
Ray Mts. 1707
Stevens Village
Eagle
Boundary
1878
Stewart
Mayo
Ross River

YUKON
Mackenzie
TERRITORIES
CANADA

St. Lawrence I.
Gambell
Nome
Elim
Nulato
Galena
Ruby
Tanana
Minto
Fairbanks
Clinton Creek
Mt. Harper 1986
Dawson
Stewart
Pelly
Carmacks

Southeast C.
Norton Sound
Stuart I.
St. Michael
Unalakleet
Shaktolik
Kaltag
Poorman
Nenana
Rex
Tanana
Delta Junction
Tetlin Junction
Northway Junction
Nubesna
Minto
Yukon
Whitehorse
TERRITORY
Ross River
2301

Kwiguk
Hamilton
Anvik
Ophir
McGrath
MT. McKINLEY NATIONAL PARK
Kantishna
Summit
Mt. Hayes 4176
Tetlin
Northway
Carmacks
Johnsons Crossing
Teslin L.
Lower Post

BERING SEA
Hooper Bay
Scammon Bay
Chevak
Aniak
Holy Cross
Farewell
Mt. McKinley 6194
Alaska Range
Gold Creek
Gulkana
Wrangell Mts.
5036
Mt. Blackburn
McCarthy
Kluane L.
Whitehorse
Tagish L.
Haines Junction
Teslin L.
Watson L.
Liard

Nunivak I.
C. Romanzof
Mountain Village
Russian Mission
Talkeetna
Talkeetna Mts. 2697
Copper
Chitina
5036
Destruction Bay
BRITISH
Liard

C. Mendenhall
Mekoryuk
Nelson I.
Baird Inlet
Bethel
Kwethluk
2944
3840
Palmer
Chugach
Valdez
Cordova
St. Elias Mountains
Mt. Logan
6050
Haines
Skagway
Atlin L.
Atlin
COLUMBIA
Cassiar Mts.
Stikine

Kipnuk
Eek
Quinhagak
1266
Anchorage
Seward
Whittier
Pr. William Sd.
Mt. St. Elias 5489
Gustavus
Juneau
2616

Kwigillingok
Kuskokwim Bay
Platinum
Napamute
Stony River
Kijik
Kenai
Katalla
Kayak I.
Yakataga
Mt. Fairweather 4663
Elfin Cove
Hoonah
Hawk Inlet
Admiralty
Angoon
3041

Kanakanak
Iliamna L.
Newhalen
Dillingham
Homer
Kenai Mts.
Seward
Yakutat
Cross Sd.
Pelican
Chichagof I.
Chatham
Sitka
Koke
Kupreanof
Petersburg
Wrangell

Hagemeister I.
Naknek
King Salmon
KATMAI NATIONAL MONUMENT
Middleton I.
ALEXANDER
Mount Edgecumbe
Baranof
Sitka
Port Alexander
Pt. of Wales
Craig
Ketchikan

Bristol Bay
Becharof L.
Uyak
GULF OF ALASKA
Baranof I.
Pr. of Wales I.
Hydaburg
Metlakatla
Annette

Alaska Peninsula
Port Moller
Port Heiden
Chignik
Uyak
KODIAK
Kodiak I.
Old Harbor
ARCHIPELAGO
150
140

Aleutian Ra.
Shelikof Str.
Cook Inlet
Barren Is.
Shuyak I.
Afognak I.

Unimak I.
C. Sarichef 2857
Cold Bay
Sand Point
Perryville
Ferryville
Chignik
Sitinak I.
Semidi Is.
Tugidak I.
Chirikof I.

Akun I.
Unimak Pass
Tigalda I.
Deer I.
Pavlof Is.
Sanak I.
Shumagin Is.

Akutan I.
Unalaska I.

---

### HAWAIIAN ISLANDS
### 1:5 000 000
50  0  50  100  150km

160
158
22
156

KAUAI
Wainiha
Kilauea
Kapaa
Waialua
Lihue
1548
Lehua
Mana
Nonopapa
Kii
Elecele
Makahuena Pt.
Kaulakahi Chan.
Kamalino
Niihau
Kawaihoa Pt.

Kauai Channel

OAHU
Kaena Pt.
Kahuku Pt.
Kahuku
Waialua
1227
Wahiawa
Kahana
Kaneohe
Waipahu
Pearl City
Kailua
Pearl Harbor
Honolulu
Kepuhi
Makapuu Hd.
Ilio Pt.
Molokai
Halawa

Kaiwi Channel
Laau Pt.
Kamalo
Pailolo Channel
Maunaloa
Kaunakakai
Nakalele Pt.
Wailuku
Kahului
Paia
Keanae
Hana

Lanai
Lanai City
Lahaina
MAUI
Makena
3055
Haleakala Crater

Kahoolawe

PACIFIC OCEAN

Alenuihaha Channel
Upolu Pt.
Makapala
Mahukona
Kawaihae
Kaupulehu
Mauna Kea 4205
Pepeekeo
Papaikou
Hilo
Kailua
Mauna Loa 4169
1247
Glenwood
Keaau
HAWAII
Kilauea Crater
Pahala
Milolii
Kauna Pt.
Naalehu
Kaalualu
Ka Lae (South Cape)
Kumukahi

156

---

### PUERTO RICO AND VIRGIN ISLANDS
### 1:5 000 000

ATLANTIC OCEAN

Arecibo
Manati
Vega Baja
San Juan
Carolina
Anegada
Virgin Gorda
Jost Van Dyke
Tortola
(U.K.)
Peter I.

Isabela
Aguadilla
Pta. Higüero
Bayamón
Caguas
1074
Fajardo
Charlotte Amalie
St. Thomas
(U.S.)

Mayagüez
Cerro de Punta 1338
Coamo
Cayey
Culebra
Virgin Is.

San Germán
PUERTO RICO (U.S.)
Humacao
Vieques

Isla Mona (Puerto Rico)
C. Rojo
Guánica
Ponce
Guayama
18

Frederiksted
Christiansted
St. Croix (U.S.)

West from Greenwich
60
18

---

### ALEUTIAN ISLANDS
### 1:15 000 000
100  0  100  200  300  400  500km

Attu I.
Near Is.
Agattu
Semichi Is.
Buldir I.
Kiska I.
Rat Is.
Amchitka I.
Semisopochnoi I.
Segula I.
Little Sitkin I.
Kanaga I.
Tanaga I.
1806
Adak I.
Andreanof
Amchitka Pass
Amukta Passage
Garelo I.
Great Sitkin I.
Atka I.
Amlia I.
Amukta I.
Chuginadak I.
Herbert I.
Islands of the Four Mountains
Nikolski

Akun I.
Unimak I.
Unimak Pass
Sanak I.
Unalaska I.
Dutch Harbor
2036
Fox Islands
Umnak I.
Yunaska I.
Seguam I.

BERING SEA

Projection: Conical with two standard parallels

175
East from Greenwich
180
Amatignak I.
175
West from Greenwich
170
165

West from Greenwich
156
COPYRIGHT GEORGE PHILIP & SON. LTD.

m
3000
2000
1500
1000
400
200
0
200
2000
m

Projection: Bonne

## ALASKA
### 1 : 30 000 000

100   0   100   200   300 miles
100   0       200       400 km

West from Greenwich

m
3000
2000
1500
1000
400
200
0
200
2000
m

1:15 000 000

100    0    100   200   300   400   500   600 km

ATLANTIC    OCEAN

Devon Island
Lancaster Sound

Baffin Bay

GREENLAND

Angmagssalik

Arctic Bay
Bylot I.
Pond Inlet
Brodeur
Peninsula
Milne
Inlet

2136

Svartenhuk
Halvø

Disko
B.
Disko

Christianshåb

Sandre Strømfjord

Kong Frederik VI.s Kyst

2850

Holsteinsborg

Sukkertoppen

Godthåb

C. Dyer

Fury & Hecla Str.
Igloolik
Island
Hall
Lake

Melville
Peninsula

Prince
Charles

Foxe
Basin

Cumberland
Peninsula

2591

Padloping
Island
C. Dyer
Cape
Dyer

Davis Strait

Frederikshåb

Ivigtut

Julianehåb
Sydprøven

Home B.

Pangnirtung

Broughton
Island

Nanortalik
Kap Farvel

Rae Isthmus
Repulse
Bay
Wager
B.

C. Dorchester

Southampton
I.

Foxe
Channel

Coral Harbour

Bell
Pen.

Coats
I.

Mansel
I.

Digges Is.

Invujivik

Saglouc
(Sugluk)

Maricourt
(Wakeham)

Koartac
(Notre Dame
de Koartac)

Akpatok
I.

Amadjuak
L.

Foxe
Penin.

Cape Dorset

Lake
Harbour

Frobisher
Bay

Nettilling
L.

Cumberland Sd.

C. Mercy

Resolution I.

C. Chidley

Hudson Strait

Ungava

Arnaud
(Payne Bay)
Bellin

Ungava Bay

3809

1676
Port Nouveau Quebec
(George R.)
Hebron

Hudson

Bay

Ottawa
Is.

257

Portland
Promontory

Peninsula

Payne L.

Feuilles

Ft. Chimo

George

Whale

Koksoak

Kaniapiskau

Meleze

Nutak

Nain

NEW

Inoucdjouac
(Port Harrison)

Sleeper Is.

King
George I.

King George Is.

Baker's
Dozen
Is.

Belcher
Is.

La à L'Eau Claire

Lac Bienville

L. Minto

Hopedale

Harrison

Indian Harbour

COAST OF LABRADOR

Scheffervile
Petitsikapau
L.

Smallwood
Reservoir

North West R.

Rigolet

Battle Harb.

Belle Isle

Leville

Cortwright

C. Harrison

Severn

C. Henrietta
Maria

Pte.
Louis-XIV

A

Poste-de-
la-Baleine
(Great Whale River)
Grand Baleine

Kanaaupscow

La Grande

Ashuanipi

Churchill
Falls
Churchill

Lobstick L.

Notre Dame B.
Twillingate
Lewisporte
Gander

Bonavista

Trinity B.

NEWFOUNDLAND

Winisk

D

Ft. George

Nouveau Comptoir
(Paint Hills)

1128

Gagnon

Eastmain

Kaniapiskau

Moisie

Nitashquan

St-Augustin
Saguenay

Str. of Belle Isle

Corner Brook
Buchans

Grand
Falls

Harbour Grace
Carbonear

St. John's

Big
Trout L.

James Bay

Akimiski
I.

Attawapiskat

Eastmain

Fort Rupert
(Rupert
House)

Rupert

Mistassini

L. Albanel

L.

Nottaway

Petronca

814

Moisie

Mingan

Moisie
Sept Iles
Port-Cartier

i. d'Anticosti

Placentia B.
P. aux Basques

Trepassey
C. Race

Severn

Big L.

ARIO

Albany

Ft. Albany

Charlton
I.

Moosonee

Harricana

Nottaway

Chibougamau

Manicouagan

Betsiamites

Baie-Comeau

R. St. Lawrence

de Gaspé

Gulf of

St. Lawrence

Cabot Str.

St. Lawrence

Ray

P. aux Basques

St. Joseph

Nakina

Longlac

Kenogami

Hearst

Matagami

Rés. de Gouin

Dolbeau

L. Mistassini

Matane
Rimouski

Pén. de Gaspé

C. Gaspé

Campbellton

Îs. de
la Madeleine

Tignish

PR. EDWARD I.

Summerside

C. North

Cape Breton
Glace Bay

Sydney

Thunder Bay

Michipicoten

Heron Bay

Oba

Cochrane

L. Abitibi

Senneterre

Roberval

Lac St-Jean

Jonquière
Chicoutimi

Saguenay

1190

Tadoussac

Rivière-
du-Loup

St-Léonard

Edmund

Dalhousie
Bathurst

Newcastle

Chatham

Pictou

New Glasgow

Northumberland Str.

Charlottetown

Port Hawkesbury

Mulgrave

Sault Ste. Marie

Sudbury

Copper Cliff

Timmins

Kirkland Lake

Noranda
Rouyn

Val d'Or

La Tuque

Shawinigan

Trois-Rivières

Quebec

Lévis

Thetford Mines

Woodstock

Fredericton

NEW
BRUNSWICK

Moncton

Springhill

Amherst

Truro

Windsor

NOVA

New Glasgow

Sable I.
(Nova Scotia)

Michipicoten

Haileybury
Cobalt

Témiscamingue

Rés. de
Cabonga

Joliette

Sorel
St. Hyacinthe

MAINE

Saint
John

B. of Fundy

Digby

Bridgewater

Halifax

Dartmouth

6309

Calumet
Keweenaw
Pt.

Sault Ste. Marie

North Chan.

Georgian
Bay

North
Bay

Pembroke

Arnprior

Hull

Ottawa

Cornwall

St. Lawrence

Sherbrooke

Bangor

Augusta

Lewiston

Yarmouth

Shelburne

Liverpool

C. Sable

Ironwood
Marquette

Escanaba

Menominee

Manistique
Cheboygan
Petoskey

Parry
Sound

Orillia

Belleville

Kingston

Burlington

L. Champlain

VERMONT

1917

Concord
Manchester

Lowell

Portland

C. Cod

Wausau
Green
Bay

Appleton

Manitowoc

Cadillac

Saginaw

Owen Sound

Peterboro

Cobourg

Oshawa

TORONTO

Guelph

Kitchener
Stratford

Hamilton

L. Ontario

Rochester

Syracuse

Utica

Worcester

MASS.

Boston

NEW
HAMPSHIRE

Glens
Falls

Albany

Springfield

Providence

RHODE I.

New Haven

Milwaukee

Racine

Kenosha

SIN

Grand
Rapids

Muskegon

L. Michigan

Saugatuck

London

Brantford

Niagara
Falls

Buffalo

NEW YORK

Binghamton

Scranton

Bridgeport

Elmira

Waterbury

CONN.

New York

Evanston

CAGO

Gary

INDIANA

South Bend

DETROIT

Toledo

OHIO

Windsor

Lake Erie

Cleveland

Akron

Youngstown

Jamestown

Williamsport

PENNSYLVANIA

Allentown

Reading

Newark

Jersey City

NEW YORK

NEW JERSEY

Trenton

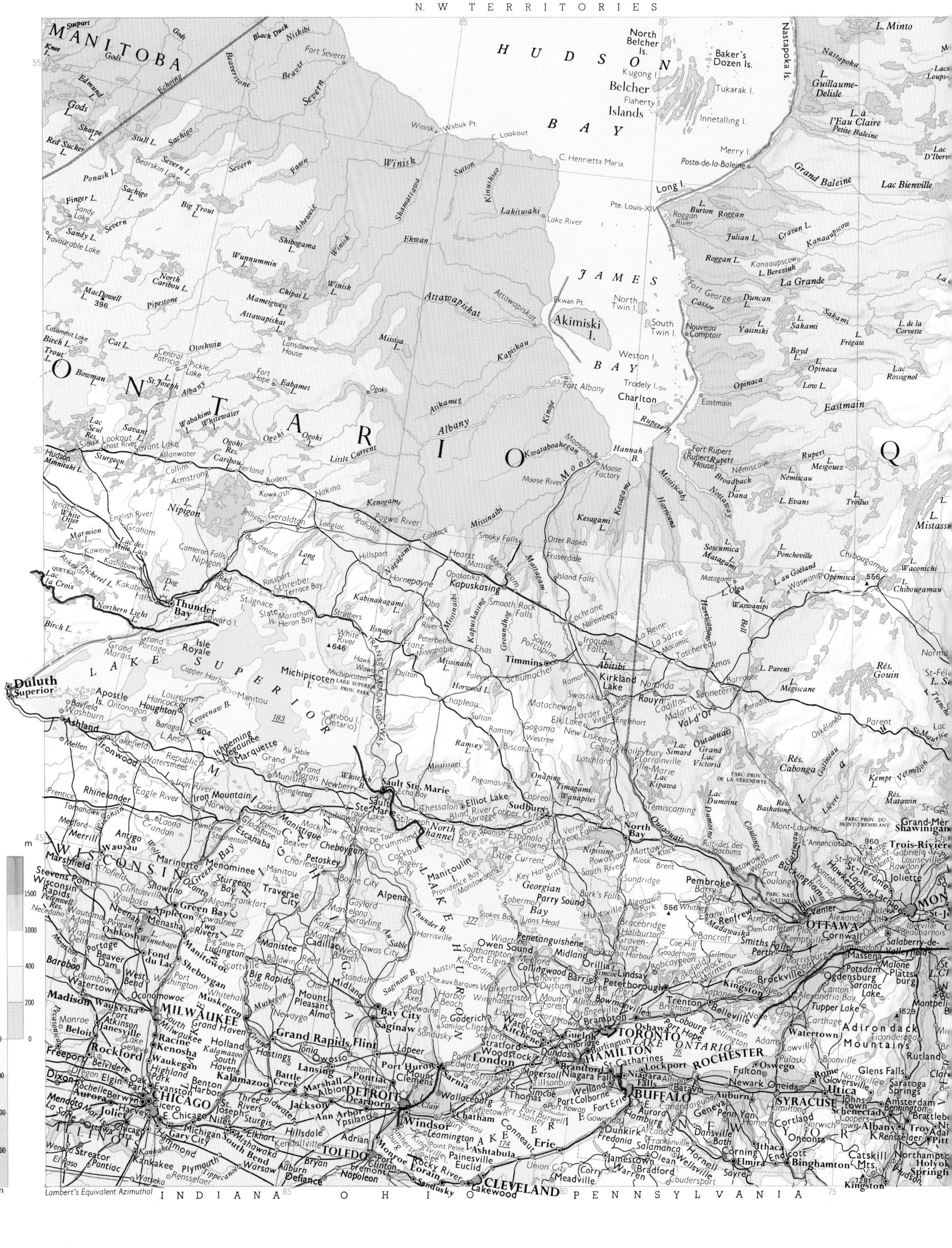

N.W  TERRITORIES

MANITOBA

HUDSON  BAY

JAMES  BAY

Belcher Islands

North Belcher Is.
Kugong I.
Baker's Dozen Is.
Tukarak I.
Flaherty I.
Innetalling I.

Akimiski I.
North Twin I.
South Twin I.
Weston I.
Trodely I.
Charlton I.

ONTARIO

QUÉBEC

Attawapiskat

Albany

Winisk

Moose Factory
Moosonee

Kapuskasing
Hearst
Mattice
Cochrane
Timmins
Kirkland Lake
Noranda
Rouyn
Val-d'Or

Thunder Bay

Geraldton
Longlac
Nipigon

LAKE SUPERIOR

Isle Royale

Duluth
Superior

Sault Ste. Marie

Sudbury
North Bay
Elliot Lake

Georgian Bay
Parry Sound

LAKE HURON

Manitoulin

WISCONSIN

Green Bay
Milwaukee
Madison
Rockford
CHICAGO

MICHIGAN

Grand Rapids
Flint
Lansing
Saginaw
Bay City
Kalamazoo

DETROIT
Windsor
Dearborn
Ann Arbor

LAKE MICHIGAN

Traverse City
Alpena
Owen Sound
Barrie
Midland
Orillia
TORONTO
Hamilton
Brampton
Guelph
Kitchener
Cambridge
London
Sarnia
St. Catharines
Niagara Falls
BUFFLO
Welland

LAKE ERIE

CLEVELAND

OTTAWA
Cornwall
Kingston
Brockville
Ogdensburg
Belleville
Peterborough
Lindsay

Pembroke
Renfrew

ROCHESTER
SYRACUSE
Utica
Albany

Adirondack Mountains

ILLINOIS

INDIANA

OHIO

PENNSYLVANIA

NEW YORK

Lambert's Equivalent Azimuthal

1:7 000 000

50   0   50   100   150   200   250   300 km

NEW

COAST OF

Erlandson   Whale   George   Fraser   South Aulatsivik I.
Fort   Nachicapau   High I.
McKenzie   L. de la   Kogaluk   Nain
Chakonipau L.   Hutte   Mistastin   Paul I.
Otelnuk L.   Sauvage   L.   Voisey B.   Tunungayualok I.
Whitegull   Davis Inlet
610   L.   Nunaksaluk I.
Sérigny   Wakuach   Big Bay   Hopedale
L.   Harp L.   Katpokok B.
Attikamagen L.   Aillik
Schefferville   Makkovik
Kanairiktok   C. Harrison
Lac Verneuil   Naskaupi   Holton
Lac Petitsikapau   Seal L.   Rigolet   Indian Harbour
L. Néret   Clairambault   Nipishish   Grôswater
Lac Delorme   Woods   L.   B.
L.   Smallwood   Grand   Hamilton Inlet
Kaniapiskau   Reservoir   L.   L. Melville   1128   Cartwright
Churchill Falls   North-West River   Meaty Mts.   Sandwich B.
L. Bermen   Shabogamo   Goose   Separation   Island of Ponds
Opiscoteo   Opiskottish L.   Goose Bay   Point   Square Islands
Nitchequon   L. Naococane   Labrador City   Happy Valley   Eagle
Wabush   Churchill   Alexis
1128   Ashuanipi   Winokapau   C. St. Lewis   Battle Harbour
Mouchalagane L.   Lac   L.   Mary's   Belle I.
Plétipi   Joseph   LABRADOR   Minipi   Harbour   Str. of Belle Isle
L.   Atikonak   L.   Red   Lunaire-Griquet
Petit Lac   L.   Burnt   Little   Bay   St. Anthony
Manicouagan   L.   Mecatina   Bradore Bay   Flower's Cove
Gagnon   QUEBEC   Lourdes-de-   Groais I.
Rés. Manicouagan   Blanc-Sablon   Conche
1048   Manie   St-Augustin   Englee   Bell I.
Manouane   Nipissis   L. Manitou   Saguenay   Outer I.   Roddickton   Horse Is.
Ouiatchouan   Romaine   Natashquan   Port
Ste-Marguerite   St-Jean   Aguanus   I. du   Saunders   White B.   C. St. John
Magpie L.   L.   Petit-Mécatina   Great   La Scie
Péribonca   Clarke   L.   Allard   Harrington Harbour   Harbour   Deep   Notre Dame   Twillingate   Fogo I.
City   Moisie   Musquaro   Daniel's   Seal Cove   Baie   Carmanville
Rés.   Walker   Sept-Îles   Harbour   Verte
Péribonca   Pipmuacan   Port-Cartier   Sheldrake   Etamamu   Sop's   Springdale
Godbout   Rivière-Pentecôte   Mingan   Aguanish   Arm   Notre Dame
Hauterive   Baie-Trinité   Natashquan   Gethsémani   Trout River   Deer   South Brook   Glenwood   Gander
Baie-   Pte. des Monts   Pte. Ouest   Lake   Howley   Botwood
Comeau   Port-Menier   Î. d'Anticosti   Bay of Islands   Cox's   Buchans   Lewisporte   Glovertown
Godbout   Cap-Chat   Mont-Louis   Jupiter   Corner Brook   Cove   Windsor   Grand   Dark Cove
Mont-St-Pierre   Dét.   Heath Pt.   Red Indian   Falls   Bishop's Falls   Wesleyville
Forestville   Mts. Chic-Chocs   Vallée   Port au Port B.   L.   Bonavista
Béthsiamites   Mt. Jacques-   Grande Vallée   Stephenville   Victoria   Grand Falls   C. Bonavista
PARC PROV   1310   Cartier   Ouest   572   St. George's B.   Res.   Clarenville   Catalina
L. au   Mont-   DE LA   Petit-Cap   GULF OF   St. David's   Long   Grey Res.   Trinity B.   Bay de Verde
Bersimis   Joli   GASPÉSIE   Rivière-   ST. LAWRENCE   St. George's   Range   White   Content   Bonavista
Forestville   Pén. de Gaspé   au-Renard   Cape Breton   St. Andrew's   Victoria Res.   Bear   Salmon   Carbonear   Conception B.
Alma   Matane   Gaspé   C. de Gaspé   St. George   Res.   381   Grace   St.
Arvida   Sayabec   Percé   Î. Brion   C. Ray   Rose Blanche   Res.   St. Alban's   Terrenceville   Spaniard's B.   John's
Chicoutimi   Amqui   Douglastown   Grande-Rivière   Channel-Port   Burgeo   Belleoram   Harbour   Mt. Pearl
Tadoussac   Causapscal   Bonaventure   Grande-Entrée   aux Basques   Rameo   Grand   Holyrood
Grandes-   Matapedia   Chandler   Miscou I.   Îs. de la   Bank   Fortune   Avalon
Bergeronnes   Rimouski   Shippegan   Madeleine   Cap-aux-Meules   Harbour Breton   Marystown   Plaisance   Peninsula
Port Alfred   Trois-Pistoles   Chaleur Bay   (Quebec)   Havre-Aubert   Burin   Ferryland
Saguenay   Dalhousie   Belledune   St. Paul   Miquelon   C. St. Mary's   Bulls
La Malbaie   Rivière-du-Loup   Campbellton   Tracadie   Fatima   C. North   Langlade   St. Pierre   C. Race
Baie-   Cabano   Atholville   Cap-aux-Meules   Pleasant Bay   SAINT-PIERRE
PARC PROV   St-Paul   St. Arthur   Bathurst   North Pt.   Havre-Aubert   NAT.   Chéticamp   ET MIQUELON   C. Trepassey
LAURENTIDES   Kedgwick   Tignish   PRINCE EDWARD   PARK   Ingonish   (Fr.)
1190   Edmundston   Grand Falls   819   Newcastle   Alberton   ISLAND   East Pt.   Sydney Mines
Ste. Anne   St-Pascal   Van Buren   NEW   Chatham   Kensington   Souris   Inverness   New Waterford
Île d'Orléans   St-Jean-Port-Joli   Caribou   Plaster   Richibucto   Summerside   Charlottetown   East Pt.   N. Sydney   Glace Bay
Quebec   Allagash   St. Leonard   Rock   Blackville   Peters   Bras d'Or   Sydney
Montmagny   Ashland   Grand Falls   BRUNSWICK   Buctouche   Cape   Murray Hr.   Louisbourg
Lauzon   Presqu'Isle   Miramichi B.   Montagne   Pt. Aux   L.
Lévis   Eagle   Hartland   Chipman   Notre   Mts.   Morts   Whycocomagh   Cape Breton
Pamphile   L.   Houlton   Dame   Northumberland   Aspy   Chéticamp   Island
Beauceville   Island Falls   Stanley   Havelock   Shediac   Tormentine   Antigonish   St. Madame
Ste-Marie   Chesuncook   Woodstock   Petitcodiac   Moncton   Springhill   St. Peters   Port Hawkesbury
Plessisville   L.   1606   Fredericton   Gagetown   Amherst   New Glasgow   Mulgrave
Thetford Mines   Patten   Millinocket   Oromocto   Elgin   Pictou   Stellarton   Mira   Chedabucto B.
St-Georges   Moosehead   Sussex   Joggins   Harrisboro   Canso
Asbestos   Lac-Mégantic   Mattawamkeag   Lincoln   Rothesay   Minas   Sherbrooke
Greenville   Gage   George   Basin   Truro   NOVA SCOTIA
Sherbrooke   East Angus   MAINE   town   St. Chipecto   Upper   Musquodoboit
Coaticook   Moosehead   Skowhegan   Blacks   Saint   Bay   Musquodoboit   ATLANTIC
Island   L.   Dover-Foxcroft   Hr.   John   St. Martins   Windsor
Pond   Binghame   Calais   Fundy   Middleton   Dartmouth   Musquodoboit Hr.
Stanstead   Mooselook-   Old Town   Bridgetown   Grand   Kentville
Berlin   meguntic L.   Brewer   Eastport   Manan I.   Annapolis   Halifax
1917   Waterville   Bangor   Machias   Royal   Bay   Stewiacke
Augusta   Ellsworth   Digby   Mahone   Sable I.
Washington   Belfast   Jonesport   St. Mary's   Weymouth   Bay   Lunenburg   (Nova Scotia)
Auburn   Camden   Bar Harbor   B.   Bridgewater
Conway   Rumford   Lewiston   Rockland   Mt. Desert I.   Freeport   Rossignol   Liverpool
Sebago   Bethel   Bath   Yarmouth   L.   Port Mouton
Rochester   Brunswick   Wedgeport   St. Mary's   Shelburne
Con   Sanford   Saco   Portland   Clark's Harbour   C. Sable   Lockeport
cord   Biddeford
Dover   OCEAN
Rochester   Portsmouth
Manchester
Nashua   Haverhill   Ann
Lawrence   Gloucester
Lowell   Lynn
Waltham   BOSTON
Brockton

St. Lawrence

FOUND LAND

Cabot Strait

Str. of Belle Isle

GULF OF ST. LAWRENCE

70   West from Greenwich   65   60

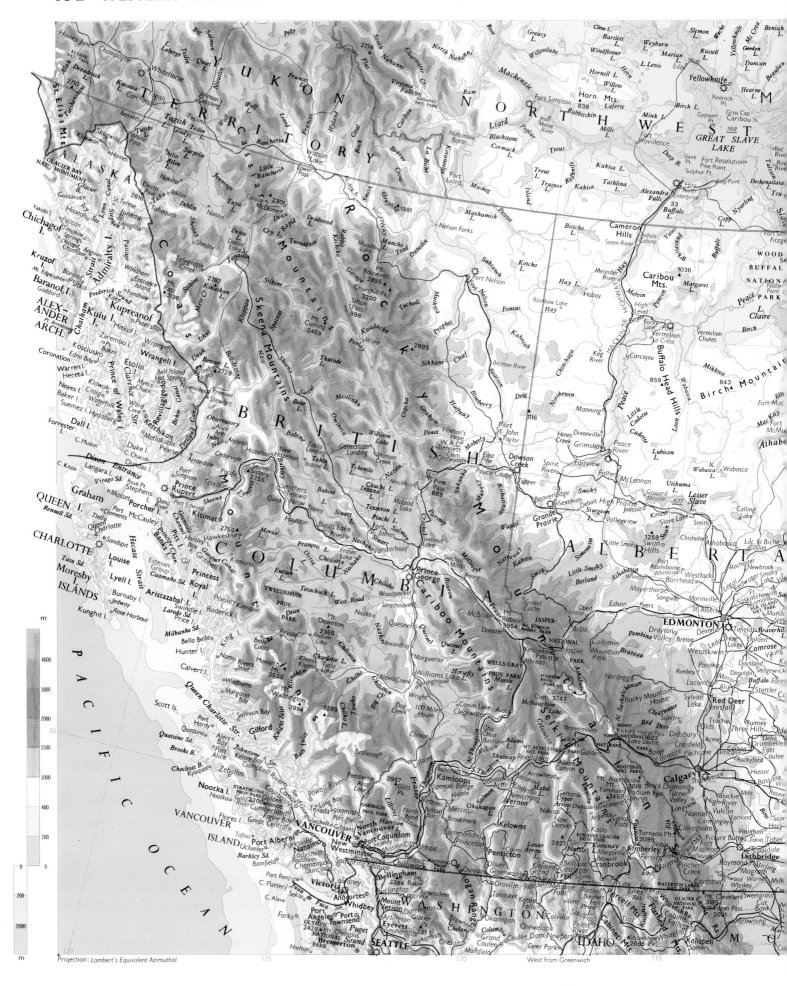

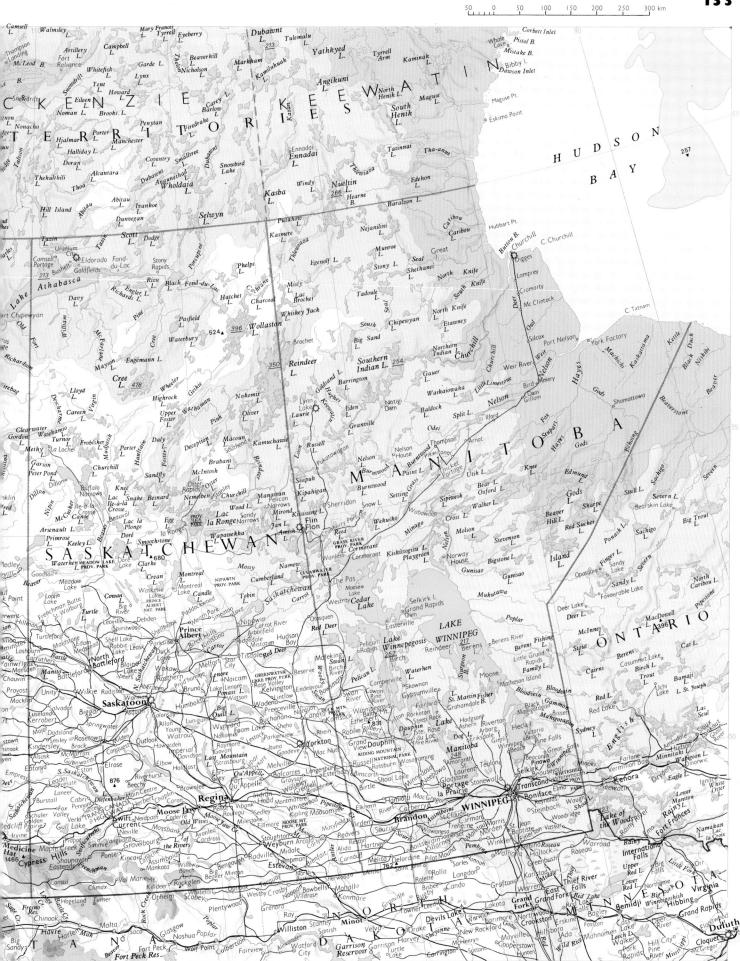

1 : 7 000 000

50    0    50    100    150    200    250    300 km

HUDSON

BAY

MA CKENZIE

TERRITORIES KEEWATIN

Dubawnt

Yathkyed

Corbett Inlet

Angikuni

North Henik L.
South Henik L.

Maguse

Maguse Pt.

Eskimo Point

Ennadai

Nueltin L.

Hearne

Baralzon L.

Button B.
Churchill
C. Churchill
Digges

Caribou

Hubbart Pt.

C. Tatnam

York Factory

Port Nelson

Nelson

SASKATCHEWAN

Lake Athabasca

MANITOBA

ONTARIO

LAKE
WINNIPEG

Lake
Winnipegosis

Prince
Albert

Saskatoon

Yorkton

Dauphin

Manitoba

Selkirk

Transcona

WINNIPEG
Boniface

Kenora

Regina

Moose Jaw
Swift
Current

Brandon

Souris

Lake of
the Woods

Medicine
Hat
Cypress Hills

Weyburn

Estevan

International
Falls

Duluth

MONTANA

NORTH DAKOTA

Williston

Minot

Devils Lake

Garrison
Reservoir

Grand
Forks

MINNESOTA

Hibbing

Grand Rapids

Fort Peck Res.

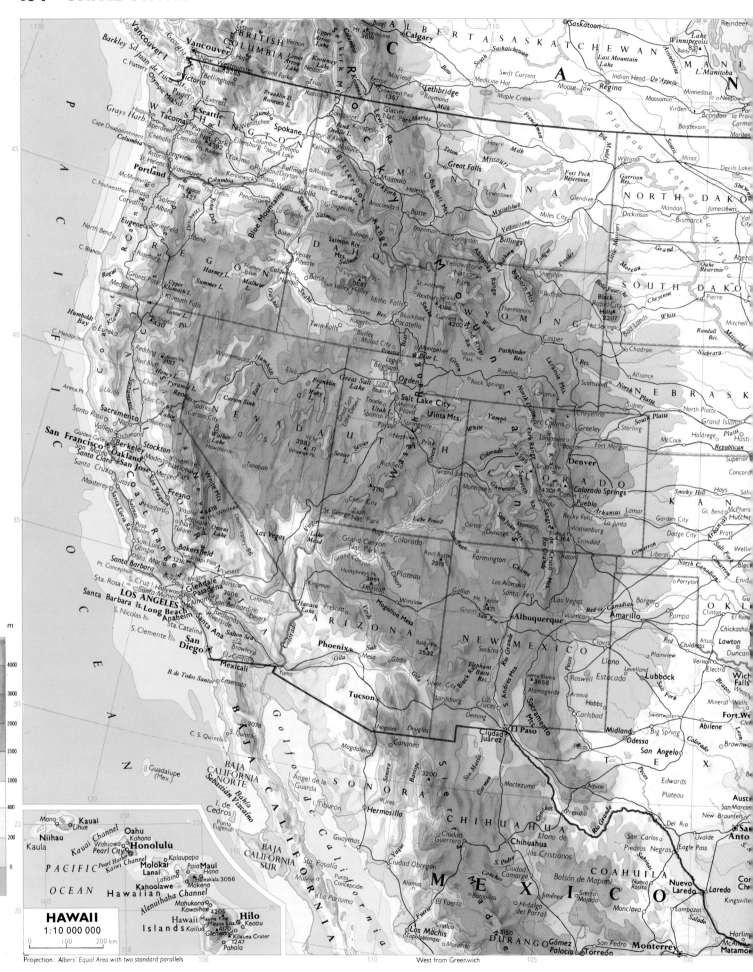

**HAWAII**
1:10 000 000

0      100      200 km

Projection: Albers' Equal Area with two standard parallels

West from Greenwich

1:12 000 000

100   0   100   200   300   400   500 km

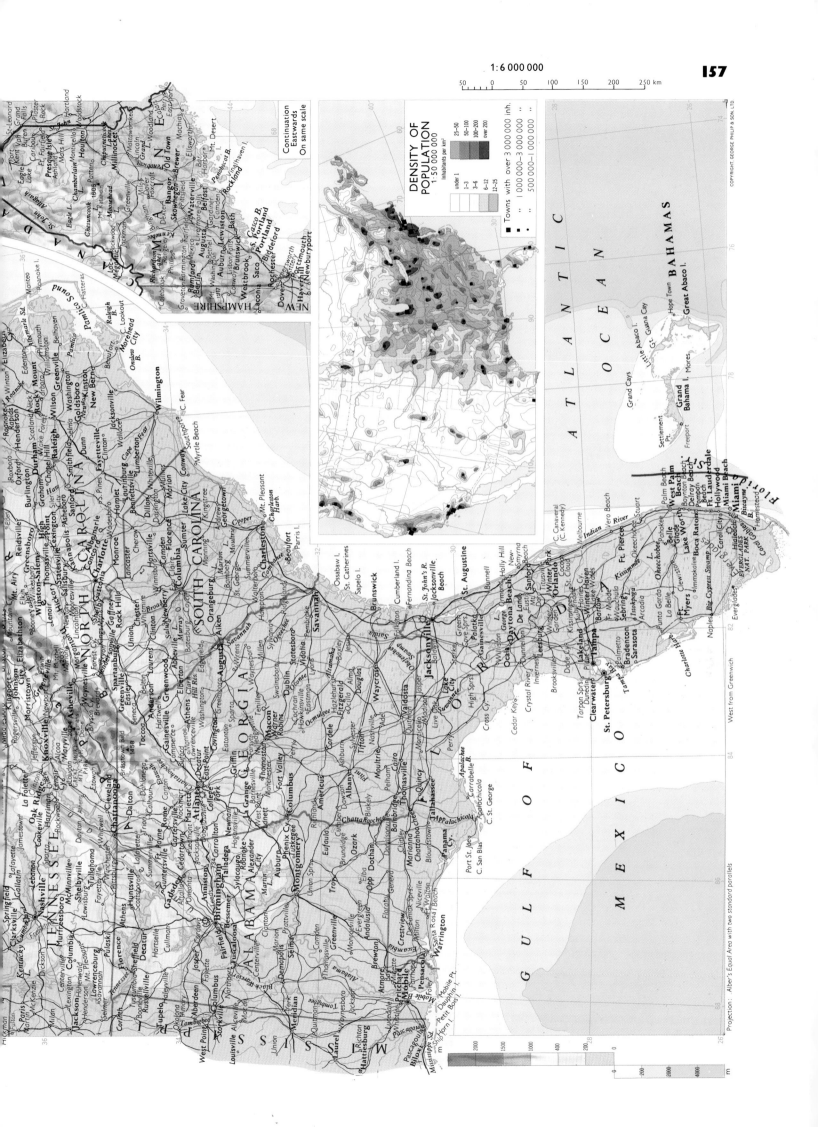

1:6 000 000

50    0    50    100    150    200    250 km

Continuation
Eastwards
On same scale

DENSITY OF
POPULATION
1:50 000 000

Inhabitants per km²

under 1
1-3
3-6
6-12
12-25

25-50
50-100
100-200
over 200

Towns with over 3 000 000 inh.

1 000 000-3 000 000
500 000-1 000 000

MAINE

Madawaska
St-Leonard
Grand Falls
Plaster Rock
Presque Isle
Eagle L.
St. John R.
Allagash
Ft. Kent
Van Buren
Caribou
Ashland
Patten
Millinocket
Mt. Katahdin
1605
Moosehead L.
Greenville
Brewer
Bangor
Old Town
Dover-Foxcroft
Skowhegan
Waterville
Augusta
Lewiston
Auburn
Brunswick
Bath
Portland
S. Portland
Casco B.
Biddeford
Saco
Westbrook
Kennebec
Rockland
Belfast
Camden
Rockland I.
Mt. Desert
Bar Hbr.
Ellsworth
Machias

NEW HAMPSHIRE
Berlin
Lisbon Falls
Conway
Laconia
Rochester
Dover
Portsmouth
Haverhill
Newburyport

N O R T H   C A R O L I N A

NORTH CAROLINA
Roanoke Rapids
Rocky Mount
Winton
Elizabeth City
Manteo
Roanoke I.
Edenton
Plymouth
Washington
Greenville
New Bern
Pamlico Sd.
C. Hatteras
Albemarle Sd.
Raleigh
Durham
Chapel Hill
Goldsboro
Kinston
Jacksonville
Wilmington
Southport
C. Fear
Myrtle Beach
Conway

S O U T H   C A R O L I N A

SOUTH CAROLINA
Columbia
Charleston
Charleston Harb.
Beaufort
Parris I.
Georgetown
Florence
Sumter
Orangeburg
Aiken

G E O R G I A

GEORGIA
Atlanta
Macon
Columbus
Savannah
Augusta
Albany
Valdosta
Brunswick

F L O R I D A

FLORIDA
Jacksonville
Tallahassee
Gainesville
Ocala
Orlando
Tampa
St. Petersburg
Clearwater
Lakeland
Daytona Beach
St. Augustine
C. Canaveral (C. Kennedy)
Melbourne
Vero Beach
Ft. Pierce
West Palm Beach
Ft. Lauderdale
Miami
Miami Beach
Hollywood
Key West
EVERGLADES NAT. PARK
Naples
Ft. Myers
Sarasota
Bradenton

A L A B A M A

ALABAMA
Birmingham
Montgomery
Mobile
Tuscaloosa
Gadsden
Dothan

T E N N E S S E E

TENNESSEE
Nashville
Knoxville
Chattanooga
Memphis

M I S S I S S I P P I

MISSISSIPPI
Biloxi
Gulfport
Pascagoula
Hattiesburg
Laurel
Meridian

A T L A N T I C   O C E A N

B A H A M A S

BAHAMAS
Great Abaco I.
Little Abaco I.
Grand Bahama I.
Freeport
Grand Cays
Hope Town
Gt. Guana Cay

G U L F   O F   M E X I C O

Projection: Alber's Equal Area with two standard parallels

West from Greenwich

m    4000   2000   1500   1000   400   200   0   0   200   2000   4000   m

COPYRIGHT GEORGE PHILIP & SON, LTD.

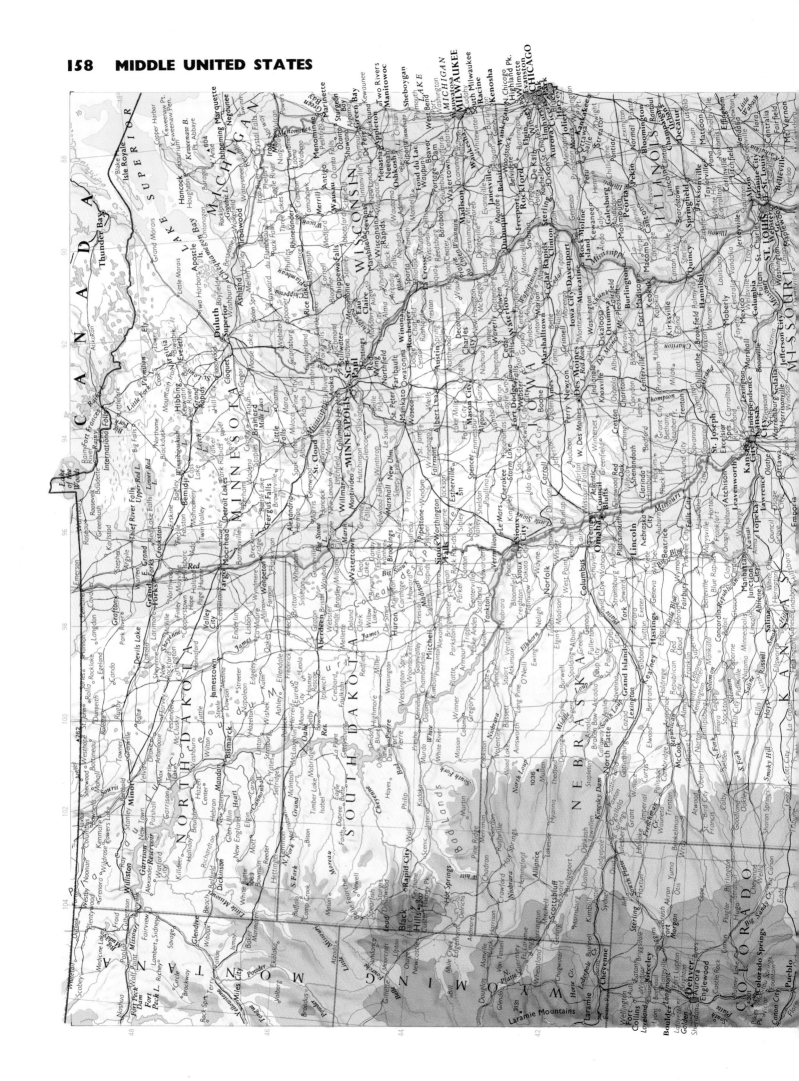

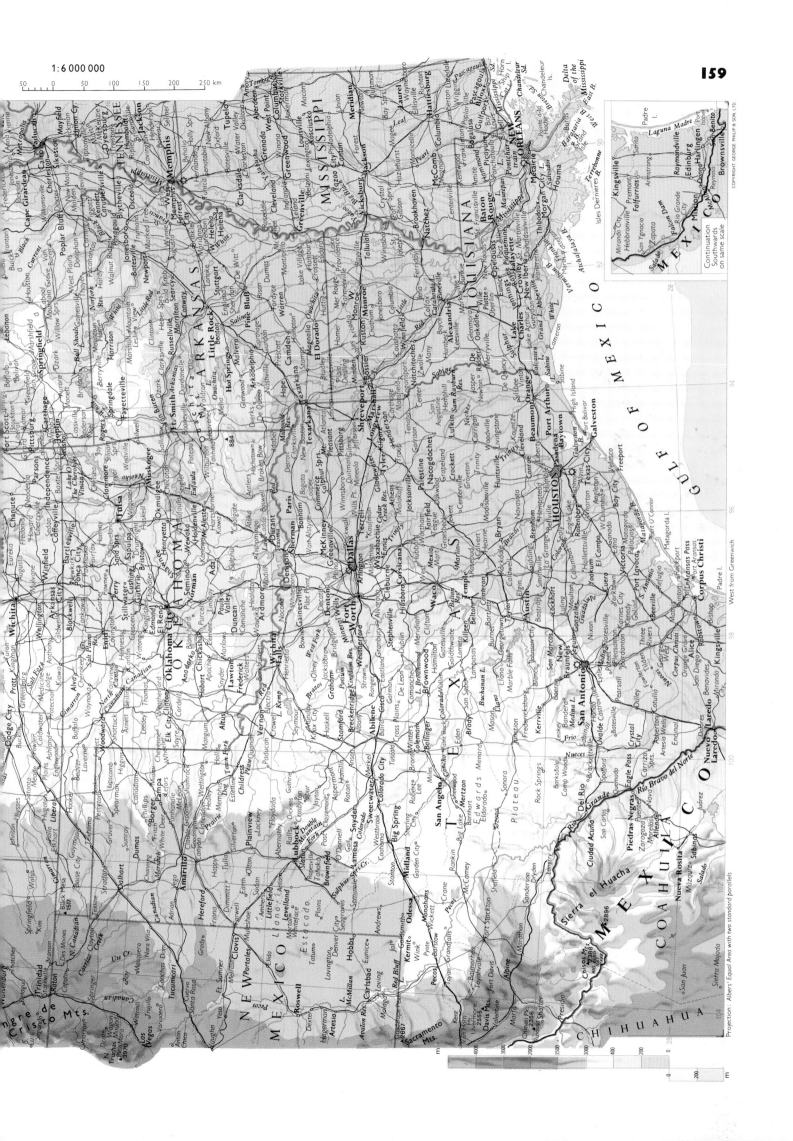

1:6 000 000

50   0   50   100   150   200   250 km

Projection: Albers' Equal Area with two standard parallels

West from Greenwich

COPYRIGHT GEORGE PHILIP & SON LTD

1 : 6 000 000

50    0    50    100    150    200    250 km

1 : 3 000 000

20  0  20  40  60  80  100  120 km

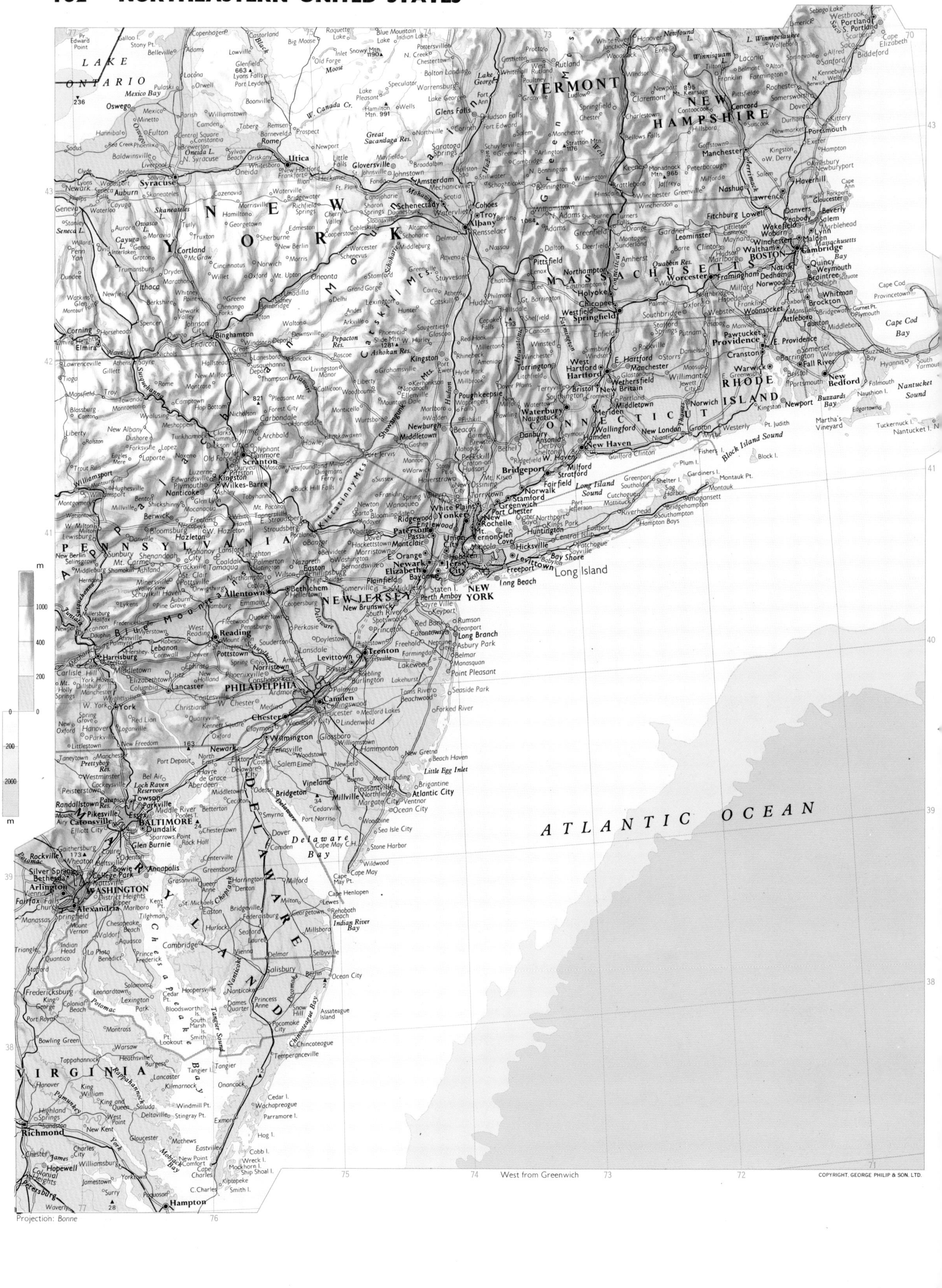

LAKE ONTARIO

NEW YORK

VERMONT

NEW HAMPSHIRE

MASSACHUSETTS

RHODE ISLAND

CONNECTICUT

PENNSYLVANIA

NEW JERSEY

NEW YORK

Long Island

Long Island Sound

DELAWARE

MARYLAND

VIRGINIA

Delaware Bay

Chesapeake Bay

Cape Cod

Cape Cod Bay

Nantucket Sound

Martha's Vineyard

ATLANTIC OCEAN

m
1000
400
200
0
200
2000
m

West from Greenwich

COPYRIGHT. GEORGE PHILIP & SON. LTD.

Projection: Bonne

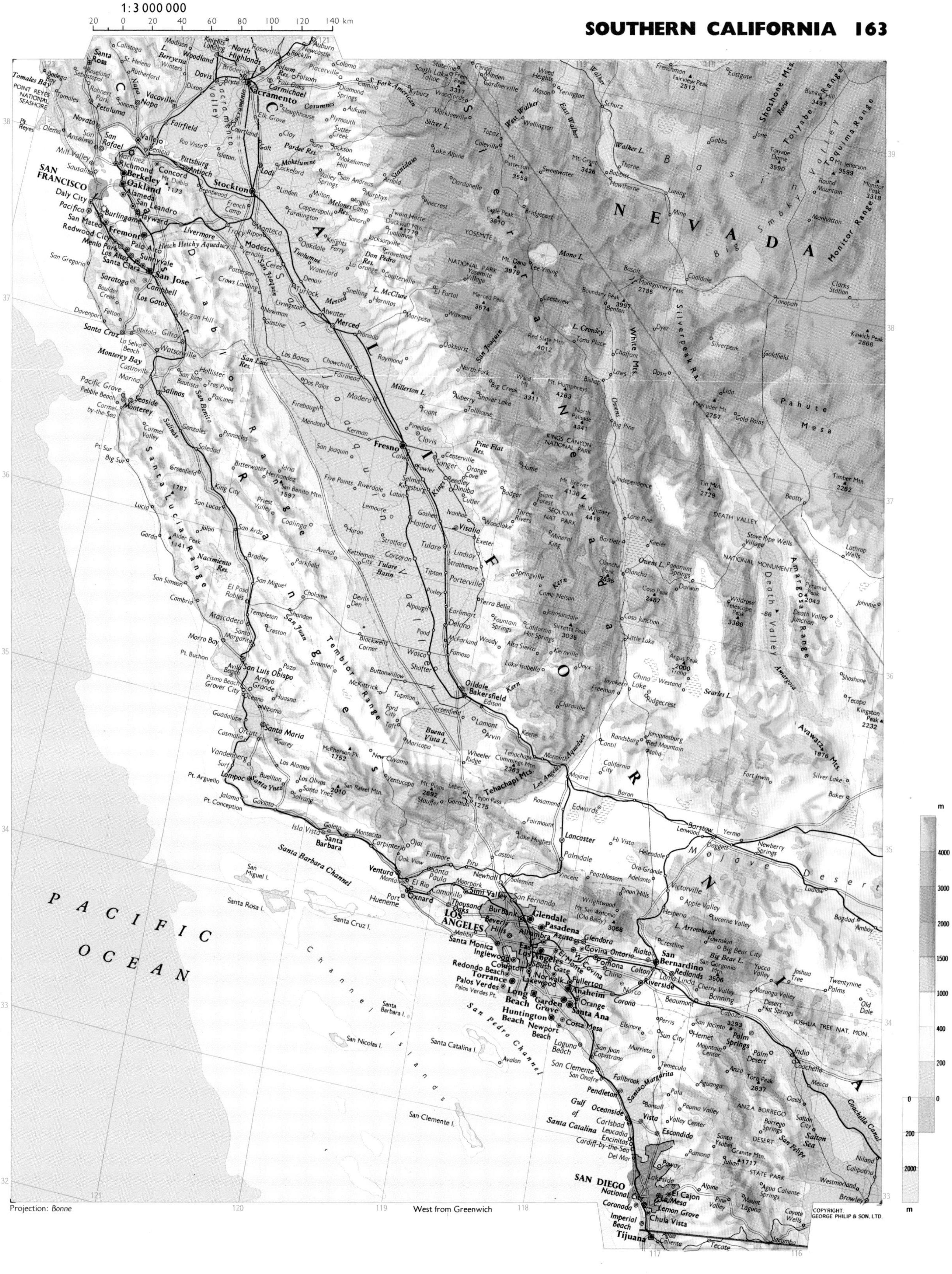

1:3 000 000

20   0   20   40   60   80   100   120   140 km

NEVADA

PACIFIC OCEAN

SAN FRANCISCO
Oakland
San Jose
Sacramento
Stockton
Modesto
Fresno
Bakersfield
LOS ANGELES
San Diego
Tijuana

Projection: Bonne

West from Greenwich

COPYRIGHT. GEORGE PHILIP & SON, LTD.

m
4000
3000
2000
1500
1000
400
200
0
200
2000
m

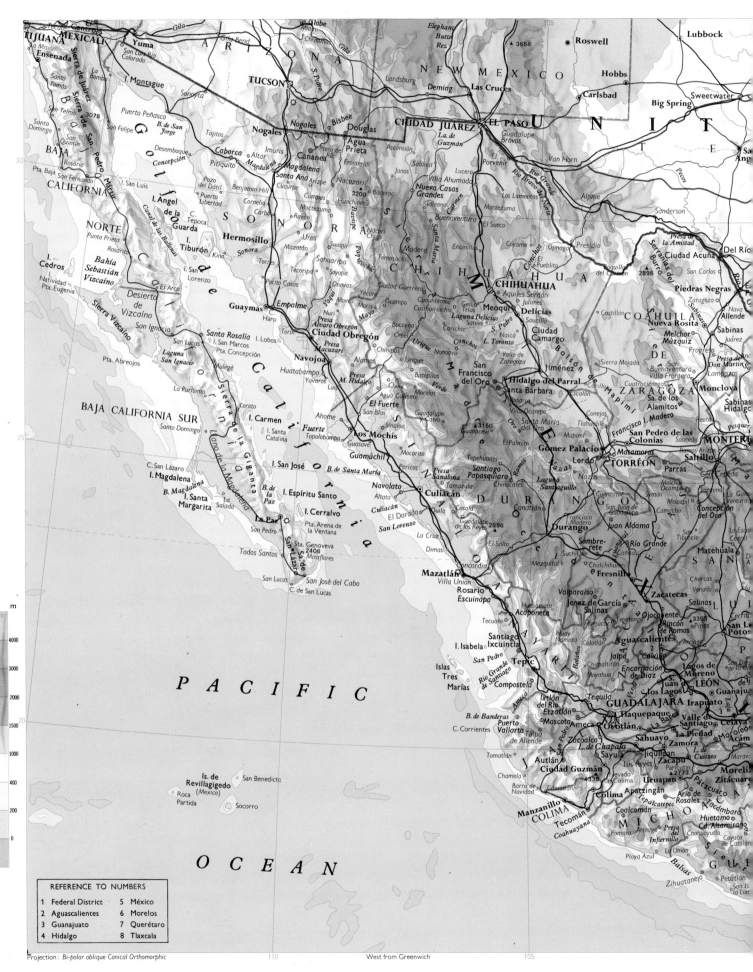

El Centro
TIJUANA MEXICALI Yuma
Ensenada
La Misión
Santo Tomás
Sierra del Juárez
San Telmo 3078
San Felipe
Santo Domingo
San Quintín
Rosario
Pta. Baja
San Fernando
BAJA
CALIFORNIA
NORTE
Punta Prieta
Rosarito
I. Cedros
I. Natividad
Pta. Eugenia
Bahía
Sebastián
Vizcaíno
Desierta
de
Vizcaíno
Sierra Vizcaíno
San Ignacio
El Arco
Santo Domingo
BAJA CALIFORNIA SUR
La Purísima
Loreto
C. San Lázaro
I. Magdalena
B. Magdalena
I. Santa
Margarita
La Salada
Mulegé
Santa Rosalía
Laguna
San Ignacio
San Lucas
I. San Marcos
Pta. Concepción
Sierra de la Giganta
Llano de la Magdalena
Todos Santos
San Lucas
San José del Cabo
C. de San Lucas
La Paz
San Pedro
Sta. Genoveva 2406
Miraflores
Pta. Arena de la Ventana
I. Cerralvo
I. Espíritu Santo
B. de la Paz
I. San José
B. de Santa María
I. Santa Catalina
I. Carmen
Fuerte
Topolobampo

Gila
Gila Bend
Globe
Miami
Christmas
Elephant
Butte Res.
▲ 3658
Roswell
Lubbock
ARIZONA
NEW MEXICO
Hobbs
Lordsburg
Deming
Las Cruces
Carlsbad
Big Spring
Sweetwater
TUCSON
Bisbee
Douglas
CIUDAD JUAREZ
EL PASO
UNIT
San Angelo
S. Pedro
Nogales
Nogales
Agua Prieta
La. de Guzmán
Guadalupe Bravos
El Porvenir
Van Horn
Alpine
Sanderson
Pecos
Puerto Peñasco
Imuris
Presa del Cananea
Ascensión
Janos
Sabinal
Lucero
Rio Grande
S.
Caborca
Altar
Magdalena
Fronteras
Villa Ahumada
Los Lamentos
Del Rí
Desemboque
Concepción
Pitiquito
Santa Ana
Anzpe
Nacozari
Galeana
Carmen
Moctezuma
Presidio
Presa de la Amistad
Serranías del Burro
Ciudad Acuña
Tajitos
Cumpas
3200 ▲
Bacerac
Nueva Casas
Grandes
El Sueco
Coyame
Ojinaga
El Pueblito
Boquilla
del Carmen 2896
San Carlos
B. de San Jorge
Cornelia
Carbó
Moctezuma
Buenaventura
Encinillas
Cuchillo
Piedras Negras
I. San Luis
Benjamin Hill
Rayón
Huachinera
Madera
Santa María
Conchos
SONORA
HERMOSILLO
Ures
Suaqui
Bavispe
Temosachic
Ciudad Guerrero
Aquiles Serdán
Julimes
CHIHUAHUA
COAHUILA
Kino
Sonora
Mazatán
Sahuaripa
Papigochic
Cuauhtémoc
Gen.
Trias
Meoqui
Castillón
Nova
Allende
Sabinas
I. Tiburón
Torres
Tecoripa
Soyopa
Onavas
Ciudad
Guerrero
Cusihuiriáchic
Carichic
Laguna Delicias
Satevó
S. Pedro
Delicias
Saucillo
Valle de Zaragoza
Nueva Rosita
Sabinas
Juárez
DE
I. San Lorenzo
Pocito Casas
Yaqui
Moris
Ocampo
Creel
L. Toronto
Ciudad Camargo
Sierra Mojada
San
Buenaventura
Villa Frontera
Progreso
Melchor
Múzquiz
Guaymas
Empalme
Nuri
Movas
Bocoyna
Urique
Nonoavá
Naica
Jiménez
Mapimí
ZARAGOZA
Alamitos
Monclova
Haro
Presa Álvaro Obregón
Torin
Urique
Conchos
San
Francisco
del Oro
Hidalgo del Parral
Santa Bárbara
Escalón
Conejos
Cuatrociénegas
San Pedro de las Colonias
Ciudad Obregón
I. Lobos
Alamos
Batopilas
Morelos
Rosario
Villa Ocampo
Tlahualilo
Francisco I. Madero
Saucedo
Navojoa
Presa Macuzari
Huatabampo
Yavaros
Luis
Presa M. Hidalgo
Ahome
San Blas
Choix
Guadalupe Calvo
▲ 3150
Guanaceví
Santa María
del Oro
El Palmito
Mapimí
Gómez Palacio
Matamoros
Lerdo
TORREÓN
Parras
Saltillo
MONTER
Los Mochis
Guasave
Sinaloa
Morcito
Tepehuanes
Ramos
Santiago
Papasquiaro
Laguna
Santaguillo
Cuencamé
Symón
Mazapil
Ceped
Guamúchil
Pericos
Coneto
Tamazula
DURANGO
Catalán
San Juan de Guadalupe
Concepción
del Oro
La Escond
Cedra
Navolato
Altata
El Dorado
Culiacán
Presa Sanalona
Cosalá
Quila
El Salto
Chinacates
Juan Aldama
Tiburcio
Rio Grande
Melchor Ocampo
Tazminal
Culiacán
El Dorado
San Lorenzo
La Cruz
Guadalupe
de los Reyes 2696 ▲
Durango
Sombrerete
Nazas
Fresnillo
Matehuala
SANT
San Pedro
Dimas
Concordia
Mazatlán
Villa Unión
Rosario
Escuinapa
Mezquital
Chalchihuites
Valparaiso
Zacatecas
Charcas
Venado
Salinas
SAN L
POTOS
Huajuquilla
Acaponeta
Tecuala
Huey
Nomoto
Colotlán
Jerez de García
Salinas
Ojocaliente
Rincón de Romos
▲3358
Pinos
Santiago
Ixcuintla
San Pedro
Huejúcar
Calvillo
Aguascalientes
I. Isabela
Rio Grande de Santiago
Jalpa
Chimaltitán
Tepic
Moyahua
Encarnación
de Diaz
Lagos de Moreno
San L
Islas
Tres
Marías
Compostela
Ixtlán
del Río
Etzatlán
Ameca
Tequila
Teocaltiche
San Juan
de los Lagos
León
Guanaj
B. de Banderas
Puerto
Vallarta
Mascota
Ahualulco
GUADALAJARA
Irapuato
Talpa de Allende
C. Corrientes
Cocula
Tlaquepaque
Ocotlán
Valle de
Santiago
Celaya
Tomatlán
L. de Chapala
Sahuayo
La Piedad
Acámb
Autlán
Sayula
Zamora
Zacoalco
Jiquilpan
Los Reyes
Zacapu
Morelia
Cuitzeo
Chamela
Ciudad Guzmán
Parícutin
▲2775
Uruapan
Zitácuaro
Barra de Navidad
Nevado de Colima
▲4335
Pátzcuaro
Coalcomán
Ario de Rosales
Tacámbaro
Manzanillo
Tecomán
Colima
Apatzingán
Huetamo
Cd. Altamirano
MICHO
Coahuayana
COLIMA
Pómaro
Arteaga
Presa del Infiernillo
Coyuca de Catalán
La Unión
Balsas
Playa Azul
SIE
Zihuatanejo
Petatlán

PACIFIC

OCEAN

Is. de
Revillagigedo
(Mexico)
San Benedicto
Roca
Partida
Socorro

REFERENCE TO NUMBERS

| 1 | Federal District | 5 | México |
|---|---|---|---|
| 2 | Aguascalientes | 6 | Morelos |
| 3 | Guanajuato | 7 | Querétaro |
| 4 | Hidalgo | 8 | Tlaxcala |

m
4000
3000
2000
1500
1000
400
200
0
200
2000
4000
m

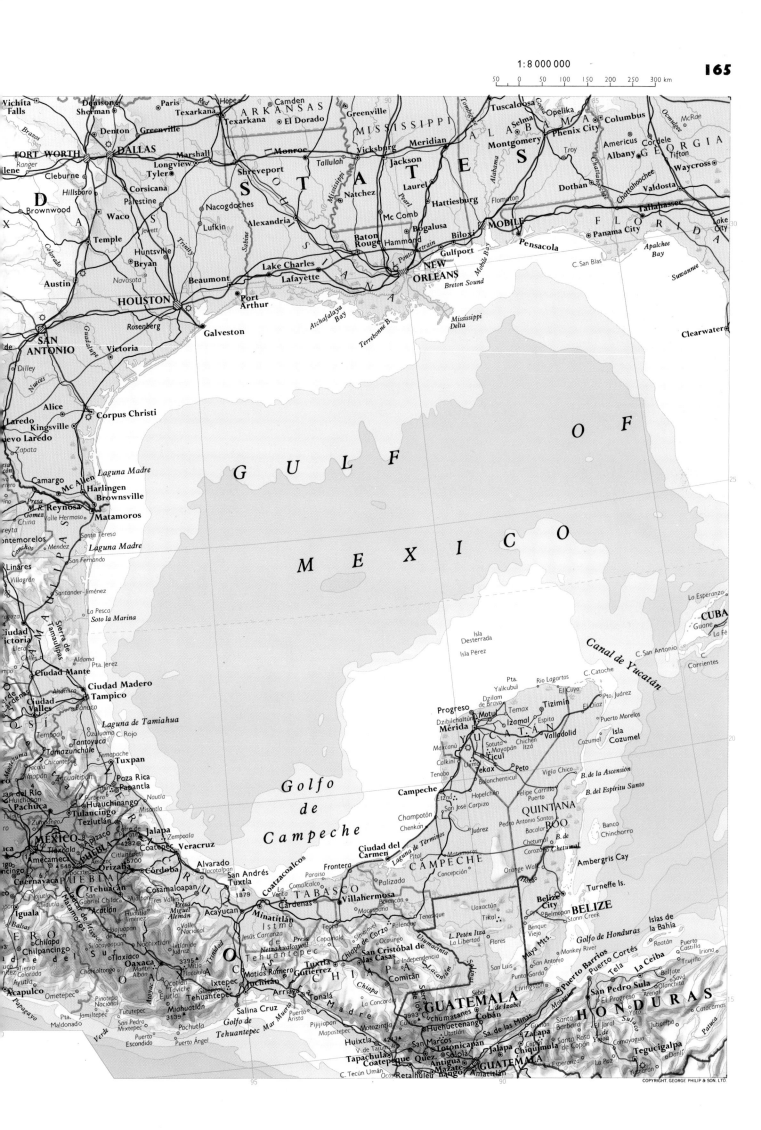

50    0    50    100    150    200    250    300 km

## UNITED STATES

FORT WORTH
Wichita Falls
Denison
Sherman
Paris
Hope
Camden
ARKANSAS
Greenville
Tuscaloosa
Opelika
Columbus
McRae
Ocmulgee
Denton
Greenville
Texarkana
Texarkana
El Dorado
MISSISSIPPI
ALABAMA
Montgomery
Phenix City
Americus
Cordele
Tifton
GEORGIA
DALLAS
Marshall
Monroe
Vicksburg
Meridian
Jackson
Selma
Troy
Albany
Waycross
Longview
Tyler
Shreveport
Tallulah
Natchez
Laurel
Hattiesburg
Dothan
Chattahoochee
Valdosta
Tallahassee
Corsicana
Palestine
Nacogdoches
Alexandria
Mc Comb
Flomaton
FLORIDA
Ranger
Cleburne
Hillsboro
Lufkin
Baton Rouge
Bogalusa
MOBILE
Panama City
Lake City
Brownwood
Waco
Jewett
Trinity
Sabine
Hammond
Biloxi
Pensacola
Apalchee Bay
Temple
Huntsville
Bryan
Lake Charles
Lafayette
Gulfport
C. San Blas
Suwannee
Austin
Navasota
Beaumont
NEW ORLEANS
Mississippi Delta
Clearwater
HOUSTON
Port Arthur
Atchafalaya Bay
Terrebonne B.
Breton Sound
SAN ANTONIO
Rosenberg
Galveston
Dilley
Victoria
Nueces
Alice
Corpus Christi
Laredo
Kingsville
Nuevo Laredo
Zapata
Camargo
Mc Allen
Harlingen
Brownsville
M.R. Reynosa
Matamoros
GULF    OF
Valle Hermoso
Santa Teresa
Mendez
Laguna Madre
ntemorelos
Conchos
San Fernando
MEXICO
Linares
Villagrán
Santander-Jiménez
La Pesca
Soto la Marina
Ciudad Victoria
Aldama
Pta. Jerez
CUBA
Guane
La Fé
Ciudad Mante
Corrientes
Ciudad Madero
Tampico
Isla Desterrada
Isla Pérez
C. San Antonio
Ciudad Valles
Ahoma
Pánuco
Laguna de Tamiahua
Canal de Yucatán
C. Catoche
La Esperanza
Ozuluama
C. Rojo
Pta. Yalkubul
Rio Lagartos
El Cuyo
Pto. Juárez
Tempoal
Tantoyuca
Progreso
Dzilam de Bravo
Motul
Temax
Tizimín
El Diaz
Tamazunchale
Tuxpan
Dzibilchaltún
Izamal
Espita
Puerto Morelos
Poza Rica
Papantla
Mérida
Sotuta
Chichén Itzá
Valladolid
Isla Cozumel
Nautla
Maxcanú
Mayapán
Cozumel
Pachuca
Huauchinango
Calkini
Uman
Ticul
Peto
Vigía Chico
B. de la Ascensión
Tulancingo
Teziutlán
Golfo
Tekax
Tenabo
Bolonchenticul
B. del Espíritu Santo
MEXICO
Apizaco
Jalapa
de
Campeche
Hopelchén
Felipe Carrillo Puerto
Banco Chinchorro
PUEBLA
Coatepec
Veracruz
Campeche
San José Carpizo
QUINTANA
Tlaxcala
Citlaltepetl 4282
Orizaba 5700
Champotón
Chenkán
Juárez
Bacalar
B. de Chetumal
Amecameca
Orizaba
Alvarado
Ciudad del Carmen
Laguna de Términos
Pedro Antonio Santos
Corozal
Chetumal
ROO
Cuernavaca
Tehuacán
San Andrés Tuxtla
Matamoros
Ambergris Cay
Iguala
Acatlán
Cosamaloapan
Frontera
CAMPECHE
Orange Walk
Turneffe Is.
Coatzacoalcos
Concepción
Palizada
Uaxactún
Chilpancingo
Matías Romero
Villahermosa
Belize City
BELIZE
Acayucan
Cárdenas
TABASCO
Benque Viejo
Belmopán
Stann Creek
Islas de la Bahía
Minatitlán
Palenque
Tikal
Golfo de Honduras
Roatán
Jesús Carranza
L. Petén Itzá
La Libertad
Flores
Monkey River
Puerto Cortés
La Ceiba
Oaxaca
OAXACA
Tuxtla Gutiérrez
San Cristóbal de las Casas
Comitán
San Luis
San Antonio
Punta Gorda
Puerto Barrios
Tela
Ixtepec
Juchitán
CHIAPAS
San Marcos
Livingston
San Pedro Sula
Tehuantepec
Arriaga
Tonalá
Sebol
Cobán
Zacapa
HONDURAS
Salina Cruz
Golfo de Tehuantepec
GUATEMALA
Cuchumatanes
Chiquimula
Tegucigalpa
Huixtla
Tapachula
Huehuetenango
Totonicapán
Jalapa
El Progreso
Coatepeque
Quiez
GUATEMALA
Amatitlán
La Paz
C. Tecún Umán
Retalhuleu
Antigua

GULF OF

MEXICO

Isla
Desterrada

Isla Pérez

Canal de Yucatán

L. Okeechobee
West Palm Beach
Fort Myers
The
Naples
C. Romano
Everglades
C. Sable
Florida Bay
Dry Tortugas
Key West
Florida Keys
Straits of Florida
Florida
Fort Lauderdale
Boca Raton
Hialeah
MIAMI
Florida City
Everglades

West End
Grand Bahama I.
Northwest Providence Channel
Bimini Is.
Berry Is.
Northeast Providence Channel
Nassau
New Providence I.
Andros Town
Andros Island

Little Abaco I.
Normans Castle
Hope Town
Abaco I.
Great Abaco I.
Nicolls Town
Eleuthera
Adelaide

GREAT BAHAMA BANK

Governor
Great Exuma I.

Progreso
Pta.
Yalkubul
Dzilam de Bravo
Dzibilchaltún
Motul
MÉRIDA
Izamal
Sotuta
Mayapán
Ticul
Tekax
Peto
Bolonchenticul

Temax
Espita
Tizimín
El Cuyo
C. Catoche
Pto. Juárez
Valladolid
Isla Cozumel
Cozumel

Río Lagartos
El Díaz

(Havana)LA HABANA
MARIANAO
San Antonio de los Baños
Guanajay
Bahía Honda
La Esperanza
Pinar del Río
Guane
La Fé
San Luis
Los Palacios
Nueva Gerona
I. de Pinos
Corrientes
C. San Antonio

Güines
Jagüey Grande
Playa Larga
Batabanó
Cienfuegos
Archipiélago de los Canarreos

Guanabacoa
Santa Cruz del Norte
Canal Nicolás
Matanzas
Cárdenas
Jovellanos
Colón
Sagua la Grande
Santa Clara
Caibarién
Placetas
Trinidad
Sancti-Spíritus
Archi. de los Jardines de la Reina
Tunas de Zaza

Cay Sal Bank
Santaren Channel

Cayo Romano
Morón
Ciego de Ávila
Júcaro
Golfo de Guacanayabo

Canal Viejo de Bahama
Nuevitas
Florida
Camagüey
Victoria de las Tunas
Manzanillo
Sierra Maestra

GREATER

Jument
Cays
Duncan T

Puerto Manc
Puerto P
Gibara
HOLGU
Bayamo
Palma
Soriano
SANTIA
DE CU
2000

Campeche
Champotón
San José Carpizo
Chenkan
Ciudad del Carmen
Laguna de Términos
Pital
Palizada
Butancan
Matamoros
Escárcega
Xpujil
CAMPECHE
Hopelchén
Bolonchén de Rejón
Calkiní
Tenabo
Maxcanú
Muna
Oxkutzcab
Calkini

Felipe Carrillo Puerto
Vigía Chico
B. de la Ascensión
B. del Espíritu Santo
Banco Chinchorro
Isla Contoy
Isla Mujeres
Puerto Morelos

Pedro Antonio Santos
Bacalar
QUINTANA
ROO
Chetumal
B. de Chetumal
Corozal
Concepción
Orange Walk
Hondo
Ambergris Cay

Cayman Islands (Br.)
Georgetown
Grand Cayman
Cayman Brac
Little Cayman

Montego Bay
Luceo
Falmouth
South Negril Pt.
Savanna la Mar
Black River
Mandeville
May Pen
St. Ann's Bay
Annotto B
Port Mari
JAMAI
KINGST
Spanish Town

CARI

Bajo Nuevo
(Colombia)

Palenque
Tenosique
Uaxactún
Ocosingo
L. Petén Itzá
La Libertad
Tikal
Flores
Comitán
La Independencia
Lacantún
Usumacinta
Sebol
San Luis
Benque Viejo
Middlesex
Stann Creek
Maya Mts.
San Antonio
Punta Gorda
Livingston
Monkey River
Golfo de Honduras

Belmopan
Belize City
Turneffe Is.
BELIZE
Islas de la Bahía
Roatán

Swan Islands
(U.S.A. & Honduras)

GUATEMALA
Cobán
4993
Cuchumatanes
Sa. de los
Huehuetenango
San Marcos
Totonicapán
Sololá
Antigua
Quezaltenango
Mazatenango
Retalhuleu
Coatepeque
Ayutla
GUATEMALA
Jalapa
Zacapa
Chiquimula
Copán
Santa Rosa de Copán
L. de Izabal
Sa. de las Minas
Santa Bárbara
El Progreso
San Pedro Sula
Puerto Barrios
Puerto Cortés
Tela
La Ceiba
Balfate
Trujillo
Puerto Castilla
Iriona
C. Camarón
Pta. Patuca
Brus Laguna

Laguna Caratasca
C. Falso
C. Gracias á Dios
Puerto Cabo Gracias á Dios
Kisalaya

Mosquitia

Escuintla
Amatitlán
Santa Ana
Suchitoto
Cojutepeque
Zacatecoluca
SAN SALVADOR
Usulután
San Miguel
La Unión
Golfo de Fonseca
SAN SALVADOR
Ahuachapán
Acajutla
Sonsonate
Nueva San Salvador
La Libertad
EL SALVADOR

HONDURAS
Copán
Gracias
La Esperanza
Santa Rosa
L. de Yojoa
El Jaral
Comayagua
Yoro
Juticalpa
Olanchito
Catacamas
Patuca
Tegucigalpa
Danlí
Yuscarán
Nacaome
Choluteca
Coco
San Pedro del Norte
Somoto
Estelí
Ocotal
Coco
Segovia
Cord. Isabella
Siuna
Bonanza
Prinzapolca
Río Grande
Puerto Cabezas
Cayos Miskitos
(Nicaragua)
Pta. Gorda

Bajo Nuevo
(Colombia)

I. de Providencia
(Colombia)

NICARAGUA
Chinandega
León
Corinto
La Paz Centro
Managua
L. de Managua
MANAGUA
Masaya
Granada
Diriamba
Jinotepe
Rivas
Boaco
Juigalpa
Matagalpa
Jinotega
Muy Muy
Santo Domingo
Rama
Siquia
Tuma
Jinotega
Tungla
San Pedro del Norte
Bluefields
El Bluff
Pta. Mico
Bahía de San Juan del Norte
Islas del Maíz
(Nicaragua, U.S.A.)

Cayos de Albuquerque
(Colombia)
I. de San Andrés
(Colombia)
Cayos Roncador
(U.S.A. & Colombia)

Lago de Nicaragua
Isla de Ometepe
San Juan del Sur
B. de Salinas
C. Sta. Elena
Golfo de Papagayo
Liberia
Nicoya
Santa Cruz
C. Velas
Pen. de Nicoya
Puntarenas
C. Blanco
Golfo de Nicoya
San Carlos
San Juan
San Juan del Norte

Cord. de Guanacaste
Cord. Central
COSTA RICA
Guápiles
Siquirres
Alajuela
San José
Cartago
Espartza
Limón
Pta. Mona
Pta.
Esparta
Cord. de Talamanca
3887
Vesta
San Isidro
Puerto Quepos
Boruca
Buenos Aires
Golfito
Bahía de Coronado
Cortes
Puerto Cortes
Pen. de Osa
Golfo Dulce
Puerto Armuelles
Pta. Burica
Golfo de Chiriquí
I. de Coiba
I. de Cebaco
I. Jicarón
Pta. Mariato

Bocas del Toro
Almirante
1 de Chiriquí
3374
Boquete
Remedios
Santiago
David
Soná
Remedios
Agua dulce
Río Hato
Chitré
Las Tablas
Pocrí
Pen. de Azuero
Tonosí
Pta. Mala

Laguna de Chiriquí
Golfo de los Mosquitos
Serranía de Tabasará
CANAL ZONE
(U.S.A.)
Gatun L.
La Chorrera
PANAMÁ
Chepo
Chimán
Penonomé
San Miguel
I. del Rey
Arch. de las Perlas
Golfo de Panamá

Colón
Nombre de Dios
Portobelo
Archipiélago de las Mulatas
Sierranía del Darién
Golfo del Darién

Pta. Manzanillo
Is. de San Bernar
G.
Morros

CARTA

Turba
G. de Uraba
El Real
La Palma
Garachine
Jaque
Monte

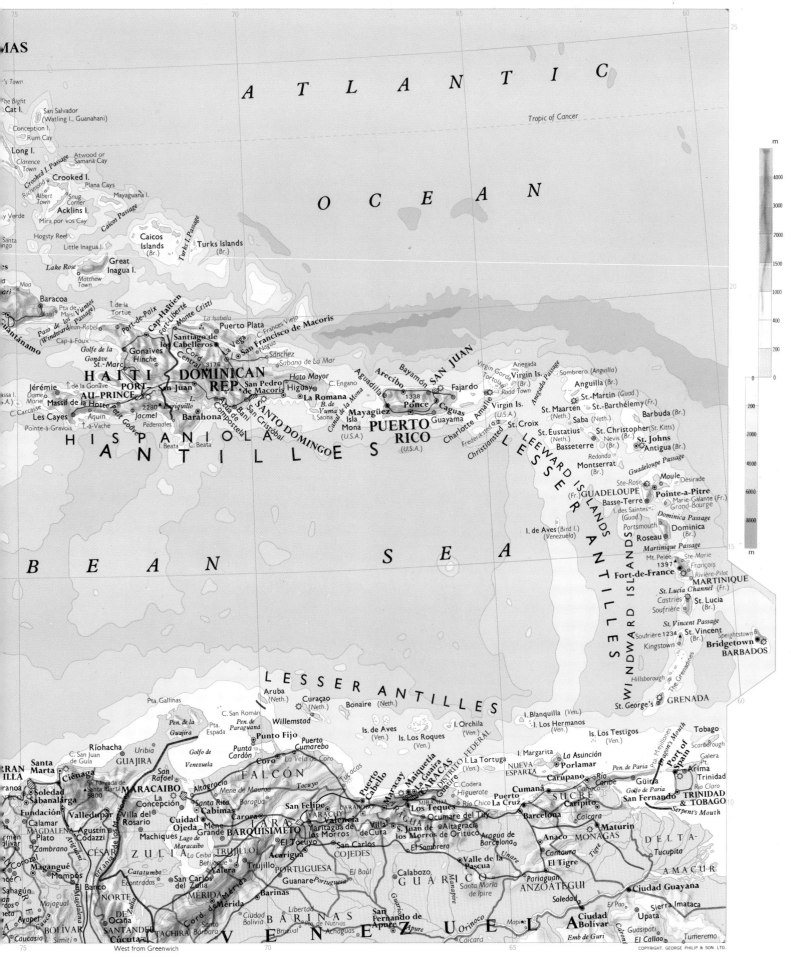

1 : 8 000 000

**167**

50 0 50 100 150 200 250 300 km

A T L A N T I C

Tropic of Cancer

O C E A N

MAS

's Town

The Bight
Cat I.
San Salvador
(Watling I., Guanahani)
Conception I.
Rum Cay
Long I.
Clarence Town
Crooked I. Passage
Crooked I.
Plana Cays
Albert Town
Snug Corner
Mayaguana I.
y Verde
Acklins I.
Mira por vos Cay
Santa
ngo
Hogsty Reef
Little Inagua I.
Lake Rose
Great Inagua I.
Matthew Town
Moa
ari
Baracoa
Pta. de Maisí
Caicos Islands (Br.)
Turks Islands (Br.)
Caicos Passage
Turks I. Passage

uantánamo
Paso de los Vientos (Windward) Passage
Î. de la Tortue
Port-de-Paix
Cap-Haïtien
Fort-Liberté
Monte Cristi
La Isabela
Puerto Plata
C. Frances Viejo
San Francisco de Macorís
Sánchez
Sabana de La Mar

Cap-à-Foux
Santiago de Cabelleros
La Vega
Nagua
Cord.
Central
3175
C. Engaño
Hato Mayor
Aguadilla
Arecibo
Bayamón
SAN JUAN
Virgin Gorda
Anegada
Sombrero (Anguilla)
Anguilla (Br.)

Golfe de la Gonâve
Gonaïves
St.-Marc
Hinche
HAITI
DOMINICAN REP.
San Pedro de Macorís
Higuay
La Romana
B. de Yuma
1338
Ponce
Caguas
Fajardo
Tortola
Road Town
Virgin Is. (U.S.A.)
St.-Martin (Guad.)
St. Maarten (Neth.)
St.-Barthélemy (Fr.)

Jérémie
Î. de la Gonâve
PORT-AU-PRINCE
San Juan
2280
Enriquillo
Barahona
Azua de Compostela
Baní
San Cristóbal
SANTO DOMINGO
Canal de la Mona
Mayagüez
Isla Mona (U.S.A.)
PUERTO RICO
(U.S.A.)
Guayama
Charlotte Amalie
Virgin Is. (U.S.A.)
St. Croix
Saba (Neth.)
St. Eustatius (Neth.)
Barbuda (Br.)
St. Christopher (St. Kitts)
Nevis (Br.)
St. Johns
Antigua (Br.)

Les Cayes
Aquin
Î.-à-Vache
Jacmel
Pedernales
HISPANIOLA
C. Beata
I. Beata
A N T I L L E S
Frederiksted
Christiansted
L E S S E R
Redonda
Montserrat (Br.)
Guadeloupe Passage
Ste-Rose
Moule
Désirade
I. des Saintes (Guad.)
Basse-Terre
GUADELOUPE (Fr.)
Pointe-a-Pitre
Marie-Galante
Grand-Bourge

C. Carcasse
Pointe-à-Gravois

B E A N
S E A
L E E W A R D   I S L A N D S
I. de Aves (Bird I.) (Venezuela)
Portsmouth
Roseau
Dominica Passage
Dominica (Br.)

Martinique Passage
Ste-Marie
Mt. Pelée 1397
François
Rivière-Pilot
Fort-de-France
MARTINIQUE (Fr.)
St. Lucia Channel (Fr.)
Castries
St. Lucia (Br.)
Soufrière

L E S S E R   A N T I L L E S
St. Vincent Passage
Soufrière 1234
St. Vincent (Br.)
Speightstown
Kingstown
Bridgetown
BARBADOS

Aruba (Neth.)
Curaçao (Neth.)
Bonaire (Neth.)
Hillsborough
The Grenadines
St. George's
GRENADA
W I N D W A R D   I S L A N D S

Pta. Gallinas
Pta. Espada
I. Blanquilla (Ven.)
I. Los Hermanos (Ven.)
Tobago
Scarborough
C. San Roman
Pen. de Paraguaná
Willemstad
Is. de Aves (Ven.)
I. Orchila (Ven.)
Is. Los Roques (Ven.)
Is. Los Testigos (Ven.)
Port of Spain
Pen. de la Guajira
Pta. Cardón
Punta Fijo
Puerto Cumarebo
I. Margarita
La Asunción
La Tortuga (Ven.)
Arima
Ríohacha
Uribia
Golfo de Venezuela
Coro
La Vela de Coro
NUEVA ESPARTA
Porlamar
Pen. de Paria
Pta. de Peñas
Dragon's Mouth
Trinidad
GUAJIRA
San Juan de Guía
Punta Cardón
FALCÓN
Tucacas
Puerto Cabello
Maiquetía
La Guaira
CARACAS
DISTRITO FEDERAL
Carúpano
Río Caribe
Güiria
Serpent's Mouth
San Fernando
TRINIDAD & TOBAGO
Santa Marta
Ciénaga
Maracay
MIRANDA
Cumaná
Golfo de Paria
Rio Claro
San Rafael
Altagracia
Mene de Mauroa
Tocuyo
Los Teques
Cariaco
SUCRE
Cariaco
Caripito
Soledad
Sabanalarga
MARACAIBO
La Concepción
Santa Rita
Cabimas
Baragua
San Felipe
YARACUY
Valencia
ARAGUA
S. Juan de los Morros
Higuerote
Río Chico
Puerto La Cruz
Barcelona
Maturín
MONAGAS
Fundación
Calamar
Cuidad Ojeda
Mene Grande
Carora
LARA
Yaritagua de los Morros
deCura
Ocumare del Tuy
Anaco
Caicara
DELTA
Tucupita
MAGDALENA
Agustín Codazzi
Plato
Machiques
Lago de Maracaibo
BARQUISIMETO
El Tocuyo
San Carlos
COJEDES
Altagracia de Orituco
Aragua de Barcelona
Cantaura
El Tigre
AMACUR
Zambrano
CÉSAR
ZULIA
La Ceiba
TRUJILLO
Acarigua
Valle de la Pascua
Ciudad Guayana
Magangué
Mompós
San Carlos del Zulia
Valera
PORTUGUESA
Guanare
Portuguesa
GUÁRICO
Pariaguán
Santa María de Ipire
Sierra Imataca
Sahagún
NORTE
El Banco
Catatumbo
MÉRIDA
Barinas
El Baúl
Calabozo
Upata
DE
Ocaña
Cord. de Mérida
Libertad
Soledad
El Pao
Ciudad Guayana
Majagual
SANTANDER
BOLÍVAR
Simití
TÁCHIRA
Cúcuta
BARINAS
Ciudad Bolivia
San Fernando de Apure
Guasipati
Caucasia
V E N E Z U E L A
San Barbara
Río de Nutrias
Achaguas
Apure
Orinoco
Ciudad Bolívar
El Callao
Tumeremo
Emb de Guri

West from Greenwich

COPYRIGHT. GEORGE PHILIP & SON. LTD.

m
4000
3000
2000
1500
1000
400
200
0
200
2000
4000
6000
8000
m

1:30 000 000

200   0   200   400   600   800   1000 km

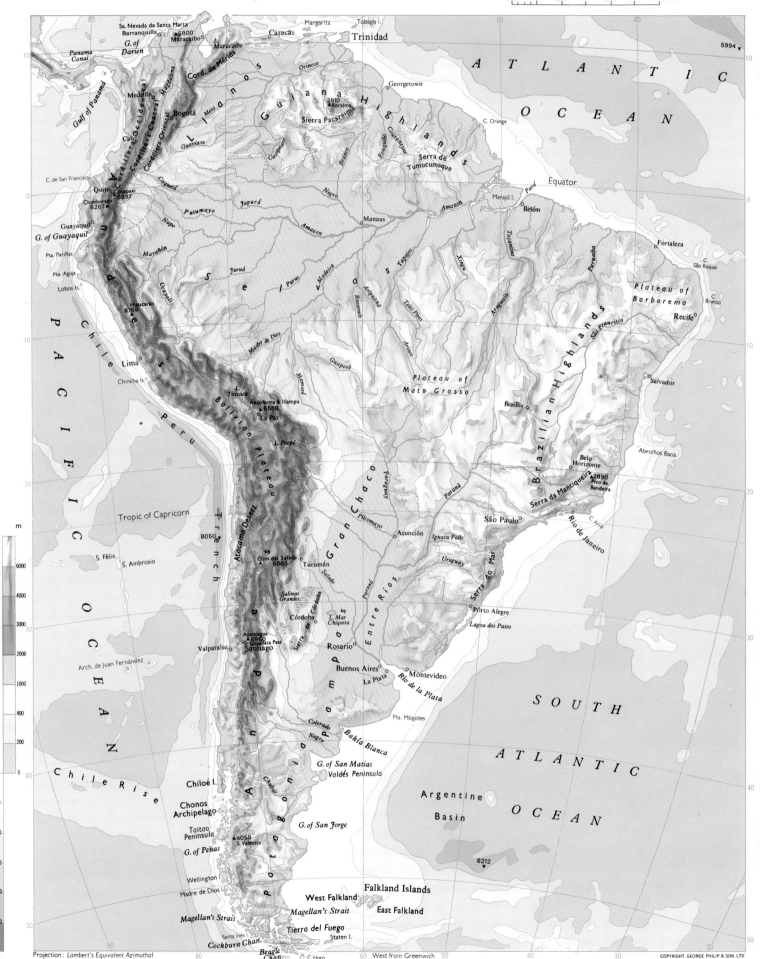

m
6000
4000
3000
2000
1000
400
200
0

m
0
200
2000
4000
6000
8000

Projection: *Lambert's Equivalent Azimuthal*

West from Greenwich

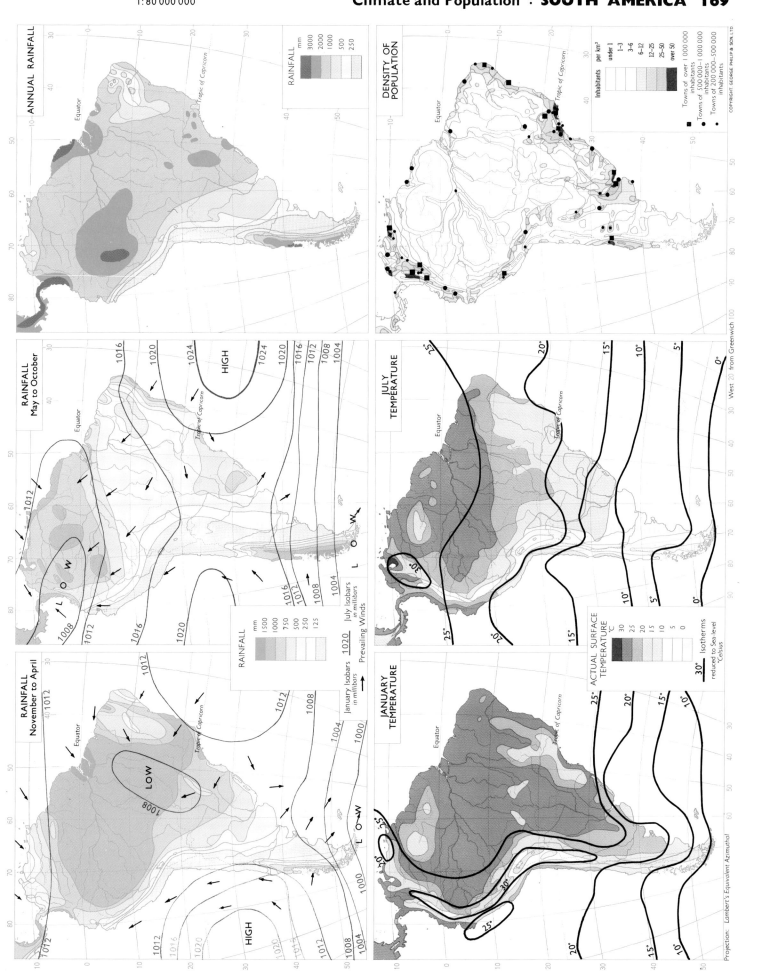

ATLANTIC OCEAN

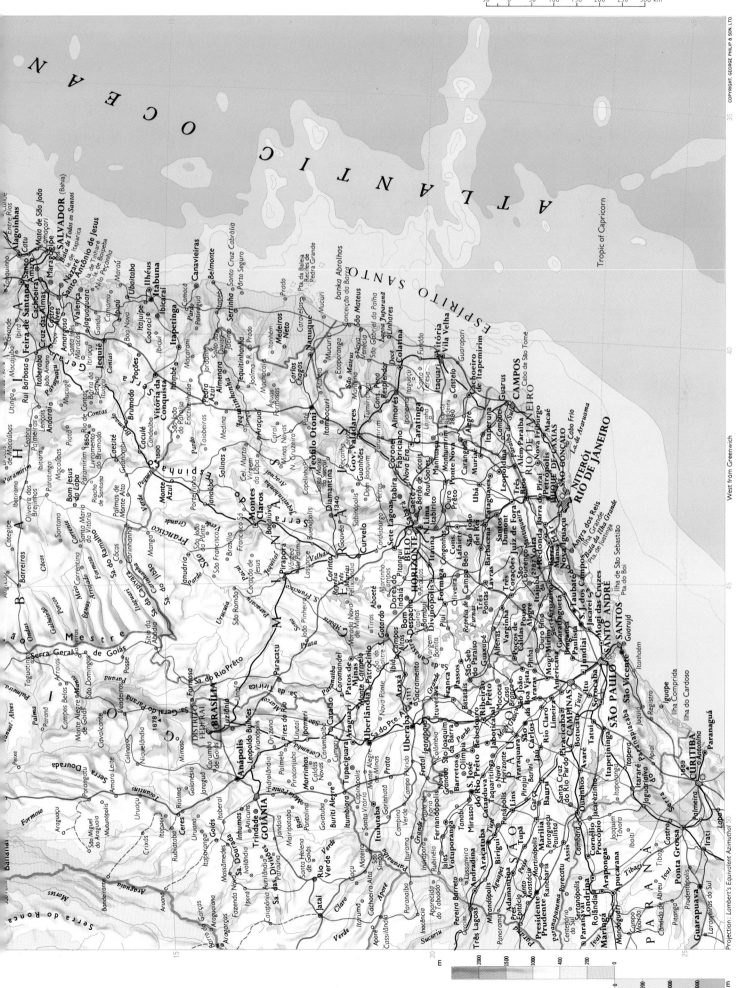

1 : 8 000 000

50   0   50   100   150   200   250   300 km

ATLANTIC OCEAN

Tropic of Capricorn

West from Greenwich

Projection: Lambert's Equivalent Azimuthal

BAHIA

ESPÍRITO SANTO

MINAS GERAIS

GOIÁS

SÃO PAULO

PARANÁ

SALVADOR (Bahia)

BELO HORIZONTE

RIO DE JANEIRO

NITERÓI

SÃO PAULO

CURITIBA

BRASÍLIA

DISTRITO FEDERAL

GOIÂNIA

CAMPOS

SANTOS

SANTO ANDRÉ

CAMPINAS

m  2000  1500  1000  400  200  0

0  200  2000  4000  m

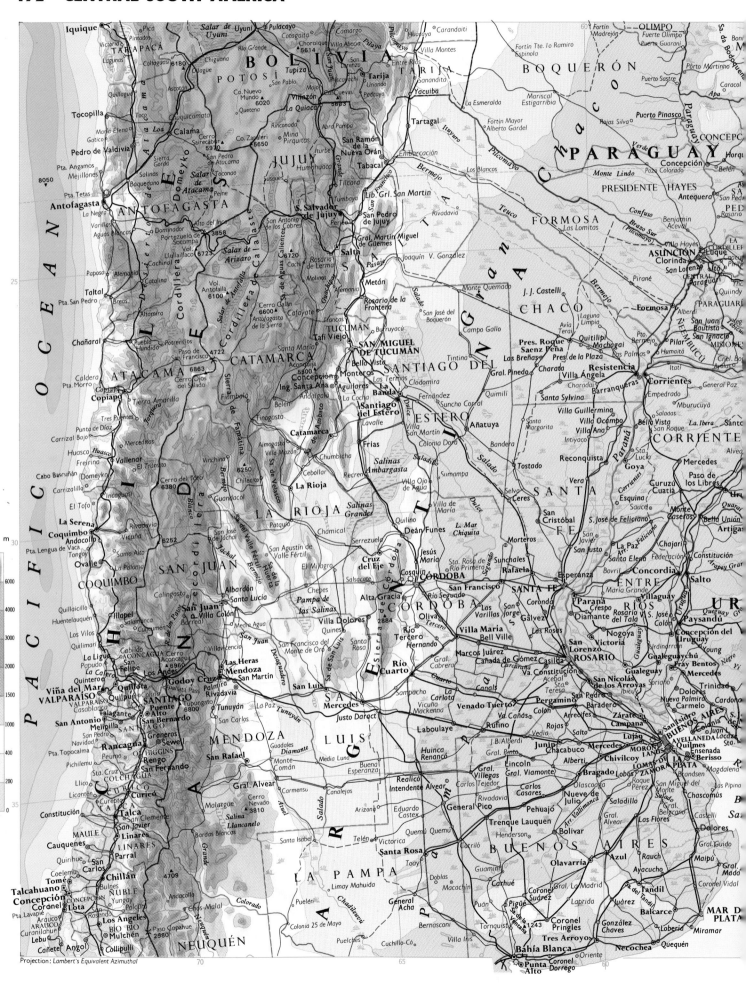

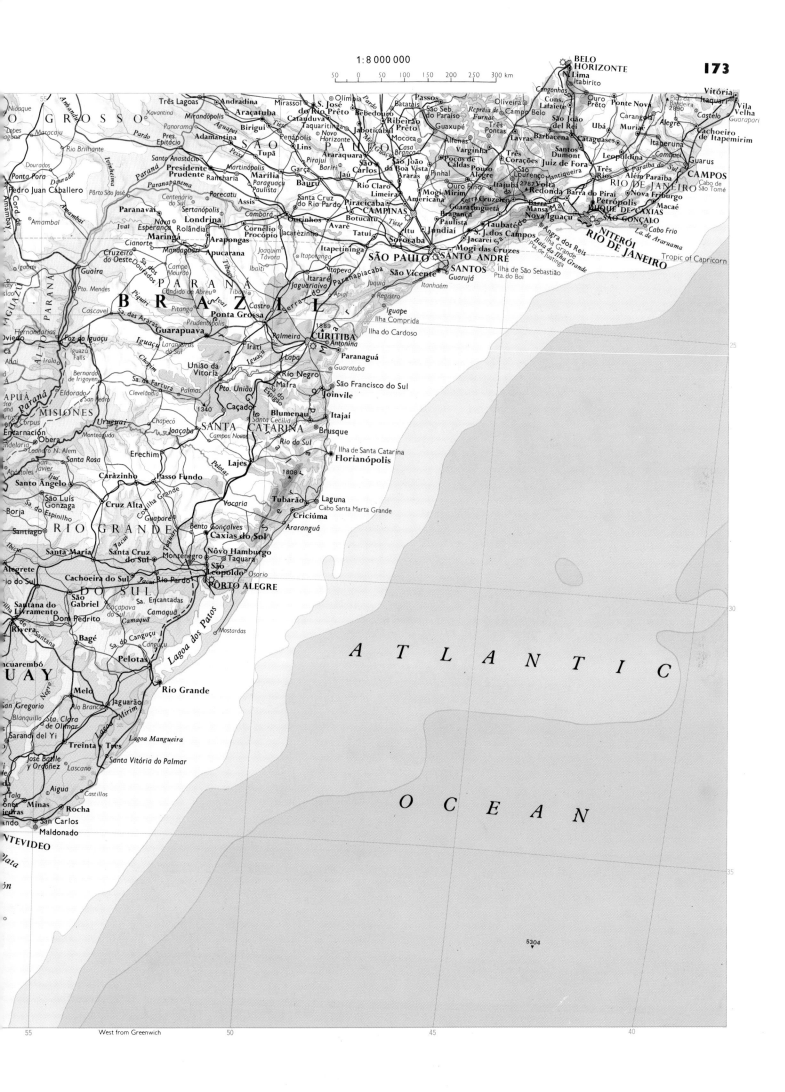

1:8 000 000

50  0  50  100  150  200  250  300 km

BELO
HORIZONTE
Lima
Itabirito

Vitória
Itaquari
Vila
Velha
Guarapari

MATO GROSSO

Três Lagoas
Andradina
Mirassol
S. José
do Rio Prêto
Batatais
Passos
Oliveira
Cons.
Lafaiete
Ouro
Prêto
Ponte Nova
Castelo

Xavantina
Mirandópolis
Araçatuba
Catanduva
Bebedouro
Ribeirão
Prêto
São Seb.
do Paraíso
Represa de
Furnas
Campo Belo
Carangola
Alegre
Cachoeiro
de Itapemirim

Maracaju
Panorama
Biriguí
Penápolis
Taquaritinga
Jaboticabal
Guaxupé
Três
Pontas
São João
del Rei
Ubá
Muriaé
Itaperuna

Rio Brilhante
Pres.
Epitácio
Adamantina
SÃO
Tupã
Lins
Novo
Horizonte
Mococa
Casa
Branca
Alfenas
Varginha
Lavras
Barbacena
Cataguases
Campos

Ponta Porã
Dourados
Pôrto São José
Presidente
Prudente
Rancharia
Marília
Garça
Bariri
Jaú
Araraquara
São
Carlos
São João
da Boa Vista
Poços de
Caldas
Pouso
Alegre
Três
Corações
Juiz de Fora
Leopoldina
Além Paraíba
Cabo de
São Tomé

Pedro Juan Caballero
Paranavaí
Nova
Esperança
Rolândia
Assis
Sertanópolis
Porecatu
Piracicaba
Limeira
Rio Claro
Araras
Pinhal
Ouro Fino
Itajubá 2787 Volta
Redonda
Mantiqueira
São
Lourenço
Macaé

Amambaí
Cianorte
Maringá
Londrina
Apucarana
Cambará
CAMPINAS
Americana
Mogi-Mirim
Serra
Cruzeiro
Guaratinguetá
Bragança
Barra do Pirai
Nova Friburgo

Guaíra
Campo
Mourão
Arapongas
Cornélio
Procópio
Jacarèzinho
Avaré
Botucatu
Itu
Paulista
Jundiaí
S. J. dos Campos
Taubaté
Jacarei
Petrópolis
RIO DE JANEIRO

Cruzeiro
do Oeste
Mandaguari
Ibaití
Itapeva
Tatuí
Sorocaba
Jaguariaíva
Itararé
São Paulo
SANTO ANDRÉ
São
Vicente
Angra dos Reis
Ilha Grande
Baía da Ilha Grande
NITERÓI
RIO DE
JANEIRO
Cabo Frio

BRAZIL
PARANÁ
Pitanga
Castro
Ponta Grossa
Palmeira
1889
CURITIBA
Antonina
SANTOS
Guarujá
Ilha de São Sebastião
Pta. do Boi

Foz do Iguaçu
Iguaçú
Falls
Guarapuava
Irati
Laranjeiras
do Sul
Lapa
Paranaguá
Guaratuba

União da
Vitória
Pto. União
Rio Negro
Mafra
São Francisco do Sul

MISIONES
Palmas
Clevelândia
Caçado
Joinvile
Itajaí

Chapecó
Joaçaba
SANTA
Campos Novos
Blumenau
Santa Cecília
Brusque

Erechim
Lajes
Rio do Sul
CATARINA
1808
Ilha de Santa Catarina
Florianópolis

Carázinho
Passo Fundo
Vacaria
Tubarão
Laguna
Cabo Santa Marta Grande

RIO GRANDE
Bento Gonçalves
Guaporé
Criciúma

Santa Maria
Cruz Alta
Caxias do Sul
Araranguá

Alegrete
Cachoeira do Sul
Santa Cruz
do Sul
Montenegro
Nôvo Hamburgo
Taquara
São
Leopoldo
Osorio

URUGUAY
Santana do
Livramento
DO
São
Gabriel
SUL
Encantadas
PÔRTO ALEGRE

Rivera
Dom Pedrito
Camaquã
Lagoa dos Patos
Mostardas

Bagé
Pelotas

Melo
Rio Grande

Jaguarão
Lagoa
Mirim

ATLANTIC

Treinta y Tres
Lagoa Mangueira

Santa Vitória do Palmar

Rocha

San Carlos
Maldonado

OCEAN

5304

Tropic of Capricorn

25

30

35

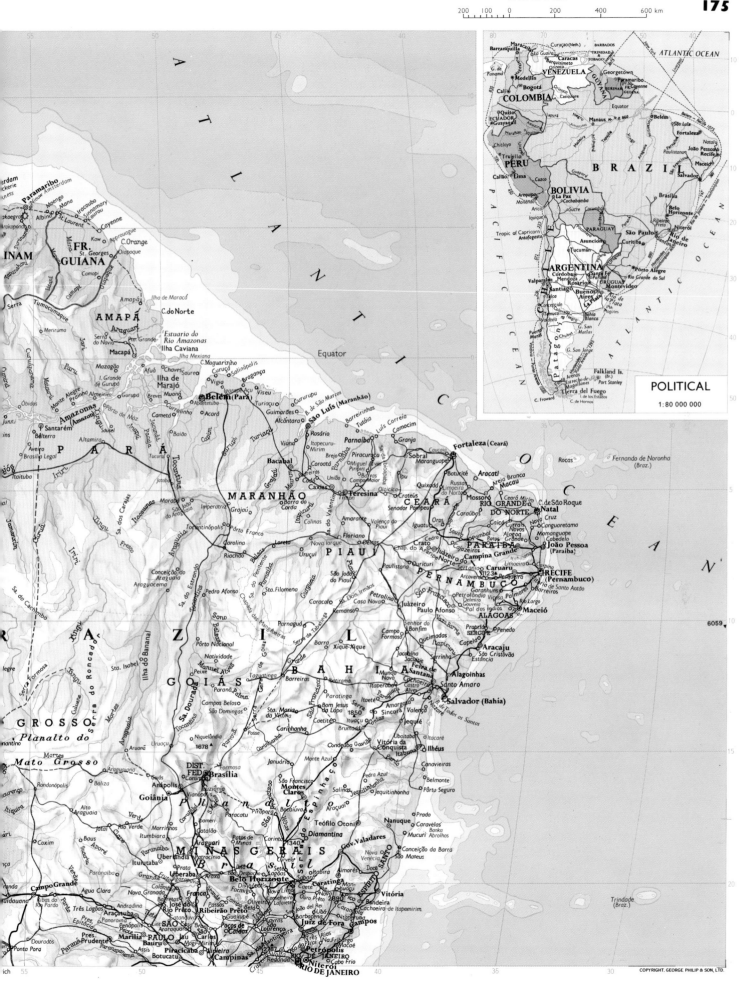

1:16 000 000

200  100  0    200    400    600 km

ATLANTIC OCEAN

VENEZUELA

Georgetown

Barranquilla
Maracaibo      Curaçao (Neth.)    BARBADOS
                                  TRINIDAD
                                  TOBAGO
Caracas

G. de
Panamá

Medellín
Bogotá

COLOMBIA

Quito
ECUADOR
Guayaquil

Manaus

Belém

São Luís
Fortaleza

PERU

Natal
João Pessoa
Recife

Truijillo
Lima
Callao    Cuzco

BRAZIL

Arequipa

BOLIVIA
La Paz    Cochabamba

Sucre

Maceió

Salvador

Brasília

Belo
Horizonte

Antofagasta

Tropic of Capricorn

PARAGUAY
Asunción

São Paulo
Rio de Janeiro

Curitiba

Niterói

Tucumán

Valparaíso
Santiago    Córdoba
Talca    Rosario
         Buenos
         Aires
ARGENTINA

URUGUAY
Montevideo

Pôrto Alegre
Rio Grande do Sul

Bahía Blanca

San
Matias

PACIFIC OCEAN

Patagonia

G. San Jorge

Estrecho de
Magallanes

Tierra del Fuego

Falkland Is.
(Br.)
Port Stanley

ATLANTIC OCEAN

**POLITICAL**

1:80 000 000

**A T L A N T I C**    **O C E A N**

Paramaribo
Nieuw Amsterdam

FR.
GUIANA

Cayenne

AMAPÁ

Macapá

C. do Norte

Estuario do
Rio Amazonas
Ilha Caviana

Ilha de
Marajó

Equator

Belém (Pará)

São Luís (Maranhão)

Parnaíba

Fortaleza (Ceará)

Fernando de Noronha
(Braz.)

P A R Á

Santarém

Amazonas (Amazon)

Óbidos

MARANHÃO

Teresina

CEARÁ

Sobral

Natal

RIO GRANDE
DO NORTE

Mossoró
Macau

C. de São Roque

Rocas

PIAUÍ

PARAÍBA

João Pessoa
(Paraíba)

Campina Grande
Caruaru

PERNAMBUCO

RECIFE
(Pernambuco)

B R A Z I L

G O I Á S

B A H I A

Feira de
Santana

Alagoinhas

Santo Amaro

Salvador (Bahia)

Juàzeiro

Paulo Afonso

ALAGOAS
Maceió

SERGIPE
Aracaju

São Cristóvão

O C E A N

6059

GROSSO

Planalto do

Mato Grosso

DIST.
FED.
Brasília

Anápolis

Goiânia

P l a n a l t o

Montes
Claros

Vitória da
Conquista

Ilhéus

Teófilo Otoni

Diamantina

Gov. Valadares

Nanuque

Conceição da Barra

Pôrto Seguro

CampoGrande

M I N A S   G E R A I S

Uberlândia

Uberaba

Belo Horizonte

ESPIRITO
SANTO

Vitória

SÃO
PAULO

Ribeirão Preto

Campinas

Juiz de Fora  Campos

Petrópolis

RIO DE JANEIRO

Niterói

Trindade
(Braz.)

COPYRIGHT, GEORGE PHILIP & SON, LTD.

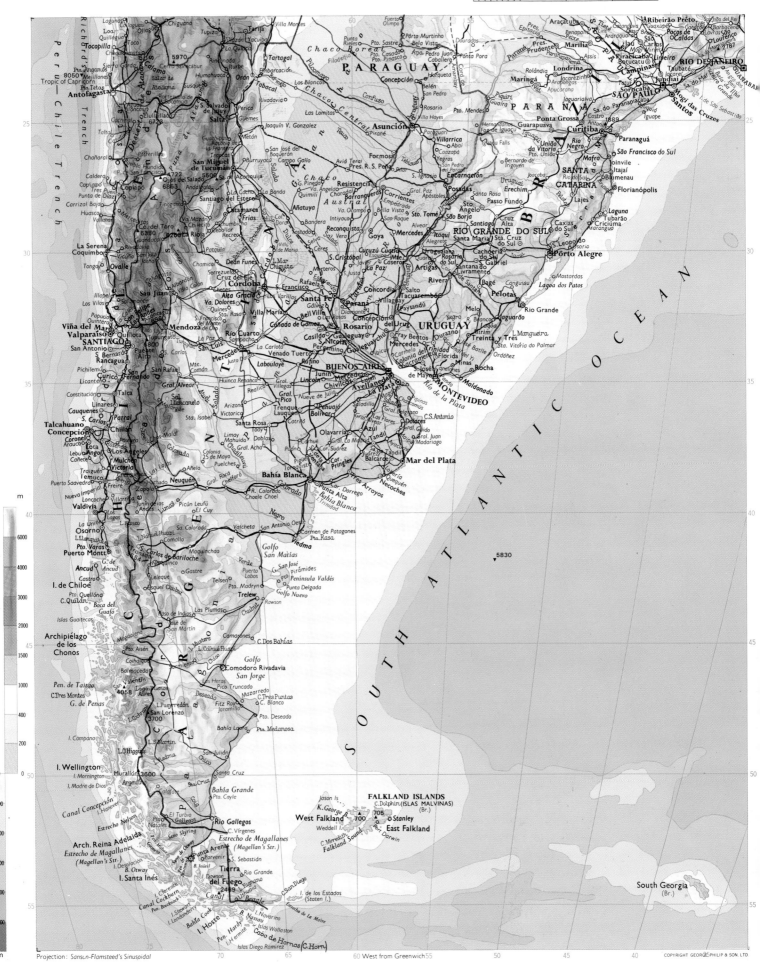

1:16 000 000

200 100 0 200 400 600 km

Projection: Sanson-Flamsteed's Sinusoidal

60 West from Greenwich 55

COPYRIGHT GEORGE PHILIP & SON, LTD.

Equatorial Scale 1:160 000 000

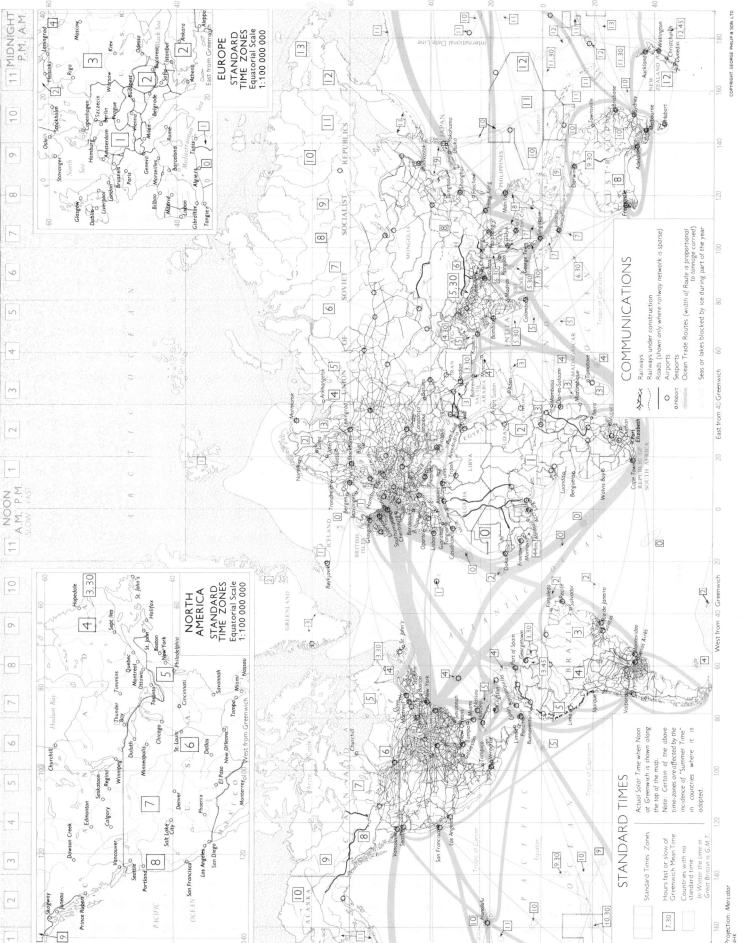

EUROPE
STANDARD
TIME ZONES
Equatorial Scale
1:100 000 000

East from Greenwich

NORTH
AMERICA
STANDARD
TIME ZONES
Equatorial Scale
1:100 000 000

West from Greenwich

## COMMUNICATIONS

Railways
Railways under construction
Roads (shown only where railway network is sparse)
o Hobart    Airports
Seaports
Ocean Trade Routes (width of Route is proportional to tonnage carried)
Seas or lakes blocked by ice during part of the year

## STANDARD TIMES

Standard Times Zones

Hours fast or slow of Greenwich Mean Time

Countries with no standard time

7.30    In Winter the time in Great Britain is G.M.T.

Actual Solar Time when Noon at Greenwich is shown along the top of the map.

Note: Certain of the above time-zones are affected by the incidence of "Summer Time" in countries where it is adopted.

East from 40 Greenwich

West from 40 Greenwich

Projection. Mercator
N·H·K

i

# THE WORLD : Wheat, Oats, Rice and Spices

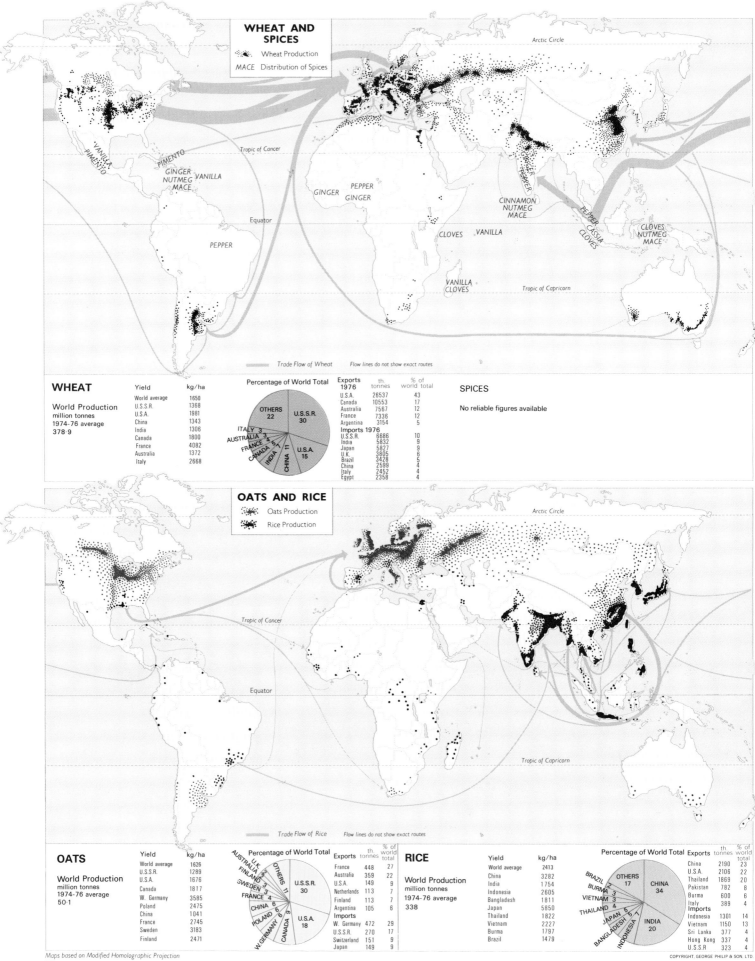

**WHEAT AND SPICES**

- Wheat Production
- *MACE* Distribution of Spices

*Trade Flow of Wheat* — Flow lines do not show exact routes

## WHEAT

World Production
million tonnes
1974-76 average
378·9

| Yield | kg/ha |
|---|---|
| World average | 1650 |
| U.S.S.R. | 1368 |
| U.S.A. | 1981 |
| China | 1343 |
| India | 1306 |
| Canada | 1800 |
| France | 4082 |
| Australia | 1372 |
| Italy | 2668 |

**Percentage of World Total**

OTHERS 22 · U.S.S.R. 30 · ITALY 3 · AUSTRALIA 3 · FRANCE 4 · CANADA 5 · INDIA 7 · CHINA 11 · U.S.A. 15

| Exports 1976 | th. tonnes | % of world total |
|---|---|---|
| U.S.A. | 26537 | 43 |
| Canada | 10553 | 17 |
| Australia | 7567 | 12 |
| France | 7336 | 12 |
| Argentina | 3154 | 5 |
| **Imports 1976** | | |
| U.S.S.R. | 6686 | 10 |
| India | 5832 | 9 |
| Japan | 5827 | 9 |
| U.K. | 3805 | 6 |
| Brazil | 3428 | 5 |
| China | 2599 | 4 |
| Italy | 2452 | 4 |
| Egypt | 2358 | 4 |

### SPICES

No reliable figures available

---

**OATS AND RICE**

- Oats Production
- Rice Production

*Trade Flow of Rice* — Flow lines do not show exact routes

## OATS

World Production
million tonnes
1974-76 average
50·1

| Yield | kg/ha |
|---|---|
| World average | 1626 |
| U.S.S.R. | 1289 |
| U.S.A. | 1676 |
| Canada | 1817 |
| W. Germany | 3585 |
| Poland | 2475 |
| China | 1041 |
| France | 2745 |
| Sweden | 3183 |
| Finland | 2471 |

**Percentage of World Total**

AUSTRALIA · U.K. · FINLAND · OTHERS 11 · U.S.S.R. 30 · SWEDEN 3 · FRANCE 4 · CHINA 6 · POLAND 6 · W.GERMANY 6 · CANADA 9 · U.S.A. 18

| Exports | th. tonnes | % of world total |
|---|---|---|
| France | 448 | 27 |
| Australia | 359 | 22 |
| U.S.A. | 149 | 9 |
| Netherlands | 113 | 7 |
| Finland | 113 | 7 |
| Argentina | 105 | 6 |
| **Imports** | | |
| W. Germany | 472 | 29 |
| U.S.S.R. | 270 | 17 |
| Switzerland | 151 | 9 |
| Japan | 149 | 9 |

## RICE

World Production
million tonnes
1974-76 average
338

| Yield | kg/ha |
|---|---|
| World average | 2413 |
| China | 3282 |
| India | 1754 |
| Indonesia | 2605 |
| Bangladesh | 1811 |
| Japan | 5850 |
| Thailand | 1822 |
| Vietnam | 2227 |
| Burma | 1797 |
| Brazil | 1479 |

**Percentage of World Total**

OTHERS 17 · CHINA 34 · BRAZIL 2 · BURMA 3 · VIETNAM 4 · THAILAND 4 · JAPAN 5 · BANGLADESH 6 · INDONESIA 5 · INDIA 20

| Exports | th. tonnes | % of world total |
|---|---|---|
| China | 2190 | 23 |
| U.S.A. | 2106 | 22 |
| Thailand | 1869 | 20 |
| Pakistan | 782 | 8 |
| Burma | 600 | 6 |
| Italy | 389 | 4 |
| **Imports** | | |
| Indonesia | 1301 | 14 |
| Vietnam | 1150 | 13 |
| Sri Lanka | 377 | 4 |
| Hong Kong | 337 | 4 |
| U.S.S.R | 323 | 4 |

*Maps based on Modified Homolographic Projection*

Equatorial Scale 1:170 000 000

# Rye, Barley, Rubber, Tea and Coffee : THE WORLD

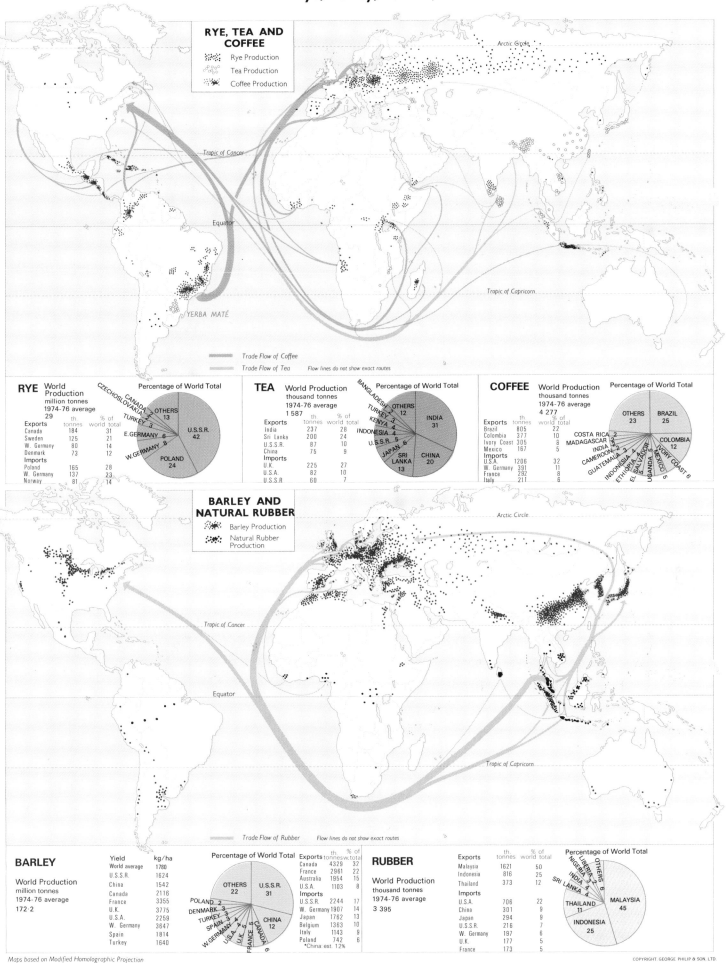

**RYE, TEA AND COFFEE**
- Rye Production
- Tea Production
- Coffee Production

*Arctic Circle*

*Tropic of Cancer*

*Equator*

*Tropic of Capricorn*

YERBA MATÉ

Trade Flow of Coffee
Trade Flow of Tea    Flow lines do not show exact routes

## RYE
World Production million tonnes 1974-76 average 29

Percentage of World Total

| Exports | th. tonnes | % of world total |
|---|---|---|
| Canada | 184 | 31 |
| Sweden | 125 | 21 |
| W. Germany | 80 | 14 |
| Denmark | 73 | 12 |
| Imports | | |
| Poland | 165 | 28 |
| W. Germany | 137 | 23 |
| Norway | 81 | 14 |

Pie: U.S.S.R. 42, POLAND 24, OTHERS 13, E.GERMANY 6, W.GERMANY 8, TURKEY 3, CANADA 2, CZECHOSLOVAKIA 2

## TEA
World Production thousand tonnes 1974-76 average 1 587

Percentage of World Total

| Exports | th. tonnes | % of world total |
|---|---|---|
| India | 237 | 28 |
| Sri Lanka | 200 | 24 |
| U.S.S.R. | 87 | 10 |
| China | 75 | 9 |
| Imports | | |
| U.K. | 225 | 27 |
| U.S.A. | 82 | 10 |
| U.S.S.R | 60 | 7 |

Pie: INDIA 31, CHINA 20, SRI LANKA 13, OTHERS 12, JAPAN 6, U.S.S.R. 5, INDONESIA 4, KENYA 3, TURKEY 3, BANGLADESH

## COFFEE
World Production thousand tonnes 1974-76 average 4 277

Percentage of World Total

| Exports | th. tonnes | % of world total |
|---|---|---|
| Brazil | 805 | 22 |
| Colombia | 377 | 10 |
| Ivory Coast | 305 | 8 |
| Mexico | 167 | 5 |
| Imports | | |
| U.S.A. | 1206 | 32 |
| W. Germany | 391 | 11 |
| France | 292 | 8 |
| Italy | 211 | 6 |

Pie: BRAZIL 25, OTHERS 23, COLOMBIA 12, IVORY COAST 6, MEXICO 5, UGANDA 5, EL SALVADOR 5, ETHIOPIA 4, INDONESIA 4, GUATEMALA 3, CAMEROON 3, INDIA 2, MADAGASCAR 2, COSTA RICA 2

---

**BARLEY AND NATURAL RUBBER**
- Barley Production
- Natural Rubber Production

*Arctic Circle*

*Tropic of Cancer*

*Equator*

*Tropic of Capricorn*

Trade Flow of Rubber    Flow lines do not show exact routes

## BARLEY
World Production million tonnes 1974-76 average 172·2

| Yield | kg/ha |
|---|---|
| World average | 1780 |
| U.S.S.R. | 1624 |
| China | 1542 |
| Canada | 2116 |
| France | 3355 |
| U.K. | 3775 |
| U.S.A. | 2259 |
| W. Germany | 3647 |
| Spain | 1814 |
| Turkey | 1640 |

Percentage of World Total

Pie: U.S.S.R. 31, OTHERS 22, CHINA 12, CANADA 6, FRANCE, U.K. 5, U.S.A. 4, W.GERMANY 3, SPAIN 3, TURKEY 3, DENMARK 3, POLAND 2

| Exports | th. tonnes | % of total |
|---|---|---|
| Canada | 4329 | 32 |
| France | 2961 | 22 |
| Australia | 1954 | 15 |
| U.S.A. | 1103 | 8 |
| Imports | | |
| U.S.S.R. | 2244 | 17 |
| W. Germany | 1907 | 14 |
| Japan | 1762 | 13 |
| Belgium | 1363 | 10 |
| Italy | 1143 | 9 |
| Poland | 742 | 6 |
| *China: est. 12% | | |

## RUBBER
World Production thousand tonnes 1974-76 average 3 395

| Exports | th. tonnes | % of world total |
|---|---|---|
| Malaysia | 1621 | 50 |
| Indonesia | 816 | 25 |
| Thailand | 373 | 12 |
| Imports | | |
| U.S.A. | 706 | 22 |
| China | 301 | 9 |
| Japan | 294 | 9 |
| U.S.S.R. | 216 | 7 |
| W. Germany | 197 | 6 |
| U.K. | 177 | 5 |
| France | 173 | 5 |

Percentage of World Total

Pie: MALAYSIA 45, INDONESIA 25, THAILAND 11, OTHERS 6, SRI LANKA, INDIA 4, NIGERIA 4, LIBERIA 3

Equatorial Scale 1:170 000 000

# THE WORLD : Maize, Sago, Potatoes and Millets

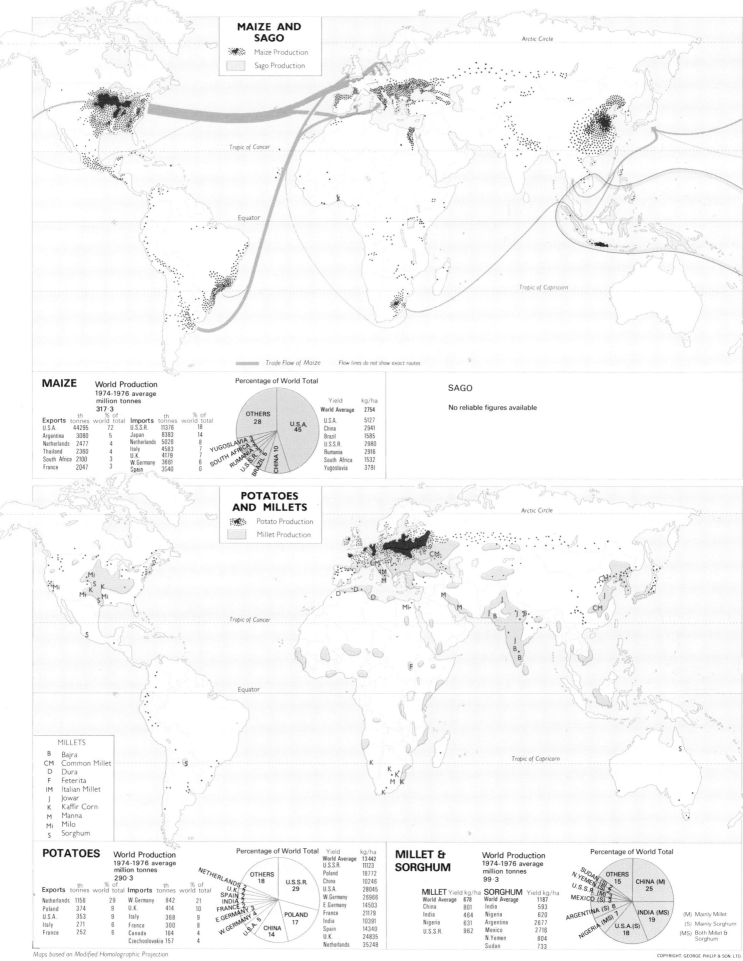

**MAIZE AND SAGO**

- Maize Production
- Sago Production

Arctic Circle

Tropic of Cancer

Equator

Tropic of Capricorn

Trade Flow of Maize    Flow lines do not show exact routes

## MAIZE

World Production
1974-1976 average
million tonnes
317·3

| Exports | th tonnes | % of world total | Imports | th tonnes | % of world total |
|---|---|---|---|---|---|
| U.S.A. | 44295 | 72 | U.S.S.R. | 11376 | 18 |
| Argentina | 3080 | 5 | Japan | 8383 | 14 |
| Netherlands | 2477 | 4 | Netherlands | 5028 | 8 |
| Thailand | 2360 | 4 | Italy | 4583 | 7 |
| South Africa | 2100 | 3 | U.K. | 4179 | 7 |
| France | 2047 | 3 | W.Germany | 3661 | 6 |
| | | | Spain | 3540 | 0 |

**Percentage of World Total**

OTHERS 28
U.S.A. 45
YUGOSLAVIA 3
SOUTH AFRICA 3
RUMANIA 3
U.S.S.R. 5
BRAZIL 5
CHINA 10

| | Yield kg/ha |
|---|---|
| World Average | 2754 |
| U.S.A. | 5127 |
| China | 2941 |
| Brazil | 1585 |
| U.S.S.R. | 2980 |
| Rumania | 2916 |
| South Africa | 1532 |
| Yugoslavia | 3791 |

## SAGO

No reliable figures available

---

**POTATOES AND MILLETS**

- Potato Production
- Millet Production

Arctic Circle

Tropic of Cancer

Equator

Tropic of Capricorn

### MILLETS

| | |
|---|---|
| B | Bajra |
| CM | Common Millet |
| D | Dura |
| F | Feterita |
| IM | Italian Millet |
| J | Jowar |
| K | Kaffir Corn |
| M | Manna |
| Mi | Milo |
| S | Sorghum |

Maps based on Modified Homolographic Projection

**iv**

## POTATOES

World Production
1974-1976 average
million tonnes
290·3

| Exports | th tonnes | % of world | Imports | th tonnes | % of world |
|---|---|---|---|---|---|
| Netherlands | 1156 | 29 | W.Germany | 842 | 21 |
| Poland | 374 | 9 | U.K. | 414 | 10 |
| U.S.A. | 353 | 9 | Italy | 368 | 9 |
| Italy | 271 | 6 | France | 300 | 8 |
| France | 252 | 6 | Canada | 164 | 4 |
| | | | Czechoslovakia | 157 | 4 |

**Percentage of World Total**

OTHERS 18
U.S.S.R. 29
POLAND 17
CHINA 14
U.S.A. 5
W.GERMANY 4
E.GERMANY 3
FRANCE 2
INDIA 2
SPAIN 2
U.K. 2
NETHERLANDS 2

| Yield | kg/ha |
|---|---|
| World Average | 13442 |
| U.S.S.R. | 11123 |
| Poland | 18772 |
| China | 10246 |
| U.S.A. | 28045 |
| W.Germany | 26966 |
| E.Germany | 14503 |
| France | 21179 |
| India | 10391 |
| Spain | 14340 |
| U.K. | 24835 |
| Netherlands | 35248 |

## MILLET & SORGHUM

World Production
1974-1976 average
million tonnes
99·3

| MILLET | Yield kg/ha | SORGHUM | Yield kg/ha |
|---|---|---|---|
| World Average | 678 | World Average | 1187 |
| China | 801 | India | 593 |
| India | 464 | Nigeria | 620 |
| Nigeria | 631 | Argentina | 2677 |
| U.S.S.R. | 962 | Mexico | 2718 |
| | | N.Yemen | 804 |
| | | Sudan | 733 |

**Percentage of World Total**

OTHERS 15
CHINA (M) 25
SUDAN (S) 3
N.YEMEN (S) 3
U.S.S.R. (M) 3
MEXICO (S) 3
ARGENTINA (S) 6
NIGERIA (MS) 7
U.S.A.(S) 18
INDIA (MS) 19

(M) Mainly Millet
(S) Mainly Sorghum
(MS) Both Millet & Sorghum

COPYRIGHT. GEORGE PHILIP & SON. LTD.

Equatorial Scale 1:170 000 000

# Grapes, Cacao, Date Palms, Cane and Beet Sugar : THE WORLD

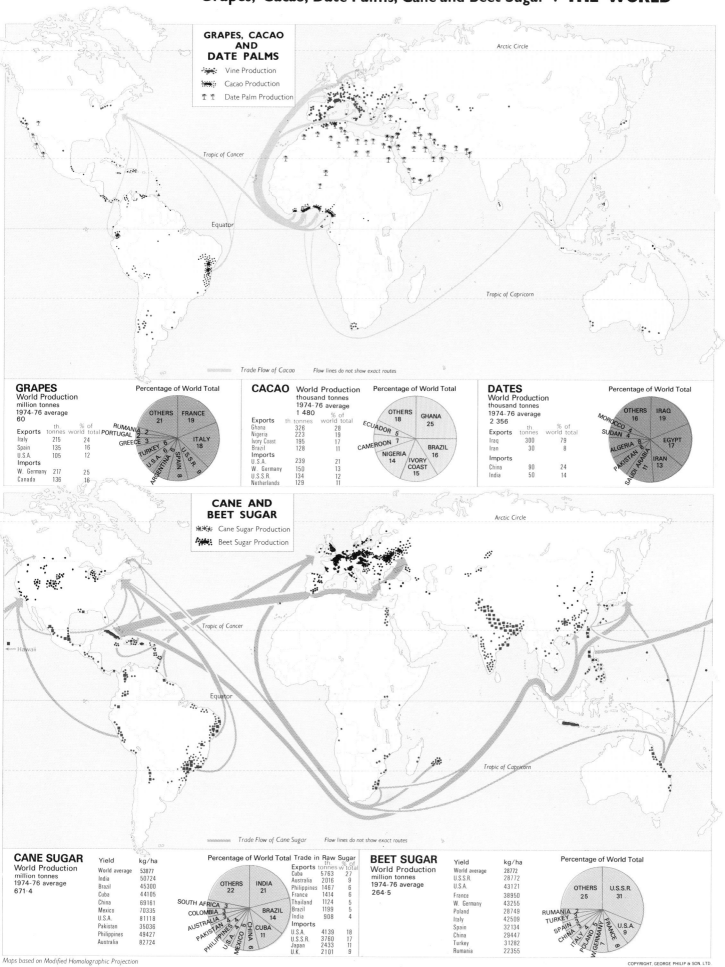

**GRAPES, CACAO AND DATE PALMS**

- Vine Production
- Cacao Production
- Date Palm Production

*Arctic Circle*

*Tropic of Cancer*

*Equator*

*Tropic of Capricorn*

Trade Flow of Cacao    Flow lines do not show exact routes

## GRAPES

World Production
million tonnes
1974-76 average
60

| Exports | th. tonnes | % of world total |
|---|---|---|
| Italy | 215 | 24 |
| Spain | 135 | 16 |
| U.S.A. | 105 | 12 |
| Imports | | |
| W. Germany | 217 | 25 |
| Canada | 136 | 16 |

Percentage of World Total

- FRANCE 19
- OTHERS 21
- RUMANIA 2
- PORTUGAL 2
- GREECE 3
- TURKEY 6
- U.S.A. 6
- ARGENTINA 6
- SPAIN 8
- U.S.S.R. 9
- ITALY 18

## CACAO

World Production
thousand tonnes
1974-76 average
1 480

| Exports | th. tonnes | % of world total |
|---|---|---|
| Ghana | 326 | 28 |
| Nigeria | 223 | 19 |
| Ivory Coast | 195 | 17 |
| Brazil | 128 | 11 |
| Imports | | |
| U.S.A. | 239 | 21 |
| W. Germany | 150 | 13 |
| U.S.S.R. | 134 | 12 |
| Netherlands | 129 | 11 |

Percentage of World Total

- GHANA 25
- OTHERS 18
- ECUADOR 5
- CAMEROON 7
- NIGERIA 14
- IVORY COAST 15
- BRAZIL 16

## DATES

World Production
thousand tonnes
1974-76 average
2 356

| Exports | th. tonnes | % of world total |
|---|---|---|
| Iraq | 300 | 79 |
| Iran | 30 | 8 |
| Imports | | |
| China | 90 | 24 |
| India | 50 | 14 |

Percentage of World Total

- IRAQ 19
- OTHERS 16
- MOROCCO 4
- SUDAN 4
- EGYPT 17
- ALGERIA 8
- PAKISTAN 8
- SAUDI ARABIA 11
- IRAN 13

---

**CANE AND BEET SUGAR**

- Cane Sugar Production
- Beet Sugar Production

*Arctic Circle*

← Hawaii

*Tropic of Cancer*

*Equator*

*Tropic of Capricorn*

Trade Flow of Cane Sugar    Flow lines do not show exact routes

## CANE SUGAR

World Production
million tonnes
1974-76 average
671·4

| Yield | kg/ha |
|---|---|
| World average | 53877 |
| India | 50724 |
| Brazil | 45300 |
| Cuba | 44105 |
| China | 69161 |
| Mexico | 70335 |
| U.S.A. | 81118 |
| Pakistan | 35036 |
| Philippines | 49427 |
| Australia | 82724 |

Percentage of World Total

- INDIA 21
- OTHERS 22
- SOUTH AFRICA 3
- COLOMBIA 3
- AUSTRALIA 4
- PAKISTAN 4
- PHILIPPINES 4
- U.S.A. 5
- MEXICO 6
- CHINA 6
- CUBA 11
- BRAZIL 14

### Trade in Raw Sugar

| Exports | th. tonnes | % of total |
|---|---|---|
| Cuba | 5763 | 27 |
| Australia | 2016 | 9 |
| Philippines | 1467 | 6 |
| France | 1414 | 6 |
| Thailand | 1124 | 5 |
| Brazil | 1199 | 5 |
| India | 908 | 4 |
| Imports | | |
| U.S.A. | 4139 | 18 |
| U.S.S.R. | 3760 | 17 |
| Japan | 2433 | 11 |
| U.K. | 2101 | 9 |

## BEET SUGAR

World Production
million tonnes
1974-76 average
264·5

| Yield | kg/ha |
|---|---|
| World average | 28772 |
| U.S.S.R. | 28772 |
| U.S.A. | 43121 |
| France | 38950 |
| W. Germany | 43255 |
| Poland | 28749 |
| Italy | 42509 |
| Spain | 32134 |
| China | 29447 |
| Turkey | 31282 |
| Rumania | 22355 |

Percentage of World Total

- U.S.S.R. 31
- OTHERS 25
- U.S.A. 9
- FRANCE 8
- W. GERMANY 7
- POLAND 4
- ITALY 4
- CHINA 3
- SPAIN 3
- TURKEY 3
- RUMANIA 2

*Maps based on Modified Homolographic Projection*

Equatorial Scale 1:170 000 000

**V**

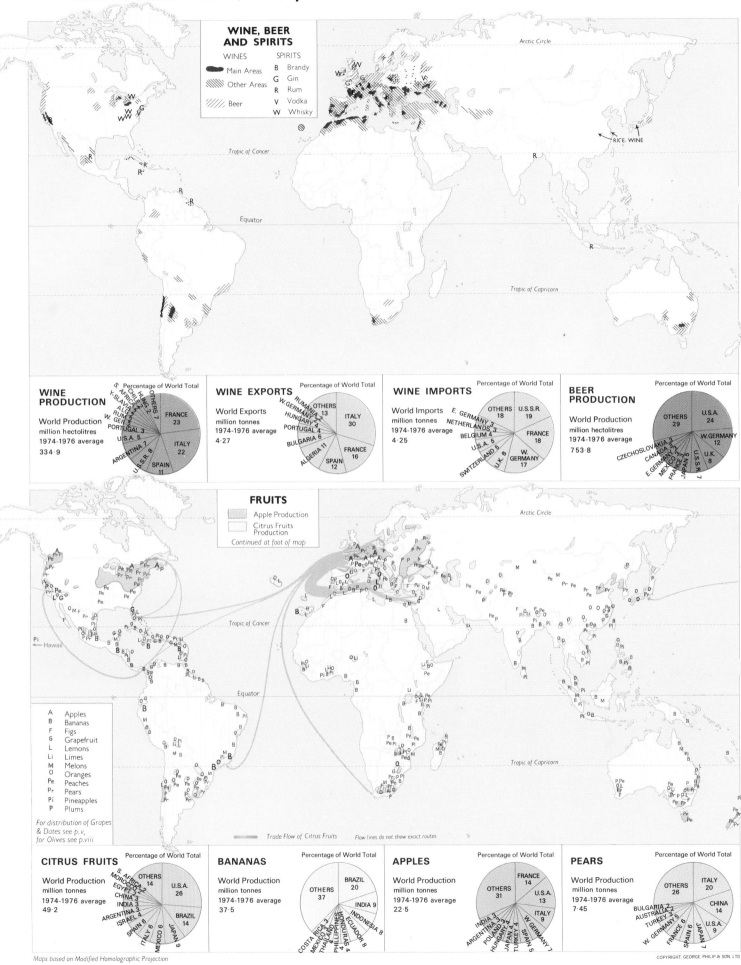

# THE WORLD : Wine, Beer, Spirits and Fruits

## WINE, BEER AND SPIRITS

WINES
- Main Areas
- Other Areas
- Beer

SPIRITS
- B Brandy
- G Gin
- R Rum
- V Vodka
- W Whisky

RICE WINE

### WINE PRODUCTION
World Production
million hectolitres
1974-1976 average
334·9

Percentage of World Total
- FRANCE 23
- ITALY 22
- SPAIN 11
- U.S.S.R. 8
- ARGENTINA 7
- U.S.A. 5
- PORTUGAL 4
- W. GER. 
- RUM.
- ALG.
- Y-SLAV.
- S. AFRICA
- CHILE
- HUNG.
- OTHERS 7

### WINE EXPORTS
World Exports
million tonnes
1974-1976 average
4·27

Percentage of World Total
- ITALY 30
- FRANCE 16
- SPAIN 12
- ALGERIA 11
- BULGARIA 6
- PORTUGAL 4
- HUNGARY 4
- W. GERMANY 
- RUMANIA 2
- OTHERS 13

### WINE IMPORTS
World Imports
million tonnes
1974-1976 average
4·25

Percentage of World Total
- U.S.S.R. 19
- FRANCE 18
- W. GERMANY 17
- U.K. 8
- SWITZERLAND 5
- U.S.A. 5
- BELGIUM 4
- NETHERLANDS 
- E. GERMANY 3
- OTHERS 18

### BEER PRODUCTION
World Production
million hectolitres
1974-1976 average
753·8

Percentage of World Total
- U.S.A. 24
- W.GERMANY 12
- U.K. 8
- U.S.S.R. 7
- JAPAN 
- FRANCE 
- MEXICO 
- E.GERMANY 
- CANADA 3
- CZECHOSLOVAKIA 3
- OTHERS 29

## FRUITS
- Apple Production
- Citrus Fruits Production

*Continued at foot of map*

- A Apples
- B Bananas
- F Figs
- G Grapefruit
- L Lemons
- Li Limes
- M Melons
- O Oranges
- Pe Peaches
- Pr Pears
- Pi Pineapples
- P Plums

*For distribution of Grapes & Dates see p.v, for Olives see p.viii*

← Hawaii

Trade Flow of Citrus Fruits    Flow lines do not show exact routes

### CITRUS FRUITS
World Production
million tonnes
1974-1976 average
49·2

Percentage of World Total
- U.S.A. 26
- BRAZIL 14
- JAPAN 9
- MEXICO 6
- ITALY 6
- SPAIN 6
- ISRAEL 4
- ARGENTINA 3
- INDIA 3
- CHINA 3
- EGYPT 2
- MOROCCO 
- S. AFRICA 
- OTHERS 14

### BANANAS
World Production
million tonnes
1974-1976 average
37·5

Percentage of World Total
- BRAZIL 20
- INDIA 9
- INDONESIA 8
- ECUADOR 8
- HONDURAS 4
- PHILIPPINES 4
- THAILAND 4
- MEXICO 3
- COSTA RICA 3
- OTHERS 37

### APPLES
World Production
million tonnes
1974-1976 average
22·5

Percentage of World Total
- FRANCE 14
- U.S.A. 13
- ITALY 9
- W. GERMANY 7
- SPAIN 
- TURKEY 
- JAPAN 4
- HUNGARY 
- POLAND 
- ARGENTINA 
- INDIA 
- OTHERS 31

### PEARS
World Production
million tonnes
1974-1976 average
7·45

Percentage of World Total
- ITALY 20
- CHINA 14
- U.S.A. 9
- JAPAN 7
- SPAIN 6
- FRANCE 6
- W. GERMANY 5
- TURKEY 
- AUSTRALIA 
- BULGARIA 2
- OTHERS 26

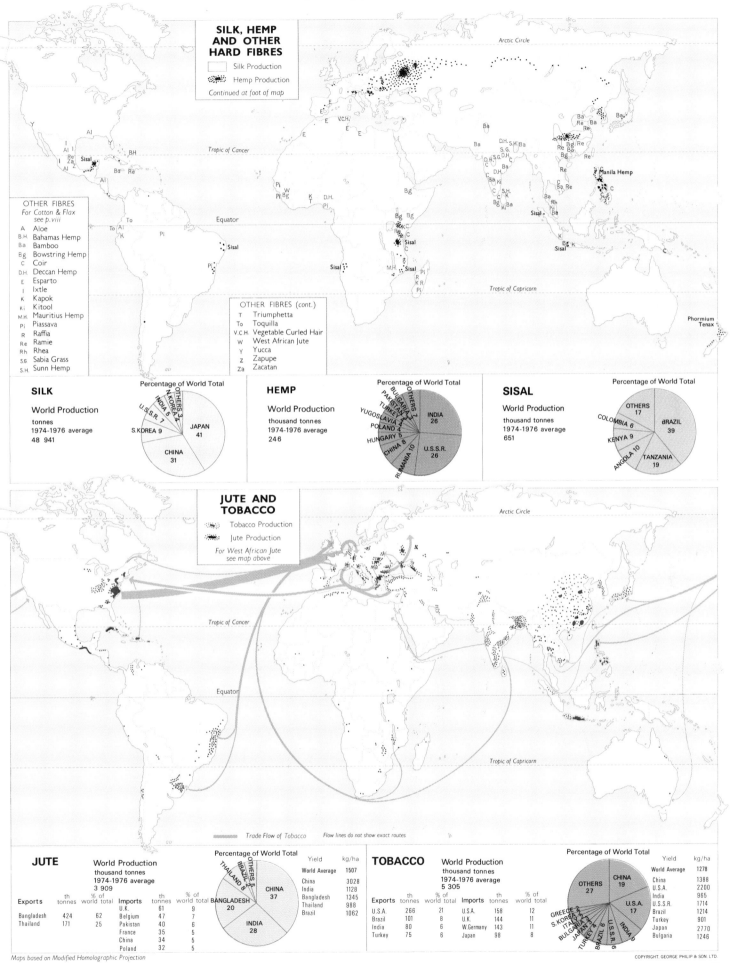

**SILK, HEMP AND OTHER HARD FIBRES**

☐ Silk Production
⠿ Hemp Production
*Continued at foot of map*

**OTHER FIBRES**
*For Cotton & Flax see p.viii*

A   Aloe
B.H. Bahamas Hemp
Ba  Bamboo
Bg  Bowstring Hemp
C   Coir
D.H. Deccan Hemp
E   Esparto
I   Ixtle
K   Kapok
Ki  Kitool
M.H. Mauritius Hemp
Pi  Piassava
R   Raffia
Re  Ramie
Rh  Rhea
S.G. Sabia Grass
S.H. Sunn Hemp

**OTHER FIBRES (cont.)**

T    Triumphetta
To   Toquilla
V.C.H. Vegetable Curled Hair
W    West African Jute
Y    Yucca
Z    Zapupe
Za   Zacatan

Arctic Circle
Tropic of Cancer
Equator
Tropic of Capricorn

Manila Hemp
Sisal
Phormium Tenax

**SILK**

World Production

tonnes
1974-1976 average
48 941

Percentage of World Total

JAPAN 41
CHINA 31
S.KOREA 9
U.S.S.R. 7
INDIA 5
N.KOREA 3
OTHERS 4

**HEMP**

World Production

thousand tonnes
1974-1976 average
246

Percentage of World Total

INDIA 26
U.S.S.R. 26
RUMANIA 10
CHINA 8
HUNGARY 5
POLAND 4
YUGOSLAVIA 4
TURKEY 4
PAKISTAN 4
BULGARIA 4
OTHERS 2

**SISAL**

World Production

thousand tonnes
1974-1976 average
651

Percentage of World Total

BRAZIL 39
TANZANIA 19
ANGOLA 10
KENYA 9
COLOMBIA 6
OTHERS 17

---

**JUTE AND TOBACCO**

⠿ Tobacco Production
⠿ Jute Production

*For West African Jute see map above*

Arctic Circle
Tropic of Cancer
Equator
Tropic of Capricorn

▬▬▬ *Trade Flow of Tobacco*   *Flow lines do not show exact routes*

**JUTE**

World Production
thousand tonnes
1974-1976 average
3 909

| Exports | th tonnes | % of world total | Imports | th tonnes | % of world total |
|---|---|---|---|---|---|
| Bangladesh | 424 | 62 | U.K. | 61 | 9 |
| Thailand | 171 | 25 | Belgium | 47 | 7 |
| | | | Pakistan | 40 | 6 |
| | | | France | 35 | 5 |
| | | | China | 34 | 5 |
| | | | Poland | 32 | 5 |

Percentage of World Total

CHINA 37
INDIA 28
BANGLADESH 20
THAILAND 8
BRAZIL 5
OTHERS 2

| Yield | kg/ha |
|---|---|
| World Average | 1507 |
| China | 3028 |
| India | 1128 |
| Bangladesh | 1345 |
| Thailand | 988 |
| Brazil | 1062 |

**TOBACCO**

World Production
thousand tonnes
1974-1976 average
5 305

| Exports | th tonnes | % of world total | Imports | th tonnes | % of world total |
|---|---|---|---|---|---|
| U.S.A. | 266 | 21 | U.S.A. | 158 | 12 |
| Brazil | 101 | 8 | U.K. | 144 | 11 |
| India | 80 | 6 | W.Germany | 143 | 11 |
| Turkey | 75 | 6 | Japan | 98 | 8 |

Percentage of World Total

CHINA 19
U.S.A. 17
OTHERS 27
GREECE
S.KOREA
ITALY
BULGARIA 4
JAPAN 4
TURKEY 4
BRAZIL 6
U.S.S.R. 6
INDIA 9

| Yield | kg/ha |
|---|---|
| World Average | 1278 |
| China | 1388 |
| U.S.A. | 2200 |
| India | 965 |
| U.S.S.R. | 1714 |
| Brazil | 1214 |
| Turkey | 901 |
| Japan | 2770 |
| Bulgaria | 1246 |

*Maps based on Modified Homolographic Projection*

Equatorial Scale 1:170 000 000

# THE WORLD : Cotton, Flax, Oil Seeds and Vegetable Oils

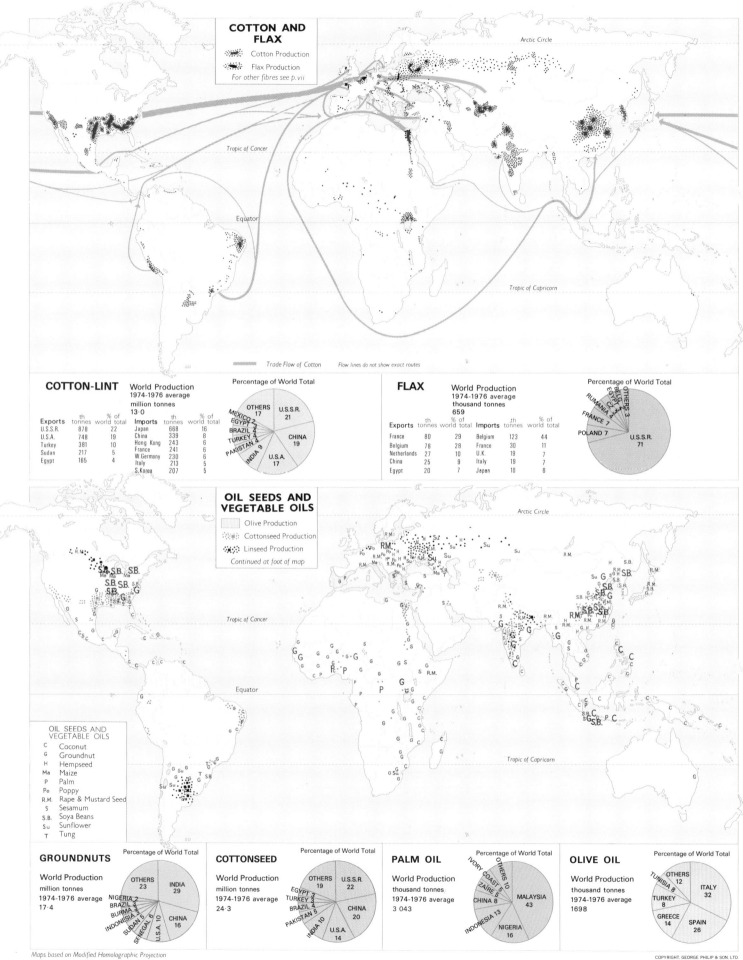

**COTTON AND FLAX**

- Cotton Production
- Flax Production

*For other fibres see p.vii*

Arctic Circle
Tropic of Cancer
Equator
Tropic of Capricorn

─────── Trade Flow of Cotton    Flow lines do not show exact routes

## COTTON-LINT

World Production
1974-1976 average
million tonnes
13·0

| Exports | th tonnes | % of world total | Imports | th tonnes | % of world total |
|---|---|---|---|---|---|
| U.S.S.R. | 878 | 22 | Japan | 668 | 16 |
| U.S.A. | 748 | 19 | China | 339 | 8 |
| Turkey | 381 | 10 | Hong Kong | 243 | 6 |
| Sudan | 217 | 5 | France | 241 | 6 |
| Egypt | 165 | 4 | W.Germany | 230 | 6 |
| | | | Italy | 213 | 5 |
| | | | S.Korea | 207 | 5 |

**Percentage of World Total**

OTHERS 17 · U.S.S.R. 21 · MEXICO 2 · EGYPT 2 · BRAZIL 4 · TURKEY 4 · PAKISTAN 4 · INDIA 9 · CHINA 19 · U.S.A. 17

## FLAX

World Production
1974-1976 average
thousand tonnes
659

| Exports | th tonnes | % of world total | Imports | th tonnes | % of world total |
|---|---|---|---|---|---|
| France | 80 | 29 | Belgium | 123 | 44 |
| Belgium | 78 | 28 | France | 30 | 11 |
| Netherlands | 27 | 10 | U.K. | 19 | 7 |
| China | 25 | 9 | Italy | 19 | 7 |
| Egypt | 20 | 7 | Japan | 10 | 8 |

**Percentage of World Total**

RUMANIA 2 · EGYPT 2 · BELG. 2 · CZ. 2 · OTHERS 3 · FRANCE 7 · POLAND 7 · U.S.S.R. 71

**OIL SEEDS AND VEGETABLE OILS**

- Olive Production
- Cottonseed Production
- Linseed Production

*Continued at foot of map*

Arctic Circle
Tropic of Cancer
Equator
Tropic of Capricorn

### OIL SEEDS AND VEGETABLE OILS

| | |
|---|---|
| C | Coconut |
| G | Groundnut |
| H | Hempseed |
| Ma | Maize |
| P | Palm |
| Po | Poppy |
| R.M. | Rape & Mustard Seed |
| S | Sesamum |
| S.B. | Soya Beans |
| Su | Sunflower |
| T | Tung |

## GROUNDNUTS

World Production
million tonnes
1974-1976 average
17·4

**Percentage of World Total**

OTHERS 23 · INDIA 29 · NIGERIA 2 · BRAZIL 3 · BURMA 3 · INDONESIA 3 · SUDAN 5 · SENEGAL 6 · U.S.A. 10 · CHINA 16

## COTTONSEED

World Production
million tonnes
1974-1976 average
24·3

**Percentage of World Total**

OTHERS 19 · U.S.S.R. 22 · EGYPT 3 · TURKEY 3 · BRAZIL 5 · PAKISTAN 5 · INDIA 10 · U.S.A. 14 · CHINA 20

## PALM OIL

World Production
thousand tonnes
1974-1976 average
3 043

**Percentage of World Total**

IVORY COAST 5 · ZAIRE 5 · OTHERS 10 · CHINA 8 · MALAYSIA 43 · INDONESIA 13 · NIGERIA 16

## OLIVE OIL

World Production
thousand tonnes
1974-1976 average
1698

**Percentage of World Total**

TUNISIA 8 · OTHERS 12 · ITALY 32 · TURKEY 8 · GREECE 14 · SPAIN 26

*Maps based on Modified Homolographic Projection*

Equatorial Scale 1:170 000 000

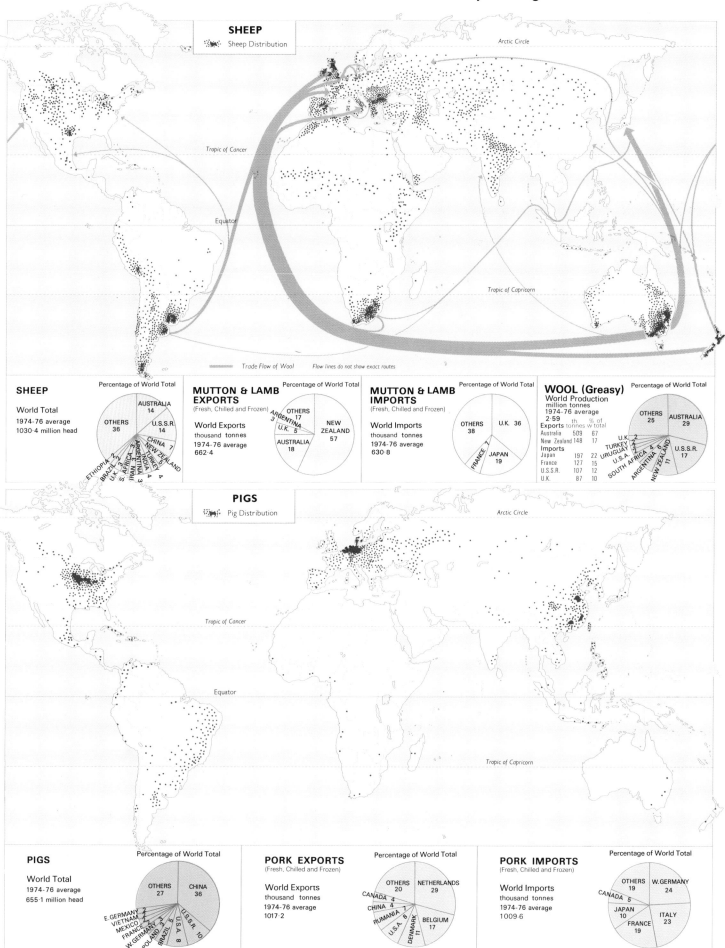

**SHEEP**
Sheep Distribution

Trade Flow of Wool    Flow lines do not show exact routes

**SHEEP**

World Total
1974-76 average
1030·4 million head

Percentage of World Total

AUSTRALIA 14
OTHERS 36
U.S.S.R. 14
CHINA 7
NEW ZEALAND 4
INDIA 4
ARGENTINA 3
IRAN 3
S. AFRICA 2
U.K. 3
TURKEY 5
BRAZIL 2
ETHIOPIA 2

**MUTTON & LAMB EXPORTS**
(Fresh, Chilled and Frozen)

World Exports
thousand tonnes
1974-76 average
662·4

Percentage of World Total

OTHERS 3
ARGENTINA 17
U.K. 5
AUSTRALIA 18
NEW ZEALAND 57

**MUTTON & LAMB IMPORTS**
(Fresh, Chilled and Frozen)

World Imports
thousand tonnes
1974-76 average
630·8

Percentage of World Total

OTHERS 38
U.K. 36
FRANCE 7
JAPAN 19

**WOOL (Greasy)**
World Production
million tonnes
1974-76 average
2·59

| Exports | th. tonnes | % of w. total |
|---|---|---|
| Australia | 509 | 67 |
| New Zealand | 148 | 17 |

| Imports | | |
|---|---|---|
| Japan | 197 | 22 |
| France | 127 | 15 |
| U.S.S.R. | 107 | 12 |
| U.K. | 87 | 10 |

Percentage of World Total

OTHERS 25
AUSTRALIA 29
U.K. 2
TURKEY 2
URUGUAY 2
U.S.A. 2
SOUTH AFRICA 4
ARGENTINA 6
NEW ZEALAND 11
U.S.S.R. 17

**PIGS**
Pig Distribution

**PIGS**

World Total
1974-76 average
655·1 million head

Percentage of World Total

OTHERS 27
CHINA 36
E.GERMANY
VIETNAM
MEXICO
FRANCE
W.GERMANY
POLAND 3
BRAZIL 5
U.S.A. 8
U.S.S.R. 10

**PORK EXPORTS**
(Fresh, Chilled and Frozen)

World Exports
thousand tonnes
1974-76 average
1017·2

Percentage of World Total

OTHERS 20
NETHERLANDS 29
CANADA 4
CHINA 4
RUMANIA 7
U.S.A. 8
DENMARK 11
BELGIUM 17

**PORK IMPORTS**
(Fresh, Chilled and Frozen)

World Imports
thousand tonnes
1974-76 average
1009·6

Percentage of World Total

OTHERS 19
W.GERMANY 24
CANADA 5
JAPAN 10
ITALY 23
FRANCE 19

Maps based on Modified Homolographic Projection

Equatorial Scale 1:170 000 000

# THE WORLD : Cattle and Dairy Produce

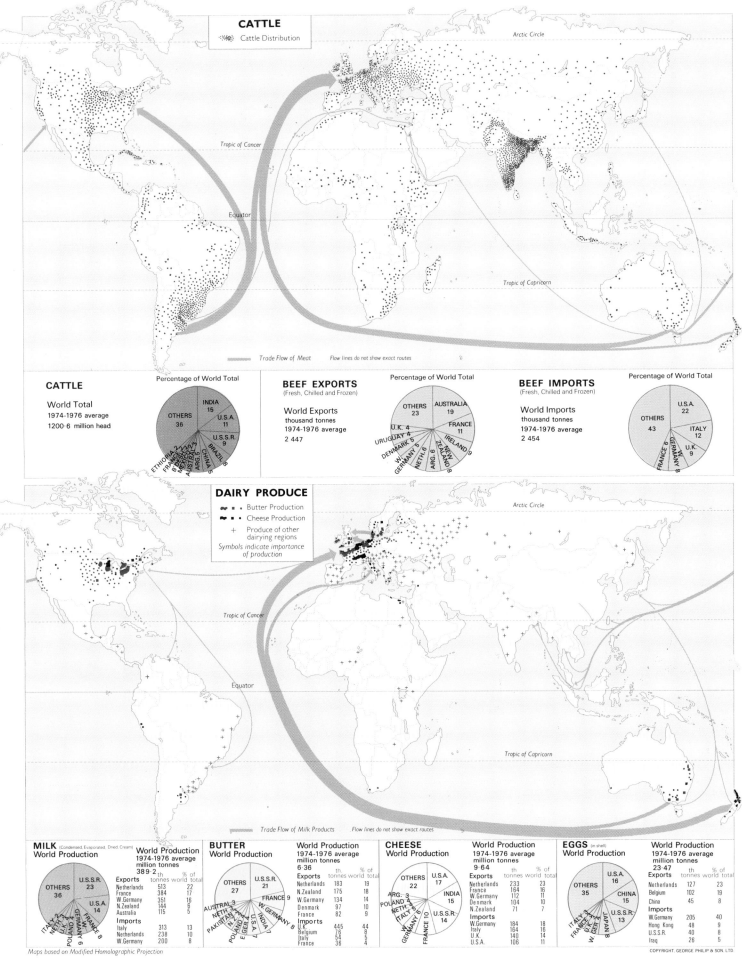

**CATTLE**
:::: Cattle Distribution

*Trade Flow of Meat*   *Flow lines do not show exact routes*

**CATTLE**

World Total
1974-1976 average
1200·6 million head

Percentage of World Total

- INDIA 15
- OTHERS 36
- U.S.A. 11
- U.S.S.R. 9
- BRAZIL 8
- CHINA 5
- ARG. 5
- AUSTRAL. 5
- MEXICO 3
- B.ECOL 2
- FRANCE 2
- ETHIOPIA 2

**BEEF EXPORTS**
(Fresh, Chilled and Frozen)

World Exports
thousand tonnes
1974-1976 average
2 447

Percentage of World Total

- OTHERS 23
- AUSTRALIA 19
- FRANCE 11
- U.K. 4
- URUGUAY 4
- DENMARK 5
- W.GERMANY 6
- NETH. 6
- ARG. 6
- NEW ZEALAND 8
- IRELAND 9

**BEEF IMPORTS**
(Fresh, Chilled and Frozen)

World Imports
thousand tonnes
1974-1976 average
2 454

Percentage of World Total

- OTHERS 43
- U.S.A. 22
- ITALY 12
- U.K. 9
- W.GERMANY 8
- FRANCE 6

**DAIRY PRODUCE**

- 🐄▪ Butter Production
- 🐄▪ Cheese Production
- + Produce of other dairying regions

*Symbols indicate importance of production*

*Trade Flow of Milk Products*   *Flow lines do not show exact routes*

**MILK** (Condensed, Evaporated, Dried, Cream)
World Production

World Production
1974-1976 average
million tonnes
389·2

- OTHERS 36
- U.S.S.R. 23
- U.S.A. 14
- FRANCE 8
- W.GERMANY 6
- POLAND 6
- U.K. 4
- NETH. 3
- ITALY 2

| Exports | th. tonnes | % of world total |
|---|---|---|
| Netherlands | 513 | 22 |
| France | 384 | 17 |
| W.Germany | 351 | 16 |
| N.Zealand | 144 | 6 |
| Australia | 115 | 5 |
| **Imports** | | |
| Italy | 313 | 13 |
| Netherlands | 238 | 10 |
| W.Germany | 200 | 8 |

**BUTTER**
World Production

World Production
1974-1976 average
million tonnes
6·36

- OTHERS 27
- U.S.S.R. 21
- FRANCE 9
- W.GERMANY 8
- INDIA 7
- U.S.A. 6
- E.GER. 5
- POLAND 4
- PAKISTAN 4
- N.Z. 4
- NETH. 3
- AUSTRAL. 3

| Exports | th. tonnes | % of world total |
|---|---|---|
| Netherlands | 183 | 19 |
| N.Zealand | 175 | 18 |
| W.Germany | 134 | 14 |
| Denmark | 97 | 10 |
| France | 82 | 9 |
| **Imports** | | |
| U.K. | 445 | 44 |
| Belgium | 76 | 8 |
| Italy | 54 | 5 |
| France | 36 | 4 |

**CHEESE**
World Production

World Production
1974-1976 average
million tonnes
9·64

- OTHERS 22
- U.S.A. 17
- INDIA 15
- U.S.S.R. 14
- FRANCE 10
- GERMANY 6
- ITALY 5
- NETH. 3
- POLAND 4
- ARG. 3

| Exports | th. tonnes | % of world total |
|---|---|---|
| Netherlands | 233 | 23 |
| France | 164 | 16 |
| W.Germany | 112 | 11 |
| Denmark | 104 | 10 |
| N.Zealand | 71 | 7 |
| **Imports** | | |
| W.Germany | 184 | 18 |
| Italy | 164 | 16 |
| U.K. | 140 | 14 |
| U.S.A. | 106 | 11 |

**EGGS** (in shell)
World Production

World Production
1974-1976 average
million tonnes
23·47

- OTHERS 35
- U.S.A. 16
- CHINA 15
- U.S.S.R. 13
- JAPAN 8
- W.GER. 3
- FRANCE 3
- U.K. 3
- ITALY 3

| Exports | th. tonnes | % of world total |
|---|---|---|
| Netherlands | 127 | 23 |
| Belgium | 102 | 19 |
| China | 45 | 8 |
| **Imports** | | |
| W.Germany | 205 | 40 |
| Hong Kong | 48 | 9 |
| U.S.S.R. | 40 | 8 |
| Iraq | 26 | 5 |

*Maps based on Modified Homolographic Projection*

Equatorial Scale 1:170 000 000

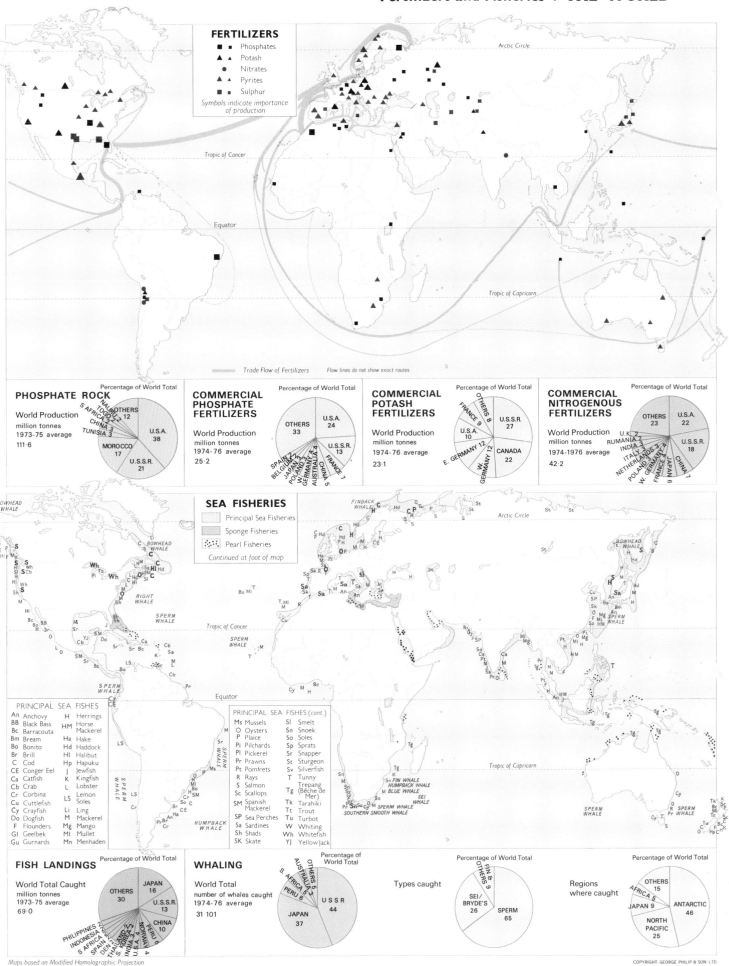

### FERTILIZERS

- ■ Phosphates
- ▲ Potash
- ● Nitrates
- ▲ Pyrites
- ■ Sulphur

*Symbols indicate importance of production*

Trade Flow of Fertilizers    Flow lines do not show exact routes

### PHOSPHATE ROCK

World Production
million tonnes
1973-75 average
111·6

*Percentage of World Total*

- NAURU 2
- OTHERS 12
- TOGO 3
- S AFRICA 3
- CHINA 3
- TUNISIA 3
- U.S.A. 38
- MOROCCO 17
- U.S.S.R. 21

### COMMERCIAL PHOSPHATE FERTILIZERS

World Production
million tonnes
1974-76 average
25·2

*Percentage of World Total*

- OTHERS 33
- U.S.A. 24
- U.S.S.R. 13
- FRANCE 7
- CHINA 5
- AUSTRALIA 4
- W.GERMANY 3
- POLAND 3
- JAPAN 3
- BELGIUM 2
- SPAIN 2

### COMMERCIAL POTASH FERTILIZERS

World Production
million tonnes
1974-76 average
23·1

*Percentage of World Total*

- OTHERS 8
- FRANCE 9
- U.S.A. 10
- E. GERMANY 12
- W. GERMANY 12
- U.S.S.R. 27
- CANADA 22

### COMMERCIAL NITROGENOUS FERTILIZERS

World Production
million tonnes
1974-1976 average
42·2

*Percentage of World Total*

- OTHERS 23
- U.K. 2
- RUMANIA 3
- INDIA 3
- ITALY 3
- NETHERLANDS 3
- POLAND 3
- W. GERMANY 4
- FRANCE 4
- JAPAN 6
- CHINA 7
- U.S.A. 22
- U.S.S.R. 18

### SEA FISHERIES

- Principal Sea Fisheries
- Sponge Fisheries
- Pearl Fisheries

*Continued at foot of map*

### PRINCIPAL SEA FISHES

| | | | |
|---|---|---|---|
| An | Anchovy | H | Herrings |
| BB | Black Bass | HM | Horse Mackerel |
| Bc | Barracouta | | |
| Bm | Bream | Ha | Hake |
| Bo | Bonito | Hd | Haddock |
| Br | Brill | Hl | Halibut |
| C | Cod | Hp | Hapuku |
| CE | Conger Eel | J | Jewfish |
| Ca | Catfish | K | Kingfish |
| Cb | Crab | L | Lobster |
| Cr | Corbina | LS | Lemon Soles |
| Cu | Cuttlefish | Li | Ling |
| Cy | Crayfish | M | Mackerel |
| Do | Dogfish | Mg | Mango |
| F | Flounders | Ml | Mullet |
| Gl | Geelbek | Mn | Menhaden |
| Gu | Gurnards | | |

### PRINCIPAL SEA FISHES (cont.)

| | | | |
|---|---|---|---|
| Ms | Mussels | Sl | Smelt |
| O | Oysters | Sn | Snoek |
| P | Plaice | So | Soles |
| Pi | Pilchards | Sp | Sprats |
| Pl | Pickerel | Sr | Snapper |
| Pr | Prawns | St | Sturgeon |
| Pt | Pomfrets | Sv | Silverfish |
| R | Rays | T | Tunny |
| S | Salmon | Tg | Trepang (Bêche de Mer) |
| Sc | Scallops | | |
| SM | Spanish Mackerel | Tk | Tarahiki |
| | | Tt | Trout |
| SP | Sea Perches | Tu | Turbot |
| Sa | Sardines | W | Whiting |
| Sh | Shads | Wh | Whitefish |
| SK | Skate | YJ | Yellow Jack |

### FISH LANDINGS

World Total Caught
million tonnes
1973-75 average
69·0

*Percentage of World Total*

- OTHERS 30
- JAPAN 16
- U.S.S.R. 13
- CHINA 10
- NORWAY 3
- INDIA 4
- S. KOREA 3
- THAILAND 3
- DENMARK 2
- SPAIN 2
- S AFRICA 2
- INDONESIA 2
- PHILIPPINES 2
- PERU 8

### WHALING

World Total
number of whales caught
1974-76 average
31 101

*Percentage of World Total*

- OTHERS 5
- S AFRICA 3
- AUSTRALIA 5
- PERU 6
- USSR 44
- JAPAN 37

*Types caught*

*Percentage of World Total*

- FIN 8
- OTHERS 1
- SEI/BRYDE'S 26
- SPERM 65

*Regions where caught*

*Percentage of World Total*

- OTHERS 15
- AFRICA 5
- JAPAN 9
- NORTH PACIFIC 25
- ANTARCTIC 46

Maps based on Modified Homolographic Projection

Equatorial Scale 1:170 000 000

# THE WORLD : Timber

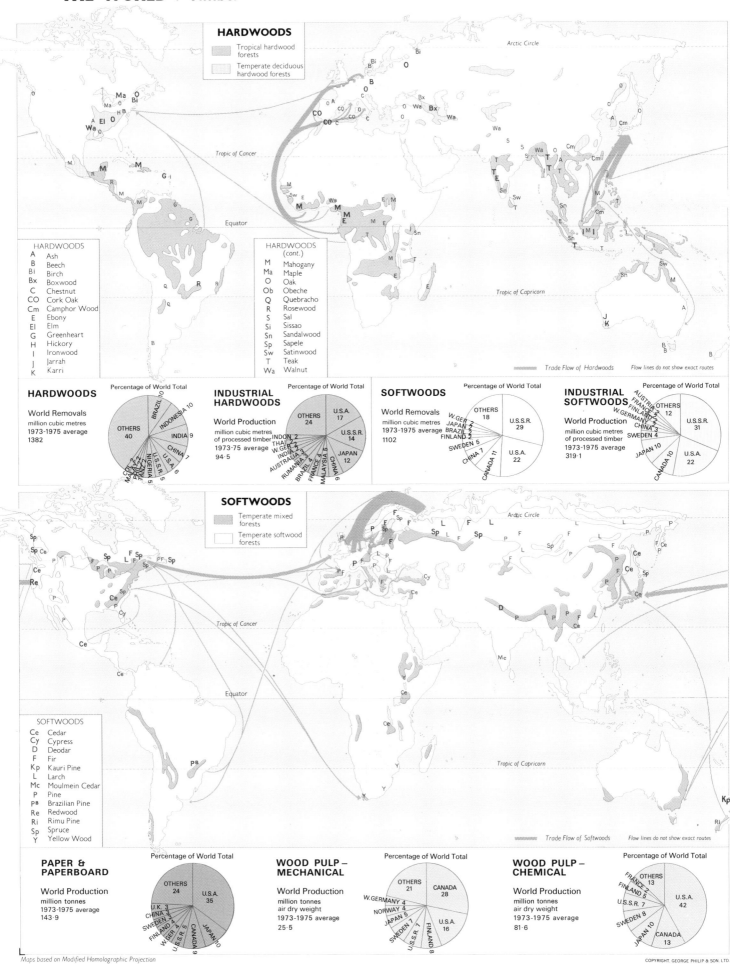

## HARDWOODS
- Tropical hardwood forests
- Temperate deciduous hardwood forests

### HARDWOODS
| | |
|---|---|
| A | Ash |
| B | Beech |
| Bi | Birch |
| Bx | Boxwood |
| C | Chestnut |
| CO | Cork Oak |
| Cm | Camphor Wood |
| E | Ebony |
| El | Elm |
| G | Greenheart |
| H | Hickory |
| I | Ironwood |
| J | Jarrah |
| K | Karri |

### HARDWOODS (cont.)
| | |
|---|---|
| M | Mahogany |
| Ma | Maple |
| O | Oak |
| Ob | Obeche |
| Q | Quebracho |
| R | Rosewood |
| S | Sal |
| Si | Sissao |
| Sn | Sandalwood |
| Sp | Sapele |
| Sw | Satinwood |
| T | Teak |
| Wa | Walnut |

Trade Flow of Hardwoods — Flow lines do not show exact routes

### HARDWOODS
World Removals
million cubic metres
1973-1975 average
1382

Percentage of World Total
BRAZIL 10 / INDONESIA 10 / INDIA 9 / CHINA 7 / U.S.S.R. 6 / NIGERIA 5 / THAI. 3 / PHIL. 3 / M.C.D. 2 / OTHERS 40

### INDUSTRIAL HARDWOODS
World Production
million cubic metres
of processed timber
1973-75 average
94·5

Percentage of World Total
U.S.A. 17 / U.S.S.R. 14 / JAPAN 12 / CHINA 6 / MALAYSIA 4 / FRANCE 4 / BRAZIL 4 / RUMANIA / AUSTRALIA / INDIA / W.GER. / THAI. / INDON. 2 / OTHERS 24

### SOFTWOODS
World Removals
million cubic metres
1973-1975 average
1102

Percentage of World Total
U.S.S.R. 29 / U.S.A. 22 / CANADA 11 / CHINA 7 / SWEDEN 5 / FINLAND 2 / JAPAN 2 / W.GER. 2 / OTHERS 18

### INDUSTRIAL SOFTWOODS
World Production
million cubic metres
of processed timber
1973-1975 average
319·1

Percentage of World Total
U.S.S.R. 31 / U.S.A. 22 / CANADA 10 / JAPAN 10 / SWEDEN 4 / CHINA 3 / W.GERMANY 3 / FINLAND 2 / FRANCE 2 / AUSTRIA 2 / OTHERS 12

## SOFTWOODS
- Temperate mixed forests
- Temperate softwood forests

### SOFTWOODS
| | |
|---|---|
| Ce | Cedar |
| Cy | Cypress |
| D | Deodar |
| F | Fir |
| Kp | Kauri Pine |
| L | Larch |
| Mc | Moulmein Cedar |
| P | Pine |
| PB | Brazilian Pine |
| Re | Redwood |
| Ri | Rimu Pine |
| Sp | Spruce |
| Y | Yellow Wood |

Trade Flow of Softwoods — Flow lines do not show exact routes

### PAPER & PAPERBOARD
World Production
million tonnes
1973-1975 average
143·9

Percentage of World Total
U.S.A. 35 / JAPAN 10 / CANADA 9 / U.S.S.R. 6 / W.GER. 4 / FINLAND 3 / SWEDEN 3 / CHINA 3 / U.K. 3 / OTHERS 24

### WOOD PULP – MECHANICAL
World Production
million tonnes
air dry weight
1973-1975 average
25·5

Percentage of World Total
CANADA 28 / U.S.A. 16 / FINLAND 8 / U.S.S.R. 7 / SWEDEN 5 / JAPAN 7 / NORWAY 4 / W.GERMANY 4 / OTHERS 21

### WOOD PULP – CHEMICAL
World Production
million tonnes
air dry weight
1973-1975 average
81·6

Percentage of World Total
U.S.A. 42 / CANADA 13 / JAPAN 10 / SWEDEN 8 / U.S.S.R. 7 / FINLAND 5 / FRANCE 2 / OTHERS 13

Maps based on Modified Homolographic Projection

Equatorial Scale 1:170 000 000

# Coal, Oil, Natural Gas, Water Power and Uranium : **THE WORLD**

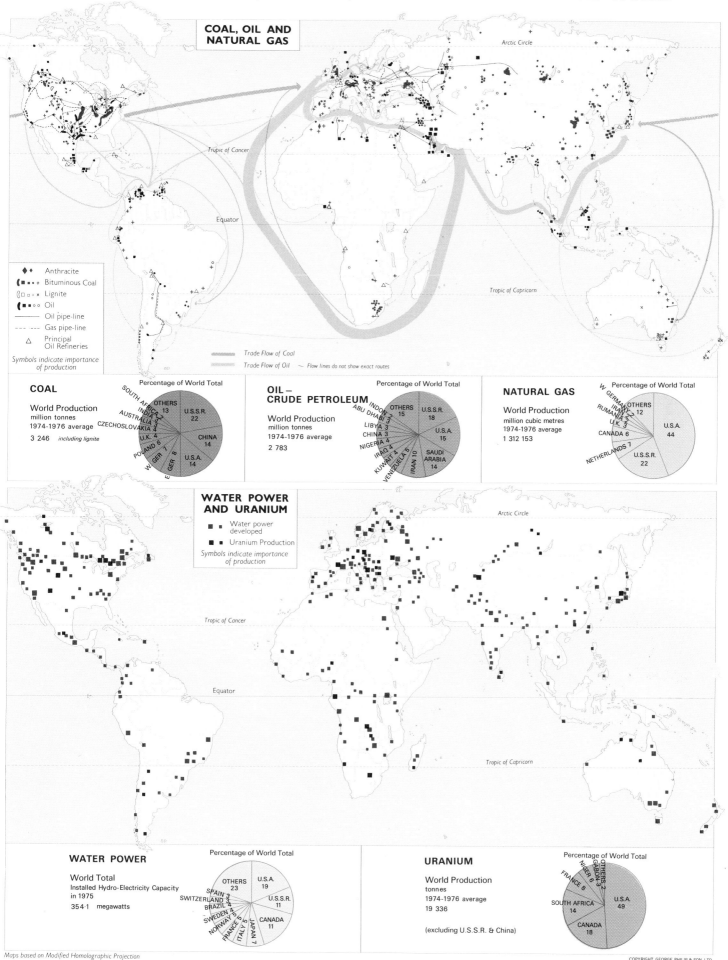

**COAL, OIL AND NATURAL GAS**

Arctic Circle

Tropic of Cancer

Equator

Tropic of Capricorn

♦ ♦ Anthracite
◖ ■ ■ ▪ ✱ Bituminous Coal
◖ □ ▫ ✕ Lignite
◖ ■ ▪ ○ Oil
—— Oil pipe-line
----- Gas pipe-line
△ Principal Oil Refineries

*Symbols indicate importance of production*

Trade Flow of Coal
Trade Flow of Oil — *Flow lines do not show exact routes*

## COAL

World Production
million tonnes
1974-1976 average

3 246 *including lignite*

Percentage of World Total

SOUTH AFRICA 3
INDIA 2
OTHERS 13
AUSTRALIA 2
CZECHOSLOVAKIA 4
U.K. 4
POLAND 6
W GER 7
E GER 8
U.S.A. 14
CHINA 14
U.S.S.R. 22

## OIL — CRUDE PETROLEUM

World Production
million tonnes
1974-1976 average

2 783

Percentage of World Total

INDON 2
ABU DHABI 3
LIBYA 3
CHINA 3
NIGERIA 4
IRAQ 4
KUWAIT 4
VENEZUELA 5
IRAN 10
OTHERS 15
U.S.S.R. 18
U.S.A. 15
SAUDI ARABIA 14

## NATURAL GAS

World Production
million cubic metres
1974-1976 average

1 312 153

Percentage of World Total

W GERMANY 2
IRAN 2
RUMANIA 3
U.K. 3
NETHERLANDS 7
CANADA 6
OTHERS 12
U.S.A. 44
U.S.S.R. 22

**WATER POWER AND URANIUM**

Arctic Circle

Tropic of Cancer

Equator

Tropic of Capricorn

■ ▪ Water power developed
■ ▪ Uranium Production

*Symbols indicate importance of production*

## WATER POWER

World Total
Installed Hydro-Electricity Capacity
in 1975

354·1 megawatts

Percentage of World Total

OTHERS 23
SPAIN 3
SWITZERLAND 4
BRAZIL 4
SWEDEN 4
NORWAY 5
FRANCE 5
ITALY 5
JAPAN 7
U.S.A. 19
U.S.S.R. 11
CANADA 11

## URANIUM

World Production
tonnes
1974-1976 average

19 336

(excluding U.S.S.R. & China)

Percentage of World Total

FRANCE 8
NIGER 6
GABON 3
OTHERS 2
SOUTH AFRICA 14
CANADA 18
U.S.A. 49

*Maps based on Modified Homolographic Projection*

Equatorial Scale 1:170 000 000

# THE WORLD : Iron, Manganese and other Ferro-Alloys

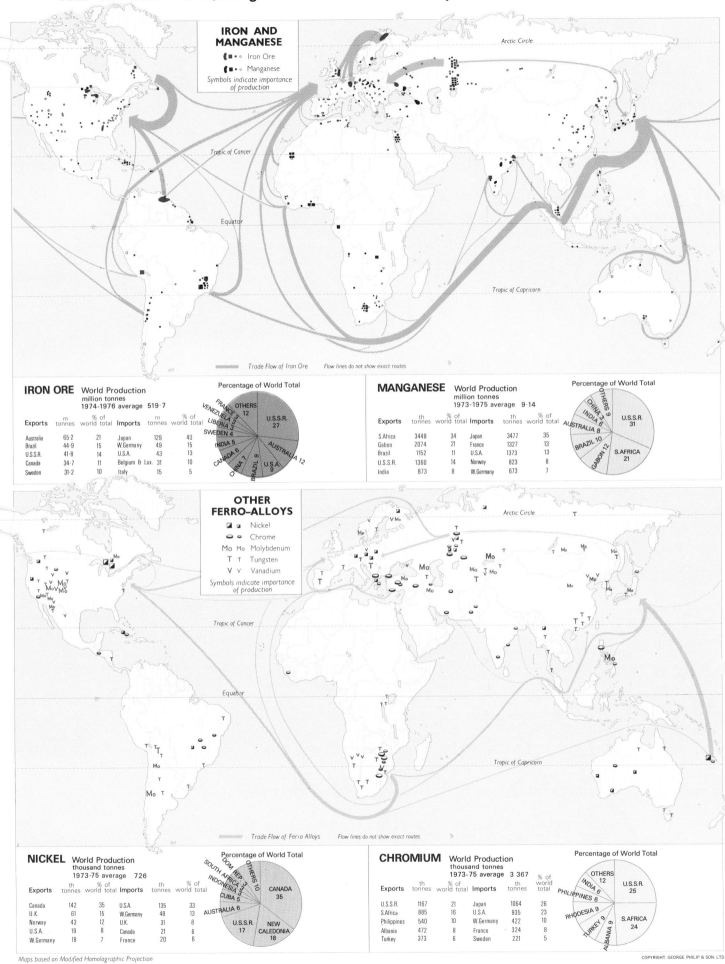

**IRON AND MANGANESE**

■● Iron Ore
■● Manganese

Symbols indicate importance of production

Arctic Circle
Tropic of Cancer
Equator
Tropic of Capricorn

Trade Flow of Iron Ore    Flow lines do not show exact routes

## IRON ORE World Production
million tonnes
1974-1976 average 519·7

| Exports | m tonnes | % of world total | Imports | m tonnes | % of world total |
|---|---|---|---|---|---|
| Australia | 65·2 | 21 | Japan | 129 | 40 |
| Brazil | 44·9 | 15 | W.Germany | 49 | 15 |
| U.S.S.R. | 41·8 | 14 | U.S.A. | 43 | 13 |
| Canada | 34·7 | 11 | Belgium & Lux. | 31 | 10 |
| Sweden | 31·2 | 10 | Italy | 15 | 5 |

Percentage of World Total

FRANCE 3
VENEZUELA 3
LIBERIA 3
SWEDEN 4
INDIA 5
CANADA 6
CHINA 7
BRAZIL 9
U.S.A. 9
AUSTRALIA 12
OTHERS 12
U.S.S.R. 27

## MANGANESE World Production
million tonnes
1973-1975 average 9·14

| Exports | th tonnes | % of world total | Imports | th tonnes | % of world total |
|---|---|---|---|---|---|
| S.Africa | 3449 | 34 | Japan | 3477 | 35 |
| Gabon | 2074 | 21 | France | 1327 | 13 |
| Brazil | 1152 | 11 | U.S.A. | 1373 | 13 |
| U.S.S.R. | 1360 | 14 | Norway | 823 | 8 |
| India | 873 | 8 | W.Germany | 673 | 7 |

Percentage of World Total

OTHERS 9
CHINA 3
INDIA 8
AUSTRALIA 3
BRAZIL 10
GABON 12
S.AFRICA 21
U.S.S.R. 31

---

# OTHER FERRO–ALLOYS

■▲ Nickel
●○ Chrome
Mo Mo Molybdenum
T T Tungsten
V v Vanadium

Symbols indicate importance of production

Arctic Circle
Tropic of Cancer
Equator
Tropic of Capricorn

Trade Flow of Ferro Alloys    Flow lines do not show exact routes

## NICKEL World Production
thousand tonnes
1973-75 average 726

| Exports | th tonnes | % of world total | Imports | th tonnes | % of world total |
|---|---|---|---|---|---|
| Canada | 142 | 35 | U.S.A. | 135 | 33 |
| U.K. | 61 | 15 | W.Germany | 48 | 13 |
| Norway | 43 | 12 | U.K. | 31 | 8 |
| U.S.A. | 19 | 8 | Canada | 21 | 6 |
| W.Germany | 18 | 7 | France | 20 | 6 |

Percentage of World Total

DOM. REP. 3
SOUTH AFRICA 5
INDONESIA 5
CUBA 5
AUSTRALIA 6
OTHERS 10
CANADA 35
U.S.S.R. 17
NEW CALEDONIA 18

## CHROMIUM World Production
thousand tonnes
1973-75 average 3 367

| Exports | th tonnes | % of world total | Imports | th tonnes | % of world total |
|---|---|---|---|---|---|
| U.S.S.R. | 1167 | 21 | Japan | 1064 | 26 |
| S.Africa | 885 | 16 | U.S.A. | 935 | 23 |
| Philippines | 540 | 10 | W.Germany | 422 | 10 |
| Albania | 472 | 8 | France | 324 | 8 |
| Turkey | 373 | 6 | Sweden | 221 | 5 |

Percentage of World Total

OTHERS 12
INDIA 6
PHILIPPINES 6
RHODESIA 9
TURKEY 9
ALBANIA 9
U.S.S.R. 25
S.AFRICA 24

Maps based on Modified Homolographic Projection

Equatorial Scale 1:170 000 000

# Copper, Lead, Tin, Zinc, Bauxite, Antimony, Mercury and Mica : THE WORLD

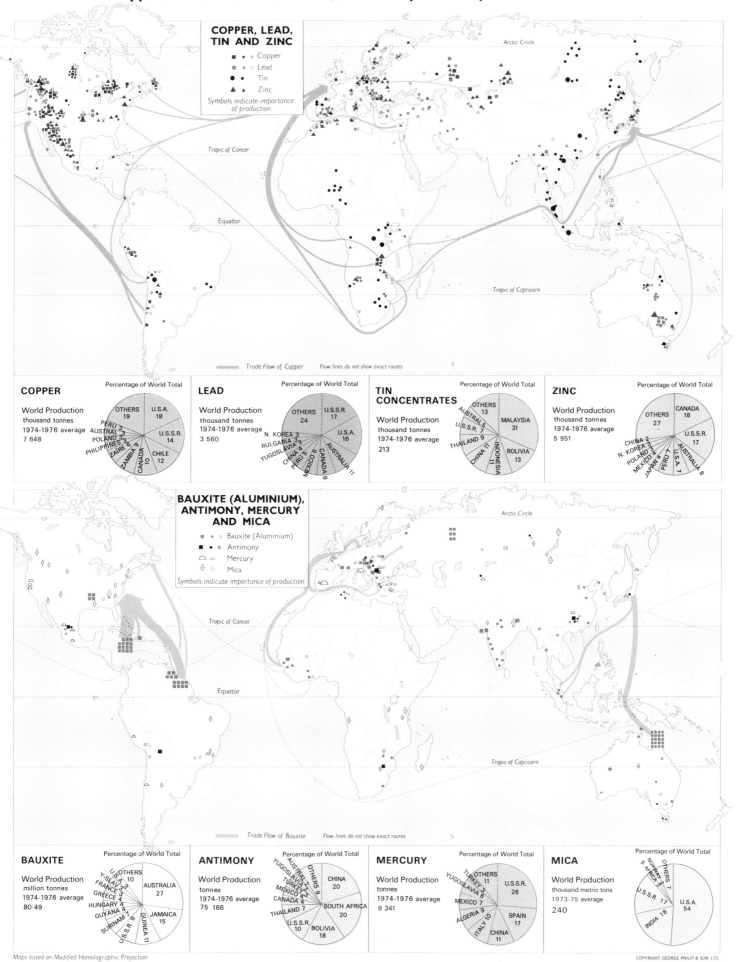

## COPPER, LEAD, TIN AND ZINC

- ■ □ ○ Copper
- ■ □ ○ Lead
- ● ○ Tin
- ▲ △ Zinc

Symbols indicate importance of production

Trade Flow of Copper    Flow lines do not show exact routes

### COPPER
World Production
thousand tonnes
1974-1976 average
7 648

Percentage of World Total

OTHERS 19 · U.S.A. 18 · U.S.S.R. 14 · CHILE 12 · CANADA 10 · ZAMBIA 9 · ZAIRE 6 · PHILIPPINES 5 · POLAND 3 · AUSTRAL 3 · PERU 3

### LEAD
World Production
thousand tonnes
1974-1976 average
3 560

Percentage of World Total

OTHERS 24 · U.S.S.R. 17 · U.S.A. 16 · AUSTRALIA 11 · CANADA 8 · MEXICO 6 · PERU 5 · CHINA 4 · YUGOSLAVIA 3 · BULGARIA 3 · N. KOREA 3

### TIN CONCENTRATES
World Production
thousand tonnes
1974-1976 average
213

Percentage of World Total

OTHERS 13 · MALAYSIA 31 · BOLIVIA 13 · INDONESIA 11 · CHINA 11 · THAILAND 9 · U.S.S.R. 7 · AUSTRAL 5

### ZINC
World Production
thousand tonnes
1974-1976 average
5 951

Percentage of World Total

OTHERS 27 · CANADA 18 · U.S.S.R. 17 · AUSTRALIA 8 · U.S.A. 7 · PERU 7 · JAPAN 4 · MEXICO 4 · POLAND 4 · N. KOREA 3 · CHINA 2

## BAUXITE (ALUMINIUM), ANTIMONY, MERCURY AND MICA

- ■ ● ○ Bauxite (Aluminium)
- ■ ● ○ Antimony
- ◠ ◠ Mercury
- ◇ ◇ Mica

Symbols indicate importance of production

Trade Flow of Bauxite    Flow lines do not show exact routes

### BAUXITE
World Production
million tonnes
1974-1976 average
80·49

Percentage of World Total

OTHERS 10 · AUSTRALIA 27 · JAMAICA 15 · GUINEA 11 · U.S.S.R. 9 · SURINAM 7 · GUYANA 4 · HUNGARY 4 · GREECE 3 · FRANCE 3 · Y-SLAV 3 · U.S. 3

### ANTIMONY
World Production
tonnes
1974-1976 average
75 166

Percentage of World Total

OTHERS 9 · CHINA 20 · SOUTH AFRICA 20 · BOLIVIA 18 · U.S.S.R. 10 · THAILAND 7 · CANADA 4 · MEXICO 4 · TURKEY 3 · YUGOSLAVIA 2 · AUSTRAL 3

### MERCURY
World Production
tonnes
1974-1976 average
9 341

Percentage of World Total

OTHERS 11 · U.S.S.R. 26 · SPAIN 17 · CHINA 11 · ITALY 10 · ALGERIA 9 · MEXICO 7 · YUGOSLAVIA 3 · TURKEY 6

### MICA
World Production
thousand metric tons
1973-75 average
240

Percentage of World Total

OTHERS 7 · U.S.A. 54 · INDIA 18 · U.S.S.R. 17 · S AFRICA 2 · NORWAY 2

Equatorial Scale 1:170 000 000

# THE WORLD : Gold, Silver, Platinum and Precious Stones

**GOLD, SILVER AND PLATINUM**

■ ● ○ Gold
■ ● ○ Silver
■ ● ○ Platinum

Symbols indicate importance of production

Mainly recovered from nickel matte

Arctic Circle
Tropic of Cancer
Equator
Tropic of Capricorn

## GOLD

World Production
tonnes
1974-1976 average
1047

Percentage of World Total

OTHERS 6
AUSTRALIA 2
PH. 2
PAPUA N.G. 2
GHANA 3
JAPAN 3
U.S.A. 4
CANADA 5
SOUTH AFRICA 74

## SILVER

World Production
tonnes
1974-1976 average
9 491

Percentage of World Total

U.S.S.R. 16
OTHERS 24
CANADA 13
JAPAN 3
AUSTRALIA 8
MEXICO 13
U.S.A. 11
PERU 12

## PLATINUM

World Production
tonnes
1973-75 average
174

Percentage of World Total

OTHERS 1
CANADA 7
S. AFRICA 47
U.S.S.R. 45

**PRECIOUS STONES**

▲ ▲ △ Diamonds
E E Emeralds
R R Rubies
S S Sapphires

Symbols indicate importance of production

Arctic Circle
Tropic of Cancer
Equator
Tropic of Capricorn

## DIAMONDS

World Production
million metric carats
1974-1976 average
44·2

Percentage of World Total

SIERRA LEONE 4
OTHERS 12
NAMIBIA 4
GHANA 5
BOTSWANA 6
ZAÏRE 30
SOUTH AFRICA 17
U.S.S.R. 22

## EMERALDS, RUBIES & SAPPHIRES

No reliable figures available

Equatorial Scale 1:170 000 000

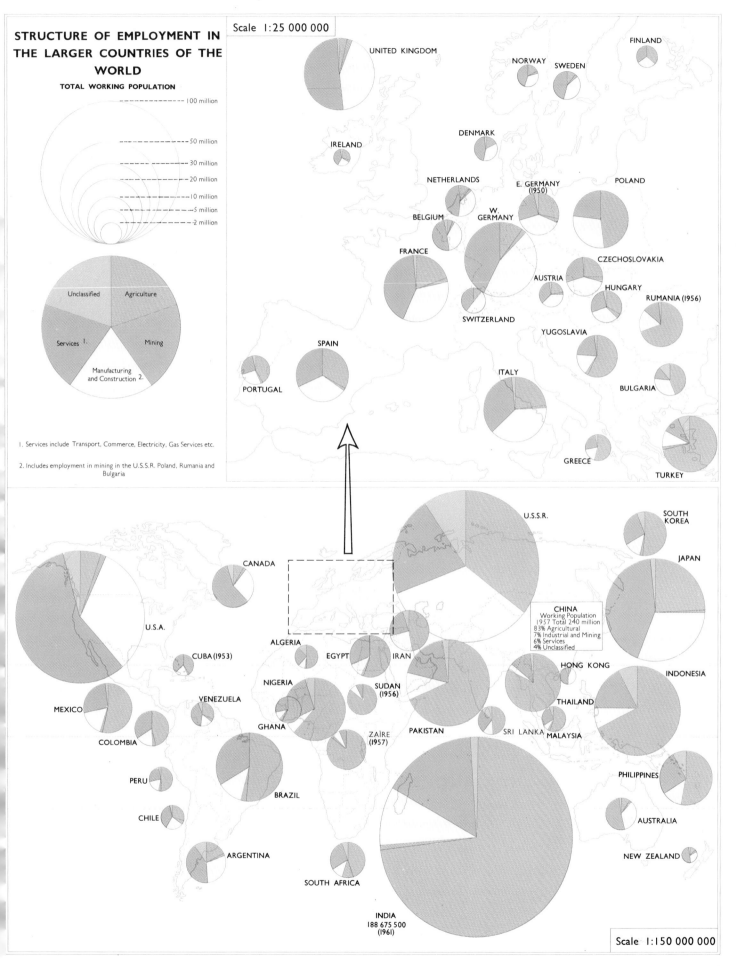

Scale 1:25 000 000

## STRUCTURE OF EMPLOYMENT IN THE LARGER COUNTRIES OF THE WORLD

### TOTAL WORKING POPULATION

- 100 million
- 50 million
- 30 million
- 20 million
- 10 million
- 5 million
- 2 million

Unclassified
Agriculture
Services 1.
Mining
Manufacturing and Construction 2.

1. Services include Transport, Commerce, Electricity, Gas Services etc.

2. Includes employment in mining in the U.S.S.R. Poland, Rumania and Bulgaria

UNITED KINGDOM
NORWAY
SWEDEN
FINLAND
IRELAND
DENMARK
NETHERLANDS
E. GERMANY (1950)
POLAND
BELGIUM
W. GERMANY
FRANCE
CZECHOSLOVAKIA
AUSTRIA
HUNGARY
SWITZERLAND
RUMANIA (1956)
SPAIN
YUGOSLAVIA
ITALY
BULGARIA
PORTUGAL
GREECE
TURKEY

U.S.S.R.
SOUTH KOREA
JAPAN
CANADA
U.S.A.
ALGERIA
EGYPT
IRAN

CHINA
Working Population
1957 Total 240 million
83% Agricultural
7% Industrial and Mining
6% Services
4% Unclassified

CUBA (1953)
NIGERIA
SUDAN (1956)
HONG KONG
INDONESIA
VENEZUELA
THAILAND
MEXICO
GHANA
ZAÏRE (1957)
PAKISTAN
SRI LANKA
MALAYSIA
COLOMBIA
PHILIPPINES
PERU
AUSTRALIA
CHILE
ARGENTINA
NEW ZEALAND
SOUTH AFRICA
INDIA
188 675 500
(1961)

Scale 1:150 000 000

# THE WORLD : Transport

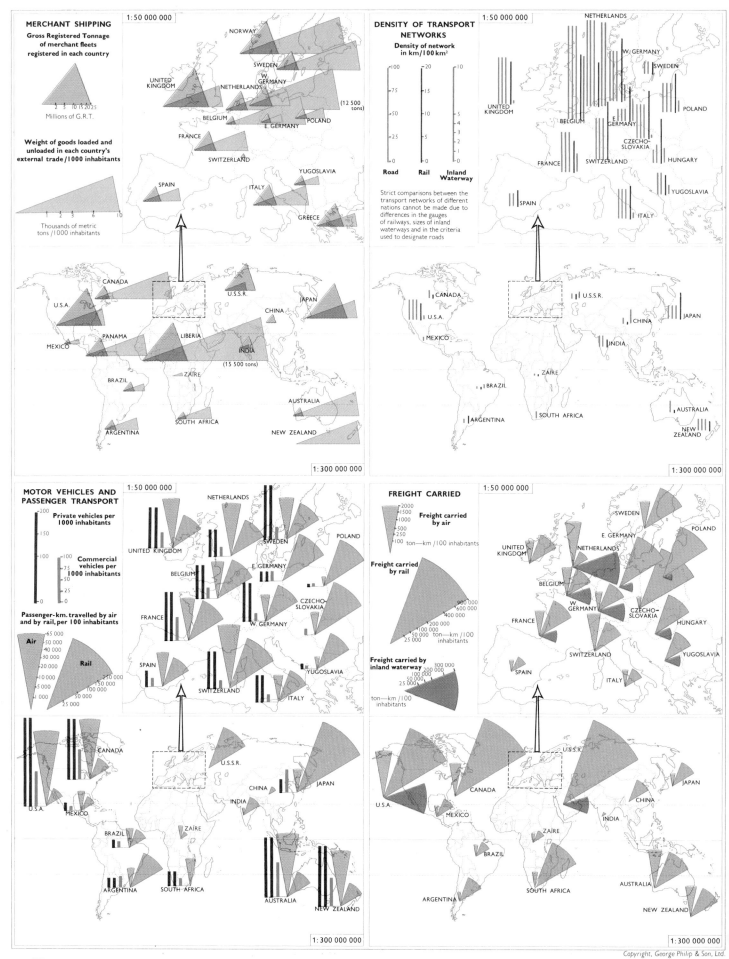

## MERCHANT SHIPPING

**Gross Registered Tonnage of merchant fleets registered in each country**

Millions of G.R.T.
2 3 10 15 20 25

**Weight of goods loaded and unloaded in each country's external trade/1000 inhabitants**

Thousands of metric tons /1000 inhabitants

1:50 000 000

1:300 000 000

## DENSITY OF TRANSPORT NETWORKS

**Density of network in km/100 km²**

Road   Rail   Inland Waterway

Strict comparisons between the transport networks of different nations cannot be made due to differences in the gauges of railways, sizes of inland waterways and in the criteria used to designate roads.

1:50 000 000

1:300 000 000

## MOTOR VEHICLES AND PASSENGER TRANSPORT

**Private vehicles per 1000 inhabitants**

**Commercial vehicles per 1000 inhabitants**

**Passenger-km. travelled by air and by rail, per 100 inhabitants**

Air        Rail

1:50 000 000

1:300 000 000

## FREIGHT CARRIED

**Freight carried by air**
ton—km /100 inhabitants

**Freight carried by rail**
ton—km /100 inhabitants

**Freight carried by inland waterway**
ton—km /100 inhabitants

1:50 000 000

1:300 000 000

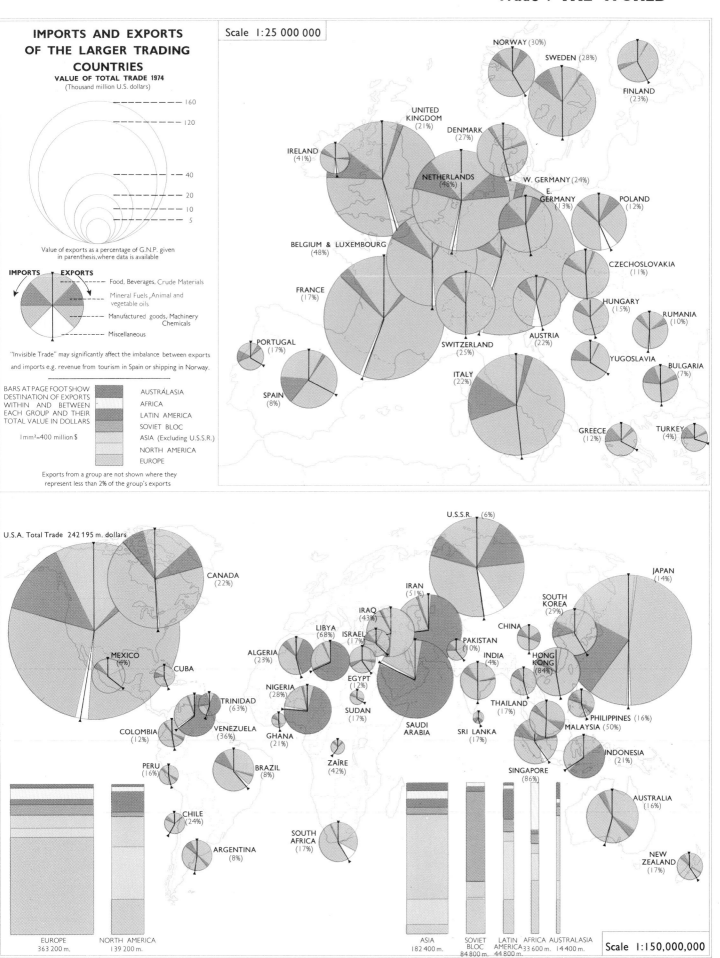

# IMPORTS AND EXPORTS OF THE LARGER TRADING COUNTRIES

**VALUE OF TOTAL TRADE 1974**
(Thousand million U.S. dollars)

Scale 1:25 000 000

Scale 1:150,000,000

**xix**

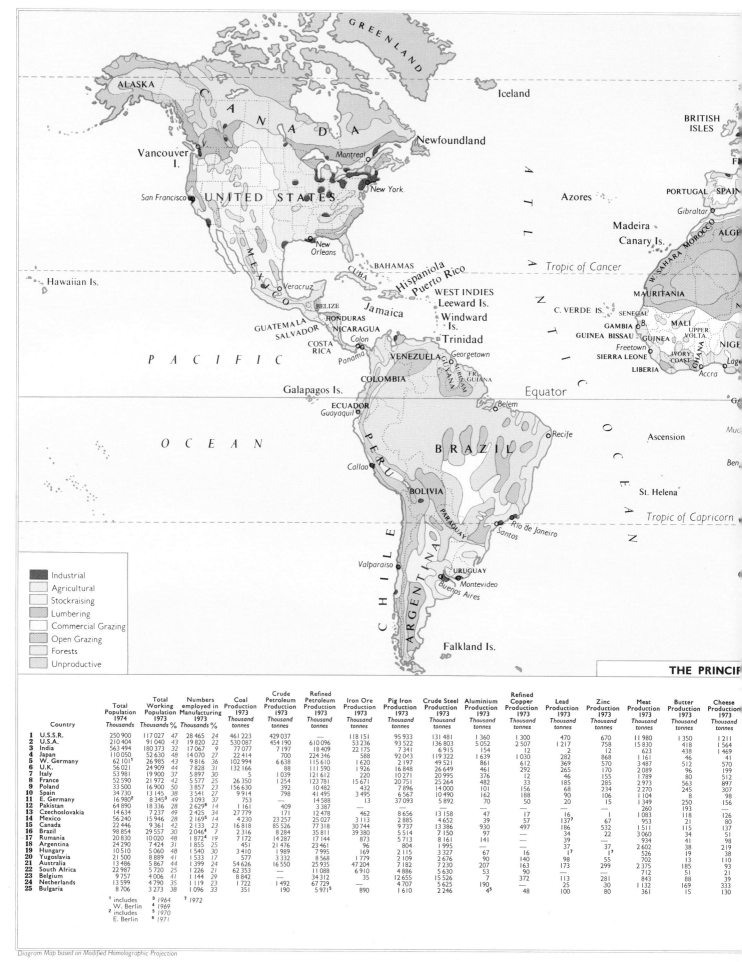

Legend:
- Industrial
- Agricultural
- Stockraising
- Lumbering
- Commercial Grazing
- Open Grazing
- Forests
- Unproductive

THE PRINCIP

| | Country | Total Population 1974 Thousands | Total Working Population 1973 Thousands | % | Numbers employed in Manufacturing 1973 Thousands | % | Coal Production 1973 Thousand tonnes | Crude Petroleum Production 1973 Thousand tonnes | Refined Petroleum Production 1973 Thousand tonnes | Iron Ore Production 1973 Thousand tonnes | Pig Iron Production 1973 Thousand tonnes | Crude Steel Production 1973 Thousand tonnes | Aluminium Production 1973 Thousand tonnes | Refined Copper Production 1973 Thousand tonnes | Lead Production 1973 Thousand tonnes | Zinc Production 1973 Thousand tonnes | Meat Production 1973 Thousand tonnes | Butter Production 1973 Thousand tonnes | Cheese Production 1973 Thousand tonnes |
|---|---|---|---|---|---|---|---|---|---|---|---|---|---|---|---|---|---|---|---|
| 1 | U.S.S.R. | 250 900 | 117 027 | 47 | 28 465 | 24 | 461 223 | 429 037 | — | 118 151 | 95 933 | 131 481 | 1 360 | 1 300 | 470 | 670 | 11 980 | 1 350 | 1 211 |
| 2 | U.S.A. | 210 404 | 91 040 | 43 | 19 820 | 22 | 530 087 | 454 190 | 610 096 | 53 236 | 93 522 | 136 803 | 5 052 | 2 507 | 1 217 | 758 | 15 830 | 418 | 1 564 |
| 3 | India | 563 494 | 180 373 | 32 | 17 067 | 9 | 77 077 | 7 197 | 18 409 | 22 175 | 7 341 | 6 915 | 154 | 12 | 2 | 12 | 623 | 438 | 1 469 |
| 4 | Japan | 110 050 | 52 630 | 48 | 14 070 | 27 | 22 414 | 700 | 224 346 | 588 | 92 043 | 119 322 | 1 639 | 1 030 | 282 | 868 | 1 161 | 46 | 41 |
| 5 | W. Germany | 62 101[1] | 26 985 | 43 | 9 816 | 36 | 102 994 | 6 638 | 115 610 | 1 620 | 2 197 | 49 521 | 861 | 612 | 369 | 570 | 3 487 | 512 | 570 |
| 6 | U.K. | 56 021 | 24 909 | 44 | 7 828 | 31 | 132 166 | 88 | 111 590 | 1 926 | 16 848 | 26 649 | 461 | 292 | 265 | 170 | 2 089 | 96 | 199 |
| 7 | Italy | 53 981 | 19 900 | 37 | 5 897 | 30 | 5 | 1 039 | 121 612 | 220 | 10 271 | 20 995 | 376 | 12 | 46 | 155 | 1 789 | 80 | 512 |
| 8 | France | 52 590 | 21 972 | 42 | 5 577 | 25 | 26 350 | 1 254 | 123 781 | 15 671 | 20 751 | 25 264 | 482 | 33 | 185 | 285 | 2 973 | 563 | 897 |
| 9 | Poland | 33 500 | 16 900 | 50 | 3 857 | 23 | 156 630 | 392 | 10 482 | 432 | 7 896 | 14 000 | 101 | 156 | 68 | 234 | 2 270 | 245 | 512 |
| 10 | Spain | 34 730 | 13 145 | 38 | 3 541 | 27 | 9 914 | 798 | 41 495 | 3 495 | 6 567 | 10 490 | 162 | 188 | 90 | 106 | 1 104 | 8 | 98 |
| 11 | E. Germany | 16 980[2] | 8 345[3] | 49 | 3 093 | 37 | 753 | — | 14 588 | 13 | 37 093 | 5 892 | 70 | 50 | 20 | 15 | 1 349 | 250 | 156 |
| 12 | Pakistan | 64 890 | 18 336 | 28 | 2 629[6] | 14 | 1 161 | 409 | 3 387 | — | | | | | | | 260 | 193 | |
| 13 | Czechoslovakia | 14 634 | 7 237 | 49 | 2 425 | 34 | 27 779 | 171 | 12 478 | 462 | 8 656 | 13 158 | 47 | 17 | 16 | 1 | 1 083 | 118 | 126 |
| 14 | Mexico | 56 240 | 15 946 | 28 | 2 169[5] | 14 | 4 230 | 23 257 | 25 027 | 3 113 | 2 885 | 4 652 | 39 | 57 | 137[7] | 67 | 953 | 21 | 80 |
| 15 | Canada | 22 446 | 9 361 | 42 | 2 133 | 23 | 16 818 | 85 526 | 77 318 | 30 744 | 9 737 | 13 386 | 930 | 497 | 186 | 532 | 1 511 | 115 | 137 |
| 16 | Brazil | 98 854 | 29 557 | 30 | 2 046[4] | 7 | 2 316 | 8 284 | 35 811 | 39 380 | 5 514 | 7 150 | 97 | — | 34 | 42 | 3 060 | 34 | 219 |
| 17 | Rumania | 20 830 | 10 020 | 48 | 1 872[4] | 19 | 7 172 | 14 287 | 17 144 | 873 | 5 713 | 8 161 | 141 | — | 39 | — | 934 | 41 | 51 |
| 18 | Argentina | 24 290 | 7 424 | 31 | 1 855 | 25 | 451 | 21 476 | 23 461 | 96 | 804 | 1 995 | — | — | 37 | 37 | 2 602 | 38 | 219 |
| 19 | Hungary | 10 510 | 5 060 | 48 | 1 540 | 30 | 3 410 | 1 989 | 7 995 | 169 | 2 115 | 3 327 | 67 | 16 | [7] | [7] | 526 | 19 | 38 |
| 20 | Yugoslavia | 21 500 | 8 889 | 41 | 1 533 | 17 | 577 | 3 332 | 8 568 | 1 779 | 2 109 | 2 676 | 90 | 140 | 98 | 55 | 702 | 13 | 110 |
| 21 | Australia | 13 486 | 5 867 | 44 | 1 399 | 24 | 54 626 | 16 550 | 25 935 | 47 204 | 7 182 | 7 230 | 207 | 163 | 173 | 299 | 2 375 | 185 | 93 |
| 22 | South Africa | 22 987 | 5 720 | 25 | 1 226 | 21 | 62 353 | — | 11 088 | 6 910 | 4 886 | 5 630 | 53 | 90 | — | — | 712 | 51 | 21 |
| 23 | Belgium | 9 757 | 4 006 | 41 | 1 144 | 29 | 8 842 | — | 34 312 | 35 | 12 655 | 15 526 | 7 | 372 | 113 | 281 | 843 | 88 | 39 |
| 24 | Netherlands | 13 599 | 4 790 | 35 | 1 119 | 23 | 1 722 | 1 492 | 67 729 | — | 4 707 | 5 625 | 190 | — | 25 | 30 | 1 132 | 169 | 333 |
| 25 | Bulgaria | 8 706 | 3 273 | 38 | 1 096 | 33 | 351 | 190 | 5 971[5] | 890 | 1 610 | 2 246 | 4[5] | 48 | 100 | 80 | 361 | 15 | 130 |

1 includes W. Berlin
2 includes E. Berlin
3 1964
4 1969
5 1970
6 1971
7 1972

Diagram Map based on Modified Homolographic Projection

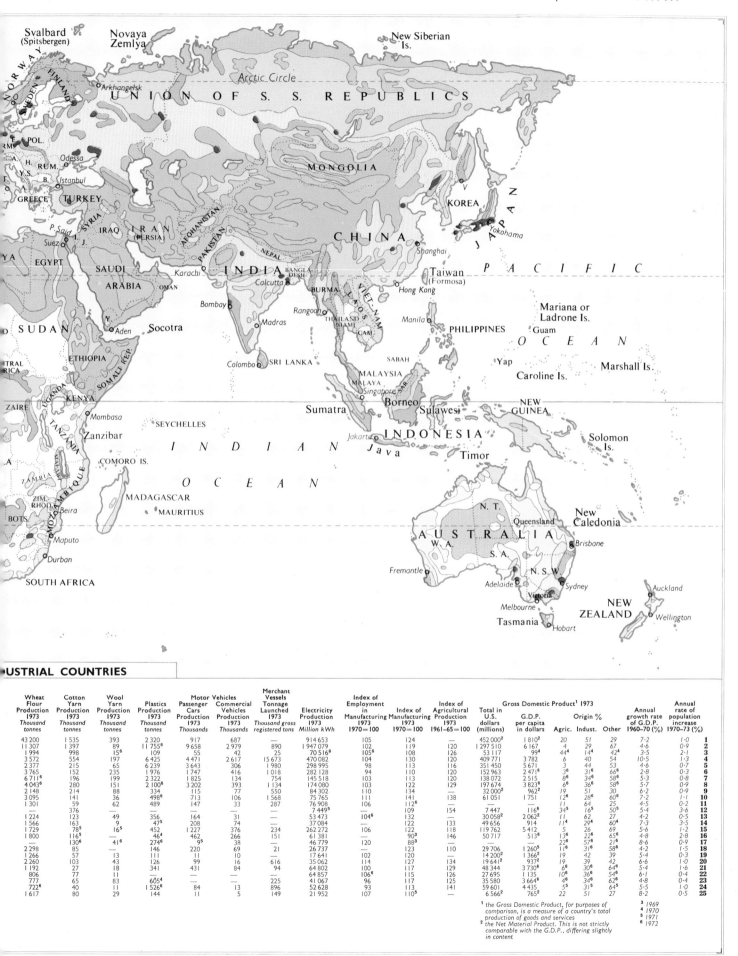

## USTRIAL COUNTRIES

| Wheat Flour Production 1973 Thousand tonnes | Cotton Yarn Production 1973 Thousand tonnes | Wool Yarn Production 1973 Thousand tonnes | Plastics Production 1973 Thousand tonnes | Motor Vehicles Passenger Cars Production 1973 Thousands | Motor Vehicles Commercial Vehicles Production 1973 Thousands | Merchant Vessels Tonnage Launched 1973 Thousand gross registered tons | Electricity Production 1973 Million kWh | Index of Employment in Manufacturing 1973 1970=100 | Index of Manufacturing 1973 1970=100 | Index of Agricultural Production 1973 1961–65=100 | G.D.P. Total in U.S. dollars (millions) | G.D.P. per capita in dollars | Origin % Agric. | Origin % Indust. | Origin % Other | Annual growth rate of G.D.P. 1960–70 (%) | Annual rate of population increase 1970–73 (%) | |
|---|---|---|---|---|---|---|---|---|---|---|---|---|---|---|---|---|---|---|
| 43 200 | 1 535 | 393 | 2 320 | 917 | 687 | — | 914 653 | 105 | 124 | — | 452 000[2] | 1 810[2] | 20 | 51 | 29 | 7·2 | 1·0 | 1 |
| 11 307 | 1 397 | 89 | 11 755[6] | 9 658 | 2 979 | 890 | 1 947 079 | 102 | 119 | 120 | 1 297 510 | 6 167 | 4 | 29 | 67 | 4·6 | 0·9 | 2 |
| 1 994 | 998 | 15[6] | 109 | 55 | 42 | 25 | 70 516[6] | 105[6] | 108 | 126 | 53 117 | 99[4] | 44[4] | 14[4] | 42[4] | 3·5 | 2·1 | 3 |
| 3 572 | 554 | 197 | 6 425 | 4 471 | 2 617 | 15 673 | 470 082 | 104 | 130 | 120 | 409 771 | 3 782 | 6 | 40 | 54 | 10·5 | 1·3 | 4 |
| 2 377 | 215 | 65 | 6 239 | 3 643 | 306 | 1 980 | 298 995 | 98 | 113 | 116 | 351 450 | 5 671 | 3 | 44 | 53 | 4·6 | 0·7 | 5 |
| 3 765 | 152 | 235 | 1 976 | 1 747 | 416 | 1 018 | 282 128 | 94 | 110 | 120 | 152 963 | 2 471[6] | 3[6] | 31[6] | 66[6] | 2·8 | 0·3 | 6 |
| 6 711[6] | 196 | 199 | 2 322 | 1 825 | 134 | 754 | 145 518 | 103 | 113 | 120 | 138 072 | 2 515 | 8[6] | 34[6] | 58[6] | 5·3 | 0·8 | 7 |
| 4 043[6] | 280 | 151 | 2 100[6] | 3 202 | 393 | 1 134 | 174 080 | 103 | 122 | 129 | 197 674 | 3 823[6] | 6[6] | 36[6] | 58[6] | 5·7 | 0·9 | 8 |
| 2 148 | 214 | 88 | 334 | 115 | 77 | 550 | 84 302 | 110 | 134 | — | 32 000[2] | 962[2] | 19 | 51 | 30 | 6·2 | 0·9 | 9 |
| 3 095 | 141 | 36 | 498[6] | 713 | 106 | 1 568 | 75 765 | 111 | 141 | 138 | 61 051 | 1 751 | 12[6] | 28[6] | 60[6] | 7·2 | 1·1 | 10 |
| 1 301 | 59 | 62 | 489 | 147 | 33 | 287 | 76 908 | 106 | 112[6] | — | — | — | 11 | 64 | 25 | 4·5 | 0·2 | 11 |
| — | 376 | — | — | — | — | — | 7 449[5] | — | 109 | 154 | 7 447 | 1 116[6] | 34[5] | 16[5] | 50[5] | 5·4 | 3·6 | 12 |
| 1 224 | 123 | 49 | 356 | 164 | 31 | — | 53 473 | 104[6] | 132 | — | 30 058[2] | 2 062[2] | 11 | 62 | 27 | 4·2 | 0·5 | 13 |
| 1 566 | 163 | 9 | 475 | 208 | 74 | — | 37 084 | — | 122 | 133 | 49 656 | 914 | 11[4] | 29[4] | 60[4] | 7·3 | 3·5 | 14 |
| 1 729 | 78[5] | 16[5] | 452 | 1 227 | 376 | 234 | 262 272 | 106 | 122 | 118 | 119 762 | 5 412 | 5 | 26 | 69 | 5·6 | 1·2 | 15 |
| 1 800 | 116[5] | — | 46[4] | 462 | 266 | 151 | 61 381 | — | 90[3] | 146 | 50 717 | 513[6] | 13[6] | 22[6] | 65[6] | 4·8 | 2·8 | 16 |
| — | 130[6] | 41[6] | 274[6] | 9[5] | 38 | — | 46 779 | 120 | — | 88[3] | — | — | 22[6] | 57[6] | 21[6] | 8·6 | 0·9 | 17 |
| 2 298 | 85 | — | 146 | 220 | 69 | 21 | 26 737 | — | 123 | 110 | 29 706 | 1 260[5] | 11[6] | 31[6] | 58[6] | 4·2 | 1·5 | 18 |
| 1 266 | 57 | 13 | 111 | 11 | 10 | — | 17 641 | 102 | 120 | — | 14 200[2] | 1 366[2] | 19 | 42 | 39 | 5·4 | 0·3 | 19 |
| 2 260 | 103 | 43 | 126 | 99 | 16 | 616 | 35 062 | 114 | 127 | 134 | 19 641[2] | 937[2] | 19 | 39 | 42 | 6·6 | 1·0 | 20 |
| 1 192 | 27 | 18 | 341 | 431 | 84 | 94 | 64 802 | 100 | 117 | 129 | 48 344 | 3 730[6] | 6[6] | 30[6] | 64[6] | 5·4 | 1·6 | 21 |
| 806 | 77 | 11 | — | — | — | — | 64 857 | 106[6] | 115 | 126 | 27 695 | 1 135 | 10[6] | 36[6] | 54[6] | 6·1 | 0·4 | 22 |
| 777 | 65 | 83 | 605[4] | — | — | 225 | 41 067 | 96 | 115 | 125 | 35 580 | 3 664[6] | 4[6] | 34[6] | 62[6] | 4·8 | 0·4 | 23 |
| 722[6] | 40 | 11 | 1 526[6] | 84 | 13 | 896 | 52 628 | 93 | 113 | 141 | 59 601 | 4 435 | 5[5] | 31[5] | 64[5] | 5·5 | 1·0 | 24 |
| 1 617 | 80 | 29 | 144 | 11 | 5 | 149 | 21 952 | 107 | 110[5] | — | 6 566[2] | 765[2] | 22 | 51 | 27 | 8·2 | 0·5 | 25 |

[1] the Gross Domestic Product, for purposes of comparison, is a measure of a country's total production of goods and services
[2] the Net Material Product. This is not strictly comparable with the G.D.P., differing slightly in content
[3] 1969
[4] 1970
[5] 1971
[6] 1972

# EUROPE : Land Use and Agriculture

## LAND USE

- Industrial
- Forest
- Desert or Alpine wastes
- Open grazing
- Pastoral
- Arable
- Arboriculture

## AGRICULTURAL PRODUCTS

| | |
|---|---|
| Wheat | Sugar Beet |
| Maize | Tobacco |
| Barley | Vine |
| Oats | Olive |
| Rye | Fruit |
| Flax | E Esparto |
| Hops | Cattle |
| Potatoes | Dairying |
| Cotton | Sheep |
| Lumbering | Pigs |

Projection: *Bonne*

West from Greenwich 0 East from Greenwich

1:17 000 000

OCEAN

Murmansk

UNION OF SOVIET

S.F.S.R.

Omsk

Tampere

Perm
Sverdlovsk
Chelyabinsk

Helsinki
Leningrad

Estonia

Gorki

Riga

Moscow

Kuybyshev

Latvia

R  u  s  s  i  a

Lithuania

SOCIALIST   REPUBLICS

White

Saratov

Russia

K  a  z  a  k  h  s  t  a  n

Warsaw

Volgograd

Kiev

Kharkov

U  k  r  a  i  n  e

Lvov

Dnepropetrovsk

Rostov

Uzbekistan

Nikolayev

C A S P I A N

S E A

BLACK   SEA

Turkmenistan

RUMANIA

Ashkhabad

Georgia
Tbilisi
Baku

Bucharest

Azerbaijan

BULGARIA

Armenia

Sofia

Tabriz

Tehran

Istanbul

Ankara

T  U  R  K  E  Y

I  R  A  N

REECE

Aleppo

Athens

S  Y  R  I  A

Baghdad

I   R   A   Q

Shiraz

LEBANON

Basra

SEA

JORDAN

200   0        200        400        600        800 km

# BRITISH ISLES : Land Use and Agriculture

LAND USE

- Urban and Industrial
- Forest
- Heath, Moor and Marsh
- Hill Pasture
- Pastoral
- Mixed Farming
- Arable
- Market Gardening
- National Parks

AGRICULTURAL PRODUCTS

- Wheat
- Barley
- Oats
- Hops
- Sugar Beet
- Potatoes
- Fruit
- Dairying
- Cattle
- Sheep

ATLANTIC OCEAN

NORTH SEA

IRISH SEA

English Channel

SCOTLAND

NORTHERN IRELAND

IRELAND

ENGLAND

Inverness
Aberdeen
Ft. William
Oban
Dundee
Perth
Stirling
Edinburgh
Glasgow
Kilmarnock
Galashiels
Ayr
Dumfries
Newcastle
Stranraer
Carlisle
Darlington
Middlesbrough
Barrow-in-Furness
Lancaster
York
Blackpool
Bradford
Leeds
Hull
Liverpool
Manchester
Sheffield
Lincoln
Stoke
Derby
Nottingham
Shrewsbury
Leicester
Peterborough
Norwich
Aberystwyth
Ludlow
Birmingham
Coventry
Northampton
Cambridge
Ipswich
Worcester
Luton
Colchester
Hereford
Cheltenham
Gloucester
Oxford
Aylesbury
London
Maidstone
Carmarthen
Reading
Basingstoke
Dover
Swansea
Cardiff
Bristol
Salisbury
Southampton
Hastings
Taunton
Brighton
Bude
Launceston
Exeter
Plymouth
Falmouth

Londonderry
Belfast
Sligo
Galway
Athlone
Dublin
Kildare
Limerick
Tralee
Wexford
Waterford
Cork

Projection: Conical with two standard parallels

West from Greenwich  0  East from Greenwich
COPYRIGHT. GEORGE. PHILIP & SON. LTD.

1 : 4 000 000    50    0    50    100    150 km

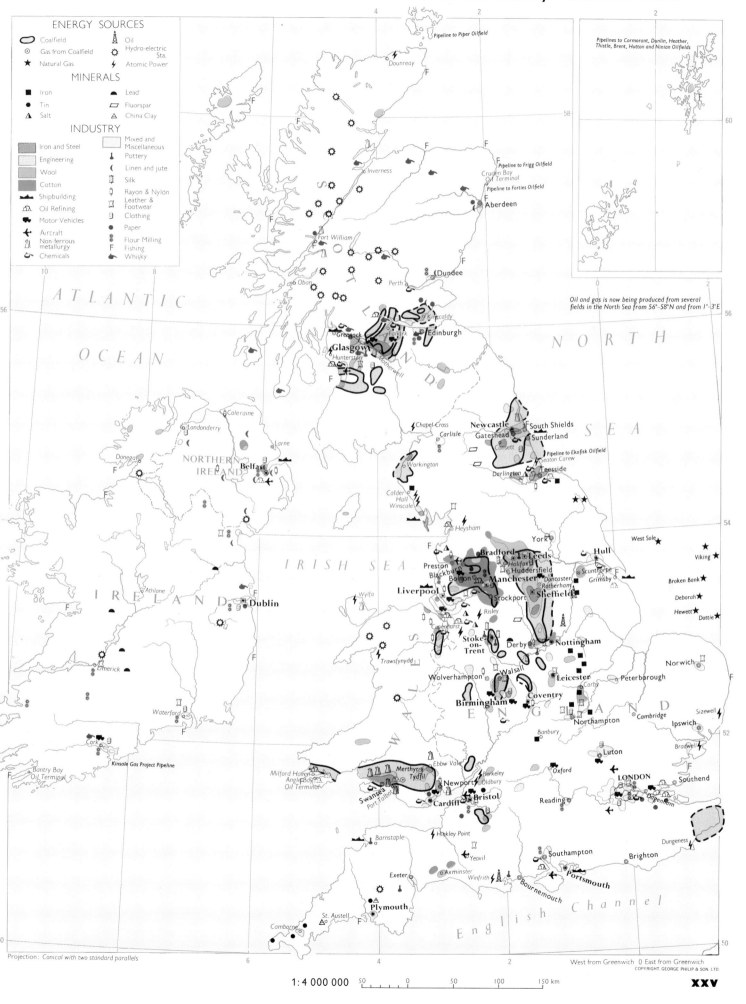

ENERGY SOURCES

- Coalfield
- Gas from Coalfield
- Natural Gas
- Oil
- Hydro-electric Sta.
- Atomic Power

MINERALS

- Iron
- Tin
- Salt
- Lead
- Fluorspar
- China Clay

INDUSTRY

- Iron and Steel
- Engineering
- Wool
- Cotton
- Mixed and Miscellaneous
- Pottery
- Linen and jute
- Silk
- Rayon & Nylon
- Leather & Footwear
- Clothing
- Paper
- Flour Milling
- Fishing
- Whisky
- Shipbuilding
- Oil Refining
- Motor Vehicles
- Aircraft
- Non-ferrous metallurgy
- Chemicals

Pipeline to Piper Oilfield

Pipelines to Cormorant, Dunlin, Heather, Thistle, Brent, Hutton and Ninian Oilfields

Oil and gas is now being produced from several fields in the North Sea from 56°–58°N and from 1°–3°E

Dounreay

Inverness

Fort William

Oban

Perth

Dundee

Kirkcaldy

Greenock

Falkirk

Edinburgh

**Glasgow**

Motherwell

Hunterston

Pipeline to Frigg Oilfield

Cruden Bay Oil Terminal

Pipeline to Forties Oilfield

Aberdeen

A T L A N T I C

O C E A N

S C O T L A N D

N O R T H   S E A

Coleraine

Londonderry

Larne

Donegal

NORTHERN IRELAND

**Belfast**

Chapel Cross

Carlisle

**Newcastle**

Gateshead

**South Shields**

Sunderland

Consett

Pipeline to Ekofisk Oilfield

Seaton Carew

Workington

Teesside

Darlington

Calder Hall Winscale

Heysham

York

Hull

West Sole

Viking

I R I S H   S E A

Athlone

I R E L A N D

Wylfa

**Dublin**

Limerick

Preston

Blackburn

Bolton

**Bradford** **Leeds**

Halifax

Huddersfield

**Manchester**

Stockport

Doncaster

Rotherham

**Sheffield**

Scunthorpe

Grimsby

Broken Bank

Deborah

Hewett

Dottie

**Liverpool**

Risley

**Stoke-on-Trent**

Trawsfynydd

Derby

**Nottingham**

Norwich

Wolverhampton

Walsall

**Leicester**

Corby

Peterborough

**Birmingham**

**Coventry**

Northampton

Banbury

Cambridge

Ipswich

Sizewell

Waterford

Cork

W A L E S

E N G L A N D

Bantry Bay Oil Terminal

Kinsale Gas Project Pipeline

Milford Haven Angle Bay Oil Terminal

Ebbw Vale

**Merthyr Tydfil**

**Newport**

Berkeley

Oldbury

Oxford

Luton

Bradwell

**Swansea**

Port Talbot

**Cardiff**

**Bristol**

Reading

**LONDON**

Dagenham

**Southend**

Dungeness

Barnstaple

Hinkley Point

Yeovil

Southampton

Brighton

Exeter

Axminster

Winfrith

Bournemouth

**Portsmouth**

**Plymouth**

St. Austell

Camborne

E n g l i s h   C h a n n e l

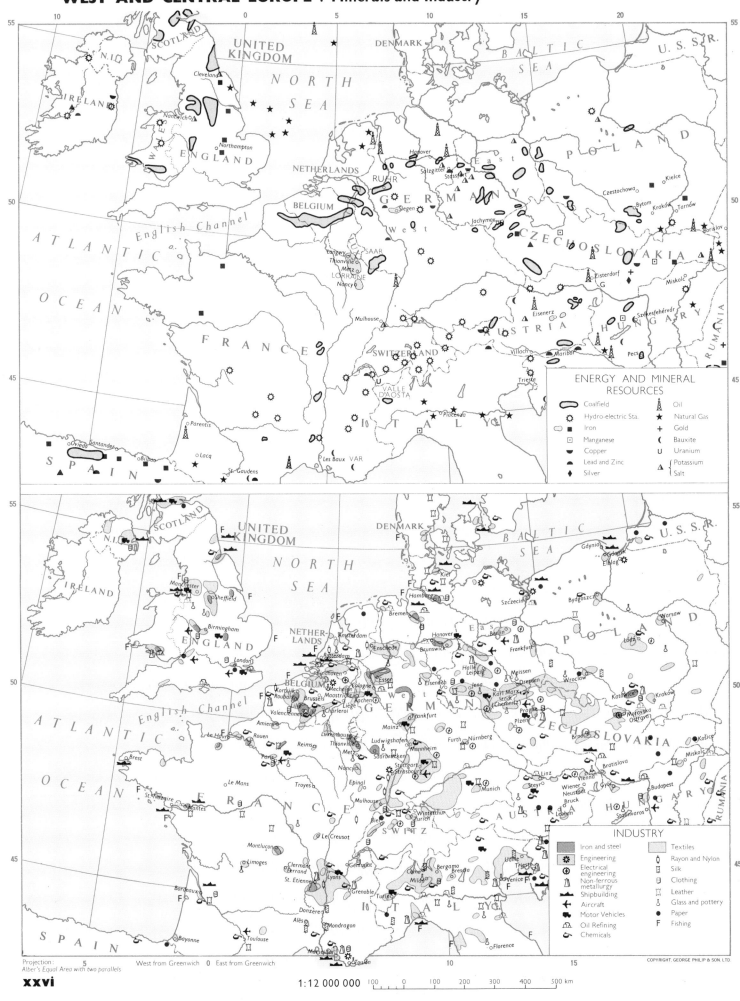

# WEST AND CENTRAL EUROPE : Minerals and Industry

## ENERGY AND MINERAL RESOURCES

- Coalfield
- Hydro-electric Sta.
- Iron
- Manganese
- Copper
- Lead and Zinc
- Silver
- Oil
- Natural Gas
- Gold
- Bauxite
- Uranium
- Potassium
- Salt

## INDUSTRY

- Iron and steel
- Engineering
- Electrical engineering
- Non-ferrous metallurgy
- Shipbuilding
- Aircraft
- Motor Vehicles
- Oil Refining
- Chemicals
- Textiles
- Rayon and Nylon
- Silk
- Clothing
- Leather
- Glass and pottery
- Paper
- Fishing

Projection:
Alber's Equal Area with two parallels

West from Greenwich   0   East from Greenwich

1:12 000 000

COPYRIGHT. GEORGE PHILIP & SON. LTD.

**xxvi**

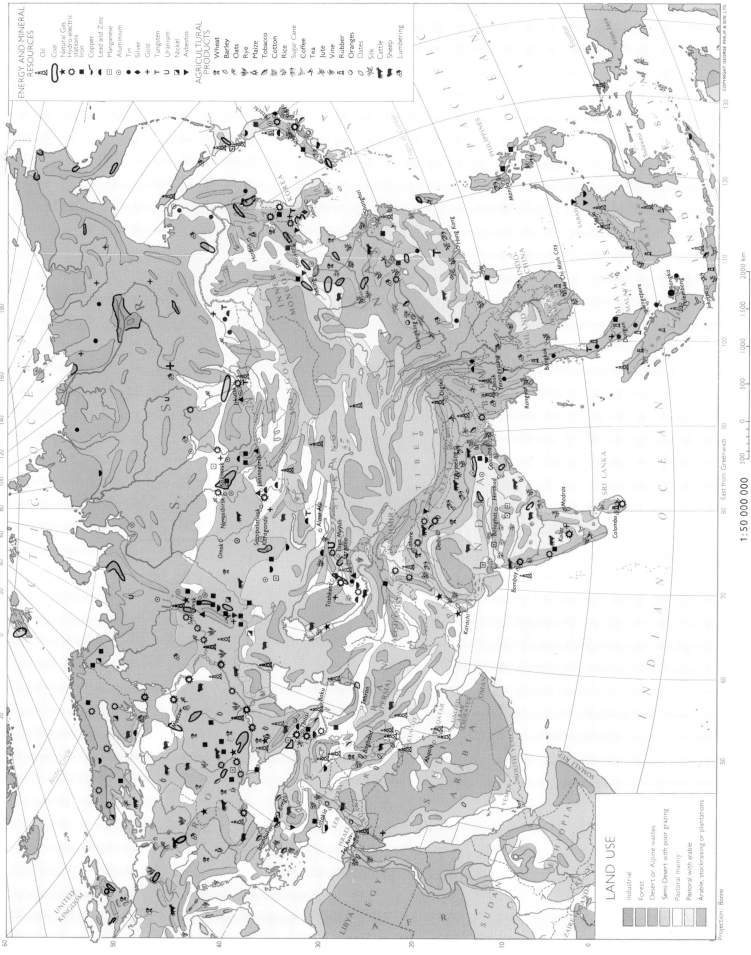

ENERGY AND MINERAL
RESOURCES

Oil
Coal
Natural Gas
Hydro-electric
stations
Iron
Copper
Lead and Zinc
Manganese
Aluminium
Tin
Silver
Gold
Tungsten
Uranium
Nickel
Asbestos

AGRICULTURAL
PRODUCTS

Wheat
Barley
Oats
Rye
Maize
Tobacco
Cotton
Rice
Sugar Cane
Coffee
Tea
Jute
Vine
Rubber
Oranges
Dates
Silk
Cattle
Sheep
Lumbering

LAND USE

Industrial
Forest
Desert or Alpine wastes
Semi-Desert with poor grazing
Pastoral mainly
Pastoral with arable
Arable, stockraising or plantations

Projection: Bonne

1:50 000 000

East from Greenwich

2000 km

COPYRIGHT GEORGE PHILIP & SON LTD

# AUSTRALIA AND NEW ZEALAND : Land Use, Agriculture and Minerals

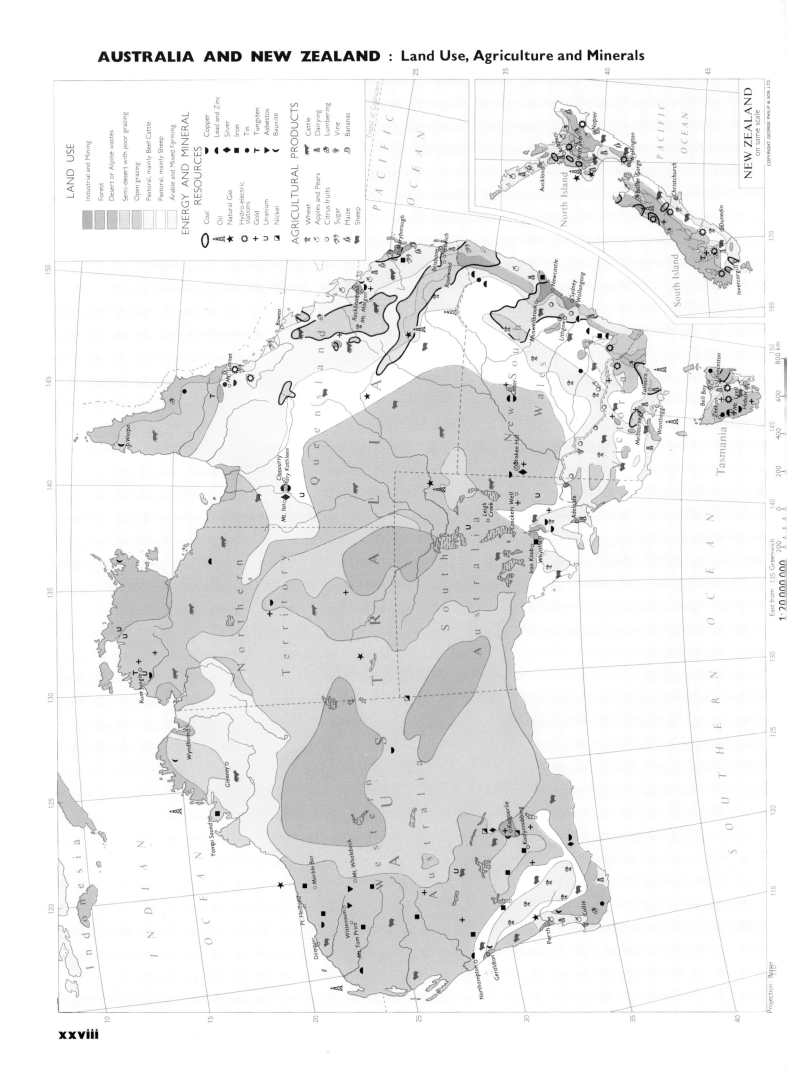

LAND USE

Industrial and Mining
Forest
Desert or Alpine wastes
Semi-desert with poor grazing
Open grazing
Pastoral, mainly Beef Cattle
Pastoral, mainly Sheep
Arable and Mixed Farming

ENERGY AND MINERAL RESOURCES

Coal
Oil
Natural Gas
Hydro-electric stations
Gold
Uranium
Nickel

Copper
Lead and Zinc
Silver
Iron
Tin
Tungsten
Asbestos
Bauxite

AGRICULTURAL PRODUCTS

Wheat
Apples and Pears
Citrus fruits
Sugar
Maize
Sheep

Cattle
Dairying
Lumbering
Vine
Bananas

NEW ZEALAND
on same scale

COPYRIGHT GEORGE PHILIP & SON LTD.

Projection Bonne

1:20 000 000

East from 135 Greenwich

xxviii

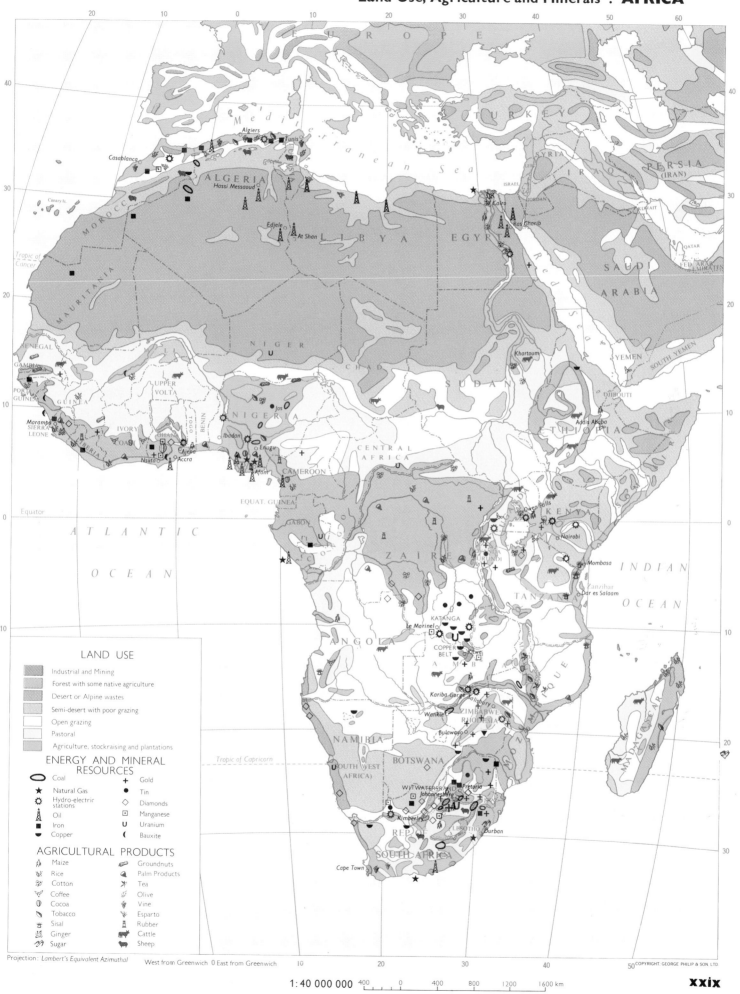

# Land Use, Agriculture and Minerals : **AFRICA**

## LAND USE

- Industrial and Mining
- Forest with some native agriculture
- Desert or Alpine wastes
- Semi-desert with poor grazing
- Open grazing
- Pastoral
- Agriculture, stockraising and plantations

## ENERGY AND MINERAL RESOURCES

- Coal
- Natural Gas
- Hydro-electric stations
- Oil
- Iron
- Copper
- Gold
- Tin
- Diamonds
- Manganese
- Uranium
- Bauxite

## AGRICULTURAL PRODUCTS

- Maize
- Rice
- Cotton
- Coffee
- Cocoa
- Tobacco
- Sisal
- Ginger
- Sugar
- Groundnuts
- Palm Products
- Tea
- Olive
- Vine
- Esparto
- Rubber
- Cattle
- Sheep

Projection: Lambert's Equivalent Azimuthal

West from Greenwich 0 East from Greenwich

1:40 000 000

400    0    400    800    1200    1600 km

COPYRIGHT: GEORGE PHILIP & SON LTD.

**xxix**

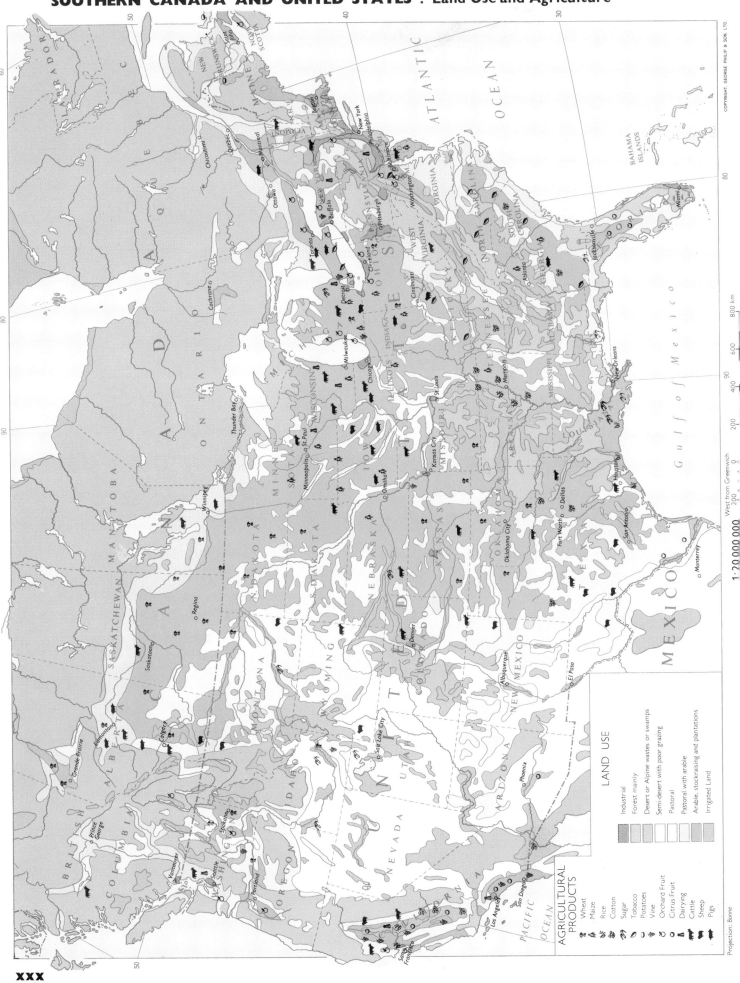

# SOUTHERN CANADA AND UNITED STATES : Land Use and Agriculture

West from Greenwich

1 : 70 000 000

200   0   200   400   600   800 km

Projection: Bonne

## LAND USE

Industrial

Forest mainly

Desert or Alpine wastes or swamps

Semi-desert with poor grazing

Pastoral

Pastoral with arable

Arable, stockraising and plantations

Irrigated Land

## AGRICULTURAL PRODUCTS

Wheat
Maize
Rice
Cotton
Sugar
Tobacco
Potatoes
Vine
Orchard Fruit
Citrus Fruit
Dairying
Cattle
Sheep
Pigs

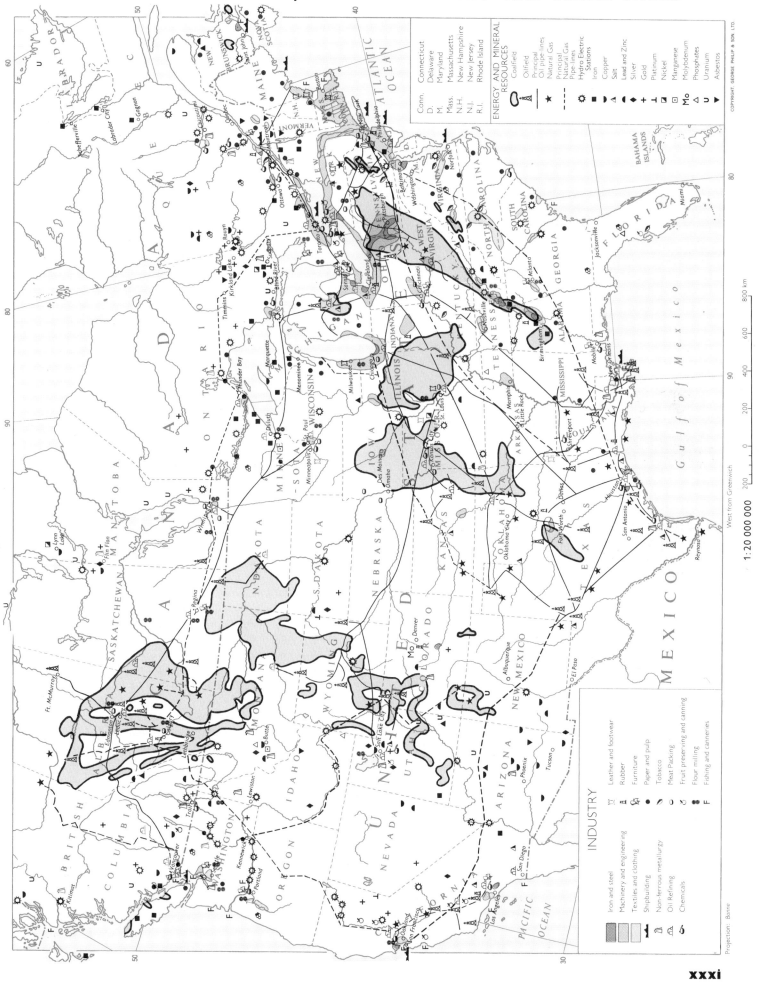

**ENERGY AND MINERAL RESOURCES**

| | |
|---|---|
| Conn. | Connecticut |
| D. | Delaware |
| M. | Maryland |
| Mass. | Massachusetts |
| N.H. | New Hampshire |
| N.J. | New Jersey |
| R.I. | Rhode Island |

Coalfield
Oilfield
Principal Oil pipe lines
Natural Gas
Principal Natural Gas Pipe lines
Hydro Electric Stations
Iron
Copper
Salt
Lead and Zinc
Silver
Gold
Platinum
Manganese
Nickel
Molybdenum
Phosphates
Uranium
Asbestos

COPYRIGHT. GEORGE PHILIP & SON LTD.

**INDUSTRY**

Iron and steel
Machinery and engineering
Textiles and clothing
Shipbuilding
Non-ferrous metallurgy
Oil Refining
Chemicals
Leather and footwear
Rubber
Furniture
Paper and pulp
Tobacco
Meat Packing
Fruit preserving and canning
Flour milling
Fishing and canneries

1 : 20 000 000

800 km

West from Greenwich

Projection: Bonne

**xxxi**

# SOUTH AMERICA : Land Use, Agriculture and Minerals

Maracaibo
Caracas
Trinidad
VENEZUELA
Medellin
Cuidad Bolivar
Georgetown
Bogota
Paramaribo
SURINAM
FRENCH
Cali
COLOMBIA
GUIANA

Quito
ECUADOR
Belém
Manaus
Guayaquil
Fortaleza

PERU
Cerro de Pasco
Recife
Lima
B R A Z I L
Salvador

La Paz
BOLIVIA
Belo Horizonte
Itabira
Potosi
Chuquicamata
PARAGUAY
São Paulo
Rio de Janeiro
Tropic of Capricorn
Asuncion
Potrerillos
Tucuman
Porto Alegre
ARGENTINA
Cordoba
URUGUAY
Valparaiso
Rosario
Santiago
El Teniente
Buenos Aires
Montevideo
Bahia Blanca

PACIFIC

OCEAN

ATLANTIC

OCEAN

Comodoro
Rivadavia

Falkland Islands

Equator

## ENERGY AND MINERAL RESOURCES

| | |
|---|---|
| | Oil |
| | Coal |
| | Hydro Electric Stations |
| | Natural Gas |
| | Iron |
| | Copper |
| | Lead and Zinc |
| | Tin |
| | Silver |
| | Manganese |
| V | Vanadium |
| + | Gold |
| | Platinum |
| | Bauxite |
| | Diamonds |
| | Salt |
| | Nitrates |
| G | Guano |

## AGRICULTURAL PRODUCTS

| | |
|---|---|
| | Wheat |
| | Maize |
| | Cotton |
| | Rice |
| | Sugar |
| | Coffee |
| | Cocoa |
| | Vine |
| | Tobacco |
| | Dairying |
| | Cattle |
| | Sheep |
| | Bananas |

## LAND USE

| | |
|---|---|
| | Industrial |
| | Forest with primitive cultivation |
| | Forest with some agriculture |
| | Desert or Alpine wastes |
| | Semi-desert with grazing |
| | Pastoral with arable |
| | Arable |

Projection: Bonne

**xxxii**

60 West from Greenwich

1:30 000 000    200  0   200  400   600   800   1000 km

COPYRIGHT. GEORGE PHILIP & SON. LTD.

# INDEX

The number printed in bold type against each index entry indicates the map page where the feature will be found. The geographical coordinates which follow the name are sometimes only approximate but are close enough for the place name to be located.

An open square ☐ signifies that the name refers to an administrative subdivision of a country while a solid square ■ follows the name of a country. (☐) follows the old county names of the U.K.

The alphabetical order of names composed of two or more words is governed primarily by the first word and then by the second. This rule applies even if the second word is a description or its abbreviation, R.,L.,I. for example. Names composed of a proper name (Gibraltar) and a description (Strait of) are positioned alphabetically by the proper name. If the same place name occurs twice or more times in the index and all are in the same country, each is followed by the name of the administrative subdivision in which it is located. The names are placed in the alphabetical order of the subdivisions. If the same place name occurs twice or more in the index and the places are in different countries they will be followed by their country names, the latter governing the alphabetical order. In a mixture of these situations the primary order is fixed by the alphabetical sequence of the countries and the secondary order by that of the country subdivisions.

FHK

Aabenraa-Sønderborg Amt □ Afognak I

# A


Aabenraa-Sønderborg Amt □ 73 55 0N 9 30E
Aachen 48 50 47N 6 4E
Aadorf 15 47 30N 8 55E
Aaiun 116 27 9N 13 12W
Aal 73 55 39N 8 18E
Aâlâ en Nîl □ 123 8 50N 29 55E
Aalen 49 48 49N 10 6E
Aalma ech Chaab 90 33 7N 35 9E
Aalsmeer 46 52 17N 4 43E
Aalsö 73 56 23N 10 52E
Aalst, Belg. 47 50 56N 4 2E
Aalst, Neth. 152 50 57N 4 20E
Aalten 46 51 56N 6 35E
Aalter 47 51 5N 3 28E
Aarau 50 47 23N 8 4E
Aarburg 50 47 2N 7 16E
Aardenburg 47 51 16N 3 28E
Aare, R. 50 47 33N 8 14E
Aareavaara 74 67 27N 23 29E
Aargau □ 50 47 26N 8 10E
Aarhus Amt □ 73 56 15N 10 15E
Aarle 47 51 30N 5 38E
Aarschot 47 50 59N 4 49E
Aarsele 47 51 0N 3 26E
Aartrijke 47 51 7N 3 6E
Aarwangen 50 47 15N 7 46E
Aasleagh 38 53 37N 9 40W
Aastrup 73 55 34N 8 49E
Aba, Congo 126 3 58N 30 17E
Aba, Nigeria 121 5 10N 7 19E
Âbâ, Jazîrat 123 13 30N 32 31E
Abadan 92 30 22N 48 20E
Abade, Ethiopia 123 9 22N 38 3E
Abade, Iran 93 31 8N 52 40E
Abadin 56 43 21N 7 29W
Abadla 118 31 2N 2 45W
Abaeté 171 19 9S 45 27W
Abaeté, R. 171 18 2S 45 12W
Abaetetuba 170 1 40S 48 50W
Abai 173 25 58S 55 54W
Abak 121 4 58N 7 50E
Abakaliki 121 6 22N 8 2E
Abakan 77 53 40N 91 10E
Abal Nam 122 25 20N 38 37E
Abalemma 121 16 12N 7 50E
Aballetuba 170 1 40S 51 15W
Abanilla 59 38 12N 1 3W
Abano Terme 63 45 22N 11 46E
Abarán 59 38 12N 1 23W
Abarqu 93 31 10N 53 20E
Abasan 90 31 19N 34 21E
Abasberes 123 11 33N 35 23E
Abashiri 112 44 0N 144 15E
Abashiri-Wan 112 44 0N 144 30E
Abau 135 10 11S 148 46E
Abaújszántó 53 48 16N 21 12E
Abaya L. 123 6 30N 37 50E
Abbadia San Salvatore 63 42 53N 11 40E
Abbay, R., (Nîl el Azraq) 123 10 17N 35 22E
Abbaye, Pt. 156 46 58N 88 4W
Abbetorp 73 56 57N 16 8E
Abbeville, France 43 50 6N 1 49E
Abbeville, La., U.S.A. 159 30 0N 92 7W
Abbeville, S.C., U.S.A. 157 34 12N 82 21W
Abbey 39 53 7N 8 25W
Abbey Town 32 54 50N 3 18W
Abbeydorney 39 52 21N 9 40W
Abbeyfeale 39 52 23N 9 20W
Abbeyleix 39 52 55N 7 20W
Abbeyside 39 52 5N 7 36W
Abbiategrasso 62 45 23N 8 55E
Abbieglassie 139 27 15S 147 28E
Abbotabad 94 34 10N 73 15E
Abbots Bromley 28 52 50N 1 52W
Abbots Langley 29 51 43N 0 25W
Abbotsbury 28 50 40N 2 36W
Abbotsford, Can. 152 49 0N 122 10W
Abbotsford, U.S.A. 158 44 55N 90 20W
Abcoude 46 52 17N 4 59E
'Abd al Kuri 91 12 5N 52 20E
Abdulino 84 53 42N 53 40E
Abe, L. 123 11 8N 41 47E
Abéché 117 13 50N 20 35E
Abejar 58 41 48N 2 47W
Abekr 123 12 45N 28 50E
Abêlessa 118 22 58N 4 47E
Abelti 123 8 10N 37 30E
Abengourou 120 6 42N 3 27W
Åbenrå 73 55 3N 9 25E
Abeokuta 121 7 3N 3 19E
Aber 126 2 12N 32 25E
Aber-soch 31 52 50N 4 31W
Aberaeron 31 52 15N 4 16W
Aberayron = Aberaeron 31 52 15N 4 16W
Abercarn 31 51 39N 3 9W
Aberchirder 37 57 34N 2 40W
Abercorn 139 25 12S 151 5E
Abercorn = Mbala 127 8 46S 31 17E
Abercrave 31 51 48N 3 42W
Aberdare 31 51 43N 3 27W
Aberdare Ra. 126 0 15S 36 50E
Aberdaron 31 52 48N 4 41W
Aberdeen, Austral. 141 32 9S 150 56E
Aberdeen, Can. 153 52 20N 106 8W
Aberdeen, S. Afr. 128 32 28S 24 2E
Aberdeen, U.K. 37 57 9N 2 6W
Aberdeen, Md., U.S.A. 162 39 30N 76 14W
Aberdeen, S.D., U.S.A. 158 45 30N 98 30W
Aberdeen, Wash., U.S.A. 160 47 0N 123 50W
Aberdeen (□) 26 57 18N 2 30W
Aberdour 35 56 2N 3 18W
Aberdovey 31 52 33N 4 3W
Aberdulais 31 51 41N 3 46W
Aberfeldy, Austral. 141 37 42S 146 22E
Aberfeldy, U.K. 37 56 37N 3 50W
Aberffraw 31 53 11N 4 28W
Aberfoyle 34 56 10N 4 23W
Abergaria-a-Velha 56 40 41N 8 32W
Abergavenny 31 51 49N 3 1W
Abergele 31 53 17N 3 35W
Abergwili 31 51 52N 4 18W
Abergynolwyn 31 52 39N 3 58W
Aberkenfig 31 51 33N 3 36W
Aberlady 35 56 0N 2 51W
Abernathy 159 33 49N 101 49W
Abernethy 35 56 19N 3 18W
Aberporth 31 52 8N 4 32W
Abersychan 31 51 44N 3 3W
Abertillery 31 51 44N 3 9W
Aberystwyth 31 52 25N 4 6W
Abha 122 18 0N 42 34E
Abhayapuri 98 26 24N 90 38E
Abidiya 122 18 18N 34 3E
Abidjan 120 5 26N 3 58W
Abilene, Kans., U.S.A. 158 39 0N 97 16W
Abilene, Texas, U.S.A. 159 32 22N 99 40W
Abingdon, U.K. 28 51 40N 1 17W
Abingdon, Ill., U.S.A. 158 40 53N 90 23W
Abingdon, Va., U.S.A. 157 36 46N 81 56W
Abington 35 55 30N 3 42W
Abington Reef 138 18 0S 149 35E
Abitan L. 153 60 27N 107 15W
Abitan, R. 153 59 53N 109 3W
Abitibi L. 150 48 40N 79 40W
Abiy Adi 123 13 39N 39 3E
Abkhaz A.S.S.R. □ 83 43 0N 41 0E
Abkit 77 64 10N 157 10E
Âbnûb 122 27 18N 31 4E
Åbo = Turku 75 60 27N 22 14E
Abo, Massif d' 119 21 41N 16 8E
Abocho 121 7 35N 6 56E
Abohar 94 30 10N 74 10E
Aboisso 120 5 30N 3 5W
Abomey 121 7 10N 2 5E
Abondance 45 46 18N 6 42E
Abong Mbang 124 4 0N 13 8E
Abonnema 121 4 41N 6 49E
Abony 53 47 12N 20 3E
Aboso 120 5 23N 1 57W
Abou Deïa 117 11 20N 19 20E
Aboyne 37 57 4N 2 48W
Abqaiq 92 26 0N 49 45E
Abra Pampa 172 22 43S 65 42W
Abrantes 57 39 24N 8 7W
Abraveses 56 40 41N 7 55E
Abreojos, Pta. 164 26 50N 113 40W
Abreschviller 43 48 39N 7 6E
Abrets, Les 45 45 32N 5 35E
Abri, Esh Shimâliya, Sudan 123 20 50N 30 27E
Abri, Kordofân, Sudan 123 11 40N 30 21E
Abrolhos, Arquipélago dos 171 18 0S 38 30W
Abrolhos, banka 171 18 0S 38 0W
Abrud 70 46 19N 23 5E
Abruzzi □ 63 42 15N 14 0E
Absaroka Ra. 160 44 40N 110 0W
Abû al Khasib 92 30 25N 48 0E
Abû 'Ali 92 27 20N 49 27E
Abu Arish 91 16 53N 42 48E
Abû Ballas 122 24 26N 27 36E
Abu Deleiq 123 15 57N 33 48E
Abū Dhabī 93 24 28N 54 36E
Abû Dis 90 31 47N 35 16E
Abu Dis 122 19 12N 33 38E
Abu Dom 123 16 18N 32 25E
Abû Gabra 123 11 2N 26 50E
Abū Ghōsh 90 31 48N 35 6E
Abû Gubeiha 123 11 30N 31 15E
Abu Habl, W. 123 12 37N 31 0E
Abu Hamed 122 19 32N 33 13E
Abû Haraz, Esh Shimâliya, Sudan 122 19 8N 32 18E
Abû Haraz, Nîl el Azraq, Sudan 123 14 35N 34 30E
Abû Higar 123 12 50N 33 59E
Abu Kamal 92 34 30N 41 0E
Abu Markha 92 25 4N 38 22E
Abu Qîr 122 31 18N 30 0E
Abu Qireiya 122 24 5N 35 28E
Abu Qurqâs 122 28 1N 30 44E
Abu Salama 122 27 10N 35 51E
Abû Simbel 122 22 18N 31 40E
Abu Tig 122 27 4N 31 15E
Abu Tiga 123 12 47N 34 12E
Abû Zabad 123 12 25N 29 10E
Abu Zenîma 122 29 0N 33 15E
Abuja 121 9 16N 7 2E
Abunã 174 9 40S 65 20W
Abunã, R. 174 9 41S 65 20W
Aburatsu 110 31 34N 131 24E
Aburo, Mt. 126 2 4N 30 53E
Abut Hd. 143 43 7S 170 15E
Abwong 123 9 2N 32 14E
Åby 73 58 40N 16 10E
Aby, Lagune 120 5 15N 3 14W
Acacías 174 3 59N 73 46W
Acajutla 166 13 36N 89 50W
Açailândia 170 5 0S 47 50W
Acámbaro 164 20 0N 100 40W
Acaponeta 164 22 30N 105 20W
Acapulco de Juárez 165 16 51N 99 56W
Acaraí, Serra 175 1 50N 57 50W
Acaraú 170 2 53S 40 7W
Acari 170 6 31S 36 38W
Acarigua 174 9 33N 69 12W
Acatlan 165 18 10N 98 3W
Acayucán 165 17 59N 94 58W
Accéglio 62 44 28N 6 59E
Accomac 156 37 43N 75 40W
Accra 121 5 35N 0 6W
Accrington 32 53 46N 2 22W
Acebal 172 33 20S 60 50W
Aceh □ 102 4 0N 97 30E
Acerenza 65 40 50N 15 58E
Acerra 65 40 57N 14 22E
Aceuchal 57 38 39N 6 30W
Achaguas 174 7 46N 68 14W
Achak Gomba 99 33 30N 96 25E
Achalpur 96 21 22N 77 32E
Achavanich 37 58 22N 3 25W
Achel 47 51 15N 5 29E
A'ch'eng 107 45 33N 127 0E
Achenkirch 52 47 32N 11 45E
Achensee 52 47 26N 11 45E
Acher 94 23 10N 72 32E
Achern 49 48 37N 8 5E
Acheron, R. 143 42 16S 173 4E
Achill 38 53 56N 9 55W
Achill Hd. 38 53 59N 10 15W
Achill I. 38 53 58N 10 5W
Achill Sd. 38 53 53N 9 55W
Achillbeg I. 38 53 51N 9 58W
Achim 48 53 1N 9 2E
Achimota 121 5 35N 0 15W
Achinsk 77 56 20N 90 20E
Achisay 85 43 35N 68 53E
Achit 84 56 48N 57 54E
Achnasheen 36 57 35N 5 5W
Achnashellach 36 57 28N 5 20W
Achol 123 6 35N 31 32E
A'Chralaig, Mt. 36 57 11N 5 10W
Acireale 65 37 37N 15 9E
Ackerman 159 33 20N 89 8W
Acklin's I. 167 22 30N 74 0W
Acland, Mt. 133 24 50S 148 20E
Aclare 38 54 4N 8 54W
Acle 29 52 38N 1 32E
Acme 152 51 33N 113 30W
Aconcagua 172 32 50S 70 0W
Aconcagua □ 172 32 15S 70 30W
Aconcagua, Cerro 172 32 39S 70 0W
Aconquija, Mt. 172 27 0S 66 0W
Acopiara 170 6 6S 39 27W
Açores, Is. dos 14 38 44N 29 0W
Acquapendente 63 42 45N 11 50E
Acquasanta 63 42 46N 13 24E
Acquaviva delle Fonti 65 40 53N 16 50E
Acqui 62 44 40N 8 28E
Acre = 'Akko 90 32 35N 35 4E
Acre □ 174 9 1S 71 0W
Acre, R. 174 10 45S 68 25W
Acri 65 39 29N 16 23E
Acs 53 47 42N 18 0E
Acton Burnell 28 52 37N 2 41W
Açu 170 5 34S 36 54W
Ad Dam 91 20 33N 44 45E
Ad Dammam 92 26 20N 50 5E
Ad Dar al Hamra 92 27 20N 37 45E
Ad Dawhah 93 25 15N 51 35E
Ad Dilam 92 23 55N 47 10E
Ada, Ethiopia 123 8 48N 38 51E
Ada, Ghana 121 5 44N 0 40E
Ada, Minn., U.S.A. 158 47 20N 96 30W
Ada, Okla., U.S.A. 159 34 50N 96 45W
Ada, Yugo. 66 45 49N 20 9E
Adair C. 12 71 50N 71 0W
Adaja, R. 56 41 15N 4 50W
Adale 91 2 58N 46 27E
Ådalslinden 72 63 27N 16 55E
Adam 93 22 15N 57 28E
Adamantina 171 21 42S 51 4W
Adamaoua, Massif de l' 121 7 20N 12 20E
Adamawa Highlands = Adamaoua 121 7 20N 12 20E
Adamello, Mt. 62 46 10N 10 34E
Adami Tulu 123 7 53N 38 41E
Adaminaby 141 36 0S 148 45E
Adamovka 84 51 32N 59 56E
Adams, Mass., U.S.A. 162 42 38N 73 8W
Adams, N.Y., U.S.A. 162 43 50N 76 3W
Adams, Wis., U.S.A. 158 43 59N 89 50W
Adam's Bridge 97 9 15N 79 40E
Adams L. 152 51 10N 119 40W
Adams Mt. 160 46 10N 121 28W
Adam's Peak 97 6 55N 80 45E
Adamuz 57 38 2N 4 32W
Adana 92 37 0N 35 16E
Adanero 56 40 56N 4 36W
Adapazari 92 40 48N 30 25E
Adarama 123 17 10N 34 52E
Adare 39 52 34N 8 48W
Adare, C. 13 71 0S 171 0E
Adavale 139 25 52S 144 32E
Adayio 123 14 29N 40 50E
Adda, R. 62 45 25N 9 30E
Addis Ababa = Addis Abeba 123 9 2N 38 42E
Addis Abeba 123 9 2N 38 42E
Addis Alem 123 9 0N 38 17E
Addlestone 29 51 22N 0 30W
Addo 29 33 32S 25 44E
Addu Atoll 87 0 30S 73 0E
Adebour 121 13 17N 11 50E
Adel 157 31 10N 83 28W
Adelaide, Austral. 140 34 52S 138 30E
Adelaide, Bahamas 166 25 0N 77 31W
Adelaide I. 13 67 15S 68 30W
Adelaide Pen. 148 68 15N 97 30W
Adelaide River 136 13 15S 131 7E
Adelanto 163 34 35N 117 22W
Adelboden 50 46 29N 7 33E
Adele, I. 136 15 32S 123 9E
Adélie, Terre 13 67 0S 140 0E
Ademuz 58 40 5N 1 13W
Aden 91 12 50N 45 0E
Aden, G. of 91 13 0N 50 0E
Adendorp 128 33 25S 24 30E
Adhoi 94 23 26N 70 32E
Adi 103 4 15S 133 30E
Adi Daro 123 14 20N 38 14E
Adi Keyih 123 14 51N 39 22E
Adi Kwala 123 14 38N 38 48E
Adi Ugri 123 14 58N 38 48E
Adieu, C. 137 32 0S 132 10E
Adieu Pt. 136 15 14S 124 35E
Adigala 123 10 24N 42 15E
Adige, R. 63 45 9N 11 25E
Adigrat 123 14 20N 39 26E
Adilabad 96 19 33N 78 35E
Adin 160 41 10N 121 0W
Adin Khel 93 32 45N 68 5E
Adinkerke 47 51 5N 2 36E
Adirampattinam 97 10 28N 79 20E
Adirondack Mts. 156 44 0N 74 15W
Adis Dera 123 10 12N 38 46E
Adjohon 121 6 41N 2 32E
Adjud 70 46 7N 27 10E
Adjumani 126 3 20N 31 50E
Adlavik Is. 151 55 2N 58 45W
Adler 83 43 28N 39 52E
Adliswil 51 47 19N 8 32E
Admer 119 20 21N 5 27E
Admer, Erg d' 119 24 0N 9 5E
Admiralty B. 13 62 0S 59 0W
Admiralty G. 136 14 20S 125 55E
Admiralty I. 147 57 40N 134 35W
Admiralty Inlet 160 48 0N 122 40W
Admiralty Is. 135 2 0S 147 0E
Admiralty Ra. 13 72 0S 164 0E
Ado 121 6 36N 2 56E
Ado Ekiti 121 7 38N 5 12E
Adok 123 8 10N 30 20E
Adola 123 11 14N 41 44E
Adonara 103 8 15S 123 5E
Adoni 97 15 33N 77 18W
Adony 53 47 6N 18 52E
Adour, R. 44 43 32N 1 32W
Adra, India 95 23 30N 86 42E
Adra, Spain 59 36 43N 3 3W
Adraj 91 20 1N 51 0E
Adrano 65 37 40N 14 49E
Adrar 118 27 51N 0 11W
Adrar des Iforhas 121 19 40N 1 40E
Adrasman 85 40 38N 69 58E
Adré 117 13 40N 22 20E
Adri 119 27 32N 13 2E
Ádria 63 45 4N 12 3E
Adrian, Mich., U.S.A. 156 41 55N 84 0W
Adrian, Tex., U.S.A. 159 35 19N 102 37W
Adriatic Sea 60 43 0N 16 0E
Adrigole 39 51 44N 9 42W
Adua 103 1 45S 129 50E
Aduku 126 2 03N 32 45E
Adula 51 46 30N 9 3E
Adung Long 98 28 7N 97 42E
Adur 97 9 8N 76 40E
Adwa, Ethiopia 123 14 15N 38 52E
Adwa, Si Arab. 92 27 15N 42 35E
Adwick le Street 33 53 35N 1 12W
Adzhar A.S.S.R. □ 83 42 0N 42 0E
Adzopé 120 6 7N 3 49W
Æbelø I. 73 55 39N 10 10E
Æbeltoft 73 56 12N 10 41E
Æbeltoft Vig. B. 73 56 9N 10 35E
Ægean Is. 61 38 0N 25 0E
Ægean Sea 61 37 0N 25 0E
Aenemuiden 47 51 30N 3 40E
Ænes 71 60 5N 6 8E
Æolian Is. = Eólie, I. 65 38 40N 15 7E
Aerhchin Shanmo 105 38 0N 88 0E
Aerhshan 105 47 93N 119 59E
Aerht'ai Shan 105 48 0N 90 0E
Æro 73 54 53N 10 20E
Ærø 73 54 52N 10 25E
Ærøskøbing 73 54 53N 10 24E
Aesch 50 47 28N 7 36E
Aëtós 69 37 15N 21 50E
Afafi, Massif d' 119 22 11N 14 48E
Afanasyevo 84 58 52N 53 15E
Afándou 69 36 18N 28 12E
Afarag, Erg 118 23 50N 2 47E
Afdera, Mt. 123 13 16N 41 5E
Affreville = Khemis Miliania 118 36 11N 2 14E
Affric, L. 36 57 15N 5 5W
Affric, R. 37 57 15N 4 50W
Afghanistan ■ 93 33 0N 65 0E
Afgoi 91 2 7N 45 0E
Afif 92 23 53N 42 56E
Afikpo 121 5 53N 7 54E
Aflisses, O. 118 28 30N 0 50E
Aflou 118 34 7N 2 3E
Afodo 123 10 18N 34 49E
Afogados da Ingàzeira 170 7 45S 37 39W
Afognak I. 147 58 10N 152 50W

Afragola Al Wakrah

Afragola 65 40 54N 14 15 E
Africa 114 10 0N 20 0 E
Afton 162 42 14N 75 31W
Aftout 118 26 50N 3 45W
Afuá 170 0 15 S 50 10W
Afula 90 32 37N 35 17 E
Afyon Karahisar 92 38 20N 30 15 E
Agadès 121 16 58N 7 59 E
Agadir 118 30 28N 9 35W
Agadir Tissint 118 29 57N 7 16W
Agano, R. 112 37 50N 139 30 E
Agapa 77 71 27N 89 15 E
Agapovka 84 53 18N 59 8 E
Agar 94 23 40N 76 2 E
Agaro 123 7 50N 36 38 E
Agartala 98 23 50N 91 23 E
Agassiz 152 49 14N 121 46W
Agat 123 15 38N 38 16 E
Agattu I. 147 52 25N 172 30 E
Agbelouvé 121 6 35N 1 14 E
Agboville 120 5 55N 4 15W
Agdam 83 40 0N 46 58 E
Agdash 83 40 44N 47 22 E
Agde 44 43 19N 3 28 E
Agde, C. d' 44 43 16N 3 28 E
Agdz 118 30 47N 6 30W
Agen 44 44 12N 0 38 E
Ageo 111 35 58N 139 36 E
Ager Tay 119 20 0N 17 41 E
Agersø 73 55 13N 11 12 E
Agger 73 56 47N 8 13 E
Aggersborg 73 57 0N 9 16 E
Aggius 64 40 56N 9 4 E
Aghalee 38 54 32N 6 17W
Aghavannagh 39 52 55N 6 25W
Aghern 39 52 5N 8 10W
Aghil Mts. 93 36 0N 77 0 E
Aghil Pass 93 36 15N 76 35 E
Aginskoye 77 51 6N 114 32 E
Agira 65 37 40N 14 30 E
Aglou 118 29 50N 9 50W
Agly, R. 44 42 46N 3 3 E
Agna Branca 170 7 57 S 47 19W
Agnes 137 28 0 S 120 30 E
Agnew 137 28 1 S 120 30 E
Agnews Hill 38 54 51N 5 55W
Agnibilékrou 120 7 10N 3 11W
Agnita 70 45 59N 24 40 E
Agnone 65 41 49N 14 20 E
Ago 111 33 36N 135 29 E
Agofie 121 8 27N 0 15 E
Agogna, R. 62 45 8N 8 42 E
Agogo, Ghana 121 6 50N 1 1W
Agogo, Sudan 123 7 50N 28 45 E
Agon 42 49 2N 1 34W
Agön 72 61 33N 17 25 E
Agon I. 72 61 34N 17 23 E
Agordo 63 46 18N 12 2 E
Agout, R. 44 43 47N 1 41 E
Agra 94 27 17N 77 58 E
Agrado 174 2 15N 75 46W
Agramunt 58 41 48N 1 6 E
Agreda 58 41 51N 1 55W
Agri 73 56 14N 10 32 E
Ağri Daği 92 39 50N 44 15 E
Agri, R. 65 40 17N 16 15 E
Agrigento 64 37 19N 13 33 E
Agrinion 69 38 37N 21 27 E
Agropoli 65 40 23N 14 59 E
Agryz 84 56 33N 53 2 E
Agua Caliente, Mexico 164 26 30N 108 20W
Agua Caliente, U.S.A. 163 32 29N 116 59W
Agua Caliente Springs 163 32 56N 116 19W
Agua Clara 175 20 25 S 52 45W
Agua Prieta 164 31 20N 109 32W
Aguadas 174 5 40N 75 38W
Aguadilla 147 18 27N 67 10W
Aguadulce 166 8 15N 80 32W
Aguanaval, R. 164 23 45N 103 10W
Aguanga 163 33 27N 116 51W
Aguanus, R. 151 50 13N 62 5W
Aguapeí, R. 171 21 0 S 51 0W
Aguapey, R. 172 29 7 S 56 36W
Aguaray Guazú, R. 172 24 47 S 57 19W
Aguarico, R. 174 0 0 77 30W
Aguas Blancas 172 24 15 S 69 55W
Aguas Calientes, Sierra de 172 25 26 S 67 27W
Aguas Formosas 171 17 5 S 40 57W
Aguas, R. 58 41 20N 0 30W
Aguascalientes 164 22 0N 102 12W
Aguascalientes □ 164 22 0N 102 20W
Agudo 57 38 59N 4 52W
Agueda 56 40 34N 8 27W
Agueda, R. 56 40 45N 6 37W
Aguelt el Kadra 118 25 3N 7 6W
Agueni N'Ikko 118 32 29N 5 47W
Aguié 121 13 31N 7 46 E
Aguilafuente 56 41 13N 4 7W
Aguilar 57 37 31N 4 40W
Aguilar de Campóo 56 42 47N 4 15W
Aguilares 172 27 26 S 65 35W
Aguilas 59 37 23N 1 35W
Aguja, C. de la 174 11 18N 74 12W
Aguja, Pta. 174 6 0 S 81 0W
Agulaa 123 13 40N 39 40 E
Agulhas, Kaap 128 34 52 S 20 0 E
Agung 102 8 20 S 115 28 E
Agur, Israel 90 31 42N 34 55 E
Agur, Uganda 126 2 28N 32 55 E
Agŭš 70 46 28N 26 15 E
Agusan, R. 103 9 20N 125 50 E
Agvali 83 42 36N 46 8 E
Aha Mts. 128 19 45 S 21 0 E
Ahaggar 119 23 0N 6 30 E
Ahamansu 121 7 38N 0 35 E
Ahar 92 38 35N 47 0 E
Ahascragh 38 53 24N 8 20W
Ahaura 143 42 20 S 171 32 E
Ahaura, R. 143 42 21 S 171 34 E
Ahaus 48 52 4N 7 1 E
Ahelledjem 119 26 37N 6 58 E
Ahimanawa Ra. 130 39 5 S 176 30 E
Ahipara B. 142 35 5 S 173 5 E
Ahiri 96 19 30N 80 0 E
Ahlen 48 51 45N 7 52 E
Ahmad Wal 94 29 18N 65 58 E
Ahmadabad (Ahmedabad) 94 23 0N 72 40 E
Ahmadnagar (Ahmednagar) 96 19 7N 74 46 E
Ahmadpur 94 29 12N 71 10 E
Ahmar Mts. 123 9 20N 41 15 E
Ahoada 121 5 8N 6 36 E
Ahoghill 38 54 52N 6 23W
Ahome 164 25 55N 109 11W
Ahr, R. 48 50 25N 6 52 E
Ahrensbök 48 54 0N 10 34 E
Ahrweiler 48 50 31N 7 3 E
Ahsā, Wahatāal 92 25 50N 49 0 E
Ahuachapán 166 13 54N 89 52W
Ahuriri, R. 143 44 31 S 170 12 E
Åhus 73 55 56N 14 18 E
Ahvāz 92 31 20N 48 40 E
Ahvenanmaa 75 60 15N 20 0 E
Ahzar 121 15 30N 3 20 E
Aibaq 93 36 15N 68 5 E
Aichach 49 48 28N 11 9 E
Aichi-ken □ 111 35 0N 137 15 E
Aidone 65 37 26N 14 26 E
Aiello Cálabro 65 39 6N 16 12 E
Aigle 50 46 18N 6 58 E
Aignay-le-Duc 43 47 40N 4 43 E
Aigre 44 45 54N 0 1 E
Aigua 173 34 13 S 54 46W
Aigueperse 44 46 3N 3 13 E
Aigues-Mortes 45 43 35N 4 12 E
Aiguilles 45 44 47N 6 51 E
Aiguillon 44 44 18N 0 21 E
Aiguillon, L' 44 46 20N 1 16W
Aigurande 44 46 27N 1 49 E
Aihui 105 50 16N 127 28 E
Aija 174 9 50 S 77 45W
Aijal 98 23 40N 92 44 E
Aiken 157 33 34N 81 50W
Ailao Shan 108 24 0N 101 30 E
Aillant-sur-Tholon 43 47 52N 3 20 E
Aillik 151 55 11N 59 18W
Ailly-sur-Noye 43 49 45N 2 20 E
Ailsa Craig, I. 34 55 15N 5 7W
Aim 77 59 0N 133 55 E
Aimere 103 8 45 S 121 3 E
Aimogasta 172 28 33 S 66 50W
Aimorés 171 19 30 S 41 4W
Aimorés, Serra dos 171 17 50 S 40 30W
Ain □ 45 46 5N 5 20 E
Ain Banaiyah 93 23 0N 51 0 E
Aïn-Beïda 119 35 50N 7 35 E
Ain ben Khellil 118 33 15N 0 49W
Ain Ben Tili 118 25 59N 9 27W
Aïn Benian 118 36 48N 2 55 E
'Ain Dalla 122 27 20N 27 23 E
Ain Dar 92 25 55N 49 10 E
Ain el Mafki 122 27 30N 28 15 E
Ain Girba 122 29 20N 25 14 E
Aïn M'lila 119 36 2N 6 35 E
Ain Qeiqab 122 29 42N 24 55 E
Ain, R. 45 45 52N 5 11 E
Aïn Rich 118 34 38N 24 55 E
Aïn-Sefra 118 32 47N 0 37W
Ain Sheikh Murzûk 122 26 47N 27 45 E
Ain Sukhna 122 29 32N 32 20 E
Aïn Tédelès 118 36 0N 0 21 E
Aïn-Témouchent 118 35 16N 1 8W
Aïn Touta 119 35 26N 5 54 E
Ain Zeitûn 122 29 10N 25 48 E
Aïn Zorah 118 34 37N 3 32W
Ainabo 91 9 0N 46 25 E
Ainazi 80 57 50N 24 24 E
Aine Galakka 117 18 10N 18 30 E
Ainos Óros 69 38 10N 20 35 E
Ainsdale 32 53 37N 3 2W
Ainsworth 158 42 33N 99 52W
Aioi 110 34 48N 134 28 E
Aion 77 69 50N 169 0 E
Aipe 174 3 13N 75 15W
Aïr 121 18 30N 8 0 E
Airaines 43 49 58N 1 55 E
Aird Brenish, C. 36 58 8N 7 8W
Aird, The, dist. 37 57 26N 4 30W
Airdrie 35 55 53N 3 57W
Aire 43 50 37N 2 22 E
Aire, Isla del 58 39 48N 4 16 E
Aire, R. 43 49 18N 5 0 E
Aire-sur-l'Adour 44 43 42N 0 15W
Aireys Inlet 140 38 29 S 144 5 E
Airolo 51 46 32N 8 37 E
Airvault 42 46 50N 0 8W
Aisgill 32 54 23N 2 21W
Aishihik 147 61 40N 137 46W
Aisne □ 43 49 42N 3 40 E
Aisne, R. 43 49 26N 2 50 E
Aït Melloul 118 30 25N 9 29W
Aitana, Sierra de 59 38 35N 0 24W
Aitape 135 3 11 S 142 22 E
Aith 37 59 8N 2 38W
Aitkin 158 46 32N 93 43W
Aitolía Kai Akarnanía □ 69 38 45N 21 18 E
Aitolikón 69 38 26N 21 21 E
Aitoska Planina 67 42 45N 27 30 E
Aiuaba 170 6 38 S 40 7W
Aiud 70 46 19N 23 44 E
Aix-en-Provence 45 43 32N 5 27 E
Aix-la-Chapelle = Aachen 48 50 47N 6 4 E
Aix-les-Bains 45 45 41N 5 53 E
Aix-les-Thermes 44 42 43N 1 51 E
Aix-sur-Vienne 44 45 48N 1 8 E
Aiyang, Mt. 135 5 10 S 141 20 E
Aiyangpienmen 107 40 55N 124 30 E
Aiyansh 152 55 17N 129 2W
Aiyina 69 37 45N 23 26 E
Aiyinion 68 40 28N 22 28 E
Aiyion 69 38 15N 22 5 E
Aizenay 42 46 44N 1 38W
Aizpute 80 56 43N 21 40 E
Aizuwakamatsu 112 37 30N 139 56 E
Ajaccio 45 41 55N 8 40 E
Ajaccio, G. d' 45 41 52N 8 40 E
Ajalpán 165 18 22N 97 15W
Ajana 137 27 56 S 114 35 E
Ajanta Ra. 96 20 28N 75 50 E
Ajax, Mt. 143 42 35 S 172 5 E
Ajdabiyah 119 30 54N 20 4 E
Ajdîr, Raîs 119 33 4N 11 44 E
AjdovTUina 63 45 54N 13 54 E
Ajibar 123 10 35N 38 36 E
'Ajlun 90 32 18N 35 47 E
Ajman 93 25 25N 55 30 E
Ajmer 94 26 28N 74 37 E
Ajo 161 32 18N 112 54W
Ajoie 50 47 22N 7 0 E
Ajok 123 9 15N 28 28 E
Ajua 120 4 50N 1 55W
Ak Dağ 92 36 30N 30 0 E
Akaba 121 8 10N 1 2 E
Akabli 118 26 49N 1 31 E
Akaishi-Dake 111 35 27N 138 9 E
Akaishi-Sammyaku 111 35 25N 138 10 E
Akaki Beseka 123 8 55N 38 45 E
Akala 123 15 39N 36 13 E
Akaroa 143 43 49 S 172 59 E
Akaroa Harb. 131 43 54 S 172 59 E
Akasha 122 21 10N 30 32 E
Akashi 110 34 45N 135 0 E
Akbou 119 36 31N 4 31 E
Akbulak 84 51 1N 55 37 E
Akdala 85 45 2N 74 35 E
Akechi 111 35 18N 137 23 E
Akegbe 121 6 17N 7 28 E
Akelamo 103 1 35N 129 40 E
Akershus Fylke □ 71 60 10N 11 15 E
Akeru, R. 96 17 25N 80 0 E
Aketi 124 2 38N 23 47 E
Akhaïa □ 69 38 5N 21 45 E
Akhalkalaki 83 41 27N 43 25 E
Akhaltsikhe 83 41 40N 43 0 E
Akharnai 69 38 5N 23 44 E
Akhelóös, R. 69 39 5N 21 25 E
Akhendriá 69 34 58N 25 16 E
Akhéron, R. 68 39 31N 20 29 E
Akhisar 92 38 56N 27 48 E
Akhladhókambos 69 37 31N 22 35 E
Akhmîm 122 26 31N 31 47 E
Akhnur 95 32 52N 74 45 E
Akhtopol 67 42 6N 27 56 E
Akhtubinsk (Petropavlovskiy) 83 48 27N 46 7 E
Akhty 83 41 30N 47 45 E
Akhtyrka 80 50 25N 35 0 E
Aki 110 33 30N 133 54 E
Aki-Nada 110 34 5N 132 40 E
Akiak 147 60 50N 161 12W
Akimiski I. 150 52 50N 81 30W
Akimovka 82 46 44N 35 0 E
Akincilar 69 37 57N 27 25 E
Akinum 138 6 15 S 149 30 E
Åkirkeby 73 55 4N 14 55 E
Akita 112 39 45N 140 0 E
Akita-ken □ 112 39 40N 140 30 E
Akjoujt 120 19 45N 14 15W
Akka 118 29 28N 8 9W
'Akko 90 32 35N 35 4 E
Akkol, Kazakh, U.S.S.R. 85 45 0N 75 39 E
Akkol, Kazakh, U.S.S.R. 85 43 36N 70 45 E
Akköy 69 37 30N 27 18 E
Akkrum 46 53 3N 5 50 E
Aklampa 121 8 15N 2 10 E
Aklavik, Can. 147 68 12N 135 0W
Aklavik, N.W.T., Can. 147 68 12N 135 0W
Akmuz 85 41 15N 76 10 E
Aknoul 118 34 40N 3 55W
Akō 110 34 45N 134 24 E
Ako 121 10 19N 10 48 E
Akobo, R. 123 7 10N 34 25 E
Akola 96 20 42N 77 2 E
Akonolinga 121 3 50N 12 18 E
Akordat 123 15 30N 37 40 E
Akosombo Dam 121 6 20N 0 5 E
Ak'osu 105 41 15N 80 14 E
Akot, India 96 21 10N 77 10 E
Akot, Sudan 123 6 31N 30 9 E
Akpatok I. 149 60 25N 68 8W
Akranes 74 64 19N 22 6W
Åkrehamn 71 59 15N 5 10 E
Akreïjit 120 18 19N 9 11W
Akrítas Venétiko, Ákra 69 36 43N 21 54 E
Akron, Colo., U.S.A. 158 40 13N 103 15W
Akron, Ohio, U.S.A. 156 41 7N 81 31W
Akrotiri, Ákra 68 40 26N 25 27W
Aksai Chih, L. 95 35 15N 79 55 E
Aksaray 92 38 25N 34 2 E
Aksarka 76 66 31N 67 50 E
Aksehir 92 38 18N 31 30 E
Aksenovo Zilovskoye 77 53 20N 117 40 E
Aksuat, Ozero 84 51 32N 64 34 E
Aksum 123 14 5N 38 40 E
Aktash, R.S.F.S.R., U.S.S.R. 84 52 2N 52 7 E
Aktash, Uzbek S.S.R., U.S.S.R. 85 39 55N 65 55 E
Aktobe 84 52 55N 62 22 E
Aktogay 85 44 25N 76 44 E
Aktyubinsk 79 50 17N 57 10 E
Aktyuz 85 42 54N 76 7 E
Aku 121 6 40N 7 18 E
Akulurak 147 62 40N 164 35W
Akun I. 147 54 15N 165 30W
Akune 110 32 1N 130 12 E
Akure 121 7 15N 5 5 E
Akureyri 74 65 40N 18 6W
Akusha 83 42 18N 47 30 E
Akutan I. 147 53 30N 166 0W
Akzhar 85 43 8N 71 37 E
Al Abyār 119 32 9N 20 29 E
Al Amadiyah 92 37 5N 43 30 E
Al Amārah 92 31 55N 47 15 E
Al Aqabah 92 29 37N 35 0 E
Al Ashkhara 93 21 50N 59 30 E
Al Ayn al Mugshin 91 19 35N 54 40 E
Al 'Azīzīyah 119 32 30N 13 1 E
Al Badi 92 22 0N 46 35 E
Al Barah 90 31 55N 35 12 E
Al Barkāt 119 24 56N 10 14 E
Al Basrah 92 30 30N 47 50 E
Al Baydā 117 32 30N 21 40 E
Al Bu'ayrāt 119 31 24N 15 44 E
Al Buqay'ah 90 32 15N 35 30 E
Al Dīwaniyah 92 32 0N 45 0 E
Al Fallujah 92 33 20N 43 55 E
Al Fāw 92 30 0N 48 30 E
Al Hadithan 92 34 0N 41 13 E
Al Hamad 92 31 30N 39 30 E
Al Hamar 92 22 23N 46 6 E
Al Hariq 92 23 29N 46 27 E
Al Hasakah 92 36 35N 40 45 E
Al Hauta 91 16 5N 48 20 E
Al Havy 92 32 5N 46 5 E
Al Hillah, Iraq 92 32 30N 44 25 E
Al Hillah, Si Arab. 92 23 35N 46 50 E
Al Hilwah 92 23 24N 46 48 E
Al Hindiya 92 32 30N 44 10 E
Al Hoceïma 118 35 8N 3 58W
Al Hufrah, Awbārī, Libya 119 25 32N 14 1 E
Al Hufrah, Misrātah, Libya 119 29 5N 18 3 E
Al Hufuf 92 25 25N 49 45 E
Al Husayyāt 119 30 24N 20 37 E
Al Husn 90 32 29N 35 52 E
Al Irq 117 29 5N 21 35 E
Al Ittihad = Madinat al Shaab 91 12 50N 45 0 E
Al Jahrah 92 29 25N 47 40 E
Al Jalāmid 92 31 20N 39 45 E
Al Jarzirah 117 26 10N 21 20 E
Al Jawf 117 24 10N 23 24 E
Al Jazir 91 18 30N 56 31 E
Al Jubail 92 27 0N 49 50 E
Al Juwara 91 19 0N 57 13 E
Al Khābūrah 93 23 57N 57 5 E
Al Khalih 90 31 32N 35 6 E
Al Khums (Homs) 119 32 40N 14 17 E
Al Kut 92 32 30N 46 0 E
Al Kuwayt 92 29 20N 48 0 E
Al Ladhiqiyah 92 35 30N 35 45 E
Al Līth 122 20 9N 40 15 E
Al Madīnah 92 24 35N 39 52 E
Al-Mafraq 90 32 17N 36 14 E
Al Majma'ah 92 25 57N 45 22 E
Al Manamah 93 26 10N 50 30 E
Al Marj 117 32 25N 20 30 E
Al Masīrah 91 20 25N 58 50 E
Al Mawsil 92 36 15N 43 5 E
Al Miqdadīyah 92 34 0N 45 0 E
Al Mubarraz 92 25 30N 49 40 E
Al Muharraq 93 26 15N 50 40 E
Al Mukha 91 13 18N 43 15 E
Al Musayyib 92 32 40N 44 25 E
Al Muwaylih 92 27 40N 35 30 E
Al Qaddāhīyah 119 31 15N 15 9 E
Al Qamishli 92 37 10N 41 10 E
Al Qaryah ash Sharqīyah 119 30 28N 13 40 E
Al Qaşabāt 119 32 39N 14 1 E
Al Qatif 92 26 35N 50 0 E
Al Qaţrun 119 24 56N 15 3 E
Al Quaisūmah 92 28 10N 46 20 E
Al Quds 90 31 47N 35 10 E
Al Qunfidha 122 19 3N 41 4 E
Al Quraiyat 93 23 17N 58 53 E
Al Qurnah 92 31 1N 47 25 E
Al 'Ula 92 26 35N 38 0 E
Al Uqaylah 119 30 12N 19 10 E
Al Uqayr 92 25 40N 50 15 E
Al' Uwayqilah 92 30 30N 42 10 E
Al 'Uyūn 92 26 30N 43 50 E
Al Wajh 122 26 10N 36 30 E
Al Wakrah 93 25 10N 51 40 E

Al Warīah Almaden


Al Warīah 92 27 50N 47 30 E
Al Wātīyah 119 32 28N 11 57 E
Ala, Italy 62 45 46N 11 0 E
Ala, Sweden 72 61 13N 17 9 E
Ala Shan 105 40 0N 104 0 E
Alabama □ 157 31 0N 87 0W
Alabama, R. 157 31 30N 87 35W
Alaçati 69 38 16N 26 23 E
Alaejos 56 41 18N 5 13W
Alagna Valsésia 62 45 51N 7 56 E
Alagôa Grande 170 7 3 S 35 35W
Alagôas □ 170 9 0 S 36 0W
Alagoinhas 171 12 0 S 38 20W
Alagón 58 41 46N 1 12W
Alagón, R. 56 39 50N 6 50W
Alajuela 166 10 2N 84 8W
Alakamisy 129 21 19 S 47 14 E
Alakurtti 78 67 0N 30 30 E
Alam Ajaib 122 25 55N 27 14 E
Alameda, Spain 57 37 12N 4 39W
Alameda, Calif., U.S.A. 163 37 46N 122 15W
Alameda, N. Mex., U.S.A. 161 35 10N 106 43W
Alameda, S.D., U.S.A. 160 43 2N 112 30W
Alamitos, Sierra de los 164 26 30N 102 20W
Alamo 161 37 21N 115 10W
Alamogordo 161 32 59N 106 0W
Alamos 164 27 0N 109 0W
Alamosa 161 37 30N 106 0W
Åland 75 60 15N 20 0 E
Aland 96 17 36N 76 35 E
Alandroal 57 38 41N 7 24W
Ålands hav 75 60 10N 19 30 E
Alange, Presa de 57 38 45N 6 18W
Alangouassou 120 7 30N 4 34W
Alanis 57 38 3N 5 43W
Alanya 92 36 38N 32 0 E
Alaotra, L. 129 17 30 S 48 30 E
Alapayevsk 84 57 52N 61 42 E
Alar del Rey 56 42 38N 4 20W
Alaraz 56 40 45N 5 17W
Alaşehir 79 38 23N 28 30 E
Alashantsoch'i 106 38 59N 105 45 E
Alaska □ 147 65 0N 150 0W
Alaska, G. of 147 58 0N 145 0W
Alaska Highway 152 60 0N 130 0W
Alaska Pen. 147 56 0N 160 0W
Alaska Range 147 62 50N 151 0W
Alássio 62 44 1N 8 10 E
Alatri 64 41 44N 13 21 E
Alatyr 81 54 45N 46 35 E
Alatyr, R. 81 54 45N 45 30 E
Alausí 174 2 0 S 78 50W
Álava □ 58 42 48N 2 28W
Alava, C. 160 48 10N 124 40W
Alaverdi 83 41 2N 44 37 E
Alawoona 140 34 45 S 140 30 E
Alaykel 85 40 15N 74 25 E
Alayor 58 39 57N 4 8 E
Alayskiy Khrebet 85 39 45N 72 0 E
Alazan, R. 83 41 25N 46 35 E
Alba 62 44 41N 8 1 E
Alba □ 70 46 10N 23 30 E
Alba de Tormes 56 40 50N 5 30W
Alba-Iulia 70 46 8N 23 39 E
Albac 70 46 28N 23 1 E
Albacete 59 39 0N 1 50W
Albacete □ 59 38 50N 2 0W
Albacutya, L. 140 35 45 S 141 58 E
Albæk 73 57 36N 10 25 E
Albæk Bugt 73 57 35N 10 40 E
Albaida 59 38 51N 0 31W
Albalate de las Nogueras 58 40 22N 2 18W
Albalate del Arzobispo 58 41 6N 0 31W
Albania ■ 68 41 0N 20 0 E
Albano Laziale 64 41 44N 12 40 E
Albany, Austral. 137 35 1 S 117 58 E
Albany, Ga., U.S.A. 157 31 40N 84 10W
Albany, Minn., U.S.A. 158 45 37N 94 38W
Albany, N.Y., U.S.A. 162 42 29N 73 47W
Albany, Oreg., U.S.A. 160 44 41N 123 0W
Albany, Tex., U.S.A. 159 32 45N 99 20W
Albany, R. 150 52 17N 81 31W
Albardón 172 31 20 S 68 30W
Albarracín 58 40 25N 1 26W
Albarracín, Sierra de 58 40 30N 1 30W
Albatross B. 138 12 45 S 141 30 E
Albatross Pt. 142 38 7 S 174 44 E
Albegna, R. 63 42 40N 11 28 E
Albemarle 157 35 27N 80 15W
Albemarle Sd. 157 36 0N 76 30W
Albenga 62 44 3N 8 12 E
Alberche, R. 56 40 10N 4 30W
Alberdi 172 26 14 S 58 20W
Alberes, Mts. 58 42 28N 2 56W
Alberga 139 27 12 S 135 28 E
Alberga, R. 136 26 50 S 133 40 E
Alberique 59 39 7N 0 31W
Alberni 152 49 20N 124 50W
Albersdorf 48 54 8N 9 19 E
Albert, Austral. 141 32 22 S 147 30 E
Albert, Can. 151 45 51N 64 38W
Albert, France 43 50 0N 2 38 E
Albert Canyon 152 51 8N 117 41W
Albert Edward, Mt. 135 8 20 S 147 24 E
Albert Edward Ra. 136 18 17 S 127 57 E
Albert L., Austral. 140 35 30 S 139 10 E
Albert L., U.S.A. 160 42 40N 120 8W
Albert Lea 158 43 32N 93 20W
Albert, L. = Mobutu Sese Seko, L. 126 1 30N 31 0 E
Albert Nile, R. 126 3 16N 31 38 E
Albert Town 167 22 37N 74 33 E
Alberta □ 152 54 40N 115 0W
Alberti 172 35 1 S 60 16W
Albertinia 128 34 11 S 21 34 E
Albertirsa 53 47 14N 19 37 E
Albertkanaal 47 51 14N 4 26 E
Alberton 151 46 50N 64 0W
Albertville 45 45 40N 6 22 E
Albertville = Kalemie 126 5 55 S 29 9 E
Albi 44 43 56N 2 9 E
Albia 158 41 0N 92 50W
Albina 175 5 37N 54 15W
Albina, Pta. 128 15 52 S 11 44 E
Albino 62 45 47N 9 48 E
Albion, Idaho, U.S.A. 160 42 21N 113 37W
Albion, Mich., U.S.A. 156 42 15N 84 45W
Albion, Nebr., U.S.A. 158 41 47N 98 0W
Alblasserdam 46 51 52N 4 40 E
Albocácer 58 40 21N 0 1 E
Alböke 73 56 57N 16 47 E
Alborán, I. 57 35 57N 3 0W
Alborea 59 39 17N 1 24W
Ålborg 73 57 2N 9 54 E
Ålborg Bugt 73 56 50N 10 35 E
Alborz, Reshteh-Ye Kūkhā-Ye 93 36 0N 52 0 E
Albox 59 37 23N 2 8W
Albreda 152 52 35N 119 10W
Albrighton 28 52 38N 2 17W
Albuera, La 57 38 45N 6 49W
Albufeira 57 37 5N 8 15W
Albula, R. 51 46 38N 9 30 E
Albuñol 59 36 48N 3 11W
Albuquerque 161 35 5N 106 47W
Albuquerque, Cayos de 166 12 10N 81 50W
Alburno, Mte. 65 40 32N 15 20 E
Alburquerque 57 39 15N 6 59W
Albury 141 36 3 S 146 56 E
Albuskjell, oilfield 19 56 40N 3 0 E
Alby 72 62 30N 15 28 E
Alcácer do Sal 57 38 22N 8 33W
Alcalá de Chisvert 58 40 19N 0 13 E
Alcalá de Guadaira 57 37 20N 5 50W
Alcalá de Henares 58 40 28N 3 22W
Alcalá de los Gazules 57 36 29N 5 43W
Alcalá la Real 57 37 27N 3 57W
Alcamo 64 37 59N 12 55 E
Alcanadre 58 42 24N 2 7W
Alcanadre, R. 58 41 43N 0 12W
Alcanar 58 40 33N 0 28 E
Alcanede 57 39 25N 8 49W
Alcanena 57 39 27N 8 40W
Alcañices 57 41 41N 6 21W
Alcaníz 58 41 2N 0 8W
Alcântara 170 2 20 S 44 30W
Alcántara 57 39 41N 6 57W
Alcantara L. 153 60 57N 108 9W
Alcantarilla 57 37 59N 1 12W
Alcaracejos 57 38 24N 4 58W
Alcaraz 59 38 40N 2 29W
Alcaraz, Sierra de 59 38 40N 2 20W
AlcáRovas 57 38 23N 8 9W
Alcarria, La 58 40 31N 2 45W
Alcaudete 57 37 35N 4 5W
Alcázar de San Juan 59 39 24N 3 12W
Alcester 28 52 13N 1 52W
Alcira 59 39 9N 0 30W
Alcoa 157 35 50N 84 0W
Alcobaça, Brazil 171 17 30 S 39 13W
Alcobaça, Port. 57 39 32N 9 0W
Alcobendas 58 40 32N 3 38W
Alcolea del Pinar 58 41 2N 2 28W
Alcora 58 40 5N 0 14W
Alcoutim 57 37 25N 7 28W
Alcova 160 42 37N 106 52W
Alcoy 59 38 43N 0 30W
Alcubierre, Sierra de 58 41 45N 0 22W
Alcublas 58 39 48N 0 43W
Alcudia 58 39 51N 3 9 E
Alcudia, Bahía de 58 39 45N 3 14 E
Alcudia, Sierra de la 57 38 34N 4 30W
Aldabra Is. 11 9 22 S 46 28 E
Aldama 165 22 25N 98 4W
Aldan 77 58 40N 125 30 E
Aldan, R. 77 62 30N 135 10 E
Aldborough 33 54 6N 1 21W
Aldbourne 28 51 28N 1 38W
Aldbrough 33 53 50N 0 7W
Aldeburgh 29 52 9N 1 35 E
Aldeia Nova 57 37 55N 7 24W
Alden I. 71 61 19N 4 45 E
Alder 160 45 27N 112 3W
Alder Pk. 163 35 53N 12 22W
Alderbury 28 51 4N 1 45W
Alderley Edge 32 53 18N 2 15W
Aldermaston 28 51 23N 1 9W
Alderney, I. 42 49 42N 2 12W
Aldershot 29 51 15N 0 43W
Aldersyde 152 50 40N 113 53W
Aldingham 32 54 8N 3 3W
Aledo 158 41 10N 90 50W
Alefa 123 11 55N 36 55 E
Aleg 120 17 3N 13 55W
Alegre 173 20 50 S 41 30W
Alegrete 173 29 40 S 56 0W
Aleisk 76 52 40N 83 0 E
Alejandro Selkirk, I. 131 33 50 S 80 15W
Aleksandriya, U.S.S.R. 79 50 45N 26 22 E
Aleksandriya, U.S.S.R. 82 48 42N 33 3 E
Aleksandriyskaya 83 43 59N 47 0 E
Aleksandrov 81 56 23N 38 44 E
Aleksandrov Gay. 81 50 15N 48 35 E
Aleksandrovac 66 44 28N 21 13 E
Aleksandrovka 82 48 55N 32 20 E
Aleksandrovo 67 43 14N 24 51 E
Aleksandrovsk 84 59 9N 57 33 E
Aleksandrovsk-Sakhaliniskiy 77 50 50N 142 20 E
Aleksandrovskiy Zavod 77 50 40N 117 50 E
Aleksandrovskoye 76 60 35N 77 50 E
Aleksandrów Kujawski 54 52 53N 18 43 E
Aleksandrów Łódzki 54 51 49N 19 17 E
Alekseyevka, R.S.F.S.R., U.S.S.R. 81 50 43N 38 40 E
Alekseyevka, R.S.F.S.R., U.S.S.R. 84 52 35N 51 17 E
Aleksin 81 54 31N 37 9 E
Aleksinac 66 43 31N 21 42 E
Além Paraíba 173 21 52 S 42 41W
Alemania, Argent. 172 25 40 S 65 30W
Alemania, Chile 172 25 10 S 69 55W
Ålen 71 62 51N 11 17 E
Alençon 42 48 27N 0 4 E
Alentejo, Alto- 55 39 0N 7 40W
Alentejo, Baixo- 55 38 0N 8 30W
Alenuihaha Chan. 147 20 25N 156 0W
Aleppo 92 36 10N 37 15 E
Aléria 45 42 5N 9 26 E
Alert B. 152 50 30N 127 35W
Alès 45 44 9N 4 5 E
Aleşd 70 47 3N 22 22 E
Alessándria 62 44 54N 8 37 E
Ålestrup 73 56 42N 9 29 E
Ålesund 71 62 28N 6 12 E
Alet 123 8 14N 29 2 E
Alet-les-Bains 44 43 0N 2 14 E
Aletschgletscher 50 46 28N 8 2 E
Aletschhorn 50 46 28N 8 0 E
Aleutian Is. 147 52 0N 175 0W
Aleutian Ra. 147 55 0N 155 0W
Alexander 158 47 51N 103 40W
Alexander Arch. 147 57 0N 135 0W
Alexander B. 128 28 36 S 16 33 E
Alexander City 157 32 58N 85 57W
Alexander I. 13 69 0 S 70 0W
Alexander, Mt. 137 28 58 S 120 16 E
Alexandra, Austral. 141 37 8 S 145 40 E
Alexandra, N.Z. 143 45 14 S 169 25 E
Alexandra Falls 152 60 29N 116 18W
Alexandria, Austral. 138 19 5 S 136 40 E
Alexandria, Brazil 171 6 25 S 38 1W
Alexandria, B.C., Can. 152 52 35N 122 27W
Alexandria, Ont., Can. 150 45 19N 74 38W
Alexandria, Rumania 70 43 57N 25 24 E
Alexandria, S. Afr. 128 33 38 S 26 28 E
Alexandria, U.K. 34 55 59N 4 40W
Alexandria, Ind., U.S.A. 156 40 18N 85 40W
Alexandria, La., U.S.A. 159 31 20N 92 30W
Alexandria, Minn., U.S.A. 158 45 50N 95 20W
Alexandria, S.D., U.S.A. 158 43 40N 97 45W
Alexandria, Va., U.S.A. 162 38 47N 77 1W
Alexandria = El Iskandarîya 122 31 0N 30 0 E
Alexandria Bay 156 44 20N 75 52W
Alexandrina, L. 140 35 25 S 139 10 E
Alexandroúpolis 68 40 50N 25 54 E
Alexis Creek 152 52 0N 123 20W
Alexis, R. 151 52 33N 56 8W
Alfambra 58 40 33N 1 5W
Alfândega da Fé 56 41 20N 6 59W
Alfaro 58 42 10N 1 50W
Alfatar 67 43 59N 27 13 E
Alfeld 48 52 0N 9 49 E
Alfenas 173 21 40 S 44 0W
Alfiós, R. 69 37 36N 21 54 E
Alfonsine 63 44 30N 12 1 E
Alford, Grampian, U.K. 37 57 13N 2 42W
Alford, Lincs., U.K. 33 53 16N 0 10 E
Alfred 162 43 28N 70 40W
Alfred Town 141 35 8 S 147 30 E
Alfredton 142 40 41 S 175 54 E
Alfreton 33 53 6N 1 22W
Alfriston 29 50 48N 0 10 E
Alfta 72 61 21N 16 4 E
Alftanes 74 64 29N 22 10W
Alga 84 49 53N 57 20 E
Algaba, La 57 37 27N 6 1W
Algar 57 36 40N 5 39W
Ålgård 71 58 46N 5 53 E
Algård 71 58 46N 5 53 E
Algarinejo 57 37 19N 4 9W
Algarve 57 37 15N 8 10W
Algeciras 57 36 9N 5 28W
Algemesí 59 39 11N 0 27W
Alger 118 36 42N 3 8 E
Algeria ■ 118 35 10N 3 11 E
Alghero 64 40 34N 8 20 E
Algiers = Alger 118 36 42N 3 8 E
Algoabaai 128 33 50 S 25 45 E
Algodonales 57 36 54N 5 24W
Algodor, R. 56 39 51N 3 48W
Algoma, Mich., U.S.A. 156 44 35N 87 27W
Algoma, Oreg., U.S.A. 160 42 25N 121 54W
Algonquin Prov. Pk. 150 45 50N 78 30W
Alhama de Almeria 59 36 57N 2 34W
Alhama de Aragón 58 41 18N 1 54W
Alhama de Granada 57 37 0N 3 59W
Alhama de Murcia 59 37 51N 1 25W
Alhambra, Spain 59 38 54N 3 4W
Alhambra, U.S.A. 163 34 8N 118 10W
Alhaurín el Grande 57 36 39N 4 41W
Alhucemas = Al-Hoceïma 118 35 8N 3 58W
Ali al Gharbi 92 32 30N 46 45 E
Ali Bayramly 83 39 43N 48 52 E
Ali Khel 94 33 56N 69 35 E
Ali Sabieh 123 11 10N 42 44 E
Ália 64 37 47N 13 42 E
Aliabad 93 28 10N 57 35 E
Aliaga 58 40 40N 0 42W
Aliakmon, R. 68 40 10N 22 0 E
Alibag 96 18 38N 72 56 E
Alibo 123 9 52N 37 5 E
Alibunar 66 45 5N 20 57 E
Alicante 59 38 23N 0 30W
Alicante □ 59 38 30N 0 37W
Alice, S. Afr. 128 32 48 S 26 55 E
Alice, U.S.A. 159 27 47N 98 1W
Alice Arm 152 55 29N 129 31W
Alice Downs 136 17 45 S 127 56 E
Alice, Punta dell' 65 39 23N 17 10 E
Alice, R., Queens., Austral. 138 15 35 S 142 20 E
Alice, R., Queens., Austral. 138 24 2 S 144 50 E
Alice Springs 138 23 40 S 135 50 E
Alicedale 128 33 15 S 26 4 E
Aliceville 157 33 9N 88 10W
Alick Cr. 138 20 35 S 142 10 E
Alicudi, I. 65 38 33N 14 20 E
Alida 153 49 25N 101 55W
Aligarh, India 93 27 55N 78 10 E
Aligarh, Raj., India 94 25 55N 76 15 E
Aligarh, Ut. P., India 94 27 55N 78 10 E
Aligudarz 92 33 25N 49 45 E
Alijó 56 41 16N 7 27W
Alimena 65 37 42N 14 4 E
Alimnía 69 36 16N 27 43 E
Aling Kangri 99 31 45N 84 45 E
Alingaabro 73 56 56N 10 32 E
Alingsås 73 57 56N 12 31 E
Alipore 95 22 32N 88 24 E
Alipur 94 29 25N 70 55 E
Alipur Duar 98 26 30N 89 35 E
Aliquippa 156 40 38N 80 18W
Aliste, R. 56 41 48N 6 14W
Alivérion 69 38 24N 24 2 E
Aliwal North 128 30 45 S 26 45 E
Alix 152 52 24N 113 11W
Aljezur 57 37 18N 8 49W
Aljustrel 57 37 55N 8 10W
Alkamari 121 13 27N 11 10 E
Alken 47 50 53N 5 18 E
Alkhalaf 91 20 30N 58 13 E
Alkmaar 46 52 37N 4 45 E
All American Canal 161 32 45N 115 0W
Allada 121 6 41N 2 9 E
Allah Dad 94 25 38N 67 34 E
Allahabad 95 25 25N 81 58 E
Allakaket 147 66 30N 152 45W
Allakh Yun 77 60 50N 137 5 E
Allal Razi 118 34 30N 6 39W
Allan 153 51 53N 106 4W
Allanche 44 45 14N 2 57 E
Allanmyo 98 19 16N 95 17 E
Allanridge 128 27 45 S 26 40 E
Allansford 140 38 26 S 142 39 E
Allanton 143 45 55 S 170 15 E
Allanwater 150 50 14N 90 10W
Allaqi, Wadi 122 22 15N 34 55 E
Allard Lake 151 50 40N 63 10W
Allariz 56 42 11N 7 50W
Allassac 44 45 15N 1 29 E
Alle 47 49 51N 4 58 E
Allegan 156 42 32N 85 52W
Allegheny Mts. 156 38 0N 80 0W
Allegheny, R. 156 41 14N 79 50W
Allègre 44 45 12N 3 41 E
Allen, Bog of 39 53 15N 7 0W
Allen, L. 38 54 30N 8 5W
Allen R. 35 54 53N 2 13W
Allenby (Hussein) Bridge 90 31 53N 35 33 E
Allendale 35 54 55N 2 15W
Allende 164 28 20N 100 50W
Allenheads 35 54 49N 2 12W
Allentown 162 40 36N 75 30W
Allentsteig 52 48 41N 15 20 E
Allenwood 39 53 16N 6 53W
Alleppey 97 9 30N 76 28 E
Alleröd 73 55 54N 12 19 E
Alleur 47 50 39N 5 31 E
Allevard 45 45 24N 6 5 E
Alliance, Nebr., U.S.A. 158 42 10N 102 50W
Alliance, Ohio, U.S.A. 156 40 53N 81 7W
Allier □ 44 46 25N 3 0 E
Allier, R. 43 46 57N 3 4 E
Alligator Cr., Queens., Austral. 138 21 20 S 149 12 E
Alligator Cr., Queens., Austral. 138 19 23 S 146 58 E
Allihies 39 51 39N 10 4W
Allingåbrl 73 56 28N 10 20 E
Allingåbro 73 56 28N 10 20 E
Allinge 73 55 17N 14 50 E
Alliston 150 44 9N 79 52W
Alloa 35 56 7N 3 49W
Allonby 32 54 45N 3 27W
Allos 45 44 15N 6 38 E
Alma, Can. 151 48 35N 71 40W
Alma, Kans., U.S.A. 158 39 1N 96 22W
Alma, Mich., U.S.A. 156 43 25N 84 40W
Alma, Nebr., U.S.A. 158 40 10N 99 25W
Alma, Wis., U.S.A. 158 44 19N 91 54W
Alma Ata 85 43 15N 76 57 E
Almada 57 38 40N 9 9W
Almaden 138 17 22 S 144 40 E

Almadén Amungen


Almadén 57 38 49N 4 52W
Almagro 57 38 50N 3 45W
Almalyk 85 40 50N 69 35E
Almanor, L. 160 40 15N 121 11W
Almansa 59 38 51N 1 5W
Almanza 56 42 39N 5 3W
Almanzor, Pico de 56 40 15N 5 18W
Almanzora, R. 59 37 22N 2 21W
Almarcha, La 58 39 41N 2 24W
Almas 171 11 33S 47 9W
Almaş, Mţii 70 44 49N 22 12E
Almazán 58 41 30N 2 30W
Almazora 58 39 57N 0 3W
Almeirim, Brazil 175 1 30S 52 0W
Almeirim, Port. 57 39 12N 8 37W
Almelo 46 52 22N 6 42E
Almenar 58 41 43N 2 12W
Almenara, Brazil 171 16 11S 40 42W
Almenara, Spain 58 39 46N 0 14W
Almenara, Sierra de 59 37 34N 1 32W
Almendralejo 57 38 41N 6 26W
Almería 59 36 52N 2 32W
Almería □ 59 37 20N 2 20W
Almería, G. de 59 36 41N 2 28W
Almetyevsk 84 54 53N 52 20E
Almhult 73 56 32N 14 10E
Almirante 166 9 10N 82 30W
Almiropótamos 69 38 16N 24 11E
Almirós 69 39 11N 22 45E
Almodôvar 57 37 31N 8 2W
Almodóvar del Campo 57 38 43N 4 10W
Almogia 57 36 50N 4 32W
Almonaster la Real 57 37 52N 6 48W
Almond R. 35 56 27N 3 27W
Almondsbury 28 51 33N 2 34W
Almonte, R. 57 39 41N 6 12W
Almora 95 29 38N 79 4E
Almoradi 59 38 7N 0 46W
Almorox 56 40 14N 4 24W
Almoustarat 121 17 35N 0 8E
Älmult 73 56 33N 14 8E
Almuñécar 57 36 43N 3 41W
Almunia, La de Doña Godina 58 41 29N 1 23W
Almvik 73 57 49N 16 30E
Aln, R. 35 55 24N 1 35W
Alness 37 57 41N 4 15W
Alness R. 37 57 45N 4 20W
Alnif 118 31 10N 5 8W
Alnmouth 35 55 24N 1 37W
Alnön I. 72 62 26N 17 33E
Alnwick 35 55 25N 1 42W
Aloi 126 2 16N 33 10E
Alon 98 22 12N 95 5E
Alonsa 153 50 50N 99 0W
Alor, I. 103 8 15S 124 30E
Alor Setar 101 6 7N 100 22E
Alora 57 36 49N 4 46W
Alosno 57 37 33N 7 7W
Alot'ai 105 47 52N 88 7E
Alotau 135 10 16S 150 30E
Alougoum 118 30 17N 6 56W
Aloysius Mt. 137 26 0S 128 38E
Alpaugh 163 35 53N 119 29W
Alpedrinha 56 40 6N 7 27W
Alpena 156 45 6N 83 24W
Alpercatas, R. 170 6 2S 44 19W
Alpes-de-Haute-Provence □ 45 44 8N 6 10E
Alpes-Maritimes □ 45 43 55N 7 10E
Alpes Valaisannes 50 46 4N 7 30E
Alpha 138 23 39S 146 37E
Alphen 47 51 29N 4 58E
Alphen aan den Rijn 46 52 7N 4 40E
Alphington 30 50 41N 3 32W
Alpi Apuan 62 44 7N 10 14E
Alpi Craie 43 45 40N 7 0E
Alpi Lepontine 51 46 22N 8 27E
Alpi Orobie 62 46 7N 10 0E
Alpi Retiche 51 46 45N 10 0E
Alpiarça 57 39 15N 8 35W
Alpine, Ariz., U.S.A. 161 33 57N 109 4W
Alpine, Calif., U.S.A. 163 32 50N 116 46W
Alpine, Tex., U.S.A. 159 30 35N 103 35W
Alpnach 51 46 57N 8 17E
Alrewas 28 52 43N 1 44W
Alrø 73 55 52N 10 5E
Alroy Downs 138 19 20S 136 5E
Als 73 56 46N 10 18E
Alsace 43 48 15N 7 25E
Alsager 32 53 7N 2 20W
Alsask 153 51 21N 109 59W
Alsásua 58 42 54N 2 10W
Alseda 73 57 27N 15 20E
Alsen 72 63 23N 13 56E
Alsfeld 48 50 44N 9 19E
Alsh, L. 36 57 15N 5 39W
Alsónémedi 53 47 34N 19 15E
Alsten 74 65 58N 12 40E
Alston 32 54 48N 2 26W
Alta 74 69 57N 23 10E
Alta Gracia 172 31 40S 64 30W
Alta Lake 152 50 10N 123 0W
Alta, Sierra 58 40 31N 1 30W
Alta Sierra 163 35 42N 118 33W
Altaelva 74 69 46N 23 45E
Altafjorden 74 70 5N 23 5E
Altagracia 174 10 45N 71 30W
Altai = Aerht'ai Shan 105 48 0N 90 0E
Altamaha, R. 157 31 50N 82 0W
Altamira, Brazil 175 3 0S 52 10W
Altamira, Chile 172 25 47S 69 51W
Altamira, Colomb. 174 2 3N 75 47W
Altamira, Mexico 165 22 24N 97 55W
Altamira, Cuevas de 56 43 20N 4 5W
Altamont 162 42 43N 74 3W
Altamura 65 40 50N 16 33E
Altanbulag 54 50 19N 106 30E
Altar 164 30 40N 111 50W
Altarnun 30 50 35N 4 30W
Altata 164 24 30N 108 0W
Altavista 156 37 9N 79 22W
Altdorf 51 46 52N 8 36E
Altea 59 38 38N 0 2W
Altenberg 48 50 46N 13 47E
Altenbruch 48 53 48N 8 44E
Altenburg 48 50 59N 12 28E
Altenkirchen 48 50 41N 7 38E
Altenmarkt 52 47 43N 14 39E
Alter do Chão 57 39 12N 7 40W
Altkirch 43 47 37N 7 15E
Altnaharra 37 58 17N 4 27W
Alto Adige = Trentino-Alto Adige 62 46 5N 11 0E
Alto Araguaia 175 17 15S 53 20W
Alto Chindio 127 16 19S 35 25E
Alto Cuchumatanes 164 15 30N 91 10W
Alto del Inca 172 24 10S 68 10W
Alto Ligonha 127 15 30S 38 11E
Alto Molocue 127 15 50S 37 35E
Alto Paraná □ 173 25 0S 54 50W
Alto Parnaíba 170 9 6S 45 57W
Alto Santo 170 5 31S 38 15W
Alto Turi 170 2 54S 45 38W
Alto Uruguay, R. 173 27 0S 53 30W
Alton, U.K. 29 51 8N 0 59W
Alton, Ill., U.S.A. 158 38 55N 90 5W
Alton, N.H., U.S.A. 162 43 27N 71 13W
Alton Downs 139 26 7S 138 57E
Altona 48 53 32N 9 56E
Altoona 156 40 32N 78 24W
Altopáscio 62 43 50N 10 40E
Altos 170 5 3S 42 28W
Altrincham 32 53 25N 2 21W
Altstätten 51 47 22N 9 33E
Alturas 160 41 36N 120 37W
Altus 159 34 30N 99 25W
Alucra 83 40 22N 38 47E
Aluksône 80 57 24N 27 3E
Alula 91 11 50N 50 45E
Alupka 82 44 23N 34 2E
Alushta 82 44 40N 34 25E
Alusi 103 7 35S 131 40E
Alustante 58 40 36N 1 40W
Alva, U.K. 35 56 9N 3 49W
Alva, U.S.A. 159 36 50N 98 50W
Alvaiázere 56 39 49N 8 23W
Alvangen 73 58 0N 12 7E
Älvängen 73 57 58N 12 8E
Alvarado, Mexico 165 18 40N 95 50W
Alvarado, U.S.A. 159 32 25N 97 15W
Alvaro Obregón, Presa 164 27 55N 109 52W
Alvastra 73 58 20N 14 44E
Alvdal 71 62 6N 10 37E
Alvear 172 29 5S 56 30W
Alvechurch 28 52 22N 1 58W
Alverca 57 38 56N 9 1W
Alveringen 47 51 1N 2 43E
Alvesta 73 56 54N 14 35E
Älvho 72 61 30N 14 45E
Alvie, Austral. 140 38 14S 143 30E
Alvie, U.K. 37 57 10N 3 50W
Alvin 159 29 23N 95 12W
Alvito 57 38 15N 8 0W
Älvkarleby 75 60 32N 17 40E
Alvra, Pic d' 51 46 35N 9 50E
Älvros 72 62 3N 14 38E
Älvsborgs län □ 73 58 30N 12 30E
Älvsby 74 65 42N 20 52E
Älvsbyn 74 65 40N 20 0E
Alvsered 73 57 14N 12 51E
Alwar 94 27 38N 76 34E
Alwaye 97 10 8N 76 24E
Alwinton 35 55 20N 2 7W
Alwyn, oilfield 19 60 30N 1 45E
Alyangula 133 13 55S 136 30E
Alyaskitovyy 77 64 45N 141 30E
Alyata 83 39 58N 49 25E
Alyth 37 56 38N 3 15W
Alzada 158 45 3N 104 22W
Alzano Lombardo 62 45 44N 9 43E
Alzette, R. 47 49 45N 6 6E
Alzey 49 49 48N 8 4E
Am-Dam 117 12 40N 20 35E
Am Djeress 117 16 15N 22 50E
Am Guereda 117 12 53N 21 14E
Am Timan 117 11 0N 20 10E
Am-Zoer 124 14 13N 21 23E
Amadeus, L. 137 24 54S 131 0E
Amadi, Congo 126 3 40N 26 40E
Amadi, Sudan 123 5 29N 30 25E
Amadi, Zaïre 126 3 40N 26 40E
Amadia 92 37 6N 43 30E
Amadjuak 149 64 0N 72 39W
Amadjuak L. 149 65 0N 71 8W
Amadora 57 38 45N 9 13W
Amaga 174 6 3N 75 42W
Amagansett 162 40 58N 72 8W
Amagasaki 111 34 42N 135 20E
Amager 73 55 37N 12 35E
Amagi 110 33 25N 130 39E
Amagunze 121 6 20N 7 40E
Amaimon 135 5 12S 145 30E
Amakusa-Nada 110 32 35N 130 5E
Amakusa-Shotō 110 32 15N 130 10E
Amâl 72 59 2N 12 40E
Åmål 72 59 3N 12 42E
Amalapuram 96 16 35N 81 55E
Amalfi, Colomb. 174 6 55N 75 4W
Amalfi, Italy 65 40 39N 14 34E
Amaliás 69 37 47N 21 22E
Amalner 96 21 5N 75 5E
Amambaí 173 23 5S 55 13W
Amambai, R. 173 23 22S 53 56W
Amambay □ 173 23 0S 56 0W
Amambay, Cordillera de 173 20 30S 56 0W
Amami-O-Shima 112 28 0N 129 0E
Amanab 135 3 40S 141 14E
Amandola 63 42 59N 13 21E
Amanfrom 121 7 20N 0 25E
Amangeldy 76 50 10N 65 10E
Amantea 65 39 8N 16 3E
Amapá 170 2 5N 50 50W
Amapá □ 170 1 40N 52 0W
Amar Gedid 123 14 27N 25 13E
Amara, Iraq 92 31 57N 47 12E
Amara, Sudan 123 10 25N 34 10E
Amarante, Brazil 170 6 14S 42 50W
Amarante, Port. 56 41 16N 8 5W
Amarante do Maranhão 170 5 36S 46 45W
Amaranth 153 50 36N 98 43W
Amarapura 98 21 54N 96 3E
Amaravati, R. 97 10 50N 77 42E
Amaravati = Amraoti 96 20 55N 77 45E
Amareleja 57 38 12N 7 13W
Amargosa 171 13 2S 39 36W
Amargosa, R. 163 36 14N 116 51W
Amargosa Ra., mts 163 36 25N 116 40W
Amarillo 159 35 14N 101 46W
Amaro Leite 171 13 58S 49 9W
Amaro, Mt. 63 42 5N 14 6E
Amarpur, India 99 23 30N 91 45E
Amarpur, Bihar, India 95 25 5N 87 0E
Amarpur, Tripura, India 99 23 30N 91 45E
Amasra 92 41 45N 32 30E
Amassama 121 5 1N 6 2E
Amasya 92 40 40N 35 50E
Amatignak I. 147 51 19N 179 10W
Amatikulu 129 29 3S 31 33E
Amatitlán 166 14 29N 90 38W
Amatrice 63 42 38N 13 16E
Amay 47 50 33N 5 19E
Amazon, R. 175 2 0S 53 30W
Amazonas □, Brazil 174 4 20S 64 0W
Amazonas □, Colomb. 174 1 0S 72 0W
Amazonas □, Venez. 174 3 30N 66 0W
Amazonas, R. 175 2 0S 53 30W
Ambad 96 19 38N 75 50E
Ambahakily 129 21 36S 43 41E
Ambala 94 30 23N 76 56E
Ambalangoda 97 6 15N 80 5E
Ambalapuzha 97 9 25N 76 25E
Ambalavao 129 21 50S 46 56E
Ambalindum 138 23 23S 134 40E
Ambam 124 2 20N 11 15E
Ambanifilao 129 12 48S 49 47E
Ambanja 129 13 40S 48 27E
Ambararata 129 13 41S 48 27E
Ambarchik 77 69 40N 162 20E
Ambarijeby 129 14 56S 47 41E
Ambarnath 96 19 12N 73 22E
Ambaro, B. d' 129 13 23S 48 38E
Ambasamudram 97 8 43N 77 25E
Ambato 174 1 5S 78 42W
Ambato-Boéni 129 16 28S 46 43E
Ambato, Sierra de 172 28 25N 66 10W
Ambatolampy 129 19 20S 47 35E
Ambatondrazaka 129 17 55S 48 28E
Ambatosoratra 129 17 37S 48 31E
Ambenja 129 15 17S 46 58E
Ambeno 103 9 20S 124 30E
Amberg 49 49 25N 11 52E
Ambergris Cay 165 18 0N 88 0W
Ambérieu-en-Bugey 45 45 57N 5 20E
Amberley 143 43 9S 172 44E
Ambert 44 45 33N 3 44E
Ambevongo 129 15 25S 42 26E
Ambia 129 16 11S 45 33E
Ambidédi 120 14 35N 11 47W
Ambikapur 95 23 15N 83 15E
Ambikol 122 21 20N 30 50E
Ambilobé 125 13 10S 49 3E
Ambinanindrano 129 20 5S 48 23E
Ambjörnarp 73 57 25N 13 17E
Amble 35 55 20N 1 36W
Ambler 162 40 9N 75 13W
Ambleside 32 54 26N 2 58W
Amblève 47 50 21N 6 10E
Amblève, R. 47 50 25N 5 45E
Ambo, Begemdir & Simen, Ethiopia 123 12 20N 37 30E
Ambo, Shewa, Ethiopia 123 9 0N 37 48E
Ambo, Peru 174 10 5S 76 10W
Ambodifototra 129 16 59S 49 52E
Ambodilazana 129 18 6S 49 10E
Ambohimahasoa 129 21 7S 47 13E
Ambohimanga du Sud 129 20 52S 47 36E
Ambon 103 3 35S 128 20E
Ambongao, Cones d' 129 17 0S 45 0E
Amboseli L. 126 2 40S 37 10E
Ambositra 129 20 31S 47 25E
Amboy 163 34 33N 115 51W
Ambre, C. d' 129 12 40S 49 10E
Ambre, Mt. d' 125 12 30S 49 10E
Ambriz 124 7 48S 13 8E
Ambrizete 124 7 10S 12 52E
Ambunti 135 4 13S 142 52E
Ambut 97 12 48N 78 43E
Amby 139 26 30S 148 11E
Amchitka I. 147 51 30N 179 0W
Amchitka P. 147 51 30N 179 0W
Amderma 76 69 45N 61 30E
Ameca 164 20 30N 104 0W
Ameca, R. 164 20 40N 105 15W
Amecameca 165 19 10N 98 57W
Ameland 46 53 27N 5 45E
Amélia 63 42 34N 12 25E
Amèlie-les-Bains-Palalda 44 42 29N 2 41E
Amen 77 68 45N 180 0E
Amendolaro 65 39 58N 16 34E
Amenia 162 41 51N 73 33W
America 47 51 27N 5 59E
American Falls 160 42 46N 112 56W
American Falls Res. 160 43 0N 112 50W
American Highland 13 73 0S 75 0E
Americana 173 22 45S 47 20W
Americus 157 32 0N 84 10W
Amersfoort, Neth. 46 52 9N 5 23E
Amersfoort, S. Afr. 129 26 59S 29 53E
Amersham 29 51 40N 0 38W
Amery, Austral. 137 31 9S 117 5E
Amery, Can. 153 56 34N 94 3W
Ames 158 42 0N 93 40W
Amesbury, U.K. 28 51 10N 1 46W
Amesbury, U.S.A. 162 42 50N 70 52W
Amesdale 153 50 2N 92 55W
Ameson 150 49 50N 84 35W
Amethyst, gasfield 19 53 38N 0 40E
Amfíklia 69 38 38N 22 35E
Amfilokhia 69 38 52N 21 9E
Amfípolis 68 40 48N 23 52E
Ámfissa 69 38 32N 22 22E
Amga, R. 77 61 0N 132 0E
Amgu 77 45 45N 137 15E
Amherst, Burma 99 16 2N 97 20E
Amherst, Can. 151 45 48N 64 8W
Amherst, Mass., U.S.A. 162 42 21N 72 30W
Amherst, Tex., U.S.A. 159 34 0N 102 24W
Amherst, Mt. 136 18 11S 126 59E
Amherstburg 150 42 6N 83 6W
Amiata Mte. 63 42 54N 11 40E
Amiens 43 49 54N 2 16E
Amigdhalokefáli 69 35 23N 23 30E
Amili 98 28 25N 95 52E
Amindaion 68 40 42N 21 42E
Amirante Is. 11 6 0S 53 0E
Amisk L. 153 54 35N 102 15W
Amistati, Presa 164 29 24N 101 0W
Amite 159 30 47N 90 31W
Åmli 71 58 45N 8 32E
Amlia I. 147 52 5N 173 30W
Amlwch 31 53 24N 4 21W
Amm Adam 123 16 20N 36 1E
'Ammān 90 32 0N 35 52E
Ammanford 31 51 48N 4 0W
Ammerån 72 63 9N 16 13E
Ammerån 72 63 9N 16 13E
Ammersee 49 48 0N 11 7E
Ammerzoden 46 51 45N 5 13E
Ammi'ad 90 32 55N 35 32E
Amnat Charoen 100 15 51N 104 38E
Amne Machin 105 34 30N 100 0E
Amnéville 43 49 16N 6 9E
Amo Chiang, R. 108 22 56N 101 47E
Amorebieta 58 43 13N 2 44W
Amorgós 69 36 50N 25 57E
Amory 57 33 59N 88 30W
Amos 150 48 35N 78 5W
Åmot 71 59 54N 9 54E
Åmot 71 59 34N 8 0E
Åmotsdal 71 59 37N 8 26E
Amour, Djebel 118 33 42N 1 37E
Amoy = Hsiamen 109 24 25N 118 4E
Amozoc 165 19 2N 98 3W
Ampang 101 3 8N 101 45E
Ampanihy 129 24 40S 44 45E
Amparihy Est. 129 23 57S 47 20E
Ampasindava, B. d' 129 13 40S 48 15E
Ampasindava, Presqu'île d' 129 13 42S 47 55W
Amper 121 9 25N 9 40E
Ampère 119 35 44N 5 27E
Ampleforth 33 54 13N 1 8W
Ampombiantambo 129 12 42S 48 57E
Amposta 58 40 43N 0 34E
Ampotaka 129 25 3S 44 41E
Ampoza 129 22 20S 44 44E
Ampthill 29 52 3N 0 30W
Amqa 90 32 59N 35 10E
Amqui 151 48 28N 67 27W
Amraoti 96 20 55N 77 45E
Amreli 94 21 35N 71 17E
Amrenene el Kasba 118 22 10N 0 30E
Amriswil 51 47 33N 9 18E
Amritsar 94 31 35N 74 57E
Amroha 95 28 53N 78 30E
Amrum 48 54 37N 8 21E
Amsel 119 22 47N 5 29E
Amsterdam, Neth. 46 52 23N 4 54E
Amsterdam, U.S.A. 162 42 58N 74 10W
Amsterdam, Î. 11 37 30S 77 30E
Amstetten 52 48 7N 14 51E
Amu Darya, R. 76 37 50N 65 0E
Amuay 174 11 50N 70 10W
Amukta I. 147 52 29N 171 20W
Amund Ringnes I. 12 78 20N 96 25W
Amundsen Gulf 148 71 0N 124 0W
Amundsen Sea 13 72 0S 115 0W
Amungen 72 61 10N 15 40E

Amuntai Anza


| | | | |
|---|---|---|---|
| Amuntai | 102 | 2 28 S | 115 25 E |
| Amur, R. | 77 | 53 30N | 122 30 E |
| Amurang | 103 | 1 5N | 124 40 E |
| Amuri Pass | 143 | 42 31 S | 172 11 E |
| Amurrio | 58 | 43 3N | 3 0W |
| Amurzet | 77 | 47 50N | 131 5 E |
| Amusco | 56 | 42 10N | 4 28W |
| Amvrakikós Kólpos | 69 | 39 0N | 20 55 E |
| Amvrosiyvka | 83 | 47 43N | 38 30 E |
| Amzeglouf | 118 | 26 50N | 0 1 E |
| An | 98 | 22 29N | 96 54 E |
| An Bien | 101 | 9 45N | 105 0 E |
| An Geata Mór, (Binghamstown) | 38 | 54 13N | 10 0W |
| An Hoa | 100 | 15 30N | 108 20 E |
| An Loc | 101 | 11 40N | 106 50 E |
| An Nafud | 92 | 28 15N | 41 0 E |
| An Najaf | 92 | 32 3N | 44 15 E |
| An-Nâqûrah | 90 | 33 7N | 35 8 E |
| An Nasiriyah | 92 | 31 0N | 46 15 E |
| An Nawfaliyah | 119 | 30 54N | 17 58 E |
| An Nhon (Binh Dinh) | 100 | 13 55N | 109 7 E |
| An Nîl □ | 123 | 17 30N | 33 0 E |
| An Nîl el Abyad □ | 123 | 14 0N | 32 15 E |
| An Nu'ayriyah | 92 | 27 30N | 48 30 E |
| An Teallach, Mt. | 36 | 57 49N | 5 18W |
| An Thoi, Dao | 101 | 9 58N | 104 0 E |
| An Tuc | 100 | 13 57N | 108 39 E |
| An Uaimh | 38 | 53 39N | 6 40W |
| Åna-Sira | 71 | 58 17N | 6 25 E |
| Anabta | 90 | 32 19N | 35 7 E |
| Anabuki | 110 | 34 2N | 134 11 E |
| Anaco | 174 | 9 27N | 64 28W |
| Anaconda | 160 | 46 7N | 113 0W |
| Anacortes | 160 | 48 30N | 122 40W |
| Anadarko | 159 | 35 4N | 98 15W |
| Anadia, Brazil | 170 | 9 42 S | 36 18W |
| Anadia, Port. | 56 | 40 26N | 8 27W |
| Anadolu | 92 | 38 0N | 29 0 E |
| Anadyr | 77 | 64 35N | 177 20 E |
| Anadyr, R. | 77 | 66 50N | 171 0 E |
| Anadyrskiy Zaliv | 77 | 64 0N | 180 0 E |
| Anáfi | 69 | 36 22N | 25 48 E |
| Anafópoulo | 69 | 36 17N | 25 50 E |
| Anagni | 64 | 41 44N | 13 8 E |
| Anah | 92 | 34 25N | 42 0 E |
| Anaheim | 163 | 33 50N | 118 0W |
| Anahim Lake | 152 | 52 28N | 125 18W |
| Anáhuac | 164 | 27 14N | 100 9W |
| Anai Mudi, Mt. | 97 | 10 12N | 77 20 E |
| Anaimalai Hills | 97 | 10 20N | 76 40 E |
| Anajás | 170 | 0 59 S | 49 57W |
| Anajatuba | 170 | 3 16 S | 44 37W |
| Anakapalle | 96 | 17 42N | 83 06 E |
| Anakie | 138 | 23 32 S | 147 45 E |
| Anaklia | 83 | 42 22N | 41 35 E |
| Analalava | 129 | 14 35 S | 48 0 E |
| Analapasy | 129 | 25 11 S | 46 40 E |
| Anam | 121 | 6 19N | 6 41 E |
| Anambar, R. | 94 | 30 10N | 68 50 E |
| Anambas, Kepulauan | 102 | 3 20N | 106 30 E |
| Anamoose | 158 | 47 55N | 100 7W |
| Anamosa | 158 | 42 7N | 91 17W |
| Anamur | 92 | 36 8N | 32 58 E |
| Anan | 110 | 33 54N | 134 40 E |
| Anand | 94 | 22 32N | 72 59 E |
| Anandpur | 96 | 21 16N | 86 13 E |
| Anánes | 69 | 36 33N | 24 9 E |
| Anantapur | 97 | 14 39N | 77 42 E |
| Anantnag | 95 | 33 45N | 75 10 E |
| Ananyev | 82 | 47 44N | 29 57 E |
| Anapa | 82 | 44 55N | 37 25 E |
| Anápolis | 171 | 16 15 S | 48 50W |
| Anar | 93 | 30 55N | 55 13 E |
| Anarak | 93 | 33 25N | 53 40 E |
| Anatolia = Anadolu | 92 | 38 0N | 29 0 E |
| Anatone | 160 | 46 9N | 117 4W |
| Añatuya | 172 | 28 20 S | 62 50W |
| Anaunethad L. | 153 | 60 55N | 104 25W |
| Anaye | 117 | 19 15N | 12 50 E |
| Anbyŏn | 107 | 39 1N | 127 35 E |
| Ancaster | 33 | 52 59N | 0 32W |
| Ancenis | 42 | 47 21N | 1 10W |
| Anch'i | 109 | 25 3N | 118 13 E |
| Anch'ing | 109 | 30 37N | 117 0 E |
| Anch'iu | 107 | 36 25N | 119 10 E |
| Ancholme, R. | 33 | 53 42N | 0 32W |
| Anchorage | 147 | 61 10N | 149 50W |
| Ancião | 56 | 39 56N | 8 27W |
| Ancohuma, Nevada | 174 | 16 0 S | 68 50W |
| Ancon | 164 | 8 57N | 79 33W |
| Ancón | 174 | 11 50 S | 77 10W |
| Ancona | 63 | 43 37N | 13 30 E |
| Ancrum | 35 | 55 31N | 2 35W |
| Ancud | 176 | 42 0 S | 73 50W |
| Ancud, G. de | 176 | 42 0 S | 73 0W |
| Andacollo, Argent. | 172 | 37 10 S | 70 42W |
| Andacollo, Chile | 172 | 30 15 S | 71 10W |
| Andado | 138 | 25 25 S | 135 15 E |
| Andalgalá | 172 | 27 40 S | 66 30W |
| Åndalsnes | 71 | 62 35N | 7 43 E |
| Andalucía | 57 | 37 35N | 5 0W |
| Andalusia | 157 | 31 51N | 86 30W |
| Andalusia = Andalucía | 57 | 37 35N | 5 0W |
| Andaman Is. | 101 | 12 30N | 92 30 E |
| Andaman Sea | 101 | 13 0N | 96 0 E |
| Andaman Str. | 101 | 12 15N | 92 20 E |
| Andara | 128 | 18 2 S | 21 9 E |
| Andaraí | 171 | 12 48 S | 41 20W |
| Andeer | 51 | 46 36N | 9 26 E |
| Andelfingen | 51 | 47 36N | 8 41 E |
| Andelot | 43 | 46 51N | 5 56 E |
| Andelys, Les | 42 | 49 15N | 1 25 E |
| Andenne | 47 | 50 30N | 5 5 E |
| Andéranboukane | 121 | 15 26N | 3 2 E |
| Anderlecht | 47 | 50 50N | 4 19 E |
| Anderlues | 47 | 50 25N | 4 16 E |
| Andermatt | 51 | 46 38N | 8 35 E |
| Andernach | 48 | 50 24N | 7 25 E |
| Andernos | 44 | 44 44N | 1 6W |
| Anderslöv | 73 | 55 26N | 13 19 E |
| Anderson, Austral. | 141 | 38 32 S | 145 27 E |
| Anderson, Calif., U.S.A. | 160 | 40 30N | 122 19W |
| Anderson, Ind., U.S.A. | 156 | 40 5N | 85 40W |
| Anderson, Mo., U.S.A. | 159 | 36 43N | 94 29W |
| Anderson, S.C., U.S.A. | 157 | 34 32N | 82 40W |
| Anderson, Mt. | 129 | 25 5 S | 30 42 E |
| Anderson, R. | 147 | 69 42N | 129 0W |
| Anderstorp | 73 | 57 19N | 13 39 E |
| Andes | 162 | 42 12N | 74 47W |
| Andes, mts. | 174 | 20 0 S | 68 0W |
| Andfjorden | 74 | 69 10N | 16 20 E |
| Andhra, L. | 96 | 18 30N | 73 32 E |
| Andhra Pradesh □ | 97 | 15 0N | 80 0 E |
| Andikíthira | 69 | 35 52N | 23 15 E |
| Andímilos | 69 | 36 47N | 24 12 E |
| Andíparos | 69 | 37 0N | 25 3 E |
| Andípaxoi | 69 | 39 9N | 20 13 E |
| Andípsara | 69 | 38 30N | 25 29 E |
| Andizhan | 76 | 41 10N | 72 0 E |
| Andkhui | 93 | 36 52N | 65 8 E |
| Andohararo | 129 | 22 58 S | 43 45 E |
| Andol | 96 | 17 51N | 78 4 E |
| Andong | 107 | 36 40N | 128 43 E |
| Andorra ■ | 58 | 42 30N | 1 30 E |
| Andorra La Vella | 58 | 42 31N | 1 32 E |
| Andover, U.K. | 28 | 51 13N | 1 29W |
| Andover, U.S.A. | 162 | 40 59N | 74 44W |
| Andradina | 171 | 20 54 S | 51 23W |
| Andrahary, Mt. | 129 | 13 37 S | 49 17 E |
| Andraitx | 58 | 39 35N | 2 25 E |
| Andramasina | 129 | 19 11 S | 47 35 E |
| Andrano-Velona | 129 | 18 10 S | 46 52 E |
| Andranopasy | 129 | 21 17 S | 43 44 E |
| Andreanof Is. | 147 | 51 0N | 178 0W |
| Andreapol | 80 | 56 40N | 32 17 E |
| Andreas | 32 | 54 23N | 4 25W |
| Andrespol | 54 | 51 45N | 19 34 E |
| Andrew, oilfield | 19 | 58 4N | 1 24 E |
| Andrews, S.C., U.S.A. | 157 | 33 29N | 79 30W |
| Andrews, Tex., U.S.A. | 159 | 32 18N | 102 33W |
| Andreyevka | 84 | 52 19N | 51 55 E |
| Ándria | 65 | 41 13N | 16 17 E |
| Andrian | 65 | 46 30N | 11 13 E |
| Andriba | 129 | 17 30 S | 46 58 E |
| Andrijevica | 66 | 42 45N | 19 48 E |
| Andrítsaina | 69 | 37 29N | 21 52 E |
| Androka | 129 | 24 58 S | 44 2 E |
| Ándros | 69 | 37 50N | 24 50 E |
| Andros I. | 166 | 24 30N | 78 0W |
| Andros Town | 166 | 24 43N | 77 47W |
| Andrychów | 54 | 49 51N | 19 18 E |
| Andújar | 57 | 38 3N | 4 5W |
| Aneby | 73 | 57 48N | 14 49 E |
| Anécho | 121 | 6 12N | 1 34 E |
| Anegada I. | 147 | 18 45N | 64 20W |
| Anergane | 118 | 31 4N | 7 14W |
| Aneto, Pico de | 58 | 42 37N | 0 40 E |
| Anfeg | 119 | 22 29N | 5 58 E |
| Anfu | 109 | 27 23N | 114 37 E |
| Ang Thong | 100 | 14 35N | 100 31 E |
| Anga | 77 | 60 35N | 132 0 E |
| Angamos, Punta | 172 | 23 1 S | 70 32W |
| Anganch'i | 98 | 47 9N | 123 48 E |
| Angara, R. | 77 | 58 30N | 97 0 E |
| Angarsk | 77 | 52 30N | 104 0 E |
| Angas Downs | 137 | 24 49 S | 132 14 E |
| Angas Ra. | 137 | 23 0 S | 127 50 E |
| Angaston | 140 | 34 30 S | 139 8 E |
| Ånge | 72 | 62 31N | 15 35 E |
| Ångebo | 72 | 61 58N | 16 22 E |
| Angel de la Guarda, I. | 164 | 29 30N | 113 30W |
| Ängelholm | 73 | 56 15N | 12 58 E |
| Angellala | 139 | 26 24 S | 146 54 E |
| Angels Camp | 163 | 38 8N | 120 30W |
| Ängelsberg | 72 | 59 58N | 16 0 E |
| Angenong | 99 | 31 57N | 94 10 E |
| Anger, R. | 123 | 9 30N | 36 35 E |
| Angereb | 123 | 13 11N | 37 7 E |
| Angereb, R. | 123 | 14 0N | 36 0 E |
| Ångermanälven | 72 | 62 40N | 18 0 E |
| Angermünde | 48 | 53 1N | 14 0 E |
| Angers | 42 | 47 30N | 0 35W |
| Angerville | 43 | 48 19N | 2 0 E |
| Ängesån | 74 | 66 50N | 22 15 E |
| Anghiari | 63 | 43 32N | 12 3 E |
| Angical | 171 | 12 0 S | 44 42W |
| Angical do Piauí | 171 | 6 5 S | 42 44W |
| Angikuni L. | 153 | 62 0N | 100 0W |
| Angkor | 100 | 13 22N | 103 50 E |
| Angle | 31 | 51 40N | 5 3W |
| Anglem Mt. | 143 | 46 45 S | 167 53 E |
| Anglés | 58 | 41 57N | 2 38 E |
| Anglesey (□) | 26 | 53 17N | 4 20W |
| Anglesey, I. | 31 | 53 17N | 4 20W |
| Anglet | 44 | 43 29N | 1 31W |
| Angleton | 159 | 29 12N | 95 23W |
| Angleur | 47 | 50 36N | 5 35 E |
| Anglure | 43 | 48 35N | 3 50 E |
| Angmagssalik | 12 | 65 40N | 37 20W |
| Angmering | 29 | 50 48N | 0 28W |
| Ango | 126 | 4 10N | 26 5 E |
| Angoche | 127 | 16 8 S | 40 0 E |
| Angoche, I. | 127 | 16 20 S | 39 50 E |
| Angol | 172 | 37 56 S | 72 45W |
| Angola | 156 | 41 40N | 85 0W |
| Angola ■ | 125 | 12 0 S | 18 0 E |
| Angoon | 147 | 57 40N | 134 40W |
| Angoram | 135 | 4 4 S | 144 4 E |
| Angoulême | 44 | 45 39N | 0 10 E |
| Angoumois | 44 | 45 30N | 0 25 E |
| Angra dos Reis | 173 | 23 0 S | 44 10W |
| Angra-Juntas | 128 | 27 39 S | 15 31 E |
| Angran | 76 | 80 59N | 69 3 E |
| Angren | 85 | 41 1N | 70 12 E |
| Angtassom | 101 | 11 1N | 104 41 E |
| Angu | 126 | 3 25N | 24 28 E |
| Anguilla, I. | 167 | 18 14N | 63 5W |
| Angurugu | 138 | 14 0 S | 136 25 E |
| Angus (□) | 26 | 56 45N | 2 55W |
| Angus, Braes of | 37 | 56 51N | 3 0W |
| Anhanduí, R. | 173 | 21 46 S | 52 9W |
| Anhée | 47 | 50 18N | 4 53 E |
| Anholt | 73 | 56 42N | 11 33 E |
| Anhsi | 105 | 40 30N | 96 0 E |
| Anhsiang | 109 | 29 24N | 112 9 E |
| Anhua, Hunan, China | 109 | 28 22N | 111 10 E |
| Anhua, Kwangsi-Chuang, China | 108 | 25 10N | 108 21 E |
| Anhwei □ | 109 | 33 15N | 116 50 E |
| Ani, Kiangsi, China | 109 | 28 50N | 115 32 E |
| Ani, Shansi, China | 106 | 35 3N | 111 2 E |
| Aniak | 147 | 61 58N | 159 50W |
| Anicuns | 171 | 16 28 S | 49 58W |
| Ánidhros | 69 | 36 38N | 25 43 E |
| Anié | 121 | 7 42N | 1 8 E |
| Animas | 161 | 31 58N | 108 58W |
| Ånimskog | 73 | 58 53N | 12 35 E |
| Anin | 101 | 15 36N | 97 50 E |
| Anivorano | 129 | 18 44 S | 48 58 E |
| Anjangaon | 96 | 21 10N | 77 20 E |
| Anjar | 94 | 23 6N | 70 10 E |
| Anjen | 109 | 26 42N | 113 19 E |
| Anjiabé | 129 | 12 7 S | 49 20 E |
| Anjidiv I. | 97 | 14 40N | 74 10 E |
| Anjō | 111 | 34 57N | 137 5 E |
| Anjou | 42 | 47 20N | 0 15W |
| Anjozorobe | 129 | 18 22 S | 47 52 E |
| Anju | 107 | 39 36N | 125 40 E |
| Anka | 121 | 12 13N | 5 58 E |
| Ank'ang | 108 | 32 38N | 109 5 E |
| Ankara | 92 | 40 0N | 32 54 E |
| Ankaramena | 129 | 21 57 S | 46 39 E |
| Ankazoabo | 129 | 22 18 S | 44 31 E |
| Ankazobé | 129 | 18 20 S | 47 10 E |
| Ankazotokana | 129 | 21 20 S | 48 9 E |
| Ankisabé | 129 | 19 17 S | 46 29 E |
| Anklesvar | 96 | 21 38N | 73 3 E |
| Ankober | 123 | 9 35N | 39 40 E |
| Ankoro | 126 | 6 45 S | 26 55 E |
| Ankuang | 107 | 45 19N | 123 40 E |
| Ankuo | 106 | 38 25N | 115 19 E |
| Anlu | 109 | 31 12N | 113 38 E |
| Anlung | 108 | 25 6N | 106 31 E |
| Anmyŏn Do | 107 | 36 25N | 126 25 E |
| Ånn | 72 | 63 19N | 12 34 E |
| Ann Arbor | 156 | 42 17N | 83 45W |
| Ann C., Antarct. | 13 | 66 30 S | 50 30 E |
| Ann C., U.S.A. | 162 | 42 39N | 70 37W |
| Ann, gasfield | 19 | 53 40N | 2 5 E |
| Ånn L. | 72 | 63 15N | 12 35 E |
| Anna, U.S.A. | 159 | 37 28N | 89 10W |
| Anna, U.S.S.R. | 81 | 51 38N | 40 23 E |
| Anna Branch, R. | 139 | 34 2 S | 141 50 E |
| Anna Plains | 136 | 19 17 S | 121 37 E |
| Annaba | 119 | 36 50N | 7 46 E |
| Annaberg-Buchholz | 48 | 50 34N | 12 58 E |
| Annagassan | 38 | 53 53N | 6 20W |
| Annagh Hd. | 38 | 54 15N | 10 5W |
| Annaka | 111 | 36 19N | 138 54 E |
| Annalee, R. | 38 | 54 3N | 7 15W |
| Annalong | 38 | 54 7N | 5 55W |
| Annam = Trung-Phan | 101 | 16 30N | 107 30 E |
| Annamitique, Chaîne | 100 | 17 0N | 106 0 E |
| Annan | 35 | 55 0N | 3 17W |
| Annan, R. | 35 | 54 58N | 3 18W |
| Annanberg | 135 | 4 52 S | 144 42 E |
| Annandale | 35 | 55 10N | 3 25W |
| Annapolis | 162 | 39 0N | 76 30W |
| Annapolis Royal | 151 | 44 44N | 65 32W |
| Annapurna | 95 | 28 34N | 83 50 E |
| Annascaul | 39 | 52 10N | 10 3W |
| Anne, oilfield | 19 | 55 24N | 5 7 E |
| Annean, L. | 137 | 26 54 S | 118 14 E |
| Anneberg | 73 | 57 32N | 12 6 E |
| Annecy | 45 | 45 55N | 6 8 E |
| Annecy, L. d' | 45 | 45 52N | 6 10 E |
| Annemasse | 45 | 46 12N | 6 16 E |
| Annestown | 39 | 52 8N | 7 18W |
| Annette | 147 | 55 2N | 131 35W |
| Annfield Plain | 33 | 54 52N | 1 45W |
| Annie Peak | 137 | 33 53 S | 119 59 E |
| Anning | 108 | 24 58N | 102 30 E |
| Anningle | 136 | 21 50 S | 133 7 E |
| Anniston | 157 | 33 45N | 85 50W |
| Annobón = Pagalu | 114 | 1 35 S | 3 35 E |
| Annonay | 45 | 45 15N | 4 40 E |
| Annonciation, L' | 150 | 46 25N | 74 55W |
| Annot | 45 | 43 58N | 6 38 E |
| Annotto Bay | 166 | 18 17N | 77 3W |
| Annuello | 140 | 34 53 S | 142 55 E |
| Annville | 162 | 40 18N | 76 32W |
| Áno Arkhánai | 69 | 35 16N | 25 11 E |
| Áno Porróia | 68 | 41 17N | 23 2 E |
| Áno Viánnos | 69 | 35 2N | 25 21 E |
| Anoka | 158 | 45 10N | 93 26W |
| Anorotsangana | 129 | 13 56 S | 47 55 E |
| Anp'ing, Hopei, China | 106 | 38 13N | 115 31 E |
| Anp'ing, Liaoning, China | 107 | 41 10N | 123 30 E |
| Ans | 47 | 50 39N | 5 32 E |
| Ansai | 106 | 36 54N | 109 10 E |
| Ansbach | 49 | 49 17N | 10 34 E |
| Anse au Loup, L' | 151 | 51 32N | 56 50W |
| Anse, L' | 150 | 46 47N | 88 28W |
| Anseba, R. | 123 | 16 15N | 37 45 E |
| Anserma | 174 | 5 13N | 75 48W |
| Anseroeul | 47 | 50 43N | 3 32 E |
| Anshan | 107 | 41 3N | 122 58 E |
| Anshun | 105 | 26 2N | 105 57 E |
| Ansley | 158 | 41 19N | 99 24W |
| Ansó | 58 | 42 51N | 0 48W |
| Anson | 159 | 32 46N | 99 54W |
| Anson B. | 136 | 13 20 S | 130 6 E |
| Ansongo | 121 | 15 25N | 0 35 E |
| Ansonia | 162 | 41 21N | 73 6W |
| Ansonville | 150 | 48 46N | 80 43W |
| Anstey | 28 | 52 41N | 1 14W |
| Anstey Hill | 109 | 34 51 S | 138 44 E |
| Anstruther | 35 | 56 14N | 2 40W |
| Ansudu | 103 | 2 11 S | 139 22 E |
| Antabamba | 174 | 14 40 S | 73 0W |
| Antakya | 92 | 36 14N | 36 10 E |
| Antalaha | 129 | 14 57 S | 50 20 E |
| Antalya | 92 | 36 52N | 30 45 E |
| Antalya Körfezi | 92 | 36 15N | 31 30 E |
| Antananrivo | 125 | 18 55 S | 47 35 E |
| Antanimbaribé | 129 | 21 30 S | 44 48 E |
| Antarctic Pen. | 13 | 67 0 S | 60 0W |
| Antarctica | 125 | 90 0 S | 0 0 |
| Antela, Laguna | 56 | 42 7N | 7 40W |
| Antelope | 127 | 21 2 S | 28 31 E |
| Anten | 73 | 58 5N | 12 22 E |
| Antenor Navarro | 170 | 6 44 S | 38 27W |
| Antequera, Parag. | 172 | 24 8 S | 57 7W |
| Antequera, Spain | 57 | 37 5N | 4 33W |
| Antero Mt. | 161 | 38 45N | 106 43W |
| Anthemoús | 68 | 40 31N | 23 15 E |
| Anthony, Kans., U.S.A. | 159 | 37 8N | 98 2W |
| Anthony, N. Mex., U.S.A. | 161 | 32 1N | 106 37W |
| Anthony Lagoon | 138 | 18 0 S | 135 30 E |
| Anti Atlas, Mts. | 118 | 30 30N | 6 30W |
| Antibes | 45 | 43 34N | 7 6 E |
| Antibes, C. d' | 45 | 43 31N | 7 7 E |
| Anticosti, Î. de | 151 | 49 30N | 63 0W |
| Antifer, C. d' | 42 | 49 41N | 0 10 E |
| Antigo | 158 | 45 8N | 89 5W |
| Antigonish | 151 | 45 38N | 61 58W |
| Antigua | 166 | 14 34N | 90 41W |
| Antigua Bahama, Canal de la | 166 | 22 10N | 77 30W |
| Antigua, I. | 167 | 17 0N | 61 50W |
| Antilla | 166 | 20 40N | 75 50W |
| Antimony | 161 | 38 7N | 112 0W |
| Antioch | 163 | 38 7N | 121 45W |
| Antioquia | 174 | 6 40N | 75 55W |
| Antioquia □ | 174 | 7 0N | 75 30W |
| Antipodes Is. | 130 | 49 45 S | 178 40 E |
| Antler | 158 | 48 58N | 101 18W |
| Antler, R. | 153 | 49 8N | 101 0W |
| Antlers | 159 | 34 15N | 95 35W |
| Antofagasta | 172 | 23 50 S | 70 30W |
| Antofagasta □ | 172 | 24 0 S | 69 0W |
| Antofagasta de la Sierra | 172 | 26 5 S | 67 20W |
| Antofallá | 172 | 25 30 S | 68 5W |
| Antofalla, Salar de | 172 | 25 40 S | 67 45W |
| Antoing | 47 | 50 34N | 3 27 E |
| Anton | 159 | 33 49N | 102 5W |
| Anton Chico | 161 | 35 12N | 105 5W |
| Antongil, B. d' | 129 | 15 30 S | 49 50 E |
| Antonibe | 129 | 15 7 S | 47 24 E |
| Antonibe, Presqu'île d' | 129 | 15 30 S | 49 50 E |
| Antonina | 173 | 25 26 S | 48 42W |
| Antonito | 161 | 37 4N | 106 1W |
| Antonovo | 83 | 49 25N | 51 42 E |
| Antony | 30 | 50 22N | 4 13W |
| Antrain | 42 | 48 28N | 1 30W |
| Antrim | 38 | 54 43N | 6 13W |
| Antrim □ | 38 | 54 42N | 6 20W |
| Antrim Co. | 38 | 54 58N | 6 20W |
| Antrim, Mts. of | 38 | 54 57N | 6 8W |
| Antrim Plateau | 136 | 18 8 S | 128 20 E |
| Antrodoco | 63 | 42 25N | 13 4 E |
| Antropovo | 81 | 58 26N | 42 51 E |
| Antsalova | 129 | 18 40 S | 44 37 E |
| Antse | 106 | 36 15N | 112 15 E |
| Antsirabé | 129 | 19 55 S | 47 2 E |
| Antsohihy | 129 | 14 50 S | 47 50 E |
| Ant'u | 107 | 43 6N | 128 54 E |
| Antung | 107 | 40 10N | 124 18 E |
| Antungwei | 107 | 35 10N | 119 20 E |
| Antwerp | 140 | 36 17 S | 142 4 E |
| Antwerp = Antwerpen | 47 | 51 13N | 4 25 E |
| Antwerpen | 47 | 51 13N | 4 25 E |
| Antwerpen □ | 47 | 51 15N | 4 40 E |
| Antz'u | 106 | 39 31N | 116 41 E |
| Anupgarh | 94 | 29 10N | 73 10 E |
| Anuradhapura | 97 | 8 22N | 80 28 E |
| Anvaing | 47 | 50 41N | 3 34 E |
| Anvers = Antwerp(en) | 47 | 51 13N | 4 25 E |
| Anvers I. | 13 | 64 30 S | 63 40W |
| Anvik | 147 | 62 37N | 160 20W |
| Anxious B. | 139 | 33 24 S | 134 45 E |
| Anyama | 120 | 5 30N | 4 3W |
| Anyang | 106 | 36 7N | 114 26 E |
| Anyer-Lor | 103 | 6 6 S | 105 56 E |
| Anyüan | 109 | 25 9N | 115 21 E |
| Anza, Jordan | 90 | 32 22N | 35 12 E |
| Anza, U.S.A. | 163 | 33 35N | 116 39W |

**Anza Borrego Desert State Park** **Arizpe**


| | | | |
|---|---|---|---|
| Anza Borrego Desert State Park | 163 | 33 0N | 116 26W |
| Anzhero-Sudzhensk | 76 | 56 10N | 83 40E |
| Anzio | 64 | 41 28N | 12 37E |
| Aoga-Shima | 111 | 32 28N | 139 46E |
| Aoiz | 58 | 42 46N | 1 22W |
| Aomori | 112 | 40 45N | 140 45E |
| Aomori-ken □ | 112 | 40 45N | 140 40E |
| Aonla | 95 | 28 16N | 79 11E |
| Aono-Yama | 110 | 34 28N | 131 48E |
| Aorangi Mts. | 142 | 41 49S | 175 22E |
| Aoreora | 118 | 28 51N | 10 53W |
| Aosta | 62 | 45 43N | 7 20E |
| Aoudéras | 121 | 17 45N | 8 20E |
| Aouinet Torkoz | 118 | 28 31N | 9 46W |
| Aoukar □ | 118 | 23 50N | 2 45W |
| Aouker | 120 | 23 48N | 4 0W |
| Aoulef el Arab | 118 | 26 55N | 1 2E |
| Aoullouz | 118 | 30 44N | 8 1W |
| Apa | 108 | 32 55N | 101 40E |
| Apa, R. | 172 | 22 6S | 58 2W |
| Apache, Ariz., U.S.A. | 161 | 31 46N | 109 6W |
| Apache, Okla., U.S.A. | 159 | 34 53N | 98 22W |
| Apahanuerhch'i | 106 | 43 58N | 116 2E |
| Apalachee B. | 157 | 30 0N | 84 0W |
| Apalachicola | 157 | 29 40N | 85 0W |
| Apalachicola, R. | 157 | 30 0N | 85 0W |
| Apapa | 121 | 6 25N | 3 25E |
| Apaporis, R. | 174 | 0 30S | 70 30W |
| Aparecida do Taboado | 171 | 20 5S | 51 5W |
| Aparri | 103 | 18 22N | 121 38E |
| Aparurén | 174 | 5 6N | 62 8W |
| Apateu | 70 | 46 36N | 21 47E |
| Apatin | 66 | 45 40N | 19 0E |
| Apatzingán | 164 | 19 0N | 102 20W |
| Apeldoorn | 46 | 52 13N | 5 57E |
| Apeldoornsch Kanal | 46 | 52 29N | 6 5E |
| Apen | 48 | 53 12N | 7 47E |
| Apenam | 102 | 8 35S | 116 13E |
| Apennines | 16 | 44 20N | 10 20E |
| Apía | 174 | 5 5N | 75 58W |
| Apiacás, Serra dos | 174 | 9 50S | 57 0W |
| Apiaí | 174 | 24 31S | 48 50W |
| Apinajé | 171 | 11 31S | 48 18W |
| Apiti | 142 | 39 58S | 175 54E |
| Apizaco | 165 | 19 26N | 98 9W |
| Aplahoué | 121 | 6 56N | 1 41E |
| Aplao | 174 | 16 0S | 72 40W |
| Apo, Mt. | 103 | 6 53N | 125 14E |
| Apodi | 170 | 5 39S | 37 48W |
| Apolda | 48 | 51 1N | 11 30E |
| Apollo Bay | 140 | 38 45S | 143 40E |
| Apollonia, Greece | 69 | 36 58N | 24 43E |
| Apollonia, Libya | 117 | 32 52N | 21 59E |
| Apolo | 174 | 14 30S | 68 30W |
| Aporé, R. | 171 | 19 27S | 50 57W |
| Aporema | 170 | 1 14N | 50 49W |
| Apostle Is. | 158 | 46 50N | 90 30W |
| Apóstoles | 173 | 28 0S | 56 0W |
| Apostolovo | 82 | 47 39N | 33 39E |
| Apoteri | 174 | 4 2N | 58 32W |
| Appalachian Mts. | 156 | 38 0N | 80 0W |
| Appelscha | 46 | 52 57N | 6 21E |
| Appeninni | 65 | 41 0N | 15 0E |
| Appeninno Ligure | 62 | 44 30N | 9 0E |
| Appenzell | 51 | 47 20N | 9 25E |
| Appenzell-Ausser Rhoden □ | 51 | 47 23N | 9 23E |
| Appenzell-Inner Rhoden □ | 51 | 47 20N | 9 25E |
| Appiano | 63 | 46 27N | 11 17E |
| Appingedam | 46 | 53 19N | 6 51E |
| Apple Valley | 163 | 34 30N | 117 11W |
| Appleby | 32 | 54 35N | 2 29W |
| Applecross | 36 | 57 26N | 5 50W |
| Applecross For. | 36 | 57 27N | 5 40W |
| Appledore, Devon, U.K. | 30 | 51 3N | 4 12W |
| Appledore, Kent, U.K. | 29 | 51 2N | 0 47E |
| Appleton | 156 | 44 17N | 88 25W |
| Approuague | 170 | 4 20N | 52 0W |
| Apreivka | 81 | 55 33N | 37 4E |
| Apricena | 65 | 41 47N | 15 25E |
| Aprigliano | 65 | 39 17N | 16 19E |
| Aprilia | 64 | 41 38N | 12 38E |
| Apsheronsk | 83 | 44 28N | 39 42E |
| Apsley Str. | 136 | 11 35S | 130 28E |
| Apt | 45 | 43 53N | 5 24E |
| Apucarana | 173 | 23 55S | 51 33W |
| Apulia = Puglia | 65 | 41 0N | 16 30E |
| Apure □ | 174 | 7 10N | 68 50W |
| Apure, R. | 174 | 8 0N | 69 20W |
| Apurimac, R. | 174 | 12 10S | 73 30W |
| Apurito, R. | 174 | 7 50N | 67 0W |
| Apuseni, Munţii | 70 | 46 30N | 22 45E |
| Aq Chah | 93 | 37 0N | 66 5E |
| 'Aqaba | 122 | 29 31N | 35 0E |
| 'Aqaba, Khalīj al | 92 | 28 15N | 33 20E |
| Aqiq | 122 | 18 14N | 38 12E |
| Aqiq, Khalîg | 122 | 18 20N | 38 10E |
| 'Aqraba | 90 | 32 9N | 35 20E |
| 'Aqrah | 92 | 36 46N | 43 45E |
| Aquanish | 151 | 50 14N | 62 2W |
| Aquasco | 162 | 38 35N | 76 43W |
| Aquidaba | 171 | 10 17S | 37 2W |
| Aquidauana | 175 | 20 30S | 55 50W |
| Aquila, L' | 63 | 42 21N | 13 24E |
| Aquiles Serdán | 164 | 28 37N | 105 54W |
| Aquin | 167 | 18 16N | 73 24W |
| Ar Ramadi | 92 | 33 25N | 43 20E |
| Ar-Ramthā | 90 | 32 34N | 36 0E |
| Ar Rass | 92 | 25 50N | 43 40E |
| Ar Rifai | 92 | 31 50N | 46 10E |
| Ar Riyād | 92 | 24 41N | 46 42E |
| Ar Rub 'al Khālī | 91 | 21 0N | 51 0E |
| Ar Rutbah | 92 | 33 0N | 40 15E |
| Arab, Khalîg el | 122 | 30 55N | 29 0E |
| Arab, Shott al | 92 | 30 0N | 48 31E |
| Araba | 121 | 13 7N | 5 0E |
| Arabatskaya Strelka | 82 | 45 40N | 35 0E |
| Arabba | 63 | 46 30N | 11 51E |
| Arabelo | 174 | 4 55N | 64 13W |
| Arabia | 86 | 25 0N | 45 0E |
| Arabian Desert | 122 | 28 0N | 32 20E |
| Arabian Sea | 86 | 16 0N | 65 0E |
| Aracajú | 170 | 10 55S | 37 4W |
| Aracataca | 174 | 10 38N | 74 9W |
| Aracati | 170 | 4 30S | 37 44W |
| Araçatuba | 173 | 21 10S | 50 30W |
| Aracena | 57 | 37 53N | 6 38W |
| Aracruz | 171 | 19 49S | 40 16W |
| Araçuaí | 171 | 16 52S | 42 4W |
| Araçuaí, R. | 171 | 16 46S | 42 2W |
| Arad | 66 | 46 10N | 21 20E |
| Arada | 117 | 15 0N | 20 20E |
| Aradu Nou | 66 | 46 8N | 21 20E |
| Arafura Sea | 103 | 10 0S | 135 0E |
| Aragats | 83 | 40 30N | 44 15E |
| Aragón | 58 | 41 25N | 1 0W |
| Aragón, R. | 58 | 42 35N | 0 50W |
| Aragona | 64 | 37 24N | 13 36E |
| Aragua □ | 174 | 10 0N | 67 10W |
| Aragua de Barcelona | 174 | 9 28N | 64 49W |
| Araguacema | 170 | 8 50S | 49 20W |
| Araguaçu | 171 | 12 49S | 49 51W |
| Araguaia, R. | 170 | 7 0S | 49 15W |
| Araguaína | 170 | 7 12S | 48 12W |
| Araguari | 171 | 18 38S | 48 11W |
| Araguari, R. | 170 | 1 0N | 51 40W |
| Araguatins | 170 | 5 38S | 48 7W |
| Araioses | 170 | 2 53S | 41 55W |
| Arak | 118 | 25 20N | 3 45E |
| Arāk | 92 | 34 0N | 49 40E |
| Arakan □ | 98 | 19 0N | 94 15E |
| Arakan Coast | 99 | 19 0N | 94 0E |
| Arakan Yoma | 98 | 20 0N | 94 30E |
| Arákhova | 69 | 38 28N | 22 35E |
| Araks, R. = Aras, Rud-e | 92 | 39 10N | 47 10E |
| Aral Sea = Aralskoye More | 76 | 44 30N | 60 0E |
| Aralsk | 76 | 46 50N | 61 20E |
| Aralskoye More | 76 | 44 30N | 60 0E |
| Aramac | 138 | 22 58S | 145 14E |
| Arambagh | 95 | 22 53N | 87 48E |
| Aramū, Mţii de | 70 | 47 10N | 22 30E |
| Aran Fawddwy, Mt. | 31 | 52 48N | 3 40W |
| Aran, I. | 38 | 55 0N | 8 30W |
| Aran Is. | 39 | 53 5N | 9 42W |
| Aranci | 64 | 41 5N | 3 40W |
| Aranci, Golfo | 64 | 41 0N | 9 35E |
| Aranda de Duero | 58 | 41 39N | 3 42W |
| Aranđelovac | 66 | 44 18N | 20 37E |
| Aranga | 142 | 35 44S | 173 40E |
| Aranjuez | 56 | 40 1N | 3 40W |
| Aranos | 125 | 24 9S | 19 7E |
| Aransas Pass | 159 | 28 0N | 97 9W |
| Aranyaprathet | 101 | 13 41N | 102 30E |
| Aranzazu | 174 | 5 16N | 75 30W |
| Arao | 110 | 32 59N | 130 25E |
| Araouane | 120 | 18 55N | 3 30W |
| Arapahoe | 158 | 40 22N | 99 53W |
| Arapari | 170 | 5 34S | 49 15W |
| Arapawa I. | 131 | 41 13S | 174 20E |
| Arapey Grande, R. | 172 | 30 55S | 57 49W |
| Arapiraca | 170 | 9 45S | 36 39W |
| Arapkir | 92 | 39 5N | 38 30E |
| Arapongas | 173 | 23 29S | 51 28W |
| Arapuni | 130 | 38 3S | 175 37E |
| Araranguá | 173 | 29 0S | 49 30W |
| Araraquara | 171 | 21 50S | 48 0W |
| Araras | 173 | 5 15S | 60 35W |
| Ararás, Serra dos | 173 | 25 0S | 53 10W |
| Ararat, Austral. | 140 | 37 16S | 143 0E |
| Ararat, Turkey | 92 | 39 50N | 44 15E |
| Ararat, Mt. = Ağri Daği | 92 | 39 50N | 44 15E |
| Arari | 170 | 3 28S | 44 47W |
| Araria | 95 | 26 9N | 87 33E |
| Araripe | 171 | 7 12S | 40 8W |
| Araripe, Chapada do | 170 | 7 20S | 40 0W |
| Araripina | 170 | 7 33S | 40 34W |
| Araro | 123 | 4 41N | 38 50E |
| Araruama, Lagoa de | 173 | 22 53S | 42 12W |
| Araruna | 170 | 6 52S | 35 44W |
| Åras | 71 | 59 42N | 10 31E |
| Aras, Rud-e | 92 | 39 10N | 47 10E |
| Araticu | 170 | 1 58S | 49 51W |
| Arauca | 174 | 7 0N | 70 40W |
| Arauca □ | 174 | 6 40N | 71 0W |
| Arauca, R. | 174 | 7 30N | 69 0W |
| Arauco | 172 | 37 16S | 73 25W |
| Arauco □ | 172 | 37 40S | 73 25W |
| Araújos | 171 | 19 56S | 45 14W |
| Arauquita | 174 | 7 2N | 71 25W |
| Araure | 174 | 9 34N | 69 13W |
| Arawa | 123 | 9 57N | 41 58E |
| Arawhata | 143 | 43 59S | 168 38E |
| Arawhata, R. | 143 | 44 0S | 168 40E |
| Araxá | 171 | 19 35S | 46 55W |
| Araya, Pen. de | 174 | 10 40N | 64 0W |
| Arba | 123 | 9 0N | 40 20E |
| Arba Jahan | 126 | 2 5N | 39 2E |
| Arba, L' | 118 | 36 40N | 3 9E |
| Arba Minch | 123 | 6 0N | 37 30E |
| Arbah, Wadi al | 90 | 30 30N | 35 5E |
| Arbatax | 64 | 39 57N | 9 42E |
| Arbedo | 51 | 46 12N | 9 3E |
| Arbeláez | 174 | 4 17N | 74 26W |
| Arbīl | 92 | 36 15N | 44 5E |
| Arboga | 72 | 59 24N | 15 52E |
| Arbois | 43 | 46 55N | 5 46E |
| Arbon | 51 | 47 31N | 9 26E |
| Arbore | 123 | 5 3N | 36 50E |
| Arborea | 64 | 39 46N | 8 34E |
| Arborfield | 153 | 53 6N | 103 39W |
| Arborg | 153 | 50 54N | 97 13W |
| Arbrå | 72 | 61 28N | 16 22E |
| Arbresle, L' | 45 | 45 50N | 4 26E |
| Arbroath | 37 | 56 34N | 2 35W |
| Arbuckle | 160 | 39 3N | 122 2W |
| Arbus | 64 | 39 30N | 8 33E |
| Arbuzinka | 82 | 47 52N | 31 25E |
| Arc | 43 | 47 28N | 5 34E |
| Arcachon | 44 | 44 40N | 1 10W |
| Arcachon, Bassin d' | 44 | 44 42N | 1 10W |
| Arcadia, Fla., U.S.A. | 157 | 27 20N | 81 50W |
| Arcadia, La., U.S.A. | 159 | 32 34N | 92 53W |
| Arcadia, Nebr., U.S.A. | 158 | 41 29N | 99 4W |
| Arcadia, Wis., U.S.A. | 158 | 44 13N | 91 29W |
| Arcata | 160 | 40 55N | 124 4W |
| Arcévia | 63 | 43 29N | 12 58E |
| Archangel = Arkhangelsk | 78 | 64 40N | 41 0E |
| Archar | 66 | 43 50N | 22 54E |
| Archbald | 162 | 41 30N | 75 31W |
| Archena | 59 | 38 9N | 1 16W |
| Archer B. | 138 | 13 20S | 141 30E |
| Archer, R. | 138 | 13 25S | 142 50E |
| Archers Post | 126 | 0 35N | 37 35E |
| Archidona | 57 | 37 6N | 4 22W |
| Archiestown | 37 | 57 28N | 3 20W |
| Arci, Monte | 64 | 39 47N | 8 44E |
| Arcidosso | 63 | 42 51N | 11 30E |
| Arcila = Asilah | 118 | 35 29N | 6 0W |
| Arcis-sur-Aube | 43 | 48 32N | 4 10E |
| Arckaringa | 139 | 27 56S | 134 45E |
| Arckaringa Cr. | 139 | 28 10S | 135 22E |
| Arco, Italy | 62 | 45 55N | 10 54E |
| Arco, U.S.A. | 160 | 43 45N | 113 16W |
| Arcola | 153 | 49 40N | 102 30W |
| Arcoona | 140 | 31 2S | 137 1E |
| Arcos, Brazil | 171 | 20 17S | 45 32W |
| Arcos, Spain | 58 | 41 12N | 2 16W |
| Arcos de los Frontera | 57 | 36 45N | 5 49W |
| Arcot | 97 | 12 53N | 79 20E |
| Arcoverde | 170 | 8 25S | 37 4W |
| Arctic Ocean | 12 | 78 0N | 160 0W |
| Arctic Red, R. | 147 | 66 0N | 132 0W |
| Arctic Red River | 147 | 67 15N | 134 0W |
| Arctic Village | 147 | 68 5N | 145 45W |
| Arda, R., Bulg. | 67 | 41 40N | 25 40E |
| Arda, R., Italy | 62 | 44 53N | 9 52E |
| Ardabil | 92 | 38 15N | 48 18E |
| Ardagh | 39 | 52 30N | 9 5W |
| Ardakan | 93 | 30 20N | 52 5E |
| Årdal | 71 | 59 9N | 6 13E |
| Ardales | 57 | 36 53N | 4 51W |
| Årdalstangen | 71 | 61 14N | 7 43E |
| Ardara | 38 | 54 47N | 8 25W |
| Ardatov | 81 | 54 51N | 46 15E |
| Ardavasar | 36 | 57 3N | 5 54E |
| Ardbeg | 34 | 55 38N | 6 6W |
| Ardcath | 38 | 53 36N | 6 21W |
| Ardcharnich | 36 | 57 52N | 5 5W |
| Ardchyle | 34 | 56 26N | 4 24W |
| Ardèche □ | 45 | 44 42N | 4 16E |
| Ardee | 38 | 53 51N | 6 32W |
| Arden Stby. | 73 | 56 46N | 9 52E |
| Ardennes | 47 | 49 30N | 5 10E |
| Ardennes □ | 43 | 49 35N | 4 40E |
| Ardentes | 43 | 46 45N | 1 50E |
| Ardentinny | 34 | 56 3N | 4 56E |
| Arderin, Mt. | 39 | 53 3N | 7 40W |
| Ardestan | 93 | 33 20N | 52 25E |
| Ardfert | 39 | 52 20N | 9 49W |
| Ardfinnan | 39 | 52 20N | 7 53W |
| Ardglass | 38 | 54 16N | 5 38W |
| Ardgour | 36 | 56 45N | 5 25W |
| Ardgroom | 39 | 51 44N | 9 53W |
| Ardhas, R. | 68 | 41 36N | 26 25E |
| Ardhasig | 36 | 57 55N | 6 51W |
| Ardhéa | 68 | 40 58N | 22 3E |
| Ardila, R. | 57 | 38 10N | 7 20W |
| Ardingly | 29 | 51 3N | 0 3W |
| Ardino | 67 | 41 34N | 25 9E |
| Ardivachar Pt. | 36 | 57 23N | 7 25W |
| Ardkearagh | 39 | 51 48N | 10 11W |
| Ardkeen | 38 | 54 27N | 5 31W |
| Ardlethan | 141 | 34 22S | 146 53E |
| Ardlui | 34 | 56 19N | 4 43W |
| Ardmore, Austral. | 138 | 21 39S | 139 11E |
| Ardmore, Okla., U.S.A. | 159 | 34 10N | 97 5W |
| Ardmore, Pa., U.S.A. | 162 | 39 58N | 75 18W |
| Ardmore, S.D., U.S.A. | 158 | 43 0N | 103 40W |
| Ardmore Hd. | 39 | 51 58N | 7 43W |
| Ardmore Pt. | 34 | 55 40N | 6 0W |
| Ardnacrusha | 39 | 52 43N | 8 38W |
| Ardnamurchan, Pen. | 36 | 56 43N | 6 0W |
| Ardnamurchan Pt. | 36 | 56 44N | 6 14W |
| Ardnaree | 38 | 54 6N | 9 8W |
| Ardnave Pt. | 34 | 55 54N | 6 20W |
| Ardooie | 47 | 50 59N | 3 13E |
| Ardore Marina | 65 | 38 11N | 16 10E |
| Ardrahan | 39 | 53 10N | 8 48W |
| Ardres | 43 | 50 50N | 2 0E |
| Ardrishaig | 34 | 56 0N | 5 27W |
| Ardrossan, Austral. | 140 | 34 26S | 137 53E |
| Ardrossan, U.K. | 34 | 55 39N | 4 50W |
| Ards □ | 38 | 54 35N | 5 30W |
| Ards Pen. | 38 | 54 30N | 5 25W |
| Ardud | 70 | 47 37N | 22 52E |
| Ardunac | 83 | 41 8N | 42 5E |
| Ardvoulie Castle | 36 | 58 0N | 6 45W |
| Ardwell | 37 | 57 20N | 3 5W |
| Åre | 72 | 63 22N | 13 15E |
| Arecibo | 147 | 18 29N | 66 42W |
| Areia Branca | 170 | 5 0S | 37 0W |
| Aremark | 71 | 59 15N | 11 42E |
| Arena de la Ventana, Punta | 164 | 24 4N | 109 52W |
| Arenales, Cerro | 176 | 47 5S | 73 40W |
| Arenas | 56 | 43 17N | 4 50W |
| Arenas de San Pedro | 56 | 40 12N | 5 5W |
| Arenas, Pta. | 174 | 10 20N | 62 39W |
| Arendal | 71 | 58 28N | 8 46E |
| Arendonk | 47 | 51 19N | 5 5E |
| Arendsee | 48 | 52 52N | 11 27E |
| Arenig Fach, Mt. | 31 | 52 55N | 3 45E |
| Arenig Fawr, Mt. | 31 | 52 56N | 3 45W |
| Arenys de Mar | 58 | 41 35N | 2 33E |
| Arenzano | 62 | 44 24N | 8 40E |
| Areópolis | 69 | 36 40N | 22 22E |
| Arequipa | 174 | 16 20S | 71 30W |
| Arero | 123 | 4 41N | 38 50E |
| Arês | 171 | 6 11S | 35 9W |
| Arès | 44 | 44 47N | 1 8W |
| Arévalo | 56 | 41 3N | 4 43W |
| Arezzo | 63 | 43 28N | 11 50E |
| Arga, R. | 58 | 42 30N | 1 50W |
| Argalastí | 68 | 39 13N | 23 13E |
| Argamasilla de Alba | 59 | 39 8N | 3 5W |
| Arganda | 58 | 40 19N | 3 26W |
| Arganil | 56 | 40 13N | 8 3W |
| Argayash | 84 | 55 29N | 60 52E |
| Argelès-Gazost | 44 | 43 0N | 0 6W |
| Argelès-sur-Mer | 44 | 42 34N | 3 1E |
| Argent-sur-Sauldre | 43 | 47 33N | 2 25E |
| Argenta, Can. | 152 | 50 20N | 116 55W |
| Argenta, Italy | 63 | 44 37N | 11 50E |
| Argentan | 42 | 48 45N | 0 1W |
| Argentário, Mte. | 63 | 42 23N | 11 11E |
| Argentat | 44 | 45 6N | 1 56E |
| Argentera | 62 | 44 23N | 6 58E |
| Argenteuil | 43 | 48 57N | 2 14E |
| Argentia | 151 | 47 18N | 53 58W |
| Argentiera, C. dell' | 64 | 40 44N | 8 8E |
| Argentière, Aiguilles d' | 50 | 45 58N | 7 2E |
| Argentina | 174 | 0 34N | 74 17W |
| Argentina ■ | 176 | 35 0S | 66 0W |
| Argentino, L. | 176 | 50 10S | 73 0W |
| Argenton-sur-Creuse | 44 | 46 36N | 1 30E |
| Argentré | 42 | 48 5N | 0 40W |
| Argeş □ | 70 | 45 0N | 24 45E |
| Argeş, R. | 70 | 44 30N | 25 50E |
| Arghandab, R. | 94 | 32 15N | 66 23E |
| Argo | 122 | 19 28N | 30 30E |
| Argo, I. | 122 | 19 28N | 30 30E |
| Argolikós Kólpos | 69 | 37 20N | 22 52E |
| Argolis □ | 69 | 37 38N | 22 50E |
| Argonne | 43 | 49 0N | 5 20E |
| Argos | 69 | 37 40N | 22 43E |
| Argos Orestikón | 68 | 40 27N | 21 26E |
| Argostólion | 69 | 38 12N | 20 33E |
| Arguedas | 58 | 42 11N | 1 36W |
| Arguello, Pt. | 163 | 34 34N | 120 40W |
| Argun, R. | 77 | 53 20N | 121 28E |
| Argungu | 121 | 12 40N | 4 31E |
| Argus Pk. | 163 | 35 52N | 117 26W |
| Argyle | 158 | 48 23N | 96 49W |
| Argyle Downs | 136 | 16 17S | 128 47E |
| Argyle, L. | 136 | 16 20S | 128 40E |
| Argyll (□) | 26 | 56 18N | 5 15W |
| Argyll, Dist. | 34 | 56 14N | 5 10W |
| Argyll, oilfield | 19 | 56 8N | 3 5E |
| Argyrádhes | 68 | 39 27N | 19 58E |
| Århus | 73 | 56 8N | 10 11E |
| Aria | 142 | 38 33S | 175 0E |
| Ariamsvlei | 128 | 28 9S | 19 51E |
| Ariana | 119 | 36 52N | 10 12E |
| Ariano Irpino | 65 | 41 10N | 15 4E |
| Ariano nel Polèsine | 63 | 44 56N | 12 5E |
| Aribinda | 121 | 14 17N | 0 52W |
| Arica, Chile | 174 | 18 32S | 70 20W |
| Arica, Colomb. | 174 | 2 0S | 71 50W |
| Arica, Peru | 174 | 1 30S | 75 30W |
| Arid, C. | 137 | 34 1S | 123 10E |
| Arida | 111 | 33 29N | 135 44E |
| Ariège □ | 44 | 42 56N | 1 30E |
| Ariège, R. | 44 | 42 56N | 1 25E |
| Arieş, R. | 70 | 46 24N | 23 20E |
| Arilje | 66 | 43 44N | 20 7E |
| Arima | 167 | 10 38N | 61 17W |
| Arinagour | 34 | 56 38N | 6 31W |
| Arinos, R. | 174 | 11 15S | 57 0W |
| Ario de Rosales | 164 | 19 12N | 101 42W |
| Aripuanã | 174 | 9 25S | 60 30W |
| Aripuanã, R. | 174 | 7 30S | 60 25W |
| Ariquemes | 174 | 9 55S | 63 6W |
| Arisaig | 36 | 56 55N | 5 50W |
| Arisaig, Sd. of | 36 | 56 50N | 5 50W |
| Arîsh, W. el | 122 | 30 25N | 34 52E |
| Arismendi | 174 | 8 29N | 68 22W |
| Arissa | 123 | 11 10N | 41 35E |
| Aristazabal, I. | 152 | 52 40N | 129 10W |
| Arita | 110 | 33 11N | 129 54E |
| Arivaca | 161 | 31 37N | 111 25W |
| Arivonimamo | 129 | 19 1S | 47 11E |
| Ariyalur | 97 | 11 8N | 79 8E |
| Ariza | 58 | 41 19N | 2 3W |
| Arizaro, Salar de | 172 | 24 40S | 67 50W |
| Arizona | 172 | 35 45S | 65 25W |
| Arizona □ | 161 | 34 20N | 111 30W |
| Arizpe | 164 | 30 20N | 110 11W |

Arjang Atalaia


Arjang 72 59 24N 12 9E
Arjäng 72 59 24N 12 8E
Arjeplog 74 66 3N 18 2E
Arjona, Colomb. 174 10 14N 75 22W
Arjona, Spain 57 37 56N 4 4W
Arjuno 103 7 49S 112 19E
Arka 77 60 15N 142 0E
Arkadak 81 51 58N 43 19E
Arkadelphia 159 34 5N 93 0W
Arkadhia □ 69 37 30N 22 20E
Arkaig, L. 36 56 58N 5 10W
Arkansas □ 159 35 0N 92 30W
Arkansas City 159 37 4N 97 3W
Arkansas, R. 159 35 20N 93 30W
Árkathos, R. 68 39 20N 21 4E
Arkhángelos 69 36 13N 28 7E
Arkhangelsk 78 64 40N 41 0E
Arkhangelskoye 81 51 32N 40 58E
Arkiko 123 15 33N 39 30E
Arkle R. 32 54 25N 2 0W
Arklow 39 52 48N 6 10W
Arklow Hd. 39 52 46N 6 10W
Arkoi 69 37 24N 26 44E
Arkona, Kap 48 54 41N 13 26E
Arkonam 97 13 7N 79 43E
Arkösund 73 58 29N 16 56E
Arkoúdhi 69 38 33N 20 43E
Arkticheskiy, Mys 77 81 10N 95 0E
Arkul 84 57 17N 50 3E
Arkville 162 42 9N 74 37W
Arlanc 44 45 25N 3 42E
Arlanza, R. 56 42 6N 4 0W
Arlanzón, R. 56 42 12N 4 0W
Arlberg Pass 49 49 9N 10 12E
Arlee 160 47 10N 114 4W
Arles 45 43 41N 4 40E
Arlesheim 50 47 30N 7 37E
Arless 39 52 53N 7 1W
Arlington, S. Afr. 129 28 1S 27 53E
Arlington, Oreg., U.S.A. 160 45 48N 120 6W
Arlington, S.D., U.S.A. 158 44 25N 97 4W
Arlington, Va., U.S.A. 162 38 52N 77 5W
Arlington, Vt., U.S.A. 162 43 5N 73 9W
Arlington, Wash., U.S.A. 160 48 11N 122 4W
Arlon 47 49 42N 5 49E
Arlöv 73 55 38N 13 5E
Arly 121 11 35N 1 28E
Armadale, Austral. 137 32 12S 116 0E
Armadale, Lothian, U.K. 35 55 54N 3 42W
Armadale, Skye, U.K. 36 57 24N 5 54W
Armagh, Can. 137 46 41N 70 32W
Armagh, U.K. 38 54 22N 6 40W
Armagh □ 38 54 18N 6 37W
Armagh Co. 38 54 16N 6 35W
Armagnac 44 43 44N 0 10E
Armançon, R. 43 47 51N 4 7E
Armavir 83 45 2N 41 7E
Armenia 174 4 35N 75 45W
Armenian S.S.R. □ 83 40 0N 41 0E
Armeniş 70 45 13N 22 17E
Armentières 43 50 40N 2 50E
Armero 174 4 58N 74 54W
Armidale 141 30 30S 151 40E
Armour 158 43 20N 98 25W
Armoy 38 55 8N 6 20W
Arms 150 49 34N 86 3W
Armstead 160 45 0N 112 56W
Armstrong, B.C., Can. 152 50 25N 119 10W
Armstrong, Ont., Can. 150 50 18N 89 4W
Armstrong, U.S.A. 159 26 59N 90 48W
Armstrong Cr. 136 16 35S 131 40E
Armur 96 18 48N 78 16E
Arnaia 68 40 30N 23 40E
Arnarfjörður 74 65 48N 23 40W
Arnay-le-Duc 43 47 10N 4 27E
Arnedillo 58 42 13N 2 14W
Arnedo 58 42 12N 2 5W
Årnes 74 66 1N 21 31W
Årnes 71 60 7N 11 28E
Arnett 159 36 9N 99 44W
Arney 38 54 17N 7 41W
Arnhem 46 51 58N 5 55E
Arnhem B. 138 12 20S 136 10E
Arnhem, C. 138 12 20S 137 0E
Arnhem Ld. 138 13 10S 135 0E
Arni 97 12 43N 79 19E
Árnissa 68 40 47N 21 49E
Arno Bay 140 33 54S 136 34E
Arno, R. 62 43 44N 10 20E
Arnold, N.Z. 143 42 29S 171 25E
Arnold, U.K. 33 53 0N 1 8W
Arnold, Calif., U.S.A. 163 38 15N 120 20W
Arnold, Nebr., U.S.A. 158 41 29N 100 10W
Arnoldstein 52 46 33N 13 43E
Arnot 153 55 46N 96 41W
Arnøy 74 70 9N 20 40E
Arnprior 150 45 26N 76 21W
Arnsberg 48 51 25N 8 10E
Arnside 32 54 12N 2 49W
Arnstadt 48 50 50N 10 56E
Aroa 174 10 26N 68 54W
Aroab 125 26 41S 19 39E
Aroánia Óri 69 37 56N 22 12E
Aroche 57 37 56N 6 57W
Aroeiras 170 7 31S 35 41W
Arolla 50 46 2N 7 29E
Arolsen 48 51 23N 9 1E
Arona 62 45 45N 8 32E
Arosa 51 46 47N 9 41E
Arosa, Ría de 56 42 28N 8 57W
Arpajon, Cantal, France 44 44 54N 2 28E
Arpajon, Seine et Oise, France 43 48 37N 2 12E
Arpino 64 41 40N 13 35E
Arra Mts. 39 52 50N 8 22W
Arrabury 139 26 45S 141 0E
Arrah 95 25 35N 84 32E
Arraias 171 12 56S 46 57W
Arraias, R. 170 7 30S 49 20W
Arraiolos 57 38 44N 7 59W
Arran, I. 34 55 34N 5 12W
Arrandale 152 54 57N 130 0W
Arras 43 50 17N 2 46E
Arreau 44 42 54N 0 22E
Arrecife 116 28 59N 13 40W
Arrecifes 172 34 06S 60 9W
Arrée, Mts. d' 42 48 26N 3 55W
Arriaga, Chiapas, Mexico 165 16 15N 93 52W
Arriaga, San Luis de Potosi, Mexico 164 21 55N 101 23W
Arrild 73 55 8N 8 58E
Arrililah P.O. 138 23 43S 143 54E
Arrino 137 29 30S 115 40E
Arrochar 34 56 12N 4 45W
Arrojado, R. 171 13 24S 44 20W
Arromanches-les-Bains 42 49 20N 0 38W
Arronches 57 39 8N 7 16W
Arrou 42 48 6N 1 8E
Arrow L. 38 54 3N 8 20W
Arrow Rock Res. 160 43 45N 115 50W
Arrowhead 152 50 40N 117 55W
Arrowhead, L. 163 34 16N 117 10W
Arrowsmith, Mt. 143 30 7N 141 38E
Arrowtown 143 44 57S 168 50E
Arroyo de la Luz 57 39 30N 6 38W
Arroyo Grande 163 35 9N 120 32W
Års 73 56 48N 9 30E
Ars 44 46 13N 1 30W
Ars-sur-Moselle 43 49 5N 6 4E
Arsenault L. 153 53 6N 108 32W
Arsiero 63 45 49N 11 22E
Arsikere 97 13 15N 76 15E
Arsk 81 56 10N 49 50E
Årskogen 72 62 8N 17 20E
Árta 69 39 8N 21 2E
Artá 58 39 40N 3 20E
Árta □ 68 39 15N 26 0E
Arteaga 164 18 50N 102 20W
Arteijo 56 43 19N 8 29W
Artem,Os. 83 40 28N 50 20E
Artémou 120 15 38N 12 16W
Artemovsk 82 48 35N 37 55E
Artemovski 83 54 45N 93 35E
Artemovskiy 84 57 21N 61 54E
Artenay 43 48 5N 1 50E
Artern 48 51 22N 11 18E
Artesa de Segre 58 41 54N 1 3E
Artesia 159 32 55N 104 25W
Artesia Wells 159 28 17N 99 18W
Artesian 158 44 2N 97 54W
Arth 51 47 4N 8 31E
Arthez-de-Béarn 44 43 29N 0 38W
Arthington 120 6 35N 10 45W
Arthur Cr. 138 22 30S 136 25E
Arthur Pt. 138 22 7S 150 3E
Arthur, R. 138 41 2S 144 40E
Arthur's Pass 143 42 54S 171 35E
Arthur's Town 167 24 38N 75 42W
Arthurstown 39 52 15N 6 58W
Artigas 172 30 20S 56 30W
Artigavan 38 54 51N 7 24W
Artik 83 40 38N 44 50E
Artillery L. 153 63 9N 107 52W
Artois 43 50 20N 2 30E
Artotína 69 38 42N 22 2E
Artvin 92 41 14N 41 44E
Aru, Kepulauan 103 6 0S 134 30E
Arua 126 3 1N 30 58E
Aruanã 171 15 0S 51 10W
Aruba I. 167 12 30N 70 0W
Arudy 44 43 7N 0 28W
Arumpo 140 33 48S 142 55E
Arun, R. 95 27 30N 87 15E
Arun R. 29 50 48N 0 33W
Arunachal Pradesh □ 98 28 0N 95 0E
Arundel 29 50 52N 0 32W
Aruppukottai 97 9 31N 78 8E
Arusha 126 3 20S 36 40E
Arusha □ 126 4 0S 36 30E
Arusha Chini 126 3 32S 37 20E
Arusi □ 123 7 45N 39 00E
Aruvi,Aru 97 8 48N 79 53E
Aruwimi, R. 126 1 30N 25 0E
Arva 38 53 57N 7 35W
Arvada 160 44 43N 106 6W
Arvaklu 97 8 20N 79 58E
Arvayheer 105 46 15N 102 48E
Arve, R. 45 46 11N 6 8E
Arvi 96 20 59N 78 16E
Arvida 151 48 25N 71 14W
Arvidsjaur 74 65 35N 19 10E
Arvika 72 59 40N 12 36E
Arvin 163 35 12N 118 50W
Arys 85 42 26N 68 48E
Arys, R. 85 42 45N 68 15E
Arzachena 64 41 5N 9 27E
Arzamas 81 55 27N 43 55E
Arzew 118 35 50N 0 23W
Arzgir 83 45 18N 44 23E
Arzignano 63 45 30N 11 20E
As 47 51 1N 5 35E
Aš 52 50 13N 12 12E
As Salt 90 32 2N 35 43E
As Samawah 92 31 15N 45 15E
As-Samū 90 31 24N 35 4E
As Sulaimānīyah 92 35 35N 45 29E
As Sultbn 119 31 4N 17 8E
As Suwaih 93 22 10N 59 33E
As Suwayda 92 32 40N 36 30E
As Suwayrah 92 32 55N 45 0E
Asab 128 25 30S 18 0E
Asaba 121 6 12N 6 38E
Asadabad 92 34 50N 48 10E
Asafo 120 6 20N 2 40W
Asahi 111 35 43N 140 39E
Asahi-Gawa, R. 110 34 36N 133 58E
Asahikawa 112 43 45N 142 30E
Asale, L. 123 14 0N 40 20E
Asama-Yama 111 36 24N 138 31E
Asamankese 121 5 50N 0 40W
Asankrangwa 120 5 45N 2 30W
Asansol 95 23 40N 87 1E
Åsarna 72 62 40N 14 20E
Åsarna 72 62 39N 14 22E
Asbe Teferi 123 9 4N 40 49E
Asbesberge 128 29 0S 23 0E
Asbest 84 57 0N 61 30E
Asbestos 151 45 47N 71 58W
Asbury Park 162 40 15N 74 1W
Ascensión 164 31 6N 107 59W
Ascensión, B. de la 165 19 50N 87 20W
Ascension, I. 15 8 0S 14 15W
Aschach 49 48 23N 14 0E
Aschaffenburg 49 49 58N 9 8E
Aschendorf 48 53 2N 7 22E
Aschersleben 48 51 45N 11 28E
Asciano 63 43 14N 11 32E
Áscoli Piceno 63 42 51N 13 34E
Áscoli Satriano 65 41 11N 15 32E
Ascona 51 46 9N 8 46E
Ascope 174 7 46S 79 8W
Ascot 29 51 24N 0 41W
Ascotán 172 21 45S 68 17W
Aseb 123 13 0N 42 40E
Åseda 73 57 10N 15 20E
Åseda 73 57 10N 15 20E
Asedjrad 118 24 51N 1 29E
Asela 123 8 0N 39 0E
Asenovgrad 67 42 1N 24 51E
Åseral 71 58 37N 7 25E
Åseral 71 58 38N 7 26E
Asfeld 43 49 27N 4 5E
Asfordby 29 52 45N 0 57W
Asfûn el Matâ'na 122 25 26N 32 30E
Åsgårdstrand 71 59 22N 10 27E
Ash 29 51 17N 1 16E
Ash Fork 161 35 14N 112 32W
Ash Grove 159 37 21N 93 36W
Ash Shām,Bādiyat 92 31 30N 40 0E
Ash Shāmīyah 92 31 55N 44 35E
Ash Shatrah 92 31 30N 46 10E
Ash Shuna 90 32 32N 35 34E
Asha 84 55 0N 57 16E
Ashaira 122 21 40N 40 40E
Ashanti 121 7 30N 2 0W
Ashau 100 16 6N 107 22E
Ashbourne, Ireland 38 53 31N 6 24W
Ashbourne, U.K. 33 53 2N 1 44W
Ashburn 157 31 42N 83 40W
Ashburton, N.Z. 143 43 53S 171 48E
Ashburton, U.K. 30 50 31N 3 45W
Ashburton Downs 136 23 25S 117 4E
Ashburton, R., Austral. 136 21 40S 114 56E
Ashburton, R., N.Z. 131 44 2S 171 50E
Ashby-de-la-Zouch 28 52 45N 1 29W
Ashchurch 28 52 0N 2 7W
Ashcroft 152 50 40N 121 20W
Ashdod 90 31 49N 34 35E
Ashdot Ya'aqov 90 32 39N 35 35E
Ashdown Forest 29 51 4N 0 2E
Asheboro 157 35 43N 79 46W
Asherton 159 28 25N 99 43W
Asheville 157 35 39N 82 30W
Asheweig, R. 150 54 17N 87 12W
Ashford, Austral. 139 29 15S 151 3E
Ashford, Derby., U.K. 33 53 13N 1 43W
Ashford, Kent, U.K. 29 51 8N 0 53E
Ashford, U.S.A. 160 46 45N 122 2W
Ashikaga 111 36 28N 139 29E
Ashington 35 55 12N 1 35W
Ashio 111 36 38N 139 27E
Ashizuri-Zaki 110 32 35N 132 50E
Ashkarkot 94 33 3N 67 58E
Ashkhabad 76 38 0N 57 50E
Ashland, Kans., U.S.A. 159 37 13N 99 43W
Ashland, Ky., U.S.A. 156 38 25N 82 40W
Ashland, Me., U.S.A. 151 46 34N 68 26W
Ashland, Mont., U.S.A. 160 45 41N 106 12W
Ashland, Nebr., U.S.A. 158 41 5N 96 27W
Ashland, Ohio, U.S.A. 156 40 52N 82 20W
Ashland, Oreg., U.S.A. 160 42 10N 122 38W
Ashland, Pa., U.S.A. 162 40 45N 76 22W
Ashland, Va., U.S.A. 156 37 46N 77 30W
Ashland, Wis., U.S.A. 158 46 40N 90 52W
Ashley, N.D., U.S.A. 158 46 3N 99 23W
Ashley, Pa., U.S.A. 162 41 14N 75 53W
Ashmont 152 54 7N 111 29W
Ashmore Is. 136 12 14S 123 50E
Ashmore Reef 136 12 14S 123 5E
Ashmûn 122 30 18N 30 55E
Ashokan Res. 162 41 56N 74 13W
Ashquelon 90 31 42N 34 55E
Ashtabula 156 41 52N 80 50W
Ashti 96 18 50N 75 15E
Ashton, S. Afr. 128 33 50S 20 5E
Ashton, U.S.A. 160 44 6N 111 30W
Ashton-in-Makerfield 32 53 29N 2 39W
Ashton-u.-Lyne 32 53 30N 2 8E
Ashuanipi, L. 151 52 45N 66 15W
Ashurst 142 40 16S 175 45E
Ashurstwood 29 51 6N 0 2E
Ashwater 30 50 43N 4 18W
Ashwick 28 51 13N 2 31W
Asia 86 45 0N 75 0E
Asia, Kepulauan 103 1 0N 131 13E
Asiago 63 45 52N 11 30E
Asifabad 96 19 30N 79 24E
Asilah 118 35 29N 6 0W
Asinara 64 41 5N 8 15E
Asinara, G. dell' 64 41 0N 8 30E
Asinara I. 64 41 5N 8 15E
Asino 76 57 0N 86 0E
Asir 91 18 40N 42 30E
Asir, Ras 91 11 55N 51 10E
Aska 96 19 37N 84 42E
Askeaton 39 52 37N 8 58W
Asker 71 59 50N 10 26E
Askersund 73 58 53N 14 55E
Askim 71 59 35N 11 10E
Askino 84 56 5N 56 34E
Askja 74 65 3N 16 48W
Åskloster 73 57 13N 12 11E
Askrigg 32 54 19N 2 6W
Asl 122 29 33N 32 44E
Aslackby 33 52 53N 0 23W
Asmar 93 35 10N 71 27E
Asmera (Asmara) 123 15 19N 38 55E
Asnæs 73 55 40N 11 0E
Åsnen 73 56 35N 15 45E
Åsnes 71 60 37N 11 59E
Asni 118 31 17N 7 58W
Aso 110 33 0N 130 42E
Aso-Zan 110 32 53N 131 6E
Asoa 126 4 35N 25 48E
Asola 62 45 12N 10 25E
Asotin 60 46 14N 117 2W
Aspatria 32 54 45N 3 20W
Aspe 59 38 20N 0 40W
Aspen 161 39 12N 106 56W
Aspermont 159 33 11N 100 15W
Aspiring, Mt. 143 44 23S 168 46E
Aspres 45 44 32N 5 44E
Aspur 94 23 58N 74 7E
Asquith 153 52 8N 107 13W
Assa 118 28 35N 9 6W
Assaba, Massif de l' 120 16 10N 11 45W
Assam □ 98 25 45N 92 30E
Assamakka 121 19 21N 5 38E
Assateague I. 162 38 5N 75 6W
Asse 47 50 54N 4 6E
Assebroek 47 51 11N 3 17E
Assekrem 119 23 16N 5 49E
Assémini 64 39 18N 9 0E
Assen 46 53 0N 6 35E
Assendelft 46 52 29N 4 45E
Assenede 47 51 14N 3 46E
Assens, Odense, Denmark 73 56 41N 10 3E
Assens, Randers, Denmark 73 55 16N 9 55E
Assesse 47 50 22N 5 2E
Assiniboia 153 49 40N 105 59W
Assiniboine, R. 153 49 53N 97 8W
Assinica L. 150 50 30N 75 20W
Assinie 120 5 9N 3 17W
Assis 173 22 40S 50 20W
Assisi 63 43 4N 12 36E
Ássos 69 38 22N 20 33E
Assynt 36 58 25N 5 10W
Assynt, L. 36 58 25N 5 15W
Astakidha 69 35 53N 26 50E
Astalfort 44 44 4N 0 40E
Astara 79 38 30N 48 50E
Astee 39 52 33N 9 36W
Asten 47 51 24N 5 45E
Asti 62 44 54N 8 11E
Astillero 56 43 24N 3 49W
Astipálaia 69 36 32N 26 22E
Aston, C. 149 70 10N 67 40W
Aston Clinton 29 51 48N 0 44W
Astorga 56 42 29N 6 8W
Astoria 160 46 16N 123 50W
Åstorp 73 56 6N 12 55E
Astrakhan 83 46 25N 48 5E
Astudillo 56 42 12N 4 22W
Asturias 56 43 15N 6 0W
Astwood Bank 28 52 15N 1 55W
Asunción 172 25 21S 57 30W
Asunción, La 174 11 2N 63 53W
Åsunden 73 57 47N 13 18E
Asutri 123 15 25N 35 45E
Aswa, R. 126 2 30N 33 5E
Aswad,Rasal 122 21 20N 39 0E
Aswân 122 24 4N 32 57E
Aswân High Dam = Sadd el Aali 122 24 5N 32 54E
Asyût 122 27 11N 31 4E
Asyûti, Wadi 122 27 18N 31 20E
Aszód 53 47 39N 19 28E
At Tafilah 92 30 45N 35 30E
At Ta'if 122 21 5N 40 27E
Atacama 172 25 40S 67 40W
Atacama □ 172 27 30S 70 0W
Atacama, Desierto de 176 24 0S 69 20W
Atacama, Salar de 172 24 0S 68 20W
Ataco 174 3 35N 75 23W
Atakor 119 23 27N 5 31E
Atakpamé 121 7 31N 1 13E
Atalaia 114 9 25S 36 0W

Atalándi Ayutla


Atalándi 69 38 39N 22 58 E
Atalaya 174 10 45 S 73 50W
Ataléia 171 18 3 S 41 6W
Atami 111 35 0N 139 55 E
Atankawng 98 25 50N 97 47 E
Atar 116 20 30N 13 5W
Atara 77 63 10N 129 10 E
Ataram, Erg d' 118 23 57N 2 0 E
Atarfe 57 37 13N 3 40W
Atascadero 163 35 32N 120 44W
Atasu 76 48 30N 71 0 E
Atauro 103 8 10 S 125 30 E
Atbara 122 17 42N 33 59 E
Atbara, R. 122 17 40N 33 56 E
Atbashi 85 41 10N 75 48 E
Atbashi, Khrebet 85 40 50N 75 30 E
Atchafalaya B. 159 29 30N 91 20W
Atchison 158 39 40N 95 0W
Atebubu 121 7 47N 1 0W
Ateca 58 41 20N 1 49W
Aterno, R. 63 42 18N 13 45 E
Atesine, Alpi 62 46 55N 11 30 E
Atessa 63 42 5N 14 27 E
Ath 47 50 38N 3 47 E
Ath Thamami 92 27 45N 35 30 E
Athabasca 152 54 45N 113 20W
Athabasca, L. 153 59 15N 109 15W
Athabasca, R. 153 58 40N 110 50W
Athboy 38 53 37N 6 55W
Athea 39 52 27N 9 18W
Athenry 39 53 18N 8 45W
Athens, Ala., U.S.A. 157 34 49N 86 58W
Athens, Ga., U.S.A. 157 33 56N 83 24W
Athens, N.Y., U.S.A. 162 42 15N 73 48W
Athens, Ohio, U.S.A. 156 39 52N 82 6W
Athens, Pa., U.S.A. 162 41 57N 76 36W
Athens, Tex., U.S.A. 159 32 11N 95 48W
Athens = Athínai 69 37 58N 23 46 E
Atherstone 28 52 35N 1 32W
Atherton, Austral. 138 17 17 S 145 30 E
Atherton, U.K. 32 53 32N 2 30W
Athiéme 121 6 37N 1 40 E
Athínai 69 37 58N 23 46 E
Athleague 38 53 34N 8 17W
Athlone 38 53 26N 7 57W
Athni 96 16 44N 75 6 E
Athol 143 45 30 S 168 35 E
Atholl, Forest of 37 56 51N 3 50W
Atholville 151 47 59N 66 43W
Áthos, Mt. 68 40 9N 24 22 E
Athus 47 49 34N 5 50 E
Athy 39 53 0N 7 0W
Ati 123 13 5N 29 2 E
Atiak 126 3 12N 32 2 E
Atiamuri 142 38 24 S 176 5 E
Atico 174 16 14 S 73 40W
Atienza 58 41 12N 2 52W
Atikokan 150 48 45N 91 37W
Atikonak L. 151 52 40N 64 32W
Atka, U.S.A. 147 52 5N 174 40W
Atka, U.S.S.R. 77 60 50N 151 48 E
Atkarsk 81 51 55N 45 2 E
Atkasuk (Meade River) 147 70 30N 157 20W
Atkinson 158 42 35N 98 59W
Atlanta, Ga., U.S.A. 157 33 50N 84 24W
Atlanta, Tex., U.S.A. 159 33 7N 94 8W
Atlantic 158 41 25N 95 0W
Atlantic City 162 39 25N 74 25W
Atlantic Ocean 14 0 0 20 0W
Atlántico □ 174 10 45N 75 0W
Atlas, Great, Mts. 114 33 0N 5 0W
Atlin 147 59 31N 133 41W
Atlin Lake 147 59 26N 133 45W
'Atlit 90 32 42N 34 56 E
Atløy 71 61 21N 4 58 E
Atmakur 97 14 37N 79 40 E
Atmore 157 31 2N 87 30W
Atnarko 152 52 25N 126 0W
Atō 110 34 25N 131 40 E
Atoka 159 34 22N 96 10W
Atókos 69 38 28N 20 49 E
Atolia 163 35 19N 117 37W
Atotonilco el Alto 164 20 20N 98 40W
Atouguia 57 39 20N 9 20W
Atoyac, R. 165 16 30N 97 31W
Atrafors 73 57 02N 12 40 E
Atrak, R. 93 37 50N 57 0 E
Atran 73 57 7N 12 57 E
Atrato, R. 174 6 40N 77 0W
Atrauli 94 28 2N 78 20 E
Atri 63 42 35N 14 0 E
Atsbi 122 13 52N 39 50 E
Atsumi 111 34 35N 137 4 E
Atsumi-Wan 111 34 44N 137 13 E
Atsuta 112 43 24N 141 26 E
Attalla 157 34 2N 86 5W
Attawapiskat 150 52 56N 82 24W
Attawapiskat, L. 150 52 18N 87 54W
Attawapiskat, R. 150 52 57N 82 18W
Attendorn 48 51 8N 7 54 E
Attersee 52 47 55N 13 31 E
Attert 47 49 45N 5 47 E
Attica 156 40 20N 87 15W
Attichy 43 49 25N 3 3 E
Attigny 43 49 28N 4 35 E
Attikamagen L. 151 55 0N 66 30W
Attikí Kai Arkhipélagos □ 69 38 10N 23 40 E
Attil 90 32 23N 35 4 E
Attleboro 162 41 56N 71 18W
Attleborough 29 52 32N 1 1 E
Attock 94 33 52N 72 20 E
Attopeu 100 14 48N 106 50 E
Attu 147 52 55N 173 10W
Attunga 141 30 55 S 150 50 E
Attur 97 11 35N 78 30 E
Attymon 39 53 20N 8 37W
Atuel, R. 172 36 17 S 66 50W
Atvidaberg 73 58 12N 16 0 E
Atwater 163 37 21N 120 37W
Atwood 158 39 52N 101 3W
Au Sable Pt. 150 46 0N 86 0W
Au Sable, R. 156 44 25N 83 20W
Aubagne 45 43 17N 5 37 E
Aubange 47 49 34N 5 48 E
Aubarede Pt. 103 17 15N 122 20 E
Aube □ 43 48 15N 4 0 E
Aubel 47 50 42N 5 51 E
Aubenas 45 44 37N 4 24 E
Aubenton 43 49 50N 4 12 E
Auberry 163 37 7N 119 29W
Aubigny-sur-Nère 43 47 30N 2 24 E
Aubin 44 44 33N 2 15 E
Aubrac, Mts. d' 44 44 38N 2 58 E
Auburn, Ala., U.S.A. 157 32 37N 85 30W
Auburn, Calif., U.S.A. 160 38 50N 121 4W
Auburn, Ind., U.S.A. 156 41 20N 85 0W
Auburn, Nebr., U.S.A. 158 40 25N 95 50W
Auburn, N.Y., U.S.A. 162 42 57N 76 39W
Auburn, Penn., U.S.A. 162 40 36N 76 6W
Auburn Range 139 25 15 S 150 30 E
Auburndale 157 28 5N 81 45W
Aubusson 44 45 57N 2 11 E
Auch 44 43 39N 0 36 E
Auchel 43 50 30N 2 29 E
Auchenblae 37 56 54N 2 26W
Auchencairn 35 54 51N 3 52W
Auchi 121 7 6N 6 13 E
Auchinleck 34 55 28N 4 18W
Auchness 37 58 0N 4 36W
Auchterarder 35 56 18N 3 43W
Auchterderran 35 56 8N 3 16W
Auchtermuchty 35 56 18N 3 15W
Auchtertyre 36 57 17N 5 35W
Auckland 142 36 52 S 174 46 E
Auckland □ 142 38 35 S 177 0 E
Auckland Is. 142 51 0 S 166 0 E
Aude □ 44 43 8N 2 28 E
Aude, R. 44 44 13N 3 15 E
Auden 150 50 14N 87 53W
Auderghem 47 50 49N 4 26 E
Auderville 42 49 43N 1 57W
Audierne 42 48 1N 4 34W
Audincourt 43 47 30N 6 50 E
Audlem 32 52 59N 2 31W
Audo Ra. 123 6 20N 41 50 E
Audrey, gasfield 19 53 35N 2 0 E
Audubon 158 41 43N 94 56W
Aue 48 50 34N 12 43 E
Auerbach 48 50 30N 12 25 E
Auffay 42 49 43N 1 07 E
Augathella 139 25 48 S 146 35 E
Augher 38 54 25N 7 10W
Aughnacloy 38 54 25N 6 58W
Aughrim, Clare, Ireland 39 53 0N 8 57W
Aughrim, Galway, Ireland 39 53 18N 8 19W
Aughrim, Wicklow, Ireland 39 52 52N 6 20W
Aughrus More 38 53 34N 10 10W
Augrabies Falls 128 28 35 S 20 20 E
Augsburg 49 48 22N 10 54 E
Augusta, Italy 65 37 14N 15 12 E
Augusta, Ark., U.S.A. 159 35 17N 91 25W
Augusta, Ga., U.S.A. 157 33 29N 81 59W
Augusta, Kans., U.S.A. 159 37 40N 97 0W
Augusta, Me., U.S.A. 151 44 20N 69 46 E
Augusta, Mont., U.S.A. 160 47 30N 112 29W
Augusta, Wis., U.S.A. 158 44 41N 91 8W
Augustenborg 73 54 57N 9 53 E
Augustine 159 31 30N 94 37W
Augusto Cardosa 127 12 40 S 34 50 E
Augustów 54 53 51N 23 00 E
Augustus Downs 138 18 35 S 139 55 E
Augustus I. 136 15 20 S 124 30 E
Augustus, Mt. 137 24 20 S 116 50 E
Auk, oilfield 19 56 25N 2 15 E
Aukan 123 15 29N 40 50 E
Aukum 163 38 34N 120 43W
Auld, L. 136 22 32 S 123 44 E
Auldearn 37 57 34N 3 50W
Aulla 62 44 12N 9 57 E
Aulnay 44 46 2N 0 22W
Aulne, R. 42 48 17N 4 16W
Ault 158 40 40N 104 42W
Ault-Onival 42 50 5N 1 29 E
Aultbea 36 57 50N 5 36W
Aulus-les-Bains 44 42 49N 1 19 E
Aumale 43 49 46N 1 46 E
Aumont-Aubrac 44 44 43N 3 17 E
Auna 121 10 9N 4 42 E
Aundh 96 17 33N 74 23 E
Aunis 44 46 0N 0 50W
Auponhia 103 1 58 S 125 27 E
Aups 45 43 37N 6 15 E
Aur, P. 101 2 35N 104 10 E
Aura 98 26 59N 97 57 E
Aurahorten, Mt. 71 59 15N 6 53 E
Auraiya 95 26 28N 79 33 E
Aurangabad, Bihar, India 95 24 45N 84 18 E
Aurangabad, Maharashtra, India 96 19 50N 75 23 E
Auray 42 47 40N 3 0W
Aurès 119 35 8N 6 30 E
Aurich 48 53 28N 7 30 E
Aurilândia 171 16 44 S 50 28W
Aurillac 44 44 55N 2 26 E
Aurlandsvangen 71 60 55N 7 12 E
Auronza 63 46 33N 12 27 E
Aurora, Brazil 171 6 57 S 38 58W
Aurora, S. Afr. 128 32 40 S 18 29 E
Aurora, Colo., U.S.A. 158 39 44N 104 55W
Aurora, Ill., U.S.A. 156 41 42N 88 12W
Aurora, Mo., U.S.A. 159 36 58N 93 42W
Aurora, Nebr., U.S.A. 158 40 55N 98 0W
Aurora, N.Y., U.S.A. 162 42 45N 76 42W
Aurskog 71 59 55N 11 26 E
Aurukun Mission 138 13 20 S 141 45 E
Aus 128 26 35 S 16 12 E
Auskerry I. 37 59 2N 2 35W
Aust-Agder fylke □ 75 58 55N 7 40 E
Austad 71 58 58N 7 37 E
Austerlitz = Slavikov 53 49 10N 16 52 E
Austevoll 71 60 5N 5 13 E
Austin, Austral. 137 27 40 S 117 50 E
Austin, Minn., U.S.A. 158 43 37N 92 59W
Austin, Nev., U.S.A. 160 39 30N 117 1W
Austin, Tex., U.S.A. 159 30 20N 97 45W
Austin, L. 137 27 40 S 118 0 E
Austral Downs 138 20 30 S 137 45 E
Austral Is. = Tubuai, Îles 143 25 0 S 150 0 E
Australia ■ 133 23 0 S 135 0 E
Australian Alps 141 36 30 S 148 8 E
Australian Cap. Terr. 139 35 15 S 149 8 E
Australian Dependency 13 73 0 S 90 0 E
Austria ■ 52 47 0N 14 0 E
Austvågøy 74 68 20N 14 40 E
Autelbas 47 49 39N 5 52 E
Auterive 44 43 21N 1 29 E
Authie, R. 43 50 22N 1 38 E
Autlan 164 19 40N 104 30W
Autun 43 46 58N 4 17 E
Auvelais 47 50 27N 4 38 E
Auvergne, Austral. 136 15 39 S 130 1 E
Auvergne, France 44 45 20N 3 0 E
Auxerre 43 47 48N 3 32 E
Auxi-le-Château 43 50 15N 2 8 E
Auxonne 43 47 10N 5 20 E
Auzances 44 46 2N 2 30 E
Avaldsnes 71 59 21N 5 20 E
Avallon 43 47 30N 3 53 E
Avalon 163 33 21N 118 20W
Avalon Pen. 151 47 30N 53 20W
Avalon Res. 159 32 30N 104 30W
Avanigadda 97 16 0N 80 56 E
Avaré 173 23 4 S 48 58W
Avas 68 40 57N 25 56 E
Avawata Mts. 163 35 30N 116 20W
Avebury 28 51 25N 1 52W
Aveh 92 35 40N 49 15 E
Aveiro, Brazil 175 3 10 S 55 5W
Aveiro, Port. 56 40 37N 8 38W
Aveiro □ 56 40 40N 8 35W
Avelgem 47 50 47N 3 27 E
Avellaneda 172 34 50 S 58 10W
Avellino 65 40 54N 14 46 E
Avenal 163 36 0N 120 8W
Avenchen 50 46 53N 7 2 E
Averøya 71 63 0N 7 35 E
Aversa 65 40 58N 14 11 E
Avery 160 47 22N 115 56W
Aves, Islas de 174 12 0N 67 40W
Avesnes-sur-Helpe 43 50 8N 3 55 E
Avesta 72 60 9N 16 10 E
Aveton Gifford 30 50 17N 3 51W
Aveyron □ 44 44 22N 2 45 E
Avezzano 63 42 2N 13 24 E
Avgó 69 35 33N 25 37 E
Aviá Terai 172 26 45 S 60 50W
Aviano 63 46 3N 12 35 E
Avich, L. 34 56 17N 5 25W
Aviemore 37 57 11N 3 50W
Avigliana 62 45 7N 7 13 E
Avigliano 65 40 44N 15 41 E
Avignon 45 43 57N 4 50 E
Ávila 56 40 39N 4 43W
Ávila □ 56 40 30N 5 0W
Avila Beach 163 35 11N 120 44W
Ávila, Sierra de 56 40 40N 5 0W
Avilés 56 43 35N 5 57W
Avionárion 69 38 31N 24 8 E
Avisio, R. 63 46 14N 11 18 E
Aviz 57 39 4N 7 53W
Avize 43 48 59N 4 0 E
Avoca, Austral. 139 37 5 S 143 26 E
Avoca, Ireland 39 52 52N 6 13W
Avoca, R., Austral. 140 35 40 S 143 43 E
Avoca, R., Ireland 39 52 48N 6 10W
Avoch 37 57 34N 4 10W
Avola, Can. 152 51 45N 119 19W
Avola, Italy 65 36 56N 15 7 E
Avon 158 43 0N 98 3W
Avon □ 28 51 30N 2 40W
Avon Downs 133 19 58 S 137 25 E
Avon Is. 133 19 37 S 158 17 E
Avon, R., Austral. 137 31 40 S 116 7 E
Avon, R., Avon, U.K. 28 51 30N 2 43W
Avon, R., Grampian, U.K. 37 57 25N 3 25W
Avon, R., Hants., U.K. 28 50 44N 1 45W
Avon, R., Warwick, U.K. 28 52 0N 2 9W
Avondale, N.Z. 142 36 54 S 174 42 E
Avondale, Rhod. 127 17 43 S 30 58 E
Avonlea 153 50 0N 105 0W
Avonmouth 28 51 30N 2 42W
Avranches 42 48 40N 1 20W
Avrig 70 45 43N 24 21 E
Avrillé 44 46 28N 1 28W
Avtovac 66 43 9N 18 35 E
Avu Meru □ 126 3 20 S 36 50 E
Awag el Baqar 123 10 10N 33 10 E
Awaji 111 34 32N 135 1 E
Awaji-Shima 110 34 30N 134 50 E
Awali 93 26 0N 50 30 E
Awantipur 95 33 55N 75 3 E
Awanui 142 35 4 S 173 17 E
Awarja, R. 96 18 0N 76 15 E
Awarta 90 32 10N 35 17 E
Awarua Pt. 143 44 15 S 168 5 E
Awasa, L. 123 7 0N 38 30 E
Awash 123 9 1N 40 10 E
Awash, R. 123 11 30N 42 0 E
Awaso 120 6 15N 2 22W
Awatere, R. 143 41 37 S 174 10 E
Awbarī 119 26 46N 12 57 E
Awe, L. 34 56 15N 5 15W
Aweil 123 8 42N 27 20 E
Awgu 121 6 4N 7 24 E
Awjilah 117 29 8N 21 7 E
Aworro 135 7 43 S 143 11 E
Ax-les-Thermes 44 42 44N 1 50 E
Axarfjörður 74 66 15N 16 45W
Axbridge 28 51 17N 2 50W
Axe Edge 32 53 14N 2 2W
Axe R. 28 51 17N 2 52W
Axel 47 51 16N 3 55 E
Axel Heiberg I. 12 80 0N 90 0W
Axelfors 73 57 26N 13 7 E
Axholme, Isle of 33 53 30N 1 10 E
Axim 120 4 51N 2 15W
Axintele 70 44 37N 26 47 E
Axiós, R. 68 40 57N 22 35 E
Axmarsbruk 72 61 3N 17 10 E
Axminster 30 50 47N 3 1W
Axmouth 30 50 43N 3 2W
Axstedt 48 53 26N 8 43 E
Axvall 73 58 23N 13 34 E
Ay 43 49 3N 4 0 E
Ay, R. 84 56 8N 57 40 E
Ayabaca 174 4 40 S 79 53W
Ayabe 111 35 20N 135 20 E
Ayacucho, Argent. 172 37 5 S 58 20W
Ayacucho, Peru 174 13 0 S 74 0W
Ayaguz 76 48 10N 80 0 E
Ayakkuduk 85 41 12N 65 12 E
Ayakok'umu Hu 105 37 30N 89 20 E
Ayakudi 97 10 57N 77 6 E
Ayamonte 57 37 12N 7 24W
Ayan 77 56 30N 138 16 E
Ayancık 82 41 57N 34 18 E
Ayapel 174 8 19N 75 9W
Ayapel, Sa. de 174 7 45N 75 30W
Ayaş 82 40 10N 32 14 E
Ayaviri 174 14 50 S 70 35W
Aydın □ 92 37 40N 27 40 E
Aye 47 50 14N 5 18 E
Ayenngré 121 8 40N 1 1 E
Ayer Hitam 101 1 55N 103 11 E
Ayeritam 101 5 24N 100 15 E
Ayers Rock 136 25 23 S 131 5 E
Ayiá 68 39 43N 22 45 E
Ayía Anna 69 38 52N 23 24 E
Ayía Marína, Kásos, Greece 69 35 27N 26 53 E
Ayía Marína, Leros, Greece 69 37 11N 26 48 E
Ayía Paraskeví 68 39 14N 26 16 E
Ayía Rouméli 69 35 14N 23 58 E
Ayiássos 69 39 5N 26 23 E
Áyios Andréas 69 37 21N 22 45 E
Áyios Evstrátios 68 39 34N 24 58 E
Áyios Ioánnis, Ákra 69 35 20N 25 40 E
Áyios Kírikos 69 37 34N 26 17 E
Áyios Matthaíos 68 39 30N 19 47 E
Áyios Míron 69 35 15N 25 1 E
Áyios Nikólaos 69 35 11N 25 41 E
Áyios Pétros 69 38 38N 20 33 E
Áyios Yeóryios 69 37 28N 23 57 E
Aykathonisi 69 37 28N 27 0 E
Ayke, Ozero 84 51 57N 61 36 E
Aylesbury 29 51 48N 0 49W
Aylesford 29 51 18N 0 29 E
Aylmer L. 148 64 0N 108 30W
Aylsham 29 52 48N 1 16 E
Ayn Zālah 92 36 45N 42 35 E
'Ayn Zaqqūt 119 29 0N 19 30 E
Ayna 59 38 34N 2 3W
Aynho 28 51 59N 1 15W
Ayni 85 39 23N 68 32 E
Ayolas 172 27 10 S 56 59W
Ayom 123 7 49N 28 23 E
Ayon, Ostrov 77 69 50N 169 0 E
Ayora 59 39 3N 1 3W
Ayr, Austral. 138 19 35 S 147 25 E
Ayr, U.K. 34 55 28N 4 37W
Ayr (□) 26 55 25N 4 25W
Ayr, Heads of 34 55 25N 4 43W
Ayr, R. 34 55 29N 4 40W
Ayre, Pt. of 37 58 55N 2 43W
Ayre, Pt. of I.o.M. 32 54 27N 4 21W
Aysgarth 32 54 18N 2 0W
Aysha 123 10 50N 42 23 E
Ayton 138 15 45 S 145 25 E
Ayton, Borders, U.K. 35 55 51N 2 6W
Ayton, N. Yorks., U.K. 33 54 15N 0 29W
Aytos 67 42 47N 27 16 E
Aytoska Planina 67 42 45N 27 30 E
Ayu, Kepulauan 103 0 35N 131 5 E
Ayutla, Guat. 166 14 40N 92 10W

Ayutla Balasore


Ayutla, Mexico 165 16 58N 99 17W
Ayutthaya = Phra Nakhon Si A. 101 14 25N 100 30 E
Aywalık 92 39 20N 26 46 E
Aywaille 47 50 28N 5 40 E
Az Zahiriya 90 31 25N 34 58 E
Az Zahran 92 26 10N 50 7 E
Az-Zarqā 90 32 5N 36 4 E
Az Zāwiyah 119 32 52N 12 56 E
Az-Zilfī 92 26 12N 44 52 E
Az Zintān 119 31 59N 12 9 E
Az Zubayr 92 30 20N 47 50 E
Azambuja 57 39 4N 8 51W
Azamgarh 95 26 35N 83 13 E
Azaouak, Vallée de l' 121 15 50N 3 20 E
Azārbāijān □ 92 37 0N 44 30 E
Azare 121 11 55N 10 10 E
Azay-le-Rideau 42 47 16N 0 30 E
Azazga 119 36 48N 4 22 E
Azbine = Aïr 121 18 0N 8 0 E
Azeffoun 119 36 51N 4 26 E
Azemmour 118 33 14N 9 20W
Azerbaijan S.S.R. □ 83 40 20N 48 0 E
Azezo 123 12 28N 37 15 E
Azilal,Beni Mallal 118 32 0N 6 30W
Azimganj 95 24 14N 84 16 E
Aznalcóllar 57 37 32N 6 17W
Azogues 174 2 35 S 78 0W
Azor 90 32 2N 34 48 E
Azores, Is. 14 38 44N 29 0W
Azov 83 47 3N 39 25 E
Azov Sea = Azovskoye More 82 46 0N 36 30 E
Azovskoye More 82 46 0N 36 30 E
Azovy 76 64 55N 64 35 E
Azpeitia 58 43 12N 2 19W
Azrou 118 33 28N 5 19W
Aztec 161 36 54N 108 0W
Azúa de Compostela 167 18 25N 70 44W
Azuaga 57 38 16N 5 39W
Azuara 58 41 15N 0 53W
Azuara, R. 58 41 12N 0 55W
Azúcar, Presa del 165 26 0N 99 5W
Azuer, R. 57 38 50N 3 15W
Azuero, Pen. de 166 7 30N 80 30W
Azul 172 36 42 S 59 43W
Azusa 163 34 8N 117 52W
Azzaba 119 36 48N 7 6 E
Azzano Décimo 63 45 53N 12 46 E

# B

B. Curri 68 42 22N 20 5 E
Ba Don 100 17 45N 106 26 E
Ba Dong 101 9 40N 106 33 E
Ba Ngoi = Cam Lam 101 11 50N 109 10 E
Ba, R. 56 13 5N 109 0 E
Ba Tri 101 10 2N 106 36 E
Baa 103 10 50 S 123 0 E
Baamonde 56 43 7N 7 44W
Baar 51 47 12N 8 32 E
Baarle Nassau 47 51 27N 4 56 E
Baarlo 47 51 20N 6 6 E
Baarn 46 52 12N 5 17 E
Bāb el Māndeb 91 12 35N 43 25 E
Baba Burnu 68 39 29N 26 2 E
Baba dag 83 41 0N 48 55 E
Baba, Mt. 67 42 44N 23 59 E
Babaçulândia 170 7 13 S 47 46W
Babadag 70 44 53N 28 44 E
Babaeski 67 41 26N 27 6 E
Babahoyo 174 1 40 S 79 30W
Babakin 137 32 7 S 118 1 E
Babana 121 10 31N 3 46 E
Babar, Alg. 119 35 10N 7 6 E
Babar, Pak. 94 31 7N 69 32 E
Babar, I. 103 8 0 S 129 30 E
Babarkach 94 29 45N 68 0 E
Babayevo 81 59 24N 35 55 E
Babb 160 48 56N 113 27W
Babbitt 163 38 32N 118 39W
Babenhausen 49 49 57N 8 56 E
Babi Besar, P. 101 2 25N 103 59 E
Babia Gora 54 49 38N 19 38 E
Babile 123 9 16N 42 11 E
Babinda 138 17 20 S 145 56 E
Babine 152 55 20N 126 35W
Babine L. 152 54 48N 126 0W
Babine, R. 152 55 45N 127 44W
Babo 103 2 30 S 133 30 E
Babócsa 53 46 2N 17 21 E
Babol 93 36 40N 52 50 E
Babol Sar 93 36 45N 52 45 E
Baboma 126 2 30N 28 10 E
Baborówo Kietrz 53 50 7N 18 1 E
Baboua 124 5 49N 14 58 E
Babuna, mts. 66 41 30N 21 40 E
Babura 121 12 51N 8 59 E
Babusar Pass 95 35 12N 73 59 E
Babushkin 81 55 45N 37 40 E
Babušnica 66 43 7N 22 27 E
Babylon, Iraq 92 32 40N 44 30 E
Babylon, U.S.A. 162 40 42N 73 20W
Bač 66 45 29N 19 17 E
Bac Can 100 22 08N 105 49 E
Bac Giang 100 21 16N 106 11 E
Bac Kan 101 22 5N 105 50 E
Bac Lieu = Vinh Loi 101 9 17N 105 43 E
Bac Ninh 100 21 13N 106 4 E
Bac Phan 100 22 0N 105 0 E
Bac Quang 100 22 30N 104 48 E
Bacabal 170 4 15N 44 45W
Bacalar 165 18 12N 87 53W
Bacan,Pulau 103 0 50 S 127 30 E
Bacarès, Le 44 42 47N 3 3 E
Bacarra 103 18 15N 120 37 E
Baccarat 43 48 28N 6 42 E
Bacchus Marsh 140 37 43 S 144 27 E
Bacerac 164 30 18N 108 50W
Bach Long Vi,Dao 100 20 10N 107 40 E
Bachaquero 174 9 56N 71 8W
Bacharach 49 50 3N 7 46 E
Bachclina 76 57 45N 67 20 E
Bachok 101 6 4N 102 25 E
Bachuma 123 6 31N 36 1 E
Bačina 66 43 42N 21 23 E
Back 36 58 17N 6 20W
Back, R. 148 65 10N 104 0W
Bačka Palanka 66 45 17N 19 27 E
Bačka Topola 66 45 49N 19 39 E
Bäckefors 73 58 48N 12 9 E
Bački Petrovac 66 45 29N 19 32 E
Backnang 49 48 57N 9 26 E
Backstairs Passage 133 35 40 S 138 5 E
Bacolod 103 10 40N 122 57 E
Bacqueville 42 49 47N 1 0 E
Bacs-Kiskun □ 53 46 43N 19 30 E
Bácsalmás 53 46 8N 19 17 E
Bacton 29 52 50N 1 29 E
Bacuit 103 11 20N 119 20 E
Bacup 32 53 42N 2 12W
Bacŭu 70 46 35N 26 55 E
Bacŭu □ 70 46 30N 26 45 E
Bad Aussee 52 47 43N 13 45 E
Bad Axe 150 43 48N 82 59W
Bad Bergzabern 49 49 6N 8 0 E
Bad Bramstedt 48 53 56N 9 53 E
Bad Doberan 48 54 6N 11 55 E
Bad Driburg 48 51 44N 9 0 E
Bad Ems 49 50 22N 7 44 E
Bad Frankenhausen 48 51 21N 11 3 E
Bad Freienwalde 52 52 46N 14 2 E
Bad Godesberg 48 50 41N 7 4 E
Bad Hersfeld 48 50 52N 9 42 E
Bad Hofgastein 52 47 17N 13 6 E
Bad Homburg 49 50 17N 8 33 E
Bad Honnef 48 50 39N 7 13 E
Bad Ischl 52 47 44N 13 38 E
Bad Kissingen 49 50 11N 10 5 E
Bad Kreuznach 49 49 47N 7 47 E
Bad Lands 158 43 40N 102 10W
Bad Lauterberg 48 51 38N 10 29 E
Bad Leonfelden 52 48 31N 14 18 E
Bad Lippspringe 48 51 47N 8 46 E
Bad Mergentheim 49 49 29N 9 47 E
Bad Münstereifel 48 50 33N 6 46 E
Bad Nauheim 49 50 24N 8 45 E
Bad Oeynhausen 48 52 16N 8 45 E
Bad Oldesloe 48 53 56N 10 17 E
Bad Orb 49 50 16N 9 21 E
Bad Pyrmont 48 51 59N 9 5 E
Bad, R. 158 44 10N 100 50W
Bad Ragaz 51 47 0N 9 30 E
Bad St. Peter 48 54 23N 8 32 E
Bad Salzuflen 48 52 8N 8 44 E
Bad Segeberg 48 53 58N 10 16 E
Bad Tölz 49 47 43N 11 34 E
Bad Waldsee 49 47 56N 9 46 E
Bad Wildungen 48 51 7N 9 10 E
Bad Wimpfen 49 49 12N 9 10 E
Bad Windsheim 49 49 29N 10 25 E
Badagara 97 11 35N 75 40 E
Badagri 121 6 25N 2 55 E
Badajoz 57 38 50N 6 59W
Badajoz □ 57 38 40N 6 30W
Badakhshan □ 93 36 30N 71 0 E
Badalona 58 41 26N 2 15 E
Badalzai 94 29 50N 65 35 E
Badampahar 96 22 10N 86 10 E
Badanah 92 30 58N 41 30 E
Badas 102 4 33N 114 25 E
Badas, Kepulauan 102 0 45N 107 5 E
Baddo, R. 93 28 15N 65 0 E
Bade 103 7 10 S 139 35 E
Baden, Austria 53 48 1N 16 13 E
Baden, Switz. 51 47 28N 8 18 E
Baden-Baden 49 48 45N 8 15 E
Baden Park 140 32 8 S 144 12 E
Baden-Württemberg □ 49 48 40N 9 0 E
Badenoch 37 58 16N 4 5W
Badenscoth 37 57 27N 2 30W
Badeso 123 9 58N 40 52 E
Badgastein 52 47 7N 13 9 E
Badger, Can. 151 49 0N 56 4W
Badger, U.S.A. 163 36 38N 119 1W
Badghis □ 93 35 0N 63 0 E
Badgom 95 34 1N 74 45 E
Badhoevedorp 46 52 20N 4 47 E
Badia Polesine 63 45 6N 11 30 E
Badin 94 24 38N 68 54 E
Badnera 96 20 48N 77 44 E
Badogo 120 11 2N 8 13W
Badrinath 95 30 45N 79 30 E
Baduen 91 7 15N 47 40 E
Badulla 97 7 1N 81 7 E
Badupi 98 21 36N 93 27 E
Bække 73 55 35N 9 6 E
Baena 57 37 37N 4 20W
Baerami Creek 141 32 27 S 150 27 E
Baetas 174 6 5 S 62 15W
Baexem 47 51 13N 5 53 E
Baeza, Ecuador 174 0 25 S 77 45W
Baeza, Spain 59 37 57N 3 25W
Bafa 93 31 40N 55 25 E
Bafa Gölü 69 37 30N 27 29 E
Bafatá 120 12 8N 15 20W
Baffin Bay 12 72 0N 64 0W
Baffin I. 149 68 0N 75 0W
Bafia 121 4 40N 11 10 E
Bafilo 121 9 22N 1 22 E
Bafing, R. 120 11 40N 10 45W
Baflo 46 53 22N 6 31 E
Bafoulabé 120 13 50N 10 55W
Bafq 93 31 40N 55 20 E
Bafra 82 41 34N 35 54 E
Baft 93 29 15N 56 38 E
Bafut 121 6 6N 10 2 E
Bafwakwandji 126 1 12N 26 52 E
Bafwasende 126 1 3N 27 5 E
Bagalkot 96 16 10N 75 40 E
Bagamoyo 126 6 28 S 38 55 E
Bagamoyo □ 126 6 20 S 38 30 E
Bagan Datok 101 3 59N 100 47 E
Bagan Serai 101 5 1N 100 32 E
Bagan Siapiapi 102 2 12N 100 50 E
Baganga 103 7 34N 126 33 E
Bagasra 94 21 59N 71 77 E
Bagawi 123 12 20N 34 18 E
Bagdad 163 34 35N 115 53W
Bagdarin 77 54 26N 113 36 E
Bagé 173 31 20 S 54 15W
Bagenalstown = Muine Bheag 39 52 42N 6 57W
Baggs 160 41 8N 107 46W
Baggy Pt. 30 51 11N 4 12W
Bagh 95 33 59N 73 45 E
Bagh nam Faoileann, B. 36 57 22N 7 13W
Baghdād 92 33 20N 44 30 E
Bagherhat 98 22 40N 89 47 E
Bagheria 64 38 5N 13 30 E
Baghin 93 30 12N 56 45 E
Baghlan 93 36 12N 69 0 E
Baghlan □ 93 36 0N 68 30 E
Baginbun Hd. 39 52 10N 6 50W
Bagley 158 47 30N 95 22W
Bagnacavallo 63 44 25N 11 58 E
Bagnara Cálabra 65 38 16N 15 49 E
Bagnères-de-Bigorre 44 43 5N 0 9 E
Bagnères-de-Luchon 44 42 47N 0 38 E
Bagni di Lucca 62 44 1N 10 37 E
Bagno di Romagna 63 43 50N 11 59 E
Bagnoles-de-l'Orne 42 48 32N 0 25W
Bagnolo Mella 62 45 27N 10 14 E
Bagnols-les-Bains 44 44 30N 3 40 E
Bagnols-sur-Cèze 45 44 10N 4 36 E
Bagnorégio 63 42 38N 12 7 E
Bagolino 62 45 49N 10 28 E
Bagotville 151 48 22N 70 54W
Bagrdan 66 44 5N 21 11 E
Bagshot 29 51 22N 0 41W
Baguio 103 16 26N 120 34 E
Bahabón de Esgueva 58 41 52N 3 43W
Bahadurabad 98 25 11N 89 44 E
Bahadurgarh 94 28 40N 76 57 E
Bahama, Canal Viejo de 166 22 10N 77 30W
Bahama Is. 167 24 40N 74 0W
Bahamas ■ 167 24 0N 74 0W
Baharîya,El Wâhât el 122 28 0N 28 50 E
Bahau 101 2 48N 102 26 E
Bahawalnagar 94 30 0N 73 15 E
Bahawalpur 94 29 37N 71 40 E
Bahawalpur □ 94 29 5N 71 3 E
Baheri 95 28 45N 79 34 E
Baheta 123 13 27N 42 10 E
Bahi 126 5 58 S 35 21 E
Bahi Swamp 126 6 10 S 35 0 E
Bahía = Salvador 171 13 0 S 38 30W
Bahía □ 171 12 0N 42 0W
Bahía Blanca 172 38 35 S 62 13W
Bahía de Caráquez 174 0 40 S 80 27W
Bahía Honda 166 22 54N 83 10W
Bahía, Islas de la 166 16 45N 86 15W
Bahía Laura 176 48 10 S 66 30W
Bahía Negra 174 20 5 S 58 5W
Bahir Dar Giyorgis 123 11 33N 37 25 E
Bahmer 118 27 32N 0 10W
Bahönye 53 46 25N 17 28 E
Bahr Aouk 124 9 20N 20 40 E
Bahr Dar 123 11 37N 37 10 E
Bahr el Abiad 123 9 30N 31 40 E
Bahr el Ahmer □ 122 20 0N 35 0 E
Bahr el Arab 123 9 50N 27 10 E
Bahr el Azraq 123 10 30N 35 0 E
Bahr el Ghazâl □ 123 7 0N 28 0 E
Bahr el Ghazâl, R. 123 9 0N 30 0 E
Bahr el Jebel 123 7 30N 30 30 E
Bahr Salamat 124 10 0N 19 0 E
Bahr Yûsef 122 28 25N 30 35 E
Bahra 92 21 25N 39 32 E
Bahra el Burullus 122 31 28N 30 48 E
Bahra el Manzala 122 31 28N 32 01 E
Bahraich 95 27 38N 81 50 E
Bahrain ■ 93 26 0N 50 35 E
Bahramabad 93 30 28N 56 2 E
Bahu Kalat 93 25 50N 61 20 E
Bai 120 13 35N 3 28W
Bai Bung, Mui 101 8 38N 104 44 E
Bai Duc 100 18 3N 105 49 E
Bai Thuong 100 19 54N 105 23 E
Baia-Mare 70 47 40N 23 17 E
Baia-Sprie 70 47 41N 23 43W
Baião 170 2 40 S 49 40W
Baïbokoum 117 7 40N 14 45 E
Baidoa 91 3 8N 43 30 E
Baie Comeau 151 49 12N 68 10W
Baie de l'Abri 151 50 3N 67 0W
Baie Johan Beetz 151 50 18N 62 50W
Baie St. Paul 151 47 28N 70 32W
Baie Trinité 151 49 25N 67 20W
Baie Verte 151 49 55N 56 12W
Baignes 44 45 28N 0 25W
Baigneux-les-Juifs 43 47 31N 4 39 E
Ba'ījī 92 35 0N 43 30 E
Baikal, L. 77 53 0N 108 0 E
Bailadila, Mt. 96 18 43N 81 15 E
Baildon 33 53 52N 1 46W
Baile Atha Cliath = Dublin 39 53 20N 6 18W
Bailei 123 6 44N 40 18 E
Bailén 57 38 8N 3 48W
Baileux 47 50 2N 4 23 E
Bailhongal 97 15 55N 74 53 E
Bailique, Ilha 170 1 2N 49 58W
Bailleul 43 50 44N 2 41 E
Baillieborough 38 53 55N 7 0W
Baimuru 135 7 35 S 144 51 E
Bain-de-Bretagne 42 47 50N 1 40W
Bainbridge, U.K. 32 54 18N 2 7W
Bainbridge, Ga., U.S.A. 157 30 53N 84 34W
Bainbridge, N.Y., U.S.A. 162 42 17N 75 29W
Baing 103 10 14 S 120 34 E
Bainville 158 48 8N 104 10W
Bainyik 135 3 40 S 143 4 E
Baird 159 32 25N 99 25W
Baird Inlet 147 64 49N 164 18W
Baird Mts. 147 67 10N 160 15W
Bairnsdale 141 37 48 S 147 36 E
Baissa 121 7 14N 10 38 E
Baitadi 95 29 35N 80 25 E
Baixa Grande 171 11 57 S 40 11W
Baiyuda 122 17 35N 32 07 E
Baja 53 46 12N 18 59 E
Baja California 164 32 10N 115 12W
Baja, Pta. 164 29 50N 116 0W
Bajah, Wadi 122 23 14N 39 20 E
Bajana 94 23 7N 71 49 E
Bajimba 139 29 22 S 152 0 E
Bajimba, Mt. 139 29 17 S 152 6 E
Bajina Bašta 66 43 58N 19 35 E
Bajitpur 95 24 13N 91 0 E
Bajmok 66 45 57N 19 24 E
Bajo Boquete 167 8 49N 82 27W
Bajoga 121 10 57N 11 20 E
Bajool 138 23 40 S 150 35 E
Bak 53 46 43N 16 51 E
Bakal 84 54 56N 58 48 E
Bakala 117 6 15N 20 20 E
Bakanas 85 44 50N 76 15 E
Bakar 63 45 18N 14 32 E
Bakel, Neth. 47 51 30N 5 45 E
Bakel, Senegal 120 14 56N 12 20W
Baker, Calif., U.S.A. 163 35 16N 116 8W
Baker, Mont., U.S.A. 158 46 22N 104 12W
Baker, Nev., U.S.A. 160 38 59N 114 7W
Baker, Oreg., U.S.A. 160 44 50N 117 55W
Baker Is. 130 0 10N 176 35 E
Baker, L., Austral. 137 26 54 S 126 5 E
Baker, L., Can. 148 64 0N 96 0W
Baker Lake 148 64 20N 96 3W
Baker Mt. 160 48 50N 121 49W
Baker's Dozen Is. 150 56 45N 78 45W
Bakersfield 163 35 25N 119 0W
Bakewell 33 53 13N 1 40W
Bakhchisaray 82 44 40N 33 45 E
Bakhmach 80 51 10N 32 45 E
Bakhtiari □ 92 32 0N 49 0 E
Bakia 123 5 18N 25 45 E
Bakinskikh Komissarov 92 39 20N 49 15 E
Bakırköy 67 40 59N 28 53 E
Bakkafjörðr 74 66 2N 14 48W
Bakkagerði 74 65 31N 13 49W
Bakke 71 58 25N 6 39 E
Bakony Forest = Bakony Hegység 53 47 10N 17 30 E
Bakony Hegység 53 47 10N 17 30 E
Bakony, R. 53 47 35N 17 54 E
Bakori 121 11 34N 7 25 E
Bakouma 117 5 40N 22 56 E
Bakov 52 50 27N 14 55 E
Bakpakty 85 44 35N 76 40 E
Bakr Uzyak 84 52 59N 58 38 E
Baku 83 40 25N 49 45 E
Bakwanga = Mbuji Mayi 124 6 9 S 23 40 E
Bal'a 90 32 20N 35 6 E
Bala, L. = Tegid, L. 31 52 53N 3 38W
Balabac I. 102 8 0N 117 0 E
Balabac, Selat 102 7 53N 117 5 E
Balabagh 94 34 25N 70 12 E
Balabakk 92 34 0N 36 10 E
Balabalangan, Kepulauan 102 2 20 S 117 30 E
Balaghat 96 21 49N 80 12 E
Balaghat Ra. 96 18 50N 76 30 E
Balaguer 58 41 50N 0 50 E
Balakhna 81 56 35N 43 32 E
Balaklava, Austral. 140 34 7 S 138 22 E
Balaklava, U.S.S.R. 82 44 30N 33 30 E
Balakleya 82 49 28N 36 55 E
Balakovo 81 52 4N 47 55 E
Balallan 36 58 5N 6 35W
Balancán 165 17 48N 91 32W
Balanda 81 51 30N 44 40 E
Balangir 96 20 43N 83 35 E
Balapur 96 21 22N 76 45 E
Balashikha 81 55 49N 37 59 E
Balashov 81 51 30N 43 10 E
Balasinor 94 22 57N 73 23 E
Balasore 96 21 35N 87 3 E

Balassagyarmat Bangor


Balassagyarmat **53** 48 4N 19 15 E
Balât **122** 25 36N 29 19 E
Balaton **53** 46 50N 17 40 E
Balatonfüred **53** 46 58N 17 54 E
Balatonszentgyörgy **53** 46 41N 17 19 E
Balazote **59** 38 54N 2 09W
Balbeggie **35** 56 26N 3 19W
Balbi, Mt. **135** 5 55 S 154 58 E
Balblair **37** 57 39N 4 11W
Balboa **166** 9 0N 79 30W
Balbriggan **38** 53 35N 6 10W
Balcarce **172** 38 0 S 58 10W
Balcarres **153** 50 50N 103 35W
Balchik **67** 43 28N 28 11 E
Balclutha **143** 46 15 S 169 45 E
Bald Hd. **137** 35 6 S 118 1 E
Bald Hill, W. Australia, Austral. **137** 31 36 S 116 13 E
Bald Hill, W. Australia, Austral. **137** 24 55 S 119 57 E
Bald I. **137** 34 57 S 118 27 E
Bald Knob **159** 35 20N 91 35W
Baldegger-See **51** 47 12N 8 17 E
Balder, oilfield **19** 59 10N 2 20 E
Balderton **33** 53 3N 0 46W
Baldock **29** 51 59N 0 11W
Baldock L. **153** 56 33N 97 57W
Baldoyle **38** 53 24N 6 10W
Baldwin, Fla., U.S.A. **156** 30 15N 82 10W
Baldwin, Mich., U.S.A. **156** 43 54N 85 53W
Baldwinsville **162** 43 10N 76 19W
Bale **63** 45 4N 13 46 E
Baleares ☐ **58** 39 30N 3 0 E
Baleares, Islas **58** 39 30N 3 0 E
Balearic Is. = Baleares, Islas **58** 39 30N 3 0 E
Baleia,Ponta da **171** 17 40 S 39 7W
Balen **47** 51 10N 5 10 E
Baler **103** 15 46N 121 34 E
Balerna **51** 45 52N 9 0 E
Baleshare I. **36** 57 30N 7 21W
Balezino **84** 58 2N 53 6 E
Balfate **166** 15 48N 86 25W
Balfe's Creek **138** 20 12 S 145 55 E
Balfour, S. Afr. **129** 26 38 S 28 35 E
Balfour, U.K. **37** 59 2N 2 54W
Balfour Downs **137** 22 45 S 120 50 E
Balfouriyya **90** 32 38N 35 18 E
Balfron **34** 56 4N 4 20W
Bali **121** 5 54N 10 0 E
Bali ☐ **102** 8 20 S 115 0 E
Bali, I. **102** 8 20 S 115 0 E
Bali, Selat **103** 8 30 S 114 35 E
Baligród **54** 49 20N 22 17 E
Balikesir **92** 39 35N 27 58 E
Balikpapan **102** 1 10 S 116 55 E
Balimbing **103** 5 10N 120 3 E
Balimo **135** 8 6 S 142 57 E
Baling **101** 5 41N 100 55 E
Balintore **37** 57 45N 3 55W
Balipara **99** 26 50N 92 45 E
Balit **95** 36 15N 74 40 E
Baliza **175** 16 0 S 52 20W
Balk **46** 52 54N 5 35 E
Balkan Mts. = Stara Planina **67** 43 15N 23 0 E
Balkan Pen. **16** 42 0N 22 0 E
Balkh = Wazirabad **93** 36 44N 66 47 E
Balkh ☐ **93** 36 30N 67 0 E
Balkhash **76** 46 50N 74 50 E
Balkhash, Ozero **76** 40 0N 74 50 E
Balla, Ireland **38** 53 48N 9 7W
Balla, Pak. **99** 24 10N 91 35 E
Ballachulish **36** 56 40N 5 10W
Balladonia **137** 32 27 S 123 51 E
Ballagan Pt. **38** 54 0N 6 6W
Ballaghaderreen **38** 53 55N 8 35W
Ballantrae **34** 55 6N 5 0W
Ballara **140** 32 19 S 140 45 E
Ballarat **139** 37 33 S 143 50 E
Ballard, L. **137** 29 20 S 120 10 E
Ballarpur **96** 19 50N 79 23 E
Ballater **37** 57 2N 3 2W
Ballaugh **32** 54 20N 4 32W
Balldale **141** 36 20N 146 33 E
Ballenas, Canal de las **164** 29 10N 113 45W
Balleni **70** 45 48N 27 51 E
Balleny Is. **13** 66 30 S 163 0 E
Ballia **95** 25 46N 84 12 E
Ballickmoyler **39** 52 54N 7 2W
Ballidu **137** 30 35 S 116 45 E
Ballina, Austral. **139** 28 50 S 153 31 E
Ballina, Mayo, Ireland **38** 54 7N 9 10W
Ballina, Tipp., Ireland **39** 52 49N 8 27W
Ballinagar **39** 53 15N 7 21W
Ballinagh = Bellananagh **38** 53 55N 7 25W
Ballinalack **38** 53 38N 7 28W
Ballinalea **39** 53 0N 6 8W
Ballinalee **38** 53 46N 7 40W
Ballinamallard **38** 54 30N 7 36W
Ballinameen **38** 53 54N 8 19W
Ballinamore **38** 54 3N 7 48W
Ballinamore Bridge **38** 53 30N 8 24W
Ballinascarty **39** 51 40N 8 52W
Ballinasloe **39** 53 20N 8 12W
Ballincollig **39** 51 52N 8 35W
Ballindaggin **39** 52 33N 6 43W
Ballinderry **38** 53 2N 8 13W
Ballinderry R. **38** 54 40N 6 32W
Ballindine **38** 53 40N 8 57W
Ballineen **39** 51 43N 8 57W
Balling **73** 56 38N 8 51 E
Ballingarry, Lim., Ireland **39** 53 1N 8 3W
Ballingarry, Tipp., Ireland **39** 52 29N 8 50W
Ballingarry, Tipp., Ireland **39** 52 35N 7 32W
Ballingeary **39** 51 51N 9 13W
Ballinger **159** 31 45N 99 58W
Ballinhassig **39** 51 48N 8 33W
Ballinlough **38** 53 45N 8 39W
Ballinluig **37** 56 40N 3 40W
Ballinrobe **38** 53 36N 9 13W
Ballinskelligs **39** 51 50N 10 17W
Ballinskelligs B. **39** 51 46N 10 11W
Ballintober **38** 53 43N 8 25W
Ballintoy **38** 55 13N 6 20W
Ballintra **38** 54 35N 8 9W
Ballinunty **39** 52 36N 7 40W
Ballinure **39** 52 34N 7 46W
Ballivian **172** 22 41 S 62 10W
Ballivor **38** 53 32N 6 50W
Ballo Pt. **79** 8 55N 13 18W
Balloch **34** 56 0N 4 35W
Ballon **39** 48 10N 0 16 E
Ballston Spa **162** 43 0N 73 51W
Ballybay **38** 54 8N 6 52W
Ballybofey **38** 54 48N 7 47W
Ballyboghil **38** 53 32N 6 16W
Ballybogy **38** 55 8N 6 33W
Ballybunion **39** 52 30N 9 40W
Ballycanew **39** 52 37N 6 18W
Ballycarney **39** 52 35N 6 44W
Ballycastle **38** 55 12N 6 15W
Ballycastle B. **38** 55 12N 6 15W
Ballyclare, Ireland **38** 53 40N 8 0W
Ballyclare, U.K. **38** 54 46N 6 0W
Ballyclerahan **39** 52 25N 7 48W
Ballycolla **39** 52 53N 7 27W
Ballyconneely **38** 53 27N 10 5W
Ballyconneely B. **38** 53 23N 10 8W
Ballyconnell **38** 54 7N 7 35W
Ballycotton **39** 51 50N 8 0W
Ballycroy **38** 54 2N 9 49W
Ballydavid **39** 53 12N 8 28W
Ballydavid Hd. **39** 52 15N 10 20W
Ballydehob **39** 51 34N 9 28W
Ballydonegan **39** 51 37N 10 12W
Ballydonegan B. **39** 51 38N 10 6W
Ballyduff, Kerry, Ireland **39** 52 27N 9 40W
Ballyduff, Waterford, Ireland **39** 52 9N 8 2W
Ballyforan **39** 53 29N 8 18W
Ballygar **38** 53 33N 8 20W
Ballygarrett **39** 52 34N 6 15W
Ballygawley **38** 54 27N 7 2W
Ballyglass **38** 53 45N 9 9W
Ballygorman **38** 55 23N 7 20W
Ballyhahill **39** 52 33N 9 13W
Ballyhaise **38** 54 3N 7 20W
Ballyhalbert **38** 54 30N 5 28W
Ballyhaunis **38** 53 47N 8 47W
Ballyheige I. **39** 52 22N 9 51W
Ballyhoura Hills **39** 52 18N 8 33W
Ballyjamesduff **38** 53 52N 7 11W
Ballylanders **39** 52 25N 8 21W
Ballylaneen **39** 52 10N 7 25W
Ballylongford **39** 52 34N 9 30W
Ballylooby **39** 52 20N 7 59W
Ballylynan **39** 52 57N 7 02W
Ballymacoda **39** 51 53N 7 56W
Ballymagorry **38** 54 52N 7 26W
Ballymahon **39** 53 35N 7 45W
Ballymena **38** 54 53N 6 18W
Ballymena ☐ **38** 54 53N 6 18W
Ballymoe **38** 53 41N 8 28W
Ballymoney **38** 55 5N 6 30W
Ballymoney ☐ **38** 55 5N 6 23W
Ballymore **39** 53 30N 7 40W
Ballymore Eustace **39** 53 8N 6 38W
Ballymote **38** 54 5N 8 30W
Ballymurphy **39** 52 33N 6 52W
Ballymurray **38** 53 36N 8 8W
Ballynabola **39** 52 21N 6 50W
Ballynacally **39** 52 42N 9 7W
Ballynacargy **38** 53 35N 7 32W
Ballynacorra **39** 51 53N 8 10W
Ballynagore **38** 53 24N 7 29W
Ballynahinch **38** 54 24N 5 55W
Ballynahown **38** 53 21N 7 52W
Ballynameen **38** 54 58N 6 41W
Ballynamona **39** 52 5N 8 39W
Ballynure **38** 54 47N 5 59W
Ballyquintin, Pt. **38** 54 20N 5 30W
Ballyragget **39** 52 47N 7 20W
Ballyroan **39** 52 57N 7 20W
Ballyronan **38** 54 43N 6 32W
Ballyroney **38** 54 17N 6 8W
Ballysadare **38** 54 12N 8 30W
Ballyshannon **38** 54 30N 8 10W
Ballyvaughan **39** 53 7N 9 10W
Ballyvourney **39** 51 57N 9 10W
Ballyvoy **38** 55 11N 6 11W
Ballywalter **38** 54 33N 5 30W
Ballywilliam **39** 52 27N 6 52W
Balmaceda **176** 46 0 S 71 50W
Balmaclellan **35** 55 6N 4 5W
Balmazújváros **53** 47 37N 21 21 E
Balmedie **37** 57 14N 2 4W
Balmhorn **50** 46 26N 7 42 E
Balmoral **140** 37 15 S 141 48 E
Balmoral For. **37** 57 0N 3 15W
Balmorhea **159** 31 2N 103 41W
Balnapaling **37** 57 42N 4 2W
Balonne, R. **139** 28 47 S 147 56 E
Balovale **125** 13 30 S 23 15 E
Balquhidder **34** 56 22N 4 22W
Balrampur **95** 27 30N 82 20 E
Balranald **140** 34 38 S 143 33 E
Balş **70** 44 22N 24 5 E
Balsas **165** 18 0N 99 40W
Balsas, R., Goias, Brazil **170** 9 0 S 48 0W
Balsas, R., Maranhão, Brazil **170** 7 15 S 44 35W
Balsas, R., Mexico **164** 18 30N 101 20W
Bålsta **72** 59 35N 17 30 E
Balsthal **50** 47 19N 7 41 E
Balta, Rumania **70** 44 54N 22 38 E
Balta, U.S.A. **158** 48 12N 100 7W
Balta, U.S.S.R. **82** 48 2N 29 45 E
Balta, I. **36** 60 44N 0 49W
Baltanás **56** 41 56N 4 15W
Baltasound **36** 60 47N 0 53W
Baltic Sea **75** 56 0N 20 0 E
Baltiisk **75** 54 38N 19 55 E
Baltim **122** 31 35N 31 10 E
Baltimore, Ireland **39** 51 29N 9 22W
Baltimore, U.S.A. **162** 39 18N 76 37W
Baltinglass **39** 52 57N 6 42W
Baltrum **48** 53 43N 7 25 E
Baluchistan ☐ **93** 27 30N 65 0 E
Balurghat **95** 25 15N 88 44 E
Balvicar **34** 56 17N 5 38W
Balygychan **77** 63 56N 154 12 E
Bam **93** 29 7N 58 14 E
Bam La **99** 29 25N 98 35 E
Bama **121** 11 33N 13 33 E
Bamako **120** 12 34N 7 55W
Bamba **121** 17 5N 1 0W
Bambari **117** 5 40N 20 35 E
Bambaroo **107** 18 50 S 146 11 E
Bamberg, Ger. **49** 49 54N 10 53 E
Bamberg, U.S.A. **157** 33 19N 81 1W
Bambesi **123** 9 45N 34 40 E
Bambey **120** 14 42N 16 28W
Bambili **126** 3 40N 26 0 E
Bamboo **138** 14 34 S 143 20 E
Bambouti **126** 5 25N 27 12 E
Bambuí **171** 20 1 S 45 58W
Bamburgh **35** 55 36N 1 42W
Bamenda **121** 5 57N 10 11 E
Bamfield **152** 48 45N 125 10W
Bamford **33** 53 21N 1 41W
Bamian ☐ **93** 35 0N 67 0 E
Bamkin **121** 6 3N 11 27 E
Bampton, Devon, U.K. **30** 50 59N 3 29W
Bampton, Oxon., U.K. **28** 51 44N 1 33W
Bampur **93** 27 15N 60 21 E
Bampur, R. **93** 27 20N 59 30 E
Ban Aranyaprathet **100** 13 41N 102 30 E
Ban Ban **100** 19 31N 103 15 E
Ban Bang Hin **101** 9 32N 98 35 E
Ban Bua Chum **101** 15 11N 101 12 E
Ban Bua Yai **100** 15 33N 102 26 E
Ban Chiang Klang **100** 19 15N 100 55 E
Ban Chik **100** 17 15N 102 22 E
Ban Choho **100** 15 2N 102 9 E
Ban Dan Lan Hoi **100** 17 0N 99 35 E
Ban Don **100** 12 53N 107 48 E
Ban Don = Surat Thani **101** 9 8N 99 20 E
Ban Don, Go **101** 9 20N 99 25 E
Ban Dong **100** 19 14N 100 3 E
Ban Hong **100** 18 18N 98 50 E
Ban Houei Sai **100** 20 22N 100 32 E
Ban Kaeng **100** 17 29N 100 7 E
Ban Kantang **101** 7 25N 99 31 E
Ban Keun **100** 18 22N 102 35 E
Ban Khai **100** 12 46N 101 18 E
Ban Khe Bo **101** 19 10N 104 39 E
Ban Kheun **100** 20 13N 101 7 E
Ban Khlong Kua **101** 6 57N 100 8 E
Ban Khuan Mao **101** 7 50N 99 37 E
Ban Khun Yuam **100** 18 49N 97 57 E
Ban Ko Yai Chim **101** 11 17N 99 26 E
Ban Kok **100** 16 40N 103 40 E
Ban Laem **100** 13 13N 99 59 E
Ban Lao Ngam **100** 15 28N 106 10 E
Ban Le Kathe **100** 15 49N 98 53 E
Ban Mae Chedi **100** 19 11N 99 31 E
Ban Mae Laeng **100** 20 1N 99 17 E
Ban Mae Sariang **100** 18 0N 97 56 E
Ban Me Thuot **100** 12 40N 108 3 E
Ban Mi **100** 15 3N 100 32 E
Ban Muong Mo **100** 19 4N 103 58 E
Ban Na Mo **100** 17 7N 105 40 E
Ban Na San **101** 8 33N 99 52 E
Ban Na Tong **100** 20 56N 101 47 E
Ban Nam Bac **100** 20 38N 102 20 E
Ban Nam Ma **100** 22 2N 101 37 E
Ban Ngang **100** 15 59N 106 11 E
Ban Nong Bok **100** 17 5N 104 48 E
Ban Nong Boua **100** 15 40N 106 33 E
Ban Nong Pling **100** 15 40N 100 10 E
Ban Pak Chan **101** 10 32N 98 51 E
Ban Phai **100** 16 4N 102 44 E
Ban Pong **100** 13 50N 99 55 E
Ban Ron Phibun **101** 8 9N 99 51 E
Ban Sanam Chai **101** 7 33N 100 25 E
Ban Sangkha **100** 14 37N 103 52 E
Ban Tak **100** 17 2N 99 4 E
Ban Tako **100** 14 5N 102 40 E
Ban Takua Pa **101** 8 55N 98 25 E
Ban Tha Dua **100** 17 59N 98 39 E
Ban Tha Li **100** 17 37N 101 25 E
Ban Tha Nun **101** 8 12N 98 18 E
Ban Thahine **100** 14 12N 105 33 E
Ban Thateng **101** 15 25N 106 27 E
Ban Xien Kok **100** 20 54N 100 39 E
Ban Yen Nhan **100** 20 57N 106 2 E
Baña, La, Punta de **58** 40 33N 0 40 E
Banadar Daryay Oman ☐ **93** 25 30N 56 0 E
Banadia **174** 6 54N 71 49W
Banagher **39** 53 12N 8 0W
Banalia **126** 1 32N 25 5 E
Banam **101** 11 20N 105 17 E
Banamba **120** 13 29N 7 22W
Banana **138** 24 28 S 150 8 E
Bananal, I. do **171** 11 30 S 50 30W
Banaras = Varanasi **95** 25 22N 83 8 E
Banas, R., Gujarat, India **94** 24 25N 72 30 E
Banas, R., Madhya Pradesh, India **95** 24 15N 81 30 E
Bânâs, Ras. **122** 23 57N 35 50 E
Banat ☐ **66** 45 45N 21 15 E
Banbridge **38** 54 21N 6 17W
Banbridge ☐ **38** 54 21N 6 16W
Banbury **28** 52 4N 1 21W
Banchory **37** 57 3N 2 30W
Bancroft **150** 45 3N 77 51W
Bancroft = Chililabombwe **127** 12 18 S 27 43 E
Band **67** 46 30N 24 25 E
Band-i-Turkistan, Ra. **93** 35 2N 64 0 E
Banda **95** 25 30N 80 26 E
Banda Aceh **102** 5 35N 95 20 E
Banda Banda, Mt. **141** 31 10 S 152 28 E
Banda Elat **103** 5 40 S 133 5 E
Banda, Kepulauan **103** 4 37 S 129 50 E
Banda, La **172** 27 45 S 64 10W
Banda, Punta **164** 31 47N 116 50W
Banda Sea **103** 6 0 S 130 0 E
Bandama, R. **120** 6 32N 5 30W
Bandanwara **94** 26 9N 74 38 E
Bandar = Masulipatnam **97** 16 12N 81 12 E
Bandar 'Abbās **93** 27 15N 56 15 E
Bandar-e Būshehr **93** 28 55N 50 55 E
Bandar-e Chārak **93** 26 45N 54 20 E
Bandar-e Deylam **92** 30 5N 50 10 E
Bandar-e Lengeh **93** 26 35N 54 58 E
Bandar-e Ma'shur **92** 30 35N 49 10 E
Bandar-e-Nakhīlu **93** 26 58N 53 30 E
Bandar-e Rīg **93** 29 30N 50 45 E
Bandar-e Shah **93** 37 0N 54 10 E
Bandar-e-Shahpur **92** 30 30N 49 5 E
Bandar-i-Pahlavi **92** 37 30N 49 30 E
Bandar Maharani = Muar **101** 2 3N 102 34 E
Bandar Penggaram = Batu Pahat **101** 1 50N 102 56 E
Bandar Seri Begawan **102** 4 52N 115 0 E
Bandawe **127** 11 58 S 34 5 E
Bande, Belg. **47** 50 10N 5 25 E
Bande, Spain **56** 42 3N 7 58W
Bandeira, Pico da **173** 20 26 S 41 47W
Bandeirante **171** 13 41 S 50 48W
Bandera, Argent. **172** 28 55 S 62 20W
Bandera, U.S.A. **159** 29 45N 99 3W
Banderas, Bahía de **164** 20 40N 105 30W
Bandi-San **112** 37 36N 140 4 E
Bandia, R. **96** 19 30N 80 25 E
Bandiagara **120** 14 12N 3 29W
Bandirma **92** 40 20N 28 0 E
Bandon **39** 51 44N 8 45W
Bandon, R. **39** 51 40N 8 11W
Bandula **127** 19 0 S 33 7 E
Bandundu **124** 3 15 S 17 22 E
Bandung **103** 6 36 S 107 48 E
Bandya **137** 27 40 S 122 5 E
Bañeres **59** 38 44N 0 38W
Banes **167** 21 0N 75 42W
Bañeza, La **56** 42 17N 5 54W
Banff, Can. **152** 51 10N 115 34W
Banff, U.K. **37** 57 40N 2 32W
Banff Nat. Park **152** 51 30N 116 15W
Banfora **120** 10 40N 4 40W
Bang Fai, R. **100** 16 57N 104 45 E
Bang Hieng, R. **100** 16 24N 105 40 E
Bang Krathum **100** 16 34N 100 18 E
Bang Lamung **100** 13 3N 100 56 E
Bang Mun Nak **100** 16 2N 100 23 E
Bang Pa In **100** 14 14N 100 35 E
Bang Rakam **100** 16 45N 100 7 E
Bang Saphan **101** 11 14N 99 28 E
Bangala Dam **127** 21 7 S 31 25 E
Bangalore **97** 12 59N 77 40 E
Bangangte **121** 5 8N 10 32 E
Bangaon **95** 23 0N 88 47 E
Bangassou **124** 4 55N 23 55 E
Bangeta, Mt. **135** 6 21 S 147 3 E
Banggai **103** 1 40 S 123 30 E
Banggi, P. **102** 7 50N 117 0 E
Banghāzī **119** 32 11N 20 3 E
Bangil **103** 7 36 S 112 50 E
Bangjang **123** 11 23N 32 41 E
Bangka, Pulau, Celebes, Indon. **103** 1 50N 125 5 E
Bangka, Pulau, Sumatera, Indon. **102** 2 0 S 105 50 E
Bangka, Selat **102** 3 30 S 105 30 E
Bangkalan **103** 7 2 S 112 46 E
Bangkinang **102** 0 18N 100 5 E
Bangko **102** 2 5 S 102 9 E
Bangkok = Krung Thep **100** 13 45N 100 31 E
Bangladesh ■ **98** 24 0N 90 0 E
Bangolo **120** 7 1N 7 29W
Bangor, Me., U.S.A. **151** 44 48N 68 42W

Bangor Bassevelde


Bangor, Pa., U.S.A. **162** 40 51N 75 13W
Bangor, N.I., U.K. **38** 54 40N 5 40W
Bangor, Wales, U.K. **31** 53 13N 4 9W
Bangued **103** 17 40N 120 37E
Bangui **124** 4 23N 18 35E
Banguru **126** 0 30N 27 10E
Bangweulu, L. **127** 11 0S 30 0E
Bangweulu Swamp **127** 11 20S 30 15E
Banham **29** 52 27N 1 3E
Bani **167** 18 16N 70 22W
Bani Bangou **121** 15 3N 2 42E
Bani, Djebel **118** 29 16N 8 0W
Bani Na'im **90** 31 31N 35 10E
Bani, R. **120** 12 40N 6 30W
Bani Suhayla **90** 31 21N 34 19E
Bania **120** 9 4N 3 6W
Baniara **135** 9 44S 149 54E
Banihal Pass **95** 33 30N 75 12E
Banīnah **119** 32 0N 20 12E
Baniyas **92** 35 10N 36 0E
Banja Luka **66** 44 49N 17 26E
Banjak, Kepulauan **102** 2 10N 97 10E
Banjar **103** 7 24S 108 30E
Banjarmasin **102** 3 20S 114 35E
Banjarnegara **103** 7 24S 109 42E
Banjul **120** 13 28N 16 40W
Banka Banka **138** 18 50S 134 0E
Bankend **35** 55 2N 3 31W
Bankeryd **73** 57 53N 14 6E
Banket **127** 17 27S 30 19E
Bankfoot **35** 56 30N 3 31W
Bankhead **37** 57 11N 2 10W
Bankilaré **121** 14 35N 0 44E
Bankipore **95** 25 35N 85 10E
Banks I., B.C., Can. **152** 53 20N 130 0W
Banks I., N. W. Terr., Can. **12** 73 15N 121 30W
Banks I., P.N.G. **135** 10 10S 142 15E
Banks Peninsula **143** 43 45S 173 15E
Banks Str. **138** 40 40S 148 10E
Bankura **95** 23 11N 87 18E
Bankya **66** 42 43N 23 8E
Bann R., Down, U.K. **38** 54 30N 6 31W
Bann R., Londonderry, U.K. **38** 55 10N 6 34W
Bannalec **42** 47 57N 3 42W
Bannang Sata **101** 6 16N 101 16E
Bannerton **140** 34 42S 142 47E
Banning, Can. **150** 48 44N 91 56W
Banning, U.S.A. **163** 33 58N 116 58W
Banningville = Bandundu **124** 3 15S 17 22E
Bannockburn, Rhod. **127** 20 17S 29 48E
Bannockburn, U.K. **35** 56 5N 3 55W
Bannow **39** 52 12N 6 50W
Bannow B. **39** 52 13N 6 48W
Bannu **93** 33 0N 70 18E
Bañolas **58** 42 16N 2 44E
Banon **45** 44 2N 5 38E
Baños de la Encina **57** 38 10N 3 46W
Baños de Molgas **56** 42 15N 7 40W
Bánovce **53** 48 44N 18 16E
Banská Bystrica **53** 48 46N 19 14E
Banská Stiavnica **53** 48 25N 18 55E
Bańsko **67** 41 52N 23 28E
Banswara **94** 23 32N 74 24E
Bantama **121** 7 48N 0 42W
Bante **121** 8 25N 1 53E
Banteer **39** 52 8N 8 53W
Banten **103** 6 5S 106 8E
Bantry **39** 51 40N 9 28W
Bantry, B. **39** 51 35N 9 50W
Bantul **103** 7 55S 110 19E
Bantva **94** 21 29N 70 12E
Bantval **97** 12 55N 75 0E
Banu **93** 35 35N 69 5E
Banwell **28** 51 19N 2 51W
Banya **67** 42 33N 24 50E
Banyo **121** 6 52N 11 45E
Banyuls **44** 42 29N 3 8E
Banyumas **103** 7 32S 109 18E
Banyuwangi **103** 8 13S 114 21E
Banzare Coast **13** 66 30S 125 0E
Banzyville = Mobayi **124** 4 15N 21 8E
Bao Ha **100** 22 11N 104 21E
Bao Lac **100** 22 57N 105 40E
Bao Loc **101** 11 32N 107 48E
Bap **94** 27 23N 72 18E
Bapatla **97** 15 55N 80 30E
Bapaume **43** 50 7N 2 50E
Bâqa el Gharbiya **90** 32 25N 35 2E
Baqūbah **92** 33 45N 44 50E
Baquedano **172** 23 20S 69 52W
Bar, U.S.S.R. **82** 49 4N 27 40E
Bar, Yugo. **66** 42 8N 19 8E
Bar Harbor **151** 44 15N 68 20W
Bar-le-Duc **43** 48 47N 5 10E
Bar-sur-Aube **43** 48 14N 4 40E
Bar-sur-Seine **43** 48 7N 4 20E
Barabai **102** 2 32S 115 34E
Barabinsk **76** 55 20N 78 20E
Baraboo **158** 43 28N 89 46W
Baracoa **167** 20 20N 74 30W
Baradero **172** 33 52S 59 29W
Baradine **141** 30 56S 149 4E
Baraga **158** 46 49N 88 29W
Barahona, Dom. Rep. **167** 18 13N 71 7W
Barahona, Spain **58** 41 17N 2 39W
Barail Range **99** 25 15N 93 20E
Barakhola **99** 25 0N 92 45E
Barakot **95** 21 33N 84 59E
Barakula **139** 26 30S 150 33E
Baralaba **138** 24 13S 149 50E
Baralzon L. **153** 60 0N 98 3W
Baramati **96** 18 11N 74 33E
Baramba **96** 20 25N 85 23E
Barameiya **122** 18 32N 36 38E
Baramula **95** 34 15N 74 20E
Baran **94** 25 9N 76 40E
Baranoa **174** 10 48N 74 55W
Baranof I. **147** 57 0N 135 10W
Baranovichi **80** 53 10N 26 0E
Baranów Sandomierski **54** 50 29N 21 30E
Baranya □ **53** 46 0N 18 15E
Barão de Cocais **171** 19 56S 43 28W
Barão de Grajaú **170** 6 45S 43 1W
Barão de Melgaço **174** 11 50S 60 45W
Baraolt **70** 46 5N 25 34E
Barapasi **103** 2 15S 137 5E
Barapina **135** 6 21S 155 25E
Barasat **95** 22 46N 88 31E
Barasoli **123** 13 38N 42 0W
Barat Daya, Kepuluan **103** 7 30S 128 0E
Barataria B. **159** 29 15N 89 45W
Baraut **94** 29 13N 77 7E
Baraya **174** 3 10N 75 4W
Barbacena **173** 21 15S 43 56W
Barbacoas, Colomb. **174** 1 45N 78 0W
Barbacoas, Venez. **174** 9 29N 66 58W
Barbados ■ **167** 13 0N 59 30W
Barbalha **170** 7 19S 39 17W
Barban **63** 45 0N 14 4E
Barbastro **58** 42 2N 0 5E
Barbate **57** 36 13N 5 56W
Barberton, S. Afr. **129** 25 42S 31 2E
Barberton, U.S.A. **156** 41 0N 81 40W
Barbigha **95** 25 21N 85 47E
Barbourville **157** 36 57N 83 52W
Barbuda I. **167** 17 30N 61 40W
Barca d'Alva **56** 41 0N 7 0W
Barca, La **164** 20 20N 102 40W
Barcaldine **138** 23 33S 145 13E
Barcarrota **57** 38 31N 6 51W
Barce = Al Marj **117** 32 25N 20 40E
Barcellona Pozzo di Gotto **65** 38 8N 15 15E
Barcelona, Spain **58** 41 21N 2 10E
Barcelona, Venez. **174** 10 10N 64 40W
Barcelona □ **58** 41 30N 2 0E
Barcelonette **45** 44 23N 6 40E
Barcelos **174** 1 0S 63 0W
Barcin **54** 52 52N 17 55E
Barcoo, R. **138** 28 29S 137 46E
Barcs **53** 45 58N 17 28E
Barczewo **54** 53 50N 20 42E
Bard, Hd. **36** 60 6N 1 5W
Barda **83** 40 25N 47 10E
Bardai **119** 21 25N 17 0E
Bardas Blancas **172** 35 49S 69 45W
Bardejov **53** 49 18N 21 15E
Bardera **91** 2 20N 42 27E
Bardi **62** 44 38N 9 43E
Bardiyah **117** 31 45N 25 0E
Bardney **33** 53 13N 0 19W
Bardo **54** 50 31N 16 42E
Bardoc **137** 30 18S 121 12E
Bardoli **96** 21 12N 73 5E
Bardsey, I. **31** 52 46N 4 47W
Bardsey Sound **31** 52 47N 4 46W
Bardstown **156** 37 50N 85 29W
Bareilly **95** 28 22N 79 27E
Barellan **141** 34 16S 146 24E
Barengapara **98** 25 14N 90 14E
Barentin **42** 49 33N 0 58E
Barenton **42** 48 38N 0 50W
Barents Sea **12** 73 0N 39 0E
Barentu **123** 15 2N 37 35E
Barfleur **42** 49 40N 1 17W
Barford **28** 52 15N 1 35W
Barga **62** 44 5N 10 30E
Bargal **91** 11 25N 51 0E
Bargara **138** 24 50S 152 25E
Barge **62** 44 43N 7 19E
Barge, La **160** 41 12N 110 4W
Bargnop **123** 9 32N 28 25E
Bargo **141** 34 18S 150 35E
Bargoed **31** 51 42N 3 22W
Bargteheide **48** 53 42N 10 13E
Barguzin **77** 53 37N 109 37E
Barh **95** 25 29N 85 46E
Barhaj **95** 26 18N 83 44E
Barham **29** 51 12N 1 10E
Barhi **95** 24 15N 85 25E
Bari, India **94** 26 39N 77 39E
Bari, Italy **65** 41 6N 16 52E
Bari Doab **94** 30 20N 73 0E
Baria = Phuoc Le **101** 10 39N 107 19E
Bariadi □ **126** 2 45S 34 40E
Barika **118** 35 23N 5 22E
Barinas **174** 8 36N 70 15W
Barinas □ **174** 8 10N 69 50W
Baring C. **148** 70 0N 117 30W
Baringo **126** 0 47N 36 16E
Baringo □ **126** 0 55N 36 0E
Baringo, L. **126** 0 47N 36 16E
Barinitas **174** 8 45N 70 25W
Baripada **96** 21 57N 86 45E
Bariri **171** 22 4S 48 44W
Bârîs **122** 24 42N 30 31E
Barisal **98** 22 30N 90 20E
Barisan, Bukit **102** 3 30S 102 15E
Barito, R. **102** 2 50S 114 50E
Barjac **45** 44 20N 4 22E
Barjols **45** 43 34N 6 2E
Barjūji, W. **119** 25 26N 12 12E
Bark L. **150** 46 58N 82 25W
Barka **122** 17 30N 37 34E
Barkah **93** 23 40N 58 0E
Barker, Mt. **139** 35 4S 138 55E
Barking **29** 51 31N 0 10E
Barkley Sound **152** 48 50N 125 10W
Barkly Downs **138** 20 30S 138 30E
Barkly East **129** 30 58S 27 33E
Barkly Tableland **138** 19 50S 138 40E
Barkly West **128** 28 5S 24 31E
Barkol, Wadi **122** 17 40N 32 0E
Barksdale **159** 29 47N 100 2W
Barlborough **33** 53 17N 1 17W
Barlby **33** 53 48N 1 3W
Barlee, L. **137** 29 15S 119 30E
Barlee, Mt. **137** 24 35S 128 10E
Barlee Ra. **137** 23 30S 116 0E
Barlett **163** 36 29N 118 2W
Barletta **65** 41 20N 16 17E
Barlinek **54** 53 0N 15 15E
Barlingbo **73** 57 35N 18 27E
Barlow L. **153** 62 00N 103 0W
Barmby Moor **33** 53 55N 0 47W
Barmedman **141** 34 9S 147 21E
Barmer **94** 25 45N 71 20E
Barmera **140** 34 15S 140 28E
Barmoor **35** 55 38N 2 0W
Barmouth **31** 52 44N 4 3W
Barmstedt **48** 53 47N 9 46E
Barna **39** 53 14N 9 10W
Barnaderg **38** 53 29N 8 43W
Barnagar **94** 23 7N 75 19E
Barnard Castle **32** 54 33N 1 55W
Barnato **141** 31 38S 145 0E
Barnaul **76** 53 20N 83 40E
Barnby Moor **33** 53 21N 1 0W
Barne Inlet **13** 80 15S 160 0E
Barnes **141** 36 2S 144 47E
Barnesville **157** 33 6N 84 9W
Barnet **29** 51 37N 0 15W
Barnetby le Wold **33** 53 34N 0 24W
Barneveld, Neth. **96** 52 7N 5 36E
Barneveld, U.S.A. **162** 43 16N 75 14W
Barneville **42** 49 23N 1 46W
Barney, Mt. **133** 28 17S 152 44E
Barngo **138** 25 3S 147 20E
Barnhart **159** 31 10N 101 8W
Barnoldswick **32** 53 55N 2 11W
Barnsley **33** 53 33N 1 29W
Barnstaple **30** 51 5N 4 3W
Barnstaple B. **30** 51 5N 4 25W
Barnsville **158** 46 43N 96 28W
Baro **121** 8 35N 6 18E
Baro, R. **123** 8 25N 33 40E
Baroda **94** 25 29N 76 35E
Baroda = Vadodara, India **93** 22 20N 73 10E
Baroda = Vadodara, Gujarat, India **94** 22 20N 73 10E
Baron Ra. **136** 23 30S 127 45E
Barpali **96** 21 11N 83 35E
Barpathar **98** 26 17N 93 53E
Barpeta **95** 26 20N 91 10E
Barqa **117** 27 0N 20 0E
Barqin **119** 27 33N 13 34E
Barques, Pte. aux **156** 44 5N 82 55W
Barquinha **57** 39 28N 8 25W
Barquísimeto **174** 9 58N 69 13W
Barr, France **43** 48 25N 7 28E
Barr, U.K. **34** 55 13N 4 44W
Barr Smith Ra. **137** 27 10S 120 15E
Barra, Brazil **170** 11 5S 43 10W
Barra, Gambia **120** 13 21N 16 36W
Barra da Estiva **171** 13 38S 41 19W
Barra de Navidad **164** 19 12N 104 41W
Barra do Corda **170** 5 30S 45 10W
Barra do Mendes **171** 11 43S 42 4W
Barra do Piraí **173** 22 30S 43 50W
Barra Falsa, Pta. da **129** 22 58S 35 37E
Barra Hd. **36** 56 47N 7 40W
Barra, I. **36** 57 0N 7 30W
Barra Mansa **173** 22 35S 44 12W
Barra, Sd. of **36** 57 4N 7 25W
Barraba **141** 30 21S 150 35E
Barrackpur **95** 22 44N 88 30E
Barrafranca **65** 37 22N 14 10E
Barranca, Lima, Peru **174** 10 45S 77 50W
Barranca, Loreto, Peru **174** 4 50S 76 50W
Barrancabermeja **174** 7 0N 73 50W
Barrancas, Colomb. **174** 10 57N 72 50W
Barrancas, Venez. **174** 8 55N 62 5W
Barrancos **57** 38 10N 6 58W
Barranqueras **172** 27 30S 59 0W
Barranquilla, Atlántico, Colomb. **174** 11 0N 74 50W
Barranquilla, Vaupés, Colomb. **174** 1 39N 72 19W
Barras, Brazil **170** 4 15S 42 18W
Barras, Colomb. **174** 1 45S 73 13W
Barraute **150** 48 26N 77 38W
Barre, U.S.A. **156** 44 15N 72 30W
Barre, U.S.A. **162** 42 26N 72 6W
Barreal **172** 31 33S 69 28W
Barreiras **171** 12 8S 45 0W
Barreirinhas **170** 2 30S 42 50W
Barreiro **57** 38 40N 9 6W
Barreiros **170** 8 49S 35 12W
Barrême **45** 43 57N 6 23E
Barren I. **101** 12 17N 95 50E
Barren Is., Madag. **129** 18 25S 43 40E
Barren Is., U.S.A. **147** 58 45N 152 0W
Barren Junc. **139** 30 5S 149 0E
Barretos **171** 20 30S 48 35W
Barrhead, Can. **152** 54 10N 114 24W
Barrhead, U.K. **34** 55 48N 4 23W
Barrhill **34** 55 7N 4 46W
Barrie **150** 44 24N 79 40W
Barrier, C. **142** 36 25S 175 32E
Barrier Ra., Austral. **140** 31 0S 141 30E
Barrier Ra., N.Z. **143** 44 5S 169 42E
Barrier Rf., Gt. **138** 19 0S 149 0E
Barrière **152** 51 12N 120 7W
Barrington, Austral. **133** 31 58S 151 55E
Barrington, Ill., U.S.A. **156** 42 8N 88 5W
Barrington, R.I., U.S.A. **162** 41 43N 71 20W
Barrington L. **153** 56 55N 100 15W
Barrington Tops. **141** 32 6S 151 28E
Barringun **139** 29 1S 145 41E
Barrow **147** 71 16N 156 50W
Barrow Creek T.O. **138** 21 30S 133 55E
Barrow I. **136** 20 45S 115 20E
Barrow-in-Furness **32** 54 8N 3 15W
Barrow Pt. **138** 14 20S 144 40E
Barrow, Pt. **147** 71 22N 156 30W
Barrow, R. **39** 52 10N 6 57W
Barrow Ra. **137** 26 0S 127 40E
Barrow Strait **12** 74 20N 95 0W
Barrow upon Humber **33** 53 41N 0 22W
Barrowford **32** 53 51N 2 14W
Barruecopardo **56** 41 4N 6 40W
Barruelo **56** 42 54N 4 17W
Barry, S. Glam., U.K. **31** 51 23N 3 19W
Barry, Tayside, U.K. **35** 56 29N 2 45W
Barry I. **31** 51 23N 3 17W
Barry's Bay **150** 45 29N 77 41W
Barry's Pt. **39** 51 36N 8 40W
Barsalogho **121** 13 25N 1 3W
Barsat **95** 36 10N 72 45E
Barsi **96** 18 10N 75 50E
Barsø **73** 55 7N 9 33E
Barsoi **99** 25 48N 87 57E
Barstow, Calif., U.S.A. **163** 34 58N 117 2W
Barstow, Tex., U.S.A. **170** 31 30N 103 25W
Barthélemy, Col **100** 19 26N 104 6E
Bartica **174** 6 25N 58 40W
Bartle Frere, Mt. **138** 17 27S 145 50E
Bartlesville **159** 36 50N 95 58W
Bartlett **159** 30 46N 97 30W
Bartlett, L. **152** 63 5N 118 20W
Bartolomeu Dias **127** 21 10S 35 8E
Barton **33** 54 28N 1 38W
Barton Siding **137** 30 31S 132 39E
Barton-upon-Humber **33** 53 41N 0 27W
Bartoszyce **54** 54 15N 20 55E
Bartow **157** 27 53N 81 49W
Barú, I. de **174** 10 15N 75 35W
Baruth **48** 52 3N 13 31E
Barvas **36** 58 21N 6 31W
Barvaux **47** 50 21N 5 29E
Barvenkovo **82** 48 57N 37 0E
Barwani **94** 22 2N 74 57E
Barwell **28** 52 35N 1 22W
Barysh **81** 49 2N 25 18E
Bas-Rhin □ **43** 48 40N 7 30E
Bašaid **66** 45 38N 20 25E
Basa'idu **93** 26 35N 55 20E
Basal **94** 33 33N 72 13E
Basalt **163** 38 0N 118 15W
Basankusa **124** 1 5N 19 50E
Basawa **94** 34 15N 70 50E
Bascharage **47** 49 34N 5 55E
Bascuñán, Cabo **172** 28 52S 71 35W
Basècles **47** 50 32N 3 39E
Basel (Basle) **50** 47 35N 7 35E
Basel Landschaft □ **50** 47 26N 7 45E
Basel-Stadt □ **50** 47 35N 7 35E
Basento, R. **65** 40 35N 16 10E
Bashi Channel **105** 21 15N 122 0E
Bashkir A.S.S.R. □ **84** 54 0N 57 0E
Basilaki, I. **135** 10 35S 151 0E
Basilan, Selat **103** 6 50N 122 0E
Basilanl, I. **103** 6 35N 122 0E
Basildon **29** 51 34N 0 29E
Basilicata □ **65** 40 30N 16 0E
Basim **96** 20 3N 77 0E
Basin **160** 44 22N 108 2W
Basing **28** 51 16N 1 3W
Basingstoke **28** 51 15N 1 5W
Basirhat **98** 22 40N 88 54E
Baskatong Res. **150** 46 46N 75 50W
Baskerville C. **136** 17 10S 122 15E
Basle = Basel **50** 47 35N 7 35E
Basmat **96** 19 15N 77 12E
Basoda **94** 23 52N 77 54E
Basodino **51** 46 25N 8 28E
Basoka **126** 1 16N 23 40E
Basongo **124** 4 15S 20 20E
Basque Provinces = Vascongadas **58** 42 50N 2 45W
Basra = Al Basrah **92** 30 30N 47 50E
Bass Rock **35** 56 5N 2 40W
Bass Strait **138** 39 15S 146 30E
Bassano, del Grappa **63** 45 45N 11 45E
Bassari **121** 9 19N 0 57E
Bassas da India **125** 22 0S 39 0E
Basse **120** 13 13N 14 15W
Basse-Terre, I. **167** 16 0N 61 40W
Bassecourt **50** 47 20N 7 15E
Bassée, La **43** 50 31N 2 49E
Bassein, Burma **98** 16 30N 94 30E
Bassein, India **96** 19 26N 72 48E
Bassein Myit **99** 16 45N 94 30E
Bassenthwaite, L. **32** 54 40N 3 14W
Basseterre **167** 17 17N 62 43W
Bassett, Nebr., U.S.A. **158** 42 37N 99 30W
Bassett, Va., U.S.A. **157** 36 48N 79 59W
Bassevelde **47** 51 15N 3 41E

Bassi 94 30 44N 76 21 E
Bassigny 43 48 0N 5 10 E
Bassikounou 120 15 55N 6 1W
Bassilly 47 50 40N 3 56 E
Bassum 48 52 50N 8 42 E
Båstad 73 56 25N 12 51 E
Båstad 73 56 25N 12 51 E
Bastak 93 27 15N 54 25 E
Bastar 96 19 25N 81 40 E
Basti 95 26 52N 82 55 E
Bastia 45 42 40N 9 30 E
Bastia Umbra 63 43 4N 12 34 E
Bastide, La 44 44 35N 3 55 E
Bastogne 47 50 1N 5 43 E
Baston 29 52 43N 0 19W
Bastrop 159 30 5N 97 22W
Basuto 128 19 50 S 26 25 E
Basutoland = Lesotho 129 29 0 S 28 0 E
Basyanovskiy 84 58 19N 60 44 E
Bat Yam 90 32 2N 34 44 E
Bata, Eq. Guin. 124 1 57N 9 50 E
Bata, Rumania 70 46 1N 22 4 E
Bataan 103 14 40N 120 25 E
Bataan Pen. 103 14 38N 120 30 E
Batabanó 166 22 40N 82 20W
Batabanó, G. de 167 22 30N 82 30W
Batac 103 18 3N 120 34 E
Batagoy 77 67 38N 134 38 E
Batak 67 41 57N 24 12 E
Batalha 57 39 40N 8 50W
Batama 126 0 58N 26 33 E
Batamay 77 63 30N 129 15 E
Batamshinskiy 84 50 36N 58 16 E
Batang 103 6 55 S 109 40 E
Batangafo 117 7 25N 18 20 E
Batangas 103 13 35N 121 10 E
Batanta, I. 103 0 55N 130 40 E
Bataszék 66 46 10N 18 44 E
Batatais 173 20 54 S 47 37W
Batavia 156 43 0N 78 10W
Bataysk 83 47 3N 39 45 E
Batchelor 136 13 4 S 131 1 E
Bateman's B. 141 35 40 S 150 12 E
Batemans Bay 141 35 44 S 150 11 E
Bates Ra. 137 27 25 S 121 0 E
Batesburg 157 33 54N 81 32W
Batesville, Ark., U.S.A. 159 35 48N 91 40W
Batesville, Miss., U.S.A. 159 34 17N 89 58W
Batesville, Tex., U.S.A. 159 28 59N 99 38W
Batetski 80 58 47N 30 16 E
Bath, U.K. 28 51 22N 2 22W
Bath, Maine, U.S.A. 151 43 50N 69 49W
Bath, N.Y., U.S.A. 156 42 20N 77 17W
Batheay 101 11 59N 104 57 E
Bathford 28 51 23N 2 18W
Bathgate 35 55 54N 3 38W
Bâthie, La 46 45 37N 6 28 E
Bathmen 46 52 15N 6 29 E
Bathurst, Austral. 141 33 25 S 149 31 E
Bathurst, Can. 151 47 37N 65 43W
Bathurst B. 138 14 16 S 144 25 E
Bathurst C. 147 70 30N 128 30W
Bathurst, C. 147 70 34N 128 0W
Bathurst, Gambia = Banjul 120 13 28N 16 40W
Bathurst Harb. 138 43 15 S 146 10 E
Bathurst I., Austral. 136 11 30 S 130 10 E
Bathurst I., Can. 12 76 30N 130 10W
Bathurst Inlet 148 66 50N 108 1W
Batie 120 9 53N 2 53W
Batley 33 53 43N 1 38W
Batlow 141 35 31 S 148 9 E
Batman 92 37 55N 41 5 E
Batna 119 35 34N 6 15 E
Batoka 127 16 45 S 27 15 E
Baton Rouge 159 30 30N 91 5W
Batong, Ko 101 6 32N 99 12 E
Batopilas 164 27 45N 107 45W
Batouri 124 4 30N 14 25 E
Battambang 100 13 7N 103 12 E
Batticaloa 97 7 43N 81 45 E
Battice 47 50 39N 5 50 E
Battipáglia 65 40 38N 15 0 E
Battir 90 31 44N 35 8 E
Battle, Can. 153 52 58N 110 52W
Battle, U.K. 29 50 55N 0 30 E
Battle Camp 138 15 20 S 144 40 E
Battle Creek 156 42 20N 85 36W
Battle Harbour 151 52 16N 55 35W
Battle Lake 158 46 20N 95 43W
Battle Mountain 160 40 45N 117 0W
Battle, R. 153 52 43N 108 15W
Battlefields 127 18 37 S 29 47 E
Battleford 153 52 45N 108 15W
Battonya 53 46 16N 21 3 E
Batu Caves 101 3 15N 101 40 E
Batu Gajah 101 4 28N 101 3 E
Batu, Kepulauan 102 0 30 S 98 25 E
Batu, Mt. 123 6 55N 39 45 E
Batu Pahat 101 1 50N 102 56 E
Batuata, P. 103 6 30 S 122 20 E
Batulaki 103 5 40N 125 30 E
Batumi 83 41 30N 41 30 E
Baturadja 102 4 11 S 104 15 E
Baturité 170 4 28 S 38 45W
Baturité, Serra de 170 4 25 S 39 0W
Baubau 103 5 25 S 123 50 E
Bauchi 121 10 22N 9 48 E
Bauchi □ 121 10 0N 10 0 E
Baud 42 47 52N 3 1W
Baudette 158 48 46N 94 35W
Baudouinville = Moba 126 7 0 S 29 48 E
Baudour 47 50 29N 3 50 E
Bauer, C. 139 32 44 S 134 4 E
Baugé 42 47 31N 0 8W
Bauhinia Downs 138 24 35 S 149 18 E
Baule, La 42 47 18N 2 23W
Bauma 51 47 3N 8 53 E
Baume les Dames 43 47 22N 6 22 E
Baunei 64 40 2N 9 41 E
Bauru 173 22 10 S 49 0W
Baús 175 18 22 S 52 47W
Bauska 80 56 25N 25 15 E
Bautzen 48 51 11N 14 25 E
Baux, Les 45 43 45N 4 51 E
BavaniŠte 66 44 49N 20 53 E
Bavaria = Bayern 49 49 7N 11 30 E
Båven 72 59 35N 17 30 E
Bavispe, R. 164 29 30N 109 11W
Bawdsey 29 52 1N 1 27 E
Bawdwin 98 23 5N 97 50 E
Bawean 102 5 46 S 112 35 E
Bawku 121 11 3N 0 19W
Bawlake 98 19 11N 97 21 E
Bawnboy 38 54 8N 7 40W
Bawtry 33 53 25N 1 1W
Baxley 157 31 43N 82 23W
Baxter Springs 159 37 3N 94 45W
Bay Bulls 151 47 19N 52 50W
Bay City, Mich., U.S.A. 156 43 35N 83 51W
Bay City, Oreg., U.S.A. 160 45 45N 123 58W
Bay City, Tex., U.S.A. 159 28 59N 95 55W
Bay de Verde 151 48 5N 52 54W
Bay, Laguna de 103 14 20N 121 11 E
Bay of Islands 142 35 15 S 174 6 E
Bay St. Louis 159 30 18N 89 22W
Bay Shore 162 40 44N 73 15W
Bay Springs 159 31 58N 89 18W
Bay View 142 39 25 S 176 50 E
Baya 127 11 53 S 27 25 E
Bayamo 166 20 20N 76 40W
Bayamón 147 18 24N 66 10W
Bayan Kara Shan 99 34 0N 98 0 E
Bayan-Ovoo 106 47 47N 112 5 E
Bayana 94 26 55N 77 18 E
Bayanaul 76 50 45N 75 45 E
Bayandalay 106 43 30N 103 29 E
Bayanga 124 2 53N 16 19 E
Bayanhongor 105 46 8N 100 43 E
Bayard 158 41 48N 103 17W
Baybay 103 10 40N 124 55 E
Bayble 36 58 12N 6 13W
Bayburt 92 40 15N 40 20 E
Bayerischer Wald 49 49 0N 13 0 E
Bayern □ 49 49 7N 11 30 E
Bayeux 42 49 17N 0 42W
Bayfield 158 46 50N 90 48W
Bayir 92 30 45N 36 55 E
Baykadam 85 43 48N 69 58 E
Baykal, Oz. 77 53 0N 108 0 E
Baykit 77 61 50N 95 50 E
Baykonur 76 47 48N 65 50 E
Baymak 84 52 36N 58 19 E
Baynes Mts. 128 17 15 S 13 0 E
Bayombong 103 16 30N 121 10 E
Bayon 43 48 30N 6 20 E
Bayona 56 42 6N 8 52W
Bayonne, France 44 43 30N 1 28W
Bayonne, U.S.A. 162 40 41N 74 7W
Bayovar 174 5 50 S 81 0W
Baypore, R. 97 11 10N 75 47 E
Bayram-Ali 76 37 37N 62 10 E
Bayreuth 49 49 56N 11 35 E
Bayrischzell 49 47 39N 12 1 E
Bayrūt 92 33 53N 35 31 E
Baysun 85 38 12N 67 12 E
Bayt Aula 90 31 37N 35 2 E
Bayt Fajjar 90 31 38N 35 9 E
Bayt Fūrīk 90 32 11N 35 20 E
Bayt Jala 90 31 43N 35 11 E
Bayt Lahm 90 31 43N 35 12 E
Bayt Rīma 90 32 2N 35 6 E
Bayt Sāhūr 90 31 42N 35 13 E
Bayt Ummar 90 31 38N 35 7 E
Bayta at Tahtā 90 32 9N 35 18 E
Baytin 90 31 56N 35 14 E
Baytown 159 29 42N 94 57W
Bayzhansay 85 43 14N 69 54 E
Bayzo 121 13 52N 4 35 E
Baza 59 37 30N 2 47W
Bazar Dyuzi 83 41 12N 48 10 E
Bazarny Karabulak 81 52 30N 46 20 E
Bazarnyy Syzgan 81 53 45N 46 40 E
Bazartobe 83 49 26N 51 45 E
Bazaruto, I. do 129 21 40 S 35 28 E
Bazas 44 44 27N 0 13W
Bazuriye 90 33 15N 35 16 E
Beabula 141 34 26 S 145 9 E
Beach 158 46 57N 104 0W
Beach Haven 162 39 34N 74 14W
Beachley 28 51 37N 2 39W
Beachport 140 37 29 S 140 0 E
Beachwood 162 39 55N 74 8W
Beachy Head 29 50 44N 0 16 E
Beacon, Austral. 137 30 26 S 117 52 E
Beacon, U.S.A. 162 41 32N 73 58W
Beaconia 153 50 25N 96 31W
Beaconsfield, Austral. 133 41 11 S 146 48 E
Beaconsfield, U.K. 29 51 36N 0 39W
Beadnell 35 55 33N 1 38W
Beagle Bay 136 16 32 S 122 54 E
Beagle, Canal 176 55 0 S 68 30W
Bealanana 129 14 33N 48 44 E
Bealey 143 43 2 S 171 36 E
Beaminster 28 50 48N 2 44W
Bear I. 39 51 38N 9 50W
Bear I. (Nor.) 12 74 30N 19 0 E
Bear L., B.C., Can. 152 56 10N 126 52W
Bear L., Man., Can. 153 55 8N 96 0W
Bear L., U.S.A. 160 42 0N 111 20W
Bearcreek 160 45 11N 109 6W
Beardmore 150 49 36N 87 57W
Beardmore Glacier 13 84 30 S 170 0 E
Beardstown 158 40 0N 90 25W
Bearn 44 43 28N 0 36W
Bearpaw Mt. 160 48 15N 109 55W
Bearsden 34 55 55N 4 21W
Bearskin Lake 150 53 58N 91 2W
Bearsted 29 51 15N 0 35 E
Beas de Segura 59 38 15N 2 53W
Beasain 58 43 3N 2 11W
Beata, C. 167 17 40N 71 30W
Beata, I. 167 17 34N 71 31W
Beatrice, Rhod. 127 18 15 S 30 55 E
Beatrice, U.S.A. 158 40 20N 96 40W
Beatrice, C. 138 14 20 S 136 55 E
Beatrice, oilfield 19 58 7N 3 6W
Beattock 35 55 19N 3 27W
Beatton, R. 152 56 15N 120 45W
Beatton River 152 57 26N 121 20W
Beatty 163 36 58N 116 46W
Beaucaire 45 43 48N 4 39 E
Beauce, Plaines de 43 48 10N 2 0 E
Beauceville 151 46 13N 70 46W
Beaudesert 139 27 59 S 153 0 E
Beaufort, Austral. 140 37 25 S 143 25 E
Beaufort, Malay. 102 5 30N 115 40 E
Beaufort, N.C., U.S.A. 157 34 45N 76 40W
Beaufort, S.C., U.S.A. 157 32 25N 80 40W
Beaufort Sea 12 72 0N 140 0W
Beaufort-West 128 32 18 S 22 36 E
Beaugency 43 47 47N 1 38 E
Beauharnois 150 45 20N 73 52W
Beaujeu 45 46 10N 4 35 E
Beaujolais 45 46 0N 4 25 E
Beaulieu, Loiret, France 44 47 31N 2 49 E
Beaulieu, Vendée, France 45 46 41N 1 37W
Beaulieu, U.K. 28 50 49N 1 27W
Beaulieu, R. 152 62 3N 113 11W
Beauly 37 57 29N 4 27W
Beauly Firth 37 57 30N 4 20W
Beauly, R. 37 57 26N 4 28W
Beaumaris 31 53 16N 4 7W
Beaumetz-les-Loges 43 50 15N 2 40 E
Beaumont, Belg. 47 50 15N 4 14 E
Beaumont, France 44 44 45N 0 46 E
Beaumont, N.Z. 143 45 50 S 169 33 E
Beaumont, Calif., U.S.A. 163 33 56N 116 58W
Beaumont, Tex., U.S.A. 159 30 5N 94 8W
Beaumont-le-Roger 42 49 4N 0 47 E
Beaumont-sur-Oise 43 49 9N 2 17 E
Beaune 43 47 2N 4 50 E
Beaune-la-Rolande 43 48 4N 2 25 E
Beauraing 47 50 7N 4 57 E
Beausejour 153 50 5N 96 35 E
Beausset, Le 45 43 10N 5 46 E
Beauvais 43 49 25N 2 8 E
Beauval 153 55 9N 107 37W
Beauvoir, Deux Sèvres, France 44 46 12N 0 30W
Beauvoir, Vendée, France 42 46 55N 2 1W
Beaver, Alaska, U.S.A. 147 66 20N 147 30W
Beaver, Okla., U.S.A. 159 36 52N 100 31W
Beaver, Utah, U.S.A. 161 38 20N 112 45W
Beaver City 158 40 13N 99 50W
Beaver Dam 158 43 28N 88 50W
Beaver Falls 156 40 44N 80 20W
Beaver Hill L. 153 54 16N 94 59W
Beaver I. 150 45 40N 85 31W
Beaver, R. 152 59 52N 124 20W
Beaver, R 150 55 55N 87 48W
Beaver, R. 153 55 26N 107 45W
Beaverhill L., Man., Can. 153 54 5N 94 50W
Beaverhill L., N.W.T., Can. 153 63 2N 111 22W
Beaverhill L., Alb., 152 53 27N 112 32W
Beaverlodge 152 55 11N 119 29W
Beavermouth 152 51 32N 117 23W
Beaverstone, R. 150 54 59N 89 25W
Beawar 94 26 3N 74 18 E
Bebedouro 173 21 0 S 48 25W
Bebington 32 53 23N 3 1W
Beboa 129 17 22 S 44 33 E
Bebra 48 50 59N 9 48 E
Beccles 29 52 27N 1 33 E
Bečej 66 45 36N 20 3 E
Beceni 70 45 23N 26 48 E
Becerreá 56 42 51N 7 10W
Béchar 118 31 38N 2 18 E
Becharof L. 147 58 0N 156 30W
Bechuanaland = Botswana 125 23 0 S 24 0 E
Bechyně 52 49 17N 14 29 E
Beckermet 32 54 26N 3 31W
Beckfoot 32 54 50N 3 25W
Beckingham 33 53 24N 0 49W
Beckley 156 37 50N 81 8W
Bécon 42 47 30N 0 50W
Bečva, R. 53 49 31N 17 40 E
Bedale 33 54 18N 1 35W
Bédar 59 37 11N 1 59W
Bédarieux 44 43 37N 3 10 E
Bédarrides 45 44 2N 4 54 E
Beddone, Mt. 138 25 50 S 134 20 E
Bedele 123 8 31N 35 44 E
Bedel,Pereval 85 41 26N 78 26 E
Bederkesa 48 53 37N 8 50 E
Bedford, Can. 150 45 7N 72 59W
Bedford, S. Afr. 128 32 40 S 26 10 E
Bedford, U.K. 29 52 8N 0 29W
Bedford, Ind., U.S.A. 156 38 50N 86 30W
Bedford, Iowa, U.S.A. 158 40 40N 94 41W
Bedford, Ohio, U.S.A. 156 41 23N 81 32W
Bedford, Va., U.S.A. 156 37 25N 79 30W
Bedford □ 29 52 4N 0 28W
Bedford, C. 138 15 14 S 145 21 E
Bedford Downs 136 17 19 S 127 20 E
Bedford Level 29 52 25N 0 5 E
Bedków 54 51 36N 19 44 E
Bedlington 35 55 8N 1 35W
Bednesti 152 53 50N 123 10W
Bednja, R. 63 46 12N 16 25 E
Bednodemyanovsk 81 53 55N 43 15 E
Bedourie 138 24 30 S 139 30 E
Bedretto 51 46 31N 8 31 E
Bedum 47 53 18N 6 36 E
Bedwas 31 51 36N 3 10W
Bedworth 28 52 28N 1 29W
Bedzin 54 50 19N 19 7 E
Bee L. 36 57 22N 7 21W
Beebyn 137 27 0 S 117 48 E
Beech Grove 156 39 40N 86 2W
Beechey Point 147 70 27N 149 18W
Beechworth 141 36 22 S 146 43 E
Beechy 153 50 53N 107 24W
Beeford 33 53 58N 0 18W
Beek, Gelderland, Neth. 46 51 55N 6 11 E
Beek, Limburg, Neth. 47 50 57N 5 48 E
Beek, Noord Brabant, Neth. 47 51 32N 5 38 E
Beekbergen 46 52 10N 5 58 E
Beelitz 48 52 14N 12 58 E
Beemem 47 51 9N 3 21 E
Beenleigh 139 27 43 S 153 10 E
Beer 30 50 41N 3 5W
Be'er Sheva' 90 31 15N 34 48 E
Be'er Sheva', N. 90 31 12N 34 40 E
Be'er Toviyyao 90 31 44N 34 42 E
Be'eri 90 31 25N 34 30 E
Be'erotayim 90 32 19N 34 59 E
Beersheba = Be'er Sheva' 90 31 15N 34 48 E
Beerta 46 53 11N 7 6 E
Beerze, R. 46 51 39N 5 20 E
Beesd 46 51 53N 5 11 E
Beesel 47 51 16N 6 2 E
Beeskow 48 52 9N 14 14 E
Beeston 33 52 55N 1 11W
Beetaloo 138 17 15 S 133 50 E
Beetsterzwaag 46 53 4N 6 5 E
Beetzendorf 48 52 42N 11 6 E
Beeville 159 28 27N 97 44W
Befale 124 0 25N 20 45 E
Befandriana 125 21 55 S 44 0 E
Befotaka, Diégo-Suarez, Madag. 129 14 30 S 48 0 E
Befotaka, Fianarantsoa, Madag. 129 23 49 S 47 0 E
Beg, L. 38 54 48N 6 28W
Bega 141 36 41 S 149 51 E
Bega, Canalul 66 45 37N 20 46 E
Begelly 31 51 45N 4 44W
Begemdir & Simen □ 123 13 55N 37 30 E
Begna 71 60 41N 9 42 E
Begonte 56 43 10N 7 40W
Begu-Sarai 95 25 24N 86 9 E
Beguildy 31 52 25N 3 11W
Béhagle = Lai 117 9 25N 16 30 E
Behara 125 24 55 S 46 20 E
Behbehan 92 30 30N 50 15 E
Behror 94 27 51N 76 20 E
Behshahr 93 36 45N 53 35 E
Beida (Al Bayda) 117 32 30N 21 40 E
Beighton 33 53 21N 1 21W
Beilen 46 52 52N 6 27 E
Beilngries 49 49 1N 11 27 E
Beilpajah 140 32 54 S 143 52 E
Beilul 123 13 2N 42 20 E
Beinn a' Ghlo, Mt. 37 56 51N 3 42W
Beinn Mhor, Mt. 36 57 59N 6 39W
Beira 127 19 50 S 34 52 E
Beira-Alta 55 40 35N 7 35W
Beira-Baixa 55 40 2N 7 30W
Beira-Litoral 55 40 5N 8 30W
Beirut = Bayrūt 92 33 53N 35 31 E
Beit Bridge 127 14 58 S 30 15 E
Beit Hanum 90 31 32N 34 32 E
Beit Lahiya 90 31 32N 34 30 E
Beit 'Ur et Tahta 90 31 54N 35 5 E
Beit Yosef 90 32 34N 35 33 E
Beitbridge 127 22 12 S 30 0 E
Beith 34 55 45N 4 38W
Beituniya 90 31 54N 35 10 E
Beiuş 70 46 40N 22 21 E
Beja 57 38 2N 7 53W
Béja 119 36 43N 9 12 E
Beja □ 57 37 55N 7 55W
Béjaïa 119 36 42N 5 2 E
Béjar 56 40 23N 5 46W
Bejestan 93 34 30N 58 5 E
Bekabad 85 40 13N 69 14 E
Bekasi 103 6 20 S 107 0 E
Békés 53 46 47N 21 9 E
Békés □ 53 46 45N 21 0 E
Békéscsaba 53 46 40N 21 10 E
Bekily 129 24 13 S 45 19 E
Bekkevoort 47 50 57N 4 58 E
Bekkjarvik 71 60 1N 5 13 E

Bekoji Berghem


| Name | Page | Lat. | Long. |
|---|---|---|---|
| Bekoji | 123 | 7 40N | 38 20E |
| Bekok | 101 | 2 20N | 103 7E |
| Bekopaka | 129 | 19 9S | 44 45E |
| Bekwai | 121 | 6 30N | 1 34W |
| Bel Air | 162 | 39 32N | 76 21W |
| Bela, India | 95 | 25 50N | 82 0E |
| Bela, Pak. | 94 | 26 12N | 66 20E |
| Bela Crkva | 66 | 44 55N | 21 27E |
| Bela Palanka | 66 | 43 13N | 22 17E |
| Bela Vista, Brazil | 173 | 22 12S | 56 20W |
| Bela Vista, Mozam. | 129 | 26 10S | 32 44E |
| Bélâbre | 44 | 46 34N | 1 8E |
| Belaia, Mt. | 123 | 11 25N | 36 8E |
| Belalcázar | 57 | 38 35N | 5 10W |
| Belanovica | 66 | 44 15N | 20 23E |
| Belavenona | 129 | 24 50S | 47 4E |
| Belawan | 102 | 3 33N | 98 32E |
| Belaya Glina | 83 | 46 5N | 40 48E |
| Belaya Kalitva | 83 | 48 13N | 40 50E |
| Belaya Kholunitsa | 84 | 58 41N | 50 13E |
| Belaya, R. | 84 | 55 54N | 53 33E |
| Belaya Tserkov | 80 | 49 45N | 30 10E |
| Belbroughton | 28 | 52 23N | 2 5W |
| Belceşti | 70 | 47 19N | 27 7E |
| Bełchatów | 54 | 51 21N | 19 22E |
| Belcher, C. | 12 | 75 0N | 160 0W |
| Belcher Is. | 150 | 56 15N | 78 45W |
| Belchite | 58 | 41 18N | 0 43W |
| Belclare | 38 | 53 29N | 8 55W |
| Belcoo | 38 | 54 18N | 7 52W |
| Belderg | 38 | 54 18N | 9 33W |
| Beldringe | 73 | 55 28N | 10 21E |
| Belebey | 84 | 54 7N | 54 7E |
| Belém de São Francisco | 170 | 8 46S | 38 58W |
| Belém (Pará) | 170 | 1 20S | 48 30W |
| Belén, Argent. | 172 | 27 40S | 67 5W |
| Belén, Colomb. | 174 | 1 26N | 75 56W |
| Belén, Parag. | 172 | 23 30S | 57 6W |
| Belen | 161 | 34 40N | 106 50W |
| Belene | 67 | 43 39N | 25 10E |
| Bélesta | 44 | 42 55N | 1 56E |
| Belet Uen | 91 | 4 30N | 45 5E |
| Belev | 81 | 53 50N | 36 5E |
| Belfast, N.Z. | 143 | 43 27S | 172 39E |
| Belfast, S. Afr. | 129 | 25 42S | 30 2E |
| Belfast, U.K. | 38 | 54 35N | 5 56W |
| Belfast, U.S.A. | 151 | 44 30N | 69 0W |
| Belfast □ | 38 | 54 35N | 5 56W |
| Belfast, L. | 38 | 54 40N | 5 50W |
| Belfeld | 47 | 51 18N | 6 6E |
| Belfeoram | 151 | 47 32N | 55 30W |
| Belfield | 158 | 46 54N | 103 11W |
| Belford | 35 | 55 36N | 1 50W |
| Belfort | 43 | 47 38N | 6 50E |
| Belfort □ | 43 | 47 38N | 6 52E |
| Belfry | 160 | 45 10N | 109 2W |
| Belgaum | 97 | 15 55N | 74 35E |
| Belgioioso | 62 | 45 9N | 9 21E |
| Belgium ■ | 47 | 51 30N | 5 0E |
| Belgooly | 138 | 51 44N | 8 30W |
| Belgorod | 82 | 50 35N | 36 35E |
| Belgorod Dnestrovskiy | 82 | 46 11N | 30 23E |
| Belgrade | 160 | 45 50N | 111 10W |
| Belgrade = Beograd | 66 | 44 50N | 20 37E |
| Belgrove | 143 | 41 27S | 172 59E |
| Belhaven | 157 | 35 34N | 76 35W |
| Beli | 121 | 7 52N | 10 58E |
| Beli Drim, R. | 66 | 42 25N | 20 34E |
| Beli Manastir | 66 | 45 45N | 18 36E |
| Beli Timok, R. | 66 | 43 39N | 22 14E |
| Belice, R. | 64 | 37 44N | 12 58E |
| Belinga | 124 | 1 10N | 13 2E |
| Belingwe | 127 | 20 29S | 29 57E |
| Belingwe, N., mt. | 127 | 20 37S | 29 55E |
| Belinsky (Chembar) | 81 | 53 0N | 43 25E |
| Belinţ | 66 | 45 48N | 21 54E |
| Belinyu | 102 | 1 35S | 105 50E |
| Beliton, Is. | 102 | 3 10S | 107 50E |
| Belitung, I. | 102 | 3 10S | 107 50E |
| Beliu | 70 | 46 30N | 22 0E |
| Belize ■ | 165 | 17 0N | 88 30W |
| Belize City | 165 | 17 25N | 88 0W |
| Beljanica | 66 | 44 08N | 21 43E |
| Bell | 151 | 53 50N | 53 10E |
| Bell Bay | 138 | 41 6S | 146 53E |
| Bell I. | 151 | 50 46N | 55 35W |
| Bell Irving, R. | 152 | 56 12N | 129 5W |
| Bell Peninsula | 149 | 63 50N | 82 0W |
| Bell, R. | 150 | 49 48N | 77 38W |
| Bell Rock = Inchcape Rock | 35 | 56 26N | 2 24W |
| Bell Ville | 172 | 32 40S | 62 40W |
| Bella Bella | 152 | 52 10N | 128 10W |
| Bella Coola | 152 | 52 25N | 126 40W |
| Bella Unión | 172 | 30 15S | 57 40W |
| Bella Vista, Corrientes, Argent. | 172 | 28 33S | 59 0W |
| Bella Vista, Tucuman, Argent. | 172 | 27 10S | 65 25W |
| Bella Yella | 120 | 7 24N | 10 9W |
| Bellacorick | 38 | 54 8N | 9 35W |
| Bellaghy | 38 | 54 50N | 6 31W |
| Bellágio | 62 | 45 59N | 9 15E |
| Bellaire | 156 | 40 1N | 80 46W |
| Bellananagh | 38 | 53 55N | 7 25W |
| Bellarena | 38 | 55 7N | 6 57W |
| Bellarwi | 141 | 34 6S | 147 13E |
| Bellary | 97 | 15 10N | 76 56E |
| Bellata | 139 | 29 53S | 149 46E |
| Bellavary | 38 | 53 54N | 9 9W |
| Belle Fourche | 158 | 44 43N | 103 52W |
| Belle Fourche, R. | 158 | 44 25N | 105 0W |
| Belle Glade | 157 | 26 43N | 80 38W |
| Belle Ile | 42 | 47 20N | 3 10W |
| Belle Isle | 151 | 51 57N | 55 25W |
| Belle-Isle-en-Terre | 42 | 48 33N | 3 23W |
| Belle Isle, Str. of | 151 | 51 30N | 56 30W |
| Belle, La | 157 | 26 45N | 81 22W |
| Belle Plaine, Iowa, U.S.A. | 158 | 41 51N | 92 18W |
| Belle Plaine, Minn., U.S.A. | 158 | 44 35N | 93 48W |
| Belledonne | 45 | 45 11N | 6 0E |
| Belledune | 151 | 47 55N | 65 50W |
| Belleek | 38 | 54 30N | 8 6W |
| Bellefontaine | 156 | 40 20N | 83 45W |
| Bellefonte | 156 | 40 56N | 77 45W |
| Bellegarde, Ain, France | 45 | 46 4N | 5 49E |
| Bellegarde, Creuse, France | 43 | 45 59N | 2 19E |
| Bellegarde, Loiret, France | 43 | 48 0N | 2 26E |
| Belleoram | 151 | 47 31N | 55 25W |
| Belleville, Can. | 150 | 44 10N | 77 23W |
| Belleville, Rhône, France | 45 | 46 7N | 4 45E |
| Belleville, Vendée, France | 42 | 46 48N | 1 28W |
| Belleville, Ill., U.S.A. | 158 | 38 30N | 90 0W |
| Belleville, Kans., U.S.A. | 158 | 39 51N | 97 38W |
| Belleville, N.Y., U.S.A. | 162 | 43 46N | 76 10W |
| Bellevue, Can. | 152 | 49 35N | 114 22W |
| Bellevue, U.S.A. | 160 | 43 25N | 144 23W |
| Belley | 45 | 45 46N | 5 41E |
| Bellin (Payne Bay) | 149 | 60 0N | 70 0W |
| Bellingen | 141 | 30 25S | 152 50E |
| Bellingham, U.K. | 35 | 55 09N | 2 16W |
| Bellingham, U.S.A. | 160 | 48 45N | 122 27W |
| Bellingshausen Sea | 13 | 66 0S | 80 0W |
| Bellinzona | 51 | 46 11N | 9 1E |
| Bello | 174 | 6 20N | 75 33W |
| Bellona Reefs | 133 | 21 26S | 159 0E |
| Bellows Falls | 162 | 43 10N | 72 30W |
| Bellpat | 94 | 29 0N | 68 5E |
| Bellpuig | 58 | 41 37N | 1 1E |
| Belluno | 63 | 46 8N | 12 6E |
| Bellville | 159 | 29 58N | 96 18W |
| Belmar | 162 | 40 10N | 74 2W |
| Bélmez | 57 | 38 17N | 5 17W |
| Belmont, Austral. | 141 | 33 4S | 151 42E |
| Belmont, U.S.A. | 162 | 43 27N | 71 29W |
| Belmonte, Brazil | 171 | 16 0S | 39 0W |
| Belmonte, Port. | 56 | 40 21N | 7 20W |
| Belmonte, Spain | 58 | 39 34N | 2 43W |
| Belmopan | 165 | 17 18N | 88 30W |
| Belmore | 140 | 33 34S | 141 13E |
| Belmullet | 38 | 54 13N | 9 58W |
| Belo Horizonte | 171 | 19 55S | 43 56W |
| Belo Jardim | 170 | 8 20S | 36 26W |
| Belo-sur-Mer | 129 | 20 42S | 44 33E |
| Belo-sur-Tsiribihana | 129 | 19 40S | 43 30E |
| Belogorsk, R.S.F.S.R., U.S.S.R. | 77 | 51 0N | 128 20E |
| Belogorsk, Ukraine, U.S.S.R. | 82 | 45 3N | 34 35E |
| Belogradchik | 66 | 43 37N | 22 40E |
| Belogradets | 67 | 43 22N | 27 18E |
| Beloha | 129 | 25 10S | 45 3E |
| Beloit, Kans., U.S.A. | 158 | 39 32N | 98 9W |
| Beloit, Wis., U.S.A. | 158 | 42 35N | 89 0W |
| Belokholunitskiy | 81 | 58 55N | 50 43E |
| Belomorsk | 78 | 64 35N | 34 30E |
| Belonia | 98 | 23 15N | 91 30E |
| Belopolye | 80 | 51 14N | 34 20E |
| Beloretsk | 84 | 53 58N | 58 24E |
| Belovo | 76 | 54 30N | 86 0E |
| Beloyarskiy | 84 | 56 45N | 61 24E |
| Beloye More | 78 | 66 0N | 38 0E |
| Beloye, Oz. | 78 | 60 10N | 37 35E |
| Beloye Ozero | 83 | 45 15N | 46 50E |
| Belozersk | 81 | 60 0N | 37 30E |
| Belpasso | 65 | 37 37N | 15 0E |
| Belper | 33 | 53 2N | 1 29W |
| Belsay | 35 | 55 6N | 1 53W |
| Belsele | 47 | 51 9N | 4 6E |
| Belsito | 64 | 37 50N | 13 47E |
| Beltana | 140 | 30 48S | 138 25E |
| Belterra | 175 | 2 45S | 55 0W |
| Beltinci | 63 | 46 37N | 16 20E |
| Belton, Humberside, U.K. | 33 | 53 33N | 0 49W |
| Belton, Norfolk, U.K. | 29 | 52 35N | 1 39E |
| Belton, S.C., U.S.A. | 157 | 34 31N | 82 39W |
| Belton, Tex., U.S.A. | 159 | 31 4N | 97 30W |
| Beltra, Mayo, Ireland | 38 | 53 57N | 9 24W |
| Beltra, Sligo, Ireland | 38 | 54 12N | 8 36W |
| Beltra L. | 38 | 53 56N | 9 28W |
| Beltsy | 82 | 47 48N | 28 0E |
| Belturbet | 38 | 54 6N | 7 28W |
| Belukha | 76 | 49 50N | 86 50E |
| Beluran | 102 | 5 48N | 117 35E |
| Beluša | 53 | 49 5N | 18 27E |
| Belušić | 66 | 43 50N | 21 10E |
| Belvedere Marittimo | 65 | 39 37N | 15 52E |
| Belvès | 44 | 44 46N | 1 0E |
| Belvidere, Ill., U.S.A. | 158 | 42 15N | 88 55W |
| Belvidere, N.J., U.S.A. | 162 | 40 48N | 75 5W |
| Belville | 38 | 54 40N | 9 22W |
| Belvis de la Jara | 57 | 39 45N | 4 57W |
| Belyando, R. | 138 | 21 38S | 146 50E |
| Belyj Jar | 76 | 58 26N | 84 39E |
| Belyy | 80 | 55 48N | 32 51E |
| Belyy, Ostrov | 76 | 73 30N | 71 0E |
| Belyye Vody | 85 | 42 25N | 69 50E |
| Belz | 80 | 50 23N | 24 1E |
| Belzig | 48 | 52 8N | 12 36E |
| Belzoni | 159 | 33 12N | 90 30W |
| Bemaraha, Plat. du | 129 | 18 40S | 44 45E |
| Bemarivo, Majunga, Madag. | 129 | 17 6S | 44 31E |
| Bemarivo, Tuléar, Madag. | 129 | 21 45S | 44 45E |
| Bemarivo, R. | 129 | 21 45S | 44 45E |
| Bemavo | 129 | 21 33S | 45 25E |
| Bembéréke | 121 | 10 11N | 2 43E |
| Bembesi | 127 | 20 0S | 28 58E |
| Bembesi, R. | 127 | 20 0S | 28 58E |
| Bembézar, R. | 57 | 38 0N | 5 20W |
| Bembridge | 28 | 50 41N | 1 4W |
| Bemidji | 158 | 47 30N | 94 50W |
| Bemmel | 46 | 51 54N | 5 54E |
| Ben Alder | 37 | 55 59N | 4 30W |
| Ben Avon | 37 | 57 6N | 3 28W |
| Ben Bheigeir, Mt. | 34 | 55 43N | 6 6W |
| Ben Bullen | 141 | 33 12S | 150 2E |
| Ben Chonzine | 35 | 56 27N | 4 0W |
| Ben Cruachan, Mt. | 34 | 56 26N | 5 8W |
| Ben Dearg | 37 | 57 47N | 4 58W |
| Ben Dearg, mt. | 37 | 56 54N | 3 49W |
| Ben Dhorain | 37 | 58 7N | 3 50W |
| Ben Dorian | 34 | 56 30N | 4 42W |
| Ben Gardane | 119 | 33 11N | 11 11E |
| Ben Hee | 37 | 58 16N | 4 43W |
| Ben Hope, mt. | 37 | 58 24N | 4 36W |
| Ben Klibreck | 37 | 58 14N | 4 25W |
| Ben Lawers, mt. | 37 | 56 33N | 4 13W |
| Ben Lomond, mt. | 139 | 30 1S | 151 43E |
| Ben Lomond mt. | 138 | 41 38S | 147 42E |
| Ben Lomond, mt. | 34 | 56 12N | 4 39W |
| Ben Loyal | 37 | 58 25N | 4 25W |
| Ben Luc | 101 | 10 39N | 106 29E |
| Ben Lui, mt. | 34 | 56 24N | 4 50W |
| Ben Macdhui | 37 | 57 4N | 3 40W |
| Ben Mhor | 36 | 57 16N | 7 21W |
| Ben More, Mull, U.K. | 34 | 56 26N | 6 2W |
| Ben More, Perth, U.K. | 34 | 56 23N | 4 31W |
| Ben More Assynt | 37 | 58 7N | 4 51W |
| Ben Nevis, mt., N.Z. | 143 | 45 15S | 169 0E |
| Ben Nevis, mt., U.K. | 36 | 56 48N | 5 0W |
| Ben Ohau Ra. | 143 | 44 1S | 170 4E |
| Ben Quang | 100 | 17 3N | 106 55E |
| Ben Stack | 36 | 58 20N | 4 58W |
| Ben Tharsiunn | 37 | 57 47N | 4 20W |
| Ben Venue | 34 | 56 13N | 4 28W |
| Ben Vorlich | 34 | 56 22N | 4 15W |
| Ben Wyvis, mt. | 37 | 57 40N | 4 35W |
| Bena | 121 | 11 20N | 5 50E |
| Bena Dibele | 124 | 4 4S | 22 50E |
| Benagalbón | 57 | 36 45N | 4 15W |
| Benagerie | 140 | 31 25S | 140 22E |
| Benahmed | 118 | 33 4N | 7 9W |
| Benalla | 141 | 36 30S | 146 0E |
| Benambra, Mt. | 141 | 36 31S | 147 34E |
| Benamejí | 57 | 37 16N | 4 33W |
| Benanee | 140 | 34 31S | 142 52E |
| Benares = Varanasi | 95 | 25 22N | 83 8E |
| Benavente, Port. | 57 | 38 59N | 8 49W |
| Benavente, Spain | 56 | 42 2N | 5 43W |
| Benavides, Spain | 56 | 42 30N | 5 54W |
| Benavides, U.S.A. | 159 | 27 35N | 98 28W |
| Benbane Hd. | 38 | 55 15N | 6 30W |
| Benbaun, Mt. | 38 | 53 30N | 9 50W |
| Benbecula, I. | 36 | 57 26N | 7 21W |
| Benbonyathe, Mt. | 140 | 30 25S | 139 11E |
| Benburb | 38 | 54 25N | 6 42W |
| Bencubbin | 137 | 30 48S | 117 52E |
| Bend | 160 | 44 2N | 121 15W |
| Bendel □ | 121 | 6 0N | 6 0E |
| Bender Beila | 91 | 9 30N | 50 48E |
| Bender Cassim | 91 | 11 12N | 49 18E |
| Bendering | 137 | 32 23S | 118 18E |
| Bendery | 82 | 46 50N | 29 50E |
| Bendigo | 140 | 36 40S | 144 15E |
| Beneden Knijpe | 46 | 52 58N | 5 59E |
| Benedick | 162 | 38 31N | 76 41W |
| Beneditinos | 170 | 5 27S | 42 22W |
| Benedito Leite | 170 | 7 13S | 44 34W |
| Benei Beraq | 129 | 32 5N | 34 50E |
| Bénéna | 120 | 13 9N | 4 17W |
| Beneraird, Mt. | 34 | 55 4N | 4 57W |
| Benešov | 52 | 49 46N | 14 41E |
| Bénestroff | 43 | 48 54N | 6 45E |
| Benet | 44 | 46 22N | 0 35W |
| Benevento | 65 | 41 7N | 14 45E |
| Benfeld | 43 | 48 22N | 7 34E |
| Beng Lovea | 100 | 12 36N | 105 34E |
| Benga | 127 | 16 11S | 33 40E |
| Bengal, Bay of | 65 | 15 0N | 00 90E |
| Bengawan Solo | 103 | 7 5S | 112 25E |
| Benghazi = Banghāzī | 119 | 32 11N | 20 3E |
| Bengkalis | 102 | 1 30N | 102 10E |
| Bengkulu | 102 | 3 50S | 102 12E |
| Bengkulu □ | 102 | 3 48S | 102 16E |
| Bengough | 153 | 49 25N | 105 10W |
| Benguela | 125 | 12 37S | 13 25E |
| Benguerir | 118 | 32 16N | 7 56W |
| Benguérua, Î. | 129 | 21 58S | 35 28E |
| Benha | 122 | 30 26N | 31 8E |
| Beni | 126 | 0 30N | 29 27E |
| Beni Abbès | 118 | 30 5N | 2 5W |
| Beni Haoua | 118 | 36 30N | 1 30E |
| Benî Mazâr | 122 | 28 32N | 30 44E |
| Beni Mellal | 118 | 32 21N | 6 21W |
| Beni Ounif | 118 | 32 0N | 1 10W |
| Beni, R. | 174 | 10 30S | 66 0W |
| Beni Saf | 118 | 35 17N | 1 15W |
| Benî Suêf | 122 | 29 5N | 31 6E |
| Beniah L. | 152 | 63 23N | 112 17W |
| Benicarló | 58 | 40 23N | 0 23E |
| Benicia | 163 | 38 3N | 122 9W |
| Benidorm | 59 | 38 33N | 0 9W |
| Benidorm, Islote de | 59 | 38 31N | 0 9W |
| Benin ■ | 121 | 10 0N | 2 0E |
| Benin, Bight of | 121 | 5 0N | 3 0E |
| Benin City | 121 | 6 20N | 5 31E |
| Benington | 33 | 52 59N | 0 5E |
| Benisa | 59 | 38 43N | 0 03E |
| Benjamin Aceval | 172 | 24 58S | 57 34W |
| Benjamin Constant | 174 | 4 40S | 70 15W |
| Benjamin Hill | 164 | 30 10N | 111 10W |
| Benkelman | 158 | 40 7N | 101 32W |
| Benlidi | 138 | 24 35S | 144 50E |
| Benmore Pk. | 143 | 44 25S | 170 8E |
| Bennane Hd. | 34 | 55 9N | 5 2W |
| Bennebroek | 46 | 52 19N | 4 36E |
| Bennekom | 46 | 52 0N | 5 41E |
| Bennett | 147 | 59 56N | 134 53W |
| Bennettsbridge | 39 | 52 36N | 7 12W |
| Bennettsville | 157 | 34 38N | 79 39W |
| Bennington | 162 | 42 52N | 73 12W |
| Benoa | 102 | 8 50S | 115 20E |
| Bénodet | 42 | 47 53N | 4 7W |
| Benoni | 129 | 26 11S | 28 18E |
| Benoud | 118 | 32 20N | 0 16E |
| Benque Viejo | 165 | 17 5N | 89 8W |
| Bensheim | 49 | 49 40N | 8 38E |
| Benson, U.K. | 28 | 51 37N | 1 6W |
| Benson, U.S.A. | 161 | 31 59N | 110 19W |
| Bent | 93 | 26 20N | 59 25E |
| Benteng | 103 | 6 10S | 120 30E |
| Bentinck I. | 138 | 17 3S | 139 35E |
| Bentiu | 123 | 9 10N | 29 55E |
| Bentley, Hants., U.K. | 29 | 51 12N | 0 52W |
| Bentley, S. Yorks, U.K. | 33 | 53 33N | 1 9W |
| Bento Gonçalves | 173 | 29 10S | 51 31W |
| Benton, Ark., U.S.A. | 159 | 34 30N | 92 35W |
| Benton, Calif., U.S.A. | 163 | 37 48N | 118 32W |
| Benton, Ill., U.S.A. | 158 | 38 0N | 88 55W |
| Benton, Pa., U.S.A. | 162 | 41 12N | 76 23W |
| Benton Harbor | 156 | 42 10N | 86 28W |
| Bentong | 101 | 3 31N | 101 55E |
| Bentu Liben | 123 | 8 32N | 38 21E |
| Benue □ | 121 | 7 30N | 7 30E |
| Benue Plateau □ | 121 | 8 0N | 8 30E |
| Benue, R. | 121 | 7 50N | 6 30E |
| Benwee Hd. | 38 | 54 20N | 9 50W |
| Beo | 103 | 4 25N | 126 50E |
| Beograd | 66 | 44 50N | 20 37E |
| Beowawe | 160 | 40 45N | 117 0W |
| Beppu | 110 | 33 15N | 131 30E |
| Beppu-Wan | 110 | 33 18N | 131 34E |
| Ber Dagan | 90 | 32 1N | 34 49E |
| Bera | 98 | 24 5N | 89 37E |
| Beragh | 38 | 54 34N | 7 10W |
| Berakit | 123 | 14 38N | 39 29E |
| Berati | 68 | 40 43N | 19 59E |
| Berber | 122 | 18 0N | 34 0E |
| Berbéra | 117 | 10 30N | 16 35E |
| Berbera | 91 | 10 30N | 45 2E |
| Berbérati | 124 | 4 15N | 15 40E |
| Berberia, Cabo | 59 | 38 39N | 1 24E |
| Berbice, R. | 174 | 5 20N | 58 10W |
| Berceto | 62 | 44 30N | 10 0E |
| Berchtesgaden | 49 | 47 37N | 13 1E |
| Berck-sur-Mer | 43 | 50 25N | 1 36E |
| Berdichev | 82 | 49 57N | 28 30E |
| Berdsk | 76 | 54 47N | 83 2E |
| Berdyansk | 82 | 46 45N | 36 50E |
| Berdyaush | 84 | 55 9N | 59 9E |
| Bere Alston | 30 | 50 29N | 4 11W |
| Bere Regis | 28 | 50 45N | 2 13W |
| Berea | 156 | 37 35N | 84 18W |
| Berebere | 103 | 2 25N | 128 45E |
| Bereda | 91 | 11 45N | 51 0E |
| Bereina | 135 | 8 39S | 146 30E |
| Berekum | 120 | 7 29N | 2 34W |
| Berenice | 122 | 24 2N | 35 25E |
| Berens I. | 153 | 52 18N | 97 18W |
| Berens, R. | 153 | 51 21N | 97 0W |
| Berens River | 153 | 52 25N | 97 0W |
| Berestechko | 80 | 50 22N | 25 5E |
| Bereşti | 70 | 46 6N | 27 50E |
| Berettyo, R. | 53 | 47 32N | 21 47E |
| Berettyóújfalu | 53 | 47 13N | 21 33E |
| Beretău, R. | 70 | 47 30N | 22 7E |
| Berevo | 129 | 19 44S | 44 58E |
| Berevo-sur-Ranobe | 129 | 17 14S | 44 17E |
| Bereza | 80 | 52 31N | 24 51E |
| Berezhany | 80 | 49 26N | 24 58E |
| Berezina, R. | 80 | 54 10N | 28 10E |
| Berezna | 80 | 51 35N | 30 46E |
| Berezniki | 84 | 59 24N | 56 46E |
| Berezovka | 82 | 47 25N | 30 55E |
| Berezovo | 76 | 64 0N | 65 0E |
| Berg | 71 | 59 10N | 11 18E |
| Berga, Spain | 58 | 42 6N | 1 48E |
| Berga, Kalmar, Sweden | 73 | 57 14N | 16 3E |
| Berga, Kronoberg, Sweden | 73 | 56 55N | 14 0E |
| Bergama | 92 | 39 8N | 27 15E |
| Bergambacht | 46 | 51 56N | 4 48E |
| Bérgamo | 62 | 45 42N | 9 40E |
| Bergantiños | 56 | 43 20N | 8 40W |
| Bergedorf | 48 | 53 28N | 10 12E |
| Bergeijk | 47 | 51 19N | 5 21E |
| Bergen, Ger. | 48 | 54 24N | 13 26E |
| Bergen, Norway | 71 | 60 23N | 5 20E |
| Bergen-Binnen | 46 | 52 40N | 4 43E |
| Bergen-op-Zoom | 47 | 51 30N | 4 18E |
| Bergerac | 44 | 44 51N | 0 30E |
| Bergheim | 48 | 50 57N | 6 38E |
| Berghem | 46 | 51 46N | 5 33E |

Bergisch-Gladbach Billesdon


Bergisch-Gladbach 48 50 59N 7 9E
Bergkvara 73 56 23N 16 5E
Bergschenhoek 46 51 59N 4 30E
Bergsjö 72 61 59N 17 3E
Berguent 118 34 1N 2 0W
Bergues 43 50 58N 2 24E
Bergum 46 53 13N 5 59E
Bergvik 72 61 16N 16 50E
Berhala, Selat 102 1 0S 104 15E
Berhampore 95 24 2N 88 27E
Berhampur 96 19 15N 84 54E
Berheci, R. 70 46 7N 27 19E
Berhungra 139 34 46S 147 52E
Bering Sea 130 58 0N 167 0E
Bering Str. 147 66 0N 170 0W
Beringarra 137 26 0S 116 55E
Beringen, Belg. 47 51 3N 5 14E
Beringen, Switz. 51 47 38N 8 34E
Beringovskiy 77 63 3N 179 19E
Berislav 82 46 50N 33 30E
Berisso 172 34 40S 58 0W
Berja 59 36 50N 2 56W
Berkane 118 34 52N 2 20W
Berkel, R. 46 52 8N 6 12E
Berkeley 163 37 52N 122 20W
Berkeley Springs 156 39 38N 78 12W
Berkhamsted 29 51 45N 0 33W
Berkhout 46 52 38N 4 59E
Berkner I. 13 79 30S 50 0W
Berkovitsa 67 43 16N 23 8E
Berkshire 162 42 19N 76 11W
Berkshire □ 28 51 30N 1 20W
Berkshire Downs 28 51 30N 1 30W
Berkyk 71 62 50N 9 59E
Berlaar 47 51 7N 4 39E
Berland, R. 152 54 0N 116 50W
Berlanga 57 38 17N 5 50W
Berlave 47 51 2N 4 0E
Berleburg 48 51 3N 8 22E
Berlenga, I. 75 39 25N 9 30W
Berlick 47 51 22N 6 9E
Berlin, Ger. 48 52 32N 13 24E
Berlin, Md., U.S.A. 162 38 19N 75 12W
Berlin, N.H., U.S.A. 156 44 29N 71 10W
Berlin, N.Y., U.S.A. 162 42 42N 73 23W
Berlin, E. □ 48 52 30N 13 30E
Berlin, W. □ 48 52 30N 13 20E
Bermeja, Sierra 57 36 45N 5 11W
Bermejo, R., Formosa, Argent. 172 26 30S 58 50W
Bermejo, R., San Juan, Argent. 172 30 0S 68 0W
Bermeo 58 43 25N 2 47W
Bermillo de Sayago 56 41 22N 6 8W
Bermuda, I. 10 32 45N 65 0W
Bern (Berne) 50 46 57N 7 28E
Bern (Berne) □ 50 46 45N 7 40E
Bernalda 65 40 24N 16 44E
Bernalillo 161 35 17N 106 37W
Bernam, R. 101 3 45N 101 5E
Bernardo de Irigoyen 173 26 15S 53 40W
Bernardsville 162 40 43N 74 34W
Bernasconi 172 37 55S 63 44W
Bernau 49 47 53N 12 20E
Bernay 42 49 5N 0 35E
Berndorf 52 47 59N 16 1E
Berne = Bern 50 46 57N 7 28E
Berner Alpen 50 46 27N 7 35E
Berneray, I. 36 56 47N 7 38W
Bernese Oberland = Oberland • 50 46 27N 7 35E
Bernier I. 137 24 50S 113 12E
Bernina Pass 51 46 22N 9 54E
Bernina, Piz 51 46 20N 9 54E
Bernissart 47 50 28N 3 39E
Beroroha 125 21 40S 45 10E
Béroubouey 121 10 34N 2 46E
Beroun 52 49 57N 14 5E
Berounka, R. 52 50 0N 13 47E
Berovo 66 41 42N 22 51E
Berrahal 119 36 54N 7 33E
Berre 45 43 28N 5 11E
Berre, Étang de 45 43 27N 5 5E
Berrechid 118 33 18N 7 36W
Berri 140 34 14S 140 35E
Berriedale 37 58 12N 3 30W
Berriew 31 52 36N 3 12W
Berrigan 141 35 38S 145 49E
Berrouaghia 118 36 10N 2 53E
Berrwillock 140 35 36S 142 59E
Berry, Austral. 141 34 46S 150 43E
Berry, France 43 47 0N 2 0E
Berry Hd. 30 50 24N 3 29W
Berry Is. 166 25 40N 77 50W
Berryville 159 36 23N 93 35W
Bersenbrück 48 52 33N 7 56E
Berst Ness 37 59 16N 3 0W
Berthaund 158 40 21N 105 5W
Berthier Is. 136 14 29S 124 59E
Berthold 158 48 19N 101 45W
Bertincourt 43 50 5N 2 58E
Bertoua 124 4 30N 13 45E
Bertraghboy, B. 38 53 22N 9 54W
Bertrand 158 40 35N 99 38W
Bertrange 47 49 37N 6 3E
Bertrix 47 49 51N 5 15E
Beruas 101 4 30N 100 47E
Berufjörður 74 64 48N 14 29W
Berur Hayil 90 31 34N 34 38E
Berwick 162 41 4N 76 17W
Berwick (□) 26 55 46N 2 30W
Berwick-upon-Tweed 35 55 47N 2 0W
Berwyn Mts. 31 52 54N 3 26W
Beryl N., oilfield 19 59 37N 1 30E
Beryl, oilfield 19 59 28N 1 30E
Beryl W., oilfield 19 59 32N 1 20E
Berzasca 66 44 39N 21 58E
Berzence 53 46 12N 17 11E
Besal 95 35 4N 73 56E
Besalampy 129 16 43S 44 29E
Besançon 43 47 9N 6 0E
Besar 102 2 40S 116 0E
Beserah 101 3 50N 103 21E
Beshenkovichi 80 55 2N 29 29E
Beška 66 45 8N 20 6E
Beskids, Mts. 53 49 35N 18 40E
Beslan 83 43 22N 44 28E
Besna Kobila 66 42 31N 22 10E
Besnard L. 153 55 25N 106 0W
Beşparmak Daği 69 37 32N 27 30E
Bessarabiya 70 46 20N 29 0E
Bessarabka 82 46 21N 28 51E
Bessbrook 38 54 12N 6 25W
Bessèges 45 44 18N 4 8E
Bessemer 158 46 27N 90 0W
Bessin 42 49 21N 1 0W
Bessines-sur-Gartempe 42 46 6N 1 22E
Best 47 51 31N 5 23E
Bet Alfa 90 32 31N 35 25E
Bet Guvrin 90 31 37N 34 54E
Bet Hashitta 90 32 31N 35 27E
Bet Ha'tmeq 90 32 58N 35 8E
Bet Qeshet 90 32 41N 35 21E
Bet She'an 90 32 30N 35 30E
Bet Tadjine, Djebel 118 29 0N 3 30W
Bet Yosef 90 32 34N 35 33E
Betafo 129 19 50S 46 51E
Betanzos 56 43 15N 8 12W
Bétaré-Oya 124 5 40N 14 5E
Betekom 47 50 59N 4 47E
Bétera 58 39 35N 0 28W
Bethal 129 26 27S 29 28E
Bethanien 125 26 31S 17 8E
Bethany, S. Afr. 128 29 34S 25 59E
Bethany, U.S.A. 158 40 18N 94 0W
Bethany = Eizarilya 90 31 47N 35 15E
Bethel, U.S.A. 147 60 50N 161 50W
Bethel, Conn., U.S.A. 162 41 22N 73 25W
Bethesda, U.K. 31 53 11N 4 3W
Bethesda, U.S.A. 162 38 59N 77 6W
Bethlehem, S. Afr. 129 28 14S 28 18E
Bethlehem, U.S.A. 162 40 39N 75 24W
Bethlehem = Bayt Lahm 90 31 43N 35 12E
Bethulie 128 30 30S 25 59E
Béthune 43 50 30N 2 38E
Béthune, R. 42 49 56N 1 5E
Bethungra 141 34 45S 147 51E
Betijoque 174 9 23N 70 44W
Betim 171 19 58S 44 13W
Betioky 129 23 48S 44 20E
Beton Bazoches 43 48 42N 3 15E
Betong 101 5 45N 101 5E
Betoota 138 25 40S 140 42E
Betroka 129 23 16S 46 0E
Betsiamites 151 48 56N 68 40W
Betsiamites, R. 151 48 56N 68 40W
Betsiboka, R. 129 17 0S 47 0E
Betsjoeanaland 128 26 30S 22 30E
Bettembourg 47 49 31N 6 6E
Betterton 162 39 52N 76 4W
Betteshanger 29 51 14N 1 20E
Bettiah 95 26 48N 84 33E
Bettles 147 66 54N 150 50W
Bèttola 62 44 46N 9 35E
Bettws Bledrws 31 52 9N 4 2W
Bettyhill 37 58 31N 4 12W
Betul 96 21 48N 77 59E
Betung 102 2 0S 103 10E
Betws-y-Coed 31 53 4N 3 49W
Beuca 70 44 14N 24 56E
Beuil 45 44 6N 7 0E
Beulah, Can. 153 50 16N 101 02W
Beulah, U.S.A. 158 47 18N 101 47W
Beuvronne, La 46 48 59N 2 41E
Bevensen 48 53 5N 10 34E
Beveren 47 51 12N 4 16E
Beverley, Austral. 137 32 9S 116 56E
Beverley, U.K. 33 53 52N 0 26W
Beverlo 47 51 7N 5 13E
Beverly, Can. 152 53 36N 113 21W
Beverly, Mass., U.S.A. 162 42 32N 70 50W
Beverly, Wash., U.S.A. 160 46 55N 119 59W
Beverly Hills 163 34 4N 118 29W
Beverwijk 46 52 28N 4 38E
Bewdley 28 52 23N 2 19W
Bex 50 46 15N 7 0E
Bexhill 29 50 51N 0 29E
Bexley 29 51 26N 0 10E
Beyin 120 5 1N 2 41W
Beykoz 67 41 8N 29 7E
Beyla 120 8 30N 8 38W
Beynat 44 45 8N 1 44E
Beyneu 76 45 10N 55 3E
Beypazai 92 40 10N 31 48E
Beyşehir Gölü 92 37 40N 31 45E
Bezdan 66 45 28N 18 57E
Bezerros 171 8 14S 35 45W
Bezet 90 33 4N 35 8E
Bezhitsa 80 53 19N 34 17E
Béziers 44 43 20N 3 12E
Bezwada = Vijayawada 97 16 31N 80 39E
Bhachau 93 23 20N 70 16E
Bhadarwah 95 32 58N 75 46E
Bhadra, R. 97 13 0N 76 0E
Bhadrakh 96 21 10N 86 30E
Bhadravati 97 13 49N 76 15E
Bhagalpur 95 25 10N 87 0E
Bhairab 98 22 51N 89 34E
Bhairab Bazar 98 24 4N 90 58E
Bhaisa 96 19 10N 77 58E
Bhakkar 94 31 40N 71 5E
Bhakra Dam 95 31 30N 76 45E
Bhamo 98 24 15N 97 15E
Bhamragarh 96 19 30N 80 40E
Bhandara 96 21 5N 79 42E
Bhanrer Ra. 94 23 40N 79 45E
Bharat = India 93 24 0N 78 0E
Bharatpur 94 27 15N 77 30E
Bharuch 96 21 47N 73 0E
Bhatghar L. 96 18 10N 73 48E
Bhatiapara Ghat 98 23 13N 89 42E
Bhatkal 97 13 58N 74 35E
Bhatpara 95 22 50N 88 25E
Bhattiprolu 97 16 7N 80 45E
Bhaun 94 32 55N 72 40E
Bhaunagar = Bhavnagar 94 21 45N 72 10E
Bhavani 97 11 27N 77 43E
Bhavani, R. 97 11 30N 77 15E
Bhavnagar 94 21 45N 72 10E
Bhawanipatna 96 19 55N 83 30E
Bhera 94 32 29N 72 57E
Bhilsa = Vidisha 94 23 28N 77 53E
Bhilwara 94 25 25N 74 38E
Bhima, R. 96 17 20N 76 30E
Bhimber 95 32 59N 74 3E
Bhimvaram 96 16 30N 81 30E
Bhind 95 26 30N 78 46E
Bhir 96 19 4N 75 58E
Bhiwandi 96 19 15N 73 0E
Bhiwani 94 28 50N 76 9E
Bhola 98 22 45N 90 35E
Bhongir 96 17 30N 78 56E
Bhopal 94 23 20N 77 53E
Bhor 96 18 12N 73 53E
Bhubaneswar 96 20 15N 85 50E
Bhuj 94 23 15N 69 49E
Bhumibol Dam 100 17 15N 98 58E
Bhusaval 96 21 15N 69 49E
Bhutan ■ 98 27 25N 89 50E
Biafra, B. of = Bonny, Bight of 121 3 30N 9 20E
Biak 103 1 0S 136 0E
Biała 54 50 24N 17 40E
Biała Piska 54 53 37N 22 5E
Biała Podlaska 54 52 4N 23 6E
Biała Podlaska □ 54 52 0N 23 0E
Biała, R. 54 49 46N 20 53E
Białogard 54 54 2N 15 58E
Biały Bór 54 53 53N 16 51E
Białystok 54 53 10N 23 10E
Białystok □ 54 53 9N 23 10E
Biancavilla 65 37 39N 14 50E
Biano Plateau = Manika Plateau 127 9 55S 26 24E
Biaro 103 2 5N 125 26E
Biarritz 44 43 29N 1 33W
Biasca 51 46 22N 8 58E
Biba 122 28 55N 31 0E
Bibaī 112 43 19N 141 52E
Bibby I. 153 61 55N 93 0W
Biberach 49 48 5N 9 49E
Biberist 50 47 11N 7 34E
Bibey, R. 56 42 24N 7 13W
Bibiani 120 6 30N 2 8W
Bibile 97 7 10N 81 25E
Biboohra 138 16 56S 145 25E
Bibungwa 126 2 40S 28 15E
Bibury 28 51 46N 1 50W
Bic 151 48 20N 68 41W
Bicaj 68 42 0N 20 25E
Bicaz 70 46 53N 26 5E
Biccari 65 41 23N 15 12E
Bicester 28 51 53N 1 9W
Biche, La, R. 152 59 57N 123 50W
Bichena 123 10 28N 38 10E
Bickerton I. 138 13 45S 136 10E
Bicknell, Ind., U.S.A. 156 38 50N 87 20W
Bicknell, Utah, U.S.A. 161 38 16N 111 35W
Bicsad 70 47 56N 23 28E
Bicton 28 52 43N 2 47W
Bida 121 9 3N 5 58E
Bidar 96 17 55N 77 35E
Biddeford 151 43 30N 70 28W
Biddenden 29 51 7N 0 40E
Biddu 90 31 50N 35 8E
Biddulph 32 53 8N 2 11W
Biddwara 123 5 11N 38 34E
Biddya 90 32 7N 35 4E
Bideford 30 51 1N 4 13W
Bideford Bay 30 51 5N 4 20W
Bidford on Avon 28 52 9N 1 53W
Bidor 101 4 6N 101 15E
Bidura 140 34 10S 143 21E
Bié 125 12 22S 16 55E
Bié Plateau 125 12 0S 16 0E
Bieber 160 41 4N 121 6W
Biel (Bienne) 50 47 8N 7 14E
Bielawa 54 50 43N 16 37E
Bielė Karpaty 53 49 5N 18 0E
Bielefeld 48 52 2N 8 31E
Bielersee 50 47 6N 7 5E
Biella 62 45 33N 8 3E
Bielsk Podlaski 54 52 47N 23 12E
Bielsko-Biała 54 49 50N 19 8E
Bielsko-Biała □ 54 49 45N 19 15E
Bien Hoa 101 10 57N 106 49E
Bienfait 153 49 10N 102 50W
Bienne = Biel 50 47 8N 7 14E
Bienvenida 57 38 18N 6 12W
Bienville, L. 150 55 5N 72 40W
Biescas 58 42 37N 0 20W
Biesiesfontein 128 30 57S 17 58E
Bietigheim 49 48 57N 9 8E
Bievre 47 49 57N 5 1E
Biferno, R. 65 41 40N 14 38E
Big B. 151 55 43N 60 35W
Big Bear City 163 34 16N 116 51W
Big Bear L. 163 34 15N 116 56W
Big Beaver 153 49 10N 105 10W
Big Beaver House 150 52 59N 89 50W
Big Bell 137 27 21S 117 40E
Big Belt Mts. 160 46 50N 111 30W
Big Bend 129 26 50S 32 2E
Big Bend Nat. Park 159 29 15N 103 15W
Big Black, R. 159 32 35N 90 30W
Big Blue, R. 158 40 20N 96 40W
Big Cr. 152 51 42N 122 41W
Big Creek 163 37 11N 119 14W
Big Cypress Swamp 157 26 12N 81 10W
Big Delta 147 64 15N 145 0W
Big Falls 158 48 11N 93 48W
Big Horn 160 46 11N 107 25W
Big Horn Mts. = Bighorn Mts. 160 44 30N 107 30W
Big Horn R. 160 45 30N 108 10W
Big Lake 159 31 12N 101 25W
Big Moose 162 43 49N 74 58W
Big Muddy, R. 158 48 25N 104 45W
Big Pine 163 37 12N 118 17W
Big Piney 160 42 32N 110 3W
Big Quill L. 153 51 55N 105 22W
Big, R. 151 54 50N 58 55W
Big Rapids 156 43 42N 85 27W
Big River 153 53 50N 107 0W
Big Sable Pt. 156 44 5N 86 30W
Big Salmon 147 61 50N 136 0W
Big Sand L. 153 57 45N 99 45W
Big Sandy 160 48 12N 110 9W
Big Sandy Cr. 158 38 52N 103 11W
Big Sioux, R. 158 44 20N 96 53W
Big Smoky Valley 163 38 30N 117 15W
Big Snowy Mt. 160 46 50N 109 15W
Big Spring 159 32 10N 101 25W
Big Springs 158 41 4N 102 3W
Big Stone City 158 45 20N 96 30W
Big Stone Gap 157 36 52N 82 45W
Big Stone L. 158 44 25N 96 35W
Big Sur 163 36 15N 121 48W
Big Trout L. 150 53 40N 90 0W
Biganos 44 44 39N 0 59W
Bigbury 30 50 17N 3 52W
Bigbury B. 30 50 18N 3 58W
Bigerymunal, Mt. 137 27 25S 120 40E
Bigfork 160 48 3N 114 2W
Biggar 153 52 4N 108 0W
Bigge I. 136 14 35S 125 10E
Biggenden 139 25 31S 152 4E
Biggleswade 29 52 6N 0 16W
Bighorn Mts. 160 44 30N 107 30W
Bignona 120 12 52N 16 23W
Bigorre 44 43 5N 0 2E
Bigstone L. 153 53 42N 95 44W
Bigtimber 160 45 53N 110 0W
Bigwa 126 7 10S 39 10E
Bihaó 63 44 49N 15 57E
Bihar 95 25 5N 85 40E
Bihar □ 95 25 0N 86 0E
Biharamulo 126 2 25S 31 25E
Biharamulo □ 126 2 30S 31 20E
Biharkeresztes 53 47 8N 21 44E
Bihé Plateau 125 12 0S 16 0E
Bihor □ 70 47 0N 22 10E
Bihor, Munţii 70 46 29N 22 47E
Bijagós, Arquipélago dos 120 11 15N 16 10W
Bijaipur 94 26 2N 77 36E
Bijapur, Mad. P., India 96 18 50N 80 50E
Bijapur, Mysore, India 96 16 50N 75 55E
Bijar 92 35 52N 47 35E
Bijeljina 66 44 46N 19 17E
Bijni 98 26 30N 90 40E
Bijnor 94 29 27N 78 11E
Bikaner 94 28 2N 73 18E
Bikapur 95 26 30N 82 7E
Bikin 77 46 50N 134 20E
Bikini, atoll 130 12 0N 167 30E
Bikoro 124 0 48S 18 15E
Bikoué 121 5 55S 11 50E
Bilād Banī Bū 'Ali 93 22 0N 59 20E
Bilara 94 26 14N 73 53E
Bilaspara 98 26 13N 90 14E
Bilaspur, India 99 22 2N 82 15E
Bilaspur, Mad. P., India 95 22 2N 82 15E
Bilaspur, Punjab, India 94 31 19N 76 50E
Bilauk Taungdan 100 13 0N 99 0E
Bilbao 58 43 16N 2 56W
Bilbor 70 47 18N 25 30E
Bildudalur 74 65 41N 23 36W
Bilecik 92 40 5N 30 5E
Bileóa 66 42 53N 18 27E
Bilibino 77 68 3N 166 20E
Bilibiza 127 12 30S 40 20E
Bilin 98 17 14N 97 15E
Bilir 77 65 40N 131 20E
Bilishti 68 40 37N 20 59E
Bill 158 43 18N 105 18W
Billa 121 8 55N 12 15E
Billabalong 137 27 25S 115 49E
Billericay 29 51 38N 0 25E
Billesdon 29 52 38N 0 56W

Billiluna Blenheim


Billiluna 136 19 37 S 127 41 E
Billimari 71 33 41 S 148 37 E
Billingham 33 54 36 N 1 18 W
Billinghay 33 53 5 N 0 17 W
Billings 160 45 43 N 108 29 W
Billingsfors 72 58 59 N 12 15 E
Billingshurst 29 51 2 N 0 28 W
Billom 44 45 43 N 3 20 E
Bilma 117 18 50 N 13 30 E
Bilo Gora 66 45 53 N 17 15 E
Biloela 138 24 24 S 150 31 E
Biloxi 159 30 30 N 89 0 W
Bilpa Morea Claypan 138 25 0 S 140 0 E
Bilston 28 52 34 N 2 5 W
Bilthoven 46 52 8 N 5 12 E
Biltine 117 14 40 N 20 50 E
Bilugyun 98 16 24 N 97 32 E
Bilyana 138 18 5 S 145 50 E
Bilyarsk 84 54 58 N 50 22 E
Bilzen 47 50 52 N 5 31 E
Bima 103 8 22 S 118 49 E
Bimban 122 24 24 N 32 54 E
Bimberi Peak, mt. 141 35 44 S 148 51 E
Bimbila 121 8 54 N 0 5 E
Bimbo 124 4 15 N 18 33 E
Bina-Etawah 94 24 13 N 78 14 E
Binačka Morava, R. 66 42 30 N 19 35 E
Binalbagan 103 10 12 N 122 50 E
Binalong 141 34 40 S 148 39 E
Binatang 102 2 10 N 111 40 E
Binbrook 33 53 26 N 0 9 W
Binche 47 50 26 N 4 10 E
Binda 139 27 52 S 147 21 E
Bindi Bindi 137 30 37 S 116 22 E
Bindle 139 27 40 S 148 45 E
Bindura 127 17 18 S 31 18 E
Bingara, N.S.W., Austral. 139 29 52 S 150 36 E
Bingara, Queens., Austral. 139 28 10 S 144 37 E
Bingen 49 49 57 N 7 53 E
Bingerville 120 5 18 N 3 49 W
Bingham, U.K. 33 52 57 N 0 55 W
Bingham, U.S.A. 151 45 5 N 69 50 W
Bingham Canyon 160 40 31 N 112 10 W
Binghamton 38 42 9 N 75 54 W
Bingley 32 53 51 N 1 50 W
Bingöl 92 39 20 N 41 0 E
Binh Dinh = An Nhon 100 13 55 N 109 7 E
Binh Khe 100 13 57 N 108 51 E
Binh Son 100 15 20 N 108 40 E
Binjai 102 3 50 N 98 30 E
Binnaway 141 31 28 S 149 24 E
Binongko 103 5 55 S 123 55 E
Binscarth 153 50 37 N 101 17 W
Bint 93 26 22 N 59 25 E
Bint Jaibail 90 33 8 N 35 25 E
Bintan 102 1 0 N 104 0 E
Bintulu 102 3 10 N 113 0 E
Binyamina 90 32 32 N 34 56 E
Binza 123 5 25 N 28 40 E
Binzert = Bizerte 119 37 15 N 9 50 E
Bío-Bío □ 172 37 35 S 72 0 W
Bio Culma 123 7 20 N 42 15 E
Biograd 63 43 56 N 15 29 E
Biokovo 66 43 23 N 17 0 E
Biougra 118 30 15 N 9 14 W
Biq'at Bet Netofa 90 32 49 N 35 22 E
Bir 93 19 0 N 75 54 E
Bîr Abû Hashim 122 23 42 N 34 6 E
Bîr Abû M'nqar 122 26 33 N 27 33 E
Bir Adal Deib 122 22 35 N 36 10 E
Bir al Malfa 119 31 58 N 15 18 E
Bir 'Asal 122 25 55 N 34 20 E
Bir Autrun 117 18 15 N 26 40 E
Bir Dhu'fān 119 31 59 N 14 32 E
Bîr Diqnash 122 31 3 N 25 23 E
Bir el Abbes 118 26 7 N 6 9 W
Bir-el-Ater 119 34 46 N 8 3 E
Bîr el Basur 122 29 51 N 25 49 E
Bîr el Gellaz 122 30 50 N 26 40 E
Bîr el Shaqqa 122 30 54 N 25 1 E
Bir Fuad 122 30 35 N 26 28 E
Bir Haimur 122 22 45 N 33 40 E
Bîr Kanayis 122 24 59 N 33 15 E
Bîr Kerawein 122 27 10 N 28 25 E
Bir Lemouissat 118 25 0 N 10 32 W
Bîr Maql 122 23 7 N 33 40 E
Bîr Misaha 122 22 13 N 27 59 E
Bir Mogreïn, (Fort Trinquet) 116 25 10 N 11 25 W
Bîr Murr 122 23 28 N 30 10 E
Bir Nabala 90 31 52 N 35 12 E
Bîr Nakheila 122 24 1 N 30 50 E
Bîr Qâtrani 122 30 55 N 26 10 E
Bîr Ranga 122 24 25 N 35 15 E
Bir Ras 123 12 0 N 44 0 E
Bir Sahara 122 22 54 N 28 40 E
Bîr Seiyâla 122 25 10 N 34 50 E
Bir Semguine 118 30 1 N 5 39 W
Bîr Shalatein 122 23 5 N 35 25 E
Bîr Shebb 122 22 25 N 29 40 E
Bîr Shût 122 23 50 N 35 15 E
Bîr Terfawi 122 22 57 N 28 55 E
Bîr Umm Qubûr 122 24 35 N 34 2 E
Bîr Ungât 122 22 8 N 33 48 E
Bîr Za'farâna 122 29 10 N 32 40 E
Bîr Zāmus 119 24 16 N 15 6 E
Bîr Zeidûn 122 25 45 N 34 40 E
Bir Zeit 90 31 59 N 35 11 E
Bira 103 2 3 S 132 2 E
Bîra 70 47 2 N 27 3 E
Biramfero 120 11 40 N 9 10 W
Birao 117 10 20 N 22 40 E
Birawa 126 2 20 S 28 48 E
Bîrca 70 43 59 N 23 36 E
Birch 29 51 50 N 0 54 E
Birch Hills 153 52 59 N 105 25 W
Birch I. 153 52 26 N 99 54 W
Birch L., N.W.T., Can. 152 62 4 N 116 33 W
Birch L., Ont., Can. 150 51 23 N 92 18 W
Birch L., U.S.A. 150 47 48 N 91 43 W
Birch Mts. 152 57 30 N 113 10 W
Birch River 153 52 24 N 101 6 W
Birchington 29 51 22 N 1 18 E
Birchip 140 35 56 S 142 55 E
Birchiş 70 45 58 N 22 0 E
Birchwood 143 45 55 S 167 53 E
Bird 153 56 30 N 94 13 W
Bird City 158 39 48 N 101 33 W
Bird I., Austral. 133 22 10 S 155 28 E
Bird I., S. Afr. 128 32 3 S 18 17 E
Birdaard 46 53 18 N 5 53 E
Birdhip 139 35 52 S 142 50 E
Birdlip 28 51 50 N 2 7 W
Birdsville 138 25 51 S 139 20 E
Birdum 136 15 39 S 133 13 E
Birecik 92 37 0 N 38 0 E
Bireuen 102 5 14 N 96 39 E
Birhan 123 10 45 N 37 55 E
Birifo 120 13 30 N 14 0 E
Birigui 173 21 18 S 50 16 W
Birimgan 138 22 41 S 147 25 E
Birjand 93 32 57 N 59 10 E
Birk 122 18 8 N 41 30 E
Birka 122 22 11 N 40 38 E
Birkdale 32 53 38 N 3 2 W
Birkenhead, N.Z. 142 36 49 S 174 46 E
Birkenhead, U.K. 32 53 24 N 3 1 W
Birket Qârûn 122 29 30 N 30 40 E
Birkfeld 52 47 21 N 15 45 E
Birkhadem 118 36 43 N 3 3 E
Bîrlad 70 46 15 N 27 38 E
Birmingham, U.K. 28 52 30 N 1 55 W
Birmingham, U.S.A. 157 33 31 N 86 50 W
Birmitrapur 96 22 30 N 84 10 E
Birni Ngaouré 121 13 5 N 2 51 E
Birni Nkonni 121 13 55 N 5 15 E
Birnin Gwari 121 11 0 N 6 45 E
Birnin Kebbi 121 12 32 N 4 12 E
Birnin Kudu 121 11 30 N 9 29 E
Birobidzhan 77 48 50 N 132 50 E
Birqin 90 32 23 N 35 15 E
Birr 39 53 7 N 7 55 W
Birrie, R. 139 29 43 S 146 37 E
Birs, R. 50 47 24 N 7 32 E
Birsilpur 94 28 11 N 72 58 E
Birsk 84 55 25 N 55 30 E
Birtin 70 46 59 N 22 31 E
Birtle 153 50 30 N 101 5 W
Birtley, Northumberland, U.K. 35 55 5 N 2 12 W
Birtley, Tyne & Wear, U.K. 35 54 53 N 1 34 W
Birur 93 13 30 N 75 55 E
Biryuchiy, Ostrov 82 46 10 N 35 0 E
Birzai 80 56 11 N 24 45 E
Bîrzava 70 46 7 N 21 59 E
Bisa 103 1 10 S 127 40 E
Bisáccia 65 41 0 N 15 20 E
Bisacquino 64 37 42 N 13 13 E
Bisai 111 35 16 N 136 44 E
Bisalpur 95 28 14 N 79 48 E
Bisbal, La 58 41 58 N 3 2 E
Bisbee 161 31 30 N 110 0 W
Biscay, B. of 14 45 0 N 2 0 W
Biscayne B. 157 25 40 N 80 12 W
Biscéglie 65 41 14 N 16 30 E
Bischofshofen 52 47 26 N 13 14 E
Bischofswerda 48 51 8 N 14 11 E
Bischofszell 51 47 29 N 9 15 E
Bischwiller 43 48 41 N 7 50 E
Biscoe I. 13 66 0 S 67 0 W
Biscostasing 150 47 18 N 82 9 W
Biscucuy 174 9 22 N 69 59 W
Biševo, I. 63 42 57 N 16 3 E
Bisha 123 15 30 N 37 31 E
Bisha, Wadi 122 20 30 N 43 0 E
Bishop, Calif., U.S.A. 163 37 20 N 118 26 W
Bishop, Tex., U.S.A. 159 27 35 N 97 49 W
Bishop Auckland 33 54 40 N 1 40 W
Bishop's Castle 28 52 29 N 3 0 W
Bishop's Cleeve 28 51 56 N 2 3 W
Bishop's Falls 151 49 2 N 55 30 W
Bishop's Frome 28 52 8 N 2 29 W
Bishops Lydeard 28 51 4 N 3 12 W
Bishop's Nympton 30 50 58 N 3 44 W
Bishop's Stortford 29 51 52 N 0 11 E
Bishop's Waltham 28 50 57 N 1 13 W
Bishopsteignton 30 50 32 N 3 32 W
Bishopstoke 28 50 58 N 1 19 W
Bisignano 65 30 30 N 16 17 E
Bisina, L. 126 1 38 N 33 56 E
Biskra 119 34 50 N 5 44 E
Biskupiec 54 53 53 N 20 58 E
Bislig 103 8 15 N 126 27 E
Bismarck 158 46 49 N 100 49 W
Bismarck Arch. 135 2 30 S 150 0 E
Bismarck Ra. 135 5 35 S 145 0 E
Bismarck Sea 135 4 10 S 146 50 E
Bismark 48 52 39 N 11 31 E
Biso 126 1 44 N 31 26 E
Bison 158 45 34 N 102 28 W
Bispfors 74 63 1 N 16 39 E
Bispgarden 72 63 2 N 16 40 E
Bissagos = Bijagós 120 11 15 N 16 10 W
Bissau 120 11 45 N 15 45 W
Bissett 153 51 2 N 95 41 W
Bissikrima 120 10 50 N 10 58 W
Bistcho L. 152 59 45 N 118 50 W
Bistreţu 70 43 54 N 23 23 E
Bistrica = Ilirska Bistrica 63 45 34 N 14 14 E
Bistriţa 70 47 9 N 24 35 E
Bistriţa Năsăud □ 70 47 15 N 24 30 E
Bistriţa, R. 70 47 10 N 24 30 E
Bistriţei, Munţii 70 47 15 N 25 40 E
Biswan 95 27 29 N 81 2 E
Bisztynek 54 54 8 N 20 53 E
Bitam 124 2 5 N 11 25 E
Bitche 43 48 58 N 7 25 E
Bitkine 124 11 59 N 18 13 E
Bitlis 92 38 20 N 42 3 E
Bitola (Bitolj) 66 41 5 N 21 21 E
Bitonto 65 41 7 N 16 40 E
Bitter Creek 160 41 39 N 108 36 W
Bitter L., Gt. 122 30 15 N 32 40 E
Bitter L. = Buheirat-Murrat el Kubra 122 30 15 N 32 40 E
Bitterfeld 48 51 36 N 12 20 E
Bitterfontein 128 31 0 S 18 32 E
Bitteroot, R. 160 46 30 N 114 20 W
Bitterroot Range 160 46 0 N 114 20 W
Bitterwater 163 36 23 N 121 0 W
Bitti 64 40 29 N 9 20 E
Bitton 28 51 25 N 2 27 W
Bittou 121 11 17 N 0 18 W
Bitumount 152 57 26 N 112 40 W
Biu 121 10 40 N 12 3 E
Bivolari 70 47 31 N 27 27 E
Bivolu 70 47 16 N 25 58 E
Biwa-Ko 111 35 15 N 135 45 E
Biwabik 158 47 33 N 92 19 W
Biylikol, Ozero 85 43 5 N 70 45 E
Biysk 76 52 40 N 85 0 E
Bizana 129 30 50 S 29 52 E
Bizen 110 34 43 N 134 8 E
Bizerte (Binzert) 119 37 15 N 9 50 E
Bjandovan, Mys 83 39 45 N 49 28 E
Bjargtangar 74 65 30 N 24 30 W
Bjärka-Säby 73 58 16 N 15 44 E
Bjarnanes 74 64 20 N 15 6 W
Bjelasica 66 42 50 N 19 40 E
Bjelo Polje 66 43 1 N 19 45 E
Bjelovar 66 45 56 N 16 49 E
Bjerringbro 73 56 23 N 9 39 E
Björbo 72 60 27 N 14 44 E
Björkhamre 72 61 24 N 16 25 E
Björkhult 73 57 50 N 15 40 E
Björneborg 72 59 14 N 14 16 E
Bjuv 73 56 5 N 12 55 E
Bla Bheinn 36 57 14 N 6 7 W
Blaby 28 52 34 N 1 10 W
Blace 66 43 18 N 21 17 E
Blachownia 54 50 49 N 18 56 E
Black Combe, mt. 32 54 16 N 3 20 W
Black Diamond 152 50 45 N 114 14 W
Black Esk R. 35 55 14 N 3 13 W
Black Forest = Schwarzwald 49 48 0 N 8 0 E
Black Hd., Ireland 39 53 9 N 9 18 W
Black Hd., Antrim, U.K. 38 54 56 N 5 42 W
Black Hd., Cornwall, U.K. 30 50 1 N 5 6 W
Black Hills 158 44 0 N 103 50 W
Black I. 153 51 12 N 96 30 W
Black Island Sd. 162 41 10 N 71 45 W
Black Isle, Reg. 37 57 35 N 4 15 W
Black L., Can. 153 59 12 N 105 15 W
Black L., U.S.A. 156 45 28 N 84 15 W
Black Mesa, Mt. 159 36 57 N 102 55 W
Black Mt. = Mynydd Du 31 51 45 N 3 45 W
Black Mountain 141 30 18 S 151 39 E
Black Mts. 31 51 52 N 3 5 W
Black Pt. 137 34 30 S 119 25 E
Black R. 38 53 54 N 7 42 W
Black, R., Ark., U.S.A. 159 36 15 N 90 45 W
Black, R., N.Y., U.S.A. 162 43 59 N 76 40 W
Black, R., Wis., U.S.A. 158 44 18 N 90 52 W
Black, R., Vietnam = Da, R. 100 21 15 N 105 20 E
Black Range, Mts. 161 33 30 N 107 55 W
Black River 166 18 0 N 77 50 W
Black Rock 140 32 50 S 138 44 E
Black Sea 21 43 30 N 35 0 E
Black Volta, R. 120 9 0 N 2 40 W
Black Warrior, R. 157 33 0 N 87 45 W
Blackall 138 24 25 S 145 45 E
Blackball 143 42 22 S 171 26 E
Blackbull 138 17 55 S 141 45 E
Blackburn 32 53 44 N 2 30 W
Blackburn, Mt. 147 61 5 N 142 3 W
Blackbutt 139 26 51 S 152 6 E
Blackdown Hills 28 50 57 N 3 15 W
Blackduck 158 47 43 N 94 32 W
Blackfoot 160 43 13 N 112 12 W
Blackfoot, R. 160 47 0 N 113 35 W
Blackford 35 56 15 N 3 48 W
Blackie 152 50 36 N 113 37 W
Blackmoor Gate 30 51 9 N 3 55 W
Blackmoor Vale 28 50 54 N 2 28 W
Blackpool 32 53 48 N 3 3 W
Blackridge 138 22 35 S 147 35 E
Blackrock 39 53 18 N 6 11 W
Blacks Harbour 151 45 3 N 66 49 W
Blacksburg 156 37 17 N 80 23 W
Blacksod B. 38 54 6 N 10 0 W
Blacksod Pt. 38 54 7 N 10 5 W
Blackstairs Mt. 39 52 33 N 6 50 W
Blackstone 156 37 6 N 78 0 W
Blackstone, R. 152 61 5 N 122 55 W
Blackstone Ra. 137 26 00 S 129 00 E
Blackville 151 46 44 N 65 50 W
Blackwater, Austral. 138 23 35 S 148 53 E
Blackwater, Can. 152 53 20 N 123 0 W
Blackwater, Ireland 39 52 26 N 6 20 W
Blackwater Cr. 139 25 56 S 144 30 E
Blackwater, R., Limerick, Ireland 39 51 55 N 7 50 W
Blackwater, R., Meath, Ireland 38 53 40 N 6 40 W
Blackwater, R., Essex, U.K. 29 51 44 N 0 53 E
Blackwater, R., Ulster, U.K. 38 54 31 N 6 35 W
Blackwater Res. 37 56 42 N 4 45 W
Blackwell 159 36 55 N 97 20 W
Blackwells Corner 163 35 37 N 119 47 W
Blackwood 35 55 40 N 3 56 W
Blackwood, C. 135 7 49 S 144 31 E
Bladel 47 51 22 N 5 13 E
Bladinge 73 56 52 N 14 29 E
Blädinge 73 56 52 N 14 29 E
Blaenau Ffestiniog 31 53 0 N 3 57 W
Blaenavon 31 51 46 N 3 5 W
Blagaj 66 43 16 N 17 55 E
Blagdon 28 51 19 N 2 42 W
Blagnac 44 43 38 N 1 24 E
Blagodarnoye 83 45 7 N 43 37 E
Blagoevgrad (Gorna Dzhumayo) 66 42 2 N 23 5 E
Blagoveshchensk, Amur, U.S.S.R. 77 50 20 N 127 30 E
Blagoveshchensk, Urals, U.S.S.R. 84 55 1 N 55 59 E
Blagoveshchenskoye 85 43 18 N 74 12 E
Blaina 31 51 46 N 3 10 W
Blaine 160 48 59 N 122 43 W
Blaine Lake 153 52 51 N 106 52 W
Blainville 43 48 33 N 6 23 E
Blair 158 41 38 N 96 10 W
Blair Athol 138 22 42 S 147 31 E
Blair Atholl 37 56 46 N 3 50 W
Blairgowrie 37 56 36 N 3 20 W
Blairmore 152 49 40 N 114 25 W
Blaj 70 46 10 N 23 57 E
Blake Pt. 158 48 12 N 88 27 W
Blakely 157 31 22 N 85 0 W
Blakeney, Glos., U.K. 28 51 45 N 2 29 W
Blakeney, Norfolk, U.K. 29 52 57 N 1 1 E
Blâmont 43 48 35 N 6 50 E
Blanc, C., Maurit. 116 20 50 N 17 0 W
Blanc, C., Tunisia 119 37 15 N 9 56 E
Blanc, Le 44 46 37 N 1 3 E
Blanc, Mont 45 45 48 N 6 50 E
Blanc Sablon 151 51 24 N 57 8 W
Blanca, Bahía 176 39 10 S 61 30 W
Blanca Peak 161 37 35 N 105 29 W
Blanchard 159 35 8 N 97 40 W
Blanche, C. 139 33 1 S 134 9 E
Blanche L., S. Austral., Austral. 139 29 15 S 139 40 E
Blanche L., W. Austral., Austral. 136 22 25 S 123 17 E
Blanco, S. Afr. 128 33 55 S 22 23 E
Blanco, U.S.A. 159 30 7 N 98 30 W
Blanco, C., C. Rica 166 9 34 N 85 8 W
Blanco, C., Peru 174 4 10 S 81 10 W
Blanco, C., Spain 59 39 21 N 2 51 E
Blanco, C., U.S.A. 160 42 50 N 124 40 W
Blanco, R. 172 31 54 S 69 42 W
Blanda 74 65 20 N 19 40 W
Blandford Forum 28 50 52 N 2 10 W
Blanding 161 37 35 N 109 30 W
Blanes 58 41 40 N 2 48 E
Blangy 43 49 14 N 0 17 E
Blanice, R. 52 49 10 N 14 5 E
Blankenberge 47 51 20 N 3 9 E
Blankenburg 48 51 46 N 10 56 E
Blanquefort 44 44 55 N 0 38 W
Blanquilla, La 174 11 51 N 64 37 W
Blanquillo 173 32 53 S 55 37 W
Blansko 53 49 22 N 16 40 E
Blantyre 127 15 45 S 35 0 E
Blaricum 46 52 16 N 5 14 E
Blarney 39 51 57 N 8 35 W
Błaski 54 51 38 N 18 30 E
Blatná 52 49 25 N 13 52 E
Blatnitsa 67 43 41 N 28 32 E
Blatten 50 46 16 N 8 0 E
Blåvands Huk 75 55 33 N 8 4 E
Blaydon 35 54 56 N 1 47 W
Blaye 44 45 8 N 0 40 W
Blaye-les-Mines 44 44 1 N 2 8 E
Blayney 141 33 32 S 149 14 E
Blaze, Pt. 136 12 56 S 130 11 E
Błazowa 54 49 53 N 22 7 E
Bleadon 28 51 18 N 2 57 W
Blean 29 51 18 N 1 3 E
Bleasdale Moors 32 53 57 N 2 40 W
Bleckede 48 53 18 N 10 43 E
Bled 63 46 27 N 14 7 E
Blednaya, Gora 76 65 50 N 65 30 E
Bléharis 47 50 31 N 3 25 E
Bleiburg 52 46 35 N 14 49 E
Blejeşti 70 44 19 N 25 27 E
Blekinge län □ 73 56 20 N 15 20 E
Blenheim 143 41 38 S 174 5 E

Bléone, R Booral

Bléone, R. 45 44 5N 6 0E
Bletchingdon 28 51 51N 1 16W
Bletchley 29 51 59N 0 44W
Bleymard, Le 44 44 30N 3 42E
Blidet Amor 119 32 59N 5 58E
Blidö 72 59 37N 18 53E
Blidsberg 73 57 56N 13 30E
Bligh Sound 143 44 47S 167 32E
Blind River 150 46 10N 82 58W
Blinishti 68 41 52N 19 58E
Blinnenhorn 51 46 26N 8 19E
Blisworth 29 52 11N 0 56W
Blitar 103 8 5S 112 11E
Blitta 121 8 23N 1 6E
Block I. 162 41 11N 71 35W
Blockley 28 52 1N 1 45W
Bloemendaal 46 52 24N 4 39E
Bloemfontein 128 29 6S 26 14E
Bloemhof 128 27 38S 25 32E
Blofield 29 52 38N 1 25E
Blois 42 47 35N 1 20E
Blokziji 46 52 43N 5 58E
Blomskog 72 59 16N 12 2E
Blonduös 74 65 40N 20 12W
Bloodsworth Is. 162 38 9N 76 3W
Bloodvein, R. 153 51 47N 96 43W
Bloody Foreland 38 55 10N 8 18W
Bloomer 158 45 8N 91 30W
Bloomfield, Iowa, U.S.A. 158 40 44N 92 26W
Bloomfield, N. Mexico, U.S.A. 161 36 46N 107 59W
Bloomfield, Nebr., U.S.A. 158 42 38N 97 15W
Bloomfield R. 138 15 56S 145 22E
Bloomingdale 162 41 33N 74 26W
Bloomington, Ill., U.S.A. 158 40 49N 89 0W
Bloomington, Ind., U.S.A. 156 39 10N 86 30W
Bloomsburg 162 41 0N 76 30W
Blora 103 6 57S 111 25E
Blossburg 162 41 40N 77 4W
Blouberg 129 23 8S 29 0E
Blountstown 157 30 28N 85 5W
Bloxham 28 52 1N 1 22W
Bludenz 52 47 10N 9 50E
Blue I. 156 41 40N 87 40W
Blue Lake 160 40 53N 124 0W
Blue Mesa Res. 161 38 30N 107 15W
Blue Mountain Lake 162 43 52N 74 30W
Blue Mountain Peak 167 18 0N 76 40W
Blue Mts., Austral. 133 33 40S 150 0E
Blue Mts., Jamaica 167 18 0N 76 40W
Blue Mts., Ore., U.S.A. 160 45 15N 119 0W
Blue Mts., Pa., U.S.A. 156 40 30N 76 0W
Blue Mud B. 138 13 30S 136 0E
Blue Nile = Nîl el Azraq 123 12 30N 34 30E
Blue Nile □ = An Nîl el Azraq □ 123 12 30N 34 30E
Blue Nile, R. = Nîl el Azraq 123 10 30N 35 0E
Blue Ridge, Mts. 157 36 30N 80 15W
Blue Stack Mts. 38 54 46N 8 5W
Blueberry, R. 152 56 45N 120 49W
Bluefield 156 37 18N 81 14W
Bluefields 166 12 0N 83 50W
Bluemull Sd. 36 60 45N 1 0W
Blueskin B. 143 45 44S 170 38E
Bluff, Austral. 138 23 35S 149 4E
Bluff, N.Z. 143 46 37S 168 20E
Bluff, U.S.A. 147 64 50N 147 15W
Bluff Downs 138 19 37S 145 30E
Bluff Harbour 143 46 36S 168 21E
Bluff Knoll, Mt. 137 34 24S 118 15E
Bluff Pt. 137 27 50S 114 5E
Bluffton 156 40 43N 85 9W
Blumenau 173 27 0S 49 0W
Blumenthal 48 53 5N 12 20E
Blümisalphorn 50 46 30N 7 47E
Blundeston 29 52 33N 1 42E
Blunt 158 44 32N 100 0W
Bly 160 42 23N 121 0W
Blyberg 72 61 9N 14 11E
Blyth, Austral. 140 33 49S 138 28E
Blyth, Northumberland, U.K. 35 55 8N 1 32W
Blyth, Notts., U.K. 33 53 22N 1 2W
Blyth Bridge 35 55 41N 3 22W
Blyth, R. 35 55 8N 1 30W
Blythburgh 29 52 19N 1 36E
Blythe 161 33 40N 114 33W
Blyton 33 53 25N 0 42W
Bo, Norway 71 59 25N 9 3E
Bo, S. Leone 120 7 55N 11 50W
Bo Duc 101 11 58N 106 50E
Bō-no-Misaki 110 31 15N 130 13E
Boa I. 38 54 30N 7 50W
Boa Nova 171 14 22S 40 10W
Boa Viagem 170 5 7S 39 44W
Boa Vista 174 2 48N 60 30W
Boaco 166 12 29N 85 35W
Boal 56 43 25N 6 49W
Boat of Garten 37 57 15N 3 45W
Boatman 139 27 16S 146 55E
Bobadah 141 32 19S 146 41E
Bobbili 96 18 35N 83 30E
Bóbbio 62 44 47N 9 22E
Bobcaygeon 150 44 33N 78 33W
Böblingen 57 48 41N 9 1E
Bobo-Dioulasso 120 11 8N 4 13W
Boboc 67 45 13N 26 59E
Bobolice 54 53 58N 16 37E
Boboshevo 66 42 9N 23 0E
Bobov Dol 66 42 20N 23 0E
Bóbr, R. 54 51 50N 15 15E
Bobrinets 82 48 4N 32 5E
Bobrov 81 51 5N 40 2E
Bobruysk 80 53 10N 29 15E
Bobures 174 9 15N 71 11W
Boca de Uracoa 174 9 8N 62 20W
Bôca do Acre 174 8 50S 67 27W
Bocage 41 49 0N 1 0W
Bocaiúva 171 17 7S 43 49W
Bocanda 120 7 5N 4 31W
Bocaranga 117 7 0N 15 35E
Bocas del Dragon 174 11 0N 61 50W
Bocas del Toro 166 9 15N 82 20W
Bocdam 36 59 55N 1 16W
Boceguillas 58 41 20N 3 39W
Bochnia 54 49 58N 20 27E
Bocholt, Belg. 47 51 10N 5 35E
Bocholt, Ger. 48 51 50N 6 35E
Bochov 52 50 9N 13 3E
Bochum 48 51 28N 7 12E
Bockenem 48 52 1N 10 8E
Bocoyna 164 27 52N 107 35W
Bocq, R. 47 50 20N 4 55E
Boçsa Montanŭ 66 45 21N 21 47E
Boda 124 4 19N 17 26E
Böda 73 57 15N 17 3E
Boda 74 57 15N 17 0E
Bodaybo 77 57 50N 114 0E
Boddam 37 57 28N 1 46W
Boddington 137 32 50S 116 30E
Bodedern 31 53 17N 4 29W
Bodegraven 46 52 5N 4 46E
Boden 74 65 50N 21 42E
Bodenham 28 52 9N 2 41W
Bodensee 51 47 35N 9 25E
Bodenteich 48 52 49N 10 41E
Boderg, L. 38 53 52N 8 0W
Bodhan 96 18 40N 77 55E
Bodiam 29 51 1N 0 33E
Bodinayakkanur 97 10 2N 77 10E
Bodinga 121 12 58N 5 10E
Bodinnick 30 50 20N 4 37W
Bodio 51 46 23N 8 55E
Bodmin 30 50 28N 4 44W
Bodmin Moor 30 50 33N 4 36W
Bodø 74 67 17N 14 24E
Bodrog, R. 53 48 15N 21 35E
Bodrum 92 37 5N 27 30E
Bódva, R. 53 48 19N 20 45E
Bodyke 39 52 53N 8 38W
Boechout 47 51 10N 4 30E
Boegoebergdam 128 29 7S 22 9E
Boekelo 46 52 12N 6 49E
Boelenslaan 46 53 10N 6 10E
Boën 45 45 44N 4 0E
Boende 124 0 24S 21 12E
Boerne 159 29 48N 98 41W
Boertange 46 53 1N 7 12E
Boezinge 47 50 54N 2 52E
Boffa 120 10 16N 14 3W
Bofin L. 38 53 51N 7 55W
Bofors 72 59 19N 14 34E
Bogale 98 21 16N 92 24E
Bogalusa 159 30 50N 89 55W
Bogan Gate 141 33 7S 147 49E
Bogan, R. 141 32 45S 148 8E
Bogantungan 138 23 41S 147 17E
Bogata 159 33 26N 95 10W
Bogatió 66 44 51N 19 30E
Bogdan, Mt. 67 42 37N 24 20E
Bogdanovitch 84 56 47N 62 1E
Bogenfels 125 27 25S 15 25E
Bogense 73 55 34N 10 5E
Boggabilla 139 28 36S 150 24E
Boggabri 141 30 45S 150 0E
Boggeragh Mts. 39 52 2N 8 55W
Boghari = Ksar el Boukhari 118 35 51N 2 52E
Bogia 135 4 9S 145 0E
Bognor Regis 29 50 47N 0 40W
Bogø 73 54 55N 12 2E
Bogo 103 11 3N 124 0E
Bogodukhov 80 50 9N 35 33E
Bogong, Mt. 141 36 47S 147 17E
Bogor 103 6 36S 106 48E
Bogoro 121 9 37N 9 29E
Bogoroditsk 81 53 47N 38 8E
Bogorodsk 81 56 4N 43 30E
Bogorodskoye 77 52 22N 140 30E
Bogoso 120 5 38N 2 3W
Bogotá 174 4 34N 74 0W
Bogotol 76 56 15N 89 50E
Bogra 98 24 51N 89 22E
Boguchany 77 58 40N 97 30E
Boguchar 83 49 55N 40 32E
Bogué 120 16 45N 14 10W
Boguslav 82 49 47N 30 53E
Boguszów Lubawka 54 50 43N 15 56E
Bohain 43 49 59N 3 28E
Bohemia 52 50 0N 14 0E
Bohemia Downs 136 18 53S 126 14E
Bohemian Forest = Böhmerwald 49 49 30N 12 40E
Bohena Cr. 139 30 17S 149 42E
Boheraphuca 39 53 1N 7 45W
Bohinjska Bistrica 63 46 17N 14 1E
Böhmerwald 49 49 30N 12 40E
Bohmte 48 52 24N 8 20E
Bohola 38 53 54N 9 4W
Boholl, I. 103 9 50N 124 10E
Bohotleh 91 8 20N 46 25E
Boi 121 9 35N 9 27E
Boi, Pta. de 173 23 55S 45 15W
Boiano 65 41 28N 14 29E
Boiestown 151 46 27N 66 26W
Boigu I. 138 9 15S 143 30E
Boileau, C. 136 17 40S 122 7E
Boipeba, I. de 171 13 39S 38 55W
Bois, Les 50 47 11N 6 50E
Bois, R. 171 18 35S 50 2W
Boischot 47 51 3N 4 47E
Boisdale L. 36 57 9N 7 19W
Boise 160 43 43N 116 9W
Boise City 159 36 45N 102 30W
Boissevain 153 49 15N 100 0W
Boite, R. 63 46 24N 12 13E
Boitzenburg 48 55 16N 13 36E
Boizenburg 48 53 22N 10 42E
Bojador C. 116 26 0N 14 30W
Bojanow 54 51 43N 16 42E
Bøjden 73 55 6N 10 7E
Bojnurd 93 37 30N 57 20E
Bojonegoro 103 7 11S 111 54E
Boju 121 7 22N 7 55E
Boka 66 45 22N 20 52E
Boka Kotorska 66 42 23N 18 32E
Bokala 120 8 31N 4 33W
Boké 120 10 56N 14 17W
Bokhara, R. 139 29 55S 146 42E
Bokkos 121 9 17N 9 1E
Boknafjorden 71 59 14N 5 40E
Bokombayevskoye 85 47 7N 77 0E
Bokoro 117 12 25N 17 14E
Bokote 124 0 12S 21 8E
Bokpyin 101 11 18N 98 42E
Boksitogorsk 80 59 32N 33 56E
Bokungu 124 0 35S 22 50E
Bol, Chad 124 13 30N 15 0E
Bol, Yugo. 63 43 18N 16 38E
Bolama 120 11 30N 15 30W
Bolan Pass 93 29 50N 67 20E
Bolangum 140 36 42S 142 54E
Bolaños, R. 164 22 0N 104 10W
Bolbec 42 49 30N 0 30E
Bolchereche 76 56 4N 74 45E
Boldeşti 70 45 3N 26 2E
Bole 123 6 36N 37 20E
Bolekhov 80 49 0N 24 0E
Bolesławiec 54 51 17N 15 37E
Bolgary 78 55 3N 48 50E
Bolgatanga 121 10 44N 0 53W
Bolgrad 82 45 40N 28 32E
Boli 123 6 2N 28 48E
Bolinao C. 103 16 30N 119 55E
Bolívar, Argent. 172 36 15S 60 53W
Bolívar, Antioquía, Colomb. 174 5 50N 76 1W
Bolívar, Cauca, Colomb. 174 2 0N 77 0W
Bolivar, Mo., U.S.A. 159 37 38N 93 22W
Bolivar, Tenn., U.S.A. 159 35 14N 89 0W
Bolívar □ 174 9 0N 74 40W
Bolivia ■ 174 17 6S 64 0W
Boljevac 66 43 51N 21 58E
Bolkhov 81 53 25N 36 0E
Bollène 45 44 18N 4 45E
Bollington 32 53 18N 2 8W
Bollnäs 72 61 21N 16 24E
Bollon 139 28 2S 147 29E
Bollstabruk 72 63 1N 17 40E
Bollullos 57 37 19N 6 32W
Bolmen 73 56 55N 13 40E
Bolney 29 50 59N 0 11W
Bolo Silase 123 8 51N 39 27E
Bolobo 124 2 6S 16 20E
Bologna 63 44 30N 11 20E
Bologne 43 48 10N 5 8E
Bologoye 80 57 55N 34 0E
Bolomba 124 0 35N 19 0E
Bolonchenticul 165 20 0N 89 49W
Bolong 103 6 6N 122 16E
Bolotovskoye 84 58 31N 62 28E
Boloven, Cao Nguyen 100 15 10N 106 30E
Bolpur 95 23 40N 87 45E
Bolsena 63 42 40N 11 58E
Bolsena, L. di 63 42 35N 11 55E
Bolshaya Glushitsa 81 52 24N 50 29E
Bolshaya Khobda, R. 84 50 50N 54 53E
Bolshaya Kinel, R. 84 53 14N 50 30E
Bolshaya Lepetrikha 82 47 11N 33 57E
Bolshaya Martynovka 83 47 12N 41 46E
Bolshaya Shatan, Gora 84 53 37N 58 3E
Bolshevik, Ostrov 77 78 30N 102 0E
Bolshezemelskaya Tundra 78 67 0N 56 0E
Bolshoi Kavkas 83 42 50N 44 0E
Bolshoi Tuters, O. 80 59 44N 26 57E
Bolshoy Atlym 76 62 25N 66 50E
Bolshoy Tokmak 82 47 16N 35 42E
Bol'soj T'uters, O. 80 59 44N 26 57E
Bolsover 33 53 14N 1 18W
Bolsward 46 53 3N 5 32E
Bolt Head 30 50 13N 3 48W
Bolt Tail 30 50 13N 3 55W
Boltaña 58 42 28N 0 4E
Boltigen 50 46 38N 7 24E
Bolton 32 53 35N 2 26W
Bolton Abbey 32 53 59N 1 53W
Bolton by Bowland 32 53 56N 2 21W
Bolton Landing 162 43 32N 73 35W
Bolton le Sands 32 54 7N 2 49W
Bolton-on-Dearne 33 53 31N 1 19W
Bolu 92 40 45N 31 35E
Bolubolu 135 9 21S 150 20E
Bolus Hd. 39 51 48N 10 20W
Bolvadin 92 38 45N 31 57E
Bolzano (Bozen) 63 46 30N 11 20E
Bom Conselho 170 9 42S 37 26W
Bom Despacho 171 19 43S 45 15W
Bom Jardim 171 7 47S 35 35W
Bom Jesus 170 9 4S 44 22W
Bom Jesus da Gurguéia, Serra 170 9 0S 43 0W
Bom Jesus da Lapa 171 13 15S 43 25W
Boma 124 5 50S 13 4E
Bomaderry 141 34 52S 150 37E
Bömba, Khalīj 117 32 20N 23 15E
Bomba, La 164 31 53N 115 2W
Bombala 141 36 56S 149 15E
Bombarral 57 39 15N 9 9W
Bombay 96 18 55N 72 50E
Bomboma 124 2 25N 18 55E
Bombombwa 126 2 18N 19 3E
Bomi Hills 120 7 1N 10 38E
Bomili 126 1 45N 27 5E
Bomokandi, R. 126 3 10N 28 15E
Bomongo 124 1 27N 18 21E
Bomu, R. 124 4 40N 23 30E
Bon C. 119 37 1N 11 2E
Bon Sar Pa 100 12 24N 107 35E
Bonaduz 15 46 49N 9 25E
Bonaire, I. 167 12 10N 68 15W
Bonang 141 37 11S 148 41E
Bonanza 166 13 54N 84 35W
Bonaparte Archipelago 136 14 0S 124 30E
Boñar 56 42 52N 5 19W
Bonarbridge 37 57 53N 4 20W
Bonäset 72 63 16N 18 45E
Bonaventure 151 48 5N 65 32W
Bonavista 151 48 40N 53 5W
Bonavista, C. 151 48 42N 53 5W
Bonchester Bri. 35 55 23N 2 36W
Bonchurch 28 50 36N 1 11W
Bondeno 63 44 53N 11 22E
Bondo 124 3 55N 23 53E
Bondoukoro 120 9 51N 4 25W
Bondoukou 120 8 2N 2 47W
Bondowoso 120 7 56S 113 49E
Bondyug 84 60 29N 55 56E
Bone Rate, I. 103 7 25S 121 5E
Bone Rate, Kepulauan 103 6 30S 121 10E
Bone, Teluk 103 4 10S 120 50E
Bonefro 65 41 42N 14 55E
Bo'ness 35 56 0N 3 38W
Bong Son = Hoai Nhon 100 14 26N 109 1E
Bongandanga 124 1 24N 21 3E
Bonge 123 6 5N 37 16E
Bongor 117 10 35N 15 20E
Bongouanou 120 6 42N 4 15W
Bonham 159 33 30N 96 10W
Bonherden 47 51 1N 4 32E
Bonifacio 45 41 24N 9 10E
Bonifacio, Bouches de 64 41 12N 9 15E
Bonin Is. 130 27 0N 142 0E
Bonito de Santa Fé 171 7 19S 38 31W
Bonn 48 50 43N 7 6E
Bonnat 44 46 20N 1 53E
Bonne B. 151 40 31N 58 0W
Bonne Espérance, I. 151 51 24N 57 40W
Bonne Terre 159 37 55N 90 38W
Bonners Ferry 160 48 38N 116 21W
Bonnert 47 49 43N 5 49E
Bonnétable 42 48 11N 0 25E
Bonneuil Matours 42 46 41N 0 34E
Bonneville 45 46 5N 6 24E
Bonney, L. 140 37 50S 140 20E
Bonnie Doon 141 37 2S 145 53E
Bonnie Rock 137 30 29S 118 22E
Bonny, France 43 47 34N 2 50E
Bonny, Nigeria 121 4 25N 7 13E
Bonny, Bight of 121 3 30N 9 20E
Bonny, R. 121 4 20N 7 14E
Bonnyrigg 35 55 52N 3 8W
Bonnyville 153 54 20N 110 45W
Bonoi 103 1 45S 137 41E
Bonorva 64 40 25N 8 47E
Bonsall 163 33 16N 117 14W
Bontang 102 0 10N 117 30E
Bonthain 103 5 34S 119 56E
Bonthe 120 7 30N 12 33W
Bonyeri 120 5 1N 2 46W
Bonyhád 53 46 18N 18 32E
Bonython Ra. 136 23 40S 128 45E
Boogardie 137 28 2S 117 45E
Bookabie P.O. 137 31 50S 132 41E
Booker 159 36 29N 100 30W
Boolaboolka, L. 140 32 38S 143 10E
Boolarra 141 38 20S 146 20E
Boolathanna 137 21 40S 113 41E
Boolcoomata 140 31 57S 140 33E
Booleroo Centre 140 32 53S 138 21E
Booligal 141 33 58S 144 53E
Booloo Downs 137 23 52S 119 33E
Boom 47 51 6N 4 20E
Boonah 139 27 58S 152 41E
Boondall 108 27 20S 153 4E
Boone, Iowa, U.S.A. 158 42 5N 93 53W
Boone, N.C., U.S.A. 157 36 14N 81 43W
Booneville, Ark., U.S.A. 159 35 10N 93 54W
Booneville, Miss., U.S.A. 157 34 39N 88 34W
Boongoondoo 138 22 55S 145 55E
Boonville, Ind., U.S.A. 156 38 3N 87 13W
Boonville, Mo., U.S.A. 158 38 57N 92 45W
Boonville, N.Y., U.S.A. 162 43 31N 75 20W
Booral 141 32 30S 151 56E

FHK

**Boorindal** **Bramminge**

Boorindal 139 30 22S 146 11E
Booroomugga 141 31 17S 146 27E
Boorowa 141 34 28S 148 44E
Boot 32 54 24N 3 18W
Boothia, Gulf of 149 71 0N 91 0W
Boothia Pen. 148 71 0N 94 0W
Bootle, Cumb., U.K. 32 54 17N 3 24W
Bootle, Merseysude, U.K. 32 53 28N 3 1W
Boué 124 0 5S 11 55E
Bopeechee 139 29 36S 137 22E
Bophuthatswana □ 126 26 0S 26 0E
Bopo 79 7 33N 7 50E
Boppard 49 50 13N 7 36E
Boquete 166 8 46N 82 27W
Boquillas 164 29 17N 102 53W
Bor 52 49 41N 12 45E
Bôr 123 6 10N 31 40E
Bor, Sweden 73 57 9N 14 10E
Bor, Yugo. 66 44 8N 22 7E
Borah, Mt. 160 44 19N 113 46W
Borang 123 4 50N 30 59E
Borås 73 57 43N 12 56E
Borås 73 57 43N 12 56E
Borazjan 93 29 22N 51 10E
Borba, Brazil 174 4 12S 59 34W
Borba, Port. 57 38 50N 7 26W
Borborema, Planalto da 170 7 0S 37 0W
Borçka 83 41 25N 41 41E
Borculo 46 52 7N 6 31E
Borda, C. 140 35 45S 136 34E
Bordeaux 44 44 50N 0 36W
Borden, Austral. 137 34 3S 118 12E
Borden, Can. 151 46 18N 63 47W
Borden I. 12 78 30N 111 30W
Borders □ 35 55 45N 2 50W
Bordertown 140 36 19S 140 45E
Borðeyri 74 65 12N 21 6W
Bordighera 62 43 47N 7 40E
Bordj bou Arridj 119 36 4N 4 45E
Bordj Djeneiene 119 31 47N 10 3E
Bordj el Hobra 119 32 9N 4 51E
Bordj Fly Ste. Marie 118 27 19N 2 32W
Bordj-in-Eker 119 24 9N 5 3E
Bordj Ménaiel 119 36 46N 3 43E
Bordj Nili 118 33 28N 3 2E
Bordj Zelfana 119 32 27N 4 15E
Bordoba 85 39 31N 73 16E
Bordon Camp 29 51 6N 0 52W
Borea Creek 141 35 5S 146 35E
Borehamwood 29 51 40N 0 15W
Borek Wlkp. 54 51 54N 17 11E
Boreland 35 55 12N 3 16W
Boremore 141 33 15S 149 0E
Borensberg 73 58 34N 15 17E
Borgarnes 74 64 32N 21 55W
Borgefjellet 74 65 20N 13 45E
Borger, Neth. 46 52 54N 6 33E
Borger, U.S.A. 159 35 40N 101 20W
Borgerhout 47 51 12N 4 28E
Borghamn 73 58 23N 14 41E
Borgholm 73 56 52N 16 39E
Bórgia 65 38 50N 16 30E
Borgie R. 37 58 28N 4 20W
Borgo San Dalmazzo 62 44 19N 7 29E
Borgo San Lorenzo 63 43 57N 11 21E
Borgo Val di Taro 62 44 29N 9 47E
Borgomanero 62 45 41N 8 28E
Borgonovo Val Tidone 62 45 1N 9 28E
Borgorose 63 42 12N 13 14E
Borgosésia 62 45 43N 8 17E
Borgvattnet 72 63 26N 15 48E
Borhaug 71 58 6N 6 33E
Borikhane 100 18 33N 103 43E
Borisoglebsk 81 51 27N 42 5E
Borisoglebskiy 81 56 28N 43 59E
Borisov 80 54 17N 28 28E
Borisovka 85 43 15N 68 10E
Borisovo-Sudskoye 81 59 58N 35 57E
Borispol 80 50 21N 30 59E
Borja, Peru 174 4 20S 77 40W
Borja, Spain 58 41 48N 1 34W
Borjas Blancas 58 41 31N 0 52E
Borkou 117 18 15N 18 50E
Borlänge 72 60 29N 15 26E
Borley, C. 13 66 15S 52 30E
Bormida, R. 62 44 35N 8 10E
Bórmio 62 46 28N 10 22E
Born 47 51 2N 5 49E
Borna 48 51 8N 12 31E
Borndiep, Str. 46 53 27N 5 35E
Borne 46 52 18N 6 46E
Bornem 47 51 6N 4 14E
Borneo, I. 102 1 0N 115 0E
Bornholm, I. 73 55 10N 15 0E
Bornholmsgattet 73 55 15N 14 20E
Borno □ 121 12 30N 12 30E
Bornos 57 36 48N 5 42W
Bornu Yassa 121 12 14N 12 25E
Borodino 80 55 31N 35 40E
Borogontsy 77 62 42N 131 8E
Boromo 120 11 45N 2 58W
Boron 163 35 0N 117 39W
Boronga Is. 98 19 58N 93 6E
Borongan 103 11 37N 125 26E
Bororen 138 24 13S 151 33E
Borotangba Mts. 123 6 30N 25 0E
Boroughbridge 33 54 6N 1 23W
Borovan 67 43 27N 23 45E
Borovichi 80 58 25N 33 55E
Borovsk, Moscow, U.S.S.R. 81 55 12N 36 24E
Borovsk, Urals, U.S.S.R. 84 59 43N 56 40E
Borovskoye 84 53 48N 64 12E
Borradaile, Mt. 136 12 5S 132 51E
Borrby 73 55 27N 14 10E
Borrego Springs 163 33 15N 116 23W
Borriol 58 40 4N 0 4W
Borris 39 32 36N 6 57W
Borris-in-Ossory 39 52 57N 7 40W
Borrisokane 39 53 0N 8 8W
Borrisoleigh 39 52 48N 7 58W
Borroloola 138 16 4S 136 17E
Borrowdale 32 54 31N 3 10W
Borsa 70 47 41N 24 50E
Borsod-Abaúj-Zemplén □ 53 48 20N 21 0E
Borssele 47 51 26N 3 45E
Bort-les-Orgues 44 45 24N 2 29E
Borth 31 52 29N 4 3W
Borujerd 92 33 55N 48 50E
Borve 36 58 25N 6 28W
Borzhomi 83 41 48N 43 28E
Borzna 80 51 18N 32 26E
Borzya 77 50 24N 116 31E
Bos. Dubica 63 45 10N 16 50E
Bos. Gradiška 66 45 10N 17 15E
Bos. Grahovo 63 44 12N 16 26E
Bos. Kostajnica 63 45 11N 16 33E
Bos. Krupa 63 44 53N 16 10E
Bos. Novi 63 45 2N 16 22E
Bos. Petrovac 63 44 35N 16 21E
Bos. Samac 66 45 3N 18 29E
Bosa 64 40 17N 8 32E
Bosaga 85 37 33N 65 41E
Bosanska Brod 66 45 10N 18 0E
Bosanski Novi 63 45 2N 16 22E
Bosavi, Mt. 135 6 30S 142 49E
Bosbury 28 52 5N 2 27W
Boscastle 30 50 42N 4 42W
Boscotrecase 65 40 46N 14 28E
Bosham 29 50 50N 0 51W
Boshoek 128 25 30S 27 9E
Boshof 128 28 31S 25 13E
Boshrūyeh 93 33 50N 57 30E
Bosilegrad 66 42 30N 22 27E
Boskoop 46 52 4N 4 40E
Boskovice 53 49 29N 16 40E
Bosna i Hercegovina □ 66 44 0N 18 0E
Bosna, R. 66 44 50N 18 10E
Bosnia = Bosna 66 44 0N 18 0E
Bosnik 103 1 5S 136 10E
Bōsō-Hantō 111 35 20N 140 20E
Bosobolo 124 4 15N 19 50E
Bosporus = Karadeniz Boğazı 92 41 10N 29 10E
Bossangoa 117 6 35N 17 30E
Bossekop 74 69 57N 23 15E
Bossembélé 117 5 25N 17 40E
Bossier City 159 32 28N 93 38W
Bosso 121 13 43N 13 19E
Bossut C. 136 18 42S 121 35E
Boston, U.K. 33 52 59N 0 2W
Boston, U.S.A. 162 42 20N 71 0W
Boston Bar 152 49 52N 121 22W
Bosut, R. 66 45 5N 19 2E
Boswell, Can. 152 49 28N 116 45W
Boswell, U.S.A. 159 34 1N 95 30W
Botad 94 22 15N 71 40E
Botany Bay 139 34 0S 151 14E
Botene 100 17 35N 101 12E
Botevgrad 67 42 55N 23 47E
Bothaville 128 27 23S 26 34E
Bothel 32 54 43N 3 16W
Bothnia, G. of 74 63 0N 21 0E
Bothwell 138 42 20S 147 1E
Boticas 56 41 41N 7 40W
Botletle R. 128 20 10S 24 10E
Botoroaga 70 44 8N 25 32E
Botoşani 70 47 42N 26 41E
Botoşani □ 70 47 50N 26 50E
Botro 120 7 51N 5 19W
Botswana ■ 125 22 0S 24 0E
Bottesford 33 52 57N 0 48W
Bottineau 158 48 49N 100 25W
Bottrop 48 51 34N 6 59E
Botucatu 173 22 55S 48 30W
Botwood 151 49 6N 55 23W
Bou Alam 118 33 50N 1 26E
Bou Ali 118 27 11N 0 4W
Bou Djébéha 120 18 25N 2 45W
Bou Garfa 118 27 4N 7 59W
Bou Guema 118 28 49N 0 19E
Bou Iblane, Djebel 118 33 50N 4 0W
Bou Ismail 118 36 38N 2 42E
Bou Izakarn 118 29 12N 9 46W
Bou Kahil, Djebel 118 34 22N 9 23E
Bou Saâda 119 35 11N 4 9E
Bou Salem 119 36 45N 9 2E
Bouaké 120 7 40N 5 2W
Bouar 124 6 0N 15 40E
Bouârfa 118 32 32N 1 58E
Bouca 117 6 45N 18 25E
Boucau 44 43 32N 1 29W
Boucaut B. 138 12 0S 134 25E
Bouches-du-Rhône □ 45 43 37N 5 2E
Bouda 118 27 50N 0 27W
Boudenib 118 31 59N 3 31W
Boudry 50 46 57N 6 50E
Boufarik 118 36 34N 2 58E
Bougainville C. 136 13 57S 126 4E
Bougainville I. 135 6 0S 155 0E
Bougainville Reef 138 15 30S 147 5E
Bougaroun, C. 119 37 6N 6 30E
Bougie = Béjaïa 119 36 42N 5 2E
Bougouni 120 11 30N 7 20W
Bouillon 47 49 44N 5 3E
Bouïra 119 36 20N 3 59E
Boujad 118 32 46N 6 24W
Bouladuff 39 52 42N 7 55W
Boulder, Austral. 132 30 46S 121 30E
Boulder, Colo., U.S.A. 158 40 3N 105 10W
Boulder, Mont., U.S.A. 160 46 14N 112 4W
Boulder City 161 36 0N 114 50W
Boulder Creek 163 37 7N 122 7W
Boulder Dam = Hoover Dam 161 36 0N 114 45W
Bouleau, Lac au 150 47 40N 77 35W
Boulhaut 118 33 30N 7 1W
Boulia 138 22 52S 139 51E
Bouligny 43 49 17N 5 45E
Boulogne, R. 42 46 50N 1 25W
Boulogne-sur-Gesne 44 43 18N 0 38E
Boulogne-sur-Mer 43 50 42N 1 36E
Boulsa 121 12 39N 0 34W
Boultoum 121 14 45N 10 25E
Boumalne 118 31 25N 6 0W
Boun Neua 100 21 38N 101 54E
Boun Tai 100 21 23N 101 58E
Bouna 120 9 10N 3 0W
Boundary 147 64 11N 141 2W
Boundary Pk. 163 37 51N 118 21W
Boundiali 120 9 30N 6 20W
Bountiful 160 40 57N 111 58W
Bounty I. 130 46 0S 180 0E
Bour Khaya 77 71 50N 133 10E
Bourbon-l'Archambault 44 46 36N 3 4E
Bourbon-Lancy 44 46 37N 3 45E
Bourbonnais 44 46 28N 3 0E
Bourbonne 43 47 59N 5 45E
Bourem 121 17 0N 0 24W
Bourg 44 45 3N 0 34W
Bourg-Argental 45 45 18N 4 32E
Bourg-de-Péage 45 45 2N 5 3E
Bourg-en-Bresse 45 46 13N 5 12E
Bourg-St.-Andéol 45 44 23N 4 39E
Bourg-St.-Maurice 45 45 35N 6 46E
Bourg-St.-Pierre 50 45 57N 7 12E
Bourganeuf 44 45 57N 1 45E
Bourges 43 47 9N 2 25E
Bourget, L. du 45 45 44N 5 52E
Bourgneuf 42 47 2N 1 58W
Bourgneuf, B. de 42 47 3N 2 10W
Bourgneuf, Le 42 48 10N 0 59W
Bourgogne 43 47 0N 4 30E
Bourgoin-Jallieu 45 45 36N 5 17E
Bourke 139 30 8S 145 55E
Bourlamaque 150 48 5N 77 56W
Bourne 29 52 46N 0 22W
Bournemouth 28 50 43N 1 53W
Bourriot-Bergonce 44 44 7N 0 14W
Bourton-on-the-Water 28 51 53N 1 45W
Bouscat, Le 44 44 53N 0 32W
Boussac 44 46 22N 2 13E
Boussens 44 43 12N 0 58E
Bousso 117 10 34N 16 52E
Boussu 47 50 26N 3 48E
Bouthillier, Le 151 47 47N 64 55W
Boutilimit 120 17 45N 14 40W
Bouvet I. 15 55 0S 3 30E
Bouznika 118 33 46N 7 6W
Bouzonville 43 49 17N 6 32E
Bova Marina 65 37 59N 15 56E
Bovalino Marina 65 38 9N 16 10E
Bovec 63 46 20N 13 33E
Bovenkarspel 46 52 41N 5 14E
Bòves 62 44 19N 7 29E
Boves 62 44 19N 7 33E
Bovey Tracey 30 50 36N 3 40W
Bovigny 47 50 12N 5 55E
Bovill 160 46 58N 116 27W
Bovino 65 41 15N 15 20E
Bow Island 152 49 50N 111 23W
Bow, R. 152 51 10N 115 0W
Bowbells 158 48 47N 102 19W
Bowdle 158 45 30N 100 2W
Bowelling 137 33 25S 116 30E
Bowen 138 20 0S 148 16E
Bowen Mts. 141 37 0S 148 0E
Bowen, R. 138 20 24S 147 20E
Bowes 32 54 31N 1 59W
Bowie, U.S.A. 162 39 0N 76 47W
Bowie, Ariz., U.S.A. 161 32 15N 109 30W
Bowie, Tex., U.S.A. 159 33 33N 97 50W
Bowland, Forest of 32 54 0N 2 30W
Bowling Green, Ky., U.S.A. 156 37 0N 86 25W
Bowling Green, Ohio, U.S.A. 156 41 22N 83 40W
Bowling Green, Va., U.S.A. 162 38 3N 77 21W
Bowling Green, C. 138 19 19S 147 25E
Bowman 158 46 12N 103 21W
Bowman, I. 13 65 0S 104 0E
Bowmans 140 34 10S 138 17E
Bowmanville 150 43 55N 78 41W
Bowmore 34 55 45N 6 18W
Bowness, Can. 152 50 55N 114 25W
Bowness, Solway, U.K. 32 54 57N 3 13W
Bowness, Windermere, U.K. 32 54 22N 2 56W
Bowral 141 34 26S 150 27E
Bowraville 139 30 37S 152 52E
Bowron, R. 152 54 3N 121 50W
Bowser L. 152 56 30N 129 30W
Bowsman 153 52 14N 101 12W
Bowutu Mts. 135 7 45S 147 10E
Bowwood 127 17 5S 26 20E
Box 28 51 24N 2 16W
Box Hill 29 51 16N 0 16W
Boxelder Creek 160 47 20N 108 30W
Boxholm 73 58 12N 15 3E
Boxley 29 51 17N 0 34E
Boxmeer 47 51 38N 5 56E
Boxtel 47 51 36N 5 9E
Boyabat 82 41 28N 34 42E
Boyacá □ 174 5 30N 72 30W
Boyanup 137 33 30S 115 40E
Boyce 159 31 25N 92 39W
Boyd L. 150 61 30N 103 20W
Boyer, R. 152 58 27N 115 57W
Boyle 38 53 58N 8 19W
Boyne City 156 45 13N 85 1W
Boyne, R. 38 53 40N 6 34W
Boynton Beach 157 26 31N 80 3W
Boyoma, Chutes 124 0 12N 25 25E
Boyup Brook 137 33 50S 116 23E
Bozburun 69 36 43N 28 8E
Bozcaada 68 39 49N 26 3E
Bozeat 29 52 14N 0 41W
Bozeman 160 45 40N 111 0W
Bozepole Wlk. 54 54 33N 17 56E
Bozevac 66 44 32N 21 24E
Bozouls 44 44 28N 2 43E
Bozoum 117 6 25N 16 35E
Bozovici 70 44 56N 22 1E
Bra 62 44 41N 7 50E
Brabant □ 47 50 46N 4 30E
Brabant L. 153 54 18N 108 5W
Brabrand 73 56 9N 10 7E
BraC 63 43 20N 16 40E
Bracadale 36 57 22N 6 24W
Bracadale, L. 36 57 20N 6 30W
Bracciano 63 42 6N 12 10E
Bracciano, L. di 63 42 8N 12 11E
Bracebridge 150 45 2N 79 19W
Bracebridge Heath 33 53 13N 0 32W
Brach 119 27 31N 14 20E
Bracieux 43 47 30N 1 30E
Bräcke 72 62 45N 15 26E
Brackettville 159 29 21N 100 20W
Brackley 28 52 3N 1 9W
Bracknell 29 51 24N 0 45W
Braco 35 56 16N 3 55W
Brad 70 46 10N 22 50E
Brădano, R. 65 40 41N 16 20E
Bradda Hd. 32 54 6N 4 46W
Bradenton 157 27 25N 82 35W
Bradford, U.K. 33 53 47N 1 45W
Bradford, Pa., U.S.A. 156 41 58N 78 41W
Bradford, Vt., U.S.A. 162 43 59N 72 9W
Bradford-on-Avon 28 51 20N 2 15W
Brading 28 50 41N 1 9W
Bradley, Ark., U.S.A. 159 33 7N 93 39W
Bradley, Calif., U.S.A. 163 35 52N 120 48W
Bradley, S.D., U.S.A. 158 45 10N 97 40W
Bradley Institute 127 17 7S 31 25E
Bradore Bay 151 51 27N 57 18W
Bradshaw 136 15 21S 130 16E
Bradwell-on-Sea 29 51 44N 0 55E
Bradworthy 30 50 54N 4 22W
Brady 159 31 8N 99 25W
Brae 36 60 23N 1 20W
Brae, oilfield 19 58 45N 1 18E
Brædstrup 73 55 58N 9 37E
Braemar, Queens., Austral. 139 25 35S 152 20E
Braemar, S. Austral., Austral. 140 33 12S 139 35E
Braemar, U.K. 37 57 2N 3 20W
Braemar, dist. 37 57 2N 3 20W
Braemore, Grampian, U.K. 37 58 16N 3 33W
Braemore, Highland, U.K. 36 57 45N 5 2W
Braeriach Mt. 37 57 4N 3 44W
Braga 56 41 35N 8 25W
Braga □ 56 41 30N 8 30W
Bragado 172 35 2S 60 27W
Bragança, Brazil 170 1 0S 47 2W
Bragança, Port. 56 41 48N 6 50W
Bragança □ 56 41 30N 6 45W
Bragança Paulista 173 22 55S 46 32W
Brahmanbaria 98 23 50N 91 15E
Brahmani, R. 96 21 0N 85 15E
Brahmaputra, R. 98 26 30N 93 30E
Brahmaur 93 32 28N 76 32E
Braich-y-Pwll 31 52 47N 4 46W
Braidwood 141 35 27S 149 49E
Brailsford 33 52 58N 1 35W
Braine-l'Alleud 47 50 42N 4 23E
Braine-le-Comte 47 50 37N 4 8E
Brainerd 158 46 20N 94 10W
Braintree, U.K. 29 51 53N 0 34E
Braintree, U.S.A. 162 42 11N 71 0W
Braithwaite Pt. 138 12 5S 133 50E
Brak, R. 128 29 50S 23 10E
Brake 48 53 19N 8 30E
Brakel 46 51 49N 5 5E
Brakne-Hoby 73 56 12N 15 8E
Bräkne-Hoby 73 56 14N 15 6E
Brakpan 129 26 13S 28 20E
Brakwater 128 22 28S 17 3E
Brålanda 73 58 34N 12 21E
Brålanda 73 58 34N 12 21E
Brăila 70 45 19N 27 59E
Brăila □ 70 45 5N 27 30E
Bralorne 152 50 50N 123 15W
Bramford 29 52 5N 1 6E
Bramminge 73 55 28N 8 42E

**Bramon** **Brøttum**


| | | | |
|---|---|---|---|
| Bramon | 72 | 62 14N | 17 40 E |
| Brampton, Can. | 150 | 43 45N | 79 45W |
| Brampton, Cambs., U.K. | 29 | 52 19N | 0 13W |
| Brampton, Cumb., U.K. | 32 | 54 56N | 2 43W |
| Bramsche | 48 | 52 25N | 7 58 E |
| Bramshott | 29 | 51 5N | 0 47W |
| Bramwell | 138 | 12 8 S | 142 37 E |
| Brancaster | 29 | 52 58N | 0 40 E |
| Branco, Cabo | 170 | 7 9 S | 34 47W |
| Branco, R. | 174 | 0 0 | 61 15W |
| Brande | 73 | 55 57N | 9 8 E |
| Brandenburg | 48 | 52 24N | 12 33 E |
| Brander, Pass of | 34 | 56 25N | 5 10W |
| Branderburgh | 37 | 57 43N | 3 17W |
| Brandfort | 128 | 28 40 S | 26 30 E |
| Brandon, Can. | 153 | 49 50N | 99 57W |
| Brandon, Durham, U.K. | 33 | 54 46N | 1 37W |
| Brandon, Suffolk, U.K. | 29 | 52 27N | 0 37 E |
| Brandon, U.S.A. | 156 | 43 48N | 73 4W |
| Brandon, U.S.A. | 162 | 44 2N | 73 5W |
| Brandon B. | 39 | 52 17N | 10 8W |
| Brandon, Mt. | 39 | 52 15N | 10 15W |
| Brandon Pt. | 39 | 52 18N | 10 10W |
| Brandsen | 172 | 35 10 S | 58 15W |
| Brandval | 71 | 60 19N | 12 1 E |
| Brandvlei | 128 | 30 25 S | 20 30 E |
| Brandýs | 52 | 50 10N | 14 40 E |
| Branford | 162 | 41 15N | 72 48W |
| Braniewo | 54 | 54 25N | 19 50 E |
| Brännarp | 73 | 56 46N | 12 38 E |
| Bransby | 139 | 28 10 S | 142 0 E |
| Bransfield Str. | 13 | 63 0 S | 59 0W |
| Branson, Colo., U.S.A. | 159 | 37 4N | 103 53W |
| Branson, Mo., U.S.A. | 159 | 36 40N | 93 18W |
| Branston | 33 | 53 13N | 0 28W |
| Brantford | 150 | 43 15N | 80 15W |
| Brantôme | 44 | 45 22N | 0 39 E |
| Branxholme | 140 | 37 52 S | 141 49 E |
| Branxton | 141 | 32 38 S | 151 21 E |
| Branzi | 62 | 46 0N | 9 46 E |
| Bras d'or, L. | 151 | 45 50N | 60 50W |
| Brasiléia | 174 | 11 0 S | 68 45W |
| Brasilia | 171 | 15 47 S | 47 55 E |
| Braslav | 80 | 55 38N | 27 0 E |
| Braslovče | 63 | 46 21N | 15 3 E |
| Braşov | 70 | 45 38N | 25 35 E |
| Braşov □ | 70 | 45 45N | 25 15 E |
| Brass | 121 | 4 35N | 6 14 E |
| Brass, R. | 121 | 4 15N | 6 13 E |
| Brasschaat | 47 | 51 19N | 4 27 E |
| Brassey, Barisan | 102 | 5 0N | 117 15 E |
| Brassey Ra. | 137 | 25 8 S | 122 15 E |
| Brasstown Bald, Mt. | 157 | 34 54N | 83 45W |
| Brassus, Le | 50 | 46 35N | 6 13 E |
| Brasted | 29 | 51 16N | 0 8 E |
| Bratislava | 53 | 48 10N | 17 7 E |
| Bratsk | 77 | 56 10N | 101 30 E |
| Bratteborg | 73 | 57 37N | 14 4 E |
| Brattleboro | 162 | 42 53N | 72 37W |
| Brattvær | 71 | 63 25N | 7 48 E |
| Braţul Chilia, R. | 70 | 45 25N | 29 20 E |
| Braţul Sfîntu Gheorghe, R. | 70 | 45 0N | 29 20 E |
| Braţul Sulina, R. | 70 | 45 10N | 29 20 E |
| Bratunac | 66 | 44 13N | 19 21 E |
| Braunau | 52 | 48 15N | 13 3 E |
| Braunschweig | 48 | 52 17N | 10 28 E |
| Braunton | 30 | 51 6N | 4 9W |
| Brava | 91 | 1 20N | 44 8 E |
| Bråvikeh | 72 | 58 38N | 16 32 E |
| Bravo del Norte, R. | 164 | 30 30N | 105 0W |
| Brawley | 163 | 32 58N | 115 30W |
| Bray, France | 43 | 49 15N | 1 40 E |
| Bray, Ireland | 39 | 53 12N | 6 6W |
| Bray, U.K. | 29 | 51 30N | 0 42W |
| Bray Hd. | 39 | 51 52N | 10 26W |
| Bray, Mt. | 138 | 14 0N | 134 30 E |
| Bray-sur-Seine | 43 | 48 25N | 3 14 E |
| Brazeau, R. | 152 | 52 55N | 115 14W |
| Brazil | 156 | 39 30N | 87 8W |
| Brazil ■ | 174 | 5 0N | 20 0W |
| Brazilian Highlands | 170 | 18 0 S | 46 30W |
| Brazo Sur, R. | 172 | 25 30 S | 58 0W |
| Brazos, R. | 159 | 30 30N | 96 20W |
| Brazzaville | 124 | 4 9 S | 15 12 E |
| Brčko | 66 | 44 54N | 18 46 E |
| Breadalbane, Austral. | 138 | 23 50 S | 139 35 E |
| Breadalbane, U.K. | 34 | 56 30N | 4 15W |
| Breaden, L. | 137 | 25 51 S | 125 28 E |
| Breage | 30 | 50 6N | 5 17W |
| Breaksea Sd. | 143 | 45 35 S | 166 35 E |
| Bream Bay | 142 | 35 56 S | 174 28 E |
| Bream Head | 142 | 35 51 S | 174 36 E |
| Bream Tail | 142 | 36 3 S | 174 36 E |
| Breamish, R. | 35 | 55 30N | 1 55W |
| Breas | 172 | 25 29 S | 70 24W |
| Brebes | 103 | 6 52 S | 109 3 E |
| Brechin | 37 | 56 44N | 2 40W |
| Brecht | 47 | 51 21N | 4 38 E |
| Breckenridge, Colo., U.S.A. | 160 | 39 30N | 106 2W |
| Breckenridge, Minn., U.S.A. | 158 | 46 20N | 96 36W |
| Breckenridge, Tex., U.S.A. | 159 | 32 48N | 98 55W |
| Breckland | 23 | 52 30N | 0 40 E |
| Brecknock (□) | 26 | 51 58N | 3 25W |
| Břeclav | 53 | 48 46N | 16 53 E |
| Brecon | 31 | 51 57N | 3 23W |
| Brecon Beacons | 31 | 51 53N | 3 27W |
| Breda | 47 | 51 35N | 4 45 E |
| Bredaryd | 73 | 57 10N | 13 45 E |
| Bredasdorp | 128 | 34 33 S | 20 2 E |
| Bredbo | 141 | 35 58 S | 149 10 E |
| Brede | 29 | 50 56N | 0 37 E |
| Bredene | 47 | 51 14N | 2 59 E |
| Bredon Hill | 28 | 52 3N | 2 2W |
| Bredy | 84 | 52 26N | 60 21 E |
| Bree | 47 | 51 8N | 5 35 E |
| Breezand | 46 | 52 53N | 4 49 E |
| Bregalnica, R. | 66 | 41 50N | 22 20 E |
| Bregenz | 52 | 47 30N | 9 45 E |
| Bregning | 73 | 56 8N | 8 30 E |
| Bréhal | 42 | 48 53N | 1 30W |
| Bréhat, I. de | 42 | 48 51N | 3 0W |
| Breiðafjörður | 74 | 65 15N | 23 15W |
| Breil | 45 | 43 56N | 7 31 E |
| Breisach | 49 | 48 2N | 7 37 E |
| Brejinho de Nazaré | 170 | 11 1 S | 48 34W |
| Brejo | 170 | 3 41 S | 42 47W |
| Brekke | 71 | 61 1N | 5 26 E |
| Bremangerlandet | 71 | 61 51N | 5 0 E |
| Bremangerpollen | 71 | 61 51N | 5 0 E |
| Bremen | 48 | 53 4N | 8 47 E |
| Bremen □ | 48 | 53 6N | 8 46 E |
| Bremer I. | 138 | 12 5 S | 136 45 E |
| Bremerhaven | 48 | 53 34N | 8 35 E |
| Bremerton | 160 | 47 30N | 122 38W |
| Bremervörde | 48 | 53 28N | 9 10 E |
| Bremgarten | 51 | 47 21N | 8 21 E |
| Bremnes | 71 | 59 47N | 5 8 E |
| Bremsnes | 71 | 63 6N | 7 40 E |
| Brendon Hills | 28 | 51 6N | 3 25W |
| Brenes | 57 | 37 32N | 5 54W |
| Brenham | 159 | 30 5N | 96 27W |
| Brenner Pass | 52 | 47 0N | 11 30 E |
| Breno | 62 | 45 57N | 10 20 E |
| Brent, Can. | 150 | 46 2N | 78 29W |
| Brent, U.K. | 29 | 51 33N | 0 18W |
| Brent, oil and gasfield | 19 | 61 0N | 1 45 E |
| Brenta, R. | 63 | 45 11N | 12 18 E |
| Brentwood, U.K. | 29 | 51 37N | 0 19W |
| Brentwood, U.S.A. | 163 | 37 55N | 121 42W |
| Bréscia | 65 | 45 33N | 10 13 E |
| Breskens | 47 | 51 23N | 3 33 E |
| Breslau = Wrocław | 54 | 51 5N | 17 5 E |
| Bresle, R. | 43 | 50 4N | 1 21 E |
| Bresles | 43 | 49 25N | 2 13 E |
| Bressanone | 63 | 46 43N | 11 40 E |
| Bressay | 36 | 60 10N | 1 6W |
| Bressay I. | 36 | 60 10N | 1 5W |
| Bressay Sd. | 36 | 60 8N | 1 10W |
| Bresse, La | 43 | 48 0N | 6 53 E |
| Bresse, Plaine de | 43 | 46 20N | 5 10 E |
| Bressuire | 42 | 46 51N | 0 30W |
| Brest, France | 42 | 48 24N | 4 31W |
| Brest, U.S.S.R. | 80 | 52 10N | 23 40 E |
| Bretagne | 42 | 48 0N | 3 0W |
| Bretçu | 70 | 46 7N | 26 18 E |
| Breteuil | 43 | 49 38N | 2 18 E |
| Breton | 152 | 53 7N | 114 28W |
| Breton Sd. | 159 | 29 40N | 89 12W |
| Brett, C. | 142 | 35 10 S | 174 20 E |
| Bretten | 49 | 49 2N | 8 43 E |
| Bretuil | 42 | 48 50N | 0 53 E |
| Breukelen | 46 | 52 10N | 5 0 E |
| Brevard | 157 | 35 19N | 82 42W |
| Breves | 170 | 1 40 S | 50 29W |
| Brevik | 71 | 59 4N | 9 42 E |
| Brewarrina | 139 | 30 0 S | 146 51 E |
| Brewer | 151 | 44 43N | 68 50W |
| Brewer, Mt. | 163 | 36 44N | 118 28W |
| Brewerton | 162 | 43 14N | 76 9W |
| Brewood | 28 | 52 41N | 2 10W |
| Brewster, N.Y., U.S.A. | 162 | 41 23N | 73 37W |
| Brewster, Wash., U.S.A. | 160 | 48 10N | 119 51W |
| Brewster, Kap | 12 | 70 7N | 22 0W |
| Brewton | 157 | 31 9N | 87 2W |
| Breyten | 129 | 26 16 S | 30 0 E |
| Breytovo | 81 | 58 18N | 37 50 E |
| Brézina | 118 | 33 4N | 1 14 E |
| Březnice | 52 | 49 32N | 13 57 E |
| Breznik | 66 | 42 44N | 22 50 E |
| Brezno | 53 | 48 50N | 19 40 E |
| Bria | 117 | 6 30N | 21 58 E |
| Briançon | 45 | 44 54N | 6 39 E |
| Briare | 43 | 47 38N | 2 45 E |
| Bribbaree | 141 | 34 10 S | 147 51 E |
| Bribie I. | 139 | 27 0 S | 152 58 E |
| Brickaville | 129 | 18 49 S | 49 4 E |
| Bricon | 43 | 48 5N | 5 0 E |
| Bricquebec | 42 | 49 29N | 1 39W |
| Bride | 32 | 54 24N | 4 23W |
| Bridestowe | 30 | 50 41N | 4 7W |
| Bridge | 29 | 51 14N | 1 8 E |
| Bridge of Allan | 35 | 56 9N | 3 57W |
| Bridge of Don | 37 | 57 10N | 2 8W |
| Bridge of Earn | 35 | 56 20N | 3 25W |
| Bridge of Orchy | 34 | 56 29N | 4 48W |
| Bridge of Weir | 34 | 55 51N | 4 35W |
| Bridge, R. | 152 | 50 50N | 122 40W |
| Bridgehampton | 162 | 40 56N | 72 18W |
| Bridgend, Islay, U.K. | 34 | 55 46N | 6 15W |
| Bridgend, Mid Glam., U.K. | 31 | 51 30N | 3 35W |
| Bridgeport, Calif., U.S.A. | 163 | 38 14N | 119 15W |
| Bridgeport, Conn., U.S.A. | 162 | 41 12N | 73 12W |
| Bridgeport, Nebr., U.S.A. | 158 | 41 42N | 103 10W |
| Bridgeport, Tex., U.S.A. | 159 | 33 15N | 97 45W |
| Bridger | 160 | 45 20N | 108 58W |
| Bridgeton | 162 | 39 29N | 75 10W |
| Bridgetown, Austral. | 137 | 33 58 S | 116 7 E |
| Bridgetown, Barbados | 167 | 13 0N | 59 30W |
| Bridgetown, Can. | 151 | 44 55N | 65 18W |
| Bridgetown, Ireland | 39 | 52 13N | 6 33W |
| Bridgeville | 162 | 38 45N | 75 36W |
| Bridgewater, Austral. | 140 | 36 36 S | 143 59 E |
| Bridgewater, Can. | 151 | 44 25N | 64 31W |
| Bridgewater, Mass., U.S.A. | 162 | 41 59N | 70 56W |
| Bridgewater, N.Y., U.S.A. | 162 | 42 58N | 75 15W |
| Bridgewater, S.D., U.S.A. | 158 | 43 34N | 97 29W |
| Bridgewater, C. | 140 | 38 23 S | 141 23 E |
| Bridgnorth | 28 | 52 33N | 2 25W |
| Bridgwater | 28 | 51 7N | 3 0W |
| Bridgwater B. | 28 | 51 15N | 3 15W |
| Bridlington | 33 | 54 6N | 0 11W |
| Bridlington B. | 33 | 54 4N | 0 10W |
| Bridport, Austral. | 138 | 40 59 S | 147 23 E |
| Bridport, U.K. | 28 | 50 43N | 2 45W |
| Brie-Comte-Robert | 43 | 48 40N | 2 35 E |
| Brie, Plaine de | 43 | 48 35N | 3 10 E |
| Briec | 42 | 48 6N | 4 0W |
| Brielle | 46 | 51 54N | 4 10 E |
| Brienne-le-Château | 43 | 48 24N | 4 30 E |
| Brienon | 43 | 48 0N | 3 35 E |
| Brienz | 50 | 46 46N | 8 2 E |
| Brienzersee | 50 | 46 44N | 7 53 E |
| Brierfield | 32 | 53 49N | 2 15W |
| Brierley Hill | 28 | 52 29N | 2 7W |
| Briey | 43 | 49 14N | 5 57 E |
| Brig | 50 | 46 18N | 7 59 E |
| Brigantine | 162 | 39 24N | 74 22W |
| Brigg | 33 | 53 33N | 0 30W |
| Briggsdale | 158 | 40 40N | 104 20W |
| Brigham City | 160 | 41 30N | 112 1W |
| Brighouse | 33 | 53 42N | 1 47W |
| Brighstone | 29 | 50 38N | 1 36W |
| Bright | 141 | 36 42 S | 146 56 E |
| Brightlingsea | 29 | 51 49N | 1 1 E |
| Brighton, Austral. | 140 | 35 5 S | 138 30 E |
| Brighton, Can. | 150 | 44 2N | 77 44W |
| Brighton, U.K. | 29 | 50 50N | 0 9W |
| Brighton, U.S.A. | 158 | 39 59N | 104 50W |
| Brightstone | 28 | 50 38N | 1 23W |
| Brightwater | 143 | 41 22 S | 173 9 E |
| Brignogan-Plage | 42 | 48 40N | 4 20W |
| Brignoles | 45 | 43 25N | 6 5 E |
| Brigstock | 29 | 52 27N | 0 38W |
| Brihuega | 58 | 40 45N | 2 52W |
| Brikama | 120 | 13 15N | 16 45W |
| Brill | 28 | 51 49N | 1 3W |
| Brilliant | 152 | 49 19N | 117 38W |
| Brilon | 48 | 51 23N | 8 32 E |
| Brim | 140 | 36 3 S | 142 27 E |
| Brimfield | 28 | 52 18N | 2 42W |
| Bríndisi | 65 | 40 39N | 17 55 E |
| Brinkley | 159 | 34 55N | 91 15W |
| Brinklow | 28 | 52 25N | 1 22W |
| Brinkworth, Austral. | 140 | 33 42 S | 138 26 E |
| Brinkworth, U.K. | 28 | 51 33N | 1 59W |
| Brinyan | 37 | 59 8N | 3 0W |
| Brion I. | 151 | 47 46N | 61 26W |
| Brionne | 42 | 49 11N | 0 43 E |
| Brionski, I. | 63 | 44 55N | 13 45 E |
| Brioude | 44 | 45 18N | 3 23 E |
| Briouze | 42 | 48 42N | 0 23W |
| Brisbane | 139 | 27 25 S | 153 2 E |
| Brisbane, R. | 139 | 27 24 S | 153 9 E |
| Brisignella | 63 | 44 14N | 11 46 E |
| Bristol, U.K. | 28 | 51 26N | 2 35W |
| Bristol, Conn., U.S.A. | 162 | 41 44N | 72 57W |
| Bristol, Pa., U.S.A. | 162 | 40 6N | 74 52W |
| Bristol, R.I., U.S.A. | 162 | 41 40N | 71 15W |
| Bristol, S.D., U.S.A. | 158 | 45 25N | 97 43W |
| Bristol B. | 147 | 58 0N | 160 0W |
| Bristol Channel | 30 | 51 18N | 4 30W |
| Bristol I. | 13 | 58 45 S | 28 0W |
| Bristol L. | 161 | 34 23N | 116 0W |
| Briston | 29 | 52 52N | 1 4 E |
| Bristow | 159 | 35 5N | 96 28W |
| British Antarctic Territory | 13 | 66 0 S | 45 0W |
| British Columbia □ | 152 | 55 0N | 125 15W |
| British Guiana = Guyana | 174 | 5 0N | 59 0W |
| British Honduras = Belize | 165 | 17 0N | 88 30W |
| British Isles | 16 | 55 0N | 4 0W |
| Briton Ferry | 31 | 51 37N | 3 50W |
| Brits | 129 | 25 37 S | 27 48 E |
| Britstown | 128 | 30 37 S | 23 30 E |
| Britt | 150 | 45 46N | 80 34W |
| Brittany = Bretagne | 42 | 48 0N | 3 0W |
| Brittas | 39 | 53 14N | 6 29W |
| Brittatorp | 73 | 57 3N | 14 58 E |
| Britton | 158 | 45 50N | 97 47W |
| Brive-la-Gaillarde | 44 | 45 10N | 1 32 E |
| Briviesca | 58 | 42 32N | 3 19W |
| Brixham | 30 | 50 24N | 3 31W |
| Brixton | 138 | 23 32 S | 144 57 E |
| Brixworth | 29 | 52 20N | 0 54W |
| Brize Norton | 28 | 51 46N | 1 35W |
| Brlik, U.S.S.R. | 76 | 44 0N | 74 5 E |
| Brlik, Kazakh S.S.R., U.S.S.R. | 85 | 44 5N | 73 31 E |
| Brlik, Kazakh S.S.R., U.S.S.R. | 85 | 43 40N | 73 49 E |
| Brno | 53 | 49 10N | 16 35 E |
| Bro | 72 | 59 13N | 13 2 E |
| Broach = Bharuch | 96 | 21 47N | 73 0 E |
| Broad Arrow | 137 | 30 23 S | 121 15 E |
| Broad B. | 36 | 58 14N | 6 16W |
| Broad Chalke | 28 | 51 2N | 1 54W |
| Broad Clyst | 30 | 50 46N | 3 27W |
| Broad Haven, Ireland | 38 | 54 20N | 9 55W |
| Broad Haven, U.K. | 31 | 51 46N | 5 6W |
| Broad Law, Mt. | 35 | 55 30N | 3 22W |
| Broad, R. | 157 | 34 30N | 81 26W |
| Broad Sd., Austral. | 138 | 22 0 S | 149 45 E |
| Broad Sd., U.K. | 30 | 49 56N | 6 19W |
| Broadalbin | 162 | 43 3N | 74 12W |
| Broadford, Austral. | 141 | 37 14 S | 145 4 E |
| Broadford, Clare, Ireland | 39 | 52 48N | 8 38W |
| Broadford, Limerick, Ireland | 39 | 52 21N | 8 59W |
| Broadford, U.K. | 36 | 57 14N | 5 55W |
| Broadhembury | 30 | 50 49N | 3 16W |
| Broadhurst Ra. | 136 | 22 30 S | 122 30 E |
| Broads, The | 29 | 52 45N | 1 30 E |
| Broadsound Ra. | 133 | 22 50 S | 149 30 E |
| Broadstairs | 29 | 51 21N | 1 28 E |
| Broadus | 158 | 45 28N | 105 27W |
| Broadview | 153 | 50 22N | 102 35W |
| Broadway, Ireland | 39 | 52 13N | 6 23W |
| Broadway, U.K. | 28 | 52 2N | 1 51W |
| Broadwindsor | 28 | 50 49N | 2 49W |
| Broager | 73 | 54 53N | 9 40 E |
| Broaryd | 73 | 57 7N | 13 15 E |
| Brochet, Man., Can. | 153 | 57 53N | 101 40W |
| Brochet, Manitoba, Can. | 153 | 57 55N | 101 40W |
| Brochet, Québec, Can. | 150 | 47 12N | 72 42W |
| Brochet, L. | 153 | 58 36N | 101 35W |
| Brock | 153 | 51 26N | 108 43W |
| Brocken | 48 | 51 48N | 10 40 E |
| Brockenhurst | 28 | 50 49N | 1 34W |
| Brocklehurst | 141 | 32 9 S | 148 38 E |
| Brockman Mt. | 137 | 22 25 S | 117 15 E |
| Brockville | 150 | 44 35N | 75 41W |
| Brockway | 158 | 47 18N | 105 46W |
| Brockworth | 28 | 51 51N | 2 9W |
| Brod | 66 | 41 35N | 21 17 E |
| Brodarevo | 66 | 43 14N | 19 44 E |
| Brodeur Pen. | 149 | 72 30N | 88 10W |
| Brodick | 34 | 55 34N | 5 9W |
| Brodnica | 54 | 53 15N | 19 25 E |
| Brodokalmak | 84 | 55 35N | 62 6 E |
| Brody | 80 | 50 5N | 25 10 E |
| Broechem | 47 | 51 11N | 4 38 E |
| Broek | 46 | 52 26N | 5 0 E |
| Broek op Langedijk | 46 | 52 41N | 4 49 E |
| Brogan | 160 | 44 14N | 117 32W |
| Broglie | 42 | 49 0N | 0 30 E |
| Brok | 54 | 52 43N | 21 52 E |
| Broke Inlet | 137 | 34 55 S | 116 25 E |
| Broken Bank, gasfield | 19 | 53 20N | 2 4 E |
| Broken Bow, Nebr., U.S.A. | 158 | 41 25N | 99 35W |
| Broken Bow, Okla., U.S.A. | 159 | 34 2N | 94 43W |
| Broken Hill | 140 | 31 58 S | 141 29 E |
| Broken Hill = Kabwe | 127 | 14 27 S | 28 28 E |
| Brokind | 73 | 58 13N | 15 42 E |
| Bromborough | 32 | 53 20N | 3 0W |
| Bromham | 28 | 51 23N | 2 3W |
| Bromhead | 153 | 49 18N | 103 40W |
| Bromley | 29 | 51 20N | 0 5 E |
| Bromölla | 73 | 56 5N | 14 28 E |
| Brompton | 33 | 54 22N | 1 25W |
| Bromsgrove | 28 | 52 20N | 2 3W |
| Bromyard | 28 | 52 12N | 2 30W |
| Brønderslev | 73 | 57 16N | 9 57 E |
| Brong Ahafo | 120 | 7 50N | 2 0 E |
| Bronkhorstspruit | 129 | 25 46 S | 28 45 E |
| Bronnitsy | 81 | 55 27N | 38 10 E |
| Bronte, Italy | 65 | 37 48N | 14 49 E |
| Bronte, U.S.A. | 159 | 31 54N | 100 18W |
| Bronte Park | 138 | 42 8 S | 146 30 E |
| Brookeborough | 38 | 54 19N | 7 23W |
| Brookfield | 158 | 39 50N | 93 4W |
| Brookhaven | 159 | 31 40N | 90 25W |
| Brookings, Oreg., U.S.A. | 160 | 42 4N | 124 10W |
| Brookings, S.D., U.S.A. | 158 | 44 20N | 96 45W |
| Brooklands | 138 | 18 5 S | 144 0 E |
| Brookmere | 152 | 49 52N | 120 53W |
| Brooks | 152 | 50 35N | 111 55W |
| Brooks B. | 152 | 50 15N | 127 55W |
| Brooks L. | 153 | 61 55N | 106 35W |
| Brooks Ra. | 147 | 68 40N | 147 0W |
| Brooksville | 157 | 28 32N | 82 21W |
| Brookton | 137 | 32 22 S | 116 57 E |
| Brookville | 156 | 39 25N | 85 0W |
| Brooloo | 139 | 26 30 S | 152 43 E |
| Broom, L. | 36 | 57 55N | 5 15W |
| Broome | 136 | 18 0 S | 122 15 E |
| Broomehill | 137 | 31 51 S | 117 39 E |
| Broomfield | 28 | 51 46N | 0 28 E |
| Broomhill | 35 | 55 19N | 1 36W |
| Broons | 42 | 48 20N | 2 16W |
| Brora | 37 | 58 0N | 3 50W |
| Brora L. | 37 | 58 3N | 3 58W |
| Brora, R. | 37 | 58 4N | 3 52W |
| Brosarp | 73 | 55 44N | 14 8 E |
| Brösarp | 73 | 55 43N | 14 6 E |
| Broseley | 28 | 52 36N | 2 30W |
| Brosna, R. | 39 | 53 8N | 8 0W |
| Broşteni | 70 | 47 14N | 25 43 E |
| Brotas de Macaúbas | 171 | 12 0 S | 42 38W |
| Brothers | 160 | 43 56N | 120 39W |
| Brothertoft | 33 | 53 0N | 0 5W |
| Brotton | 33 | 54 34N | 0 55W |
| Brøttum | 71 | 61 2N | 10 34 E |

Brough Bura


| | | | |
|---|---|---|---|
| Brough, Cumbria, U.K. | 32 | 54 32N | 2 19W |
| Brough, Humberside, U.K. | 33 | 53 44N | 0 35W |
| Brough Hd. | 37 | 59 8N | 3 20W |
| Broughams Gate | 140 | 30 51S | 140 59E |
| Broughshane | 38 | 54 54N | 6 12W |
| Broughton, Austral. | 138 | 20 10S | 146 20E |
| Broughton, Borders, U.K. | 35 | 55 37N | 3 25W |
| Broughton, Humberside, U.K. | 33 | 53 33N | 0 36W |
| Broughton, Northampton, U.K. | 29 | 52 22N | 0 45W |
| Broughton, Yorkshire, U.K. | 33 | 54 26N | 1 8W |
| Broughton-in-Furness | 32 | 54 17N | 3 12W |
| Broughty Ferry | 35 | 56 29N | 2 50W |
| Broumov | 53 | 50 35N | 16 20E |
| Brouwershaven | 46 | 51 45N | 3 55E |
| Brouwershavensche Gat | 46 | 51 46N | 3 50E |
| Brovary | 80 | 50 34N | 30 48E |
| Brovst | 73 | 57 6N | 9 31E |
| Browerville | 158 | 46 3N | 94 50W |
| Brown, Mt. | 140 | 32 30S | 138 0E |
| Brown, Pt. | 139 | 32 32S | 133 50E |
| Brown Willy, Mt. | 30 | 50 35N | 4 34W |
| Brownfield | 159 | 33 10N | 102 15W |
| Browngrove | 38 | 53 33N | 8 49W |
| Brownhills | 28 | 52 38N | 1 57W |
| Browning | 160 | 48 35N | 113 10W |
| Brownlee | 153 | 50 43N | 106 1W |
| Browns Bay | 142 | 36 40S | 174 40E |
| Brownstown Hd. | 39 | 52 8N | 7 8W |
| Brownsville, Oreg., U.S.A. | 160 | 44 29N | 123 0W |
| Brownsville, Tenn., U.S.A. | 159 | 35 35N | 89 15W |
| Brownsville, Tex., U.S.A. | 159 | 25 56N | 97 25W |
| Brownwood | 159 | 31 45N | 99 0W |
| Brownwood, L. | 159 | 31 51N | 98 35W |
| Browse I. | 136 | 14 7S | 123 33E |
| Broxburn | 35 | 55 56N | 3 23W |
| Broye, R. | 50 | 46 52N | 6 58E |
| Brozas | 57 | 39 37N | 6 47W |
| Bruas | 101 | 4 31N | 100 46E |
| Bruay-en-Artois | 43 | 50 29N | 2 33E |
| Bruce Bay | 143 | 43 35S | 169 42E |
| Bruce, gasfield | 19 | 59 45N | 1 32E |
| Bruce Mines | 150 | 46 20N | 83 45W |
| Bruce, Mt. | 136 | 22 37S | 118 8E |
| Bruce Rock | 137 | 31 52S | 118 8E |
| Bruchsal | 49 | 49 9N | 8 39E |
| Bruck a.d. Leitha | 53 | 48 1N | 16 47E |
| Bruck a.d. Mur | 52 | 47 24N | 15 16E |
| Brückenau | 49 | 50 17N | 9 48E |
| Brŭdiceni | 70 | 45 3N | 23 4E |
| Brue, R. | 28 | 51 10N | 2 59W |
| Bruernish Pt. | 36 | 57 0N | 7 22W |
| Bruff | 39 | 52 29N | 8 35W |
| Brugelette | 47 | 50 35N | 3 52E |
| Bruges = Brugge | 47 | 51 13N | 3 13E |
| Brugg | 50 | 47 29N | 8 11E |
| Brugge | 47 | 51 13N | 3 13E |
| Brühl | 48 | 50 49N | 6 51E |
| Bruinisse | 47 | 51 40N | 4 5E |
| Brûlé | 152 | 53 15N | 117 58W |
| Brûlon | 42 | 47 58N | 0 15W |
| Brûly | 47 | 49 58N | 4 32E |
| Brumado | 171 | 14 14S | 41 40W |
| Brumado, R. | 171 | 14 13S | 41 40W |
| Brumath | 43 | 48 43N | 7 40E |
| Brummen | 46 | 52 5N | 6 10E |
| Brumunddal | 71 | 60 53N | 10 56E |
| Brunchilly | 138 | 18 50S | 134 30E |
| Brundidge | 157 | 31 43N | 85 45W |
| Bruneau | 160 | 42 57N | 115 55W |
| Bruneau, R. | 160 | 42 45N | 115 50W |
| Brunei = Bandar Seri Begawan | 102 | 4 52N | 115 0E |
| Brunei ■ | 102 | 4 50N | 115 0E |
| Brunette Downs | 138 | 18 40S | 135 55E |
| Brunflo | 72 | 63 5N | 14 50E |
| Brunico | 63 | 46 50N | 11 55E |
| Brünig, Col de | 50 | 46 46N | 8 8E |
| Bruhkeberg | 71 | 59 26N | 8 28E |
| Brunna | 72 | 59 52N | 17 25E |
| Brunnen | 51 | 46 59N | 8 37E |
| Brunner | 143 | 42 27S | 171 20E |
| Brunner, L. | 143 | 42 27S | 171 20E |
| Brunnsvik | 72 | 60 12N | 15 8E |
| Bruno | 153 | 52 20N | 105 30W |
| Brunsberg | 72 | 59 38N | 12 52E |
| Brunsbüttelkoog | 48 | 53 52N | 9 13E |
| Brunssum | 47 | 50 57N | 5 59E |
| Brunswick, Ga., U.S.A. | 157 | 31 10N | 81 30W |
| Brunswick, Md., U.S.A. | 156 | 39 20N | 77 38W |
| Brunswick, Me., U.S.A. | 151 | 43 53N | 69 50W |
| Brunswick, Mo., U.S.A. | 158 | 39 26N | 93 10W |
| Brunswick = Braunschweig | 48 | 52 17N | 10 28E |
| Brunswick B. | 136 | 15 15S | 124 50E |
| Brunswick Junction | 137 | 33 15S | 115 50E |
| Brunswick, Pen. de | 176 | 53 30S | 71 30W |
| Bruntál | 53 | 50 0N | 17 27E |
| Brunton | 35 | 55 2N | 2 6W |
| Bruny I. | 138 | 43 20S | 147 15E |
| Bruree | 39 | 52 25N | 8 40W |
| Brus Laguna | 166 | 15 47N | 84 35W |
| Brusartsi | 66 | 43 40N | 23 5E |
| Brush | 158 | 40 17N | 103 33W |
| Brusio | 51 | 46 14N | 10 8E |
| Brusque | 173 | 27 5S | 49 0W |
| Brussel | 47 | 50 51N | 4 21E |
| Brussels = Bruxelles | 47 | 50 51N | 4 21E |
| Brustem | 47 | 50 48N | 5 14E |
| Bruthen | 141 | 37 42S | 147 50E |
| Bruton | 28 | 51 6N | 2 28W |
| Bruvik | 71 | 60 29N | 5 40E |
| Bruxelles | 47 | 50 51N | 4 21E |
| Bruyères | 43 | 48 10N | 6 40E |
| Brwinow | 54 | 52 9N | 20 40E |
| Bryagovo | 67 | 41 58N | 25 8E |
| Bryan, Ohio, U.S.A. | 156 | 41 30N | 84 30W |
| Bryan, Texas, U.S.A. | 159 | 30 40N | 96 27W |
| Bryan, Mt. | 140 | 33 30S | 139 0E |
| Bryansk | 80 | 53 13N | 34 25E |
| Bryanskoye | 83 | 44 9N | 47 10E |
| Bryant | 58 | 44 39N | 97 26W |
| Bryggja | 71 | 61 56N | 5 27E |
| Bryher I. | 30 | 49 57N | 6 21W |
| Brymbo | 31 | 53 4N | 3 5W |
| Brynamman | 31 | 51 49N | 3 52W |
| Bryncethin | 31 | 51 33N | 3 34W |
| Bryne | 71 | 58 44N | 5 38E |
| Brynmawr | 31 | 51 48N | 3 11W |
| Bryrup | 73 | 56 2N | 9 30E |
| Bryson City | 157 | 35 28N | 83 25W |
| Bryte | 163 | 38 35N | 121 33W |
| Brza Palanka | 66 | 44 28N | 22 37E |
| Brzava, R. | 66 | 45 21N | 20 45E |
| Brzeg | 54 | 50 52N | 17 30E |
| Brzeg Dln | 54 | 51 16N | 16 41E |
| Brzesko | 54 | 49 59N | 20 34E |
| Brześć Kujawski | 54 | 52 36N | 18 55E |
| Brzeszcze | 54 | 49 59N | 19 10E |
| Brzeziny | 54 | 51 49N | 19 42E |
| Brzozów | 54 | 49 41N | 22 3E |
| Bu Athiah | 119 | 30 1N | 15 30E |
| Bu Craa | 116 | 26 45N | 17 2E |
| Buapinang | 103 | 4 40S | 121 30E |
| Buayan | 103 | 5 3N | 125 28E |
| Buba | 120 | 11 40N | 14 59W |
| Bubanza | 126 | 3 6S | 29 23E |
| Bucaramanga | 174 | 7 0N | 73 0W |
| Buccaneer Arch. | 136 | 16 7S | 123 20E |
| Bucchiánico | 63 | 42 20N | 14 10E |
| Bucecea | 70 | 47 47N | 26 28E |
| Bŭceşti | 70 | 46 50N | 27 11E |
| Buchach | 80 | 49 5N | 25 25E |
| Buchan, Austral. | 141 | 37 30S | 148 12E |
| Buchan, U.K. | 37 | 57 32N | 2 8W |
| Buchan Ness | 37 | 57 29N | 1 48W |
| Buchan, oilfield | 19 | 57 55N | 0 0 |
| Buchanan, Can. | 153 | 51 40N | 102 45W |
| Buchanan, Liberia | 120 | 5 57N | 10 2W |
| Buchanan Cr. | 138 | 17 10S | 138 6E |
| Buchanan, L., Queens., Austral. | 138 | 21 35S | 145 52E |
| Buchanan, L., W. Australia, Austral. | 137 | 25 33S | 123 2E |
| Buchanan, L., U.S.A. | 159 | 30 50N | 98 25W |
| Buchans | 151 | 49 50N | 56 52W |
| Bucharest = Bucureşti | 70 | 44 27N | 26 10E |
| Buchholz | 48 | 53 19N | 9 51E |
| Buchloe | 49 | 48 3N | 10 45E |
| Buchlyvie | 34 | 56 7N | 4 20W |
| Buchon, Pt. | 163 | 35 15N | 120 54W |
| Buchs | 51 | 47 10N | 9 28E |
| Buck Hill Falls | 162 | 41 11N | 75 16W |
| Buck, The, mt. | 37 | 57 19N | 3 0W |
| Buckden | 29 | 52 17N | 0 16W |
| Bückeburg | 48 | 52 16N | 9 2E |
| Buckeye | 161 | 33 28N | 112 40W |
| Buckfastleigh | 30 | 50 28N | 3 47W |
| Buckhannon | 156 | 39 2N | 80 10W |
| Buckhaven | 35 | 56 10N | 3 2W |
| Buckie | 37 | 57 40N | 2 58W |
| Buckingham, Can. | 150 | 45 37N | 75 24W |
| Buckingham, U.K. | 29 | 52 0N | 0 59W |
| Buckingham □ | 29 | 51 50N | 0 55W |
| Buckingham B. | 138 | 12 10S | 135 40E |
| Buckingham Can. | 97 | 14 0N | 80 5E |
| Buckinguy | 139 | 31 3S | 147 30E |
| Buckland | 147 | 66 0N | 161 5W |
| Buckland Brewer | 30 | 50 56N | 4 14W |
| Buckle Hd. | 136 | 14 26S | 127 52E |
| Buckleboo | 140 | 32 54S | 136 12E |
| Buckley, U.K. | 31 | 53 10N | 3 5W |
| Buckley, U.S.A. | 160 | 47 10N | 122 2W |
| Bucklin | 159 | 37 37N | 99 40W |
| Bucksburn | 37 | 57 10N | 2 10W |
| Bucquoy | 43 | 50 9N | 2 43E |
| Buctouche | 151 | 46 30N | 64 45W |
| Bucureşti | 70 | 44 27N | 26 10E |
| Bucyrus | 156 | 40 48N | 83 0W |
| Budacul, Munte | 41 | 47 5N | 25 40E |
| Budafok | 53 | 47 26N | 19 2E |
| Budalin | 98 | 22 20N | 95 10E |
| Budapest | 53 | 47 29N | 19 5E |
| Budaun | 95 | 28 5N | 79 10E |
| Budd Coast | 13 | 67 0S | 112 0E |
| Buddabadah | 141 | 31 56S | 147 14E |
| Buddon Ness | 35 | 56 29N | 2 42W |
| Buddusò | 64 | 40 35N | 9 18E |
| Bude | 30 | 50 49N | 4 33W |
| Bude Bay | 30 | 50 50N | 4 40W |
| Budel | 47 | 51 17N | 5 34E |
| Budeşti | 70 | 44 13N | 26 30E |
| Budge Budge | 95 | 22 30N | 88 25E |
| Budgewoi Lake | 141 | 33 13S | 151 34E |
| Budia | 58 | 40 38N | 2 46W |
| Búdir | 74 | 64 49N | 23 23W |
| Budjala | 124 | 2 50N | 19 40E |
| Budle B. | 35 | 55 37N | 1 45W |
| Budleigh Salterton | 30 | 50 37N | 3 19W |
| Búdrio | 63 | 44 31N | 11 31E |
| Budva | 66 | 42 17N | 18 50E |
| Budzyn | 54 | 52 54N | 16 59E |
| Buea | 121 | 4 10N | 9 9E |
| Buellton | 163 | 34 37N | 120 12W |
| Buena | 162 | 39 31N | 74 56W |
| Buena Vista, Colo., U.S.A. | 161 | 38 56N | 106 6W |
| Buena Vista, Va., U.S.A. | 156 | 37 47N | 79 23W |
| Buena Vista L. | 163 | 35 15N | 119 21W |
| Buenaventura | 164 | 29 50N | 107 30W |
| Buenaventura, B. de | 174 | 3 48N | 77 17W |
| Buendia, Pantano de | 58 | 40 25N | 2 43W |
| Buenópolis | 171 | 17 54S | 44 11W |
| Buenos Aires, Argent. | 172 | 34 30S | 58 20W |
| Buenos Aires, Colomb. | 174 | 1 36N | 73 18W |
| Buenos Aires, C. Rica | 166 | 9 10N | 83 20W |
| Buenos Aires □ | 172 | 36 30S | 60 0W |
| Buenos Aires, Lago | 176 | 46 35S | 72 30W |
| Buesaco | 174 | 1 23N | 77 9W |
| Buffalo, Can. | 153 | 50 49N | 110 42W |
| Buffalo, Mo., U.S.A. | 159 | 37 40N | 93 5W |
| Buffalo, Okla., U.S.A. | 159 | 36 55N | 99 42W |
| Buffalo, S.D., U.S.A. | 159 | 45 39N | 103 31W |
| Buffalo, Wyo., U.S.A. | 160 | 44 25N | 106 50W |
| Buffalo Center | 147 | 64 2N | 145 50W |
| Buffalo Head Hills | 152 | 57 25N | 115 55W |
| Buffalo L. | 152 | 52 27N | 112 54W |
| Buffalo Narrows | 153 | 55 51N | 108 29W |
| Buffalo, R. | 152 | 57 50N | 117 1W |
| Buffels, R. | 129 | 29 36S | 17 15E |
| Buford | 157 | 34 5N | 84 0W |
| Bug, R., Poland | 54 | 51 20N | 23 40E |
| Bug, R., U.S.S.R. | 82 | 48 0N | 31 0E |
| Buga | 174 | 4 0N | 77 0W |
| Buganda □ | 126 | 0 0N | 31 30E |
| Buganga | 126 | 0 25N | 32 0E |
| Bugeat | 44 | 45 36N | 1 55E |
| Buggenhout | 47 | 51 1N | 4 12E |
| Buggs I. L. | 157 | 36 20N | 78 30W |
| Buglawton | 32 | 53 12N | 2 11W |
| Bugle | 30 | 50 23N | 4 46W |
| Bugojno | 66 | 44 2N | 17 25E |
| Bugsuk, I. | 102 | 8 15N | 117 15E |
| Bugue, Le | 44 | 44 55N | 0 56E |
| Bugulma | 84 | 54 33N | 52 48E |
| Buguma | 121 | 4 42N | 6 55E |
| Bugun Shara | 105 | 49 0N | 104 0E |
| Buguruslan | 84 | 53 39N | 52 26E |
| Buheirat-Murrat-el-Kubra | 122 | 30 15N | 32 40E |
| Buhl, Idaho, U.S.A. | 160 | 42 35N | 114 54W |
| Buhl, Minn., U.S.A. | 158 | 47 30N | 92 46W |
| Buhûeşti | 70 | 46 47N | 27 32E |
| Buhuşi | 70 | 46 41N | 26 45E |
| Buick | 159 | 37 8N | 91 2W |
| Bŭicoi | 70 | 45 3N | 25 52E |
| Buie L. | 34 | 56 20N | 5 55W |
| Bŭileşti | 70 | 44 01N | 23 20E |
| Builth Wells | 31 | 52 10N | 3 26W |
| Buina Qara | 93 | 36 20N | 67 0E |
| Buinsk | 81 | 55 0N | 48 18E |
| Buíque | 170 | 8 37S | 37 9W |
| Buis-les-Baronnies | 45 | 44 17N | 5 16E |
| Buit, L. | 151 | 50 59N | 63 13W |
| Buitenpost | 46 | 53 15N | 6 9E |
| Buitrago | 56 | 41 0N | 3 38W |
| Bujalance | 57 | 37 54N | 4 23W |
| Buján | 56 | 42 59N | 8 36W |
| Bujaraloz | 58 | 41 29N | 0 10W |
| Buje | 63 | 45 24N | 13 39E |
| Buji | 135 | 9 8S | 142 11E |
| Bujnurd | 93 | 37 35N | 57 15E |
| Bujumbura (Usumbura) | 126 | 3 16S | 29 18E |
| Bük | 53 | 47 22N | 16 45E |
| Buk | 54 | 52 21N | 16 17E |
| Buka I. | 135 | 5 10S | 154 35E |
| Bukachacha | 77 | 52 55N | 116 50E |
| Bukama | 127 | 9 10S | 25 50E |
| Bukandula | 126 | 0 13N | 31 50E |
| Bukavu | 126 | 2 20S | 28 52E |
| Bukene | 126 | 4 15S | 32 48E |
| Bukhara | 85 | 39 48N | 64 25E |
| Bukima | 126 | 1 50S | 33 25E |
| Bukit Mertajam | 101 | 5 22N | 100 28E |
| Bukittinggi | 102 | 0 20S | 100 20E |
| Bukkapatnam | 97 | 14 14N | 77 46E |
| Buklyan | 84 | 55 42N | 52 10E |
| Bukoba | 126 | 1 20S | 31 49E |
| Bukoba □ | 126 | 1 30S | 32 0E |
| Bukowno | 54 | 50 17N | 19 35E |
| Bukrale | 123 | 4 32N | 42 0E |
| Bukuru | 121 | 9 42N | 8 48E |
| Bukuya | 126 | 0 40N | 31 52E |
| Bula | 120 | 12 7N | 15 43W |
| Bülach | 51 | 47 31N | 8 32E |
| Bulahdelah | 141 | 32 23S | 152 13E |
| Bulan | 103 | 12 40N | 123 52E |
| Bulanash | 84 | 57 16N | 62 0E |
| Bulandshahr | 94 | 28 28N | 77 58E |
| Bulanovo | 84 | 52 27N | 55 10E |
| Bulantai | 99 | 36 33N | 92 18E |
| Bûlâq | 122 | 25 10N | 30 38E |
| Bulawayo | 127 | 20 7S | 28 32E |
| Buldana | 96 | 20 30N | 76 18E |
| Buldir I. | 147 | 52 20N | 175 55E |
| Bulford | 28 | 51 11N | 1 45W |
| Bulgan | 105 | 48 45N | 103 34E |
| Bulgaria ■ | 67 | 42 35N | 25 30E |
| Bulgroo | 138 | 25 47S | 143 58E |
| Bulgunnia | 139 | 30 10S | 134 53E |
| Bulhar | 91 | 10 25N | 44 30E |
| Buli, Teluk | 103 | 1 5N | 128 25E |
| Buliluyan, C. | 102 | 8 20N | 117 15E |
| Bulki | 123 | 6 11N | 36 31E |
| Bulkington | 163 | 52 29N | 1 25W |
| Bulkley, R. | 152 | 55 15N | 127 40W |
| Bulkur | 77 | 71 50N | 126 30E |
| Bull Shoals L. | 159 | 36 40N | 93 5W |
| Bullabulling | 137 | 31 1S | 120 32E |
| Bullange | 47 | 50 24N | 6 15E |
| Bullaque, R. | 57 | 39 20N | 4 13W |
| Bullara | 136 | 22 40S | 114 3E |
| Bullaring | 137 | 32 30S | 117 45E |
| Bullas | 59 | 38 2N | 1 40W |
| Bulle | 50 | 46 37N | 7 3E |
| Buller Gorge | 143 | 41 40S | 172 10E |
| Buller, Mt. | 141 | 37 10S | 146 28E |
| Buller, R. | 143 | 41 44S | 171 36E |
| Bullfinch | 137 | 30 58S | 119 3E |
| Bulli | 141 | 34 15S | 150 57E |
| Bullock Cr. | 138 | 17 51S | 143 45E |
| Bulloo Downs, Queens., Austral. | 139 | 28 31S | 142 57E |
| Bulloo Downs, W.A., Austral. | 137 | 24 0S | 119 32E |
| Bulloo L. | 139 | 28 43S | 142 25E |
| Bulloo, R. | 139 | 28 43S | 142 30E |
| Bulls | 142 | 40 10S | 175 24E |
| Bully-les-Mines | 43 | 50 27N | 2 44E |
| Bulnes | 172 | 36 42S | 72 19W |
| Bulo Burti | 91 | 3 50N | 45 33E |
| Bulolo | 135 | 7 10S | 146 40E |
| Bulpunga | 140 | 33 47S | 141 45E |
| Bulqiza | 68 | 40 30N | 20 21E |
| Bulsar | 96 | 20 40N | 72 58E |
| Bultfontein | 128 | 28 18S | 26 10E |
| Bulu Karakelong | 103 | 4 35N | 126 50E |
| Buluan | 103 | 9 0N | 125 30E |
| Bŭlŭciţa | 70 | 44 23N | 23 8E |
| Bulukumba | 103 | 5 33S | 120 11E |
| Bulun | 77 | 70 37N | 127 30E |
| Bulwell | 33 | 53 1N | 1 12W |
| Bumba | 124 | 2 13N | 22 30E |
| Bumbiri I. | 126 | 1 40S | 31 55E |
| Bumble Bee | 161 | 34 8N | 112 18W |
| Bumbum | 121 | 14 10N | 8 10E |
| Bumhkang | 98 | 26 51N | 97 40E |
| Bumhpa Bum | 98 | 26 51N | 97 14E |
| Bumi, R. | 127 | 17 30S | 28 30E |
| Bumtang, R. | 98 | 26 56N | 90 53E |
| Buna, Kenya | 124 | 2 58N | 39 30E |
| Buna, P.N.G. | 135 | 8 42S | 148 27E |
| Bunaiyin | 92 | 23 10N | 51 8E |
| Bunaw | 39 | 51 47N | 9 50W |
| Bunazi | 126 | 1 3S | 31 23E |
| Bunbeg | 38 | 55 4N | 8 18W |
| Bunbury | 132 | 33 20S | 115 35E |
| Bunclody | 39 | 52 40N | 6 40W |
| Buncrana | 38 | 55 8N | 7 28W |
| Bundaberg | 139 | 24 54S | 152 22E |
| Bünde | 48 | 52 11N | 8 33E |
| Bundey, R. | 138 | 21 46S | 135 37E |
| Bundi | 94 | 25 30N | 75 35E |
| Bundooma | 138 | 24 54S | 134 16E |
| Bundoran | 38 | 54 24N | 8 17W |
| Bundukia | 123 | 5 14N | 30 55E |
| Bundure | 141 | 35 10S | 146 1E |
| Bŭneasa | 70 | 45 56N | 27 55E |
| Bunessan | 34 | 56 18N | 6 15W |
| Bung Kan | 100 | 18 23N | 103 37E |
| Bungay | 29 | 52 27N | 1 26E |
| Bungendore | 141 | 35 14S | 149 30E |
| Bungil Cr. | 138 | 27 5S | 149 5E |
| Bungō-Suidō | 110 | 33 0N | 132 15E |
| Bungoma | 126 | 0 34N | 34 34E |
| Bungotakada | 110 | 33 35N | 131 25E |
| Bungu | 126 | 7 35S | 39 0E |
| Bunguran N. Is. | 102 | 4 45N | 108 0E |
| Bunia | 126 | 1 35N | 30 20E |
| Bunji | 95 | 35 45N | 74 40E |
| Bunju | 102 | 3 35N | 117 50E |
| Bunker Hill | 163 | 39 15N | 117 8W |
| Bunkerville | 161 | 36 47N | 114 6W |
| Bunkie | 159 | 31 1N | 92 12W |
| Bunmahon | 39 | 52 8N | 7 22W |
| Bunnanaddan | 38 | 54 3N | 8 35W |
| Bunnell | 157 | 29 28N | 81 12W |
| Bunnik | 46 | 52 4N | 5 12E |
| Bunnyconnellan | 38 | 54 7N | 9 1W |
| Bunnythorpe | 142 | 40 16S | 175 39E |
| Buñol | 59 | 39 25N | 0 47W |
| Bunsbeek | 47 | 50 50N | 4 56E |
| Bunschoten | 46 | 52 14N | 5 22E |
| Buntingford | 29 | 51 57N | 0 1W |
| Buntok | 102 | 1 40S | 114 58E |
| Bununu | 121 | 9 51N | 9 32E |
| Bununu Doss | 121 | 10 6N | 9 25E |
| Bunwell | 29 | 52 30N | 1 9E |
| Bunyoro □ = Western □ | 126 | 1 45N | 31 30E |
| Bunza | 121 | 12 8N | 4 0E |
| Bûoareyri | 74 | 65 2N | 14 13W |
| Buol | 103 | 1 15N | 121 32E |
| Buon Brieng | 100 | 13 9N | 108 12E |
| Buong Long | 100 | 13 44N | 106 59E |
| Buorkhaya, Mys | 77 | 71 50N | 133 10E |
| Buqbuq | 122 | 31 29N | 25 29E |
| Buqei'a | 90 | 32 58N | 35 20E |
| Bur Acaba | 91 | 3 12N | 44 20E |
| Bûr Fuad | 122 | 31 15N | 32 20E |
| Bûr Safâga | 122 | 26 43N | 33 57E |
| Bûr Sa'îd | 122 | 31 16N | 32 18E |
| Bûr Sûdân | 122 | 19 32N | 37 9E |
| Bûr Taufiq | 122 | 29 54N | 32 32E |
| Bura | 126 | 1 4S | 39 58E |

**Buraidah** **Caithness, Ord of, C**


| | | | |
|---|---|---|---|
| Buraidah | **92** | 26 20N | 44 8 E |
| Buraimī, Al Wāhāt al | **93** | 24 15N | 55 43 E |
| Burak Sulayman | **90** | 31 42N | 35 7 E |
| Burama | **91** | 9 55N | 43 7 E |
| Burao | **91** | 9 32N | 45 32 E |
| Buras | **159** | 29 20N | 89 33W |
| Burayevo | **84** | 55 50N | 55 24 E |
| Burbage, Derby, U.K. | **32** | 53 15N | 1 55W |
| Burbage, Leics., U.K. | **28** | 52 31N | 1 20W |
| Burbage, Wilts., U.K. | **28** | 51 21N | 1 40W |
| Burbank | **163** | 34 9N | 118 23W |
| Burcher | **141** | 33 30 S | 147 16 E |
| Burdekin, R. | **138** | 19 38 S | 147 25 E |
| Burdett | **152** | 49 50N | 111 32W |
| Burdur | **92** | 37 45N | 30 22 E |
| Burdwan | **95** | 23 16N | 87 54 E |
| Bure | **123** | 10 40N | 37 4 E |
| Bure, R. | **29** | 52 38N | 1 45 E |
| Bureba, La | **58** | 42 36N | 3 24W |
| Buren | **46** | 51 55N | 5 20 E |
| Burfell | **74** | 64 5N | 20 56W |
| Burford | **28** | 51 48N | 1 38W |
| Burg, Magdeburg, Ger. | **48** | 52 16N | 11 50 E |
| Burg, Schleswig-Holstein, Ger. | **48** | 54 25N | 11 10 E |
| Burg el Arab | **122** | 30 54N | 29 32 E |
| Burg et Tuyur | **122** | 20 55N | 27 56 E |
| Burgan | **92** | 29 0N | 47 57 E |
| Burgas | **67** | 42 33N | 27 29 E |
| Burgaski Zaliv | **67** | 42 30N | 27 39 E |
| Burgdorf, Ger. | **48** | 52 27N | 10 0 E |
| Burgdorf, Switz. | **50** | 47 3N | 7 37 E |
| Burgenland □ | **53** | 47 20N | 16 20 E |
| Burgeo | **151** | 47 37N | 57 38W |
| Burgersdorp | **128** | 31 0 S | 26 20 E |
| Burges, Mt. | **137** | 30 50 S | 121 5 E |
| Burgess | **162** | 37 53N | 76 21W |
| Burgess Hill | **29** | 50 57N | 0 7W |
| Burgh-le-Marsh | **33** | 53 10N | 0 15 E |
| Burghclere | **28** | 51 19N | 1 20W |
| Burghead | **37** | 57 42N | 3 30W |
| Burghead B. | **37** | 57 40N | 3 33W |
| Búrgio | **64** | 37 35N | 13 18 E |
| Bürglen | **51** | 46 53N | 8 40 E |
| Burglengenfeld | **49** | 49 11N | 12 2 E |
| Burgo de Osma | **58** | 41 35N | 3 4W |
| Burgohondo | **56** | 40 26N | 4 47W |
| Burgos | **58** | 42 21N | 3 41W |
| Burgos □ | **58** | 42 21N | 3 42W |
| Burgstädt | **48** | 50 55N | 12 49 E |
| Burgsteinfurt | **48** | 52 9N | 7 23 E |
| Burgsvik | **73** | 57 3N | 18 19 E |
| Burguillos del Cerro | **57** | 38 23N | 6 35W |
| Burgundy = Bourgogne | **43** | 47 0N | 4 30 E |
| Burhanpur | **96** | 21 18N | 76 20 E |
| Burhou Rocks | **42** | 49 45N | 2 15W |
| Buri Pen. | **123** | 15 25N | 39 55 E |
| Burias, I. | **103** | 12 55N | 123 5 E |
| Buribay | **84** | 51 57N | 58 10 E |
| Burica, Punta | **166** | 8 3N | 82 51W |
| Burigi, L. | **126** | 2 2 S | 31 22 E |
| Burin, Can. | **151** | 47 1N | 55 14W |
| Burin, Jordan | **90** | 32 11N | 35 15 E |
| Buriram | **100** | 15 0N | 103 0 E |
| Buriti Alegre | **171** | 18 9 S | 49 3W |
| Buriti Bravo | **170** | 5 50 S | 43 50W |
| Buriti dos Lopes | **170** | 3 10 S | 41 52W |
| Burji | **123** | 5 29N | 37 51 E |
| Burkburnett | **159** | 34 7N | 98 35W |
| Burke | **160** | 47 31N | 115 56W |
| Burke, R. | **138** | 23 12 S | 139 33 E |
| Burketown | **138** | 17 45 S | 139 33 E |
| Burk's Falls | **150** | 45 37N | 79 24W |
| Burley, Hants, U.K. | **28** | 50 49N | 1 41W |
| Burley, N. Yorks., U.K. | **33** | 53 55N | 1 46W |
| Burley, U.S.A. | **160** | 42 37N | 113 55W |
| Burlingame | **163** | 37 35N | 122 21W |
| Burlington, Colo., U.S.A. | **158** | 39 21N | 102 18W |
| Burlington, Iowa, U.S.A. | **158** | 40 50N | 91 5W |
| Burlington, Kans., U.S.A. | **158** | 38 15N | 95 47W |
| Burlington, N.C., U.S.A. | **157** | 36 7N | 79 27W |
| Burlington, N.J., U.S.A. | **162** | 40 5N | 74 50W |
| Burlington, Wash., U.S.A. | **160** | 48 29N | 122 19W |
| Burlington, Wis., U.S.A. | **156** | 42 41N | 88 18W |
| Burlyu-Tyube | **76** | 46 30N | 79 10 E |
| Burma ■ | **98** | 21 0N | 96 30 E |
| Burnabbie | **137** | 32 7 S | 126 21 E |
| Burnaby I. | **152** | 52 25N | 131 19W |
| Burnamwood | **141** | 31 7 S | 144 53 E |
| Burnet | **159** | 30 45N | 98 11W |
| Burnett, R. | **133** | 24 45 S | 152 23 E |
| Burney | **160** | 40 56N | 121 41W |
| Burnfoot | **38** | 55 4N | 7 15W |
| Burngup | **137** | 33 2 S | 118 42 E |
| Burnham, Essex, U.K. | **29** | 51 37N | 0 50 E |
| Burnham, Somerset, U.K. | **28** | 51 14N | 3 0W |
| Burnham Market | **29** | 52 57N | 0 43 E |
| Burnie | **138** | 41 4 S | 145 56 E |
| Burnley | **32** | 53 47N | 2 15W |
| Burnmouth | **35** | 55 50N | 2 4W |
| Burnoye | **85** | 42 36N | 70 47 E |
| Burns, Oreg., U.S.A. | **160** | 43 40N | 119 4W |
| Burns, Wyo., U.S.A. | **158** | 41 13N | 104 18W |
| Burns Lake | **152** | 54 20N | 125 45W |
| Burnside, L. | **137** | 25 25 S | 123 0 E |
| Burnt Paw | **147** | 67 2N | 142 43W |
| Burntisland | **35** | 56 4N | 3 14W |
| Burntwood L. | **153** | 55 22N | 100 26W |
| Burntwood, R. | **153** | 56 8N | 96 34W |
| Burqa | **90** | 32 18N | 35 11 E |
| Burra | **140** | 33 40 S | 138 55 E |
| Burragorang, L. | **141** | 33 52 S | 150 37 E |
| Burramurra | **138** | 20 25N | 137 15 E |
| Burravoe | **36** | 60 30N | 1 3W |
| Burray I. | **37** | 58 50N | 2 54W |
| Burreli | **68** | 41 36N | 20 1 E |
| Burrelton | **35** | 56 30N | 3 16W |
| Burren | **39** | 53 9N | 9 5W |
| Burren Junction | **139** | 30 7 S | 148 59 E |
| Burrendong Dam | **139** | 32 39 S | 149 6 E |
| Burrendong Res. | **141** | 32 45 S | 149 10 E |
| Burriana | **58** | 39 50N | 0 4W |
| Burrinjuck Res. | **141** | 35 0 S | 148 36 E |
| Burro, Serranias del | **164** | 29 0N | 102 0W |
| Burrow Hd. | **34** | 54 40N | 4 23W |
| Burrundie | **136** | 13 32 S | 131 42 E |
| Burruyacú | **172** | 26 30 S | 64 40W |
| Burry Port | **31** | 51 41N | 4 17W |
| Bursa | **92** | 40 15N | 29 5 E |
| Burseryd | **73** | 57 12N | 13 17 E |
| Burstall | **153** | 50 39N | 109 54W |
| Burstwick | **33** | 53 43N | 0 6W |
| Burton | **33** | 54 10N | 2 43W |
| Burton Agnes | **33** | 54 4N | 0 18W |
| Burton Bradstock | **28** | 50 41N | 2 43W |
| Burton Fleming | **33** | 54 8N | 0 20W |
| Burton L. | **150** | 54 45N | 78 20W |
| Burton Latimer | **29** | 52 23N | 0 41W |
| Burton upon Stather | **33** | 53 39N | 0 41W |
| Burton-upon-Trent | **28** | 52 48N | 1 39W |
| Burtonport | **38** | 54 59N | 8 26W |
| Burtundy | **140** | 33 45 S | 142 15 E |
| Burtville | **137** | 28 42 S | 122 33 E |
| Buru, I. | **103** | 3 30 S | 126 30 E |
| Burufu | **120** | 10 25N | 2 50W |
| Burujird | **92** | 33 58N | 48 41 E |
| Burullus, Bahra el | **122** | 31 25N | 31 0 E |
| Burunday | **85** | 43 20N | 76 51 E |
| Burundi ■ | **126** | 3 15 S | 30 0 E |
| Burung | **102** | 0 21N | 108 25 E |
| Bururi | **126** | 3 57 S | 29 37 E |
| Burutu | **121** | 5 20N | 5 29 E |
| Burwash | **29** | 50 59N | 0 24 E |
| Burwash Landing | **147** | 61 21N | 139 0W |
| Burwell, U.K. | **29** | 52 17N | 0 20 E |
| Burwell, U.S.A. | **158** | 41 49N | 99 8W |
| Bury | **32** | 53 36N | 2 19W |
| Bury St. Edmunds | **29** | 52 15N | 0 42 E |
| Buryat A.S.S.R. □ | **77** | 53 0N | 110 0 E |
| Burzenin | **54** | 51 28N | 18 47 E |
| Busalla | **62** | 44 34N | 8 58 E |
| Busango Swamp | **127** | 14 15 S | 25 45 E |
| Busayyah | **92** | 30 0N | 46 10 E |
| Busby | **152** | 53 55N | 114 0W |
| Bushati | **68** | 41 58N | 19 34 E |
| Bushell | **153** | 59 31N | 108 45W |
| Bushenyi | **126** | 0 35 S | 30 10 E |
| Bushey | **29** | 51 38N | 0 20W |
| Bushman Land | **128** | 29 30 S | 19 30 E |
| Bushmills | **38** | 55 14N | 6 32W |
| Bushnell, Ill., U.S.A. | **158** | 40 32N | 90 30W |
| Bushnell, Nebr., U.S.A. | **158** | 41 18N | 103 50W |
| Busia □ | **126** | 0 25N | 34 6 E |
| Busie | **120** | 10 29N | 2 22W |
| Businga | **124** | 3 16N | 20 59 E |
| Buskerud fylke □ | **75** | 60 13N | 9 0 E |
| Busko Zdrój | **54** | 50 28N | 20 42 E |
| Busovača | **66** | 44 6N | 17 53 E |
| Busra | **92** | 32 30N | 36 25 E |
| Bussa | **121** | 10 11N | 4 32 E |
| Bussang | **43** | 47 50N | 6 50 E |
| Busselton | **137** | 33 42 S | 115 15 E |
| Bussigny | **50** | 46 33N | 6 33 E |
| Bussum | **46** | 52 16N | 5 10 E |
| Bustard Hd. | **133** | 24 0 S | 151 48 E |
| Busto Arsizio | **62** | 45 40N | 8 50 E |
| Busto, C. | **56** | 43 34N | 6 28W |
| Busu-Djanoa | **124** | 1 50N | 21 5 E |
| Busuangal, I. | **103** | 12 10N | 120 0 E |
| Büsum | **48** | 54 7N | 8 50 E |
| Buta | **126** | 2 50N | 24 53 E |
| Butare | **126** | 2 31 S | 29 52 E |
| Bute | **140** | 33 51 S | 138 2 E |
| Bute (□) | **26** | 55 40N | 5 10W |
| Bute, I. | **34** | 55 48N | 5 2W |
| Bute Inlet | **152** | 50 40N | 124 53W |
| Bute, Kyles of | **34** | 55 55N | 5 10W |
| Bute, Sd. of | **34** | 55 43N | 5 8W |
| Butemba | **126** | 1 9N | 31 37 E |
| Butembo | **126** | 0 9N | 29 18 E |
| Butera | **65** | 37 10N | 14 10 E |
| Bütgenbach | **47** | 50 26N | 6 12 E |
| Buthidaung | **98** | 20 52N | 92 32 E |
| Butiaba | **126** | 1 50N | 31 20 E |
| Butler | **158** | 38 17N | 94 18W |
| Bütschwil | **51** | 47 23N | 9 5 E |
| Butte, Mont., U.S.A. | **160** | 46 0N | 112 31W |
| Butte, Nebr., U.S.A. | **158** | 42 56N | 98 54W |
| Butterfield, Mt. | **137** | 24 45 S | 128 7 E |
| Buttermere | **32** | 54 32N | 3 17W |
| Butterworth | **101** | 5 24N | 100 23 E |
| Buttevant | **39** | 52 14N | 8 40 E |
| Buttfield, Mt. | **137** | 24 45 S | 128 9 E |
| Button B. | **153** | 58 45N | 94 23W |
| Buttonwillow | **163** | 35 24N | 119 28W |
| Butty Hd. | **137** | 33 54 S | 121 39 E |
| Butuan | **103** | 8 57N | 125 33 E |
| Butuku-Luba | **121** | 3 29N | 8 33 E |
| Butung, I. | **103** | 5 0 S | 122 45 E |
| Buturlinovka | **81** | 50 50N | 40 35 E |
| Butzbach | **48** | 50 24N | 8 40 E |
| Buxar | **95** | 25 34N | 83 58 E |
| Buxton, S. Afr. | **128** | 27 38 S | 24 42 E |
| Buxton, U.K. | **32** | 53 16N | 1 54W |
| Buxy | **43** | 46 44N | 4 40 E |
| Buyaga | **77** | 59 50N | 127 0 E |
| Buynaksk | **83** | 42 36N | 47 42 E |
| Buyr Nuur | **105** | 47 50N | 117 42 E |
| Büyük çekmece | **67** | 41 2N | 28 35 E |
| Büyük Kemikli Burun | **68** | 40 20N | 26 15 E |
| Büyük Menderes, R. | **79** | 37 45N | 27 40 E |
| Buzançais | **42** | 46 54N | 1 25 E |
| Buzau, Pasul | **70** | 45 35N | 26 12 E |
| Buzaymah | **117** | 24 35N | 22 0 E |
| Buzen | **110** | 33 35N | 131 5 E |
| Buzet | **63** | 45 24N | 13 58 E |
| Buzi, R. | **127** | 19 52 S | 34 30 E |
| Buziaş | **66** | 45 38N | 21 36 E |
| Buzuluk | **84** | 52 48N | 52 12 E |
| Buzuluk, R. | **81** | 50 50N | 52 12 E |
| Buzŭu | **70** | 45 10N | 26 50 E |
| Buzŭu □ | **70** | 45 20N | 26 30 E |
| Buzŭu, R. | **70** | 45 10N | 27 20 E |
| Buzzards Bay | **162** | 41 45N | 70 38W |
| Bwagaoia | **135** | 10 40 S | 152 52 E |
| Bwana Mkubwe | **127** | 13 8 S | 28 38 E |
| Byala, Ruse, Bulg. | **67** | 43 28N | 25 44 E |
| Byala, Varna, Bulg. | **67** | 42 53N | 27 55 E |
| Byala Slatina | **67** | 43 26N | 23 55 E |
| Byandovan, Mys | **83** | 39 45N | 49 28 E |
| Bychawa | **54** | 51 1N | 22 36 E |
| Byczyha | **54** | 51 7N | 18 12 E |
| Bydgoszcz | **54** | 53 10N | 18 0 E |
| Bydgoszcz □ | **54** | 53 16N | 17 33 E |
| Byelorussian S.S.R. □ | **80** | 53 30N | 27 0 E |
| Byers | **158** | 39 46N | 104 13W |
| Byfield | **28** | 52 10N | 1 15W |
| Bygland | **71** | 58 50N | 7 48 E |
| Byglandsfjord | **71** | 58 40N | 7 50 E |
| Byglandsfjorden | **71** | 58 44N | 7 50 E |
| Byhalia | **159** | 34 53N | 89 41W |
| Bykhov | **80** | 53 31N | 30 14 E |
| Bykle | **71** | 59 20N | 7 22 E |
| Bykovo | **83** | 49 50N | 45 25 E |
| Bylas | **161** | 33 11N | 110 9W |
| Bylchau | **31** | 53 9N | 3 32W |
| Bylderup | **73** | 54 57N | 9 6 E |
| Bylot I. | **149** | 73 13N | 78 34W |
| Byrd Land = Marie Byrd Land | **13** | 79 30 S | 125 0W |
| Byrd Sub-Glacial Basin | **13** | 82 0 S | 120 0W |
| Byro | **137** | 26 5 S | 116 11 E |
| Byrock | **141** | 30 40 S | 146 27 E |
| Byron B. | **151** | 54 42N | 57 40W |
| Byron, C. | **133** | 28 38 S | 153 40W |
| Byrranga, Gory | **77** | 75 0N | 100 0 E |
| Byrum | **73** | 57 16N | 11 0 E |
| Byske | **74** | 64 57N | 21 11 E |
| Byske, R. | **74** | 65 20N | 20 0 E |
| Bystrovka | **85** | 42 47N | 75 42 E |
| Bystrzyca Kłodzka | **54** | 50 19N | 16 39 E |
| Byten | **80** | 52 50N | 25 27 E |
| Bytom | **54** | 50 25N | 19 0 E |
| Bytom Ordz. | **54** | 51 44N | 15 48 E |
| Bytów | **54** | 54 10N | 17 30 E |
| Byumba | **126** | 1 35 S | 30 4 E |
| Byvalla | **72** | 61 22N | 16 27 E |
| Bzéma | **117** | 24 50N | 22 20 E |
| Bzenec | **53** | 48 58N | 17 18 E |


# C


| | | | |
|---|---|---|---|
| Ca Mau = Quan Long | **101** | 9 7N | 105 8 E |
| Ca Mau, Mui = Bai Bung | **101** | 8 35N | 104 42 E |
| Ca Na | **101** | 11 20N | 108 54 E |
| Ca, R. | **100** | 18 45N | 105 45 E |
| Caacupé | **172** | 25 23N | 57 5W |
| Caamano Sd. | **152** | 52 55N | 129 25W |
| Caatingas | **170** | 7 0 S | 52 30W |
| Caazapá | **172** | 26 8 S | 56 19W |
| Caazapá □ | **173** | 26 10 S | 56 0W |
| Caballeria, Cabo de | **58** | 40 5N | 4 5 E |
| Cabañaquinta | **56** | 43 10N | 5 38W |
| Cabanatuan | **103** | 15 30N | 121 5 E |
| Cabanes | **58** | 40 9N | 0 2 E |
| Cabano | **151** | 47 40N | 68 56 E |
| Cabazon | **163** | 33 55N | 116 47W |
| Cabbage Tree Hd. | **108** | 27 20 S | 153 5 E |
| Cabedelo | **170** | 7 0 S | 34 50W |
| Cabeza del Buey | **57** | 38 44N | 5 13W |
| Cabildo | **172** | 32 30 S | 71 5W |
| Cabimas | **174** | 10 30N | 71 25W |
| Cabinda | **124** | 5 40 S | 12 11 E |
| Cabinda □ | **124** | 5 0 S | 12 30 E |
| Cabinet Mts. | **160** | 48 0N | 115 30W |
| Cables | **137** | 27 55 S | 123 25 E |
| Cableskill | **162** | 42 39N | 74 30W |
| Cabo Blanco | **176** | 47 56 S | 65 47W |
| Cabo Delgado □ | **127** | 10 35 S | 40 35 E |
| Cabo Frio | **173** | 22 51 S | 42 3W |
| Cabo Pantoja | **174** | 1 0 S | 75 10W |
| Cabonga Reservoir | **150** | 47 20N | 76 40W |
| Cabool | **159** | 37 10N | 92 8W |
| Caboolture | **139** | 27 5 S | 152 58 E |
| Cabora Bassa Dam | **127** | 15 20 S | 32 50 E |
| Caborca (Heroica) | **164** | 30 40N | 112 10W |
| Cabot Strait | **151** | 47 15N | 59 40W |
| Cabra | **57** | 37 30N | 4 28W |
| Cabra del Santo Cristo | **59** | 37 42N | 3 16W |
| Cabrach | **37** | 57 20N | 3 0W |
| Cabras | **64** | 39 57N | 8 30 E |
| Cabrera, I. | **59** | 39 6N | 2 59 E |
| Cabrera, Sierra | **56** | 42 12N | 6 40W |
| Cabri | **153** | 50 35N | 108 25W |
| Cabriel, R. | **59** | 39 20N | 1 20W |
| Cabruta | **174** | 7 50N | 66 10W |
| Caburan | **103** | 6 3N | 125 45 E |
| Cabuyaro | **174** | 4 18N | 72 49W |
| Çacabelos | **56** | 42 36N | 6 44W |
| ČaCak | **66** | 43 54N | 20 20 E |
| Cáceres, Brazil | **174** | 16 5 S | 57 40W |
| Cáceres, Colomb. | **174** | 7 35N | 75 20W |
| Cáceres, Spain | **57** | 39 26N | 6 23W |
| Cáceres □ | **57** | 39 45N | 6 0W |
| Cache B. | **150** | 46 26N | 80 1W |
| Cache Bay | **150** | 46 22N | 80 0W |
| Cachepo | **57** | 37 20N | 7 49W |
| Cacheu | **120** | 12 14N | 16 8W |
| Cachi | **172** | 25 5 S | 66 10W |
| Cachimbo, Serra do | **175** | 9 30 S | 55 0W |
| Cáchira | **174** | 7 21N | 73 17W |
| Cachoeira | **171** | 12 30 S | 39 0W |
| Cachoeira Alta | **171** | 18 48 S | 50 58W |
| Cachoeira de Itapemirim | **173** | 20 51 S | 41 7W |
| Cachoeira do Sul | **173** | 30 3 S | 52 53W |
| Cachoeiro do Arari | **170** | 1 1 S | 48 58W |
| Cachopo | **57** | 37 20N | 7 49W |
| Cacolo | **124** | 10 9 S | 19 21 E |
| Caconda | **125** | 13 48 S | 15 8 E |
| Caçu | **171** | 18 37 S | 51 4W |
| Caculé | **171** | 14 30 S | 42 13W |
| Cadamstown | **39** | 53 7N | 7 39W |
| Cadarga | **139** | 26 8 S | 150 58 E |
| Çadaux | **137** | 30 48 S | 117 15 E |
| Čadca | **53** | 49 26N | 18 45 E |
| Caddo | **159** | 34 8N | 96 18W |
| Cadenazzo | **51** | 46 9N | 8 57 E |
| Cader Idris | **31** | 52 43N | 3 56W |
| Cadereyta Jiménez | **165** | 25 36N | 100 0W |
| Cadí, Sierra del | **58** | 42 17N | 1 42 E |
| Cadibarrawirracanna, L. | **139** | 28 52 S | 135 27 E |
| Cadillac, Can. | **150** | 48 14N | 78 23W |
| Cadillac, France | **44** | 44 38N | 0 20W |
| Cadillac, U.S.A. | **156** | 44 16N | 85 25W |
| Cadiz | **103** | 11 30N | 123 15 E |
| Cádiz | **57** | 36 30N | 6 20W |
| Cádiz □ | **57** | 36 36N | 5 45W |
| Cádiz, G. de | **57** | 36 40N | 7 0W |
| Cadomin | **152** | 53 2N | 117 20W |
| Cadotte, R. | **152** | 56 43N | 117 10W |
| Cadours | **44** | 43 44N | 1 2 E |
| Cadoux | **137** | 30 46 S | 117 7 E |
| Caen | **42** | 49 10N | 0 22W |
| Caenby Corner | **33** | 53 23N | 0 32W |
| Caergwrle | **29** | 53 6N | 3 3W |
| Caerhun | **31** | 53 14N | 3 50W |
| Caerleon | **31** | 51 37N | 2 57W |
| Caernarfon | **31** | 53 8N | 4 17W |
| Caernarfon B. | **31** | 53 4N | 4 40W |
| Caernarvon = Caernarfon | **31** | 53 8N | 4 17W |
| Caernarvon (□) | **26** | 53 8N | 4 17W |
| Caerphilly | **31** | 51 34N | 3 13W |
| Caersws | **31** | 52 32N | 3 27W |
| Caerwent | **31** | 51 37N | 2 47W |
| Cæsarea = Qesari | **90** | 32 30N | 34 53 E |
| Caeté | **171** | 20 0 S | 43 40W |
| Caetité | **171** | 13 50 S | 42 50W |
| Cafayate | **172** | 26 2 S | 66 0W |
| Cafu | **128** | 16 30 S | 15 8 E |
| Cagayan de Oro | **103** | 8 30N | 124 40 E |
| Cagayan, R. | **103** | 18 25N | 121 42 E |
| Cagli | **63** | 43 32N | 12 38 E |
| Cágliari | **64** | 39 15N | 9 6 E |
| Cágliari, G. di | **64** | 39 8N | 9 10 E |
| Cagnano Varano | **65** | 41 49N | 15 47 E |
| Cagnes-sur-Mer | **45** | 43 40N | 7 9 E |
| Caguas | **147** | 18 14N | 66 4W |
| Caha Mts. | **39** | 51 45N | 9 40W |
| Caher I. | **38** | 53 44N | 10 1W |
| Caherconlish | **39** | 52 36N | 8 30W |
| Cahermore | **39** | 51 35N | 10 2W |
| Cahir | **39** | 52 23N | 7 56W |
| Cahirciveen | **39** | 51 57N | 10 13W |
| Cahore Pt. | **39** | 52 34N | 6 11W |
| Cahors | **44** | 44 27N | 1 27 E |
| Cahuapanas | **174** | 5 15 S | 77 0W |
| Cai Ban, Dao | **100** | 21 10N | 107 27 E |
| Cai Nuoc | **101** | 8 56N | 105 1 E |
| Caianda | **127** | 11 29 S | 23 31 E |
| Caibarién | **166** | 22 30N | 79 30W |
| Caicara | **174** | 7 38N | 66 10W |
| Caicó | **170** | 6 20 S | 37 0W |
| Caicos Is. | **167** | 21 40N | 71 40W |
| Caicos Passage | **167** | 22 45N | 72 45W |
| Caihaique | **176** | 45 30 S | 71 45W |
| Caird Coast | **13** | 75 0 S | 25 0W |
| Cairn Gorm | **37** | 57 7N | 3 40W |
| Cairn Table | **35** | 55 30N | 4 0W |
| Cairngorm Mts. | **37** | 57 6N | 3 42W |
| Cairnryan | **34** | 54 59N | 5 0W |
| Cairns | **138** | 16 57 S | 145 45 E |
| Cairo, Ga., U.S.A. | **157** | 30 52N | 84 12W |
| Cairo, Illinois, U.S.A. | **159** | 37 0N | 89 10W |
| Cairo, N.Y., U.S.A. | **162** | 42 18N | 74 0W |
| Cairo = El Qâhira | **122** | 30 1N | 31 14 E |
| Cairo Montenotte | **62** | 44 23N | 8 16 E |
| Caister-on-Sea | **29** | 52 38N | 1 43 E |
| Caistor | **33** | 53 29N | 0 20W |
| Caithness (□) | **26** | 58 25N | 3 25W |
| Caithness, Ord of, C. | **37** | 58 35N | 3 37W |

**Caiundo** **Canton**


Caiundo 125 15 50S 17 52E
Caiza 174 20 2S 65 40W
Cajamarca 174 7 5S 78 28W
Cajapió 170 2 58S 44 48W
Cajarc 44 44 29N 1 50E
Cajàzeiros 170 7 0S 38 30W
Čajetina 66 43 47N 19 42E
Čajniče 66 43 34N 19 5E
Çakirgöl 83 40 33N 39 40E
Cala 57 37 59N 6 21W
Cala Cadolar 59 38 38N 1 35E
Cala, R. 57 37 50N 6 8W
Calabar 121 4 57N 8 20E
Calabozo 174 9 0N 67 20W
Calábria □ 65 39 24N 16 30E
Calaburras, Pta. de 57 36 30N 4 38W
Calaceite 58 41 1N 0 11E
Calafat 70 43 58N 22 59E
Calafate 176 50 25S 72 25W
Calahorra 58 42 18N 1 59W
Calais, France 43 50 57N 1 56E
Calais, U.S.A. 151 45 5N 67 20W
Calais, Pas de 160 50 57N 1 20E
Calalaste, Sierra de 172 25 0S 67 0W
Calama, Brazil 174 8 0S 62 50W
Calama, Chile 172 22 30S 68 55W
Calamar, Bolívar, Colomb. 174 10 15N 74 55W
Calamar, Vaupés, Colomb. 174 1 58N 72 32W
Calamian Group 103 11 50N 119 55E
Calamocha 58 40 50N 1 17W
Calanaque 174 0 5S 64 0W
Calañas 57 37 40N 6 53W
Calanda 58 40 56N 0 15W
Calang 102 4 30N 95 43E
Calangiánus 64 40 56N 9 12E
Calapan 103 13 25N 121 7E
Calasparra 59 38 14N 1 41W
Calatafimi 64 37 56N 12 50E
Calatayud 58 41 20N 1 40W
Calauag 103 13 55N 122 15E
Calavà, C. 65 38 11N 14 55E
Calavite, Cape 103 13 26N 120 10E
Calbe 48 51 57N 11 47E
Calca 174 13 10S 72 0W
Calci 62 43 44N 10 31E
Calcidica = Khalkidhiki □ 170 40 25N 23 40E
Calcutta 95 22 36N 88 24E
Caldaro 63 46 23N 11 15E
Caldas □ 174 5 15N 75 30W
Caldas da Rainha 57 39 24N 9 8W
Caldas de Reyes 56 42 36N 8 39W
Caldas Novas 171 17 45S 48 38W
Caldbeck 32 54 45N 3 3W
Calder Bridge 32 54 27N 3 31W
Calder Hall 32 54 26N 3 31W
Calder, R. 33 53 44N 1 21W
Caldera 172 27 5S 70 55W
Caldew R. 32 54 54N 2 59W
Caldiran 92 39 7N 44 0E
Caldwell, Idaho, U.S.A. 160 43 45N 116 42W
Caldwell, Kans., U.S.A. 159 37 5N 97 37W
Caldwell, Texas, U.S.A. 159 30 30N 96 42W
Caldy I. 31 51 38N 4 42W
Caledon, S. Afr. 128 34 14S 19 26E
Caledon, U.K. 38 54 22N 6 50W
Caledon B. 138 12 45S 137 0E
Caledon, R. 128 30 0S 26 46E
Caledonian Can. 37 56 50N 5 6W
Calella 58 41 37N 2 40E
Calemba 128 16 0S 15 38E
Calera, La 172 32 50S 71 10W
Calexico 161 32 40N 115 33W
Calf of Man 32 54 4N 4 48W
Calgary, Can. 152 51 0N 114 10W
Calgary, U.K. 34 56 34N 6 17W
Calhoun 157 34 30N 84 55W
Cali 174 3 25N 76 35W
Caliach Pt. 34 56 37N 6 20W
Calicoan, I. 103 10 59N 125 50E
Calicut 93 11 15N 75 43E
Calicut, (Kozhikode) 97 11 15N 75 43E
Caliente 161 37 43N 114 34W
California 158 38 37N 92 30W
California □ 160 37 25N 120 0W
California, Baja 164 32 10N 115 12W
California, Baja, T.N. □ 164 30 0N 115 0W
California, Baja, T.S. □ 164 25 50N 111 50W
California City 163 35 7N 117 57W
California, Golfo de 164 27 0N 111 0W
California Hot Springs 163 35 51N 118 41W
California, Lr. = California, Baja 164 25 50N 111 50W
Calilegua 172 23 45S 64 42W
Călimăneşti 70 45 14N 24 20E
Calingasta 172 31 15S 69 30W
Calipatria 161 33 8N 115 30W
Calistoga 160 38 36N 122 32W
Calitri 65 40 54N 15 25E
Calkini 165 20 21N 90 3W
Callabonna, L. 139 29 40S 140 5E
Callac 42 48 25N 3 27W
Callafo 91 6 48N 43 47E
Callan 39 52 33N 7 25W
Callanish 36 58 12N 6 43W
Callantsoog 46 52 50N 4 42E
Callao 174 12 0S 77 0W
Callaway 158 41 20N 99 56W
Calles 165 23 2N 98 42W
Callicoon 162 41 46N 75 3W
Callide 138 24 18S 150 28E
Calling Lake 152 55 15N 113 12W
Callington 30 56 30N 4 19W
Calliope 138 24 0S 151 16E
Callosa de Ensarriá. 59 38 40N 0 8W
Callosa de Segura 59 38 1N 0 53W
Callow 38 53 58N 9 2W
Calne 28 51 26N 2 0W
Calola 128 16 25S 17 48E
Calore, R. 65 41 8N 14 45E
Caloundra 139 26 45S 153 10E
Calpe 59 38 39N 0 3E
Calshot 28 50 49N 1 18W
Calstock, Can. 150 49 47N 84 9W
Calstock, U.K. 30 50 30N 4 13W
Caltabellotta 64 37 36N 13 11E
Caltagirone 65 37 13N 14 30E
Caltanissetta 65 37 30N 14 3E
Caluire-et-Cuire 45 45 49N 4 51E
Calulo 124 10 1S 14 56E
Calumbo 124 9 0S 13 20E
Caluso 62 45 18N 7 52E
Calvados □ 42 49 5N 0 15W
Calvert 159 30 59N 96 50W
Calvert Hills 138 17 15S 137 20E
Calvert I. 152 51 30N 128 0W
Calvert, R. 138 16 17S 137 44E
Calvert Ra. 136 24 0S 122 30E
Calvillo 164 21 51N 102 43W
Calvinia 128 31 28S 19 45E
Calwa 163 36 42N 119 46W
Calzada Almuradiel 59 38 32N 3 28W
Calzada de Calatrava 57 38 42N 3 46W
Cam Lam 101 11 54N 109 10E
Cam Pha 100 21 1N 107 18E
Cam, R. 29 52 21N 0 16E
Cam Ranh 101 11 54N 109 12E
Cam Xuyen 100 18 15N 106 0E
Camabatela 124 8 20S 15 26E
Camacã 171 15 24S 39 30W
Camaçari 171 12 41S 38 18W
Camacho 164 24 25N 102 18W
Camaguán 174 8 6N 67 36W
Camagüey 166 21 20N 78 0W
Camaiore 62 43 57N 10 18E
Camamu 171 13 57S 39 7W
Camaná 174 16 30S 72 50W
Camaquã, R. 173 30 50S 52 50W
Camaret 42 48 16N 4 37W
Camargo 174 20 38S 65 15E
Camargue 45 43 34N 4 34E
Camarillo 163 34 13N 119 2W
Camariñas 56 43 8N 9 12W
Camarón, C. 166 16 0N 85 0W
Camarones, Argent. 176 44 50S 65 40W
Camarones, Chile 174 19 0S 69 58W
Camas 160 45 35N 122 24W
Camas Valley 160 43 0N 123 46W
Cambados 56 42 31N 8 49W
Cambará 173 23 2S 50 5W
Cambay 94 22 23N 72 33E
Cambay, G. of 94 20 45N 72 30E
Camberley 29 51 20N 0 44W
Cambil 59 37 40N 3 33W
Cambo 35 55 9N 1 57W
Cambo-les-Bains 44 43 22N 1 23W
Cambodia ■ 100 12 15N 105 0E
Camborne 30 50 13N 5 18W
Cambrai 43 50 11N 3 14E
Cambria 163 35 44N 121 6W
Cambrian Mts. 31 52 25N 3 52W
Cambridge, Can. 150 43 23N 80 15W
Cambridge, Jamaica 166 18 18N 77 54W
Cambridge, N.Z. 142 37 54S 175 29E
Cambridge, U.K. 29 52 13N 0 8E
Cambridge, Idaho, U.S.A. 160 44 36N 116 52W
Cambridge, Mass., U.S.A. 162 42 20N 71 8W
Cambridge, Md., U.S.A. 162 38 33N 76 2W
Cambridge, Minn., U.S.A. 158 45 34N 93 15W
Cambridge, Nebr., U.S.A. 158 40 20N 100 12W
Cambridge, N.Y., U.S.A. 162 43 2N 73 22W
Cambridge, Ohio, U.S.A. 156 40 1N 81 22W
Cambridge Bay 148 69 10N 105 0W
Cambridge Gulf 136 14 45S 128 0E
Cambridgeshire □ 29 52 12N 0 7E
Cambrils 58 41 8N 1 3E
Cambuci 173 21 35S 41 55W
Camden, Austral. 141 34 1S 150 43E
Camden, U.K. 29 51 33N 0 10W
Camden, Ala., U.S.A. 157 31 59N 87 15W
Camden, Ark., U.S.A. 159 33 30N 92 50W
Camden, Del., U.S.A. 162 39 7N 75 33W
Camden, Me., U.S.A. 151 44 14N 69 6W
Camden, N.J., U.S.A. 162 39 57N 75 1W
Camden, N.Y., U.S.A. 162 43 20N 75 45W
Camden, S.C., U.S.A. 157 34 17N 80 34W
Camden, B. 147 71 0N 145 0W
Camden Sound 136 15 27S 124 25E
Camel R. 30 50 28N 4 49W
Camelford 30 50 37N 4 41W
Camembert 42 48 53N 0 10E
Cámeri 62 45 30N 8 40E
Camerino 63 43 10N 13 4E
Cameron, Ariz., U.S.A. 161 35 55N 111 31W
Cameron, La., U.S.A. 159 29 50N 93 18W
Cameron, Mo., U.S.A. 158 39 42N 94 14W
Cameron, Tex., U.S.A. 159 30 53N 97 0W
Cameron Falls 150 49 8N 88 19W
Cameron Highlands 101 4 27N 101 22E
Cameron Hills 152 59 48N 118 0W
Cameron Mts. 143 46 1S 167 0E
Cameroon ■ 124 3 30N 12 30E
Camerota 65 40 2N 15 21E
Cameroun, Mt. 121 4 45N 8 55E
Cameroun, R. 121 4 0N 9 35E
Camerton 28 51 18N 2 27W
Cametá 170 2 0S 49 30W
Caminha 56 41 50N 8 50W
Camino 163 38 47N 120 40W
Camira Creek 139 29 15S 152 58E
Camiranga 170 1 48S 46 17W
Cammachmore 37 57 2N 2 9W
Camocim 170 2 55S 40 50W
Camogli 62 44 21N 9 9E
Camolin 39 52 37N 6 26W
Camooweal 138 19 56S 138 7E
Camopi, R. 175 3 12N 52 17W
Camp Crook 158 45 36N 103 59W
Camp Hill 162 40 15N 76 56W
Camp Nelson 163 36 8N 118 39W
Camp Wood 159 29 47N 100 0W
Campagna 65 40 40N 15 5E
Campana 172 34 10S 58 55W
Campana, I. 176 48 20S 75 10W
Campanario 57 38 52N 5 36W
Campania □ 65 40 50N 14 45E
Campbell 163 37 17N 121 57W
Campbell, C. 143 41 47S 174 18E
Campbell I. 142 52 30S 169 0E
Campbell L. 153 63 14N 106 55W
Campbell River 152 50 5N 125 20W
Campbell Town 138 41 52S 147 30E
Campbellpur 94 33 46N 72 20E
Campbellsville 156 37 23N 85 12W
Campbellton, Alta., Can. 152 53 32N 113 15W
Campbellton, N.B., Can. 151 47 57N 66 43W
Campbelltown, Austral. 141 34 4S 150 49E
Campbelltown, U.K. 37 57 34N 4 2W
Campbeltown 34 55 25N 5 36W
Campeche 165 19 50N 90 32W
Campeche □ 165 19 50N 90 32W
Campeche, Golfo de 165 19 30N 93 0W
Camperdown 140 38 14S 143 9E
Camperville 153 51 59N 100 9W
Campi Salentina 65 40 22N 18 2E
Campidano 64 39 30N 8 40E
Campillo de Altobuey 58 39 36N 1 49W
Campillo de Llerena 57 38 30N 5 50W
Campillos 57 37 4N 4 51W
Campina Grande 170 7 20S 35 47W
Campiña, La 57 37 45N 4 45W
Campina Verde 171 19 31S 49 28W
Campinas 173 22 50S 47 0W
Campine 47 51 8N 5 20E
Campinho 170 14 30S 39 10W
Campli 63 42 44N 13 40E
Campo 124 2 15N 9 58E
Campo Beló 171 21 0S 45 30W
Campo de Criptana 59 39 25N 3 7W
Campo de Gibraltar 57 36 15N 5 25W
Campo Flórido 171 19 47S 48 35W
Campo Formoso 170 10 30S 40 20W
Campo Grande 175 20 25S 54 40W
Campo Maior, Brazil 170 4 50S 42 12W
Campo Maior, Port. 57 38 59N 7 7W
Campo Mourão 171 24 3S 52 22W
Campo Tencia 51 46 26N 8 43E
Campo Túres 63 46 53N 11 55E
Campoalegre 174 2 41N 75 20W
Campobasso 65 41 34N 14 40E
Campobello di Licata 64 37 16N 13 55E
Campobello di Mazara 64 37 38N 12 45E
Campofelice 64 37 54N 13 53E
Camporeale 64 37 53N 13 3E
Campos 173 21 50S 41 20W
Campos Altos 171 19 41S 46 10W
Campos Belos 171 13 10S 46 45W
Campos del Puerto 59 39 26N 3 1E
Campos Novos 173 27 21S 51 20W
Campos Sales 170 7 4S 40 23W
Camprodón 58 42 19N 2 23E
Campsie Fells 23 56 2N 4 20W
Camptown 162 41 44N 76 14W
Campuya, R. 174 1 10S 74 0W
Camrose, Can. 152 53 0N 112 50W
Camrose, U.K. 31 51 50N 5 2W
Camsall L. 153 72 32N 106 47W
Camsell Portage 153 59 37N 109 15W
Camurra 139 29 21S 149 52E
Can Gio 101 10 25N 106 58E
Can Tho 101 10 2N 105 46E
Canada ■ 148 60 0N 100 0W
Cañada de Gómez 73 32 55S 61 30W
Canadian 159 35 56N 100 25W
Canadian, R. 159 36 0N 98 45W
Canairiktok, R. 151 54 30N 62 30W
Canajoharie 162 42 54N 74 35W
Çanakkale 68 40 8N 26 30E
Çanakkale Boğazi 68 40 0N 26 0E
Canal de l'Est 43 48 45N 5 35E
Canal Flats 152 50 10N 115 48W
Canal latéral à la Garonne 44 44 25N 0 15E
Canalejas 172 35 15S 66 34W
Canals 172 33 35S 62 40W
Canáls 59 38 58N 0 35W
Canandaigua 156 42 55N 77 18W
Cananea 164 31 0N 110 20W
Canarias, Islas 116 29 30N 17 0W
Canarreos, Arch. de los 166 21 35N 81 40W
Canary Is. = Canarias, Islas 116 29 30N 17 0W
Canastra, Serra da 171 20 0S 46 20W
Canatlán 164 24 31N 104 47W
Canaveral, C. 157 28 28N 80 31W
Cañaveras 58 40 27N 2 14W
Canavieiras 171 15 39S 39 0W
Canbelego 141 31 32S 146 18E
Canberra 141 35 15S 149 8E
Canby, Calif., U.S.A. 160 41 26N 120 58W
Canby, Minn., U.S.A. 158 44 44N 96 15W
Canby, Oregon, U.S.A. 160 45 24N 122 45W
Cancale 42 48 40N 1 50W
Candala 91 11 30N 49 58E
Candas 56 43 35N 5 45W
Candé 42 47 34N 1 0W
Candea = Iráklion 69 35 20N 25 12E
Candela 65 41 8N 15 31E
Candelaria 173 27 29S 55 44W
Candelaria, Pta. de la 56 43 45N 8 0W
Candeleda 56 40 10N 5 14W
Candelo 141 36 47S 149 43E
Candia = Iráklion 69 35 20N 25 12E
Cândido de Abreu 171 24 35S 51 20W
Cândido Mendes 170 1 27S 45 43W
Candle L. 153 53 50N 105 18W
Cando 158 48 30N 99 14W
Canea = Khaniá 69 35 30N 24 4E
Canela 170 10 15S 48 25W
Canelli 62 44 44N 8 18E
Canelones 172 34 32S 56 10W
Canet-Plage 44 42 41N 3 2E
Cañete, Chile 172 37 50S 73 30W
Cañete, Cuba 167 20 36N 74 43W
Cañete, Peru 174 13 0S 76 30W
Cañete, Spain 58 40 3N 1 54W
Cañete de las Torres 57 37 53N 4 19W
Canfranc 58 42 42N 0 31W
Cangamba 125 13 40S 19 54E
Cangas 56 42 16N 8 47W
Cangas de Narcea 56 43 10N 6 32W
Cangas de Onís 56 43 21N 5 8W
Canguaretama 170 6 20S 35 5W
Canguçu 173 31 22S 52 43W
Canhotinho 171 8 53S 36 12W
Cani, Is. 119 36 21N 10 5E
Canicado 125 24 2S 33 2E
Canicatti 64 37 21N 13 50E
Canicattini 65 37 1N 15 3E
Canim, L. 152 51 45N 120 50W
Canim Lake 152 51 17N 120 54W
Canindé 170 4 22S 39 19W
Canindé, R. 170 6 15S 42 52W
Canipaan 102 8 33N 117 15E
Canisbay 37 58 38N 3 6W
Canisp Mt. 36 58 8N 5 5W
Cañitas 164 23 36N 102 43W
Cañiza, La 56 42 13N 8 16W
Cañizal 56 41 20N 5 22W
Canjáyar 59 37 1N 2 44W
Cankırı 92 40 40N 33 30E
Cankuzo 126 3 10S 30 31E
Canlaon, Mt. 103 9 27N 118 25E
Canmore 152 51 7N 115 18W
Cann River 141 37 35S 149 7E
Canna I. 36 57 3N 6 33W
Canna, Sd. of 36 57 1N 6 30W
Cannanore 97 11 53N 75 27E
Cannes 45 43 32N 7 0E
Cannich 37 57 20N 4 48W
Canning Basin 136 19 50S 124 0E
Canning Town 95 22 23N 88 40E
Cannington 28 51 8N 3 4W
Cannock 28 52 42N 2 2W
Cannock Chase, hills 23 52 43N 2 0W
Cannon Ball, R. 158 46 20N 101 20W
Cannondale, Mt. 138 25 13S 148 57E
Caño Colorado 174 2 18N 68 22W
Canoe L. 153 55 10N 108 15W
Canol 147 65 15N 126 50W
Canon City 158 39 30N 105 20W
Canonbie 35 55 4N 2 58W
Canopus 140 33 29S 140 42E
Canora 153 51 40N 102 30W
Canosa di Púglia 65 41 13N 16 4E
Canourgue, Le 44 44 26N 3 13E
Canowindra 141 33 35S 148 38E
Canso 151 45 20N 61 0W
Cantabria, Sierra de 58 42 40N 2 30W
Cantabrian Mts. = Cantábrica 56 43 0N 5 10W
Cantábrica, Cordillera 56 43 0N 5 10W
Cantal □ 44 45 4N 2 45E
Cantanhede 56 40 20N 8 36W
Cantaura 174 9 19N 64 21W
Cantavieja 58 40 31N 0 25W
Čantavir 66 45 55N 19 46E
Canterbury, Austral. 138 25 23S 141 53E
Canterbury, U.K. 29 51 17N 1 5E
Canterbury □ 143 43 45S 171 19E
Canterbury Bight 143 44 16S 171 55E
Canterbury Plains 143 43 55S 171 22E
Cantil 163 35 18N 117 58W
Cantillana 57 37 36N 5 50W
Canto do Buriti 170 8 7S 42 58W
Canton, Ga., U.S.A. 157 34 13N 84 29W
Canton, Ill., U.S.A. 158 40 32N 90 0W
Canton, Mass., U.S.A. 162 42 9N 71 9W
Canton, Miss., U.S.A. 159 32 40N 90 1W
Canton, Mo., U.S.A. 158 40 10N 91 33W
Canton, Ohio, U.S.A. 156 40 47N 81 22W
Canton, Okla., U.S.A. 159 36 5N 98 36W

**Canton** **Cascade**

Canton, Pa., U.S.A. 162 41 39N 76 51W
Canton, S.D., U.S.A. 158 43 20N 96 35W
Canton = Kuangchou 109 23 10N 113 10 E
Canton I. 130 2 30 S 172 0W
Canton L. 159 36 12N 98 40W
Cantù 62 45 44N 9 8 E
Canudos 174 7 13 S 58 5W
Canulloit 161 31 58N 106 36W
Canutama 174 6 30 S 64 20W
Canvey 29 51 32N 0 35 E
Canyon, Can. 147 47 25N 84 36W
Canyon, Texas, U.S.A. 159 35 0N 101 57W
Canyon, Wyo., U.S.A. 160 44 43N 110 36W
Canyonlands Nat. Park 161 38 25N 109 30W
Canyonville 160 42 55N 123 14W
Canzo 62 45 54N 9 18 E
Cao Bang 100 22 40N 106 15 E
Cao Lanh 101 10 27N 105 38 E
Caoles 34 56 32N 6 43W
Caolisport, Loch 34 55 54N 5 40W
Cáorle 63 45 36N 12 51 E
Cap-aux-Meules 151 47 23N 61 52W
Cap Chat 151 49 6N 66 40W
Cap-de-la-Madeleine 150 46 22N 72 31W
Cap Haïtien 167 19 40N 72 20W
Cap St.-Jacques = Vung Tau 101 10 21N 107 4 E
Capa Stilo 65 38 25N 16 25 E
Capáccio 65 40 26N 15 4 E
Capaia 124 8 27 S 20 13 E
Capanaparo, R. 174 7 0N 67 30W
Capanema 170 1 12 S 47 11W
Caparo, R. 174 7 30N 70 30W
Capatárida 174 11 11N 70 37W
Capbreton 44 43 39N 1 26W
Capdenac 44 44 34N 2 5 E
Cape Barren I. 138 40 25 S 148 15 E
Cape Breton Highlands Nat. Park 151 46 50N 60 40W
Cape Breton I. 151 46 0N 60 30W
Cape Charles 162 37 15N 75 59W
Cape Coast 121 5 5N 1 15W
Cape Cod B. 162 41 50N 70 18W
Cape Dorset 149 64 14N 76 32W
Cape Dyer 149 66 40N 61 22W
Cape Fear, R. 157 34 30N 78 25W
Cape Girardeau 159 37 20N 89 30W
Cape Jervis 140 35 40 S 138 5 E
Cape May 162 39 1N 74 53W
Cape May C.H. 162 39 5N 74 50W
Cape May Pt. 162 38 56N 74 56W
Cape Montague 151 46 5N 62 25W
Cape Palmas 120 4 25N 7 49W
Cape Preston 136 20 51 S 116 12 E
Cape Province □ 128 32 0 S 23 0 E
Cape, R. 138 20 37 S 147 1 E
Cape Tormentine 151 46 8N 63 47W
Cape Town (Kaapstad) 128 33 55 S 18 22 E
Cape Verde Is. 14 17 10N 25 20W
Cape York Peninsula 138 33 34 S 115 33 E
Capel 29 51 8N 0 18W
Capel Curig 31 53 6N 3 55W
Capela 170 10 30 S 37 0W
Capela de Campo 170 4 40 S 41 55W
Capelinha 171 17 42 S 42 31W
Capella 138 23 2 S 148 1 E
Capella, G. 138 4 45 S 140 50 E
Capella, Mt. 135 5 4 S 141 8 E
Capelle, La 43 49 59N 3 50 E
Capendu 44 43 11N 2 31 E
Capernaum = Kefar Nahum 90 32 54N 35 32 E
Capestang 44 43 20N 3 2 E
Capim 170 1 41 S 47 47W
Capim, R. 170 3 0 S 48 0W
Capinópolis 171 18 41 S 49 35W
Capitan 161 33 40N 105 41W
Capitola 163 36 59N 121 57W
Capivara, Serra da 171 14 35 S 45 0W
Çapizzi 65 37 50N 14 26 E
Čapljina 66 43 35N 17 43 E
Capoche, R. 127 15 0 S 32 45 E
Cappamore 39 52 38N 8 20W
Cappoquin 39 52 9N 7 46W
Capraia, I. 62 43 2N 9 50 E
Caprarola 63 42 21N 12 11 E
Capreol 150 46 43N 80 56W
Caprera, I. 64 41 12N 9 28 E
Capri, I. 65 40 34N 14 15 E
Capricorn, C. 133 23 30 S 151 13 E
Capricorn Group 138 23 30 S 151 55 E
Capricorn Ra. 136 23 20 S 117 0 E
Caprino Veronese 62 45 37N 10 47 E
Caprivi Strip 128 18 0 S 23 0 E
Captainganj 95 26 55N 83 45 E
Captain's Flat 141 35 35 S 149 27 E
Captieux 44 44 18N 0 16W
Cápua 65 41 7N 14 15 E
Capulin 159 36 48N 103 59W
Caquetá □ 174 1 0N 74 0W
Caquetá, R. 174 1 0N 76 20W
Cáqueza 174 4 25N 73 57W
Carabobo 174 10 10N 68 5W
Caracal 70 44 8N 24 22 E
Caracarai 174 1 50N 61 8W
Caracas 174 10 30N 66 55W
Caracol, Piaui, Brazil 170 9 15 S 43 45W
Caracol, Rondonia, Brazil 174 9 15 S 64 20W
Caradoc 140 30 35 S 143 5 E
Caragabal 141 33 49 S 147 45 E
Caragh L. 39 52 3N 9 50W
Caráglio 62 44 25N 7 25 E
Caraí 171 17 12 S 41 42W
Carajás, Serra dos 170 6 0 S 51 30W
Caramanta 174 5 33N 75 38W
Carangola 173 20 50 S 42 5W
Carani 137 30 57 S 116 28 E
Caransebeş 70 45 28N 22 18 E
Carapelle, R. 65 41 20N 15 35 E
Caraş Severin □ 66 45 10N 22 10 E
Caraşova 66 45 11N 21 51 E
Caratasca, Laguna 166 15 30N 83 40W
Caratec 42 48 40N 3 55W
Caratinga 171 19 50 S 42 10W
Caratunk 151 45 13N 69 55W
Caraúbas 170 7 43 S 36 31W
Caravaca 59 38 8N 1 52W
Caravággio 62 45 30N 9 39 E
Caravelas 171 17 45 S 39 15W
Caraveli 174 15 45 S 73 25W
Caràzinho 173 28 0 S 53 0W
Carballino 56 42 26N 8 5W
Carballo 56 43 13N 8 41W
Carberry 153 49 50N 99 25W
Carbia 56 42 48N 8 14W
Carbó 164 29 42N 110 58W
Carbon 152 51 30N 113 9W
Carbonara, C. 64 39 8N 9 30 E
Carbondale, Colo, U.S.A. 160 39 30N 107 10W
Carbondale, Ill., U.S.A. 159 37 45N 89 10W
Carbondale, Pa., U.S.A. 162 41 37N 75 30W
Carbonear 151 47 42N 53 13W
Carboneras 59 37 0N 1 53W
Carboneras de Guadazaón 58 39 54N 1 50W
Carbonia 64 39 10N 8 30 E
Carbost 36 57 19N 6 21W
Carbury 38 53 22N 6 58W
Carcabuey 57 37 27N 4 17W
Carcagente 59 39 8N 0 28W
Carcajou 152 57 47N 117 6W
Carcasse, C. 167 18 30N 74 28W
Carcassonne 44 43 13N 2 20 E
Carche 59 38 26N 1 9W
Carcoar 141 33 36 S 149 8 E
Carcross 147 60 13N 134 45W
Cardabia 136 23 2 S 113 55 E
Cardamom Hills 97 9 30N 77 15 E
Cárdenas, Cuba 166 23 0N 81 30W
Cárdenas, San Luis Potosí, Mexico 166 22 0N 99 41W
Cárdenas, Tabasco, Mexico 165 17 59N 93 21W
Cardenete 58 39 46N 1 41W
Cardiff 31 51 28N 3 11W
Cardiff-by-the-Sea 163 33 1N 117 17W
Cardigan 31 52 6N 4 41W
Cardigan (□) 26 52 6N 4 41W
Cardigan B. 31 52 30N 4 30W
Cardington 29 52 7N 0 23W
Cardón 174 11 37N 70 14W
Cardona, Spain 58 41 56N 1 40 E
Cardona, Uruguay 172 33 53 S 57 18W
Cardoner, R. 58 42 0N 1 33 E
Cardross 153 49 50N 105 40W
Cardston 152 49 15N 113 20W
Cardwell 138 18 14 S 146 2 E
Careen L. 153 57 0N 108 11W
Carei 70 47 40N 22 29 E
Carentan 42 49 19N 1 15W
Carey, Idaho, U.S.A. 160 43 19N 113 58W
Carey, Ohio, U.S.A. 156 40 58N 83 22W
Carey, L. 137 29 0 S 122 15 E
Carey L. 153 62 12N 102 55W
Careysburg 120 6 34N 10 30W
Cargados Garajos, Is. 11 17 0 S 59 0 E
Cargelligo, L. 139 33 17 S 146 24 E
Cargèse 45 42 7N 8 35 E
Carhaix-Plouguer 42 48 18N 3 36W
Carhué 172 37 10 S 62 50W
Cariacica 171 20 16 S 40 25W
Cariaco 174 10 29N 63 33W
Caribaná, Pta. 174 8 37N 76 52W
Caribbean Sea 167 15 0N 75 0W
Cariboo Mts. 152 53 0N 121 0W
Caribou, Can. 153 53 15N 121 55W
Caribou, U.S.A. 151 46 55N 68 0W
Caribou I. 150 47 22N 85 49W
Caribou Is. 152 61 55N 113 15W
Caribou L., Man., Can. 153 59 21N 96 10W
Caribou L., Ont., Can. 150 50 25N 89 5W
Caribou Mts. 152 59 12N 115 40W
Caribou, R., Man., Can. 153 59 20N 94 44W
Caribou, R., N.W.T., Can. 152 61 27N 125 45W
Carichic 164 27 56N 107 3W
Carignan 43 49 38N 5 10 E
Carignano 62 44 55N 7 40 E
Carillo 164 26 50N 103 55W
Carinda 141 30 28 S 147 41 E
Cariñena 58 41 20N 1 13W
Carinhanha 171 14 15 S 44 0W
Carinhanha, R. 171 14 20 S 43 47W
Carini 64 38 9N 13 10 E
Carinish 36 57 31N 7 20W
Carinola 64 41 11N 13 58 E
Carinthia □ = Kärnten 52 46 52N 13 30 E
Caripito 174 10 8N 63 6W
Caririacu 171 7 2 S 39 17W
Carisbrooke 28 50 42N 1 19W
Caritianas 174 9 20 S 63 0W
Cark 32 54 11N 2 59W
Carlentini 65 37 15N 15 2 E
Carleton Place 150 45 8N 76 9W
Carleton Rode 29 52 30N 1 6 E
Carletonville 128 26 23 S 27 22 E
Carlin 160 40 50N 116 5W
Carlingford 38 54 3N 6 10W
Carlingford, L. 38 54 0N 6 5W
Carlinville 158 39 20N 89 55W
Carlisle, U.K. 32 54 54N 2 55W
Carlisle, U.S.A. 162 40 12N 77 10W
Carlitte, Pic 44 42 35N 1 43 E
Carloforte 64 39 10N 8 18 E
Carlops 35 55 47N 3 20W
Carlos Casares 172 35 53 S 61 20W
Carlos Chagas 171 17 43 S 40 45W
Carlos Tejedor 172 35 25 S 62 25W
Carlota, La 172 33 30 S 63 20W
Carlow 39 52 50N 6 58W
Carlow □ 39 52 43N 6 50W
Carloway 36 58 17N 6 48W
Carlsbad, Calif., U.S.A. 163 33 11N 117 25W
Carlsbad, N. Mex., U.S.A. 159 32 20N 104 7W
Carlton 33 52 58N 1 6W
Carlton Colville 29 52 27N 1 41 E
Carlton Miniott 33 54 13N 1 22W
Carluke 35 55 44N 3 50W
Carlyle, Can. 153 49 40N 102 20W
Carlyle, U.S.A. 158 38 38N 89 23W
Carmacks 147 62 5N 136 16W
Carmagnola 62 44 50N 7 42 E
Carman 153 49 30N 98 0W
Carmangay 152 50 10N 113 10W
Carmanville 151 49 23N 54 19W
Carmarthen 31 51 52N 4 20W
Carmarthen (□) 26 53 40N 4 18W
Carmarthen B. 31 51 40N 4 30W
Carmaux 44 44 3N 2 10 E
Carmel, Calif., U.S.A. 163 36 38N 121 55W
Carmel, N.Y., U.S.A. 162 41 25N 73 38W
Carmel Hd. 31 53 24N 4 34W
Carmel Mt. 90 32 45N 35 3 E
Carmel Valley 163 36 29N 121 43W
Carmelo 172 34 0 S 58 10W
Carmen, Colomb. 174 9 43N 75 8W
Carmen, Parag. 173 27 13 S 56 12W
Carmen de Patagones 176 40 50 S 63 0W
Carmen, I. 164 26 0N 111 20W
Carmen, R. 164 30 42N 106 29W
Cármenes 56 42 58N 5 34W
Carmensa 172 35 15 S 67 40W
Carmi 156 38 6N 88 10W
Carmichael 163 38 38N 121 19W
Carmila 138 21 55 S 149 24 E
Carmo do Paranaiba 171 18 59 S 46 21W
Carmona 57 37 28N 5 42W
Carmyllie 37 56 36N 2 41W
Carn Ban 37 57 6N 4 15W
Carn Eige 36 57 17N 5 9W
Carn Glas Chorie 37 57 20N 3 50W
Carn Mor 37 57 14N 3 13W
Carn na Saobhaidh 37 57 12N 4 20W
Carna 39 53 20N 9 50W
Carnarvon, Queens., Austral. 138 24 48 S 147 45 E
Carnarvon, W. Austral., Austral. 137 24 51 S 113 42 E
Carnarvon, S. Afr. 128 30 56 S 22 8 E
Carnarvon Ra., Queensland, Austral. 138 25 15 S 148 30 E
Carnarvon Ra., W.A., Austral. 137 25 0 S 120 45 E
Carnaxide 57 38 43N 9 14W
Carncastle 38 54 55N 5 52W
Carndonagh 38 55 15N 7 16W
Carnduff 153 49 10N 101 50W
Carnedd Llewelyn, Mt. 31 53 9N 3 58W
Carnegie, L. 137 26 5 S 122 30 E
Carnew 39 52 43N 6 30W
Carney 38 54 20N 8 30W
Carnforth 32 54 8N 2 47W
Carnic Alps = Karnische Alpen 63 46 34N 12 50 E
Carnlough 38 55 0N 6 0W
Carno 31 52 34N 3 31W
Carnon 44 43 32N 3 59 E
Carnot 124 4 59N 15 56 E
Carnot B. 136 17 20 S 121 30 E
Carnoustie 35 56 30N 2 41W
Carnsore Pt. 39 52 10N 6 20W
Carnwath 35 55 42N 3 38W
Caro 156 43 29N 83 27W
Carolina, Brazil 170 7 10 S 47 30W
Carolina, S. Afr. 129 26 5 S 30 6 E
Carolina, La 57 38 17N 3 38W
Caroline I. 131 9 15 S 150 3W
Caroline Is. 130 8 0N 150 0 E
Caroline Pk. 143 45 57 S 167 15 E
Carolside 152 51 20N 111 40W
Caron 153 50 30N 105 50W
Caroni, R. 174 6 0N 62 40W
Carora 174 10 11N 70 5W
Carovigno 65 40 42N 17 40 E
Carpathians, Mts. 53 46 20N 26 0 E
Carpaţii Meridionali 70 45 30N 25 0 E
Carpenédolo 62 45 22N 10 25 E
Carpentaria Downs 138 18 44 S 144 20 E
Carpentaria, G. of 133 14 0 S 139 0 E
Carpentras 45 44 3N 5 2 E
Carpi 62 44 47N 10 52 E
Carpina 170 7 51 S 35 15W
Carpino 65 41 50N 15 51 E
Carpinteria 163 34 25N 119 31W
Carpio 56 41 13N 5 7W
Carpolac = Morea 140 36 45 S 141 18 E
Carr Boyd Ra. 136 16 15 S 128 35 E
Carra L. 38 53 41N 9 12W
Carrabelle 157 29 52N 84 40W
Carracastle 38 53 57N 8 42W
Carradale 34 55 35N 5 30W
Carraipia 174 11 16N 72 22W
Carrara 62 44 5N 10 7 E
Carrascosa del Campo 58 40 2N 2 45W
Carrauntohill, Mt. 39 52 0N 9 49W
Carraweena 139 29 10 S 140 0 E
Carrbridge 37 57 17N 3 50W
Carriacou, I. 167 12 30N 61 28W
Carribee 140 35 7 S 136 57 E
Carrick 38 54 40N 8 39W
Carrick, dist. 34 55 12N 4 38W
Carrick-on-Shannon 38 53 57N 8 7W
Carrick-on-Suir 39 52 22N 7 30W
Carrick Ra. 143 45 15 S 169 8 E
Carrickart 38 55 10N 7 47W
Carrickbeg 39 52 20N 7 25W
Carrickboy 38 53 36N 7 40W
Carrickfergus 36 54 43N 5 50W
Carrickfergus □ 38 54 43N 5 49W
Carrickmacross 38 54 0N 6 43W
Carrieton 140 32 25 S 138 31 E
Carrigaholt 39 52 37N 9 42W
Carrigahorig 39 53 4N 8 10W
Carrigaline 39 51 49N 8 22W
Carrigallen 38 53 59N 7 40W
Carrigan Hd. 38 54 38N 8 40W
Carrignavar 39 52 0N 8 29W
Carrigtwohill 39 51 55N 8 15W
Carrington 158 47 30N 99 7W
Carrión de los Condes 56 42 20N 4 37W
Carrión, R. 56 42 42N 4 47W
Carrizal 174 12 1N 72 11W
Carrizal Bajo 172 28 5 S 71 20W
Carrizalillo 172 29 0 S 71 30W
Carrizo Cr. 159 36 30N 103 40W
Carrizo Springs 159 28 28N 99 50W
Carrizozo 161 33 40N 105 57W
Carroll 158 42 2N 94 55W
Carrollton, Ga., U.S.A. 157 33 36N 85 5W
Carrollton, Ill., U.S.A. 158 39 20N 90 25W
Carrollton, Ky., U.S.A. 156 38 40N 85 10W
Carrollton, Mo., U.S.A. 158 39 19N 93 24W
Carron L. 36 57 22N 5 35W
Carron R., U.K. 36 57 30N 5 30W
Carron R., U.K. 37 57 51N 4 21W
Carrot, R. 153 53 50N 101 17W
Carrot River 153 53 17N 103 35W
Carrouges 42 48 34N 0 10W
Carrowkeel 38 55 7N 7 12W
Carrowmore L. 38 54 12N 9 48W
Carruthers 153 52 52N 109 16W
Carryduff 38 54 32N 5 52W
Çarşamba 92 41 15N 36 45 E
Carsoli 63 42 7N 13 3 E
Carson 158 46 27N 101 29W
Carson City 160 39 12N 119 46W
Carson Sink 160 39 50N 118 40W
Carsonville 156 43 25N 82 39W
Carsphairn 34 55 13N 4 15W
Carstairs 35 55 42N 3 41W
Cartagena, Colomb. 174 10 25N 75 33W
Cartagena, Spain 59 37 38N 0 59W
Cartago, Colomb. 174 4 45N 75 55W
Cartago, C. Rica 166 9 50N 84 0W
Cartaret 42 49 23N 1 47W
Cartaxo 57 39 10N 8 47W
Cartaya 57 37 16N 7 9W
Cartersville 157 34 11N 84 48W
Carterton 142 41 2 S 175 31 E
Carthage, Ark., U.S.A. 159 34 4N 92 32W
Carthage, Ill., U.S.A. 158 40 25N 91 10W
Carthage, Mo., U.S.A. 159 37 10N 94 20W
Carthage, N.Y., U.S.A. 156 43 59N 75 37W
Carthage, S.D., U.S.A. 158 44 14N 97 38W
Carthage, Texas, U.S.A. 159 32 8N 94 20W
Cartier I. 136 12 31 S 123 29 E
Cartmel 32 54 13N 2 57W
Cartwright 151 53 41N 56 58W
Caruaru 170 8 15 S 35 55W
Carúpano 174 10 45N 63 15W
Carutapera 170 1 13 S 46 1W
Caruthersville 159 36 10N 89 40W
Carvarzere 63 45 8N 12 7 E
Carvin 43 50 30N 2 57 E
Carvoeiro 174 1 30 S 61 59W
Carvoeiro, Cabo 57 39 21N 9 24W
Casa Agapito 174 2 3N 73 58W
Casa Branca, Brazil 171 21 46 S 47 4W
Casa Branca, Port. 57 38 29N 8 12W
Casa Grande 161 32 53N 111 51W
Casa Nova 170 9 10 S 41 5W
Casablanca, Chile 172 33 20 S 71 25W
Casablanca, Moroc. 118 33 36N 7 36W
Casacalenda 65 41 45N 14 50 E
Casalbordino 63 42 10N 14 34 E
Casale Monferrato 62 45 8N 8 28 E
Casalmaggiore 62 44 59N 10 25 E
Casalpusterlengo 62 45 10N 9 40 E
Casamance, R. 120 12 54N 15 0W
Casamássima 65 40 58N 16 55 E
Casanare, R. 174 6 30N 71 20W
Casarano 65 40 0N 18 10 E
Casares 57 36 27N 5 16W
Casas Grandes 164 30 22N 108 0W
Casas IbáPez 59 39 17N 1 30W
Casasimarro 59 39 22N 2 3W
Casatejada 56 39 54N 5 40W
Casavieja 56 40 17N 4 46W
Cascade, Idaho, U.S.A. 160 44 30N 116 2W

**Cascade** **Cepin**

Cascade, Mont., U.S.A. 160 47 16N 111 46W
Cascade Locks 160 45 44N 121 54W
Cascade Pt. 143 44 1S 168 20E
Cascade Ra. 160 45 0N 121 30W
Cascais 57 38 41N 9 25W
Cascina 62 43 40N 10 32E
Caselle Torinese 62 45 12N 7 39E
Caserta 65 41 5N 14 20E
Cashel 39 52 31N 7 53W
Cashla B. 39 53 12N 9 37W
Cashmere 160 47 31N 120 30W
Cashmere Downs 137 28 57S 119 35E
Casigua 174 11 2N 71 1W
Casiguran 103 16 15N 122 15E
Casilda 172 33 10S 61 10W
Casimcea 70 44 45N 28 23E
Casino 139 28 52S 153 3E
Casiquiare, R. 174 2 45N 66 20W
Caslan 152 54 38N 112 31W
Casma 174 9 30S 78 20W
Casmalia 163 34 50N 120 32W
Casola Valsenio 63 44 12N 11 40E
Cásoli 63 42 7N 14 18E
Caspe 58 41 14N 0 1W
Casper 160 42 52N 106 27W
Caspian Sea 79 43 0N 50 0E
Casquets 42 49 46N 2 15W
Cass City 156 43 34N 83 15W
Cass Lake 158 47 23N 94 38W
Cassá de la Selva 58 41 53N 2 52E
Cassano Iónio 65 39 47N 16 20E
Cassel 43 50 48N 2 30E
Casselton 158 47 0N 97 15W
Cássia 171 20 36S 46 56W
Cassiar 152 59 16N 129 40W
Cassiar Mts. 152 59 30N 130 30W
Cassils 152 50 29N 112 15W
Cassinga 125 15 5S 16 23E
Cassino 64 41 30N 13 50E
Cassiporé, C. 170 3 50N 51 5W
Cassis 45 43 14N 5 32E
Cassville 159 36 45N 93 59W
Cástagneto Carducci 62 43 9N 10 36E
Castaic 163 34 30N 118 38W
Castanhal 170 1 18S 47 55W
Castanheiro 174 0 17S 65 38W
Casteau 47 50 32N 4 2E
Castéggio 62 45 1N 9 8E
Castejón de Monegros 58 41 37N 0 15W
Castel di Sangro 65 41 41N 14 5E
Castel San Giovanni 62 45 4N 9 25E
Castel San Pietro 63 44 23N 11 30E
Castelbuono 65 37 56N 14 4E
Casteldelfino 62 44 35N 7 4E
Castelfiorentino 62 43 36N 10 58E
Castelfranco Emília 62 44 37N 11 2E
Castelfranco Veneto 63 45 40N 11 56E
Casteljaloux 44 44 19N 0 6E
Castellabate 65 40 18N 14 55E
Castellammare del Golfo 64 38 2N 12 53E
Castellammare di Stábia 65 40 47N 14 29E
Castellammare, G. di 64 38 5N 12 55E
Castellamonte 62 45 23N 7 42E
Castellana Grotte 65 40 53N 17 10E
Castellane 45 43 50N 6 31E
Castellaneta 65 40 40N 16 57E
Castellar de Santisteban 59 38 16N 3 8W
Castelleone 62 45 19N 9 47E
Castelli 172 36 7S 57 47W
Castelló de Ampurias 58 42 15N 3 4E
Castellón □ 58 40 15N 0 5W
Castellón de la Plana 58 39 58N 0 3W
Castellote 58 40 48N 0 15W
Castelltersol 58 41 45N 2 8E
Castelmáuro 65 41 50N 14 40E
Castelnau-de-Médoc 44 45 2N 0 48W
Castelnaudary 44 43 20N 1 58E
Castelnovo ne' Monti 62 44 27N 10 26E
Castelnuovo di Val di Cécina 62 43 12N 10 54E
Castelo 173 20 53S 41 42E
Castelo Branco 56 39 50N 7 31W
Castelo Branco □ 56 39 52N 7 45W
Castelo de Paiva 56 41 2N 8 16W
Castelo de Vide 57 39 25N 7 27W
Castelo do Piauí 170 5 20S 41 33W
Castelsarrasin 44 44 2N 1 7E
Casteltérmini 64 37 32N 13 38E
Castelvetrano 64 37 40N 12 46E
Casterton 140 37 30S 141 30E
Castets 44 43 52N 1 6W
Castiglione del Lago 63 43 7N 12 3E
Castiglione della Pescáia 62 42 46N 10 53E
Castiglione della Stiviere 62 45 23N 10 30E
Castiglione Fiorentino 63 43 20N 11 55E
Castilblanco 57 39 17N 5 5W
Castilla La Nueva 57 39 45N 3 20W
Castilla La Vieja 56 41 55N 4 0W
Castilla, Playa de 57 37 0N 6 33W
Castille = Castilla 56 40 0N 3 30W
Castilletes 174 11 51N 71 19W
Castillón 164 28 20N 103 38W
Castillon-en-Couserans 44 42 56N 1 1E
Castillon-la-Bataille 44 44 51N 0 2W
Castillonès 44 44 39N 0 37E
Castillos 173 34 12S 53 52W
Castle Acre 29 52 42N 0 42W
Castle Cary 28 51 5N 2 32W
Castle Dale 160 39 11N 111 1W
Castle Donington 28 52 50N 1 20W
Castle Douglas 35 54 57N 3 57W
Castle Eden 54 54 45N 1 20W
Castle Point 142 40 54N 176 15E
Castle Rock, Colo., U.S.A. 158 39 26N 104 50W
Castle Rock, Wash., U.S.A. 160 46 20N 122 58W
Castlebar 38 53 52N 9 17W
Castlebay 36 56 57N 7 30W
Castlebellingham 38 53 53N 6 22W
Castleblakeney 38 53 26N 8 28W
Castleblayney 38 54 7N 6 44W
Castlebridge 39 52 23N 6 28W
Castlecliff 142 39 57S 174 59E
Castlecomer 39 52 49N 7 13W
Castleconnell 39 52 44N 8 30W
Castledawson 38 54 47N 6 35W
Castlederg 38 54 43N 7 35W
Castledermot 39 52 55N 6 50W
Castlefinn 38 54 47N 7 35W
Castleford 33 53 43N 1 21W
Castlegar 152 49 20N 117 40W
Castlegate 160 39 45N 110 57W
Castlegregory 39 52 16N 10 0W
Castlehill 38 51 1N 9 49W
Castleisland 39 52 14N 9 28W
Castlemaine, Austral. 140 37 2S 144 12E
Castlemaine, Ireland 39 52 10N 9 42W
Castlemaine Harb. 39 52 8N 9 50W
Castlemartyr 39 51 54N 8 3W
Castlepollard 38 53 40N 7 20W
Castlereagh 38 53 47N 8 30W
Castlereagh □ 38 54 33N 5 33W
Castlereagh B. 138 12 10S 135 10E
Castlereagh, R. 141 30 12S 147 32E
Castleside 32 54 50N 1 52W
Castleton, Derby., U.K. 33 53 20N 1 47W
Castleton, N. Yorks., U.K. 33 54 27N 0 57W
Castleton, U.S.A. 162 43 37N 73 11W
Castletown, Geoghegan, Ireland 38 53 27N 7 30W
Castletown, Laois, Ireland 38 52 58N 7 31W
Castletown, Meath, Ireland 39 53 47N 6 41W
Castletown, I. of Man 32 54 4N 4 40W
Castletown, U.K. 37 58 35N 3 22W
Castletown Bearhaven 39 51 40N 9 54W
Castletownroche 39 52 10N 8 28W
Castletownshend 39 51 31N 9 11W
Castlevale 138 24 30S 146 48E
Castlewellan 38 54 16N 5 57W
Castor 152 52 15N 111 50W
Castorland 162 43 53N 75 31W
Castres 44 43 37N 2 13E
Castricum 46 52 33N 4 40E
Castries 167 14 0N 60 50W
Castril 59 37 48N 2 46W
Castro, Brazil 173 24 45S 50 0W
Castro, Chile 176 42 30S 73 50W
Castro Alves 171 12 46S 39 26W
Castro del Río 57 37 41N 4 29W
Castro Marim 57 37 13N 7 26W
Castro Urdiales 58 43 23N 3 19W
Castro Verde 57 37 41N 8 4W
Castrojeriz 56 42 17N 4 9W
Castropol 56 43 32N 7 0W
Castroreale 65 38 5N 15 15E
Castrovíllari 65 39 49N 16 11E
Castroville, Calif., U.S.A. 163 36 46N 121 45W
Castroville, Tex, U.S.A. 159 29 20N 98 53W
Castuera 57 38 43N 5 37W
Casummit L. 150 51 29N 92 22W
Cat Ba 100 20 50N 107 0E
Cat I., Bahamas 167 24 30N 75 30W
Cat I., U.S.A. 159 30 15N 89 7W
Cat L. 150 51 40N 91 50W
Čata 53 47 58N 18 38E
Catacamas 166 14 54N 85 56W
Catacaos 174 5 20S 80 45W
Cataguases 173 21 23S 42 39W
Catahoula L. 159 31 30N 92 5W
Catalão 171 18 10S 47 57W
Çatalca 92 41 9N 28 28E
Catalina 151 48 31N 53 4W
Catalonia = Cataluña 58 41 40N 1 15E
Cataluña 58 41 40N 1 15E
Catamarca 172 28 30S 65 50W
Catamarca □ 172 28 30S 65 50W
Catanduanas, Is. 103 13 50N 124 20E
Catanduva 173 21 5S 48 58W
Catánia 65 37 31N 15 4E
Catánia, G. di 65 37 25N 15 8E
Catanzaro 65 38 54N 16 38E
Catarman 103 12 28N 124 1E
Catastrophe C. 136 34 59S 136 0E
Catcleugh 35 55 19N 2 22W
Cateau, Le 43 50 6N 3 30E
Cateel 103 7 47N 126 24E
Catende 170 8 40S 35 43W
Caterham 29 51 16N 0 4W
Cathcart, Austral. 141 36 2S 149 24E
Cathcart, S. Afr. 128 32 18S 27 10E
Catine 41 46 30N 0 15W
Catio 120 11 17N 15 15W
Catismiña 174 4 5N 63 52W
Catita 170 9 31S 43 1W
Catlettsburg 156 38 23N 82 38W
Cato I. 133 23 15S 155 32E
Catoche, C. 165 21 40N 87 0W
Catolé 171 7 19S 36 1W
Catolé do Rocha 170 6 21S 37 45W
Caton 32 54 5N 2 41W
Catonsville 162 39 16N 76 44W
Catral 59 38 10N 0 47W
Catria, Mt. 63 43 28N 12 42E
Catrimani 174 0 27N 61 41W
Catrine 34 55 30N 4 20W
Catsfield 29 50 53N 0 28E
Catskill 162 42 14N 73 52W
Catskill Mts. 162 42 15N 74 15W
Catt, Mt. 138 13 49S 134 23E
Catterick 33 54 23N 1 38W
Cattólica 63 43 58N 12 43E
Cattólica Eraclea 64 37 27N 13 24E
Catton 35 54 56N 2 16W
Catu 171 12 21S 38 23W
Catuala 128 16 25S 19 2E
Catur 127 13 45S 35 30E
Catwick Is. 101 10 0N 109 0E
Cauca □ 174 2 30N 76 50W
Cauca, R. 174 7 25N 75 30W
Caucasia 174 8 0N 75 12W
Caucasus Mts. = Bolshoi Kavkas 83 42 50N 44 0E
Caucaia 170 3 40S 38 35W
Caudebec-en-Caux 42 49 30N 0 42E
Caudete 59 38 42N 1 2W
Caudry 43 50 7N 3 22E
Caulkerbush 35 54 54N 3 40W
Caulnes 42 48 18N 2 10W
Caulónia 65 38 23N 16 25E
Caungula 124 8 15S 18 50E
Cáuquenes 172 36 0S 72 30W
Caura, R. 174 6 20N 64 30W
Cauresi, R. 127 17 40S 33 10E
Causapscal 151 48 19N 67 12W
Causeway 39 52 25N 9 45W
Caussade 44 44 10N 1 33E
Cauterets 44 42 52N 0 8W
Cauvery, R. 93 12 0N 77 45E
Caux 42 49 38N 0 35E
Cava dei Tirreni 65 40 42N 14 42E
Cávado, R. 56 41 37N 8 15W
Cavaillon 45 43 50N 5 2E
Cavalaire-sur-Mer 45 43 10N 6 33E
Cavalcante 171 13 48S 47 30W
Cavalerie, La 44 44 0N 3 10E
Cavalese 63 46 17N 11 29E
Cavalier 158 48 50N 97 39W
Cavalli Is. 142 35 0S 173 58E
Cavallo, I. 45 41 22N 9 16E
Cavally, R. 120 5 0N 7 40W
Cavan 38 54 0N 7 22W
Cavan □ 38 53 58N 7 10W
Cavanagh Ra. 137 26 10S 122 50E
Cavárzere 63 45 8N 12 6E
Cave City 156 37 13N 85 57W
Cavenagh Range 137 26 12S 127 55E
Cavendish 140 37 31S 142 2E
Cavers 150 48 55N 87 41W
Caviana, Ilha 170 0 15N 50 0W
Cavite 103 14 20N 120 55E
Cavour 62 44 47N 7 22E
Cavtat 66 42 35N 18 13E
Cawdor 37 57 31N 3 56W
Cawkers Well 140 31 41S 142 57E
Cawndilla, L. 140 32 30S 142 15E
Cawnpore = Kanpur 95 26 35N 80 20E
Cawood 33 53 50N 1 7W
Cawston 29 52 47N 1 10E
Caxias 174 5 0S 43 27W
Caxias do Sul 173 29 10S 51 10W
Caxine, C. 118 35 56N 0 27W
Caxito 124 8 30S 13 30E
Cay Sal Bank 166 23 45N 80 0W
Cayambe 174 0 3N 78 22W
Cayce 157 33 59N 81 2W
Cayenne 175 5 0N 52 18W
Cayes, Les 167 18 15N 73 46W
Cayeux-sur-Mer. 43 50 10N 1 30E
Cayey 147 18 7N 66 10W
Caylus 44 44 15N 1 47E
Cayman Brac, I. 166 19 43N 79 49W
Cayman Is. 166 19 40N 79 50W
Cayo 165 17 10N 89 0W
Cayo Romano, I. 167 22 0N 73 30W
Cayuga 162 42 28N 76 30W
Cayuga L. 162 42 45N 76 45W
Cazalla de la Sierra 57 37 56N 5 45W
Cazaux et de Sanguinet, Étang de 44 44 29N 1 10W
Cazenovia 162 42 56N 75 51W
Cazères 44 43 13N 1 5E
Çazin 63 44 57N 15 57E
Čazma 63 45 45N 16 39E
Cazombo 125 12 0S 22 48E
Cazorla, Spain 59 37 55N 3 2W
Cazorla, Venez. 174 8 1N 67 0W
Cazorla, Sierra de 59 38 5N 2 55W
Cea, R. 56 42 40N 5 5W
Ceamurlia de Jos 67 44 43N 28 47E
Ceanannas Mor 38 53 42N 6 53W
Ceará = Fortaleza 170 3 35S 38 35W
Ceará □ 170 5 0S 40 0W
Ceará Mirim 170 5 38S 35 25W
Ceauru, L. 70 44 58N 23 11E
Cebaco, I. 166 7 33N 81 9W
Cebollar 172 29 10S 66 35W
Cebollera, Sierra de 58 42 0N 2 30W
Cebreros 56 40 27N 4 28W
Cebú 103 10 18N 123 54E
Cebú, I. 103 10 15N 123 40E
Ceccano 64 41 34N 13 18E
Cece 53 46 46N 18 39E
Cechi 120 6 15N 4 25W
Cecil Plains 139 27 30S 151 11E
Cecilton 162 39 24N 75 52W
Cécina 62 43 19N 10 33E
Cécina, R. 62 43 19N 10 40E
Ceclavin 56 39 50N 6 45W
Cedar City 161 37 41N 113 3W
Cedar Creek Res. 159 32 15N 96 0W
Cedar Falls 158 42 39N 92 29W
Cedar I. 162 37 35N 75 32W
Cedar Key 157 29 9N 83 5W
Cedar L. 153 53 20N 100 10W
Cedar Pt. 162 38 18N 76 25W
Cedar, R. 158 41 50N 91 20W
Cedar Rapids 158 42 0N 91 38W
Cedarburg 156 43 18N 87 55W
Cedartown 157 34 1N 85 15W
Cedarvale 152 55 1N 128 22W
Cedarville 160 41 37N 120 13W
Cedeira 56 43 39N 8 2W
Cedral 164 23 50N 100 42W
Cedrino, R. 64 40 8N 9 25E
Cedro 170 6 34S 39 3W
Cedros, I. de 164 28 10N 115 20W
Ceduna 139 32 7S 133 46E
Cedynia 54 52 53N 14 12E
Ceepeecee 152 49 52N 126 42W
Cefalù 65 38 3N 14 1E
Cega, R. 56 41 17N 4 10W
Cegléd 53 47 11N 19 47E
Céglie Messápico 65 40 39N 17 31E
Cehegín 59 38 6N 1 48W
Cehu-Silvaniei 70 47 24N 23 9E
Ceiba, La 166 15 40N 86 50W
Ceica 70 46 53N 22 10E
Ceira, R. 56 40 15N 7 55W
Cekhira 119 34 20N 10 5E
Celano 63 42 6N 13 30E
Celanova 56 42 9N 7 58W
Celaya 164 20 31N 100 37W
Celbridge 39 53 20N 6 33W
Celebes I. = Sulawesi 103 2 0S 120 0E
Celebes Sea 103 3 0N 123 0E
Celga 123 12 38N 37 3E
Celina 156 40 32N 84 31W
Čelić 66 44 43N 18 47E
Celje 63 46 16N 15 18E
Cellar Hd. 36 58 25N 6 10W
Celldömölk 53 47 16N 17 10E
Celle 48 52 37N 10 4E
Celles 47 50 42N 3 28E
Celorica da Beira 56 40 38N 7 24W
Cemaes Bay 31 53 24N 4 27W
Cemaes Hd. 31 52 7N 4 44W
Cement 159 34 56N 98 8W
Čemerno 66 43 26N 20 26E
Cemmaes Road 31 52 39N 3 41W
Cenarth 31 52 3N 4 32W
Cenis, Col du Mt. 45 45 15N 6 55E
Ceno, R. 62 44 40N 9 52E
Cenon 44 44 50N 0 33W
Centallo 62 44 30N 7 35E
Centenário do Sul 171 22 48S 51 57W
Center, N.D., U.S.A. 158 47 9N 101 17W
Center, Texas, U.S.A. 159 31 50N 94 10W
Centerfield 160 39 9N 111 56W
Centerville, Ala., U.S.A. 157 32 55N 87 7W
Centerville, Calif., U.S.A. 163 36 44N 119 30W
Centerville, Iowa, U.S.A. 158 40 45N 92 57W
Centerville, Miss., U.S.A. 159 31 10N 91 3W
Centerville, S.D., U.S.A. 158 43 10N 96 58W
Centerville, Tenn., U.S.A. 157 35 46N 87 29W
Centerville, Tex., U.S.A. 159 31 15N 95 56W
Cento 63 44 43N 11 16E
Central 170 11 8S 42 8W
Central □, Kenya 126 0 30S 33 30E
Central □, Malawi 126 13 30S 33 30E
Central □, U.K. 34 56 0N 4 30W
Central □, Zambia 127 14 25S 28 50E
Central African Empire ■ 124 7 0N 20 0E
Central Auckland □ 142 37 30S 175 30E
Central City, Ky., U.S.A. 156 37 20N 87 7W
Central City, Nebr., U.S.A. 158 41 8N 98 0W
Central, Cordillera, C. Rica 166 10 10N 84 5W
Central, Cordillera, Dom. Rep. 167 19 15N 71 0W
Central I., L. Turkana 126 3 30N 36 0E
Central Islip 162 40 49N 73 13W
Central Makran Range 93 26 30N 64 15E
Central Patricia 150 51 30N 90 9W
Central Ra. 135 5 0S 143 0E
Central Russian Uplands 16 54 0N 36 0E
Central Siberian Plateau 77 65 0N 105 0E
Central Square 162 43 17N 76 9W
Centralia, Ill., U.S.A. 158 38 32N 89 5W
Centralia, Mo., U.S.A. 158 39 12N 92 6W
Centralia, Wash., U.S.A. 160 46 46N 122 59W
Centúripe 65 37 37N 14 41E
Cephalonia = Kefallinía 69 38 28N 20 30E
Cepin 66 45 32N 18 34E

Ceprano Château d'Oex


Ceprano 64 41 33N 13 30 E
Ceptura 70 45 1N 26 21 E
Ceram I. = Seram I. 103 3 10S 129 0 E
Ceram Sea 103 2 30S 128 30 E
Cerbère 44 42 26N 3 10 E
Cerbicales, Îles 45 41 33N 9 22 E
Cerbu 70 44 46N 24 46 E
Cercal 57 37 48N 8 40W
Cercemaggiore 65 41 27N 14 43 E
Cerdaña 58 42 22N 1 35 E
Cerdedo 56 42 33N 8 23W
Cerea 63 45 12N 11 13 E
Ceres, Argent. 172 29 55S 61 55W
Ceres, Brazil 171 15 17S 49 35W
Ceres, Italy 62 45 19N 7 22 E
Ceres, S. Afr. 128 33 21S 19 18 E
Ceres, U.K. 35 56 18N 2 57W
Ceres, U.S.A. 163 37 35N 120 57W
Céret 44 42 30N 2 42 E
Cereté 174 8 53N 75 48W
Cerfontaine 47 50 11N 4 26 E
Cerignola 65 41 17N 15 53 E
Cerigo = Kíthira 69 36 9N 23 0 E
Cérilly 44 46 37N 2 50 E
Cerisiers 43 48 8N 3 30 E
Cerizay 42 46 50N 0 40W
Çerkeş 92 40 40N 32 58 E
Cerknica 63 45 48N 14 21 E
Çermerno 66 43 35N 20 25 E
Cerna 70 44 4N 28 17 E
Cerna, R. 70 44 45N 24 0 E
Cernavodă 70 44 22N 28 3 E
Cernay 43 47 44N 7 10 E
Cerne Abbas 28 50 49N 2 29W
Cernik 66 45 17N 17 22 E
Cerralvo, I. 164 24 20N 109 45 E
Cerreto Sannita 65 41 17N 14 34 E
Cerrig-y-druidion 31 53 2N 3 34W
Cerritos 164 22 20N 100 20W
Cerro 161 36 47N 105 36W
Cêrro Corá 171 6 3S 36 21W
Cerro de Punta, Mt. 147 18 10N 67 0W
Certaldo 62 43 32N 11 2 E
Cervaro, R. 65 41 21N 15 30 E
Cervera 58 41 40N 1 16 E
Cervera de Pisuerga 56 42 51N 4 30W
Cervera del Río Alhama 58 42 2N 1 58W
Cérvia 63 44 15N 12 20 E
Cervignano del Friuli 63 45 49N 13 20 E
Cervinara 65 41 2N 14 36 E
Cervo 56 43 40N 7 24W
Cervoine 45 42 20N 9 29 E
Cesanâtico 63 44 12N 12 22 E
César □ 174 9 0N 73 30W
Cesaro 65 37 50N 14 38 E
Cesena 63 44 9N 12 14 E
Cesenático 63 44 12N 12 22 E
Cēsis 80 57 17N 25 28 E
Česká Třebová 53 49 54N 16 27 E
Česke Budějovice 52 48 55N 14 25 E
České Velenice 52 48 45N 15 1 E
Českézemě 52 50 0N 14 0 E
Ceskomoravská Vrchovina 52 49 20N 15 45 E
Český Brod 52 50 4N 14 52 E
Český Krumlov 52 48 43N 14 21 E
Český Těšin 53 49 45N 18 39 E
Çeşme 69 38 20N 26 23 E
Cess, R. 120 5 25N 9 35W
Cessnock 141 32 50S 151 21 E
Cestos, R. 120 5 30N 9 30W
Cetate 70 44 7N 23 2 E
Cetina, R. 63 43 50N 16 30 E
Cetinje 66 42 23N 18 59 E
Cetraro 65 39 30N 15 56 E
Ceuta 118 35 52N 5 18W
Ceva 62 44 23N 8 0 E
Cévennes, mts. 44 44 10N 3 50 E
Ceylon = Sri Lanka ■ 97 7 30N 80 50 E
Cha-am 100 12 48N 99 58 E
Cha Pa 100 22 21N 103 50 E
Chaam 47 51 30N 4 52 E
Chabeuil 45 44 54N 5 1 E
Chabjuwardoo B. 137 23 0S 113 30 E
Chablais 45 46 20N 6 36 E
Chablis 43 47 47N 3 48 E
Chabounia 118 35 30N 2 38 E
Chacabuco 172 34 40S 60 27W
Chacewater 30 50 15N 5 8W
Chachapoyas 174 6 15S 77 50W
Chachoengsao 100 13 42N 101 5 E
Chachran 93 28 55N 70 30 E
Chachro 94 25 5N 70 15 E
Chaco □ 172 25 0S 61 0W
Chaco Austral 176 27 30S 61 40W
Chaco Boreal 172 22 30S 60 10W
Chaco Central 176 24 0S 61 0W
Chad ■ 117 12 30N 17 15 E
Chadan 77 51 17N 91 35 E
Chadileuvú, R. 172 37 0S 65 55W
Chadiza 127 14 10S 33 34 E
Chadron 158 42 50N 103 0W
Chadyr-Lunga 82 46 3N 28 51 E
Chae Hom 100 18 43N 99 35 E
Chaem, R. 100 18 11N 98 38 E
Chaeryŏng 107 38 24N 125 36 E
Chafurray 174 3 10N 73 14W
Chagai 93 29 30N 63 0 E
Chagai Hills 93 29 30N 63 0 E
Chagda 77 58 45N 130 30 E
Chagford 30 50 40N 3 50W
Chagny 43 46 57N 4 45 E
Chagoda 80 59 10N 35 25 E
Chagos Arch. 86 6 0S 72 0 E
Chāh Bahār 93 25 20N 60 40 E
Ch'ahaerhyuichungch'i 106 41 18N 112 48 E
Ch'ahanch'elo 106 41 41N 114 15 E
Chahar Buriak 93 30 15N 62 0 E
Chāhr-e Babak 93 30 10N 55 20 E
Chahsikiang 105 32 32N 79 41 E
Chahtung 98 26 41N 98 10 E
Chai-nat 100 15 11N 100 8 E
Chaibasa 99 22 42N 85 49 E
Chaillé-les-Marais 44 46 25N 1 2W
Chaise Dieu, La 44 45 20N 3 40 E
Chaiya 101 9 23N 99 14 E
Chaiyaphum 100 15 48N 102 2 E
Chaize-le-Vicomté, La 42 46 40N 1 18W
Chaj Doab 94 32 0N 73 0 E
Chajari 172 30 42N 58 0W
Chakaria 98 21 45N 92 5 E
Chake Chake 126 5 15S 39 45 E
Chakhansur 93 31 10N 62 0 E
Chaklashi 94 22 40N 72 52 E
Chakonipau, L. 151 56 18N 68 30W
Chakradharpur 95 22 45N 85 40 E
Chakwadam 98 27 29N 98 31 E
Chakwal 94 32 50N 72 45 E
Chala 174 15 48S 74 20W
Chalais 44 45 16N 0 3 E
Chalakudi 97 10 18N 76 20 E
Chalcatongo 165 17 4N 97 34W
Chalchihuites 164 23 29N 103 53W
Chalcis = Khalkís 69 38 27N 23 42 E
Chale 28 50 35N 1 19W
Chaleur B. 151 47 55N 65 30W
Chalfant 163 37 32N 118 21W
Chalfont St. Peter 29 51 36N 0 33W
Chalhuanca 174 14 15S 73 5W
Ch'aling 109 26 47N 113 45 E
Chaling Hu 105 34 55N 98 0 E
Chalisgaon 96 20 30N 75 10 E
Chalkar 83 50 35N 51 52 E
Chalkar Oz. 83 50 33N 51 45 E
Chalky Inlet 143 46 3S 166 31 E
Challans 42 46 50N 1 52W
Challapata 174 19 0S 66 50W
Challerange 43 49 18N 4 46 E
Challis 160 44 32N 114 25W
Chalna 95 22 36N 89 35 E
Chalon-sur-Saône 43 46 48N 4 50 E
Chalonnes 42 47 20N 0 45W
Châlons-sur-Marne 43 48 58N 4 20 E
Châlus 44 45 39N 0 58 E
Cham, Ger. 49 49 12N 12 40 E
Cham, Switz. 51 47 11N 8 28 E
Cham, Cu Lao 100 15 57N 108 30 E
Chama, R. 127 36 57N 106 37W
Chaman 93 30 58N 66 25 E
Chamarajanagar-Ramasamudram 97 11 52N 76 52 E
Chamartin de la Rosa 58 40 28N 3 40W
Chamba, India 94 32 35N 76 10 E
Chamba, Tanz. 125 11 37S 37 0 E
Chambal, R. 94 26 0N 76 55 E
Chamberlain, Austral. 136 15 58S 127 54 E
Chamberlain, U.S.A. 158 43 50N 99 21W
Chambers 161 35 13N 109 30W
Chambersburg 156 39 53N 77 41W
Chambéry 45 45 34N 5 55 E
Chambeshi 127 12 39S 28 1 E
Chambeshi, R. 124 10 20S 31 58 E
Chambois 42 48 48N 0 6 E
Chambon-Feugerolles, Le 45 45 24N 4 18 E
Châmbon, Le 45 45 35N 4 26 E
Chambord 151 48 25N 72 6W
Chamboulive 44 45 26N 1 42 E
Chambri L. 135 4 15S 143 10 E
Chamela 164 19 32N 105 5W
Chamical 172 30 22S 66 27W
Chamkar Luong 101 11 0N 103 45 E
Chamonix 45 45 55N 6 51 E
Champa 95 22 2N 82 43 E
Champagne, Can. 152 60 49N 136 30W
Champagne, France 43 49 0N 4 40 E
Champagnole 43 46 45N 5 55 E
Champaign 156 40 8N 88 14W
Champassak 100 14 53N 105 52 E
Champaubert 43 48 50N 3 45 E
Champdeniers 44 46 29N 0 25W
Champeix 44 45 37N 3 8 E
Champerico 166 14 18N 91 55W
Champier 50 45 27N 5 17 E
Champion B. 137 28 44S 114 36 E
Champlain 151 46 27N 72 24W
Champotón 165 19 20N 90 50W
Chamusca 57 39 21N 8 29W
Chana 101 6 55N 100 44 E
Chañaral 172 26 15S 70 50W
Chanasma 94 23 44N 72 5 E
Chanca, R. 57 37 49N 7 15W
Chanchiang 109 21 15N 110 20 E
Chancy 50 46 8N 6 0 E
Chanda 96 19 57N 79 25 E
Chandalar 147 67 30N 148 35W
Chandausi 95 28 27N 78 49 E
Chandeleur Is. 159 29 45N 88 53W
Chandeleur Sd. 159 29 58N 88 40W
Chandernagore 95 22 52N 88 24 E
Chandigarh 94 30 30N 76 58 E
Chandler, Can. 151 48 18N 64 46W
Chandler, Ariz., U.S.A. 161 33 20N 111 56W
Chandler, Okla., U.S.A. 159 35 43N 97 20W
Chandler's Ford 28 50 59N 1 23W
Chandlers Peak 141 30 24S 152 10 E
Chandmani 105 45 20N 97 59 E
Chandpur, Bangla. 98 22 8N 90 55 E
Chandpur, India 94 29 8N 78 19 E
Chang 94 26 59N 68 30 E
Ch'ang Chiang, R. 109 31 40N 121 50 E
Chang, Ko 101 12 0N 102 23 E
Changa 95 33 53N 77 35 E
Changanacheri 97 9 25N 76 31 E
Changane, R. 125 23 30S 33 50 E
Ch'anganpao 108 26 9N 109 42 E
Changchiak'ou 106 40 50N 114 53 E
Ch'angchiang 100 19 19N 108 43 E
Ch'angchih 106 36 11N 113 6 E
Ch'angchou 109 31 47N 119 58 E
Changchou 109 24 31N 117 40 E
Ch'angch'un 107 43 58N 125 19 E
Ch'angch'unling 107 45 22N 125 28 E
Changdori 107 38 30N 127 40 E
Ch'angfeng 109 32 27N 117 9 E
Changhsing 109 31 0N 119 56 E
Ch'anghua 109 30 10N 119 15 E
Changhua 109 24 2N 120 30 E
Changhŭng 107 34 41N 126 52 E
Changhŭngni 107 40 24N 128 19 E
Ch'angi 107 36 51N 119 23 E
Changjin 107 40 23N 127 15 E
Changjin-chŏsuji 107 40 30N 127 15 E
Changkuangts'ai Ling 107 45 50N 128 50 E
Changli 107 39 40N 119 19 E
Ch'angling 107 44 16N 123 57 E
Ch'anglo, Fukien, China 109 25 58N 119 31 E
Ch'anglo, Fukien, China 109 26 40N 117 20 E
Ch'anglo, Kwangtung, China 109 24 4N 115 37 E
Changlun 101 6 25N 100 26 E
Changming 108 31 44N 104 44 E
Ch'angning, Hunan, China 109 26 25N 112 15 E
Ch'angning, Szechwan, China 108 28 38N 104 57 E
Ch'angning, Yunnan, China 108 24 50N 99 36 E
Ch'angpai 107 41 26N 128 0 E
Ch'angpai Shan 107 42 25N 129 0 E
Changpei 106 41 7N 114 51 E
Ch'angp'ing 106 40 12N 116 12 E
Changp'ing 109 25 18N 117 24 E
Changpu 109 24 2N 117 31 E
Ch'angsha 109 28 15N 113 0 E
Ch'angshan 109 28 57N 118 31 E
Ch'angshou 108 29 50N 107 2 E
Ch'angshu 109 31 33N 120 45 E
Ch'angshun 108 25 59N 106 25 E
Ch'angt'ai 109 24 34N 117 50 E
Ch'angte 109 29 5N 111 42 E
Ch'angt'ing 109 25 52N 116 20 E
Ch'angt'u 107 42 47N 124 0 E
Ch'angtu 108 31 10N 97 14 E
Ch'angt'u Shan 109 30 15N 122 20 E
Ch'angwu 106 35 9N 107 42 E
Changwu 107 42 24N 122 30 E
Ch'angyang 109 30 28N 111 9 E
Ch'angyatien 106 40 40N 108 46 E
Changyeh 105 38 56N 100 37 E
Changyŏn 107 38 15N 125 6 E
Ch'angyüan 106 35 17N 114 50 E
Chanhanga 128 16 0S 14 8 E
Chanhua 107 37 42N 118 8 E
Chani 108 25 36N 103 49 E
Channapatna 97 12 40N 77 15 E
Channel Is. 42 49 30N 2 40W
Channel Islands 163 33 30N 119 0W
Channing, Mich., U.S.A. 156 46 9N 88 1W
Channing, Tex., U.S.A. 159 35 45N 102 20W
Chantada 56 42 36N 7 46W
Chanthaburi 100 12 38N 102 12 E
Chantilly 43 49 12N 2 29 E
Chantonnay 42 46 40N 1 3W
Chantrey Inlet 148 67 48N 96 20W
Chanute 159 37 45N 85 25W
Chanyü 107 44 39N 122 45 E
Chanza, R. 57 37 49N 7 15W
Ch'ao Hu 109 31 40N 117 30 E
Chao Phraya Lowlands 100 15 30N 100 0 E
Chao Phraya, R. 100 13 32N 100 36 E
Ch'aoan 109 23 41N 116 33 E
Chaoan 109 23 47N 117 5 E
Chaoch'eng, Shansi, China 106 36 26N 111 43 E
Chaoch'eng, Shantung, China 106 36 3N 115 35 E
Chaochiao 108 28 1N 102 49 E
Chaoch'ing 109 23 7N 112 24 E
Chaohsien 106 37 45N 114 46 E
Ch'aohsien 109 31 41N 117 49 E
Chaop'ing 109 24 1N 110 59 E
Chaot'ung 108 27 19N 103 42 E
Ch'aoyang, Kwangtung, China 109 23 10N 116 30 E
Ch'aoyang, Liaoning, China 107 41 46N 120 16 E
Chaoyüan, Heilungkiang, China 107 45 30N 125 8 E
Chaoyüan, Shantung, China 107 37 22N 120 24 E
Chap Kuduk 76 48 45N 55 5 E
Chapala 127 15 50S 37 35 E
Chapala, Lago de 164 20 10N 103 20W
Chaparmukh 98 26 12N 92 31 E
Chapayevo 83 50 25N 51 10 E
Chapayevsk 81 53 0N 49 40 E
Chapecó 173 27 14S 52 41W
Chapel-en-le-Frith 32 53 19N 1 54W
Chapel Hill 157 35 53N 79 3W
Chapelle-d'Angillon, La 43 47 21N 2 25 E
Chapelle Glain, La 42 47 38N 1 11W
Chapeyevo 84 50 12N 51 10 E
Chapleau 150 47 50N 83 24W
Chaplin 153 50 28N 106 40W
Chaplino 82 48 8N 36 15 E
Chaplygin 81 53 15N 39 55 E
Chapra 95 25 48N 84 50 E
Char 116 21 40N 12 45W
Chara 77 56 54N 118 12 E
Charadai 172 27 35S 60 0W
Charagua 174 19 45S 63 10W
Charak 93 26 46N 54 18 E
Charalá 174 6 17N 73 10W
Charaña 174 17 30S 69 35W
Charapita 174 0 37S 74 21W
Charata 172 27 13S 61 14W
Charcas 164 23 10N 101 20W
Charcoal L. 153 58 49N 102 22W
Charcot I. 13 70 0S 75 0W
Chard, Can. 153 55 55N 111 10W
Chard, U.K. 28 50 52N 2 59W
Chardara 76 41 16N 67 59 E
Chardara, Step 85 42 20N 68 0 E
Charduar 98 26 51N 92 46 E
Chardzhou 85 39 6N 63 34 E
Charente-Maritime □ 44 45 50N 0 35W
Charente □ 44 45 50N 0 16W
Charente, R. 44 45 41N 0 30W
Charentsavan 83 40 35N 44 41 E
Chârib, G. 122 28 6N 32 54 E
Charikar 93 35 0N 69 10 E
Charing 29 51 12N 0 49 E
Charité, La 43 47 10N 3 0 E
Chariton R. 158 39 19N 92 58W
Charkhari 95 25 24N 79 45 E
Charkhi Dadri 94 28 37N 76 17 E
Charlbury 28 51 52N 1 29W
Charlemont 38 54 26N 6 40W
Charleroi 47 50 24N 4 27 E
Charles, C. 162 37 10N 75 52W
Charles City, Iowa, U.S.A. 158 43 2N 92 41W
Charles City, Va., U.S.A. 162 37 20N 77 4W
Charles L. 153 59 50N 110 33W
Charles, Pk. 137 32 53S 121 8 E
Charles Town 156 39 20N 77 50W
Charleston, Miss., U.S.A. 159 34 2N 90 3W
Charleston, Mo., U.S.A. 159 36 52N 89 20W
Charleston, S.C., U.S.A. 157 32 47N 79 56W
Charleston, W. Va., U.S.A. 157 38 24N 81 36W
Charlestown, Ireland 38 53 58N 8 48W
Charlestown, S. Afr. 129 27 26S 29 53 E
Charlestown, Ind., U.S.A. 156 38 29N 85 40W
Charlestown, N.H., U.S.A. 162 43 14N 72 24W
Charlestown of Aberlour 37 57 27N 3 13W
Charlesville 124 5 27S 20 59 E
Charleville 139 26 24S 146 15 E
Charleville-Mézières 43 49 44N 4 40 E
Charleville = Rath Luirc 39 52 21N 8 40W
Charlevoix 156 45 19N 85 14W
Charlieu 45 46 10N 4 10 E
Charlotte, Mich., U.S.A. 156 42 36N 84 48W
Charlotte, N.C., U.S.A. 157 35 16N 80 46W
Charlotte Amalie 147 18 22N 64 56W
Charlotte Harb. 157 26 45N 82 10W
Charlotte Waters 136 25 56N 134 54 E
Charlottenberg 72 59 54N 12 17 E
Charlottesville 156 38 1N 78 30W
Charlottetown 151 46 14N 63 8W
Charlton, Austral. 140 36 16S 143 24 E
Charlton, U.S.A. 158 40 59N 93 20W
Charlton I. 150 52 0N 79 20W
Charlton Kings 28 51 52N 2 3W
Charlwood 29 51 8N 0 12W
Charmes 43 48 22N 6 17 E
Charminster 28 50 43N 2 28W
Charmouth 28 50 45N 2 54W
Charnwood Forest 23 52 43N 1 18W
Charny 151 46 43N 71 15W
Charolles 45 46 27N 4 16 E
Charost 43 47 0N 2 7 E
Charouine 118 29 0N 0 15W
Charre 127 17 19S 35 10 E
Charroux 44 46 9N 0 25 E
Charsadda 94 34 7N 71 45 E
Charters Towers 138 20 5S 146 13 E
Chartham 29 51 14N 1 1 E
Chartre, La 42 47 42N 0 34 E
Chartres 42 48 29N 1 30 E
Chascomús 172 35 30S 58 0W
Chasefu 127 11 55N 32 58 E
Chaslands Mistake 143 46 38S 169 22 E
Chasseneuil-sur-Bonnieure 44 45 52N 0 29 E
Chata 94 27 42N 77 30 E
Châtaigneraie, La 42 46 38N 0 45W
Chatal Balkan = Udvoy Balkan 67 42 50N 26 50 E
Château-Chinon 43 47 4N 3 56 E
Château d'Oex 50 46 28N 7 8 E

Château-du-Loir Ch'iench'engchen


| | | | |
|---|---|---|---|
| Château-du-Loir | 42 | 47 40N | 0 25 E |
| Château Gontier | 42 | 47 50N | 0 42W |
| Château-la-Vallière | 42 | 47 30N | 0 20 E |
| Château-Landon | 43 | 48 8N | 2 40 E |
| Château, Le | 44 | 45 52N | 1 12W |
| Château Porcien | 43 | 49 31N | 4 13 E |
| Château Renault | 42 | 47 36N | 0 56 E |
| Château-Salins | 43 | 48 50N | 6 30 E |
| Château-Thierry | 43 | 49 3N | 3 20 E |
| Châteaubourg | 43 | 48 7N | 1 25W |
| Châteaubriant | 42 | 47 43N | 1 23W |
| Châteaudun | 42 | 48 3N | 1 20 E |
| Châteaugiron | 42 | 48 3N | 1 30W |
| Châteaulin | 42 | 48 11N | 4 8W |
| Châteaumeillant | 44 | 46 35N | 2 12 E |
| Châteauneuf | 42 | 48 35N | 1 15 E |
| Châteauneuf-du-Faou | 42 | 48 11N | 3 50W |
| Châteauneuf-sur-Charente | 44 | 45 36N | 0 3W |
| Châteauneuf-sur-Cher | 44 | 46 52N | 2 18 E |
| Châteauneuf-sur-Loire | 43 | 47 52N | 2 13 E |
| Châteaurenard | 45 | 43 53N | 4 51 E |
| Châteauroux | 43 | 46 50N | 1 40 E |
| Châtel-Guyon | 44 | 45 55N | 3 4 E |
| Châtel St. Denis | 50 | 46 32N | 6 54 E |
| Châtelaillon-Plage | 44 | 46 5N | 1 5W |
| Châtelard, Le | 50 | 46 4N | 6 57 E |
| Châtelaudren | 42 | 48 33N | 2 59W |
| Chatelet | 47 | 50 24N | 4 32 E |
| Châtelet, Le, Cher, France | 44 | 46 40N | 2 20 E |
| Châtelet, Le, Seine et Marne, France | 43 | 48 30N | 2 47 E |
| Châtellerault | 42 | 46 50N | 0 30 E |
| Châtelus-Malvaleix | 44 | 46 18N | 2 1 E |
| Chatham, N.B., Can. | 151 | 47 2N | 65 28W |
| Chatham, Ont., Can. | 150 | 42 24N | 82 11W |
| Chatham, U.K. | 29 | 51 22N | 0 32 E |
| Chatham, Alaska, U.S.A. | 147 | 57 30N | 135 0W |
| Chatham, La., U.S.A. | 159 | 32 22N | 92 26W |
| Chatham, N.Y., U.S.A. | 162 | 42 21N | 73 32W |
| Chatham Is. | 130 | 44 0 S | 176 40W |
| Chatham Str. | 152 | 57 0N | 134 40W |
| Châtillon, Loiret, France | 43 | 47 36N | 2 44 E |
| Châtillon, Marne, France | 43 | 49 5N | 3 43 E |
| Chatillon | 62 | 45 45N | 7 40 E |
| Châtillon-Coligny | 43 | 47 50N | 2 51 E |
| Châtillon-en-Bazois | 43 | 47 3N | 3 39 E |
| Châtillon-en-Diois | 45 | 44 41N | 5 29 E |
| Châtillon-sur-Seine | 43 | 47 50N | 4 33 E |
| Châtillon-sur-Sèvre | 42 | 46 56N | 0 45W |
| Chatkal, R. | 85 | 41 38N | 70 1 E |
| Chatkalskiy Khrebet | 85 | 41 30N | 70 45 E |
| Chatmohar | 95 | 24 15N | 89 26 E |
| Chatra | 95 | 24 12N | 84 56 E |
| Chatrapur | 96 | 19 22N | 85 2 E |
| Châtre, La | 44 | 46 35N | 1 59 E |
| Chatsworth | 127 | 19 32 S | 30 46 E |
| Chatta-Hantō | 111 | 34 45N | 136 55 E |
| Chattahoochee | 157 | 30 43N | 84 51W |
| Chattanooga | 157 | 35 2N | 85 17W |
| Chatteris | 29 | 52 27N | 0 3 E |
| Chatton | 35 | 55 34N | 1 55W |
| Chaturat | 100 | 15 34N | 101 51 E |
| Chatyrkel, Ozero | 85 | 40 40N | 75 18 E |
| Chatyrtash | 85 | 40 55N | 76 25 E |
| Chau Phu | 101 | 10 42N | 105 7 E |
| Chaudes-Aigues | 44 | 44 51N | 3 1 E |
| Chauffailes | 44 | 46 13N | 4 20 E |
| Chauk | 98 | 20 53N | 94 49 E |
| Chaukan La | 99 | 27 0N | 97 15 E |
| Chaukan Pass | 98 | 27 8N | 97 10 E |
| Chaulnes | 43 | 49 48N | 2 47 E |
| Chaumont | 43 | 48 7N | 5 8 E |
| Chaumont-en-Vexin | 43 | 49 16N | 1 53 E |
| Chaumont-sur-Loire | 42 | 47 29N | 1 11 E |
| Chaunay | 44 | 46 13N | 0 9 E |
| Chauny | 43 | 49 37N | 3 12 E |
| Chausey, Îs. | 42 | 48 52N | 1 49W |
| Chaussin | 43 | 46 59N | 5 22 E |
| Chauvin | 153 | 52 45N | 110 10W |
| Chaux de Fonds, La | 50 | 47 7N | 6 50 E |
| Chaves, Brazil | 170 | 0 15 S | 49 55W |
| Chaves, Port. | 56 | 41 45N | 7 32W |
| Chavuma | 125 | 13 10 S | 22 55 E |
| Chawang | 101 | 8 25N | 99 30 E |
| Ch'aya | 108 | 30 35N | 98 3 E |
| Chayan | 85 | 43 5N | 69 25 E |
| Chayek | 85 | 41 55N | 74 30 E |
| Chaykovskiy | 84 | 56 47N | 54 9 E |
| Chazelles-sur-Lyon | 45 | 45 39N | 4 22 E |
| Cheadle, Gr. Manchester, U.K. | 32 | 53 23N | 2 14W |
| Cheadle, Staffs., U.K. | 32 | 52 59N | 1 59W |
| Cheadle Hulme | 32 | 53 22N | 2 12W |
| Cheb (Eger) | 52 | 50 9N | 12 20 E |
| Chebarkul | 84 | 55 0N | 60 25 E |
| Cheboksary | 81 | 56 8N | 47 30 E |
| Cheboygan | 156 | 45 38N | 84 29W |
| Chebsara | 81 | 59 10N | 38 45 E |
| Chech, Erg | 118 | 25 0N | 2 15W |
| Chechaouen | 118 | 35 9N | 5 15W |
| Chechen | 83 | 43 59N | 47 40 E |
| Chech'eng | 106 | 34 4N | 115 13 E |
| Checheno-Ingush, A.S.S.R. □ | 83 | 43 30N | 45 29 E |
| Chechon | 107 | 37 8N | 128 12 E |
| Checiny | 54 | 50 46N | 20 37 E |
| Checleset B. | 152 | 50 5N | 127 35W |
| Checotah | 159 | 35 31N | 95 30W |
| Chedabucto B. | 151 | 45 25N | 61 8W |
| Cheddar | 28 | 51 16N | 2 47W |
| Cheddleton | 32 | 53 5N | 2 2W |
| Cheduba I. | 98 | 18 45N | 93 40 E |
| Cheepie | 139 | 26 43 S | 144 59 E |
| Ch'eerhch'en Ho, R. | 105 | 39 30N | 88 15 E |
| Chef-Boutonne | 44 | 46 7N | 0 4W |
| Chefoo = Yent'ai | 107 | 37 30N | 121 12 E |
| Chefornak | 147 | 60 10N | 164 15W |
| Chegdomyn | 77 | 51 7N | 132 52 E |
| Chegga | 118 | 25 15N | 5 40W |
| Chehalis | 160 | 46 44N | 122 59W |
| Cheju | 107 | 33 28N | 126 30 E |
| Cheju Do | 107 | 33 29N | 126 34 E |
| Chejung | 109 | 27 13N | 119 52 E |
| Chekalin | 81 | 54 10N | 36 10 E |
| Chekao | 109 | 31 46N | 117 45 E |
| Chekiang □ | 109 | 29 30N | 120 0 E |
| Chela, Sa. da | 128 | 16 20 S | 13 20 E |
| Chelan, Can. | 153 | 52 38N | 103 22 E |
| Chelan, U.S.A. | 160 | 47 49N | 120 0W |
| Chelan, L. | 152 | 48 5N | 120 30W |
| Cheleken | 76 | 39 26N | 53 7 E |
| Chelforó | 176 | 39 0 S | 66 40W |
| Chéliff, O. | 118 | 36 0N | 0 8 E |
| Chelkar | 76 | 47 40N | 59 32 E |
| Chelkar Tengiz, Solonchak | 76 | 48 0N | 62 30 E |
| Chellala Dahrania | 118 | 33 2N | 0 1 E |
| Chelles | 43 | 48 52N | 2 33 E |
| Chełm | 54 | 51 8N | 23 30 E |
| Chełm □ | 54 | 51 15N | 23 30 E |
| Chelmarsh | 28 | 52 29N | 2 25W |
| Chełmek | 54 | 50 6N | 19 16 E |
| Chelmer, R. | 29 | 51 45N | 0 42 E |
| Chełmno | 54 | 53 20N | 18 30 E |
| Chelmsford | 29 | 51 44N | 0 29 E |
| Chełmża | 54 | 53 10N | 18 39 E |
| Chelsea, Austral. | 141 | 38 5 S | 145 8 E |
| Chelsea, Okla., U.S.A. | 159 | 36 35N | 95 25W |
| Chelsea, Vermont, U.S.A. | 162 | 43 59N | 72 27W |
| Cheltenham | 28 | 51 55N | 2 5W |
| Chelva | 58 | 39 45N | 1 0W |
| Chelyabinsk | 84 | 55 10N | 61 24 E |
| Chelyuskin, C. | 86 | 77 30N | 103 0 E |
| Chemainus | 152 | 48 55N | 123 48W |
| Chemikovsk | 78 | 56 31N | 58 11 E |
| Chemillé | 42 | 47 14N | 0 45W |
| Chemnitz = Karl-Marx-Stadt | 48 | 50 50N | 12 55 E |
| Chemor | 101 | 4 44N | 101 6 E |
| Chemult | 160 | 43 14N | 121 54W |
| Chen, Gora | 77 | 65 10N | 141 20 E |
| Chenab, R. | 94 | 30 40N | 73 30 E |
| Chenachane, O. | 118 | 25 30N | 3 30W |
| Chenan | 106 | 33 16N | 109 1 E |
| Chenango Forks | 162 | 42 15N | 75 51W |
| Chencha | 123 | 6 15N | 37 32 E |
| Ch'ench'i | 109 | 28 1N | 110 13 E |
| Ch'enchiachiang | 107 | 34 25N | 119 50 E |
| Chenchiang | 109 | 32 12N | 119 27 E |
| Chenchieh | 108 | 23 15N | 107 9 E |
| Chênée | 47 | 50 37N | 5 37 E |
| Cheney | 160 | 47 38N | 117 34W |
| Chenfeng | 108 | 25 25N | 105 51 E |
| Chengan | 108 | 28 30N | 107 30 E |
| Ch'engch'eng | 106 | 35 6N | 109 52 E |
| Ch'engchiang | 108 | 24 40N | 102 55 E |
| Chengchou | 106 | 34 38N | 113 43 E |
| Chengchow = Chengchou | 106 | 34 38N | 113 43 E |
| Chengelee | 98 | 28 47N | 96 16 E |
| Chengho | 109 | 27 25N | 118 46 E |
| Ch'enghsi Hu | 109 | 32 22N | 116 12 E |
| Ch'enghsien, Chekiang, China | 109 | 29 30N | 120 48 E |
| Ch'enghsien, Kansu, China | 106 | 33 42N | 105 36 E |
| Ch'engk'ou | 108 | 31 58N | 108 48 E |
| Ch'engku | 106 | 33 9N | 107 22 E |
| Ch'engkung | 108 | 24 53N | 102 45 E |
| Ch'engmai | 100 | 19 44N | 109 59 E |
| Ch'engpu | 109 | 26 12N | 110 5 E |
| Ch'engte | 107 | 41 0N | 117 58 E |
| Chengting | 106 | 38 8N | 114 37 E |
| Ch'engtu | 108 | 30 45N | 104 0 E |
| Ch'engtung Hu | 109 | 32 17N | 116 23 E |
| Ch'engtzut'uan | 107 | 39 30N | 122 30 E |
| Ch'engwu | 106 | 35 0N | 115 56 E |
| Ch'engyang | 107 | 36 20N | 120 16 E |
| Chengyang | 109 | 32 36N | 114 23 E |
| Chengyangkuan | 109 | 32 29N | 116 37 E |
| Chenhai | 109 | 29 57N | 121 42 E |
| Ch'enhsien | 109 | 25 48N | 113 2 E |
| Chenhsiung | 108 | 27 27N | 104 50 E |
| Chenhsü | 109 | 27 6N | 120 16 E |
| Chenkán | 165 | 19 8N | 90 58W |
| Chenk'ang | 108 | 24 4N | 99 18 E |
| Chenlai | 107 | 45 52N | 123 12 E |
| Chenning | 108 | 25 57N | 105 51 E |
| Chenp'ing | 106 | 33 2N | 112 14 E |
| Ch'enp'ing | 108 | 31 52N | 109 31 E |
| Chenyüan, Kansu, China | 106 | 35 59N | 107 2 E |
| Chenyüan, Kweichow, China | 108 | 27 0N | 108 20 E |
| Cheo Reo = Hau Bon | 101 | 13 25N | 108 28 E |
| Cheom Ksan | 100 | 14 13N | 104 56 E |
| Chepelare | 67 | 41 44N | 24 40 E |
| Chepén | 174 | 7 10 S | 79 15W |
| Chepes | 172 | 31 20 S | 66 35W |
| Chepo | 166 | 9 10N | 79 6W |
| Chepstow | 31 | 51 38N | 2 40W |
| Cheptsa, R. | 81 | 58 36N | 50 4 E |
| Cheptulil, Mt. | 126 | 1 25N | 35 35 E |
| Chequamegon B. | 158 | 46 40N | 90 30W |
| Chequeche | 127 | 14 13 S | 38 30 E |
| Cher □ | 43 | 47 10N | 2 30 E |
| Cher, R. | 43 | 47 10N | 2 10 E |
| Cheran | 98 | 25 45N | 90 44 E |
| Cherasco | 62 | 44 39N | 7 50 E |
| Cheratte | 47 | 50 40N | 5 41 E |
| Cheraw | 157 | 34 42N | 79 54W |
| Cherbourg | 42 | 49 39N | 1 40W |
| Cherchell | 118 | 36 35N | 2 12 E |
| Cherdakly | 81 | 54 25N | 48 50 E |
| Cherdyn | 84 | 60 24N | 56 29 E |
| Cheremkhovo | 77 | 53 32N | 102 40 E |
| Cherepanovo | 76 | 54 15N | 83 30 E |
| Cherepovets | 81 | 59 5N | 37 55 E |
| Chergui, Chott Ech | 118 | 34 10N | 0 25 E |
| Cheri | 121 | 13 26N | 11 21 E |
| Cherikov | 80 | 53 32N | 31 20 E |
| Cheriton | 28 | 51 3N | 1 9W |
| Cheriton Fitzpaine | 30 | 50 51N | 3 38W |
| Cherkessk | 83 | 44 25N | 42 10 E |
| Cherlak | 76 | 54 15N | 74 55 E |
| Chermoz | 84 | 58 46N | 56 10 E |
| Chernak | 85 | 43 24N | 68 2 E |
| Chernaya Kholunitsa | 84 | 58 51N | 51 52 E |
| Cherni, Mt. | 67 | 42 35N | 23 18 E |
| Chernigov | 80 | 51 28N | 31 20 E |
| Chernikovsk | 84 | 54 48N | 56 8 E |
| Chernobyl | 80 | 51 13N | 30 15 E |
| Chernogorsk | 77 | 54 5N | 91 10 E |
| Chernomorskoye | 82 | 45 31N | 32 46 E |
| Chernovskoye | 81 | 58 48N | 47 20 E |
| Chernovtsy | 82 | 48 0N | 26 0 E |
| Chernoye | 77 | 70 30N | 89 10 E |
| Chernushka | 84 | 56 29N | 56 3 E |
| Chernyakhovsk | 80 | 54 29N | 21 48 E |
| Chernyshevskiy | 77 | 62 40N | 112 30 E |
| Chernyshkovskiy | 83 | 48 30N | 42 28 E |
| Cherokee, Iowa, U.S.A. | 158 | 42 40N | 95 30W |
| Cherokee, Okla., U.S.A. | 159 | 36 45N | 98 25W |
| Cherokees, L. of the | 159 | 36 50N | 95 12W |
| Cherquenco | 176 | 38 35 S | 72 0W |
| Cherrapunji | 99 | 25 17N | 91 47 E |
| Cherry Creek | 160 | 39 50N | 114 58W |
| Cherry Valley, U.S.A. | 162 | 42 48N | 74 45W |
| Cherry Valley, U.S.A. | 163 | 33 59N | 116 57W |
| Cherryvale | 159 | 37 20N | 95 33W |
| Cherskiy | 77 | 68 45N | 161 18 E |
| Cherskogo Khrebet | 77 | 65 0N | 143 0 E |
| Chertkovo | 83 | 49 25N | 40 19 E |
| Chertsey | 29 | 51 23N | 0 30W |
| Cherven | 80 | 53 45N | 28 13 E |
| Cherven-Bryag | 67 | 43 17N | 24 7 E |
| Cherwell, R. | 28 | 51 46N | 1 18W |
| Chesapeake Bay | 162 | 38 0N | 76 12W |
| Chesapeake Beach | 162 | 38 41N | 76 32W |
| Chesha B. = Cheshskaya G. | 78 | 67 20N | 47 0 E |
| Chesham | 29 | 51 42N | 0 36W |
| Cheshire □ | 32 | 53 14N | 2 30W |
| Cheshunt | 29 | 51 42N | 0 1W |
| Chesil Beach | 23 | 50 37N | 2 33W |
| Cheslatta L. | 152 | 53 49N | 125 20W |
| Chesne, Le | 43 | 49 30N | 4 45 E |
| Cheste | 59 | 39 30N | 0 41W |
| Chester, U.K. | 32 | 53 12N | 2 53W |
| Chester, Calif., U.S.A. | 160 | 40 22N | 121 22W |
| Chester, Ill., U.S.A. | 158 | 37 58N | 89 50W |
| Chester, Mont., U.S.A. | 160 | 48 31N | 111 0W |
| Chester, Pa., U.S.A. | 162 | 39 54N | 75 20W |
| Chester, S.C., U.S.A. | 157 | 34 44N | 81 13W |
| Chester, Va., U.S.A. | 162 | 37 21N | 77 27W |
| Chester, Vt., U.S.A. | 162 | 43 16N | 72 36W |
| Chester-le-Street | 33 | 54 53N | 1 34W |
| Chesterfield, Can. | 148 | 63 0N | 91 0W |
| Chesterfield, U.K. | 33 | 53 14N | 1 26W |
| Chesterfield, U.S.A. | 162 | 37 23N | 77 31W |
| Chesterfield I. | 129 | 16 20 S | 43 58 E |
| Chesterfield, Îles | 133 | 19 52 S | 158 15 E |
| Chesterfield Inlet | 148 | 63 30N | 90 45W |
| Chesterton Range | 138 | 25 30 S | 147 27 E |
| Chestertown | 162 | 39 13N | 76 4W |
| Chesuncook L. | 151 | 46 0N | 69 10W |
| Chetaibi | 119 | 37 1N | 7 20 E |
| Cheticamp | 151 | 46 37N | 60 59W |
| Chetumal | 165 | 18 30N | 88 20W |
| Chetumal, Bahía de | 165 | 18 40N | 88 10W |
| Chetwynd | 152 | 55 45N | 121 45W |
| Chevanceaux | 44 | 45 18N | 0 14W |
| Cheviot Hills | 35 | 55 20N | 2 30W |
| Cheviot Ra. | 138 | 25 20 S | 143 45 E |
| Cheviot, The | 35 | 55 29N | 2 8W |
| Chew Bahir | 123 | 4 40N | 30 50 E |
| Chew Magna | 28 | 51 21N | 2 37W |
| Chewelah | 160 | 48 17N | 117 43W |
| Cheyenne, Okla., U.S.A. | 159 | 35 40N | 99 40W |
| Cheyenne, Wyo., U.S.A. | 158 | 41 9N | 104 49W |
| Cheyenne, R. | 158 | 44 50N | 101 0W |
| Cheyenne Wells | 158 | 38 51N | 102 23W |
| Cheylard, Le | 45 | 44 55N | 4 25 E |
| Cheyne B. | 137 | 34 35 S | 118 50 E |
| Chhabra | 94 | 24 40N | 76 54 E |
| Chhang | 100 | 12 15N | 104 14 E |
| Chhatak | 95 | 25 5N | 91 37 E |
| Chhatarpur | 95 | 24 55N | 79 43 E |
| Chhep | 100 | 13 45N | 105 24 E |
| Chhindwara | 95 | 22 2N | 78 59 E |
| Chhlong | 101 | 12 15N | 105 58 E |
| Chhuk | 101 | 10 46N | 104 8 E |
| Chi, R. | 100 | 15 11N | 104 43 E |
| Chiaho | 109 | 25 33N | 112 15 E |
| Chiahsiang | 106 | 35 25N | 116 21 E |
| Chiahsien, Hensi, China | 106 | 38 6N | 110 28 E |
| Chiahsien, Honan, China | 106 | 33 58N | 113 13 E |
| Chiahsing | 109 | 30 45N | 120 43 E |
| Chiai | 109 | 23 29N | 120 25 E |
| Chiali | 109 | 23 10N | 120 11 E |
| Chialing Chiang, R. | 108 | 30 2N | 106 19 E |
| Chiamussu | 105 | 46 50N | 130 21 E |
| Chian, Kiangsi, China | 109 | 27 8N | 115 0 E |
| Chian, Kirin, China | 107 | 41 6N | 126 10 E |
| Chiang Dao | 100 | 19 22N | 98 58 E |
| Chiang Kham | 100 | 19 32N | 100 18 E |
| Chiang Khan | 100 | 17 52N | 101 36 E |
| Chiang Khong | 100 | 20 17N | 100 24 E |
| Chiang Mai | 100 | 18 47N | 98 59 E |
| Chiang Saen | 100 | 20 16N | 100 5 E |
| Chiangch'eng | 108 | 22 36N | 101 50 E |
| Chiangchiat'un | 107 | 40 54N | 120 36 E |
| Chiangching | 108 | 29 13N | 106 15 E |
| Chiangchun | 109 | 23 5N | 120 5 E |
| Chianghua | 109 | 25 2N | 111 45 E |
| Chiangk'ou | 108 | 27 42N | 108 50 E |
| Chiangling | 109 | 30 21N | 112 5 E |
| Chiangmen | 109 | 22 37N | 113 3 E |
| Chiangpei | 108 | 29 47N | 106 29 E |
| Chiangp'ing | 108 | 21 36N | 108 8 E |
| Chiangshan | 109 | 28 45N | 118 37 E |
| Chiangta | 108 | 31 28N | 99 12 E |
| Chiangti | 108 | 27 1N | 103 37 E |
| Chiangyin | 109 | 31 50N | 120 18 E |
| Chiangyü | 108 | 31 47N | 104 45 E |
| Chiangyung | 109 | 25 16N | 111 20 E |
| Chianie | 125 | 15 35 S | 13 40 E |
| Ch'iaochia | 108 | 26 57N | 103 3 E |
| Chiaochou Wan | 107 | 36 10N | 120 15 E |
| Chiaoho, Hopei, China | 106 | 38 1N | 116 17 E |
| Chiaoho, Kirin, China | 107 | 43 42N | 127 19 E |
| Chiaohsien | 107 | 36 20N | 120 0 E |
| Chiaoling | 109 | 24 40N | 117 10 E |
| Chiaotso | 106 | 35 17N | 113 18 E |
| Chiapa de Corzo | 165 | 16 42N | 93 0W |
| Chiapa, R. | 165 | 16 42N | 93 0W |
| Chiapas □ | 165 | 17 0N | 92 45W |
| Chiaramonte Gulfi | 65 | 37 1N | 14 41 E |
| Chiaravalle | 63 | 38 41N | 16 24 E |
| Chiaravalle Centrale | 65 | 38 41N | 16 25 E |
| Chiari | 62 | 45 31N | 9 55 E |
| Chiashan | 109 | 32 37N | 118 8 E |
| Chiasso | 51 | 45 50N | 9 0 E |
| Chiating | 109 | 31 21N | 121 15 E |
| Chiautla | 165 | 18 18N | 98 34W |
| Chiávari | 62 | 44 20N | 9 20 E |
| Chiavenna | 62 | 46 18N | 9 23 E |
| Chiawang | 107 | 34 30N | 117 22 E |
| Chiayü | 109 | 29 59N | 113 54 E |
| Chiba | 111 | 35 30N | 140 7 E |
| Chiba-ken □ | 111 | 35 30N | 140 20 E |
| Chibabava | 129 | 20 25 S | 33 35 E |
| Chibemba | 125 | 15 48 S | 14 8 E |
| Chibougamau | 150 | 49 56N | 74 24W |
| Chibougamau L. | 150 | 49 50N | 74 20W |
| Chibougamau, R. | 150 | 49 50N | 75 40W |
| Chibuk | 121 | 10 52N | 12 50 E |
| Chibuto | 129 | 24 40 S | 33 33 E |
| Chic-Chocs, Mts. | 151 | 48 55N | 66 0W |
| Chic-Chocs, Parc Prov. des | 151 | 48 55N | 66 20W |
| Chicacole = Srikakulam | 97 | 18 14N | 84 4 E |
| Chicago | 156 | 41 53N | 87 40W |
| Chicago Heights | 156 | 41 29N | 87 37W |
| Chicago North | 156 | 42 20N | 87 50W |
| Chichagof I. | 152 | 58 0N | 136 0W |
| Chichaoua | 118 | 31 32N | 8 44W |
| Chichén Itzá | 165 | 20 40N | 88 32W |
| Chichester | 29 | 50 50N | 0 47W |
| Chichester Ra. | 136 | 21 35 S | 117 45 E |
| Chich'i | 109 | 30 4N | 118 34 E |
| Ch'ichiang | 108 | 29 0N | 106 40 E |
| Chichibu | 111 | 36 5N | 139 10 E |
| Ch'ich'ihaerh | 105 | 47 22N | 123 57 E |
| Chichiriviche | 174 | 10 56N | 68 16W |
| Ch'ich'un | 109 | 30 14N | 115 25 E |
| Chickasha | 159 | 35 0N | 98 0W |
| Chicken Hd. | 31 | 58 10N | 6 15W |
| Chiclana de la Frontera | 57 | 36 26N | 6 9W |
| Chiclayo | 174 | 6 42 S | 79 50W |
| Chico | 160 | 39 45N | 121 54W |
| Chico, R., Chubut, Argent. | 160 | 44 0 S | 67 0W |
| Chico, R., Santa Cruz, Argent. | 176 | 49 30 S | 69 30W |
| Chicoa | 125 | 15 35 S | 32 20 E |
| Chicomo | 129 | 24 31 S | 34 6 E |
| Chicontepec | 165 | 20 58N | 98 10W |
| Chicopee | 162 | 42 6N | 72 37W |
| Chicoutimi | 151 | 48 28N | 71 5W |
| Chidambaram | 97 | 11 20N | 79 45 E |
| Chiddingfold | 29 | 51 6N | 0 37W |
| Chidenguele | 129 | 24 55 S | 34 2 E |
| Chidley C. | 149 | 60 23N | 64 26W |
| Chiehhsiu | 106 | 37 0N | 111 55 E |
| Ch'iehmo | 105 | 38 8N | 85 32 E |
| Chiehshou | 106 | 33 20N | 115 24 E |
| Chiehyang | 109 | 23 37N | 116 19 E |
| Chiem Hoa | 100 | 22 12N | 105 17 E |
| Chiemsee | 49 | 47 53N | 12 27 E |
| Chiench'ang | 107 | 41 16N | 124 28 E |
| Chiench'angying | 107 | 40 8N | 118 50 E |
| Ch'iench'engchen | 108 | 27 12N | 109 50 E |

Ch'ienchiang

Chomen Swamp

Ch'ienchiang, Hupeh, China 109 30 25N 112 51 E
Ch'ienchiang, Kwangsi-Chuang, China 108 23 40N 108 58 E
Ch'ienchiang, Szechwan, China 108 29 31N 108 46 E
Chiench'uan 108 26 28N 99 52 E
Chiengi 124 8 45 S 29 10 E
Chienho 108 26 39N 108 35 E
Ch'ienhsi 108 27 3N 106 0 E
Ch'ienhsien 106 34 30N 108 10 E
Chienko 108 32 0N 105 23 E
Chienli 109 29 49N 112 53 E
Chienou 109 27 5N 118 20 E
Ch'ienshan, Anhwei, China 109 30 41N 116 35 E
Ch'ienshan, Kiangsi, China 109 28 18N 117 40 E
Chienshih 108 30 40N 109 43 E
Chienshui 108 23 37N 102 49 E
Chiente 109 29 29N 119 16 E
Chienti, R. 63 43 15N 13 30 E
Chienwei 108 29 13N 103 56 E
Chienyang 109 27 21N 118 5 E
Ch'ienyang, Hunan, China 109 27 18N 110 10 E
Ch'ienyang, Kansu, China 106 34 35N 107 2 E
Chienyang 108 30 24N 104 33 E
Chierhkalang 107 43 6N 122 54 E
Chieri 62 45 0N 7 50 E
Chiese, R. 62 45 45N 10 35 E
Chieti 63 42 22N 14 10 E
Chièvres 47 50 35N 3 48 E
Chigasaki 111 35 19N 139 24 E
Chignecto B. 151 45 48N 64 40W
Chignik 147 56 15N 158 27W
Chigorodó 174 7 41N 76 42W
Chiguana 172 21 0 S 67 50W
Chihari 107 38 40N 126 30 E
Ch'ihch'i 109 21 59N 112 58 E
Chihchiang, Hunan, China 108 27 27N 109 41 E
Chihchiang, Hupei, China 109 30 19N 111 30 E
Chihchin 108 26 42N 105 45 E
Ch'ihfeng 107 42 18N 118 57 E
Chihkou 107 35 55N 119 13 E
Chihli, G. of = Po Hai 107 38 40N 119 0 E
Ch'ihshui 108 29 29N 105 38 E
Ch'ihshui Ho, R. 108 28 53N 105 48 E
Chihsi 107 45 20N 130 55 E
Ch'ihsien 106 34 33N 114 47 E
Chihsien, Honan, China 106 35 25N 114 5 E
Chihsien, Hopei, China 106 37 34N 115 34 E
Chihsien, Shansi, China 106 36 8N 110 39 E
Chihtan 106 36 56N 108 47 E
Chihte 109 30 9N 117 0 E
Chihuahua 164 28 40N 106 3W
Chihuahua □ 164 28 40N 106 3W
Chihuatlán 164 19 14N 104 35W
Chiili 85 44 20N 66 15 E
Chik Ballapur 97 13 25N 77 45 E
Chikawawa 127 16 2 S 34 50 E
Chikhli 96 20 20N 76 18 E
Chikmagalur 97 13 15N 75 45 E
Chikodi 96 16 26N 74 38 E
Chikonde 127 12 16 S 31 38 E
Ch'ik'ou 107 38 37N 117 35 E
Chikugo 110 33 14N 130 28 E
Chikuma-Gawa, R. 111 36 59N 138 35 E
Chilac 165 18 20N 97 24W
Chilako, R. 152 53 53N 122 57W
Chilam Chavki 95 35 5N 75 5 E
Chilanga 127 15 33 S 28 16 E
Chilant'ai 106 39 45N 105 45 E
Chilapa 165 17 40N 99 20W
Chilas 95 35 25N 74 5 E
Chilaw 93 7 30N 79 50 E
Chilcotin, R. 152 51 44N 122 23W
Childers 139 25 15 S 152 17 E
Childress 159 34 30N 100 50W
Chile ■ 176 35 0 S 71 15W
Chilecito 172 29 0 S 67 40W
Chilete 174 7 10 S 78 50W
Chilham 29 51 15N 0 59 E
Chilik, Kazakh S.S.R., U.S.S.R. 84 51 7N 53 55 E
Chilik, Kirgiz S.S.R., U.S.S.R. 85 43 33N 78 17 E
Chililabombwe (Bancroft) 125 12 18 S 27 43 E
Chilin 105 43 53N 126 38 E
Ch'ilin Hu 105 31 50N 89 0 E
Chilka L. 96 19 40N 85 25 E
Chilko, L. 152 52 60N 124 10W
Chilko, R. 152 52 6N 124 9W
Chillagoe 138 17 14 S 144 33 E
Chillán 172 36 40 S 72 10W
Chillicothe, Ill., U.S.A. 158 40 55N 89 32W
Chillicothe, Mo., U.S.A. 158 39 45N 93 30W
Chillicothe, Ohio, U.S.A. 156 39 53N 82 58W
Chilliwack 152 49 10N 122 0W
Chilo 94 27 12N 73 32 E
Chiloane, I. 129 20 40 S 34 55 E
Chiloé, I. de 176 42 50 S 73 45W
Chilpancingo 165 17 30N 99 40W
Chiltern 141 36 10 S 146 36 E
Chiltern Hills 29 51 44N 0 42W
Chilton 156 44 1N 88 12W
Chiluage 124 9 15 S 21 42 E
Chilubula 127 10 14 S 30 51 E
Chilumba 127 10 28 S 34 12 E
Chilung 109 25 3N 121 45 E
Chilwa, L. (Shirwa) 127 15 15 S 35 40 E
Chimacum 160 48 1N 122 53W
Chimaltitán 164 21 46N 103 50W
Chimán 166 8 45N 78 40W
Chimay 47 50 3N 4 20 E
Chimbay 76 42 57N 59 47 E
Chimborazo 174 1 20 S 78 55W
Chimbote 174 9 0 S 78 35W
Ch'imen 109 29 56N 117 47 E
Chimion 85 40 15N 71 32 E
Chimishliya 70 46 34N 28 44 E
Chimkent 85 42 18N 69 36 E
Chimo 107 36 23N 120 27 E
Chimpembe 127 9 31 S 29 33 E
Chin □ 98 22 0N 93 0 E
Chin Chiang, R. 109 28 23N 115 48 E
Chin Hills 98 22 30N 93 30 E
Chin Ho, R. 106 35 2N 113 25 E
Chin Ling Shan 106 34 0N 107 0 E
Ch'in Shui, R. 106 35 40N 112 15 E
China 164 25 40N 99 20W
China ■ 105 30 0N 110 0 E
China Lake 163 35 44N 117 37W
Chinacates 164 25 0N 105 14W
Chinacota 174 7 37N 72 36W
Ch'inan 106 34 50N 105 35 E
Chinan 106 36 32N 117 0 E
Chinandega 166 12 30N 87 0W
Chinati Pk. 159 30 0N 104 25W
Chincha Alta 174 13 20 S 76 0W
Chinch'eng 106 35 30N 112 50 E
Chinchi 106 37 57N 106 6 E
Chinch'i 109 27 54N 116 44 E
Chinchiang, Fukien, China 109 24 54N 118 35 E
Chinchiang, Kiangsi, China 109 29 44N 115 59 E
Chinchiang, Yunnan, China 108 26 14N 100 34 E
Chinchilla 139 26 45 S 150 38 E
Chinchilla de Monte Aragón 59 38 53N 1 40W
Chinchón 58 40 9N 3 26W
Chinchorro, Banco 165 18 35N 87 20W
Ch'inchou 108 21 58N 108 35 E
Chinchou 107 41 8N 121 6 E
Chinch'uan 108 31 30N 101 55 E
Chincoteague 162 37 58N 75 21W
Chincoteague B. 162 38 5N 75 8W
Chinde 127 18 45 S 36 30 E
Chindo 107 34 28N 126 15 E
Chindwin, R. 98 21 26N 95 15 E
Chineni 95 33 2N 75 15 E
Ch'ing Chiang, R. 109 29 51N 112 22 E
Ch'ing Hai 105 37 0N 100 20 E
Ching Ho, R. 106 34 29N 109 5 E
Ching Shan 109 31 40N 111 30 E
Chinga 127 15 13 S 38 35 E
Chingan 109 28 52N 115 22 E
Ch'ingchen 108 26 32N 106 30 E
Ch'ingch'eng 107 37 11N 117 42 E
Chingchiang 109 32 2N 120 16 E
Ch'ingchiang, Kiangsi, China 109 28 5N 115 30 E
Ch'ingchiang, Kiangsu, China 107 33 33N 119 4 E
Ch'ingchien 106 37 12N 110 6 E
Chingch'uan 106 35 15N 107 22 E
Ch'ingfeng 106 35 54N 115 7 E
Chinghai 106 38 56N 116 55 E
Ch'inghomen 107 41 45N 121 25 E
Chinghsi 108 23 8N 106 25 E
Ch'inghsien 106 38 35N 116 48 E
Chinghsien 109 30 42N 118 23 E
Ch'inghsü 106 37 40N 112 20 E
Chinghung 108 22 0N 100 49 E
Chingi Chiang, R. 108 29 32N 103 44 E
Chingku 108 23 28N 100 42 E
Chingleput 97 12 42N 79 58 E
Ch'ingliu 109 26 12N 116 48 E
Chinglo 106 38 24N 111 54 E
Ch'inglung 108 25 48N 105 14 E
Chingmen 109 30 58N 112 6 E
Chingning, Chekiang, China 109 27 58N 119 38 E
Chingning, Kansu, China 106 35 30N 105 45 E
Chingola 127 12 31 S 27 53 E
Chingole 127 13 4 S 34 17 E
Chingpien 106 37 24N 108 36 E
Chingpo Hu 107 43 50N 128 50 E
Ch'ingp'u 109 31 9N 121 6 E
Chingshan 109 31 2N 113 3 E
Chingshih 109 29 40N 111 50 E
Ch'ingshui 106 34 44N 106 2 E
Chingsing 106 38 5N 114 8 E
Chingt'ai 106 37 10N 104 8 E
Ch'ingtao 107 36 5N 120 25 E
Chingte 109 30 19N 118 31 E
Chingtechen 109 29 19N 117 15 E
Ch'ingt'ien 109 28 9N 120 17 E
Chingtung 108 24 22N 100 50 E
Chingtzukuan 106 33 13N 111 2 E
Chinguar 125 12 18 S 16 45 E
Chinguetti 116 20 25N 12 15W
Chingune 129 20 33 S 35 0 E
Ch'ingyang 105 36 5N 107 40 E
Chingyang 106 34 32N 108 52 E
Ch'ingyang, Anhwei, China 109 30 38N 117 50 E
Ch'ingyang, Ningsia Hui, China 106 36 5N 107 40 E
Chingyü 107 42 22N 126 45 E
Chingyüan 106 36 35N 104 40 E
Ch'ingyüan, Chekiang, China 109 27 37N 119 3 E
Ch'ingyüan, Kwangtung, China 109 23 42N 112 58 E
Ch'ingyüan, Liaoning, China 107 42 6N 124 55 E
Ch'ingyün 107 37 53N 117 23 E
Chinhae 107 35 9N 128 40 E
Chinhanguanine 129 25 21 S 32 30 E
Chinhsi 107 40 49N 120 55 E
Chinhsiang 106 35 5N 116 18 E
Chinhsien, Hopei, China 106 38 2N 115 2 E
Chinhsien, Kiangsi, China 109 28 22N 116 14 E
Chinhsien, Liaoning, China 107 39 6N 121 3 E
Chinhua 109 29 9N 119 41 E
Ch'inhuangtao 107 39 57N 119 40 E
Chining, Inner Mongolia, China 106 41 2N 113 8 E
Chining, Shantung, China 106 35 19N 116 36 E
Chiniot 94 31 45N 73 0 E
Chinipas 164 27 22N 108 32W
Chinju 107 35 12N 128 2 E
Chink'ou 109 30 20N 114 7 E
Chinle 161 36 14N 109 38W
Chinmen 109 24 27N 118 21 E
Chinmen Tao, I. 109 24 25N 118 25 E
Chinnamanur 97 9 50N 77 16 E
Chinnampo 107 38 52N 125 28 E
Chinning 108 24 40N 102 35 E
Chinnur 96 18 57N 79 43 E
Chino, Japan 111 35 59N 138 9 E
Chino, U.S.A. 163 34 1N 117 41W
Chino Valley 161 34 54N 112 28W
Chinon 42 47 10N 0 15 E
Chinook, Can. 153 51 28N 110 59W
Chinook, U.S.A. 160 48 35N 109 19W
Chinp'ing, Kweichow, China 108 26 40N 109 7 E
Chinp'ing, Yunnan, China 108 22 46N 103 15 E
Chinsali 124 10 30 S 32 2 E
Chinsha 108 27 29N 106 15 E
Chinsha Chiang, R. = Yangtze Chiang, R. 108 27 30N 99 30 E
Chinshan 109 30 3N 121 13 E
Ch'inshui 106 35 41N 112 11 E
Chintamani 97 13 26N 78 3 E
Chint'an 109 31 45N 119 35 E
Chint'ang 108 30 51N 104 27 E
Chinwangtao = Ch'inhuangtao 107 39 57N 119 40 E
Ch'inyang 106 35 5N 112 55 E
Ch'inyüan 106 36 31N 112 15 E
Chióggia 63 45 13N 12 15 E
Chíos = Khíos 69 38 27N 26 9 E
Chip Lake 152 53 35N 115 35W
Chipai L. 150 52 56N 87 53W
Chipata (Ft. Jameson) 127 13 38 S 32 28 E
Chipewyan L. 153 58 0N 98 27W
Chipinga 127 20 13 S 32 36 E
Chipiona 57 36 44N 6 26W
Chipley 157 30 45N 85 32W
Chiplun 96 17 31N 73 34 E
Chipman 151 46 6N 65 53W
Chipoka 127 13 57 S 34 28 E
Chiporovtsi 66 43 24N 22 52 E
Chippenham 28 51 27N 2 7W
Chippewa Falls 158 44 55N 91 22W
Chippewa, R. 158 44 45N 91 55W
Chipping Campden 28 52 4N 1 48W
Chipping Norton 28 51 56N 1 32W
Chipping Ongar 29 51 43N 0 15 E
Chipping Sodbury 28 51 31N 2 23W
Chiquian 174 10 10 S 77 0W
Chiquimula 166 14 51N 89 37W
Chiquinquirá 174 5 37N 73 50W
Chir, R. 83 48 45N 42 10 E
Chirala 97 15 50N 80 20 E
Chiramba 127 16 55 S 34 39 E
Chiran 110 31 22N 130 27 E
Chiras 93 35 14N 65 40 E
Chirawa 94 28 14N 75 42 E
Chirayinkil 97 8 41N 76 49 E
Chirbury 28 52 35N 3 6W
Chirchik 85 41 29N 69 35 E
Chirfa 117 20 55N 12 14 E
Chiricahua Pk. 161 31 53N 109 14W
Chirikof I. 147 55 50N 155 40W
Chiriquí, Golfo de 166 8 0N 82 10W
Chiriquí, Lago de 166 9 10N 82 0W
Chiriquí, Vol. 166 8 55N 82 35W
Chirivira Falls 127 21 10 S 32 12 E
Chirk 31 52 57N 3 4W
Chirmiri 99 23 15N 82 20 E
Chirnogi 70 44 7N 26 32 E
Chirnside 35 55 47N 2 11W
Chiromo 125 16 30 S 35 7 E
Chirpan 67 42 10N 25 19 E
Chirripó Grande, cerro 166 9 29N 83 29W
Chisamba 127 14 55 S 28 20 E
Chisapani Garhi 99 27 30N 84 2 E
Ch'ishan 106 34 28N 107 35 E
Chishan 106 35 36N 110 59 E
Ch'ishan 109 22 44N 120 31 E
Chishmy 84 54 35N 55 23 E
Chisholm 152 54 55N 114 10W
Chishou 108 28 12N 109 43 E
Chishui 109 27 14N 115 10 E
Chisimba Falls 127 10 12 S 30 56 E
Chisineu Criş 66 46 32N 21 37 E
Chisledon 28 51 30N 1 44W
Chisone, R. 62 45 0N 7 5 E
Chisos Mts. 159 29 20N 103 15W
Chistian Mandi 94 29 50N 72 55 E
Chistopol 81 55 25N 50 38 E
Chita, Colomb. 174 6 11N 72 28W
Chita, U.S.S.R. 77 52 0N 113 25 E
Chitado 125 17 10 S 14 8 E
Ch'it'ai 105 44 1N 89 28 E
Chitapur 96 17 10N 76 50 E
Chitembo 125 13 30 S 16 50 E
Chitina 147 61 30N 144 30W
Chitinghsilin 105 32 51N 92 28 E
Chitipa 127 9 41 S 33 19 E
Chitokoloki 125 13 43 S 23 4 E
Chitorgarh 94 24 52N 74 43 E
Chitrakot 96 19 20N 81 40 E
Chitral 93 35 50N 71 56 E
Chitravati, R. 97 14 30N 78 0 E
Chitré 167 7 59N 80 27W
Chitse 106 36 54N 114 52 E
Chittagong 98 22 19N 91 55 E
Chittagong □ 98 24 5N 91 25 E
Chittoor 97 13 15N 79 5 E
Chittur 97 10 40N 76 45 E
Chitu 123 8 38N 37 58 E
Ch'itung, Hunan, China 109 26 47N 112 7 E
Ch'itung, Kiangsu, China 109 31 49N 121 40 E
Chiuant'u 107 42 33N 128 19 E
Chiuchaohua 108 32 20N 105 45 E
Chiuch'engch'i 108 27 10N 108 42 E
Chiuchiang, Kiangsi, China 109 29 43N 115 55 E
Chiuchiang, Kwangtung, China 109 22 50N 112 50 E
Chiuch'üan 105 39 46N 98 34 E
Chiuhsiangch'eng 109 33 13N 114 50 E
Chiukuanch'eng 106 35 50N 115 22 E
Chiuling Shan 109 28 50N 114 20 E
Chiuliuch'eng 108 24 32N 109 15 E
Chiulung 108 28 59N 101 32 E
Ch'iungchou Haihsia 100 20 10N 110 15 E
Ch'iunghai 100 19 15N 110 26 E
Chiunglai 108 30 25N 103 30 E
Chiunglai Shan 108 31 20N 102 50 E
Ch'iungshan 100 19 51N 110 26 E
Chiuningkang 109 26 48N 114 6 E
Ch'iupei 108 24 3N 104 12 E
Chiushench'iu 106 33 10N 115 8 E
Chiushengch'i 108 27 31N 109 12 E
Chiusi 63 43 1N 11 58 E
Chiut'ai 107 44 10N 125 49 E
Chiutaosha 106 35 39N 103 45 E
Chiuwuch'ing 106 39 23N 116 53 E
Chiva 59 39 27N 0 41W
Chivasso 62 45 10N 7 52 E
Chivilcoy 172 35 0 S 60 0W
Chiwanda 127 11 23 S 34 55 E
Chiwefwe 127 13 37 S 29 31 E
Chiyang 107 37 0N 117 13 E
Ch'iyang 109 20 35N 111 52 E
Chiyüan 106 35 5N 112 39 E
Chiyün 109 28 35N 120 2 E
Chizera 127 13 10 S 25 0 E
Chkalov = Orenburg 78 52 0N 55 5 E
Chkolovsk 81 56 50N 43 10 E
Chlumec 52 50 9N 15 29 E
Chmielnik 54 50 37N 20 43 E
Cho Bo 100 20 46N 105 10 E
Cho Do 107 38 30N 124 40 E
Cho Phuoc 101 10 26N 107 18 E
Choba 126 2 30N 38 5 E
Chobe National Park 128 21 30 S 25 0 E
Chobe, R. 128 18 10 S 24 10 E
Chobol 121 11 53N 13 1 E
Chochiwŏn 107 36 37N 127 18 E
Chocianów 54 51 35N 15 33 E
Chociwel 54 53 29N 15 21 E
Chocó □ 174 6 0N 77 0W
Chocontá 174 5 9N 73 41W
Chodaków 54 52 16N 20 18 E
Chodavaram 96 17 40N 82 50 E
Chodecz 54 52 56N 19 2 E
Chodziez 54 52 58N 17 0 E
Choele Choel 176 39 11 S 65 40W
Chōfu 111 35 39N 139 33 E
Chohsien 106 39 30N 116 0 E
Choiseul I. 130 7 0 S 156 40 E
Choisy-le-Roi 43 48 45N 2 24 E
Choix 164 26 40N 108 10W
Chojna 54 52 58N 14 25 E
Chojnice 54 53 42N 17 40 E
Chojnów 54 51 25N 15 58 E
Choke Mts. 123 11 18N 37 15 E
Chokurdakh 77 70 38N 147 55 E
Cholame 163 35 44N 120 18W
Cholet 42 47 4N 0 52W
Chollerton 35 55 4N 2 7W
Cholpon-Ata 85 42 40N 77 6 E
Cholsey 28 51 34N 1 10W
Cholu 106 40 19N 115 5 E
Choluteca 166 13 20N 87 14W
Choluteca, R. 166 13 5N 87 20W
Chom Bung 100 13 37N 99 36 E
Chom Thong 100 18 25N 98 41 E
Choma 127 16 48 S 26 59 E
Chomen Swamp 123 9 20N 37 10 E

**Chomu** **Clee Hills**


| | | | |
|---|---|---|---|
| Chomu | **94** | 27 15N | 75 40E |
| Chomutov | **52** | 50 28N | 13 23E |
| Chon Buri | **100** | 13 22N | 100 59E |
| Chon Thanh | **101** | 11 24N | 106 36E |
| Chŏnan | **107** | 36 48N | 127 9E |
| Chonburi | **101** | 13 21N | 101 1E |
| Chone | **174** | 0 40S | 80 0W |
| Chong Kai | **100** | 13 57N | 103 35E |
| Chong Mek | **100** | 15 10N | 105 27E |
| Chŏngdo | **107** | 35 38N | 128 42E |
| Chŏngha | **107** | 36 12N | 129 21E |
| Chŏngjin | **107** | 41 47N | 129 50E |
| Chŏngju | **107** | 39 40N | 125 5E |
| Chŏngŭp | **107** | 35 35N | 126 50E |
| Chŏnju | **107** | 35 50N | 127 4E |
| Chonos, Arch. de los | **176** | 45 0S | 75 0W |
| Chopda | **96** | 21 20N | 75 15E |
| Chopim, R. | **173** | 25 35S | 53 5W |
| Choptank, R. | **162** | 38 41N | 76 0W |
| Chorbat La | **95** | 34 42N | 76 37E |
| Chorley | **32** | 53 39N | 2 39W |
| Chormet el Melah | **119** | 30 11N | 16 29E |
| Chorolque, Cerro | **172** | 20 59S | 66 5W |
| Choroszcz | **54** | 53 10N | 22 59E |
| Chortkov | **80** | 49 2N | 25 46E |
| Chorul Tso | **95** | 32 30N | 82 30E |
| Chŏrwŏn | **107** | 38 15N | 127 10E |
| Chorzele | **54** | 53 15N | 21 2E |
| Chorzów | **54** | 50 18N | 19 0E |
| Chos-Malal | **172** | 37 15S | 70 5W |
| Chosan | **107** | 40 50N | 125 47E |
| Choshi | **111** | 35 45N | 140 45E |
| Choszczno | **54** | 53 7N | 15 25E |
| Choteau | **160** | 47 50N | 112 10W |
| Chotila | **94** | 22 30N | 71 15E |
| Chotzu | **106** | 40 52N | 112 33E |
| Chou Shan | **109** | 30 2N | 122 6E |
| Chouchih | **106** | 34 8N | 108 14E |
| Chouch'ü | **106** | 33 46N | 104 18E |
| Chouning | **109** | 27 15N | 119 13E |
| Chouts'un | **107** | 36 48N | 117 52E |
| Ch'ouyang | **108** | 23 14N | 104 35E |
| Chowchilla | **163** | 37 11N | 120 12W |
| Chowkham | **98** | 20 52N | 97 28E |
| Choybalsan | **105** | 48 4N | 114 30E |
| Christchurch, N.Z. | **143** | 43 33S | 172 47E |
| Christchurch, U.K. | **28** | 50 44N | 1 47W |
| Christiana, S. Afr. | **128** | 27 52S | 25 8E |
| Christiana, U.S.A. | **162** | 39 40N | 75 40W |
| Christiansfeld | **73** | 55 21N | 9 29E |
| Christiansö, I. | **73** | 55 19N | 15 12E |
| Christiansted | **147** | 17 45N | 64 42W |
| Christie B. | **153** | 62 32N | 111 10W |
| Christina, R. | **153** | 56 40N | 111 3W |
| Christmas Cr. | **136** | 18 53S | 125 55E |
| Christmas Creek | **136** | 18 29S | 125 23E |
| Christmas I., Ind. Oc. | **142** | 10 0S | 105 40E |
| Christmas I., Pac. Oc. | **131** | 1 58N | 157 27W |
| Christopher L. | **137** | 24 49S | 127 42E |
| Chrudim | **52** | 49 58N | 15 43E |
| Chrzanów | **54** | 50 10N | 19 21E |
| Chtimba | **127** | 10 35S | 34 13E |
| Chu | **85** | 43 36N | 73 42E |
| Ch'u Chiang, R. | **108** | 30 2N | 106 19E |
| Chu Chua | **152** | 51 22N | 120 10W |
| Chu Lai | **100** | 15 28N | 108 45E |
| Chu, R., U.S.S.R. | **85** | 45 0N | 67 44E |
| Chu, R., Viet. | **100** | 19 53N | 105 45E |
| Chuadanga | **98** | 23 38N | 88 51E |
| Ch'üanchou, Fukien, China | **109** | 24 56N | 118 35E |
| Ch'üanchou, Kwangsi-Chuang, China | **109** | 25 59N | 111 4E |
| Chuangho | **107** | 39 42N | 123 0E |
| Chüannan | **109** | 24 50N | 114 40E |
| Chūbu □ | **112** | 36 45N | 137 30E |
| Chubut, R. | **176** | 43 0S | 70 0W |
| Chuch'eng | **107** | 36 0N | 119 16E |
| Chuch'i | **108** | 32 19N | 109 52E |
| Chuchi, Chekiang, China | **109** | 29 43N | 120 14E |
| Chuchi, Honan, China | **106** | 34 27N | 115 39E |
| Chuchi L. | **152** | 55 12N | 124 30W |
| Ch'uching | **108** | 25 34N | 103 45E |
| Chuchou | **109** | 27 50N | 113 10E |
| Chudleigh | **30** | 50 35N | 3 36W |
| Chudovo | **80** | 59 10N | 31 30E |
| Chudskoye, Oz. | **80** | 58 13N | 27 30E |
| Ch'üehshan | **109** | 32 48N | 114 1E |
| Chugach Mts. | **147** | 62 0N | 146 0W |
| Chugiak | **147** | 61 7N | 149 10W |
| Chuginadak I. | **147** | 52 50N | 169 45W |
| Chūgoku □ | **110** | 35 0N | 133 0E |
| Chūgoku-Sanchi | **110** | 35 0N | 133 0E |
| Chuguyev | **82** | 49 55N | 36 45E |
| Chugwater | **158** | 41 48N | 104 47W |
| Chuhai | **109** | 22 17N | 113 34E |
| Chühsien | **107** | 35 35N | 118 49E |
| Ch'uhsien, China | **109** | 28 57N | 118 58E |
| Ch'uhsien, China | **109** | 32 18N | 118 18E |
| Chuhsien | **105** | 28 57N | 118 58E |
| Ch'ühsien | **108** | 30 51N | 107 1E |
| Ch'uhsiung | **108** | 25 2N | 101 32E |
| Chüjung | **109** | 31 56N | 119 10E |
| Chukai | **101** | 4 13N | 103 25E |
| Chukhloma | **81** | 58 45N | 42 40E |
| Chūkō | **111** | 36 44N | 139 27E |
| Chukotskiy Khrebet | **77** | 68 0N | 175 0E |
| Chukotskiy, Mys | **77** | 66 10N | 169 3E |
| Chukotskoye More | **77** | 68 0N | 175 0W |
| Chula Vista | **163** | 32 39N | 117 8W |
| Chulak-Kurgan | **85** | 43 46N | 69 9E |
| Chülu | **106** | 37 13N | 115 1E |
| Chulucanas | **174** | 5 0S | 80 0W |
| Chum Phae | **100** | 16 32N | 102 6E |
| Chum Saeng | **100** | 15 55N | 100 15E |
| Chumar | **95** | 32 40N | 78 35E |
| Chumatien | **109** | 33 0N | 114 4E |
| Chumbicha | **172** | 29 0S | 66 10W |
| Chumerna | **67** | 42 45N | 25 55E |
| Chumikan | **77** | 54 40N | 135 10E |
| Chumphon | **101** | 10 35N | 99 14E |
| Chumuare | **127** | 14 31S | 31 50E |
| Chumunjin | **107** | 37 55N | 127 44E |
| Chunchŏn | **107** | 37 58N | 127 44E |
| Chunga | **127** | 15 0S | 26 2E |
| Ch'ungan | **109** | 27 45N | 118 0E |
| Ch'ungch'ing, Szechwan, China | **108** | 29 30N | 106 30E |
| Ch'ungch'ing, Szechwan, China | **108** | 30 27N | 103 43E |
| Chungch'üantzu | **106** | 39 22N | 102 42E |
| Chunggang ŭp | **107** | 41 48N | 126 48E |
| Chunghsiang | **109** | 31 10N | 112 35E |
| Chunghsien | **108** | 30 17N | 108 4E |
| Chunghwa | **107** | 38 52N | 125 47E |
| Ch'ungi | **109** | 25 42N | 114 19E |
| Ch'ungjen | **109** | 27 44N | 116 2E |
| Chungju | **107** | 36 58N | 127 58E |
| Chungkang | **107** | 43 42N | 127 37E |
| Chungking = Ch'ungch'ing | **108** | 29 30N | 106 30E |
| Ch'ungli | **106** | 40 5N | 115 12E |
| Chungli | **109** | 24 57N | 121 13E |
| Ch'ungming | **109** | 31 27N | 121 24E |
| Ch'ungming Tao, I. | **109** | 31 35N | 121 40E |
| Chungmu | **107** | 34 50N | 128 20E |
| Chungning | **106** | 35 22N | 105 40E |
| Chungshan, Kwangsi-Chuang, China | **109** | 24 30N | 111 17E |
| Chungshan, Kwangtung, China | **109** | 22 31N | 113 20E |
| Ch'ungshuiho | **106** | 39 54N | 111 34E |
| Ch'ungte | **109** | 30 32N | 120 26E |
| Chungt'iaoshan | **106** | 35 0N | 111 30E |
| Chungtien | **108** | 27 51N | 99 42E |
| Ch'ungtso | **108** | 22 20N | 107 20E |
| Chungtu | **108** | 24 41N | 109 42E |
| Chungwei | **106** | 37 35N | 105 10E |
| Chungyang | **106** | 37 24N | 111 10E |
| Chungyang Shanmo | **109** | 23 10N | 121 0E |
| Chungyüan | **100** | 19 9N | 110 28E |
| Chünhsien | **109** | 32 40N | 111 15E |
| Chunian | **94** | 31 10N | 74 0E |
| Chunya | **127** | 8 30S | 33 27E |
| Chunya □ | **126** | 7 48S | 33 0E |
| Ch'unyang | **107** | 43 42N | 129 26E |
| Chuquibamba | **174** | 15 47N | 72 44W |
| Chuquicamata | **172** | 22 15S | 69 0W |
| Chuquisaca □ | **172** | 23 30S | 63 30W |
| Chur | **51** | 46 52N | 9 32E |
| Churachandpur | **98** | 24 20N | 93 40E |
| Church Hill | **38** | 55 0N | 7 53W |
| Church House | **152** | 50 20N | 125 10W |
| Church Stretton | **28** | 52 32N | 2 49W |
| Churchdown | **28** | 51 53N | 2 9W |
| Churchill | **153** | 58 47N | 94 11W |
| Churchill, C. | **153** | 58 46N | 93 12W |
| Churchill Falls | **151** | 53 36N | 64 19W |
| Churchill L. | **153** | 55 55N | 108 20W |
| Churchill Pk. | **152** | 58 10N | 125 10W |
| Churchill, R., Man., Can. | **153** | 58 47N | 94 12W |
| Churchill, R., Newf., Can. | **151** | 53 19N | 60 10W |
| Churchill, R., Sask., Can. | **153** | 58 47N | 94 12W |
| Churchtown | **39** | 52 12N | 6 20W |
| Churfisten | **51** | 47 8N | 9 17E |
| Churston Ferrers | **30** | 50 23N | 3 32W |
| Churu | **94** | 28 20N | 75 0E |
| Churuguaro | **174** | 10 49N | 69 32W |
| Churwalden | **51** | 46 47N | 9 33E |
| Chusan | **109** | 32 13N | 110 24E |
| Chushul | **95** | 33 40N | 78 40E |
| Chusovaya, R. | **84** | 58 18N | 56 22E |
| Chusovoy | **84** | 58 15N | 57 40E |
| Chust | **85** | 41 0N | 71 13E |
| Ch'ützu | **106** | 36 24N | 107 27E |
| Chuuronjang | **107** | 41 35N | 129 40E |
| Chuvash A.S.S.R. □ | **81** | 55 30N | 48 0E |
| Chuwassu | **108** | 28 48N | 97 27E |
| Ch'üwu | **106** | 35 35N | 111 23E |
| Ch'üyang | **106** | 38 37N | 114 41E |
| Chüyeh | **106** | 35 23N | 116 6E |
| Ciacova | **66** | 45 35N | 21 10E |
| Cicero | **156** | 41 48N | 87 48W |
| Cicero Dantas | **170** | 10 36S | 38 23W |
| Cidacos, R. | **58** | 42 15N | 2 10W |
| Cide | **82** | 41 40N | 32 50E |
| Ciechanów | **54** | 52 52N | 20 38E |
| Ciechanów □ | **54** | 53 0N | 20 30E |
| Ciechocinek | **54** | 52 53N | 18 45E |
| Ciego de Avila | **166** | 21 50N | 78 50W |
| Ciénaga | **174** | 11 1N | 74 15W |
| Ciénaga de Oro | **174** | 8 53N | 75 37W |
| Cienfuegos | **166** | 22 10N | 80 30W |
| Cieplice Slaskie Zdrój | **54** | 50 50N | 15 40E |
| Cierp | **44** | 42 55N | 0 40E |
| Cíes, Islas | **56** | 42 12N | 8 55W |
| Cieszyn | **54** | 49 45N | 18 35E |
| Cieza | **59** | 38 17N | 1 23W |
| Cifuentes | **58** | 40 47N | 2 37W |
| Ciha Pa. | **101** | 22 20N | 103 47E |
| Cijara, Pantano de | **57** | 39 18N | 4 52W |
| Cijulang | **103** | 7 42S | 108 27E |
| Cikampek | **103** | 6 23S | 107 28E |
| Cilacap | **103** | 7 43S | 109 0E |
| Cıldır | **83** | 41 10N | 43 20E |
| Cilgerran | **31** | 52 4N | 4 39W |
| Cilician Gates P. | **92** | 37 20N | 34 52E |
| Cilician Taurus | **92** | 36 40N | 34 0E |
| Cîlnicu | **70** | 44 54N | 23 4E |
| Cimarron, Kans., U.S.A. | **159** | 37 50N | 100 20W |
| Cimarron, N. Mex., U.S.A. | **159** | 36 30N | 104 52W |
| Cimarron, R. | **159** | 37 10N | 102 10W |
| Cîmpia Turzii | **70** | 46 34N | 23 53E |
| Cîmpina | **70** | 45 10N | 25 45E |
| Cîmpulung, Argeş, Rumania | **70** | 45 17N | 25 3E |
| Cîmpulung, Suceava, Rumania | **70** | 47 32N | 25 30E |
| Cîmpuri | **67** | 46 0N | 26 50E |
| Cinca, R. | **58** | 42 20N | 0 9E |
| Cincer | **66** | 43 55N | 17 5E |
| Cinch, R. | **157** | 36 0N | 84 15W |
| Cincinnati | **156** | 39 10N | 84 26W |
| Cincinnatus | **162** | 42 33N | 75 54W |
| Cinderford | **28** | 51 49N | 2 30W |
| Cîndeşti | **70** | 45 15N | 26 42E |
| Ciney | **47** | 50 18N | 5 5E |
| Cinigiano | **63** | 42 53N | 11 23E |
| Cinogli | **63** | 43 23N | 13 10E |
| Cinto, Mt. | **45** | 42 24N | 8 54E |
| Cioranii | **70** | 44 45N | 26 25E |
| Çiotat, La | **45** | 43 12N | 5 36E |
| Čiovo | **63** | 43 30N | 16 17E |
| Cipó | **171** | 11 6S | 38 31W |
| Circle, Alaska, U.S.A. | **147** | 65 50N | 144 10W |
| Circle, Montana, U.S.A. | **158** | 47 26N | 105 35W |
| Circleville, Ohio, U.S.A. | **156** | 39 35N | 82 57W |
| Circleville, Utah, U.S.A. | **161** | 38 12N | 112 24W |
| Cirebon | **103** | 6 45S | 108 32E |
| Cirencester | **28** | 51 43N | 1 59W |
| Cireşu | **70** | 44 47N | 22 31E |
| Cirey-sur-Vezouze | **43** | 48 35N | 6 57E |
| Ciriè | **62** | 45 14N | 7 35E |
| Cirò | **65** | 39 23N | 17 3E |
| Cisco | **159** | 32 25N | 99 0W |
| Cislǎu | **70** | 45 14N | 26 33E |
| Cisna | **54** | 49 12N | 22 20E |
| Cisneros | **174** | 6 33N | 75 4W |
| Cisnădie | **70** | 45 42N | 24 9E |
| Cisterna di Latina | **64** | 41 35N | 12 50E |
| Cisternino | **65** | 40 45N | 17 26E |
| Cité de Cansado | **116** | 20 51N | 17 0W |
| Citega (Kitega) | **126** | 3 30S | 29 58E |
| Citeli-Ckaro | **83** | 41 33N | 46 0E |
| Citlaltépetl, mt. | **165** | 19 0N | 97 20W |
| Citrusdal | **128** | 32 35S | 19 0E |
| Città della Pieve | **63** | 42 57N | 12 0E |
| Città di Castello | **63** | 43 27N | 12 14E |
| Città Sant' Angelo | **63** | 42 32N | 14 5E |
| Cittadella | **63** | 45 39N | 11 48E |
| Cittaducale | **63** | 42 24N | 12 58E |
| Cittanova | **65** | 38 22N | 16 0E |
| Ciucaş, mt. | **70** | 45 31N | 25 56E |
| Ciudad Acuña | **164** | 29 20N | 101 10W |
| Ciudad Altamirano | **164** | 18 20N | 100 40W |
| Ciudad Bolívar | **174** | 8 5N | 63 30W |
| Ciudad Camargo | **164** | 27 41N | 105 10W |
| Ciudad de Valles | **165** | 22 0N | 98 30W |
| Ciudad del Carmen | **165** | 18 20N | 97 50W |
| Ciudad Delicias = Delicias | **164** | 28 10N | 105 30W |
| Ciudad Guerrero | **164** | 28 33N | 107 28W |
| Ciudad Guzmán | **164** | 19 40N | 103 30W |
| Ciudad Juárez | **164** | 31 40N | 106 28W |
| Ciudad Madero | **165** | 22 19N | 97 50W |
| Ciudad Mante | **165** | 22 50N | 99 0W |
| Ciudad Obregón | **164** | 27 28N | 109 59W |
| Ciudad Piar | **174** | 7 27N | 63 19W |
| Ciudad Real | **57** | 38 59N | 3 55W |
| Ciudad Real □ | **57** | 38 50N | 4 0W |
| Ciudad Rodrigo | **56** | 40 35N | 6 32W |
| Ciudad Trujillo = Sto. Domingo | **167** | 18 30N | 70 0W |
| Ciudad Victoria | **165** | 23 41N | 99 9W |
| Ciudadela | **58** | 40 0N | 3 50E |
| Ciulniţa | **70** | 44 26N | 27 22E |
| Civa, B. | **82** | 41 20N | 36 40E |
| Cividale del Friuli | **63** | 46 6N | 13 25E |
| Cívita Castellana | **63** | 42 18N | 12 24E |
| Civitanova Marche | **63** | 43 18N | 13 41E |
| Civitavécchia | **63** | 42 6N | 11 46E |
| Civitella del Tronto | **63** | 42 48N | 13 40E |
| Civray | **44** | 46 10N | 0 17E |
| Çivril | **92** | 38 20N | 29 55E |
| Cixerri, R. | **64** | 39 45N | 8 40E |
| Cizre | **92** | 37 19N | 42 10E |
| Clabach | **34** | 56 38N | 6 36W |
| Clabby | **38** | 54 24N | 7 22W |
| Clach Leathad | **34** | 56 36N | 7 52W |
| Clachan, N. Uist., U.K. | **36** | 57 33N | 7 20W |
| Clachan, Strathclyde, U.K. | **34** | 55 45N | 5 35W |
| Clackline | **137** | 31 40S | 116 32E |
| Clackmannan | **35** | 56 10N | 3 50W |
| Clackmannan (□) | **26** | 56 10N | 3 47W |
| Clacton-on-Sea | **29** | 51 47N | 1 10E |
| Cladich | **34** | 56 21N | 5 5W |
| Claire, L. | **152** | 58 35N | 112 5W |
| Clairemont | **159** | 33 9N | 100 44W |
| Clairvaux-les-Laes | **45** | 46 35N | 5 45E |
| Clamecy | **43** | 47 28N | 3 30E |
| Clane | **39** | 53 18N | 6 40W |
| Clanfield | **29** | 50 56N | 1 0W |
| Clanton | **157** | 32 48N | 86 36W |
| Clanwilliam | **128** | 32 11S | 18 52E |
| Clar, L. nan | **37** | 58 17N | 4 8W |
| Clara | **39** | 53 20N | 7 38W |
| Clara, R. | **138** | 19 8S | 142 30E |
| Claraville | **163** | 35 24N | 118 20W |
| Clare, N.S.W., Austral. | **140** | 33 24S | 143 54E |
| Clare, S. Austral., Austral. | **140** | 33 50S | 138 37E |
| Clare, N. Ireland, U.K. | **38** | 54 25N | 6 19W |
| Clare, Suffolk, U.K. | **29** | 52 5N | 0 36E |
| Clare, U.S.A. | **156** | 43 47N | 84 45W |
| Clare □ | **39** | 52 20N | 7 38W |
| Clare I. | **38** | 53 48N | 10 0W |
| Clare, R. | **38** | 53 20N | 9 0W |
| Clarecastle | **39** | 52 50N | 8 58W |
| Clareen | **39** | 53 4N | 7 49W |
| Claregalaway | **39** | 53 20N | 8 57W |
| Claremont | **162** | 43 23N | 72 20W |
| Claremont Pt. | **138** | 14 1S | 143 41E |
| Claremore | **159** | 36 20N | 95 20W |
| Claremorris | **38** | 53 45N | 9 0W |
| Clarence I. | **13** | 61 30S | 53 50W |
| Clarence, I. | **176** | 54 0S | 72 0W |
| Clarence, R., Austral. | **139** | 29 25S | 153 22E |
| Clarence, R., N.Z. | **143** | 42 10S | 173 56E |
| Clarence Str., Austral. | **136** | 12 0S | 131 0E |
| Clarence Str., U.S.A. | **152** | 55 40N | 132 10W |
| Clarence Town | **167** | 23 6N | 74 59W |
| Clarendon, Ark., U.S.A. | **159** | 34 41N | 91 20W |
| Clarendon, Tex., U.S.A. | **159** | 34 58N | 100 54W |
| Clarenville | **151** | 48 10N | 54 1W |
| Claresholm | **152** | 50 0N | 113 45W |
| Clarie Coast | **13** | 67 0S | 135 0E |
| Clarinbridge | **39** | 53 13N | 8 55W |
| Clarinda | **158** | 40 45N | 95 0W |
| Clarion | **158** | 42 41N | 93 46W |
| Clark | **158** | 44 55N | 97 45W |
| Clark Fork | **160** | 48 9N | 116 9W |
| Clark Fork, R. | **160** | 48 0N | 115 40W |
| Clark Hill Res. | **157** | 33 45N | 82 20W |
| Clarkdale | **161** | 34 53N | 112 3W |
| Clarke City | **151** | 50 12N | 66 38W |
| Clarke, I. | **138** | 40 32S | 148 10E |
| Clarke L. | **153** | 54 24N | 106 54W |
| Clarke Ra. | **138** | 20 45S | 148 20E |
| Clarks Fork, R. | **160** | 45 0N | 109 30W |
| Clark's Harbour | **151** | 43 25N | 65 38W |
| Clarks Station | **163** | 38 8N | 116 42W |
| Clarks Summit | **162** | 41 31N | 75 44W |
| Clarksburg | **156** | 39 18N | 80 21W |
| Clarksdale | **159** | 34 12N | 90 33W |
| Clarkston | **160** | 46 28N | 117 2W |
| Clarksville, Ark., U.S.A. | **159** | 35 29N | 93 27W |
| Clarksville, Tenn., U.S.A. | **157** | 36 32N | 87 20W |
| Clarksville, Tex., U.S.A. | **159** | 33 37N | 94 59W |
| Claro, R. | **171** | 19 8S | 50 40W |
| Clashmore | **37** | 57 53N | 4 8W |
| Clatskanie | **160** | 46 9N | 123 12W |
| Clatteringshaws L. | **34** | 55 3N | 4 17W |
| Claude | **159** | 35 8N | 101 22W |
| Claudio | **171** | 20 26S | 44 46W |
| Claudy | **38** | 54 55N | 7 10W |
| Claunie L. | **36** | 57 8N | 5 6W |
| Claveria | **103** | 18 37N | 121 15E |
| Claverley | **28** | 52 32N | 2 19W |
| Clay | **163** | 38 17N | 121 10W |
| Clay Center | **158** | 39 27N | 97 9W |
| Clay Cross | **33** | 53 11N | 1 26W |
| Clay Hd. | **32** | 54 13N | 4 23W |
| Claydon | **29** | 52 6N | 1 7E |
| Clayette, La | **45** | 46 17N | 4 19E |
| Claymont | **162** | 39 48N | 75 28W |
| Claymore, oilfield | **19** | 58 30N | 0 15W |
| Claypool | **161** | 33 27N | 110 55W |
| Clayton, Idaho, U.S.A. | **160** | 44 12N | 114 31W |
| Clayton, N. Mex., U.S.A. | **159** | 36 30N | 103 10W |
| Cle Elum | **160** | 47 15N | 120 57W |
| Cleady | **39** | 51 53N | 9 32W |
| Clear C. | **39** | 51 26N | 9 30W |
| Clear I. | **39** | 51 26N | 9 30W |
| Clear Lake, Calif., U.S.A. | **160** | 39 5N | 122 47W |
| Clear Lake, S.D., U.S.A. | **158** | 44 48N | 96 41W |
| Clear Lake, Wash., U.S.A. | **160** | 48 27N | 122 15W |
| Clear Lake Res. | **160** | 41 55N | 121 10W |
| Clearfield, Pa., U.S.A. | **156** | 41 0N | 78 27W |
| Clearfield, Utah, U.S.A. | **160** | 41 10N | 112 0W |
| Clearmont | **160** | 44 43N | 106 29W |
| Clearwater, Can. | **152** | 51 38N | 120 2W |
| Clearwater, U.S.A. | **157** | 27 58N | 82 45W |
| Clearwater Cr. | **152** | 61 36N | 125 30W |
| Clearwater L. | **150** | 56 10N | 75 0W |
| Clearwater, Mts. | **160** | 46 20N | 115 30W |
| Clearwater Prov. Park | **153** | 54 0N | 101 0W |
| Clearwater, R., Alta., Can. | **152** | 52 22N | 114 57W |
| Clearwater, R., Alta., Can. | **153** | 56 44N | 111 23W |
| Clearwater, R., B.C., Can. | **152** | 51 38N | 120 3W |
| Cleat | **37** | 58 45N | 2 56W |
| Cleator Moor | **32** | 54 30N | 3 32W |
| Cleburne | **159** | 32 18N | 97 25W |
| Cleddau R. | **31** | 51 46N | 4 44W |
| Clee Hills | **23** | 52 26N | 2 35W |

Cleethorpes Columbia

Cleethorpes 33 53 33N 0 2W
Cleeve Cloud 28 51 56N 2 0W
Cleggan 38 53 33N 10 7W
Clelles 45 44 50N 5 38E
Clemency 47 49 35N 5 53E
Clent 28 52 25N 2 6W
Cleobury Mortimer 28 52 23N 2 28W
Clerke Reef 136 17 22S 119 20E
Clerks Rocks 13 56 0S 36 30W
Clermont 133 22 49S 147 39E
Clermont-en-Argonne 43 49 5N 5 4E
Clermont-Ferrand 44 45 46N 3 4E
Clermont-l'Hérault 44 43 38N 3 26E
Clerval 43 47 25N 6 30E
Cléry-Saint-André 43 47 50N 1 46E
Cles 62 46 21N 11 4E
Clevedon 28 51 26N 2 52W
Cleveland, Austral. 139 27 30S 153 15E
Cleveland, Miss., U.S.A. 159 33 43N 90 43W
Cleveland, Ohio, U.S.A. 156 41 28N 81 43W
Cleveland, Okla., U.S.A. 159 36 21N 96 33W
Cleveland, Tenn., U.S.A. 157 35 9N 84 52W
Cleveland, Tex., U.S.A. 159 30 18N 95 0W
Cleveland □ 33 54 35N 1 8E
Cleveland, C. 138 19 11S 147 1E
Cleveland Hills 33 54 25N 1 11W
Clevelândia 173 26 24S 52 23W
Clevvaux 47 50 4N 6 2E
Clew Bay 38 53 54N 9 50W
Clewiston 157 26 44N 80 50W
Cley 29 52 57N 1 3E
Clifden, Ireland 38 53 30N 10 2W
Clifden, N.Z. 143 46 1S 167 42E
Clifden B. 38 53 29N 10 5W
Cliff 161 33 0N 108 44W
Cliffe 29 51 27N 0 31E
Cliffony 38 54 25N 8 28W
Clifford 28 52 6N 3 6W
Clift Sound 36 60 4N 1 17W
Clifton, Austral. 139 27 59S 151 53E
Clifton, Ariz., U.S.A. 161 33 8N 109 23W
Clifton, Tex., U.S.A. 159 31 46N 97 35W
Clifton Forge 156 37 49N 79 51W
Climax 153 49 10N 108 20W
Clingmans Dome 157 35 35N 83 30W
Clint 161 31 37N 106 11W
Clinton, B.C., Can. 152 51 6N 121 35W
Clinton, Ont., Can. 150 43 37N 81 32W
Clinton, N.Z. 143 46 12S 169 23E
Clinton, Ark., U.S.A. 159 35 37N 92 30W
Clinton, Conn., U.S.A. 162 41 17N 72 32W
Clinton, Ill., U.S.A. 158 40 8N 89 0W
Clinton, Ind., U.S.A. 156 39 40N 87 22W
Clinton, Iowa, U.S.A. 158 41 50N 90 12W
Clinton, Mass., U.S.A. 162 42 26N 71 40W
Clinton, Mo., U.S.A. 158 38 20N 93 46W
Clinton, N.C., U.S.A. 157 35 5N 78 15W
Clinton, Okla., U.S.A. 159 35 30N 99 0W
Clinton, S.C., U.S.A. 157 34 30N 81 54W
Clinton, Tenn., U.S.A. 157 36 6N 84 10W
Clinton C. 138 22 30S 150 45E
Clinton Colden L. 148 64 58N 107 27W
Clintonville 158 44 35N 88 46W
Clipperton, I. 143 10 18N 109 13W
Clipston 29 52 26N 0 58W
Clisson 42 47 5N 1 16W
Clitheroe 32 53 52N 2 23W
Clive 142 39 36S 176 58E
Clive L. 152 63 13N 118 54W
Cloates, Pt. 136 22 43S 113 40E
Clocolan 129 28 55S 27 34E
Clodomira 172 27 35S 64 14W
Clogh 39 52 51N 7 11W
Cloghan, Donegal, Ireland 38 54 50N 7 56W
Cloghan, Offaly, Ireland 39 53 13N 7 53W
Cloghan, W'meath, Ireland 38 53 33N 7 15W
Clogheen 39 52 17N 8 0W
Clogher 38 54 25N 7 10W
Clogher Hd. 38 53 48N 6 15W
Cloghjordan 39 52 57N 8 2W
Cloghran 38 53 26N 6 14W
Clonakilty 39 51 37N 8 53W
Clonakilty B. 39 51 33N 8 50W
Clonbur 38 53 32N 9 21W
Cloncurry, Austral. 138 20 40S 140 28E
Cloncurry, Ireland 38 53 26N 6 47W
Cloncurry, R. 138 18 37S 140 40E
Clondalkin 39 53 20N 6 25W
Clonee 38 53 25N 6 28W
Cloneen 39 52 28N 7 36W
Clones 38 54 10N 7 13W
Clonkeen 39 51 59N 9 20W
Clonmany 38 55 16N 7 24W
Clonmel 39 52 22N 7 42W
Clonmore 39 52 49N 6 35W
Clonroche 39 52 27N 6 42W
Clontarf 38 53 22N 6 10W
Cloonakool 38 54 6N 8 47W
Cloone 38 53 57N 7 47W
Cloonfad 38 53 41N 8 45W
Cloppenburg 48 52 50N 8 3E
Cloquet 158 46 40N 92 30W
Clorinda 172 25 16S 57 45W
Closeburn 35 55 13N 3 45W
Cloud Peak 160 44 30N 107 10W
Cloudcroft 161 33 0N 105 48W
Cloudy B. 143 41 25S 174 10E
Clough, Ballymena, U.K. 38 54 58N 6 16W
Clough, Down, U.K. 38 54 18N 5 50W
Cloughton 33 54 20N 0 27W
Clova 37 56 50N 3 4W
Clovelly 30 51 0N 4 25W
Cloverdale 160 38 49N 123 0W
Clovis, Calif., U.S.A. 163 36 54N 119 45W
Clovis, N. Mex., U.S.A. 159 34 20N 103 10W
Clowne 33 53 18N 1 16W
Cloyne 39 51 52N 8 7W
Club Terrace 141 37 35S 148 58E
Cluj 70 46 47N 23 38E
Cluj □ 70 46 45N 23 30E
Clun 28 52 26N 3 2W
Clun Forest 28 52 27N 3 7W
Clunbury 28 52 25N 2 55W
Clunes, Austral. 140 37 20S 143 45E
Clunes, U.K. 36 56 57N 4 58W
Cluny 45 46 26N 4 38E
Cluses 45 46 5N 6 35E
Clusone 62 45 54N 9 58E
Clutha, R. 143 46 20S 169 49E
Clwyd □ 31 53 5N 3 20W
Clwyd, R. 31 53 12N 3 30W
Clwydian Ra. 31 53 10N 3 15W
Clydach 31 51 42N 3 54W
Clyde, Austral. 139 28 48S 143 40E
Clyde, Can. 149 70 30N 68 30W
Clyde, N.Z. 143 45 12S 169 20E
Clyde, Firth of 34 55 20N 5 0W
Clyde, R. 34 55 46N 4 58W
Clydebank 34 55 54N 4 25W
Clydesdale 35 55 42N 3 50W
Clynnog-fawr 31 53 2N 4 22W
Côa, R. 56 40 45N 7 0W
Coachella 163 33 44N 116 13W
Coachella Canal 163 32 43N 114 57W
Coachford 39 51 54N 8 48W
Coachman's Cove 151 50 6N 56 20W
Coagh 38 54 39N 6 37W
Coahoma 159 32 17N 101 20W
Coahuayana, R. 164 18 41N 103 45W
Coahuayutla 164 18 19N 101 42W
Coahuila □ 164 27 0N 112 30W
Coal Creek Flat 143 45 27S 169 19E
Coal I. 143 46 8S 166 40E
Coal, R. 152 59 39N 126 57W
Coalane 127 17 48S 37 2E
Coalbrookdale 28 52 38N 2 30W
Coalburn 35 55 35N 3 55W
Coalcomán 164 18 40N 103 10W
Coaldale, Can. 152 49 45N 112 35W
Coaldale, U.S.A. 163 38 2N 117 55W
Coaldale, Pa., U.S.A. 162 40 50N 75 54W
Coalgate 159 34 35N 96 13W
Coalinga 163 36 10N 120 21W
Coalisland 38 54 33N 6 42W
Coalspur 152 53 15N 117 0W
Coalville, U.K. 28 52 43N 1 21W
Coalville, U.S.A. 160 40 58N 111 24W
Coamo 147 18 5N 66 22W
Coaraci 171 14 38S 39 32W
Coari 174 4 8S 63 7W
Coast □ 126 2 40S 39 45E
Coast Mts. 152 52 0N 126 0W
Coast Range 163 40 0N 124 0W
Coastal Plains Basin 137 30 10S 115 30E
Coatbridge 35 55 52N 4 2W
Coatepec 165 19 27N 96 58W
Coatepeque 166 14 46N 91 55W
Coatesville 162 39 59N 75 30W
Coaticook 151 45 10N 71 46W
Coats I. 149 62 30N 83 0W
Coats Land 13 77 0S 25 0W
Coatzacoalcos 165 18 7N 94 35W
Cobadin 70 44 5N 28 13E
Cobalt 150 47 25N 79 42W
Cobán 166 15 30N 90 21W
Cobar 141 31 27S 145 48E
Cobb I. 162 37 17N 75 42W
Cobbannah 141 37 37S 147 12E
Cobberas, Mt. 141 36 53S 148 12E
Cobden 140 38 20S 143 3E
Cóbh 39 51 50N 8 18W
Cobija 174 11 0S 68 50W
Cobourg 150 43 58N 78 10W
Cobourg Pen. 136 11 20S 132 15E
Cobram 141 35 54S 145 40E
Cobre 160 41 6N 114 25W
Cóbué 125 12 0S 34 58E
Coburg 49 50 15N 10 58E
Coca 56 41 13N 4 32W
Coca, R. 174 0 25S 77 5W
Cocal 170 3 28S 41 34W
Cocanada = Kakinada 96 16 55N 82 20E
Cocentaina 59 38 45N 0 27W
Cocha, La 172 27 50S 65 40W
Cochabamba 174 17 15S 66 20W
Coche, I. 174 10 47N 63 56W
Cochem 49 50 8N 7 7E
Cochemane 127 17 0S 32 54E
Cochilha Grande de Albardão 173 28 30S 51 30W
Cochin 97 9 55N 76 22E
Cochin China 101 10 30N 106 0E
Cochin China = Nam-Phan 101 10 30N 106 0E
Cochise 161 32 6N 109 58W
Cochran 157 32 25N 83 23W
Cochrane, Alta., Can. 152 51 11N 114 30W
Cochrane, Ont., Can. 150 49 0N 81 0W
Cochrane, L. 176 47 10S 72 0W
Cochrane, R. 153 57 53N 101 34W
Cockatoo I. 136 16 6S 123 37E
Cockburn 140 32 5S 141 0E
Cockburn, Canal 176 54 30S 72 0W
Cockburn, C. 136 11 20S 132 52E
Cockburn I. 150 45 55N 83 22W
Cockburn Ra. 136 15 46S 128 0E
Cockburnspath 35 55 56N 2 23W
Cockenzie 35 55 58N 2 59W
Cockerham 32 53 58N 2 49W
Cockermouth 32 54 40N 3 22W
Cockeysville 162 39 29N 76 39W
Cockfield 29 52 8N 0 47E
Cocklebiddy 137 32 0S 126 3E
Coco Chan. 101 13 50N 93 25E
Coco Is. 101 14 0N 93 12E
Coco, Pta. 174 2 58N 77 43W
Coco, R. (Wanks) 166 14 10N 85 0W
Cocoa 157 28 22N 80 40W
Cocobeach 124 0 59N 9 34E
Cocoli, R. 120 12 0N 14 0W
Cocora 70 44 45N 27 3E
Côcos 171 14 10S 44 33W
Cocos (Keeling) Is. 11 12 12S 96 54E
Côcos, R. 171 12 44S 44 48W
Cod, C. 162 42 8N 70 10W
Cod, gasfield 19 57 8N 2 35E
Codajás 174 3 40S 62 0W
Coddenham 29 52 8N 1 8E
Codera, C. 174 10 35N 66 4W
Coderre 153 50 11N 106 31W
Codigoro 63 44 50N 12 5E
Codó 170 4 30S 43 55W
Codogno 62 45 10N 9 42E
Codróipo 63 45 57N 13 0E
Codru, Munţii 70 46 30N 22 15E
Cods Hd. 39 51 40N 10 7W
Cody 160 44 35N 109 0W
Coe Hill 150 44 52N 77 50W
Coelemu 172 36 30S 72 48W
Coelho Neto 170 4 15S 43 0W
Coen 138 13 52S 143 12E
Coesfeld 48 51 56N 7 10E
Coeur d'Alene 160 47 45N 116 51W
Coevorden 46 52 40N 6 44E
Coffeyville 159 37 0N 95 40W
Coffin B. Pen. 136 34 20S 135 10E
Coffs Harbour 141 30 16S 153 5E
Cofre de Perote, Cerro 165 19 30N 97 10W
Cofrentes 59 39 13N 1 5W
Cogealac 70 44 36N 28 36E
Coggeshall 29 51 53N 0 41E
Coghinas, R. 64 40 55N 8 48E
Cognac 44 45 41N 0 20W
Cogne 62 45 37N 7 21E
Cogolludo 58 40 59N 3 10W
Cohagen 160 47 2N 106 45W
Cohoes 162 42 47N 73 42W
Cohuna 140 35 45S 144 15E
Coiba I. 166 7 30N 81 40W
Coig, R. 176 51 0S 70 20W
Coigach, dist. 36 58 0N 5 10W
Coillore 36 57 21N 6 23W
Coimbatore 97 11 2N 76 59E
Coimbra 56 40 15N 8 27W
Coimbra □ 56 40 12N 8 25W
Coín 57 36 40N 4 48W
Cojedes □ 174 9 20N 68 20W
Cojimies 174 0 20N 80 0W
Cojocna 70 46 45N 23 50E
Cojutepequé 166 13 41N 88 54W
Čoka 66 45 57N 20 12E
Cokeville 160 42 4N 111 0W
Col di Tenda 62 44 7N 7 36E
Colaba Pt. 96 18 54N 72 47E
Colac 140 38 21S 143 35E
Colachel 97 8 10N 77 15E
Colares 57 38 48N 9 30W
Colatina 171 19 32S 40 37W
Colbinabbin 141 36 38S 144 48E
Colby, U.K. 32 54 6N 4 42W
Colby, U.S.A. 158 39 27N 101 2W
Colchagua □ 172 34 30S 71 0W
Colchester 29 51 54N 0 55E
Cold Fell 32 54 54N 2 40W
Coldingham 35 55 53N 2 10W
Coldstream 35 55 39N 2 14W
Coldwater 159 37 18N 99 24W
Coldwell 150 48 45N 86 30W
Colebrook 138 42 31S 147 12E
Colebrooke 30 50 45N 3 44W
Coleford 28 51 46N 2 38W
Coleman, Can. 152 49 40N 114 30W
Coleman, U.S.A. 159 31 52N 99 30W
Coleman, R. 138 15 6S 141 38E
Colenso 129 28 44S 29 50E
Coleraine, Austral. 140 37 36S 141 40E
Coleraine, U.K. 38 55 8N 6 40E
Coleraine □ 38 55 8N 6 40E
Coleridge, L. 143 43 17S 171 30E
Coleroon, R. 97 11 0N 79 0E
Colesberg 128 30 45S 25 5E
Coleshill 28 52 30N 1 42W
Coleville 163 38 44N 119 30W
Colfax, La., U.S.A. 159 31 35N 92 39W
Colfax, Wash., U.S.A. 160 46 57N 117 28W
Colgrave Sd. 36 60 35N 1 0W
Colhué Huapi, L. 176 45 30S 69 0W
Cólico 62 46 8N 9 22E
Coligny 128 46 24N 5 21E
Colima 164 19 10N 103 40W
Colima □ 164 19 10N 103 40W
Colima, Nevado de 164 19 30N 103 40W
Colina 172 33 13S 70 45W
Colina do Norte 120 12 28N 15 0W
Colinas, Goiás, Brazil 171 14 15S 48 2W
Colinas, Maranhão, Brazil 170 6 0S 44 10W
Colinton, Austral. 141 35 50S 149 10E
Colinton, U.K. 35 55 54N 3 17W
Coll, I. 34 56 40N 6 35W
Collaguasi 172 21 5S 68 45W
Collarada, Peña 58 42 43N 0 29W
Collarenebri 139 29 33S 148 36E
Collbran 161 39 16N 107 58W
Colle Salvetti 62 43 34N 10 27E
Colle Sannita 65 41 22N 14 48E
Colléchio 62 44 23N 10 10E
Colleen Bawn 127 21 0S 29 12E
College Park, Ga., U.S.A. 157 33 42N 84 27W
College Park, Md., U.S.A. 162 39 0N 76 55W
Collette 151 46 40N 65 30W
Collie, N.S.W., Austral. 141 31 41S 148 18E
Collie, W. Austral., Austral. 137 33 22S 116 8E
Collier B. 136 16 10S 124 15E
Collier Law Pk. 32 54 47N 1 59W
Collier Ra. 137 24 45S 119 10E
Collin 35 55 4N 3 30W
Colline Metallifere 62 43 10N 11 0E
Collingbourne 28 51 16N 1 39W
Collingswood 162 39 55N 75 4W
Collingwood, Austral. 138 22 20S 142 31E
Collingwood, Can. 150 44 29N 80 13W
Collingwood, N.Z. 143 40 25S 172 40E
Collingwood B. 138 9 30S 149 30E
Collins 150 50 17N 89 27W
Collinsville 138 20 30S 147 56E
Collipulli 172 37 55S 72 30W
Collison Ra. 136 14 49S 127 25E
Collo 119 36 58N 6 37E
Collon 38 53 46N 6 29W
Collonges 45 46 9N 5 52E
Collooney 38 54 11N 8 28W
Colmar 43 48 5N 7 20E
Colmars 45 44 11N 6 39E
Colmenar 57 36 54N 4 20W
Colmenar de Oreja 58 40 6N 3 25W
Colmenar Viejo 56 40 39N 3 47W
Colmor 159 36 18N 104 36W
Colne 32 53 51N 2 11W
Colne, R., Essex, U.K. 29 51 55N 0 50E
Colne, R., Herts., U.K. 29 51 36N 0 30W
Colnett, Cabo 164 31 0N 116 20W
Colo, R. 141 33 25S 150 52E
Cologna Véneta 63 45 19N 11 21E
Colomb-Béchar = Béchar 118 31 38N 2 18E
Colombey-les-Belles 43 48 32N 5 54E
Colombey-les-deux Églises 43 48 20N 4 50E
Colômbia 171 20 10S 48 40W
Colombia 174 3 23N 79 49W
Colombia ■ 174 3 45N 73 0W
Colombier 50 46 58N 6 53E
Colombo 97 6 56N 79 58E
Colombus, Kans., U.S.A. 159 37 15N 94 30W
Colombus, Nebr., U.S.A. 158 41 30N 97 25W
Colombus, N.Mex., U.S.A. 161 31 54N 107 43W
Colome 158 43 20N 99 44W
Colón, Argent. 172 32 12S 58 30W
Colón, Cuba 166 22 42N 80 54W
Colón, Panama 166 9 20N 80 0W
Colonel Hill 167 22 50N 74 21W
Colonella 63 42 52N 13 50E
Colonia del Sacramento 173 34 25S 57 50W
Colonia Dora 172 28 34S 62 59W
Colonia Las Heras 176 46 30S 69 0W
Colonia Sarmiento 176 45 30S 68 15W
Colonial Hts. 162 37 15N 77 25W
Colonne, C. delle 65 39 2N 17 11E
Colonsay 153 51 59N 105 52W
Colonsay, I. 34 56 4N 6 12W
Colorado □ 154 37 40N 106 0W
Colorado Aqueduct 161 34 17N 114 10W
Colorado City 159 32 25N 100 50W
Colorado Desert 154 34 20N 116 0W
Colorado Plateau 161 36 40N 110 30W
Colorado, R., Argent. 172 37 30S 69 0W
Colorado, R., Ariz., U.S.A. 161 33 30N 114 30W
Colorado, R., Calif., U.S.A. 161 34 0N 114 33W
Colorado, R., Tex., U.S.A. 159 29 40N 96 30W
Colorado Springs 158 38 55N 104 50W
Colorno 62 44 55N 10 21E
Colossal 141 30 52S 147 3E
Colotepec 165 15 47N 97 3W
Colotlán 164 22 6N 103 16W
Colpy 37 57 23N 2 35W
Colsterworth 29 52 48N 0 37W
Coltishall 29 52 44N 1 21E
Colton, Calif., U.S.A. 163 34 4N 117 20W
Colton, Wash., U.S.A. 160 46 41N 117 6W
Columbia, La., U.S.A. 159 32 7N 92 5W
Columbia, Miss., U.S.A. 159 31 16N 89 50W
Columbia, Mo., U.S.A. 158 38 58N 92 20W
Columbia, Pa., U.S.A. 162 40 2N 76 30W
Columbia, S.C., U.S.A. 157 34 0N 81 0W

| | | | |
|---|---|---|---|
| Columbia, Tenn., U.S.A. | **157** | 35 40N | 87 0W |
| Columbia, C. | **12** | 83 0N | 70 0W |
| Columbia City | **156** | 41 8N | 85 30W |
| Columbia, District of □ | **156** | 38 55N | 77 0W |
| Columbia Falls | **160** | 48 25N | 114 16W |
| Columbia Heights | **158** | 45 5N | 93 10W |
| Columbia, Mt. | **152** | 52 8N | 117 20W |
| Columbia Plateau | **160** | 47 30N | 118 30W |
| Columbia, R. | **160** | 45 49N | 120 0W |
| Columbretes, Is. | **58** | 39 50N | 0 50E |
| Columbus, Ga., U.S.A. | **157** | 32 30N | 84 58W |
| Columbus, Ind., U.S.A. | **156** | 39 14N | 85 55W |
| Columbus, Miss., U.S.A. | **157** | 33 30N | 88 26W |
| Columbus, Mont., U.S.A. | **160** | 45 45N | 109 14W |
| Columbus, N.D., U.S.A. | **158** | 48 52N | 102 48W |
| Columbus, Ohio, U.S.A. | **156** | 39 57N | 83 1W |
| Columbus, Tex., U.S.A. | **159** | 29 42N | 96 33W |
| Columbus, Wis., U.S.A. | **158** | 43 20N | 89 2W |
| Colunda | **125** | 12 7S | 23 36E |
| Colunga | **56** | 43 29N | 5 16W |
| Colusa | **160** | 39 15N | 122 1W |
| Colville | **160** | 48 33N | 117 54W |
| Colville, C. | **142** | 36 29S | 175 21E |
| Colville, R. | **147** | 69 15N | 152 0W |
| Colwell | **35** | 55 4N | 2 4W |
| Colwich | **28** | 52 48N | 1 58W |
| Colwyn | **31** | 53 17N | 3 43W |
| Colwyn Bay | **31** | 53 17N | 3 44W |
| Colyton | **30** | 50 44N | 3 4W |
| Comácchio | **63** | 44 41N | 12 10E |
| Comalcalco | **165** | 18 16N | 93 13W |
| Comallo | **176** | 41 0S | 70 5W |
| Comana | **70** | 44 10N | 26 10E |
| Comanche, Okla., U.S.A. | **159** | 34 27N | 97 58W |
| Comanche, Tex., U.S.A. | **159** | 31 55N | 98 35W |
| Comăneşti | **70** | 46 25N | 26 26E |
| Comayagua | **166** | 14 25N | 87 37W |
| Combahee, R. | **157** | 32 45N | 80 50W |
| Combara | **141** | 31 10S | 148 22E |
| Combe Martin | **30** | 51 12N | 4 2W |
| Combeaufontaine | **43** | 47 38N | 5 54E |
| Comber | **38** | 54 33N | 5 45W |
| Combermere Bay | **98** | 19 37N | 93 34E |
| Comblain | **47** | 50 29N | 5 35E |
| Combles | **43** | 50 0N | 2 50E |
| Combourg | **42** | 48 25N | 1 46W |
| Comboyne | **141** | 31 34S | 152 34E |
| Combronde | **44** | 45 58N | 3 5E |
| Comeragh Mts. | **39** | 52 17N | 7 35W |
| Comercinho | **171** | 16 19S | 41 47W |
| Comet | **138** | 23 36S | 148 38E |
| Comet Vale | **137** | 29 55S | 121 4E |
| Comilla | **98** | 23 28N | 91 10E |
| Comines | **47** | 50 46N | 3 0E |
| Comino, C. | **64** | 40 28N | 9 47E |
| Cómiso | **65** | 36 57N | 14 35E |
| Comitán | **165** | 16 18N | 92 9W |
| Commentry | **44** | 46 20N | 2 46E |
| Commerce, Ga., U.S.A. | **157** | 34 10N | 83 25W |
| Commerce, Tex., U.S.A. | **159** | 33 15N | 95 50W |
| Commercy | **43** | 48 40N | 5 34E |
| Committee B. | **149** | 68 30N | 86 30W |
| Commonwealth B. | **13** | 67 0S | 144 0E |
| Commoron Cr., R. | **139** | 28 22S | 150 8E |
| Communism Pk. = Kommunizma, Pk. | **93** | 38 40N | 72 20E |
| Como | **62** | 45 48N | 9 5E |
| Como, L. di | **62** | 46 5N | 9 17E |
| Comodoro Rivadavia | **176** | 45 50S | 67 40W |
| Comores, Arch. des | **11** | 10 0S | 50 0E |
| Comores, Is. | **11** | 12 10S | 44 15E |
| Comorin, C. | **97** | 8 3N | 77 40E |
| Comorişte | **70** | 45 10N | 21 35E |
| Comoro Is. | **11** | 12 10S | 44 15E |
| Comox | **152** | 49 42N | 124 55W |
| Compiègne | **43** | 49 24N | 2 50E |
| Compiglia Marittima | **62** | 43 4N | 10 37E |
| Comporta | **57** | 38 22N | 8 46W |
| Compostela | **164** | 21 15N | 104 53W |
| Comprida, I. | **173** | 24 50S | 47 42W |
| Compton, U.K. | **28** | 51 2N | 1 19W |
| Compton, U.S.A. | **163** | 33 54N | 118 13W |
| Compton Downs | **139** | 30 28S | 146 30E |
| Comrie | **35** | 56 22N | 4 0W |
| Con Cuong | **100** | 19 2N | 104 54E |
| Côn Dao | **101** | 8 45N | 106 45E |
| Con Son, Is. | **101** | 8 41N | 106 37E |
| Conakry | **120** | 9 29N | 13 49W |
| Conara Junction | **138** | 41 50S | 147 26E |
| Conargo | **141** | 35 16S | 145 10E |
| Conatlán | **164** | 24 30N | 104 42W |
| Concarneau | **42** | 47 52N | 3 56W |
| Conceição, Brazil | **170** | 7 33S | 38 31W |
| Conceição, Mozam. | **127** | 18 47S | 36 7E |
| Conceição da Barra | **171** | 18 35S | 39 45W |
| Conceição do Araguaia | **170** | 8 0S | 49 2W |
| Conceição do Canindé | **170** | 7 54S | 41 34W |
| Conceição do Mato Dentro | **171** | 19 1S | 43 25W |
| Concepcián | **165** | 18 15N | 90 5W |
| Concepción, Argent. | **172** | 27 20S | 65 35W |
| Concepción, Boliv. | **174** | 15 50S | 61 40W |
| Concepción, Chile | **172** | 36 50S | 73 0W |
| Concepción, Colomb. | **174** | 0 5N | 75 37W |
| Concepción, Parag. | **172** | 23 30S | 57 20W |
| Concepción, Venez. | **174** | 10 48N | 71 46W |
| Concepción □ | **172** | 37 0S | 72 30W |
| Concepcion, C. | **154** | 34 30N | 120 34W |
| Concepción del Oro | **164** | 24 40N | 101 30W |
| Concepción del Uruguay | **172** | 32 35S | 58 20W |
| Concepción, L. | **174** | 17 20S | 61 10W |
| Concepción, La = Ri-Aba | **121** | 3 28N | 84 0E |
| Concepción, Punta | **164** | 26 55N | 111 50W |
| Concepción, R. | **164** | 30 32N | 113 2W |
| Conception B. | **128** | 23 55S | 14 22E |
| Conception I. | **167** | 23 52N | 75 9W |
| Conception, Pt. | **163** | 34 27N | 120 28W |
| Concession | **127** | 17 27S | 30 56E |
| Conchas Dam | **159** | 35 25N | 104 10W |
| Conche | **151** | 50 48N | 55 58W |
| Conches-en-Ouche | **50** | 48 58N | 0 58E |
| Concho | **161** | 34 32N | 109 43W |
| Concho, R. | **159** | 31 30N | 100 8W |
| Conchos, R., Chihnahua, Mexico | **164** | 29 20N | 105 0W |
| Conchos, R., Tamaulipas, Mexico | **165** | 25 0N | 97 32W |
| Concon | **172** | 32 56S | 71 33W |
| Concord, Calif., U.S.A. | **163** | 37 59N | 122 2W |
| Concord, N.C., U.S.A. | **157** | 35 28N | 80 35W |
| Concord, N.H., U.S.A. | **162** | 43 12N | 71 30W |
| Concórdia, Argent. | **172** | 31 20S | 58 2W |
| Concórdia, Brazil | **174** | 4 36S | 66 36W |
| Concordia, Colomb. | **174** | 2 39N | 72 47W |
| Concordia, Mexico | **164** | 23 18N | 106 2W |
| Concordia, U.S.A. | **158** | 39 35N | 97 40W |
| Concordia, La | **165** | 16 8N | 92 38W |
| Concots | **44** | 44 26N | 1 40E |
| Concrete | **160** | 48 35N | 121 49W |
| Condah | **140** | 37 57S | 141 44E |
| Condamine, R. | **133** | 27 7S | 149 48E |
| Condat | **44** | 45 21N | 2 46E |
| Conde | **171** | 11 49S | 37 37W |
| Condé | **43** | 50 26N | 3 34E |
| Conde | **158** | 45 13N | 98 5W |
| Condé-sur-Noireau | **42** | 48 51N | 0 33W |
| Condeúba | **171** | 15 0S | 42 0W |
| Condobolin | **141** | 33 4S | 147 6E |
| Condom | **44** | 43 57N | 0 22E |
| Condon | **160** | 45 15N | 120 8W |
| Condove | **62** | 45 8N | 7 19E |
| Condover | **28** | 52 39N | 2 46W |
| Conegliano | **63** | 45 53N | 12 18E |
| Conejera, I. | **59** | 39 11N | 2 58E |
| Conejos | **164** | 26 14N | 103 53W |
| Conflans-en-Jarnisy | **43** | 49 10N | 5 52E |
| Confolens | **44** | 46 2N | 0 40E |
| Confuso, R. | **172** | 24 10S | 59 0W |
| Congleton | **32** | 53 10N | 2 12W |
| Congo | **170** | 7 48S | 36 40W |
| Congo ■ | **124** | 1 0S | 16 0E |
| Congo Basin | **114** | 0 10S | 24 30E |
| Congo, Democratic Rep. of = Zaïre ■ | **124** | 3 0S | 22 0E |
| Congo (Kinshasa) ■ = Zaïre ■ | **124** | 1 0S | 16 0E |
| Congo, R. = Zaïre, R. | **124** | 1 30N | 28 0E |
| Congonhas | **173** | 20 30S | 43 52W |
| Congresbury | **28** | 51 20N | 2 49W |
| Congress | **161** | 34 11N | 112 56W |
| Congucu | **113** | 31 25S | 52 30W |
| Conil | **57** | 36 17N | 6 10W |
| Coningsby | **33** | 53 7N | 0 9W |
| Conisbrough | **33** | 53 29N | 1 12W |
| Coniston, Can. | **150** | 46 29N | 80 51W |
| Coniston, U.K. | **32** | 54 22N | 3 6W |
| Coniston Water | **32** | 54 20N | 3 5W |
| Conjeevaram = Kancheepuram | **97** | 12 52N | 79 45E |
| Conjuboy | **138** | 18 35S | 144 45E |
| Conklin | **153** | 55 38N | 111 5W |
| Conlea | **139** | 30 7S | 144 35E |
| Conn, L. | **38** | 54 3N | 9 15W |
| Conna | **39** | 52 5N | 8 8W |
| Connacht | **38** | 53 23N | 8 40W |
| Connah's Quay | **31** | 53 13N | 3 6W |
| Conneaut | **156** | 41 55N | 80 32W |
| Connecticut □ | **162** | 41 40N | 72 40W |
| Connecticut, R. | **162** | 41 17N | 72 21W |
| Connel | **34** | 56 27N | 5 24W |
| Connel Park | **34** | 55 22N | 4 15W |
| Connell | **160** | 46 45N | 118 58W |
| Connemara | **38** | 53 29N | 9 45W |
| Conner, La | **160** | 48 22N | 122 27W |
| Connersville | **156** | 39 40N | 85 10W |
| Connonagh | **39** | 51 35N | 9 8W |
| Connor, Mt. | **136** | 14 34S | 126 4E |
| Connors Ra. | **138** | 21 40S | 149 10E |
| Conoble | **141** | 32 55S | 144 42E |
| Cononaco, R. | **174** | 1 20S | 76 30W |
| Conquest | **153** | 51 32N | 107 14W |
| Conquet, Le | **42** | 48 21N | 4 46W |
| Conrad | **160** | 48 11N | 112 0W |
| Conran, C. | **141** | 37 49S | 148 44E |
| Conroe | **159** | 30 15N | 95 28W |
| Conselheiro Lafaiete | **173** | 20 40S | 43 48W |
| Conselheiro Pena | **171** | 19 10S | 41 30W |
| Consett | **32** | 54 52N | 1 50W |
| Conshohocken | **162** | 40 5N | 75 18W |
| Consort | **153** | 52 1N | 110 46W |
| Constance = Konstanz | **49** | 47 39N | 9 10E |
| Constance, L. = Bodensee | **51** | 47 35N | 9 25E |
| Constanţa | **70** | 44 14N | 28 38E |
| Constanţa □ | **70** | 44 15N | 28 15E |
| Constantia | **162** | 43 15N | 76 1W |
| Constantina | **57** | 37 51N | 5 40W |
| Constantine | **119** | 36 25N | 6 42E |
| Constitución, Chile | **172** | 35 20S | 72 30W |
| Constitución, Uruguay | **172** | 31 0S | 58 10W |
| Consuegra | **57** | 39 28N | 3 43W |
| Consul | **153** | 49 20N | 109 30W |
| Contact | **160** | 41 50N | 114 56W |
| Contai | **95** | 21 54N | 87 55E |
| Contamana | **174** | 7 10S | 74 55W |
| Contarina | **63** | 45 2N | 12 13E |
| Contas, R. | **171** | 13 5S | 41 53W |
| Contes | **45** | 43 49N | 7 19E |
| Conthey | **50** | 46 14N | 7 28E |
| Contin | **37** | 57 34N | 4 35W |
| Contoocook | **162** | 43 13N | 71 45W |
| Contra Costa | **129** | 25 9S | 33 30E |
| Contres | **43** | 47 24N | 1 26E |
| Contrexéville | **43** | 48 6N | 5 53E |
| Convención | **174** | 8 28N | 73 21W |
| Conversano | **65** | 40 57N | 17 8E |
| Convoy | **38** | 54 52N | 7 40W |
| Conway, Ark., U.S.A. | **159** | 35 5N | 92 30W |
| Conway, N.H., U.S.A. | **162** | 43 58N | 71 8W |
| Conway, S.C., U.S.A. | **157** | 33 49N | 79 2W |
| Conway = Conwy | **31** | 53 17N | 3 50W |
| Conway, L. | **139** | 28 17S | 135 35E |
| Conwy | **31** | 53 17N | 3 50W |
| Conwy Bay | **31** | 53 17N | 3 57W |
| Conwy, R. | **31** | 53 18N | 3 50W |
| Coober Pedy | **136** | 29 1S | 134 43E |
| Coobina | **137** | 23 22S | 120 10E |
| Cooch Behar | **98** | 26 22N | 89 29E |
| Cook, Austral. | **137** | 30 37S | 130 25E |
| Cook, U.S.A. | **158** | 47 49N | 92 39W |
| Cook, Bahia | **176** | 55 10S | 70 0W |
| Cook Inlet | **147** | 59 0N | 151 0W |
| Cook Is. | **131** | 20 0S | 160 0W |
| Cook, Mount | **143** | 43 36S | 170 9E |
| Cook Strait | **143** | 41 15S | 174 29E |
| Cooke Plains | **140** | 35 23S | 139 34E |
| Cookeville | **157** | 36 12N | 85 30W |
| Cookham | **29** | 51 33N | 0 42W |
| Cookhouse | **128** | 32 44S | 25 47E |
| Cookstown | **38** | 54 40N | 6 43W |
| Cookstown □ | **38** | 54 40N | 6 43W |
| Cooktown | **138** | 15 30S | 145 16E |
| Coolabah | **141** | 31 1S | 146 43E |
| Cooladdi | **139** | 26 37S | 145 23E |
| Coolah | **141** | 31 48S | 149 41E |
| Coolamon | **141** | 34 46S | 147 8E |
| Coolaney | **38** | 54 10N | 8 36W |
| Coolangatta | **139** | 28 11S | 153 29E |
| Coole | **38** | 53 42N | 7 23W |
| Coolgardie | **137** | 30 55S | 121 8E |
| Coolgreany | **39** | 52 46N | 6 14W |
| Coolibah | **136** | 15 33S | 130 56E |
| Coolidge | **161** | 33 1N | 111 35W |
| Coolidge Dam | **161** | 33 10N | 110 30W |
| Coolmore | **38** | 54 33N | 8 12W |
| Cooma | **141** | 36 12S | 149 8E |
| Coomacarrea Mts. | **39** | 51 59N | 10 0W |
| Coonabarabran | **141** | 31 14S | 149 18E |
| Coonalpyn | **140** | 35 43S | 139 52E |
| Coonamble | **141** | 30 56S | 148 27E |
| Coonana | **137** | 31 0S | 123 0E |
| Coondapoor | **97** | 13 42N | 74 40E |
| Coongie | **139** | 27 9S | 140 8E |
| Coongoola | **139** | 27 43S | 145 47E |
| Cooninie, L. | **139** | 26 4S | 139 59E |
| Coonoor | **97** | 11 10N | 76 45E |
| Cooper | **159** | 33 20N | 95 40W |
| Cooper Cr. | **139** | 28 29S | 137 46E |
| Cooper, R. | **157** | 33 0N | 79 55W |
| Coopersburg | **162** | 40 31N | 75 23W |
| Cooperstown, N.D., U.S.A. | **158** | 47 30N | 98 14W |
| Cooperstown, New York, U.S.A. | **162** | 42 42N | 74 57W |
| Coorabie P.O. | **137** | 31 54S | 132 18E |
| Coorabulka | **138** | 23 41S | 140 20E |
| Coorong, The | **133** | 35 50S | 139 20E |
| Coorow | **137** | 29 53S | 116 2E |
| Cooroy | **139** | 26 22S | 152 54E |
| Coos Bay | **160** | 43 26N | 124 7W |
| Cootamundra | **141** | 34 36S | 148 1E |
| Cootehill | **38** | 54 5N | 7 5W |
| Cooyar | **139** | 26 59S | 151 51E |
| Cooyeana | **138** | 24 29S | 138 45E |
| Copahué, Paso | **172** | 37 49S | 71 8W |
| Copainalá | **165** | 17 8N | 93 11W |
| Copake Falls | **162** | 42 7N | 73 31W |
| Copán | **166** | 14 50N | 89 9W |
| Cope | **158** | 39 44N | 102 50W |
| Cope, Cabo | **59** | 37 26N | 1 28W |
| Cope Cope | **140** | 36 27S | 143 5E |
| Copeland I. | **38** | 54 38N | 5 33W |
| Copenhagen | **162** | 43 54N | 75 41W |
| Copenhagen = København | **73** | 55 41N | 12 34E |
| Copertino | **65** | 40 17N | 18 2W |
| Copeville | **140** | 34 47S | 139 51E |
| Copiapó | **172** | 27 15S | 70 20E |
| Copiapó, R. | **172** | 27 19S | 70 56W |
| Copinsay I. | **37** | 58 54N | 2 40W |
| Coplay | **162** | 40 44N | 75 29W |
| Copley | **140** | 30 24S | 138 26E |
| Copp L. | **152** | 60 14N | 114 40W |
| Copparo | **63** | 44 52N | 11 49E |
| Copper Center | **147** | 62 10N | 145 25W |
| Copper Cliff | **150** | 46 28N | 81 4W |
| Copper Harbor | **156** | 47 31N | 87 55W |
| Copper Mountain | **152** | 49 20N | 120 30W |
| Copper Queen | **127** | 17 29S | 29 18E |
| Copper R. | **147** | 61 30N | 144 30W |
| Copperbelt □ | **127** | 13 15N | 27 30E |
| Copperfield | **137** | 29 1S | 120 26E |
| Coppermine | **148** | 67 50N | 115 5W |
| Coppermine, R. | **148** | 67 49N | 115 4W |
| Copperopolis | **163** | 37 58N | 120 38W |
| Cöppingen | **49** | 48 42N | 9 40E |
| Copythorne | **28** | 50 56N | 1 34W |
| Coquet, I. | **35** | 55 21N | 1 30W |
| Coquet, R. | **35** | 55 18N | 1 45W |
| Coquilhatville = Mbandaka | **124** | 0 1N | 18 18E |
| Coquille | **160** | 43 15N | 124 6W |
| Coquimbo | **172** | 30 0S | 71 20W |
| Coquimbo □ | **172** | 31 0S | 71 0W |
| Cora, oilfield | **19** | 55 45N | 4 45E |
| Corabia | **70** | 43 48N | 24 30E |
| Coração de Jesus | **171** | 11 39S | 39 56W |
| Coracora | **174** | 15 5S | 73 45W |
| Coradi, Is. | **65** | 40 27N | 71 10E |
| Coral Harbour | **149** | 64 8N | 83 10W |
| Coral Rapids | **150** | 50 20N | 81 40W |
| Coral Sea | **142** | 15 0S | 150 0E |
| Coral Sea Islands Terr. | **133** | 20 0S | 155 0E |
| Corato | **65** | 41 12N | 16 22E |
| Corbeil-Essonnes | **43** | 48 36N | 2 26E |
| Corbie | **43** | 49 54N | 2 30E |
| Corbières, mts. | **44** | 42 55N | 2 35E |
| Corbigny | **43** | 47 16N | 3 40E |
| Corbin | **156** | 37 0N | 84 3W |
| Corbion | **47** | 49 48N | 5 0E |
| Corbones, R. | **57** | 37 25N | 5 35W |
| Corbridge | **35** | 54 58N | 2 0W |
| Corby, Lincs., U.K. | **29** | 52 49N | 0 31W |
| Corby, Northants., U.K. | **29** | 52 29N | 0 41W |
| Corcoles, R. | **59** | 39 12N | 2 40W |
| Corcoran | **163** | 36 6N | 119 35W |
| Corcubión | **56** | 42 56N | 9 12W |
| Cord. de Caravaya | **174** | 14 0S | 70 30W |
| Cordele | **157** | 31 55N | 83 49W |
| Cordell | **159** | 35 18N | 99 0W |
| Cordenons | **63** | 45 59N | 12 42E |
| Cordes | **44** | 44 5N | 1 57E |
| Cordillera Oriental | **174** | 5 0N | 74 0W |
| Cordisburgo | **171** | 19 7S | 44 21W |
| Córdoba | **172** | 31 20S | 64 10W |
| Cordoba | **164** | 26 20N | 103 20W |
| Córdoba, Mexico | **165** | 18 50N | 97 0W |
| Córdoba, Spain | **57** | 37 50N | 4 50W |
| Córdoba □, Argent. | **172** | 31 22S | 64 15W |
| Córdoba □, Colomb. | **174** | 8 20N | 75 40W |
| Córdoba □, Spain | **57** | 38 5N | 5 0W |
| Córdoba, Sierra de | **172** | 31 10S | 64 25W |
| Cordon | **103** | 16 42N | 121 32E |
| Cordova, Ala., U.S.A. | **157** | 33 45N | 87 12W |
| Cordova, Alaska, U.S.A. | **147** | 60 36N | 145 45W |
| Corella | **58** | 42 7N | 1 48W |
| Corella, R. | **138** | 19 34S | 140 47E |
| Coremas | **170** | 7 1S | 37 58W |
| Corfe Castle | **28** | 50 58N | 2 3W |
| Corfe Mullen | **28** | 50 45N | 2 0W |
| Corfield | **138** | 21 40S | 143 21E |
| Corfu = Kerkira | **68** | 39 38N | 19 50E |
| Corgo | **56** | 42 56N | 7 25W |
| Cori | **64** | 41 39N | 12 53E |
| Coria | **56** | 40 0N | 6 33W |
| Coricudgy, Mt. | **141** | 32 51S | 150 24E |
| Corigliano Cálabro | **65** | 39 36N | 16 31E |
| Coringa Is. | **138** | 16 58S | 149 58E |
| Corinna | **138** | 41 35S | 145 10E |
| Corinth, Miss., U.S.A. | **157** | 34 54N | 88 30W |
| Corinth, N.Y., U.S.A. | **162** | 43 15N | 73 50W |
| Corinth = Korinthos | **69** | 37 56N | 22 55E |
| Corinth Canal | **69** | 37 48N | 23 0E |
| Corinth, G. of = Korinthiakós | **69** | 38 16N | 22 30E |
| Corinto, Brazil | **171** | 18 20S | 44 30W |
| Corinto, Nic. | **166** | 12 30N | 87 10W |
| Corj □ | **70** | 45 5N | 23 25E |
| Cork | **39** | 51 54N | 8 30W |
| Cork □ | **39** | 51 50N | 8 50W |
| Cork Harbour | **39** | 51 46N | 8 16W |
| Corlay | **42** | 48 20N | 3 5W |
| Corleone | **64** | 37 48N | 13 16E |
| Corleto Perticara | **65** | 40 23N | 16 2E |
| Çorlu | **67** | 41 11N | 27 49E |
| Cormack L. | **152** | 60 56N | 121 37W |
| Cormóns | **63** | 45 58N | 13 29E |
| Cormorant | **153** | 54 14N | 100 35W |
| Cormorant L. | **153** | 54 15N | 100 50W |
| Cormorant, oilfield | **19** | 61 0N | 1 10E |
| Corn Hill, Mt. | **38** | 53 48N | 7 43W |
| Corn Is. | **167** | 12 0N | 83 0W |
| Cornelio | **164** | 29 55N | 111 8W |
| Cornélio Procópio | **173** | 23 7S | 50 40W |
| Cornell | **158** | 45 10N | 91 8W |
| Corner Brook | **151** | 48 57N | 57 58W |
| Corner Inlet | **133** | 38 45S | 146 20E |
| Cornforth | **33** | 54 42N | 1 28W |
| Corniglio | **62** | 44 29N | 10 5E |
| Corning, Ark., U.S.A. | **159** | 36 27N | 90 34W |
| Corning, Calif., U.S.A. | **160** | 39 56N | 122 9W |
| Corning, Iowa, U.S.A. | **158** | 40 57N | 94 40W |
| Corning, N.Y., U.S.A. | **162** | 42 10N | 77 3W |
| Cornwall, Austral. | **138** | 41 33S | 148 7E |
| Cornwall, Can. | **150** | 45 2N | 74 44W |
| Cornwall, U.S.A. | **162** | 40 17N | 76 25W |
| Cornwall □ | **30** | 50 26N | 4 40W |
| Cornwall, C. | **30** | 50 8N | 5 42W |
| Cornwallis I. | **12** | 75 8N | 95 0W |
| Corny Pt. | **140** | 34 55S | 137 0E |
| Coro | **174** | 11 25N | 69 41W |
| Coroaci | **171** | 18 35S | 42 17W |

Crookwell Dalandzadgad


| | | | |
|---|---|---|---|
| Crookwell | 141 | 34 28 S | 149 24 E |
| Croom | 39 | 52 32 N | 8 43 W |
| Crosby, Cumb., U.K. | 32 | 54 45 N | 3 25 W |
| Crosby, Merseyside, U.K. | 32 | 53 30 N | 3 2 W |
| Crosby, Minn., U.S.A. | 158 | 46 28 N | 93 57 W |
| Crosby, N.D., U.S.A. | 153 | 48 55 N | 103 18 W |
| Crosby Ravensworth | 32 | 54 34 N | 2 35 W |
| Crosbyton | 159 | 33 37 N | 101 12 W |
| Cross City | 157 | 29 35 N | 83 5 W |
| Cross Fell | 32 | 54 44 N | 2 29 W |
| Cross L. | 153 | 54 45 N | 97 30 W |
| Cross Plains | 159 | 32 8 N | 99 7 W |
| Cross, R. | 121 | 4 46 N | 8 20 E |
| Cross River □ | 121 | 6 0 N | 8 0 E |
| Cross Sound | 147 | 58 20 N | 136 30 W |
| Crossakiel | 38 | 53 43 N | 7 2 W |
| Crossbost | 36 | 58 8 N | 6 27 W |
| Crossdoney | 38 | 53 57 N | 7 27 W |
| Crosse, La, Kans., U.S.A. | 158 | 38 33 N | 99 20 W |
| Crosse, La, Wis., U.S.A. | 158 | 43 48 N | 91 13 W |
| Crossett | 159 | 33 10 N | 91 57 W |
| Crossfarnoge Pt. | 39 | 52 10 N | 6 37 W |
| Crossfield | 152 | 51 25 N | 114 0 W |
| Crossgar | 38 | 54 22 N | 5 46 W |
| Crosshaven | 39 | 51 48 N | 8 19 W |
| Crosshill | 34 | 55 19 N | 4 39 W |
| Crossley, Mt. | 143 | 42 50 S | 172 5 E |
| Crossmaglen | 38 | 54 5 N | 6 37 W |
| Crossmolina | 38 | 54 6 N | 9 21 W |
| Croton-on-Hudson | 162 | 41 12 N | 73 55 W |
| Crotone | 65 | 39 5 N | 17 6 E |
| Crouch, R. | 29 | 51 37 N | 0 53 E |
| Crow Agency | 160 | 45 40 N | 107 30 W |
| Crow Hd. | 39 | 51 34 N | 10 9 W |
| Crow, R. | 152 | 59 41 N | 124 20 W |
| Crow Sound | 30 | 49 56 N | 6 16 W |
| Crowborough | 29 | 51 3 N | 0 9 E |
| Crowell | 159 | 33 59 N | 99 45 W |
| Crowl Creek | 141 | 32 0 S | 145 30 E |
| Crowland | 29 | 52 41 N | 0 10 W |
| Crowle | 33 | 53 36 N | 0 49 W |
| Crowley | 159 | 30 15 N | 92 20 W |
| Crowley, L. | 163 | 37 53 N | 118 42 W |
| Crowlin Is. | 36 | 57 20 N | 5 50 W |
| Crown Point | 156 | 41 24 N | 87 23 W |
| Crows Landing | 163 | 37 23 N | 121 6 W |
| Crows Nest | 139 | 27 16 S | 152 4 E |
| Crowsnest Pass | 152 | 49 40 N | 114 40 W |
| Croyde | 30 | 51 7 N | 4 13 W |
| Croydon, Austral. | 138 | 18 13 S | 142 14 E |
| Croydon, U.K. | 29 | 51 18 N | 0 5 W |
| Crozet, Île | 11 | 46 27 S | 52 0 E |
| Crozon | 42 | 48 15 N | 4 30 W |
| Cruces, Pta. | 174 | 6 39 N | 77 32 W |
| Cruden Bay | 37 | 57 25 N | 1 50 W |
| Crudgington | 28 | 52 46 N | 2 33 W |
| Crumlin | 38 | 54 38 N | 6 12 W |
| Crummer Peaks | 138 | 6 40 S | 144 0 E |
| Crummock Water L. | 32 | 54 33 N | 3 18 W |
| Crusheen | 39 | 52 57 N | 8 52 W |
| Cruz, C. | 166 | 19 50 N | 77 50 W |
| Cruz das Almas | 171 | 12 40 S | 39 6 W |
| Cruz de Malta | 170 | 8 15 S | 40 20 W |
| Cruz del Eje | 172 | 30 45 S | 64 50 W |
| Cruz, La, Colomb. | 174 | 1 35 N | 76 58 W |
| Cruz, La, C. Rica | 166 | 11 4 N | 85 39 W |
| Cruz, La, Mexico | 164 | 23 55 N | 106 54 W |
| Cruzeiro | 173 | 22 50 S | 45 0 W |
| Cruzeiro do Oeste | 173 | 23 46 S | 53 4 W |
| Cruzeiro do Sul | 174 | 7 35 S | 72 35 W |
| Cry L. | 152 | 58 45 N | 128 5 W |
| Cryfow Sl. | 54 | 51 2 N | 15 24 E |
| Crymmych | 31 | 51 59 N | 4 40 W |
| Crystal Brook | 140 | 33 21 S | 138 12 E |
| Crystal City, Mo., U.S.A. | 158 | 38 15 N | 90 23 W |
| Crystal City, Tex., U.S.A. | 159 | 28 40 N | 99 50 W |
| Crystal Falls | 156 | 46 9 N | 88 11 W |
| Crystal River | 157 | 28 54 N | 82 35 W |
| Crystal Springs | 159 | 31 59 N | 90 25 W |
| Čáslav | 52 | 49 54 N | 15 22 E |
| Csongrád | 53 | 46 43 N | 20 12 E |
| Csongrád □ | 53 | 46 32 N | 20 15 E |
| Csorna | 53 | 47 38 N | 17 18 E |
| Csurgo | 53 | 46 16 N | 17 9 E |
| Ctesiphon | 92 | 33 9 N | 44 35 E |
| Cu Lao Hon | 101 | 10 54 N | 108 18 E |
| Cua Rao | 100 | 19 16 N | 104 27 E |
| Cuácua, R. | 127 | 18 0 S | 36 0 E |
| Cuamato | 128 | 17 2 S | 15 7 E |
| Cuamba = Nova Preixo | 127 | 14 45 S | 36 22 E |
| Cuando | 128 | 16 25 S | 22 2 E |
| Cuando Cubango □ | 128 | 16 25 S | 20 0 E |
| Cuando, R. | 125 | 14 0 S | 19 30 E |
| Cuangar | 128 | 17 28 S | 14 40 E |
| Cuango | 124 | 6 15 S | 16 35 E |
| Cuarto, R. | 172 | 33 25 S | 63 2 W |
| Cuatrociénegas de Carranza | 164 | 26 59 N | 102 5 W |
| Cuauhtémoc | 164 | 28 25 N | 106 52 W |
| Cuba, Port. | 57 | 38 10 N | 7 54 W |
| Cuba, U.S.A. | 161 | 36 0 N | 107 0 W |
| Cuba ■ | 166 | 22 0 N | 79 0 W |
| Cuballing | 137 | 32 50 S | 117 10 E |
| Cubango, R. | 128 | 16 15 S | 17 45 E |
| Cuchi | 125 | 14 37 S | 17 10 E |
| Cuchumatanes, Sierra de los | 166 | 15 35 N | 91 25 W |
| Cuckfield | 29 | 51 0 N | 0 8 W |
| Cucurpe | 164 | 30 20 N | 110 43 W |
| Cucurrupí | 174 | 4 23 N | 76 56 W |
| Cúcuta | 174 | 7 54 N | 72 31 W |
| Cudahy | 156 | 42 54 N | 87 50 W |
| Cudalbi | 70 | 45 46 N | 27 41 E |
| Cuddalore | 97 | 11 46 N | 79 45 E |
| Cuddapah | 97 | 14 30 N | 78 47 E |
| Cuddapan, L. | 138 | 25 45 S | 141 26 E |
| Cudgewa | 141 | 36 10 S | 147 42 E |
| Cudillero | 56 | 43 33 N | 6 9 W |
| Cudworth | 33 | 53 35 N | 1 25 W |
| Cue | 137 | 27 25 S | 117 54 E |
| Cuéllar | 56 | 41 23 N | 4 21 W |
| Cuenca, Ecuador | 174 | 2 50 S | 79 9 W |
| Cuenca, Spain | 58 | 40 5 N | 2 10 W |
| Cuenca □ | 58 | 40 0 N | 2 0 W |
| Cuenca, Serranía de | 58 | 39 55 N | 1 50 W |
| Cuencamé | 164 | 24 53 N | 103 41 W |
| Cuerda del Pozo, Pantano de la | 58 | 41 51 N | 2 44 W |
| Cuernavaca | 165 | 18 50 N | 99 20 W |
| Cuero | 159 | 29 5 N | 97 17 W |
| Cuers | 45 | 43 14 N | 6 5 E |
| Cuervo | 159 | 35 5 N | 104 25 W |
| Cuesmes | 47 | 50 26 N | 3 56 E |
| Cuevas de Altamira | 56 | 43 20 N | 4 5 W |
| Cuevas del Almanzora | 59 | 37 18 N | 1 58 W |
| Cuevo | 174 | 20 25 N | 63 30 W |
| Cugir | 70 | 43 48 N | 23 25 E |
| Cugno | 123 | 6 14 N | 42 31 E |
| Cuhimbre | 174 | 0 10 S | 75 23 W |
| Cuiabá | 175 | 15 30 S | 56 0 W |
| Cuiabá, R. | 175 | 16 50 S | 56 30 W |
| Cuidad Bolivar | 174 | 8 21 N | 70 34 W |
| Cuilcagh, Mt. | 38 | 54 12 N | 7 50 W |
| Cuilco | 166 | 15 24 N | 91 58 W |
| Cuillin Hills | 36 | 57 14 N | 6 15 W |
| Cuillin Sd. | 36 | 57 4 N | 6 20 W |
| Cuima | 125 | 13 0 S | 15 45 E |
| Cuiseaux | 45 | 46 30 N | 5 22 E |
| Cuité | 170 | 6 29 S | 36 9 W |
| Cuito, R. | 128 | 16 50 S | 19 30 E |
| Cuitzeo, L. | 164 | 19 55 N | 101 5 W |
| Cujmir | 70 | 44 13 N | 22 57 E |
| Culan | 44 | 46 34 N | 2 20 E |
| Cǔlaraşi | 43 | 44 14 N | 27 23 E |
| Culbertson | 158 | 48 9 N | 104 30 W |
| Culburra | 140 | 35 50 S | 139 58 E |
| Culcairn | 141 | 35 41 S | 147 3 E |
| Culdaff | 38 | 55 17 N | 7 10 W |
| Culebra, I. | 147 | 18 19 N | 65 17 W |
| Culebra, Sierra de la | 56 | 41 55 N | 6 20 W |
| Culemborg | 46 | 51 58 N | 5 14 E |
| Culgoa | 140 | 35 44 S | 143 6 E |
| Culgoa, R. | 139 | 29 56 S | 146 20 E |
| Culiacán | 164 | 24 50 N | 107 40 W |
| Culiacán, R. | 164 | 24 30 N | 107 42 W |
| Cǔlimani, Munţii | 70 | 47 12 N | 25 0 E |
| Cǔlineşti | 70 | 45 21 N | 24 18 E |
| Culion, I. | 103 | 11 54 N | 120 1 E |
| Cúllar de Baza | 59 | 37 35 N | 2 34 W |
| Cullarin Range | 141 | 34 30 S | 149 30 E |
| Cullaville | 38 | 54 4 N | 6 40 W |
| Cullen, Austral. | 136 | 13 58 S | 131 54 E |
| Cullen, U.K. | 37 | 57 45 N | 2 50 W |
| Cullen Pt. | 138 | 11 57 S | 141 54 E |
| Cullera | 59 | 39 9 N | 0 17 W |
| Cullin L. | 38 | 53 58 N | 9 12 W |
| Cullivoe | 36 | 60 43 N | 1 0 W |
| Cullman | 157 | 34 13 N | 86 50 W |
| Culloden Moor | 37 | 57 29 N | 4 7 W |
| Cullompton | 30 | 50 52 N | 3 23 W |
| Cullyhanna | 38 | 54 8 N | 6 35 W |
| Culm, R. | 30 | 50 46 N | 3 31 W |
| Culoz | 45 | 45 47 N | 5 46 E |
| Culpataro | 140 | 33 40 S | 144 22 E |
| Culpeper | 156 | 38 29 N | 77 59 W |
| Culrain | 37 | 57 55 N | 4 25 W |
| Culross | 35 | 56 4 N | 3 38 W |
| Cults | 37 | 57 8 N | 2 10 W |
| Culuene, R. | 175 | 12 15 S | 53 10 W |
| Culvain Mt. | 36 | 56 55 N | 5 19 W |
| Culver, Pt. | 137 | 32 54 S | 124 43 E |
| Culverden | 143 | 42 47 S | 172 49 E |
| Cumali | 69 | 36 42 N | 27 28 E |
| Cumaná | 174 | 10 30 N | 64 5 W |
| Cumari | 171 | 18 16 S | 48 11 W |
| Cumberland, Can. | 152 | 49 40 N | 125 0 W |
| Cumberland, Md., U.S.A. | 156 | 39 40 N | 78 43 W |
| Cumberland, Wis., U.S.A. | 158 | 45 32 N | 92 3 W |
| Cumberland (□) | 26 | 54 44 N | 2 55 W |
| Cumberland I. | 157 | 30 52 N | 81 30 W |
| Cumberland Is. | 138 | 20 35 S | 149 10 E |
| Cumberland L. | 153 | 54 3 N | 102 18 W |
| Cumberland Pen. | 149 | 67 0 N | 64 0 W |
| Cumberland Plat. | 157 | 36 0 N | 84 30 W |
| Cumberland, R. | 157 | 36 15 N | 87 0 W |
| Cumberland Sd. | 149 | 65 30 N | 66 0 W |
| Cumborah | 139 | 29 40 S | 147 45 E |
| Cumbrae Is. | 34 | 55 46 N | 4 54 W |
| Cumbres Mayores | 57 | 38 4 N | 6 39 W |
| Cumbria □ | 32 | 54 35 N | 2 55 W |
| Cumbrian Mts. | 32 | 54 30 N | 3 0 W |
| Cumbum | 97 | 15 40 N | 79 10 E |
| Cuminestown | 37 | 57 32 N | 2 17 W |
| Cummerower See | 48 | 53 47 N | 12 52 E |
| Cummertrees | 35 | 55 0 N | 3 20 W |
| Cummings Mtn. | 163 | 35 2 N | 118 34 W |
| Cummins | 139 | 34 16 S | 135 43 E |
| Cumnock, Austral. | 141 | 32 59 S | 148 46 E |
| Cumnock, U.K. | 34 | 55 27 N | 4 18 W |
| Cumnor | 28 | 51 44 N | 1 20 W |
| Cumpas | 164 | 30 0 N | 109 48 W |
| Cumuruxatiba | 171 | 17 6 S | 39 13 W |
| Cumwhinton | 32 | 54 51 N | 2 49 W |
| Cuñaré | 174 | 0 49 N | 72 32 W |
| Cuncumén | 172 | 31 53 S | 70 38 W |
| Cunderdin | 137 | 31 37 S | 117 12 E |
| Cundinamarca □ | 174 | 5 0 N | 74 0 W |
| Cunene, R. | 128 | 17 0 S | 15 0 E |
| Cúneo | 62 | 44 23 N | 7 31 E |
| Cunillera, I. | 59 | 38 59 N | 1 13 E |
| Cunlhat | 44 | 45 38 N | 3 32 E |
| Cunnamulla | 139 | 28 2 S | 145 38 E |
| Cunninghame, Reg. | 34 | 55 38 N | 4 35 W |
| Cuorgnè | 62 | 45 23 N | 7 39 E |
| Cupar, Can. | 153 | 50 57 N | 104 10 W |
| Cupar, U.K. | 35 | 56 20 N | 3 0 W |
| Cupica | 174 | 6 50 N | 77 30 W |
| Cupica, Golfo de | 174 | 6 25 N | 77 30 W |
| Ćuprija | 66 | 43 57 N | 21 26 E |
| Curaçá | 170 | 8 59 S | 39 54 W |
| Curaçao, I. | 167 | 12 10 N | 69 0 W |
| Curanilahue | 172 | 37 29 S | 73 28 W |
| Curaray, R. | 174 | 1 30 S | 75 30 W |
| Curatabaca | 174 | 6 19 N | 62 51 W |
| Curbarado | 174 | 7 3 N | 76 54 W |
| Curbur | 137 | 26 28 S | 115 55 E |
| Cure, La | 50 | 46 28 N | 6 4 E |
| Curepto | 172 | 35 8 S | 72 1 W |
| Curiapo | 174 | 8 33 N | 61 5 W |
| Curicó | 172 | 34 55 S | 71 20 W |
| Curicó □ | 172 | 34 50 S | 71 15 W |
| Curimatá | 170 | 10 2 S | 44 17 W |
| Curiplaya | 174 | 0 16 N | 74 52 W |
| Curitiba | 173 | 25 20 S | 49 10 W |
| Curlew Mts. | 38 | 54 0 N | 8 20 W |
| Curoca Norte | 128 | 16 15 S | 12 58 E |
| Currabubula | 141 | 31 16 S | 150 44 E |
| Curracunya | 139 | 28 29 S | 144 9 E |
| Curraglass | 39 | 52 5 N | 8 4 W |
| Currais Novos | 170 | 6 13 S | 36 30 W |
| Curralinho | 170 | 1 35 S | 49 30 W |
| Curran, L. = Terewah, L. | 139 | 29 50 S | 147 24 E |
| Currane L. | 39 | 51 50 N | 10 8 W |
| Currant | 160 | 38 51 N | 115 32 W |
| Curranyalpa | 141 | 30 53 S | 144 39 E |
| Curraweena | 141 | 30 47 S | 145 54 E |
| Currawilla | 138 | 25 10 S | 141 20 E |
| Current, R. | 159 | 37 15 N | 91 10 W |
| Currie, Austral. | 138 | 39 56 S | 143 53 E |
| Currie, U.K. | 35 | 55 53 N | 3 17 W |
| Currie, U.S.A. | 160 | 40 16 N | 114 45 W |
| Currie, Mt. | 129 | 30 29 S | 29 21 E |
| Currituck Sd. | 157 | 36 20 N | 75 50 W |
| Curry Rivel | 28 | 51 2 N | 2 52 W |
| Curryglass | 39 | 51 40 N | 9 50 W |
| Curtea-de-Argeş | 70 | 45 12 N | 24 42 E |
| Curtis, Spain | 56 | 43 7 N | 8 4 W |
| Curtis, U.S.A. | 158 | 40 41 N | 100 32 W |
| Curtis, I. | 138 | 23 35 S | 151 10 E |
| Curtis, Pt. | 138 | 23 53 S | 151 21 E |
| Curuá, I. | 170 | 0 48 N | 50 10 W |
| Curuapanema, R. | 175 | 7 0 S | 54 30 W |
| Curuçá | 170 | 0 35 S | 47 50 W |
| Curuguaty | 173 | 24 19 S | 55 49 W |
| Curupira, Serra | 174 | 1 25 N | 64 30 W |
| Cururupu | 170 | 1 50 S | 44 50 W |
| Curuzú Cuatiá | 172 | 29 50 S | 58 5 W |
| Curvelo | 171 | 18 45 S | 44 27 W |
| Curyo | 140 | 35 50 S | 142 47 E |
| Cushendall | 38 | 55 5 N | 6 3 W |
| Cushendun | 38 | 55 8 N | 6 3 W |
| Cushina | 39 | 53 11 N | 7 10 W |
| Cushing, Mt. | 152 | 57 35 N | 126 57 W |
| Cusihuiriáchic | 164 | 28 10 N | 106 50 W |
| Cussabat | 119 | 32 39 N | 14 1 E |
| Cusset | 44 | 46 8 N | 3 28 E |
| Custer | 158 | 43 45 N | 103 38 W |
| Cut Bank | 160 | 48 40 N | 112 15 W |
| Cutchogue | 162 | 41 1 N | 72 30 W |
| Cuthbert | 157 | 31 47 N | 84 47 W |
| Cutler | 163 | 36 31 N | 119 17 W |
| Cutra L. | 39 | 53 2 N | 8 48 W |
| Cutro | 65 | 39 1 N | 16 58 E |
| Cuttaburra, R. | 139 | 29 43 S | 144 22 E |
| Cuttack | 96 | 20 25 N | 85 57 E |
| Cuvier, C. | 137 | 23 14 S | 113 22 E |
| Cuvier I. | 142 | 36 27 S | 175 50 E |
| Cuxhaven | 48 | 53 51 N | 8 41 E |
| Cuyabeno | 174 | 0 16 S | 75 53 W |
| Cuyahoga Falls | 156 | 41 8 N | 81 30 W |
| Cuyo | 103 | 10 50 N | 121 5 E |
| Cuyuni, R. | 175 | 7 0 N | 59 30 W |
| Cuzco | 174 | 13 32 S | 72 0 W |
| Cuzco, Mt. | 174 | 20 0 S | 66 50 W |
| Çuzŭneşti | 70 | 44 36 N | 27 3 E |
| Čvrsnica, Mt. | 66 | 43 36 N | 17 35 E |
| Cwmbran | 31 | 51 39 N | 3 0 W |
| Cwrt | 31 | 52 35 N | 3 55 W |
| Cyangugu | 126 | 2 29 S | 28 54 E |
| Cybinka | 54 | 52 12 N | 14 46 E |
| Cyclades = Kikladhes | 69 | 37 20 N | 24 30 E |
| Cygnet | 138 | 43 8 S | 147 1 E |
| Cymmer | 31 | 51 37 N | 3 38 W |
| Cynthiana | 156 | 38 23 N | 84 10 W |
| Cynwyl Elfed | 31 | 51 55 N | 4 22 W |
| Cypress Hills | 153 | 49 40 N | 109 30 W |
| Cyprus ■ | 92 | 35 0 N | 33 0 E |
| Cyrenaica □ | 117 | 27 0 N | 20 0 E |
| Cyrene | 117 | 32 39 N | 21 18 E |
| Czaplinek | 54 | 53 34 N | 16 14 E |
| Czar | 153 | 52 27 N | 110 50 W |
| Czarne | 54 | 53 42 N | 16 58 E |
| Czarnków | 54 | 52 55 N | 16 38 E |
| Czechoslovakia ■ | 53 | 49 0 N | 17 0 E |
| Czechowice-Dziedzice | 54 | 49 54 N | 18 59 E |
| Czeladz | 54 | 50 16 N | 19 2 E |
| Czempin | 54 | 52 9 N | 16 33 E |
| Czersk | 54 | 53 46 N | 17 58 E |
| Czerwiensk | 54 | 52 1 N | 15 13 E |
| Czerwionka | 54 | 50 7 N | 18 37 E |
| Częstochowa | 54 | 50 49 N | 19 7 E |
| Częstochowa □ | 54 | 50 45 N | 19 0 E |
| Człopa | 54 | 53 6 N | 16 6 E |
| Człuchów | 54 | 53 41 N | 17 22 E |


# D


| | | | |
|---|---|---|---|
| Da Lat | 101 | 11 56 N | 108 25 E |
| Da Nang | 100 | 16 4 N | 108 13 E |
| Da, R. | 100 | 21 15 N | 105 20 E |
| Daarlerveen | 46 | 52 26 N | 6 34 E |
| Dab'a, Ras el | 122 | 31 3 N | 28 31 E |
| Dabai | 121 | 11 25 N | 5 15 E |
| Dabajuro | 174 | 11 2 N | 70 40 W |
| Dabakala | 120 | 8 15 N | 4 20 W |
| Dabatou | 120 | 11 50 N | 9 20 W |
| Dabburiya | 90 | 32 42 N | 35 22 E |
| Daberas | 128 | 25 27 S | 18 30 E |
| Dabhoi | 94 | 22 10 N | 73 20 E |
| Dabie | 54 | 53 27 N | 14 45 E |
| Dabola | 120 | 10 50 N | 11 5 W |
| Dabong | 101 | 5 23 N | 103 1 E |
| Dabou | 120 | 5 20 N | 4 23 W |
| Daboya | 121 | 9 30 N | 1 20 W |
| Dabra Berhan | 123 | 9 42 N | 39 15 E |
| Dabra Sina | 123 | 9 51 N | 39 45 E |
| Dabra Tabor | 123 | 11 50 N | 37 58 E |
| Dabra Zabit | 123 | 11 48 N | 38 30 E |
| Dabrowa Górnicza | 54 | 50 15 N | 19 10 E |
| Dabrowa Tarnówska | 54 | 50 10 N | 20 59 E |
| Dabrówno | 54 | 53 27 N | 20 2 E |
| Dabus, R. | 123 | 10 12 N | 35 0 E |
| Dacca | 98 | 23 43 N | 90 26 E |
| Dacca □ | 98 | 24 0 N | 90 25 E |
| Dachau | 49 | 48 16 N | 11 27 E |
| Dadanawa | 174 | 3 0 N | 59 30 W |
| Daday | 82 | 41 28 N | 33 35 E |
| Daddato | 123 | 12 24 N | 42 45 E |
| Dade City | 157 | 28 20 N | 82 12 W |
| Dadiya | 121 | 9 35 N | 11 24 E |
| Dadra and Nagar Haveli □ | 96 | 20 5 N | 73 0 E |
| Dadri = Charkhi Dadri | 94 | 28 37 N | 76 17 E |
| Dadu | 94 | 26 45 N | 67 45 E |
| Daer R. | 35 | 55 23 N | 3 39 W |
| Daet | 103 | 14 2 N | 122 55 E |
| Dagaio | 123 | 6 8 N | 40 40 E |
| Dagana | 120 | 16 30 N | 15 20 W |
| Dagash | 122 | 19 19 N | 33 25 E |
| Dagestan, A.S.S.R. □ | 83 | 42 30 N | 47 0 E |
| Daggett | 163 | 34 43 N | 116 52 W |
| Daggs Sd. | 143 | 45 23 S | 166 45 E |
| Daghfeli | 122 | 19 18 N | 32 40 E |
| Daghirie | 123 | 11 40 N | 41 50 E |
| Dagö = Hiiumaa | 80 | 58 50 N | 22 45 E |
| Dagoreti | 126 | 1 18 S | 36 4 E |
| Dagua | 135 | 3 27 S | 143 20 E |
| Dagupan | 103 | 16 3 N | 120 20 E |
| Dahab | 122 | 28 30 N | 34 31 E |
| Dahlak Kebir | 123 | 15 50 N | 40 10 E |
| Dahlenburg | 48 | 53 11 N | 10 43 E |
| Dahlonega | 157 | 34 35 N | 83 59 W |
| Dahme | 48 | 51 51 N | 13 25 E |
| Daho | 121 | 10 28 N | 11 18 E |
| Dahomey ■ = Benin ■ | 121 | 8 0 N | 2 0 E |
| Dahra | 120 | 15 22 N | 15 30 W |
| Dahra, Massif de | 118 | 36 7 N | 1 21 E |
| Dai Hao | 100 | 18 1 N | 106 25 E |
| Dai-Sen | 110 | 35 22 N | 133 32 E |
| Daigo | 111 | 36 46 N | 140 21 E |
| Dailly | 34 | 55 16 N | 4 44 W |
| Daimanji-San | 110 | 36 14 N | 133 20 E |
| Daimiel | 59 | 39 5 N | 3 35 W |
| Daintree | 138 | 16 20 S | 145 20 E |
| Daiō-Misaki | 111 | 34 15 N | 136 45 E |
| Dairen = Lüta | 107 | 38 55 N | 121 40 E |
| Dairût | 122 | 27 34 N | 30 43 E |
| Dairymple | 34 | 55 24 N | 4 36 W |
| Daisetsu-Zan | 112 | 43 30 N | 142 57 E |
| Daitari | 96 | 21 10 N | 85 46 E |
| Daitō | 110 | 35 19 N | 132 58 E |
| Dajarra | 138 | 21 42 S | 139 30 E |
| Dak Dam | 100 | 12 20 N | 107 21 E |
| Dak Nhe | 100 | 15 28 N | 107 48 E |
| Dak Pek | 100 | 15 4 N | 107 44 E |
| Dak Song | 101 | 12 19 N | 107 35 E |
| Dak Sui | 100 | 14 55 N | 107 43 E |
| Dakala | 121 | 14 27 N | 2 27 E |
| Dakar | 120 | 14 34 N | 17 29 W |
| Dakhla | 116 | 23 50 N | 15 53 W |
| Dakhla, El Wâhât el- | 122 | 25 30 N | 28 50 E |
| Dakhovskaya | 83 | 44 13 N | 40 13 E |
| Dakingari | 121 | 11 37 N | 4 1 E |
| Dakor | 94 | 22 45 N | 73 11 E |
| Dakoro | 121 | 14 31 N | 6 46 E |
| Dakota City | 158 | 42 27 N | 96 28 W |
| Dakota, North | 158 | 47 30 N | 100 0 W |
| Đakovica | 66 | 42 22 N | 20 26 E |
| Dakovo | 66 | 45 19 N | 18 24 E |
| Dakra | 120 | 15 22 N | 15 30 W |
| Dalaba | 120 | 10 42 N | 12 15 W |
| Dalälven, L. | 72 | 61 27 N | 17 15 E |
| Dalandzadgad | 106 | 43 27 N | 104 30 E |

Dalarö Degeh-Bur


Dalarö 75 59 8N 18 24 E
Dalat 101 12 3N 108 32 E
Dalbandin 93 29 0N 4 23 E
Dalbeattie 35 54 55N 3 50W
Dalbosjön, L. 73 58 40N 12 45 E
Dalby, Austral. 139 27 10 S 151 17 E
Dalby, Sweden 73 55 42N 13 22 E
Dale, Sogn og Fjordane, Norway 71 61 27N 7 28 E
Dale, Sogn og Fjordane, Norway 71 61 22N 5 23 E
Dale, U.K. 31 51 42N 5 11W
Dalen, Neth. 46 52 42N 6 46 E
Dalen, Norway 71 59 26N 8 0 E
Dalet 98 19 59N 93 51 E
Daletme 98 21 36N 92 46 E
Dalfsen 46 52 31N 6 16 E
Dalga 122 27 39N 30 41 E
Dalgaranger, Mt. 137 27 50 S 117 5 E
Dalhalvaig 37 58 28N 3 53W
Dalhart 159 36 0N 102 30W
Dalhousie, Can. 151 48 0N 66 26W
Dalhousie, India 94 32 38N 76 0 E
Daliburgh 36 57 10N 7 23W
Dalj 174 45 28N 18 58 E
Dalkeith 35 55 54N 3 5W
Dalkey 39 53 16N 6 7W
Dall I. 152 54 59N 133 25W
Dallarnil 139 25 19 S 152 2 E
Dallas, U.K. 37 57 33N 3 32W
Dallas, Oregon, U.S.A. 160 45 0N 123 15W
Dallas, Texas, U.S.A. 159 32 50N 96 50W
Dallol 123 14 14N 40 17 E
Dalmacija 66 43 20N 17 0 E
Dalmally 34 56 25N 5 0W
Dalmatia = Dalmacija 66 43 20N 17 0 E
Dalmatovo 84 56 16N 62 56 E
Dalmellington 34 55 20N 4 25W
Dalneretchensk 77 45 50N 133 40 E
Daloa 120 7 0N 6 30W
Dalry 34 55 44N 4 42W
Dalrymple, Mt. 133 21 1 S 148 39 E
Dalsjöfors 73 57 46N 18 5 E
Dalskog 73 58 44N 12 18 E
Dalton, Can. 150 48 11N 84 1W
Dalton, Cumbria, U.K. 33 54 9N 3 11W
Dalton, Dumfries, U.K. 35 55 3N 3 22W
Dalton, N. Yorks., U.K. 33 54 28N 1 32W
Dalton, Ga., U.S.A. 103 34 45N 85 0W
Dalton, Mass., U.S.A. 162 42 28N 73 11W
Dalton, Nebr., U.S.A. 158 41 27N 103 0W
Dalton Post 152 66 42N 137 0W
Daltonganj 95 24 0N 84 4 E
Dalvik 74 65 58N 18 32W
Dalwhinnie 37 56 56N 4 14W
Daly City 163 37 42N 122 28W
Daly L. 153 56 32N 105 39W
Daly, R. 136 13 21 S 130 18 E
Daly Waters 138 16 15 S 133 24 E
Dalystown 38 53 26N 7 23W
Dam 170 4 45N 55 0W
Dam Doi 101 8 59N 105 12 E
Dam Gillan 153 56 20N 94 40W
Dam Ha 100 21 21N 107 36 E
Dama, Wadi 122 27 12N 35 50 E
Daman 96 20 25N 72 57 E
Daman □ 96 20 25N 72 58 E
Damanhûr 122 31 0N 30 30 E
Damar, I. 103 7 15 S 128 30 E
Damaraland 128 21 0 S 17 0 E
Damascus = Dimashq 92 33 30N 36 18 E
Damaturu 121 11 45N 11 55 E
Damâvand 93 36 0N 52 0 E
Damâvand, Qolleh-ye 93 35 45N 52 10 E
Damba, Angola 124 6 44 S 15 29 E
Damba, Ethiopia 123 15 10N 38 47 E
Dâmbovnic, R. 70 44 28N 25 18 E
Dame Marie 167 18 36N 74 26W
Damerham 28 50 57N 1 52W
Dames Quarter 162 38 11N 75 54W
Damghan 93 36 10N 54 17 E
Damietta = Dumyât 122 31 24N 31 48 E
Damin 93 27 30N 60 40 E
Damiya 90 32 6N 35 34 E
Damman 92 26 25N 50 2 E
Dammarie 43 48 20N 1 30 E
Dammartin 43 49 3N 2 41 E
Dammastock 51 46 38N 8 24 E
Damme 48 52 32N 8 12 E
Damodar, R. 95 23 17N 87 35 E
Damoh 95 23 50N 79 28 E
Dampier 136 20 41 S 116 42 E
Dampier Arch. 136 20 38 S 116 32 E
Dampier Downs 136 18 24 S 123 5 E
Dampier, Selat 103 0 40 S 131 0 E
Dampier Str. 135 5 50 S 148 0 E
Damrei, Chuor Phnum 101 12 30N 103 0 E
Damville 42 48 51N 1 5 E
Damvillers 43 49 20N 5 21 E
Dan Chadi 121 12 47N 5 17 E
Dan Dume 121 11 28N 7 8 E
Dan Gora 121 11 30N 8 7 E
Dan Gulbi 121 11 40N 6 15 E
Dan, oilfield 19 55 30N 5 10 E
Dan Sadau 121 11 25N 6 20 E
Dana 103 11 0 S 122 52 E
Dana, Lac 150 50 53N 77 20W
Dana, Mt 163 37 54N 119 12W
Danakil Depression 123 12 45N 41 0 E
Danao 103 10 31N 124 1 E
Danbury 162 41 23N 73 29W
Danby L. 161 34 17N 115 0W
Dand 94 31 28N 65 32 E
Dandaragan 137 30 40 S 115 40 E
Dandeldhura 95 29 20N 80 35 E
Dandeli 93 15 5N 74 30 E
Dandenong 141 38 0 S 145 15 E
Dandkandi 98 23 32N 90 43 E
Danforth 151 45 39N 67 57W
Dang Raek 101 14 40N 104 0 E
Dangara 85 38 6N 69 22 E
Danger Is. 131 10 53 S 165 49W
Danger Pt. 128 34 40 S 19 17 E
Dangla 123 11 18N 36 56 E
Dangora 121 11 30N 8 7 E
Dangrek, Phnom 100 14 15N 105 0 E
Daniel 160 42 56N 110 2W
Daniel's Harbour 151 50 13N 57 35W
Danielskull 128 28 11 S 23 33 E
Danielson 162 41 50N 71 52W
Danilov 81 58 16N 40 13 E
Danilovgrad 66 42 38N 19 9 E
Danilovka 81 50 25N 44 12 E
Danissa 126 3 15N 40 58 E
Danja 121 11 29N 7 30 E
Dankalwa 121 11 52N 12 12 E
Dankama 121 13 20N 7 44 E
Dankhar Gompa 93 32 10N 78 10 E
Dankov 81 53 20N 39 5 E
Danlí 166 14 4N 86 35W
Dannemora 75 60 12N 17 51 E
Dannenberg 48 53 7N 11 4 E
Dannevirke 142 40 12 S 176 8 E
Dannhauser 129 28 0 S 30 3 E
Dansalan 103 8 2N 124 30 E
Dansville 156 42 32N 77 41W
Dantan 95 21 57N 87 20 E
Danube, R. 53 45 0N 28 20W
Danubyo 98 17 15N 95 35 E
Danvers 162 42 34N 70 55 E
Danville, Ill., U.S.A. 156 40 10N 87 40W
Danville, Ky., U.S.A. 156 37 40N 84 45W
Danville, Pa., U.S.A. 162 40 58N 76 37W
Danville, Va., U.S.A. 157 36 40N 79 20W
Danzig = Gdansk 54 54 22N 18 40 E
Dão 103 10 30N 122 6 E
Dão, R. 56 40 28N 8 0W
Daosa 94 26 52N 76 20 E
Daoud = Aïn Beida 119 35 50N 7 29 E
Daoulas 42 48 22N 4 17W
Dapango 121 10 55N 0 16 E
Dar al Hamra, Ad 92 27 22N 37 43 E
Dar es Salaam 126 6 50 S 39 12 E
Dar'ā 90 32 36N 36 7 E
Darab 93 28 50N 54 30 E
Darabani 70 48 10N 26 39 E
Daraj 119 30 10N 10 28 E
Daraut Kurgan 85 39 33N 72 11 E
Daravica 66 42 32N 20 8 E
Daraw 121 24 22N 32 51 E
Darazo 121 11 1N 10 24W
Darband 94 34 30N 72 50 E
Darbhanga 95 26 15N 86 8 E
Darby 160 46 2N 114 7W
D'Arcy 152 50 35N 122 30W
Darda 66 45 40N 18 41 E
Dardanelle 163 38 2N 119 50W
Dardanelles = Canakkale Boğlazi 92 40 0N 26 20 E
Dardenelle 159 35 12N 93 9W
Darent, R. 29 51 22N 0 12 E
Darfield 143 43 29 S 172 7 E
Darfo 62 45 43N 10 11 E
Dargai 94 34 25N 71 45 E
Dargan Ata 76 40 40N 62 20 E
Dargaville 142 35 57 S 173 52 E
Darharala 120 8 23N 4 20W
Dari 123 5 48N 30 26 E
Darién, G. del 174 9 0N 77 0W
Darién, Serrania del 174 8 30N 77 30W
Dariganga 106 45 5N 113 45 E
Darinskoye 84 51 20N 51 44 E
Darjeeling 95 27 3N 88 18 E
Dark Cove 151 48 47N 54 13W
Darkan 137 33 20 S 116 43 E
Darke Peak 140 33 27 S 136 12 E
Darkot Pass 95 36 45N 73 26 E
Darlaston 28 52 35N 2 1W
Darling Downs 139 28 30 S 152 0 E
Darling, R. 140 34 4 S 141 54 E
Darling Ra. 137 32 30 S 116 0 E
Darlington, U.K. 33 54 33N 1 33W
Darlington, S.C., U.S.A. 157 34 18N 79 50W
Darlington, Wis., U.S.A. 158 42 43N 90 7W
Darlot, L. 137 27 48 S 121 35 E
Darłowo 54 54 25N 16 25 E
Darmstadt 49 49 51N 8 40 E
Darnall 129 29 23 S 31 18 E
Darnétal 42 49 25N 1 10 E
Darney 43 48 5N 6 0 E
Darnick 140 32 48 S 143 38 E
Darnley B. 147 69 30N 123 30W
Darnley, C. 13 68 0 S 69 0 E
Daroca 58 41 9N 1 25W
Darr 138 23 13 S 144 7 E
Darr, R. 138 23 39 S 143 50 E
Darragh 39 52 47N 9 7W
Darran Mts. 143 44 37 S 167 59 E
Darrington 160 48 14N 121 37W
Darror, R. 91 10 30N 50 0 E
Darsana 98 23 35N 88 48 E
Darsi 97 15 46N 79 44 E
Darsser Ort 48 44 27N 12 30 E
Dart, R., N.Z. 143 44 20 S 168 20 E
Dart, R., U.K. 30 50 24N 3 36W
Dartford 29 51 26N 0 15 E
Dartington 30 50 26N 3 42W
Dartmoor, Austral. 140 37 56N 141 19 E
Dartmoor, U.K. 30 50 36N 4 0W
Dartmouth, Austral. 138 23 31 S 144 44 E
Dartmouth, Can. 151 44 40N 63 30W
Dartmouth, U.K. 30 50 21N 3 35W
Dartmouth, L. 139 26 4 S 145 18 E
Darton 33 53 36N 1 32W
Dartuch, C. 58 39 55N 3 49 E
Daru, P.N.G. 135 9 3 S 143 13 E
Daru, S. Leone 120 8 0N 10 52W
Darvel 34 55 37N 4 20W
Darvel Bay 103 4 50N 118 20 E
Darwen 32 53 42N 2 29W
Darwha 96 20 15N 77 45 E
Darwin, Austral. 136 12 25 S 130 51 E
Darwin, U.S.A. 163 36 15N 117 35W
Darwin, Mt. 127 16 45 S 31 33 E
Darwin River 136 12 50 S 130 58 E
Daryacheh-ye-Sistan 93 31 0N 61 0 E
Daryapur 96 20 55N 77 20 E
Dase 123 14 53N 37 15 E
Dashato, R. 123 7 25N 42 40 E
Dashkesan 83 40 40N 46 0 E
Dasht-e Kavīr 93 34 30N 55 0 E
Dasht-e Lut 93 31 30N 58 0 E
Dasht-i-Khash 93 32 0N 62 0 E
Dasht-i-Margo 93 30 40N 62 30 E
Dasht-i-Nawar 94 33 52N 68 0 E
Dasht, R. 93 25 40N 62 20 E
Daska 94 32 20N 74 20 E
Dassa-Zoume 121 7 46N 2 14 E
Dasseneiland 128 33 37 S 18 3 E
Datça 69 36 46N 27 40 E
Datia 95 25 39N 78 27 E
Dattapur 96 20 45N 78 15 E
Daugava 80 57 0N 24 0 E
Daugavpils 80 55 53N 26 32 E
Daulat Yar 93 34 30N 65 45 E
Daulatabad 96 19 57N 75 15 E
Daun 49 50 5N 6 53 E
Dauphin, Can. 153 51 9N 100 5W
Dauphin, U.S.A. 162 40 22N 76 56W
Dauphin I. 157 30 16N 88 10W
Dauphin L. 153 51 20N 99 45W
Dauphiné 45 45 15N 5 25 E
Dauqa 122 19 30N 41 0 E
Daura, Kano, Nigeria 121 13 2N 8 21 E
Daura, N.-E., Nigeria 121 11 31N 11 24 E
Davadi 120 14 10N 16 3W
Davangere 97 14 25N 75 50 E
Davao 103 7 0N 125 40 E
Davao, G. of 103 6 30N 125 48 E
Davar Panab 93 27 25N 62 15 E
Dave 74 52 55N 1 50W
Davenport, Calif., U.S.A. 163 37 1N 122 12W
Davenport, Iowa, U.S.A. 158 41 30N 90 40W
Davenport, Wash., U.S.A. 160 47 40N 118 5W
Davenport Downs 138 24 8 S 141 7 E
Davenport Ra. 138 20 28 S 134 0 E
Daventry 28 52 16N 1 10W
David 166 8 30N 82 30W
David City 158 41 18N 97 10W
David Gorodok 80 52 4N 27 8 E
Davidson 153 51 16N 105 59W
Davik 71 61 53N 5 33 E
Davis 163 38 33N 121 45W
Davis Dam 161 35 11N 114 35W
Davis Inlet 151 55 50N 60 45W
Davis Mts. 159 30 42N 104 15W
Davis Str. 149 65 0N 58 0W
Davlekanovo 84 54 13N 55 3 E
Davos 51 46 48N 9 49 E
Davy L. 153 58 53N 108 18W
Davyhurst 137 30 2 S 120 40 E
Dawa, R. 123 5 0N 39 5 E
Dawaki, Jos, Nigeria 121 9 25N 9 33 E
Dawaki, Kano, Nigeria 121 12 5N 8 23 E
Dawayima 90 31 33N 34 55 E
Dawes Ra. 138 24 40 S 150 40 E
Dawley 28 52 40N 2 29W
Dawlish 30 50 34N 3 28W
Dawna Range 98 16 30N 98 30 E
Dawnyein 98 15 54N 95 36 E
Dawros Hd. 38 54 48N 8 32W
Dawson, Can. 147 64 10N 139 30W
Dawson, Ga., U.S.A. 157 31 45N 84 28W
Dawson, N.D., U.S.A. 158 46 56N 99 45W
Dawson Creek 152 55 45N 120 15W
Dawson, I. 176 53 50 S 70 50W
Dawson Inlet 153 61 50N 93 25W
Dawson, R. 133 23 25 S 150 10 E
Dawson Range 138 24 30 S 149 48 E
Dawson's 127 17 0 S 30 57 E
Daylesford 140 37 21 S 144 9 E
Dayr al-Ghusūn 90 32 21N 35 4 E
Dayr az Zawr 92 35 20N 40 5 E
Daysland 152 52 50N 112 20W
Dayton, Ohio, U.S.A. 156 39 45N 84 10W
Dayton, Tenn., U.S.A. 157 35 30N 85 1W
Dayton, Wash., U.S.A. 160 46 20N 118 0W
Daytona Beach 157 29 14N 81 0W
Dayville 160 44 33N 119 37W
De Aar 128 30 39 S 24 0 E
De Bilt 46 52 6N 5 11 E
De Funiak Springs 157 30 42N 86 10W
De Grey 136 20 12 S 119 12 E
De Grey, R. 136 20 0 S 119 13 E
De Kalb 158 41 55N 88 45W
De Koog 46 53 6N 4 46 E
De Land 157 29 1N 81 19W
De Leon 159 32 9N 98 35W
De Long Mts. 147 68 10N 163 0W
De Long, Ostrova 77 76 40N 149 20 E
De Panne 47 51 6N 2 34 E
De Pere 156 44 28N 88 1W
De Queen 159 34 3N 94 24W
De Quincy 159 30 30N 93 27W
De Ridder 159 30 48N 93 15W
De Rijp 46 52 33N 4 51 E
De Smet 158 44 25N 97 35W
De Tour Village 156 45 49N 83 56W
De Witt 159 34 19N 91 20W
Dead Sea = Miyet, Bahr el 92 31 30N 35 30 E
Deadwood 58 44 25N 103 43W
Deadwood L. 152 59 10N 128 30W
Deaf Adder Cr. 136 13 0 S 132 47 E
Deakin 137 30 46 S 129 58 E
Deal 29 51 13N 1 25 E
Dealesville 128 28 41 S 25 44 E
Dean, Forest of 28 51 50N 2 35W
Deán Funes 172 30 20 S 64 20W
Dearborn 150 42 18N 83 15W
Dearham 32 54 43N 3 28W
Dease L. 152 58 40N 130 5W
Dease Lake 152 58 25N 130 6W
Dease, R. 152 59 56N 128 32W
Death Valley 163 36 27N 116 52W
Death Valley Junc. 163 36 21N 116 30W
Death Valley Nat. Monument 163 36 30N 117 0W
Deauville 42 49 23N 0 2 E
Deba Habe 121 10 14N 11 20 E
Debaltsevo 82 48 22N 38 26 E
Debar 66 41 21N 20 37 E
Debba 123 14 20N 41 18 E
Debden 153 53 30N 106 50W
Debdou 118 33 59N 3 0W
Debeeti 128 23 45 S 26 32 E
Deben, R. 29 52 4N 1 19 E
Debenham 29 52 14N 1 10 E
Debessy 84 57 39N 53 49 E
Dębica 54 50 2N 21 25 E
Deblin 54 51 34N 21 50 E
Debo, L. 120 15 14N 3 57W
Debolt 152 55 12N 118 1W
Deborah, gasfield 19 53 4N 1 50 E
Deborah, L. 137 30 45 S 119 0 E
Debrc 66 44 38N 19 53 E
Debre Birhan 123 9 41N 39 31 E
Debre Markos 123 10 20N 37 40 E
Debre May 123 11 20N 37 25 E
Debre Sina 123 9 51N 39 50 E
Debre Tabor 123 11 50N 38 26 E
Debrecen 53 47 33N 21 42 E
Dečani 66 42 30N 20 10 E
Decatur, Ala., U.S.A. 157 34 35N 87 0W
Decatur, Ga., U.S.A. 157 33 47N 84 17W
Decatur, Ill., U.S.A. 158 39 50N 89 0W
Decatur, Ind., U.S.A. 156 40 52N 85 28W
Decatur, Texas, U.S.A. 159 33 15N 97 35W
Decazeville 44 44 34N 2 15 E
Deccan 97 14 0N 77 0 E
Deception I. 13 63 0 S 60 15W
Deception L. 153 56 33N 104 13W
Deception, Mt. 140 30 42 S 138 16 E
Decize 43 46 50N 3 28 E
Decollatura 65 39 2N 16 21 E
Decorah 158 43 20N 91 50W
Deda 70 46 56N 24 50 E
Dedaye 98 16 24N 95 53 E
Deddington 28 51 58N 1 19W
Dedemsvaavt 46 52 36N 6 28 E
Dedham 162 42 14N 71 10W
Dedilovo 81 53 59N 37 50 E
Dédougou 120 12 30N 3 35W
Deduru Oya 97 7 32N 81 45 E
Dedza 127 14 20 S 34 20 E
Dee, R., Eng.-Wales, U.K. 31 53 15N 3 7W
Dee, R., Scot., U.K. 37 57 4N 2 7W
Deel R. 38 53 35N 7 9W
Deelish 39 51 41N 9 18W
Deep B. 152 61 15N 116 35W
Deep Lead 140 37 0 S 142 43 E
Deep Well 138 24 20 S 134 0 E
Deepdale 136 26 22 S 114 20 E
Deeping Fen 29 52 45N 0 15W
Deeping, St. Nicholas 29 52 44N 0 11W
Deepwater 139 29 25 S 151 51 E
Deer I. 147 54 55N 162 20W
Deer Lake, Newf., Can. 151 49 11N 57 27W
Deer Lake, Ontario, Can. 153 52 36N 94 20W
Deer Lodge 160 46 25N 112 40W
Deer Park 160 47 55N 117 21W
Deer, R. 153 58 23N 94 13W
Deer River 158 47 21N 93 44W
Deer Sound 37 58 58N 2 50W
Deeral 138 17 14 S 145 55 E
Deerdepoort 128 24 37 S 26 27 E
Deering 147 66 5N 162 50W
Deerlijk 47 50 51N 3 22 E
Deerness 37 58 57N 2 44W
Deesa 94 24 18N 72 10 E
Deferiet 162 44 2N 75 41W
Defiance 156 41 20N 84 20W
Deganwy 31 53 18N 3 49W
Deganya 90 32 43N 35 34 E
Degebe, R. 57 38 21N 7 37W
Degeh-Bur 91 8 11N 43 31 E


FHK

| | | | |
|---|---|---|---|
| Degema | **121** | 4 50N | 6 48 E |
| Degerfors | **74** | 64 16N | 19 46 E |
| Degersfor | **73** | 59 20N | 14 28 E |
| Degersheim | **51** | 47 23N | 9 12 E |
| Degersiö | **72** | 63 13N | 18 3 E |
| Deggendorf | **49** | 48 49N | 12 59 E |
| Degloor | **96** | 18 34N | 77 33 E |
| Deh Bīd | **93** | 30 39N | 53 11 E |
| Deh Kheyr | **93** | 28 45N | 54 40 E |
| Deh Titan | **93** | 33 45N | 63 50 E |
| Dehibat | **119** | 32 0N | 10 47 E |
| Dehiwala | **97** | 6 50N | 79 51 E |
| Dehkhvareqan | **92** | 37 50N | 45 55 E |
| Dehra Dun | **94** | 30 20N | 78 4 E |
| Dehri | **95** | 24 50N | 84 15 E |
| Deinze | **47** | 50 59N | 3 32 E |
| Deir Abu Sa'id | **90** | 32 30N | 38 42 E |
| Deir Dibwan | **90** | 31 55N | 35 15 E |
| Dej | **70** | 47 10N | 23 52 E |
| Deje | **72** | 59 35N | 13 29 E |
| Dekar | **128** | 18 30 S | 23 10 E |
| Dekemhare | **123** | 15 6N | 39 0 E |
| Dekese | **124** | 3 24 S | 21 24 E |
| Dekhkanabad | **85** | 38 21N | 66 30 E |
| Del Mar | **163** | 32 58N | 117 16W |
| Del Norte | **161** | 37 47N | 106 27W |
| Del Rey, Rio | **121** | 4 30N | 8 48 E |
| Del Rio, Mexico | **164** | 29 22N | 100 54W |
| Del Rio, U.S.A. | **159** | 29 15N | 100 50W |
| Delabole | **30** | 50 37N | 4 45W |
| Delagoa B. | **129** | 25 50 S | 32 45 E |
| Delagua | **159** | 32 35N | 104 40W |
| Delai | **122** | 17 21N | 36 6 E |
| Delambre I. | **136** | 20 27 S | 117 4 E |
| Delano | **163** | 35 48N | 119 13W |
| Delareyville | **128** | 26 41 S | 25 26 E |
| Delavan | **158** | 42 40N | 88 39W |
| Delaware | **156** | 40 20N | 83 0W |
| Delaware □ | **162** | 39 0N | 75 40W |
| Delaware B. | **162** | 38 50N | 75 0W |
| Delaware City | **162** | 39 34N | 75 36W |
| Delaware, R. | **162** | 39 20N | 75 25W |
| Del čevo | **66** | 41 58N | 22 46 E |
| Delchirach | **37** | 57 23N | 3 20W |
| Delegate | **141** | 37 4 S | 148 56 E |
| Delémont | **50** | 47 22N | 7 20 E |
| Delft | **46** | 52 1N | 4 22 E |
| Delft I. | **97** | 9 30N | 79 40 E |
| Delfzijl | **46** | 53 20N | 6 55 E |
| Delgado, C. | **127** | 10 45 S | 40 40 E |
| Delgerhet | **106** | 45 50N | 110 30 E |
| Delgo | **122** | 20 6N | 30 40 E |
| Delhi, India | **94** | 28 38N | 77 17 E |
| Delhi, U.S.A. | **162** | 42 17N | 74 56W |
| Deli Jovan | **66** | 44 13N | 22 9 E |
| Delia | **152** | 51 38N | 112 23W |
| Delice, R. | **92** | 39 45N | 34 15 E |
| Delicias | **164** | 28 10N | 105 30W |
| Delicias, Laguna | **164** | 28 7N | 105 40W |
| Delimiro Gouveia | **170** | 9 23 S | 37 59W |
| Delitzsch | **48** | 51 32N | 12 22 E |
| Dell City | **161** | 31 58N | 105 19W |
| Dell Rapids | **158** | 43 53N | 96 44W |
| Delle | **43** | 47 30N | 7 2 E |
| Dellys | **119** | 36 50N | 3 57 E |
| Delmar, Del., U.S.A. | **162** | 38 27N | 75 34W |
| Delmar, N.Y., U.S.A. | **162** | 42 5N | 73 50W |
| Delmenhorst | **48** | 53 3N | 8 37 E |
| Delmiro | **170** | 9 24 S | 38 6W |
| Delnice | **63** | 45 23N | 14 50 E |
| Deloraine, Austral. | **138** | 41 30 S | 146 40 E |
| Deloraine, Can. | **153** | 49 15N | 100 29W |
| Delorme, L. | **151** | 54 31N | 69 52W |
| Delovo | **66** | 44 55N | 20 52 E |
| Delphi | **156** | 40 37N | 86 40W |
| Delphos | **156** | 40 51N | 84 17W |
| Delportshoop | **128** | 28 22 S | 24 20 E |
| Delray Beach | **157** | 26 27N | 80 4W |
| Delsbo | **72** | 61 48N | 16 32 E |
| Delta, Colo., U.S.A. | **161** | 38 44N | 108 5W |
| Delta, Utah, U.S.A. | **160** | 39 21N | 112 29W |
| Delta Amacuro □ | **174** | 8 30N | 61 30W |
| Deltaville | **162** | 37 33N | 76 20W |
| Delungra | **139** | 29 39 S | 150 51 E |
| Delvin | **38** | 53 37N | 7 8W |
| Delvina | **68** | 39 59N | 20 4 E |
| Delvinákion | **68** | 39 57N | 20 32 E |
| Demak | **103** | 6 50 S | 110 40 E |
| Demanda, Sierra de la | **58** | 42 15N | 3 0W |
| Demba | **124** | 5 28 S | 22 15 E |
| Dembecha | **123** | 10 32N | 37 30 E |
| Dembi | **123** | 8 5N | 36 25 E |
| Dembia | **126** | 3 33N | 25 48 E |
| Dembidolo | **123** | 8 34N | 34 50 E |
| Demchok | **93** | 32 40N | 79 29 E |
| Demer, R. | **47** | 51 0N | 5 8 E |
| Demerais, L. | **150** | 47 35N | 77 0W |
| Demerara, R. | **174** | 7 0N | 58 0W |
| Demidov | **80** | 55 10N | 31 30 E |
| Deming | **161** | 32 10N | 107 50W |
| Demini, R. | **174** | 0 46N | 62 56W |
| Demmin | **48** | 53 54N | 13 2 E |
| Demmit | **152** | 55 20N | 119 50W |
| Demnate | **118** | 31 44N | 6 59W |
| Demonte | **62** | 44 18N | 7 18 E |
| Demopolis | **157** | 32 30N | 87 48W |
| Dempo, Mt. | **102** | 4 10 S | 103 15 E |
| Demyansk | **80** | 57 30N | 32 27 E |
| Den Bemmel | **46** | 51 43N | 4 26 E |
| Den Burg | **46** | 53 3N | 4 47 E |
| Den Chai | **100** | 17 59N | 100 4 E |
| Den Dungen | **47** | 51 41N | 5 22 E |
| Den Haag ='s Gravenhage | **46** | 52 7N | 4 17 E |
| Den Ham | **46** | 52 28N | 6 30 E |
| Den Helder | **46** | 52 57N | 4 45 E |
| Den Hulst | **46** | 52 36N | 6 16 E |
| Den Oever | **46** | 52 56N | 5 2 E |
| Denain | **43** | 50 20N | 3 22 E |
| Denair | **163** | 37 32N | 120 48W |
| Denau | **85** | 38 16N | 67 54 E |
| Denbigh | **31** | 53 12N | 3 26W |
| Denbigh (□) | **26** | 53 8N | 3 30W |
| Denby Dale | **33** | 53 35N | 1 40W |
| Denchin | **99** | 31 35N | 95 15 E |
| Dendang | **102** | 3 7 S | 107 56 E |
| Dender, R. | **47** | 51 2N | 4 6 E |
| Denderhoutem | **47** | 50 53N | 4 2 E |
| Denderleeuw | **47** | 50 54N | 4 5 E |
| Dendermonde | **47** | 51 2N | 4 5 E |
| Deneba | **123** | 9 47N | 39 10 E |
| Denekamp | **46** | 52 22N | 7 1 E |
| Denezhkin Kamen, Gora | **84** | 60 25N | 59 32 E |
| Denge | **121** | 12 52N | 5 21 E |
| Dengi | **121** | 9 25N | 9 55 E |
| Denham | **137** | 25 56 S | 113 31 E |
| Denham Ra. | **138** | 21 55 S | 147 46 E |
| Denham Sd. | **137** | 25 45 S | 113 15 E |
| Denholm | **153** | 52 40N | 108 0W |
| Denia | **59** | 38 49N | 0 8 E |
| Denial B. | **139** | 32 14 S | 133 32 E |
| Deniliquin | **141** | 35 30 S | 144 58 E |
| Denison, Iowa, U.S.A. | **158** | 42 0N | 95 18W |
| Denison, Texas, U.S.A. | **159** | 33 50N | 96 40W |
| Denison Plains | **136** | 18 35 S | 128 0 E |
| Denison Range | **136** | 28 30 S | 136 5 E |
| Denisovka | **84** | 52 28N | 61 46 E |
| Denizli | **92** | 37 42N | 29 2 E |
| Denkez Iyesus | **123** | 12 27N | 37 43 E |
| Denman | **141** | 32 24 S | 150 42 E |
| Denmark | **137** | 34 59 S | 117 18 E |
| Denmark ■ | **73** | 55 30N | 9 0 E |
| Denmark Str. | **14** | 66 0N | 30 0W |
| Dennis Hd. | **37** | 59 23N | 2 26W |
| Denniston | **143** | 41 45 S | 171 49 E |
| Denny | **35** | 56 1N | 3 55W |
| Denpasar | **102** | 8 45 S | 115 5 E |
| Dent | **32** | 54 17N | 2 28W |
| Denton, E. Sussex, U.K. | **29** | 50 48N | 0 5 E |
| Denton, Gr. Manchester, U.K. | **32** | 53 26N | 2 10W |
| Denton, Lincs., U.K. | **33** | 52 52N | 0 42W |
| Denton, Md., U.S.A. | **162** | 38 53N | 75 50W |
| Denton, Mont., U.S.A. | **160** | 47 25N | 109 56W |
| Denton, Texas, U.S.A. | **159** | 33 12N | 97 10W |
| D'Entrecasteaux, C. | **137** | 34 50 S | 115 59 E |
| D'Entrecasteaux Is. | **135** | 9 0 S | 151 0 E |
| D'Entrecasteaux Pt. | **137** | 34 50 S | 115 57 E |
| Dents du Midi | **50** | 46 10N | 6 56 E |
| Denu | **121** | 6 4N | 1 8 E |
| Denver, Colo., U.S.A. | **158** | 39 45N | 105 0W |
| Denver, Pa., U.S.A. | **162** | 40 14N | 76 8W |
| Denver City | **159** | 32 58N | 102 48W |
| Deoband | **94** | 29 42N | 77 43 E |
| Deobhog | **96** | 19 53N | 82 44 E |
| Deogarh | **96** | 21 32N | 84 45 E |
| Deoghar | **95** | 24 30N | 86 59 E |
| Deolali | **96** | 19 50N | 73 50 E |
| Deoli | **94** | 25 50N | 75 50 E |
| Deoria | **95** | 26 31N | 83 48 E |
| Deosai, Mts. | **95** | 35 40N | 75 0 E |
| Deposit | **162** | 42 5N | 75 23W |
| Depot Spring | **137** | 27 55 S | 120 3 E |
| Depuch I. | **136** | 20 35 S | 117 44 E |
| Deputatskiy | **77** | 69 18N | 139 54 E |
| Dera Ghazi Khan | **94** | 30 5N | 70 43 E |
| Dera Ismail Khan | **94** | 31 50N | 70 50 E |
| Dera Ismail Khan □ | **94** | 32 30N | 70 0 E |
| Derati Wells | **126** | 3 52N | 36 37 E |
| Derbent | **74** | 42 5N | 48 15 E |
| Derby, Austral. | **136** | 17 18 S | 123 38 E |
| Derby, U.K. | **33** | 52 55N | 1 28W |
| Derby, U.S.A. | **162** | 41 20N | 73 5W |
| Derby □ | **33** | 52 55N | 1 28W |
| Derecske | **53** | 47 20N | 21 33 E |
| Derg, L. | **39** | 53 0N | 8 20W |
| Derg, R. | **38** | 54 42N | 7 26W |
| Dergachi | **81** | 50 3N | 36 3 E |
| Dergaon | **99** | 26 45N | 94 0 E |
| Dermantsi | **67** | 43 8N | 24 17 E |
| Derna | **117** | 32 40N | 22 35 E |
| Dernieres Isles | **159** | 29 0N | 90 45W |
| Derriana, L. | **39** | 51 54N | 10 1W |
| Derrinallum | **140** | 37 57 S | 143 15 E |
| Derry R. | **39** | 52 43N | 6 35W |
| Derrybrien | **39** | 53 4N | 8 38W |
| Derrygonnelly | **38** | 54 25N | 7 50W |
| Derrygrogan | **39** | 53 19N | 7 23W |
| Derrykeighan | **38** | 55 8N | 6 30W |
| Derrylin | **38** | 54 12N | 7 34W |
| Derry = Londonderry | **38** | 55 0N | 7 19W |
| Derrynasaggart Mts. | **39** | 51 58N | 9 15W |
| Derryrush | **38** | 53 23N | 9 40W |
| Derryveagh Mts. | **38** | 55 0N | 8 40W |
| Derudub | **122** | 17 31N | 36 7 E |
| Dervaig | **34** | 56 35N | 6 13W |
| Derval | **42** | 47 40N | 1 41W |
| Dervéni | **69** | 38 8N | 22 25 E |
| Derwent | **153** | 53 41N | 110 58W |
| Derwent, R., Derby, U.K. | **33** | 52 53N | 1 17W |
| Derwent, R., N. Yorks., U.K. | **33** | 53 45N | 0 57W |
| Derwent, R., Tyne & Wear, U.K. | **35** | 54 58N | 1 40W |
| Derwentwater, L. | **32** | 53 34N | 3 9W |
| Des Moines, Iowa, U.S.A. | **158** | 41 35N | 93 37W |
| Des Moines, N. Mex., U.S.A. | **159** | 36 50N | 103 51W |
| Des Moines, R. | **158** | 40 23N | 91 25W |
| Desaguadero, R., Argent. | **172** | 33 28 S | 67 15W |
| Desaguadero, R., Boliv. | **174** | 17 30 S | 68 0W |
| Desborough | **29** | 52 27N | 0 50W |
| Deschaillons | **151** | 46 32N | 72 7W |
| Descharme, R. | **153** | 56 51N | 109 13W |
| Deschutes, R. | **160** | 45 30N | 121 0W |
| Dese | **123** | 11 5N | 39 40 E |
| Deseado, R. | **176** | 40 0 S | 69 0W |
| Desemboque | **164** | 30 30N | 112 27W |
| Desenzano del Gardo | **62** | 45 28N | 10 32 E |
| Desert Center | **161** | 33 45N | 115 27W |
| Desert Hot Springs | **163** | 33 58N | 116 30W |
| Desertmartin | **38** | 54 47N | 6 40W |
| Desford | **28** | 52 38N | 1 19W |
| Désirade, I. | **167** | 16 18N | 61 3W |
| Deskenatlata L. | **152** | 60 55N | 112 3W |
| Desna, R. | **80** | 52 0N | 33 15 E |
| Desnǔtui, R. | **70** | 44 15N | 23 27 E |
| Desolación, I. | **176** | 53 0 S | 74 0W |
| Despeñaperros, Paso | **59** | 38 24N | 3 30W |
| Despotovac | **66** | 44 6N | 21 30 E |
| Dessa | **121** | 14 44N | 1 6 E |
| Dessau | **48** | 51 49N | 12 15 E |
| Dessel | **47** | 51 15N | 5 7 E |
| Dessye = Dese | **123** | 11 5N | 39 40 E |
| D'Estress B. | **140** | 35 55 S | 137 45 E |
| Desuri | **94** | 25 18N | 73 35 E |
| Desvrès | **43** | 50 40N | 1 48 E |
| Det Udom | **100** | 14 54N | 105 5 E |
| Detinjá, R. | **66** | 43 51N | 19 45 E |
| Detmold | **48** | 51 55N | 8 50 E |
| Detour Pt. | **156** | 45 37N | 86 35W |
| Detroit, Mich., U.S.A. | **150** | 42 13N | 83 22W |
| Detroit, Tex., U.S.A. | **159** | 33 40N | 95 10W |
| Detroit Lakes | **158** | 46 50N | 95 50W |
| Dett | **127** | 18 32 S | 26 57 E |
| Dettifoss | **74** | 65 49N | 16 24W |
| Děčin | **52** | 50 47N | 14 12 E |
| Deurne, Belg. | **47** | 51 12N | 4 24 E |
| Deurne, Neth. | **47** | 51 27N | 5 49 E |
| Deutsche Bucht | **48** | 54 10N | 7 51 E |
| Deutschlandsberg | **52** | 46 49N | 15 14 E |
| Deux-Acren, Les | **47** | 50 44N | 3 51 E |
| Deux-Sèvres □ | **42** | 46 35N | 0 20W |
| Deva | **70** | 45 53N | 22 55 E |
| Devakottai | **97** | 9 55N | 78 45 E |
| Devaprayag | **95** | 30 13N | 78 35 E |
| Dévaványa | **53** | 47 2N | 20 59 E |
| Deveci Daği | **82** | 40 10N | 36 0 E |
| Devecser | **53** | 47 6N | 17 26 E |
| Deventer | **46** | 52 15N | 6 10 E |
| Deveron, R. | **37** | 57 40N | 2 31W |
| Devesel | **70** | 44 28N | 22 41 E |
| Devgad, I. | **97** | 14 48N | 74 5 E |
| Devil R., Pk. | **143** | 40 56 S | 172 37 E |
| Devils Bridge | **31** | 52 23N | 3 50W |
| Devils Den | **163** | 35 46N | 119 58W |
| Devils Lake | **158** | 48 5N | 98 50W |
| Devils Paw, mt. | **152** | 58 47N | 134 0W |
| Devils Pt. | **97** | 9 26N | 80 6 E |
| Devilsbit Mt. | **39** | 52 50N | 7 58W |
| Devin | **67** | 41 44N | 24 24 E |
| Devizes | **28** | 51 21N | 2 0W |
| Devnya | **67** | 43 13N | 27 33 E |
| Devolli, R. | **68** | 40 57N | 20 15 E |
| Devon | **152** | 53 24N | 113 44W |
| Devon I. | **12** | 75 47N | 88 0W |
| Devonport, Austral. | **138** | 41 10 S | 146 22 E |
| Devonport, N.Z. | **142** | 36 49 S | 174 49 E |
| Devonport, U.K. | **30** | 50 23N | 4 11W |
| Devonshire □ | **30** | 50 50N | 3 40W |
| Dewas | **94** | 22 59N | 76 3 E |
| Dewetsdorp | **128** | 29 33 S | 26 39 E |
| Dewgad Baria | **94** | 22 40N | 73 55 E |
| Dewsbury | **33** | 53 42N | 1 38W |
| Dexter, Mo., U.S.A. | **159** | 36 50N | 90 0W |
| Dexter, N. Mex., U.S.A. | **159** | 33 15N | 104 25W |
| Dey-Dey, L. | **137** | 29 12 S | 131 4 E |
| Deyhuk | **93** | 33 15N | 104 25W |
| Deyyer | **93** | 27 55N | 51 55 E |
| Dezadeash L. | **152** | 60 28N | 136 58W |
| Dezfūl | **92** | 32 20N | 48 30 E |
| Dezh Shanpur | **92** | 35 30N | 46 25 E |
| Dezhneva, Mys | **77** | 66 10N | 169 3 E |
| Dhaba | **92** | 27 25N | 35 40 E |
| Dháfni | **69** | 37 48N | 22 1 E |
| Dhahaban | **122** | 21 58N | 39 3 E |
| Dhahiriya = Qz Zahiriya | **90** | 31 25N | 34 58 E |
| Dhahran | **92** | 26 9N | 50 10 E |
| Dhama Dzong | **99** | 28 15N | 91 15 E |
| Dhamási | **68** | 39 43N | 22 11 E |
| Dhampur | **95** | 29 19N | 78 33 E |
| Dhamtari | **96** | 20 42N | 81 35 E |
| Dhanbad | **95** | 23 50N | 86 30 E |
| Dhangarhi | **99** | 28 55N | 80 40 E |
| Dhankuta | **95** | 26 55N | 87 20 E |
| Dhanora | **96** | 20 20N | 80 22 E |
| Dhar | **94** | 22 35N | 75 26 E |
| Dharampur, Mad. P., India | **94** | 22 13N | 75 18 E |
| Dharampur, Maharashtra, India | **96** | 20 32N | 73 17 E |
| Dharapuram | **97** | 10 45N | 77 34 E |
| Dharmapuri | **97** | 12 10N | 78 10 E |
| Dharmavaram | **97** | 14 29N | 77 44 E |
| Dharmsala, (Dharamsala) | **94** | 32 16N | 73 23 E |
| Dhaulagiri Mt. | **95** | 28 45N | 83 45 E |
| Dhebar, L. | **94** | 24 10N | 74 0 E |
| Dhenkanal | **96** | 20 45N | 85 35 E |
| Dhenoúsa | **69** | 37 8N | 25 48 E |
| Dhesfina | **69** | 38 25N | 22 31 E |
| Dheskáti | **68** | 39 55N | 21 49 E |
| Dhespotikó | **69** | 36 57N | 24 58 E |
| Dhidhimótikhon | **68** | 41 22N | 26 29 E |
| Dhikti, Mt. | **69** | 35 8N | 25 29 E |
| Dhilianáta | **69** | 38 15N | 20 34 E |
| Dhílos | **69** | 37 23N | 25 15 E |
| Dhimitsána | **69** | 37 36N | 22 3 E |
| Dhirfis, Mt. | **69** | 38 40N | 23 54 E |
| Dhodhekánisos | **69** | 36 35N | 27 0 E |
| Dhofar | **91** | 17 0N | 54 10 E |
| Dhokós | **69** | 37 20N | 23 20 E |
| Dholiana | **68** | 39 54N | 20 32 E |
| Dholka | **94** | 22 44N | 72 29 E |
| Dholpur | **94** | 26 45N | 77 59 E |
| Dhomokós | **69** | 39 10N | 22 18 E |
| Dhond | **96** | 18 26N | 74 40 E |
| Dhoraji | **94** | 21 45N | 70 37 E |
| Dhoxáthon | **68** | 41 9N | 24 16 E |
| Dhragonisi | **69** | 37 27N | 25 29 E |
| Dhrangadhra | **94** | 22 59N | 71 31 E |
| Dhriopós | **69** | 37 35N | 24 35 E |
| Dhrol | **94** | 22 40N | 70 25 E |
| Dhubaibah | **93** | 23 25N | 54 35 E |
| Dhubri | **98** | 26 2N | 90 2 E |
| Dhulasar | **98** | 21 52N | 90 14 E |
| Dhulia | **96** | 20 58N | 74 50 E |
| Dhupdhara | **98** | 25 58N | 91 4 E |
| Dhurm | **122** | 20 18N | 42 53 E |
| Di Linh | **101** | 11 35N | 108 4 E |
| Di Linh, Cao Nguyen | **101** | 11 30N | 108 0 E |
| Día, I. | **69** | 35 26N | 25 13 E |
| Diable, Mt. | **163** | 37 53N | 121 56W |
| Diablerets, Les | **50** | 46 22N | 7 10 E |
| Diablo Range | **163** | 37 0N | 121 5W |
| Diafarabé | **120** | 14 17N | 4 57W |
| Diala | **120** | 13 59N | 10 0W |
| Dialakoro | **120** | 12 18N | 7 54W |
| Diallassagou | **120** | 13 47N | 3 41W |
| Diamante | **172** | 32 5 S | 60 40W |
| Diamante, R. | **172** | 34 31 S | 66 56W |
| Diamantina | **171** | 18 5 S | 43 40W |
| Diamantina, R. | **138** | 22 25 S | 142 20 E |
| Diamantino | **175** | 14 30 S | 56 30W |
| Diamond Harbour | **95** | 22 11N | 88 14 E |
| Diamond Is. | **138** | 17 25 S | 151 5 E |
| Diamond Mts. | **160** | 40 0N | 115 58W |
| Diamond Springs | **163** | 38 42N | 120 49W |
| Diamondville | **160** | 41 51N | 110 30W |
| Diano Marina | **62** | 43 55N | 8 3 E |
| Dianópolis | **171** | 11 38 S | 46 50W |
| Dianra | **120** | 8 45N | 6 14W |
| Diaole, Î. du. | **170** | 5 15N | 52 45W |
| Diapaga | **121** | 12 5N | 1 46 E |
| Diapangou | **121** | 12 5N | 0 10 E |
| Diapur | **140** | 36 19 S | 141 29 E |
| Diariguila | **120** | 10 35N | 10 2W |
| Dibai (Dubai) | **93** | 25 15N | 55 20 E |
| Dibaya | **124** | 6 20 S | 22 0 E |
| Dibaya Lubue | **124** | 4 12 S | 19 54 E |
| Dibba | **93** | 25 45N | 56 16 E |
| Dibbi | **123** | 4 10N | 41 52 E |
| Dibden | **28** | 50 53N | 1 24W |
| Dibega | **92** | 35 50N | 43 46 E |
| Dibër | **68** | 41 38N | 20 15 E |
| Dibete | **128** | 23 45 S | 26 32 E |
| Dibi | **123** | 4 10N | 41 52 E |
| Dibrugarh | **98** | 27 29N | 94 55 E |
| Dibulla | **174** | 11 17N | 73 19W |
| Dickinson | **158** | 46 50N | 102 40W |
| Dickson | **157** | 36 5N | 87 22W |
| Dickson City | **162** | 41 29N | 75 40W |
| Dicomano | **63** | 43 53 S | 11 30 E |
| Didam | **46** | 51 57N | 6 8 E |
| Didcot | **28** | 51 36N | 1 14W |
| Didesa, W. | **123** | 9 40N | 35 50 E |
| Didiéni | **120** | 14 5N | 7 50W |
| Didsbury | **152** | 51 35N | 114 10W |
| Didwana | **94** | 27 17N | 74 25 E |
| Die | **45** | 44 47N | 5 22 E |
| Diébougou | **120** | 11 0N | 3 15W |
| Diefenbaker L. | **153** | 51 0N | 106 55W |
| Diego Garcia, I. | **11** | 9 50 S | 75 0 E |
| Diégo Suarez | **129** | 12 25 S | 49 20 E |
| Diekirch | **47** | 49 52N | 6 10 E |
| Diélette | **42** | 49 33N | 1 52W |
| Diéma | **120** | 14 32N | 9 3W |
| Diemen | **46** | 52 21N | 4 58 E |
| Dieméring | **120** | 12 29N | 16 47W |
| Dien Ban | **100** | 15 53N | 108 16 E |
| Diên Biên Phu | **100** | 21 20N | 103 0 E |
| Dien Khanh | **101** | 12 15N | 109 6 E |
| Diepenheim | **46** | 52 12N | 6 33 E |
| Diepenveen | **46** | 52 18N | 6 9 E |
| Diepholz | **48** | 52 37N | 8 22 E |
| Diepoldsau | **51** | 47 23N | 9 40 E |
| Dieppe | **42** | 49 54N | 1 4 E |
| Dieren | **46** | 52 3N | 6 6 E |
| Dierks | **159** | 34 9N | 94 0W |
| Diessen | **47** | 51 29N | 5 10 E |
| Diessenhofen | **51** | 47 42N | 8 46 E |
| Diest | **47** | 50 58N | 5 4 E |
| Dietikon | **51** | 47 24N | 8 24 E |
| Dieulefit | **45** | 44 32N | 5 4 E |
| Dieuze | **43** | 48 30N | 6 40 E |

Diever Donskoy


| | | | |
|---|---|---|---|
| Diever | 46 | 52 51N | 6 19 E |
| Diffa | 121 | 13 34N | 12 33 E |
| Differdange | 47 | 49 81N | 5 54 E |
| Dig | 94 | 27 28N | 77 20 E |
| Digba | 126 | 4 25N | 25 42 E |
| Digboi | 98 | 27 23N | 95 38 E |
| Digby | 151 | 44 41N | 65 50W |
| Digges | 153 | 58 40N | 94 0W |
| Digges Is. | 149 | 62 40N | 77 50W |
| Digges Lamprey | 153 | 58 33N | 94 8W |
| Dighinala | 98 | 23 15N | 92 5 E |
| Dighton | 158 | 38 30N | 100 26W |
| Digne | 45 | 44 5N | 6 12 E |
| Digoin | 44 | 46 29N | 3 58 E |
| Digos | 103 | 6 45N | 125 20 E |
| Digranes | 74 | 66 4N | 14 44 E |
| Digras | 96 | 20 6N | 77 45 E |
| Dihang, R. | 99 | 27 30N | 96 30 E |
| Dijlah | 92 | 37 0N | 42 30 E |
| Dijle, R. | 47 | 50 58N | 4 41 E |
| Dijon | 43 | 47 20N | 5 0 E |
| Dikala | 123 | 4 45N | 31 28 E |
| Dikhal | 123 | 11 8N | 42 20 E |
| Dikomu di Kai, Mt. | 128 | 24 51 S | 24 36 E |
| Diksmuide | 47 | 51 2N | 2 52 E |
| Dikson | 76 | 73 40N | 80 5 E |
| Dikumbiya | 123 | 14 45N | 37 30 E |
| Dikwa | 121 | 12 4N | 13 30 E |
| Dila | 123 | 6 14N | 38 22 E |
| Dilam | 92 | 23 55N | 47 10 E |
| Dilbeek | 47 | 50 51N | 4 17 E |
| Dili | 103 | 8 39 S | 125 34 E |
| Dilizhan | 83 | 41 46N | 44 57 E |
| Dillenburg | 48 | 50 44N | 8 17 E |
| Dilley | 159 | 28 40N | 99 12W |
| Dilling | 123 | 12 3N | 29 35 E |
| Dillingen | 49 | 49 22N | 6 42 E |
| Dillingham | 147 | 59 5N | 158 30W |
| Dillon, Can. | 153 | 55 56N | 108 56W |
| Dillon, Mont., U.S.A. | 160 | 45 9N | 112 36W |
| Dillon, S.C., U.S.A. | 157 | 34 26N | 79 20W |
| Dillon, R. | 153 | 55 56N | 108 56W |
| Dillsburg | 162 | 40 7N | 77 2W |
| Dilolo | 14 | 10 28 S | 22 18 E |
| Dilsen | 47 | 51 2N | 5 44 E |
| Dilston | 138 | 41 22 S | 147 10 E |
| Dima | 123 | 6 19N | 36 15 E |
| Dimapur | 98 | 25 54N | 93 45 E |
| Dimas | 164 | 23 43N | 106 47W |
| Dimashq | 92 | 33 30N | 36 18 E |
| Dimbelenge | 124 | 4 30S | 23 0 E |
| Dimbokro | 120 | 6 45N | 4 30W |
| Dimboola | 140 | 36 28 S | 142 0 E |
| Dîmboviţa □ | 70 | 45 0N | 25 30 E |
| Dîmbovita, R. | 70 | 44 40N | 26 0 E |
| Dimbulah | 138 | 17 2 S | 145 4 E |
| Dimitriya Lapteva, Proliv | 77 | 73 0N | 140 0 E |
| Dimitrovgrad, Bulg. | 67 | 42 5N | 25 35 E |
| Dimitrovgrad, U.S.S.R. | 84 | 54 25N | 49 33 E |
| Dimitrovgrad, Yugo. | 66 | 43 0N | 22 48 E |
| Dimmitt | 159 | 34 36N | 102 16W |
| Dimo | 123 | 5 19N | 29 10 E |
| Dimona | 90 | 31 2N | 35 1 E |
| Dimovo | 66 | 43 43N | 22 50 E |
| Dinagat I. | 103 | 10 10N | 125 40 E |
| Dinajpur | 98 | 25 33N | 88 43 E |
| Dinan | 42 | 48 28N | 2 2W |
| Dinant | 47 | 50 16N | 4 55 E |
| Dinapore | 95 | 25 38N | 85 5 E |
| Dinar | 92 | 38 5N | 30 15 E |
| Dinard | 42 | 48 38N | 2 6W |
| Dinaric Alps | 16 | 44 0N | 17 30 E |
| Dinas Hd. | 31 | 52 2N | 4 56W |
| Dinas Mawddwy | 31 | 52 44N | 3 41W |
| Dinas Powis | 31 | 51 25N | 3 14W |
| Dinder, Nahr ed | 123 | 12 32N | 35 0 E |
| Dindi, R. | 96 | 16 24N | 78 15 E |
| Dindigul | 97 | 10 25N | 78 0 E |
| Dingelstädt | 48 | 51 19N | 10 19 E |
| Dingila | 126 | 3 25N | 26 25 E |
| Dingle | 39 | 52 9N | 10 17W |
| Dingle B. | 39 | 52 3N | 10 20W |
| Dingle Harbour | 39 | 52 7N | 10 12W |
| Dingmans Ferry | 162 | 41 13N | 74 55W |
| Dingo | 138 | 23 38 S | 149 19 E |
| Dingolfing | 49 | 48 38N | 12 30 E |
| Dinguiraye | 120 | 11 30N | 10 35W |
| Dingwall | 37 | 57 36N | 4 26W |
| Dingyadi | 121 | 13 0N | 0 53 E |
| Dinh Lap | 100 | 21 33N | 107 6 E |
| Dinh, Mui | 101 | 11 22N | 109 1 E |
| Dinhata | 98 | 26 8N | 89 27 E |
| Dinkel | 46 | 52 30N | 6 58 E |
| Dinokwe (Palla Road) | 128 | 23 29 S | 26 37 E |
| Dinosaur National Monument | 160 | 40 30N | 108 45W |
| Dinslaken | 47 | 51 34N | 6 41 E |
| Dintel, R. | 47 | 51 39N | 4 22 E |
| Dinuba | 163 | 36 37N | 119 22W |
| Dinxperlo | 46 | 51 52N | 6 30 E |
| Dio | 73 | 56 37N | 14 15 E |
| Diosgyör | 53 | 48 7N | 20 43 E |
| Diosig | 70 | 47 18N | 22 2 E |
| Dioundiou | 121 | 12 37N | 3 33 E |
| Diourbel | 120 | 14 39N | 16 12W |
| Diphu Pass | 98 | 28 9N | 97 20 E |
| Diplo | 94 | 24 25N | 69 35 E |
| Dipolog | 103 | 8 36N | 123 20 E |
| Dipşa | 70 | 46 58N | 24 27 E |
| Dipton | 143 | 45 54 S | 168 22 E |
| Dir | 93 | 35 08N | 71 59 E |
| Diré | 120 | 15 20N | 3 25W |
| Dire Dawa | 123 | 9 35N | 41 45 E |
| Direction, C. | 138 | 12 51 S | 143 32 E |
| Diriamba | 166 | 11 51N | 86 19W |
| Dirico | 125 | 17 50 S | 20 42 E |
| Dirk Hartog I. | 137 | 25 50 S | 113 5 E |
| Dirranbandi | 139 | 28 33 S | 148 17 E |
| Disa | 123 | 12 5N | 34 15 E |
| Disappointment, C. | 160 | 46 20N | 124 0W |
| Disappointment L. | 136 | 23 20 S | 122 40 E |
| Disaster B. | 141 | 37 15 S | 150 0 E |
| Discovery | 148 | 63 0N | 115 0W |
| Discovery B. | 140 | 38 10 S | 140 40 E |
| Disentis | 51 | 46 42N | 8 50 E |
| Dishna | 122 | 26 9N | 32 32 E |
| Disina | 121 | 11 35N | 9 50 E |
| Disko | 12 | 69 45N | 53 30W |
| Disko Bugt | 12 | 69 10N | 52 0W |
| Disna | 80 | 55 32N | 28 11 E |
| Disna, R. | 80 | 55 20N | 27 30 E |
| Dison | 47 | 50 37N | 5 51 E |
| Diss | 29 | 52 23N | 1 6 E |
| Disteghil Sar | 95 | 36 20N | 75 5 E |
| Distington | 32 | 54 35N | 3 33W |
| District Heights | 162 | 38 51N | 76 53W |
| District of Columbia □ | 162 | 38 55N | 77 0W |
| Distrito Federal □, Brazil | 171 | 15 45 S | 47 45W |
| Distrito Federal □, Venez. | 174 | 10 30N | 66 55W |
| Disûq | 122 | 31 8N | 30 35 E |
| Ditchingham | 29 | 52 28N | 1 26 E |
| Ditchling & Beacon | 29 | 50 59N | 0 7W |
| Ditinn | 120 | 10 53N | 12 11W |
| Dittisham | 30 | 50 22N | 3 36W |
| Ditton Priors | 28 | 52 30N | 2 33W |
| Diu, I. | 94 | 20 45N | 70 58 E |
| Diver | 150 | 46 44N | 79 30W |
| Dives | 42 | 49 18N | 0 8W |
| Dives, R. | 42 | 49 18N | 0 7W |
| Divi Pt. | 97 | 15 59N | 81 9 E |
| Divichi | 83 | 41 15N | 48 57 E |
| Divide | 160 | 45 48N | 112 47W |
| Dividing Ra. | 137 | 27 45 S | 116 0 E |
| Divinopólis | 171 | 20 10 S | 44 54W |
| Divisões, Serra dos | 171 | 17 0 S | 51 0W |
| Divnoye | 83 | 45 55N | 43 27 E |
| Divo | 120 | 5 48N | 5 15W |
| Diwal Kol | 94 | 34 23N | 67 52 E |
| Dixie | 160 | 45 37N | 115 27W |
| Dixon, Calif., U.S.A. | 163 | 38 27N | 121 49W |
| Dixon, Ill., U.S.A. | 158 | 41 50N | 89 30W |
| Dixon, Mont., U.S.A. | 160 | 47 19N | 114 25W |
| Dixon, N. Mex., U.S.A. | 161 | 36 15N | 105 57W |
| Dixon Entrance | 153 | 54 30N | 132 0W |
| Dixonville | 152 | 56 32N | 117 40W |
| Diyarbakir | 92 | 37 55N | 40 18 E |
| Dizzard Pt. | 30 | 50 46N | 4 38W |
| Djabotaoure | 121 | 8 35N | 0 58 E |
| Djado | 119 | 21 4N | 12 14 E |
| Djado, Plateau du | 119 | 21 29N | 12 21 E |
| Djakarta = Jakarta | 103 | 6 9 S | 106 49 E |
| Djakovo | 66 | 45 19N | 18 24 E |
| Djamâa | 119 | 33 32N | 5 59 E |
| Djamba | 128 | 16 45 S | 13 58 E |
| Djambala | 124 | 2 20 S | 14 30 E |
| Djanet | 119 | 24 35N | 9 32 E |
| Djang | 121 | 5 30N | 10 5 E |
| Djaul I. | 135 | 2 58 S | 150 57 E |
| Djawa = Jawa | 103 | 7 0 S | 110 0 E |
| Djebiniana | 119 | 35 1N | 11 0 E |
| Djelfa | 118 | 34 40N | 3 15 E |
| Djema | 126 | 6 9N | 25 15 E |
| Djeneïene | 119 | 31 45N | 10 9 E |
| Djenné | 120 | 14 0N | 4 30W |
| Djenoun, Garet el | 119 | 25 4N | 5 31 E |
| Djerba | 119 | 33 52N | 10 51 E |
| Djerba, Île de | 119 | 33 56N | 11 0 E |
| Djerid, Chott | 119 | 33 42N | 8 30 E |
| Djibo | 121 | 14 15N | 1 35W |
| Djibouti | 123 | 11 30N | 43 5 E |
| Djibouti ■ | 123 | 11 30N | 42 15 E |
| Djidjelli | 119 | 36 52N | 5 50 E |
| Djirlange | 101 | 11 44N | 108 15 E |
| Djofra | 119 | 28 59N | 15 47 E |
| Djolu | 124 | 0 45N | 22 5 E |
| Djorf el Youdi | 118 | 32 14N | 9 8W |
| Djougou | 121 | 9 40N | 1 45 E |
| Djoum | 124 | 2 41N | 12 35 E |
| Djourab, Erg du | 117 | 16 40N | 18 50 E |
| Djugu | 126 | 1 55N | 30 35 E |
| Djúpivogur | 74 | 64 39N | 14 17W |
| Djursholm | 72 | 59 25N | 18 6 E |
| Djursland | 73 | 56 27N | 10 45 E |
| Dmitriev-Lgovskiy | 80 | 52 10N | 35 0 E |
| Dmitriya Lapteva, Proliv | 77 | 73 0N | 140 0 E |
| Dmitrov | 81 | 56 25N | 37 32 E |
| Dmitrovsk Orlovskiy | 80 | 52 29N | 35 10 E |
| Dneiper, R. = Dnepr | 82 | 52 29N | 35 10 E |
| Dnepr, R. | 82 | 50 0N | 31 0 E |
| Dneprodzerzhinsk | 82 | 48 32N | 34 30 E |
| Dneprodzerzhinskoye Vdkhr. | 77 | 49 0N | 34 0 E |
| Dnepropetrovsk | 82 | 48 30N | 35 0 E |
| Dneprorudnoye | 82 | 47 21N | 34 58 E |
| Dnestr, R. | 82 | 48 30N | 26 30 E |
| Dnestrovski = Belgorod | 82 | 50 35N | 36 35 E |
| Dniester = Dnestr | 82 | 48 30N | 26 30 E |
| Dno | 80 | 57 50N | 29 58 E |
| Doan Hung | 100 | 21 38N | 105 10 E |
| Doba | 117 | 8 40N | 16 50 E |
| Dobané | 126 | 6 20N | 24 39 E |
| Dobbiaco | 63 | 46 44N | 12 13 E |
| Dobbyn | 138 | 19 44 S | 139 59 E |
| Dobczyce | 54 | 49 52N | 20 25 E |
| Döbeln | 48 | 51 7N | 13 10 E |
| Doberai, Jazirah | 103 | 1 25 S | 133 0 E |
| Dobiegniew | 54 | 52 59N | 15 45 E |
| Doblas | 172 | 37 5 S | 64 0W |
| Dobo | 103 | 5 45 S | 134 15 E |
| Doboj | 66 | 44 46N | 18 6 E |
| Dobra, Poland | 54 | 53 34N | 15 20 E |
| Dobra, Dîmboviţa, Rumania | 67 | 44 52N | 25 40 E |
| Dobra, Hunedoara, Rumania | 70 | 45 54N | 22 36 E |
| Dobre Miasto | 54 | 53 58N | 20 26 E |
| Dobrinishta | 67 | 41 49N | 23 34 E |
| Dobriš | 52 | 49 46N | 14 10 E |
| Dobrodzien | 54 | 50 45N | 18 25 E |
| Dobrogea | 70 | 44 30N | 28 15 E |
| Dobruja = Dobrogea | 70 | 44 30N | 28 15 E |
| Dobrush | 80 | 52 28N | 30 35 E |
| Dobryanka | 84 | 58 27N | 56 25 E |
| Dobrzyn n. Wisła | 54 | 52 39N | 19 22 E |
| Dobtong | 123 | 6 25N | 31 40 E |
| Doc, Mui | 100 | 17 58N | 106 30 E |
| Doce, R. | 171 | 19 37 S | 39 49W |
| Docking | 29 | 52 55N | 0 39 E |
| Doda | 95 | 33 10N | 75 34 E |
| Döda Fallet | 72 | 63 4N | 16 35 E |
| Doddington | 29 | 52 29N | 0 3 E |
| Dodecanese = Dhodhekánisos | 69 | 36 35N | 27 0 E |
| Dodewaard | 46 | 51 55N | 5 39 E |
| Dodge Center | 158 | 44 1N | 92 57W |
| Dodge City | 159 | 37 42N | 100 0W |
| Dodge L. | 153 | 59 50N | 105 36W |
| Dodgeville | 158 | 42 55N | 90 8W |
| Dodman Pt. | 30 | 50 13N | 4 49W |
| Dodo | 123 | 5 10N | 29 57 E |
| Dodola | 123 | 6 59N | 39 11 E |
| Dodoma | 126 | 6 8 S | 35 45 E |
| Dodoma □ | 126 | 6 0 S | 36 0 E |
| Dodsland | 153 | 51 50N | 108 45W |
| Dodson | 160 | 48 23N | 108 4W |
| Doesburg | 46 | 52 1N | 6 9 E |
| Doetinchem | 46 | 51 59N | 6 18 E |
| Doftana | 70 | 45 17N | 25 45 E |
| Dog Creek | 152 | 51 35N | 122 14W |
| Dog L., Man., Can. | 152 | 51 2N | 98 31W |
| Dog L., Ont., Can. | 150 | 48 12N | 89 16W |
| Dog, R. | 152 | 57 50N | 94 40W |
| Doganbey | 69 | 37 40N | 27 10 E |
| Dogi | 93 | 32 20N | 62 50 E |
| Dogliani | 62 | 44 35N | 7 55 E |
| Dōgo | 110 | 36 15N | 133 16 E |
| Dōgo-San | 110 | 35 2N | 133 13 E |
| Dògondoutchi | 121 | 13 38N | 4 2 E |
| Dogoraoua | 121 | 14 0N | 5 31 E |
| Dogran | 94 | 31 48N | 73 35 E |
| Dohad | 94 | 22 50N | 74 15 E |
| Dohazari | 99 | 22 10N | 92 5 E |
| Doheny | 150 | 47 4N | 72 35W |
| Doherty | 150 | 46 58N | 79 44W |
| Doi, I. | 103 | 2 21N | 127 49 E |
| Doi Luang | 101 | 18 20N | 101 30 E |
| Doi Saket | 100 | 18 52N | 99 9 E |
| Doig, R., Alta., Can. | 152 | 56 57N | 120 0W |
| Doig, R., B.C., Can. | 152 | 56 25N | 120 40W |
| Dois Irmãos, Serra | 171 | 8 30 S | 41 5W |
| Dokka | 71 | 60 49N | 10 7 E |
| Dokka, R. | 71 | 61 7N | 10 0 E |
| Dokkum | 46 | 53 20N | 5 59 E |
| Dokkumer Ee, R. | 46 | 53 18N | 5 52 E |
| Dokri Mohenjodaro | 94 | 27 25N | 68 7 E |
| Dol | 42 | 48 34N | 1 47W |
| Dolak, Pulau = Kolepom, P. | 103 | 8 0 S | 138 30 E |
| Doland | 158 | 44 55N | 98 5W |
| Dolbeau | 151 | 48 53N | 72 18W |
| Dôle | 43 | 47 7N | 5 31 E |
| Doleib, W. | 123 | 10 30N | 33 15 E |
| Dolgarrog | 31 | 53 11N | 3 50W |
| Dolgellau | 31 | 52 44N | 3 53W |
| Dolgelly = Dolgellau | 31 | 52 44N | 3 53W |
| Dolginovo | 80 | 54 39N | 27 29 E |
| Dolianovo | 64 | 39 23N | 9 11 E |
| Dolinskaya | 82 | 48 16N | 32 36 E |
| Dolisie | 124 | 4 0 S | 13 10 E |
| Dolj □ | 70 | 44 10N | 23 30 E |
| Dolla | 39 | 52 47N | 8 12W |
| Dollar | 35 | 56 9N | 3 41W |
| Dollart | 46 | 53 20N | 7 10 E |
| Dolna Banya | 67 | 42 18N | 23 44 E |
| Dolni Dubnik | 67 | 43 24N | 24 26 E |
| Dolo | 63 | 45 25N | 12 4 E |
| Dolo Bay | 123 | 4 11N | 42 3 E |
| Dolomites = Dolomiti | 63 | 46 30N | 11 40 E |
| Dolomiti | 63 | 46 30N | 11 40 E |
| Dolores, Argent. | 172 | 36 20 S | 57 40W |
| Dolores, Mexico | 164 | 28 53N | 108 27W |
| Dolores, Uruguay | 172 | 33 34 S | 58 15W |
| Dolores, Colo., U.S.A. | 161 | 37 30N | 108 30W |
| Dolores, Tex., U.S.A. | 159 | 27 40N | 99 38W |
| Dolores, R. | 159 | 38 30N | 108 55W |
| Đolovo | 66 | 44 55N | 20 52 E |
| Dolphin and Union Str. | 148 | 69 5N | 114 45W |
| Dolphin C. | 176 | 51 10 S | 50 0W |
| Dolphinton | 35 | 55 42N | 3 28W |
| Dolsk | 54 | 51 59N | 17 3 E |
| Dolton | 30 | 50 53N | 4 2W |
| Dolwyddelan | 31 | 53 3N | 3 53W |
| Dom | 50 | 46 6N | 7 50 E |
| Dom Joaquim | 171 | 18 57 S | 43 16W |
| Dom Pedrito | 173 | 31 0 S | 54 40W |
| Dom Pedro | 170 | 4 29 S | 44 27W |
| Doma | 121 | 8 25N | 8 18 E |
| Domasi | 127 | 15 22 S | 35 10 E |
| Domat Ems | 51 | 46 50N | 9 27 E |
| Domazlice | 52 | 49 28N | 13 0 E |
| Dombarovskiy | 84 | 50 46N | 59 32 E |
| Dombås | 71 | 62 6N | 9 4 E |
| Dombasle | 43 | 49 8N | 5 10 E |
| Dombe Grande | 125 | 12 56 S | 13 8 E |
| Dombes | 45 | 46 3N | 5 0 E |
| Dombóvár | 53 | 46 21N | 18 9 E |
| Dombrád | 53 | 48 13N | 21 54 E |
| Domburg | 47 | 51 34N | 3 30 E |
| Domel, I = Letsok-aw-kyun | 101 | 11 30N | 98 25 E |
| Domérat | 44 | 46 21N | 2 32 E |
| Domett | 143 | 42 53 S | 173 12 E |
| Domeyko | 172 | 29 0 S | 71 30W |
| Domeyko, Cordillera | 172 | 24 30 S | 69 0W |
| Domfront | 42 | 48 37N | 0 40W |
| Dominador | 172 | 24 21 S | 69 20W |
| Dominica I. | 167 | 15 20N | 61 20W |
| Dominica Passage | 167 | 15 10N | 61 20W |
| Dominican Rep. ■ | 167 | 19 0N | 70 30W |
| Dömitz | 48 | 53 9N | 11 13 E |
| Domme | 44 | 44 48N | 1 12 E |
| Dommel, R. | 47 | 51 30N | 5 20 E |
| Dommerby | 73 | 56 33N | 9 5 E |
| Domo | 91 | 7 50N | 47 10 E |
| Domodossóla | 62 | 46 6N | 8 19 E |
| Dompaire | 43 | 48 14N | 6 14 E |
| Dompierre | 44 | 46 31N | 3 41 E |
| Dompin | 120 | 5 10N | 2 5W |
| Domrémy | 43 | 48 26N | 5 40 E |
| Domsjö | 72 | 63 16N | 18 41 E |
| Domville, Mt. | 139 | 28 1 S | 151 15 E |
| Domvraina | 69 | 38 15N | 22 59 E |
| Domzale | 63 | 46 9N | 3 6 E |
| Don Benito | 57 | 38 53N | 5 51W |
| Don, C. | 136 | 11 18 S | 131 46 E |
| Don Duong | 101 | 11 51N | 108 35 E |
| Don Martín, Presa de | 164 | 27 30N | 100 50W |
| Don Pedro Res. | 163 | 37 43N | 120 24W |
| Don, R., India | 97 | 16 40N | 75 55W |
| Don, R., Eng., U.K. | 33 | 53 41N | 0 51W |
| Don, R., Scot., U.K. | 37 | 57 14N | 2 5W |
| Don, R., U.S.S.R. | 83 | 49 35N | 41 40 E |
| Dona Ana | 127 | 17 25 S | 35 17 E |
| Donabate | 38 | 53 30N | 6 9W |
| Donadea | 38 | 53 20N | 6 45W |
| Donaghadee | 38 | 54 38N | 5 32W |
| Donaghmore, Ireland | 39 | 52 54N | 7 37W |
| Donaghmore, U.K. | 38 | 54 33N | 6 50W |
| Donald | 140 | 36 23 S | 143 0 E |
| Donalda | 152 | 52 35N | 112 34W |
| Donaldsonville | 159 | 30 2N | 91 50W |
| Donalsonville | 157 | 31 3N | 84 52W |
| Donard | 39 | 53 1N | 6 37W |
| Donau-Kanal | 49 | 49 1N | 11 27 E |
| Donau, R. | 53 | 47 55N | 17 20 E |
| Donaueschingen | 49 | 47 57N | 8 30 E |
| Donawitz | 52 | 47 22N | 15 4 E |
| Doncaster | 33 | 53 31N | 1 9W |
| Dondo, Angola | 74 | 9 45 S | 14 25 E |
| Dondo, Mozam. | 127 | 19 33 S | 34 46 E |
| Dondo, Teluk | 103 | 0 29N | 120 45 E |
| Dondra Head | 97 | 5 55N | 80 40 E |
| Donegal | 38 | 54 39N | 8 8W |
| Donegal □ | 38 | 54 53N | 8 0W |
| Donegal B. | 38 | 54 30N | 8 35W |
| Donegal Har. | 38 | 54 35N | 8 15W |
| Donegal Pt. | 39 | 52 44N | 9 38W |
| Doneraile | 39 | 52 13N | 8 37W |
| Donets, R. | 81 | 48 50N | 38 45 E |
| Donetsk | 82 | 48 0N | 37 45 E |
| Dong | 121 | 9 20N | 12 15 E |
| Dong Ba Thin | 101 | 12 8N | 109 13 E |
| Dong Dang | 100 | 21 4N | 106 57 E |
| Dong Giam | 100 | 19 15N | 105 31 E |
| Dong Ha | 100 | 16 49N | 107 8 E |
| Dong Hene | 100 | 16 16N | 105 18 E |
| Dong Hoi | 100 | 17 29N | 106 36 E |
| Dong Khe | 100 | 22 26N | 106 27 E |
| Dong Van | 100 | 23 16N | 105 22 E |
| Dong Xoai | 101 | 11 32N | 106 55 E |
| Donga | 121 | 7 45N | 10 2 E |
| Dongara | 137 | 29 14 S | 114 57 E |
| Dongargarh | 96 | 21 10N | 80 40 E |
| Dongen | 47 | 51 38N | 4 56 E |
| Donges | 42 | 47 18N | 2 4W |
| Donggala | 103 | 0 30 S | 119 40 E |
| Dongola | 122 | 19 9N | 30 22 E |
| Dongou | 124 | 2 0N | 18 5 E |
| Donhead | 28 | 51 1N | 2 8W |
| Donington | 33 | 52 54N | 0 12W |
| Donington, C. | 140 | 34 45 S | 136 0 E |
| Doniphan | 159 | 36 40N | 90 50W |
| Donja Stubica | 63 | 45 59N | 16 0 E |
| Donji Dušnik | 66 | 43 12N | 22 5 E |
| Donji Miholjac | 66 | 45 45N | 18 10 E |
| Donji Milanovac | 66 | 44 28N | 22 6 E |
| Donji Vakuf | 66 | 44 8N | 17 24 E |
| Donjon, Le | 44 | 46 22N | 3 48 E |
| Donna | 74 | 66 6N | 12 30 E |
| Donna | 74 | 66 6N | 12 30 E |
| Donna | 159 | 26 12N | 98 2W |
| Donna Nook, Pt. | 33 | 53 29N | 0 9 E |
| Donnaconna | 151 | 46 41N | 71 41W |
| Donnelly's Crossing | 142 | 35 42 S | 173 38 E |
| Donnybrook | 137 | 33 34 S | 115 48 E |
| Donor's Hills | 138 | 18 42 S | 140 33 E |
| Donoughmore | 39 | 52 0N | 8 42W |
| Donskoy | 81 | 53 55N | 38 15W |

Donya Lendava Duncan Town


| | | | |
|---|---|---|---|
| Donya Lendava | 63 | 46 35N | 16 25 E |
| Donzère | 45 | 44 28N | 4 43 E |
| Donzy | 43 | 47 20N | 3 6 E |
| Dooagh | 38 | 53 59N | 10 7W |
| Doochary | 38 | 54 54N | 8 10W |
| Doodlakine | 137 | 31 34 S | 117 51 E |
| Dooega Hd. | 38 | 53 54N | 10 3W |
| Doon L. | 34 | 55 15N | 4 22W |
| Doon, R. | 34 | 55 26N | 4 41W |
| Doonbeg | 39 | 52 44N | 9 31W |
| Doonbeg R. | 39 | 52 42N | 9 20W |
| Doorn | 46 | 52 2N | 5 20 E |
| Dor (Tantura) | 90 | 32 37N | 34 55 E |
| Dora Báltea, R. | 62 | 45 42N | 7 25 E |
| Dora, L. | 136 | 22 0 S | 123 0 E |
| Dora Riparia, R. | 62 | 45 7N | 7 24 E |
| Dorada, La | 174 | 5 30N | 74 40W |
| Dorading | 123 | 8 30N | 33 5 E |
| Doran L. | 153 | 61 13N | 108 6W |
| Dorat, Le | 44 | 46 14N | 1 5 E |
| Dörby | 73 | 56 20N | 16 12 E |
| Dorchester, Dorset, U.K. | 28 | 50 42N | 2 28W |
| Dorchester, Oxon., U.K. | 28 | 51 38N | 1 10W |
| Dorchester, C. | 149 | 65 27N | 77 27W |
| Dordogne □ | 44 | 45 5N | 0 40 E |
| Dordogne, R. | 44 | 45 2N | 0 36W |
| Dordrecht, Neth. | 46 | 51 48N | 4 39 E |
| Dordrecht, S. Afr. | 128 | 31 20 S | 27 3 E |
| Doré L. | 153 | 54 46N | 107 17W |
| Doré Lake | 153 | 54 38N | 107 54W |
| Dore, Mt. | 44 | 45 32N | 2 50 E |
| Dore, R. | 44 | 45 59N | 3 28 E |
| Dores | 37 | 57 22N | 4 20W |
| Dores do Indaiá | 171 | 19 27 S | 45 36W |
| Dorfen | 49 | 48 16N | 12 10 E |
| Dorgali | 64 | 40 18N | 9 35 E |
| Dori | 121 | 14 3N | 0 2W |
| Doring, R. | 128 | 32 30 S | 19 30 E |
| Dorion | 150 | 45 23N | 74 3W |
| Dorking | 29 | 51 14N | 0 20W |
| Dormaa-Ahenkro | 120 | 7 15N | 2 52W |
| Dormo, Ras | 123 | 13 14N | 42 35 E |
| Dornach | 50 | 47 29N | 7 37 E |
| Dornberg | 63 | 45 45N | 13 50 E |
| Dornbirn | 52 | 47 25N | 9 45 E |
| Dornes | 43 | 46 48N | 3 18 E |
| Dornie | 36 | 57 17N | 5 30W |
| Dornoch | 37 | 57 52N | 4 0W |
| Dornoch, Firth of | 37 | 57 52N | 4 0W |
| Dornogovi □ | 106 | 44 0N | 110 0 E |
| Doro | 121 | 16 9N | 0 51W |
| Dorog | 53 | 47 42N | 18 45 E |
| Dorogobuzh | 80 | 54 50N | 33 10 E |
| Dorohoi | 70 | 47 56N | 26 30 E |
| Döröö Nuur | 105 | 47 40N | 93 30 E |
| Dorre I. | 137 | 25 13 S | 113 12 E |
| Dorrigo | 141 | 30 20 S | 152 44 E |
| Dorris | 160 | 41 59N | 121 58W |
| Dorset □ | 28 | 50 48N | 2 25W |
| Dorsten | 48 | 51 40N | 6 55 E |
| Dorstone | 28 | 52 4N | 3 0W |
| Dortmund | 48 | 51 32N | 7 28 E |
| Dörtyol | 92 | 36 52N | 36 12 E |
| Dorum | 48 | 53 40N | 8 33 E |
| Doruma | 126 | 4 42N | 27 33 E |
| Dorya, W. | 123 | 5 15N | 41 30 E |
| Dos Bahías, C. | 176 | 44 58 S | 65 32W |
| Dos Cabezas | 161 | 32 1N | 109 37W |
| Dos Hermanas | 57 | 37 16N | 5 55W |
| Dos Palos | 163 | 36 59N | 120 37W |
| Dosara | 121 | 12 20N | 6 5 E |
| Doshi | 93 | 35 35N | 68 50 E |
| Dosso | 121 | 13 0N | 3 13 E |
| Döstrup | 73 | 56 41N | 9 42 E |
| Dot | 152 | 50 12N | 121 25W |
| Dothan | 157 | 31 10N | 85 25W |
| Dottignies | 47 | 50 44N | 3 19 E |
| Dotty, gasfield | 19 | 53 3N | 1 48 E |
| Douai | 43 | 50 21N | 3 4 E |
| Douala | 121 | 4 0N | 9 45 E |
| Douarnenez | 42 | 48 6N | 4 21W |
| Double Island Pt. | 139 | 25 56 S | 153 11 E |
| Doubrava, R. | 52 | 49 40N | 15 30 E |
| Doubs □ | 43 | 47 10N | 6 20 E |
| Doubs, R. | 43 | 46 53N | 5 1 E |
| Doubtful B. | 137 | 34 15 S | 119 28 E |
| Doubtful Sd. | 143 | 45 20 S | 166 49 E |
| Doubtless B. | 142 | 34 55 S | 173 26 E |
| Doucet | 150 | 48 15N | 76 35W |
| Doudeville | 42 | 49 43N | 0 47 E |
| Doué | 42 | 47 11N | 0 20W |
| Douentza | 120 | 14 58N | 2 48W |
| Douglas, S. Afr. | 128 | 29 4 S | 23 46 E |
| Douglas, U.K. | 32 | 54 9N | 4 29W |
| Douglas, U.K. | 35 | 55 33N | 3 50W |
| Douglas, Alaska, U.S.A. | 147 | 58 23N | 134 32W |
| Douglas, Ariz., U.S.A. | 161 | 31 21N | 109 30W |
| Douglas, Ga., U.S.A. | 157 | 31 32N | 82 52W |
| Douglas, Wyo., U.S.A. | 158 | 42 45N | 105 20W |
| Douglas Hd. | 32 | 54 9N | 4 28W |
| Douglastown | 151 | 48 46N | 64 24W |
| Douglasville | 157 | 33 46N | 84 43W |
| Douirat | 118 | 33 2N | 4 11W |
| Doukáton, Ákra | 69 | 38 34N | 20 30 E |
| Doulevant | 43 | 48 22N | 4 53 E |
| Doullens | 43 | 50 10N | 2 20 E |
| Doulus Hd. | 39 | 51 57N | 10 19W |
| Doumé | 124 | 4 15N | 13 25 E |
| Douna | 120 | 12 40N | 6 0W |
| Dounby | 37 | 59 4N | 3 13W |
| Doune | 35 | 56 12N | 4 3W |
| Dounreay | 37 | 58 40N | 3 28W |
| Dour | 47 | 50 24N | 3 46 E |
| Dourada, Serra | 171 | 13 10 S | 48 45W |
| Dourados | 173 | 22 9 S | 54 50W |
| Dourados, R. | 173 | 21 58 S | 54 18W |
| Dourdan | 43 | 48 30N | 2 0 E |
| Douro Litoral □ | 55 | 41 10N | 8 20W |
| Douro, R. | 56 | 41 1N | 8 16W |
| Douŭzeci Si Trei August | 70 | 43 50N | 28 40 E |
| Douvaine | 45 | 46 19N | 6 16 E |
| Douz | 119 | 33 25N | 9 0 E |
| Dove | 32 | 52 51N | 1 36W |
| Dove Brook | 151 | 53 40N | 57 40W |
| Dove Creek | 161 | 37 53N | 108 59W |
| Dove Dale | 33 | 53 10N | 1 47W |
| Dove, R. | 33 | 54 20N | 0 55W |
| Dover, Austral. | 138 | 43 18 S | 147 2 E |
| Dover, U.K. | 29 | 51 7N | 1 19 E |
| Dover, Del., U.S.A. | 162 | 39 10N | 75 31W |
| Dover, N.H., U.S.A. | 162 | 43 5N | 70 51W |
| Dover, N.J., U.S.A. | 162 | 40 53N | 74 34W |
| Dover, Ohio, U.S.A. | 156 | 40 32N | 81 30W |
| Dover-Foxcroft | 151 | 45 14N | 69 14W |
| Dover Plains | 162 | 41 43N | 73 35W |
| Dover, Pt. | 137 | 32 32 S | 125 32 E |
| Dover, Str. of | 16 | 51 0N | 1 30 E |
| Doveridge | 32 | 52 54N | 1 49 E |
| Dovey, R. | 31 | 52 32N | 4 0W |
| Dovre | 71 | 62 0N | 9 15 E |
| Dovrefjell | 71 | 62 15N | 9 33 E |
| Dowa | 127 | 13 38 S | 33 58 E |
| Dowagiac | 156 | 42 0N | 86 8W |
| Dowlatabad | 93 | 28 20N | 50 40 E |
| Down □ | 38 | 54 20N | 5 50W |
| Down, Co. | 38 | 54 20N | 6 0W |
| Downey | 160 | 42 29N | 112 3W |
| Downham | 29 | 52 26N | 0 15 E |
| Downham Market | 29 | 52 36N | 0 22 E |
| Downhill | 38 | 55 10N | 6 48W |
| Downieville | 160 | 39 34N | 120 50W |
| Downpatrick | 38 | 54 20N | 5 43W |
| Downpatrick Hd. | 38 | 54 20N | 9 21W |
| Downs Division | 139 | 27 10 S | 150 44 E |
| Downs, The | 38 | 53 30N | 7 15W |
| Downsville | 162 | 42 5N | 74 60W |
| Downton | 28 | 51 0N | 1 44W |
| Dowra | 38 | 54 11N | 8 2W |
| Doylestown | 162 | 40 21N | 75 10W |
| Doyung | 99 | 33 40N | 99 25 E |
| Dra, Cap | 118 | 28 58N | 11 0W |
| Draa, O. | 118 | 30 29N | 6 1W |
| Drachten | 46 | 53 7N | 6 5 E |
| Drăgăneşti | 70 | 44 9N | 24 32 E |
| Drăgăneşti-Viaşca | 70 | 44 5N | 25 33 E |
| Dragaš | 66 | 42 5N | 20 35 E |
| Drăgăsani | 70 | 44 39N | 24 17 E |
| Dragina | 66 | 44 30N | 19 25 E |
| Dragocvet | 66 | 44 0N | 21 15 E |
| Dragonera, I. | 58 | 39 35N | 2 19 E |
| Dragon's Mouth | 174 | 11 0N | 61 50W |
| Dragovistica, (Berivol) | 66 | 42 22N | 22 39 E |
| Draguignan | 45 | 43 30N | 6 27 E |
| Drain | 160 | 43 45N | 123 17W |
| Drake, Austral. | 139 | 28 55 S | 152 25 E |
| Drake, U.S.A. | 158 | 47 56N | 100 31W |
| Drake Passage | 13 | 58 0 S | 68 0W |
| Drakensberg | 129 | 31 0 S | 25 0 E |
| Dráma | 68 | 41 9N | 24 10 E |
| Dráma □ | 68 | 41 10N | 24 0 E |
| Drammen | 71 | 59 42N | 10 12 E |
| Drangajökull | 74 | 66 9N | 22 15W |
| Drangan | 39 | 52 32N | 7 36W |
| Drangedal | 71 | 59 6N | 9 3 E |
| Dranov, Ostrov | 70 | 44 55N | 29 30 E |
| Draperstown | 38 | 54 48N | 6 47 E |
| Dras | 95 | 34 25N | 75 48 E |
| Drau, R. | 52 | 47 46N | 13 33 E |
| Drava, R. | 66 | 45 50N | 18 0W |
| Draveil | 43 | 48 41N | 2 25 E |
| Dravograd | 63 | 46 36N | 15 5 E |
| Drawa, R. | 54 | 53 6N | 15 56 E |
| Drawno | 54 | 53 13N | 15 46 E |
| Drawsko Pom | 54 | 53 35N | 15 50 E |
| Drayton Valley | 152 | 53 25N | 114 58W |
| Dreghorn | 34 | 55 36N | 4 30W |
| Dreibergen | 46 | 52 3N | 5 17 E |
| Drejö | 73 | 54 58N | 10 25 E |
| Dren | 66 | 43 8N | 20 44 E |
| Drenagh | 38 | 55 3N | 6 55W |
| Drenthe □ | 54 | 52 52N | 6 40 E |
| Drentsche Hoofdvaart | 46 | 52 39N | 6 4 E |
| Dresden | 48 | 51 2N | 13 45 E |
| Dresden □ | 48 | 51 12N | 14 0 E |
| Dreumel | 47 | 51 51N | 5 26 E |
| Dreux | 42 | 48 44N | 1 23 E |
| Drezdenko | 54 | 52 50N | 15 49 E |
| Driel | 46 | 51 57N | 5 49 E |
| Driffield | 33 | 54 0N | 0 25W |
| Driftwood | 150 | 49 8N | 81 23 E |
| Drigana | 119 | 20 51N | 12 17 E |
| Driggs | 160 | 43 50N | 111 8W |
| Drimnin | 36 | 56 36N | 6 0W |
| Drimoleague | 39 | 51 40N | 9 15W |
| Drin-i-zi, R. | 68 | 41 37N | 20 28 E |
| Drina, R. | 66 | 44 30N | 19 10 E |
| Drincea, R. | 70 | 44 20N | 22 55 E |
| Drînceni | 70 | 46 49N | 28 10 E |
| Drini, R. | 68 | 42 20N | 20 0 E |
| Drinjača, R. | 66 | 44 20N | 19 0 E |
| Driva | 71 | 62 33N | 9 38 E |
| Driva, R. | 71 | 62 34N | 9 33 E |
| Drivstua | 71 | 62 26N | 9 37 E |
| Drniš | 63 | 43 51N | 16 10 E |
| Drøbak | 71 | 59 39N | 10 39 E |
| Dröbak | 75 | 59 39N | 10 48 E |
| Drobbakk | 71 | 59 39N | 10 39 E |
| Drobin | 54 | 52 42N | 19 58 E |
| Drogheda | 38 | 53 45N | 6 20W |
| Drogichin | 80 | 52 15N | 25 8 E |
| Drogobych | 80 | 49 20N | 23 30 E |
| Droichead Nua | 39 | 53 11N | 6 50W |
| Droitwich | 28 | 52 16N | 2 10W |
| Dromahair | 38 | 54 13N | 8 18W |
| Dromara | 38 | 54 21N | 6 1W |
| Dromard | 38 | 54 14N | 8 40W |
| Drôme □ | 45 | 44 38N | 5 15 E |
| Drôme, R. | 45 | 44 46N | 4 46 E |
| Dromedary, C. | 141 | 36 17 S | 150 10 E |
| Dromiskin | 38 | 53 56N | 6 25W |
| Dromod | 38 | 53 52N | 7 55W |
| Dromore, Down, U.K. | 38 | 54 24N | 6 10W |
| Dromore, Tyrone, U.K. | 38 | 54 31N | 7 28W |
| Dromore West | 38 | 54 15N | 8 50W |
| Dronero | 62 | 44 29N | 7 22 E |
| Dronfield, Austral. | 138 | 21 12 S | 140 3 E |
| Dronfield, U.K. | 33 | 53 18N | 1 29W |
| Dronninglund | 73 | 57 10N | 10 19 E |
| Dronrijp | 46 | 53 11N | 5 39 E |
| Drosendorf | 52 | 48 52N | 15 37 E |
| Drouin | 141 | 38 10 S | 145 53 E |
| Drouzhba | 67 | 43 22N | 28 0 E |
| Drum | 38 | 54 6N | 7 9W |
| Drumbeg, N. Ire., U.K. | 38 | 54 33N | 6 0W |
| Drumbeg, Scot., U.K. | 36 | 58 15N | 5 12W |
| Drumcard | 38 | 54 14N | 7 42W |
| Drumcliffe | 38 | 54 20N | 8 30W |
| Drumcondra | 38 | 53 50N | 6 40W |
| Drumheller | 152 | 51 25N | 112 40W |
| Drumjohn | 34 | 55 14N | 4 15W |
| Drumkeerin | 38 | 54 10N | 8 8W |
| Drumlish | 38 | 53 50N | 7 47W |
| Drummond | 160 | 46 46N | 113 4W |
| Drummond I. | 150 | 46 0N | 83 40W |
| Drummond Pt. | 139 | 34 9 S | 135 16 E |
| Drummond Ra. | 138 | 23 45 S | 147 10 E |
| Drummondville | 150 | 45 55N | 72 25W |
| Drummore | 34 | 54 41N | 4 53W |
| Drumquin | 38 | 54 38N | 7 30W |
| Drumright | 159 | 35 59N | 96 38W |
| Drumshanbo | 38 | 54 2N | 8 4W |
| Drumsna | 38 | 53 57N | 8 0W |
| Drunen | 47 | 51 41N | 5 8 E |
| Druridge B. | 35 | 55 16N | 1 32W |
| Druskinankaj | 80 | 54 3N | 23 58 E |
| Drut, R. | 80 | 52 32N | 30 0 E |
| Druten | 46 | 51 53N | 5 36 E |
| Druya | 80 | 55 45N | 27 15 E |
| Druzhina | 77 | 68 14N | 145 18 E |
| Drvar | 63 | 44 21N | 16 2 E |
| Drvenik | 63 | 43 27N | 16 3 E |
| Dry Tortugas | 166 | 24 38N | 82 55W |
| Dryanovo | 67 | 42 59N | 25 28 E |
| Dryden, Can. | 153 | 49 50N | 92 50W |
| Dryden, N.Y., U.S.A. | 162 | 42 30N | 76 18W |
| Dryden, Tex., U.S.A. | 159 | 30 3N | 102 3W |
| Drygalski I. | 13 | 66 0 S | 92 0 E |
| Drygarn Fawr | 31 | 52 13N | 3 39W |
| Drymen | 70 | 56 4N | 4 28W |
| Drynoch | 36 | 57 17N | 6 18W |
| Drysdale I. | 138 | 11 41 S | 136 0 E |
| Drysdale, R. | 136 | 13 59 S | 126 51 E |
| Dschang | 121 | 5 32N | 10 3 E |
| Du | 121 | 10 26N | 1 34W |
| Du Bois | 156 | 41 8N | 78 46W |
| Du Quoin | 158 | 38 0N | 89 10W |
| Duanesburg | 162 | 42 45N | 74 11W |
| Duaringa | 138 | 23 42 S | 149 42 E |
| Duba | 92 | 27 10N | 35 40 E |
| Dubai = Dubayy | 93 | 24 10N | 55 20 E |
| Dubawnt, L. | 153 | 63 4N | 101 42W |
| Dubawnt, R. | 153 | 64 33N | 100 6W |
| Dubbayy | 93 | 24 10N | 55 20 E |
| Dubbeldam | 46 | 51 47N | 4 43 E |
| Dubbo | 141 | 32 11 S | 148 35 E |
| Dubele | 126 | 2 56N | 29 35 E |
| Dübendorf | 51 | 47 24N | 8 37 E |
| Dubenskiy | 84 | 51 27N | 56 38 E |
| Dubh Artach | 34 | 56 8N | 6 40W |
| Dubica | 63 | 45 17N | 16 48 E |
| Dublin, Ireland | 38 | 53 20N | 6 18W |
| Dublin, Ga., U.S.A. | 157 | 32 30N | 83 0W |
| Dublin, Tex., U.S.A. | 159 | 32 0N | 98 20W |
| Dublin □ | 38 | 53 24N | 6 20W |
| Dublin, B. | 39 | 53 24N | 6 20W |
| Dubna | 81 | 54 8N | 36 52 E |
| Dubno | 80 | 50 25N | 25 45 E |
| Dubois | 160 | 44 7N | 112 9W |
| Dubossary | 82 | 47 15N | 29 10 E |
| Dubossasy Vdkhr. | 82 | 47 30N | 29 0 E |
| Dubovka | 83 | 49 5N | 44 50 E |
| Dubovskoye | 83 | 47 28N | 42 40 E |
| Dubrajpur | 95 | 23 48N | 87 25 E |
| Dubrékah | 120 | 9 46N | 13 31W |
| Dubrovitsa | 80 | 51 31N | 26 35 E |
| Dubrovnik | 66 | 42 39N | 18 6 E |
| Dubrovskoye | 77 | 58 55N | 111 0 E |
| Dubuque | 158 | 42 30N | 90 41W |
| Duchesne | 160 | 40 14N | 110 22W |
| Duchess | 138 | 21 20 S | 139 50 E |
| Ducie I. | 131 | 24 47 S | 124 40W |
| Duck Cr., N.S.W., Austral. | 139 | 31 4 S | 147 6 E |
| Duck Cr., W. Australia, Austral. | 136 | 22 37 S | 116 53 E |
| Duck Lake | 153 | 52 50N | 106 16W |
| Duck, Mt. | 153 | 51 27N | 100 35W |
| Duck Mt. Prov. Parks | 153 | 51 45N | 101 0W |
| Duckwall Mtn. | 163 | 37 58N | 120 7W |
| Duddington | 29 | 52 36N | 0 32W |
| Duddon R. | 32 | 54 12N | 3 15W |
| Düdelange | 47 | 49 29N | 6 5 E |
| Duderstadt | 48 | 51 30N | 10 15 E |
| Dudhi | 99 | 24 15N | 83 10 E |
| Dudhnai | 98 | 25 59N | 90 47 E |
| Düdingen | 50 | 46 52N | 7 12 E |
| Dudinka | 77 | 69 30N | 86 0 E |
| Dudley | 28 | 52 30N | 2 5W |
| Dudna, R. | 96 | 19 36N | 76 20 E |
| Dueñas | 56 | 41 52N | 4 33W |
| Duéni | 70 | 44 51N | 28 10 E |
| Dueodde | 73 | 54 59N | 15 4 E |
| Dueré | 171 | 11 20 S | 49 17W |
| Duero, R. | 56 | 41 37N | 4 25W |
| Duff Is. | 142 | 9 0 S | 167 0 E |
| Duffel | 47 | 51 6N | 4 30 E |
| Duffield | 33 | 52 59N | 1 30W |
| Dufftown | 37 | 57 26N | 3 9W |
| Dufourspitz | 50 | 45 56N | 7 52 E |
| Dugi, I. | 63 | 44 0N | 15 0 E |
| Dugo Selo | 63 | 45 51N | 16 18 E |
| Duhak | 93 | 33 20N | 57 30 E |
| Duifken Pt. | 138 | 12 33 S | 141 38 E |
| Duisburg | 48 | 51 27N | 6 42 E |
| Duitama | 174 | 5 50N | 73 2W |
| Duiveland | 47 | 51 38N | 4 0 E |
| Duiwelskloof | 129 | 23 42 S | 30 10 E |
| Dukana | 126 | 3 59N | 37 20 E |
| Dukati | 68 | 40 16N | 19 32 E |
| Duke I. | 152 | 54 50N | 131 20W |
| Dukhan | 93 | 25 25N | 50 50 E |
| Dukhovshchina | 80 | 55 15N | 32 27 E |
| Duki | 93 | 30 14N | 68 25 E |
| Dukla | 54 | 49 30N | 21 35 E |
| Duku, North-Eastern, Nigeria | 121 | 10 43N | 10 43 E |
| Duku, North-Western, Nigeria | 121 | 11 11N | 4 55 E |
| Dulas B. | 31 | 53 22N | 4 16W |
| Dulawan | 103 | 7 5N | 124 20 E |
| Dulce, Golfo | 166 | 8 40N | 83 20W |
| Dulce, R. | 172 | 29 30 S | 63 0W |
| Duleek | 38 | 53 40N | 6 24W |
| Dŭlgopol | 67 | 43 3N | 27 22 E |
| Dullewala | 94 | 31 50N | 71 25 E |
| Dülmen | 48 | 51 49N | 7 18 E |
| Dulnain Bridge | 37 | 57 19N | 3 40W |
| Dulovo | 67 | 43 48N | 27 9 E |
| Dululu | 138 | 23 48 S | 150 15 E |
| Duluth | 158 | 46 48N | 92 10W |
| Dulverton | 28 | 51 2N | 3 33W |
| Dum Dum | 95 | 22 39N | 88 26 E |
| Dum Duma | 99 | 27 40N | 95 40 E |
| Dumaguete | 103 | 9 17N | 123 15 E |
| Dumai | 102 | 1 35N | 101 20 E |
| Dumaran I. | 103 | 10 33N | 119 50 E |
| Dumaring | 103 | 1 46N | 118 10 E |
| Dumas, Ark., U.S.A. | 159 | 33 52N | 91 30W |
| Dumas, Okla., U.S.A. | 159 | 35 50N | 101 58W |
| Dūmat al Jandal | 92 | 29 55N | 39 40 E |
| Dumba I. | 71 | 61 43N | 4 50 E |
| Dumbarton | 34 | 55 58N | 4 35W |
| Dumbleyung | 137 | 33 17 S | 117 42 E |
| Dumbrŭveni | 70 | 46 14N | 24 34 E |
| Dumfries | 35 | 55 4N | 3 37W |
| Dumfries & Galloway □ | 35 | 54 30N | 4 0W |
| Dumfries (□) | 26 | 55 0N | 3 30W |
| Dŭmienesti | 70 | 46 44N | 27 1 E |
| Dumka | 95 | 24 0N | 87 22 E |
| Dumoine L. | 150 | 46 55N | 77 55W |
| Dumoine, R. | 150 | 46 13N | 77 51W |
| Dumraon | 95 | 25 33N | 84 8 E |
| Dumyât | 122 | 31 24N | 31 48 E |
| Dumyât, Masabb | 122 | 31 28N | 32 0 E |
| Dun Laoghaire, (Dunleary) | 39 | 53 17N | 6 9W |
| Dun-le-Palestel | 44 | 46 18N | 1 39 E |
| Dun-sur-Auron | 43 | 46 53N | 2 33 E |
| Duna, R. | 53 | 45 51N | 18 48 E |
| Dunaff Hd. | 38 | 55 18N | 7 30W |
| Dunaföldvár | 53 | 46 50N | 18 57 E |
| Dunai, R. | 53 | 47 50N | 18 52 E |
| Dunaj, R. | 67 | 45 17N | 29 32 E |
| Dunajec, R. | 54 | 50 12N | 20 52 E |
| Dunajska Streda | 53 | 48 0N | 17 37 E |
| Dunamanagh | 38 | 54 53N | 7 20W |
| Dunans | 34 | 56 4N | 5 9W |
| Dunany Pt. | 38 | 53 51N | 6 15W |
| Dunapatai | 53 | 46 39N | 19 4 E |
| Dunaszekcsö | 53 | 46 22N | 18 45 E |
| Dunaújváros | 53 | 47 0N | 18 57 E |
| Dunav, R. | 66 | 45 0N | 20 21 E |
| Dunavtsi | 66 | 43 57N | 22 53 E |
| Dunback | 143 | 45 23 S | 170 36 E |
| Dunbar, Austral. | 138 | 16 0 S | 142 22 E |
| Dunbar, U.K. | 35 | 56 0N | 2 32W |
| Dunbarton (□) | 26 | 56 4N | 4 42W |
| Dunbeath | 37 | 58 15N | 3 25W |
| Dunblane | 35 | 56 10N | 3 58W |
| Dunboyne | 38 | 53 25N | 6 30W |
| Duncan, Can. | 152 | 48 45N | 123 40W |
| Duncan, Ariz., U.S.A. | 161 | 32 46N | 109 6W |
| Duncan, Okla., U.S.A. | 159 | 34 25N | 98 0W |
| Duncan L. | 152 | 62 51N | 113 58W |
| Duncan, L., Brit. Col., Can. | 150 | 50 20N | 117 0W |
| Duncan, L., Qué., Can. | 152 | 53 29N | 77 58W |
| Duncan Pass. | 101 | 11 0N | 92 30 E |
| Duncan Town | 166 | 22 15N | 75 45W |

**Duncansby** **Ecoporanga**


Duncansby 37 58 37N 3 3W
Duncansby Head 37 58 39N 3 0W
Dunchurch 28 52 21N 1 19W
Duncormick 39 53 14N 6 40W
Dundalk, Ireland 38 53 55N 6 45W
Dundalk, U.S.A. 162 39 15N 76 31W
Dundalk, B. 38 53 55N 6 15W
Dundas 150 43 17N 79 59W
Dundas I. 152 54 30N 130 50W
Dundas, L. 137 32 35 S 121 50 E
Dundas Str. 136 11 15 S 131 35 E
Dundee, S. Afr. 129 28 11 S 30 15 E
Dundee, U.K. 35 56 29N 3 0W
Dundee, U.S.A. 162 42 32N 76 59W
Dundgovi □ 106 45 10N 106 0 E
Dundo 124 7 23 S 20 48 E
Dundonald 38 54 37N 5 50W
Dundoo 139 27 40 S 144 37 E
Dundrennan 35 54 49N 3 56W
Dundrum, Ireland 39 53 17N 6 15W
Dundrum, U.K. 38 54 17N 5 50W
Dundwara 95 27 48N 79 9 E
Dunedin, N.Z. 143 45 50 S 170 33 E
Dunedin, U.S.A. 157 28 1N 82 45W
Dunedin, R. 152 59 30N 124 5W
Dunfanaghy 38 55 10N 7 59W
Dunfermline 35 56 5N 3 28W
Dungannon 38 54 30N 6 47W
Dungannon □ 38 54 30N 6 55W
Dungarpur 94 23 52N 73 45 E
Dungarvan 39 52 6N 7 40W
Dungarvan Harb. 39 52 5N 7 35W
Dungas 121 13 4N 9 20 E
Dungavel 35 55 37N 4 7W
Dungbura La 99 34 41N 93 18 E
Dungeness 29 50 54N 0 59 E
Dungiven 38 54 55N 6 56W
Dunglow 38 54 57N 8 20W
Dungo, L. do 128 17 15 S 19 0 E
Dungog 141 32 22 S 151 40 E
Dungourney 39 51 58N 8 5W
Dungu 124 2 32N 28 22 E
Dungunâb 122 21 10N 37 9 E
Dungunâb, Khalîg 122 21 5N 37 12 E
Dunhinda Falls 97 7 5N 81 6 E
Dunières 45 45 13N 4 20 E
Dunk I. 138 17 59 S 146 14 E
Dunkeld, Austral. 140 37 40 S 142 22 E
Dunkeld, U.K. 37 56 34N 3 36W
Dunkerque 43 51 2N 2 20 E
Dunkery Beacon 28 51 15N 3 37W
Dunkineely 38 54 38N 8 22W
Dunkirk 156 42 30N 79 18W
Dunkirk = Dunkerque 43 51 2N 2 20 E
Dunkuj 123 11 15N 33 0 E
Dunkur 123 11 58N 35 58 E
Dunkwa, Central, Ghana 120 6 0N 1 47W
Dunkwa, Central, Ghana 121 5 30N 1 0W
Dunlap 158 41 50N 95 30W
Dunlavin 39 53 3N 6 40W
Dunleary = Dun Laoghaire 39 53 17N 6 8W
Dunleer 38 53 50N 6 23W
Dunlin, oilfield 19 61 12N 1 40 E
Dunloe, Gap of 39 52 2N 9 40W
Dunlop 34 55 43N 4 32W
Dunloy 38 55 1N 6 25W
Dunmanus B. 39 51 31N 9 50W
Dunmanway 39 51 43N 9 8W
Dunmara 138 16 42 S 133 25 E
Dunmod 105 47 45N 106 58 E
Dunmore, Ireland 38 53 37N 8 44W
Dunmore, U.S.A. 162 41 27N 75 38W
Dunmore East 39 52 9N 7 0W
Dunmore Town 166 25 30N 76 39W
Dunmurry 38 54 33N 6 0W
Dunn 157 35 18N 78 36W
Dunnellon 157 29 4N 82 28W
Dunnet 37 58 37N 3 20W
Dunnet B. 37 58 37N 3 23W
Dunnet Hd. 37 58 38N 3 22W
Dunning, U.K. 35 56 18N 3 37W
Dunning, U.S.A. 158 41 52N 100 4W
Dunolly 140 36 51 S 143 44 E
Dunoon 34 55 57N 4 56W
Dunqul 122 23 40N 31 10 E
Duns 35 55 47N 2 20W
Dunscore 35 55 8N 3 48W
Dunseith 158 48 49N 100 2W
Dunsford 30 50 41N 3 40W
Dunshaughlin 38 53 31N 6 32W
Dunsmuir 160 41 0N 122 10W
Dunstable 29 51 53N 0 31W
Dunstan Mts. 143 44 53 S 169 35 E
Dunster, Can. 152 53 8N 119 50W
Dunster, U.K. 28 51 11N 3 28W
Dunston 28 52 46N 2 7W
Duntelchaig, L. 37 57 20N 4 18W
Dunton Green 29 51 17N 0 11 E
Duntroon 143 44 51 S 170 40 E
Dunûrea, R. 70 45 0N 29 40 E
Dunvegan 36 57 26N 6 35W
Dunvegan Hd. 36 57 30N 6 42W
Dunvegan L. 153 60 8N 107 10W
Duong Dong 101 10 13N 103 58 E
Dupree 158 45 4N 101 35W
Dupuyer 160 48 11N 112 31W
Duque de Caxias 173 22 45 S 43 19W
Dura 90 31 31N 35 1 E
Durack 136 15 33 S 127 52 E
Durack Ra. 136 16 50 S 127 40 E
Durance, R. 45 43 55N 4 45 E
Durand 156 42 54N 83 58W
Durango, Mexico 164 24 3N 104 39W
Durango, Spain 58 43 13N 2 40W
Durango, U.S.A. 161 37 10N 107 50W
Durango □ 164 25 0N 105 0W
Duranillin 137 33 30 S 116 45 E
Durant 159 34 0N 96 25W
Duratón, R. 56 41 27N 4 0W
Durazno 172 33 25 S 56 38W
Durazzo = Durrësi 68 41 19N 19 28 E
Durban, France 44 43 0N 2 49W
Durban, S. Afr. 129 29 49 S 31 1 E
Dúrcal 57 37 0N 3 34W
Đurdevac 66 46 2N 17 3 E
Düren 48 50 48N 6 30 E
Durg 96 21 15N 81 22 E
Durgapur 95 23 30N 87 9 E
Durham, Can. 150 44 10N 80 49W
Durham, U.K. 33 54 47N 1 34W
Durham, N.C., U.S.A. 157 36 0N 78 55W
Durham, N.H., U.S.A. 162 43 8N 70 56W
Durham □ 32 54 42N 1 45W
Durham Downs 139 26 6 S 149 3 E
Durlstone Hd. 28 50 35N 1 58W
Durmitor Mt. 66 43 18N 19 0 E
Dŭrmŭneşti 70 46 21N 26 33 E
Durness 37 58 34N 4 45W
Durness, Kyle of 37 58 35N 4 55W
Durrandella 138 24 3 S 146 35 E
Durrësi 68 41 19N 19 28 E
Durrie 138 25 40 S 140 15 E
Durrington 28 51 12N 1 47W
Durrow 39 53 20N 7 31W
Durrus 39 51 37N 9 32W
Dursey Hd. 39 51 34N 10 41W
Dursey I. 39 51 36N 10 12W
Dursley 28 51 41N 2 21W
Durtal 42 47 40N 0 18W
Duru 126 4 20N 28 50 E
Durup 73 56 45N 8 57 E
D'Urville Island 143 40 50 S 173 55 E
Duryea 162 41 20N 75 45W
Dusa Mareb 91 5 40N 46 33 E
Dûsh 122 24 35N 30 41 E
Dushak 76 37 20N 60 10 E
Dushanbe 85 38 33N 68 48 E
Dusheti 83 42 0N 44 55 E
Dushore 162 41 31N 76 24W
Dusky Sd. 143 45 47 S 166 30 E
Dussejour, C. 136 14 45 S 128 13 E
Düsseldorf 48 51 15N 6 46 E
Dussen 46 51 44N 4 59 E
Duszniki Zdrój 54 51 26N 16 22 E
Dutch Harbour 147 53 54N 166 35W
Dutlhe 128 23 58 S 23 46 E
Dutsan Wai 121 10 50N 8 10 E
Dutton, R. 138 20 44 S 143 10 E
Duvan 84 55 42N 57 54 E
Duved 72 63 24N 12 55 E
Duvno 66 43 42N 17 13 E
Duwadami 92 24 35N 44 15 E
Duzdab = Zāhedān 93 29 30N 60 50 E
Dve Mogili 67 43 47N 25 55 E
Dvina, Sev. 78 56 30N 24 0 E
Dvina, Zap. 80 61 40N 45 30 E
Dvinsk = Daugavpils 80 55 33N 26 32 E
Dvinskaya Guba 78 65 0N 39 0 E
Dvor 63 45 4N 16 22 E
Dvorce 53 49 50N 17 34 E
Dvur Králové 52 50 27N 15 50 E
Dwarka 94 22 18N 69 8 E
Dwellingup 137 32 43 S 116 4 E
Dwight 156 41 5N 88 25W
Dyakovskoya 81 60 5N 41 12 E
Dyatkovo 80 53 48N 34 27 E
Dyaul, I. 138 3 0 S 150 55 E
Dyce 37 57 12N 2 11W
Dyer 163 37 40N 118 5W
Dyer, C. 149 67 0N 61 0W
Dyerbeldzhin 85 41 13N 74 54 E
Dyersburg 159 36 2N 89 20W
Dyfed □ 31 52 0N 4 30W
Dyje, R. 53 48 50N 16 45 E
Dyke Acland Bay 138 8 45 S 148 45 E
Dykehead 37 56 43N 3 0W
Dyle, R. 47 50 58N 4 41 E
Dymchurch 29 51 2N 1 0 E
Dymock 28 51 58N 2 27W
Dynevor Downs 139 28 10 S 144 20 E
Dynów 54 49 50N 22 11 E
Dypvag 71 79 40N 9 8 E
Dyrnes 71 63 25N 7 52 E
Dysart, Can. 153 50 57N 104 2W
Dysart, U.K. 35 56 8N 3 8W
Dysjön 72 62 38N 15 31 E
Dyulgeri 67 42 18N 27 23 E
Dyurtyuli 84 55 9N 54 4 E
Dzambeyty 83 50 15N 52 30 E
Dzaudzhikau = Ordzhonikidze 83 43 0N 44 35 E
Dzerzhinsk 80 53 40N 27 7 E
Dzhailma 76 51 30N 61 50 E
Dzhalal-Abad 84 40 56N 73 0 E
Dzhalinda 77 53 40N 124 0 E
Dzhambeyty 84 50 16N 52 35 E
Dzhambul 85 42 54N 71 22 E
Dzhambul, Gora 85 44 54N 73 0 E
Dzhankoi 82 45 40N 34 30 E
Dzhanybek 83 49 25N 46 50 E
Dzhardzhan 77 68 10N 123 5 E
Dzharkurgan 85 37 31N 67 25 E
Dzhelinde 77 70 0N 114 20 E
Dzherzhinsk 80 53 48N 27 19 E
Dzhetygara 84 52 11N 61 12 E
Dzhetym, Khrebet 85 41 30N 77 0 E
Dzhezkazgan 76 47 10N 67 40 E
Dzhizak 85 40 6N 67 50 E
Dzhugdzur, Khrebet 77 57 30N 138 0 E
Dzhuma 85 39 42N 66 40 E
Dzhumgoltau, Khrebet 85 42 15N 74 30 E
Dzhungarskiye Vorota 76 45 0N 82 0 E
Dzhvari 83 42 42N 42 4 E
Działdowo 54 53 15N 20 15 E
Działoszyce 54 50 22N 20 20 E
Działoszyn 54 51 6N 18 50 E
Dzibilchaltún 165 21 5N 89 36W
Dzierzgon 54 53 58N 19 20 E
Dzierzoniow 54 50 45N 16 39 E
Dzilam de Bravo 165 21 24N 88 53W
Dzioua 119 33 14N 5 14 E
Dziwnów 54 54 2N 14 45 E
Dzungaria 105 44 10N 88 0 E
Dzungarian Gates = Dzhungarskiye V. 105 45 0N 82 0 E


# E


Eabamet, L. 150 51 30N 87 46W
Eads 158 38 30N 102 46W
Eagle, Alaska, U.S.A. 147 64 44N 141 29W
Eagle, Colo., U.S.A. 160 39 45N 106 55W
Eagle Butt 158 45 1N 101 12W
Eagle Grove 158 42 37N 93 53W
Eagle L., Calif., U.S.A. 160 40 35N 120 50W
Eagle L., Me., U.S.A. 151 46 23N 69 22W
Eagle Lake 159 29 35N 96 21W
Eagle Nest 161 36 33N 105 13W
Eagle Pass 159 28 45N 100 35W
Eagle Pk. 163 38 10N 119 25W
Eagle Pt. 136 16 11 S 124 23 E
Eagle, R. 151 53 36N 57 26W
Eagle River 158 45 55N 89 17W
Eaglehawk 140 36 43 S 144 16 E
Eagles Mere 162 41 25N 76 33W
Eaglesfield 35 55 3N 3 12W
Eagleshan 34 55 44N 4 18W
Eakring 33 53 9N 0 59W
Ealing 29 51 30N 0 19W
Earaheedy 137 25 34 S 121 29 E
Earby 32 53 55N 2 8W
Eardisland 28 52 14N 2 50W
Eardisley 28 52 8N 3 0W
Earith 29 52 21N 0 1 E
Earl Grey 153 50 57N 104 43W
Earl Shilton 28 52 35N 1 20W
Earl Soham 29 52 14N 1 15 E
Earle 159 35 18N 90 26W
Earlimart 163 35 53N 119 16W
Earls Barton 29 52 16N 0 44W
Earl's Colne 29 51 56N 0 43 E
Earlsferry 35 56 11N 2 50W
Earlston 35 55 39N 2 40W
Earn, L. 34 56 23N 4 14W
Earn, R. 35 56 20N 3 19W
Earnslaw, Mt. 143 44 32 S 168 27 E
Earoo 137 29 34 S 118 22 E
Earsdon 35 55 4N 1 30W
Earth 159 34 18N 102 30W
Easebourne 29 51 0N 0 42W
Easington, Durham, U.K. 33 54 50N 1 24W
Easington, Yorks., U.K. 33 54 40N 0 7W
Easington Colliery 33 54 49N 1 19W
Easingwold 33 54 8N 1 11W
Easky 38 54 17N 8 58W
Easley 157 34 52N 82 35W
East Aberthaw 31 51 23N 3 23W
East Anglian Hts. 29 52 10N 0 17 E
East Angus 151 45 30N 71 40W
East, B. 159 29 2N 89 16W
East Barming 29 51 15N 0 29 E
East Bathurst 151 47 35N 65 40W
East Bengal 99 24 0N 90 0 E
East Bergholt 29 51 58N 1 2 E
East Beskids, mts. 53 49 30N 18 45 E
East Brent 28 51 14N 2 55W
East C., N.Z. 142 37 42 S 178 35 E
East C., P.N.G. 135 10 13 S 150 53 E
East Chicago 156 41 40N 87 30W
East China Sea 105 30 5N 126 0 E
East Coulee 152 51 23N 112 27W
East Cowes 28 50 45N 1 17W
East Dereham 29 52 40N 0 57 E
East Falkland 176 51 30 S 58 30W
East Fen 33 53 4N 0 5 E
East Florenceville 151 46 26N 67 36W
East Grand Forks 158 47 55N 97 5W
East Greenwich 162 41 40N 71 27W
East Grinstead 29 51 8N 0 1W
East Harling 29 52 26N 0 55 E
East Hartford 162 41 46N 72 39W
East Helena 160 46 37N 111 58W
East Ilsley 28 51 33N 1 15W
East Indies 102 0 0 120 0 E
East Jordan 156 45 10N 85 7W
East Kilbride 35 55 46N 4 10W
East Kirkby 33 53 5N 1 15W
East Lansing 156 42 44N 84 37W
East Linton 35 56 0N 2 40W
East Liverpool 156 40 39N 80 35W
East London 129 33 0 S 27 55 E
East Looe 30 50 22N 4 28W
East Los Angeles 163 34 1N 118 9W
East Lynne 141 35 35 S 150 16 E
East Main (Eastmain) 151 52 20N 78 30W
East Markham 33 53 15N 0 53W
East Midlands, oilfield 19 53 20N 0 45W
East Moor 33 53 15N 1 30W
East, Mt. 137 29 0 S 122 30 E
East Orange 162 40 46N 74 13W
East P. 151 46 27N 61 58W
East Pakistan = Bangladesh 99 24 0N 90 0 E
East Pine 152 55 48N 120 5W
East Point 157 33 40N 84 28W
East Providence 162 41 49N 71 23W
East Retford 33 53 19N 0 55W
East St. Louis 158 38 36N 90 10W
East Schelde, R. 47 51 38N 3 40 E
E. Siberian Sea 77 73 0N 160 0 E
East Stroudsburg 162 41 0N 75 11W
East Sussex □ 29 50 55N 0 20 E
East Tawas 156 44 17N 83 31W
East Toorale 139 30 27 S 145 28 E
East Walker, R. 163 38 52N 119 10W
East Wemyss 35 56 8N 3 5W
East Woodhay 28 51 21N 1 26W
Eastbourne, N.Z. 142 41 19 S 174 55 E
Eastbourne, U.K. 29 50 46N 0 18 E
Eastchurch 29 51 23N 0 53 E
Eastend 153 49 32N 108 50W
Easter Islands 143 27 0 S 109 0W
Easter Ross, dist. 37 57 50N 4 35W
Easter Skeld 36 60 12N 1 27W
Eastern □ 126 0 0 S 38 30 E
Eastern Cr. 138 20 40 S 141 35 E
Eastern Ghats 97 15 0N 80 0 E
Eastern Group, Is. 137 33 30 S 124 30 E
Eastern Province □ 120 8 15N 11 0W
Easterville 153 53 8N 99 49W
Easthampton 162 42 16N 72 40W
Eastland 159 32 26N 98 45W
Eastleigh 28 50 58N 1 21W
Eastmain (East Main) 150 52 20N 78 30W
Eastmain, R. 150 52 27N 72 26W
Eastman 157 32 13N 83 41W
Eastnor 28 52 2N 2 22W
Easton, Dorset, U.K. 28 50 32N 2 27W
Easton, Northants., U.K. 29 52 37N 0 31W
Easton, Somerset, U.K. 28 51 28N 2 42W
Easton, Md., U.S.A. 162 38 47N 76 7W
Easton, Pa., U.S.A. 162 40 41N 75 15W
Easton, Wash., U.S.A. 160 47 14N 121 8W
Eastport, Maine, U.S.A. 151 44 57N 67 0W
Eastport, N.Y., U.S.A. 162 40 50N 72 44W
Eastry 29 51 15N 1 19 E
Eastview 150 45 27N 75 40W
Eastville 162 37 21N 75 57W
Eastwood 33 53 2N 1 17W
Eaton, U.K. 29 52 52N 0 46W
Eaton, U.S.A. 158 40 35N 104 42W
Eaton, L. 136 22 55 S 130 57 E
Eaton Socon 29 52 13N 0 18W
Eatonia 153 51 13N 109 25W
Eatonton 157 33 22N 83 24W
Eatontown 162 40 18N 74 7W
Eau Claire, S.C., U.S.A. 157 34 5N 81 2W
Eau Claire, Wis., U.S.A. 158 44 46N 91 30W
Eauze 44 43 53N 0 7 E
Eaval, Mt. 36 57 33N 7 12W
Ebagoola 138 14 15 S 143 12 E
Eban 121 9 40N 4 50 E
Ebberston 33 54 14N 0 35W
Ebbw Vale 31 51 47N 3 12W
Ebeggui 119 26 2N 6 0 E
Ebeltoft 75 56 12N 10 41 E
Ebensee 52 47 48N 13 46 E
Eberbach 49 49 27N 8 59 E
Eberswalde 48 52 49N 13 50 E
Ebikon 51 47 5N 8 21 E
Ebingen 49 48 13N 9 1 E
Ebino 110 32 2N 130 48 E
Ebnat-Kappel 51 47 16N 9 7 E
Eboli 65 40 39N 15 2 E
Ebolowa 121 2 55N 11 10 E
Ebony 128 22 6 S 15 15 E
Ébrié, Lagune 120 5 12N 4 40W
Ebro, Pantano del 56 43 0N 3 58W
Ebro, R. 58 41 49N 1 5W
Ebstorf 48 53 2N 10 23 E
Ecaussines-d'Enghien 47 50 35N 4 11 E
Ecclefechan 35 55 3N 3 18W
Eccleshall 28 52 52N 2 14W
Eceabat 68 40 11N 26 21 E
Éceuillé 42 47 10N 1 19 E
Ech Chebbi 118 26 41N 0 29 E
Echallens 50 46 38N 6 38 E
Echaneni 77 27 33 S 32 6 E
Echelles, Les 45 45 27N 5 45 E
Echizen-Misaki 111 35 59N 135 57 E
Echmiadzin 83 40 12N 44 19 E
Echo Bay, N.W.T., Can. 148 66 10N 117 40W
Echo Bay, Ont., Can. 153 46 29N 84 4W
Echoing, R. 153 55 51N 92 5W
Echt, Neth. 47 51 7N 5 52 E
Echt, U.K. 37 57 8N 2 26W
Echternach 47 49 49N 6 3 E
Echuca 141 36 3 S 144 46 E
Ecija 57 37 30N 5 10W
Eck L. 34 56 5N 5 0W
Eckernförde 48 54 26N 9 50 E
Eckington 33 53 19N 1 21W
Eclipse Is. 136 13 54 S 126 19 E
Écommoy 42 47 50N 0 17 E
Ecoporanga 171 18 23 S 40 50W

Écos Eldorado


| | | | |
|---|---|---|---|
| Écos | 43 | 49 9N | 1 35E |
| Écouché | 42 | 48 42N | 0 10W |
| Ecuador ■ | 174 | 2 0S | 78 0W |
| Ed | 73 | 58 55N | 11 55E |
| Ed Dabbura | 122 | 17 40N | 34 15E |
| Ed Damer | 122 | 17 27N | 34 0E |
| Ed Debba | 122 | 18 0N | 30 51E |
| Ed-Déffa | 122 | 30 40N | 26 30E |
| Ed Deim | 123 | 10 10N | 28 20E |
| Ed Dueim | 123 | 14 0N | 32 10E |
| Ed Dzong | 99 | 32 11N | 90 12E |
| Edah | 137 | 28 16S | 117 10E |
| Edam, Can. | 153 | 53 11N | 108 46W |
| Edam, Neth. | 46 | 52 31N | 5 3E |
| Edapally | 97 | 11 19N | 78 3E |
| Eday, I. | 37 | 59 11N | 2 47W |
| Eday Sd. | 37 | 59 12N | 2 45W |
| Edd | 123 | 14 0N | 41 30E |
| Edda, oilfield | 19 | 56 25N | 3 15E |
| Edderton | 37 | 57 50N | 4 10W |
| Eddrachillis B. | 36 | 58 16N | 5 10W |
| Eddystone | 30 | 50 11N | 4 16W |
| Eddystone Pt. | 138 | 40 59S | 148 20E |
| Ede, Neth. | 46 | 52 4N | 5 40E |
| Ede, Nigeria | 121 | 7 45N | 4 29E |
| Ede, Sweden | 72 | 62 10N | 16 50E |
| Édea | 121 | 3 51N | 10 9E |
| Edegem | 47 | 51 10N | 4 27E |
| Edehon L. | 153 | 60 25N | 97 15W |
| Edekel, Adrar | 119 | 23 56N | 6 47E |
| Eden, Austral. | 141 | 37 3S | 149 55E |
| Eden, U.K. | 38 | 54 44N | 5 47W |
| Eden, Tex., U.S.A. | 159 | 31 16N | 99 50W |
| Eden, Wyo., U.S.A. | 160 | 42 2N | 109 27W |
| Eden L. | 153 | 56 38N | 100 15W |
| Eden, R. | 32 | 54 57N | 3 2W |
| Edenbridge | 29 | 51 12N | 0 4E |
| Edenburg | 128 | 29 43S | 25 58E |
| Edendale | 143 | 46 19S | 168 48E |
| Edenderry | 39 | 53 21N | 7 3W |
| Edenton | 157 | 36 5N | 76 36W |
| Edenville | 129 | 27 37S | 27 34E |
| Ederny | 38 | 54 32N | 7 40W |
| Edgar | 158 | 40 25N | 98 0W |
| Edgartown | 162 | 41 22N | 70 28W |
| Edge Hill | 28 | 52 7N | 1 28W |
| Edge I. | 12 | 77 45N | 22 30E |
| Edgecumbe | 142 | 37 59S | 176 47E |
| Edgefield | 157 | 33 43N | 81 59W |
| Edgeley | 158 | 46 27N | 98 41W |
| Edgemont | 158 | 43 15N | 103 53W |
| Edgeøya | 12 | 77 45N | 22 30E |
| Edgeworthstown = Mostrim | 38 | 53 42N | 7 36W |
| Edhessa | 68 | 40 48N | 22 5E |
| Edievale | 143 | 45 49S | 169 22E |
| Edina, Liberia | 120 | 6 0N | 10 19W |
| Edina, U.S.A. | 158 | 40 6N | 92 10W |
| Edinburg | 159 | 26 22N | 98 10W |
| Edinburgh | 35 | 55 57N | 3 12W |
| Edington | 28 | 51 17N | 2 6W |
| Edirne | 67 | 41 40N | 26 45E |
| Edison | 163 | 35 21N | 118 52W |
| Edithburgh | 140 | 35 5S | 137 43E |
| Edjeleh | 119 | 28 25N | 9 40E |
| Edjudina | 137 | 29 48S | 122 23E |
| Edmeston | 162 | 42 42N | 75 15W |
| Edmond | 159 | 35 37N | 97 30W |
| Edmondbyers | 32 | 54 50N | 1 59W |
| Edmonds | 160 | 47 47N | 122 22W |
| Edmonton, Austral. | 138 | 17 2S | 145 46E |
| Edmonton, Can. | 152 | 53 30N | 113 30W |
| Edmund L. | 153 | 54 45N | 93 17W |
| Edmundston | 151 | 47 23N | 68 20W |
| Edna | 159 | 29 0N | 96 40W |
| Edna Bay | 152 | 55 55N | 133 40W |
| Edolo | 62 | 46 10N | 10 21E |
| Edouard, L. | 126 | 0 25S | 29 40E |
| Edremit | 92 | 39 40N | 27 0E |
| Edsbyn | 72 | 61 23N | 15 49E |
| Edsel Ford Ra. | 13 | 77 0S | 143 0W |
| Edsele | 72 | 63 25N | 16 32E |
| Edson | 152 | 53 40N | 116 28W |
| Eduardo Castex | 172 | 35 50S | 64 25W |
| Edward I. | 150 | 48 22N | 88 37W |
| Edward, L. = Idi Amin Dada, L. | 126 | 0 25S | 29 40E |
| Edward, R. | 140 | 35 0S | 143 30E |
| Edward VII Pen. | 13 | 80 0S | 160 0W |
| Edwards | 163 | 34 55N | 117 51W |
| Edwards Plat. | 159 | 30 30N | 101 5W |
| Edwardsville | 162 | 41 15N | 75 56W |
| Edzell | 37 | 56 49N | 2 40W |
| Edzo | 152 | 62 49N | 116 4W |
| Eefde | 46 | 52 10N | 6 13E |
| Eek | 147 | 60 10N | 162 0W |
| Eekloo | 47 | 51 11N | 3 33E |
| Eelde | 46 | 53 8N | 6 34E |
| Eem, R. | 46 | 52 16N | 5 20E |
| Eems Kanaal | 46 | 53 18N | 6 46E |
| Eems, R. | 46 | 53 26N | 6 57E |
| Eenrum | 46 | 53 22N | 6 28E |
| Eernegem | 47 | 51 8N | 3 2E |
| Eerste Valthermond | 46 | 52 53N | 6 58E |
| Eersterivier | 128 | 34 0S | 18 45E |
| Efate, I. (Vate) | 46 | 17 40S | 168 25E |
| Eferding | 52 | 48 18N | 14 1E |
| Eferi | 119 | 24 30N | 9 28E |
| Effingham | 156 | 39 8N | 88 30W |
| Effiums | 121 | 6 35N | 8 0E |
| Effretikon | 51 | 47 25N | 8 42E |
| Efiduasi | 121 | 6 45N | 1 25W |
| Eforie Sud | 70 | 44 1N | 28 37E |
| Ega, R. | 58 | 42 32N | 1 58W |
| Égadi, Ísole | 64 | 37 55N | 12 10E |
| Eganville | 150 | 45 32N | 77 5W |
| Egeland | 158 | 48 42N | 99 6W |
| Egenolf L. | 153 | 59 3N | 100 0W |
| Eger | 53 | 47 53N | 20 27E |
| Eger, R. | 53 | 47 43N | 20 32E |
| Egersund = Eigersund | 75 | 58 26N | 6 1E |
| Egerton, Mt. | 137 | 24 42S | 117 44E |
| Egg L. | 153 | 55 5N | 105 30W |
| Eggenburg | 52 | 48 38N | 15 50E |
| Eggiwil | 50 | 46 52N | 7 47E |
| Egham | 29 | 51 25N | 0 33W |
| Egilsay I. | 37 | 59 10N | 2 56W |
| Eginbah | 136 | 20 53S | 119 47E |
| Egletons | 44 | 45 24N | 2 3E |
| Eglisau | 51 | 47 35N | 8 31E |
| Egmond-aan-Zee | 46 | 52 37N | 4 38E |
| Egmont, C. | 142 | 39 16S | 173 45E |
| Egmont, Mt. | 142 | 39 17S | 174 5E |
| Egogi Bad | 123 | 13 10N | 41 30E |
| Egremont | 32 | 54 28N | 3 33W |
| Eğridir Gölü | 92 | 37 53N | 30 50E |
| Egton | 33 | 54 27N | 0 45W |
| Egtved | 73 | 55 38N | 9 18E |
| Egua | 174 | 5 5N | 68 0W |
| Éguas, R. | 171 | 13 26S | 44 14W |
| Egume | 121 | 7 30N | 7 14E |
| Éguzon | 44 | 46 27N | 1 33E |
| Egvekinot | 77 | 66 19N | 179 50W |
| Egyek | 53 | 47 39N | 20 52E |
| Egypt ■ | 122 | 28 0N | 31 0E |
| Eha Amufu | 121 | 6 30N | 7 40E |
| Ehime-ken □ | 110 | 33 30N | 132 40E |
| Ehingen | 49 | 48 16N | 9 43E |
| Ehrwald | 52 | 47 24N | 10 56E |
| Eibar | 58 | 43 11N | 2 28W |
| Eibergen | 46 | 52 6N | 6 39E |
| Eichstätt | 49 | 48 53N | 11 12E |
| Eidanger | 71 | 59 7N | 9 43E |
| Eide | 71 | 60 31N | 6 44E |
| Eider, R. | 48 | 54 15N | 8 50E |
| Eidsberg | 71 | 59 32N | 11 16E |
| Eidsfoss | 71 | 59 36N | 10 2E |
| Eidsvold | 139 | 25 25S | 151 12E |
| Eidsvoll | 75 | 60 19N | 11 14E |
| Eifel | 49 | 50 10N | 6 45E |
| Eiffel Flats | 127 | 18 20S | 30 0E |
| Eigersund | 71 | 58 26N | 6 1E |
| Eigg, I. | 36 | 56 54N | 6 10W |
| Eigg, Sd. of | 36 | 56 52N | 6 15W |
| Eighty Mile Beach | 136 | 19 30S | 120 40E |
| Eil | 91 | 8 0N | 49 50E |
| Eil, L. | 36 | 56 50N | 5 15W |
| Eilat | 90 | 29 30N | 34 56E |
| Eildon | 141 | 37 14S | 145 55E |
| Eildon, L. | 139 | 37 10S | 146 0E |
| Eileen L. | 153 | 62 16N | 107 37W |
| Eilenburg | 48 | 51 28N | 12 38E |
| Ein 'Arik | 90 | 31 54N | 35 8E |
| Ein el Luweiqa | 123 | 14 5N | 33 50E |
| Einasleigh | 138 | 18 32S | 144 5E |
| Einasleigh, R. | 138 | 17 30S | 142 17E |
| Einbeck | 48 | 51 48N | 9 50E |
| Eindhoven | 47 | 51 26N | 5 30E |
| Einsiedeln | 51 | 47 7N | 8 46E |
| Eiríksjökull | 74 | 64 46N | 20 24W |
| Eirlandsche Gat | 46 | 53 12N | 4 54E |
| Eirunepé | 174 | 6 35S | 70 0W |
| Eisden | 47 | 50 59N | 5 42E |
| Eisenach | 48 | 50 58N | 10 18E |
| Eisenberg | 48 | 50 59N | 11 50E |
| Eisenerz | 52 | 47 32N | 15 54E |
| Eisenhüttenstadt | 48 | 52 9N | 14 41E |
| Eisenkappel | 52 | 46 29N | 14 36E |
| Eisenstadt | 53 | 47 51N | 16 31E |
| Eiserfeld | 47 | 50 50N | 8 0E |
| Eisfeld | 49 | 50 25N | 10 54E |
| Eishort, L. | 36 | 57 9N | 6 0W |
| Eisleben | 48 | 51 31N | 11 31E |
| Eizariya (Bethany) | 90 | 31 47N | 35 15E |
| Ejby | 73 | 55 25N | 9 56E |
| Eje, Sierra del | 56 | 42 24N | 6 54W |
| Ejea de los Caballeros | 58 | 42 7N | 1 9W |
| Ejido | 174 | 8 33N | 71 14W |
| Ejura | 121 | 7 25N | 1 25E |
| Ejutla | 165 | 16 34N | 96 44W |
| Ekalaka | 158 | 45 55N | 104 30E |
| Ekawasaki | 110 | 33 13N | 132 46E |
| Ekeryd | 73 | 57 37N | 14 6E |
| Eket | 121 | 4 38N | 7 56W |
| Eketahuna | 142 | 40 38S | 175 43E |
| Ekhinos | 68 | 41 16N | 25 1W |
| Ekibastuz | 76 | 51 40N | 75 22E |
| Ekimchan | 77 | 53 0N | 133 0W |
| Ekofisk, oilfield | 19 | 56 35N | 3 30E |
| Ekofisk, W., oilfield | 19 | 56 35N | 3 5E |
| Ekoli | 126 | 0 23S | 24 13E |
| Ekoln, I. | 72 | 59 45N | 17 40E |
| Eksjö | 73 | 57 40N | 14 58W |
| Ekwan Pt. | 150 | 53 16N | 82 7W |
| Ekwan, R. | 150 | 53 12N | 82 15W |
| El Abiodh | 118 | 32 53N | 0 31E |
| El Aïoun | 118 | 34 33N | 2 30W |
| El 'Aiyat | 122 | 29 36N | 31 15E |
| El Alamein | 122 | 30 48N | 28 58E |
| El Aqaba | 90 | 29 31N | 35 0E |
| El Arahal | 57 | 37 15N | 5 33W |
| El Araq | 122 | 28 40N | 26 20E |
| El Arba | 118 | 36 28N | 3 12E |
| El Arba du Rharb | 118 | 34 50N | 5 59W |
| El Aricha | 118 | 34 13N | 1 16W |
| El Arīhā | 90 | 31 52N | 35 27E |
| El Arish | 138 | 17 49S | 146 1E |
| El 'Arîsh | 122 | 31 8N | 33 50E |
| El Arnaud | 119 | 36 7N | 5 49E |
| El Arrouch | 119 | 36 37N | 6 53E |
| El Asnam | 118 | 36 10N | 1 20E |
| El Astillero | 56 | 43 24N | 3 49W |
| El Badâri | 122 | 27 4N | 31 25E |
| El Bahrein | 122 | 28 30N | 26 25E |
| El Ballâs | 122 | 26 2N | 32 43E |
| El Balyana | 122 | 26 10N | 32 3E |
| El Baqeir | 122 | 18 40N | 33 40E |
| El Barco de Ávila | 56 | 40 21N | 5 31W |
| El Barco de Valdeorras | 56 | 42 23N | 7 0W |
| El Bauga | 122 | 18 18N | 33 52E |
| El Baúl | 174 | 8 57N | 68 17W |
| El Bawiti | 122 | 28 25N | 28 45E |
| El Bayadh | 118 | 33 40N | 1 1E |
| El Bierzo | 56 | 42 45N | 6 30W |
| El Biodh | 118 | 26 0N | 6 32W |
| El Bluff | 166 | 11 59N | 83 40W |
| El Bonillo | 59 | 38 57N | 2 35W |
| El Cajon | 163 | 32 49N | 117 0W |
| El Callao | 174 | 7 25N | 61 50W |
| El Camp | 58 | 41 5N | 1 10E |
| El Campo | 159 | 29 10N | 96 20W |
| El Carmen | 174 | 1 16N | 66 52W |
| El Castillo | 57 | 37 41N | 6 19W |
| El Centro | 161 | 32 50N | 115 40W |
| El Cerro, Boliv. | 174 | 17 30S | 61 40W |
| El Cerro, Spain | 57 | 37 45N | 6 57W |
| El Cocuy | 174 | 6 25N | 72 27W |
| El Coronil | 57 | 37 5N | 5 38W |
| El Cuy | 176 | 39 55S | 68 25W |
| El Cuyo | 165 | 21 30N | 87 40W |
| El Dab'a | 122 | 31 0N | 28 27E |
| El Dátil | 164 | 30 7N | 112 15W |
| El Deir | 122 | 25 25N | 32 20E |
| El Dere | 91 | 3 50N | 47 8E |
| El Díaz | 165 | 21 1N | 87 17W |
| El Difícul | 174 | 9 51N | 74 14W |
| El Díos | 164 | 20 40N | 87 20W |
| El Diviso | 174 | 1 22N | 78 14W |
| El Djouf | 120 | 20 0N | 11 30E |
| El Dorado, Colomb. | 174 | 1 11N | 71 52W |
| El Dorado, Ark., U.S.A. | 159 | 33 10N | 92 40W |
| El Dorado, Kans., U.S.A. | 159 | 37 55N | 96 56W |
| El Dorado, Venez. | 174 | 6 55N | 61 30W |
| El Dorado Springs | 159 | 37 54N | 93 59W |
| El Eglab | 118 | 26 20N | 4 30W |
| El Escorial | 56 | 40 35N | 4 7W |
| El Faiyûm | 122 | 29 19N | 30 50E |
| El Fâsher | 123 | 13 33N | 25 26E |
| El Fashn | 122 | 28 50N | 30 54E |
| El Ferrol | 56 | 43 29N | 3 14W |
| El Fifi | 123 | 10 4N | 25 0E |
| El Fuerte | 164 | 26 30N | 108 40W |
| El Gal | 91 | 10 58N | 50 20E |
| El Gebir | 123 | 13 40N | 29 40E |
| El Gedida | 122 | 25 40N | 28 30E |
| El Geneina | 117 | 13 27N | 22 45E |
| El Geteina | 123 | 14 50N | 32 27E |
| El Gezira | 123 | 14 0N | 33 0E |
| El Gezira □ | 123 | 15 0N | 33 0E |
| El Gîza | 122 | 30 0N | 31 10E |
| El Goléa | 118 | 30 30N | 2 50E |
| El Guettar | 119 | 34 5N | 4 38E |
| El Hadjire | 119 | 32 36N | 5 30E |
| El Hagiz | 123 | 15 15N | 35 50E |
| El Hajeb | 118 | 33 41N | 5 23W |
| El Hammâm | 122 | 30 52N | 29 25E |
| El Hank, Alg. | 118 | 25 38N | 5 29W |
| El Hank, Maurit. | 118 | 24 37N | 7 0W |
| El Haql | 122 | 29 15N | 34 59E |
| El Hawata | 123 | 13 25N | 34 42E |
| El Heiz | 122 | 27 50N | 28 40E |
| El 'Idisât | 122 | 25 30N | 32 35E |
| El Iskandarîya | 122 | 31 0N | 30 0E |
| El Istwâ'ya □ | 123 | 5 0N | 30 0E |
| El Jadida | 118 | 33 16N | 9 31W |
| El Jorf Lasfar, C. | 118 | 33 5N | 8 54W |
| El Kab | 122 | 19 27N | 32 46E |
| El Kala | 119 | 36 50N | 8 30E |
| El Kamlin | 123 | 15 3N | 33 11E |
| El Kantara, Alg. | 119 | 35 14N | 5 45E |
| El Kantara, Tunisia | 119 | 33 45N | 10 58E |
| El Karaba | 122 | 18 32N | 33 41E |
| El Kef | 119 | 36 12N | 8 47E |
| El Kelâa des Srarhna | 118 | 32 4N | 7 27W |
| El Khandaq | 122 | 18 30N | 30 30E |
| El Khârga | 122 | 25 30N | 30 33E |
| El Khartûm | 123 | 15 31N | 32 35E |
| El Khartûm Bahrî | 123 | 15 40N | 32 31E |
| El-Khroubs | 119 | 36 10N | 6 55E |
| El Khureiba | 122 | 28 3N | 35 10E |
| El Kseur | 119 | 36 46N | 4 49E |
| El Ksiba | 118 | 32 45N | 6 1W |
| El Kuntilla | 122 | 30 1N | 34 45E |
| El Ladhiqiya | 92 | 35 20N | 35 30E |
| El Laqeita | 122 | 25 50N | 33 15E |
| El Leiya | 123 | 16 15N | 35 28E |
| El Mafâza | 123 | 13 38N | 34 30E |
| El Mahalla el Kubra | 122 | 31 0N | 31 0E |
| El Mahâriq | 122 | 25 35N | 30 35E |
| El Maiz | 118 | 28 19N | 0 9W |
| El-Maks el-Bahari | 122 | 24 30N | 30 40E |
| El Manshâh | 122 | 26 26N | 31 50E |
| El Mansour | 118 | 27 47N | 0 14W |
| El Mansûra | 122 | 31 0N | 31 19E |
| El Mantico | 174 | 7 27N | 62 32W |
| El Manzala | 122 | 31 10N | 31 50E |
| El Marâgha | 122 | 26 35N | 31 10E |
| El Masid | 123 | 15 15N | 33 0E |
| El Matariya | 122 | 31 15N | 32 0E |
| El Meghaier | 119 | 33 55N | 5 58E |
| El Melfa | 119 | 31 58N | 15 18E |
| El Meraguen | 118 | 28 0N | 0 7W |
| El Metemma | 123 | 16 50N | 33 10E |
| El Miamo | 174 | 7 39N | 61 46W |
| El Milagro | 172 | 30 59S | 65 59W |
| El Milheas | 118 | 25 27N | 6 57W |
| El Milia | 119 | 36 51N | 6 13E |
| El Minyâ | 122 | 28 7N | 30 33E |
| El Molar | 58 | 40 42N | 3 45W |
| El Monte | 163 | 34 4N | 118 2W |
| El Mreyye | 120 | 18 0N | 6 0W |
| El Obeid | 123 | 13 8N | 30 10E |
| El Oro = Sta. María del Oro | 164 | 25 50N | 105 20W |
| El Oro de Hidalgo | 165 | 19 48N | 100 8W |
| El Oued | 119 | 33 20N | 6 58E |
| El Ouig | 120 | 19 31N | 0 27E |
| El Palmar | 174 | 7 58N | 61 53W |
| El Palmito, Presa | 164 | 25 40N | 105 3W |
| El Panadés | 58 | 41 10N | 1 30E |
| El Pao | 174 | 9 38N | 68 8W |
| El Pardo | 56 | 40 31N | 3 47W |
| El Paso | 161 | 31 50N | 106 30W |
| El Paso Robles | 163 | 35 38N | 120 41W |
| El Pedernoso | 59 | 39 29N | 2 45W |
| El Pedroso | 57 | 37 51N | 5 45W |
| El Pilar | 174 | 10 32N | 63 9W |
| El Pobo de Dueñas | 58 | 40 46N | 1 39W |
| El Portal | 163 | 37 44N | 119 49W |
| El Porvenir, Mexico | 164 | 31 15N | 105 51W |
| El Porvenir, Venez. | 174 | 4 42N | 71 19W |
| El Prat de Llobregat | 58 | 41 18N | 2 3E |
| El Progreso | 166 | 15 26N | 87 51W |
| El Provencio | 59 | 39 23N | 2 35W |
| El Pueblito | 164 | 29 3N | 105 4W |
| El Qahîra | 122 | 30 1N | 31 14E |
| El Qantara | 122 | 30 51N | 32 20E |
| El Qasr | 122 | 25 44N | 28 42E |
| El Qubba | 123 | 11 10N | 27 5E |
| El Quseima | 122 | 30 40N | 34 15E |
| El Qusîya | 122 | 27 29N | 30 44E |
| El Râshda | 122 | 25 36N | 28 57E |
| El Reno | 159 | 35 30N | 98 0W |
| El Rheauya | 118 | 25 52N | 6 30W |
| El Ribero | 56 | 42 30N | 8 30W |
| El Ridisiya | 122 | 24 56N | 32 51E |
| El Rio | 163 | 34 14N | 119 10W |
| El Ronquillo | 57 | 37 44N | 6 10W |
| El Rubio | 57 | 37 22N | 5 0W |
| El Saff | 122 | 29 34N | 31 16E |
| El Salado | 174 | 8 56N | 73 55W |
| El Salto | 164 | 23 47N | 105 22W |
| El Salvador ■ | 166 | 13 50N | 89 0W |
| El Sancejo | 57 | 37 4N | 5 6W |
| El Sauce | 166 | 13 0N | 86 40W |
| El Shallal | 122 | 24 0N | 32 53E |
| El Suweis | 122 | 29 58N | 32 31E |
| El Temblador | 174 | 8 59N | 62 44W |
| El Thamad | 122 | 29 40N | 34 28E |
| El Tigre | 174 | 8 55N | 64 15W |
| El Tocuyo | 174 | 9 47N | 69 48W |
| El Tofo | 172 | 29 22S | 71 18W |
| El Tránsito | 172 | 28 52S | 70 17W |
| El Tûr | 122 | 28 14N | 33 36E |
| El Turbio | 176 | 51 30S | 72 40W |
| El Uqsur | 122 | 25 41N | 32 38E |
| El Vado | 58 | 41 2N | 3 18W |
| El Vallés | 58 | 41 35N | 2 20E |
| El Vigía | 174 | 8 38N | 71 39W |
| El Wak | 124 | 2 49N | 40 56E |
| El Waqf | 122 | 25 45N | 32 15E |
| El Wâsta | 122 | 29 19N | 31 12E |
| El Weguet | 123 | 5 28N | 42 17E |
| Ela | 123 | 12 50N | 42 20E |
| Elafónisos | 69 | 36 29N | 22 56E |
| Elaine | 140 | 37 44S | 144 2E |
| Elamanchili = Yellamanchilli | 96 | 17 26N | 82 50E |
| Elan R. | 31 | 52 17N | 3 40W |
| Elan Village | 31 | 52 18N | 3 34W |
| Elands | 141 | 31 37S | 152 20E |
| Elandsvlei | 128 | 32 19S | 19 31E |
| Elassa | 69 | 35 18N | 26 21E |
| Elassón | 68 | 39 53N | 22 12E |
| Elat | 103 | 5 40S | 133 5E |
| Elateia | 69 | 38 37N | 22 46E |
| Elâziğ | 92 | 38 37N | 39 22E |
| Elba | 157 | 31 27N | 86 4W |
| Elba, I. | 62 | 42 48N | 10 15E |
| Elbasani | 68 | 41 9N | 20 9E |
| Elbasani-Berati | 68 | 40 58N | 20 0E |
| Elbe, R. | 48 | 53 15N | 10 7E |
| Elbert, Mt. | 161 | 39 12N | 106 36W |
| Elberta | 155 | 44 35N | 86 14W |
| Elberton | 157 | 34 7N | 82 51W |
| Elbeuf | 42 | 49 17N | 1 2E |
| Elbląg □ | 54 | 54 15N | 19 30E |
| Elblag (Elbing) | 54 | 54 10N | 19 25E |
| Elbow | 153 | 51 7N | 106 35W |
| Elbrus, Mt. | 83 | 43 30N | 42 30E |
| Elburg | 46 | 52 26N | 5 50E |
| Elburz Mts. = Alborz | 93 | 36 0N | 52 0E |
| Elche | 59 | 38 15N | 0 42W |
| Elche de la Sierra | 59 | 38 27N | 2 3W |
| Elcho I. | 138 | 11 55S | 135 45E |
| Elda | 59 | 38 29N | 0 47W |
| Eldfisk, oilfield | 19 | 56 25N | 3 30E |
| Eldon, Iowa, U.S.A. | 97 | 40 50N | 92 12W |
| Eldon, Mo., U.S.A. | 158 | 38 20N | 92 38W |
| Eldora | 158 | 42 20N | 93 5W |
| Eldorado, Argent. | 173 | 26 28S | 54 43W |

Eldorado Ermelo


Eldorado, Ont., Can. 97 44 40N 77 32W
Eldorado, Sask., Can. 153 59 35N 108 30W
Eldorado, Mexico 164 24 0N 107 30W
Eldorado, Ill., U.S.A. 156 37 50N 88 25W
Eldorado, Tex., U.S.A. 159 30 52N 100 35W
Eldoret 126 0 30N 35 25E
Electra 159 34 0N 99 0W
Eleele 147 21 54N 159 35W
Elefantes, R. 129 24 0S 32 30E
Elektrogorsk 81 55 56N 38 50E
Elektrostal 81 55 41N 38 32E
Elele 121 5 5N 6 50E
Elena 67 42 55N 25 53E
Elephant Butte Res. 161 33 45N 107 30W
Elephant I. 13 61 0S 55 0W
Elephant Pass 97 9 35N 80 25E
Elesbão Veloso 170 6 13S 42 8W
Eleshnitsa 67 41 52N 23 36E
Eleuthera I. 166 25 0N 76 20W
Elevsís 69 38 4N 23 26E
Elevtheroúpolis 68 40 52N 24 20E
Elfin Cove 147 58 11N 136 20W
Elgåhogna, Mt. 72 62 7N 12 7E
Elgepiggen 71 62 10N 11 21E
Elgeyo-Marakwet □ 126 0 45N 35 30E
Elgg 51 47 29N 8 52E
Elgin, Can. 151 45 48N 65 10W
Elgin, U.K. 37 57 39N 3 20W
Elgin, Ill., U.S.A. 156 42 0N 88 20W
Elgin, N.D., U.S.A. 158 46 24N 101 46W
Elgin, Nebr., U.S.A. 158 41 58N 98 3W
Elgin, Nev., U.S.A. 161 37 27N 114 36W
Elgin, Oreg., U.S.A. 160 45 37N 118 0W
Elgin, Texas, U.S.A. 159 30 21N 97 22W
Elgol 36 57 9N 6 6W
Elgon, Mt. 126 1 10N 34 30E
Elham 29 51 9N 1 7E
Eliase 103 8 10S 130 55E
Elida 159 33 56N 103 41W
Elie 153 49 48N 97 52W
Elie de Beaumont, Mt. 143 43 30S 170 20E
Elikón, Mt. 69 38 18N 22 45E
Elim 147 64 35N 162 20W
Elin Pelin 126 42 40N 23 38E
Elisabethville = Lubumbashi 127 11 32S 27 38E
Eliseu Martins 170 8 13S 43 42W
Elishaw 35 55 16N 2 14W
Elista 83 46 16N 44 14E
Elit 123 15 10N 37 0E
Elizabeth, Austral. 140 34 42S 138 41E
Elizabeth, U.S.A. 162 40 37N 74 12W
Elizabeth City 157 36 18N 76 16W
Elizabetha 126 1 3N 23 37E
Elizabethton 157 36 20N 82 13W
Elizabethtown, Ky., U.S.A. 156 37 40N 85 54W
Elizabethtown, Pa., U.S.A. 162 40 8N 76 36W
Elizondo 58 43 12N 1 30W
Elk City 159 35 25N 99 25W
Elk Grove 163 38 25N 121 22W
Elk Island Nat. Park 152 53 47N 112 59W
Elk Lake 150 47 40N 80 25W
Elk Point 153 53 54N 110 55W
Elk River, Idaho, U.S.A. 160 46 50N 116 8W
Elk River, Minn., U.S.A. 158 45 17N 93 34W
Elkedra 138 21 9S 135 26E
Elkedra, R. 138 21 8S 136 22E
Elkhart, Ind., U.S.A. 156 41 42N 85 55W
Elkhart, Kans., U.S.A. 159 37 3N 101 54W
Elkhorn 153 49 59N 101 14W
Elkhorn, R. 158 42 0N 98 15W
Elkhotovo 83 43 19N 44 15E
Elkhovo 67 42 10N 26 40E
Elkin 157 36 17N 80 50W
Elkins 156 38 53N 79 53W
Elko, Can. 152 49 20N 115 10W
Elko, U.S.A. 160 40 40N 115 50W
Elkton 162 39 36N 75 50W
Ell, L. 137 29 13S 127 46E
Elland 33 53 41N 1 49W
Ellecom 46 52 2N 6 6E
Ellef Ringnes I. 12 78 30N 102 2W
Ellen, Mt. 161 38 4N 110 56W
Ellen R. 32 54 44N 3 24W
Ellendale, Austral. 136 17 56S 124 48E
Ellendale, U.S.A. 158 46 3N 98 30W
Ellensburg 160 47 0N 120 30W
Ellenville 162 41 42N 74 23W
Eller Beck Bri. 33 54 23N 0 40W
Ellerston 141 31 49S 151 20E
Ellery, Mt. 141 37 28S 148 40E
Ellesmere 32 52 55N 2 53W
Ellesmere I. 12 79 30N 80 0W
Ellesmere, L. 131 43 46S 172 27E
Ellesmere Port 32 53 17N 2 55W
Ellesworth Land 13 74 0S 85 0W
Ellezelles 47 50 44N 3 42E
Ellice Is. 130 8 0S 176 0E
Ellicott City 162 39 16N 76 48W
Ellington 35 55 14N 1 34W
Ellinwood 158 38 27N 98 37W
Elliot, Austral. 138 17 33S 133 32E
Elliot, S. Afr. 129 31 22S 27 48E
Elliot Lake 150 46 35N 82 35W
Ellis 158 39 0N 99 39W
Ellisville 157 31 38N 89 12W
Ellon 37 57 21N 2 5W
Ellore = Eluru 96 16 48N 81 8E
Ells, R. 152 57 18N 111 40W
Ellsworth 158 38 47N 98 15W
Ellsworth Land 13 76 0S 89 0W
Ellwangen 49 48 57N 10 9E
Ellwood City 156 40 52N 80 19W
Elm 51 46 54N 9 10E
Elma, Can. 153 49 52N 95 55W
Elma, U.S.A. 160 47 0N 123 30E
Elmer 162 39 36N 75 10W
Elmhurst 156 41 52N 87 58W
Elmina 121 5 5N 1 21W
Elmira, Can. 151 46 30N 61 59W
Elmira, U.S.A. 162 42 8N 76 49W
Elmira Heights 162 42 8N 76 50W
Elmore, Austral. 140 36 30S 144 37E
Elmore, U.S.A. 163 33 7N 115 49W
Elmshorn 48 53 44N 9 40E
Elmswell 29 52 14N 0 53E
Elorza 174 7 3N 69 31W
Eloy 161 32 46N 111 46W
Eloyes 43 48 6N 6 36E
Elphin, Ireland 38 53 50N 8 11W
Elphin, U.K. 36 58 4N 5 3W
Elphinstone 138 21 30S 148 17E
Elrose 153 51 12N 108 0W
Elsas 150 48 32N 82 55W
Elsinore, Austral. 141 31 35S 145 11E
Elsinore, Cal., U.S.A. 163 33 40N 117 15W
Elsinore, Utah, U.S.A. 161 38 40N 112 2W
Elsinore = Helsingør 73 56 2N 12 35E
Elspe 48 51 10N 8 1E
Elspeet 46 52 17N 5 48E
Elst 46 51 55N 5 51E
Elsterwerda 48 51 27N 13 32E
Elstree 29 51 38N 0 16W
Elten 46 51 52N 6 9E
Eltham, Austral. 141 37 43S 145 12E
Eltham, N.Z. 142 39 26S 174 19E
Elton 83 49 5N 46 52E
Eluru 96 16 48N 81 8E
Elvas 57 38 50N 7 17W
Elven 42 47 44N 2 36W
Elverum 71 60 53N 11 34E
Elvire, Mt. 137 21 52S 116 50E
Elvire, R. 136 17 51S 128 11E
Elvo, R. 62 45 32N 8 14E
Elvran 71 63 24N 11 3E
Elwood, Ind., U.S.A. 156 40 20N 85 50W
Elwood, Nebr., U.S.A. 158 40 38N 99 51W
Ely, U.K. 29 52 24N 0 16E
Ely, Minn., U.S.A. 158 47 54N 91 52W
Ely, Nev., U.S.A. 160 39 10N 114 50W
Elyashiv 90 32 23N 34 55E
Elyria 156 41 22N 82 8W
Emådalen 72 61 20N 14 44E
Emaiygi, R. 80 58 30N 26 30E
Emba 76 48 50N 58 8E
Embarcación 172 23 10S 64 0W
Embarras Portage 153 58 27N 111 28W
Embleton 35 55 30N 1 38W
Embo 37 57 55N 4 0W
Embóna 69 36 13N 27 51E
Embrach 51 47 30N 8 36E
Embrun 45 44 34N 6 30E
Embu 126 0 32S 37 38E
Embu □ 126 0 30S 37 35E
Emden 48 53 22N 7 12E
Emeq Hula 90 33 5N 35 8E
'Emeq Yizre'el 90 32 35N 35 12E
Emerald 138 23 32S 148 10E
Emerson 153 49 0N 97 10W
Emery 161 38 59N 111 17W
Emery Park 161 32 10N 110 59W
Emi Koussi, Mt. 117 20 0N 18 55E
Emilia-Romagna □ 62 44 33N 10 40E
Emilius, Mt. 62 45 41N 7 23E
Eminabad 94 32 2N 74 8E
Emine 67 42 40N 27 56E
Emlichheim 48 52 37N 6 51E
Emly 39 52 28N 8 20W
Emmaboda 73 56 37N 15 32E
Emmaus 162 40 32N 75 30W
Emme, R. 50 47 0N 7 42E
Emmeloord 46 52 44N 5 46E
Emmen, Neth. 47 52 48N 6 57E
Emmen, Switz. 51 47 4N 8 17E
Emmendingen 49 48 7N 7 51E
Emmental 50 47 0N 7 35E
Emmer-Compascum 46 52 49N 7 2E
Emmerich 48 51 50N 6 12E
Emmet 138 24 45S 144 30E
Emmetsburg 158 43 3N 94 40W
Emmett 160 43 51N 116 33W
Emőd 53 47 57N 20 47E
Emona 67 42 43N 27 53E
Empalme 164 28 1N 110 49W
Empangeni 129 28 50S 31 52E
Empedrado 172 28 0S 58 46W
Empoli 62 43 43N 10 57E
Emporia, Kans., U.S.A. 158 38 25N 96 16W
Emporia, Va., U.S.A. 157 36 41N 77 32W
Emporium 156 41 30N 78 17W
Empress 153 50 57N 110 0W
Emptinne 47 50 19N 5 8E
Ems, R. 48 52 37N 7 16E
Emsdetten 48 52 11N 7 31E
Emsworth 29 50 51N 0 56E
Emu 140 36 44S 143 26E
Emu Park 138 23 13S 150 50E
Emu Ra. 136 23 0S 122 0E
Emyvale 38 54 20N 6 57W
En Gedi 90 31 28N 35 25E
En Harod 90 32 33N 35 22E
'En Kerem 90 31 47N 35 6E
En Nahud 123 12 45N 28 25E
en Namous, O. 118 31 15N 0 10W
Ena 111 35 25N 137 25E
Ena-San 111 35 26N 137 36E
Enafors 72 63 17N 12 20E
Enambú 174 1 1N 70 17W
Enana 128 17 30S 16 23E
Enånger 72 61 30N 17 9E
Enard B. 36 58 5N 5 20W
Enbetsu 112 44 44N 141 47E
Encantadas, Serra 173 30 40S 53 0W
Encanto, Cape 103 20 20N 121 40E
Encarnación 173 27 15S 56 0W
Encarnación de Diaz 164 21 30N 102 20W
Ench'eng 106 37 9N 116 16E
Enchi 120 5 53N 2 48W
Encinal 159 28 3N 99 25W
Encinillas 164 33 3N 117 17W
Encinitas 163 33 3N 117 17W
Encino 161 34 46N 106 16W
Encounter B. 140 35 45S 138 45E
Encruzilhada 171 15 31S 40 54W
Endau 101 2 40N 103 38E
Endau, R. 101 2 30N 103 30E
Ende 103 8 45S 121 30E
Endeavour 153 52 10N 102 39W
Endeavour Str. 138 10 45S 142 0E
Endelave 73 55 46N 10 18E
Enderbury I. 131 3 8S 171 5W
Enderby, Can. 152 50 35N 119 10W
Enderby, U.K. 28 52 35N 1 15W
Enderby I. 136 20 35S 116 30E
Enderby Land 13 66 0S 53 0E
Enderlin 158 46 45N 97 41W
Endicott, N.Y., U.S.A. 162 42 6N 76 2W
Endicott, Wash., U.S.A. 160 47 0N 117 45W
Endicott Mts. 147 68 0N 152 30W
Endröd 53 46 55N 20 47E
Endyalgout I. 136 11 40S 132 35E
Enebakk 71 59 46N 11 9E
Enez 68 40 45N 26 5E
Enfida 119 36 6N 10 28E
Enfield, U.K. 29 51 39N 0 4W
Enfield, U.S.A. 162 43 34N 71 57W
Engadin 51 46 45N 10 10E
Engadine, Lower = Engiadina Bassa 51 46 51N 10 18E
Engadine, Upper = Engiadin 'Ota 51 46 38N 10 0E
Engano, C. 167 18 30N 68 20W
Engaño, C. 103 18 35N 122 23E
Engeddi 90 31 28N 35 25E
Engelberg 51 46 48N 8 26E
Engels 81 51 28N 46 6E
Engemann L. 153 55 55N 106 55W
Enger 71 60 35N 10 20E
Enggano, I. 102 5 20S 102 40E
Enghien 47 50 37N 4 2E
Engiadin 'Ota 51 46 38N 10 0E
Engiadina Bassa 51 46 51N 10 18E
Engkilili 102 1 3N 111 42E
England 159 34 30N 91 58W
England □ 27 53 0N 2 0W
Englee 151 50 45N 56 5W
Englefield 140 37 21S 141 48E
Englehart 150 47 49N 79 52W
Engler L. 153 59 8N 106 52W
Englewood, Colo., U.S.A. 158 39 40N 105 0W
Englewood, Kans., U.S.A. 159 37 7N 99 59W
Englewood, N.J., U.S.A. 162 40 54N 73 59W
English Bazar 95 24 58N 88 21E
English Channel 42 50 0N 2 0W
English Company Is. 133 12 0S 137 0E
English, R. 153 50 30N 93 50W
English River 150 49 20N 91 0W
Enid 159 36 26N 97 52W
Enipévs, R. 68 39 22N 22 17E
Eniwetok 131 11 30N 152 16E
Enjil 118 33 12N 4 32W
Enkeldoorn 127 19 2S 30 52E
Enkhuizen 46 52 42N 5 17E
Enköping 72 59 37N 17 4E
Enlo 108 24 0N 107 7E
Enna 65 37 34N 14 15E
Ennadai 153 61 8N 100 53W
Ennadai L. 153 61 0N 101 0W
Ennedi 117 17 15N 22 0E
Ennell L. 38 53 29N 7 25W
Ennerdale Water 32 54 32N 3 24W
Enngonia 139 29 21S 145 50E
Enningdal 71 58 59N 11 33E
Ennis, Ireland 39 52 51N 8 59W
Ennis, Mont., U.S.A. 160 45 27N 111 48W
Ennis, Texas, U.S.A. 159 32 15N 96 40W
Enniscorthy 39 52 30N 6 35W
Enniskean 39 51 44N 8 56W
Enniskerry 39 53 12N 6 10W
Enniskillen 38 54 20N 7 40W
Ennistimon 39 52 56N 9 18W
Enns 52 48 12N 14 28E
Enns, R. 52 48 8N 14 27E
Enoggera Range 108 27 26S 152 56E
Enoggera Res. 109 27 27S 152 55E
Enontekiö 74 68 23N 23 37E
Enp'ing 109 22 11N 112 18E
Enriquillo, L. 167 18 20N 72 5W
Ens 46 52 38N 5 50E
Enschede 46 52 13N 6 53E
Ensenada, Argent. 172 34 55S 57 55W
Ensenada, Mexico 164 31 50N 116 50W
Enshih 108 30 18N 109 27E
Enshū-Nada 111 34 27N 137 38E
Ensisheim 43 47 50N 7 20E
Enstone 28 51 55N 1 25W
Entebbe 126 0 4N 32 28E
Enter 46 52 17N 6 35E
Enterprise, Can. 152 60 47N 115 45W
Enterprise, Oreg., U.S.A. 160 45 30N 117 11W
Enterprise, Utah, U.S.A. 161 37 37N 113 36W
Entlebuch 50 46 59N 8 4E
Entrance 152 53 25N 117 50W
Entre Rios, Boliv. 172 21 30S 64 25W
Entre Rios, Mozam. 127 14 57S 37 20E
Entre Rios □ 172 30 30S 58 30W
Entre Rios, Bahia 171 11 56S 38 5W
Entrecasteaux, Pt. d' 137 34 50S 115 56E
Entrepeñas, Pantano de 58 40 34N 2 42W
Entwistle 152 53 30N 115 0W
Enugu 121 6 30N 7 30E
Enugu Ezike 121 7 0N 7 29E
Enumclaw 160 47 12N 122 0W
Envermeu 42 49 53N 1 15E
Envigado 174 6 10N 75 35W
Enza, R. 62 44 33N 10 22E
Enzan 111 35 42N 138 44E
Eólie o Lípari, Is. 65 38 30N 14 50E
Epa 138 8 28S 146 52E
Epanomí 68 40 25N 22 59E
Epe, Neth. 47 52 21N 5 59E
Epe, Nigeria 121 6 36N 3 59E
Epernay 43 49 3N 3 56E
Epernon 43 48 35N 1 40E
Ephesus 92 38 0N 27 30E
Ephraim 160 39 30N 111 37W
Ephrata, Pa., U.S.A. 162 40 11N 76 11W
Ephrata, Wash., U.S.A. 160 47 28N 119 32W
Epila 58 41 36N 1 17W
Epinac-les-Mines 43 46 59N 4 31E
Epinal 43 48 19N 6 27E
Episcopia Bihorului 70 47 12N 21 55E
Epitálion 69 37 37N 21 30E
Eport L. 36 57 33N 7 10W
Epping 29 51 42N 0 8E
Epping Forest 29 51 40N 0 5E
Epsom 29 51 19N 0 16W
Epukiro 125 21 30S 19 0E
Epworth 33 53 30N 0 50W
Equatorial Guinea ■ 124 2 0S 78 0W
Equeurdreville-Hainneville 42 49 40N 1 40W
Er Rahad 123 12 45N 30 32E
Er Rif 118 35 1N 4 1W
Er Roseires 123 11 55N 34 30E
Er Rumman 90 32 9N 35 48E
Eradu 137 28 40S 115 2E
Erandol 96 20 56N 75 20E
Erap 135 6 37S 146 51E
Erāwadī Myit, R. = Irrawaddy, R. 98 19 30N 95 15E
Erba, Italy 62 45 49N 9 12E
Erba, Sudan 122 19 5N 36 40E
Ercha 77 69 45N 147 20E
Erciyas Daği 92 38 30N 35 30E
Erdene 106 44 30N 111 10E
Erding 49 48 18N 11 55E
Erebus, Mt. 13 77 35S 167 0E
Erechim 173 27 35S 52 15W
Ereğli 92 41 15N 31 30E
Erei, Monti 65 37 20N 14 20E
Erembodegem 47 50 56N 4 4E
Eresma, R. 56 41 13N 4 30W
Eressós 69 39 11N 25 57E
Erewadi Myitwanya 99 15 30N 95 0E
Erfenis Dam 128 28 30S 26 50E
Erfjord 71 59 20N 6 14E
Erfoud 118 31 30N 4 15W
Erfurt 48 50 58N 11 2E
Erfurt □ 48 51 10N 10 30E
Ergani 92 38 26N 39 49E
Ergene, R. 67 41 20N 27 0E
Ergeni Vozyshennost 83 47 0N 44 0E
Erhlien 106 43 42N 112 2E
Erhlin 109 23 54N 120 22E
Erhtao Chiang, R. 107 42 35N 128 10E
Erhyüan 108 26 7N 99 57E
Eria, R. 56 42 10N 6 8W
Eriba 123 16 40N 36 10E
Eriboll, L. 37 58 28N 4 41W
Erica 46 52 43N 6 56E
Erice 64 38 4N 12 34E
Ericht, L. 37 56 50N 4 25W
Erie 156 42 10N 80 7W
Erigavo 91 10 35N 47 35E
Erikoúsa 68 39 55N 19 14E
Eriksdale 153 50 52N 98 7W
Erikslund 72 62 31N 15 54E
Erímanthos 69 37 57N 21 50E
Erimo-misaki 112 41 50N 143 15E
Eriskay I. 36 57 4N 7 18W
Eriskay, Sd. of 36 57 5N 7 20W
Erisort L. 36 58 5N 6 30W
Eriswil 50 47 5N 7 46E
Erith 152 53 25N 116 46W
Erithraí 69 38 13N 23 20E
Eritrea □ 123 14 0N 41 0E
Erjas, R. 56 39 45N 6 52W
Erker, L. 72 59 51N 18 29E
Erlangen 49 49 35N 11 0E
Erldunda 138 25 14S 133 12E
Ermelo, Neth. 46 52 35N 5 35E
Ermelo, S. Afr. 129 26 31S 29 59E

Ermenak Fairmount


Ermenak 92 36 44N 33 0E
Ermióni 69 37 23N 23 15E
Ermoúpolis = Siros 69 37 28N 24 57E
Ernakulam 97 9 59N 76 19E
Erne, Lough 38 54 26N 7 46W
Erne, R. 38 54 30N 8 16W
Ernée 42 48 18N 0 56W
Ernest Giles Ra. 137 27 0S 123 45E
Erode 97 11 24N 77 45E
Eromanga 139 26 40S 143 11E
Erongo 128 21 39S 15 58E
Erongoberg 128 21 45S 15 32E
Erp 47 51 36N 5 37E
Erquelinnes 47 50 19N 4 8E
Erquy 42 48 38N 2 29W
Erquy, Cap d' 42 48 39N 2 29W
Err, Piz d' 51 46 34N 9 43E
Errabiddy 137 25 25S 117 5E
Erramala Hills 97 15 30N 78 15E
Errer, R. 123 42 35N 8 40E
Errigal, Mt. 38 55 2N 8 8W
Errill 39 52 52N 7 40W
Erris Hd. 38 54 19N 10 0W
Errochty, L. 37 56 45N 4 10W
Errogie 37 57 16N 4 23W
Errol 35 56 24N 3 13W
Erseka 68 40 22N 20 40E
Erskine 158 47 37N 96 0W
Erstein 43 48 25N 7 38E
Erstfeld 51 46 50N 8 38E
Ertil 81 51 55N 40 50E
Ertvågøy 71 63 12N 8 25E
Ertvelde 47 51 11N 3 45E
Erundu 128 20 39S 16 26E
Eruwa 121 7 33N 3 26E
Ervalla 72 59 28N 15 16E
Ervy-le-Châtel 43 48 2N 3 55E
Erwin 157 36 10N 82 28W
Erzgebirge 48 50 25N 13 0E
Erzin 77 50 15N 95 10E
Erzincan 92 39 46N 39 30E
Erzurum 92 39 57N 41 15E
Es Sahrâ' Esh Sharqîya 122 26 0N 33 30E
Es Sider 119 30 50N 18 21E
Es Sînâ' 122 29 0N 34 0E
Es Souk 121 18 48N 1 2E
Es Sûkî 123 13 20N 34 58E
Esa'ala 135 9 45S 150 49E
Esambo 126 3 48S 23 30E
Esan-misaki 112 41 40N 141 10E
Esbjerg 73 55 29N 8 29E
Escada 170 8 22S 35 14W
Escalante 161 37 47N 111 37W
Escalante, R. 161 37 45N 111 0W
Escalón 164 26 40N 104 20W
Escalona 56 40 9N 4 29W
Escambia, R. 157 30 45N 87 15W
Escanaba 156 45 44N 87 5W
Escant, R. 47 51 2N 3 45E
Esch-sur-Alzette 47 49 32N 6 0E
Eschallens 50 46 39N 6 38E
Eschede 48 52 44N 10 13E
Escholzmatt 50 46 55N 7 56E
Eschwege 48 51 10N 10 3E
Eschweiler 48 50 49N 6 14E
Escondida, La 164 24 6N 99 55W
Escondido 163 33 9N 117 4W
Escrick 33 53 53N 1 3W
Escuinapa 164 22 50N 105 50W
Escuintla 166 14 20N 90 48W
Escuminac 151 48 0N 67 0W
Escutillas = Ceba 174 6 33N 70 24W
Eséka 121 3 41N 10 44E
Esens 48 53 40N 7 35E
Esera, R. 58 42 24N 0 22E
Esfahan □ 93 33 0N 53 0E
Esgueva, R. 56 41 46N 4 14W
Esh Sham = Dimashq 92 33 30N 36 18E
Esh Shamâliya □ 122 19 0N 31 0E
Esha Ness 36 60 30N 1 36W
Eshowe 129 28 50S 31 30E
Eshta' ol 90 31 47N 35 0E
Esiama 120 4 48N 2 25W
Esino, R. 63 43 28N 13 8E
Esk R. 32 54 23N 3 21W
Esk, R., Dumfries, U.K. 35 54 58N 3 4W
Esk, R., N. Yorks., U.K. 33 54 27N 0 36W
Eskdale 35 55 12N 3 4W
Eskifjördur 74 65 3N 13 55W
Eskilstuna 72 59 22N 16 32E
Eskimo Ls. 147 69 15N 132 17W
Eskimo Pt. 153 61 10N 94 3W
Eskişehir 92 39 50N 30 35E
Esla, R. 56 41 45N 5 50W
Eslöv 73 55 50N 13 20E
Esmeralda, La 172 22 16S 62 33W
Esmeraldas 174 1 0N 79 40W
Esneux 47 50 32N 5 33E
Espa 71 60 35N 11 15E
Espada, Pta. 174 12 5N 71 7W
Espalion 44 44 32N 2 47E
Espalmador, I. 59 38 48N 1 26E
Espanola 150 46 15N 81 46W
Espardell, I. del 59 38 47N 1 25E
Esparraguera 58 41 33N 1 52E
Esparta 166 9 59N 84 40W
Espejo 57 37 40N 4 34W
Espenberg, C. 147 66 35N 163 40W
Esperança 170 7 1S 35 51W
Esperance 137 33 45S 121 55E
Esperance B. 137 33 48S 121 55E
Esperantinópolis 170 4 53S 44 53W
Esperanza 172 31 29S 61 3W
Esperanza, La, Argent. 172 24 9S 64 52W
Esperanza, La, Boliv. 174 14 20S 62 0W
Esperanza, La, Cuba 166 22 46N 83 44W
Esperanza, La, Hond. 166 14 15N 88 10W
Espéraza 44 42 56N 2 14E
Espevær Lt. Ho. 71 59 35N 5 7E
Espichel, C. 57 38 22N 9 16W
Espiel 57 38 11N 5 1W
Espigão, Serra do 173 26 35S 50 30W
Espinal 174 4 9N 74 53W
Espinazo, Sierra del = Espinhaço, Serra do 171 17 30S 43 30W
Espinhaço, Serra do 171 17 30S 43 30W
Espinho 56 41 1N 8 38W
Espinilho, Serra do 173 28 30S 55 0W
Espino 174 8 34N 66 1W
Espinosa de los Monteros 56 43 5N 3 34W
Espírito Santo □ 171 20 0S 40 45W
Espíritu Santo, B. del 165 19 15N 79 40W
Espíritu Santo, I. 164 24 30N 110 23W
Espita 165 21 1N 88 19W
Esplanada 171 11 47S 37 57W
Espluga de Francolí 58 41 24N 1 7E
Espuña, Sierra de 59 37 51N 1 35W
Espungabera 129 20 29S 32 45E
Esquel 176 42 40S 71 20W
Esquimalt 148 48 30N 123 23W
Esquina 172 30 0S 59 30W
Essaouira (Mogador) 118 31 32N 9 42W
Essarts, Les 42 46 47N 1 12W
Essebie 126 2 58N 30 40E
Essen, Belg. 47 51 28N 4 28E
Essen, Ger. 48 51 28N 6 59E
Essendon, Mt. 137 25 0S 120 30E
Essequibo, R. 174 5 45N 58 50W
Essex 162 39 18N 76 29W
Essex □ 29 51 48N 0 30E
Esslingen 49 48 43N 9 19E
Essonne □ 43 48 30N 2 20E
Essvik 72 62 18N 17 24E
Estadilla 58 42 4N 0 16E
Estados, I. de los 176 54 40S 64 30W
Estagel 44 42 47N 2 40E
Estância 170 11 16S 37 26W
Estancia 161 34 50N 106 1W
Estarreja 56 40 45N 8 35W
Estats, P. d' 44 42 40N 1 40E
Estavayer le Lac 50 46 51N 6 51E
Estcourt 129 28 58S 29 53E
Este 63 45 12N 11 40E
Esteban 56 43 33N 6 5W
Esteli 166 13 9N 86 22W
Estella 58 42 40N 2 0W
Estelline, S.D., U.S.A. 158 44 39N 96 52W
Estelline, Texas, U.S.A. 159 34 35N 100 27W
Estena, R. 57 39 23N 4 44W
Estepa 57 37 17N 4 52W
Estepona 57 36 24N 5 7W
Esterhazy 153 50 37N 102 5W
Esternay 43 48 44N 3 33E
Esterri de Aneu 58 42 38N 1 5E
Estevan 153 49 10N 102 59W
Estevan Group 152 53 3N 129 38W
Estherville 158 43 25N 94 50W
Estissac 43 48 16N 3 48E
Eston, Can. 153 51 8N 108 40W
Eston, U.K. 33 54 33N 1 6W
Estonian S.S.R. □ 80 48 30N 25 30E
Estoril 57 38 42N 9 23W
Estrada, La 56 42 43N 8 27W
Estrêla, Serra da 56 40 10N 7 45W
Estrella 59 38 25N 3 35W
Estremadura 57 39 0N 9 0W
Estremoz 57 38 51N 7 39W
Estrondo, Serra do 170 7 20S 48 0W
Esztergom 53 47 47N 18 44E
Et Tieta 118 29 37N 9 15W
Et Turra 90 32 39N 35 39E
Étables-sur-Mer 42 48 38N 2 51W
Etah 95 27 35N 78 40E
Étain 43 49 13N 5 38E
Etalle 47 49 40N 5 36E
Etamamu 151 50 18N 59 59W
Étampes 43 48 26N 2 10E
Etang 43 46 52N 4 10E
Etanga 128 17 55S 13 00E
Étaples 43 50 30N 1 39E
Etawah 95 26 48N 79 6E
Etawah, R. 157 34 20N 84 15W
Etawney L. 153 57 50N 96 50W
Etchingham 29 51 0N 0 27E
Eteh 121 7 2N 7 28E
Etelia 121 19 10N 0 55E
Ethe 47 49 35N 5 35E
Ethel Creek 136 22 55S 120 11E
Ethel, Oued el 118 28 31N 3 37W
Ethelbert 153 51 32N 100 25W
Ethiopia ■ 91 8 0N 40 0E
Ethiopian Highlands 114 10 0N 37 0E
Etive, L. 34 56 30N 5 12W
Etna, Mt. 65 37 45N 15 0E
Etne 71 59 40N 5 56E
Etoile 127 11 33S 27 30E
Etolin I. 152 56 5N 132 20W
Eton 29 51 29N 0 37W
Etoshapan 128 18 40S 16 30E
Etowah 157 35 20N 84 30W
Étrépagny 42 49 18N 1 36E
Étretat 42 49 42N 0 12E
Etroits, Les 151 47 24N 68 54W
Etropole 68 43 50N 24 0E
Ettelbrüch 47 49 50N 6 5E
Ettelbruck 47 49 51N 6 5E
Etten 47 51 34N 4 38E
Ettington 28 52 8N 1 38W
Ettlingen 49 48 58N 8 25E
Ettrick Forest 35 55 30N 3 0W
Ettrick Water 35 55 31N 2 55W
Etuku 126 3 42S 25 45E
Etzatlán 164 20 48N 104 5W
Etzna 165 19 35N 90 15W
Eu 42 50 3N 1 26E
Euboea = Évvoia 69 38 40N 23 40E
Euchareena 141 32 57S 149 6E
Eucla Basin 137 31 19S 126 9E
Euclid 156 41 32N 81 31W
Euclides da Cunha 170 10 31S 39 1W
Eucumbene, L. 141 36 2S 148 40E
Eudora 159 33 5N 91 17W
Eudunda 140 34 12S 139 7E
Eufaula, Ala., U.S.A. 157 31 55N 85 11W
Eufaula, Okla., U.S.A. 159 35 20N 95 33W
Eufaula, L. 159 35 15N 95 28W
Eugene 160 44 0N 123 8W
Eugenia, Punta 164 27 50N 115 5W
Eugowra 141 33 22S 148 24E
Eulo 139 28 10S 145 3E
Eumungerie 141 31 56N 148 36E
Eunice, La., U.S.A. 159 30 35N 92 28W
Eunice, N. Mex., U.S.A. 159 32 30N 103 10W
Eupen 47 50 37N 6 3E
Euphrates = Furat, Nahr al 92 33 30N 43 0E
Eure □ 42 49 6N 1 0E
Eure-et-Loir □ 42 48 22N 1 30E
Eureka, Can. 12 80 0N 85 56W
Eureka, Calif., U.S.A. 160 40 50N 124 0W
Eureka, Kans., U.S.A. 159 37 50N 96 20W
Eureka, Mont., U.S.A. 160 48 53N 115 6W
Eureka, Nev., U.S.A. 160 39 32N 116 2W
Eureka, S.D., U.S.A. 158 45 49N 99 38W
Eureka, Utah, U.S.A. 160 40 0N 112 0W
Eureka, Mt. 137 26 35S 121 35E
Eurelia 140 32 33S 138 35E
Euroa 141 36 44S 145 35E
Europa, Île 125 22 20S 40 22E
Europa, Picos de 56 43 10N 5 0W
Europa Pt. 55 36 2N 6 32W
Europa Pt. = Europa, Pta. de 57 36 3N 5 21W
Europa, Pta. de 57 36 3N 5 21W
Europe 16 20 0N 20 0E
Europoort 46 51 57N 4 10E
Euskirchen 48 50 40N 6 45E
Eustis 157 28 54N 81 36W
Eutin 48 54 7N 10 38E
Eutsuk L. 152 53 20N 126 45W
Euxton 32 53 41N 2 42W
Eva Downs 138 18 1S 134 52E
Eval, Mt. 90 32 15N 35 15E
Evanger 71 60 39N 6 7E
Evans 158 40 25N 104 43W
Evans Head 139 29 7S 153 27E
Evans L. 150 50 50N 77 0W
Evans P. 158 41 0N 105 35W
Evanston, Ill., U.S.A. 156 42 0N 87 40W
Evanston, Wy., U.S.A. 160 41 10N 111 0W
Evansville, Ind., U.S.A. 156 38 0N 87 35W
Evansville, Wis., U.S.A. 158 42 47N 89 18W
Evanton 37 57 40N 4 20W
Evato 129 20 37S 47 10E
Évaux-les-Bains 44 46 12N 2 29E
Eveleth 158 47 35N 92 40W
Even Yahuda 90 32 16N 34 53E
Evensk 77 61 57N 159 14E
Evenstad 71 61 25N 11 7E
Everard, C. 141 37 49S 149 17E
Everard, L. 139 31 30S 135 0E
Everard Ras. 137 27 5S 132 28E
Evercreech 28 51 8N 2 30W
Everdale 141 31 52S 144 46E
Evere 47 50 52N 4 25E
Everest, Mt. 95 28 5N 86 58E
Everett 160 48 0N 122 10W
Evergem 47 51 7N 3 43E
Everglades 157 26 0N 80 30W
Evergreen 157 31 28N 86 55W
Everöd 73 55 53N 14 5E
Everson 160 48 57N 122 22W
Everton 141 36 25S 146 33E
Evesham 28 52 6N 1 57W
Evian-les-Bains 45 46 24N 6 35E
Evinayong 124 1 50N 10 35E
Évinos, R. 69 38 27N 21 40E
Évisa 45 42 15N 8 48E
Évora 57 38 33N 7 57W
Évora □ 57 38 33N 7 50W
Évreux 42 49 0N 1 8E
Évritania □ 69 39 5N 21 30E
Évron 42 48 23N 1 58W
Évros □ 68 41 10N 26 0E
Evrótas, R. 69 36 50N 22 40E
Évvoia 69 38 30N 24 0E
Évvoia □ 69 38 40N 23 40E
Ewe, L. 36 57 49N 5 38W
Ewell 29 51 20N 0 15W
Ewhurst 29 51 9N 0 25W
Ewing 158 42 18N 98 22W
Ewo 124 0 48S 14 45E
Exaltación 174 13 10S 65 20W
Excelsior 139 33 6S 149 59W
Excelsior Springs 158 39 20N 94 10W
Excideuil 44 45 20N 1 4E
Exe, R. 30 50 38N 3 27W
Exeter, U.K. 30 50 43N 3 31W
Exeter, Calif., U.S.A. 163 36 17N 119 9W
Exeter, Nebr., U.S.A. 158 40 43N 97 30W
Exeter, N.H., U.S.A. 162 43 0N 70 58W
Exford 28 51 8N 3 39W
Exloo 46 52 53N 6 52E
Exmes 42 48 45N 0 10E
Exminster 30 50 40N 3 29W
Exmoor 30 51 10N 3 59W
Exmore 162 37 32N 75 50W
Exmouth, Austral. 136 22 6S 114 0E
Exmouth, U.K. 30 50 37N 3 26W
Exmouth G. 136 22 15S 114 15E
Expedition Range 138 24 30S 149 12E
Exton 29 52 42N 0 38W
Extremadura 57 39 30N 6 5W
Exu 171 7 31S 39 43W
Exuma Sound 166 24 30N 76 20W
Eyam 33 53 17N 1 40W
Eyasi, L. 126 3 30S 35 0E
Eyawaddi Myii 98 15 50N 95 6E
Eye, Camb., U.K. 29 52 36N 0 11W
Eye, Norfolk, U.K. 29 52 19N 1 9E
Eye Pen. 36 58 13N 6 10W
Eyeberry L. 153 63 8N 104 43W
Eyemouth 35 55 53N 2 5W
Eygurande 44 45 40N 2 26E
Eyhatten 47 50 43N 6 1E
Eyisen 82 41 0N 36 50E
Eyjafjorður 74 66 15N 18 30W
Eymet 44 44 40N 0 25E
Eymoutiers 44 45 40N 1 45E
Eynhallow Sd. 37 59 8N 3 7W
Eynort, L. 36 57 13N 7 18W
Eynsham 28 51 47N 1 21W
Eyrarbakki 74 63 52N 21 9W
Eyre 137 32 15S 126 18E
Eyre Cr. 138 26 40S 139 0E
Eyre, L. 133 29 30S 137 26E
Eyre L., (North) 139 28 30S 137 20E
Eyre L., (South) 139 29 18S 137 25E
Eyre Mts. 143 45 25S 168 25E
Eyre Pen. 139 33 30S 137 17E
Eyrecourt 39 53 12N 8 8W
Ez Zeidab 122 17 25N 33 55E
Ez Zergoun, W. 118 32 45N 2 25E
Ezcaray 58 42 19N 3 0W
Ezine 68 39 48N 26 12E


# F


Fabens 161 31 30N 106 8W
Fåborg 73 55 6N 10 15E
Fabriano 63 43 20N 12 52E
Fabrizia 43 38 29N 16 19E
Făcăeni 70 44 32N 27 53E
Facatativá 174 4 49N 74 22W
Facture 44 44 39N 0 58W
Fada 117 17 13N 21 34E
Fada-n-Gourma 121 12 10N 0 30E
Fadd 53 46 28N 18 49E
Faddeyevski, Ostrov 77 76 0N 150 0E
Fadhili 92 26 55N 49 10E
Fadlab 122 17 42N 34 2E
Faenza 63 44 17N 11 53E
Fafa 121 15 22N 0 48E
Fafe 56 41 27N 8 11W
Fagam 121 11 1N 10 1E
Fågelsjö 72 61 50N 14 35E
Fagerhult 73 57 8N 15 40E
Fagernes 75 60 59N 9 14E
Fagersta 72 60 1N 15 46E
Fåglavik 73 58 6N 13 6E
Fagnano Castello 65 39 31N 16 4E
Fagnano, L. 176 54 30S 68 0W
Fagnières 43 48 58N 4 20E
Fahral 93 29 0N 59 0E
Fahūd 93 22 18N 56 28E
Faid 92 27 1N 42 52E
Faido 51 46 29N 8 48E
Fair, C. 138 12 24S 143 16E
Fair Hd. 38 55 14N 6 10W
Fair Isle 23 59 30N 1 40W
Fair Oaks 163 38 39N 121 16W
Fairbank 161 31 44N 110 12W
Fairbanks 147 64 59N 147 40W
Fairbourne 31 52 42N 4 3W
Fairbury 158 40 5N 97 5W
Fairfax, Okla., U.S.A. 159 36 37N 96 45W
Fairfax, Va., U.S.A. 162 38 51N 77 18W
Fairfield, Austral. 141 33 53S 150 57E
Fairfield, Ala., U.S.A. 157 33 30N 87 0W
Fairfield, Calif., U.S.A. 163 38 14N 122 1W
Fairfield, Conn., U.S.A. 162 41 8N 73 16W
Fairfield, Idaho, U.S.A. 160 43 27N 114 52W
Fairfield, Ill., U.S.A. 156 38 20N 88 20W
Fairfield, Iowa, U.S.A. 158 41 0N 91 58W
Fairfield, Mont., U.S.A. 160 47 40N 112 0W
Fairfield, Texas, U.S.A. 159 31 40N 96 0W
Fairford, Can. 153 51 37N 98 38W
Fairford, U.K. 28 51 42N 1 48W
Fairhope 157 30 35N 87 50W
Fairlie, N.Z. 143 44 5S 170 49E
Fairlie, U.K. 34 55 44N 4 52W
Fairlight 29 50 53N 0 40E
Fairmead 163 37 5N 120 10W
Fairmont, Minn., U.S.A. 158 43 37N 94 30W
Fairmont, W. Va., U.S.A. 156 39 29N 80 10W
Fairmont Hot Springs 152 50 20N 115 56W
Fairmount 163 34 45N 118 26W

**Fairplay** **Field**


| | | | |
|---|---|---|---|
| Fairplay | 161 | 39 9N | 107 0W |
| Fairport | 156 | 43 8N | 77 29W |
| Fairview, Austral. | 138 | 15 31S | 144 17E |
| Fairview, Can. | 152 | 56 5N | 118 25W |
| Fairview, N. Dak., U.S.A. | 158 | 47 49N | 104 7W |
| Fairview, Okla., U.S.A. | 159 | 36 19N | 98 30W |
| Fairview, Utah, U.S.A. | 160 | 39 50N | 111 0W |
| Fairweather, Mt. | 147 | 58 55N | 137 45W |
| Faith | 158 | 45 2N | 102 4W |
| Faither, The, C. | 36 | 60 34N | 1 30W |
| Faizabad, Afghan. | 93 | 37 7N | 70 33E |
| Faizabad, India | 95 | 26 45N | 82 10E |
| Faizpur | 96 | 21 14N | 75 49E |
| Fajardo | 147 | 18 20N | 65 39W |
| Fakenham | 29 | 52 50N | 0 51E |
| Fakfak | 103 | 3 0S | 132 15E |
| Fakiya | 170 | 42 10N | 27 4E |
| Fakobli | 120 | 7 23N | 7 23W |
| Fakse | 73 | 55 15N | 12 8E |
| Fakse B. | 73 | 55 11N | 12 15E |
| Fakse Ladeplads | 73 | 55 16N | 12 9E |
| Fak'u | 107 | 42 31N | 123 26E |
| Falaise | 42 | 48 54N | 0 12W |
| Falaise, Mui | 100 | 19 6N | 105 45E |
| Falakrón Óros | 68 | 41 15N | 23 58E |
| Falam | 98 | 23 0N | 93 45E |
| Falcarragh | 38 | 55 8N | 8 8W |
| Falces | 58 | 42 24N | 1 48W |
| Falcón □ | 174 | 11 0N | 69 50W |
| Falcon, C. | 118 | 35 50N | 0 50W |
| Falcón Dam | 159 | 26 50N | 99 20W |
| Falconara Marittima | 63 | 43 37N | 13 23E |
| Faldingworth | 33 | 53 21N | 0 22W |
| Faléa | 120 | 12 16N | 11 17W |
| Falelatai | 84 | 13 55S | 171 59W |
| Falenki | 84 | 58 22N | 51 35E |
| Faleshty | 82 | 47 32N | 27 44E |
| Falfurrias | 159 | 27 8N | 98 8W |
| Falher | 152 | 55 44N | 117 15W |
| Falkenberg, Ger. | 48 | 51 34N | 13 13E |
| Falkenberg, Sweden | 73 | 56 54N | 12 30E |
| Falkensee | 48 | 52 35N | 13 6E |
| Falkenstein | 48 | 50 27N | 12 24E |
| Falkirk | 35 | 56 0N | 3 47W |
| Falkland | 35 | 56 15N | 3 13W |
| Falkland Is. | 176 | 51 30S | 59 0W |
| Falkland Is. Dep. | 13 | 57 0S | 40 0W |
| Falkland Sd. | 176 | 52 0S | 60 0W |
| Falkonéra | 69 | 36 50N | 23 52E |
| Falköping | 73 | 58 12N | 13 33E |
| Fall Brook | 161 | 33 25N | 117 12W |
| Fall River | 162 | 41 45N | 71 5W |
| Fall River Mills | 160 | 41 1N | 121 30W |
| Fallbrook | 163 | 33 23N | 117 15W |
| Fallmore | 38 | 54 6N | 10 5W |
| Fallon, Mont., U.S.A. | 158 | 46 52N | 105 8W |
| Fallon, Nev., U.S.A. | 160 | 39 31N | 118 51W |
| Falls Church | 162 | 38 53N | 77 11W |
| Falls City, Nebr., U.S.A. | 158 | 40 0N | 95 40W |
| Falls City, Oreg., U.S.A. | 160 | 44 54N | 123 29W |
| Falmey | 121 | 12 36N | 2 51E |
| Falmouth, Jamaica | 166 | 18 30N | 77 40W |
| Falmouth, U.K. | 30 | 50 9N | 5 5W |
| Falmouth, Ky., U.S.A. | 156 | 38 40N | 84 20W |
| Falmouth, Mass., U.S.A. | 162 | 41 34N | 70 38W |
| Falmouth B. | 30 | 50 7N | 5 3E |
| False B. | 128 | 34 15S | 18 40E |
| False Divi Pt. | 97 | 15 35N | 80 50E |
| Falset | 58 | 41 7N | 0 50E |
| Falso, C. | 166 | 15 12N | 83 21W |
| Falster | 73 | 54 45N | 11 55E |
| Falsterbo | 73 | 55 23N | 12 50E |
| Falsterbokanalen | 73 | 55 25N | 12 56E |
| Falstone | 35 | 55 10N | 2 26W |
| Faluja | 90 | 31 48N | 31 37E |
| Falun | 72 | 60 37N | 15 37E |
| Famagusta | 92 | 35 8N | 33 55E |
| Famaka | 123 | 11 24N | 34 52E |
| Famatina, Sierra, de | 172 | 29 5S | 68 0W |
| Family L. | 153 | 51 54N | 95 27W |
| Famoso | 163 | 35 37N | 119 12W |
| Fampotabe | 129 | 15 56S | 50 8E |
| Fan i Madh, R. | 68 | 41 56N | 20 16E |
| Fana, Mali | 120 | 13 0N | 6 56W |
| Fana, Norway | 71 | 60 16N | 5 20E |
| Fanad Hd. | 38 | 55 17N | 7 40W |
| Fanambana | 129 | 13 34S | 50 0E |
| Fanárion | 68 | 39 24N | 21 47E |
| Fanch'ang | 109 | 31 2N | 118 13E |
| Fanchiat'un | 107 | 43 42N | 125 5E |
| Fanchih | 106 | 39 14N | 113 19E |
| Fandriana | 129 | 20 14S | 47 21E |
| Fang | 100 | 19 55N | 99 13E |
| Fangch'eng, Honan, China | 106 | 33 16N | 112 59E |
| Fangch'eng, Kwangsi-Chuang, China | 108 | 21 46N | 108 21E |
| Fanghsien | 109 | 32 0N | 111 0E |
| Fangliao | 109 | 22 22N | 130 35E |
| Fangshan | 106 | 38 0N | 111 16E |
| Fangtzu | 107 | 36 39N | 119 15E |
| Fannich, L. | 36 | 57 40N | 5 0W |
| Fanning I. | 131 | 3 51N | 159 22W |
| Fanny Bay | 152 | 49 27N | 124 48W |
| Fanø | 73 | 55 25N | 8 25E |
| Fano | 63 | 43 50N | 13 0E |
| Fanø, I. | 73 | 55 25N | 8 25E |
| Fanshaw | 152 | 57 11N | 133 30W |
| Fao (Al Fāw) | 92 | 30 0N | 48 30E |
| Faqirwali | 94 | 29 27N | 73 0E |
| Fara in Sabina | 63 | 42 13N | 12 44E |
| Farab | 85 | 39 9N | 63 36E |
| Faraday Seamount Group | 14 | 50 0N | 27 0W |
| Faradje | 126 | 3 50N | 29 45E |
| Farafangana | 129 | 22 49S | 47 50E |
| Farâfra, El Wâhât el- | 122 | 27 15N | 28 20E |
| Farah | 93 | 32 20N | 62 7E |
| Farah □ | 93 | 32 25N | 62 10E |
| Farahalana | 129 | 14 26S | 50 10E |
| Faraid, Gebel | 122 | 23 33N | 35 19E |
| Faraid Hd. | 37 | 58 35N | 4 48W |
| Faramana | 120 | 11 56N | 4 45W |
| Faranah | 120 | 10 3N | 10 45W |
| Farasān, Jazā'ir | 91 | 16 45N | 41 55E |
| Farasan Kebir | 91 | 16 40N | 42 0E |
| Faratsiho | 129 | 19 24S | 46 57E |
| Fardes, R. | 59 | 37 25N | 3 10W |
| Fareham | 28 | 50 52N | 1 11W |
| Farewell | 147 | 62 30N | 154 0W |
| Farewell, C. | 143 | 40 29S | 172 43E |
| Farewell C. = Farvel, K. | 12 | 59 48N | 43 55W |
| Farewell Spit | 143 | 40 35S | 173 0E |
| Farfán | 174 | 0 16N | 76 41W |
| Fargo | 158 | 47 0N | 97 0W |
| Faria, R. | 90 | 32 12N | 35 27E |
| Faribault | 158 | 44 15N | 93 19W |
| Faridkot | 94 | 30 44N | 74 45E |
| Faridpur, Bangla. | 98 | 23 15N | 90 0E |
| Faridpur, India | 95 | 18 14N | 79 34E |
| Farila | 72 | 61 48N | 15 50E |
| Färila | 72 | 61 48N | 15 50E |
| Farim | 120 | 12 27N | 15 17W |
| Farimān | 93 | 35 40N | 60 0E |
| Farina | 139 | 30 3S | 138 15E |
| Faringdon | 28 | 51 39N | 1 34W |
| Faringe | 72 | 59 55N | 18 7E |
| Farinha, R. | 170 | 6 15S | 47 30W |
| Färjestaden | 73 | 56 38N | 16 25E |
| Farmakonisi | 69 | 37 17N | 27 8E |
| Farmerville | 159 | 32 48N | 92 23W |
| Farmingdale | 162 | 40 12N | 74 10W |
| Farmington, Calif., U.S.A. | 163 | 37 56N | 121 0W |
| Farmington, N. Mex., U.S.A. | 161 | 36 45N | 108 28W |
| Farmington, N.H., U.S.A. | 162 | 43 25N | 71 3W |
| Farmington, Utah, U.S.A. | 160 | 41 0N | 111 58W |
| Farmington, R. | 162 | 41 51N | 72 38W |
| Farmville | 156 | 37 19N | 78 22W |
| Farnborough | 29 | 51 17N | 0 46W |
| Farne Is. | 35 | 55 38N | 1 37W |
| Farnham | 29 | 51 13N | 0 49W |
| Farnham, Mt. | 152 | 45 20N | 72 55W |
| Farnworth | 32 | 53 33N | 2 24W |
| Faro, Brazil | 175 | 2 0S | 56 45W |
| Faro, Port. | 57 | 37 2N | 7 55W |
| Fårö | 75 | 58 0N | 19 10E |
| Faro □ | 57 | 37 12N | 8 10W |
| Faroe Is. | 16 | 62 0N | 7 0W |
| Farquhar, C. | 137 | 23 38S | 113 36E |
| Farquhar, Mt. | 136 | 22 18S | 116 53E |
| Farr | 37 | 57 21N | 4 13W |
| Farranfore | 39 | 52 10N | 9 32W |
| Farrars, Cr. | 138 | 25 35S | 140 43E |
| Farrashband | 93 | 28 57N | 52 5E |
| Farrell | 156 | 41 13N | 80 29W |
| Farrell Flat | 140 | 33 48S | 138 48E |
| Farrukhabad | 95 | 27 30N | 79 32E |
| Fars □ | 93 | 29 30N | 55 0E |
| Fársala | 68 | 39 17N | 22 23E |
| Farsø | 73 | 56 46N | 9 19E |
| Farsö | 73 | 56 48N | 9 20E |
| Farstrup | 73 | 56 59N | 9 28E |
| Farsund | 71 | 58 5N | 6 55E |
| Fartura, Serra da | 173 | 26 21S | 52 52W |
| Faru | 121 | 12 48N | 6 12E |
| Farum | 73 | 55 49N | 12 21E |
| Farvel, Kap | 12 | 59 48N | 43 55W |
| Farwell | 159 | 34 25N | 103 0W |
| Faryab | 93 | 28 7N | 57 14E |
| Fasa | 93 | 29 0N | 53 32E |
| Fasag | 36 | 57 33N | 5 32W |
| Fasano | 65 | 40 50N | 17 20E |
| Fashoda | 123 | 9 50N | 32 2E |
| Faskari | 79 | 11 42N | 6 58E |
| Faslane | 34 | 56 3N | 4 49W |
| Fastnet Rock | 39 | 51 22N | 9 37W |
| Fastov | 80 | 50 7N | 29 57E |
| Fatehgarh | 95 | 27 25N | 79 35E |
| Fatehpur, Raj., India | 94 | 28 0N | 75 4E |
| Fatehpur, Ut. P., India | 95 | 27 8N | 81 7E |
| Fatick | 120 | 14 19N | 16 27W |
| Fatima | 151 | 47 24N | 61 53W |
| Fátima | 57 | 39 37N | 8 39W |
| Fatoya | 120 | 11 37N | 9 10W |
| Faucilles, Monts | 43 | 48 5N | 5 50E |
| Fauldhouse | 35 | 55 50N | 3 44W |
| Faulkton | 158 | 45 4N | 99 8W |
| Faulquemont | 43 | 49 3N | 6 36E |
| Fauquembergues | 43 | 50 36N | 2 5E |
| Faure I. | 137 | 25 52S | 113 50E |
| Fauresmith | 128 | 29 44S | 25 17E |
| Fauske | 74 | 67 17N | 15 25E |
| Fauvillers | 47 | 49 51N | 5 40E |
| Faux-Cap | 129 | 25 33S | 45 32E |
| Favara | 64 | 37 19N | 13 39E |
| Faversham | 29 | 51 18N | 0 54E |
| Favignana | 64 | 37 56N | 12 18E |
| Favone | 45 | 41 47N | 9 26E |
| Favourable Lake | 150 | 52 50N | 93 39W |
| Fawley | 28 | 50 49N | 1 20W |
| Fawn, R. | 150 | 52 22N | 88 20W |
| Fawnskin | 163 | 34 16N | 116 56W |
| Faxaflói | 74 | 64 29N | 23 0W |
| Faxälven | 72 | 63 13N | 17 13E |
| Faya = Largeau | 117 | 17 58N | 19 6E |
| Fayence | 45 | 43 38N | 6 42E |
| Fayette, Ala., U.S.A. | 157 | 33 40N | 87 50W |
| Fayette, La., U.S.A. | 156 | 40 22N | 86 52W |
| Fayette, Mo., U.S.A. | 158 | 39 10N | 92 40W |
| Fayetteville, Ark., U.S.A. | 159 | 36 0N | 94 5W |
| Fayetteville, N.C., U.S.A. | 157 | 35 0N | 78 58W |
| Fayetteville, Tenn., U.S.A. | 157 | 35 0N | 86 30W |
| Fayón | 58 | 41 15N | 0 20E |
| Fazeley | 28 | 52 36N | 1 42W |
| Fazenda Nova | 171 | 16 11S | 50 48W |
| Fazilka | 94 | 30 27N | 74 2E |
| Fazilpur | 94 | 29 18N | 70 29E |
| F'Derik | 116 | 22 40N | 12 45W |
| Fé, La | 166 | 22 2N | 84 15W |
| Feakle | 39 | 52 56N | 8 41W |
| Feale, R. | 39 | 52 26N | 9 28W |
| Fear, C. | 157 | 33 45N | 78 0W |
| Fearn | 37 | 57 47N | 4 0W |
| Fearnan | 37 | 56 34N | 4 6W |
| Feather, R. | 160 | 39 30N | 121 20W |
| Featherston | 142 | 41 6S | 175 20E |
| Featherstone | 127 | 18 42S | 30 55E |
| Fécamp | 42 | 49 45N | 0 22E |
| Fedala = Mohammeda | 118 | 33 44N | 7 21W |
| Fedamore | 39 | 52 33N | 8 36W |
| Federación | 172 | 31 0S | 57 55W |
| Federalsburg | 162 | 38 42N | 75 47W |
| Fedjadj, Chott el | 119 | 33 52N | 9 14E |
| Fedje | 71 | 60 47N | 4 43E |
| Fedorovka | 84 | 53 38N | 62 42E |
| Feeagh L. | 38 | 53 56N | 9 35W |
| Feeny | 38 | 54 54N | 7 0W |
| Fehérgyarmat | 53 | 48 0N | 22 30E |
| Fehmarn | 48 | 54 26N | 11 10E |
| Fehmarn Bælt | 73 | 54 35N | 11 20E |
| Feihsiang | 106 | 36 32N | 114 47E |
| Feihsien | 107 | 35 12N | 118 0E |
| Feilding | 142 | 40 13S | 175 35E |
| Feira | 65 | 15 35S | 30 16E |
| Feira de Santana | 171 | 12 15S | 38 57W |
| Fejér □ | 53 | 47 9N | 18 30E |
| Fejø | 73 | 54 55N | 11 30E |
| Felanitx | 59 | 39 27N | 3 7E |
| Feldbach | 52 | 46 57N | 15 52E |
| Feldberg | 48 | 53 20N | 13 26E |
| Feldberg, mt. | 49 | 47 51N | 7 58E |
| Feldis | 51 | 46 48N | 9 26E |
| Feldkirch | 52 | 47 15N | 9 37E |
| Feldkirchen | 52 | 46 44N | 14 6E |
| Felhit | 123 | 16 40N | 38 1E |
| Felipe Carrillo Puerto | 165 | 19 38N | 88 3W |
| Felixlândia | 171 | 18 47S | 44 55W |
| Felixstowe | 29 | 51 58N | 1 22W |
| Felletin | 44 | 45 53N | 2 11E |
| Felpham | 29 | 50 47N | 0 38W |
| Felton, U.K. | 35 | 55 18N | 1 42W |
| Felton, U.S.A. | 163 | 37 3N | 122 4W |
| Feltre | 63 | 46 1N | 11 55E |
| Feltwell | 29 | 52 29N | 0 32E |
| Femø | 73 | 54 58N | 11 53E |
| Femunden | 71 | 62 10N | 11 53E |
| Fen Ho, R. | 106 | 35 36N | 110 42E |
| Fench'ing | 108 | 24 35N | 99 54E |
| Fénérive | 129 | 17 22S | 49 25E |
| Fenerwa | 123 | 13 5N | 39 3E |
| Fengári | 68 | 40 25N | 25 32E |
| Fengchen | 106 | 40 30N | 113 0E |
| Fengch'eng, Kiangsi, China | 109 | 28 10N | 115 43E |
| Fengch'eng, Liaoning, China | 107 | 40 30N | 124 2E |
| Fengchieh | 108 | 31 3N | 109 28E |
| Fengch'iu | 106 | 35 2N | 114 24E |
| Fenghsiang | 106 | 34 26N | 107 18E |
| Fenghsien, Kiangsu, China | 106 | 34 42N | 116 34E |
| Fenghsien, Shanghai, China | 109 | 30 55N | 121 27E |
| Fenghsien, Shensi, China | 106 | 33 56N | 106 41E |
| Fenghsin | 109 | 28 42N | 115 23E |
| Fenghua | 109 | 29 40N | 121 24E |
| Fenghuang | 108 | 27 58N | 109 19E |
| Fenghuangtsui | 106 | 33 30N | 109 27E |
| Fengi | 108 | 25 35N | 100 18E |
| Fengjun | 107 | 39 51N | 118 8E |
| Fengk'ai | 109 | 23 26N | 111 30E |
| Fengkang | 108 | 27 58N | 107 47E |
| Fengloho | 109 | 31 29N | 112 29E |
| Fengning | 106 | 41 12N | 116 32E |
| Fengshan, Hopei, China | 107 | 41 13N | 117 6E |
| Fengshan, Kwangsi-Chuang, China | 108 | 24 32N | 107 3E |
| Fengt'ai, Anhwei, China | 109 | 32 44N | 116 43E |
| Fengt'ai, Peip'ing, China | 106 | 39 51N | 116 17E |
| Fengteng | 106 | 36 25N | 114 14E |
| Fengtu | 108 | 29 58N | 107 59E |
| Fengyuang | 109 | 32 52N | 117 32E |
| Fenhsi | 106 | 36 38N | 111 31E |
| Feni | 109 | 27 48N | 114 41E |
| Feni Is. | 135 | 4 0S | 153 40E |
| Fenit | 39 | 52 17N | 9 51W |
| Fennagh | 39 | 52 42N | 6 50W |
| Fennimore | 158 | 42 58N | 90 41W |
| Fenny | 98 | 22 55N | 91 32E |
| Fenny Bentley | 33 | 53 4N | 1 43W |
| Fenny Compton | 28 | 52 9N | 1 20W |
| Fenny Stratford | 29 | 51 59N | 0 42W |
| Feno, C. de | 45 | 41 58N | 8 33E |
| Fenoarivo | 129 | 18 26S | 46 34E |
| Fens, The | 29 | 52 45N | 0 2E |
| Fenton, Can. | 153 | 53 0N | 105 35W |
| Fenton, U.S.A. | 156 | 42 47N | 83 44W |
| Fenwick | 34 | 55 38N | 4 25W |
| Fenyang | 106 | 37 19N | 111 46E |
| Feodosiya | 82 | 45 2N | 35 28E |
| Fer, C. de | 119 | 37 3N | 7 10E |
| Ferbane | 39 | 53 17N | 7 50W |
| Ferdows | 93 | 33 58N | 58 2E |
| Fère-Champenoise | 43 | 48 45N | 4 0E |
| Fère-en-Tardenois | 43 | 49 10N | 3 30E |
| Fère, La | 43 | 49 40N | 3 20E |
| Ferentino | 64 | 41 42N | 13 14E |
| Ferfer | 91 | 5 18N | 45 20E |
| Fergana | 85 | 40 23N | 71 46E |
| Ferganskaya Dolina | 85 | 40 50N | 71 30E |
| Ferganskiy Khrebet | 85 | 41 0N | 73 50E |
| Fergus | 150 | 43 43N | 80 24W |
| Fergus Falls | 158 | 46 25N | 96 0W |
| Fergus, R. | 39 | 52 45N | 9 0W |
| Ferguson | 150 | 47 50N | 73 30W |
| Fergusson I. | 135 | 9 30S | 150 45E |
| Fériana | 119 | 34 59N | 8 33E |
| FeriCanci | 66 | 45 32N | 18 0E |
| Ferkane | 119 | 34 37N | 7 26E |
| Ferkéssédougou | 120 | 9 35N | 5 6W |
| Ferlach | 52 | 46 32N | 14 18E |
| Ferland | 150 | 50 19N | 88 27W |
| Ferlo, Vallée du | 120 | 15 15N | 14 15W |
| Fermanagh (□) | 38 | 54 21N | 7 40W |
| Fermo | 63 | 43 10N | 13 42E |
| Fermoselle | 56 | 41 19N | 6 27W |
| Fermoy | 39 | 52 4N | 8 18W |
| Fernagh | 38 | 54 2N | 7 51W |
| Fernan Nuñ,z | 57 | 37 40N | 4 44W |
| Fernández | 172 | 27 55S | 63 50W |
| Fernandina | 157 | 30 40N | 81 30W |
| Fernando de Noronha, I. | 170 | 4 0S | 33 10W |
| Fernando do Noronho □ | 170 | 4 0S | 33 10W |
| Fernando Póo = Macias Nguema Biyoga | 113 | 3 30N | 8 40E |
| Fernandópolis | 171 | 20 16S | 50 14W |
| Ferndale, Calif., U.S.A. | 160 | 40 37N | 124 12W |
| Ferndale, Wash., U.S.A. | 160 | 48 51N | 122 41W |
| Ferness | 37 | 57 28N | 3 44W |
| Fernhurst | 29 | 51 3N | 0 43W |
| Fernie | 152 | 49 30N | 115 5W |
| Fernilea | 36 | 57 18N | 6 24W |
| Fernlees | 138 | 23 51S | 148 7E |
| Fernley | 160 | 39 42N | 119 20W |
| Feroke | 97 | 11 9N | 75 46E |
| Ferozepore | 94 | 30 55N | 74 40E |
| Férrai | 68 | 40 53N | 26 10E |
| Ferrandina | 65 | 40 30N | 16 28E |
| Ferrara | 63 | 44 50N | 11 36E |
| Ferrato, C. | 64 | 39 18N | 9 39E |
| Ferreira do Alentejo | 57 | 38 4N | 8 6W |
| Ferreñafe | 174 | 6 35S | 79 50W |
| Ferret, C. | 44 | 44 38N | 1 15W |
| Ferrette | 43 | 47 30N | 7 20E |
| Ferriday | 159 | 31 35N | 91 33W |
| Ferrières | 43 | 48 5N | 2 48E |
| Ferriete | 62 | 44 40N | 9 30E |
| Ferrol | 56 | 43 29N | 8 15W |
| Ferron | 160 | 39 3N | 111 3W |
| Ferros | 171 | 19 14S | 43 2W |
| Ferryhill | 33 | 54 42N | 1 32W |
| Ferryland | 151 | 47 2N | 52 53W |
| Ferté Bernard, La | 42 | 48 10N | 0 40E |
| Ferté, La | 43 | 48 57N | 3 6E |
| Ferté-Mace, La | 42 | 48 35N | 0 21W |
| Ferté-St. Aubin, La | 43 | 47 42N | 1 57E |
| Ferté-Vidame, La | 42 | 48 37N | 0 53E |
| Fertile | 158 | 47 37N | 96 18W |
| Fertília | 64 | 40 37N | 8 13E |
| Fertöszentmiklós | 53 | 47 35N | 16 53E |
| Fès | 118 | 34 0N | 5 0W |
| Feschaux | 47 | 50 9N | 4 54E |
| Feshi | 124 | 6 0S | 18 10E |
| Fessenden | 158 | 47 42N | 99 44W |
| Fet | 71 | 59 57N | 11 12E |
| Feteşti | 70 | 44 22N | 27 51E |
| Fethaland, Pt. | 36 | 60 39N | 1 20W |
| Fethard | 39 | 52 29N | 7 42W |
| Fethiye | 92 | 36 36N | 29 10E |
| Fetlar, I. | 36 | 60 36N | 0 52W |
| Fettercairn | 37 | 56 50N | 2 33W |
| Feuerthalen | 51 | 47 32N | 8 38E |
| Feurs | 45 | 45 45N | 4 13E |
| Fezzan | 117 | 27 0N | 15 0E |
| Ffestiniog | 31 | 52 58N | 3 56W |
| Fforest Fawr, mt. | 31 | 51 52N | 3 35W |
| Fiambalá | 172 | 27 45S | 67 37W |
| Fianarantsoa | 125 | 21 20S | 46 45E |
| Fianarantsoa □ | 129 | 19 30S | 47 0E |
| Fianga | 117 | 9 55N | 15 20E |
| Fibiş | 66 | 45 57N | 21 26E |
| Fichot, I. | 151 | 51 12N | 55 40W |
| Fichtelgebirge | 49 | 50 10N | 12 0E |
| Ficksburg | 129 | 28 51S | 27 53E |
| Fiddown | 39 | 52 20N | 7 20W |
| Fidenza | 62 | 44 51N | 10 3E |
| Field | 150 | 46 31N | 80 1W |

Field I Fort Garland


| | | | |
|---|---|---|---|
| Field I. | 136 | 12 5S | 132 23E |
| Field, R. | 138 | 23 48S | 138 0E |
| Fields Finds | 137 | 29 0S | 117 10E |
| Fierenana | 129 | 18 29S | 48 24E |
| Fiéri | 68 | 40 43N | 19 33E |
| Fiesch | 50 | 46 25N | 8 12E |
| Fife □ | 35 | 56 13N | 3 2W |
| Fife Ness | 35 | 56 17N | 2 35W |
| Fifth Cataract | 123 | 18 15N | 33 50E |
| Figeac | 44 | 44 37N | 2 2E |
| Figline Valdarno | 63 | 43 37N | 11 28E |
| Figtree | 127 | 20 22S | 28 20E |
| Figueira da Foz | 56 | 40 7N | 8 54W |
| Figueiró dos Vinhos | 56 | 39 55N | 8 16W |
| Figueras | 58 | 42 18N | 2 58E |
| Figuig | 118 | 32 5N | 1 11W |
| Fihaonana | 129 | 18 36S | 47 12E |
| Fiherenana, R. | 129 | 22 50S | 44 0E |
| Fiji ■ | 142 | 17 20S | 179 0E |
| Fiji Is. | 130 | 17 20S | 179 0E |
| Fik | 90 | 32 46N | 35 41E |
| Fika | 121 | 11 15N | 11 13E |
| Filabres, Sierra de los | 59 | 37 13N | 2 20W |
| Filadélfia, Brazil | 170 | 7 21S | 47 30W |
| Filadélfia, Italy | 65 | 38 47N | 16 17E |
| Filadelfia | 172 | 22 25S | 60 0W |
| Fil'akovo | 53 | 48 17N | 19 50E |
| Filby | 29 | 52 40N | 1 39E |
| Filchner Ice Shelf | 13 | 78 0S | 60 0W |
| Filer | 160 | 42 30N | 114 35W |
| Filey | 33 | 54 13N | 0 18W |
| Filey B. | 33 | 54 12N | 0 15W |
| Filiaşi | 70 | 44 32N | 23 31E |
| Filiátes | 68 | 39 38N | 20 16E |
| Filiatrá | 69 | 37 9N | 21 35E |
| Filicudi, I. | 65 | 38 35N | 14 33E |
| Filiouri, R. | 68 | 41 15N | 25 40E |
| Filipstad | 72 | 59 43N | 14 9E |
| Filisur | 51 | 46 41N | 9 40E |
| Fillmore, Can. | 153 | 49 50N | 103 25W |
| Fillmore, U.S.A. | 163 | 34 23N | 118 58W |
| Filottrano | 63 | 43 28N | 13 20E |
| Filton | 28 | 51 29N | 2 34E |
| Filyos | 82 | 41 34N | 32 4E |
| Filyos çayi | 82 | 41 35N | 32 10E |
| Finale Ligure | 62 | 44 10N | 8 21E |
| Finale nell' Emília | 63 | 44 50N | 11 18E |
| Fiñana | 59 | 37 10N | 2 50W |
| Fincham | 29 | 52 38N | 0 30E |
| Findhorn | 37 | 57 39N | 3 36W |
| Findhorn, R. | 37 | 57 38N | 3 38W |
| Findlay | 156 | 41 0N | 83 41W |
| Findon | 29 | 50 53N | 0 24W |
| Finea | 38 | 53 46N | 7 23W |
| Finedon | 29 | 52 20N | 0 40W |
| Finger L. | 153 | 53 9N | 93 30W |
| Fingest | 29 | 51 35N | 0 52W |
| Finglas | 38 | 53 22N | 6 18W |
| Fingõe | 127 | 15 12S | 31 50E |
| Finike | 92 | 36 21N | 30 10E |
| Finistère □ | 42 | 48 20N | 4 0W |
| Finisterre | 56 | 42 54N | 9 16W |
| Finisterre, C. | 56 | 42 50N | 9 19W |
| Finisterre Ra. | 135 | 6 0S | 146 30E |
| Finke | 138 | 25 34S | 134 35E |
| Finke, R. | 138 | 24 54S | 134 16E |
| Finland ■ | 78 | 70 0N | 27 0E |
| Finland, G. of | 78 | 60 0N | 26 0E |
| Finlay, R. | 152 | 55 50N | 125 10W |
| Finley, Austral. | 141 | 35 38S | 145 35E |
| Finley, U.S.A. | 158 | 47 35N | 97 50W |
| Finn, R. | 38 | 54 50N | 7 55W |
| Finnart | 34 | 56 7N | 4 48W |
| Finnigan, Mt. | 138 | 15 49S | 145 17E |
| Finniss | 140 | 35 24S | 138 48E |
| Finniss, C. | 139 | 33 38S | 134 51E |
| Finnmark fylke □ | 74 | 69 30N | 25 0E |
| Finschhafen | 135 | 6 33S | 147 50E |
| Finse | 71 | 60 36N | 7 30E |
| Finspång | 73 | 58 45N | 15 43E |
| Finsta | 72 | 59 45N | 18 34E |
| Finsteraarhorn | 50 | 46 31N | 8 10E |
| Finsterwalde | 48 | 51 37N | 13 42E |
| Finsterwolde | 46 | 53 12N | 7 6E |
| Finstown | 37 | 59 0N | 3 8W |
| Fintona | 38 | 54 30N | 7 20W |
| Fintown | 38 | 54 52N | 8 8W |
| Finucanel I. | 132 | 20 19S | 118 30E |
| Finvoy | 38 | 55 0N | 6 29W |
| Fionn L. | 36 | 57 46N | 5 30W |
| Fionnphort | 34 | 56 19N | 6 23W |
| Fiora, R. | 63 | 42 25N | 11 35E |
| Fiordland National Park | 143 | 45 0S | 167 50E |
| Fiorenzuola d'Arda | 62 | 44 56N | 9 54E |
| Fiq | 90 | 32 46N | 35 41E |
| Fire River | 150 | 48 47N | 83 36W |
| Firebag, R. | 153 | 57 45N | 111 21W |
| Firebaugh | 163 | 36 52N | 120 27W |
| Firedrake L. | 153 | 61 25N | 104 30W |
| Firenze | 63 | 43 47N | 11 15E |
| Firkessédougou | 120 | 9 35N | 5 6W |
| Firmi | 44 | 44 32N | 2 19E |
| Firminy | 45 | 45 23N | 4 18E |
| Firoz Kohi | 93 | 34 45N | 63 0E |
| Firozabad | 95 | 27 10N | 78 25E |
| First Cataract | 122 | 24 1N | 32 51E |
| Firūzābād | 93 | 28 52N | 52 35E |
| Firuzkuh | 93 | 35 50N | 52 40E |
| Firvale | 152 | 52 27N | 126 13W |
| Fish, R. | 128 | 27 40S | 17 30E |
| Fisher | 137 | 30 30S | 131 0E |
| Fisher B. | 153 | 51 35N | 97 13W |
| Fishguard | 31 | 51 59N | 4 59W |
| Fishguard B. | 31 | 52 2N | 4 58W |
| Fishing L. | 153 | 52 10N | 95 24W |
| Fishkill | 162 | 41 32N | 73 53W |
| Fishtoft | 33 | 52 27N | 0 2E |
| Fishtown | 120 | 4 24N | 7 45E |
| Fiskivötn | 74 | 64 50N | 20 45W |
| Fiskum | 71 | 59 42N | 9 46E |
| Fismes | 43 | 49 20N | 3 40E |
| Fister | 71 | 59 10N | 6 5E |
| Fitchburg | 162 | 42 35N | 71 47W |
| Fitero | 58 | 42 4N | 1 52W |
| Fitful Hd. | 36 | 59 54N | 1 20W |
| Fitjar | 71 | 59 55N | 5 17E |
| Fitri, L. | 124 | 12 50N | 17 28E |
| Fitz Roy | 176 | 47 10S | 67 0W |
| Fitzgerald, Can. | 152 | 59 51N | 111 36W |
| Fitzgerald, U.S.A. | 157 | 31 45N | 83 10W |
| Fitzmaurice, R. | 136 | 14 50S | 129 50E |
| Fitzpatrick | 150 | 47 29N | 72 46W |
| Fitzroy Crossing | 136 | 18 9S | 125 38E |
| Fitzroy, R., Queens., Austral. | 138 | 23 32S | 150 52E |
| Fitzroy, R., W. Australia, Austral. | 136 | 17 25S | 124 0E |
| Fiume = Rijeka | 63 | 45 20N | 14 21E |
| Fiumefreddo Brúzio | 65 | 39 14N | 16 4E |
| Five Alley | 39 | 53 9N | 7 51W |
| Five Points | 163 | 36 26N | 120 6W |
| Fivemiletown | 38 | 54 23N | 7 20W |
| Fizi | 126 | 4 17S | 28 55E |
| Fjæra | 71 | 59 52N | 6 22E |
| Fjaere | 71 | 58 23N | 8 36E |
| Fjellerup | 73 | 56 29N | 10 34E |
| Fjerritslev | 73 | 57 5N | 9 15E |
| Fkih ben Salah | 118 | 32 45N | 6 45W |
| Fla | 71 | 60 25N | 9 26E |
| Flå | 71 | 63 13N | 10 18E |
| Flagler | 158 | 39 20N | 103 4W |
| Flagstaff | 161 | 35 10N | 111 40W |
| Flagstone | 152 | 49 4N | 115 10W |
| Flaherty, I. | 150 | 56 15N | 79 15W |
| Flåm | 75 | 60 52N | 7 14E |
| Flambeau, R. | 158 | 45 40N | 90 50W |
| Flamborough | 33 | 54 7N | 0 7W |
| Flamborough Hd. | 33 | 54 8N | 0 4W |
| Flaming Gorge Dam | 160 | 40 50N | 109 25W |
| Flaming Gorge L. | 160 | 41 15N | 109 30W |
| Flamingo, Teluk | 103 | 5 30S | 138 0E |
| Flanders = Flandres | 47 | 51 10N | 3 15E |
| Flandre Occidental □ | 47 | 51 0N | 3 0E |
| Flandre Orientale □ | 47 | 51 0N | 4 0E |
| Flandreau | 158 | 44 5N | 96 38W |
| Flandres, Plaines des | 47 | 51 10N | 3 15E |
| Flannan Is. | 23 | 58 9N | 7 52W |
| Flaren L. | 73 | 57 2N | 14 5E |
| Flåsjön | 74 | 64 5N | 15 50E |
| Flat, R. | 152 | 61 51N | 128 0W |
| Flat River | 159 | 37 50N | 90 30W |
| Flatey, Barðastrandarsýsla, Iceland | 74 | 66 10N | 17 52W |
| Flatey, Suður-þingeyjarsýsla, Iceland | 74 | 65 22N | 22 56W |
| Flathead L. | 160 | 47 50N | 114 0W |
| Flattery, C., Austral. | 138 | 14 58S | 145 21E |
| Flattery, C., U.S.A. | 160 | 48 21N | 124 43W |
| Flavy-le-Martel | 43 | 49 43N | 3 12E |
| Flawil | 51 | 47 26N | 9 11E |
| Flaxton | 158 | 48 52N | 102 24W |
| Flèche, La | 42 | 47 42N | 0 5W |
| Fleeming, C. | 136 | 11 15S | 131 21E |
| Fleet | 29 | 51 16N | 0 50W |
| Fleetwood, U.K. | 32 | 53 55N | 3 1W |
| Fleetwood, U.S.A. | 162 | 40 27N | 75 49W |
| Flekkefjord | 71 | 58 18N | 6 39E |
| Flémalle | 47 | 50 36N | 5 28E |
| Flensborg Fjord | 73 | 54 50N | 9 40E |
| Flensburg | 48 | 54 46N | 9 28E |
| Flers | 42 | 48 47N | 0 33W |
| Flesberg | 71 | 59 51N | 9 22E |
| Fletton | 29 | 52 34N | 0 13W |
| Fleurance | 44 | 43 52N | 0 40E |
| Fleurier | 50 | 46 54N | 6 35E |
| Fleurus | 47 | 50 29N | 4 32E |
| Flickerbäcken | 72 | 61 47N | 12 34E |
| Flims | 51 | 46 50N | 9 17E |
| Flin Flon | 153 | 54 46N | 101 53W |
| Flinders B. | 137 | 34 19S | 115 9E |
| Flinders Group, Is. | 138 | 14 11S | 144 15E |
| Flinders I. | 138 | 40 0S | 148 0E |
| Flinders, R. | 138 | 17 36S | 140 36E |
| Flinders Ranges | 140 | 31 30S | 138 30E |
| Flinders Reefs | 138 | 17 37S | 148 31E |
| Flint | 156 | 43 5N | 83 19W |
| Flint (□) | 26 | 53 15N | 3 12W |
| Flint, I. | 131 | 11 26S | 151 48W |
| Flint, R. | 157 | 31 20N | 84 10W |
| Flinton | 139 | 27 55S | 149 32E |
| Fliseryd | 73 | 57 6N | 16 15E |
| Flitwick | 29 | 51 59N | 0 30W |
| Flix | 58 | 41 14N | 0 32E |
| Flixecourt | 43 | 50 0N | 2 5E |
| Flobecq | 47 | 50 44N | 3 45E |
| Floda | 72 | 60 30N | 14 53E |
| Flodden | 35 | 55 37N | 2 8W |
| Floodwood | 158 | 46 55N | 92 55W |
| Flora, N. Tröndelag, Norway | 71 | 63 27N | 11 22E |
| Flora, Sogn & Fjordane, Norway | 71 | 61 35N | 5 1E |
| Flora, U.S.A. | 156 | 38 40N | 88 30W |
| Florac | 44 | 44 20N | 3 37E |
| Florala | 157 | 31 0N | 86 20W |
| Florânia | 170 | 6 8S | 36 49W |
| Floreffe | 47 | 50 26N | 4 46E |
| Florence, Ala., U.S.A. | 157 | 34 50N | 87 50W |
| Florence, Ariz., U.S.A. | 161 | 33 0N | 111 25W |
| Florence, Colo., U.S.A. | 158 | 38 26N | 105 0W |
| Florence, Oreg., U.S.A. | 160 | 44 0N | 124 3W |
| Florence, S.C., U.S.A. | 157 | 34 5N | 79 50W |
| Florence = Firenze | 63 | 43 47N | 11 15E |
| Florence, L. | 139 | 28 53S | 138 9E |
| Florennes | 47 | 50 15N | 4 35E |
| Florensac | 44 | 43 23N | 3 28E |
| Florenville | 47 | 49 40N | 5 19E |
| Flores, Azores | 16 | 39 13N | 31 13W |
| Flores, Brazil | 170 | 7 51S | 37 59W |
| Flores, Guat. | 166 | 16 50N | 89 40W |
| Flores I. | 152 | 49 20N | 126 10W |
| Flores, I. | 103 | 8 35S | 121 0E |
| Flores Sea | 102 | 6 30S | 124 0E |
| Floresta | 170 | 9 46S | 37 26W |
| Floresville | 159 | 29 10N | 98 10W |
| Floriano | 170 | 6 50S | 43 0W |
| Florianópolis | 173 | 27 30S | 48 30W |
| Florida, Cuba | 166 | 21 32N | 78 14W |
| Florida, Uruguay | 173 | 34 7S | 56 10W |
| Florida □ | 157 | 28 30N | 82 0W |
| Florida B. | 167 | 25 0N | 81 20W |
| Florida Keys | 167 | 25 0N | 80 40W |
| Florida, Strait of | 167 | 25 0N | 80 0W |
| Floridia | 65 | 37 6N | 15 9E |
| Flórina | 68 | 40 48N | 21 26E |
| Flórina □ | 68 | 40 45N | 21 20E |
| Florningen | 72 | 61 50N | 12 16E |
| Florø | 71 | 61 35N | 5 1E |
| Flosta | 71 | 58 32N | 8 56E |
| Flower's Cove | 151 | 51 14N | 56 46W |
| Floydada | 159 | 33 58N | 101 18W |
| Flüela Pass | 51 | 46 45N | 9 57E |
| Fluk | 103 | 1 42S | 127 38E |
| Flumen, R. | 58 | 41 50N | 0 25W |
| Flumendosa, R. | 64 | 39 30N | 9 25E |
| Fluminimaggiore | 64 | 39 25N | 8 30E |
| Flums | 51 | 47 6N | 9 21E |
| Flushing = Vlissingen | 47 | 51 26N | 3 34E |
| Fluviá, R. | 58 | 42 12N | 3 7E |
| Fly, R. | 135 | 8 25S | 143 0E |
| Foam Lake | 153 | 51 40N | 103 32W |
| Foča | 66 | 43 31N | 18 47E |
| Focşani | 70 | 45 41N | 27 15E |
| Fofo Fofo | 138 | 8 9S | 147 6E |
| Foggaret el Arab | 118 | 27 3N | 2 59E |
| Foggaret ez Zoua | 118 | 27 20N | 3 0E |
| Fóggia | 65 | 41 28N | 15 31E |
| Foggo | 121 | 11 21N | 9 57E |
| Foglia, R. | 63 | 43 50N | 12 32E |
| Fogo | 151 | 49 43N | 54 17W |
| Fogo I. | 151 | 49 40N | 54 5W |
| Fohnsdorf | 52 | 47 12N | 14 40E |
| Föhr | 48 | 54 40N | 8 30E |
| Foia, Cerro da | 57 | 37 19N | 8 10W |
| Foix | 44 | 42 58N | 1 38E |
| Fojnica | 66 | 43 59N | 17 51E |
| Fokang | 109 | 23 52N | 113 31E |
| Fokino | 80 | 53 30N | 34 10E |
| Fokis □ | 69 | 38 30N | 22 15E |
| Fokstua | 71 | 62 8N | 9 16E |
| Folda, Nord-Trøndelag, Norway | 74 | 64 41N | 10 50E |
| Folda, Nordland, Norway | 74 | 67 38N | 14 50E |
| Földeák | 53 | 46 19N | 20 30E |
| Folette, La | 157 | 36 23N | 84 9W |
| Foley | 128 | 30 25N | 87 40W |
| Foleyet | 150 | 48 15N | 82 25W |
| Folgefonni | 71 | 60 23N | 6 34E |
| Foligno | 63 | 42 58N | 12 40E |
| Folkestone | 29 | 51 5N | 1 11E |
| Folkston | 157 | 30 55N | 82 0W |
| Follett | 159 | 36 30N | 100 12W |
| Follónica | 62 | 42 55N | 10 45E |
| Folsom | 160 | 38 41N | 121 7W |
| Fond-du-Lac | 153 | 59 19N | 107 12W |
| Fond du lac | 158 | 43 46N | 88 26W |
| Fond-du-Lac, R. | 153 | 59 17N | 106 0W |
| Fondak | 118 | 35 34N | 5 35W |
| Fondi | 64 | 41 21N | 13 25E |
| Fonfría | 56 | 41 37N | 6 9W |
| Fongen | 71 | 63 11N | 11 38E |
| Fonni | 64 | 40 5N | 9 16E |
| Fonsagrada | 56 | 43 8N | 7 4W |
| Fonseca, G. de | 166 | 13 10N | 87 40W |
| Fontaine-Française | 43 | 47 32N | 5 21E |
| Fontainebleau | 43 | 48 24N | 2 40E |
| Fontas, R. | 152 | 58 14N | 121 48W |
| Fonte Boa | 174 | 2 25S | 66 0W |
| Fontem | 121 | 5 32N | 9 52E |
| Fontenay-le-Comte | 44 | 46 28N | 0 48W |
| Fontenelle | 151 | 48 54N | 64 33W |
| Fontur | 74 | 66 23N | 14 32W |
| Fonyód | 53 | 46 44N | 17 33E |
| Foochow = Fuchou | 109 | 26 5N | 119 18E |
| Foping | 106 | 33 22N | 108 19E |
| Foppiano | 62 | 46 21N | 8 24E |
| Föra | 73 | 57 1N | 16 51E |
| Forbach | 43 | 49 10N | 6 52E |
| Forbes | 141 | 33 22S | 148 0E |
| Forbesganj | 95 | 26 17N | 87 18E |
| Forcados | 121 | 5 26N | 5 26E |
| Forcados, R. | 121 | 5 25N | 5 20E |
| Forcall, R. | 58 | 40 40N | 0 12W |
| Forcalquier | 45 | 43 58N | 5 47E |
| Forchheim | 49 | 49 42N | 11 4E |
| Forclaz, Col de la | 50 | 46 3N | 7 1E |
| Ford City | 163 | 35 9N | 119 27W |
| Førde | 71 | 61 27N | 5 53E |
| Fordingbridge | 28 | 50 56N | 1 48W |
| Fordongianus | 44 | 40 0N | 8 50E |
| Fords Bridge | 139 | 29 41S | 145 29E |
| Fordyce | 159 | 33 50N | 92 20W |
| Forécariah | 120 | 9 20N | 13 10W |
| Forel | 12 | 66 52N | 36 55W |
| Foremost | 152 | 49 26N | 111 25W |
| Forenza | 65 | 40 50N | 15 50E |
| Forest, Belg. | 47 | 50 49N | 4 20E |
| Forest, U.S.A. | 159 | 32 21N | 89 27W |
| Forest City, Ark., U.S.A. | 159 | 35 0N | 90 50W |
| Forest City, Iowa, U.S.A. | 158 | 43 12N | 93 39W |
| Forest City, N.C., U.S.A. | 157 | 35 23N | 81 50W |
| Forest Grove | 160 | 45 31N | 123 4W |
| Forest Lawn | 152 | 51 4N | 114 0W |
| Forest Row | 29 | 51 6N | 0 3E |
| Forestburg | 152 | 52 35N | 112 1W |
| Forestier Pen. | 138 | 43 0S | 148 0E |
| Forestville, Can. | 151 | 48 48N | 69 20W |
| Forestville, U.S.A. | 156 | 44 41N | 87 29W |
| Forez, Mts. du | 44 | 45 40N | 3 50E |
| Forfar | 37 | 56 40N | 2 53W |
| Forges-les-Eaux | 43 | 49 37N | 1 30E |
| Forget | 150 | 49 40N | 102 50W |
| Forked River | 162 | 39 50N | 74 12W |
| Forks | 160 | 47 56N | 124 23W |
| Forksville | 162 | 41 29N | 76 35W |
| Forlì | 63 | 44 14N | 12 2E |
| Forman | 158 | 46 9N | 97 43W |
| Formazza | 62 | 46 23N | 8 26E |
| Formby Pt. | 32 | 53 33N | 3 7W |
| Formentera, I. | 59 | 38 40N | 1 30E |
| Formentor, C. de | 58 | 39 58N | 3 13E |
| Fórmia | 64 | 41 15N | 13 34E |
| Formiga | 171 | 20 27S | 45 25W |
| Formigine | 62 | 44 37N | 10 51E |
| Formiguères | 44 | 42 37N | 2 5E |
| Formosa, Argent. | 172 | 26 15S | 58 10W |
| Formosa, Brazil | 171 | 15 32S | 47 20W |
| Formosa = Taiwan ■ | 109 | 24 0N | 121 0E |
| Formosa □ | 172 | 26 5S | 58 10W |
| Formosa Bay | 126 | 2 40S | 40 20E |
| Formosa Strait | 109 | 24 40N | 120 0E |
| Formoso, R. | 171 | 10 34S | 49 56W |
| Fornaes, C. | 73 | 56 27N | 10 58E |
| Fornells | 58 | 40 4N | 4 4E |
| Fornos de Algodres | 56 | 40 38N | 7 32W |
| Fornovo di Taro | 62 | 44 42N | 10 7E |
| Forres | 37 | 57 37N | 3 38W |
| Forrest, Vic., Austral. | 140 | 38 22S | 143 40E |
| Forrest, W. Australia, Austral. | 137 | 30 51S | 128 6E |
| Forrest Lakes | 137 | 29 12S | 128 46E |
| Forrest, Mt. | 137 | 24 48S | 127 45E |
| Forrières | 47 | 50 8N | 5 17E |
| Fors, Jämtland, Sweden | 72 | 63 0N | 16 40E |
| Fors, Kopparberg, Sweden | 72 | 60 14N | 16 20E |
| Forsa | 72 | 61 44N | 16 55E |
| Forsand | 71 | 58 54N | 6 5E |
| Forsayth | 138 | 18 33S | 143 34E |
| Forsbacka | 72 | 60 39N | 16 54E |
| Forse | 72 | 63 8N | 17 1E |
| Forserum | 73 | 57 42N | 14 30E |
| Forshaga | 72 | 59 33N | 13 29E |
| Forshem | 73 | 58 38N | 13 30E |
| Forsmo | 72 | 63 16N | 17 11E |
| Forst | 48 | 51 43N | 14 37E |
| Forster | 141 | 32 12S | 152 31E |
| Forsyth, Ga., U.S.A. | 157 | 33 4N | 83 55W |
| Forsyth, Mont., U.S.A. | 160 | 46 14N | 106 37W |
| Forsyth I. | 143 | 40 58S | 174 5E |
| Fort Albany | 150 | 52 15N | 81 35W |
| Fort Ann | 162 | 43 25N | 73 30W |
| Fort Apache | 161 | 33 50N | 110 0W |
| Fort Archambault = Sarh | 117 | 9 5N | 18 23E |
| Fort Assiniboine | 152 | 54 20N | 114 45W |
| Fort Augustus | 37 | 57 9N | 4 40W |
| Fort Babine | 152 | 55 22N | 126 37W |
| Fort Beaufort | 128 | 32 46S | 26 40E |
| Fort Benton | 160 | 47 50N | 110 40W |
| Fort Bragg | 160 | 39 28N | 123 50W |
| Fort Bretonnet = Bousso | 117 | 10 34N | 16 52E |
| Fort Bridger | 160 | 41 22N | 110 20W |
| Fort Charlet = Djanet | 121 | 24 35N | 9 32E |
| Fort Chimo | 149 | 58 6N | 68 25W |
| Fort Chipewyan | 153 | 58 42N | 111 8W |
| Fort Collins | 158 | 40 30N | 105 4W |
| Fort Coulonge | 150 | 45 50N | 76 45W |
| Fort Crampel = Crampel | 117 | 7 8N | 19 18E |
| Fort-Dauphin | 129 | 25 2S | 47 0E |
| Fort Davis | 159 | 30 38N | 103 53W |
| Fort-de-France | 167 | 14 36N | 61 2W |
| Fort de Polignac = Illizi | 119 | 26 31N | 8 32E |
| Fort de Possel = Possel | 124 | 5 5N | 19 10E |
| Fort Defiance | 161 | 35 47N | 109 4W |
| Fort Dodge | 158 | 42 29N | 94 10W |
| Fort Flatters = Zaouiet El-Khala | 119 | 27 10N | 6 40E |
| Fort Foureau = Kousseri | 117 | 12 0N | 14 55E |
| Fort Frances | 153 | 48 35N | 93 25W |
| Fort Franklin | 148 | 65 30N | 123 45W |
| Fort Garland | 161 | 37 28N | 105 30W |

Fort George Frýdek-Místek

Fort George 151 53 50N 79 0W
Fort George, R. 150 53 50N 77 0W
Fort Good-Hope 147 66 14N 128 40W
Fort Gouraud = F'Dérik 116 22 40N 12 45W
Fort Grahame 152 56 30N 124 35W
Fort Hancock 161 31 19N 105 56W
Fort Hauchuca 161 31 32N 110 30W
Fort Hertz (Putao) 99 27 28N 97 30 E
Fort Hope 150 51 30N 88 10W
Fort Irwin 163 35 16N 116 34W
Fort Jameson = Chipata 127 13 38 S 32 38 E
Fort Johnston 127 14 25 S 35 16 E
Fort Kent 151 47 12N 68 30W
Fort Klamath 160 42 45N 122 0W
Fort Lallemand 119 31 13N 6 17 E
Fort-Lamy = Ndjamena 117 12 4N 15 8 E
Fort Lapperrine = Tamanrasset 119 22 56N 5 30 E
Fort Laramie 158 42 15N 104 30W
Fort Lauderdale 157 26 10N 80 5W
Fort Liard 152 60 20N 123 30W
Fort Liberté 167 19 42N 71 51W
Fort Lupton 158 40 8N 104 48W
Fort Mackay 152 57 12N 111 41W
Fort McKenzie 151 57 20N 69 0W
Fort Macleod 152 49 45N 113 30W
Fort MacMahon 118 29 51N 1 45 E
Fort McMurray 152 56 44N 111 23W
Fort McPherson 147 67 30N 134 55W
Fort Madison 158 40 39N 91 20W
Fort Meade 157 27 45N 81 45W
Fort Miribel 118 29 31N 2 55 E
Fort Morgan 158 40 10N 103 50W
Fort Myers 157 26 30N 82 0W
Fort Nelson 152 58 50N 122 38W
Fort Nelson, R. 152 59 32N 124 0W
Fort Norman 147 64 57N 125 30W
Fort Pacot (Chirfa) 119 20 55N 12 14 E
Fort Payne 157 34 25N 85 44W
Fort Peck 160 47 1N 105 30W
Fort Peck Dam 160 48 0N 106 20W
Fort Peck Res. 160 47 40N 107 0W
Fort Pierce 158 27 29N 80 19W
Fort Pierre 158 44 25N 100 25W
Fort Pierre Bordes 118 20 0N 2 55 E
Fort Portal 126 0 40N 30 20 E
Fort Providence 152 61 21N 117 40W
Fort Qu'Appelle 153 50 45N 103 50W
Fort Randall 147 55 10N 162 48W
Fort Reliance 153 63 0N 109 20W
Fort Resolution 152 61 10N 113 40W
Fort Rixon 127 20 2 S 29 17 E
Fort Roseberry = Mansa 127 11 10 S 28 50 E
Fort Rupert (Rupert House) 150 51 30N 78 40W
Fort Saint 119 30 13N 9 31 E
Fort St. James 152 54 30N 124 10W
Fort St. John 152 56 15N 120 50W
Fort Sandeman 94 31 20N 69 25 E
Fort Saskatchewan 152 53 40N 113 15W
Fort Scott 159 38 0N 94 40W
Fort Selkirk 147 62 43N 137 22W
Fort Severn 150 56 0N 87 40W
Fort Shevchenko 83 44 30N 50 10W
Fort Sibut = Sibut 117 5 52N 19 10 E
Fort Simpson 152 61 45N 121 23W
Fort Smith, Can. 152 60 0N 111 51W
Fort Smith, U.S.A. 159 35 25N 94 25W
Fort Stanton 161 33 33N 105 36W
Fort Stockton 159 30 48N 103 2W
Fort Sumner 159 34 24N 104 8W
Fort Thomas 161 33 2N 109 59W
Fort Trinquet = Bir Mogrein 116 25 10N 11 25W
Fort Valley 157 32 33N 83 52W
Fort Vermilion 152 58 24N 116 0W
Fort Victoria 127 20 8 S 30 55 E
Ft. Walton Beach 157 30 25N 86 40W
Fort Wayne 156 41 5N 85 10W
Fort William 36 56 48N 5 8W
Fort William = Thunder Bay 150 48 20N 89 10W
Fort Worth 159 32 45N 97 25W
Fort Yates 158 46 8N 100 38W
Fort Yukon 147 66 35N 145 12W
Fortaleza 170 3 35 S 38 35W
Forte Coimbra 174 19 55 S 57 48W
Forte Rocadas 125 16 38 S 15 22 E
Forteau 151 51 28N 57 1W
Fortescue 136 21 4 S 116 4 E
Fortescue, R. 136 21 20 S 116 5 E
Forth, Firth of 35 56 5N 2 55W
Forthassa Rharbia 118 32 52N 1 11W
Forties, oilfield 19 57 40N 1 0 E
Fortín Corrales 174 22 21 S 60 35W
Fortín Guachalla 174 22 22 S 62 23W
Fortín Rojas Silva 174 22 40 S 59 3W
Fortín Siracuas 174 21 3 S 61 46W
Fortín Teniente Montania 172 22 1 S 59 45W
Fortore, R. 63 41 40N 15 0 E
Fortrose 143 46 38 S 168 45 E
Fortuna, Spain 59 38 11N 1 7W
Fortuna, Cal., U.S.A. 160 48 38N 124 8W
Fortuna, N.D., U.S.A. 158 48 55N 103 48W
Fortune Bay 151 47 30N 55 22W
Forty Mile 147 64 20N 140 30W
Forūr 93 26 20N 54 30 E
Fos 62 43 20N 4 57 E
Fos do Jordâo 174 9 30 S 72 14W
Fos-sur-Mer 45 43 26N 4 56 E
Foshan 109 23 4N 113 5 E
Fossacesia 63 42 15N 14 30 E
Fossano 62 44 39N 7 40 E
Fosses-la-Ville 47 50 24N 4 41 E
Fossil 160 45 0N 120 9W
Fossilbrook 138 17 47 S 144 29 E
Fossombrone 63 43 41N 12 49 E
Fosston 158 47 33N 95 39W
Foster, R. 153 55 47N 105 49W
Fosters Ra. 138 21 35 S 133 48 E
Fostoria 156 41 8N 83 25W
Fou Chiang, R. 108 30 3N 106 21 E
Fouch'eng 106 37 52N 116 8 E
Fougamou 124 1 38 S 11 39 E
Fougères 42 48 21N 1 14W
Fouhsinshih 107 42 13N 121 51 E
Foul Pt. 97 8 35N 81 25 E
Foula, I. 23 60 10N 2 5W
Fouling 108 29 40N 107 20 E
Foulpointe 129 17 41 S 49 31 E
Foum el Alba 118 20 45N 3 0W
Foum el Kreneg 118 29 0N 0 58W
Foum Tatahouine 119 32 57N 10 29 E
Foum Zguid 118 30 2N 6 59W
Foumban 121 5 45N 10 50 E
Foundiougne 120 14 5N 16 32W
Founing 107 33 47N 119 48 E
Fountain, Colo., U.S.A. 158 38 42N 104 40W
Fountain, Utah, U.S.A. 160 39 41N 111 50W
Fountain Springs 163 35 54N 118 51W
Foup'ing 106 38 55N 114 13 E
Four Mts., Is. of the 147 52 0N 170 30W
Fourchambault 43 47 0N 3 3 E
Fourchu 151 45 43N 60 17W
Fourcroy, C. 136 11 45 S 130 2 E
Fourmies 43 50 1N 4 2 E
Fournás 69 39 3N 21 52 E
Foúrnoi 69 37 36N 26 32 E
Fours 43 46 50N 3 42 E
Foushan 106 35 58N 111 51 E
Fouta Djalon 120 11 20N 12 10W
Foux, Cap-à- 167 19 43N 73 27W
Fouyang 109 32 55N 115 52 E
Foveaux Str. 143 46 42 S 168 10 E
Fowler, Calif., U.S.A. 163 36 41N 119 41W
Fowler, Colo., U.S.A. 158 38 10N 104 0W
Fowler, Kans., U.S.A. 159 37 28N 100 7W
Fowlers B. 137 31 59 S 132 34 E
Fowlers Bay 137 32 0 S 132 29 E
Fowlerton 159 28 26N 98 50W
Fox Is. 147 52 30N 166 0W
Fox, R. 153 56 3N 93 18W
Fox Valley 153 50 30N 109 25W
Foxboro 162 42 4N 71 16W
Foxe Basin 149 68 30N 77 0W
Foxe Channel 149 66 0N 80 0W
Foxe Pen. 149 65 0N 76 0W
Foxen, L. 72 59 25N 11 55 E
Foxhol 46 53 10N 6 43 E
Foxpark 160 41 4N 106 6W
Foxton 142 40 29 S 175 18 E
Foyle, Lough 38 55 6N 7 8W
Foynes 38 52 30N 9 5W
Foz 56 43 33N 7 20W
Foz do Cunene 128 17 15 S 11 55 E
Foz do Gregório 174 6 47 S 71 0W
Foz do Iguaçu 173 25 30 S 54 30W
Frackville 162 40 46N 76 15W
Fraga 58 41 32N 0 21 E
Fraire 47 50 16N 4 31 E
Frameries 47 50 24N 3 54 E
Framlingham 29 52 14N 1 20 E
Franca 171 20 25 S 47 30W
Francavilla al Mare 63 42 25N 14 16 E
Francavilla Fontana 65 40 32N 17 35 E
France ■ 41 47 0N 3 0 E
Frances 140 36 41 S 140 55 E
Frances Creek 136 13 25 S 132 3 E
Frances L. 152 61 23N 129 30W
Frances, R. 152 60 16N 129 10W
Francés Viejo, C. 167 19 40N 70 0W
Franceville 124 1 40 S 13 32 E
Franche Comté □ 43 46 30N 5 50 E
Franches Montagnes 50 47 10N 7 0 E
Francis-Garnier 118 36 30N 1 30 E
Francis Harbour 151 52 34N 55 44W
Francisco I. Madero, Coahuila, Mexico 164 25 48N 103 18W
Francisco I. Madero, Durango, Mexico 164 24 32N 104 22W
Francisco Sá 171 16 28 S 43 30W
Francistown 125 21 7 S 27 33 E
Francofonte 65 37 13N 14 50 E
François 151 47 35N 56 45W
François L. 152 54 0N 125 30W
François, Le 167 14 38N 60 57W
Francorchamps 47 50 27N 5 57 E
Franeker 46 53 12N 5 33 E
Frankado 123 12 30N 43 12 E
Frankenberg 48 51 3N 8 47 E
Frankenthal 49 49 32N 8 21 E
Frankford = Kilcormac 39 53 10N 7 43W
Frankfort, Ind., U.S.A. 156 40 20N 86 33W
Frankfort, Kans., U.S.A. 158 39 42N 96 26W
Frankfort, Ky., U.S.A. 156 38 12N 84 52W
Frankfort, Mich., U.S.A. 156 44 38N 86 14W
Frankfort, N.Y., U.S.A. 162 43 2N 75 4W
Frankfurt □ 48 52 30N 14 0 E
Frankfurt am Main 49 50 7N 8 40 E
Frankfurt an der Oder 48 52 50N 14 31 E
Fränkische Alb 49 49 20N 11 30 E
Fränkische Saale 49 50 7N 9 49 E
Fränkische Saale, R. 49 50 7N 9 49 E
Fränkische Schweiz 49 49 45N 11 10 E
Frankland, R. 137 35 0 S 116 48 E
Franklin, Ky., U.S.A. 157 36 40N 86 30W
Franklin, La., U.S.A. 159 29 45N 91 30W
Franklin, Mass., U.S.A. 162 42 4N 71 23W
Franklin, Nebr., U.S.A. 158 40 9N 98 55W
Franklin, N.H., U.S.A. 162 43 28N 71 39W
Franklin, N.J., U.S.A. 162 41 9N 74 38W
Franklin, Pa., U.S.A. 156 41 22N 79 45W
Franklin, Tenn., U.S.A. 157 35 54N 86 53W
Franklin, Va., U.S.A. 157 36 40N 76 58W
Franklin, W. Va., U.S.A. 156 38 38N 79 21W
Franklin □ 149 71 0N 99 0W
Franklin B. 147 69 45N 126 0W
Franklin D. Roosevelt L. 160 48 30N 118 16W
Franklin I. 13 76 10 S 168 30 E
Franklin, L. 160 40 20N 115 26W
Franklin Mts., Can. 148 66 0N 125 0W
Franklin Mts., N.Z. 143 44 55 S 167 45 E
Franklin Str. 148 72 0N 96 0W
Franklinton 159 30 53N 90 10W
Franklyn Mt. 143 42 4 S 172 42 E
Franks Peak 160 43 50N 109 5W
Frankston 141 38 8 S 145 8 E
Frankton Junc. 142 37 47 S 175 16 E
Fränsta 72 62 30N 16 11 E
Frant 29 51 5N 0 17 E
Frantsa Josifa, Zemlya 76 76 0N 62 0 E
Franz 150 48 25N 84 30W
Franz Josef Fd. 12 73 20N 22 0 E
Franz Josef Land = Frantsa Josifa 76 76 0N 62 0 E
Franzburg 48 54 9N 12 52 E
Frascati 64 41 48N 12 41 E
Fraser I. 139 25 15 S 153 10 E
Fraser L. 152 54 0N 124 50W
Fraser, Mt. 137 25 35 S 118 20 E
Fraser, R., B.C., Can. 152 49 7N 123 11W
Fraser, R., Newf., Can. 151 56 39N 63 10W
Fraserburg 128 31 55 S 21 30 E
Fraserburgh 37 57 41N 2 0W
Fraserdale 150 49 55N 81 37W
Frasertown 142 38 58 S 177 28 E
Frashëri 68 40 23N 20 26 E
Frasne 43 46 50N 6 10 E
Frater 150 47 20N 84 25W
Frauenfeld 51 47 34N 8 54 E
Fray Bentos 172 33 10 S 58 15W
Frazier Downs P.O. 136 18 48 S 121 42 E
Frechilla 56 42 8N 4 50W
Fredericia 73 55 34N 9 45 E
Frederick, Md., U.S.A. 162 39 25N 77 23W
Frederick, Okla., U.S.A. 159 34 22N 99 0W
Frederick, S.D., U.S.A. 158 45 55N 98 29W
Frederick Reef 133 20 58 S 154 23 E
Frederick Sd. 153 57 10N 134 0W
Fredericksburg, Tex., U.S.A. 159 30 17N 98 55W
Fredericksburg, Va., U.S.A. 162 38 16N 77 29W
Frederickstown 159 37 35N 90 15W
Fredericton 151 45 57N 66 40W
Fredericton Junc. 151 45 41N 66 40W
Frederiksberg 72 60 12N 14 25 E
Frederiksborg Amt □ 73 55 50N 12 10 E
Frederikshåb 12 62 0N 49 30W
Frederikshavn 73 57 28N 10 31 E
Frederikssund 73 55 50N 12 3 E
Frederiksted 147 17 43N 64 53W
Fredonia, Ariz., U.S.A. 161 36 59N 112 36W
Fredonia, Kans., U.S.A. 159 37 34N 95 50W
Fredonia, N.Y., U.S.A. 156 42 26N 79 20W
Fredrikstad 71 59 13N 10 57 E
Freehold 162 40 15N 74 18W
Freel Pk. 163 38 52N 119 53W
Freeland 162 41 3N 75 48W
Freeling, Mt. 136 22 35 S 133 06 E
Freels, C. 151 49 15N 53 30W
Freeman, Calif., U.S.A. 163 35 35N 117 53W
Freeman, S.D., U.S.A. 158 43 25N 97 20W
Freeport, Bahamas 167 25 45N 88 30 E
Freeport, Can. 151 44 15N 66 20W
Freeport, Ill., U.S.A. 158 42 18N 89 40W
Freeport, N.Y., U.S.A. 162 40 39N 73 35W
Freeport, Tex., U.S.A. 159 28 55N 95 22W
Freetown 120 8 30N 13 10W
Freevater Forest 37 57 51N 4 45W
Fregenal de la Sierra 57 38 10N 6 39W
Fregene 64 41 50N 12 12 E
Fregeneda, La 56 40 58N 6 54W
Fréhel C. 42 48 40N 2 20W
Freiberg 48 50 55N 13 20 E
Freibourg = Fribourg 50 46 49N 7 9 E
Freiburg, Baden, Ger. 49 48 0N 7 52 E
Freiburg, Sachsen, Ger. 48 53 49N 9 17 E
Freiburger Alpen 50 46 37N 7 10 E
Freire 176 39 0 S 72 50W
Freirina 172 28 30 S 70 27W
Freising 49 48 24N 11 47 E
Freistadt 52 48 30N 14 30 E
Freital 48 51 0N 13 40 E
Fréjus 45 43 25N 6 44 E
Fremantle 137 32 1 S 115 47 E
Fremont, Calif., U.S.A. 163 37 32N 122 57W
Fremont, Mich., U.S.A. 156 43 29N 85 59W
Fremont, Nebr., U.S.A. 158 41 30N 96 30W
Fremont, Ohio, U.S.A. 156 41 20N 83 5W
Fremont, L. 160 43 0N 109 50W
Fremont, R. 161 38 15N 110 20W
French Camp 163 37 53N 121 16W
French Cr. 156 41 30N 80 2W
French Guiana ■ 175 4 0N 53 0W
French I. 141 38 20 S 145 22 E
French Terr. of Afars & Issas □ = Djibouti 123 11 30N 42 15 E
Frenchglen 160 42 56N 119 0W
Frenchman Butte 153 53 36N 109 36W
Frenchman Creek, R. 158 40 34N 101 35W
Frenchman, R. 160 49 25N 108 20W
Frenchpark 38 53 53N 8 25W
Frenda 118 35 2N 1 1 E
Fresco, R. 175 7 15 S 51 30W
Freshfield, C. 13 68 25 S 151 10 E
Freshford 39 52 45N 7 25W
Freshwater 28 50 42N 1 31W
Fresnillo 164 23 10N 103 0W
Fresno 163 36 47N 119 50W
Fresno Alhandiga 56 40 42N 5 37W
Fresno Res. 160 48 47N 110 0W
Freswick 37 58 35N 3 5W
Freuchie 35 56 14N 3 8W
Freudenstadt 49 48 27N 8 25 E
Freux 47 49 59N 5 27 E
Frévent 43 50 15N 2 17 E
Frew, R. 138 20 0 S 135 38 E
Frewena 138 19 50 S 135 50 E
Freycinet, C. 137 34 9 S 115 0 E
Freycinet Pen. 138 42 10 S 148 25 E
Fria 120 10 27N 13 32W
Fria, La 174 8 13N 72 15W
Friant 163 36 59N 119 43W
Frías 172 28 40 S 65 5W
Fribourg 50 46 49N 7 9 E
Fribourg □ 50 45 40N 7 0 E
Frick 50 47 31N 8 1 E
Fridafors 73 56 25N 14 39 E
Fridaythorpe 33 54 2N 0 40W
Friedberg, Bayern, Ger. 49 48 21N 10 59 E
Friedberg, Hessen, Ger. 10 50 19N 8 45 E
Friedland 49 53 40N 13 33 E
Friedrichshafen 49 47 39N 9 29 E
Friedrichskoog 48 54 1N 8 52 E
Friedrichsort 48 54 24N 10 11 E
Friedrichstadt 48 54 23N 9 6 E
Friendly (Tonga) Is. 130 19 50 S 174 30W
Friesach 52 46 57N 14 24 E
Friesack 48 52 43N 12 35 E
Friesche Wad 46 53 22N 5 44 E
Friesland □ 46 53 5N 5 50 E
Friesoythe 48 53 1N 7 51 E
Frigate, L. 150 53 15N 74 45W
Frigg E., gasfield 19 59 50N 2 20 E
Frigg, gasfield 19 59 50N 2 15 E
Frigg N.E., gasfield 19 60 0N 2 17 E
Frillesås 73 57 20N 12 12 E
Frimley 29 51 18N 0 43W
Frinnaryd 73 57 55N 14 50 E
Frinton-on-Sea 29 51 50N 1 16 E
Frio, C. 128 18 0 S 12 0 E
Frio, R. 159 29 40N 99 40W
Friockheim 37 56 39N 2 40W
Friona 159 34 40N 102 42W
Frisa, Loch 34 56 34N 6 5W
Frisian Is. 48 53 30N 6 0 E
Fristad 73 57 50N 13 0 E
Fritch 159 35 40N 101 35W
Fritsla 73 57 33N 12 47 E
Fritzlar 48 51 8N 9 19 E
Friuli-Venezia-Giulia □ 63 46 0N 13 0 E
Frizington 32 54 33N 3 30W
Frobisher B. 149 63 0N 67 0W
Frobisher L. 153 56 20N 108 15W
Frobisher Sd. 149 62 30N 66 0W
Frodsham 32 53 17N 2 45W
Frogmore 141 34 15 S 148 52 E
Frohavet 74 64 5N 9 35 E
Froid 158 48 20N 104 29W
Froid-Chapelle 47 50 9N 4 19 E
Frolovo 83 49 45N 43 30 E
Fromberg 160 45 19N 108 58W
Frombork 54 54 21N 19 41 E
Frome 28 51 16N 2 17W
Frome Downs 140 31 13 S 139 46 E
Frome, L. 140 30 45 S 139 45 E
Frome, R. 28 50 44N 2 5W
Fromentine 42 46 53N 2 9W
Frómista 56 42 16N 4 25W
Front Range 160 40 0N 105 10W
Front Royal 156 38 55N 78 10W
Fronteira 57 39 3N 7 39W
Fronteiras 170 7 5 S 40 37W
Frontera 165 18 30N 92 40W
Frontignan 44 43 27N 3 45 E
Frosinone 64 41 38N 13 20 E
Frosolone 65 41 34N 14 27 E
Frostburg 156 39 43N 78 57W
Frostisen 74 68 14N 17 10 E
Frouard 43 48 47N 6 8 E
Frövi 72 59 28N 15 24 E
Frower Pt. 39 51 40N 8 30W
Froya 71 63 43N 8 40 E
Frøya 71 63 43N 8 40 E
Fröya I. 74 63 45N 8 45 E
Fruges 43 50 30N 2 8 E
Frumoasa 70 46 28N 25 48 E
Frunze 85 42 54N 74 36 E
Fruška Gora 66 45 7N 19 30 E
Frutal 171 20 0 S 49 0W
Frutigen 50 46 35N 7 38 E
Frýdek-Místek 53 49 40N 18 20 E

Frýdlant Garibaldi Prov. Park


Frýdlant, Severočeský, Czech. 52 50 56N 15 9 E
Frýdlant, Severomoravsky, Czech. 53 49 35N 18 20 E
Fryvaldov = Jesenik 53 50 0N 17 8 E
Fthiótis □ 69 38 50N 22 25 E
Fu 72 60 57N 14 44 E
Fuan 109 27 9N 119 38 E
Fucécchio 62 43 44N 10 51 E
Fuch'ing 109 25 43N 119 22 E
Fuchou, Fukien, China 109 26 5N 119 18 E
Fuchou, Liaoning, China 107 39 45N 121 45 E
Fuchū 110 34 34N 133 14 E
Fūchū 111 35 40N 139 29 E
Fuch'üan 108 26 42N 107 33 E
Fuch'uan 109 24 50N 111 16 E
Fucino, L. 44 42 0N 13 30 E
Fuencaliente 57 38 25N 4 18W
Fuengirola 57 36 32N 4 41W
Fuente-Alamo 59 38 44N 1 24W
Fuente de Cantos 57 38 15N 6 18W
Fuente de San Esteban, La 56 40 49N 6 15W
Fuente del Maestre 57 38 31N 6 28W
Fuente el Fresno 57 39 14N 3 46W
Fuente Ovejuna 57 38 15N 5 25W
Fuentes de Andalucía 57 37 28N 5 20W
Fuentes de Ebro 58 41 31N 0 38W
Fuentes de León 57 38 5N 6 32W
Fuentes de Oñoro 56 40 33N 6 52W
Fuentesaúco 56 41 15N 5 30W
Fuerte Olimpo 172 21 0S 58 0W
Fuerte, R. 164 26 0N 109 0W
Fuerteventura, I. 116 28 30N 14 0W
Fuertey 38 53 37N 8 16W
Fufeng 106 34 20N 107 51 E
Fŭget 70 45 52N 22 10 E
Fŭget, Munţii 70 45 50N 22 9 E
Fugløysund 74 70 15N 20 20 E
Fŭgŭraş 70 45 48N 24 58 E
Fŭgŭraş, Munţii 70 45 40N 24 40 E
Fuhai 105 47 6N 87 23 E
Fuhsien, Liaoning, China 107 39 38N 122 0 E
Fuhsien, Shensi, China 106 36 2N 109 20 E
Fuhsingchen 108 22 47N 101 5 E
Fujaira 93 25 7N 56 18 E
Fuji 111 35 9N 138 39 E
Fuji-no-miya 111 35 20N 138 40 E
Fuji-San 111 35 22N 138 44 E
Fuji-yoshida 111 35 50N 138 46 E
Fujieda 111 34 52N 138 16 E
Fujioka 111 36 15N 139 5 E
Fujisawa 111 35 22N 139 29 E
Fukien □ 109 26 0N 117 30 E
Fukou 106 34 3N 114 27 E
Fuku 106 39 2N 111 3 E
Fukuchiyama 111 35 25N 135 9 E
Fukui 111 36 0N 136 10 E
Fukui-ken □ 111 36 0N 136 12 E
Fukuma 110 33 46N 130 28 E
Fukung 108 26 58N 98 54 E
Fukuoka 110 33 30N 130 30 E
Fukuoka-ken □ 110 33 30N 131 0 E
Fukuroi 111 34 45N 137 55 E
Fukushima 112 37 30N 140 15 E
Fukushima-ken □ 112 37 30N 140 15 E
Fukuyama 110 34 35N 133 20 E
Fŭlciu 70 46 17N 28 7 E
Fulda 48 50 32N 9 41 E
Fullerton, Calif., U.S.A. 163 33 52N 117 58W
Fullerton, Nebr., U.S.A. 158 41 25N 98 0W
Fulmar, oilfield 19 56 30N 2 8 E
Fülöpszállás 53 46 49N 19 16 E
Fŭlticeni 70 47 21N 26 20W
Fulton, Mo., U.S.A. 158 38 50N 91 55W
Fulton, N.Y., U.S.A. 162 43 20N 76 22W
Fuluälven 72 61 18N 13 4 E
Fulufjället 72 61 32N 12 41 E
Fulungch'üan 107 44 24N 124 37 E
Fülüpszállás 53 46 49N 19 16 E
Fumay 43 50 0N 4 40 E
Fumbusi 121 10 25N 1 20W
Fumel 44 44 30N 0 58 E
Fumin 108 25 14N 102 29 E
Funabashi 111 35 45N 140 0 E
Funafuti, I. 130 8 30S 179 0 E
Funchal 116 32 45N 16 55W
Fundación 174 10 31N 74 11W
Fundão, Brazil 171 19 55S 40 24W
Fundão, Port. 56 40 8N 7 30W
Fundu 127 14 58S 30 14 E
Fundy, B. of 151 45 0N 56 0W
Funes 174 1 0N 77 28W
Funing, Hopei, China 107 39 54N 119 12 E
Funing, Yunnan, China 108 23 37N 105 36 E
Funiu Shan 106 33 40N 112 30 E
Funsi 120 10 21N 1 54W
Funtua 121 11 30N 7 18 E
Fupien 108 31 18N 102 27 E
Fup'ing 106 34 47N 109 7 E
Fur 73 56 50N 9 0 E
Furat, Nahr al 92 33 30N 43 0 E
Furbero 165 20 22N 97 31W
Furka Pass 51 46 34N 8 35 E
Furmanov 81 57 25N 41 3 E
Furmanovka 85 44 17N 72 57 E
Furmanovo 83 49 42N 49 25 E
Furnas, Represa de 173 20 50S 45 0W
Furneaux Group 138 40 10S 147 50 E
Furness, Pen. 32 54 12N 3 10W
Fürstenau 48 52 32N 7 40 E
Fürstenfeld 52 47 3N 16 3 E
Fürstenfeldbruck 49 48 10N 11 15 E
Fürstenwalde 48 52 20N 14 3 E
Fürth 49 49 29N 11 0 E
Fürth i. Wald 49 49 19N 12 51 E
Furtwangen 49 48 3N 8 14 E
Furudal 72 61 10N 15 11 E
Furukawa 111 36 14N 137 11 E
Furusund 72 59 40N 18 55 E
Fury and Hecla Str. 149 69 56N 84 0W
Fusa 71 60 12N 5 37 E
Fusagasugá 174 4 21N 74 22W
Fuscaldo 65 39 25N 16 1 E
Fushan 107 37 30N 121 5 E
Fushë Arrëzi 68 42 4N 20 2 E
Fushun, Liaoning, China 107 41 50N 123 55 E
Fushun, Szechwan, China 108 29 13N 105 0 E
Fush'un Chiang, R. 109 30 5N 120 5 E
Fusio 51 46 27N 8 40 E
Füssen 49 47 35N 10 43 E
Fusui 108 22 35N 107 58 E
Fusung 107 42 15N 127 20 E
Futago-Yama 110 33 35N 131 36 E
Futing 109 27 15N 120 10 E
Futuk 121 9 45N 10 56 E
Futuna I. 130 14 25S 178 20 E
Fŭurei 70 45 6N 27 19 E
Fuwa 122 31 12N 30 33 E
Fuyang 109 30 5N 119 56 E
Fuyang Ho, R. 106 38 14N 116 5 E
Fuyü 107 45 10N 124 50 E
Fuyüan 105 47 40N 132 30 E
Füzesgyarmat 53 47 6N 21 14 E
Fwaka 125 12 5S 29 25 E
Fylde 32 53 50N 2 58W
Fylingdales Moor 33 54 22N 0 32W
Fyn 73 55 20N 10 30 E
Fyne, L. 34 56 0N 5 20W
Fyns Amt □ 73 55 15N 10 30 E
Fynshav 73 54 59N 9 59 E
Fyresvatn 71 59 6N 8 10 E
Fyvie 37 57 26N 2 24W


# G


Gaanda 121 10 10N 12 27 E
Gaba 123 6 20N 35 7 E
Gaba Tula 82 0 20N 38 35 E
Gabah, C. 91 8 0N 50 0 E
Gabarin 121 11 8N 10 27 E
Gabbs 163 38 52N 117 55W
Gabela 124 11 0S 14 37 E
Gaberones = Gaborone 128 24 37S 25 57 E
Gabès 119 33 53N 10 2 E
Gabès, Golfe de 119 34 0N 10 30 E
Gabgaba, W. 122 22 10N 33 5 E
Gabin 54 52 23N 19 41 E
Gabon ■ 124 0 10S 10 0 E
Gaborone 128 24 37S 25 57 E
Gabrovo 67 42 52N 25 27 E
Gacé 42 48 49N 0 20 E
Gach Saran 93 30 15N 50 45 E
Gacko 66 43 10N 18 33 E
Gada 121 13 38N 5 36 E
Gadag 97 15 30N 75 45 E
Gadamai 123 17 11N 36 10 E
Gadap 94 25 5N 67 28 E
Gadarwara 95 22 50N 78 50 E
Gäddede 74 64 30N 14 15 E
Gadebusch 48 53 41N 11 6 E
Gadein 123 8 10N 28 45 E
Gadhada 94 22 0N 71 35 E
Gadmen 51 46 45N 8 16 E
Gádor, Sierra de 59 36 57N 2 45W
Gadsden, Ala., U.S.A. 157 34 1N 86 0W
Gadsden, Ariz., U.S.A. 161 32 35N 114 47W
Gadwal 96 16 10N 77 50 E
Gaerwen 31 53 13N 4 17W
Gaeta 64 41 12N 13 35 E
Gaeta, G. di 64 41 0N 13 25 E
Gaffney 157 35 10N 81 31W
Gafsa 119 34 24N 8 51 E
Gagarin (Gzhatsk) 80 55 30N 35 0 E
Gagetown 151 45 46N 66 29W
Gagino 81 55 15N 45 10 E
Gagliano del Capo 65 39 50N 18 23 E
Gagnef 72 60 36N 15 5 E
Gagnoa 120 6 4N 5 55W
Gagnon 151 51 50N 68 5W
Gagnon, L. 153 62 3N 110 27W
Gagra 83 43 20N 40 10 E
Gah 44 43 12N 0 27W
Gahini 126 1 50S 30 30 E
Gahmar 95 25 27N 83 55 E
Gaibandha 98 25 20N 89 36 E
Gaïdhouronísi 69 34 53N 25 41 E
Gail 159 32 48N 101 25W
Gail, R. 52 46 37N 13 15 E
Gaillac 44 43 54N 1 54 E
Gaillon 42 49 10N 1 20 E
Gaima 135 8 9S 142 59 E
Gainesville, Fla., U.S.A. 157 29 38N 82 20W
Gainesville, Ga., U.S.A. 157 34 17N 83 47W
Gainesville, Mo., U.S.A. 159 36 35N 92 26W
Gainesville, Tex., U.S.A. 159 33 40N 97 10W
Gainford 33 54 34N 1 44W
Gainsborough 33 53 23N 0 46W
Gairdner L. 140 31 30S 136 0 E
Gairloch 36 57 42N 5 40W
Gairloch L. 36 57 43N 5 45W
Gairlochy 36 56 55N 5 0W
Gairsay, I. 37 59 4N 2 59W
Gais 51 47 22N 9 27 E
Gaithersburg 162 39 9N 77 12W
Gaj 66 45 28N 17 3 E
Gajale 121 11 25N 8 10 E
Gajiram 121 12 29N 13 9 E
Gakuch 95 36 7N 73 45 E
Gal Oya Res. 97 8 5N 80 55 E
Galachipa 98 22 8N 90 26 E
Galadi 121 13 5N 6 20 E
Galán, Cerro 172 25 55S 66 52W
Galana, R. 126 3 0S 39 10 E
Galangue 125 13 48S 16 3 E
Galanta 53 48 11N 17 45 E
Galápagos, Is. 131 0 0 89 0W
Galas, R. 101 4 55N 101 57 E
Galashiels 35 55 37N 2 50W
Galatás 69 37 30N 23 26 E
Galatea 142 38 24S 176 45 E
Galaţi 70 45 27N 28 2 E
Galaţi □ 70 45 45N 27 30 E
Galatina 65 40 10N 18 10 E
Galátone 65 40 8N 18 3 E
Galax 157 36 42N 80 57W
Galaxídhion 69 38 22N 22 23 E
Galbally 39 52 24N 8 17W
Galbraith 138 16 25S 141 30 E
Galdhøpiggen 71 61 38N 8 18 E
Galeana 164 24 50N 100 4W
Galela 103 1 50N 127 55 E
Galena, Austral. 137 27 48S 114 42 E
Galena, U.S.A. 147 64 42N 157 0W
Galeota Point 167 10 8N 61 0W
Galera 59 37 45N 2 33W
Galera, Pta. de la 174 10 48N 75 16W
Galesburg 158 40 57N 90 23W
Galey R. 39 52 30N 9 23W
Galgate 32 53 59N 2 47W
Galheirão, R. 171 12 23S 45 5W
Galheiros 171 13 18S 46 25W
Galicea Mare 70 44 4N 23 19 E
Galich, R.S.F.S.R., U.S.S.R. 81 58 23N 42 18 E
Galich, Uk., U.S.S.R. 80 49 10N 24 40 E
Galiche 67 43 34N 23 50 E
Galicia 56 42 43N 8 0W
Galijp 46 53 10N 5 58 E
Galilee = Hagalil 90 32 53N 35 18 E
Galilee, L. 138 22 20S 145 50 E
Galite, Is. de la 119 37 30N 8 59 E
Galivro Mts. 161 32 40N 110 30W
Gallan Hd. 36 58 14N 7 0W
Gallarate 62 45 40N 8 48 E
Gallatin 157 36 24N 86 27W
Galle 97 6 5N 80 10 E
Gallego 164 29 49N 106 22W
Gállego, R. 58 42 23N 0 30W
Gallegos, R. 176 51 50S 71 0W
Galley Hd. 39 51 32N 8 56W
Galliate 62 45 27N 8 44 E
Gallinas, Pta. 174 12 28N 71 40W
Gallipoli 65 40 8N 18 0 E
Gallipoli = Gelibolu 68 40 28N 26 43 E
Gallipolis 156 38 50N 82 10W
Gällivare 74 67 9N 20 40 E
Gällö 72 62 56N 15 15 E
Gallo, C. di 64 38 13N 13 19 E
Gallocanta, Laguna de 58 40 58N 1 30W
Galloway 34 55 0N 4 25W
Galloway, Mull of 34 54 38N 4 50W
Gallup 161 35 30N 108 54W
Gallur 58 41 52N 1 19W
Gallyaaral 85 40 2N 67 35 E
Galmi 121 13 58N 5 41 E
Gal'on 90 31 38N 34 51 E
Galong 141 34 37S 148 34 E
Galoya 93 8 10N 80 55 E
Galston 34 55 36N 4 22W
Galt, Can. 150 43 21N 80 19W
Galt, U.S.A. 163 38 15N 121 18W
Galtström 72 62 10N 17 30 E
Galtür 52 46 58N 10 11 E
Galty Mts. 39 52 22N 8 10W
Galtymore, Mt. 39 52 22N 8 12W
Galva 158 41 10N 90 0W
Galve de Sorbe 58 41 13N 3 10W
Galveston 159 29 15N 94 48W
Galveston B. 159 29 30N 94 50W
Gálvez, Argent. 172 32 0S 61 20W
Gálvez, Spain 57 39 42N 4 16W
Galway 39 53 16N 9 4W
Galway □ 38 53 16N 9 3W
Galway B. 39 53 10N 9 20W
Gam, R. 100 21 55N 105 12 E
Gamagōri 111 34 50N 137 14 E
Gamare, L. 123 11 32N 41 40 E
Gamarra 174 8 20N 73 45W
Gamawa 121 12 10N 10 31 E
Gambaga 121 10 30N 0 28W
Gambat 94 27 17N 68 26 E
Gambela 123 8 14N 34 38 E
Gambell 147 63 55N 171 50W
Gambia ■ 120 13 25N 16 0W
Gambia, R. 120 13 20N 15 45W
Gambier, C. 136 11 56S 130 57 E
Gambier Is. 140 35 3S 136 30 E
Gamboli 94 29 53N 68 24 E
Gamboma 124 1 55S 15 52 E
Gamboola 138 16 29S 143 43 E
Gameleira 170 7 50S 50 0W
Gamerco 161 35 33N 108 56W
Gamleby 73 57 54N 16 20W
Gamlingay 29 52 9N 0 11W
Gammelgarn 171 57 24N 18 49 E
Gammon, R. 153 51 24N 95 44W
Gamōda-Saki 110 33 50N 134 45 E
Gan (Addu Atoll) 87 0 10S 71 10 E
Gan Shemu'el 90 32 28N 34 56 E
Gan Yavne 90 31 48N 34 42 E
Ganado, Ariz., U.S.A. 161 35 46N 109 41W
Ganado, Tex., U.S.A. 159 29 4N 96 31W
Gananoque 150 44 20N 76 10W
Ganaveh 93 29 35N 50 35 E
Gand 47 51 2N 3 37 E
Gandak, R. 95 27 0N 84 8 E
Gandava 94 28 32N 67 32 E
Gander 151 48 18N 54 29W
Gander L. 151 48 58N 54 35W
Ganderowe Falls 127 17 20S 29 10 E
Gandesa 58 41 3N 0 26 E
Gand = Gent 47 51 2N 3 37 E
Gandhi Sagar 94 24 40N 75 40 E
Gandi 121 12 55N 5 49 E
Gandía 59 38 58N 0 9W
Gandino 62 45 50N 9 52 E
Gandole 121 8 28N 11 35 E
Gandu 171 13 45S 39 30W
Ganedidalem = Gani 103 0 48S 128 14 E
Ganetti 122 18 0N 31 10 E
Ganga, Mouths of the 95 21 30N 90 0 E
Ganga, R. 95 25 0N 88 0 E
Ganganagar 94 29 56N 73 56 E
Gangapur 94 26 32N 76 37 E
Gangara 121 14 35N 8 40 E
Gangavati 97 15 30N 76 36 E
Gangaw 98 22 5N 94 15 E
Ganges 44 43 56N 3 42 E
Ganges = Ganga, R. 95 25 0N 88 0 E
Gangoh 94 29 46N 77 18 E
Gangtok 98 27 20N 88 37 E
Ganj 95 27 45N 78 47 E
Ganmain 141 34 47S 147 1 E
Gannat 44 46 7N 3 11 E
Gannett Pk. 160 43 15N 109 47W
Gannvalley 158 44 3N 98 57W
Ganserdorf 53 48 20N 16 43 E
Ganta (Gompa) 120 7 15N 8 59W
Gantheaume B. 137 27 40S 114 10 E
Gantheaume, C. 140 36 4S 137 25 E
Gantsevichi 80 52 42N 26 30 E
Ganyushkino 83 46 35N 49 20 E
Ganzi 123 4 30N 31 15 E
Gao □ 121 18 0N 1 0 E
Gao Bang 101 22 37N 106 18 E
Gaoua 120 10 20N 3 8W
Gaoual 120 11 45N 13 25W
Gaouz 118 31 52N 4 20W
Gap 45 44 33N 6 5 E
Gar Dzong 93 32 20N 79 55 E
Gara, L. 38 53 57N 8 26W
Garachiné 166 8 0N 78 12W
Garanhuns 170 8 50S 36 30W
Garawe 120 4 35N 8 0W
Garba Tula 126 0 30N 38 32 E
Garber 159 36 30N 97 36W
Garberville 160 40 11N 123 50W
Garboldisham 29 52 24N 0 57 E
Garça 171 22 14S 49 37W
Garças, R. 170 8 43S 39 41W
Gard □ 45 44 2N 4 10 E
Garda, L. di 62 45 40N 10 40 E
Gardanne 45 43 27N 5 27 E
Garde L. 153 62 50N 106 13W
Gardelegen 48 52 32N 11 21 E
Garden City, Kans., U.S.A. 159 38 0N 100 45W
Garden City, Tex., U.S.A. 159 31 52N 101 28W
Garden Grove 163 33 47N 117 55W
Gardenstown 37 57 40N 2 20W
Gardez 94 33 31N 68 59 E
Gardhiki 69 38 50N 21 55 E
Gardian 117 15 45N 19 40 E
Gardiner, Can. 150 49 19N 81 2W
Gardiner, Mont., U.S.A. 160 45 3N 110 53W
Gardiner, New Mexico, U.S.A. 159 36 55N 104 29W
Gardiners I. 162 41 4N 72 5W
Gardner 162 42 35N 72 0W
Gardner Canal 152 53 27N 128 8W
Gardnerville 160 38 59N 119 47W
Gardo 91 9 18N 49 20 E
Gare, L. 34 56 1N 4 50W
Garelochhead 34 56 7N 4 50W
Gareloi I. 147 51 49N 178 50W
Gareśnica 66 45 36N 16 56 E
Garéssio 62 44 12N 8 1 E
Garey 163 34 53N 120 19W
Garfield, Utah, U.S.A. 160 40 45N 112 15W
Garfield, Wash., U.S.A. 160 47 3N 117 8W
Garforth 33 53 48N 1 22W
Gargaliánoi 69 37 4N 21 38 E
Gargano, Mte. 65 41 43N 15 43 E
Gargans, Mt. 44 45 37N 1 39 E
Gargantua, C. 150 47 35N 85 0W
Gargoune 121 15 56N 0 13 E
Gargrave 32 53 58N 2 7W
Garhshankar 94 31 13N 76 11 E
Gari 84 59 26N 62 21 E
Garibaldi 152 49 56N 123 15W
Garibaldi Prov. Park 152 49 50N 122 40W

Garies Ghent


Garies **125** 30 32 S 17 59 E
Garigliano, R. **64** 41 13N 13 44 E
Garissa **126** 0 25 S 39 40 E
Garissa □ **126** 0 20 S 40 0 E
Garkida **121** 10 27N 12 36 E
Garko **121** 11 45N 8 53 E
Garland **160** 41 47N 112 10W
Garlasco **62** 45 11N 8 55 E
Garlieston **34** 54 47N 4 22W
Garm **85** 39 0N 70 20 E
Garmab **94** 32 50N 65 30 E
Garmisch-Partenkirchen **49** 47 30N 11 5 E
Garmo **126** 61 51N 8 48 E
Garmouth **37** 57 40N 3 8W
Garmsar **93** 35 20N 52 25 E
Garner **158** 43 4N 93 37W
Garnett **158** 38 18N 95 12W
Garo Hills **95** 25 30N 90 30 E
Garoe **91** 8 35N 48 40 E
Garoke **139** 36 45 S 141 30 E
Garona, R. **58** 42 55N 0 45 E
Garonne, R. **44** 45 2N 0 36W
Garoua (Garwa) **121** 9 19N 13 21 E
Garraway **120** 4 35N 8 0W
Garrel **48** 52 58N 7 59 E
Garrigues **44** 43 40N 3 30 E
Garrison, Ireland **38** 54 25N 8 5W
Garrison, Mont., U.S.A. **160** 46 37N 112 56W
Garrison, N.D., U.S.A. **158** 31 50N 94 28W
Garrison, Tex., U.S.A. **159** 47 39N 101 27W
Garrison Res. **158** 47 30N 102 0W
Garron Pt. **38** 55 3N 6 0W
Garrovillas **57** 39 40N 6 33W
Garrucha **59** 37 11N 1 49W
Garry L., Can. **148** 65 58N 100 18W
Garry L., U.K. **37** 57 5N 4 52W
Garry, R. **37** 56 47N 3 47W
Garsdale Head **32** 54 19N 2 19W
Garsen **124** 2 20 S 40 5 E
Garson L., Alta., Can. **153** 56 19N 110 2W
Garson L., Sask., Can. **153** 56 20N 110 1W
Garstang **32** 53 53N 2 47W
Garston **32** 53 21N 2 55W
Gartempe, R. **44** 46 47N 0 49 E
Gartok **93** 31 59N 80 30 E
Gartz **48** 54 17N 13 21 E
Garu, Ghana **121** 10 55N 0 20W
Garu, Nigeria **121** 13 35N 5 25 E
Garub **128** 26 37 S 16 0 E
Garupá **170** 1 25 S 51 35W
Garut **103** 7 14 S 107 53 E
Garvagh **38** 55 0N 6 41W
Garvaghey **38** 54 29N 7 8W
Garvald **35** 55 55N 2 39W
Garváo **57** 37 42N 8 21W
Garvellachs, Is. **34** 56 14N 5 48W
Garvie Mts. **143** 45 30 S 168 50 E
Garwa **95** 24 11N 83 47 E
Garwolin **54** 51 55N 21 38 E
Gary **156** 41 35N 87 20W
Garzón **174** 2 10N 75 40W
Gasan Kuli **76** 37 40N 54 20 E
Gascogne **44** 43 45N 0 20 E
Gascogne, G. de **58** 44 0N 2 0W
Gascony = Gascogne **44** 43 45N 0 20 E
Gascoyne Junc. Teleg. Off. **137** 25 2 S 115 17 E
Gascoyne, R. **137** 24 52 S 113 37 E
Gascueña **58** 40 18N 2 31W
Gash, W. **123** 15 0N 37 15 E
Gashaka **121** 7 20N 11 29 E
Gasherbrum **95** 35 40N 76 40 E
Gashua **121** 12 54N 11 0 E
Gasmata **138** 6 15 S 150 30 E
Gaspé **151** 48 52N 64 30W
Gaspé, C. **151** 48 48N 64 7W
Gaspé Pass. **151** 49 10N 64 0W
Gaspé Pen. **151** 48 45N 65 40W
Gaspésie, Parc Prov. de la **151** 48 55N 65 50W
Gaspesian Prov. Park **151** 49 0N 66 45W
Gassaway **156** 38 42N 80 43W
Gasselte **46** 52 58N 6 48 E
Gasselternijveen **46** 52 59N 6 51 E
Gássino Torinese **62** 45 8N 7 50 E
Gassol **121** 8 34N 10 25 E
Gastonia **157** 35 17N 81 10W
Gastoúni **69** 37 51N 21 15 E
Gastoúri **68** 39 34N 19 54 E
Gastre **176** 42 10 S 69 15W
Gata, C. de **59** 36 41N 2 13W
Gata, Sierra de **56** 40 20N 6 20W
Gataga, R. **152** 58 35N 126 59W
Gatchina **80** 59 35N 30 0 E
Gatehouse of Fleet **34** 54 53N 4 10W
Gateshead **35** 54 57N 1 37W
Gatesville **159** 31 29N 97 45W
Gaths **127** 26 2 S 30 32 E
Gatico **172** 22 40 S 70 20W
Gatinais **43** 48 5N 2 40 E
Gâtine, Hauteurs de **44** 46 35N 0 45W
Gatineau, Parc de la **150** 45 20N 76 0W
Gatineau, R. **150** 45 27N 75 42W
Gatley **32** 53 25N 2 15W
Gatooma **125** 18 20 S 29 52 E
Gattinara **62** 45 37N 8 22 E
Gatun, L. **166** 9 7N 79 56W
Gaucín **57** 36 31N 5 19W
Gaud-i-Zirreh **93** 29 45N 62 0 E
Gauer L. **153** 57 0N 97 50W
Gauhati **98** 26 10N 91 45 E
Gauja, R. **80** 57 10N 24 45 E
Gaula, R. **71** 62 57N 11 0 E
Gaurain-Ramecroix **47** 50 36N 3 30 E
Gaurdak **85** 37 50N 66 4 E
Gaussberg, Mt. **13** 66 45 S 89 0 E
Gausta **71** 59 50N 8 37 E
Gausta, Mt. **75** 59 48N 8 40 E
Gavá **58** 41 18N 2 0 E
Gavarnie **44** 42 44N 0 3W
Gavater **93** 25 10N 61 23 E
Gavdhopoúla **69** 34 56N 24 0 E
Gávdhos **69** 34 50N 24 5 E
Gavere **47** 50 55N 3 40 E
Gavião **57** 39 28N 7 50W
Gaviota **163** 34 29N 120 13W
Gavle **72** 60 41N 17 13 E
Gävle **72** 60 40N 17 9 E
Gävleborgs Lan □ **72** 61 20N 16 15 E
Gavorrano **62** 42 55N 10 55 E
Gavray **42** 49 55N 1 20W
Gavrilov Yam **81** 57 10N 39 37 E
Gávrion **69** 37 54N 24 44 E
Gawachab **128** 27 4 S 17 55 E
Gawai **98** 27 56N 97 40 E
Gawilgarh Hills **96** 21 15N 76 45 E
Gawler **140** 34 30 S 138 42 E
Gawler Ranges **136** 32 30 S 135 45 E
Gawthwaite **32** 54 16N 3 6W
Gay **84** 51 27N 58 27 E
Gaya, India **95** 24 47N 85 4 E
Gaya, Niger **121** 11 58N 3 28 E
Gaya, Nigeria **121** 11 57N 9 0 E
Gaylord **156** 45 1N 84 35W
Gayndah **139** 25 35 S 151 39 E
Gayny **84** 60 18N 54 19 E
Gaysin **82** 48 57N 28 25 E
Gayton **29** 52 45N 0 35 E
Gayvoron **82** 48 22N 29 45 E
Gaywood **29** 52 46N 0 26 E
Gaza **90** 31 30N 34 28 E
Gaza □ **129** 23 10 S 32 45 E
Gaza Strip **90** 31 29N 34 25 E
Gazaoua **121** 13 32N 7 55 E
Gazelle Pen. **135** 4 40 S 152 0 E
Gazi **126** 1 3N 24 30 E
Gaziantep **92** 37 6N 37 23 E
Gbanga **120** 7 19N 9 13W
Gbekebo **121** 6 26N 4 48 E
Gboko **121** 7 17N 9 4 E
Gbongan **121** 7 28N 4 20 E
Gcuwa **129** 32 20 S 28 11 E
Gdansk **54** 54 22N 18 40 E
Gdansk □ **54** 54 10N 18 30 E
Gdanska, Zatoka **54** 54 30N 19 20 E
Gdov **80** 58 40N 27 55 E
Gdynia **54** 54 35N 18 33 E
Geashill **39** 53 14N 7 20W
Gebe, I. **103** 0 5N 129 25 E
Gebeit Mine **122** 21 3N 36 29 E
Gecoa **123** 7 30N 35 18 E
Gedaref **123** 14 2N 35 28 E
Gedera **90** 31 49N 34 46 E
Gedinne **47** 49 59N 4 56 E
Gedney **29** 52 47N 0 5W
Gedo **123** 9 2N 37 25 E
Gèdre **44** 42 47N 0 2 E
Gedser **73** 54 35N 11 55 E
Gedser Odde, C. **73** 54 30N 12 5 E
Geel **47** 51 10N 4 59 E
Geelong **140** 38 10 S 144 22 E
Geelvink Chan. **137** 28 30 S 114 0 E
Geer, R. **47** 50 51N 5 42 E
Geestenseth **48** 53 31N 8 51 E
Geesthacht **48** 53 25N 10 20 E
Geffen **46** 51 44N 5 28 E
Geh **126** 26 10N 60 0 E
Geia **90** 31 38N 34 37 E
Geidam **121** 12 57N 11 57 E
Geikie, R. **153** 57 45N 103 52W
Geilenkirchen **48** 50 58N 6 8 E
Geili **123** 16 1N 32 37 E
Geilo **71** 60 32N 8 14 E
Geinica **53** 48 51N 20 55 E
Geisingen **49** 47 55N 8 37 E
Geita **126** 2 48 S 32 12 E
Geita □ **126** 2 50 S 32 10 E
Gel, R. **123** 7 5N 29 10 E
Gel River **123** 7 5N 29 10 E
Gela, Golfo di **65** 37 0N 14 8 E
Geladi **91** 6 59N 46 30 E
Gelderland □ **46** 52 5N 6 10 E
Geldermalsen **46** 51 53N 5 17 E
Geldern **48** 51 32N 6 18 E
Geldrop **47** 51 25N 5 32 E
Geleen **47** 50 57N 5 49 E
Gelehun **120** 8 20N 11 40W
Gelendzhik **82** 44 33N 38 17 E
Gelibolu **68** 40 28N 26 43 E
Gelnhausen **49** 50 12N 9 12 E
Gelsenkirchen **48** 51 30N 7 5 E
Gelting **48** 54 43N 9 53 E
Gemas **101** 2 37N 102 36 E
Gembloux **47** 50 34N 4 43 E
Gembu **121** 8 58N 12 31 E
Gemena **124** 3 20N 19 40 E
Gemerek **92** 39 15N 36 10 E
Gemert **47** 51 33N 5 41 E
Gemiston **128** 26 15 S 28 10 E
Gemlik **92** 40 26N 29 13 E
Gemmi **49** 46 25N 7 37 E
Gemona del Friuli **63** 46 16N 13 7 E
Gemsa **122** 27 39N 33 35 E
Gemu-Gofa □ **123** 5 40N 36 40 E
Gemünden **49** 50 3N 9 43 E
Genale **123** 6 0N 39 30 E
Genappe **47** 50 37N 4 27 E
Gençay **44** 46 23N 0 23 E
Gendringen **46** 51 52N 6 21 E
Gendt **46** 51 53N 5 59 E
Geneina, Gebel **122** 29 2N 33 55 E
Genemuiden **46** 52 38N 6 2 E
General Acha **172** 37 20 S 64 38W
General Alvear, B. A., Argent. **172** 36 0 S 60 0W
General Alvear, Mend., Argent. **172** 35 0 S 67 40W
General Artigas **172** 26 52 S 56 16W
General Belgrano **172** 36 0 S 58 30W
General Cabrera **172** 32 53 S 63 58W
General Cepeda **164** 25 23N 101 27W
General Guido **172** 36 40 S 57 50W
General Juan Madariaga **172** 37 0 S 57 0W
General La Madrid **172** 37 30 S 61 10W
General MacArthur **103** 11 18N 125 28 E
General Martin Mignuel de Güemes **172** 24 50 S 65 0W
General Paz **172** 27 45 S 57 36W
General Paz, L. **176** 44 0 S 72 0W
General Pico **172** 35 45 S 63 50W
General Pinedo **172** 27 15 S 61 30W
General Pinto **172** 34 45 S 61 50W
General Roca **176** 30 0 S 67 40W
General Sampaio **170** 4 2 S 39 29W
General Santos **103** 6 12N 125 14 E
General Toshevo **67** 43 42N 28 6 E
General Treviño **165** 26 14N 99 29W
General Trías **164** 28 21N 106 22W
General Viamonte **172** 35 1 S 61 3W
General Villegas **172** 35 0 S 63 0W
Generoso, Mte. **51** 45 56N 9 2 E
Genesee **160** 46 31N 116 59W
Genesee, R. **156** 41 35N 78 0W
Geneseo, Ill., U.S.A. **158** 41 25N 90 10W
Geneseo, Kans., U.S.A. **158** 38 32N 98 8W
Geneva, Ala., U.S.A. **157** 31 2N 85 52W
Geneva, Nebr., U.S.A. **158** 40 35N 97 35W
Geneva, N.Y., U.S.A. **162** 42 53N 77 0W
Geneva, Ohio, U.S.A. **156** 41 49N 80 58W
Geneva = Genève **50** 46 12N 6 9 E
Geneva, L. **156** 42 38N 88 30W
Geneva, L. = Léman, Lac **50** 46 26N 6 30 E
Genève **50** 46 12N 6 9 E
Genève □ **50** 46 10N 6 10 E
Gengenbach **49** 48 25N 8 0 E
Genichesk **82** 46 12N 34 50 E
Genil, R. **57** 37 12N 3 50W
Génissiat, Barrage de **45** 46 1N 5 48 E
Genk **47** 50 58N 5 32 E
Genkai-Nada **110** 34 0N 130 0 E
Genlis **43** 47 15N 5 12 E
Gennargentu, Mt. del **64** 40 0N 9 10 E
Gennep **47** 51 41N 5 59 E
Gennes **42** 47 20N 0 17W
Genoa, Austral. **141** 37 29 S 149 35 E
Genoa, Nebr., U.S.A. **158** 41 31N 97 44W
Genoa, N.Y., U.S.A. **162** 42 40N 76 32W
Genoa = Génova **62** 44 24N 8 57 E
Génova **62** 44 24N 8 56 E
Génova, Golfo di **62** 44 0N 9 0 E
Gent **47** 51 2N 3 37 E
Gentbrugge **47** 51 3N 3 47 E
Genteng **103** 7 25 S 106 23 E
Genthin **48** 52 24N 12 10 E
Gentio do Ouro **170** 11 25 S 42 30W
Geographe B. **137** 33 30 S 113 20 E
Geographe Chan. **137** 24 30 S 113 0 E
Geokchay **83** 40 42N 47 43 E
George, Can. **151** 46 12N 62 32W
George, S. Afr. **128** 33 58 S 22 29 E
George, L., New South Wales, Austral. **141** 35 10 S 149 25 E
George, L., S. Austral., Austral. **140** 37 25 S 140 0 E
George, L., W. A., Austral. **137** 22 45 S 123 40 E
George, L., Uganda **126** 0 5N 30 10 E
George, L., Fla., U.S.A. **157** 29 15N 81 35W
George, L., N.Y., U.S.A. **162** 43 30N 73 30W
George, Mt. **137** 25 17 S 119 0 E
George, R. **151** 58 49N 66 10W
George River = Port Nouveau **149** 58 30N 65 50W
George Sound **143** 44 52 S 167 25 E
George Town, Austral. **138** 41 5 S 146 49 E
George Town, Bahamas **166** 23 33N 75 47W
George Town, Malay. **101** 5 25N 100 19 E
George V Coast **13** 67 0 S 148 0 E
George West **159** 28 18N 98 5W
Georgetown, Austral. **133** 18 17 S 143 33 E
Georgetown, Ont., Can. **150** 43 40N 80 0W
Georgetown, P.E.I., Can. **151** 46 13N 62 24W
Georgetown, Cay. Is. **166** 19 20N 81 24W
Georgetown, Gambia **120** 13 30N 14 47W
Georgetown, Guyana **174** 6 50N 58 12W
Georgetown, Colo., U.S.A. **160** 39 46N 105 49W
Georgetown, Del., U.S.A. **162** 38 42N 75 23W
Georgetown, N.Y., U.S.A. **162** 42 46N 75 44W
Georgetown, Ohio, U.S.A. **156** 38 50N 83 50W
Georgetown, S.C., U.S.A. **157** 33 22N 79 15W
Georgetown, Tex., U.S.A. **159** 30 45N 98 10W
Georgi Dimitrov **67** 42 15N 23 54 E
Georgia □ **156** 32 0N 82 0W
Georgia, Str. of **152** 49 25N 124 0W
Georgian B. **150** 45 15N 81 0W
Georgian S.S.R. □ **83** 41 0N 45 0 E
Georgievsk **83** 44 12N 43 28 E
Georgina Downs **138** 21 10 S 137 40 E
Georgina, R. **138** 23 30 S 139 47 E
Georgiu-Dezh **81** 51 3N 39 20 E
Georgiyevka **85** 43 3N 74 43 E
Gera **48** 50 53N 12 5 E
Gera □ **48** 50 45N 11 30 E
Geraardsbergen **47** 50 45N 3 53 E
Geral de Goias, Serra **171** 12 0 S 46 0W
Geral do Paranã Serra **171** 15 0 S 47 0W
Geral, Serra, Bahia, Brazil **171** 14 0 S 41 0W
Geral, Serra, Goiás, Brazil **170** 11 15 S 46 30W
Geral, Serra, Santa Catarina, Brazil **173** 26 25 S 50 0W
Geraldine, N.Z. **143** 44 5 S 171 15 E
Geraldine, U.S.A. **160** 47 45N 110 18W
Geraldton, Austral. **137** 28 48 S 114 32 E
Geraldton, Can. **150** 49 44N 86 59W
Geranium **140** 35 23 S 140 11 E
Gerardmer **43** 48 3N 6 50 E
Gerdine, Mt. **147** 61 32N 152 30W
Gerede **82** 40 45N 32 10 E
Gérgal **59** 37 7N 2 31W
Geriban **91** 7 10N 48 55 E
Gerik **101** 5 25N 100 8 E
Gering **158** 41 51N 103 40W
Gerizim **90** 32 13N 35 15 E
Gerlach **160** 40 43N 119 27W
Gerlachovka, Mt. **53** 49 11N 20 7 E
Gerlafingen **50** 47 10N 7 34 E
Gerlev **73** 56 36N 10 9 E
Gerlogubi **91** 6 53N 45 3 E
German Planina **66** 42 33N 22 0 E
Germansen Landing **152** 55 43N 124 40W
Germany, East ■ **48** 52 0N 12 0 E
Germany, West ■ **48** 52 0N 9 0 E
Germersheim **49** 49 13N 8 0 E
Germiston **125** 26 11 S 28 10 E
Gernsheim **49** 49 44N 8 29 E
Gero **111** 35 48N 137 14 E
Gerogery **141** 35 50 S 147 1 E
Gerolstein **49** 50 12N 6 24 E
Gerona **58** 41 58N 2 46 E
Gerona □ **58** 42 11N 2 30 E
Gérouville **47** 49 37N 5 26 E
Gerrans B. **30** 50 12N 4 57W
Gerrard **152** 50 30N 117 17W
Gerrards Cross **29** 51 35N 0 32W
Gerrild **73** 56 30N 10 50 E
Gerringong **141** 34 46 S 150 47 E
Gers □ **44** 43 35N 0 38 E
Gersau **51** 47 0N 8 32 E
Gersoppa Falls **97** 14 12N 74 46 E
Gerufa **128** 19 8 S 26 0 E
Gerze **92** 41 45N 35 10 E
Geseke **48** 51 38N 8 29 E
Geser **103** 3 50N 130 35 E
Gesso, R. **62** 44 21N 7 20 E
Gesves **47** 50 24N 5 4 E
Getafe **56** 40 18N 3 44W
Gethsémani **151** 50 13N 60 40W
Gettysburg, Pa., U.S.A. **156** 39 47N 77 18W
Gettysburg, S.D., U.S.A. **158** 45 3N 99 56W
Getz Ice Shelf **13** 75 0 S 130 0W
Geul, R. **47** 50 53N 5 43 E
Geurie **141** 32 22 S 148 50 E
Gevaudan **44** 44 40N 3 40 E
Gevgelija **66** 41 9N 22 30 E
Gévora, R. **57** 38 53N 6 57W
Gex **45** 46 21N 6 3 E
Geyikli **68** 39 50N 26 12 E
Geyser **160** 47 17N 110 30W
Geysir **74** 64 19N 20 18W
Geyve **82** 40 32N 30 18 E
Ghaghara, R. **95** 26 0N 84 20 E
Ghail **92** 21 40N 46 20 E
Ghalla, Wadi el **123** 12 0N 28 58 E
Ghana ■ **121** 6 0N 1 0W
Ghandhi Dam **93** 24 30N 75 35 E
Ghansor **95** 22 39N 80 1 E
Ghanzi **128** 21 50 S 21 45 E
Ghanzi □ **128** 21 50 S 21 45 E
Gharbîya, Es Sahrâ el **122** 27 40N 26 30 E
Ghard Abû Muharik **122** 26 50N 30 0 E
Ghardaïa **118** 32 31N 3 37 E
Gharyān **119** 32 10N 13 0 E
Ghāt **119** 24 59N 10 19 E
Ghat Ghat **92** 26 0N 45 5 E
Ghatal **95** 22 40N 87 46 E
Ghatampur **95** 26 8N 80 13 E
Ghatprabha, R. **96** 16 15N 75 20 E
Ghazal, Bahr el **117** 15 0N 17 0 E
Ghazaouet **118** 35 8N 1 50W
Ghaziabad **94** 28 42N 77 35 E
Ghazipur **95** 25 38N 83 35 E
Ghazni **94** 33 30N 68 17 E
Ghazni □ **93** 33 0N 68 0 E
Ghedi **62** 45 24N 10 16 E
Ghelari **70** 45 42N 22 45 E
Ghelinsor **91** 6 35N 46 55 E
Ghent = Gand **47** 51 4N 3 43 E

Gheorghe Gheorghiu-Dej Gobo


Gheorghe Gheorghiu-Dej 70 46 17N 26 47 E
Gheorgheni 70 46 43N 25 41 E
Ghergani 70 44 37N 25 37 E
Gherla 70 47 0N 23 57 E
Ghilarza 64 40 8N 8 50 E
Ghisonaccia 45 42 1N 9 26 E
Ghizao 94 33 30N 65 59 E
Ghizar, R. 95 36 10N 73 4 E
Ghod, R. 96 18 40N 74 15 E
Ghorat □ 93 34 0N 64 20 E
Ghost River, Can. 150 50 10N 91 27W
Ghost River, Ont., Can. 150 51 25N 83 20W
Ghot Ogrein 122 31 10N 25 20 E
Ghotaru 94 27 20N 70 1 E
Ghotki 94 28 5N 69 30 E
Ghudāmis 119 30 11N 9 29 E
Ghugri 95 22 39N 80 41 E
Ghugus 96 20 0N 79 0 E
Ghulam Mohammad Barrage 94 25 30N 67 0 E
Ghuriān 93 34 17N 61 25 E
Gia Dinh 101 10 49N 106 42 E
Gia Lai = Pleiku 101 14 3N 108 0 E
Gia Nghia 101 12 0N 107 42 E
Gia Ngoc 100 14 50N 108 58 E
Gia Vuc 100 14 42N 108 34 E
Giamda Dzong 99 30 3N 93 2 E
Giannutri, I. 62 42 16N 11 5 E
Giant Forest 163 36 36N 118 43W
Giant Mts. = Krkonose 52 50 50N 16 10 E
Giant's Causeway 38 55 15N 6 30W
Giarabub = Jaghbub 117 29 42N 24 38 E
Giarre 65 37 44N 15 10 E
Giaveno 62 45 3N 7 20 E
Gibara 166 21 0N 76 20W
Gibbon 158 40 49N 98 45W
Gibe, R. 123 6 25N 36 10 E
Gibellina 64 37 48N 13 0 E
Gibeon 128 25 7 S 17 45 E
Gibraléon 57 37 23N 6 58W
Gibraltar 57 36 7N 5 22W
Gibraltar Pt. 33 53 6N 0 20 E
Gibraltar, Str. of 57 35 55N 5 40W
Gibson Des. 136 24 0 S 126 0 E
Gibsons 152 49 24N 123 32W
Gida. G. 12 72 30N 77 0 E
Giddalur 97 15 20N 78 57 E
Gidde 123 5 40N 37 25 E
Giddings 159 30 11N 96 58W
Gide 123 9 52N 35 5 E
Gien 43 47 40N 2 36 E
Giessen 48 50 34N 8 40 E
Gieten 46 53 0N 6 46 E
Gif-sur-Yvette 46 48 42N 2 8 E
Gifatin, Geziret 122 27 10N 33 50 E
Gifford 35 55 54N 2 45W
Gifford Creek 137 24 3 S 116 16 E
Gifhorn 48 52 29N 10 32 E
Gifu 111 35 30N 136 45 E
Gifu-ken □ 111 36 0N 137 0 E
Gigant 83 46 28N 41 30 E
Giganta, Sa. de la 164 25 30N 111 30W
Gigen 67 43 40N 24 28 E
Giggleswick 32 54 5N 2 19W
Gigha, I. 39 55 42N 5 45W
Giglio, I. 62 42 20N 10 52 E
Gignac 44 43 39N 3 32 E
Gigüela, R. 58 39 47N 3 0W
Gijón 56 43 32N 5 42W
Gil I. 152 53 12N 129 15W
Gila Bend 161 33 0N 112 46W
Gila Bend Mts. 161 33 15N 113 0W
Gila, R. 161 33 5N 108 40W
Gilau 138 5 38 S 149 3 E
Gilbedi 121 13 40N 5 45 E
Gilbert Is. 130 1 0 S 176 0 E
Gilbert Plains 153 51 9N 100 28W
Gilbert, R. 138 16 35 S 141 15 E
Gilbert River 138 18 9 S 142 52 E
Gilberton 138 19 16 S 143 35 E
Gilbués 170 9 50 S 45 21W
Gilford 38 54 23N 6 20W
Gilford I. 152 50 40N 126 30W
Gilgai 137 31 15 S 119 56 E
Gilgandra 141 31 43 S 148 39 E
Gilgil 126 0 30 S 36 20 E
Gilgit 95 35 50N 74 15 E
Gilgit, R. 95 35 50N 74 25 E
Gilgunnia 141 32 26 S 146 2 E
Giligulgul 139 26 26 S 150 0 E
Gilima 126 3 53N 28 15 E
Giljeva Planina 66 43 9N 20 0 E
Gill L. 38 54 15N 8 25W
Gillam 153 56 20N 94 40W
Gilleleje 73 56 8N 12 19 E
Gillen, L. 137 26 11 S 124 38 E
Gilles, L. 140 32 50 S 136 45 E
Gillespie Pt. 143 43 24 S 169 49 E
Gillett 162 41 57N 76 48W
Gillette 158 44 20N 105 38W
Gilliat 138 20 40 S 141 28 E
Gillingham, Dorset, U.K. 28 51 2N 2 15W
Gillingham, Kent, U.K. 29 51 23N 0 34 E
Gilmer 159 32 44N 94 55W
Gilmore 141 35 14 S 148 12 E
Gilmore, L. 137 32 29 S 121 37 E
Gilmour 150 44 48N 77 37W
Gilo 123 7 35N 34 30 E
Gilo, R. 161 33 5N 108 40W
Gilort, R. 70 44 38N 23 32 E
Gilroy 163 37 1N 121 37W
Gilsland 32 55 0N 2 34W
Gilŭu 70 46 45N 23 23W
Giluwe, Mt. 135 6 8 S 143 52 E
Gilwern 31 51 49N 3 5W
Gilze 47 51 32N 4 57 E
Gimåfors 72 62 40N 16 25 E
Gimbi 123 9 3N 35 42 E
Gimigliano 65 38 53N 16 32 E
Gimli 153 50 40N 97 10W
Gimmi 123 9 0N 37 20 E
Gimo 72 60 11N 18 12 E
Gimont 44 43 38N 0 52 E
Gimzo 90 31 56N 34 56 E
Gin Ganga 97 6 5N 80 7 E
Gin Gin 139 25 0 S 151 44 E
Ginâh 122 25 21N 30 30 E
Gindie 138 23 44 S 148 8 E
Gineta, La 59 39 8N 2 1W
Gingin 137 31 22 S 115 54 E
Gîngiova 70 43 54N 23 50 E
Ginir 123 7 12N 40 40 E
Ginosa 65 40 35N 16 45 E
Ginowan 112 26 15N 127 47 E
Ginzo de Limia 56 42 3N 7 47W
Giohar 91 2 20N 45 15 E
Gióia del Colle 65 40 49N 16 55 E
Gióia, G. di 65 38 30N 15 50 E
Gióia Táuro 65 38 26N 15 53 E
Gioiosa Jónica 65 38 20N 16 19 E
Gióna, Óros 69 38 38N 22 14 E
Giong, Teluk 103 4 50N 118 20 E
Giovi, P. dei 45 44 30N 8 55 E
Giovinazzo 65 41 10N 16 40 E
Gippsland 133 37 45 S 147 15 E
Gir Hills 94 21 0N 71 0 E
Girab 94 26 2N 70 38 E
Giralla 136 22 31 S 114 15 E
Giraltovce 53 49 7N 21 32 E
Girard 159 37 30N 94 50W
Girardot 174 4 18N 74 48W
Girdle Ness 37 57 9N 2 2W
Giresun 92 40 45N 38 30 E
Girga 122 26 17N 31 55 E
Girgir, C. 135 3 50 S 144 35 E
Giridih 95 24 10N 86 21 E
Girifalco 65 38 49N 16 25 E
Girilambone 141 31 16 S 146 57 E
Girishk 93 31 47N 64 24 E
Giro 121 11 7N 4 42 E
Giromagny 43 47 44N 6 50 E
Gironde □ 44 44 45N 0 30W
Gironde, R. 44 45 27N 0 53W
Gironella 58 42 2N 1 53 E
Giru 138 19 30 S 147 5 E
Girvan 34 55 15N 4 50W
Girvan R. 34 55 18N 4 51W
Gisborne 142 38 39 S 178 5 E
Gisburn 32 53 56N 2 16W
Gisenyi 126 1 41 S 29 30 E
Giske 71 62 30N 6 3 E
Gisla 36 58 7N 6 53W
Gislaved 73 57 19N 13 32 E
Gisors 43 49 15N 1 40 E
Gissarskiy, Khrebet 85 39 0N 69 0 E
Gistel 47 51 9N 2 59 E
Giswil 50 46 50N 8 11 E
Gitega (Kitega) 126 3 26 S 29 56 E
Gits 47 51 0N 3 6 E
Giubiasco 51 46 11N 9 1 E
Giugliano in Campania 65 40 55N 14 12 E
Giulianova 63 42 45N 13 58 E
Giurgeni 70 44 45N 27 38 E
Giurgiu 70 43 52N 25 57 E
Giv'at Brenner 90 31 52N 34 47 E
Give 73 55 51N 9 13 E
Givet 43 50 8N 4 49 E
Givors 45 45 35N 4 45 E
Givry, Belg. 47 50 23N 4 2 E
Givry, France 43 46 41N 4 46 E
Giza (El Giza) 122 30 1N 31 11 E
Gizhduvan 85 40 6N 64 41 E
Gizhiga 77 62 0N 150 27 E
Gizhiginskaya, Guba 77 61 0N 158 0 E
Gizycko 54 54 2N 21 48 E
Gizzeria 65 38 57N 16 10 E
Gjegjan 68 41 58N 20 3 E
Gjerpen 71 59 15N 9 33 E
Gjerstad 71 58 54N 9 0 E
Gjiri-i-Vlorës 68 40 29N 19 27 E
Gjirokastër 68 40 7N 20 16 E
Gjoa Haven 148 68 20N 96 0W
Gjovdal 71 58 52N 8 19 E
Gjøvik 71 60 47N 10 43 E
Glace Bay 151 46 11N 59 58W
Glacier B. 152 58 30N 136 10W
Glacier Nat. Park 152 51 15N 117 30W
Glacier National Park 160 48 35N 113 40W
Glacier Peak Mt. 160 48 7N 121 7W
Gladewater 159 32 30N 94 58W
Gladstone, Queens., Austral. 74 23 52 S 151 16 E
Gladstone, S.A., Austral. 140 33 15 S 138 22 E
Gladstone, W. Australia, Austral. 137 25 57 S 114 17 E
Gladstone, Can. 153 50 13N 98 57W
Gladstone, U.S.A. 156 45 52N 87 1W
Gladwin 156 43 59N 84 29W
Gladys L. 152 59 50N 133 0W
Glafsfjorden 72 59 30N 12 45 E
Głagów Małapolski 53 50 10N 21 56 E
Glåma 74 65 48N 23 0W
Glåma, R. 71 60 30N 12 8 E
Glamis 37 56 37N 3 0W
Glamorgan (□) 26 51 37N 3 35W
Glamorgan, Vale of 23 50 45N 3 15W
Glan, Phil. 103 5 45N 125 20 E
Glan, Sweden 73 58 37N 16 0 E
Glanaman 31 51 48N 3 56W
Glanaruddery Mts. 39 52 20N 9 27W
Glandore 39 51 33N 9 7W
Glandore Harb. 39 51 33N 9 8W
Glanerbrug 46 52 13N 6 58 E
Glanton 35 55 25N 1 54W
Glanworth 39 52 10N 8 25W
Glarner Alpen 51 46 50N 9 0 E
Glärnisch 51 47 0N 9 0 E
Glarus 51 47 3N 9 4 E
Glarus □ 51 47 0N 9 5 E
Glas Maol 37 56 52N 3 20W
Glasco, Kans., U.S.A. 158 39 25N 97 50W
Glasco, N.Y., U.S.A. 162 42 3N 73 57W
Glasgow, U.K. 34 55 52N 4 14W
Glasgow, Ky., U.S.A. 156 37 2N 85 55W
Glasgow, Mont., U.S.A. 160 48 12N 106 35W
Glasnevin 38 53 22N 6 18W
Glassboro 162 39 42N 75 7W
Glasslough 38 54 20N 6 53W
Glastonbury, U.K. 28 51 9N 2 42W
Glastonbury, U.S.A. 162 41 42N 72 27W
Glatt, R. 51 47 28N 8 32 E
Glattfelden 51 47 33N 8 30 E
Glauchau 48 50 50N 12 33 E
Glazov 81 58 9N 52 40 E
Glbovo 67 42 1N 24 43 E
Gleichen 152 50 50N 113 0W
Gleisdorf 52 47 6N 15 44 E
Glemsford 29 52 6N 0 41 E
Glen Affric 36 57 15N 5 0W
Glen Afton 142 37 46 S 175 4 E
Glen Almond 35 56 28N 3 50W
Glen B. 38 54 43N 8 45W
Glen Burnie 162 39 10N 76 37W
Glen Canyon Dam 161 37 0N 111 25W
Glen Canyon Nat. Recreation Area 161 37 30N 111 0W
Glen Coe 23 56 40N 5 0W
Glen Cove 162 40 51N 73 37W
Glen Esk 37 56 53N 2 50W
Glen Etive 34 56 37N 5 0W
Glen Florrie 136 22 55 S 115 59 E
Glen Garry, Inv., U.K. 36 57 3N 5 7W
Glen Garry, Per., U.K. 37 56 47N 4 5W
Glen Gowrie 140 31 4 S 143 10 E
Glen Helen 32 54 14N 4 35W
Glen Innes 139 29 40 S 151 39 E
Glen Lyon, U.K. 37 56 35N 4 20W
Glen Lyon, U.S.A. 162 41 10N 76 7W
Glen Massey 142 37 38 S 175 2 E
Glen Mor 37 57 12N 4 37 E
Glen Moriston 36 57 10N 4 58W
Glen Orchy 34 56 27N 4 52W
Glen Orrin 37 57 30N 4 45W
Glen Oykel 37 58 5N 4 50W
Glen, R. 29 52 50N 0 7W
Glen Shee 37 56 45N 3 25W
Glen Shiel 36 57 8N 5 20W
Glen Spean 37 56 53N 4 40W
Glen Trool Lodge 34 55 5N 4 30W
Glen Ullin 158 46 48N 101 46W
Glen Valley 141 36 54 S 147 28 E
Glenade 38 54 22N 8 17W
Glenamoy 38 54 14N 9 40W
Glénans, Is. de 42 47 42N 4 0W
Glenariff 141 30 50 S 146 33 E
Glenarm 38 54 58N 5 58W
Glenart Castle 39 52 48N 6 12W
Glenavy, N.Z. 143 44 54 S 171 7 E
Glenavy, U.K. 38 54 36N 6 12W
Glenbarr 34 55 34N 5 40W
Glenbeigh 39 52 3N 9 57W
Glenbrittle 36 57 13N 6 18W
Glenbrook 142 33 46 S 150 37 E
Glenburn 141 37 27 S 145 26 E
Glencoe, S. Afr. 129 28 11 S 30 11 E
Glencoe, U.S.A. 158 44 45N 94 10W
Glencolumbkille 38 54 43N 8 41W
Glendale, Can. 150 46 45N 84 2W
Glendale, Rhod. 127 17 22 S 31 5 E
Glendale, Ariz., U.S.A. 161 33 40N 112 8W
Glendale, Calif., U.S.A. 163 34 7N 118 18W
Glendale, Oreg., U.S.A. 160 42 44N 123 29W
Glendive 158 47 7N 104 40W
Glendo 158 42 30N 105 0W
Glendora 163 34 8N 117 52W
Gleneagles 35 56 16N 3 44W
Glenealy 39 52 59N 6 10W
Gleneely 38 52 14N 7 8W
Glenelg, Austral. 140 34 58 S 138 31 E
Glenelg, U.K. 36 57 13N 5 37W
Glenelg, R. 140 38 4 S 140 59 E
Glenfarne 38 54 17N 8 0W
Glenfield 162 43 43N 75 24W
Glenfinnan 36 56 52N 5 28W
Glengad Hd. 38 55 19N 7 11W
Glengariff 39 51 45N 9 33W
Glengormley 38 54 41N 5 57W
Glengyle 138 24 48 S 139 37 E
Glenham 143 46 26 S 168 52 E
Glenhope 143 41 40 S 172 39 E
Glenisland 38 53 54N 9 24W
Glenkens, The 34 55 10N 4 15W
Glenluce 34 54 53N 4 50W
Glenmary, Mt. 143 44 0 S 169 55 E
Glenmaye 32 54 11N 4 42W
Glenmora 159 31 1N 92 34W
Glenmorgan 139 27 14 S 149 42 E
Glenn, oilfield 19 57 55N 0 15 E
Glennagevlagh 38 53 36N 9 41W
Glennamaddy 38 53 37N 8 33W
Glenn's Ferry 160 43 0N 115 15W
Glenoe 38 54 47N 5 50W
Glenorchy, S. Austral., Austral. 140 31 55 S 139 46 E
Glenorchy, Tas., Austral. 138 42 49 S 147 18 E
Glenorchy, Vic., Austral. 140 36 55 S 142 41 E
Glenore 138 17 50 S 141 12 E
Glenormiston 138 22 55 S 138 50 E
Glenreagh 139 30 2 S 153 1 E
Glenrock 160 42 53N 105 55W
Glenrothes 35 56 12N 3 11W
Glenrowan 141 36 29 S 146 13 E
Glenroy, S. Australia, Austral. 140 37 13 S 140 48 E
Glenroy, W. Australia, Austral. 136 17 16 S 126 14 E
Glenroy, S. Afr. 132 26 23 S 28 17 E
Glens Falls 162 43 19N 73 39W
Glentane 38 53 25N 8 30W
Glenties 38 54 48N 8 18W
Glenville 156 38 56N 80 50W
Glenwood, Alta., Can. 152 49 21N 113 31W
Glenwood, Newf., Can. 151 49 0N 54 47W
Glenwood, Ark., U.S.A. 159 34 20N 93 30W
Glenwood, Hawaii, U.S.A. 147 19 29N 155 10W
Glenwood, Iowa, U.S.A. 158 41 7N 95 41W
Glenwood, Minn., U.S.A. 158 45 38N 95 21W
Glenwood Sprs. 160 39 39N 107 15W
Gletsch 51 46 34N 8 22 E
Glettinganes 51 65 30N 13 37W
Glin 39 52 34N 9 17W
Glina 63 45 20N 16 6 E
Glinojeck 54 52 49N 20 21 E
Glinsk 39 53 23N 9 49W
Glittertind 71 61 40N 8 32 E
Gliwice (Gleiwitz) 54 50 22N 18 41 E
Globe 161 33 25N 110 53W
Glodeanu-Siliştea 70 44 50N 26 48 E
Glödnitz 52 46 53N 14 7 E
Glodyany 70 47 45N 27 31 E
Gloggnitz 52 47 41N 15 56 E
Głogów 54 51 37N 16 5 E
Głogowek 54 50 21N 17 53 E
Gloria, La 174 8 37N 73 48W
Glorieuses, Îs. 129 11 30 S 47 20 E
Glossop 32 53 27N 1 56W
Gloucester, Austral. 141 32 0 S 151 59 E
Gloucester, U.K. 28 51 52N 2 15W
Gloucester, U.S.A. 162 42 38N 70 39W
Gloucester, Va., U.S.A. 162 37 25N 76 32W
Gloucester, C. 135 5 26 S 148 21 E
Gloucester City 162 39 54N 75 8W
Gloucester, I. 138 20 0 S 148 30 E
Gloucestershire □ 28 51 44N 2 10W
Gloversville 162 43 5N 74 18W
Glovertown 151 48 40N 54 03W
Głubczyce 54 50 13N 17 52 E
Glubokiy 83 48 35N 40 25 E
Glubokoye 80 55 10N 27 45 E
Głucholazy 54 50 19N 17 24 E
Glücksburg 48 54 48N 9 34 E
Glückstadt 48 53 46N 9 28 E
Gluepot 140 33 45 S 140 0 E
Glukhov 80 51 40N 33 50 E
Glussk 80 52 53N 28 41 E
Główno 54 51 59N 19 42 E
Glyn-ceiriog 31 52 56N 3 12W
Glyn Neath 31 51 45N 3 37W
Glyncorrwg 31 51 40N 3 39W
Glyngøre 73 56 46N 8 52 E
Glynn 39 52 29N 6 55W
Gmünd, Kärnten, Austria 52 46 54N 13 31 E
Gmünd, Niederösterreich, Austria 52 48 45N 15 0 E
Gmunden 52 47 55N 13 48 E
Gnarp 72 62 3N 17 16 E
Gnesta 72 59 3N 17 17 E
Gniew 54 53 50N 18 50 E
Gniewkowo 54 52 54N 18 25 E
Gniezno 54 52 30N 17 35 E
Gnoien 48 53 58N 12 41 E
Gnopp 123 8 47N 29 50 E
Gnosall 28 52 48N 2 15W
Gnosjö 73 57 22N 13 43 E
Gnowangerup 137 33 58 S 117 59 E
Go Cong 101 10 22N 106 40 E
Gō-no-ura 110 33 44N 129 40 E
Goa 97 15 33N 73 59 E
Goa □ 97 15 33N 73 59 E
Goageb 128 26 49 S 17 15 E
Goalen Hd. 141 36 33 S 150 4 E
Goalpara 98 26 10N 90 40 E
Goalundo 95 23 50N 89 47 E
Goaso 120 6 48N 2 30W
Goat Fell 34 55 37N 5 11W
Goba, Ethiopia 123 7 1N 39 59 E
Goba, Mozam. 125 26 15 S 32 13 E
Gobabis 128 22 16 S 19 0 E
Gobi, desert 105 44 0N 111 0 E
Gobichettipalayam 97 11 31N 77 21 E
Gobō 111 33 53N 135 10 E
Gobo 123 5 40N 30 10 E

**Goch** **Grand Bassa**


| | | | |
|---|---|---|---|
| Goch | **48** | 51 40N | 6 9E |
| Gochas | **125** | 24 59S | 19 25E |
| Godalming | **29** | 51 12N | 0 37W |
| Godavari Point | **96** | 17 0N | 82 20E |
| Godavari, R. | **96** | 19 5N | 79 0E |
| Godbout | **151** | 49 20N | 67 38W |
| Godda | **95** | 24 50N | 87 20E |
| Goddua | **119** | 26 26N | 14 19E |
| Godech | **66** | 43 1N | 23 4E |
| Godegård | **73** | 58 43N | 15 8E |
| Goderich | **150** | 43 45N | 81 41W |
| Goderville | **42** | 49 38N | 0 22E |
| Godhavn | **12** | 69 15N | 53 38W |
| Godhra | **94** | 22 49N | 73 40E |
| Godmanchester | **29** | 52 19N | 0 11W |
| Gödöllö | **53** | 47 38N | 19 25E |
| Godoy Cruz | **172** | 32 56S | 68 52W |
| Godrevy Pt. | **30** | 50 15N | 5 24W |
| Gods L. | **153** | 54 40N | 94 15W |
| Gods, R. | **153** | 56 22N | 92 51W |
| Godshill | **28** | 50 38N | 1 13W |
| Godstone | **29** | 51 15N | 0 3W |
| Godthåb | **12** | 64 10N | 51 46W |
| Godwin Austen (K2) | **93** | 36 0N | 77 0E |
| Goeie Hoop, Kaap die | **128** | 34 24S | 18 30E |
| Goeland, L. | **150** | 49 50N | 76 48W |
| Goeree | **46** | 51 50N | 4 0E |
| Goes | **47** | 51 30N | 3 55E |
| Goffstown | **162** | 43 1N | 71 36W |
| Gogama | **150** | 47 35N | 81 43W |
| Gogango | **138** | 23 40S | 150 2E |
| Gogebic, L. | **158** | 46 30N | 89 34W |
| Gogha | **94** | 21 32N | 72 9E |
| Gogolin | **54** | 50 30N | 18 0E |
| Gogra, R. = Ghaghara | **99** | 26 0N | 84 20E |
| Gogriâl | **123** | 8 30N | 28 0E |
| Goiana | **170** | 7 33S | 34 59W |
| Goiandira | **171** | 11 46S | 46 40W |
| Goianésia | **171** | 15 18S | 49 7W |
| Goiânia | **171** | 16 35S | 49 20W |
| Goiás | **171** | 15 55S | 50 10W |
| Goiás □ | **170** | 12 10S | 48 0W |
| Goiatuba | **171** | 18 1S | 49 23W |
| Goil L. | **34** | 56 8N | 4 52W |
| Goirle | **47** | 51 31N | 5 4E |
| Góis | **56** | 40 10N | 8 6W |
| Goisern | **52** | 47 38N | 13 38E |
| Gojam □ | **123** | 10 55N | 36 30E |
| Gojeb, W. | **123** | 7 12N | 36 40E |
| Gojō | **111** | 34 21N | 135 42E |
| Gojra | **94** | 31 10N | 72 40E |
| Gokak | **97** | 16 11N | 74 52E |
| Gokarannath | **95** | 27 57N | 80 39E |
| Gokarn | **97** | 14 33N | 74 17E |
| Gökçeada | **68** | 40 10N | 26 0E |
| Gokteik | **99** | 22 26N | 97 0E |
| Gokurt | **94** | 29 47N | 67 26E |
| Gøl | **73** | 57 4N | 9 42E |
| Gola | **95** | 28 3N | 80 32E |
| Gola I. | **38** | 55 4N | 8 20W |
| Golaghat | **98** | 26 30N | 94 0E |
| Golakganj | **95** | 26 8N | 89 52E |
| Golaya Pristen | **82** | 46 29N | 32 23E |
| Golchikha | **12** | 71 45N | 84 0E |
| Golconda | **160** | 40 58N | 117 32W |
| Gold Beach | **160** | 42 25N | 124 25W |
| Gold Coast, Austral. | **139** | 28 0S | 153 25E |
| Gold Coast, W. Afr. | **121** | 4 0N | 1 40W |
| Gold Creek | **147** | 62 45N | 149 45W |
| Gold Hill | **160** | 42 28N | 123 2W |
| Gold Point | **163** | 37 21N | 117 21W |
| Gold River | **152** | 49 40N | 126 10E |
| Goldach | **51** | 47 28N | 9 28E |
| Goldau | **51** | 47 3N | 8 33E |
| Goldberg | **48** | 53 34N | 12 6E |
| Golden, Can. | **152** | 51 20N | 117 0W |
| Golden, Ireland | **39** | 52 30N | 8 0W |
| Golden, U.S.A. | **158** | 39 42N | 105 30W |
| Golden Bay | **143** | 40 40S | 172 50E |
| Golden Gate | **160** | 37 54N | 122 30W |
| Golden Hinde, mt. | **152** | 49 40N | 125 44W |
| Golden Prairie | **153** | 50 13N | 109 37W |
| Golden Rock | **97** | 10 45N | 78 48E |
| Golden Vale | **39** | 52 33N | 8 17W |
| Goldendale | **160** | 45 53N | 120 48W |
| Goldfield | **163** | 37 45N | 117 13W |
| Goldfields | **153** | 59 28N | 108 29W |
| Goldpines | **153** | 50 45N | 93 05W |
| Goldsand L. | **153** | 57 2N | 101 8W |
| Goldsboro | **157** | 35 24N | 77 59W |
| Goldsmith | **159** | 32 0N | 102 40W |
| Goldsworthy | **136** | 20 21S | 119 30E |
| Goldsworthy, Mt. | **136** | 20 23S | 119 31E |
| Goldthwaite | **159** | 31 25N | 98 32W |
| Goleen | **39** | 51 30N | 9 43W |
| Golegã | **57** | 39 24N | 8 29W |
| Goleniów | **54** | 53 35N | 14 50E |
| Goleta | **163** | 34 27N | 119 50W |
| Golfito | **166** | 8 41N | 83 5W |
| Golfo degli Aranci | **65** | 41 0N | 9 38E |
| Goliad | **159** | 28 40N | 97 22W |
| Golija | **66** | 43 22N | 20 15E |
| Golija, Mts. | **66** | 43 5N | 18 45E |
| Golina | **54** | 52 15N | 18 4E |
| Golo, R. | **45** | 42 31N | 9 32E |
| Golovanesvsk | **82** | 48 25N | 30 30E |
| Gölpazari | **82** | 40 17N | 30 17E |
| Golra | **94** | 33 37N | 72 56E |
| Golspie | **37** | 57 58N | 3 58W |
| Golub Dobrzyn | **54** | 53 7N | 19 2E |
| Golubac | **66** | 44 38N | 21 38E |
| Golyama Kamchiya, R. | **67** | 43 2N | 27 18E |
| Goma, Ethiopia | **123** | 8 29N | 36 53E |
| Goma, Rwanda | **126** | 2 11S | 29 18E |
| Goma, Zaïre | **126** | 1 37S | 29 10E |
| Gomare | **128** | 19 25S | 22 8E |
| Gomati, R. | **95** | 26 30N | 81 50E |
| Gombari | **126** | 2 45N | 29 3E |
| Gombe | **121** | 10 19N | 11 2E |
| Gombe, R. | **126** | 4 30S | 32 50E |
| Gombi | **121** | 10 12N | 12 45E |
| Gomel | **80** | 52 28N | 31 0E |
| Gomera, I. | **116** | 28 10N | 17 5W |
| Gometra I. | **34** | 56 30N | 6 18W |
| Gómez Palacio | **164** | 25 40N | 104 40W |
| Gommern | **48** | 52 54N | 11 47E |
| Gomogomo | **103** | 6 25S | 134 53E |
| Gomoh | **99** | 23 52N | 86 10E |
| Gomotartsi | **66** | 44 6N | 22 57E |
| Goms | **50** | 46 30N | 8 15E |
| Gonābād | **93** | 34 15N | 58 45E |
| Gonaïves | **167** | 19 20N | 72 50W |
| Gonâve, G. de la | **167** | 19 29N | 72 42W |
| Gonâve, I. de la | **167** | 18 45N | 73 0W |
| Gönc | **53** | 48 28N | 21 14E |
| Gonda | **95** | 27 9N | 81 58E |
| Gondab-e Kāvūs | **93** | 37 20N | 55 25E |
| Gondal | **94** | 21 58N | 70 52E |
| Gonder | **123** | 12 23N | 37 30E |
| Gondia | **96** | 21 30N | 80 10E |
| Gondola | **127** | 19 4S | 33 37E |
| Gondomar, Port. | **56** | 41 10N | 8 35W |
| Gondomar, Spain | **56** | 42 7N | 8 45W |
| Gondrecourt-le-Château | **43** | 48 26N | 5 30E |
| Gongola □ | **121** | 8 0N | 12 0E |
| Gongola, R. | **121** | 10 30N | 10 22E |
| Goniadz | **54** | 53 30N | 22 44E |
| Goniri | **121** | 11 30N | 12 15E |
| Gonnesa | **64** | 39 17N | 8 27E |
| Gonno-Altaysk | **76** | 51 50N | 86 5E |
| Gonnos | **68** | 39 52N | 22 29E |
| Gonnosfanadiga | **64** | 39 30N | 8 39E |
| Gonzales, Calif., U.S.A. | **163** | 36 35N | 121 30W |
| Gonzales, Tex., U.S.A. | **159** | 29 30N | 97 30W |
| González Chaves | **172** | 38 02S | 60 05W |
| Good Hope, C. of = Goeie Hoop | **128** | 34 24S | 18 30E |
| Goode | **139** | 31 58S | 133 45E |
| Goodenough I. | **135** | 9 20S | 150 15E |
| Gooderham | **150** | 44 54N | 78 21W |
| Goodeve | **153** | 51 4N | 103 10W |
| Gooding | **160** | 43 0N | 114 50W |
| Goodland | **158** | 39 22N | 101 44W |
| Goodnight | **159** | 35 4N | 101 13W |
| Goodooga | **139** | 29 1S | 147 28E |
| Goodrich | **28** | 51 52N | 2 38W |
| Goodsoil | **153** | 54 24N | 109 13W |
| Goodsprings | **161** | 35 51N | 115 30W |
| Goodwick | **31** | 52 0N | 5 0W |
| Goodwin, Mt. | **136** | 14 13S | 129 52E |
| Goodwood | **29** | 50 53N | 0 44W |
| Goole | **33** | 53 42N | 0 52W |
| Goolgowi | **141** | 33 58S | 145 41E |
| Goolwa | **140** | 35 30S | 138 47E |
| Goomalling | **137** | 31 15S | 116 42E |
| Goombalie | **139** | 29 59S | 145 26E |
| Goonalga | **140** | 31 45S | 143 37E |
| Goonda | **127** | 19 48S | 33 57E |
| Goondiwindi | **139** | 28 30S | 150 21E |
| Goongarrie | **137** | 30 2S | 121 8E |
| Goonumbla | **141** | 32 59S | 148 11E |
| Goonyella | **138** | 21 47S | 147 58E |
| Goor | **46** | 52 13N | 6 33E |
| Gooray | **139** | 28 25S | 150 2E |
| Goose Bay | **151** | 53 15N | 60 20W |
| Goose L. | **160** | 42 0N | 120 30W |
| Goose R. | **151** | 53 20N | 60 35W |
| Goothinga | **138** | 17 36S | 140 50E |
| Gooty | **97** | 15 7N | 77 41E |
| Gop | **93** | 22 5N | 69 50E |
| Gopalganj, Bangla. | **98** | 23 1N | 89 50E |
| Gopalganj, India | **95** | 26 28N | 84 30E |
| Goppenstein | **50** | 46 23N | 7 46E |
| Göppingen | **49** | 48 42N | 9 40E |
| Gor | **59** | 37 23N | 2 58W |
| Góra | **54** | 51 40N | 16 31E |
| Gorakhpur | **95** | 26 47N | 83 32E |
| Gorbatov | **81** | 56 12N | 43 2E |
| Gorbea, Peña | **58** | 43 1N | 2 50W |
| Gorda | **163** | 35 53N | 121 26W |
| Gorda, Punta | **166** | 14 10N | 83 10W |
| Gordon, Austral. | **140** | 32 7S | 138 20E |
| Gordon, U.K. | **35** | 55 41N | 2 32W |
| Gordon, U.S.A. | **158** | 42 49N | 102 6W |
| Gordon B. | **136** | 11 35S | 130 10E |
| Gordon Downs | **136** | 18 48S | 128 40E |
| Gordon L., Alta., Can. | **153** | 56 30N | 110 25W |
| Gordon L., N.W.T., Can. | **152** | 63 5N | 113 11W |
| Gordon, R. | **138** | 42 27S | 145 30E |
| Gordon River | **137** | 34 10S | 117 15E |
| Gordonia | **128** | 28 13S | 21 10E |
| Gordonvale | **138** | 17 5S | 145 50E |
| Gore | **139** | 28 17S | 151 30E |
| Goré | **117** | 7 59N | 16 49E |
| Gore, Ethiopia | **123** | 8 12N | 35 32E |
| Gore, N.Z. | **143** | 46 5S | 168 58E |
| Gore B. | **150** | 45 57N | 82 28W |
| Gorebridge | **35** | 55 51N | 3 2W |
| Goresbridge | **39** | 52 38N | 7 0W |
| Gorey | **39** | 52 41N | 6 18W |
| Gorgan | **93** | 36 55N | 54 30E |
| Gorge, The | **138** | 18 27S | 145 30E |
| Gorgona, I. | **174** | 3 0N | 78 10W |
| Gorgona I. | **62** | 43 27N | 9 52E |
| Gorgora | **123** | 12 15N | 37 17E |
| Gori | **83** | 42 0N | 44 7E |
| Gorinchem | **46** | 51 50N | 4 59E |
| Goring, Oxon, U.K. | **28** | 51 31N | 1 8W |
| Goring, Sussex, U.K. | **29** | 50 49N | 0 26W |
| Gorinhatã | **171** | 19 15S | 49 45W |
| Goritsy | **81** | 57 4N | 36 43E |
| Gorízia | **63** | 45 56N | 13 37E |
| Gorka | **54** | 51 39N | 16 58E |
| Gorki = Gorkiy | **81** | 56 20N | 44 0E |
| Gorkiy | **81** | 57 20N | 44 0E |
| Gorkovskoye Vdkhr. | **81** | 57 2N | 43 4E |
| Gorleston | **29** | 52 35N | 1 44E |
| Gorlev | **73** | 55 30N | 11 15E |
| Gorlice | **54** | 49 35N | 21 11E |
| Görlitz | **54** | 51 10N | 14 59E |
| Gorlovka | **81** | 48 25N | 37 58E |
| Gorman, Calif., U.S.A. | **163** | 34 47N | 118 51W |
| Gorman, Tex., U.S.A. | **159** | 32 15N | 98 43W |
| Gorna Oryakhovitsa | **67** | 43 7N | 25 40E |
| Gorna Radgona | **63** | 46 40N | 16 2E |
| Gornja Tuzla | **66** | 44 35N | 18 46E |
| Gornji Grad | **63** | 46 20N | 14 52E |
| Gornji Milanovac | **66** | 44 00N | 20 29E |
| Gornji Vafuk | **66** | 43 57N | 17 34E |
| Gorno Ablanovo | **67** | 43 37N | 25 43E |
| Gorno Filinskoye | **76** | 60 5N | 70 0E |
| Gornyy | **81** | 51 50N | 48 30E |
| Gorodenka | **82** | 48 41N | 25 29E |
| Gorodets | **81** | 56 38N | 43 28E |
| Gorodische | **81** | 53 13N | 45 40E |
| Gorodnitsa | **80** | 50 46N | 27 26E |
| Gorodnya | **80** | 51 55N | 31 33E |
| Gorodok, Byelorussia, U.S.S.R. | **80** | 55 30N | 30 3E |
| Gorodok, Ukraine, U.S.S.R. | **80** | 49 46N | 23 32E |
| Goroka | **135** | 6 7S | 145 25E |
| Goroke | **140** | 36 43S | 141 29E |
| Gorokhov | **80** | 50 15N | 24 45E |
| Gorokhovets | **81** | 56 13N | 42 39E |
| Gorom Gorom | **121** | 14 26N | 0 14W |
| Goromonzi | **127** | 17 52S | 31 22E |
| Gorong, Kepulauan | **103** | 4 5S | 131 15E |
| Gorongosa, Sa. da | **127** | 18 27S | 32 2E |
| Gorongose, R. | **129** | 20 40S | 34 30E |
| Gorontalo | **103** | 0 35N | 123 13E |
| Goronyo | **121** | 13 29N | 5 39E |
| Gorredijk | **46** | 53 0N | 6 3E |
| Gorron | **42** | 48 25N | 0 50W |
| Gorseinon | **31** | 51 40N | 4 2W |
| Gorssel | **46** | 52 12N | 6 12E |
| Gort | **39** | 53 4N | 8 50W |
| Gortin | **38** | 54 43N | 7 13W |
| Gorumahisani | **96** | 22 20N | 86 24E |
| Gorumna I. | **39** | 53 15N | 9 44W |
| Gorzkowice | **54** | 51 13N | 19 36E |
| Gorzno | **54** | 53 12N | 19 38E |
| Gorzów Slaski | **54** | 51 3N | 18 22E |
| Gorzów Wielkopolski | **54** | 52 43N | 15 15E |
| Gorzów Wielkopolski □ | **54** | 52 45N | 15 30E |
| Gosainthan, Mt. | **99** | 28 20N | 85 45E |
| Gosberton | **33** | 52 52N | 0 10W |
| Göschenen | **51** | 46 40N | 8 36E |
| Gōse | **111** | 34 27N | 135 44E |
| Gosford | **141** | 33 23N | 151 18E |
| Gosforth | **32** | 54 24N | 3 27W |
| Goshen, S. Afr. | **128** | 25 50S | 25 0E |
| Goshen, Calif., U.S.A. | **163** | 36 21N | 119 25W |
| Goshen, Ind., U.S.A. | **156** | 41 36N | 85 46W |
| Goshen, N.Y., U.S.A. | **162** | 41 23N | 74 21W |
| Goslar | **48** | 51 55N | 10 23E |
| Gospič | **63** | 44 35N | 15 23E |
| Gosport | **28** | 50 48N | 1 8W |
| Gossa, I. | **71** | 62 52N | 6 50E |
| Gossau | **51** | 47 25N | 9 15E |
| Gosse, R. | **138** | 19 32S | 134 37E |
| Gostivar | **66** | 41 48N | 20 57E |
| Gostyn | **54** | 51 50N | 17 3E |
| Gostynin | **54** | 52 26N | 19 29E |
| Göta | **73** | 58 6N | 12 10E |
| Göta älv | **73** | 57 42N | 11 54E |
| Göta Kanal | **73** | 58 35N | 14 15E |
| Götaland, reg. | **73** | 58 0N | 14 0E |
| Göteborg | **73** | 57 43N | 11 59E |
| Göteborg & Bohus □ | **73** | 58 20N | 11 50E |
| Gotemba | **111** | 35 18N | 138 56E |
| Götene | **73** | 58 32N | 13 30E |
| Gotha | **48** | 50 56N | 10 42E |
| Gothenburg | **158** | 40 58N | 100 8W |
| Gothenburg = Göteborg | **73** | 57 43N | 11 59E |
| Gotse Delchev (Nevrokop) | **67** | 41 43N | 23 46E |
| Gotska Sandön | **75** | 58 24N | 19 15E |
| Götsu | **110** | 35 0N | 132 14E |
| Göttingen | **48** | 51 31N | 9 55E |
| Gottwaldov (Zlin) | **53** | 49 14N | 17 40E |
| Gouda | **46** | 52 1N | 4 42E |
| Goudhurst | **29** | 51 7N | 0 28E |
| Goudiry | **120** | 14 15N | 12 45E |
| Gough I. | **15** | 40 10S | 9 45W |
| Gouin Res. | **150** | 48 35N | 74 40W |
| Gouitafla | **120** | 7 30N | 5 53W |
| Goula Touila | **118** | 21 50N | 1 57E |
| Goulburn | **141** | 34 44S | 149 44E |
| Goulburn Is. | **138** | 11 40S | 133 20E |
| Gould, mt. | **137** | 25 46S | 117 18E |
| Goulia | **120** | 10 1N | 7 11W |
| Goulimine | **118** | 28 50N | 10 0W |
| Goulmima | **118** | 31 41N | 4 57W |
| Gouménissa | **68** | 40 56N | 22 37E |
| Goumeur | **119** | 20 40N | 18 30E |
| Goundam | **135** | 16 25N | 3 45W |
| Gounou-Gaya | **124** | 9 38N | 15 31E |
| Goûra | **69** | 37 56N | 22 20E |
| Gourara | **118** | 29 0N | 0 30E |
| Gouraya | **118** | 36 31N | 1 56E |
| Gourdon, France | **44** | 44 44N | 1 23E |
| Gourdon, U.K. | **37** | 56 50N | 2 15W |
| Gouré | **121** | 14 0N | 10 10E |
| Gourits, R. | **128** | 34 15S | 21 45E |
| Gourma Rharous | **121** | 16 55N | 2 5W |
| Gournay-en-Bray | **43** | 49 29N | 1 44E |
| Gouro | **117** | 19 30N | 19 30E |
| Gourock | **34** | 55 58N | 4 49W |
| Gourock Ra. | **141** | 36 0S | 149 25E |
| Gourselik | **121** | 13 31N | 10 52E |
| Goursi | **120** | 12 42N | 2 37W |
| Gouvêa | **171** | 18 27S | 43 44W |
| Gouzon | **44** | 46 12N | 2 14E |
| Govan | **153** | 51 20N | 105 0W |
| Gove | **133** | 12 25S | 136 55E |
| Goverla | **82** | 49 9N | 24 30E |
| Governador Valadares | **171** | 18 15S | 41 57W |
| Governor's Harbour | **166** | 25 10N | 76 14W |
| Gowan | **138** | 25 0S | 145 0E |
| Gowanda | **156** | 42 29N | 78 58W |
| Gower, The | **31** | 51 35N | 4 10W |
| Gowerton | **31** | 51 38N | 4 2W |
| Gowna, L. | **38** | 53 52N | 7 35W |
| Gowran | **39** | 52 38N | 7 5W |
| Goya | **172** | 29 10S | 59 10W |
| Goyder's Lagoon | **139** | 27 3S | 139 58E |
| Goyllarisquizga | **174** | 10 19S | 76 31W |
| Goz Beïda | **117** | 12 20N | 21 30E |
| Goz Regeb | **123** | 16 3N | 35 33E |
| Gozdnica | **54** | 51 28N | 15 4E |
| Gozo (Ghaudex) | **60** | 36 0N | 14 13E |
| Graaff-Reinet | **128** | 32 13S | 24 32E |
| Graasten | **73** | 54 57N | 9 34E |
| Grabow | **48** | 53 17N | 11 31E |
| Grabów | **54** | 51 31N | 18 7E |
| Grabs | **51** | 47 11N | 9 27E |
| Gračac | **63** | 44 18N | 15 57E |
| Gračanica | **66** | 44 43N | 18 18E |
| Graçay | **43** | 47 10N | 1 50E |
| Grace | **160** | 42 38N | 111 46W |
| Grace, L., (North) | **137** | 33 10S | 118 20E |
| Grace, L., (South) | **137** | 33 15S | 118 25E |
| Graceville | **158** | 45 36N | 96 23W |
| Grachevka | **84** | 52 55N | 52 52E |
| Gracias a Dios, C. | **166** | 15 0N | 83 20W |
| Gradačac | **66** | 44 52N | 18 26E |
| Gradaús | **170** | 7 43S | 51 11W |
| Gradaús, Serra dos | **170** | 8 0S | 50 45W |
| Gradeska Planina | **66** | 41 30N | 22 15E |
| Gradets | **67** | 42 46N | 26 30E |
| Gradignan | **66** | 44 47N | 0 36W |
| Gradnitsa | **67** | 42 57N | 24 58E |
| Grado, Italy | **63** | 45 40N | 13 20E |
| Grado, Spain | **56** | 43 23N | 6 4W |
| Gradule | **139** | 28 32S | 149 15E |
| Grady | **159** | 34 52N | 103 15W |
| Graeca, Lacul | **70** | 44 5N | 26 10E |
| Graemsay I. | **37** | 58 56N | 3 17W |
| Graénalon, L. | **74** | 64 10N | 17 20W |
| Grafham Water | **29** | 52 18N | 0 17W |
| Grafton, Austral. | **139** | 29 38S | 152 58E |
| Grafton, U.S.A. | **158** | 48 30N | 97 25W |
| Grafton, C. | **133** | 16 51S | 146 0E |
| Gragnano | **65** | 40 42N | 14 30E |
| Graham, Can. | **150** | 49 20N | 90 30W |
| Graham, N.C., U.S.A. | **157** | 36 5N | 79 22W |
| Graham, Tex., U.S.A. | **159** | 33 7N | 98 38W |
| Graham Bell, Os. | **76** | 80 5N | 70 0E |
| Graham I. | **152** | 53 40N | 132 30W |
| Graham Land | **13** | 65 0S | 64 0W |
| Graham Mt. | **161** | 32 46N | 109 58W |
| Graham, R. | **152** | 56 31N | 122 17W |
| Grahamdale | **153** | 51 23N | 98 30W |
| Grahamstown | **128** | 33 19S | 26 31E |
| Grahamsville | **162** | 41 51N | 74 33W |
| Grahovo | **66** | 42 40N | 18 4E |
| Graïba | **119** | 34 30N | 10 13E |
| Graide | **47** | 49 58N | 5 4E |
| Graigue | **39** | 52 51N | 6 56W |
| Graiguenamanagh | **39** | 52 32N | 6 58W |
| Grain Coast | **120** | 4 20N | 10 0W |
| Grainthorpe | **33** | 53 27N | 0 5E |
| Graivoron | **80** | 50 29N | 35 39E |
| Grajaú | **170** | 5 50S | 46 30W |
| Grajaú, R. | **170** | 3 41S | 44 48W |
| Grajewo | **54** | 53 39N | 22 30E |
| Gramada | **66** | 43 49N | 22 39E |
| Gramat | **44** | 44 48N | 1 43E |
| Gramisdale | **36** | 57 29N | 7 18W |
| Grammichele | **65** | 37 12N | 14 37E |
| Grampian □ | **37** | 57 0N | 3 0W |
| Grampians, Mts. | **140** | 37 0S | 142 20E |
| Gran Canaria | **116** | 27 55N | 15 35W |
| Gran Chaco | **156** | 25 0S | 61 0W |
| Gran Paradiso | **62** | 49 33N | 7 17E |
| Gran Sabana, La | **174** | 5 30N | 61 30W |
| Gran Sasso d'Italia, Mt. | **44** | 42 25N | 13 30E |
| Granada, Nic. | **166** | 11 58N | 86 0W |
| Granada, Spain | **59** | 37 10N | 3 35W |
| Granada, U.S.A. | **158** | 38 5N | 102 13W |
| Granada □ | **57** | 37 5N | 4 30W |
| Granard | **38** | 53 47N | 7 30W |
| Granbo | **72** | 61 16N | 16 33E |
| Granbury | **159** | 32 28N | 97 48W |
| Granby | **150** | 45 25N | 72 45W |
| Grand Bahama I. | **166** | 26 40N | 78 30W |
| Grand Bank | **151** | 47 6N | 55 48W |
| Grand Bassa | **120** | 6 0N | 10 2W |

Grand Bassam Grillby


Grand Bassam 120 5 10N 3 49W
Grand Béréby 120 4 38N 6 55W
Grand-Bourg 167 15 53N 61 19W
Grand Canal 39 53 15N 8 10W
Grand Canyon National Park 161 36 15N 112 20W
Grand Cayman 166 19 20N 81 20W
Grand Cess 120 4 40N 8 12W
Grand 'Combe, La 45 44 13N 4 2 E
Grand Coulee 160 47 48N 119 1W
Grand Coulee Dam 160 48 0N 118 50W
Grand Erg Occidental 118 30 20N 1 0 E
Grand Erg Oriental 119 30 0N 6 30 E
Grand Falls 151 47 2N 67 46W
Grand Forks, Can. 152 49 0N 118 30W
Grand Forks, U.S.A. 158 48 0N 97 3W
Grand-Fougeray 42 47 43N 1 44W
Grand Fougeray, Le 42 47 44N 1 43W
Grand Haven 156 43 3N 86 13W
Grand I. 150 46 30N 86 40W
Grand Island 158 40 59N 98 25W
Grand Isle 159 29 15N 89 58W
Grand Junction 161 39 0N 108 30W
Grand L., N.B., Can. 151 45 57N 66 7W
Grand L., Newf., Can. 151 48 45N 57 45W
Grand L., Newf., Can. 151 53 40N 60 30W
Grand L., Newf., Can. 151 49 0N 57 30W
Grand L., U.S.A. 159 29 55N 92 45W
Grand Lac 150 47 35N 77 35W
Grand Lahou 120 5 10N 5 0W
Grand Lake 160 40 20N 105 54W
Grand-Leez 47 50 35N 4 45 E
Grand Lieu, Lac de 42 47 6N 1 40W
Grand Manan I. 151 44 45N 66 52W
Grand Marais, Can. 158 47 45N 90 25W
Grand Marais, U.S.A. 156 46 39N 85 59W
Grand Mère 150 46 36N 72 40W
Grand Motte, La 45 48 35N 1 4 E
Grand Popo 121 6 15N 1 44 E
Grand Portage 150 47 58N 89 41W
Grand Pressigny, Le 42 46 55N 0 48 E
Grand, R., Mo., U.S.A. 160 39 23N 93 27W
Grand, R., S.D., U.S.A. 160 45 45N 101 30W
Grand Rapids, Can. 153 53 12N 99 19W
Grand Rapids, Mich., U.S.A. 156 42 57N 85 40W
Grand Rapids, Minn., U.S.A. 158 47 19N 93 29W
Grand St.-Bernard, Col. du 50 45 53N 7 11 E
Grand Teton 160 43 45N 110 57W
Grand Valley 160 39 30N 108 2W
Grand View 153 51 11N 100 51W
Grandas de Salime 56 43 13N 6 53W
Grande 170 11 30 S 44 30W
Grande, B. 176 50 30 S 68 20W
Grande Baie 151 48 19N 70 52W
Grande Cache 152 53 53N 119 8W
Grande, Coxilha 173 28 18 S 51 30W
Grande de Santiago, R. 164 21 20N 105 50W
Grande Dixence, Barr. de la 50 46 5N 7 23 E
Grande-Entrée 151 47 30N 61 40W
Grande, I. 171 23 9 S 44 14W
Grande, La 160 45 15N 118 0W
Grande Prairie 152 55 15N 118 50W
Grande, R., Jujuy, Argent. 172 23 9 S 65 52W
Grande, R., Mendoza, Argent. 172 36 52 S 69 45W
Grande R. 174 18 35 S 63 0W
Grande, R., Brazil 171 20 0 S 50 0W
Grande, R., Spain 59 39 6N 0 48W
Grande, R., U.S.A. 159 29 20N 100 40W
Grande Rivière 151 48 26N 64 30W
Grande, Serra, Goiás, Brazil 170 11 15 S 46 30W
Grande, Serra, Maranhao, Brazil 170 4 30 S 41 20W
Grande, Serra, Piauí, Brazil 170 8 0 S 45 0W
Grande Vallée 151 49 14N 65 8W
Grandes Bergeronnes 151 48 16N 69 35W
Grandfalls 159 31 21N 102 51W
Grandglise 47 50 30N 3 42 E
Grandoe Mines 152 56 29N 129 54W
Grândola 57 38 12N 8 35W
Grandpré 43 49 20N 4 50 E
Grandson 50 46 49N 6 39 E
Grandview, Can. 153 51 10N 100 42W
Grandview, U.S.A. 160 46 13N 119 58W
Grandvilliers 43 49 40N 1 57 E
Graneros 172 34 5 S 70 45W
Graney L. 39 53 0N 8 40W
Grange 38 54 24N 8 32W
Grange, La, Austral. 136 18 45 S 121 43 E
Grange, La, U.S.A. 163 37 42N 120 27W
Grange, La, Ga., U.S.A. 157 33 4N 85 0W
Grange, La, Ky., U.S.A. 156 38 20N 85 20W
Grange, La, Tex., U.S.A. 159 29 54N 96 52W
Grange-over-Sands 32 54 12N 2 55W
Grangemouth 35 56 1N 3 43W
Granger 160 46 25N 120 5W
Grangesberg 72 60 6N 15 1 E
Grängesberg 72 60 6N 15 1 E
Grangetown 33 54 36N 1 7W
Grangeville 160 45 57N 116 4W
Granite City 158 38 45N 90 3W
Granite Falls 158 44 45N 95 35W
Granite Mtn. 163 33 5N 116 28W
Granite Peak 137 25 40 S 121 20 E
Granite Pk., mt. 160 45 8N 109 52W
Granitnyy, Pik 85 39 32N 70 20 E
Granity 143 41 39 S 171 51 E
Granja 170 3 17 S 40 50W
Granja de Moreruela 56 41 48N 5 44W
Granja de Torrehermosa 57 38 19N 5 35W
Gränna 73 58 1N 14 28 E
Granollers 58 41 39N 2 18 E
Gransee 48 53 0N 13 10 E
Grant, Can. 150 50 6N 86 18W
Grant, U.S.A. 158 40 53N 101 42W
Grant City 158 40 30N 94 25W
Grant, I. 136 11 10 S 132 52 E
Grant, Mt. 163 38 34N 118 48W
Grant Range Mts. 161 38 30N 115 30W
Grantham 33 52 55N 0 39W
Grantown-on-Spey 37 57 19N 3 36W
Grants 161 35 14N 107 57W
Grant's Pass 160 42 30N 123 22W
Grantsburg 158 45 46N 92 44W
Grantshouse 35 55 53N 2 17W
Grantsville 160 40 35N 112 32W
Granville, France 42 48 50N 1 35W
Granville, U.K. 38 54 30N 6 47W
Granville, N.D., U.S.A. 158 48 18N 100 48W
Granville, N.Y., U.S.A. 162 43 24N 73 16W
Granville L. 153 56 18N 100 30W
Grao de Gandia 59 39 0N 0 27W
Grapeland 159 31 30N 95 25W
Gras, L. de 148 64 30N 110 30W
Graskop 129 24 56 S 30 49 E
Gräsmark 72 59 58N 12 44 E
Grasmere, Austral. 139 35 1 S 117 45 E
Grasmere, U.K. 32 54 28N 3 2W
Gräsö 72 60 21N 18 28 E
Graso 72 60 28N 18 35 E
Grasonville 162 38 57N 76 13W
Grass, R. 153 56 3N 96 33W
Grass Range 160 47 0N 109 0W
Grass River Prov. Park 153 54 40N 100 50W
Grass Valley, Calif., U.S.A. 160 39 18N 121 0W
Grass Valley, Oreg., U.S.A. 160 45 28N 120 48W
Grassano 65 40 38N 16 17 E
Grasse 45 43 38N 6 56 E
Grassington 32 54 5N 2 0W
Grassmere 140 31 24 S 142 38 E
Grate's Cove 151 48 8N 53 0W
Graubünden (Grisons) □ 51 46 45N 9 30 E
Graulhet 44 43 45N 1 58 E
Graus 58 42 11N 0 20 E
Gravatá 170 6 59 S 35 29W
Grave 46 51 46N 5 44 E
Grave, Pte. de 44 45 34N 1 4W
's-Graveland 46 52 15N 5 7 E
Gravelbourg 153 49 50N 106 35W
Gravelines 43 51 0N 2 10 E
's-Gravendeel 46 51 47N 4 37 E
's-Gravenhage 46 52 7N 4 17 E
's-Gravenpolder 47 51 28N 3 54 E
's-Gravensance 46 52 0N 4 9 E
Graversfors 73 58 42N 16 8 E
Gravesend, Austral. 139 29 35 S 150 20 E
Gravesend, U.K. 29 51 25N 0 22 E
Gravina di Pùglia 65 40 48N 16 25 E
Gravir 36 58 2N 6 25W
Gravois, Pointe-à 167 16 15N 73 45W
Gravone, R. 45 42 3N 8 54 E
Grävsnäs 73 58 5N 12 29 E
Gray 43 47 27N 5 35 E
Grayling 156 44 40N 84 42W
Grayling, R. 152 59 21N 125 0W
Grayrigg 32 54 22N 2 40W
Grays Harbor 160 46 55N 124 8W
Grays L. 160 43 8N 111 30W
Grays Thurrock 29 51 28N 0 23 E
Grayson 153 50 45N 102 40W
Grayvoron 80 50 29N 35 39 E
Graz 52 47 4N 15 27 E
Grazalema 57 36 46N 5 23W
Grdelica 66 42 55N 22 3 E
Greasy L. 152 62 55N 122 12W
Great Abaco I. 166 26 15N 77 10W
Great Australia Basin 133 26 0 S 140 0 E
Great Australian Bight 137 33 30 S 130 0 E
Great Ayton 33 54 29N 1 8W
Great Baddow 29 51 43N 0 31 E
Great Bahama Bank 166 23 15N 78 0W
Great Barrier I. 142 36 11 S 175 25 E
Great Barrier Reef 138 19 0 S 149 0 E
Great Barrington 162 42 11N 73 22W
Great Basin 154 40 0N 116 30W
Great Bear L. 148 65 0N 120 0W
Great Bear, R. 148 65 0N 124 0W
Great Belt 73 55 20N 11 0 E
Great Bena 162 41 57N 75 45W
Great Bend 158 38 25N 98 55W
Great Bentley 29 51 51N 1 5 E
Great Bernera, I. 137 58 15N 6 50W
Great Bitter Lake 122 30 15N 32 40 E
Great Blasket, I. 39 52 5N 10 30W
Great Britain 16 54 0N 2 15W
Great Bushman Land 128 29 20 S 19 20 E
Great Central 152 49 20N 125 10W
Great Chesterford 29 52 4N 0 11 E
Great Clifton 32 54 39N 3 29W
Great Coco I. 101 14 10N 93 25 E
Great Divide 141 23 0 S 146 0 E
Great Dunmow 29 51 52N 0 22 E
Great Exuma I. 166 23 30N 75 50W
Great Falls, Can. 153 50 27N 96 1W
Great Falls, U.S.A. 160 47 27N 111 12W
Great Fish R., S. Afr. 128 33 28 S 27 5 E
Great Fish R., S. Afr. 128 31 30 S 20 16 E
Great Gonerby 33 52 56N 0 40W
Great Guana Cay 166 24 0N 76 20W
Great Hanish 123 13 40N 43 0 E
Great Harbour Deep 151 50 35N 56 25W
Great Harwood 32 52 41N 2 49W
Great I., Can. 153 58 53N 96 35W
Great I., Ireland 39 51 52N 8 15W
Great Inagua I. 167 21 0N 73 20W
Gt. Indian Desert = Thar Desert 94 28 0N 72 0 E
Great Jarvis 151 47 39N 57 12W
Great Karoo = Groot Karoo 128 32 30 S 23 0 E
Great Lake 138 41 50 S 146 30 E
Great Lakes 153 44 0N 82 0W
Great Malvern 28 52 7N 2 19W
Great Massingham 29 52 47N 0 41 E
Great Missenden 29 51 42N 0 42W
Gt. Namaqualand = Groot Namakwaland 128 26 0 S 18 0 E
Great Orme's Head 31 53 20N 3 52W
Great Ouse, R. 29 52 20N 0 8 E
Great Palm I. 138 18 45 S 146 40 E
Great Papuan Plateau 135 6 30 S 142 25 E
Great Plains 50 45 0N 100 0W
Great Ruaha, R. 126 7 30 S 35 0 E
Great Salt Lake 160 41 0N 112 30W
Great Salt Lake Desert 160 40 20N 113 50W
Great Salt Plains Res. 159 36 40N 98 15W
Great Sandy Desert 136 21 0 S 124 0 E
Great Sandy I. = Fraser I. 139 25 15 S 153 0 E
Great Scarcies, R. 120 9 30N 12 40W
Great Shefford 28 51 29N 1 27W
Great Shelford 29 52 9N 0 9 E
Great Shunner Fell 32 54 22N 2 16W
Great Sitkin I. 147 52 0N 176 10W
Great Slave L. 152 61 23N 115 38W
Great Stour, R. 29 51 21N 1 15 E
Gt. Sugar Loaf, mt. 39 53 10N 6 10W
Great Torrington 30 50 57N 4 9W
Gt. Victoria Des. 137 29 30 S 126 30 E
Great Wall 106 38 30N 109 30 E
Gt. Waltham 29 51 47N 0 29 E
Great Whale, R. 150 55 20N 75 30W
Great Whernside, mt. 147 54 9N 1 59W
Great Winterhoek, mt. 128 33 07 S 19 10 E
Great Wyrley 28 52 40N 2 1W
Great Yarmouth 29 52 40N 1 45 E
Great Yeldham 29 52 1N 0 33 E
Greater Antilles 167 17 40N 74 0W
Greater Manchester □ 32 53 30N 2 15W
Greatham 33 54 38N 1 14W
Grebbestad 73 58 42N 11 15 E
Grebenka 80 50 9N 32 22 E
Greco, Mt. 64 41 48N 14 0 E
Gredos, Sierra de 56 40 20N 5 0W
Greece ■ 68 40 0N 23 0 E
Greeley, Colo., U.S.A. 158 40 30N 104 40W
Greeley, Nebr., U.S.A. 158 41 36N 98 32W
Green B. 156 45 0N 87 30W
Green Bay 156 44 30N 88 0W
Green C. 141 37 13 S 150 1 E
Green Cove Springs 157 29 59N 81 40W
Green Hammerton 33 54 2N 1 17W
Green Hd. 137 30 5 S 114 56 E
Green Is. 135 4 35 S 154 10 E
Green Island 143 45 55 S 170 26 E
Green Lowther, Mt. 35 55 22N 3 44W
Green R., Ky., U.S.A. 156 37 54N 87 30W
Green R., Utah, U.S.A. 161 39 0N 110 6W
Green R., Wyo., U.S.A. 160 43 2N 110 2W
Green R., Wyo., U.S.A. 160 41 44N 109 28W
Greenbush 158 48 46N 96 10W
Greencastle, U.K. 38 54 2N 6 5W
Greencastle, U.S.A. 156 39 40N 86 48W
Greene 162 42 20N 75 45W
Greenfield, Calif., U.S.A. 163 35 15N 119 0W
Greenfield, Calif., U.S.A. 163 36 19N 121 15W
Greenfield, Ind., U.S.A. 156 39 47N 85 51W
Greenfield, Iowa, U.S.A. 158 41 18N 94 28W
Greenfield, Mass., U.S.A. 162 42 38N 72 38W
Greenfield, Miss., U.S.A. 159 37 28N 93 50W
Greenhead 35 54 58N 2 31W
Greening 150 48 10N 74 55W
Greenisland 38 54 42N 5 50W
Greenland 12 66 0N 45 0W
Greenland Sea 12 73 0N 10 0W
Greenlaw 35 55 42N 2 28W
Greenock 34 55 57N 4 46W
Greenodd 32 54 14N 3 3W
Greenore 38 54 2N 6 8W
Greenore Pt. 39 52 15N 6 20W
Greenough, R. 137 28 54 S 115 36 E
Greenport 162 41 5N 72 23W
Greensboro, Ga., U.S.A. 157 33 34N 83 12W
Greensboro, Md., U.S.A. 162 38 59N 75 48W
Greensboro, N.C., U.S.A. 157 36 7N 79 46W
Greensburg, Ind., U.S.A. 156 39 20N 85 30W
Greensburg, Kans., U.S.A. 159 37 38N 99 20W
Greensburg, Pa., U.S.A. 156 40 18N 79 31W
Greenstone Pt. 36 57 55N 5 38W
Greenville, Liberia 120 5 7N 9 6W
Greenville, Ala., U.S.A. 157 31 50N 86 37W
Greenville, Calif., U.S.A. 160 40 8N 121 0W
Greenville, Ill., U.S.A. 158 38 53N 89 22W
Greenville, Me., U.S.A. 151 45 30N 69 32W
Greenville, Mich., U.S.A. 156 43 12N 85 14W
Greenville, Miss., U.S.A. 159 33 25N 91 0W
Greenville, N.C., U.S.A. 157 35 37N 77 26W
Greenville, N.H., U.S.A. 162 42 46N 71 49W
Greenville, N.Y., U.S.A. 162 42 25N 74 1W
Greenville, Ohio, U.S.A. 156 40 5N 84 38W
Greenville, Pa., U.S.A. 156 41 23N 80 22W
Greenville, S.C., U.S.A. 157 34 54N 82 24W
Greenville, Tenn., U.S.A. 157 36 13N 82 51W
Greenville, Tex., U.S.A. 159 33 5N 96 5W
Greenwater Lake Prov. Park 153 52 32N 103 30W
Greenway 31 51 56N 4 49W
Greenwich, U.K. 29 51 28N 0 0
Greenwich, Conn., U.S.A. 162 41 1N 73 38W
Greenwich, N.Y., U.S.A. 162 43 2N 73 36W
Greenwood, Can. 152 49 10N 118 40W
Greenwood, Miss., U.S.A. 159 33 30N 90 4W
Greenwood, S.C., U.S.A. 157 34 13N 82 13W
Greenwood, Mt. 136 13 48 S 130 4 E
Gregory 158 43 14N 99 20W
Gregory Downs 138 18 35 S 138 45 E
Gregory, L. 139 28 55 S 139 0 E
Gregory L. 136 20 5 S 127 0 E
Gregory, L. 137 25 38 S 119 58 E
Gregory Lake 136 20 10 S 127 30 E
Gregory, R. 138 17 53 S 139 17 E
Gregory Ra., Queens., Austral. 138 19 30 S 143 40 E
Gregory Ra., W. Austral., Austral. 136 21 20 S 121 12 E
Greian Hd. 36 57 1N 7 30W
Greiffenberg 48 53 6N 13 57 E
Greifswald 48 54 6N 13 23 E
Greifswalder Bodden 48 54 12N 13 35 E
Greifswalder Oie 48 54 15N 13 55 E
Grein 52 48 14N 14 51 E
Greiner Wald 52 48 30N 15 0 E
Greiz 48 50 39N 12 12 E
Gremikha 78 67 50N 39 40 E
Grenå 73 56 25N 10 53 E
Grenada 159 33 45N 89 50W
Grenada I. ■ 167 12 10N 61 40W
Grenade 44 43 47N 1 17 E
Grenadines 167 12 40N 61 20W
Grenchen 50 47 12N 7 24 E
Grenen 73 57 44N 10 40 E
Grenfell, Austral. 141 33 52 S 148 8 E
Grenfell, Can. 153 50 30N 102 56W
Grenoble 45 45 12N 5 42 E
Grenora 158 48 38N 103 54W
Grenville, C. 138 12 0 S 143 13 E
Grenville Chan. 152 53 40N 129 46W
Gréoux-les-Bains 45 43 45N 5 52 E
Gresham 160 45 30N 122 31W
Gresik 103 9 13 S 112 38 E
Gressoney St. Jean 62 45 49N 7 47 E
Greta 32 54 9N 2 36W
Greta R. 32 54 36N 3 5W
Gretna, U.K. 35 54 59N 3 4W
Gretna, U.S.A. 159 30 0N 90 2W
Gretna Green 35 55 0N 3 3W
Gretton 29 52 33N 0 40W
Grevelingen Krammer 46 51 44N 4 0 E
Greven 48 52 7N 7 36 E
Grevená 68 40 4N 21 25 E
Grevená □ 68 40 2N 21 25 E
Grevenbroich 48 51 6N 6 32 E
Grevenmacher 47 49 41N 6 26 E
Grevesmühlen 48 53 51N 11 10 E
Grevie 73 56 22N 12 46 E
Grevinge 73 55 48N 11 34 E
Grey, C. 138 13 0 S 136 35 E
Grey, R. 143 42 27 S 171 12 E
Grey Range 133 27 0 S 143 30 E
Grey Res. 151 48 20N 56 30W
Greyabbey 38 54 32N 5 35W
Greybull 160 44 30N 108 3W
Greystone 32 54 39N 2 52W
Greystones 39 53 9N 6 4W
Greytown, N.Z. 142 41 5 S 175 29 E
Greytown, S. Afr. 129 29 1 S 30 36 E
Gribanovskiy 81 51 28N 41 50 E
Gribbell I. 152 53 23N 129 0W
Gribbin Head 30 50 18N 4 41W
Gridley 160 39 27N 121 47W
Griekwastad 128 28 49 S 23 15 E
Griffin 157 33 17N 84 14W
Griffith 141 34 18 S 146 2 E
Griffith Mine 153 50 47N 93 25W
Grigoryevka 84 50 48N 58 18 E
Grijalva, R. 164 16 20N 92 20W
Grijpskerk 46 53 16N 6 18 E
Grillby 72 59 38N 17 15 E

Grim, C Gus


Grim, C. 133 40 45S 144 45E
Grimaïlov 80 49 20N 26 5E
Grimari 117 5 43N 20 0E
Grimbergen 47 50 56N 4 22E
Grimeton 73 57 6N 12 25E
Griminish Pt. 36 57 40N 7 30W
Grimma 48 51 14N 12 44E
Grimmen 48 54 6N 13 2E
Grimsay I. 36 57 29N 7 12W
Grimsby 33 53 35N 0 5W
Grimsel Pass 51 46 34N 8 23E
Grímsey 74 66 33N 18 0W
Grimshaw 152 56 10N 117 40W
Grimstad 71 58 22N 8 35E
Grindelwald 50 46 38N 8 2E
Grindsted 73 55 46N 8 55E
Grindstone Island 151 47 25N 62 0W
Grindu 70 44 44N 26 50E
Grinduşul, Mt. 70 46 40N 26 7E
Griñón 56 40 13N 3 51W
Grinnell 158 41 45N 92 43W
Grip 71 63 16N 7 37E
Griqualand East 129 30 30S 29 0E
Griqualand West 128 28 40S 23 30E
Griquet 151 51 30N 55 35W
Grisolles 44 43 49N 1 19E
Grisons □ 49 46 40N 9 30E
Grisslehamm 72 60 5N 18 49E
Grita, La 174 8 8N 71 59W
Gritley 37 58 56N 2 45W
Grivegnée 47 50 37N 5 36E
Griz Nez 43 50 50N 1 35E
Grizebeck 32 54 16N 3 10W
Grmeč Planina 63 44 43N 16 16E
Groais I. 151 50 55N 55 35W
Groblersdal 129 25 15S 29 25E
Grobming 52 47 27N 13 54E
Grocka 66 44 40N 20 42E
Grodek 80 52 46N 23 38E
Grodkow 54 50 43N 17 40E
Grodno 80 53 42N 23 52E
Grodzisk Mazowiecki 54 52 7N 20 37E
Grodzisk Wlkp. 54 52 15N 16 22E
Grodzyanka 80 53 31N 28 42E
Groenlo 46 52 2N 6 37E
Groesbeck 159 31 32N 96 34W
Groesbeek 46 51 47N 5 58E
Groix 42 47 38N 3 29W
Groix, I. de 42 47 38N 3 28W
Grójec 54 51 50N 20 58E
Grolloo 46 52 56N 6 41E
Gronau 48 52 13N 7 2E
Grong 74 64 25N 12 8E
Groningen 46 53 15N 6 35E
Groningen □ 46 53 16N 6 40E
Groninger Wad 46 53 27N 6 30E
Grönskåra 73 57 5N 15 43E
Gronsveld 47 50 49N 5 44E
Groom 159 35 12N 100 59W
Groomsport 38 54 41N 5 37W
Groot Berg, R. 128 32 50S 18 20E
Groot-Brakrivier 128 34 2S 22 18E
Groot Karoo 128 32 35S 23 0E
Groot Namakwaland = Namaland 128 26 0S 18 0E
Groot, R. 128 33 10S 23 35E
Groote Eylandt 138 14 0S 136 50E
Grootebroek 46 52 41N 5 13E
Grootfontein 128 19 31S 18 6E
Grootlaagte, R. 128 21 10S 21 20E
Gros C. 152 61 59N 113 32W
Grosa, Punta 59 39 6N 1 36E
Grósio 62 46 18N 10 17E
Grosne, R. 45 46 30N 4 40E
Gross Glockner 52 47 5N 12 40E
Gross Ottersleben 48 52 5N 11 33E
Grossa, Pta. 170 1 20N 50 0W
Grossenbrode 48 54 21N 11 4E
Grossenhain 48 51 17N 13 32E
Grosseto 62 42 45N 11 7E
Grossgerungs 52 48 34N 14 57E
Grosswater B. 151 54 20N 57 40W
Grote Gette, R. 47 50 51N 5 6E
Grote Nete, R. 47 51 8N 4 34E
Groton, U.S.A. 162 41 22N 72 12W
Groton, U.S.A. 162 42 36N 76 22W
Grottaglie 65 40 32N 17 25E
Grottaminarda 65 41 5N 15 4E
Grouard Mission 152 55 33N 116 9W
Grouin, Pointe du 42 48 43N 1 51W
Groundhog, R. 150 48 45N 82 20W
Grouse Creek 160 41 51N 113 57W
Grouw 46 53 5N 5 51E
Groveland 163 37 50N 120 14W
Grovelsjön 72 62 6N 12 16E
Grover City 163 35 7N 120 37W
Groveton 159 31 5N 95 4W
Groznjan 63 45 22N 13 43E
Groznyy 83 43 20N 45 45E
Grubbenvorst 47 51 25N 6 9E
Grubišno Polje 66 45 44N 17 12E
Grudusk 54 53 3N 20 38E
Grudziadz 54 53 30N 18 47E
Gruinard B. 36 57 56N 5 35W
Gruissan 44 43 8N 3 7E
Grumo Áppula 65 41 2N 16 43E
Grums 72 59 22N 13 5E
Grünau 125 27 45S 18 26E
Grünberg 48 50 37N 8 55E
Grundy Center 158 42 22N 92 45W
Grungedal 71 59 44N 7 43E
Gruting Voe 36 60 12N 1 32W
Gruver 159 36 19N 101 20W
Gruyères 50 46 35N 7 4E
Gruza 66 43 54N 20 46E
Gryazi 81 52 30N 39 58E
Gryazovets 81 58 50N 40 20E
Grybów 54 49 36N 20 55E
Grycksbo 72 60 40N 15 29E
Gryfice 54 53 55N 15 13E
Gryfino 54 53 16N 14 29E
Grytgöl 73 58 49N 15 33E
Grythyttan 72 59 41N 14 32E
Grytviken 13 53 50S 37 10W
Gstaad 50 46 28N 7 18E
Gua 99 22 18N 85 20E
Gua Musang 101 4 53N 101 58E
Guacanayabo, Golfo de 166 20 40N 77 20W
Guacara 174 10 14N 67 53W
Guachípas 172 25 40S 65 30W
Guachiría, R. 174 5 30N 71 30W
Guadajoz, R. 57 37 50N 4 51W
Guadalajara, Mexico 164 20 40N 103 20W
Guadalajara, Spain 58 40 37N 3 12W
Guadalajara □ 58 40 47N 3 0W
Guadalcanal 57 38 5N 5 52W
Guadalcanal, I. 130 9 32S 160 12E
Guadalén, R. 59 38 30N 3 7W
Guadales 172 34 30S 67 55W
Guadalete, R. 57 36 45N 5 47W
Guadalhorce, R. 57 36 50N 4 42W
Guadalimar, R. 59 38 10N 2 53W
Guadalmena, R. 59 38 31N 2 50W
Guadalmez, R. 57 38 33N 4 42W
Guadalope, R. 58 41 0N 0 13W
Guadalquivir, R. 57 38 0N 4 0W
Guadalupe, Brazil 170 6 44S 43 47W
Guadalupe, Spain 57 39 27N 5 17W
Guadalupe, U.S.A. 163 34 59N 120 33W
Guadalupe Bravos 164 31 20N 106 10W
Guadalupe de los Reyes 164 25 23N 104 15W
Guadalupe I. 143 21 20N 118 50W
Guadalupe Pk. 161 31 50N 105 30W
Guadalupe, R. 159 29 25N 97 30W
Guadalupe, Sierra de 55 39 28N 5 30W
Guadalupe y Calvo 164 26 6N 106 58W
Guadarrama, Sierra de 56 41 0N 4 0W
Guadeloupe, I. 167 16 20N 61 40W
Guadeloupe Passage 167 16 50N 68 15W
Guadiamar, R. 57 37 9N 6 20W
Guadiana Menor, R. 59 37 45N 3 7W
Guadiana, R. 57 37 45N 7 35W
Guadiaro, R. 57 36 39N 5 17W
Guadiato, R. 57 37 55N 4 53W
Guadiela, R. 58 40 30N 2 23W
Guadix 59 37 18N 3 11W
Guafo, Boca del 176 43 35S 74 0W
Guaina 174 5 9N 63 36W
Guainía □ 174 2 30N 69 00W
Guaira 173 24 5S 54 10W
Guaira, La 174 10 36N 66 56W
Guaitecas, Islas 176 44 0S 74 30W
Guajará-Mirim 174 10 50S 65 20W
Guajira, La □ 174 11 30N 72 30W
Guajira, Pen. de la 167 12 0N 72 0W
Gualan 166 15 8N 89 22W
Gualdo Tadino 63 43 14N 12 46E
Gualeguay 172 33 10S 59 20W
Gualeguaychú 172 33 3S 58 31W
Guam I. 130 13 27N 144 45E
Guamá 170 1 37S 47 29W
Guama 174 10 16N 68 49W
Guamá, R. 170 1 29S 48 30W
Guamareyes 174 0 30S 73 0W
Guaminí 172 37 1S 62 28W
Guampí, Sierra de 174 6 0N 65 35W
Guamuchil 164 25 25N 108 3W
Guanabacoa 166 23 8N 82 18W
Guanabara □ 173 23 0S 43 25W
Guanacaste 166 10 40N 85 30W
Guanacaste, Cordillera del 166 10 40N 85 4W
Guanacevío 164 25 40N 106 0W
Guanajay 166 22 56N 82 42W
Guanajuato 164 21 0N 101 20W
Guanajuato □ 164 20 40N 101 20W
Guanambi 171 14 13S 42 47W
Guanare 174 8 42N 69 12W
Guanare, R. 174 8 50N 68 50W
Guandacol 172 29 30S 68 40W
Guane 166 22 10N 84 0W
Guanhães 171 18 47S 42 57W
Guanica 147 17 58N 66 55W
Guanipa, R. 174 9 20N 63 30W
Guanta 174 10 14N 64 36W
Guantánamo 167 20 10N 75 20W
Guapí 174 2 36N 77 54W
Guápiles 166 10 10N 83 46W
Guaporé 173 12 0S 64 0W
Guaporé, R. 174 13 0S 63 0W
Guaqui 174 16 41S 68 54W
Guara, Sierra de 58 42 19N 0 15W
Guarabira 170 6 51S 35 29W
Guarapari 173 20 40S 40 30W
Guarapuava 171 25 20S 51 30W
Guaratinguetá 173 22 49S 45 9W
Guaratuba 173 25 53S 48 38W
Guard Bridge 35 56 21N 2 52W
Guarda 56 40 32N 7 20W
Guarda □ 56 40 40N 7 20W
Guardafui, C. = Asir, Ras 91 11 55N 51 10E
Guardamar del Segura 59 38 5N 0 39W
Guardavalle 65 38 31N 16 30E
Guardia, La 56 41 56N 8 52W
Guardiagrele 63 42 11N 14 11E
Guardo 56 42 47N 4 50W
Guareña 57 38 51N 6 6W
Guareña, R. 56 41 25N 5 25W
Guaría □ 172 25 45N 56 30W
Guárico □ 174 8 40N 66 35W
Guarujá 173 24 2S 46 25W
Guarus 173 21 30S 41 20W
Guasave 164 25 34N 108 27W
Guasdualito 174 7 15N 70 44W
Guasipati 174 7 28N 61 54W
Guasopa 135 9 12S 152 56E
Guastalla 62 44 55N 10 40E
Guatemala 166 14 40N 90 30W
Guatemala ■ 166 15 40N 90 30W
Guatire 174 10 28N 66 32W
Guaviare, R. 174 3 30N 71 0W
Guaxupé 173 21 10S 47 5W
Guayabal 174 4 43N 71 37W
Guayama 147 17 59N 66 7W
Guayaquil 174 2 15S 79 52W
Guayaquil, Golfo de 174 3 10S 81 0W
Guaymallen 172 32 50S 68 45W
Guaymas 164 27 50N 111 0W
Guba, Ethiopia 123 4 52N 39 18E
Guba, Zaïre 127 10 38S 26 27E
Gubakha 84 58 52N 57 36E
Gubam 135 8 39S 141 53E
Gúbbio 63 43 20N 12 34E
Gubio 121 12 30N 12 42E
Gubkin 81 51 17N 37 32E
Guča 66 43 46N 20 15E
Guchil 101 5 35N 102 10E
Gudalur 97 11 30N 76 29E
Gudata 83 43 7N 40 32E
Gudbransdal 75 61 33N 10 0E
Guddu Barrage 93 28 30N 69 50E
Gudenå 73 56 27N 9 40E
Gudermes 83 43 24N 46 20E
Gudhjem 73 55 12N 14 58E
Gudiña, La 56 42 4N 7 8W
Gudivada 96 16 30N 81 15E
Gudiyatam 97 12 57N 78 55E
Gudmundra 72 62 56N 17 47E
Gudrun, gasfield 19 58 50N 1 48E
Gudur 97 14 12N 79 55E
Guebwiller 43 47 55N 7 12E
Guecho 58 43 21N 2 59W
Guéckédou 120 8 40N 10 5W
Guelma 119 36 25N 7 29E
Guelph 150 43 35N 80 20W
Guelt es Stel 118 35 12N 3 1E
Guelttara 118 29 23N 2 10W
Guemar 119 33 30N 6 57E
Guéméné-Penfao 42 47 38N 1 50W
Guéméné-sur-Scorff 42 48 4N 3 13W
Güemes 172 24 50S 65 0W
Guéné 121 11 44N 3 16E
Guer 42 47 54N 2 8W
Guérande 42 47 20N 2 26W
Guerche, La 42 47 57N 1 16W
Guerche-sur-l'Aubois, La 43 46 58N 2 56E
Guercif 118 34 14N 3 21W
Guéréda 124 14 31N 22 5E
Guéret 44 46 11N 1 51E
Guérigny 43 47 6N 3 10E
Guernica 58 43 19N 2 40W
Guernsey 158 42 19N 104 45W
Guernsey I. 42 49 30N 2 35W
Guerrara, Oasis, Alg. 119 32 51N 4 35E
Guerrara, Saoura, Alg. 118 28 5N 0 8W
Guerrero □ 165 17 30N 100 0W
Guerzim 118 29 45N 1 47W
Güeşti 70 44 48N 25 19E
Guestling Green 29 50 53N 0 40E
Gueugnon 45 45 36N 4 3E
Gueydan 159 30 3N 92 30W
Guezendi = Ghesendor 119 21 14N 18 14E
Guglia, P. dal 51 46 28N 9 45E
Guglionesi 63 51 55N 14 54E
Guhra 93 27 36N 56 8E
Guia Lopes da Laguna 173 21 26S 56 7W
Guiana Highlands 174 5 0N 60 0W
Guibes 128 26 41S 16 49E
Guider 121 9 55N 13 59E
Guidimouni 121 13 42N 9 31E
Guiglo 120 6 45N 7 30W
Guija 125 34 35S 33 15E
Guijo de Coria 56 40 6N 6 28W
Guildford 29 51 14N 0 34W
Guilford, Conn., U.S.A. 162 41 15N 72 40W
Guilford, Me., U.S.A. 151 45 12N 69 25W
Guillaumes 45 44 5N 6 52E
Guillestre 45 44 39N 6 40E
Guilsfield 31 52 42N 3 9W
Guilvinec 42 47 48N 4 17W
Guimarães 170 2 9S 44 35W
Guimarãis 56 41 28N 8 24W
Guimaras I. 103 10 35N 122 37E
Guinea ■ 120 10 20N 10 0W
Guinea Bissau ■ 120 12 0N 15 0W
Guinea, Gulf of 121 3 0N 2 30E
Guinea, Port. = Guinea Bissau 120 12 0N 15 0W
Güines 166 22 50N 82 0W
Guingamp 42 48 34N 3 10W
Guipavas 42 48 26N 4 29W
Guipúzcoa □ 58 43 12N 2 15W
Guir, O. 118 39 29N 2 58W
Guirgo 121 11 54N 1 21W
Güiria 174 10 32N 62 18W
Guisborough 33 54 32N 1 2W
Guiscard 43 49 40N 3 0E
Guise 43 49 52N 3 35E
Guitiriz 56 43 11N 7 50W
Guivan 103 11 5N 125 55E
Gujan-Mestras 44 44 38N 1 4W
Gujar Khan 84 33 15N 73 21E
Gujarat □ 94 23 20N 71 0E
Gujranwala 94 32 10N 74 12E
Gujrat 94 32 40N 74 2E
Gukhothae 101 17 2N 99 50E
Gukovo 83 48 1N 39 58E
Gulak 121 10 50N 13 30E
Gulargambone 141 31 20S 148 30E
Gulbahar 93 35 5N 69 10E
Gulbargâ 96 17 20N 76 50E
Gulbene 80 57 8N 26 52E
Gulcha 85 40 19N 73 26E
Guldborg Sd. 73 54 39N 11 50E
Guledgud 97 16 3N 75 48E
Gulf Basin 136 15 20S 129 0E
Gulfport 159 30 28N 89 3W
Gulgong 141 32 20S 149 30E
Gulistan, Pak. 94 30 30N 66 35E
Gulistan, U.S.S.R. 85 40 29N 68 46E
Gulkana 147 62 15N 145 48W
Gull Lake 153 50 10N 108 29W
Gullane 35 56 2N 2 50W
Gullegem 47 50 51N 3 13E
Gullringen 73 57 48N 15 44E
Güllük 69 37 12N 27 36E
Gulma 121 12 40N 4 23E
Gulmarg 95 34 3N 74 25E
Gulnam 123 6 55N 29 30E
Gulnare 140 33 27S 138 27E
Gulpaigan 92 33 26N 50 20E
Gulpen 47 50 49N 5 53E
Gülpinar 68 39 32N 26 10E
Gulshad 76 46 45N 74 25E
Gulsvik 71 60 24N 9 38E
Gulu 126 2 48N 32 17E
Gulwe 126 6 30S 36 25E
Gulyaypole 82 47 45N 36 21E
Gum Lake 140 32 42S 143 9E
Gumal, R. 94 32 5N 70 5E
Gumbaz 94 30 2N 69 0E
Gumel 121 12 39N 9 22E
Gumiel de Hizán 58 41 46N 3 41W
Gumlu 138 19 53S 147 41E
Gumma-ken □ 111 36 30N 138 20E
Gummersbach 48 51 2N 7 32E
Gummi 121 12 4N 5 9E
Gümüsane 92 40 30N 39 30E
Gümüşhaciköy 82 40 50N 35 18E
Gumzai 103 5 28S 134 42E
Guna 94 24 40N 77 19E
Guna Mt. 123 11 50N 37 40E
Gundagai 141 35 3S 148 6E
Gundih 103 7 10S 110 56E
Gundlakamma, R. 97 15 30N 80 15E
Gunebang 141 33 5S 146 38E
Gungal 141 32 17S 150 32E
Gungi 123 10 20N 38 3E
Gungu 124 5 43S 19 20E
Gunisao L. 153 53 33N 96 15W
Gunisao, R. 153 53 56N 97 53W
Gunnedah 141 30 59S 150 15E
Gunniguldrie 141 33 12S 146 8E
Gunningbar Cr. 141 31 14S 147 6E
Gunnison, Colo., U.S.A. 161 38 32N 106 56W
Gunnison, Utah, U.S.A. 160 39 11N 111 48W
Gunnison, R. 161 38 50N 108 30W
Gunnworth 153 51 20N 108 9W
Guntakal 97 15 11N 77 27E
Guntersville 157 34 18N 86 16W
Guntong 101 4 36N 101 3E
Guntur 96 16 23N 80 30E
Gunungapi 103 6 45S 126 30E
Gunungsitoli 102 1 15N 97 30E
Gunungsugih 102 4 58S 105 7E
Gunupur 96 19 5N 83 50E
Gunworth 153 51 20N 108 10W
Gunza 124 10 50S 13 50E
Gunzenhausen 49 49 6N 10 45E
Gupis 95 36 15N 73 20E
Gura 94 25 12N 71 39E
Gura Humorului 70 47 35N 25 53E
Gura Teghii 70 45 30N 26 25E
Gurage, mt. 123 8 20N 38 20E
Gurchan 92 34 55N 49 25E
Gurdaspur 94 32 5N 75 25E
Gurdon 159 33 55N 93 10W
Gurdzhaani 83 41 43N 45 52E
Gurgan 93 36 51N 54 25E
Gurgaon 94 28 33N 77 10E
Gurghiu, Munţii 70 46 41N 25 15E
Gurguéia, R. 170 6 50S 43 24W
Guria 62 44 30N 9 0E
Gurk, R. 52 46 48N 14 20E
Gurkha 95 28 5N 84 40E
Gurla Mandhata 95 30 30N 81 10E
Gurley 139 29 45S 149 48E
Gurnard's Head 30 50 12N 5 37W
Gurnet Pt. 162 42 1N 70 34W
Gurrumbah 138 17 30S 144 55E
Gurun 101 5 49N 100 27E
Gürün 92 38 41N 37 22E
Gurupá 175 1 20S 51 45W
Gurupá, I. Grande de 175 1 0S 51 45W
Gurupi 171 11 43S 49 4W
Gurupi, R. 170 3 20S 47 20W
Gurupi, Serra do 170 5 0S 47 30W
Guryev 83 47 5N 52 0E
Gus 126 3 2N 36 57E

Gus-Khrsutalnyy Han Chiang, R

Gus-Khrsutalnyy 81 55 42N 40 35 E
Gusau 121 12 18N 6 31 E
Gusev 80 54 35N 22 20 E
Gushiago 121 9 55N 0 15W
Gusinje 66 42 35N 19 50 E
Gúspini 64 39 32N 8 38 E
Gusselby 72 59 38N 15 14 E
Güssing 53 47 3N 16 20 E
Gustanj 63 46 36N 14 49 E
Gustavus 147 58 25N 135 58W
Gustine 163 37 21N 121 0W
Güstrow 48 53 47N 12 12 E
Gusum 73 58 16N 16 30 E
Gŭtaia 70 45 26N 21 30 E
Gütersloh 48 51 54N 8 25 E
Gutha 137 28 58 S 115 55 E
Guthalungra 138 19 52 S 147 50 E
Guthrie 159 35 55N 97 30W
Guttannen 51 46 38N 8 18 E
Guttenberg 158 42 46N 91 10W
Guyana ■ 174 5 0N 59 0W
Guyenne 44 44 30N 0 40 E
Guyman 159 36 45N 101 30W
Guyra 139 30 15 S 151 40 E
Guzar 85 38 36N 66 15 E
Guzmán, Laguna de 164 31 25N 107 25W
Gwa 98 17 30N 94 40 E
Gwaai 127 19 15 S 27 45 E
Gwabegar 141 30 31 S 149 0 E
Gwadabawa 121 13 20N 5 15 E
Gwādar 93 25 10N 62 18 E
Gwagwada 121 10 15N 7 15 E
Gwalchmai 31 53 16N 4 23W
Gwalia 137 28 54 S 121 20 E
Gwalior 94 26 12N 78 10 E
Gwanara 121 18 55N 3 10 E
Gwanda 127 20 55 S 29 0 E
Gwandu 121 12 30N 4 41 E
Gwane 126 4 45N 25 48 E
Gwaram 121 11 15N 9 51 E
Gwarzo 121 12 20N 8 55 E
Gwasero 121 9 30N 8 30 E
Gwaun-Cae-Gurwen 31 51 46N 3 51W
Gweebarra B. 38 54 52N 8 21W
Gweedore 38 55 4N 8 15W
Gweek 30 50 6N 5 12W
Gwelo 125 19 28 S 29 45 E
Gwennap 30 50 12N 5 9W
Gwent □ 31 51 45N 2 55W
Gweta 128 20 12 S 25 17 E
Gwi 121 9 0N 7 10 E
Gwinn 156 46 15N 87 29W
Gwio Kura 121 12 40N 11 2 E
Gwolu 120 10 58N 1 59W
Gwoza 121 11 12N 13 40 E
Gwyddelwern 31 53 2N 3 23W
Gwydir, R. 139 29 27 S 149 48 E
Gwynedd □ 31 53 0N 4 0W
Gya La 95 28 45N 84 45 E
Gyangtse 99 28 50N 89 33 E
Gydanskiy P-ov. 76 70 0N 78 0 E
Gyland 71 58 24N 6 45 E
Gympie 139 26 11 S 152 38 E
Gyobingauk 98 18 13N 95 39 E
Gyoda 111 36 10N 139 30 E
Gyoma 53 46 56N 20 58 E
Gyöngyös 53 47 48N 20 15 E
Györ 53 47 41N 17 40 E
Györ-Sopron □ 53 47 40N 17 20 E
Gypsum Palace 140 32 37 S 144 9 E
Gypsum Pt. 152 61 53N 114 35W
Gypsumville 153 51 45N 98 40W
Gyttorp 72 59 31N 14 58 E
Gyula 53 46 38N 21 17 E
Gzhatsk = Gagarin 80 55 30N 35 0 E

# H

Ha Coi 100 21 26N 107 46 E
Ha Dong 100 20 58N 105 46 E
Ha Giang 100 22 50N 104 59 E
Ha Nam = Phu-Ly 100 20 35N 105 50 E
Ha Tien 101 10 23N 104 29 E
Ha Tinh 100 18 20N 105 54 E
Ha Trung 100 20 0N 105 50 E
Haa, The 36 60 20N 1 0 E
Haacht 47 50 59N 4 37 E
Haag 49 48 11N 12 12 E
Haaksbergen 46 52 9N 6 45 E
Haaltert 47 50 55N 4 1 E
Haamstede 47 51 42N 3 45 E
Haapamäki 74 62 18N 24 28 E
Haapsalu 80 58 56N 23 30 E
Haarby 73 55 13N 10 8 E
Haarlem 46 52 23N 4 39 E
Haast 143 43 51 S 169 1 E
Haast P. 143 44 6 S 169 21 E
Haast, R. 143 43 50 S 169 2 E
Haastrecht 46 52 0N 4 47 E
Hab Nadi Chauki 94 25 0N 66 50 E
Hab, R. 93 25 15N 67 8 E
Haba 92 27 10N 47 0 E
Habana, La 166 23 8N 82 22W
Habaswein 126 1 2N 39 30 E
Habay 152 58 50N 118 44W
Habay-la-Neuve 47 49 44N 5 38 E
Habiganj 98 24 24N 91 30 E
Hablingbo 73 57 12N 18 16 E
Habo 73 57 55N 14 6 E
Haccourt 47 50 44N 5 40 E
Hachenburg 48 50 40N 7 49 E
Hachijō-Jima 111 33 5N 139 45 E
Hachinohe 112 40 30N 141 29 E
Hachiōji 111 35 30N 139 30 E
Hachŏn 107 40 29N 129 2 E
Hachy 47 49 42N 5 41 E
Hacketstown 39 52 52N 6 35W
Hackett 152 52 9N 112 28W
Hackettstown 162 40 51N 74 50W
Hackney 29 51 33N 0 2W
Hackthorpe 32 54 37N 2 42W
Hadali 94 32 16N 72 11 E
Hadarba, Ras 122 22 4N 36 51 E
Hadd, Ras al 93 22 35N 59 50 E
Haddenham 29 51 46N 0 56W
Haddington 35 55 57N 2 48W
Haddon Rig 141 31 27 S 147 52 E
Hadeija 121 12 30N 10 5 E
Hadeija, R. 121 12 20N 9 30W
Haden 139 27 13 S 151 54 E
Hadera 90 32 27N 34 55 E
Haderslev 73 55 15N 9 30 E
Hadhra 122 20 10N 41 5 E
Hadhramaut = Hadramawt 91 15 30N 49 30 E
Hadibu 91 12 35N 54 2 E
Hadjeb el Aïoun 119 35 21N 9 32 E
Hadleigh 29 52 3N 0 58 E
Hadley 28 52 42N 2 28W
Hadlow 29 51 12N 0 20 E
Hadong 107 35 5N 127 44 E
Hadramawt 91 15 30N 49 30 E
Hadrians Wall 35 55 0N 2 30W
Hadsten 73 56 19N 10 3 E
Hadsund 73 56 44N 10 8 E
Haeju 107 38 3N 125 45 E
Haenam 107 34 34N 126 15 E
Haerhpin 107 45 45N 126 45 E
Hafar al Batin 92 28 25N 46 50 E
Hafizabad 94 32 5N 73 40 E
Haflong 98 25 10N 93 5 E
Hafnarfjörður 74 64 4N 21 57W
Haft-Gel 92 31 30N 49 32 E
Hafun 91 10 25N 51 16 E
Hafun, Ras 91 10 29N 51 20 E
Hagalil 90 32 53N 35 18 E
Hagar Banga 117 10 40N 22 45 E
Hagari, R. 97 14 0N 76 45 E
Hagemeister I. 147 58 42N 161 0W
Hagen 48 51 21N 7 29 E
Hagenow 48 53 25N 11 10 E
Hagerman 159 33 5N 104 22W
Hagerstown 156 39 39N 77 46W
Hagetmau 44 43 39N 0 37W
Hagfors 72 60 3N 13 45 E
Häggenås 72 63 24N 14 55 E
Hagi, Iceland 74 65 28N 23 25W
Hagi, Japan 110 34 30N 131 30 E
Hagion Evstratios 68 39 30N 25 0 E
Hagion Óros 68 40 37N 24 6 E
Hags Hd. 39 52 57N 9 30W
Hague, C. de la 42 49 44N 1 56W
Hague, The = s'-Gravenhage 47 52 7N 4 17 E
Haguenau 43 48 49N 7 47 E
Hai □ 126 3 10 S 37 10 E
Hai Duong 100 20 56N 106 19 E
Haian, Kiangsu, China 109 32 37N 120 33 E
Haian, Kwangtung, China 109 20 18N 110 11 E
Haich'eng, Fukien, China 109 24 24N 117 51 E
Haich'eng, Liaoning, China 107 40 52N 122 45 E
Haichou 107 34 34N 119 6 E
Haichou Wan 107 35 0N 119 30 E
Haidar Khel 94 33 58N 68 38 E
Haifa 90 32 46N 35 0 E
Haifeng 109 22 59N 115 21 E
Haig 137 30 55 S 126 10 E
Haiger 48 50 44N 8 12 E
Haik'ang 109 20 56N 110 4 E
Haik'ou 100 20 5N 110 20 E
Hā'il 92 27 28N 42 2 E
Hailaerh 105 49 12N 119 42 E
Hailakandi 98 24 42N 92 34 E
Hailey 160 43 30N 114 15W
Haileybury 150 47 30N 79 38W
Hailin 107 44 32N 129 24 E
Hailing Tao 109 21 37N 111 65 E
Hailsham 29 50 52N 0 17 E
Hailun 105 47 27N 126 56 E
Hailung 107 42 30N 125 40 E
Hailuoto 74 65 3N 24 45 E
Haimen, Chekiang, China 109 28 39N 121 25 E
Haimen, Kwangtung, China 109 23 15N 116 35 E
Hainan 100 19 0N 110 0 E
Hainan Str. = Ch'iungcho Haihsia 100 20 10N 110 15 E
Hainaut □ 47 50 30N 4 0 E
Hainburg 53 48 9N 16 56 E
Haines, Alaska, U.S.A. 147 59 20N 135 36W
Haines, Oreg., U.S.A. 160 44 51N 117 59W
Haines City 157 28 6N 81 35W
Haines Junction 147 60 45N 137 30W
Hainfeld 52 48 3N 15 48 E
Haining 109 30 23N 120 30 E
Hainton 33 53 21N 0 13W
Haiphong 100 20 47N 106 35 E
Hait'an Tao 109 25 35N 119 45 E
Haiti ■ 167 19 0N 72 30W
Haiya Junc. 122 18 20N 36 40 E
Haiyang 107 36 45N 121 15 E
Haiyen 109 30 28N 120 57 E
Haiyüan, Kwangsi-Chuang, China 108 22 6N 107 25 E
Haiyüan, Ningsia Hui, China 106 36 32N 105 40 E
Haja 103 3 19 S 129 37 E
Hajdú-Bihar □ 53 47 30N 21 30 E
Hajdúböszörmény 53 47 40N 21 30 E
Hajdúdurog 53 47 48N 21 30 E
Hajdúhadház 53 47 40N 21 40 E
Hajdúnánás 53 47 50N 21 26 E
Hajdúsámson 53 47 37N 21 42 E
Hajdúszobaszló 53 47 27N 21 22 E
Haji Langar 93 35 50N 79 20 E
Hajiganj 98 23 15N 90 50 E
Hajipur 95 25 45N 85 20 E
Hajr 93 24 0N 56 34 E
Haka 98 22 39N 93 37 E
Hakansson, Mts. 127 8 40 S 25 45 E
Hakantorp 73 58 18N 12 55 E
Håkantorp 73 58 18N 12 55 E
Hakataramea 143 44 30 S 170 30 E
Hakataramea, R. 143 44 35 S 170 40 E
Hakken-Zan 111 34 10N 135 54 E
Hakodate 112 41 45N 140 44 E
Hakota 111 36 5N 140 30 E
Haku-San 111 36 9N 136 46 E
Hakun 98 26 46N 95 42 E
Hala 93 25 43N 68 20 E
Hala Hu 105 38 15N 97 40 E
Halab = Aleppo 92 36 10N 37 15 E
Halabjah 92 35 10N 45 58 E
Halaib 122 22 5N 36 30 E
Halanzy 47 49 33N 5 44 E
Halawa 147 21 9N 156 47W
Halbe 122 19 40N 42 15 E
Halberstadt 48 51 53N 11 2 E
Halberton 30 50 55N 3 24W
Halcombe 142 40 8 S 175 30 E
Halcyon, Mt. 103 13 0N 121 30 E
Halden 72 59 7N 11 23 E
Haldensleben 48 52 17N 11 30 E
Haldia 99 22 5N 88 3 E
Haldwani 95 29 25N 79 30 E
Hale 32 53 24N 2 21W
Hale, R. 138 24 56 S 135 53 E
Haleakala Crater 147 20 43N 156 12W
Halen 47 50 57N 5 6 E
Halesowen 28 52 27N 2 2W
Halesworth 29 52 21N 1 30 E
Haleyville 157 34 15N 87 40W
Half Assini 120 5 1N 2 50W
Halfmoon B. 143 46 50 S 168 5 E
Halfway 160 44 56N 117 8W
Halfway, R. 152 56 12N 121 32W
Halhul 90 31 35N 35 7 E
Hali 122 18 40N 41 15 E
Haliburton 150 45 3N 78 30W
Halibut, oilfield 19 61 20N 1 36 E
Halifax, Austral. 138 18 32 S 146 22 E
Halifax, Can. 151 44 38N 63 35W
Halifax, U.K. 32 53 43N 1 51W
Halifax, U.S.A. 162 40 25N 76 55W
Halifax B. 138 18 50 S 147 0 E
Halifax I. 128 26 38 S 15 4 E
Halil, R. 93 27 40N 58 30 E
Halkirk 37 58 30N 3 30W
Hall 52 47 17N 11 30 E
Hall Land 12 81 20N 60 0W
Hall Pt. 136 15 40 S 124 23 E
Hallabro 73 56 22N 15 5 E
Halland 73 56 55N 12 50 E
Hallands län □ 73 56 50N 12 50 E
Hallands Väderö 73 56 27N 12 34 E
Hallandsås 73 56 22N 13 0 E
Halle, Belg. 47 50 44N 4 13W
Halle, Nordrhein-Westfalen, Ger. 48 52 4N 8 20 E
Halle, Sachsen-Anhalt, Ger. 48 51 29N 12 0 E
Halle □ 48 51 28N 11 58 E
Hällefors 72 59 47N 14 31 E
Hallein 52 47 40N 13 5 E
Hällekis 73 58 38N 13 27 E
Hallett 140 33 25 S 138 55 E
Hallettsville 159 29 28N 96 57W
Hällevadsholm 73 58 37N 11 33 E
Hällevadsholm 73 58 35N 11 33 E
Halley Bay 13 75 31 S 26 36W
Hallia, R. 96 16 55N 79 10 E
Halliday 158 47 20N 102 25W
Halliday L. 153 61 21N 108 56W
Hallim 107 33 24N 126 15 E
Hallingdal, R. 75 60 34N 9 12 E
Hallingskeid 71 60 40N 7 17 E
Hällnäs 74 64 19N 19 36 E
Hallock 153 48 47N 97 57W
Hallow 28 52 14N 2 15W
Hall's Creek 136 18 16 S 127 46 E
Hallsberg 72 59 5N 15 7 E
Hallstahammar 72 59 38N 16 15 E
Hallstatt 52 47 33N 13 38 E
Hallstavik 72 60 5N 18 37 E
Hallstead 162 41 56N 75 45W
Hallwiler See 50 47 16N 8 12 E
Hallworthy 30 50 38N 4 34W
Halmahera, I. 103 0 40N 128 0 E
Halmeu 70 47 57N 23 2 E
Halmstad 73 56 41N 12 52 E
Halq el Oued 119 36 53N 10 10 E
Hals 73 56 59N 10 18 E
Halsa 71 63 3N 8 14 E
Halsafjorden 71 63 5N 8 10 E
Hälsingborg = Helsingborg 73 56 3N 12 42 E
Halstad 158 47 21N 96 41W
Halstead 29 51 59N 0 39 E
Haltdalen 71 62 56N 11 8 E
Haltern 48 51 44N 7 10 E
Haltwhistle 35 54 58N 2 27W
Ham 128 49 44N 3 3 E
Ham Tan 101 10 40N 107 45 E
Ham Yen 100 22 4N 105 3 E
Hamā 92 35 5N 36 40 E
Hamab 128 28 7 S 19 16 E
Hamad 123 15 20N 33 32 E
Hamada 110 34 50N 132 10 E
Hamadān 92 34 52N 48 32 E
Hamadān □ 92 35 0N 49 0 E
Hamadh 122 24 55N 39 3 E
Hamadia 118 35 28N 1 57 E
Hamakita 111 34 45N 137 47 E
Hamale 120 10 56N 2 45W
Hamamatsu 111 34 45N 137 45 E
Hamar 71 60 48N 11 7 E
Hamar Koke 123 51 5N 36 45 E
Hamarøy 74 68 5N 15 38 E
Hamâta, Gebel 122 24 17N 35 0 E
Hambantota 93 6 10N 81 10 E
Hamber Prov. Park 152 52 20N 118 0W
Hambledon 28 50 56N 1 6W
Hambleton Hills 33 54 17N 1 12W
Hamburg, Ger. 48 53 32N 9 59 E
Hamburg, Ark., U.S.A. 159 33 15N 91 47W
Hamburg, Iowa, U.S.A. 158 40 37N 95 38W
Hamburg, Pa., U.S.A. 162 40 33N 76 0W
Hamburg □ 48 53 30N 10 0 E
Hamden 162 41 21N 72 56W
Hame 75 61 30N 24 0 E
Hämeen Lääni 75 61 24N 24 10 E
Hämeenlinna 75 61 0N 24 28 E
Hamelin Pool 137 26 22 S 114 20 E
Hamelin Pool Bay 137 26 10 S 114 5 E
Hameln 48 52 7N 9 24 E
Hamersley 136 22 20 S 117 37 E
Hamersley Ra. 136 22 0 S 117 45 E
Hamhung 107 40 0N 127 30 E
Hami 105 42 47N 93 32 E
Hamilton, Austral. 140 37 45 S 142 2 E
Hamilton, Can. 150 43 20N 79 50W
Hamilton, N.Z. 142 37 47 S 175 19 E
Hamilton, U.K. 35 55 47N 4 2W
Hamilton, Alas., U.S.A. 147 62 55N 164 0W
Hamilton, Mont., U.S.A. 160 46 20N 114 6W
Hamilton, N.Y., U.S.A. 162 42 49N 75 31W
Hamilton, Ohio, U.S.A. 156 39 20N 84 35W
Hamilton, Tex., U.S.A. 159 31 40N 98 5W
Hamilton Downs 106 21 25 S 142 23 E
Hamilton, gasfield 19 56 54N 2 13 E
Hamilton Hotel 138 22 45 S 140 40 E
Hamilton Inlet 151 54 0N 57 30W
Hamilton Mt. 162 43 25N 74 22W
Hamilton, R., Queens., Austral. 138 23 30 S 139 47 E
Hamilton, R., S. Austral., Austral. 136 26 40 S 134 20 E
Hamiota 153 50 11N 100 38W
Hamlet 157 34 56N 79 40W
Hamley Bridge 140 34 17 S 138 35 E
Hamlin 159 32 58N 100 8W
Hamm 48 51 40N 7 58 E
Hammam bou Hadjar 118 35 23N 0 58W
Hammamet 119 36 24N 10 38 E
Hammamet, G. de 119 36 10N 10 48 E
Hammarö, I. 72 59 20N 13 30 E
Hammarstrand 72 63 7N 16 20 E
Hamme 47 51 6N 4 8 E
Hamme-Mille 47 50 47N 4 43 E
Hammel 73 56 16N 9 52 E
Hammelburg 49 50 7N 9 54 E
Hammenton 156 39 40N 74 47W
Hammeren 73 55 18N 14 47 E
Hammerfest 74 70 39N 23 41 E
Hammersmith 29 51 30N 0 15W
Hammond, Ind., U.S.A. 156 41 40N 87 30W
Hammond, La., U.S.A. 159 30 32N 90 30W
Hammonton 162 39 38N 74 48W
Hamnavoe 36 60 25N 1 5W
Hamneda 73 56 41N 13 51 E
Hamoir 47 50 25N 5 32 E
Hamont 47 51 15N 5 32 E
Hampden 143 45 18 S 170 50 E
Hampshire □ 28 51 3N 1 20W
Hampshire Downs 28 51 10N 1 10W
Hampton, Ark., U.S.A. 159 33 35N 92 29W
Hampton, Iowa, U.S.A. 158 42 42N 93 12W
Hampton, N.H., U.S.A. 162 42 56N 70 48W
Hampton, S.C., U.S.A. 157 32 52N 81 2W
Hampton, Va., U.S.A. 162 37 4N 76 18W
Hampton Bays 162 40 53N 72 31W
Hampton Harbour 136 20 30 S 116 30 E
Hampton in Arden 28 52 26N 1 42W
Hampton Tableland 137 32 0N 127 0 E
Hamra 92 24 2N 38 55 E
Hamrange 72 60 59N 17 5 E
Hamrat esh Sheykh 123 14 45N 27 55 E
Hamre 71 60 33N 5 20 E
Hamun Helmand 93 31 15N 61 15 E
Hamun-i-Lora, Pak. 93 29 38N 64 58 E
Hamun-i-Lora, Pak. 93 29 38N 64 58 E
Hamun-i-Mashkel 93 28 30N 63 0 E
Hamyang 107 35 32N 127 42 E
Han Chiang, R., Hupeh, China 109 30 35N 114 15 E

Han Chiang, R Hawzen

Han Chiang, R., Kwangtung, China 109 23 30N 116 48 E
Hana 147 20 45N 155 59W
Hanak 122 25 32N 37 0 E
Hanamaki 112 39 23N 141 7 E
Hanang □ 126 4 10 S 35 40 E
Hanang, mt. 126 4 30 S 35 25 E
Hanau 49 50 8N 8 56 E
Hanbogd 106 43 11N 107 10 E
Hanch'eng 106 35 30N 110 30 E
Hanchiang 109 25 29N 119 5 E
Hanch'uan 109 30 39N 113 46 E
Hanchuang 107 34 36N 117 22 E
Hanchung 106 33 10N 107 2 E
Hancock, Mich., U.S.A. 158 47 10N 88 35W
Hancock, Minn., U.S.A. 158 45 26N 95 46W
Hancock, Pa., U.S.A. 162 41 57N 75 19W
Handa, Japan 111 34 53N 137 0 E
Handa, Somalia 91 10 37N 51 2 E
Handa I. 36 58 23N 5 10W
Handen 72 59 12N 18 12 E
Handeni 124 5 25 S 38 2 E
Handeni □ 126 5 30 S 38 0 E
Handlová 155 48 45N 18 35 E
Handub 122 19 15N 37 25 E
Handwara 95 34 21N 74 20 E
Handzame 47 51 2N 3 0 E
Hanegev 90 30 50N 35 0 E
Haney 152 49 12N 122 40W
Hanford 163 36 25N 119 39W
Hang Chat 100 18 20N 99 21 E
Hang Dong 100 18 41N 98 55 E
Hangang, R. 107 37 50N 126 30 E
Hangayn Nuruu 105 47 30N 100 0 E
Hangchinch'i 106 39 54N 108 56 E
Hangchinhouch'i 106 41 55N 107 15 E
Hangchou 109 30 15N 120 8 E
Hangchou Wan 109 30 30N 121 30 E
Hanger 73 57 6N 13 58 E
Hangklip, K. 128 34 26 S 18 48 E
Hangö (Hanko) 75 59 59N 22 57 E
Hanhongor 106 43 55N 104 28 E
Hanish J. 91 13 45N 42 46 E
Hanita 90 33 5N 35 10 E
Hankinson 158 46 9N 96 58W
Hanko = Hangö 75 59 59N 22 57 E
Hank'ou 109 30 40N 114 18 E
Hankow = Hank'ou 109 30 40N 114 18 E
Hanksville 161 38 19N 110 45W
Hanku 107 39 16N 117 50 E
Hanle 95 32 42N 79 4 E
Hanmer 143 42 32 S 172 50 E
Hann, Mt. 136 16 0 S 126 0 E
Hann, R. 136 17 26 S 126 17 E
Hanna 152 51 40N 111 54W
Hannaford 158 47 23N 98 18W
Hannah 158 48 58N 98 42W
Hannah B. 150 51 40N 80 0W
Hannahs Bridge 141 31 55 S 149 41 E
Hannibal, Mo., U.S.A. 158 39 42N 91 22W
Hannibal, N.Y., U.S.A. 162 43 19N 76 35W
Hannik 122 18 12N 32 20 E
Hanningfield Water 29 51 40N 0 30 E
Hannover 48 52 23N 9 43 E
Hannut 47 50 40N 5 4 E
Hanö 73 56 0N 14 50 E
Hanö, I. 73 56 2N 14 50 E
Hanöbukten 73 55 35N 14 30 E
Hanoi 100 21 5N 105 55 E
Hanover, S. Afr. 128 31 4 S 24 29 E
Hanover, N.H., U.S.A. 162 43 43N 72 17W
Hanover, Pa., U.S.A. 162 39 46N 76 59W
Hanover, Va., U.S.A. 162 37 46N 77 22W
Hanover = Hannover 48 52 23N 9 43 E
Hanover, I. 176 51 0 S 74 50W
Hanpan, C. 135 5 0 S 154 35 E
Hans Meyer Ra. 135 4 20 S 152 55 E
Hansholm 73 57 8N 8 38 E
Hanshou 109 28 55N 111 58 E
Hansi 94 29 10N 75 57 E
Hansjö 72 61 10N 14 40 E
Hanson, L. 140 31 0 S 136 15 E
Hanson Range 136 27 0 S 136 30 E
Hansted 73 57 8N 8 36 E
Hantan 105 36 42N 114 30 E
Hante 47 50 19N 4 11 E
Hanton 106 36 42N 114 30 E
Hanwood 141 34 26 S 146 3 E
Hanyang 109 30 35N 114 0 E
Hanyin 108 32 53N 108 37 E
Hanyü 111 36 10N 139 32 E
Hanyüan 108 29 21N 102 43 E
Haoch'ing 108 26 34N 100 12 E
Haokang 105 47 25N 132 8 E
Haopi 106 35 57N 114 13 E
Haparanda 74 65 52N 24 8 E
Hapert 47 51 22N 5 15 E
Happy 159 34 47N 101 50W
Happy Camp 160 41 52N 123 30W
Happy Valley 151 53 15N 60 20W
Hapsu 107 41 13N 128 51 E
Hapur 94 28 45N 77 45 E
Haql 92 29 10N 35 0 E
Har 103 5 16 S 133 14 E
Har-Ayrag 106 45 47N 109 16 E
Har Tuv 90 31 46N 35 0 E
Har Us Nuur 105 48 0N 92 10 E
Har Yehuda 90 31 35N 34 57 E
Harad 92 24 15N 49 0 E
Haradera 91 4 33N 47 38 E
Haradh 92 24 15N 49 0 E
Haramsøya 71 62 39N 6 12 E
Haran 92 36 48N 39 0 E
Harat 123 16 5N 39 26 E
Haraze 117 14 20N 19 12 E
Haraze-Mangueigne 117 7 22N 17 3 E
Harbin = Haerhpin 107 45 45N 126 45 E
Harboør 73 56 38N 8 10 E
Harbor Beach 156 43 50N 82 38W
Harbor Springs 156 45 28N 85 0W
Harbour Breton 151 47 29N 55 50W
Harbour Deep 151 50 25N 56 30W
Harbour Grace 151 47 40N 53 22W
Harburg 48 53 27N 9 58 E
Hårby 73 55 13N 10 7 E
Harcourt 138 24 17 S 149 55 E
Harda 94 22 27N 77 5 E
Hardangerfjorden. 71 60 15N 6 0 E
Hardangerjøkulen 71 60 30N 7 0 E
Hardangervidda 71 60 20N 7 20 E
Hardap Dam 128 24 32 S 17 50 E
Hardegarijp 46 53 13N 5 57 E
Harden 141 34 32 S 148 24 E
Hardenberg 46 52 34N 6 37 E
Harderwijk 46 52 21N 5 38 E
Hardey, R. 136 22 45 S 116 8 E
Hardin 160 45 50N 107 35W
Harding 129 30 22 S 29 55 E
Harding Ra. 136 16 17 S 124 55 E
Hardisty 152 52 40N 111 18W
Hardman 160 45 12N 119 49W
Hardoi 95 27 26N 80 15 E
Hardwar 94 29 58N 78 16 E
Hardy 159 36 20N 91 30W
Hardy, Pen. 176 55 30 S 68 20W
Hare B. 151 51 15N 55 45W
Hare Gilboa 90 32 31N 35 25 E
Hare Meron 90 32 59N 35 24 E
Harelbeke 47 50 52N 3 20 E
Haren, Ger. 48 52 47N 7 18 E
Haren, Neth. 46 53 11N 6 36 E
Harer 123 9 20N 42 8 E
Harer □ 123 7 12N 42 0 E
Hareto 123 9 23N 37 6 E
Harfleur 42 49 30N 0 10 E
Hargeisa 91 9 30N 44 2 E
Hargshamn 72 60 12N 18 30 E
Hari, R., Afghan. 93 34 20N 64 30 E
Hari, R., Indon. 102 1 10 S 101 50 E
Haricha, Hamada el 118 22 40N 3 15W
Harihar 97 14 32N 75 44 E
Harim, J. al 60 26 0N 56 10 E
Harima-Nada 110 34 30N 134 35 E
Haringey 29 51 35N 0 7W
Haringhata, R. 98 22 0N 89 58 E
Haringvliet 46 51 48N 4 10 E
Haripad 97 9 14N 76 28 E
Harirúd 93 35 0N 61 0 E
Harkat 122 20 25N 39 40 E
Harlan, Iowa, U.S.A. 158 41 37N 95 20W
Harlan, Tenn., U.S.A. 157 36 58N 83 20W
Harlech 31 52 52N 4 7W
Harlem 160 48 29N 108 39W
Harleston 29 52 25N 1 18 E
Harlingen, Neth. 46 53 11N 5 25 E
Harlingen, U.S.A. 159 26 30N 97 50W
Harlow 29 51 47N 0 9 E
Harlowton 160 46 30N 109 54W
Harmånger 72 61 55N 17 20 E
Harmil 123 16 30N 40 10 E
Harney Basin 160 43 30N 119 0W
Harney L. 160 43 0N 119 0W
Harney Pk. 158 43 52N 103 33W
Härnön 72 62 36N 18 0 E
Härnösand 72 62 38N 18 5 E
Haro 58 42 35N 2 55W
Haro, C. 164 27 50N 110 55W
Haroldswick 36 60 48N 0 50W
Håroy 73 55 13N 10 8 E
Harp L. 151 55 5N 61 50W
Harpe, La 158 40 30N 91 0W
Harpenden 29 51 48N 0 20W
Harpenhalli 97 14 47N 76 2 E
Harper 120 4 25N 7 43 E
Harper Mt. 147 64 15N 143 57W
Harplinge 73 56 45N 12 45 E
Harport L. 36 57 20N 6 20W
Harput 92 38 48N 39 15 E
Harrand 94 29 28N 70 3 E
Harrat al Kishb 92 22 30N 40 15 E
Harrat al Umuirid 92 26 50N 38 0 E
Harrat Khaibar 122 25 45N 40 0 E
Harrat Nawāsīf 122 21 30N 42 0 E
Harray, L. of 37 59 0N 3 15W
Harricana, R. 150 50 30N 79 10W
Harrietsham 29 51 15N 0 41 E
Harriman 157 36 0N 84 35W
Harrington, U.K. 32 54 37N 3 55W
Harrington, U.S.A. 162 38 56N 75 35W
Harrington Harbour 151 50 31N 59 30W
Harris 36 57 50N 6 55W
Harris L. 136 31 10 S 135 10 E
Harris Mts. 143 44 49 S 168 49 E
Harris, Sd. of 36 57 44N 7 6W
Harrisburg, Ill., U.S.A. 159 37 42N 88 30W
Harrisburg, Nebr., U.S.A. 158 41 36N 103 46W
Harrisburg, Oreg., U.S.A. 160 44 25N 123 10W
Harrisburg, Pa., U.S.A. 162 40 18N 76 52W
Harrismith 129 28 15 S 29 8 E
Harrison, Ark., U.S.A. 159 36 10N 93 4W
Harrison, Idaho, U.S.A. 160 47 30N 116 51W
Harrison, Nebr., U.S.A. 158 42 42N 103 52W
Harrison B. 147 70 25N 151 0W
Harrison, C. 151 55 0N 58 0W
Harrison L. 152 49 33N 121 50W
Harrisonburg 156 38 28N 78 52W
Harrisonville 158 38 45N 93 45W
Harriston 150 43 57N 80 53W
Harrisville 150 44 40N 83 19W
Harrogate 33 53 59N 1 32W
Harrow 29 51 35N 0 15W
Harry, L. 139 29 23 S 138 19 E
Harsefeld 48 53 26N 9 31 E
Harskamp 46 52 8N 5 46 E
Harstad 74 68 48N 16 30 E
Hart 156 43 42N 86 21W
Hart, L. 140 31 10 S 136 25 E
Hartbees, R. 128 29 8 S 20 48 E
Hartberg 52 47 17N 15 58 E
Harteigen, Mt. 71 60 11N 7 5 E
Hartest 29 52 7N 0 41 E
Hartford, Conn., U.S.A. 162 41 47N 72 41W
Hartford, Ky., U.S.A. 156 37 26N 86 50W
Hartford, S.D., U.S.A. 158 43 40N 96 58W
Hartford, Wis., U.S.A. 158 43 18N 88 25W
Hartford City 156 40 22N 85 20W
Harthill 35 55 52N 3 45W
Hartland, Can. 151 46 20N 67 32W
Hartland, U.K. 30 50 59N 4 29W
Hartland Pt. 30 51 2N 4 32W
Hartlebury 28 52 20N 2 13W
Hartlepool 33 54 42N 1 11W
Hartley, Rhod. 127 18 10 S 30 7 E
Hartley, U.K. 35 55 5N 1 27W
Hartley Bay 152 53 25N 129 15W
Hartmannberge 128 17 0 S 13 0 E
Hartney 153 49 30N 100 35W
Hartpury 28 51 55N 2 18W
Hartselle 157 34 25N 86 55W
Hartshorne 159 34 51N 95 30W
Hartsville 157 34 23N 80 2W
Hartwell 157 34 21N 82 52W
Harunabad 94 29 35N 73 2 E
Harur 97 12 3N 78 29 E
Harvard, Mt. 161 39 0N 106 5W
Harvey, Austral. 137 33 5 S 115 54 E
Harvey, Ill., U.S.A. 156 41 40N 87 50W
Harvey, N.D., U.S.A. 158 47 50N 99 58W
Harwell 28 51 40N 1 17W
Harwich 29 51 56N 1 18 E
Harwood 33 53 54N 1 30W
Haryana □ 94 29 0N 76 10 E
Harz 48 51 40N 10 40 E
Harzé 47 50 27N 5 40 E
Harzgerode 48 51 38N 11 8 E
Hasa 92 26 0N 49 0 E
Hasaheisa 123 14 25N 33 20 E
Hasani 122 25 0N 37 8 E
Hasanpur 94 28 51N 78 9 E
Haselünne 48 52 40N 7 30 E
Hasharon 90 32 12N 34 49 E
Hashefela 90 31 30N 34 43 E
Hashima 111 35 20N 136 40 E
Hashimoto 111 34 19N 135 37 E
Hasjö 72 63 2N 16 20 E
Håsjö 72 63 1N 16 5 E
Haskell, Kans., U.S.A. 159 35 51N 95 40W
Haskell, Tex., U.S.A. 159 33 10N 99 45W
Haskier Is. 36 57 42N 7 40W
Haslach 49 48 16N 8 7 E
Hasle 73 55 11N 14 44 E
Haslemere 29 51 5N 0 41W
Haslev 73 55 18N 11 57 E
Haslingden 32 53 43N 2 20W
Hasparren 44 43 24N 1 18W
Hassan 92 13 0N 76 5 E
Hasselt, Belg. 47 50 56N 5 21 E
Hasselt, Neth. 46 52 36N 6 6 E
Hassene, Ad. 118 21 0N 4 0 E
Hassfurt 49 50 2N 10 30 E
Hassi Berrekrem 119 33 45N 5 16 E
Hassi Daoula 119 33 4N 5 38 E
Hassi el Biod 119 28 30N 6 0 E
Hassi el Heïda 74 29 34N 0 14W
Hassi Inifel 118 29 50N 3 41 E
Hassi Marroket 119 30 10N 3 0 E
Hassi Messaoud 119 31 43N 6 8 E
Hassi Taguenza 172 29 8N 0 23W
Hassi Zerzour 118 30 51N 3 56W
Hässleby 73 57 37N 15 30 E
Hässleholmen 73 56 9N 13 45 E
Hastière-Lavaux 47 50 13N 4 49 E
Hastigrow 37 58 32N 3 15W
Hastings, Austral. 141 38 18 S 145 12 E
Hastings, N.Z. 142 39 39 S 176 52 E
Hastings, U.K. 29 50 51N 0 36 E
Hastings, Mich., U.S.A. 156 42 40N 82 20W
Hastings, Minn., U.S.A. 158 44 41N 92 51W
Hastings, Nebr., U.S.A. 158 40 34N 98 22W
Hastings Ra. 141 31 15 S 152 14 E
Hästveda 73 56 17N 13 55 E
Hat Nhao 101 14 46N 106 32 E
Hat Yai 101 7 1N 100 27 E
Hatanbulag 106 43 8N 109 14 E
Hatano 111 35 22N 139 14 E
Hatch 161 32 45N 107 8W
Hatches Creek 138 20 56 S 135 12 E
Hatchet L. 153 58 36N 103 40W
Haţeg 70 45 36N 22 55 E
Haţeg, Mţii 70 45 25N 23 0 E
Hatert 46 51 49N 5 50 E
Hatfield 29 51 46N 0 11W
Hatfield Broad Oak 29 51 48N 0 16 E
Hatfield Post Office 140 33 54N 143 49 E
Hatgal 105 50 26N 100 9 E
Hatherleigh 30 50 49N 4 4W
Hathersage 33 53 20N 1 39W
Hathras 94 27 36N 78 6 E
Hatia 99 22 30N 91 5 E
Hato de Corozal 174 6 11N 71 45W
Hato Mayor 167 18 46N 69 15W
Hattah 140 34 48N 142 17 E
Hattem 46 52 28N 6 4 E
Hatteras, C. 157 35 10N 75 30W
Hattiesburg 159 31 20N 89 20W
Hatton, Can. 153 50 2N 109 50W
Hatton, U.K. 37 57 24N 1 57W
Hatvan 53 47 40N 19 45 E
Hau Bon (Cheo Reo) 100 13 25N 108 28 E
Hau Duc 100 15 20N 108 13 E
Hauchinango 164 20 12N 97 45W
Haug 71 60 23N 10 26 E
Haugastøl 71 60 30N 7 50 E
Haugesund 71 59 23N 5 13 E
Haugh of Urr 35 55 0N 3 51W
Haughangaroa Ra. 142 38 42 S 175 40 E
Haughley 29 52 13N 0 59 E
Haukelisæter 71 59 51N 7 9 E
Haulerwijk 46 53 4N 6 20 E
Haultain, R. 153 55 51N 106 46W
Haungpa 98 25 29N 96 7 E
Haura 91 13 50N 47 35 E
Hauraki Gulf 142 36 35 S 175 5 E
Hausruck 52 48 6N 13 30 E
Haut Atlas 118 32 0N 7 0W
Haut-Rhin □ 43 48 0N 7 15 E
Haut Zaïre □ 126 2 20N 26 0 E
Hauta Oasis 92 23 40N 47 0 E
Hautah, Wahāt al 92 23 40N 47 0 E
Haute-Corse □ 45 42 30N 9 30 E
Haute-Garonne □ 44 43 28N 1 30 E
Haute-Loire □ 44 45 5N 3 50 E
Haute-Marne □ 43 48 10N 5 20 E
Haute-Saône □ 43 47 45N 6 10 E
Haute-Savoie □ 45 46 0N 6 20 E
Haute-Vienne □ 44 45 50N 1 10 E
Hauterive 151 49 10N 68 16W
Hautes-Alpes □ 45 44 42N 6 20 E
Hautes Fagnes 47 50 34N 6 6 E
Hautes-Pyrénées □ 44 43 0N 0 10 E
Hauteville-Lompnes 45 45 59N 5 35 E
Hautmont 43 50 15N 3 55 E
Hautrage 47 50 29N 3 46 E
Hauts-de-Seine □ 43 48 52N 2 15 E
Hauts Plateaux 118 34 14N 1 0 E
Hauxley 35 55 21N 1 35W
Havana 158 40 19N 90 3W
Havana = La Habana 166 23 8N 82 22W
Havant 29 50 51N 0 59W
Havasu, L. 161 34 18N 114 8W
Havdhem 73 57 10N 18 20 E
Havelange 47 50 23N 5 15 E
Havelian 94 34 2N 73 10 E
Havelock, N.B., Can. 151 46 2N 65 24W
Havelock, Ont., Can. 150 44 26N 77 53W
Havelock, N.Z. 143 41 17 S 173 48 E
Havelock I. 101 11 55N 93 2 E
Havelte 46 52 46N 6 14 E
Haverfordwest 31 51 48N 4 59W
Haverhill, U.K. 29 52 6N 0 27 E
Haverhill, U.S.A. 162 42 50N 71 2W
Haveri 97 14 53N 75 24 E
Haverigg 32 54 12N 3 16W
Havering 29 51 33N 0 20 E
Haverstraw 162 41 12N 73 58W
Håverud 73 58 50N 12 28 E
Havîrna 70 48 4N 26 43 E
Havlíčkuv Brod 52 49 36N 15 33 E
Havnby 73 55 5N 8 34 E
Havre 160 48 40N 109 34W
Havre-Aubert 151 47 12N 62 0W
Havre de Grace 162 39 33N 76 6W
Havre, Le 42 49 30N 0 5 E
Havre St. Pierre 151 50 18N 63 33W
Havza 92 41 0N 35 35 E
Haw, R. 157 37 43N 80 52W
Hawaii □ 147 20 30N 157 0W
Hawaii I. 147 20 0N 155 0W
Hawaiian Is. 147 20 30N 156 0W
Hawarden, Can. 153 51 25N 106 36W
Hawarden, U.K. 31 53 11N 3 2W
Hawarden, U.S.A. 158 43 2N 96 28W
Hawea Flat 143 44 40 S 169 19 E
Hawea Lake 143 44 28 S 169 19 E
Hawera 142 39 35 S 174 19 E
Hawes 32 54 18N 2 12W
Hawes Water, L. 32 54 32N 2 48W
Hawick 35 55 25N 2 48W
Hawk Junction 150 48 30N 84 38W
Hawkchurch 30 50 47N 2 56W
Hawkdun Ra. 143 44 53 S 170 5 E
Hawke B. 142 39 25N 177 20 E
Hawker 28 31 59 S 138 22 E
Hawke's Bay □ 142 39 45 S 176 35 E
Hawke's Harbour 151 53 2N 55 50W
Hawkesbury 150 45 35N 74 40W
Hawkesbury I. 152 53 37N 129 3W
Hawkesbury Pt. 138 11 55 S 134 5 E
Hawkesbury River 133 33 50 S 151 44W
Hawkesbury Upton 28 51 34N 2 19W
Hawkhurst 29 51 2N 0 31 E
Hawkinsville 157 32 17N 83 30W
Hawkshead 32 54 23N 3 0W
Hawkwood 139 25 45 S 150 50 E
Hawley, Minn., U.S.A. 158 46 53N 96 20W
Hawley, Pa., U.S.A. 162 41 28N 75 11W
Haworth 32 53 50N 1 57W
Hawsker 33 54 27N 0 34W
Hawthorne 163 38 31N 118 37W
Hawzen 123 13 58N 39 28 E

Haxby Higashiōsaka


Haxby 33 54 1N 1 4W
Haxtun 158 40 40N 102 39W
Hay, Austral. 141 34 30S 144 51E
Hay, U.K. 31 52 4N 3 9W
Hay, C. 136 14 5S 129 29E
Hay L. 152 58 50N 118 50W
Hay Lakes 152 53 12N 113 2W
Hay, R., Austral. 138 24 10S 137 20E
Hay, R., Can. 152 60 0N 116 56W
Hay River 152 60 51N 115 44W
Hay Springs 158 42 40N 102 38W
Hayange 43 49 20N 6 2E
Hayato 110 31 40N 130 43E
Hayburn Wyke 33 54 22N 0 28W
Haycock 147 65 10N 161 20W
Hayden, Ariz., U.S.A. 161 33 2N 110 54W
Hayden, Wyo., U.S.A. 160 40 30N 107 22W
Haydenville 162 42 22N 72 42W
Haydon 138 18 0S 141 30E
Haydon Bridge 35 54 58N 2 15W
Haye Descartes, La 42 46 58N 0 42E
Haye-du-Puits, La 42 49 17N 1 33W
Hayes 158 44 22N 101 1W
Hayes Pen. 12 75 30N 65 0W
Hayes, R. 153 57 3N 92 12W
Hayle 30 50 12N 5 25W
Haymana 92 39 30N 32 35E
Haynesville 159 33 0N 93 7W
Hays, Can. 152 50 6N 111 48W
Hays, U.S.A. 158 38 55N 99 25W
Hayton 32 54 55N 2 45W
Hayward, Calif., U.S.A. 163 37 40N 122 5W
Hayward, Wis., U.S.A. 158 46 2N 91 30W
Hayward's Heath 29 51 0N 0 5W
Hazard 156 37 18N 83 10W
Hazaribagh 95 23 58N 85 26E
Hazaribagh Road 95 24 12N 85 57E
Hazebrouck 43 50 42N 2 31E
Hazelton, Can. 152 55 20N 127 42W
Hazelton, U.S.A. 158 46 30N 100 15W
Hazen 160 39 37N 119 2W
Hazerswoude 46 52 5N 4 36E
Hazlehurst 157 31 50N 82 35W
Hazleton 156 40 58N 76 0W
Hazlett, L. 136 21 30S 128 48E
Hazrat Imam 93 37 15N 68 50E
Heacham 29 52 55N 0 30E
Head of Bight 137 31 30S 131 25E
Headcorn 29 51 10N 0 39E
Headford 38 53 28N 9 6W
Headington 28 51 46N 1 13W
Headlands 127 18 15S 32 2E
Healdsburg 160 38 33N 122 51W
Healdton 159 34 16N 97 31W
Healesville 141 37 35S 145 30E
Heanor 33 53 1N 1 20W
Heard I. 11 53 0S 74 0E
Hearne 159 30 54N 96 35W
Hearne B. 153 60 10N 99 10W
Hearne L. 152 62 20N 113 10W
Hearst 150 49 40N 83 41W
Heart, R. 158 46 40N 101 30W
Heart's Content 151 47 54N 53 27W
Heath Mts. 143 45 39S 167 9E
Heath Pt. 151 49 8N 61 40W
Heath Steele 151 47 17N 66 5W
Heathcote 141 36 56S 144 45E
Heather, oilfield 19 60 55N 0 50E
Heathfield 29 50 58N 0 18E
Heathsville 162 37 55N 76 28W
Heavener 159 34 54N 94 36W
Hebbronville 159 27 20N 98 40W
Hebburn 35 54 59N 1 30W
Hebden Bridge 32 53 45N 2 0W
Hebel 139 28 58S 147 47E
Heber Springs 159 35 29N 91 39W
Hebgen, L. 160 44 50N 111 15W
Hebrides, U.K. 36 57 30N 7 0W
Hebrides, Inner Is., U.K. 36 57 20N 6 40W
Hebrides, Outer Is., U.K. 36 57 50N 7 25W
Hebron, Can. 149 58 12N 62 38W
Hebron, N.D., U.S.A. 158 46 56N 102 2W
Hebron, Nebr., U.S.A. 158 40 15N 97 33W
Hebron (Al Khalil) 90 31 32N 35 6E
Heby 72 59 56N 16 53E
Hecate Str. 152 53 10N 130 30W
Hechingen 49 48 20N 8 58E
Hechtel 47 51 8N 5 22E
Heckington 33 52 59N 0 17W
Hecla 158 45 56N 98 8W
Hecla I. 153 51 10N 96 43W
Hecla Mt. 36 57 18N 7 15W
Heddal 71 59 36N 9 20E
Heddon 35 55 0N 1 47W
Hédé 42 48 18N 1 49W
Hede 72 62 23N 13 30E
Hedemora 72 60 18N 15 58E
Hedgehope 143 46 12S 168 34E
Hedley 159 34 53N 100 39W
Hedmark □ 75 61 17N 11 40E
Hedmark fylke □ 71 61 17N 11 40E
Hednesford 28 52 43N 2 0W
Hedon 33 53 44N 0 11W
Hedrum 71 59 7N 10 5E
Heeg 46 52 58N 5 37E
Heegermeer 46 52 56N 5 32E
Heemskerk 46 52 31N 4 40E
Heemstede 46 52 22N 4 37E
Heer 47 50 50N 5 43E
Heerde 46 52 24N 6 2E
's Heerenburg 46 51 53N 6 16E
's Heerenloo 46 52 19N 5 36E
Heerenveen 46 52 57N 5 55E
Heerhugowaard 46 52 40N 4 51E
Heerlen 47 50 55N 6 0E
Heerlerheide 47 50 54N 5 58E
Heers 47 50 45N 5 18E
Heesch 46 51 44N 5 32E
Heestert 47 50 47N 3 25E
Heeze 47 51 23N 5 35E
Hegyalja, Mts. 53 48 25N 21 25E
Heich'engchen 106 36 16N 106 19E
Heide 48 54 10N 9 7E
Heide, oilfield 19 54 5N 9 5E
Heidelberg, Ger. 49 49 23N 8 41E
Heidelberg, C. Prov., S. Afr. 128 34 6S 20 59E
Heidelberg, Trans., S. Afr. 129 26 30S 28 23E
Heidenheim 49 48 40N 10 10E
Heigun-To 110 33 47N 132 14E
Heikant 47 51 15N 4 1E
Heilam 37 58 31N 4 40W
Heilbron 129 27 16S 27 59E
Heilbronn 49 49 8N 9 13E
Heiligenblut 52 47 2N 12 51E
Heiligenhafen 48 54 21N 10 58E
Heiligenstadt 48 51 22N 10 9E
Heilungkiang □ 46 48 0N 128 0E
Heim 71 63 26N 9 5E
Heimdal, gasfield 19 59 35N 2 15E
Heino 46 52 26N 6 14E
Heinola 75 61 13N 26 24E
Heinsburg 153 53 50N 110 30W
Heinsch 47 49 42N 5 44E
Heinsun 98 25 52N 95 35E
Heinze Is. 101 14 25N 97 45E
Heirnkut 98 25 14N 94 44E
Heishan 107 41 40N 122 3E
Heishui, Liaoning, China 107 42 6N 119 22E
Heishui, Szechwan, China 108 32 15N 103 0E
Heist 47 51 20N 3 15E
Heist-op-den-Berg 47 51 5N 4 44E
Heistad 71 59 35N 9 40E
Hejaz = Hijāz 92 26 0N 37 30E
Hekelegem 47 50 55N 4 7E
Hekimhan 92 38 50N 38 0E
Hekinan 111 34 52N 137 0E
Hekla 74 63 56N 19 35W
Hel 60 54 38N 18 50E
Helagsfjället 72 62 54N 12 25E
Helchteren 47 51 4N 5 22E
Helden 47 51 19N 6 0E
Helechosa 57 39 22N 4 53W
Helena, Ark., U.S.A. 159 34 30N 90 35W
Helena, Mont., U.S.A. 160 46 40N 112 0W
Helendale 163 34 45N 117 19W
Helensburgh, Austral. 141 34 11S 151 1E
Helensburgh, U.K. 34 56 0N 4 44W
Helensville 142 36 41S 174 29E
Helets 90 31 36N 34 39E
Helgasjön 73 57 0N 14 50E
Helgeland 74 66 20N 13 30E
Helgeroa 71 59 0N 9 45E
Helgoland, I. 48 54 10N 7 51E
Helgum 72 63 25N 16 50E
Heligoland = Helgoland 48 54 10N 7 51E
Heliopolis 122 30 6N 31 17E
Hell-Ville 129 13 25S 48 16E
Hellebæk 73 56 4N 12 32E
Helleland 71 58 33N 6 7E
Hellendoorn 46 52 24N 6 27E
Hellertown 162 40 35N 75 21W
Hellevoetsluis 46 51 50N 4 8E
Helli Ness 36 60 3N 1 10W
Hellick Kenyon Plateau 13 82 0S 110 0W
Hellifield 32 54 0N 2 13W
Hellin 59 38 31N 1 40W
Hellum 73 57 16N 10 10E
Helmand □ 93 31 20N 64 0E
Helmand, R. 94 34 0N 67 0E
Helmond 47 51 29N 5 41E
Helmsdale 37 58 7N 3 40W
Helmsley 33 54 15N 1 2W
Helmstedt 48 52 16N 11 0E
Helnæs 73 55 9N 10 0E
Helper 160 39 44N 110 56W
Helperby 33 54 8N 1 20W
Helsby 32 53 16N 2 47W
Helsingborg 73 56 3N 12 42E
Helsinge 73 56 2N 12 12E
Helsingfors = Helsinki 75 60 15N 25 3E
Helsingør 73 56 2N 12 35E
Helsinki (Helsingfors) 75 60 15N 25 3E
Helston 30 50 7N 5 17W
Helvick Hd. 39 52 3N 7 33W
Helvoirt 47 51 38N 5 14E
Helwân 122 29 50N 31 20E
Hem 71 59 26N 10 0E
Hemavati, R. 97 12 50N 67 0E
Hemel Hempstead 29 51 45N 0 28W
Hemet 163 33 45N 116 59W
Hemingford 158 42 21N 103 4W
Hemphill 159 31 21N 93 49W
Hempstead 159 30 5N 96 5W
Hempton 29 52 50N 0 49E
Hemse 73 57 15N 18 22E
Hemsö, I. 72 62 43N 18 5E
Hemsön 72 62 42N 18 5E
Hemsworth 33 53 37N 1 21W
Hemyock 30 50 55N 1 13W
Hen & Chicken Is. 142 35 58S 174 45E
Henares, R. 58 40 55N 3 0W
Hendaye 44 43 23N 1 47W
Henderson, Argent. 172 36 18S 61 43W
Henderson, U.K. 36 57 42N 5 47W
Henderson, Ky., U.S.A. 156 37 50N 87 38W
Henderson, Nev., U.S.A. 161 36 2N 115 0W
Henderson, Pa., U.S.A. 157 35 25N 88 40W
Henderson, Tex., U.S.A. 159 32 5N 94 49W
Hendersonville 157 35 21N 82 28W
Hendon 139 28 5S 151 50E
Hendorf 70 46 4N 24 5E
Henfield 29 50 56N 0 17W
Hengch'eng 106 38 26N 106 26E
Hengelo, Gelderland, Neth. 46 52 3N 6 19E
Hengelo, Overijssel, Neth. 46 52 16N 6 48E
Hengfeng 109 28 25N 117 35E
Henghsien 108 22 36N 109 16E
Hengoed 31 51 39N 3 14W
Hengshan, Hunan, China 109 27 15N 112 51E
Hengshan, Shansi, China 106 37 56N 108 53E
Hengshui 106 37 43N 115 42E
Hengtaohotze 107 44 55N 129 3E
Hengyang 109 26 51N 112 30E
Hengyanghsien 109 26 58N 112 21E
Hénin-Beaumont 43 50 25N 2 58E
Henley 29 51 32N 0 53W
Henley-in-Arden 28 52 18N 1 47W
Henllan 31 53 13N 3 29W
Henlopen, C. 162 38 48N 75 5W
Henlow 29 51 2N 0 18W
Hennan, L. 72 62 3N 15 55E
Henne 73 55 44N 8 11E
Hennebont 42 47 49N 3 19W
Hennenman 128 27 59S 27 1E
Hennessy 159 36 8N 97 53W
Hennigsdorf 48 52 38N 13 13E
Henribourg 153 53 25N 105 38W
Henrichemont 43 47 20N 2 21E
Henrietta 159 33 50N 98 15W
Henrietta Maria C. 150 55 9N 82 20W
Henry 158 41 5N 89 20W
Henryetta 159 35 2N 96 0W
Henstridge 28 50 59N 2 24W
Hentiyn Nuruu 105 48 30N 108 30E
Henty 141 35 30S 147 0E
Henzada 98 17 38N 95 35E
Heppner 160 45 27N 119 34W
Herad 71 58 8N 6 47E
Héraðsflói 74 65 42N 14 12W
Héradsvötn 74 65 25N 19 5W
Herald Cays 138 16 58S 149 9E
Herāt 93 34 20N 62 7E
Herāt □ 93 35 0N 62 0E
Hérault □ 44 43 34N 3 15E
Hérault, R. 44 43 20N 3 32E
Herbert 153 50 30N 107 10W
Herbert Downs 138 23 7S 139 9E
Herbert I. 147 52 49N 170 10W
Herbert, R. 138 18 31S 146 17E
Herberton 138 17 28S 145 25E
Herbertstown 39 52 32N 8 29W
Herbiers, Les 42 46 52N 1 0W
Herbignac 42 47 27N 2 18W
Herborn 48 50 40N 8 19E
Herby 54 50 45N 18 50E
Hercegnovi 66 42 30N 18 33E
Herðubreið 74 65 11N 16 21W
Herdla 71 60 34N 4 56E
Hereford, U.K. 28 52 4N 2 42W
Hereford, U.S.A. 159 34 50N 102 28W
Hereford and Worcester □ 28 52 10N 2 30W
Herefordshire □ 26 52 15N 2 50W
Herefoss 71 58 32N 8 32E
Herekino 142 35 18S 173 11E
Herent 47 50 54N 4 40E
Herentals 47 51 12N 4 51E
Herenthout 47 51 8N 4 45E
Herfølge 73 55 26N 12 9E
Herford 48 52 7N 8 40E
Héricourt 43 47 32N 6 55E
Herington 158 38 43N 97 0W
Herisau 51 47 22N 9 17E
Hérisson 44 46 32N 2 42E
Herjehogna 75 61 43N 12 7E
Herk, R. 47 50 56N 5 12E
Herkenbosch 47 51 9N 6 4E
Herkimer 162 43 0N 74 59W
Herm I. 42 49 30N 2 28W
Herma Ness 36 60 50N 0 54W
Hermagor 52 46 38N 13 23E
Herman 158 45 51N 96 8W
Hermandez 163 36 24N 120 46W
Hermann 158 38 40N 91 25W
Hermannsburg 48 52 49N 10 6E
Hermannsburg Mission 136 23 57S 132 45E
Hermanus 128 34 27S 19 12E
Herment 44 45 45N 2 24E
Hermidale 141 31 30S 146 42E
Hermiston 160 45 50N 119 16W
Hermitage 143 43 44S 170 5E
Hermitage B. 151 47 33N 56 10W
Hermite, Is. 176 55 50S 68 0W
Hermon, Mt. = Sheikh, J. ash 92 33 20N 36 0E
Hermosillo 164 29 10N 111 0W
Hernad, R. 53 48 20N 21 15E
Hernandarias 173 25 20S 54 40W
Hernando, Argent. 172 32 28S 63 40W
Hernando, U.S.A. 159 34 50N 89 59W
Herndon 162 40 43N 76 51W
Herne, Belg. 47 50 44N 4 2E
Herne, Ger. 48 51 33N 7 12E
Herne Bay 29 51 22N 1 8E
Herne Hill 137 31 45S 116 5E
Herning 73 56 8N 8 58E
Heroica Nogales 164 31 14N 110 56W
Heron Bay 150 48 40N 85 25W
Heröy 71 62 18N 5 45E
Herreid 158 45 53N 100 5W
's Herrenbroek 46 52 32N 6 1E
Herrera 57 39 12N 4 50W
Herrera de Alcántar 57 39 39N 7 25W
Herrera de Pisuerga 56 42 35N 4 20W
Herrera del Duque 57 39 10N 5 3W
Herrero, Punta 165 19 17N 87 27W
Herrick 138 41 5S 147 55E
Herrin 159 37 50N 89 0W
Herrljunga 73 58 5N 13 1E
Hersbruck 49 49 30N 11 25E
Herschel I. 147 69 35N 139 5W
Herseaux 47 50 43N 3 15E
Herselt 47 51 3N 4 53E
Herserange 47 49 30N 5 48E
Hershey 162 40 17N 76 39W
Herstal 47 50 40N 5 38E
Herstmonceux 29 50 53N 0 21E
Hersvik 71 61 10N 4 53E
Hertford 29 51 47N 0 4W
Hertford □ 29 51 51N 0 5W
's Hertogenbosch 47 51 42N 5 18E
Hertzogville 128 28 9S 25 30E
Hervás 56 40 16N 5 52W
Herve 47 50 38N 5 48E
Hervey B. 133 25 0S 152 52E
Hervey Is. 131 19 30S 159 0W
Hervey Junction 150 46 50N 72 29W
Herwijnen 46 51 50N 5 7E
Herzberg, Cottbus, Ger. 48 51 40N 13 13E
Herzberg, Niedersachsen, Ger. 48 51 38N 10 20E
Herzele 47 50 53N 3 53E
Herzliyya 90 32 10N 34 50E
Herzogenbuchsee 50 47 11N 7 42E
Herzogenburg 52 48 17N 15 41E
Hesdin 43 50 21N 2 0E
Hesel 48 53 18N 7 36E
Heskestad 71 58 28N 6 22E
Hesperange 47 49 35N 6 10E
Hesperia 163 34 25N 117 18W
Hesse = Hessen 48 50 57N 9 20E
Hessen □ 48 50 57N 9 20E
Hessle 33 53 44N 0 28E
Hetch Hetchy Aqueduct 163 37 36N 121 25W
Heteren 46 51 58N 5 46E
Hethersett 29 52 35N 1 10E
Hettinger 158 46 8N 102 38W
Hetton-le-Hole 35 54 49N 1 26W
Hettstedt 48 51 39N 11 30E
Heugem 47 50 49N 5 42E
Heule 47 50 51N 3 15E
Heusden, Belg. 47 51 2N 5 17E
Heusden, Neth. 46 51 44N 5 8E
Hève, C. de la 42 49 30N 0 5E
Heverlee 47 50 52N 4 42E
Heves □ 53 47 50N 20 0E
Hevron, N. 90 31 28N 34 52E
Hewett, C. 149 70 16N 67 45W
Hewett, gasfield 19 53 5N 1 50E
Hex River 128 33 30S 19 35E
Hexham 35 54 58N 2 7W
Heybridge 29 51 44N 0 42E
Heyfield 141 37 59S 146 47E
Heysham 32 54 5N 2 53W
Heytesbury 28 51 11N 2 7W
Heythuysen 47 51 15N 5 55E
Heywood, Austral. 140 38 8S 141 37E
Heywood, U.K. 32 53 36N 2 13W
Hi-no-Misaki 110 35 26N 132 38E
Hi Vista 163 34 44N 117 46W
Hiamen 109 31 52N 121 15E
Hiawatha, Kans., U.S.A. 158 39 55N 95 33W
Hiawatha, Utah, U.S.A. 160 39 37N 111 1W
Hibbing 158 47 30N 93 0W
Hibbs B. 138 42 35S 145 15E
Hibbs, Pt. 138 42 38S 145 15E
Hibernia Reef 136 12 0S 123 23E
Hibiki-Nada 110 34 0N 130 0E
Hickman 159 36 35N 89 8W
Hickory 157 35 46N 81 17W
Hicks Bay 142 37 34S 178 21E
Hicksville 162 40 46N 73 30W
Hida-Gawa 70 47 10N 23 9E
Hida-Gawa, R. 111 35 26N 137 3E
Hida-Sammyaku 111 36 30N 137 40E
Hida-Sanchi 111 36 10N 137 0E
Hidaka 110 35 30N 134 44E
Hidalgo □ 164 20 30N 99 10W
Hidalgo del Parral 164 26 58N 105 40W
Hidalgo, Presa M. 164 26 30N 108 35W
Hiddensee 48 54 30N 13 6E
Hidrolândia 171 17 0S 49 15W
Hieflau 52 47 36N 14 46E
Hiendelaencina 58 41 5N 3 0W
Hierro I. 116 27 57N 17 56E
Higashi-matsuyama 111 36 2N 139 25E
Higashiōsaka 111 34 40N 135 37E

Higasi-Suidō  Hong Kong ■


| | | | |
|---|---|---|---|
| Higasi-Suidō | **110** | 34 0N | 129 30 E |
| Higgins | **159** | 36 9N | 100 1W |
| Higginsville | **137** | 31 42 S | 121 38 E |
| Higgs I. L. | **157** | 36 20N | 78 30W |
| High Atlas = Haut Atlas | **118** | 32 30N | 5 0W |
| High Bentham | **32** | 54 8N | 2 31W |
| High Borrow Bri. | **32** | 54 26N | 2 43W |
| High Bridge | **162** | 40 40N | 74 54W |
| High Ercall | **28** | 52 46N | 2 37W |
| High Hesket | **32** | 54 47N | 2 49W |
| High I. | **151** | 56 40N | 61 10W |
| High Island | **159** | 29 32N | 94 22W |
| High Level | **152** | 58 31N | 117 8W |
| High Pike, mt. | **32** | 54 43N | 3 4W |
| High Point | **157** | 35 57N | 79 58W |
| High Prairie | **152** | 55 30N | 116 30W |
| High River | **152** | 50 30N | 113 50W |
| High Springs | **157** | 29 50N | 82 40W |
| High Tatra | **53** | 49 30N | 20 00 E |
| High Veld = Hoëveld | **129** | 26 30 S | 30 0 E |
| High Willhays, hill | **30** | 50 41N | 3 59W |
| High Wycombe | **29** | 51 37N | 0 45W |
| Higham Ferrers | **29** | 52 18N | 0 36W |
| Highbank | **138** | 47 34 S | 171 45 E |
| Highbridge | **28** | 51 13N | 2 59W |
| Highbury | **138** | 16 25 S | 143 9 E |
| Highclere | **28** | 51 20N | 1 22W |
| Highland □ | **36** | 57 30N | 5 0W |
| Highland Pk. | **156** | 42 10N | 87 50W |
| Highland Springs | **162** | 37 33N | 77 20W |
| Highley | **28** | 52 25N | 2 23W |
| Highmore | **158** | 44 35N | 99 26W |
| Highrock L. | **153** | 57 5N | 105 32W |
| Hightae | **35** | 55 5N | 3 27W |
| Hightstown | **162** | 40 16N | 74 31W |
| Highworth | **28** | 51 38N | 1 42W |
| Higley | **161** | 33 27N | 111 46W |
| Higüay | **167** | 18 37N | 68 42W |
| Higüero, Pta. | **147** | 18 22N | 67 16W |
| Hiiumaa | **80** | 58 50N | 22 45 E |
| Hijar | **58** | 41 10N | 0 27W |
| Hijāz | **91** | 26 0N | 37 30 E |
| Hiji | **110** | 33 22N | 131 32 E |
| Hijken | **46** | 52 54N | 6 30 E |
| Hikari | **110** | 33 58N | 131 58 E |
| Hiketa | **110** | 34 13N | 134 24 E |
| Hiko | **161** | 37 30N | 115 13W |
| Hikone | **111** | 35 15N | 136 10 E |
| Hikurangi, East Court | **142** | 37 55 S | 178 4 E |
| Hikurangi, Mt. | **142** | 37 55 S | 178 4 E |
| Hilawng | **98** | 21 23N | 93 48 E |
| Hildburghhausen | **49** | 50 24N | 10 43 E |
| Hildesheim | **48** | 52 9N | 9 55 E |
| Hilgay | **29** | 52 34N | 0 23 E |
| Hill | **150** | 45 40N | 74 45W |
| Hill City, Idaho, U.S.A. | **160** | 43 20N | 115 2W |
| Hill City, Kans., U.S.A. | **158** | 39 25N | 99 51W |
| Hill City, Minn., U.S.A. | **158** | 46 57N | 93 35W |
| Hill City, S.D., U.S.A. | **158** | 43 58N | 103 35W |
| Hill End | **141** | 38 1 S | 146 9 E |
| Hill Island L. | **153** | 60 30N | 109 50W |
| Hill, R. | **137** | 30 23 S | 115 3 E |
| Hilla, Iraq | **92** | 32 30N | 44 27 E |
| Hilla, Si Arab. | **92** | 23 35N | 46 50 E |
| Hillared | **73** | 57 37N | 13 10 E |
| Hillegom | **46** | 52 18N | 4 35 E |
| Hillerød | **73** | 55 56N | 12 19 E |
| Hillerstorp | **73** | 57 20N | 13 52 E |
| Hilli | **98** | 25 17N | 89 1 E |
| Hillingdon | **29** | 51 33N | 0 29W |
| Hillman | **156** | 45 5N | 83 52W |
| Hillmond | **153** | 53 26N | 109 41W |
| Hillsboro, Kans., U.S.A. | **158** | 38 28N | 97 10W |
| Hillsboro, N. Mex., U.S.A. | **161** | 33 0N | 107 35W |
| Hillsboro, N. Mex., U.S.A. | **161** | 33 0N | 107 35W |
| Hillsboro, N.D., U.S.A. | **158** | 47 23N | 97 9W |
| Hillsboro, N.H., U.S.A. | **156** | 43 8N | 71 56W |
| Hillsboro, Oreg., U.S.A. | **160** | 45 31N | 123 0W |
| Hillsboro, Tex., U.S.A. | **159** | 32 0N | 97 10W |
| Hillsborough, U.K. | **38** | 54 28N | 6 6W |
| Hillsborough, W. Indies | **167** | 12 28N | 61 28W |
| Hillsdale, Mich., U.S.A. | **156** | 41 55N | 84 40W |
| Hillsdale, N.Y., U.S.A. | **162** | 42 11N | 73 30W |
| Hillside | **136** | 21 45 S | 119 23 E |
| Hillsport | **150** | 49 27N | 85 34W |
| Hillston | **141** | 33 30 S | 145 31 E |
| Hillswick | **36** | 60 29N | 1 28W |
| Hilltown | **38** | 54 12N | 6 8W |
| Hilo | **147** | 19 44N | 155 5W |
| Hilonghilong, mt. | **103** | 9 10N | 125 45 E |
| Hilpsford Pt. | **32** | 54 4N | 3 12W |
| Hilvarenbeek | **47** | 51 29N | 5 8 E |
| Hilversum | **46** | 52 14N | 5 10 E |
| Himachal Pradesh □ | **94** | 31 30N | 77 0 E |
| Himalaya | **99** | 29 0N | 84 0 E |
| Himara | **68** | 40 8N | 19 43 E |
| Himatnagar | **93** | 23 37N | 72 57 E |
| Hime-Jima | **110** | 33 43N | 131 40 E |
| Himeji | **110** | 34 50N | 134 40 E |
| Himi | **111** | 36 50N | 137 0 E |
| Himmerland | **73** | 56 45N | 9 30 E |
| Hims = Homs | **92** | 34 40N | 36 45 E |
| Hinako, Kepulauan | **102** | 0 50N | 97 20 E |
| Hinche | **167** | 19 9N | 72 1W |
| Hinchinbrook I. | **138** | 18 20 S | 146 15 E |
| Hinckley, U.K. | **28** | 52 33N | 1 21W |
| Hinckley, U.S.A. | **160** | 39 18N | 112 41W |
| Hindås | **73** | 57 42N | 12 27 E |
| Hindaun | **94** | 26 44N | 77 5 E |
| Hinde Rapids (Hells Gate) | **126** | 5 25 S | 27 3 E |
| Hinderwell | **33** | 54 32N | 0 45W |
| Hindhead | **29** | 51 6N | 0 42W |
| Hindley | **32** | 53 32N | 2 35W |
| Hindmarsh L. | **140** | 36 5 S | 141 55 E |
| Hindol | **95** | 20 40N | 85 10 E |
| Hinds | **143** | 43 59 S | 171 36 E |
| Hindsholm | **73** | 55 30N | 10 40 E |
| Hindu Bagh | **94** | 30 56N | 67 57 E |
| Hindu Kush | **93** | 36 0N | 71 0 E |
| Hindubagh | **93** | 30 56N | 67 57 E |
| Hindupur | **97** | 13 49N | 77 32 E |
| Hines Creek | **152** | 56 20N | 118 40W |
| Hinganghat | **96** | 20 30N | 78 59 E |
| Hingeon | **47** | 50 32N | 4 59 E |
| Hingham, U.K. | **29** | 52 35N | 0 59 E |
| Hingham, U.S.A. | **160** | 48 40N | 110 29W |
| Hingol, R. | **93** | 25 30N | 65 30 E |
| Hingoli | **96** | 19 41N | 77 15 E |
| Hinkley Pt. | **28** | 50 59N | 3 32W |
| Hinlopenstretet | **12** | 79 35N | 18 40 E |
| Hinna | **121** | 10 25N | 11 28 E |
| Hinnøy | **74** | 68 40N | 16 28 E |
| Hino | **111** | 35 0N | 136 15 E |
| Hinojosa | **55** | 38 30N | 5 17W |
| Hinojosa del Duque | **57** | 38 30N | 5 17W |
| Hinokage | **110** | 32 39N | 131 24 E |
| Hinsdale | **160** | 48 26N | 107 2W |
| Hinstock | **28** | 52 50N | 2 28W |
| Hinterrhein, R. | **51** | 46 40N | 9 25 E |
| Hinton, Can. | **152** | 53 26N | 117 34W |
| Hinton, U.S.A. | **156** | 37 40N | 80 51W |
| Hinwil | **51** | 47 18N | 8 51 E |
| Hippolytushoef | **46** | 52 54N | 4 58 E |
| Hirado | **110** | 33 22N | 129 33 E |
| Hirado-Shima | **110** | 33 20N | 129 30 E |
| Hirakarta | **111** | 34 48N | 135 40 E |
| Hirakud | **96** | 21 32N | 83 51 E |
| Hirakud Dam | **96** | 21 32N | 83 45 E |
| Hirara | **112** | 24 48N | 125 17 E |
| Hirata | **110** | 35 24N | 132 49 E |
| Hiratsuka | **111** | 35 19N | 139 21 E |
| Hirhafok | **119** | 23 49N | 5 45 E |
| Hirlŭu | **70** | 47 23N | 27 0 E |
| Hiromi | **110** | 33 13N | 132 36 E |
| Hirosaki | **112** | 40 34N | 140 28 E |
| Hiroshima | **110** | 34 30N | 132 30 E |
| Hiroshima-ken □ | **112** | 34 50N | 133 0 E |
| Hiroshima-Wan | **110** | 34 5N | 132 20 E |
| Hirsoholmene | **73** | 57 30N | 10 36 E |
| Hirson | **43** | 49 55N | 4 4 E |
| Hîrşova | **70** | 44 40N | 27 59 E |
| Hirtshals | **73** | 57 36N | 9 57 E |
| Hirwaun | **31** | 51 43N | 3 30W |
| Hisoy | **71** | 58 26N | 8 44 E |
| Hispaniola, I. | **165** | 19 0N | 71 0W |
| Hissar | **94** | 29 12N | 75 45 E |
| Histon | **29** | 52 15N | 0 6 E |
| Hita | **110** | 33 20N | 130 58 E |
| Hitachi | **111** | 36 36N | 140 39 E |
| Hitachiota | **111** | 36 30N | 140 30 E |
| Hitchin | **29** | 51 57N | 0 16W |
| Hitoyoshi | **110** | 32 13N | 130 45 E |
| Hitra | **71** | 63 30N | 8 45 E |
| Hitzacker | **48** | 53 9N | 11 1 E |
| Hiuchi-Nada | **110** | 34 5N | 133 20 E |
| Hjalmar L. | **153** | 61 33N | 109 25W |
| Hjälmare Kanal | **72** | 59 20N | 15 59 E |
| Hjälmaren | **72** | 59 18N | 15 40 E |
| Hjartdal | **71** | 59 37N | 8 41 E |
| Hjärtsäter | **73** | 58 35N | 12 3 E |
| Hjerkinn | **71** | 62 13N | 9 33 E |
| Hjerpsted | **73** | 55 2N | 8 39 E |
| Hjo | **73** | 58 22N | 4 17 E |
| Hjørring | **73** | 57 29N | 9 59 E |
| Hjorted | **73** | 57 37N | 16 19 E |
| Hjortkvarn | **73** | 58 54N | 15 26 E |
| Hko-ut | **98** | 21 40N | 97 46 E |
| Hkyenhpa | **98** | 27 43N | 97 25 E |
| Hlaingbwe | **98** | 17 8N | 97 50 E |
| Hlinsko | **52** | 49 45N | 15 54 E |
| Hlohovec | **53** | 48 26N | 17 49 E |
| Hlwaze | **98** | 18 54N | 96 37 E |
| Ho | **121** | 6 37N | 0 27 E |
| Ho Chi Minh, Phanh Bho | **101** | 10 58N | 106 40 E |
| Ho Thuong | **100** | 19 32N | 105 48 E |
| Hoa Binh | **100** | 20 50N | 105 20 E |
| Hoa Da (Phan Ri) | **100** | 11 16N | 108 40 E |
| Hoa Hiep | **101** | 11 34N | 105 51 E |
| Hoadley | **152** | 52 45N | 114 30W |
| Hoai Nhon (Bon Son) | **100** | 14 28N | 109 1 E |
| Hoare B. | **149** | 65 17N | 62 55W |
| Hobart, Austral. | **138** | 42 50 S | 147 21 E |
| Hobart, U.S.A. | **159** | 35 0N | 99 5W |
| Hobbs | **159** | 32 40N | 103 3W |
| Hobjærg | **73** | 56 19N | 9 32 E |
| Hobo | **174** | 2 35N | 75 30W |
| Hoboken, Belg. | **47** | 51 11N | 4 21 E |
| Hoboken, U.S.A. | **162** | 40 45N | 74 4W |
| Hobro | **73** | 56 39N | 9 46 E |
| Hobscheid | **47** | 49 42N | 5 57 E |
| Hoburg C. | **73** | 56 54N | 18 8 E |
| Hoburgen | **73** | 56 55N | 18 7 E |
| Hochang | **108** | 27 8N | 104 45 E |
| Hochatown | **159** | 34 11N | 94 39W |
| Hochdorf | **51** | 47 10N | 8 17 E |
| Hochiang | **108** | 28 48N | 105 48 E |
| Hochien | **106** | 38 26N | 116 5 E |
| Hoch'ih | **108** | 24 43N | 108 2 E |
| Hoching | **106** | 35 37N | 110 43 E |
| Hoch'iu | **109** | 32 21N | 116 13 E |
| Höchst | **49** | 50 6N | 8 33 E |
| Hoch'ü | **106** | 39 26N | 111 8 E |
| Hoch'uan | **108** | 30 2N | 106 18 E |
| Hockenheim | **49** | 49 18N | 8 33 E |
| Hod, oilfield | **19** | 56 10N | 3 25 E |
| Hodaka-Dake | **111** | 36 17N | 137 39 E |
| Hodde | **73** | 55 42N | 8 39 E |
| Hodder R. | **32** | 53 57N | 2 27W |
| Hoddesdon | **29** | 51 45N | 0 1W |
| Hodeïda | **91** | 14 50N | 43 0 E |
| Hodge, R. | **33** | 54 14N | 0 55W |
| Hodgson | **153** | 51 13N | 97 36W |
| Hódmezővásárhely | **53** | 46 28N | 20 22 E |
| Hodna, Chott el | **119** | 35 30N | 5 0 E |
| Hodonin | **53** | 48 50N | 17 0 E |
| Hodsager | **73** | 56 19N | 8 51 E |
| Hoeamdong | **107** | 42 30N | 130 16 E |
| Hoëdic, I. | **42** | 47 21N | 2 52W |
| Hoegaarden | **47** | 50 47N | 4 53 E |
| Hoek van Holland | **46** | 52 0N | 4 7 E |
| Hoeksche Waard | **46** | 51 46N | 4 25 E |
| Hoenderloo | **46** | 52 7N | 5 52 E |
| Hoengsŏng | **107** | 37 29N | 127 59 E |
| Hoensbroek | **47** | 50 55N | 5 55 E |
| Hoeryong | **107** | 42 30N | 129 58 E |
| Hoeselt | **47** | 50 51N | 5 29 E |
| Hoëveld | **129** | 26 30 S | 30 0 E |
| Hoeven | **47** | 51 35N | 4 35 E |
| Hoeyang | **107** | 38 43N | 127 36 E |
| Hof, Ger. | **49** | 50 18N | 11 55 E |
| Hof, Iceland | **74** | 64 33N | 14 40W |
| Höfðakaupstaður | **74** | 65 50N | 20 19W |
| Hofei | **109** | 31 52N | 117 15 E |
| Hoff | **32** | 54 34N | 2 31W |
| Hofgeismar | **48** | 51 29N | 9 23 E |
| Hofors | **72** | 60 35N | 16 15 E |
| Hofsjökull | **74** | 64 49N | 18 48W |
| Hofsós | **74** | 65 53N | 19 26W |
| Hōfu | **110** | 34 3N | 131 34 E |
| Hofuf | **92** | 25 20N | 49 40 E |
| Hög-Gia, Mt. | **71** | 62 23N | 10 7 E |
| Hog I. | **162** | 37 26N | 75 42W |
| Hogan Group | **139** | 39 13 S | 147 1 E |
| Höganäs | **73** | 56 13N | 12 34 E |
| Hogansville | **157** | 33 14N | 84 50W |
| Hogarth, Mt. | **138** | 21 50 S | 137 0 E |
| Hogeland | **160** | 48 51N | 108 40W |
| Högen | **72** | 61 47N | 14 11 E |
| Hogenaki Falls | **97** | 12 6N | 77 50 E |
| Högfors, Örebro, Sweden | **72** | 59 58N | 15 3 E |
| Högfors, Västmanlands, Sweden | **72** | 60 2N | 16 3 E |
| Hoggar = Ahaggar | **119** | 23 0N | 6 30 E |
| Hōgo-Kaikyo | **110** | 33 20N | 131 58 E |
| Hog's Back, hill | **29** | 51 13N | 0 40W |
| Hogs Hd. | **39** | 51 46N | 10 13W |
| Högsäter | **73** | 58 38N | 12 5 E |
| Högsby | **73** | 57 10N | 16 1 E |
| Högsjo | **72** | 59 4N | 15 44 E |
| Hogsthorpe | **33** | 53 13N | 0 19 E |
| Hogsty Reef | **167** | 21 41N | 73 48W |
| Hohe Rhön | **49** | 50 24N | 9 58 E |
| Hohe Tauern | **52** | 47 11N | 12 40 E |
| Hohenau | **53** | 48 36N | 16 55 E |
| Hohenems | **52** | 47 22N | 9 42 E |
| Hohenstein Ernstthal | **48** | 50 48N | 12 43 E |
| Hohenwald | **157** | 35 35N | 87 30W |
| Hohenwestedt | **48** | 54 6N | 9 40 E |
| Hohoe | **121** | 7 8N | 0 32 E |
| Hohsi | **108** | 24 9N | 102 38 E |
| Hohsien, Anhwei, China | **109** | 31 43N | 118 22 E |
| Hohsien, Kwangsi-Chuang, China | **109** | 24 25N | 111 31 E |
| Hohsüeh | **109** | 30 2N | 112 25 E |
| Hôi An | **100** | 15 30N | 108 19 E |
| Hoi Xuan | **100** | 20 25N | 105 9 E |
| Hoisington | **158** | 38 33N | 98 50W |
| Højer | **73** | 54 58N | 8 42 E |
| Hōjō | **110** | 33 58N | 132 46 E |
| Hok | **73** | 57 31N | 14 16 E |
| Hokensås | **73** | 58 0N | 14 5 E |
| Hökensås | **73** | 58 0N | 14 5 E |
| Hökerum | **73** | 57 51N | 13 16 E |
| Hokianga Harbour | **142** | 35 31 S | 173 22 E |
| Hokitika | **143** | 42 42 S | 171 0 E |
| Hokkaidō | **112** | 43 30N | 143 0 E |
| Hokkaidō □ | **112** | 43 30N | 143 0 E |
| Hokksund | **71** | 59 44N | 9 59 E |
| Hok'ou, Kansu, China | **106** | 36 9N | 103 29 E |
| Hok'ou, Kwantang, China | **109** | 23 13N | 112 45 E |
| Hok'ou, Yunnan, China | **108** | 22 39N | 103 57 E |
| Hokow | **101** | 22 39N | 103 57 E |
| Hol-Hol. | **123** | 11 20N | 42 50 E |
| Holan Shan | **106** | 38 50N | 105 50 E |
| Holbæk | **73** | 55 43N | 11 43 E |
| Holbeach | **29** | 52 48N | 0 1 E |
| Holbeach Marsh | **29** | 52 52N | 0 5 E |
| Holborn Hd. | **37** | 58 37N | 3 30W |
| Holbrook, Austral. | **141** | 35 42 S | 147 18 E |
| Holbrook, U.S.A. | **161** | 35 0N | 110 0W |
| Holden | **152** | 53 13N | 112 11W |
| Holden Fillmore | **160** | 39 0N | 112 26W |
| Holdenville | **159** | 35 5N | 96 25W |
| Holder | **140** | 34 21 S | 140 0 E |
| Holderness | **33** | 53 45N | 0 5W |
| Holdfast | **153** | 50 58N | 105 25W |
| Holdrege | **153** | 40 25N | 99 30W |
| Hole | **71** | 60 6N | 10 12 E |
| Hole-Narsipur | **97** | 12 48N | 76 16 E |
| Holešov | **53** | 49 20N | 17 35 E |
| Holguín | **166** | 20 50N | 76 20W |
| Holinkoerh | **106** | 40 23N | 111 53 E |
| Holič | **53** | 48 49N | 17 10 E |
| Holkham | **29** | 52 57N | 0 48 E |
| Holla, Mt. | **123** | 7 5N | 36 35 E |
| Hollabrunn | **52** | 48 34N | 16 5 E |
| Hollams Bird I. | **128** | 24 40 S | 14 30 E |
| Holland | **156** | 42 47N | 86 7W |
| Holland Fen | **33** | 53 0N | 0 8W |
| Holland-on-Sea | **29** | 51 48N | 1 12 E |
| Hollandia = Jajapura | **103** | 2 28 S | 140 38 E |
| Hollands Bird I. | **128** | 24 40 S | 14 30 E |
| Hollandsch Diep | **47** | 51 41N | 4 30 E |
| Hollandsch IJssel, R. | **46** | 51 55N | 4 34 E |
| Hollandstoun | **37** | 59 22N | 2 25W |
| Höllen | **71** | 58 6N | 7 49 E |
| Holleton | **137** | 31 55 S | 119 0 E |
| Hollidaysburg | **156** | 40 26N | 78 25W |
| Hollis | **159** | 34 45N | 99 55W |
| Hollister | **161** | 36 51N | 121 24W |
| Hollum | **46** | 53 26N | 5 38 E |
| Holly | **158** | 38 7N | 102 7W |
| Holly Hill | **157** | 29 15N | 81 3W |
| Holly Springs | **159** | 34 45N | 89 25W |
| Hollymount | **38** | 53 40N | 9 7W |
| Hollywood, Ireland | **39** | 53 6N | 6 35W |
| Hollywood, Calif., U.S.A. | **154** | 34 7N | 118 25W |
| Hollywood, Fla., U.S.A. | **157** | 26 0N | 80 9W |
| Holm | **72** | 62 40N | 16 40 E |
| Holman Island | **148** | 71 0N | 118 0W |
| Hólmavík | **74** | 65 42N | 21 40W |
| Holme, Humberside,, U.K. | **33** | 53 50N | 0 48W |
| Holme, N. Yorks., U.K. | **32** | 53 34N | 1 50W |
| Holmedal | **71** | 59 46N | 5 50 E |
| Holmedal, Fjordane | **71** | 61 22N | 5 11 E |
| Holmegil | **72** | 59 10N | 11 44 E |
| Holmes Chapel | **32** | 53 13N | 2 21W |
| Holmes Reefs | **138** | 16 27 S | 148 0 E |
| Holmestrand | **71** | 59 31N | 10 14 E |
| Holmfirth | **33** | 53 34N | 1 48W |
| Holmsbu | **71** | 59 32N | 10 27 E |
| Holmsjön | **72** | 62 26N | 15 20 E |
| Holmsland Klit | **73** | 56 0N | 8 5 E |
| Holmsund | **74** | 63 41N | 20 20 E |
| Holmwood | **29** | 51 12N | 0 19W |
| Hölö | **72** | 59 3N | 17 36 E |
| Holo Ho, R. | **107** | 44 54N | 122 22 E |
| Holod | **70** | 46 49N | 22 8 E |
| Holon | **90** | 32 2N | 34 47 E |
| Holroyd, R. | **138** | 14 10 S | 141 36 E |
| Holsen | **71** | 61 25N | 6 8 E |
| Holstebro | **73** | 56 22N | 8 37 E |
| Holsworthy | **30** | 50 48N | 4 21W |
| Holt, Iceland | **74** | 63 33N | 19 48W |
| Holt, Clwyd, U.K. | **31** | 53 4N | 2 52W |
| Holt, Norfolk, U.K. | **29** | 52 55N | 1 4 E |
| Holte | **73** | 55 50N | 12 29 E |
| Holten | **46** | 52 17N | 6 26 E |
| Holton Harbour | **151** | 54 31N | 57 12W |
| Holton le Clay | **33** | 53 29N | 0 3W |
| Holtville | **161** | 32 50N | 115 27W |
| Holum | **71** | 58 6N | 7 32 E |
| Holwerd | **46** | 53 22N | 5 54 E |
| Holy Cross | **147** | 62 10N | 159 52W |
| Holy I., England, U.K. | **35** | 55 42N | 1 48W |
| Holy I., Scotland, U.K. | **34** | 55 31N | 5 4W |
| Holy I., Wales, U.K. | **31** | 53 17N | 4 37W |
| Holyhead | **31** | 53 18N | 4 38W |
| Holyhead B. | **31** | 53 20N | 4 35W |
| Holyoke, Mass., U.S.A. | **162** | 42 14N | 72 37W |
| Holyoke, Nebr., U.S.A. | **158** | 40 39N | 102 18W |
| Holyrood | **151** | 47 27N | 53 8W |
| Holywell | **31** | 53 16N | 3 14W |
| Holywood | **38** | 54 38N | 5 50W |
| Holzminden | **48** | 51 49N | 9 31 E |
| Homa Bay | **126** | 0 36 S | 34 22 E |
| Homa Bay □ | **126** | 0 50 S | 34 30 E |
| Homalin | **98** | 24 55N | 95 0 E |
| Homberg | **48** | 51 2N | 9 20 E |
| Hombori | **121** | 15 20N | 1 38W |
| Homburg | **49** | 49 19N | 7 21 E |
| Home B. | **149** | 68 40N | 67 10W |
| Home Hill | **138** | 19 43 S | 147 25 E |
| Homedale | **160** | 43 42N | 116 59W |
| Homer, Alaska, U.S.A. | **147** | 59 40N | 151 35W |
| Homer, La., U.S.A. | **159** | 32 50N | 93 4W |
| Homestead, Austral. | **138** | 20 20 S | 145 40 E |
| Homestead, U.S.A. | **157** | 25 29N | 80 27W |
| Hominy | **159** | 36 26N | 96 24W |
| Homnabad | **96** | 17 45N | 77 5 E |
| Homoine | **129** | 23 55 S | 35 8 E |
| Homorod | **70** | 46 5N | 25 15 E |
| Homs = Al Khums | **119** | 32 40N | 14 17 E |
| Homs (Hims) | **92** | 34 40N | 36 45 E |
| Hon Chong | **101** | 10 16N | 104 38 E |
| Hon Me | **100** | 19 23N | 105 56 E |
| Honan □ | **106** | 34 10N | 113 10 E |
| Honbetsu | **112** | 43 7N | 143 37 E |
| Honda | **174** | 5 12N | 74 45W |
| Hondeklipbaai | **125** | 30 19 S | 17 17 E |
| Hondo, Japan | **110** | 32 27N | 130 12 E |
| Hondo, U.S.A. | **159** | 29 22N | 99 6W |
| Hondo, R. | **165** | 18 25N | 88 21W |
| Honduras ■ | **166** | 14 40N | 86 30W |
| Honduras, Golfo de | **166** | 16 50N | 87 0W |
| Hönefoss | **71** | 60 10N | 10 12 E |
| Honey L. | **160** | 40 13N | 120 14W |
| Honfleur | **42** | 49 25N | 0 13 E |
| Höng | **73** | 55 30N | 11 14 E |
| Hong Gai | **100** | 20 57N | 107 5 E |
| Hong Kong ■ | **109** | 22 11N | 114 14 E |

Hong, R Hsiushui


Hong, R. 100 20 17N 106 34 E
Hongchŏn 107 37 44N 127 53 E
Hongha, R. 101 22 0N 104 0 E
Hongor 106 45 56N 112 50 E
Hongsa 100 19 43N 101 20 E
Hongsŏng 107 36 37N 126 38 E
Honguedo, Détroit d' 151 49 15N 64 0W
Hongwon 107 40 0N 127 56 E
Honiara 142 9 30S 160 0 E
Honington 33 52 58N 0 35W
Honiton 30 50 48N 3 11W
Honjo, Akita, Japan 112 39 23N 140 3 E
Honjo, Gumma, Japan 111 36 14N 139 11 E
Honkawane 111 35 5N 138 5 E
Honkorâb, Ras 122 24 35N 35 10 E
Honolulu 147 21 19N 157 52W
Honshū 112 36 0N 138 0 E
Hontoria del Pinar 58 41 50N 3 10W
Hoo 29 51 25N 0 33 E
Hood Mt. 160 45 15N 122 0W
Hood, Pt. 137 34 23S 119 34 E
Hood Pt. 135 10 4S 147 45 E
Hood River 160 45 45N 121 37W
Hoodsport 160 47 24N 123 7W
Hooge 48 54 31N 8 36 E
Hoogerheide 47 51 26N 4 20 E
Hoogeveen 46 52 44N 6 30 E
Hoogeveensche Vaart 46 52 42N 6 12 E
Hoogezand 46 53 11N 6 45 E
Hooghly-Chinsura 95 22 53N 88 27 E
Hooghly, R. 95 21 59N 88 10 E
Hoogkerk 46 53 13N 6 30 E
Hooglede 47 50 59N 3 5 E
Hoogstraten 47 51 24N 4 46 E
Hoogvliet 46 51 52N 4 21 E
Hook 29 51 17N 0 55W
Hook Hd. 39 52 8N 6 57W
Hook I. 138 20 4S 149 0 E
Hook of Holland = Hoek v. Holland 47 52 0N 4 7 E
Hooker 159 36 55N 101 10W
Hooker Cr. 136 18 23S 130 50 E
Hoonah 147 58 15N 135 30W
Hooper Bay 147 61 30N 166 10W
Hoopersville 162 38 16N 76 11W
Hoopeston 156 40 30N 87 40W
Hoopstad 128 27 50S 25 55 E
Höör 73 55 55N 13 33 E
Hoorn 46 52 38N 5 4 E
Hoover Dam 161 36 0N 114 45W
Hop Bottom 162 41 41N 75 47W
Hopà 83 41 28N 41 30 E
Hope, Can. 152 49 25N 121 25 E
Hope, U.K. 31 53 7N 3 2W
Hope, Ark., U.S.A. 159 33 40N 93 30W
Hope, N.D., U.S.A. 158 47 21N 97 42W
Hope Bay 13 65 0S 55 0W
Hope, L. 139 28 24S 139 18 E
Hope L. 37 58 24N 4 38W
Hope Pt. 147 68 20N 166 50W
Hope Town 157 26 30N 76 30W
Hopedale, Can. 151 55 28N 60 13W
Hopedale, U.S.A. 162 42 8N 71 33W
Hopefield 128 33 3S 18 22 E
Hopei □ 107 39 25N 116 45 E
Hopelchén 165 19 46N 89 50W
Hopeman 37 57 42N 3 26W
Hopen 71 63 27N 8 2 E
Hopetoun 137 33 57S 120 7 E
Hopetown, Austral. 140 35 42S 142 22 E
Hopetown, S. Afr. 128 29 34S 24 3 E
Hopewell 162 37 18N 77 17W
Hopien-Ts'un 108 27 40N 101 55 E
Hopin 98 21 14N 96 53 E
Hop'ing 109 24 26N 114 56 E
Hopkins 158 40 31N 94 45W
Hopkins, L. 136 24 15S 128 35 E
Hopkinsville 157 36 52N 87 26W
Hopland 160 39 0N 123 7W
Hopo 108 31 24N 99 0 E
Hoptrup 73 55 11N 9 28 E
Hop'u 108 21 41N 109 10 E
Hoquiam 160 46 50N 123 55W
Hōrai 111 34 58N 137 32 E
Horazdovice 52 49 19N 13 42 E
Hörby 73 55 50N 13 44 E
Horcajo de Santiago 58 39 50N 3 1W
Hordaland fylke □ 71 60 25N 6 15 E
Horden 33 54 45N 1 17W
Hordern Hills 136 20 40S 130 20 E
Hordio 91 10 36N 51 8 E
Horezu 70 45 6N 24 0 E
Horgen 51 47 15N 8 35 E
Horgoš 66 46 10N 20 0 E
Horice 52 50 21N 15 39 E
Horley 29 51 10N 0 10W
Horlick Mts. 13 84 0S 102 0W
Hormoz 93 27 35N 55 0 E
Hormuz, I. 93 27 8N 56 28 E
Hormuz Str. 93 26 30N 56 30 E
Horn, Austria 52 48 39N 15 40 E
Horn, Isafjarðarsýsla, Iceland 74 66 28N 22 28W
Horn, Suður-Múlasýsla, Iceland 74 65 10N 13 31W
Horn, Neth. 47 51 12N 5 57 E
Horn, Cape = Hornos, C. de 176 55 50S 67 30W
Horn Head 38 55 13N 8 0W
Horn I., Austral. 138 10 37S 142 17 E
Horn I., P.N.G. 135 10 35S 142 20 E
Horn, I. 157 30 17N 88 40W
Horn Mts. 152 62 15N 119 15W
Horn, R. 152 61 30N 118 1W
Hornachuelos 57 37 50N 5 14W
Hornavan 74 66 15N 17 30 E
Hornbæk, Frederiksborg, Denmark 73 56 5N 12 26 E
Hornbæk, Viborg, Denmark 73 56 28N 9 58 E
Hornbeck 159 31 22N 93 20W
Hornbrook 160 41 58N 122 37W
Hornburg 48 52 2N 10 36 E
Hornby 143 43 33S 172 33 E
Horncastle 33 53 13N 0 8W
Horndal 72 60 18N 16 23 E
Horndean 29 50 56N 1 5W
Hornell 156 42 23N 77 41W
Hornell L. 152 62 20N 119 25W
Hornepayne 150 49 14N 84 48W
Hornindal 71 61 58N 6 30 E
Horningsham 28 51 11N 2 16W
Hornitos 163 37 30N 120 14W
Hornnes 71 58 34N 7 45 E
Hornos, Cabo de 176 55 50S 67 30 E
Hornoy 43 49 50N 1 54 E
Hornsberg, Jamtland, Sweden 72 63 14N 14 40 E
Hornsberg, Kronobergs, Sweden 72 56 37N 13 47 E
Hornsby 141 33 42S 151 2 E
Hornsea 33 53 55N 0 10W
Hornslandet Pen. 72 61 35N 17 37 E
Hornslet 73 56 18N 10 19 E
Hornu 47 50 26N 3 50 E
Hörnum 73 54 44N 8 18 E
Horovice 52 49 48N 13 53 E
Horqueta 172 23 15S 56 55W
Horra, La 56 41 44N 3 53W
Horred 73 57 22N 12 28 E
Horse Cr. 158 41 33N 104 45W
Horse Is. 151 50 15N 55 50W
Horsefly L. 152 52 25N 121 0W
Horseheads 162 42 10N 76 49W
Horseleap 38 53 25N 7 34W
Horsens 73 55 52N 9 51 E
Horsens Fjord 73 55 50N 10 0 E
Horseshoe 137 25 27S 118 31 E
Horseshoe Dam 161 33 45N 111 35W
Horsforth 33 53 50N 1 39W
Horsham, Austral. 140 36 44S 142 13 E
Horsham, U.K. 29 51 4N 0 20W
Horsham St. Faith 29 52 41N 1 15 E
Horsovsky Tyn 52 49 31N 12 58 E
Horst 47 51 27N 6 3 E
Horsted Keynes 29 51 2N 0 1W
Horten 71 59 25N 10 32 E
Hortobágy, R. 53 47 30N 21 6 E
Horton 158 39 42N 95 30W
Horton-in-Ribblesdale 32 54 9N 2 19W
Horton, R. 147 69 56N 126 52W
Hörvik 73 56 2N 14 45 E
Horw 51 47 1N 8 19 E
Horwich 32 53 37N 2 33W
Horwood, L. 150 48 10N 82 20W
Hosaina 123 7 30N 37 47 E
Hosdurga 97 13 40N 76 17 E
Hose, Pegunungan 102 2 5N 114 6 E
Hoshan 109 31 24N 116 20 E
Hoshangabad 94 22 45N 77 45 E
Hoshiarpur 94 31 30N 75 58 E
Hoshui 106 36 0N 107 59 E
Hoshun 106 37 19N 113 34 E
Hosingen 47 50 1N 6 6 E
Hoskins 135 5 29S 150 27 E
Hosmer 158 45 36N 99 29W
Hososhima 110 32 26N 131 40 E
Hospental 51 46 37N 8 34 E
Hospet 97 15 15N 76 20 E
Hospital 39 52 30N 8 28W
Hospitalet de Llobregat 58 41 21N 2 6 E
Hospitalet, L' 44 42 36N 1 47 E
Hoste, I. 176 55 0S 69 0W
Hostens 44 44 30N 0 40W
Hoswick 36 60 0N 1 15W
Hot 100 18 8N 98 29 E
Hot Creek Ra. 160 39 0N 116 0W
Hot Springs, Ark, U.S.A. 159 34 30N 93 0W
Hot Springs, S.D., U.S.A. 158 43 25N 103 30W
Hotagen, L. 74 63 50N 14 30 E
Hotazel 128 27 17S 23 00 E
Hotchkiss 161 38 55N 107 47W
Hotham, C. 136 12 2S 131 18 E
Hot'ien 105 37 7N 79 55 E
Hoting 74 64 8N 16 15 E
Hotolishti 68 41 10N 20 25 E
Hotse 106 35 14N 115 27 E
Hotte, Massif de la 167 18 30N 73 45W
Hottentotsbaai 128 26 8S 14 59 E
Hotton 47 50 16N 5 26 E
Houat, I. 42 47 24N 2 58W
Houck 161 35 15N 109 15W
Houdan 43 48 48N 1 35 E
Houdeng-Goegnies 47 50 29N 4 10 E
Houei Sai 100 20 18N 100 26 E
Houffalize 47 50 8N 5 48 E
Houghton 158 47 9N 88 39W
Houghton L. 156 44 20N 84 40W
Houghton-le-Spring 35 54 51N 1 28W
Houghton Regis 29 51 54N 0 32W
Houhora 142 34 49S 173 9 E
Houille, R. 47 50 8N 4 50 E
Houlton 151 46 5N 68 0W
Houma 159 29 35N 90 50W
Houmt Souk = Djerba 119 33 53N 10 37 E
Houndé 120 11 34N 3 31W
Hounslow 29 51 29N 0 20W
Hourn L. 36 57 7N 5 35W
Hourtin 44 45 11N 1 4W
Housatonic, R. 162 41 10N 73 7W
Houston, Can. 152 54 25N 126 30W
Houston, Mo., U.S.A. 159 37 20N 92 0W
Houston, Tex., U.S.A. 159 29 50N 95 20W
Houten 46 52 2N 5 10 E
Houthalen 47 51 2N 5 23 E
Houthem 47 50 48N 2 57 E
Houthulst 47 50 59N 2 57 E
Houtman Abrolhos 137 28 43S 113 48 E
Houyet 47 50 11N 5 1 E
Hova 73 58 53N 14 14 E
Høvag 71 58 10N 8 15 E
Hövåg 71 58 10N 8 16 E
Hovd 105 48 1N 91 39 E
Hovden 71 59 33N 7 22 E
Hove 29 50 50N 0 10W
Hoveton 29 52 45N 1 23 E
Hovingham 33 54 10N 0 59W
Hovmantorp 73 56 47N 15 7 E
Hövsgöl 106 43 37N 109 39 E
Hovsta 72 59 22N 15 15 E
Howakil 123 15 10N 40 16 E
Howar, W., (Shau) 123 17 0N 25 30 E
Howard, Austral. 139 25 16S 152 32 E
Howard, Kans., U.S.A. 159 37 30N 96 16W
Howard, S.D., U.S.A. 158 44 2N 97 30W
Howard I. 138 12 10S 135 24 E
Howard L. 153 62 15N 105 57W
Howatharra 137 28 29S 114 33 E
Howden 33 53 45N 0 52W
Howe 160 43 48N 113 0W
Howe, C. 141 37 30S 150 0 E
Howell 156 42 38N 84 0W
Howick, N.Z. 142 36 54S 174 48 E
Howick, S. Afr. 129 29 28S 30 14 E
Howick Group 138 14 20S 145 30 E
Howitt, L. 139 27 40S 138 40 E
Howley 151 49 12N 57 2W
Howmore 36 57 18N 7 23W
Howrah 95 22 37N 88 27 E
Howth 38 53 23N 6 3W
Howth Hd. 38 53 21N 6 0W
Hoxne 29 52 22N 1 11 E
Höxter 48 51 45N 9 26 E
Hoy I. 37 58 50N 3 15W
Hoy Sd. 37 58 57N 3 20W
Hoya 48 52 47N 9 10 E
Høyanger 71 61 25N 6 50 E
Höydalsmo 71 59 30N 8 15 E
Hoyerswerda 48 51 26N 14 14 E
Hoylake 32 53 24N 3 11W
Höyland 71 58 50N 5 43 E
Hoyleton 140 34 2S 138 34 E
Hoyos 56 40 9N 6 45W
Hoyüan 109 23 50N 114 40 E
Hpawlum 98 27 12N 98 12 E
Hpettintha 98 24 14N 95 23 E
Hpizow 98 26 57N 98 24 E
Hpungan Pass 99 27 30N 96 55 E
Hrádec Králové 52 50 15N 15 50 E
Hrádek 53 48 46N 16 16 E
Hranice 53 49 34N 17 45 E
Hron, R. 53 48 0N 18 4 E
Hrubieszów 54 50 49N 23 51 E
Hrubý Nízký Jeseník 53 50 7N 17 10 E
Hrvatska 63 45 20N 16 0 E
Hsenwi 98 23 22N 97 55 E
Hsi Chiang, R. 109 22 20N 113 20 E
Hsiach'engtzu, Heilungkiang, China 107 44 41N 130 27 E
Hsiach'engtzu, Schechwan, China 108 29 24N 101 46 E
Hsiachiang 109 27 33N 115 10 E
Hsiaching 106 36 57N 115 59 E
Hsiach'uan Shan 109 21 40N 112 37 E
Hsiahsien 106 35 12N 111 11 E
Hsiai 106 34 17N 116 11 E
Hsiakuan 108 25 39N 100 9 E
Hsiamen 109 24 30N 118 7 E
Hsian 106 34 17N 109 0 E
Hsiang Chiang, R. 109 29 30N 113 10 E
Hsiangch'eng, Honan, China 106 33 50N 113 29 E
Hsiangch'eng, Honan, China 106 33 13N 114 50 E
Hsiangch'eng, Szechwan, China 108 29 0N 99 46 E
Hsiangchou 108 23 58N 109 41 E
Hsiangfan 109 32 7N 112 9 E
Hsianghsiang 109 27 46N 112 30 E
Hsiangning 106 36 1N 110 47 E
Hsiangshan 109 29 18N 121 37 E
Hsiangshuik'ou 107 34 12N 119 34 E
Hsiangt'an 109 27 55N 112 52 E
Hsiangtu 108 23 14N 106 57 E
Hsiangyang 109 32 2N 112 6 E
Hsiangyin 109 28 40N 112 53 E
Hsiangyüan 106 36 32N 113 2 E
Hsiangyün 108 25 29N 100 35 E
Hsiaochin 108 31 1N 102 23 E
Hsiaofeng 109 30 36N 119 33 E
Hsiaohsien 106 34 2N 116 56 E
Hsiaohsinganling Shanmo 105 48 45N 127 0 E
Hsiaoi 106 37 7N 111 46 E
Hsiaokan 109 30 57N 113 53 E
Hsiaoshan 109 30 10N 120 15 E
Hsiaot'ai Shan 107 36 18N 116 38 E
Hsiap'u 109 26 58N 119 57 E
Hsiawa 107 42 38N 120 31 E
Hsich'ang 108 27 50N 102 18 E
Hsichieht'o 108 30 24N 108 13 E
Hsich'uan 109 33 0N 111 24 E
Hsich'ung 108 31 0N 105 48 E
Hsiehch'eng 107 34 48N 117 15 E
Hsiehmaho 109 31 38N 111 12 E
Hsienchü 109 28 51N 120 44 E
Hsienfeng 108 29 40N 109 7 E
Hsienhsien 106 38 2N 116 12 E
Hsienning 109 29 51N 114 15 E
Hsienshui Ho, R. 108 30 5N 101 5 E
Hsienyang 106 34 22N 108 48 E
Hsienyu 109 25 24N 118 40 E
Hsifei Ho, R. 109 32 38N 116 39 E
Hsifeng, Kweichow, China 108 27 5N 106 42 E
Hsifeng, Liaoning, China 107 42 44N 124 42 E
Hsifengchen 106 35 40N 107 42 E
Hsifengk'ou 107 40 24N 118 19 E
Hsiho 106 34 2N 105 12 E
Hsihsia, Honan, China 106 33 30N 111 30 E
Hsihsia, Shantung, China 107 37 25N 120 48 E
Hsihsiang 108 33 1N 107 40 E
Hsihsien, Honan, China 109 32 24N 114 52 E
Hsihsien, Shensi, China 106 36 41N 110 56 E
Hsihua 106 33 47N 114 31 E
Hsilamunlun Ho, R. 107 43 24N 123 42 E
Hsiliao Ho, R. 107 43 24N 123 42 E
Hsilin 108 24 30N 105 3 E
Hsin Chiang, R. 109 28 50N 116 40 E
Hsin Ho, R. 107 43 33N 123 31 E
Hsinchan 107 43 52N 127 20 E
Hsinch'ang 109 29 30N 120 54 E
Hsincheng 106 34 25N 113 46 E
Hsinch'eng, Hopei, China 106 39 15N 115 59 E
Hsinch'eng, Kwangsi-Chuang, China 108 24 4N 108 40 E
Hsinchiang 106 35 40N 111 15 E
Hsinchien 108 23 58N 102 47 E
Hsinchin 107 39 25N 121 59 E
Hsinching 108 30 25N 103 49 E
Hsinchi'u 107 41 53N 119 40 E
Hsinchou 109 30 52N 114 48 E
Hsinchu 109 24 48N 120 58 E
Hsinfeng, Kiangsi, China 109 25 27N 114 58 E
Hsinfeng, Kiangsi, China 109 26 7N 116 11 E
Hsinfeng, Kwangtung, China 109 24 4N 114 12 E
Hsingan 109 25 39N 110 39 E
Hsingch'eng 107 40 40N 120 48 E
Hsingho 106 40 52N 113 58 E
Hsinghsien 106 38 31N 111 4 E
Hsinghua 107 32 55N 119 52 E
Hsinghua Wan 109 25 20N 119 20 E
Hsingi 108 25 5N 104 55 E
Hsinging 109 26 25N 110 44 E
Hsingjen 108 25 25N 105 13 E
Hsingjenp'ao 106 37 0N 105 0 E
Hsingkuo 109 26 26N 115 16 E
Hsinglung 107 40 29N 117 32 E
Hsingning 109 24 8N 115 43 E
Hsingp'ing 106 34 18N 108 26 E
Hsingshan 109 31 10N 110 51 E
Hsingt'ai 106 37 5N 114 38 E
Hsingyeh 108 22 45N 109 52 E
Hsinhailien = Lienyünchiangshih 107 34 37N 119 13 E
Hsinhsiang 106 35 15N 113 54 E
Hsinhsien, Shansi, China 106 38 24N 112 47 E
Hsinhsien, Shantung, China 106 36 15N 115 40 E
Hsinhsing 109 22 45N 112 11 E
Hsinhua 109 27 43N 111 18 E
Hsinhui 109 22 30N 113 0 E
Hsini 109 22 12N 110 53 E
Hsining 105 36 37N 101 46 E
Hsink'ai Ho, R. 107 41 10N 122 5 E
Hsinkan 109 27 45N 115 21 E
Hsinkao Shan 109 23 25N 120 52 E
Hsinlit'un 107 42 2N 122 19 E
Hsinlo 106 38 15N 114 40 E
Hsinmin 107 42 0N 122 52 E
Hsinpaoan 106 40 27N 115 23 E
Hsinpin 107 41 43N 125 2 E
Hsinp'ing 108 24 6N 101 58 E
Hsinshao 109 27 20N 111 26 E
Hsint'ai 107 35 54N 117 44 E
Hsint'ien 109 25 56N 112 13 E
Hsints'ai 109 32 44N 114 59 E
Hsinyang 109 32 10N 114 6 E
Hsinyeh 109 37 31N 112 21 E
Hsinyü 109 27 48N 114 56 E
Hsipaw 98 22 37N 97 18 E
Hsip'ing, Honan, China 106 33 34N 110 45 E
Hsip'ing, Honan, China 106 33 23N 114 2 E
Hsishni 109 30 27N 115 13 E
Hsitalahai 106 40 38N 109 38 E
Hsiu Shui, R. 109 29 13N 116 0 E
Hsiujen 109 24 26N 110 14 E
Hsiunghsien 106 38 50N 116 11 E
Hsiungyüeh 107 40 12N 122 12 E
Hsiuning 109 29 51N 118 15 E
Hsiushan 108 28 27N 108 59 E
Hsiushui 109 29 2N 114 34 E

**Hsiuwen** **Ibara**


Hsiuwen **108** 26 52N 106 35 E
Hsiuyen **107** 40 19N 123 15 E
Hsiyang **106** 37 27N 113 46 E
Hsüanch'eng **109** 30 54N 118 41 E
Hsüanen **108** 29 59N 109 24 E
Hsüanhan **108** 31 25N 107 38 E
Hsüanhua **106** 40 38N 115 5 E
Hsüanwei **108** 26 13N 104 5 E
Hsüch'ang **106** 34 1N 113 53 E
Hsüchou **107** 34 15N 117 10 E
Hsüehfeng Shan **109** 27 0N 110 30 E
Hsüehweng Shan **109** 24 24N 121 12 E
Hsun Chiang, R. **109** 23 30N 111 30 E
Hsünhsien **106** 35 40N 114 32 E
Hsüni **106** 35 6N 108 20 E
Hsüntien **108** 25 33N 103 15 E
Hsünwu **109** 24 57N 115 28 E
Hsünyang **108** 32 48N 109 27 E
Hsüp'u **109** 27 56N 110 36 E
Hsüshui **106** 39 1N 115 39 E
Hsüwen **109** 20 20N 110 9 E
Hsüyung **108** 28 6N 105 21 E
Htawgaw **98** 25 57N 98 23 E
Hua Hin **100** 12 34N 99 58 E
Huaan **109** 25 1N 117 33 E
Huachacalla **164** 18 45 S 68 17W
Huachinera **164** 30 9N 108 55W
Huachipato **172** 36 45 S 73 09W
Huacho **174** 11 10 S 77 35W
Huachón **174** 10 35 S 76 0W
Huachou **109** 21 38N 110 35 E
Huacrachuco **174** 8 35 S 76 50W
Huahsien, Honan, China **106** 35 33N 114 34 E
Huahsien, Shensi, China **106** 34 31N 109 46 E
Huai Yot **101** 7 45N 99 37 E
Huaiachen **106** 40 33N 114 30 E
Huaian, Hopei, China **106** 40 33N 114 30 E
Huaian, Kiangsu, China **107** 33 31N 119 8 E
Huaichi **109** 24 0N 112 8 E
Huaihua **109** 27 34N 109 56 E
Huaijen **106** 39 50N 113 7 E
Huaijou **106** 40 20N 116 37 E
Huainan **109** 32 39N 117 2 E
Huaining **109** 30 21N 116 42 E
Huaite **107** 43 30N 124 50 E
Huaitechen **107** 43 52N 124 45 E
Huaiyang **106** 33 50N 115 2 E
Huaiyüan, Anhwei, China **109** 32 58N 117 13 E
Huaiyüan, Kwangsi-Chuang, China **108** 24 36N 108 27 E
Huajuapan **165** 17 50N 98 0W
Huajung **109** 29 34N 112 34 E
Hualien **109** 24 0N 121 30 E
Huallaga, R. **174** 5 30 S 76 10W
Hualpai Pk. **161** 35 8N 113 58W
Huan Chiang, R. **106** 36 4N 107 40 E
Huancabamba **174** 5 10 S 79 15W
Huancané **174** 15 10 S 69 50W
Huancapi **174** 13 25 S 74 0W
Huancavelica **174** 12 50 S 75 5W
Huancayo **174** 12 5 S 75 0W
Huanchiang **108** 24 50N 108 15 E
Huang Ho, R. **107** 36 50N 118 20 E
Huangchiakopa **106** 40 20N 109 18 E
Huangch'uan **109** 32 8N 115 4 E
Huanghsien, Hunen, China **108** 27 22N 109 10 E
Huanghsien, Shantung, China **107** 37 38N 120 30 E
Huangkang **109** 30 27N 114 50 E
Huanglienp'u **108** 25 32N 99 44 E
Huangling **106** 35 36N 109 17 E
Huangliu **108** 18 20N 108 50 E
Huanglung **106** 35 37N 109 58 E
Huanglungt'an **109** 32 38N 110 33 E
Huangmei **109** 30 4N 115 56 E
Huangshih **109** 30 10N 115 2 E
Huangt'uan **107** 36 55N 121 41 E
Huangyang **109** 26 37N 111 42 E
Huangyen **109** 28 37N 121 12 E
Huanhsien **106** 36 32N 107 10 E
Huaning **108** 24 12N 102 55 E
Huanjen **107** 41 16N 125 21 E
Huanp'ing **108** 26 54N 107 55 E
Huant'ai **107** 36 57N 118 5 E
Huánuco **174** 9 55 S 76 15W
Huap'ing **108** 26 37N 101 13 E
Huap'itientzu **107** 43 30N 130 2 E
Huaraz **174** 9 30 S 77 32W
Huarmey **174** 10 5 S 78 5W
Huasamota **164** 22 30N 104 30W
Huascarán **174** 9 0 S 77 30W
Huasco **172** 28 24 S 71 15W
Huasco, R. **172** 28 27 S 71 13W
Huasna **163** 35 6N 120 24W
Huatabampo **164** 26 50N 109 50W
Huate **106** 41 57N 114 4 E
Huatien **107** 42 58N 126 50 E
Huauchinango **165** 20 11N 98 3W
Huautla **164** 18 20N 96 50W
Huautla de Jiménez **165** 18 8N 96 51W
Huay Namota **164** 21 56N 104 30W
Huayin **106** 34 36N 110 2 E
Huayllay **174** 11 03 S 76 21W
Huayüan **108** 28 30N 109 25 E
Hubbard **159** 31 50N 96 50W
Hubbart Pt. **153** 59 21N 94 41W
Hubli-Dharwar **97** 15 22N 75 15 E
Huchang **107** 41 25N 127 2 E
Huchuetenango **164** 15 25N 91 30W
Hückelhoven-Ratheim **48** 51 6N 6 3 E
Hucknall **33** 53 3N 1 12W
Huddersfield **33** 53 38N 1 49W
Hudi **122** 17 43N 34 28 E
Hudiksvall **72** 61 43N 17 10 E
Hudson, Can. **153** 50 6N 92 09W
Hudson, Mich., U.S.A. **156** 41 50N 84 20W
Hudson, N.H., U.S.A. **162** 42 46N 71 26W
Hudson, N.Y., U.S.A. **162** 42 15N 73 46W
Hudson, Wis., U.S.A. **158** 44 57N 92 45W
Hudson, Wyo., U.S.A. **160** 42 54N 108 37W
Hudson B. **153** 59 0N 91 0W
Hudson Bay, Can. **149** 60 0N 86 0W
Hudson Bay, Sask., Can. **153** 52 51N 102 23W
Hudson Falls **162** 43 18N 73 34W
Hudson, R. **162** 40 42N 74 2W
Hudson Str. **148** 62 0N 70 0W
Hudson's Hope **152** 56 0N 121 54W
Hué **100** 16 30N 107 35 E
Huebra, R. **56** 40 54N 6 28W
Huedin **70** 46 52N 23 2 E
Huehuetenango **166** 15 20N 91 28W
Huejúcar **164** 22 21N 103 13W
Huelgoat **42** 48 22N 3 46W
Huelma **59** 37 39N 3 28W
Huelva **57** 37 18N 6 57W
Huelva □ **57** 37 40N 7 0W
Huelva, R. **57** 37 46N 6 15W
Huentelauquén **172** 31 38 S 71 33W
Huércal Overa **59** 37 23N 1 57W
Huerta, Sa. de la **172** 31 10 S 67 30W
Huertas, C. de las **59** 38 21N 0 24W
Huerva, R. **58** 41 13N 1 15W
Huesca **58** 42 8N 0 25W
Huesca □ **58** 42 20N 0 1 E
Huéscar **59** 37 44N 2 35W
Huétamo **164** 18 36N 100 54W
Huete **58** 40 10N 2 43W
Hugh, R. **138** 25 1 S 134 10 E
Hugh Town **30** 49 55N 6 19W
Hughenden **138** 20 52 S 144 10 E
Hughes, Austral. **137** 30 42 S 129 31 E
Hughes, U.S.A. **147** 66 0N 154 20W
Hughesville **162** 41 14N 76 44W
Hugo, Colo., U.S.A. **158** 39 12N 103 27W
Hugo, Okla., U.S.A. **159** 34 0N 95 30W
Hugoton **159** 37 18N 101 22W
Huhehot = Huhohaot'e **106** 40 50N 110 39 E
Huhohaot'e **106** 40 50N 110 39 E
Huhsien **106** 34 8N 108 34 E
Huian **109** 25 4N 118 47 E
Huianp'u **106** 37 30N 106 40 E
Huiarau Ra. **142** 38 45 S 176 55 E
Huich'ang **109** 25 32N 115 45 E
Huichapán **165** 20 24N 99 40W
Huichou **109** 23 5N 114 24 E
Huifa Ho, R. **107** 43 6N 126 53 E
Huihsien, Honan, China **106** 35 32N 113 54 E
Huihsien, Kansu, China **106** 33 46N 106 6 E
Huila **128** 15 30 S 15 0 E
Huila □ **174** 2 30N 75 45W
Huila, Nevado del **174** 3 0N 76 0W
Huilai **109** 23 4N 116 18 E
Huili **108** 26 39N 102 11 E
Huimin **107** 37 29N 117 29 E
Huinan **107** 42 40N 126 5 E
Huinca Renancó **172** 34 51 S 64 22W
Huining **106** 35 41N 105 8 E
Huinung **106** 39 0N 106 45 E
Huiroa **142** 39 15 S 174 30 E
Huise **47** 50 54N 3 36 E
Huishui **108** 26 8N 106 35 E
Huissen **46** 51 57N 5 57 E
Huiting **106** 34 6N 116 4 E
Huitse **108** 26 22N 103 15 E
Huit'ung **108** 26 56N 109 36 E
Huixtla **165** 15 9N 92 28W
Huiya **92** 24 40N 49 15 E
Huizen **46** 52 18N 5 14 E
Hukawng Valley **99** 26 30N 96 30 E
Hukou **109** 29 45N 116 13 E
Hukuma **123** 14 55N 36 2 E
Hukuntsi **128** 23 58 S 21 45 E
Hula **123** 6 33N 38 30 E
Hulaifa **92** 25 58N 41 0 E
Hulan **105** 46 0N 126 44 E
Huld **106** 45 5N 105 30 E
Hülda **90** 31 50N 34 51 E
Hull, Can. **150** 45 20N 75 40W
Hull, U.K. **33** 53 45N 0 20W
Hullavington **28** 51 31N 2 9W
Hulme End **32** 53 8N 1 51W
Hulst **47** 51 17N 4 2 E
Hultsfred **73** 57 30N 15 52 E
Hulun Ch'ih **105** 49 1N 117 32 E
Humacao **147** 18 9N 65 50W
Humahuaca **172** 23 10 S 65 25W
Humaitá **174** 7 35 S 62 40W
Humaita **172** 27 2 S 58 31W
Humansdorp **128** 34 2 S 24 46 E
Humber, Mouth of **33** 53 32N 0 8 E
Humber, R. **33** 53 40N 0 10W
Humberside □ **33** 53 50N 0 30W
Humbert River **136** 16 30 S 130 45 E
Humble **159** 29 59N 95 10W
Humboldt, Can. **153** 52 15N 105 9W
Humboldt, Iowa, U.S.A. **158** 42 42N 94 15W
Humboldt, Tenn., U.S.A. **157** 35 50N 88 55W
Humboldt Gletscher **12** 79 30N 62 0W
Humboldt, R. **160** 40 55N 116 0W
Humbolt Mts. **143** 44 30 S 168 15 E
Hume **163** 36 48N 118 54W
Hume, L. **141** 36 0 S 147 0 E
Humenné **53** 48 55N 21 50 E
Humphreys, Mt. **163** 37 17N 118 40W
Humphreys Pk. **161** 35 24N 111 38W
Humpolec **52** 49 31N 15 20 E
Humshaugh **35** 55 3N 2 8W
Humula **141** 35 30 S 147 46 E
Hün **119** 29 2N 16 0 E
Hun Chiang, R. **107** 40 52N 125 42 E
Huna Floi **74** 65 50N 20 50W
Hunan □ **109** 27 30N 111 30 E
Hunch'un **107** 42 52N 130 21 E
Hundested **73** 55 58N 11 52 E
Hundred House **31** 52 11N 3 17W
Hundred Mile House **152** 51 38N 121 18W
Hundshögen, mt. **72** 62 57N 13 46 E
Hunedoara **70** 45 40N 22 50 E
Hunedoara □ **70** 45 45N 22 54 E
Hünfeld **48** 50 40N 9 47 E
Hung Chiang, R. **108** 27 7N 109 57 E
Hung Ho, R. **109** 32 24N 115 32 E
Hung Liu Ho, R. **106** 38 3N 109 10 E
Hung Yen **100** 20 39N 106 4 E
Hungan **109** 31 18N 114 33 E
Hungary ■ **53** 47 20N 19 20 E
Hungary, Plain of **16** 47 0N 20 0 E
Hungchiang **109** 27 6N 110 0 E
Hungerford, Austral. **139** 28 58 S 144 24 E
Hungerford, U.K. **28** 51 25N 1 30W
Hunghai Wan **109** 22 45N 115 15 E
Hunghu **109** 29 49N 113 30 E
Hüngnam **107** 39 55N 127 45 E
Hungshui Ho, R. **108** 23 24N 110 12 E
Hungtech'eng **106** 36 48N 107 6 E
Hungt'ou Hsü **109** 22 4N 121 25 E
Hungt'se Hu **107** 33 15N 118 45 E
Hungtung **106** 36 15N 111 37 E
Hungya **108** 29 56N 103 25 E
Hungyüan **108** 32 46N 102 42 E
Huni Valley **120** 5 33N 1 56W
Hunmanby **33** 54 12N 0 19W
Hunsberge **128** 27 58 S 17 5 E
Hunsrück, mts. **49** 50 0N 7 30 E
Hunstanton **29** 52 57N 0 30 E
Hunsur **97** 12 16N 76 16 E
Hunte, R. **48** 52 47N 8 28 E
Hunter, N.Z. **143** 44 36 S 171 2 E
Hunter, N.D., U.S.A. **158** 47 12N 97 17W
Hunter, N.Y., U.S.A. **162** 42 13N 74 13W
Hunter Hills, The **143** 44 26 S 170 46 E
Hunter, I. **138** 40 30 S 144 54 E
Hunter I. **152** 51 55N 128 0W
Hunter Mts. **143** 45 43 S 167 25 E
Hunter, R. **143** 44 21 S 169 27 E
Hunter Ra. **141** 32 45 S 150 15 E
Hunters Road **127** 19 9 S 29 49 E
Hunterston **34** 55 43N 4 55W
Hunterton **139** 26 12 S 148 30 E
Hunterville **142** 39 56 S 175 35 E
Huntingburg **156** 38 20N 86 58W
Huntingdon, Can. **150** 45 10N 74 10W
Huntingdon, U.K. **29** 52 20N 0 11W
Huntingdon, N.Y., U.S.A. **162** 40 52N 73 25W
Huntingdon, Pa., U.S.A. **156** 40 28N 78 1W
Huntingdon & Peterborough (□) **26** 52 23N 0 10W
Huntingdon I. **151** 53 48N 56 45W
Huntington, U.K. **33** 54 0N 1 4W
Huntington, Id., U.S.A. **160** 44 22N 117 21W
Huntington, Ind., U.S.A. **156** 40 52N 85 30W
Huntington, Ut., U.S.A. **160** 39 24N 111 1W
Huntington, W. Va., U.S.A. **156** 38 20N 82 30W
Huntington Beach **163** 33 40N 118 0W
Huntington Park **161** 34 58N 118 15W
Huntly, N.Z. **142** 37 34 S 175 11 E
Huntly, U.K. **37** 57 27N 2 48W
Huntsville, Can. **150** 45 20N 79 14W
Huntsville, Ala., U.S.A. **157** 34 45N 86 35W
Huntsville, Tex., U.S.A. **159** 30 50N 95 35W
Hunyani Dams. **127** 18 0 S 31 10 E
Hunyani, R. **127** 18 0 S 31 10 E
Hunyüan **106** 39 44N 113 42 E
Hunza, R. **95** 36 24N 75 50 E
Huohsien **106** 36 38N 111 43 E
Huon, G. **135** 7 0 S 147 30 E
Huon Pen. **135** 6 20 S 147 30 E
Huong Hoa **106** 16 37N 106 45 E
Huong Khe **100** 18 13N 105 41 E
Huonville **138** 43 0 S 147 5 E
Huoshaop'u **107** 43 23N 130 26 E
Hupei □ **109** 31 5N 113 5 E
Hurbanovo **53** 47 51N 18 11 E
Hurezani **70** 44 49N 23 40 E
Hurghada **122** 27 15N 33 50 E
Hŭrghita □ **70** 46 30N 25 30 E
Hŭrghita Mţii **70** 46 25N 25 35 E
Hurley, N. Mex., U.S.A. **161** 32 45N 108 7W
Hurley, Wis., U.S.A. **158** 46 26N 90 10W
Hurlford **34** 55 35N 4 29W
Hurliness **37** 58 47N 3 15W
Hurlock **162** 38 38N 75 52W
Huron, Calif., U.S.A. **163** 36 12N 120 6W
Huron, S.D., U.S.A. **158** 44 30N 98 20W
Hurricane **161** 37 10N 113 12W
Hursley **28** 51 1N 1 23W
Hurso **123** 9 35N 41 33 E
Hurstbourne Tarrant **28** 51 17N 1 27W
Hurstpierpoint **29** 50 56N 0 11W
Hurum, Buskerud, Norway **71** 59 36N 10 23 E
Hurum, Oppland, Norway **71** 61 9N 8 46 E
Hurunui, R. **143** 42 54 S 173 18 E
Hurup **73** 56 46N 8 25 E
Husaby **73** 58 35N 13 25 E
Húsavík **74** 66 3N 17 21W
Husband's Bosworth **28** 52 27N 1 3W
Husi **70** 46 41N 28 7 E
Husinish Pt. **36** 57 59N 7 6W
Huskvarna **73** 57 47N 14 15 E
Huslia **147** 65 40N 156 30W
Husøy **71** 61 3N 4 44 E
Hussar **152** 51 3N 112 41W
Hussein (Allenby) Br. **90** 31 53N 35 33 E
Hustopéce **53** 48 57N 16 43 E
Husum, Ger. **48** 54 27N 9 3 E
Husum, Sweden **72** 63 21N 19 12 E
Hutchinson, Kans., U.S.A. **159** 38 3N 97 59W
Hutchinson, Minn, U.S.A. **158** 44 50N 94 22W
Huttenberg **52** 46 56N 14 33 E
Hüttental **47** 50 53N 8 1 E
Huttig **159** 33 5N 92 10W
Hutton, Mt. **139** 25 51 S 148 20 E
Hutton, oilfield **19** 61 0N 1 30 E
Hutton Ra. **137** 24 45 S 124 30 E
Huttwil **50** 47 7N 7 50 E
Huwarā **90** 32 9N 35 15 E
Huwun **123** 4 23N 40 6 E
Huy **47** 50 31N 5 15 E
Huyton **32** 53 25N 2 52W
Hvaler **71** 59 4N 11 1 E
Hvammsfjörður **74** 65 4N 22 5W
Hvammur **74** 65 13N 21 49W
Hvar **63** 43 10N 16 45 E
Hvar, I. **63** 43 11N 16 28 E
Hvarski Kanal **63** 43 15N 16 35 E
Hvítá, Arnessýsla, Iceland **74** 64 0N 20 58W
Hvítá, Mýrasýsla, Iceland **74** 64 40N 21 5W
Hvítárvatn **74** 63 37N 19 50W
Hvitsten **71** 59 35N 10 42 E
Hwachon-chōsuji **107** 38 5N 127 50 E
Hwang Ho = Huang Ho, R. **107** 36 50N 118 20 E
Hwekum **98** 26 7N 95 22 E
Hyannis, Mass., U.S.A. **162** 41 39N 70 17W
Hyannis, Nebr., U.S.A. **158** 41 60N 101 45W
Hyargas Nuur **105** 49 12N 93 34 E
Hyattsville **162** 38 59N 76 55W
Hybo **72** 61 49N 16 15 E
Hydaburg **147** 55 15N 132 45W
Hyde, N.Z. **143** 45 18 S 170 16 E
Hyde, U.K. **32** 53 26N 2 6W
Hyde Park **162** 41 47N 73 56W
Hyden **137** 32 24 S 118 46 E
Hyderabad, India **96** 17 10N 78 29 E
Hyderabad, Pak. **94** 25 23N 68 36 E
Hyderabad □ **94** 25 3N 68 24 E
Hyères **45** 43 8N 6 9 E
Hyères, Is. d' **45** 43 0N 6 28 E
Hyesan **107** 41 20N 128 10 E
Hyland Post **139** 57 40N 128 10W
Hyland, R. **152** 59 52N 128 12W
Hylestad **71** 59 6N 7 29 E
Hyllested **71** 56 17N 10 46 E
Hyltebruk **73** 56 59N 13 15 E
Hymia **95** 33 40N 78 2 E
Hyndman Pk. **160** 44 4N 114 0W
Hynish **34** 56 27N 6 54W
Hynish B. **34** 56 29N 6 40W
Hyōgo-ken □ **110** 35 15N 135 0 E
Hyrum **160** 41 35N 111 56W
Hysham **160** 46 21N 107 11W
Hythe **29** 51 4N 1 5 E
Hyūga **110** 32 25N 131 35 E
Hyvinkä **75** 60 38N 24 50 E


# I


I Ho, R. **107** 34 10N 118 4 E
I-n-Azaoua **119** 20 45N 7 31 E
I-n-Echaïe **118** 20 10N 2 5W
I-n-Gall **121** 6 51N 7 1 E
I-n-Tabedog **118** 19 54N 1 3 E
Iabès, Erg **118** 27 30N 2 2W
Iaco, R. **174** 10 25 S 70 30W
Iaçu **171** 12 45 S 40 13W
Iakora **129** 23 6 S 46 40 E
Ialomiţa □ **70** 44 30N 27 30 E
Ianca **70** 45 6N 27 29 E
Iar Connacht **39** 53 20N 9 20W
Iara **70** 46 31N 23 35 E
Iaşi □ **70** 47 20N 27 0 E
Iaşi (Jassy) **70** 47 10N 27 40 E
Iauaretê **174** 0 30N 69 5W
Iaucdjovac, (Port Harrison) **149** 58 25N 78 15W
Iba **103** 15 22N 120 0 E
Ibadan **121** 7 22N 3 58 E
Ibagué **174** 4 27N 73 14W
Ibaiti **171** 23 50 S 50 10W
Iballja **68** 42 12N 20 0 E
Ibar, R. **66** 43 15N 20 40 E
Ibara **110** 34 36N 133 28 E

| Ibaraki-ken □ | 111 36 10N 140 10 E |
| Ibararaki | 111 34 49N 135 34 E |
| Ibarra | 174 0 21N 78 7W |
| Ibba | 123 4 49N 29 2 E |
| Ibba, Bahr el | 123 5 30N 28 55 E |
| Ibbenbüren | 48 52 16N 7 41 E |
| Ibembo | 126 2 35N 23 35 E |
| Ibera, Laguna | 172 28 30 S 57 9W |
| Iberian Peninsula | 16 40 0N 5 0W |
| Iberville | 150 45 19N 73 17W |
| Iberville, Lac d' | 150 55 55N 73 15W |
| Ibi | 121 8 15N 9 50 E |
| Ibiá | 171 19 30 S 46 30W |
| Ibicaraí | 171 14 51 S 39 36W |
| Ibicuí | 171 14 51 S 39 59W |
| Ibicuy | 172 33 55 S 59 10W |
| Ibioapaba, Serra da | 170 20 14 S 40 25W |
| Ibipetuba | 171 11 0 S 44 32W |
| Ibiracu | 171 19 50 S 40 30W |
| Ibitiara | 171 12 39 S 42 13W |
| Ibiza | 59 38 54N 1 26 E |
| Ibiza, I. | 59 39 0N 1 30 E |
| Iblei, Monti | 65 37 15N 14 45 E |
| Ibo | 127 12 22 S 40 32 E |
| Ibonma | 103 3 22 S 133 31 E |
| Ibotirama | 171 12 13 S 43 12W |
| Ibriktepe | 68 41 2N 26 33 E |
| Ibshawâi | 122 29 21N 30 40 E |
| Ibstock | 28 52 42N 1 23W |
| Ibu | 103 1 35N 127 25 E |
| Ibuki-Sanchi | 111 35 25N 136 34 E |
| Ibuneşti | 70 46 45N 24 50 E |
| Iburg | 48 52 10N 8 3 E |
| Ibusuki | 110 31 12N 130 32 E |
| Ibwe Munyama | 127 16 5 S 28 31 E |
| Ica | 174 14 0 S 75 30W |
| Ica, R. | 174 2 55 S 69 0W |
| Icabarú | 174 4 20N 61 45W |
| Içana | 174 1 21N 69 0W |
| Icatu | 170 2 46 S 44 4W |
| Iceland, I. ■ | 74 65 0N 19 0W |
| Icha | 77 55 30N 156 0 E |
| Ichang | 109 25 25N 112 55 E |
| Ich'ang | 109 30 40N 111 20 E |
| Ichchapuram | 96 19 10N 84 40 E |
| Icheng | 109 32 16N 119 12 E |
| Ich'eng, Hupeh, China | 109 31 43N 112 12 E |
| Ich'eng, Shansi, China | 106 35 42N 111 40 E |
| Ichihara | 111 35 28N 140 5 E |
| Ichikawa | 111 35 44N 139 55 E |
| Ichilo, R. | 174 16 30 S 64 45W |
| Ichinomiya, Gifu, Japan | 111 35 18N 136 48 E |
| Ichinomiya, Kumamoto, Japan | 110 32 58N 131 5 E |
| Ichinoseki | 112 38 55N 141 8 E |
| Ichôn | 107 37 17N 127 27 E |
| Icht | 118 29 6N 8 54W |
| Ichtegem | 47 51 5N 3 1 E |
| Ich'uan | 106 36 4N 110 6 E |
| Ich'un | 105 47 42N 128 54 E |
| Ichün | 106 35 23N 109 7 E |
| Ich'un, Heilungkiang, China | 105 47 42N 128 54 E |
| Ich'un, Kiangsi, China | 109 27 47N 114 22 E |
| Icó | 170 6 24 S 38 51W |
| Icoraci | 170 1 18 S 48 28W |
| Icy C. | 12 70 25N 162 0W |
| Icy Str. | 153 58 20N 135 30W |
| Ida Grove | 158 42 20N 95 25W |
| Ida Valley | 137 28 42 S 120 29 E |
| Idabel | 159 33 53N 94 50W |
| Idaga Hamus | 123 14 13N 39 35 E |
| Idah | 121 6 10N 6 40 E |
| Idaho □ | 160 44 10N 114 0W |
| Idaho City | 160 43 50N 115 52W |
| Idaho Falls | 160 43 30N 112 10W |
| Idaho Springs | 160 39 49N 105 30W |
| Idanha-a-Nova | 56 39 50N 7 15W |
| Idanre | 121 7 8N 5 5 E |
| Idar-Oberstein | 49 49 43N 7 19 E |
| Idd el Ghanam | 117 11 30N 24 25 E |
| Iddan | 91 6 10N 49 5 E |
| Idehan | 119 27 10N 11 30 E |
| Idehan Marzūq | 119 24 50N 13 51 E |
| Idelès | 119 23 58N 5 53 E |
| Idfû | 122 25 0N 32 49 E |
| Idhi Oros | 69 35 15N 24 45 E |
| Idhra | 69 37 20N 23 28 E |
| Idi | 102 4 55N 97 45 E |
| Idi Amin Dada, L. | 93 0 25 S 29 40 E |
| Idiofa | 124 4 55 S 19 42 E |
| Idkerberget | 72 60 22N 15 15 E |
| Idle | 33 53 50N 1 45W |
| Idle, R. | 33 53 22N 0 49W |
| Idmiston | 28 51 8N 1 43W |
| Idna | 90 31 34N 34 58 E |
| Idria | 163 36 25N 120 41W |
| Idrija | 63 46 0N 14 5 E |
| Idritsa | 80 56 25N 28 57 E |
| Idstein | 49 50 13N 8 17 E |
| Idsworth | 29 50 56N 0 56W |
| Idutywa | 125 32 8 S 28 18 E |
| Ieper | 47 50 51N 2 53 E |
| Ierápetra | 69 35 0N 25 44 E |
| Ierissós | 68 40 22N 23 52 E |
| Ierissóu Kólpos | 68 40 27N 23 57 E |
| Ierzu | 64 39 48N 9 32 E |
| Ieshima-Shotō | 110 34 40N 134 32 E |
| Iesi | 63 43 32N 13 12 E |
| Ifach, Punta | 59 38 38N 0 5 E |
| Ifanadiana | 129 21 29 S 47 39 E |
| Ife | 121 7 30N 4 31 E |
| Iférouâne | 121 19 5N 8 35 E |

| Ifni | 118 29 25N 10 10W |
| Ifon | 121 6 58N 5 40 E |
| Iga | 111 34 45N 136 10 E |
| Iganga | 126 0 30N 33 28 E |
| Igarapava | 171 20 3 S 47 47W |
| Igarapé Açu | 170 1 4 S 47 33W |
| Igarapé-Mirim | 170 1 59 S 48 58W |
| Igarka | 77 67 30N 87 20 E |
| Igatimi | 173 24 5 S 55 30W |
| Igatpuri | 96 19 40N 73 35 E |
| Igbetti | 121 8 44N 4 8 E |
| Igbo-Ora | 121 7 10N 3 15 E |
| Igboho | 121 8 40N 3 50 E |
| Iggesund | 72 61 39N 17 10 E |
| Igherm | 118 30 7N 8 18W |
| Ighil Izane | 118 35 44N 0 31 E |
| Iglene | 118 22 57N 4 58 E |
| Iglésias | 64 39 19N 8 27 E |
| Igli | 118 30 25N 2 12W |
| Iglino | 84 54 50N 56 26 E |
| Igloolik Island | 149 69 20N 81 30W |
| Igma | 118 29 9N 6 11W |
| Igma, Gebel el | 122 28 55N 34 0 E |
| Ignace | 150 49 30N 91 40W |
| Igoshevo | 81 59 25N 42 35 E |
| Igoumenitsa | 68 39 32N 20 18 E |
| Igra | 84 57 33N 53 7 E |
| Iguaçu, Cat. del | 173 25 41N 54 26W |
| Iguaçu, R. | 173 25 30 S 53 10W |
| Iguala | 165 18 20N 99 40W |
| Igualada | 58 41 37N 1 37 E |
| Iguape | 171 24 43 S 47 33W |
| Iguape, R. | 173 24 40 S 48 0W |
| Iguassu = Iguaçu | 173 25 41N 54 26W |
| Iguatu | 170 6 20 S 39 18W |
| Iguéla | 124 2 0 S 9 16 E |
| Igumale | 121 6 47N 7 55 E |
| Igunga □ | 126 4 20 S 33 45 E |
| Ihiala | 121 5 40N 6 55 E |
| Ihosy | 129 22 24 S 46 8 E |
| Ihotry, L. | 129 21 56 S 43 41 E |
| Ihsien, Anwhei, China | 109 29 53N 117 57 E |
| Ihsien, Hopeh, China | 106 39 21N 115 29 E |
| Ihsien, Liaoning, China | 107 41 34N 121 15 E |
| Ihsien, Shantung, China | 107 37 11N 119 55 E |
| Ihuang | 109 27 32N 115 57 E |
| Ii | 74 65 15N 25 30 E |
| Iida | 111 35 35N 138 0 E |
| Iiey | 138 18 53 S 141 12 E |
| Iijoki | 74 65 20N 26 15 E |
| Iisalmi | 74 63 32N 27 10 E |
| Iizuka | 110 33 38N 130 42 E |
| Ijebu-Igbo | 121 6 56N 4 1 E |
| Ijebu-Ode | 121 6 47N 3 52 E |
| IJmuiden | 46 52 28N 4 35 E |
| IJssel, R. | 46 52 35N 5 50 E |
| IJsselmeer | 46 52 45N 5 20 E |
| IJsselmuiden | 46 52 34N 5 57 E |
| IJsselstein | 46 52 1N 5 2 E |
| Ijuí, R. | 173 27 58 S 55 20W |
| Ijüin | 110 31 37N 130 24 E |
| IJzendijke | 47 51 19N 3 37 E |
| IJzer, R. | 47 51 9N 2 44 E |
| Ik, R. | 84 55 55N 52 36 E |
| Ikamatua | 41 42 15 S 171 41 E |
| Ikare | 121 7 18N 5 40 E |
| Ikaria, I. | 69 37 35N 26 10 E |
| Ikast | 73 56 8N 9 10 E |
| Ikawa | 111 35 13N 138 15 E |
| Ikeda | 111 34 1N 133 48 E |
| Ikeja | 121 6 28N 3 45 E |
| Ikela | 124 1 0 S 23 35 E |
| Ikerre | 121 7 25N 5 19 E |
| Ikhtiman | 67 42 27N 23 48 E |
| Iki | 110 33 45N 129 42 E |
| Iki-Kaikyō | 110 33 40N 129 45 E |
| Ikimba L. | 126 1 30 S 31 20 E |
| Ikire | 121 7 10N 4 15 E |
| Ikirun | 121 7 54N 4 40 E |
| Ikitsuki-Shima | 110 33 23N 129 26 E |
| Ikole | 121 7 40N 5 37 E |
| Ikom | 121 6 0N 8 42 E |
| Ikopa, R. | 129 17 45 S 46 40 E |
| Ikot Ekpene | 121 5 12N 7 40 E |
| Ikungu | 126 1 33 S 33 42 E |
| Ikuno | 110 35 10N 134 48 E |
| Ila | 121 8 0N 4 51 E |
| Ilam | 95 26 58N 87 58 E |
| Ilan, China | 105 46 14N 129 33 E |
| Ilan, Taiwan | 109 24 45N 121 44 E |
| Ilanskiy | 77 56 14N 96 3 E |
| Ilanz | 51 46 46N 9 12 E |
| Ilaomita, R. | 47 44 47N 27 0 E |
| Ilaro Agege | 121 6 53 S 3 3 E |
| Ilayangudi | 97 9 34N 78 37 E |
| Ilbilbie | 138 21 45 S 149 20 E |
| Ilchester | 28 51 0N 2 41W |
| Ile-à-la-Crosse | 153 55 27N 107 53W |
| Ile-à-la-Crosse, Lac | 153 55 40N 107 45W |
| Ile Bouchard, L' | 42 47 7N 0 26 E |
| Ile de France □ | 43 49 0N 2 20 E |
| Ilebo | 124 4 17 S 20 47 E |
| Ileje □ | 127 9 30 S 33 25 E |
| Ilek | 84 51 32N 53 21 E |
| Ilek, R. | 84 51 30N 53 22 E |
| Ilen R. | 39 51 38N 9 19W |
| Ilero | 121 8 0N 3 20 E |
| Ilesha, West-Central, Nigeria | 121 7 37N 4 40 E |

| Ilesha, Western, Nigeria | 121 8 57N 3 28 E |
| Ilford | 153 56 4N 95 35W |
| Ilfov □ | 70 44 20N 26 0 E |
| Ilfracombe, Austral. | 138 23 30 S 144 30 E |
| Ilfracombe, U.K. | 30 51 13N 4 8W |
| Ilha Grande, Baia da | 171 23 9 S 44 30W |
| Ílhavo | 56 40 33N 8 43W |
| Ilheus | 171 14 49 S 39 2W |
| Ili | 85 45 53N 77 10 E |
| Ilia | 70 45 57N 22 40 E |
| Ilia □ | 69 37 45N 21 35 E |
| Iliamna L. | 147 59 35N 155 30W |
| Iliang, Yunnan, China | 108 24 54N 103 9 E |
| Iliang, Yunnan, China | 108 27 35N 104 1 E |
| Ilich | 85 40 50N 68 27 E |
| Ilico | 172 34 50 S 72 20W |
| Iliff | 158 40 50N 103 3W |
| Iliki | 69 38 24N 23 15 E |
| Ilio Pt. | 147 21 13N 157 16W |
| Iliodhrómia | 68 39 12N 23 50 E |
| Ilion | 162 43 0N 75 3W |
| Ilirska Bistrica | 63 45 34N 14 14 E |
| Iliysk | 76 44 10N 77 20 E |
| Ilkal | 97 15 57N 76 8 E |
| Ilkeston | 33 52 59N 1 19W |
| Ilkley | 21 53 56N 1 49W |
| Illana B. | 103 7 35N 123 45 E |
| Illapel | 172 32 0 S 71 10W |
| 'Illar | 90 32 23N 35 7 E |
| Ille | 44 42 40N 2 37 E |
| Ille-et-Vilaine □ | 42 48 10N 1 30W |
| Iller, R. | 49 47 53N 10 10 E |
| Illescás | 56 40 8N 3 51W |
| Illig | 91 7 47N 49 45 E |
| Illimani, Mte. | 174 16 30 S 67 50W |
| Illinois □ | 155 40 15N 89 30W |
| Illinois, R. | 155 40 10N 90 20W |
| Illizi | 119 26 31N 8 32 E |
| Illora | 57 37 17N 3 53W |
| Ilmen, Oz. | 80 58 15N 31 10 E |
| Ilmenau | 48 50 41N 10 55 E |
| Ilminster | 28 50 55 S 2 56W |
| Ilo | 174 17 40 S 71 20W |
| Ilobu | 121 7 45N 4 25 E |
| Ilohuli Shan | 105 51 20N 124 20 E |
| Iloilo | 103 10 45N 122 33 E |
| Ilok | 66 45 15N 19 20 E |
| Ilora | 121 7 45N 3 50 E |
| Ilorin | 121 8 30N 4 35 E |
| Ilovatka | 81 50 30N 46 50 E |
| Ilovlya | 83 49 15N 44 2 E |
| Ilovlya, R. | 83 49 38N 44 20 E |
| Ilowa | 54 51 30N 15 10 E |
| Ilubabor □ | 123 7 25N 35 0 E |
| Ilukste | 80 55 55N 26 20 E |
| Ilung | 108 31 34N 106 24 E |
| Ilva Micá | 70 47 17N 24 40 E |
| Ilwaki | 103 7 55 S 126 30 E |
| Ilyichevsk | 82 46 10N 30 35 E |
| Imabari | 110 34 4N 133 0 E |
| Imadahane | 118 32 8N 7 0W |
| Imaichi | 111 36 6N 139 16 E |
| Imaloto, R. | 129 23 10 S 45 15 E |
| Iman = Dalneretchensk | 77 45 50N 133 40 E |
| Imari | 110 33 15N 129 52 E |
| Imasa | 122 18 0N 36 12 E |
| Imathía □ | 68 40 30N 22 15 E |
| Imbâbah | 122 30 5N 31 12 E |
| Imbler | 160 45 31N 118 0W |
| Imbros = Imroz | 68 40 10N 26 0 E |
| Imen | 108 24 40N 102 9 E |
| Imeni Panfilova | 85 43 23N 77 7 E |
| Imeni Poliny Osipenko | 77 55 25N 136 29 E |
| Imeri, Serra | 174 0 50N 65 25W |
| Imerimandroso | 129 17 26 S 48 35 E |
| Imi (Hinna) | 123 6 35N 42 30 E |
| Imi n'Tanoute | 118 31 13N 8 51 E |
| Imienp'o | 107 45 0N 128 16 E |
| Imishly | 83 39 49N 48 4 E |
| Imiteg | 118 29 43N 8 10W |
| Imlay | 160 40 45N 118 9W |
| Immingham | 33 53 37N 0 12W |
| Immokalee | 157 26 25N 81 20W |
| Imo □ | 121 5 15N 7 20 E |
| Imola | 63 44 20N 11 42 E |
| Imotski | 66 43 27N 17 21 E |
| Imperatriz | 170 5 30 S 47 29W |
| Impéria | 62 43 52N 8 0 E |
| Imperial, Can. | 153 51 21N 105 28W |
| Imperial, Calif., U.S.A. | 161 32 52N 115 34W |
| Imperial, Nebr., U.S.A. | 158 40 38N 101 39W |
| Imperial Beach | 163 32 35N 117 8W |
| Imperial Dam | 161 32 50N 114 30W |
| Imperial Valley | 163 32 55N 115 30W |
| Imperieuse Reef | 136 17 36 S 118 50 E |
| Impfondo | 124 1 40N 18 0 E |
| Imphal | 98 24 48N 93 56 E |
| Imphy | 43 46 56N 3 15 E |
| Imroz = Gökçeada | 68 40 10N 26 0 E |
| Imst | 52 47 15N 10 44 E |
| Imuruan B. | 103 10 40N 119 10 E |
| In Belbel | 118 27 55N 1 12 E |
| In Delimane | 121 15 52N 1 31 E |
| In-Gall | 121 16 51N 7 1 E |
| In Rhar | 118 27 10N 1 59 E |
| In Salah | 118 27 10N 2 32 E |
| In Tallak | 121 16 19N 3 15 E |
| Ina | 111 35 50N 138 0 E |
| Ina-Bonchi | 111 35 45N 137 58 E |

| Inagh | 39 52 53N 9 11W |
| Inajá | 170 8 54 S 37 49W |
| Inangahua Junc. | 143 41 52 S 171 59 E |
| Inanwatan | 103 2 10 S 132 5 E |
| Iñapari | 174 11 0 S 69 40W |
| Inari | 74 68 54N 27 5 E |
| Inari, L. | 74 69 0N 28 0 E |
| Inazawa | 111 35 15N 136 47 E |
| Inca | 58 39 43N 2 54 E |
| Incaguasi | 172 29 12 S 71 5W |
| Ince | 32 53 32N 2 38W |
| Ince Burnu | 92 42 2N 35 0 E |
| Inch | 39 52 42N 8 8W |
| Inch Br. | 39 52 49N 9 6W |
| Inchard, Loch | 36 58 28N 5 2W |
| Inchcape Rock | 35 56 26N 2 24W |
| Inchigeelagh | 39 51 50N 9 8W |
| Inchini | 123 8 55N 37 37 E |
| Inchkeith, I. | 35 56 2N 3 8W |
| Inchnadamph | 36 58 9N 5 0W |
| Inch'ŏn | 107 37 27N 126 40 E |
| Inchture | 35 56 26N 3 8W |
| Incio | 56 42 39N 7 21W |
| Incomáti, R. | 129 25 15 S 32 35 E |
| Incudine, Mte. l' | 45 41 50N 9 12 E |
| Inda Silase | 123 14 10N 38 15 E |
| Indaal, L. | 34 55 44N 6 20W |
| Indalsälven | 72 62 36N 17 30 E |
| Indaw | 98 24 15N 96 5 E |
| Indbir | 123 8 7N 37 52 E |
| Indefatigable, gasfield | 19 53 20N 2 40 E |
| Independence, Calif., U.S.A. | 163 36 51N 118 7W |
| Independence, Iowa, U.S.A. | 158 42 27N 91 52W |
| Independence, Kans., U.S.A. | 159 37 10N 95 50W |
| Independence, Mo., U.S.A. | 158 39 3N 94 25W |
| Independence, Oreg., U.S.A. | 160 44 53N 123 6W |
| Independence Fjord | 12 82 10N 29 0W |
| Independence Mts. | 160 41 30N 116 2W |
| Independência | 170 5 23 S 40 19W |
| Independencia, La | 165 16 31N 91 47W |
| Independenţa | 70 45 25N 27 42 E |
| Inderborskly | 83 48 30N 51 42 E |
| India ■ | 87 20 0N 80 0 E |
| Indian Cabins | 152 59 52N 117 2W |
| Indian Harbour | 151 54 27N 57 13W |
| Indian Head | 153 50 30N 103 35W |
| Indian House L. | 151 56 30N 64 30W |
| Indian Lake | 162 43 47N 74 16W |
| Indian Ocean | 11 5 0 S 75 0 E |
| Indian River B. | 162 38 36N 75 4W |
| Indiana | 156 40 38N 79 9W |
| Indiana □ | 156 40 0N 86 0W |
| Indianapolis | 156 39 42N 86 10W |
| Indianola, Iowa, U.S.A. | 158 41 20N 93 38W |
| Indianola, Miss., U.S.A. | 159 33 27N 90 40W |
| Indiápolis | 171 19 2 S 47 55 E |
| Indiapora | 171 19 57 S 50 17W |
| Indiaroba | 171 11 32 S 37 31W |
| Indiga | 78 67 50N 48 50 E |
| Indigirka, R. | 77 69 0N 147 0 E |
| Indija | 66 45 6N 20 7 E |
| Indio | 163 33 46N 116 15W |
| Indonesia ■ | 102 5 0 S 115 0 E |
| Indore | 94 22 42N 75 53 E |
| Indramaju | 103 6 21 S 108 20 E |
| Indramaju, Tg. | 103 6 20 S 108 20 E |
| Indravati, R. | 96 19 0N 81 15 E |
| Indre □ | 43 47 12N 1 39 E |
| Indre-et-Loire □ | 42 47 12N 0 40 E |
| Indre, R. | 42 47 2N 1 8 E |
| Indre Söndeled | 71 58 46N 9 5 E |
| Indus, Mouth of the | 94 24 00N 68 00 E |
| Indus, R. | 94 28 40N 70 10 E |
| Inebolu | 92 41 55N 33 40 E |
| Infante, Kaap | 128 34 27 S 20 51 E |
| Infantes | 59 38 43N 3 1W |
| Infiernillo, Presa del | 164 18 9N 102 0W |
| Infiesto | 56 43 21N 5 21W |
| Ingá | 171 7 17 S 35 36W |
| Ingatestone | 29 51 40N 0 23W |
| Ingelmunster | 47 50 56N 3 16 E |
| Ingende | 124 0 12 S 18 57 E |
| Ingenio Santa Ana | 172 27 25 S 65 40W |
| Ingesvang | 73 56 10N 9 20 E |
| Ingham | 138 18 43 S 146 10 E |
| Ingichka | 85 39 47N 65 58 E |
| Ingleborough, mt. | 32 54 11N 2 23W |
| Inglefield Land | 143 78 30N 70 0W |
| Ingleton | 32 54 9N 2 29W |
| Inglewood, Queensland, Austral. | 139 28 25 S 151 8 E |
| Inglewood, Vic., Austral. | 140 36 29 S 143 53 E |
| Inglewood, N.Z. | 142 39 9 S 174 14 E |
| Inglewood, U.S.A. | 163 33 58N 118 21W |
| Ingoldmells, Pt. | 33 53 11N 0 21 E |
| Ingólfshöfði | 74 63 48N 16 39W |
| Ingolstadt | 49 48 45N 11 26 E |
| Ingomar | 160 46 43N 107 37W |
| Ingonish | 151 46 42N 60 18W |
| Ingore | 120 12 24N 15 48W |
| Ingul, R. | 82 47 30N 33 25 E |
| Ingulec | 82 47 42N 33 4 E |
| Ingulets, R. | 82 47 20N 33 20 E |
| Inguri, R. | 83 42 58N 42 17 E |
| Inhaca, I. | 129 26 1 S 32 57 E |
| Inhafenga | 129 20 36 S 33 47 E |
| Inhambane | 125 23 54 S 35 30 E |

**Inhambane □** **Itaueira**


| | | | |
|---|---|---|---|
| Inhambane □ | **129** | 22 30 S | 34 20 E |
| Inhambupe | **171** | 11 47 S | 38 21 W |
| Inhaminga | **127** | 18 26 S | 35 0 E |
| Inharrime | **129** | 24 30 S | 35 0 E |
| Inharrime, R. | **129** | 24 30 S | 35 0 E |
| Inhassoro | **127** | 21 50 S | 35 15 E |
| Inhuma | **170** | 6 40 S | 41 42 W |
| Inhumas | **171** | 16 22 S | 49 30 W |
| Iniesta | **59** | 39 27 N | 1 45 W |
| Ining, Kwangsi-Chuang, China | **109** | 25 8 N | 109 57 E |
| Ining, Sinkiang-Uigur, China | **105** | 43 54 N | 81 21 E |
| Inírida, R. | **174** | 3 0 N | 68 40 W |
| Inishark | **38** | 53 36 N | 10 17 W |
| Inishark I. | **38** | 53 38 N | 10 17 W |
| Inishbofin I., Donegal, Ireland | **38** | 55 10 N | 8 10 W |
| Inishbofin I., Galway, Ireland | **38** | 53 35 N | 10 12 W |
| Inisheer | **39** | 53 3 N | 9 32 W |
| Inishfree B. | **38** | 55 4 N | 8 20 W |
| Inishkea Is. | **38** | 54 8 N | 10 10 W |
| Inishmaan I. | **39** | 53 5 N | 9 35 W |
| Inishmore, I. | **39** | 53 8 N | 9 45 W |
| Inishmurray I. | **38** | 54 26 N | 8 40 W |
| Inishowen Hd. | **38** | 55 14 N | 6 56 W |
| Inishowen, Pen. | **38** | 55 14 N | 7 15 W |
| Inishrush | **38** | 54 52 N | 6 32 W |
| Inishtooskert I. | **39** | 52 10 N | 10 35 W |
| Inishturk I. | **38** | 53 42 N | 10 8 W |
| Inishvickillane | **39** | 52 3 N | 10 37 W |
| Inistioge | **39** | 52 30 N | 7 5 W |
| Injune | **139** | 25 46 S | 148 32 E |
| Inkberrow | **28** | 52 13 N | 1 59 W |
| Inklin | **152** | 58 56 N | 133 5 W |
| Inklin, R. | **152** | 58 50 N | 133 10 W |
| Inkom | **160** | 42 51 N | 112 7 W |
| Inkpen Beacon | **28** | 51 22 N | 1 28 W |
| Inle Aing | **98** | 20 30 N | 96 58 E |
| Inn, R. | **49** | 48 35 N | 13 28 E |
| Innamincka | **139** | 27 44 S | 140 46 E |
| Innellan | **34** | 55 54 N | 4 58 W |
| Inner Mongolia □ | **106** | 44 50 N | 117 40 E |
| Inner Sound | **36** | 57 30 N | 5 55 W |
| Innerleithen | **35** | 55 37 N | 3 4 W |
| Innertkirchen | **50** | 46 43 N | 8 14 E |
| Innetalling I. | **150** | 56 0 N | 79 0 W |
| Innfield | **38** | 53 25 N | 6 50 W |
| Inniscrone | **38** | 54 13 N | 69 0 W |
| Innisfail, Austral. | **138** | 17 33 S | 146 5 E |
| Innisfail, Can. | **152** | 52 0 N | 113 57 W |
| Innishannon | **39** | 51 45 N | 8 40 W |
| Inniskeen | **38** | 54 0 N | 6 35 W |
| In'no-shima | **110** | 34 19 N | 133 10 E |
| Innsbruck | **52** | 47 16 N | 11 23 E |
| Ino | **110** | 33 33 N | 133 26 E |
| Inocência | **171** | 19 47 S | 51 48 W |
| Inongo | **124** | 1 35 S | 18 30 E |
| Inosu | **174** | 12 22 N | 71 38 W |
| Inoucdjouac (Port Harrison) | **149** | 58 27 N | 78 6 W |
| Inowrocław | **54** | 52 50 N | 18 20 E |
| Inpundong | **107** | 41 25 N | 126 34 E |
| Inquisivi | **174** | 16 50 S | 66 45 W |
| Ins | **50** | 47 1 N | 7 7 E |
| Insch | **37** | 57 20 N | 2 39 W |
| Inscription, C. | **137** | 25 29 S | 112 59 E |
| Insein | **98** | 17 15 N | 96 0 E |
| Însurăţei | **70** | 44 50 N | 27 40 E |
| Intendente Alvear | **172** | 35 12 S | 63 32 W |
| Interior | **158** | 43 46 N | 101 59 W |
| Interlaken, Switz. | **50** | 46 41 N | 7 50 E |
| Interlaken, U.S.A. | **162** | 42 37 N | 76 43 W |
| International Falls | **158** | 48 36 N | 93 25 W |
| Interview I. | **101** | 12 55 N | 92 42 E |
| Inthanon, Mt. | **101** | 18 35 N | 98 29 E |
| Intiyaco | **172** | 28 50 S | 60 0 W |
| Intragna | **51** | 46 11 N | 8 42 E |
| Inubō-Zaki | **111** | 35 42 N | 140 52 E |
| Inútil, B. | **176** | 53 30 S | 70 15 W |
| Inuvik | **147** | 68 16 N | 133 40 W |
| Inuyama | **111** | 35 23 N | 136 56 E |
| Inver B. | **38** | 54 35 N | 8 28 W |
| Inverallochy | **37** | 57 40 N | 1 56 W |
| Inveran, Ireland | **39** | 53 14 N | 9 28 W |
| Inveran, U.K. | **37** | 57 58 N | 4 26 W |
| Inveraray | **34** | 56 13 N | 5 5 W |
| Inverbervie | **37** | 56 50 N | 2 17 W |
| Invercargill | **143** | 46 24 S | 168 24 E |
| Inverell | **139** | 29 45 S | 151 8 E |
| Invergarry | **37** | 57 5 N | 4 48 W |
| Invergordon | **37** | 57 41 N | 4 10 W |
| Invergowrie | **35** | 56 29 N | 3 5 W |
| Inverie | **36** | 57 2 N | 5 40 W |
| Inverkeilor | **37** | 56 38 N | 2 33 W |
| Inverkeithing | **35** | 56 2 N | 3 24 W |
| Inverleigh | **140** | 38 6 S | 144 3 E |
| Invermere | **152** | 50 30 N | 116 2 W |
| Invermoriston | **37** | 57 13 N | 4 38 W |
| Inverness, Can. | **151** | 46 15 N | 61 19 W |
| Inverness, U.K. | **37** | 57 29 N | 4 12 W |
| Inverness, U.S.A. | **157** | 28 50 N | 82 20 W |
| Inverness (□) | **26** | 57 6 N | 4 40 W |
| Invershiel | **36** | 57 13 N | 5 25 W |
| Inverurie | **37** | 57 15 N | 2 21 W |
| Inverway | **136** | 17 50 S | 129 38 E |
| Investigator Group | **136** | 34 45 S | 134 20 E |
| Investigator Str. | **140** | 35 30 S | 137 0 E |
| Inyanga | **127** | 18 12 S | 32 40 E |
| Inyangahi, mt. | **127** | 18 20 S | 32 20 E |
| Inyantue | **127** | 18 30 S | 26 40 E |
| Inyazura | **127** | 18 40 S | 31 40 E |
| Inyo Range | **161** | 37 0 N | 118 0 W |
| Inyokern | **163** | 35 37 N | 117 54 W |
| Inywa | **98** | 22 4 N | 94 44 E |
| Inza | **81** | 53 55 N | 46 25 E |
| Inzell | **49** | 47 48 N | 12 15 E |
| Inzer | **84** | 54 14 N | 57 34 E |
| Inzhavino | **81** | 52 22 N | 42 23 E |
| Ioánnina (Janinà) □ | **68** | 39 39 N | 20 57 E |
| Iōhen | **110** | 32 58 N | 132 32 E |
| Iola | **159** | 38 0 N | 95 20 W |
| Ioma | **135** | 8 19 S | 147 52 E |
| Ion Corvin | **70** | 44 7 N | 27 50 E |
| Iona I. | **34** | 56 20 N | 6 25 W |
| Ionava | **80** | 55 8 N | 24 12 E |
| Ione, Calif., U.S.A. | **163** | 38 20 N | 121 0 W |
| Ione, Wash., U.S.A. | **160** | 48 44 N | 117 29 W |
| Ionia | **156** | 42 59 N | 85 7 W |
| Ionian Is. = Ionioi Nisoi | **69** | 38 40 N | 20 0 E |
| Ionian Sea | **61** | 37 30 N | 17 30 E |
| Iónioi Nísoi | **69** | 38 40 N | 20 8 E |
| Ioniškis | **80** | 56 13 N | 23 35 E |
| Iori, R. | **83** | 41 12 N | 46 10 E |
| Ios, I. | **69** | 36 41 N | 25 20 E |
| Iowa □ | **158** | 42 18 N | 93 30 W |
| Iowa City | **158** | 41 40 N | 91 35 W |
| Iowa Falls | **158** | 42 30 N | 93 15 W |
| Ipala | **126** | 4 30 S | 33 5 E |
| Ipameri | **171** | 17 44 S | 48 9 W |
| Ipanema | **75** | 9 48 S | 41 45 W |
| Ipáti | **69** | 38 52 N | 22 14 E |
| Ipatovo | **83** | 45 45 N | 42 50 E |
| Ipel, R. | **53** | 48 10 N | 19 35 E |
| Ipiales | **174** | 0 50 N | 77 37 W |
| Ipiaú | **171** | 14 8 S | 39 44 W |
| Ipin | **108** | 28 48 N | 104 33 E |
| Ipinlang | **108** | 25 5 N | 101 58 E |
| Ipirá | **171** | 12 10 S | 39 44 W |
| Ipiros □ | **68** | 39 30 N | 20 30 E |
| Ipixuna | **174** | 7 0 S | 71 40 W |
| Ipoh | **101** | 4 35 N | 101 5 E |
| Iporá | **171** | 16 28 S | 51 7 W |
| Ippy | **117** | 6 5 N | 21 7 E |
| Ipsárion Óros | **68** | 40 40 N | 24 40 E |
| Ipswich, Austral. | **139** | 27 35 S | 152 46 E |
| Ipswich, U.K. | **29** | 52 4 N | 1 9 E |
| Ipswich, N.H., U.S.A. | **162** | 42 40 N | 70 50 W |
| Ipswich, S.D., U.S.A. | **158** | 45 28 N | 99 20 W |
| Ipu | **170** | 4 23 S | 40 44 W |
| Ipueiras | **170** | 4 33 S | 40 43 W |
| Ipupiara | **171** | 11 49 S | 42 37 W |
| Iput, R. | **80** | 53 0 N | 32 10 E |
| Iquique | **174** | 20 19 S | 70 5 W |
| Iquitos | **174** | 3 45 S | 73 10 W |
| Iracoubo | **175** | 5 30 N | 53 10 W |
| Iráklia, I. | **69** | 36 50 N | 25 28 E |
| Iráklion | **69** | 35 20 N | 25 12 E |
| Iráklion □ | **69** | 35 10 N | 25 10 E |
| Irako-Zaki | **111** | 34 35 N | 137 1 E |
| Irala | **173** | 25 55 S | 54 35 W |
| Iramba □ | **126** | 4 30 S | 34 30 E |
| Iran ■ | **93** | 33 0 N | 53 0 E |
| Iran, Pegunungan | **102** | 2 20 N | 114 50 E |
| Iran, Plateau of | **43** | 33 00 N | 55 0 E |
| Iranamadu Tank | **97** | 9 23 N | 80 29 E |
| Iranshahr | **93** | 27 75 N | 60 40 E |
| Irapa | **174** | 10 34 N | 62 35 W |
| Irapuato | **164** | 20 40 N | 101 40 W |
| Iraq ■ | **92** | 33 0 N | 44 0 E |
| Irarrar, W. | **118** | 20 10 N | 1 30 E |
| Irati | **173** | 25 25 S | 50 38 W |
| Irbid | **90** | 32 35 N | 35 48 E |
| Irbit | **84** | 57 41 N | 63 3 E |
| Irchester | **29** | 52 17 N | 0 40 W |
| Irebu | **124** | 0 40 S | 17 55 E |
| Irecê | **170** | 11 18 S | 41 52 W |
| Iregua, R. | **58** | 42 22 N | 2 24 E |
| Ireland ■ | **38** | 53 0 N | 8 0 W |
| Ireland's Eye | **38** | 53 25 N | 6 4 W |
| Irele | **121** | 7 40 N | 5 40 E |
| Iremel, Gora | **84** | 54 33 N | 58 50 E |
| Iret | **77** | 60 10 N | 154 5 E |
| Irgiz, Bol. | **81** | 52 10 N | 49 10 E |
| Irharharene | **119** | 27 37 N | 7 30 E |
| Irharrhar, O. | **119** | 27 30 N | 6 0 E |
| Irhyangdong | **107** | 41 15 N | 129 30 E |
| Iri | **107** | 35 59 N | 127 0 E |
| Irian Jaya □ | **103** | 4 0 S | 137 0 E |
| Iriba | **124** | 15 7 N | 22 15 E |
| Irié | **120** | 8 15 N | 9 10 W |
| Iriklinskiy | **84** | 51 39 N | 58 38 E |
| Iringa | **126** | 7 48 S | 35 43 E |
| Iringa □, Tanz. | **126** | 7 48 S | 35 43 E |
| Iringa □, Tanz. | **127** | 9 0 S | 35 0 E |
| Irinjalakuda | **97** | 10 21 N | 76 14 E |
| Iriomote-Jima | **112** | 24 19 N | 123 48 E |
| Iriona | **166** | 15 57 N | 85 11 W |
| Irish Sea | **32** | 54 0 N | 5 0 W |
| Irish Town | **93** | 40 55 S | 145 9 E |
| Irkeshtam | **85** | 39 41 N | 73 55 E |
| Irkutsk | **77** | 52 10 N | 104 20 E |
| Irlam | **32** | 53 26 N | 2 27 W |
| Irma | **153** | 52 55 N | 111 14 W |
| Irmak | **92** | 39 58 N | 33 25 E |
| Irō-Zaki | **111** | 34 36 N | 138 51 E |
| Iroise | **42** | 48 15 N | 4 45 W |
| Iron Baron | **140** | 33 3 S | 137 11 E |
| Iron Gate = Porţile de Fier | **70** | 44 42 N | 22 30 E |
| Iron Knob | **140** | 32 46 S | 137 8 E |
| Iron, L. | **38** | 53 37 N | 7 34 W |
| Iron Mountain | **156** | 45 49 N | 88 4 W |
| Iron River | **158** | 46 6 N | 88 40 W |
| Ironbridge | **28** | 52 38 N | 2 29 W |
| Ironhurst | **138** | 18 5 S | 143 28 E |
| Ironstone Kopje, Mt. | **128** | 25 17 S | 24 5 E |
| Ironton, Mo., U.S.A. | **159** | 37 40 N | 90 40 W |
| Ironton, Ohio, U.S.A. | **156** | 38 35 N | 82 40 W |
| Ironwood | **158** | 46 30 N | 90 10 W |
| Iroquois Falls | **150** | 48 46 N | 80 41 W |
| Irpen | **80** | 50 30 N | 30 8 E |
| Irrara Cr. | **139** | 29 35 S | 145 31 E |
| Irrawaddy | **98** | 17 0 N | 95 0 E |
| Irrawaddy □ | **98** | 17 0 N | 95 0 E |
| Irrawaddy, R. | **98** | 15 50 N | 95 6 E |
| Irsina | **65** | 40 45 N | 16 15 E |
| Irt R. | **32** | 54 24 N | 3 25 W |
| Irthing R. | **35** | 54 25 N | 2 48 W |
| Irthlingborough | **29** | 52 20 N | 0 37 W |
| Irtysh, R. | **76** | 53 36 N | 75 30 E |
| Irumu | **126** | 1 32 N | 29 53 E |
| Irún | **58** | 43 20 N | 1 52 W |
| Irurzun | **58** | 42 55 N | 1 50 W |
| Irvine, Can. | **153** | 49 57 N | 110 16 W |
| Irvine, U.K. | **34** | 55 37 N | 4 40 W |
| Irvine, U.S.A. | **156** | 37 42 N | 83 58 W |
| Irvinestown | **38** | 54 28 N | 7 38 W |
| Irwin, Pt. | **137** | 35 5 S | 116 55 E |
| Irwin, R. | **137** | 29 15 S | 114 54 E |
| Irymple | **140** | 34 14 S | 142 8 E |
| Is-sur-Tille | **43** | 47 30 N | 5 10 E |
| Isa | **121** | 13 14 N | 6 24 E |
| Isaac, R. | **138** | 22 55 S | 149 20 E |
| Isabel | **158** | 45 27 N | 101 22 W |
| Isabela, Dom. Rep. | **167** | 19 58 N | 71 2 W |
| Isabela, Pto Rico | **147** | 18 30 N | 67 01 W |
| Isabela, Cord. | **166** | 13 30 N | 85 25 W |
| Isabela, I. | **164** | 21 51 N | 105 55 W |
| Isabella Ra. | **136** | 21 0 S | 121 4 E |
| Ísafjarðardjúp | **74** | 66 10 N | 23 0 W |
| Ísafjörður | **74** | 66 5 N | 23 9 W |
| Isagarh | **94** | 24 48 N | 77 51 E |
| Isahaya | **110** | 32 52 N | 130 2 E |
| Isaka | **126** | 3 56 S | 32 59 E |
| Isakly | **84** | 54 8 N | 51 32 E |
| Isangi | **124** | 0 52 N | 24 10 E |
| Isar, R. | **49** | 48 40 N | 12 30 E |
| Isarco, R. | **63** | 46 40 N | 11 35 E |
| Isari | **69** | 37 22 N | 22 0 E |
| Isbergues | **43** | 50 36 N | 2 24 E |
| Isbiceni | **70** | 43 45 N | 24 40 E |
| Ischia, I. | **64** | 40 45 N | 13 51 E |
| Iscuandé | **174** | 2 28 N | 77 59 W |
| Isdell, R. | **136** | 16 27 S | 124 51 E |
| Ise | **111** | 34 25 N | 136 45 E |
| Ise-Heiya | **111** | 34 40 N | 136 30 E |
| Ise-Wan | **111** | 34 43 N | 136 43 E |
| Isefjord | **73** | 55 53 N | 11 50 E |
| Iseltwald | **50** | 46 43 N | 7 58 E |
| Isenthal | **51** | 46 55 N | 8 34 E |
| Iseo | **62** | 45 40 N | 10 3 E |
| Iseo, L. di | **62** | 45 45 N | 10 3 E |
| Iseramagazi | **126** | 4 37 S | 32 10 E |
| Isère □ | **45** | 45 15 N | 5 40 E |
| Isère, R. | **44** | 45 15 N | 5 30 E |
| Iserlohn | **48** | 51 22 N | 7 40 E |
| Isérnia | **65** | 41 35 N | 14 12 E |
| Isesaki | **111** | 36 19 N | 139 12 E |
| Iset, R. | **84** | 56 36 N | 66 24 E |
| Iseyin | **121** | 8 0 N | 3 36 E |
| Isfara | **85** | 40 7 N | 70 38 E |
| Ishan | **108** | 24 30 N | 108 41 E |
| Ishara | **121** | 6 40 N | 3 40 E |
| Ishigaki | **112** | 24 20 N | 124 10 E |
| Ishikari-Wan | **112** | 43 20 N | 141 20 E |
| Ishikawa | **112** | 26 25 N | 127 48 E |
| Ishikawa-ken □ | **111** | 36 30 N | 136 30 E |
| Ishim | **76** | 56 10 N | 69 18 E |
| Ishim, R. | **76** | 57 45 N | 71 10 E |
| Ishimbay | **84** | 53 28 N | 56 2 E |
| Ishinomaki | **112** | 38 32 N | 141 20 E |
| Ishioka | **111** | 36 11 N | 140 16 E |
| Ishizuchi-Yama | **110** | 33 45 N | 133 6 E |
| Ishkashim | **85** | 36 44 N | 71 37 E |
| Ishkuman | **95** | 36 30 N | 73 50 E |
| Ishmi | **68** | 41 33 N | 19 34 E |
| Ishpeming | **156** | 46 30 N | 87 40 W |
| Ishua | **121** | 7 15 N | 5 50 E |
| Ishui | **107** | 35 50 N | 118 32 E |
| Ishurdi | **98** | 24 9 N | 89 3 E |
| Isigny-sur-Mer | **42** | 49 19 N | 1 6 W |
| Işik | **82** | 40 40 N | 32 35 E |
| Isil Kul | **76** | 54 55 N | 71 16 E |
| Isili | **44** | 39 45 N | 9 6 E |
| Isiolo | **126** | 0 24 N | 37 33 E |
| Isipingo | **129** | 30 00 S | 30 57 E |
| Isipingo Beach | **129** | 30 00 S | 30 57 E |
| Isiro | **126** | 2 53 N | 27 58 E |
| Iskander | **85** | 41 36 N | 69 41 E |
| İskenderun | **92** | 36 32 N | 36 10 E |
| İskilip | **82** | 40 50 N | 34 20 E |
| Iskut, R. | **152** | 56 45 N | 131 49 W |
| Iskyr, R. | **67** | 43 35 N | 24 20 E |
| Isla Cristina | **57** | 37 13 N | 7 17 W |
| Isla, La | **174** | 6 51 N | 76 56 W |
| Isla, R. | **37** | 56 32 N | 3 20 W |
| Islamabad | **94** | 33 40 N | 73 0 E |
| Islamkot | **94** | 24 42 N | 70 13 E |
| Islampur | **96** | 17 2 N | 72 9 E |
| Island Falls, Can. | **150** | 49 35 N | 81 20 W |
| Island Falls, U.S.A. | **151** | 46 0 N | 68 25 W |
| Island L. | **153** | 53 47 N | 94 25 W |
| Island Lagoon | **140** | 31 30 S | 136 40 E |
| Island Pt. | **137** | 30 20 S | 115 1 E |
| Island Pond | **156** | 44 50 N | 71 50 W |
| Island, R. | **152** | 60 25 N | 121 12 W |
| Islands, B. of, Can. | **151** | 49 11 N | 58 15 W |
| Islands, B. of, N.Z. | **142** | 35 20 S | 174 20 E |
| Islay, I. | **34** | 55 46 N | 6 10 W |
| Islay Sound | **34** | 55 45 N | 6 5 W |
| Isle-Adam, L' | **43** | 49 6 N | 2 14 E |
| Isle aux Morts | **151** | 47 35 N | 59 0 W |
| Isle-Jourdain, L', Gers, France | **44** | 43 36 N | 1 5 E |
| Isle-Jourdain, L', Vienne, France | **42** | 46 13 N | 0 31 E |
| Isle, L', Tarn, France | **44** | 43 52 N | 1 49 E |
| Isle, L', Vaucluse, France | **45** | 43 55 N | 5 3 E |
| Isle of Whithorn | **34** | 54 42 N | 4 22 W |
| Isle of Wight □ | **28** | 50 40 N | 1 20 W |
| Isle Ornsay | **36** | 57 9 N | 5 50 W |
| Isle Royale | **158** | 48 0 N | 88 50 W |
| Isle-sur-la-Sorgue, L' | **45** | 43 55 N | 5 2 E |
| Isle-sur-le-Doubs, L' | **43** | 47 26 N | 6 34 E |
| Isle Vista | **163** | 34 27 N | 119 52 W |
| Isleham | **29** | 52 21 N | 0 24 E |
| Islet, L' | **151** | 47 4 N | 70 23 W |
| Isleta | **161** | 34 58 N | 106 46 W |
| Isleton | **163** | 38 10 N | 121 37 W |
| Islip | **28** | 51 49 N | 1 12 W |
| Ismail | **82** | 45 22 N | 28 46 E |
| Ismâ'ilîya | **122** | 30 37 N | 32 18 E |
| Ismay | **158** | 46 33 N | 104 44 W |
| Isna | **122** | 25 17 N | 32 30 E |
| Isogstalo | **95** | 34 15 N | 78 46 E |
| Isola del Liri | **64** | 41 39 N | 13 32 E |
| Isola della Scala | **62** | 45 16 N | 11 0 E |
| Isola di Capo Rizzuto | **65** | 38 56 N | 17 5 E |
| Isparta | **92** | 37 47 N | 30 30 E |
| Isperikh | **67** | 43 43 N | 26 50 E |
| Ispica | **65** | 36 47 N | 14 53 E |
| Israel ■ | **90** | 32 0 N | 34 50 E |
| Isseka | **137** | 28 22 S | 114 35 E |
| Issia | **120** | 6 33 N | 3 50 W |
| Issoire | **44** | 45 32 N | 3 15 E |
| Issoudun | **43** | 46 57 N | 2 0 E |
| Issyk-Kul, Ozero | **85** | 42 25 N | 77 15 E |
| İstanbul | **92** | 41 0 N | 29 0 E |
| Istmina | **174** | 5 10 N | 76 39 W |
| Istok | **66** | 42 45 N | 20 24 E |
| Istokpoga, L. | **157** | 27 22 N | 81 14 W |
| Istra, U.S.S.R. | **81** | 55 55 N | 36 50 E |
| Istra, Yugo. | **63** | 45 10 N | 14 0 E |
| Istranca Dağlari | **67** | 41 48 N | 27 30 E |
| Istres | **45** | 43 31 N | 4 59 E |
| Istria = Istra | **63** | 45 10 N | 14 0 E |
| Itá | **172** | 25 29 N | 57 21 W |
| Itabaiana, Paraíba, Brazil | **170** | 7 18 S | 35 19 W |
| Itabaiana, Sergipe, Brazil | **170** | 10 41 S | 37 26 W |
| Itabaianinha | **170** | 11 16 S | 37 47 W |
| Itaberaba | **171** | 12 32 S | 40 18 W |
| Itaberaí | **171** | 16 2 S | 49 48 W |
| Itabira | **171** | 19 37 S | 43 13 W |
| Itabirito | **173** | 20 15 S | 43 48 W |
| Itabuna | **171** | 14 48 S | 39 16 W |
| Itacaiunas, R. | **170** | 5 21 S | 49 8 W |
| Itacajá | **170** | 8 19 S | 47 46 W |
| Itaete | **171** | 13 0 S | 41 5 W |
| Itaguaçu | **171** | 19 48 S | 40 51 W |
| Itaguari, R. | **171** | 14 11 S | 44 40 W |
| Itaguatins | **170** | 5 47 S | 47 29 W |
| Itaim, R. | **170** | 7 2 S | 42 2 W |
| Itainópolis | **170** | 7 24 S | 41 31 W |
| Itaituba | **175** | 4 10 S | 55 50 W |
| Itajaí | **173** | 27 0 S | 48 45 W |
| Itajubá | **173** | 22 24 S | 45 30 W |
| Itajuípe | **171** | 14 41 S | 39 22 W |
| Itaka | **127** | 8 50 S | 32 49 E |
| Itako | **111** | 35 56 N | 140 33 E |
| Italy ■ | **60** | 42 0 N | 13 0 E |
| Itamataré | **170** | 2 16 S | 46 24 W |
| Itambacuri | **171** | 18 1 S | 41 42 W |
| Itambé | **171** | 15 15 S | 40 37 W |
| Itambe, mt. | **170** | 18 30 S | 43 15 W |
| Itampolo | **129** | 24 41 S | 43 57 E |
| Itanhaém | **121** | 24 9 S | 46 47 W |
| Itanhém | **171** | 17 9 S | 40 20 W |
| Itano | **110** | 34 1 N | 134 28 E |
| Itapaci | **171** | 14 57 S | 49 34 W |
| Itapagé | **170** | 3 41 S | 39 34 W |
| Itaparica, I. de | **171** | 12 54 S | 38 42 W |
| Itapebi | **171** | 15 56 S | 39 32 W |
| Itapecerica | **171** | 20 28 S | 45 7 W |
| Itapecuru-Mirim | **170** | 3 24 S | 44 20 W |
| Itapecuru, R. | **170** | 3 20 S | 44 15 W |
| Itaperuna | **171** | 21 10 S | 42 0 W |
| Itapetinga | **171** | 15 15 S | 40 15 W |
| Itapetininga | **173** | 23 36 S | 48 7 W |
| Itapeva | **173** | 23 59 S | 48 59 W |
| Itapicuru | **170** | 10 50 S | 38 40 W |
| Itapicuru, R. | **170** | 5 40 S | 44 30 W |
| Itapipoca | **170** | 3 30 S | 39 35 W |
| Itapiúna | **170** | 4 33 S | 38 57 W |
| Itaporanga | **171** | 7 18 S | 38 10 W |
| Itapuá □ | **173** | 26 40 S | 55 40 W |
| Itapuranga | **171** | 15 35 S | 49 59 W |
| Itaquari | **173** | 20 12 S | 40 25 W |
| Itaquatiana | **174** | 2 58 S | 58 30 W |
| Itaquí | **172** | 29 0 S | 56 30 W |
| Itararé | **173** | 24 6 S | 49 23 W |
| Itarsi | **94** | 22 36 N | 77 51 E |
| Itarumã | **171** | 18 42 S | 51 25 W |
| Itati | **172** | 27 16 S | 58 15 W |
| Itatira | **170** | 4 30 S | 39 37 W |
| Itatuba | **174** | 5 40 S | 63 20 W |
| Itaueira | **170** | 7 36 S | 43 2 W |

Itaueira, R Jedrzejów

Itaueira, R. 170 6 41S 42 55W
Itaúna 171 20 4S 44 34W
Itchen, R. 28 50 57N 1 20W
Itéa 69 38 25N 22 25E
Ithaca 162 42 25N 76 30W
Ithaca = Itháki 69 38 25N 20 43E
Itháki, I. 69 38 25N 20 40E
Ithon R. 31 52 16N 3 23W
It'iaoshan 106 37 10N 104 2E
Itinga 171 16 36S 41 47W
Itiruçu 171 13 31S 40 9W
Itiúba 171 10 43S 39 51W
Ito 111 34 58N 139 5E
Itonamas, R. 174 13 0S 64 25W
Itsa 122 29 15N 30 40E
Itsukaichi 110 34 22N 132 8E
Itsuki 110 32 24N 130 50E
Itteville 46 48 31N 2 21E
Ittiri 64 40 38N 8 32E
Itu, Brazil 173 23 10S 47 15W
Itu, Hupeh, China 109 30 24N 111 26E
Itu, Shantung, China 107 36 41N 118 28E
Itu, Nigeria 121 5 10N 7 58E
Ituaçu 171 13 50S 41 18W
Ituango 174 7 4N 75 45W
Ituiutaba 171 19 0S 49 25W
Itumbiara 171 18 20S 49 10W
Ituna 153 51 10N 103 30W
It'ung 107 43 20N 125 17E
Itunge Port 127 9 40S 33 55E
Itupiranga 170 5 9S 49 20W
Iturama 171 19 44S 50 11W
Iturbe 172 23 0S 65 25W
Ituri, R. 126 1 45N 26 45E
Iturup, Ostrov 77 45 0N 148 0E
Ituverava 171 20 20S 47 47W
Ituyuro, R. 172 22 40S 63 50W
Itzehoe 48 53 56N 9 31E
Ivalo 74 68 38N 27 35E
Ivalojoki 74 68 30N 27 0E
Ivanaj 68 42 17N 19 25E
Ivanhoe, N.S.W., Austral. 140 32 56S 144 20E
Ivanhoe, N.T., Austral. 136 15 41S 128 41E
Ivanhoe, U.S.A. 163 36 23N 119 13W
Ivanhoe L. 153 60 25N 106 30W
Ivanió Grad 63 45 41N 16 25E
Ivanjica 66 43 35N 20 12E
Ivanjscie 63 46 12N 16 13E
Ivankovskoye Vdkhr. 81 56 48N 36 55E
Ivano-Frankovsk, (Stanislav) 80 49 0N 24 40E
Ivanovka 84 52 34N 53 23E
Ivanovo, Byelorussia, U.S.S.R. 80 52 7N 25 29E
Ivanovo, R.S.F.S.R., U.S.S.R. 81 57 5N 41 0E
Ivato 129 20 37S 47 10E
Ivaylovgrad 67 41 32N 26 8E
Ivinghoe 29 51 50N 0 38W
Ivinheima, R. 173 21 48S 54 15W
Iviza = Ibiza 59 39 0N 1 30E
Ivohibe 129 22 31S 46 57E
Ivolândia 171 16 34S 50 51W
Ivory Coast ■ 120 7 30N 5 0W
Ivösjön 73 56 8N 14 25E
Ivrea 62 45 30N 7 52E
Ivugivik, (N.D. d'Ivugivic) 149 62 24N 77 55W
Ivybridge 30 50 24N 3 56W
Iwahig 102 8 35N 117 32E
Iwai-Jima 110 33 47N 131 58E
Iwaki 112 37 3N 140 55E
Iwakuni 110 34 15N 132 8E
Iwami 110 35 32N 134 15E
Iwamisawa 112 43 12N 141 46E
Iwanai 112 42 58N 140 30E
Iwanuma 112 38 7N 140 58E
Iwase 110 36 21N 140 6E
Iwata 111 34 49N 137 59E
Iwate-ken □ 112 39 30N 141 30E
Iwate-San 112 39 51N 141 0E
Iwo 121 7 39N 4 9E
Iwonicz-Zdroj 54 49 37N 21 47E
Ixiamas 174 13 50S 68 5W
Ixopo 129 30 11S 30 5E
Ixtepec 165 16 40N 95 10W
Ixtlán de Juárez 165 17 23N 96 28W
Ixtlán del Rio 164 21 5N 104 28W
Ixworth 29 52 18N 0 50E
Iyang, Honan, China 106 34 9N 112 25E
Iyang, Hunan, China 109 28 36N 112 20E
Iyang, Kiangsi, China 109 28 23N 117 25E
Iyo 110 33 45N 132 45E
Iyo-mishima 110 33 58N 133 30E
Iyo-Nada 110 33 40N 132 20E
Izabal, L. 166 15 30N 89 10W
Izamal 165 20 56N 89 1W
Izberbash 83 42 35N 47 45E
Izbica Kujawski 54 52 25N 18 30E
Izegem 47 50 55N 3 12E
Izgrev 67 43 36N 26 58E
Izh, R. 84 55 58N 52 38E
Izhevsk 84 56 51N 53 14E
Izmail 82 45 22N 28 46E
Izmir (Smyrna) 79 38 25N 27 8E
Izmit 92 40 45N 29 50E
Izola 63 45 32N 13 39E
Izu-Hantō 111 34 45N 139 0E
Izuhara 110 34 12N 129 17E
Izumi 110 32 5N 130 22E
Izumiotsu 111 34 30N 135 24E
Izumisano 111 34 40N 135 43E
Izumo 110 35 20N 132 55E
Izyaslav 80 50 5N 25 50E
Izyum 82 49 12N 37 28E

## J

Jaba 123 6 20N 35 7E
Jaba' 90 32 20N 35 13E
Jabaliya 90 31 32N 34 27E
Jabalón, R. 59 38 45N 3 35W
Jabalpur 95 23 9N 79 58E
Jablah 92 35 20N 36 0E
Jablanac 63 44 42N 14 56E
Jablonec 52 50 43N 15 10E
Jablonica 53 48 37N 17 26E
Jabłonowo 54 53 23N 19 10E
Jaboatão 170 8 7S 35 1W
Jaboticabal 173 21 15S 48 17W
Jabukovac 66 44 22N 22 21E
Jaburu 174 5 30S 64 0W
Jaca 58 42 35N 0 33W
Jacala 165 21 1N 99 11W
Jacaré, R. 170 10 3S 42 13W
Jacareí 173 23 20S 46 0W
Jacarèzinho 173 23 5S 50 0W
Jáchal 172 30 5S 69 0W
Jáchymov 52 50 22N 12 55E
Jacinto 171 16 10S 40 17W
Jack Lane B. 151 55 45N 60 35W
Jackfish 150 48 45N 87 0W
Jackman 151 45 35N 70 17W
Jacksboro 159 33 14N 98 15W
Jackson, Austral. 139 26 39S 149 39E
Jackson, Ala., U.S.A. 157 31 32N 87 53W
Jackson, Calif., U.S.A. 159 37 25N 89 42W
Jackson, Ill., U.S.A. 163 38 25N 120 47W
Jackson, Ky., U.S.A. 156 37 35N 83 22W
Jackson, Mich., U.S.A. 156 42 18N 84 25W
Jackson, Minn., U.S.A. 158 43 35N 95 30W
Jackson, Miss., U.S.A. 159 32 20N 90 10W
Jackson, Ohio, U.S.A. 156 39 0N 82 40W
Jackson, Tenn., U.S.A. 157 35 40N 88 50W
Jackson, Wyo., U.S.A. 160 43 30N 110 49W
Jackson Bay, Can. 152 50 32N 125 57W
Jackson Bay, N.Z. 143 43 58S 168 42E
Jackson, C. 143 40 59S 174 20E
Jackson, L. 160 43 55N 110 40W
Jacksons 143 42 46S 171 32E
Jacksonville, Ala., U.S.A. 157 33 49N 85 45W
Jacksonville, Calif., U.S.A. 163 37 52N 120 24W
Jacksonville, Fla., U.S.A. 157 30 15N 81 38W
Jacksonville, Ill., U.S.A. 158 39 42N 90 15W
Jacksonville, N.C., U.S.A. 157 34 50N 77 29W
Jacksonville, Oreg., U.S.A. 160 42 13N 122 56W
Jacksonville, Tex., U.S.A. 159 31 58N 95 12W
Jacksonville Beach 157 30 19N 81 26W
Jacmel 167 18 20N 72 40W
Jacob Lake 161 36 45N 112 12W
Jacobabad 94 28 20N 68 29E
Jacobeni 70 47 25N 25 20E
Jacobina 170 11 11S 40 30W
Jacob's Well 90 32 13N 35 13E
Jacques Cartier, Mt. 151 48 57N 66 0W
Jacques Cartier Pass 151 49 50N 62 30W
Jacqueville 120 5 12N 4 25W
Jacuí, R. 173 30 2S 51 15W
Jacuipe, R. 171 12 30S 39 5W
Jacundá, R. 170 1 57S 50 26W
Jade 48 53 22N 8 14E
Jadebusen, B. 48 53 30N 8 15E
Jadoigne 47 50 43N 4 52E
Jadotville = Likasi 127 10 55S 26 48E
Jadovnik 66 43 20N 19 45E
Jadraque 58 40 55N 2 55W
Jädū 119 32 0N 12 0E
Jaén, Peru 174 5 25S 78 40W
Jaén, Spain 57 37 44N 3 43W
Jaén □ 57 37 50N 3 30W
Jafène 118 20 35N 5 30W
Jaffa = Tel Aviv-Yafo 90 32 4N 34 48E
Jaffa, C. 140 36 58S 139 40E
Jaffna 97 9 45N 80 2E
Jaffrey 162 42 50N 72 4W
Jagadhri 94 30 10N 77 20E
Jagadishpur 95 25 30N 84 21E
Jagdalpur 96 19 3N 82 6E
Jagersfontein 128 29 44S 25 27E
Jaghbub 117 29 42N 24 38E
Jagraon 93 30 50N 75 25E
Jagst, R. 49 49 13N 10 0E
Jagtial 96 18 50N 79 0E
Jaguaquara 171 13 32S 39 58W
Jaguariaiva 173 24 10S 49 50W
Jaguaribe 170 5 53S 38 37W
Jaguaribe, R. 170 6 0S 38 35W
Jaguaruana 170 4 50S 37 47W
Jagüey 166 22 35N 81 7W
Jagungal, Mt. 141 36 8S 148 22E
Jahangirabad 94 28 19N 78 4E
Jahrom 92 28 30N 53 31E
Jaicós 170 7 21S 41 8W
Jainti 98 26 45N 89 40E
Jaintiapur 98 25 8N 92 7E
Jaipur 94 27 0N 76 10E
Jajarm 93 37 5N 56 20E
Jajce 66 44 19N 17 17E
Jajere 121 11 58N 11 25E
Jajpur 96 20 53N 86 22E
Jakarta 103 6 9S 106 49E
Jakobstad (Pietarsaari) 74 63 40N 22 43E
Jakupica 66 41 45N 21 22E
Jal 159 32 8N 103 8W
Jala 93 27 30N 62 40E
Jalalabad, Afghan. 94 34 30N 70 29E
Jalalabad, India 95 26 41N 79 42E
Jalalpur Jattan 94 32 38N 74 19E
Jalama 163 34 29N 120 29W
Jalapa, Guat. 166 14 45N 89 59W
Jalapa, Mexico 165 19 30N 96 50W
Jalas, Jabal al 92 27 30N 36 30E
Jalaun 95 26 8N 79 25E
Jales 171 20 16S 50 33W
Jaleswar 95 26 38N 85 48E
Jalgaon, Maharashtra, India 96 21 2N 76 31E
Jalgaon, Maharashtra, India 96 21 0N 75 42E
Jalhay 47 50 33N 5 58E
Jalingo 121 8 55N 11 25E
Jalisco □ 164 20 0N 104 0W
Jalkot 95 35 20N 73 24E
Jallas, R. 56 42 57N 9 0W
Jallumba 140 36 55N 141 57E
Jalna 96 19 48N 75 57E
Jalón, R. 58 41 20N 1 40W
Jalpa 164 21 38N 102 58W
Jalpaiguri 98 26 32N 88 46E
Jalq 93 27 35N 62 33E
Jaluit I. 130 6 0N 169 30E
Jamaari 121 11 44N 9 53E
Jamaica, I. ■ 166 18 10N 77 30W
Jamalpur, Bangla. 98 24 52N 90 2E
Jamalpur, India 95 25 18N 86 28E
Jamalpurganj 95 23 2N 88 1E
Jamanxim, R. 175 6 30S 55 50W
Jambe 103 1 15S 132 10E
Jambes 47 50 27N 4 52E
Jambi 102 1 38S 103 30E
Jambusar 94 22 3N 72 51E
Jamdena, I. = Yamdena 103 7 45S 131 20E
James B. 150 53 30N 80 0W
James, R., Dak., U.S.A. 158 44 50N 98 0W
James, R., Va., U.S.A. 162 37 0N 76 27W
James Ranges 136 24 10S 132 0E
James Ross I. 13 63 58S 50 94W
Jamestown, Austral. 140 33 10S 138 32E
Jamestown, S. Afr. 128 31 6S 26 45E
Jamestown, Ky., U.S.A. 156 37 0N 85 5W
Jamestown, N.D., U.S.A. 158 47 0N 98 30W
Jamestown, N.Y., U.S.A. 156 42 5N 79 18W
Jamestown, Tenn., U.S.A. 157 36 25N 85 0W
Jamestown, Va., U.S.A. 162 37 12N 76 46W
Jamiltepec 165 16 17N 97 49W
Jamkhandi 97 16 30N 75 15E
Jamma'in 90 32 8N 35 12E
Jammalamadugu 97 14 51N 78 25E
Jammerbugt 73 57 15N 9 20E
Jammu 94 32 43N 74 54E
Jammu & Kashmir □ 95 34 25N 77 0E
Jamnagar 94 22 30N 70 0E
Jamner 96 20 45N 75 45E
Jamoigne 47 49 41N 5 24E
Jampur 94 29 39N 70 32E
Jamrud 94 34 2N 71 24E
Jamshedpur 95 22 44N 86 20E
Jamtara 95 23 59N 86 41E
Jämtlands län □ 72 62 40N 13 50E
Jamuna, R. 98 23 51N 89 45E
Jamurki 98 24 9N 90 2E
Jan Kemp 128 27 55S 24 51E
Jan L. 153 54 56N 102 55W
Jan Mayen Is. 12 71 0N 11 0W
Janaúba 171 15 48S 43 19W
Janaucu, I. 170 0 30N 50 10W
Jand 94 33 30N 72 0E
Janda, Laguna de la 57 36 15N 5 45W
Jandaia 171 17 6S 50 7W
Jandaq 92 34 3N 54 22E
Jandola 94 32 20N 70 9E
Jandowae 139 26 45S 151 7E
Jandrain-Jandrenouilles 47 50 40N 4 58E
Jándula, R. 57 38 25N 3 55W
Jane Pk. 142 45 15S 168 20E
Janesville 158 42 39N 89 1W
Janga 121 10 5N 1 0W
Jangaon 96 17 44N 79 5E
Janhtang Ga 98 26 32N 96 38E
Jani Khel 93 32 45N 68 25E
Janja 66 44 40N 19 17E
Janjevo 66 42 35N 21 19E
Janjina 66 42 58N 17 25E
Janos 164 30 45N 108 10W
Jánoshalma 53 46 18N 19 21E
Jánosháza 53 47 8N 17 12E
Jánossomorja 53 47 47N 17 11E
Janów 54 50 43N 22 30E
Janów Lubelski 54 50 48N 22 23E
Janów Podlaski 54 52 11N 23 11E
Janowiec Wlkp. 54 52 45N 17 30E
Januária 171 15 25S 44 25W
Janub Dârfûr □ 123 11 0N 25 0E
Janub Kordofân □ 123 12 0N 30 0E
Janville 43 48 10N 1 50E
Janzé 42 47 55N 1 28W
Jaop'ing 109 23 43N 117 0E
Jaora 94 23 40N 75 10E
Jaoyang 106 38 14N 115 44E
Japan ■ 112 36 0N 136 0E
Japan, Sea of 112 40 0N 135 0E
Japan Trench 142 28 0N 145 0E
Japara 103 6 30S 110 40E
Japen, I. = Yapen 103 1 50S 136 0E
Japero 103 4 59S 137 11E
Japurá 174 1 48S 66 30W
Japurá, R. 174 3 8S 64 46W
Jaque 174 7 27N 78 15W
Jaques Cartier, Détroit de 151 50 0N 63 30W
Jara, La 161 37 16N 106 0W
Jaraguá 171 15 45S 49 20W
Jaraicejo 57 39 40N 5 49W
Jaraiz 56 40 4N 5 45W
Jarales 161 34 44N 106 51W
Jarama, R. 58 40 50N 3 20W
Jarandilla 56 40 8N 5 39W
Jaranwala 94 31 15N 73 20E
Jarash 90 32 17N 35 54E
Järbo 72 60 42N 16 38E
Jarbridge 160 41 56N 115 27W
Jardim 172 21 28S 56 9W
Jardín, R. 59 38 50N 2 10W
Jardines de la Reina, Is. 166 20 50N 78 50W
Jargalant = Hovd 105 48 1N 91 38E
Jargeau 43 47 50N 2 7E
Jarmen 48 53 56N 13 20E
Järna, Kopp., Sweden 72 60 33N 14 26E
Järna, Stockholm, Sweden 72 59 7N 17 35E
Jarnac 44 45 40N 0 11W
Jarny 43 49 9N 5 53E
Jarocin 54 51 59N 17 29E
Jaroměr 52 50 22N 15 52E
Jarosław 54 50 2N 22 42E
Järpås 73 58 23N 12 57E
Järpås 73 58 23N 12 57E
Järpen 72 63 21N 13 26E
Jarrahdale 137 32 24S 116 5E
Jarres, Plaine des 100 19 27N 103 10E
Jarrow 35 54 58N 1 28W
Jarso 123 5 15N 37 30E
Järved 72 63 16N 18 43E
Jarvis I. 131 0 15S 159 55W
Jarvornik 53 50 23N 17 2E
Jarwa 95 27 45N 82 30E
Jaša Tomió 66 45 26N 20 50E
Jasien 54 51 46N 15 0E
Jasin 101 2 20N 102 26E
Jäsk 93 25 38N 57 45E
Jasło 54 49 45N 21 30E
Jasper, Can. 152 52 55N 118 5W
Jasper, Ala., U.S.A. 157 33 48N 87 16W
Jasper, Ark., U.S.A. 97 36 0N 93 10W
Jasper, Fla., U.S.A. 157 30 31N 82 58W
Jasper, La., U.S.A. 159 30 59N 93 58W
Jasper, S.D., U.S.A. 158 43 52N 96 22W
Jasper Nat. Park 152 52 50N 118 8W
Jasper Place 152 53 33N 113 25W
Jastrebarsko 63 45 41N 15 39E
Jastrowie 54 53 26N 16 49E
Jastrzebie Zdroj 54 49 57N 18 35E
Jászapáti 53 47 32N 20 10E
Jászárokszállás 53 47 39N 20 1E
Jászberény 53 47 30N 19 55E
Jászkiser 53 47 27N 20 20E
Jászladány 53 47 23N 20 18E
Jatai 171 17 50S 51 45W
Jati 94 24 27N 68 19E
Jatibarang 103 6 28S 108 18E
Jatinegara 103 6 13S 106 52E
Játiva 59 39 0N 0 32W
Jatobal 170 4 35S 49 33W
Jatt 90 32 24N 35 2E
Jaú 173 22 10S 48 30W
Jau al Milah 91 15 15N 45 40E
Jauche 47 50 41N 4 57E
Jauja 174 11 45S 75 30W
Jaunelgava 80 56 35N 25 0E
Jaunpur 95 25 46N 82 44E
Java = Jawa 103 7 0S 110 0E
Java Sea 102 4 35S 107 15E
Javadi Hills 97 12 40N 78 40E
Jávea 59 38 48N 0 10E
Javhlant = Ulyasutay 105 47 45N 96 49E
Javla 96 17 18N 75 9E
Javron 42 48 25N 0 25W
Jawa 103 7 0S 110 0E
Jawor 54 51 4N 16 11E
Jaworzno 54 50 13N 19 22E
Jay 159 33 17N 94 46W
Jayawijaya, Pengunungan 103 7 0S 139 0E
Jaydot 153 49 15N 110 15W
Jaynagar 99 26 43N 86 9E
Jayton 159 33 17N 100 35W
Jazminal 164 24 56N 101 25W
Jean 161 35 47N 115 20W
Jean Marie River 152 61 32N 120 38W
Jean Rabel 167 19 50N 73 30W
Jeanerette 159 29 52N 91 38W
Jebba, Moroc. 118 35 11N 4 43W
Jebba, Nigeria 121 9 9N 4 48E
Jebel 66 40 35N 21 15E
Jebel Aulia 123 15 10N 32 31E
Jebel Qerri 123 16 16N 32 50E
Jedburgh 35 55 28N 2 33W
Jedlicze 54 49 43N 21 40E
Jedlnia-Letnisko 54 51 25N 21 19E
Jedrzejów 54 50 35N 20 15E

Jedway Kaboudia, Rass


| | | | |
|---|---|---|---|
| Jedway | **152** | 52 17N | 131 14W |
| Jeetze, R. | **48** | 52 58N | 11 6E |
| Jefferson, Iowa, U.S.A. | **158** | 42 3N | 94 25W |
| Jefferson, Tex., U.S.A. | **159** | 32 45N | 94 23W |
| Jefferson, Wis., U.S.A. | **158** | 43 0N | 88 49W |
| Jefferson City | **157** | 36 8N | 83 30W |
| Jefferson, Mt., Calif., U.S.A. | **163** | 38 51N | 117 0W |
| Jefferson, Mt., Oreg., U.S.A. | **160** | 44 45N | 121 50W |
| Jeffersonville | **156** | 38 20N | 85 42W |
| Jega | **121** | 12 15N | 4 23E |
| Jekabpils | **80** | 56 29N | 25 57E |
| Jelenia Góra | **54** | 50 50N | 15 45E |
| Jelenia Góra □ | **54** | 51 0N | 15 30E |
| Jelgava | **80** | 56 41N | 22 49E |
| Jelica | **66** | 43 50N | 20 17E |
| Jelli | **123** | 5 25N | 31 45E |
| Jellicoe | **150** | 49 40N | 87 30W |
| Jelšava | **53** | 48 37N | 20 15E |
| Jemaja | **103** | 3 5N | 105 45E |
| Jemaluang | **101** | 2 16N | 103 52E |
| Jemappes | **47** | 50 27N | 3 54E |
| Jember | **103** | 8 11S | 113 41E |
| Jembongan, I. | **102** | 6 45N | 117 20E |
| Jemmapes = Azzaba | **119** | 36 48N | 7 6E |
| Jemnice | **52** | 49 1N | 15 34E |
| Jena, Ger. | **48** | 50 56N | 11 33E |
| Jena, U.S.A. | **159** | 31 41N | 92 7W |
| Jench'iu | **106** | 38 43N | 116 5E |
| Jendouba | **119** | 36 29N | 8 47E |
| Jenhochieh | **108** | 26 29N | 101 45E |
| Jenhsien | **106** | 37 8N | 114 37E |
| Jenhua | **109** | 25 5N | 113 45E |
| Jenhuai | **108** | 27 53N | 106 17E |
| Jenin | **90** | 32 28N | 35 18E |
| Jenkins | **156** | 37 13N | 82 41W |
| Jennings | **159** | 30 10N | 92 45W |
| Jennings, R. | **152** | 59 38N | 132 5W |
| Jenny | **73** | 57 47N | 16 35E |
| Jeparit | **140** | 36 8S | 142 1E |
| Jequié | **171** | 13 51S | 40 5W |
| Jequitaí, R. | **171** | 17 4S | 44 50W |
| Jequitinhonha | **171** | 16 30S | 41 0W |
| Jequitinhonha, R. | **171** | 15 51S | 38 53W |
| Jerada | **118** | 34 40N | 2 10W |
| Jerantut | **101** | 3 56N | 102 22E |
| Jérémie | **167** | 18 40N | 74 10W |
| Jeremoabo | **170** | 10 4S | 38 21W |
| Jerez de García Salinas | **164** | 22 39N | 103 0W |
| Jerez de la Frontera | **57** | 36 41N | 6 7W |
| Jerez de los Caballeros | **57** | 38 20N | 6 45W |
| Jerez, Punta | **165** | 22 58N | 97 40W |
| Jericho | **138** | 23 38S | 146 6E |
| Jericho = El Arīhā | **90** | 31 52N | 35 27E |
| Jerichow | **48** | 52 30N | 12 2E |
| Jerilderie | **141** | 35 20S | 145 41E |
| Jermyn | **162** | 41 31N | 75 31W |
| Jerome | **161** | 34 50N | 112 0W |
| Jersey City | **162** | 40 41N | 74 8W |
| Jersey, I. | **42** | 49 13N | 2 7W |
| Jersey Shore | **156** | 41 17N | 77 18W |
| Jerseyville | **158** | 39 5N | 90 20W |
| Jerumenha | **171** | 7 5S | 43 30W |
| Jerusalem | **90** | 31 47N | 35 10E |
| Jervaulx | **33** | 54 19N | 1 41W |
| Jervis B. | **141** | 35 8S | 150 46E |
| Jervis, C. | **139** | 35 38S | 138 6E |
| Jesenice | **63** | 46 28N | 14 3E |
| Jesenik | **53** | 50 0N | 17 8E |
| Jeseník (Frývaldov) | **53** | 50 15N | 17 11E |
| Jesenske | **53** | 48 20N | 20 10E |
| Jesselton = Kota Kinabalu | **102** | 6 0N | 116 12E |
| Jessnitz | **48** | 51 42N | 12 19E |
| Jessore | **98** | 23 10N | 89 10E |
| Jesup | **157** | 31 30N | 82 0W |
| Jesús Carranza | **165** | 17 28N | 95 1W |
| Jesús María | **172** | 30 59S | 64 5W |
| Jetmore | **159** | 38 10N | 99 57W |
| Jetpur | **94** | 21 45N | 70 10E |
| Jette | **47** | 50 53N | 4 20E |
| Jevnaker | **71** | 60 15N | 10 26E |
| Jewett | **159** | 31 20N | 96 8W |
| Jewett City | **162** | 41 36N | 72 0W |
| Jeypore | **96** | 18 50N | 82 38E |
| Jeziorany | **54** | 53 58N | 20 46E |
| J.F. Rodrigues | **170** | 2 55S | 50 20W |
| Jhajjar | **94** | 28 37N | 76 14E |
| Jhal Jhao | **93** | 26 20N | 65 35E |
| Jhalakati | **98** | 22 39N | 90 12E |
| Jhalawar | **94** | 24 35N | 76 10E |
| Jhang Maghiana | **94** | 31 15N | 72 15E |
| Jhansi | **95** | 25 30N | 78 36E |
| Jharia | **95** | 23 45N | 86 18E |
| Jharsaguda | **99** | 21 50N | 84 5E |
| Jharsuguda | **96** | 21 50N | 84 5E |
| Jhelum | **94** | 33 0N | 73 45E |
| Jhelum, R. | **95** | 31 50N | 72 10E |
| Jhunjhunu | **94** | 28 10N | 75 20E |
| Jiangshan | **95** | 28 45N | 118 37E |
| Jibão, Serra do | **171** | 14 48S | 45 0W |
| Jibiya | **121** | 13 5N | 7 12E |
| Jibou | **70** | 47 15N | 23 17E |
| Jicín | **52** | 50 25N | 15 20E |
| Jicarón, I. | **166** | 7 10N | 81 50W |
| Jiddah | **92** | 21 29N | 39 16E |
| Jido | **99** | 29 2N | 94 58E |
| Jifna | **90** | 31 58N | 35 13E |
| Jiggalong | **136** | 23 24S | 120 47E |
| Jihk'atse | **107** | 29 15N | 88 53E |
| Jihlava | **52** | 49 28N | 15 35E |
| Jihočeský □ | **52** | 49 8N | 14 35E |
| Jihomoravský □ | **53** | 49 5N | 16 30E |
| Jiht'u | **105** | 33 27N | 79 42E |
| Jijiga | **91** | 9 20N | 42 50E |
| Jijona | **59** | 38 34N | 0 30W |
| Jikamshi | **121** | 12 12N | 7 45E |
| Jiloca, R. | **58** | 41 0N | 1 20W |
| Jílové | **52** | 49 52N | 14 29E |
| Jim Jim Cr. | **136** | 12 50S | 132 32E |
| Jima | **123** | 7 40N | 36 55E |
| Jimbolia | **66** | 45 47N | 20 57E |
| Jimena de la Frontera | **57** | 36 27N | 5 24W |
| Jimenbuen | **141** | 36 42S | 148 53E |
| Jiménez | **164** | 27 10N | 105 0W |
| Jind | **94** | 29 19N | 76 16E |
| Jindabyne | **141** | 36 25S | 148 35E |
| Jindrichuv Hradeç | **52** | 49 10N | 15 2E |
| Jinja | **126** | 0 25N | 33 12E |
| Jinjang | **101** | 3 13N | 101 39E |
| Jinjini | **120** | 7 20N | 3 42W |
| Jinnah Barrage | **93** | 32 58N | 71 33E |
| Jinotega | **166** | 13 6N | 85 59W |
| Jinotepe | **166** | 11 50N | 86 10W |
| Jiparaná (Machado), R. | **174** | 8 45S | 62 20W |
| Jipijapa | **174** | 1 0S | 80 40W |
| Jiquilpán | **164** | 19 57N | 102 42W |
| Jisresh Shughur | **92** | 35 49N | 36 18E |
| Jitarning | **137** | 32 48S | 117 57E |
| Jitra | **101** | 6 16N | 100 25E |
| Jiu, R. | **70** | 44 50N | 23 20E |
| Jiuchin | **109** | 25 53N | 116 0E |
| Jiuli | **108** | 24 6N | 97 54E |
| Jizera, R. | **52** | 50 21N | 14 48E |
| Jizl Wadi | **122** | 26 30N | 38 0E |
| Jizō-zaki | **110** | 35 34N | 133 20E |
| Joaçaba | **173** | 27 5S | 51 31W |
| Joaíma | **171** | 16 39S | 41 2W |
| João | **170** | 2 46S | 50 59W |
| João Amaro | **171** | 12 46S | 40 22W |
| João Câmara | **170** | 5 32S | 35 48W |
| João de Almeida | **125** | 15 10S | 13 50E |
| João Pessoa | **170** | 7 10S | 34 52W |
| João Pinheiro | **171** | 17 45S | 46 10W |
| Joaquim Távora | **171** | 23 30S | 49 58W |
| Joaquín V. González | **172** | 25 10S | 64 0W |
| Jobourg, Nez de | **42** | 49 41N | 1 57W |
| Joch'iang | **105** | 39 2N | 88 0E |
| Jódar | **59** | 37 50N | 3 21W |
| Jodhpur | **94** | 26 23N | 73 2E |
| Joe Batt's Arm | **151** | 49 44N | 54 10W |
| Joensuu | **78** | 62 37N | 29 49E |
| Joeuf | **43** | 49 12N | 6 1E |
| Jofane | **125** | 21 15S | 34 18E |
| Joggins | **151** | 45 42N | 64 27W |
| Jogjakarta = Yogyakarta | **103** | 7 49S | 110 22E |
| Jōhana | **111** | 36 37N | 136 57E |
| Johannesburg, S. Afr. | **129** | 26 10S | 28 8E |
| Johannesburg, U.S.A. | **163** | 35 22N | 117 38W |
| Johannisnäs | **72** | 62 45N | 16 15E |
| Johansfors, Halland, Sweden | **73** | 56 50N | 12 58E |
| Johansfors, Kronoberg, Sweden | **73** | 56 42N | 15 32E |
| John Days, R. | **160** | 45 0N | 120 0W |
| John o' Groats | **37** | 58 39N | 3 3W |
| Johnshaven | **37** | 56 48N | 2 20W |
| Johnson | **159** | 37 35N | 101 48W |
| Johnson City, N.Y., U.S.A. | **162** | 42 7N | 75 57W |
| Johnson City, Tenn., U.S.A. | **157** | 36 18N | 82 21W |
| Johnson City, Tex., U.S.A. | **159** | 30 15N | 98 24W |
| Johnson Cy. | **156** | 42 9N | 67 0W |
| Johnson Ra. | **137** | 29 40S | 119 15E |
| Johnsondale | **163** | 35 58N | 118 32W |
| Johnsons Crossing | **152** | 60 29N | 133 18W |
| Johnsonville | **142** | 41 13S | 174 48E |
| Johnston | **31** | 51 45N | 5 5W |
| Johnston Falls = Mambilima Falls | **127** | 10 31S | 28 45E |
| Johnston I. | **131** | 17 10N | 169 8E |
| Johnston Lakes | **137** | 32 20S | 120 45E |
| Johnston Ra. | **137** | 29 40S | 119 20E |
| Johnstone | **34** | 55 50N | 4 31W |
| Johnstone Str. | **152** | 50 28N | 126 0W |
| Johnstown, Ireland | **39** | 52 46N | 7 34W |
| Johnstown, N.Y., U.S.A. | **162** | 43 1N | 74 20W |
| Johnstown, Pa., U.S.A. | **156** | 40 19N | 78 53W |
| Johnstown Bridge | **38** | 53 23N | 6 53W |
| Johor □ | **101** | 2 5N | 103 20E |
| Johor Baharu | **101** | 1 28N | 103 46E |
| Johor, S. | **101** | 1 45N | 103 47E |
| Joigny | **43** | 48 0N | 3 20E |
| Joinvile | **173** | 26 15S | 48 55E |
| Joinville | **43** | 48 27N | 5 10E |
| Joinville I. | **13** | 63 15N | 55 30W |
| Jojutla | **165** | 18 37N | 99 11W |
| Jokkmokk | **74** | 66 35N | 19 50E |
| Jökulsá á Brú | **74** | 65 40N | 14 16W |
| Jökulsá Fjöllum | **74** | 65 30N | 16 15W |
| Jökulsa R. | **74** | 65 30N | 16 15W |
| Jolan | **163** | 35 58N | 121 9W |
| Joliet | **156** | 41 30N | 88 0W |
| Joliette | **150** | 46 3N | 73 24W |
| Jolo I. | **103** | 6 0N | 121 0E |
| Jome, I. | **103** | 1 16S | 127 30E |
| Jönåker | **73** | 58 44N | 16 40E |
| Jönaker | **73** | 58 44N | 16 43E |
| Jones C. | **150** | 54 33N | 79 35W |
| Jones Sound | **12** | 76 0N | 89 0W |
| Jonesboro, Ark., U.S.A. | **159** | 35 50N | 90 45W |
| Jonesboro, Ill., U.S.A. | **159** | 37 26N | 89 18W |
| Jonesboro, La., U.S.A. | **159** | 32 15N | 92 41W |
| Jonesport | **151** | 44 32N | 67 38W |
| Jönköping | **73** | 57 45N | 14 10E |
| Jönköpings län □ | **75** | 57 30N | 14 30E |
| Jonquière | **151** | 48 27N | 71 14W |
| Jonsberg | **73** | 58 30N | 16 48E |
| Jonsered | **73** | 57 45N | 12 10E |
| Jonzac | **44** | 45 27N | 0 28W |
| Joplin | **159** | 37 0N | 94 25W |
| Jordan, Phil. | **103** | 10 41N | 122 38E |
| Jordan, Mont., U.S.A. | **160** | 47 25N | 106 58W |
| Jordan, N.Y., U.S.A. | **162** | 43 4N | 76 29W |
| Jordan ■ | **92** | 31 0N | 36 0E |
| Jordan, R. | **90** | 32 10N | 35 32E |
| Jordan Valley | **160** | 43 0N | 117 2W |
| Jordânia | **171** | 15 45S | 40 11W |
| Jordanów | **54** | 49 41N | 19 49E |
| Jorhat | **98** | 26 45N | 94 20E |
| Jörn | **74** | 65 4N | 20 1E |
| Jørpeland | **71** | 59 3N | 6 1E |
| Jorquera, R. | **172** | 28 3S | 69 58W |
| Jos | **121** | 9 53N | 8 51E |
| Jošanička Banja | **66** | 43 24N | 20 47E |
| José Batlle y OrdóPez | **173** | 33 20S | 55 10W |
| Josefow | **54** | 52 10N | 21 11E |
| Joseni | **70** | 47 42N | 25 29E |
| Joseph | **160** | 45 27N | 117 13W |
| Joseph Bonaparte G. | **136** | 14 35S | 128 50E |
| Joseph City | **161** | 35 0N | 110 16W |
| Joseph, Lac | **151** | 52 45N | 65 18W |
| Josephine, oilfield | **19** | 58 35N | 2 45E |
| Joshua Tree | **163** | 34 8N | 116 19W |
| Joshua Tree Nat. Mon. | **163** | 33 56N | 116 5W |
| Josselin | **42** | 47 57N | 2 33W |
| Jostedal | **71** | 61 35N | 7 15E |
| Jostedalsbre, Mt. | **71** | 61 45N | 7 0E |
| Jotunheimen | **71** | 61 35N | 8 25E |
| Jounieh | **92** | 33 59N | 35 30E |
| Jourdanton | **159** | 28 54N | 98 32W |
| Journe | **46** | 52 58N | 5 48E |
| Joussard | **152** | 55 22N | 115 57W |
| Joux, Lac de | **50** | 46 39N | 6 18E |
| Jouzjan □ | **93** | 36 10N | 66 0E |
| Jovellanos | **166** | 22 40N | 81 10W |
| Jowai | **98** | 25 26N | 92 12E |
| Joyce's Country, dist. | **38** | 53 32N | 9 30W |
| Joyeuse | **45** | 44 29N | 4 16E |
| Jozini Dam | **129** | 27 27S | 32 7E |
| Ju Shui, R. | **109** | 28 36N | 116 4E |
| Juan Aldama | **164** | 24 20N | 103 23W |
| Juan Bautista | **161** | 36 55N | 121 33W |
| Juan Bautista Alberdi | **172** | 34 26S | 61 48W |
| Juan de Fuca Str. | **160** | 48 15N | 124 0W |
| Juan de Nova, I. | **129** | 17 3S | 42 45E |
| Juan Fernández, Arch. de | **131** | 33 50S | 80 0W |
| Juan José Castelli | **172** | 25 57S | 60 37W |
| Juan L. Lacaze | **172** | 34 26S | 57 25W |
| Juárez, Argent. | **172** | 37 40S | 59 43W |
| Juárez, Mexico | **164** | 27 37N | 100 44W |
| Juárez, Sierra de | **164** | 32 0N | 116 0W |
| Juatinga, Ponta de | **171** | 23 17S | 44 30W |
| Juàzeiro | **170** | 9 30S | 40 30W |
| Juàzeiro do Norte | **170** | 7 10S | 39 18W |
| Jûbâ | **123** | 4 57N | 31 35E |
| Juba, R. | **91** | 1 30N | 42 35E |
| Jubaila | **92** | 24 55N | 46 25E |
| Jûbâl | **122** | 27 30N | 34 0E |
| Jubbulpore = Jabalpur | **95** | 23 9N | 79 58E |
| Jübek | **48** | 54 31N | 9 24E |
| Jubga | **83** | 44 19N | 38 48E |
| Jubilee L. | **137** | 29 0S | 126 50E |
| Juby, C. | **116** | 28 0N | 12 59W |
| Júcar, R. | **58** | 40 8N | 2 13W |
| Júcaro | **166** | 21 37N | 78 51W |
| Juch'eng | **109** | 25 32N | 113 39E |
| Juchitán | **165** | 16 27N | 95 5W |
| Judaea = Yehuda | **90** | 31 35N | 34 57E |
| Judenburg | **52** | 47 12N | 14 38E |
| Judith Gap | **160** | 46 48N | 109 46W |
| Judith Pt. | **162** | 41 20N | 71 30W |
| Judith, R. | **160** | 47 30N | 109 30W |
| Juian | **109** | 27 45N | 120 38E |
| Juich'ang | **109** | 29 40N | 115 39E |
| Juigalpa | **166** | 12 6N | 85 26W |
| Juillac | **44** | 45 20N | 1 19E |
| Juist, I. | **48** | 53 40N | 7 0E |
| Juiz de Fora | **171** | 21 43S | 43 19W |
| Jujuy | **172** | 24 10S | 65 25W |
| Jujuy □ | **172** | 23 20S | 65 40W |
| Jukao | **109** | 32 24N | 120 35E |
| Julesberg | **158** | 41 0N | 102 20W |
| Juli | **174** | 16 10S | 69 25W |
| Julia Cr. | **138** | 20 0S | 141 11E |
| Julia Creek | **138** | 20 39S | 141 44E |
| Juliaca | **174** | 15 25S | 70 10W |
| Julian | **163** | 33 4N | 116 38W |
| Julian Alps = Julijske Alpe | **63** | 46 15N | 14 1E |
| Julianakanaal | **47** | 51 6N | 5 52E |
| Julianehåb | **12** | 60 43N | 46 0W |
| Julianstown | **38** | 53 40N | 6 16W |
| Jülich | **48** | 50 55N | 6 20E |
| Julier P. | **51** | 46 28N | 9 32E |
| Julijske Alpe | **63** | 46 15N | 14 1E |
| Julimes | **164** | 28 25N | 105 27W |
| Jullundur | **94** | 31 20N | 75 40E |
| Jumbo | **127** | 17 30S | 30 58E |
| Jumento, Cayos | **167** | 23 0N | 75 40E |
| Jumet | **47** | 50 27N | 4 25E |
| Jumilla | **59** | 38 28N | 1 19W |
| Jumla | **95** | 29 15N | 82 13E |
| Jumna, R. = Yamuna | **94** | 27 0N | 78 30E |
| Junagadh | **94** | 21 30N | 70 30E |
| Junan | **109** | 32 58N | 114 31E |
| Junction, Tex., U.S.A. | **159** | 30 29N | 99 48W |
| Junction, Utah, U.S.A. | **161** | 38 10N | 112 15W |
| Junction B. | **138** | 11 52S | 133 55E |
| Junction City, Kans., U.S.A. | **158** | 39 4N | 96 55W |
| Junction City, Oreg., U.S.A. | **160** | 44 20N | 123 12W |
| Jundah | **138** | 24 46S | 143 2E |
| Jundiaí | **173** | 23 10S | 47 0W |
| Juneau | **147** | 58 26N | 134 30W |
| Junee | **141** | 34 53S | 147 35E |
| Jung Chiang, R. | **108** | 23 25N | 110 0E |
| Jungan | **108** | 25 14N | 109 23E |
| Jungch'ang | **108** | 29 27N | 105 33E |
| Jungch'eng | **107** | 37 9N | 122 23E |
| Jungchiang | **108** | 25 56N | 108 31E |
| Jungching | **108** | 29 49N | 102 55E |
| Jungfrau | **50** | 46 32N | 7 58E |
| Jungho | **106** | 35 21N | 110 32E |
| Junghsien, Kwangsi-Chuang, China | **109** | 22 52N | 110 33E |
| Junghsien, Szechwan, China | **108** | 29 29N | 104 22E |
| Junglinster | **47** | 49 43N | 6 15E |
| Jungshahi | **94** | 24 52N | 67 44E |
| Jungshui | **108** | 24 14N | 109 23E |
| Juniata, R. | **162** | 40 30N | 77 40W |
| Junín | **172** | 34 33S | 60 57W |
| Junín de los Andes | **176** | 39 45S | 71 0W |
| Junnar | **96** | 19 12N | 73 58E |
| Junquera, La | **58** | 42 25N | 2 53E |
| Junta, La | **159** | 38 0N | 103 30W |
| Juntura | **160** | 43 44N | 119 4W |
| Juparanã, Lagoa | **171** | 19 35S | 40 18W |
| Jupiter, R. | **151** | 49 29N | 63 37W |
| Juquiá | **171** | 24 19S | 47 38W |
| Jur, Nahr el | **123** | 8 45N | 29 0E |
| Jura | **43** | 46 35N | 6 5E |
| Jura □ | **43** | 46 47N | 5 45E |
| Jura, I. | **34** | 56 0N | 5 50W |
| Jura, Paps of, mts. | **34** | 55 55N | 6 0W |
| Jura, Sd. of | **34** | 55 57N | 5 45W |
| Jura Suisse | **50** | 47 10N | 7 0E |
| Jurado | **174** | 7 7N | 77 46W |
| Jurby Hd. | **32** | 54 23N | 4 31W |
| Jurien B. | **132** | 30 17S | 115 0E |
| Jurilovca | **70** | 44 46N | 28 52W |
| Jurm | **93** | 36 50N | 70 45E |
| Juruá, R. | **174** | 2 30S | 66 0W |
| Juruena, R. | **174** | 7 20S | 58 3W |
| Juruti | **175** | 2 9S | 56 4W |
| Jushan | **107** | 36 54N | 121 30E |
| Jussey | **43** | 47 50N | 5 55E |
| Justo Daract | **172** | 33 52S | 65 12W |
| Jüterbog | **48** | 51 59N | 13 6E |
| Juticalpa | **166** | 14 40N | 85 50W |
| Jutland | **16** | 56 0N | 8 0E |
| Jutphaas | **46** | 52 2N | 5 6E |
| Jutung | **109** | 32 19N | 121 14E |
| Juvigny-sous-Andaine | **42** | 48 32N | 0 30W |
| Juvisy | **43** | 48 43N | 2 23E |
| Juwain | **93** | 31 45N | 61 30E |
| Juyüan | **109** | 24 46N | 113 16E |
| Juzennecourt | **43** | 48 10N | 5 0E |
| Jye-kundo | **99** | 33 0N | 96 50E |
| Jylhama | **74** | 64 34N | 26 40E |
| Jylland | **73** | 56 15N | 9 20E |
| Jylland (Jutland) | **73** | 56 25N | 9 30E |
| Jyväskylä | **74** | 62 14N | 25 44E |


# K


| | | | |
|---|---|---|---|
| K. Sedili Besar | **101** | 1 55N | 104 5E |
| K2, Mt. | **95** | 36 0N | 77 0E |
| Ka Lae (South C.) | **147** | 18 55N | 155 41W |
| Kaaia, Mt. | **147** | 21 31N | 158 9W |
| Kaap die Goeie Hoop | **128** | 34 24S | 18 30E |
| Kaap Plato | **128** | 28 30S | 24 0E |
| Kaapkruis | **128** | 21 43S | 14 0E |
| Kaapstad = Cape Town | **125** | 33 56S | 18 27E |
| Kaatsheuvel | **47** | 51 39N | 5 2E |
| Kabaena, I. | **103** | 5 15S | 122 0E |
| Kabala | **120** | 9 38N | 11 37W |
| Kabale | **126** | 1 15S | 30 0E |
| Kabalo | **126** | 6 0S | 27 0E |
| Kabambare | **126** | 4 41S | 27 39E |
| Kabango | **127** | 8 35S | 28 30E |
| Kabanjahe | **102** | 8 2N | 98 27E |
| Kabara | **120** | 16 40N | 2 50W |
| Kabardinka | **82** | 44 40N | 37 57E |
| Kabardino-Balkar, A.S.S.R. □ | **83** | 43 30N | 43 30E |
| Kabarega Falls | **126** | 2 15N | 31 38E |
| Kabasalan | **103** | 7 47N | 122 44E |
| Kabba | **121** | 7 57N | 6 3E |
| Kabe | **110** | 34 31N | 132 31E |
| Kabi | **121** | 13 30N | 12 35E |
| Kabin Buri | **100** | 13 57N | 101 43E |
| Kabinakagami L. | **150** | 48 54N | 84 25W |
| Kabinda | **126** | 6 23S | 24 28E |
| Kablungu, C. | **135** | 6 20S | 150 1E |
| Kabna | **122** | 19 6N | 32 40E |
| Kabompo | **127** | 13 30S | 24 14E |
| Kabompo, R. | **127** | 13 50S | 24 10E |
| Kabondo | **127** | 8 58S | 25 40E |
| Kabongo | **126** | 7 22S | 25 33E |
| Kabou | **121** | 9 28N | 0 55E |
| Kaboudia, Rass | **119** | 35 13N | 11 10E |

Kabra Kandalakshkiyzaliv


Kabra 138 23 25 S 150 25 E
Kabūd Gonbad 93 37 5N 59 45 E
Kabuiri 121 11 30N 13 30 E
Kabul 94 34 28N 69 18 E
Kabul □ 93 34 0N 68 30 E
Kabul, R. 94 34 30N 69 13 E
Kabunga 126 1 38 S 28 3 E
Kaburuang 103 3 50N 126 30 E
Kabushiya 123 16 54N 33 41 E
Kabwe 127 14 30 S 28 29 E
Kabwum 135 6 11 S 147 15 E
Kačanik 66 42 13N 21 12 E
Kachanovo 80 57 25N 27 38 E
Kachebera 127 13 56 S 32 50 E
Kachin □ 98 26 0N 97 0 E
Kachira, Lake 126 0 40 S 31 0 E
Kachiry 76 53 10N 75 50 E
Kachisi 123 9 40N 37 57 E
Kachkanar 84 58 42N 59 33 E
Kachot 101 11 30N 103 3 E
Kaçkar 83 40 45N 41 30 E
Kadaingti 98 17 37N 97 32 E
Kadan Kyun, I. 101 12 30N 98 20 E
Kadanai, R. 94 32 0N 66 10 E
Kadarkút 53 46 13N 17 39 E
Kadayanallur 97 9 3N 77 22 E
Kaddi 121 13 40N 5 40 E
Kade 121 6 7N 0 56W
Kadgo, L. 137 25 30 S 125 30 E
Kadi 94 23 18N 72 23 E
Kadina 140 34 0 S 137 43 E
Kadiri 97 14 12N 78 13 E
Kadiyevka 83 48 35N 38 30 E
Kadoka 158 43 50N 101 31W
Kadom 81 54 37N 42 24 E
Kaduna 121 10 30N 7 21 E
Kaduna □ 121 11 0N 7 30 E
Kaduna, R. 121 10 5N 8 10 E
Kadyoha 120 8 58N 5 53W
Kadzhi-Say 85 42 8N 77 10 E
Kaedi 120 16 9N 13 28W
Kaelé 121 10 15N 14 15 E
Kaena Pt. 147 21 35N 158 17W
Kaeng Khoï 100 14 35N 101 0 E
Kaeo 142 35 6 S 173 49 E
Kaerh, China 105 31 45N 80 22 E
Kaerh, Sudan 123 5 35N 31 20 E
Kaesŏng 107 37 58N 126 35 E
Kaf 92 31 25N 37 20 E
Kafakumba 124 9 38 S 23 46 E
Kafan 79 39 18N 46 15 E
Kafanchan 121 9 40N 8 20 E
Kafareti 121 10 25N 11 12 E
Kaffrine 120 14 8N 15 36W
Kafia Kingi 117 9 20N 24 25 E
Kafinda 127 12 32 S 30 20 E
Kafirévs, Ákra 69 38 9N 24 8 E
Kafiristan 93 35 0N 70 30 E
Kafr Ana 70 32 2N 34 48 E
Kafr 'Ein 90 32 3N 35 7 E
Kafr el Dauwâr 122 31 8N 30 8 E
Kafr Kama 90 32 44N 35 26 E
Kafr Kannā 90 32 45N 35 20 E
Kafr Malik 90 32 0N 35 18 E
Kafr Mandā 90 32 49N 35 15 E
Kafr Quaddum 90 32 14N 35 7 E
Kafr Ra'i 90 32 23N 35 9 E
Kafr Sir 90 33 19N 35 23 E
Kafr Yasif 90 32 58N 35 10 E
Kafue 127 15 46 S 28 9 E
Kafue Flats 127 15 32 S 27 0 E
Kafue Gorge 127 16 0 S 28 0 E
Kafue Hook 127 14 58 S 26 0 E
Kafue Nat. Park 65 15 30 S 25 40 E
Kafue, R. 125 15 30 S 26 0 E
Kafulwe 127 9 0 S 29 1 E
Kaga, Afghan. 94 34 14N 70 10 E
Kaga, Japan 111 36 16N 136 15 E
Kagamil I. 147 53 0N 169 40W
Kagan 85 39 43N 64 33 E
Kagawa-ken □ 110 34 15N 134 0 E
Kagera R. 126 1 15 S 31 20 E
Kagoshima 110 31 36N 130 40 E
Kagoshima-ken □ 110 30 0N 130 0 E
Kagoshima-Wan 110 31 0N 130 40 E
Kagul 82 45 50N 28 15 E
Kahajan, R. 102 2 10 S 114 0 E
Kahama 126 4 8 S 32 30 E
Kahama □ 126 3 40 S 32 0 E
Kahang 101 2 12N 103 32 E
Kahe 126 3 30 S 37 25 E
Kahemba 124 7 18 S 18 55 E
Kaherekoua Mts. 143 45 45 S 167 15 E
Kahniah, R. 152 58 15N 120 55W
Kahnuj 93 27 55N 57 40 E
Kahoka 158 40 25N 91 42W
Kahoolawe, I. 147 20 33N 156 35W
Kahuku & Pt. 147 21 41N 157 57W
Kahulai 147 20 54N 156 28W
Kahurangi, Pt. 143 40 50 S 172 10 E
Kahuta 94 33 35N 73 24 E
Kai Kai 128 19 52 S 21 15 E
Kai, Kepulauan 103 5 55 S 132 45W
Kaiama 121 9 36N 4 1 E
Kaiapit 135 6 18 S 146 18 E
Kaiapoi 143 42 24 S 172 40 E
Kaibara 111 35 8N 135 5 E
K'aichien 109 23 45N 111 47 E
K'aifeng 106 34 50N 114 27 E
Kaihsien 107 40 25N 122 25 E
K'aihsien 108 31 12N 108 25 E
K'aihua 109 29 9N 118 24 E
Kaiingveld 128 30 0 S 22 0 E
Kaikohe 142 35 25 S 173 49 E
Kaikoura 143 42 25 S 173 43 E
Kaikoura Pen. 143 42 25 S 173 43 E
Kaikoura Ra. 143 41 59 S 173 41 E
Kailahun 120 8 18N 10 39W
Kailashahar 98 25 19N 92 0 E
Kaili 108 26 32N 107 57 E
K'ailu 107 43 35N 121 12 E
Kailua 147 19 39N 156 0W
Kaimana 103 3 30 S 133 45 E
Kaimanawa Mts. 142 39 15 S 175 56 E
Kaimata 143 42 34 S 171 28 E
Kaimganj 95 27 33N 79 24 E
Kaimon-Dake 110 31 11N 130 32 E
Kaimur Hill 95 24 30N 82 0 E
Kainan 110 34 9N 135 12 E
Kainantu 135 6 18 S 145 52 E
Kaingaroa Forest 142 38 30 S 176 30 E
Kainji Res. 121 10 1N 4 40 E
Kaipara Harb. 142 36 25 S 174 14 E
K'aip'ing 109 22 31N 112 32 E
Kaipokok B. 151 54 54N 59 47W
Kairana 94 29 33N 77 15 E
Kairiru, I. 138 3 20 S 143 20 E
Kaironi 103 0 47 S 133 40 E
Kairouan 119 35 45N 10 5 E
Kairuku 135 8 51 S 146 35 E
Kaiserslautern 49 49 30N 7 43 E
Kaitaia 142 35 8 S 173 17 E
Kaitangata 143 46 17 S 169 51 E
Kaithal 94 29 48N 76 26 E
Kaitu, R. 94 33 20N 70 20 E
Kaiwi Channel 147 21 13N 157 30W
K'aiyang 108 27 4N 106 55 E
K'aiyüan, Liaoning, China 107 42 33N 124 4 E
K'aiyüan, Yunnan, China 108 23 47N 103 10 E
Kaiyuh Mts. 147 63 40N 159 0W
Kajaani 74 64 17N 27 46 E
Kajabbi 138 20 0 S 140 1 E
Kajan, R. 102 2 40N 116 40 E
Kajang 101 2 59N 101 48 E
Kajeli 103 3 20 S 127 10 E
Kajiado 126 1 53 S 36 48 E
Kajiki 110 31 44N 130 40 E
Kajo Kaji 123 3 58N 31 40 E
Kajoa, I. 103 0 1N 127 28 E
Kajuagung 102 3 8 S 104 46 E
Kakabeka Falls 150 48 24N 89 37W
Kakamas 125 28 45 S 20 33 E
Kakamega 126 0 20N 34 46 E
Kakamega □ 126 0 20N 34 46 E
Kakamigahara 111 35 28N 136 48 E
Kakanj 66 44 9N 18 7 E
Kakanui Mts. 143 45 10 S 170 30 E
Kakapotahi 143 43 0 S 170 45 E
Kake, Japan 110 34 36N 132 19 E
Kake, U.S.A. 147 57 0N 134 0W
Kakegawa 111 34 45N 138 1 E
Kakhib 83 42 28N 46 34 E
Kakhovskoye Vdkhr. 82 47 5N 34 16 E
Kakia 125 24 48 S 23 22 E
Kakinada = Cocanada 99 16 50N 82 11 E
Kakinada (Cocanada) 96 16 50N 82 11 E
Kakisa L. 152 60 56N 117 43W
Kakisa, R. 152 61 3N 117 10W
Kakogawa 110 34 46N 134 51 E
Kaktovik 147 70 8N 143 50W
Kakwa, R. 152 54 37N 118 28W
Kala 121 12 2N 14 40 E
Kala Oya. 97 8 15N 80 0 E
Kala Shank'ou 95 35 42N 78 20 E
Kalaa-Kebira 119 35 59N 10 32 E
Kalabagh 94 33 0N 71 28 E
Kalabáka 68 39 42N 21 39 E
Kalabo 125 14 58 S 22 33 E
Kalach 81 50 22N 41 0 E
Kaladan, R. 99 21 30N 92 45 E
Kalahari, Des. 128 24 0 S 22 0 E
Kalahari Gemsbok Nat. Pk. 128 26 0 S 20 30 E
Kalahasti 97 13 45N 79 44 E
Kalai-Khumb 85 38 28N 70 46 E
Kalaja e Turrës 68 41 10N 19 28 E
Kalakamati 129 20 40 S 27 25 E
Kalakan 77 55 15N 116 45 E
K'alak'unlun Shank'ou 95 35 33N 77 46 E
Kalam 95 35 34N 72 30 E
Kalama, U.S.A. 160 46 0N 122 55W
Kalama, Zaïre 126 2 52 S 28 35 E
Kalamariá 68 40 33N 22 55 E
Kalamata 69 37 3N 22 10 E
Kalamazoo 156 42 20N 85 35W
Kalamazoo, R. 156 42 40N 86 12W
Kalamb 96 18 3N 74 48 E
Kalambo Falls 127 8 37 S 31 35 E
Kálamos, I. 69 38 37N 20 55 E
Kalamoti 69 38 15N 26 4 E
Kalamunda 137 32 0 S 116 0 E
Kalangadoo 140 37 34 S 140 41 E
Kalannie 137 30 22 S 117 5 E
Kalao, I. 103 7 21 S 121 0 E
Kalaotoa, I. 103 7 20 S 121 50 E
Kälarne 72 62 59N 16 8 E
Kalárovo 53 47 54N 18 0 E
Kalasin 100 16 26N 103 30 E
Kalat 93 29 8N 66 31 E
Kalat □ 93 27 0N 64 30 E
Kalat-i-Ghilzai 93 32 15N 66 58 E
Kálathos (Calato) 69 36 9N 28 8 E
Kalaupapa 147 21 12N 156 59W
Kalaus, R. 83 45 40N 43 30 E
Kalávrita 69 38 3N 22 8 E
Kalaw 98 16 24N 97 30 E
Kalba 120 9 30N 2 42W
Kalbarri 137 27 40 S 114 10 E
Kaldhovd 71 60 5N 8 20 E
Kalecik 82 40 4N 33 26 E
Kalegauk Kyun 99 15 33N 97 35 E
Kalehe 126 2 6 S 28 50 E
Kalema 126 1 12 S 31 55 E
Kalemie 124 5 55 S 29 9 E
Kalemyo 98 23 11N 94 4 E
Kalety 54 50 35N 18 52 E
Kalewa 98 22 41N 95 32 E
Kálfafellsstaður 74 64 11N 15 53W
Kalgan = Changchiak'ou 106 40 50N 114 53 E
Kalgoorlie 137 30 40 S 121 22 E
Kaliakra, Nos 67 43 21N 28 30 E
Kalianda 102 5 50 S 105 45 E
Kalibo 103 11 43N 122 22 E
Kaliganj Town 98 23 25N 89 8 E
Kalima 126 2 33 S 26 32 E
Kalimantan Barat □ 102 0 0 110 30 E
Kalimantan Selatan □ 102 4 10 S 115 30 E
Kalimantan Tengah □ 102 2 0 S 113 30 E
Kalimantan Timor □ 102 1 30N 116 30 E
Kálimnos, I. 69 37 0N 27 0 E
Kalimpong 95 27 4N 88 35 E
Kalinadi, R. 97 14 50N 74 20 E
Kalinin 81 56 55N 35 55 E
Kaliningrad 80 54 42N 20 32 E
Kalinino 83 45 12N 38 59 E
Kalininskoye 85 42 50N 73 49 E
Kalinkovichi 80 52 12N 29 20 E
Kalinovik 66 43 31N 18 29 E
Kalipetrovo (Starčevo) 67 44 5N 27 14 E
Kaliro 126 0 56N 33 30 E
Kalirrákhi 68 40 40N 24 35 E
Kalispell 160 48 10N 114 22W
Kalisz 54 51 45N 18 8 E
Kalisz □ 54 51 30N 18 0 E
Kalisz Pom 54 53 17N 15 55 E
Kaliua 126 5 5 S 31 48 E
Kaliveli Tank 97 12 5N 79 50 E
Kalix R. 74 67 0N 22 0 E
Kalka 94 30 56N 76 57 E
Kalkaroo 140 31 12 S 143 54 E
Kalkaska 150 44 44N 85 11W
Kalkfeld 128 20 57 S 16 14 E
Kalkfontein 128 22 4 S 20 57 E
Kalkfontein Dam 128 29 30 S 24 15 E
Kalkrand 128 24 1 S 17 35 E
Kall L. 72 63 35N 13 10 E
Kallakurichi 97 11 44N 79 1 E
Kållandsö 73 58 40N 13 5 E
Källby 73 58 30N 13 8 E
Kallia 86 31 46N 35 30 E
Kallidaikurichi 97 8 38N 77 31 E
Kallinge 73 56 15N 15 18 E
Kallithéa 69 37 55N 23 41 E
Kallmeti 68 41 51N 19 41 E
Kallonis, Kólpos 69 39 10N 26 10 E
Kallsjön 74 63 38N 13 0 E
Kalltorp 73 58 23N 13 20 E
Kalmalo 121 13 40N 5 20 E
Kalmar 73 56 40N 16 20 E
Kalmar län □ 73 57 25N 16 15 E
Kalmar sund 73 56 40N 16 25 E
Kalmthout 47 51 23N 4 29 E
Kalmyk A.S.S.R. □ 83 46 5N 46 1 E
Kalmykovo 83 49 0N 51 35 E
Kalna 95 23 13N 88 25 E
Kalo 135 10 1 S 147 48 E
Kalocsa 53 46 32N 19 0 E
Kalofer 67 42 37N 24 59 E
Kalol, Gujarat, India 94 23 15N 72 33 E
Kalol, Gujarat, India 94 22 37N 73 31 E
Kalola 127 10 0 S 28 0 E
Kalolímnos 69 37 4N 27 8 E
Kalomo 127 17 0 S 26 30 E
Kalonerón 69 37 20N 21 38 E
Kalpi 95 26 8N 79 47 E
Kalrayan Hills 97 11 45N 78 40 E
Kalsubai, Mt. 96 17 35N 73 45 E
Kaltbrunn 51 47 13N 9 2 E
Kaltungo 121 9 48N 11 19 E
Kalu 94 25 5N 67 39 E
Kaluga 81 54 35N 36 10 E
Kalulushi 127 12 50 S 28 3 E
Kalundborg 73 55 41N 11 5 E
Kalush 80 42 9N 24 12 E
Kałuszyn 54 52 13N 21 52 E
Kalutara 97 6 35N 80 0 E
Kalwaria 54 49 53N 19 41 E
Kalya 84 60 15N 59 59 E
Kalyan, Austral. 140 34 55 S 139 49 E
Kalyan, India 96 20 30N 74 3 E
Kalyani 174 17 53N 76 59 E
Kalyazin 81 57 15N 37 45 E
Kam Keut 101 18 20N 104 48 E
Kama, Burma 98 22 10N 95 10 E
Kama, Zaïre 126 3 30 S 27 5 E
Kama, R. 84 60 0N 53 0 E
Kamachumu 126 1 37 S 31 37 E
Kamae 110 32 48N 131 56 E
Kamaguenam 121 13 36N 10 30 E
Kamaing 98 24 26N 94 55 E
Kamaishi 112 39 20N 142 0 E
Kamakura 111 35 19N 139 33 E
Kamalia 94 30 44N 72 42 E
Kamalino 147 21 50N 160 14W
Kamamaung 98 17 21N 97 40 E
Kamango 126 0 40N 29 52 E
Kamapanda 127 12 5 S 24 0 E
Kamaran 91 15 28N 42 35 E
Kamashi 85 38 51N 65 23 E
Kamativi 127 18 15 S 0 27 E
Kamba 121 11 50N 3 45 E
Kambalda 137 31 10 S 121 37 E
Kambam 97 9 45N 77 16 E
Kambar 94 27 37N 68 1 E
Kambarka 84 56 15N 54 11 E
Kambia 120 9 3N 12 53W
Kambolé 127 8 47 S 30 48 E
Kambove 127 10 51 S 26 33 E
Kamchatka, P-ov. 77 57 0N 160 0 E
Kamde 138 8 0 S 140 58 E
Kamen 76 53 50N 81 30 E
Kamen Kashirskiy 80 51 39N 24 56 E
Kamenica 66 44 25N 19 40 E
Kamenice 52 49 18N 15 2 E
Kamenjak, Rt. 63 44 47N 13 55 E
Kamenka, R.S.F.S.R., U.S.S.R. 78 65 58N 44 0 E
Kamenka, R.S.F.S.R., U.S.S.R. 81 50 47N 39 20 E
Kamenka Bugskaya 80 50 8N 24 16 E
Kamenka Dneprovskaya 82 47 29N 34 14 E
Kamensk 76 56 25N 62 45 E
Kamensk Shakhtinskiy 83 48 23N 40 20 E
Kamensk-Uralskiy 84 56 25N 62 2 E
Kamenskiy 81 50 48N 45 25 E
Kamenskoye 77 62 45N 165 30 E
Kamenyak 67 43 24N 26 57 E
Kamenz 48 51 17N 14 7 E
Kameoka 111 35 0N 135 35 E
Kames 34 55 53N 5 15W
Kameyama 111 34 51N 136 27 E
Kami 68 42 17N 20 18 E
Kami-Jima 110 32 27N 130 20 E
Kami-koshiki-Jima 110 31 50N 129 52 E
Kamiah 160 46 12N 116 2W
Kamien Krajenskie 54 53 32N 17 32 E
Kamien Pomorski 54 53 57N 14 43 E
Kamiensk 54 51 12N 19 29 E
Kamiita 110 34 6N 134 22 E
Kamilonísion 69 35 50N 26 15 E
Kamilukuak, L. 153 62 22N 101 40W
Kamina 127 8 45 S 25 0 E
Kaminak L. 153 62 10N 95 0W
Kamioka 111 36 25N 137 15 E
Kamitüga Mungombe 126 3 2 S 28 10 E
Kamiyaku 112 30 25N 130 30 E
Kamloops 152 50 40N 120 20W
Kamo 143 35 42 S 174 20 E
Kamogawa 111 35 5N 140 5 E
Kamoke 94 32 4N 74 4 E
Kamono 124 3 10 S 13 20 E
Kamp, R. 52 48 35N 15 26 E
Kampala 126 0 20N 32 30 E
Kampar 101 4 18N 101 9 E
Kampar, R. 102 0 30N 102 0 E
Kampen 46 52 33N 5 53 E
Kamperland 47 51 34N 3 43 E
Kamphaeng Phet 100 16 28N 99 30 E
Kampolombo, L. 127 11 30 S 29 35 E
Kampong Ayer Puteh 101 4 15N 103 10 E
Kampong Jerangau 101 4 50N 103 10 E
Kampong Raja 101 5 45N 102 35 E
Kampong Sedili Besar 101 1 56N 104 8 E
Kampong To 101 6 3N 101 13 E
Kampot 101 10 36N 104 10 E
Kamptee 94 21 9N 79 19 E
Kampti 120 10 7N 3 25W
Kampuchea ■ = Cambodia 100 12 15N 105 0 E
Kamrau, Teluk 103 3 30 S 133 45 E
Kamsack 153 51 34N 101 54W
Kamskoye Ustye 81 55 10N 49 20 E
Kamskoye Vdkhr. 78 58 0N 56 0 E
Kamuchawie L. 153 56 18N 101 59W
Kamui-Misaki 112 45 3N 142 30 E
Kamyshin 81 50 10N 45 30 E
Kamyshlov 84 56 50N 62 33 E
Kamyzyak 83 46 4N 48 10 E
Kan 98 20 53N 93 49 E
Kan Chiang, R. 109 29 45N 116 10 E
Kanaaupscow 150 54 2N 76 30W
Kanab 161 37 3N 112 29W
Kanab Creek 161 37 0N 112 40W
Kanaga I. 147 51 45N 177 22W
Kanagawa-ken □ 111 35 20N 139 20 E
Kanairiktok, R. 151 55 2N 60 18W
Kanakanak 147 59 0N 158 58W
Kanakapura 97 12 33N 77 28 E
Kanália 68 39 30N 22 53 E
Kananga 124 5 55 S 22 18 E
Kanarraville 161 37 34N 113 12W
Kanash 81 55 48N 47 32 E
Kanawha, R. 156 39 40N 82 0W
Kanayis, Ras el 122 31 30N 28 5 E
Kanazawa 111 36 30N 136 38 E
Kanbalu 98 17 55N 85 24 E
Kanchanaburi 100 14 8N 99 31 E
Kanchenjunga, Mt. 95 27 50N 88 10 E
Kanchipuram (Conjeeveram) 97 12 52N 79 45 E
Kanchou 109 25 51N 114 59 E
Kanch'üan 106 36 19N 109 19 E
Kanda Kanda 124 6 52 S 23 48 E
Kandagach 79 49 20N 57 15 E
Kandahar 94 31 32N 65 30 E
Kandahar □ 94 31 0N 65 0 E
Kandalaksha 78 67 9N 32 30 E
Kandalakshkiyzaliv 78 66 0N 35 0 E

**Kandalu** **Kástron**


Kandalu 93 29 55N 63 20E
Kandangan 102 2 50S 115 20E
Kandanos 69 35 19N 23 44E
Kandé 121 9 57N 1 53E
Kandep 135 5 54S 143 32E
Kander, R. 50 46 33N 7 38E
Kandersteg 50 46 30N 7 40E
Kandewu 127 14 1S 26 16E
Kandhíla 69 37 46N 22 22E
Kandhkot 94 28 16N 69 8E
Kandhla 94 29 18N 77 19E
Kandi, Benin 121 11 7N 2 55E
Kandi, India 95 23 58N 88 5E
Kandinduna 127 13 58S 24 19E
Kandira 92 41 5N 30 10E
Kandla 94 23 0N 70 10E
Kandos 141 32 45S 149 58E
Kandrach 93 25 30N 65 30E
Kandrian 135 6 14S 149 37E
Kandukur 95 15 12N 79 57E
Kandy 97 7 18N 80 43E
Kane 156 41 39N 78 53W
Kane Bassin 12 79 30N 68 0W
Kanel 120 13 18N 14 35W
Kaneohe 147 21 25N 157 48W
Kanevskaya 83 46 3N 39 3E
Kanfanar 63 45 7N 13 50E
Kang 93 30 55N 61 55E
Kangaba 120 11 56N 8 25W
Kangar 101 6 27N 100 12E
Kangaroo I. 140 35 45S 137 0E
Kangaroo Mts. 138 23 25S 142 0E
Kangavar 92 34 40N 48 0E
Kangean, Kepulauan 102 6 55S 115 23E
Kangerdlugsuaé 12 68 10N 32 20W
Kanggye 107 41 0N 126 35E
Kanggyŏng 107 36 10N 126 0E
Kanghwa 107 37 45N 126 30E
K'angkang 108 32 46N 101 3E
Kangnŭng 107 37 45N 128 54E
Kango 124 0 11N 10 5E
K'angp'ing 107 43 45N 123 20E
Kangpokpi 98 25 8N 93 58E
K'angting 108 30 2N 102 0E
Kangtissu Shan 95 31 0N 82 0E
Kangto, Mt. 99 27 50N 92 35E
Kangyao 107 44 15N 126 40E
Kangyidaung 98 16 56N 94 54E
Kanhangad 97 12 21N 74 58E
Kanheri 96 19 13N 72 50E
Kani, China 99 29 25N 95 25E
Kani, Ivory C. 120 8 29N 6 36W
Kaniama 126 7 30S 24 12E
Kaniapiskau L. 151 54 10N 69 55W
Kaniapiskau, R. 151 57 40N 69 30E
Kanibadam 85 40 17N 70 25E
Kanin Nos, Mys 78 68 45N 43 20E
Kanin, P-ov. 78 68 0N 45 0E
Kanina 68 40 23N 19 30E
Kaniva 140 36 22S 141 18E
Kanjiza 66 46 3N 20 4E
Kanjut Sar 95 36 15N 75 25E
Kankakee 156 41 6N 87 50W
Kankakee, R. 156 41 13N 87 0W
Kankan 120 10 30N 9 15W
Kanker 96 20 10N 81 40E
Kankouchen 107 40 30N 119 27E
Kanku 106 34 45N 105 12E
Kankunskiy 77 57 37N 126 8E
Kanmuri-Yama 110 34 30N 132 4E
Kannabe 110 34 32N 133 23E
Kannapolis 157 35 32N 80 37W
Kannauj 95 27 3N 79 26E
Kannod 93 22 45N 76 40E
Kano 121 12 2N 8 30E
Kano □ 121 12 30N 9 0E
Kan'onji 110 34 7N 133 39E
Kanoroba 120 9 7N 6 8W
Kanowit 102 2 14N 112 20E
Kanowna 137 30 32S 121 31E
Kanoya 110 31 25N 130 50E
Kanózuga 54 49 58N 22 25E
Kanpetlet 98 21 10N 93 59E
Kanpur 95 26 35N 80 20E
Kansas □ 158 38 40N 98 0W
Kansas City, Kans., U.S.A. 158 39 0N 94 40W
Kansas City, Mo., U.S.A. 158 39 3N 94 30W
Kansas, R. 158 39 15N 96 20W
Kansenia 127 10 20S 26 0E
Kansk 77 56 20N 95 37E
Kansŏng 107 38 24N 128 30E
Kansu □ 105 35 30N 104 30E
Kant 85 42 53N 74 51E
Kant'angtzu 106 37 28N 104 33E
Kantché 121 13 31N 8 30E
Kantemirovka 83 49 43N 39 55E
Kantharalak 100 14 39N 104 39E
Kantishna 147 63 31N 151 5W
Kantō □ 111 36 0N 140 0E
Kantō-Heiya 111 36 0N 139 30E
Kantō-Sanchi 111 35 50N 138 50E
Kantu-long 98 19 57N 97 36E
Kanturk 39 52 10N 8 55W
Kantzu 108 31 37N 100 0E
Kanuma 111 36 44N 139 42E
Kanus 128 27 50S 18 39E
Kanye 128 25 0S 25 28E
Kanyu 128 20 7S 24 37E
Kanyü 107 34 53N 119 9E
Kanzene 127 10 30S 25 12E
Kanzi, Ras 126 7 1S 39 33E
Kaoan 109 28 25N 115 22E
Kaochou 109 21 55N 110 52E
Kaohofu 109 30 43N 116 49E
Kaohsien 108 28 21N 104 31E
Kaohsiung 109 22 35N 120 16E
Kaok'eng 109 27 39N 114 4E
Kaoko Otavi 125 18 12S 13 45E
Kaokoveld 128 19 0S 13 0E
Kaolack 120 14 5N 16 8W
Kaolan Shan 109 21 55N 113 15E
Kaolikung Shan 108 26 0N 98 55E
Kaomi 107 36 25N 119 45E
Kaopao Hu 109 32 50N 119 15E
Kaop'ing 106 35 48N 112 55E
K'aoshant'un 107 44 25N 124 27E
Kaot'ang 106 36 51N 116 13E
Kaoyang 106 38 42N 115 47E
Kaoyu 109 32 46N 119 32E
Kaoyüan 107 37 7N 118 0E
Kapaa 147 22 5N 159 19W
Kapadvanj 94 23 5N 73 0E
Kapagere 135 9 46S 147 42E
Kapanga 124 8 30S 22 40E
Kapanovka 83 47 28N 46 50E
Kapata 127 14 16S 26 15E
Kapellen 47 51 19N 4 25E
Kapello, Ákra 69 36 9N 23 3E
Kapema 127 10 45S 28 22E
Kapfenberg 52 47 26N 15 18E
Kapiri Mposhi 127 13 59S 28 43E
Kapiskau 150 52 50N 82 1W
Kapiskau, R. 150 52 47N 81 55W
Kapit 102 2 0N 113 5E
Kapiti I. 142 40 50S 174 56E
Kaplice 52 48 42N 14 30E
Kapoe 101 9 34N 98 32E
Kapoeta 123 4 50N 33 35E
Kápolnásnyék 53 47 16N 18 41E
Kaponga 143 39 29S 174 9E
Kapos, R. 53 46 30N 18 20E
Kaposvár 53 46 25N 17 47E
Kappeln 48 54 37N 9 56E
Kapps 128 22 32S 17 18E
Kaprije 63 43 42N 15 43E
Kaprijke 47 51 13N 3 38E
Kapsan 107 41 4N 128 19E
Kapsukas 80 54 33N 23 19E
Kapuas Hulu, Pegunungan 102 1 30N 113 30E
Kapuas, R. 102 0 20N 111 40E
Kapuka 127 10 30S 32 55E
Kapulo 127 8 18S 29 15E
Kapunda 140 34 20S 138 56E
Kapurthala 94 31 23N 75 25E
Kapuskasing 150 49 25N 82 30W
Kapuskasing, R. 150 49 49N 82 0W
Kapustin Yar 83 48 37N 45 40E
Kaputar, Mt. 139 30 15S 150 10E
Kaputir 126 2 5N 35 28E
Kapuvár 53 47 36N 17 1E
Kara, Turkey 69 38 29N 26 19E
Kara, U.S.S.R. 76 69 10N 65 25E
Kara Bogaz Gol, Zaliv 76 41 0N 53 30E
Kara Burun 69 38 41N 26 28E
Kara, I. 69 36 58N 27 30E
Kara Kalpak A.S.S.R. □ 76 43 0N 60 0E
Kara Kum 76 39 30N 60 0E
Kara-Saki 110 34 41N 129 30E
Kara Sea 76 75 0N 70 0E
Kara Su 85 40 44N 72 53E
Kara, Wadi 122 20 40N 42 0E
Karabash 84 55 29N 60 14E
Karabekaul 85 38 30N 64 8E
Karabük 82 41 10N 32 30E
Karabulak 85 44 54N 78 30E
Karaburuni 68 40 25N 19 20E
Karabutak 84 49 59N 60 14E
Karachala 83 39 45N 48 53E
Karachayevsk 83 43 50N 42 0E
Karachev 80 53 10N 35 5E
Karachi 94 24 53N 67 0E
Karachi □ 94 25 30N 67 0E
Karad 96 17 15N 74 10E
Karadeniz Boğazı 92 41 10N 29 5E
Karadeniz Dağlari 92 41 30N 35 0E
Karaga 121 9 58N 0 28W
Karagajly 76 49 26N 76 0E
Karaganda 76 49 50N 73 0E
Karaginskiy, Ostrov 77 58 45N 164 0E
Karagwe □ 126 2 0S 31 0E
Karaikal 97 10 59N 79 50E
Karaikkudi 97 10 0N 78 45E
Karaitivu I. 97 9 45N 79 52E
Karaj 93 35 4N 51 0E
Karak, Jordan 90 31 14N 35 40E
Karak, Malay. 101 3 25N 102 2E
Karakas 76 48 20N 83 30E
Karakitang 103 3 14N 125 28E
Karakobis 128 22 3S 20 37E
Karakoram 95 35 20N 76 0E
Karakoram P. = K'alak'unlun Shank'ou 95 35 33N 77 46E
Karakoram Pass 93 35 20N 78 0E
Karakul, Tadzhik, S.S.R., U.S.S.R. 85 39 2N 73 33E
Karakul, Uzbek S.S.R., U.S.S.R. 85 39 22N 63 50E
Karakuldzha 85 40 39N 73 26E
Karakulino 84 56 1N 53 43E
Karalon 77 57 5N 115 50E
Karaman 92 37 14N 33 13E
Karambu 102 3 53S 116 6E
Karamea 143 41 14S 172 6E
Karamea Bight 143 41 22S 171 40E
Karamea, R. 143 41 13S 172 26E
Karamet Niyaz 85 37 45N 64 34E
Karamoja □ 126 3 0N 34 15E
Karamsad 94 22 35N 72 50E
Karanganjar 103 7 38S 109 37E
Karanja 96 20 29N 77 31E
Karapoit 142 37 53S 175 32E
Karaşar 82 40 21N 31 55E
Karasburg 128 28 0S 18 44E
Karasino 76 66 50N 86 50E
Karasjok 74 69 27N 25 30E
Karasuk 76 53 44N 78 2E
Karasuk □ 126 2 12N 35 15E
Karasuyama 111 36 39N 140 9E
Karatau 85 43 10N 70 28E
Karatau, Khrebet 85 43 30N 69 30E
Karativu, I. 97 8 22N 79 52E
Karatiya 90 31 39N 34 43E
Karatobe 84 49 44N 53 30E
Karatoya, R. 98 24 7N 89 36E
Karaturuk 85 43 35N 78 0E
Karaul-Bazar 85 39 30N 64 48E
Karauli 94 26 30N 77 4E
Karavasta •68 40 53N 19 28E
Karawa 124 3 18N 20 17E
Karawanken 52 46 30N 14 40E
Karazhal 76 48 2N 70 49E
Karbala 92 32 47N 44 3E
Kårböle 72 61 59N 15 22E
Karcag 53 47 19N 21 1E
Karcha, R. 95 34 15N 75 57E
Kärda 73 57 10N 13 49E
Kardeljevo 66 43 2N 17 27E
Kardhámila 69 38 35N 26 5E
Kardhítsa 68 39 23N 21 54E
Kardhítsa □ 68 39 15N 21 50E
Kärdla 80 58 50N 22 40E
Kareeberge 128 30 50S 22 0E
Kareima 122 18 30N 31 49E
Karelian A.S.S.R. □ 78 65 30N 32 30E
Karema, P.N.G. 135 9 12S 147 18E
Karema, Tanz. 126 6 49S 30 24E
Karen 101 12 49N 92 53E
Karganrud 92 37 55N 49 0E
Kargapolye 84 55 57N 64 24E
Kargasok 76 59 3N 80 53E
Kargat 76 55 10N 80 15E
Kargı 82 41 11N 34 30E
Kargil 95 34 32N 76 12E
Kargowa 54 52 5N 15 51E
Karguéri 121 13 36N 10 30E
Kariai 69 40 14N 24 19E
Kariba 127 16 28S 28 36E
Kariba Dam 125 16 30S 28 35E
Kariba Gorge 127 16 30S 28 50E
Kariba Lake 127 16 40S 28 25E
Karibib 128 21 0S 15 56E
Karikal 97 10 59N 79 50E
Karikkale 92 39 55N 33 30E
Karimata, Kepulauan 102 1 40S 109 0E
Karimata, Selat 102 2 0S 108 20E
Karimnagar 96 18 26N 79 10E
Karimundjawa, Kepulauan 102 5 50S 110 30E
Karin 91 10 50N 45 52E
Káristos 69 38 1N 24 29E
Karitane 51 45 38S 170 39E
Kariya 111 34 58N 137 1E
Karkal 97 13 15N 74 56E
Karkar I. 135 4 40S 146 0E
Karkinitskiy Zaliv 82 45 36N 32 35E
Karkur 90 32 29N 34 57E
Karkur Tohl 122 22 5N 25 5E
Karl Libknekht 80 51 40N 35 45E
Karl-Marx-Stadt 48 50 50N 12 55E
Karl-Marx-Stadt □ 48 50 45N 13 0E
Karla, L = Voiviis, Limni 68 39 35N 22 45E
Karlino 54 54 3N 15 53E
Karlobag 63 44 32N 15 5E
Karlovac 63 45 31N 15 36E
Karlovka 82 49 29N 35 8E
Karlovy Vary 52 50 13N 12 51E
Karlsborg 73 58 33N 14 33E
Karlshamn 73 56 10N 14 51E
Karlskoga 72 59 22N 14 33E
Karlskrona 73 56 10N 15 35E
Karlsruhe 49 49 3N 8 23E
Karlstad, Sweden 72 59 23N 13 30E
Karlstad, U.S.A. 158 48 38N 96 30W
Karmøy 71 59 15N 5 15E
Karnal 94 29 42N 77 2E
Karnali, R. 95 29 0N 82 0E
Karnaphuli Res. 98 22 40N 92 20E
Karnataka □ 97 13 15N 77 0E
Karnes City 159 28 53N 97 53W
Karni 120 10 45N 2 40W
Karnische Alpen 52 46 36N 13 0E
Karnobat 67 42 40N 27 0E
Kärnten □ 52 46 52N 13 30E
Karo 120 12 16N 2 22W
Karoi 127 16 48S 29 45E
Karonga 127 9 57S 33 55E
Karoonda 140 35 1S 139 59E
Karos, Is. 69 36 54N 25 40E
Karousâdhes 68 39 47N 19 45E
Karpalund 73 56 4N 14 5E
Kárpathos, I. 69 35 37N 27 10E
Kárpathos, Stenón 69 36 0N 27 30E
Karpinsk 84 59 45N 60 1E
Karpogory 78 63 59N 44 27E
Karrebaek 73 55 12N 11 39E
Kars 92 40 40N 43 5E
Karsakpay 76 47 55N 66 40E
Karsha 83 49 45N 51 35E
Karshi 85 38 53N 65 48E
Karsun 81 54 14N 46 57E
Kartál Óros 68 41 15N 25 13E
Kartaly 84 53 3N 60 40E
Kartapur 94 31 27N 75 32E
Kartuzy 54 54 22N 18 10E
Karuah 141 32 37S 151 56E
Karufa 103 3 50S 133 20E
Karumba 138 17 31S 140 50E
Karumo 126 2 25S 32 50E
Karumwa 126 3 12S 32 38E
Karungu 126 0 50S 34 10E
Karunjie 136 16 18S 127 12E
Karup 73 56 19N 9 10E
Karur 97 10 59N 78 2E
Karviná 53 49 53N 18 25E
Karwar 93 14 55N 74 13E
Karwi 95 25 12N 80 57E
Kas Kong 101 11 27N 102 12E
Kasache 127 13 25S 34 20E
Kasai 110 34 55N 134 52E
Kasai Occidental □ 127 6 30S 22 30E
Kasai Oriental □ 126 5 0S 24 30E
Kasai, R. 124 8 20S 22 0E
Kasaji 127 10 25S 23 27E
Kasama, Japan 111 36 23N 140 16E
Kasama, Zambia 127 10 16S 31 9E
Kasandong 107 41 18N 126 55E
Kasane 128 17 34S 24 50E
Kasanga 127 8 30S 31 10E
Kasangulu 124 4 15S 15 15E
Kasaoka 110 34 30N 133 30E
Kasaragod 97 12 30N 74 58E
Kasat 98 15 56N 98 13E
Kasba 98 25 51N 87 37E
Kasba L. 153 60 20N 102 10W
Kasba Tadla 118 32 36N 6 17W
Kaschmar 93 35 16N 58 26E
Kaseberga 73 55 24N 14 8E
Kaseda 110 31 25N 130 19E
Kasempa 127 13 30S 25 44E
Kasenga 127 10 20S 28 45E
Kasese 126 0 13N 30 3E
Kasewa 127 14 28S 28 53E
Kasganj 95 27 48N 78 42E
Kashabowie 150 48 40N 90 26W
Kashan 93 34 5N 51 30E
Kashgar = K'oshin 105 39 29N 75 58E
Kashihara 111 34 35N 135 37E
Kashima, Ibaraki, Japan 111 35 58N 140 38E
Kashima, Saga, Japan 110 33 7N 130 6E
Kashima-Nada 111 36 0N 140 45E
Kashimbo 127 11 12S 26 19E
Kashin 81 57 20N 37 36E
Kashipur, Orissa, India 96 19 16N 83 3E
Kashipur, Ut. P., India 95 29 15N 79 0E
Kashira 81 54 45N 38 10E
Kashiwa 111 35 52N 139 59E
Kashiwazaki 112 37 22N 138 33E
Kashkasu 85 39 54N 72 44E
Kashmir □ 95 32 44N 74 54E
Kashmor 94 28 28N 69 32E
Kashpirovka 81 53 0N 48 30E
Kashum Tso 99 34 45N 86 0E
Kashun Noerh 105 42 25N 101 0E
Kasimov 81 54 55N 41 20E
Kasing 126 6 15S 26 58E
Kaskaskia, R. 158 37 58N 89 57W
Kaskattama, R. 153 57 3N 90 4W
Kaskelan 85 43 20N 76 35E
Kaskinen (Kaskö) 74 62 22N 21 15E
Kaskö (Kaskinen) 74 62 22N 21 15E
Kasli 84 55 53N 60 46E
Kaslo 152 49 55N 117 0W
Kasmere L. 153 59 34N 101 10W
Kasonawedjo 127 1 50S 137 41E
Kasongo 126 4 30S 26 33E
Kasongo Lunda 124 6 35S 17 0E
Kásos, I. 69 35 20N 26 55E
Kásos, Stenón 69 35 30N 26 30E
Kaspi 83 41 54N 44 17E
Kaspiysk 83 42 45N 47 40E
Kaspiyskiy 83 45 22N 47 23E
Kassab ed Doleib 123 13 30N 33 35E
Kassaba 122 22 40N 29 55E
Kassala 123 15 23N 36 26E
Kassala □ 123 15 20N 36 26E
Kassan 85 39 2N 65 35E
Kassandra 68 40 0N 23 30E
Kassansay 85 41 15N 71 31E
Kassel 48 51 19N 9 32E
Kassinger 122 18 46N 31 51E
Kassiópi 80 39 48N 19 53E
Kassue 103 6 58S 139 21E
Kastamonu 92 41 25N 33 43E
Kastav 63 45 22N 14 20E
Kastélli 69 35 29N 23 38E
Kastéllion 69 35 12N 25 20E
Kastellorizon = Megiste 61 36 8N 29 34E
Kastellou, Ákra 69 35 30N 27 15E
Kasterlee 47 51 15N 4 59E
Kastlösa 73 56 26N 16 25E
Kastó, I. 69 38 35N 20 55E
Kastóri 69 37 10N 22 17E
Kastoria 68 40 30N 21 19E
Kastoria □ 68 40 30N 21 15E
Kastorías 68 40 30N 21 20E
Kastornoye 81 51 55N 38 2E
Kástron 68 39 53N 25 8E

Kastrosikiá Kerman


Kastrosikiá 69 39 6N 20 36 E
Kasugai 111 35 12N 136 59 E
Kasukabe 111 35 58N 139 49 E
Kasulu 126 4 37 S 30 5 E
Kasulu □ 126 4 37 S 30 5 E
Kasumi 110 35 38N 134 38 E
Kasumiga-Ura 111 36 0N 140 25 E
Kasumkent 83 41 47N 48 15 E
Kasungu 127 13 0 S 33 29 E
Kasur 94 31 5N 74 25 E
Kata 77 58 46N 102 40 E
Kataba 127 16 10 S 25 10 E
Katako Kombe 126 3 25 S 24 20 E
Katákolon 69 37 38N 21 19 E
Katale 126 4 52 S 31 7 E
Katalla 147 60 10N 144 35W
Katama 123 9 35N 38 36 E
Katamatite 141 36 6 S 145 41 E
Katanda 126 0 55 S 29 21 E
Katanga = Shaba 126 8 0 S 25 0 E
Katanghan □ 93 36 0N 69 0 E
Katangi 96 21 56N 79 50 E
Katangli 77 51 42N 143 14 E
Katanich 123 6 0N 33 40 E
Katanning 132 33 40 S 117 33 E
Katastári 69 37 50N 20 45 E
Katav Ivanovsk 84 54 45N 58 12 E
Katavi Swamps 126 6 50 S 31 10 E
Kateríni 68 40 18N 22 37 E
Katesbridge 38 54 18N 6 8W
Katha 99 24 10N 96 30 E
Katherina, Gebel 122 28 30N 33 57 E
Katherine 136 14 27 S 132 20 E
Kathiawar, dist. 93 22 20N 71 0 E
Kathua 95 32 23N 75 30 E
Kati 120 12 41N 8 4W
Katiet 102 2 21 S 99 44 E
Katihar 95 25 34N 87 36 E
Katima Mulilo 125 17 28 S 24 13 E
Katima Mulilo Rapids 128 17 28 S 24 13 E
Katimbira 127 12 40 S 34 0 E
Katiola 120 8 10N 5 10W
Katkopberg 128 30 0 S 20 0 E
Katlanovo 66 41 52N 21 40 E
Katmai Nat. Monument 147 58 30N 155 0W
Katmai, vol. 147 58 20N 154 59W
Katmandu 95 27 45N 85 12 E
Kato Akhaïa 69 38 8N 21 33 E
Kato Stazros 68 40 39N 23 43 E
Katol 96 21 17N 78 38 E
Katompi 124 6 2 S 26 23 E
Katonga, R. 126 0 15N 31 50 E
Katoomba 141 33 41 S 150 19 E
Katowice 54 50 17N 19 5 E
Katowice □ 53 50 15N 19 0 E
Katrine L. 34 56 15N 4 30W
Katrineholm 72 59 9N 16 12 E
Katsepe 129 15 45 S 46 15 E
Katsina 121 7 10N 9 20 E
Katsina Ala, R. 121 6 52N 9 40 E
Katsumoto 110 33 51N 129 42 E
Katsuta 111 36 25N 140 31 E
Katsuura 111 35 15N 140 20 E
Katsuyama 111 36 3N 136 30 E
Kattakurgan 85 39 55N 66 15 E
Kattawaz 93 32 48N 68 23 E
Kattawaz-Urgun □ 93 32 10N 62 20 E
Kattegat 73 57 0N 11 20 E
Katumba 126 7 40 S 25 17 E
Katungu 126 2 55 S 40 3 E
Katwa 95 23 30N 89 25 E
Katwijk-aan-Zee 46 52 12N 4 24 E
Katy 54 51 2N 16 45 E
Kau Tao 101 10 6N 99 48 E
Kauai Chan. 147 21 45N 158 50W
Kauai, I. 147 19 30N 155 30W
Kaufakha 90 31 29N 34 40 E
Kaufbeuren 49 47 42N 10 37 E
Kaufman 159 32 35N 96 20W
Kaukauna 156 44 20N 88 13W
Kaukauveld 128 20 0 S 20 15 E
Kaukonen 74 67 31N 24 53 E
Kaulille 47 51 11N 5 31 E
Kauliranta 74 66 27N 23 41 E
Kaunas 80 54 54N 23 54 E
Kaunghein 98 25 41N 95 26 E
Kaupulehu 147 19 43N 155 53W
Kaura Namoda 121 12 37N 6 33 E
Kautokeino 74 69 0N 23 4 E
Kavacha 77 60 16N 169 51 E
Kavadarci 66 41 26N 22 3 E
Kavaja 68 41 11N 19 33 E
Kavali 97 14 55N 80 1 E
Kavála 68 40 57N 24 28 E
Kavála □ 68 41 05N 24 30 E
Kavála Kólpos 68 40 50N 24 25 E
Kavanayén 174 5 38N 61 48W
Kavarna 67 43 26N 28 22 E
Kavieng 135 2 36 S 150 51 E
Kavkaz, Bolshoi 83 42 50N 44 0 E
Kavousi 69 35 7N 25 51 E
Kaw = Caux 175 4 30N 52 15W
Kawa 123 13 42N 32 34 E
Kawachi-Nagano 111 34 28N 135 31 E
Kawagoe 111 35 55N 139 29 E
Kawaguchi 111 35 52N 138 45 E
Kawaihae 147 20 3N 155 50W
Kawaihoa Pt. 147 21 47N 160 12W
Kawaikini, Mt. 147 22 0N 159 30W
Kawakawa 142 35 23 S 174 6 E
Kawama 127 9 30 S 28 30 E
Kawambwa 127 9 48 S 29 3 E
Kawanoe 110 34 1N 133 34 E
Kawarau 143 45 3 S 169 0 E
Kawardha 95 22 0N 81 17 E
Kawasaki 111 35 35N 138 42 E
Kawau I. 142 36 25 S 174 52 E
Kawene 150 48 45N 91 15W
Kawerau 142 38 7 S 176 42 E
Kawhia Harbour 142 38 5 S 174 51 E
Kawick Peak 163 37 58N 116 57W
Kawkareik 98 16 33N 98 14 E
Kawlin 98 23 47N 95 41 E
Kawnro 99 22 48N 99 8 E
Kawthaung 101 10 5N 98 36 E
Kawthoolei □ = Kawthuk 98 18 0N 97 30 E
Kawthuk □ 98 18 0N 97 30 E
Kawya 98 16 40N 97 50 E
Kay 84 59 57N 52 59 E
Kaya 121 13 25N 1 10W
Kayah □ 98 19 15N 97 15 E
Kayaho 107 43 5N 129 46 E
Kayak I. 147 60 0N 144 30W
Kayan 98 16 54N 96 34 E
Kayangulam 97 9 10N 76 33 E
Kaycee 160 43 45N 106 46W
Kayenta 161 36 46N 110 15W
Kayes 120 14 25N 11 30W
Kayima 120 8 54N 11 15W
Kayl 47 49 29N 6 2 E
Kayomba 127 13 11 S 24 2 E
Kayoro 121 11 0N 1 28W
Kayrakkumskoye Vdkhr. 85 40 20N 70 0 E
Kayrunnera 139 30 40 S 142 30 E
Kaysatskoye 83 49 47N 46 49 E
Kayseri 92 38 45N 35 30 E
Kaysville 160 41 2N 111 58W
Kazachinskoye 77 56 16N 107 36 E
Kazachye 77 70 52N 135 58 E
Kazakh S.S.R. □ 85 50 0N 58 0 E
Kazakhstan 84 51 11N 53 0 E
Kazan 81 55 48N 49 3 E
Kazan, R. 153 64 2N 95 30W
Kazanluk 67 42 38N 25 35 E
Kazanskaya 83 49 50N 40 30 E
Kazarman 85 41 24N 73 59 E
Kazatin 82 49 45N 28 50 E
Kazerun 93 29 38N 51 40 E
Kazhim 84 60 21N 51 33 E
Kazi Magomed 83 40 3N 49 0 E
Kazimierza Wielki 54 50 15N 20 30 E
Kazincbarcika 53 48 17N 20 36 E
Kazo 111 36 7N 139 36 E
Kaztalovka 83 49 47N 48 43 E
Kazu 98 25 27N 97 46 E
Kazumba 124 6 25 S 22 5 E
Kazvin 92 36 15N 50 0 E
Kazym, R. 76 63 40N 68 30 E
Kcynia 54 53 0N 17 30 E
Ké 120 13 58N 5 18W
Ke-hsi Mansam 98 21 56N 97 50 E
Ke-Macina 120 14 5N 5 20W
Kéa 69 37 35N 24 22 E
Kea 30 50 13N 5 4W
Kéa, I. 69 37 30N 24 22 E
Keaau 147 19 37N 155 3W
Keady 38 54 15N 6 42W
Keal, Loch na 34 56 30N 6 5W
Kealkill 39 51 45N 9 20W
Keams Canyon 161 35 53N 110 9W
Keanae 147 20 52N 156 9W
Kearney 158 40 45N 99 3W
Kearsage, Mt. 162 43 25N 71 51W
Keban 92 38 50N 38 50 E
Kebele 123 12 52N 40 40 E
Kebi 120 9 18N 6 37W
Kebili 119 33 47N 9 0 E
Kebkabiya 117 13 50N 24 0 E
Kebnekaise, mt. 74 67 54N 18 33 E
Kebock Hd. 36 58 1N 6 20W
Kebri Dehar 91 6 45N 44 17 E
Kebumen 103 7 42 S 109 40 E
Kecel 53 46 31N 19 16 E
Kechika, R. 152 59 41N 127 12W
Kecskemét 53 46 57N 19 35 E
Kedada 123 5 30N 35 58 E
Kedah □ 101 5 50N 100 40 E
Kedainiai 80 55 15N 23 57 E
Kedgwick 151 47 40N 67 20W
Kedia Hill 128 21 28 S 24 37 E
Kediri 103 7 51 S 112 1 E
Kédougou 120 12 35N 12 10W
Kedzierzyn 54 50 20N 18 12 E
Keefers 152 50 0N 121 40W
Keel 38 53 59N 10 2W
Keelby 33 53 34N 0 15W
Keele 32 53 0N 2 17W
Keele, R. 147 64 15N 127 0W
Keeler 163 36 29N 117 52W
Keeley L. 153 54 54N 108 8W
Keeling Is. = Cocos Is. 142 12 12 S 96 54 E
Keelung = Chilung 109 25 3N 121 45 E
Keen, Mt. 37 56 58N 2 54W
Keenagh 38 53 36N 7 50W
Keene, Calif., U.S.A. 163 35 13N 118 33W
Keene, N.H., U.S.A. 162 42 57N 72 17W
Keeper, Mt. 39 52 46N 8 17W
Keer-Weer, C. 138 14 0 S 141 32 E
Keerbergen 47 51 1N 4 38 E
Keeten Mastgat 47 51 36N 4 0 E
Keetmanshoop 128 26 35 S 18 8 E
Keewatin 158 47 23N 93 0W
Keewatin □ 153 63 20N 94 40W
Keewatin, R. 153 56 29N 100 46W
Kefa □ 123 6 55N 36 30 E
Kefallinía, I. 69 38 28N 20 30 E
Kefamenanu 103 9 28 S 124 38 E
Kefar Ata 90 32 48N 35 7 E
Kefar Etsyon 90 31 39N 35 7 E
Kefar Hasidim 90 32 47N 35 5 E
Kefar Hittim B. 90 32 48N 35 27 E
Kefar Nahum 90 32 54N 35 22 E
Kefar Sava 90 32 11N 34 54 E
Kefar Szold 90 33 11N 35 34 E
Kefar Vitkin 90 32 22N 34 53 E
Kefar Yehezqel 90 32 34N 35 22 E
Kefar Yona 90 32 20N 34 54 E
Kefar Zekharya 90 31 43N 34 57 E
Keffi 121 8 55N 7 43 E
Keflavik 74 64 2N 22 35W
Keg River 152 57 54N 117 7W
Kegalla 97 7 15N 80 21 E
Kegashka 151 50 14N 61 18W
Kegworth 28 52 50N 1 17W
Kehl 49 48 34N 7 50 E
Keighley 32 53 52N 1 54W
Keimaneigh, P. of 39 51 49N 9 17W
Keimoes 128 28 41 S 21 0 E
Keiss 37 58 33N 3 6W
Keïta 121 14 46N 5 56 E
Keith, Austral. 140 36 0 S 140 20 E
Keith, U.K. 37 57 33N 2 58W
Keith Arm 148 65 20N 122 15W
Kekaygyr 85 40 42N 75 32 E
Kekri 94 26 0N 75 10 E
Kël 77 69 30N 124 10 E
Kelamet 123 16 0N 38 20 E
Kelang 101 3 2N 101 26 E
Kelani Ganga, R. 97 6 58N 79 50 E
Kelantan □ 101 5 10N 102 0 E
Kelantan, R. 101 6 13N 102 14 E
Këlcyra 68 40 22N 20 12 E
Keld 32 54 24N 2 11W
Keles, R. 85 41 1N 68 37 E
Kelheim 49 48 58N 11 57 E
Kelibia 119 36 50N 11 3 E
Kellas 37 57 33N 3 23W
Kellé, Congo 124 0 8 S 14 38 E
Kellé, Niger 121 14 18N 10 10 E
Keller 160 48 2N 118 44W
Kellerberrin 137 31 36 S 117 38 E
Kellett C. 12 72 0N 126 0W
Kellogg 160 47 30N 116 5W
Kelloselkä 74 66 56N 28 53 E
Kells, Ireland 39 52 33N 7 18W
Kells, U.K. 38 54 48N 6 13W
Kells = Ceanannas Mor 38 53 42N 6 53W
Kells, Rhinns of 34 55 9N 4 22W
Kelmentsy 80 48 30N 26 50 E
Kélo 124 9 10N 15 45 E
Kelowna 152 49 50N 119 25W
Kelsale 29 52 15N 1 30 E
Kelsall 32 53 14N 2 44W
Kelsey Bay 152 50 25N 126 0W
Kelso, N.Z. 143 45 54 S 169 15 E
Kelso, U.K. 35 55 36N 2 27W
Kelso, U.S.A. 160 46 10N 122 57W
Keltemashat 85 42 25N 70 8 E
Keluang 101 2 3N 103 18 E
Kelvedon 29 51 50N 0 43 E
Kelvington 153 52 10N 103 30W
Kem 78 65 0N 34 38 E
Kem-Kem 118 30 40N 4 30W
Kem, R. 78 64 45N 32 20 E
Kema 103 1 22N 125 8 E
Kemah 92 39 32N 39 5 E
Kemano 152 53 35N 128 0W
Kemapyu 98 18 49N 97 19 E
Kemasik 101 4 25N 103 25 E
Kembolcha 123 11 29N 39 42 E
Kemenets-Podolskiy 82 48 40N 26 30 E
Kemerovo 76 55 20N 85 50 E
Kemi 74 65 44N 24 34 E
Kemi älv = Kemijoki 74 65 47N 24 32 E
Kemijärvi 74 66 43N 27 22 E
Kemijoki 74 65 47N 24 32 E
Kemmel 47 50 47N 2 50 E
Kemmerer 160 41 52N 110 30W
Kemnay 37 57 14N 2 28W
Kemp Coast 13 69 0S 55 0 E
Kemp L. 159 33 45N 99 15W
Kempsey, Austral. 141 31 1 S 152 50 E
Kempsey, U.K. 28 52 8N 2 11W
Kempston 29 52 7N 0 30W
Kempt, L. 150 47 25N 74 22W
Kempten 49 47 42N 10 18 E
Kemptville 150 45 0N 75 38W
Ken L. 35 55 0N 4 8W
Kenadsa 118 31 48N 2 26W
Kenai 147 60 35N 151 20W
Kenai Mts. 147 60 0N 150 0W
Kendal, Indon. 103 6 56 S 110 14 E
Kendal, U.K. 32 54 19N 2 44W
Kendall 141 31 35 S 152 44 E
Kendall, R. 138 14 4 S 141 35 E
Kendallville 156 41 25N 85 15W
Kendari 103 3 50 S 122 30 E
Kendawangan 102 2 32 S 110 17 E
Kende 121 11 30N 4 12 E
Kendenup 137 34 30 S 117 38 E
Kendrapara 96 20 35N 86 30 E
Kendrick 160 46 43N 116 41W
Kendriki Kai Dhitiki Makedhonia □ 68 40 30N 22 0 E
Kene Thao 100 17 44N 101 25 E
Kenema 120 7 50N 11 14W
Keng Kok 100 16 26N 105 12 E
Keng Tawng 98 20 45N 98 18 E
Keng Tung, Burma 99 21 0N 99 30 E
Keng Tung, Burma 99 21 0N 99 30 E
Kenge 124 4 50 S 16 55 E
Kengeja 126 5 26 S 39 45 E
Kengma 108 23 34N 99 24 E
Kenhardt 128 29 19 S 21 12 E
Kenilworth 28 52 22N 1 35W
Kenimekh 85 40 16N 65 7 E
Kéninkoumou 120 15 17N 12 18W
Kénitra (Port Lyautey) 118 34 15N 6 40W
Kenmare, Ireland 39 51 52N 9 35W
Kenmare, U.S.A. 158 48 40N 102 4W
Kenmare, R. 39 51 40N 10 0W
Kenmore 37 56 35N 4 0W
Kenn Reef 133 21 12 S 155 46 E
Kennebec 158 43 56N 99 54W
Kennedy 127 18 52 S 27 10 E
Kennedy, C. = Canaveral, C. 157 28 28N 80 31W
Kennedy, Mt. 148 60 19N 139 0W
Kennedy Ra. 137 24 45 S 115 10 E
Kennedy Taungdeik 99 23 35N 94 4 E
Kennet, R. 28 51 24N 1 7W
Kenneth Ra. 137 23 50 S 117 8 E
Kennett 159 36 7N 90 0W
Kennett Square 162 39 51N 75 43W
Kennewick 160 46 11N 119 2W
Kenninghall 29 52 26N 1 0 E
Kénogami 151 48 25N 71 15W
Kenogami, R. 150 51 6N 84 28W
Kenora 153 49 50N 94 35W
Kenosha 156 42 33N 87 48W
Kensington, Can. 151 46 28N 63 34W
Kensington, U.S.A. 158 39 48N 99 2W
Kensington Downs 138 22 31 S 144 19 E
Kent, Ohio, U.S.A. 156 41 8N 81 20W
Kent, Oreg., U.S.A. 160 45 11N 120 45W
Kent, Tex., U.S.A. 159 31 5N 104 12W
Kent □ 29 51 12N 0 40 E
Kent Gr. 138 39 30 S 147 20 E
Kent Pen. 148 68 30N 107 0W
Kent Pt. 162 38 50N 76 22W
Kent, Vale of 23 51 12N 0 30 E
Kentau 85 43 32N 68 36 E
Kentdale 137 34 54 S 117 3 E
Kentisbeare 30 50 51N 3 18W
Kentland 156 40 45N 87 25W
Kenton, U.K. 30 50 37N 3 28W
Kenton, U.S.A. 156 40 40N 83 35W
Kentucky 141 30 45 S 151 28 E
Kentucky □ 156 37 20N 85 0W
Kentucky Dam 156 37 2N 88 15W
Kentucky L. 157 36 0N 88 0W
Kentucky, R. 156 38 41N 85 11W
Kentville 151 45 6N 64 29W
Kentwood 159 31 0N 90 30W
Kenya ■ 126 2 20N 38 0 E
Kenya, Mt. 126 0 10 S 37 18 E
Keo Nena, Deo 100 18 23N 105 10 E
Keokuk 158 40 25N 91 24W
Kep, Camb. 101 10 29N 104 19 E
Kep, Viet. 100 21 24N 106 16 E
Kep-i-Gjuhëzës 68 40 28N 19 15 E
Kep-i-Palit 68 41 25N 19 21 E
Kep-i-Rodonit 68 41 32N 19 30 E
Kepi 103 6 32 S 139 19 E
Kepice 54 54 16N 16 51 E
Kepler Mts. 143 45 25 S 167 20 E
Kepno 54 51 18N 17 58 E
Keppel B. 133 23 21 S 150 55 E
Kepsut 92 39 40N 28 15 E
Kepuhi 147 22 13N 159 21W
Kepulauan, R. 103 5 30 S 139 0 E
Kepulauan Sunda, Ketjil Barat □ 102 8 50 S 117 30 E
Kepulauan Sunda, Ketjil Timor □ 103 9 30 S 122 0 E
Kerala □ 97 11 0N 76 15 E
Kerama-Shotō 112 26 12N 127 22 E
Keran 95 34 35N 73 59 E
Kerang 140 35 40 S 143 55 E
Keratéa 69 37 48N 23 58 E
Keraudren, C., Tas., Austral. 136 40 22 S 144 47 E
Keraudren, C., W. Austral., Austral. 138 19 58 S 119 45 E
Keravat 135 4 17 S 152 2 E
Keray 93 26 15N 57 30 E
Kerch 82 45 20N 36 20 E
Kerchinskiy Proliv 82 45 10N 36 30 E
Kerchoual 121 17 20N 0 20 E
Kerem Maharal 90 32 39N 34 59 E
Kerema 135 7 58 S 145 50 E
Keren 123 15 45N 38 28 E
Kerewan 120 13 35N 16 10W
Kerguelen I. 11 48 15 S 69 10 E
Kerhonkson 162 41 46N 74 11W
Keri 69 37 40N 20 49 E
Keri Kera 123 12 21N 32 37 E
Kericho 126 0 22 S 35 15 E
Kericho □ 126 0 30 S 35 15 E
Kerikeri 143 35 12 S 173 59 E
Kerinci 102 2 5 S 101 0 E
Kerkdriel 46 51 47N 5 20 E
Kerkenna, Iles 119 34 48N 11 1 E
Kerki 85 37 50N 65 12 E
Kérkira 68 39 38N 19 50 E
Kerkrade 47 50 53N 6 4 E
Kerma 122 19 33N 30 32 E
Kermadec Is. 130 31 8 S 175 16W
Kermân 93 30 15N 57 1 E
Kerman 163 36 43N 120 4W

Kermān □ Killavullen


Kermân □ 93 30 0N 57 0E
Kermanshah 92 34 23N 47 0E
Kermanshah □ 92 34 0N 46 30E
Kerme Körfezi 69 36 55N 27 50E
Kermen 67 42 30N 26 16E
Kermit 159 31 56N 103 3W
Kern, R. 163 35 16N 119 18W
Kerns 51 46 54N 8 17E
Kernville 163 35 45N 118 26W
Keroh 101 5 43N 101 1E
Kerr, Pt. 142 34 25S 173 5E
Kerrera I. 34 56 24N 5 32W
Kerrobert 157 52 0N 109 11W
Kerrville 159 30 1N 99 8W
Kerry 31 52 28N 3 16W
Kerry □ 39 52 7N 9 35W
Kerry Hd. 39 52 26N 9 56W
Kerrysdale 36 57 41N 5 39W
Kersa 123 9 28N 41 48E
Kerstinbo 72 60 16N 16 58E
Kerteminde 73 55 28N 10 39E
Kertosono 103 7 38S 112 9E
Keru 123 15 40N 37 5E
Kerulen, R. 105 48 48N 117 0E
Kerzaz 118 29 29N 1 25W
Kerzers 50 46 59N 7 12E
Kesagami L. 150 50 23N 80 15W
Kesagami, R. 150 51 4N 79 45W
Kesan 68 41 49N 26 38E
Kesch, Piz 51 46 38N 9 53E
Kesh 38 54 31N 7 43W
Keski Suomen □ 74 62 45N 25 15E
Kessel, Belg. 47 51 8N 4 38E
Kessel, Neth. 47 51 17N 6 3E
Kessel-Lo 47 50 53N 4 43E
Kessingland 29 52 25N 1 41E
Kestell 129 28 17S 28 42E
Kestenga 78 66 0N 31 50E
Kesteren 46 51 56N 5 34E
Keswick 32 54 35N 3 9W
Keszthely 53 46 50N 17 15E
Keta 121 5 49N 1 0E
Ketapang 102 1 55S 110 0E
Ketchikan 147 55 25N 131 40W
Ketchum 160 43 50N 114 27W
Kete Krachi 121 7 55N 0 1W
Ketef, Khalîg Umm el 122 23 40N 35 35E
Ketelmeer 46 32 36N 5 46E
Keti Bandar 94 24 8N 67 27E
Ketri 94 28 1N 75 50E
Ketrzyn 54 54 7N 21 22E
Kettering 29 52 24N 0 44W
Kettla, Ness 36 60 3N 1 20W
Kettle Falls 160 48 41N 118 2W
Kettle Ness 33 54 32N 0 41W
Kettle, R. 153 56 23N 94 34W
Kettleman City 163 36 1N 119 58W
Kettlewell 32 54 8N 2 2W
Kety 54 49 51N 19 16E
Kevin 160 48 45N 111 58W
Kewanee 158 41 18N 90 0W
Kewaunee 156 44 27N 87 30W
Keweenaw B. 156 46 56N 88 23W
Keweenaw Pen. 156 47 30N 88 0W
Keweenaw Pt. 156 47 26N 87 40W
Kexby 33 53 21N 0 41W
Key Harbour 150 45 50N 80 45W
Key, L. 38 54 0N 8 15W
Key West 166 24 40N 82 0W
Keyingham 33 53 42N 0 7W
Keyling Inlet 136 14 50S 129 40E
Keymer 29 50 55N 0 5W
Keynsham 28 51 25N 2 30W
Keynshamburg 127 19 15S 29 40E
Keyport 162 40 26N 74 12W
Keyser 156 39 26N 79 0W
Keystone, S.D., U.S.A. 158 43 54N 103 27W
Keystone, W. Va., U.S.A. 156 37 30N 81 30W
Keyworth 28 52 52N 1 8W
Kez 84 57 55N 53 46E
Kezhma 77 59 15N 100 57E
Kezmarok 53 49 10N 20 28E
Khabarovo 76 69 30N 60 30E
Khabarovsk 77 48 20N 135 0E
Khachmas 83 41 31N 48 42E
Khachraud 94 23 25N 75 20E
Khadari, W. el 123 10 35N 26 16E
Khadro 94 26 11N 68 50E
Khadyzhensk 83 44 26N 39 32E
Khadzhilyangar 95 35 45N 79 20E
Khagaria 95 25 18N 86 32E
Khaibar 92 25 38N 39 28E
Khaibor 122 25 49N 39 16E
Khaipur, Bahawalpur, Pak. 94 29 34N 72 17E
Khaipur, Hyderabad, Pak. 94 27 32N 68 49E
Khair 94 27 57N 77 46E
Khairabad 95 27 33N 80 47E
Khairagarh 95 21 27N 81 2E
Khairpur 93 27 32N 68 49E
Khairpur □ 94 23 30N 69 8E
Khakhea 125 24 48S 23 22E
Khalach 85 38 4N 64 52E
Khalfallah 118 34 33N 0 16E
Khalij-e-Fars □ 93 28 20N 51 45E
Khalilabad 95 26 48N 83 5E
Khálki 68 39 36N 22 30E
Khálki, I. 69 36 15N 27 35E
Khalkidhiki □ 68 40 25N 23 20E
Khalkis 69 38 27N 23 42E
Khalmer-Sede = Tazovskiy 76 67 30N 78 30E
Khalmer Yu 76 67 58N 65 1E
Khalturin 81 58 40N 48 50E
Kham Kent 100 18 15N 104 43E
Khamaria 96 23 10N 80 52E
Khama's Country 128 21 45S 26 30E
Khamba Dzong 99 28 25N 88 30W
Khambhalia 94 22 14N 69 41E
Khamgaon 96 20 42N 76 37E
Khammam 96 17 11N 80 6E
Khân Yûnis 90 31 21N 34 18E
Khan Yunus 90 31 21N 34 18E
Khanabad, Afghan. 93 36 45N 69 5E
Khanabad, U.S.S.R. 85 40 59N 70 38E
Khānaqin 92 34 23N 45 25E
Khandrá 69 35 3N 26 8E
Khandwa 96 21 49N 76 22E
Khandyga 77 62 30N 134 50E
Khanewal 94 30 20N 71 55E
Khanga Sidi Nadji 119 34 50N 6 50E
Khanh Duong 100 12 44N 108 44E
Khanh Hung 101 9 36N 105 58E
Khaniá 69 35 30N 24 4E
Khaniá □ 69 35 0N 24 0E
Khanion Kólpos 69 35 33N 23 55E
Khanka, Oz. 76 45 0N 132 30E
Khanna 94 30 42N 76 16E
Khanpur 94 28 42N 70 35E
Khantau 85 44 13N 73 48E
Khanty-Mansiysk 76 61 0N 69 0E
Khapalu 95 35 10N 76 20E
Kharagpur 95 22 20N 87 25E
Kharaij 122 21 25N 41 0E
Kharan Kalat 93 28 34N 65 21E
Kharanaq 93 32 20N 54 45E
Kharda 96 18 40N 75 40E
Khardung La 95 34 20N 77 43E
Kharfa 92 22 0N 46 35E
Kharg, Jazireh 92 29 15N 50 28E
Khârga, El Wâhât el 122 25 0N 30 0E
Khargon, India 93 21 45N 75 35E
Khargon, India 96 21 45N 75 40E
Kharit, Wadi el 122 24 5N 34 10E
Kharkov 82 49 58N 36 20E
Kharmanli 67 41 55N 25 55E
Kharovsk 81 59 56N 40 13E
Kharsaniya 92 27 10N 49 10E
Khartoum = El Khartûm 123 15 31N 32 35E
Khartoum □ 123 16 0N 33 0E
Khasab 93 26 14N 56 15E
Khasavyurt 83 43 30N 46 40E
Khasebake 128 20 42S 24 29E
Khash 93 28 15N 61 5E
Khashm el Girba 123 14 59N 35 58E
Khasi Hills 98 25 30N 91 30E
Khaskovo 67 41 56N 25 30E
Khatanga 77 72 0N 102 20E
Khatanga, Zaliv 12 66 0N 112 0E
Khatauli 94 29 17N 77 43E
Khatyrchi 85 40 2N 65 58E
Khatyrka 77 62 3N 175 15E
Khavar □ 92 37 20N 46 0E
Khavast 85 40 10N 68 49E
Khawa 122 29 45N 40 25E
Khaydarken 85 39 57N 71 20E
Khazzân Jabal el Awliyâ 123 15 24N 32 20E
Khe Bo 100 19 8N 104 41E
Khe Long 100 21 29N 104 46E
Khed, Maharashtra, India 96 18 51N 73 56E
Khed, Maharashtra, India 96 17 43N 73 27E
Khed Brahma 93 24 7N 73 5E
Khekra 94 28 52N 77 20E
Khemarak Phouminville 101 11 37N 102 59E
Khemis Miliana 118 36 11N 2 14E
Khemisset 118 33 50N 6 1W
Khemmarat 100 16 10N 105 15E
Khenchela 119 35 28N 7 11E
Khenifra 118 32 58N 5 46W
Khenmarak Phouminville 102 11 40N 102 58E
Kherrata 119 36 27N 5 13E
Kherson 82 46 35N 32 35E
Khersónisos Akrotíri 69 35 30N 24 10E
Khetinsiring 99 32 54N 92 50E
Khiliomódhion 69 37 48N 22 51E
Khilok 77 51 30N 110 45E
Khimki 81 55 50N 37 20E
Khingan, mts. 86 47 0N 119 30E
Khíos 69 38 27N 26 9E
Khisar-Momina Banya 67 42 30N 24 44E
Khiuma = Hiiumaa 80 58 50N 22 45E
Khiva 76 41 30N 60 18E
Khiyav 92 38 30N 47 45E
Khlaouia 118 25 50N 6 32W
Khlong Khlung 100 16 12N 99 43E
Khlong, R. 101 15 30N 98 50E
Khmelnitsky 82 49 23N 27 0E
Khmer Republic ■ = Cambodia 100 12 15N 105 0E
Khoai, Hon 101 8 26N 104 50E
Khodzhent 85 40 14N 69 37E
Khoi 92 38 40N 45 0E
Khojak P. 93 30 55N 66 30E
Khok Kloi 101 8 17N 98 19E
Khok Pho 101 6 43N 101 6E
Khokholskiy 81 51 35N 38 50E
Kholm 80 57 10N 31 15E
Kholmsk 77 35 5N 139 48E
Khomas Hochland 128 22 40S 16 0E
Khomayn 92 33 40N 50 7E
Khomo 128 21 7S 24 35E
Khon Kaen 100 16 30N 102 47E
Khong, Camb. 101 13 55N 105 56E
Khong, Laos 100 14 7N 105 51E
Khong, R., Laos 101 15 0N 106 50E
Khong, R., Thai. 101 17 45N 104 20E
Khong Sedone 100 15 34N 105 49E
Khonh Hung (Soc Trang) 101 9 37N 105 50E
Khonu 77 66 30N 143 25E
Khoper, R. 81 52 0N 43 20E
Khor el 'Atash 123 13 20N 34 15E
Khóra 69 37 3N 21 42E
Khóra Sfákion 69 35 15N 24 9E
Khorasan □ 93 34 0N 58 0E
Khorat = Nakhon Ratchasima 100 14 59N 102 12E
Khorat, Cao Nguyen 100 15 30N 102 50E
Khorat Plat. 101 15 30N 102 50E
Khorb el Ethel 118 28 44N 6 11W
Khorog 85 37 30N 71 36E
Khorol 82 49 48N 33 15E
Khorramabad 92 33 30N 48 25E
Khorramshahr 92 30 29N 48 15E
Khota Kota 127 12 55S 34 15E
Khotan = Hot'ien 105 37 7N 79 55E
Khotin 82 48 31N 26 27E
Khouribga 118 32 58N 6 50W
Khowai 98 24 5N 91 40E
Khoyniki 80 51 54N 29 55E
Khrami, R. 83 41 30N 44 30E
Khrenovoye 81 51 4N 40 6E
Khristianá, I. 69 36 14N 25 13E
Khromtau 84 50 17N 58 27E
Khtapodhiá, I. 69 37 24N 25 34E
Khu Khan 100 14 42N 104 12E
Khufaifiya 92 24 50N 44 35E
Khugiani 94 31 28N 66 14E
Khulna 98 22 45N 89 34E
Khulna □ 98 22 45N 89 35E
Khulo 83 41 33N 42 19E
Khunzakh 83 42 35N 46 42E
Khur 93 32 55N 58 18E
Khurai 94 24 3N 78 23E
Khurais 92 24 55N 48 5E
Khurja 94 28 15N 77 58E
Khurma 92 21 58N 42 3E
Khūryān Mūryān, Jazā 'ir 91 17 30N 55 58E
Khush 93 32 55N 62 10E
Khushab 94 32 20N 72 20E
Khuzdar 94 27 52N 66 30E
Khuzestan □ 92 31 0N 50 0E
Khvalynsk 81 52 30N 48 2E
Khvatovka 81 52 24N 46 32E
Khvor 93 33 45N 55 0E
Khvormuj 93 28 40N 51 30E
Khvoy 92 38 35N 45 0E
Khvoynaya 80 58 49N 34 28E
Khwaja Muhammad 93 36 0N 70 0E
Khyber Pass 94 34 10N 71 8E
Kiabukwa 127 8 40S 24 48E
Kiadho, R. 96 19 50N 76 55E
Kiama 141 34 40S 150 50E
Kiamba 126 6 0N 124 40E
Kiambi 126 7 15S 28 0E
Kiambu 126 1 8S 36 50E
Kiangsi □ 109 27 20N 115 40E
Kiangsu □ 109 33 0N 119 50E
Kiania 129 20 18S 47 8E
Kiaohsien = Chiaohsien 107 36 20N 120 0E
Kibæk 73 56 2N 8 51E
Kibanga Port 126 0 10S 32 58E
Kibangou 124 3 18S 12 22E
Kibara 126 2 8S 33 30E
Kibara, Mts. 126 8 25S 27 10E
Kibombo 126 3 57S 25 53E
Kibondo 126 3 35S 30 45E
Kibondo □ 126 4 0S 30 55E
Kibumbu 126 3 32S 29 45E
Kibungu 126 2 10S 30 32E
Kibuye, Burundi 126 3 39S 29 59E
Kibuye, Rwanda 126 2 3S 29 21E
Kibwesa 126 6 30S 29 58E
Kibwezi 124 2 27S 37 57E
Kibworth Beauchamp 29 52 33N 0 59W
Kičevo 66 41 34N 20 59E
Kichiga 77 59 50N 163 5E
Kicking Horse Pass 152 51 27N 116 25W
Kidal 121 17 50N 1 22E
Kidderminster 28 52 24N 2 13W
Kidete 126 6 25S 37 17E
Kidira 120 14 28N 12 13W
Kidlington 28 51 49N 1 18W
Kidnappers, C. 142 39 38S 177 5E
Kidsgrove 32 53 6N 2 15W
Kidston 138 18 52S 144 8E
Kidstones 32 54 15N 2 2W
Kidugalle 126 6 49S 38 15E
Kidwelly 31 51 44N 4 20W
Kiel 48 54 16N 10 8E
Kiel Canal = Nord-Ostee-Kanal 48 54 15N 9 40E
Kielce 54 50 58N 20 42E
Kielce □ 54 51 0N 20 40E
Kielder 35 55 14N 2 35W
Kieldrecht 47 51 17N 4 11E
Kieler Bucht 48 54 30N 10 30E
Kien Binh 101 9 55N 105 19E
Kien Hung 101 9 43N 105 17E
Kien Tan 101 10 7N 105 17E
Kienchwan 99 26 30N 99 45E
Kienge 127 10 30S 27 30E
Kiessé 121 13 29N 4 1E
Kieta 135 6 12S 155 36E
Kiev = Kiyev 80 50 30N 30 28E
Kiffa 120 16 50N 11 15W
Kifisiá 69 38 4N 23 49E
Kifissós, R. 69 38 30N 23 0E
Kifri 92 34 45N 45 0E
Kigali 126 1 5S 30 4E
Kigarama 126 1 1S 31 50E
Kigoma □ 126 5 0S 30 0E
Kigoma-Ujiji 126 5 30S 30 0E
Kigomasha, Ras 126 4 58S 38 58E
Kihee 139 27 23S 142 37E
Kihikihi 142 38 2S 175 22E
Kii-Hantō 111 34 0N 135 45E
Kii-Sanchi 111 34 20N 136 0E
Kijik 147 60 20N 154 20W
Kikai-Jima 112 28 19N 129 58E
Kikinda 66 45 50N 20 30E
Kikládhes □ 69 37 0N 25 0E
Kikládhes, Is. 69 37 20N 24 30E
Kikoira 141 33 59S 146 40E
Kikori 135 7 13S 144 15E
Kikori, R. 135 7 5S 144 0E
Kikuchi 110 32 59N 130 47E
Kikwit 124 5 5S 18 45E
Kil 72 59 30N 13 20E
Kilafors 72 61 14N 16 36E
Kilakarai 97 9 12N 78 47E
Kilauea 147 22 13N 159 25W
Kilauea Crater 147 19 24N 155 17W
Kilbaha 39 52 35N 9 51W
Kilbeggan 38 53 22N 7 30W
Kilbeheny 39 52 18N 8 13W
Kilbennan 38 53 33N 8 54W
Kilbirnie 34 55 46N 4 42W
Kilbrannan Sd. 34 55 40N 5 23W
Kilbride 39 52 56N 6 5W
Kilbrien 39 52 12N 7 40W
Kilbrittain 39 51 40N 8 42W
Kilbuck Mts. 147 60 30N 160 0W
Kilchberg 51 47 18N 8 33E
Kilchoan 36 56 42N 6 8W
Kilcock 38 53 24N 6 40W
Kilcoe 39 51 33N 9 26W
Kilcogan 39 53 13N 8 52W
Kilconnell 39 53 20N 8 25W
Kilcoo 38 54 14N 6 1W
Kilcormac 39 53 11N 7 44W
Kilcoy 139 26 59S 152 30E
Kilcreggan 34 55 59N 4 50W
Kilcrohane 39 51 35N 9 44W
Kilcullen 39 53 8N 6 45W
Kilcurry 38 54 3N 6 26W
Kildare 39 53 10N 6 50W
Kildare □ 39 53 10N 6 50W
Kildavin 39 52 41N 6 42W
Kildemo 39 52 37N 8 50W
Kildonan 37 58 10N 3 50W
Kildorrery 39 52 15N 8 25W
Kilembe 126 0 15N 30 3E
Kilfenora 39 53 0N 9 13W
Kilfinan 34 55 57N 5 19W
Kilfinnane 39 52 21N 8 30W
Kilgarvan 39 51 54N 9 28W
Kilgore 159 32 22N 94 40W
Kilham 33 54 4N 0 22W
Kilian Qurghan 93 36 52N 78 3E
Kilifi 126 3 40S 39 48E
Kilifi □ 126 3 30S 39 40E
Kilimanjaro □ 126 4 0S 38 0E
Kilimanjaro, Mt. 126 3 7S 37 20E
Kilinailau, Is. 135 4 45S 155 20E
Kilindini 126 4 4S 39 40E
Kilis 92 36 50N 37 10E
Kiliya 82 45 28N 29 16E
Kilju 107 40 57N 129 25E
Kilkea 39 52 57N 6 55W
Kilkee 39 52 41N 9 40W
Kilkeel 38 54 4N 6 0W
Kilkelly 38 53 53N 8 50W
Kilkenny 39 52 40N 7 17W
Kilkenny □ 39 52 35N 7 15W
Kilkerrin 38 52 32N 8 36W
Kilkhampton 30 50 53N 4 30W
Kilkieran 39 53 20N 9 45W
Kilkieran B. 38 53 18N 9 45W
Kilkis 68 40 58N 22 57E
Kilkis □ 68 41 5N 22 50E
Kilkishen 39 52 49N 8 45W
Kilknock 38 53 42N 8 53W
Kill 39 52 11N 7 20W
Killadoon 38 53 44N 9 53W
Killadysert 39 52 40N 9 7W
Killala 38 54 13N 9 12W
Killala B. 38 54 20N 9 12W
Killaloe 39 52 48N 8 28W
Killam 152 52 47N 111 51W
Killane 39 53 20N 7 6W
Killard, Pt. 38 54 18N 5 31W
Killare 38 53 28N 7 34W
Killarney, Man., Can. 150 49 10N 99 40W
Killarney, Ont., Can. 153 45 55N 81 30W
Killarney, Ireland 39 52 2N 9 30W
Killarney, L's. of 39 52 0N 9 30W
Killary Harb. 38 53 38N 9 52W
Killashandra 38 54 1N 7 32W
Killashee 38 53 40N 7 52W
Killavally 38 53 22N 7 23W
Killavullen 39 52 8N 8 32W

Killchianaig Kíthnos


Killchianaig 34 56 2N 5 48W
Killdeer, Can. 153 49 6N 106 22W
Killdeer, U.S.A. 158 47 26N 102 48W
Killeagh 39 51 56N 8 0W
Killean 34 55 38N 5 40W
Killeen 159 31 7N 97 45W
Killeenleigh 39 51 58N 8 49W
Killeigh 39 53 14N 7 27W
Killenaule 39 52 35N 7 40W
Killianspick 39 52 21N 7 18W
Killiecrankie P. 37 56 44N 3 46W
Killimor 39 53 10N 8 17W
Killin 34 56 28N 4 20W
Killiney 39 53 15N 6 8W
Killingdal 71 62 47N 11 26 E
Killinghall 33 54 1N 1 33W
Killini 69 37 55N 21 8 E
Killini, Mts. 69 37 54N 22 25 E
Killinick 39 52 15N 6 29W
Killorglin 39 52 6N 9 48W
Killough 38 54 16N 5 40W
Killtullagh 39 53 17N 8 37W
Killucan 38 53 30N 7 10W
Killurin 39 52 23N 6 35W
Killybegs 38 54 38N 8 26W
Killyleagh 38 54 24N 5 40W
Kilmacolm 34 55 54N 4 39W
Kilmacthomas 39 52 13N 7 27W
Kilmaganny 39 52 26N 7 20W
Kilmaine 38 53 33N 9 10W
Kilmaley 39 52 50N 9 11W
Kilmallock 39 52 22N 8 35W
Kilmaluag 36 57 40N 6 18W
Kilmanagh 39 52 38N 7 28W
Kilmarnock, U.K. 34 55 36N 4 30W
Kilmarnock, U.S.A. 162 37 43N 76 23W
Kilmartin 34 56 8N 5 29W
Kilmaurs 34 55 37N 4 33W
Kilmeaden 39 52 15N 7 15W
Kilmeedy 39 52 25N 8 55W
Kilmelford 34 56 16N 5 30W
Kilmez 84 56 58N 50 55 E
Kilmez, R. 84 56 58N 50 28 E
Kilmichael 39 51 49N 9 4W
Kilmichael Pt. 39 52 44N 6 8W
Kilmihill 39 52 44N 9 18W
Kilmore, Austral. 141 37 25 S 144 53 E
Kilmore, Ireland 39 52 12N 6 35W
Kilmore Quay 39 52 10N 6 36W
Kilmuir 37 57 44N 4 7W
Kilmurry 39 52 47N 9 30W
Kilmurvy 39 53 9N 9 46W
Kilnaleck 38 53 52N 7 21W
Kilninver 34 56 20N 5 30W
Kilombero □ 127 8 0 S 37 0 E
Kilondo 127 9 45 S 34 20 E
Kilosa 126 6 48 S 37 0 E
Kilosa □ 126 6 48 S 37 0 E
Kilpatrick 39 51 46N 8 42W
Kilrea 38 54 58N 6 34W
Kilrenny 35 56 15N 2 40W
Kilronan 39 53 8N 9 40W
Kilrush 39 52 39N 9 30W
Kilsby 28 52 20N 1 11W
Kilsheelan 39 52 23N 7 37W
Kilsmo 72 59 6N 15 35 E
Kilsyth 35 55 58N 4 3W
Kiltamagh 38 53 52N 9 0W
Kiltealy 39 52 34N 6 45W
Kiltegan 39 52 53N 6 35W
Kiltoom 38 53 30N 8 0W
Kilwa □ 127 9 0 S 39 0 E
Kilwa Kisiwani 127 8 58 S 39 32 E
Kilwa Kivinje 127 8 45 S 39 25 E
Kilwa Masoko 127 8 55 S 39 30 E
Kilwinning 34 55 40N 4 41W
Kilworth 39 52 10N 8 15W
Kilworth, mts. 39 52 10N 8 15W
Kim 159 37 18N 103 20W
Kimamba 126 6 45 S 37 10 E
Kimba 140 33 8 S 136 23 E
Kimball, Nebr., U.S.A. 158 41 17N 103 20W
Kimball, S.D., U.S.A. 158 43 47N 98 57W
Kimbe 135 5 33 S 150 11 E
Kimbe B. 135 5 15 S 150 30 E
Kimberley, N.S.W., Austral. 140 32 50 S 141 4 E
Kimberley, W. Australia, Austral. 136 16 20 S 127 0 E
Kimberley, Can. 152 49 40N 115 59W
Kimberley, S. Afr. 128 28 43 S 24 46 E
Kimberley, dist. 132 16 20 S 127 0 E
Kimberley Downs 136 17 24 S 124 22 E
Kimberly 160 42 33N 114 25W
Kimbolton 29 52 17N 0 23W
Kimchŏn 107 36 11N 128 4 E
Kími 69 38 38N 24 6 E
Kimje 107 35 48N 126 45 E
Kimmeridge, oilfield 19 50 36N 2 6W
Kimolos 69 36 48N 24 37 E
Kimolos, I. 69 36 48N 24 35 E
Kimovsk 81 54 0N 38 29 E
Kimparana 120 12 48N 5 0W
Kimry 81 56 55N 37 15 E
Kimsquit 152 52 45N 126 57W
Kimstad 73 58 35N 15 58 E
Kinabalu, mt. 102 6 0N 116 0 E
Kínaros, I. 69 36 59N 26 15 E
Kinaskan L. 152 57 38N 130 8W
Kinawley 38 54 14N 7 40W
Kinbrace 37 58 16N 3 56W
Kincaid 153 49 40N 107 0W
Kincardine, Can. 150 44 10N 81 40W
Kincardine, Fife, U.K. 35 56 4N 3 43W
Kincardine, Highland, U.K. 37 57 52N 4 20W
Kincardine (□) 26 56 56N 2 28W
Kincraig 37 57 8N 3 57W
Kindersley 153 51 30N 109 10W
Kindia 120 10 0N 12 52W
Kindu 126 2 55 S 25 50 E
Kinel 84 53 15N 50 40 E
Kineshma 81 57 30N 42 5 E
Kinesi 126 1 25 S 33 50 E
Kineton 28 52 10N 1 30W
King and Queen 162 37 42N 76 50W
King City 163 36 11N 121 8W
King Cr. 138 24 35 S 139 30 E
King Edward, R. 136 14 14 S 126 35 E
King Frederick VI Land 12 63 0N 43 0W
King Frederick VIII Land 12 77 30N 25 0W
King George 162 38 15N 77 10W
King George B. 176 51 30 S 60 30W
King George I. 13 60 0 S 60 0W
King George Is. 149 53 40N 80 30W
King George Sd. 132 35 5 S 118 0 E
King I., Austral. 138 39 50 S 144 0 E
King I., Can. 152 52 10N 127 40W
King I. = Kadah Kyun 101 12 30N 98 20 E
King, L. 137 33 10 S 119 35 E
King Leopold Ranges 136 17 20 S 124 20 E
King, Mt. 138 25 10 S 147 30 E
King Sd. 136 16 50 S 123 20 E
King William I. 148 69 10N 97 25W
King William, L. 50 42 14 S 146 15 E
King William's Town 128 32 51 S 27 22 E
Kingairloch, dist. 36 56 37N 5 30W
Kingaroy 139 26 32 S 151 51 E
Kingarrow 38 54 55N 8 5W
Kingarth 34 55 45N 5 2W
Kingfisher 159 35 50N 97 55W
Kinghorn 35 56 4N 3 10W
Kingisepp 80 59 25N 28 40 E
Kingisepp (Kuressaare) 80 58 15N 22 15 E
Kingman, Ariz., U.S.A. 161 35 12N 114 2W
Kingman, Kans., U.S.A. 159 37 41N 96 9W
Kings B. 12 78 0N 15 0 E
Kings Canyon National Park 163 37 0N 118 35W
King's Lynn 29 52 45N 0 25 E
Kings Mountain 157 35 13N 81 20W
Kings Park 162 40 53N 73 16W
King's Peak 160 40 46N 110 27W
King's, R. 39 52 32N 7 12W
Kings, R. 163 36 10N 119 50W
King's Sutton 28 52 1N 1 16W
King's Worthy 28 51 6N 1 18W
Kingsbarns 35 56 18N 2 40W
Kingsbridge 30 50 17N 3 46W
Kingsburg 163 36 35N 119 36W
Kingsbury 28 52 33N 1 41W
Kingscote 140 35 33 S 137 31 E
Kingscourt 38 53 55N 6 48W
Kingskerswell 30 50 30N 3 34W
Kingsland 28 52 15N 2 49W
Kingsley 158 42 37N 95 58W
Kingsley Dam 158 41 20N 101 40W
Kingsport 157 36 33N 82 36W
Kingsteignton 30 50 32N 3 35W
Kingston, Can. 150 44 14N 76 30W
Kingston, Jamaica 166 18 0N 76 50W
Kingston, N.Z. 143 45 20 S 168 43 E
Kingston, U.K. 28 51 23N 1 40W
Kingston, N.Y., U.S.A. 162 41 55N 74 0W
Kingston, Pa., U.S.A. 162 41 19N 75 58W
Kingston, R.I., U.S.A. 162 41 29N 71 30W
Kingston South East 140 36 51 S 139 55 E
Kingston-upon-Thames 29 51 23N 0 20W
Kingstown, Austral. 141 30 29 S 151 6 E
Kingstown, St. Vinc. 167 13 10N 61 10W
Kingstree 157 33 40N 79 48W
Kingsville, Can. 150 42 2N 82 45W
Kingsville, U.S.A. 159 27 30N 97 53W
Kingswear 30 50 21N 3 33W
Kingswood 28 51 26N 2 31W
Kington 28 52 12N 3 2W
Kingtung 99 24 30N 100 50 E
Kingussie 37 47 5N 4 2W
Kinistino 153 52 57N 105 2W
Kinkala 124 4 18 S 14 49 E
Kinki □ 111 35 0N 135 30 E
Kinleith 142 38 20 S 175 56 E
Kinloch, N.Z. 143 44 51 S 168 20 E
Kinloch, L. More, U.K. 37 58 17N 4 50W
Kinloch, Rhum, U.K. 36 57 0N 6 18W
Kinloch Rannoch 37 56 41N 4 12W
Kinlochbervie 36 58 28N 5 5W
Kinlochewe 36 57 37N 5 20W
Kinlochiel 36 56 52N 5 20W
Kinlochleven 36 56 42N 4 59W
Kinlochmoidart 36 56 47N 5 43W
Kinloss 37 57 38N 3 37W
Kinlough 38 54 27N 8 16W
Kinn 71 61 34N 4 45 E
Kinna 73 57 32N 12 42 E
Kinnaird 152 49 17N 117 39W
Kinnaird's Hd. 37 57 40N 2 0W
Kinnared 73 57 2N 13 7 E
Kinnegad 38 53 28N 7 8W
Kinneret 90 32 44N 35 34 E
Kinneret, Yam 90 32 45N 35 35 E
Kinneviken, B. 73 58 38N 18 20 E
Kinnitty 39 53 6N 7 44W
Kino 164 28 45N 111 59W
Kinoje, R. 150 52 8N 81 25W
Kinomoto 111 35 30N 136 13 E
Kinoni, C. Afr. Emp. 123 5 40N 26 10 E
Kinoni, Uganda 126 0 41 S 30 28 E
Kinping 101 22 56N 103 15 E
Kinrooi 47 51 9N 5 45 E
Kinross 35 56 13N 3 25W
Kinross (□) 26 56 13N 3 25W
Kinsale 39 51 42N 8 31W
Kinsale Harbour 39 51 40N 8 30W
Kinsale Head, gasfield 19 51 20N 8 0W
Kinsale Old Hd. 39 51 37N 8 32W
Kinsarvik 71 60 22N 6 43 E
Kinshasa 124 4 20 S 15 15 E
Kinsley 159 37 57N 99 30W
Kinston 157 35 18N 77 35W
Kintampo 121 8 5N 1 41W
Kintap 102 3 51 S 115 13 E
Kintaravay 36 58 4N 6 42W
Kintore 37 57 14N 2 20W
Kintore Ra. 137 23 15 S 128 47 E
Kintyre, Mull of 34 55 17N 5 4W
Kintyre, pen. 34 55 30N 5 35W
Kinu 98 22 46N 95 37 E
Kinu-Gawa, R. 111 35 36N 139 57 E
Kinushseo, R. 150 55 15N 83 45W
Kinuso 152 55 25N 115 25W
Kinvara 39 53 8N 8 57W
Kinyangiri 126 4 35 S 34 37 E
Kióni 69 38 27N 20 41 E
Kiosk 150 46 6N 78 53W
Kiowa, Kans., U.S.A. 159 37 3N 98 30W
Kiowa, Okla., U.S.A. 159 34 45N 95 50W
Kipahigan L. 153 55 20N 101 55W
Kipanga 126 6 15 S 35 20 E
Kiparissia 69 37 15N 21 40 E
Kiparissiakós Kólpos 69 37 25N 21 25 E
Kipawa Res. Prov. Park 150 47 0N 78 30W
Kipembawe 124 7 38 S 33 27 E
Kipengere Ra. 127 9 12 S 34 15 E
Kipili 126 7 28 S 30 32 E
Kipini 126 2 30 S 40 32 E
Kipling 153 50 6N 102 38W
Kipnuk 147 59 55N 164 7W
Kippen 34 56 8N 4 12W
Kippure, Mt. 39 53 11N 6 23W
Kipushi 127 11 48 S 27 12 E
Kir 124 1 29 S 19 25 E
Kirandul 96 18 33N 81 10 E
Kiratpur 94 29 32N 78 12 E
Kirchberg 50 47 5N 7 35 E
Kirchhain 48 50 49N 8 54 E
Kirchheim 49 48 38N 9 20 E
Kirchheim Bolanden 49 49 40N 8 0 E
Kirchschlag 53 47 30N 16 19 E
Kircubbin 38 54 30N 5 33W
Kirensk 77 57 50N 107 55 E
Kirgiz S.S.R. □ 85 42 0N 75 0 E
Kirgiziya Steppe 79 50 0N 55 0 E
Kiri 124 1 29 S 19 25 E
Kiriburu 96 22 0N 85 0 E
Kirikkale 92 39 51N 33 32 E
Kirikopuni 142 35 50 S 174 1 E
Kirillov 81 59 51N 38 14 E
Kirin □ 107 43 50N 125 45 E
Kirindi, R. 97 6 15N 81 20 E
Kirishi 80 51 28N 31 59 E
Kirishima-Yama 110 31 58N 130 55 E
Kiriwina Is. = Trobriand Is. 138 8 40 S 151 0 E
Kirk Michael 32 54 17N 4 35W
Kirkbean 35 54 56N 3 35W
Kirkbride 32 54 54N 3 13W
Kirkburton 33 53 36N 1 42W
Kirkby 32 53 29N 2 54W
Kirkby-in-Ashfield 33 53 6N 1 15W
Kirkby Lonsdale 32 54 13N 2 36W
Kirkby Malzeard 33 54 10N 1 38W
Kirkby Moorside 33 54 16N 0 56W
Kirkby Steven 32 54 27N 2 23W
Kirkby Thore 32 54 38N 2 34W
Kirkcaldy 35 56 7N 3 10W
Kirkcolm 34 54 59N 5 4W
Kirkconnel 35 55 23N 4 0W
Kirkcowan 34 54 53N 4 38W
Kirkcudbright 35 54 50N 4 3W
Kirkcudbright (□) 26 55 4N 4 0W
Kirkcudbright B. 35 54 46N 4 0W
Kirkeby 73 55 7N 8 33 E
Kirkee 96 18 34N 73 56 E
Kirkenær 71 60 27N 12 3 E
Kirkenes 74 69 40N 30 5 E
Kirkham 32 53 47N 2 52W
Kirkinner 34 54 59N 4 28W
Kirkintilloch 35 55 57N 4 10W
Kirkjubæjarklaustur 74 63 47N 18 4W
Kirkland, Ariz., U.S.A. 161 34 29N 112 46W
Kirkland, Wash., U.S.A. 160 47 40N 122 10W
Kirkland Lake 150 48 9N 80 2W
Kirklareli 67 41 44N 27 15 E
Kirkliston 35 55 55N 3 27W
Kirkliston Ra. 143 44 25 S 170 34 E
Kirkmichael 37 56 43N 3 31W
Kirkoswald 32 54 46N 2 41W
Kirkoswold 34 55 19N 4 48W
Kirkstone P. 32 54 29N 2 55W
Kirksville 158 40 8N 92 35W
Kirkuk 92 35 30N 44 21 E
Kirkwall 37 58 59N 2 59W
Kirkwhelpington 35 55 9N 2 0W
Kirkwood 128 33 22 S 25 15 E
Kirlampudi 96 17 12N 82 12 E
Kirn 49 49 46N 7 29 E
Kirov, R.S.F.S.R., U.S.S.R. 81 54 3N 34 12 E
Kirov, R.S.F.S.R., U.S.S.R. 84 58 35N 49 40 E
Kirovabad 83 40 45N 46 10 E
Kirovakan 83 41 0N 44 0 E
Kirovo 85 40 26N 70 36 E
Kirovo-Chepetsk 81 58 28N 50 0 E
Kirovograd 82 48 35N 32 20 E
Kirovsk, R.S.F.S.R., U.S.S.R. 78 67 48N 33 50 E
Kirovsk, Ukraine, U.S.S.R. 83 48 35N 38 30 E
Kirovski 83 45 51N 48 11 E
Kirovskiy 85 44 52N 78 12 E
Kirovskoye 85 42 39N 71 35 E
Kirriemuir, Can. 153 51 56N 110 20W
Kirriemuir, U.K. 37 56 41N 3 0W
Kirs 84 59 21N 52 14 E
Kirsanov 81 52 35N 42 40 E
Kirşehir 92 39 14N 34 5 E
Kirstonia 128 25 30 S 23 45 E
Kirtachi 121 12 52N 2 30 E
Kirthar Range 93 27 0N 67 0 E
Kirtling 29 52 11N 0 27 E
Kirtlington 28 51 54N 1 9W
Kirton 39 52 56N 0 3W
Kirton-in-Lindsey 33 53 29N 0 35W
Kiruna 74 67 52N 20 15 E
Kirundu 124 0 50 S 25 35 E
Kirup 137 33 40 S 115 50 E
Kiryū 111 36 24N 139 20 E
Kiryu 81 55 5N 46 45 E
Kirzhach 81 56 12N 38 50 E
Kisa 73 58 0N 15 39 E
Kisaga 126 4 30 S 34 23 E
Kisalaya 166 14 40N 84 3W
Kisámou, Kólpos 69 35 30N 23 38 E
Kisanga 126 2 30N 26 35 E
Kisangani 126 0 35N 25 15 E
Kisar, I. 103 8 5 S 127 10 E
Kisaran 102 2 47N 99 29 E
Kisarawe 126 6 53 S 39 0 E
Kisarawe □ 126 7 3 S 39 0 E
Kisarazu 111 35 23N 139 55 E
Kisbér 53 47 30N 18 0 E
Kiselevsk 76 54 5N 86 6 E
Kishanganga, R. 95 34 50N 74 15 E
Kishanganj 95 26 3N 88 14 E
Kishangarh 94 27 50N 70 30 E
Kishi 121 9 1N 3 45 E
Kishinev 82 47 0N 28 50 E
Kishinoi 82 47 1N 28 50 E
Kishiwada 111 34 28N 135 22 E
Kishkeam 39 52 15N 9 12 E
Kishon 90 32 33N 35 12 E
Kishorganj 98 24 26N 90 40 E
Kishorn L. 36 57 22N 5 40W
Kishtwar 95 33 20N 75 48 E
Kisii 126 0 40 S 34 45 E
Kisii □ 126 0 40 S 34 45 E
Kisiju 124 7 23 S 39 19 E
Kısır, Dağ 83 41 0N 43 5 E
Kisizi 126 1 0 S 29 58 E
Kiska I. 147 52 0N 177 30 E
Kiskatinaw, R. 152 56 8N 120 10W
Kiskittogisu L. 153 54 13N 98 20W
Kiskomárom = Zalakomár 53 46 33N 17 10 E
Kiskőrös 53 46 37N 19 20 E
Kiskundorozsma 53 46 16N 20 5 E
Kiskunfelégyháza 53 46 42N 19 53 E
Kiskunhalas 53 46 28N 19 37 E
Kiskunmajsa 53 46 30N 19 48 E
Kislovodsk 83 43 50N 42 45 E
Kismayu 113 0 20 S 42 30 E
Kiso-Gawa, R. 111 35 2N 136 45 E
Kiso-Sammyaku 111 35 30N 137 45 E
Kisofukushima 111 35 52N 137 43 E
Kisoro 126 1 17 S 29 48 E
Kispest 53 47 27N 19 9 E
Kissidougou 120 9 5N 10 0W
Kissimmee 157 28 18N 81 22W
Kissimmee, R. 157 27 20N 81 0W
Kississing L. 153 55 34N 100 47W
Kistanje 63 43 58N 15 55 E
Kisterenye 53 48 3N 19 50 E
Kisújszállás 53 47 12N 20 50 E
Kisuki 110 35 17N 132 54 E
Kisumu 126 0 3 S 34 45 E
Kisvárda 53 48 14N 22 4 E
Kiswani 126 4 5 S 37 57 E
Kiswere 127 9 27 S 39 30 E
Kit Carson 158 38 48N 102 45W
Kita 120 13 5N 9 25W
Kita-Ura 111 36 0N 140 34 E
Kitab 85 39 7N 66 52 E
Kitakami, R. 112 38 25N 141 19 E
Kitakyūshū 110 33 50N 130 50 E
Kitale 126 1 0N 35 12 E
Kitami 112 43 48N 143 54 E
Kitangiri, L. 126 4 5 S 34 20 E
Kitano-Kaikyō 110 34 17N 134 58 E
Kitaya 127 10 38 S 40 8 E
Kitchener, Austral. 137 30 55 S 124 8 E
Kitchener, Can. 150 43 27N 80 29W
Kitchigami, R. 150 50 35N 78 5W
Kitega = Citega 126 3 30 S 29 58 E
Kiteto □ 126 5 0 S 37 0 E
Kitgum Matidi 126 3 17N 32 52 E
Kíthira 69 36 9N 23 0 E
Kíthira, I. 69 36 15N 23 0 E
Kíthnos 69 37 26N 24 27 E

| | | | |
|---|---|---|---|
| Kíthnos, I. | **69** | 37 25N | 24 25E |
| Kitimat | **152** | 54 3N | 128 38W |
| Kitinen, R. | **74** | 67 34N | 26 40E |
| Kitiyab | **123** | 17 13N | 33 35E |
| Kítros | **68** | 40 22N | 22 34E |
| Kitsuki | **110** | 33 35N | 131 37E |
| Kittakittaooloo, L. | **139** | 28 3S | 138 14E |
| Kittanning | **156** | 40 49N | 79 30W |
| Kittatinny Mts. | **162** | 41 0N | 75 0W |
| Kittery | **162** | 43 7N | 70 42W |
| Kitui | **126** | 1 17S | 38 0E |
| Kitui □ | **126** | 1 30S | 38 25E |
| Kitwe | **127** | 12 54S | 28 7E |
| Kitzbühel | **52** | 47 27N | 12 24E |
| Kitzingen | **49** | 49 44N | 10 9E |
| Kivalina | **147** | 67 45N | 164 40W |
| Kivalo | **74** | 66 18N | 26 0E |
| Kivarli | **94** | 24 33N | 72 46E |
| Kivotós | **68** | 40 13N | 21 26E |
| Kivu □ | **126** | 3 10S | 27 0E |
| Kivu, L. | **126** | 1 48S | 29 0E |
| Kiwai I. | **135** | 8 35S | 143 30E |
| Kiyev | **80** | 50 30N | 30 28E |
| Kiyevskoye Vdkhr. | **80** | 51 0N | 30 0E |
| Kizel | **84** | 59 3N | 57 40E |
| Kiziguru | **126** | 1 46S | 30 23E |
| Kizil Jilga | **95** | 35 26N | 79 50E |
| Kizil Kiya | **76** | 40 20N | 72 35E |
| Kızılcahaman | **82** | 40 30N | 32 30E |
| Kızılırmak | **83** | 39 15N | 36 0E |
| Kizilskoye | **84** | 52 44N | 58 54E |
| Kizimkazi | **126** | 6 28S | 39 30E |
| Kizlyar | **83** | 43 51N | 46 40E |
| Kizyl-Arvat | **76** | 38 58N | 56 15E |
| Kjellerup | **73** | 56 17N | 9 25E |
| Klabat, Teluk | **102** | 1 30S | 105 40E |
| Kladanj | **66** | 44 14N | 18 42E |
| Kladnica | **66** | 43 23N | 20 2E |
| Kladno | **52** | 50 10N | 14 7E |
| Kladovo | **66** | 44 36N | 22 33E |
| Klaeng | **100** | 12 47N | 101 39E |
| Klagenfurt | **52** | 46 38N | 14 20E |
| Klagerup | **73** | 55 36N | 13 17E |
| Klagshamn | **73** | 55 32N | 12 53E |
| Klagstorp | **73** | 55 22N | 13 23E |
| Klaipeda | **80** | 55 43N | 21 10E |
| Klakring | **73** | 55 42N | 9 59E |
| Klamath Falls | **160** | 42 20N | 121 50W |
| Klamath Mts. | **160** | 41 20N | 123 0W |
| Klamath, R. | **160** | 41 40N | 123 30W |
| Klang = Kelang | **101** | 3 1N | 101 33E |
| Klangklang | **98** | 22 41N | 93 26E |
| Klanjec | **63** | 46 3N | 15 45E |
| Klappan, R. | **152** | 58 0N | 129 43W |
| Klarälven | **72** | 60 32N | 13 15E |
| Klaten | **103** | 7 43S | 110 36E |
| Klatovy | **52** | 49 23N | 13 18E |
| Klawak | **152** | 55 35N | 133 0W |
| Klawer | **128** | 31 44S | 18 36E |
| Klazienaveen | **46** | 52 44N | 7 0E |
| Kłecko | **54** | 52 38N | 17 25E |
| Kleczew | **54** | 52 22N | 18 9E |
| Kleena Kleene | **152** | 52 0N | 124 50W |
| Klein | **160** | 46 26N | 108 31W |
| Klein-Karas | **128** | 27 33S | 18 7E |
| Klein Karoo | **128** | 33 45S | 21 30E |
| Kleine Gette, R. | **47** | 50 51N | 5 6E |
| Kleine Nete, R. | **47** | 51 12N | 4 46E |
| KlekovaCa, mt. | **63** | 44 25N | 16 32E |
| Klemtu | **152** | 52 35N | 128 55W |
| Klenovec, Czech. | **53** | 48 36N | 19 54E |
| Klenovec, Yugo. | **66** | 31 32N | 20 49E |
| Klepp | **71** | 59 48N | 5 36E |
| Klerksdorp | **128** | 26 51S | 26 38E |
| Kletnya | **80** | 53 30N | 33 2E |
| Kletsk | **80** | 53 5N | 26 45E |
| Kletskiy | **83** | 49 20N | 43 0E |
| Kleve | **48** | 51 46N | 6 10E |
| Klickitat | **160** | 45 50N | 12 10W |
| Klimovichi | **80** | 53 36N | 32 0E |
| Klin | **81** | 56 28N | 36 48E |
| Klinaklini, R. | **152** | 51 21N | 125 40W |
| Klinte | **73** | 53 35N | 10 12E |
| Klintehamn | **73** | 57 22N | 18 12E |
| Klintsey | **80** | 52 50N | 32 10E |
| Klipplaat | **128** | 33 0S | 24 22E |
| Klisura | **67** | 42 40N | 24 28E |
| Klitmøller | **73** | 57 3N | 8 30E |
| Kljajićevo | **66** | 45 45N | 19 17E |
| Ključ | **63** | 44 32N | 16 48E |
| Kłobuck | **54** | 50 55N | 19 5E |
| Kłodzko | **54** | 50 28N | 16 38E |
| Kloetinge | **47** | 51 30N | 3 56E |
| Klondike | **147** | 64 0N | 139 26W |
| Kloosterzande | **47** | 51 22N | 4 1E |
| Klosi | **68** | 41 28N | 20 10E |
| Klosterneuburg | **53** | 48 18N | 16 19E |
| Klosters | **51** | 46 52N | 9 52E |
| Kloten, Sweden | **72** | 59 54N | 15 19E |
| Kloten, Switz. | **51** | 47 27N | 8 35E |
| Klötze | **48** | 52 38N | 11 9E |
| Klouto | **121** | 6 57N | 0 44E |
| Klovborg | **73** | 55 56N | 9 30E |
| Klövsjöfj, mt. | **72** | 62 36N | 13 57E |
| Kluane, L. | **147** | 61 15N | 138 40W |
| Kluang = Keluang | **101** | 1 59N | 103 20E |
| Kluczbork | **54** | 50 58N | 18 12E |
| Klundert | **47** | 51 40N | 4 32E |
| Klyuchevskaya, Guba | **83** | 55 50N | 160 30E |
| Kmelnitski | **80** | 49 23N | 27 0E |
| Knapdale, dist. | **34** | 55 55N | 5 30W |
| Knaresborough | **33** | 54 1N | 1 29W |
| Knebworth | **29** | 51 52N | 0 11W |
| Knee L., Man., Can. | **153** | 55 3N | 94 45W |
| Knee L., Sask., Can. | **153** | 55 51N | 107 0W |
| Knesselare | **47** | 51 9N | 3 26E |
| Knezha | **67** | 43 30N | 23 56E |
| Knic | **66** | 43 53N | 20 45E |
| Knight Inlet | **152** | 50 45N | 125 40W |
| Knighton | **31** | 52 21N | 3 2W |
| Knights Ferry | **163** | 37 50N | 120 40W |
| Knight's Landing | **160** | 38 50N | 121 43W |
| Knin | **63** | 44 1N | 16 17E |
| Knittelfeld | **52** | 47 13N | 14 51E |
| Knjazevac | **66** | 43 35N | 22 18E |
| Knob, C. | **137** | 34 32S | 119 16E |
| Knock | **38** | 53 48N | 8 55W |
| Knockananna | **39** | 52 52N | 6 34W |
| Knockhoy Mt. | **39** | 51 49N | 9 27W |
| Knocklayd Mt. | **38** | 55 10N | 6 15W |
| Knocklofty | **39** | 52 20N | 7 49W |
| Knockmahon | **39** | 52 8N | 7 21W |
| Knockmealdown Mts. | **39** | 52 16N | 8 0W |
| Knocknaskagh Mt. | **39** | 52 7N | 8 25W |
| Knokke | **47** | 51 20N | 3 17E |
| Knott End | **32** | 53 55N | 3 0W |
| Knottingley | **33** | 53 42N | 1 15W |
| Knowle | **28** | 52 23N | 1 43W |
| Knox | **156** | 41 18N | 86 36W |
| Knox, C. | **152** | 54 11N | 133 5W |
| Knox City | **159** | 33 26N | 99 38W |
| Knox Coast | **13** | 66 30S | 108 0E |
| Knoxville, Iowa, U.S.A. | **158** | 41 20N | 93 5W |
| Knoxville, Pa., U.S.A. | **157** | 41 57N | 77 26W |
| Knoxville, Tenn., U.S.A. | **157** | 35 58N | 83 57W |
| Knoydart, dist. | **36** | 57 3N | 5 33W |
| Knurów | **54** | 50 13N | 18 38E |
| Knutsford | **32** | 53 18N | 2 22W |
| Knutshø | **71** | 62 18N | 9 41E |
| Knysna | **128** | 34 2S | 23 2E |
| Knyszyn | **54** | 53 20N | 22 56E |
| Ko Chang | **101** | 12 0N | 102 20E |
| Ko Ho, R. | **109** | 32 58N | 117 13E |
| Ko Kha | **100** | 18 11N | 99 24E |
| Ko Kut | **101** | 11 40N | 102 32E |
| Ko Phangan | **101** | 9 45N | 100 10E |
| Ko Phra Thong | **101** | 9 6N | 98 15E |
| Kō-Saki | **110** | 34 5N | 129 13E |
| Ko Samui | **101** | 9 30N | 100 0E |
| Koartac (Notre Dame de Koartac) | **149** | 61 5N | 69 36E |
| Koba, Aru, Indon. | **103** | 6 37S | 134 37E |
| Koba, Bangka, Indon. | **102** | 2 26S | 106 14E |
| Kobarid | **63** | 46 15N | 13 30E |
| Kobayashi | **110** | 31 56N | 130 59E |
| Kōbe | **111** | 34 45N | 135 10E |
| Kobelyaki | **82** | 49 11N | 34 9E |
| København | **73** | 55 41N | 12 34E |
| Koblenz, Ger. | **49** | 50 21N | 7 36E |
| Koblenz, Switz. | **50** | 47 37N | 8 14E |
| Kobo | **123** | 12 2N | 39 56E |
| Kobrin | **80** | 52 15N | 24 22E |
| Kobroor, Kepulauan | **103** | 6 10S | 134 30E |
| Kobuchizawa | **111** | 35 52N | 138 19E |
| Kobuk | **147** | 66 55N | 157 0W |
| Kobuk, R. | **147** | 66 55N | 157 0W |
| Kobuleti | **83** | 41 55N | 41 45E |
| Kobylin | **54** | 51 43N | 17 12E |
| Kobyłka | **54** | 52 21N | 21 10E |
| Kobylkino | **81** | 54 8N | 43 46E |
| Kobylnik | **80** | 54 58N | 26 39E |
| Kočani | **66** | 41 55N | 22 25E |
| Koçarli | **69** | 37 45N | 27 43E |
| Koceljevo | **66** | 44 28N | 19 50E |
| Kočevje | **63** | 45 39N | 14 50E |
| Kochang | **107** | 35 41N | 127 55E |
| Kochas | **95** | 25 15N | 83 56E |
| Kōchi | **110** | 33 30N | 133 35E |
| Kōchi-Heiya | **110** | 33 28N | 133 30E |
| Kōchi-ken □ | **110** | 33 40N | 133 30E |
| Kochiu | **108** | 23 25N | 103 7E |
| Kochkor-Ata | **85** | 41 1N | 72 29E |
| Kochkorka | **85** | 42 13N | 75 46E |
| Kodaikanai | **97** | 10 13N | 77 32E |
| Kodaira | **111** | 35 44N | 139 29E |
| Koddiyar Bay | **97** | 8 33N | 81 15E |
| Kodiak | **147** | 57 30N | 152 45W |
| Kodiak I. | **147** | 57 30N | 152 45W |
| Kodiang | **101** | 6 21N | 100 18E |
| Kodinar | **94** | 20 46N | 70 46E |
| Kodori, R. | **83** | 43 0N | 41 40E |
| Koekelare | **47** | 51 5N | 2 59E |
| K'oerch'inyuich-'iench'i | **107** | 46 5N | 122 5E |
| Koerhmu | **105** | 36 22N | 94 55E |
| Koersel | **47** | 51 3N | 5 17E |
| Koes | **125** | 26 0S | 19 15E |
| Köflach | **13** | 47 4N | 15 4E |
| Koforidua | **121** | 6 3N | 0 17W |
| Kōfu | **111** | 35 40N | 138 30E |
| Koga | **111** | 36 11N | 139 43E |
| Kogaluk, R. | **151** | 56 12N | 61 44W |
| Kogan | **139** | 27 2S | 150 40E |
| Kogin Baba | **121** | 7 55N | 11 35E |
| Kogizman | **92** | 40 5N | 43 10E |
| Kogon | **121** | 11 20N | 14 32W |
| Kogota | **112** | 38 33N | 141 3E |
| Koh-i-Bab, mts. | **94** | 34 30N | 67 0E |
| Koh-i-Khurd | **94** | 33 30N | 65 59E |
| Koh-i-Mazar | **94** | 32 30N | 66 25E |
| Kohat | **94** | 33 40N | 71 29E |
| Kohima | **98** | 25 35N | 94 10E |
| Kohler Ra. | **13** | 77 0N | 110 0W |
| Kohtla-Järve | **80** | 59 20N | 27 20E |
| Kohukohu | **142** | 36 31S | 173 38E |
| Koindong | **107** | 40 28N | 126 18E |
| Kojabuti | **103** | 2 36S | 140 37E |
| Kojetin | **53** | 49 21N | 17 20E |
| Kojima | **110** | 34 20N | 133 38E |
| Kōjo | **110** | 34 33N | 133 55E |
| Kojō | **107** | 38 58N | 127 58E |
| Kojonup | **137** | 33 48S | 117 10E |
| Kok Yangak | **85** | 41 2N | 73 12E |
| Koka | **122** | 20 5N | 30 35E |
| Kokand | **85** | 40 30N | 70 57E |
| Kokanee Glacier Prov. Park | **152** | 49 47N | 117 10W |
| Kokas | **103** | 2 42S | 132 26E |
| Kokava | **53** | 48 35N | 19 50E |
| Kokchetav | **76** | 53 20N | 69 10E |
| Kokemäenjoki | **75** | 61 32N | 21 44E |
| Kokemäenjoki = Kumo älv | **75** | 61 32N | 21 44E |
| Kokhma | **81** | 56 55N | 41 18E |
| Kokkola (Gamlakarleby) | **74** | 63 50N | 23 8E |
| Koko, Mid-Western, Nigeria | **121** | 6 5N | 5 28E |
| Koko, North-Western, Nigeria | **121** | 11 28N | 4 29E |
| Koko Kyunzu | **101** | 14 10N | 93 25E |
| Koko-Nor = Ch'ing Hai | **105** | 37 0N | 100 20E |
| Koko Shili | **99** | 35 20N | 91 0E |
| Kokoda | **135** | 8 54S | 147 47E |
| Kokolopozo | **120** | 5 8N | 6 5W |
| Kokomo | **156** | 40 30N | 86 6W |
| Kokopo | **135** | 4 22S | 152 19E |
| Kokoro | **121** | 14 12N | 0 55E |
| Kokoura | **77** | 71 35N | 144 50E |
| Koksan | **107** | 38 46N | 126 40E |
| Koksengir, Gora | **85** | 44 21N | 65 6E |
| Koksoak, R. | **149** | 54 5N | 64 10W |
| Kokstad | **125** | 30 32S | 29 29E |
| Kokubu | **110** | 31 44N | 130 46E |
| Kola | **78** | 68 45N | 33 8E |
| Kola, I. | **103** | 5 35S | 134 30E |
| Kola Pen. = Kolskiy P-ov. | **78** | 67 30N | 38 0E |
| Kolagede | **103** | 7 54S | 110 26E |
| Kolahoi | **95** | 34 12N | 75 22E |
| Kolahun | **120** | 8 15N | 10 4W |
| Kolaka | **103** | 4 3S | 121 46E |
| K'olamai | **105** | 45 30N | 84 55E |
| K'olan | **106** | 38 43N | 111 32E |
| Kolar | **97** | 13 12N | 78 15E |
| Kolar Gold Fields | **97** | 12 58N | 78 16E |
| Kolari | **74** | 67 20N | 23 48E |
| Kolarovgrad | **67** | 43 27N | 26 42E |
| Kolarovo | **53** | 47 56N | 18 0E |
| Kolašin | **66** | 42 50N | 19 31E |
| Kolayat | **93** | 27 50N | 72 50E |
| Kolby | **73** | 55 49N | 10 33E |
| Kolby Kås | **73** | 55 48N | 10 32E |
| Kolchugino | **81** | 56 17N | 39 22E |
| Kolda | **120** | 12 55N | 14 50W |
| Koldewey I. | **12** | 77 0N | 18 0W |
| Kolding | **73** | 55 30N | 9 29E |
| Kole | **124** | 3 16S | 22 42E |
| Koléa | **118** | 36 38N | 2 46E |
| Kolepom, Pulau | **103** | 8 0S | 138 30E |
| Kölfors | **72** | 62 9N | 16 30E |
| Kolguyev, Ostrov | **78** | 69 20N | 48 30E |
| Kolham | **46** | 53 11N | 6 44E |
| Kolhapur | **96** | 16 43N | 74 15E |
| Kolia | **120** | 9 46N | 6 28W |
| Kolín | **52** | 50 2N | 15 9E |
| Kolind | **73** | 56 21N | 10 34E |
| Kölleda | **48** | 51 11N | 11 14E |
| Kollegal | **97** | 12 9N | 77 9E |
| Kolleru L. | **96** | 16 40N | 81 10E |
| Kollum | **46** | 53 17N | 6 10E |
| Kolmanskop | **128** | 26 45S | 15 14E |
| Köln | **48** | 50 56N | 9 58E |
| Koło | **54** | 52 14N | 18 40E |
| Kołobrzeg | **54** | 54 10N | 15 35E |
| Kologriv | **81** | 58 48N | 44 25E |
| Kolokani | **120** | 13 35N | 7 45W |
| Kolomna | **81** | 55 8N | 38 45E |
| Kolomyya | **82** | 48 31N | 25 2E |
| Kolondiéba | **120** | 11 5N | 6 54W |
| Kolonodale | **103** | 2 3S | 121 25E |
| Kolosib | **98** | 24 15N | 92 45E |
| Kolpashevo | **76** | 58 20N | 83 5E |
| Kolpino | **80** | 59 44N | 30 39E |
| Kolpny | **81** | 52 12N | 37 10E |
| Kolskiy Poluostrov | **78** | 67 30N | 38 0E |
| Kolskiy Zaliv | **78** | 69 23N | 34 0E |
| Koltubanovskiy | **84** | 52 57N | 52 2E |
| Kolubara, R. | **66** | 44 35N | 20 15E |
| Kolumna | **54** | 51 36N | 19 14E |
| Koluszki | **54** | 51 45N | 19 46E |
| Kolwezi | **124** | 10 40S | 25 25E |
| Kolyberovo | **81** | 55 15N | 38 40E |
| Kolyma, R. | **77** | 64 40N | 153 0E |
| Kolymskoye, Okhotsko | **77** | 63 0N | 157 0E |
| Kôm Ombo | **122** | 24 25N | 32 52E |
| Komagene | **111** | 35 44N | 137 58E |
| Komaki | **111** | 35 17N | 136 55E |
| Komandorskiye Ostrava | **77** | 55 0N | 167 0E |
| Komárno | **53** | 47 49N | 18 5E |
| Komárom | **53** | 47 43N | 18 7E |
| Komárom □ | **53** | 47 35N | 18 20E |
| Komarovo | **80** | 58 38N | 33 40E |
| Komatsu | **111** | 36 25S | 136 30E |
| Komatsukima | **110** | 34 0N | 134 35E |
| Kombissiri | **121** | 12 4N | 1 20W |
| Kombori | **120** | 13 26N | 3 56W |
| Kombóti | **69** | 39 6N | 21 5E |
| Komen | **63** | 45 49N | 13 45E |
| Komenda | **121** | 5 4N | 1 28W |
| Komi, A.S.S.R. □ | **84** | 64 0N | 55 0E |
| Komiza | **63** | 43 3N | 16 11E |
| Komló | **53** | 46 15N | 18 16E |
| Kommamur Canal | **97** | 16 0N | 80 25E |
| Kommunarsk | **83** | 48 30N | 38 45E |
| Kommunizma, Pik | **85** | 39 0N | 72 2E |
| Komnes | **71** | 59 30N | 9 55E |
| Komodo | **103** | 8 37S | 119 20E |
| Komoé | **120** | 5 12N | 3 44W |
| Komono | **124** | 3 15S | 13 20E |
| Komoran, Pulau | **103** | 8 18S | 138 45E |
| Komoro | **111** | 36 19N | 138 26E |
| Komorze | **54** | 62 8N | 17 38E |
| Komotiri | **68** | 41 9N | 25 26E |
| Kompong Bang | **101** | 12 24N | 104 40E |
| Kompong Cham | **101** | 11 54N | 105 30E |
| Kompong Chhnang | **101** | 12 20N | 104 35E |
| Kompong Chikreng | **100** | 13 5N | 104 18E |
| Kompong Kleang | **101** | 13 6N | 104 8E |
| Kompong Luong | **101** | 11 49N | 104 48E |
| Kompong Pranak | **101** | 13 35N | 104 55E |
| Kompong Som | **101** | 10 38N | 103 30E |
| Kompong Som, Chhung | **101** | 10 50N | 103 32E |
| Kompong Speu | **101** | 11 26N | 104 32E |
| Kompong Sralao | **100** | 14 5N | 105 46E |
| Kompong Thom | **100** | 12 35N | 104 51E |
| Kompong Trabeck, Camb. | **100** | 13 6N | 105 14E |
| Kompong Trabeck, Camb. | **101** | 11 9N | 105 28E |
| Kompong Trach, Camb. | **101** | 11 25N | 105 48E |
| Kompong Trach, Camb. | **118** | 10 34N | 104 28E |
| Kompong Tralach | **101** | 11 54N | 104 47E |
| Komrat | **82** | 46 18N | 28 40E |
| Komsberge | **128** | 32 40S | 20 45E |
| Komsomolabad | **85** | 38 50N | 69 55E |
| Komsomolets | **84** | 53 45N | 62 2E |
| Komsomolets, Ostrov | **77** | 80 30N | 95 0E |
| Komsomolsk, R.S.F.S.R., U.S.S.R. | **77** | 50 30N | 137 0E |
| Komsomolsk, Turkmen S.S.R., U.S.S.R. | **85** | 39 2N | 63 36E |
| Komsomolskiy | **81** | 53 30N | 49 40E |
| Kona, Niger | **121** | 13 33N | 8 3E |
| Kona, Nigeria | **121** | 8 58N | 11 15E |
| Konakovo | **81** | 56 52N | 36 45E |
| Konam Dzong | **99** | 29 5N | 93 0E |
| Konawa | **159** | 34 59N | 96 46W |
| Kondagaon | **96** | 19 35N | 81 35E |
| Konde | **126** | 4 57S | 39 45E |
| Kondiá | **68** | 39 52N | 25 10E |
| Kondinin | **137** | 32 34S | 118 8E |
| Kondoa | **126** | 4 55S | 35 50E |
| Kondoa □ | **126** | 5 0S | 36 0E |
| Kondratyevo | **77** | 57 30N | 98 30E |
| Konduga | **121** | 11 35N | 13 26E |
| Kong | **120** | 8 54N | 4 36W |
| Kong Christian IX.s Land | **12** | 68 0N | 36 0W |
| Kong Christian X.s Land | **12** | 74 0N | 29 0W |
| Kong Frederik VIII.s Land | **12** | 78 30N | 26 0W |
| Kong Frederik VI.s Kyst | **12** | 63 0N | 43 0W |
| Kong, Koh | **101** | 11 20N | 103 0E |
| Kong Oscar Fjord | **12** | 72 20N | 24 0W |
| Kong, R. | **100** | 13 32N | 105 58E |
| Konga | **73** | 56 30N | 15 6E |
| Kongeå | **73** | 55 24N | 8 39E |
| Kongju | **107** | 36 30N | 127 0E |
| Konglu | **98** | 27 13N | 97 57E |
| Kongolo | **126** | 5 22S | 27 0E |
| Kongoussi | **121** | 13 19N | 1 32W |
| Kongsberg | **71** | 59 39N | 9 39E |
| Kongsvinger | **71** | 60 12N | 12 2E |
| Kongsvoll | **71** | 62 20N | 9 36E |
| Kongwa | **126** | 6 11S | 36 26E |
| Koni | **127** | 10 40S | 27 11E |
| Koni, Mts. | **127** | 10 36S | 27 10E |
| Koniecpol | **54** | 50 46N | 19 40E |
| Königsberg = Kaliningrad | **80** | 54 42N | 20 32E |
| Königslutter | **48** | 52 14N | 10 50E |
| Königswusterhausen | **48** | 52 19N | 13 38E |
| Konin | **54** | 52 12N | 18 15E |
| Konin □ | **54** | 52 15N | 18 30E |
| Konispol | **68** | 39 42N | 20 10E |
| Kónitsa | **68** | 40 5N | 20 48E |
| Köniz | **50** | 46 56N | 7 25E |
| Konjic | **66** | 43 42N | 17 58E |
| Konjice | **63** | 46 20N | 15 28E |
| Konkouré, R. | **120** | 10 30N | 13 40W |
| Könnern | **48** | 51 40N | 11 45E |
| Konnur | **96** | 16 14N | 74 49E |
| Kono | **120** | 8 30N | 11 5W |
| Konoğlu | **82** | 40 35N | 31 50E |
| Konolfingen | **50** | 46 54N | 7 38E |
| Konongo | **121** | 6 40N | 1 15W |
| Konos | **135** | 3 10S | 151 44E |
| Konosha | **78** | 61 0N | 40 5E |
| Kōnosu | **111** | 36 3N | 139 31E |
| Konotop | **80** | 51 12N | 33 7E |
| Konskaya, R. | **82** | 47 30N | 35 0E |
| Konskie | **54** | 51 15N | 20 23E |
| Konsmo | **71** | 58 16N | 7 23E |
| Konstantinovka | **82** | 48 32N | 37 39E |
| Konstantinovski, R.S.F.S.R., U.S.S.R. | **81** | 57 45N | 39 35E |

FHK

Konstantinovski Krokom


Konstantinovski, R.S.F.S.R., U.S.S.R. 83 47 33N 41 10 E
Konstantynów Łódzki 54 51 45N 19 20 E
Konstanz 49 47 39N 9 10 E
Kontagora 121 10 23N 5 27 E
Kontich 47 51 8N 4 26 E
Kontum 100 14 24N 108 0 E
Kontum, Plat. du 100 14 30N 108 0 E
Konya 92 37 52N 32 35 E
Konyin 98 22 58N 94 42 E
Konz Karthaus 49 49 41N 6 36 E
Konza 124 1 45 S 37 0 E
Konzhakovskiy Kamen, Gora 84 59 38N 59 8 E
Koog 12 52 27N 4 49 E
Kookynie 137 29 17 S 121 22 E
Koolan I. 136 16 0 S 123 45 E
Kooline 136 22 57 S 116 20 E
Kooloonong 140 34 48 S 143 10 E
Koolyanobbing 137 30 48 S 119 36 E
Koolymilka P.O. 140 30 58 S 136 32 E
Koondrook 140 35 33 S 144 8 E
Koorawatha 141 34 2 S 148 33 E
Koorda 137 30 48 S 117 35 E
Kooskia 160 46 9N 115 59W
Koostatak 153 51 26N 97 26W
Kootenai, R. 160 48 30N 115 30W
Kootenay L. 153 49 45N 117 0W
Kootenay Nat. Park 152 51 0N 116 0W
Kootingal 173 31 1 S 151 3 E
Kopa 85 43 31N 75 50 E
Kopaonik Planina 66 43 10N 21 0 E
Kopargaon 96 19 51N 74 28 E
Kópavogur 74 64 6N 21 55W
Koper 63 45 31N 13 44 E
Kopervik 71 59 17N 5 17 E
Kopeysk 84 55 7N 61 37 E
Kopi 139 33 24 S 135 40 E
Köping 72 59 31N 16 3 E
Kopiste 63 42 48N 16 42 E
Kopliku 68 42 15N 19 25 E
Köpmanholmen 72 63 10N 18 35 E
Köpmannebro 73 58 45N 12 30 E
Koppal 97 15 23N 76 5 E
Koppang 71 61 34N 11 3 E
Kopparberg 75 59 52N 15 0 E
Kopparbergs län □ 147 61 20N 14 15 E
Koppeh Dāgh 93 38 0N 58 0 E
Kopperå 71 63 24N 11 50 E
Kopperå 71 63 24N 11 52 E
Koppio 140 34 26 S 135 51 E
Koppom 72 59 43N 12 10 E
Koprivlen 67 41 36N 23 53 E
Koprivnica 63 46 12N 16 45 E
Koprivshtitsa 67 42 40N 24 19 E
Kopychintsy 80 49 7N 25 58 E
Korab, mt. 66 41 44N 20 40 E
Korakiána 68 39 42N 19 45 E
Koraput 96 18 50N 82 40 E
Korba 95 22 20N 82 45 E
Korbach 48 51 17N 8 50 E
Korbu, G. 101 4 41N 101 18 E
Korça 68 40 37N 20 50 E
Korça □ 68 40 40N 20 50 E
Korčula 63 42 57N 17 8 E
Korčula, I. 63 42 57N 17 0 E
Korčulanski Kanal 63 43 3N 16 40 E
Kordestān □ 92 36 0N 47 0 E
Korea 107 40 0N 127 0 E
Korea Bay 107 39 0N 124 0 E
Korea, South ■ 107 36 0N 128 0 E
Korea Strait 107 34 0N 129 30 E
Koregaon 96 17 40N 74 10 E
Korenevo 80 51 27N 34 55 E
Korenovsk 83 45 12N 39 22 E
Korets 80 50 40N 27 5 E
Korgus 122 19 16N 33 48 E
Korhogo 120 9 29N 5 28W
Koribundu 120 7 41N 11 46W
Koridina 139 29 42 S 143 25 E
Korim 103 0 58 S 136 10 E
Korinthía □ 69 37 50N 22 35 E
Korinthiakós Kólpos 69 38 16N 22 30 E
Kórinthos 69 37 56N 22 55 E
Korioumé 120 16 35N 3 0W
Kōriyama 112 37 24N 140 23 E
Korkino 84 54 54N 61 23 E
Körmend 53 47 5N 16 35 E
Kornat, I. 63 43 50N 15 20 E
Korneshty 82 47 21N 28 1 E
Korneuburg 53 48 20N 16 20 E
Korning 73 56 30N 9 44 E
Kornsjø 71 58 57N 11 39 E
Kornstad 71 62 59N 7 27 E
Koro, Ivory C. 120 8 32N 7 30W
Koro, Mali 120 14 1N 2 58W
Koroba 135 5 44 S 142 47 E
Korocha 81 50 55N 37 30 E
Korogwe 124 5 5 S 38 25 E
Korogwe □ 126 5 0 S 38 20 E
Koroit 140 38 18 S 142 24 E
Korong Vale 140 36 22 S 143 45 E
Koróni 69 36 48N 21 57 E
Korónia, Limni 68 40 47N 23 37 E
Koronis 69 37 12N 25 35 E
Koronowo 54 53 19N 17 55 E
Koror 103 7 20N 134 28 E
Körös, R. 53 46 45N 20 20 E
Köröstarcsa 53 46 53N 21 3 E
Korosten 80 50 57N 28 25 E
Korotoyak 81 51 1N 39 2 E
Korraraika, B. de 129 17 45 S 43 57 E
Korsakov 77 46 30N 142 42 E
Korshavn 71 58 2N 7 0 E
Korshunovo 77 58 37N 110 10 E
Korsör 73 55 20N 11 9 E
Korsze 54 54 11N 21 9 E
Kortemark 47 51 2N 3 3 E
Kortessem 47 50 52N 5 23 E
Korti 122 18 0N 31 40 E
Kortrijk 47 50 50N 3 17 E
Korumburra 141 38 26 S 145 50 E
Korwai 94 24 7N 78 5 E
Koryakskiy Khrebet 77 61 0N 171 0 E
Koryŏng 107 35 44N 128 15 E
Kos 69 36 52N 27 19 E
Kos, I. 69 36 50N 27 15 E
Kosa, Ethiopia 123 7 50N 36 50 E
Kosa, U.S.S.R. 84 59 56N 55 0 E
Kosa, R. 84 60 11N 55 10 E
Kosaya Gora 81 54 10N 37 30 E
Koschagy 79 46 40N 54 0 E
Kosciusko 159 33 3N 89 34W
Kosciusko, I. 152 56 0N 133 40W
Kosciusko, Mt. 141 36 27 S 148 16 E
Kösély, R. 53 47 25N 21 30 E
Kosgi 96 16 58N 77 43 E
Kosha 122 20 50N 30 30 E
Koshigaya 111 35 54N 139 48 E
K'oshih 105 39 29N 75 58 E
K'oshihk'ot'engch'i 107 43 17N 117 24 E
Koshiki-Rettō 110 31 45N 129 49 E
Kōshoku 111 36 38N 138 6 E
Koshtëbë 85 41 5N 74 15 E
Kosi 94 27 48N 77 29 E
Kosi-meer 129 27 0 S 32 50 E
Košice 53 48 42N 21 15 E
Kosjerič 66 44 0N 19 55 E
Koslan 78 63 28N 48 52 E
Kosŏng 107 38 48N 128 24 E
Kosovska-Mitrovica 66 42 54N 20 52 E
Kosścian 54 52 5N 16 40 E
Kosścierzyna 54 54 8N 17 59 E
Kosso 120 5 3N 5 47W
Kostajnica 63 45 17N 16 30 E
Kostanjevica 63 45 51N 15 27 E
Kostelec 53 50 14N 16 35 E
Kostenets 67 42 15N 23 52 E
Koster 128 25 52 S 26 54 E
Kôstî 123 13 8N 32 43 E
Kostolac 66 44 43N 21 15 E
Kostroma 81 57 50N 41 58 E
Kostromskoye Vdkhr. 81 57 52N 40 49 E
Kostrzyn 54 52 24N 17 14 E
Kostyukovichi 80 53 10N 32 4 E
Koszalin 54 54 12N 16 8 E
Koszalin □ 54 54 10N 16 10 E
Kószeg 53 47 23N 16 33 E
Kot Adu 94 30 30N 71 0 E
Kot Moman 94 32 13N 73 0 E
Kota 94 25 14N 75 49 E
Kota Baharu 101 6 7N 102 14 E
Kota Kinabalu 102 6 0N 116 12 E
Kota-Kota = Khota Kota 127 12 55 S 34 15 E
Kota Tinggi 101 1 44N 103 53 E
Kotaagung 102 5 38 S 104 29 E
Kotabaru 102 3 20 S 116 20 E
Kotabumi 102 4 49 S 104 46 E
Kotamobagu 103 0 57N 124 31 E
Kotaneelee, R. 152 60 11N 123 42W
Kotawaringin 102 2 28 S 111 27 E
Kotchandpur 98 23 24N 89 1 E
Kotcho L. 152 59 7N 121 12W
Kotel 67 42 52N 26 26 E
Kotelnich 81 58 20N 48 10 E
Kotelnikovo 83 47 45N 43 15 E
Kotelnyy, Ostrov 77 75 10N 139 0 E
Kothagudam 96 17 30N 80 40 E
Kothapet 96 19 21N 79 28 E
Köthen 48 51 44N 11 59 E
Kothi 95 24 45N 80 40 E
Kotiro 94 26 17N 67 13 E
Kotka 75 60 28N 26 58 E
Kotlas 78 61 15N 47 0 E
Kotlenska Planina 67 42 56N 26 30 E
Kotli 94 33 30N 73 55 E
Kotmul 95 35 32N 75 10 E
Kotohira 110 34 11N 133 49 E
Kotonkoro 121 11 3N 5 58 E
Kotor 66 42 25N 18 47 E
Kotor Varoš 66 44 38N 17 22 E
Kotoriba 63 46 23N 16 48 E
Kotovo 81 50 22N 44 45 E
Kotovsk 82 47 55N 29 35 E
Kotputli 94 27 43N 76 12 E
Kotri 94 25 22N 68 22 E
Kotri, R. 96 19 45N 80 35 E
Kótronas 69 36 38N 22 29 E
Kötschach-Mauthern 52 46 41N 13 1 E
Kottayam 97 9 35N 76 33 E
Kottur 97 10 34N 76 56 E
Kotturu 93 14 45N 76 10 E
Kotuy, R. 77 70 30N 103 0 E
Kotzebue 147 66 50N 162 40W
Kotzebue Sd. 147 66 30N 164 0W
Kouango 124 5 0N 20 10 E
Koudekerke 47 51 29N 3 33 E
Koudougou 120 12 10N 2 20W
Koufonísi, I. 69 34 56N 26 8 E
Koufonísia, I. 69 36 57N 25 35 E
Kougaberge 128 33 48 S 24 20 E
Kouibli 120 7 15N 7 14W
Kouilou, R. 124 4 10 S 12 5 E
Kouki 124 7 22N 17 3 E
Koula Moutou 124 1 15 S 12 25 E
Koulen 100 13 50N 104 40 E
Koulikoro 120 12 40N 7 50W
Koumala 138 21 38 S 149 15 E
Koumankoun 120 11 58N 6 6W
Koumbia, Guin. 120 11 54N 13 40W
Koumbia, Upp. Vol. 120 11 10N 3 50W
Koumboum 120 10 25N 13 0W
Koumpenntoum 120 13 59N 14 34W
Koumra 117 8 50N 17 35 E
Koumradskiy 76 47 20N 75 0 E
Koundara 120 12 29N 13 18W
Kountze 159 30 20N 94 22W
Koupangtzu 107 41 22N 121 46 E
Koupéla 121 12 11N 0 21 E
Kourizo, Passe de 119 22 28N 15 27 E
Kouroussa 120 10 45N 9 45W
Koussané 120 14 53N 11 14W
Kousseri 117 12 0N 14 55 E
Koutiala 120 12 25N 5 35W
Kouto 120 9 53N 6 25W
Kouvé 121 6 25N 0 59 E
KovaCica 66 45 5N 20 38 E
Kovel 80 51 10N 24 20 E
Kovilpatti 97 9 10N 77 50 E
Kovin 66 44 44N 20 59 E
Kovrov 81 56 25N 41 25 E
Kovur, Andhra Pradesh, India 96 17 3N 81 39 E
Kovur, Andhra Pradesh, India 97 14 30N 80 1 E
Kowal 54 52 32N 19 7 E
Kowalewo Pomorskie 54 53 10N 18 52 E
Kowkash 150 50 20N 87 20W
Kowloon 109 22 20N 114 15 E
Kowŏn 107 39 26N 127 14 E
Kōyama 110 31 20N 130 56 E
Koyan, Pegunungan 102 3 15N 114 30 E
Koyang 106 33 31N 116 11 E
Koytash 85 40 11N 67 19 E
Koyuk 147 64 55N 161 20W
Koyukuk, R. 147 65 45N 156 30W
Koyulhisar 82 40 20N 37 52 E
Koza 112 26 19N 127 46 E
Kozan 92 37 35N 35 50 E
Kozàni 68 40 19N 21 47 E
Kozàni □ 68 40 18N 21 45 E
Kozara, Mts. 63 45 0N 17 0 E
Kozarac 63 44 58N 16 48 E
Kozelsk 80 54 2N 35 38 E
Kozhikode = Calicut 97 11 15N 75 43 E
Kozhva 78 65 10N 57 0 E
Koziegłowy 54 50 37N 19 8 E
Kozje 63 46 5N 15 35 E
Kozle 54 50 20N 18 8 E
Kozlodui 67 43 45N 23 42 E
Kozlovets 67 43 30N 25 20 E
Kozmin 54 51 48N 17 27 E
Kōzu-Shima 111 34 13N 139 10 E
Kozuchów 54 51 45N 15 31 E
Kpabia 121 9 10N 0 20W
Kpandae 121 8 30N 0 2W
Kpandu 121 7 2N 0 18 E
Kpessi 121 8 4N 1 16 E
Kra Buri 101 10 22N 98 46 E
Kra, Isthmus of = Kra, Kho Khot 101 10 15N 99 30 E
Kra, Kho Khot 101 10 15N 99 30 E
Krabbendijke 47 51 26N 4 7 E
Krabi 101 8 4N 98 55 E
Kragan 103 6 43 S 111 38 E
Kragerø 71 58 52N 9 25 E
Kragujevac 66 44 2N 20 56 E
Krajenka 54 53 18N 16 59 E
Krakatau = Rakata, Pulau 102 6 10 S 105 20 E
Krakor 100 12 32N 104 12 E
Kraków 54 50 4N 19 57 E
Kraków □ 53 50 0N 20 0 E
Kraksaan 103 7 43 S 113 23 E
Kraksmala 73 57 2N 15 20 E
Kråkstad 71 59 40N 10 50 E
Kråkstad 71 59 39N 10 55 E
Kralanh 100 13 35N 103 25 E
Králiky 53 50 6N 16 45 E
Kraljevo 66 43 44N 20 41 E
Kralovice 52 49 59N 13 29 E
Královsky Chlmec 53 48 27N 22 0 E
Kralupy 52 50 13N 14 20 E
Kramatorsk 82 48 50N 37 30 E
Kramer 161 35 0N 117 38W
Kramfors 72 62 55N 17 48 E
Kramis, C. 118 36 26N 0 45 E
Krångede 72 63 9N 16 10 E
Krångede 72 63 9N 16 6 E
Kraniá 68 39 53N 21 18 E
Kranidhion 69 37 20N 23 10 E
Kranj 63 46 16N 14 22 E
Kranjska Gora 63 46 29N 13 48 E
Kranzberg 128 21 59 S 15 37 E
Krapina 63 46 10N 15 52 E
Krapina, R. 63 46 0N 15 55 E
Krapivna 81 53 58N 37 10 E
Krapkowice 54 50 29N 17 56 E
Kras Polyana 83 43 40N 40 25 E
Krashyy Klyuch 84 55 23N 56 39 E
Kraskino 77 42 44N 130 48 E
Krāslāva 80 55 52N 27 12 E
Kraslice 52 50 19N 12 31 E
Krasnaya Gorbatka 81 55 52N 41 45 E
Krasnik Fabryezny 54 50 58N 22 11 E
Krasnoarmeisk 82 48 18N 37 11 E
Krasnoarmeysk, R.S.F.S.R., U.S.S.R. 81 50 32N 45 50 E
Krasnoarmeysk, R.S.F.S.R., U.S.S.R. 83 48 30N 44 25 E
Krasnodar 83 45 5N 38 50 E
Krasnodonetskaya 83 48 5N 40 50 E
Krasnog Dardeiskoye 82 45 32N 34 16 E
Krasnogorskiy 81 56 10N 48 28 E
Krasnograd 82 49 27N 35 27 E
Krasnogvardeysk 85 39 46N 67 16 E
Krasnogvardeyskoye 83 45 52N 41 33 E
Krasnoïarsk 77 56 8N 93 0 E
Krasnokamsk 84 58 4N 55 48 E
Krasnokutsk 80 50 10N 34 50 E
Krasnoperekopsk 82 46 0N 33 54 E
Krasnoselkupsk 76 65 20N 82 10 E
Krasnoslobodsk 83 48 42N 44 33 E
Krasnoturinsk 84 59 46N 60 12 E
Krasnoufimsk 84 56 57N 57 46 E
Krasnouralsk 84 58 21N 60 3 E
Krasnousolskiy 84 53 54N 56 27 E
Krasnovishersk 84 60 23N 57 3 E
Krasnovodsk 79 40 0N 52 52 E
Krasnoyarsk 77 56 8N 93 0 E
Krasnoyarskiy 84 51 58N 59 55 E
Krasnoye, Kal., U.S.S.R. 83 46 16N 45 0 E
Krasnoye, R.S.F.S.R., U.S.S.R. 81 59 15N 47 40 E
Krasnoye, Ukr., U.S.S.R. 80 49 56N 24 42 E
Krasnozavodsk 81 56 38N 38 16 E
Krasny Liman 82 48 58N 37 50 E
Krasny Sulin 83 47 52N 40 8 E
Krasnystaw 54 50 57N 23 5 E
Krasnyy 80 49 56N 24 42 E
Krasnyy Kholm, R.S.F.S.R., U.S.S.R. 81 58 10N 37 10 E
Krasnyy Kholm, R.S.F.S.R., U.S.S.R. 84 51 35N 54 9 E
Krasnyy Kut 81 50 50N 47 0 E
Krasnyy Luch 83 48 13N 39 0 E
Krasnyy Yar, Kal., U.S.S.R. 83 46 43N 48 23 E
Krasnyy Yar, R.S.F.S.R., U.S.S.R. 81 50 42N 44 45 E
Krasnyy Yar, R.S.F.S.R., U.S.S.R. 81 53 30N 50 22 E
Krasnyyoskolskoye, Vdkhr. 82 49 30N 37 30 E
Kraśnik 54 50 55N 22 5 E
Kraszna, R. 53 48 0N 22 20 E
Kratie 100 12 32N 106 10 E
Kratke Ra. 135 6 45 S 146 0 E
Kratovo 66 42 6N 22 10 E
Kravanh, Chuor Phnum 101 12 0N 103 32 E
Krawang 103 6 19N 107 18 E
Krefeld 48 51 20N 6 22 E
Kremaston, Limni 69 38 52N 21 30 E
Kremenchug 82 49 5N 33 25 E
Kremenchugskoye Vdkhr. 82 49 20N 32 30 E
Kremenets 82 50 8N 25 43 E
Kremenica 66 40 55N 21 25 E
Kremennaya 82 49 1N 38 10 E
Kremikovtsi 67 42 46N 23 28 E
Kremmen 48 52 45N 13 1 E
Kremmling 160 40 10N 106 30W
Kremnica 53 48 45N 18 50 E
Krems 52 48 25N 15 36 E
Kremsmünster 52 48 3N 14 8 E
Kretinga 80 55 53N 21 15 E
Krettamia 118 28 47N 3 27W
Krettsy 80 58 15N 32 30 E
Kreuzlingen 51 47 38N 9 10 E
Kribi 121 2 57N 9 56 E
Krichem 67 46 16N 24 28 E
Krichev 80 53 45N 31 50 E
Kriens 51 47 2N 8 17 E
Krim, mt. 63 45 53N 14 30 E
Krimpen 46 51 55N 4 34 E
Krionéri 69 38 20N 21 35 E
Krishna, R. 96 16 30N 77 0 E
Krishnagiri 97 12 32N 78 16 E
Krishnanagar 95 23 24N 88 33 E
Krishnaraja Sagara 97 12 20N 76 30 E
Kristianopel 73 56 12N 16 0 E
Kristiansand 71 58 9N 8 1 E
Kristianstad 73 56 2N 14 9 E
Kristianstad □ 75 56 15N 14 0 E
Kristiansund 71 63 7N 7 45 E
Kristiinankaupunki 74 62 16N 21 21 E
Kristinehamn 72 59 18N 14 13 E
Kristinestad 74 62 16N 21 21 E
Kriti, I. 69 35 15N 25 0 E
Kritsá 69 35 10N 25 41 E
Kriva Palanka 66 42 11N 22 19 E
Kriva, R. 66 42 12N 22 18 E
Krivaja, R. 66 44 15N 18 22 E
Krivelj 66 44 8N 22 5 E
Krivoy Rog 82 47 51N 33 20 E
Krizevci 63 46 3N 16 32 E
Krk 63 45 5N 14 36 E
Krk, I. 63 45 8N 14 40 E
Krka, R. 63 45 50N 15 30 E
Krkonoše 52 50 50N 16 10 E
Krnov 53 50 5N 17 40 E
Krobia 54 51 47N 16 59 E
Kročehlavy 52 50 8N 14 9 E
Kroeng Krai 101 14 55N 98 30 E
Krokawo 54 54 47N 18 9 E
Krokeaí 69 36 53N 22 32 E
Kroken, Norway 71 58 57N 9 8 E
Kroken, Sweden 71 59 2N 11 23 E
Krokom 72 63 20N 14 30 E

Krolevets Kuybyshevskoye Vdkhr


Krolevets 80 51 35N 33 20 E
Kroměříz 53 49 18N 17 21 E
Krommenie 46 52 30N 4 46 E
Krompachy 53 48 54N 20 52 E
Kromy 80 52 40N 35 48 E
Kronobergs län □ 73 56 45N 14 30 E
Kronprins Harald Kyst 13 70 0 S 35 1 E
Kronprins Olav Kyst 13 69 0 S 42 0 E
Kronprinsesse Märtha Kyst 13 73 30 S 10 0W
Kronshtadt 80 60 5N 29 35 E
Kroonstad 125 27 43 S 27 19 E
Kröpelin 48 54 4N 11 48 E
Kropotkin 77 45 25N 40 35 E
Kropp 48 54 24N 9 32 E
Krośniewice 54 52 15N 19 11 E
Krosno 54 49 35N 21 56 E
Krosno □ 54 49 30N 22 0 E
Krosno Odrz 54 52 3N 15 7 E
Krosścienko 54 49 29N 20 25 E
Krotoszyn 54 51 42N 17 23 E
Krotovka 84 53 18N 51 10 E
Krraba 68 41 13N 20 0 E
Krško 63 45 57N 15 30 E
Krstača, mt. 66 42 57N 20 8 E
Kruger Nat. Pk. 129 24 0 S 31 40 E
Krugersdorp 129 26 5 S 27 46 E
Kruidfontein 128 32 48 S 21 59 E
Kruiningen 47 51 27N 4 2 E
Kruis, Kaap 128 21 55 S 13 57 E
Kruishoutem 47 50 54N 3 32 E
Kruisland 47 51 34N 4 25 E
Kruja 68 41 32N 19 46 E
Krulevshchina 80 55 5N 27 45 E
Kruma 68 42 37N 20 28 E
Krumovgrad 67 41 29N 25 38 E
Krung Thep 100 13 45N 100 35 E
Krupanj 66 44 25N 19 22 E
Krupina 53 48 22N 19 5 E
Krupinica, R. 53 48 15N 19 5 E
Kruševac 66 43 35N 21 28 E
Krušovo 66 41 23N 21 19 E
Kruszwica 54 52 40N 18 20 E
Kruzof I. 152 57 10N 135 40W
Krylbo 72 60 7N 16 15 E
Krymsk Abinsk 82 44 50N 38 0 E
Krymskaya 82 45 0N 34 0 E
Krynica 54 49 25N 20 57 E
Krynica Morska 54 54 23N 19 28 E
Krynki 54 53 17N 23 43 E
Kryulyany 70 47 12N 29 9 E
Krzepice 54 50 58N 18 50 E
Krzeszowice 54 50 8N 19 37 E
Krzywin 54 51 58N 16 50 E
Krzyz 54 52 52N 16 0 E
Ksabi, Alg. 118 29 8N 0 58W
Ksabi, Moroc. 118 32 51N 4 13W
Ksar Chellala 118 35 13N 2 19 E
Ksar el Boukhari 118 35 51N 2 52 E
Ksar el Kebir 118 35 0N 6 0W
Ksar es Souk 118 31 58N 4 20W
Ksar Rhilane 119 33 0N 9 39 E
Ksiba 118 32 46N 6 0W
Ksour, Mts. des 118 32 45N 0 30W
Kstovo 81 56 12N 44 13 E
Kuachou 109 32 14N 119 24 E
Kuala 102 2 46N 105 47 E
Kuala Berang 101 5 5N 103 1 E
Kuala Dungun 101 4 45N 103 25 E
Kuala Kangsar 101 4 46N 100 56 E
Kuala Kerai 101 5 30N 102 12 E
Kuala Klawang 101 2 56N 102 5 E
Kuala Kubu Baharu 101 3 34N 101 39 E
Kuala Lipis 101 4 10N 102 3 E
Kuala Lumpur 101 3 9N 101 41 E
Kuala Marang 101 5 12N 103 13 E
Kuala Nerang 101 6 16N 100 37 E
Kuala Pilah 101 2 45N 102 15 E
Kuala Rompin 101 2 49N 103 29 E
Kuala Selangor 101 3 20N 101 15 E
Kuala Terengganu 101 5 20N 103 8 E
Kuala Trengganu 101 5 20N 103 8 E
Kualakahi Chan 147 22 2N 159 53W
Kualakapuas 102 2 55 S 114 20 E
Kualakurun 102 1 10 S 113 50 E
Kualapembuang, Indon. 102 3 14 S 112 38 E
Kualapembuang, Indon. 102 2 52 S 111 45 E
Kuanaan 107 34 8N 119 24 E
Kuanch'eng 107 40 39N 118 32 E
Kuandang 103 0 56N 123 1 E
Kuangan 108 30 30N 106 35 E
Kuangch'ang 109 26 50N 116 15 E
Kuangchou 109 23 12N 113 12 E
Kuangfeng 109 28 26N 118 12 E
Kuanghan 108 30 56N 104 15 E
Kuanghua 109 32 22N 111 43 E
Kuangjao 107 37 5N 118 25 E
Kuangling 106 39 47N 114 10 E
Kuangnan 108 24 3N 105 3 E
Kuangning 109 23 40N 112 23 E
Kuangshi 109 29 55N 115 25 E
Kuangshun 108 26 5N 106 16 E
Kuangte 109 30 54N 119 26 E
Kuangtse 109 27 30N 117 24 E
Kuangwuch'eng 106 37 49N 108 51 E
Kuangyüan 108 32 22N 105 50 E
Kuanhsien 108 31 0N 103 40 E
Kuanling 108 25 55N 105 35 E
Kuanp'ing 109 31 39N 110 16 E
Kuantan 101 3 49N 103 20 E
Kuant'ao 106 36 31N 115 16 E
Kuantaok'ou 106 34 18N 111 1 E
K'uantien 107 40 47N 124 43 E
Kuanyang 109 25 29N 111 9 E
Kuanyün 107 34 17N 119 15 E
Kuaram 123 12 25N 39 30 E
Kuba 83 41 21N 48 32 E
Kubak 93 27 10N 63 10 E
Kuban, R. 82 45 5N 38 0 E
Kubenskoye, Oz. 81 59 40N 39 25 E
Kuberle 83 47 0N 42 20 E
Kubokawa 110 33 12N 133 8 E
Kubor 135 6 10 S 144 44 E
Kubrat 67 43 49N 26 31 E
Kučevo 66 44 30N 21 40 E
Kucha Gompa 95 34 25N 76 56 E
Kuchaman 94 27 13N 74 47 E
Kuch'ang 108 24 58N 102 45 E
Kuchang 109 28 37N 109 56 E
K'uche K'uerhlo 105 41 43N 82 54 E
Kuchenspitze 49 47 3N 10 14 E
Kuchiang 109 27 11N 114 47 E
Kuching 102 1 33N 110 25 E
Kuchinoerabu-Jima 112 30 28N 130 11 E
Kuchinotsu 110 32 36N 130 11 E
Kuçove = Qytet Stalin 68 40 47N 19 57 E
Kud, R. 94 26 30N 66 12 E
Kuda 93 23 10N 71 15 E
Kudalier, R. 96 18 20N 78 40 E
Kudamatsu 110 34 0N 131 52 E
Kudara 85 38 25N 72 39 E
Kudat 102 6 55N 116 55 E
Kudremukh, Mt. 97 13 15N 75 20 E
Kuduarra Well 136 20 38 S 126 20 E
Kudus 103 6 48 S 110 51 E
Kudymkar 84 59 1N 54 39 E
Kuei Chiang, R. 109 23 33N 111 18 E
Kueich'i 109 28 17N 117 11 E
Kueich'ih 109 30 42N 117 30 E
Kueichu 108 26 25N 106 40 E
Kueihsien 108 23 6N 109 36 E
Kueilin 109 25 20N 110 18 E
Kueip'ing 108 23 24N 110 5 E
Kueiting 108 26 30N 107 17 E
Kueitung 109 26 12N 114 0 E
Kueiyang, Hunan, China 109 25 44N 112 43 E
Kueiyang, Kweichow, China 108 26 35N 106 43 E
K'uerhlo 105 41 44N 86 9 E
Kufra, El Wâhât el 117 24 17N 23 15 E
Kufrinja 90 32 20N 35 41 E
Kufstein 52 47 35N 12 11 E
Kugmallit B. 147 29 0N 134 0W
Kugong, I. 150 56 18N 79 50W
Kūh-e-Alijuq 93 31 30N 51 41 E
Kūh-e-Dinar 93 30 10N 51 0 E
Kūh-e-Hazaran 93 29 35N 57 20 E
Kūh-e-Jebel Barez 93 29 0N 58 0 E
Kūh-e-Sorkh 93 35 30N 58 45 E
Kūh-e-Taftan 93 28 40N 61 0 E
Kūhak 93 27 12N 63 10 E
Kūhha-ye-Bashakerd 93 26 45N 59 0 E
Kūhha-ye Sabalān 93 38 15N 47 45 E
Kuhnsdorf 52 46 37N 14 38 E
Kuhpayeh 93 32 44N 52 20 E
Kui Buri 101 12 3N 99 52 E
Kuinre 46 52 47N 5 51 E
Kuiseb, R. 125 23 40 S 15 30 E
Kuiu I. 147 56 40N 134 15W
Kujangdong 107 39 57N 126 1 E
Kuji 112 40 11N 141 46 E
Kujū-San 110 33 5N 131 15 E
Kujukuri-Heiya 111 35 45N 140 30 E
Kukavica, mt. 66 42 48N 21 57 E
Kukawa 121 12 58N 13 27 E
Kukerin 137 33 13 S 118 0 E
Kukësi 68 42 5N 20 20 E
Kukësi □ 68 42 25N 20 15 E
Kukko 123 8 26N 41 35 E
Kukmor 84 56 11N 50 54 E
Kukup 101 1 20N 103 27 E
K'uk'ushihli Shanmo 105 35 20N 91 0 E
Kukvidze 81 50 40N 43 15 E
Kula, Bulg. 66 43 52N 22 36 E
Kula, Yugo. 66 45 37N 19 32 E
Kulai 101 1 44N 103 35 E
Kulal, Mt. 126 2 42N 36 57 E
Kulaly, O. 83 45 0N 50 0 E
Kulanak 85 41 22N 75 30 E
Kulasekharapattanam 97 8 20N 78 0 E
Kuldiga 80 56 58N 21 59 E
Kuldja = Ining 105 43 54N 81 21 E
Kuldu 123 12 50N 28 30 E
Kulebaki 81 55 22N 42 25 E
Kulen Vakuf 63 44 35N 16 2 E
Kulgam 95 33 36N 75 2 E
Kuli 83 42 2N 46 12 E
Kulim 101 5 22N 100 34 E
Kulin 137 32 40 S 118 2 E
Kulja 137 30 28 S 117 18 E
Küllük 69 37 12N 27 36 E
Kulm 158 46 22N 98 58W
K'uloch'akonnoerh 106 43 25N 114 50 E
Kulsary 76 46 59N 54 1 E
Kultay 76 45 5N 51 40 E
Kulti 95 23 43N 86 50 E
Kulu 93 37 12N 115 2 E
Kulumadau 138 9 15 S 152 50 E
K'ulunch'i 107 42 44N 121 44 E
Kulunda 76 52 45N 79 15 E
Kulungar 94 34 0N 69 2 E
Kulwin 140 35 0 S 142 42 E
Kulyab 85 37 55N 69 50 E
Kum Tekei 76 43 10N 79 30 E
Kuma 110 33 39N 132 54 E
Kuma, R. 83 44 55N 45 57 E
Kumaganum 121 13 8N 10 38 E
Kumagaya 111 36 9N 139 22 E
Kumak 84 51 10N 60 8 E
Kumamoto 110 32 45N 130 45 E
Kumamoto-ken □ 110 32 30N 130 40 E
Kumano 111 33 54N 136 5 E
Kumano-Nada 111 33 47N 136 20 E
Kumanovo 66 42 9N 21 42 E
Kumara 143 42 37 S 171 12 E
Kumarkhali 98 23 51N 89 15 E
Kumarl 137 32 47 S 121 33 E
Kumasi 120 6 41N 1 38W
Kumba 121 4 36N 9 24 E
Kumbakonam 97 10 58N 79 25 E
Kumbarilla 139 27 15 S 150 55 E
Kumbo 121 6 15N 10 36 E
Kumbukkan Oya 97 6 35N 81 40 E
Kümchön 107 38 10N 126 29 E
Kumdok 95 33 32N 78 10 E
Kumeny 81 58 10N 49 47 E
Kümhwa 107 38 17N 127 28 E
Kumi 126 1 30N 33 58 E
Kumkale 68 40 30N 26 13 E
Kumla 72 59 8N 15 10 E
Kumo 121 10 1N 11 12 E
Kumon Bum 98 26 30N 97 15 E
Kumotori-Yama 111 35 51N 138 57 E
Kumta 97 14 29N 74 32 E
Kumtorkala 83 43 2N 46 50 E
Kumukahi, C. 147 19 31N 154 49W
Kumusi, R. 135 8 16 S 148 13 E
Kumylzhenskaya 83 49 51N 42 38 E
Kunágota 53 46 26N 21 3 E
Kunama 141 35 35 S 148 4 E
Kunar 93 34 30N 71 3 E
Kunashir, Ostrov 77 44 0N 146 0 E
Kunch 95 26 0N 79 10 E
Kunda 80 59 30N 26 34 E
Kundiawa 135 6 2 S 145 1 E
Kundip 137 33 42 S 120 10 E
Kundla 94 21 21N 71 25 E
Kunduz 93 36 50N 68 50 E
Kunduz □ 93 36 50N 68 50 E
Kunene, R. 128 17 15 S 13 40 E
Kungala 139 29 58 S 153 7 E
Kungälv 73 57 53N 11 59 E
Kungan 109 30 4N 112 12 E
Kungch'eng 109 24 50N 110 49 E
K'ungch'iao Ho 105 41 48N 86 47 E
Kŭngdong 107 39 9N 126 5 E
Kungey Alatau, Khrebet 85 42 50N 77 0 E
Kunghit I. 152 52 6N 131 3W
Kungho 105 36 28N 100 45 E
Kungka 108 28 44N 100 22 E
Kungkuan 108 21 51N 109 33 E
Kungrad 76 43 6N 58 54 E
Kungsbacka 73 57 30N 12 5 E
Kungshan 108 27 41N 97 37 E
Kungt'an 108 28 49N 108 38 E
Kungur 84 57 25N 56 57 E
Kungurri 138 21 3 S 148 46 E
Kungyangon 98 16 27N 96 1 E
Kungyingtzu 107 43 38N 121 0 E
Kunhar, R. 95 35 0N 73 40 E
Kunhegyes 53 47 22N 20 36 E
Kunimi-Dake 110 32 33N 131 1 E
Kuningan 103 6 59 S 108 29 E
Kunisaki 110 33 33N 131 45 E
Kunlara 140 34 54 S 139 55 E
Kunlong 98 23 20N 98 50 E
Kunlun Shan 105 36 0N 86 30 E
Kunmadaras 53 47 28N 20 45 E
K'unming 108 25 5N 102 40 E
Kunnamkulam 97 10 38N 76 7 E
Kunrade 47 50 53N 5 57 E
Kunsan 107 35 59N 126 45 E
K'unshan 109 31 22N 121 0 E
Kunszentmárton 53 46 50N 20 20 E
Kununurra 136 15 40 S 128 39 E
Kunwarara 138 22 55 S 150 9 E
Kuohsien 106 38 57N 112 46 E
Kuopio 74 62 53N 27 35 E
Kuopion Lääni □ 74 63 25N 27 10 E
Kupa, R. 63 45 30N 16 10 E
Kupang 103 10 19 S 123 39 E
Kupeik'ou 107 40 42N 117 9 E
Kupiano 135 10 4 S 148 14 E
Kupreanof I. 147 56 50N 133 30W
Kupres 66 44 1N 17 15 E
Kupyansk 82 49 45N 37 35 E
Kupyansk-Uzlovoi 82 49 52N 37 34 E
Kur, R. 98 26 50N 91 0 E
Kura, R. 83 40 20N 47 30 E
Kurahashi-Jima 110 34 8N 132 31 E
Kuranda 138 16 48 S 145 35 E
Kurandvad 96 16 45N 74 39 E
Kurashiki 110 34 40N 133 50 E
Kurayoshi 110 35 26N 133 50 E
Kurday 85 43 21N 74 59 E
Kurdistan, reg. 92 37 30N 42 0 E
Kurduvadi 96 18 8N 75 29 E
Kure 110 34 14N 132 32 E
Kuressaare = Kingisepp 80 58 15N 22 15 E
Kurgaldzhino 76 50 35N 70 20 E
Kurgan, R.S.F.S.R., U.S.S.R. 77 64 5N 172 50W
Kurgan, R.S.F.S.R., U.S.S.R. 84 55 26N 65 18 E
Kurgan-Tyube 85 37 50N 68 47 E
Kuria Muria I = Khyryān Muryān J. 91 17 30N 55 58 E
Kurichchi 97 11 36N 77 35 E
Kuridala 138 21 16 S 140 29 E
Kurigram 98 25 49N 89 39 E
Kurihashi 111 36 8N 139 42 E
Kuril Trench 142 44 0N 153 0 E
Kurilskiye Ostrova 77 45 0N 150 0 E
Kuring Kuru 128 17 42 S 18 32 E
Kuringen 47 50 56N 5 18 E
Kurino 110 31 57N 130 43 E
KüRKkkuyu 68 39 35N 26 27 E
Kurkur 122 23 50N 32 0 E
Kurkûrah 119 31 30N 20 1 E
Kurla 96 19 5N 72 52 E
Kurlovski 81 55 25N 40 40 E
Kurma 123 13 55N 24 40 E
Kurmuk 123 10 33N 34 21 E
Kurnalpi 137 30 29 S 122 16 E
Kurnool 97 15 45N 78 0 E
Kurobe-Gawe, R. 111 36 55N 137 25 E
Kurogi 110 33 12N 130 40 E
Kurovskoye 81 55 35N 38 55 E
Kurow 143 44 4 S 170 29 E
Kurrajong, N.S.W., Austral. 141 33 33 S 150 42 E
Kurrajong, W.A., Austral. 137 28 39 S 120 59 E
Kurram, R. 94 33 30N 70 15 E
Kurri Kurri 141 32 50 S 151 28 E
Kuršenai 80 56 1N 23 3 E
Kurseong 95 26 56N 88 18 E
Kursk 81 51 42N 36 11 E
Kuršumlija 66 43 9N 21 19 E
Kuršumlijska Banja 66 43 3N 21 11 E
Kurtalon 92 37 55N 41 40 E
Kurtamysh 84 54 55N 64 27 E
Kurty, R. 85 44 16N 76 42 E
Kuru (Chel), Bahr el 123 8 10N 26 50 E
Kuruman 128 27 28 S 23 28 E
Kurume 110 33 15N 130 30 E
Kurunegala 97 7 30N 80 18 E
Kurya 77 61 15N 108 10 E
Kusa 84 55 20N 59 29 E
Kuşadası 69 37 52N 27 15 E
Kuşadası Körfezı 69 37 56N 27 0 E
Kusatsu, Gumma, Japan 111 36 37N 138 36 E
Kusatsu, Shiga, Japan 111 34 58N 136 5 E
Kusawa L. 152 60 20N 136 13W
Kusel 49 49 31N 7 25 E
Kushchevskaya 83 46 33N 39 35 E
Kushikino 110 31 44N 130 16 E
Kushima 110 31 29N 131 14 E
Kushimoto 111 33 28N 135 47 E
Kushin 109 32 12N 115 48 E
Kushiro 112 43 0N 144 25 E
Kushiro, R. 112 42 59N 144 23 E
Kushk 93 34 55N 62 30 E
Kushka 76 35 20N 62 18 E
Kushmurun 84 52 27N 64 36 E
Kushmurun, Ozero 84 52 40N 64 48 E
Kushnarenkovo 84 55 6N 55 22 E
Kushol 95 33 40N 76 36 E
Kushrabat 85 40 18N 66 32 E
Kushtia 98 23 55N 89 5 E
Kushum, R. 83 50 40N 50 20 E
Kushva 84 58 18N 59 45 E
Kuskokwim Bay 147 59 50N 162 56W
Kuskokwim Mts. 147 63 0N 156 0W
Kuskokwim, R. 147 61 48N 157 0W
Küsnacht 51 47 19N 8 15 E
Kussa 123 4 9N 38 58 E
Küssnacht 51 47 5N 8 26 E
Kustanay 84 53 10N 63 35 E
Kusu 110 33 16N 131 9 E
Kusung 108 28 25N 105 12 E
Kut, Ko 101 11 40N 102 35 E
Kutá Horq 52 49 57N 15 16 E
Kutahya 92 39 30N 30 2 E
Kutaisi 83 42 19N 42 40 E
Kutaradja = Banda Aceh 102 5 35N 95 20 E
Kutatjane 102 3 45N 97 50 E
Kutch, G. of 94 22 50N 69 15 E
Kutch, Rann of 94 24 0N 70 0 E
Kut'ien 109 26 36N 118 48 E
Kutina 63 45 29N 16 48 E
Kutiyana 94 21 36N 70 2 E
Kutjevo 66 45 23N 17 55 E
Kutkai 98 23 27N 97 56 E
Kutkashen 83 40 58N 47 47 E
Kutná Hora 52 49 57N 15 16 E
Kutno 54 52 15N 19 23 E
Kuttabul 138 21 5 S 148 48 E
Kutu 124 2 40 S 18 11 E
Kutum 123 14 20N 24 10 E
Kúty 53 48 40N 17 3 E
Kuŭptong 107 40 45N 126 1 E
Kuurne 47 50 51N 3 18 E
Kuvandyk 84 51 28N 57 21 E
Kuvasay 85 40 18N 71 59 E
Kuvshinovo 80 57 2N 34 11 E
Kuwait = Al Kuwayt 92 29 30N 47 30 E
Kuwait ■ 92 29 30N 47 30 E
Kuwana 111 35 0N 136 43 E
Kuyang 106 41 8N 110 1 E
Kuybyshev 81 55 27N 78 19 E
Kuybyshevo, Ukraine S.S.R., U.S.S.R. 82 47 25N 36 40 E
Kuybyshevo, Uzbek S.S.R., U.S.S.R. 85 40 20N 71 15 E
Kuybyshevskiy 85 37 52N 68 44 E
Kuybyshevskoye Vdkhr. 81 55 2N 49 30 E

Kuyeh Ho, R — Lambay I

Kuyeh Ho, R. 106 38 30N 110 44 E
Kuylyuk 85 41 14N 69 17 E
Kuyto, Oz. 78 64 40N 31 0 E
Kuyüan, Hopeh, China 106 41 34N 115 38 E
Kuyüan, Ningsia Hui, China 106 36 1N 106 17 E
Kuzhithura 97 8 18N 77 11 E
Kuzino 84 57 1N 59 27 E
Kuzmin 66 45 2N 19 25 E
Kuznetsk 81 53 12N 46 40 E
Kuzomen 78 66 22N 36 50 E
Kvænangen 74 69 55N 21 15 E
Kvam 71 61 40N 9 42 E
Kvamsøy 71 61 7N 6 28 E
Kvarken 74 63 30N 21 0 E
Kvarner 63 44 50N 14 10 E
Kvarnerič 63 44 43N 14 37 E
Kvarnsveden 72 60 32N 15 25 E
Kvarntorp 72 59 8N 15 17 E
Kvås 71 58 16N 7 14 E
Kvernes 71 63 1N 7 44 E
Kvillsfors 73 57 24N 15 29 E
Kvina, R. 71 58 43N 6 52 E
Kvinesdal 71 58 18N 6 59 E
Kviteseid 71 59 24N 8 29 E
Kwabhaca 129 30 51 S 29 0 E
Kwadacha, R. 152 57 28N 125 38W
Kwakhanai 128 21 39 S 21 16 E
Kwakoegron 175 5 25N 55 25W
Kwale, Kenya 126 4 15 S 39 31 E
Kwale, Nigeria 121 6 18N 5 28 E
Kwale □ 126 4 15 S 39 10 E
Kwamouth 124 3 9 S 16 20 E
Kwando, R. 128 16 48 S 22 45 E
Kwangdaeri 107 40 31N 127 32 E
Kwangju 107 35 9N 126 54 E
Kwangsi-Chuang A.R. □ 109 24 0N 109 0 E
Kwangtung □ 109 23 45N 114 0 E
Kwara □ 121 8 0N 5 0 E
Kwaraga 128 20 26 S 24 32 E
Kwataboahegan, R. 150 51 9N 80 50W
Kwatisore 103 3 7 S 139 59 E
Kweichow □ 108 27 20N 107 0 E
Kweiyang = Kueiyang 108 26 35N 106 43 E
Kwethluk 147 60 45N 161 34W
Kwidzyn 54 54 45N 18 58 E
Kwigillingok 147 59 50N 163 10W
Kwiguk 147 63 45N 164 35W
Kwikila 135 9 49 S 147 38 E
Kwimba □ 126 3 0 S 33 0 E
Kwinana 137 32 15 S 115 47 E
Kwitaba 126 3 56 S 29 39 E
Kya-in-Seikkyi 98 16 2N 98 8 E
Kyabe 117 9 30N 19 0 E
Kyabra Cr. 139 25 36 S 142 55 E
Kyabram 139 36 19 S 145 4 E
Kyaiklat 98 16 46N 96 52 E
Kyaikmaraw 98 16 23N 97 44 E
Kyaikthin 98 23 32N 95 40 E
Kyaikto 100 17 20N 97 3 E
Kyakhta 77 50 30N 106 25 E
Kyangin 98 18 20N 95 20 E
Kyaring Tso 99 31 5N 88 25 E
Kyaukhnyat 98 18 15N 97 31 E
Kyaukpadaung 99 20 52N 95 8 E
Kyaukpyu 99 19 28N 93 30 E
Kyaukse 98 21 36N 96 10 E
Kyauktaw 98 21 16N 96 44 E
Kyawkku 98 21 48N 96 56 E
Kyburz 163 38 47N 120 18W
Kybybolite 140 36 53 S 140 55 E
Kyegegwa 126 0 30N 31 0 E
Kyeintali 98 18 0N 94 29 E
Kyela □ 127 9 45 S 34 0 E
Kyenjojo 126 0 40N 30 37 E
Kyidaunggan 98 19 53N 96 12 E
Kyle Dam 127 20 15 S 31 0 E
Kyle, dist. 34 55 32N 4 25W
Kyle of Lochalsh 36 57 17N 5 43W
Kyleakin 36 57 16N 5 44W
Kyneton 140 37 10 S 144 29 E
Kynuna 138 21 37 S 141 55 E
Kyō-ga-Saki 111 35 45N 135 15 E
Kyoga, L. 126 1 35N 33 0 E
Kyogle 139 28 40 S 153 0 E
Kyongju 107 35 51N 129 14 E
Kyongpyaw 99 17 12N 95 10 E
Kyŏngsŏng 107 41 35N 129 36 E
Kyōto 111 35 0N 135 45 E
Kyōto-fu □ 111 35 15N 135 30 E
Kyrinia 92 35 20N 33 20 E
Kyritz 48 52 57N 12 25 E
Kyrkebyn 72 59 18N 13 3 E
Kyrping 71 59 45N 6 5 E
Kyshtym 84 55 42N 60 34 E
Kystatyam 77 67 20N 123 10 E
Kytalktakh 77 65 30N 123 40 E
Kytlym 84 59 30N 59 12 E
Kyu-hkok 98 24 4N 98 4 E
Kyulyunken 77 64 10N 137 5 E
Kyunhla 98 23 25N 95 15 E
Kyuquot 152 50 3N 127 25W
Kyuquot Sd. 83 50 0N 127 25W
Kyurdamir 83 40 25N 48 3 E
Kyūshū 110 33 0N 131 0 E
Kyūshū □ 110 33 0N 131 0 E
Kyūshū-Sanchi 110 32 45N 131 40 E
Kyustendil 66 42 25N 22 41 E
Kyusyur 77 70 39N 127 15 E
Kywong 141 34 58 S 146 44 E
Kyzyl 77 51 50N 94 30 E
Kyzyl-Kiya 85 40 16N 72 8 E
Kyzyl Orda 85 44 56N 65 30 E
Kyzyl Rabat 76 37 45N 74 55 E
Kyzylkum 84 42 30N 65 0 E
Kyzylsu, R. 85 39 11N 72 2 E
Kzyl-orda 85 44 48N 65 28 E

# L

Laa 53 48 43N 16 23 E
Laage 48 53 55N 12 21 E
Laasphe 48 50 56N 8 23 E
Laau Pt. 147 21 57N 159 40W
Laba, R. 83 45 0N 40 30 E
Laban, Burma 98 25 52N 96 40 E
Laban, Ireland 39 53 8N 8 50W
Labasheeda 39 52 37N 9 15W
Labastide 44 43 28N 2 39 E
Labastide-Murat 44 44 39N 1 33 E
Labbézenga 121 15 2N 0 48 E
Labdah = Leptis Magna 119 32 40N 14 12 E
Labé 120 11 24N 12 16W
Labe, R. 52 50 3N 15 20 E
Laberec, R. 53 21 57N 49 7 E
Laberge, L. 152 61 11N 135 12W
Labin 63 45 5N 14 8 E
Labinsk 83 44 40N 40 48W
Labis 101 2 22N 103 2 E
Labiszyn 54 52 57N 17 54 E
Laboa 103 8 6 S 122 50 E
Laboe 48 54 25N 10 13 E
Labouheyre 44 44 13N 0 55W
Laboulaye 172 34 10 S 63 30W
Labrador City 151 52 57N 66 55W
Labrador, Coast of ■ 149 53 20N 61 0W
Labranzagrande 174 5 33N 72 34W
Lábrea 174 7 15 S 64 51W
Labrède 44 44 41N 0 32W
Labuan, I. 102 5 15N 115 38W
Labuha 103 0 30 S 127 30 E
Labuhan 103 6 26 S 105 50 E
Labuhanbajo 103 8 28 S 120 1 E
Labuissière 47 50 19N 4 11 E
Labuk, Telok 102 6 10N 117 50 E
Labutta 98 16 9N 94 46 E
Labytnangi 78 66 29N 66 40 E
Lac Allard 151 50 33N 63 24W
Lac Bouchette 151 48 16N 72 11W
Lac du Flambeau 158 46 1N 89 51W
Lac Édouard 151 47 40N 72 16W
Lac la Biche 152 54 45N 111 58W
Lac-Mégantic 151 45 35N 70 53W
Lac Seul 153 50 28N 92 0W
Lac Thien 100 12 25N 108 11 E
Lacanau, Étang de 44 44 58N 1 7W
Lacanau Médoc 44 44 59N 1 5W
Lacantum, R. 165 16 36N 90 40W
Lacara, R. 57 39 7N 6 25W
Lacaune 44 43 43N 2 40 E
Lacaune, Mts. de 44 43 43N 2 50 E
Laccadive Is. = Lakshadweep Is. 86 10 0N 72 30 E
Laceby 33 53 32N 0 10W
Lacepede B. 140 36 40 S 139 40 E
Lacepede Is. 136 16 55 S 122 0 E
Lacerdónia 127 18 3 S 35 35 E
Lachen, Sikkim 98 47 12N 8 51 E
Lachen, Switz. 51 47 12N 8 51 E
Lachi 94 33 25N 71 20 E
Lachine 150 45 30N 73 40W
Lachlan 139 42 50 S 147 3 E
Lachlan, R. 140 34 22 S 143 55 E
Lachmangarh 94 27 50N 75 4 E
Lachute 150 45 39N 74 21 E
Lackagh Hills 38 54 14N 8 0W
Lackawanna 156 42 49N 78 50W
Lackawaxen 162 41 29N 74 59W
Lacock 28 51 24N 2 8W
Lacombe 152 52 30N 113 44W
Lacona 162 43 37N 76 5W
Láconi 64 39 54N 9 4 E
Laconia 162 43 32N 71 30W
Lacq 44 43 25N 0 35W
Lacrosse 160 46 51N 117 58W
Ladainha 171 17 39 S 41 44W
Ladakh Ra. 95 34 0N 78 0 E
Ladder Hills 37 57 14N 3 13W
Ladhar Bheinn 36 57 5N 5 37W
Ladhon, R. 69 37 40N 21 50 E
Lâdik 82 40 57N 35 58 E
Ladismith 128 33 28 S 21 15 E
Lādiz 93 28 55N 61 15 E
Ladnun 94 27 38N 74 25 E
Ladock 30 50 19N 4 58W
Ladoga, L. = Ladozhskoye Oz. 78 61 15N 30 30 E
Ladon 43 48 0N 2 30 E
Ladozhskoye Ozero 76 61 15N 30 30 E
Ladrone Is. = Mariana Is. 130 17 0N 145 0 E
Lady Babbie 127 18 30 S 29 20 E
Lady Beatrix L. 150 5 20N 76 50W
Lady Edith Lagoon 136 20 36 S 126 47 E
Lady Grey 128 30 43 S 27 13 E
Ladybank 35 56 16N 3 8W
Ladybrand 128 29 9 S 27 29 E
Lady's I. Lake 39 52 12N 6 23W
Ladysmith, Can. 152 49 0N 123 49W
Ladysmith, S. Afr. 129 28 32 S 29 46 E
Ladysmith, U.S.A. 158 45 27N 91 4W
Lae 135 6 40 S 147 2 E
Laem Ngop 101 12 10N 102 26 E
Laem Pho 101 6 55N 101 19 E
Læsø 73 57 15N 10 53 E
Læsø Rende 73 57 20N 10 45 E
Lafayette, Colo., U.S.A. 158 40 0N 105 2W
Lafayette, Ga., U.S.A. 157 34 44N 85 15W
Lafayette, La., U.S.A. 159 30 18N 92 0W
Lafayette, Tenn., U.S.A. 157 36 35N 86 0W
Laferté 150 48 37N 78 48W
Laferte, R. 152 61 53N 117 44W
Laffan's Bridge 39 52 36N 7 45W
Lafia 121 8 30N 8 34 E
Lafiagi 121 8 52N 5 20 E
Lafleche 153 49 45N 106 40W
Lafon 123 5 5N 32 29 E
Laforest 150 47 4N 81 12W
Laforsen 72 61 56N 15 3 E
Lagaip, R. 135 5 4 S 141 52 E
Lagan 73 56 32N 12 58 E
Lagan, R. 38 54 35N 5 55W
Lagarfljót 74 65 40N 14 18W
Lagarto 170 10 54 S 37 41W
Lagarto, Serra do 173 23 0 S 57 15W
Lage, Ger. 48 52 0N 8 47 E
Lage, Spain 56 43 13N 9 0W
Lage-Mierde 47 51 25N 5 9 E
Lågen 71 61 29N 10 2 E
Lågen, R. 75 61 30N 10 20 E
Lägerdorf 48 53 53N 9 35 E
Lagg 34 56 57N 5 50W
Laggan, Grampian, U.K. 37 57 24N 3 6W
Laggan, Highland, U.K. 37 57 3N 4 48W
Laggan B. 34 55 40N 6 20W
Laggan L. 37 56 57N 4 30W
Laggers Pt. 139 30 52 S 153 4 E
Laghman □ 93 34 20N 70 0 E
Laghouat 118 33 50N 2 59 E
Laghy 38 54 37N 8 7W
Lagnieu 45 45 55N 5 20 E
Lagny 43 48 52N 2 40 E
Lago 65 39 9N 16 8 E
Lagôa 57 37 8N 8 27W
Lagoaça 56 41 11N 6 44W
Lagodekhi 83 41 50N 46 22 E
Lagónegro 65 40 8N 15 45 E
Lagonoy Gulf 103 13 50N 123 50 E
Lagos, Nigeria 121 6 25N 3 27 E
Lagos, Port. 57 37 5N 8 41W
Lagos de Moreno 164 21 21N 101 55W
Lagrange 136 14 13 S 125 46 E
Lagrange B. 136 18 38 S 121 42 E
Laguardia 58 42 33N 2 35W
Laguépie 44 44 8N 1 57 E
Laguna, Brazil 173 28 30 S 48 50W
Laguna, U.S.A. 161 35 3N 107 28W
Laguna Beach 163 33 31N 117 52W
Laguna Dam 161 32 55N 114 30W
Laguna de la Janda 57 36 15N 5 45W
Laguna Limpia 172 26 32 S 59 45W
Laguna Madre 165 27 0N 97 20W
Laguna Veneta 63 45 23N 12 25 E
Lagunas, Chile 172 21 0 S 69 45W
Lagunas, Peru 174 5 10 S 75 35W
Lagunillas 174 10 8N 71 16W
Lahad Datu 103 5 0N 118 30 E
Lahaina 147 20 52N 156 41W
Lahan Sai 100 14 25N 102 52 E
Lahanam 100 16 16N 105 16 E
Lahardaun 38 54 2N 9 20W
Laharpur 95 27 43N 80 56 E
Lahat 102 3 45 S 103 30 E
Lahe 98 19 18N 93 36 E
Lahewa 102 1 22N 97 12 E
Lahijan 93 37 10N 50 6 E
Lahn, R. 48 50 52N 8 35 E
Laholm 73 56 30N 13 2 E
Laholmsbukten 73 56 30N 12 45 E
Lahontan Res. 160 39 28N 118 58W
Lahore 94 31 32N 74 22 E
Lahore □ 94 31 55N 74 5 E
Lahpongsel 98 27 7N 98 25 E
Lahr 49 48 20N 7 52 E
Lahti 75 60 58N 25 40 E
Lai (Béhagle) 117 9 25N 16 30 E
Lai Chau 100 22 5N 103 3 E
Lai-hka 98 21 16N 97 40 E
Laiagam 135 5 33 S 143 30 E
Laian 109 32 27N 118 25 E
Laichou Wan 107 37 30N 119 30 E
Laidley 139 27 39 S 152 20 E
Laidon L. 37 56 40N 4 40W
Laifeng 108 29 31N 109 18 E
Laigle 42 48 46N 0 38 E
Laignes 43 47 50N 4 20 E
Laihsi 107 36 51N 120 30 E
Laikipia □ 126 0 30N 36 30 E
Laila 92 22 10N 46 40 E
Laillahue, Mt. 174 17 0 S 69 30W
Laingsburg 128 33 9 S 20 52 E
Laipin 108 23 42N 109 16 E
Lairg 37 58 1N 4 24W
Lais 102 3 35 S 102 0 E
Laishui 106 39 23N 115 42 E
Laiwu 107 36 12N 117 38 E
Laiyang 107 36 58N 120 41 E
Laiyüan 106 39 19N 114 41 E
Laja, R. 164 20 55N 100 46W
Lajes, Rio Grande d. N., Brazil 170 5 41 S 36 14W
Lajes, Sta. Catarina, Brazil 173 27 48 S 50 20W
Lajinha 171 20 9 S 41 37W
Lajkovac 66 44 27N 20 14 E
Lajosmizse 53 47 3N 19 32 E
Lak Sao 100 18 11N 104 59 E
Laka Chih 95 30 40N 81 10 E
Lakaband 94 31 2N 69 15 E
Lakar 103 8 15 S 128 17 E
Lake Alpine 163 38 29N 120 0W
Lake Andes 158 43 10N 98 32W
Lake Anse 156 46 42N 88 25W
Lake Arthur 159 30 8N 92 40W
Lake Brown 137 30 56 S 118 20 E
Lake Cargelligo 141 33 15 S 146 22 E
Lake Charles 159 31 10N 93 10W
Lake City, Colo, U.S.A. 161 38 3N 107 27W
Lake City, Fla., U.S.A. 157 30 10N 82 40W
Lake City, Iowa, U.S.A. 158 42 12N 94 42W
Lake City, Mich., U.S.A. 156 44 20N 85 10W
Lake City, Minn., U.S.A. 158 44 28N 92 21W
Lake City, S.C., U.S.A. 157 33 51N 79 44W
Lake Coleridge 143 43 17 S 171 30 E
Lake District 23 54 30N 3 10W
Lake George 162 43 25N 73 43W
Lake Grace 137 33 7 S 118 28 E
Lake Harbour 149 62 30N 69 50W
Lake Havasu City 161 34 25N 114 29W
Lake Hughes 163 34 41N 118 26W
Lake Isabella 163 35 38N 118 28W
Lake King 137 33 5 S 119 45 E
Lake Lenore 153 52 24N 104 59W
Lake Louise 152 51 30N 116 10W
Lake Mason 137 27 30 S 119 30 E
Lake Mead Nat. Rec. Area 161 36 0N 114 30W
Lake Mills 158 43 23N 93 33W
Lake Murray 135 6 48 S 141 29 E
Lake Nash 138 20 57 S 138 0 E
Lake of the Woods 155 49 0N 95 0W
Lake Pleasant 162 43 28N 74 25W
Lake Providence 159 32 49N 91 12W
Lake River 150 54 22N 82 31W
Lake Superior Prov. Park 150 47 45N 84 45W
Lake Tekapo 143 43 55 S 170 30 E
Lake Traverse 150 45 56N 78 4W
Lake Varley 137 32 48 S 119 30 E
Lake Village 159 33 20N 91 19W
Lake Wales 157 27 55N 81 32W
Lake Worth 157 26 36N 80 3W
Lakefield 150 44 25N 78 16W
Lakehurst 162 40 1N 74 19W
Lakeland 157 28 0N 82 0W
Lakenheath 29 52 25N 0 30 E
Lakes Entrance 141 37 50 S 148 0 E
Lakeside, Ariz., U.S.A. 161 34 12N 109 59W
Lakeside, Calif., U.S.A. 163 32 52N 116 55W
Lakeside, Nebr., U.S.A. 158 42 5N 102 24W
Lakeview, N.Y., U.S.A. 156 42 43N 78 57W
Lakeview, Oreg., U.S.A. 160 42 15N 120 22W
Lakewood, Calif., U.S.A. 163 33 51N 118 8W
Lakewood, N.J., U.S.A. 162 40 5N 74 13W
Lakhaniá 69 35 58N 27 54 E
Lákhi 69 35 24N 23 27 E
Lakhimpur 95 27 14N 94 7 E
Lakhipur, Assam, India 98 24 48N 93 0 E
Lakhipur, Assam, India 98 26 2N 90 18 E
Lakhonpheng 100 15 54N 105 34 E
Lakhpat 94 23 48N 68 47 E
Laki 74 64 4N 18 14W
Lakin 159 37 58N 101 18W
Lakitusaki, R. 150 54 21N 82 25W
Lakki 93 32 38N 70 50 E
Lakonía □ 69 36 55N 22 30 E
Lakonikós Kólpos 69 36 40N 22 40 E
Lakor, I. 103 8 15 S 128 17 E
Lakota, Ivory C. 120 5 50N 5 30W
Lakota, U.S.A. 158 48 0N 98 22W
Laksefjorden 74 70 45N 26 50 E
Lakselv 74 70 2N 24 56 E
Lakselvbukt 74 69 26N 19 40 E
Lakshadweep Is. 86 10 0N 72 30 E
Laksham 98 23 14N 91 8 E
Lakshmi Kantapur 95 22 5N 88 20 E
Lakshmipur 98 22 38N 88 16 E
Lakuramau 135 2 54 S 151 15 E
Lala Ghat 99 24 30N 92 40 E
Lala Musa 94 32 40N 73 57 E
Lalago 126 3 28 S 33 58 E
Lalapanzi 127 19 20 S 30 15 E
Lalganj 95 25 52N 85 13 E
Lalibala 123 12 8N 39 10 E
Lalin 107 45 14N 126 52 E
Lalin 56 42 40N 8 5W
Lalin Ho, R. 107 45 28N 125 43 E
Lalinde 44 44 50N 0 44 E
Lalitapur 99 26 36N 85 32 E
Lalitpur 95 24 42N 78 28 E
Lam 100 21 21N 106 31 E
Lam Pao Res. 100 16 50N 103 15 E
Lama Kara 121 9 30N 1 15 E
Lamaing 99 15 25N 97 53 E
Lamaipum 98 25 40N 97 57 E
Lamar, Colo., U.S.A. 158 38 9N 102 35W
Lamar, Mo., U.S.A. 159 37 30N 94 20W
Lamas 174 6 28 S 76 31W
Lamastre 45 44 59N 4 35 E
Lamaya 108 29 50N 99 56 E
Lamb Hd. 37 59 5N 2 32W
Lambach 52 48 6N 13 51 E
Lamballe 42 48 29N 2 31W
Lambaréné 124 0 20 S 10 12 E
Lambay I. 38 53 30N 6 0W

**Lambayeque □** **Lawrenceville**


Lambayeque □ **174** 6 45S 80 0W
Lamberhurst **29** 51 5N 0 21E
Lambert **158** 47 44N 104 39W
Lambert, C. **135** 4 11S 151 31E
Lambert Land **12** 79 12N 20 30W
Lambesc **45** 43 39N 5 16E
Lambeth **29** 51 27N 0 7W
Lambi Kyun, (Sullivan I.) **101** 10 50N 98 20E
Lámbia **69** 37 52N 21 53E
Lambley **35** 54 56N 2 30W
Lambon **135** 4 45S 152 48E
Lambourn **28** 51 31N 1 31W
Lambro, R. **62** 45 18N 9 20E
Lambs Hd. **39** 51 44N 10 10W
Lame **121** 10 27N 9 12E
Lame Deer **160** 45 45N 106 40W
Lamego **56** 41 5N 7 52W
Lameque **151** 47 45N 64 38W
Lameroo **140** 35 19S 140 33E
Lamesa **159** 32 45N 101 57W
Lamhult **73** 57 12N 14 36E
Lamia **69** 38 55N 22 41E
Lamitan **103** 6 40N 122 10E
Lammermuir **35** 55 50N 2 25W
Lammermuir Hills **35** 55 50N 2 40W
Lamoille **160** 40 47N 115 31W
Lamon Bay **103** 14 30N 122 20E
Lamont, Can. **152** 53 46N 112 50W
Lamont, U.S.A. **163** 35 15N 118 55W
Lampa **174** 15 10S 70 30W
Lampang **100** 18 18N 99 31E
Lampasas **159** 31 5N 98 10W
Lampaul **42** 48 28N 5 7W
Lampazos de Naranjo **164** 27 2N 100 32W
Lampedusa, I. **60** 35 36N 12 40E
Lampeter **31** 52 6N 4 6W
Lampione, I. **119** 35 33N 12 20E
Lampman **153** 49 25N 102 50W
Lamprechtshausen **52** 48 0N 12 58E
Lampung **102** 1 48S 115 0E
Lamu, Burma **98** 19 14N 94 10E
Lamu, Kenya **126** 2 10S 40 55E
Lamy **161** 35 30N 105 58W
Lan Tsan Kiang (Mekong) **87** 18 0N 104 15E
Lanai City **147** 20 50N 156 56W
Lanai I. **147** 20 50N 156 55W
Lanak La **95** 34 27N 79 32E
Lanaken **47** 50 53N 5 39E
Lanak'o Shank'ou = Lanak La **95** 34 27N 79 32E
Lanao, L. **103** 7 52N 124 15E
Lanark **35** 55 40N 3 48W
Lanark (□) **26** 55 37N 3 50W
Lancashire □ **32** 53 40N 2 30W
Lancaster, Can. **151** 45 17N 66 10W
Lancaster, U.K. **32** 54 3N 2 48W
Lancaster, Calif., U.S.A. **163** 34 47N 118 8W
Lancaster, Ky., U.S.A. **156** 37 40N 84 40W
Lancaster, Pa., U.S.A. **162** 40 4N 76 19W
Lancaster, S.C., U.S.A. **157** 34 45N 80 47W
Lancaster, Va., U.S.A. **162** 37 46N 76 28W
Lancaster, Wis., U.S.A. **158** 42 48N 90 43W
Lancaster Sd. **12** 74 13N 84 0W
Lancer **153** 50 48N 108 53W
Lanchester **33** 54 50N 1 44W
Lanch'i **109** 29 11N 119 30E
Lanchou **106** 36 5N 103 55E
Lanciano **63** 42 15N 14 22E
Lancing **29** 50 49N 0 19W
Łancut **54** 50 10N 22 20E
Lancy **50** 46 12N 6 8E
Lándana **124** 5 11S 12 5E
Landau **49** 49 12N 8 7E
Landeck **52** 47 9N 10 34E
Landen **47** 50 45N 5 3E
Lander, Austral. **136** 20 25S 132 0E
Lander, U.S.A. **160** 42 50N 108 49W
Landerneau **42** 48 28N 4 17W
Landeryd **73** 57 7N 13 15E
Landes □ **44** 43 57N 0 48W
Landes, Les **44** 44 20N 1 0W
Landete **58** 39 56N 1 25W
Landi Kotal **94** 34 7N 71 6E
Landivisiau **42** 48 31N 4 6W
Landkey **30** 51 2N 4 0W
Landor **137** 25 10S 117 0E
Landquart **51** 46 58N 9 32E
Landquart, R. **51** 46 50N 9 47E
Landrecies **43** 50 7N 3 40E
Land's End, Can. **12** 76 10N 123 0W
Land's End, U.K. **30** 50 4N 5 43W
Landsberg **49** 48 3N 10 52E
Landsborough Cr. **138** 22 28S 144 35E
Landsbro **73** 57 24N 14 56E
Landschaft **50** 47 28N 7 40E
Landshut **48** 48 31N 12 10E
Landskrona **73** 56 53N 12 50E
Landvetter **73** 57 41N 12 17E
Lane **73** 58 25N 12 3E
Laneffe **47** 50 17N 4 35E
Lanesboro **162** 41 57N 75 34W
Lanesborough **38** 53 40N 8 0W
Lanett **157** 33 0N 85 15W
Lang Bay **152** 49 17N 124 21W
Lang Qua **100** 22 16N 104 27E
Lang Shan **106** 41 0N 106 20E
Lang Suan **101** 9 57N 99 4E
Langaa **73** 56 23N 9 51E
Långadhás **68** 40 46N 23 2E
Langádhia **69** 37 43N 22 1E
Långan **72** 63 19N 14 44E
Langara I. **152** 54 14N 133 1W
Langavat L. **36** 58 4N 6 48W
Langchen Khambah (Sutlej) **95** 31 25N 80 0E
Langch'i **109** 31 10N 119 10E
Langchung **108** 31 31N 105 58E
Langdon **158** 48 47N 98 24W
Langdorp **47** 50 59N 4 52E
Langeac **44** 45 7N 3 29E
Langeb, R. **122** 17 28N 36 50E
Langeberge, C. Prov., S. Afr. **128** 28 15S 22 33E
Langeberge, C. Prov., S. Afr. **128** 33 55S 21 20E
Langeland **73** 54 56N 10 48E
Langelands Bælt **73** 54 55N 10 56E
Langemark **47** 50 55N 2 55E
Langen **49** 53 36N 8 36E
Langenburg **153** 50 51N 101 43W
Langeness **48** 54 34N 8 35E
Langenlois **52** 48 29N 15 40E
Langensalza **48** 51 6N 10 40E
Langenthal **50** 47 13N 7 47E
Langeoog **48** 53 44N 7 33E
Langeskov **73** 55 22N 10 35E
Langesund **71** 59 0N 9 45E
Langhem **73** 57 36N 13 14E
Länghem **73** 57 36N 13 14E
Langhirano **62** 44 39N 10 16E
Langholm **35** 55 9N 2 59W
Langidoon **140** 31 36S 142 2E
Langjökull **74** 64 39N 20 12W
Langkawi I. **101** 6 20N 99 45E
Langkawi, P. **101** 6 25N 99 45E
Langkon **102** 6 30N 116 40E
Langk'ouhsü **109** 26 8N 115 10E
Langlade, Can. **150** 48 14N 76 10W
Langlade, St. P. & M. **151** 46 50N 56 20W
Langlo **139** 26 26S 146 5E
Langlois **160** 42 54N 124 26W
Langnau **50** 46 56N 7 47E
Langness **32** 54 3N 4 37W
Langogne **44** 44 43N 3 50E
Langon **44** 44 33N 0 16W
Langøya **74** 68 45N 15 10E
Langport **28** 51 2N 2 51W
Langres **43** 47 52N 5 20E
Langres, Plateau de **43** 47 45N 5 20E
Langsa **102** 4 30N 97 57E
Långsele **72** 63 12N 17 4E
Långshyttan **72** 60 27N 16 2E
Langson **100** 21 52N 106 42E
Langstrothdale Chase **32** 54 14N 2 13W
Langtai **108** 26 6N 105 20E
Langtao **98** 27 15N 97 34E
Langting **98** 25 31N 93 7E
Langtoft **29** 52 42N 0 19W
Langtree **30** 50 55N 4 11W
Langtry **159** 29 50N 101 33W
Langu **101** 6 53N 99 47E
Languedoc □ **44** 43 58N 3 22E
Langwies **51** 46 50N 9 44E
Lanhsien **106** 38 17N 111 38E
Lanigan **153** 51 51N 105 2W
Lank'ao **106** 34 50N 114 49E
Lanna **72** 59 16N 14 56E
Lannemezan **44** 43 8N 0 23E
Lannercost **138** 18 35S 146 0E
Lannilis **42** 48 35N 4 32W
Lannion **42** 48 46N 3 29W
Lanouaille **44** 45 24N 1 9E
Lanp'ing **108** 26 25N 99 24E
Lansdale **162** 40 14N 75 18W
Lansdowne **141** 31 48S 152 30E
Lansdowne House **150** 52 14N 87 53W
Lansford **162** 40 48N 75 55W
Lanshan **109** 25 18N 112 6E
Lansing **156** 42 47N 84 32W
Lanslebourg-Mont-Cenis **45** 45 17N 6 52E
Lanta Yai, Ko **101** 7 35N 99 3E
Lant'ien **106** 34 3N 109 20E
Lants'ang **108** 22 40N 99 58E
Lants'ang Chiang, R. **108** 30 0N 98 0E
Lantsien **99** 32 4N 96 6E
Lants'un **107** 36 24N 120 10E
Lantuna **103** 8 19S 124 8E
Lanus **172** 34 44S 58 27W
Lanusei **64** 39 53N 9 31E
Lanzarote, I. **116** 29 0N 13 40W
Lanzo Torinese **62** 45 16N 7 29E
Lao Bao **100** 16 35N 106 30E
Lao Cai **100** 22 30N 103 57E
Lao, R. **65** 39 45N 15 45E
Laoag **103** 18 7N 120 34E
Laoang **103** 12 32N 125 8E
Laoha Ho, R. **107** 43 24N 120 39E
Laois □ **39** 53 0N 7 20W
Laon **43** 49 33N 3 35E
Laona **156** 45 32N 88 41W
Laos ■ **100** 17 45N 105 0E
Lapa **173** 25 46S 49 44W
Lapalisse **44** 46 15N 3 44E
Laparan Cap, I. **103** 6 0N 120 0E
Lapeer **156** 43 3N 83 20W
Lapford **30** 50 52N 3 49W
Lapi □ **74** 67 0N 27 0E
Lapland = Lappland **74** 68 7N 24 0E
Laporte **162** 41 27N 76 30W
Lapovo **66** 44 10N 21 2E
Lappland **74** 68 7N 24 0E
Laprida **172** 37 34S 60 45W
Laptev Sea **77** 76 0N 125 0E
Lapush **160** 47 56N 124 33W
Lăpuşu, R. **70** 47 25N 23 40E
Lar **93** 27 40N 54 14E
Lara **140** 38 2S 144 26E
Lara □ **174** 10 10N 69 50W
Larabanga **120** 9 16N 1 56W
Laracha **56** 43 15N 8 35W
Larache **118** 35 10N 6 5W
Laragh **39** 53 0N 6 20W
Laragne-Montéglin **45** 44 18N 5 49E
Laramie **158** 41 15N 105 29W
Laramie Mts. **158** 42 0N 105 30W
Laranjeiras **170** 10 48S 37 10W
Laranjeiras do Sul **173** 25 23S 52 23W
Larantuka **103** 8 5S 122 55E
Larap **103** 14 18N 122 39E
Larat, I. **103** 7 0S 132 0E
Larbert **35** 56 2N 3 50W
Lärbro **73** 57 47N 18 50E
Larch, R. **149** 57 30N 71 0W
Lårdal **71** 59 20N 8 25E
Lårdal **71** 59 25N 8 10E
Larde **127** 16 28S 39 43E
Larder Lake **150** 48 5N 79 40W
Lárdhos, Ákra **69** 36 4N 28 10E
Laredo, Spain **58** 43 26N 3 28W
Laredo, U.S.A. **159** 27 34N 99 29W
Laredo Sd. **152** 52 30N 128 53W
Laren **46** 52 16N 5 14E
Largeau (Faya) **117** 17 58N 19 6E
Largentière **45** 44 34N 4 18E
Largs **34** 55 48N 4 51W
Lari **62** 43 34N 10 35E
Lariang **103** 1 35S 119 25E
Larimore **158** 47 55N 97 35W
Larino **65** 41 48N 14 54E
Lárisa **68** 39 38N 22 28E
Lárisa □ **68** 39 39N 22 24E
Larkana **94** 27 32N 68 2E
Larkollen **71** 59 20N 10 41E
Larnaca **92** 35 0N 33 35E
Lárnax **92** 35 0N 33 35E
Larne **38** 54 52N 5 50W
Larne L. **38** 54 52N 5 50W
Larned **158** 38 15N 99 10W
Laroch **36** 56 40N 5 9W
Larochette **47** 49 47N 6 13E
Laroquebrou **44** 44 58N 2 12E
Larrey, Pt. **136** 19 55S 119 7E
Larrimah **136** 15 35S 133 12E
Larsen Ice Shelf **13** 67 0S 62 0W
Larteh **121** 5 50N 0 5W
Laru **126** 2 54N 24 25E
Larvik **71** 59 4N 10 0E
Laryak **76** 61 15N 80 0E
Larzac, Causse du **44** 44 0N 3 17E
Las Animas **159** 38 8N 103 18W
Las Anod **91** 8 26N 47 19E
Las Blancos **59** 37 38N 0 49W
Las Bonitas **174** 7 50N 65 40W
Las Brenãs **172** 27 5S 61 7W
Las Cabezas de San Juan **57** 37 0N 5 58W
Las Cruces **161** 32 25N 106 50W
Las Flores **172** 36 0S 59 0W
Las Heras, Mendoza, Argent. **173** 32 51S 68 49W
Las Heras, Santa Cruz, Argent. **176** 46 30S 69 0W
Las Huertas, Cabo de **59** 38 22N 0 24W
Las Khoreh **91** 11 4N 48 20E
Las Lajas **176** 38 30S 70 25W
Las Lajitas **174** 6 55N 65 39W
Las Lomitas **172** 24 35S 60 50W
Las Marismas **57** 37 5N 6 20W
Las Mercedes **174** 9 7N 66 24W
Las Navas de la Concepción **57** 37 56N 5 30W
Las Navas de Tolosa **57** 38 18N 3 38W
Las Palmas, Argent. **172** 27 8S 58 45W
Las Palmas, Canary Is. **116** 28 10N 15 28W
Las Palmas □ **116** 28 10N 15 28W
Las Piedras **173** 34 35S 56 20W
Las Plumas **176** 43 40S 67 15W
Las Rosas **172** 32 30S 61 40W
Las Tablas **166** 7 49N 80 14W
Las Termas **172** 27 29S 64 52W
Las Tres Marías, Is. **164** 20 12N 106 30W
Las Varillas **172** 32 0S 62 50W
Las Vegas, Nev., U.S.A. **161** 36 10N 115 5W
Las Vegas, N.M., U.S.A. **161** 35 35N 105 10W
Lascano **173** 33 35S 54 18W
Lascaux **44** 45 5N 1 10E
Lashburn **153** 53 10N 109 40W
Lashio **98** 22 56N 97 45E
Lashkar **94** 26 10N 78 10E
Łasin **54** 53 30N 19 2E
Lasithi □ **69** 35 5N 25 50E
Lask **54** 51 34N 19 8E
Laskill **33** 54 19N 1 6W
Laško **63** 46 10N 15 16E
Lassance **171** 17 54S 44 34W
Lassay **42** 48 27N 0 30W
Lassen, Pk. **160** 40 20N 121 0W
Lasswade **35** 55 53N 3 8W
Last Mountain L. **153** 51 5N 105 14W
Lastoursville **124** 0 55S 12 38E
Lastovo **63** 42 46N 16 55E
Lastovo, I. **63** 42 46N 16 55E
Lastovski Kanal **63** 42 50N 17 0E
Lat Yao **100** 15 45N 99 48E
Latacunga **174** 0 50S 78 35W
Latakia = Al Ladhiqiya **92** 35 30N 35 45E
Latchford **150** 47 20N 79 50W
Laterza **65** 40 38N 16 47E
Latham **137** 29 44S 116 20E
Lathen **48** 52 51N 7 21E
Latheron **37** 58 17N 3 20W
Lathrop Wells **163** 36 39N 116 24W
Latiano **65** 40 33N 17 43E
Latina **64** 41 26N 12 53E
Latisana **63** 45 47N 13 1E
Latium = Lazio **63** 42 0N 12 30E
Laton **163** 36 26N 119 41W
Latorica, R. **53** 48 31N 22 0E
Latouche **147** 60 0N 148 0W
Latouche Treville, C. **136** 18 27S 121 49E
Latrobe **138** 38 8S 146 44E
Latrobe, Mt. **139** 39 0S 146 23E
Latrónico **65** 40 5N 16 0E
Latrun **90** 31 50N 34 58E
Latur **96** 18 25N 76 40E
Latvia, S.S.R. □ **80** 56 50N 24 0E
Latzu **105** 29 10N 87 45E
Lauchhammer **48** 51 35N 13 40E
Laudal **71** 58 15N 7 30E
Lauder **35** 55 43N 2 45W
Lauderdale **35** 55 43N 2 44W
Lauenburg **48** 53 23N 10 33E
Läufelfingen **50** 47 24N 7 52E
Laufen **50** 47 25N 7 30E
Laugarbakki **74** 65 20N 20 55W
Laugharne **31** 51 45N 4 28W
Laujar **59** 37 0N 2 54W
Launceston, Austral. **138** 41 24S 147 8E
Launceston, U.K. **30** 50 38N 4 21W
Laune, R. **39** 52 5N 9 40W
Launglon Bok **101** 13 50N 97 54E
Laupheim **49** 48 13N 9 53E
Laura, Queens., Austral. **133** 15 32S 144 32E
Laura, S.A., Austral. **140** 33 10S 138 18E
Lauragh **39** 51 46N 9 46W
Laureana di Borrello **65** 38 28N 16 5E
Laurel, Del., U.S.A. **162** 38 33N 75 34W
Laurel, Md., U.S.A. **162** 39 6N 76 51W
Laurel, Miss., U.S.A. **159** 31 50N 89 0W
Laurel, Mont., U.S.A. **160** 45 46N 108 49W
Laurencekirk **37** 56 50N 2 30W
Laurencetown **39** 53 14N 8 11W
Laurens **157** 34 32N 82 2W
Laurentian Plat. **151** 52 0N 70 0W
Laurentides, Parc Prov. des **151** 47 45N 71 15W
Lauria **65** 40 3N 15 50E
Laurie I. **13** 60 0S 46 0W
Laurie L. **153** 56 35N 101 57W
Lauriestion **35** 54 57N 4 2W
Laurinburg **157** 34 50N 79 25W
Laurium **156** 47 14N 88 26W
Lausanne **50** 46 32N 6 38E
Laut Kecil, Kepulauan **102** 4 45S 115 40E
Laut, Kepulauan **102** 4 45N 108 0E
Lauterbach **48** 50 39N 9 23E
Lauterbrunnen **50** 46 36N 7 55E
Lauterecken **49** 49 38N 7 35E
Lauwe **47** 50 47N 3 12E
Lauwers **46** 53 32N 6 23E
Lauwers Zee **46** 53 21N 6 13E
Lauzon **151** 46 48N 71 10W
Lava Hot Springs **160** 42 38N 112 1W
Lavadores **56** 42 14N 8 41W
Lavagna **62** 44 18N 9 22E
Laval **42** 48 4N 0 48W
Lavalle **172** 28 15S 65 15W
Lavandou, Le **45** 43 8N 6 22E
Lâvara **68** 41 19N 26 22E
Lavardac **44** 44 12N 0 20E
Lavaur **44** 43 42N 1 49E
Lavaux **50** 46 30N 6 45E
Lavaveix **44** 46 5N 2 8E
Lavelanet **44** 42 57N 1 51E
Lavello **65** 41 4N 15 47E
Lavendon **29** 52 11N 0 39W
Lavenham **29** 52 7N 0 48E
Laverendrye Prov. Park **150** 46 15N 17 15W
Laverne **159** 36 43N 99 58W
Lavers Hill **140** 38 40S 143 25E
Laverton **137** 28 44S 122 29E
Lavi **90** 32 47N 35 25E
Lavik **71** 61 6N 5 25E
Lávkos **69** 39 9N 23 14E
Lavos **56** 40 6N 8 49W
Lavras **173** 21 20S 45 0W
Lavre **57** 38 46N 8 22W
Lavrentiya **77** 65 35N 171 0W
Lávrion **69** 37 40N 24 4E
Lavumisa **129** 27 20S 31 55E
Lawas **102** 4 55N 115 40E
Lawele **103** 5 16S 123 3E
Lawers **35** 56 31N 4 9W
Lawksawk **98** 21 15N 96 52E
Lawn Hill **138** 18 36S 138 33E
Lawng Pit **99** 26 45N 98 35E
Lawra **120** 10 39N 2 51W
Lawrence, Austral. **173** 29 30S 153 8E
Lawrence, Kans., U.S.A. **158** 39 0N 95 10W
Lawrence, Mass., U.S.A. **162** 42 40N 71 9W
Lawrenceburg, Ind., U.S.A. **156** 39 5N 84 50W
Lawrenceburg, Tenn., U.S.A. **157** 35 12N 87 19W
Lawrenceville, Ga., U.S.A. **157** 33 55N 83 59W

Lawrenceville | Lexington


| | | | |
|---|---|---|---|
| Lawrenceville, Pa., U.S.A. | **162** | 42 0N | 77 8W |
| Laws | **163** | 37 24N | 118 20W |
| Lawton | **159** | 34 33N | 98 25W |
| Lawu Mt. | **103** | 7 40S | 111 13E |
| Laxa | **72** | 59 0N | 14 37E |
| Laxey | **32** | 54 15N | 4 23W |
| Laxfield | **29** | 52 18N | 1 23E |
| Laxford, L. | **36** | 58 25N | 5 10W |
| Laxmeshwar | **97** | 15 9N | 75 28E |
| Laysan I. | **143** | 25 30N | 167 0W |
| Laytonville | **160** | 39 44N | 123 29W |
| Laytown | **38** | 53 40N | 6 15W |
| Laza | **98** | 26 30N | 97 38E |
| Lazarevac | **66** | 44 23N | 20 17E |
| Lazio □ | **63** | 42 10N | 12 30E |
| Lazonby | **32** | 54 45N | 2 42W |
| Łazy | **54** | 50 27N | 19 24E |
| Łbzenica | **54** | 53 18N | 17 15E |
| Lea | **33** | 53 22N | 0 45W |
| Lea, R. | **29** | 51 40N | 0 3W |
| Leach | **101** | 12 21N | 103 46E |
| Lead | **158** | 44 20N | 103 40W |
| Leadenham | **33** | 53 5N | 0 33W |
| Leader | **153** | 50 50N | 109 30W |
| Leadhills | **35** | 55 25N | 3 47W |
| Leadville | **161** | 39 17N | 106 23W |
| Leaf, R., Can. | **149** | 58 47N | 70 4W |
| Leaf, R., U.S.A. | **159** | 31 45N | 89 20W |
| Leakey | **159** | 29 45N | 99 45W |
| Leaksville | **157** | 36 30N | 79 49W |
| Lealui | **125** | 15 10S | 23 2E |
| Leamington, Can. | **150** | 42 3N | 82 36W |
| Leamington, N.Z. | **130** | 37 55S | 175 29E |
| Leamington, U.K. | **28** | 52 18N | 1 32W |
| Leamington, U.S.A. | **160** | 39 37N | 112 17W |
| Leandro Norte Alem | **173** | 27 34S | 55 15W |
| Leane L. | **39** | 52 2N | 9 32W |
| Leaoto, Mt. | **70** | 45 20N | 25 20E |
| Leap | **39** | 51 34N | 9 11W |
| Learmonth | **136** | 22 40S | 114 10E |
| Leask | **153** | 53 5N | 106 45W |
| Leatherhead | **29** | 51 18N | 0 20W |
| Leavenworth, Mo., U.S.A. | **158** | 39 25N | 95 0W |
| Leavenworth, Wash., U.S.A. | **160** | 47 44N | 120 37W |
| Łeba | **54** | 54 45N | 17 32E |
| Lebak | **103** | 6 32N | 124 5E |
| Lebane | **66** | 42 56N | 21 44E |
| Lebanon, Ind., U.S.A. | **156** | 40 3N | 86 55W |
| Lebanon, Kans., U.S.A. | **158** | 39 50N | 98 35W |
| Lebanon, Ky., U.S.A. | **156** | 37 35N | 85 15W |
| Lebanon, Mo., U.S.A. | **159** | 37 40N | 92 40W |
| Lebanon, Oreg., U.S.A. | **160** | 44 31N | 122 57W |
| Lebanon, Pa., U.S.A. | **162** | 40 20N | 76 28W |
| Lebanon, Tenn., U.S.A. | **157** | 36 15N | 86 20W |
| Lebanon ■ | **92** | 34 0N | 36 0E |
| Lebbeke | **47** | 51 0N | 4 8E |
| Lebec | **163** | 34 36N | 118 59W |
| Lebedin | **80** | 50 35N | 34 30E |
| Lebedyan | **81** | 53 0N | 39 10E |
| Lebomboberge | **129** | 24 30S | 32 0E |
| Łebork | **54** | 54 33N | 17 46E |
| Lebrija | **57** | 36 53N | 6 5W |
| Lebu | **172** | 37 40S | 73 47W |
| Lecce | **65** | 40 20N | 18 10E |
| Lecco | **62** | 45 50N | 9 27E |
| Lecco, L. di. | **62** | 45 51N | 9 22E |
| Lécera | **58** | 41 13N | 0 43W |
| Lech | **52** | 47 13N | 10 9E |
| Lech, R. | **49** | 48 45N | 10 45E |
| Lechlade | **28** | 51 42N | 1 40W |
| Lechtaler Alpen | **52** | 47 15N | 10 30E |
| Lectoure | **44** | 43 56N | 0 38E |
| Łeczyca | **54** | 52 5N | 19 45E |
| Ledbury | **28** | 52 3N | 2 25W |
| Lede | **47** | 50 58N | 3 59E |
| Ledeberg | **47** | 51 2N | 3 45E |
| Ledec | **52** | 49 41N | 15 18E |
| Ledesma | **56** | 41 6N | 5 59W |
| Leduc | **152** | 53 20N | 113 30W |
| Ledyczek | **54** | 53 33N | 16 59E |
| Lee, U.K. | **28** | 50 47N | 1 11W |
| Lee, U.S.A. | **160** | 40 35N | 115 36W |
| Lee Vining | **163** | 37 58N | 119 7W |
| Leech L. | **158** | 47 9N | 94 23W |
| Leedey | **159** | 35 53N | 99 24W |
| Leeds, U.K. | **33** | 53 48N | 1 34W |
| Leeds, U.S.A. | **157** | 33 32N | 86 30W |
| Leek, Neth. | **46** | 53 10N | 6 24E |
| Leek, U.K. | **32** | 53 7N | 2 2W |
| Leende | **47** | 51 21N | 5 33E |
| Leer | **48** | 53 13N | 7 29E |
| Leerdam | **46** | 51 54N | 5 6E |
| Leersum | **46** | 52 0N | 5 26E |
| Leesburg | **157** | 28 47N | 81 52W |
| Leeston | **143** | 43 45N | 172 19E |
| Leesville | **159** | 31 12N | 93 15W |
| Leeton | **141** | 34 23S | 146 23E |
| Leeuwarden | **46** | 53 15N | 5 48E |
| Leeuwin, C. | **137** | 34 20S | 115 9E |
| Leeward Is. | **167** | 16 30N | 63 30W |
| Lefors | **159** | 35 30N | 100 50W |
| Lefroy, L. | **137** | 31 21S | 121 40E |
| Legal | **152** | 53 55N | 113 45W |
| Legendre I. | **136** | 20 22S | 116 55E |
| Leghorn = Livorno | **62** | 43 32N | 10 18E |
| Legion | **127** | 21 25S | 28 30E |
| Legionowo | **54** | 52 25N | 20 50E |
| Léglise | **47** | 49 48N | 5 32E |
| Legnago | **63** | 45 10N | 11 19E |
| Legnano | **62** | 45 35N | 8 55E |
| Legnica | **54** | 51 12N | 16 10E |
| Legnica □ | **54** | 51 30N | 16 0E |
| Legoniel | **38** | 54 38N | 6 0W |
| Legrad | **63** | 46 17N | 16 51E |
| Legume | **139** | 28 20S | 152 12E |
| Leh | **95** | 34 15N | 77 35E |
| Lehi | **160** | 40 20N | 112 0W |
| Lehighton | **162** | 40 50N | 75 44W |
| Lehinch | **39** | 52 56N | 9 21E |
| Lehliu | **70** | 44 29N | 26 20E |
| Lehrte | **48** | 52 22N | 9 58E |
| Lehua, I. | **147** | 22 1N | 160 6W |
| Lehututu | **128** | 23 54S | 21 55E |
| Lei Shui, R. | **109** | 26 56N | 112 39E |
| Leiah | **94** | 30 58N | 70 58E |
| Leibnitz | **52** | 46 47N | 15 34E |
| Leicester | **28** | 52 39N | 1 9W |
| Leicester □ | **28** | 52 40N | 1 10W |
| Leichhardt, R. | **133** | 17 50S | 139 49E |
| Leichhardt Ra. | **138** | 20 46S | 147 40E |
| Leichou Chiang, R. | **109** | 20 52N | 110 10E |
| Leichou Pantao | **108** | 20 40N | 110 10E |
| Leiden | **46** | 52 9N | 4 30E |
| Leiderdorp | **46** | 52 9N | 4 32E |
| Leidschendam | **46** | 52 5N | 4 24E |
| Leie, R. | **47** | 51 2N | 3 45E |
| Leigh, Gr. Manch., U.K. | **32** | 53 29N | 2 31W |
| Leigh, Here. & Worcs., U.K. | **28** | 52 10N | 2 21W |
| Leigh Creek | **140** | 30 28S | 138 24E |
| Leighlinbridge | **39** | 52 45N | 7 2W |
| Leighton Buzzard | **29** | 51 55N | 0 39W |
| Leignon | **47** | 50 16N | 5 7E |
| Leiktho | **98** | 19 13N | 96 35E |
| Leinster, Mt. | **39** | 52 38N | 6 47W |
| Leinster, prov. | **39** | 53 0N | 7 10W |
| Leintwardine | **28** | 52 22N | 2 51W |
| Leipo | **108** | 28 15N | 103 34E |
| Leipzig | **48** | 51 20N | 12 23E |
| Leipzig □ | **48** | 51 20N | 12 30E |
| Leiria | **57** | 39 46N | 8 53W |
| Leiria □ | **57** | 39 46N | 8 53W |
| Leisler, Mt. | **136** | 23 23S | 129 30E |
| Leiston | **29** | 52 13N | 1 35E |
| Leith | **35** | 55 59N | 3 10W |
| Leith Hill | **29** | 51 10N | 0 23W |
| Leitha, R. | **53** | 47 57N | 17 5E |
| Leitholm | **35** | 55 42N | 2 16W |
| Leitrim | **38** | 54 0N | 8 5W |
| Leitrim □ | **38** | 54 8N | 8 0W |
| Leiyang | **109** | 26 24N | 112 51E |
| Leiza | **58** | 43 5N | 1 55W |
| Lek, R. | **46** | 51 54N | 4 38E |
| Lekáni | **68** | 41 10N | 24 35E |
| Leke | **47** | 51 6N | 2 54E |
| Lekhainá | **69** | 37 57N | 21 16E |
| Lekkerkerk | **46** | 51 54N | 4 41E |
| Leknice | **61** | 51 34N | 14 45E |
| Leksula | **103** | 3 46S | 126 31E |
| Leland | **159** | 33 25N | 90 52W |
| Leland Lakes | **153** | 60 0N | 110 59W |
| Lelant | **30** | 50 11N | 5 26W |
| Leleque | **176** | 42 15S | 71 0W |
| Lelu | **98** | 19 4N | 95 30E |
| Lelystad | **46** | 52 30N | 5 25E |
| Lema | **121** | 12 58N | 4 13E |
| Lemagrut, mt. | **123** | 3 9S | 35 22E |
| Leman Bank, gasfield | **19** | 53 5N | 2 20E |
| Léman, Lac | **50** | 46 26N | 6 30E |
| Lemelerveld | **46** | 52 26N | 6 20E |
| Lemera | **126** | 3 0S | 28 55E |
| Lemery | **103** | 13 58N | 120 56E |
| Lemesós | **92** | 34 42N | 33 1E |
| Lemgo | **48** | 52 2N | 8 52E |
| Lemhi Ra. | **160** | 44 30N | 113 30W |
| Lemmer | **46** | 52 51N | 5 43E |
| Lemmon | **158** | 45 59N | 102 10W |
| Lemon Grove | **163** | 32 45N | 117 2W |
| Lemoore | **163** | 36 23N | 119 46W |
| Lempdes | **44** | 45 22N | 3 17E |
| Lemvig | **73** | 56 33N | 8 20E |
| Lemyethna | **98** | 21 10N | 95 52E |
| Lena, R. | **77** | 64 30N | 127 0E |
| Lenadoon Pt. | **38** | 54 19N | 9 3W |
| Lencloître | **42** | 46 50N | 0 20E |
| Lençóis | **171** | 12 35S | 41 43W |
| Lendalfoot | **34** | 55 12N | 4 55W |
| Lendelede | **47** | 50 53N | 3 16E |
| Lendinara | **63** | 45 4N | 11 37E |
| Lene L. | **38** | 53 40N | 7 12W |
| Lengau de Vaca, Punta | **172** | 30 14S | 71 38W |
| Lenger | **85** | 42 12N | 69 54E |
| Lengerich | **48** | 52 12N | 7 50E |
| Lenggong | **101** | 5 6N | 100 58E |
| Lengyeltóti | **53** | 46 40N | 17 40E |
| Lenham | **29** | 51 14N | 0 44E |
| Lenhovda | **73** | 57 0N | 15 16E |
| Lenia | **123** | 4 10N | 37 25E |
| Lenin | **83** | 48 20N | 40 56E |
| Lenina, Pik | **85** | 39 20N | 72 55E |
| Leninabad | **85** | 40 17N | 69 37E |
| Leninakan | **83** | 41 0N | 42 50E |
| Leningrad | **80** | 59 55N | 30 20E |
| Leninogorsk, Kazakh S.S.R., U.S.S.R. | **76** | 50 20N | 83 30E |
| Leninogorsk, R.S.F.S.R., U.S.S.R. | **84** | 54 36N | 52 30E |
| Leninpol | **85** | 42 29N | 71 55E |
| Leninsk, R.S.F.S.R., U.S.S.R. | **83** | 48 40N | 45 15E |
| Leninsk, Uzbek S.S.R., U.S.S.R. | **85** | 40 38N | 72 15E |
| Leninsk-Kuznetskiy | **76** | 55 10N | 86 10E |
| Leninskaya | **81** | 56 7N | 44 29E |
| Leninskoye, R.S.F.S.R., U.S.S.R. | **77** | 47 56N | 132 38E |
| Leninskoye, R.S.F.S.R., U.S.S.R. | **81** | 58 23N | 47 3E |
| Leninskoye, Uzbek S.S.R., U.S.S.R. | **85** | 41 45N | 69 23E |
| Lenk | **50** | 46 27N | 7 28E |
| Lenkoran | **79** | 39 45N | 48 50E |
| Lenmalu | **103** | 1 58S | 130 0E |
| Lennard, R. | **136** | 17 22S | 124 20E |
| Lennox Hills | **34** | 56 3N | 4 12W |
| Lennoxtown | **34** | 55 58N | 4 14W |
| Leno | **62** | 45 24N | 10 14E |
| Lenoir | **157** | 35 55N | 81 36W |
| Lenoir City | **157** | 35 40N | 84 20W |
| Lenora | **158** | 39 39N | 100 1W |
| Lenore L. | **153** | 52 30N | 104 59W |
| Lenox | **162** | 42 20N | 73 18W |
| Lens, Belg. | **47** | 50 33N | 3 54E |
| Lens, France | **43** | 50 26N | 2 50E |
| Lens St. Remy | **47** | 50 39N | 5 7E |
| Lensk (Mukhtuya) | **77** | 60 48N | 114 55E |
| Lenskoye | **82** | 45 3N | 34 1E |
| Lent | **46** | 51 52N | 5 52E |
| Lentini | **65** | 37 18N | 15 0E |
| Lenwood | **163** | 34 53N | 117 7W |
| Lenzburg | **50** | 47 23N | 8 11E |
| Lenzen | **48** | 53 6N | 11 26E |
| Lenzerheide | **51** | 46 44N | 9 34E |
| Léo | **120** | 11 3N | 2 2W |
| Leoben | **52** | 47 22N | 15 5E |
| Leola | **158** | 45 47N | 98 58W |
| Leominster, U.K. | **28** | 52 15N | 2 43W |
| Leominster, U.S.A. | **162** | 42 32N | 71 45W |
| Léon | **44** | 43 53N | 1 18W |
| León, Mexico | **164** | 21 7N | 101 30W |
| León, Nic. | **166** | 12 20N | 86 51W |
| León, Spain | **56** | 42 38N | 5 34W |
| Leon | **158** | 40 40N | 93 40W |
| León □ | **56** | 42 40N | 5 55W |
| León, Montañas de | **56** | 42 30N | 6 18W |
| Leonardtown | **162** | 38 19N | 76 39W |
| Leonel, Mte. | **50** | 46 15N | 8 5E |
| Leonforte | **65** | 37 39N | 14 22E |
| Leongatha | **141** | 38 30S | 145 58E |
| Leonídhion | **69** | 37 9N | 22 52E |
| Leonora | **137** | 28 49S | 121 19E |
| Leonora Downs | **140** | 32 29S | 142 5E |
| Léopold II, Lac = Mai-Ndombe | **124** | 2 0S | 18 0E |
| Leopoldina | **173** | 21 28S | 42 40W |
| Leopoldo Bulhões | **171** | 16 37S | 48 46W |
| Leopoldsburg | **47** | 51 7N | 5 13E |
| Léopoldville = Kinshasa | **124** | 4 20S | 15 15E |
| Leoti | **158** | 38 31N | 101 19W |
| Leoville | **153** | 53 39N | 107 33W |
| Lépa, L. do | **128** | 17 0S | 19 0E |
| Lepe | **57** | 37 15N | 7 12W |
| Lepel | **80** | 54 50N | 28 40E |
| Lephin | **36** | 57 26N | 6 43W |
| Lepikha | **77** | 64 45N | 125 55E |
| Lépo, L. do | **128** | 17 0S | 19 0E |
| Lepontine Alps | **62** | 46 22N | 8 27E |
| Lepsény | **53** | 47 0N | 18 15E |
| Leptis Magna | **119** | 32 40N | 14 12E |
| Lequeitio | **58** | 43 20N | 2 32W |
| Lerbäck | **72** | 58 56N | 15 2E |
| Lercara Friddi | **64** | 37 42N | 13 36E |
| Lerdo | **164** | 25 32N | 103 32W |
| Léré | **124** | 9 39N | 14 13E |
| Lere | **121** | 9 43N | 9 18E |
| Leribe | **129** | 28 51S | 28 3E |
| Lérici | **62** | 44 4N | 9 48E |
| Lérida | **58** | 41 37N | 0 39E |
| Lérida □ | **58** | 42 6N | 1 0E |
| Lérins, Is. de | **45** | 43 31N | 7 3E |
| Lerma | **56** | 42 0N | 3 47W |
| Léros, I. | **69** | 37 10N | 26 50E |
| Lérouville | **43** | 48 50N | 5 30E |
| Lerrig | **39** | 52 22N | 9 47W |
| Lerwick | **36** | 60 10N | 1 10W |
| Les | **70** | 46 58N | 21 50E |
| Lesbos, I. = Lésvos | **69** | 39 0N | 26 20E |
| Lesbury | **35** | 55 25N | 1 37W |
| Lésina, L. di | **63** | 41 53N | 15 25E |
| Lesja | **71** | 62 7N | 8 51E |
| Lesjaverk | **71** | 62 12N | 8 34E |
| Lesko | **54** | 49 30N | 22 23E |
| Leskov, I. | **13** | 56 0S | 28 0W |
| Leskovac | **68** | 43 0N | 21 58E |
| Leskovec | **68** | 40 10N | 20 34E |
| Leslie, U.K. | **35** | 56 12N | 3 12W |
| Leslie, U.S.A. | **159** | 35 50N | 92 35W |
| Lesmahagow | **35** | 55 38N | 3 55W |
| Lesna | **54** | 51 0N | 15 15E |
| Lesneven | **42** | 48 35N | 4 20W |
| Lesnič a | **66** | 44 39N | 19 20E |
| Lesnoy | **84** | 59 47N | 52 9E |
| Lesnoye | **80** | 58 15N | 35 31E |
| Lesotho ■ | **129** | 29 40S | 28 0E |
| Lesozavodsk | **77** | 45 30N | 133 20E |
| Lesparre-Médoc | **44** | 45 18N | 0 57W |
| Lessay | **42** | 49 14N | 1 30W |
| Lesse, R. | **47** | 50 15N | 4 54E |
| Lesser Antilles | **167** | 12 30N | 61 0W |
| Lesser Slave L. | **152** | 55 30N | 115 25W |
| Lessines | **47** | 50 42N | 3 50E |
| Lestock | **153** | 51 19N | 103 59W |
| Lesuer I. | **136** | 13 50S | 127 17E |
| Lesuma | **128** | 17 58S | 25 12E |
| Lésvos, I. | **69** | 39 0N | 26 20E |
| Leswalt | **34** | 54 56N | 5 6W |
| Leszno | **54** | 51 50N | 16 30E |
| Leszno □ | **54** | 51 45N | 16 30E |
| Letchworth | **29** | 51 58N | 0 13W |
| Letea, Ostrov | **70** | 45 18N | 29 20E |
| Lethbridge | **152** | 49 45N | 112 45W |
| Lethero | **140** | 33 33S | 142 30E |
| Lethlhakeng | **128** | 24 0S | 24 59E |
| Leti | **103** | 8 10S | 127 40E |
| Leti, Kepulauan | **103** | 8 10S | 128 0E |
| Letiahau, R. | **128** | 21 40S | 23 30E |
| Leticia | **174** | 4 0S | 70 0W |
| Letpadan | **98** | 17 45N | 96 0E |
| Letpan | **98** | 19 28N | 93 52E |
| Letsôk-aw-Kyun (Domel I.) | **101** | 11 30N | 98 25E |
| Letterbreen | **38** | 54 18N | 7 43W |
| Letterfrack | **38** | 53 33N | 9 58W |
| Letterkenny | **38** | 54 57N | 7 42W |
| Lettermacaward | **38** | 54 51N | 8 18W |
| Lettermore I. | **39** | 53 18N | 9 40W |
| Lettermullan | **39** | 53 15N | 9 44W |
| Letterston | **31** | 51 56N | 5 0W |
| Lettoch | **37** | 57 22N | 3 30W |
| Leu | **70** | 44 10N | 24 0E |
| Leucadia | **163** | 33 4N | 117 18W |
| Leucate | **44** | 42 56N | 3 3E |
| Leucate, Étang de | **44** | 42 50N | 3 0E |
| Leuchars | **35** | 56 23N | 2 53W |
| Leuk | **50** | 46 19N | 7 37E |
| Leukerbad | **50** | 46 24N | 7 36E |
| Leupegem | **47** | 50 50N | 3 36E |
| Leuser, G. | **102** | 4 0N | 96 51E |
| Leutkirch | **49** | 47 49N | 10 1E |
| Leuven (Louvain) | **47** | 50 52N | 4 42E |
| Leuze, Hainaut, Belg. | **47** | 50 36N | 3 37E |
| Leuze, Namur, Belg. | **47** | 50 33N | 4 54E |
| Lev Tolstoy | **81** | 53 13N | 39 29E |
| Levádhia | **69** | 38 27N | 22 54E |
| Levan | **160** | 39 37N | 111 32W |
| Levanger | **74** | 63 45N | 11 19E |
| Levani | **68** | 40 40N | 19 28E |
| Lévanto | **62** | 44 10N | 9 37E |
| Levanzo, I. | **64** | 38 0N | 12 19E |
| Levelland | **159** | 33 38N | 102 17W |
| Leven, Fife, U.K. | **35** | 56 12N | 3 0W |
| Leven, Humb., U.K. | **33** | 53 54N | 0 18W |
| Leven, Banc du | **129** | 12 30S | 47 45E |
| Leven, L. | **35** | 56 12N | 3 22W |
| Leven R. | **33** | 54 27N | 1 15W |
| Levens | **45** | 43 50N | 7 12E |
| Leveque C. | **136** | 16 20S | 123 0E |
| Leverano | **65** | 40 16N | 18 0E |
| Leverburgh | **36** | 57 46N | 7 0W |
| Leverkusen | **48** | 51 2N | 6 59E |
| Levet | **43** | 46 56N | 2 22E |
| Levice | **53** | 48 13N | 18 35E |
| Levick, Mt. | **13** | 75 0S | 164 0E |
| Levico | **63** | 46 0N | 11 18E |
| Levie | **45** | 41 40N | 9 7E |
| Levier | **43** | 46 58N | 6 8E |
| Levin | **142** | 40 37S | 175 18E |
| Levis | **151** | 46 48N | 71 9W |
| Levis, L. | **152** | 62 37N | 117 58W |
| Levítha, I. | **69** | 37 0N | 26 28E |
| Levittown, N.Y., U.S.A. | **162** | 40 41N | 73 31W |
| Levittown, Pa., U.S.A. | **162** | 40 10N | 74 51W |
| Levka | **67** | 41 52N | 26 15E |
| Lévka, Mt. | **69** | 35 18N | 24 3E |
| Levkás | **69** | 38 48N | 20 43E |
| Levkás, I. | **69** | 38 40N | 20 43E |
| Levkimmi | **68** | 39 25N | 20 3E |
| Levkôsia = Nicosia | **92** | 35 10N | 33 25E |
| Levoč a | **53** | 48 59N | 20 35E |
| Levroux | **43** | 47 0N | 1 38E |
| Levski | **67** | 43 21N | 25 10E |
| Levskigrad | **67** | 42 38N | 24 47E |
| Lewe | **98** | 19 38N | 96 7E |
| Lewellen | **158** | 41 22N | 102 5W |
| Lewes, U.K. | **29** | 50 53N | 0 2E |
| Lewes, U.S.A. | **156** | 38 45N | 75 8W |
| Lewes, L. | **148** | 60 30N | 134 20W |
| Lewin Brzeski | **54** | 50 45N | 17 37E |
| Lewis, Butt of | **36** | 58 30N | 6 12W |
| Lewis, I. | **36** | 58 10N | 6 40W |
| Lewis, R. | **160** | 48 0N | 113 15W |
| Lewis Ra. | **136** | 20 3S | 128 50E |
| Lewisburg, Pa., U.S.A. | **162** | 40 57N | 76 57W |
| Lewisburg, Tenn., U.S.A. | **157** | 35 29N | 86 46W |
| Lewisham | **29** | 51 27N | 0 1W |
| Lewisporte | **151** | 49 15N | 55 3W |
| Lewiston, U.K. | **37** | 57 19N | 4 30W |
| Lewiston, Idaho, U.S.A. | **160** | 45 58N | 117 0W |
| Lewiston, Utah, U.S.A. | **160** | 42 0N | 111 56W |
| Lewistown, Mont., U.S.A. | **160** | 47 0N | 109 25W |
| Lewistown, Pa., U.S.A. | **156** | 40 37N | 77 33W |
| Lexington, Ill., U.S.A. | **158** | 40 37N | 88 47W |
| Lexington, Ky., U.S.A. | **156** | 38 6N | 84 30W |
| Lexington, Md., U.S.A. | **162** | 38 16N | 76 27W |
| Lexington, Miss., U.S.A. | **159** | 33 8N | 90 2W |
| Lexington, Mo., U.S.A. | **158** | 39 7N | 93 55W |
| Lexington, N.C., U.S.A. | **157** | 35 50N | 80 13W |
| Lexington, Nebr., U.S.A. | **158** | 40 48N | 99 45W |
| Lexington, N.Y., U.S.A. | **162** | 42 15N | 74 22W |
| Lexington, Oreg., U.S.A. | **160** | 45 29N | 119 46W |

| | | | | |
|---|---|---|---|---|
| Lexington, Tenn., U.S.A. | 157 | 35 38N | 88 25W |
| Leyburn | 33 | 54 19N | 1 50W |
| Leyland | 32 | 53 41N | 2 42W |
| Leysdown on Sea | 29 | 51 23N | 0 57 E |
| Leysin | 50 | 46 21N | 7 0 E |
| Leyte, I. | 103 | 11 0N | 125 0 E |
| Lezay | 44 | 46 17N | 0 0 E |
| Lèze, R. | 44 | 43 28N | 1 25 E |
| Lezha | 68 | 41 47N | 19 42 E |
| Lézignan-Corbières | 44 | 43 13N | 2 43 E |
| Lezoux | 44 | 45 49N | 3 21 E |
| Lgov | 80 | 51 42N | 35 10 E |
| Lhanbryde | 37 | 57 38N | 3 12W |
| Lhariguo | 99 | 30 29N | 93 4 E |
| Lhasa | 105 | 29 39N | 91 6 E |
| Lhokseumawe | 102 | 5 20N | 97 10 E |
| Lhuntsi Dzong | 98 | 27 39N | 91 10 E |
| Li, Finland | 74 | 65 20N | 25 20 E |
| Li, Thai. | 100 | 17 48N | 98 57 E |
| Li Shui, R. | 109 | 29 24N | 112 1 E |
| Liádhoi, I. | 69 | 36 50N | 26 11 E |
| Liang Liang | 103 | 5 58N | 121 30 E |
| Liang Shan | 108 | 23 42N | 99 48 E |
| Lianga | 103 | 8 38N | 126 6 E |
| Liangch'eng, Inner Mongolia, China | 106 | 40 26N | 112 14 E |
| Liangch'eng, Shantung, China | 107 | 35 35N | 119 32 E |
| Lianghok'ou | 108 | 29 10N | 108 44 E |
| Lianghsiang | 106 | 39 44N | 116 8 E |
| Liangp'ing | 108 | 30 41N | 107 49 E |
| Liangpran, Gunong | 102 | 1 0N | 114 23 E |
| Liangtang | 106 | 33 56N | 106 12 E |
| Liao Ho, R. | 107 | 40 39N | 122 12 E |
| Liaoch'eng | 106 | 36 26N | 115 58 E |
| Liaochung | 107 | 41 30N | 122 42 E |
| Liaoning □ | 107 | 41 15N | 122 0 E |
| Liaotung Pantao | 107 | 40 0N | 122 22 E |
| Liaotung Wan | 107 | 40 30N | 121 30 E |
| Liaoyang | 107 | 41 17N | 123 11 E |
| Liaoyüan | 107 | 42 55N | 125 10 E |
| Liapádhes | 68 | 39 42N | 19 40 E |
| Liard, R. | 152 | 61 51N | 121 18W |
| Liari | 94 | 25 37N | 66 30 E |
| Libau = Liepaja | 80 | 56 30N | 21 0 E |
| Libby | 160 | 48 20N | 115 10W |
| Libenge | 124 | 3 40N | 18 55 E |
| Liberal, Kans., U.S.A. | 159 | 37 4N | 101 0W |
| Liberal, Mo., U.S.A. | 159 | 37 35N | 94 30W |
| Liberec | 52 | 50 47N | 15 7 E |
| Liberia | 166 | 10 40N | 85 30W |
| Liberia ■ | 120 | 6 30N | 9 30W |
| Libertad | 174 | 8 20N | 69 37W |
| Libertad, La | 166 | 16 47N | 90 7W |
| Liberty, Mo., U.S.A. | 158 | 39 15N | 94 24W |
| Liberty, N.Y., U.S.A. | 162 | 41 48N | 74 45W |
| Liberty, Pa., U.S.A. | 162 | 41 34N | 77 6W |
| Liberty, Tex., U.S.A. | 159 | 30 5N | 94 50W |
| Libiaz | 53 | 50 7N | 19 21 E |
| Libin | 47 | 49 59N | 5 15 E |
| Lîbîya, Sahrâ' | 114 | 27 35N | 25 0 E |
| Libohava | 68 | 40 3N | 20 10 E |
| Libourne | 44 | 44 55N | 0 14W |
| Libramont | 47 | 49 55N | 5 23 E |
| Librazhdi | 68 | 41 12N | 20 22 E |
| Libreville | 124 | 0 25N | 9 26 E |
| Libya ■ | 117 | 28 30N | 17 30 E |
| Libyan Plateau = Ed-Déffa | 122 | 30 40N | 26 30 E |
| Licantén | 172 | 34 55 S | 72 0W |
| Licata | 64 | 37 6N | 13 55 E |
| Lich'eng | 106 | 36 59N | 113 31 E |
| Lichfield | 28 | 52 40N | 1 50W |
| Lichiang | 108 | 26 54N | 100 12 E |
| Lichin | 107 | 37 32N | 118 20 E |
| Lichtaart | 47 | 51 13N | 4 55 E |
| Lichtenburg | 128 | 26 8 S | 26 8 E |
| Lichtenfels | 49 | 50 7N | 11 4 E |
| Lichtenvoorde | 46 | 51 59N | 6 34 E |
| Lichtervelde | 47 | 51 2N | 3 9 E |
| Lich'uan, Hupeh, China | 109 | 30 18N | 108 51 E |
| Lich'uan, Kiangsi, China | 109 | 27 14N | 116 51 E |
| Licosa, Punta | 65 | 40 15N | 14 53 E |
| Lida, U.S.A. | 163 | 37 30N | 117 30W |
| Lida, U.S.S.R. | 80 | 53 53N | 25 15 E |
| Lidhult | 73 | 56 50N | 13 27 E |
| Lidingö | 73 | 59 22N | 18 8 E |
| Lidköping | 73 | 58 31N | 13 14 E |
| Lido, Italy | 63 | 45 25N | 12 23 E |
| Lido, Niger | 121 | 12 54N | 3 44 E |
| Lido di Óstia | 64 | 41 44N | 12 14 E |
| Lidzbark | 54 | 53 15N | 19 49 E |
| Lidzbark Warminski | 54 | 54 7N | 20 34 E |
| Liebenwalde | 48 | 52 51N | 13 23 E |
| Lieberose | 48 | 51 59N | 14 18 E |
| Liebling | 66 | 45 36N | 21 20 E |
| Liechtenstein ■ | 49 | 47 8N | 9 35 E |
| Liederkerke | 47 | 50 52N | 4 5 E |
| Liège | 47 | 50 38N | 5 35 E |
| Liège □ | 47 | 50 32N | 5 35 E |
| Liegnitz = Legnica | 54 | 51 12N | 16 10 E |
| Liempde | 47 | 51 35N | 5 23 E |
| Lienart | 126 | 3 3N | 25 31 E |
| Lienartville | 126 | 3 3N | 25 31 E |
| Liench'eng | 109 | 25 47N | 116 48 E |
| Lienchiang, Fukien, China | 109 | 26 11N | 119 32 E |
| Lienchiang, Kwangtung, China | 109 | 21 36N | 110 16 E |
| Lienhsien | 109 | 24 50N | 112 23 E |
| Lienp'ing | 109 | 24 22N | 114 30 E |
| Lienshan, Kwangtung, China | 109 | 24 37N | 112 2 E |
| Lienshan, Yunnan, China | 108 | 24 48N | 97 54 E |
| Lienshankuan | 107 | 40 58N | 123 46 E |
| Lienshui | 107 | 33 46N | 119 18 E |
| Lienyüan | 109 | 27 41N | 111 40 E |
| Lienyünchiang | 107 | 34 47N | 119 30 E |
| Lienyünchiangshih | 107 | 34 37N | 119 13 E |
| Lienz | 52 | 46 50N | 12 46 E |
| Liepāja | 80 | 56 30N | 21 0 E |
| Lier | 47 | 51 7N | 4 34 E |
| Lierneux | 47 | 50 17N | 5 47 E |
| Lieshout | 47 | 51 31N | 5 36 E |
| Liesta | 70 | 45 38N | 27 34 E |
| Liestal | 50 | 47 29N | 7 44 E |
| Liesti | 70 | 45 38N | 27 34 E |
| Liévin | 43 | 50 24N | 2 47 E |
| Lièvre, R. | 150 | 45 31N | 75 26W |
| Liezen | 52 | 47 34N | 14 15 E |
| Liffey, R. | 39 | 53 21N | 6 20W |
| Lifford | 38 | 54 50N | 7 30W |
| Liffré | 42 | 48 12N | 1 30W |
| Lifjell | 71 | 59 27N | 8 45 E |
| Lightning Ridge | 139 | 29 22 S | 148 0 E |
| Lignano | 63 | 45 42N | 13 8 E |
| Ligny-er-Barrois | 43 | 48 36N | 5 20 E |
| Ligny-le-Châtel | 43 | 47 54N | 3 45 E |
| Ligoúrion | 69 | 37 37N | 23 2 E |
| Ligua, La | 172 | 32 30 S | 71 16W |
| Liguria □ | 62 | 44 30N | 9 0 E |
| Ligurian Sea | 62 | 43 20N | 9 0 E |
| Lihir Group | 135 | 3 0 S | 152 35 E |
| Lihou Reefs and Cays | 138 | 17 25 S | 151 40 E |
| Lihsien, Hopeh, China | 106 | 38 29N | 115 34 E |
| Lihsien, Hunan, China | 109 | 29 38N | 111 45 E |
| Lihsien, Kansu, China | 106 | 34 11N | 105 2 E |
| Lihsien, Szechwan, China | 108 | 31 28N | 103 17 E |
| Lihue | 147 | 21 59N | 159 24W |
| Lihwa | 99 | 30 4N | 100 18 E |
| Likasi | 127 | 10 55 S | 26 48 E |
| Likati | 124 | 3 20N | 24 0 E |
| Likhoslavl | 80 | 57 12N | 35 30 E |
| Likhovski | 83 | 48 10N | 40 10 E |
| Likoma I. | 127 | 12 3 S | 34 45 E |
| Likumburu | 127 | 9 43 S | 35 8 E |
| Liling | 109 | 27 40N | 113 30 E |
| Lill | 47 | 51 15N | 4 50 E |
| Lille | 43 | 50 38N | 3 3 E |
| Lille Bælt | 73 | 55 30N | 9 45 E |
| Lillebonne | 42 | 49 30N | 0 32 E |
| Lillehammer | 71 | 61 8N | 10 30 E |
| Lillers | 43 | 50 35N | 2 28 E |
| Lillesand | 71 | 58 15N | 8 23 E |
| Lillestrøm | 71 | 59 58N | 11 5 E |
| Lillian Point, Mt. | 137 | 27 40 S | 126 6 E |
| Lillo | 58 | 39 45N | 3 20W |
| Lillooet, R. | 152 | 49 15N | 121 57W |
| Lilongwe | 127 | 14 0 S | 33 48 E |
| Liloy | 103 | 8 4N | 122 39 E |
| Lilun | 108 | 28 3N | 100 27 E |
| Lim, R. | 66 | 43 0N | 19 40 E |
| Lima, Indon. | 103 | 3 37 S | 128 4 E |
| Lima, Peru | 174 | 12 0 S | 77 0W |
| Lima, Sweden | 72 | 60 55N | 13 20 E |
| Lima, Mont., U.S.A. | 160 | 44 41N | 112 38W |
| Lima, Ohio, U.S.A. | 156 | 40 42N | 84 5W |
| Lima, R. | 56 | 41 50N | 8 18W |
| Limanowa | 54 | 49 42N | 20 22 E |
| Limassol | 92 | 34 42N | 33 1 E |
| Limavady | 38 | 55 3N | 6 58W |
| Limavady □ | 38 | 55 0N | 6 55W |
| Limay Mahuida | 172 | 37 10 S | 66 45W |
| Limay, R. | 176 | 39 40 S | 69 45W |
| Limbang | 102 | 4 42N | 115 6 E |
| Limbara, Monti | 64 | 40 50N | 9 10 E |
| Limbdi | 94 | 22 34N | 71 51 E |
| Limbourg | 47 | 50 37N | 5 56 E |
| Limbourg □ | 47 | 51 2N | 5 25 E |
| Limbri | 141 | 31 3 S | 151 5 E |
| Limbunya | 136 | 17 14 S | 129 50 E |
| Limburg | 49 | 50 22N | 8 4 E |
| Limburg □ | 47 | 51 20N | 5 55 E |
| Limedsforsen | 72 | 60 52N | 13 25 E |
| Limeira | 173 | 22 35 S | 47 28W |
| Limenária | 68 | 40 38N | 24 32 E |
| Limerick | 39 | 52 40N | 8 38W |
| Limerick □ | 39 | 52 30N | 8 50W |
| Limerick Junction | 39 | 52 30N | 8 12W |
| Limestone, R. | 153 | 56 31N | 94 7W |
| Limfjorden | 73 | 56 55N | 9 0 E |
| Limia, R. | 56 | 41 55N | 8 8W |
| Limmared | 73 | 57 34N | 13 20 E |
| Limmat, R. | 51 | 47 26N | 8 20 E |
| Limmen | 46 | 52 34N | 4 42 E |
| Limmen Bight | 138 | 14 40 S | 135 35 E |
| Limmen Bight R. | 138 | 15 7 S | 135 44 E |
| Límni | 69 | 38 43N | 23 18 E |
| Limnos, I. | 68 | 39 50N | 25 5 E |
| Limoeiro | 170 | 7 52 S | 25 27W |
| Limoeiro do Norte | 170 | 5 5 S | 38 0W |
| Limoges | 44 | 45 50N | 1 15 E |
| Limón | 167 | 10 0N | 83 2W |
| Limon | 158 | 39 18N | 103 38W |
| Limone | 62 | 44 12N | 7 32 E |
| Limousin | 44 | 46 0N | 1 0 E |
| Limousin, Plateau de | 44 | 46 0N | 1 0 E |
| Limoux | 44 | 43 4N | 2 12 E |
| Limpopo, R. | 129 | 23 15 S | 32 5 E |
| Limpsfield | 29 | 51 15N | 0 1 E |
| Limu Ling, mts. | 100 | 19 0N | 109 20 E |
| Limuru | 126 | 1 2 S | 36 35 E |
| Lin | 68 | 41 4N | 20 38 E |
| Linan | 109 | 30 13N | 119 40 E |
| Linares | 172 | 35 50 S | 71 40W |
| Linares, Mexico | 165 | 24 50N | 99 40W |
| Linares, Spain | 59 | 38 10N | 3 40W |
| Linares □ | 172 | 36 0 S | 71 0W |
| Linas Mte. | 64 | 39 25N | 8 38 E |
| Linchenchen | 106 | 36 28N | 110 0 E |
| Linch'eng | 106 | 37 26N | 114 34 E |
| Linch'i | 106 | 35 46N | 113 53 E |
| Linchiang | 107 | 41 50N | 126 55 E |
| Linchin | 106 | 35 6N | 110 33 E |
| Linch'ing | 106 | 36 56N | 115 45 E |
| Linch'ü | 107 | 36 30N | 118 32 E |
| Linch'uan | 109 | 28 0N | 116 20 E |
| Lincluden | 35 | 55 5N | 3 40W |
| Lincoln, Argent. | 172 | 34 55N | 61 30W |
| Lincoln, N.Z. | 143 | 43 38 S | 172 30 E |
| Lincoln, N.Z. | 33 | 53 14N | 0 32W |
| Lincoln, Ill., U.S.A. | 158 | 40 10N | 89 20W |
| Lincoln, Kans., U.S.A. | 158 | 39 6N | 98 9W |
| Lincoln, Maine, U.S.A. | 151 | 45 27N | 68 29W |
| Lincoln, N. Mex., U.S.A. | 161 | 33 30N | 105 26W |
| Lincoln, Nebr., U.S.A. | 158 | 40 50N | 96 42W |
| Lincoln, N.H., U.S.A. | 162 | 44 3N | 71 40W |
| Lincoln □ | 33 | 53 14N | 0 32W |
| Lincoln Wolds | 33 | 53 20N | 0 5W |
| Lincoln Sea | 12 | 84 0N | 55 0W |
| Lincolnton | 157 | 35 30N | 81 15W |
| Lind, Austral. | 138 | 18 58 S | 144 30 E |
| Lind, U.S.A. | 160 | 47 0N | 118 33W |
| Lindale | 32 | 54 14N | 2 54W |
| Lindås, Norway | 71 | 60 44N | 5 10 E |
| Lindås, Sweden | 73 | 56 38N | 15 35 E |
| Lindau | 49 | 47 33N | 9 41 E |
| Linde | 46 | 52 50N | 6 57 E |
| Linden, Guyana | 174 | 6 0N | 58 10W |
| Linden, Calif., U.S.A. | 163 | 38 1N | 121 5W |
| Linden, Tex., U.S.A. | 159 | 33 0N | 94 20W |
| Lindenheuvel | 47 | 50 59N | 5 48 E |
| Lindenwold | 162 | 39 49N | 72 59W |
| Linderöd | 73 | 55 56N | 13 47 E |
| Linderödsåsen | 73 | 55 53N | 13 53 E |
| Lindesberg | 72 | 59 36N | 15 15 E |
| Lindesnes | 71 | 57 58N | 7 3 E |
| Lindfield | 29 | 51 2N | 0 5W |
| Lindi | 127 | 9 58 S | 39 38 E |
| Lindi □ | 127 | 9 40 S | 38 30 E |
| Lindi, R. | 126 | 1 25N | 25 56 E |
| Lindoso | 56 | 41 52N | 8 11W |
| Lindow | 48 | 52 58N | 12 58 E |
| Lindsay, Can. | 150 | 44 22N | 78 43W |
| Lindsay, Calif., U.S.A. | 163 | 36 14N | 119 6W |
| Lindsay, Okla., U.S.A. | 159 | 34 51N | 97 37W |
| Lindsborg | 158 | 38 35N | 97 40W |
| Línea de la Concepción, La | 55 | 36 15N | 5 23W |
| Línea de la Concepción, La | 57 | 36 15N | 5 23W |
| Linfen | 106 | 36 5N | 111 32 E |
| Lingakok | 99 | 29 55N | 87 38 E |
| Lingayer | 103 | 16 1N | 120 14 E |
| Lingayer G. | 103 | 16 10N | 120 15 E |
| Lingch'iu | 106 | 39 28N | 114 10 E |
| Lingch'uan, Kwangsi Chuang, China | 109 | 25 25N | 110 20 E |
| Lingch'uan, Shansi, China | 106 | 35 46N | 113 26 E |
| Lingen | 48 | 52 32N | 7 21 E |
| Lingfield | 29 | 51 11N | 0 1W |
| Lingga, Kepulauan | 102 | 0 10 S | 104 30 E |
| Linghed | 72 | 60 48N | 15 55 E |
| Linghsien, Hunan, China | 109 | 26 26N | 113 45 E |
| Linghsien, Shantung, China | 106 | 37 21N | 116 34 E |
| Lingle | 158 | 42 10N | 104 18W |
| Lingling | 109 | 26 13N | 111 37 E |
| Lingpi | 107 | 33 33N | 117 33 E |
| Lingshan | 108 | 22 26N | 109 17 E |
| Lingshih | 106 | 36 51N | 111 47 E |
| Lingshou | 106 | 38 18N | 114 22 E |
| Lingshui | 100 | 18 27N | 110 0 E |
| Lingt'ai | 106 | 35 4N | 107 37 E |
| Linguéré | 120 | 15 25N | 15 5W |
| Lingwu | 106 | 38 5N | 106 20 E |
| Lingyün | 108 | 24 24N | 106 31 E |
| Linh Cam | 100 | 18 31N | 105 31 E |
| Linhai | 109 | 28 51N | 121 7 E |
| Linhares | 171 | 19 25 S | 40 4W |
| Linho | 106 | 40 50N | 107 30 E |
| Linhsi | 107 | 43 37N | 118 8 E |
| Linhsia | 105 | 35 36N | 103 5 E |
| Linhsiang | 109 | 29 29N | 113 30 E |
| Linhsien | 106 | 37 57N | 110 57 E |
| Lini | 107 | 35 5N | 118 20 E |
| Linju | 106 | 34 14N | 112 45 E |
| Link | 68 | 41 4N | 20 38 E |
| Linkao | 100 | 19 56N | 109 42 E |
| Linkinhorne | 30 | 50 31N | 4 22W |
| Linköping | 73 | 58 28N | 15 36 E |
| Link'ou | 107 | 45 18N | 130 15 E |
| Linli | 109 | 29 27N | 111 39 E |
| Linlithgow | 35 | 55 58N | 3 38W |
| Linn, Mt. | 160 | 40 0N | 123 0W |
| Linney Head | 31 | 51 37N | 5 4W |
| Linnhe, L. | 34 | 56 36N | 5 25W |
| Linosa | 119 | 35 51N | 12 50 E |
| Lins | 173 | 21 40 S | 49 44W |
| Linshui | 108 | 30 18N | 106 55 E |
| Linslade | 29 | 51 55N | 0 40W |
| Lint'ao | 106 | 35 20N | 104 0 E |
| Linth, R. | 49 | 46 54N | 9 0 E |
| Linthal | 51 | 46 54N | 9 0 E |
| Lintlaw | 153 | 52 4N | 103 14W |
| Linton, Can. | 151 | 47 15N | 72 16W |
| Linton, U.K. | 29 | 52 6N | 0 19 E |
| Linton, Ind., U.S.A. | 156 | 39 0N | 87 10W |
| Linton, N. Dak., U.S.A. | 158 | 46 21N | 100 12W |
| Lints'ang | 108 | 23 54N | 100 0 E |
| Lint'ung | 106 | 34 24N | 109 13 E |
| Linville | 139 | 26 50 S | 152 11 E |
| Linwu | 109 | 25 17N | 112 33 E |
| Linxe | 44 | 43 56N | 1 13W |
| Linyanti, R. | 128 | 18 10 S | 24 10 E |
| Linyüan | 107 | 41 18N | 119 15 E |
| Linz, Austria | 52 | 48 18N | 14 18 E |
| Linz, Ger. | 48 | 50 33N | 7 18 E |
| Lion-d'Angers, Le | 42 | 47 37N | 0 43W |
| Lion, G. du | 44 | 43 0N | 4 0 E |
| Lioni | 65 | 40 52N | 15 10 E |
| Lion's Den | 127 | 17 15 S | 30 5 E |
| Lion's Head | 150 | 44 58N | 81 15W |
| Liozno | 80 | 55 0N | 30 50 E |
| Lipali | 127 | 15 50 S | 35 50 E |
| Lipari | 65 | 38 26N | 14 58 E |
| Lipari, Is. | 65 | 38 40N | 15 0 E |
| Lipetsk | 81 | 52 45N | 39 35 E |
| Lipiany | 54 | 53 2N | 14 58 E |
| Lip'ing | 108 | 26 16N | 109 0 E |
| Lipkany | 82 | 48 14N | 26 25 E |
| Lipljan | 66 | 42 31N | 21 7 E |
| Lipnik | 53 | 49 32N | 17 36 E |
| Lipno | 54 | 52 49N | 19 15 E |
| Lipo | 108 | 25 25N | 107 53 E |
| Lipova | 66 | 46 8N | 21 42 E |
| Lipovets | 82 | 49 12N | 29 1 E |
| Lippstadt | 48 | 51 40N | 8 19 E |
| Lipsco | 54 | 51 10N | 21 36 E |
| Lipscomb | 159 | 36 16N | 100 28W |
| Lipsko | 54 | 51 9N | 21 40 E |
| Lipsói, I. | 69 | 37 19N | 26 50 E |
| Liptovsky Svaty Milkula | 53 | 49 6N | 19 35 E |
| Liptrap C. | 141 | 38 50 S | 145 55 E |
| Lip'u | 109 | 24 30N | 110 23 E |
| Lira | 126 | 2 17N | 32 57 E |
| Liri, R. | 64 | 41 25N | 13 45 E |
| Liria | 58 | 39 37N | 0 35W |
| Lisala | 124 | 2 12N | 21 38 E |
| Lisbellaw | 38 | 54 20N | 7 32W |
| Lisboa | 57 | 38 42N | 9 10W |
| Lisboa □ | 57 | 39 0N | 9 12W |
| Lisbon | 158 | 46 30N | 97 46W |
| Lisbon = Lisboa | 57 | 38 42N | 9 10W |
| Lisburn | 38 | 54 30N | 6 9W |
| Lisburne, C. | 147 | 68 50N | 166 0W |
| Liscannor | 39 | 52 57N | 9 24W |
| Liscannor, B. | 39 | 52 57N | 9 24W |
| Liscarroll | 39 | 52 15N | 8 44W |
| Liscia, R. | 64 | 41 5N | 9 17 E |
| Liscomb | 151 | 45 2N | 62 0W |
| Lisdoonvarna | 39 | 53 2N | 9 18W |
| Lishe Ho, R. | 108 | 24 18N | 101 32 E |
| Lishih | 106 | 37 30N | 111 7 E |
| Lishu | 107 | 43 20N | 124 37 E |
| Lishuchen | 107 | 45 5N | 130 40 E |
| Lishui, Chekiang, China | 109 | 28 27N | 119 54 E |
| Lishui, Kiangsu, China | 109 | 31 38N | 119 2 E |
| Lisianski I. | 130 | 25 30N | 174 0W |
| Lisieux | 42 | 49 10N | 0 12 E |
| Lisischansk | 83 | 48 55N | 38 30 E |
| Liskeard | 30 | 50 27N | 4 29W |
| Lismore, N.S.W., Austral. | 139 | 28 44 S | 153 21 E |
| Lismore, Vic., Austral. | 133 | 37 58 S | 143 21 E |
| Lismore, Ireland | 39 | 52 8N | 7 58W |
| Lismore I. | 34 | 56 30N | 5 30W |
| Lisnacree | 38 | 54 4N | 6 5W |
| Lisnaskea | 38 | 54 15N | 7 27W |
| Liss | 29 | 51 3N | 0 53W |
| Lissatinning Bri. | 39 | 51 55N | 10 1W |
| Lisse | 46 | 52 16N | 4 33 E |
| Lisselton | 39 | 52 30N | 9 34W |
| Lissycasey | 39 | 52 44N | 9 12W |
| List | 48 | 55 1N | 8 26 E |
| Lista, Norway | 71 | 58 7N | 6 39 E |
| Lista, Sweden | 75 | 59 19N | 16 16 E |
| Lister, Mt. | 13 | 78 0 S | 162 0 E |
| Liston | 139 | 28 39 S | 152 6 E |
| Listowel, Can. | 150 | 43 44N | 80 58W |
| Listowel, Ireland | 39 | 52 27N | 9 30W |
| Listowel Dns. | 139 | 25 10 S | 145 12 E |
| Lit-et-Mixe | 44 | 44 2N | 1 15W |
| Lit'ang, Kwangsi-Chuang, China | 108 | 23 11N | 109 5 E |
| Lit'ang, Szechwan, China | 108 | 30 4N | 100 18 E |
| Litang | 103 | 5 27N | 118 31 E |
| Lit'ang Ho, R. | 108 | 28 5N | 101 28 E |
| Litcham | 29 | 52 43N | 0 47 E |
| Litchfield, Austral. | 140 | 36 18 S | 142 52 E |
| Litchfield, Conn., U.S.A. | 162 | 41 44N | 73 12W |
| Litchfield, Ill., U.S.A. | 158 | 39 10N | 89 40W |
| Litchfield, Minn., U.S.A. | 158 | 45 5N | 95 0W |
| Liteni | 70 | 47 32N | 26 32 E |
| Litherland | 32 | 53 29N | 3 0W |
| Lithgow | 141 | 33 25 S | 150 8 E |
| Lithínon, Ákra | 69 | 34 55N | 24 44 E |
| Lithuania S.S.R. □ | 80 | 55 30N | 24 0 E |
| Litija | 63 | 46 3N | 14 50 E |

Lititz Londonderry


| | | | |
|---|---|---|---|
| Lititz | 162 | 40 9N | 76 18W |
| Litókhoron | 68 | 40 8N | 22 34E |
| Litomĕrice | 52 | 50 33N | 14 10E |
| Litomysi | 53 | 49 52N | 16 20E |
| Litschau | 52 | 48 58N | 15 4E |
| Little Abaco I. | 157 | 26 50N | 77 30W |
| Little Aden | 91 | 12 41N | 45 6E |
| Little America | 13 | 79 0N | 160 0W |
| Little Andaman I. | 101 | 10 40N | 92 15E |
| Little Barrier I. | 142 | 36 12S | 175 8E |
| Little Belt | 72 | 55 8N | 9 55E |
| Little Belt Mts. | 160 | 46 50N | 111 0W |
| Little Blue, R. | 158 | 40 18N | 97 45W |
| Little Bushman Land | 128 | 29 10S | 18 10E |
| Little Cadotte, R. | 152 | 56 41N | 117 6W |
| Little Cayman, I. | 166 | 19 41N | 80 3W |
| Little Churchill, R. | 153 | 57 30N | 95 22W |
| Little Coco I. | 101 | 14 0N | 93 15E |
| Little Colorado, R. | 161 | 36 0N | 111 31W |
| Little Current | 150 | 45 55N | 82 0W |
| Little Current, R. | 150 | 50 57N | 84 36W |
| Little Egg Inlet | 162 | 39 30N | 74 20W |
| Little Falls, Minn., U.S.A. | 158 | 45 58N | 94 19W |
| Little Falls, N.Y., U.S.A. | 162 | 43 3N | 74 50W |
| Lit. Grand Rapids | 153 | 52 0N | 95 29W |
| Lit. Humbaldt, R. | 160 | 41 20N | 117 27W |
| Lit. Inagua I. | 167 | 21 40N | 73 50W |
| Little Lake | 163 | 35 58N | 117 58W |
| Little Longlac | 150 | 49 42N | 86 58W |
| Little Marais | 158 | 47 24N | 91 8W |
| Little Mecatiná I. | 151 | 50 30N | 59 25W |
| Little Minch | 36 | 57 35N | 6 45W |
| Lit. Miquelon I. | 151 | 46 45N | 56 25W |
| Lit. Missouri R. | 158 | 46 40N | 103 50W |
| Little Namaqualand | 128 | 29 0S | 17 9E |
| Little Ormes Hd. | 31 | 53 19N | 3 47W |
| Little Ouse, R. | 29 | 52 25N | 0 50E |
| Little Para, R. | 109 | 34 47S | 138 25E |
| Little Rann of Kutch | 94 | 23 25N | 71 25E |
| Little Red, R. | 159 | 35 40N | 92 15W |
| Little River | 143 | 43 45S | 172 49E |
| Little Rock | 159 | 34 41N | 92 10W |
| Little Ruaha, R. | 126 | 7 50S | 35 30E |
| Little Sable Pt. | 156 | 43 40N | 86 32W |
| Little Scarcies, R. | 125 | 9 30N | 12 25W |
| Little Sioux, R. | 147 | 42 20N | 95 55W |
| Little Smoky | 152 | 54 44N | 117 11W |
| Little Smoky River | 152 | 55 40N | 117 38W |
| Little Snake, R. | 160 | 40 45N | 108 15W |
| Little Wabash, R. | 156 | 38 40N | 88 20W |
| Little Walsingham | 29 | 52 53N | 0 51E |
| Little Whale, R. | 150 | 55 50N | 75 0W |
| Littleborough | 32 | 53 38N | 2 8W |
| Littlefield | 159 | 33 57N | 102 17W |
| Littlefork | 158 | 48 24N | 93 35W |
| Littlehampton, Austral. | 109 | 35 3S | 138 52E |
| Littlehampton, U.K. | 29 | 50 48N | 0 32W |
| Littlemill | 37 | 57 31N | 3 49W |
| Littleport | 29 | 52 27N | 0 18E |
| Littlestone-on-Sea | 29 | 50 59N | 0 59E |
| Littlestown | 162 | 39 45N | 77 3W |
| Littleton Common | 162 | 42 32N | 71 28W |
| Litu | 108 | 28 24N | 101 16E |
| Liuan | 109 | 31 45N | 116 30E |
| Liuch'eng | 108 | 24 39N | 109 14E |
| Liuchou | 108 | 24 15N | 109 22E |
| Liuchuang | 107 | 33 9N | 120 18E |
| Liuheng Tao | 109 | 29 43N | 122 8E |
| Liuho, Kiangsu, China | 109 | 32 20N | 118 51E |
| Liuho, Kirin, China | 107 | 42 16N | 125 42E |
| Liukou | 107 | 40 57N | 118 18E |
| Liuli | 127 | 11 3S | 34 38E |
| Liupa | 106 | 33 40N | 107 0E |
| Liuwa Plain | 125 | 14 20S | 22 30E |
| Liuyang | 109 | 28 9N | 113 38E |
| Livada | 70 | 47 52N | 23 5E |
| Livadherón | 68 | 40 2N | 21 57E |
| Livanovka | 84 | 52 6N | 61 59E |
| Livarot | 42 | 49 0N | 0 9E |
| Live Oak | 157 | 30 17N | 83 0W |
| Liveringa | 136 | 18 3S | 124 10E |
| Livermore | 163 | 37 41N | 121 47W |
| Livermore, Mt. | 159 | 30 45N | 104 8W |
| Liverpool, Austral. | 141 | 33 54S | 150 58E |
| Liverpool, Can. | 151 | 44 5N | 64 41W |
| Liverpool, U.K. | 32 | 53 25N | 3 0W |
| Liverpool, U.S.A. | 162 | 43 6N | 76 13W |
| Liverpool Bay, Can. | 147 | 70 0N | 128 0W |
| Liverpool Bay, U.K. | 23 | 53 30N | 3 20W |
| Liverpool Plains | 141 | 31 15S | 150 15E |
| Liverpool Ra. | 141 | 31 50S | 150 30E |
| Livingston, Guat. | 166 | 15 50N | 88 50W |
| Livingston, U.K. | 45 | 55 52N | 3 33W |
| Livingston, Calif., U.S.A. | 163 | 37 23N | 120 43W |
| Livingston, Mont., U.S.A. | 160 | 45 40N | 110 40W |
| Livingstone | 159 | 30 44N | 94 54W |
| Livingstone Falls | 126 | 5 25S | 13 35E |
| Livingstone I. | 13 | 63 0S | 60 15W |
| Livingstone (Maramba) | 127 | 17 46S | 25 52E |
| Livingstone Memorial | 127 | 12 20S | 30 18E |
| Livingstone Mts., N.Z. | 143 | 45 15S | 168 9E |
| Livingstone Mts., Tanz. | 127 | 9 40S | 34 20E |
| Livingstonia | 127 | 10 38S | 34 5E |
| Livno | 66 | 43 50N | 17 0E |
| Livny | 81 | 52 30N | 37 30E |
| Livorno | 62 | 43 32N | 10 18E |
| Livramento | 173 | 30 55S | 55 30W |
| Livramento do Brumado | 171 | 13 39S | 41 50W |
| Livron-sur-Drôme | 45 | 44 46N | 4 51E |
| Liwale | 127 | 9 48S | 37 58E |
| Liwale □ | 127 | 9 0S | 38 0E |
| Liwale Chini | 127 | 9 40S | 38 0E |
| Lixnaw | 39 | 52 24N | 9 37W |
| Lixoúrion | 69 | 38 14N | 20 24E |
| Liyang | 109 | 31 22N | 119 30E |
| Lizard | 30 | 49 58N | 5 10W |
| Lizard I. | 138 | 14 42S | 145 30E |
| Lizard Pt. | 30 | 49 57N | 5 11W |
| Lizarda | 170 | 9 36S | 46 41W |
| Lizzano | 65 | 40 23N | 17 25E |
| Ljig | 66 | 44 13N | 20 18E |
| Ljubija | 63 | 44 55N | 16 35E |
| Ljubinje | 66 | 42 58N | 18 5E |
| Ljubljana | 63 | 46 4N | 14 33E |
| Ljubno | 63 | 46 25N | 14 46E |
| Ljubovija | 66 | 44 11N | 19 22E |
| Ljubuški | 66 | 43 12N | 17 34E |
| Ljung | 73 | 58 1N | 13 3E |
| Ljungan | 72 | 62 18N | 17 23E |
| Ljungan, R. | 74 | 62 30N | 14 30E |
| Ljungaverk | 72 | 62 30N | 16 5E |
| Ljungby | 73 | 56 49N | 13 55E |
| Ljusdal | 72 | 61 46N | 16 3E |
| Ljusnan | 72 | 61 12N | 17 8E |
| Ljusnan, R. | 75 | 62 0N | 15 20E |
| Ljusne | 72 | 61 13N | 17 7E |
| Ljutomer | 63 | 46 31N | 16 11E |
| Lki | 67 | 41 28N | 23 43E |
| Llagostera | 58 | 41 50N | 2 54E |
| Llanaber | 31 | 52 45N | 4 5W |
| Llanaelhaiarn | 31 | 52 59N | 4 24W |
| Llanafan-fawr | 31 | 52 12N | 3 29W |
| Llanarmon Dyffryn Ceiriog | 31 | 52 53N | 3 15W |
| Llanarth | 31 | 52 12N | 4 19W |
| Llanarthney | 31 | 51 51N | 4 9W |
| Llanbedr | 31 | 52 40N | 4 7W |
| Llanbedrog | 31 | 52 52N | 4 29W |
| Llanberis | 31 | 53 7N | 4 7W |
| Llanbister | 31 | 52 22N | 3 19W |
| Llanbrynmair | 31 | 52 36N | 3 19W |
| Llancanelo, Salina | 172 | 35 40S | 69 8W |
| Llandaff | 31 | 51 29N | 3 13W |
| Llanddewi-Brefi | 31 | 52 11N | 3 57W |
| Llandilo | 31 | 51 45N | 4 0W |
| Llandogo | 31 | 51 44N | 2 40W |
| Llandovery | 31 | 51 59N | 3 49W |
| Llandrillo | 31 | 52 56N | 3 27W |
| Llandrindod Wells | 31 | 52 15N | 3 23W |
| Llandudno | 31 | 53 19N | 3 51W |
| Llandybie | 31 | 51 49N | 4 0W |
| Llandyfriog | 31 | 52 2N | 4 26W |
| Llandygwydd | 31 | 52 3N | 4 33W |
| Llandyrnog | 31 | 53 10N | 3 19W |
| Llandyssul | 31 | 52 3N | 4 20W |
| Llanelli | 31 | 51 41N | 4 11W |
| Llanelltyd | 31 | 52 45N | 3 54W |
| Llanenddwyn | 31 | 52 48N | 4 7W |
| Llanerchymedd | 31 | 53 20N | 4 22W |
| Llanes | 56 | 43 25N | 4 50W |
| Llanfaelog | 31 | 53 13N | 4 29W |
| Llanfair Caereinion | 31 | 52 39N | 3 20W |
| Llanfair Talhaiarn | 31 | 53 13N | 3 37W |
| Llanfairfechan | 31 | 53 15N | 3 58W |
| Llanfechell | 31 | 52 23N | 4 25W |
| Llanfyllin | 31 | 52 47N | 3 17W |
| Llangadog | 31 | 51 56N | 3 53W |
| Llangefni | 31 | 53 15N | 4 20W |
| Llangelynin | 31 | 52 39N | 4 7W |
| Llangennech | 31 | 51 41N | 4 10W |
| Llangerniew | 31 | 53 12N | 3 41W |
| Llangollen | 31 | 52 58N | 3 10W |
| Llangranog | 31 | 52 11N | 4 29W |
| Llangurig | 31 | 52 25N | 3 36W |
| Llangynog | 31 | 52 50N | 3 24W |
| Llanharan | 31 | 51 32N | 3 28W |
| Llanidloes | 31 | 52 28N | 3 31W |
| Llanilar | 31 | 52 22N | 4 2W |
| Llanllyfni | 31 | 53 2N | 4 18W |
| Llannor | 31 | 52 55N | 4 23W |
| Llano Estacado | 154 | 34 0N | 103 0W |
| Llano R. | 159 | 30 50N | 99 0W |
| Llanon | 31 | 52 17N | 4 9W |
| Llanos | 174 | 3 25N | 71 35W |
| Llanpumpsaint | 31 | 51 56N | 4 19W |
| Llanrhaedr-ym-Mochnant | 31 | 52 50N | 3 18W |
| Llanrhidian | 31 | 51 36N | 4 11W |
| Llanrhystyd | 31 | 52 19N | 4 9W |
| Llanrwst | 31 | 53 8N | 3 49W |
| Llansannan | 31 | 53 10N | 3 35W |
| Llansawel | 31 | 52 0N | 4 1W |
| Llanstephan | 31 | 51 46N | 4 24W |
| Llanthony | 31 | 51 57N | 3 2W |
| Llantrisant | 31 | 51 33N | 3 22W |
| Llanuwchllyn | 31 | 52 52N | 3 41W |
| Llanvihangel Crucorney | 31 | 51 53N | 2 58W |
| Llanwenog | 31 | 52 6N | 4 11W |
| Llanwrda | 31 | 51 58N | 3 52W |
| Llanwrtyd Wells | 31 | 52 6N | 3 39W |
| Llanyblodwel | 28 | 52 47N | 3 8W |
| Llanybyther | 31 | 52 4N | 4 10W |
| Llanymynech | 28 | 52 48N | 3 6W |
| Llanystymdwy | 31 | 52 56N | 4 17W |
| Llera | 165 | 23 19N | 99 1W |
| Llerena | 57 | 38 17N | 6 0W |
| Llethr Mt. | 31 | 52 47N | 3 58W |
| Lleyn Peninsula | 31 | 52 55N | 4 35W |
| Llico | 172 | 34 46S | 72 5W |
| Llobregat, R. | 58 | 41 19N | 2 9E |
| Lloret de Mar | 58 | 41 41N | 2 53E |
| Lloyd B. | 138 | 12 45S | 143 27E |
| Lloyd Barrage | 95 | 27 46N | 68 50E |
| Lloyd L. | 153 | 57 22N | 108 57W |
| Lloydminster | 153 | 53 20N | 110 0W |
| Lluchmayor | 59 | 39 29N | 2 53E |
| Llullaillaco, volcán | 172 | 24 30S | 68 30W |
| Llwyngwril | 31 | 52 41N | 4 6W |
| Llyswen | 31 | 52 2N | 3 18W |
| Lo | 47 | 50 59N | 2 45E |
| Lo Ho, Honan, China | 106 | 34 48N | 113 4E |
| Lo Ho, Shensi, China | 106 | 34 41N | 110 6E |
| Lo, R. | 100 | 21 18N | 105 25E |
| Loa | 161 | 38 18N | 111 46W |
| Loa, R. | 172 | 21 30S | 70 0W |
| Loan | 109 | 27 24N | 115 49E |
| Loanhead | 35 | 55 53N | 3 10W |
| Loano | 62 | 44 8N | 8 14E |
| Loans | 34 | 55 33N | 4 39W |
| Lobatse | 125 | 25 12S | 25 40E |
| Löbau | 48 | 51 5N | 14 42E |
| Lobaye, R. | 128 | 4 30N | 17 0E |
| Lobbes | 47 | 50 21N | 4 16E |
| Lobenstein | 48 | 50 25N | 11 39E |
| Loberia | 172 | 38 10S | 58 40W |
| Łobez | 54 | 53 38N | 15 39E |
| Lobito | 125 | 12 18S | 13 35E |
| Lobón, Canal de | 57 | 38 50N | 6 55W |
| Lobos | 172 | 35 2S | 59 0W |
| Lobos, I. | 164 | 21 27N | 97 13W |
| Lobos, Is. | 168 | 6 35S | 80 45W |
| Lobstick L. | 151 | 54 0N | 65 12W |
| Lobva | 84 | 59 10N | 60 30E |
| Lobva, R. | 84 | 59 8N | 60 48E |
| Loc Binh | 100 | 21 46N | 106 54E |
| Loc Ninh | 101 | 11 50N | 106 34E |
| Locarno | 51 | 46 10N | 8 47E |
| Loch Raven Res. | 162 | 39 26N | 76 33W |
| Lochaber | 36 | 56 55N | 5 0W |
| Lochailort | 36 | 56 53N | 5 40W |
| Lochaline | 36 | 56 32N | 5 47W |
| Loch'ang | 109 | 25 10N | 113 20E |
| Lochans | 34 | 54 52N | 5 1W |
| Lochboisdale | 36 | 57 10N | 7 20W |
| Lochbuie | 34 | 56 21N | 5 52W |
| Lochcarron | 36 | 57 25N | 5 30W |
| Lochdonhead | 34 | 56 27N | 5 40W |
| Loche L., La | 153 | 56 40N | 109 30W |
| Loche, La | 153 | 56 29N | 109 26W |
| Lochearnhead | 34 | 56 24N | 4 19W |
| Lochem | 46 | 52 9N | 6 26E |
| Loch'eng | 108 | 24 47N | 108 54E |
| Loches | 42 | 47 7N | 1 0E |
| Lochgelly | 35 | 56 7N | 3 18W |
| Lochgilphead | 34 | 56 2N | 5 37W |
| Lochgoilhead | 34 | 56 10N | 4 54W |
| Lochiang | 108 | 31 21N | 104 28E |
| Lochih | 108 | 30 18N | 105 0E |
| Loch'ing | 109 | 28 8N | 120 57E |
| Loch'ing Wan | 109 | 28 4N | 121 5E |
| Lochinver | 36 | 58 9N | 5 15W |
| Lochlaggan Hotel | 37 | 56 59N | 4 25W |
| Lochmaben | 35 | 55 8N | 3 27W |
| Lochmaddy | 36 | 57 36N | 7 10W |
| Lochnagar, Queens., Austral. | 138 | 24 34S | 144 52E |
| Lochnagar, Queens., Austral. | 138 | 23 33S | 145 38E |
| Lochnagar, Mt. | 37 | 56 57N | 3 14W |
| Łochow | 54 | 52 33N | 21 42E |
| Lochranza | 34 | 55 42N | 5 18W |
| Lochs Park, Reg. | 36 | 58 7N | 6 33W |
| Loch'uan | 106 | 35 48N | 109 35E |
| Lochwinnoch | 34 | 55 47N | 4 39W |
| Lochy, L. | 37 | 56 58N | 4 55W |
| Lochy, R. | 36 | 56 52N | 5 3W |
| Lock | 139 | 33 34S | 135 46E |
| Lock Haven | 156 | 41 7N | 77 31W |
| Lockeford | 163 | 38 10N | 121 9W |
| Lockeport | 151 | 43 47N | 65 4W |
| Lockerbie | 35 | 55 7N | 3 21W |
| Lockhart, Austral. | 141 | 35 14S | 146 40E |
| Lockhart, U.S.A. | 159 | 29 55N | 97 40W |
| Lockhart, L. | 137 | 33 15S | 119 3E |
| Lockington | 140 | 36 16S | 144 34E |
| Lockport | 156 | 43 12N | 78 42W |
| Locle, Le | 50 | 47 3N | 6 44E |
| Locminé | 42 | 47 54N | 2 51W |
| Locri | 65 | 38 14N | 16 14E |
| Locronan | 42 | 48 7N | 4 15W |
| Loctudy | 42 | 47 50N | 4 12W |
| Lod | 90 | 31 57N | 34 54E |
| Lodalskåpa | 71 | 61 47N | 7 13E |
| Loddon | 29 | 52 32N | 1 29E |
| Lodève | 44 | 43 44N | 3 19E |
| Lodge Grass | 160 | 45 21N | 107 27W |
| Lodgepole | 158 | 41 12N | 102 40W |
| Lodgepole Cr. | 158 | 41 20N | 104 30W |
| Lodhran | 94 | 29 32N | 71 30E |
| Lodi, Italy | 62 | 45 19N | 9 30E |
| Lodi, U.S.A. | 163 | 38 12N | 121 16W |
| Lodja | 124 | 3 30S | 23 23E |
| Lodji | 103 | 1 38S | 127 28E |
| Lodosa | 58 | 42 25N | 2 4W |
| Lodose | 73 | 58 5N | 12 10E |
| Lödöse | 73 | 58 2N | 12 9E |
| Lodwar | 126 | 3 10N | 35 40E |
| Łodz | 54 | 51 45N | 19 27E |
| Łodz □ | 54 | 51 45N | 19 27E |
| Loengo | 126 | 4 48S | 26 30E |
| Lofer | 52 | 47 35N | 12 41E |
| Lofoten | 74 | 68 10N | 13 0E |
| Lofoten Is. | 74 | 68 30N | 15 0E |
| Lofsen | 72 | 62 7N | 13 57E |
| Loftahammar | 73 | 57 54N | 16 41E |
| Loftsdalen | 72 | 62 10N | 13 20E |
| Loftus | 33 | 54 33N | 0 52W |
| Lofty Ra. | 136 | 24 15S | 119 30E |
| Loga | 121 | 13 37N | 3 14E |
| Logan, Kans., U.S.A. | 158 | 39 23N | 99 35W |
| Logan, Ohio, U.S.A. | 156 | 39 25N | 82 22E |
| Logan, Utah, U.S.A. | 160 | 41 45N | 111 50W |
| Logan, Mt. | 147 | 60 41N | 140 22W |
| Logan Pass | 152 | 48 41N | 113 44W |
| Logansport | 156 | 31 58N | 93 58W |
| Loganville | 162 | 39 51N | 76 42W |
| Logo | 123 | 5 20N | 30 18E |
| Logo Dergo | 123 | 6 10N | 29 18E |
| Logroño | 58 | 42 28N | 2 32W |
| Logroño □ | 58 | 42 28N | 2 27W |
| Logrosán | 57 | 39 20N | 5 32W |
| Løgstør | 73 | 56 58N | 9 14E |
| Lohardaga | 95 | 23 27N | 84 45E |
| Loheia | 91 | 15 45N | 42 40E |
| Lohja | 75 | 60 12N | 24 5E |
| Loho | 106 | 33 33N | 114 5E |
| Lohr | 49 | 50 0N | 9 35E |
| Loikaw | 98 | 19 40N | 97 17E |
| Loimaa | 75 | 60 50N | 23 5E |
| Loir-et-Cher □ | 43 | 47 40N | 1 20E |
| Loire □ | 45 | 45 40N | 4 5E |
| Loire-Atlantique □ | 42 | 47 25N | 1 40W |
| Loire, R. | 42 | 47 16N | 2 10W |
| Loiret □ | 43 | 47 58N | 2 10E |
| Loitz | 48 | 53 58N | 13 8E |
| Loja, Ecuador | 174 | 3 59S | 79 16W |
| Loja, Spain | 57 | 37 10N | 4 10W |
| Lojung | 108 | 24 27N | 109 36E |
| Loka | 123 | 4 13N | 31 0E |
| Lokandu | 124 | 2 30S | 25 45E |
| Løken | 71 | 59 48N | 11 29E |
| Lokerane | 128 | 24 54S | 24 42E |
| Lokeren | 47 | 51 6N | 3 59E |
| Lokhvitsa | 80 | 50 25N | 33 18E |
| Lokichokio | 126 | 4 19N | 34 13E |
| Lokitaung | 124 | 4 12N | 35 48E |
| Lokka | 74 | 67 49N | 27 45E |
| Løkken, Denmark | 73 | 57 22N | 9 41E |
| Løkken, Norway | 71 | 63 8N | 9 45E |
| Loknya | 80 | 56 49N | 30 4E |
| Lokobo | 123 | 4 20N | 30 30E |
| Lokoja | 121 | 7 47N | 6 45E |
| Lokolama | 124 | 2 35S | 19 50E |
| Loktung | 100 | 18 41N | 109 5E |
| Lokuti | 123 | 4 21N | 33 15E |
| Lokwei | 100 | 19 12N | 110 30E |
| Lol | 123 | 5 28N | 29 36E |
| Lol, R. | 123 | 9 0N | 28 10E |
| Lola | 120 | 7 52N | 8 29W |
| Lolibai, Gebel | 123 | 3 50N | 33 50E |
| Lolimi | 123 | 4 35N | 34 0E |
| Loliondo | 124 | 2 2S | 35 39E |
| Lolland | 73 | 54 45N | 11 30E |
| Lollar | 48 | 50 39N | 8 43E |
| Lolo | 160 | 46 50N | 114 8W |
| Lolodorf | 121 | 3 16N | 10 49E |
| Lolungchung | 126 | 30 43N | 96 7E |
| Lom | 67 | 43 48N | 23 20E |
| Lom Kao | 100 | 16 53N | 101 14E |
| Lom, R. | 66 | 43 45N | 23 7E |
| Lom Sak | 100 | 16 47N | 101 15E |
| Loma | 160 | 47 59N | 110 29W |
| Loma Linda | 163 | 34 3N | 117 16W |
| Lomami, R. | 126 | 1 0S | 24 40E |
| Lomas de Zamóra | 172 | 34 45S | 58 25W |
| Lombadria | 136 | 16 31S | 122 54E |
| Lombard | 160 | 46 7N | 111 28W |
| Lombardia □ | 62 | 45 35N | 9 45E |
| Lombardy = Lombardia | 62 | 45 35N | 9 45E |
| Lombez | 44 | 43 29N | 0 55E |
| Lomblen, I. | 103 | 8 30S | 123 32E |
| Lombok, I. | 102 | 8 35S | 116 20E |
| Lomé | 121 | 6 9N | 1 20E |
| Lomela | 124 | 2 5S | 23 52E |
| Lomela, R. | 124 | 1 30S | 22 50E |
| Lomello | 62 | 45 11N | 8 46E |
| Lometa | 159 | 31 15N | 98 25W |
| Lomie | 124 | 3 13N | 13 38E |
| Loming | 123 | 4 27N | 33 40W |
| Lomma | 73 | 55 43N | 13 6E |
| Lomme, R. | 47 | 50 8N | 5 10E |
| Lommel | 47 | 51 14N | 5 19E |
| Lomond | 152 | 50 24N | 112 36W |
| Lomond, gasfield | 19 | 57 18N | 1 12E |
| Lomond, L. | 34 | 56 8N | 4 38W |
| Lomond, mt. | 139 | 30 0S | 151 45E |
| Lomphat | 101 | 13 30N | 106 59E |
| Lompobatang, mt. | 103 | 5 24S | 119 56E |
| Lompoc | 163 | 34 41N | 120 32W |
| Lomsegga | 71 | 61 49N | 8 21E |
| Łomza | 54 | 53 10N | 22 2E |
| Łomza □ | 54 | 53 0N | 22 30E |
| Lonan | 106 | 34 6N | 110 10E |
| Lonavla | 96 | 18 46N | 73 29E |
| Loncoche | 176 | 39 20S | 72 50W |
| Londa | 97 | 15 30N | 74 30E |
| Londe, La | 45 | 43 8N | 6 14E |
| Londerzeel | 47 | 51 0N | 4 19E |
| Londiani | 126 | 0 10S | 35 33E |
| Londinières | 42 | 49 50N | 1 25E |
| London, Can. | 150 | 43 0N | 81 15W |
| London, U.K. | 29 | 51 30N | 0 5W |
| London, Ky., U.S.A. | 156 | 37 11N | 84 5W |
| London, Ohio, U.S.A. | 156 | 39 54N | 83 28W |
| London □ | 29 | 51 30N | 0 5W |
| Londonderry | 38 | 55 0N | 7 20W |

**Londonderry, C** **Lugano, L. di**

Londonderry, C. **136** 13 45S 126 55E
Londonderry, Co. **38** 55 0N 7 20W
Londonderry, I. **176** 55 0S 71 0W
Londrina **173** 23 0S 51 10W
Lone Pine **163** 36 35N 118 2W
Long Beach, Calif., U.S.A. **163** 33 46N 118 12W
Long Beach, N.Y., U.S.A. **162** 40 35N 73 40W
Long Beach, Wash., U.S.A. **160** 46 20N 124 1W
Long Bennington **33** 52 59N 0 45W
Long Branch **162** 40 19N 74 0W
Long Clawson **29** 52 51N 0 56W
Long Crendon **29** 51 47N 1 0W
Long Eaton **33** 52 54N 1 16W
Long Gully **109** 35 1S 138 40E
Long I., Austral. **138** 22 8S 149 53E
Long I., Bahamas **167** 23 20N 75 10W
Long I., Can. **150** 44 23N 66 19W
Long I., Ireland **39** 51 30N 9 35W
Long I., P.N.G. **135** 5 20S 147 5E
Long I., U.S.A. **162** 40 50N 73 20W
Long I. Sd. **162** 41 10N 73 0W
Long Itchington **28** 52 16N 1 24W
Long L. **150** 49 30N 86 50W
Long, L. **34** 56 4N 4 50W
Long L. **162** 43 57N 74 25W
Long Melford **29** 52 5N 0 44E
Long Mt. **31** 52 38N 3 7W
Long Mynd **23** 52 35N 2 50W
Long Pine **158** 43 33N 99 50W
Long Pocket **138** 18 30S 146 0E
Long Pt., Can. **151** 48 47N 58 46W
Long Pt., N.Z. **143** 46 34S 169 36E
Long Preston **32** 54 0N 2 16W
Long Ra. **151** 49 30N 57 30W
Long Range Mts **151** 48 0N 58 30W
Long Reef **136** 13 55S 125 45E
Long Str. **12** 70 0N 175 0E
Long Sutton **29** 52 47N 0 9E
Long Thanh **101** 10 47N 106 57E
Long Xuyen **101** 10 19N 105 28E
Longá **69** 36 53N 21 55E
Longa I. **36** 57 45N 5 50W
Longarone **63** 46 15N 12 18E
Longburn **142** 40 23S 175 35E
Longdam **99** 28 12N 98 16E
Longeau **43** 47 47N 5 20E
Longford, Austral. **138** 41 32S 147 3E
Longford, Ireland **38** 53 43N 7 50W
Longford, U.K. **28** 51 53N 2 14W
Longford □ **38** 53 42N 7 45W
Longforgan **35** 56 28N 3 8W
Longframlington **35** 55 18N 1 47W
Longhawan **102** 2 15N 114 55E
Longhorsley **35** 55 15N 1 46W
Longhoughton **35** 55 26N 1 38W
Longido **126** 2 43S 36 35E
Longiram **102** 0 5S 115 45E
Longkin **98** 25 39N 96 22E
Longlac **150** 49 45N 86 25W
Longlier **47** 49 52N 5 27E
Longling **99** 24 42N 98 58E
Longmont **158** 40 10N 105 4W
Longnawan **102** 21 50N 114 55E
Longobucco **65** 39 27N 16 37E
Longone, R. **117** 10 0N 15 40E
Longreach **138** 23 28S 144 14E
Longridge **32** 53 50N 2 37W
Long's Peak **160** 40 20N 105 50W
Longside **37** 57 30N 1 57W
Longton, Austral. **138** 21 0S 145 55E
Longton, Lancs., U.K. **32** 53 43N 2 48W
Longton, Stafford, U.K. **32** 53 00N 2 8W
Longtown **32** 55 1N 2 59W
Longué **42** 47 22N 0 8W
Longueau **42** 49 52N 2 22E
Longuyon **43** 49 27N 5 35E
Longview, Can. **152** 50 32N 114 10W
Longview, Tex., U.S.A. **159** 32 30N 94 45W
Longview, Wash., U.S.A. **160** 46 9N 122 58W
Longvilly **47** 50 2N 5 50E
Longwy **43** 49 30N 5 45E
Lonigo **63** 45 23N 11 22E
Loning **106** 34 28N 111 42E
Löningen **48** 54 43N 7 44E
Lonja, R. **63** 45 30N 16 40E
Lonkor Tso **95** 32 40N 83 15E
Lonoke **159** 34 48N 91 57W
Lonouaille **44** 46 30N 1 35E
Lons-le-Saunier **43** 46 40N 5 31E
Lønsdal **74** 66 46N 15 26E
Lønstrup **73** 57 29N 9 47E
Looc **103** 12 20N 112 5E
Lookout, C., Can. **150** 55 18N 83 56W
Lookout, C., U.S.A. **157** 34 30N 76 30W
Lookout, Pt. **162** 38 2N 76 21W
Loolmalasin, mt. **126** 3 0S 35 53E
Loomis **153** 49 15N 108 45W
Loon L. **153** 44 50N 77 15W
Loon Lake **153** 54 2N 109 10W
Loon-op-Zand **47** 51 38N 5 5E
Loon, R., Alta., Can. **152** 57 8N 115 3W
Loon, R., Man., Can. **153** 55 53N 101 59W
Loongana **137** 30 52S 127 5E
Loop Hd. **39** 52 34N 9 55W
Loosduinen **46** 52 3N 4 14E
Lop Buri **100** 14 48N 100 37E
Lop Nor **105** 40 20N 90 10E
Lopare **66** 44 39N 18 46E
Lopatin **83** 43 50N 47 35E
Lopatina, G. **77** 50 0N 143 30E
Lopaye **123** 6 37N 33 40E
Lopera **57** 37 56N 4 14W
Lopez **162** 41 27N 76 20W
Lopez C. **124** 0 47S 8 40E
Lop'ing, Kiangsi, China **109** 28 57N 117 5E
Lop'ing, Yunnan, China **108** 24 56N 104 20E
Lopodi **123** 5 5N 33 15E
Loppem **47** 51 9N 3 12E
Loppersum **46** 53 20N 6 44E
Lopphavet **74** 70 27N 21 15E
Lora Cr. **139** 28 10S 135 22E
Lora del Río **57** 37 39N 5 33W
Lora, La **56** 42 45N 4 0W
Lora, R. **93** 32 0N 67 15E
Lorain **156** 41 20N 82 5W
Loralai **94** 30 29N 68 30E
Lorca **59** 37 41N 1 42W
Lord Howe I. **130** 31 33S 159 6E
Lordsburg **161** 32 15N 108 45W
Lorengau **135** 2 1S 147 15E
Loreto, Brazil **170** 7 5S 45 30W
Loreto, Italy **63** 43 26N 13 36E
Loreto, Mexico **164** 26 1N 111 21W
Loreto Aprutina **63** 42 24N 13 59E
Lorgues **45** 43 28N 6 22E
Lorica **174** 9 14N 75 49W
Lorient **42** 47 45N 3 23W
Lorne, Austral. **140** 38 33S 143 59E
Lorne, U.K. **34** 56 26N 5 10W
Lorne, Firth of **34** 56 20N 5 40W
Lörrach **49** 47 36N 7 38E
Lorraine **43** 49 0N 6 0E
Lorrainville **150** 47 21N 79 23W
Los Alamos, Calif., U.S.A. **163** 34 44N 120 17W
Los Alamos, N. Mex., U.S.A. **161** 35 57N 106 17W
Los Altos **163** 37 23N 122 7W
Los Andes **172** 32 50S 70 40W
Los Ángeles **172** 37 28S 72 23W
Los Angeles **163** 34 0N 118 10W
Los Angeles Aqueduct **163** 35 25N 118 0W
Los Banos **163** 37 8N 120 56W
Los Barrios **57** 36 11N 5 30W
Los Blancos, Argent. **172** 23 45S 62 30W
Los Blancos, Spain **59** 37 38N 0 49W
Los Gatos **163** 37 15N 121 59W
Los, Îles de **120** 9 30N 13 50W
Los Lamentos **164** 30 36N 105 50W
Los Lunas **161** 34 55N 106 47W
Los Mochis **164** 25 45N 109 5W
Los Monegros **58** 41 29N 0 3W
Los Muertos, Punta de **59** 36 57N 1 54W
Los Olivos **163** 34 40N 120 7W
Los Palacios **166** 22 35N 83 15W
Los Palacios y Villafranca **57** 37 10N 5 55W
Los Reyes **164** 19 21N 99 7W
Los Roques, Is. **167** 11 50N 66 45W
Los Santos de Maimona **57** 38 37N 6 22W
Los Testigos, Is. **174** 11 23N 63 6W
Los Vilos **172** 32 0S 71 30W
Los Yébenes **57** 39 36N 3 55W
Loshan, Honan, China **109** 32 12N 114 32E
Loshan, Szechwan, China **108** 29 34N 103 44E
Loshkalakh **77** 62 45N 147 20E
Lošinj, I. **63** 44 55N 14 45E
Losser **46** 52 16N 7 1E
Lossiemouth **37** 57 43N 3 17W
Lostwithiel **30** 50 24N 4 41W
Losuia **135** 8 30S 151 4E
Lot □ **44** 44 39N 1 40E
Lot-et-Garonne □ **44** 44 22N 0 30E
Lot, R. **44** 44 18N 0 20E
Lota, Austral. **108** 27 28S 153 11E
Lota, Chile **172** 37 5S 73 10W
Løten **71** 60 51N 11 21E
Lothian, (□) **26** 55 55N 3 35W
Lothiers **43** 46 42N 1 33E
Lotien **108** 25 29N 106 39E
Lot'ien **109** 30 47N 115 20E
Lot'ing **107** 39 26N 118 56E
Loting **109** 22 46N 111 34E
Lötschberg **49** 46 25N 7 53E
Lotschbergtunnel **50** 46 26N 7 43E
Lottefors **72** 61 25N 16 24E
Lotung, China **100** 18 44N 109 9E
Lotung, Taiwan **109** 24 41N 121 46E
Lotz'u **108** 25 19N 102 18E
Lotzukou **107** 43 44N 130 20E
Lotzwil **50** 47 12N 7 48E
Loudéac **42** 48 11N 2 47W
Loudon **157** 35 41N 84 22W
Loudun **42** 47 0N 0 5E
Loué **42** 47 59N 0 9W
Loue, R. **42** 47 4N 6 10E
Louga **120** 15 45N 16 5W
Loughborough **28** 52 46N 1 11W
Loughbrickland **38** 54 19N 6 19W
Loughmore **39** 52 45N 7 50W
Loughor **31** 51 39N 4 5W
Loughrea **39** 53 11N 8 33W
Loughros More, B. **38** 54 48N 8 30W
Louhans **45** 46 38N 5 12E
Louis Gentil **118** 32 16N 8 31W
Louis Trichardt **125** 23 0S 29 55E
Louis XIV, Pte. **150** 54 37N 79 45W
Louisa **156** 38 5N 82 40W
Louisbourg **151** 45 55N 60 0W
Louisbourg Nat. Historic Park **151** 45 58N 60 20W
Louisburgh **38** 53 46N 9 49W
Louise I. **152** 52 55N 131 40W
Louiseville **150** 46 20N 73 0W
Louisiade Arch. **135** 11 10S 153 0E
Louisiana **158** 39 25N 91 0W
Louisiana □ **159** 30 50N 92 0W
Louisville, Ky., U.S.A. **156** 38 15N 85 45W
Louisville, Miss., U.S.A. **159** 33 7N 89 3W
Loulay **44** 46 3N 0 30W
Loulé **57** 37 9N 8 0W
Lount L. **153** 50 10N 94 20W
Louny **52** 50 20N 13 48E
Loup City **158** 41 19N 98 57W
Loupe, La **42** 48 29N 1 1E
Lourdes **44** 43 6N 0 3W
Lourdes-de-Blanc-Sablon **151** 51 24N 57 12W
Lourenço-Marques, B. de **129** 25 50S 32 45E
Lourenço-Marques = Maputo **129** 25 58S 32 32E
Loures **57** 38 50N 9 9W
Lourinhã **57** 39 14N 9 17W
Louroux Béconnais, Le **42** 47 30N 0 55W
Lousã **56** 40 7N 8 14W
Louth, Austral. **141** 30 30S 145 8E
Louth, Ireland **38** 53 47N 6 33W
Louth, U.K. **33** 53 23N 0 0W
Louth □ **38** 53 55N 6 30W
Louti **109** 27 45N 111 58E
Loutrá Aidhipsoú **69** 38 54N 23 2E
Loutráki **69** 38 0N 22 57E
Louveigné **47** 50 32N 5 42E
Louvière, La **47** 50 27N 4 10E
Louviers **42** 49 12N 1 10E
Lovat, R. **80** 56 30N 31 20E
Love **153** 53 29N 104 10W
Loveland **158** 40 27N 105 4W
Lovell **160** 44 51N 108 20W
Lovelock **160** 40 17N 118 25W
Lóvere **62** 45 50N 10 4E
Loviisa = Lovisa **75** 60 31N 26 20E
Loving **159** 32 17N 104 4W
Lovington **159** 33 0N 103 20W
Lovios **56** 41 55N 8 4W
Lovisa (Loviisa) **75** 60 28N 26 12E
Lovosice **52** 50 30N 14 2E
Lovran **63** 45 18N 14 15E
Lovrin **66** 45 58N 20 48E
Lövstabukten **72** 60 35N 17 45E
Low Pt. **137** 32 25S 127 25E
Low Rocky Pt. **133** 42 59S 145 29E
Lowa **124** 1 25S 25 47E
Lowa, R. **126** 1 15S 27 40E
Lowell **162** 42 38N 71 19W
Lower Arrow L. **152** 49 40N 118 5W
Lower Austria = Niederösterreich **52** 48 25N 15 40E
Lower Beeding **29** 51 2N 0 15W
Lower Hermitage **109** 34 49S 138 46E
Lower Hutt **142** 41 10S 174 55E
Lower L. **160** 41 17N 120 3W
Lower Lake **160** 38 56N 122 36W
Lower Neguac **151** 47 20N 65 10W
Lower Post **152** 59 58N 128 30W
Lower Sackville **151** 44 45N 63 43W
Lower Saxony = Niedersachsen **48** 52 45N 9 0E
Lower Seal, L. **150** 56 30N 74 23W
Lower Woolgar **138** 19 47S 143 27E
Lowes Water L. **32** 54 35N 3 23W
Lowestoft **29** 52 29N 1 44E
Lowick **35** 55 38N 1 57W
Łowicz **54** 52 6N 19 55E
Lowther Hills **35** 55 20N 3 40W
Lowville **162** 43 48N 75 30W
Loxton **140** 34 28S 140 31E
Loyal L. **37** 58 24N 4 20W
Loyalty Is. **130** 21 0S 167 30E
Loyang **106** 34 41N 112 28E
Loyauté, Îles **130** 21 0S 167 30E
Loyeh **108** 24 48N 106 34E
Loyev **80** 57 7N 30 40E
Loyoro **126** 3 22N 34 14E
Loyüan **109** 26 30N 119 33E
Loz **63** 45 43N 14 14E
Lozère □ **44** 44 35N 3 30E
Loznica **66** 44 32N 19 14E
Lozovaya **82** 49 0N 36 27E
Lozva, R. **84** 59 36N 62 20E
Lu **98** 45 0N 8 29E
Lü-Tao **109** 22 47N 121 20E
Luabo **147** 18 30S 36 10E
Luacano **124** 11 15S 21 37E
Lualaba, R. **126** 5 45S 26 50E
Luampa **127** 15 4S 24 20E
Luan **103** 6 10N 124 25E
Luan Chau **100** 21 38N 103 24E
Luan Ho, R. **107** 39 25N 119 15E
Luanch'eng **106** 37 53N 114 39E
Luanda **124** 8 58S 13 9E
Luang Doi **100** 18 30N 101 0E
Luang Prabang **100** 19 45N 102 10E
Luang Thale **101** 7 30N 100 15E
Luangwa, R. **125** 14 25S 30 25E
Luangwa Val. **127** 13 30S 31 30E
Luanho **107** 40 56N 117 42E
Luanhsien **107** 39 45N 118 44E
Luanping **107** 40 56N 117 42E
Luanshya **127** 13 3S 28 28E
Luapula □ **127** 11 0S 29 0E
Luapula, R. **127** 12 0S 28 50E
Luarca **56** 43 32N 6 32W
Luashi **127** 10 50S 23 36E
Lubalo **124** 9 10S 19 15E
Luban **54** 51 5N 15 15E
Lubana, Osero **80** 56 45N 27 0E
Lubang Is. **103** 13 50N 120 12E
Lubartów **54** 51 28N 22 42E
Lubawa **54** 53 30N 19 48E
Lubban **90** 32 9N 35 14E
Lubbeek **47** 50 54N 4 50E
Lübben **48** 51 56N 13 54E
Lübbenau **48** 51 49N 13 59E
Lubbock **159** 33 40N 102 0W
Lubcroy **37** 57 58N 4 47W
Lübeck **48** 53 52N 10 41E
Lübecker Bucht **48** 54 3N 11 0E
Lubefu **126** 4 47S 24 27E
Lubefu, R. **126** 4 47S 24 27E
Lubero = Luofu **126** 0 1S 29 15E
Lubicon L. **152** 56 23N 115 56W
Lubien Kujawski **54** 52 23N 19 9E
Lubin **54** 51 24N 16 11E
Lublin **54** 51 12N 22 38E
Lublin □ **54** 51 5N 22 30E
Lubliniec **54** 50 43N 18 45E
Lubny **80** 50 3N 32 58E
Lubok Antu **102** 1 3N 111 50E
Lubon **54** 52 21N 16 51E
Lubongola **126** 2 35S 27 50E
Lubotin **53** 49 17N 20 53E
Lubraniec **54** 52 33N 18 50E
Lubsko **54** 51 45N 14 57E
Lübtheen **48** 53 18N 11 4E
Lubuagan **103** 17 21N 121 10E
Lubudi **124** 6 50S 21 20E
Lubudi, R. **127** 9 30S 25 0E
Lubuhanbilik **102** 2 33N 100 14E
Lubuk Linggau **102** 3 15S 102 55E
Lubuk Sikaping **102** 0 10N 100 15E
Lubumbashi **127** 11 32S 27 28E
Lubunda **126** 5 12S 26 41E
Lubungu **127** 14 35S 26 24E
Lubutu **126** 0 45S 26 30E
Luc An Chau **100** 22 6N 104 43E
Luc-en-Diois **45** 44 36N 5 28E
Luc, Le **45** 43 23N 6 21E
Lucan **38** 53 21N 6 27W
Lucania, Mt. **147** 60 48N 141 25W
Lucca **62** 43 50N 10 30E
Luccens **50** 46 43N 6 51E
Luce Bay **138** 54 45N 4 48W
Lucea **166** 18 25N 78 10W
Lucedale **157** 30 55N 88 34W
Lucena, Phil. **103** 13 56N 121 37E
Lucena, Spain **57** 37 27N 4 31W
Lucena del Cid **58** 40 9N 0 17W
Lučenec **53** 48 18N 19 42E
Lucera **65** 41 30N 15 20E
Lucerne = Luzern **51** 47 3N 8 18E
Lucerne Valley **163** 34 27N 116 57W
Lucero **164** 30 49N 106 30W
Luchai **108** 24 33N 109 48E
Luchena, R. **59** 37 50N 2 0W
Luch'eng **106** 36 18N 113 15E
Lucheringo, R. **127** 12 0S 36 5E
Luch'i **109** 28 17N 110 10E
Luchiang, China **109** 31 14N 117 17E
Luchiang, Taiwan **109** 24 1N 120 22E
Luchou **108** 28 53N 105 22E
Lüchow **48** 52 58N 11 8E
Luch'uan **109** 22 20N 110 14E
Lucindale **93** 36 59S 140 23E
Lucira **125** 14 0S 12 35E
Luckau **48** 51 50N 13 43E
Luckenwalde **48** 52 5N 13 11E
Lucknow **95** 26 50N 81 0E
Lucomagno, Paso del **51** 46 34N 8 49E
Luçon **44** 46 28N 1 10W
Luda Kamchiya, R. **67** 42 50N 27 0E
Ludbreg **63** 46 15N 16 38E
Lüdenscheid **48** 51 13N 7 37E
Lüderitz **128** 26 41S 15 8E
Ludewa □ **127** 10 0S 34 50E
Ludgershall **28** 51 15N 1 38W
Ludgvan **30** 50 9N 5 30W
Ludhiana **94** 30 57N 75 56E
Lüdinghausen **48** 51 46N 7 28E
Ludington **156** 43 58N 86 27W
Ludlow, U.K. **28** 52 23N 2 42W
Ludlow, Calif., U.S.A. **163** 34 43N 116 10W
Ludlow, Vt., U.S.A. **162** 43 25N 72 40W
Luduş **70** 46 29N 24 5E
Ludvika **72** 60 8N 15 14E
Ludwigsburg **49** 48 53N 9 11E
Ludwigshafen **49** 49 27N 8 27E
Ludwigslust **48** 53 19N 11 28E
Ludza **80** 56 32N 27 43E
Lue **141** 32 38S 149 50E
Luebo **124** 5 21S 21 17E
Lüehyang **106** 33 20N 106 3E
Lueki **126** 3 20S 25 48E
Luena, Zaîre **127** 9 28S 25 43E
Luena, Zambia **127** 10 40S 30 25E
Luepa **174** 5 43N 61 31W
Lufeng, Kwangtung, China **109** 23 2N 115 37E
Lufeng, Yunnan, China **108** 25 10N 102 5E
Lufira R. **124** 9 30S 27 0E
Lufkin **159** 31 25N 94 40W
Lufupa **127** 10 32S 24 50E
Luga **80** 58 40N 29 55E
Luga, R. **80** 59 5N 28 30E
Lugano **51** 46 0N 8 57E
Lugano, L. di **51** 46 0N 9 0E

Lugansk McIlwraith Ra


| | | | |
|---|---|---|---|
| Lugansk = Voroshilovgrad | 83 | 48 35N | 39 29 E |
| Lugard's Falls | 126 | 3 6S | 38 41 E |
| Lugela | 127 | 16 25S | 36 43 E |
| Lugenda, R. | 127 | 12 35S | 36 50 E |
| Lugh Ganana | 91 | 3 48N | 42 40 E |
| Lugnaquilla, Mt. | 39 | 52 48N | 6 28W |
| Lugnvik | 72 | 62 56N | 17 55 E |
| Lugo, Italy | 63 | 44 25N | 11 53 E |
| Lugo, Spain | 56 | 43 2N | 7 35W |
| Lugo □ | 56 | 43 0N | 7 30W |
| Lugoj | 66 | 45 42N | 21 57 E |
| Lugones | 56 | 43 26N | 5 50W |
| Lugovoy | 76 | 43 0N | 72 20 E |
| Lugovoye | 85 | 42 55N | 72 43 E |
| Lugwardine | 28 | 52 4N | 2 38W |
| Luhe, R. | 48 | 53 7N | 10 0 E |
| Luhsi, Yunan, China | 108 | 24 31N | 103 46 E |
| Luhsi, Yunnan, China | 108 | 24 27N | 98 36 E |
| Luhuo | 108 | 31 24N | 100 41 E |
| Lui | 106 | 33 52N | 115 28 E |
| Luiana | 125 | 17 25S | 22 30W |
| Luichart L. | 37 | 57 36N | 4 43W |
| Luichow Pen. = Leichou Pantao | 108 | 20 40N | 110 5 E |
| Luing I. | 34 | 56 15N | 5 40W |
| Luino | 62 | 46 0N | 8 42 E |
| Luís | 164 | 26 36N | 109 11W |
| Luís Correia | 170 | 3 0S | 41 35W |
| Luís Gomes | 171 | 6 25S | 38 23W |
| Luís Gonçalves | 170 | 5 37S | 50 25W |
| Luisa | 124 | 7 40S | 22 30 E |
| Luiza | 124 | 7 40S | 22 30 E |
| Luizi | 126 | 6 0S | 27 25 E |
| Luján | 172 | 34 45S | 59 5W |
| Lukanga Swamp | 127 | 14 30S | 27 40 E |
| Lukenie, R. | 124 | 3 0S | 18 50 E |
| Lukhisaral | 95 | 27 11N | 86 5 E |
| Lukolela | 124 | 1 10S | 17 12 E |
| Lukosi | 127 | 18 30S | 26 30 E |
| Lukovit | 67 | 43 13N | 24 11 E |
| Lukoyanov | 81 | 55 2N | 44 20 E |
| Lukuhu | 108 | 27 46N | 100 50 E |
| Lukulu | 125 | 14 35S | 23 25 E |
| Lula | 126 | 0 30N | 25 10 E |
| Lule, R. | 74 | 65 35N | 22 10 E |
| Luleå | 74 | 65 35N | 22 10 E |
| Lüleburgaz | 67 | 41 23N | 27 28 E |
| Luliang | 108 | 25 3N | 103 39 E |
| Luling | 159 | 29 45N | 97 40W |
| Lulonga, R. | 124 | 1 0N | 19 0 E |
| Lulua, R. | 124 | 6 30S | 22 50 E |
| Luluabourg = Kananga | 124 | 5 55S | 22 18 E |
| Lulung | 107 | 39 55N | 118 57 E |
| Lumai | 125 | 13 20S | 21 25 E |
| Lumajang | 103 | 8 8S | 113 16 E |
| Lumbala, Angola | 125 | 12 36S | 22 30 E |
| Lumbala, Angola | 125 | 14 18S | 21 18 E |
| Lumberton, Miss., U.S.A. | 159 | 31 4N | 89 28W |
| Lumberton, N. Mex., U.S.A. | 161 | 36 58N | 106 57W |
| Lumberton, N.C., U.S.A. | 157 | 34 37N | 78 59W |
| Lumbres | 43 | 50 40N | 2 5 E |
| Lumbwa | 126 | 0 12S | 35 28 E |
| Lumby | 152 | 50 10N | 118 50W |
| Lumding | 98 | 25 46N | 93 10 E |
| Lumege | 125 | 11 45S | 20 50 E |
| Lumeyen | 123 | 4 55N | 33 28 E |
| Lumi | 135 | 3 30S | 142 2 E |
| Lummen | 47 | 50 59N | 5 12 E |
| Lumphanan | 37 | 57 8N | 2 41W |
| Lumsden, N.Z. | 143 | 45 44S | 168 27 E |
| Lumsden, U.K. | 37 | 57 16N | 2 51W |
| Lumut | 101 | 4 13N | 100 37 E |
| Lumut, Tg. | 102 | 3 50S | 105 58 E |
| Lunan | 108 | 24 47N | 103 16 E |
| Lunan B. | 37 | 56 40N | 2 25W |
| Lunavada | 94 | 23 8N | 73 37 E |
| Lunca | 70 | 47 22N | 25 1 E |
| Lund, Norway | 74 | 68 42N | 18 9 E |
| Lund, Sweden | 73 | 55 41N | 13 12 E |
| Lund, U.S.A. | 160 | 38 53N | 115 0W |
| Lunda | 124 | 9 40S | 20 12 E |
| Lundazi | 125 | 12 20S | 33 7 E |
| Lunde | 71 | 59 17N | 9 5 E |
| Lunderskov | 73 | 55 29N | 9 19 E |
| Lundi, R. | 127 | 21 15S | 31 25 E |
| Lundu | 102 | 1 40N | 109 50 E |
| Lundy, I. | 30 | 51 10N | 4 41W |
| Lune, R. | 32 | 54 0N | 2 51W |
| Lüneburg | 48 | 53 15N | 10 23 E |
| Lüneburg Heath = Lüneburger Heide | 48 | 53 0N | 10 0 E |
| Lüneburger Heide | 48 | 53 0N | 10 0 E |
| Lunel | 45 | 43 39N | 4 9 E |
| Lünen | 48 | 51 36N | 7 31 E |
| Lunenburg | 151 | 44 22N | 64 18W |
| Lunéville | 43 | 48 36N | 6 30 E |
| Lung Chiang, R. | 108 | 24 30N | 109 15 E |
| Lunga, R. | 127 | 13 0S | 26 33 E |
| Lungan | 108 | 23 11N | 107 41 E |
| Lungch'ang | 108 | 29 20N | 105 19 E |
| Lungch'ih | 108 | 29 25N | 103 24 E |
| Lungchou | 108 | 22 24N | 106 50 E |
| Lungch'üan | 109 | 28 5N | 119 7 E |
| Lungch'uan, Kwangtung, China | 109 | 24 6N | 115 15 E |
| Lungch'uan, Yunnan, China | 108 | 24 16N | 97 58 E |
| Lungern | 50 | 46 48N | 8 10 E |
| Lungholt | 74 | 63 35N | 18 10 E |
| Lunghsi | 106 | 35 3N | 104 38 E |
| Lunghsien | 106 | 34 47N | 107 0 E |
| Lunghua | 107 | 41 18N | 117 42 E |
| Lunghui | 109 | 27 18N | 110 52 E |
| Lungi Airport | 120 | 8 40N | 16 47 E |
| Lungk'ou | 107 | 37 42N | 120 21 E |
| Lungkuan | 106 | 40 45N | 115 43 E |
| Lungkukang | 108 | 32 18N | 99 7 E |
| Lungleh | 98 | 22 55N | 92 45 E |
| Lungli | 108 | 26 27N | 106 58 E |
| Lunglin | 108 | 24 43N | 105 26 E |
| Lungling | 108 | 24 38N | 98 35 E |
| Lungmen | 109 | 23 44N | 114 15 E |
| Lungming | 108 | 23 4N | 107 14 E |
| Lungnan | 109 | 24 54N | 114 47 E |
| Lungngo | 98 | 21 57N | 93 36 E |
| Lungshan | 108 | 29 27N | 109 23 E |
| Lungsheng | 109 | 25 48N | 110 0 E |
| Lungte | 106 | 35 38N | 106 6 E |
| Lungyen | 109 | 25 9N | 117 0 E |
| Lungyu | 109 | 29 2N | 119 10 E |
| Luni | 94 | 26 0N | 73 6 E |
| Luni, R. | 94 | 25 40N | 72 20 E |
| Luninets | 80 | 52 15N | 27 0 E |
| Luning | 163 | 38 30N | 118 10W |
| Lunino | 81 | 53 35N | 45 6 E |
| Lunna Ness | 36 | 60 27N | 1 4W |
| Lunner | 71 | 60 19N | 10 35 E |
| Lunsemfwa Falls | 127 | 14 30S | 29 6 E |
| Lunsemfwa, R. | 127 | 14 50S | 30 10 E |
| Lunteren | 46 | 52 5N | 5 38 E |
| Luofu | 126 | 0 1S | 29 15 E |
| Luozi | 124 | 4 54S | 14 0 E |
| Lupeni | 70 | 45 21N | 23 13 E |
| Łupków | 53 | 49 15N | 22 4 E |
| Lupundu | 127 | 14 18S | 26 45 E |
| Luque, Parag. | 172 | 25 19S | 57 25W |
| Luque, Spain | 57 | 37 35N | 4 16W |
| Luray | 156 | 38 39N | 78 26W |
| Lure | 43 | 47 40N | 6 30 E |
| Luremo | 124 | 8 30S | 17 50 E |
| Lurgainn L. | 36 | 58 1N | 5 15W |
| Lurgan | 38 | 54 28N | 6 20W |
| Luristan | 92 | 33 20N | 47 0 E |
| Lusaka | 127 | 15 28S | 28 16 E |
| Lusambo | 126 | 4 58S | 23 28 E |
| Luseland | 153 | 52 5N | 109 24W |
| Lushan, Honan, China | 106 | 33 45N | 113 10 E |
| Lushan, Kweichow, China | 108 | 26 33N | 107 58 E |
| Lushan, Szechwan, China | 108 | 30 10N | 102 59 E |
| Lushih | 106 | 34 4N | 110 2 E |
| Lushnja | 68 | 40 55N | 19 41 E |
| Lushoto | 126 | 4 47S | 38 20 E |
| Lushoto □ | 126 | 4 45S | 38 20 E |
| Lushui | 108 | 25 51N | 98 55 E |
| Lüshun | 107 | 38 48N | 121 16 E |
| Lusignan | 44 | 46 26N | 0 8 E |
| Lusigny-sur-Barse | 43 | 48 16N | 4 15 E |
| Lusk, Ireland | 38 | 53 32N | 6 10W |
| Lusk, U.S.A. | 158 | 42 47N | 104 27W |
| Luss | 34 | 56 6N | 4 40W |
| Lussac-les-Châteaux | 44 | 46 24N | 0 43 E |
| Lussanvira | 171 | 20 42S | 51 7W |
| Lüta | 107 | 38 55N | 121 40 E |
| Luti | 108 | 7 14S | 157 0 E |
| Luting | 108 | 29 56N | 102 12 E |
| Luton | 29 | 51 53N | 0 24W |
| Lutong | 102 | 4 30N | 114 0 E |
| Lutry | 50 | 46 31N | 6 42 E |
| Lutsk | 80 | 50 50N | 25 15 E |
| Lutterworth | 28 | 52 28N | 1 12W |
| Luverne | 158 | 43 35N | 96 12W |
| Luvua | 127 | 8 48S | 25 17 E |
| Luwegu, R. | 127 | 9 30S | 36 20 E |
| Luwingu, Mt. | 124 | 10 15S | 30 2 E |
| Luwuk | 103 | 10 0S | 122 40 E |
| Luxembourg | 47 | 49 37N | 6 9 E |
| Luxembourg □ | 47 | 49 58N | 5 30 E |
| Luxembourg ■ | 47 | 50 0N | 6 0 E |
| Luxeuil-les-Bains | 43 | 47 49N | 6 24 E |
| Luxor = El Uqsur | 122 | 25 41N | 32 38 E |
| Luy de Béarn, R. | 44 | 43 39N | 0 48W |
| Luy de France, R. | 44 | 43 39N | 0 48W |
| Luy, R. | 44 | 43 39N | 1 9W |
| Luyksgestel | 47 | 51 17N | 5 20 E |
| Luz, Brazil | 171 | 19 48S | 45 40W |
| Luz, France | 44 | 42 53N | 0 1 E |
| Luzern | 51 | 47 3N | 8 18 E |
| Luzern □ | 50 | 47 2N | 7 55 E |
| Luzerne | 162 | 41 17N | 75 54W |
| Luziânia | 171 | 16 20S | 48 0W |
| Luzilândia | 170 | 3 28S | 42 22W |
| Luzon, I. | 103 | 16 0N | 121 0 E |
| Luzy | 43 | 46 47N | 3 58 E |
| Luzzi | 65 | 39 28N | 16 17 E |
| Lvov | 80 | 49 40N | 24 0 E |
| Lwówek | 54 | 52 28N | 16 10 E |
| Lwówek Śląski | 54 | 51 7N | 15 38 E |
| Lyakhovichi | 80 | 53 2N | 26 32 E |
| Lyakhovskiye, Ostrova | 77 | 73 40N | 141 0 E |
| Lyaki | 83 | 40 34N | 47 22 E |
| Lyall Mt. | 142 | 45 16S | 167 32 E |
| * Lyallpur | 94 | 31 30N | 73 5 E |
| Lyalya, R. | 84 | 59 9N | 61 29 E |
| Lyaskovets | 67 | 43 6N | 25 44 E |
| Lybster | 37 | 58 18N | 3 16W |
| Lychen | 48 | 53 13N | 13 20 E |
| Lyckeby | 73 | 56 12N | 15 37 E |
| Lycksele | 74 | 64 38N | 18 40 E |
| Lydd | 29 | 50 57N | 0 56 E |
| Lydda = Lod | 90 | 31 57N | 34 54 E |
| Lydenburg | 129 | 25 10S | 30 29 E |
| Lydford | 30 | 50 38N | 4 7W |
| Lydham | 28 | 52 31N | 2 59W |
| Lyell | 143 | 41 48S | 172 4 E |
| Lyell I. | 152 | 52 40N | 131 35W |
| Lyell, oilfield | 19 | 60 55N | 1 12 E |
| Lyell Range | 143 | 41 38S | 172 20 E |
| Lygnern | 73 | 57 30N | 12 15 E |
| Lykens | 162 | 40 34N | 76 42W |
| Lykling | 71 | 59 42N | 5 12 E |
| Lyman | 160 | 41 24N | 110 15W |
| Lyme Bay | 23 | 50 36N | 2 55W |
| Lyme Regis | 30 | 50 44N | 2 57W |
| Lyminge | 29 | 51 7N | 1 6 E |
| Lymington | 28 | 50 46N | 1 32W |
| Lymm | 32 | 53 23N | 2 30W |
| Lympne | 29 | 51 4N | 1 2 E |
| Lynchburg | 156 | 37 23N | 79 10W |
| Lynd, R. | 138 | 16 28S | 143 18 E |
| Lynd Ra. | 139 | 25 30S | 149 20 E |
| Lynden | 160 | 48 56N | 122 32W |
| Lyndhurst, N.S.W., Austral. | 138 | 33 41S | 149 2 E |
| Lyndhurst, Queens., Austral. | 138 | 19 12S | 144 20 E |
| Lyndhurst, S. Australia, Austral. | 139 | 30 15S | 138 18 E |
| Lyndhurst, U.K. | 28 | 50 53N | 1 33W |
| Lyndon, R. | 137 | 23 29S | 114 6 E |
| Lyneham | 28 | 51 30N | 1 57W |
| Lyngdal, Agder, Norway | 71 | 58 8N | 7 7 E |
| Lyngdal, Buskerud, Norway | 71 | 59 54N | 9 32 E |
| Lynher Reef | 136 | 15 27S | 121 55 E |
| Lynmouth | 30 | 51 14N | 3 50W |
| Lynn | 162 | 42 28N | 70 57W |
| Lynn Canal | 152 | 58 50N | 135 20W |
| Lynn L. | 153 | 56 30N | 101 40W |
| Lynn Lake | 153 | 56 51N | 101 3W |
| Lynton | 30 | 51 14N | 3 50W |
| Lyntupy | 80 | 55 4N | 26 23 E |
| Lynx L. | 153 | 62 25N | 106 15W |
| Lyø | 73 | 55 3N | 10 9 E |
| Lyon | 45 | 45 46N | 4 50 E |
| Lyonnais | 45 | 45 45N | 4 15 E |
| Lyons, Colo., U.S.A. | 158 | 40 17N | 105 15W |
| Lyons, Ga., U.S.A. | 157 | 32 10N | 82 15W |
| Lyons, Kans., U.S.A. | 158 | 38 24N | 98 13W |
| Lyons, N.Y., U.S.A. | 162 | 43 3N | 77 0W |
| Lyons = Lyon | 45 | 45 46N | 4 50 E |
| Lyons Falls | 162 | 43 37N | 75 22W |
| Lyons, R. | 137 | 25 2S | 115 9 E |
| Lyrestad | 73 | 58 48N | 14 4 E |
| Lysá | 52 | 50 11N | 14 51 E |
| Lysekil | 73 | 58 17N | 11 26 E |
| Lyskovo | 81 | 56 0N | 45 3 E |
| Lyss | 50 | 47 4N | 7 19 E |
| Lysva | 84 | 58 07N | 57 49 E |
| Lysvik | 72 | 60 1N | 13 9 E |
| Lytchett Minster | 28 | 50 44N | 2 3W |
| Lytham St. Anne's | 32 | 53 45N | 2 58W |
| Lythe | 33 | 54 30N | 0 40W |
| Lytle | 159 | 29 14N | 98 46W |
| Lyttelton | 143 | 43 35S | 172 44 E |
| Lytton | 152 | 50 13N | 121 31W |
| Lyuban | 80 | 59 16N | 31 18 E |
| Lyubim | 81 | 58 20N | 40 50 E |
| Lyubimets | 67 | 41 50N | 26 5 E |
| Lyubomi | 81 | 51 10N | 24 2 E |
| Lyubotin | 82 | 50 0N | 36 4 E |
| Lyubytino | 80 | 58 50N | 33 16 E |
| Lyudinovo | 80 | 53 52N | 34 28 E |


# M


| | | | |
|---|---|---|---|
| Ma, R. | 100 | 19 47N | 105 56 E |
| Ma'ad | 90 | 32 37N | 35 36 E |
| Maam Cross | 38 | 53 23N | 9 32W |
| Maamba | 128 | 17 17S | 26 28 E |
| Ma'an | 92 | 30 12N | 35 44 E |
| Maanshan | 109 | 31 40N | 118 30 E |
| Maarheeze | 47 | 51 19N | 5 36 E |
| Maarianhamina | 75 | 60 5N | 19 55 E |
| Maarn | 47 | 52 3N | 5 22 E |
| Maarssen | 46 | 52 9N | 5 2 E |
| Maartensdijk | 46 | 52 9N | 5 10 E |
| Maas | 38 | 54 49N | 8 21W |
| Maas, R. | 47 | 51 48N | 4 55 E |
| Maasbracht | 47 | 51 9N | 5 54 E |
| Maasbree | 47 | 51 22N | 6 3 E |
| Maasdan | 46 | 51 48N | 4 34 E |
| Maasdijk | 46 | 51 58N | 4 13 E |
| Maaseik | 47 | 51 6N | 5 45 E |
| Maasin | 102 | 10 5N | 124 55 E |
| Maasland | 46 | 51 57N | 4 16 E |
| Maasniel | 47 | 51 12N | 6 1 E |
| Maassluis | 47 | 51 56N | 4 16 E |
| Maastricht | 47 | 50 50N | 5 40 E |
| Maatin-es-Sarra | 117 | 21 45N | 22 0 E |
| Maave | 129 | 21 4S | 34 47 E |
| Mabein | 98 | 23 29N | 96 37 E |
| Mabel L. | 152 | 50 35N | 118 43W |
| Mabel, oilfield | 19 | 58 6N | 1 36 E |
| Mabenge | 126 | 4 15N | 24 12 E |
| Mablethorpe | 33 | 53 21N | 0 14 E |
| Mabrouk | 121 | 19 29N | 1 15W |
| Mabton | 127 | 46 13N | 120 1W |
| Mac Bac | 101 | 9 46N | 106 7 E |
| Mc Grath | 147 | 62 58N | 155 40W |
| Macachin | 172 | 37 10S | 63 43W |
| Macadam Ra. | 136 | 14 40S | 129 50 E |
| Macaé | 173 | 22 20S | 41 55W |
| Macaguane | 174 | 6 35N | 71 43W |
| Macaíba | 170 | 5 15S | 35 21W |
| Macajuba | 171 | 12 9S | 40 22W |
| McAlester | 159 | 34 57N | 95 40W |
| Macamic | 150 | 48 45N | 79 0W |
| Macão | 57 | 39 35N | 7 59W |
| Macao = Macau ■ | 109 | 22 16N | 113 35 E |
| Macapá | 175 | 0 5N | 51 10W |
| Macarani | 171 | 15 33S | 40 24W |
| Macarena, Serranía de la | 174 | 2 45N | 73 55W |
| Macarthur | 140 | 38 5S | 142 0 E |
| McArthur, R. | 136 | 16 45S | 136 0 E |
| McArthur River | 138 | 16 27S | 137 7 E |
| Macau | 170 | 5 0S | 36 40W |
| Macau ■ | 109 | 22 16N | 113 35 E |
| Macaúbas | 171 | 13 2S | 42 42W |
| McBride | 152 | 53 20N | 120 10W |
| McCamey | 159 | 31 8N | 102 15W |
| McCammon | 160 | 42 41N | 112 11W |
| McCarthy | 147 | 61 25N | 143 0W |
| McCauley I. | 152 | 53 40N | 130 15W |
| Macclesfield | 32 | 53 16N | 2 9W |
| McClintock | 153 | 57 50N | 94 10W |
| McClintock Chan. | 148 | 72 0N | 102 0W |
| McClintock Ra., Mts. | 136 | 18 44S | 127 38 E |
| McCloud | 160 | 41 14N | 122 5W |
| McCluer Gulf | 103 | 2 20S | 133 0 E |
| McCluer I. | 136 | 11 5S | 133 0 E |
| McClure, L. | 163 | 37 35N | 120 16W |
| McClusky | 158 | 47 30N | 100 31W |
| McComb | 159 | 31 20N | 90 30W |
| McConnell Creek | 152 | 56 53N | 126 30W |
| McCook | 158 | 40 15N | 100 35W |
| McCulloch | 152 | 49 45N | 119 15W |
| McCusker, R. | 153 | 55 32N | 108 39W |
| McDame | 152 | 59 44N | 128 59W |
| McDermitt | 160 | 42 0N | 117 45W |
| McDonald I. | 11 | 54 0S | 73 0 E |
| Macdonald L. | 137 | 23 30S | 129 0 E |
| Macdonald Ra. | 136 | 15 35S | 124 50 E |
| Macdonnell Ranges | 136 | 23 40S | 133 0 E |
| McDouall Peak | 139 | 29 51S | 134 55 E |
| Macdougall L. | 148 | 66 00N | 98 27W |
| McDougalls Well | 140 | 31 8S | 141 15 E |
| MacDowell L. | 150 | 52 15N | 92 45W |
| Macduff | 37 | 57 40N | 2 30W |
| Mace | 150 | 48 55N | 80 0W |
| Maceda | 56 | 42 16N | 7 39W |
| Macedo da Cavaleiros | 124 | 11 25S | 16 45 E |
| Macedo de Cavaleiros | 56 | 41 31N | 6 57W |
| Macedonia = Makedonija | 66 | 41 53N | 21 40 E |
| Macedonia = Makhedonia | 68 | 40 39N | 22 0 E |
| Maceió | 170 | 9 40S | 35 41W |
| Maceira | 57 | 39 41N | 8 55W |
| Macenta | 120 | 8 35N | 9 20W |
| Macerata | 63 | 43 19N | 13 28 E |
| McFarland | 163 | 35 41N | 119 14W |
| Macfarlane, L. | 140 | 32 0S | 136 40 E |
| McFarlane, R. | 153 | 59 12N | 107 58W |
| McGehee | 159 | 33 40N | 91 25W |
| McGill | 160 | 39 27N | 114 50W |
| Macgillycuddy's Reeks, mts. | 39 | 52 2N | 9 45W |
| McGraw | 162 | 42 35N | 76 4W |
| MacGregor | 153 | 49 57N | 98 48W |
| McGregor, Iowa, U.S.A. | 158 | 42 58N | 91 15W |
| McGregor, Minn., U.S.A. | 158 | 46 37N | 93 17W |
| McGregor, R. | 152 | 55 10N | 122 0W |
| McGregor Ra. | 139 | 27 0S | 142 45 E |
| Mach | 93 | 29 50N | 67 20 E |
| Machacalis | 171 | 17 5S | 40 45W |
| Machachi | 174 | 0 30S | 78 15W |
| Machado, R. = Jiparana | 174 | 8 45S | 62 20W |
| Machagai | 172 | 26 56S | 60 2W |
| Machakos | 126 | 1 30S | 37 15 E |
| Machakos □ | 126 | 1 30S | 37 15 E |
| Machala | 174 | 3 10S | 79 50W |
| Machanga | 129 | 20 59S | 35 0 E |
| Machar Marshes | 123 | 9 28N | 33 21 E |
| Machattie, L. | 138 | 24 50S | 139 48 E |
| Machava | 129 | 25 54S | 32 28 E |
| Machece | 127 | 19 15S | 35 32 E |
| Machecoul | 42 | 47 0N | 1 49W |
| Machelen | 47 | 50 55N | 4 26 E |
| Mach'eng | 109 | 31 11N | 115 2 E |
| Mcherrah | 118 | 27 0N | 4 30W |
| Machevna | 77 | 61 20N | 172 20 E |
| Machezo, mt. | 57 | 39 21N | 4 20W |
| Machiang | 108 | 26 30N | 107 35 E |
| Mach'iaoho | 107 | 44 41N | 130 32 E |
| Machias | 151 | 44 40N | 67 34W |
| Machichaco, Cabo | 58 | 43 28N | 2 47W |
| Machichi, R. | 153 | 57 3N | 92 6W |
| Machida | 111 | 35 28N | 139 23 E |
| Machilipatnam | 99 | 16 12N | 81 12 E |
| Machilipatnam = Masulipatnam | 96 | 16 12N | 131 15 E |
| Machine, La | 43 | 46 54N | 3 27 E |
| Mchinja | 127 | 9 44S | 39 45 E |
| Mchinji | 127 | 13 47S | 32 58 E |
| Machiques | 174 | 10 4N | 72 34W |
| Machrihanish | 34 | 55 25N | 5 42W |
| Machupicchu | 174 | 13 8S | 72 30W |
| Machynlleth | 31 | 52 36N | 3 51W |
| Macias Nguema Biyoga | 113 | 3 30N | 8 40 E |
| McIlwraith Ra. | 138 | 13 50S | 143 20 E |


* Renamed Shah Faisalabad

Makhachkala Manitou I

Makhachkala 83 43 0N 47 15 E
Makharadze 83 41 55N 42 2 E
Makian, I. 103 0 12N 127 20 E
Makin, I. 130 3 30N 174 0 E
Makindu 124 2 7 S 37 40 E
Makinsk 76 52 37N 70 26 E
Makkah 122 21 30N 39 54 E
Makkovik 151 55 0N 59 10W
Makkum 46 53 3N 5 25 E
Maklakovo 77 58 16N 92 29 E
Makó 53 46 14N 20 33 E
Makokou 124 0 40N 12 50 E
Makongo 126 3 15N 26 17 E
Makoro 126 3 10N 29 59 E
Makoua 124 0 5 S 15 50 E
Maków Podhal 54 49 43N 19 45 E
Makrá, I. 69 36 15N 25 54 E
Makrai 93 22 2N 77 0 E
Makran 93 26 13N 61 30 E
Makran Coast Range 93 25 40N 4 0 E
Makrana 94 27 2N 74 46 E
Mákri 68 40 52N 25 40 E
Maksimkin Yar 76 58 58N 86 50 E
Maktar 119 35 48N 9 12 E
Mākū 92 39 15N 44 31 E
Makuan 108 23 2N 104 24 E
Makum 98 27 30N 95 23 E
Makumbe 128 20 15 S 24 26 E
Makumbi 124 5 50 S 20 43 E
Makunda 128 22 30 S 20 7 E
Makurazaki 110 31 15N 130 20 E
Makurdi 120 7 43N 8 28 E
Makwassie 128 27 17 S 26 0 E
Mal 98 26 51N 86 45 E
Mal B. 39 52 50N 9 30W
Mal-i-Gjalicës së Lumës 68 42 2N 20 25 E
Mal i Gribës 68 40 17N 9 45 E
Mal i Nemërçkës 68 40 15N 20 15 E
Mal i Tomorit 68 40 42N 20 11 E
Mala Kapela 63 44 45N 15 30 E
Mala, Pta. 166 7 28N 80 2W
Malabang 103 7 36N 124 3 E
Malabar Coast 97 11 0N 75 0 E
Malacca = Melaka 101 2 15N 102 15 E
Malacca, Str. of 101 3 0N 101 0 E
Malacky 53 48 27N 17 0 E
Malad City 160 41 10N 112 20 E
Maladetta, Mt. 59 42 40N 0 30 E
Malafaburi 123 10 37N 40 30 E
Málaga, Colomb. 174 6 42N 72 44W
Málaga, Spain 57 36 43N 4 23W
Malaga 159 32 12N 104 2W
Málaga □ 57 36 38N 4 58W
Malagarasi 126 5 5 S 30 50 E
Malagarasi, R. 126 3 50 S 30 30 E
Malagasy Rep. ■ = Madagascar ■ 129 20 0 S 47 0 E
Malagón 57 39 11N 3 52W
Malagón, R. 57 37 40N 7 20W
Malahide 38 53 26N 6 10W
Malaimbandy 129 20 20 S 45 36 E
Malakâl 123 9 33N 31 50 E
Malakand 94 34 40N 71 55 E
Malakoff 159 32 10N 95 55W
Malakwa 152 50 55N 118 50W
Malamyzh 77 50 0N 136 50 E
Malang 103 7 59 S 112 35 E
Malanje 124 9 30 S 16 17 E
Mälaren 72 59 30N 17 10 E
Malargüe 172 35 40 S 69 30W
Malartic 150 48 9N 78 9W
Malatya 92 38 25N 38 20 E
Malawi ■ 127 13 0 S 34 0 E
Malawi, L. (Lago Niassa) 127 12 30 S 34 30 E
Malay Pen. 101 7 25N 100 0 E
Malaya □ 101 4 0N 102 0 E
Malaya Belözerka 82 47 12N 34 56 E
Malaya Vishera 80 58 55N 32 25 E
Malaybalay 103 8 5N 125 15 E
Malayer 92 34 19N 48 51 E
Malaysia ■ 102 5 0N 110 0 E
Malaysia, Western □ 101 5 0N 102 0 E
Malazgirt 92 39 10N 42 33 E
Malbaie, La 151 47 40N 70 10W
Malbon 138 21 5 S 140 17 E
Malbooma 139 30 41 S 134 11 E
Malbork 54 54 3N 19 10 E
Malca Dube 123 6 40N 41 52 E
Malchin 48 53 43N 12 44 E
Malchow 48 53 29N 12 25 E
Malcolm 137 28 51 S 121 25 E
Malcolm, Pt., S. Australia, Austral. 109 34 52 S 138 29 E
Malcolm, Pt., W. Australia, Austral. 137 33 48 S 123 45 E
Malczyce 54 51 14N 16 29 E
Maldegem 47 51 14N 3 26 E
Malden, Mass., U.S.A. 162 42 26N 71 5W
Malden, Mo., U.S.A. 159 36 35N 90 0W
Malden I. 143 4 3 S 155 1W
Maldive Is. ■ 86 2 0N 73 0W
Maldon, Austral. 140 37 0 S 144 6 E
Maldon, U.K. 29 51 43N 0 41 E
Maldonado 173 35 0 S 55 0W
Maldonado, Punta 165 16 19N 98 35W
Malé 62 46 20N 10 55 E
Malé Karpaty 53 48 30N 17 20 E
Malea, Ákra 69 36 28N 23 7 E
Malegaon 96 20 30N 74 30 E
Malei 127 17 12 S 36 58 E
Malela 126 4 22 S 26 8 E
Malenge 127 12 40 S 26 42 E
Mälerås 73 56 54N 15 34 E
Malerkotla 94 30 32N 75 58 E
Mâles 69 36 6N 25 35 E
Malesherbes 43 48 15N 2 24 E
Maleske Planina 66 41 38N 23 7 E
Malestroit 42 47 49N 2 25W
Malfa 65 38 35N 14 50 E
Malgobek 83 43 30N 44 52 E
Malgomaj L. 74 64 40N 16 30 E
Malgrat 58 41 39N 2 46 E
Malham Tarn 32 54 6N 2 11W
Malhão, Sa. do 55 37 25N 8 0W
Malheur L. 160 43 19N 118 42W
Malheur, R. 160 43 55N 117 55W
Mali 120 12 10N 12 20W
Mali ■ 121 15 0N 10 0W
Mali H Ka R. 98 25 42N 97 30 E
Mali Kanal 66 45 36N 19 24 E
Mali Kyun, I. 101 13 0N 98 20 E
Mali, R. 99 26 20N 97 40 E
Malibu 163 34 2N 118 41W
Malih, Nahr al 90 32 20N 35 29 E
Malik 103 0 39 S 123 16 E
Malili 103 2 42 S 121 23 E
Malimba, Mts. 126 7 30 S 29 30 E
Malin, Ireland 38 55 18N 7 16W
Malin, U.S.S.R. 80 50 46N 29 15 E
Malin Hd. 38 55 18N 7 16W
Malin Pen. 38 55 20N 7 17W
Malinau 102 3 35N 116 30 E
Malindi 126 3 12 S 40 5 E
Maling, Mt. 103 1 0N 121 0 E
Malingping 103 6 45 S 106 2 E
Malinyi 127 8 56 S 36 0 E
Maliqi 68 40 45N 20 48 E
Malita 103 6 19N 125 39 E
Malkapur, Maharashtra, India 96 16 57N 74 0W
Malkapur, Maharashtra, India 96 20 53N 76 17 E
Małkinia Grn. 54 52 42N 21 58 E
Malko Turnovo 67 41 59N 27 31 E
Mallacoota 141 37 40 S 149 40 E
Mallacoota Inlet 141 37 40 S 149 40 E
Mallaha 90 33 6N 35 35 E
Mallaig 36 57 0N 5 50W
Mallala 140 34 26 S 138 30 E
Mallawan 95 27 4N 80 12 E
Mallawi 122 27 44N 30 44 E
Mallemort 45 43 44N 5 11 E
Málles Venosta 62 46 42N 10 32 E
Mállia 69 35 17N 25 27 E
Mallina P.O. 136 20 53 S 118 2 E
Mallorca, I. 58 39 30N 3 0 E
Mallow 39 52 8N 8 40W
Malltraeth B. 31 53 7N 4 30W
Mallwyd 31 52 43N 3 41W
Malmbäck 73 57 34N 14 28 E
Malmberget 74 67 11N 20 40 E
Malmèdy 47 50 25N 6 2 E
Malmesbury, S. Afr. 128 33 28 S 18 41 E
Malmesbury, U.K. 28 51 35N 2 5W
Malmö 75 55 36N 12 59 E
Malmöhus län □ 73 55 45N 13 30 E
Malmslätt 73 58 27N 15 33 E
Malmyzh 84 56 31N 50 41 E
Malmyzh Mozhga 81 56 35N 50 30 E
Malnaş 70 46 2N 25 49 E
Malo Konare 67 42 12N 24 24 E
Maloarkhangelsk 81 52 28N 36 30 E
Maloja 51 46 25N 9 35 E
Maloja Pass 51 46 23N 9 42 E
Malolos 103 14 50N 121 2 E
Malomalsk 84 58 45N 59 53 E
Malombe L. 127 14 40 S 35 15 E
Malomir 67 42 16N 26 30 E
Malone 156 44 50N 74 19W
Malorad 67 43 28N 23 41 E
Malorita 80 51 41N 24 3 E
Maloyaroslovets 81 55 2N 36 20 E
Malozemelskaya Tundra 78 67 0N 50 0 E
Malpartida 57 39 26N 6 30W
Malpas 32 53 3N 2 47W
Malpelo I. 174 4 3N 80 35W
Malpica 56 43 19N 8 50W
Malprabha, R. 97 15 40N 74 50 E
Malta, Brazil 170 6 54 S 37 31W
Malta, Idaho, U.S.A. 160 42 15N 113 50W
Malta, Mont., U.S.A. 160 48 20N 107 55W
Malta Channel 64 36 40N 14 0 E
Maltahöhe 125 24 55 S 17 0 E
Maltby 33 53 25N 1 12W
Malters 50 47 3N 8 11 E
Malton 33 54 9N 0 48W
Maluku □ 103 3 0 S 128 0 E
Maluku, Kepulauan 103 3 0 S 128 0 E
Malumfashi 121 11 48N 7 39 E
Malung, China 108 25 18N 103 20 E
Malung, Sweden 72 60 42N 13 44 E
Malvalli 97 12 28N 77 8 E
Malvan 97 16 2N 73 30 E
Malvern, U.K. 28 52 7N 2 19W
Malvern, U.S.A. 159 34 22N 92 50W
Malvern Hills 28 52 0N 2 19W
Malvern Wells 28 52 4N 2 19W
Malvérnia 129 22 6 S 31 42 E
Malvik 71 63 25N 10 40 E
Malvinas Is. = Falkland Is. 174 51 30 S 59 0W
Malya 126 3 5 S 33 38 E
Malybay 85 43 30N 78 25 E
Mama 77 58 18N 112 54 E
Mamadysh 81 55 44N 51 23 E
Mamaia 70 44 18N 28 37 E
Mamaku 142 38 5 S 176 8 E
Mamanguape 170 6 50 S 35 4W
Mamasa 103 2 55 S 119 20 E
Mambasa 126 1 22N 29 3 E
Mamberamo, R. 103 2 0 S 137 50 E
Mambilima Falls 127 10 31 S 28 45 E
Mambirima 127 11 25 S 27 33 E
Mambo 126 4 52 S 38 22 E
Mambrui 126 3 5 S 40 5 E
Mameigwess L. 150 52 35N 87 50W
Mamer 47 49 38N 6 2 E
Mamers 42 48 21N 0 22 E
Mamfe 121 5 50N 9 15 E
Mammamattawa 150 50 25N 84 23W
Mámmola 65 38 23N 16 13 E
Mammoth 161 32 46N 110 43W
Mamoré, R. 175 9 55 S 65 20W
Mamou 120 10 15N 12 0W
Mampatá 120 11 54N 14 53W
Mampawah 102 0 30N 109 5 E
Mampong 121 7 6N 1 26W
Mamuju 103 2 50 S 118 50 E
Man 120 7 30N 7 40W
Man, I. of 32 54 15N 4 30W
Man Na 98 23 27N 97 19 E
Man O' War Peak 151 56 58N 61 40W
Man, R. 96 17 20N 75 0 E
Man Tun 98 23 2N 98 38 E
Mana, Fr. Gui. 175 5 45N 53 55W
Mana, U.S.A. 147 22 3N 159 45W
Mana, R. 123 6 20N 40 41 E
Måna, R. 71 59 55N 8 50 E
Manaar, Gulf of 97 8 30N 79 0 E
Manacacias, R. 174 4 23N 72 4W
Manacapuru 174 3 10 S 60 50W
Manacles, The 30 50 3N 5 5W
Manacor 58 39 32N 3 12 E
Manage 47 50 31N 4 15 E
Managua 166 12 0N 86 20W
Managua, L. 166 12 20N 86 30W
Manaia 142 39 33 S 174 8 E
Manakana 129 13 45 S 50 4 E
Manakara 129 22 8 S 48 1 E
Manakau Mt. 143 42 15 S 173 42 E
Manam I. 135 4 5 S 145 0 E
Manamâh, Al 93 26 11N 50 35 E
Manambao, R. 129 17 35 S 44 45 E
Manambato 129 13 43 S 49 7 E
Manambolo, R. 129 19 20 S 45 0 E
Manambolosy 129 16 2 S 49 40 E
Mananara 129 16 10 S 49 30 E
Mananara, R. 129 23 25 S 48 10 E
Mananjary 129 21 13 S 48 20 E
Manantenina 129 24 17 S 47 19 E
Manaos = Manaus 174 3 0 S 60 0W
Manapouri 143 45 34 S 167 39 E
Manapouri, L. 143 45 32 S 167 32 E
Manar, R. 96 18 50N 77 20 E
Manas, Gora 85 42 22N 71 2 E
Manas, R. 99 26 12N 90 40 E
Manasarowar, L. 105 30 45N 81 20 E
Manasarowar L. 105 30 45N 81 20 E
Manasir 93 24 30N 51 10 E
Manaslu, Mt. 95 28 33N 84 33 E
Manasquan 162 40 7N 74 3W
Manassa 161 37 12N 105 58W
Manassas 162 38 45N 77 28W
Manassu 105 44 18N 86 13 E
Manati 147 18 26N 66 29W
Manaung Kyun 98 18 45N 93 40 E
Manaus 174 3 0 S 60 0W
Manawan L. 153 55 24N 103 14W
Manawatu, R. 142 40 28 S 175 12 E
Manay 103 7 17N 126 33 E
Manby 33 53 22N 0 6 E
Mancelona 156 44 54N 85 5W
Mancha, La 59 39 10N 2 54W
Mancha Real 57 37 48N 3 39W
Manchester, L. 108 27 29 S 152 46 E
Manche □ 42 49 10N 1 20W
Manchester, U.K. 32 53 30N 2 15W
Manchester, Conn., U.S.A. 162 41 47N 72 30W
Manchester, Ga., U.S.A. 157 32 53N 84 32W
Manchester, Iowa, U.S.A. 158 42 28N 91 27W
Manchester, Ky., U.S.A. 156 38 40N 83 45W
Manchester, N.H., U.S.A. 162 42 58N 71 29W
Manchester, Pa., U.S.A. 162 40 4N 76 43W
Manchester, Vt., U.S.A. 162 43 10N 73 5W
Manchester L. 153 61 28N 107 29W
Manchouli 105 49 46N 117 24 E
Manchuria = Tung Pei 107 44 0N 126 0 E
Manciano 63 42 35N 11 30 E
Mancifa 123 6 53N 41 50 E
Mand, R. 93 28 20N 52 30 E
Manda, Chunya, Tanz. 127 6 51 S 32 29 E
Manda, Jombe, Tanz. 127 10 30 S 34 40 E
Mandabé 125 21 0 S 44 55 E
Mandaguari 173 23 32 S 51 42W
Mandah 106 44 27N 108 20 E
Mandal 71 58 2N 7 25 E
Mandalay 99 22 0N 96 10 E
Mandalay = Mandale 98 22 0N 96 10 E
Mandale 99 22 0N 96 10 E
Mandalgovi 106 45 45N 106 20 E
Mandali 92 33 52N 45 28 E
Mandalya Körfezi 69 37 15N 27 20 E
Mandan 158 46 50N 101 0W
Mandapeta 96 16 47N 81 56 E
Mandar, Teluk 103 3 35 S 119 4 E
Mandas 64 39 40N 9 8 E
Mandasaur 93 24 3N 75 8 E
Mandasor (Mandsaur) 94 24 3N 75 8 E
Mandawai (Katingan), R. 102 1 30 S 113 0 E
Mandelieu-la-Napoule 45 43 34N 6 57 E
Mandera 126 3 55N 41 42 E
Mandera □ 126 3 30N 41 0 E
Manderfeld 47 50 20N 6 20 E
Mandi, India 94 31 39N 76 58 E
Mandi, Zambia 127 14 30 S 23 45 E
Mandimba 125 14 20 S 35 40 E
Mandioli 103 0 40 S 127 20 E
Mandla 95 22 39N 80 30 E
Mandø 73 55 18N 8 33 E
Mandoto 129 19 34 S 46 17 E
Mandoúdhion 69 38 48N 23 29 E
Mandra 94 33 23N 73 12 E
Mandráki 69 36 36N 27 11 E
Mandrase, R. 129 25 10 S 46 30 E
Mandritsara 129 15 50 S 48 49 E
Mandsaur (Mandasor) 94 24 3N 75 8 E
Mandurah 137 32 36 S 115 48 E
Mandúria 65 40 25N 17 38 E
Mandvi 96 22 51N 69 22 E
Mandya 97 12 30N 77 0 E
Mandzai 94 30 55N 67 6 E
Mané 121 12 59N 1 21W
Manea 29 52 29N 0 10 E
Maner, R. 97 18 30N 79 40 E
Maneroo 138 23 22 S 143 53 E
Maneroo Cr. 138 23 21 S 143 53 E
Manfalût 122 27 20N 30 52 E
Manfred 140 33 19 S 143 45 E
Manfredónia 65 41 40N 15 55 E
Manfredónia, G. di 65 41 30N 16 10 E
Manga, Brazil 171 14 46 S 43 56W
Manga, Upp. Vol. 121 11 40N 1 4W
Mangabeiras, Chapada das 170 10 0 S 46 30W
Mangahan 142 40 26 S 175 48 E
Mangalagiri 96 16 26N 80 36 E
Mangaldai 98 26 26N 92 2 E
Mangalia 70 43 50N 28 35 E
Mangalore, Austral. 141 36 56 S 145 10 E
Mangalore, India 97 12 55N 74 47 E
Manganeses 56 41 45N 5 43W
Mangaon 96 18 15N 73 20 E
Manger 71 60 38N 5 3W
Mangerton Mt. 39 51 59N 9 30W
Manggar 102 2 50 S 108 10 E
Manggawitu 103 4 8 S 133 32 E
Mangin Range 98 24 15N 95 45 E
Mangla Dam 95 33 32N 73 50 E
Manglaur 94 29 44N 77 49 E
Mangoche 125 14 25 S 35 16 E
Mangoky, R. 129 21 55 S 44 40 E
Mangole I. 103 1 50 S 125 55 E
Mangombe 126 1 20 S 26 48 E
Mangonui 142 35 1 S 173 32 E
Mangotsfield 28 51 29N 2 29W
Mangualde 56 40 38N 7 48W
Mangueigne 117 10 40N 21 5 E
Mangueira, Lagoa da 173 33 0 S 52 50W
Manguéni, Hamada 119 22 47N 12 56 E
Mangum 159 34 50N 99 30W
Mangyai 105 37 50N 91 38 E
Mangyshlak P-ov. 83 43 40N 52 30 E
Manhattan, Kans., U.S.A. 158 39 10N 96 40W
Manhattan, Nev., U.S.A. 163 38 31N 117 3W
Manhiça 129 25 23 S 32 49 E
Manhuaçu 171 20 15 S 42 2W
Manhui 106 41 1N 107 14 E
Manhumirim 171 20 22 S 41 57W
Mani 99 34 52N 87 11 E
Mani 174 4 49N 72 17W
Mania, R. 129 19 55 S 46 10 E
Maniago 63 46 11N 12 40 E
Manica 127 18 58 S 32 59 E
Manica e Sofala □ 129 19 10 S 33 45 E
Manicaland □ 127 19 0 S 32 30 E
Manicoré 174 6 0 S 61 10W
Manicouagan L. 151 51 25N 68 15W
Manicouagan, R. 151 49 30N 68 30W
Manifah 92 27 30N 49 0 E
Manifold 138 22 41 S 150 40 E
Manigotagan 153 51 6N 96 8W
Manigotagan L. 153 50 52N 95 37W
Manihiki I. 131 10 24 S 161 1W
Manika, Plat. de 127 10 0 S 25 5 E
Manikganj 98 23 52N 90 0 E
Manila, Phil. 103 14 40N 121 3 E
Manila, U.S.A. 160 41 0N 109 44W
Manila B. 103 14 0N 120 0 E
Manilla 141 30 45 S 150 43 E
Manimpé 120 14 11N 5 28W
Maningory 129 17 9 S 49 30 E
Manipur □ 98 24 30N 94 0 E
Manipur, R. 98 23 45N 93 40 E
Manisa 92 38 38N 27 30 E
Manistee 156 44 15N 86 20W
Manistee, R. 156 44 15N 86 21W
Manistique 156 45 59N 86 18W
Manito L. 153 52 43N 109 43W
Manitoba □ 153 55 30N 97 0W
Manitoba, L. 153 51 0N 98 45W
Manitou 153 49 15N 98 32W
Manitou I. 150 47 22N 87 30W

Manitou Is Marosakoa


Manitou Is. 156 45 8N 86 0W
Manitou L., Ont., Can. 153 49 15N 93 0W
Manitou L., Qué., Can. 151 50 55N 65 17W
Manitoulin I. 150 45 40N 82 30W
Manitowaning 150 45 46N 81 49W
Manitowoc 156 44 8N 87 40W
Manizales 174 5 5N 75 32W
Manja 129 21 26S 44 20E
Manjacaze 125 24 45S 34 0E
Manjakandriana 129 18 55S 47 47E
Manjeri 97 11 7N 76 11E
Manjhand 94 25 50N 68 10E
Manjil 92 36 46N 49 30E
Manjimup 137 34 15S 116 6E
Manjra, R. 96 18 20N 77 20E
Mankaiana 129 26 38S 31 6E
Mankato, Kans., U.S.A. 158 39 49N 98 11W
Mankato, Minn., U.S.A. 158 44 8N 93 59W
Mankono 120 8 10N 6 10W
Mankota 153 49 25N 107 5W
Manlay 106 44 9N 106 50E
Manlleu 58 42 2N 2 17E
Manly, N.S.W., Austral. 141 33 48S 151 17E
Manly, Queens., Austral. 108 27 27S 153 11E
Manmad 96 20 18N 74 28E
Mann Ranges, Mts. 137 26 6S 130 5E
Manna 102 4 25S 102 55E
Mannahill 140 32 25S 140 0E
Mannar 97 9 1N 79 54E
Mannar, G. of 97 8 30N 79 0E
Mannar I. 97 9 5N 79 45E
Mannargudi 97 10 45N 79 32E
Männedorf 51 47 15N 8 43E
Mannheim 49 49 28N 8 29E
Manning, Can. 152 56 53N 117 39W
Manning, U.S.A. 157 33 40N 80 9W
Manning Prov. Park 152 49 5N 120 45W
Mannington 156 39 35N 80 25W
Manningtree 29 51 56N 1 3E
Mannu, C. 64 40 2N 8 24E
Mannu, R. 64 39 35N 8 56E
Mannum 140 34 57S 139 12E
Mano 120 8 3N 12 12W
Manokwari 103 0 54S 134 0E
Manolás 69 38 4N 21 21E
Manombo 129 22 57S 43 28E
Manono 124 7 15S 27 25E
Manorbier 31 51 38N 4 48W
Manorhamilton 38 54 19N 8 11W
Manosque 45 43 49N 5 47E
Manouane L. 151 50 45N 70 45W
Manpojin 107 41 6N 126 24E
Manresa 58 41 48N 1 50E
Mans, Le 42 48 0N 0 10E
Mansa, Gujarat, India 94 23 27N 72 45E
Mansa, Punjab, India 94 30 0N 75 27E
Mansa, Zambia 127 11 13S 28 55E
Mansel I. 149 62 0N 79 50W
Mansenra 94 34 20N 73 11E
Mansfield, Austral. 141 37 4S 146 6E
Mansfield, U.K. 33 53 8N 1 12W
Mansfield, La., U.S.A. 159 32 2N 93 40W
Mansfield, Mass., U.S.A. 162 42 2N 71 12W
Mansfield, Ohio, U.S.A. 156 40 45N 82 30W
Mansfield, Pa., U.S.A. 162 41 48N 77 4W
Mansfield, Wash., U.S.A. 160 47 51N 119 44W
Mansfield Woodhouse 33 53 11N 1 11W
Mansi 98 24 40N 95 44E
Mansidão 170 10 43S 44 2W
Mansilla de las Mulas 56 42 30N 5 25W
Mansle 44 45 52N 0 9E
Manso, R. 171 14 0S 52 0W
Mansôa 120 12 0N 15 20W
Manson Cr. 152 55 37N 124 25W
Mansoura, Djebel 119 36 1N 4 31E
Manta 174 1 0S 80 40W
Mantalingajan, Mt. 102 8 55N 117 45E
Mantare 126 2 42S 33 13E
Manteca 163 37 50N 121 12W
Mantecal 174 7 34N 69 17W
Mantekomu Hu 99 34 40N 89 0E
Mantena 171 18 47S 40 59W
Manteo 157 35 55N 75 41W
Mantes-la-Jolie 43 49 0N 1 41E
Manthani 96 18 40N 79 35E
Manthelan 42 47 9N 0 47E
Manti 160 39 23N 111 32W
Mantiqueira, Serra da 173 22 0S 44 0W
Manton, U.K. 29 52 37N 0 41W
Manton, U.S.A. 156 44 23N 85 25W
Mantorp 73 58 21N 15 20E
Mántova 62 45 10N 10 47E
Mänttä 74 62 0N 24 40E
Mantua = Mántova 62 45 10N 10 47E
Mantung 140 34 35S 140 3E
Manturova 81 58 10N 44 30E
Manu 174 12 10S 71 0W
Manucan 103 8 14N 123 3E
Manuel Alves Grande, R. 170 7 27S 47 35W
Manuel Alves, R. 171 11 19S 48 28W
Manui I. 103 3 35S 123 5E
Manukau 142 37 1S 174 55E
Manukau Harbour 142 37 3S 174 45E
Manunui 142 38 54S 175 21E
Manus I. 135 2 0S 147 0E
Manvi 97 15 57N 76 59E
Manville, R.I., U.S.A. 162 41 58N 71 28W
Manville, Wyo., U.S.A. 158 42 48N 104 36W
Manwath 96 19 19N 76 32E
Many 159 31 36N 93 28W
Manyane 128 23 21S 21 42E
Manyara L. 126 3 40S 35 50E
Manych-Gudilo, Oz. 83 46 24N 42 38E
Manych, R. 83 47 0N 41 15E
Manyonga, R. 126 4 5S 34 0E
Manyoni 126 5 45S 34 55E
Manyoni □ 126 6 30S 34 30E
Manzai 94 32 20N 70 15E
Manzala, Bahra el 122 31 10N 31 56E
Manzanares 59 39 0N 3 22W
Manzaneda, Cabeza de 56 42 12N 7 15W
Manzanillo, Cuba 166 20 20N 77 10W
Manzanillo, Mexico 164 19 0N 104 20W
Manzanillo, Pta. 166 9 30N 79 40W
Manzano Mts. 161 34 30N 106 45W
Manzini 129 26 30S 31 25E
Mao 117 14 4N 15 19E
Maohsing 107 45 31N 124 32E
Maoke, Pengunungan 102 3 40S 137 30E
Maolin 107 43 55N 123 25E
Maoming 109 21 39N 110 54E
Maopi T'ou 109 21 56N 120 43E
Maoping 109 30 51N 110 54E
Maowen 108 31 41N 103 52E
Mapastepec 165 15 26N 92 54W
Mapia, Kepulauan 103 0 50N 134 20E
Mapien 108 28 48N 103 39E
Mapimí 164 25 50N 103 31W
Mapimí, Bolsón de 164 27 30N 103 15W
Map'ing 109 31 36N 113 33E
Mapinga 126 6 40S 39 12E
Mapinhane 129 22 20S 35 0E
Maple Creek 153 49 55N 109 29W
Mapleton 160 44 4N 123 58W
Maplewood 158 38 33N 90 18W
Mappinga 109 34 58S 138 52E
Maprik 135 3 44S 143 3E
Mapuca 97 15 36N 73 46E
Mapuera, R. 174 0 30S 58 25W
Maputo 129 25 58S 32 32E
Maqnā 92 28 25N 34 50E
Maquela do Zombo 124 6 0S 15 15E
Maquinchao 176 41 15S 68 50W
Maquoketa 158 42 4N 90 40W
Mar Chiquita, L. 172 30 40S 62 50W
Mar del Plata 172 38 0S 57 30W
Mar Menor, L. 59 37 40N 0 45W
Mar, Reg. 37 57 11N 2 53W
Mar, Serra do 173 25 30S 49 0W
Mara, Bangla. 98 28 11N 94 7E
Mara, Tanz. 126 1 30S 34 32E
Mara □, Tanz. 126 1 45S 34 20E
Mara □, Tanz. 126 1 30S 34 32E
Maraã 174 1 43S 65 25W
Marabá 170 5 20S 49 5W
Maracá, I. de 170 2 10N 50 30W
Maracaibo 174 10 40N 71 37W
Maracaibo, Lago de 174 9 40N 71 30W
Maracaju 173 21 38S 55 9W
Maracanã 170 0 46S 47 27W
Maracás 171 13 26S 40 27W
Maracay 174 10 15N 67 36W
Marādah 119 29 4N 19 4E
Maradi 121 13 35N 8 10E
Maradun 121 12 35N 6 18E
Marāgheh 92 37 30N 46 12E
Maragogipe 171 12 46S 38 55W
Marajó, B. de 170 1 0S 48 30W
Marajó, Ilha de 170 1 0S 49 30W
Maralal 124 1 0N 36 38E
Maralinga 137 29 45S 131 15E
Marama 140 35 10S 140 10E
Marampa 120 8 45N 12 28W
Maramureş □ 70 47 45N 24 0E
Maran 101 3 35N 102 45E
Marana 161 32 30N 111 9W
Maranboy 136 14 40S 132 40E
Maranchón 58 41 6N 2 15W
Marand 92 38 30N 45 45E
Marandellas 127 18 5S 31 42E
Maranguape 170 3 55S 38 50W
Maranhão = São Luis 170 2 31S 44 16W
Maranhão □ 170 5 0S 46 0W
Marañ ó n, R. 174 4 50S 75 35W
Marano, L. di 63 45 42N 13 13E
Maranoa R. 139 27 50S 148 37E
Maraş 92 37 37N 36 53E
Marașești 70 45 52N 27 5E
Maratea 65 39 59N 15 43E
Marateca 57 38 34N 8 40W
Marathókambos 69 37 43N 26 42E
Marathon, Austral. 138 20 51S 143 32E
Marathon, Can. 150 48 44N 86 23W
Marathón 69 38 11N 23 58E
Marathon, N.Y., U.S.A. 162 42 25N 76 3W
Marathon, Tex., U.S.A. 159 30 15N 103 15W
Maratua, I. 103 2 10N 118 35E
Maraú 171 14 6S 39 0W
Marazion 30 50 8N 5 29W
Marbat 91 17 0N 54 45E
Marbella 57 36 30N 4 57W
Marble Bar 136 21 9S 119 44E
Marble Falls 159 30 30N 98 15W
Marblehead 162 42 29N 70 51W
Marburg 48 50 49N 8 44E
Marby 72 63 7N 14 18E
Marcal, R. 53 47 21N 17 15E
Marcali 53 46 35N 17 25E
Marcaria 62 45 7N 10 34E
March 29 52 33N 0 5E
Marchand = Rommani 118 33 20N 6 40W
Marché 44 46 0N 1 20E
Marche □ 63 43 22N 13 10E
Marche-en-Famenne 47 50 14N 5 19E
Marchena 57 37 18N 5 23W
Marches = Marche 63 43 22N 13 10E
Marciana Marina 62 42 44N 10 12E
Marcianise 65 41 3N 14 16E
Marcigny 45 46 17N 4 2E
Marcillac-Vallon 44 44 29N 2 27E
Marcillat 44 46 12N 2 38E
Marcinelle 47 50 24N 4 26E
Marck 43 50 57N 1 57E
Marckolsheim 43 48 10N 7 30E
Marcos Juárez 172 32 42S 62 5W
Marcus I. 130 24 0N 153 45E
Mardan 94 34 20N 72 0E
Marden 28 52 7N 2 42W
Mardie 136 21 12S 115 59E
Mardin 92 37 20N 40 36E
Marechal Deodoro 170 9 43S 35 54W
Maree L. 36 57 40N 5 30W
Mareeba 138 16 59S 145 28E
Mareham le Fen 33 53 7N 0 3W
Marek 103 4 41S 120 24E
Marek = Stanke Dimitrov 66 42 27N 23 9E
Maremma 62 42 45N 11 15E
Maréna 120 14 0N 7 30W
Marenberg 63 46 38N 15 13E
Marengo 158 41 42N 92 5W
Marennes 126 45 49N 1 5W
Marenyi 126 4 22S 39 8E
Marerano 129 21 23S 44 52E
Marèttimo, I. 64 37 58N 12 5E
Mareuil-sur-Lay 44 46 32N 1 14W
Marfa 159 30 15N 104 0W
Marfleet 33 53 45N 0 15W
Margable 123 12 54N 42 38E
Margam 31 51 33N 3 45W
Marganets 82 47 40N 34 40E
Margao 97 14 12N 73 58E
Margaree Harbour 151 46 26N 61 8W
Margaret Bay 152 51 20N 127 20W
Margaret L. 152 58 56N 115 25W
Margaret, R. 136 12 57S 131 16E
Margaret River 137 33 57S 115 7E
Margarita, Isla de 174 11 0N 64 0W
Margarítion 68 39 22N 20 26E
Margate, S. Afr. 129 30 50S 30 20E
Margate, U.K. 29 51 23N 1 24E
Margate City 162 39 20N 74 31W
Margelan 85 40 27N 71 42E
Margeride, Mts. de la 44 44 43N 3 38E
Margherita 98 27 16N 95 40E
Margherita di Savola 65 41 25N 16 5E
Marghita 70 47 22N 22 22E
Margonin 54 52 58N 17 5E
Margreten 47 50 49N 5 49E
Marguerite 152 52 30N 122 25W
Marhoum 118 34 27N 0 11W
Mari, A.S.S.R. □ 81 56 30N 48 0E
Maria Elena 172 22 18S 69 40W
Maria Grande 172 31 45S 59 55W
Maria, I. 138 14 52S 135 45E
Maria I. 138 42 35S 148 0E
Maria van Diemen, C. 142 34 29S 172 40E
Mariager 73 56 40N 10 0E
Mariager Fjord 73 56 42N 10 19E
Mariakani 126 3 50S 39 27E
Marian L. 152 63 0N 116 15W
Mariana 171 20 23S 43 25W
Mariana Is. 130 17 0N 145 0E
Mariana Trench 130 13 0N 145 0W
Marianao 166 23 8N 82 24W
Mariani 98 26 39N 94 19E
Marianna, Ark., U.S.A. 159 34 48N 90 48W
Marianna, Fla., U.S.A. 157 30 45N 85 15W
Mariannelund 73 57 37N 15 35E
Mariánské Lázně 52 49 57N 12 41E
Marias, R. 160 48 26N 111 40W
Mariato, Punta 166 7 12N 80 52W
Mariazell 52 47 47N 15 19E
Marib 91 15 25N 45 20E
Maribo 73 54 48N 11 30E
Maribor 63 46 36N 15 40E
Marico, R. 128 24 25S 26 30E
Maricopa, Ariz., U.S.A. 161 33 5N 112 2W
Maricopa, Calif., U.S.A. 163 35 7N 119 27W
Marîdî 123 4 55N 29 25E
Marîdî, W. 123 5 25N 29 21E
Marie Galante, I. 167 15 56N 61 16W
Mariecourt 149 61 30N 72 0W
Mariefred 72 59 15N 17 12E
Mariehamn (Maarianhamina) 75 60 5N 19 57E
Marienberg, Ger. 48 50 40N 13 10E
Marienberg, Neth. 47 52 30N 6 35E
Marienberg, P.N.G. 138 3 54S 144 10E
Marienbourg 47 50 6N 4 31E
Mariental 128 24 36S 18 0E
Mariestad 73 58 43N 13 50E
Marietta, Ga., U.S.A. 157 34 0N 84 30W
Marietta, Ohio, U.S.A. 156 39 27N 81 27W
Marignane 45 43 25N 5 13E
Mariinsk 76 56 10N 87 20E
Mariinskiy Posad 81 56 10N 47 45E
Marília 173 22 0S 50 0W
Marillana 136 22 37S 119 24E
Marín 56 42 23N 8 42W
Marina 163 36 41N 121 48W
Marina di Cirò 65 39 22N 17 8E
Mariña, La 56 43 30N 7 40W
Marina Plains 138 14 37S 143 57E
Marinduque, I. 103 13 25N 122 0E
Marine City 156 42 45N 82 29W
Marinel, Le 127 10 25S 25 17E
Marineo 64 37 57N 13 23E
Marinette, Ariz., U.S.A. 161 33 41N 112 16W
Marinette, Wis., U.S.A. 156 45 4N 87 40W
Maringá 173 23 35S 51 50W
Marinha Grande 57 39 45N 8 56W
Marino 109 35 3S 138 31E
Marino Rocks 109 35 3S 138 31E
Marion, Austral. 109 34 59S 138 33E
Marion, Ala., U.S.A. 157 32 33N 87 20W
Marion, Ill., U.S.A. 159 37 45N 88 55W
Marion, Ind., U.S.A. 156 40 35N 85 40W
Marion, Iowa, U.S.A. 158 42 2N 91 36W
Marion, Kans., U.S.A. 158 38 25N 97 2W
Marion, Mich., U.S.A. 156 44 7N 85 8W
Marion, N.C., U.S.A. 157 35 42N 82 0W
Marion, Ohio, U.S.A. 156 40 38N 83 8W
Marion, S.C., U.S.A. 157 34 11N 79 22W
Marion, Va., U.S.A. 157 36 51N 81 29W
Marion Bay 140 35 12S 136 59E
Marion, L. 157 33 30N 80 15W
Marion Reef 138 19 10S 152 17E
Maripa 174 7 26N 65 9W
Mariposa 163 37 31N 119 59W
Mariscal Estigarribia 172 22 3S 60 40W
Maritime Alps = Alpes Maritimes 62 44 10N 7 10E
Maritsa 67 42 1N 25 50E
Maritsá 69 36 22N 28 10E
Maritsa, R. 67 42 15N 24 0E
Mariyampole = Kapsukas 80 54 33N 23 19E
Marjan 93 32 5N 68 20E
Mark 34 55 2N 5 1W
Marka 122 18 14N 41 19E
Markapur 97 15 44N 79 19E
Markaryd 73 56 28N 13 35E
Marke 47 50 48N 3 14E
Marked Tree 159 35 35N 90 24W
Markelo 46 52 14N 6 30E
Markelsdorfer Huk 48 54 33N 11 0E
Marken 46 52 26N 5 12E
Markerwaard 46 52 33N 5 15E
Market Bosworth 28 52 37N 1 24W
Market Deeping 29 52 40N 0 20W
Market Drayton 32 52 55N 2 30W
Market Harborough 29 52 29N 0 55W
Market Lavington 28 51 17N 1 59W
Market Rasen 33 53 24N 0 20W
Market Weighton 33 53 52N 0 40W
Markethill 38 54 18N 6 31W
Markfield 28 52 42N 1 18W
Markham I. 12 84 0N 0 45W
Markham L. 153 62 30N 102 35W
Markham Mts. 13 83 0S 164 0E
Markham, R. 135 6 41S 147 2E
Marki 54 52 20N 21 2E
Markinch 35 56 12N 3 9W
Markleeville 163 38 42N 119 47W
Markoupoulon 69 37 53N 23 57E
Markovac 66 44 14N 21 7E
Markovo 77 64 40N 169 40E
Markoye 121 14 39N 0 2E
Marks 81 51 45N 46 50E
Marks Tey 29 51 53N 0 48E
Marksville 159 31 10N 92 2W
Markt Schwaben 49 48 14N 11 49E
Marktredwitz 49 50 1N 12 2E
Marlboro, Can. 152 53 30N 116 50W
Marlboro, U.S.A. 162 42 19N 71 33W
Marlboro, N.Y., U.S.A. 162 41 36N 73 58W
Marlborough, Austral. 138 22 46S 149 52E
Marlborough, U.K. 28 51 26N 1 44W
Marlborough □ 143 41 45S 173 33E
Marlborough Downs 28 51 25N 1 55W
Marle 43 49 43N 3 47E
Marlin 159 31 25N 96 50W
Marlow, Austral. 141 35 17S 149 55E
Marlow, Ger. 48 54 8N 12 34E
Marlow, U.K. 29 51 34N 0 47W
Marlow, U.S.A. 159 34 40N 97 58W
Marly-le-Grand 50 46 47N 7 10E
Marmagao 97 15 25N 73 56E
Marmande 44 44 30N 0 10E
Marmara denizi 92 40 45N 28 15E
Marmara, I. 82 40 35N 27 38E
Marmara, Sea of = Marmara denizi 92 40 45N 28 15E
Marmaris 92 36 50N 28 14E
Marmarth 158 46 21N 103 52W
Marmion L. 150 48 55N 91 30W
Marmion Mt. 137 29 16S 119 50E
Marmolada, Mte. 63 46 25N 11 55E
Marmolejo 57 38 3N 4 13W
Marmora 150 44 28N 77 41W
Marnay 43 47 20N 5 48E
Marne 48 53 57N 9 1E
Marne □ 43 49 0N 4 10E
Marne, R. 43 48 53N 4 25E
Marnhull 28 50 58N 2 20W
Maro 124 8 30N 19 0E
Maroa 174 2 43N 67 33W
Maroala 129 15 23S 47 59E
Maroantsetra 129 15 26S 49 44E
Marocco ■ 129 32 0N 5 50W
Maromandia 129 14 13S 48 5E
Maroni, R. 175 4 0N 52 0W
Marónia 68 40 53N 25 24E
Maroochydore 139 26 29S 153 5E
Maroona 140 37 27S 142 54E
Maros, R. 53 46 25N 20 20E
Marosakoa 129 15 26S 46 38E

Marostica Maya, R

Marostica 63 45 44N 11 40 E
Maroua 121 10 40N 14 20 E
Marovoay 129 16 6S 46 39 E
Marple 32 53 23N 2 5W
Marquard 128 28 40S 27 28 E
Marqueira 57 38 41N 9 9W
Marquesas Is. = Marquises 131 9 30S 140 0W
Marquette 156 46 30N 87 21W
Marquise 43 50 50N 1 40 E
Marquises, Is. 131 9 30S 140 0W
Marra 139 31 12S 144 10 E
Marra, Gebet 123 7 20N 27 35 E
Marradi 63 44 5N 11 37 E
Marrakech 118 31 40N 8 0W
Marrat 92 25 0N 45 35 E
Marrawah 138 40 55S 144 42 E
Marrecas, Serra das 170 9 0S 41 0W
Marree 139 29 39S 138 1 E
Marrimane 129 22 58S 33 34 E
Marromeu 125 18 40S 36 25 E
Marroqui, Punta 56 36 0N 5 37W
Marrowie Creek 141 33 23S 145 40 E
Marrubane 127 18 0S 37 0 E
Marrum 46 53 19N 5 48 E
Marrupa 127 13 8S 37 30 E
Mars, Le 158 43 0N 96 0W
Marsa Susa (Apollonia) 117 32 52N 21 59 E
Marsabit 126 2 18N 38 0 E
Marsabit □ 126 2 45N 37 45 E
Marsala 64 37 48N 12 25 E
Marsciano 63 42 54N 12 20 E
Marsden 141 33 47N 147 32 E
Marsdiep 46 52 58N 4 46 E
Marseillan 44 43 23N 3 31 E
Marseille 45 43 18N 5 23 E
Marseilles = Marseille 45 43 18N 5 23 E
Marsh I. 159 29 35N 91 50W
Marshall, Liberia 120 6 8N 10 22W
Marshall, Ark., U.S.A. 159 35 58N 92 40W
Marshall, Mich., U.S.A. 156 42 17N 84 59W
Marshall, Minn., U.S.A. 158 44 25N 95 45W
Marshall, Mo., U.S.A. 158 39 8N 93 15W
Marshall, Tex., U.S.A. 159 32 29N 94 20W
Marshall Is. 130 9 0N 171 0 E
Marshall, R. 138 22 59S 136 59 E
Marshalltown 158 42 0N 93 0W
Marshfield, U.K. 28 51 27N 2 18W
Marshfield, Mo., U.S.A. 159 37 20N 92 58W
Marshfield, Wis., U.S.A. 158 44 42N 90 10W
Mársico Nuovo 65 40 26N 15 43 E
Marske by the sea 33 54 35N 1 0W
Märsta 72 59 37N 17 52 E
Marstal 73 54 51N 10 30 E
Marston Moor 33 53 58N 1 17W
Marstrand 73 57 53N 11 35 E
Mart 159 31 34N 96 51W
Marta, R. 63 42 18N 11 47 E
Martaban 98 16 30N 97 35 E
Martaban, G. of 98 15 40N 96 30 E
Martano 65 40 14N 18 18 E
Martapura 102 3 22S 114 56 E
Marte 121 12 23N 13 46 E
Martebo 73 57 45N 18 30 E
Martelange 47 49 49N 5 43 E
Martés, Sierra 59 39 20N 1 0W
Marthaguy Creek 141 30 50S 147 45 E
Martham 29 52 42N 1 38 E
Martha's Vineyard 162 41 25N 70 35W
Martigné Ferchaud 42 47 50N 1 20W
Martigny 50 46 6N 7 3 E
Martigues 45 43 24N 5 4 E
Martil 118 35 36N 5 15W
Martin, Czech. 53 49 6N 18 48 E
Martin, S.D., U.S.A. 158 43 11N 101 45W
Martin, Tenn., U.S.A. 159 36 23N 88 51W
Martin, L. 157 32 45N 85 50W
Martin, R. 58 41 2N 0 43W
Martina 51 46 53N 10 28 E
Martina Franca 65 40 42N 17 20 E
Martinborough 142 41 14S 175 29 E
Martinez 163 38 1N 122 8W
Martinho Campos 171 19 20S 45 13W
Martinique, I. 167 14 40N 61 0W
Martinique Passage 167 15 15N 61 0W
Martinon 69 38 25N 23 15 E
Martinópolis 173 22 11S 51 12W
Martins 171 6 5S 37 55W
Martinsberg 52 48 22N 15 9 E
Martinsburg 156 39 30N 77 57W
Martinsville, Ind., U.S.A. 156 39 29N 86 23W
Martinsville, Va., U.S.A. 157 36 41N 79 52W
Martley 28 52 14N 2 22W
Martock 28 50 58N 2 47W
Marton 142 40 4S 175 23 E
Martorell 58 41 28N 1 56 E
Martos 57 37 44N 3 58W
Martre, La, L. 148 63 8N 117 16W
Martre, La, R. 148 63 0N 118 0W
Martuk 84 50 46N 56 31 E
Martuni 83 40 9N 45 10 E
Maru 121 12 22N 6 22 E
Marudi 102 4 10N 114 25 E
Maruf 93 31 30N 67 0 E
Marugame 110 34 15N 133 55 E
Maruggio 65 40 20N 17 33 E
Marui 135 4 4S 143 2 E
Maruim 170 10 45S 37 5W
Marulan 141 34 43S 150 3 E
Marum 46 53 9N 6 16 E
Marunga 128 17 20S 20 2 E
Marungu, Mts. 126 7 30S 30 0 E
Maruoka 111 36 9N 136 16 E
Marvejols 44 44 33N 3 19 E
Marvine Mt. 161 38 44N 111 40W
Marwar 94 25 43N 73 45 E
Mary 76 37 40N 61 50 E
Mary Frances L. 153 63 19N 106 13W
Mary Kathleen 138 20 35S 139 48 E
Maryborough, Queens., Austral. 139 25 31S 152 37 E
Maryborough, Vic., Austral. 140 37 0S 143 44 E
Maryets 81 56 17N 49 47 E
Maryfield 153 49 50N 101 35W
Marykirk 37 56 47N 2 30W
Maryland □ 156 39 10N 76 40W
Maryland Jc. 127 12 45S 30 31 E
Maryport 32 54 43N 3 30W
Mary's Harbour 151 52 18N 55 51W
Marystown 151 47 10N 55 10W
Marysvale 161 38 25N 112 17W
Marysville, Can. 152 49 35N 116 0W
Marysville, Calif., U.S.A. 160 39 14N 121 40W
Marysville, Kans., U.S.A. 158 39 50N 96 38W
Marysville, Ohio, U.S.A. 156 40 15N 83 20W
Marytavy 30 50 34N 4 6W
Maryvale 139 28 4S 152 12 E
Maryville 157 35 50N 84 0W
Marywell 37 56 35N 2 31W
Marzo, Punta 174 6 50N 77 42W
Marzuq 119 25 53N 14 10 E
Masada = Mesada 90 31 20N 35 19 E
Masafa 127 13 50S 27 30 E
Masai 101 1 29N 103 55 E
Masai Steppe 126 4 30S 36 30 E
Masaka 126 0 21S 31 45 E
Masakali 121 13 2N 12 32 E
Masalima, Kepulauan 102 5 10S 116 50 E
Masamba 103 2 30S 120 15 E
Masan 107 35 11N 128 32 E
Masanasa 59 39 25N 0 25W
Masandam, Ras 93 26 30N 56 30 E
Masasi 127 10 45S 38 52 E
Masasi □ 127 10 45S 38 50 E
Masaya 166 12 0N 86 7W
Masba 121 10 35N 13 1 E
Mascara 118 35 26N 0 6 E
Mascota 164 20 30N 104 50W
Masela 103 8 9S 129 51 E
Maseme 147 18 46S 25 3 E
Maseru 128 29 18S 27 30 E
Mashaba 127 20 2S 30 29 E
Mashabih 92 25 35N 36 30 E
Masham 33 54 15N 1 40W
Mashan 108 23 44N 108 14 E
Masherbrum, mt. 95 35 38N 76 18 E
Mashhad 93 36 20N 59 35 E
Mashi 121 13 0N 7 54 E
Mashiki 110 32 51N 130 53 E
Mashki Chah 93 29 5N 62 30 E
Mashkode 150 47 2N 84 7W
Mashonaland, North, □ 127 16 30S 30 0 E
Mashonaland, South, □ 127 18 0S 31 30 E
Mashtagi 83 40 35N 50 0 E
Masi 74 69 26N 23 50 E
Masi-Manimba 124 4 40S 18 5 E
Masindi 126 1 40N 31 43 E
Masindi Port 126 1 43N 32 2 E
Masirah 91 20 25N 58 50 E
Masisea 174 8 35S 74 15W
Masisi 126 1 23S 28 49 E
Masjed Solyman 92 31 55N 49 25 E
Mask, L. 38 53 36N 9 24W
Maski 97 15 56N 76 46 E
Maslen Nos 67 42 18N 27 48 E
Maslinica 63 43 24N 16 13 E
Masnou 58 41 28N 2 20 E
Masoala, C. 129 15 59S 50 13 E
Masoarivo 129 19 3S 44 19 E
Masohi 103 3 2S 128 15 E
Masomeloka 129 20 17S 48 37 E
Mason, Nev., U.S.A. 163 38 56N 119 8W
Mason, S.D., U.S.A. 158 45 12N 103 27W
Mason, Tex., U.S.A. 159 30 45N 99 15W
Mason B. 143 46 55S 167 45 E
Mason City 160 48 0N 119 0W
Masqat 93 23 37N 58 36 E
Massa 62 44 2N 10 7 E
Massa Maríttima 62 43 3N 10 52 E
Massa, O. 118 30 0N 9 30W
Massachusetts □ 162 42 25N 72 0W
Massachusetts B. 162 42 30N 70 0W
Massada 90 33 12N 35 45 E
Massafra 65 40 35N 17 8 E
Massaguet 124 12 28N 15 26 E
Massakory 117 13 0N 15 49 E
Massangena 129 21 34S 33 0 E
Massapê 170 3 31S 40 19W
Massarosa 62 43 53N 10 17 E
Massat 44 42 53N 1 21 E
Massava 84 60 40N 62 6 E
Massawa = Mitsiwa 123 15 35N 39 25 E
Massena 156 44 52N 74 55W
Massenya 117 11 30N 16 25 E
Masset 152 54 0N 132 0W
Massiac 44 45 15N 3 11 E
Massif Central 44 44 30N 2 21 E
Massillon 156 40 47N 81 30W
Massinga 125 23 15S 35 22 E
Massingir 129 23 46S 32 4 E
Mässlingen 98 62 42N 12 48 E
Massman 138 16 25S 145 25 E
Masson I. 13 66 10S 93 20 E
Mastaba 122 20 52N 39 30 E
Mastanli = Momchilgrad 21 41 33N 25 23 E
Masterton 142 40 56S 175 39 E
Mástikho, Ákra 68 38 10N 26 2 E
Mastuj 95 36 20N 72 36 E
Mastung 93 29 50N 66 42 E
Mastura 122 23 7N 38 52 E
Masuda 110 34 40N 131 51 E
Masulipatam 96 16 12N 81 12 E
Maswa □ 126 1 20S 34 0 E
Mat, R. 68 41 40N 20 0 E
Mata de São João 171 12 31S 38 17W
Matabeleland North □ 127 20 0S 28 0 E
Matabeleland South □ 127 19 0S 29 0 E
Mataboor 103 1 41S 138 3 E
Matachel, R. 57 38 32N 6 0W
Matachewan 150 47 56N 80 39W
Matad 105 47 12N 115 29 E
Matadi 124 5 52S 13 31 E
Matador 153 50 49N 107 56W
Matagalpa 166 13 10N 85 40W
Matagami 150 49 45N 77 34W
Matagami, L. 150 49 50N 77 40W
Matagorda 159 28 43N 96 0W
Matagorda, B. 159 28 30N 96 15W
Matagorda I. 159 28 10N 96 40W
Matak, P. 101 3 18N 106 16 E
Matakana 141 32 59S 145 54 E
Matale 97 7 30N 80 44 E
Matam 120 15 34N 13 17W
Matamata 142 37 48S 175 47 E
Matameye 121 13 26N 8 28 E
Matamoros, Campeche, Mexico 165 25 53N 97 30W
Matamoros, Coahuila, Mexico 164 25 45N 103 1W
Matamoros, Puebla, Mexico 165 18 2N 98 17W
Matamoros, Tamaulipas, Mexico 165 25 50N 97 30W
Matana, D. 103 2 30S 121 25 E
Matandu, R. 127 8 35S 39 40 E
Matane 151 48 50N 67 33W
Mat'ang, Szechwan, China 108 31 54N 102 55 E
Mat'ang, Yunnan, China 108 23 30N 104 4 E
Matankari 121 13 46N 4 1 E
Matanuska 148 61 38N 149 0W
Matanzá 174 7 22N 73 2W
Matanzas 166 23 0N 81 40W
Matapá, Ákra 69 36 22N 22 27 E
Matapedia 151 48 0N 66 59W
Matara 97 5 58N 80 30 E
Mataram 102 8 41S 116 10 E
Matarani 174 16 50S 72 10W
Mataranka 136 14 55S 133 4 E
Mataró 58 41 32N 2 29 E
Matarraña, R. 58 40 55N 0 8 E
Mataruška Banja 66 43 40N 20 45 E
Matata 142 37 54S 176 48 E
Matatiele 129 30 20S 28 49 E
Mataura 143 46 11S 168 51 E
Mataura, R. 143 45 49S 168 44 E
Matehuala 164 23 40N 100 50W
Mateira 171 18 54S 50 30W
Mateke Hills 127 21 48S 31 0 E
Matélica 63 43 15N 13 0 E
Matera 65 40 40N 16 37 E
Mátészalka 53 47 58N 22 20 E
Matetsi 127 18 12S 26 0 E
Mateur 119 37 0N 9 48 E
Mateyev Kurgan 83 47 35N 38 47 E
Matfors 72 62 21N 17 2 E
Matha 44 45 52N 0 20W
Matheson I. 153 51 45N 96 56W
Mathews 162 37 26N 76 19W
Mathias Pass 143 43 7S 171 6 E
Mathis 159 28 4N 97 48W
Mathoura 141 35 50S 144 55 E
Mathry 31 51 56N 5 6W
Mathura 94 27 30N 77 48 E
Mati 103 6 55N 126 15 E
Mati, R. 68 41 40N 20 0 E
Matías Romero 165 16 53N 95 2W
Matibane 127 14 49S 40 45 E
Matien 109 32 55N 116 26 E
Matlock 33 53 8N 1 32W
Matmata 119 33 30N 9 59 E
Matna 123 13 49N 35 10 E
Mato Grosso □ 175 14 0S 55 0W
Mato Grosso, Planalto do 174 15 0S 54 0W
Mato Verde 171 15 23S 42 52W
Matochkin Shar 76 73 10N 56 40 E
Matong 135 5 36S 151 50 E
Matopo Hills 127 20 36S 28 20 E
Matopos 127 20 20S 28 29 E
Matour 45 46 19N 4 29 E
Matozinhos 56 41 11N 8 42W
Matrah 93 23 37N 58 30 E
Matrûh 122 31 19N 27 9 E
Matsang Tsangpo (Brahmaputra), R. 99 29 25N 88 0 E
Matsena 121 13 5N 10 5 E
Matsesta 83 43 34N 39 44 E
Matsu Tao 109 26 9N 119 56 E
Matsubara 111 34 33N 135 34 E
Matsudo 111 35 47N 139 54 E
Matsue 110 35 25N 133 10 E
Matsumae 112 41 26N 140 7 E
Matsumoto 111 36 15N 138 0 E
Matsusaka 111 34 34N 136 32 E
Matsutō 111 36 31N 136 34 E
Matsuura 110 33 20N 129 49 E
Matsuyama 110 33 45N 132 45 E
Mattagami, R. 150 50 43N 81 29W
Mattancheri 97 9 50N 76 15 E
Mattawa 150 46 20N 78 45W
Mattawamkeag 151 45 30N 68 30W
Matterhorn, mt. 50 45 58N 7 39 E
Mattersburg 53 47 44N 16 24 E
Matthew Town 167 20 57N 73 40W
Matthew's Ridge 174 7 37N 60 10W
Mattice 150 49 40N 83 20W
Mattituck 162 40 58N 72 32W
Mattmar 72 63 18N 13 54 E
Mattoon 156 39 30N 88 20W
Matua 102 2 58S 110 52 E
Matuba 129 24 28S 32 49 E
Matucana 174 11 55S 76 15W
Matun 94 33 22N 69 58 E
Maturín 174 9 45N 63 11W
Matutina 171 19 13S 45 58W
Matuzaki 111 34 43N 138 50 E
Mau-é-ele 129 24 18S 34 2 E
Mau Escarpment 126 0 40S 36 0 E
Mau Ranipur 95 25 16N 79 8 E
Mauagami, R. 150 49 30N 82 0W
Maubeuge 43 50 17N 3 57 E
Maubourguet 44 43 29N 0 1 E
Mauchline 34 55 31N 4 23W
Maud 37 57 30N 2 8W
Maud, Pt. 137 23 6S 113 45 E
Maude 140 34 29S 144 18 E
Maudheim 13 71 5S 11 0W
Maudin Sun 99 16 0N 94 30 E
Mauês 174 3 20S 57 45W
Mauganj 99 24 50N 81 55 E
Maughold 32 54 18N 4 17W
Maughold Hd. 32 54 18N 4 17W
Maui I. 147 20 45N 156 20 E
Maulamyaing 99 16 30N 97 40 E
Maule □ 172 36 5S 72 30W
Mauleon 44 43 14N 0 54W
Maulvibazar 98 24 29N 91 42 E
Maum 38 53 31N 9 35W
Maumee 156 41 35N 83 40W
Maumee, R. 156 41 42N 83 28W
Maumere 103 8 38S 122 13 E
Maumturk Mts. 38 53 32N 9 42W
Maun 128 20 0S 23 26 E
Mauna Kea, Mt. 147 19 50N 155 28W
Mauna Loa, Mt. 147 19 50N 155 28W
Maunath Bhanjan 95 25 56N 83 33 E
Maungaturoto 142 36 6S 174 23 E
Maungdow 98 21 14N 94 5 E
Maungmagan Is. 99 14 0S 97 48 E
Maungmagan Kyunzu 101 14 0N 97 48 E
Maupin 160 45 12N 121 9W
Maure-de-Bretagne 42 47 53N 2 0W
Maureen, oilfield 19 58 5N 1 45 E
Maurepas L. 159 30 18N 90 35W
Maures, mts. 45 43 15N 6 15 E
Mauriac 44 45 13N 2 19 E
Maurice L. 137 29 30S 131 0 E
Mauriceville 142 40 45S 175 35 E
Maurienne 45 45 15N 6 20 E
Mauritania ■ 116 20 50N 10 0W
Mauritius ■ 11 20 0S 57 0 E
Mauron 42 48 9N 2 18W
Maurs 44 44 43N 2 12 E
Maurthe, R. 43 48 47N 6 9 E
Mauston 158 43 48N 90 5W
Mauterndorf 52 47 9N 13 40 E
Mauvezin 44 43 44N 0 53 E
Mauzé-sur le Mignon 44 46 12N 0 41W
Mavelikara 97 9 14N 76 32 E
Mavinga 125 15 50S 20 10 E
Mavli 94 24 45N 73 55 E
Mavqi'im 90 31 38N 34 32 E
Mavrova 68 40 26N 19 32 E
Mavuradonha Mts. 127 16 30S 31 30 E
Mawa 126 2 45N 26 33 E
Mawana 94 29 6N 77 58 E
Mawand 94 29 33N 68 38 E
Mawer 153 50 46N 106 22W
Mawgan 30 50 4N 5 10W
Mawkmai 98 20 14N 97 50 E
Mawlaik 98 23 40N 94 26 E
Mawlawkho 98 17 50N 97 38 E
Mawson Base 13 67 30S 65 0 E
Max 158 47 50N 101 20W
Maxcanú 165 20 40N 90 10W
Maxhamish L. 152 59 50N 123 17W
Maxixe 129 23 54S 35 17 E
Maxwellheugh 35 55 35N 2 23W
Maxwelltown 142 39 51S 174 49 E
Maxwelton, Queens., Austral. 138 15 45S 142 30 E
Maxwelton, Queens., Austral. 138 20 43S 142 41 E
May Downs 138 22 38S 148 55 E
May, I. of 35 56 11N 2 32W
May Nefalis 123 15 0N 38 12 E
May Pen 166 17 58N 77 15W
May River 135 4 19S 141 58 E
Maya 58 43 12N 1 29W
Maya Gudo, Mt. 123 7 30N 37 8 E
Maya Mts. 165 16 30N 89 0W
Maya, R. 77 58 20N 135 0 E

Mayaguana Island Menglien


Mayaguana Island 167 21 30N 72 44W
Mayagüez 147 18 12N 67 9W
Mayahi 121 13 58N 7 40E
Mayals 58 41 22N 0 30E
Mayang 108 27 53N 109 48E
Mayanup 137 33 58S 116 25E
Mayapán 165 20 38N 89 27W
Mayarf 167 20 40N 75 39W
Mayarí 167 20 40N 75 41W
Mayavaram = Mayuram 97 11 3N 79 42E
Maybell 160 40 30N 108 4W
Maybole 34 55 21N 4 41W
Maychew 123 12 50N 39 42E
Maydena 138 42 45S 146 39E
Maydos 68 40 13N 26 20E
Mayen 49 50 18N 7 10E
Mayenne 42 48 20N 0 38W
Mayenne □ 42 48 10N 0 40W
Mayer 161 34 28N 112 17W
Mayerthorpe 152 53 57N 115 8W
Mayfield, Derby., U.K. 33 53 1N 1 47W
Mayfield, E. Sussex, U.K. 29 51 1N 0 17E
Mayfield, Ky., U.S.A. 157 36 45N 88 40W
Mayfield, N.Y., U.S.A. 162 43 6N 74 16W
Mayhill 161 32 58N 105 30W
Maykop 83 44 35N 40 25E
Mayli-Say 85 41 17N 72 24E
Maymyo 100 22 2N 96 28E
Maynard 162 42 30N 71 33W
Maynard Hills 137 28 35S 119 50E
Mayne, Le, L. 151 57 5N 68 30W
Mayne, R. 138 23 40S 142 10E
Maynooth, Can. 150 45 14N 77 56W
Maynooth, Ireland 38 53 22N 6 38W
Mayo 147 63 38N 135 57W
Mayo □ 139 53 47N 9 7W
Mayo Bridge 38 54 11N 6 13W
Mayo L. 147 63 45N 135 0W
Mayo, R. 164 26 45N 109 47W
Mayon, Mt. 103 13 15N 123 42E
Mayor I. 142 37 16S 176 17E
Mayorga 56 42 10N 5 16W
Mays Landing 162 39 27N 74 44W
Mayskiy 83 43 47N 43 59E
Mayson L. 153 57 55N 107 10W
Maysville 156 38 43N 84 16W
Mayu, I. 103 1 30N 126 30E
Mayuram 97 11 3N 79 42E
Mayville 158 47 30N 97 23W
Mayya 77 61 44N 130 18E
Mazabuka 127 15 52S 27 44E
Mazagán = El Jadida 118 33 11N 8 17W
Mazagão 175 0 20S 51 50W
Mazama 152 49 43N 120 8W
Mazamet 44 43 30N 2 20E
Mazán 174 3 15S 73 0W
Mazapil 164 24 38N 101 34W
Mazar-i-Sharif 93 36 41N 67 0E
Mazar, O. 118 32 0N 1 38E
Mazara del Vallo 64 37 40N 12 34E
Mazarredo 176 47 10S 66 50W
Mazarrón 59 37 38N 1 19W
Mazarrón, Golfo de 59 37 27N 1 19W
Mazaruni, R. 174 6 15N 60 0W
Mazatán 164 29 0N 110 8W
Mazatenango 166 14 35N 91 30W
Mazatlán 164 23 10N 106 30W
Māzhān 93 32 30N 59 0E
Mazheikyai 80 56 20N 22 20E
Mazīnān 93 36 25N 56 48E
Mazoe 127 17 28S 30 58E
Mazoe R. 125 16 45S 32 30E
Mazoi 127 16 42S 33 7E
Mazrûb 123 14 0N 29 20E
Mazurian Lakes = Mazurski, Pojezierze 54 53 50N 21 0E
Mazurski, Pojezierze 54 53 50N 21 0E
Mazzarino 65 37 19N 14 12E
Mbaba 120 14 59N 16 44W
Mbabane 129 26 18S 31 6E
Mbagne 120 16 6N 14 47W
M'bahiakro 120 7 33N 4 19W
M'Baiki 124 3 53N 18 1E
Mbala 127 8 46S 31 17E
Mbale 126 1 8N 34 12E
Mbalmayo 121 3 33N 11 33E
Mbamba Bay 127 11 13S 34 49E
Mbandaka 124 0 1S 18 18E
Mbanga 121 4 30N 9 33E
Mbanza Congo 124 6 18S 14 16E
Mbanza Ngungu 124 5 12S 14 53E
Mbarara 126 0 35S 30 25E
Mbatto 120 6 28N 4 22W
Mbenkuru, R. 127 9 25S 39 50E
Mberubu 121 6 10N 7 38E
Mbesuma 127 10 0S 32 2E
Mbeya 127 8 54S 33 29E
Mbeya □ 126 8 15S 33 30E
Mbia 123 6 15N 29 18E
Mbimbi 127 13 25S 23 2E
Mbinga 127 10 50S 35 0E
Mbinga □ 127 10 50S 35 0E
Mbini □ 124 1 30N 10 0E
Mbiti 123 5 42N 28 3E
Mboki 123 5 19N 25 58E
Mboro 120 15 9N 16 54W
Mboune 120 14 42N 13 34W
Mbour 120 14 22N 16 54W
Mbout 120 16 1N 12 38W
Mbozi □ 127 9 0S 32 50E
Mbuji-Mayi 126 6 9S 23 40E
Mbulu 124 3 45S 35 30E
Mbulu □ 126 3 52S 35 33E
Mbumbi 128 18 26S 19 59E
Mburucuyá 172 28 1S 58 14W
M'chounech 119 34 57N 6 1E
M'Clure Str., Can. 10 75 0N 118 0W
M'Clure Str., Can. 12 74 0N 120 0W
Mdennah 118 24 37N 6 0W
Mead L. 161 36 1N 114 44W
Meade, Can. 150 49 26N 83 51W
Meade, U.S.A. 159 37 18N 100 25W
Meadow 137 26 35S 114 40E
Meadow Lake 153 54 10N 108 26W
Meadow Lake Prov. Park 153 54 27N 109 0W
Meadville 156 41 39N 80 9W
Meaford 150 44 36N 80 35W
Mealfuarvonie, Mt. 37 57 15N 4 34W
Mealhada 56 40 22N 8 27W
Mealsgate 32 54 46N 3 14W
Mealy Mts. 151 53 10N 60 0W
Meander, R. = Menderes, Büyük 92 37 45N 27 40E
Meander River 152 59 2N 117 42W
Meare's, C. 160 45 37N 124 0W
Mearim, R. 170 3 4S 44 35W
Mearns, Howe of the 37 56 52N 2 26W
Measham 28 52 43N 1 30W
Meath □ 38 53 32N 6 40W
Meath Park 153 53 27N 105 22W
Meatian 140 35 34S 143 21E
Meaulne 44 46 36N 2 28E
Meaux 43 48 58N 2 50E
Mecanhelas 127 15 12S 35 54E
Mecca 163 33 37N 116 3W
Mecca = Makkah 122 21 30N 39 54E
Mechanicsburg 162 40 12N 77 0W
Mechanicville 162 42 54N 73 41W
Mechara 123 8 36N 40 20E
Mechelen, Anvers, Belg. 47 51 2N 4 29E
Mechelen, Limbourg, Belg. 47 50 58N 5 41E
Méchéria 118 33 35N 0 18W
Mechernich 48 50 35N 6 39E
Mechetinskaya 83 46 45N 40 32E
Mecidiye 68 40 38N 26 32E
Mecitözü 82 40 32N 35 25E
Mecklenburg B. 48 54 20N 11 40E
Meconta 127 14 59S 39 50E
Meda 56 40 57N 7 18W
Meda P.O. 136 17 22S 123 59E
Meda, R. 136 17 20S 124 30E
Medaguine 118 33 41N 3 26E
Medak 96 18 1N 78 15E
Medan 102 3 40N 98 38E
Medanosa, Pta. 176 48 0S 66 0W
Medawachchiya 97 8 30N 80 30E
Medouza, cap 118 32 33N 9 9W
Médéa 118 36 12N 2 50E
Mededa 66 43 44N 19 15E
Medeiros Neto 171 17 20S 40 14W
Medel, Pic 51 46 37N 8 55E
Medellín 174 6 15N 75 35W
Medemblik 46 52 46N 5 8E
Meder 123 14 42N 40 44E
Mederdra 120 17 0N 15 38W
Medford, Oreg., U.S.A. 160 42 20N 122 52W
Medford, Wis., U.S.A. 158 45 9N 90 21W
Medford Lakes 162 39 52N 74 48W
Medgidia 70 44 15N 28 19E
Medi 123 5 4N 30 42E
Media 162 39 55N 75 23W
Media Agua 172 31 58S 68 25W
Media Luna 172 34 45S 66 44W
Mediaş 70 46 9N 24 22E
Medical Lake 160 47 41N 117 42W
Medicina 63 44 29N 11 38E
Medicine Bow 160 41 56N 106 11W
Medicine Hat 153 50 0N 110 45W
Medicine Lake 158 48 30N 104 30W
Medicine Lodge 159 37 20N 98 37W
Medina, Brazil 171 16 15S 41 29W
Medina, Colomb. 174 4 30N 73 21W
Medina, N.D., U.S.A. 158 46 57N 99 20W
Medina, N.Y., U.S.A. 156 43 15N 78 27W
Medina, Ohio, U.S.A. 156 41 9N 81 50W
Medina = Al Madīnah 92 24 35N 39 52E
Medina de Ríoseco 56 41 53N 5 3W
Medina del Campo 56 41 18N 4 55W
Medina L. 159 29 35N 98 58W
Medina, R. 159 29 10N 98 20W
Medina-Sidonia 57 36 28N 5 57W
Medinaceli 58 41 12N 2 30W
Mediterranean Sea 60 35 0N 15 0E
Medjerda, O. 119 36 35N 8 30E
Medkovets 67 43 37N 23 10E
Medley 153 54 25N 110 16W
Mednogorsk 84 51 24N 57 37E
Médoc 44 45 10N 0 56W
Medstead, Can. 153 53 19N 108 5W
Medstead, U.K. 28 51 7N 1 4W
Medulin 63 44 49N 13 55E
Medveda 66 42 50N 21 32E
Medveditsa, R. 81 50 30N 44 0E
Medvedok 81 57 20N 50 1E
Medvezhi, Ostrava 77 71 0N 161 0E
Medvezhyegorsk 78 63 0N 34 25E
Medway, R. 29 51 12N 0 23E
Medyn 81 54 59N 35 56E
Medzev 53 48 43N 20 55E
Medzilaborce 53 49 17N 21 52E
Meeandh 108 27 26S 153 6E
Meeberrie 137 26 57S 116 0E
Meekatharra 137 26 32S 118 29E
Meeker 160 40 1N 107 58W
Meelpaeg L. 151 48 18N 56 35W
Meeniyan 141 38 35S 146 0E
Meer 47 51 27N 4 45E
Meerane 48 50 51N 12 30E
Meerbeke 47 50 50N 4 3E
Meerle 47 51 29N 4 48E
Meerssen 47 50 53N 5 50E
Meerut 94 29 1N 77 50E
Meeteetsa 160 44 10N 108 56W
Meeuwen 47 51 6N 5 31E
Mega 123 3 57N 38 30E
Megálo Khorío 69 36 27N 27 24E
Megálo Petalí, I. 69 38 0N 24 15E
Megalópolis 69 37 25N 22 7E
Meganisi, I. 69 38 39N 20 48E
Mégantic 151 45 36N 70 56W
Mégara 69 37 58N 23 22E
Megarine 119 33 14N 6 2E
Megdhova, R. 69 39 10N 21 45E
Megen 46 51 49N 5 34E
Mégève 45 45 51N 6 37E
Meghalaya □ 98 25 50N 91 0E
Meghalayap 99 25 40N 89 55E
Meghezez, Mt. 123 9 18N 39 26E
Meghna, R. 98 23 45N 90 40E
Megiddo 90 32 36N 35 11E
Mégiscane, L. 150 48 35N 75 55W
Megiste 61 36 8N 29 34E
Mehadia 70 44 56N 22 23E
Mehaigne, R. 47 50 32N 5 13E
Mehaïguene, O. 118 32 20N 2 45E
Meharry, Mt. 132 22 59S 118 35E
Mehedinti □ 70 44 40N 22 45E
Meheisa 122 19 38N 32 57E
Mehndawal 95 26 58N 83 5E
Mehsana 94 23 39N 72 26E
Mehun-sur-Yèvre 43 47 10N 2 13E
Mei Chiang, R. 109 24 24N 116 35E
Meia Ponte, R. 171 18 32S 49 36W
Meichuan 109 30 9N 115 33E
Meidrim 31 51 51N 4 3W
Meiganga 124 6 20N 14 10E
Meigh 38 54 8N 6 22W
Meihsien, Kwangtung, China 109 24 18N 116 7E
Meihsien, Shensi, China 106 34 16N 107 42E
Meijel 47 51 21N 5 53E
Meiktila 98 21 0N 96 0E
Meilen 51 47 16N 8 39E
Meiningen 48 50 32N 10 25E
Meio, R. 171 13 36S 49 7W
Meira, Sierra de 56 43 15N 7 15W
Meiringen 50 46 43N 8 12E
Meishan 108 30 3N 103 51E
Meissen 48 51 10N 13 29E
Meit'an 108 27 48N 107 28E
Meithalun 90 32 21N 35 16E
Méjean 44 44 15N 3 30E
Mejillones 172 23 10S 70 30W
Meka 137 27 25S 116 48E
Mekambo 124 1 2N 14 5E
Mekdela 123 11 24N 39 10E
Mekhtar 93 30 30N 69 15E
Meklong = Samut Songkhram 101 13 24N 100 1E
Meknès 118 33 57N 5 33W
Meko 121 7 27N 2 52E
Mekong, R. 101 18 0N 104 15E
Mekongga 103 3 50S 121 30E
Mekoryok 147 60 20N 166 20W
Melagiri Hills 97 12 20N 77 30E
Melah, Sebkhet el 118 29 20N 1 30W
Melaka 101 2 15N 102 15E
Melaka □ 101 2 20N 102 15E
Melalap 102 5 10N 116 5E
Mélambes 69 35 8N 24 40E
Melanesia 130 4 0S 155 0E
Melapalaiyam 97 8 39N 77 44E
Melbost 36 58 12N 6 20W
Melbourn 29 52 5N 0 1E
Melbourne, Austral. 141 37 50S 145 0E
Melbourne, U.K. 28 52 50N 1 25W
Melbourne, U.S.A. 157 28 13N 80 14W
Melcésine 62 45 46N 10 48E
Melchor Múzquiz 164 27 50N 101 40W
Melchor Ocampo (San Pedro Ocampo) 164 24 52N 101 40W
Méldola 63 44 7N 12 3E
Meldorf 48 54 5N 9 5E
Mêle-sur-Sarthe, Le 42 48 31N 0 22E
Melegnano 62 45 21N 9 20E
Melekess = Dimitrovgrad 81 54 25N 49 33E
Melenci 66 45 32N 20 20E
Melenki 81 55 20N 41 37E
Meleuz 84 52 58N 55 55E
Melfi, Chad 117 11 0N 17 59E
Melfi, Italy 65 41 0N 15 40E
Melfort, Can. 153 52 50N 104 37W
Melfort, Rhod. 127 18 0S 31 25E
Melfort, Loch 34 56 13N 5 33W
Melgaço 56 42 7N 8 15W
Melgar de Fernamental 56 42 27N 4 17W
Melhus 71 63 17N 10 18E
Melick 47 51 10N 6 1E
Melide 51 45 57N 8 57E
Meligalá 69 37 15N 21 59E
Melilla 118 35 21N 2 57W
Melilot 42 31 22N 34 37E
Melipilla 172 33 42S 71 15W
Mélissa Óros 69 37 32N 26 4E
Melita 153 49 15N 101 5W
Mélito di Porto Salvo 65 37 55N 15 47E
Melitopol 82 46 50N 35 22E
Melk 52 48 13N 15 20E
Melksham 28 51 22N 2 9W
Mellan-Fryken 72 59 45N 13 10E
Mellansel 74 63 25N 18 17E
Melle, Belg. 47 51 0N 3 49E
Melle, France 44 46 14N 0 10W
Melle, Ger. 48 52 12N 8 20E
Mellégue, O. 119 36 32N 8 51E
Mellen 158 46 19N 90 36W
Mellerud 73 58 41N 12 28E
Mellette 158 45 11N 98 29W
Mellid 56 42 55N 8 1W
Mellish Reef 133 17 25S 155 50E
Mellit 123 14 15N 25 40E
Mellon Charles 36 57 52N 5 37W
Melmerby 32 54 44N 2 35W
Melnik 67 40 58N 23 25E
Mělník 52 50 22N 14 23E
Melo 173 32 20S 54 10W
Melolo 103 9 53S 120 40E
Melones Res. 163 37 57N 120 31W
Melouprey 100 13 48N 105 16E
Melovoye 83 49 25N 40 5E
Melrhir, Chott 119 34 25N 6 24E
Melrose, N.S.W., Austral. 141 32 42S 146 57E
Melrose, W. Australia, Austral. 137 27 50S 121 15E
Melrose, U.K. 35 55 35N 2 44W
Melrose, U.S.A. 159 34 27N 103 33W
Mels 51 47 3N 9 25E
Melsele 47 51 13N 4 17E
Melsonby 33 54 28N 1 41W
Melstone 160 46 45N 108 0W
Melsungen 48 51 8N 9 34E
Melton 29 52 51N 1 1E
Melton Constable 29 52 52N 1 1E
Melton Mowbray 29 52 46N 0 52W
Melun 43 48 32N 2 39E
Melunga 128 17 15S 16 22E
Melur 97 10 2N 78 23E
Melut 123 10 30N 32 20E
Melvaig 36 57 48N 5 49W
Melvich 37 58 33N 3 55W
Melville 153 50 55N 102 50W
Melville B. 138 12 0S 136 45E
Melville, C. 138 14 11S 144 30E
Melville I., Austral. 136 11 30S 131 0E
Melville I., Can. 12 75 30N 111 0W
Melville, L., Newf., Can. 151 53 45N 59 40W
Melville, L., Newf., Can. 151 59 30N 53 40W
Melville Pen. 149 68 0N 84 0W
Melvin L. 38 54 26N 8 10W
Melvin, R. 152 59 11N 117 31W
Mélykút 53 46 11N 19 25E
Memaliaj 68 40 25N 19 58E
Memba 127 14 11S 40 30E
Memboro 103 9 30S 119 30E
Membrilla 59 38 59N 3 21W
Memel 129 27 38S 29 36E
Memel = Klaipeda 80 55 43N 21 10E
Memmingen 49 47 59N 10 12E
Memphis, Tenn., U.S.A. 159 35 7N 90 0W
Memphis, Tex., U.S.A. 159 34 45N 100 30W
Mena 159 34 40N 94 15W
Menai Bridge 31 53 14N 4 11W
Menai Strait 31 53 7N 4 20W
Ménaka 121 15 59N 2 18E
Menaldum 46 53 13N 5 40E
Menamurtee 140 31 25S 143 11E
Menarandra, R. 129 25 0S 44 50E
Menard 159 30 57N 99 58W
Menasha 156 44 13N 88 27W
Menate 102 0 12S 112 47E
Mendawai, R. 102 1 30S 113 0E
Mende 44 44 31N 3 30E
Mendebo Mts. 123 7 0N 39 22E
Mendenhall, C. 147 59 44N 166 10W
Menderes, R. 92 37 25N 28 45E
Mendez 165 25 7N 98 34W
Mendhar 95 33 35N 74 10E
Mendi, Ethiopia 123 9 47N 35 4E
Mendi, P.N.G. 135 6 11S 143 47E
Mendip Hills 28 51 17N 2 40W
Mendlesham 29 52 15N 1 4E
Mendocino 160 39 26N 123 50W
Mendong Gompa 95 31 16N 85 11E
Mendota, Calif., U.S.A. 163 36 46N 120 24W
Mendota, Ill., U.S.A. 158 41 35N 89 5W
Mendoza 172 32 50S 68 52W
Mendoza □ 172 33 0S 69 0W
Mendrisio 51 45 52N 8 59E
Mene Grande 174 9 49N 70 56W
Menemen 92 38 18N 27 10E
Menen 47 50 47N 3 7E
Menfi 64 37 36N 12 57E
Meng-pan 99 23 5N 100 19E
Meng-so 101 22 33N 99 31E
Meng-wang 99 22 17N 100 32E
Meng Wang 101 22 18N 100 31E
Mengch'eng 106 33 17N 116 34E
Mengeš 63 46 24N 14 35E
Menggala 102 4 20S 105 15E
Menghai 108 21 58N 100 28E
Menghsien 106 34 54N 112 47E
Mengíbar 57 37 58N 3 48W
Mengla 108 21 28N 101 35E
Menglien 108 22 21N 99 36E

Mengoub Mikołajki


Mengoub **118** 29 49N 5 26W
Mengpolo **108** 24 24N 99 14 E
Mengshan **109** 24 12N 110 31 E
Mengting **108** 23 33N 98 5 E
Mengtz = Mengtzu **108** 23 25N 103 20 E
Mengtzu **108** 23 25N 103 20 E
Mengyin **107** 35 40N 117 55 E
Menihek L. **151** 54 0N 67 0W
Menin **47** 50 47N 3 7 E
Menindee **140** 32 20N 142 25 E
Menindee, L. **140** 32 20N 142 25 E
Meningie **140** 35 43 S 139 20 E
Menkúng **99** 28 38N 98 24 E
Menlo Park **163** 37 27N 122 12W
Menominee **156** 45 9N 87 39W
Menominee, R. **156** 45 30N 87 50W
Menomonie **158** 44 50N 91 54W
Menor, Mar **59** 37 43N 0 48W
Menorca, I. **58** 40 0N 4 0 E
Mentawai, Kepulauan **102** 2 0 S 99 0 E
Mentekab **101** 3 29N 102 21 E
Menton **45** 43 50N 7 29 E
Menyamya **135** 7 10 S 145 59 E
Menzel-Bourguiba **119** 39 9N 9 49 E
Menzel Chaker **119** 35 0N 10 26 E
Menzelinsk **84** 55 53N 53 1 E
Menzies **137** 29 40 S 120 58 E
Me'ona (Tarshiha) **90** 33 1N 35 15 E
Meoqui **164** 28 17N 105 29W
Mepaco **127** 15 57 S 30 48 E
Meppel **47** 52 42N 6 12 E
Meppen **48** 52 41N 7 20 E
Mequinenza **58** 41 22N 0 17 E
Mer Rouge **159** 32 47N 91 48W
Merabéllou, Kólpos **69** 35 10N 25 50 E
Merai **135** 4 52 S 152 19 E
Merak **103** 5 55 S 106 1 E
Meramangye, L. **137** 28 25 S 132 13 E
Merano (Meran) **63** 46 40N 11 10 E
Merate **62** 45 42N 9 23 E
Merauke **103** 8 29 S 140 24 E
Merbabu, Mt. **103** 7 30 S 110 40 E
Merbein **140** 34 10 S 142 2 E
Merca **91** 1 48N 44 50 E
Mercadal **58** 39 59N 4 5 E
Mercara **97** 12 30N 75 45 E
Mercato Saraceno **63** 43 57N 12 11 E
Merced **163** 37 18N 120 30W
Merced Pk. **163** 37 36N 119 24W
Merced, R. **163** 37 21N 120 58W
Mercedes, Buenos Aires, Argent. **172** 34 40 S 59 30W
Mercedes, Corrientes, Argent. **172** 29 10 S 58 5W
Mercedes, San Luis, Argent. **172** 33 5 S 65 21W
Mercedes, Uruguay **172** 33 12 S 58 0W
Merceditas **172** 28 20 S 70 35W
Mercer **142** 37 16 S 175 5 E
Merchtem **47** 50 58N 4 14 E
Mercy C. **149** 65 0N 62 30W
Merdrignac **42** 48 11N 2 27W
Mere, Belg. **47** 50 55N 3 58 E
Mere, U.K. **28** 51 5N 2 16W
Meredith C. **176** 52 15 S 60 40W
Meredith, L. **159** 35 30N 101 35W
Merei **70** 45 7N 26 43 E
Merelbeke **47** 51 0N 3 45 E
Méréville **43** 48 20N 2 5 E
Merewa **123** 7 40N 36 54 E
Mergenevo **84** 49 56N 51 18 E
Mergenevskiy **83** 49 59N 51 15 E
Mergui **101** 12 30N 98 35 E
Mergui Arch. = Myeik Kyunzu **101** 11 30N 97 30 E
Meribah **140** 34 43 S 140 51 E
Mérida, Mexico **165** 20 50N 89 40W
Mérida, Spain **57** 38 55N 6 25W
Mérida, Venez. **174** 8 36N 71 8W
Mérida □ **174** 8 30N 71 10W
Mérida, Cord. de **174** 9 0N 71 0W
Meriden, U.K. **28** 52 27N 1 36W
Meriden, U.S.A. **162** 41 33N 72 47W
Meridian, Idaho, U.S.A. **160** 43 41N 116 25W
Meridian, Miss., U.S.A. **157** 32 20N 88 42W
Meridian, Tex., U.S.A. **159** 31 55N 97 37W
Mering **49** 48 15N 11 0 E
Merioneth (□) **26** 52 49N 3 55W
Merirumã **175** 1 15N 54 50W
Merke **85** 42 52N 73 11 E
Merkel **159** 32 30N 100 0W
Merkem **47** 50 57N 2 51 E
Merksem **47** 51 16N 4 25 E
Merksplas **47** 51 22N 4 52 E
Merlebach **43** 49 5N 6 52 E
Merlerault, Le **42** 48 41N 0 16 E
Mermaid Mt. **108** 27 29 S 152 49 E
Mermaid Reef **136** 17 6 S 119 36 E
Mern **73** 55 3N 12 3 E
Merowe **122** 18 29N 31 46 E
Merredin **137** 31 28 S 118 18 E
Merrick, Mt. **34** 55 8N 4 30W
Merrill, Oregon, U.S.A. **160** 42 2N 121 37W
Merrill, Wis., U.S.A. **158** 45 11N 89 41W
Merrimack, R. **162** 42 49N 70 49W
Merritt **152** 50 10N 120 45W
Merriwa **141** 32 6 S 150 22 E
Merriwagga **141** 33 47 S 145 43 E
Merroe **137** 27 53 S 117 50 E
Merry I. **150** 55 29N 77 31W
Merrygoen **141** 31 51 S 149 12 E
Merryville **159** 30 47N 93 31W
Mersa Fatma **123** 14 57N 40 17 E
Mersch **47** 49 44N 6 7 E
Merse, dist. **35** 55 40N 2 30W
Mersea I. **29** 51 48N 0 55 E
Merseburg **48** 51 20N 12 0 E
Mersey, R. **32** 53 20N 2 56W
Merseyside □ **32** 53 25N 2 55W
Mersin **92** 36 51N 34 36 E
Mersing **101** 2 25N 103 50 E
Merta **94** 26 39N 74 4 E
Mertert **47** 49 43N 6 29 E
Merthyr Tydfil **31** 51 45N 3 23W
Mértola **57** 37 40N 7 40 E
Merton **29** 51 25N 0 13W
Mertzig **47** 49 51N 6 1 E
Mertzon **159** 31 17N 100 48W
Méru **43** 49 13N 2 8 E
Meru **126** 0 3N 37 40 E
Meru □ **126** 0 3N 37 46 E
Meru, mt. **126** 3 15 S 36 46 E
Merville **43** 50 38N 2 38 E
Méry-sur-Seine **43** 48 31N 3 54 E
Merzifon **82** 40 53N 35 32 E
Merzig **49** 49 26N 6 37 E
Merzouga, Erg Tin **119** 24 0N 11 4 E
Mesa **161** 33 20N 111 56W
Mesa, La, Colomb. **174** 4 38N 74 28W
Mesa, La, Calif., U.S.A. **163** 32 48N 117 5W
Mesa, La, N. Mex., U.S.A. **161** 32 6N 106 48W
Mesach Mellet **119** 24 30N 11 30 E
Mesada **90** 31 20N 35 19 E
Mesagne **65** 40 34N 17 48 E
Mesaras, Kólpos **69** 35 6N 24 47 E
Meschede **48** 51 20N 8 17 E
Mesfinto **123** 13 30N 37 22 E
Mesgouez, L. **150** 51 20N 75 0W
Meshchovsk **80** 54 22N 35 17 E
Meshed = Mashhad **93** 36 20N 59 35 E
Meshoppen **162** 41 36N 76 3W
Mesick **156** 44 24N 85 42W
Mesilinka, R. **152** 56 6N 124 30W
Mesilla **161** 32 20N 107 0W
Meslay-du-Maine **42** 47 58N 0 33W
Mesocco **51** 46 23N 9 12 E
Mesolóngion **69** 38 27N 21 28 E
Mesopotamia, reg. **92** 33 30N 44 0 E
Mesoraca **65** 39 5N 16 47 E
Mésou Volímais **69** 37 53N 27 35 E
Mess Cr. **152** 57 55N 131 14W
Messac **42** 47 49N 1 50W
Messad **118** 34 8N 3 30 E
Méssaména **121** 3 48N 12 49 E
Messancy **47** 49 36N 5 49 E
Messeix **44** 45 37N 2 33 E
Messina, Italy **65** 38 10N 15 32 E
Messina, S. Afr. **129** 22 20 S 30 12 E
Messina, Str. di **65** 38 5N 15 35 E
Messini **69** 37 4N 22 1 E
Messinia □ **69** 37 10N 22 0 E
Messiniakós, Kólpos **69** 36 45N 22 5 E
Mestá, Ákra **69** 38 16N 25 53 E
Mesta, R. **67** 41 30N 24 0 E
Mestanza **57** 38 35N 4 4W
Město Teplá **52** 49 59N 12 52 E
Mestre **63** 45 30N 12 13 E
Mestre, Espigão **171** 12 30 S 46 10W
Městys Zelezná Ruda **52** 49 8N 13 15 E
Meta □ **174** 3 30N 73 0W
Meta, R. **174** 6 20N 68 5W
Metagama **150** 47 0N 81 55W
Metaline Falls **160** 48 52N 117 22W
Metán **172** 25 30 S 65 0W
Metauro, R. **63** 43 45N 12 59 E
Metchosin **152** 48 15N 123 37W
Metehara **123** 8 58N 39 57 E
Metema **123** 12 56N 36 13 E
Metengobalame **127** 14 49 S 34 30 E
Méthana **69** 37 35N 23 23 E
Metheringham **33** 53 9N 0 22W
Methlick **37** 57 26N 2 13W
Methóni **69** 36 49N 21 42 E
Methuen, Mt. **136** 15 54 S 124 44 E
Methven, N.Z. **143** 43 38 S 171 40 E
Methven, U.K. **35** 56 25N 3 35W
Methwin, Mt. **137** 25 3 S 120 45 E
Methwold **29** 52 30N 0 33 E
Methy L. **153** 56 28N 109 30W
Metil **125** 16 24 S 39 0 E
Metkovets **67** 43 37N 23 10 E
Metkovió **66** 43 6N 17 39 E
Metlakatla **147** 55 10N 131 33W
Metlaoui **119** 34 24N 8 24 E
Metlika **63** 45 40N 15 20 E
Metowra **139** 25 3 S 146 15 E
Metropolis **159** 37 10N 88 47W
Métsovon **68** 39 48N 21 12 E
Mettet **47** 50 19N 4 41 E
Mettuppalaiyam **97** 11 18N 76 59 E
Mettur **97** 11 48N 77 47 E
Mettur Dam **95** 11 45N 77 45 E
Metulla **90** 33 17N 35 34 E
Metz **43** 49 8N 6 10 E
Meulaboh **102** 4 11N 96 3 E
Meulan **43** 49 0N 1 52 E
Meung-sur-Loire **43** 47 50N 1 40 E
Meureudu **102** 5 19N 96 10 E
Meurthe-et-Moselle □ **43** 48 52N 6 0 E
Meuse □ **43** 49 8N 5 25 E
Meuse, R. **47** 50 45N 5 41 E
Meuselwitz **48** 51 3N 12 18 E
Mevagissey **30** 50 16N 4 48W
Mevagissey Bay **30** 50 15N 4 40W
Mexborough **33** 53 29N 1 18W
Mexia **159** 31 38N 96 32W
Mexiana, I. **170** 0 0 49 30W
Mexicali **164** 32 40N 115 30W
México **165** 19 20N 99 10W
Mexico, Me., U.S.A. **156** 44 35N 70 30W
Mexico, Mo., U.S.A. **158** 39 10N 91 55W
Mexico, N.Y., U.S.A. **162** 43 28N 76 18W
Mexico ■ **164** 20 0N 100 0W
México □ **164** 19 20N 99 10W
Mexico, G. of **165** 25 0N 90 0W
Mey **37** 58 38N 3 14W
Meyenburg **48** 53 19N 12 15 E
Meymac **44** 45 32N 2 10 E
Meyrargues **45** 43 38N 5 32 E
Meyrueis **44** 44 12N 3 27 E
Meyssac **44** 45 3N 1 40 E
Mezdra **67** 43 12N 23 35 E
Mèze **44** 43 27N 3 36 E
Mezen **78** 65 50N 44 20 E
Mezha, R. **80** 55 50N 31 45 E
Mezhdurechenskiy **84** 59 36N 65 56 E
Mezidon **42** 49 5N 0 1W
Mézières **43** 49 45N 4 42 E
Mézilhac **45** 44 49N 4 21 E
Mézin **44** 44 4N 0 16 E
Mezöberény **53** 46 49N 21 3 E
Mezöfalva **53** 46 55N 18 49 E
Mezöhegyes **53** 46 19N 20 49 E
Mezokövácsháza **53** 46 25N 20 57 E
Mezökövesd **53** 47 49N 20 35 E
Mézos **44** 44 5N 1 10W
Mezötúr **53** 47 0N 20 41 E
Mezquital **164** 23 29N 104 23W
Mezzolombardo **62** 46 13N 11 5 E
Mgeta **127** 8 22 S 38 6 E
Mglin **80** 53 2N 32 50 E
Mhlaba Hills **127** 18 30 S 30 30 E
Mhow **94** 22 33N 75 50 E
Mi-Shima **110** 34 46N 131 9 E
Miahuatlán **165** 16 21N 96 36W
Miajadas **57** 39 9N 5 54W
Mialar **94** 26 15N 70 20 E
Miallo **138** 16 28 S 145 22 E
Miami, Ariz., U.S.A. **161** 33 25N 111 0W
Miami, Fla., U.S.A. **157** 25 52N 80 15W
Miami, Tex., U.S.A. **159** 35 44N 100 38W
Miami Beach **157** 25 49N 80 6W
Miami, R. **156** 39 20N 84 40W
Miamisburg **156** 39 40N 84 11W
Miandowāb **92** 37 0N 46 5 E
Miandrivazo **125** 19 50 S 45 56 E
Miāneh **92** 37 30N 47 40 E
Mianwali **94** 32 38N 71 28 E
Miaoli **109** 24 34N 120 48 E
Miarinarivo **129** 18 57 S 46 55 E
Miass **84** 54 59N 60 6 E
Miass, R. **84** 56 6N 64 30 E
Miasteczko Kraj **54** 53 7N 17 1 E
Miastko **54** 54 0N 16 58 E
Mica Dam **152** 52 5N 118 32W
Mica Res. **152** 51 55N 118 00W
Michael, Mt. **135** 6 27 S 145 22 E
Michalovce **29** 48 44N 21 54 E
Micheldever **28** 51 7N 1 17W
Michelson, Mt. **147** 69 20N 144 20W
Michelstadt **49** 49 40N 9 0 E
Michigan □ **155** 44 40N 85 40W
Michigan City **156** 41 42N 86 56W
Michigan, L. **156** 44 0N 87 0W
Michih **106** 37 49N 110 7 E
Michikamau L. **151** 54 0N 64 0W
Michipicoten **150** 47 55N 84 55W
Michipicoten I. **150** 47 40N 85 50W
Michoacan □ **164** 19 0N 102 0W
Michurin **67** 42 9N 27 51 E
Michurinsk **81** 52 58N 40 27 E
Mickle Fell **32** 54 38N 2 16W
Mickleover **33** 52 55N 1 32W
Mickleton, Oxon., U.K. **28** 52 5N 1 45W
Mickleton, Yorks., U.K. **32** 54 36N 2 3W
Miclere **138** 22 34 S 147 32 E
Micronesia **130** 17 0N 160 0 E
Micŭsasa **70** 46 7N 24 7 E
Mid Calder **35** 55 53N 3 23W
Mid Glamorgan □ **31** 51 40N 3 25W
Mid Yell **36** 60 36N 1 5W
Midai, P. **101** 3 0N 107 47 E
Midale **153** 49 25N 103 20W
Midas **160** 41 14N 116 56W
Middagsfjället **72** 63 27N 12 19 E
Middelbeers **47** 51 28N 5 15 E
Middelburg, Neth. **47** 51 30N 3 36 E
Middelburg, C. Prov., S. Afr. **128** 31 30 S 25 0 E
Middelburg, Trans., S. Afr. **129** 25 49N 29 28 E
Middelfart **73** 55 30N 9 43 E
Middelharnis **46** 51 46N 4 10 E
Middelkerke **47** 51 11N 2 49 E
Middelrode **47** 51 41N 5 26 E
Middelveld **128** 29 45 S 22 30 E
Middle Alkali L. **160** 41 30N 120 3W
Middle Andaman I. **101** 12 30N 92 30 E
Middle Brook **151** 48 40N 54 20W
Middle I. **137** 28 55 S 113 55 E
Middle River **162** 39 19N 76 25W
Middle Zoy **28** 51 5N 2 54W
Middleboro **162** 41 49N 70 55W
Middleburg, N.Y., U.S.A. **162** 42 36N 74 19W
Middleburg, Pa., U.S.A. **162** 40 47N 77 3W
Middlebury **162** 44 0N 73 9W
Middleham **33** 54 17N 1 49W
Middlemarch **143** 45 30 S 170 9 E
Middlemarsh **28** 50 51N 2 29W
Middleport **156** 39 0N 82 5W
Middlesbrough **33** 54 35N 1 14W
Middlesex, Belize **165** 17 2N 88 31W
Middlesex, U.S.A. **162** 40 36N 74 30W
Middleton, Can. **151** 44 57N 65 4W
Middleton, Gr. Manchester, U.K. **32** 53 33N 2 12W
Middleton, Norfolk, U.K. **29** 52 43N 0 29 E
Middleton Cheney **28** 52 4N 1 17W
Middleton Cr. **138** 22 35 S 141 51 E
Middleton I. **147** 59 30N 146 28W
Middleton-in-Teesdale **32** 54 38N 2 5W
Middleton in the Wolds **33** 53 56N 0 35W
Middleton P.O. **138** 22 22 S 141 32 E
Middletown, U.K. **38** 54 18N 6 50W
Middletown, Conn., U.S.A. **162** 41 37N 72 40W
Middletown, Del., U.S.A. **162** 39 30N 84 21W
Middletown, N.Y., U.S.A. **162** 41 28N 74 28W
Middletown, Pa., U.S.A. **162** 40 12N 76 44W
Middlewich **32** 53 12N 2 28W
Midelt **118** 32 46N 4 44W
Midhurst, N.Z. **142** 39 17 S 174 18 E
Midhurst, U.K. **29** 50 59N 0 44W
Midi, Canal du **44** 43 45N 1 21 E
Midi d'Ossau **58** 42 50N 0 25W
Midland, Austral. **137** 31 54 S 115 59 E
Midland, Can. **150** 44 45N 79 50W
Midland, Mich., U.S.A. **156** 43 37N 84 17W
Midland, Tex., U.S.A. **159** 32 0N 102 3W
Midland Junc. **137** 31 50 S 115 58 E
Midlands □ **127** 19 40 S 29 0 E
Midleton **39** 51 52N 8 12W
Midlothian, Austral. **138** 17 10 S 141 12 E
Midlothian, U.S.A. **159** 32 30N 97 0W
Midlothian (□) **26** 55 45N 3 15W
Midnapore **95** 22 25N 87 21 E
Midongy du Sud **129** 23 35 S 47 1 E
Midongy, Massif de **129** 23 30 S 47 0 E
Midskog **73** 58 56N 14 5 E
Midsomer Norton **28** 51 17N 2 29W
Midvale **160** 40 39N 111 58W
Midway Is. **130** 28 13N 177 22W
Midwest **160** 43 27N 106 11W
Midwolda **46** 53 12N 6 52 E
Midzur **66** 43 24N 22 40 E
Mie-ken □ **111** 34 30N 136 10 E
Miechów **54** 50 21N 20 5 E
Miedzyborz **54** 51 39N 17 24 E
Miedzychód **54** 52 35N 15 53 E
Miedzylesie **54** 50 41N 16 40 E
Miedzyrzec Podlaski **54** 51 58N 22 45 E
Miedzyrzecz **54** 52 26N 15 35 E
Miedzyzdroje **54** 53 56N 14 26 E
Miejska Górka **54** 51 39N 16 58 E
Miélan **44** 43 27N 0 19 E
Mielelek **138** 6 1 S 148 58 E
Mienchʻih **106** 34 48N 111 40 E
Mienchu **108** 31 22N 104 7 E
Mienga **128** 17 12 S 19 48 E
Mienhsien **106** 33 11N 106 36 E
Mienning **108** 28 30N 102 10 E
Mienyang, Hupei, China **109** 30 10N 113 20 E
Mienyang, Szechwan, China **108** 31 28N 104 46 E
Miercurea Ciuc **70** 46 21N 25 48 E
Mieres **56** 43 18N 5 48W
Mierlo **47** 51 27N 5 37 E
Mieso **123** 9 15N 40 43 E
Mieszkowice **54** 52 47N 14 30 E
Migdal **90** 32 51N 35 30 E
Migdal Afeq **90** 32 5N 34 58 E
Migennes **43** 47 58N 3 31 E
Migliarino **63** 44 54N 11 56 E
Miguel Alemán, Presa **165** 18 15N 96 40W
Miguel Alves **170** 4 11 S 42 55W
Miguel Calmon **170** 11 26 S 40 36W
Mihara **110** 34 24N 133 5 E
Mihara-Yama **111** 34 43N 139 23 E
Mihsien **106** 34 31N 113 22 E
Mii **108** 26 50N 102 3 E
Mijares, R. **58** 40 15N 0 50W
Mijas **57** 36 36N 4 40W
Mijdrecht **46** 52 13N 4 53 E
Mijilu **121** 10 22N 13 19 E
Mikese **126** 6 48 S 37 55 E
Mikha Tskhakaya **83** 42 15N 42 7 E
Mikhailovgrad **67** 43 27N 23 16 E
Mikhailovka **82** 47 16N 35 27 E
Mikhaylov **81** 54 20N 39 0 E
Mikhaylovka, Azerbaijan, U.S.S.R. **83** 41 31N 48 52 E
Mikhaylovka, R.S.F.S.R., U.S.S.R. **81** 50 3N 43 5 E
Mikhaylovski **84** 56 27N 59 7 E
Mikhnevo **81** 55 4N 37 59 E
Miki, Hyōgō, Japan **110** 34 48N 134 59 E
Miki, Kagawa, Japan **110** 34 12N 134 7 E
Mikinai **69** 37 43N 22 46 E
Mikindani **127** 10 15 S 40 2 E
Mikkeli **75** 61 43N 27 25 E
Mikkeli □ **74** 62 0N 28 0 E
Mikkelin Lääni □ **74** 61 56N 28 0 E
Mikkwa, R. **152** 58 25N 114 46W
Mikniya **123** 17 0N 33 45 E
Mikołajki **54** 53 49N 21 37 E

Mikol Mjømna


Mikołów 53 50 10N 18 50 E
Mikonos, I. 69 37 30N 25 25 E
Mikrón Dhérion 68 41 19N 26 6 E
Mikulov 53 48 48N 16 39 E
Mikumi 126 7 26 S 37 9 E
Mikun 78 62 20N 50 0 E
Mikuni 111 36 13N 136 9 E
Mikuni-Tōge 111 36 50N 138 40 E
Mikura-Jima 111 33 52N 139 36 E
Mila 119 36 27N 6 16 E
Milaca 158 45 45N 93 40W
Milagro 174 2 0 S 79 30W
Milan, Mo., U.S.A. 158 40 10N 93 5W
Milan, Tenn., U.S.A. 157 35 55N 88 45W
Milan = Milano 62 45 28N 9 10 E
Milang, S. Australia, Austral. 139 32 2 S 139 10 E
Milang, S. Australia, Austral. 140 35 24 S 138 58 E
Milange 127 16 3 S 35 45 E
Milano 62 45 28N 9 10 E
Milâs 92 37 20N 27 50 E
Milazzo 65 38 13N 15 13 E
Milbank 158 45 17N 96 38W
Milborne Port 28 50 58N 2 28W
Milden 153 51 29N 107 32W
Mildenhall 29 52 20N 0 30 E
Mildura 140 34 13 S 142 9 E
Miléai 68 39 20N 23 9 E
Miles, Austral. 139 26 40 S 150 23 E
Miles, U.S.A. 159 31 39N 100 11W
Miles City 158 46 30N 105 50W
Milestone 153 49 59N 104 31W
Mileto 65 38 37N 16 3 E
Miletto, Mte. 65 41 26N 14 23 E
Mileurà 137 26 22 S 117 20 E
Milevsko 52 49 27N 14 21 E
Milford, Ireland 39 52 20N 8 52W
Milford, Conn., U.S.A. 162 41 13N 73 4W
Milford, Del., U.S.A. 162 38 52N 75 27W
Milford, Mass., U.S.A. 162 42 8N 71 30W
Milford, N.H., U.S.A. 162 42 50N 71 39W
Milford, Pa., U.S.A. 162 41 20N 74 47W
Milford, Utah, U.S.A. 161 38 20N 113 0W
Milford Haven 31 51 43N 5 2W
Milford Haven, B. 31 51 40N 5 10W
Milford on Sea 28 50 44N 1 36W
Milford Sd. 143 44 34 S 167 47 E
Milgun 137 25 6 S 118 18 E
Milh, Ras el 117 32 0N 24 55 E
Miliana, Aïn Salah, Alg. 118 27 20N 2 32 E
Miliana, Médéa, Alg. 118 36 12N 2 15 E
Milicz 54 51 31N 17 19 E
Miling 137 30 30 S 116 17 E
Militello in Val di Catánia 65 37 16N 14 46 E
Milk, R. 160 48 40N 107 15W
Milk River 152 49 10N 112 5W
Mill 47 51 41N 5 48 E
Mill City 160 44 45N 122 28W
Mill, I. 13 66 0 S 101 30 E
Mill Valley 163 37 54N 122 32W
Millau 44 44 8N 3 4 E
Millbrook, U.K. 30 50 19N 4 12W
Millbrook, U.S.A. 162 41 47N 73 42W
Millbrook Res. 109 34 50 S 138 49 E
Mille Lacs, L. 158 46 10N 93 30W
Mille Lacs, L. des 150 48 45N 90 35W
Milledgeville 157 33 7N 83 15W
Millen 157 32 50N 81 57W
Miller 158 44 35N 98 59W
Millerovo 83 48 57N 40 28 E
Miller's Flat 143 45 39 S 169 23 E
Millersburg 162 40 32N 76 58W
Millerton, N.Z. 143 41 39 S 171 54 E
Millerton, U.S.A. 162 41 57N 73 32W
Millerton, L. 163 37 0N 119 42W
Milleur Pt. 34 55 2N 5 5W
Millevaches, Plat. de 44 45 45N 2 0 E
Millicent 140 37 34 S 140 21 E
Millingen 46 51 52N 6 2 E
Millinocket 151 45 45N 68 45W
Millisle 38 54 38N 5 33W
Millmerran 139 27 53 S 151 16 E
Millom 32 54 13N 3 16W
Millport 34 55 45N 4 55W
Mills L. 152 61 30N 118 20W
Millsboro 162 38 36N 75 17W
Millstreet 39 52 4N 9 5W
Milltown, Galway, Ireland 38 53 37N 8 54W
Milltown, Kerry, Ireland 39 52 9N 9 42W
Milltown, U.K. 37 57 33N 4 48W
Milltown Malbay 39 52 51N 9 25W
Millville, N.J., U.S.A. 162 39 22N 75 0W
Millville, Pa., U.S.A. 162 41 7N 76 32W
Millwood Res. 159 33 45N 94 0W
Milly 43 48 24N 2 20 E
Milly Milly 137 26 4 S 116 43 E
Milna 63 43 20N 16 28 E
Milnathort 35 56 14N 3 25W
Milne Inlet 149 72 30N 80 0W
Milne, R. 138 21 10 S 137 33 E
Milngavie 34 55 57N 4 20W
Milnor 158 46 19N 97 29W
Milnthorpe 32 54 14N 2 47W
Milo, Can. 152 50 34N 112 53W
Milo, China 108 24 28N 103 23 E
Milolii 147 22 8N 159 42W
Milos 69 36 44N 24 25 E
Milos, I. 69 36 44N 24 25 E
Miloševo 66 45 42N 20 20 E
Miłosław 54 52 12N 17 32 E
Milovaig 36 57 27N 6 45W
Milparinka P.O. 139 29 46 S 141 57 E
Miltenberg 49 49 41N 9 13 E
Milton, N.Z. 143 46 7 S 169 59 E
Milton, Dumf. & Gall., U.K. 34 55 18N 4 50W
Milton, Hants., U.K. 28 50 45N 1 40W
Milton, Northants, U.K. 29 52 12N 0 55W
Milton, Calif., U.S.A. 163 38 3N 120 51W
Milton, Del., U.S.A. 162 38 47N 75 19W
Milton, Fla., U.S.A. 157 30 38N 87 0W
Milton, Pa., U.S.A. 162 41 0N 76 53W
Milton Abbot 30 50 35N 4 16W
Milton-Freewater 160 45 57N 118 24W
Milton Keynes 29 52 3N 0 42W
Milverton 28 51 2N 3 15W
Milwaukee 156 43 9N 87 58W
Milwaukie 160 45 27N 122 39W
Mim 120 6 57N 2 33W
Mimizan 44 44 12N 1 13W
Mimon 52 50 38N 14 43 E
Mimoso 171 15 10 S 48 5W
Min Chiang, R., China 105 28 48N 104 33 E
Min Chiang, R., Fukien, China 109 26 5N 119 37 E
Min Chiang, R., Szechwan, China 108 28 48N 104 33 E
Min-Kush 85 41 4N 74 28 E
Mina 161 38 21N 118 9W
Mina Pirquitas 172 22 40 S 66 40W
Mina Saud 92 28 45N 48 20 E
Minā'al Ahmadī 92 29 5N 48 10 E
Mīnāb 93 27 10N 57 1 E
Minago, R. 153 54 33N 98 13W
Minakami 111 36 49N 138 59 E
Minaki 153 50 0N 94 40W
Minakuchi 111 34 58N 136 10 E
Minamata 110 32 10N 130 30 E
Minamitane 112 30 25N 130 54 E
Minas Basin 151 45 20N 64 12W
Minas de Rio Tinto 57 37 42N 6 22W
Minas de San Quintín 57 38 49N 4 23W
Minas Gerais □ 171 18 50 S 46 0W
Minas Novas 171 17 15 S 42 36W
Minas, Sierra de las 166 15 9N 89 31W
Minatitlán 165 17 58N 94 35W
Minbu 98 20 10N 95 0 E
Minbya 98 20 22N 93 16 E
Mincha 140 36 1 S 144 6 E
Minch'in 106 38 42N 103 11 E
Minch'ing 109 26 13N 118 51 E
Minchinhampton 28 51 42N 2 10W
Mincio, R. 62 45 8N 10 55 E
Mindanao, I. 103 8 0N 125 0 E
Mindanao Sea 103 9 0N 124 0 E
Mindanao Trench 103 8 0N 128 0 E
Mindelheim 49 48 4N 10 30 E
Minden, Ger. 48 52 18N 8 54 E
Minden, U.S.A. 159 32 40N 93 20W
Mindiptana 103 5 45 S 140 22 E
Mindon 98 19 21N 94 44 E
Mindoro, I. 103 13 0N 121 0 E
Mindoro Strait 103 12 30N 120 30 E
Mindouli 124 4 12 S 14 28 E
Mine 110 34 12N 131 7 E
Mine Hd. 39 52 0N 7 37W
Minehead 28 51 12N 3 29W
Mineola, N.Y., U.S.A. 162 40 45N 73 38W
Mineola, Tex., U.S.A. 159 32 40N 95 30W
Minera 31 53 3N 3 7W
Mineral King 163 36 27N 118 36W
Mineral Wells 159 32 50N 98 5W
Mineralnyye Vody 83 44 18N 43 15 E
Minersville, Pa., U.S.A. 162 40 40N 76 17W
Minersville, Utah, U.S.A. 161 38 14N 112 58W
Minervino Murge 65 41 6N 16 4 E
Minette 157 30 54N 87 43W
Minetto 162 43 24N 76 28W
Mingan 151 50 20N 64 0W
Mingary, Austral. 140 32 8 S 140 45 E
Mingary, U.K. 36 56 42N 6 5W
Mingch'i 109 26 24N 117 12 E
Mingchiang 109 32 28N 114 8 E
Mingechaur 83 40 52N 47 0 E
Mingechaurskoye Vdkhr. 83 40 56N 47 20 E
Mingela 138 19 52 S 146 38 E
Mingenew 137 29 12 S 115 21 E
Mingera Cr. 138 20 38 S 138 10 E
Mingin 98 22 50N 94 30 E
Minginish, Dist. 36 57 14N 6 15W
Minglanilla 58 39 34N 1 38W
Mingulay I. 36 56 50N 7 40W
Minho □ 55 41 25N 8 20W
Minho, R. 55 41 58N 8 40W
Minhou 109 26 0N 119 18 E
Minhow = Fuchou 109 26 5N 119 18 E
Minhsien 106 34 26N 104 2 E
Minidoka 160 42 47N 113 34W
Minigwal L. 137 29 31 S 123 14 E
Minilya 137 23 55 S 114 0 E
Minilya, R. 137 23 45 S 114 0 E
Mininera 140 37 37 S 142 58 E
Minićevo 66 43 42N 22 18 E
Minipi, L. 151 52 25N 60 45W
Minj 135 5 54 S 144 30 E
Mink L. 152 61 54N 117 40W
Minlaton 140 34 45 S 137 35 E
Minna 121 9 37N 6 30 E
Minneapolis, Kans., U.S.A. 158 39 11N 97 40W
Minneapolis, Minn., U.S.A. 158 44 58N 93 20W
Minnesota □ 158 46 40N 94 0W
Minnesund 71 60 23N 11 14 E
Minnie Creek 137 24 3 S 115 42 E
Minnigaff 34 54 58N 4 30W
Minnitaki L. 150 49 47N 91 5W
Mino 111 35 32N 136 55 E
Mino-Kamo 111 35 23N 137 2 E
Mino-Mikawa-Kōgen 111 35 10N 137 30 E
Miño, R. 56 41 58N 8 40W
Minobu 111 35 22N 138 26 E
Minobu-Sanchi 111 35 14N 138 20 E
Minorca = Menorca 58 40 0N 4 0 E
Minore 141 32 14 S 148 27 E
Minot 158 48 10N 101 15W
Minquiers, Les 42 48 58N 2 8W
Minsen 48 53 43N 7 58 E
Minsk 80 53 52N 27 30 E
Minsk Mazowiecki 54 52 10N 21 33 E
Minster 29 51 20N 1 20 E
Minster-on-Sea 29 51 25N 0 50 E
Minsterley 28 52 38N 2 56W
Mintaka Pass 93 37 0N 74 58 E
Minthami 98 23 55N 94 16 E
Mintlaw 37 57 32N 1 59W
Minto 147 64 55N 149 20W
Minto L. 150 48 0N 84 45W
Minton 153 49 10N 104 35W
Minturn 160 39 45N 106 25W
Minturno 64 41 15N 13 43 E
Minûf 122 30 26N 30 52 E
Minusinsk 77 53 50N 91 20 E
Minutang 98 28 15N 96 30 E
Minvoul 124 2 9N 12 8 E
Minya Konka 108 29 34N 101 53 E
Minyar 84 55 4N 57 33 E
Minyip 140 36 29 S 142 36 E
Mionica 66 44 14N 20 6 E
Mios Num, I. 103 1 30 S 135 10 E
Miquelon 151 47 3N 56 20W
Miquelon, St. Pierre et, □ 151 47 8N 56 24W
Mir-Bashir 83 40 11N 46 58 E
Mira, Italy 63 45 26N 12 9 E
Mira, Port. 56 40 26N 8 44W
Mira, R. 57 37 30N 8 30W
Mirabella Eclano 65 41 3N 14 59 E
Miracema do Norte 170 9 33 S 48 24W
Mirador 170 6 22 S 44 22W
Miraflores 164 23 21N 109 45W
Miraj 96 16 50N 74 45 E
Miram 138 21 15 S 148 55 E
Miram Shah 94 33 0N 70 0 E
Miramar, Argent. 172 38 15 S 57 50W
Miramar, Mozam. 129 23 50 S 35 35 E
Miramas 45 43 33N 4 59 E
Mirambeau 44 45 23N 0 35W
Miramichi B. 151 47 15N 65 0W
Miramont-de-Guyenne 44 44 37N 0 21 E
Miranda 175 20 10 S 56 15W
Miranda de Ebro 58 42 41N 2 57W
Miranda do Corvo 56 40 6N 8 20W
Miranda do Douro 56 41 30N 6 16W
Mirando City 159 27 28N 98 59W
Mirandola 62 44 53N 11 2 E
Mirandópolis 173 21 9 S 51 6W
Mirango 127 13 32 S 34 58 E
Mirano 63 45 29N 12 6 E
Miraporvos, I. 167 22 9N 74 30W
Mirassol 173 20 46 S 49 28W
Mirboo North 141 38 24 S 146 10 E
Mirear, I. 122 23 15N 35 41 E
Mirebeau, Côte d'Or, France 43 47 25N 5 20 E
Mirebeau, Vienne, France 42 46 49N 0 10 E
Mirecourt 43 48 20N 6 10 E
Mirgorod 80 49 58N 33 50 E
Miri 102 4 18N 114 0 E
Miriam Vale 138 24 20 S 151 33 E
Mirim, Lagoa 173 32 45 S 52 50W
Mirimire 174 11 10N 68 43W
Mirny 13 66 0 S 95 0 E
Mirnyy 77 62 33N 113 53 E
Mirond L. 153 55 6N 102 47W
Mirosławiec 54 53 20N 16 5 E
Mirpur 95 33 15N 73 50 E
Mirpur Bibiwari 94 28 33N 67 44 E
Mirpur Khas 94 25 30N 69 0 E
Mirpur Sakro 94 24 33N 67 41 E
Mirrool 141 34 19 S 147 10 E
Mirror 152 52 30N 113 7W
Mîrsani 70 44 1N 23 59 E
Mirsk 54 50 58N 15 23 E
Miryang 107 35 31N 128 44 E
Mirzaani 83 41 24N 46 5 E
Mirzapur 95 25 10N 82 45 E
Misantla 165 19 56N 96 50W
Miscou I. 151 47 57N 64 31W
Misery, Mt. 108 34 52 S 138 48 E
Mish'ab, Ra'as al 92 28 15N 48 43 E
Mishan 105 45 31N 132 2 E
Mishawaka 156 41 40N 86 8W
Mishbih, Gebel 122 22 48N 34 38 E
Mishima 111 35 10N 138 52 E
Mishkino 84 55 20N 63 55 E
Mishmar Aiyalon 90 31 52N 34 57 E
Mishmar Ha' Emeq 90 32 37N 35 7 E
Mishmar Ha Negev 90 31 22N 34 48 E
Mishmar Ha Yarden 90 33 0N 35 56 E
Mishmi Hills 98 29 0N 96 0 E
Misilmeri 64 38 2N 13 25 E
Misima I. 135 10 40 S 152 45 E
Misión, La 164 32 5N 116 50W
Misiones □, Argent. 173 27 0 S 55 0W
Misiones □, Parag. 172 27 0 S 56 0W
Miskin 93 23 44N 56 52 E
Miskitos, Cayos 166 14 26N 82 50W
Miskolc 53 48 7N 20 50 E
Misoke 126 0 42 S 28 2 E
Misoöl, I. 103 2 0 S 130 0 E
Misrātah 119 32 18N 15 3 E
Missanabie 150 48 20N 84 6W
Missão Velha 170 7 15 S 39 10W
Misserghin 118 35 44N 0 49W
Missinaibi L. 150 48 23N 83 40W
Missinaibi, R. 150 50 30N 82 40W
Mission, S.D., U.S.A. 158 43 21N 100 36W
Mission, Tex., U.S.A. 159 26 15N 98 30W
Mission City 152 49 10N 122 15W
Missisa L. 150 52 20N 85 7W
Mississagi 150 46 15N 83 9W
Mississippi, R. 159 35 30N 90 0W
Mississippi Sd. 159 30 25N 89 0W
Missoula 160 47 0N 114 0W
Missouri □ 158 38 25N 92 30W
Missouri, Little, R. 160 46 0N 111 35W
Missouri, R. 158 40 20N 95 40W
Mistake B. 153 62 8N 93 0W
Mistassini L. 150 51 0N 73 40W
Mistassini, R. 151 48 42N 72 20W
Mistastin L. 151 55 57N 63 20W
Mistatim 153 52 52N 103 22W
Mistelbach 53 48 34N 16 34 E
Misterbianco 65 37 32N 15 0 E
Misterton, Notts., U.K. 33 53 27N 0 49W
Misterton, Som., U.K. 28 50 51N 2 46W
Mistretta 65 37 56N 14 20 E
Misty L. 153 58 53N 101 40W
Misugi 111 34 31N 136 16 E
Misumi 110 32 37N 130 27 E
Mît Ghamr 122 30 42N 31 12 E
Mitaka 111 35 40N 139 33 E
Mitan 85 40 0N 66 35 E
Mitatib 123 15 59N 36 12 E
Mitcham 109 34 59 S 138 37 E
Mitchel Troy 31 51 46N 2 45W
Mitcheldean 28 51 51N 2 29W
Mitchell, Austral. 139 26 29 S 147 58 E
Mitchell, Ind., U.S.A. 156 38 42N 86 25W
Mitchell, Nebr., U.S.A. 158 41 58N 103 45W
Mitchell, Oreg., U.S.A. 160 44 31N 120 8W
Mitchell, S.D., U.S.A. 158 43 40N 98 0W
Mitchell, Mt. 157 35 40N 82 20W
Mitchell, R. 138 15 12 S 141 35 E
Mitchelstown 39 52 16N 8 18W
Mitchelton 108 27 25 S 152 59 E
Mitha Tiwana 94 32 13N 72 6 E
Míthimna 68 39 20N 26 12 E
Mitiamo 140 36 12 S 144 15 E
Mitilini 69 39 6N 26 35 E
Mitilini = Lesvos 68 39 0N 26 20 E
Mitilinoi 69 37 42N 26 56 E
Mitla 165 16 55N 96 24W
Mito 111 36 20N 140 30 E
Mitsinjo 129 16 1 S 45 52 E
Mitsiwa 123 15 35N 39 25 E
Mitsiwa Channel 123 15 30N 40 0 E
Mitsukaidō 111 36 1N 139 59 E
Mittagong 141 34 28 S 150 29 E
Mittelland 50 46 50N 7 23 E
Mittelland Kanal 48 52 23N 7 45 E
Mittenwalde 48 52 16N 13 33 E
Mittweida 48 50 59N 13 0 E
Mitu 108 25 21N 100 32 E
Mitú 174 1 8N 70 3W
Mituas 174 3 52N 68 49W
Mitumba 126 7 8 S 31 2 E
Mitumba, Chaîne des 126 10 0 S 26 20 E
Mitwaba 127 8 2N 27 17 E
Mityana 126 0 23N 32 2 E
Mitzick 124 0 45N 11 40 E
Miura 111 35 12N 139 40 E
Mius, R. 83 47 30N 39 0 E
Mixteco, R. 165 18 11N 98 30W
Miyagi-Ken □ 112 38 15N 140 45 E
Miyâh, W. el 122 25 10N 33 30 E
Miyake-Jima 111 34 0N 139 30 E
Miyako 112 39 40N 141 75 E
Miyako-Jima 112 24 45N 125 20 E
Miyakonojō 110 31 32N 131 5 E
Miyanojō 110 31 54N 130 27 E
Miyanoura-Dake 112 30 20N 130 26 E
Miyata 110 33 49N 130 42 E
Miyazaki 110 31 56N 131 30 E
Miyazaki-ken □ 110 32 0N 131 30 E
Miyazu 110 35 35N 135 10 E
Miyet, Bahr el 92 31 30N 35 30 E
Miyoshi 110 34 48N 132 51 E
Miyün 106 40 22N 116 49 E
Mizamis = Ozamiz 103 8 15N 123 50 E
Mizdah 119 31 30N 13 0 E
Mizen Hd., Cork, Ireland 39 51 27N 9 50W
Mizen Hd., Wick., Ireland 39 52 52N 6 4W
Mizil 70 44 59N 26 29 E
Mizoram □ 98 23 0N 92 40 E
Mizuho 111 35 6N 135 17 E
Mizunami 111 35 22N 137 15 E
Mjöbäck 73 57 28N 12 53 E
Mjölby 73 58 20N 15 10 E
Mjømna 71 60 55N 4 55 E

Mjörn Montcornet


Mjörn 73 57 55N 12 25 E
Mjøsa 71 60 40N 11 0 E
Mkata 126 5 45 S 38 20 E
Mkokotoni 126 5 55 S 39 15 E
Mkomazi 126 4 40 S 38 7 E
Mkulwe 127 8 37 S 32 20 E
Mkumbi, Ras 126 7 38 S 39 55 E
Mkushi 127 14 25 S 29 15 E
Mkushi River 127 13 40 S 29 30 E
Mkuze, R. 129 27 45 S 32 30 E
Mkwaya 126 6 17 S 35 40 E
Mladá Boleslav 52 50 27N 14 53 E
Mladenovac 66 44 28N 20 44 E
Mlala Hills 126 6 50 S 31 40 E
Mlange 127 16 2 S 35 33 E
Mlava, R. 66 44 35N 21 18 E
Mława 54 53 9N 20 25 E
Mliniŝte 63 44 15N 16 50 E
Mljet, I. 66 42 43N 17 30 E
Młynary 54 54 12N 19 46 E
Mme 121 6 18N 10 14 E
Mo, Hordaland, Norway 71 60 49N 5 48 E
Mo, Telemark, Norway 71 59 28N 7 50 E
Mo, Sweden 72 61 19N 16 47 E
Mo i Rana 74 66 15N 14 7 E
Moa, I. 103 8 0 S 128 0 E
Moa, R. 120 7 0N 11 40W
Moab 161 38 40N 109 35W
Moabi 124 2 24 S 10 59 E
Moalie Park 139 29 42 S 143 3 E
Moaña 56 42 18N 8 43W
Moanda 124 1 28 S 13 21 E
Moapo 161 36 45N 114 37W
Moate 39 53 25N 7 43W
Moba 126 7 0 S 29 48 E
Mobara 111 35 25N 140 18 E
Mobaye 124 4 25N 21 5 E
Mobayi 124 4 15N 21 8 E
Moberley 158 39 25N 92 25W
Moberly, R. 152 56 12N 120 55W
Mobert 150 48 41N 85 40W
Mobile 157 30 41N 88 3W
Mobile B. 157 30 30N 88 0W
Mobile, Pt. 157 30 15N 88 0W
Mobjack B. 162 37 16N 76 22W
Möborg 73 56 24N 8 21 E
Mobridge 158 45 40N 100 28W
Mobutu Sese Seko, L. 126 1 30N 31 0 E
Moc Chav 100 20 50N 104 38 E
Moc Hoa 101 10 46N 105 56 E
Mocabe Kasari 127 9 58 S 26 12 E
Mocajuba 170 2 35 S 49 30W
Moçambique 127 15 3 S 40 42 E
Moçambique □ 127 14 45 S 38 30 E
Mocanaqua 162 41 9N 76 8W
Mochiang 108 23 25N 101 44 E
Mochiara Grove 128 20 43 S 21 50 E
Mochudi 128 24 27 S 26 7 E
Mocimboa da Praia 127 11 25 S 40 20 E
Mociu 70 46 46N 24 3 E
Möckeln 73 56 40N 14 15 E
Mockhorn I. 162 37 10N 75 52W
Moclips 160 47 14N 124 10W
Moçâmedes □ 128 16 35 S 12 30 E
Mocoa 174 1 15N 76 45W
Mococa 173 21 28 S 47 0W
Mocorito 164 25 20N 108 0W
Moctezuma 164 30 12N 106 26W
Moctezuma, R. 165 21 59N 98 34W
Mocuba 125 16 54 S 37 25 E
Moda 98 24 22N 96 29 E
Modane 45 45 12N 6 40 E
Modasa 94 23 30N 73 21 E
Modave 47 50 27N 5 18 E
Modbury, Austral. 109 34 50 S 138 41 E
Modbury, U.K. 30 50 21N 3 53W
Modder, R. 128 28 50 S 24 50 E
Modderrivier 128 29 2 S 24 38 E
Módena 62 44 39N 10 55 E
Modena 161 37 55N 113 56W
Modesto 163 37 43N 121 0W
Módica 65 36 52N 14 45 E
Modigliana 63 44 9N 11 48 E
Modjokerto 103 7 29 S 112 25 E
Modlin 54 52 24N 20 41 E
Mödling 53 48 5N 16 17 E
Modo 123 5 31N 30 33 E
Modra 53 48 19N 17 20 E
Modreeny 39 52 57N 8 6W
Modriča 66 44 57N 18 17 E
Moe 141 38 12 S 146 19 E
Moebase 127 17 3 S 38 41 E
Moei, R. 101 17 25N 98 10 E
Moëlan-s-Mer 42 47 49N 3 38W
Moelfre 31 53 21N 4 15W
Moengo 175 5 45N 54 20W
Moergestel 47 51 33N 5 11 E
Moësa, R. 51 46 12N 9 10 E
Moffat 35 55 20N 3 27W
Moga 94 30 48N 75 8 E
Mogadiscio = Mogadishu 91 2 2N 45 25 E
Mogadishu 91 2 2N 45 25 E
Mogador = Essaouira 118 31 32N 9 42W
Mogadouro 56 41 22N 6 47W
Mogami-gawa, R. 112 38 45N 140 0 E
Mogaung 98 25 20N 97 0 E
Møgeltønder 73 54 57N 8 48 E
Mogente 59 38 52N 0 45W
Moggil 108 27 34 S 152 52 E
Mogho 123 4 54N 40 16 E
Mogi das Cruzes 173 23 45 S 46 20W
Mogi-Guaçu, R. 173 20 53 S 48 10W
Mogi-Mirim 173 22 20 S 47 0W
Mogielnica 54 51 42N 20 41 E
Mogilev 80 53 55N 30 18 E
Mogilev Podolskiy 82 48 20N 27 40 E
Mogilno 54 52 39N 17 55 E
Mogincual 125 15 35 S 40 25 E
Mogliano Veneto 63 45 33N 12 15 E
Mogocha 77 53 40N 119 50 E
Mogoi 103 1 55 S 133 10 E
Mogok 98 23 0N 96 40 E
Mogollon 161 33 25N 108 55W
Mogollon Mesa 161 43 40N 111 0W
Mogriguy 141 32 3 S 148 40 E
Moguer 57 37 15N 6 52W
Mogumber 137 31 2 S 116 3 E
Mohács 53 45 58N 18 41 E
Mohaka, R. 142 39 7 S 177 12 E
Mohall 158 48 46N 101 30W
Mohammadābād 93 37 30N 59 5 E
Mohammedia 118 33 44N 7 21W
Mohave Desert 161 35 0N 117 30W
Mohawk 161 32 45N 113 50W
Mohawk, R. 162 42 47N 73 42W
Moheda 73 57 1N 14 35 E
Mohembo 125 18 15 S 21 43 E
Moher, Cliffs of 39 52 58N 9 30W
Mohican, C. 147 60 10N 167 30W
Mohill 38 53 57N 7 52W
Möhne, R. 48 51 29N 8 10 E
Mohnyin 98 24 47N 96 22 E
Moholm 73 58 37N 14 5 E
Mohon 43 49 45N 4 44 E
Mohoro 126 8 6 S 39 8 E
Moia 123 5 3N 28 2 E
Moidart, L. 36 56 47N 5 40W
Moinabad 96 17 44N 77 16 E
Moineşti 70 46 28N 26 21 E
Mointy 76 47 40N 73 45 E
Moira 38 54 28N 6 16W
Moirais 69 35 4N 24 56 E
Moirans 45 45 20N 5 33 E
Moirans-en-Montagne 45 46 26N 5 43 E
Moisäkula 80 58 3N 24 38 E
Moisie 151 50 7N 66 1W
Moisie, R. 151 50 6N 66 5W
Moissac 44 44 7N 1 5 E
Moita 57 38 38N 8 58W
Mojácar 59 37 6N 1 55W
Mojados 56 41 26N 4 40W
Mojave 163 35 8N 118 8W
Mojave Desert 163 35 0N 116 30W
Mojo, Boliv. 172 21 48 S 65 33W
Mojo, Ethiopia 123 8 35N 39 5 E
Mojo, I. 102 8 10 S 117 40 E
Moju, R. 170 1 40 S 48 25W
Mokai 142 38 32 S 175 56 E
Mokambo 127 12 25 S 28 20 E
Mokameh 95 25 24N 85 55 E
Mokau, R. 142 38 35 S 174 55 E
Mokelumne Hill 163 38 18N 120 43W
Mokelumne, R. 163 38 23N 121 25W
Mokhós 69 35 16N 25 27 E
Mokhotlong 129 29 22 S 29 2 E
Mokihinui 143 41 33 S 171 58 E
Moknine 119 35 35N 10 58 E
Mokokchung 99 26 15N 94 30 E
Mokpalin 98 17 26N 96 53 E
Mokpo 107 34 50N 126 30 E
Mokra Gora 66 42 50N 20 30 E
Mokronog 63 45 57N 15 9 E
Moksha, R. 81 54 45N 43 40 E
Mokshan 81 52 25N 44 35 E
Mokta Spera 120 16 38N 9 6W
Moktama Kwe 99 15 40N 96 30 E
Mol 47 51 11N 5 5 E
Mola, C. de la 58 39 53N 4 20 E
Mola di Bari 65 41 3N 17 5 E
Moland 71 59 11N 8 6 E
Moláoi 69 36 49N 22 56 E
Molat, I. 63 44 15N 14 50 E
Molchanovo 76 57 40N 83 50 E
Mold 31 53 10N 3 10W
Moldava nad Bodvou 53 48 38N 21 0 E
Moldavia = Moldova 70 46 30N 27 0 E
Moldavian S.S.R. □ 82 47 0N 28 0 E
Molde 71 62 45N 7 9 E
Moldotau, Khrebet 85 41 35N 75 0 E
Moldova 70 46 30N 27 0 E
Moldova Nouă 70 44 45N 21 41 E
Moldoveanu, mt. 67 45 36N 24 45 E
Mole Creek 138 41 32 S 146 24 E
Mole, R. 29 51 13N 0 15W
Molepolole 125 24 28 S 25 28 E
Moléson 50 46 33N 7 1 E
Molesworth 143 42 5 S 173 16 E
Molfetta 65 41 12N 16 35 E
Molina de Aragón 58 40 46N 1 52W
Moline 158 41 30N 90 30W
Molinella 63 44 38N 11 40 E
Molinos 172 25 28 S 66 15W
Moliro 126 8 12 S 30 30 E
Molise □ 63 41 45N 14 30 E
Moliterno 65 40 14N 15 50 E
Mollahat 98 22 56N 89 48 E
Mölle 73 56 17N 12 31 E
Molledo 56 43 8N 4 6W
Mollendo 174 17 0 S 72 0W
Mollerin, L. 137 30 30 S 117 35 E
Mollerusa 58 41 37N 0 54 E
Mollina 57 37 8N 4 38W
Mölln 48 53 37N 10 41 E
Mollösund 73 58 4N 11 30 E
Mölltorp 73 58 30N 14 26 E
Mölndal 73 57 40N 12 3 E
Mölnlycke 73 57 40N 12 8 E
Molo 98 23 22N 96 53 E
Molochansk 82 47 15N 35 23 E
Molochaya, R. 82 47 0N 35 30 E
Molodechno 80 54 20N 26 50 E
Molokai, I. 147 21 8N 157 0W
Moloma, R. 81 59 0N 48 15 E
Molong 141 33 5 S 148 54 E
Molopo, R. 125 25 40 S 24 30 E
Mólos 69 38 47N 22 37 E
Molotov, Mys 77 81 10N 95 0 E
Moloundou 124 2 8N 15 15 E
Molsheim 43 48 33N 7 29 E
Molson L. 153 54 22N 95 32W
Molteno 128 31 22 S 26 22 E
Molu, I. 103 6 45 S 131 40 E
Molucca Sea 103 4 0 S 124 0 E
Moluccas = Maluku, Is. 103 1 0 S 127 0 E
Molusi 128 20 21 S 24 29 E
Moma, Mozam. 127 16 47 S 39 4 E
Moma, Zaïre 126 1 35 S 23 52 E
Momanga 128 18 7 S 21 41 E
Momba 140 30 58 S 143 30 E
Mombaça 170 15 43 S 48 43W
Mombasa 126 4 2 S 39 43 E
Mombetsu, Hokkaido, Japan 112 42 27N 142 4 E
Mombetsu, Hokkaido, Japan 112 44 21N 143 22 E
Mombuey 56 42 3N 6 20W
Momchilgrad 67 41 33N 25 23 E
Momi 126 1 42 S 27 0 E
Momignies 47 50 2N 4 10 E
Mompós 174 9 14N 74 26W
Møn 73 54 57N 12 15 E
Mon, R. 99 20 25N 94 30 E
Mona, Canal de la 167 18 30N 67 45W
Mona, I. 167 18 5N 67 54W
Mona Passage 167 18 0N 67 40W
Mona, Punta, C. Rica 166 9 37N 82 36W
Mona, Punta, Spain 57 36 43N 3 45W
Monach Is. 36 57 32N 7 40W
Monach, Sd. of 36 57 34N 7 26W
Monaco ■ 44 43 46N 7 23 E
Monadhliath Mts. 37 57 10N 4 4W
Monadnock Mt. 162 42 52N 72 7W
Monagas □ 174 9 20N 63 0W
Monaghan 38 54 15N 6 58W
Monaghan □ 38 54 10N 7 0W
Monahans 159 31 35N 102 50W
Monapo 127 14 50 S 40 12 E
Monar For. 36 57 27N 5 10W
Monar L. 36 57 26N 5 8W
Monarch Mt. 152 51 55N 125 57W
Monasterevan 39 53 10N 7 5W
Monastier-sur-Gazeille, Le 44 44 57N 3 59 E
Monastir 119 35 50N 10 49 E
Monastyriska 80 49 8N 25 14 E
Monavullagh Mts. 39 52 14N 7 35W
Moncada 58 39 30N 0 24W
Moncalieri 62 45 0N 7 40 E
Moncalvo 62 45 3N 8 15 E
Moncarapacho 57 37 5N 7 46W
Moncayo, Sierra del 58 41 48N 1 50W
Mönchengladbach 48 51 12N 6 23 E
Monchique 57 37 19N 8 38W
Monchique, Sa. de, 55 37 18N 8 39W
Monclova 164 26 50N 101 30W
Monção 56 42 4N 8 27W
Moncontant 42 46 43N 0 36W
Moncontour 42 48 22N 2 38W
Moncton 151 46 7N 64 51W
Mondego, Cabo 56 40 11N 8 54W
Mondego, R. 56 40 28N 8 0W
Mondeodo 103 3 21 S 122 9 E
Mondolfo 63 43 45N 13 8 E
Mondoñedo 56 43 25N 7 23W
Mondovi 62 44 23N 7 56 E
Mondovi 158 44 37N 91 40W
Mondragon 45 44 13N 4 44 E
Mondragone 64 41 8N 13 52 E
Mondrain I. 137 34 9 S 122 14 E
Monduli □ 126 3 0 S 36 0 E
Monemvasía 69 36 41N 23 3 E
Monessen 156 40 9N 79 50W
Monesterio 57 38 6N 6 15W
Monestier-de-Clermont 45 44 55N 5 38 E
Monet 150 48 10N 75 40W
Monêtier-les-Bains, Le 45 44 58N 6 30 E
Monett 159 36 55N 93 56W
Moneygall 39 52 54N 7 59W
Moneymore 38 54 42N 6 40W
Monfalcone 63 45 49N 13 32 E
Monflanquin 44 44 32N 0 47 E
Monforte 57 39 6N 7 25W
Monforte de Lemos 56 42 31N 7 33W
Mong Cai 101 21 27N 107 54 E
Möng Hsu 99 21 54N 98 30 E
Mong Hta 98 19 50N 98 35 E
Mong Ket 98 23 8N 98 22 E
Möng Kung 98 21 35N 97 35 E
Mong Kyawt 98 19 56N 98 45 E
Mong Lang 101 20 29N 97 52 E
Möng Nai 98 20 32N 97 55 E
Möng Pai 98 19 40N 97 15 E
Mong Pawk 99 22 4N 99 16 E
Mong Ping 98 21 22N 99 2 E
Mong Pu 98 20 55N 98 44 E
Mong Ton 98 20 25N 98 45 E
Mong Tung 98 22 2N 97 41 E
Mong Wa 99 21 26N 100 27 E
Mong Yai 98 22 28N 98 3 E
Mongalla 123 5 8N 31 55 E
Monger, L. 137 29 25 S 117 5 E
Monghyr 95 25 23N 86 30 E
Mongla 98 22 8N 89 35 E
Mongngaw 98 22 47N 96 59 E
Mongo 117 12 14N 18 43 E
Mongolia ■ 105 47 0N 103 0 E
Mongonu 121 12 40N 13 32 E
Mongororo 124 12 22N 22 26 E
Mongoumba 124 3 33N 18 40 E
Mongpang 101 23 5N 100 25 E
Mongu 125 15 16 S 23 12 E
Mongua 128 16 43 S 15 20 E
Moniaive 35 55 11N 3 55W
Monifieth 35 56 30N 2 48W
Monistral-St.-Loire 45 45 17N 4 11 E
Monitor, Pk. 163 38 52N 116 35W
Monitor, Ra. 163 38 30N 116 45W
Monivea 38 53 22N 8 42W
Monk 153 47 7N 69 59W
Monkey Bay 127 14 7 S 35 1 E
Monkey River 165 16 22N 88 29W
Monki 54 53 23N 22 48 E
Monkira 138 24 46 S 140 30 E
Monkoto 124 1 38 S 20 35 E
Monmouth, U.K. 31 51 48N 2 43W
Monmouth, U.S.A. 158 40 50N 90 40W
Monmouth (□) 26 51 34N 3 5W
Monnow R. 28 51 54N 2 48W
Mono, L. 163 38 0N 119 9W
Mono, Punta del 166 12 0N 83 30W
Monolith 163 35 7N 118 22W
Monópoli 65 40 57N 17 18 E
Monor 53 47 21N 19 27 E
Monóvar 59 38 28N 0 53W
Monowai 143 45 53 S 167 25 E
Monowai, L. 143 45 53 S 167 25 E
Monreal del Campo 58 40 47N 1 20W
Monreale 64 38 6N 13 16 E
Monroe, La., U.S.A. 159 32 32N 92 4W
Monroe, Mich., U.S.A. 156 41 55N 83 26W
Monroe, N.C., U.S.A. 157 35 2N 80 37W
Monroe, Utah, U.S.A. 161 38 45N 111 39W
Monroe, Wis., U.S.A. 158 42 38N 89 40W
Monroe City 158 39 39N 91 40W
Monroeton 162 41 43N 76 29W
Monroeville 157 31 33N 87 15W
Monrovia, Liberia 120 6 18N 10 47W
Monrovia, U.S.A. 161 34 7N 118 1W
Mons 47 50 27N 3 58 E
Møns Klint 73 54 57N 12 33 E
Monsaraz 57 38 28N 7 22W
Monse 103 4 0 S 123 10 E
Monségur 44 44 38N 0 4 E
Monsélice 63 43 13N 11 45 E
Monster 46 52 1N 4 10 E
Mont-aux-Sources 129 28 44 S 28 52 E
Mont-de-Marsin 44 43 54N 0 31W
Mont d'Or, Tunnel 43 46 45N 6 18 E
Mont-Dore, Le 44 45 35N 2 50 E
Mont Joli 151 48 37N 68 10W
Mont Laurier 150 46 35N 75 30W
Mont Luis 151 42 31N 2 6 E
Mont St. Michel 42 48 40N 1 30W
Mont-sur-Marchienne 47 50 23N 4 24 E
Mont Tremblant Prov. Park 150 46 30N 74 30W
Montabaur 48 50 26N 7 49 E
Montacute 109 34 53 S 138 45 E
Montagnac 44 43 29N 3 28 E
Montagnana 63 45 13N 11 29 E
Montagu 128 33 45 S 20 8 E
Montagu, I. 164 58 30 S 26 15W
Montague, Can. 151 46 10N 62 39W
Montague, Calif., U.S.A. 160 41 47N 122 30W
Montague, Mass., U.S.A. 162 42 31N 72 33W
Montague, I. 164 31 40N 144 46W
Montague I. 147 60 0N 147 0W
Montague Ra. 137 29 15 S 119 30 E
Montague Sd. 136 14 28 S 125 20 E
Montaigu 42 46 59N 1 18W
Montalban 58 40 50N 0 45W
Montalbano di Elicona 65 38 1N 15 0 E
Montalbano Iónico 65 40 17N 16 33 E
Montalbo 58 39 53N 2 42W
Montalcino 63 43 4N 11 30 E
Montalegre 56 41 49N 7 47W
Montalto di Castro 63 42 20N 11 36 E
Montalto Uffugo 65 39 25N 16 9 E
Montalvo 163 34 15N 119 12W
Montamarta 56 41 39N 5 49W
Montaña 174 6 0 S 73 0W
Montana 50 46 19N 7 29 E
Montana □ 154 47 0N 110 0W
Montánchez 57 39 15N 6 8W
Montañita 174 1 30N 75 28W
Montargis 43 48 0N 2 43 E
Montauban 44 44 0N 1 21 E
Montauk 162 41 3N 71 57W
Montauk Pt. 162 41 4N 71 52W
Montbard 43 47 38N 4 20 E
Montbéliard 43 47 31N 6 48 E
Montblanch 58 41 23N 1 4 E
Montbrison 45 45 36N 4 3 E
Montcalm, Pic de 44 42 40N 1 25 E
Montceau-les-Mines 43 46 40N 4 23 E
Montchanin 62 46 47N 4 30 E
Montclair 162 40 53N 74 49W
Montcornet 43 49 40N 4 0 E

Montcuq Morvan, Mts. du

Montcuq 44 44 21N 1 13 E
Montdidier 43 49 38N 2 35 E
Monte Albán 165 17 2N 96 45W
Monte Alegre 175 2 0S 54 0W
Monte Alegre de Goiás 171 13 14S 47 10W
Monte Alegre de Minas 171 18 52S 48 52W
Monte Azul 171 15 9S 42 53W
Monte Bello Is. 136 20 30S 115 45 E
Monte Carlo 45 43 46N 7 23 E
Monte Carmelo 171 18 43S 47 29W
Monte Caseros 172 30 10S 57 50W
Monte Comán 172 34 40S 68 0W
Monte Cristi 167 19 52N 71 39W
Monte Libano 16 8 5N 75 29W
Monte Lindo, R. 172 25 30S 58 40W
Monte Quemado 172 25 53S 62 41W
Monte Redondo 56 39 53N 8 50W
Monte San Savino 63 43 20N 11 42 E
Monte Sant' Angelo 65 41 42N 15 59 E
Monte Santo, C. di 64 40 5N 9 42 E
Monte Visto 161 37 40N 106 8W
Monteagudo 173 27 14S 54 8W
Montealegre 59 38 48N 1 17W
Montebello 150 45 40N 74 55W
Montebelluna 63 45 47N 12 3 E
Montebourg 42 49 30N 1 20W
Montecastrilli 63 42 40N 12 30 E
Montecatini Terme 62 43 55N 10 48 E
Montecito 163 34 26N 119 40W
Montecristi 174 1 0S 80 40W
Montecristo, I. 62 42 20N 10 20 E
Montefalco 63 42 53N 12 38 E
Montefiascone 63 42 31N 12 2 E
Montefrio 57 37 20N 3 39W
Montegnée 47 50 38N 5 31 E
Montego B. 166 18 30N 78 0W
Montegranaro 63 43 13N 13 38 E
Monteiro 170 7 22S 37 38W
Monteith 140 35 11S 139 23 E
Montejicar 59 37 33N 3 30W
Montejinnie 136 16 40S 131 45 E
Montekomu Hu 99 34 40N 89 0 E
Montelíbano 174 8 5N 75 29W
Montélimar 45 44 33N 4 45 E
Montella 65 40 50N 15 0 E
Montellano 57 36 59N 5 36W
Montello 158 43 49N 89 21W
Montelupo Fiorentino 62 43 44N 11 2 E
Montemór-o-Novo 57 38 40N 8 12W
Montemór-o-Velho 56 40 11N 8 40W
Montemorelos 165 25 11N 99 42W
Montendre 44 45 16N 0 26W
Montenegro 173 29 39S 51 29W
Montenegro □ 66 42 40N 19 20 E
Montenero di Bisaccia 63 42 0N 14 47 E
Montepuez 127 13 8S 38 59 E
Montepuez, R. 127 12 40S 40 15 E
Montepulciano 63 43 5N 11 46 E
Montereale 63 42 31N 13 13 E
Montereau 43 48 22N 2 57 E
Monterey 163 36 35N 121 57W
Monterey, B. 163 36 50N 121 55W
Montería 174 8 46N 75 53W
Monteros 172 27 11S 65 30W
Monterotondo 63 42 3N 12 36 E
Monterrey 164 25 40N 100 30W
Montes Altos 170 5 50S 47 4W
Montes Claros 171 16 30S 43 50W
Montes de Toledo 57 39 35N 4 30W
Montesano 160 47 0N 123 39W
Montesárchio 65 41 5N 14 37 E
Montescaglioso 65 40 34N 16 40 E
Montesilvano 63 42 30N 14 8 E
Montevarchi 63 43 30N 11 32 E
Monteverde 124 8 45S 16 45 E
Montevideo 173 34 50S 56 11W
Montezuma 158 41 32N 92 35W
Montfaucon, Haute-Loire, France 45 45 11N 4 20 E
Montfaucon, Meuse, France 43 49 16N 5 8 E
Montfort 47 51 7N 5 58 E
Montfort-l'Amaury 43 48 47N 1 49 E
Montfort-sur-Meu 42 48 8N 1 58W
Montgenèvre 45 44 56N 6 42 E
Montgomery, U.K. 31 52 34N 3 9W
Montgomery, Ala., U.S.A. 157 32 20N 86 20W
Montgomery, Pa., U.S.A. 162 41 10N 76 53W
Montgomery, W. Va., U.S.A. 156 38 9N 81 21W
Montgomery = Sahiwal 94 30 45N 73 8 E
Montgomery (□) 26 52 34N 3 9W
Montgomery Pass 163 37 58N 118 20W
Montguyon 44 45 12N 0 12W
Monthey 50 46 15N 6 56 E
Monticelli d'Ongina 62 45 3N 9 56 E
Monticello, Ark., U.S.A. 159 33 40N 91 48W
Monticello, Fla., U.S.A. 157 30 35N 83 50W
Monticello, Ind., U.S.A. 156 40 40N 86 45W
Monticello, Iowa, U.S.A. 158 42 18N 91 18W
Monticello, Ky., U.S.A. 157 36 52N 84 50W
Monticello, Minn., U.S.A. 158 45 17N 93 52W
Monticello, Miss., U.S.A. 159 31 35N 90 8W
Monticello, N.Y., U.S.A. 162 41 37N 74 42W
Monticello, Utah, U.S.A. 161 37 55N 109 27W
Montichiari 62 45 28N 10 29 E
Montieri 43 48 30N 4 45 E
Montignac 44 45 4N 1 10 E
Montignies-sur-Sambre 47 50 24N 4 29 E
Montigny-les-Metz 43 49 7N 6 10 E
Montigny-sur-Aube 43 47 57N 4 45 E
Montijo 57 38 52N 6 39W
Montijo, Presa de 57 38 55N 6 26W
Montilla 57 37 36N 4 40W
Montivideo 158 44 55N 95 40W
Montlhéry 43 48 39N 2 15 E
Montluçon 44 46 22N 2 36 E
Montmagny 151 46 58N 70 34W
Montmarault 53 46 11N 2 54 E
Montmartre 153 50 14N 103 27W
Montmédy 43 49 30N 5 20 E
Montmélian 45 45 30N 6 4 E
Montmirail 43 48 51N 3 30 E
Montmoreau-St.-Cybard 44 45 23N 0 8 E
Montmorency 151 46 53N 71 11W
Montmorillon 44 46 26N 0 50 E
Montmort 43 48 55N 3 49 E
Monto 138 24 52S 151 12 E
Montório al Vomano 63 42 35N 13 38 E
Montoro 57 38 1N 4 27W
Montour Falls 162 42 20N 76 51W
Montpelier, Idaho, U.S.A. 160 42 15N 111 29W
Montpelier, Ohio, U.S.A. 156 41 34N 84 40W
Montpelier, Vt., U.S.A. 156 44 15N 72 38W
Montpellier 44 43 37N 3 52 E
Montpezat-de-Quercy 44 44 15N 1 30 E
Montpon-Ménestrol 44 45 2N 0 11 E
Montréal, Can. 150 45 31N 73 34W
Montréal, France 44 43 13N 2 8 E
Montréal L. 153 54 20N 105 45W
Montreal Lake 153 54 3N 105 46W
Montredon-Labessonnié 44 43 45N 2 18 E
Montréjeau 44 43 6N 0 35 E
Montrésor 42 47 10N 1 10 E
Montreuil 43 50 27N 1 45 E
Montreuil-Bellay 42 47 8N 0 9W
Montreux 50 46 26N 6 55 E
Montrevault 42 47 17N 1 2W
Montrevel-en-Bresse 45 46 21N 5 8 E
Montrichard 42 47 20N 1 10 E
Montrose, U.K. 37 56 43N 2 28W
Montrose, Col., U.S.A. 161 38 30N 107 52W
Montrose, Pa., U.S.A. 162 41 50N 75 55W
Montrose, oilfield 19 57 20N 1 35 E
Montross 162 38 6N 76 50W
Monts, Pte des 151 49 27N 67 12W
Montsalvy 44 44 41N 2 30 E
Montsant, Sierra de 58 41 17N 0 1 E
Montsauche 43 47 13N 4 0 E
Montsech, Sierra del 58 42 0N 0 45 E
Montseny 58 42 29N 1 2 E
Montserrat, I. 167 16 40N 62 10W
Montserrat, mt. 58 41 36N 1 49 E
Montuenga 56 41 3N 4 38W
Montuiri 58 39 34N 2 59 E
Monveda 124 2 52N 21 30 E
Monymusk 37 57 13N 2 32W
Monyo 98 17 59N 95 30 E
Mônywa 98 22 7N 95 11 E
Monza 62 45 35N 9 15 E
Monze 127 16 17S 27 29 E
Monze, C. 94 24 47N 66 37 E
Monzón 58 41 52N 0 10 E
Mook 46 51 46N 5 54 E
Mo'oka 111 36 26N 140 1 E
Moolawatana 139 29 55S 139 45 E
Mooleulooloo 140 31 36S 140 32 E
Mooliabeenee 137 31 20S 116 2 E
Mooloogool 137 26 2S 119 5 E
Moomin, Cr. 139 29 44S 149 20 E
Moonah, R. 138 22 3S 138 33 E
Moonbeam 150 49 20N 82 10W
Mooncoin 39 52 18N 7 17W
Moonie 139 27 46S 150 20 E
Moonie, R. 139 27 45S 150 0 E
Moonta 140 34 6S 137 32 E
Moora 137 30 37S 115 58 E
Moorabeerree 138 25 13S 140 54 E
Moorarie 137 25 56S 117 35 E
Moorcroft 158 44 17N 104 58W
Moore, L. 137 29 50S 117 35 E
Moore, R. 137 31 22S 115 30 E
Moore Reefs 138 16 0S 149 5 E
Moore River Native Settlement 137 31 1S 115 56 E
Moorebank 47 33 56S 150 56 E
Moorefield 156 39 5N 78 59W
Mooresville 157 35 36N 80 45W
Moorfoot Hills 35 55 44N 3 8W
Moorhead 158 47 0N 97 0W
Moorland 141 31 46S 152 38 E
Mooroopna 141 36 25S 145 22 E
Moorpark 163 34 17N 118 53W
Moorreesburg 128 33 6S 18 38 E
Moorslede 47 50 54N 3 4 E
Moosburg 49 48 28N 11 57 E
Moose Factory 150 51 20N 80 40W
Moose I. 153 51 42N 97 10W
Moose Jaw 153 50 24N 105 30W
Moose Jaw R. 153 50 34N 105 18W
Moose Lake, Can. 153 53 43N 100 20W
Moose Lake, U.S.A. 158 46 27N 92 48W
Moose Mountain Cr. 153 49 13N 102 12W
Moose Mtn. Prov. Park 153 49 48N 102 25W
Moose, R. 150 51 20N 80 25W
Moose River 150 50 48N 81 17W
Moosehead L. 151 45 40N 69 40W
Moosomin 153 50 9N 101 40W
Moosonee 150 51 17N 80 39W
Moosup 162 41 44N 71 52W
Mopeia 125 17 30S 35 40 E
Mopipi 128 21 6S 24 55 E
Mopoi 123 5 6N 26 54 E
Moppin 139 29 12S 146 45 E
Mopti 120 14 30N 4 0W
Moqatta 123 14 38N 35 50 E
Moquegua 174 17 15S 70 46W
Mór 53 47 25N 18 12 E
Móra 57 38 55N 8 10W
Mora, Sweden 72 61 2N 14 38 E
Mora, Minn., U.S.A. 158 45 52N 93 19W
Mora, N. Mex., U.S.A. 161 35 58N 105 21W
Mora de Ebro 58 41 6N 0 38 E
Mora de Rubielos 58 40 15N 0 45W
Mora la Nueva 58 41 7N 0 39 E
Morača, R. 66 42 40N 19 20 E
Morada Nova 170 5 7S 38 23W
Morada Nova de Minas 171 18 37S 45 22W
Moradabad 94 28 50N 78 50 E
Morafenobe 129 17 50S 44 53 E
Morag 54 53 55N 19 56 E
Moral de Calatrava 59 38 51N 3 33W
Moraleja 56 40 6N 6 43W
Morales 174 2 45N 76 38W
Moramanga 125 18 56S 48 12 E
Moran, Kans., U.S.A. 159 37 53N 94 35W
Moran, Wyo., U.S.A. 160 43 53N 110 37W
Morano Cálabro 65 39 51N 16 8 E
Morant Cays 166 17 22N 76 0W
Morant Pt. 166 17 55N 76 12W
Morar 36 56 58N 5 49W
Morar L. 36 56 57N 5 40W
Moratalla 59 38 14N 1 49W
Moratuwa 97 6 45N 79 55 E
Morava, R. 53 49 50N 16 50 E
Moravatío 164 19 51N 100 25W
Moravia, Iowa, U.S.A. 158 40 50N 92 50W
Moravia, N.Y., U.S.A. 162 42 43N 76 25W
Moravian Hts. = Ceskemoravská V. 52 49 30N 15 40 E
Moravica, R. 66 43 40N 20 8 E
Moravice, R. 53 49 50N 17 43 E
Moravita 66 45 17N 21 14 E
Moravska Trebová 53 49 45N 16 40 E
Moravské Budějovice 52 49 4N 15 49 E
Morawa 137 29 13S 116 0 E
Morawhanna 174 8 30N 59 40W
Moray (□) 26 57 32N 3 25W
Moray Firth 37 57 50N 3 30W
Morbach 49 49 48N 7 7 E
Morbegno 62 46 8N 9 34 E
Morbihan □ 42 47 55N 2 50W
Morcenx 44 44 0N 0 55W
Mordelles 42 48 5N 1 52W
Morden 153 49 15N 98 10W
Mordovian S.S.R. □ 81 54 20N 44 30 E
Mordovo 81 52 13N 40 50 E
More L. 37 58 18N 4 52W
Møre og Romsdal □ 71 63 0N 9 0 E
Morea 140 36 45S 141 18 E
Moreau, R. 158 45 15N 102 45W
Morebattle 35 55 30N 2 20W
Morecambe 32 54 5N 2 52W
Morecambe B. 32 54 7N 3 0W
Morecambe, gasfield 19 53 57N 3 40W
Moree 139 29 28S 149 54 E
Morehead, P.N.G. 135 8 41S 141 41 E
Morehead, U.S.A. 156 38 12N 83 22W
Morehead City 157 34 46N 76 44W
Moreira 174 0 34S 63 26W
Morelia 164 19 40N 101 11W
Morella, Austral. 138 23 0S 143 47 E
Morella, Spain 58 40 35N 0 2 E
Morelos 164 26 42N 107 40W
Morelos □ 165 18 40N 99 10W
Morena, Sierra 57 38 20N 4 0W
Morenci 161 33 7N 109 20W
Moreni 70 44 59N 25 36 E
Moreno 171 8 7S 35 6W
Mores, I. 157 26 15N 77 35W
Moresby I. 152 52 30N 131 40W
Morestel 45 45 40N 5 28 E
Moret 43 48 22N 2 48 E
Moreton B. 133 27 10S 153 10 E
Moreton, I. 139 27 10S 153 25 E
Moreton-in-Marsh 28 51 59N 1 42W
Moreton Telegraph Office 138 12 22S 142 30 E
Moretonhampstead 30 50 39N 3 45W
Moreuil 43 49 46N 2 30 E
Morez 45 46 31N 6 2 E
Morgan, Austral. 140 34 0S 139 35 E
Morgan, U.S.A. 160 41 3N 111 44W
Morgan City 159 29 40N 91 15W
Morgan Hill 163 37 8N 121 39W
Morganfield 156 37 40N 87 55W
Morganton 157 35 46N 81 48W
Morgantown 156 39 39N 79 58W
Morganville, Queens., Austral. 139 25 10S 152 0 E
Morganville, S. Australia, Austral. 140 33 10S 140 32 E
Morgat 42 48 15N 4 32 E
Morgenzon 129 26 45S 29 36 E
Morges 50 46 31N 6 29 E
Morhange 43 48 55N 6 38 E
Mori 62 45 51N 10 59 E
Morialmée 47 50 17N 4 30 E
Morialta Falls Reserve 109 34 54S 138 43 E
Moriarty 161 35 3N 106 2W
Morice L. 152 53 50N 127 40W
Morichal 174 2 10N 70 34W
Morichal Largo, R. 174 8 55N 63 0W
Moriguchi 111 34 44N 135 34 E
Moriki 121 12 52N 6 30 E
Morinville 152 53 49N 113 41W
Morioka 112 39 45N 141 8 E
Moris 164 28 8N 108 32W
Morisset 141 33 6S 151 30 E
Morkalla 140 34 23S 141 10 E
Morlaàs 44 43 21N 0 18W
Morlaix 42 48 36N 3 52W
Morlanwelz 47 50 28N 4 15 E
Morley 33 53 45N 1 36W
Mormanno 65 39 53N 15 59 E
Mormant 43 48 37N 2 52 E
Morney 139 25 22S 141 23 E
Morningside 108 27 28S 153 4 E
Mornington, Victoria, Austral. 141 38 15S 145 5 E
Mornington, W. Australia, Austral. 136 17 31S 126 6 E
Mornington, Ireland 38 53 42N 6 17W
Mornington I. 138 16 30S 139 30 E
Mornington, I. 176 49 50S 75 30W
Mórnos, R. 69 38 30N 22 0 E
Moro 123 10 50N 30 9 E
Moro G. 103 6 30N 123 0 E
Morobe 135 7 49S 147 38 E
Morocco ■ 118 32 0N 5 50W
Morococha 174 11 40S 76 5W
Morogoro 126 6 50S 37 40 E
Morogoro □ 126 8 0S 37 0 E
Morokweng 125 26 12S 23 45 E
Moroleón 164 20 8N 101 32W
Morombé 129 21 45S 43 22 E
Moron 172 34 39S 58 37W
Morón 166 22 0N 78 30W
Morón de Almazán 58 41 29N 2 27W
Morón de la Frontera 57 37 6N 5 28W
Morondava 129 20 17S 44 17 E
Morondo 120 8 57N 6 47W
Morongo Valley 163 34 3N 116 37W
Moronou 120 6 16N 4 59W
Morotai, I. 103 2 10N 128 30 E
Moroto 124 2 28N 34 42 E
Moroto Summit, Mt. 126 2 30N 34 43 E
Morozov (Bratan), mt. 67 42 30N 25 10 E
Morozovsk 83 48 25N 41 50 E
Morpeth 35 55 11N 1 41W
Morrelganj 98 22 28N 89 51 E
Morrilton 159 35 10N 92 45W
Morrinhos, Ceara, Brazil 170 3 14S 40 7W
Morrinhos, Minas Gerais, Brazil 171 17 45S 49 10W
Morrinsville 142 37 40S 175 32 E
Morris, Can. 153 49 25N 97 22W
Morris, Ill., U.S.A. 156 41 20N 88 20W
Morris, Minn., U.S.A. 158 45 33N 95 56W
Morris, N.Y., U.S.A. 162 42 33N 75 15W
Morris, Mt. 137 26 9S 131 4 E
Morrisburg 150 44 55N 75 7W
Morrison 158 41 47N 90 0W
Morristown, Ariz., U.S.A. 161 33 54N 112 45W
Morristown, N.J., U.S.A. 162 40 48N 74 30W
Morristown, S.D., U.S.A. 158 45 57N 101 44W
Morristown, Tenn., U.S.A. 157 36 18N 83 20W
Morrisville, N.Y., U.S.A. 162 42 54N 75 39W
Morrisville, Pa., U.S.A. 162 40 13N 74 47W
Morro Agudo 171 20 44S 48 4W
Morro Bay 163 35 27N 120 54W
Morro do Chapéu 171 11 33S 41 9W
Morro, Pta. 172 27 6S 71 0W
Morros 170 2 52S 44 3W
Morrosquillo, Golfo de 167 9 35N 75 40W
Morrum 73 56 12N 14 45 E
Morrumbene 125 23 31S 35 16 E
Mors 73 56 50N 8 45 E
Morshank 81 53 28N 41 50 E
Mörsil 72 63 19N 13 40 E
Mortagne, Charente Maritime, France 44 45 28N 0 49W
Mortagne, Orne, France 42 48 30N 0 32 E
Mortagne, Vendée, France 42 46 59N 0 57W
Mortagne-au-Perche 42 48 31N 0 33 E
Mortagne, R. 43 48 30N 6 30 E
Mortain 42 48 40N 0 57W
Mortara 62 45 15N 8 43 E
Morte Bay 30 51 10N 4 13W
Morte Pt. 30 51 13N 4 14W
Morteau 43 47 3N 6 35 E
Mortehoe 30 51 21N 4 12W
Morteros 172 30 50S 62 0W
Mortes, R. das 171 11 45S 50 44W
Mortimer's Cross 28 52 17N 2 50W
Mortlake 140 38 5S 142 50 E
Morton, Tex., U.S.A. 159 33 39N 102 49W
Morton, Wash., U.S.A. 160 46 33N 122 17W
Morton Fen 29 52 45N 0 23W
Mortsel 47 51 11N 4 27 E
Morundah 141 34 57S 146 19 E
Moruya 141 35 58N 150 3 E
Morvan, Mts. du 43 47 5N 4 0 E

**Morven** **Mukden**

Morven, Austral. **139** 26 22S 147 5E
Morven, N.Z. **143** 44 50S 171 6E
Morven, dist. **34** 56 38N 5 44W
Morven, mt., Grampian, U.K. **37** 57 8N 3 1W
Morven, mt., Highland, U.K. **37** 58 15N 3 40W
Morvern **36** 56 38N 5 44W
Morwell **141** 38 10S 146 22E
Moryn **54** 52 51N 14 22E
Mosalsk **80** 54 30N 34 55E
Mosbach **49** 49 21N 9 9E
Mosciano Sant' Ángelo **63** 42 42N 13 52E
Moscos Is. **101** 14 0N 97 30E
Moscow, Idaho, U.S.A. **160** 46 45N 116 59W
Moscow, Pa., U.S.A. **162** 41 20N 75 31W
Moscow = Moskva **81** 55 45N 37 35E
Mosel, R. **49** 50 22N 7 36E
Moselle □ **43** 48 59N 6 33E
Moselle, R. **47** 50 22N 7 36E
Moses Lake **160** 47 16N 119 17W
Mosgiel **143** 45 53S 170 21E
Moshi **126** 3 22S 37 18E
Moshi □ **126** 3 22S 37 18E
Moshupa **128** 24 46S 25 29E
Mósina **54** 52 15N 16 50E
Mosjøen **74** 65 51N 13 12E
Moskenesøya **74** 67 58N 13 0E
Moskenstraumen **74** 67 47N 13 0E
Moskva **81** 55 45N 37 35E
Moskva, R. **81** 55 5N 38 51E
Moslavačka Gora **63** 45 40N 16 37E
Mošóenice **63** 45 17N 14 16E
Mosomane (Artesia) **128** 24 2S 26 19E
Mosonmagyaróvár **53** 47 52N 17 18E
Mo orin **66** 45 19N 20 4E
Mospino **82** 47 52N 38 0E
Mosquera **174** 2 35N 78 30W
Mosquero **159** 35 48N 103 57W
Mosqueruela **58** 40 21N 0 27W
Mosquitia **166** 15 20N 84 10W
Mosquitos, Golfo de los **166** 9 15N 81 10W
Moss **71** 59 27N 10 40E
Moss Vale **141** 34 32S 150 25E
Mossaka **124** 1 15S 16 45E
Mossâmedes, Angola **125** 15 7S 12 11E
Mossâmedes, Brazil **171** 16 7S 50 11W
Mossbank **153** 49 56N 105 56W
Mossburn **143** 45 41S 168 15E
Mosselbaai **128** 34 11S 22 8E
Mossendjo **124** 2 55S 12 42E
Mosses, Col des **50** 46 25N 7 7E
Mossgiel **140** 33 15S 144 30E
Mossley **32** 53 31N 2 1W
Mossman **138** 16 28S 145 23E
Mossoró **170** 5 10S 37 15W
Mossuril **127** 14 58S 40 42E
Mossy, R. **153** 54 5N 102 58W
Most **52** 50 31N 13 38E
Mostar **66** 43 22N 17 50E
Mostardas **173** 31 2S 50 51W
Mostefa, Rass **119** 36 55N 11 3E
Mosterøy **71** 59 5N 5 37E
Mostiska **80** 49 48N 23 4E
Mostrim **38** 53 42N 7 38W
Mosty **80** 53 27N 24 38E
Mostyn **31** 53 18N 3 14W
Mosul = Al Mawsil **92** 36 20N 43 5E
Mosulpo **107** 33 20N 126 17E
Mosvatn, L. **71** 59 52N 8 5E
Mota del Cuervo **58** 39 30N 2 52W
Mota del Marqués **56** 41 38N 5 11W
Motagua, R. **166** 15 44N 88 14W
Motala **73** 58 32N 15 1E
Motcombe **28** 51 1N 2 12W
Motegi **111** 36 32N 140 11E
Mothe-Achard, La **42** 46 37N 1 40W
Motherwell **35** 55 48N 4 0W
Motihari **95** 26 37N 85 1E
Motilla del Palancar **58** 39 34N 1 55W
Motnik **63** 46 14N 14 54E
Motocurunya **174** 4 24N 64 5W
Motovun **63** 45 20N 13 50E
Motozintea de Mendoza **165** 15 21N 92 14W
Motril **59** 36 44N 3 37W
Motrul, R. **70** 44 44N 22 59E
Mott **158** 46 25N 102 14W
Motte-Chalançon, La **45** 44 30N 5 21E
Motte, La **45** 44 20N 6 3E
Mottisfont **28** 51 22N 1 32W
Mottola **65** 40 38N 17 0E
Motueka **143** 41 7S 173 1E
Motul **165** 21 0N 89 20W
Motupena Pt. **135** 6 30S 155 10E
Mouchalagane, R. **151** 50 56N 68 41W
Moúdhros **68** 39 50N 25 18E
Moudjeria **120** 17 50N 12 15W
Moudon **50** 46 40N 6 49E
Mouila **124** 1 50S 11 0E
Moulamein **140** 35 3S 144 1E
Moule, Le **167** 16 20N 61 22W
Moulins **44** 46 35N 3 19E
Moulmein **98** 16 30N 97 40E
Moulmeingyun **98** 16 23N 95 16E
Moulouya, O. **118** 35 8N 2 22W
Moulton, U.K. **29** 52 17N 0 51W
Moulton, U.S.A. **159** 29 35N 97 8W
Moultrie **157** 31 11N 83 47W
Moultrie, L. **157** 33 25N 80 10W
Mound City, Mo., U.S.A. **158** 40 2N 95 25W
Mound City, S.D., U.S.A. **158** 45 46N 100 3W
Moúnda, Ákra **69** 38 5N 20 45E
Moundou **117** 8 40N 16 10E
Moundsville **156** 39 53N 80 43W
Moung **100** 12 46N 103 27E
Mount Airy **162** 36 31N 80 37W
Mount Amherst **136** 18 24S 126 58E
Mount Angel **160** 45 4N 122 46W
Mount Augustus **137** 24 20S 116 56E
Mount Barker, S.A., Austral. **140** 35 5S 138 52E
Mount Barker, W.A., Austral. **137** 34 38S 117 40E
Mount Barker Junc. **109** 35 1S 138 52E
Mount Beauty **141** 36 47S 147 10E
Mount Bellew Bridge **38** 53 28N 8 30W
Mount Buckley **138** 20 6S 148 0E
Mount Carmel, Ill., U.S.A. **156** 38 20N 87 48W
Mount Carmel, Pa., U.S.A. **162** 40 46N 76 25W
Mount Clemens **150** 42 35N 82 50W
Mount Coolon **138** 21 25S 147 25E
Mount Cootatha Park **108** 27 29S 152 57E
Mount Crosby **108** 27 32S 152 48E
Mount Darwin **125** 16 47S 31 38E
Mount Desert I. **151** 44 25N 68 25W
Mount Dora **157** 28 49N 81 32W
Mount Douglas **138** 21 35S 146 50E
Mount Edgecumbe **147** 57 8N 135 22W
Mount Elizabeth **136** 16 0S 125 50E
Mount Enid **136** 21 42S 116 26E
Mount Forest **150** 43 59N 80 43W
Mount Fox **138** 18 45S 145 45E
Mount Gambier **140** 37 50S 140 46E
Mount Garnet **138** 17 37S 145 6E
Mount Goldsworthy **132** 20 25S 119 39E
Mount Gravatt **108** 27 32S 153 5E
Mount Hagen **135** 5 52S 144 16E
Mount Hope, N.S.W., Austral. **141** 32 51S 145 51E
Mount Hope, S.A., Austral. **139** 34 7S 135 23E
Mount Hope, U.S.A. **156** 37 52N 81 9W
Mount Horeb **158** 43 0N 89 42W
Mount Howitt **139** 26 31S 142 16E
Mount Isa **138** 20 42S 139 26E
Mount Ive **140** 32 25S 136 5E
Mount Keith **137** 27 15S 120 30E
Mount Kisco **162** 41 12N 73 44W
Mount Laguna **163** 32 52N 116 25W
Mount Larcom **138** 23 48S 150 59E
Mount Lavinia **93** 6 50N 79 50E
Mount Lofty Ra. **133** 34 35S 139 5E
Mount McKinley Nat. Pk. **147** 64 0N 150 0W
Mount Magnet **137** 28 2S 117 47E
Mount Manara **140** 32 29S 143 58E
Mount Margaret **139** 26 54S 143 21E
Mount Maunganui **142** 37 40S 176 14E
Mount Monger **137** 31 0S 122 0E
Mount Morgan **138** 23 40S 150 25E
Mount Morris **156** 42 43N 77 50W
Mount Mulligan **138** 16 45S 144 47E
Mount Narryer **137** 26 30S 115 55E
Mount Newman **136** 23 18S 119 45E
Mount Nicholas **137** 22 54S 120 27E
Mount Oxide **138** 19 30S 139 29E
Mount Pearl **151** 47 31N 52 47W
Mount Penn **162** 40 20N 75 54W
Mount Perry **139** 25 13S 151 42E
Mount Phillips **137** 24 25S 116 15E
Mount Pleasant, Iowa, U.S.A. **158** 41 0N 91 35W
Mount Pleasant, Mich., U.S.A. **156** 43 35N 84 47W
Mount Pleasant, S.C., U.S.A. **157** 32 45N 79 48W
Mount Pleasant, Tenn., U.S.A. **157** 35 31N 87 11W
Mount Pleasant, Tex., U.S.A. **159** 33 5N 95 0W
Mount Pleasant, Ut., U.S.A. **160** 39 40N 111 29W
Mount Pocono **162** 41 8N 75 21W
Mount Rainier Nat. Park. **160** 46 50N 121 43W
Mount Revelstoke Nat. Park **152** 51 5N 118 30W
Mount Robson **152** 52 56N 119 15W
Mount Robson Prov. Park **152** 53 0N 119 0W
Mount Samson **108** 27 18S 152 51E
Mount Sandiman **137** 24 25S 115 30E
Mount Shasta **160** 41 20N 122 18W
Mount Somers **143** 43 45S 171 27E
Mount Sterling, Ill., U.S.A. **158** 40 0N 90 40W
Mount Sterling, Ky., U.S.A. **158** 38 0N 84 0W
Mount Surprise **138** 18 10S 144 17E
Mount Talbot **38** 53 31N 8 18W
Mount Tom Price **137** 22 50S 117 40E
Mount Upton **162** 42 26N 75 23W
Mount Vernon, Austral. **137** 24 15S 118 15E
Mount Vernon, D.C., U.S.A. **162** 38 47N 77 10W
Mount Vernon, Ill., U.S.A. **162** 38 17N 88 57W
Mount Vernon, Ind., U.S.A. **158** 38 17N 88 57W
Mount Vernon, N.Y., U.S.A. **156** 40 57N 73 49W
Mount Vernon, Ohio, U.S.A. **156** 40 20N 82 30W
Mount Vernon, Wash., U.S.A. **160** 48 27N 122 18W
Mount Victor **140** 32 11S 139 44E
Mount Whaleback **132** 23 18S 119 44E
Mount Willoughby **139** 27 58S 134 8E
Mountain Ash **31** 51 42N 3 22W
Mountain Center **163** 33 42N 116 44W
Mountain City, Nev., U.S.A. **160** 41 54N 116 0W
Mountain City, Tenn., U.S.A. **157** 36 30N 81 50W
Mountain Dale **162** 41 41N 74 32W
Mountain Grove **159** 37 5N 92 20W
Mountain Home, Ark., U.S.A. **159** 36 20N 92 25W
Mountain Home, Idaho, U.S.A. **160** 43 11N 115 45W
Mountain Iron **158** 47 30N 92 87W
Mountain Park. **152** 52 50N 117 15W
Mountain View, Ark., U.S.A. **159** 35 52N 92 10W
Mountain View, Calif., U.S.A. **161** 37 26N 122 5W
Mountain Village **147** 62 10N 163 50W
Mountainair **161** 34 35N 106 15W
Mountcharles **38** 54 37N 8 12W
Mountfield **38** 54 34N 7 10W
Mountmellick **39** 53 7N 7 20W
Mountnorris **38** 54 15N 6 29W
Mountnorris B. **136** 11 25S 132 45E
Mountrath **39** 53 0N 7 30W
Mounts Bay **30** 50 3N 5 27W
Mountsorrel **28** 52 43N 1 9W
Mountvernon **152** 48 25N 122 20W
Mouping **107** 37 24N 121 35E
Moura, Austral. **138** 24 35S 149 58E
Moura, Brazil **174** 1 25S 61 45W
Moura, Port. **57** 38 7N 7 30W
Mourão **57** 38 22N 7 22W
Mourdi, Depression du **117** 18 10N 23 0E
Mourdiah **120** 14 35N 7 25W
Moure, La **158** 46 27N 98 17W
Mourenx **44** 43 23N 0 36W
Mouri **121** 5 6N 1 14W
Mourilyan **138** 17 35S 146 3E
Mourmelon-le-Grand **43** 49 8N 4 22E
Mourne Mts. **38** 54 10N 6 0W
Mourne, R. **38** 54 45N 7 39W
Mouroubra **137** 29 42S 117 52E
Mourzouq **119** 25 53N 14 10W
Mousa I. **36** 60 0N 1 10W
Mouscron **47** 50 45N 3 12E
Moussoro **117** 13 50N 16 35E
Mouthe **43** 46 44N 6 12E
Moutier **50** 47 16N 7 21E
Moutiers **45** 45 29N 6 31E
Mouting **108** 25 22N 101 32E
Moutong **103** 0 28N 121 13E
Mouy **43** 49 18N 2 20E
Mouzáki **68** 39 25N 21 37E
Movas **164** 28 10N 109 25W
Moville **38** 55 11N 7 3W
Moxhe **47** 50 38N 5 5E
Moxotó, R. **170** 9 19S 38 14W
Moy, Inverness, U.K. **37** 57 22N 4 3W
Moy, Ulster, U.K. **38** 54 27N 6 40W
Moy, R. **38** 54 5N 8 50W
Moyagee **137** 27 48S 117 48E
Moyahua **164** 21 16N 103 10W
Moyale, Ethiopia **123** 3 34N 39 4E
Moyale, Kenya **126** 3 30N 39 0E
Moyamba **120** 8 15N 12 30W
Moyasta **39** 52 40N 9 31W
Moycullen **39** 53 20N 9 10W
Moyie **152** 49 17N 115 50W
Moyle □ **38** 55 10N 6 15W
Moylett **38** 53 57N 7 7W
Moynalty **38** 53 48N 6 52W
Moyne **39** 52 45N 7 43W
Moyobamba **174** 6 0S 77 0W
Moyvalley **38** 53 26N 6 55W
Moza **90** 31 48N 35 8E
Mozambique = Moçambique **125** 15 3S 40 42E
Mozambique ■ **129** 19 0S 35 0E
Mozambique Chan. **129** 20 0S 39 0E
Mozdok **83** 43 45N 44 48E
Mozhaisk **81** 55 30N 36 2E
Mozhga **84** 56 26N 52 15E
Mozirje **63** 46 22N 14 58E
Mozua **126** 3 57N 24 2E
Mozyr **80** 52 0N 29 15E
Mpanda **126** 6 23S 31 40E
Mpanda □ **126** 6 23S 31 40E
Mpésoba **120** 12 31N 5 39W
Mpika **127** 11 51S 31 25E
Mpraeso **121** 6 50N 0 50W
Mpulungu **127** 8 51S 31 5E
Mpwapwa **124** 6 30S 36 30E
Mpwapwa □ **126** 6 30S 36 20E
Mragowo **54** 53 57N 21 18E
Mrakovo **84** 52 43N 56 38E
Mramor **66** 43 20N 21 45E
Mrhaïer **119** 33 55N 5 58E
Mrimina **118** 29 50N 7 9W
Mrkonjió Grad **66** 44 26N 17 4E
Mrkopalj **63** 45 21N 14 52E
Mrocza **54** 53 16N 17 35E
Msab, Oued en **119** 32 35N 5 20E
Msaken **119** 35 49N 10 33E
M'Salu, R. **127** 12 25S 39 15E
Msambansovu, mt. **127** 15 50S 30 3E
M'sila **119** 35 46N 4 30E
Msoro **125** 13 35S 31 50E
Msta, R. **80** 58 30N 33 30E
Mstislavl **80** 54 0N 31 50E
Mszana Dolna **54** 49 41N 20 5E
Mszczonów **54** 51 58N 20 33E
Mtama **127** 10 17S 39 21E
Mtilikwe, R. **127** 21 0S 31 12E
Mtsensk **81** 53 25N 36 30E
Mtskheta **83** 41 52N 44 45E
Mtwara **124** 10 20S 40 20E
Mtwara □ **126** 1 0S 39 0E
Mtwara-Mikindani **127** 10 20S 40 20E
Mu Gia, Deo **100** 17 40N 105 47E
Mu Ness **36** 60 41N 0 50W
Mu, R. **98** 21 56N 95 38E
Muaná **170** 1 25S 49 15W
Muanda **124** 6 0S 12 20E
Muang Chiang Rai **100** 19 52N 99 50E
Muang Kalasin **101** 16 26N 103 30E
Muang Lampang **101** 18 16N 99 32E
Muang Lamphun **100** 18 40N 98 53E
Muang Nan **101** 18 52N 100 42E
Muang Phetchabun **101** 16 23N 101 12E
Muang Phichit **101** 16 29N 100 21E
Muang Ubon **101** 15 15N 104 50E
Muang Yasothon **101** 15 50N 104 10E
Muar **101** 2 3N 102 34E
Muar, R. **101** 2 15N 102 48E
Muarabungo **102** 1 40S 101 10E
Muaradjuloi **102** 0 12S 114 3E
Muaraenim **102** 3 40S 103 50E
Muarakaman **102** 0 2S 116 45E
Muaratebo **102** 1 30S 102 26E
Muaratembesi **102** 1 42S 103 2E
Muaratewe **102** 0 50S 115 0E
Mubairik **92** 23 22N 39 8E
Mubarakpur **95** 26 12N 83 24E
Mubende **126** 0 33N 31 22E
Mubi **121** 10 18N 13 16E
Mubur, P. **101** 3 20N 106 12E
Mucajaí, Serra do **174** 2 23N 61 10W
Much Dewchurch **28** 51 58N 2 45W
Much Marcle **28** 51 59N 2 27W
Much Wenlock **28** 52 36N 2 34W
Muchalls **37** 57 2N 2 10W
Mücheln **48** 51 18N 11 49E
Muchinga Mts. **127** 11 30S 31 30E
Muchkapskiy **81** 51 52N 42 28E
Mŭcin **70** 45 16N 28 8E
Muck, I. **36** 56 50N 6 15W
Muckadilla **139** 26 35S 148 23E
Muckle Roe I. **36** 60 22N 1 22W
Muckross Hd. **38** 54 37N 8 35W
Mucubela **129** 16 53S 37 49E
Mucugê **171** 13 5S 37 49E
Mucuri **171** 18 0S 40 0W
Mucurici **171** 18 6S 40 31W
Mud I. **108** 27 20S 153 14E
Mud L. **160** 40 15N 120 15W
Mudanya **82** 40 25N 28 50E
Muddy, R. **161** 38 30N 110 55W
Mudgee **141** 32 32S 149 31E
Mudhnib **92** 25 50N 44 18E
Mudjatik, R. **153** 56 1N 107 36W
Mudon **98** 16 15N 97 44E
Muecate **127** 14 55S 39 34E
Muêda **127** 11 36S 39 28E
Muela, La **58** 41 36N 1 7W
Mueller Ra., Mts. **136** 18 18S 126 46E
Muerto, Mar **165** 16 10N 94 10W
Muff **38** 55 4N 7 16W
Mufindi □ **127** 8 30S 35 20E
Mufou Shan **109** 29 15N 114 20E
Mufulira **127** 12 32S 28 15E
Mufumbiro Range **126** 1 25S 29 30E
Mugardos **56** 43 27N 8 15W
Muge **57** 39 3N 8 40W
Muge, R. **57** 39 15N 8 18W
Múggia **63** 45 36N 13 47E
Mugi **110** 33 40N 134 25E
Mugia **56** 43 3N 9 17W
Mugila, Mts. **126** 7 0S 28 50E
Muğla **92** 37 15N 28 28E
Múglizh **67** 42 37N 25 32E
Mugu **95** 29 45N 82 30E
Muhammad Qol **122** 20 53N 37 9E
Muhammad Râs **122** 27 50N 34 0E
Muhammadabad **95** 26 4N 83 25E
Muharraqa = Sa'ad **90** 31 28N 34 33E
Muhesi, R. **126** 6 40S 35 5E
Muheza □ **126** 5 0S 39 0E
Mühldorf **49** 48 14N 12 23E
Mühlhausen **48** 51 12N 10 29E
Mühlig-Hofmann-fjella **13** 72 30S 5 0E
Muhutwe **126** 1 35S 31 45E
Mui Bai Bung **101** 8 35N 104 42E
Mui Ron **101** 18 7N 106 27E
Muiden **46** 52 20N 5 4E
Muine Bheag **39** 52 42N 6 59W
Muiños **56** 41 58N 7 59W
Muir, L. **137** 34 30S 116 40E
Muir of Ord **37** 57 30N 4 35W
Muirdrum **35** 56 31N 2 40W
Muirkirk **35** 55 31N 4 6W
Muja **123** 12 2N 39 30E
Mukachevo **80** 48 27N 22 45E
Mukah **102** 2 55N 112 5E
Mukalla **91** 14 33N 49 2E
Mukawwa, Geziret **122** 23 55N 35 53E
Mukdahan **100** 16 32N 104 43E
Mukden = Shenyang **107** 41 48N 123 27E

**Mukeiras** **Nabari**


| | | | |
|---|---|---|---|
| Mukeiras | **91** | 13 59N | 45 52 E |
| Mukhtolovo | **81** | 55 29N | 43 15 E |
| Mukinbudin | **137** | 30 55 S | 118 5 E |
| Mukombwe | **127** | 15 48 S | 26 32 E |
| Mukomuko | **102** | 2 20 S | 101 10 E |
| Mukomwenze | **126** | 6 49 S | 27 15 E |
| Mukry | **85** | 37 54N | 65 12 E |
| Muktsar | **94** | 30 30N | 74 30 E |
| Muktsar Bhatinda | **94** | 30 15N | 74 57 E |
| Mukur | **94** | 32 50N | 67 50 E |
| Mukutawa, R. | **153** | 53 10N | 97 24W |
| Mukwela | **127** | 17 0 S | 26 40 E |
| Mula | **59** | 38 3N | 1 33W |
| Mula, R. | **96** | 19 16N | 74 20 E |
| Mulanay | **103** | 13 30N | 122 30 E |
| Mulange | **126** | 3 40 S | 27 10 E |
| Mulatas, Arch. de las | **166** | 6 51N | 78 31W |
| Mulchén | **172** | 37 45 S | 72 20W |
| Mulde, R. | **48** | 50 55N | 12 42 E |
| Mule Creek | **158** | 43 19N | 104 8W |
| Muleba | **126** | 1 50 S | 31 37 E |
| Muleba □ | **126** | 2 0 S | 31 30 E |
| Mulegé | **164** | 26 53N | 112 1W |
| Mulegns | **51** | 46 32N | 9 38 E |
| Mulengchen | **107** | 44 32N | 130 14 E |
| Muleshoe | **159** | 34 17N | 102 42W |
| Mulga Valley | **140** | 31 8 S | 141 3 E |
| Mulgathing | **139** | 30 15 S | 134 0 E |
| Mulgrave | **151** | 45 38N | 61 31W |
| Mulgrave I. | **135** | 10 5 S | 142 10 E |
| Mulhacén | **59** | 37 4N | 3 20W |
| Mülheim | **48** | 51 26N | 6 53W |
| Mulhouse | **43** | 47 40N | 7 20 E |
| Muli, China | **99** | 28 21N | 100 40 E |
| Muli, China | **108** | 27 50N | 101 15 E |
| Mull Head | **37** | 59 23N | 2 53W |
| Mull I. | **34** | 56 27N | 6 0W |
| Mull, Ross of, dist. | **34** | 56 20N | 6 15W |
| Mull, Sound of | **34** | 56 30N | 5 50W |
| Mullagh | **39** | 53 13N | 8 25W |
| Mullaghareirk Mts. | **39** | 52 20N | 9 10W |
| Mullaittvu | **97** | 9 15N | 80 55 E |
| Mullardoch L. | **36** | 57 30N | 5 0W |
| Mullen | **158** | 42 5N | 101 0W |
| Mullengudgery | **141** | 31 43 S | 147 29 E |
| Mullens | **156** | 37 34N | 81 22W |
| Muller, Pegunungan | **102** | 0 30N | 113 30 E |
| Muller Ra. | **138** | 5 30 S | 143 0 E |
| Mullet Pen. | **38** | 54 10N | 10 2W |
| Mullewa | **137** | 28 29 S | 115 30 E |
| Mullheim | **49** | 47 48N | 7 37 E |
| Mulligan, R. | **138** | 26 40 S | 139 0 E |
| Mullin | **159** | 31 33N | 98 38W |
| Mullinahone | **39** | 52 30N | 7 31W |
| Mullinavat | **39** | 52 23N | 7 10W |
| Mullingar | **38** | 53 31N | 7 20W |
| Mullins | **157** | 34 12N | 79 15W |
| Mullion | **30** | 50 1N | 5 15W |
| Mullsjö | **73** | 57 56N | 13 55 E |
| Mullumbimby | **139** | 28 30 S | 153 30 E |
| Mulobezi | **127** | 16 45 S | 25 7 E |
| Mulrany | **38** | 53 54N | 9 47W |
| Mulroy B. | **38** | 55 15N | 7 45W |
| Mulshi L. | **96** | 18 30N | 73 20 E |
| Multai | **96** | 21 39N | 78 15 E |
| Multan | **94** | 30 15N | 71 30 E |
| Multan □ | **94** | 30 29N | 72 29 E |
| Multrå | **72** | 63 10N | 17 24 E |
| Mulumbe, Mts. | **127** | 8 40 S | 27 30 E |
| Mulungushi Dam | **127** | 14 48 S | 28 48 E |
| Mulvane | **159** | 37 30N | 97 15W |
| Mulwad | **122** | 18 45N | 30 39 E |
| Mulwala | **141** | 35 59 S | 146 0 E |
| Mumbles | **31** | 51 34N | 4 0W |
| Mumbles Hd. | **31** | 51 33N | 4 0W |
| Mumbwa | **125** | 15 0 S | 27 0 E |
| Mumeng | **135** | 7 1 S | 146 37 E |
| Mumra | **83** | 45 45N | 47 41 E |
| Mun | **101** | 15 17N | 103 0 E |
| Mun, R. | **100** | 15 19N | 105 30 E |
| Muna, I. | **103** | 5 0 S | 122 30 E |
| Muna Sotuta | **165** | 20 29N | 89 43W |
| Munawwar | **95** | 32 47N | 74 27 E |
| Münchberg | **49** | 50 11N | 11 48 E |
| Müncheberg | **48** | 52 30N | 14 9 E |
| München | **49** | 48 8N | 11 33 E |
| Munchen-Gladbach = Mönchengladbach | **48** | 51 12N | 6 23 E |
| Muncho Lake | **152** | 59 0N | 125 50W |
| Munchŏn | **107** | 39 14N | 127 19 E |
| Münchwilen | **51** | 47 38N | 8 59 E |
| Muncie | **156** | 40 10N | 85 20W |
| Mundakayam | **97** | 9 30N | 76 32 E |
| Mundala, Puncak | **103** | 4 30 S | 141 0 E |
| Mundare | **152** | 53 35N | 112 20W |
| Munday | **159** | 33 26N | 99 39W |
| Münden | **48** | 51 25N | 9 42 E |
| Mundesley | **29** | 52 53N | 1 24 E |
| Mundiwindi | **136** | 23 47 S | 120 9 E |
| Mundo Novo | **171** | 11 50 S | 40 29W |
| Mundo, R. | **59** | 38 30N | 2 15W |
| Mundra | **94** | 22 54N | 69 26 E |
| Mundrabilla | **137** | 31 52 S | 127 51 E |
| Munera | **59** | 39 2N | 2 29W |
| Muneru, R. | **96** | 16 45N | 80 3 E |
| Mungallala | **139** | 26 25 S | 147 34 E |
| Mungallala Cr. | **139** | 28 53 S | 147 5 E |
| Mungana | **138** | 17 8 S | 144 27 E |
| Mungaoli | **94** | 24 24N | 78 7 E |
| Mungari | **127** | 17 12 S | 33 42 E |
| Mungbere | **124** | 2 36N | 28 28 E |
| Mungindi | **139** | 28 58 S | 149 1 E |
| Munhango | **125** | 12 10 S | 18 38 E |
| Munhango R. | **125** | 11 30 S | 19 30 E |
| Munich = München | **49** | 48 8N | 11 35 E |
| Munising | **156** | 46 25N | 86 39W |
| Munjiye | **122** | 18 47N | 41 20W |
| Munka-Ljungby | **73** | 56 16N | 12 58 E |
| Munkedal | **73** | 58 28N | 11 40 E |
| Munkfors | **72** | 59 50N | 13 30 E |
| Muñoz Gamero, Pen. | **176** | 52 30 S | 73 5 E |
| Munro | **141** | 37 56 S | 147 11 E |
| Munroe L. | **153** | 59 13N | 98 35W |
| Munsan | **107** | 37 51N | 126 48 E |
| Munshiganj | **98** | 23 33N | 90 32 E |
| Münsingen | **50** | 46 52N | 7 32 E |
| Munster | **43** | 48 2N | 7 8 E |
| Münster, Niedersachsen, Ger. | **48** | 52 59N | 10 5 E |
| Münster, Nordrhein-Westfalen, Ger. | **48** | 51 58N | 7 37 E |
| Münster, Switz. | **51** | 46 30N | 8 17 E |
| Munster □ | **39** | 52 20N | 8 40W |
| Muntadgin | **137** | 31 45 S | 118 33 E |
| Muntele Mare | **70** | 46 30N | 23 12 E |
| Muntok | **102** | 2 5 S | 105 10 E |
| Muon Pak Beng | **101** | 19 51N | 101 4 E |
| Muong Beng | **100** | 20 23N | 101 46 E |
| Muong Boum | **100** | 22 24N | 102 49 E |
| Muong Er | **100** | 20 49N | 104 1 E |
| Muong Hai | **100** | 21 3N | 101 49 E |
| Muong Hiem | **100** | 20 5N | 103 22 E |
| Muong Houn | **100** | 20 8N | 101 23 E |
| Muong Hung | **100** | 20 56N | 103 53 E |
| Muong Kau | **100** | 15 6N | 105 47 E |
| Muong Khao | **100** | 19 47N | 103 29 E |
| Muong Khoua | **100** | 21 5N | 102 31 E |
| Muong La | **101** | 20 52N | 102 5 E |
| Muong Liep | **100** | 18 29N | 101 40 E |
| Muong May | **100** | 14 49N | 106 56 E |
| Muong Ngeun | **100** | 20 36N | 101 3 E |
| Muong Ngoi | **100** | 20 43N | 102 41 E |
| Muong Nhie | **100** | 22 12N | 102 28 E |
| Muong Nong | **100** | 16 22N | 106 30 E |
| Muong Ou Tay | **100** | 22 7N | 101 48 E |
| Muong Oua | **100** | 18 18N | 101 20 E |
| Muong Pak Bang | **100** | 19 54N | 101 8 E |
| Muong Penn | **100** | 20 13N | 103 52 E |
| Muong Phalane | **100** | 16 39N | 105 34 E |
| Muong Phieng | **100** | 19 6N | 101 32 E |
| Muong Phine | **100** | 16 32N | 106 2 E |
| Muong Sai | **100** | 20 42N | 101 59 E |
| Muong Saiapoun | **100** | 18 24N | 101 31 E |
| Muong Sen | **100** | 19 24N | 104 8 E |
| Muong Sing | **100** | 21 11N | 101 9 E |
| Muong Son | **100** | 20 27N | 103 19 E |
| Muong Soui | **100** | 19 33N | 102 52 E |
| Muong Va | **100** | 21 53N | 102 19 E |
| Muong Xia | **100** | 20 19N | 104 50 E |
| Muonio | **74** | 67 57N | 23 40 E |
| Muonio älv | **74** | 67 48N | 23 25 E |
| Muotathal | **51** | 46 58N | 8 46 E |
| Muotohora | **142** | 38 18 S | 177 40 E |
| Mupa | **125** | 16 5 S | 15 50 E |
| Muqaddam, Wadi | **123** | 17 0N | 32 0 E |
| Mur-de-Bretagne | **42** | 48 12N | 3 0W |
| Mur, R. | **52** | 47 7N | 13 55 E |
| Mura, R. | **63** | 46 37N | 16 9 E |
| Murallón, Cuerro | **176** | 49 55 S | 73 30W |
| Muralto | **51** | 46 11N | 8 49 E |
| Muranda | **126** | 1 52 S | 29 20 E |
| Murang'a | **126** | 0 45 S | 37 9 E |
| Murashi | **81** | 59 30N | 49 0 E |
| Murat | **44** | 45 7N | 2 53 E |
| Murau | **52** | 47 6N | 14 10 E |
| Muravera | **64** | 39 25N | 9 35 E |
| Murça | **56** | 41 24N | 7 28W |
| Murchison | **143** | 41 49 S | 172 21 E |
| Murchison Downs | **137** | 26 45 S | 118 55 E |
| Murchison Falls = Kabarega Falls | **126** | 2 15N | 31 38 E |
| Murchison House | **137** | 27 39 S | 114 14 E |
| Murchison Mts. | **143** | 45 13 S | 167 23 E |
| Murchison, oilfield | **19** | 61 25N | 1 40 E |
| Murchison, R. | **137** | 26 45 S | 116 15 E |
| Murchison Ra. | **138** | 20 0 S | 134 10 E |
| Murchison Rapids | **127** | 15 55 S | 34 35 E |
| Murcia | **59** | 38 2N | 1 10W |
| Murcia □ | **59** | 37 50N | 1 30W |
| Murdo | **158** | 43 56N | 100 43W |
| Murdoch Pt. | **138** | 14 37 S | 144 55 E |
| Murdock Hill | **109** | 34 59 S | 138 55 E |
| Mure, La | **45** | 44 55N | 5 48 E |
| Mureş □ | **70** | 46 45N | 24 40 E |
| Mureşul, R. | **70** | 46 15N | 20 13 E |
| Muret | **44** | 43 30N | 1 20 E |
| Murfatlar | **70** | 44 10N | 28 26 E |
| Murfreesboro | **157** | 35 50N | 86 21W |
| Murg | **51** | 47 8N | 9 13 E |
| Murgab | **85** | 38 10N | 73 59 E |
| Murgeni | **70** | 46 12N | 28 1 E |
| Murgenthal | **50** | 47 16N | 7 50 E |
| Murgon | **139** | 26 15 S | 151 54 E |
| Murgoo | **137** | 27 24 S | 116 28 E |
| Muri | **51** | 47 17N | 8 21 E |
| Muriaé | **173** | 21 8 S | 42 23W |
| Murias de Paredes | **56** | 42 52N | 6 19W |
| Murici | **170** | 9 19 S | 35 56W |
| Muriel Mine | **127** | 17 14 S | 30 40 E |
| Muritiba | **171** | 12 55 S | 39 15W |
| Murits see | **48** | 53 25N | 12 40 E |
| Murjo Mt. | **103** | 6 36 S | 110 53 E |
| Murka | **126** | 3 27 S | 38 0 E |
| Murmansk | **78** | 68 57N | 33 10 E |
| Murmerwoude | **46** | 53 18N | 6 0 E |
| Murnau | **49** | 47 40N | 11 11 E |
| Muro, France | **45** | 42 34N | 8 54 E |
| Muro, Spain | **58** | 39 45N | 3 3 E |
| Muro, C. di | **45** | 41 44N | 8 37 E |
| Muro Lucano | **65** | 40 45N | 15 30 E |
| Murom | **81** | 55 35N | 42 3 E |
| Muroran | **112** | 42 25N | 141 0 E |
| Muros | **56** | 42 45N | 9 5W |
| Muros y de Noya, Ria de | **56** | 42 45N | 9 0W |
| Muroto | **110** | 33 18N | 134 9 E |
| Muroto-Misaki | **110** | 33 15N | 134 10 E |
| Murowana Gośślina | **54** | 52 35N | 17 0 E |
| Murphy | **160** | 43 11N | 116 33W |
| Murphys | **163** | 38 8N | 120 28W |
| Murphysboro | **159** | 37 50N | 89 20W |
| Murrat | **122** | 18 51N | 29 33 E |
| Murray, Ky., U.S.A. | **157** | 36 40N | 88 20W |
| Murray, Utah, U.S.A. | **160** | 40 41N | 111 58W |
| Murray Bridge | **140** | 35 6 S | 139 14 E |
| Murray Downs | **138** | 21 4 S | 134 40 E |
| Murray Harb. | **151** | 46 0N | 62 28W |
| Murray, L., P.N.G. | **135** | 7 0 S | 141 35 E |
| Murray, L., U.S.A. | **157** | 34 8N | 81 30W |
| Murray, R., S. Australia, Austral. | **140** | 35 20 S | 139 22 E |
| Murray, R., W. Australia, Austral. | **133** | 32 33 S | 115 45 E |
| Murray, R., Can. | **152** | 56 11N | 120 45W |
| Murraysburg | **128** | 31 58 S | 23 47 E |
| Murree | **94** | 33 56N | 73 28 E |
| Murrieta | **163** | 33 33N | 117 13W |
| Murrin Murrin | **137** | 28 50 S | 121 45 E |
| Murrough | **39** | 53 7N | 9 18W |
| Murrumbidgee, R. | **140** | 34 40 S | 143 0 E |
| Murrumburrah | **141** | 34 32 S | 148 22 E |
| Murrurundi | **141** | 31 42 S | 150 51 E |
| Murshid | **122** | 21 40N | 31 10 E |
| Murshidabad | **95** | 24 11N | 88 19 E |
| Murska Sobota | **63** | 46 39N | 16 12 E |
| Murtazapur | **96** | 20 40N | 77 25 E |
| Murten | **50** | 46 56N | 6 7 E |
| Murten-see | **50** | 46 56N | 7 4 E |
| Murtle L. | **152** | 52 8N | 119 38W |
| Murtoa | **140** | 36 35 S | 142 28 E |
| Murton | **33** | 54 51N | 1 22W |
| Murtosa | **56** | 40 44N | 8 40W |
| Muru | **123** | 6 36N | 29 16 E |
| Murungu | **126** | 4 12 S | 31 10 E |
| Murupara | **142** | 38 28 S | 176 42 E |
| Murwara | **95** | 23 46N | 80 28 E |
| Murwillumbah | **139** | 28 18 S | 153 27 E |
| Mürz, R. | **52** | 47 30N | 15 25 E |
| Mürzzuschlag | **52** | 47 36N | 15 41 E |
| Muş | **92** | 38 45N | 41 30 E |
| Musa, Gebel (Sinai) | **122** | 28 32N | 33 59 E |
| Musa Khel | **94** | 30 29N | 69 52 E |
| Musa Qala (Musa Kala) | **93** | 32 20N | 64 50 E |
| Musa, R. | **135** | 9 3 S | 148 55 E |
| Musaffargarh | **93** | 30 10N | 71 10 E |
| Musairik, Wadi | **122** | 19 30N | 43 10 E |
| Musala, I. | **102** | 1 41N | 98 28 E |
| Musalla, mt. | **67** | 42 13N | 23 37 E |
| Musan | **107** | 42 12N | 129 12 E |
| Musangu | **127** | 10 28 S | 23 55 E |
| Musasa | **126** | 3 25 S | 31 30 E |
| Musashino | **111** | 35 42N | 139 34 E |
| Muscat = Masqat | **93** | 23 37N | 58 36 E |
| Muscat & Oman = Oman | **91** | 23 0N | 58 0 E |
| Muscatine | **158** | 41 25N | 91 5W |
| Musel | **56** | 43 34N | 5 42W |
| Musetula | **127** | 14 28 S | 24 1 E |
| Musgrave Ras. | **137** | 26 0 S | 132 0 E |
| Mushie | **124** | 2 56 S | 17 4 E |
| Mushin | **121** | 6 32N | 3 21 E |
| Musi, R., India | **96** | 17 10N | 79 25 E |
| Musi, R., Indon. | **102** | 2 55 S | 103 40 E |
| Muskeg, R. | **152** | 60 20N | 123 20W |
| Muskegon | **156** | 43 15N | 86 17W |
| Muskegon Hts. | **156** | 43 12N | 86 17W |
| Muskegon, R. | **156** | 43 25N | 86 0W |
| Muskogee | **159** | 35 50N | 95 25W |
| Muskwa, R. | **152** | 58 47N | 122 48W |
| Musmar | **122** | 18 6N | 35 40 E |
| Musofu | **127** | 13 30 S | 29 0 E |
| Musoma | **126** | 1 30 S | 33 48 E |
| Musoma □ | **126** | 1 50 S | 34 30 E |
| Musquaro, L. | **151** | 50 38N | 61 5W |
| Musquodoboit Harbour | **151** | 44 50N | 63 9W |
| Mussau I. | **135** | 1 30 S | 149 40 E |
| Musselburgh | **35** | 55 57N | 3 3W |
| Musselkanaal | **46** | 52 57N | 7 0 E |
| Musselshell, R. | **160** | 46 30N | 108 15W |
| Mussidan | **44** | 45 2N | 0 22 E |
| Mussomeli | **64** | 37 35N | 13 43 E |
| Musson | **47** | 49 33N | 5 42 E |
| Mussooree | **94** | 30 27N | 78 6 E |
| Mussuco | **128** | 17 2 S | 19 3 E |
| Mustafa Kemalpaşa | **92** | 40 3N | 28 25 E |
| Mustajidda | **92** | 26 30N | 41 50 E |
| Mustang | **95** | 29 10N | 83 55 E |
| Mustapha, C. | **119** | 36 55N | 11 3 E |
| Musters, L. | **176** | 45 20 S | 69 25W |
| Musudan | **107** | 40 50N | 129 43 E |
| Muswellbrook | **141** | 32 16 S | 150 56 E |
| Muszyna | **53** | 49 22N | 20 55 E |
| Mût | **122** | 25 28N | 28 58 E |
| Mut | **92** | 36 40N | 33 28 E |
| Mutan Chiang, R. | **107** | 46 18N | 129 31 E |
| Mutanchiang | **107** | 44 40N | 129 35 E |
| Mutanda, Mozam. | **129** | 21 0 S | 33 34 E |
| Mutanda, Zambia | **127** | 12 15 S | 26 13 E |
| Muthill | **35** | 56 20N | 3 50W |
| Mutis | **174** | 1 4N | 77 25W |
| Mutooroo | **140** | 32 26 S | 140 55 E |
| Mutshatsha | **127** | 10 35 S | 24 20 E |
| Mutsu-Wan | **112** | 41 5N | 140 55 E |
| Muttaburra | **138** | 22 38 S | 144 29 E |
| Muttama | **141** | 34 46 S | 148 8 E |
| Mutton Bay | **151** | 50 50N | 59 2W |
| Mutton I. | **39** | 52 50N | 9 31W |
| Mutuáli | **127** | 14 55 S | 37 0 E |
| Mutung | **108** | 29 35N | 106 51 E |
| Mutunópolis | **171** | 13 40 S | 49 15W |
| Muvatupusha | **97** | 9 53N | 76 35 E |
| Muxima | **124** | 9 25 S | 13 52 E |
| Muy, Le | **45** | 43 28N | 6 34 E |
| Muy Muy | **166** | 12 39N | 85 36W |
| Muya | **77** | 56 27N | 115 39 E |
| Muyaga | **126** | 3 14 S | 30 33 E |
| Muyunkum, Peski | **85** | 44 12N | 71 0 E |
| Muzaffarabad | **95** | 34 25N | 73 30 E |
| Muzaffargarh | **94** | 30 5N | 71 14 E |
| Muzaffarnagar | **94** | 29 26N | 77 40 E |
| Muzaffarpur | **95** | 26 7N | 85 32 E |
| Muzhi | **76** | 65 25N | 64 40 E |
| Muzillac | **42** | 47 35N | 2 30W |
| Muzkol, Khrebet | **85** | 38 22N | 73 20 E |
| Muzo | **174** | 5 32N | 74 6W |
| Muzon C. | **152** | 54 40N | 132 40W |
| Mvôlô | **123** | 6 10N | 29 53 E |
| Mwadui | **126** | 3 35 S | 33 40 E |
| Mwandi Mission | **127** | 17 30 S | 24 51 E |
| Mwango | **126** | 6 48 S | 24 12 E |
| Mwanza, Katanga, Congo | **126** | 7 55 S | 26 43 E |
| Mwanza, Kwango, Congo | **127** | 5 29 S | 17 43 E |
| Mwanza, Malawi | **126** | 16 58 S | 24 28 E |
| Mwanza, Tanz. | **126** | 2 30 S | 32 58 E |
| Mwanza □ | **126** | 2 0 S | 33 0 E |
| Mwaya | **126** | 9 32 S | 33 55 E |
| Mweelrea, Mt. | **38** | 53 37N | 9 48W |
| Mweka | **124** | 4 50 S | 21 40 E |
| Mwenga | **126** | 3 1 S | 28 21 E |
| Mwepo | **127** | 11 50 S | 26 10 E |
| Mweru, L. | **127** | 9 0 S | 29 0 E |
| Mweza Range | **127** | 21 0 S | 30 0 E |
| Mwimbi | **127** | 8 38 S | 31 39 E |
| Mwinilunga | **127** | 11 43 S | 24 25 E |
| Mwinilunga, Mt. | **127** | 11 43 S | 24 25 E |
| My Tho | **101** | 10 29N | 106 23 E |
| Mya, O. | **119** | 30 46N | 4 44 E |
| Myadh | **124** | 1 16N | 13 10 E |
| Myanaung | **98** | 18 25N | 95 10 E |
| Myaungmya | **98** | 16 30N | 95 0 E |
| Mybster | **37** | 58 27N | 3 24W |
| Myddfai | **31** | 51 59N | 3 47W |
| Myddle | **28** | 52 49N | 2 47W |
| Myerstown | **162** | 40 22N | 76 18W |
| Myingyan | **98** | 21 30N | 95 30 E |
| Myitkyina | **98** | 25 30N | 97 26 E |
| Myittha, R. | **98** | 16 15N | 94 34 E |
| Myjava | **53** | 48 41N | 17 37 E |
| Mylor | **109** | 35 3 S | 138 46 E |
| Mymensingh | **98** | 24 45N | 90 24 E |
| Myndmere | **158** | 46 23N | 97 7W |
| Mynydd Bach, Hills | **31** | 52 16N | 4 6W |
| Mynydd Eppynt, Mts. | **31** | 52 4N | 3 30W |
| Mynydd Prescelly, mt. | **31** | 51 57N | 4 48W |
| Mynzhilgi, Gora | **85** | 43 48N | 68 51 E |
| Myogi | **101** | 21 24N | 96 28 E |
| Myrdal | **71** | 60 43N | 7 10 E |
| Mýrdalsjökull | **74** | 63 40N | 19 6W |
| Myrrhee | **136** | 36 46 S | 146 17 E |
| Myrtle Beach | **157** | 33 43N | 78 50W |
| Myrtle Creek | **160** | 43 0N | 123 19W |
| Myrtle Point | **160** | 43 0N | 124 4W |
| Myrtleford | **141** | 36 34 S | 146 44 E |
| Myrtletown | **108** | 27 23 S | 153 8 E |
| Mysen | **71** | 59 33N | 11 20 E |
| Myslenice | **54** | 49 51N | 19 57 E |
| Myslibórz | **54** | 52 55N | 14 50 E |
| Mysłowice | **54** | 50 15N | 19 12 E |
| Mysore | **97** | 12 17N | 76 41 E |
| Mysore □ = Karnataka | **142** | 13 15N | 77 0 E |
| Mystic | **162** | 41 21N | 71 58W |
| Mystishchi | **81** | 55 50N | 37 50 E |
| Myszkow | **54** | 50 45N | 19 22 E |
| Mythen | **51** | 47 2N | 8 42 E |
| Myton | **160** | 40 10N | 110 2W |
| Mývatn | **74** | 65 36N | 17 0W |
| Mze, R. | **52** | 49 47N | 12 50 E |
| Mzimba | **127** | 11 48 S | 33 33 E |
| Mzuzu | **127** | 11 30 S | 33 55 E |


## N


| | | | |
|---|---|---|---|
| N' Dioum | **120** | 16 31N | 14 39W |
| Na-lang | **98** | 22 42N | 97 33 E |
| Na Noi | **100** | 18 19N | 100 43 E |
| Na Phao | **100** | 17 35N | 105 44 E |
| Na Sam | **100** | 22 3N | 106 37 E |
| Na San | **100** | 21 12N | 104 2 E |
| Naaldwijk | **46** | 51 59N | 4 13 E |
| Naalehu | **147** | 19 4N | 155 35W |
| Na'am | **123** | 9 42N | 28 27 E |
| Na'an | **90** | 31 53N | 34 52 E |
| Naantali | **75** | 60 29N | 22 2 E |
| Naarden | **46** | 52 18N | 5 9 E |
| Naas | **39** | 53 12N | 6 40W |
| Nababeep | **128** | 29 36 S | 17 46 E |
| Nabadwip | **95** | 23 34N | 88 20 E |
| Nabari | **111** | 34 37N | 136 5 E |

Nabas Nashville


Nabas 103 11 47N 122 6 E
Nabberu, L. 137 25 30 S 120 30 E
Naberezhnyye Chelny 84 55 42N 52 19 E
Nabesna 147 62 33N 143 10W
Nabeul 119 36 30N 10 51 E
Nabha 94 30 26N 76 14 E
Nabi Rubin 90 31 56N 34 44 E
Nabire 103 3 15 S 136 27 E
Nabisar 94 25 8N 69 40 E
Nabispi, R. 151 50 14N 62 13W
Nabiswera 126 1 27N 32 15 E
Nablus = Nābulus 90 32 14N 35 15 E
Naboomspruit 129 24 32 S 28 40 E
Nābulus 90 32 14N 35 15 E
Nabúri 127 16 53 S 38 59 E
Nacala-Velha 127 14 32 S 40 34 E
Nacaome 166 13 31N 87 30W
Nacaroa 127 14 22 S 39 56 E
Naches 160 46 48N 120 49W
Nachikatsuura 111 33 33N 135 58 E
Nachingwea 127 10 49 S 38 49 E
Nachingwea □ 127 10 30 S 38 30 E
Nachna 94 27 34N 71 41 E
Náchod 53 50 25N 16 8 E
Nacimento Res. 163 35 46N 120 53W
Nacka 72 59 17N 18 12 E
Nackara 140 32 48 S 139 12 E
Naco, Mexico 164 31 20N 109 56W
Naco, U.S.A. 161 31 24N 109 58W
Nacogdoches 159 31 33N 95 30W
Nácori Chico 164 29 39N 109 1W
Nacozari 164 30 30N 109 50W
Nadi 122 18 40N 33 41 E
Nadiad 94 22 41N 72 56 E
Nador 118 35 14N 2 58W
Nadushan 93 32 2N 53 35 E
Nadvornaya 80 48 40N 24 35 E
Nadym 76 63 35N 72 42 E
Nadym, R. 76 65 30N 73 0 E
Nærbø 71 58 40N 5 39 E
Næstved 73 55 13N 11 44 E
Nafada 121 11 8N 11 20 E
Näfels 51 47 6N 9 4 E
Nafferton 33 54 1N 0 24W
Naft Shāh 92 34 0N 45 30 E
Nafūd ad Dahy 92 22 0N 45 0 E
Nafūsah, Jabal 119 32 12N 12 30 E
Nag Hammâdi 122 26 2N 32 18 E
Naga 103 13 38N 123 15 E
Naga Hills 99 26 0N 94 30 E
Naga, Kreb en 118 24 12N 6 0W
Naga-Shima, Kagoshima, Japan 110 32 10N 130 9 E
Naga-Shima, Yamaguchi, Japan 110 33 55N 132 5 E
Nagagami, R. 150 49 40N 84 40W
Nagahama, Ehime, Japan 111 33 36N 132 29 E
Nagahama, Shiga, Japan 111 35 23N 136 16 E
Nagai Parkar 94 24 28N 70 46 E
Nagaland □ 98 26 0N 94 30 E
Nagambie 141 36 47 S 145 10 E
Nagano 111 36 40N 138 10 E
Nagano-ken □ 111 36 15N 138 0 E
Nagaoka 112 37 27N 138 50 E
Nagappattinam 97 10 46N 79 51 E
Nagar Parkar 93 24 30N 70 35 E
Nagara-Gawa, R. 111 35 1N 136 43 E
Nagari Hills 97 15 30N 79 45 E
Nagarjuna Sagar 96 16 35N 79 17 E
Nagasaki 110 32 47N 129 50 E
Nagasaki-ken □ 110 32 50N 129 40 E
Nagato 110 34 19N 131 5 E
Nagaur 94 27 15N 73 45 E
Nagbhir 96 20 34N 79 42 E
Nagchu Dzong 99 31 22N 91 54 E
Nagercoil 97 8 12N 77 33 E
Nagina 95 29 30N 78 30 E
Nagineh 93 34 20N 57 15 E
Nagold 49 48 38N 8 40 E
Nagoorin 138 24 17 S 151 15 E
Nagorsk 81 59 18N 50 48 E
Nagorum 126 4 1N 34 33 E
Nagoya 111 35 10N 136 50 E
Nagpur 96 21 8N 79 10 E
Nagrong 99 32 46N 84 16 E
Nagua 167 19 23N 69 50W
Nagyatád 53 46 14N 17 22 E
Nagyecsed 53 47 53N 22 24 E
Nagykanizsa 53 46 28N 17 0 E
Nagykörös 53 46 55N 19 48 E
Nagyléta 53 47 23N 21 55 E
Naha 112 26 13N 127 42 E
Nahalal 90 32 41N 35 12 E
Nahanni Butte 152 61 2N 123 20W
Nahanni Nat. Pk. 152 61 15N 125 0W
Naharayim 90 32 28N 35 33 E
Nahariyya 90 33 1N 35 5 E
Nahāvand 92 34 10N 48 30 E
Nahe, R. 49 49 48N 7 33 E
Nahf 90 32 56N 35 18 E
Nahîya, Wadi 122 27 37N 32 0 E
Nahlin 152 58 55N 131 38W
Nahud 122 18 12N 41 40 E
Naiapu 70 44 12N 25 47 E
Naicá 164 27 53N 105 31W
Naicam 153 52 30N 104 30W
Na'ifah 91 19 59N 50 46 E
Naila 49 50 19N 11 43 E
Nailsea 28 51 25N 2 44W
Nailsworth 28 51 41N 2 12W
Nain 151 56 34N 61 40W
Na'in 93 32 54N 53 0 E
Naini Tal 95 29 23N 79 30 E
Nainpur 93 22 30N 80 10 E
Naintré 42 46 46N 0 29 E
Naira, I. 103 4 28 S 130 0 E
Nairn 37 57 35N 3 54W
Nairn (□) 26 57 28N 3 52W
Nairn R. 37 57 32N 3 58W
Nairobi 126 1 17 S 36 48 E
Naivasha 126 0 40 S 36 30 E
Naivasha □ 126 0 40 S 36 30 E
Naivasha L. 126 0 48 S 36 20 E
Najac 44 44 14N 1 58 E
Najafābād 93 32 40N 51 15 E
Najd 92 26 30N 42 0 E
Nájera 58 42 26N 2 48W
Najerilla, R. 58 42 15N 2 45W
Najibabad 94 29 40N 78 20 E
Najin 107 42 12N 130 15 E
Naju 107 35 3N 126 43 E
Naka-Gawa, R. 111 36 20N 140 36 E
Naka-no-Shima 112 29 51N 129 46 E
Nakalagba 126 2 50N 27 58 E
Nakama 110 33 56N 130 43 E
Nakaminato 111 36 21N 140 36 E
Nakamura 110 33 0N 133 0 E
Nakanai Mts. 135 5 40 S 151 0 E
Nakano 111 36 45N 138 22 E
Nakanojō 111 36 35N 138 51 E
Nakatane 112 30 31N 130 57 E
Nakatsu 110 33 40N 131 15 E
Nakatsugawa 111 35 29N 137 30 E
Nakelele Pt. 147 21 2N 156 35W
Nakfa 123 16 40N 38 25 E
Nakhichevan, A.S.S.R. □ 79 39 14N 45 30 E
Nakhl 122 29 55N 33 43 E
Nakhl Mubarak 92 24 10N 38 10 E
Nakhodka 77 43 10N 132 45 E
Nakhon Nayok 100 14 12N 101 13 E
Nakhon Pathom 100 13 49N 100 3 E
Nakhon Phanom 100 17 23N 104 43 E
Nakhon Ratchasima (Khorat) 100 14 59N 102 12 E
Nakhon Sawan 100 15 35N 100 10 E
Nakhon Si Thammarat 100 8 29N 100 0 E
Nakhon Thai 100 17 17N 100 50 E
Nakina, B.C., Can. 152 59 12N 132 52W
Nakina, Ont., Can. 150 50 10N 86 40W
Nakło n. Noteoja 54 53 9N 17 38 E
Naknek 147 58 45N 157 0W
Nakodar 94 31 8N 75 31 E
Nakomis 127 39 19N 89 19W
Nakskov 73 54 50N 11 8 E
Näkten 72 62 48N 14 38 E
Naktong, R. 107 35 7N 128 57 E
Nakur 94 30 2N 77 32 E
Nakuru 126 0 15 S 35 5 E
Nakuru □ 126 0 15 S 35 5 E
Nakuru, L. 126 0 23 S 36 5 E
Nakusp 152 50 20N 117 45W
Nal, R. 94 27 0N 65 50 E
Nalchik 83 43 30N 43 33 E
Nälden 72 63 21N 14 14 E
Näldsjön 72 63 25N 14 15 E
Nalerigu 121 10 35N 0 25W
Nalgonda 96 17 6N 79 15 E
Nalhati 95 24 17N 87 52 E
Nalinnes 47 50 19N 4 27 E
Nallamalai Hills 97 15 30N 78 50 E
Nalón, R. 56 43 35N 6 10W
Nālūt 119 31 54N 11 0 E
Nam Can 101 8 46N 104 59 E
Nam Dinh 100 20 25N 106 5 E
Nam Du, Hon 101 9 41N 104 21 E
'Nam', gasfields 19 53 17N 3 36 E
Nam Ngum 100 18 35N 102 34 E
'Nam', oilfield 19 54 50N 4 40 E
Nam-Phan 101 10 30N 106 0 E
Nam Phong 100 16 42N 102 52 E
Nam Tha 100 20 58N 101 30 E
Nam Tok 100 14 14N 99 4 E
Nam Tso = Namu Hu 105 30 45N 90 30 E
Namacurra 125 17 30 S 36 50 E
Namakkal 97 11 13N 78 13 E
Namaland, Africa 128 26 0 S 18 0 E
Namaland, S. Afr. 128 30 0 S 18 0 E
Namangan 85 41 0N 71 40 E
Namapa 127 13 43 S 39 50 E
Namasagali 126 1 2N 33 0 E
Namatanai 135 3 40 S 152 29 E
Nambala 120 14 1N 5 58W
Namber 103 1 2 S 134 57 E
Nambour 139 26 32 S 152 58 E
Nambucca Heads 141 30 37 S 153 0 E
Namcha Barwa 105 29 40N 95 10 E
Namche Bazar 95 27 51N 86 47 E
Namchonjŏm 107 38 15N 126 26 E
Namêche 47 50 28N 5 0 E
Namecund 127 14 54 S 37 37 E
Nameh 102 2 34N 116 21 E
Nameponda 127 15 50 S 39 50 E
Namerikawa 111 36 46N 137 20 E
Nåmestovo 53 49 24N 19 25 E
Nametil 127 15 40 S 39 15 E
Náměšt nad Oslavou 53 49 12N 16 10 E
Namew L. 153 54 14N 101 56W
Namhsan 98 22 48N 97 42 E
Nami 101 6 2N 100 46 E
Namib Desert = Namib Woestyn 128 22 30 S 15 0 E
Namib-Woestyn 128 22 30 S 15 0 E
Namibia □ 128 22 0 S 18 9 E
Namiquipa 164 29 15N 107 25W
Namja Pass 95 30 0N 82 25 E
Namkhan 98 23 50N 97 41 E
Namlea 103 3 10 S 127 5 E
Namoi, R. 141 30 12 S 149 30 E
Namous, O. 118 30 44N 0 18W
Nampa 160 43 40N 116 40W
Nampula 127 15 6 S 39 7 E
Namrole 103 3 46 S 126 46 E
Namsen 74 64 27N 11 42 E
Namsen, R. 74 64 40N 12 45 E
Namsos 74 64 28N 11 0 E
Namtu 98 23 5N 97 28 E
Namtumbo 127 10 30 S 36 4 E
Namu 152 51 52N 127 41W
Namu Hu 105 30 45N 90 30 E
Namur 47 50 27N 4 52 E
Namur □ 47 50 17N 5 0 E
Namutoni 128 18 49 S 16 55 E
Namwala 127 15 44 S 26 30 E
Namwŏn 107 35 23N 127 23 E
Namysłow 54 51 6N 17 42 E
Nan 100 18 48N 100 46 E
Nan Ling 109 25 0N 112 30 E
Nan, R. 100 15 42N 100 9 E
Nan Shan 105 38 30N 99 0 E
Nana 70 44 17N 26 34 E
Nānā, W. 119 30 0N 15 24 E
Nanaimo 152 49 10N 124 0W
Nanam 107 41 44N 129 40 E
Nan'an 109 24 58N 118 23 E
Nanango 139 26 40 S 152 0 E
Nanao 109 23 26N 117 1 E
Nanch'ang 109 28 40N 115 50 E
Nanchang, Fukien, China 109 24 26N 117 18 E
Nanchang, Hupei, China 109 31 47N 111 42 E
Nanch'eng 109 27 33N 116 35 E
Nancheng = Hanchung 106 33 10N 107 2 E
Nanchiang 108 32 21N 106 50 E
Nanchiao 108 22 2N 100 15 E
Nanchien 106 25 5N 100 30 E
Nanching 109 32 3N 118 47 E
Nanchishan Liehtao 108 27 28N 121 4 E
Nanch'uan 108 29 7N 107 16 E
Nanch'ung 108 30 50N 106 4 E
Nancy 43 48 42N 6 12 E
Nanda Devi, Mt. 95 30 30N 80 30 E
Nandan 110 34 10N 134 42 E
Nander 96 19 10N 77 20 E
Nandewar Ra. 139 30 15 S 150 35 E
Nandi □ 126 0 15N 35 0 E
Nandikotkur 97 15 52N 78 18 E
Nandura 96 20 52N 76 25 E
Nandurbar 96 21 20N 74 15 E
Nandyal 97 15 30N 78 30 E
Nanfeng 109 27 10N 116 24 E
Nanga 137 26 7 S 113 45 E
Nanga Eboko 121 4 41N 12 22 E
Nanga Parbat, mt. 95 35 10N 74 35 E
Nangade 127 11 5 S 39 36 E
Nangapinoh 102 0 20 S 111 14 E
Nangarhar □ 93 34 20N 70 0 E
Nangatajap 102 1 32 S 110 34 E
Nangeya Mts. 126 3 30N 33 30 E
Nangis 43 48 33N 3 0 E
Nangodi 121 10 58N 0 42W
Nangola 120 12 41N 6 35W
Nangwarry 140 37 33 S 140 48 E
Nanhsien 109 29 22N 112 25 E
Nanhsiung 109 25 10N 114 18 E
Nanhua 108 25 10N 101 20 E
Nanhui 109 31 3N 121 46 E
Nani Hu 109 31 10N 118 55 E
Nanjangud 97 12 6N 76 43 E
Nanjeko 127 5 31 S 23 30 E
Nanjirinji 127 9 41 S 39 5 E
Nankana Sahib 94 31 27N 73 38 E
Nank'ang 109 25 38N 114 45 E
Nanking = Nanching 109 32 5N 118 45 E
Nankoku 110 33 29N 133 38 E
Nankung 106 37 22N 115 20 E
Nanling 109 30 56N 118 19 E
Nannine 137 26 51 S 118 18 E
Nanning 108 22 48N 108 20 E
Nannup 137 33 59 S 115 48 E
Nanpa 108 32 13N 104 51 E
Nanp'an Chiang, R. 108 25 0N 106 11 E
Nanpara 95 27 52N 81 33 E
Nanp'i 106 38 4N 116 34 E
Nanp'ing, Fukien, China 109 26 38N 118 10 E
Nanp'ing, Hupeh, China 109 29 55N 112 2 E
Nanpu 108 31 19N 106 2 E
Nanripe 127 13 52 S 38 52 E
Nansei-Shotō 112 26 0N 128 0 E
Nansen Sd. 12 81 0N 91 0W
Nansio 126 2 3 S 33 4 E
Nanson 137 28 35 S 114 45 E
Nant 44 44 1N 3 18 E
Nantes 42 47 12N 1 33W
Nanteuil-le-Haudouin 43 49 9N 2 48 E
Nantiat 44 46 1N 1 11 E
Nanticoke 162 41 12N 76 1W
Nanticoke, R. 162 38 16N 75 56W
Nanton, Can. 152 50 21N 113 46W
Nanton, China 108 24 59N 107 32 E
Nantua 45 46 10N 5 35 E
Nantucket 162 41 17N 70 6W
Nantucket I. 155 41 16N 70 3W
Nantucket Sd. 162 41 30N 70 15W
Nant'ung 109 32 0N 120 55 E
Nantwich 32 53 5N 2 31W
Nanuque 171 17 50 S 40 21W
Nanutarra 136 22 32 S 115 30 E
Nanyang 106 33 0N 112 32 E
Nan'yō 110 34 3N 131 49 E
Nanyüan 106 39 48N 116 24 E
Nanyuki 126 0 2N 37 4 E
Nao, C. de la 59 38 44N 0 14 E
Nao Chou Tao 109 20 55N 110 35 E
Nao, La, Cabo de 59 38 44N 0 14 E
Naococane L. 151 52 50N 70 45W
Naogaon 98 24 52N 88 52 E
Napa 163 38 18N 122 17W
Napa, R. 163 38 10N 122 19W
Napamute 147 61 30N 158 45W
Napanee 150 44 15N 77 0W
Napanoch 162 41 44N 74 2W
Nape 100 18 18N 105 6 E
Nape Pass = Keo Neua, Deo 100 18 23N 105 10 E
Napf 50 47 1N 7 56 E
Napiéolédougou 120 9 18N 5 35W
Napier 142 39 30 S 176 56 E
Napier Broome B. 136 14 2 S 126 37 E
Napier Downs 136 17 11 S 124 36 E
Napier Pen. 138 12 4 S 135 43 E
Naples 157 26 10N 81 45W
Naples = Nápoli 65 40 50N 14 5 E
Nap'o 108 23 44N 106 49 E
Napo □ 174 0 30 S 77 0W
Napo, R. 174 3 5 S 73 0W
Napoleon, N. Dak., U.S.A. 158 46 32N 99 49W
Napoleon, Ohio, U.S.A. 156 41 24N 84 7W
Nápoli 65 40 50N 14 5 E
Nápoli, G. di 65 40 40N 14 10 E
Napopo 126 4 15N 28 0 E
Napoule, La 45 43 31N 6 56 E
Nappa 32 53 58N 2 14W
Nappa Merrie 139 27 36 S 141 7 E
Naqâda 122 25 53N 32 42 E
Nara, Japan 111 34 40N 135 49 E
Nara, Mali 120 15 25N 7 20W
Nara, Canal 94 26 0N 69 20 E
Nara-ken □ 111 34 30N 136 0 E
Nara Visa 159 35 39N 103 10W
Naracoorte 140 36 58 S 140 45 E
Naradhan 141 33 34 S 146 17 E
Narasapur 96 16 26N 81 50 E
Narasaropet 96 16 14N 80 4 E
Narathiwat 101 6 40N 101 55 E
Narayanganj 98 23 31N 90 33 E
Narayanpet 96 16 45N 77 30 E
Narberth 31 51 48N 4 45W
Narbonne 44 43 11N 3 0 E
Narborough 28 52 34N 1 12W
Narcea, R. 56 43 15N 6 30W
Nardò 65 40 10N 18 0 E
Nare Head 30 50 12N 4 55W
Narembeen 137 32 7 S 118 17 E
Naretha 137 31 0 S 124 45 E
Nari, R. 94 29 10N 67 50 E
Narin 93 36 5N 69 0 E
Narinda, B. de 129 14 55 S 47 30 E
Narino □ 174 1 30N 78 0W
Narita 111 35 47N 140 19 E
Narmada, R. 94 22 40N 77 30 E
Narnaul 94 28 5N 76 11 E
Narni 63 42 30N 12 30 E
Naro, Ghana 120 10 22N 2 27W
Naro, Italy 64 37 18N 13 48 E
Naro Fominsk 81 55 23N 36 32 E
Narodnaya, G. 78 65 5N 60 0 E
Narok 126 1 20 S 33 30 E
Narok □ 126 1 20 S 33 30 E
Narón 56 43 32N 8 9W
Narooma 141 36 14 S 150 4 E
Narowal 94 32 6N 74 52 E
Narrabri 139 30 19 S 149 46 E
Narran, R. 139 28 37 S 148 12 E
Narrandera 141 34 42 S 146 31 E
Narraway, R. 152 55 44N 119 55W
Narrogin 137 32 58 S 117 14 E
Narromine 141 32 12 S 148 12 E
Narrows, str. 36 57 20N 6 5W
Narsampet 96 17 57N 79 58 E
Narsinghpur 95 22 54N 79 14 E
Naruto 110 34 11N 134 37 E
Narutō 111 35 36N 140 25 E
Naruto-Kaikyō 110 34 14N 134 39 E
Narva 80 59 10N 28 5 E
Narva, R. 80 59 10N 27 50 E
Narvik 74 68 28N 17 26 E
Narvskoye Vdkhr. 80 59 10N 28 5 E
Narwana 94 29 39N 76 6 E
Naryan-Mar 78 68 0N 53 0 E
Naryilco 139 28 37 S 141 53 E
Narym 76 59 0N 81 58 E
Narymskoye 76 49 10N 84 15 E
Naryn 85 41 26N 75 58 E
Naryn, R. 85 40 52N 71 36 E
Nasa 74 66 29N 15 23 E
Nasa, mt. 74 66 32N 15 23 E
Nasarawa 121 8 32N 7 41 E
Naseby, N.Z. 143 45 1 S 170 10 E
Naseby, U.K. 29 52 24N 0 59W
Naser, Buheirat en 122 23 0N 32 30 E
Nash Pt. 31 51 24N 3 34W
Nashua, Iowa, U.S.A. 158 42 55N 92 34W
Nashua, Mont., U.S.A. 160 48 10N 106 25W
Nashua, N.H., U.S.A. 162 42 50N 71 25W
Nashville, Ark., U.S.A. 159 33 56N 93 50W

**Nashville** **Nevillé-Pont-Pierre**


| | | | |
|---|---|---|---|
| Nashville, Ga., U.S.A. | **157** | 31 13N | 83 15W |
| Nashville, Tenn., U.S.A. | **157** | 36 12N | 86 46W |
| Našice | **66** | 45 32N | 18 4E |
| Nasielsk | **54** | 52 35N | 20 50E |
| Nasik | **96** | 20 2N | 73 50E |
| Nasirabad, Bangla. | **95** | 24 42N | 90 30E |
| Nasirabad, India | **94** | 26 15N | 74 45E |
| Nasirabad, Pak. | **96** | 28 25N | 68 25E |
| Naskaupi, R. | **151** | 53 47N | 60 51W |
| Naso | **65** | 38 8N | 14 46E |
| Nass, R. | **152** | 55 0N | 129 40W |
| Nassau, Bahamas | **166** | 25 0N | 77 30W |
| Nassau, U.S.A. | **162** | 42 30N | 73 34W |
| Nassau, Bahia | **176** | 55 20S | 68 0W |
| Nasser City = Kôm Ombo | **122** | 24 25N | 32 52E |
| Nasser, L. = Naser, Buheiret en | **122** | 23 0N | 32 30E |
| Nassian | **120** | 7 58N | 2 57W |
| Nässjö | **73** | 57 38N | 14 45E |
| Nastopoka Is. | **150** | 57 0N | 77 0W |
| Näsum | **73** | 56 10N | 14 29E |
| Näsviken | **72** | 61 46N | 16 52E |
| Nata, Bots. | **128** | 20 7S | 26 4E |
| Nata, China | **100** | 19 37N | 109 17E |
| Nata, Si Arab. | **92** | 27 15N | 48 35E |
| Nata, Tanz. | **125** | 2 0S | 34 25E |
| Natagaima | **174** | 3 37N | 75 6W |
| Natal, Brazil | **170** | 5 47S | 35 13W |
| Natal, Can. | **152** | 49 43N | 114 51W |
| Natal, Indon. | **102** | 0 35N | 99 0E |
| Natal □ | **129** | 28 30S | 30 30E |
| Natalinci | **66** | 44 15N | 20 49E |
| Natanz | **93** | 33 30N | 51 55E |
| Natashquan | **151** | 50 14N | 61 46W |
| Natashquan Pt. | **151** | 50 8N | 61 40W |
| Natashquan, R. | **151** | 50 7N | 61 50W |
| Natchez | **159** | 31 35N | 91 25W |
| Natchitoches | **159** | 31 47N | 93 4W |
| Naters | **50** | 46 19N | 8 0E |
| Nathalia | **141** | 36 1S | 145 7E |
| Nathdwara | **94** | 24 55N | 73 50E |
| Natick | **162** | 42 16N | 71 19W |
| Natih | **93** | 22 25N | 56 30E |
| Natimuk | **140** | 36 42S | 142 0E |
| Nation, R. | **152** | 55 30N | 123 32W |
| National City | **163** | 32 45N | 117 7W |
| National Mills | **153** | 52 52N | 101 40W |
| Natitingou | **121** | 10 20N | 1 26E |
| Natividad, I. de | **164** | 27 50N | 115 10W |
| Natkyizin | **101** | 14 57N | 97 59E |
| Natogyi | **98** | 21 25N | 95 39E |
| Natoma | **158** | 39 14N | 99 0W |
| Natron L. | **126** | 2 20S | 36 0E |
| Natrûn, W. el. | **122** | 30 25N | 30 0E |
| Natuna Besar, Kepulauan | **101** | 4 0N | 108 15E |
| Natuna Selatan, Kepulauan | **101** | 2 45N | 109 0E |
| Naturaliste, C. | **132** | 33 32S | 115 0E |
| Naturaliste C. | **138** | 40 50S | 148 15E |
| Naturaliste Channel | **137** | 25 20S | 113 0E |
| Natya | **140** | 34 57S | 143 13E |
| Nau | **85** | 40 9N | 69 22E |
| Nau-Nau | **128** | 18 57S | 21 4E |
| Nau Qala | **94** | 34 5N | 68 5E |
| Naubinway | **150** | 46 7N | 85 27W |
| Naucelle | **44** | 44 13N | 2 20E |
| Nauders | **52** | 46 54N | 10 30E |
| Nauen | **48** | 52 36N | 12 52E |
| Naujoji Vilnia | **80** | 54 48N | 25 27E |
| Naumburg | **48** | 51 10N | 11 48E |
| Nauru I. | **130** | 0 25N | 166 0E |
| Naurzum | **84** | 51 32N | 64 34E |
| Naushahra | **93** | 34 0N | 72 0E |
| Nauta | **174** | 4 20S | 73 35W |
| Nautanwa | **99** | 27 20N | 83 25E |
| Nautla | **165** | 20 20N | 96 50W |
| Nava | **164** | 28 25N | 100 46W |
| Nava del Rey | **56** | 41 22N | 5 6W |
| Navacerrada, Puerto de | **56** | 40 47N | 4 0W |
| Navahermosa | **57** | 39 41N | 4 28W |
| Navalcarnero | **56** | 40 17N | 4 5W |
| Navalmoral de la Mata | **56** | 39 52N | 5 16W |
| Navalvillar de Pela | **57** | 39 9N | 5 24W |
| Navan = An Uaimh | **38** | 53 39N | 6 40W |
| Navarino, I. | **176** | 55 0S | 67 30W |
| Navarra □ | **58** | 42 40N | 1 40W |
| Navarre | **44** | 43 15N | 1 20E |
| Navarreux | **44** | 43 20N | 0 47W |
| Navasota | **159** | 30 20N | 96 5W |
| Navassa I. | **167** | 18 30N | 75 0W |
| Nave | **62** | 45 35N | 10 17E |
| Navenby | **33** | 53 7N | 0 32W |
| Naver L. | **37** | 58 18N | 4 20W |
| Naver, R. | **37** | 58 34N | 4 15W |
| Navia | **56** | 43 24N | 6 42W |
| Navia de Suarna | **56** | 42 58N | 6 59W |
| Navia, R. | **56** | 43 15N | 6 50W |
| Navidad | **172** | 33 57S | 71 50W |
| Navlya | **80** | 52 53N | 34 15E |
| Navoi | **85** | 40 9N | 65 22E |
| Navojoa | **164** | 27 0N | 109 30W |
| Navolato | **164** | 24 47N | 107 42W |
| Navolok | **78** | 62 33N | 39 57E |
| Návpaktos | **69** | 38 23N | 21 42E |
| Návplion | **69** | 37 33N | 22 50E |
| Navrongo | **121** | 10 57N | 0 58W |
| Navsari | **96** | 20 57N | 72 59E |
| Nawa Kot | **94** | 28 21N | 71 24E |
| Nawabganj | **98** | 24 35N | 81 14E |
| Nawabganj, Bara Banki | **95** | 26 56N | 81 14E |
| Nawabganj, Bareilly | **95** | 28 32N | 79 40E |
| Nawabshah | **94** | 26 15N | 68 25E |
| Nawada | **95** | 24 50N | 85 25E |
| Nawakot | **95** | 28 0N | 85 10E |
| Nawalgarh | **96** | 27 50N | 75 15E |
| Nawansnahr | **95** | 32 33N | 74 48E |
| Nawapara | **95** | 20 52N | 82 33E |
| Nawi | **122** | 18 32N | 30 50E |
| Nawng Hpa | **98** | 21 52N | 97 52E |
| Náxos | **69** | 37 8N | 25 25E |
| Náxos, I. | **69** | 37 5N | 25 30E |
| Nay | **44** | 43 10N | 0 18W |
| Nay Band | **93** | 27 20N | 52 40E |
| Naya | **174** | 3 13N | 77 22W |
| Naya, R. | **174** | 3 13N | 77 22W |
| Nayakhan | **77** | 62 10N | 159 0E |
| Nayarit □ | **164** | 22 0N | 105 0W |
| Nayé | **120** | 14 28N | 12 12W |
| Nayung | **108** | 26 50N | 105 17E |
| Nazaré, Bahia, Brazil | **171** | 13 0S | 39 0W |
| Nazaré, Goiás, Brazil | **170** | 6 23S | 47 40W |
| Nazaré, Port. | **57** | 39 36N | 9 4W |
| Nazaré Antônio de Jesus | **171** | 13 2S | 39 0W |
| Nazaré da Mata | **171** | 7 44S | 35 14W |
| Nazareth, Israel | **90** | 32 42N | 35 17E |
| Nazareth, U.S.A. | **162** | 40 44N | 75 19W |
| Nazas | **164** | 25 10N | 104 0W |
| Nazas, R. | **164** | 25 20N | 104 4W |
| Naze | **112** | 28 22N | 129 27E |
| Naze, The | **29** | 51 43N | 1 19E |
| Nazeret | **123** | 8 45N | 39 15E |
| Nazir Hat | **98** | 22 35N | 91 55E |
| Nazko | **152** | 53 1N | 123 37W |
| Nazko, R. | **152** | 53 7N | 123 34W |
| Nchacoongo | **129** | 24 20S | 35 9E |
| Nchanga | **127** | 12 30S | 27 49E |
| Ncheu | **127** | 14 50S | 34 37E |
| Ndala | **126** | 4 45S | 33 23E |
| Ndali | **121** | 9 50N | 2 46E |
| Ndareda | **126** | 4 12S | 35 30E |
| Ndélé | **117** | 8 25N | 20 36E |
| Ndendeé | **124** | 2 29S | 10 46E |
| Ndjamena | **117** | 12 4N | 15 8E |
| Ndjolé | **124** | 0 10S | 10 45E |
| Ndola | **127** | 13 0S | 28 34E |
| Ndoto Mts. | **126** | 2 0N | 37 0E |
| Ndrhamcha, Sebkra de | **120** | 18 30N | 15 55W |
| Nduguti | **126** | 4 18S | 34 41E |
| NE Frt. Agency = Arun. Pradesh □ | **98** | 28 0N | 95 0E |
| Nea | **71** | 63 15N | 11 0E |
| Néa Epidhavros | **69** | 37 40N | 23 7E |
| Néa Filippiás | **68** | 39 12N | 20 53W |
| Néa Kallikrátiá | **68** | 40 21N | 23 1E |
| Néa Vissi | **68** | 41 34N | 26 33E |
| Neagari | **111** | 36 26N | 136 25E |
| Neagh, Lough | **38** | 54 35N | 6 25W |
| Neah Bay | **160** | 48 25N | 124 40W |
| Neale L. | **137** | 24 15S | 130 0E |
| Neamarrói | **127** | 15 58S | 36 50E |
| Neamţ □ | **70** | 47 0N | 26 20E |
| Neápolis, Kozan, Greece | **68** | 40 20N | 21 24E |
| Neápolis, Kriti, Greece | **69** | 35 15N | 25 36E |
| Neápolis, Lakonia, Greece | **69** | 36 27N | 23 8E |
| Near Is. | **147** | 53 0N | 172 0W |
| Neath | **31** | 51 39N | 3 49W |
| Neath, R. | **23** | 51 46N | 3 35W |
| Nebbou | **121** | 11 9N | 1 51W |
| Nebine Cr. | **139** | 29 7S | 146 56E |
| Nebo | **138** | 21 42S | 148 42E |
| Nebolchy | **81** | 59 12N | 32 58E |
| Nebraska □ | **158** | 41 30N | 100 0W |
| Nebraska City | **158** | 40 40N | 95 52W |
| Necedah | **158** | 44 2N | 90 7W |
| Nechako, R. | **152** | 53 30N | 122 44W |
| Neches, R. | **159** | 31 80N | 94 20W |
| Neckar, R. | **49** | 48 43N | 9 15E |
| Necochea | **172** | 38 30S | 58 50W |
| Nectar Brook | **140** | 32 43S | 137 57E |
| Nedelišće | **63** | 46 23N | 16 22E |
| Neder Rijn, R. | **46** | 51 57N | 6 2E |
| Nederbrakel | **47** | 50 48N | 3 46E |
| Nederlandsöy I. | **71** | 62 20N | 5 35E |
| Nederweert | **47** | 51 17N | 5 45E |
| Nedha, R. | **69** | 37 25N | 21 45E |
| Nedroma | **118** | 35 1N | 1 45W |
| Nedstrand | **71** | 59 21N | 5 49E |
| Neede | **46** | 52 8N | 6 37E |
| Needham Market | **29** | 52 9N | 1 2E |
| Needilup | **137** | 33 55S | 118 45E |
| Needles | **161** | 34 50N | 114 35W |
| Needles, Pt. | **142** | 36 3S | 175 25E |
| Needles, The | **28** | 50 48N | 1 19W |
| Ñeembucú □ | **172** | 27 0S | 58 0W |
| Neemuch (Nimach) | **94** | 24 30N | 74 50E |
| Neenah | **156** | 44 10N | 88 30W |
| Neepawa | **153** | 50 20N | 99 30W |
| Neer | **47** | 51 16N | 5 59E |
| Neerheylissem | **47** | 51 5N | 5 42E |
| Neeroeteren | **47** | 50 44N | 4 58E |
| Neerpelt | **47** | 51 13N | 5 26E |
| Nefta | **119** | 33 53N | 7 58E |
| Neftah Sidi Boubekeur | **118** | 35 1N | 0 4E |
| Neftegorsk | **83** | 44 25N | 39 45E |
| Neftenbach | **51** | 47 32N | 8 41E |
| Neftyannye Kamni | **79** | 40 20N | 50 55E |
| Nefyn | **31** | 52 57N | 4 29W |
| Negapatam = Nagappattinam | **97** | 10 46N | 79 38E |
| Negaunee | **156** | 46 30N | 87 36W |
| Negba | **90** | 31 40N | 34 41E |
| Negele | **123** | 5 20N | 39 30E |
| Negeri Sembilan □ | **101** | 2 50N | 102 10E |
| Negev = Hanegev | **90** | 30 50N | 35 0E |
| Negolu | **70** | 45 48N | 24 32E |
| Negombo | **97** | 7 12N | 79 50E |
| Negotin | **66** | 44 16N | 22 37E |
| Negotino | **66** | 41 29N | 22 9E |
| Negra, La | **172** | 23 46S | 70 18W |
| Negra, Peña | **56** | 42 11N | 6 30W |
| Negra Pt. | **103** | 18 40N | 120 50E |
| Negrais C. | **98** | 16 0N | 94 30E |
| Negreira | **56** | 42 54N | 8 45W |
| Negreşti | **70** | 46 50N | 27 30E |
| Négrine | **119** | 34 30N | 7 30E |
| Negro, C. | **118** | 35 40N | 5 11W |
| Negro, R., Argent. | **176** | 40 0S | 64 0W |
| Negro, R., Brazil | **174** | 0 25S | 64 0W |
| Negro, R., Uruguay | **173** | 32 30S | 55 30W |
| Negros, I. | **103** | 10 0N | 123 0E |
| Negru Vodů | **70** | 43 47N | 28 21E |
| Nehbandān | **93** | 31 35N | 60 5E |
| Neheim-Hüsten | **48** | 51 27N | 7 58E |
| Nehoiaşu | **70** | 45 24N | 26 20E |
| Neichiang | **108** | 29 35N | 105 0E |
| Neich'iu | **106** | 37 17N | 114 31E |
| Neidpath | **153** | 50 12N | 107 20W |
| Neihart | **160** | 47 0N | 110 52W |
| Neihsiang | **106** | 33 3N | 111 53E |
| Neilrex | **141** | 31 44S | 149 20E |
| Neilston | **34** | 55 47N | 4 27W |
| Neilton | **160** | 47 24N | 123 59W |
| Neira de Jusá | **56** | 42 53N | 7 14W |
| Neisse, R. | **48** | 51 0N | 15 0E |
| Neiva | **174** | 2 56N | 75 18W |
| Nejanilini L. | **153** | 59 33N | 97 48W |
| Nejo | **123** | 9 30N | 35 28E |
| Nekemte | **123** | 9 4N | 36 30E |
| Nêkheb | **122** | 25 10N | 33 0E |
| Neksø | **73** | 55 4N | 15 8E |
| Nelas | **56** | 40 32N | 7 52W |
| Nelaug | **71** | 58 39N | 8 40E |
| Nelgowrie | **141** | 30 54S | 148 7E |
| Nelia | **138** | 20 39S | 142 12E |
| Nelidovo | **80** | 56 13N | 32 49E |
| Neligh | **158** | 42 11N | 98 2W |
| Nelkan | **77** | 57 50N | 136 15E |
| Nellikuppam | **97** | 11 46N | 79 43E |
| Nellore | **97** | 14 27N | 79 59E |
| Nelma | **77** | 47 30N | 139 0E |
| Nelson, Can. | **152** | 49 30N | 117 20W |
| Nelson, N.Z. | **143** | 41 18S | 173 16E |
| Nelson, U.K. | **32** | 53 50N | 2 14W |
| Nelson, Ariz., U.S.A. | **161** | 35 35N | 113 24W |
| Nelson, Nev., U.S.A. | **161** | 35 46N | 114 55W |
| Nelson □ | **143** | 42 11S | 172 15E |
| Nelson, C., Austral. | **140** | 38 26S | 141 32E |
| Nelson, C., P.N.G. | **135** | 9 0S | 149 20E |
| Nelson, Estrecho | **176** | 51 30S | 75 0W |
| Nelson Forks | **152** | 59 30N | 124 0W |
| Nelson House | **153** | 55 47N | 98 51W |
| Nelson I. | **147** | 60 40N | 164 40W |
| Nelson L. | **153** | 55 48N | 100 7W |
| Nelson, R. | **153** | 54 33N | 98 2W |
| Nelspruit | **126** | 25 29S | 30 59E |
| Néma | **120** | 16 40N | 7 15W |
| Neman (Nemunas), R. | **80** | 53 30N | 25 10E |
| Neméa | **69** | 37 49N | 22 40E |
| Nemegos | **150** | 47 40N | 83 15W |
| Nemeiben L. | **153** | 55 20N | 105 20W |
| Nemira, Mt. | **70** | 46 17N | 26 19E |
| Nemiscau | **150** | 49 30N | 111 15W |
| Nemours | **43** | 48 16N | 2 40E |
| Nemunas, R. | **80** | 55 25N | 21 10E |
| Nemuro | **112** | 43 20N | 145 35E |
| Nemuro-Kaikyō | **112** | 43 30N | 145 30E |
| Nemuy | **77** | 55 40N | 135 55E |
| Nenagh | **39** | 52 52N | 8 11W |
| Nenana | **147** | 64 30N | 149 0W |
| Nenasi | **101** | 3 9N | 103 23E |
| Nenchiang | **105** | 49 11N | 125 13E |
| Nene, R. | **29** | 52 38N | 0 7E |
| Neno | **127** | 15 25S | 34 40E |
| Nenusa, Kepulauan | **103** | 4 45N | 127 1E |
| Neodesha | **159** | 37 30N | 95 37W |
| Néon Petrítsi | **68** | 41 16N | 23 15E |
| Neópolis | **170** | 10 18S | 36 35W |
| Neosho | **159** | 36 56N | 94 28W |
| Neosho, R. | **159** | 35 59N | 95 10W |
| Nepal ■ | **95** | 28 0N | 84 30E |
| Nepalganj | **95** | 28 0N | 81 40E |
| Nephi | **160** | 39 43N | 111 52W |
| Nephin Beg Ra. | **38** | 54 0N | 9 40W |
| Nephin, Mt. | **38** | 54 1N | 9 21W |
| Nepomuk | **52** | 49 29N | 13 35E |
| Neptune City | **162** | 40 13N | 74 4W |
| Néra, R. | **66** | 44 52N | 21 45E |
| Nerac | **44** | 44 19N | 0 20E |
| Nerchinsk | **77** | 52 0N | 116 39E |
| Nerchinskiy Zavod | **77** | 51 10N | 119 30E |
| Nereju | **70** | 45 43N | 26 43E |
| Nerekhta | **81** | 57 26N | 40 38E |
| Neret L. | **151** | 54 45N | 70 44W |
| Neretva, R. | **66** | 43 30N | 17 50E |
| Neretvanski | **66** | 43 7N | 17 10E |
| Neringa | **80** | 55 21N | 21 5E |
| Nerja | **57** | 36 43N | 3 55W |
| Nerl, R. | **81** | 56 30N | 40 30E |
| Nerokoúrou | **69** | 35 29N | 24 3E |
| Nerpio | **59** | 38 11N | 2 16W |
| Nerva | **57** | 37 42N | 6 30W |
| Nes, Iceland | **74** | 65 53N | 17 24W |
| Nes, Neth. | **46** | 53 26N | 5 47E |
| Nes Ziyyona | **90** | 31 56N | 34 48W |
| Nesbyen | **71** | 60 34N | 9 6E |
| Nescopeck | **162** | 41 3N | 76 12W |
| Nesebyr | **67** | 42 41N | 27 46E |
| Nesflaten | **71** | 59 38N | 6 48E |
| Neskaupstaður | **74** | 65 9N | 13 42W |
| Nesland | **71** | 59 31N | 7 59E |
| Neslandsvatn | **71** | 58 57N | 9 10E |
| Nesle | **43** | 49 45N | 2 53E |
| Nesodden | **71** | 59 48N | 10 40E |
| Ness, dist. | **36** | 58 27N | 6 20W |
| Ness, Loch | **37** | 57 15N | 4 30W |
| Nesslau | **51** | 47 14N | 9 13E |
| Neston | **32** | 53 17N | 3 3W |
| Nestórion Óros | **68** | 40 24N | 21 16E |
| Néstos, R. | **68** | 41 20N | 24 35E |
| Nesttun | **71** | 60 19N | 5 21E |
| Nesvizh | **80** | 53 14N | 26 38E |
| Netanya | **90** | 32 20N | 34 51E |
| Nèthe, R. | **47** | 51 5N | 4 55E |
| Netherdale | **138** | 21 10S | 148 33E |
| Netherlands ■ | **47** | 52 0N | 5 30E |
| Netherlands Guiana = Surinam | **170** | 4 0N | 56 0W |
| Nethy Bridge | **37** | 57 15N | 3 40W |
| Netley | **28** | 50 53N | 1 21W |
| Netley Gap | **28** | 32 43S | 139 59E |
| Netley Marsh | **28** | 50 55N | 1 32W |
| Neto, R. | **65** | 39 10N | 16 58E |
| Netrakong | **98** | 24 53N | 90 47E |
| Nettancourt | **43** | 48 51N | 4 57E |
| Nettilling L. | **149** | 66 30N | 71 0W |
| Nettlebed | **29** | 51 34N | 0 54W |
| Nettleham | **33** | 53 15N | 0 28W |
| Nettuno | **64** | 41 29N | 12 40E |
| Netzahualcoyotl, Presa | **165** | 17 10N | 93 30W |
| Neu-Isenburg | **49** | 50 3N | 8 42E |
| Neu Ulm | **49** | 48 23N | 10 2E |
| Neubrandenburg | **48** | 53 33N | 13 17E |
| Neubrandenburg □ | **48** | 53 30N | 13 20E |
| Neubukow | **48** | 54 1N | 11 40E |
| Neuburg | **49** | 48 43N | 11 11E |
| Neuchâtel | **50** | 47 0N | 6 55E |
| Neuchâtel □ | **50** | 47 0N | 6 55E |
| Neuchâtel, Lac de | **50** | 46 53N | 6 50E |
| Neudau | **52** | 47 11N | 16 6E |
| Neuenegg | **50** | 46 54N | 7 18E |
| Neuenhaus | **48** | 52 30N | 6 55E |
| Neuf-Brisach | **43** | 48 0N | 7 30E |
| Neufchâteau, Belg. | **47** | 49 50N | 5 25E |
| Neufchâteau, France | **43** | 48 21N | 5 40E |
| Neufchâtel | **43** | 49 43N | 1 30E |
| Neufchâtel-sur-Aisne | **43** | 49 26N | 4 0E |
| Neuhaus | **48** | 53 16N | 10 54E |
| Neuhausen | **51** | 47 41N | 8 37E |
| Neuilly-St. Front | **43** | 49 10N | 3 15E |
| Neukalen | **49** | 53 49N | 12 48E |
| Neumarkt | **49** | 49 16N | 11 28E |
| Neumünster | **48** | 54 4N | 9 58E |
| Neung-sur-Beuvron | **43** | 47 30N | 1 50E |
| Neunkirchen, Austria | **52** | 47 43N | 16 4E |
| Neunkirchen, Ger. | **49** | 49 23N | 7 6E |
| Neuquén | **176** | 38 0S | 68 0E |
| Neuquén □ | **172** | 38 0S | 69 50W |
| Neuruppin | **48** | 52 56N | 12 48E |
| Neuse, R. | **157** | 35 5N | 77 40W |
| Neusiedl | **53** | 47 57N | 16 50E |
| Neusiedler See | **53** | 47 50N | 16 47E |
| Neuss | **48** | 51 12N | 6 39E |
| Neussargues-Moissac | **44** | 45 9N | 3 1E |
| Neustadt, Bay., Ger. | **49** | 49 42N | 12 10E |
| Neustadt, Bay., Ger. | **49** | 48 48N | 11 47E |
| Neustadt, Bay., Ger. | **49** | 49 34N | 10 37E |
| Neustadt, Bay., Ger. | **49** | 50 23N | 11 0E |
| Neustadt, Gera, Ger. | **48** | 50 45N | 11 43E |
| Neustadt, Hessen, Ger. | **48** | 50 51N | 9 9E |
| Neustadt, Niedersachsen, Ger. | **48** | 52 30N | 9 30E |
| Neustadt, Potsdam, Ger. | **48** | 52 50N | 12 27E |
| Neustadt, Rhld-Pfz., Ger. | **49** | 49 21N | 8 10E |
| Neustadt, S.-Holst., Ger. | **48** | 54 6N | 10 49E |
| Neustrelitz | **48** | 53 22N | 13 4E |
| Neuveville, La | **50** | 47 4N | 7 6E |
| Neuvic | **44** | 45 23N | 2 16E |
| Neuville, Belg. | **95** | 50 11N | 4 32E |
| Neuville, France | **43** | 45 52N | 4 51E |
| Neuville-aux-Bois | **43** | 48 4N | 2 3E |
| Neuvy-St.-Sépulchure | **44** | 46 35N | 1 48E |
| Neuvy-sur-Barangeon | **43** | 47 20N | 2 15E |
| Neuwerk, I. | **48** | 53 55N | 8 30E |
| Neuwied | **48** | 50 26N | 7 29E |
| Neva, R. | **78** | 59 50N | 30 30E |
| Nevada | **159** | 37 20N | 94 40W |
| Nevada □ | **160** | 39 20N | 117 0W |
| Nevada City | **163** | 39 20N | 121 0W |
| Nevada de Sta. Marta, Sa. | **174** | 10 55N | 73 50W |
| Nevada, Sierra, Spain | **59** | 37 3N | 3 15W |
| Nevada, Sierra, U.S.A. | **160** | 39 0N | 120 30W |
| Nevado, Cerro | **172** | 35 30S | 68 20W |
| Nevado de Colima, Mt. | **164** | 19 35N | 103 45W |
| Nevanka | **77** | 56 45N | 98 55E |
| Nevasa | **94** | 19 34N | 75 0E |
| Nevel | **80** | 56 0N | 29 55E |
| Nevele | **47** | 51 3N | 3 28E |
| Nevern | **31** | 52 2N | 4 49W |
| Nevers | **43** | 47 0N | 3 9E |
| Nevertire | **141** | 31 50S | 147 44E |
| Neville | **153** | 49 58N | 107 39W |
| Nevillé-Pont-Pierre | **42** | 47 33N | 0 33E |

**Nevinnomyssk** **Nîl el Abyad, Bahr**


| | | | |
|---|---|---|---|
| Nevinnomyssk | **83** | 44 40N | 42 0E |
| Nevis I. | **167** | 17 0N | 62 30W |
| Nevis, L. | **36** | 57 0N | 5 43W |
| Nevlunghavn | **71** | 58 58N | 9 53E |
| Nevoria | **137** | 31 25S | 119 25E |
| Nevrokop = Gotse Delchev | **67** | 41 43N | 23 46E |
| Nevşehir | **92** | 38 33N | 34 40E |
| Nevyansk | **84** | 57 30N | 60 13E |
| New Abbey | **35** | 54 59N | 3 38W |
| New Aberdour | **37** | 57 39N | 2 12W |
| New Adawso | **121** | 6 50N | 0 2W |
| New Albany, Ind., U.S.A. | **156** | 38 20N | 85 50W |
| New Albany, Miss., U.S.A. | **159** | 34 30N | 89 0W |
| New Albany, Pa., U.S.A. | **162** | 41 35N | 76 28W |
| New Alresford | **28** | 51 6N | 1 10W |
| New Amsterdam | **174** | 6 15N | 57 30W |
| New Angledool | **139** | 29 10S | 147 55E |
| New Bedford | **162** | 41 40N | 70 52W |
| New Berlin, N.Y., U.S.A. | **162** | 42 38N | 75 20W |
| New Berlin, Pa., U.S.A. | **162** | 40 50N | 76 57W |
| New Bern | **157** | 35 8N | 77 3W |
| New Birmingham | **39** | 52 36N | 7 38W |
| New Boston | **159** | 33 27N | 94 21W |
| New Braunfels | **159** | 29 43N | 98 9W |
| New Brighton, N.Z. | **143** | 43 29S | 172 43E |
| New Brighton, U.K. | **32** | 53 27N | 3 2W |
| New Britain | **162** | 41 41N | 72 47W |
| New Britain, I. | **135** | 5 50S | 150 20E |
| New Brunswick | **162** | 40 30N | 74 28W |
| New Brunswick □ | **151** | 46 50N | 66 30W |
| New Buildings | **38** | 54 57N | 7 21W |
| New Bussa | **121** | 9 53N | 4 31E |
| New Byrd | **13** | 80 0S | 120 0W |
| New Caledonia, I. | **130** | 21 0S | 165 0E |
| New Castile = Castilla La Neuva | **57** | 39 45N | 3 20W |
| New Castle, Del., U.S.A. | **162** | 39 40N | 75 34W |
| New Castle, Ind., U.S.A. | **156** | 39 55N | 85 23W |
| New Castle, Pa., U.S.A. | **156** | 41 0N | 80 20W |
| New Chapel Cross | **39** | 51 51N | 10 12W |
| New City | **162** | 41 8N | 74 0W |
| New Cumnock | **34** | 55 24N | 4 13W |
| New Cuyama | **163** | 34 57N | 119 38W |
| New Deer | **37** | 57 30N | 2 10W |
| New Delhi | **94** | 28 37N | 77 13E |
| New Denver | **152** | 50 0N | 117 25W |
| New England | **158** | 46 36N | 102 47W |
| New England Ra. | **139** | 30 20S | 151 45E |
| New Forest | **28** | 50 53N | 1 40W |
| New Freedom | **162** | 39 44N | 76 42W |
| New Galloway | **35** | 55 4N | 4 10W |
| New Glasgow | **151** | 45 35N | 62 36W |
| New Gretna | **162** | 39 35N | 74 28W |
| New Guinea, I. | **135** | 4 0S | 136 0E |
| New Hampshire □ | **156** | 43 40N | 71 40W |
| New Hampton | **158** | 43 2N | 92 20W |
| New Hanover | **129** | 29 22S | 30 31E |
| New Hanover I. | **135** | 2 30S | 150 10E |
| New Hartford | **162** | 43 4N | 75 18W |
| New Haven | **162** | 41 20N | 72 54W |
| New Hazelton | **152** | 55 20N | 127 30W |
| New Hebrides, Is. | **130** | 15 0S | 168 0E |
| New Holland, U.K. | **33** | 53 42N | 0 22W |
| New Holland, U.S.A. | **162** | 40 6N | 76 5W |
| New Iberia | **159** | 30 2N | 91 54W |
| New Inn | **39** | 53 5N | 7 10W |
| New Ireland, I. | **135** | 3 20S | 151 50E |
| New Jersey □ | **162** | 39 50N | 74 10W |
| New Kensington | **156** | 40 36N | 79 43W |
| New Kent | **162** | 37 31N | 76 59W |
| New Lexington | **156** | 39 40N | 82 15W |
| New Liskeard | **150** | 47 31N | 79 41W |
| New London, Conn., U.S.A. | **162** | 41 23N | 72 8W |
| New London, Minn., U.S.A. | **158** | 45 17N | 94 55W |
| New London, Wis., U.S.A. | **158** | 44 23N | 88 43W |
| New Luce | **34** | 54 57N | 4 50W |
| New Madrid | **159** | 36 40N | 89 30W |
| New Meadows | **160** | 45 0N | 116 10W |
| New Mexico □ | **154** | 34 30N | 106 0W |
| New Milford, Conn., U.S.A. | **162** | 41 35N | 73 25W |
| New Milford, Pa., U.S.A. | **162** | 41 50N | 75 45W |
| New Mills | **32** | 53 22N | 2 0W |
| New Norcia | **137** | 30 57S | 116 13E |
| New Norfolk | **138** | 42 46S | 147 2E |
| New Orleans | **159** | 30 0N | 90 5W |
| New Oxford | **162** | 39 52N | 77 4W |
| New Philadelphia | **156** | 40 29N | 81 25W |
| New Pitsligo | **37** | 57 35N | 2 11W |
| New Plymouth, Bahamas | **166** | 26 56N | 77 20W |
| New Plymouth, N.Z. | **142** | 39 4S | 174 5E |
| New Point Comfort | **162** | 37 18N | 76 15W |
| New Providence I. | **166** | 25 0N | 77 30W |
| New Quay | **31** | 52 13N | 4 21W |
| New Radnor | **31** | 52 15N | 3 10W |
| New Richmond | **158** | 45 6N | 92 34W |
| New Roads | **159** | 30 43N | 91 30W |
| New Rockford | **158** | 47 44N | 99 7W |
| New Romney | **29** | 50 59N | 0 57E |
| New Ross | **39** | 52 24N | 6 58W |
| New Rossington | **33** | 53 30N | 1 4W |
| New Salem | **158** | 46 51N | 101 25W |
| New Siberian Is. = Novosibirskiye Os. | **77** | 75 0N | 140 0E |
| New Smyrna Beach | **157** | 29 0N | 80 50W |
| New South Wales □ | **139** | 33 0S | 146 0E |
| New Springs | **137** | 25 49S | 120 1E |
| New Tamale | **121** | 9 10N | 1 10W |
| New Tredegar | **31** | 51 43N | 3 15W |
| New Ulm | **158** | 44 15N | 94 30W |
| New Waterford | **151** | 46 13N | 60 4W |
| New Westminster | **152** | 49 10N | 122 52W |
| New York □ | **156** | 42 40N | 76 0W |
| New York City | **162** | 40 45N | 74 0W |
| New Zealand ■ | **143** | 40 0S | 176 0E |
| Newala | **127** | 10 58S | 39 10E |
| Newala □ | **127** | 10 46S | 39 20E |
| Newark, U.K. | **33** | 53 6N | 0 48W |
| Newark, Del., U.S.A. | **162** | 39 42N | 75 45W |
| Newark, N.J., U.S.A. | **162** | 40 41N | 74 12W |
| Newark, N.Y., U.S.A. | **162** | 43 2N | 77 10W |
| Newark, Ohio, U.S.A. | **156** | 40 5N | 82 30W |
| Newark Valley | **162** | 42 14N | 76 11W |
| Newberg | **160** | 45 22N | 123 0W |
| Newberry | **156** | 46 20N | 85 32W |
| Newberry Springs | **163** | 34 50N | 116 41W |
| Newbiggin-by-the-Sea | **35** | 55 12N | 1 31W |
| Newbigging | **35** | 55 42N | 3 33W |
| Newbliss | **38** | 54 10N | 7 8W |
| Newborough | **31** | 53 10N | 4 22W |
| Newbridge, Kildare, Ireland | **39** | 53 11N | 6 50W |
| Newbridge, Limerick, Ireland | **38** | 52 33N | 9 0W |
| Newbridge-on-Wye | **31** | 52 13N | 3 27W |
| Newbrook | **152** | 54 24N | 112 57W |
| Newburgh, Fife, U.K. | **35** | 56 21N | 3 15W |
| Newburgh, Grampian, U.K. | **37** | 57 19N | 2 0W |
| Newburgh, U.S.A. | **162** | 41 30N | 74 1W |
| Newburn | **35** | 54 57N | 1 45W |
| Newbury | **28** | 51 24N | 1 19W |
| Newburyport | **162** | 42 48N | 70 50W |
| Newby Bridge | **32** | 54 16N | 2 59W |
| Newbyth | **37** | 57 35N | 2 17W |
| Newcastle, Austral. | **141** | 33 0S | 151 40E |
| Newcastle, Can. | **151** | 47 1N | 65 38W |
| Newcastle, Ireland | **39** | 53 5N | 6 4W |
| Newcastle, S. Afr. | **125** | 27 45S | 29 58E |
| Newcastle, U.K. | **38** | 54 13N | 5 54W |
| Newcastle, U.S.A. | **158** | 43 50N | 104 12W |
| Newcastle Emlyn | **31** | 52 2N | 4 29W |
| Newcastle Ra. | **136** | 15 45S | 130 15E |
| Newcastle-under-Lyme | **32** | 53 2N | 2 15W |
| Newcastle-upon-Tyne | **35** | 54 59N | 1 37W |
| Newcastle Waters | **136** | 17 30S | 133 28E |
| Newcastle West | **38** | 52 27N | 9 3W |
| Newcastleton | **35** | 55 10N | 2 50W |
| Newchurch | **31** | 52 9N | 3 10W |
| Newdegate | **137** | 33 6S | 119 0E |
| Newe Etan | **90** | 32 30N | 35 32E |
| Newe Sha'anan | **90** | 32 47N | 34 59E |
| Newe Zohar | **90** | 31 9N | 35 21E |
| Newell | **158** | 44 48N | 103 25W |
| Newenham, C. | **147** | 58 40N | 162 15W |
| Newent | **28** | 51 56N | 2 24W |
| Newfield, N.J., U.S.A. | **162** | 39 33N | 75 1W |
| Newfield, N.Y., U.S.A. | **162** | 42 18N | 76 33W |
| Newfound L. | **162** | 43 40N | 71 47W |
| Newfoundland | **151** | 48 30N | 56 0W |
| Newfoundland □ | **151** | 48 28N | 56 0W |
| Newhalem | **152** | 48 41N | 121 16W |
| Newhalen | **147** | 59 40N | 155 0W |
| Newhall | **163** | 34 23N | 118 32W |
| Newham | **29** | 51 31N | 0 2E |
| Newhaven | **29** | 50 47N | 0 4E |
| Newington, N. Kent, U.K. | **29** | 51 21N | 0 40E |
| Newington, S. Kent, U.K. | **29** | 51 5N | 1 8E |
| Newinn | **39** | 52 28N | 7 54W |
| Newkirk | **159** | 36 52N | 97 3W |
| Newlyn | **30** | 50 6N | 5 33W |
| Newlyn East | **30** | 50 22N | 5 3W |
| Newmachar | **37** | 57 16N | 2 11W |
| Newman | **163** | 37 19N | 121 1W |
| Newman, Mt. | **137** | 23 20S | 119 34E |
| Newmarket, Ireland | **39** | 52 13N | 9 0W |
| Newmarket, Lewis, U.K. | **36** | 58 14N | 6 24W |
| Newmarket, Norfolk, U.K. | **29** | 52 15N | 0 23E |
| Newmarket, U.S.A. | **162** | 43 4N | 70 57W |
| Newmarket-on-Fergus | **39** | 52 46N | 8 54W |
| Newmill | **37** | 57 34N | 2 58W |
| Newmills | **38** | 54 56N | 7 49W |
| Newmilns | **34** | 55 36N | 4 20W |
| Newnan | **157** | 33 22N | 84 48W |
| Newnes | **139** | 33 9S | 150 16E |
| Newnham | **28** | 51 48N | 2 27W |
| Newport, Essex, U.K. | **29** | 51 58N | 0 13E |
| Newport, Gwent, U.K. | **31** | 51 35N | 3 0W |
| Newport, I. of W., U.K. | **28** | 50 42N | 1 18W |
| Newport, Salop, U.K. | **28** | 52 47N | 2 22W |
| Newport, Ark., U.S.A. | **159** | 35 38N | 91 15W |
| Newport, Ky., U.S.A. | **156** | 39 5N | 84 23W |
| Newport, N.H., U.S.A. | **162** | 43 23N | 72 8W |
| Newport, Oreg., U.S.A. | **160** | 44 41N | 124 2W |
| Newport, R.I., U.S.A. | **162** | 41 30N | 71 19W |
| Newport, Tenn., U.S.A. | **157** | 35 39N | 83 12W |
| Newport, Wash., U.S.A. | **160** | 48 11N | 117 2W |
| Newport B. | **38** | 53 52N | 9 38W |
| Newport Beach | **163** | 33 40N | 117 58W |
| Newport News | **162** | 37 2N | 76 54W |
| Newport on Tay | **35** | 56 27N | 2 56W |
| Newport Pagnell | **29** | 52 5N | 0 42W |
| Newquay | **30** | 50 24N | 5 6W |
| Newry | **38** | 54 10N | 6 20W |
| Newry & Mourne □ | **38** | 54 10N | 6 15W |
| Newton, Iowa, U.S.A. | **158** | 41 40N | 93 3W |
| Newton, Kans., U.S.A. | **159** | 38 2N | 97 30W |
| Newton, Mass., U.S.A. | **156** | 42 21N | 71 10W |
| Newton, N.C., U.S.A. | **157** | 35 42N | 81 10W |
| Newton, N.J., U.S.A. | **162** | 41 3N | 74 46W |
| Newton, Texas, U.S.A. | **159** | 30 54N | 93 42W |
| Newton Abbot | **30** | 50 32N | 3 37W |
| Newton Arlosh | **32** | 54 53N | 3 15W |
| Newton-Aycliffe | **33** | 54 36N | 1 33W |
| Newton Boyd | **139** | 29 45S | 152 16E |
| Newton Ferrers | **30** | 50 19N | 4 3W |
| Newton le Willows | **32** | 53 28N | 3 27W |
| Newton St. Cyres | **30** | 50 46N | 3 35W |
| Newton Stewart | **34** | 54 57N | 4 30W |
| Newtonabbey □ | **38** | 54 45N | 6 0W |
| Newtongrange | **35** | 55 52N | 3 4W |
| Newtonhill | **37** | 57 1N | 20 52E |
| Newtonmore | **37** | 57 4N | 4 7W |
| Newtown, Ireland | **39** | 52 20N | 8 47W |
| Newtown, Scot, U.K. | **35** | 55 34N | 2 38W |
| Newtown, Wales, U.K. | **31** | 52 31N | 3 19W |
| Newtown Crommelin | **38** | 54 59N | 6 13W |
| Newtown Cunningham | **38** | 55 0N | 7 32W |
| Newtown Forbes | **38** | 53 46N | 7 50W |
| Newtown Gore | **38** | 54 3N | 7 41W |
| Newtown Hamilton | **38** | 54 12N | 6 35W |
| Newtownabbey | **38** | 54 40N | 5 55W |
| Newtownards | **38** | 54 37N | 5 40W |
| Newtownbutler | **38** | 54 12N | 7 22W |
| | **39** | 53 5N | 6 7W |
| Newtownstewart | **38** | 54 43N | 7 22W |
| Nexon | **48** | 45 41N | 1 10E |
| Neya | **81** | 58 21N | 43 49E |
| Neyland | **31** | 51 43N | 4 58W |
| Neyrīz | **93** | 29 15N | 54 55E |
| Neyshābūr | **93** | 36 10N | 58 20E |
| Neyyattinkara | **97** | 8 26N | 77 5E |
| Nezhin | **80** | 51 5N | 31 55E |
| Nezperce | **160** | 46 13N | 116 15W |
| Ngabang | **102** | 0 30N | 109 55E |
| Ngaiphaipi | **98** | 22 14N | 93 15E |
| Ngambé | **121** | 5 48N | 11 29E |
| Ngami Depression | **128** | 20 30S | 22 46E |
| Ngamo | **127** | 19 3S | 27 25E |
| Ngandjuk | **103** | 7 32S | 111 55E |
| Ngao | **100** | 18 46N | 99 59E |
| Ngaoundéré | **124** | 7 15N | 13 35E |
| Ngapara | **143** | 44 57S | 170 46E |
| Ngara | **126** | 2 29S | 30 40E |
| Ngara □ | **126** | 2 29S | 30 40E |
| Ngaruawahia | **142** | 37 42S | 175 11E |
| Ngatapa | **142** | 38 32S | 177 45E |
| Ngathainggyaung | **98** | 17 24N | 95 5E |
| Ngauruhoe, Mt. | **142** | 39 13S | 175 45E |
| Ngawi | **103** | 7 24S | 111 26E |
| Ngetera | **121** | 12 40S | 12 46E |
| Ngha Lo | **101** | 21 33N | 104 28E |
| Nghia Lo | **100** | 21 33N | 104 28E |
| Ngoma | **127** | 13 8S | 33 45E |
| Ngomahura | **127** | 20 33S | 30 57E |
| Ngomba | **127** | 8 20S | 32 53E |
| Ngonye Falls | **128** | 16 35S | 23 30E |
| Ngop | **123** | 6 17N | 30 9E |
| Ngorkou | **120** | 15 40N | 3 41W |
| Ngorongoro | **126** | 3 11S | 35 32E |
| Ngozi | **126** | 2 54S | 29 50E |
| Ngudu | **126** | 2 58S | 33 25E |
| N'Guigrai | **117** | 14 20N | 13 20E |
| Nguna, I. | **100** | 17 26S | 168 21E |
| Ngunga | **126** | 3 37S | 33 37E |
| Ngungu | **143** | 6 15N | 28 16E |
| Ngunguru | **94** | 35 37S | 174 30E |
| Nguru | **121** | 12 56N | 10 29E |
| Nguru Mts. | **126** | 6 0S | 37 30E |
| Nguyen Binh | **100** | 22 39N | 105 56E |
| Ngwenya | **129** | 26 5S | 31 7E |
| Nha Trang | **101** | 12 16N | 109 10E |
| Nhacoongo | **129** | 24 18S | 35 14E |
| Nhangutazi, Lago | **129** | 24 0S | 34 30E |
| Nhill | **140** | 36 18S | 141 40E |
| Nho Quan | **100** | 20 18N | 105 45E |
| Nhulunbuy | **138** | 12 10S | 136 45E |
| Nia-nia | **126** | 1 30N | 27 40E |
| Niafounké | **120** | 16 0N | 4 5W |
| Niagara | **156** | 45 45N | 88 0W |
| Niagara Falls, Can. | **150** | 43 7N | 79 5W |
| Niagara Falls, N. Amer. | **150** | 43 5N | 79 5W |
| Niah | **102** | 3 58N | 113 46E |
| Niamey | **121** | 13 27N | 2 6E |
| Nianforando | **120** | 9 37N | 10 36W |
| Nianfors | **72** | 61 36N | 16 46E |
| Niangara | **126** | 3 50N | 27 50E |
| Niantic | **162** | 41 19N | 72 12W |
| Nias, I. | **102** | 1 0N | 97 40E |
| Niassa □ | **127** | 13 30S | 36 0E |
| Niassa, Lago | **127** | 12 30S | 34 30E |
| Nibbiano | **62** | 44 54N | 9 20E |
| Nibe | **73** | 56 59N | 9 38E |
| Nibong Tebal | **101** | 5 10N | 100 29E |
| Nicaragua ■ | **166** | 11 40N | 85 30W |
| Nicaragua, Lago de | **166** | 12 50N | 85 30W |
| Nicastro | **65** | 39 0N | 16 18E |
| Nice | **45** | 43 42N | 7 14E |
| Niceville | **157** | 30 30N | 86 30W |
| Nichinan | **110** | 31 38N | 131 23E |
| Nicholas, Chan. | **166** | 23 30N | 80 30W |
| Nicholasville | **156** | 37 54N | 84 31W |
| Nichols | **162** | 42 1N | 76 22W |
| Nicholson, Austral. | **136** | 18 2S | 128 54E |
| Nicholson, Can. | **150** | 47 58N | 83 47W |
| Nicholson, U.S.A. | **162** | 41 37N | 75 47W |
| Nicholson, R. | **138** | 17 31S | 139 36E |
| Nicholson Ra. | **137** | 27 15S | 116 30E |
| Nicobar Is. | **86** | 9 0N | 93 0E |
| Nicoclí | **174** | 8 26N | 76 48W |
| Nicola | **152** | 50 8N | 120 40W |
| Nicolet | **150** | 46 17N | 72 35W |
| Nicolls Town | **166** | 25 8N | 78 0W |
| Nicosia, Cyprus | **92** | 35 10N | 33 25E |
| Nicosia, Italy | **65** | 37 45N | 14 22E |
| Nicótera | **65** | 38 33N | 15 57E |
| Nicoya | **166** | 10 9N | 85 27W |
| Nicoya, Golfo de | **166** | 10 0N | 85 0W |
| Nicoya, Pen. de | **166** | 9 45N | 85 40W |
| Nidau | **50** | 47 7N | 7 15E |
| Nidd, R. | **33** | 54 1N | 1 32W |
| Nidda | **48** | 50 24N | 9 2E |
| Nidda, R. | **49** | 50 25N | 9 2E |
| Nidderdale | **33** | 54 5N | 1 46W |
| Nidzica | **54** | 53 25N | 20 28E |
| Niebüll | **48** | 54 47N | 8 49E |
| Niederaula | **48** | 50 48N | 9 37E |
| Niederbipp | **50** | 47 16N | 7 42E |
| Niederbronn | **43** | 48 57N | 7 39E |
| Niedere Tauern | **93** | 47 18N | 14 0E |
| Niedermarsberg | **48** | 51 28N | 8 52E |
| Niederösterreich □ | **52** | 48 25N | 15 40E |
| Niedersachsen □ | **48** | 54 45N | 9 0E |
| Niel | **47** | 51 7N | 4 20E |
| Niellé | **120** | 10 5N | 5 38W |
| Niemba | **126** | 5 58S | 28 24E |
| Niemcza | **54** | 50 42N | 16 47E |
| Niemodlin | **54** | 50 38N | 17 38E |
| Niemur | **140** | 35 17S | 144 9E |
| Nienburg | **48** | 52 38N | 9 15E |
| Nienchʼingtʼangkula Shan | **105** | 30 10N | 90 0E |
| Niepołomice | **54** | 50 3N | 20 13E |
| Niesen | **50** | 46 38N | 7 39E |
| Niesky | **48** | 51 18N | 14 48E |
| Nieszawa | **54** | 52 52N | 18 42E |
| Nieuw Amsterdam | **46** | 52 43N | 6 52E |
| Nieuw Beijerland | **46** | 51 49N | 4 20E |
| Nieuw-Buinen | **46** | 52 58N | 6 56E |
| Nieuw-Dordrecht | **46** | 52 45N | 6 59E |
| Nieuw Hellevoet | **46** | 51 51N | 4 8E |
| Nieuw Loosdrecht | **46** | 52 12N | 5 8E |
| Nieuw Nickerie | **175** | 6 0N | 57 10W |
| Nieuw-Schoonebeek | **46** | 52 39N | 7 0E |
| Nieuw-Vassemeer | **47** | 51 34N | 4 12E |
| Nieuw-Vennep | **46** | 52 16N | 4 38E |
| Nieuw-Weerdinge | **46** | 52 51N | 6 59E |
| Nieuwe-Niedorp | **46** | 52 44N | 4 54E |
| Nieuwe-Pekela | **46** | 53 5N | 6 58E |
| Nieuwe-Schans | **46** | 53 11N | 7 12E |
| Nieuwe-Tonge | **47** | 51 43N | 4 10E |
| Nieuwendijk | **46** | 51 46N | 4 55E |
| Nieuwerkerken | **47** | 50 52N | 5 12E |
| Nieuwkoop | **46** | 52 9N | 4 48E |
| Nieuwleusen | **46** | 52 34N | 6 17E |
| Nieuwnamen | **47** | 51 18N | 4 9E |
| Nieuwolda | **46** | 53 15N | 6 58E |
| Nieuwpoort | **47** | 51 8N | 2 45E |
| Nieuwveen | **46** | 52 12N | 4 46E |
| Nieves | **56** | 42 7N | 8 26W |
| Nièvre □ | **43** | 47 10N | 5 40E |
| Nigata | **110** | 34 13N | 132 39E |
| Nigde | **92** | 38 0N | 34 40E |
| Nigel | **129** | 26 27S | 28 25E |
| Niger □ | **121** | 10 0N | 5 0E |
| Niger ■ | **121** | 13 30N | 10 0E |
| Niger, R. | **121** | 10 0N | 4 40E |
| Nigeria ■ | **121** | 8 30N | 8 0E |
| Nigg B. | **37** | 57 41N | 4 5W |
| Nightcaps | **143** | 45 57S | 168 14E |
| Nigrita | **68** | 40 56N | 23 29E |
| Nihtaur | **94** | 29 27N | 78 23E |
| Nii-Jima | **111** | 34 20N | 139 15E |
| Niigata | **112** | 37 58N | 139 0E |
| Niigata-ken □ | **112** | 37 15N | 138 45E |
| Niihama | **110** | 33 55N | 133 10E |
| Niihau, I. | **147** | 21 55N | 160 10W |
| Niimi | **110** | 34 59N | 133 28E |
| Níjar | **59** | 36 53N | 2 15W |
| Nijkerk | **47** | 52 13N | 5 30E |
| Nijlen | **47** | 51 10N | 4 40E |
| Nijmegen | **47** | 51 50N | 5 52E |
| Nijverdal | **46** | 52 22N | 6 28E |
| Nike | **121** | 6 26N | 7 29E |
| Nikel | **74** | 69 30N | 30 5E |
| Nikiniki | **103** | 9 40S | 124 30E |
| Nikitas | **68** | 40 17N | 23 34E |
| Nikki | **121** | 9 58N | 3 21E |
| Nikkō | **111** | 36 45N | 139 35E |
| Nikolayev | **82** | 46 58N | 32 7E |
| Nikolayevsk-na-Amur | **77** | 53 40N | 140 50E |
| Nikolayevski | **81** | 50 10N | 45 35E |
| Nikolsk | **81** | 59 30N | 45 28E |
| Nikolski | **147** | 53 0N | 168 50W |
| Nikolskoye, Amur, U.S.S.R. | **77** | 47 50N | 131 5E |
| Nikolskoye, Kamandorskiye, U.S.S.R. | **77** | 55 12N | 166 0E |
| Nikopol, Bulg. | **67** | 43 43N | 24 54E |
| Nikopol, U.S.S.R. | **82** | 47 35N | 34 25E |
| Niksar | **82** | 40 31N | 37 2E |
| Nīkshah | **93** | 26 15N | 60 10E |
| Nikšió | **66** | 42 50N | 18 57E |
| Nîl el Abyad, Bahr | **123** | 9 30N | 31 40E |

Nîl el Azraq □ N. Taranaki Bt


Nîl el Azraq □ 123 12 30N 34 30 E
Nîl el Azraq, Bahr 123 10 30N 35 0 E
Nîl, Nahr el 122 27 30N 30 30 E
Nila 103 8 24 S 120 29 E
Niland 161 33 16N 115 30W
Nile □ 126 2 0N 31 30 E
Nile Delta 122 31 40N 31 0 E
Nile, R. = Nîl, Nahr el 122 27 30N 30 30 E
Niles 156 41 8N 80 40W
Nilgiri Hills 97 11 30N 76 30 E
Nilo Peçanha 171 13 37 S 39 6W
Nilpena 140 30 58 S 138 20 E
Nimach = Neemuch 94 24 30N 74 50 E
Nimar 96 21 49N 76 22 E
Nimba, Mt. 120 7 39N 8 30W
Nimbahera 94 24 37N 74 45 E
Nîmes 45 43 50N 4 23 E
Nimfaion, Ákra 68 40 5N 24 20 E
Nimingarra 132 20 31 S 119 55 E
Nimmitabel 141 36 29 S 149 15 E
Nimneryskiy 77 58 0N 125 10 E
Nimule 123 3 32N 32 3 E
Nimy 47 50 28N 3 57 E
Nin 63 44 16N 15 12 E
Nindigully 139 28 21 S 148 50 E
Ninemile 152 56 0N 130 7W
Ninemilehouse 39 52 28N 7 29W
Ninety Mile Beach 130 34 45 S 173 0 E
Ninety Mile Beach, The 133 38 15 S 147 24 E
Nineveh 92 36 25N 43 10 E
Ninfield 29 50 53N 0 26 E
Ningaloo 136 22 41 S 113 41 E
Ningan 107 44 23N 129 26 E
Ningch'eng 107 41 34N 119 20 E
Ningch'iang 106 32 49N 106 13 E
Ningchin 106 37 37N 114 55 E
Ningching Shan 108 31 45N 97 15 E
Ninghai 109 29 18N 121 25 E
Ninghsiang 109 28 15N 112 30 E
Ninghsien 106 35 35N 107 58 E
Ninghua 109 26 14N 116 36 E
Ningkang 109 26 45N 113 58 E
Ningkuo 109 30 38N 118 58 E
Ninglang 108 27 19N 100 53 E
Ningling 106 34 27N 115 19 E
Ningming 108 22 12N 107 5 E
Ningnan 108 27 7N 102 42 E
Ningpo 109 29 53N 121 33 E
Ningshan 106 33 12N 108 29 E
Ningsia Hui A.R. □ 106 37 45N 106 0 E
Ningte 109 26 45N 120 0 E
Ningtsin 99 29 44N 98 28 E
Ningtu 109 26 22N 115 48 E
Ningwu 106 29 2N 112 15 E
Ningyang, Fukien, China 109 25 44N 117 8 E
Ningyang, Shantung, China 106 35 46N 116 47 E
Ningyüan 109 25 36N 111 54 E
Ninh Binh 100 20 15N 105 55 E
Ninh Giang 100 20 44N 106 24 E
Ninh Hoa 100 12 30N 109 7 E
Ninh Ma 100 12 48N 109 21 E
Ninian, oilfield 19 60 42N 1 30 E
Ninove 47 50 51N 4 2 E
Nioaque 173 21 5 S 55 50W
Niobrara 158 42 48N 97 59W
Niobrara R. 158 42 30N 103 0W
Nioki 124 2 47 S 17 40 E
Niono 120 14 15N 6 0W
Nioro 120 15 30N 9 30W
Nioro du Rip 120 13 40N 15 50W
Nioro du Sahel 120 15 30N 9 30W
Niort 44 46 19N 0 29W
Niou 121 12 42N 2 1W
Nipa 135 6 9 S 143 29 E
Nipan 138 24 45 S 150 0 E
Nipani 96 16 20N 74 25 E
Nipawin 153 53 20N 104 0W
Nipawin Prov. Park 153 54 0N 104 37W
Nipigon 150 49 0N 88 17W
Nipigon, L. 150 49 50N 88 30W
Nipin, R. 153 55 46N 109 2W
Nipishish L. 151 54 12N 60 45W
Nipissing L. 150 46 20N 80 0W
Nipomo 163 35 4N 120 29W
Niquelândia 171 14 33 S 48 23W
Nira, R. 96 18 5N 74 25 E
Nirasaki 111 35 42N 138 27 E
Nirmal 96 19 3N 78 20 E
Nirmali 95 26 20N 86 35 E
Niš 66 43 19N 21 58 E
Nisa 57 39 30N 7 41W
Nisab 91 14 25N 46 29 E
Nišava, R. 66 43 20N 22 10 E
Niscemi 65 37 8N 14 21 E
Nishi-Sonogi-Hantō 110 32 55N 129 45 E
Nishinomiya 111 34 45N 135 20 E
Nishinoomote 112 30 43N 130 59 E
Nishio 111 34 52N 137 3 E
Nishiwaki 110 34 59N 134 48 E
Nisíros, I. 69 36 35N 27 12 E
Niskibi, R. 150 56 29N 88 9W
Nisko 54 50 35N 22 7 E
Nispen 47 51 29N 4 28 E
Nisporeny 70 47 4N 28 10 E
Nissafors 73 57 25N 13 37 E
Nissan 73 56 40N 12 51 E
Nissan I. 138 4 30 S 154 10 E
Nissedal 71 59 10N 8 30 E
Nisser 71 59 7N 8 28 E
Nissum Fjord 73 56 20N 8 11 E
Nistelrode 47 51 42N 5 34 E
Nisutlin, R. 152 60 14N 132 34W
Nitchequon 151 53 10N 70 58W
Niterói 173 22 52 S 43 0W
Nith, R. 35 55 20N 3 5W
Nithsdale 35 55 14N 3 50W
Niton 28 50 35N 1 14W
Nitra 53 48 19N 18 4 E
Nitra, R. 53 48 30N 18 7 E
Nitsa, R. 84 57 29N 64 33 E
Nittedal 71 60 1N 10 57 E
Niuchieh 108 27 47N 104 16 E
Niuchuang 107 40 58N 122 38 E
Niue I. (Savage I.) 130 19 2 S 169 54W
Niulan Chiang, R. 108 27 24N 103 9 E
Niut, Mt. 102 0 55N 109 30 E
Nivelles 47 50 35N 4 20 E
Nivernais 43 47 0N 3 40 E
Nixon, Nev., U.S.A. 160 39 54N 119 22W
Nixon, Tex., U.S.A. 159 29 17N 97 45W
Nizam Sagar 96 18 10N 77 58 E
Nizamabad 96 18 45N 78 7 E
Nizamghat 98 28 20N 95 45 E
Nizhanaya Tunguska 77 64 20N 93 0 E
Nizhiye Sergi 84 56 40N 59 18 E
Nizhne Kolymsk 77 68 40N 160 55 E
Nizhne-Vartovskoye 76 60 56N 76 38 E
Nizhneangarsk 77 56 0N 109 30 E
Nizhnegorskiy 82 45 27N 34 38 E
Nizhneudinsk 77 55 0N 99 20 E
Nizhniy Lomov 81 53 34N 43 38 E
Nizhniy Novgorod = Gorkiy 81 56 20N 44 0 E
Nizhniy Pyandzh 85 37 12N 68 35 E
Nizhniy Tagil 84 57 55N 59 57 E
Nizhny Salda 84 58 8N 60 42 E
Nizké Tatry 53 48 55N 20 0 E
Nizza Monferrato 62 44 46N 8 22 E
Njakwa 127 11 1 S 33 56 E
Njinjo 127 8 34 S 38 44 E
Njombe 124 9 20 S 34 50 E
Njombe □ 127 9 20 S 34 49 E
Njombe, R. 126 7 15 S 34 30 E
Nkambe 121 6 35N 10 40 E
Nkana 127 13 0 S 28 8 E
Nkawkaw 121 6 36N 0 49W
Nkhata Bay 124 11 33 S 34 16 E
Nkhota Kota 127 12 56 S 34 15 E
Nkongsamba 121 4 55N 9 55 E
Nkunka 127 14 57 S 25 58 E
Nkwanta 120 6 10N 2 10W
Nmai Pit, R. 99 25 30N 98 0 E
Nmai, R. 99 25 30N 98 0 E
Nmaushahra 95 33 11N 74 15 E
Nnewi 121 6 0N 6 59 E
Noakhali = Maijdi 98 22 50N 90 45 E
Noatak 147 67 32N 163 10W
Noatak, R. 147 68 0N 161 0W
Nobber 38 53 49N 6 45W
Nobeoka 110 32 36N 131 41 E
Nōbi-Heiya 111 35 15N 136 45 E
Noblejas 58 39 58N 3 26W
Noblesville 156 40 1N 85 59W
Noce, R. 62 46 22N 11 0 E
Nocera Inferiore 65 40 45N 14 37 E
Nocera Terinese 65 39 2N 16 9 E
Nocera Umbra 63 43 8N 12 47 E
Nochixtlán 165 17 28N 97 14W
Noci 65 40 47N 17 7 E
Nockatunga 139 27 42 S 142 42 E
Nocona 159 33 48N 97 45W
Nocrich 70 45 55N 24 26 E
Noda, Japan 111 35 56N 139 52 E
Noda, U.S.S.R. 77 47 30N 142 5 E
Noel 159 36 36N 94 29W
Nogales, Mexico 164 31 36N 94 29W
Nogales, U.S.A. 161 31 33N 115 50W
Nōgata 110 33 48N 130 54 E
Nogent-en-Bassigny 43 48 0N 5 20 E
Nogent-le-Rotrou 42 48 20N 0 50 E
Nogent-sur-Seine 43 48 30N 3 30 E
Noggerup 137 33 32 S 116 5 E
Noginsk, Moskva, U.S.S.R. 81 55 50N 38 25 E
Noginsk, Sib., U.S.S.R. 77 64 30N 90 50 E
Nogoa, R. 138 23 33 S 148 32 E
Nogoyá 172 32 24 S 59 48W
Nógrád □ 53 48 0N 19 30 E
Nogueira de Ramuin 56 42 21N 7 43W
Noguera Pallaresa, R. 58 42 15N 1 0 E
Noguera Ribagorzana, R. 58 42 15N 0 45 E
Nohar 94 29 11N 74 49 E
Noi, R. 101 14 50N 100 15 E
Noire, Mts. 42 48 11N 3 40W
Noirétable 44 45 48N 3 46 E
Noirmoutier 42 47 0N 2 15W
Noirmoutier, Î. de 42 46 58N 2 10W
Nojane 128 23 15 S 20 14 E
Nojima-Zaki 111 34 54N 139 53 E
Nok Kundi 93 28 50N 62 45 E
Nokaneng 128 19 47 S 22 17 E
Nokhtuysk 77 60 0N 117 45 E
Nokomis 153 51 35N 105 0W
Nokomis L. 153 57 0N 103 0W
Nokou 124 14 35N 14 47 E
Nol 73 57 56N 12 5 E
Nola, C. Afr. Emp. 124 3 35N 16 10 E
Nola, Italy 65 40 54N 14 29 E
Nolay 43 46 58N 4 35 E
Nolby 72 62 17N 17 26 E
Noli, C. di 62 44 12N 8 26 E
Nolinsk 84 57 28N 49 57 E
Noma Omuramba, R. 128 19 6 S 20 30 E
Noma-Saki 110 31 25N 130 7 E
Nomad 135 6 19 S 142 13 E
Noman L. 153 62 15N 108 55W
Nombre de Dios 166 9 34N 79 28W
Nome 147 64 30N 165 30W
Nomo-Zaki 110 32 35N 129 44 E
Nonacho L. 153 61 57N 109 28W
Nonancourt 42 48 47N 1 11 E
Nonant-le-Pin 42 48 42N 0 12 E
Nonda 138 20 40 S 142 28 E
Nong Chang 100 15 23N 99 51 E
Nong Het 100 19 29N 103 59 E
Nong Khae 101 14 29N 100 53 E
Nong Khai 100 17 50N 102 46 E
Nonoava 164 27 22N 106 38W
Nonopapa 147 21 50N 160 15W
Nonthaburi 100 13 51N 100 34 E
Nontron 44 45 31N 0 40 E
Noonamah 136 12 40 S 131 4 E
Noonan 158 48 51N 102 59W
Noondoo 139 28 35 S 148 30 E
Noonkanbah 102 18 30 S 124 50 E
Noord-Bergum 46 53 14N 6 1 E
Noord Brabant □ 47 51 40N 5 0 E
Noord Holland □ 46 52 30N 4 45 E
Noordbeveland 47 51 45N 3 50 E
Noordeloos 46 51 55N 4 56 E
Noordhollandsch Kanaal 46 52 55N 4 48 E
Noordhorn 46 53 16N 6 24 E
Noordoostpolder 46 52 45N 5 45 E
Noordwijk aan Zee 46 52 14N 4 26 E
Noordwijk-Binnen 46 52 14N 4 27 E
Noordwijkerhout 46 52 16N 4 30 E
'Noordwinning', gasfield 19 53 13N 3 10 E
Noordzee Kanaal 46 52 28N 4 35 E
Noorvik 147 66 50N 161 14W
Noorwolde 46 52 54N 6 8 E
Nootka 152 49 38N 126 38W
Nootka I. 152 49 40N 126 50W
Noqui 124 5 55 S 13 30 E
Nora, Ethiopia 123 16 6N 40 4 E
Nora, Sweden 72 59 32N 15 2 E
Noranda 150 48 20N 79 0W
Norberg 72 60 4N 15 56 E
Norbottens län □ 74 66 58N 20 0 E
Nórcia 63 42 50N 13 5 E
Norco 163 33 56N 117 33W
Nord □ 43 50 15N 3 30 E
Nord-Ostee Kanal 48 54 5N 9 15 E
Nord-Süd Kanal 48 53 0N 10 32 E
Nord-Trondelag Fylke □ 74 64 20N 12 0 E
Nordagutu 71 59 25N 9 20 E
Nordaustlandet 12 79 55N 23 0 E
Nordborg 73 55 5N 9 50 E
Nordby, Fanø, Denmark 73 55 27N 8 24 E
Nordby, Samsø, Denmark 73 55 58N 10 32 E
Norddal 71 62 15N 7 14 E
Norddalsfjord kpl. 71 61 39N 5 23 E
Norddeich 48 53 37N 7 10 E
Nordegg 152 52 29N 116 5W
Nordelph 29 52 34N 0 18 E
Norden 48 53 35N 7 12 E
Nordenham 48 53 29N 8 28 E
Norderhov 71 60 7N 10 17 E
Norderney 48 53 42N 7 9 E
Norderney, I. 48 53 42N 7 15 E
Nordfjord 71 61 55N 5 30 E
Nordfriesische Inseln 48 54 40N 8 20 E
Nordhausen 48 51 29N 10 47 E
Nordhorn 48 52 27N 7 4 E
Nordjyllands Amt □ 73 57 0N 10 0 E
Nordkapp, Norway 74 71 10N 25 44 E
Nordkapp, Svalb. 12 80 31N 20 0 E
Nordkinn 16 71 3N 28 0 E
Nordland Fylke □ 74 65 40N 13 0 E
Nördlingen 49 48 50N 10 30 E
Nordrhein-Westfalen □ 48 51 45N 7 30 E
Nordstrand, I. 48 54 27N 8 50 E
Nordvik 77 73 40N 110 57 E
Nore 71 60 10N 9 0 E
Nore R. 39 52 40N 7 20W
Noreena Cr. 136 22 20 S 120 25 E
Norefjell 71 60 16N 9 29 E
Norembega 150 48 59N 80 43W
Noresund 71 60 11N 9 37 E
Norfolk, Nebr., U.S.A. 158 42 3N 97 25W
Norfolk, Va., U.S.A. 156 36 52N 76 15W
Norfolk □ 29 52 39N 1 0 E
Norfolk Broads 29 52 30N 1 15 E
Norfolk I. 130 28 58 S 168 3 E
Norfork Res. 159 36 25N 92 0W
Norg 46 53 4N 6 28 E
Norham 35 55 44N 2 9W
Norilsk 77 69 20N 88 0 E
Norley 139 27 45 S 143 48 E
Normal 158 40 30N 89 0W
Norman 159 35 12N 97 30W
Norman, R. 138 19 20 S 142 35 E
Norman Wells 147 65 17N 126 45W
Normanby 142 39 32 S 174 18 E
Normanby I. 135 10 55 S 151 5 E
Normanby, R. 138 14 23 S 144 10 E
Normandie 42 48 45N 0 10 E
Normandie, Collines de 42 48 55N 0 45W
Normandin 150 48 49N 72 31W
Normandy = Normandie 42 48 45N 0 10 E
Normanhurst, Mt. 137 25 13 S 122 30 E
Normanton, Austral. 138 17 40 S 141 10 E
Normanton, U.K. 33 53 41N 1 26W
Normanville 140 35 27 S 138 18 E
Norna, Mt. 138 20 55 S 140 42 E
Nornalup 137 35 0 S 116 48 E
Norquay 153 51 53N 102 5W
Ñorquinco 176 41 51 S 70 55W
Norrahammar 73 57 43N 14 7 E
Norrbottens län □ 74 66 50N 18 0 E
Norrby 74 64 55N 18 15 E
Nørre Åby 73 55 27N 9 52 E
Nørre Nebel 73 55 47N 8 17 E
Nørresundby 73 57 5N 9 52 E
Norris 160 45 40N 111 48W
Norristown 162 40 9N 75 15W
Norrköping 73 58 37N 16 11 E
Norrland □ 74 66 50N 18 0 E
Norrtälje 72 59 46N 18 42 E
Norseman 137 32 8 S 121 43 E
Norsholm 73 58 31N 15 59 E
Norsk 77 52 30N 130 0 E
Norte de Santander □ 174 8 0N 73 0W
North Adams 162 42 42N 73 6W
North America 50 40 0N 70 0W
North Andaman I. 101 13 15N 92 40 E
North Atlantic Ocean 14 30 0N 50 0W
North Ballachulish 36 56 42N 5 9W
North Battleford 153 52 50N 108 17W
North Bay 150 46 20N 79 30W
North Belcher Is. 150 56 50N 79 50W
North Bend, Can. 152 49 50N 121 35W
North Bend, U.S.A. 160 43 28N 124 7W
North Bennington 162 42 56N 73 15W
North Berwick, U.K. 35 56 4N 2 44W
North Berwick, U.S.A. 162 43 18N 70 43W
North Br., Ashburton R. 143 43 30 S 171 30 E
North Buganda □ 126 1 0N 32 0 E
North Canadian, R. 159 36 48N 103 0W
North C., Antarct. 13 71 0N 166 0 E
North C., Can. 151 47 2N 60 20W
North, Cape 151 47 2N 60 25W
North C., N.Z. 142 34 23 S 173 4 E
North C., P.N.G. 135 2 32 S 150 50 E
North C., Spitsbergen 12 80 40N 20 0 E
North Caribou L. 150 52 50N 90 40W
North Carolina □ 157 35 30N 80 0W
North Cerney 28 51 45N 1 58W
North Channel, Br. Is. 34 55 0N 5 30W
North Channel, Can. 150 46 0N 83 0W
North Chicago 156 42 19N 87 50W
North Collingham 33 53 8N 0 46W
North Dakota □ 158 47 30N 100 0W
North Dandalup 137 32 30 S 116 2 E
N. Dorset Downs 28 50 50N 2 30W
North Down □ 38 54 40N 5 45W
North Downs 29 51 17N 0 30W
North East 162 39 36N 75 56W
North Eastern □ 126 1 30N 40 0 E
North Esk, R. 37 56 44N 2 25W
North European Plain 16 55 0N 20 0 E
N. Foreland, Pt. 29 51 22N 1 28 E
North Fork 163 37 14N 119 29W
N. Frisian Is. = Nordfr'sche Inseln 48 54 50N 8 20 E
N. Harris, dist. 36 58 0N 6 55W
North Henik L. 153 61 45N 97 40W
North Hill 30 50 33N 4 26W
North Horr 126 3 20N 37 8 E
North Hykeham 33 53 10N 0 35W
North I., Kenya 126 4 5N 36 5 E
North I., N.Z. 143 38 0 S 175 0 E
North Kamloops 152 50 40N 120 25W
North Kessock 37 57 30N 4 15W
North Knife L., Can. 153 58 0N 97 0W
North Knife L., Man., Can. 153 58 5N 97 5W
North Knife, R. 153 58 53N 94 45W
North Koel, R. 95 23 50N 84 5 E
North Korea ■ 105 40 0N 127 0 E
N. Lakhimpur 99 27 15N 94 10 E
N. Las Vegas 161 36 15N 115 6W
North Mara □ 126 1 20 S 34 20 E
North Minch 36 58 5N 5 55W
North Molton 30 51 3N 3 48W
North Nahanni, R. 152 62 15N 123 20W
North Ossetian A.S.S.R. □ 83 43 30N 44 30 E
North Palisade 163 37 6N 118 32W
North Petherton 28 51 6N 3 1W
North Platte 158 41 10N 100 50W
North Platte, R. 160 42 50N 106 50W
North Pt., Austral. 108 27 23 S 153 14 E
North Pt., Can. 151 47 5N 65 0W
North Pole 12 90 0N 0 0 E
North Portal 153 49 0N 102 33W
North Powder 160 45 2N 117 59W
North Queensferry 35 56 1N 3 22W
North Riding (□) 26 54 22N 1 30W
North Roe, dist. 36 60 40N 1 22W
North Ronaldsay, I. 37 59 20N 2 30W
North Sea 19 56 0N 4 0 E
North Sentinel, I. 101 11 35N 92 15 E
North Somercotes 33 53 28N 0 9 E
North Sound 39 53 10N 9 48W
North Sound, The 37 59 18N 2 45W
North Sporades = Voríai Sporádhes 69 39 0N 24 10 E
North Stradbroke I. 133 27 35 S 153 28 E
North Sunderland 35 55 35N 1 40W
North Sydney 151 46 12N 60 21W
North Syracuse 162 43 8N 76 7W
N. Taranaki Bt. 82 38 45 S 174 20 E

**North Tawton** **Nyirbátor**


| | | | |
|---|---|---|---|
| North Tawton | **30** | 50 48N | 3 55W |
| North Thompson, R. | **152** | 50 40N | 120 20W |
| North Thoresby | **33** | 53 27N | 0 3W |
| North Tidworth | **28** | 51 14N | 1 40W |
| North Tolsta | **36** | 58 21N | 6 13W |
| N. Tonawanda | **156** | 43 5N | 78 50W |
| N. Truchas Pk. | **161** | 36 0N | 105 30W |
| North Twin I. | **150** | 53 20N | 80 0W |
| North Tyne, R. | **35** | 54 59N | 2 7W |
| North Uist I. | **36** | 57 40N | 7 15W |
| North Vancouver | **152** | 49 25N | 123 20W |
| North Vermilion | **152** | 58 25N | 116 0W |
| North Vernon | **156** | 39 0N | 85 35W |
| North Vietnam ■ | **100** | 22 0N | 105 0E |
| North Wabasca L. | **152** | 56 0N | 113 55W |
| North Walsham | **29** | 52 49N | 1 22E |
| North West C. | **136** | 21 45S | 114 9E |
| North West Highlands | **36** | 57 35N | 5 2W |
| North West River | **151** | 53 30N | 60 10W |
| North Western □ | **127** | 13 30S | 25 30E |
| North York Moors | **33** | 54 25N | 0 50W |
| North Yorkshire □ | **33** | 54 15N | 1 25W |
| Northallerton | **33** | 54 20N | 1 26W |
| Northam, Austral. | **132** | 31 35S | 116 42E |
| Northam, S. Afr. | **137** | 24 55S | 27 15E |
| Northam, U.K. | **30** | 51 2N | 4 13W |
| Northampton, Austral. | **137** | 28 21S | 114 33E |
| Northampton, U.K. | **29** | 52 14N | 0 54W |
| Northampton, Mass., U.S.A. | **162** | 42 22N | 72 39W |
| Northampton, Pa., U.S.A. | **162** | 40 38N | 75 24W |
| Northampton □ | **29** | 52 16N | 0 55W |
| Northampton Downs | **138** | 24 35S | 145 48E |
| Northbridge | **162** | 42 12N | 71 40W |
| Northcliffe | **137** | 34 39S | 116 7E |
| N.E. Land | **12** | 80 0N | 24 0E |
| N.E. Providence Chan. | **166** | 26 0N | 76 0W |
| Northeast Providence Channel | **166** | 26 0N | 76 0W |
| Northeim | **48** | 51 42N | 10 0E |
| Northern □, Malawi | **127** | 11 0S | 34 0E |
| Northern □, Uganda | **126** | 3 5N | 32 30E |
| Northern □, Zambia | **127** | 10 30S | 31 0E |
| Northern Circars | **96** | 17 30N | 82 30E |
| Northern Indian L. | **153** | 57 20N | 97 20W |
| Northern Ireland □ | **38** | 54 45N | 7 0W |
| Northern Light, L. | **150** | 48 15N | 90 39W |
| Northern Province □ | **120** | 9 0S | 11 30W |
| Northern Territory □ | **136** | 16 0S | 133 0E |
| Northfield, Minn., U.S.A. | **158** | 44 37N | 93 10W |
| Northfield, N.J., U.S.A. | **162** | 39 22N | 74 33W |
| Northfleet | **29** | 51 26N | 0 20E |
| Northiam | **29** | 50 59N | 0 39E |
| Northland □ | **143** | 35 30S | 173 30E |
| Northleach | **28** | 51 49N | 1 50W |
| Northome | **158** | 47 53N | 94 15W |
| Northop | **31** | 53 13N | 3 8W |
| Northport, Ala., U.S.A. | **157** | 33 15N | 87 35W |
| Northport, Mich., U.S.A. | **156** | 45 8N | 85 39W |
| Northport, N.Y., U.S.A. | **162** | 40 53N | 73 20W |
| Northport, Wash., U.S.A. | **160** | 48 55N | 117 48W |
| Northrepps | **29** | 52 53N | 1 20E |
| Northumberland □ | **35** | 55 12N | 2 0W |
| Northumberland, C. | **140** | 38 5S | 140 40E |
| Northumberland Is. | **138** | 21 30S | 149 50E |
| Northumberland Str. | **151** | 46 20N | 64 0W |
| Northville | **162** | 43 13N | 74 11W |
| Northway Junction | **147** | 63 0N | 141 55W |
| N.W. Providence Chan. | **166** | 26 0N | 78 0W |
| Northwest Terr. | **148** | 65 0N | 100 0W |
| N.W.Basin | **137** | 25 45S | 115 0E |
| Northwich | **32** | 53 16N | 2 30W |
| Northwold | **29** | 52 33N | 0 37E |
| Northwood, Iowa, U.S.A. | **158** | 43 27N | 93 12W |
| Northwood, N.D., U.S.A. | **158** | 47 44N | 97 30W |
| Norton, Rhod. | **127** | 17 52S | 30 40E |
| Norton, N. Yorks., U.K. | **33** | 54 9N | 0 48W |
| Norton, Suffolk, U.K. | **29** | 52 15N | 0 52E |
| Norton, U.S.A. | **158** | 39 50N | 100 0W |
| Norton B. | **147** | 64 40N | 162 0W |
| Norton Fitzwarren | **28** | 51 1N | 3 10W |
| Norton Sd. | **147** | 64 0N | 165 0W |
| Norton Summit | **109** | 34 56S | 138 43E |
| Nortorf | **48** | 54 14N | 9 47E |
| Norwalk, Calif., U.S.A. | **163** | 33 54N | 118 5W |
| Norwalk, Conn., U.S.A. | **162** | 41 9N | 73 25W |
| Norwalk, Ohio, U.S.A. | **156** | 41 13N | 82 38W |
| Norway | **156** | 45 46N | 87 57W |
| Norway ■ | **74** | 67 0N | 11 0E |
| Norway House | **153** | 53 59N | 97 50W |
| Norwegian Dependency | **13** | 66 0N | 15 0E |
| Norwegian Sea | **14** | 66 0N | 1 0E |
| Norwich, U.K. | **29** | 52 38N | 1 17E |
| Norwich, Conn., U.S.A. | **162** | 41 33N | 72 5W |
| Norwich, N.Y., U.S.A. | **162** | 42 32N | 75 30W |
| Norwood, Austral. | **109** | 34 56S | 138 39E |
| Norwood, U.S.A. | **162** | 42 10N | 71 10W |
| Noshiro | **112** | 40 12N | 140 0E |
| Noshiro, R. | **112** | 40 15N | 140 15E |
| Nosok | **76** | 70 10N | 82 20E |
| Nosovka | **80** | 50 50N | 31 30E |
| Nosratābād | **93** | 29 55N | 60 0E |
| Noss Hd. | **37** | 58 29N | 3 4W |
| Noss, I. of | **36** | 60 8N | 1 1W |
| Nossa Senhora da Glória | **170** | 10 14S | 37 25W |
| Nossa Senhora das Dores | **170** | 10 29S | 37 13W |
| Nossebro | **73** | 58 12N | 12 43E |
| Nossob | **128** | 22 15S | 17 48E |
| Nossob, R. | **128** | 25 15S | 20 30E |
| Nosy Bé, I. | **125** | 13 25S | 48 15E |
| Nosy Mitsio, I. | **125** | 12 54S | 48 36E |
| Nosy Varika | **125** | 20 35S | 48 32E |
| Notigi Dam | **153** | 56 40N | 99 10W |
| Notikewin | **152** | 56 55N | 117 50W |
| Notikewin, R. | **152** | 56 59N | 117 38W |
| Notios Evvoïkós Kólpos | **69** | 38 20N | 24 0E |
| Noto | **65** | 36 52N | 15 4E |
| Noto, G. di | **65** | 36 50N | 15 10E |
| Notodden | **71** | 59 35N | 9 17E |
| Notre Dame | **151** | 46 18N | 64 46W |
| Notre Dame B. | **151** | 49 45N | 55 30W |
| Notre Dame de Koartac | **149** | 60 55N | 69 40W |
| Notre Dame d'Ivugivic | **149** | 62 20N | 78 0W |
| Nottaway, R. | **150** | 51 22N | 78 55W |
| Nøtterøy | **71** | 59 14N | 10 24E |
| Nottingham | **33** | 52 57N | 1 10W |
| Nottingham □ | **33** | 53 10N | 1 0W |
| Nottoway, R. | **156** | 37 0N | 77 45W |
| Notwani, R. | **128** | 24 14S | 26 20E |
| Nouadhibou | **116** | 21 0N | 17 0W |
| Nouakchott | **120** | 18 20N | 15 50W |
| Nouméa | **130** | 22 17S | 166 30E |
| Noup Hd. | **37** | 59 20N | 3 2W |
| Noupoort | **128** | 31 10S | 24 57E |
| Nouveau Comptoir (Paint Hills) | **150** | 53 0N | 78 49W |
| Nouvelle Calédonie | **142** | 21 0S | 165 0E |
| Nouzonville | **43** | 49 48N | 4 44E |
| Nova-Annenskiy | **81** | 50 32N | 42 39E |
| Nová Bana | **53** | 48 28N | 18 39E |
| Nová Bystrice | **52** | 49 2N | 15 8E |
| Nova Chaves | **124** | 10 50S | 21 15E |
| Nova Cruz | **170** | 6 28S | 35 25W |
| Nova Era | **171** | 19 45S | 43 3W |
| Nova Esperança | **173** | 23 8S | 52 13W |
| Nova Friburgo | **173** | 22 10S | 42 30W |
| Nova Gaia | **124** | 10 10S | 17 35E |
| Nova Gradiška | **66** | 45 17N | 17 28E |
| Nova Granada | **171** | 20 30S | 49 20W |
| Nova Iguaçu | **173** | 22 45S | 43 28W |
| Nova Iorque | **170** | 7 0S | 44 5W |
| Nova Lamego | **120** | 12 19N | 14 11W |
| Nova Lima | **173** | 19 59S | 43 51W |
| Nova Lisboa = Huambo | **125** | 12 42S | 15 54E |
| Nova Lusitânia | **127** | 19 50S | 34 34E |
| Nova Mambone | **129** | 21 0S | 35 3E |
| Nova Mesto | **63** | 45 47N | 15 12E |
| Nova Paka | **52** | 50 29N | 15 30E |
| Nova Ponte | **171** | 19 8S | 47 41W |
| Nova Preixo | **127** | 14 45S | 36 22E |
| Nova Scotia □ | **151** | 45 10N | 63 0W |
| Nova Sofala | **129** | 20 7S | 34 48E |
| Nova Varoš | **66** | 43 29N | 19 48E |
| Nova Venécia | **171** | 18 45S | 40 24W |
| Nova Zagora | **67** | 42 32N | 25 59E |
| Novaci, Rumania | **70** | 45 10N | 23 42E |
| Novaci, Yugo. | **66** | 41 5N | 21 29E |
| Novaleksandrovskaya | **83** | 45 29N | 41 17E |
| Novalorque | **171** | 6 48S | 44 0W |
| Novara | **62** | 45 27N | 8 36E |
| Novato | **163** | 38 6N | 122 35W |
| Novaya Kakhovka | **82** | 46 42N | 33 27E |
| Novaya Ladoga | **78** | 60 7N | 32 16E |
| Novaya Lyalya | **84** | 58 50N | 60 35E |
| Novaya Sibir, O. | **77** | 75 10N | 150 0E |
| Novaya Zemlya | **76** | 75 0N | 56 0E |
| Novelda | **59** | 38 24N | 0 45W |
| Novellara | **62** | 44 50N | 10 43E |
| Noventa Vicentina | **63** | 45 18N | 11 30E |
| Novgorod | **80** | 58 30N | 31 25E |
| Novgorod Severskiy | **80** | 52 2N | 33 10E |
| Novgorod Volynski | **80** | 50 38N | 27 47E |
| Novi Bečej. | **66** | 45 36N | 20 10E |
| Novi Grad | **63** | 45 19N | 13 33E |
| Novi Knezeva | **66** | 46 4N | 20 8E |
| Novi Krichim | **67** | 42 22N | 24 31E |
| Novi Ligure | **62** | 44 45N | 8 47E |
| Novi-Pazar | **67** | 43 25N | 27 15E |
| Novi Pazar | **66** | 43 12N | 20 28E |
| Novi Sad | **66** | 45 18N | 19 52E |
| Novi Vinodolski | **63** | 45 10N | 14 48E |
| Novigrad | **63** | 44 10N | 15 32E |
| Noville | **47** | 50 4N | 5 46E |
| Novo Acôrdo | **170** | 13 10S | 46 48W |
| Nôvo Cruzeiro | **171** | 17 29S | 41 53W |
| Novo Freixo | **127** | 14 49S | 36 30E |
| Nôvo Hamburgo | **173** | 29 37S | 51 7W |
| Novo Horizonte | **171** | 21 25S | 49 10W |
| Novo Luso | **103** | 4 3S | 126 6E |
| Novo Redondo | **124** | 11 10S | 13 48E |
| Novo Selo | **66** | 44 11N | 22 47E |
| Novo-Sergiyevskiy | **84** | 52 5N | 53 38E |
| Novo-Zavidovskiy | **81** | 56 32N | 36 29E |
| Novoalekseyevka | **84** | 50 8N | 55 39E |
| Novoataysk | **76** | 53 30N | 84 0E |
| Novoazovsk | **82** | 47 15N | 38 4E |
| Novobelitsa | **80** | 52 27N | 31 2E |
| Novobogatinskoye | **83** | 47 26N | 51 17E |
| Novocherkassk | **83** | 47 27N | 40 5E |
| Novodevichye | **81** | 53 37N | 48 58E |
| Novograd Volynskiy | **80** | 50 40N | 27 35E |
| Novogrudok | **80** | 53 40N | 25 50E |
| Novokayakent | **83** | 42 45N | 42 52E |
| Novokazalinsk | **76** | 45 40N | 61 40E |
| Novokhopersk | **81** | 51 5N | 41 50E |
| Novokuybyshevsk | **84** | 53 7N | 49 58E |
| Novokuznetsk | **76** | 54 0N | 87 10E |
| Novomirgorod | **82** | 48 57N | 31 33E |
| Novomoskovsk, R.S.F.S.R., U.S.S.R. | **81** | 54 5N | 38 15E |
| Novomoskovsk, Ukrainian S.S.R., U.S.S.R. | **81** | 48 33N | 35 17E |
| Novoorsk | **84** | 51 21N | 59 2E |
| Novopolotsk | **80** | 55 38N | 28 37E |
| Novorossiysk | **82** | 44 43N | 37 52E |
| Novorzhev | **80** | 57 3N | 29 25E |
| Novoselitsa | **82** | 48 14N | 26 15E |
| Novoshakhtinsk | **83** | 47 39N | 39 58E |
| Novosibirsk | **76** | 55 0N | 83 5E |
| Novosibirskiye Ostrava | **77** | 75 0N | 140 0E |
| Novosil | **81** | 52 58N | 36 58E |
| Novosokolniki | **80** | 56 33N | 28 42E |
| Novotroitsk | **84** | 51 10N | 58 15E |
| Novotroitskoye | **85** | 43 42N | 73 46E |
| Novotulskiy | **81** | 54 10N | 37 36E |
| Novoukrainka | **82** | 48 25N | 31 30E |
| Novouzensk | **81** | 50 32N | 48 17E |
| Novovolynsk | **80** | 50 45N | 24 4E |
| Novovyatsk | **84** | 58 24N | 49 45E |
| Novozybkov | **80** | 52 30N | 32 0E |
| Novska | **66** | 45 19N | 17 0E |
| Novy Bug | **82** | 47 34N | 34 29E |
| Nový Bydzov | **52** | 50 14N | 15 29E |
| Novy Dwór Mazowiecki | **54** | 52 26N | 20 44E |
| Nový Jičin | **53** | 49 15N | 18 0E |
| Novyy Oskol | **81** | 50 44N | 37 55E |
| Novyy Port | **76** | 67 40N | 72 30E |
| Novyye Aneny | **70** | 46 51N | 29 13E |
| Now Shahr | **93** | 36 40N | 51 40E |
| Nowa Deba | **54** | 50 26N | 21 41E |
| Nowa Nowa | **141** | 37 44S | 148 3E |
| Nowa Skalmierzyce | **54** | 51 43N | 18 0E |
| Nowa Sól | **54** | 51 48N | 15 44E |
| Nowe | **54** | 53 41N | 18 44E |
| Nowe Miasteczko | **54** | 51 42N | 15 42E |
| Nowe Miasto | **54** | 51 38N | 20 34E |
| Nowe Miasto Lubawskie | **54** | 53 27N | 19 33E |
| Nowe Warpno | **54** | 53 42N | 14 18E |
| Nowen Hill | **39** | 51 42N | 9 15W |
| Nowendoc | **141** | 31 32S | 151 44E |
| Nowgong | **98** | 26 20N | 92 50E |
| Nowingi | **140** | 34 33S | 142 15E |
| Nowogard | **54** | 53 41N | 15 10E |
| Nowogród | **54** | 53 14N | 21 53E |
| Nowra | **141** | 34 53S | 150 35E |
| Nowthanna Mt. | **137** | 27 0S | 118 40E |
| Nowy Dwór | **54** | 53 40N | 23 0E |
| Nowy Korczyn | **54** | 50 19N | 20 48E |
| Nowy Sącz | **54** | 49 40N | 20 41E |
| Nowy Sącz □ | **54** | 49 30N | 20 30E |
| Nowy Staw | **54** | 54 13N | 19 2E |
| Nowy Targ | **53** | 49 30N | 20 2E |
| Nowy Tomyśl | **54** | 52 19N | 16 10E |
| Noxen | **162** | 41 25N | 76 4W |
| Noxon | **160** | 48 0N | 115 54W |
| Noya | **56** | 42 48N | 8 53W |
| Noyant | **42** | 47 30N | 0 6E |
| Noyers | **43** | 47 40N | 4 0E |
| Noyes, I. | **152** | 55 30N | 133 40W |
| Noyon | **43** | 49 34N | 3 0E |
| Nriquinha | **125** | 16 0S | 21 25E |
| Nsa, O. en | **119** | 32 23N | 5 20E |
| Nsanje | **127** | 16 55S | 35 12E |
| Nsawam | **121** | 5 50N | 0 24W |
| Nsomba | **127** | 10 45S | 29 59E |
| Nsopzup | **98** | 25 51N | 97 30E |
| Nsukka | **121** | 7 0N | 7 50E |
| Nuanetsi | **125** | 21 15S | 30 48E |
| Nuanetsi, R. | **127** | 21 10S | 31 20E |
| Nuatja | **121** | 7 0N | 1 10E |
| Nuba Mts. = Nubāh, Jibālan | **123** | 12 0N | 31 0E |
| Nubāh, Jibālan | **123** | 12 0N | 31 0E |
| Nûbîya, Es Sahrâ En | **122** | 21 30N | 33 30E |
| Nuble □ | **172** | 37 0S | 72 0W |
| Nuboai | **103** | 2 10S | 136 30E |
| Nubra, R. | **95** | 34 50N | 77 25E |
| Nudgee | **108** | 27 22S | 153 5E |
| Nudgee Beach | **108** | 27 21S | 153 6E |
| Nüdlac | **66** | 46 10N | 20 50E |
| Nudo Ausangate, Mt. | **174** | 13 45S | 71 10W |
| Nudo de Vilcanota | **174** | 14 30S | 70 0W |
| Nueces, R. | **159** | 28 18N | 98 39W |
| Nueltin L. | **153** | 60 30N | 99 30W |
| Nuenen | **47** | 51 29N | 5 33E |
| Nueva Antioquia | **174** | 6 5N | 69 26W |
| Nueva Casas Grandes | **164** | 30 25N | 107 55W |
| Nueva Esparta □ | **174** | 11 0N | 64 0W |
| Nueva Gerona | **166** | 21 53N | 82 49W |
| Nueva Imperial | **176** | 38 45S | 72 58W |
| Nueva Palmira | **172** | 33 52S | 58 20W |
| Nueva Rosita | **164** | 28 0N | 101 20W |
| Nueva San Salvador | **166** | 13 40N | 89 25W |
| Nuéve de Julio | **172** | 35 30S | 61 0W |
| Nuevitas | **166** | 21 30N | 77 20W |
| Nuevo, Golfo | **176** | 43 0S | 64 30W |
| Nuevo Guerrero | **165** | 26 34N | 99 15W |
| Nuevo Laredo | **165** | 27 30N | 99 40W |
| Nuevo León □ | **164** | 25 0N | 100 0W |
| Nuevo Rocafuerte | **174** | 0 55S | 76 50W |
| Nugget Pt. | **143** | 46 27S | 169 50E |
| Nugrus Gebel | **122** | 24 58N | 39 34E |
| Nuhaka | **142** | 39 3S | 177 45E |
| Nuhurowa, I. | **103** | 5 30S | 132 45E |
| Nuits | **43** | 47 10N | 4 56E |
| Nuits-St.-Georges | **43** | 47 10N | 4 56E |
| Nukey Bluff, Mt. | **132** | 32 32S | 135 40E |
| Nukheila (Merga) | **122** | 19 1N | 26 21E |
| Nukus | **76** | 42 20N | 59 40E |
| Nuland | **46** | 51 44N | 5 26E |
| Nulato | **147** | 64 40N | 158 10W |
| Nules | **58** | 39 51N | 0 9W |
| Nullagine | **136** | 21 53S | 120 6E |
| Nullagine, R. | **136** | 21 20S | 120 20E |
| Nullarbor | **137** | 31 28S | 130 55E |
| Nullarbor Plain | **137** | 30 45S | 129 0E |
| Numalla, L. | **139** | 28 43S | 144 20E |
| Numan | **121** | 9 29N | 12 3E |
| Numansdorp | **46** | 51 43N | 4 26E |
| Numata | **111** | 36 45N | 139 4E |
| Numatinna, W. | **123** | 6 38N | 27 15E |
| Numazu | **111** | 35 7N | 138 51E |
| Numbulwar | **138** | 14 15S | 135 45E |
| Numfoor, I. | **103** | 1 0S | 134 50E |
| Numurkah | **141** | 36 0S | 145 26E |
| Nun, R. | **105** | 47 30N | 124 40E |
| Nunaksaluk, I. | **151** | 55 49N | 60 20W |
| Nundah | **108** | 27 24S | 152 54E |
| Nuneaton | **28** | 52 32N | 1 29W |
| Nungo | **127** | 13 23S | 37 43E |
| Nungwe | **126** | 2 48S | 32 2E |
| Nunivak I. | **147** | 60 0N | 166 0W |
| Nunkun, Mt. | **95** | 33 57N | 76 8E |
| Nunney | **28** | 51 13N | 2 20W |
| Nunspeet | **46** | 52 21N | 5 45E |
| Nuoro | **64** | 40 20N | 9 20E |
| Nŭousa | **68** | 40 42N | 22 9E |
| Nuqayy, Jabal | **119** | 23 11N | 19 30E |
| Nuquí | **174** | 5 42N | 77 17W |
| Nurata | **85** | 40 33N | 65 41E |
| Nuratau, Khrebet | **85** | 40 40N | 66 30E |
| Nure, R. | **62** | 44 40N | 9 32E |
| Nuremburg = Nürnberg | **49** | 49 26N | 11 5E |
| Nuri | **164** | 28 2N | 109 22W |
| Nurina | **137** | 30 44S | 126 23E |
| Nuriootpa | **140** | 34 27S | 139 0E |
| Nurlat | **84** | 54 29N | 50 45E |
| Nürnberg | **49** | 49 26N | 11 5E |
| Nurrari Lakes | **137** | 29 1S | 130 5E |
| Nurri | **64** | 39 43N | 9 13E |
| Nusa Barung | **103** | 8 22S | 113 20E |
| Nusa Kambangan | **103** | 7 47S | 109 0E |
| Nusa Tenggara □ | **102** | 7 30S | 117 0E |
| Nusa Tenggara Barat | **102** | 8 50S | 117 30E |
| Nusa Tenggara Timur | **103** | 9 30S | 122 0E |
| Nushki | **94** | 29 35N | 65 65E |
| Nŭsŭud | **70** | 47 19N | 24 29E |
| Nutak | **149** | 57 28N | 61 52W |
| Nuth | **47** | 50 55N | 5 53E |
| Nutwood Downs | **138** | 15 49S | 134 10E |
| Nuwaiba | **122** | 28 58N | 34 40E |
| Nuwakot | **95** | 28 10N | 83 55E |
| Nuwara Eliya | **97** | 6 58N | 80 55E |
| Nuwefontein | **128** | 28 1S | 19 6E |
| Nuweveldberge | **128** | 32 10S | 21 45E |
| Nuyts Arch. | **139** | 32 12S | 133 20E |
| Nuyts, C. | **137** | 32 2S | 132 21E |
| Nuyts, Pt. | **132** | 35 4S | 116 38E |
| Nuzvid | **96** | 16 47N | 80 53E |
| NW Tor, oilfield | **19** | 56 42N | 3 13E |
| Nyaake (Webo) | **120** | 4 52N | 7 37W |
| Nyabing | **137** | 33 30S | 118 7E |
| Nyack | **162** | 41 5N | 73 57W |
| Nyadal | **72** | 62 48N | 17 59E |
| Nyagyn | **76** | 62 8N | 63 36E |
| Nyah West | **140** | 35 11S | 143 21E |
| Nyahanga | **126** | 2 20S | 33 37E |
| Nyahua | **126** | 5 25S | 33 23E |
| Nyahururu | **126** | 0 2N | 36 27E |
| Nyahururu Falls | **126** | 0 2N | 36 27E |
| Nyakanazi | **126** | 3 2S | 31 10E |
| Nyakasu | **126** | 3 58S | 30 6E |
| Nyakrom | **121** | 5 40N | 0 50W |
| Nyâlâ | **123** | 12 2N | 24 58E |
| Nyamandhlovu | **127** | 19 55S | 28 16E |
| Nyambiti | **126** | 2 48S | 33 27E |
| Nyamwaga | **126** | 1 27S | 34 33E |
| Nyandekwa | **126** | 3 57S | 32 32E |
| Nyanga, L. | **137** | 29 57S | 126 10E |
| Nyangana | **128** | 18 0S | 20 40E |
| Nyanguge | **126** | 2 30S | 33 12E |
| Nyangwena | **127** | 15 18S | 28 45E |
| Nyanji | **127** | 14 25S | 31 46E |
| Nyankpala | **121** | 9 21N | 0 58W |
| Nyanza, Burundi | **126** | 4 21S | 29 36E |
| Nyanza, Rwanda | **126** | 2 20S | 29 42E |
| Nyanza □ | **126** | 0 10S | 34 15E |
| Nyarling, R. | **152** | 60 41N | 113 23W |
| Nyasa, L. = Malawi, L. | **127** | 12 0S | 34 30E |
| Nyaunglebin | **98** | 17 52N | 96 42E |
| Nyazepetrovsk | **84** | 56 3N | 59 36E |
| Nyazwidzi, R. | **127** | 19 35S | 32 0E |
| Nyborg | **73** | 55 18N | 10 47E |
| Nybro | **73** | 56 44N | 15 55E |
| Nybster | **37** | 58 34N | 3 6W |
| Nyda | **76** | 66 40N | 73 10E |
| Nyenchen Tanglha Shan | **99** | 30 30N | 95 0E |
| Nyeri | **126** | 0 23S | 36 56E |
| Nyeri □ | **126** | 0 25S | 36 55E |
| Nyerol | **123** | 8 41N | 32 1E |
| Nyhem | **72** | 62 54N | 15 37E |
| Nyiel | **123** | 6 9N | 31 4E |
| Nyika Plat. | **127** | 10 30S | 36 0E |
| Nyilumba | **127** | 10 30S | 40 22E |
| Nyinahin | **120** | 6 43N | 2 3W |
| Nyirbátor | **53** | 47 49N | 22 9E |

Nyíregyháza Oldmeldrum


Nyiregyháza 53 48 0N 21 47 E
Nykarleby (Uusikaarlepyy) 74 63 32N 22 31 E
Nykobing 73 54 56N 11 52 E
Nykøbing, Falster, Denmark 73 54 56N 11 52 E
Nykøbing, Mors, Denmark 73 56 48N 8 51 E
Nykøbing, Sjælland, Denmark 73 55 55N 11 40 E
Nyköbing 73 56 49N 8 50 E
Nyköping 73 58 45N 17 0 E
Nykroppa 72 59 37N 14 18 E
Nykvarn 72 59 11N 17 25 E
Nyland 72 63 1N 17 45 E
Nylstroom 129 24 42 S 28 22 E
Nymagee 141 32 7 S 146 20 E
Nymburk 52 50 10N 15 1 E
Nymindegab 73 55 50N 8 12 E
Nynäshamn 72 58 54N 17 57 E
Nyngan 141 31 30 S 147 8 E
Nyon 50 46 23N 6 14 E
Nyons 45 44 22N 5 10 E
Nyora 141 38 20 S 145 41 E
Nyord 73 55 4N 12 13 E
Nysa 54 50 40N 17 22 E
Nysa, R. 54 52 4N 14 46 E
Nyssa 160 43 56N 117 2W
Nysted 73 54 40N 11 44 E
Nytva 84 57 56N 55 20 E
Nyūgawa 110 33 56N 133 5 E
Nyunzu 126 5 57 S 27 58 E
Nyurba 77 63 17N 118 20 E
Nzega 126 4 10 S 33 12 E
Nzega □ 126 4 10 S 33 10 E
N'Zérékoré 120 7 49N 8 48W
Nzilo, Chutes de 127 10 18 S 25 27 E
Nzubuka 126 4 45 S 32 50 E

## O

O-Shima, Fukuoka, Japan 110 33 54N 130 25 E
O-Shima, Nagasaki, Japan 110 33 29N 129 33 E
O-Shima, Shizuoka, Japan 111 34 44N 139 24 E
Oa, Mull of 34 55 35N 6 20W
Oa, The, Pen. 34 55 36N 6 17W
Oacoma 158 43 50N 99 26W
Oadby 28 52 37N 1 7W
Oahe 158 44 33N 100 29W
Oahe Dam 158 44 28N 100 25W
Oahe Res 158 45 30N 100 15W
Oahu I. 147 21 30N 158 0W
Oak Creek 160 40 15N 106 59W
Oak Harb. 160 48 20N 122 38W
Oak Lake 153 49 45N 100 45W
Oak Park 156 41 55N 87 45W
Oak Ridge 157 36 1N 84 5W
Oak View 163 34 24N 119 18W
Oakbank, S. Australia, Austral. 109 34 59 S 138 51 E
Oakbank, S. Australia, Austral. 140 33 4 S 140 33 E
Oakdale, Calif., U.S.A. 163 37 49N 120 56W
Oakdale, La., U.S.A. 159 30 50N 92 38W
Oakengates 28 52 42N 2 29W
Oakes 158 46 14N 98 4W
Oakesdale 160 47 11N 117 9W
Oakey 139 27 25 S 151 43 E
Oakham 29 52 40N 0 43W
Oakhill 156 38 0N 81 7W
Oakhurst 163 37 19N 119 40W
Oakland 163 37 50N 122 18W
Oakland City 156 38 20N 87 20W
Oaklands, N.S.W., Austral. 141 35 34 S 146 10 E
Oaklands, S. Australia, Austral. 109 35 1 S 138 32 E
Oakley 160 42 14N 113 55W
Oakley Creek 141 31 37 S 149 46 E
Oakover, R. 136 20 43 S 120 33 E
Oakridge 160 43 47N 122 31W
Oakwood 159 31 35N 95 47W
Oamaru 143 45 5 S 170 59 E
Oamishirasato 111 35 23N 140 18 E
Oarai 111 36 21N 140 40 E
Oasis, Calif., U.S.A. 163 33 28N 116 6W
Oasis, Nev., U.S.A. 163 37 29N 117 55W
Oates Coast 13 69 0 S 160 0 E
Oatman 161 35 1N 114 19W
Oaxaca 165 17 2N 96 40W
Oaxaca □ 165 17 0N 97 0W
Ob, R. 76 62 40N 66 0 E
Oba 150 49 4N 84 7W
Obala 121 4 9N 11 32 E
Obama, Eukui, Japan 111 35 30N 135 45 E
Obama, Nagasaki, Japan 110 32 43N 130 13 E
Oban, N.Z. 143 46 55 S 168 10 E
Oban, U.K. 34 56 25N 5 30W
Obatogamau L. 150 49 34N 74 26W
Obbia 91 5 25N 48 30 E
Obdam 46 52 41N 4 55 E
Obed 152 53 30N 117 10W
Obeh 93 34 28N 63 10 E
Ober-Aagau 50 47 10N 7 45 E
Obera 173 27 21 S 55 2W
Oberalppass 51 46 39N 8 35 E
Oberalpstock 51 46 45N 8 47 E
Oberammergau 49 47 35N 11 3 E
Oberdrauburg 52 46 44N 12 58 E
Oberengadin 51 46 35N 9 55 E
Oberentfelden 50 47 21N 8 2 E
Oberhausen 48 51 28N 6 50 E
Oberkirch 49 48 31N 8 5 E
Oberland 50 46 30N 7 30 E
Oberlin, Kans., U.S.A. 158 39 52N 100 31W
Oberlin, La., U.S.A. 159 30 42N 92 42W
Obernai 43 48 28N 7 30 E
Oberndorf 49 48 17N 8 35 E
Oberon 141 33 45 S 149 52 E
Oberösterreich □ 52 48 10N 14 0 E
Oberpfalzer Wald 49 49 30N 12 25 E
Oberseebach 51 48 53N 7 58 E
Obersiggenthal 51 47 29N 8 18 E
Oberstdorf 49 47 25N 10 16 E
Oberwil 50 47 32N 7 33 E
Obi, Kepulauan 103 1 30 S 127 30 E
Ọbiaruku 121 5 51N 6 9 E
Óbidos, Brazil 175 1 50 S 55 30W
Óbidos, Port. 57 39 19N 9 10W
Obihiro 112 42 25N 143 12 E
Obilnoye 83 47 32N 44 30 E
Öbisfelde 48 52 27N 10 57 E
Objat 44 45 16N 1 24 E
Obluchye 77 49 10N 130 50 E
Obninsk 81 55 8N 36 13 E
Obo, C. Afr. Emp. 123 5 20N 26 32 E
Obo, Ethiopia 123 3 34N 38 52 E
Oboa, Mt. 126 1 45N 34 45 E
Obock 123 12 0N 43 20 E
Oborniki 54 52 39N 16 59 E
Oborniki Śl. 54 51 17N 16 53 E
Obot 123 4 32N 37 13 E
Obout 121 3 28N 11 47 E
Oboyan 81 51 20N 36 28 E
Obrenovac 66 44 40N 20 11 E
O'Briensbridge 39 52 46N 8 30W
Obrovac 63 44 11N 15 41 E
Observatory Inlet 152 55 25N 129 45W
Obshchi Syrt 16 52 0N 53 0 E
Obskaya Guba 76 70 0N 73 0 E
Obuasi 121 6 17N 1 40W
Obubra 121 6 8N 8 20 E
Obyachevo 84 60 20N 49 37 E
Obzor 67 42 50N 27 52 E
Ocala 157 29 11N 82 5W
Ocampo 164 28 9N 108 8W
Ocaña 58 39 55N 3 30W
Ocanomowoc 158 43 7N 88 30W
Ocate 159 36 12N 104 59W
Occidental, Cordillera 174 5 0N 76 0W
Ocean City, Md., U.S.A. 162 38 20N 75 5W
Ocean City, N.J., U.S.A. 162 39 18N 74 34W
Ocean Falls 152 52 25N 127 40W
Ocean I. 130 0 45 S 169 50 E
Ocean Park 160 46 30N 124 2W
Oceanlake 160 45 0N 124 0W
Oceano 163 35 6N 120 37W
Oceanside 163 33 13N 117 26W
Ochagavia 58 42 55N 1 5W
Ochakov 82 46 35N 31 30 E
Ochamchire 83 42 46N 41 32 E
Ochamps 47 49 56N 5 16 E
Och'eng 109 30 20N 114 51 E
Ocher 84 57 53N 54 42 E
Ochiai 110 35 1N 133 45 E
Ochil Hills 35 56 14N 3 40W
Ochiltree 34 55 26N 4 23W
Ochre River 153 51 4N 99 47W
Ochsenfurt 49 49 38N 10 3 E
Ocilla 157 31 35N 83 12W
Ockelbo 72 60 54N 16 45 E
Ocmulgee, R. 157 32 0N 83 19W
Ocna Mureș 70 46 23N 23 49 E
Ocna-Sibiului 70 45 52N 24 2 E
Ocnele Mari 70 45 8N 24 18 E
Oconee, R. 157 32 30N 82 55W
Oconto 156 44 52N 87 53W
Oconto Falls 156 44 52N 88 10W
Ocós 166 14 31N 92 11W
Ocosingo 165 18 4N 92 15W
Ocotal 166 13 41N 86 41W
Ocotlán 164 20 21N 102 42W
Ocquier 47 50 24N 5 24 E
Ọcreza, R. 56 39 50N 7 35W
Öcsa 53 47 17N 19 15 E
Octave 161 34 10N 112 43W
Octeville 42 49 38N 1 40W
Octyabrskoy Revolyutsii, Os. 77 79 30N 97 0 E
Ocumare del Tuy 174 10 7N 66 46W
Ocussi 103 9 20 S 124 30 E
Oda, Ghana 121 5 50N 1 5W
Oda, Ehime, Japan 110 33 36N 132 53 E
Ọda, Shimane, Japan 110 35 11N 132 30 E
Ödåkra 73 56 9N 12 45 E
Ödåkra 73 56 7N 12 45 E
Ọdanakumadona 128 20 55 S 24 46 E
Ódáðahraun 74 65 5N 17 0W
Odate 112 40 16N 140 34 E
Odawara 111 35 20N 139 6 E
Odda 71 60 3N 6 35 E
Odder 73 55 58N 10 10 E
Oddobo 123 12 21N 42 6 E
Ọddur 91 4 0N 43 35 E
Ödeborg 73 58 32N 11 58 E
Odei, R. 153 56 6N 96 54W
Ọdemira 57 37 35N 8 40W
Ödemiș 92 38 15N 28 0 E
Odense 73 55 22N 10 23 E
Odenton 162 39 5N 76 42W
Odenwald 48 49 18N 9 0 E
Oder, R. 48 53 0N 14 12 E
Oderzo 63 45 47N 12 29 E
Odessa, Del., U.S.A. 162 39 27N 75 40W
Odessa, Tex., U.S.A. 159 31 51N 102 23W
Odessa, Wash., U.S.A. 160 47 25N 118 35W
Odessa, U.S.S.R. 82 46 30N 30 45 E
Odiel, R. 57 37 30N 6 55W
Odienné 120 9 30N 7 34W
Odiham 29 51 16N 0 56W
Odin, gasfield 19 60 5N 2 10 E
Odoben 121 5 38N 0 56W
Odobeşti 70 45 43N 27 4 E
Odolanów 54 51 34N 17 40 E
O'Donnell 159 33 0N 101 48W
Odoorn 46 52 51N 6 51 E
Odorheiul Secuiesc 70 46 21N 25 21 E
Odoyevo 81 53 56N 36 42 E
Odra, R., Czech. 53 49 43N 17 47 E
Odra, R., Poland 54 52 40N 14 28 E
Odra, R., Spain 56 42 30N 4 15W
Odzaci 66 45 30N 19 17 E
Odzak 66 45 3N 18 18 E
Odzi 125 19 0 S 32 20 E
Oedelem 47 51 10N 3 21 E
Oegstgeest 46 52 11N 4 29 E
Oeiras, Brazil 170 7 0 S 42 8W
Oeiras, Port. 57 38 41N 9 18W
Oelrichs 158 43 11N 103 14W
Oelsnitz 48 50 24N 12 11 E
Oenpelli 136 12 20 S 133 4 E
Oensingen 50 47 17N 7 43 E
Oerhtossu, reg. 106 39 20N 108 30 E
Ofanto, R. 65 41 8N 15 50 E
Ofen Pass 51 46 37N 10 17 E
Offa 121 8 13N 4 42 E
Offaly □ 39 53 15N 7 30W
Offenbach 49 50 6N 8 46 E
Offenbeek 47 51 17N 6 5 E
Offenburg 126 48 27N 7 56 E
Offerdal 72 63 28N 14 0 E
Offida 63 42 56N 13 40 E
Offranville 42 49 52N 1 0 E
Ofidhousa, I. 69 36 33N 26 8 E
Ofotfjorden 74 68 27N 16 40 E
Oga-Hantō 111 39 58N 139 59 E
Ọgahalla 150 50 6N 85 51W
Ōgaki 111 35 21N 136 37 E
Ogallala 158 41 12N 101 40W
Ogbomosho 121 8 1N 3 29 E
Ogden, Iowa, U.S.A. 158 42 3N 94 0W
Ogden, Utah, U.S.A. 160 41 13N 112 1W
Ogdensburg 156 44 40N 75 27W
Ogeechee, R. 157 32 30N 81 32W
Oglio, R. 62 45 15N 10 15 E
Ogmore 138 22 37 S 149 35 E
Ogmore, R. 31 51 29N 3 37W
Ogmore Vale 30 51 35N 3 32W
Ogna 71 58 31N 5 48 E
Ognon, R. 43 47 43N 6 32 E
Ogoja 121 6 38N 8 39 E
Ogoki 150 51 35N 86 0W
Ogoki L. 150 50 50N 87 10W
Ogoki, R. 150 51 38N 85 57W
Ogoki Res. 150 50 45N 88 15W
Ogooué, R. 124 1 0 S 10 0 E
Ogori 110 34 6N 131 24 E
Ogosta, R. 67 43 35N 23 35 E
Ogowe, R. = Ogooué, R. 124 1 0 S 10 0 E
Ograzden 66 41 30N 22 50 E
Ogrein 122 17 55N 34 50 E
Ogulin 63 45 16N 15 16 E
Ogun □ 121 7 0N 3 0 E
Oguni 110 33 4N 131 2 E
Oguta 121 5 44N 6 44 E
Ogwashi-Uku 121 6 15N 6 30 E
Ogwe 121 5 0N 7 14 E
Ohai 143 44 55 S 168 0 E
Ohakune 142 39 24 S 175 24 E
Ohara 111 35 15N 140 23 E
Ohau, L. 143 44 15 S 169 53 E
Ohaupo 142 37 56 S 175 20 E
Ohey 47 50 26N 5 8 E
O'Higgins □ 172 34 15 S 71 1W
Ohio □ 156 40 20N 83 0W
Ohio, R. 156 38 0N 86 0W
Ohiwa Harbour 142 37 59 S 177 10 E
Ohre, R. 52 50 10N 12 30 E
Ohrid 66 41 8N 20 52 E
Ohridsko, Jezero 66 41 8N 20 52 E
Ọhrigstad 129 24 41 S 30 36 E
Öhringen 49 49 11N 9 31 E
Oi Ho 108 28 37N 98 16 E
Oignies 47 50 28N 3 0 E
Oil City 156 41 26N 79 40W
Oildale 163 35 25N 119 1W
Oilgate 39 52 25N 6 30W
Oinousa, I. 69 38 33N 26 14 E
Oirschot 47 51 30N 5 18 E
Oise □ 43 49 28N 2 30 E
Oise, R. 43 49 53N 3 50 E
Oisterwijk 47 51 35N 5 12 E
Oita 110 33 14N 131 36 E
Oita-ken □ 110 33 15N 131 30 E
Oiticica 170 5 3 S 41 5W
Ojai 163 34 28N 119 16W
Ojinaga 164 29 34N 104 25W
Ojocaliente 164 30 25N 106 30W
Ojos del Salado 172 27 0 S 68 40W
Oka, R. 81 56 20N 43 59 E
Okahandja 128 22 0 S 16 59 E
Okahukura 142 38 48N 175 14 E
Okaihau 142 35 19 S 173 36 E
Okakune 142 39 26 S 175 24 E
Okanagan L. 152 50 0N 119 30W
Okanogan 160 48 22N 119 35W
Okanogan, R. 160 48 40N 119 24W
Okány 53 46 52N 21 21 E
Okapa 135 6 38 S 145 39 E
Okaputa 128 20 5 S 17 0 E
Okara 94 30 50N 73 25 E
Okarito 143 43 15 S 170 9 E
Okato 142 39 12 S 173 53 E
Okaukuejo 125 19 10 S 16 0 E
Okavango, R. = Cubango, R. 125 16 15 S 18 0 E
Okavango Swamp 128 19 30 S 23 0 E
Okawa 110 33 9N 130 21 E
Okaya 111 36 0N 138 10 E
Okayama 110 34 40N 133 54 E
Okayama-ken □ 110 35 0N 133 50 E
Okazaki 111 34 57N 137 10 E
Oke-Iho 121 8 1N 3 18 E
Okeechobee 157 27 16N 80 46W
Okeechobee L. 157 27 0N 80 50W
Okefenokee Swamp 157 30 50N 82 15W
Okehampton 30 50 44N 4 1W
Okene 121 7 32N 6 11 E
Oker, R. 48 52 7N 10 34 E
Ọkha 77 53 40N 143 0 E
Ókhi Óros 69 38 5N 24 25 E
Okhotsk 77 59 20N 143 10 E
Okhotsk, Sea of 77 55 0N 145 0 E
Okhotskiy Perevoz 77 61 52N 135 35 E
Okhotsko Kolymskoy 77 63 0N 157 0 E
Oki-no-Shima 110 32 44N 132 33 E
Oki-Shotō 110 36 15N 133 15 E
Okiep 128 29 39 S 17 53 E
Okigwi 121 5 52N 7 20 E
Okija 121 5 54N 6 55 E
Okinawa-Jima 112 26 32N 128 0 E
Okinawa-Shotō 112 27 0N 128 0 E
Okinoerabu-Jima 112 27 21N 128 33 E
Okitipupa 121 6 31N 4 50 E
Oklahoma □ 159 35 20N 97 30W
Oklahoma City 159 35 25N 97 30W
Okmulgee 159 35 38N 96 0W
Oknitsa 82 48 25N 27 20 E
Okolo 126 2 37N 31 8 E
Okondeka 128 21 38 S 15 37 E
Okondja 124 0 35 S 13 45 E
Okonek 54 53 32N 16 51 E
Okrika 121 4 47N 7 4 E
Oksby 73 55 33N 8 8 E
Oktyabr 85 43 41N 77 12 E
Oktyabrskiy 84 54 28N 53 28 E
Okuchi 110 32 4N 130 37 E
Okulovka 80 58 19N 33 28 E
Okuru 143 43 55 S 168 55 E
Okushiri-Tō 112 42 15N 139 30 E
Okuta 121 9 14N 3 12 E
Okwa, R. 128 22 25 S 22 30 E
Okwoga 121 7 3N 7 42 E
Ọla 159 35 2N 93 10W
Ọlafsfjörður 74 66 4N 18 39W
Ólafsvík 74 64 53N 23 43W
Olancha 163 36 15N 118 1W
Olancha Pk. 163 36 15N 118 7W
Ọlanchito 167 15 30N 86 30W
Öland 73 56 45N 16 50 E
Olargues 44 43 34N 2 53 E
Olary 140 32 18 S 140 19 E
Olascoaga 172 35 15 S 60 39W
Olathe 158 38 50N 94 50W
Olavarría 172 36 55 S 60 20W
Ọława 54 50 57N 17 20 E
Ọlbia 64 40 55N 9 30 E
Olbia, G. di 64 40 55N 9 35 E
Old Bahama Chan. 166 22 10N 77 30W
Old Baldy Pk = San Antonio, Mt. 163 34 17N 117 38W
Old Castile = Castilla la Vieja 56 41 55N 4 0W
Old Castle 38 53 46N 7 10W
Old Cork 138 22 57 S 142 0 E
Old Dale 163 34 8N 115 47W
Old Deer 37 57 30N 2 3W
Old Dongola 122 18 11N 30 44 E
Old Factory 150 52 36N 78 43W
Old Forge, N.J., U.S.A. 162 43 43N 74 58W
Old Forge, N.Y., U.S.A. 162 43 43N 74 58W
Old Forge, Pa., U.S.A. 162 41 20N 75 46W
Old Fort, R. 153 58 36N 110 24W
Old Harbor 147 57 12N 153 22W
Old Kilpatrick 34 55 56N 4 34W
Old Leake 33 53 2N 0 6 E
Old Leighlin 39 52 46N 7 2W
Old Man of Hoy 37 58 53N 3 25W
Old Point Comfort 162 37 0N 76 20W
Old Radnor 31 52 14N 3 7W
Old Serenje 127 13 7 S 30 45 E
Old Shinyanga 126 3 33 S 33 27 E
Old Town 151 45 0N 68 50W
Old Wives L. 153 50 5N 106 0W
Oldbury 28 52 30N 2 0W
Oldeani 126 3 22 S 35 35 E
Oldenburg, Niedersachsen, Ger. 48 53 10N 8 10 E
Oldenburg, S.-Holst, Ger. 48 54 16N 10 53 E
Oldenzaal 46 52 19N 6 53 E
Oldham 32 53 33N 2 8W
Oldman, R. 152 49 57N 111 42W
Oldmeldrum 37 57 20N 2 19W

Olds Örken, L

Olds 152 51 50N 114 10W
Olean 156 42 8N 78 25W
Oléggio 62 45 36N 8 38 E
Oleiros 56 39 56N 7 56W
Olekma, R. 77 58 0N 121 30 E
Olekminsk 77 60 40N 120 30 E
Olema 163 38 3N 122 47W
Olen 47 51 9N 4 52 E
Olenek 77 68 20N 112 30 E
Olenek, R. 77 71 0N 123 50 E
Olenino 80 56 15N 33 20 E
Oléron, I. d' 44 45 55N 1 15W
Olesno 54 50 51N 18 26 E
Oleśnica 54 51 13N 17 22 E
Olevsk 80 51 18N 27 39 E
Olga 77 43 50N 135 0 E
Olga, L. 150 49 47N 77 15W
Olga, Mt. 137 25 20 S 130 40 E
Olgastretet 12 78 35N 25 0 E
Ølgod 73 55 49N 8 36 E
Olgrinmole 37 58 29N 3 33W
Olhão 57 37 3N 7 48W
Olib 63 44 23N 14 44 E
Olib, I. 63 44 23N 14 44 E
Oliena 64 40 18N 9 22 E
Oliete 58 41 1N 0 41W
Olifants, R. 125 24 5 S 31 20 E
Olifantshoek 128 27 57 S 22 42 E
Ólimbos 69 35 44N 27 11 E
Ólimbos, Óros 68 40 6N 22 23 E
Olímpia 173 20 44 S 48 54W
Olimpo □ 172 20 30 S 58 45W
Olinda 170 8 1 S 34 51W
Olindiná 170 11 22 S 38 21W
Oling Hu 105 34 52N 97 30 E
Olite 58 42 29N 1 40W
Oliva, Argent. 172 32 0 S 63 38W
Oliva, Spain 59 38 58N 0 15W
Oliva de la Frontera 57 38 17N 6 54W
Oliva, Punta del 56 43 37N 5 28W
Olivares 58 39 46N 2 20W
Oliveira, Bahia, Brazil 171 12 23 S 38 35W
Oliveira, Minas Gerais, Brazil 171 20 50 S 44 50W
Oliveira de Azemeis 56 40 49N 8 29W
Oliveira dos Brejinhos 171 12 19 S 42 54W
Olivença 127 11 47 S 35 13 E
Olivenza 57 38 41N 7 9W
Oliver 152 49 20N 119 30W
Oliver L. 153 56 56N 103 22W
Olivine Ra. 143 44 15 S 168 30 E
Olivone 51 46 32N 8 57 E
Olkhovka 83 49 48N 44 32 E
Olkusz 54 50 18N 19 33 E
Ollagüe 172 21 15 S 68 10W
Ollerton 33 53 12N 1 1W
Olloy 47 50 5N 4 36 E
Olmedo 56 41 20N 4 43W
Olmos, L. 172 33 25 S 63 19W
Olney, U.K. 29 52 9N 0 42W
Olney, Ill., U.S.A. 156 38 40N 88 0W
Olney, Tex., U.S.A. 159 33 25N 98 45W
Olofström 73 56 17N 14 32 E
Oloma 121 3 29N 11 19 E
Olomane, R. 151 50 14N 60 37W
Olomouc 53 49 38N 17 12 E
Olonets 78 61 10N 33 0 E
Olongapo 103 14 50N 120 18 E
Oloron-Ste.-Marie 44 43 11N 0 38W
Olot 58 42 11N 2 30 E
Olovo 66 44 8N 18 35 E
Olovyannaya 77 50 50N 115 10 E
Olpe 48 51 2N 7 50 E
Olsene 47 50 58N 3 28 E
Olshanka 82 48 16N 30 58 E
Olst 46 52 20N 6 7 E
Olsztyn 54 53 48N 20 29 E
Olsztyn □ 54 54 0N 21 0 E
Olsztynek 54 53 34N 20 19 E
Olt □ 70 44 20N 24 30 E
Olt, R. 70 43 50N 24 40 E
Olten 50 47 21N 7 53 E
Oltenita 70 44 7N 26 42 E
Olton 159 34 16N 102 7W
Oltu 92 40 35N 41 50 E
Oluanpi 109 21 54N 120 51 E
Oluego 58 41 47N 2 0W
Olvera 57 36 55N 5 18W
Olympia, Greece 69 37 39N 21 39 E
Olympia, U.S.A. 160 47 0N 122 58W
Olympic Mts. 160 47 50N 123 45W
Olympic Nat. Park 160 47 48N 123 30W
Olympus, Mt. 160 47 52N 123 40W
Olympus, Mt. = Olimbos, Oros 68 40 6N 22 23 E
Olyphant 162 41 28N 75 37W
Om Hajer 123 14 20N 36 41 E
Om Koï 100 17 48N 98 22 E
Omachi 111 36 30N 137 50 E
Omae-Zaki 111 34 36N 138 14 E
Omagh 38 54 36N 7 20W
Omagh □ 38 54 35N 7 15W
Omaha 158 41 15N 96 0W
Omak 160 48 24N 119 31W
Oman ■ 92 23 0N 58 0 E
Oman, G. of 93 24 30N 58 30 E
Omaruru 128 21 26 S 16 0 E
Omaruru, R. 128 21 44 S 14 30 E
Omate 174 16 45 S 71 0W
Ombai, Selat 103 8 30 S 124 50 E
Ombersley 28 52 17N 2 12W
Ombo 71 59 18N 6 0 E
Ombombo 128 18 43 S 13 57 E
Omboué 124 1 35 S 9 15 E
Ombrone, R. 62 42 48N 11 15 E
Omchi 119 21 22N 17 53 E
Omdraai 128 20 5 S 21 56 E
Omdurmân 121 15 40N 32 28 E
Ome 111 35 47N 139 15 E
Omegna 62 45 52N 8 23 E
Omeonga 126 3 40 S 24 22 E
Ometepe, Isla de 166 11 32N 85 35W
Ometepec 165 16 39N 98 23W
Omez 90 32 22N 35 0 E
Omi-Shima, Ehime, Japan 110 34 15N 133 0 E
Omi-Shima, Yamaguchi, Japan 110 34 15N 131 9 E
Omihachiman 111 35 7N 136 3 E
Omineca, R. 152 56 3N 124 16W
Omiš 63 43 28N 16 40 E
Omisalj 63 45 13N 14 32 E
Omitara 128 22 16 S 18 2 E
Ōmiya 111 35 54N 139 38 E
Omme 73 55 56N 8 32 E
Ommen 46 52 31N 6 26 E
Ömnögovi □ 106 43 15N 104 0 E
Omono, R. 112 39 46N 140 3 E
Omsk 76 55 0N 73 38 E
Omsukchan 77 62 32N 155 48 E
Omul, Mt. 70 45 27N 25 29 E
Omura 110 33 8N 130 0 E
Omura-Wan 110 32 57N 129 52 E
Omuramba, R. 125 19 10 S 19 20 E
Omurtag 67 43 8N 26 26 E
Ōmuta 110 33 0N 130 26 E
Omutninsk 84 58 45N 52 4 E
On 47 50 11N 5 18 E
On-Take 110 31 35N 130 39 E
Oña 58 42 43N 3 25W
Onaga 158 39 32N 96 12W
Onalaska 158 43 53N 91 14W
Onamia 158 46 4N 93 38W
Onancock 162 37 42N 75 49W
Onang 103 3 2 S 118 55 E
Onaping L. 150 47 3N 81 30W
Onarheim 71 59 57N 5 35 E
Oñate 58 43 3N 2 25W
Onavas 164 28 28N 109 30W
Onawa 158 42 2N 96 2W
Onaway 156 45 21N 84 11W
Oncesti 70 43 56N 25 52 E
Onchan 32 54 11N 4 27W
Oncocua 128 16 30 S 13 40 E
Onda 58 39 55N 0 17W
Ondaejin 107 41 34N 129 40 E
Ondangua 128 17 57 S 16 4 E
Ondárroa 58 43 19N 2 25W
Ondas, R. 171 12 8 S 45 0W
Ondava, R. 53 48 50N 21 40 E
Onderdijk 46 52 45N 5 8 E
Ondo, Japan 110 24 11N 132 32 E
Ondo, Nigeria 121 7 4N 4 47 E
Ondo □ 121 7 0N 5 0 E
Ondombo 128 21 3 S 16 5 E
Öndörhaan 105 47 19N 110 39 E
Ondörshil 106 45 33N 108 5 E
Ondverdarnes 74 64 52N 24 0W
One Tree Hill 109 34 43 S 138 46 E
Onega 78 64 0N 38 10 E
Onega, G. of = Onezhskaya G. 78 64 30N 37 0 E
Onega, L. = Onezhskoye Oz. 78 62 0N 35 30 E
Onega, R. 78 63 0N 39 0 E
Onehunga 142 36 55 S 174 30 E
Oneida 162 43 5N 75 40W
Oneida L. 162 43 12N 76 0W
O'Neill 158 42 30N 98 38W
Onekotan, Ostrov 77 49 59N 154 0 E
Onema 126 4 35 S 24 30 E
Oneonta, Ala., U.S.A. 157 33 58N 86 29W
Oneonta, N.Y., U.S.A. 162 42 26N 75 5W
Onerahi 142 35 45 S 174 22 E
Onezhskaya Guba 78 64 30N 37 0 E
Onezhskoye Ozero 78 62 0N 35 30 E
Ongarue 142 38 42 S 175 19 E
Ongerup 137 33 58 S 118 28 E
Ongjin 107 37 56N 125 21 E
Ongkharak 100 14 8N 101 1 E
Ongoka 126 1 20 S 26 0 E
Ongole 97 15 33N 80 2 E
Ongon 106 45 41N 113 5 E
Onhaye 47 50 15N 4 50 E
Oni 83 42 33N 43 26 E
Onida 158 44 42N 100 5W
Onilahy, R. 129 23 30 S 44 0 E
Onitsha 121 6 6N 6 42 E
Onkaparinga, R. 109 35 2 S 138 47 E
Onmaka 98 22 17N 96 41 E
Onny, R. 28 52 30N 2 50W
Ono, Japan 110 34 51N 134 56 E
Ono, Japan 111 35 55N 136 29 E
Onoda 110 33 59N 131 11 E
Onomichi 110 34 25N 133 12 E
Onpyŏngni 107 33 25N 126 55 E
Ons, Islas de 56 42 23N 8 55W
Onsala 73 57 26N 12 0 E
Onslow 136 21 40 S 115 0 E
Onslow B. 157 34 10N 77 0W
Onstwedde 46 52 2N 7 4 E
Ontake-San 111 35 53N 137 29 E
Ontaneda 56 43 12N 3 57W
Ontario, Calif., U.S.A. 163 34 2N 117 40W
Ontario, Oreg., U.S.A. 160 44 1N 117 1W
Ontario □ 150 52 0N 88 10W
Ontario, L. 150 43 40N 78 0W
Onteniente 59 38 50N 0 35W
Ontonagon 158 46 52N 89 19W
Ontur 59 38 38N 1 29W
Onyx 163 35 41N 118 14W
Oodnadatta 139 27 33 S 135 30 E
Ooglaamie 12 72 1N 157 0W
Ookala 147 20 1N 155 17W
Ooldea 137 30 27 S 131 50 E
Ooltgensplaat 47 51 41N 4 21 E
Oona River 152 53 57N 130 16W
Oordegem 47 50 58N 3 54 E
Oorindi 138 20 40 S 141 1 E
Oost-Vlaanderen □ 47 51 5N 3 50 E
Oost-Vlieland 46 53 18N 5 4 E
Oostakker 47 51 6N 3 46 E
Oostburg 47 51 19N 3 30 E
Oostduinkerke 47 51 7N 2 41 E
Oostelijk-Flevoland 46 52 31N 5 38 E
Oostende 47 51 15N 2 50 E
Oosterbeek 46 51 59N 5 51 E
Oosterdijk 46 52 44N 5 14 E
Oosterend, Frise, Neth. 46 53 24N 5 23 E
Oosterend, Holl. Sept., Neth. 46 53 5N 4 52 E
Oosterhout, Brabank, Neth. 47 51 39N 4 52 E
Oosterhout, Gueldre, Neth. 46 51 53N 5 50 E
Oosterschelde 47 51 33N 4 0 E
Oosterwolde 46 53 0N 6 17 E
Oosterzele 47 50 57N 3 48 E
Oostkamp 47 51 9N 3 14 E
Oostmalle 47 51 18N 4 44 E
Oostrozebekke 47 50 55N 3 21 E
Oostvleteven 47 50 56N 2 45 E
Oostvoorne 46 51 55N 4 5 E
Oostzaan 46 52 26N 4 52 E
Ootacamund 97 11 30N 76 44 E
Ootha 141 33 6 S 147 29 E
Ootmarsum 46 52 24N 6 54 E
Ootsa L. 152 53 50N 126 20W
Ootsi 128 25 2 S 25 45 E
Opaka 67 43 28N 26 10 E
Opala, U.S.S.R. 77 52 15N 156 15 E
Opala, Zaïre 124 1 11 S 24 45 E
Opalenica 54 52 18N 16 24 E
Opalton 138 23 15 S 142 46 E
Opan 67 42 13N 25 41 E
Opanake 97 6 35N 80 40 E
Opapa 142 39 47 S 176 42 E
Opasatika 150 49 30N 82 50W
Opasquia 153 53 16N 93 34W
Opatija 63 45 21N 14 17 E
Opatów 54 50 50N 21 27 E
Opava 53 49 57N 17 58 E
Opawica, L. 150 49 35N 75 55W
Opeinde 46 53 8N 6 4 E
Opelousas 159 30 35N 92 0W
Opémisca L. 150 50 0N 75 0W
Open Bay Is. 143 43 51 S 168 51 E
Opglabbeek 47 51 3N 5 35 E
Opheim 160 48 52N 106 30W
Ophir, U.K. 147 58 56N 3 11W
Ophir, U.S.A. 147 63 10N 156 40W
Ophthalmia Ra. 136 23 15 S 119 30 E
Opi 121 6 36N 7 28 E
Opien 108 29 15N 103 24 E
Opinaca L. 150 52 39N 76 20W
Opinaca, R. 150 52 15N 78 2W
Opioo 47 51 37N 5 54 E
Opiskotish, L. 151 53 10N 67 50W
Opmeer 46 52 42N 4 57 E
Opobo 121 4 35N 7 34 E
Opochka 80 56 42N 28 45 E
Opoczno 54 51 22N 20 18 E
Opole 54 50 42N 17 58 E
Opole □ 54 50 40N 17 56 E
Oporto = Porto 56 41 8N 8 40W
Opotiki 142 38 1 S 177 19 E
Opp 157 31 19N 86 13W
Oppegård 71 59 48N 10 48 E
Oppenheim 49 49 50N 8 22 E
Opperdoes 46 52 45N 5 4 E
Oppido Mamertina 65 38 16N 15 59 E
Oppland fylke □ 71 61 15N 9 30 E
Oppstad 71 60 17N 11 40 E
Opua 142 35 19 S 174 9 E
Opunake 142 39 26 S 173 52 E
Opuzen 66 43 1N 17 34 E
Or Yehuda 90 32 2N 34 50 E
Ora 63 46 20N 11 19 E
Ora Banda 137 30 20 S 121 0 E
Oracle 161 32 45N 110 46W
Oradea 70 47 2N 21 58 E
Öræfajökull 74 64 2N 16 39W
Orahovac 66 42 24N 20 40 E
Orahovica 66 45 35N 17 52 E
Orai 95 25 58N 79 30 E
Oraison 45 43 55N 5 55 E
Oran, Alg. 118 35 37N 0 39W
Oran, Argent. 172 23 10 S 64 20W
Oran, Ireland 38 53 40N 8 20W
Orange, Austral. 141 33 15 S 149 7 E
Orange, France 45 44 8N 4 47 E
Orange, Calif., U.S.A. 163 33 47N 117 51W
Orange, Mass., U.S.A. 162 42 35N 72 15W
Orange, Tex., U.S.A. 159 30 0N 93 40W
Orange, Va., U.S.A. 156 38 17N 78 5W
Orange, C. 175 4 20N 51 30W
Orange Cove 163 36 38N 119 19W
Orange Free State = Oranje Vrystaat 128 28 30 S 27 0 E
Orange Free State □ 128 28 30 S 27 0 E
Orange Grove 159 27 57N 97 57W
Orange, R. = Oranje, R. 128 28 30 S 18 0 E
Orange Walk 165 18 6N 88 33W
Orangeburg 157 33 27N 80 53W
Orangerie B. 138 10 30 S 149 30 E
Orangeville 150 43 55N 80 5W
Oranienburg 48 52 45N 13 15 E
Oranje, R. 128 28 30 S 18 0 E
Oranje Vrystaat □ 128 28 30 S 27 0 E
Oranjemund (Orange Mouth) 128 28 32 S 16 29 E
Oranmore 39 53 16N 8 57W
Orapa 128 21 13 S 25 25 E
Oras 103 12 9N 125 22 E
Orašje 66 45 1N 18 42 E
Oraşul Stalin = Braşov 70 45 7N 25 39 E
Orava, R. 53 49 24N 19 20 E
Oraviţa 66 45 6N 21 43 E
Orb, R. 44 43 28N 3 5 E
Orba, R. 62 44 45N 8 40 E
Ørbæk 73 55 17N 10 39 E
Orbe 50 46 43N 6 32 E
Orbec 42 49 1N 0 23 E
Orbetello 63 42 26N 11 11 E
Órbigo, R. 56 42 40N 5 45W
Orbost 141 37 40 S 148 29 E
Örbyhus 72 60 15N 17 43 E
Orbyhus 72 60 13N 17 43 E
Orce 59 37 44N 2 28W
Orce, R. 59 37 45N 2 30W
Orchies 43 50 28N 3 14 E
Orchila, Isla 167 11 48N 66 10W
Orco, R. 62 45 20N 7 45 E
Orcutt 163 34 52N 120 27W
Ord 136 17 23 S 128 51 E
Ord, Mt. 136 17 20 S 125 34 E
Ord, R. 136 15 33 S 128 35 E
Ordenes 56 43 5N 8 29W
Orderville 161 37 18N 112 43W
Ordhead 37 57 10N 2 31W
Ordie 37 57 6N 2 54W
Ordos (Oerhtossu) 106 39 0N 108 0 E
Ordu 92 40 55N 37 53 E
Orduña 58 42 58N 2 58W
Orduña, Mte. 59 37 20N 3 30W
Ordway 158 38 15N 103 42W
Ordzhonikidze, R.S.F.S.R., U.S.S.R. 83 43 0N 44 35 E
Ordzhonikidze, Ukraine S.S.R., U.S.S.R. 82 47 32N 34 3 E
Ordzhonikidze, Uzbek S.S.R., U.S.S.R. 85 41 21N 69 22 E
Ordzhonikidzeabad 85 38 34N 69 1 E
Ore, Sweden 72 61 8N 15 10 E
Ore, Zaïre 126 3 17N 29 30 E
Ore Mts. = Erzgebirge 49 50 25N 13 0 E
Orebic 66 43 0N 17 11 E
Örebro 72 59 20N 15 18 E
Örebro län □ 72 59 27N 15 0 E
Oregon 158 42 1N 89 20W
Oregon □ 160 44 0N 120 0W
Oregon City 160 45 21N 122 35W
Öregrund 72 60 21N 18 30 E
Öregrundsgrepen 72 60 25N 18 15 E
Orekhov 82 47 30N 35 32 E
Orekhovo-Zuyevo 81 55 50N 38 55 E
Orel 81 52 57N 36 3 E
Orel, R. 82 49 5N 35 25 E
Orellana, Canal de 57 39 2N 6 0W
Orellana la Vieja 57 39 1N 5 32W
Orellana, Pantano de 57 39 5N 5 10W
Orem 160 40 27N 111 45W
Oren 69 37 3N 27 57 E
Orenburg 84 51 45N 55 6 E
Orense 56 42 19N 7 55W
Orense □ 56 42 15N 7 30W
Orepuki 143 46 19 S 167 46 E
Orestiás 68 41 30N 26 33 E
Øresund 73 55 45N 12 45 E
Oreti, R. 143 45 39 S 168 14 E
Orford 29 52 6N 1 31 E
Orford Ness 29 52 6N 1 31 E
Orgañá 58 42 13N 1 20 E
Orgaz 57 39 39N 3 53W
Orgeyev 82 47 9N 29 10 E
Orgon 45 43 47N 5 3 E
Orhon Gol, R. 105 50 21N 106 5 E
Oria 65 40 30N 17 38 E
Orient 139 28 7 S 143 3 E
Orient Bay 150 49 20N 88 10W
Oriente 172 38 44 S 60 37W
Origny 43 49 50N 3 30 E
Origny-Ste.-Benoîte 43 49 50N 3 30 E
Orihuela 59 38 7N 0 55W
Orihuela del Tremedal 58 40 33N 1 39W
Oriku 68 40 20N 19 30 E
Orinoco, Delta del 167 8 30N 61 0W
Orinoco, R. 174 5 45N 67 40W
Orion 153 49 28N 110 49W
Oriskany 162 43 9N 75 20W
Orissa □ 96 21 0N 85 0 E
Oristano 64 39 54N 8 35 E
Oristano, Golfo di 64 39 50N 8 22 E
Orizaba 165 18 50N 97 10W
Orizare 67 42 44N 27 39 E
Orizona 171 17 3 S 48 18W
Ørje 71 59 29N 11 39 E
Orjen, mt. 66 42 35N 18 34 E
Orjiva 59 36 53N 3 24W
Orkanger 71 63 18N 9 52 E
Orkelljunga 73 56 17N 13 17 E
Örken, L. 73 57 11N 15 0 E

Owen Falls Pang-Yang

Owen Falls 126 0 30N 33 5E
Owen Mt. 143 41 35S 152 33E
Owen Sound 150 44 35N 80 55W
Owen Stanley Range 135 8 30S 147 0E
Owendo 124 0 17N 9 30E
Oweniny R. 38 54 13N 9 32W
Owenkillew R. 38 54 44N 7 15W
Owens L. 163 36 20N 118 0W
Owens, R. 163 36 32N 117 59W
Owensboro 156 37 40N 87 5W
Owensville 158 38 20N 91 30W
Owerri 121 5 29N 7 0E
Owhango 142 39 51S 175 20E
Owl, R. 153 57 51N 92 44W
Owo 121 7 18N 5 30E
Owosso 156 43 0N 84 10W
Owston Ferry 33 53 28N 0 47W
Owyhee 160 42 0N 116 3W
Owyhee, R. 160 43 10N 117 37W
Owyhee Res. 160 43 30N 117 30W
Ox Mts. 38 54 6N 9 0W
Oxberg 72 61 7N 14 11E
Oxelösund 73 58 43N 17 15E
Oxford, N.Z. 143 43 18S 172 11E
Oxford, U.K. 28 51 45N 1 15W
Oxford, Mass., U.S.A. 162 42 7N 71 52W
Oxford, Miss., U.S.A. 159 34 22N 89 30W
Oxford, N.C., U.S.A. 157 36 19N 78 36W
Oxford, N.Y., U.S.A. 162 42 27N 75 36W
Oxford, Ohio, U.S.A. 156 39 30N 84 40W
Oxford, Pa., U.S.A. 162 39 47N 75 59W
Oxford □ 28 51 45N 1 15W
Oxford L. 153 54 51N 95 37W
Oxilithos 69 38 35N 24 7E
Oxley 140 34 11S 144 6E
Oxley Cr. 108 27 35S 153 0E
Oxnard 163 34 10N 119 14W
Oya 102 2 55N 111 55E
Oyabe 111 36 47N 136 56E
Oyama 111 36 18N 139 48E
Oyana 110 32 32N 130 18E
Oyem 124 1 42N 11 43E
Oyen 153 51 22N 110 28W
Øyeren 71 59 48N 11 14E
Oyeren 71 59 50N 11 15E
Oykel Bridge 37 57 58N 4 45W
Oykell, R. 37 57 55N 4 26W
Oymyakon 77 63 25N 143 10E
Oyo 121 7 46N 3 56E
Oyo □ 121 8 0N 3 30E
Oyonnax 45 46 16N 5 40E
Oyster B. 138 42 15S 148 5E
Oystese 71 60 22N 6 9E
Øystese 71 60 24N 6 12E
Oytal 85 42 54N 73 17E
Ozamis (Mizamis) 103 8 15N 123 50E
Ozark, Ala., U.S.A. 157 31 29N 85 39W
Ozark, Ark., U.S.A. 159 35 30N 93 50W
Ozark, Mo., U.S.A. 159 37 0N 93 15W
Ozark Plateau 159 37 20N 91 40W
Ozarks, L. of 158 38 10N 93 0W
Ózd 53 48 14N 20 15E
Ozerhinsk 80 53 40N 27 7E
Ozërnyy 84 51 8N 60 50E
Ozieri 64 40 35N 9 0E
Ozimek 54 50 41N 18 11E
Ozona 159 30 43N 101 11W
Ozorków 54 51 57N 19 16E
Ozren, Mt. 66 43 55N 18 29E
Ozu 110 33 30N 132 33E
Ozu Kumamoto 110 32 52N 130 52E
Ozuluama 165 21 40N 97 50W
Ozun 70 45 47N 25 50E

# P

Pa 120 11 33N 3 19W
Pa-an 98 16 45N 97 40E
Pa Mong Dam 100 18 0N 102 22E
Pa Sak, R. 101 15 30N 101 0E
Paal 47 51 2N 5 10E
Paar, R. 49 48 42N 11 27E
Paarl 128 33 45S 18 56E
Paatsi, R. 74 68 55N 29 0E
Paauilo 147 20 3N 155 22W
Pab Hills 94 26 30N 66 45E
Pabbay I. 36 57 46N 7 12W
Pabbay, Sd. of 36 57 45N 7 4W
Pabianice 54 51 40N 19 20E
Pabna 98 24 1N 89 18E
Pabo 126 2 56N 32 3E
Pacajá, R. 170 1 56S 50 50W
Pacajus 170 4 10S 38 38W
Pacasmayo 174 7 20S 79 35W
Pacaudière, La 43 46 11N 3 52E
Paceco 64 37 59N 12 32E
Pachhar 94 24 40N 77 42E
Pachino 65 36 43N 15 4E
Pacho 174 5 8N 74 10W
Pachora 96 20 38N 75 29E
Pachpadra 93 25 58N 72 10E
Pachuca 165 20 10N 98 40W
Pachung 108 31 58N 106 40E
Pacific 152 54 48N 128 28W
Pacific Grove 163 36 38N 121 58W
Pacific Ocean 143 10 0N 140 0W
Pacifica 163 37 36N 122 30W
Packsaddle 140 30 36S 141 58E
Pacoh 152 53 0N 132 30W
Pacov 52 49 27N 15 0E
Pacsa 53 46 44N 17 2E
Pacuí, R. 171 16 46S 45 1W
Pacy-sur-Eure 171 49 1N 1 23E
Paczkow 54 50 28N 17 0E
Padaido, Kepulauan 103 1 5S 138 0E
Padalarang 103 7 50S 107 30E
Padang 102 1 0S 100 20E
Padang, I. 102 1 0S 100 10E
Padangpanjang 102 0 30S 100 20E
Padangsidimpuan 102 1 30N 99 15E
Padatchuang 98 19 41N 96 35E
Padborg 73 54 49N 9 21E
Paddock Wood 29 51 13N 0 24E
Paddockwood 153 53 30N 105 30W
Paderborn 48 51 42N 8 44E
Padesul 70 45 40N 22 22E
Padiham 32 53 48N 2 20W
Padina 70 44 50N 27 8E
Padlei 153 62 10N 97 5W
Padloping Island 149 67 0N 63 0W
Padma, R. 98 23 22N 90 32E
Padmanabhapuram 97 8 16N 77 17E
Pádova 63 45 24N 11 52E
Padra 94 22 15N 73 7E
Padrauna 95 26 54N 83 59E
Padre I. 159 27 0N 97 20W
Padrón 56 42 41N 8 39W
Padstow 32 50 33N 4 57W
Padstow Bay 30 50 35N 4 58W
Padua = Pádova 63 45 24N 11 52E
Paducah, Ky., U.S.A. 156 37 0N 88 40W
Paducah, Tex., U.S.A. 159 34 3N 100 16W
Padul 57 37 1N 3 38W
Padula 65 40 20N 15 40E
Padwa 96 18 27N 82 37E
Paekakariki 142 40 59S 174 58E
Paektu-san 107 42 0N 128 3E
Paengaroa 142 37 49S 176 29E
Paengnyŏng Do 107 37 57N 124 40E
Paeroa 142 37 23S 175 41E
Paesana 62 44 40N 7 18E
Pag 63 44 27N 15 5E
Pag, I. 63 44 50N 15 0E
Paga 121 11 1N 1 8W
Pagadian 103 7 55N 123 30E
Pagai Selatan, I. 102 3 0S 100 15W
Pagai Utara, I. 102 2 35S 100 0E
Pagalu, I. 114 1 35S 3 35E
Pagaralam 102 4 0S 103 17E
Pagastikós Kólpos 68 39 15N 23 12E
Pagatan 102 3 33S 115 59E
Page 158 47 11N 97 37W
Paglieta 63 42 10N 14 30E
Pagnau 123 8 15N 34 7E
Pagny-sur-Moselle 43 48 59N 6 2E
Pagosa Springs 161 37 16N 107 4W
Pagwa River 150 50 2N 85 14W
Pahala 147 20 25N 156 0W
Pahang □ 101 3 40N 102 20E
Pahang, R. 101 3 30N 103 9E
Pahang, st. 101 3 30N 103 9E
Pahiatua 142 40 27S 175 50E
Pahoa 147 19 30N 154 57W
Pahokee 157 26 50N 80 30W
Pahrump 161 36 15N 116 0W
Pahsien 106 39 10N 116 20E
Pahsientung 107 43 11N 120 57E
Pai 100 19 19N 98 27E
Paia 147 20 54N 156 22W
Paible 36 57 35N 7 30W
Paich'eng 105 45 40N 122 52E
Paich'i 109 28 2N 111 18E
P'aichou 109 30 12N 113 56E
Paicines 163 36 44N 121 17W
Paide 80 58 57N 25 31E
Paignton 30 50 26N 3 33W
Paiho, China 109 32 49N 110 3E
Paiho, Taiwan 109 23 21N 120 25E
Paihok'ou 109 31 46N 110 13E
Päijänne 75 61 30N 25 30E
Pailin 101 12 46N 102 36E
Pailolo Chan. 147 21 5N 156 42W
Paimbœuf 42 47 17N 2 0W
Paimboeuf 44 47 17N 2 2W
Paimpol 42 48 48N 3 4W
Painan 102 1 15S 100 40E
Painesville 156 41 42N 81 18W
Painiu 109 32 51N 112 10E
Painscastle 31 52 7N 3 13W
Painswick 28 51 47N 2 11W
Paint l. 153 55 28N 97 57W
Painted Desert 161 36 40N 112 0W
Paintsville 156 37 50N 82 50W
Paipa 174 5 47N 73 7W
Paise 108 23 55N 106 28E
Paisha 106 34 23N 112 32E
Paisley, U.K. 34 55 51N 4 27W
Paisley, U.S.A. 160 42 43N 120 40W
Paita 174 5 5S 81 0W
Paiva, R. 56 40 50N 7 55W
Paiyin 105 36 45N 104 4E
Paiyü 99 31 12N 98 45E
Paiyunopo 106 41 46N 109 58E
Pajares 56 39 57N 1 48W
Pak Lay 100 18 15N 101 27E
Pak Phanang 101 8 21N 100 12E
Pak Sane 100 18 22N 103 39E
Pak Song 100 15 11N 106 14E
Pak Suong 100 19 58N 102 15E
Pakala 97 13 29N 79 8E
Pakanbaru 102 0 30N 101 15E
Pakaraima, Sierra 174 6 0N 60 0W
Pakemba 127 13 3S 29 58E
Pakenham 141 38 6S 145 30E
Pakhoi = Peihai 108 21 30N 109 5E
Pakhtakor 85 40 2N 65 46E
Pakistan ■ 93 30 0N 70 0E
Pakistan, East = Bangladesh ■ 99 24 0N 90 0E
Pakkading 100 18 19N 103 59E
Paknam = Samut Prakan 100 13 36N 100 36E
P'ako 105 30 52N 81 19E
Pakokku 98 21 30N 95 0E
Pakpattan 94 30 25N 73 16E
Pakrac 66 45 27N 17 12E
Paks 53 46 38N 18 55E
Pakse 100 15 5N 105 52E
Paksikori 107 42 27N 130 31E
Paktya □ 93 33 0N 69 15E
Pakwach 126 2 28N 31 27E
Pal 93 33 45N 79 33E
Pala, Chad 117 9 25N 15 5E
Pala, U.S.A. 163 33 22N 117 5W
Pala, Zaïre 126 6 45S 29 30E
Palabek 126 3 22N 32 33E
Palacious 159 28 44N 96 12W
Palafrugell 58 41 55N 3 10E
Palagiano 65 40 35N 17 0E
Palagonia 65 37 20N 14 43E
Palagruza 63 42 24N 16 15E
Palaiókastron 69 35 12N 26 18E
Palaiokhora 69 35 16N 23 39E
Pálairos 69 38 45N 20 51E
Palais, Le 42 47 20N 3 10W
Palakol 96 16 31N 81 46E
Palam 96 19 0N 77 0E
Palamás 68 39 26N 22 4E
Palamós 58 41 50N 3 10E
Palampur 94 32 10N 76 30E
Palana, Austral. 138 39 45S 147 55E
Palana, U.S.S.R. 77 59 10N 160 10E
Palanan 103 17 8N 122 29E
Palandri 95 33 42N 73 40E
Palanpur 94 24 10N 72 25E
Palapye 128 22 30S 27 7E
Palar, R. 97 12 27N 80 13E
Palas 95 35 4N 73 4E
Palatka 157 29 40N 81 40W
Palau Is. 130 7 30N 134 30E
Palauig 103 15 26N 119 54E
Palauk 101 13 10N 98 40E
Palavas 44 43 32N 3 56E
Palawan, I. 102 10 0N 119 0E
Palayancottai 97 8 45N 77 45E
Palazzo San Gervásio 65 40 53N 15 58E
Palazzolo Acreide 65 37 4N 14 43E
Paldiski 80 59 23N 24 9E
Pale 66 43 50N 18 38E
Palel 98 24 27N 94 2E
Paleleh 103 1 10N 121 50E
Palembang 102 3 0S 104 50E
Palencia 56 42 1N 4 34W
Palencia □ 56 42 31N 4 33W
Palermo, Colomb. 174 2 54N 75 26W
Palermo, Italy 64 38 8N 13 20E
Palermo, U.S.A. 160 39 30N 121 37W
Palestine, Asia 90 32 0N 35 0E
Palestine, U.S.A. 159 31 42N 95 35W
Palestrina 64 41 50N 12 52E
Paletwa 98 21 30N 92 50E
Palghat 97 10 46N 76 42E
Palgrave 29 52 22N 1 7E
Palgrave, Mt. 136 23 22S 115 58E
P'ali 105 27 45N 89 10E
Pali 94 25 50N 73 20E
Palik'un 105 43 35N 92 51E
Palimé 121 6 57N 0 37E
Palintaoch'i 107 43 59N 119 20E
Palinuro, C. 65 40 1N 15 14E
Palinyuch'i (Tapanshang) 107 43 40N 118 20E
Palisade 158 40 35N 101 10W
Paliseul 47 49 54N 5 8E
Palitana 94 21 32N 71 49E
Palizada 165 18 18N 92 8W
Palizzi 65 37 58N 15 59E
Palk Bay 97 9 30N 79 30E
Palk Strait 97 10 0N 80 0E
Palkonda 96 18 36N 83 48E
Palkonda Ra. 97 13 50N 79 20E
Pallasgreen 39 52 35N 8 22W
Pallaskenry 39 52 39N 8 53W
Pallasovka 81 50 4N 47 0E
Palleru, R. 96 17 30N 79 40E
Pallinup 137 34 0S 117 55E
Pallisa 126 1 12N 33 43E
Palliser Bay 142 41 26S 175 5E
Palliser, C. 142 41 37S 175 14E
Pallu 94 28 59N 74 14E
Palm Beach 157 26 46N 80 0W
Palm Desert 163 33 43N 116 22W
Palm Is. 138 18 40S 146 35E
Palm Springs 163 33 51N 116 35W
Palma, Canary Is. 16 28 40N 17 50W
Palma, Mozam. 127 10 46S 40 29E
Palma, Spain 58 39 33N 2 39E
Palma, Bahía de 59 39 30N 2 39E
Palma del Río 57 37 43N 5 17W
Palma di Montechiaro 64 37 12N 13 46E
Palma, I. 116 28 45N 17 50W
Palma, La, Panama 166 8 15N 78 0W
Palma, La, Spain 57 37 21N 6 38W
Palma, R. 171 10 10N 71 50W
Palma Soriano 166 20 15N 76 0W
Palmanova 63 45 54N 13 18E
Palmares 170 8 41S 35 36W
Palmarito 174 7 37N 70 10W
Palmarola, I. 64 40 57N 12 50E
Palmas 173 26 29S 52 0W
Palmas, C. 120 4 27N 7 46W
Palmas de Monte Alto 171 14 16S 43 10W
Pálmas, G. di 64 39 0N 8 30E
Palmdale 163 34 36N 118 7W
Palmeira 171 25 25S 50 0W
Palmeira dos Indios 170 9 25S 36 37W
Palmeirais 170 12 31S 41 34W
Palmeiras, R. 171 12 22S 47 8W
Palmeirinhas, Pta. das 124 9 2S 12 57E
Palmela 57 38 32N 8 57W
Palmelo 171 17 20S 48 27W
Palmer, Alaska, U.S.A. 147 61 35N 149 10W
Palmer, Mass., U.S.A. 162 42 9N 72 21W
Palmer Arch 13 64 15S 65 0W
Palmer Lake 158 39 10N 104 52W
Palmer Pen. 13 73 0S 60 0W
Palmer, R., N. Terr., Austral. 138 24 30S 133 0E
Palmer, R., Queens., Austral. 138 16 5S 142 43E
Palmerston 142 45 29S 170 43E
Palmerston, C. 133 21 32S 149 29E
Palmerston North 143 40 21S 175 39E
Palmerton 162 40 47N 75 36W
Palmetto 157 27 33N 82 33W
Palmi 65 38 21N 15 51E
Palmira, Argent. 172 32 59S 68 25W
Palmira, Colomb. 174 3 32N 76 16W
Palmyra, Mo., U.S.A. 158 39 45N 91 30W
Palmyra, N.J., U.S.A. 162 40 0N 75 1W
Palmyra, Pa., U.S.A. 162 40 18N 76 36W
Palmyra = Tadmor 92 34 30N 37 55E
Palni 97 10 30N 77 30E
Palni Hills 97 10 14N 77 33E
Palo Alto 163 37 25N 122 8W
Palo del Colle 65 41 4N 16 43E
Paloe 103 8 20S 121 43E
Paloma, La 172 30 35S 71 0W
Palombara Sabina 63 42 4N 12 45E
Palopo 103 3 0S 120 16E
Palos, Cabo de 59 37 38N 0 40W
Palos Verdes 163 33 48N 118 23W
Palos Verdes, Pt. 163 33 43N 118 26W
Palouse 160 46 59N 117 5W
Palparara 138 24 47S 141 22E
Pålsboda 73 59 3N 15 22E
Palu, Indon. 103 1 0S 119 59E
Palu, Turkey 92 38 45N 40 0E
Paluan 103 13 35N 120 29E
Palwal 94 28 8N 77 19E
Pama, China 108 24 9N 107 15E
Pama, Upp. Vol. 121 11 19N 0 44E
Pamanukan 103 6 16S 107 49E
Pamban I. 97 9 24N 79 35E
Pamekasan 103 7 10S 113 29E
Pameungpeuk 103 7 38S 107 44E
Pamiench'eng 107 43 13N 124 2E
Pamiers 44 43 7N 1 39E
Pamir, R. 85 37 1N 72 41E
Pamirs, Ra. 85 37 40N 73 0E
Pamlico, R. 157 35 25N 76 40W
Pamlico Sd. 157 35 20N 76 0W
Pampa 159 35 35N 100 58W
Pampa de las Salinas 172 32 1S 66 58W
Pampa, La □ 172 36 50S 66 0W
Pampanua 103 4 22S 120 14E
Pamparato 62 44 16N 7 54E
Pampas, Argent. 172 34 0S 64 0W
Pampas, Peru 174 12 20S 74 50W
Pamplona, Colomb. 174 7 23N 72 39W
Pamplona, Spain 58 42 48N 1 38W
Pampoenpoort 128 31 3S 22 40E
Pamunkey, R. 162 37 32N 76 50W
Pana 158 39 25N 89 0W
Panaca 161 37 51N 114 50W
Panagyurishte 67 42 49N 24 15E
Panaitan, I. 103 6 35S 105 10E
Panaji (Panjim) 97 15 25N 73 50E
Panamá 166 9 0N 79 25W
Panama ■ 166 8 48N 79 55W
Panama Canal 166 9 10N 79 56W
Panama Canal Zone 166 9 10N 79 56W
Panama City 157 30 10N 85 41W
Panamá, Golfo de 166 8 4N 79 20W
Panamint Mts. 161 36 15N 117 20W
Panamint Springs 163 36 20N 117 28W
Panão 174 9 55S 75 55W
Panare 101 6 51N 101 30E
Panarea, I. 65 38 38N 15 3E
Panaro, R. 62 44 48N 11 5E
Panarukan 103 7 40S 113 52E
Panay, G. 103 11 0N 122 30E
Panay I. 103 11 10N 122 30E
Pancake Ra. 161 38 30N 116 0W
Pančevo 66 44 52N 20 41E
Panciu 70 45 54N 27 8E
Pancorbo, Paso 58 42 32N 3 5W
Pandan 103 11 45N 122 10E
Pandangpanjang 102 0 40S 100 20E
Pandeglang 103 6 25S 106 0E
Pandharpur 96 17 41N 75 20E
Pandhurna 96 21 36N 78 35E
Pandilla 58 41 32N 3 43W
Pando 173 34 30S 56 0W
Pando, L. = Hope L. 139 28 24S 139 18E
Panevězys 80 55 42N 24 25E
Panfilov 76 44 30N 80 0E
Panfilovo 81 50 25N 42 46E
Pang-Long 99 23 11N 98 45E
Pang-Yang 99 22 7N 98 48E

Panga Paulista

Panga 126 1 52N 26 18 E
Pangaíon Óros 68 40 50N 24 0 E
Pangalanes, Canal des 129 22 48 S 47 50 E
Pangani 126 5 25 S 38 58 E
Pangani □ 126 5 25 S 39 0 E
Pangani, R. 126 4 40 S 37 50 E
Pangbourne 28 51 28N 1 5W
P'angchiang 106 42 50N 113 1 E
Pangfou 109 32 55N 117 25 E
Pangi 126 3 10 S 26 35 E
Pangkai 98 22 40N 97 31 E
Pangkalanberandan 102 4 1N 98 20 E
Pangkalansusu 102 4 2N 98 42 E
Pangkoh 102 3 5 S 114 8 E
Pangnirtung 149 66 0N 66 0W
Pangong Tso, L. 95 34 0N 78 20 E
Pangrango 103 6 46 S 107 1 E
Pangsau Pass 98 27 15N 96 10 E
Pangta 105 30 14N 97 24 E
Pangtara 98 20 57N 96 40 E
Panguitch 161 37 52N 112 30W
Pangutaran Group 103 6 18N 120 34 E
Panhandle 159 35 23N 101 23W
P'anhsien 108 25 46N 104 39 E
Pani Mines 94 22 29N 73 50 E
Panipat 94 29 25N 77 2 E
Panjal Range 94 32 30N 76 50 E
Panjgur 93 27 0N 64 5 E
Panjim = Panaji 93 15 25N 73 50 E
Panjinad Barrage 93 29 22N 71 15 E
Panjwai 94 31 26N 65 27 E
Pankadjene 103 4 46 S 119 34 E
Pankal Pinang 102 2 0 S 106 0 E
Pankshin 121 9 25N 9 25 E
P'anlung Chiang, R. 108 21 18N 105 25 E
Panmunjŏm 107 37 59N 126 38 E
Panna 95 24 40N 80 15 E
Panna Hills 95 24 40N 81 15 E
Pannuru 97 16 5N 80 34 E
Panorama 173 21 21 S 51 51W
Panruti 97 11 46N 79 35 E
P'anshan 107 41 12N 122 4 E
P'anshih 107 42 55N 126 3 E
Pant'anching 106 39 7N 103 52 E
Pantano 161 32 0N 110 32W
Pantar, I. 103 8 28 S 124 10 E
Pantelleria 64 36 52N 12 0 E
Pantelleria, I. 64 36 52N 12 0 E
Pantha 98 24 7N 94 17 E
Pantin Sakan 98 18 38N 97 33 E
Pantjo 103 8 42 S 118 40 E
Pantón 56 42 31N 7 37W
Pantukan 103 7 17N 125 58 E
Panuco 165 22 0N 98 25W
Panyam 121 9 27N 9 8 E
P'anyü 109 23 2N 113 20 E
Pão de AçIcar 171 9 45 S 37 26W
Paoan 109 22 32N 114 8 E
Paoch'eng 106 33 14N 106 56 E
Paochi 106 34 25N 107 11 E
Paochiatun 107 33 56N 120 12 E
Paoching 108 28 41N 109 35 E
Paok'ang 109 31 57N 111 20 E
Paokuot'u 107 42 20N 120 42 E
Páola 65 39 21N 16 2 E
Paola 158 38 36N 94 50W
Paonia 161 38 56N 107 37W
Paoshan, Shanghai, China 109 31 25N 121 29 E
Paoshan, Yunnan, China 105 25 7N 99 9 E
Paote 106 39 7N 111 13 E
Paoti 107 39 44N 117 18 E
Paoting 106 38 50N 115 30 E
Paot'ou 106 40 35N 110 3 E
Paoua 117 7 25N 16 30 E
Paoying 107 33 15N 119 20 E
Papá 53 47 22N 17 30 E
Papa Sd. 37 59 20N 2 56W
Papa, Sd. of 36 60 19N 1 40W
Papa Stour I. 36 60 20N 1 40W
Papa Stronsay I. 37 59 10N 2 37W
Papa Westray I. 37 59 20N 2 55W
Papagayo, Golfo de 166 10 4N 85 50W
Papagayo, R., Brazil 164 12 30 S 58 10W
Papagayo, R., Mexico 165 16 36N 99 43W
Papagni R. 97 14 10N 78 30 E
Papaikou 147 19 47N 155 6W
Papakura 142 37 4 S 174 59 E
Papaloapan, R. 164 18 2N 96 51W
Papantla 165 20 45N 97 21W
Papar 102 5 45N 116 0 E
Paparoa 142 36 6 S 174 16 E
Paparoa Range 143 42 5 S 171 35 E
Pápas, Ákra 69 38 13N 21 6 E
Papatoetoe 142 36 59 S 174 51 E
Papenburg 48 53 7N 7 25 E
Papien Chiang, R. (Da) 108 22 56N 101 47 E
Papigochic, R. 164 29 9N 109 40W
Paposo 172 25 0 S 70 30W
Paps, The, mts. 39 52 0N 9 15W
Papua, Gulf of 135 9 0 S 144 50 E
Papua New Guinea ■ 135 8 0 S 145 0 E
PapuCa 63 44 22N 15 30 E
Papudo 172 32 29 S 71 27W
Papuk, mts. 66 45 30N 17 30 E
Papun 98 18 0N 97 30 E
Pará = Belém 170 1 20 S 48 30W
Pará □ 175 3 20 S 52 0W
Parábita 65 40 3N 18 8 E
Paracatú 171 17 10 S 46 50W
Paracatu, R. 171 16 30 S 45 4W
Paracel Is. 102 16 49N 111 2 E
Parachilna 140 31 10 S 138 21 E
Parachinar 94 34 0N 70 5 E
Paracombe 109 34 51 S 138 47 E
Paracuru 170 3 24 S 39 4W
Paradas 57 37 18N 5 29W
Paradela 56 42 44N 7 37W
Paradip 95 20 15N 86 35 E
Paradise 160 47 27N 114 54W
Paradise, R. 151 53 27N 57 19W
Paradise Valley 160 41 30N 117 28W
Parado 103 8 42 S 118 30 E
Paradyz 54 51 19N 20 2 E
Parafield 109 34 47 S 138 38 E
Parafield Airport 109 34 48 S 138 38 E
Paragould 159 36 5N 90 30W
Paragua, La 174 6 50N 63 20W
Paragua, R. 174 6 30N 63 30W
Paraguaçu Paulista 173 22 22 S 50 35W
Paraguaçu, R. 171 12 45 S 38 54W
Paraguai, R. 174 16 0 S 57 52W
Paraguaipoa 174 11 21N 71 57W
Paraguana, Pen. de 174 12 0N 70 0W
Paraguarí 172 25 36 S 57 0W
Paraguarí □ 172 26 0 S 57 10W
Paraguay ■ 172 23 0 S 57 0W
Paraguay, R. 172 27 18 S 58 38W
Paraíba = Joéo Pessoa 164 7 10 S 35 0W
Paraiba □ 170 7 0 S 36 0W
Paraíba do Sul, R. 173 21 37 S 41 3W
Paraibano 171 6 30 S 44 1W
Parainen 75 60 18N 22 18 E
Paraíso 165 19 3 S 52 59W
Paraiso 165 18 24N 93 14W
Parakhino Paddubye 80 58 46N 33 10 E
Parakou 121 9 25N 2 40 E
Parakylia 140 30 24 S 136 25 E
Paralion-Astrous 69 37 25N 22 45 E
Paramagudi 97 9 31N 78 39 E
Paramaribo 175 5 50N 55 10W
Parambu 170 6 13 S 40 43W
Paramillo, Nudo del 174 7 4N 75 55W
Paramirim 171 13 26 S 42 15W
Paramirim, R. 171 11 34 S 43 18W
Paramithiá 68 39 30N 20 35 E
Paramushir, Ostrov 77 40 24N 156 0 E
Paran, N. 90 30 14N 34 48 E
Paraná 172 32 0 S 60 30W
Paranã 171 12 30 S 47 40W
Paraná □ 173 24 30 S 51 0W
Paraná, R. 172 33 43 S 59 15W
Paranã, R. 171 22 25 S 53 1W
Paranaguá 173 25 30 S 48 30W
Paranaíba, R. 171 18 0 S 49 12W
Paranapanema, R. 173 22 40 S 53 9W
Paranapiacaba, Serra do 173 24 31 S 48 35W
Paranavaí 173 23 4 S 52 28W
Parang, Jolo, Phil. 103 5 55N 120 54 E
Parang, Mindanao, Phil. 103 7 23N 124 16 E
Parangaba 170 3 45 S 38 33W
Paraóin 66 43 54N 21 27 E
Paraparanma 143 40 57 S 175 3 E
Parapóla, I. 69 36 55N 23 27 E
Paraspóri, Ákra 69 35 55N 27 15 E
Paratinga 171 12 40 S 43 10W
Paratoo 140 32 42 S 139 22 E
Parattah 138 42 22 S 147 23 E
Paraúna 171 17 2 S 50 26W
Paray-le-Monial 45 46 27N 4 7 E
Parbati, R. 94 25 51N 76 34 E
Parbatipur 98 25 39N 88 55 E
Parbhani 96 19 8N 76 52 E
Parchim 48 53 25N 11 50 E
Parczew 54 51 9N 22 52 E
Pardee Res. 163 38 16N 120 51W
Pardes Hanna 90 32 28N 34 57 E
Pardilla 56 41 33N 3 43W
Pardo, R., Bahia, Brazil 171 15 40 S 39 0W
Pardo, R., Mato Grosso, Brazil 171 21 0 S 53 25W
Pardo, R., Minas Gerais, Brazil 171 15 48 S 44 48W
Pardo, R., São Paulo, Brazil 171 20 45 S 48 0W
Pardubice 52 50 3N 15 45 E
Pare 103 7 43 S 112 12 E
Pare □ 126 4 10 S 38 0 E
Pare Mts. 126 4 0 S 37 45 E
Pare Pare 103 4 0 S 119 45 E
Parecis, Serra dos 174 13 0 S 60 0W
Paredes de Nava 56 42 9N 4 42W
Parelhas 170 6 41 S 36 39W
Paren 77 62 45N 163 0 E
Parengarenga Harbour 142 34 31 S 173 0 E
Parent 150 47 55N 74 35W
Parent, Lac. 150 48 31N 77 1W
Parentis-en-Born 44 44 21N 1 4W
Parepare 103 4 0 S 119 40 E
Parfino 80 57 59N 31 34 E
Parfuri 129 22 28 S 31 17 E
Paria, Golfo de 174 10 20N 62 0W
Paria, Pen. de 174 10 50N 62 30W
Pariaguán 174 8 51N 64 43W
Pariaman 102 0 47 S 100 11 E
Paricutín, Cerro 164 19 28N 102 15W
Parigi 103 0 50 S 120 5 E
Parika 174 6 50N 58 20W
Parima, Serra 174 2 30N 64 0W
Parinari 174 4 35 S 74 25W
Parincea 70 46 27N 27 9 E
Parîng, mt. 70 45 20N 23 37 E
Parintins 175 2 40 S 56 50W
Pariparit Kyun 99 14 55 S 93 45 E
Paris, Can. 150 43 12N 80 25W
Paris, France 43 48 50N 2 20 E
Paris, Idaho, U.S.A. 160 42 13N 111 30W
Paris, Ky., U.S.A. 156 38 12N 84 12W
Paris, Tenn., U.S.A. 157 36 20N 88 20W
Paris, Tex., U.S.A. 159 33 40N 95 30W
Parish 162 43 24N 76 9W
Pariti 103 9 55 S 123 30 E
Park City 160 40 42N 111 35W
Park Falls 158 45 58N 90 27 E
Park Range 160 40 0N 106 30W
Park Rapids 158 46 56N 95 0W
Park River 158 48 25N 97 17W
Park Rynie 129 30 25 S 30 35 E
Park View 161 36 45N 106 37W
Parkent 85 41 18N 69 40 E
Parker, Ariz., U.S.A. 161 34 8N 114 16W
Parker, S.D., U.S.A. 158 43 25N 97 7W
Parker Dam 161 34 13N 114 5W
Parkersburg 156 39 18N 81 31W
Parkerview 153 51 21N 103 18W
Parkes, A.C.T., Austral. 133 35 18 S 149 8 E
Parkes, N.S.W., Austral. 141 33 9 S 148 11 E
Parkfield 163 35 54N 120 26W
Parkhar 85 37 30N 69 34 E
Parknasilla 39 51 49N 9 50W
Parkside 153 53 10N 106 33W
Parkston 158 43 25N 98 0W
Parksville 152 49 20N 124 21W
Parkville 162 39 23N 76 33W
Parlakimedi 96 18 45N 84 5 E
Parma, Italy 62 44 50N 10 20 E
Parma, U.S.A. 160 43 49N 116 59W
Parna, R. 62 44 27N 10 3 E
Parnaguá 170 10 10 S 44 10W
Parnaíba, Piauí, Brazil 170 3 0 S 41 40W
Parnaíba, São Paulo, Brazil 170 19 34 S 51 14W
Parnaíba, R. 170 3 35 S 43 0W
Parnamirim 170 8 5 S 39 34W
Parnarama 170 5 41 S 43 6W
Parnassós, mt. 69 38 17N 21 30 E
Parnassus 143 42 42 S 173 23 E
Párnis, mt. 69 38 14N 23 45 E
Párnon Óros 69 37 15N 22 45 E
Pärnu 80 58 12N 24 33 E
Parola 96 20 47N 75 7 E
Paroo Chan. 133 30 50 S 143 35 E
Paroo, R. 139 30 0 S 144 5 E
Paropamisus Range = Fī roz Kohi 93 34 45N 63 0 E
Páros 69 37 5N 25 9 E
Páros, I. 69 37 5N 25 12 E
Parowan 161 37 54N 112 56W
Parpaillon, mts. 45 44 30N 6 40 E
Parracombe 30 51 11N 3 55W
Parral 172 36 10 S 72 0W
Parramatta 141 33 48 S 151 1 E
Parramore I. 162 37 32N 75 39W
Parras 164 25 30N 102 20W
Parrett, R. 28 51 7N 2 58W
Parris I. 157 32 20N 80 30W
Parrsboro 151 45 30N 64 10W
Parry 153 49 47N 104 41W
Parry, C. 147 70 20N 123 38W
Parry Is. 12 77 0N 110 0W
Parry Sound 150 45 20N 80 0W
Parshall 158 47 56N 102 11W
Parsnip, R. 152 55 10N 123 2W
Parsons 159 37 20N 95 10W
Parsons Ra., Mts. 138 13 30 S 135 15 E
Partabpur 96 20 0N 80 42 E
Partanna 64 37 43N 12 51 E
Partapgarh 94 24 2N 74 40 E
Parthenay 42 46 38N 0 16W
Partille 73 57 48N 12 18 E
Partinico 64 38 3N 13 6 E
Partney 33 53 12N 0 7 E
Parton 32 54 34N 3 35W
Partry Mts. 38 53 40N 9 28W
Partur 96 19 40N 76 14 E
Paru, R. 175 0 20 S 53 30W
Parur 97 10 13N 76 14 E
Paruro 174 13 45 S 71 50W
Parvatipuram 96 18 50N 83 25 E
Parwan □ 93 35 0N 69 0 E
Påryd 73 56 34N 15 55 E
Parys 128 26 52 S 27 29 E
Parys, Mt. 31 53 23N 4 18W
Pas-de-Calais □ 43 50 30N 2 30 E
Pasadena, Calif., U.S.A. 163 34 5N 118 9W
Pasadena, Tex., U.S.A. 159 29 45N 95 14W
Pasaje 174 3 10 S 79 40W
Pasaje, R. 172 25 35 S 64 57W
Pascagoula 159 30 30N 88 30W
Pascagoula, R. 159 30 40N 88 35W
Paşcani 70 47 14N 26 45 E
Pasco 160 46 10N 119 0W
Pasco, Cerro de 174 10 45 S 76 10W
Pascoag 162 41 57N 71 42W
Pascoe, Mt. 137 27 25 S 120 40 E
Pasewalk 48 53 30N 14 0 E
Pasfield L. 153 58 24N 105 20W
Pasha, R. 80 60 20N 33 0 E
Pashiwari 95 34 40N 75 10 E
Pashiya 84 58 33N 58 26 E
Pashmakli = Smolyan 67 41 36N 24 38 E
Pasighat 98 28 4N 95 21 E
Pasir Mas 101 6 2N 102 8 E
Pasir Puteh 101 5 50N 102 24 E
Pasirian 103 8 13 S 113 8 E
Pasley, C. 137 33 52 S 123 35 E
Pasman I. 63 43 58N 15 20 E
Pasmore, R. 140 31 5 S 139 49 E
Pasni 93 25 15N 63 27 E
Paso de Indios 176 43 55 S 69 0W
Paso de los Libres 172 29 44 S 57 10W
Paso de los Toros 172 32 36 S 56 37W
Paso Robles 161 35 40N 120 45W
Paspebiac 151 48 3N 65 17W
Pasrur 94 32 16N 74 43 E
Passage East 39 52 15N 7 0W
Passage West 39 51 52N 8 20W
Passaic 162 40 50N 74 8W
Passau 49 48 34N 13 27 E
Passendale 47 50 54N 3 2 E
Passero, C. 65 36 42N 15 8 E
Passo Fundo 173 28 10 S 52 30W
Passos 171 20 45 S 46 37W
Passow 48 53 13N 14 3 E
Passwang 50 47 22N 7 41 E
Passy 43 45 55N 6 41 E
Pastaza, R. 174 2 45 S 76 50W
Pastek 54 54 3N 19 41 E
Pasto 174 1 13N 77 17W
Pasto Zootécnico do Cunene 128 16 20 S 15 20 E
Pastos Bons 170 6 36 S 44 5W
Pastrana 58 40 27N 2 53W
Pasuruan 103 7 40 S 112 53 E
Pasym 54 53 48N 20 49 E
Pásztó 53 47 52N 19 43 E
Patagonia, Argent. 176 45 0 S 69 0W
Patagonia, U.S.A. 161 31 35N 110 45W
Patan, India 93 23 54N 72 14 E
Patan, Gujarat, India 96 17 22N 73 48 E
Patan, Maharashtra, India 94 23 54N 72 14 E
Patan (Lalitapur) 99 27 40N 85 20 E
Pat'ang Szechwan 105 30 2N 98 58 E
Patani 103 0 20N 128 50 E
Pataohotzu 107 43 5N 127 33 E
Patapsco Res. 162 39 27N 76 55W
Pataudi 94 28 18N 76 48 E
Patay 43 48 2N 1 40 E
Patcham 29 50 52N 0 9W
Patchewollock 140 35 22 S 142 12 E
Patchogue 162 40 46N 73 1W
Patea 142 39 45 S 174 30 E
Pategi 121 8 50N 5 45 E
Pateley Bridge 33 54 5N 1 45W
Patensie 128 33 46 S 24 49 E
Paternò 65 37 34N 14 53 E
Paternoster, Kepulauan 102 7 5 S 118 15 E
Pateros 160 48 4N 119 58W
Paterson, Austral. 141 32 37 S 151 39 E
Paterson, U.S.A. 162 40 55N 74 10W
Paterson Inlet 143 46 56 S 168 12 E
Paterson Ra. 136 21 45 S 122 10 E
Paterswolde 46 53 9N 6 34 E
Pathankot 94 32 18N 75 45 E
Patharghata 98 22 2N 89 58 E
Pathfinder Res. 160 42 0N 107 0W
Pathiu 101 10 42N 99 19 E
Pathum Thani 100 14 1N 100 32 E
Páti 103 6 45 S 111 3 E
Patiala 94 30 23N 76 26 E
Patine Kouta 120 12 45N 13 45W
Patjitan 103 8 12 S 111 8 E
Patkai Bum 98 27 0N 95 30 E
Pátmos 69 37 21N 26 36 E
Pátmos, I. 69 37 21N 26 36 E
Patna, India 95 25 35N 85 18 E
Patna, U.K. 34 55 21N 4 30W
Patonga 126 2 45N 33 15 E
Patos 170 7 1 S 37 16W
Patos de Minas 171 18 35 S 46 32W
Patos, Lag. dos 173 31 20 S 51 0 E
Patosi 68 40 42N 19 38 E
Patquía 172 30 0 S 66 55W
Pátrai 69 38 14N 21 47 E
Pátraikos, Kólpos 69 38 17N 21 30 E
Patrick 32 54 13N 4 41W
Patrocínio 171 18 57 S 47 0W
Patta 126 2 10 S 41 0 E
Patta, I. 126 2 10 S 41 0 E
Pattada 64 40 35N 9 7 E
Pattanapuram 97 9 6N 76 33 E
Pattani 101 6 48N 101 15 E
Patten 151 45 59N 68 28W
Patterdale 32 54 33N 2 55W
Patterson, Calif., U.S.A. 163 37 30N 121 9W
Patterson, La., U.S.A. 159 29 44N 91 20W
Patterson, Mt. 163 38 29N 119 20W
Patti 94 31 17N 74 54 E
Patti Castroreale 65 38 8N 14 57 E
Pattoki 94 31 5N 73 52 E
Pattukkottai 97 10 25N 79 20 E
Patu 170 6 6 S 37 38W
Patuakhali 98 22 20N 90 25 E
Patuca, Punta 166 15 49N 84 14W
Patuca, R. 166 15 20N 84 40W
Patung 109 31 0N 110 30 E
Pâturages 47 50 25N 3 52 E
Patutahi 142 38 38 S 177 55 E
Pátzcuaro 164 19 30N 101 40W
Pau 44 43 19N 0 25W
Pau d' Arco 170 7 30 S 49 22W
Pau dos Ferros 170 6 7 S 38 10W
Pauillac 44 45 11N 0 46W
Pauini, R. 174 1 42 S 62 50W
Pauk 98 21 55N 94 30 E
Paul I. 151 56 30N 61 20W
Paulatuk 147 69 25N 124 0W
Paulhan 44 43 33N 3 28 E
Paulis = Isiro 126 2 53N 27 58 E
Paulista 170 7 57 S 34 53W

Paulistana Perryton


| | | | |
|---|---|---|---|
| Paulistana | 170 | 8 9S | 41 9W |
| Paull | 33 | 53 42N | 0 12W |
| Paullina | 158 | 42 55N | 95 40W |
| Paulo Afonso | 170 | 9 21S | 38 15W |
| Paulo de Faria | 171 | 20 2S | 49 24W |
| Paulpietersburg | 129 | 27 23S | 30 50E |
| Paul's Valley | 159 | 34 40N | 97 17W |
| Pauma Valley | 163 | 33 16N | 116 58W |
| Paungde | 98 | 18 29N | 95 30E |
| Pauni | 96 | 20 48N | 79 40E |
| Pavelets | 81 | 53 49N | 39 14E |
| Pavia | 62 | 45 10N | 9 10E |
| Pavlikeni | 67 | 43 14N | 25 20E |
| Pavlodar | 76 | 52 33N | 77 0E |
| Pavlof Is. | 147 | 55 30N | 161 30W |
| Pavlograd | 82 | 48 30N | 35 52E |
| Pavlovo, Gorkiy, U.S.S.R. | 81 | 55 58N | 43 5E |
| Pavlovo, Yakut A.S.S.R., U.S.S.R. | 77 | 63 5N | 115 25E |
| Pavlovsk | 81 | 50 26N | 40 5E |
| Pavlovskaya | 83 | 46 17N | 39 47E |
| Pavlovskiy Posad | 81 | 55 37N | 38 42E |
| Pavullo nel Frignano | 62 | 44 20N | 10 50E |
| Pawahku | 98 | 26 11N | 98 40E |
| Pawhuska | 159 | 36 40N | 96 25W |
| Pawling | 162 | 41 35N | 73 37W |
| Pawnee | 159 | 36 24N | 96 50W |
| Pawnee City | 158 | 40 8N | 96 10W |
| Pawtucket | 162 | 41 51N | 71 22W |
| Paximádhia | 69 | 35 0N | 24 35E |
| Paxoi, I. | 68 | 39 14N | 20 12E |
| Paxton, Ill., U.S.A. | 156 | 40 25N | 88 0W |
| Paxton, Nebr., U.S.A. | 158 | 41 12N | 101 27W |
| Paya Bakri | 101 | 2 3N | 102 44E |
| Payakumbah | 102 | 0 20S | 100 35E |
| Payenhaot'e (Alashantsoch'i) | 106 | 38 50N | 105 32E |
| Payenk'ala Shan | 105 | 34 20N | 97 0E |
| Payerne | 50 | 46 49N | 6 56E |
| Payette | 160 | 44 0N | 117 0W |
| Paymogo | 57 | 37 44N | 7 21W |
| Payne L. | 149 | 59 30N | 74 30W |
| Payne, R. | 149 | 60 0N | 70 0W |
| Payneham | 109 | 34 54S | 138 39E |
| Paynes Find | 137 | 29 15S | 117 42E |
| Paynesville, Liberia | 120 | 6 20N | 10 45W |
| Paynesville, U.S.A. | 158 | 45 21N | 94 44W |
| Paysandú | 172 | 32 19S | 58 8W |
| Payson, Ariz., U.S.A. | 161 | 34 17N | 111 15W |
| Payson, Utah, U.S.A. | 160 | 40 8N | 111 41W |
| Paz, Bahía de la | 164 | 24 15N | 110 25W |
| Paz Centro, La | 166 | 12 20N | 86 41W |
| Paz, La, Entre Ríos, Argent. | 172 | 30 50S | 59 45W |
| Paz, La, San Luis, Argent. | 172 | 33 30S | 67 20W |
| Paz, La, Boliv. | 174 | 16 20S | 68 10W |
| Paz, La, Hond. | 166 | 14 20N | 87 47W |
| Paz, La, Mexico | 164 | 24 10N | 110 20W |
| Paz, La, Bahía de | 164 | 24 20N | 110 40W |
| Paz, R. | 166 | 13 44N | 90 10W |
| Pazar | 92 | 41 10N | 40 50E |
| Pazardzhik | 67 | 42 12N | 24 20E |
| Pazin | 63 | 45 14N | 13 56E |
| Pčinja, R. | 66 | 42 0N | 21 45E |
| Pe Ell | 160 | 46 30N | 123 18W |
| Peabody | 162 | 42 31N | 70 56W |
| Peace Point | 152 | 59 7N | 112 27W |
| Peace, R. | 152 | 59 0N | 111 25W |
| Peace River | 152 | 56 15N | 117 18W |
| Peace River Res. | 152 | 55 40N | 123 40W |
| Peacehaven | 29 | 50 47N | 0 1E |
| Peach Springs | 161 | 35 36N | 113 30W |
| Peak Downs | 138 | 22 55S | 148 0E |
| Peak Downs Mine | 138 | 22 17S | 148 11E |
| Peak Hill, N.S.W., Austral. | 141 | 32 39S | 148 11E |
| Peak Hill, W. A., Austral. | 137 | 25 35S | 118 43E |
| Peak Range | 138 | 22 50S | 148 20E |
| Peak, The | 32 | 53 24N | 1 53W |
| Peake | 140 | 35 25S | 140 0E |
| Peake Cr. | 139 | 28 2S | 136 7E |
| Peale Mt. | 161 | 38 25N | 109 12W |
| Pearblossom | 163 | 34 30N | 117 55W |
| Pearce | 161 | 31 57N | 109 56W |
| Pearl Banks | 97 | 8 45N | 79 45E |
| Pearl City | 147 | 2 21N | 158 0W |
| Pearl Harbor | 147 | 21 20N | 158 0W |
| Pearl, R. | 159 | 31 50N | 90 0W |
| Pearsall | 159 | 28 55N | 99 8W |
| Pearse I. | 152 | 54 52N | 130 14W |
| Peary Land | 12 | 82 40N | 33 0W |
| Pease, R. | 159 | 34 18N | 100 15W |
| Peasenhall | 29 | 52 17N | 1 24E |
| Pebane | 127 | 17 10S | 38 8E |
| Pebas | 174 | 3 10S | 71 55W |
| Pebble Beach | 163 | 36 34N | 121 57W |
| Peçanha | 171 | 18 33S | 42 34W |
| Péccioli | 62 | 43 32N | 10 43E |
| Pechea | 70 | 45 36N | 27 49E |
| Pechenezhin | 82 | 48 30N | 24 48E |
| Pechenga | 78 | 69 30N | 31 25E |
| Pechnezhskoye Vdkhr. | 81 | 50 0N | 36 50E |
| Pechora, R. | 78 | 62 30N | 56 30E |
| Pechorskaya Guba | 78 | 68 40N | 54 0E |
| Pechory | 80 | 57 48N | 27 40E |
| Pecica | 66 | 46 10N | 21 3E |
| Pečka | 66 | 44 18N | 19 33E |
| Pécora, C. | 64 | 39 28N | 8 23E |
| Pecos | 159 | 31 25N | 103 35W |
| Pecos, R. | 159 | 31 22N | 102 30W |
| Pecqueuse | 47 | 48 39N | 2 3E |
| Pécs | 53 | 46 5N | 18 15E |
| Pedasí | 166 | 7 32N | 80 3W |
| Peddapalli | 96 | 18 40N | 79 24E |
| Peddapuram | 96 | 17 6N | 82 5E |
| Peddavagu, R. | 96 | 16 33N | 79 8E |
| Pedder, L. | 138 | 42 55S | 146 10E |
| Pedernales | 167 | 18 2N | 71 44W |
| Pedirka | 139 | 26 40S | 135 14E |
| Pedjantan, I. | 102 | 0 5S | 106 15E |
| Pedra Azul | 171 | 16 2S | 41 17W |
| Pedra Grande, Recifes do | 171 | 17 45S | 38 58W |
| Pedras, Pta. de | 171 | 7 38S | 34 47W |
| Pedreiras | 170 | 4 32S | 44 40W |
| Pedrera, La | 174 | 1 18S | 69 43W |
| Pedro Afonso | 170 | 9 0S | 48 10W |
| Pedro Antonio Santos | 165 | 18 54N | 88 15W |
| Pedro Cays | 166 | 17 5N | 77 48W |
| Pedro Chico | 174 | 1 4N | 70 25W |
| Pedro de Valdivia | 172 | 22 33S | 69 38W |
| Pedro Juan Caballero | 173 | 22 30S | 55 40W |
| Pedro Muñoz | 59 | 39 25N | 2 56W |
| Pedrógão Grande | 56 | 39 55N | 8 0W |
| Peebinga | 140 | 34 52S | 140 57E |
| Peebles | 35 | 55 40N | 3 12W |
| Peebles (□) | 26 | 55 37N | 3 4W |
| Peekshill | 162 | 41 18N | 73 57W |
| Peel, Austral. | 139 | 33 20S | 149 38E |
| Peel, I. of Man | 32 | 54 14N | 4 40W |
| Peel Fell, mt. | 35 | 55 17N | 2 35W |
| Peel, R., Austral. | 141 | 30 50S | 150 29E |
| Peel, R., Can. | 147 | 67 0N | 135 0W |
| Peelwood | 141 | 34 7S | 149 27E |
| Peene, R. | 48 | 53 53N | 13 53E |
| Peera Peera Poolanna L. | 139 | 26 30S | 138 0E |
| Peers | 152 | 53 40N | 116 0W |
| Pegasus Bay | 143 | 43 20S | 173 10E |
| Peggau | 52 | 47 12N | 15 21E |
| Pego | 59 | 38 51N | 0 8W |
| Pegswood | 35 | 55 12N | 1 38W |
| Pegu | 99 | 17 20N | 96 29E |
| Pegu Yoma, mts. | 98 | 19 0N | 96 0E |
| Pegwell Bay | 29 | 51 18N | 1 22E |
| Pehčevo | 66 | 41 41N | 22 55E |
| Pehuajó | 172 | 36 0S | 62 0W |
| Pei Chiang, R. | 109 | 23 12N | 112 45E |
| Pei Wan | 107 | 36 25N | 120 45E |
| Peian | 105 | 48 16N | 126 36E |
| Peichen | 107 | 41 38N | 121 50E |
| Peichengchen | 107 | 44 30N | 123 27E |
| Peichiang | 109 | 23 0N | 120 0E |
| Peihai | 108 | 21 30N | 109 5E |
| P'eihsien, Kiangsu, China | 106 | 34 44N | 116 55E |
| P'eihsien, Kiangsu, China | 107 | 34 20N | 117 57E |
| Peiliu | 109 | 22 45N | 110 22E |
| Peine, Chile | 172 | 23 45S | 68 8W |
| Peine, Ger. | 48 | 52 19N | 10 12E |
| Peip'an Chiang, R. | 108 | 25 0N | 106 11E |
| Peip'ei | 105 | 29 49N | 106 27E |
| Peip'iao | 107 | 41 48N | 120 44E |
| Peip'ing | 106 | 39 45N | 116 25E |
| Peissenberg | 49 | 47 48N | 11 4E |
| Peitz | 48 | 51 50N | 14 23E |
| Peixe | 171 | 12 0S | 48 40W |
| Peixe, R. | 171 | 21 31S | 51 58W |
| Peize | 46 | 53 9N | 6 30E |
| Pek, R. | 66 | 44 58N | 21 55E |
| Pekalongan | 103 | 6 53S | 109 40E |
| Pekan | 101 | 3 30N | 103 25E |
| Pekin | 158 | 40 35N | 89 40W |
| Peking = Peip'ing | 106 | 39 45N | 116 25E |
| Pelabuhan Ratu, Teluk | 103 | 7 5S | 106 30E |
| Pelabuhanratu | 103 | 7 0S | 106 32E |
| Pélagos, I. | 68 | 39 17N | 24 4E |
| Pelagruza, Is. | 63 | 42 24N | 16 15E |
| Pelaihari | 102 | 3 55S | 114 45E |
| Pelczyce | 54 | 53 3N | 15 16E |
| Peleaga, mt. | 70 | 45 22N | 22 55E |
| Pelee I. | 150 | 41 47N | 82 40W |
| Pelée, Mt. | 167 | 14 40N | 61 0W |
| Pelee, Pt. | 150 | 41 54N | 82 31W |
| Pelekech, mt. | 126 | 3 52N | 35 8E |
| Peleng, I. | 103 | 1 20S | 123 30E |
| Pelham | 157 | 31 5N | 84 6W |
| Pelhrimov | 52 | 49 24N | 15 12E |
| Pelican | 147 | 58 12N | 136 28W |
| Pelican L. | 153 | 52 28N | 100 20W |
| Pelican Narrows | 153 | 55 10N | 102 56W |
| Pelican Portage | 152 | 55 51N | 113 0W |
| Pelican Rapids | 153 | 52 45N | 100 42W |
| Peligre, L. de | 167 | 19 1N | 71 58W |
| Pelkosenniemi | 74 | 67 6N | 27 28E |
| Pella | 158 | 41 20N | 93 0W |
| Pélla □ | 68 | 40 52N | 22 0E |
| Péllaro | 65 | 38 1N | 15 40E |
| Pellworm, I. | 48 | 54 30N | 8 40E |
| Pelly Bay | 149 | 68 0N | 89 50W |
| Pelly L. | 148 | 66 0N | 102 0W |
| Pelly, R. | 147 | 62 15N | 133 30W |
| Peloponnese = Pelóponnisos | 69 | 37 10N | 22 0E |
| Pelopónnisos Kai Dhitiktí Iprotikí Ellas □ | 69 | 37 10N | 22 0E |
| Peloritani, Monti | 65 | 38 2N | 15 15E |
| Peloro, C. | 65 | 38 15N | 15 40E |
| Pelorus Sound | 143 | 40 59S | 173 59E |
| Pelotas | 173 | 31 42S | 52 23W |
| Pelòvo | 67 | 43 26N | 24 17E |
| Pelvoux, Massif de | 45 | 44 52N | 6 20E |
| Pelym R. | 84 | 59 39N | 63 6E |
| Pemalang | 103 | 6 53S | 109 23E |
| Pematang Siantar | 102 | 2 57N | 99 5E |
| Pemba, Mozam. | 127 | 12 58S | 40 30E |
| Pemba, Zambia | 127 | 16 30S | 27 28E |
| Pemba Channel | 126 | 5 0S | 39 37E |
| Pemba, I. | 126 | 5 0S | 39 45E |
| Pemberton, Austral. | 137 | 34 30S | 116 0E |
| Pemberton, Can. | 152 | 50 25N | 122 50W |
| Pembina | 153 | 48 58N | 97 15W |
| Pembina, R. | 153 | 49 0N | 98 12W |
| Pembine | 156 | 45 38N | 87 59W |
| Pembrey | 31 | 51 42N | 4 17W |
| Pembroke, Can. | 150 | 45 50N | 77 7W |
| Pembroke, N.Z. | 143 | 44 33S | 169 9E |
| Pembroke, U.K. | 31 | 51 41N | 4 57W |
| Pembroke, U.S.A. | 157 | 32 5N | 81 32W |
| Pembroke (□) | 26 | 51 40N | 5 0W |
| Pembroke Dock | 31 | 51 41N | 4 57W |
| Pembury | 29 | 51 8N | 0 20E |
| Pen-y-Ghent | 32 | 54 10N | 2 15W |
| Pen-y-groes, Dyfed, U.K. | 31 | 51 48N | 4 3W |
| Pen-y-groes, Gwynedd, U.K. | 31 | 53 3N | 4 18W |
| Peñíscola | 58 | 40 22N | 0 24E |
| Peña de Francia, Sierra de | 56 | 40 32N | 6 10W |
| Peña Roya, mt. | 58 | 40 24N | 0 40W |
| Peña, Sierra de la | 58 | 42 32N | 0 45W |
| Penafiel | 56 | 41 12N | 8 17W |
| Peñafiel | 56 | 41 35N | 4 7W |
| Peñaflor | 57 | 37 43N | 5 21W |
| Peñalara, Pico | 56 | 40 51N | 3 57W |
| Penally | 31 | 51 39N | 4 44W |
| Penalva | 170 | 3 18S | 45 10W |
| Penamacôr | 56 | 40 10N | 7 10W |
| Penang = Pinang | 101 | 5 25N | 100 15E |
| Penápolis | 173 | 21 30S | 50 0W |
| Peñaranda de Bracamonte | 56 | 40 53N | 5 13W |
| Peñarroya-Pueblonuevo | 57 | 38 19N | 5 16W |
| Penarth | 31 | 51 26N | 3 11W |
| Peñas, C. de | 56 | 43 42N | 5 52W |
| Peñas de San Pedro | 59 | 38 44N | 2 0W |
| Peñas, G. de | 176 | 47 0S | 75 0W |
| Peñas, Pta. | 174 | 11 17N | 70 28W |
| Pench'i | 107 | 41 20N | 123 48E |
| Pencoed | 31 | 51 31N | 3 30W |
| Pend Oreille, L. | 160 | 48 0N | 116 30W |
| Pend Oreille, R. | 160 | 49 4N | 117 37W |
| Pendálofon | 68 | 40 14N | 21 12E |
| Pendeen | 30 | 50 11N | 5 39W |
| Pendelikón | 69 | 38 5N | 23 53E |
| Pendembu | 120 | 9 7N | 12 14W |
| Pendências | 170 | 5 15S | 36 43W |
| Pender B. | 136 | 16 45S | 122 42E |
| Pendine | 31 | 51 44N | 4 33W |
| Pendle Hill | 32 | 53 53N | 2 18W |
| Pendleton, Calif., U.S.A. | 163 | 33 16N | 117 23W |
| Pendleton, Oreg., U.S.A. | 160 | 45 35N | 118 50W |
| Pendzhikent | 85 | 39 29N | 67 37E |
| Penedo | 170 | 10 15S | 36 36W |
| Penetanguishene | 150 | 44 50N | 79 55W |
| Penfield | 109 | 34 44S | 138 38E |
| Pengalengan | 103 | 7 9S | 107 30E |
| P'engch'i | 108 | 30 50N | 105 42E |
| Penge, Kasai, Congo | 126 | 5 30S | 24 33E |
| Penge, Kivu, Congo | 126 | 4 27S | 28 25E |
| P'enghsien | 108 | 30 59N | 103 56E |
| P'enghu Liehtao | 109 | 22 30N | 119 30E |
| P'englai | 107 | 37 49N | 120 47E |
| P'engshui | 108 | 29 19N | 108 12E |
| P'engtse | 109 | 29 53N | 116 32E |
| Penguin | 138 | 41 8S | 146 6E |
| Penhalonga | 127 | 18 52S | 32 40E |
| Peniche | 57 | 39 19N | 9 22W |
| Penicuik | 35 | 55 50N | 3 14W |
| Penida, I. | 102 | 8 45S | 115 30E |
| Penistone | 33 | 53 31N | 1 38W |
| Penitentes, Serra dos | 170 | 8 45S | 46 20W |
| Penkridge | 28 | 52 44N | 2 8W |
| Penmachno | 31 | 53 2N | 3 47W |
| Penmaenmawr | 31 | 53 16N | 3 55W |
| Penmarch | 42 | 47 49N | 4 21W |
| Penmarch, Pte. de | 42 | 47 48N | 4 22W |
| Penn Yan | 162 | 42 39N | 77 7W |
| Pennabilli | 63 | 43 50N | 12 17E |
| Pennant | 153 | 50 32N | 108 14W |
| Penne | 63 | 42 28N | 13 56E |
| Penner, R. | 97 | 14 50N | 78 20E |
| Penneshaw | 140 | 35 44S | 137 56E |
| Pennines | 32 | 54 50N | 2 20W |
| Pennino, Mte. | 63 | 43 6N | 12 54E |
| Pennsburg | 162 | 40 23N | 75 30W |
| Pennsville | 162 | 39 39N | 75 31W |
| Pennsylvania □ | 156 | 40 50N | 78 0W |
| Penny | 152 | 53 51N | 121 48W |
| Peno | 80 | 57 2N | 32 33E |
| Penola | 140 | 37 25S | 140 47E |
| Penong | 139 | 31 59S | 133 5E |
| Penonomé | 166 | 8 31N | 80 21W |
| Penpont | 35 | 55 14N | 3 49W |
| Penrhyn Is. | 131 | 9 0S | 150 30W |
| Penrith, Austral. | 141 | 33 43S | 150 38E |
| Penrith, U.K. | 32 | 54 40N | 2 45W |
| Penryn | 30 | 50 10N | 5 7W |
| Pensacola | 157 | 30 30N | 87 10W |
| Pensacola Mts. | 13 | 84 0S | 40 0W |
| Pense | 153 | 50 25N | 104 59W |
| Penshurst, Austral. | 140 | 37 49S | 142 20W |
| Penshurst, U.K. | 29 | 51 10N | 0 12E |
| Pentecoste | 170 | 3 48S | 37 17W |
| Penticton | 152 | 49 30N | 119 30W |
| Pentire Pt. | 30 | 50 35N | 4 57W |
| Pentland | 138 | 20 32S | 145 25E |
| Pentland Firth | 37 | 58 43N | 3 10W |
| Pentland Hills | 35 | 55 48N | 3 25W |
| Pentland Skerries | 37 | 58 41N | 2 53W |
| Pentraeth | 31 | 53 17N | 4 13W |
| Pentre Foelas | 31 | 53 2N | 3 41W |
| Penukonda | 97 | 14 5N | 77 38E |
| Penwortham | 32 | 53 45N | 2 44W |
| Penybont | 31 | 52 17N | 3 18W |
| Penylan L. | 153 | 61 50N | 106 20W |
| Penza | 81 | 53 15N | 45 5E |
| Penzance | 30 | 50 7N | 5 32W |
| Penzberg | 49 | 47 46N | 11 23E |
| Penzhinskaya Guba | 77 | 61 30N | 163 0E |
| Penzlin | 48 | 53 32N | 13 6E |
| Peó | 66 | 42 40N | 20 17E |
| Peoria, Ariz., U.S.A. | 161 | 33 40N | 112 15W |
| Peoria, Ill., U.S.A. | 158 | 40 40N | 89 40W |
| Pepacton Res. | 162 | 42 5N | 74 58W |
| Pepingen | 47 | 50 46N | 4 10E |
| Pepinster | 47 | 50 34N | 5 47E |
| Pepmbridge | 28 | 52 13N | 2 54W |
| Pepperwood | 160 | 40 23N | 124 0W |
| Peqini | 68 | 41 4N | 19 44E |
| Pera Hd. | 138 | 12 55S | 141 37E |
| Perabumilih | 102 | 3 27S | 104 15E |
| Perakhóra | 69 | 38 2N | 22 56E |
| Peraki, R. | 101 | 5 10N | 101 4E |
| Perales de Alfambra | 58 | 40 38N | 1 0W |
| Perales del Puerto | 56 | 40 10N | 6 40W |
| Peralta | 58 | 42 21N | 1 49W |
| Pérama | 69 | 35 20N | 24 22E |
| Perast | 66 | 42 31N | 18 47E |
| Percé | 151 | 48 31N | 64 13W |
| Perche | 42 | 48 31N | 1 1E |
| Perche, Collines de la | 42 | 42 30N | 2 5E |
| Percival Lakes | 136 | 21 25S | 125 0E |
| Percy | 42 | 48 55N | 1 11W |
| Percy Is. | 138 | 21 39S | 150 16E |
| Percyville | 138 | 19 2S | 143 45E |
| Perdido, Mte. | 58 | 42 40N | 0 50E |
| Pereira | 174 | 4 49N | 75 43W |
| Pereira Barreto | 171 | 20 38S | 51 7W |
| Pereira de Eóa | 128 | 16 48S | 15 50E |
| Perekerten | 140 | 34 55S | 143 40E |
| Perenjori | 137 | 29 26S | 116 16E |
| Pereslavi-Zelesskiy | 80 | 56 45N | 38 58E |
| Pereyaslav-Khmelnitskiy | 80 | 50 3N | 31 28E |
| Perez, I. | 165 | 22 24N | 89 42W |
| Perg | 52 | 48 15N | 14 38E |
| Pergamino | 172 | 33 52S | 60 30W |
| Pergine Valsugano | 63 | 46 4N | 11 15E |
| Pérgola | 63 | 43 35N | 12 50E |
| Perham | 158 | 46 36N | 95 36W |
| Perham Down Camp | 28 | 51 14N | 1 38W |
| Perhentian, Kepulauan | 101 | 5 54N | 102 42E |
| Peri, L. | 140 | 30 45S | 143 35E |
| Periam | 66 | 46 2N | 20 59E |
| Peribonca, L. | 151 | 50 1N | 71 10W |
| Péribonca, R. | 151 | 48 45N | 72 5W |
| Perico | 172 | 24 20S | 65 5W |
| Pericos | 164 | 25 3N | 107 42W |
| Périers | 42 | 49 11N | 1 25W |
| Périgord | 44 | 45 0N | 0 40E |
| Périgueux | 44 | 45 10N | 0 42E |
| Perija, Sierra de | 174 | 9 30N | 73 3W |
| Perim, I. | 91 | 12 39N | 43 25E |
| Peristera, I. | 69 | 39 15N | 23 58E |
| Peritoró | 170 | 4 20S | 44 18W |
| Periyakulam | 97 | 10 5N | 77 30E |
| Periyar, L. | 97 | 9 25N | 77 10E |
| Periyar, R. | 97 | 10 15N | 78 10E |
| Perkam, Tg. | 103 | 1 35S | 137 50E |
| Perkasie | 162 | 40 22N | 75 18W |
| Perkovió | 63 | 43 41N | 16 10E |
| Perlas, Arch. de las | 166 | 8 41N | 79 7W |
| Perlas, Punta de | 166 | 11 30N | 83 30W |
| Perleberg | 48 | 53 5N | 11 50E |
| Perlevka | 81 | 51 56N | 38 57E |
| Perlez | 66 | 45 11N | 20 22E |
| Perlis □ | 101 | 6 30N | 100 15E |
| Perm (Molotov) | 84 | 58 0N | 57 10E |
| Përmeti | 68 | 40 15N | 20 21E |
| Pernambuco = Recife | 170 | 8 0S | 35 0W |
| Pernambuco □ | 170 | 8 0S | 37 0W |
| Pernatty Lagoon | 140 | 31 30S | 137 12E |
| Peron, C. | 137 | 25 30S | 113 30E |
| Peron Is. | 136 | 13 9S | 130 4E |
| Peron Pen. | 137 | 26 0S | 113 10E |
| Péronne | 43 | 49 55N | 2 57E |
| Péronnes | 47 | 50 27N | 4 9E |
| Perosa Argentina | 62 | 44 57N | 7 11E |
| Perouse Str., La | 86 | 45 40N | 142 0E |
| Perow | 152 | 54 35N | 126 10W |
| Perpendicular Pt. | 139 | 31 37S | 152 52E |
| Perpignan | 44 | 42 42N | 2 53E |
| Perranporth | 30 | 50 21N | 5 9W |
| Perranzabuloe | 30 | 50 18N | 5 7W |
| Perris | 163 | 33 47N | 117 14W |
| Perros-Guirec | 42 | 48 49N | 3 28W |
| Perry, Fla., U.S.A. | 157 | 30 9N | 83 10W |
| Perry, Ga., U.S.A. | 157 | 32 25N | 83 41W |
| Perry, Iowa, U.S.A. | 158 | 41 48N | 94 5W |
| Perry, Maine, U.S.A. | 157 | 44 59N | 67 20W |
| Perry, Okla., U.S.A. | 159 | 36 20N | 97 20W |
| Perry, Mt. | 139 | 25 12S | 151 41E |
| Perryton | 159 | 36 28N | 100 48W |

Perryville
Ping, R

Perryville, Alas., U.S.A. 147 55 54N 159 10W
Perryville, Mo., U.S.A. 159 37 42N 89 50W
Persberg 72 59 47N 14 15 E
Persepolis 93 29 55N 52 50 E
Pershore 28 52 7N 2 4W
Persia = Iran 93 35 0N 50 0 E
Persian Gulf 93 27 0N 50 0 E
Perstorp 73 56 10N 13 25 E
Perth, Austral. 137 31 57 S 115 52 E
Perth, N.B., Can. 150 46 43N 67 42W
Perth, Ont., Can. 150 44 55N 76 15W
Perth, U.K. 35 56 24N 3 27W
Perth (□) 26 56 30N 4 0W
Perth Amboy 162 40 30N 74 25W
Perthus, Le 44 42 30N 2 53 E
Pertuis 45 43 42N 5 30 E
Pertuis Breton 44 46 17N 1 25W
Pertuis d'Antioche 44 46 6N 1 20W
Peru, Ill., U.S.A. 158 41 18N 89 12W
Peru, Ind., U.S.A. 156 40 42N 86 0W
Peru ■ 174 8 0 S 75 0W
Perúgia 63 43 6N 12 24 E
Perušić 63 44 40N 15 22 E
Péruwelz 47 50 31N 3 36 E
Pervomayskiy 81 53 20N 40 10 E
Pervouralsk 84 56 55N 60 0 E
Perwez 47 50 38N 4 48 E
Pésaro 63 43 55N 12 53 E
Pesca, La 165 23 46N 97 47W
Pescadores Is. (P'enghu Liehtao) 109 23 30N 119 30 E
Pescara 63 42 28N 14 13 E
Peschanokopskoye 83 46 14N 41 4 E
Péscia 62 43 54N 10 40 E
Pescina 63 42 0N 13 39 E
Peseux 50 46 59N 6 53 E
Peshawar 94 34 2N 71 37 E
Peshawar □ 94 35 0N 72 50 E
Peshkopia 68 41 41N 20 25 E
Peshovka 84 59 4N 52 22 E
Peshtera 67 42 2N 24 18 E
Peshtigo 156 45 4N 87 46W
Peski 81 51 14N 42 12 E
Peskovka 81 59 9N 52 28 E
Pêso da Régua 56 41 10N 7 47W
Pesqueira 170 8 20 S 36 42W
Pesquiería 164 29 23N 110 54W
Pesquiería, R. 164 25 54N 99 11W
Pessac 44 44 48N 0 37W
Pessoux 47 50 17N 5 11 E
Pest □ 53 47 29N 19 5 E
Pestovo 80 58 33N 35 18 E
Pestravka 81 52 28N 49 57 E
Péta 69 39 10N 21 2 E
Petah Tiqwa 90 32 6N 34 53 E
Petalídhion, Khóra 69 36 57N 21 55 E
Petaling Jaya 101 3 4N 101 42 E
Petaluma 163 38 13N 122 39W
Petange 47 49 33N 5 55 E
Petatlán 164 17 31N 101 16W
Petauke 127 14 14 S 31 12 E
Petawawa 150 45 54N 77 17W
Petegem 47 50 59N 3 32 E
Petén Itza, Lago 166 16 58N 89 50W
Peter 1st, I. 13 69 0 S 91 0W
Peter Pond L. 153 55 55N 108 44W
Peterbell 150 48 36N 83 21W
Peterboro 162 42 55N 71 59W
Peterborough, S. Australia, Austral. 140 32 58 S 138 51 E
Peterborough, Victoria, Austral. 133 38 37 S 142 50 E
Peterborough, U.K. 29 52 35N 0 14W
Peterchurch 28 52 3N 2 57W
Peterculter 37 57 5N 2 18W
Peterhead 37 57 30N 1 49W
Peterlee 33 54 45N 1 18W
Petersburg, Alas., U.S.A. 152 56 50N 133 0W
Petersburg, Ind., U.S.A. 156 38 30N 87 15W
Petersburg, Va., U.S.A. 162 37 17N 77 26W
Petersburg, W. Va., U.S.A. 156 38 59N 79 10W
Petersfield 29 51 0N 0 56W
Peterswell 39 53 7N 8 46W
Petford 138 17 20 S 144 50 E
Petília Policastro 65 39 7N 16 48 E
Petit Bois I. 157 30 16N 88 25W
Petit Cap 151 48 58N 63 58W
Petit Goâve 167 18 27N 72 51W
Petit-Quevilly, Le 42 49 26N 1 0 E
Petitcodiac 151 45 57N 65 11W
Petite Saguenay 151 47 59N 70 1W
Petitsikapau, L. 151 54 37N 66 25W
Petlad 94 22 30N 72 45 E
Peto 165 20 10N 89 0W
Petone 142 41 13 S 174 53 E
Petoskey 150 45 22N 84 57W
Petra, Jordan 90 30 20N 35 22 E
Petra, Spain 58 39 37N 3 6 E
Petra, Ostrova 12 76 15N 118 30 E
Petralia 65 37 49N 14 4 E
Petrel 59 38 30N 0 46W
Petrich 67 41 24N 23 13 E
Petrijanec 63 46 23N 16 17 E
Petrikov 80 52 11N 28 29 E
Petrila 70 45 29N 23 29 E
Petrinja 63 45 28N 16 18 E
'Petroland', gasfield 19 53 35N 4 15 E
Petrolândia 170 9 5 S 38 20W
Petrolia 150 42 54N 82 9W
Petrolina 170 9 24 S 40 30W
Petropavlovsk 76 55 0N 69 0 E
Petropavlovsk-Kamchatskiy 77 53 16N 159 0 E
Petrópolis 173 22 33 S 43 9W
Petroşeni 70 45 28N 23 20 E
Petrova Gora 63 45 15N 15 45 E
Petrovac 66 42 13N 18 57 E
Petrovaradin 66 45 16N 19 55 E
Petrovsk 81 52 22N 45 19 E
Petrovsk-Zabaykalskiy 77 51 26N 108 30 E
Petrovskoye, R.S.F.S.R., U.S.S.R. 83 45 25N 42 58 E
Petrovskoye, R.S.F.S.R., U.S.S.R. 84 53 37N 56 23 E
Petrozavodsk 78 61 41N 34 20 E
Petrus Steyn 129 27 38 S 28 8 E
Petrusburg 128 29 4 S 25 26 E
Pettigo 38 54 32N 7 49W
Pettitts 141 34 56 S 148 10 E
Petworth 29 50 59N 0 37W
Peumo 172 34 21 S 71 19W
Peureulak 102 4 48N 97 45 E
Pevek 77 69 15N 171 0 E
Pevensey 29 50 49N 0 20 E
Pevensey Levels 29 50 50N 0 20 E
Peveragno 62 44 20N 7 37 E
Pewsey 28 51 20N 1 46W
Pewsey, Vale of 28 51 20N 1 46W
Peyrehorade 44 43 34N 1 7W
Peyruis 45 44 1N 5 56 E
Pézenas 44 43 28N 3 24 E
Pezinok 53 48 17N 17 17 E
Pfaffenhofen 49 48 31N 11 31 E
Pfäffikon 51 47 13N 8 46 E
Pfarrkirchen 49 48 25N 12 57 E
Pforzheim 49 48 53N 8 43 E
Pfungstadt 49 49 47N 8 36 E
Phagwara 93 31 10N 75 40 E
Phala 128 23 45 S 26 50 E
Phalodi 94 27 12N 72 24 E
Phalsbourg 43 48 46N 7 15 E
Phan 100 19 28N 99 43 E
Phan Rang 101 11 40N 109 9 E
Phan Thiet 101 11 1N 108 9 E
Phanat Nikhom 100 13 27N 101 11 E
Phangan, Ko 101 9 45N 100 0 E
Phangnga 101 8 28N 98 30 E
Phanh Bho Ho Chi Minh 101 10 58N 106 40 E
Phanom Dang Raek, mts. 100 14 45N 104 0 E
Phanom Sarakham 100 13 45N 101 21 E
Pharenda 95 27 5N 83 17 E
Phatthalung 101 7 39N 100 6 E
Phayao 100 19 11N 99 55 E
Phelps, N.Y., U.S.A. 162 42 57N 77 5W
Phelps, Wis., U.S.A. 158 46 2N 89 2W
Phelps L. 153 59 15N 103 15W
Phenix City 157 32 30N 85 0W
Phet Buri 100 13 1N 99 55 E
Phetchabun 100 16 25N 101 8 E
Phetchabun, Thiu Khao 100 16 0N 101 20 E
Phetchaburi 101 13 1N 99 55 E
Phi Phi, Ko 101 7 45N 98 46 E
Phiafay 100 14 48N 106 0 E
Phibun Mangsahan 100 15 14N 105 14 E
Phichai 100 17 22N 100 10 E
Phichit 100 16 26N 100 22 E
Philadelphia, Miss., U.S.A. 159 32 47N 89 5W
Philadelphia, Pa., U.S.A. 162 40 0N 75 10W
Philip 158 44 4N 101 42W
Philip Smith Mts. 147 68 0N 146 0W
Philippeville 47 50 12N 4 33 E
Philippi L. 138 24 20 S 138 55 E
Philippines ■ 103 12 0N 123 0 E
Philippolis 128 30 15 S 25 16 E
Philippopolis = Plovdiv 67 42 8N 24 44 E
Philipsburg 160 46 20N 113 21W
Philipstown 128 30 28 S 24 30 E
Phillip, I. 141 38 30 S 145 12 E
Phillips, Texas, U.S.A. 159 35 48N 101 17W
Phillips, Wis., U.S.A. 158 45 41N 90 22W
Phillips Ra. 136 16 53 S 125 50 E
Phillipsburg, Kans., U.S.A. 158 39 48N 99 20W
Phillipsburg, Penn., U.S.A. 162 40 43N 75 12W
Phillott 139 27 53 S 145 50 E
Philmont 162 42 14N 73 37W
Philomath 160 44 28N 123 21W
Phimai 100 15 13N 102 30 E
Phitsanulok 100 16 50N 100 12 E
Phnom Penh 101 11 33N 104 55 E
Phnom Thbeng 101 13 50N 104 56 E
Phoenicia 162 42 5N 74 14W
Phoenix, Ariz., U.S.A. 161 33 30N 112 10W
Phoenix, N.Y., U.S.A. 162 43 13N 76 18W
Phoenix Is. 130 3 30 S 172 0W
Phoenixville 162 40 12N 75 29W
Phon 100 15 49N 102 36 E
Phon Tiou 100 17 53N 104 37 E
Phong, R. 100 16 23N 102 56 E
Phong Saly 100 21 42N 102 9 E
Phong Tho 100 22 32N 103 21 E
Phongdo 99 30 14N 91 14 E
Phonhong 100 18 30N 102 25 E
Phonum 101 8 49N 98 48 E
Photharam 100 13 41N 99 51 E
Phra Chedi Sam Ong 100 15 16N 98 23 E
Phra Nakhon Si Ayutthaya 100 14 25N 100 30 E
Phra Thong, Ko 101 9 5N 98 17 E
Phrae 100 18 7N 100 9 E
Phrao 101 19 23N 99 15 E
Phrom Phiram 100 17 2N 100 12 E
Phu Dien 100 18 58N 105 31 E
Phu Doan 101 21 40N 105 10 E
Phu Loi 100 20 14N 103 14 E
Phu Ly (Ha Nam) 100 20 35N 105 50 E
Phu Qui 100 19 20N 105 20 E
Phu Tho 100 21 24N 105 13 E
Phuc Yen 100 21 16N 105 45 E
Phuket 100 8 0N 98 28 E
Phuket, Ko, I. 101 8 0N 98 22 E
Phulbari 98 21 52N 88 8 E
Phulera (Phalera) 94 26 52N 75 16 E
Phun Phin 101 9 7N 99 12 E
Phuoc Le (Baria) 101 10 39N 107 19 E
Piabia 138 25 12 S 152 45 E
Piacá 170 7 42 S 47 18W
Piacenza 62 45 2N 9 42 E
Piaçubaçu 170 10 24 S 36 25W
Piádena 62 45 8N 10 22 E
Pialba 139 25 20 S 152 45 E
Pian, Cr. 139 30 2 S 148 12 E
Piancó 171 7 12 S 37 57W
Pianella 63 42 24N 14 5 E
Piangil 140 35 5 S 143 20 E
Pianoro 63 44 20N 11 20 E
Pianosa, I., Puglia, Italy 63 42 12N 15 44 E
Pianosa, I., Toscana, Italy 62 42 36N 10 4 E
Piapot 153 49 59N 109 8W
Pias 57 38 1N 7 29W
Piaseczno 54 52 5N 21 2 E
Piassabussu 171 10 24 S 36 25W
Piastow 54 52 12N 20 48 E
Piatá 171 13 9 S 41 48W
Piatra Neamţ 70 46 56N 26 21 E
Piatra Olt 70 43 51N 25 9 E
Piauí □ 170 7 0 S 43 0W
Piaui, R. 170 6 38 S 42 42W
Piave, R. 63 45 50N 13 9 E
Piazza Armerina 65 37 21N 14 20 E
Pibor Post 123 6 47N 33 3 E
Pibor, R. 123 7 1N 33 0 E
Pica 174 20 35 S 69 25W
Picard, Plaine de 43 50 0N 2 0 E
Picardie 43 50 0N 2 15 E
Picardy = Picardie 43 50 0N 2 15 E
Picayune 159 30 40N 89 40W
Piccadilly, Austral. 109 34 59 S 138 44 E
Piccadilly, Zambia 127 14 0 S 29 30 E
Picerno 65 40 40N 15 37 E
Pichiang 108 26 40N 98 53 E
Pichieh 108 27 20N 105 20 E
Pichilemu 172 34 22 S 72 9W
Pickerel L. 150 48 40N 91 25W
Pickering 33 54 15N 0 46W
Pickering, Vale of 33 54 0N 0 45W
Pickle Lake 150 51 30N 90 12W
Pico 16 38 28N 28 18W
Pico Truncado 176 46 40 S 68 10W
Picos 170 7 5 S 41 28W
Picos Ancares, Sierra de 56 42 51N 6 52W
Picquigny 43 49 56N 2 10 E
Picton, Austral. 141 34 12 S 150 34 E
Picton, Can. 150 44 1N 77 9W
Picton, N.Z. 143 41 18 S 174 3 E
Pictou 151 45 41N 62 42W
Picture Butte 152 49 55N 112 45W
Picuí 170 6 31 S 36 21W
Picún-Leufú 176 39 30 S 69 5W
Pidley 29 52 33N 0 4W
Pidurutalagala, mt. 97 7 10N 80 50 E
Piedad, La 164 20 20N 102 1W
Piedecuesta 174 6 59N 73 3W
Piedicavallo 62 45 41N 7 57 E
Piedmont 157 33 55N 85 39W
Piedmont = Piemonte 62 45 0N 7 30 E
Piedmont Plat. 157 34 0N 81 30W
Piedmonte d'Alife 65 41 22N 14 22 E
Piedra, R. 58 41 10N 1 45W
Piedrabuena 57 39 0N 4 10W
Piedrahita 56 40 28N 5 23W
Piedras Blancas Pt. 161 35 45N 121 18W
Piedras Negras 164 28 35N 100 35W
Piedras, R. de las 174 11 40 S 70 50W
Piemonte 62 45 0N 7 30 E
Piena 45 42 15N 8 34 E
Piensk 54 51 16N 15 2 E
Pier Millan 140 35 14 S 142 40 E
Pierce 160 46 46N 115 53W
Pieria □ 68 40 13N 22 25 E
Pierowall 37 59 20N 3 0W
Pierre, France 43 46 54N 5 13 E
Pierre, U.S.A. 158 44 23N 100 20W
Pierrefeu 45 43 8N 6 9 E
Pierrefonds 43 49 20N 3 0 E
Pierrefontaine 43 47 14N 6 32 E
Pierrefort 44 44 55N 2 50 E
Pierrelatte 45 44 23N 4 43 E
Pieštany 155 48 35N 17 50 E
Piesting, R. 53 48 0N 16 19 E
Pieszyce 54 50 43N 16 33 E
Piet Retief 129 27 1 S 30 50 E
Pietarsaari 74 63 41N 22 40 E
Pietermaritzburg 129 29 35 S 30 25 E
Pietersburg 129 23 54 S 29 25 E
Pietraperzia 65 37 26N 14 8 E
Pietrasanta 62 43 57N 10 12 E
Pietrosu 70 47 12N 25 8 E
Pietrosul 70 47 35N 24 43 E
Pieve di Cadore 63 46 25N 12 22 E
Pieve di Teco 62 44 3N 7 54 E
Pievepélago 62 44 12N 10 35 E
Pigadhitsa 68 39 59N 21 23 E
Pigadia 69 35 30N 27 12 E
Pigeon I. 97 14 2N 74 20 E
Pigeon, R. 150 48 1N 89 42W
Piggott 159 36 20N 90 10W
Pigna 62 43 57N 7 40 E
Pigüe 172 37 36 S 62 25W
Pihani 95 27 36N 80 15 E
Pijnacker 46 52 1N 4 26 E
Pikalevo 80 59 37N 34 0 E
Pikes Peak 158 38 50N 105 10W
Pikesville 162 39 23N 76 44W
Piketberg 128 32 55 S 18 40 E
Pikeville 156 37 30N 82 30W
Pik'ochi 106 40 45N 111 17 E
Pikou 106 32 45N 105 22 E
Pikwitonei 153 55 35N 97 9W
Piła 54 53 10N 16 48 E
Piła □ 54 53 0N 17 0 E
Pila, mte. 59 38 16N 1 11W
Pilaia 68 40 32N 22 59 E
Pilani 94 28 22N 75 33 E
Pilão Arcado 170 10 9 S 42 26W
Pilar, Brazil 170 9 36 S 35 56W
Pilar, Parag. 172 26 50 S 58 10W
Pilas, I. 103 6 39N 121 37 E
Pilatus 51 46 59N 8 15 E
Pilbara Cr. 132 21 15 S 118 22 E
Pilbara Mining Centre 136 21 15 S 118 16 E
Pilcomayo, R. 172 25 21 S 57 42W
Píli 69 36 50N 27 15 E
Pilibhit 95 28 40N 79 50 E
Pilion, mt. 68 39 27N 23 7 E
Pilis 53 47 17N 19 35 E
Pilisvörösvár 53 47 38N 18 56 E
Pilkhawa 94 28 43N 77 42 E
Pilling 32 53 55N 2 54W
Pilltown 39 51 59N 7 49W
Pilos 69 36 55N 21 42 E
Pilot Mound 153 49 15N 98 54W
Pilot Point 159 33 26N 97 0W
Pilot Rock 160 45 30N 118 58W
Pilsen = Plzen 52 49 45N 13 22 E
Pilštanj 63 46 8N 15 39 E
Pilton 28 51 0N 2 35W
Piltown 39 52 22N 7 18W
Pilzno 54 50 0N 21 16 E
Pimba 140 31 18 S 136 46 E
Pimenta Bueno 174 11 35 S 61 10W
Pimentel 174 6 45 S 79 55W
Pimuacan, Rés. 151 49 45N 70 30W
Pina 58 41 29N 0 33W
Pinang, I. 101 5 25N 100 15 E
Pinar del Rio 166 22 26N 83 40W
Pinawa 149 50 9N 95 50W
Pince C. 151 46 38N 53 45W
Pinchbeck 29 52 48N 0 9W
Pincher Creek 152 49 30N 113 57W
Pinchi L. 152 54 38N 124 30W
Pinch'uan 108 25 51N 100 34 E
Pinckneyville 158 38 5N 89 20W
Pincota 66 46 20N 21 45 E
Pind Dadan Khan 94 32 55N 73 47 E
Pindar 137 28 30 S 115 47 E
Pindaré Mirim 170 3 37 S 45 21W
Pindaré, R. 170 3 17 S 44 47W
Pindi Gheb 94 33 14N 72 12 E
Pindiga 121 9 58N 10 53 E
Pindobal 170 3 16 S 48 25W
Pindos Óros 68 40 0N 21 0 E
Pindus Mts. = Pindos Óros 68 40 0N 21 0 E
Pine 161 34 27N 111 30W
Pine Bluff 159 34 10N 92 0W
Pine, C. 151 46 37N 53 32W
Pine City 158 45 46N 93 0W
Pine Creek, N.T., Austral. 132 13 50 S 131 49 E
Pine Creek, Queens., Austral. 138 13 13 S 142 47 E
Pine Dock 153 51 38N 96 48W
Pine Falls 153 50 34N 96 11W
Pine Flat Res. 163 36 50N 119 20W
Pine Grove 162 40 33N 76 23W
Pine Hill 138 23 42 S 147 0 E
Pine, La 160 40 53N 80 45W
Pine Pass 152 55 25N 122 42W
Pine Point 152 60 50N 114 28W
Pine, R., Austral. 108 27 18 S 153 2 E
Pine, R., Can. 153 55 20N 107 38W
Pine Ridge, Austral. 141 31 10 S 147 30 E
Pine Ridge, U.S.A. 158 42 2N 102 35W
Pine River, Can. 153 51 45N 100 30W
Pine River, U.S.A. 158 46 40N 94 20W
Pine Valley 163 32 50N 116 32W
Pinecrest 163 38 12N 120 1W
Pinedale, Ariz., U.S.A. 161 34 23N 110 16W
Pinedale, Calif., U.S.A. 163 36 50N 119 48W
Pinega 52 64 45N 43 40 E
Pinega, R. 78 64 20N 43 0 E
Pinehill 138 23 38 S 146 57 E
Pinerolo 62 44 47N 7 21 E
Pineto 63 42 36N 14 4 E
Pinetop 161 34 10N 109 57W
Pinetown 129 29 48 S 30 54 E
Pinetree 158 43 42N 105 52W
Pineville, Ky., U.S.A. 157 36 42N 83 42W
Pineville, La., U.S.A. 159 31 22N 92 30W
Pinewood 153 48 45N 94 10W
Piney, Can. 153 49 5N 96 10W
Piney, France 43 48 22N 4 21 E
Ping, R. 100 15 42N 100 9 E

**Pingaring** **Polcura**

Pingaring 137 32 40S 118 32E
P'ingch'ang 108 31 33N 107 6E
P'ingchiang 109 28 42N 113 35E
P'ingch'uan 107 41 0N 118 36E
Pingelly 137 32 29S 116 59E
P'ingho 109 24 18N 117 2E
P'inghsiang, Kiangsi, China 109 27 39N 113 50E
P'inghsiang, Kwangsi Chuang, China 108 22 6N 106 44E
P'inghu 109 30 38N 121 0E
P'ingi, Shantung, China 107 35 30N 117 36E
P'ingi, Yünnan, China 108 25 40N 104 14E
P'ingkuo 108 23 20N 107 34E
P'ingli 108 32 26N 109 22E
P'ingliang 105 35 32N 106 50E
Pinglo, Kwangsi-Chuang, China 109 24 30N 110 45E
Pinglo, Ningsia Hui, China 106 38 58N 106 30E
P'inglu 106 37 32N 112 14E
P'ingluch'eng 106 39 46N 112 6E
P'ingnan, Fukien, China 109 26 56N 119 3E
P'ingnan, Kwangsi-Chiang, China 109 23 33N 110 23E
P'ingpa 108 26 25N 106 15E
P'ingpien 108 22 54N 103 40E
Pingrup 137 33 32S 118 29E
P'ingt'an 109 25 31N 119 47E
P'ingt'ang 108 25 50N 107 19E
P'ingting 106 37 48N 113 37E
P'ingt'ingshan 106 33 43N 113 28E
P'ingtu 107 36 47N 119 56E
P'ingtung 105 22 38N 120 30E
Pingwu 105 32 27N 104 25E
P'ingwu 108 32 25N 104 36E
P'ingyang 109 27 40N 120 33E
P'ingyangchen 107 45 11N 131 15E
P'ingyao 106 37 12N 112 10E
P'ingyin 106 36 18N 116 26E
P'ingyüan, Kwangtung, China 109 24 34N 115 54E
P'ingyüan, Ningsia Hui, China 106 37 9N 116 25E
Pinhai 107 34 0N 119 50E
Pinhal 173 22 10S 46 46W
Pinheiro 170 2 31S 45 5W
Pinhel 56 40 18N 7 0W
Pinhoe 30 50 44N 3 29W
Pinhsien, Heilung Kiang, China 107 45 44N 127 27E
Pinhsien, Shensi, China 106 35 10N 108 10E
Pini, I. 102 0 10N 98 40E
Piniós, R., Ilia, Greece 69 37 38N 21 20E
Piniós, R., Trikkala, Greece 68 39 55N 22 10E
Pinjarra 137 32 37S 115 52E
Pink, R. 153 56 50N 103 50W
Pinkafeld 53 47 22N 16 9E
Pinlebu 98 24 5N 95 22E
Pinnacles, Austral. 137 28 12S 120 26E
Pinnacles, U.S.A. 163 36 33N 121 8W
Pinnaroo 140 35 13S 140 56E
Pinon Hills 163 34 26N 117 39W
Pinos 164 22 20N 101 40W
Pinos, I. de 166 21 40N 82 40W
Pinos, Mt 163 34 49N 119 8W
Pinos Pt. 161 36 50N 121 57W
Pinos Puente 57 37 15N 3 45W
Pinotepa Nacional 165 16 25N 97 55W
Pinrang 103 3 46S 119 34E
Pinsk 80 52 10N 26 8E
Pintados 174 20 35S 69 40W
Pinto Butte Mt. 153 49 22N 107 27W
Pintumba 137 31 50S 132 18E
Pinwherry 34 55 9N 4 50W
Pinyang 108 23 17N 108 47E
Pinyug 78 60 5N 48 0E
Pinzolo 62 46 9N 10 45E
Pio XII 170 3 53S 45 17W
Pioche 161 38 0N 114 35W
Piombino 62 42 54N 10 30E
Pioner, I. 77 79 50N 92 0E
Pionki 54 51 29N 21 28E
Piorini, L. 174 3 15S 62 35W
Piotrków Trybunalski 54 51 23N 19 43E
Piotrków Trybunalski □ 54 51 30N 19 45E
Piove di Sacco 63 45 18N 12 1E
Pip 93 26 45N 60 10E
Pipar 94 26 25N 73 31E
Pipariya 96 22 45N 78 23E
Piper, oilfield 19 58 30N 0 15E
Pipéri, I. 68 39 20N 24 19E
Pipestone 158 44 0N 96 20W
Pipestone Cr. 153 53 37N 109 46W
Pipestone, R. 150 52 53N 89 23W
Pipinas 172 35 30S 57 19W
Pipiriki 142 38 28S 175 5E
Pipmuacan Res. 151 49 40N 70 25W
Pippingarra 136 20 27S 118 42E
Pipriac 42 47 49N 1 58W
Piqua 156 40 10N 84 10W
Piquet Carneiro 171 5 48S 39 25W
Piquiri, R. 173 24 3S 54 14W
Piracanjuba 171 17 18S 49 1W
Piracicaba 173 22 45S 47 30W
Piracuruca 170 3 50S 41 50W
Piræus = Piraiévs 69 37 57N 23 42E
Piraiévs 69 37 57N 23 42E
Piraiévs □ 69 37 0N 23 30E
Piráino 65 38 10N 14 52E
Pirajuí 173 21 59S 49 29W
Piran (Pirano) 63 45 31N 13 33E
Pirane 172 25 25S 59 30W
Piranhas 170 9 27S 37 46W
Pirapemas 170 3 43S 44 14W
Pirapora 171 17 20S 44 56W
Piratyin 80 50 15N 32 25E
Pirbright 29 51 17N 0 40W
Pirdop 67 42 40N 24 10E
Pires do Rio 171 17 18S 48 17W
Pirganj 98 25 51S 88 24E
Pirgos, Ilia, Greece 69 37 40N 21 27E
Pirgos, Messinia, Greece 69 36 50N 22 16E
Pirgovo 67 43 44N 25 43E
Piriac-sur-Mer 42 47 22N 2 33W
Piribebuy 172 25 26S 57 2W
Pirin Planina 67 41 40N 23 30E
Pirineos, mts. 58 42 40N 1 0E
Piripiri 170 4 15S 41 46W
Piritu 174 9 23N 69 12W
Pirmasens 49 49 12N 7 30E
Pirna 48 50 57N 13 57E
Pirojpur 98 22 35N 90 1E
Pirot 66 43 9N 22 39E
Pirsagat, R. 83 40 15N 48 45E
Pirtleville 161 31 25N 109 35W
Piru 163 34 25N 118 48W
Piryí 69 38 13N 25 59E
Pisa 62 43 43N 10 23E
Pisa Ra. 143 44 52S 169 12E
Pisagua 174 19 40S 70 15W
Pisarovina 63 45 35N 15 50E
Pisciotta 65 40 7N 15 12E
Pisco 174 13 50S 76 5W
Piscu 70 45 30N 27 43E
Pisek 52 49 19N 14 10E
Pisham 108 29 37N 106 13E
P'ishan 105 37 38N 78 19E
Pishin Lora, R. 94 30 15N 66 5E
Pising 103 5 8S 121 53E
Pismo Beach 163 35 9N 120 38W
Pissos 44 44 19N 0 49W
Pisticci 65 40 24N 16 33E
Pistoia 62 43 57N 10 53E
Pistol B. 153 62 25N 92 37W
Pisuerga, R. 56 42 10N 4 15W
Pisz 54 53 38N 21 49E
Pitalito 174 1 51N 76 2W
Pitanga 171 24 46S 51 44W
Pitangui 171 19 40S 44 54E
Pitarpunga, L. 140 34 24S 143 30E
Pitcairn I. 131 25 5S 130 5W
Pite älv 74 65 44N 20 50W
Piteå 74 65 20N 21 25E
Piteşti 70 44 52N 24 54E
Pithapuram 96 17 10N 82 15E
Pithara 137 30 20S 116 35E
Pithion 68 41 24N 26 40W
Pithiviers 43 48 10N 2 13E
Pitigliano 63 42 38N 11 40E
Pitiquito 164 30 42N 112 2W
Pitlochry 37 56 43N 3 43W
Pitt I. 152 53 30N 129 50W
Pittem 47 51 1N 3 13E
Pittenweem 35 56 13N 2 43W
Pittsburg, Calif., U.S.A. 163 38 1N 121 50W
Pittsburg, Kans., U.S.A. 159 37 21N 94 43W
Pittsburg, Tex., U.S.A. 159 32 59N 94 58W
Pittsburgh 156 40 25N 79 55W
Pittsfield, Ill., U.S.A. 158 39 35N 90 46W
Pittsfield, N.H., U.S.A. 162 43 17N 71 18W
Pittston 162 41 19N 75 50W
Pittsworth 139 27 41S 151 37E
Pituri, R. 138 22 35S 138 30E
Pitzewo 107 39 28N 122 30E
Piuí 171 20 28S 45 58W
Pium 170 10 27S 49 11W
Piura 174 5 5S 80 45W
Piva, R. 66 43 15N 18 50E
Pivijay 174 10 28N 74 37W
Piwniczna 54 49 27N 20 42E
Pixariá Óros 69 38 42N 23 39E
Pixley 163 35 58N 119 18W
Piyai 68 39 17N 21 25E
Piyang 109 32 50N 113 30E
Piz Bernina 49 46 23N 9 45E
Pizarro 174 4 58N 77 22W
Pizol 51 46 57N 9 23E
Pizzo 65 38 44N 16 10E
Placentia 151 47 20N 54 0W
Placentia B. 151 47 0N 54 40W
Placerville 160 38 47N 120 51W
Placetas 166 22 15N 79 44W
'Placid', gasfield 19 53 25N 4 20E
Plačkovica, mts. 66 41 45N 22 30E
Pladda, I. 34 55 25N 5 7W
Plaffein 50 46 45N 7 17E
Plain Dealing 159 32 56N 93 41W
Plainfield 162 40 37N 74 28W
Plains, Kans., U.S.A. 159 37 20N 100 35W
Plains, Mont., U.S.A. 160 47 27N 114 57W
Plains, Tex., U.S.A. 159 33 11N 102 50W
Plainview, Nebr., U.S.A. 158 42 25N 97 48W
Plainview, Tex., U.S.A. 159 34 10N 101 40W
Plainville 158 39 18N 99 19W
Plainwell 156 42 28N 85 40W
Plaisance 44 43 36N 0 3E
Pláka 68 36 45N 24 26E
Plakhino 76 67 45N 86 5E
Planá 52 49 50N 12 44E
Plana Cays 167 22 38N 73 30W
Planada 163 37 18N 120 19W
Planaltina 171 15 30S 47 45W
Plancoët 42 48 32N 2 13W
Plandište 66 45 16N 21 10E
Planeta Rica 174 8 25N 75 36W
Planina, Slovenija, Yugo. 63 45 47N 14 19E
Planina, Slovenija, Yugo. 63 46 10N 15 12E
Plankinton 158 43 45N 98 27W
Plano 159 33 0N 96 45W
Plant City 157 28 0N 82 15W
Plant, La 158 45 11N 100 40W
Plaquemine 159 30 20N 91 15W
Plasencia 56 40 3N 6 8W
Plaški 63 45 4N 15 22E
Plassen 72 61 9N 12 30E
Plast 84 54 22N 60 50E
Plaster Rock 151 46 53N 67 22W
Plata, La, Argent. 172 35 0S 57 55W
Plata, La, U.S.A. 162 38 32N 76 59W
Plata, La, Río de 172 35 0S 56 40W
Platani, R. 64 37 28N 13 23E
Plateau 13 70 55S 40 0E
Plateau □ 121 9 0N 9 0E
Plateau du Coteau du Missouri 158 47 9N 101 5W
Platí, Ákra 68 40 27N 24 0E
Platinum 147 59 2N 161 50W
Plato 174 9 47N 74 47W
Platte 158 43 28N 98 50W
Platte, Piz 51 46 30N 9 35E
Platte, R. 158 41 0N 98 0W
Platteville 158 40 18N 104 47W
Plattling 49 48 46N 12 53E
Plattsburgh 156 44 41N 73 30W
Plattsmouth 158 41 0N 96 0W
Plau 48 53 27N 12 16E
Plauen 48 50 29N 12 9E
Plav 66 42 38N 19 57E
Plavnica 66 42 10N 19 20E
Plavsk 81 53 40N 37 18E
Playa Azul 164 17 59N 102 24W
Playa de Castilla 57 41 25N 0 12W
Playgreen L. 153 54 0N 98 15W
Pleasant Bay 151 46 51N 60 48W
Pleasant Hill 158 38 48N 94 14W
Pleasant Hills 141 35 28S 146 50E
Pleasant Mount 162 41 44N 75 26W
Pleasant Pt. 143 44 16S 171 9E
Pleasanton 159 29 0N 98 30W
Pleasantville 162 39 25N 74 30W
Pléaux 44 45 8N 2 13E
Pleiku (Gia Lai) 101 14 3N 108 0E
Plélan-le-Grand 42 48 0N 2 7W
Plémet 42 48 11N 2 36W
Pléneuf-Val-André 42 48 35N 2 32W
Plenita 70 44 14N 23 10E
Plenty, Bay of 142 37 45S 177 0E
Plenty, R. 138 23 25S 136 31E
Plentywood 158 48 45N 104 35W
Plesetsk 78 62 40N 40 10E
Plessisville 151 46 14N 71 47W
Plestin-les-Grèves 42 48 40N 3 39W
Pleszew 54 51 53N 17 47E
Pleternica 66 45 17N 17 48E
Pletipi L. 151 51 44N 70 6W
Pleven 67 43 26N 24 37E
Plevlja 66 43 21N 19 21E
Płock 54 52 32N 19 40E
Płock □ 54 52 30N 19 45E
Plöcken Passo 63 46 37N 12 57E
Plockton 36 57 20N 5 40W
Ploegsteert 47 50 44N 2 53E
Ploëmeur 42 47 44N 3 26W
Ploërmel 42 47 55N 2 26W
Ploieşti 70 44 57N 26 5E
Plomárion 69 38 58N 26 24E
Plomb du Cantal 44 45 2N 2 48E
Plombières 43 47 59N 6 27E
Plomin 63 45 8N 14 10E
Plön 48 54 8N 10 22E
Plöner See 48 53 9N 15 5E
Plonge, Lac La 153 55 8N 107 20W
Płonsk 54 52 37N 20 21E
Płoty 54 53 48N 15 18E
Plouay 42 47 55N 3 21W
Ploudalmézeau 42 48 34N 4 41W
Plougasnou 42 48 42N 3 49W
Plouha 42 48 41N 2 57W
Plouhinec 42 48 0N 4 29W
Plovdiv 67 42 8N 24 44E
Plum I. 162 41 10N 72 12W
Plumbridge 38 54 46N 7 15W
Plummer 160 47 21N 116 59W
Plumtree 127 20 27S 27 55E
Plunge 80 55 53N 21 51E
Pluvigner 42 47 46N 3 1W
Plymouth, U.K. 30 50 23N 4 9W
Plymouth, Calif., U.S.A. 163 38 29N 120 51W
Plymouth, Ind., U.S.A. 156 41 20N 86 19W
Plymouth, Mass., U.S.A. 162 41 58N 70 40W
Plymouth, N.C., U.S.A. 157 35 54N 76 55W
Plymouth, N.H., U.S.A. 162 43 44N 71 41W
Plymouth, Pa., U.S.A. 162 41 17N 76 0W
Plymouth, Wis., U.S.A. 156 43 42N 87 58W
Plymouth Sd. 30 50 20N 4 10W
Plympton 30 50 24N 4 2W
Plymstock 30 50 22N 4 6W
Plynlimon = Pumlumon Fawr 31 52 29N 3 47W
Plyussa 80 47 40N 29 0E
Plyussa, R. 80 58 40N 28 30E
Plzen 52 49 45N 13 22E
Pniewy 54 52 31N 16 16E
Pô 121 11 14N 1 5W
Po Hai 107 38 30N 119 0E
Po, R. 62 45 0N 10 45E
Poai 106 35 10N 113 4E
Pobé 121 7 0N 2 38E
Pobedino 76 49 51N 142 49E
Pobedy Pik 76 40 45N 79 58E
Pobiedziska 54 52 29N 17 19E
Pobla de Lillet, La 58 42 16N 1 59E
Pobla de Segur 58 42 15N 0 58E
Pobladura de Valle 56 42 6N 5 44W
Pocahontas, Arkansas, U.S.A. 159 37 18N 81 20W
Pocahontas, Iowa, U.S.A. 158 42 41N 94 42W
Pocatello 160 42 50N 112 25W
Pochep 80 52 58N 33 15E
Pochinki 81 54 41N 44 59E
Pochinok 80 54 28N 32 29E
Pöchlarn 52 48 12N 15 12E
Pochontas 152 53 0N 117 51W
Pochutla 165 15 50N 96 31W
Pocinhos 170 7 4S 36 3W
Pocita Casas 164 28 32N 111 6W
Pocklington 33 53 56N 0 48W
Poções 171 14 31S 40 21W
Pocomoke City 162 38 4N 75 32W
Pocomoke, R. 162 38 5N 75 34W
Poços de Caldas 173 21 50S 46 45W
Pocrane 171 19 37S 41 37W
PoC!tky 52 49 15N 15 14E
Poddebice 54 51 54N 18 58E
Poděbrady 52 50 9N 15 8E
Podensac 44 44 40N 0 22W
Podgorica = Titograd 66 42 30N 19 19E
Podkamennaya Tunguska 77 61 50N 90 26E
Podlapac 63 44 45N 15 47E
Podmokly 52 50 48N 14 10E
Podoleni 70 46 46N 26 39E
Podolínec 53 49 16N 20 31E
Podolsk 81 55 25N 37 30E
Podor 120 16 40N 14 50W
Podporozhy 78 60 55N 34 2E
Podravska Slatina 66 45 42N 17 45E
Podsreda 63 45 42N 17 41E
Podu Turcului 70 46 11N 27 25E
Podujevo 66 42 54N 21 10E
Poel, I. 48 54 0N 11 25E
Pofadder 128 29 10S 19 22E
Pogamasing 150 46 55N 81 50W
Pogiardo 65 40 3N 18 21E
Poggibonsi 63 43 27N 11 8E
Pogoanele 70 44 55N 27 0E
Pogorzela 54 51 50N 17 12E
Pogradeci 68 40 57N 20 48E
Poh 103 0 46S 122 51E
Pohang 107 36 1N 129 23E
Pohorelá 53 48 59N 20 2E
Pohorelice 53 48 59N 16 31E
Pohorje, mts. 63 46 30N 15 7E
Poiana Mare 70 43 57N 23 5E
Poiana Ruscăi, Munţii 70 45 45N 22 25E
Pt. Augusta 140 32 30S 137 50E
Point Baker 147 56 20N 133 35W
Point Cloates 137 22 40S 113 45E
Point Edward 150 43 10N 82 30W
Point Fortin 167 10 9N 61 46W
Point Hope 147 68 20N 166 50W
Point Lay 147 69 45N 163 10W
Point Pass 140 34 5S 139 5E
Point Pedro 97 9 50N 80 15E
Point Pleasant, N.J., U.S.A. 162 40 5N 74 4W
Point Pleasant, W. Va., U.S.A. 156 38 50N 82 7W
Point Reyes Nat. Seashore 163 38 0N 122 58W
Point Rock 159 31 30N 99 56W
Pointe-à-la Hache 159 29 35N 89 55W
Pointe-à-Pitre 167 16 10N 61 30W
Pointe-Noire 124 4 48S 12 0E
Poirino 62 44 55N 7 50E
Poisonbush Ra. 136 22 30S 121 30E
Poissy 43 48 55N 2 0E
Poitiers 42 46 35N 0 20W
Poitou, Plaines du 44 46 30N 0 1W
Poix 43 49 47N 2 0E
Poix-Terron 43 49 38N 4 38E
Pojoaque 161 35 55N 106 0W
Pojuca 171 12 21S 38 20W
Pokaran 93 27 0N 71 50E
Pokataroo 139 29 30S 148 34E
Poko, Sudan 123 5 41N 31 55E
Poko, Zaïre 126 3 7N 26 52E
Pok'ot'u 105 48 46N 121 54E
Pokrovka 85 42 20N 78 0E
Pokrovsk 77 61 29N 129 6E
Pokrovsk-Uralskiy 84 60 10N 59 49E
Pol 56 43 9N 7 20W
Pola 80 57 30N 32 0E
Pola de Allande 56 43 16N 6 37W
Pola de Gordón, La 56 42 51N 5 41W
Pola de Lena 56 43 10N 5 49W
Pola de Siero 56 43 24N 5 39W
Pola de Somiedo 56 43 5N 6 15W
Polacca 161 35 52N 110 25W
Polan 93 25 30N 61 10E
Poland ■ 54 52 0N 20 0E
Polanów 54 54 7N 16 41E
Polar Bear Prov. Park 150 54 30N 83 20W
Polcura 172 37 10S 71 50W

Połcyn Zdrój
Portel

Połcyn Zdrój 54 53 47N 16 5 E
Polden Hills 28 51 7N 2 50W
Polegate 29 50 49N 0 15 E
Polessk 80 54 50N 21 8 E
Polesworth 28 52 37N 1 37W
Polevskoy 84 56 26N 60 11 E
Polewali, Sulawesi, Indon. 103 4 8S 119 43 E
Polewali, Sulawesi, Indon. 103 3 21S 119 31 E
Polgar 53 47 54N 21 6 E
Pŏlgyo-ri 107 34 51N 127 21 E
Poli 124 8 34N 12 54 E
Políaigos, I. 69 36 45N 24 38 E
Policastro, Golfo di 65 39 55N 15 35 E
Police 54 53 33N 14 33 E
Polička 53 49 43N 16 15 E
Polignano a Mare 65 41 0N 17 12 E
Poligny 43 46 50N 5 42 E
Polikhnitas 69 39 4N 26 10 E
Polillo I. 103 14 56N 122 0 E
Polis 92 35 3N 32 30 E
Polístena 65 38 25N 16 4 E
Políyiros 68 40 23N 23 25 E
Polkowice 54 51 29N 16 3 E
Polla 65 40 31N 15 27 E
Pollachi 97 10 35N 77 0 E
Pollensa 58 39 54N 3 2 E
Pollensa, B. de 58 39 55N 3 5 E
Póllica 65 40 13N 15 3 E
Pollino, Mte. 65 39 54N 16 13 E
Pollock 158 45 58N 100 18W
Pollremon 38 53 40N 8 38W
Polna 80 58 31N 28 0 E
Polnovat 76 63 50N 66 5 E
Polo, Kwangtung, China 109 23 9N 114 17 E
Polo, S.-U., China 105 44 59N 81 57 E
Polo, U.S.A. 158 42 0N 89 38W
Pologi 82 47 29N 36 15 E
Polonnoye 80 50 6N 27 30 E
Polossu 108 31 12N 98 36 E
Polotsk 80 55 30N 28 50 E
Polperro 30 50 19N 4 31W
Polruan 30 50 17N 4 36W
Polski Trmbesh 67 43 20N 25 38 E
Polsko Kosovo 67 43 23N 25 38 E
Polson 160 47 45N 114 12W
Poltava 82 49 35N 34 35 E
Polur 97 12 32N 79 11 E
Polyarny 78 69 8N 33 20 E
Pomarance 62 43 18N 10 51 E
Pomarico 65 40 31N 16 33 E
Pomaro 164 18 20N 103 18W
Pombal, Brazil 170 6 55S 37 50W
Pombal, Port. 56 39 55N 8 40W
Pómbia 69 35 0N 24 51 E
Pomeroy, U.K. 38 54 36N 6 56W
Pomeroy, Ohio, U.S.A. 156 39 0N 82 0W
Pomeroy, Wash., U.S.A. 160 46 30N 117 33W
Pomio 135 5 32S 151 33 E
Pomona 163 34 2N 117 49W
Pomorie 67 42 26N 27 41 E
Pompano 157 26 12N 80 6W
Pompei 65 40 45N 14 30 E
Pompey 43 48 50N 6 2 E
Pompeys Pillar 160 46 0N 108 0W
Ponape I. 130 6 55N 158 10 E
Ponask, L. 150 54 0N 92 41W
Ponass L. 153 52 16N 103 58W
Ponca 158 42 38N 96 41W
Ponca City 159 36 40N 97 5W
Ponce 147 18 1N 66 37W
Ponchatoula 159 30 27N 90 25W
Poncheville, L. 150 50 10N 76 55W
Poncin 45 46 6N 5 25 E
Pond 163 35 43N 119 20W
Pond Inlet 149 72 30N 75 0W
Pondicherry 97 11 59N 79 50 E
Pondoland 129 31 10S 29 30W
Pondooma 140 33 29S 136 59 E
Pondrôme 47 50 6N 5 0 E
Ponds, I. of 151 53 27N 55 52W
Ponferrada 56 42 32N 6 35W
Pongaroa 142 40 33S 176 15 E
Póngo , Ponte de 127 19 0S 34 0 E
Pongo, W. 123 8 0N 27 20 E
Poniatowa 54 51 11N 22 3 E
Poniec 54 51 48N 16 50 E
Ponnaiyar, R. 97 11 50N 79 45 E
Ponnani 97 10 45N 75 59 E
Ponnani, R. 97 10 45N 75 59 E
Ponneri 97 13 20N 80 15 E
Ponnyadaung 99 22 0N 94 10 E
Ponoi 78 67 0N 41 0 E
Ponoi, R. 78 67 10N 39 0 E
Ponoka 152 52 42N 113 40W
Ponomarevka 84 53 19N 54 8 E
Ponorogo 103 7 52S 111 29 E
Pons, France 44 45 35N 0 34W
Pons, Spain 58 41 55N 1 12 E
Ponsul, R. 57 39 54N 8 45 E
Pont-à-Celles 47 50 30N 4 22 E
Pont-à-Mousson 43 45 54N 6 1 E
Pont Audemer 42 49 21N 0 30 E
Pont Aven 42 47 51N 3 47W
Pont Canavese 62 45 24N 7 33 E
Pont Château 42 47 26N 2 8W
Pont-de-Roide 43 47 23N 6 45 E
Pont-de-Salars 44 44 18N 2 44 E
Pont-de-Vaux 43 46 26N 4 56 E
Pont-de-Veyle 45 46 17N 4 53 E
Pont-l'Abbé 42 47 52N 4 15W
Pont Lafrance 151 47 40N 64 58W
Pont, Le 50 46 41N 6 20 E
Pont-l'Eveque 42 49 18N 0 11 E
Pont-St.-Esprit 45 44 16N 4 40 E
Pont-sur-Yonne 43 48 18N 3 10 E
Ponta de Pedras 170 1 23S 48 52W
Ponta Grossa 173 25 0S 50 10W
Ponta Pora 173 22 20S 55 35W
Ponta São Sebastião 129 22 2S 35 25 E
Pontacq 44 43 11N 0 8W
Pontailler 43 47 18N 5 24 E
Pontal, R. 170 9 8S 40 12W
Pontalina 171 17 31S 49 27W
Pontardawe 31 51 43N 3 51W
Pontardulais 31 51 42N 4 3W
Pontarlier 43 46 54N 6 20 E
Pontassieve 63 43 47N 11 25 E
Pontaubault 42 48 40N 1 20W
Pontaumur 44 45 52N 2 40 E
Pontcharra 45 45 26N 6 1 E
Pontchartrain, L. 159 30 12N 90 0W
Pontchâteau 42 47 25N 2 5W
Ponte Alta do Norte 170 10 45S 47 34W
Ponte Alta, Serra do 171 19 42S 47 40W
Ponte da Barca 56 41 48N 8 25W
Ponte de Sor 57 39 17N 7 57W
Ponte dell 'Olio 62 44 52N 9 39 E
Ponte di Legno 62 46 15N 10 30 E
Ponte do Lima 56 41 46N 8 35W
Ponte do Pungué 127 19 30S 34 33 E
Ponte Leccia 45 42 28N 9 13 E
Ponte nell' Alpi 63 46 10N 12 18 E
Ponte Nova 173 20 25S 42 54W
Ponte San Martino 62 45 36N 7 47 E
Ponte San Pietro 62 45 42N 9 35 E
Pontebba 63 46 30N 13 17 E
Pontecorvo 64 41 28N 13 40 E
Pontedera 62 43 40N 10 37 E
Pontefract 33 53 42N 1 19W
Ponteix 153 49 46N 107 29W
Ponteland 35 53 3N 1 45W
Pontelandolfo 65 41 17N 14 41 E
Pontemacassar Naikliu 103 9 30S 123 58 E
Pontevedra 56 42 26N 8 40W
Pontevedra □ 56 42 25N 8 39W
Pontevedra, R. de 56 42 22N 8 45W
Pontevico 62 45 16N 10 6 E
Ponthierville = Ubundi 126 0 22S 25 30 E
Pontiac, Ill., U.S.A. 158 40 50N 88 40W
Pontiac, Mich., U.S.A. 156 42 40N 83 20W
Pontian Kechil 101 1 29N 103 23 E
Pontianak 102 0 3S 109 15 E
Pontine Is. = Ponziane, Isole 64 40 55N 13 0 E
Pontine Mts. = Karadeniz D. 92 41 30N 35 0 E
Pontínia 64 41 25N 13 2 E
Pontivy 42 48 5N 3 0W
Pontoise 43 49 3N 2 5 E
Ponton, R. 152 58 27N 116 11W
Pontorson 42 48 34N 1 30W
Pontrémoli 62 44 22N 9 52 E
Pontresina 51 46 29N 9 48 E
Pontrhydfendigaid 31 52 17N 3 50W
Pontrieux 28 48 42N 3 10W
Pontrilas 28 51 56N 2 53W
Ponts-de Cé, Les 42 47 25N 0 30W
Pontypool 31 51 42N 3 1W
Pontypridd 31 51 36N 3 21W
Ponza, I. 64 40 55N 12 57 E
Ponziane, Isole 64 40 55N 13 0 E
Poochera 139 32 43S 134 51 E
Poole 28 50 42N 2 2W
Poole Harb. 28 50 41N 2 0W
Poolewe 36 57 45N 5 38W
Pooley Bridge 32 54 37N 2 49W
Pooley I. 152 52 45N 128 15W
Poonamallee 97 13 3N 80 10 E
Poona = Pune 96 18 29N 73 57 E
Pooncarie 140 33 22S 142 31 E
Poonindie 140 34 34S 135 54 E
Poopelloe, L. 140 31 40S 144 0 E
Poopó, Lago de 174 18 30S 67 35W
Poor Knights Is. 142 35 29S 174 43 E
Pooraka 109 34 50S 138 38 E
Poorman 147 64 5N 155 48W
Popai 108 22 13N 109 55 E
Popak 101 22 15N 109 56 E
Popakai, Austral. 170 32 12S 141 46 E
Popakai, Surinam 170 3 20N 55 30W
Popanyinning 137 32 40S 117 2 E
Popayán 174 2 27N 76 36W
Poperinge 47 50 51N 2 42 E
Popigay 77 71 55N 110 47 E
Popilta, L. 140 33 10S 141 42 E
Popio, L. 140 33 10S 141 52 E
Poplar 158 48 3N 105 9W
Poplar Bluff 159 36 45N 90 22W
Poplar, R., Man., Can. 153 53 0N 97 19W
Poplar, R., N.W.T., Can. 152 61 22N 121 52W
Poplarville 159 30 55N 89 30W
Popocatepetl, vol. 165 19 10N 98 40W
Popokabaka 124 5 49S 16 40 E
Pópoli 63 42 12N 13 50 E
Popondetta 135 8 48S 148 17 E
Popovača 63 45 30N 16 41 E
Popovo 67 43 21N 26 18 E
Poppel 47 51 27N 5 2 E
Poprád 53 49 3N 20 18 E
Poprád, R. 53 49 15N 20 30 E
Poquoson 162 37 7N 76 21W
Poradaha 98 23 51N 89 1 E
Porali, R. 94 27 15N 66 24 E
Porangahau 142 40 17S 176 37 E
Porangatu 171 13 26S 49 10W
Porbandar 94 21 44N 69 43 E
Porcher I. 152 53 50N 130 30W
Porcos, R. 171 12 42S 45 7W
Porcuna 57 37 52N 4 11W
Porcupine, R., Can. 153 59 11N 104 46W
Porcupine, R., U.S.A. 147 67 0N 143 0W
Pordenone 63 45 58N 12 40 E
Pordim 67 43 23N 24 51 E
Pore 174 5 43N 72 0W
Poreč 63 45 14N 13 36 E
Porecatu 171 22 43S 51 24W
Poretskoye 81 55 9N 46 21 E
Pori 75 61 29N 21 48 E
Porirua 142 41 8S 174 52 E
Porjus 74 66 57N 19 50 E
Porkhov 80 57 45N 29 38 E
Porkkala 75 59 59N 24 26 E
Porlamar 174 10 57N 63 51W
Porlezza 62 46 2N 9 8 E
Porlock 28 51 13N 3 36W
Porlock B. 28 51 14N 3 37W
Porlock Hill 28 51 12N 3 40W
Porma, R. 56 42 45N 5 21W
Pornic 42 47 7N 2 5W
Poronaysk 77 49 20N 143 0 E
Póros 69 37 30N 23 30 E
Póros, I. 69 37 30N 23 30 E
Poroshiri-Dake 112 42 41N 142 52 E
Poroszló 53 47 39N 20 40 E
Poroto Mts. 127 9 0S 33 30 E
Porraburdoo 137 23 15S 117 28 E
Porrentruy 50 47 25N 7 6 E
Porreras 58 39 29N 3 2 E
Porsangen 74 70 40N 25 40 E
Porsgrunn 71 59 10N 9 40 E
Port 43 47 43N 6 4 E
Port Adelaide 140 34 46S 138 30 E
Port Alberni 152 49 15N 124 50W
Port Albert 141 38 42S 146 42 E
Port Albert Victor 94 21 0N 71 30 E
Port Alexander 147 56 13N 134 40W
Port Alfred, Can. 151 48 18N 70 53W
Port Alfred, S. Afr. 125 33 36S 26 55 E
Port Alice 152 50 25N 127 25W
Port Allegany 156 41 49N 78 17W
Port Allen 159 30 30N 91 15W
Port Alma 138 23 38S 150 53 E
Port Angeles 160 48 7N 123 30W
Port Antonio 166 18 10N 76 30W
Port Aransas 159 27 49N 97 4W
Port Arthur, Austral. 138 43 7S 147 50 E
Port Arthur, U.S.A. 159 30 0N 94 0W
Port Arthur = Lüshun 107 38 51N 121 20 E
Port Arthur = Thunder Bay 150 48 25N 89 10W
Port Askaig 34 55 51N 6 8W
Port au Port B. 151 48 40N 58 50W
Port-au-Prince 167 18 40N 72 20W
Port Augusta West 140 32 29S 137 47 E
Port Austin 150 44 3N 82 59W
Port aux Basques 151 47 32N 59 8W
Port Awanui 142 37 50S 178 29 E
Port Bannatyne 34 55 51N 5 4W
Port Bell 126 0 18N 32 35 E
Port Bergé Vaovao 129 15 33S 47 40 E
Port Blair 101 11 40N 92 30 E
Port Blandford 151 48 30N 53 50W
Port Bolivar 159 29 20N 94 40W
Port Bou 58 42 25N 3 9 E
Port Bouet 120 5 16N 4 57W
Port Bradshaw 138 12 30S 137 0 E
Port Broughton 140 33 37S 137 56 E
Port Burwell 150 42 40N 80 48W
Port Campbell 140 35 37S 143 1 E
Port Canning 95 22 17N 88 48 E
Port Carlisle 32 54 56N 3 12W
Port-Cartier 151 50 10N 66 50W
Port Chalmers 143 45 49S 170 30 E
Port Charlotte 34 55 44N 6 22W
Port Chester 162 41 0N 73 41W
Port Clements 152 53 40N 132 10W
Port Clinton 156 41 30N 83 0W
Port Colborne 150 42 50N 79 10W
Port Coquitlam 152 49 20N 122 45W
Port Curtis 138 24 0S 151 34 E
Port Darwin, Austral. 136 12 24S 130 45 E
Port Darwin, Falk. Is. 176 51 50S 59 0W
Port Davey 138 43 16S 145 55 E
Port-de-Bouc 45 43 24N 4 59 E
Port de Paix 167 19 50N 72 50W
Port Deposit 162 39 37N 76 5W
Port Dickson 101 2 30N 101 49 E
Port Dinorwic 31 53 11N 4 12W
Port Douglas 138 16 30S 145 30 E
Port Edward 152 54 12N 130 10W
Port Elgin 150 44 25N 81 25W
Port Elizabeth 128 33 58S 25 40 E
Port Ellen 34 55 38N 6 10W
Port Erin 32 54 5N 4 45W
Port Erroll 37 57 25N 1 50W
Port Essington 136 11 15S 132 10 E
Port Étienne = Nouadhibou 116 21 0N 17 0W
Port Ewen 162 41 54N 73 59W
Port Fairy 140 38 22S 142 12 E
Port Fitzroy 142 36 8S 175 20 E
Port Fouâd = Bûr Fuad 122 31 15N 32 20 E
Port Francqui 124 4 17S 20 47 E
Port-Gentil 124 0 47S 8 40 E
Port Gibson 159 31 57N 91 0W
Port Glasgow 34 55 57N 4 40W
Port Gregory 137 27 40S 114 0 E
Port Harcourt 121 4 40N 7 10 E
Port Hardy 152 50 41N 127 30W
Port Harrison 149 58 25N 78 15W
Port Hawkesbury 151 45 36N 61 22W
Port Hedland 136 20 25S 118 35 E
Port Heiden 147 57 0N 158 40W
Port Hood 151 46 0N 61 32W
Port Hope 150 44 0N 78 20W
Port Hueneme 163 34 7N 119 12W
Port Huron 156 43 0N 82 28W
Port Isaac 30 50 35N 4 50W
Port Isaac B. 30 50 36N 4 50W
Port Isabel 159 26 12N 97 9W
Port Jackson 133 33 50S 151 18 E
Port Jefferson 162 40 58N 73 5W
Port Jervis 162 41 22N 74 42W
Port Joinville 42 46 45N 2 23W
Port Kaituma 174 8 3N 59 58W
Port Katon 83 46 27N 38 56 E
Port Kelang 101 3 0N 101 23 E
Port Kembla 141 34 29S 150 56 E
Port La Nouvelle 44 43 1N 3 3 E
Port Laoise 39 53 2N 7 20W
Port Lavaca 159 28 38N 96 38W
Port Leyden 162 43 35N 75 21W
Port Lincoln 140 34 42S 135 52 E
Port Logan 34 54 42N 4 57W
Port Loko 120 8 48N 12 46W
Port Louis 42 47 42N 3 22W
Port Lyautey = Kenitra 118 34 15N 6 40W
Port Lyttelton 143 43 37N 172 50 E
Port Macdonnell 140 38 0S 140 39 E
Port Macquarie 141 31 25S 152 54 E
Port Maitland 151 44 0N 66 2W
Port Maria 166 18 25N 76 55W
Port Mellon 152 49 32N 123 31W
Port Menier 151 49 51N 64 15W
Port Morant 166 17 54N 76 19W
Port Moresby 135 9 24S 147 8 E
Port Mouton 151 43 58N 64 50W
Port Musgrave 138 11 55S 141 50 E
Port Navalo 42 47 34N 2 54W
Port Nelson 153 57 3N 92 36W
Port Nicholson 142 41 20S 174 52 E
Port Nolloth 128 29 17S 16 52 E
Port Norris 162 39 15N 75 2W
Port Nouveau-Quebec (George R.) 149 58 30N 65 50W
Port O'Connor 159 28 26N 96 24W
Port of Ness 36 58 29N 6 13W
Port of Spain 167 10 40N 61 20W
Port Orchard 160 47 31N 122 38W
Port Oxford 160 42 45N 124 28W
Port Pegasus 143 47 12S 167 41 E
Port Perry 150 44 6N 78 56W
Port Phillip B. 139 38 10S 144 50 E
Port Pirie 140 33 10S 137 58 E
Port Pólnocny □ 54 54 25N 18 42 E
Port Radium = Echo Bay 148 66 10N 117 40W
Port Renfrew 152 48 30N 124 20W
Port Roper 138 14 45S 134 47 E
Port Rowan 150 42 40N 80 30W
Port Royal 162 38 10N 77 12W
Port Safaga = Bûr Safâga 122 26 43N 33 57 E
Port Said = Bûr Sa'îd 122 31 16N 32 18 E
Port St. Joe 157 29 49N 85 20W
Port St. Johns = Umzimvubu 129 31 38S 29 33 E
Port-St. Louis 45 43 23N 4 50 E
Port St. Louis 129 13 7S 48 48 E
Port-St.-Louis-du-Rhône 45 43 23N 4 49 E
Port St. Mary 32 54 5N 4 45W
Port St. Servain 151 51 21N 58 0W
Port Sanilac 150 43 26N 82 33W
Port Saunders 151 50 40N 57 18W
Port Shepstone 129 30 44S 30 28 E
Port Simpson 152 54 30N 130 20W
Port Stanley 150 42 40N 81 10W
Port Sudan = Bôr Sôdân 122 19 32N 37 9 E
Port Sunlight 32 53 22N 3 0W
Port Talbot 31 51 35N 3 48W
Port Taufiq = Bûr Taufiq 122 29 54N 32 32 E
Port Townsend 160 48 7N 122 50W
Port-Vendres 44 42 32N 3 8 E
Port Victoria 140 34 30S 137 29 E
Port Wakefield 140 34 12S 138 10 E
Port Washington 156 43 25N 87 52W
Port Weld 101 4 50N 100 38 E
Port William 34 54 46N 4 35W
Portachuelo 174 17 10S 63 20W
Portacloy 38 54 20N 9 48W
Portadown (Craigavon) 38 54 27N 6 26W
Portaferry 38 54 23N 5 32W
Portage, Can. 151 46 40N 64 5W
Portage, U.S.A. 158 43 31N 89 25W
Portage la Prairie 153 49 58N 98 18W
Portage Mt. Dam 152 56 0N 122 0W
Portageville 159 36 25N 89 40W
Portaguiran 36 58 15N 6 10W
Portalegre 57 39 19N 7 25W
Portalegre □ 57 39 20N 7 40W
Portales 159 34 12N 103 25W
Portarlington 39 53 10N 7 10W
Porte, La 156 41 40N 86 40W
Porteirinha 171 15 44S 43 2W
Portel, Brazil 170 1 57S 50 49W

Portel Prochowice

Portel, Port. 57 38 19N 7 41W
Porter L., N.W.T., Can. 153 61 41N 108 5W
Porter L., Sask., Can. 153 56 20N 107 20W
Porterville, S. Afr. 128 33 0S 18 57E
Porterville, U.S.A. 163 36 5N 119 0W
Portet 44 43 34N 0 11W
Porteynon 31 51 33N 4 13W
Portglenone 38 54 53N 6 30W
Portgordon 37 57 40N 3 1W
Porth Neigwl 31 52 48N 4 35W
Porth Neigwl, B. 31 52 48N 4 33W
Porthcawl 31 51 28N 3 42W
Porthill 160 49 0N 116 30W
Porthleven 30 50 5N 5 19W
Porthmadog 31 52 55N 4 13W
Portile de Fier 70 44 42N 22 30E
Portimão 57 37 8N 8 32W
Portishead 28 51 29N 2 46W
Portknockle 37 57 40N 2 52W
Portland, N.S.W., Austral. 141 33 20S 150 0E
Portland, Victoria, Austral. 140 38 20S 141 35E
Portland, Conn., U.S.A. 162 41 34N 72 39W
Portland, Me., U.S.A. 151 43 40N 70 15W
Portland, Mich., U.S.A. 156 42 52N 84 58W
Portland, Oreg., U.S.A. 160 45 35N 122 40W
Portland B. 140 38 15S 141 45E
Portland Bill 28 50 31N 2 27W
Portland, C. 133 40 46S 148 0E
Portland I. 142 39 20S 177 51E
Portland, I. of 28 50 32N 2 25W
Portland, Pa. 162 40 55N 75 6W
Portland Prom. 149 58 40N 78 33W
Portlaw 39 52 18N 7 20W
Portmagee 39 51 53N 10 22W
Portmahomack 37 57 50N 3 50W
Portmarnock 38 53 25N 6 10W
Portnacroish 34 56 34N 5 24W
Portnahaven 34 55 40N 6 30W
Portneuf 151 46 43N 71 55W
Pôrto, Brazil 170 3 54S 42 42W
Pôrto, Port. 56 41 8N 8 40W
Pôrto □ 56 41 8N 8 20W
Pôrto Alegre, Mato Grosso, Brazil 170 21 40S 53 30W
Pôrto Alegre, Rio Grande do Sul, Brazil 173 30 5S 51 3W
Porto Alexandre 128 15 55S 11 55E
Porto Amboim = Gunza 124 10 50S 13 50E
Porto Amelia = Pemba 127 12 58S 40 30E
Porto Argentera 62 44 15N 7 27E
Porto Azzurro 62 42 46N 10 24E
Porto Botte 64 39 3N 8 33E
Pôrto Calvo 171 9 4S 35 24W
Porto Civitanova 63 43 19N 13 44E
Pôrto da Fôlha 170 9 55S 37 17W
Pôrto de Moz 170 1 41S 52 22W
Pôrto de Pedras 170 9 10S 35 17W
Porto Empédocle 64 37 18N 13 30E
Pôrto Esperança 174 19 37S 57 29W
Pôrto Franco 170 6 20S 47 24W
Porto Garibaldi 63 44 41N 12 14E
Porto, G. de 45 42 17N 8 34E
Pôrto Lago 68 41 1N 25 6E
Porto Mendes 173 24 30S 54 15W
Porto Murtinho 174 21 45S 57 55W
Pôrto Nacional 170 10 40S 48 30W
Porto Novo, Benin 121 6 23N 2 42E
Porto Novo, India 97 11 30N 79 38E
Porto Recanati 63 43 26N 13 40E
Porto San Giorgio 63 43 11N 13 49E
Porto San Stéfano 68 42 26N 11 6E
Porto Santo, I. 116 33 45S 16 25W
Pôrto São José 173 22 43S 53 10W
Pôrto Seguro 171 16 26S 39 5W
Porto Tolle 63 44 57N 12 20E
Porto Tôrres 64 40 50N 8 23E
Pôrto União 173 26 10S 51 10W
Pôrto Válter 174 8 5S 72 40W
Porto-Vecchio 45 41 35N 9 16E
Pôrto Velho 174 8 46S 63 54W
Portobelo 166 9 35N 79 42W
Portoferráio 62 42 50N 10 20E
Portogruaro 63 45 47N 12 50E
Portola 160 39 49N 120 28W
Portomaggiore 63 44 41N 11 47E
Porton Camp 28 51 8N 1 42W
Portoscuso 64 39 12N 8 22E
Portovénere 62 44 2N 9 50E
Portoviejo 174 1 0S 80 20W
Portpatrick 34 54 50N 5 7W
Portree 36 57 25N 6 11W
Portroe 39 52 53N 8 20W
Portrush 38 55 13N 6 40W
Portsall 42 48 37N 4 45W
Portsalon 38 55 12N 7 37W
Portskerra 37 58 35N 3 55W
Portslade 29 50 50N 0 11W
Portsmouth, Domin. 167 15 34N 61 27W
Portsmouth, U.K. 28 50 48N 1 6W
Portsmouth, N.H., U.S.A. 162 43 5N 70 45W
Portsmouth, Ohio, U.S.A. 156 38 45N 83 0W
Portsmouth, R.I., U.S.A. 162 41 35N 71 44W
Portsmouth, Va., U.S.A. 156 36 50N 76 20W
Portsoy 37 57 41N 2 41W
Portstewart 38 55 12N 6 43W
Porttipahta 74 68 5N 26 30E
Portugal ■ 56 40 0N 7 0W
Portugalete 58 43 19N 3 4W
Portuguesa □ 174 9 10N 69 15W
Portuguese Guinea = Guinea Bissau 120 12 0N 15 0W
Portuguese Timor ■ = Timor 103 8 0S 126 30E
Portumna 39 53 5N 8 12W
Porvenir 176 53 10S 70 30W
Porvoo 75 60 24N 25 40E
Porzuna 57 39 9N 4 9W
Posada, R. 64 40 40N 9 35E
Posadas, Argent. 173 27 30S 56 0W
Posadas, Spain 57 37 47N 5 11W
Poschiavo 51 46 19N 10 4E
Posets, mt. 58 42 39N 0 25E
Poshan 107 36 30N 117 50E
Posídhio, Ákra 68 39 57N 23 30E
Poso 103 1 20S 120 55E
Poso Colorado 172 23 30S 58 45W
Poso, D. 103 1 20S 120 55E
Posong 107 34 46N 129 5E
Posse 171 14 4S 46 18W
Possel 124 5 5N 19 10E
Possession I. 13 72 4S 172 0E
Pössneck 48 50 42N 11 34E
Possut'eng Hu 105 42 0N 87 0E
Post 159 33 13N 101 21W
Post Falls 160 47 50N 116 59W
Postavy 80 55 4N 26 58E
Postbridge 30 50 36N 3 54W
Poste-de-la-Baleine 30 50 36N 3 54W
Poste Maurice Cortier (Bidon 5) 118 22 14N 1 2E
Postiljon, Kepulauan 103 6 30S 118 50E
Postmasburg 128 28 18S 23 5E
Postojna 63 45 46N 14 12E
Potamós 69 39 38N 19 53E
Potchefstroom 125 26 41S 27 7E
Potcoava 70 44 30N 24 39E
Poté 171 17 49S 41 49W
Poteau 159 35 5N 94 37W
Poteet 159 29 4N 98 35W
Potelu, Lacul 70 43 44N 24 20E
Potenza 65 40 40N 15 50E
Potenza Picena 63 43 22N 13 37E
Poteriteri, L. 143 46 5S 167 10E
Potes 56 43 15N 4 42W
Potgietersrus 129 24 10S 29 3E
Poti 83 42 10N 41 38E
Potiraguá 171 15 36S 39 53W
Potiskum 121 11 39N 11 2E
Potlogi 70 44 34N 25 34E
Potomac, R. 162 38 0N 76 23W
Potosí 174 19 38S 65 50W
Potosí □ 174 20 31S 67 0W
Pot'ou 106 37 57N 116 39E
Potrerillos 172 26 20S 69 30W
Potros, Cerro del 172 28 32S 69 0W
Potsdam, Ger. 48 52 23N 13 4E
Potsdam, U.S.A. 156 44 40N 74 59W
Potsdam □ 48 52 40N 12 50E
Potter 158 41 15N 103 20W
Potter Heigham 29 52 44N 1 33E
Potterne 28 51 19N 2 0W
Potters Bar 29 51 42N 0 11W
Potterspury 29 52 5N 0 52W
Pottery Hill = Abu Ballas 122 24 26N 27 36E
Pottstown 162 40 17N 75 40W
Pottsville 162 40 39N 76 12W
Pottuvil 93 6 55N 81 50E
P'otzu 109 23 30N 120 25E
Pouancé 42 47 44N 1 10W
Pouce Coupé 152 55 40N 120 10W
Poughkeepsie 162 41 40N 73 57W
Pouilly 43 47 18N 2 57E
Poulaphouca Res. 39 53 8N 6 30W
Pouldu, Le 42 47 41N 3 36W
Poulsbo 160 47 45N 122 39W
Poultney 162 43 31N 73 14W
Poulton le Fylde 32 53 51N 2 59W
Poundstock 30 50 44N 4 34W
Pouso Alegre, Mato Grosso, Brazil 175 11 55S 57 0W
Pouso Alegre, Minas Gerais, Brazil 173 22 14S 45 57W
Pouzages 44 46 40N 0 50W
Povenets 78 62 50N 34 50E
Poverty Bay 142 38 43S 178 2E
Póvoa de Lanhosa 56 41 33N 8 15W
Póvoa de Varzim 56 41 25N 8 46W
Povorino 81 51 12N 42 28E
Powassan 150 46 5N 79 25W
Poway 163 32 58N 117 2W
Powder, R. 158 46 47N 105 12W
Powell 160 44 45N 108 45W
Powell Creek 136 18 6S 133 46E
Powell River 152 49 22N 125 31W
Powers, Mich., U.S.A. 156 45 40N 87 32W
Powers, Oreg., U.S.A. 160 42 53N 124 2W
Powers Lake 158 48 37N 102 38W
Powick 28 52 9N 2 15W
Powis, Vale of 23 52 40N 3 10W
Powys □ 31 52 20N 3 20W
P'oyang 109 29 1N 116 38E
Poyang Hu 109 29 10N 116 10E
Poyarkovo 77 49 36N 128 41E
Poyntzpass 38 54 17N 6 22W
Poysdorf 53 48 40N 16 37E
Poza de la Sal 58 42 35N 3 31W
Poza Rica 165 20 33N 97 27W
Pozarevac 66 44 35N 21 18E
Pozega 66 45 21N 17 41E
Pozhva 84 59 5N 56 5E
Poznan 54 52 25N 17 0E
Pozo 163 35 20N 120 24W
Pozo Alcón 59 37 42N 2 56W
Pozo Almonte 174 20 10S 69 50W
Pozoblanco 57 38 23N 4 51W
Pozzallo 65 36 44N 15 40E
Pra, R. 121 5 30N 1 38W
Prabuty 54 53 47N 19 15E
Prača 66 43 47N 18 43E
Prachatice 52 49 1N 14 0E
Prachin Buri 100 14 0N 101 25E
Prachuap Khiri Khan 101 11 49N 99 48E
Pradelles 44 44 46N 3 52E
Pradera 174 3 25N 76 15W
Prades 44 42 38N 2 23E
Prado 171 17 20S 39 13W
Prado del Rey 57 36 48N 5 33W
Præstø 73 55 8N 12 2E
Pragersko 63 46 27N 15 42E
Prague = Praha 52 50 5N 14 22E
Praha 52 50 5N 14 22E
Prahecq 44 46 19N 0 26W
Prahita, R. 97 19 0N 79 55E
Prahova □ 70 44 50N 25 50E
Prahova, R. 70 44 50N 25 50E
Prahova, Reg. 70 44 50N 25 50E
Prahovo 66 44 18N 22 39E
Praid 70 46 32N 25 10E
Prainha, Amazonas, Brazil 174 7 10S 60 30W
Prainha, Pará, Brazil 175 1 45S 53 30W
Prairie, Queens., Austral. 138 20 50S 144 35E
Prairie, S. Australia, Austral. 109 34 51S 138 49E
Prairie City 160 45 27N 118 44W
Prairie du Chien 158 43 1N 91 9W
Prairie, R. 159 34 45N 101 15W
Praja 102 8 39S 116 27E
Prajeczno 54 51 10N 19 0E
Pramánda 68 39 32N 21 8E
Pran Buri 100 12 23N 99 55E
Prang 121 8 1N 0 56W
Prapat 102 2 41N 98 58E
Praszka 54 51 32N 18 31E
Prata, Minas Gerais, Brazil 171 19 25S 49 0W
Prata, Pará, Brazil 170 1 10S 47 35W
Prática di Mare 64 41 40N 12 26E
Prato 62 43 53N 11 5E
Prátola Peligna 63 42 7N 13 51E
Pratovécchio 63 43 44N 11 43E
Prats-de-Molló 44 42 25N 2 27E
Pratt 159 37 40N 98 45W
Pratteln 50 47 31N 7 41E
Prättigau 51 46 56N 9 44E
Prattville 157 32 30N 86 28W
Pravara, R. 96 19 30N 74 28E
Pravdinsk 81 56 29N 43 28E
Pravia 56 43 30N 6 12W
Prawle Pt. 30 50 13N 3 41W
Pré-en-Pail 42 48 28N 0 12W
Pré St. Didier 62 45 45N 7 0E
Precordillera 172 30 0S 69 1W
Predáppio 63 44 7N 11 58E
Predazzo 63 46 19N 11 37E
Predejane 66 42 51N 22 9E
Preeceville 153 51 57N 102 40W
Prees 32 52 54N 2 40W
Preesall 32 53 55N 2 58W
Préfailles 42 47 9N 2 11W
Pregonero 174 8 1N 71 46W
Pregrada 63 46 11N 15 45E
Preko 63 44 7N 15 14E
Prelate 153 50 51N 109 24W
Prelog 63 46 18N 16 32E
Premier 152 56 4N 129 56W
Premier Downs 137 30 30S 126 30E
Premont 159 27 19N 98 8W
Premuda, I. 63 44 20N 14 36E
Prenj, mt. 66 43 33N 17 53E
Prenjasi 68 41 6N 20 32E
Prentice 158 45 31N 90 19W
Prenzlau 48 53 19N 13 51E
Prepansko Jezero 68 40 45N 21 0E
Preparis I. 99 14 55N 93 45E
Preparis North Channel 101 15 12N 93 40E
Preparis South Channel 101 14 36N 93 40E
Prerov 53 49 28N 17 27E
Prescot 32 53 27N 2 49W
Prescott, Can. 150 44 45N 75 30W
Prescott, Ariz., U.S.A. 161 34 35N 112 30W
Prescott, Ark., U.S.A. 159 33 49N 93 22W
Preservation Inlet 143 46 8S 166 35E
Preševo 66 42 19N 21 39E
Presho 158 43 56N 100 4W
Preshute 28 51 24N 1 45W
Presicce 65 39 53N 18 13E
Presidencia de la Plaza 172 27 0S 60 0W
Presidencia Roque Sáenz Peña 172 26 45S 60 30W
Presidente Dutra 164 5 15S 44 30W
Presidente Epitácio 171 21 46S 52 6W
Presidente Hayes □ 172 24 0S 59 0W
Presidente Hermes 174 11 0S 61 55W
Presidente Prudente 173 22 5S 51 25W
Presidente Rogue Saena Peña 172 34 33S 58 30W
Presidio, Mexico 164 29 29N 104 23W
Presidio, U.S.A. 159 29 30N 104 20W
Preslav 67 43 10N 26 52E
Prespa, L. = Prepansko Jezero 68 40 45N 21 0E
Prespa, mt. 67 41 44N 25 0E
Presque Isle 151 46 40N 68 0W
Prestatyn 31 53 20N 3 24W
Prestea 120 5 22N 2 7W
Presteigne 31 52 17N 3 0W
Preštice 52 49 34N 13 20E
Preston, Borders, U.K. 35 55 48N 2 18W
Preston, Dorset, U.K. 28 50 38N 2 26W
Preston, Lancs., U.K. 32 53 46N 2 42W
Preston, Idaho, U.S.A. 160 42 0N 112 0W
Preston, Minn., U.S.A. 158 43 39N 92 3W
Preston, Nev., U.S.A. 160 38 59N 115 2W
Preston, C. 136 20 51S 116 12E
Prestonpans 35 55 58N 3 0W
Prestwich 32 53 32N 2 18W
Prestwick 34 55 30N 4 38W
Prêto, R., Bahia 170 11 21S 43 52W
Pretoria 129 25 44S 28 12E
Prettyboy Res. 162 39 37N 76 43W
Preuilly-sur-Claise 42 46 51N 0 56E
Préveza 69 38 57N 20 47E
Préveza □ 68 39 20N 20 40E
Prey-Veng 101 11 35N 105 29E
Priazovskoye 82 46 22N 35 28E
Pribilov Is. 12 56 0N 170 0W
Priboj 66 43 35N 19 32E
Pribram 52 49 41N 14 2E
Price 160 39 40N 110 48W
Price I. 152 52 23N 128 41W
Prichalnaya 83 48 57N 44 33E
Priego 58 40 38N 2 21W
Priego de Córdoba 57 37 27N 4 12W
Priekule 80 57 27N 21 45E
Prieska 128 29 40S 22 42E
Priest Gully Cr. 108 27 29S 153 11E
Priest L. 160 48 30N 116 55W
Priest River 160 48 11N 117 0W
Priest Valley 163 36 10N 120 39W
Priestly 152 54 8N 125 20W
Prievidza 53 48 46N 18 36E
Prijedor 63 44 58N 16 41E
Prijepolje 66 43 27N 19 40E
Prilep 66 41 21N 21 37E
Priluki 80 50 30N 32 15E
Prime Seal I. 138 40 3S 147 43E
Primeira Cruz 170 2 30S 43 26W
Primorsko 67 42 15N 27 44E
Primorsko-Akhtarsk 82 46 2N 38 10E
Primrose L. 153 54 55N 109 45W
Prince Albert 153 53 15N 105 50W
Prince Albert Nat. Park 153 54 0N 106 25W
Prince Albert Pen. 148 72 30N 116 0W
Prince Alfred C. 12 74 20N 124 40W
Prince Charles I. 149 67 47N 76 12W
Prince Edward I. □. 151 44 2N 77 20W
Prince Edward Is. 11 45 15S 39 0E
Prince Frederick 162 38 33N 76 35W
Prince George 152 53 50N 122 50W
Prince of Wales, C. 147 65 50N 168 0W
Prince of Wales I. 147 73 0N 99 0W
Prince of Wales, I. 147 53 30N 131 30W
Prince of Wales Is. 135 10 40S 142 10E
Prince Patrick I. 12 77 0N 120 0W
Prince Regent Inlet 12 73 0N 90 0W
Prince Rupert 152 54 20N 130 20W
Prince William Sd. 147 60 20N 146 30W
Princenhage 47 51 9N 4 45E
Princes Risborough 29 51 43N 0 50W
Princesa Isabel 170 7 44S 38 0W
Princess Anne 162 38 12N 75 41W
Princess Charlotte B. 138 14 25S 144 0E
Princess Mary Ranges 136 15 30S 125 30E
Princess Royal I. 152 53 0N 128 40W
Princeton, Can. 152 49 27N 120 30W
Princeton, Ill., U.S.A. 158 41 25N 89 25W
Princeton, Ind., U.S.A. 156 38 20N 87 35W
Princeton, Ky., U.S.A. 156 37 6N 87 55W
Princeton, Mo., U.S.A. 158 40 23N 93 35W
Princeton, N.J., U.S.A. 162 40 18N 74 40W
Princeton, W. Va., U.S.A. 156 37 21N 81 8W
Princetown 30 50 33N 4 0W
Principe Chan. 152 53 28N 130 0W
Principe da Beira 174 12 20S 64 30W
Principe, I. de 114 1 37N 7 27E
Prineville 160 44 17N 120 57W
Prins Albert 128 33 12S 22 2E
Prins Harald Kyst 13 70 0S 35 1E
Prinzapolca 166 13 20N 83 35W
Prior, C. 56 43 34N 8 17W
Pripet Marshes = Polesye 80 52 0N 28 10E
Pripet, R. = Pripyat, R. 80 51 30N 30 0E
Pripyat, R. 80 51 30N 30 0E
Prislop, Pasul 70 47 37N 25 15E
Pristen 81 51 15N 12 40E
Priština 66 42 40N 21 13E
Pritchard 157 30 47N 88 5W
Pritzwalk 48 53 10N 12 11E
Privas 45 44 45N 4 37E
Priverno 64 41 29N 13 10E
Privolzhsk 81 57 9N 14 9E
Privolzhskaya Vozvyshennest 81 51 0N 46 0E
Privolzhskiy 81 51 25N 46 3E
Privolzhye 81 52 52N 48 33E
Privutnoye 83 47 12N 43 30E
Prizren 66 42 13N 20 45E
Prizzi 64 37 44N 13 24E
Prnjavor 66 44 52N 17 43E
Probolinggo 103 7 46S 113 13E
Probus 30 50 17N 4 55W
Prochowice 54 51 17N 16 20E

Procida, I
Qattâra, Munkhafed el

Procida, I. 64 40 46N 14 0 E
Proctor 162 43 40N 73 2W
Proddatur 97 14 45N 78 30 E
Proença-a-Nova 57 39 45N 7 54W
Profondeville 47 50 23N 4 52 E
Progreso 165 21 20N 89 40W
Prokhladnyy 83 43 50N 44 2 E
Prokletije 68 42 30N 19 45 E
Prokopyevsk 76 54 0N 87 3 E
Prokuplje 66 43 16N 21 36 E
Proletarskaya 83 46 42N 41 50 E
Prome = Pyè 99 18 45N 95 30 E
Prophet, R. 152 58 48N 122 40W
Propriá 170 10 13 S 36 51W
Propriano 45 41 41N 8 52 E
Proserpine 138 20 21 S 148 36 E
Prospect, Austral. 109 34 53 S 138 36 E
Prospect, U.S.A. 162 43 18N 75 9W
Prosser 160 46 11N 119 52W
Prostějov 53 49 30N 17 9 E
Proston 139 26 14 S 151 32 E
Proszowice 54 50 13N 20 16 E
Protection 159 37 16N 99 30W
Próti, I. 69 37 5N 21 32 E
Provadija 67 43 12N 27 30 E
Proven 47 50 54N 2 40 E
Provence 45 43 40N 5 46 E
Providence, Ky., U.S.A. 156 37 25N 87 46W
Providence, R.I., U.S.A. 162 41 41N 71 15W
Providence Bay 150 45 41N 82 15W
Providence C. 143 45 59 S 166 29 E
Providence Mts. 161 35 0N 115 30W
Providencia 174 0 28 S 76 28W
Providencia, I. de 166 13 25N 81 26W
Provideniya 77 64 23N 173 18 E
Province Wellesley 101 5 15N 100 20 E
Provincetown 162 42 5N 70 11W
Provins 43 48 33N 3 15 E
Provo 160 40 16N 111 37W
Provost 153 52 25N 110 20W
Prozor 66 43 50N 17 34 E
Prudentópolis 171 25 12 S 50 57W
Prudhoe 35 54 57N 1 52W
Prudhoe Bay, Austral. 138 21 30 S 149 30W
Prudhoe Bay, U.S.A. 147 70 20N 148 20W
Prudhoe I. 138 21 23 S 149 45 E
Prudhoe Land 12 78 1N 65 0W
Prud'homme 153 52 20N 105 54W
Prudnik 54 50 20N 17 38 E
Prüm 49 50 14N 6 22 E
Pruszcz 54 54 17N 19 40 E
Pruszków 54 52 9N 20 49 E
Prut, R. 70 46 3N 28 10 E
Prvič, I. 63 44 55N 14 47 E
Prvomay 67 42 8N 25 17 E
Prydz B. 13 69 0 S 74 0 E
Pryor 159 36 17N 95 20W
Przasnysz 54 53 2N 20 45 E
Przedbórz 54 51 6N 19 53 E
Przedecz 54 52 20N 18 53 E
Przemyśl 54 49 50N 22 45 E
Przemyśl □ 54 80 0N 23 0 E
Przeworsk 54 50 6N 22 32 E
Przewóz 54 51 28N 14 57 E
Przhevalsk 85 42 30N 78 20 E
Przysucha 54 51 22N 20 38 E
Psakhná 69 38 34N 23 35 E
Psarà, I. 69 38 37N 25 38 E
Psathoúra, I. 68 39 30N 24 12 E
Psel, R. 82 49 25N 33 50 E
Pserimos, I. 69 36 56N 27 12 E
Pskem, R. 85 41 38N 70 1 E
Pskemskiy Khrebet 85 42 0N 70 45 E
Pskent 85 40 54N 69 20 E
Pskov 80 57 50N 28 25 E
Psunj, mt. 66 45 25N 17 19 E
Pszczyna 54 49 59N 18 58 E
Pteleón 69 39 3N 22 57 E
Ptich, R. 80 52 30N 28 45 E
Ptolemais 68 40 30N 21 43 E
Ptuj 63 46 28N 15 50 E
Ptujska Gora 63 46 23N 15 47 E
Pua 100 19 11N 100 55 E
Puán 172 37 30 S 63 0W
P'uan 108 25 47N 104 57 E
Puan 107 35 44N 126 7 E
Pubnico 151 43 47N 65 50W
Pucallpa 174 8 25 S 74 30W
P'uchen 107 37 21N 118 1 E
P'uch'eng 109 27 45N 118 47 E
Pucheni 70 45 12N 25 17 E
P'uch'i 109 29 43N 113 53 E
Pucisce 63 43 22N 16 43 E
Puck 54 54 45N 18 23 E
Puddletown 28 50 45N 2 21W
Pudsey 33 53 47N 1 40W
Pudukkottai 97 10 28N 78 47 E
Puebla 165 19 0N 98 10W
Puebla □ 165 18 30N 98 0W
Puebla de Alcocer 57 38 59N 5 14W
Puebla de Don Fadrique 59 37 58N 2 25W
Puebla de Don Rodrigo 57 39 5N 4 37W
Puebla de Guzmán 57 37 37N 7 15W
Puebla de los Infantes, La 57 37 47N 5 24W
Puebla de Montalbán, La 56 39 52N 4 22W
Puebla de Sanabria 56 42 4N 6 38W
Puebla de Trives 56 42 20N 7 10W
Puebla del Caramiñal 56 42 37N 8 56W
Puebla, La 58 39 50N 3 0 E
Pueblo 158 38 20N 104 40W
Pueblo Bonito 161 36 4N 107 57W
Pueblo Hundido 172 26 20 S 69 30W
Pueblo Nuevo 174 8 26N 71 26W
Pueblonuevo 55 38 16N 5 16W
Puelches 172 38 5 S 66 0W
Puelén 172 37 32 S 67 38W
Puente Alto 172 33 32 S 70 35W
Puente del Arzobispo 56 39 48N 5 10W
Puente Genil 57 37 22N 4 47W
Puente la Reina 58 42 40N 1 49W
Puentearas 56 42 10N 8 28W
Puentedeume 56 43 24N 8 10W
Puentes de García Rodríguez 56 43 27N 7 51W
Puerco, R. 161 35 10N 109 45W
Puerh 105 23 11N 100 56 E
P'uerh 108 23 5N 101 5 E
Puerhching 105 47 43N 86 53 E
Puerta, La 59 38 22N 2 45W
Puerto Aisén 176 45 10 S 73 0W
Puerto Angel 165 15 40N 96 29W
Puerto Arista 165 15 56N 93 48W
Puerto Armuelles 166 8 20N 83 10W
Puerto Ayacucho 174 5 40N 67 35W
Puerto Barrios 166 15 40N 88 40W
Puerto Bermejo 172 26 55 S 58 34W
Puerto Bermúdez 174 10 20 S 75 0W
Puerto Bolívar 174 3 10 S 79 55W
Puerto Cabello 174 10 28N 68 1W
Puerto Cabezas 166 14 0N 83 30W
Puerto Cabo Gracias a Dios 166 15 0N 83 10W
Puerto Capaz = Jebba 118 35 11N 4 43W
Puerto Carreño 174 6 12N 67 22W
Puerto Casado 172 22 19 S 57 56W
Puerto Castilla 166 16 0N 86 0W
Puerto Chicama 174 7 45 S 79 20W
Puerto Coig 176 50 54 S 69 15W
Puerto Columbia 174 10 59N 74 58W
Puerto Cortés, C. Rica 166 8 20N 82 20W
Puerto Cortés, Hond. 166 15 51N 88 0W
Puerto Cuemani 174 0 5N 73 21W
Puerto Cumarebo 174 11 29N 69 21W
Puerto de Cabras 116 28 40N 13 30W
Puerto de Morelos 165 20 49N 86 52W
Puerto de Santa María 57 36 36N 6 13W
Puerto Deseado 176 47 45 S 66 0W
Puerto Heath 174 12 25 S 68 45W
Puerto Huitoto 174 0 18N 74 3W
Puerto Juárez 165 21 11N 86 49W
Puerto La Cruz 174 10 13N 64 38W
Puerto Leguízamo 174 0 12 S 74 46W
Puerto Libertad 164 29 55N 112 41W
Puerto Limón, Meta, Colomb. 174 3 23N 73 30W
Puerto Limón, Putumayo, Colomb. 174 1 3N 76 30W
Puerto Lobos 176 42 0 S 65 3W
Puerto López 174 4 5N 72 58W
Puerto Lumbreras 59 37 34N 1 48W
Puerto Madryn 176 42 48 S 65 4W
Puerto Maldonado 174 12 30 S 69 10W
Puerto Manotí 166 21 22N 76 50W
Puerto Mazarrón 59 37 34N 1 15W
Puerto Mercedes 174 1 11N 72 53W
Puerto Montt 176 41 22 S 72 40W
Puerto Natales 176 51 45 S 72 25W
Puerto Nuevo 174 5 53N 69 56W
Puerto Ordaz 174 8 16N 62 44W
Puerto Padre 166 21 13N 76 35W
Puerto Páez 174 6 13N 67 28W
Puerto Peñasco 164 31 20N 113 33W
Puerto Pinasco 172 22 43 S 57 50W
Puerto Pirámides 176 42 35 S 64 20W
Puerto Plata 167 19 40N 70 45W
Puerto Princesa 94 9 44N 118 44 E
Puerto Quellón 176 43 7 S 73 37W
Puerto Quepos 166 9 29N 84 6W
Puerto Real 57 36 33N 6 12W
Puerto Rico 174 1 54N 75 10W
Puerto Rico ■ 147 18 15N 66 45W
Puerto Rico Trough 14 20 0N 63 0W
Puerto Sastre 172 22 25 S 57 55W
Puerto Suárez 174 18 58 S 57 52W
Puerto Tejada 174 3 14N 76 24W
Puerto Umbria 174 0 52N 76 33W
Puerto Vallarta 164 20 26N 105 15W
Puerto Villamizar 174 8 25N 72 30W
Puerto Wilches 174 7 21N 73 54W
Puertollano 57 38 43N 4 7W
Puertomarín 56 42 48N 7 37W
Pueyrredón, L. 176 47 20 S 72 0W
Puffin I., Ireland 39 51 50N 10 25W
Puffin I., U.K. 31 53 19N 4 1W
Pugachev 81 52 0N 48 55 E
Puge 126 4 45 S 33 11 E
Puget Sd. 160 47 15N 123 30W
Puget-Théniers 45 43 58N 6 53 E
Púglia 65 41 0N 16 30 E
Pugŏdong 107 42 5N 130 0 E
Pugu 126 6 55 S 39 4 E
Puha 142 38 30 S 177 50 E
P'uhsien 106 36 25N 110 4 E
Puhute Mesa 163 37 25N 116 50W
Pui 70 45 30N 23 4 E
Puieşti 70 46 25N 27 33 E
Puig Mayor, Mte. 58 39 49N 2 47 E
Puigcerdá 58 42 24N 1 50 E
Puigmal, Mt. 58 42 23N 2 7 E
Puisaye, Collines de 43 47 34N 3 28 E
Puiseaux 43 48 11N 2 30 E
Pujon-chosuji 107 40 35N 127 35 E
Puka 68 42 2N 19 53 E
Pukaki L. 143 44 4 S 170 1 E
Pukatawagan 153 55 45N 101 20W
Pukchin 107 40 12N 125 45 E
Pukchŏng 107 40 14N 128 18 E
Pukearuhe 142 38 55 S 174 31 E
Pukekohe 142 37 12 S 174 55 E
Puketeraki Ra. 143 42 58 S 172 13 E
Pukeuri 143 45 4 S 171 2 E
P'uko 108 27 27N 102 34 E
Pukoo 147 21 4N 156 48W
P'uk'ou 109 32 7N 118 43 E
Pula 64 39 0N 9 0 E
Pula (Pola) 63 44 54N 13 57 E
Pulaski, N.Y., U.S.A. 162 43 32N 76 9W
Pulaski, Tenn., U.S.A. 157 35 10N 87 0W
Pulaski, Va., U.S.A. 156 37 4N 80 49W
Pulawy 54 51 23N 21 59 E
Pulborough 29 50 58N 0 30W
Pulgaon 96 20 44N 78 21 E
Pulham Market 29 52 25N 1 15 E
Pulham St. Mary 29 52 25N 1 14 E
Pulicat, L. 97 13 40N 80 15 E
Puliyangudi 97 9 11N 77 24 E
Pullabooka 141 33 44 S 147 46 E
Pullen Cr. 108 27 33 S 152 54 E
Pullman 160 46 49N 117 10W
Pulmakong 121 11 2N 0 2 E
Pulog, Mt. 103 16 40N 120 50 E
Puloraja 102 4 55N 95 24 E
Pułtusk 54 52 43N 21 6 E
Pumlumon Fawr 31 52 29N 3 47W
Pumpsaint 31 52 3N 3 58W
Puna 174 19 45 S 65 28W
Puna de Atacama 172 25 0 S 67 0W
Puná, I. 174 2 55 S 80 5W
Punakha 98 27 42N 89 52 E
Punalur 97 9 0N 76 56 E
Punasar 94 27 6N 73 6 E
Punata 174 17 25 S 65 50W
Punch 95 33 48N 74 4 E
Pune 96 18 29N 73 57 E
Pungsan 107 40 50N 128 9 E
P'uning 109 23 19N 116 9 E
Punjab □ 94 31 0N 76 0 E
Punkatawagon 153 55 44N 101 20W
Puno 174 15 55 S 70 3W
Punt, La 51 46 35N 9 56 E
Punta Alta 176 38 53 S 62 4W
Punta Arenas 176 53 0 S 71 0W
Punta de Díaz 172 28 0 S 70 45W
Punta de Piedras 174 10 54N 64 6W
Punta del Lago Viedma 176 49 45 S 72 0W
Punta Gorda, Belize 165 16 10N 88 45W
Punta Gorda, U.S.A. 157 26 55N 82 0W
Punta Prieta 164 28 58N 114 17W
Puntabie 139 32 12 S 134 5 E
Puntarenas 166 10 0N 84 50W
Puntes de García Rodríguez 56 43 27N 7 50W
Punto Fijo 174 11 42N 70 13W
Punxsutawney 156 40 56N 79 0W
P'upei 108 22 16N 109 33 E
Puquio 174 14 45 S 74 10W
Pur, R. 76 65 30N 77 40 E
Purace, vol. 174 2 21N 76 23W
Puračić 66 44 33N 18 28 E
Purari, R. 135 7 49 S 145 0 E
Purbeck, Isle of 28 50 40N 2 5W
Purcell 159 35 0N 97 25W
Purchena Tetica 59 37 21N 2 21W
Purdy Is. 138 3 0 S 146 0 E
Purfleet 29 51 29N 0 15 E
Puri 96 19 50N 85 58 E
Purificación 174 3 51N 74 55W
Purísima, La 164 26 10N 112 4W
Purley 28 51 29N 1 4W
Purli 96 18 50N 76 35 E
Purmerend 47 52 30N 4 58 E
Purna, R. 96 19 55N 76 20 E
Purnea 95 25 45N 87 31 E
Pursat 101 12 34N 103 50 E
Puruey 174 7 35N 64 48W
Purukcahu 102 0 35 S 114 35 E
Purulia 95 23 17N 86 33 E
Purus, R. 174 5 25 S 64 0W
Purwakarta 103 6 35 S 107 29 E
Purwodadi, Jawa, Indon. 103 7 7 S 110 55 E
Purwodadi, Jawa, Indon. 103 7 51 S 110 0 E
Purworejo 103 7 43 S 110 2 E
Puryong 107 42 0N 129 43 E
Pus, R. 96 19 50N 77 45 E
Pusad 96 19 56N 77 36 E
Pusan 107 35 5N 129 0 E
Pushchino 77 54 20N 158 10 E
Pushkin 80 59 45N 30 25 E
Pushkino 81 51 16N 47 9 E
Puskitamika L. 150 49 20N 76 30W
Püspökladány 53 47 19N 21 6 E
Pussa 129 24 30 S 33 55 E
Pustoshka 80 56 11N 29 30 E
Puszczykowo 54 52 18N 16 49 E
Putahow L. 153 59 54N 100 40W
Putao 98 27 28N 97 30 E
Putaruru 142 38 2 S 175 50 E
Putbus 48 54 19N 13 29 E
Put'ehach'i 105 48 0N 122 43 E
Puţeni 70 45 49N 27 42 E
Puthein Myit, R. 99 15 56N 94 18 E
P'ut'ien 109 25 27N 118 59 E
Putignano 65 40 50N 17 5 E
P'uting 108 26 19N 105 45 E
Putlitz 48 53 15N 12 3 E
Putna 70 47 50N 25 33 E
Putna, R. 70 45 42N 27 26 E
Putnam 162 41 55N 71 55W
Putnok 53 48 18N 20 26 E
P'ut'o 109 29 58N 122 15 E
Putorana, Gory 77 69 0N 95 0 E
Putorino 142 39 4 S 177 9 E
Putta 47 51 4N 4 38 E
Puttalam 93 8 1N 79 55 E
Puttalam Lagoon 97 8 15N 79 45 E
Putte 47 51 22N 4 24 E
Putten 46 52 16N 5 36 E
Puttgarden 48 54 28N 11 15 E
Puttur 97 12 46N 75 12 E
Putty 141 32 57 S 150 42 E
Putumayo □ 174 1 30 S 70 0W
Putumayo, R. 174 1 30 S 70 0W
Putussibau, G. 102 0 45N 113 50 E
Pututahi 142 38 39 S 177 53 E
Puurs 47 51 5N 4 17 E
Puy-de-Dôme 44 45 46N 2 57 E
Puy-de-Dôme □ 44 45 47N 3 0 E
Puy-de-Sancy 44 45 32N 2 41 E
Puy Guillaume 44 45 57N 3 28 E
Puy, Le 44 45 3N 3 52 E
Puy l'Evêque 44 44 31N 1 9 E
Puyallup 160 47 10N 122 22W
P'uyang 106 35 41N 115 0 E
Puylaurens 44 43 35N 2 0 E
Puyôo 44 43 33N 0 56W
Pwalagu 121 10 38N 0 50W
Pwani □, Tanz. 126 7 0 S 39 0 E
Pwani □, Tanz. 126 7 0 S 39 30 E
Pweto 127 8 25 S 28 51 E
Pwinbyu 98 20 23N 94 40 E
Pwllheli 31 52 54N 4 26W
Pya Ozero 78 66 8N 31 22 E
Pyana, R. 81 55 30N 45 0 E
Pyandzh 85 37 14N 69 6 E
Pyandzh, R. 85 37 6N 68 20 E
Pyapon 98 16 5N 95 50 E
Pyasina, R. 77 72 30N 90 30 E
Pyatigorsk 83 44 2N 43 0 E
Pyatikhatki 82 48 28N 33 38 E
Pyaye 98 19 12N 95 10 E
Pyè 98 18 49N 95 13 E
Pyinbauk 98 19 10N 95 12 E
Pyinmana 98 19 45N 96 20 E
Pyŏktong 107 40 37N 125 26 E
Pyŏnggang 107 38 24N 127 17 E
P'yŏngtaek 107 37 1N 127 4 E
P'yŏngyang 107 39 0N 125 45 E
Pyote 159 31 34N 103 5W
Pyramid L. 160 40 0N 119 30W
Pyramid Pk. 163 36 25N 116 37W
Pyramids 122 29 58N 31 9 E
Pyrenees 44 42 45N 0 18 E
Pyrénées-Atlantiques □ 44 43 15N 1 0W
Pyrénées-Orientales □ 44 42 35N 2 26 E
Pyrzyce 54 53 10N 14 55 E
Pyshchug 81 58 57N 45 27 E
Pyshma, R. 84 57 8N 66 18 E
Pytalovo 80 57 5N 27 55 E
Python 127 17 56 S 29 10 E
Pyttegga 71 62 13N 7 42 E
Pyu 98 18 30N 96 35 E
Pyzdry 54 52 11N 17 42 E

# Q

Qaar Zeitun 122 29 10N 25 48 E
Qabalon 90 32 8N 35 17 E
Qabatiya 90 32 25N 35 16 E
Qadam 93 32 55N 66 45 E
Qadhimah 92 22 20N 39 13 E
Qadian 94 31 51N 74 19 E
Qal at Shajwa 122 25 2N 38 57 E
Qala-i-Jadid (Spin Baldak) 94 31 1N 66 25 E
Qala-i-Kirta 93 32 15N 63 0 E
Qala Nau 93 35 0N 63 5 E
Qala Punja 93 37 0N 72 40 E
Qala Yangi 94 34 20N 66 30 E
Qal'at al Akhdhar 92 28 0N 37 10 E
Qal'at Saura 122 26 10N 38 40 E
Qal'eh Shaharak 93 34 10N 64 20 E
Qalqīlya 90 32 12N 34 58 E
Qalyûb 122 30 12N 31 11 E
Qam 90 32 36N 35 43 E
Qamar, Ghubbat al 91 16 20N 52 30 E
Qamruddin Karez 94 31 45N 68 20 E
Qana 90 33 12N 35 17 E
Qâra 122 29 38N 26 30 E
Qara Qash, R. 95 35 45N 78 45 E
Qara Tagh La = Kala Shank'ou 95 35 42N 78 20 E
Qarachuk 92 37 0N 42 2 E
Qarah 92 29 55N 40 3 E
Qardud 123 10 20N 29 56 E
Qarrasa 123 14 38N 32 5 E
Qarsa 123 9 28N 41 48 E
Qaşr Bū Hadi 119 31 1N 16 45 E
Qasr-e-Qand 93 26 15N 60 45 E
Qasr Farâfra 122 27 0N 28 1 E
Qastina 90 31 44N 34 45 E
Qatar ■ 93 25 30N 51 15 E
Qattâra 122 30 12N 27 3 E
Qattara Depression = Q. Munkhafed el 122 29 30N 27 30 E
Qattâra, Munkhafed el 122 29 30N 27 30 E

Qayen Rancharia

Qayen 93 33 40N 59 10 E
Qazvin 92 36 15N 50 0 E
Qena 122 26 10N 32 43 E
Qena, Wadi 122 26 57N 32 50 E
Qendrevca 68 40 20N 19 48 E
Qesari 90 32 30N 34 53 E
Qeshm 93 26 55N 56 10 E
Qeshm, I. 93 26 50N 56 0 E
Qila Safed 93 29 0N 61 30 E
Qila Saifulla 94 30 45N 68 17 E
Qiryat 'Anivim 90 31 49N 35 7 E
Qiryat Bialik 90 32 50N 35 5 E
Qiryat 'Eqron 90 31 52N 34 49 E
Qiryat Hayyim 90 32 49N 35 4 E
Qiryat Shemona 90 33 13N 35 35 E
Qiryat Yam 90 32 51N 35 4 E
Qishon, R. 90 32 42N 35 7 E
Qishran 122 20 14N 40 2 E
Qizan 123 16 57N 42 34 E
Qom 93 34 40N 51 0 E
Quabbin Res. 162 42 17N 72 21W
Quabbo 123 12 2N 39 56 E
Quackenbrück 48 52 40N 7 59 E
Quadring 33 52 53N 0 9W
Quainton 29 51 51N 0 53W
Quairading 137 32 0 S 117 21 E
Quakerstown 162 40 27N 75 20W
Qualeup 137 33 48 S 116 48 E
Quambatook 138 35 49 S 143 34 E
Quambone 141 30 57 S 147 53 E
Quan Long 101 9 7N 105 8 E
Quanan 159 34 20N 99 45W
Quandialla 141 34 1 S 147 47 E
Quang Nam 101 15 55N 108 15 E
Quang Ngai 101 15 13N 108 58 E
Quang Yen 100 21 3N 106 52 E
Quantock Hills, The 28 51 8N 3 10W
Quaraí 172 30 15 S 56 20W
Quarré les Tombes 43 47 21N 4 0 E
Quarryville 162 39 54N 76 10W
Quartu Sant' Elena 64 39 15N 9 10 E
Quartzsite 161 33 44N 114 16W
Quatsino 152 50 30N 127 40W
Quatsino Sd. 152 50 42N 127 58W
Qubab = Mishmar Aiyalon 90 31 52N 34 57 E
Qūchān 93 37 10N 58 27 E
Que Que 127 18 58 S 29 48 E
Queanbeyan 141 35 17 S 149 14 E
Québec 151 46 52N 71 13W
Québec □ 151 50 0N 70 0W
Quedlinburg 48 51 47N 11 9 E
Queen Alexandra Ra. 13 85 0 S 170 0 E
Queen Anne 162 38 55N 75 57W
Queen Bess Mt. 152 51 13N 124 35W
Queen Charlotte 152 53 15N 132 2W
Queen Charlotte Is. 152 53 20N 132 10W
Queen Charlotte Sd. 143 41 10 S 174 15 E
Queen Charlotte Str. 152 51 0N 128 0W
Queen Elizabeth Is. 10 78 0N 95 0W
Queen Elizabeth Nat. Pk. 126 0 0 S 30 0 E
Queen Mary Coast 13 70 0 S 95 0 E
Queen Maud G. 148 68 15N 102 30W
Queenborough 29 51 24N 0 46 E
Queen's Chan. 136 15 0 S 129 30 E
Queensbury 32 53 46N 1 50W
Queenscliff 138 38 16 S 144 39 E
Queensferry 35 56 0N 3 25W
Queensland □ 138 15 0 S 142 0 E
Queenstown, Austral. 138 42 4 S 145 35 E
Queenstown, N.Z. 143 45 1 S 168 40 E
Queenstown, S. Afr. 125 31 52 S 26 52 E
Queguay Grande, R. 172 32 9 S 58 9W
Queimadas 170 11 0 S 39 38W
Quela 124 9 10 S 16 56 E
Quelimane 127 17 53 S 36 58 E
Quemado, N. Mex., U.S.A. 161 34 17N 108 28W
Quemado, Tex., U.S.A. 159 28 58N 100 35W
Quemoy, I. = Chinmen Tao, I. 109 24 25N 118 25 E
Quemú-Quemú 172 36 3 S 63 36W
Quendale, B. of 36 59 53N 1 20W
Quequén 172 38 30 S 58 30W
Querein 123 13 30N 34 50 E
Querétaro 164 20 40N 100 23W
Querétaro □ 164 20 30N 100 30W
Querfurt 48 51 22N 11 33 E
Quesada 59 37 51N 3 4W
Quesnel 152 53 5N 122 30W
Quesnel L. 152 52 30N 121 20W
Quesnel, R. 152 52 58N 122 29W
Quest, Pte. 151 49 52N 64 40W
Questa 161 36 45N 105 35W
Questembert 42 47 40N 2 28W
Quetico 150 48 45N 90 55W
Quetico Prov. Park 150 48 30N 91 45W
Quetta 93 30 15N 66 55 E
Quetta □ 93 30 15N 66 55 E
Quezaltenango 166 14 40N 91 30W
Quezon City 103 14 38N 121 0 E
Qui Nhon 101 13 40N 109 13 E
Quiaca, La 172 22 5 S 65 35W
Quibaxi 124 8 24 S 14 27 E
Quibdó 174 5 42N 76 40W
Quiberon 42 47 29N 3 9W
Quibor 174 9 56N 69 37W
Quick 152 54 36N 126 54W
Quickborn 48 53 42N 9 52 E
Quiet L. 152 61 5N 133 5W
Quiévrain 47 50 24N 3 41 E
Quiindy 172 25 58 S 57 14W
Quila 164 24 23N 107 13W
Quilán, C. 176 43 15 S 74 30W
Quilengues 125 14 12 S 14 12 E
Quilimarí 172 32 5 S 70 30W
Quilino 172 30 14 S 64 29W
Quillabamba 174 12 50 S 72 50W
Quillagua 172 21 40 S 69 40W
Quillaicillo 172 31 17 S 71 40W
Quillan 44 42 53N 2 10 E
Quillebeuf 42 49 28N 0 30 E
Quillota 172 32 54 S 71 16W
Quilmes 172 34 43 S 58 15W
Quilon 97 8 50N 76 38 E
Quilpie 139 26 35 S 144 11 E
Quilpué 172 33 5 S 71 33W
Quilty 39 52 50N 9 27W
Quilua 127 16 17 S 39 54 E
Quimilí 172 27 40 S 62 30W
Quimper 42 48 0N 4 9W
Quimperlé 42 47 53N 3 33W
Quin 39 52 50N 8 52W
Quinag 36 58 13N 5 5W
Quincy, Calif., U.S.A. 160 39 56N 121 0W
Quincy, Fla., U.S.A. 157 30 34N 84 34W
Quincy, Ill., U.S.A. 158 39 55N 91 20W
Quincy, Mass., U.S.A. 162 42 14N 71 0W
Quincy, Wash., U.S.A. 160 47 22N 119 56W
Quines 172 32 13 S 65 48W
Quinga 127 15 49 S 40 15 E
Quingey 43 47 7N 5 52 E
Quinhagak 147 59 45N 162 0W
Quintana de la Serena 57 38 45N 5 40W
Quintana Roo □ 165 19 0N 88 0W
Quintanar de la Orden 58 39 36N 3 5W
Quintanar de la Sierra 58 41 57N 2 55W
Quintanar del Rey 59 39 21N 1 56W
Quintero 172 32 45 S 71 30W
Quintin 42 48 26N 2 56W
Quinto 58 41 25N 0 32W
Quinyambie 139 30 15 S 141 0 E
Quipar, R. 59 37 58N 2 3W
Quirihue 172 36 15 S 72 35W
Quirindi 141 31 28 S 150 40 E
Quiriquire 174 9 59N 63 13W
Quiroga 56 42 28N 7 18W
Quirpon I. 151 51 32N 55 28W
Quisiro 174 10 53N 71 17W
Quissac 45 43 55N 4 0 E
Quissanga 127 12 24 S 40 28 E
Quitilipi 172 26 50 S 60 13W
Quitman, Ga., U.S.A. 157 30 49N 83 35W
Quitman, Miss., U.S.A. 157 32 2N 88 42W
Quitman, Tex., U.S.A. 159 32 48N 95 25W
Quito 174 0 15 S 78 35W
Quixadá 170 4 55 S 39 0W
Quixaxe 127 15 17 S 40 4 E
Quixeramobim 170 5 12 S 39 17W
Qul'ân, Jazâ'ir 122 24 22N 35 31 E
Qumran 90 31 43N 35 27 E
Quneitra 90 33 7N 35 48 E
Quoich L. 36 57 4N 5 20W
Quoile, R. 38 54 21N 5 40W
Quoin I. 136 14 54 S 129 32 E
Quoin Pt., N.Z. 143 46 19 S 170 11 E
Quoin Pt., S. Afr. 128 34 46 S 19 37 E
Quondong 140 33 6 S 140 18 E
Quorn, Austral. 140 32 25 S 138 0 E
Quorn, Can. 150 49 25N 90 55W
Quorndon 28 52 45N 1 10W
Qûs 122 25 55N 32 50 E
Quseir 122 26 7N 34 16 E
Qusra 90 32 5N 35 20 E
Quthing 129 30 25 S 27 36 E
Quynh Nhai 100 21 49N 103 33 E
Qytet Stalin (Kuçove) 68 40 47N 19 57 E

# R

Ra, Ko 101 9 13N 98 16 E
Raa. 73 56 0N 12 45 E
Råå 73 56 0N 12 45 E
Raahana 90 32 12N 34 52 E
Raahe 74 64 40N 24 28 E
Raalte 46 52 23N 6 16 E
Raamsdonksveer 47 51 43N 4 52 E
Raasay I. 36 57 25N 6 4W
Raasay, Sd. of 36 57 30N 6 8W
Rab 63 44 45N 14 45 E
Rab, I. 63 44 45N 14 45 E
Raba 103 8 36 S 118 55 E
Rába, R. 54 47 38N 17 38 E
Rabaçal, R. 56 41 41N 7 15W
Rabah 121 13 5N 5 30 E
Rabai 126 3 50 S 39 31 E
Rabaraba 135 9 58 S 149 49 E
Rabastens 44 43 50N 1 43 E
Rabastens, Hautes Pyrénées 44 43 25N 0 10 E
Rabat 118 34 2N 6 48W
Rabaul 135 4 24 S 152 18 E
Rabbalshede 73 58 40N 11 27 E
Rabbit L. 153 47 0N 79 38W
Rabbit Lake 153 53 8N 107 46W
Rabbit, R. 152 59 41N 127 12W
Rabbitskin, R. 152 61 47N 120 42W
Rabigh 92 22 50N 39 5 E
Rabka 54 49 37N 19 59 E
Rača 66 44 14N 21 0 E
Rácale 65 39 57N 18 6 E
Racalmuto 64 37 25N 13 41 E
Racconigi 62 44 47N 7 41 E
Race, C. 151 46 40N 53 5W
Raceview 108 27 38 S 152 47 E
Rach Gia 101 10 5N 105 5 E
Raciaz 54 52 46N 20 10 E
Racibórz (Ratibor) 54 50 7N 18 18 E
Racine 156 42 41N 87 51W
Rackheath 29 52 41N 1 22 E
Rackwick 37 58 52N 3 23W
Radama, Is. 129 14 0 S 47 47 E
Radama, Presqu'île d' 129 14 16 S 47 53 E
Radan, mt. 66 42 59N 21 29 E
Radbuza, R. 52 49 35N 13 5 E
Radcliffe, Gr. Manch., U.K. 32 53 35N 2 19W
Radcliffe, Notts., U.K. 33 52 57N 1 3W
Rade 71 59 21N 10 53 E
Radeburg 48 51 6N 13 45 E
Radeče 63 46 5N 15 14 E
Radekhov 80 50 25N 24 32 E
Radford 156 37 8N 80 32W
Radhanpur 94 23 50N 71 38 E
Radika, R. 66 41 38N 20 37 E
Radisson 153 52 30N 107 20W
Radium Hill 133 32 30 S 140 42 E
Radium Hot Springs 152 50 48N 116 12W
Radkow 54 50 30N 16 24 E
Radley 28 51 42N 1 14W
Radlin 54 50 3N 18 29 E
Radna 66 46 7N 21 41 E
Radnevo 67 42 17N 25 58 E
Radnice 52 49 51N 13 35 E
Radnor (□) 26 52 20N 3 20W
Radnor Forest 31 52 17N 3 10W
Radom 54 51 23N 21 12 E
Radom □ 54 51 30N 21 0 E
Radomir 66 42 37N 23 4 E
Radomsko 54 51 5N 19 28 E
Radomyshl 80 50 30N 29 12 E
Radomysl Wielki 54 50 14N 21 15 E
Radoszyce 54 51 4N 20 15 E
Radoviš 66 41 38N 22 28 E
Radovljica 63 46 22N 14 12 E
Radöy I. 71 60 40N 4 55 E
Radstadt 52 47 24N 13 28 E
Radstock 28 51 17N 2 25W
Radstock, C. 139 33 12 S 134 20 E
Raduša 66 42 7N 21 15 E
Radviliškis 80 55 49N 23 33 E
Radville 153 49 30N 104 15W
Radymno 54 49 59N 22 52 E
Radyr 31 51 32N 3 16W
Radzanów 54 52 56N 20 8 E
Radziejów 54 52 40N 18 30 E
Radzyn Chełminski 54 53 23N 18 55 E
Rae 152 62 50N 116 3W
Rae Bareli 95 26 18N 81 20 E
Rae Isthmus 149 66 40N 87 30W
Raeside, L. 137 29 20 S 122 0 E
Raetihi 142 39 25 S 175 17 E
Rafaela 172 31 10 S 61 30W
Rafah 122 31 18N 34 14 E
Rafai 126 4 59N 23 58 E
Raffadali 64 37 23N 13 29 E
Rafhā 92 29 35N 43 35 E
Rafid 90 32 57N 35 52 E
Rafsanjān 93 30 30N 56 5 E
Raft Pt. 136 16 4 S 124 26 E
Ragag 123 10 59N 24 40 E
Ragama 93 7 0N 79 50 E
Ragged Mt. 137 33 27 S 123 25 E
Raglan, Austral. 138 23 42 S 150 49 E
Raglan, N.Z. 142 37 55 S 174 55 E
Raglan, U.K. 31 51 46N 2 51W
Ragueneau 151 49 11N 68 18W
Ragunda 72 63 6N 16 23 E
Ragusa 65 36 56N 14 42 E
Raha 103 8 20 S 118 40 E
Rahad el Berdi 117 11 20N 23 40 E
Rahad, Nahr er 123 12 40N 35 30 E
Rahden 48 52 26N 8 36 E
Raheita 123 12 46N 43 4 E
Raheng = Tak 100 17 5N 99 10 E
Rahimyar Khan 94 28 30N 70 25 E
Rahotu 142 39 20 S 173 49 E
Raichur 96 16 10N 77 20 E
Raiganj 95 25 37N 88 10 E
Raigarh, Madhya Pradesh, India 96 21 56N 83 25 E
Raigarh, Orissa, India 96 19 51N 82 6 E
Raiis 92 23 33N 38 43 E
Raijua 103 10 37 S 121 36 E
Railton 138 41 25 S 146 28 E
Rainbow 140 35 55 S 142 0 E
Rainbow Lake 152 58 30N 119 23W
Rainham 29 51 22N 0 36 E
Rainier 160 46 4N 123 0W
Rainier, Mt. 160 46 50N 121 50W
Rainworth 33 53 8N 1 6W
Rainy L. 153 48 42N 93 10W
Rainy River 153 48 50N 94 30W
Raipur 96 21 17N 81 45 E
Raith 150 48 50N 90 0W
Raj Nandgaon 99 21 0N 81 0 E
Raja Empat, Kepulauan 103 0 30 S 129 40 E
Raja-Jooseppi 74 68 28N 28 29 E
Raja, Ujung 102 3 40N 96 25 E
Rajahmundry 96 17 1N 81 48 E
Rajang, R. 102 2 30N 113 30 E
Rajapalaiyarm 97 9 25N 77 35 E
Rajasthan □ 94 26 45N 73 30 E
Rajasthan Canal 94 30 31N 71 0 E
Rajauri 95 33 25N 74 21 E
Rajbari 98 23 47N 89 41 E
Rajgarh, Mad. P., India 94 24 2N 76 45 E
Rajgarh, Raj., India 94 28 40N 75 25 E
Rajgród 54 53 42N 22 42 E
Rajhenburg 63 46 1N 15 29 E
Rajkot 94 22 15N 70 56 E
Rajmahal Hills 95 24 30N 87 30 E
Rajnandgaon 96 21 5N 81 5 E
Rajojooseppi 74 68 25N 28 30 E
Rajpipla 96 21 50N 73 30 E
Rajpura 94 30 32N 76 32 E
Rajshahi 98 24 22N 88 39 E
Rajshahi □ 95 25 0N 89 0 E
Rakaia 143 43 45 S 172 1 E
Rakaia, R. 143 43 26 S 171 47 E
Rakan, Ras 93 26 10N 51 20 E
Rakaposhi 95 36 10N 74 0 E
Rakaposhi, mt. 93 36 20N 74 30 E
Rakha 122 18 25N 41 30 E
Rakhni 94 30 4N 69 56 E
Rakitovo 67 41 59N 24 5 E
Rakkestad 71 59 25N 11 21 E
Rakoniewice 54 52 10N 16 16 E
Rakops 128 21 1 S 24 28 E
Rákospalota 53 47 30N 19 5 E
Rakovica 63 44 59N 15 38 E
Rakovník 52 50 6N 13 42 E
Rakovski 67 42 21N 24 57 E
Raleigh, Can. 150 49 30N 92 5W
Raleigh, U.S.A. 150 35 46N 78 38W
Raleigh B. 157 34 50N 76 15W
Ralja 66 44 33N 20 34 E
Ralls 159 33 40N 101 20W
Ralston 162 41 30N 76 57W
Rām Allāh 90 31 55N 35 10 E
Ram Hd. 141 37 47 S 149 30 E
Ram, R. 152 62 1N 123 41W
Rama, Israel 90 32 56N 35 21 E
Rama, Nic. 166 12 9N 84 15W
Ramacca 65 37 24N 14 40 E
Ramachandrapuram 96 16 50N 82 4 E
Ramadi 92 33 28N 43 15 E
Ramales de la Victoria 58 43 15N 3 28W
Ramalho, Serra do 171 13 45 S 44 0W
Raman 101 6 29N 101 18 E
Ramanathapuram 97 9 25N 78 55 E
Ramanetaka, B. de 129 14 13 S 47 52 E
Ramas C. 97 15 5N 73 55 E
Ramat Gan 90 32 4N 34 48 E
Ramatlhabama 128 25 37 S 25 33 E
Ramban 95 33 14N 75 12 E
Rambervillers 43 48 20N 6 38 E
Rambipudji 103 8 12 S 113 37 E
Rambla, La 57 37 37N 4 45W
Rambouillet 43 48 40N 1 48 E
Rambre Kyun 98 19 0N 94 0 E
Ramdurg 97 15 58N 75 22 E
Rame Head 30 50 19N 4 14W
Ramechhap 95 27 25N 86 10 E
Ramelau, Mte. 103 8 55 S 126 22 E
Ramenskoye 81 55 32N 38 15 E
Ramgarh, Bihar, India 95 23 40N 85 35 E
Ramgarh, Rajasthan, India 94 27 16N 75 14 E
Ramgarh, Rajasthan, India 94 27 30N 70 36 E
Ramhormoz 92 31 15N 49 35 E
Ramla 90 31 55N 34 52 E
Ramlat Zalṭan 119 28 30N 19 30 E
Ramlu Mt. 123 13 32N 41 40 E
Ramme 73 56 30N 8 11 E
Rammun 90 31 55N 35 17 E
Ramna Stacks, Is. 36 60 40N 1 20W
Ramnad = Ramanathapuram 97 9 25N 78 55 E
Ramnagar 95 32 47N 75 18 E
Ramnäs 72 59 46N 16 12 E
Ramon 81 52 8N 39 21 E
Ramona 163 33 1N 116 56W
Ramor L. 38 53 50N 7 5W
Ramore 150 48 30N 80 25W
Ramos Arizpe 164 25 35N 100 59W
Ramos, R. 164 25 35N 105 3W
Ramoutsa 128 24 50 S 25 52 E
Rampart 147 65 0N 150 15W
Rampside 32 54 6N 3 10W
Rampur, H.P., India 94 31 26N 77 43 E
Rampur, M.P., India 94 23 25N 73 53 E
Rampur, Orissa, India 96 21 48N 83 58 E
Rampur, U.P., India 94 28 50N 79 5 E
Rampura 94 24 30N 75 27 E
Rampurhat 95 24 10N 87 50 E
Ramsbottom 32 53 36N 2 20W
Ramsbury 28 51 26N 1 37W
Ramsel 47 51 2N 4 50 E
Ramsele 74 63 31N 16 27 E
Ramsey, Can. 150 47 25N 82 20W
Ramsey, Cambs., U.K. 29 52 27N 0 6W
Ramsey, Essex, U.K. 29 51 55N 1 12 E
Ramsey, I. of M., U.K. 32 54 20N 4 21W
Ramsgate 29 51 20N 1 25 E
Ramshai 98 26 44N 88 51 E
Rämshyttan 72 60 17N 15 15 E
Ramsjö 72 62 11N 15 37 E
Ramtek 96 21 20N 79 15 E
Ramu, R. 135 4 0 S 144 41 E
Ramvik 72 62 49N 17 51 E
Ranaghat 95 23 15N 88 35 E
Ranahu 94 25 55N 69 45 E
Ranau 102 6 2N 116 40 E
Rancagua 172 34 10 S 70 50W
Rance 47 50 9N 4 16 E
Rance, R. 42 48 34N 1 59W
Rancharia 171 22 15 S 50 55W

Rancheria, R Rennell Sd


Rancheria, R. 152 60 13N 129 7W
Ranchester 160 44 57N 107 12W
Ranchi 95 23 19N 85 27 E
Rancu 70 44 32N 24 15 E
Rand 141 35 33 S 146 32 E
Randallstown 162 39 22N 76 48W
Randalstown 38 54 45N 6 20W
Randan 44 46 2N 3 21 E
Randazzo 65 37 53N 14 56 E
Randböl 73 55 43N 9 17 E
Randers 73 56 29N 10 1 E
Randers Fjord 73 56 37N 10 20 E
Randfontein 129 26 8 S 27 45 E
Randolph, Mass., U.S.A. 162 42 10N 71 3W
Randolph, Utah, U.S.A. 160 41 43N 111 10W
Randolph, Vt., U.S.A. 162 43 55N 72 39W
Randsburg 163 35 26N 117 44W
Randsfjord 71 60 15N 10 25 E
Råne älv 74 66 26N 21 10 E
Råneå 74 65 53N 22 18 E
Ranfurly 143 45 7 S 170 6 E
Rangae 101 6 19N 101 44 E
Rangamati 98 22 38 S 92 12 E
Rangataua 142 39 26 S 175 28 E
Rangaunu B. 142 34 51 S 173 15 E
Rångedala 73 57 47N 13 9 E
Rangeley 156 44 58N 70 33W
Rangely 160 40 3N 108 53W
Ranger 159 32 30N 98 42W
Rangia 98 26 15N 91 20 E
Rangiora 143 43 19 S 172 36 E
Rangitaiki 130 38 52 S 176 23 E
Rangitaiki, R. 142 37 54 S 176 49 E
Rangitata, R. 143 43 45 S 171 15 E
Rangitikei, R. 142 40 17 S 175 15 E
Rangitoto Range 142 38 25 S 175 35 E
Rangkasbitung 103 6 22 S 106 16 E
Rangon 99 16 45N 96 20 E
Rangon, R. 99 16 28N 96 40 E
Rangoon 98 16 45N 96 20 E
Rangpur 98 25 42N 89 22 E
Rangsit 100 13 59N 100 37 E
Ranibennur 97 14 35N 75 30 E
Raniganj 95 23 40N 87 15 E
Ranipet 97 12 56N 79 23 E
Raniwara 93 24 50N 72 10 E
Ranken, R. 138 20 31 S 137 36 E
Rankin 159 31 16N 101 56W
Rankin Inlet 148 62 30N 93 0W
Rankin's Springs 141 33 49 S 146 14 E
Rannes 138 24 6 S 150 11 E
Rannoch L. 37 56 41N 4 20W
Rannoch Moor 34 56 38N 4 48W
Rannoch Sta. 37 56 40N 4 32W
Ranobe, B. de 129 23 3 S 43 33 E
Ranohira 129 22 29 S 45 24 E
Ranomafana, Tamatave, Madag. 129 18 57 S 48 50 E
Ranomafana, Tuléar, Madag. 129 24 34 S 47 0 E
Ranong 101 9 56N 98 40 E
Rantau 102 4 15N 98 5 E
Rantauprapat 102 2 15N 99 50 E
Rantemario 103 3 15 S 119 57 E
Rantis 90 32 4N 35 3 E
Rantoul 156 40 18N 88 10W
Ranum 73 56 54N 9 14 E
Ranwanlenau 128 19 37 S 22 49 E
Raon-l' Étape 43 48 24N 6 50 E
Raoui, Erg er 118 29 0N 2 0W
Rapa Iti, I. 131 27 35 S 144 20W
Rapallo 62 44 21N 9 12 E
Rapang 103 3 45 S 119 55 E
Râpch 93 25 40N 59 15 E
Raphoe 38 54 52N 7 36W
Rapid City 158 44 0N 103 0W
Rapid, R. 152 59 15N 129 5W
Rapid River 156 45 55N 87 0W
Rapides des Joachims 150 46 13N 77 43W
Rapla 80 58 88N 24 52 E
Rapness 37 59 15N 2 51W
Raposos 171 19 57 S 43 48W
Rappahannock, R. 162 37 35N 76 17W
Rapperswil 51 47 14N 8 45 E
Raqqa 92 36 0N 38 55 E
Raquete 127 14 8 S 38 13 E
Raquette Lake 162 43 49N 74 40W
Rareagh 38 53 37N 8 37W
Rarotonga, I. 131 21 30 S 160 0W
Ras al Khaima 93 25 50N 56 5 E
Ra's Al-Unüf 119 30 25N 18 15 E
Ra's at Tannurah 92 26 40N 50 10 E
Ras Dashan, mt. 123 13 8N 37 45 E
Ras el Ma 118 34 26N 0 50W
Ras Gharib 122 28 6N 33 18 E
Ras Mallap 122 29 18N 32 50 E
Rasa, Punta 176 40 50 S 62 15W
Rasboda 72 60 8N 16 58 E
Raseiniai 80 55 25N 23 5 E
Rashad 123 11 55N 31 0 E
Rashîd 122 31 21N 30 22 E
Rashîd, Masabb 122 31 22N 30 17 E
Rasht 92 37 20N 49 40 E
Rasi Salai 100 15 20N 104 9 E
Rasipuram 97 11 30N 78 25 E
Raška 66 43 19N 20 39 E
Raso, C. 170 1 50N 50 0W
Rason, L. 137 28 45 S 124 25 E
Raşova 70 44 15N 27 55 E
Rasovo 67 43 42N 23 17 E
Rasra 95 25 50N 83 50 E
Rass el Oued 119 35 57N 5 2 E
Rasskazovo 81 52 35N 41 50 E
Rastatt 49 48 50N 8 12 E
Rastu 70 43 53N 23 16 E
Raszków 54 51 43N 17 40 E
Rat Buri 100 13 30N 99 54 E
Rat, Is. 147 51 50N 178 15 E
Rat, R. 152 56 0N 99 30W
Rat River 152 61 7N 112 36W
Rätan 72 62 27N 14 33 E
Ratangarh 94 28 5N 74 35 E
Rath 95 25 36N 79 37 E
Rath Luirc (Charleville) 39 52 21N 8 40W
Rathangan 39 53 13N 7 0W
Rathconrah 38 53 30N 7 32W
Rathcoole 39 53 17N 6 29W
Rathcormack 39 52 5N 8 19W
Rathdowney 39 52 52N 7 36W
Rathdrum, Ireland 39 52 57N 6 13W
Rathdrum, U.S.A. 160 47 50N 116 58W
Ratheclaung 98 20 29N 92 45 E
Rathen 37 57 38N 1 58W
Rathenow 48 52 38N 12 23 E
Rathfriland 38 54 12N 6 12W
Rathkeale 39 52 32N 8 57W
Rathkenny 38 53 45N 6 39W
Rathlin I. 38 55 18N 6 14W
Rathlin O'Birne I. 38 54 40N 8 50W
Rathmelton 38 55 3N 7 35W
Rathmolyon 38 53 30N 6 49W
Rathmore, Cork, Ireland 39 51 30N 9 21W
Rathmore, Kerry, Ireland 39 52 5N 9 12W
Rathmore, Kildare, Ireland 39 53 13N 6 35W
Rathmullen 38 55 6N 7 32W
Rathnure 39 52 30N 6 47W
Rathvilly 72 52 54N 6 42W
Ratlam 94 23 20N 75 0 E
Ratnagiri 96 16 57N 73 18 E
Ratnapura 97 6 40N 80 20 E
Ratoath 38 53 30N 6 27W
Raton 159 37 0N 104 30W
Rattaphum 101 7 8N 100 16 E
Ratten 52 47 28N 15 44 E
Rattray 37 56 36N 3 20W
Rattray Hd. 37 57 38N 1 50W
Rättvik 72 60 52N 15 7 E
Ratz, Mt. 152 57 23N 132 12W
Ratzeburg 48 53 41N 10 46 E
Raub 101 3 47N 101 52 E
Rauch 172 36 45 S 59 5W
Raufarhöfn 74 66 27N 15 57W
Raufoss 71 60 44N 10 37 E
Raukumara Ra. 142 38 5 S 177 55 E
Raul Soares 171 20 5 S 42 22W
Rauland 71 59 43N 8 0 E
Rauma 75 61 10N 21 30 E
Rauma, R. 71 62 34N 7 43 E
Raundal 71 60 40N 6 37 E
Raunds 29 52 20N 0 32W
Raung, Mt. 103 8 8 S 114 4 E
Raurkela 96 22 14N 84 50 E
Rava Russkaya 80 50 15N 23 42 E
Ravanusa 64 37 16N 13 58 E
Ravar 93 31 20N 56 51 E
Ravels 47 51 22N 5 0 E
Ravena 162 42 28N 73 49W
Ravenglass 32 54 21N 3 25W
Ravenna, Italy 63 44 28N 12 15 E
Ravenna, U.S.A. 158 41 3N 98 58W
Ravensburg 49 47 48N 9 38 E
Ravenshoe 138 17 37 S 145 29 E
Ravenstein 46 51 47N 5 39 E
Ravensthorpe 137 33 35 S 120 2 E
Ravenstonedale 32 54 26N 2 26W
Ravenswood, Austral. 138 20 6 S 146 54 E
Ravenswood, U.S.A. 156 38 58N 81 47W
Ravensworth 141 32 26 S 151 4 E
Raventasón 174 6 10 S 81 0W
Ravi, R. 94 31 0N 73 0 E
Ravna Gora 63 45 24N 14 50 E
Ravna Reka 66 43 59N 21 35 E
Ravnstrup 73 56 27N 9 17 E
Rawa Mazowiecka 54 51 46N 20 12 E
Rawalpindi 94 33 38N 73 8 E
Rawalpindi □ 93 33 10N 72 50 E
Rawāndūz 92 36 40N 44 30 E
Rawang 101 3 20N 101 35 E
Rawdon 150 46 3N 73 40W
Rawene 142 35 25 S 173 32 E
Rawicz 54 51 36N 16 52 E
Rawlinna 137 30 58 S 125 28 E
Rawlins 160 41 50N 107 20W
Rawlinson Range 137 24 40 S 128 30 E
Rawmarsh 33 53 27N 1 20W
Rawson 176 43 15 S 65 0W
Rawtenstall 32 53 42N 2 18W
Rawuya 121 12 10N 6 50 E
Ray, N. Mex., U.S.A. 159 35 57N 104 8W
Ray, N.D., U.S.A. 158 48 21N 103 6W
Ray, C. 151 47 33N 59 15W
Ray Mts. 147 66 0N 152 10W
Rayachoti 97 14 4N 78 50 E
Rayadrug 97 14 40N 76 50 E
Rayagada 96 19 15N 83 20 E
Raychikhinsk 77 49 46N 129 25 E
Rayevskiy 84 54 4N 54 56 E
Rayin 93 29 40N 57 22 E
Rayleigh 29 51 36N 0 38 E
Raymond, Can. 152 49 30N 112 35W
Raymond, Calif., U.S.A. 163 37 13N 119 54W
Raymond, Wash., U.S.A. 160 46 45N 123 48W
Raymond Terrace 141 32 45 S 151 44 E
Raymondville 159 26 30N 97 50W
Raymore 153 51 25N 104 31W
Rayne 159 30 16N 92 16W
Rayón 164 29 43N 110 35W
Rayong 100 12 40N 101 20 E
Rayville 159 32 30N 91 45W
Raz, Pte. du 42 48 2N 4 47W
Razana 66 44 6N 19 55 E
Razanj 66 43 40N 21 31 E
Razdelna 67 43 13N 27 41 E
Razelm, Lacul 70 44 50N 29 0 E
Razgrad 67 43 33N 26 34 E
Razlog 67 41 53N 23 28 E
Razmak 94 32 45N 69 50 E
Razole 96 16 56N 81 48 E
Razor Back Mt. 152 51 32N 125 0W
Ré, Île de 44 46 12N 1 30W
Rea, L. 39 53 10N 8 32W
Reading, U.K. 29 51 27N 0 57W
Reading, U.S.A. 162 40 20N 75 53W
Realicó 172 35 0 S 64 15W
Réalmont 44 43 48N 2 10 E
Ream 101 10 34N 103 39 E
Reata 164 26 8N 101 5W
Reay 37 58 33N 3 48W
Rebais 43 48 50N 3 10 E
Rebecca L. 137 30 0 S 122 30 E
Rebi 103 5 30 S 134 7 E
Rebiana 117 24 12N 22 10 E
Rebun-Tō 112 45 23N 141 2 E
Recanati 63 43 24N 13 32 E
Recaş 66 45 46N 21 30 E
Recess 38 53 29N 9 4W
Recherche, Arch. of the 137 34 15 S 122 50 E
Rechitsa 80 52 13N 30 15 E
Recht 47 50 20N 6 3 E
Recife 170 8 0 S 35 0W
Recklinghausen 48 51 36N 7 10 E
Reconquista 172 29 10 S 59 45W
Recreo 172 29 25 S 65 10W
Reculver 29 51 22N 1 12 E
Recz 54 53 16N 15 31 E
Red B. 38 55 4N 6 2W
Red Bank 162 40 21N 74 4W
Red Bay 151 51 44N 56 25W
Red Bluff 160 40 11N 122 11W
Red Bluff L. 159 31 59N 103 58W
Red Cliffs 140 34 19 S 142 11 E
Red Cloud 158 40 8N 98 33W
Red Creek 162 43 14N 76 45W
Red Deer 152 52 20N 113 50W
Red Deer L. 153 52 55N 101 20W
Red Deer, R. 152 50 58N 110 0W
Red Deer R. 153 52 53N 101 1W
Red Dial 32 54 48N 3 9W
Red Hook 162 41 55N 73 53W
Red Indian L. 151 48 35N 57 0W
Red L. 158 48 0N 95 0W
Red Lake 153 51 1N 94 1W
Red Lake Falls 158 47 54N 96 30W
Red Lion 162 39 54N 76 36W
Red Lodge 160 45 10N 109 10W
Red Mountain 163 35 37N 117 38W
Red Oak 158 41 0N 95 10W
Red Point Rock 137 32 13 S 127 32 E
Red, R., Can. 153 50 24N 96 48W
Red, R., Minn., U.S.A. 158 48 10N 97 0W
Red, R., Tex., U.S.A. 159 33 57N 95 30W
Red, R. = Hong, R. 100 20 17N 106 34 E
Red Rock 150 48 55N 88 15W
Red Rock, L. 158 41 30N 93 15W
Red Sea 91 25 0N 36 0 E
Red Slate Mtn. 163 37 31N 118 52W
Red Sucker L 153 54 9N 93 40W
Red Tower Pass = Turnu Rosu P. 70 45 33N 24 17 E
Red Wharf Bay 31 53 18N 4 10W
Red Wing 158 44 32N 92 35W
Reda 54 54 40N 18 19 E
Rédange 47 49 46N 5 52 E
Redbank 108 27 36 S 152 52 E
Redbridge 29 51 35N 0 7 E
Redcar 33 54 37N 1 4W
Redcliff 153 50 10N 110 50W
Redcliffe 139 27 12 S 153 0 E
Redcliffe, Mt. 137 28 30 S 121 30 E
Redcliffs 138 34 16 S 142 10 E
Reddersburg 128 29 41 S 26 10 E
Redding 160 40 30N 122 25W
Redditch 28 52 18N 1 57W
Rede, R. 35 55 8N 2 12W
Redenção 170 4 13 S 38 43W
Redesmouth 35 55 7N 2 12W
Redfield 158 45 0N 98 30W
Redhill 29 51 14N 0 10W
Redknife, R. 152 61 14N 119 22W
Redland 37 59 6N 3 4W
Redlands 163 34 0N 117 11W
Redlynch 28 50 59N 1 42W
Redmile 33 52 54N 0 48W
Redmire 32 54 19N 1 55W
Redmond, Austral. 137 34 55 S 117 40 E
Redmond, U.S.A. 160 44 19N 121 11W
Redon 42 47 40N 2 6W
Redonda, I. 167 16 58N 62 19W
Redondela 56 42 15N 8 38W
Redondo 57 38 39N 7 37W
Redondo Beach 163 33 52N 118 26W
Redrock Pt. 152 62 11N 115 2W
Redruth 30 50 14N 5 14W
Redvers 153 49 35N 101 40W
Redwater 152 53 55N 113 6W
Redwood City 163 37 30N 122 15W
Redwood Falls 158 44 30N 95 2W
Ree, L. 38 53 35N 8 0W
Reed City 156 43 52N 85 30W
Reed L. 153 54 38N 100 30W
Reed, Mt. 151 52 5N 68 5W
Reeder 158 47 7N 102 52W
Reedham 29 52 34N 1 33 E
Reedley 163 36 36N 119 27W
Reedsburg 158 43 34N 90 5W
Reedsport 160 43 45N 124 4W
Reedy Creek 140 36 58 S 140 2 E
Reef Pt. 142 35 10 S 173 5 E
Reefton, N.S.W., Austral. 141 34 15 S 147 27 E
Reefton, S. Australia, Austral. 109 34 57 S 138 55 E
Reefton, N.Z. 143 42 6 S 171 51 E
Reepham 29 52 46N 1 6 E
Reeth 32 54 23N 1 56W
Refsnes 71 61 9N 7 14 E
Reftele 73 57 11N 13 35 E
Refugio 159 28 18N 97 17W
Rega, R. 54 53 52N 15 16 E
Regalbuto 65 37 40N 14 38 E
Regar 85 38 30N 68 14 E
Regavim 90 32 32N 35 2 E
Regen 49 48 58N 13 9 E
Regeneração 170 6 15 S 42 41W
Regensburg 49 49 1N 12 7 E
Regensdorf 51 47 26N 8 28 E
Réggio di Calábria 65 38 7N 15 38 E
Réggio nell' Emilia 62 44 42N 10 38 E
Regina 153 50 30N 104 35W
Registan □ 93 30 15N 65 0 E
Registro 173 24 29 S 47 49W
Reguengos de Monsaraz 57 38 25N 7 32W
Rehar 95 23 36N 82 52 E
Rehoboth, Damaraland, Namibia 128 23 15 S 17 4 E
Rehoboth, Ovamboland, Namibia 128 17 55 S 15 5 E
Rehoboth Beach 162 38 43N 75 5W
Rehovot 90 31 54N 34 48 E
Reichenbach, Ger. 48 50 36N 12 19 E
Reichenbach, Switz. 50 46 38N 7 42 E
Reid 137 30 49 S 128 26 E
Reid River 138 19 40 S 146 48 E
Reiden 50 47 14N 7 59 E
Reidsville 157 36 21N 79 40W
Reigate 29 51 14N 0 11W
Reillo 58 39 54N 1 53W
Reims 43 49 15N 4 0 E
Reina 90 32 43N 35 18 E
Reina Adelaida, Arch. 176 52 20 S 74 0W
Reinach, Aargau, Switz. 50 47 14N 8 11 E
Reinach, Basel, Switz. 50 47 29N 7 35 E
Reinbeck 158 42 18N 92 40W
Reindeer I. 153 52 30N 98 0W
Reindeer L. 153 57 15N 102 15W
Reindeer, R. 153 55 36N 103 11W
Reine, La 150 48 50N 79 30W
Reinga, C. 142 34 25 S 172 43 E
Reinosa 56 43 2N 4 15W
Reinosa, Paso 56 42 56N 4 10W
Reira 123 15 25N 34 50 E
Reiss 37 58 29N 3 7W
Reisterstown 162 39 28N 76 50W
Reitdiep 46 53 20N 6 20 E
Reitz 129 27 48 S 28 29 E
Reivilo 128 27 36 S 24 8 E
Rejmyra 73 58 50N 15 55 E
Reka, R. 63 45 40N 14 0 E
Rekovac 66 43 51N 21 3 E
Remad, Ouedber 118 33 28N 1 20W
Remanso 170 9 41 S 42 4W
Remarkable, Mt. 140 32 48 S 138 10 E
Rembang 103 6 42 S 111 21 E
Remchi 118 35 2N 1 26W
Remedios, Colomb. 174 7 2N 74 41W
Remedios, Panama 166 8 15N 81 50W
Remeshk 93 26 55N 58 50 E
Remetea 70 46 45N 29 29 E
Remich 47 49 32N 6 22 E
Remiremont 43 48 0N 6 36 E
Remo 123 6 48N 41 20 E
Remontnoye 83 47 44N 43 37 E
Remoulins 45 43 55N 4 35 E
Remscheid 48 51 11N 7 12 E
Remsen 162 43 19N 75 11W
Rena 71 61 8N 11 20 E
Renda 123 14 30N 40 0 E
Rende 65 39 19N 16 11 E
Rendeux 47 50 14N 5 30 E
Rendina 69 39 4N 21 58 E
Rendsburg 48 54 18N 9 41 E
Rene 77 66 2N 179 25W
Renee, oilfield 19 58 4N 0 16 E
Renens 50 46 31N 6 34 E
Renfrew, Can. 150 45 30N 76 40W
Renfrew, U.K. 34 55 52N 4 24W
Renfrew (□) 26 55 50N 4 30W
Rengat 102 0 30 S 102 45 E
Rengo 172 34 24 S 70 50W
Reni 82 45 28N 28 15 E
Renigunta 97 13 38N 79 30 E
Renish Pt. 36 57 44N 6 59W
Renkum 46 51 58N 5 43 E
Renmark 140 34 11 S 140 43 E
Rennell Sd. 152 53 23N 132 35W

Renner Springs Teleg. Off
Riverton

Renner Springs Teleg. Off. 138 18 20S 133 47E
Rennes 42 48 7N 1 41W
Rennesøy 71 59 6N 5 43E
Reno 160 39 30N 119 50W
Reno, R. 63 44 45N 11 40E
Renovo 156 41 20N 77 47W
Rens 55 54 54N 9 5E
Rensselaer, Ind., U.S.A. 156 41 0N 87 10W
Rensselaer, N.Y., U.S.A. 162 42 38N 73 41W
Rentería 58 43 19N 1 54W
Renton 160 47 30N 122 9W
Renwicktown 143 41 30S 173 51E
Réo 120 12 28N 2 35E
Réole, La 44 44 35N 0 1W
Reotipur 95 25 33N 83 45E
Repalle 97 16 2N 80 45E
Répcelak 53 47 24N 17 1E
Repton 28 52 50N 1 32W
Republic, Mich., U.S.A. 156 46 25N 87 59W
Republic, Wash., U.S.A. 160 48 38N 118 42W
Republican City 158 40 9N 99 20W
Republican, R. 158 40 0N 98 30W
Repulse B., Antarct. 13 64 30S 99 30E
Repulse B., Austral. 133 20 31S 148 45E
Repulse Bay 149 66 30N 86 30W
Requena, Peru 174 5 5S 73 52W
Requena, Spain 59 39 30N 1 4W
Resele 72 63 20N 17 5E
Resen 66 41 5N 21 0E
Reserve, Can. 153 52 28N 102 39W
Reserve, U.S.A. 161 33 50N 108 54W
Resht = Rasht 92 37 20N 49 40E
Resistencia 172 27 30S 59 0W
Reşiţa 66 45 18N 21 53E
Resko 54 53 47N 15 25E
Resolution I., Can. 149 61 30N 65 0W
Resolution I., N.Z. 143 45 40S 166 40E
Resolven 31 51 43N 3 42W
Resplandes 170 6 17S 45 13W
Resplendor 171 19 20S 41 15W
Ressano Garcia 129 25 25S 32 0E
Rest Downs 141 31 48S 146 21E
Reston, Can. 153 49 33N 101 6W
Reston, U.K. 35 55 51N 2 11W
Restrepo 174 4 15N 73 33W
Reszel 54 54 4N 21 10E
Retalhuleu 166 14 33N 91 46W
Reteag 70 47 10N 24 0E
Retem, O. el 119 33 40N 0 40E
Retenue, Lac de 127 11 0S 27 0E
Rethel 43 49 30N 4 20E
Rethem 48 52 47N 9 25E
Réthimnon 69 35 15N 24 40E
Réthimnon □ 69 35 23N 24 28E
Retie 47 51 16N 5 5E
Rétiers 42 47 55N 1 25W
Retiro 172 35 59S 71 47W
Retortillo 56 40 48N 6 21W
Rétság 53 47 58N 19 10E
Reuland 47 50 12N 6 8E
Réunion, Î. 11 22 0S 56 0E
Reus 58 41 10N 1 5E
Reusel 47 51 21N 5 9E
Reuss, R. 51 47 16N 8 24E
Reuterstadt-Stavenhagen 48 53 41N 12 54E
Reutlingen 49 48 28N 9 13E
Reutte 52 47 29N 10 42E
Reuver 47 51 17N 6 5E
Revda 84 56 48N 59 57E
Revel 44 43 28N 2 0E
Revelganj 95 25 50N 84 40E
Revelstoke 152 51 0N 118 0W
Revigny 43 48 50N 5 0E
Revilla Gigedo, Is. de 131 18 40N 112 0W
Revillagigedo I. 152 55 50N 131 20W
Revin 43 49 55N 4 39E
Revolyutsii, Pix 85 38 31N 72 21E
Revuè, R. 127 19 30S 33 35E
Rewa 95 24 33N 81 25E
Rewari 94 28 15N 76 40E
Rex 147 64 10N 149 20W
Rexburg 160 43 45N 111 50W
Rey Bouba 117 8 40N 14 15E
Rey Malabo 121 3 45N 8 50E
Reyes, Pt. 163 37 59N 123 2W
Reykjahlið 74 65 40N 16 55W
Reykjanes 74 63 48N 22 40W
Reykjavík 74 64 10N 21 57E
Reynolds 153 49 40N 95 55W
Reynolds Ra. 136 22 30S 133 0E
Reynosa 165 26 5N 98 18W
Reza'iyeh 92 37 40N 45 0E
Rezā'iyeh, Daryācheh-ye 92 37 30N 45 30E
Rēzekne 80 56 30N 27 17E
Rezh 84 57 23N 61 24E
Rezina 70 47 45N 29 0E
Rezovo 67 42 0N 28 0E
Rgotina 67 44 1N 22 18E
Rhaeadr Ogwen 31 53 8N 4 0W
Rharis, O. 119 26 30N 5 4E
Rhayader 31 52 19N 3 30W
Rheden 46 52 0N 6 3E
Rheidol, R. 31 52 25N 3 57W
Rhein 153 51 25N 102 15W
Rhein, R. 48 51 42N 6 20E
Rheinbach 48 50 38N 6 54E
Rheine 48 52 17N 7 25E
Rheineck 51 47 28N 9 31E
Rheinfelden 50 47 32N 7 47E
Rheinland-Pfalz □ 49 50 50N 7 0E
Rheinsberg 48 53 6N 12 52E
Rheinwaldhorn 51 46 30N 9 3E
Rhenen 46 51 58N 5 33E
Rheydt 48 51 10N 6 24E
Rhin, R. 48 51 42N 6 20E
Rhinau 43 48 19N 7 43E
Rhine, R. = Rhein 47 51 42N 6 20E
Rhinebeck 162 41 56N 73 55W
Rhinelander 158 45 38N 89 29W
Rhino Camp 126 3 0N 31 22E
Rhisnes 47 50 31N 4 48E
Rhiw 31 52 49N 4 37W
Rho 62 45 31N 9 2E
Rhode Island □ 162 41 38N 71 37W
Rhodes = Ródhos 69 36 15N 28 10E
Rhodes' Tomb 127 20 30S 28 30E
* Rhodesia ■ 127 20 0S 30 0E
Rhodope Mts. = Rhodopi Planina 67 41 40N 24 20E
Rhodopi Planina 67 41 40N 24 20E
Rhondda 31 51 39N 3 30W
Rhône □ 45 45 54N 4 35E
Rhône, R. 45 43 28N 4 42E
Rhos-on-Sea 31 53 18N 3 46W
Rhosllanerchrugog 31 53 3N 3 4W
Rhossilli 31 51 34N 4 18W
Rhu Coigach, C. 36 58 6N 5 27W
Rhuddlan 31 53 17N 3 28W
Rhum, I. 36 57 0N 6 20W
Rhyl 31 53 19N 3 29W
Rhymney 31 51 45N 3 17W
Rhynie 37 57 20N 2 50W
Ri-Aba 121 3 28N 8 40E
Riachão 170 7 20S 46 37W
Riachão do Jacuípe 171 11 48S 39 21W
Riacho de Santana 171 13 37S 42 57W
Rialma 171 15 18S 49 34W
Rialto 163 34 6N 117 22W
Riang 98 27 31N 92 56E
Riaño 56 42 59N 5 0W
Rians 45 43 37N 5 44E
Riansares, R. 58 40 0N 3 0W
Riasi 95 33 10N 74 50E
Riau □ 102 0 0 102 35E
Riau, Kepulauan 102 0 30N 104 20E
Riaza 58 41 18N 3 30W
Riaza, R. 58 41 16N 3 29W
Riba de Saelices 58 40 55N 2 18E
Ribadavia 56 42 17N 8 8W
Ribadeo 56 43 35N 7 5W
Ribadesella 56 43 30N 5 7W
Ribamar 170 2 33S 44 3W
Ribas 58 42 19N 2 15E
Ribat 125 29 50N 60 55E
Ribatejo □ 55 39 15N 8 30W
Ribble, R. 32 54 13N 2 20W
Ribe 73 55 19N 8 44E
Ribe Amt □ 73 55 34N 8 30E
Ribeauvillé 43 48 10N 7 20E
Ribécourt 43 49 30N 2 55E
Ribeira 56 42 36N 8 58W
Ribeira do Pombal 170 10 50S 38 32W
Ribeirão Prêto 173 21 10S 47 50W
Ribeiro Gonçalves 170 7 32S 45 14W
Ribémont 43 49 47N 3 27E
Ribera 64 37 30N 13 13E
Ribérac 44 45 15N 0 20E
Riberalta 174 11 0S 66 0W
Ribnica 63 45 45N 14 45E
Ribnitz-Dangarten 48 54 14N 12 24E
Ričany 52 50 0N 14 40E
Riccall 33 53 50N 1 4W
Riccarton 143 43 32S 172 37E
Riccia 65 41 30N 14 50E
Riccione 63 44 0N 12 39E
Rice Lake 158 45 30N 91 42W
Rich 118 32 16N 4 30W
Rich Hill 159 38 5N 94 22W
Richards B. 129 28 48S 32 6E
Richards Deep 15 25 0S 73 0W
Richards L. 153 59 10N 107 10W
Richardson Mts. 143 44 49S 168 34E
Richardson, R. 153 58 25N 111 14W
Richardton 158 46 56N 102 22W
Riche, C. 137 34 36S 118 47E
Richelieu 42 47 0N 0 20E
Richey 158 47 42N 105 5W
Richfield, Idaho, U.S.A. 160 43 2N 114 5W
Richfield, Utah, U.S.A. 161 38 50N 112 0W
Richfield Springs 162 42 51N 74 59W
Richibucto 151 46 42N 64 54W
Richland, Ga., U.S.A. 157 32 7N 84 40W
Richland, Oreg., U.S.A. 160 44 49N 117 9W
Richland, Wash., U.S.A. 160 46 15N 119 15W
Richland Center 158 43 21N 90 22W
Richlands 156 37 7N 81 49W
Richmond, N.S.W., Austral. 141 33 35S 150 42E
Richmond, Queens., Austral. 138 20 43S 143 8E
Richmond, N.Z. 143 41 4S 173 12E
Richmond, S. Afr. 125 29 51S 30 18E
Richmond, N. Yorks., U.K. 33 54 24N 1 43W
Richmond, Surrey, U.K. 29 51 28N 0 18W
Richmond, Calif., U.S.A. 163 38 0N 122 21W
Richmond, Ind., U.S.A. 156 39 50N 84 50W
Richmond, Ky., U.S.A. 156 37 40N 84 20W
Richmond, Mo., U.S.A. 158 39 15N 93 58W
Richmond, Tex., U.S.A. 159 29 32N 95 42W
Richmond, Va., U.S.A. 162 37 33N 77 27W
Richmond Gulf 150 56 20N 75 50W
Richmond, Mt. 143 41 32S 173 22E
Richmond, Ra. 139 29 0S 152 45E
Richmond Ra. 143 41 32S 173 22E
Richterswil 51 47 13N 8 43E
Richton 157 31 23N 88 58W
Richwood 156 38 17N 80 32W
Rickmansworth 29 51 38N 0 28W
Ricla 58 41 31N 1 24W
Riddarhyttan 72 59 49N 15 33E
Ridderkerk 46 51 52N 4 35E
Riddes 50 46 11N 7 14E
Ridgecrest 163 35 38N 117 40W
Ridgedale 153 53 0N 104 10W
Ridgefield 162 41 17N 73 30W
Ridgeland 157 32 30N 80 58W
Ridgelands 138 23 16S 150 17E
Ridgetown 150 42 26N 81 52W
Ridgewood 162 40 59N 74 7W
Ridgway 156 41 25N 78 43W
Riding Mt. Nat. Park 153 50 50N 100 0W
Ridley Mt. 137 33 12S 122 7E
Ridsdale 35 55 9N 2 8W
Ried 52 48 14N 13 30E
Riehen 50 47 35N 7 39E
Riel 47 51 31N 5 1E
Rienne 47 50 0N 4 53E
Rienza, R. 63 46 49N 11 47E
Riesa 48 51 19N 13 19E
Riesi 65 37 16N 14 4E
Rietfontein 128 26 44S 20 1E
Rieti 63 42 23N 12 50E
Rieupeyroux 44 44 19N 2 12E
Rievaulx 33 54 16N 1 7W
Riez 45 43 49N 6 6E
Rifle 160 39 40N 107 50W
Rifstangi 74 66 32N 16 12W
Rift Valley 126 0 20N 36 0E
Rig Rig 117 14 13N 14 25E
Riga 80 56 53N 24 8E
Riga, G. of = Rīgas Jūras Līcis 80 57 40N 23 45E
Rīgas Jūras Līcis 80 57 40N 23 45E
Rigby 160 43 41N 111 58W
Riggins 160 45 29N 116 26W
Rignac 44 44 25N 2 16E
Rigo 138 9 41S 147 31E
Rigolet 151 54 10N 58 23W
Riihimäki 75 60 45N 24 48E
Riiser-Larsen halvøya 13 68 0S 35 0E
Riishiri-Tō 112 45 11N 141 15E
Rijau 121 11 8N 5 17E
Rijeka Crnojevica 66 42 24N 19 1E
Rijeka (Fiume) 63 45 20N 14 21E
Rijen 47 51 35N 4 55E
Rijkevorsel 47 51 21N 4 46E
Rijn, R. 47 52 5N 4 50E
Rijnsberg 46 52 11N 4 27E
Rijssbergen 47 51 31N 4 41E
Rijssen 46 52 19N 6 30E
Rijswijk 46 52 4N 4 22E
Rike 123 10 50N 39 53E
Rikita 123 5 5N 28 29E
Rila 67 42 7N 23 7E
Rila Planina 66 42 10N 23 30E
Rillington 33 54 10N 0 41W
Rilly 43 49 11N 4 3E
Rima 99 28 35N 97 5E
Rima, R. 121 13 15N 5 15E
Rimavská Sobota 53 48 22N 20 2E
Rimbey 152 52 35N 114 15W
Rimbo 72 59 44N 18 21E
Rimforsa 73 58 8N 15 42E
Rimi 121 12 58N 7 43E
Rímini 63 44 3N 12 33E
Rîmna, R. 70 45 36N 27 3E
Rîmnicu Sărat 70 45 26N 27 3E
Rîmnicu Vîlcece 70 45 9N 24 21E
Rimouski 151 48 27N 68 30W
Rinca 103 8 45S 119 35E
Rincón de Romos 164 22 14N 102 18W
Rinconada 172 22 26S 66 10W
Ringarum 73 58 21N 16 26E
Ringe 73 55 13N 10 28E
Ringel Spitz 51 46 53N 9 19E
Ringford 35 54 55N 4 3W
Ringim 121 12 13N 9 10E
Ringkøbing 73 56 5N 8 15E
Ringkøbing Amt □ 73 56 15N 8 30E
Ringling 160 46 16N 110 56W
Ringmer 29 50 53N 0 5E
Ringmoen 71 60 21N 10 6E
Ringsaker 71 60 54N 10 45E
Ringsend 38 55 2N 6 45W
Ringsjön L. 73 55 55N 13 30E
Ringsted 73 55 25N 11 46E
Ringvassøy 74 69 36N 19 15E
Ringville 39 52 3N 7 37W
Ringwood 28 50 50N 1 48W
Rinía, I. 69 37 23N 25 13E
Rinjani 65 8 20S 116 30E
Rinns, The, Reg. 34 54 52N 5 3W
Rintein 48 52 11N 9 3E
Rio Arica 174 1 35S 75 30W
Rio Branco 174 9 58S 67 49W
Río Branco 173 32 40S 53 40W
Rio Brilhante 173 21 48S 54 33W
Rio Chico 174 10 19N 65 59W
Rio Claro, Brazil 173 22 19S 47 35W
Rio Claro, Trin 167 10 20N 61 25W
Rio Colorado 176 39 0S 64 0W
Río Cuarto 172 33 10S 64 25W
Rio das Pedras 129 23 8S 35 28E
Rio de Contas 171 13 36S 41 48W
Rio de Janeiro 173 23 0S 43 12W
Rio de Janeiro □ 173 22 50S 43 0W
Rio del Rey 121 4 42N 8 37E
Rio do Prado 171 16 35S 40 34W
Rio do Sul 173 27 95S 49 37W
Río Gallegos 176 51 35S 69 15W
Río Grande 176 53 50S 67 45W
Rio Grande 173 32 0S 52 20W
Río Grande, Mexico 164 23 50N 103 2W
Río Grande, Nic. 166 12 54N 83 33W
Rio Grande City 159 26 30N 91 55W
Río Grande del Norte, R. 154 26 0N 97 0W
Rio Grande do Norte □ 170 5 40S 36 0W
Rio Grande do Sul □ 173 30 0S 53 0W
Rio Grande, R. 161 37 47N 106 15W
Río Hato 166 8 22N 80 10W
Rio Lagartos 165 21 36N 88 10W
Rio Largo 171 9 28S 35 50W
Rio Maior 57 39 19N 8 57W
Rio Marina 62 42 48N 10 25E
Río Mulatos 174 19 40S 66 50W
Rio Muni □ = Mbini □ 124 1 30N 10 0E
Rio Negro 173 26 0S 50 0W
Río Oriente 166 22 17N 81 13W
Rio Pardo, Minas Gerais, Brazil 171 15 55S 42 30W
Rio Pardo, Rio Grande do Sul, Brazil 173 30 0S 52 30W
Rio Prêto, Serra do 171 13 29S 39 55W
Rio, Punta del 59 36 49N 2 24W
Rio Real 171 11 28S 37 56W
Río Segundo 172 31 40S 63 59W
Río Tercero 172 32 15S 64 8W
Rio Tinto, Brazil 170 6 48S 35 5W
Rio Tinto, Port. 56 41 11N 8 34W
Rio Verde 170 17 50S 51 0W
Río Verde 165 21 56N 99 59W
Rio Vista 163 38 11N 121 44W
Ríobamba 174 1 50S 78 45W
Riohacha 174 11 33N 72 55W
Rioja, La, Argent. 172 29 20S 67 0W
Rioja, La, Spain 58 42 20N 2 20W
Rioja, La □ 172 29 30S 67 0W
Riom 44 45 54N 3 7E
Riom-ès-Montagnes 44 45 17N 2 39E
Rion-des-Landes 44 43 55N 0 56W
Rionegro 174 6 9N 75 22W
Rionero in Vúlture 65 40 55N 15 40E
Ríos 56 41 58N 7 16W
Riosucio, Caldas, Colomb. 174 5 30N 75 40W
Riosucio, Choco, Colomb. 174 7 27N 77 7W
Riou L. 153 59 7N 106 25W
Riparia, Dora, R. 62 45 7N 7 24E
Ripatransone 63 43 0N 13 45E
Ripley, Derby, U.K. 33 53 3N 1 24W
Ripley, N. Yorks, U.K. 33 54 3N 1 34W
Ripley, U.S.A. 159 35 43N 89 34W
Ripoll 58 42 15N 2 13E
Ripon, Calif., U.S.A. 163 37 44N 121 7W
Ripon, Wis., U.S.A. 156 43 51N 88 50W
Riposto 65 37 44N 15 12E
Risalpur 94 34 3N 71 59E
Risan 66 42 32N 18 42E
Risca 31 51 36N 3 6W
Riscle 44 43 39N 0 5W
Rishon Le Zion 90 31 58N 34 48E
Rishpon 90 32 12N 34 49E
Rishton 32 53 46N 2 26W
Riska 71 58 56N 5 52E
Risle, R. 42 48 55N 0 41E
Rîsnov 70 45 35N 25 27E
Rison 159 33 57N 92 11W
Risør 71 58 43N 9 13E
Ritchie's Archipelago 101 12 5N 94 0E
Riti 121 7 57N 9 41E
Ritzville 160 47 10N 118 21W
Riu 98 28 19N 95 3E
Riva Bella Ouistreham 42 49 17N 0 18W
Riva del Garda 62 45 53N 10 50E
Rivadavia, Buenos Aires, Argent. 172 35 29S 62 59W
Rivadavia, Mendoza, Argent. 172 33 13S 68 30W
Rivadavia, Salta, Argent. 172 24 5S 63 0W
Rivadavia, Chile 172 29 50S 70 35W
Rivarolo Canavese 62 45 20N 7 42E
Rivas 166 11 30N 85 50W
Rive-de-Gier 45 45 32N 4 37E
River Cess 120 5 30N 9 25W
Rivera 173 31 0S 55 50W
Riverchapel 39 52 38N 6 14W
Riverdale 163 36 26N 119 52W
Riverhead 162 40 53N 72 40W
Riverhurst 153 50 55N 106 50W
Riverina 136 29 45S 120 40E
Riverina, dist. 133 35 30S 145 20E
Rivers 153 50 2N 100 14W
Rivers □ 121 5 0N 6 30E
Rivers Inlet 152 51 40N 127 20W
Rivers, L. of the 153 49 49N 105 44W
Riversdal 128 34 7S 21 15E
Riverside, Calif., U.S.A. 163 34 0N 117 22W
Riverside, Wyo., U.S.A. 160 41 12N 106 57W
Riversleigh 138 19 5S 138 48E
Riverton, Austral. 140 34 10S 138 46E

* Renamed Zimbabwe Rhodesia

**Riverton** — **Ross and Cromarty (□)**


| | | | |
|---|---|---|---|
| Riverton, Can. | 153 | 51 5N | 97 0W |
| Riverton, N.Z. | 143 | 46 21S | 168 0E |
| Riverton, U.S.A. | 160 | 43 1N | 108 27W |
| Riverview | 108 | 27 36S | 152 51E |
| Rives | 45 | 45 21N | 5 31E |
| Rivesaltes | 44 | 42 47N | 2 50E |
| Riviera | 62 | 44 0N | 8 30E |
| Rivière à Pierre | 151 | 46 57N | 72 12W |
| Rivière-au-Renard | 151 | 48 59N | 64 23W |
| Rivière Bleue | 151 | 47 26N | 69 2W |
| Rivière-du-Loup | 151 | 47 50N | 69 30W |
| Rivière Pontecôte | 151 | 49 57N | 67 1W |
| Rívoli | 62 | 45 3N | 7 31E |
| Rivoli B. | 140 | 37 32S | 140 3E |
| Rivungo | 128 | 16 9S | 21 51E |
| Riwaka | 143 | 41 5S | 172 59E |
| Rixensart | 47 | 50 43N | 4 32E |
| Riyadh = Ar Riyad | 92 | 24 41N | 46 42E |
| Rize | 92 | 41 0N | 40 30E |
| Rizzuto, C. | 65 | 38 54N | 17 5E |
| Rjukan | 71 | 59 54N | 8 33E |
| Roa, Norway | 71 | 60 17N | 10 37E |
| Roa, Spain | 56 | 41 41N | 3 56W |
| Road Town | 167 | 18 27N | 64 37W |
| Road Weedon | 28 | 52 14N | 1 6W |
| Roade | 29 | 52 10N | 0 53W |
| Roadhead | 32 | 55 4N | 2 44W |
| Roag, L. | 36 | 58 10N | 6 55W |
| Roan Antelope | 127 | 13 2S | 28 19E |
| Roanne | 45 | 46 3N | 4 4E |
| Roanoke, Ala., U.S.A. | 157 | 33 9N | 85 23W |
| Roanoke, Va., U.S.A. | 156 | 37 19N | 79 55W |
| Roanoke I. | 157 | 35 55N | 75 40W |
| Roanoke, R. | 157 | 36 15N | 77 20W |
| Roanoke Rapids | 157 | 36 36N | 77 42W |
| Roaringwater B. | 39 | 51 30N | 9 30W |
| Roatán | 166 | 16 18N | 86 35W |
| Robbins I. | 138 | 40 42S | 145 0E |
| Robe, R., Austral. | 136 | 21 42S | 116 15E |
| Robe, R., Ireland | 38 | 53 38N | 9 10W |
| Röbel | 48 | 53 24N | 12 37E |
| Robert Lee | 159 | 31 55N | 100 26W |
| Robert Pt. | 137 | 32 34S | 115 40E |
| Roberton | 35 | 55 24N | 2 53W |
| Roberts | 160 | 43 44N | 112 8W |
| Robertsganj | 95 | 24 44N | 83 12E |
| Robertson, Austral. | 132 | 34 37S | 150 36E |
| Robertson, S. Afr. | 128 | 33 46S | 19 50E |
| Robertson I. | 13 | 68 0S | 75 0W |
| Robertson Ra. | 136 | 23 15S | 121 0E |
| Robertsport | 120 | 6 45N | 11 26W |
| Robertstown, Austral. | 140 | 33 58S | 139 5E |
| Robertstown, Ireland | 39 | 53 16N | 6 50W |
| Roberval | 150 | 48 32N | 72 15W |
| Robeson Kanal | 12 | 82 0N | 61 30W |
| Robesonia | 162 | 40 21N | 76 8W |
| Robin Hood's B. | 33 | 54 26N | 0 31W |
| Robinson Crusoe I. | 143 | 33 50S | 78 30W |
| Robinson, R. | 138 | 16 3S | 137 16E |
| Robinson Ranges | 137 | 25 40S | 118 0E |
| Robinson River | 138 | 16 45S | 136 58E |
| Robinvale | 140 | 34 40S | 142 45E |
| Robla, La | 56 | 42 50N | 5 41W |
| Roblin | 153 | 51 14N | 101 21W |
| Roboré | 174 | 18 10S | 59 45W |
| Robson, Mt. | 152 | 53 10N | 119 10W |
| Robstown | 159 | 27 47N | 97 40W |
| Roca, C. da | 57 | 38 40N | 9 31W |
| Roca Partida, I. | 164 | 19 1N | 112 2W |
| Roçadas | 128 | 16 45S | 15 0E |
| Rocas, I. | 170 | 4 0S | 34 1W |
| Rocca d'Aspidé | 65 | 40 27N | 15 10E |
| Rocca San Casciano | 63 | 44 3N | 11 30E |
| Roccalbegna | 63 | 42 47N | 11 30E |
| Roccastrada | 63 | 43 0N | 11 10E |
| Rocella Iónica | 65 | 38 20N | 16 24E |
| Rocester | 32 | 52 56N | 1 50W |
| Rocha | 173 | 34 30S | 54 25W |
| Rochdale | 32 | 53 36N | 2 10W |
| Roche | 30 | 50 24N | 4 50W |
| Roche-Bernard, La | 42 | 47 31N | 2 19W |
| Roche-Canillac, La | 44 | 45 12N | 1 57E |
| Roche-en-Ardenne, La | 47 | 50 11N | 5 35E |
| Roche, La, France | 45 | 46 4N | 6 19E |
| Roche, La, Switz. | 50 | 46 42N | 7 7E |
| Roche-sur-Yon, La | 42 | 46 40N | 1 25W |
| Rochechouart | 44 | 45 50N | 0 49E |
| Rochefort, Belg. | 47 | 50 9N | 5 12E |
| Rochefort, France | 44 | 45 56N | 0 57W |
| Rochefort-en-Terre | 42 | 47 42N | 2 22W |
| Rochefoucauld, La | 44 | 45 44N | 0 24E |
| Rochelle | 158 | 41 55N | 89 5W |
| Rochelle, La | 44 | 46 10N | 1 9W |
| Rocher River | 152 | 61 23N | 112 44W |
| Rocherath | 47 | 50 26N | 6 18E |
| Rocheservière | 42 | 46 57N | 1 30W |
| Rochester, Austral. | 140 | 36 22S | 144 41E |
| Rochester, Can. | 152 | 54 22N | 113 27W |
| Rochester, Kent, U.K. | 29 | 51 22N | 0 30E |
| Rochester, Northum., U.K. | 35 | 55 16N | 2 16W |
| Rochester, Ind., U.S.A. | 156 | 41 5N | 86 15W |
| Rochester, Minn., U.S.A. | 158 | 44 1N | 92 28W |
| Rochester, N.H., U.S.A. | 162 | 43 19N | 70 57W |
| Rochester, N.Y., U.S.A. | 156 | 43 10N | 77 40W |
| Rochford | 29 | 51 36N | 0 42E |
| Rochfortbridge | 38 | 53 25N | 7 19W |
| Rociana | 57 | 37 19N | 6 35W |
| Rociu | 70 | 44 43N | 25 2E |
| Rock Flat | 141 | 36 21S | 149 13E |
| Rock Hall | 162 | 39 8N | 76 14W |
| Rock Hill | 157 | 34 55N | 81 2W |
| Rock Island | 158 | 41 30N | 90 35W |
| Rock Lake | 158 | 48 50N | 99 13W |
| Rock, R. | 152 | 60 7N | 127 7W |
| Rock Rapids | 158 | 43 25N | 96 10W |
| Rock River | 160 | 41 49N | 106 0W |
| Rock Sound | 166 | 24 54N | 76 12W |
| Rock Sprs., Ariz., U.S.A. | 161 | 34 2N | 112 11W |
| Rock Sprs., Mont., U.S.A. | 160 | 46 55N | 106 11W |
| Rock Sprs., Tex., U.S.A. | 159 | 30 2N | 100 11W |
| Rock Sprs., Wyo., U.S.A. | 160 | 41 40N | 109 10W |
| Rock Valley | 158 | 43 10N | 96 17W |
| Rockall I. | 16 | 57 37N | 13 42W |
| Rockanje | 46 | 51 52N | 4 4E |
| Rockcliffe | 32 | 54 58N | 3 0W |
| Rockcorry | 38 | 54 7N | 7 0W |
| Rockdale | 159 | 30 40N | 97 0W |
| Rockefeller Plat. | 13 | 84 0S | 130 0W |
| Rockford | 158 | 42 20N | 89 0W |
| Rockglen | 153 | 49 11N | 105 57W |
| Rockhampton | 138 | 23 22S | 150 32E |
| Rockhampton Downs | 138 | 18 57S | 135 10E |
| Rockhill | 39 | 52 25N | 8 44W |
| Rockingham, Austral. | 137 | 32 15S | 115 38E |
| Rockingham, U.K. | 29 | 52 32N | 0 43W |
| Rockingham B. | 138 | 18 5S | 146 10E |
| Rockingham For. | 29 | 52 28N | 0 42W |
| Rockland, Idaho, U.S.A. | 160 | 42 37N | 112 57W |
| Rockland, Me., U.S.A. | 151 | 44 0N | 69 0W |
| Rockland, Mich., U.S.A. | 158 | 46 40N | 89 10W |
| Rockmart | 157 | 34 1N | 85 2W |
| Rockmills | 39 | 52 13N | 8 25W |
| Rockport, Mass., U.S.A. | 162 | 42 39N | 70 36W |
| Rockport, Mo., U.S.A. | 158 | 40 26N | 95 30W |
| Rockport, Tex., U.S.A. | 159 | 28 2N | 97 3W |
| Rockville, Conn., U.S.A. | 162 | 41 51N | 72 27W |
| Rockville, Md., U.S.A. | 162 | 39 7N | 77 10W |
| Rockwall | 159 | 32 55N | 96 30W |
| Rockwell City | 158 | 42 20N | 94 35W |
| Rockwood | 157 | 35 52N | 84 40W |
| Rocky Ford | 158 | 38 7N | 103 45W |
| Rocky Gully | 137 | 34 30S | 117 0E |
| Rocky Lane | 152 | 58 31N | 116 22W |
| Rocky Mount | 157 | 35 55N | 77 48W |
| Rocky Mountain House | 152 | 52 22N | 114 55W |
| Rocky Mts. | 152 | 55 0N | 121 0W |
| Rocky Pt. | 137 | 33 30S | 123 57E |
| Rockyford | 152 | 51 14N | 113 10W |
| Rocroi | 43 | 49 55N | 4 30E |
| Rod | 93 | 28 10N | 63 5E |
| Roda, La, Albacete, Spain | 59 | 39 13N | 2 15W |
| Roda, La, Sevilla, Spain | 57 | 37 12N | 4 46W |
| Rødberg | 71 | 60 17N | 8 56E |
| Rødby | 73 | 54 41N | 11 23E |
| Rødby Havn | 73 | 54 39N | 11 22E |
| Roddickton | 151 | 50 51N | 56 8W |
| Rødding | 73 | 55 23N | 9 3E |
| Rødekro | 73 | 55 4N | 9 20E |
| Rodel | 36 | 57 45N | 6 57W |
| Roden | 46 | 53 8N | 6 26E |
| Rødenes | 71 | 59 35N | 11 34E |
| Rodenkirchen | 48 | 53 24N | 8 26E |
| Roderick I. | 152 | 52 38N | 128 22W |
| Rodez | 44 | 44 21N | 2 33E |
| Rodholívas | 68 | 40 55N | 24 0E |
| Rodhópi □ | 68 | 41 10N | 25 30E |
| Ródhos | 69 | 36 15N | 28 10E |
| Ródhos, I. | 69 | 36 15N | 28 10E |
| Roding R. | 29 | 51 31N | 0 7E |
| Rödjenäs | 73 | 57 33N | 14 50E |
| Rodna | 70 | 47 25N | 24 50E |
| Rodney, C. | 142 | 36 17S | 174 50E |
| Rodniki | 81 | 57 7N | 41 37E |
| Rodriguez, I. | 11 | 20 0S | 65 0E |
| Roe, R. | 38 | 55 0N | 6 56W |
| Roebling | 162 | 40 7N | 74 45W |
| Roebourne | 136 | 20 44S | 117 9E |
| Roebuck B. | 136 | 18 5S | 122 20E |
| Roebuck Plains P.O. | 136 | 17 56S | 122 28E |
| Roelofarendsveen | 46 | 52 12N | 4 38E |
| Roer, R. | 47 | 51 12N | 5 59E |
| Roermond | 47 | 51 12N | 6 0E |
| Roes Welcome Sd. | 149 | 65 0N | 87 0W |
| Roeselare | 47 | 50 57N | 3 7E |
| Rœulx | 47 | 50 31N | 4 7E |
| Rogachev | 80 | 53 8N | 30 5E |
| Rogagua, L. | 174 | 14 0S | 66 50W |
| Rogaland fylke □ | 75 | 59 12N | 6 20E |
| Rogans Seat, Mt. | 32 | 54 25N | 2 10W |
| Rogaóica | 66 | 44 4N | 19 40E |
| Rogaška Slatina | 63 | 46 15N | 15 42E |
| Rogate | 29 | 51 0N | 0 51W |
| Rogatec | 63 | 46 15N | 21 46E |
| Rogatin | 80 | 29 24N | 24 36E |
| Rogers | 159 | 36 20N | 94 0W |
| Rogers City | 156 | 45 25N | 83 49W |
| Rogerson | 160 | 42 10N | 114 40W |
| Rogersville | 157 | 36 27N | 83 1W |
| Roggan River | 151 | 54 25N | 79 32W |
| Roggel | 47 | 51 16N | 5 56E |
| Roggeveldberge | 128 | 32 10S | 20 10E |
| Roggiano Grávina | 65 | 39 37N | 16 9E |
| Rogliano, France | 45 | 42 57N | 9 30E |
| Rogliano, Italy | 65 | 39 11N | 16 20E |
| Rogoaguado, L. | 174 | 13 0S | 65 30W |
| Rogowo | 54 | 52 43N | 17 38E |
| Rogozno | 54 | 52 45N | 16 59E |
| Rogue, R. | 160 | 42 30N | 124 0W |
| Rohan | 42 | 48 4N | 2 45W |
| Rohnert Park | 163 | 38 16N | 122 40W |
| Rohrbach | 43 | 49 3N | 7 15E |
| Rohri | 94 | 27 45N | 68 51E |
| Rohri Canal | 94 | 26 15N | 68 27E |
| Rohtak | 94 | 28 55N | 76 43E |
| Roi Et | 100 | 15 56N | 103 40E |
| Roisel | 43 | 49 58N | 3 6E |
| Rojas | 172 | 34 10S | 60 45W |
| Rojo, C., Mexico | 165 | 21 33N | 97 20W |
| Rojo, C., W. Indies | 147 | 17 56N | 67 11W |
| Rokan, R. | 102 | 1 30N | 100 50E |
| Rokeby | 138 | 13 39S | 142 40E |
| Rokiskis | 80 | 55 55N | 25 35E |
| Rokitnoye | 81 | 50 57N | 35 56E |
| Rokycany | 52 | 49 43N | 13 35E |
| Rolândia | 173 | 23 5S | 52 0W |
| Røldal | 71 | 59 47N | 6 50E |
| Rolde | 46 | 52 59N | 6 39E |
| Rolette | 158 | 48 42N | 99 50W |
| Rolfstorp | 73 | 57 11N | 12 27E |
| Rolla, Kansas, U.S.A. | 159 | 37 10N | 101 40W |
| Rolla, Missouri, U.S.A. | 159 | 38 0N | 91 42W |
| Rolla, N. Dak., U.S.A. | 158 | 48 50N | 99 36W |
| Rollag | 71 | 60 2N | 9 18E |
| Rollands Plains | 141 | 31 17S | 152 42E |
| Rolle | 50 | 46 28N | 6 20E |
| Rolleston, Austral. | 138 | 24 28S | 148 35E |
| Rolleston, N.Z. | 143 | 43 35S | 172 24E |
| Rollingstone | 138 | 19 2S | 146 24E |
| Rom | 123 | 9 54N | 32 16E |
| Roma, Austral. | 139 | 26 32S | 148 49E |
| Roma, Italy | 64 | 41 54N | 12 30E |
| Roma, Sweden | 73 | 57 32N | 18 26E |
| Roman, Bulg. | 67 | 43 8N | 23 54E |
| Roman, Rumania | 70 | 46 57N | 26 55E |
| Romana, La | 167 | 18 27N | 68 57W |
| Romang, I. | 103 | 7 30S | 127 20E |
| Rômani | 122 | 30 59N | 32 38E |
| Romanija planina | 66 | 43 50N | 18 45E |
| Romano, Cayo | 166 | 22 0N | 77 30W |
| Romano di Lombardia | 62 | 45 32N | 9 45E |
| Romanovka = Bessarabka | 82 | 46 21N | 28 51E |
| Romans | 62 | 45 3N | 5 3E |
| Romanshorn | 51 | 47 33N | 9 22E |
| Romanzof, C. | 147 | 62 0N | 165 50W |
| Rombo □ | 126 | 3 10S | 37 30E |
| Rome, U.S.A. | 162 | 41 51N | 76 21W |
| Rome, Ga., U.S.A. | 157 | 34 20N | 85 0W |
| Rome, N.Y., U.S.A. | 162 | 43 14N | 75 29W |
| Rome = Roma | 64 | 41 54N | 12 30E |
| Romeleåsen | 73 | 55 34N | 13 33E |
| Romenây | 45 | 46 30N | 5 1E |
| Romeo | 151 | 47 28N | 57 4W |
| Romerike | 71 | 60 7N | 11 10E |
| Romilly | 43 | 48 31N | 3 44E |
| Romîni | 70 | 44 59N | 24 11E |
| Rommani | 118 | 33 31N | 6 40W |
| Romney | 156 | 39 21N | 78 45W |
| Romney Marsh | 29 | 51 0N | 1 0E |
| Romny | 80 | 50 48N | 33 28E |
| Rømø | 73 | 55 10N | 8 30E |
| Romodan | 80 | 50 0N | 33 15E |
| Romodanovo | 81 | 54 26N | 45 23E |
| Romont | 50 | 46 42N | 6 54E |
| Romorantin-Lanthenay | 43 | 47 21N | 1 45E |
| Romsdal, R. | 71 | 62 25N | 8 0E |
| Romsdalen | 74 | 62 25N | 7 50E |
| Romsey | 28 | 51 0N | 1 29W |
| Ron | 100 | 17 53N | 106 27E |
| Rona I. | 36 | 57 33N | 6 0W |
| Ronan | 160 | 47 30N | 114 11W |
| Ronas Hill | 36 | 60 33N | 1 25W |
| Ronay I. | 36 | 57 30N | 7 10W |
| Roncador Cay | 166 | 13 40N | 80 4W |
| Roncador, Serra do | 171 | 12 30S | 52 30W |
| Roncesvalles, Paso | 58 | 43 1N | 1 19W |
| Ronceverte | 156 | 37 45N | 80 28W |
| Ronciglione | 63 | 42 18N | 12 12E |
| Ronco, R. | 63 | 44 26N | 12 15E |
| Ronda | 57 | 36 46N | 5 12W |
| Ronda, Serranía de | 57 | 36 44N | 5 3W |
| Rondane | 71 | 61 57N | 9 50E |
| Rondón | 174 | 6 17N | 71 6W |
| Rondônia □ | 174 | 11 0S | 63 0W |
| Rong, Koh | 101 | 10 45N | 103 15E |
| Ronge, La, Can. | 153 | 55 5N | 105 20W |
| Ronge, La, Sask., Can. | 153 | 55 6N | 105 17W |
| Ronge, Lac La | 153 | 55 10N | 105 0W |
| Rongotea | 142 | 40 19S | 175 25E |
| Rønne | 73 | 55 6N | 14 44E |
| Ronne Land | 13 | 83 0S | 70 0W |
| Ronneby | 73 | 56 12N | 15 17E |
| Ronsard, C. | 137 | 24 46S | 113 10E |
| Ronse | 47 | 50 45N | 3 35E |
| Roodepoort-Maraisburg | 125 | 26 8S | 27 52E |
| Roodeschool | 46 | 53 25N | 6 46E |
| Roof Butte | 161 | 36 29N | 109 5W |
| Roompot | 47 | 51 37N | 3 44E |
| Roorkee | 94 | 29 52N | 77 59E |
| Roosendaal | 47 | 51 32N | 4 29E |
| Roosevelt, Minn., U.S.A. | 158 | 48 51N | 95 2W |
| Roosevelt, Utah, U.S.A. | 160 | 40 19N | 110 1W |
| Roosevelt I. | 13 | 79 0S | 161 0W |
| Roosevelt, Mt. | 152 | 58 20N | 125 20W |
| Roosevelt Res. | 161 | 33 46N | 111 0W |
| Roosky | 38 | 53 50N | 7 55W |
| Ropczyce | 54 | 50 4N | 21 38E |
| Roper, R. | 138 | 14 43S | 135 27E |
| Ropesville | 159 | 33 25N | 102 10W |
| Ropsley | 33 | 52 53N | 0 31W |
| Roque Pérez | 172 | 35 25S | 59 24W |
| Roquefort | 44 | 44 2N | 0 20W |
| Roquefort-sur-Souizon | 44 | 43 58N | 2 59E |
| Roquemaure | 45 | 44 3N | 4 48E |
| Roquetas | 58 | 40 50N | 0 30E |
| Roquevaire | 45 | 43 20N | 5 36E |
| Roraima □ | 174 | 2 0N | 61 30W |
| Roraima, Mt. | 174 | 5 10N | 60 40W |
| Rorketon | 153 | 51 24N | 99 35W |
| Røros | 71 | 62 35N | 11 23E |
| Rorschach | 51 | 47 28N | 9 30E |
| Rørvik | 74 | 64 54N | 11 15E |
| Rosa, U.S.A. | 160 | 38 15N | 122 16W |
| Rosa, Zambia | 127 | 9 33S | 31 15E |
| Rosa Brook | 137 | 33 57S | 115 10E |
| Rosa, C. | 119 | 37 0N | 8 16E |
| Rosa, Monte | 50 | 45 57N | 7 53E |
| Rosal | 56 | 41 57N | 8 51W |
| Rosal de la Frontera | 57 | 37 59N | 7 13W |
| Rosalia | 160 | 47 26N | 117 25W |
| Rosamund | 163 | 34 52N | 118 10W |
| Rosans | 45 | 44 24N | 5 29E |
| Rosario | 172 | 33 0S | 60 50W |
| Rosário, Maran., Brazil | 170 | 3 0S | 44 15W |
| Rosário, Rio Grande do Sul, Brazil | 176 | 30 15S | 55 0W |
| Rosario, Baja California, Mexico | 164 | 30 0N | 116 0W |
| Rosario, Durango, Mexico | 164 | 26 30N | 105 35W |
| Rosario, Sinaloa, Mexico | 164 | 23 0N | 106 0W |
| Rosario, Venez. | 174 | 10 19N | 72 19W |
| Rosario de la Frontera | 172 | 25 50S | 65 0W |
| Rosario de Lerma | 172 | 24 59S | 65 35W |
| Rosario del Tala | 172 | 32 20S | 59 10W |
| Rosário do Sul | 173 | 30 15S | 54 55W |
| Rosarito | 164 | 28 38N | 114 4W |
| Rosarno | 65 | 38 29N | 15 59E |
| Rosas | 58 | 42 19N | 3 10E |
| Rosas, G. de, | 55 | 42 10N | 3 15E |
| Rosburgh | 143 | 45 33S | 169 19E |
| Roscoe | 162 | 41 56N | 74 55W |
| Roscoff | 42 | 48 44N | 4 0W |
| Roscommon, Ireland | 38 | 53 38N | 8 11W |
| Roscommon, U.S.A. | 156 | 44 27N | 84 35W |
| Roscommon □ | 38 | 53 40N | 8 15W |
| Roscrea | 39 | 52 58N | 7 50W |
| Rose Blanche | 151 | 47 38N | 58 45W |
| Rose Harbour | 152 | 52 15N | 131 10W |
| Rose Ness | 37 | 58 52N | 2 50W |
| Rose Pt. | 152 | 54 11N | 131 39W |
| Rose, R. | 138 | 14 16S | 135 45E |
| Rose Valley | 153 | 52 19N | 103 49W |
| Roseau, Domin. | 167 | 15 20N | 61 30W |
| Roseau, U.S.A. | 158 | 48 51N | 95 46W |
| Rosebery | 138 | 41 46S | 145 33E |
| Rosebud, Austral. | 141 | 38 21S | 144 54E |
| Rosebud, U.S.A. | 159 | 31 5N | 97 0W |
| Roseburg | 160 | 43 10N | 123 10W |
| Rosedale, Austral. | 138 | 24 38S | 151 53E |
| Rosedale, U.S.A. | 159 | 33 51N | 91 0W |
| Rosedale Abbey | 33 | 54 22N | 0 51W |
| Rosée | 47 | 50 14N | 4 41E |
| Rosegreen | 39 | 52 28N | 7 51W |
| Rosehall | 37 | 57 59N | 4 36W |
| Rosehearty | 37 | 57 42N | 2 8W |
| Rosemarkie | 37 | 57 35N | 4 8W |
| Rosemary | 152 | 50 46N | 112 5W |
| Rosenallis | 39 | 53 10N | 7 25W |
| Rosenberg | 159 | 29 30N | 95 48W |
| Rosendaël | 43 | 51 3N | 2 24E |
| Rosenheim | 49 | 47 51N | 12 9E |
| Roseto degli Abruzzi | 63 | 42 40N | 14 2E |
| Rosetown | 153 | 51 35N | 108 3W |
| Rosetta = Rashîd | 122 | 31 21N | 30 22E |
| Roseville | 160 | 38 46N | 121 17W |
| Rosewood, N.S.W., Austral. | 141 | 35 38S | 147 52E |
| Rosewood, N.T., Austral. | 136 | 16 28S | 128 58E |
| Rosewood, Queens., Austral. | 139 | 27 38S | 152 36E |
| Rosh Haniqra, Kefar | 90 | 33 5N | 35 5E |
| Rosh Pinna | 90 | 32 58N | 35 32E |
| Rosh Ze'ira | 90 | 31 14N | 35 15E |
| Roshage C. | 73 | 57 7N | 8 35E |
| Rosières | 43 | 48 36N | 6 20E |
| Rosignano Marittimo | 62 | 43 23N | 10 28E |
| Rosignol | 174 | 6 15N | 57 30W |
| Roşiorĭ-de-Vede | 70 | 44 9N | 25 0E |
| Rositsa | 67 | 43 57N | 27 57E |
| Rositsa, R. | 67 | 43 10N | 25 30E |
| Roskeeragh Pt. | 38 | 54 22N | 8 40W |
| Roskhill | 36 | 57 24N | 6 31W |
| Roskilde | 73 | 55 38N | 12 3E |
| Roskilde Amt □ | 73 | 55 35N | 12 5E |
| Roskilde Fjord | 73 | 55 50N | 12 2E |
| Roskill, Mt. | 142 | 36 55S | 174 45E |
| Roslavl | 80 | 53 57N | 32 55E |
| Roslyn | 141 | 34 29S | 149 37E |
| Rosmaninhal | 57 | 39 44N | 7 5W |
| Røsnæs | 73 | 55 44N | 10 55E |
| Rosneath | 34 | 56 1N | 4 49W |
| Rosolini | 65 | 36 49N | 14 58E |
| Rosporden | 42 | 47 57N | 3 50W |
| Ross, Austral. | 138 | 42 2S | 147 30E |
| Ross, N.Z. | 143 | 42 53S | 170 49E |
| Ross, U.K. | 28 | 51 55N | 2 34W |
| Ross and Cromarty (□) | 26 | 57 43N | 4 50W |

Ross Dependency Sabang, O

Ross Dependency 13 70 0S 170 5W
Ross I. 13 77 30S 168 0E
Ross Ice Shelf 13 80 0S 180 0W
Ross L. 160 48 50N 121 0W
Ross on Wye 28 51 55N 2 34W
Ross River, Austral. 138 19 15S 146 51E
Ross River, Can. 147 62 30N 131 30W
Ross Sea 13 74 0S 178 0E
Rossa 51 46 23N 9 8E
Rossall Pt. 32 53 55N 3 2W
Rossan Pt. 38 54 42N 8 47W
Rossano Cálabro 65 39 36N 16 39E
Rossburn 153 50 40N 100 49W
Rosscahill 38 53 23N 9 15W
Rosscarbery 39 51 39N 9 1W
Rosscarbery B. 39 51 32N 9 0W
Rossel I. 138 11 30S 154 30E
Rosses B. 38 55 2N 8 30W
Rosses Point 38 54 17N 8 34W
Rosses, The 38 55 2N 8 20W
Rossignol, L., N.S., Can. 151 44 12N 65 0W
Rossignol, L., Qué., Can. 150 52 43N 73 40W
Rossing 128 22 30S 14 50E
Rossland 152 49 6N 117 50W
Rosslare 39 52 17N 6 23W
Rosslau 48 51 52N 12 15E
Rosslea 38 54 15N 7 11W
Rosso 120 16 40N 15 45W
Rossosh 83 50 15N 39 20E
Rossport 150 48 50N 87 30W
Rossum 46 51 48N 5 20E
Røssvatnet 74 65 45N 14 5E
Rossville 138 15 48S 145 15E
Rosthern 153 52 40N 106 20W
Rostock 48 54 4N 12 9E
Rostock □ 48 54 10N 12 30E
Rostov, Don, U.S.S.R. 83 47 15N 39 45E
Rostov, Moskva, U.S.S.R. 81 57 14N 39 25E
Rostrenen 42 48 14N 3 21W
Rostrevor 38 54 7N 6 12W
Roswell 159 33 26N 104 32W
Rosyth 35 56 2N 3 26W
Rota 57 36 37N 6 20W
Rotälven 72 61 30N 14 10E
Rotan 159 32 52N 100 30W
Rotem 47 51 3N 5 45E
Rotenburg 48 53 6N 9 24E
Rothbury 35 55 19N 1 55W
Rothbury Forest 35 55 19N 1 50W
Rothenburg 51 47 6N 8 16E
Rothenburg ob der Tauber 49 49 21N 10 11E
Rother, R. 29 50 59N 0 40W
Rotherham 33 53 26N 1 21W
Rothes 37 57 31N 3 12W
Rothesay, Can. 151 45 23N 66 0W
Rothesay, U.K. 34 55 50N 5 3W
Rothhaar G., mts. 50 51 6N 8 10E
Rothienorman 37 57 24N 2 28W
Rothrist 50 47 18N 8 54E
Rothwell, Northants, U.K. 29 52 25N 0 48W
Rothwell, W. Yorks., U.K. 33 53 46N 1 29W
Roti, I. 103 10 50S 123 0E
Rotkop 128 26 44S 15 27E
Roto 141 33 0S 145 30E
Roto Aira L. 142 39 3S 175 55E
Rotoehu L. 142 38 1S 176 32E
Rotoiti L. 142 41 51S 172 49E
Rotoma L. 142 38 2S 176 35E
Rotondella 65 40 10N 16 30E
Rotoroa Lake 143 41 55S 172 39E
Rotorua 142 38 9S 176 16E
Rotorua, L. 142 38 5S 176 18E
Rotselaar 47 50 57N 4 42E
Rottal 37 56 48N 3 1W
Rotten, R. 50 46 18N 7 36E
Rottenburg 49 48 28N 8 56E
Rottenmann 52 47 31N 14 22E
Rotterdam 46 51 55N 4 30E
Rottingdean 29 50 48N 0 3W
Rottnest I. 137 32 0S 115 27E
Rottumeroog 46 53 33N 6 34E
Rottweil 49 48 9N 8 38E
Rotuma, I. 130 12 25S 177 5E
Roubaix 43 50 40N 3 10E
Roudnice 52 50 25N 14 15E
Rouen 42 49 27N 1 4E
Rouergue 45 44 20N 2 20E
Rough, gasfield 19 53 50N 0 27E
Rough Pt. 39 52 19N 10 0W
Rough Ridge 143 45 10S 169 55E
Rouillac 44 45 47N 0 4W
Rouleau 153 50 10N 104 56W
Round Mt. 139 30 26S 152 16E
Round Mountain 163 38 46N 117 3W
Roundstone 38 53 24N 9 55W
Roundup 160 46 25N 108 35W
Roundwood 39 53 4N 6 14W
Rourkela 95 22 14N 84 50E
Rousay, I. 37 59 10N 3 2W
Rousky 38 54 44N 7 10E
Rousse, L'Île 45 43 27N 8 57E
Roussillon 45 45 24N 4 49E
Rouveen 46 52 37N 6 11E
Rouxville 128 30 11S 26 50E
Rouyn 150 48 20N 79 0W
Rovaniemi 74 66 29N 25 41E
Rovato 62 45 34N 10 0E
Rovenki 83 48 5N 39 27E
Rovereto 62 45 53N 11 3E
Rovigo 63 45 4N 11 48E
Rovinari 70 46 56N 23 10E
Rovinj 63 45 18N 13 40E
Rovira 174 4 15N 75 20W
Rovno 80 50 40N 26 10E
Rovnoye 81 50 52N 46 3E
Rovuma, R. 127 11 30S 36 10E
Rowanburn 35 55 5N 2 54W
Rowena 139 29 48S 148 55E
Rowes 141 37 0S 149 6E
Rowley Shoals 136 17 40S 119 20E
Rowood 161 32 18N 112 54W
Rowrah 32 54 34N 3 26W
Roxa 120 11 15N 15 45W
Roxas 103 11 36N 122 49E
Roxboro 157 36 24N 78 59W
Roxborough Downs 138 22 20S 138 45E
Roxburgh, N.Z. 143 45 33S 169 19E
Roxburgh, U.K. 35 55 34N 2 30W
Roxburgh (□) 26 55 30N 2 30W
Roxby 33 53 38N 0 37W
Roxen 73 58 30N 15 40E
Roy 160 47 17N 109 0W
Roy Hill 136 22 37S 119 58E
Roy, Le 159 38 8N 95 35W
Roya, Peña 58 40 25N 0 40W
Royal Canal 38 53 29N 7 0W
Royal Oak 156 42 30N 83 5W
Royalla 141 35 30S 149 9E
Royan 44 45 37N 1 2W
Roybridge 37 56 53N 4 50W
Roye 43 47 40N 6 31E
Røyken 71 59 45N 10 23E
Royston 29 52 3N 0 1W
Royton 32 53 34N 2 7W
Rozaj 66 42 50N 20 15E
Rozan 54 52 52N 21 25E
Rozdol 80 49 30N 24 1E
Rozier, Le 44 44 13N 3 12E
Roznava 53 48 37N 20 35E
Rozoy 43 48 40N 2 56E
Rozoy-sur-Serre 43 49 40N 4 8E
Rozwadów 54 50 37N 22 2E
Rrësheni 68 41 47N 19 49E
Rtanj, mt. 66 43 45N 21 50W
Rtem, Oued el 119 33 40N 5 34E
Rtishchevo 81 52 35N 43 50E
Rúa 56 42 24N 7 6W
Ruacaná 128 17 20S 14 12E
Ruahine Ra. 142 39 55S 176 2E
Ruamahanga, R. 142 41 24S 175 8E
Ruapehu 142 39 17S 175 35E
Ruapuke I. 143 46 46S 168 31E
Ruatoria 142 37 55S 178 20E
Ruâus, W. 119 30 14N 15 0E
Ruawai 142 36 15S 173 59E
Rub 'al Khali 91 21 0N 51 0E
Rubeho, mts. 126 6 50S 36 25E
Rubery 28 52 24N 1 59W
Rubezhnoye 82 49 6N 38 25E
Rubha Ardvule C. 36 57 17N 7 32W
Rubha Hunish, C. 36 57 42N 6 20W
Rubh'an Dunain, C. 36 57 10N 6 20W
Rubiataba 171 15 8S 49 48W
Rubicone, R. 63 44 0N 12 20E
Rubim 171 16 23S 40 32W
Rubinéia 171 20 13S 51 2W
Rubino 120 6 4N 4 18W
Rubio 174 7 43N 72 22W
Rubona 126 0 29N 30 9E
Rubtsovsk 76 51 30N 80 50E
Ruby 147 64 40N 155 35W
Ruby L. 160 40 10N 115 28W
Ruby Mts. 160 40 30N 115 30W
Rubyvale 138 23 25S 147 45E
Rucava 80 56 9N 20 32E
Ruciane-Nida 54 53 40N 21 32E
RûcûSdia 66 44 59N 21 36E
Rud 71 60 1N 10 1E
Ruda 73 57 6N 16 7E
Ruda Slaska 53 50 16N 18 50E
Rudall 140 33 43S 136 17E
Rudbar 93 30 0N 62 30E
Ruden, I. 48 54 13N 13 47E
Rüdersdorf 48 52 28N 13 48E
Rudewa 127 10 7S 34 47E
Rudgwick 29 51 7N 0 54W
Rudkøbing 73 54 56N 10 41E
Rudna 54 51 30N 16 17E
Rudnichnyy 84 59 38N 52 26E
Rudnik, Bulg. 67 42 36N 27 30E
Rudnik, Yugo. 67 44 7N 20 35E
Rudnik, mt. 67 44 7N 20 35E
Rudnogorsk 77 57 15N 103 42E
Rudnya 80 54 55N 31 13E
Rudnyy 84 52 57N 63 7E
Rudo 66 43 41N 19 23E
Rudolstadt 48 50 44N 11 20E
Rudozem 67 41 29N 24 51E
Rudston 33 54 6N 0 19W
Rûducaneni 70 46 58N 27 54E
Rûdŭuţi 70 47 50N 25 59E
Rudyard 156 46 14N 84 35E
Rue 43 50 15N 1 40E
Ruelle 44 45 41N 0 14E
Rufa'a 123 14 44N 33 32E
Ruffec Charente 44 46 2N 0 12W
Rufi 123 5 58N 30 18E
Rufiji □ 126 8 0S 38 30E
Rufiji, R. 124 7 50S 38 15E
Rufino 172 34 20S 62 50W
Rufisque 120 14 40N 17 15W
Rufunsa 127 15 4S 29 34E
Rugby, U.K. 28 52 23N 1 16W
Rugby, U.S.A. 158 48 21N 100 0W
Rugeley 28 52 47N 1 56W
Rügen, I. 48 54 22N 13 25E
Rugezi 126 2 6S 33 18E
Rugles 42 48 50N 0 40E
Ruhâma 90 31 31N 34 43E
Ruhea 98 26 10N 88 25E
Ruhengeri 126 1 30S 29 36E
Ruhla 48 50 53N 10 21E
Ruhland 48 51 27N 13 52E
Ruhr, R. 48 51 25N 7 15E
Ruhuhu, R. 127 10 15S 34 55E
Rui Barbosa 171 12 18S 40 27W
Ruidosa 159 29 59N 104 39W
Ruidoso 161 33 19N 105 39W
Ruinen 46 52 46N 6 21E
Ruinen A Kanaal 46 52 54N 7 8E
Ruinerwold 46 52 44N 6 15E
Ruj, mt. 66 42 52N 22 42E
Rujen, mt. 66 42 9N 22 30E
Ruk 94 27 50N 68 42E
Rukwa □, Tanz. 126 7 0S 31 30E
Rukwa □, Tanz. 126 7 0S 31 30E
Rukwa L. 126 7 50S 32 10E
Rulhieres, C. 136 13 56S 127 22E
Rulles 47 49 43N 5 32E
Rully 167 46 52N 4 44E
Rum Jungle 136 13 0S 130 59E
Ruma 66 45 8N 19 50E
Rumah 92 25 35N 47 10E
Rumania ■ 61 46 0N 25 0E
Rumbalara 138 25 20S 134 29E
Rumbek 123 6 54N 29 37E
Rumbeke 47 50 56N 3 10E
Rumburk 52 50 57N 14 32E
Rumelange 47 49 27N 6 2E
Rumford 156 44 30N 70 30W
Rumia 54 54 37N 18 25E
Rumilly 45 45 53N 5 56E
Rumney 31 51 32N 3 7W
Rumoi 112 43 56N 141 39W
Rumonge 126 3 59S 29 26E
Rumsey 152 51 51N 112 48W
Rumson 162 40 23N 74 0W
Rumula 138 16 35S 145 20E
Rumuruti 126 0 17N 36 32E
Runabay Hd. 38 55 10N 6 2W
Runanga 143 42 25S 171 15E
Runaway, C. 142 37 32S 178 2E
Runcorn, Austral. 108 27 36S 153 4E
Runcorn, U.K. 32 53 20N 2 44W
Rungwa 126 6 55S 33 32E
Rungwa, R. 126 7 15S 33 10E
Rungwe 127 9 11S 33 32E
Rungwe □ 127 9 25S 33 32E
Runka 121 12 28N 7 20E
Runn 72 60 30N 15 40E
Rupa 98 27 15N 92 30E
Rupar 94 31 2N 76 38E
Rupat, I. 102 1 45N 101 40E
Rupea 61 46 2N 25 13E
Rupert House = Fort Rupert 150 51 30N 78 40W
Rupert, R. 150 51 29N 78 45W
Rupsa 98 21 44N 87 20E
Rupununi, R. 175 3 30N 59 30W
Ruquka Gie La 99 31 35N 97 55E
Rurrenabaque 174 14 30S 67 32W
Rus, R. 58 39 30N 2 30W
Rusambo 127 16 30S 32 4E
Rusape 125 18 35S 32 8E
Ruschuk = Ruse 67 43 48N 25 59E
Ruse 67 43 48N 25 59E
Rusetu 70 44 57N 27 14E
Rush 38 53 31N 6 7W
Rushden 29 52 17N 0 37W
Rushford 158 43 48N 91 46W
Rushville, Ill., U.S.A. 158 40 6N 90 35W
Rushville, Ind., U.S.A. 156 39 38N 85 22W
Rushville, Nebr., U.S.A. 158 42 43N 102 35W
Rushworth 141 36 32S 145 1E
Rusken 73 57 15N 14 20E
Ruskington 33 53 5N 0 23W
Russas 171 4 56S 38 2W
Russell, Can. 153 50 50N 101 20W
Russell, N.Z. 142 35 16S 174 10E
Russell, U.S.A. 158 38 56N 98 55W
Russell L., Man., Can. 153 56 15N 101 30W
Russell L., N.W.T., Can. 152 63 5N 115 44W
Russellkonda 96 19 57N 84 42E
Russellville, Ala., U.S.A. 157 34 30N 87 44W
Russellville, Ark., U.S.A. 159 35 15N 93 0W
Russellville, Ky., U.S.A. 157 36 50N 86 50W
Russi 63 44 21N 12 1E
Russian Mission 147 61 45N 161 25W
Russian S.F.S.R. □ 77 62 0N 105 0E
Russkoye Ustie 12 71 0N 149 0E
Rust 53 47 49N 16 42E
Rustam 94 34 25N 72 13E
Rustam Shahr 94 26 58N 66 6E
Rustavi 83 40 45N 44 30E
Rustenburg 128 25 41S 27 14E
Ruston 159 32 30N 92 40W
Ruswil 50 47 5N 8 8E
Rutana 126 3 55S 30 0E
Rutba 92 33 4N 40 15E
Rute 57 37 19N 4 29W
Ruteng 103 8 26S 120 30E
Ruth 160 39 15N 115 1W
Ruth, oilfield 19 55 33N 4 55E
Rutherglen, Austral. 141 36 5S 146 29E
Rutherglen, U.K. 34 55 50N 4 11W
Ruthin 31 53 7N 3 20W
Ruthven 37 57 4N 4 2W
Ruthwell 35 55 0N 3 24W
Rüti 51 47 16N 8 51E
Rutigliano 65 41 1N 17 0E
Rutland 162 43 38N 73 0W
Rutland (□) 26 52 38N 0 40W
Rutland I. 101 11 25N 92 40E
Rutland Plains 138 15 38S 141 49E
Rutledge L. 153 61 33N 110 47W
Rutledge, R. 153 61 4N 112 0W
Rutshuru 126 1 13S 29 25E
Ruurlo 46 52 5N 6 24E
Ruvo di Púglia 65 41 7N 16 27E
Ruvu 126 6 49S 38 43E
Ruvu, R. 126 7 25S 38 15E
Ruvuma □ 127 10 20S 36 0E
Ruvuma, R. 127 11 30S 36 10E
Ruwaidha 92 23 40N 44 40E
Ruwandiz 92 36 40N 44 32E
Ruwenzori Mts. 126 0 30N 29 55E
Ruwenzori, mt. 126 0 30N 29 55E
Ruyigi 126 3 29S 30 15E
Ruzayevka 81 54 10N 45 0E
Ruzhevo Konare 67 42 23N 24 46E
Ruzomberok 53 49 3N 19 17E
Rwanda ■ 126 2 0S 30 0E
Ryaberg 73 56 47N 13 15E
Ryakhovo 67 44 0N 26 18E
Ryan, L. 34 55 0N 5 2W
Ryazan 81 54 50N 39 40E
Ryazhsk 81 53 45N 40 3E
Rybache 76 46 40N 81 20E
Rybachi Poluostrov 78 69 43N 32 0E
Rybachye 85 42 26N 76 12E
Rybinsk (Shcherbakov) 81 58 5N 38 50E
Rybinsk Vdkhr. 81 58 30N 38 0E
Rybnik 54 50 6N 18 32E
Rybnitsa 82 47 45N 29 0E
Rychwał 54 52 4N 18 10E
Ryd 73 56 27N 14 42E
Rydal 32 54 28N 2 59W
Ryde 28 50 44N 1 9W
Rydö 73 56 58N 13 10E
Rydsnäs 73 57 47N 15 9E
Rydułtowy 54 50 4N 18 23E
Rydzyna 54 51 47N 16 39E
Rye, Denmark 73 56 5N 9 45E
Rye, U.K. 29 50 57N 0 46E
Rye Patch Res. 160 40 45N 118 20W
Rye, R. 33 54 12N 0 53W
Ryegate 160 46 21N 109 27W
Ryhope 35 54 52N 1 22W
Rylsk 80 51 30N 34 51E
Rylstone 141 32 46S 149 58E
Rymanów 54 49 35N 21 51E
Ryn 54 53 57N 21 34E
Ryningsnäs 73 57 17N 15 58E
Ryōhaku-Sanchi 111 36 0N 136 49E
Rypin 54 53 3N 19 32E
Ryton, Tyne & Wear, U.K. 35 54 58N 1 44W
Ryton, Warwick, U.K. 28 52 23N 1 25W
Ryūgasaki 111 35 54N 140 11E
Ryūkyū Is. = Nansei-Shotō 112 26 0N 128 0E
Rzepin 54 52 20N 14 49E
Rzeszów 54 50 5N 21 58E
Rzeszów □ 54 50 0N 22 0E
Rzhev 80 56 20N 34 20E

# S

s'-Hertogenbosch 47 51 42N 5 17E
Sa 100 18 34N 100 45E
Sa. da Canastra 125 19 30S 46 5W
Sa Dec 101 10 20N 105 46E
Sa-Koi 98 19 54N 97 3E
Sa'ad (Muharraga) 90 31 28N 34 33E
Sa'ādatabād 93 30 10N 53 5E
Saale, R. 48 51 25N 11 56E
Saaler Bodden 48 54 20N 12 25E
Saalfelden 70 47 26N 12 51E
Saalfield 48 50 39N 11 21E
Saane, R. 50 46 23N 7 18E
Saanen 50 46 29N 7 15E
Saar (Sarre), □ 43 49 20N 6 45E
Saarbrücken 49 49 15N 6 58E
Saarburg 49 49 36N 6 32E
Saaremaa 80 58 30N 22 30E
Saariselkä 74 68 16N 28 15E
Saarland □ 131 49 20N 6 45E
Saarlouis 49 49 19N 6 45E
Saas Fee 50 46 7N 7 56E
Saas-Grund 50 46 7N 7 57E
Saba I. 167 17 30N 63 10W
Sabac 66 44 48N 19 42E
Sabadell 58 41 28N 2 7E
Sabae 111 35 57N 136 11E
Sabagalel 102 1 36S 98 40E
Sabah □ 102 6 0N 117 0E
Sabak 100 3 46N 100 58E
Sábana de la Mar 167 19 7N 69 40W
Sábanalarga 174 10 38N 74 55W
Sabang, O. 102 5 50N 95 15E

Sabará St. Lawrence

Sabará 171 19 55S 43 55W
Sabarania 103 2 5S 138 18E
Sabari, R. 96 18 0N 81 25E
Sabastiya 90 32 17N 35 12E
Sabaudia 64 41 17N 13 2E
Sabderat 123 15 26N 36 42E
Sabhah 119 27 9N 14 29E
Sabie 129 25 4S 30 48E
Sabinal, Mexico 164 30 50N 107 25W
Sabinal, U.S.A. 159 29 20N 99 27W
Sabinal, Punta del 59 36 43N 2 44W
Sabinas 164 27 50N 101 10W
Sabinas Hidalgo 164 26 40N 100 10W
Sabinas, R. 164 27 37N 100 42W
Sabine 159 29 42N 93 54W
Sabine, R. 159 31 30N 93 35W
Sabinópolis 171 18 40S 43 6W
Sabinov 53 49 6N 21 5E
Sabirabad 83 40 0N 48 30E
Sabkhat Tawurgha 119 31 48N 15 30E
Sablayan 103 12 5N 120 50E
Sable 42 47 50N 0 21W
Sable, C., Can. 151 43 29N 65 38W
Sable, C., U.S.A. 166 25 5N 81 0W
Sable I. 151 44 0N 60 0W
Sablé-sur-Sarthe 42 47 50N 0 20W
Sables-D'Olonne, Les 44 46 30N 1 45W
Saboeiro 170 6 32S 39 54W
Sabor, R. 56 41 16N 7 10W
Sabou 120 12 1N 2 28W
Sabrātah 119 32 47N 12 29E
Sabrina Coast 13 67 0S 120 0E
Sabugal 56 40 20N 7 5W
Sabzevar 93 36 15N 57 40E
Sabzvaran 93 28 45N 57 50E
Sac City 158 42 26N 95 0W
Sacandaga Res. 162 43 6N 74 16W
Sacedón 58 40 29N 2 41W
Sachigo, L. 150 53 50N 92 12W
Sachigo, R. 150 55 6N 88 58W
Sachinbulako 106 43 5N 111 47E
Sachkhere 83 42 25N 43 28E
Sachseln 51 46 52N 8 15E
Sacile 63 45 58N 16 7E
Säckingen 49 47 34N 7 56E
Saco, Me., U.S.A. 162 43 30N 70 27W
Saco, Mont., U.S.A. 160 48 28N 107 19W
Sacquoy Hd. 37 59 12N 3 5W
Sacramento, Brazil 171 19 53S 47 27W
Sacramento, U.S.A. 163 38 39N 121 30E
Sacramento Mts. 161 32 30N 105 30W
Sacramento, R. 163 38 3N 121 56W
Sacratif, Cabo 59 36 42N 3 28W
Sacriston 33 54 49N 1 38W
Sada 56 43 22N 8 15W
Sada-Misaki-Hantō 110 33 22N 132 1E
Sadaba 58 2 19N 1 12W
Sa'dani 124 5 58S 38 35E
Sadao 101 6 38N 100 26E
Sadasivpet 96 17 38N 77 50E
Sadberge 33 54 32N 1 30W
Sadd el Aali 122 24 5N 32 54E
Saddell 34 55 31N 5 30W
Saddle, Hd. 38 54 0N 10 10W
Saddle, The 36 57 10N 5 27W
Sade 121 11 22N 10 45E
Sadiba 128 18 53S 23 1E
Sadimi 127 9 25S 23 32E
Sado 112 38 0N 138 25E
Sado, R. 57 38 10N 8 22W
Sadon, Burma 99 25 28N 98 0E
Sadon, U.S.S.R. 83 42 52N 43 58E
Sadri 94 24 28N 74 30E
Saduya 98 27 50N 95 40E
Sæby 73 57 21N 10 30E
Saelices 58 39 55N 2 49W
Safâga 122 26 42N 34 0E
Safaha 122 26 25N 39 0E
Safaniya 92 28 5N 48 42E
Safárikovo 53 48 25N 20 20E
Safed Koh, Mts. 94 34 15N 64 0E
Safford 61 32 54N 109 52W
Saffron Walden 29 52 2N 0 15E
Safi, Jordan 90 31 2N 35 28E
Safi, Moroc. 118 32 18N 9 14W
Safiah 42 31 27N 34 46E
Safonovo 80 65 40N 47 50E
Safranbolu 82 41 15N 32 34E
Sag Harbor 162 40 59N 72 17W
Sag Sag 135 5 32S 148 23E
Saga, Indon. 103 2 40S 132 55E
Saga, Kōchi, Japan 110 33 5N 133 6E
Saga, Saga, Japan 110 33 15N 130 16E
Saga-ken □ 110 33 15N 130 20E
Sagåg 71 59 46N 5 25E
Sagaing 98 23 30N 95 30E
Sagaing □ 98 22 0N 95 30E
Sagala 120 14 9N 6 38W
Sagami-Nada 111 34 58N 139 23E
Sagami-Wan 111 35 15N 139 25E
Sagamihara 111 35 33N 139 25E
Saganoseki 110 33 15N 131 53E
Sagar 93 23 50N 78 50E
Sagara, India 97 14 14N 75 6E
Sagara, Japan 111 34 41N 138 12E
Sagara, L. 126 5 20S 31 0E
Sagawa 110 33 28N 133 11E
Sågen 72 60 17N 14 10E
Sagil 105 50 20N 91 40E
Saginaw 156 43 26N 83 55W
Saginaw B. 150 43 50N 83 40W
Sagleipie 45 45 25N 7 0E
Saglouc (Sugluk) 149 62 30N 74 15W
Sagone 45 42 7N 8 42E
Sagone, G. de 45 42 4N 8 40E
Sagori 107 35 25N 126 49E
Sagra, La, Mt. 59 38 0N 2 35W
Sagres 57 37 0N 8 58W
Sagu 98 20 13N 94 46E
Sagua la Grande 166 22 50N 80 10W
Saguache 161 38 10N 106 4W
Saguenay, R. 151 48 22N 71 0W
Sagunto 58 39 42N 0 18W
Sahaba 122 18 57N 30 25E
Sahagún, Colomb. 174 8 57N 75 27W
Sahagún, Spain 56 42 18N 5 2W
Saham 90 32 42N 35 46E
Sahara 118 23 0N 5 0W
Saharanpur 94 29 58N 77 33E
Saharien Atlas 118 34 9N 3 29E
Sahasinaka 129 21 49S 47 49E
Sahaswan 95 28 5N 78 45E
Sahel, Canal du 120 14 20N 6 0W
Sahibganj 95 25 12N 87 55E
Sahiwal 94 30 45N 73 8E
Sahl Arraba 90 37 26N 35 12E
Sahtaneh, R. 152 59 2N 122 28W
Sahuaripa 164 29 30N 109 0W
Sahuarita 161 31 58N 110 59W
Sahuayo 164 20 4N 102 43W
Sahy 53 48 4N 18 55E
Sai Buri 101 6 43N 101 39E
Saibai I. 135 9 25S 142 40E
Sa'id Bundas 117 8 24N 24 48E
Saïda 118 34 50N 0 11E
Sa'idabad 93 29 30N 55 45E
Saidapet 97 13 0N 80 15E
Saidor 135 5 40S 146 29E
Saidu 95 34 50N 72 15E
Säle 72 59 8N 12 55E
Saighan 93 35 10N 67 55E
Saignelégier 50 47 15N 7 0E
Saignes 44 45 20N 2 31E
Saigō 110 36 12N 133 20E
Saigon = Phanh Bho Ho Chi Minh 101 10 58N 106 40E
Saih-al-Malih 93 23 37N 58 31E
Saihut 91 15 12N 51 10E
Saijō, Ehima, Japan 110 33 55N 133 11E
Saijō, Hiroshima, Japan 110 34 25N 132 45E
Saikhoa Ghat 99 27 50N 95 40E
Saiki 110 32 58N 131 57E
Saillans 45 44 42N 5 12E
Sailolof 103 1 7S 130 46E
Saima 107 40 59N 124 15E
Saimaa, L. 78 61 15N 28 15E
St. Abbs 35 55 54N 2 7W
St. Abb's Head 35 55 55N 2 10W
St. Aegyd 52 47 52N 15 33E
St. Affrique 44 43 57N 2 53E
St. Agnes 30 50 18N 5 13W
St. Agnes Hd. 30 50 19N 5 14W
St. Agnes I. 30 49 53N 6 20W
St.-Agrève 45 45 0N 4 23E
St.-Aignan 42 47 16N 1 22E
St. Albans, Austral. 138 24 43S 139 56E
St. Albans, Can. 151 47 51N 55 50W
St. Albans, U.K. 29 51 44N 0 19W
St. Albans, Vt., U.S.A. 156 44 49N 73 7W
St. Albans, W. Va., U.S.A. 156 38 21N 81 50W
St. Alban's Head 28 50 34N 2 3W
St. Albert 152 53 37N 113 40W
St. Amand 43 50 25N 3 6E
St.-Amand-en-Puisaye 43 47 32N 3 5E
St.-Amand-Mont-Rond 44 46 43N 2 30E
St.-Amarin 43 47 54N 7 0E
St.-Amour 45 46 26N 5 21E
St. Andrä 52 46 46N 14 50E
St. André, C. 129 16 11S 44 27E
St.-André-de-Cubzac 44 44 59N 0 26W
St. André de l'Eure 42 48 54N 1 16E
St.-André-les-Alpes 45 43 58N 6 30E
St. Andrews, Can. 151 47 45N 59 15W
St. Andrews, N.Z. 143 44 33S 171 10E
St. Andrews, U.K. 35 56 20N 2 48W
St. Ann B. 151 46 22N 60 25W
St. Anne 42 49 43N 2 11W
St. Anne's 32 53 45N 3 2W
St. Ann's 35 55 14N 3 28W
St. Ann's Bay 166 18 26N 77 15W
St. Ann's Hd. 31 51 41N 5 11W
St. Anthony, Can. 151 51 22N 55 35W
St. Anthony, U.S.A. 160 44 0N 111 49W
St.-Antonin-Noble-Val 44 44 10N 1 45E
St. Arnaud 140 36 32S 143 16E
St. Arnaud Ra. 143 42 1S 172 53E
St. Arthur 151 47 47N 67 46W
St. Asaph 31 53 15N 3 27W
St. Astier 44 45 8N 0 31E
St.-Aubin 50 46 54N 6 47E
St.-Aubin-du-Cormier 42 48 15N 1 26W
St. Augustin 129 23 33S 43 46E
St-Augustin-Saguenay 151 51 13N 58 38W
St. Augustine 157 29 52N 81 20W
St. Austell 30 50 20N 4 48W
St.-Avold 43 49 6N 6 43E
St. Barthélemy, I. 167 17 50N 62 50W
St. Bathans 143 44 53S 170 0E
St. Bathan's Mt. 143 44 45S 169 45E
St. Bees 32 54 29N 3 36W
St. Bee's Hd. 32 54 30N 3 38E
St.-Benoît-du-Sault 44 46 26N 1 24E
St. Bernard, Col du Grand 50 45 53N 7 11E
St.-Blaise 50 47 1N 6 59E
St. Blazey 32 50 22N 4 48W
St. Boniface 153 49 50N 97 10W
St. Bonnet 45 44 40N 6 5E
St. Boswells 35 55 34N 2 39W
St.-Brévin-les-Pins 42 47 14N 2 10W
St. Briavels 28 51 44N 2 39W
St.-Brice-en-Coglès 42 48 25N 1 22W
St. Bride's 151 46 56N 54 10W
St. Bride's B. 31 51 48N 5 15W
St.-Brieuc 42 48 30N 2 46W
St. Budeaux 30 50 23N 4 10W
St. Buryan 30 50 4N 5 34W
St.-Calais 42 47 55N 0 45E
St.-Cast 42 48 37N 2 18W
St. Catharines 150 43 10N 79 15W
St. Catherine's I. 157 31 35N 81 10W
St. Catherine's Pt. 28 50 34N 1 18W
St.-Céré 44 44 51N 1 54E
St. Cergue 50 46 27N 6 10E
St. Cernin 44 45 5N 2 25E
St.-Chamond 45 45 28N 4 31E
St. Charles, Ill., U.S.A. 156 41 55N 88 21W
St. Charles, Mo., U.S.A. 158 38 46N 90 30W
St.-Chély-d'Apcher 44 44 48N 3 17E
St.-Chinian 44 43 25N 2 56E
St. Christopher (St. Kitts) 167 17 20N 62 40W
St.-Ciers-sur-Gironde 44 45 17N 0 37W
St. Clair 162 40 42N 76 12W
St. Clair, L. 150 42 30N 82 45W
St.-Claud 44 45 54N 0 28E
St. Claude 153 49 40N 98 20W
St.-Claude 45 46 22N 5 52E
St. Clears 31 51 48N 4 30W
St.-Cloud 42 48 51N 2 12E
St. Cloud, Fla., U.S.A. 157 28 15N 81 15W
St. Cloud, Minn., U.S.A. 158 45 30N 94 11W
St. Coeur de Marie 151 48 39N 71 43W
St. Columb Major 30 50 26N 4 56W
St. Combs 37 57 40N 1 55W
St. Cricq, C. 137 25 17S 113 6E
St. Croix Falls 158 45 18N 92 22W
St. Croix, I. 147 17 45N 64 45W
St. Croix, R. 158 45 20N 92 50W
St. Cyprien 44 42 37N 3 0E
St.-Cyr 45 43 11N 5 43E
St. Cyrus 36 56 47N 2 25W
St. David's, Can. 151 48 12N 58 52W
St. David's, U.K. 31 51 54N 5 16W
St. David's Head 31 51 54N 5 16W
St.-Denis 43 48 56N 2 22E
St.-Denis-d'Orques 42 48 2N 0 17W
St. Dennis 30 50 23N 4 53W
St.-Dié 43 48 17N 6 56E
St. Dizier 43 48 40N 5 0E
St. Dogmaels 31 52 6N 4 42W
St. Dominick 30 50 28N 4 15W
St. Donats 31 51 23N 3 32W
St.-Egrève 45 45 14N 5 41E
St. Elias, Mt. 147 60 20N 141 59W
St. Elias Mts. 147 59 30N 137 30W
St. Eloy 44 46 10N 2 51E
St. Emilon 44 44 53N 0 9W
St. Endellion 30 50 33N 4 49W
St. Enoder 30 50 22N 4 57W
St. Erth 30 50 10N 5 26W
St. Étienne 45 45 27N 4 22E
St.-Étienne-de-Tinée 45 44 16N 6 56E
St. Eustatius I. 167 17 20N 63 0W
St. Félicien 150 48 40N 72 25W
St. Fergus 37 57 33N 1 50W
St. Fillans 35 56 25N 4 7W
St. Finian's B. 39 51 50N 10 22W
St. Fintan's 151 48 10N 58 50W
St.-Florent 45 42 41N 9 18E
St.-Florent-sur-Cher 43 46 59N 2 15E
St.-Florentin 43 48 0N 3 45E
St.-Flour 44 45 2N 3 6E
St.-Fons 45 45 42N 4 52E
St. Francis 158 39 48N 101 47W
St. Francis C. 128 34 14S 24 49E
St. Francis, R. 159 32 25N 90 36W
St.-Fulgent 42 46 50N 1 10W
St. Gabriel de Brandon 150 46 17N 73 24W
St.-Gengoux-le-National 45 46 37N 4 40E
St.-Geniez-d'Olt 44 44 27N 2 58E
St. George, Austral. 139 28 1S 148 41E
St. George, Can. 151 45 11N 66 50W
St. George, P.N.G. 135 4 10S 152 20E
St. George, S.C., U.S.A. 157 33 13N 80 37W
St. George, Utah, U.S.A. 161 37 10N 113 35W
St. George, C., Can. 151 48 30N 59 16W
St. George, C., P.N.G. 135 4 49S 152 53E
St. George, C., U.S.A. 157 29 36N 85 2W
St. George Hd. 139 35 11S 150 45E
St. George Ra., Mts. 136 18 40S 125 0E
St. George West 153 50 33N 96 7W
St.-Georges 47 50 37N 4 20E
St. George's 151 48 26N 58 31W
St. Georges, Qué., Can. 151 46 8N 70 40W
St. Georges, Quebec, Can. 150 46 42N 72 35W
St. Georges, Fr. Gui. 175 4 0N 52 0W
St. George's 167 12 5N 61 43W
St. George's B. 151 48 24N 58 53W
St. George's Channel 147 52 0N 6 0W
St. Georges-de-Didonne 44 45 36N 1 0W
St. Georges Head 141 35 12S 150 42E
St.-Gérard 47 50 21N 4 44E
St. Germain 43 48 53N 2 5E
St.-Germain-Lembron 44 45 27N 3 14E
St.-Germain-de-Calberte 44 44 13N 3 48E
St.-Germain-des-Fossés 44 46 12N 3 26E
St.-Germain-du-Plain 43 46 42N 4 58E
St.-Germain-Laval 45 45 50N 4 1E
St. Germans 30 50 24N 4 19W
St. Gervais, Haute Savoie, France 45 45 53N 6 42E
St. Gervais, Puy de Dôme, France 44 46 4N 2 50E
St.-Gervais-les-Bains 43 45 53N 6 41E
St.-Gildas, Pte. de 42 47 8N 2 14W
St.-Gilles 45 43 40N 4 26E
St. Gilles Croix-de-Vie 42 46 41N 1 55W
St.-Gingolph 50 46 24N 6 48E
St.-Girons 44 42 59N 1 8E
St. Gla, L. 72 59 35N 12 30E
St. Goar 49 50 31N 7 43E
St. Gotthard P. = San Gottardo 51 46 33N 8 33E
St. Govan's Hd. 31 51 35N 4 56W
St.-Guadens 44 43 6N 0 44E
St.-Gualtier 42 46 39N 1 26E
St.-Guénolé 42 47 49N 4 23W
St. Harmon 31 52 21N 3 29W
St. Heddinge 73 55 9N 12 26E
St. Helena 160 38 29N 122 30W
St. Helena, I. 15 15 55S 5 44W
St. Helenabaai 128 32 40S 18 10E
St. Helens, Austral. 138 41 20S 148 15E
St. Helens, I.o.W., U.K. 28 50 42N 1 6W
St. Helens, Merseyside, U.K. 32 53 28N 2 44W
St. Helens, U.S.A. 160 45 55N 122 50W
St. Helier 42 49 11N 2 6W
St. Hilaire 42 48 35N 1 7W
St. Hippolyte 43 47 20N 6 50E
St. Hippolyte-du-Fort 44 43 58N 3 52E
St.-Honoré 43 46 54N 3 50E
St.-Hubert 47 50 2N 5 23E
St. Hyacinthe 150 45 40N 72 58W
St. Ignace 156 45 53N 84 43W
St. Ignace I. 150 48 45N 88 0W
St. Ignatius 160 47 25N 114 2W
St.-Imier 50 47 9N 6 58E
St. Issey 30 50 30N 4 55W
St. Ives, Cambs., U.K. 29 52 20N 0 5W
St. Ives, Cornwall, U.K. 30 50 13N 5 29W
St. Ives Bay 30 50 15N 5 27W
St.-James 42 48 31N 1 20W
St. James 158 43 57N 94 40W
St. James C. 152 51 55N 131 0W
St. Jean 150 45 20N 73 50W
St.-Jean 45 48 57N 3 1E
St. Jean Baptiste 153 49 15N 97 20W
St. Jean, C. 124 1 5N 9 20E
St.-Jean-de-Maurienne 45 45 16N 6 28E
St.-Jean-de-Luz 44 43 23N 1 39W
St.-Jean-de-Monts 42 46 47N 2 4W
St.-Jean-du-Gard 44 47 7N 3 52E
St.-Jean-en-Royans 45 45 1N 5 18E
St.-Jean, L. 151 48 40N 72 0W
St. Jean-Port-Joli 151 47 15N 70 13W
St.-Jean, R. 151 50 17N 64 20W
St. Jérôme, Qué., Can. 150 45 47N 74 0W
St. Jérôme, Qué., Can. 151 48 26N 71 53W
St. John, Can. 151 45 20N 66 8W
St. John, Kans., U.S.A. 159 37 59N 98 45W
St. John, N.D., U.S.A. 158 48 58N 99 40W
St. John, C. 151 50 0N 55 32W
St. John, I. 147 18 20N 64 45W
St. John, R. 151 45 15N 66 4W
St. Johns 167 17 6N 61 51W
St. John's, Can. 151 47 35N 52 40W
St. John's, U.K. 32 54 13N 4 38W
St. Johns, Ariz., U.S.A. 161 34 31N 109 26W
St. Johns, Mich., U.S.A. 156 43 0N 84 38W
St. Johns Chapel 32 54 43N 2 10W
St. John's Pt., Ireland 38 54 35N 8 26W
St. John's Pt., U.K. 38 54 14N 5 40W
St. Johns, R. 157 30 20N 81 30W
St. Johnsbury 156 44 25N 72 1W
St. Johnston 38 54 56N 7 29W
St. Johnsville 162 43 0N 74 43W
St. Joseph, La., U.S.A. 159 31 55N 91 15W
St. Joseph, Mo., U.S.A. 158 39 40N 94 50W
St. Joseph, I. 150 46 12N 83 58W
St. Joseph, L. 150 51 10N 90 35W
St. Joseph, R. 156 42 7N 86 30W
St. Joseph's 156 42 5N 86 30W
St. Jovite 150 46 8N 74 38W
St. Juéry 44 43 55N 2 42E
St. Julien 45 46 8N 6 5E
St.-Julien-Chapteuil 45 45 2N 4 4E
St. Julien du Sault 43 48 1N 3 17E
St.-Junien 44 45 53N 0 55E
St. Just 30 50 7N 5 41W
St.-Just-en-Chaussée 43 49 30N 2 25E
St.-Just-en-Chevalet 44 45 55N 3 50E
St.-Justin 44 43 59N 0 14W
St. Karlsö, I. 73 57 17N 17 58E
St. Keverne 30 50 3N 5 5W
St. Kew 30 50 34N 4 48W
St. Kilda 143 45 53S 170 31E
St. Kilda, I. 23 57 40N 8 50W
St. Kitts, I. 167 17 20N 62 40W
St. Laurent 153 50 25N 97 58W
St.-Laurent-du-Pont 45 45 23N 5 45E
St.-Laurent-en-Grandvaux 45 46 35N 5 45E
St. Lawrence, Austral. 138 22 16S 149 31E
St. Lawrence, Can. 151 46 54N 55 23W

St. Lawrence, Gulf of
Sam Ngao

St. Lawrence, Gulf of 151 48 25N 62 0W
St. Lawrence, I. 147 63 0N 170 0W
St. Lawrence, R. 151 49 30N 66 0W
St.-Léger 47 49 37N 5 39E
St. Leonard 151 47 12N 67 58W
St.-Léonard-de-Noblat 44 45 49N 1 29E
St. Leonards 29 50 51N 0 34E
St. Levan 30 50 3N 5 36W
St Lewis, R. 151 52 26N 56 11W
St. Lin 150 45 44N 73 46W
St.-Lô 42 49 7N 1 5W
St. Louis, Senegal 120 16 8N 16 27W
St. Louis, Mich., U.S.A. 156 43 27N 84 38W
St. Louis, Mo., U.S.A. 158 38 40N 90 12W
St. Louis R. 158 47 15N 92 45W
St.-Loup-sur-Semouse 43 47 53N 6 16E
St. Lucia, C. 129 28 32S 32 29E
St. Lucia Channel 167 14 15N 61 0W
St. Lucia I. 167 14 0N 60 50W
St. Lucia, Lake 129 28 5S 32 30E
St. Lunaire-Griquet 151 51 31N 55 28W
St. Maarten, I. 167 18 0N 63 5W
St. Mabyn 30 50 30N 4 45W
St. Magnus B. 36 60 25N 1 35W
St.-Maixent-l'École 44 46 24N 0 12W
St.-Malo 42 48 39N 2 1W
St. Malo, G. de 42 48 50N 2 30W
St. Mandrier 45 43 4N 5 56E
St. Marc 167 19 10N 72 50W
St.-Marcellin 45 45 9N 5 20E
St. Marcouf, Is. 42 49 30N 1 10W
St.-Mard 47 49 2N 2 42E
St. Margaret's-at-Cliffe 29 51 10N 1 23E
St. Margaret's Hope 37 58 49N 2 58W
St. Maries 160 47 17N 116 34W
St. Martin 43 50 42N 1 38E
St.-Martin, I. 167 18 0N 63 0W
St. Martin L. 153 51 40N 98 30W
St. Martin-Tende-Vésubie 45 44 4N 7 15E
St. Martins 151 45 22N 65 25W
St. Martin's I. 30 49 58N 6 16W
St. Martinsville 159 30 10N 91 50W
St.-Martory 44 43 9N 0 56E
St. Mary B. 151 46 50N 53 50W
St. Mary Bourne 28 51 16N 1 24W
St. Mary C. 120 13 24N 13 10E
St. Mary Is. 97 13 20N 74 35E
St. Mary, Mt. 135 8 8S 146 54E
St. Mary Pk. 140 31 32S 138 34E
St. Marys, N.S.W., Austral. 133 33 44S 150 49E
St. Marys, Tas., Austral. 138 41 32S 148 11E
St. Mary's, Can. 151 46 56N 53 34W
St. Mary's, U.K. 37 58 53N 2 55W
St. Mary's, Ohio, U.S.A. 156 40 33N 84 20W
St. Mary's, Pa., U.S.A. 156 41 30N 78 33W
St Marys Bay 151 44 25N 66 10W
St. Mary's, C. 151 46 50N 54 12W
St. Mary's I. 30 49 55N 6 17W
St. Mary's Pk. 133 31 30S 138 33E
St. Mary's Sd. 30 49 53N 6 19W
St. Mathews I. = Zadetkyi Kyun 101 10 0N 48 25E
St.-Mathieu, Pte. de 42 48 20N 4 45W
St. Matthias Grp. 135 1 30S 150 0E
St.-Maur-des-Fosses 43 48 48N 2 30E
St. Maurice 50 46 13N 7 0E
St. Maurice R. 150 47 20N 72 50W
St. Mawes 30 50 10N 5 1W
St.-Médard-de-Guizières 44 45 1N 0 4W
St.-Méen-le-Grand 42 48 11N 2 12W
St. Merryn 30 50 31N 4 58W
St. Michael 147 63 30N 162 30W
St. Michaels, Arizona, U.S.A. 161 35 45N 109 5W
St. Michaels, Maryland, U.S.A. 162 38 47N 76 14W
St. Michael's Mt. 30 50 7N 5 30W
St. Michel 45 45 15N 6 29E
St. Mihiel 43 48 54N 5 30E
St. Minver 30 50 34N 4 52W
St. Monans 35 56 13N 2 46W
St.-Nazaire 42 47 17N 2 12W
St. Neots 29 52 14N 0 16W
St.-Nicholas-de-Port 43 48 38N 6 18E
St. Niklaus 50 46 10N 7 49E
St. Ninian's, I. 36 59 59N 1 20W
St. Olaf 73 55 40N 14 12E
St.-Omer 43 50 45N 2 15E
St. Osyth 29 51 47N 1 4E
St. Ouen 43 48 50N 2 20E
St. Pacome 151 47 24N 69 58W
St. Palais 44 45 40N 1 8W
St. Pamphile 151 46 58N 69 48W
St.-Pardoux-la-Rivière 44 45 29N 0 45E
St. Pascal 151 47 32N 69 48W
St. Patrickswell 39 52 36N 8 43W
St. Paul, Can. 152 54 59N 111 17W
St. Paul, France 44 43 44N 1 3W
St. Paul, Minn., U.S.A. 158 44 54N 93 5W
St. Paul, Nebr., U.S.A. 158 41 15N 98 30W
St. Paul-de-Fenouillet 44 42 50N 2 28E
St. Paul, I., Atl. Oc. 14 0 50N 31 40W
St. Paul, I., Can. 151 47 12N 60 9W
St. Paul, I., Ind. Oc. 11 30 40S 77 34E
St. Paul's B. 151 49 48N 57 58W
St.-Peray 45 44 57N 4 50E
St.-Père-en-Retz 42 47 11N 2 2W
St. Peter 158 44 15N 93 57W
St. Peter Port 42 49 27N 2 31W
St. Peters, N.S., Can. 151 45 40N 60 53W
St. Peters, P.E.I., Can. 151 46 25N 62 35W
St. Petersburg 157 27 45N 82 40W
St.-Philbert-de-Grand-Lieu 42 47 2N 1 39W
St Pierre 151 46 40N 56 0W
St.-Pierre-d'Oleron 44 45 57N 1 19W
St.-Pierre-Église 42 49 40N 1 24W
St.-Pierre-en-Port 42 49 48N 0 30E
Saint-Pierre et Miquelon □ 151 46 55N 56 10W
St-Pierre, L. 150 46 12N 72 52W
St.-Pierre-le-Moûtier 43 46 47N 3 7E
St. Pierre-sur-Dives 42 49 2N 0 1W
St.-Pieters Leew 47 50 47N 4 16E
St. Pol 43 50 21N 2 20E
St.-Pol-de-Léon 42 48 41N 4 0W
St.-Pol-sur-Mer 43 51 1N 2 20E
St. Pons 44 43 30N 2 45E
St.-Pourçain-sur-Sioule 43 46 18N 3 18E
St.-Quay-Portrieux 42 48 39N 2 51W
St.-Quentin 43 49 50N 3 16E
St. Rambert-d'Albon 45 45 17N 1 35E
St.-Raphaël 45 43 25N 6 46E
St. Regis 160 47 20N 115 3W
St.-Rémy-de-Provence 45 43 48N 4 50E
St.-Renan 42 48 26N 4 37W
St.-Saëns 42 49 41N 1 16E
St.-Sauveur-en-Puisaye 43 47 37N 3 12E
St.-Sauveur-le-Vicomte 42 49 23N 1 32W
St. Savin 44 46 34N 0 50E
St.-Savinien 44 45 53N 0 42W
St. Sebastien, C. 129 12 26S 48 44E
St.-Seine-l'Abbaye 43 47 26N 4 47E
St. Sernin 44 43 54N 2 35E
St.-Servan-sur-Mer 42 48 38N 2 0E
St.-Sever-Calvados 42 48 50N 1 3W
St. Simeon 151 47 51N 69 54W
St. Stephen, Can. 151 45 16N 67 17W
St. Stephen, U.K. 30 50 20N 4 52W
St.-Sulpice 44 43 46N 1 41E
St.-Sulpice-Laurière 44 46 3N 1 29E
St. Teath 30 50 34N 4 45W
St.-Thegonnec 42 48 31N 3 57W
St. Thomas 150 42 45N 81 10W
St. Thomas, I. 147 18 21N 64 55W
St. Tite 150 46 45N 72 40W
St. Tropez 45 43 17N 6 38E
St. Troud 47 50 48N 5 10E
St. Tudwal's Is. 31 52 48N 4 28W
St. Tudy 30 50 33N 4 45W
St.-Vaast-la-Hougue 42 49 35N 1 17W
St. Valéry 43 50 10N 1 38E
St.-Valéry-en-Caux 42 49 52N 0 43E
St.-Vallier 45 45 11N 4 50E
St.-Vallier-de-Thiey 45 43 42N 6 51E
St.-Varent 44 46 53N 0 13W
St. Vincent 14 18 0N 26 1W
St. Vincent C. 125 21 58S 43 20E
St. Vincent, C. = São Vincente 57 37 0N 9 0W
St. Vincent-de-Tyrosse 44 43 39N 1 18W
St. Vincent, G. 140 35 0S 138 0E
St. Vincent, I. 167 13 10N 61 10W
St. Vincent Passage 167 13 30N 61 0W
St.-Vith 47 50 17N 6 9E
St.-Yrieux-la-Perche 44 45 31N 1 12E
Ste.-Adresse 42 49 31N 0 5E
Ste.-Agathe-des-Monts 150 46 3N 74 17W
Ste. Anne 167 14 26N 60 53W
Ste. Anne de Beaupré 151 47 2N 70 58W
Ste. Anne de Portneuf 151 48 38N 69 8W
Ste.-Anne-des-Monts 151 49 8N 66 30W
Ste. Benoîte 43 49 47N 3 30E
Ste. Cecile 151 47 56N 64 34W
Ste.-Croix 43 46 49N 6 34W
Ste.-Enimie 44 44 22N 3 26E
Ste.-Foy-la-Grande 44 44 50N 0 13E
Ste. Genevieve 158 37 59N 90 2W
Ste. Germaine 151 46 24N 70 24W
Ste.-Hermine 44 46 32N 1 4W
Ste.-Livrade-sur-Lot 44 44 24N 0 36E
Ste. Marguerite, R. 151 50 9N 66 36W
Ste. Marie 167 14 48N 61 1W
Ste.-Marie-aux-Mines 43 48 10N 7 12E
Ste. Marie, C. 129 25 36S 45 8E
Ste. Marie de la Madeleine 151 46 26N 71 0W
Ste. Marie, I. 129 16 50S 49 55E
Ste.-Maure-de-Touraine 42 47 7N 0 37E
Ste.-Maxime 45 43 19N 6 39E
Ste.-Menehould 43 49 5N 4 54E
Ste.-Mère-Église 42 49 24N 1 19W
Ste. Rose 167 16 20N 61 45W
Ste. Rose du lac 153 51 41N 99 30W
Ste. Teresa 172 33 33S 60 54W
Saintes 44 45 45N 0 37W
Saintes, I. des 167 15 50N 61 35W
Saintes-Maries-de-la-Mer 45 43 26N 4 26E
Saintes Maries, Les 45 43 27N 4 25E
Saintfield 38 54 28N 5 50W
Saintonge 44 45 40N 0 50W
Sairang 99 23 50N 92 45E
Sairecábur, Cerro 172 22 43S 67 54W
Saitama-ken □ 111 36 25N 137 0E
Saito 110 32 3N 131 18E
Sajama, Nevada 174 18 0S 68 55W
Sajan 66 45 50N 20 58E
Sajószentpéter 53 48 12N 20 44E
Sajum, mt. 95 33 20N 79 0E
Saka Ilkalat 93 27 20N 64 7E
Sakai 111 34 30N 135 30E
Sakaide 110 34 15N 133 56E
Sakaiminato 110 35 38N 133 11E
Sakaka 92 30 0N 40 8E
Sakami, L. 150 53 15N 76 45W
Sâkâne, 'Erg i-n 118 20 30N 1 30W
Sakania 127 12 43S 28 30E
Sakar, I. 138 5 30S 148 0E
Sakarya, R. 82 40 5N 31 0E
Sakata 112 36 38N 138 19E
Sakchu 107 40 23N 125 2E
Sakeny, R. 129 20 0S 45 25E
Sakété 121 6 40N 2 32E
Sakhalin, Ostrov 77 51 0N 143 0E
Sakhi Gopal 96 19 58N 85 50E
Sakhnin 90 32 52N 35 12E
Saki 82 45 16N 33 34E
Sakiai 80 54 59N 23 0E
Sakmara 84 52 0N 55 20E
Sakmara, R. 84 51 46N 55 1E
Sakołow Małopolski 54 50 10N 22 9E
Sakon Nakhon 100 17 10N 104 9E
Sakrand 94 26 10N 68 15E
Sakri 96 21 2N 74 40E
Sakskøbing 73 54 49N 11 39E
Saku 111 36 11N 138 31E
Sakuma 111 35 3N 137 56E
Sakurai 111 34 30N 135 51E
Sakuru 111 35 43N 140 14E
Säkylä 75 61 4N 22 20E
Sal, R. 83 47 25N 42 20E
Sal'a 53 48 10N 17 50E
Sala 72 59 58N 16 35E
Sala Consilina 65 40 23N 15 35E
Sala-y-Gomez, I. 131 26 28S 105 28W
Salaberry-de-Valleyfield 150 45 15N 74 8W
Salada, La 164 24 30N 111 30W
Saladas 172 28 15S 58 40W
Saladillo 172 35 40S 59 55W
Salado, R., Buenos Aires, Argent. 172 35 40S 58 10W
Salado, R., Santa Fe, Argent. 172 27 0S 63 40W
Salado, R., Mexico 164 26 52N 99 19W
Salaga 121 8 31N 0 31W
Salala, Liberia 120 6 42N 10 7W
Salala, Sudan 122 21 17N 36 16E
Salalah 91 16 56N 53 59E
Salama 90 32 3N 34 48E
Salamanca, Chile 172 32 0S 71 25W
Salamanca, Spain 56 40 58N 5 39W
Salamanca, U.S.A. 156 42 10N 78 42W
Salamanca □ 56 40 57N 5 40W
Salamaua 138 7 10S 147 0E
Salamina 174 5 25N 75 29W
Salamis 69 37 56N 23 30E
Salar de Atacama 176 23 30S 68 25W
Salar de Uyuni 174 20 30S 67 45W
Salard 70 47 12N 22 3E
Salas 56 43 25N 6 15W
Salas de los Infantes 58 42 2N 3 17W
Salavat 84 53 21N 55 55E
Salaverry 174 8 15S 79 0W
Salawe 126 3 17S 32 56E
Salayar, I. 103 6 15S 120 30E
Salazar, R. 58 42 45N 1 8W
Salbohed 72 59 55N 16 22E
Salbris 43 47 25N 2 3E
Salcia 70 43 56N 24 55E
Salcombe 30 50 14N 3 47W
Salcombe Regis 30 50 41N 3 11W
Saldaña 56 42 32N 4 48W
Saldanha 128 33 0S 17 58E
Saldanhabaai 128 33 6S 18 0E
Saldus 80 56 45N 22 37E
Sale 141 38 6S 147 6E
Salé 118 34 3N 6 48W
Sale 32 53 26N 2 19W
Saléa-koïra 121 16 54N 0 46W
Salebabu 103 3 45N 125 55E
Salehabad 93 35 40N 61 2E
Salekhard 76 66 30N 66 25E
Salem, India 97 11 40N 78 11E
Salem, Ind., U.S.A. 156 38 38N 86 16W
Salem, Mass., U.S.A. 162 42 29N 70 53W
Salem, Mo., U.S.A. 159 37 40N 91 30W
Salem, N.H., U.S.A. 162 42 47N 71 12W
Salem, N.J., U.S.A. 162 39 34N 75 29W
Salem, N.Y., U.S.A. 162 43 10N 73 20W
Salem, Ohio, U.S.A. 156 40 52N 80 50W
Salem, Oreg., U.S.A. 160 45 0N 123 0W
Salem, Va., U.S.A. 156 37 19N 80 8W
Salembu, Kepulauan 102 5 35S 114 30E
Salemi 64 37 49N 12 47E
Salen, Norway 75 64 41N 11 27E
Salen, Highland, U.K. 36 56 42N 5 48W
Salen, Strathclyde, U.K. 34 56 31N 5 57W
Salernes 45 43 34N 6 15E
Salerno 65 40 40N 14 44E
Salerno, G. di 65 40 35N 14 45E
Salfit 90 32 5N 35 11E
Salford 32 53 30N 2 17W
Salford Priors 28 52 10N 1 52W
Salgir, R. 82 45 30N 34 30E
Salgótarján 53 48 5N 19 47E
Salgueiro 170 8 4S 39 6W
Salies-de-Béarn 44 43 28N 0 56W
Salima 125 13 47S 34 28E
Salin 98 20 35N 94 40E
Salina 158 38 50N 97 40W
Salina Cruz 165 16 10N 95 10W
Salina, I. 65 38 35N 14 50E
Salina, La 174 10 22N 71 27W
Salinas, Brazil 171 16 20S 42 10W
Salinas, Chile 172 23 31S 69 29W
Salinas, Ecuador 174 2 10S 80 50W
Salinas, Mexico 164 23 37N 106 8W
Salinas, U.S.A. 163 36 40N 121 31W
Salinas Ambargasta 172 29 0S 65 30W
Salinas, B. de 166 11 4N 85 45W
Salinas, Cabo de 59 39 16N 3 4E
Salinas (de Hidalgo) 164 22 30N 101 40W
Salinas Grandes 172 30 0S 65 0W
Salinas, Pampa de las 172 31 58S 66 42W
Salinas, R., Mexico 165 16 28N 90 31W
Salinas, R., U.S.A. 163 36 45N 121 48W
Saline, R. 158 39 10N 99 5W
Salines-les-Bains 43 46 58N 5 52E
Salinópolis 170 0 40S 47 20W
Salir 57 37 14N 8 2W
Salisbury, Austral. 140 34 46S 138 40E
Salisbury, Rhod. 127 17 50S 31 2E
Salisbury, U.K. 28 51 4N 1 48W
Salisbury, Md., U.S.A. 162 38 20N 75 38W
Salisbury, N.C., U.S.A. 157 35 42N 80 29W
Salisbury Plain 28 51 13N 1 50W
Salitre, R. 170 9 29S 40 39W
Salka 121 10 20N 4 58E
Salle, La 158 41 20N 89 5W
Sallent 58 41 49N 1 54E
Salles-Curan 44 44 11N 2 48E
Salling 73 56 40N 8 55E
Sallisaw 159 35 26N 94 45W
Sallom Junc. 122 19 23N 37 6E
Sally Gap, Mt. 39 53 7N 6 18W
Salmerón 58 40 33N 2 29W
Salmo 152 49 10N 117 20W
Salmon 160 45 12N 113 56W
Salmon Arm 152 50 40N 119 15W
Salmon Falls 160 42 55N 114 59W
Salmon Gums 137 32 59S 121 38E
Salmon, R., Can. 152 54 3N 122 40W
Salmon, R., U.S.A. 160 46 0N 116 30W
Salmon Res. 151 48 05N 56 00W
Salmon River Mts. 160 45 0N 114 30W
Salo 75 60 22N 23 3E
Salò 62 45 37N 10 32E
Salobreña 57 36 44N 3 35W
Salome 161 33 51N 113 37W
Salon-de-Provence 45 43 39N 5 6E
Salonica = Thessaloníki 68 40 38N 22 58E
Salonta 70 46 49N 21 42E
Salop □ 28 52 36N 2 45W
Salor, R. 57 39 39N 7 3W
Salou, Cabo 58 41 3N 1 10E
Salsacate 172 31 20S 65 5W
Salsaker 72 62 59N 18 20E
Salses 44 42 50N 2 55E
Salsette I. 96 19 5N 72 50E
Salsk 83 46 28N 41 30E
Salso, R. 65 37 6N 13 55E
Salsomaggiore 62 44 48N 9 59E
Salt 90 32 2N 35 43E
Salt Creek 140 36 8S 139 38E
Salt Creek Telegraph Office 139 36 0S 139 35E
Salt Fork R. 159 37 25N 98 40W
Salt Lake City 160 40 45N 111 58W
Salt, R., Can. 152 60 0N 112 25W
Salt, R., U.S.A. 161 33 50N 110 25W
Salt Range 94 32 30N 72 25E
Salta 172 24 47S 65 25W
Salta □ 172 24 48S 65 30W
Saltash 30 50 25N 4 13W
Saltburn by Sea 33 54 35N 0 58W
Saltcoats 34 55 38N 4 47W
Saltee Is. 39 52 7N 6 37W
Saltergate 33 54 20N 0 40W
Saltfjorden 74 67 15N 14 20E
Saltfleet 33 53 25N 0 11E
Saltfleetby 33 53 23N 0 10E
Salthill 39 53 15N 9 6W
Saltholm 73 55 38N 12 43E
Salthólmavík 74 65 24N 21 57W
Saltillo 164 25 30N 100 57W
Salto, Argent. 172 34 20S 60 15W
Salto, Uruguay 172 31 20S 57 59W
Salto □ 172 31 20S 57 59W
Salto Augusto, falls 172 8 30S 58 0W
Salto da Divisa 171 16 0S 39 57W
Salton City 163 33 21N 115 59W
Salton Sea 163 33 20N 115 50W
Saltpond 121 5 15N 1 3W
Saltsjöbaden 73 59 15N 18 20E
Saltspring 152 48 54N 123 37W
Saltwood 29 51 4N 1 5E
Saluda 162 37 36N 76 36W
Salula, R. 157 34 12N 81 45W
Salûm 122 31 31N 25 7E
Salûm, Khâlig el 122 31 30N 25 9E
Salur 96 18 27N 83 18E
Saluzzo 62 44 39N 7 29E
Salvador, Brazil 171 13 0S 38 30W
Salvador, Can. 153 52 10N 109 25W
Salvador ■ 164 13 50N 89 0W
Salvador, L. 159 29 46N 90 16W
Salvaterra 170 0 46S 48 31W
Salvaterra de Magos 57 39 1N 8 47W
Sálvora, Isla 56 42 30N 8 58W
Salwa 93 24 45N 50 55E
Salween, R. 98 16 31N 97 37E
Salza, R. 52 47 43N 15 0E
Salzach, R. 52 47 15N 12 25E
Salzburg 52 47 48N 13 2E
Salzgitter 48 52 2N 10 22E
Salzwedel 48 52 50N 11 11E
Sam Neua 100 20 29N 104 0E
Sam Ngao 100 17 18N 99 0E

**Sam Rayburn Res** **San Quintín**


Sam Rayburn Res. **159** 31 15N 94 20W
Sam Son **100** 19 44N 105 54 E
Sam Ten **100** 19 59N 104 38 E
Sama **84** 60 12N 60 22 E
Sama de Langreo **56** 43 18N 5 40W
Samales Group **103** 6 0N 122 0 E
Samalkot **96** 17 3N 82 13 E
Samâlût **122** 28 20N 30 42 E
Samana **94** 30 10N 76 13 E
Samana Cay **167** 23 3N 73 45W
Samanco **174** 9 10 S 78 30W
Samanga **127** 8 20 S 39 13 E
Samangan **93** 36 15N 67 40 E
Samangwa **126** 4 23 S 24 10 E
Samani **112** 42 7N 142 56 E
Samar, I. **103** 12 0N 125 0 E
Samara, R. **84** 53 10N 50 4 E
Samaria **135** 10 39 S 150 41 E
Samaria = Shomron **90** 32 15N 35 13 E
Samarkand **85** 39 40N 67 0 E
Samarra **92** 34 16N 43 55 E
Samastipur **95** 25 50N 85 50 E
Samatan **44** 43 29N 0 55 E
Samba, Kashmir **95** 32 32N 75 10 E
Samba, Zaïre **126** 4 38 S 26 22 E
Sambaíba **170** 7 8 S 45 21W
Sambaina **129** 19 37 S 47 8 E
Sambaise **65** 38 58N 16 16 E
Sambalpur **96** 21 28N 83 58 E
Sambas, S. **102** 1 20N 109 20 E
Sambava **129** 14 16 S 50 10 E
Sambawizi **127** 18 24 S 26 13 E
Sambhal **95** 28 35N 78 37 E
Sambhar **94** 26 52N 75 10 E
Sambonifacio **62** 45 24N 11 16 E
Sambor, Camb. **100** 12 46N 106 0 E
Sambor, U.S.S.R. **80** 49 30N 23 10 E
Sambre, R. **47** 50 27N 4 52 E
Sambuca **64** 37 39N 13 6 E
Samburu □ **126** 1 10N 37 0 E
Sambusu **128** 17 55 S 19 21 E
Samchŏk **107** 37 30N 129 10 E
Samchonpo **107** 34 54N 128 6 E
Same **126** 4 2 S 37 38 E
Samedan **51** 46 32N 9 52 E
Samer **43** 50 38N 1 44 E
Samfya **127** 11 16 S 29 31 E
Sámi **69** 38 15N 20 39 E
Samna **122** 25 12N 37 17 E
Samnager **71** 60 23N 5 39 E
Samnaun **51** 46 57N 10 22 E
Samnu **119** 27 15N 14 55 E
Samo Alto **172** 30 22 S 71 0W
Samoan Is. **10** 14 0 S 171 0W
Samobor **63** 45 47N 15 44 E
Samoëns **45** 46 5N 6 45 E
Samoorombón, Bahía **172** 36 5 S 57 20W
Samorogouan **120** 11 21N 4 57W
Samos **56** 42 44N 7 20W
Samoš **66** 45 13N 20 49 E
Sámos, I. **69** 37 45N 26 50 E
Samosir, P. **102** 2 35N 98 50 E
Samothráki **68** 40 28N 25 38 E
Samothráki, I. **68** 40 25N 25 40 E
Sampa **120** 8 0N 2 36W
Sampacho **172** 33 20 S 64 50W
Sampang **103** 7 11 S 113 13 E
Samper de Calanda **58** 41 11N 04 2W
Sampford Courtenay **30** 50 47N 3 58W
Sampit **102** 2 20 S 113 0 E
Samra **92** 25 35N 41 0 E
Samreboi **120** 5 34N 7 28 E
Samrée **47** 50 13N 5 39 E
Samrong, Camb. **100** 14 15N 103 30 E
Samrong, Thai. **100** 15 10N 100 40 E
Samsø **73** 55 50N 10 35 E
Samsø Bælt **73** 55 45N 10 45 E
Samsonovo **85** 37 53N 65 15 E
Samsun **92** 41 15N 36 15 E
Samsun Daği **69** 37 45N 27 10 E
Samtredia **83** 42 7N 42 24 E
Samui, Ko **101** 9 30N 100 0 E
Samur, R. **83** 41 30N 48 0 E
Samusole **127** 10 2 S 24 0 E
Samut Prakan **100** 13 32N 100 40 E
Samut Sakhon **100** 13 31N 100 20 E
Samut Songkhram (Mekong) **100** 13 24N 100 1 E
Samwari **94** 28 5N 66 46 E
Samyo La **99** 29 55N 84 46 E
San **120** 13 15N 4 45W
San Adrián, C. de **56** 43 21N 8 50W
San Adrián, G. de **56** 43 21N 8 50W
San Agustín **174** 1 53N 76 16W
San Agustin, C. **103** 6 20N 126 13 E
San Agustín de Valle Fértil **172** 30 35 S 67 30W
San Ambrosio, I. **131** 26 35 S 79 30W
San Andreas **163** 38 17N 120 39W
San Andrés, I. de **166** 12 42N 81 46W
San Andres Mts. **161** 33 0N 106 45W
San Andrés Tuxtla **165** 18 30N 95 20W
San Angelo **159** 31 30N 100 30W
San Anselmo **163** 37 49N 122 34W
San Antonio, Belize **165** 16 15N 89 2W
San Antonio, Chile **172** 33 40 S 71 40W
San Antonio, N. Mex., U.S.A. **161** 33 58N 106 57W
San Antonio, Tex., U.S.A. **159** 29 30N 98 30W
San Antonio, Venez. **174** 3 30N 66 44W
San Antonio Abad **59** 38 59N 1 19 E
San Antonio, C., Argent. **172** 36 15 S 56 40W
San Antonio, C., Cuba **166** 21 50N 84 57W
San Antonio, C. de **59** 38 48N 0 12 E
San Antonio de Caparo **174** 7 35N 71 27W
San Antonio de los Baños **166** 22 54N 82 31W
San Antonio de los Cobres **172** 24 16 S 66 2W
San Antonio do Zaire **124** 6 8 S 12 11 E
San Antonio, Mt. (Old Baldy Pk.) **163** 34 17N 117 38W
San Antonio Oeste **176** 40 40 S 65 0W
San Antonio, R. **159** 28 30N 97 14W
San Ardo **163** 36 1N 120 54W
San Bartolomeo in Galdo **65** 41 23N 15 2 E
San Benedetto **62** 45 2N 10 57 E
San Benedetto del Tronto **63** 42 57N 13 52 E
San Benedicto, I. **164** 19 18N 110 49W
San Benito **159** 26 5N 97 32W
San Benito Mtn. **163** 36 22N 120 37W
San Benito, R. **163** 36 53N 121 50W
San Bernardino **163** 34 7N 117 18W
San Bernardino, Paso del **51** 46 28N 9 11 E
San Bernardo **172** 33 40 S 70 50W
San Bernardo, I. de **174** 9 45N 75 50W
San Blas **164** 26 10N 108 40W
San Blas, C. **157** 29 40N 85 25W
San Blas, Cord. de **166** 9 15N 78 30W
San Borja **174** 15 0 S 67 12W
San Buenaventura **164** 27 5N 101 32W
San Buenaventura = Ventura **163** 34 17N 119 18W
San Carlos, Argent. **172** 33 50 S 69 0W
San Carlos, Mexico **164** 29 0N 101 10W
San Carlos, Nic. **166** 11 12N 84 50W
San Carlos, Phil. **103** 10 29N 123 25 E
San Carlos, Uruguay **173** 34 46 S 54 58W
San Carlos, U.S.A. **161** 33 24N 110 27W
San Carlos, Amazonas, Venez. **174** 1 55N 67 4W
San Carlos, Cojedes, Venez. **174** 9 40N 68 36W
San Carlos de Bariloche **176** 41 10 S 71 25W
San Carlos de la Rápita **58** 40 37N 0 35 E
San Carlos del Zulia **174** 9 1N 71 55W
San Carlos L. **161** 33 20N 110 10W
San Carlos = Butuku-Luba **121** 3 29N 8 33 E
San Cataldo **64** 37 30N 13 58 E
San Celoni **58** 41 42N 2 30 E
San Clemente, Chile **172** 35 30 S 71 39W
San Clemente, Spain **59** 39 24N 2 25W
San Clemente, U.S.A. **163** 33 29N 117 45W
San Clemente I. **163** 32 53N 118 30W
San Constanzo **63** 43 46N 13 5 E
San Cristóbal, Argent. **172** 30 20 S 61 10W
San Cristóbal, Dom. Rep. **167** 18 25N 70 6W
San Cristóbal, Venez. **174** 7 46N 72 14W
San Cristóbal de las Casas **165** 16 50N 92 33W
San Damiano d'Asti **62** 44 51N 8 4 E
San Daniel del Friuli **63** 46 10N 13 0 E
San Demétrio Corone **65** 39 34N 16 22 E
San Diego, Calif., U.S.A. **163** 32 43N 117 10W
San Diego, Tex., U.S.A. **159** 27 47N 98 15W
San Diego, C. **176** 54 40 S 65 10W
San Diego de la Unión **164** 21 28N 100 52W
San Donà di Piave **63** 45 38N 12 34 E
San Elpídio a Mare **63** 43 16N 13 41 E
San Estanislao **172** 24 39 S 56 26W
San Esteban de Gormaz **58** 41 34N 3 13W
San Felice sul Panaro **62** 44 51N 11 9 E
San Felipe, Chile **172** 32 43 S 70 50W
San Felipe, Mexico **164** 31 0N 114 52W
San Felipe, Venez. **174** 10 20N 68 44W
San Felipe, R. **163** 33 12N 115 49W
San Feliu de Guixols **58** 41 45N 3 1 E
San Feliu de Llobregat **58** 41 23N 2 2 E
San Félix **174** 8 20N 62 35W
San Felix, I. **131** 26 30 S 80 0W
San Fernando, Chile **172** 34 30 S 71 0W
San Fernando, Mexico **164** 30 0N 115 10W
San Fernando, Luzon, Phil. **103** 15 5N 120 37 E
San Fernando, Luzon, Phil. **103** 16 40N 120 23 E
San Fernando, Spain **57** 36 22N 6 17W
San Fernando, Trin **167** 10 20N 61 30W
San Fernando, U.S.A. **163** 34 15N 118 29W
San Fernando de Apure **174** 7 54N 67 28W
San Fernando de Atabapo **174** 4 3N 67 42W
San Fernando di Puglia **65** 41 18N 16 5 E
San Fernando, R. **164** 25 0N 99 0W
San Francisco, Córdoba, Argent. **172** 31 30 S 62 5W
San Francisco, San Luis, Argent. **172** 32 45 S 66 10W
San Francisco, U.S.A. **163** 37 47N 122 30W
San Francisco de Macorîs **167** 19 19N 70 15W
San Francisco del Monte de Oro **172** 32 36 S 66 8W
San Francisco del Oro **164** 26 52N 105 50W
San Francisco Javier **59** 38 40N 1 25 E
San Francisco, Paso de **172** 35 40 S 70 24W
San Francisco, R. **161** 33 30N 109 0W
San Francisco Solano, Pta. **174** 6 18N 77 29W
San Francisville **159** 30 48N 91 22W
San Fratello **65** 38 1N 14 33 E
San Gabriel **174** 0 36N 77 49W
San Gavino Monreale **64** 39 33N 8 47 E
San German **147** 18 5N 67 3W
San Gil **174** 6 33N 73 8W
San Gimignano **62** 43 28N 11 3 E
San Giórgio di Nogaro **63** 45 50N 13 13 E
San Giórgio Iónico **65** 40 27N 17 23 E
San Giovanni Bianco **62** 45 52N 9 40 E
San Giovanni in Fiore **65** 39 16N 16 42 E
San Giovanni in Persieceto **63** 44 39N 11 12 E
San Giovanni Rotondo **65** 41 41N 15 42 E
San Giovanni Valdarno **63** 43 32N 11 30 E
San Giuliano Terme **62** 43 45N 10 26 E
San Gorgonio Mtn. **163** 34 7N 116 51W
San Gottardo, Paso del **51** 46 33N 8 33 E
San Gregorio, Uruguay **173** 32 37 S 55 40W
San Gregorio, U.S.A. **163** 37 20N 122 23W
San Guiseppe Iato **64** 37 37N 13 11 E
San Ignacio, Boliv. **174** 16 20 S 60 55W
San Ignacio, Mexico **164** 27 27N 112 51W
San Ignacio, Parag. **172** 26 52 S 57 3W
San Ignacio, Laguna **164** 26 50N 113 11W
San Ildefonso, C. **103** 16 0N 122 10 E
San Isidro **172** 34 29 S 58 31W
San Jacinto, Colomb. **174** 9 50N 75 8W
San Jacinto, U.S.A. **163** 33 47N 116 57W
San Javier, Misiones, Argent. **173** 27 55 S 55 5W
San Javier, Santa Fe, Argent. **172** 30 40 S 59 55W
San Javier, Boliv. **174** 16 18 S 62 30W
San Javier, Chile **172** 35 40 S 71 45W
San Javier, Spain **59** 37 49N 0 50W
San Jerónimo, Sa. de **174** 8 0N 75 50W
San Joaquin **163** 36 36N 120 11W
San Joaquín **174** 10 16N 67 47W
San Joaquin R. **163** 38 4N 121 51W
San Joaquin Valley **163** 37 0N 120 30W
San Jorge **172** 31 54 S 61 50W
San Jorge, Bahía de **164** 31 20N 113 20W
San Jorge, Golfo de **176** 46 0 S 66 0W
San Jorge, G. de **58** 40 50N 0 55W
San José, Boliv. **174** 17 45 S 60 50W
San José, C. Rica **166** 10 0N 84 2W
San José, Guat. **164** 14 0N 90 50W
San José, Luzon, Phil. **103** 15 45N 120 55 E
San José, Mindoro, Phil. **103** 10 50N 122 5 E
San José, Spain **59** 38 55N 1 18 E
San Jose, Calif., U.S.A. **163** 37 20N 121 53W
San Jose, N. Mex., U.S.A. **159** 35 26N 105 30W
San José Carpizo **165** 19 26N 90 32W
San José de Feliciano **172** 30 26 S 58 46W
San José de Jáchal **172** 30 5 S 69 0W
San José de Mayo **172** 34 27 S 56 27W
San José de Ocuné **174** 4 15N 70 20W
San José del Cabo **164** 23 0N 109 50W
San José del Guaviare **174** 2 35N 72 38W
San José, I. **164** 25 0N 110 50W
San Juan, Argent. **172** 31 30 S 68 30W
San Juan, Antioquía, Colomb. **174** 8 46N 76 32W
San Juan, Meta, Colomb. **174** 3 26N 73 50W
San Juan, Dom. Rep. **147** 18 49N 71 12W
San Juan, Coahuila, Mexico **164** 29 34N 101 53W
San Juan, Jalisco, Mexico **164** 21 20N 102 50W
San Juan, Querétaro, Mexico **164** 20 25N 100 0W
San Juan, Phil. **103** 8 35N 126 20 E
San Juan, Pto Rico **147** 18 28N 66 37W
San Juan □ **172** 31 9 S 69 0W
San Juan Bautista, Parag. **172** 26 37 S 57 6W
San Juan Bautista, Spain **59** 39 5N 1 31 E
San Juan Bautista, U.S.A. **163** 36 51N 121 32W
San Juan, C. **147** 18 23N 65 37W
San Juan Capistrano **163** 33 29N 117 40W
San Juan de Guadalupe **164** 24 38N 102 44W
San Juan de los Cayos **174** 11 10N 68 25W
San Juan de los Morros **174** 9 55N 67 21W
San Juan de Norte, B. de **166** 11 30N 83 40W
San Juan del Norte **166** 10 58N 83 40W
San Juan del Puerto **57** 37 20N 6 50W
San Juan del Río **165** 24 47N 104 27W
San Juan del Sur **166** 11 20N 85 40W
San Juan Mts. **161** 38 30N 108 30W
San Juan, Presa de **164** 17 45N 95 15W
San Juan, R., Argent. **172** 32 20 S 67 25W
San Juan, R., Colomb. **174** 4 0N 77 20W
San Juan, R., Nic. **166** 11 0N 84 30W
San Juan, R., Calif., U.S.A. **163** 36 14N 121 9W
San Juan, R., Utah, U.S.A. **161** 37 20N 110 20W
San Julián **176** 49 15 S 68 0W
San Just, Sierra de **58** 40 45N 0 41W
San Justo **172** 30 55 S 60 30W
San Kamphaeng **100** 18 45N 99 8 E
San Lázaro, C. **164** 24 50N 112 18W
San Lázaro, Sa. de **164** 23 25N 110 0W
San Leandro **163** 37 40N 122 6W
San Leonardo **58** 41 51N 3 5W
San Lorenzo, Argent. **172** 32 45 S 60 45W
San Lorenzo, Ecuador **174** 1 15N 78 50W
San Lorenzo, Parag. **172** 25 20 S 57 32W
San Lorenzo, Venez. **174** 9 47N 71 4W
San Lorenzo de la Parilla **58** 39 51N 2 22W
San Lorenzo de Morunys **58** 42 8N 1 35 E
San Lorenzo, I., Mexico **164** 28 35N 112 50W
San Lorenzo, I., Peru **174** 12 20 S 77 35W
San Lorenzo, Mt. **176** 47 40 S 72 20W
San Lorenzo, R. **164** 24 15N 107 24W
San Lucas, Boliv. **174** 20 5 S 65 0W
San Lucas, Baja California S., Mexico **164** 27 10N 112 14W
San Lucas, Baja California S., Mexico **164** 22 53N 109 54W
San Lucas, U.S.A. **163** 36 8N 121 1W
San Lucas, C. de **164** 22 50N 110 0W
San Lucido **65** 39 18N 16 3 E
San Luis, Argent. **172** 33 20 S 66 20W
San Luis, Cuba **166** 22 17N 83 46W
San Luis, Guat. **166** 16 14N 89 27W
San Luis, U.S.A. **161** 37 14N 105 26W
San Luis, Venez. **174** 11 7N 69 42W
San Luis □ **172** 34 0 S 66 0W
San Luís de la Loma **164** 17 18N 100 55W
San Luís de la Paz **164** 21 19N 100 32W
San Luís de Potosí **164** 22 9N 100 59W
San Luís de Potosí □ **164** 22 10N 101 0W
San Luis, I. **164** 29 58N 114 26W
San Luis Obispo **161** 35 21N 120 38W
San Luis Res. **163** 37 4N 121 5W
San Luis Río Colorado **164** 32 29N 114 48W
San Luis, Sierra de **172** 37 25N 66 10W
San Marco Argentano **65** 39 34N 16 8 E
San Marco dei Cavoti **65** 41 20N 14 50 E
San Marco in Lámis **65** 41 43N 15 38 E
San Marcos, Guat. **166** 14 59N 91 52W
San Marcos, U.S.A. **159** 29 53N 98 0W
San Marcos, I. **164** 27 13N 112 6W
San Marino **63** 43 56N 12 25 E
San Marino ■ **63** 43 56N 12 25 E
San Martín, Argent. **172** 33 5 S 68 28W
San Martín, Colomb. **174** 3 42N 73 42W
San Martín de Valdeiglesias **56** 40 21N 4 24W
San Martín, L. **176** 48 50 S 72 50W
San Martino de Calvi **62** 45 57N 9 41 E
San Mateo, Spain **58** 40 28N 0 10 E
San Mateo, U.S.A. **163** 37 32N 122 19W
San Matías **174** 16 25 S 58 20W
San Matías, Golfo de **176** 41 30 S 64 0W
San Miguel, El Sal. **166** 13 30N 88 12W
San Miguel, Panama **166** 8 27N 78 55W
San Miguel, Spain **59** 39 3N 1 26 E
San Miguel, U.S.A. **163** 35 45N 120 42W
San Miguel, Venez. **174** 9 40N 65 11W
San Miguel de Salinas **59** 37 59N 0 47W
San Miguel de Tucumán **172** 26 50 S 65 20W
San Miguel del Monte **172** 35 23 S 58 50W
San Miguel I. **163** 34 2N 120 23W
San Miguel, R., Boliv. **174** 16 0 S 62 45W
San Miguel, R., Ecuador/Ecuador **174** 0 25N 76 30W
San Miniato **62** 43 40N 10 50 E
San Narcisco **103** 15 2N 120 3 E
San Nicolás de los Arroyas **172** 33 17 S 60 10W
San Nicolas I. **154** 33 16N 119 30W
San Onafre **163** 33 22N 117 34W
San Onofre **174** 9 44N 75 32W
San Pablo, Boliv. **172** 21 43 S 66 38W
San Pablo, Colomb. **174** 5 27N 70 56W
San Paolo di Civitate **65** 41 44N 15 16 E
San Pedro, Buenos Aires, Argent. **173** 33 43 S 59 45W
San Pedro, Jujuy, Argent. **172** 24 12 S 64 55W
San Pedro, Chile **172** 21 58 S 68 30W
San Pedro, Colomb. **174** 4 56N 71 53W
San Pedro, Dom. Rep. **167** 18 30N 69 18W
San Pedro, Ivory C. **120** 4 50N 6 33W
San Pedro, Mexico **164** 23 55N 110 17W
San Pedro □ **172** 24 0 S 57 0W
San Pedro Channel **163** 33 35N 118 25W
San Pedro de Arimena **174** 4 37N 71 42W
San Pedro de Atacama **172** 22 55 S 68 15W
San Pedro de Jujuy **172** 24 12 S 64 55W
San Pedro de las Colonias **164** 25 50N 102 59W
San Pedro de Lloc **174** 7 15 S 79 28W
San Pedro del Norte **166** 13 4N 84 33W
San Pedro del Paraná **172** 26 43 S 56 13W
San Pedro del Pinatar **59** 37 50N 0 50W
San Pedro Mártir, Sierra **164** 31 0N 115 30W
San Pedro Mixtepec **165** 16 2N 97 0W
San Pedro Ocampo = Melchor Ocampo **164** 24 52N 101 40W
San Pedro, Pta. **172** 25 30 S 70 38W
San Pedro, R., Chihuahua, Mexico **164** 28 20N 106 10W
San Pedro, R., Michoacan, Mexico **164** 19 23N 103 51W
San Pedro, R., Nayarit, Mexico **164** 21 45N 105 30W
San Pedro, R., U.S.A. **161** 32 45N 110 35W
San Pedro, Sierra de **57** 39 18N 6 40W
San Pedro Sula **166** 15 30N 88 0W
San Pedro Tututepec **165** 16 9N 97 38W
San Pedro,Pta. **172** 25 30 S 70 38W
San Pietro, I. **64** 39 9N 8 17 E
San Pietro Vernotico **65** 40 28N 18 0 E
San Quintín, Mexico **164** 30 29N 115 57W

San Quintín Santiago

San Quintín, Phil. 103 16 1N 120 56 E
San, R. 54 50 25N 22 20 E
San Rafael, Argent. 172 34 40 S 68 30W
San Rafael, Colomb. 174 6 2N 69 45W
San Rafael, Calif., U.S.A. 163 38 0N 122 32W
San Rafael, N. Mex., U.S.A. 161 35 6N 107 58W
San Rafael, Venez. 174 10 42N 71 46W
San Rafael Mtn. 163 34 41N 119 52W
San Ramón de la Nueva Orán 172 23 10 S 64 20W
San Remo 62 43 48N 7 47 E
San Román, C. 174 12 12N 70 0W
San Roque, Argent. 172 28 15 S 58 45W
San Roque, Spain 57 36 17N 5 21W
San Rosendo 172 37 10 S 72 50W
San Saba 159 31 12N 98 45W
San Salvador 166 13 40N 89 20W
San Salvador de Jujuy 172 23 30 S 65 40W
San Salvador (Watlings) I. 167 24 0N 74 40W
San Sebastián, Argent. 176 53 10 S 68 30W
San Sebastián, Spain 58 43 17N 1 58W
San Sebastián, Venez. 174 9 57N 67 11W
San Serverino 63 43 13N 13 10 E
San Severo 63 41 41N 15 23 E
San Simeon 163 35 39N 121 11W
San Simon 161 32 14N 109 16W
San Stéfano di Cadore 63 46 34N 12 33 E
San Telmo 164 30 58N 116 6W
San Tiburcio 164 24 8N 101 32W
San Valentin, Mte. 176 46 30 S 73 30W
San Vicente de Alcántara 57 39 22N 7 8W
San Vicente de la Barquera 56 43 30N 4 29W
San Vicente del Caguán 174 2 7N 74 46W
San Vicenzo 93 43 9N 10 32 E
San Vito al Tagliamento 63 45 55N 12 50 E
San Vito, C. 64 38 11N 12 41 E
San Vito Chietino 63 42 19N 14 27 E
San Vito dei Normanni 65 40 40N 17 40 E
San Yanaro 174 2 47N 69 42W
San Ygnacio 159 27 6N 92 24W
San Ysidro 161 32 33N 117 5W
San'a 91 15 27N 44 12 E
Sana, R. 63 44 40N 16 43 E
Sanaba 120 12 25N 3 47W
Sanabria, La 56 42 0N 6 30W
Sanâfir 122 27 49N 34 37 E
Sanaga, R. 121 3 35N 9 38 E
Sanak I 147 53 30N 162 30W
Sanaloa, Presa 164 24 50N 107 20W
Sanana 103 2 5 S 125 50 E
Sanand 94 22 59N 72 25 E
Sanandaj 92 35 25N 47 7 E
Sanandita 172 21 40 S 63 35W
Sanary 45 43 7N 5 48 E
Sanawad 94 22 11N 76 5 E
Sanbe-San 110 35 6N 132 38 E
Sancergues 43 47 10N 2 54 E
Sancerre 43 47 20N 2 50 E
Sanch'a Ho 108 26 55N 106 6 E
Sanch'aho 107 44 59N 126 1 E
Sánchez 167 19 15N 69 36W
Sanchiang 108 25 22N 109 26 E
Sanchor 94 24 52N 71 49 E
Sanco, Pt. 103 8 15N 126 24 E
Sancoins 43 46 47N 2 55 E
Sancti-Spíritus 166 21 52N 79 33W
Sand Lake 150 47 46N 84 31W
Sand Point 147 55 20N 160 32W
Sand, R. 129 22 25 S 30 5 E
Sand Springs 159 36 12N 96 5W
Sanda 111 34 53N 135 14 E
Sanda I. 34 55 17N 5 35W
Sandah 122 20 35N 39 32 E
Sandakan 102 5 53N 118 10 E
Sandalwood 140 34 55 S 140 9 E
Sandan 101 12 46N 106 0 E
Sandanski 67 41 35N 23 16 E
Sandaré 120 14 40N 10 15W
Sanday I. 36 57 2N 6 30W
Sanday, I. 37 59 15N 2 30W
Sanday Sd. 37 59 11N 2 31W
Sandbach 32 53 9N 2 23W
Sandbank 34 55 58N 4 57W
Sande, Möre og Romsdal, Norway 71 62 15N 5 27 E
Sande, Sogn og Fjordane, Norway 71 61 20N 5 47 E
Sandefjord 71 59 10N 10 15 E
Sandeid 71 59 33N 5 52 E
Sanders 161 35 12N 109 25W
Sanderson 159 30 5N 102 30W
Sanderston 140 34 46 S 139 15 E
Sandfell 74 63 57N 16 48W
Sandfly L. 153 55 43N 106 6W
Sandgate, Austral. 139 27 18 S 153 3 E
Sandgate, U.K. 29 51 5N 1 9 E
Sandhammaren, C. 73 55 23N 14 14 E
Sandhead 34 54 48N 4 58W
Sandhurst 29 51 21N 0 48W
Sandia 174 14 10 S 69 30W
Sandikli 92 38 30N 30 20 E
Sandiman, Mt. 137 24 21 S 115 20 E
Sandnes 71 58 50N 5 45 E
Sandness 37 60 18N 1 38W
Sandoa 124 9 48 S 23 0 E
Sandomierz 54 50 40N 21 43 E
Sandona 174 1 17N 77 28W
Sandover, R. 138 21 43 S 136 32 E
Sandoway 99 18 20N 94 30 E
Sandown 28 50 39N 1 9W
Sandpoint 160 48 20N 116 40W
Sandray, I. 36 56 53N 7 30W
Sandringham 29 52 50N 0 30 E
Sandslån 72 63 2N 17 49 E
Sandspit 152 53 14N 131 49W
Sandston 162 37 31N 77 19W
Sandstone 137 27 59 S 119 16 E
Sandusky, Mich., U.S.A. 150 43 26N 82 50W
Sandusky, Ohio, U.S.A. 156 41 25N 82 40W
Sandveld 128 32 0 S 18 15 E
Sandvig, Denmark 73 55 18N 14 48 E
Sandvig, Sweden 72 55 32N 14 47 E
Sandvika 71 59 54N 10 29 E
Sandviken 72 60 38N 16 46 E
Sandwich 29 51 16N 1 21 E
Sandwich B., Can. 151 53 40N 57 15W
Sandwich B., S. Afr. 128 23 25 S 14 20 E
Sandwich, C. 138 18 14 S 146 18 E
Sandwich Group 13 57 0 S 27 0W
Sandwip Chan. 99 22 35N 91 35 E
Sandy 29 53 8N 0 18W
Sandy Bight 137 33 50 S 123 20 E
Sandy C., Queens., Austral. 139 24 42 S 153 15 E
Sandy C., Tas., Austral. 138 41 25 S 144 45 E
Sandy Cay 167 23 13N 75 18W
Sandy Cr. 160 42 20N 109 30W
Sandy L. 150 53 2N 93 0W
Sandy Lake 150 53 0N 93 15W
Sandy Narrows 153 55 5N 103 4W
Sanford, Fla., U.S.A. 157 28 45N 81 20W
Sanford, Me., U.S.A. 162 43 28N 70 47W
Sanford, N.C., U.S.A. 157 35 30N 79 10W
Sanford, Mt. 136 16 58 S 130 32 E
Sanford Mt. 148 62 30N 143 0W
Sanford, R. 137 27 22 S 115 53 E
Sang-i-Masha 94 33 16N 67 5 E
Sanga 127 12 22 S 35 21 E
Sanga, R. 124 1 0N 16 30 E
Sanga Tolon 77 61 50N 149 40 E
Sangamner 96 19 30N 74 15 E
Sangar, Afghan. 94 32 56N 65 30 E
Sangar, U.S.S.R. 77 63 55N 127 31 E
Sangar Sarcai 94 34 27N 70 35 E
Sangasanga 102 0 29 S 117 13 E
Sangchen La 99 31 30N 84 40 E
Sangchih 109 29 25N 109 30 E
Sange 126 6 58 S 84 40 E
Sangeang, I. 103 8 12 S 119 6 E
Sanger 163 36 47N 119 35W
Sangerhausen 48 51 28N 11 18 E
Sanggau 102 0 5N 110 30 E
Sangihe, Kep. 103 3 0N 126 0 E
Sangihe, P. 103 3 45N 125 30 E
Sangju 107 36 25N 128 10 E
Sangkan Ho 106 40 24N 115 19 E
Sangkapura 102 5 52 S 112 40 E
Sangkhla 100 15 7N 98 28 E
Sangli 96 16 55N 74 33 E
Sangmélina 121 2 57N 12 1 E
Sangonera, R. 59 37 39N 2 0W
Sangpang Bum 98 26 30N 95 50 E
Sangre de Cristo Mts. 159 37 0N 105 0W
Sangro, R. 63 42 10N 14 30 E
Sangudo 152 53 50N 114 54W
Sangüesa 58 42 37N 1 17W
Sanguinaires, I. 45 41 51N 8 36 E
Sanhala 120 10 3N 6 51W
Sanho 107 39 59N 117 4 E
Sani R. 100 13 32N 105 57 E
Sanish 158 48 0N 102 30W
Sanje 126 0 49 S 31 30 E
Sankaranayinarkovil 97 9 10N 77 35 E
Sankeshwar 96 16 23N 74 23 E
Sankosh, R. 98 26 24N 89 47 E
Sankt Andra 52 46 46N 14 50 E
Sankt Antönien 51 46 58N 9 48 E
Sankt Blasien 49 47 47N 8 7 E
Sankt Gallen 51 47 26N 9 22 E
Sankt Gallen □ 51 47 25N 9 22 E
Sankt Ingbert 49 49 16N 7 6 E
Sankt Johann 52 47 22N 13 12 E
Sankt Margrethen 51 47 28N 9 37 E
Sankt Moritz 51 46 30N 9 50 E
Sankt Olof 73 55 37N 14 8 E
Sankt Pölten 52 48 12N 15 38 E
Sankt Valentin 52 48 11N 14 33 E
Sankt Veit 52 46 54N 14 22 E
Sankt Wendel 49 49 27N 7 9 E
Sankt Wolfgang 52 47 43N 13 27 E
Sankuru, R. 124 4 17 S 20 25 E
Sanlúcar de Barrameda 57 37 26N 6 18W
Sanlucár la Mayor 57 37 26N 6 18W
Sanluri 64 39 35N 8 55 E
Sanmártin 70 46 19N 25 58 E
Sanmen 109 29 5N 121 35 E
Sanmenhsia 106 34 46N 111 30 E
Sanming 109 26 13N 117 35 E
Sannan 111 35 2N 135 1 E
Sannaspos 128 29 6 S 26 34 E
Sannicandro Gargánico 65 41 50N 15 34 E
Sânnicolaul-Maré 66 46 5N 20 39 E
Sannidal 71 58 55N 9 15 E
Sannieshof 128 26 30 S 25 47 E
Sano 111 36 19N 139 35 E
Sanok 54 49 35N 22 10 E
Sanokwelle 120 7 19N 8 38W
Sanpa 108 29 43N 99 33 E
Sanpah 139 30 32 S 141 12 E
Sanquhar 35 55 21N 3 56W
Sansanding Dam 120 13 37N 6 0W
Sansanné-Mango 121 10 20N 0 30 E
Sansepolcro 63 43 34N 12 8 E
Sanshui 109 23 11N 112 53 E
Sanski Most 63 44 46N 16 40 E
Sansui 108 26 57N 108 37 E
Sant' Ágata de Gati 65 41 6N 14 30 E
Sant' Ágata di Militello 65 38 2N 14 40 E
Santa Ana, Ecuador 174 1 10 S 80 20W
Santa Ana, El Sal. 166 14 0N 89 40W
Santa Ana, Mexico 164 30 31N 111 8W
Santa Ana, U.S.A. 163 33 48N 117 55W
Santa Ana, El Beni 174 13 50 S 65 40W
Sant' Ángelo Lodigiano 62 45 14N 9 25 E
Sant' Antíoco 64 39 2N 8 30 E
Sant' Antíoco, I. 64 39 2N 8 30 E
Sant' Arcángelo di Romagna 63 44 4N 12 26 E
Santa Bárbara, Brazil 171 16 0 S 59 0W
Santa Bárbara, Colomb. 174 5 53N 75 35W
Santa Barbara 166 14 53N 88 14W
Santa Bárbara, Mexico 164 26 48N 105 50W
Santa Bárbara, Spain 58 40 42N 0 29 E
Santa Barbara 163 34 25N 119 40W
Santa Bárbara 174 7 47N 71 10W
Santa Barbara Channel 163 34 20N 120 0W
Santa Barbara I. 163 33 29N 119 2W
Santa Barbara Is. 161 33 31N 119 0W
Santa Bárbara, Mt. 59 37 23N 2 50W
Santa Catalina 174 10 36N 75 17W
Santa Catalina, G. of 163 33 0N 118 0W
Santa Catalina, I., Mexico 164 25 40N 110 50W
Santa Catalina, I., U.S.A. 163 33 20N 118 30W
Santa Catarina □ 173 27 25 S 48 30W
Santa Catarina, I. de 173 27 30 S 48 40W
Santa Caterina 65 37 37N 14 1 E
Santa Cecília 173 26 56 S 50 27W
Santa Clara, Cuba 166 22 20N 80 0W
Santa Clara, Calif., U.S.A. 163 37 21N 122 0W
Santa Clara, Utah, U.S.A. 161 37 10N 113 38W
Santa Clara de Olimar 173 32 50 S 54 54W
Santa Clotilde 174 2 25 S 73 45W
Santa Coloma de Farnés 58 41 50N 2 39 E
Santa Coloma de Gramanet 58 41 27N 2 13 E
Santa Comba 56 43 2N 8 49W
Santa Croce Camerina 65 36 50N 14 30 E
Santa Cruz, Argent. 176 50 0 S 68 50W
Santa Cruz, Boliv. 174 17 43 S 63 10W
Santa Cruz, Brazil 170 7 57 S 36 12W
Santa Cruz, Canary Is. 116 28 29N 16 26W
Santa Cruz, Chile 172 34 38 S 71 27W
Santa Cruz, C. Rica 166 10 15N 85 41W
Santa Cruz, Phil. 103 14 20N 121 30 E
Santa Cruz, Calif., U.S.A. 163 36 55N 122 1W
Santa Cruz, N. Mexico, U.S.A. 161 35 59N 106 1W
Santa Cruz □ 174 17 43 S 63 10W
Santa Cruz Cabrália 171 16 17 S 39 2W
Santa Cruz de Barahona 167 18 12N 71 6W
Santa Cruz de Mudela 59 38 39N 3 28W
Santa Cruz de Tenerife □ 72 28 10N 17 20W
Santa Cruz del Norte 166 23 9N 81 55W
Santa Cruz del Retamar 56 40 8N 4 14W
Santa Cruz del Sur 166 20 50N 78 0W
Santa Cruz do Rio Pardo 173 22 54 S 49 37W
Santa Cruz do Sul 173 29 42 S 52 25W
Santa Cruz I. 154 34 0N 119 45W
Santa Cruz, Is. 130 10 30 S 166 0 E
Santa Cruz, R. 176 50 10 S 70 0W
Santa Elena, Argent. 172 30 58 S 59 47W
Santa Elena, Ecuador 174 2 16 S 80 52W
Santa Elena C. 167 10 54N 85 56W
Santa Enimie 44 44 24N 3 26 E
Sant' Eufémia, Golfo di 65 38 50N 16 10 E
Santa Eulalia 59 40 34N 1 20W
Santa Fe, Argent. 172 31 35 S 60 41W
Santa Fe, Spain 57 37 11N 3 43W
Santa Fe, U.S.A. 161 35 40N 106 0W
Santa Fé □ 172 31 50 S 60 55W
Santa Filomena 170 9 0 S 45 50W
Santa Genoveva, Mt. 164 23 18N 109 52W
Santa Groce di Magliano 65 41 43N 14 59 E
Santa Helena 170 2 14 S 45 18W
Santa Helena de Goiás 171 17 43 S 50 35W
Santa Inês 171 13 17 S 39 48W
Santa Inés, I. 176 54 0 S 73 0W
Santa Inés, Mt. 57 38 32N 5 37W
Santa Isabel, Argent. 172 36 10 S 67 0W
Santa Isabel, Brazil 171 13 45 S 56 30W
Santa Isabel = Rey Malabo 121 3 45N 8 50 E
Santa Isabel do Araguaia 170 6 7 S 48 19W
Santa Isabel, Pico 121 4 43N 8 49 E
Santa Juliana 171 19 19 S 47 32W
Santa Lucía, Corrientes, Argent. 172 28 58 S 59 5W
Santa Lucía, San Juan, Argent. 172 31 30 S 68 45W
Santa Lucía, Spain 59 37 35N 0 58W
Santa Lucia 172 34 27 S 56 24W
Santa Lucia Range 163 36 0N 121 20W
Santa Luzia 170 6 53 S 36 56W
Santa Magdalena, I. 164 24 50N 112 15W
Santa Margarita, Argent. 172 38 18 S 61 35W
Santa Margarita, U.S.A. 163 35 23N 120 37W
Santa Margarita, I. 164 24 30N 112 0W
Santa Margarita, R. 163 33 13N 117 23W
Santa Margherita 62 44 20N 9 11 E
Santa María, Argent. 172 26 40 S 66 0W
Santa Maria, Brazil 173 29 40 S 53 40W
Santa Maria 65 41 3N 14 29 E
Santa María 164 27 40N 114 40W
Santa Maria, Spain 58 39 39N 2 45 E
Santa Maria, Switz. 51 46 36N 10 25 E
Santa Maria, U.S.A. 163 34 58N 120 29W
Santa Maria, Zambia 127 11 5 S 29 58 E
Santa Maria, Bahía de 164 25 10N 108 40W
Santa Maria, Cabo de 57 36 39N 7 53W
Santa Maria da Vitória 171 13 24 S 44 12W
Santa María del Oro 164 25 30N 105 20W
Santa Maria di Leuca, C. 65 39 48N 18 20 E
Santa Maria do Suaçuí 171 18 12 S 42 25W
Santa María la Real de Nieva 56 41 4N 4 24W
Santa María, R. 164 31 0N 107 14W
Santa Marta, Colomb. 174 11 15N 74 13W
Santa Marta, Spain 57 38 37N 6 39W
Santa Marta Grande, C. 173 28 43 S 48 50W
Santa Marta, Ría de 56 43 44N 7 45W
Santa Marta, Sierra Nevada de 147 10 55N 73 50W
Santa Monica 163 34 0N 118 30W
Santa Napa 160 38 28N 122 45W
Santa Olalla, Huelva, Spain 57 37 54N 6 14W
Santa Olalla, Toledo, Spain 56 40 2N 4 25W
Sant' Onofrio 65 38 42N 16 10 E
Santa Paula 163 34 20N 119 2W
Santa Pola 59 38 13N 0 35W
Santa Quitéria 170 4 20 S 40 10W
Santa Rita, U.S.A. 161 32 50N 108 0W
Santa Rita, Guarico, Venez. 174 8 8N 66 16W
Santa Rita, Zulia, Venez. 174 10 32N 71 32W
Santa Rosa, La Pampa, Argent. 172 36 40 S 64 30W
Santa Rosa, San Luis, Argent. 172 32 30 S 65 10W
Santa Rosa, Boliv. 174 10 25 S 67 20W
Santa Rosa, Brazil 173 27 52 S 54 29W
Santa Rosa, Colomb. 174 3 32N 69 48W
Santa Rosa, Hond. 164 14 40N 89 0W
Santa Rosa, Calif., U.S.A. 163 38 26N 122 43W
Santa Rosa, N. Mexico, U.S.A. 159 34 58N 104 40W
Santa Rosa, Amazonas, Venez. 174 1 29N 66 55W
Santa Rosa, Apure, Venez. 174 6 37N 67 57W
Santa Rosa de Cabal 174 4 52N 75 38W
Santa Rosa de Copán 166 14 47N 88 46W
Santa Rosa de Osos 174 6 39N 75 28W
Santa Rosa de Río Primero 172 31 8 S 63 20W
Santa Rosa de Viterbo 174 5 53N 72 59W
Santa Rosa I., Calif., U.S.A. 163 34 0N 120 6W
Santa Rosa I., Fla., U.S.A. 157 30 23N 87 0W
Santa Rosa Mts. 160 41 45N 117 30W
Santa Rosalia 164 27 20N 112 30W
Santa Sofia 63 43 57N 11 55 E
Santa Sylvina 172 27 50 S 61 10W
Santa Tecla = Nueva San Salvador 164 13 40N 89 25W
Santa Teresa, Argent. 172 33 25 S 60 47W
Santa Teresa, Brazil 171 19 55 S 40 36W
Santa Teresa, Mexico 165 25 17N 97 51W
Santa Teresa, Venez. 174 4 43N 61 4W
Santa Teresa di Riva 63 37 58N 15 21 E
Santa Teresa Gallura 64 41 14N 9 12 E
Santa Teresinha 170 12 45 S 39 32W
Santa Vitória 171 18 50 S 50 8W
Santa Vitória do Palmar 173 33 32 S 53 25W
Santa Ynez 163 34 37N 120 5W
Santa Ynez, R. 163 34 37N 120 41W
Santa Ysabel 163 33 7N 116 40W
Sant'ai 108 31 5N 105 2 E
Santadi 64 39 5N 8 42 E
Santahar 98 24 48N 88 59 E
Santaluz 171 11 15 S 39 22W
Santana 171 13 2 S 44 5W
Santana, Coxilha de 173 30 50 S 55 35W
Santana do Ipanema 170 9 22 S 37 14W
Santana do Livramento 173 30 55 S 55 30W
Santander, Colomb. 174 3 1N 76 28W
Santander, Spain 56 43 27N 3 51W
Santander □ 56 43 25N 4 0W
Santander Jiménez 165 24 11N 98 29W
Santañy 59 39 20N 3 5 E
Santaquin 160 40 0N 111 51W
Santarém, Brazil 175 2 25 S 54 42W
Santarém, Port. 57 39 12N 8 42W
Santarém □ 57 39 10N 8 40W
Santaren Channel 166 24 0N 79 30W
Santèramo in Colle 65 40 48N 16 45 E
Santerno, R. 63 44 10N 11 38 E
Santhia 62 45 20N 8 10 E
Santiago, Brazil 173 29 11 S 54 52W
Santiago, Chile 172 33 24 S 70 50W
Santiago, Dom. Rep. 167 19 30N 70 40W

| Name | Pg | Lat ° | ′ | N/S | Long ° | ′ | E/W |
|---|---|---|---|---|---|---|---|
| Santiago, Panama | 166 | 8 | 0N | | 81 | 0W | |
| Santiago □ | 172 | 33 | 30 s | | 70 | 50W | |
| Santiago de Compostela | 56 | 42 | 52N | | 8 | 37W | |
| Santiago de Cuba | 166 | 20 | 0N | | 75 | 49W | |
| Santiago del Estero | 172 | 27 | 50 s | | 64 | 15W | |
| Santiago del Estero □ | 172 | 27 | 50 s | | 64 | 20W | |
| Santiago do Cacém | 57 | 38 | 1N | | 8 | 42W | |
| Santiago Ixcuintla | 164 | 21 | 50N | | 105 | 11W | |
| Santiago Papasquiaro | 164 | 25 | 0N | | 105 | 20W | |
| Santiago, Punta de | 121 | 3 | 12N | | 8 | 40 E | |
| Santiaguillo, L. de | 164 | 24 | 50N | | 104 | 50W | |
| Santillana del Mar | 56 | 43 | 24N | | 4 | 6W | |
| Santipur | 95 | 23 | 17N | | 88 | 25 E | |
| Säntis | 51 | 47 | 15N | | 9 | 22 E | |
| Santisteban del Puerto | 59 | 38 | 17N | | 3 | 15W | |
| Santo Amaro | 171 | 12 | 30 s | | 38 | 50W | |
| Santo Anastácio | 173 | 21 | 58 s | | 51 | 39W | |
| Santo André | 173 | 23 | 39 s | | 46 | 29W | |
| Santo Ângelo | 173 | 28 | 15 s | | 54 | 15W | |
| Santo Antonio | 170 | 15 | 50 s | | 56 | 0W | |
| Santo Antônio de Jesus | 171 | 12 | 58 s | | 39 | 16W | |
| Santo Antonio do Zaire | 124 | 6 | 7 s | | 12 | 20 E | |
| Santo Corazón | 174 | 18 | 0 s | | 58 | 45W | |
| Santo Domingo, Dom. Rep. | 167 | 18 | 30N | | 70 | 0W | |
| Santo Domingo, Baja Calif. N., Mexico | 164 | 30 | 43N | | 115 | 56W | |
| Santo Domingo, Baja Calif. S., Mexico | 164 | 25 | 32N | | 112 | 2W | |
| Santo Domingo, Nic. | 166 | 12 | 14N | | 84 | 59W | |
| Santo Domingo de la Calzada | 58 | 42 | 26N | | 2 | 27W | |
| Santo Isabel do Morro | 171 | 11 | 34 s | | 50 | 40W | |
| Santo Stéfano di Camastro | 65 | 38 | 1N | | 14 | 22 E | |
| Santo Stino di Livenza | 63 | 45 | 45N | | 12 | 40 E | |
| Santo Tirso | 56 | 41 | 29N | | 8 | 18W | |
| Santo Tomas | 164 | 31 | 33N | | 116 | 24W | |
| Santo Tomás | 174 | 14 | 34 s | | 72 | 30W | |
| Santo Tomé | 173 | 28 | 40 s | | 56 | 5W | |
| Santoña | 56 | 43 | 29N | | 3 | 20W | |
| Santos | 173 | 24 | 0 s | | 46 | 20W | |
| Santos Dumont | 173 | 22 | 55 s | | 43 | 10W | |
| Santos, Sierra de los | 57 | 38 | 7N | | 5 | 12W | |
| Santport | 46 | 52 | 26N | | 4 | 39 E | |
| Santu | 108 | 25 | 59N | | 107 | 52 E | |
| Sanur | 90 | 32 | 22N | | 35 | 15 E | |
| Sanvignes-les-Mines | 43 | 46 | 40N | | 4 | 18 E | |
| San'yō | 110 | 34 | 2N | | 131 | 5 E | |
| Sanyuki-Sammyaku | 110 | 34 | 5N | | 133 | 0 E | |
| Sanza Pombo | 124 | 7 | 18 s | | 15 | 56 E | |
| São Anastacio | 173 | 22 | 0 s | | 51 | 40W | |
| São Bartolomeu de Messines | 57 | 37 | 15N | | 8 | 17W | |
| São Benedito | 170 | 4 | 3 s | | 40 | 53W | |
| São Bento | 170 | 2 | 42 s | | 44 | 50W | |
| São Bento do Norte | 170 | 5 | 4 s | | 36 | 2W | |
| São Borja | 173 | 28 | 45 s | | 56 | 0W | |
| São Bras d'Alportel | 57 | 37 | 8N | | 7 | 58W | |
| São Caitano | 170 | 8 | 21 s | | 36 | 6W | |
| São Carlos | 173 | 22 | 0 s | | 47 | 50W | |
| São Cristóvão | 170 | 11 | 15 s | | 37 | 15W | |
| São Domingos, Brazil | 171 | 13 | 25 s | | 46 | 10W | |
| São Domingos, Guin.-Biss. | 170 | 12 | 22N | | 16 | 8W | |
| São Domingos do Maranhão | 170 | 5 | 42 s | | 44 | 22W | |
| São Félix, Bahia, Brazil | 171 | 12 | 38 s | | 38 | 58W | |
| São Félix, Mato Grosso, Brazil | 171 | 11 | 36 s | | 50 | 39W | |
| Sao Francisco | 171 | 16 | 0 s | | 44 | 50W | |
| São Francisco do Maranhão | 170 | 6 | 15 s | | 42 | 52W | |
| São Francisco do Sul | 173 | 26 | 15 s | | 48 | 36W | |
| São Francisco, R. | 170 | 10 | 30 s | | 36 | 24W | |
| São Gabriel | 173 | 30 | 10 s | | 54 | 30W | |
| São Gabriel da Palha | 171 | 18 | 47 s | | 40 | 59W | |
| São Gonçalo | 173 | 22 | 48 s | | 43 | 5W | |
| São Gotardo | 171 | 19 | 19 s | | 46 | 3W | |
| Sao Hill | 127 | 8 | 20 s | | 35 | 18 E | |
| São João da Boa Vista | 173 | 22 | 0 s | | 46 | 52W | |
| São João da Pesqueira | 56 | 41 | 8N | | 7 | 24W | |
| São João da Ponte | 171 | 15 | 56 s | | 44 | 1W | |
| São João del Rei | 173 | 21 | 8 s | | 44 | 15W | |
| São João do Araguaia | 170 | 5 | 23 s | | 48 | 46W | |
| São João do Paraíso | 171 | 15 | 19 s | | 42 | 1W | |
| São João do Piauí | 170 | 8 | 10 s | | 42 | 15W | |
| São João dos Patos | 170 | 6 | 30 s | | 43 | 42W | |
| São João Evangelista | 171 | 18 | 32 s | | 42 | 45W | |
| São Joaquim da Barra | 171 | 20 | 35 s | | 47 | 53W | |
| São José, B. de | 170 | 2 | 38 s | | 44 | 4W | |
| São José da Laje | 170 | 9 | 1 s | | 36 | 3W | |
| São José de Mipibu | 170 | 6 | 5 s | | 35 | 15W | |
| São José do Peixe | 170 | 7 | 24 s | | 42 | 34W | |
| São José do Rio Prêto | 173 | 20 | 50 s | | 49 | 20W | |
| São José dos Campos | 173 | 23 | 7 s | | 45 | 52W | |
| São Leopoldo | 173 | 29 | 50 s | | 51 | 10W | |
| São Lourenço, Mato Grosso, Brazil | 173 | 16 | 30 s | | 55 | 5W | |
| São Lourenço, Minas Gerais, Brazil | 171 | 22 | 7 s | | 45 | 3W | |
| São Lourenço, R. | 175 | 16 | 40 s | | 56 | 0W | |
| São Luís do Curu | 170 | 3 | 40 s | | 39 | 14W | |
| São Luís Gonzaga | 173 | 28 | 25 s | | 55 | 0W | |
| São Luís (Maranhão) | 170 | 2 | 39 s | | 44 | 15W | |
| Sao Marcelino | 174 | 1 | 0N | | 67 | 12W | |
| São Marcelino | 174 | 1 | 0N | | 67 | 12W | |
| São Marcos, B. de | 170 | 2 | 0 s | | 44 | 0W | |
| São Marcos, R. | 171 | 18 | 15 s | | 47 | 37W | |
| São Martinho | 56 | 39 | 30N | | 9 | 8W | |
| São Mateus | 171 | 18 | 44 s | | 39 | 50W | |
| São Mateus, R. | 171 | 18 | 35 s | | 39 | 44W | |
| São Miguel | 16 | 37 | 33N | | 25 | 27W | |

| Name | Pg | Lat ° | ′ | N/S | Long ° | ′ | E/W |
|---|---|---|---|---|---|---|---|
| São Miguel do Araguaia | 171 | 13 | 19 s | | 50 | 13W | |
| São Miguel dos Campos | 170 | 9 | 47 s | | 36 | 5W | |
| São Nicolau, R. | 170 | 5 | 45 s | | 42 | 2W | |
| São Paulo | 173 | 23 | 40 s | | 46 | 50W | |
| São Paulo □ | 173 | 22 | 0 s | | 49 | 0W | |
| São Pedro do Piauí | 171 | 5 | 56 s | | 42 | 43W | |
| São Pedro do Sul | 56 | 40 | 46N | | 8 | 4W | |
| São Rafael | 170 | 5 | 47 s | | 36 | 55W | |
| São Raimundo das Mangabeiras | 170 | 7 | 1 s | | 45 | 29W | |
| São Raimundo Nonato | 170 | 9 | 1 s | | 42 | 42W | |
| São Romão, Amazonas, Brazil | 174 | 5 | 53 s | | 67 | 50W | |
| São Romão, Minas Gerais, Brazil | 171 | 16 | 22 s | | 45 | 4W | |
| São Roque, C. de | 170 | 5 | 30 s | | 35 | 10W | |
| São Sebastião do Paraíso | 173 | 20 | 54 s | | 46 | 59W | |
| São Sebastião, I. | 173 | 23 | 50 s | | 45 | 18W | |
| São Simão | 171 | 18 | 56 s | | 50 | 30W | |
| São Teotónio | 57 | 37 | 30N | | 8 | 42W | |
| São Tomé | 170 | 5 | 58 s | | 36 | 4W | |
| São Tomé, C. de | 173 | 22 | 0 s | | 41 | 10W | |
| São Tomé, I. | 114 | 0 | 10N | | 7 | 0 E | |
| São Vicente | 173 | 23 | 57 s | | 46 | 23W | |
| São Vicente, Cabo de | 57 | 37 | 0N | | 9 | 0W | |
| Saona, I. | 167 | 18 | 10N | | 68 | 40W | |
| Saône-et-Loire □ | 43 | 46 | 25N | | 4 | 50 E | |
| Sâone, R. | 43 | 46 | 25N | | 4 | 50 E | |
| Saonek | 103 | 0 | 28 s | | 130 | 47 E | |
| Saoura, O. | 118 | 29 | 55N | | 1 | 50W | |
| Sapai | 68 | 41 | 2N | | 25 | 43 E | |
| Sapão, R. | 170 | 11 | 1 s | | 45 | 32W | |
| Saparua, I. | 103 | 3 | 33 s | | 128 | 40 E | |
| Sapé | 170 | 7 | 6 s | | 35 | 13W | |
| Sapele | 121 | 5 | 50N | | 5 | 40 E | |
| Sapelo I. | 157 | 31 | 28N | | 81 | 15W | |
| Sapiéntza I. | 69 | 36 | 33N | | 21 | 43 E | |
| Sapodnyy Sayan | 77 | 52 | 30N | | 94 | 0 E | |
| Sapone | 121 | 12 | 3N | | 1 | 35W | |
| Saposoa | 174 | 6 | 55 s | | 76 | 30W | |
| Sapozhok | 81 | 53 | 59N | | 40 | 51 E | |
| Sappemeer | 46 | 53 | 10N | | 6 | 48 E | |
| Sapporo | 112 | 43 | 0N | | 141 | 15 E | |
| Sapri | 65 | 40 | 5N | | 15 | 37 E | |
| Sapudi, I. | 103 | 7 | 2 s | | 114 | 17 E | |
| Sapulpa | 159 | 36 | 0N | | 96 | 40W | |
| Sapur | 95 | 34 | 18N | | 74 | 27 E | |
| Saqota | 123 | 12 | 40N | | 39 | 1 E | |
| Saqqez | 92 | 36 | 15N | | 46 | 20 E | |
| Sar-i-Pul | 93 | 36 | 10N | | 66 | 0 E | |
| Sar Planina | 66 | 42 | 10N | | 21 | 0 E | |
| Sara | 120 | 11 | 40N | | 3 | 53W | |
| Sara Buri | 100 | 14 | 30N | | 100 | 55 E | |
| Sarab | 92 | 38 | 0N | | 47 | 30 E | |
| Sarada, R. | 99 | 28 | 15N | | 80 | 30 E | |
| Saragossa = Zaragoza | 58 | 41 | 39N | | 0 | 53W | |
| Saraguro | 174 | 3 | 35 s | | 79 | 16W | |
| Sarai | 70 | 44 | 43N | | 28 | 10 E | |
| Saraipalli | 96 | 21 | 20N | | 82 | 59 E | |
| Sarajevo | 66 | 43 | 52N | | 18 | 26 E | |
| Saraktash | 84 | 51 | 47N | | 56 | 22 E | |
| Saramati | 98 | 25 | 44N | | 95 | 2 E | |
| Saran | 122 | 19 | 35N | | 40 | 30 E | |
| Saran, G. | 102 | 0 | 30 s | | 111 | 25 E | |
| Saranac Lake | 156 | 44 | 20N | | 74 | 10W | |
| Saranda, Alb. | 68 | 39 | 59N | | 19 | 55 E | |
| Saranda, Tanz. | 126 | 5 | 45 s | | 34 | 59 E | |
| Sarandí del Yi | 173 | 33 | 18 s | | 55 | 38W | |
| Sarandí Grande | 172 | 33 | 20 s | | 55 | 50W | |
| Sarangani B. | 103 | 6 | 0N | | 125 | 13 E | |
| Sarangani Is. | 103 | 5 | 25N | | 125 | 25 E | |
| Sarangarh | 96 | 21 | 30N | | 82 | 57 E | |
| Saransk | 81 | 54 | 10N | | 45 | 10 E | |
| Sarapul | 84 | 56 | 28N | | 53 | 48 E | |
| Sarasota | 157 | 27 | 10N | | 82 | 30W | |
| Saratoga, Calif., U.S.A. | 163 | 37 | 16N | | 122 | 2W | |
| Saratoga, Wyo., U.S.A. | 160 | 41 | 30N | | 106 | 56W | |
| Saratoga Springs | 162 | 43 | 5N | | 73 | 47W | |
| Saratok | 102 | 3 | 5 s | | 110 | 50 E | |
| Saratov | 81 | 51 | 30N | | 46 | 2 E | |
| Saravane | 100 | 15 | 43N | | 106 | 25 E | |
| Sarawak □ | 102 | 2 | 0N | | 113 | 0 E | |
| Saraya | 120 | 12 | 50N | | 11 | 45W | |
| Sarbaz | 93 | 26 | 38N | | 61 | 19 E | |
| Sarbisheh | 93 | 32 | 30N | | 59 | 40 E | |
| Sårbogård | 53 | 46 | 55N | | 18 | 40 E | |
| Sarca, R. | 62 | 46 | 5N | | 10 | 45 E | |
| Sardalas | 119 | 25 | 50N | | 10 | 54 E | |
| Sardarshahr | 94 | 28 | 30N | | 74 | 29 E | |
| Sardegna, I. | 64 | 39 | 57N | | 9 | 0 E | |
| Sardhana | 94 | 29 | 9N | | 77 | 39 E | |
| Sardinata | 174 | 8 | 5N | | 72 | 48W | |
| Sardinia = Sardegna | 64 | 39 | 57N | | 9 | 0 E | |
| Sardo | 123 | 11 | 56N | | 41 | 14 E | |
| Sarektjåkkå | 74 | 67 | 27N | | 17 | 43 E | |
| Sarengrad | 66 | 45 | 14N | | 19 | 16 E | |
| Saréyamou | 120 | 16 | 25N | | 3 | 10W | |
| Sargasso Sea | 14 | 27 | 0N | | 72 | 0W | |
| Sargent | 158 | 41 | 42N | | 99 | 24W | |
| Sargodha | 94 | 32 | 10N | | 72 | 40 E | |
| Sargodha □ | 94 | 31 | 50N | | 72 | 0 E | |
| Sarh | 117 | 9 | 5N | | 18 | 23 E | |
| Sarhro, Jebel | 118 | 31 | 6N | | 5 | 0W | |
| Sári | 93 | 36 | 30N | | 53 | 11 E | |
| Sária, I. | 69 | 35 | 54N | | 27 | 17 E | |
| Sarichef C. | 147 | 54 | 38N | | 164 | 59W | |
| Sarida, R. | 90 | 32 | 4N | | 35 | 3 E | |
| Sarikamiş | 92 | 40 | 22N | | 42 | 35 E | |
| Sarikei | 102 | 2 | 8N | | 111 | 30 E | |
| Sarina | 138 | 21 | 22 s | | 149 | 13 E | |
| Sarine, R. | 50 | 46 | 32N | | 7 | 4 E | |
| Sariñena | 58 | 41 | 47N | | 0 | 10W | |

| Name | Pg | Lat ° | ′ | N/S | Long ° | ′ | E/W |
|---|---|---|---|---|---|---|---|
| Sarir Tibasti | 119 | 22 | 50N | | 18 | 30 E | |
| Sarita | 159 | 27 | 14N | | 90 | 49W | |
| Sariwoln | 107 | 38 | 31N | | 125 | 46 E | |
| Sariyer | 67 | 41 | 10N | | 29 | 3 E | |
| Sark, I. | 42 | 49 | 25N | | 2 | 20W | |
| Sarkad | 53 | 46 | 47N | | 21 | 17 E | |
| Sarlat-la-Canéda | 44 | 44 | 54N | | 1 | 13 E | |
| Sarles | 158 | 48 | 58N | | 98 | 57W | |
| Sarmi | 103 | 1 | 49 s | | 138 | 38 E | |
| Särna | 72 | 61 | 41N | | 12 | 58 E | |
| Sarnano | 63 | 43 | 2N | | 13 | 17 E | |
| Sarnen | 50 | 46 | 53N | | 8 | 13 E | |
| Sarnia | 150 | 42 | 58N | | 82 | 23W | |
| Sarno | 65 | 40 | 48N | | 14 | 35 E | |
| Sarnowa | 54 | 51 | 39N | | 16 | 53 E | |
| Sarny | 80 | 51 | 17N | | 26 | 40 E | |
| Särö | 73 | 57 | 31N | | 11 | 57 E | |
| Sarolangun | 102 | 2 | 30 s | | 102 | 30 E | |
| Saronikós Kólpos | 69 | 37 | 45N | | 23 | 45 E | |
| Saros Körfezi | 68 | 40 | 30N | | 26 | 15 E | |
| Sárospatak | 53 | 48 | 18N | | 21 | 33 E | |
| Sarosul Romanesc | 66 | 45 | 34N | | 21 | 43 E | |
| Sarpsborg | 71 | 59 | 16N | | 11 | 12 E | |
| Sarracín | 58 | 42 | 15N | | 3 | 45W | |
| Sarralbe | 43 | 48 | 55N | | 7 | 1 E | |
| Sarraz, La | 50 | 46 | 38N | | 6 | 30 E | |
| Sarre, La | 150 | 48 | 45N | | 79 | 15W | |
| Sarre, R. | 43 | 48 | 49N | | 7 | 0 E | |
| Sarre-Union | 43 | 48 | 55N | | 7 | 4 E | |
| Sarrebourg | 43 | 48 | 43N | | 7 | 3 E | |
| Sarreguemines | 43 | 49 | 1N | | 7 | 4 E | |
| Sarriá | 56 | 42 | 41N | | 7 | 29W | |
| Sarrión | 58 | 40 | 9N | | 0 | 49W | |
| Sarro | 120 | 13 | 40N | | 5 | 5W | |
| Sarstedt | 48 | 52 | 13N | | 9 | 50 E | |
| Sartène | 45 | 41 | 38N | | 9 | 0 E | |
| Sarthe □ | 42 | 47 | 58N | | 0 | 10 E | |
| Sarthe, R. | 42 | 47 | 33N | | 0 | 31W | |
| Sartilly | 42 | 48 | 45N | | 1 | 28W | |
| Sartynya | 76 | 63 | 30N | | 62 | 50 E | |
| Sarum | 122 | 21 | 11N | | 39 | 10 E | |
| Sarúr | 93 | 23 | 17N | | 58 | 4 E | |
| Sárvár | 53 | 47 | 15N | | 16 | 56 E | |
| Sarveston | 93 | 29 | 20N | | 53 | 10 E | |
| Särvfjället | 72 | 62 | 42N | | 13 | 30 E | |
| Sárviz, R. | 53 | 46 | 40N | | 18 | 40 E | |
| Sary Ozek | 85 | 44 | 22N | | 77 | 59 E | |
| Sary-Tash | 85 | 39 | 44N | | 73 | 15 E | |
| Saryagach | 85 | 41 | 27N | | 69 | 9 E | |
| Sarych, Mys. | 82 | 44 | 25N | | 33 | 25 E | |
| Sarykolskiy Khrebet | 85 | 38 | 30N | | 74 | 30 E | |
| Sarykopa, Ozero | 84 | 50 | 22N | | 64 | 6 E | |
| Sarymoin, Ozero | 84 | 51 | 36N | | 64 | 30 E | |
| Saryshagan | 76 | 46 | 12N | | 73 | 48 E | |
| Sarzana | 70 | 44 | 7N | | 9 | 57 E | |
| Sarzeau | 42 | 47 | 31N | | 2 | 48W | |
| Sas van Gent | 47 | 51 | 14N | | 3 | 48 E | |
| Sasa | 90 | 33 | 2N | | 35 | 23 E | |
| Sasabeneh | 91 | 7 | 59N | | 44 | 43 E | |
| Sasaram | 95 | 24 | 57N | | 84 | 5 E | |
| Sasayama | 111 | 35 | 4N | | 135 | 13 E | |
| Sasca Montanŭ | 66 | 44 | 41N | | 21 | 45 E | |
| Sasebo | 110 | 33 | 10N | | 129 | 43 E | |
| Saser Mt. | 95 | 34 | 50N | | 77 | 50 E | |
| Saskatchewan □ | 153 | 54 | 40N | | 106 | 0W | |
| Saskatchewan, R. | 153 | 53 | 12N | | 99 | 16W | |
| Saskatoon | 153 | 52 | 10N | | 106 | 38W | |
| Sasolburg | 129 | 26 | 46 s | | 27 | 49 E | |
| Sasovo | 81 | 54 | 25N | | 41 | 55 E | |
| Sassandra | 120 | 5 | 0N | | 6 | 8W | |
| Sassandra, R. | 120 | 5 | 0N | | 6 | 8W | |
| Sássari | 64 | 40 | 44N | | 8 | 33 E | |
| Sassenheim | 46 | 52 | 14N | | 4 | 31 E | |
| Sassnitz | 48 | 54 | 29N | | 13 | 39 E | |
| Sasso Marconi | 63 | 44 | 22N | | 11 | 12 E | |
| Sassocorvaro | 63 | 43 | 47N | | 12 | 30 E | |
| Sassoferrato | 63 | 43 | 26N | | 12 | 51 E | |
| Sassuolo | 62 | 44 | 31N | | 10 | 47 E | |
| Sástago | 58 | 41 | 19N | | 0 | 21W | |
| Sastown | 120 | 4 | 45N | | 8 | 27W | |
| Sasumua Dam | 126 | 0 | 54 s | | 36 | 46 E | |
| Sasyk, Ozero | 70 | 45 | 45N | | 30 | 0 E | |
| Sasykkul | 85 | 37 | 41N | | 73 | 11 E | |
| Sata-Misaki | 110 | 30 | 59N | | 130 | 40 E | |
| Satadougou | 120 | 12 | 40N | | 11 | 25W | |
| Satanta | 159 | 37 | 30N | | 101 | 0W | |
| Satara | 96 | 17 | 44N | | 73 | 58 E | |
| Satilla, R. | 157 | 31 | 15N | | 81 | 50W | |
| Satka | 84 | 55 | 3N | | 59 | 1 E | |
| Satkania | 98 | 22 | 4N | | 92 | 3 E | |
| Satkhira | 98 | 22 | 43N | | 89 | 8 E | |
| Satmala Hills | 96 | 20 | 15N | | 74 | 40 E | |
| Satna | 95 | 24 | 35N | | 80 | 50 E | |
| Sator, mt. | 63 | 44 | 11N | | 16 | 43 E | |
| Sátoraljaújhely | 53 | 48 | 25N | | 21 | 41 E | |
| Satpura Ra. | 94 | 21 | 40N | | 75 | 0 E | |
| Satrup | 48 | 54 | 39N | | 9 | 38 E | |
| Satsuma-Hantō | 110 | 31 | 25N | | 130 | 25 E | |
| Satsuna-Shotō | 112 | 30 | 0N | | 130 | 0 E | |
| Sattahip | 100 | 12 | 41N | | 100 | 54 E | |
| Sattenpalle | 96 | 16 | 25N | | 80 | 6 E | |
| Satu Mare | 70 | 47 | 46N | | 22 | 55 E | |
| Satui | 102 | 3 | 50 s | | 115 | 20 E | |
| Satumare □ | 70 | 47 | 45N | | 23 | 0 E | |
| Satun | 101 | 6 | 43N | | 100 | 2 E | |
| Saturnina, R. | 174 | 12 | 15 s | | 58 | 10W | |
| Sauce | 172 | 30 | 5 s | | 58 | 46W | |
| Sauceda | 164 | 25 | 46N | | 101 | 19W | |
| Saucillo | 164 | 28 | 1N | | 105 | 17W | |
| Sauda | 71 | 59 | 38N | | 6 | 21 E | |
| Saúde | 170 | 10 | 56 s | | 40 | 24W | |
| Sauðarkrókur | 74 | 65 | 45N | | 19 | 40W | |
| Saudi Arabia ■ | 92 | 26 | 0N | | 44 | 0 E | |

| Name | Pg | Lat ° | ′ | N/S | Long ° | ′ | E/W |
|---|---|---|---|---|---|---|---|
| Sauerland | 48 | 51 | 0N | | 8 | 0 E | |
| Saugerties | 162 | 42 | 4N | | 73 | 58W | |
| Saugues | 44 | 44 | 58N | | 3 | 32 E | |
| Sauherad | 71 | 59 | 25N | | 9 | 15 E | |
| Sauid el Amia | 118 | 25 | 57N | | 6 | 8W | |
| Saujon | 44 | 45 | 41N | | 0 | 55W | |
| Sauk Center | 158 | 45 | 42N | | 94 | 57W | |
| Sauk Rapids | 158 | 45 | 35N | | 94 | 10W | |
| Saulgau | 49 | 48 | 4N | | 9 | 32 E | |
| Saulieu | 43 | 47 | 17N | | 4 | 14 E | |
| Sault | 45 | 44 | 6N | | 5 | 24 E | |
| Sault Ste. Marie, Can. | 150 | 46 | 30N | | 84 | 20W | |
| Sault Ste. Marie, U.S.A. | 156 | 46 | 27N | | 84 | 22W | |
| Saumlaki | 103 | 7 | 55 s | | 131 | 20 E | |
| Saumur | 42 | 47 | 15N | | 0 | 5W | |
| Saunders | 152 | 52 | 58N | | 115 | 40W | |
| Saunders C. | 143 | 45 | 53 s | | 170 | 45 E | |
| Saunders I. | 13 | 57 | 30 s | | 27 | 30W | |
| Saunders Point, Mt. | 137 | 27 | 52 s | | 125 | 38 E | |
| Saundersfoot | 31 | 51 | 43N | | 4 | 42W | |
| Saurbær, Borgarfjarðarsýsla, Iceland | 74 | 64 | 24N | | 21 | 35W | |
| Saurbær, Eyjafjarðarsýsla, Iceland | 74 | 65 | 27N | | 18 | 13W | |
| Sauri | 121 | 11 | 50N | | 6 | 44 E | |
| Sausalito | 163 | 37 | 51N | | 122 | 29W | |
| Sautatá | 174 | 7 | 50N | | 77 | 4W | |
| Sauveterre, R. | 44 | 43 | 25N | | 0 | 57W | |
| Sauzé-Vaussais | 44 | 46 | 8N | | 0 | 8 E | |
| Savá | 166 | 15 | 32N | | 86 | 15W | |
| Sava | 65 | 40 | 28N | | 17 | 32 E | |
| Sava, R. | 63 | 44 | 40N | | 19 | 50 E | |
| Savage | 158 | 47 | 43N | | 104 | 20W | |
| Savalou | 121 | 7 | 57N | | 2 | 4 E | |
| Savanah Downs | 138 | 19 | 30 s | | 141 | 30 E | |
| Savane | 127 | 19 | 37 s | | 35 | 8 E | |
| Savanna | 158 | 42 | 5N | | 90 | 10W | |
| Savanna la Mar | 166 | 18 | 10N | | 78 | 10W | |
| Savannah, Ga., U.S.A. | 157 | 32 | 4N | | 81 | 4W | |
| Savannah, Mo., U.S.A. | 158 | 39 | 55N | | 94 | 46W | |
| Savannah, Tenn., U.S.A. | 157 | 35 | 12N | | 88 | 18W | |
| Savannah Downs | 138 | 19 | 28 s | | 141 | 47 E | |
| Savannah, R. | 157 | 33 | 0N | | 81 | 30W | |
| Savannakhet | 100 | 16 | 30N | | 104 | 49 E | |
| Savant L. | 150 | 50 | 14N | | 90 | 6W | |
| Savant Lake | 150 | 50 | 30N | | 90 | 25W | |
| Savantvadi | 97 | 15 | 55N | | 73 | 54 E | |
| Savanur | 97 | 14 | 59N | | 75 | 28 E | |
| Savda | 96 | 21 | 9N | | 75 | 56 E | |
| Savé | 121 | 8 | 2N | | 2 | 17 E | |
| Save R. | 125 | 21 | 16 s | | 34 | 0 E | |
| Saveh | 92 | 35 | 2N | | 50 | 20 E | |
| Savelovo | 81 | 56 | 51N | | 37 | 20 E | |
| Savelugu | 121 | 9 | 38N | | 0 | 54W | |
| Savenay | 42 | 47 | 20N | | 1 | 55W | |
| Saverdun | 44 | 43 | 14N | | 1 | 34 E | |
| Saverne | 43 | 48 | 39N | | 7 | 20 E | |
| Savièse | 50 | 46 | 17N | | 7 | 22 E | |
| Savigliano | 62 | 44 | 39N | | 7 | 40 E | |
| Savigny-sur-Braye | 44 | 47 | 53N | | 0 | 49 E | |
| Saviñao | 56 | 42 | 35N | | 7 | 38W | |
| Savio, R. | 63 | 43 | 58N | | 12 | 10 E | |
| Savnik | 66 | 42 | 59N | | 19 | 10 E | |
| Savognin | 51 | 46 | 36N | | 9 | 37 E | |
| Savoie □ | 45 | 45 | 26N | | 6 | 35 E | |
| Savona | 62 | 44 | 19N | | 8 | 29 E | |
| Savonlinna | 78 | 61 | 55N | | 28 | 55 E | |
| Sävsjö | 73 | 57 | 20N | | 14 | 40 E | |
| Sävsjöström | 73 | 57 | 1N | | 15 | 25 E | |
| Sawahlunto | 102 | 0 | 52 s | | 100 | 52 E | |
| Sawai | 103 | 3 | 0 s | | 129 | 5 E | |
| Sawai Madhopur | 94 | 26 | 0N | | 76 | 25 E | |
| Sawang Daen Din | 100 | 17 | 28N | | 103 | 28 E | |
| Sawankhalok | 100 | 17 | 19N | | 99 | 50 E | |
| Sawara | 111 | 35 | 55N | | 140 | 30 E | |
| Sawatch Mts. | 161 | 38 | 30N | | 106 | 30W | |
| Sawbridgeworth | 29 | 51 | 49N | | 0 | 10 E | |
| Sawdā, Jabal as | 119 | 28 | 51N | | 15 | 12 E | |
| Sawel, Mt. | 38 | 54 | 48N | | 7 | 5W | |
| Sawfajjin, W. | 119 | 31 | 46N | | 14 | 30 E | |
| Sawi | 101 | 10 | 14N | | 99 | 5 E | |
| Sawmills | 127 | 19 | 30 s | | 28 | 2 E | |
| Sawston | 29 | 52 | 7N | | 0 | 11 E | |
| Sawtry | 29 | 52 | 26N | | 0 | 17W | |
| Sawu, I. | 103 | 10 | 35 s | | 121 | 50 E | |
| Sawu Sea | 103 | 9 | 30 s | | 121 | 50 E | |
| Saxby, R. | 138 | 18 | 25 s | | 140 | 53 E | |
| Saxilby | 33 | 53 | 16N | | 0 | 40W | |
| Saxlingham Nethergate | 29 | 52 | 33N | | 1 | 16 E | |
| Saxmundham | 29 | 52 | 13N | | 1 | 29 E | |
| Saxon | 50 | 46 | 9N | | 7 | 11 E | |
| Saxony, Lower = Niedersachsen | 48 | 52 | 45N | | 9 | 0 E | |
| Say | 121 | 13 | 8N | | 2 | 22 E | |
| Saya | 121 | 9 | 30N | | 3 | 18 E | |
| Sayabec | 151 | 48 | 35N | | 67 | 41W | |
| Sayaboury | 100 | 19 | 15N | | 101 | 45 E | |
| Sayán | 174 | 11 | 0 s | | 77 | 25W | |
| Sayan, Vostochnyy | 77 | 54 | 0N | | 96 | 0 E | |
| Sayan, Zapadnyy | 77 | 52 | 30N | | 94 | 0 E | |
| Sayasan | 83 | 42 | 56N | | 46 | 15 E | |
| Sayda | 92 | 33 | 35N | | 35 | 25 E | |
| Sayhan Ovoo | 106 | 45 | 27N | | 103 | 54 E | |
| Sayhandulaan | 106 | 44 | 40N | | 109 | 1 E | |
| Saynshand | 106 | 44 | 55N | | 110 | 11 E | |
| Sayō | 110 | 34 | 59N | | 134 | 22 E | |
| Sayre, Okla., U.S.A. | 159 | 35 | 20N | | 99 | 40W | |
| Sayre, Pa., U.S.A. | 162 | 42 | 0N | | 76 | 30W | |
| Sayula | 164 | 19 | 50N | | 103 | 40W | |
| Sayville | 162 | 40 | 45N | | 73 | 7W | |

Sazan Semirara Is

Sazan 68 40 30N 19 20 E
Sazin 95 35 35N 73 30 E
Sazlika, R. 67 42 15N 25 50 E
Sbeïtla 119 35 12N 9 7 E
Scaër 42 48 2N 3 42W
Scalasaig 34 56 4N 6 10W
Scalby 33 54 18N 0 26W
Scalby Ness 33 54 18N 0 25W
Scalea 65 39 49N 15 47 E
Scalloway 36 60 9N 1 16W
Scalpay, I., Inner Hebrides, U.K. 36 57 18N 6 0W
Scalpay, I., Outer Hebrides, U.K. 36 57 51N 6 40W
Scamblesby 33 53 17N 0 5W
Scammon Bay 147 62 0N 165 49W
Scandia 152 50 20N 112 0W
Scandiano 62 44 36N 10 40 E
Scandinavia 16 64 0N 12 0 E
Scansano 63 42 40N 11 20 E
Scapa Flow 37 58 52N 3 6W
Scarastovore 36 57 50N 7 2W
Scarba, I. 34 56 10N 5 42W
Scarborough, Trin 167 11 11N 60 42W
Scarborough, U.K. 33 54 17N 0 24W
Scargill 143 42 56 S 172 58 E
Scariff 39 52 55N 8 32W
Scariff I. 39 51 43N 10 15W
Scarinish 34 56 30N 6 48W
Scarning 29 52 40N 0 53W
Scarp, I. 36 58 1N 7 8W
Scarpe, R. 43 50 31N 3 27 E
Scarsdale 140 37 41 S 143 39 E
Scattery I. 39 52 37N 9 30W
Scavaig, L. 36 57 8N 6 10W
Scebeli, Uebi 91 2 0N 44 0 E
Scédro, I. 63 43 6N 16 43 E
Scenic 158 43 49N 102 32W
Schaal See 48 53 40N 10 57 E
Schaan 51 47 10N 9 31 E
Schaesberg 47 50 54N 6 0 E
Schaffen 47 51 0N 5 5 E
Schaffhausen 51 47 42N 8 39 E
Schaffhausen □ 51 47 42N 8 36 E
Schagen 47 52 49N 4 48 E
Schaghticoke 162 42 54N 73 35W
Schalkhaar 46 52 17N 6 12 E
Schalkwijk 46 52 0N 5 11 E
Schangnau 50 46 50N 7 47 E
Schänis 51 47 10N 9 3 E
Schärding 52 48 27N 13 27 E
Scharhörn, I. 48 53 58N 8 24 E
Scharnitz 52 47 23N 11 15 E
Scheessel 48 53 10N 9 33 E
Schefferville 151 54 48N 66 50W
Scheibbs 52 48 1N 15 9 E
Schelde, R. 47 51 10N 4 20 E
Scheldewindeke 47 50 56N 3 46 E
Schenectady 162 42 50N 73 58W
Schenevus 162 42 33N 74 50W
Scherfede 48 51 32N 9 2 E
Scherpenheuvel 47 50 58N 4 58 E
Scherpenisse 47 51 33N 4 6 E
Scherpenzeel 46 52 5N 5 30 E
Schesaplana 51 47 5N 9 43 E
Scheveningen 46 52 6N 4 16 E
Schichallion, Mt. 37 56 40N 4 6W
Schiedam 46 51 55N 4 25 E
Schiermonnikoog 46 53 29N 6 10 E
Schiermonnikoog, I. 46 53 30N 6 15 E
Schiers 51 47 58N 9 41 E
Schifferstadt 49 49 22N 8 23 E
Schifflange 47 49 30N 6 1 E
Schijndel 47 51 37N 5 27 E
Schiltigheim 43 48 35N 7 45 E
Schio 63 45 42N 11 21 E
Schipbeek 46 52 14N 6 10 E
Schipluiden 46 51 59N 4 19 E
Schirmeck 43 48 29N 7 12 E
Schladming 52 47 23N 13 41 E
Schlei, R. 48 54 45N 9 52 E
Schleiden 48 50 32N 6 26 E
Schleswig 48 54 32N 9 34 E
Schleswig-Holstein □ 48 54 10N 9 40 E
Schlieren 51 47 26N 8 27 E
Schlüchtern 49 50 20N 9 32 E
Schmalkalden 48 50 43N 10 28 E
Schmölin 48 50 54N 12 22 E
Schneeberg, Austria 52 47 53N 15 55 E
Schneeberg, Ger. 48 50 35N 12 39 E
Schoenberg 47 50 17N 6 16 E
Schofield 158 44 54N 89 39W
Schoharie 162 42 40N 74 19W
Schoharie, R. 162 42 56N 74 18W
Schönberg, Rostock, Ger. 48 53 50N 10 55 E
Schönberg, Schleswig-Holstein, Ger. 48 54 23N 10 20 E
Schönebeck 48 52 2N 11 42 E
Schönenwerd 50 47 23N 8 0 E
Schöningen 48 52 8N 10 57 E
Schoondijke 47 51 21N 3 33 E
Schoonebeek 46 52 39N 6 52 E
Schoonebeek, oilfield 19 52 45N 6 50 E
Schoonhoven 46 51 57N 4 51 E
Schoonoord 46 52 51N 6 46 E
Schoorl 46 52 42N 4 42 E
Schors 80 51 48N 31 56 E
Schortens 48 53 37N 7 51 E
Schoten 47 51 16N 4 30 E
Schouten, Kepulauan 103 1 0 S 136 0 E
Schouter I. 138 42 20 S 148 20 E
Schouwen, I. 47 51 43N 3 45 E
Schramberg 49 48 12N 8 24 E
Schrankogl 52 47 3N 11 7 E
Schreckhorn 50 46 36N 8 7 E
Schreiber 150 48 45N 87 20W
Schroon Lake 162 43 47N 73 46W
Schruns 52 47 5N 9 56 E
Schuler 153 50 20N 110 6W
Schuls 51 46 48N 10 18 E
Schumacher 150 48 30N 81 16W
Schüpfen 50 47 2N 7 24 E
Schüpfheim 50 46 57N 8 2 E
Schurz 163 38 57N 118 48W
Schuyler 158 41 30N 97 3W
Schuylerville 162 43 5N 73 35W
Schuylkill Haven 162 40 37N 76 11W
Schuylkill, R. 162 39 53N 75 12W
Schwabach 49 49 19N 11 3 E
Schwäbisch Gmünd 49 48 49N 9 48 E
Schwäbisch Hall 49 49 7N 9 45 E
Schwäbischer Alb 49 48 30N 9 30 E
Schwanden 51 47 1N 9 5 E
Schwarzach, R. 52 50 30N 11 30 E
Schwarzenberg 48 50 31N 12 49 E
Schwarzenburg 50 46 49N 7 20 E
Schwarzwald 49 48 0N 8 0 E
Schwaz 52 47 20N 11 44 E
Schwedt 48 53 4N 14 18 E
Schweinfurt 49 50 3N 10 12 E
Schweizer Mittelland 50 47 0N 7 15 E
Schweizer Reneke 128 27 11 S 25 18 E
Schwerin 48 53 37N 11 22 E
Schwerin □ 48 53 35N 11 20 E
Schweriner See 48 53 45N 11 26 E
Schwetzingen 49 49 22N 8 35 E
Schwyz 51 47 2N 8 39 E
Schwyz □ 51 47 2N 8 39 E
Sciacca 64 37 30N 13 3 E
Scicli 65 36 48N 14 41 E
Scie, La 151 49 57N 55 36W
Scillave 91 6 22N 44 32 E
Scilly, Isles of 30 49 55N 6 15W
Scinawa 54 51 25N 16 26 E
Scioto, R. 156 39 0N 83 0W
Scituate 162 42 12N 70 44W
Sclayn 47 50 29N 5 2 E
Scobey 158 48 47N 105 30W
Scole 29 52 22N 1 10 E
Scone 141 32 0 S 150 52 E
Scopwick 33 53 6N 0 24W
Scórdia 65 37 19N 14 50 E
Score Hd. 36 60 12N 1 5W
Scoresby Sund 12 70 20N 23 0W
Scorno, Punta dello 64 41 7N 8 23 E
Scotia, Calif., U.S.A. 160 40 36N 124 4W
Scotia, N.Y., U.S.A. 162 42 50N 73 58W
Scotia Sea 13 56 5 S 56 0W
Scotland 158 43 10N 97 45W
Scotland □ 51 57 0N 4 0W
Scotland Neck 157 36 6N 77 24W
Scott 13 77 0 S 165 0 E
Scott, C., Antarct. 13 71 30 S 168 0 E
Scott, C., Austral. 136 13 30 S 129 49 E
Scott City 158 38 30N 100 52W
Scott, I. 13 67 0 S 179 0 E
Scott Inlet 149 71 0N 71 0W
Scott Is. 152 50 48N 128 40W
Scott L. 153 59 55N 106 18W
Scott Reef 136 14 0 S 121 50 E
Scottburgh 129 30 15 S 30 47 E
Scottsbluff 158 41 55N 103 35W
Scottsboro 157 34 40N 86 0W
Scottsburg 156 38 40N 85 46W
Scottsdale 138 41 9 S 147 31 E
Scottsville 157 36 48N 86 10W
Scottville, Austral. 138 20 33 S 147 49 E
Scottville, U.S.A. 156 43 57N 86 18W
Scourie 36 58 20N 5 10W
Scousburgh 36 59 58N 1 20W
Scrabby 38 53 53N 7 32W
Scrabster 37 58 36N 3 31W
Scram, gasfield 19 52 55N 2 42 E
Scramoge 38 53 46N 8 4W
Scranton 162 41 22N 75 41W
Screebe Lodge 38 53 23N 9 33W
Screggan 42 53 15N 7 32W
Scremerston 35 55 44N 1 59W
Scridain, L. 34 56 23N 6 7W
Scunthorpe 33 53 35N 0 38W
Scuol 51 46 48N 10 17 E
Scusciuban 91 10 28N 50 5 E
SE Tor, oilfield 19 56 38N 3 27 E
Sea Isle City 162 39 9N 74 42W
Seabra 171 12 25 S 41 46W
Seabrook, L. 137 30 55 S 119 40 E
Seaford, Austral. 141 38 10 S 145 11 E
Seaford, U.K. 29 50 46N 0 8 E
Seaford, U.S.A. 162 38 37N 75 36W
Seaforth 150 43 35N 81 25W
Seaforth, L. 36 57 52N 6 36W
Seagraves 159 32 56N 102 30W
Seaham 35 54 51N 1 20W
Seahouses 35 55 35N 1 39W
Seal Cove 151 49 57N 56 22W
Seal L. 151 54 20N 61 30W
Seal, R. 153 58 50N 97 30W
Sealga, L. na 36 57 50N 5 18W
Sealy 159 29 46N 96 9W
Seamer 33 54 14N 0 27W
Sean, gasfield 19 53 13N 2 50 E
Searchlight 161 35 31N 114 55W
Searcy 159 35 15N 91 45W
Searles, L. 163 35 47N 117 17W
Seascale 32 54 24N 3 29W
Seaside, Calif., U.S.A. 163 36 37N 121 50W
Seaside, Oreg., U.S.A. 160 46 12N 121 55W
Seaside Park 162 39 55N 74 5W
Seaspray 141 38 25 S 147 15 E
Seaton, U.K. 30 50 42N 3 3W
Seaton, U.K. 32 54 40N 3 31W
Seaton Delaval 35 55 5N 1 33W
Seattle 160 47 41N 122 15W
Seaview Ra. 138 18 40 S 145 45 E
Seaward Kaikouras, Mts. 143 42 10 S 173 44 E
Sebago Lake 162 43 50N 70 35W
Sebastián Vizcaíno, Bahía 164 28 0N 114 30W
Sebastopol 160 38 24N 122 49W
Sebastopol = Sevastopol 82 44 35N 33 30 E
Sebderat 123 15 26N 36 42 E
Sebdou 118 34 38N 1 19W
Sebeşului, Mţii. 70 45 56N 23 40 E
Sebewaing 156 43 45N 83 27W
Sebezh 80 56 14N 28 22 E
Sebi 120 15 50N 4 12W
Sebinkarahisar 82 40 22N 38 28 E
Sebiş 70 46 23N 22 13 E
Sebkra Azzel Mati 118 26 10N 0 43 E
Sebkra Mekerghene 118 26 21N 1 30 E
Sebou, Oued 118 34 16N 6 40W
Sebring 157 27 36N 81 47W
Sebta = Ceuta 118 35 52N 5 26W
Sebuku, I. 102 3 30 S 116 25 E
Sebuku, Teluk 102 4 0N 118 10 E
Sečanj 66 45 25N 20 47 E
Secchia, R. 62 44 30N 10 40 E
Sechelt 152 49 25N 123 42W
Sechura, Desierto de 174 6 0 S 80 30W
Seclin 43 50 33N 3 2 E
Secondigny 42 46 37N 0 26W
Sečovce 53 48 42N 21 40 E
Secretary I. 143 45 15 S 166 56 E
Secunderabad 96 17 28N 78 30 E
Seda, R. 57 39 6N 7 53W
Sedalia 158 38 40N 93 18W
Sedan, Austral. 140 34 34 S 139 19 E
Sedan, France 43 49 43N 4 57 E
Sedan, U.S.A. 159 37 10N 96 11W
Sedano 58 42 43N 3 49W
Sedbergh 32 54 20N 2 31W
Seddon 143 41 40 S 174 7 E
Seddonville 143 41 33 S 172 1 E
Sede Ya'aqov 90 32 43N 35 7 E
Sederberg, Mt. 128 32 22 S 19 7 E
Sedgefield 33 54 40N 1 27W
Sedgewick 152 52 48N 111 41W
Sedhiou 120 12 50N 15 30W
Sedičany 52 49 40N 14 25 E
Sedico 63 46 8N 12 6 E
Sedinenie 67 42 16N 24 33 E
Sedley 153 50 10N 104 0W
Sedom 90 31 5N 35 20 E
Sedova, Pik 76 73 20N 55 10 E
Sédrata 119 36 7N 7 31 E
Sedro Woolley 160 48 30N 122 15W
Sedrun 51 46 36N 8 47 E
Seduva 80 55 45N 23 45 E
Sedziszów Małapolski 54 50 5N 21 45 E
Seebad Ahlbeck 48 53 56N 14 10 E
Seefeld 52 51 53N 13 17 E
Seehausen 48 52 52N 11 43 E
Seeheim 128 26 32 S 17 52 E
Seekoe, R. 128 30 34 S 24 45 E
Seeland 50 47 0N 7 6 E
Seelaw 48 52 32N 14 22 E
Seend 28 51 20N 2 2W
Sées 42 48 38N 0 10 E
Seesen 48 51 53N 10 10 E
Sefadu 120 8 35N 10 58W
Séfeto 120 14 8N 9 49W
Sefrou 118 33 52N 4 52W
Sefton 143 43 15 S 172 41 E
Sefton Mt. 143 43 40 S 170 5 E
Sefuri-San 110 33 28N 130 18 E
Sefwi Bekwai 120 6 10N 2 25W
Seg-ozero 76 63 0N 33 10 E
Segamat 101 2 30N 102 50 E
Segarcea 70 44 6N 23 43 E
Segbwema 120 8 0N 11 0W
Segeston 31 51 41N 4 48W
Seget 103 1 24 S 130 58 E
Seggueur, O. 118 32 4N 2 4 E
Segid 123 16 55N 42 0 E
Segonzac 44 45 36N 0 14W
Segorbe 58 39 50N 0 30W
Ségou 120 13 30N 6 10W
Segovia 56 40 57N 4 10W
Segovia □ 56 40 55N 4 10W
Segré 42 47 40N 0 52W
Segre, R. 58 41 40N 0 43 E
Seguam 147 52 0N 172 30W
Seguam Pass. 147 53 0N 175 30W
Séguéla 120 7 55N 6 40W
Segula I. 147 52 0N 178 5W
Segundo 159 37 12N 104 50W
Segundo, R. 172 30 53 S 62 44W
Segura, R. 59 38 9N 0 40W
Segura, Sierra de 59 38 5N 2 45W
Sehithwa 125 20 30 S 22 30 E
Sehore 94 23 10N 77 5 E
Sehwan 94 26 28N 67 53 E
Seica Mare 70 46 1N 24 7 E
Seikpyu 98 20 54N 94 48 E
Seil, I. 34 56 17N 5 37W
Seilandsjøkelen 74 70 25N 23 16 E
Seiling 159 36 10N 99 5W
Seille, R. 45 46 31N 4 57 E
Seilles 47 50 30N 5 6 E
Sein, I. de 42 48 2N 4 52W
Seinäjoki 74 62 48N 22 43 E
Seine-Maritime □ 42 49 40N 1 0 E
Seine □ 43 49 0N 3 0 E
Seine-et-Marne □ 43 48 45N 3 0 E
Seine, R. 42 49 28N 0 15 E
Seine-Saint-Denis □ 43 48 58N 2 24 E
Seini 70 47 44N 23 21 E
Seistan 93 30 50N 61 0 E
Seiyala 122 22 57N 32 41 E
Sejal 174 2 45N 68 0W
Sejerby 73 55 54N 11 10 E
Sejerø 73 55 54N 11 15 E
Sejerø Bugt 73 55 53N 11 9 E
Seka 123 8 10N 36 52 E
Sekaju 102 2 58 S 103 58 E
Seke 126 3 20 S 33 31 E
Sekenke 126 4 18 S 34 11 E
Seki 111 35 29N 136 55 E
Sekigahara 111 35 22N 136 28 E
Sekiu 160 48 30N 124 29W
Sekkane, Erg in 118 20 30N 1 30W
Sekondi 120 5 2N 1 48W
Sekondi-Takoradi 120 5 0N 1 48W
Sekuma 128 24 36 S 23 57 E
Sela Dingay 123 9 58N 39 32 E
Selah 160 46 44N 120 30W
Selama 101 5 12N 100 42 E
Selangor □ 101 3 20N 101 30 E
Selargius 64 39 14N 9 14 E
Selaru, I. 103 8 18 S 131 0 E
Selat Bangka 102 2 30 S 105 30 E
Selawik 147 66 55N 160 10W
Selb 49 50 9N 12 9 E
Selborne 29 51 5N 0 55W
Selby, U.K. 33 53 47N 1 5W
Selby, U.S.A. 158 45 34N 99 55W
Selbyville 162 38 28N 75 13W
Selce 63 43 20N 16 50 E
Selden 158 39 24N 100 39W
Seldovia 147 59 30N 151 45W
Sele, R. 65 40 27N 15 0 E
Selenica 68 40 33N 19 39 E
Selenter See 48 54 19N 10 26 E
Selestat 43 48 10N 7 26 E
Selet 72 63 15N 15 45 E
Seletan, Tg. 102 4 10 S 114 40 E
Seletin 70 47 50N 25 12 E
Selevac 66 44 44N 20 52 E
Selfridge 158 46 3N 100 57W
Sélibaby 120 15 20N 12 15W
Seliger, Oz. 80 57 15N 33 0 E
Seligman 161 35 17N 112 56W
Selim, C. Afr. Emp. 126 5 31N 23 48 E
Selim, Turkey 83 40 15N 42 58 E
Selima, El Wâhât el 122 21 28N 29 31 E
Selinda Spillway 128 18 35 S 23 10 E
Selinoús 69 37 35N 21 37 E
Selinsgrove 162 40 48N 76 52W
Selipuk Gompa 95 31 23N 82 49 E
Selizharovo 80 57 1N 33 17 E
Selje 71 62 3N 5 22 E
Seljord 71 59 30N 8 40 E
Selkirk, Can. 153 50 10N 97 20W
Selkirk, U.K. 35 55 33N 2 50W
Selkirk (□) 26 55 30N 3 0W
Selkirk I. 153 53 20N 99 6W
Selkirk Mts. 152 51 15N 117 40W
Selles-sur-Cher 43 47 16N 1 33 E
Sellières 43 46 50N 5 32 E
Sells 161 31 57N 111 57W
Sellye 53 45 52N 17 51 E
Selma, Ala., U.S.A. 157 32 30N 87 0W
Selma, Calif., U.S.A. 163 36 39N 119 39W
Selma, N.C., U.S.A. 157 35 32N 78 15W
Selmer 157 35 9N 88 36W
Sélo, Óros 68 41 10N 126 0 E
Selongey 43 47 36N 5 10 E
Selowandoma Falls 127 21 15 S 31 50 E
Selpele 103 0 1 S 130 5 E
Selsey 29 50 44N 0 47W
Selsey Bill 29 50 44N 0 47W
Seltz 43 48 48N 8 4 E
Selu, I. 103 7 26 S 130 55 E
Selukwe 127 19 40 S 30 0 E
Sélune, R. 42 48 38N 1 22W
Selva, Argent. 172 29 50 S 62 0W
Selva, Spain 58 41 13N 1 8 E
Selva Beach, La 163 36 56N 121 51W
Selva, La 58 42 0N 2 45 E
Selvas 174 6 30 S 67 0W
Selwyn 133 21 30 S 140 29 E
Selwyn L. 153 60 0N 104 30W
Selwyn Mts. 147 63 0N 130 0W
Selwyn P.O. 138 21 32 S 140 30 E
Selwyn Ra. 138 21 10 S 140 0 E
Semani, R. 68 40 45N 19 50 E
Semarang 103 7 0 S 110 26 E
Sembabule 126 0 4 S 31 25 E
Semeih 123 12 43N 30 53 E
Semenov 81 56 43N 44 30 E
Semenovka 82 49 37N 33 2 E
Semeru, Mt. 103 8 4 S 113 3 E
Sémi 120 15 4N 13 41W
Semiluki 81 51 41N 39 10 E
Seminoe Res. 160 42 0N 107 0W
Seminole, Okla., U.S.A. 159 35 15N 96 45W
Seminole, Tex., U.S.A. 159 32 41N 102 38W
Semiozernoye 84 52 22N 64 8 E
Semipalatinsk 76 50 30N 80 10 E
Semirara Is. 103 12 0N 121 20 E

Semisopochnoi I Shawbost


Semisopochnoi I. 147 52 0N 179 40W
Semitau 102 0 29N 111 57E
Semiyarskoye 76 50 55N 78 30E
Semmering Pass. 52 47 41N 15 45E
Semnan 93 35 55N 53 25E
Semnan □ 93 36 0N 54 0E
Semois, R. 47 49 53N 4 44E
Semporna 103 4 30N 118 33E
Semuda 102 2 51S 112 58E
Semur-en-Auxois 43 47 30N 4 20E
Sen. R. 101 13 45N 105 12E
Sena Madureira 174 9 5S 68 45W
Senador Pompeu 170 5 40S 39 20W
Senai 101 1 38N 103 38E
Senaja 102 6 49S 117 2E
Senanga 128 16 2S 23 14E
Senatobia 159 34 38N 89 57W
Sendafa 123 9 11N 39 3E
Sendai, Kagoshima, Japan 110 31 50N 130 20E
Sendai, Miyagi, Japan 112 38 15N 141 0E
Sendamangalam 97 11 17N 78 17E
Sendeling's Drift 128 28 12S 16 52E
Sendenhorst 48 51 50N 7 49E
Sendurjana 96 21 32N 78 24E
Senec 53 48 12N 17 23E
Seneca, Oreg., U.S.A. 160 44 10N 119 2W
Seneca, S.C., U.S.A. 157 34 43N 82 59W
Seneca Falls 162 42 55N 76 50W
Seneca L. 162 42 40N 76 58W
Seneffe 47 50 32N 4 16E
Senegal ■ 120 14 30N 14 30W
Senegal, R. 120 16 30N 15 30W
Senekal 129 28 18S 27 36E
Senftenberg 48 51 30N 13 51E
Senga Hill 127 9 19S 31 11E
Senge Khambab (Indus), R. 94 28 40N 70 10E
Sengerema □ 126 2 10S 32 20E
Sengiley 81 53 58N 48 54E
Sengwa, R. 127 17 10S 28 15E
Senhor-do-Bonfim 170 10 30S 40 10W
Senica 53 48 41N 17 25E
Senigállia 63 43 42N 13 12E
Seniku 98 25 32N 97 48E
Senio, R. 63 44 18N 11 47E
Senj 63 45 0N 14 58E
Senja 74 69 25N 17 20E
Senlis 43 49 13N 2 35E
Senmonorom 100 12 27N 107 12E
Sennâr 123 13 30N 33 35E
Senne, R. 47 50 42N 4 13E
Sennen 30 50 4N 5 42W
Senneterre 150 48 25N 77 15W
Senno 80 54 45N 29 58E
Sennori 64 40 49N 8 36E
Senny Bridge 31 51 57N 3 35W
Seno 100 16 41N 105 1E
Senonches 42 48 34N 1 2E
Senorbi 64 39 33N 9 8E
Senožeče 63 45 43N 14 3E
Sens 43 48 11N 3 15E
Senta 66 45 55N 20 3E
Sentein 44 42 53N 0 58E
Senteny 126 5 17S 25 42E
Sentier, Le 51 46 37N 6 15E
Sentinel 161 32 56N 113 13W
Sento Sé 170 9 40S 41 18W
Sentolo 103 7 55S 110 13E
Senya Beraku 121 5 28N 0 31W
Seo de Urgel 58 42 22N 1 23E
Seohara 95 29 15N 78 33E
Seoni 95 22 5N 79 30E
Seorinayan 96 21 45N 82 34E
Separation Point 151 53 37N 57 25W
Seph, R. 33 54 17N 1 9W
Sepik, R. 135 3 49S 144 30E
Sepólno Krajenskie 54 53 26N 17 30E
Sepone 100 16 45N 106 13E
Sepopa 128 18 49S 22 12E
Sepopol 54 54 16N 21 2E
Sepori 107 38 57N 127 25E
Sept Îles 151 50 13N 66 22W
Septemvri 67 42 13N 24 6E
Septimus 138 21 13S 148 47E
Sepúlveda 56 41 18N 3 45W
Sequeros 56 40 31N 6 2W
Sequim 160 48 3N 123 9W
Sequoia Nat. Park 163 36 30N 118 30W
Serafimovich 83 49 30N 42 50E
Seraing 47 50 35N 5 32E
Seraja 101 2 41N 108 35E
Seram, I. 103 3 10S 129 0E
Serampore 95 22 44N 88 30E
Serang 103 6 8S 106 10E
Serasan 101 2 31N 109 2E
Serasan, I. 102 2 29N 109 4E
Seravezza 62 43 59N 10 13E
Serbia = Srbija 66 43 30N 21 0E
Sercaia 70 45 49N 25 9E
Serdo 123 11 56N 41 14E
Serdobsk 81 52 28N 44 10E
Seredka 80 58 12N 28 3E
Seregno 62 45 40N 9 12E
Seremban 101 2 43N 101 53E
Serena, La, Chile 172 29 55S 71 10W
Serena, La, Spain 57 38 45N 5 40W
Serengeti □ 126 2 0S 34 30E
Serengeti Plain 126 2 40S 35 0E
Serenje 125 13 14S 30 15E
Sergach 81 55 30N 45 30E
Serge, R. 58 42 5N 1 21E
Sergievsk 81 54 0N 51 10E
Sergipe □ 170 10 30S 37 30W
Seria 102 4 37N 114 30E
Serian 102 1 10N 110 40E
Seriate 62 45 42N 9 43E
Sérifontaine 43 49 20N 1 45E
Sérifos, I. 69 37 9N 24 30E
Sérignan 44 43 17N 3 17E
Serik 92 36 55N 31 10E
Seringapatam Reef 136 13 38S 122 5E
Sermaize-les-Bains 43 48 47N 4 54E
Sermata, I. 103 8 15S 128 50E
Sérmide 63 45 0N 11 17E
Sernovodsk 76 61 20N 73 28E
Sernovodsk 84 53 54N 51 16E
Sero 120 14 42N 10 59W
Serón 59 37 20N 2 29W
Serós 58 41 27N 0 24E
Serov 84 59 36N 60 35E
Serowe 128 22 25S 26 43E
Serpa 57 37 57N 7 38E
Serpeddi, Punta 64 39 19N 9 28E
Serpentara 64 39 8N 9 38E
Serpentine 137 32 23S 115 58E
Serpentine L. 137 28 30S 129 10E
Serpent's Mouth 174 10 0N 61 30W
Serpis, R. 59 38 45N 0 21W
Serpukhov 81 54 55N 37 28E
Serra 171 20 7S 40 18W
Serra Capriola 65 41 47N 15 12E
Serra do Salitre 74 19 6S 46 41W
Serra Talhada 170 7 59S 38 18W
Serradilla 56 39 50N 6 9W
Sérrai □ 68 41 5N 23 37E
Serramanna 64 39 26N 8 56E
Serranía de Cuenca 58 40 10N 1 50W
Serrat, C. 119 37 14N 9 10E
Serres 45 44 26N 5 43E
Serrezuela 172 30 40S 65 20W
Serrinha 171 11 39S 39 0W
Serrita 170 7 56S 39 19W
Serro 171 18 37S 43 23W
Sersale 65 39 1N 16 44E
Sertã 56 39 48N 8 6W
Sertânia 170 8 5S 37 20W
Sertanópolis 173 23 4S 51 2W
Sertâo 170 10 0S 40 20W
Sertig 51 46 44N 9 52E
Serua, P. 103 6 18S 130 1E
Serui 103 1 45S 136 10E
Serule 128 21 57S 27 11E
Sérvia 68 40 9N 21 58E
Sesajap Lama 102 3 32N 117 11E
Sese Is. 126 0 30S 32 30E
Sesepe 103 1 30S 127 59E
Sesfontein 128 19 7S 13 39E
Sesheke 128 17 29S 24 13E
Sesia, R. 62 45 35N 8 23E
Sesimbra 57 38 28N 9 20W
Seskanore 38 54 31N 7 15W
Sessa Aurunca 64 41 14N 13 55E
Sestao 58 43 18N 3 0W
Sesto S. Giovanni 62 45 32N 9 14E
Sestri Levante 62 44 17N 9 22E
Sestrières 62 44 58N 6 56E
Sestrunj, I. 63 44 10N 15 0E
Sestu 64 39 18N 9 6E
Sesvenna 51 46 42N 10 25E
Seta 108 32 20N 100 41E
Setaka 110 33 9N 130 28E
Setana 112 42 26N 139 51E
Sète 44 43 25N 3 42E
Sete Lagoas 171 19 27S 44 16W
Sétif 119 36 9N 5 26E
Seto 111 35 14N 137 6E
Seto Naikai 110 34 20N 133 30E
Setouchi 112 28 8N 129 19E
Setsan 98 16 3N 95 23E
Settat 118 33 0N 7 40W
Setté Cama 124 2 32S 9 57E
Séttimo Tor 62 45 9N 7 46E
Setting L. 153 55 0N 98 38W
Settle 32 54 5N 2 18W
Settlement Pt. 157 26 40N 79 0W
Setto Calende 62 45 44N 8 37E
Setúbal 57 38 30N 8 58W
Setúbal □ 57 38 25N 8 35W
Setúbal, B. de 57 38 40N 8 56W
Seul L. 150 50 25N 92 30W
Seul Reservoir, Lac 150 50 25N 92 30W
Seulimeum 102 5 27N 95 15E
Seuzach 51 47 32N 8 49E
Sevastopol 82 44 35N 33 30E
Sevelen 51 47 7N 9 30E
Seven Emu 138 16 20S 137 8E
Seven Heads 39 51 35N 8 43W
Seven Hogs, Is. 39 52 20N 10 0W
Seven, R. 33 54 11N 0 51W
Seven Sisters 31 51 46N 3 43W
Seven Sisters, mt 152 54 56N 128 10W
Sevenoaks 29 51 16N 0 11E
Sevenum 47 51 25N 6 2E
Sever, R. 57 39 40N 7 32W
Sévérac-le-Chateau 44 44 20N 3 5E
Severn Beach 28 51 34N 2 39W
Severn L. 150 53 54N 90 48W
Severn, R., Can. 150 56 2N 87 36W
Severn, R., U.K. 28 51 35N 2 38W
Severn Stoke 28 52 5N 2 13W
Severnaya Zemlya 77 79 0N 100 0E
Severnyye Uvaly 78 58 0N 48 0E
Severo-Kurilsk 77 50 40N 156 8E
Severodonetsk 83 48 50N 38 30E
Severodvinsk 78 64 27N 39 58E
Severomoravsky □ 53 49 38N 17 40E
Severouralsk 84 60 9N 59 57E
Sevier 161 38 39N 112 11W
Sevier L. 160 39 0N 113 20W
Sevier, R. 161 39 10N 112 50W
Sevilla, Colomb. 174 4 16N 75 57W
Sevilla, Spain 57 37 23N 6 0W
Sevilla □ 57 37 0N 6 0W
Seville = Sevilla 57 37 23N 6 0W
Sevnica 63 46 2N 15 19E
Sevsk 80 52 10N 34 30E
Seward 147 60 0N 149 40W
Seward Pen. 147 65 0N 164 0W
Sewell 172 34 10S 70 45W
Sewer 103 5 46S 134 40E
Sexbierum 46 53 13N 5 29E
Sexsmith 152 55 21N 118 47W
Seychelles, Is. 11 5 0S 56 0E
Seyðisfjörður 74 65 16N 14 0W
Seym, R. 80 51 45N 35 0E
Seymchan 77 62 40N 152 30E
Seymour, Austral. 141 37 0S 145 10E
Seymour, Conn., U.S.A. 162 41 23N 73 5W
Seymour, Ind., U.S.A. 156 39 0N 85 50W
Seymour, Tex., U.S.A. 159 33 35N 99 18W
Seymour, Wis., U.S.A. 156 44 30N 88 20W
Seyne 45 44 21N 6 22E
Seyne-sur-Mer, La 45 43 7N 5 52E
Sezana 63 45 43N 13 41E
Sézanne 43 48 40N 3 40E
Sezze 64 41 30N 13 3E
Sfântu Gheorghe 70 45 52N 25 48E
Sfax 119 34 49N 10 48E
Sgurr Mor 36 57 42N 5 0W
Sgurr na Ciche 36 57 0N 5 29W
Sgurr na Lapaich 36 57 23N 5 5W
Sha Ch'i, R. 109 26 35N 118 8E
Shaartuz 85 37 16N 68 8E
Shaba 126 8 0S 25 0E
Shaba Gamba 99 32 8N 88 55E
Shaballe, R. 123 5 0N 44 0E
Shabani 127 20 17S 30 2E
Shabbear 30 50 52N 4 12W
Shabla 67 43 31N 28 32E
Shabogamo L. 151 48 40N 77 0W
Shabunda 126 2 40S 27 16E
Shackleton 13 78 30S 36 1W
Shackleton Inlet 13 83 0S 160 0E
Shaddad 122 21 25N 40 2E
Shadi 95 33 24N 77 14E
Shadrinsk 84 56 5N 63 58E
Shadwân 122 27 30N 34 0E
Shaffa 121 10 30N 12 6E
Shafter 163 35 32N 119 14W
Shaftesbury 28 51 0N 2 12W
Shag Pt. 143 45 29S 170 52E
Shagamu 121 6 51N 3 39E
Shagram 95 36 24N 72 20E
Shah Bunder 94 24 13N 67 50E
Shahabad, And. P., India 96 17 10N 78 11E
Shahabad, Punjab, India 94 30 10N 76 55E
Shahabad, Raj., India 94 25 15N 77 11E
Shahabad, Uttar Pradesh, India 95 27 36N 79 56E
Shāhābād 93 37 40N 56 50E
Shahada 96 21 33N 74 30E
Shahapur 96 15 50N 74 34E
Shāhbād 92 34 10N 46 30E
Shahdād 93 30 30N 57 40E
Shahdadkot 94 27 50N 67 55E
Shahddpur 94 25 55N 68 35E
Shahganj 95 26 3N 82 44E
Shahgarh 93 27 15N 69 50E
Shahhat (Cyrene) 117 32 40N 21 35E
Shāhī 93 36 30N 52 55E
Shahjahanpur 95 27 54N 79 57E
Shaho 106 36 31N 114 35E
Shahpur, Mad. P., India 94 22 12N 77 58E
Shahpur, Mysore, India 97 16 40N 76 48E
Shahpur, Iran 92 38 12N 44 45E
Shahpur, Pak. 94 28 46N 68 27E
Shahpura 95 23 10N 80 45E
Shahr-e Babak 93 30 10N 55 20E
Shahr Kord 93 32 15N 50 55E
Shahraban 92 34 0N 45 0E
Shahreza 93 32 0N 51 55E
Shahrig 94 30 15N 67 40E
Shahriza 93 32 0N 51 50E
Shahrud 93 36 30N 55 0E
Shahrukh 93 33 50N 60 10E
Shahsavar 93 36 45N 51 12E
Shahsien 109 26 25N 117 50E
Shahuk'ou 106 40 20N 112 18E
Shaibâra 123 25 26N 36 47E
Shaikhabad 94 34 0N 68 45E
Shaim 84 60 21N 64 10E
Shajapur 94 23 20N 76 15E
Shakargarh 94 32 17N 75 43E
Shakawe 128 18 28S 21 49E
Shakhristan 85 39 47N 68 49E
Shakhrisyabz 85 39 3N 66 50E
Shakhty 83 47 40N 40 10E
Shakhunya 81 57 40N 47 0E
Shaki 121 8 41N 3 21E
Shakopee 158 44 45N 93 30W
Shaktolik 147 64 30N 161 15W
Shala Lake 123 7 30N 38 30E
Shaldon 30 50 32N 3 31W
Shalkar Karashatau, Ozero 84 50 26N 61 12E
Shalkar Yega Kara, Ozero 84 50 45N 60 54E
Sham, J. ash 93 23 10N 57 5E
Shama 121 5 1N 1 42W
Shamâl Dâfû □ 123 15 0N 25 0E
Shamâl Kordofân □ 123 15 0N 30 0E
Shamar, Jabal 92 27 40N 41 0E
Shamattawa 153 55 51N 92 5W
Shamattawa, R. 150 55 1N 85 23W
Shambe 123 7 2N 30 46E
Shambu 123 9 32N 37 3E
Shamgong Dzong 98 27 19N 90 35E
Shamil, India 94 29 32N 77 18E
Shamil, Iran 93 27 30N 56 55E
Shamkhor 83 40 56N 46 0E
Shamo, L. 123 5 45N 37 30E
Shamokin 162 40 47N 76 33W
Shamrock 159 35 15N 100 15W
Shamva 125 17 20S 31 32E
Shan □ 98 21 30N 98 30E
Shanagolden 39 52 35N 9 6W
Shanan, R. 123 8 0N 40 20E
Shanch'eng 109 31 45N 115 30E
Shandon 163 35 39N 120 23W
Shandon Downs 138 17 45S 134 50E
Shanga 121 9 1N 5 2E
Shangalowe 127 10 50S 26 30E
Shangani 127 19 1S 28 51E
Shangani, R. 127 18 35S 27 45E
Shangchih, (Chuho) 107 45 10N 127 59E
Shangching 106 33 9N 110 2E
Shangch'iu 105 34 26N 115 40E
Shangch'uan Shan, I. 109 21 45N 112 45E
Shanghai 109 31 10N 121 25E
Shanghang 109 25 5N 116 30E
Shangho 107 37 19N 117 9E
Shanghsien 106 33 30N 109 58E
Shangjao 109 28 25N 117 57E
Shangkao 109 28 16N 114 50E
Shanglin 108 23 26N 108 36E
Shangnan 106 33 35N 110 49E
Shangpanch'eng 107 40 50N 118 0E
Shangshui 106 33 42N 114 34E
Shangssu 108 22 10N 108 0E
Shangtsai 106 33 15N 114 20E
Shangtu 106 41 31N 113 35E
Shangyu 109 25 59N 114 29E
Shanhaikuan 107 40 2N 119 48E
Shanhot'un 107 44 42N 127 12E
Shanhsien 106 34 51N 116 9E
Shani 121 10 14N 12 2E
Shaniko 160 45 0N 120 15W
Shanklin 28 50 39N 1 9W
Shannon, Greenl. 12 75 10N 18 30W
Shannon, N.Z. 142 40 33S 175 25E
Shannon Airport 39 52 42N 85 7W
Shannon Bridge 39 53 17N 8 2W
Shannon I. 12 75 0N 18 0W
Shannon, Mouth of the 39 52 30N 9 55W
Shannon, R. 39 53 10N 8 10W
Shansi □ 106 37 30N 112 15E
Shantar, Ostrov Bolshoi 77 55 9N 137 40E
Shant'ou 109 23 28N 116 40E
Shantung □ 105 36 0N 117 30E
Shantung Pantao 107 37 5N 121 0E
Shanyang 106 33 39N 110 2E
Shanyin 106 39 34N 112 50E
Shaohing 109 30 0N 120 32E
Shaokuan 109 24 50N 113 35E
Shaowu 109 27 25N 117 30E
Shaoyang 109 27 10N 111 30E
Shap 32 54 32N 2 40W
Shap'ing 109 22 46N 112 57E
Shapinsay, I. 37 59 2N 2 50W
Shapinsay Sd. 37 59 0N 2 51W
Shaqra 92 25 15N 45 16E
Sharafa (Ogr) 123 11 59N 27 7E
Sharavati, R. 97 14 32N 74 0E
Sharhjui 93 32 30N 67 22E
Shari 92 27 20N 43 45E
Sharjah 93 25 23N 55 26E
Shark B., N. Territory, Austral. 132 11 20S 130 35E
Shark B., W. Australia, Austral. 137 25 55S 113 32E
Sharm el Sheikh 122 27 53N 34 15E
Sharon, Mass., U.S.A. 162 42 5N 71 11W
Sharon, Pa., U.S.A. 156 41 18N 80 30W
Sharon, Plain of = Hasharon 90 32 12N 34 49E
Sharon Springs 162 42 48N 74 37W
Sharp Pt. 138 10 58S 142 43E
Sharpe, L. 150 54 10N 93 21W
Sharpe L. 153 50 23N 95 30W
Sharpness 28 51 43N 2 28W
Sharya 81 58 12N 45 40E
Shasha 123 6 29N 35 59E
Shashemene 123 7 13N 38 33E
Shashi 125 21 15S 27 27E
Shashi, R. 127 21 40S 28 40E
Shashih 109 30 19N 112 14E
Shasta, Mt. 160 41 45N 122 0W
Shasta Res. 160 40 50N 122 15W
Shati 109 26 0N 114 51E
Shatsk 81 54 0N 41 45E
Shattuck 159 36 17N 99 55W
Shaumyani 83 41 13N 44 45E
Shaunavon 153 49 35N 108 25W
Shaver Lake 163 37 9N 119 18W
Shaw I. 138 20 30S 149 2E
Shaw, R. 136 20 21S 119 17E
Shawan 105 44 21N 85 37E
Shawangunk Mts. 162 41 40N 74 25W
Shawano 156 44 45N 88 38W
Shawbost 36 58 20N 6 40W


FHK

Shawbury Siddeburen


Shawbury 28 52 48N 2 40W
Shawinigan 150 46 35N 72 50W
Shawnee 159 35 15N 97 0W
Shaymak 85 37 33N 74 50E
Shaziz 99 33 10N 82 43E
Shchëkino 81 54 1N 37 28E
Shcherbakov = Rybinsk 81 58 5N 38 50E
Shchigri 81 51 55N 36 58E
Shchuchinsk 76 52 56N 70 12E
Shchuchye 84 55 12N 62 46E
Shchurovo 81 55 0N 38 51E
Shebekino 81 50 28N 37 0E
Shebele, Wabi 123 2 0N 44 0E
Sheboygan 156 43 46N 87 45W
Shechem 90 32 13N 35 21E
Shech'i 106 33 3N 112 57E
Shediac 151 46 14N 64 32W
Sheefry Hills 38 53 40N 9 40W
Sheelin, Lough 38 53 48N 7 20W
Sheep Haven 38 55 12N 7 55W
Sheeps Hd. 39 51 32N 9 50W
Sheerness 29 51 26N 0 47E
Sheet Harbour 151 44 56N 62 31W
Shefar'am 90 32 48N 35 10E
Shefeiya 90 32 35N 34 58E
Sheffield, U.K. 33 53 23N 1 28W
Sheffield, Ala., U.S.A. 157 34 45N 87 42W
Sheffield, Mass., U.S.A. 162 42 6N 73 23W
Sheffield, Tex., U.S.A. 159 30 42N 101 49W
Shefford 29 52 2N 0 20W
Shegaon 96 20 48N 76 59E
Sheho 153 51 35N 103 13W
Shehojele 123 10 40N 35 27E
Shehsien, Anhwei, China 109 29 52N 118 26E
Shehsien, Hopeh, China 106 36 33N 113 40E
Shehung 108 31 0N 105 12E
Shehy Mts. 39 51 47N 9 15W
Sheikhpura 95 25 9N 85 53E
Shek Hasan 123 13 5N 35 58E
Shekar Dzong 95 28 45N 87 0E
Shekhupura 94 31 42N 73 58E
Sheki 83 41 10N 47 5E
Sheksna, R. 81 59 30N 38 30E
Shelburne, N.S., Can. 151 43 47N 65 20W
Shelburne, Ont., Can. 150 44 4N 80 15W
Shelburne B. 133 11 50S 143 0E
Shelburne Falls 162 42 36N 72 45W
Shelby, Mich., U.S.A. 156 43 34N 86 27W
Shelby, Mont., U.S.A. 160 48 30N 111 59W
Shelby, N.C., U.S.A. 157 35 18N 81 34W
Shelbyville, Ill., U.S.A. 158 39 25N 88 45W
Shelbyville, Ind., U.S.A. 156 39 30N 85 42W
Shelbyville, Tenn., U.S.A. 157 35 30N 86 25W
Sheldon 158 43 6N 95 51W
Sheldon Point 147 62 30N 165 0W
Sheldrake 151 50 20N 64 51W
Shelikef, Str. 147 58 0N 154 0W
Shelikhova, Zaliv 77 59 30N 157 0E
Shell, L. 36 58 0N 6 28W
Shell Lake 153 53 19N 107 14W
Shell Lakes 137 29 20S 127 30E
Shellbrook 153 53 13N 106 24W
Shellharbour 141 34 31S 150 51E
Shelon, R. 80 58 10N 30 30E
Shelter Bay 151 50 30N 67 20W
Shelter I 162 41 5N 72 21W
Shelton, Conn., U.S.A. 162 41 18N 73 7W
Shelton, Wash., U.S.A. 160 47 15N 123 6W
Shemakha 83 40 50N 48 28E
Shenandoah, Iowa, U.S.A. 158 40 50N 95 25W
Shenandoah, Pa., U.S.A. 162 40 49N 76 13W
Shenandoah, Va., U.S.A. 156 38 30N 78 38W
Shenandoah, R. 156 38 30N 78 38W
Shencha 105 30 56N 88 38E
Shench'ih 106 39 8N 112 10E
Shenchingtzu 107 44 48N 124 32E
Shench'iu 106 33 26N 115 2E
Shencottah 97 8 59N 77 18E
Shendam 121 9 10N 9 30E
Shendî 123 16 46N 33 33E
Shendurni 96 20 39N 75 36E
Shenfield 29 51 39N 0 21E
Shengfang 106 39 5N 116 42E
Shëngjergji 68 41 2N 20 10E
Shëngjini 68 41 50N 19 35E
Shenmëria 68 42 7N 20 13E
Shenmu 106 38 54N 110 24E
Shensi □ 106 34 50N 109 25E
Shenton, Mt. 137 27 57S 123 22E
Shenyang 107 42 50N 123 25E
Sheopur Kalan 93 25 40N 76 40E
Shepetovka 80 50 10N 27 0E
Shephelah = Hashefela 90 31 30N 34 43E
Shepparton 141 36 23S 145 26E
Sheppey, I. of 29 51 23N 0 50E
Shepshed 28 52 47N 1 18W
Shepton Mallet 28 51 11N 2 31W
Sher Khan Qala 94 29 55N 66 10E
Sher Qila 95 36 7N 74 2E
Sherada 123 7 25N 36 30E
Sherborne 28 50 56N 2 31W
Sherborne St. John 28 51 18N 1 7W
Sherbro I. 120 7 30N 12 40W
Sherbrooke 151 45 8N 81 57W
Sherburn, N. Yorks., U.K. 33 54 12N 0 32W
Sherburn, N. Yorks., U.K. 33 53 47N 1 15W
Sherburne 162 42 41N 75 30W
Shercock 38 54 0N 6 54W
Sherda 119 20 7N 16 46E
Shere 29 51 13N 0 28W
Shereik 122 18 52N 33 40E
Sherfield English 28 51 1N 1 35W
Sheridan, Ark., U.S.A. 159 34 20N 92 25W
Sheridan, Col., U.S.A. 158 39 44N 105 3W
Sheridan, Wyo., U.S.A. 160 44 50N 107 0W
Sheriff Hutton 33 54 5N 1 0W
Sheriff Muir 35 56 12N 3 53W
Sheringham 29 52 56N 1 11E
Sherkin I. 39 51 38N 9 25W
Sherkot 95 29 22N 78 35E
Sherman 159 33 40N 96 35W
Sherpur 98 24 41N 89 25E
Sherridon 153 55 8N 101 5W
Sherston 28 51 35N 2 13W
Sherwood, N.D., U.S.A. 158 48 59N 101 36W
Sherwood, Tex., U.S.A. 159 31 18N 100 45W
Sherwood For. 33 53 5N 1 5W
Shesheke 125 17 14S 24 22E
Sheslay 152 58 17N 131 45W
Sheslay, R. 152 58 48N 132 5W
Shethanei L. 153 58 48N 97 50W
Shetland □ 36 60 30N 1 30W
Shetland Is. 36 60 30N 1 30W
Shevaroy Hills 97 11 58N 78 12E
Shevchenko 83 44 25N 51 20E
Shewa □ 123 9 33N 38 10E
Sheyenne 159 47 52N 99 8W
Sheyenne, R. 158 47 40N 98 15W
Shiant Is. 36 57 54N 6 20W
Shiant, Sd. of Scot. 36 57 54N 6 30W
Shibam 91 16 0N 48 36E
Shibata 112 37 57N 139 20E
Shiberghan □ 93 35 45N 66 0E
Shibetsu 112 44 10N 142 23E
Shibîn El Kôm 122 30 31N 30 55E
Shibogama L. 150 53 35N 88 15W
Shibukawa 111 36 29N 139 0E
Shibushi 110 31 25N 131 0E
Shibushi-Wan 110 31 24N 131 8E
Shickshinny 162 41 9N 76 9W
Shido 110 34 19N 134 10E
Shiel, L. 36 56 48N 5 32W
Shield, C. 138 13 20S 136 20E
Shieldaig 36 57 31N 5 39W
Shifnal 28 52 40N 2 23W
Shiga-ken □ 111 35 20N 136 0E
Shigaib 117 15 5N 23 35E
Shigaraki 111 34 57N 136 2E
Shihch'eng 109 26 19N 116 15E
Shihchiachuangi 106 38 2N 114 30E
Shihch'ien 108 27 30N 108 14E
Shihchiu Hu 109 31 28N 118 53E
Shihchu 108 30 4N 108 10E
Shihch'üan 106 33 3N 108 17E
Shihhsing 109 24 57N 114 4E
Shihku 108 26 52N 99 56E
Shihkuaikou 106 40 42N 110 20E
Shihlung 109 23 55N 113 35E
Shihmen 109 29 36N 111 23E
Shihmenchien 109 29 33N 116 47E
Shihmien 108 29 20N 102 28E
Shihping 108 27 2N 108 7E
Shihp'ing 108 23 43N 102 30E
Shihshou 109 29 43N 112 26E
Shihtai 109 30 22N 117 57E
Shihtien 108 24 44N 99 11E
Shiht'ouhotzu 107 44 52N 128 41E
Shihtsuishan 106 39 15N 106 50E
Shihtsung 108 24 51N 103 59E
Shiiba 110 32 29N 131 4E
Shijaku 68 41 21N 19 33E
Shikarpur, India 94 28 17N 78 7E
Shikarpur, Pak. 94 27 57N 68 39E
Shikine-Jima 111 34 19N 139 13E
Shikohabad 93 27 6N 78 38E
Shikoku 110 33 30N 133 30E
Shikoku □ 110 33 30N 133 30E
Shikoku-Sanchi 110 33 30N 133 30E
Shilbottle 35 55 23N 1 42W
Shilda 84 51 49N 59 47E
Shildon 33 54 37N 1 39W
Shilka 77 52 0N 115 55E
Shilka, R. 77 57 30N 93 18E
Shillelagh 39 52 46N 6 32W
Shillingstone 28 50 54N 2 15W
Shillington 162 40 18N 75 58W
Shillong 98 25 35N 91 53E
Shiloh 90 32 4N 35 10E
Shilovo 81 54 25N 40 57E
Shima-Hantō 111 34 22N 136 45E
Shimabara 110 32 48N 130 20E
Shimada 111 34 49N 138 19E
Shimane-Hantō 110 35 30N 133 0E
Shimane-ken □ 110 35 0N 132 30E
Shimenovsk 77 52 15N 127 30E
Shimizu 111 35 0N 138 30E
Shimo-Jima 110 32 15N 130 7E
Shimo-Koshiki-Jima 110 31 40N 129 43E
Shimoda 111 34 40N 138 57E
Shimodate 111 36 20N 139 55E
Shimoga 97 13 57N 75 32E
Shimoni 126 4 38S 39 20E
Shimonita 111 36 13N 138 47E
Shimonoseki 110 33 58N 131 0E
Shimotsuma 111 36 11N 139 58E
Shimpuru Rapids 128 17 45S 19 55E
Shimsha, R. 97 13 15N 76 54E
Shimsk 80 58 15N 30 50E
Shin Dand 93 33 12N 62 8E
Shin, L. 37 58 7N 4 30W
Shin, R. 37 58 0N 4 26W
Shin-Tone-Gawa 111 35 57N 140 27E
Shingbwiyang 98 26 41N 96 13E
Shingleton 150 46 33N 86 33W
Shingu 111 33 40N 135 55E
Shinji 110 35 24N 132 54E
Shinji Ko 110 35 26N 132 57E
Shinjō 112 38 46N 140 18E
Shinkafe 121 13 8N 6 29E
Shinminato 111 36 47N 137 4E
Shinonoi 111 36 35N 138 9E
Shinrone 39 53 0N 7 58W
Shinshiro 111 34 54N 137 30E
Shinyanga 126 3 45S 33 27E
Shinyanga □ 126 3 30S 33 30E
Shio-no-Misaki 111 33 25N 135 45E
Shiogama 112 38 19N 141 1E
Shiojiri 111 36 6N 137 58E
Ship I. 159 30 16N 88 55W
Ship Shoal I. 162 37 10N 75 45W
Shipbourne 29 51 13N 0 19E
Shipdham 29 52 38N 0 53E
Shipehenski Prokhod 67 42 39N 25 28E
Shipki La 93 31 45N 78 40E
Shipley 33 53 50N 1 47W
Shippegan 151 47 45N 64 45W
Shippensburg 156 40 4N 77 32W
Shiprock 161 36 51N 108 45W
Shipston-on-Stour 28 52 4N 1 38W
Shipton-under-Wychwood 28 51 51N 1 35W
Shir Kūh 93 31 45N 53 30E
Shirabad 85 37 40N 67 1E
Shirahama 111 33 41N 135 20E
Shirakawa 111 36 17N 136 56E
Shirane-San, Gumma, Japan 111 36 48N 139 22E
Shirane-San, Yamanashi, Japan 111 35 34N 138 9E
Shiraoi 112 42 33N 141 21E
Shirati 126 1 10S 34 0E
Shiraz 93 29 42N 52 30E
Shire, R. 127 16 30S 35 0E
Shirebrook 33 53 13N 1 11W
Shiresh 85 39 58N 70 59E
Shirinab, R. 94 29 30N 66 30E
Shiringushi 81 42 54N 53 56W
Shiriya-Zaki 112 41 25N 141 30E
Shirol 96 16 47N 74 41E
Shirpur 96 21 21N 74 57E
Shirvan 93 37 30N 57 50E
Shirwa L. = Chilwa L. 127 15 15S 35 40E
Shishmanova 67 42 58N 23 12E
Shishmaref 147 66 15N 166 10W
Shivali, (Sirkall) 97 11 15N 79 41E
Shivpuri 94 25 18N 77 42E
Shivta 90 30 53N 34 40E
Shiwele Ferry 127 11 25S 28 31E
Shiyata 122 29 25N 25 7E
Shizuoka 111 35 0N 138 30E
Shizuoka-ken □ 111 35 15N 138 40E
Shklov 80 54 10N 30 15E
Shkoder = Shkodra 68 42 6N 19 20E
Shkodra 68 42 6N 19 20E
Shkodra □ 68 42 5N 19 20E
Shkumbini, R. 68 41 5N 19 50E
Shmidt, O. 77 81 0N 91 0E
Shō Gawa, R. 111 36 47N 137 4E
Shoa Ghimirra, (Wota) 123 7 4N 35 51E
Shoal, C. 137 33 52S 121 10E
Shoal Lake 153 50 30N 100 35W
Shōbara 110 34 51N 133 1E
Shōdo-Shima 110 34 30N 134 15E
Shoeburyness 29 51 31N 0 49E
Shokpar 85 43 49N 74 21E
Sholapur 96 17 43N 75 56E
Shologontsy 77 66 13N 114 14E
Shomera 90 33 4N 35 17E
Shōmrōn 90 32 15N 35 13E
Shona I. 36 56 48N 5 50W
Shongopovi 161 35 49N 110 37W
Shoranur 97 10 46N 76 19E
Shorapur 96 16 31N 76 48E
Shoreham-by-Sea 29 50 50N 0 17W
Shortland I. 135 7 0S 155 45E
Shoshone, Calif., U.S.A. 163 35 58N 116 16W
Shoshone, Idaho, U.S.A. 160 43 0N 114 27W
Shoshone L. 160 44 0N 111 0W
Shoshone Mts. 160 39 30N 117 30W
Shoshong 125 22 56S 26 31E
Shoshoni 160 43 13N 108 5W
Shostka 80 51 57N 33 32E
Shotts 35 55 49N 3 47W
Shouch'ang 109 29 22N 119 13E
Shouhsien 109 32 35N 116 48E
Shoukuang 107 36 53N 118 42E
Shouning 109 27 26N 119 27E
Shouyang 106 37 59N 113 9E
Show Low 161 34 16N 110 0W
Shpola 82 49 1N 31 30E
Shreveport 159 32 30N 93 50W
Shrewsbury 28 52 42N 2 45W
Shrewton 28 51 11N 1 55W
Shrivardhan 96 18 10N 73 3E
Shrivenham 28 51 36N 1 39W
Shropshire (□) = Salop 28 52 36N 2 45W
Shrule 38 53 32N 9 7W
Shuangch'eng 107 45 25N 126 20E
Shuangchiang 108 23 33N 99 45E
Shuangfeng 109 27 26N 112 10E
Shuangfeng Tao 109 26 35N 120 8E
Shuangkou 107 34 3N 117 34E
Shuangliao 105 43 31N 123 30E
Shuangpai 108 24 50N 101 36E
Shuangshantzu 107 40 21N 119 12E
Shuangyang 107 43 32N 125 40E
Shuangyashan 105 46 37N 131 22E
Shuch'eng 109 31 27N 116 57E
Shugden Gomba 99 29 35N 96 55E
Shuguri Falls 127 8 33S 37 22E
Shuich'eng 108 26 35N 104 54E
Shuichi 109 27 28N 118 21E
Shuiyeh 106 36 8N 114 6E
Shujalpur 94 23 43N 76 40E
Shulan 107 44 27N 126 57E
Shumagin Is. 147 55 0N 159 0W
Shumerlya 81 55 30N 46 10E
Shumikha 84 55 10N 63 15E
Shunan 109 29 37N 119 0E
Shunch'ang 109 26 48N 117 47E
Shungay 83 48 30N 46 45E
Shungnak 147 66 55N 157 10W
Shunning 99 24 35N 99 50E
Shunte 109 22 48N 113 17E
Shuohsien 106 39 19N 112 25E
Shupka Kunzang 95 34 22N 78 22E
Shuqra 91 13 22N 45 34E
Shur, R. 93 28 30N 55 0E
Shurab 85 40 3N 70 33E
Shurchi 85 37 59N 67 47E
Shurkhua 98 22 15N 93 38E
Shurma 84 56 58N 50 21E
Shusf 93 31 50N 60 5E
Shūshtar 92 32 0N 48 50E
Shuswap L. 152 50 55N 119 3W
Shuweika 90 32 20N 35 1E
Shuya 81 56 50N 41 28E
Shuyak I. 147 58 35N 152 30W
Shuzenji 111 34 58N 138 56E
Shwebo 98 22 30N 95 45E
Shwegu 98 18 49N 95 26E
Shwegun 98 17 9N 97 39E
Shweli Myit 99 23 45N 96 45E
Shweli, R. 99 23 45N 96 45E
Shwenyaung 98 20 46N 96 57E
Shyok 95 34 15N 78 5E
Shyok, R. 95 34 30N 78 15E
Si Chon 101 9 0N 99 54E
Si Kiang = Hsi Chiang, R. 39 22 20N 113 20E
Si Prachan 100 14 37N 100 9E
Si Racha 101 13 10N 100 56E
Siah 92 22 0N 47 0E
Siahan Range 93 27 30N 64 40E
Siaksriinderapura 102 0 51N 102 0E
Sialkot 94 32 32N 74 30E
Sialsuk 98 23 24N 92 45E
Siam 140 32 35S 136 41E
Siam, G. of 101 11 30N 101 0E
Siam = Thailand ■ 100 16 0N 102 0E
Sian = Hsian 106 34 17N 109 0E
Siantan, P. 101 3 10N 106 15E
Siareh 93 28 5N 60 20E
Siargao, I. 103 9 52N 126 3E
Siari 95 34 55N 76 40E
Siasi 103 5 34N 120 50E
Siassi 135 5 40S 147 51E
Siátista 68 40 15N 21 33E
Siau, I. 103 2 50N 125 25E
Siauliai 80 55 56N 23 15E
Siaya □ 126 0 0N 34 20E
Siazan 83 41 3N 48 7E
Sibâi, Gebel el 122 25 45N 34 10E
Sibari 65 39 47N 16 27E
Sibay 84 52 42N 58 39E
Sibaya, L. 129 27 20S 32 45E
Sibbald 153 51 24N 110 10W
Sibenik 63 43 48N 15 54E
Siberia 77 60 0N 100 0E
Siberut, I. 102 1 30S 99 0E
Sibi 94 29 30N 67 48E
Sibil 103 4 59S 140 35E
Sibiti 124 3 38S 13 19E
Sibiu 70 45 45N 24 9E
Sibiu □ 70 45 50N 24 15E
Sible Hedingham 29 51 58N 0 37E
Sibley, Iowa, U.S.A. 158 43 21N 95 43W
Sibley, La., U.S.A. 159 32 34N 93 16W
Sibolga 102 1 50N 98 45E
Sibret 47 49 58N 5 38E
Sibsagar 98 27 0N 94 36E
Sibsey 33 53 3N 0 1E
Sibuco 103 7 20N 122 10E
Sibuguey B. 103 7 50N 122 45E
Sibuko 103 7 20N 122 10E
Sibut 117 5 52N 19 10E
Sibutu, I. 102 4 45N 119 30E
Sibutu Passage 103 4 50N 120 0E
Sibuyan, I. 103 12 25N 122 40E
Sicamous 152 50 49N 119 0W
Sicapoo 103 18 9N 121 34E
Sicasica 154 17 20S 67 45W
Siccus, R. 140 31 42S 139 25E
Sicilia, Canale di 64 37 25N 12 30E
Sicilia, I. 65 37 30N 14 30E
Sicily = Sicilia 65 37 30N 14 30E
Sicuani 174 14 10S 71 10W
Siculiana 64 37 20N 13 23E
Sid 63 45 6N 19 16E
Sidamo □ 123 5 0N 37 50E
Sidaouet 121 18 34N 8 3E
Sidaradougou 120 10 42N 4 12W
Sidbury 30 50 43N 3 12W
Siddeburen 46 53 15N 6 52E

**Siddipet** **Skaneateles**


Siddipet 96 18 0N 79 0E
Sidensjo 72 63 20N 18 20E
Sidéradougou 120 10 42N 4 12W
Siderno Marina 65 38 16N 16 17E
Sidheros, Ákra 69 35 19N 26 19E
Sidhirókastron 68 37 20N 21 46E
Sidhpur 94 23 56N 71 25E
Sîdi Abd el Rahman 122 30 55N 28 41E
Sîdi Barrâni 122 31 32N 25 58E
Sidi-Bel-Abbès 118 35 13N 0 10W
Sidi Bennour 118 32 40N 9 26W
Sidi Haneish 122 31 10N 27 35E
Sidi Ifni 118 29 29N 10 3W
Sidi Kacem 118 34 11N 5 40W
Sīdī Miftāh 119 31 8N 16 58E
Sidi Moussa, O. 118 33 0N 8 50W
Sidi Omar 122 31 24N 24 57E
Sīdī Yahya 119 30 55N 16 30E
Sidlaw Hills 35 56 32N 3 10W
Sidlesham 29 50 46N 0 46W
Sidmouth 30 50 40N 3 13W
Sidmouth, C. 138 13 25S 143 36E
Sidney, Can. 152 48 39N 123 24W
Sidney, Mont., U.S.A. 158 47 51N 104 7W
Sidney, N.Y., U.S.A. 162 42 18N 75 20W
Sidney, Ohio, U.S.A. 156 40 18N 84 6W
Sidoardjo 103 7 30S 112 46E
Sidoktaya 98 20 27N 94 15E
Sidon, (Saida) 92 33 38N 35 28E
Sidra, G. of = Khalīj Surt 61 31 40N 18 30E
Siedlce 54 52 10N 22 20E
Siedlce □ 54 52 0N 22 0E
Siegburg 48 50 48N 7 12E
Siegen 48 50 52N 8 2E
Siem Pang 100 14 7N 106 23E
Siem Reap 100 13 20N 103 52E
Siena 63 43 20N 11 20E
Sieniawa 54 50 11N 22 38E
Sieradź 54 51 37N 18 41E
Sieradź □ 54 51 30N 19 0E
Sieraków 54 52 39N 16 2E
Sierck-les-Bains 43 49 26N 6 20E
Sierpc 54 52 55N 19 43E
Sierpe, Bocas de la 174 10 0N 61 30W
Sierra Alta 58 40 31N 1 30W
Sierra Blanca 161 31 11N 105 17W
Sierra Blanca, mt. 161 33 20N 105 54W
Sierra City 160 39 34N 120 42W
Sierra Colorado 176 40 35S 67 50W
Sierra de Gädor 59 36 57N 2 45W
Sierra de Yeguas 57 37 7N 4 52W
Sierra Gorda 172 23 0S 69 15W
Sierra Leone ■ 120 9 0N 12 0W
Sierra Majada 164 27 19N 103 42W
Sierre 50 46 17N 7 31E
Sifnos 69 37 0N 24 45E
Sifton 153 51 21N 100 8W
Sifton Pass 152 57 52N 126 15W
Sig 118 35 32N 0 12W
Sigaboy 103 6 39N 126 10E
Sigdal 71 60 4N 9 38E
Sigean 44 43 2N 2 58E
Sighetul Marmatiei 70 47 57N 23 52E
Sighişoara 70 46 12N 24 50E
Sighty Crag 35 55 8N 2 37W
Sigli 102 5 25N 96 0E
Siglufjörður 74 66 12N 18 55W
Sigma 103 11 29N 122 40E
Sigmaringen 49 48 5N 9 13E
Signakhi 83 40 52N 45 57E
Signau 50 46 56N 7 45E
Signy I. 13 60 45S 46 30W
Signy-l'Abbaye 43 49 40N 4 25E
Sigsig 174 3 0S 78 50W
Sigtuna 72 59 36N 17 44E
Sigüenza 58 41 3N 2 40W
Siguiri 120 11 31N 9 10W
Sigulda 80 57 10N 24 55E
Sigurd 161 38 57N 112 0W
Sihanoukville = Kompong Som 101 10 40N 103 30E
Si'ir 90 31 35N 35 9E
Siirt 92 37 57N 41 55E
Sijarira, Ra. 127 17 36S 27 45E
Sijsele 13 51 12N 3 20E
Sikandarabad 94 28 30N 77 39E
Sikandra Rao 93 27 43N 78 24E
Sikar 94 27 39N 75 10E
Sikasso 120 11 7N 5 35W
Sikerete 128 19 0S 20 48E
Sikeston 159 36 52N 89 35W
Sikhote Alin, Khrebet 77 46 0N 136 0E
Sikiá. 68 40 2N 23 56E
Sikinos, I. 69 36 40N 25 8E
Sikionia 69 38 0N 22 44E
Sikkani Chief, R. 152 57 47N 122 15W
Sikkim ■ 98 27 50N 88 50E
Siklós 53 45 50N 18 19E
Sikoro 120 12 19N 7 8W
Sikqo 101 7 34N 99 21E
Sil, R. 56 42 23N 7 30W
Sila, La, Mts. 65 39 15N 16 35E
Silacayoapán 165 17 30N 98 9W
Silandro 62 46 38N 10 48E
Sīlat adh Dhahr 90 32 19N 35 11E
Silba 63 44 24N 14 41E
Silba, I. 63 44 24N 14 41E
Silchar 98 24 49N 92 48E
Silcox 153 57 12N 94 10W
Silenrieux 47 50 14N 4 27E
Siler City 157 35 44N 79 30W
Sileru, R. 96 18 0N 82 0E
Silesia = Slask 54 51 0N 16 30E
Silet 118 22 44N 4 37E
Silgarhi Doti 95 29 15N 82 0E
Silghat 98 26 35N 93 0E
Silifke 92 36 22N 33 58E
Siliguri 98 26 45N 88 25E
Siliqua 64 39 20N 8 49E
Silistra 67 44 6N 27 19E
Siljan, L. 72 60 55N 14 45E
Silkeborg 73 56 10N 9 32E
Sillajhuay, Cordillera 174 19 40S 68 40W
Sillé-le Guillaume 42 48 10N 0 8W
Silloth 32 54 53N 3 25W
Siloam Springs 159 36 15N 94 31W
Silogui 102 1 10S 98 46E
Silsbee 159 30 20N 94 8W
Silsden 32 53 55N 1 55W
Silute 80 55 21N 21 33E
Silva Porto = Bié 125 12 22S 16 55E
Silvaplana 51 46 28N 9 48E
Silver City, Calif., U.S.A. 160 36 19N 119 44W
Silver City, N. Mex., U.S.A. 161 32 50N 108 18W
Silver Cr., R. 160 43 30N 119 30W
Silver Creek 156 42 33N 79 9W
Silver L. 163 38 39N 120 6W
Silver Lake, Calif., U.S.A. 163 35 21N 116 7W
Silver Lake, Oreg., U.S.A. 160 43 9N 121 4W
Silver Springs 162 39 2N 77 3W
Silverhojden 72 60 2N 15 0E
Silvermine, Mts. 39 52 47N 8 15W
Silvermines 39 52 48N 8 15W
Silverpeak, Ra. 163 37 35N 117 45W
Silverstone 28 52 5N 1 3W
Silverton, Austral. 140 31 52S 141 10E
Silverton, U.K. 30 50 49N 3 29W
Silverton, Colo., U.S.A. 161 37 51N 107 45W
Silverton, Tex., U.S.A. 159 34 30N 101 16W
Silves 57 37 11N 8 26W
Silvia 174 2 37N 76 21W
Silvies, R. 160 43 57N 119 5W
Silvolde 46 51 55N 6 23E
Silvretta Gruppe 51 46 50N 10 6E
Silwa Bahari 122 24 45N 32 55E
Silwan 90 31 59N 35 15E
Silwani 93 23 18N 78 27E
Silz 52 47 16N 10 56E
Sim, C. 118 31 26N 9 51W
Simanggang 102 1 15N 111 25E
Simão Dias 170 10 44S 37 49W
Simard, L. 150 47 40N 78 40W
Simarun 93 31 16N 51 40E
Simba 126 1 41S 34 12E
Simbach 49 48 16N 13 3E
Simbo 126 4 51S 29 41E
Simcoe 150 42 50N 80 20W
Simcoe, L. 150 44 25N 79 20W
Simenga 77 62 50N 107 55E
Simeon 47 50 45N 5 36E
Simeulue, I. 102 2 45N 95 45E
Simferopol 82 44 55N 34 3E
Simi 69 36 35N 27 50E
Simi, I. 69 36 35N 27 50E
Simi Valley 163 34 16N 118 47W
Simikot 95 30 0N 81 50E
Simiti 174 7 58N 73 57W
Simitli 66 41 52N 23 7E
Simla 94 31 2N 77 15E
Simleu-Silvaniei 70 47 17N 22 50E
Simme, R. 50 46 38N 7 25E
Simmern 48 49 59N 7 32E
Simmie 153 49 56N 108 6W
Simmler 163 35 21N 119 59W
Simões 170 7 30S 40 49W
Simojärvi 74 66 5N 27 10E
Simojoki 74 65 46N 25 15E
Simojovel 165 17 12N 92 38W
Simonette, R. 152 55 9N 118 15W
Simonsbath 28 51 8N 3 45W
Simonside, Mt. 35 55 17N 2 0W
Simonstown 128 34 14S 18 26E
Simontornya 53 46 45N 18 33E
Simpang 101 4 50N 100 40E
Simpleveld 47 50 50N 5 58E
Simplicio Mendes 170 7 51S 41 54W
Simplon 50 46 12N 8 4E
Simplon Pass 50 46 15N 8 0E
Simplon Tunnel 50 46 15N 8 7E
Simpson Des. 138 25 0S 137 0E
Simpungdong 107 41 56N 129 29E
Simrishamn 73 55 33N 14 22E
Simsbury 162 41 52N 72 48W
Simunjan 102 1 25N 110 45E
Sîmŭrtin 70 46 19N 25 58E
Simushir, Ostrov 77 46 50N 152 30E
Sina, R. 97 18 25N 75 28E
Sinaai 47 51 9N 4 2E
Sinabang 102 2 30N 46 30E
Sinai = Es Sînâ' 122 29 0N 34 0E
Sinai, Mt. = Musa, G. 122 28 32N 33 59E
Sinaia 70 45 21N 25 38E
Sinaloa 164 25 50N 108 20W
Sinaloa □ 164 25 0N 107 30W
Sinalunga 63 43 12N 11 43E
Sinamaica 174 11 5N 71 51W
Sînandrei 70 45 52N 21 13E
Sînāwan 119 31 0N 10 30E
Sinbaung we 98 19 43N 95 10E
Sinbo 98 24 46N 97 3E
Sincé 174 9 15N 75 9W
Sincelejo 174 9 18N 75 24W
Sinchangni, Kor., N. 107 40 7N 128 28E
Sinchangni, Kor., N. 107 39 24N 126 8E
Sinclair 160 41 47N 107 35W
Sinclair Mills 152 54 5N 121 40W
Sinclair's B. 37 58 30N 3 0W
Sincorá, Serra do 171 13 30S 41 0W
Sind, R. 95 34 18N 75 0E
Sind Sagar Doab 94 32 0N 71 30E
Sinda 127 17 28S 25 51E
Sindal 73 57 28N 10 10E
Sindangan 103 8 10N 123 5E
Sindangbarang 103 7 27S 107 9E
Sindjai 103 5 0S 120 20E
Sinelnikovo 82 48 25N 35 30E
Sines 57 37 56N 8 51W
Sines, Cabo de 57 37 58N 8 53W
Sineu 58 39 39N 3 0E
Sinewit, Mt. 135 4 44S 152 2E
Sinfra 120 6 35N 5 56W
Sing Buri 100 14 53N 100 25E
Singa 123 13 10N 33 57E
Singanallurt 97 11 2N 77 1E
Singaparna 103 7 23S 108 4E
Singapore ■ 101 1 17N 103 51E
Singapore, Straits of 101 1 15N 104 0E
Singaraja 102 8 15S 115 10E
Singen 49 47 45N 8 50E
Singida 126 4 49S 34 48E
Singida □ 126 6 0S 34 30E
Singitikós, Kólpos 68 40 6N 24 0E
Singkaling Hkamti 98 26 0N 95 45E
Singkang 103 4 8S 120 1E
Singkawang 102 1 0N 109 5E
Singkep, I. 102 0 30S 104 20E
Singleton, Austral. 141 32 33S 151 10E
Singleton, U.K. 29 50 55N 0 45W
Singleton, Mt. 137 29 27S 117 15E
Singö 72 60 12N 18 45E
Singoli 94 25 0N 75 16E
Singora = Songkhla 101 7 12N 100 36E
Singosan 107 38 52N 127 25E
Sinhailian (Lienyünchiangshih) 107 34 31N 118 15E
Sinhung 107 40 11N 127 34E
Siniatsikon, Óros 68 40 25N 21 35E
Siniscóla 64 40 35N 9 40E
Sinj 63 43 42N 16 39E
Sinjajevina, Planina 66 42 57N 19 22E
Sinjil 90 32 3N 35 15E
Sinkat 122 18 55N 36 49E
Sinkiang-Uighur □ 105 42 0N 86 0E
Sinmark 107 38 25N 126 14E
Sinnai Sardinia 64 39 18N 9 13E
Sinnar 96 19 48N 74 0E
Sinni, R. 65 40 6N 16 15E
Sînnicolau-Maré 70 46 5N 20 39E
Sinnûris 122 29 26N 30 31E
Sinoe, L. 70 44 35N 28 50E
Sinoia 127 17 20S 30 8E
Sinop 92 42 1N 35 11E
Sinop, R. 82 42 1N 35 2E
Sinpo 107 40 0N 128 13E
Sins 51 47 12N 8 24E
Sinskoye 77 61 8N 126 48E
Sint Annaland 47 51 36N 4 6E
Sint Annaparochie 46 53 16N 5 40E
Sint-Denijs 47 50 45N 3 23E
Sint Eustatius, I. 167 17 30N 62 59W
Sint-Genesius-Rode 47 50 45N 4 22E
Sint-Gillis-Waas 47 51 13N 4 6E
Sint-Huibrechts-Lille 47 51 13N 5 29E
Sint-Katelinje-Waver 47 51 5N 4 32E
Sint-Kruis 47 51 13N 3 15E
Sint-Laureins 47 51 14N 3 32E
Sint Maarten, I. 167 18 4N 63 4W
Sint-Michiels 47 51 11N 3 15E
Sint Nicolaasga 46 52 55N 5 45E
Sint Niklaas 47 51 10N 4 9E
Sint Oedenrode 47 51 35N 5 29E
Sint Pancras 46 52 40N 4 48E
Sint-Pauwels 47 51 11N 3 57E
Sint Philipsland 47 51 37N 4 10E
Sint Truiden 47 50 48N 5 12E
Sint Willebroad 47 51 33N 4 33E
Sîntana Ano 70 46 20N 21 30E
Sintang 102 0 5N 111 35E
Sintjohannesga 46 52 55N 5 52E
Sinton 159 28 1N 97 30W
Sintra 57 38 47N 9 25W
Sinŭiju 107 40 5N 124 24E
Sinuk 147 64 42N 166 22W
Sinyang = Hsinyang 109 32 10N 114 6E
Sinyukha, R. 82 48 31N 30 31E
Siófok 53 46 54N 18 4E
Sióma 128 16 25S 23 28E
Sion 50 46 14N 7 20E
Sion Mills 38 54 47N 7 29W
Sioua, El Wâhât es 122 29 10N 25 30E
Sioux City 158 42 32N 96 25W
Sioux Falls 158 43 35N 96 40W
Sioux Lookout 150 50 10N 91 50W
Sip Song Chaw Thai, reg. 100 21 30N 103 30E
Sipan 66 42 45N 17 52E
Sipera, I. 102 2 18S 99 40E
Sipiwesk L. 153 55 5N 97 35W
Sipul 138 5 50S 148 28E
Siquia, R. 166 12 30N 84 30W
Siquijor, I. 103 9 12N 123 45E
Siquirres 166 10 6N 83 30W
Siquisique 174 10 34N 69 42W
Sir Edward Pellew Group 138 15 40S 137 10E
Sir Graham Moore Is. 136 13 53S 126 34E
Sir Samuel Mt. 137 27 45S 120 40E
Sir Thomas, Mt. 137 27 10S 129 45E
Sira 97 13 41N 76 49E
Sira, R. 71 58 43N 6 40E
Siracusa 65 37 4N 15 17E
Sirajganj 95 24 25N 89 47E
Sirake 138 9 1S 141 2E
Sirakoro 120 12 41N 9 14W
Sirasso 120 9 16N 6 6W
Siret 70 47 55N 26 5E
Siret, R. 70 47 58N 26 5E
Siria 66 46 16N 21 38E
Sirinhaém 171 8 35S 35 7W
Sirkall (Shivali) 97 11 15N 79 41E
Sírna, I. 69 36 22N 26 42E
Sirnach 51 47 28N 8 59E
Sirohi 94 24 52N 72 53E
Siroki Brijeg 66 43 21N 17 36E
Sironj 94 24 5N 77 45E
Síros 69 37 28N 24 57E
Síros, I. 69 37 28N 24 57E
Sirretta Pk. 163 35 56N 118 19W
Sirsa 94 29 33N 75 4E
Sirsi 97 14 40N 74 49E
Siruela 57 38 58N 5 3W
Sisak 63 45 30N 16 21E
Sisaket 100 15 8N 104 23E
Sisante 59 39 25N 2 12W
Sisargas, Islas 56 43 21N 8 50W
Sishen 128 27 55S 22 59E
Sisipuk I. 153 55 40N 102 0W
Sisipuk L. 153 55 45N 101 50W
Sisophon 100 13 31N 102 59E
Sissach 50 47 27N 7 48E
Sisseton 158 45 43N 97 3W
Sissonne 43 49 34N 3 51E
Sistan-Baluchistan □ 93 27 0N 62 0E
Sistema Central 56 40 40N 5 55W
Sistema Ibérico 58 41 0N 2 10W
Sisteron 45 44 12N 5 57E
Sisters 160 44 21N 121 32W
Sitamarhi 95 26 37N 85 30E
Sitapur 95 27 38N 80 45E
Siteki 129 26 32S 31 58E
Sitges 58 41 17N 1 47E
Sithoniá 68 40 0N 23 45E
Sitía 69 35 13N 26 6E
Sitio da Abadia 171 14 48S 46 16W
Sitka 147 57 9N 134 58W
Sitona 123 14 25N 37 23E
Sitoti 128 23 15S 23 40E
Sitra 122 28 40N 26 53E
Sittang Myit, R. 99 18 20N 96 45E
Sittang, R. 98 17 10N 96 58E
Sittard 47 51 0N 5 52E
Sittaung 98 24 10N 94 35E
Sittensen 48 53 17N 9 32E
Sittingbourne 29 51 20N 0 43E
Sittwe 99 20 15N 92 45E
Situbondo 103 7 45S 114 0E
Siuch'uan 109 26 20N 114 30E
Siuna 166 13 37N 84 45W
Sivaganga 97 9 50N 78 28E
Sivagiri 97 9 16N 77 26E
Sivakasi 97 9 24N 77 47E
Sivand 93 30 5N 52 55E
Sivas 92 39 43N 36 58E
Siverek 92 37 50N 39 25E
Sivrihisar 92 39 30N 31 35E
Sivry 47 50 10N 4 12E
Sîwa 122 29 11N 25 31E
Siwalik Range 95 28 0N 83 0E
Siwan 95 26 13N 84 27E
Sixmile Cross 38 54 34N 7 7W
Sixmilebridge 39 52 45N 8 46W
Siyâl, Jazâ'ir 122 22 49N 36 6E
Siyana 94 28 37N 78 6E
Sizewell 29 52 13N 1 38E
Sjaelland 73 55 30N 11 30E
Sjaellands Odde 73 56 0N 11 15E
Själevad 72 63 18N 18 36E
Sjarinska Banja 66 42 45N 21 38E
Sjenica 66 43 16N 20 0E
Sjernaröy 71 59 15N 5 50E
Sjoa 71 61 41N 9 40E
Sjöbo 73 55 37N 13 45E
Sjöholt 71 62 27N 6 52E
Sjönsta 74 67 10N 16 3E
Sjösa 73 58 47N 17 4E
Skadovsk 82 46 17N 32 52E
Skælskör 73 55 16N 11 18E
Skagafjörður 74 65 54N 19 35W
Skagastölstindane, mt. 75 61 25N 8 10E
Skagen 75 68 37N 14 27E
Skagen, pt. 73 57 43N 10 35E
Skagern 72 59 0N 14 20E
Skagerrak 73 57 30N 9 0E
Skagway 147 59 30N 135 20W
Skaidi 74 70 26N 24 30E
Skala Podolskaya 82 48 50N 26 15E
Skalat 80 49 23N 25 55E
Skalbmierz 54 56 22N 12 30E
Skalderviken 73 56 22N 12 30E
Skalicd 53 48 50N 17 15E
Skallingen, Odde 73 55 32N 8 13E
Skalni Dol = Kamenyak 67 43 24N 26 57E
Skals 73 56 34N 9 24E
Skanderborg 73 56 2N 9 55E
Skaneateles 162 42 57N 76 26W

Skaneateles L Sollentuna


Skaneateles L. 162 42 51N 76 22W
Skånevik 71 59 43N 5 53E
Skanninge 73 58 24N 15 5E
Skanör 73 55 24N 12 50E
Skanor 73 55 24N 12 50E
Skantzoúra I. 69 39 5N 24 6E
Skara 73 58 25N 13 30E
Skaraborgs län □ 73 58 20N 13 30E
Skarblacka 73 58 36N 15 50E
Skardhö 71 62 30N 8 47E
Skardu 95 35 20N 75 35E
Skaresta 73 58 26N 16 22E
Skarszewy 54 54 4N 18 25E
Skarvane, Mt. 71 63 18N 11 27E
Skarzysko Kamienna 54 51 7N 20 52E
Skatöy 71 50 50N 9 30E
Skattungbyn 72 61 10N 14 56E
Skaw (Grenen) 73 57 46N 10 34E
Skaw Taing 36 60 23N 0 57W
Skebo 72 59 58N 18 37E
Skebokvarn 72 59 7N 16 45E
Skeena Mts. 152 56 40N 128 30W
Skeena, R. 152 54 9N 130 5W
Skeggjastadir 74 66 3N 14 50W
Skegness 33 53 9N 0 20E
Skeldon 174 6 0N 57 20W
Skellefte älv 74 65 30N 18 30E
Skellefteå 74 64 45N 20 58E
Skelleftehamn 74 64 41N 21 14E
Skellig Rocks 39 51 47N 10 32W
Skellingthorpe 33 53 14N 0 37W
Skelmersdale 32 53 34N 2 49W
Skelmorlie 34 55 52N 4 53W
Skelton, Cleveland., U.K. 33 54 33N 0 59W
Skelton, Cumb., U.K. 32 54 42N 2 50W
Skender Vakuf 66 44 29N 17 22E
Skene 73 57 30N 12 37E
Skerries, Rks. 38 55 14N 6 40W
Skerries, The 31 53 27N 4 40W
Skhirra, La = Cekhira 119 34 20N 10 5E
Skhíza, I. 69 36 41N 20 40E
Skhoinoúsa, I. 69 36 53N 25 31E
Ski 71 59 43N 10 52E
Skiathos, I. 69 39 12N 23 30E
Skibbereen 39 51 33N 9 16W
Skiddaw, Mt. 32 54 39N 3 9W
Skidegate, Inlet 48 53 20N 132 0W
Skien 71 59 12N 9 35E
Skierniewice 54 51 58N 20 19E
Skikda 119 36 50N 6 58E
Skillingaryd 73 57 27N 14 5E
Skillinge 73 55 30N 14 16E
Skillingmark 72 59 48N 120 1E
Skinari, Ákra 69 37 56N 20 40E
Skipness 34 55 46N 5 20W
Skipsea 33 53 58N 0 13W
Skipton, Austral. 140 37 39S 143 21E
Skipton, U.K. 32 53 57N 2 1W
Skirild 73 55 58N 8 53E
Skirmish Pt. 138 11 59S 134 17E
Skiropoúla, I. 69 38 50N 24 21E
Skíros 69 38 55N 24 34E
Skíros, I. 69 38 55N 24 34E
Skivarp 73 55 26N 13 34E
Skive 73 56 33N 9 2E
Skjåk 71 61 52N 8 22E
Skjálfandafljót 74 65 15N 17 25W
Skjálfandi 74 66 5N 17 30W
Skjeberg 71 59 12N 11 12E
Skjern 73 55 57N 8 30E
Skjönne 71 60 16N 9 1E
Skoczów 54 49 49N 18 45E
Skodje 71 62 30N 6 43E
Skofja Loka 63 46 9N 14 19E
Skoger 71 59 42N 10 16E
Skoghall 72 59 20N 13 30E
Skoghult 73 56 59N 15 55E
Skokholm, I. 31 51 42N 5 16W
Skoki 54 52 40N 17 11E
Skole 80 49 3N 23 30E
Skomer, I. 31 51 44N 5 19W
Skonsberg 72 62 25N 17 21E
Skópelos 69 39 9N 23 47E
Skópelos, I. 69 39 9N 23 47E
Skopin 81 53 55N 39 32E
Skopje 66 42 1N 21 32E
Skorcz 54 43 47N 18 30E
Skorped 72 63 23N 17 55E
Skotfoss 71 59 12N 9 30E
Skoudas 80 56 21N 21 45E
Skövde 75 58 15N 13 59E
Skovorodino 77 54 0N 125 0E
Skowhegan 151 44 49N 69 40W
Skowman 153 51 58N 99 35W
Skradin 63 43 52N 15 53E
Skreanäs 73 56 52N 12 35E
Skudeneshavn 71 59 10N 5 10E
Skull 39 51 32N 9 40W
Skultorp 73 58 24N 13 51E
Skulyany 82 47 19N 27 39E
Skunk, R. 158 40 42N 91 7W
Skurup 73 55 28N 13 30E
Skutskär 73 60 37N 17 25E
Skvira 82 49 44N 29 32E
Skwaner, Pegunungan 102 1 0S 112 30E
Skwierzyna 54 52 46N 15 30E
Skye, I. 36 57 15N 6 10W
Skykomish 160 47 43N 121 16W
Skyros (Skíros), L. 69 38 52N 24 37E
Slagelse 73 55 23N 11 19E
Slagharen 46 52 37N 6 34E
Slaidburn 32 53 57N 2 28W
Slaley 35 54 55N 2 4W
Slamannon 140 32 1S 143 41E
Slamet, G. 102 7 16S 109 8E
Slane 38 53 42N 6 32W
Slaney, R. 39 52 52N 6 45W
Slangerup 73 55 50N 12 11E
Slănic 70 45 14N 25 58E
Slankamen 66 45 8N 20 15E
Slano 66 42 48N 17 53E
Slantsy 80 59 7N 28 5E
Slany 52 50 13N 14 6E
Slask 54 51 25N 16 0E
Slatbaken 73 58 28N 16 30E
Slate Is. 150 48 40N 87 0W
Slatina 70 44 28N 24 22E
Slatington 162 40 45N 75 37W
Slaton 159 33 27N 101 38W
Slave Coast 121 6 0N 2 30E
Slave Lake 152 55 17N 114 50W
Slave Pt. 152 61 11N 114 56W
Slave, R. 152 61 18N 113 39W
Slavgorod 76 53 10N 78 50E
Slavinja 66 43 14N 22 50E
Slavkov (Austerlitz) 53 49 10N 16 52E
Slavnoye 80 54 24N 29 15E
Slavonski Brod 66 45 11N 18 0E
Slavonski Pozega 66 45 20N 17 40E
Slavuta 80 50 15N 27 2E
Slavyans 82 48 55N 37 30E
Slavyansk 82 45 15N 38 11E
Sława 54 51 52N 16 2E
Sławno 54 54 20N 16 41E
Sławoborze 54 53 55N 15 42E
Slea Hd. 39 52 7N 10 30W
Sleaford 33 53 0N 0 22W
Sleaford B. 139 34 55S 135 45E
Sleat, Pt. of 36 57 1N 6 0W
Sleat, Sd. of 36 57 5N 5 47W
Sledmere 33 54 4N 0 35W
Sleeper, Is. 149 56 50N 80 30W
Sleepers, The 149 58 30N 81 0W
Sleepy Eye 158 44 15N 94 45W
Sleidinge 47 51 8N 3 41E
Sleights 33 54 27N 0 40W
Sleipner, gasfield 19 58 30N 1 48E
Sleman 103 7 40S 110 20E
Slemmestad 71 59 47N 10 30E
Slemon L. 152 63 13N 116 4W
Slesin 54 52 22N 18 14E
Sletterhage, Kap 73 56 7N 10 31E
Slide Mt. 162 42 0N 74 23W
Slidell 159 30 20N 89 48W
Sliedrecht 46 51 50N 4 45E
Slieve Anierin 38 54 5N 7 58W
Slieve Aughty 39 53 4N 8 30W
Slieve Bernagh 39 52 50N 8 30W
Slieve Bloom 39 53 4N 7 40W
Slieve Callan 39 52 51N 9 16W
Slieve Donard 38 54 10N 5 57W
Slieve Felim 39 52 40N 8 20W
Slieve Gamph 38 54 6N 9 0W
Slieve Gullion 38 54 8N 6 26W
Slieve League 38 54 40N 8 42W
Slieve Mish 39 52 12N 9 50W
Slieve Miskish 39 51 40N 10 10W
Slieve More 38 54 1N 10 3W
Slieve Snaght 38 54 59N 8 7W
Slieve Tooey 38 54 46N 8 39W
Slievenamon Mt. 39 52 25N 7 37W
Sligachan 36 57 17N 6 10W
Sligo 38 54 17N 8 28W
Sligo □ 38 54 10N 8 35W
Sligo B. 38 54 20N 8 40W
Slikkerveer 46 51 53N 4 36E
Slioch, mt. 36 57 40N 5 20W
Slipje 47 51 9N 2 51E
Slite 75 57 42N 18 48E
Sliven 67 42 42N 26 19E
Slivnitsa 66 42 50N 23 0E
Sljeme, mt. 63 45 57N 15 58E
Słupsk □ 54 54 15N 17 30E
Sloansville 162 42 45N 74 22W
Slobodskoy 84 58 40N 50 6E
Slobozia, Ialomiţa, Rumania 70 44 34N 27 23E
Slobozia, Valahia, Rumania 70 44 30N 25 14E
Slocan 152 49 48N 117 28W
Slochteren 46 53 12N 6 48E
Slochteren-Groningen, gasfield 19 53 10N 6 45E
Slöinge 73 56 51N 12 42E
Słomniki 54 50 16N 20 4E
Slonim 80 53 4N 25 19E
Slotermeer 46 52 55N 5 38E
Slough 29 51 30N 0 35W
Sloughhouse 163 38 26N 121 12W
Slovakia □ 53 48 30N 19 0E
Slovenia = Slovenija 63 45 58N 14 30E
Slovenija □ 63 45 58N 14 30E
Slovenska Bistrica 63 46 24N 15 35E
Slovenske Krusnohorie 53 48 45N 20 0E
Slovenské Rhudhorie 52 48 45N 19 0E
Słubice 54 52 22N 14 35E
Sluis 47 51 18N 3 23E
Slunchev Bryag 67 42 40N 27 41E
Slunj 63 45 6N 15 33E
Słupca 54 52 15N 17 52E
Słupsk 54 54 30N 17 3E
Slurry 128 25 49S 25 42E
Slyne Hd. 38 53 25N 10 10W
Slyudyanka 77 51 40N 103 30E
Smål-Taberg 73 57 42N 14 5E
Smålandsfarvandet 73 55 10N 11 20E
Smalandsstenar 73 57 9N 13 24E
Smålandstarvandet 73 55 10N 11 20E
Smalltree L. 153 61 0N 105 0W
Smallwood Reservoir 151 54 20N 63 10W
Smara 118 26 48N 11 31W
Smarje 63 46 15N 15 34E
Smart Syndicate Dam 128 30 45S 23 10E
Smeaton 153 53 30N 105 49W
Smedberg 73 58 35N 12 0E
Smederevo 66 44 40N 20 57E
Smedstorp 73 55 38N 13 58E
Smela 82 49 30N 32 0E
Smerwick Harb. 39 52 12N 10 23W
Smethwick 28 52 29N 1 58W
Smidovich 77 48 36N 133 49E
Smilde 46 52 58N 6 28E
Smiley 153 51 38N 109 29W
Smilyan 67 41 29N 24 46E
Smith 152 55 10N 114 0W
Smith Arm 152 66 15N 123 0W
Smith Center 158 39 50N 98 50W
Smith I. 162 38 0N 76 0W
Smith, R. 152 59 34N 126 30W
Smith Sund 12 78 30N 74 0W
Smithborough 38 54 13N 7 8W
Smithburne, R. 138 17 3S 140 57E
Smithers 152 54 45N 127 10W
Smithfield, U.K. 32 54 59N 2 51W
Smithfield, U.S.A. 157 35 31N 78 16W
Smith's Falls 150 44 55N 76 0W
Smithton, N.S.W., Austral. 139 31 0S 152 48E
Smithton, Tas., Austral. 138 40 53S 145 6E
Smithtown 141 30 58S 152 56E
Smithville 159 30 2N 97 12W
Smjörfjöll 74 65 30N 15 42W
Smoky Bay 139 32 22S 133 56E
Smoky Falls 150 50 4N 82 10W
Smoky Hill, R. 158 38 45N 98 0W
Smoky Lake 152 54 10N 112 30W
Smola 71 63 23N 8 3E
Smolensk 80 54 45N 32 0E
Smolikas, Óros 68 40 9N 20 58E
Smolník 53 48 43N 20 44E
Smolyan 67 41 36N 24 38E
Smooth Rock Falls 150 49 17N 81 37W
Smoothstone L. 153 54 40N 106 50W
Smorgon 80 54 28N 26 24E
Smulţi 70 45 57N 27 44E
Smyadovo 67 43 2N 27 1E
Smyrna 162 39 18N 75 36W
Smyrna = Izmir 92 38 25N 27 8E
Snaefell 30 54 18N 4 26W
Snaefells Jökull 74 64 45N 23 25W
Snainton 33 54 14N 0 33W
Snaith 33 53 42N 1 1W
Snake I. 141 38 47S 146 33E
Snake L. 153 55 32N 106 35W
Snake, R. 160 46 31N 118 50W
Snake Ra., Mts. 160 39 0N 114 30W
Snake River Plain 160 43 13N 113 0W
Snap, The 36 60 35N 0 50W
Snape 29 52 11N 1 29E
Snarum 71 60 1N 9 54E
Snasahogarha 72 63 10N 12 20E
Snedsted 73 56 55N 8 32E
Sneek 46 53 2N 5 40E
Sneeker-meer 46 53 2N 5 45E
Sneem 39 51 50N 9 55W
Snejbjerg 73 56 8N 8 54E
Snĕka 52 50 41N 15 50E
Snelling 163 37 31N 120 26W
Snettisham 29 52 52N 0 30E
Snezhnoye 83 48 0N 38 58E
Sneznik, mt. 63 45 36N 14 35E
Snigirevka 82 47 2N 32 35E
Snina 53 49 0N 22 9E
Snizort, L. 36 57 33N 6 28W
Snohetta 71 62 19N 9 16E
Snohomish 160 47 53N 122 6W
Snonuten 71 59 31N 6 50E
Snoul 101 12 4N 106 26E
Snow Hill 162 38 10N 75 21W
Snow L. 153 54 52N 100 3W
Snowbird L. 153 60 45N 103 0W
Snowdon, Mt. 31 53 4N 4 8W
Snowdrift 153 62 24N 110 44W
Snowdrift, R. 153 62 24N 110 44W
Snowflake 161 34 30N 110 4W
Snowshoe 152 53 43N 121 0W
Snowtown 140 33 46S 138 14E
Snowville 160 41 59N 112 47W
Snowy Mt. 162 43 45N 74 26W
Snowy Mts. 141 36 30S 148 20E
Snowy, R. 141 37 46S 148 30E
Snug Corner 167 22 33N 73 52W
Snyder, Okla., U.S.A. 159 34 4N 99 0W
Snyder, Tex., U.S.A. 159 32 45N 100 57W
Soacha 174 4 35N 74 13W
Soahanina 129 18 42S 44 13E
Soalala 129 16 6S 45 20E
Soan, R. 94 33 20N 72 40E
Soanierana-Ivongo 129 16 55S 49 35E
Soap Lake 160 47 29N 119 31W
Soay, I. 36 57 9N 6 13W
Soay Sd. 36 57 10N 6 15W
Sobat, Nahr 123 8 32N 32 40E
Soběslav 52 49 16N 14 45E
Sobhapur 94 22 47N 78 17E
Sobinka 81 56 0N 40 0E
Sobo-Yama 110 32 51N 131 16E
Sobótka 54 50 54N 16 44E
Sobrado 56 43 2N 8 2W
Sobral 170 3 50S 40 30W
Sobreira Formosa 57 39 46N 7 51W
Soc Giang 100 22 54N 106 1E
Soc Trang = Khonh Hung 101 9 37N 105 50E
Soča, R. 63 46 20N 13 40E
Socha 174 6 0N 72 41W
Sochaczew 54 52 15N 20 13E
Soch'e 105 38 24N 77 20E
Sochi 83 43 35N 39 40E
Société, Is. de la 131 17 0S 151 0W
Socompa, Portezuelo de 172 24 27S 68 18W
Socorro 174 6 29N 73 16W
Socorro, I. 164 18 45N 110 58W
Socotra, I. 91 12 30N 54 0E
Socúellmos 59 39 16N 2 47W
Soda Creek 152 52 25N 122 10W
Soda L. 161 35 7N 116 2W
Soda Plains 94 35 30N 79 0E
Soda Springs 160 42 4N 111 40W
Sodankylä 74 67 29N 26 40E
Söderfjärden 72 62 3N 17 25E
Söderfors 72 60 23N 17 25E
Söderhamn 72 61 18N 17 10E
Söderköping 72 58 31N 16 35E
Södermanlands län □ 72 59 10N 16 30E
Södertälje 72 59 12N 17 50E
Sodium 128 30 15S 15 45E
Sodo 123 7 0N 37 57E
Södra Vi 73 57 45N 15 45E
Sodrazica 63 45 45N 14 39E
Sodus 162 43 13N 77 5W
Soekmekaar 129 23 30S 29 55E
Soest, Ger. 48 51 34N 8 7E
Soest, Neth. 46 52 9N 5 19E
Soestdijk 46 52 11N 5 17E
Sofádhes 68 39 28N 22 4E
Sofara 120 13 59N 4 9W
Sofia = Sofiya 67 42 45N 23 20E
Sofia, R. 129 15 25S 48 40E
Sofievka 82 47 58N 34 14E
Sofikón 69 37 47N 23 3E
Sofila 67 42 45N 23 20E
Sofiya 67 42 45N 23 20E
Sogad 103 10 30N 125 0E
Sogakofe 121 6 2N 0 39E
Sogamoso 174 5 43N 72 56W
Sögel 48 52 50N 7 32E
Sogeri 135 9 26S 147 35E
Sogipo 107 33 13N 126 34E
Sogn og Fjordane fylke □ 71 61 40N 6 0E
Sogndal 71 58 20N 6 15E
Sogndalsfjøra 75 61 14N 7 5E
Sognefjorden 71 61 10N 5 50E
Sohâg 122 26 27N 31 43E
Soham 29 52 20N 0 20E
Sohano 135 5 22S 154 37E
Sŏhori 107 40 7N 128 23E
Soignies 47 50 35N 4 5E
Soira, Mt. 123 14 45N 39 30E
Soissons 43 49 25N 3 19E
Soitava, R. 53 49 30N 16 37E
Sojat 94 25 55N 73 38E
Sok, R. 84 53 24N 50 8E
Sokal 80 50 31N 24 15E
Söke 69 37 48N 27 28E
Sokhós 68 40 48N 23 22E
Sokhta Chinar 93 35 5N 67 35E
Sokna 71 60 16N 9 50E
Soknedal 71 62 57N 10 13E
Soko Banja 66 43 40N 21 51E
Sokodé 121 9 0N 1 11E
Sokó'ka 54 53 25N 23 30E
Sokol 81 59 30N 40 5E
Sokolo 120 14 42N 6 8W
Sokolov 52 50 12N 12 40E
Sokoł ó w Matopolski 53 50 12N 22 7E
Sokoł ó w Podlaski 54 52 25N 22 15E
Sokoto 121 13 2N 5 16E
Sokoto □ 121 12 30N 5 0E
Sokoto, R. 121 12 30N 6 10E
Sokuluk 85 42 52N 74 18E
Sol Iletsk 84 51 10N 55 0E
Sola 71 58 53N 5 36E
Sola, R. 126 49 38N 19 8E
Solai 126 0 2N 36 12E
Solana, La 59 38 59N 3 14W
Solano 103 16 25N 121 15E
Solares 56 43 23N 3 43W
Solberga 73 57 45N 14 43E
Solca 70 47 40N 25 50E
Solec Kujawski 54 53 5N 18 14E
Soledad, Colomb. 174 10 55N 74 46W
Soledad, U.S.A. 163 36 27N 121 16W
Soledad, Venez. 174 8 10N 63 34W
Solemint 163 34 25N 118 27W
Solent, The 28 50 45N 1 25W
Solenzara 45 41 53N 9 23E
Solesmes 43 50 10N 3 30E
Solfonn, Mt. 71 60 2N 6 57E
Soligalich 81 59 5N 42 10E
Solihull 28 52 26N 1 47W
Solikamsk 84 59 38N 56 50E
Solila 129 21 25S 46 37E
Soliman 119 36 42N 10 30E
Solimões, R. 174 2 15S 66 30W
Solingen 48 51 10N 7 4E
Sollas 36 57 39N 7 20W
Sollebrunn 73 58 8N 12 32E
Sollefteå 72 63 12N 17 20E
Sollentuna 72 59 26N 17 56E

Soller Speer

Soller **58** 39 43N 2 45 E
Sollerön **72** 60 54N 14 38 E
Solna **72** 59 22N 18 1 E
Solnechnogorsk **81** 56 10N 36 57 E
Sölnkletten, Mt. **71** 61 55N 10 18 E
Sologne **59** 47 40N 2 0 E
Solojärg **73** 56 50N 10 8 E
Solok **102** 0 55 S 100 40 E
Sololá **166** 14 49N 91 10 E
Solomon Is. **135** 6 0 S 155 0 E
Solomon, N. Fork, R. **158** 39 45N 99 0W
Solomon Sea **135** 7 0 S 150 0 E
Solomon, S. Fork, R. **158** 39 25N 99 12W
Solomon's Pools = Burak Sulayman **90** 31 42N 35 7 E
Solon Springs **158** 46 19N 91 47W
Solonópole **170** 5 44 S 39 1W
Solor, I. **103** 8 27 S 123 0 E
Solotcha **81** 54 48N 39 53 E
Solothurn **50** 47 13N 7 32 E
Solothurn □ **50** 47 18N 7 40 E
Solotobe **85** 44 37N 66 3 E
Solsona **58** 42 0N 1 31 E
Solt **53** 46 45N 19 1 E
Solta, I. **63** 43 24N 16 15 E
Soltanabad **93** 36 29N 58 5 E
Soltaniyeh **92** 36 20N 48 55 E
Soltau **48** 52 59N 9 50 E
Soltsy **80** 58 10N 30 10 E
Solun **105** 46 40N 120 40 E
Solund **71** 61 5N 4 50 E
Solund I. **71** 61 7N 4 50 E
Solunska Glava **66** 41 44N 21 31 E
Solva **31** 51 52N 5 12W
Solvang **163** 34 36N 120 8W
Solvay **162** 43 5N 76 17W
Solvesborg **73** 56 5N 14 35 E
Sölvesborg **73** 56 5N 14 35 E
Solway Firth **32** 54 45N 3 38W
Solwezi **127** 12 20 S 26 21 E
Somali Rep. ■ **91** 7 0N 47 0 E
Somaliland **123** 12 0N 43 0 E
Sombe Dzong **98** 27 13N 89 8 E
Sombernon **43** 47 20N 4 40 E
Sombor **66** 45 46N 19 17 E
Sombrerete **164** 23 40N 103 40W
Sombrero I. **167** 18 30N 63 30W
Somerby **29** 52 42N 0 49W
Someren **47** 51 23N 5 42 E
Somers **160** 48 4N 114 18W
Somerset, Austral. **138** 10 45 S 142 25 E
Somerset, Can. **153** 49 25N 98 39W
Somerset, Colo., U.S.A. **161** 38 55N 107 30W
Somerset, Ky., U.S.A. **156** 37 5N 84 40W
Somerset, Mass., U.S.A. **162** 41 45N 71 10W
Somerset □ **28** 51 9N 3 0W
Somerset East **128** 32 42 S 25 35 E
Somerset, I. **148** 73 30N 93 0W
Somerset West **128** 34 8 S 18 50 E
Somersham **29** 52 24N 0 0W
Somersworth **162** 43 15N 70 51W
Somerton, U.K. **28** 51 3N 2 45W
Somerton, U.S.A. **161** 32 41N 114 47W
Somerville **162** 40 34N 74 36W
Someş, R. **70** 47 15N 23 45 E
Someşul Mare, R. **70** 47 18N 24 30 E
Somma Lombardo **62** 45 41N 8 42 E
Somma Vesuviana **65** 40 52N 14 23 E
Sommariva **139** 26 24 S 146 36 E
Sommatino **65** 37 20N 14 0 E
Somme □ **43** 50 0N 2 20 E
Somme, B. de la **42** 5 22N 1 30 E
Sommelsdijk **46** 51 46N 4 9 E
Sommen **73** 58 12N 15 0 E
Sommen, L. **73** 58 0N 15 15 E
Sommepy-Tahure **43** 49 15N 4 31 E
Sömmerda **48** 51 10N 11 8 E
Sommersted **73** 55 19N 9 18 E
Sommesous **43** 48 44N 4 12 E
Sommières **45** 43 47N 4 6 E
Somogy □ **53** 46 19N 17 30 E
Somogyszob **53** 46 18N 17 20 E
Somoto **166** 13 28N 86 37W
Sompolno **54** 52 26N 18 45 E
Somport, Paso **58** 42 48N 0 31W
Somport, Puerto de **58** 42 48N 0 31W
Sompting **29** 50 51N 0 20W
Son, Neth. **47** 51 31N 5 30 E
Son, Norway **71** 59 32N 10 42 E
Son, Spain **56** 42 43N 8 58W
Son Hoa **100** 13 2N 108 58 E
Son La **100** 21 20N 103 50 E
Son Ma **100** 15 3N 108 34 E
Son Tay **100** 21 8N 105 30 E
Soná **166** 8 0N 81 10W
Sonamarg **95** 34 18N 75 21 E
Sonamukhi **95** 23 18N 87 27 E
Sonamura **98** 23 29N 91 15 E
Sŏnchŏn **107** 39 48N 124 55 E
Soncino **62** 45 24N 9 52 E
Sondags, R. **128** 32 10N 24 40 E
Sóndala **62** 46 20N 10 20 E
Sondar **95** 33 28N 75 56 E
Sönder Hornum **73** 56 32N 9 38 E
Sønder Omme **73** 55 50N 8 54 E
Sønderborg **73** 54 55N 9 49 E
Sonderhausen **48** 51 22N 10 50 E
Sonderjyllands Amt □ **73** 55 10N 9 10 E
Sondre Höland **71** 59 44N 11 30 E
Sondre Land **71** 60 44N 10 21 E
Söndre Stromfjord **12** 66 30N 50 52W
Sóndrio **62** 46 10N 9 53 E
Sone **127** 17 23 S 34 55 E
Sonepat **94** 29 0N 77 5 E
Sonepur **96** 20 55N 83 50 E
Song **100** 18 28N 100 11 E
Song Cau **100** 13 20N 109 18 E
Songa, R. **71** 59 57N 7 30 E
Sŏngchŏn **107** 39 12N 126 15 E
Songea **127** 10 40 S 35 40 E
Songea □ **127** 10 30 S 36 0 E
Songeons **43** 49 32N 1 50 E
Songjin **107** 40 40N 129 10 E
Songjŏngni **107** 35 8N 126 47 E
Songkhla **101** 7 13N 100 37 E
Songnim **107** 38 45N 125 39 E
Songwe, Malawi **127** 9 44 S 33 58 E
Songwe, Zaîre **127** 3 20 S 26 16 E
Sonkel, Ozero **85** 41 50N 75 12 E
Sonkovo **81** 57 50N 37 5 E
Sonmiani **94** 25 25N 66 40 E
Sonning **29** 51 28N 0 53W
Sonnino **64** 41 25N 13 13 E
Sono, R., Goias, Brazil **170** 8 58 S 48 11W
Sono, R., Minas Gerais, Brazil **171** 17 2 S 45 32W
Sonobe **111** 35 6N 135 28 E
Sonogno **51** 46 22N 8 47 E
Sonoma **163** 38 17N 122 27W
Sonora, Calif., U.S.A. **163** 37 59N 120 27W
Sonora, Texas, U.S.A. **159** 30 33N 100 37W
Sonora □ **164** 28 0N 111 0W
Sonora P. **160** 38 17N 119 35W
Sonora, R. **164** 28 30N 111 33W
Sonoyta **164** 31 51N 112 50W
Sŏnsan **107** 36 14N 128 17 E
Sonskyn **128** 30 47 S 26 28 E
Sonsonate **166** 13 43N 89 44W
Sonthofen **49** 47 31N 10 16 E
Soo Junction **156** 46 20N 85 14W
Soochow = Suchou **109** 31 15N 120 40 E
Söonder Nissum **73** 56 19N 8 11 E
Sop Hao **100** 20 33N 104 27 E
Sop Prap **100** 17 53N 99 20 E
Sopi **103** 2 40N 128 28 E
Sopo, Nahr **123** 8 40N 26 30 E
Sopot, Poland **54** 54 27N 18 31 E
Sopot, Yugo. **66** 44 29N 20 30 E
Sopotnica **66** 41 23N 21 13 E
Sopron **49** 47 41N 16 37 E
Sop's Arm **151** 49 46N 56 56W
Sör-Fron **71** 61 35N 9 59 E
Sor, R. **57** 39 7N 9 52 E
Sør-Rondane **13** 72 0 S 25 0 E
Sør Trøndelag fylke □ **71** 63 0N 11 0 E
Sora **64** 41 45N 13 36 E
Sorada **96** 19 32N 84 45 E
Sorah **94** 27 13N 68 56 E
Söråker **72** 62 30N 17 32 E
Sorano **63** 42 40N 11 42 E
Sorata **174** 15 50 S 68 50W
Sorbas **59** 37 6N 2 7W
Sorbie **34** 54 46N 4 26W
Sordale **37** 58 33N 3 26W
Sordeval **42** 48 44N 0 55W
Sorel **150** 46 0N 73 10W
Sörenberg **50** 46 50N 8 2 E
Soresina **62** 45 17N 9 51 E
Sörfold **74** 67 5N 14 20 E
Sorgues **45** 44 1N 4 53 E
Soria **58** 41 43N 2 32W
Soria □ **58** 41 46N 2 28W
Soriano **172** 33 24 S 58 19W
Soriano □ **176** 33 30 S 58 0W
Sorisdale **34** 56 40N 6 28W
Sorn **34** 55 31N 4 18W
Sorø **73** 55 26N 11 32 E
Soro **120** 10 9N 9 48W
Sorocaba **173** 23 31 S 47 35W
Sorochinsk **84** 52 26N 53 10 E
Soroki **82** 48 8N 28 12 E
Soroksár **53** 47 24N 19 9 E
Soron **94** 27 55N 78 45 E
Sorong **103** 0 55 S 131 15 E
Sororoca **174** 0 43N 61 31W
Soroti **126** 1 43N 33 35 E
Soröy Sundet **74** 70 25N 23 0 E
Soröya **74** 70 35N 22 45 E
Soroyane **71** 62 25N 5 32 E
Sorraia, R. **57** 38 55N 8 35W
Sorrento, Austral. **139** 38 22 S 144 47 E
Sorrento, Italy **65** 40 38N 14 23 E
Sorris Sorris **128** 21 0 S 14 46 E
Sorsele **74** 65 31N 17 30 E
Sorso **64** 40 50N 8 34 E
Sorsogon **103** 13 0N 124 0 E
Sortat **37** 58 32N 3 12W
Sortino **65** 37 9N 15 1 E
Sos **58** 42 30N 1 13W
Sŏsan **107** 36 47N 126 27 E
Soscumica, L. **150** 50 15N 77 27W
Sosdala **73** 56 2N 13 41 E
Sosna, R. **81** 52 30N 38 0 E
Sosnowiec **54** 50 20N 19 10 E
Sospel **45** 43 52N 7 27 E
Soštanj **63** 46 23N 15 4 E
Sŏsura **107** 42 16N 130 36 E
Sosva **84** 59 10N 61 50 E
Sosva, R. **84** 59 32N 62 20 E
Soto la Marina, R. **165** 23 40N 97 40W
Soto y Amío **56** 42 46N 5 53W
Sotra I. **71** 60 15N 5 0 E
Sotteville **42** 49 24N 1 5 E
Souanké **124** 2 10N 14 10 E
Souderton **162** 40 19N 75 19W
Soufi **120** 15 13N 12 17W
Souflíon **68** 41 12N 26 18 E
Soufrière **167** 13 51N 61 4W
Soufrière, vol. **167** 13 10N 61 10W
Sougne-Remouchamps **47** 50 29N 5 42 E
Souillac **44** 44 53N 1 29 E
Souk-Ahras **119** 36 17N 7 57 E
Souk el Arba du Rharb **118** 34 50N 5 59W
Souk el Khemis **119** 36 36N 8 58 E
Soukhouma **100** 14 38N 105 48 E
Sŏul **105** 37 31N 127 6 E
Soulac-sur-Mer **44** 45 30N 1 7W
Soultz **43** 48 57N 7 52 E
Soumagne **47** 50 37N 5 44 E
Sound, The **75** 56 7N 12 30 E
Soúnion, Ákra **69** 37 37N 24 1 E
Sour el Ghozlane **119** 36 10N 3 45 E
Sources, Mt. aux **129** 28 45 S 28 50 E
Sourdeval **42** 48 43N 0 55W
Soure, Brazil **170** 0 35 S 48 30W
Soure, Port. **56** 40 4N 8 38W
Souris, Man., Can. **153** 49 40N 100 20W
Souris, P.E.I., Can. **151** 46 21N 62 15W
Souris, R. **153** 49 40N 99 34W
Soúrpi **69** 39 6N 22 54 E
Sous, R. **118** 30 31N 9 27W
Sousa **170** 6 45 S 38 10W
Sousel, Brazil **170** 2 38 S 52 29W
Sousel, Port. **57** 38 57N 7 40W
Souss, O. **118** 30 23N 8 24W
Sousse **119** 35 50N 10 38 E
Soustons **44** 43 45N 1 19W
Souterraine, La **44** 46 15N 1 30 E
South Africa, Rep. of, ■ **125** 30 0 S 25 0 E
South Amboy **162** 40 29N 74 17W
South America **168** 10 0 S 60 0W
South Auckland & Bay of Plenty □ **142** 38 30 S 177 0 E
South Aulatsivik I. **151** 56 45N 61 30W
South Australia □ **136** 32 0 S 139 0 E
South Baldy, Mt. **161** 34 6N 107 27W
South Bend, Indiana, U.S.A. **156** 41 38N 86 20W
South Bend, Wash., U.S.A. **160** 46 44N 123 52W
South Benfleet **29** 51 33N 0 34 E
South Blackwater **138** 24 00 S 148 35 E
South Boston **157** 36 42N 78 58W
South Br. Ashburton, R. **143** 43 30 S 171 15 E
South Branch, Can. **151** 47 55N 59 2W
South Branch, U.S.A. **151** 44 30N 83 55W
South Brent **30** 50 26N 3 50W
South Brook **151** 49 26N 56 5W
South Buganda □ **126** 0 15 S 31 30 E
South Cape **147** 18 58N 155 24 E
South Carolina □ **157** 33 45N 81 0W
South Cave **33** 53 46N 0 37W
South Charleston **156** 38 20N 81 40W
South China Sea **101** 7 0N 107 0 E
South Dakota □ **158** 45 0N 100 0W
South Dell **36** 58 28N 6 20W
South Dorset Downs **28** 50 40N 2 26W
South Downs **29** 50 53N 0 10W
South East C. **138** 43 40 S 146 50 E
South East Is. **137** 34 17 S 123 30 E
South Elkington **33** 53 22N 0 5W
South Esk, R. **37** 56 44N 3 3W
South Foreland **29** 51 7N 1 23 E
S. Fork, American, R. **163** 38 45N 121 5W
South Fork, R. **160** 47 54N 113 15W
South Gamboa **164** 9 4N 79 40W
South Gate **163** 33 57N 118 12W
South Georgia **13** 54 30 S 37 0W
South Glamorgan □ **31** 51 30N 3 20W
South Grafton **139** 29 41 S 152 47 E
South Harris, district **36** 56 51N 3 10W
South Haven **156** 42 22N 86 20W
South Hayling **29** 50 47N 0 56W
South Henik, L. **153** 61 30N 97 30W
South Horr **126** 2 12N 36 56 E
South I., Kenya **126** 2 35N 36 35 E
South I., N.Z. **143** 43 0 S 170 0 E
South Invercargill **143** 46 26N 168 23 E
South Kirby **33** 53 35N 1 25W
South Knife, R. **153** 58 55N 94 37W
S. Kolok **101** 6 2N 101 58 E
South Korea ■ **107** 36 0N 128 0 E
S. Lembing **101** 3 55N 103 3 E
South Magnetic Pole **13** 66 30 S 139 30 E
South Marsh Is. **162** 38 6N 76 1W
South Milwaukee **156** 42 50N 87 52W
South Molton **30** 51 1N 3 50W
South Nahanni, R. **152** 61 3N 123 21W
South Nesting B. **36** 60 18N 1 5W
South Orkney Is. **13** 63 0 S 45 0W
South Pass **160** 42 20N 108 58W
South Passage **137** 26 07 S 113 09 E
S. Petani **101** 5 37N 100 30 E
South Petherton **28** 50 57N 2 49W
South Petherwin **30** 50 35N 4 22W
South Pines **157** 35 10N 79 25W
South Platte, R. **158** 40 50N 102 45W
South Pt. **151** 49 6N 62 11W
South Pole **13** 90 0 S 0 0 E
South Porcupine **150** 48 30N 81 12W
South Portland **162** 43 38N 70 15W
South River, Can. **150** 45 52N 79 29W
South River, U.S.A. **162** 40 27N 74 23W
South Ronaldsay, I. **37** 58 46N 2 58W
S. Sandwich Is. **15** 57 0 S 27 0W
South Saskatchewan, R. **153** 53 15N 105 5W
South Sd. **39** 53 4N 9 28W
South Seal, R. **153** 58 48N 98 8W
South Sentinel, I. **101** 11 1N 92 16 E
South Shetland Is. **13** 62 0 S 59 0W
South Shields **35** 54 59N 1 26W
South Sioux City **158** 42 30N 96 30W
South Taranaki Bight **142** 39 40 S 174 5 E
South Tawton **30** 50 44N 3 55W
South Thompson, R. **152** 50 40N 120 20W
South Twin I. **150** 53 7N 79 52W
South Tyne, R. **35** 54 46N 2 25W
South Uist, I. **37** 57 4N 7 21W
South Ulvön, I. **72** 63 0N 18 45 E
South Walls, I. **37** 58 45N 3 7W
South West Africa ■ = Namibia **128** 22 0 S 18 9 E
South West C. **138** 43 34 S 146 3 E
South West Cape **143** 47 16 S 167 31 E
South Williamsport **162** 41 14N 77 0W
South Yarmouth **162** 41 35N 70 10W
South Yemen ■ **91** 15 0N 48 0 E
South Yorkshire □ **33** 53 30N 1 20W
Southam **28** 52 16N 1 24W
Southampton, Can. **150** 44 30N 81 25W
Southampton, U.K. **28** 50 54N 1 23W
Southampton, U.S.A. **162** 40 54N 72 22W
Southampton I. **149** 64 30N 84 0W
Southampton Water **28** 50 52N 1 21W
Southborough **29** 51 10N 0 15 E
Southbridge, N.Z. **143** 43 48 S 172 16 E
Southbridge, U.S.A. **162** 42 4N 72 2W
Southeast C. **147** 62 55N 169 40W
Southend, Can. **153** 56 19N 103 14W
Southend, U.K. **34** 55 18N 5 38W
Southend-on-Sea **29** 51 32N 0 42 E
Southern □, Malawi **127** 15 0 S 35 0 E
Southern □, S. Leone **120** 0 8N 12 30 E
Southern □, Uganda **122** 0 30 S 30 30 E
Southern □, Zambia **127** 16 20 S 26 20 E
Southern Alps **143** 43 41 S 170 11 E
Southern Cross **137** 31 12 S 119 15 E
Southern Hills **137** 32 15 S 122 40 E
Southern Indian L. **153** 57 10N 98 30W
Southern Indian Lake **153** 57 0N 99 0W
Southern Ocean **13** 62 0 S 160 0W
Southern Uplands **35** 55 30N 3 3W
Southery **29** 52 32N 0 23 E
Southington **162** 41 37N 72 53W
Southland □ **143** 45 51 S 168 13 E
Southminster **29** 51 40N 0 51 E
Southold **162** 41 4N 72 26W
Southport, Austral. **139** 27 58 S 153 25 E
Southport, U.K. **32** 53 38N 3 1W
Southport, U.S.A. **157** 33 55N 78 0W
Southwark **29** 51 29N 0 5W
Southwell **33** 53 4N 0 57W
Southwick **29** 50 50N 0 14W
Southwold **29** 52 19N 1 41 E
Soutpansberge **129** 23 0 S 29 30 E
Souvigny **44** 46 33N 3 10 E
Sovata **70** 46 35N 25 3 E
Sovetsk, Lithuania, U.S.S.R. **80** 55 6N 21 50 E
Sovetsk, R.S.F.S.R., U.S.S.R. **81** 57 38N 48 53 E
Sovetskaya Gavan **77** 48 50N 140 0 E
Sovicille **63** 43 16N 11 12 E
Sovra **66** 42 44N 17 34 E
Sowerby **33** 54 13N 1 19W
Sōya-Misaki **112** 45 30N 142 0 E
Soyopa **164** 28 41N 109 37W
Sozh, R. **80** 53 50N 31 50 E
Sozopol **67** 42 23N 27 42 E
Spa **47** 50 29N 5 53 E
Spain ■ **55** 40 0N 5 0W
Spakenburg **46** 52 15N 5 22 E
Spalding, Austral. **140** 33 30 S 138 37 E
Spalding, U.K. **29** 52 47N 0 9W
Spalding, U.S.A. **158** 41 45N 98 27W
Spandet **73** 55 15N 8 54 E
Spånga **72** 59 23N 17 55 E
Spångenäs **73** 57 36N 16 7 E
Spangereid **71** 58 3N 7 9 E
Spaniard's Bay **151** 47 38N 53 20W
Spanish **150** 46 12N 82 20W
Spanish Fork **160** 40 10N 111 37W
Spanish Pt. **39** 52 51N 9 27W
Spanish Sahara □ = Western Sahara **116** 25 0N 13 0W
Spanish Town **166** 18 0N 77 20W
Sparkford **28** 51 2N 2 33W
Sparrows Point **162** 39 13N 76 29W
Sparta, Ga., U.S.A. **157** 33 18N 82 59W
Sparta, N.J., U.S.A. **162** 41 2N 74 38W
Sparta, Wis., U.S.A. **158** 43 55N 91 10W
Sparta = Spárti **69** 37 5N 22 25 E
Spartanburg **157** 35 0N 82 0W
Spartel, C. **118** 35 47N 5 56W
Spárti **69** 37 5N 22 25 E
Spartivento, C., Calabria, Italy **65** 37 56N 16 4 E
Spartivento, C., Sard., Italy **65** 38 52N 8 50 E
Spas-Demensk **80** 54 20N 34 0 E
Spas-Klepiki **81** 54 34N 40 2 E
Spassk-Dalniy **77** 44 40N 132 40 E
Spassk-Ryazanskiy **81** 54 30N 40 25 E
Spatha Ákra. **69** 35 42N 23 43 E
Spatsizi, R. **152** 57 42N 128 7W
Spean Bridge **36** 56 53N 4 55W
Spearfish **158** 44 32N 103 52W
Spearman **159** 36 15N 101 10W
Speculator **162** 43 30N 74 25W
Speed **140** 35 21 S 142 27 E
Speer **51** 47 12N 9 8 E

Speers Stíra


Speers 153 52 43N 107 34W
Speightstown 167 13 15N 59 39W
Speke 32 53 21N 2 51W
Speke Gulf, L. Victoria 126 2 20S 32 50E
Spekholzerheide 47 50 51N 6 2E
Spelve, L. 34 56 22N 5 45W
Spenard 147 61 5N 149 50W
Spencer, Idaho, U.S.A. 160 44 18N 112 8W
Spencer, Iowa, U.S.A. 158 43 5N 95 3W
Spencer, Nebr., U.S.A. 158 42 52N 98 43W
Spencer, N.Y., U.S.A. 162 42 14N 76 30W
Spencer, W. Va., U.S.A. 156 38 47N 81 24W
Spencer B. 128 25 30S 14 47E
Spencer Bay 148 69 32N 93 32W
Spencer, C. 140 35 20S 136 45E
Spencer G. 140 34 0S 137 20E
Spences Bridge 152 50 25N 121 20W
Spennymoor 33 54 43N 1 35W
Spenser Mts. 143 42 15S 172 45E
Sperkhiós, R. 69 38 57N 22 3E
Sperrin Mts. 38 54 50N 7 0W
Spessart 49 50 0N 9 20E
Spetsai 69 37 16N 23 9E
Spétsai, I. 69 37 15N 23 10E
Spey B. 37 57 41N 3 0W
Spey Bay 37 57 39N 3 4W
Spey, R. 37 57 26N 3 25W
Speyer 49 49 19N 8 26E
Speyer, R. 41 49 18N 7 52E
Spezia = La Spézia 62 44 7N 9 49E
Spézia, La 62 44 8N 9 50E
Spezzano Albanese 65 39 41N 16 19E
Spiddal 39 53 14N 9 19W
Spiekeroog, I. 48 53 45N 7 42E
Spielfeld 63 46 43N 15 38E
Spiez 50 46 40N 7 40E
Spijk 46 53 24N 6 50E
Spijkenisse 46 51 51N 4 20E
Spili 69 35 13N 24 31E
Spilimbergo 63 46 7N 12 53E
Spillimacheen 152 51 6N 117 0W
Spilsby 33 53 10N 0 6E
Spin Baldak 93 31 3N 66 16E
Spinazzola 65 40 58N 16 5E
Spincourt 43 49 20N 5 39E
Spind 71 58 6N 6 53E
Spineni 70 44 43N 24 37E
Spirit Lake 160 47 56N 116 56W
Spirit River 152 55 45N 118 50W
Spiritwood 153 53 24N 107 33W
Spišská Nová Ves 53 48 58N 20 34E
Spišské Podhradie 53 49 0N 20 48E
Spit Pt. 136 20 4S 118 59E
Spithead 29 50 43N 0 56W
Spittal 52 46 48N 13 31E
Spitzbergen (Svalbard) 12 78 0N 17 0E
Split 63 43 31N 16 26E
Split L. 153 56 8N 96 15W
Splitski Kan 63 43 31N 16 20E
Splügen 51 46 34N 9 21E
Splügenpass 51 46 30N 9 20E
Spoffard 159 29 10N 100 27W
Spofforth 33 53 57N 1 28W
Spokane 160 47 45N 117 25W
Sponvika 71 59 7N 11 15E
Spooner 158 45 49N 91 51W
Sporádhes 69 37 0N 27 0E
Sporyy Navolok, M. 76 75 50N 68 40E
Spotswood 162 40 23N 74 23W
Spragge 150 46 15N 82 40W
Sprague 160 47 25N 117 59W
Sprague River 160 42 49N 121 31W
Spratly, I. 102 8 20N 112 0E
Spray 160 44 56N 119 46W
Spree, R. 48 52 23N 13 52E
Sprimont 47 50 30N 5 40E
Spring City, Pa., U.S.A. 162 40 11N 75 33W
Spring City, Utah, U.S.A. 160 39 31N 111 28W
Spring Grove 162 39 55N 76 56W
Spring Hill 141 33 23S 149 9E
Spring Mts. 161 36 20N 115 43W
Spring Valley, Minn., U.S.A. 158 43 40N 92 30W
Spring Valley, N.Y., U.S.A. 162 41 7N 74 4W
Springbok 128 29 42S 17 54E
Springburn 143 43 40S 171 32E
Springdale, Can. 151 49 30N 56 6W
Springdale, Ark., U.S.A. 159 36 10N 94 5W
Springdale, Wash., U.S.A. 160 48 1N 117 50W
Springe 48 52 12N 9 35E
Springerville 161 34 10N 109 16W
Springfield, N.Z. 143 43 19S 171 56E
Springfield, Colo., U.S.A. 159 37 26N 102 40W
Springfield, Ill., U.S.A. 158 39 48N 89 40W
Springfield, Mass., U.S.A. 162 42 8N 72 37W
Springfield, Mo., U.S.A. 159 37 15N 93 20W
Springfield, Ohio, U.S.A. 156 39 50N 83 48W
Springfield, Oreg., U.S.A. 160 44 2N 123 0W
Springfield, Tenn., U.S.A. 157 36 35N 86 55W
Springfield, Va., U.S.A. 162 38 45N 77 13W
Springfield, Vt., U.S.A. 162 43 20N 72 30W
Springfontein 128 30 15S 25 40E
Springhill 151 45 40N 64 4W
Springhouse 152 51 56N 122 7W
Springhurst 141 36 10S 146 31E
Springs 129 26 13S 28 25E
Springsure 138 24 8S 148 6E
Springvale, Queens., Austral. 138 23 33S 140 42E
Springvale, W. Australia, Austral. 136 17 48S 127 41E
Springvale, U.S.A. 162 43 28N 70 48W
Springville, Calif., U.S.A. 163 36 8N 118 49W
Springville, N.Y., U.S.A. 156 42 31N 78 41W
Springville, Utah, U.S.A. 160 40 14N 111 35W
Springwater 153 51 58N 108 23W
Sproatley 33 53 46N 0 9W
Spur 159 33 28N 100 50W
Spurn Hd. 33 53 34N 0 8E
Spuz 66 42 32N 19 10E
Spuzzum 152 49 37N 121 23W
Spydeberg 71 59 37N 11 4E
Squam L. 162 43 45N 71 32W
Squamish 152 49 45N 123 10W
Square Islands 151 52 47N 55 47W
Squillace, Golfo di 65 38 43N 16 35E
Squinzano 65 40 27N 18 1E
Squires, Mt. 137 26 14S 127 46E
Sragen 103 7 28S 110 59E
Srbac 66 45 7N 17 30E
Srbija □ 66 43 30N 21 0E
Srbobran 66 45 32N 19 48E
Sre Khtum 101 12 10N 106 52E
Sre Umbell 101 11 8N 103 46E
Srebrnica 66 44 10N 19 18E
Sredinyy Khrebet 77 57 0N 160 0E
Središce 63 46 24N 16 17E
Sredna Gora 67 42 40N 25 0E
Sredne Tambovskoye 77 50 55N 137 45E
Srednekolymsk 77 67 20N 154 40E
Srednevilyuysk 77 63 50N 123 5E
Sredni Rodopi 67 41 40N 24 45E
Sredniy Ural, mts. 166 59 0N 59 0E
Srem 54 52 6N 17 2E
Srepok, R. 100 13 33N 106 16E
Sretensk 77 52 10N 117 40E
Sri Lanka ■ 97 7 30N 80 50E
Sriharikota, I. 97 13 40N 81 30E
Srikakulam 96 18 14N 84 4E
Srinagar 95 34 12N 74 50E
Sripur 98 24 14N 90 30E
Srirangam 97 10 54N 78 42E
Srirangapatnam 97 12 26N 76 43E
Şrivilliputtur 97 9 31N 77 40E
Šroda Wlkp. 54 52 15N 17 19E
Srpska Crnja 66 45 38N 20 44E
Srpska Itabej 66 45 35N 20 44E
Ssu Chiao 109 30 43N 122 28E
Ssuhsien 107 33 25N 117 54E
Ssuhui 109 23 20N 112 41E
Ssunan 108 27 56N 108 14E
Ssup'ing 105 43 10N 124 25E
Ssushui, Honan, China 106 34 51N 113 12E
Ssushui, Shantung, China 107 35 39N 117 15E
Ssutzuwangch'i 106 41 30N 111 37E
Staaten, R. 138 16 24S 141 17E
Stabroek 47 51 20N 4 22E
Stack's Mts. 39 52 20N 9 34W
Stad Delden 46 52 16N 6 43E
Stade 48 53 35N 9 31E
Staden 47 50 59N 3 1E
Staðarhólskirkja 74 65 23N 21 58W
Stadil 73 56 12N 8 12E
Städjan 72 61 56N 12 30E
Stadlandet 71 62 10N 5 10E
Stadsforsen 72 63 0N 16 45E
Stadskanaal 46 53 4N 6 48E
Stadthagen 48 52 20N 9 14E
Stadtlohn 48 51 59N 6 52E
Stadtroda 48 50 51N 11 44E
Stäfa 51 47 14N 8 45E
Stafafell 74 64 25N 14 52W
Staffa, I. 34 56 26N 6 21W
Stafford, U.K. 28 52 49N 2 9W
Stafford, Kansas, U.S.A. 159 38 0N 98 35W
Stafford, Va., U.S.A. 162 38 2S 77 30W
Stafford □ 28 52 53N 2 10W
Stafford Springs 162 41 58N 72 20W
Stagnone, I. 64 37 50N 12 28E
Staindrop 33 54 35N 1 49W
Staines 29 51 26N 0 30W
Stainforth 33 53 37N 0 59W
Stainmore For. 32 54 29N 2 5W
Stainton 33 53 17N 0 23W
Stainz 52 46 53N 15 17E
Staithes 33 54 33N 0 47W
Stakkroge 73 55 53N 8 51E
Stalač 66 43 43N 21 28E
Stalbridge 28 50 57N 2 22W
Stalden 50 46 14N 7 52E
Stalham 29 52 46N 1 31E
Stalingrad = Volgograd 83 48 40N 44 25E
Staliniri = Tskhinvali 83 42 14N 44 1E
Stalino = Donetsky 82 48 0N 37 45E
Stalinogorsk = Novomoskovsk 81 54 5N 38 15E
Stallingborough 33 53 36N 0 11W
Stalowa Wola 54 50 34N 22 3E
Stalybridge 32 53 29N 1 56W
Stamford, Austral. 138 21 15S 143 46E
Stamford, U.K. 29 52 39N 0 29W
Stamford, Conn., U.S.A. 162 41 5N 73 30W
Stamford, N.Y., U.S.A. 162 42 25N 74 37W
Stamford, Tex., U.S.A. 159 32 58N 99 50W
Stamford Bridge 33 53 59N 0 53W
Stamfordham 35 55 3N 1 53W
Stampersgat 47 51 37N 4 26E
Stamps 159 33 22N 93 30W
Stanberry 158 40 12N 94 32W
Standerton 129 26 55S 29 13E
Standish, U.K. 32 53 35N 2 39W
Standish, U.S.A. 156 43 58N 83 57W
Standon 29 51 53N 0 2E
Stanford 160 47 11N 110 10W
Stanford on Teme 28 52 17N 2 26W
Stange Hedmark 71 60 43N 11 11E
Stanger 129 29 18S 31 21E
Stanhope, Austral. 141 36 27S 144 59E
Stanhope, U.K. 32 54 45N 2 0W
Stanišic 53 45 53N 19 12E
Stanislaus, R. 163 37 40N 121 15W
Stanislav = Ivano-Frankovsk 80 49 0N 24 40E
Stanke Dimitrov 66 42 27N 23 9E
Stanley, Austral. 138 40 46S 145 19E
Stanley, N.B., Can. 151 46 20N 66 50W
Stanley, Sask., Can. 153 55 24N 104 22W
Stanley, Falk. Is. 176 51 40S 58 0W
Stanley, Durham, U.K. 33 54 53N 1 42W
Stanley, Tayside, U.K. 35 56 29N 3 28W
Stanley, Idaho, U.S.A. 160 44 10N 114 59W
Stanley, N.D., U.S.A. 158 48 20N 102 23W
Stanley, Wis., U.S.A. 158 44 57N 91 0W
Stanley Res. 97 11 50N 77 40E
Stanleyville = Kisangani 126 0 35N 25 15E
Stanlow 32 53 17N 2 52W
Stann Creek 165 17 0N 88 20W
Stannington 35 55 7N 1 41W
Stanovoy Khrebet 77 55 0N 130 0E
Stans 51 46 58N 8 21E
Stansmore Ra. 136 21 23S 128 33E
Stansted Mountfitchet 29 51 54N 0 13E
Stanthorpe 139 28 36S 151 59E
Stanton, Can. 147 69 45N 128 52W
Stanton, U.S.A. 159 32 8N 101 45W
Stantsiya Karshi 85 38 49N 65 47E
Stanwix 32 54 54N 2 56W
Staphorst 46 52 39N 6 12E
Stapleford 33 52 56N 1 16W
Staplehurst 29 51 9N 0 35E
Stapleton 158 41 30N 100 31W
Staporkow 54 51 9N 20 31E
Star City 153 52 55N 104 20W
Stara-minskaya 83 46 33N 39 0E
Stara Moravica 66 45 50N 19 30E
Stara Pazova 66 45 0N 20 10E
Stara Planina 67 43 15N 23 0E
Stara Zagora 67 42 26N 25 39E
Starachowice-Wierzbnik 54 51 3N 21 2E
Staraya Russa 80 57 58N 31 10E
Starbuck I. 131 5 37S 155 55W
Stargard 48 53 29N 13 19E
Stargard Szczecinski 54 53 20N 15 0E
Stari Bar 66 42 7N 19 13E
Stari Trg. 63 45 29N 15 7E
Staritsa 80 56 33N 35 0E
Starke 157 30 0N 82 10W
Starkville, Colo., U.S.A. 159 37 10N 104 31W
Starkville, Miss., U.S.A. 157 33 26N 88 48W
Starnberg 49 48 0N 11 20E
Starnberger See 49 48 0N 11 0E
Starobelsk 83 49 27N 39 0E
Starodub 80 52 30N 32 50E
Starogard 54 53 55N 18 30E
Start Bay 30 50 15N 3 35W
Start Pt., Devon, U.K. 30 50 13N 3 38W
Start Pt., Orkney, U.K. 37 59 17N 2 25W
Stary Sacz 54 49 33N 30 26E
Staryy Biryuzyak 83 44 46N 46 50E
Staryy Kheydzhan 77 60 0N 144 50E
Staryy Krym 82 44 48N 35 8E
Staryy Oskol 81 51 12N 37 55E
Stassfurt 48 51 51N 11 34E
State College 156 40 47N 77 49W
State Is. 150 48 40N 87 0W
Staten I. 162 40 35N 74 10W
Staten, I. = Los Estados, I. de 176 54 40S 64 0W
Statesboro 157 32 26N 81 46W
Statesville 157 35 48N 80 51W
Statfjord, oilfield 19 61 15N 1 50E
Stathelle 71 59 3N 9 41E
Stauffer 163 34 45N 119 3W
Staunton, U.K. 28 51 58N 2 19W
Staunton, Ill., U.S.A. 158 39 0N 89 49W
Staunton, Va., U.S.A. 156 38 7N 79 4W
Stavanger 159 58 57N 5 40E
Staveley, Cumbria, U.K. 32 54 24N 2 49W
Staveley, Derby, U.K. 33 53 16N 1 20W
Stavelot 47 50 23N 5 55E
Stavenisse 47 51 35N 4 1E
Staveren 46 52 53N 5 22E
Stavern 71 59 0N 10 1E
Stavfjord 71 61 30N 5 0E
Stavre 72 62 51N 15 19E
Stavropol 83 45 5N 42 0E
Stavroúpolis 68 41 12N 24 45E
Stavsjö 73 48 42N 16 30E
Stawell 140 37 5S 142 47E
Stawell, R. 138 20 38S 142 55E
Stawiszyn 54 51 56N 18 4E
Staxigoe 37 58 28N 3 2W
Steamboat Springs 160 40 30N 106 58W
Stebark 54 53 30N 20 10E
Stebleva 68 41 18N 20 33E
Steckborn 51 47 44N 8 59E
Steele 158 46 56N 99 52W
Steelton 162 40 17N 76 50W
Steelville 159 37 57N 91 21W
Steen, R. 152 59 35N 117 10W
Steen River 152 59 40N 117 12W
Steenbergen 47 51 35N 4 19E
Steenvoorde 43 50 48N 2 33E
Steenwijk 46 52 47N 6 7E
Steep Pt. 137 26 08S 113 8E
Steep Rock 153 51 30N 98 48W
Steep Rock Lake 150 48 50N 91 38W
Stefǎnesti 70 47 44N 27 15E
Stefanie L. = Chew Bahir 123 4 40N 30 50E
Steffisburg 50 46 47N 7 38E
Stefǔnesti 70 47 44N 27 15E
Stege 73 55 0N 12 18E
Steierdorf Anina 66 45 6N 21 51E
Steiermark □ 52 47 26N 15 0E
Steigerwald 49 49 45N 10 30E
Stein, Neth. 47 50 58N 5 45E
Stein, Switz. 51 47 40N 8 50E
Stein, U.K. 36 57 30N 6 35W
Steinbach 153 49 32N 96 40W
Steinfort 47 49 39N 5 55E
Steinheim 48 51 50N 9 6E
Steinkjer 74 63 59N 11 31E
Steinkopf 125 29 15S 17 48E
Stekene 47 51 12N 4 2E
Stella Land 128 26 45S 24 50E
Stellarton 151 45 32N 62 45W
Stellenbosch 128 33 58S 18 50E
Stellendam 46 51 49N 4 1E
Stelvio, Paso dello 51 46 32N 10 27E
Stemshaug 71 63 19N 8 44E
Stendal 48 52 36N 11 50E
Stene 47 51 12N 2 56E
Stenhousemuir 35 56 2N 3 46W
Stenmagle 73 55 49N 11 39E
Stenness, L., of 37 59 0N 3 15W
Stensele 74 65 3N 17 8E
Stenstorp 73 58 17N 13 45E
Stenungsund 73 58 6N 11 50E
Stepanakert 79 40 0N 46 25E
Stephan 158 48 30N 96 53W
Stephens Cr. 140 32 15S 141 55E
Stephens I., Can. 152 54 10N 130 45W
Stephens I., N.Z. 143 40 40S 174 1E
Stephenville, Can. 151 48 31N 58 30W
Stephenville, U.S.A. 159 32 12N 98 12W
Stepnica 54 53 38N 14 36E
Stepnoi = Elista 83 46 25N 44 17E
Stepnoye 84 54 4N 60 26E
Sterkstroom 128 31 32S 26 32E
Sterlego, Mys 12 80 30N 90 0E
Sterling, Colo., U.S.A. 158 40 40N 103 15W
Sterling, Ill., U.S.A. 158 41 45N 89 45W
Sterling, Kans., U.S.A. 158 38 17N 98 13W
Sterling City 159 31 50N 100 59W
Sterlitamak 84 53 40N 56 0E
Sternberg 48 53 42N 11 48E
Sternberk 53 49 45N 17 15E
Stettin = Szczecin 54 53 27N 14 27E
Stettiner Haff 48 53 50N 14 25E
Stettler 152 52 19N 112 40W
Steubenville 156 40 21N 80 39W
Stevenage 29 51 54N 0 11W
Stevens Port 158 44 32N 89 34W
Stevens Village 147 66 0N 149 10W
Stevenson L. 153 53 55N 95 9W
Stevenson, R. 136 46 15S 134 10E
Stevenston 34 55 38N 4 46W
Stevns Klint 73 55 17N 12 28E
Stewart 152 55 56N 129 57W
Stewart, C. 138 11 57S 134 45E
Stewart, I. 176 54 50S 71 30W
Stewart I. 143 46 58S 167 54E
Stewart River 147 63 19N 139 26W
Stewarton 34 55 40N 4 30W
Stewartstown 38 54 35N 6 40W
Stewiacke 151 45 9N 63 22W
Steyning 29 50 54N 0 19W
Steynsburg 128 31 15S 25 49E
Steyr 52 48 3N 14 25E
Steyr, R. 52 48 57N 14 15E
Steytlerville 128 33 17S 24 19E
Stia 63 43 48N 11 41E
Stiens 46 53 16N 5 46E
Stigler 159 35 19N 95 6W
Stigliano 65 40 24N 16 13E
Stigsnæs 73 55 13N 11 18E
Stigtomta 73 58 47N 16 48E
Stikine Mts. 148 59 30N 129 30W
Stikine, R. 147 58 0N 131 12W
Stilfontein 128 26 50S 26 50E
Stilis 69 38 55N 22 37E
Stillington 33 54 7N 1 5W
Stillwater, Minn., U.S.A. 158 45 3N 92 47W
Stillwater, N.Y., U.S.A. 162 42 55N 73 41W
Stillwater, Okla., U.S.A. 159 36 5N 97 3W
Stillwater Mts. 160 39 45N 118 6W
Stilwell 159 35 52N 94 36W
Stimfalías, L. 69 37 51N 22 27E
Stimson 150 48 58N 80 30W
Stinchar, R. 34 55 10N 4 50W
Stingray Pt. 162 37 35N 76 15W
Stip 66 41 42N 22 10E
Stiperstones Mt. 28 52 36N 2 57W
Stira 69 38 9N 24 14E

Stiring Wendel Sukkur


Stiring Wendel 43 49 12N 6 57 E
Stirling, Austral. 138 17 12 S 141 35 E
Stirling, Can. 152 49 30N 112 30W
Stirling, N.Z. 143 46 14 S 169 49 E
Stirling, U.K. 35 56 17N 3 57W
Stirling (□) 26 56 3N 4 10W
Stirling Ra. 137 34 0 S 118 0 E
Stjárneborg 73 57 53N 14 45 E
Stjarnsfors 72 60 2N 13 45 E
Stjördalshalsen 71 63 29N 10 51 E
Stobo 35 55 38N 3 18W
Stoborough, oilfield 19 50 38N 2 8W
Stockaryd 73 57 19N 14 36 E
Stockbridge 28 51 7N 1 30W
Stockerau 53 48 24N 16 12 E
Stockett 160 47 23N 111 7W
Stockholm 72 59 20N 18 3 E
Stockholms län □ 72 59 30N 18 20 E
Stockhorn 50 46 42N 7 33 E
Stockport 32 53 25N 2 11W
Stocksbridge 33 53 30N 1 36W
Stockton, Austral. 141 32 56 S 151 47 E
Stockton, Calif., U.S.A. 163 38 0N 121 20W
Stockton, Kans., U.S.A. 158 39 30N 99 20W
Stockton, Mo., U.S.A. 159 37 40N 93 48W
Stockton-on-Tees 33 54 34N 1 20W
Stockvik 72 62 17N 17 23 E
Stoczek Łukowski 54 51 58N 22 22 E
Stode 72 62 28N 16 35 E
Stoer 36 58 12N 5 20W
Stogovo, mts. 66 41 31N 20 38 E
Stoke, N.Z. 143 41 19N 173 14 E
Stoke, U.K. 29 51 26N 0 41 E
Stoke Ferry 29 52 34N 0 31 E
Stoke Fleming 30 50 19N 3 36W
Stoke Mandeville 29 51 46N 0 47W
Stoke Prior 28 52 18N 2 5W
Stokenham 30 50 15N 3 40W
Stokes Bay 150 45 0N 81 22W
Stokes Pt. 138 40 10 S 143 56 E
Stokes Ra. 136 15 50 S 130 50 E
Stokesley 33 54 27N 1 12W
Stokke 71 59 13N 10 17 E
Stokkem 47 51 1N 5 45 E
Stokken 71 58 31N 8 53 E
Stokkseyri 74 63 50N 20 58W
Stokksnes 74 64 14N 14 58W
Stolac 66 43 8N 17 59 E
Stolberg, Germ., E. 48 51 33N 11 0 E
Stolberg, Germ., W. 48 50 48N 6 13 E
Stolbovaya, R.S.F.S.R., U.S.S.R. 77 64 50N 153 50 E
Stolbovaya, R.S.F.S.R., U.S.S.R. 81 55 10N 37 32 E
Stolbtsy 80 53 22N 26 43 E
Stolin 80 51 53N 26 50 E
Stolnici 70 44 31N 24 48 E
Stolwijk 46 51 59N 4 47 E
Ston 66 42 51N 17 43 E
Stone, Bucks., U.K. 29 51 48N 0 52W
Stone, Stafford, U.K. 32 52 55N 2 10W
Stone Harbor 162 39 3N 74 45W
Stonecliffe 150 46 13N 77 56W
Stonehaven 37 56 58N 2 11W
Stonehenge, Austral. 138 24 22 S 143 17 E
Stonehenge, U.K. 28 51 9N 1 45W
Stonehouse, Glous., U.K. 28 51 45N 2 18W
Stonehouse, Strathclyde, U.K. 35 55 42N 4 0W
Stonewall 153 50 10N 97 19W
Stongfjord 71 61 28N 14 0 E
Stonham Aspall 29 52 11N 1 7 E
Stony L. 153 58 51N 98 40W
Stony Point 162 41 14N 73 59W
Stony Rapids 153 59 16N 105 50W
Stony River 147 61 48N 156 48W
Stony Stratford 29 52 4N 0 51W
Stony Tunguska = Tunguska, Nizhmaya 77 64 0N 95 0 E
Stopnica 54 50 27N 20 57 E
Stor Elvdal 71 61 30N 11 1 E
Stora Borge Fjell, Mt. 48 65 12N 14 0 E
Stora Gla 72 59 30N 12 30 E
Stora Karlsö 73 57 17N 17 59 E
Stora Lulevatten 74 67 10N 19 30 E
Stora Sjøfallet 74 67 29N 18 40 E
Storavan 74 65 45N 18 10 E
Stord Leirvik, I. 71 59 48N 5 27 E
Store Bælt 73 55 20N 11 0 E
Store Creek 141 32 54 S 149 6 E
Store Heddinge 73 55 18N 12 23 E
Storen 71 63 3N 10 18 E
Storfjorden 71 62 25N 6 30 E
Storm B. 138 43 10 S 147 30 E
Storm Lake 158 42 35N 95 5W
Stormberg 125 31 16 S 26 17 E
Stormsrivier 128 33 59 S 23 52 E
Stornoway 36 58 12N 6 23W
Storozhinets 82 48 14 S 25 45 E
Storr, The, mt. 36 57 30N 6 12W
Storrs 162 41 48N 72 15W
Storsjö 72 62 49N 13 5 E
Storsjöen, Hedmark, Norway 71 60 20N 11 40 E
Storsjöen, Hedmark, Norway 71 61 30N 11 14 E
Storsjön, Gavleborg, Sweden 72 60 35N 16 45 E
Storsjön, Jämtland, Sweden 72 62 50N 13 8 E
Storstroms Amt □ 73 49 50N 11 45 E
Stort, R. 29 51 50N 0 7 E
Storuman 74 65 5N 17 10 E
Storuman, L. 74 65 5N 17 10 E
Storvätteshagna, Mt. 72 62 6N 12 30 E
Storvik 72 60 35N 16 33 E
Stotfold 29 52 2N 0 13W
Stoughton 153 49 40N 103 0W
Stour, R., Dorset, U.K. 28 50 48N 2 7W
Stour, R., Heref. & Worcs., U.K. 28 52 25N 2 13W
Stour, R., Kent, U.K. 29 51 15N 0 57 E
Stour, R., Suffolk, U.K. 29 51 55N 1 5 E
Stourbridge 28 52 28N 2 8W
Stourport 28 52 21N 2 18W
Stout, L. 153 52 0N 94 40W
Stove Pipe Wells Village 163 36 35N 117 11W
Stow 35 55 41N 2 50W
Stow Bardolph 29 52 38N 0 24 E
Stow-on-the-Wold 28 51 55N 1 42W
Stowmarket 29 52 11N 1 0 E
Stowupland 29 52 12N 1 3 E
Strabane 38 54 50N 7 28W
Strabane □ 38 54 45N 7 25W
Strachan 37 57 1N 2 31W
Strachur 34 56 10N 5 5W
Stracin 66 42 13N 22 2 E
Stradbally, Kerry, Ireland 39 52 15N 10 4W
Stradbally, Laoighis, Ireland 39 53 2N 7 10W
Stradbally, Waterford, Ireland 39 52 7N 7 28W
Stradbroke 29 52 19N 1 16 E
Strade 38 53 56N 9 8W
Stradella 62 45 4N 9 20 E
Stradone 38 54 0N 7 12W
Strahan 138 42 9 S 145 20 E
Straldzha 67 42 35N 26 40 E
Stralkonice 52 49 15N 13 53 E
Stralsund 48 54 17N 13 5 E
Strand, Hedmark, Norway 71 61 18N 11 15 E
Strand, Rogaland, Norway 71 59 3N 5 56 E
Strand, S. Afr. 128 34 9 S 18 48 E
Stranda 71 62 19N 6 58 E
Strandby 73 56 47N 9 13 E
Strandebarm 71 60 17N 6 0 E
Strandhill 38 54 16N 8 34W
Strandvik 71 60 9N 5 41 E
Strangford 38 54 23N 5 34W
Strängnäs 72 59 23N 17 8 E
Stranorlar 38 54 58N 7 47W
Stranraer 34 54 54N 5 0W
Strasbourg, Can. 153 51 4N 104 55W
Strasbourg, France 43 48 35N 7 42 E
Strasburg, Ger. 48 53 30N 13 44 E
Strasburg, U.S.A. 158 46 12N 101 9W
Strassen 47 49 37N 6 4 E
Stratford, N.S.W., Austral. 141 32 7 S 151 55 E
Stratford, Vic., Austral. 141 37 59 S 147 7 E
Stratford, Can. 150 43 23N 81 0W
Stratford, N.Z. 142 39 20 S 174 19 E
Stratford, Calif., U.S.A. 163 36 10N 119 49W
Stratford, Conn., U.S.A. 162 41 13N 73 8W
Stratford, Tex., U.S.A. 159 36 20N 102 3W
Stratford-on-Avon 28 52 12N 1 42W
Stratford St. Mary 29 51 58N 0 59 E
Strath Avon 37 57 19N 3 23W
Strath Dearn 37 57 20N 4 0W
Strath Earn 35 56 20N 3 50W
Strath Glass 37 57 20N 4 40W
Strath Naver 37 58 24N 4 12W
Strath Spey 37 57 15N 3 40W
Strathalbyn 140 35 13 S 138 53 E
Strathaven 35 55 40N 4 4W
Strathbogie, Dist. 37 57 25N 2 45W
Strathclyde □ 34 56 0N 4 50W
Strathcona Prov. Park 152 49 38N 125 40W
Strathdon 37 57 12N 3 4W
Strathkanaird 36 57 58N 5 5W
Strathmore, Austral. 138 17 50 S 142 35 E
Strathmore, Can. 152 51 5N 113 25W
Strathmore, Highland, U.K. 37 58 20N 4 40W
Strathmore, Tayside, U.K. 37 56 40N 3 4W
Strathmore, U.S.A. 163 36 9N 119 4W
Strathnaver 152 53 20N 122 33W
Strathpeffer 37 57 35N 4 32W
Strathroy 150 42 58N 81 38W
Strathy 37 58 30N 4 0W
Strathy Pt. 37 58 35N 4 0W
Strathyre 34 56 14N 4 20W
Stratmiglo Scot. 35 56 16N 3 15W
Stratton, U.K. 30 50 49N 4 31W
Stratton, U.S.A. 158 39 20N 102 36W
Stratton St. Margaret 28 51 35N 1 45W
Straubing 49 48 53N 12 35 E
Straumnes 74 66 26N 23 8W
Straumsnes Åsskard 71 63 4N 8 2 E
Strausberg 48 52 40N 13 52 E
Strawberry Res. 160 40 0N 111 0W
Strawn 159 32 36N 98 30W
Strážnice 53 48 54N 17 19 E
Streaky B. 139 32 51 S 134 18 E
Streaky Bay 139 32 48 S 134 13 E
Streatley 28 51 31N 1 9W
Streator 158 41 9N 88 52W
Stredočeský □ 52 49 55N 14 30 E
Stredoslovenský □ 53 48 30N 19 15 E
Streé 47 50 17N 4 18 E
Street 28 51 7N 2 43W
Strehaia 70 44 37N 23 10 E
Strelcha 67 42 30N 24 19 E
Strelka 77 58 5N 93 10 E
Streng, R. 100 13 12N 103 37 E
Strengelvåg 74 68 58N 15 11 E
Strensall 33 54 3N 1 2W
Stretford 32 53 27N 2 19W
Stretton 32 53 21N 2 34W
Strezhevoy 76 60 42N 77 34 E
Strezhnoye 76 57 45N 84 2 E
Stribro 52 49 44N 13 0 E
Strichen 37 57 35N 2 5W
Strickland, R. 135 7 35 S 141 36 E
Strijen 46 51 45N 4 33 E
Strimón, R. 68 41 0N 23 30 E
Strimonikós Kólpos 68 40 33N 24 0 E
Striven, L. 34 55 58N 5 9W
Strofadhes, I. 69 37 15N 21 0 E
Strokestown 38 53 47N 8 6W
Strom 71 60 17N 11 44 E
Ström 72 61 52N 17 20 E
Stroma, I. of 37 58 40N 3 8W
Strombacka 72 61 58N 16 44 E
Strómboli, I. 65 38 48N 15 12 E
Stromeferry 36 57 20N 5 33W
Stromemore 36 57 22N 5 33W
Stromness 37 58 58N 3 18W
Ströms Vattudal L. 74 64 0N 15 30 E
Stromsberg 72 60 28N 17 44 E
Strömsnäsbruk 73 56 35N 13 45 E
Strömstad 72 58 55N 11 15 E
Stromsund 74 63 51N 15 35 E
Stronachlachar 34 56 15N 4 35W
Strone 34 55 59N 4 54W
Stróngoli 65 39 16N 17 2 E
Stronsay Firth 37 59 4N 2 50W
Stronsay, I. 37 59 8N 2 38W
Strontian 36 56 42N 5 32W
Strood 29 51 23N 0 30 E
Stroove 38 55 13N 6 57W
Stropkov 53 49 13N 21 39 E
Stroud 28 51 44N 2 12W
Stroud Road 141 32 18 S 151 57 E
Stroudsberg 162 40 59N 75 15W
Struer 73 56 30N 8 35 E
Struga 66 41 13N 20 44 E
Strugi Krasnye 80 58 21N 28 51 E
Struma, R. 67 41 50N 23 18 E
Strumble Hd. 31 52 3N 5 6W
Strumica 66 41 28N 22 41 E
Strumica, R. 66 41 26N 27 46 E
Strusshamn 71 60 24N 5 10 E
Struthers 150 48 41N 85 51W
Struy 37 57 25N 4 40W
Stryama 67 42 16N 24 54 E
Stryi 80 49 16N 23 48 E
Stryker 152 48 40N 114 44W
Stryków 54 51 55N 19 33 E
Strzegom 54 50 58N 16 20 E
Strzelce Krajenskie 54 52 52N 15 33 E
Strzelecki Creek 139 29 37 S 139 59 E
Strzelin 54 50 46N 17 2 E
Strzelno 54 52 35N 18 9 E
Strzyzów 54 49 52N 21 47 E
Stuart, Fla., U.S.A. 157 27 11N 80 12W
Stuart, Nebr., U.S.A. 158 42 39N 99 8W
Stuart I. 147 63 55N 164 50W
Stuart L. 152 54 30N 124 30W
Stuart Mts. 143 45 2 S 167 39 E
Stuart, R. 152 54 0N 123 35W
Stuart Range 139 29 10 S 134 56 E
Stuart's Ra. 136 29 10 S 135 0 E
Stubbekøbing 73 54 53N 12 9 E
Stuben 52 46 58N 10 31 E
Stuberhuk 48 54 23N 11 18 E
Studholme Junc. 143 44 42 S 171 9 E
Studland 28 50 39N 1 58W
Studley 28 52 16N 1 54W
Stugsund 72 61 16N 17 18 E
Stugun 72 63 10N 15 40 E
Stull, L. 153 54 24N 92 34W
Stung-Treng 100 13 31N 105 58 E
Stupart, R. 153 56 0N 93 25W
Stupino 81 54 57N 38 2 E
Sturgeon B. 153 52 0N 97 50W
Sturgeon Bay 156 44 52N 87 20W
Sturgeon Falls 150 46 25N 79 57W
Sturgeon L., Alta., Can. 152 55 6N 117 32W
Sturgeon L., Ont., Can. 150 50 0N 90 45W
Sturgis, Mich., U.S.A. 156 41 50N 85 25W
Sturgis, S.D., U.S.A. 158 44 25N 103 30W
Sturko, I. 73 56 5N 15 42 E
Sturminster Marshall 28 50 48N 2 4W
Sturminster Newton 28 50 56N 2 18W
Stúrovo 53 47 48N 18 41 E
Sturt Cr. 136 19 0 S 128 15 E
Sturt Creek 136 19 0 S 128 15 E
Sturt, R. 136 34 58 S 138 31 E
Sturton 33 53 22N 0 39W
Sturts Meadows 140 31 18 S 141 42 E
Stutterheim 128 32 33 S 27 28 E
Stuttgart, Ger. 49 48 46N 9 10 E
Stuttgart, U.S.A. 159 34 30N 91 33W
Stuyvesant 162 42 23N 73 45W
Stykkishólmur 74 65 2N 22 40W
Styr, R. 80 51 4N 25 20 E
Styria = Steiermark 52 47 26N 15 0 E
Su-no-Saki 111 34 58N 139 45 E
Suakin 122 19 0N 37 20 E
Suan 107 38 42N 126 22 E
Suaqui 164 29 12N 109 41W
Suay Rieng 101 11 9N 105 45 E
Subang 103 7 30 S 107 45 E
Subansiri, R. 98 26 48N 93 50 E
Subi 101 2 55N 108 50 E
Subi, I. 102 2 58N 108 50 E
Subiaco 63 41 56N 13 5 E
Subotica 66 46 6N 19 29 E
Success 153 50 28N 108 6W
Suceava 70 47 38N 26 16 E
Suceava □ 70 47 37N 26 18 E
Suceava, R. 70 47 38N 26 16 E
Sucha-Beskidzka 54 49 44N 19 35 E
Suchan 54 53 18N 15 18 E
Suchedniów 54 51 3N 20 49 E
Such'i 109 21 23N 110 16 E
Suchien 107 33 58N 118 17 E
Suchil 164 23 38N 103 55W
Suchitoto 166 13 56N 89 0W
Suchou 109 31 15N 120 40 E
Süchow = Hsüchou 107 34 15N 117 10 E
Suchowola 54 53 33N 23 3 E
Sucio, R. 174 6 40N 77 0W
Suck, R. 39 53 17N 8 10W
Suckling, Mt. 135 9 43 S 148 59 E
Sucre, Boliv. 174 19 0 S 65 15W
Sucre, Venez. 174 10 25N 64 5W
Sucre □, Colomb. 174 8 50N 75 40W
Sucre □, Venez. 174 10 25N 63 30W
Sŭcueni 70 47 20N 22 5 E
Sucunduri, R. 174 6 20N 58 35W
SuCuraj 63 43 10N 17 8 E
Sucuriju 170 1 39N 49 57W
Sud-Ouest, Pte. du 151 49 23N 63 36W
Sud, Pte. 151 49 3N 62 14W
Suda, R. 81 59 40N 36 30 E
Sudak 82 44 51N 34 57 E
Sudan ■ 117 15 0N 30 0 E
Sudan, The 114 11 0N 9 0 E
Suday 81 59 0N 43 15 E
Sudbury, Can. 150 46 30N 81 0W
Sudbury, Derby, U.K. 33 52 53N 1 43W
Sudbury, Suffolk, U.K. 29 52 2N 0 44 E
Sûdd 123 8 20N 29 30 E
Süderbrarup 48 54 38N 9 47 E
Süderlügum 48 54 50N 8 46 E
Sudetan Mts. = Sudety 53 50 20N 16 45 E
Sudety 53 50 20N 16 45 E
Sudi 127 10 11 S 39 57 E
Sudirman, Pengunungan 103 4 30N 137 0 E
Sudiţi 70 44 35N 27 38 E
Sudogda 81 55 55N 40 50 E
Sudr 122 29 40N 32 42 E
Sudzha 80 51 14N 34 25 E
Sueca 59 39 12N 0 21W
Sueur, Le 158 44 25N 93 52W
Suez = Suweis 122 28 40N 33 0 E
Suf 90 32 19N 35 49 E
Sufaina 92 23 6N 40 44 E
Suffield 153 50 12N 111 10W
Suffolk 156 36 47N 76 33W
Suffolk □ 29 52 16N 1 0 E
Suffolk, East, □ 29 52 16N 1 10 E
Suffolk, West, □ 29 52 16N 0 45 E
Sufi-Kurgan 85 40 2N 73 30 E
Sufuk 93 23 50N 51 50 E
Suga no-Sen 110 35 25N 134 25 E
Sugag 70 45 47N 23 37 E
Sugar City 158 38 18N 103 38W
Sugarloaf Pt. 126 32 22 S 152 30 E
Suguk = Sagloue 149 62 10N 75 40W
Sugny 47 49 49N 4 54 E
Suhaia, L. 70 43 45N 25 15 E
Suhār 93 24 20N 56 40 E
Suhbaatar 105 46 54N 113 25 E
Suhl 48 50 35N 10 40 E
Suhl □ 48 50 37N 10 43 E
Suhr 50 47 22N 8 5 E
Suhsien 106 33 40N 117 0 E
Suhum 121 6 5N 0 27W
Suian 109 29 28N 118 44 E
Suica 66 43 52N 17 11 E
Suich'ang 109 28 36N 119 16 E
Suichiang 108 28 40N 103 58 E
Suifenho 107 44 30N 131 2 E
Suihsien 109 31 41N 113 20 E
Suihua 98 46 37N 127 0 E
Suilu 108 22 20N 107 48 E
Suining, Hunan, China 108 26 21N 110 0 E
Suining, Kiangsu, China 107 33 54N 117 56 E
Suining, Szechwan, China 108 30 31N 105 34 E
Suippes 43 49 8N 4 30 E
Suir, R. 39 52 31N 7 59W
Suita 111 34 45N 135 32 E
Suiteh 106 37 35N 110 5 E
Suiyang, Heilungkiang, China 107 44 26N 130 51 E
Suiyang, Kweichow, China 108 27 57N 107 11 E
Sujangarh 94 27 42N 47 31 E
Sukabumi 103 6 56 S 106 57 E
Sukadana 102 1 10 S 110 0 E
Sukandja 102 2 28 S 110 25 E
Sukarnapura = Jajapura 103 2 28N 140 38 E
Sukarno, G. = Jaja, Puncak 103 3 57 S 137 17 E
Sukchŏn 107 39 22N 125 35 E
Sukhinichi 80 54 8N 35 10 E
Sukhona, R. 78 60 30N 45 0 E
Sukhothai 100 17 1N 99 49 E
Sukhoy Log 84 56 55N 62 1 E
Sukhumi 83 43 0N 41 0 E
Sukkur 94 27 50N 68 46 E

Sukkur Barrage Sydra, G. of


| | | | |
|---|---|---|---|
| Sukkur Barrage | 93 | 27 50N | 68 45 E |
| Sukma | 96 | 18 24N | 81 37 E |
| Sukovo | 66 | 43 4N | 22 37 E |
| Sukumo | 110 | 32 56N | 132 44 E |
| Sukunka, R. | 152 | 55 45N | 121 15W |
| Sul, Canal do | 170 | 0 10 S | 48 30W |
| Sula, Kepulauan | 103 | 1 45 S | 125 0 E |
| Sula, R. | 80 | 50 0N | 33 0 E |
| Sulaco, R. | 166 | 15 2N | 87 44W |
| Sulaiman Range | 94 | 30 30N | 69 50 E |
| Sulaimanke Headworks | 94 | 30 27N | 73 55 E |
| Sŭlaj □ | 70 | 47 15N | 23 0 E |
| Sulak, R. | 83 | 43 20N | 47 20 E |
| Sulam Tsor | 90 | 33 4N | 35 6 E |
| Sulawesi □ | 103 | 2 0 S | 120 0 E |
| Sulawesi, I. | 103 | 2 0 S | 120 0 E |
| Sulby | 32 | 54 18N | 4 29W |
| Sulechów | 54 | 52 5N | 15 40 E |
| Sulecin | 54 | 52 26N | 15 10 E |
| Sulejów | 54 | 51 26N | 19 53 E |
| Sulejówek | 54 | 52 13N | 21 17 E |
| Sulgen | 51 | 47 33N | 9 7 E |
| Sulima | 120 | 6 58N | 11 32W |
| Sulina | 70 | 45 10N | 29 40 E |
| Sulingen | 48 | 52 41N | 8 47 E |
| Sŭlişte | 70 | 45 45N | 23 56 E |
| Suliţa | 70 | 47 39N | 20 59 E |
| Sulitälma | 74 | 67 17N | 17 28 E |
| Sulitjelma | 74 | 61 7N | 16 8 E |
| Sułkowice | 54 | 49 50N | 19 49 E |
| Sullana | 174 | 5 0 S | 80 45W |
| Sullivan, Ill., U.S.A. | 158 | 39 40N | 88 40W |
| Sullivan, Ind., U.S.A. | 156 | 39 5N | 87 26W |
| Sullivan, Mo., U.S.A. | 158 | 38 10N | 91 10W |
| Sullivan Bay | 152 | 50 55N | 126 50W |
| Sullom Voe | 36 | 60 30N | 1 20W |
| Sully-sur-Loire | 43 | 47 45N | 2 20 E |
| Sulmierzyce | 57 | 51 36N | 17 30 E |
| Sulmona | 63 | 42 3N | 13 55 E |
| Sulo | 105 | 39 25N | 76 6 E |
| Sulphur, La., U.S.A. | 159 | 30 20N | 93 22W |
| Sulphur, Okla., U.S.A. | 159 | 34 35N | 97 0W |
| Sulphur Pt. | 152 | 60 56N | 114 48W |
| Sulphur Springs | 159 | 33 5N | 95 30W |
| Sulphur Springs, Cr. | 159 | 32 50N | 102 8W |
| Sultan | 150 | 47 36N | 82 47W |
| Sultanpur | 95 | 26 18N | 82 10 E |
| Sulu Arch. | 103 | 6 0N | 121 0 E |
| Sulu Sea | 103 | 8 0N | 120 0 E |
| Sululta | 123 | 9 10N | 38 43 E |
| Sulung Shan | 108 | 31 30N | 99 30 E |
| Suluq | 119 | 31 44N | 20 14 E |
| Sulyukta | 85 | 39 56N | 69 34 E |
| Sulzbach-Rosenburg | 49 | 49 30N | 11 46 E |
| Sumalata | 103 | 1 0N | 122 37 E |
| Sumampa | 172 | 29 25 S | 63 29W |
| Sumatera, I. | 102 | 0 40N | 100 20 E |
| Sumatera Selatan □ | 102 | 3 30 S | 104 0 E |
| Sumatera Tengah □ | 102 | 1 0 S | 100 0 E |
| Sumatera Utara □ | 102 | 2 0N | 99 0 E |
| Sumatra | 160 | 46 45N | 107 37W |
| Sumatra = Sumatera | 102 | 0 40N | 100 20 E |
| Sumba, I. | 103 | 9 45 S | 119 35 E |
| Sumba, Selat | 103 | 9 0 S | 118 40 E |
| Sumbawa | 102 | 8 26 S | 117 30 E |
| Sumbawa, I. | 103 | 8 34 S | 117 17 E |
| Sumbawanga □ | 126 | 8 0 S | 31 30 E |
| Sumbing, mt. | 103 | 7 19 S | 110 3 E |
| Sumburgh Hd. | 36 | 59 52N | 1 17W |
| Sumdo | 95 | 35 6N | 79 43 E |
| Sumé | 170 | 7 39 S | 36 55W |
| Sumedang | 103 | 6 49 S | 107 56 E |
| Sümeg | 53 | 46 59N | 17 20 E |
| Sumenep | 103 | 7 3 S | 113 51 E |
| Sumgait | 83 | 40 34N | 49 10 E |
| Sumisu-Jima | 111 | 31 27N | 140 3 E |
| Sumiswald | 50 | 47 2N | 7 44 E |
| Summer Is. | 36 | 58 0N | 5 27W |
| Summer L. | 160 | 42 50N | 120 50W |
| Summerhill | 38 | 53 30N | 6 44W |
| Summerland | 152 | 49 32N | 119 41W |
| Summerside | 151 | 46 24N | 63 47W |
| Summerville, Ga., U.S.A. | 157 | 34 30N | 85 20W |
| Summerville, S.C., U.S.A. | 157 | 33 2N | 80 11W |
| Summit, Can. | 150 | 47 50N | 72 20W |
| Summit, U.S.A. | 147 | 63 20N | 149 20W |
| Summit L. | 152 | 54 20N | 122 40W |
| Summit Pk. | 161 | 37 20N | 106 48W |
| Sumner, N.Z. | 143 | 43 35 S | 172 48 E |
| Sumner, U.S.A. | 158 | 42 49N | 92 7W |
| Sumner L. | 143 | 42 42 S | 172 15 E |
| Sumoto | 110 | 34 21N | 134 54 E |
| Sumperk | 53 | 49 59N | 17 0 E |
| Sumprabum | 98 | 26 33N | 97 4 E |
| Sumter | 157 | 33 55N | 80 10W |
| Sumy | 80 | 50 57N | 34 50 E |
| Sun City | 163 | 33 41N | 117 11W |
| Suna | 126 | 5 23 S | 34 48 E |
| Sunan | 107 | 39 15N | 125 40 E |
| Sunart, dist. | 36 | 56 40N | 5 40W |
| Sunart, L. | 36 | 56 42N | 5 43W |
| Sunburst | 160 | 48 56N | 111 59W |
| Sunbury, Austral. | 141 | 37 35 S | 144 44 E |
| Sunbury, U.S.A. | 162 | 40 50N | 76 46W |
| Sunchales | 172 | 30 58 S | 61 35W |
| Suncho Corral | 172 | 27 55 S | 63 14W |
| Sunchŏn | 107 | 34 52N | 127 31 E |
| Suncook | 162 | 43 8N | 71 27W |
| Sund | 71 | 60 13N | 5 10 E |
| Sunda Ketjil, Kepulauan | 102 | 7 30 S | 117 0 E |
| Sunda, Selat | 102 | 6 20 S | 105 30 E |
| Sundalsöra | 71 | 62 40N | 8 36 E |
| Sundance | 158 | 44 27N | 104 27W |
| Sundarbans, The | 98 | 22 0N | 89 0 E |
| Sundargarh | 96 | 22 10N | 84 5 E |
| Sunday Str. | 136 | 16 25 S | 123 18 E |
| Sundays, R. | 128 | 32 10 S | 24 40 E |
| Sundby | 73 | 56 53N | 8 40 E |
| Sundbyberg | 72 | 59 22N | 17 58 E |
| Sunderland, U.K. | 35 | 54 54N | 1 22W |
| Sunderland, U.S.A. | 162 | 42 27N | 72 36W |
| Sundre | 152 | 51 49N | 114 38W |
| Sundridge, Can. | 150 | 45 45N | 79 25W |
| Sundridge, U.K. | 29 | 51 15N | 0 10 E |
| Sunds | 73 | 56 13N | 9 1 E |
| Sundsjö | 72 | 62 59N | 15 9 E |
| Sundsvall | 72 | 62 23N | 17 17 E |
| Sung Hei | 101 | 10 20N | 106 2 E |
| Sungaipakning | 102 | 1 19N | 102 0 E |
| Sungaipenuh | 102 | 2 1 S | 101 20 E |
| Sungaitiram | 102 | 0 45 S | 117 8 E |
| Sungari, R. = Sunghua Chiang | 107 | 44 30N | 126 20 E |
| Sungch'i | 109 | 27 2N | 118 19 E |
| Sungchiang | 109 | 31 2N | 121 14 E |
| Sungei Lembing | 101 | 2 53N | 103 4 E |
| Sungei Patani | 101 | 5 38N | 100 29 E |
| Sungei Siput | 101 | 4 51N | 101 6 E |
| Sungfou | 109 | 31 5N | 114 42 E |
| Sungguminasa | 103 | 5 17 S | 119 30 E |
| Sunghsien | 106 | 34 10N | 112 10 E |
| Sunghua Chiang, R. | 105 | 47 42N | 132 30 E |
| Sungikai | 123 | 12 20N | 29 51 E |
| Sungk'an | 108 | 28 33N | 106 52 E |
| Sungming | 108 | 25 22N | 103 2 E |
| Sungpan | 105 | 32 50N | 103 20 E |
| Sungp'an | 108 | 32 36N | 103 36 E |
| Sungt'ao | 108 | 28 12N | 109 12 E |
| Sungtzu Hu | 109 | 30 10N | 111 45 E |
| Sungü | 129 | 21 18 S | 32 28 E |
| Sungurlu | 82 | 40 12N | 34 21 E |
| Sungyang | 109 | 28 16N | 119 29 E |
| Sunja | 63 | 45 21N | 16 35 E |
| Sunk Island | 33 | 53 38N | 0 7W |
| Sunkar, Gora | 85 | 44 15N | 73 50 E |
| Sunnäsbruk | 72 | 61 10N | 7 12 E |
| Sunne, Jamtland, Sweden | 72 | 63 7N | 14 25 E |
| Sunne, Varmland, Sweden | 72 | 59 52N | 13 12 E |
| Sunnfjord | 71 | 61 25N | 5 18 E |
| Sunnhordland | 71 | 59 50N | 5 30 E |
| Sunninghill | 29 | 51 25N | 0 40W |
| Sunnmöre | 71 | 62 15N | 6 30 E |
| Sunnyside, Utah, U.S.A. | 160 | 39 40N | 110 24W |
| Sunnyside, Wash., U.S.A. | 160 | 46 24N | 120 2W |
| Sunnyvale | 163 | 37 23N | 122 2W |
| Sunray | 159 | 36 1N | 101 47W |
| Sunshine | 141 | 37 48 S | 144 52 E |
| Sunson | 121 | 9 35N | 0 2W |
| Suntar | 77 | 62 15N | 117 30 E |
| Sunyani | 120 | 7 21N | 2 22W |
| Suō-Nada | 110 | 33 50N | 131 30 E |
| Suolahti | 74 | 62 34N | 25 52 E |
| Suonenjoki | 74 | 62 37N | 27 7 E |
| Supai | 161 | 36 14N | 112 44W |
| Supaul | 95 | 26 10N | 86 40 E |
| Supe | 123 | 8 34N | 35 35 E |
| Superior, Ariz., U.S.A. | 161 | 33 19N | 111 9W |
| Superior, Mont., U.S.A. | 160 | 47 15N | 114 57W |
| Superior, Nebr., U.S.A. | 158 | 40 3N | 98 2W |
| Superior, Wis., U.S.A. | 158 | 46 45N | 92 0W |
| Superior, L. | 155 | 47 40N | 87 0W |
| Supetar | 63 | 43 25N | 16 32 E |
| Suphan Buri | 100 | 14 30N | 100 10 E |
| Suprasśl | 54 | 53 13N | 23 19 E |
| Suq al Jumah | 119 | 32 58N | 13 12 E |
| Sür, Leb. | 90 | 33 19N | 35 16 E |
| Sür, Oman | 93 | 22 34N | 59 32 E |
| Sur, Pt. | 163 | 36 18N | 121 54W |
| Sura, R. | 81 | 55 30N | 46 20 E |
| Surab | 94 | 28 25N | 66 15 E |
| Surabaja = Surabaya | 103 | 7 17 S | 112 45 E |
| Surabaya | 103 | 7 17 S | 112 45 E |
| Surahammar | 72 | 59 43N | 16 13 E |
| Suraia | 70 | 45 40N | 27 25 E |
| Surakarta | 103 | 7 35 S | 110 48 E |
| Surakhany | 83 | 40 13N | 50 1 E |
| Surandai | 97 | 8 58N | 77 26 E |
| Surany | 53 | 48 6N | 18 10 E |
| Surat, Austral. | 139 | 27 10 S | 149 6 E |
| Surat, India | 96 | 21 12N | 72 55 E |
| Surat, Khalij | 119 | 31 40N | 18 30 E |
| Surat Thani | 101 | 9 6N | 99 14 E |
| Suratgarh | 94 | 29 18N | 73 55 E |
| Surazh | 80 | 53 5N | 32 27 E |
| Surduc | 70 | 47 15N | 23 25 E |
| Surduc Pasul | 70 | 45 21N | 23 23 E |
| Surdulica | 66 | 42 41N | 22 11 E |
| Sûre, R. | 47 | 49 51N | 6 6 E |
| Surendranagar | 94 | 22 45N | 71 40 E |
| Surf | 163 | 34 41N | 120 36W |
| Surf Inlet | 152 | 53 8N | 128 50W |
| Surgères | 44 | 46 7N | 0 47W |
| Surhuisterveen | 46 | 53 11N | 6 10 E |
| Suri | 95 | 23 50N | 87 34 E |
| Surianu, mt. | 70 | 45 33N | 23 31 E |
| Suriapet | 96 | 17 10N | 79 40 E |
| Surif | 90 | 31 40N | 35 4 E |
| Surin | 100 | 14 50N | 103 34 E |
| Surin Nua, Ko | 101 | 9 30N | 97 55 E |
| Surinam ■ | 175 | 4 0N | 56 15W |
| Suriname, R. | 170 | 4 30N | 55 30W |
| Surkhandarya, R. | 85 | 37 12N | 67 20 E |
| Sŭrmasu | 70 | 46 45N | 25 13 E |
| Sürmene | 83 | 41 0N | 40 1 E |
| Surovikino | 83 | 48 32N | 42 55 E |
| Surprise L. | 152 | 59 40N | 133 15W |
| Surrey □ | 29 | 51 16N | 0 30W |
| Surry | 162 | 37 8N | 76 50W |
| Sursee | 50 | 47 11N | 8 6 E |
| Sursk | 81 | 53 3N | 45 40W |
| Surt | 119 | 31 11N | 16 46 E |
| Surt, Al Hammādah al | 119 | 30 0N | 17 50 E |
| Surtsey | 74 | 63 20N | 20 30W |
| Surubim | 170 | 7 50 S | 35 45W |
| Suruga-Wan | 111 | 34 45N | 138 30 E |
| Surup | 103 | 6 27N | 126 17 E |
| Surur | 93 | 23 20N | 58 10 E |
| Susa | 62 | 45 8N | 7 3 E |
| Susaa, R. | 73 | 55 20N | 11 42 E |
| Sušac, I. | 63 | 42 46N | 16 30 E |
| Susak, I. | 63 | 44 30N | 14 28 E |
| Susaki | 110 | 33 22N | 133 17 E |
| Susamyr | 85 | 42 12N | 73 58 E |
| Susamyrtau, Khrebet | 85 | 42 8N | 73 15 E |
| Susangerd | 92 | 31 35N | 48 20 E |
| Susanino | 77 | 52 50N | 140 14 E |
| Susanville | 160 | 40 28N | 120 40W |
| Susch | 51 | 46 46N | 10 5 E |
| Sušice | 52 | 49 17N | 13 30 E |
| Susquehanna Depot | 162 | 41 55N | 75 36W |
| Susquehanna, R. | 156 | 41 50N | 76 20W |
| Susques | 172 | 23 35 S | 66 25W |
| Sussex, Can. | 151 | 45 45N | 65 37W |
| Sussex, U.S.A. | 162 | 41 12N | 74 38W |
| Sussex (□) | 26 | 50 55N | 0 20W |
| Sussex, E. □ | 29 | 51 0N | 0 0 E |
| Sussex, W. □ | 29 | 51 0N | 0 30W |
| Susten Pass | 51 | 46 43N | 8 26 E |
| Susteren | 47 | 51 4N | 5 51 E |
| Sustut, R. | 152 | 56 20N | 127 30W |
| Susuman | 77 | 62 47N | 148 10 E |
| Susuna | 103 | 3 20 S | 133 25 E |
| Susung | 109 | 30 9N | 116 6 E |
| Susz | 54 | 53 44N | 19 20 E |
| Suţeşti | 70 | 45 13N | 27 27 E |
| Sutherland, Austral. | 141 | 34 2 S | 151 4 E |
| Sutherland, Can. | 153 | 52 15N | 106 40W |
| Sutherland, S. Afr. | 125 | 32 33 S | 20 40 E |
| Sutherland, U.S.A. | 158 | 41 12N | 101 11W |
| Sutherland (□) | 26 | 58 10N | 4 30W |
| Sutherland Falls | 143 | 44 48 S | 167 46 E |
| Sutherland Pt. | 133 | 28 15 S | 153 35 E |
| Sutherland Ra. | 137 | 25 42 S | 125 21 E |
| Sutherlin | 160 | 43 28N | 123 16W |
| Sutivan | 63 | 43 23N | 16 30 E |
| Sutlej, R. | 94 | 30 0N | 73 0 E |
| Sutter Creek | 163 | 38 24N | 120 48W |
| Sutterton | 33 | 52 54N | 0 8W |
| Sutton, N.Z. | 143 | 45 34 S | 170 8 E |
| Sutton, U.K. | 29 | 51 22N | 0 13W |
| Sutton, U.S.A. | 158 | 40 40N | 97 50W |
| Sutton Bridge | 29 | 52 46N | 0 12 E |
| Sutton Coldfield | 28 | 52 33N | 1 50W |
| Sutton Courtenay | 28 | 51 39N | 1 16W |
| Sutton-in-Ashfield | 33 | 52 8N | 1 16W |
| Sutton-on-Sea | 33 | 53 18N | 0 18 E |
| Sutton, R. | 150 | 55 15N | 83 45W |
| Sutton Scotney | 28 | 51 9N | 1 20W |
| Suttor, R. | 138 | 20 36 S | 147 2 E |
| Sutwik I. | 147 | 56 35N | 157 10W |
| Suva | 143 | 17 40 S | 178 8 E |
| Suva Gora | 66 | 41 45N | 21 3 E |
| Suva Planina | 66 | 43 10N | 22 5 E |
| Suva Reka | 66 | 42 21N | 20 50 E |
| Suvarov Is. | 131 | 13 15 S | 163 30W |
| Suvo Rudište | 66 | 43 17N | 20 49 E |
| Suvorovo | 67 | 43 20N | 27 35 E |
| Suwa | 111 | 36 2N | 138 8 E |
| Suwa-Ko | 111 | 36 3N | 138 5 E |
| Suwałki | 54 | 54 8N | 22 59 E |
| Suwałki □ | 54 | 54 0N | 22 30 E |
| Suwannaphum | 100 | 15 33N | 105 47 E |
| Suwannee, R. | 157 | 30 0N | 83 0W |
| Suwanose-Jima | 112 | 29 38N | 129 38 E |
| Suweis, El | 122 | 29 58N | 32 31 E |
| Suweis, Khalîg es | 122 | 28 40N | 33 0 E |
| Suweis, Qanâl es | 122 | 31 0N | 32 20 E |
| Suwŏn | 107 | 37 17N | 127 1 E |
| Suykbulak | 84 | 50 25N | 62 33 E |
| Suzak | 85 | 44 9N | 68 27 E |
| Suzaka | 111 | 36 39N | 138 19 E |
| Sŭzava, R. | 52 | 49 50N | 15 0 E |
| Suzdal | 81 | 56 29N | 40 26 E |
| Suze, La | 42 | 47 54N | 0 2 E |
| Suzuka | 111 | 34 55N | 136 36 E |
| Suzuka-Sam | 111 | 35 5N | 136 30 E |
| Suzzara | 62 | 45 0N | 10 45 E |
| Svalbard, Arctica | 12 | 78 0N | 17 0 E |
| Svalbard, Iceland | 74 | 66 12N | 15 43W |
| Svalöv | 73 | 55 57N | 13 8 E |
| Svanå | 72 | 59 46N | 15 23 E |
| Svanvik | 74 | 69 38N | 30 3 E |
| Svappavaari | 74 | 67 40N | 21 03 E |
| Svarstad | 71 | 59 27N | 9 56 E |
| Svartisen | 74 | 66 40N | 14 16 E |
| Svartvik | 72 | 62 19N | 17 24 E |
| Svatovo | 82 | 49 35N | 38 5 E |
| Svay Chek | 100 | 13 48N | 102 58 E |
| Svay Rieng | 101 | 11 5N | 105 48 E |
| Svealand □ | 75 | 59 55N | 15 0 E |
| Svedala | 73 | 55 30N | 13 15 E |
| Sveg | 72 | 62 2N | 14 21 E |
| Sveio | 71 | 59 33N | 5 23 E |
| Svelvik | 71 | 59 37N | 10 24 E |
| Svendborg | 73 | 55 4N | 10 35 E |
| Svene | 71 | 59 45N | 9 31 E |
| Svenljunga | 73 | 57 29N | 13 29 E |
| Svensbro | 73 | 58 15N | 13 52 E |
| Svenstavik | 72 | 62 45N | 14 26 E |
| Svenstrup | 73 | 56 58N | 9 50 E |
| Sverdlovsk | 84 | 56 50N | 60 30 E |
| Sverdrup Is. | 12 | 79 0N | 97 0W |
| Svetac | 63 | 43 3N | 15 43 E |
| Sveti Ivan Zelina | 63 | 45 57N | 16 16 E |
| Sveti Jurij | 63 | 46 14N | 15 24 E |
| Sveti Lenart | 63 | 46 36N | 15 48 E |
| Sveti Nikola | 66 | 41 51N | 21 56 E |
| Sveti Trojica | 63 | 46 37N | 15 33 E |
| Svetlogorsk | 80 | 52 38N | 29 46 E |
| Svetlograd | 83 | 45 25N | 42 58 E |
| Svetlovodsk | 80 | 49 2N | 33 13 E |
| Svetlyy | 84 | 50 48N | 60 51 E |
| Svetozarevo | 66 | 44 0N | 21 15 E |
| Svidník | 53 | 49 20N | 21 37 E |
| Svilaja Pl. | 63 | 43 49N | 16 31 E |
| Svilajnac | 66 | 44 15N | 21 11 E |
| Svilengrad | 67 | 41 49N | 26 12 E |
| Svinö | 73 | 55 6N | 11 44 E |
| Svir, R. | 78 | 61 2N | 34 50 E |
| Svishov | 67 | 43 36N | 25 23 E |
| Svisloch | 80 | 53 26N | 24 2 E |
| Svitavy | 53 | 49 47N | 16 28 E |
| Svobodnyy | 77 | 51 20N | 128 0 E |
| Svoge | 67 | 42 59N | 23 23 E |
| Svolvær | 74 | 68 15N | 14 34 E |
| Svratka, R. | 53 | 49 27N | 16 12 E |
| Svrljig | 66 | 43 25N | 22 6 E |
| Swa | 98 | 19 15N | 96 17 E |
| Swabian Alps | 49 | 48 30N | 9 30 E |
| Swadlincote | 28 | 52 47N | 1 34W |
| Swaffham | 29 | 52 38N | 0 42 E |
| Swain Reefs | 138 | 21 45 S | 152 20 E |
| Swainsboro | 157 | 32 38N | 82 22W |
| Swakopmund | 128 | 22 37 S | 14 30 E |
| Swale, R. | 34 | 54 18N | 1 20W |
| Swallowfield | 29 | 51 23N | 0 56W |
| Swalmen | 47 | 51 13N | 6 2 E |
| Swan Hill | 140 | 35 20 S | 143 33 E |
| Swan Hills | 152 | 54 42N | 115 24W |
| Swan Islands | 166 | 17 22N | 83 57W |
| Swan L. | 153 | 52 30N | 100 50W |
| Swan Pt. | 136 | 16 22 S | 123 1 E |
| Swan, R. | 132 | 32 3 S | 115 35 E |
| Swan Reach | 140 | 34 35 S | 139 37 E |
| Swan River | 153 | 52 10N | 101 16W |
| Swanage | 28 | 50 36N | 1 59W |
| Swanlinbar | 38 | 54 11N | 7 42W |
| Swansea, Austral. | 141 | 33 3 S | 151 35 E |
| Swansea, U.K. | 31 | 51 37N | 3 57W |
| Swansea Bay | 31 | 51 34N | 3 55W |
| Swar, R. | 95 | 35 15N | 72 24 E |
| Swartberg | 128 | 30 15 S | 29 23 E |
| Swartberge | 128 | 33 20 S | 22 0 E |
| Swarte Bank, gasfield | 19 | 53 27N | 2 10 E |
| Swartruggens | 128 | 25 39 S | 26 42 E |
| Swarzedz | 54 | 52 25N | 17 4 E |
| Swastika | 150 | 48 7N | 80 6W |
| Swatow = Shant'ou | 109 | 23 28N | 116 40 E |
| Swatragh | 38 | 54 55N | 6 40W |
| Swaziland ■ | 129 | 26 30 S | 31 30 E |
| Sweden ■ | 74 | 67 0N | 15 0 E |
| Swedru | 121 | 5 32N | 0 41W |
| Sweet Home | 160 | 44 26N | 122 38W |
| Sweetwater, Nev., U.S.A. | 163 | 38 27N | 119 9W |
| Sweetwater, Tex., U.S.A. | 159 | 32 30N | 100 28W |
| Sweetwater, R. | 160 | 42 31N | 107 30W |
| Swellendam | 128 | 34 1 S | 20 26 E |
| Świdin | 54 | 53 47N | 15 49 E |
| Swidnica | 54 | 50 50N | 16 30 E |
| Swidnik | 54 | 51 13N | 22 39 E |
| Świebodzice | 54 | 50 51N | 16 20 E |
| Swiebodzin | 54 | 52 15N | 15 37 E |
| Swiecie | 54 | 53 25N | 18 30 E |
| Swietorkrzyskie, Góry | 54 | 51 0N | 20 30 E |
| Swift Current | 153 | 50 20N | 107 45W |
| Swiftcurrent Cr. | 153 | 50 38N | 107 44W |
| Swilly L. | 38 | 55 12N | 7 35W |
| Swilly, R. | 38 | 54 56N | 7 50W |
| Swindle, I. | 152 | 52 30N | 128 35W |
| Swindon | 28 | 51 33N | 1 47W |
| Swinemünde = Świnoujście | 54 | 53 54N | 14 16 E |
| Swineshead | 33 | 57 57N | 0 9W |
| Swinford | 38 | 53 57N | 8 57W |
| Świnoujście | 54 | 53 54N | 14 16 E |
| Swinton, Borders, U.K. | 35 | 55 43N | 2 14W |
| Swinton, Gr. Manch., U.K. | 32 | 53 31N | 2 21W |
| Swinton, S. Yorks., U.K. | 33 | 53 28N | 1 20W |
| Switzerland ■ | 49 | 46 30N | 8 0 E |
| Swona, I. | 37 | 58 30N | 3 3W |
| Swords | 38 | 53 27N | 6 15W |
| Syasstroy | 80 | 60 5N | 32 15 E |
| Sybil Pt. | 39 | 52 12N | 10 28W |
| Sychevka | 80 | 55 45N | 34 10 E |
| Syców | 54 | 51 19N | 17 40 E |
| Sydney, Austral. | 141 | 33 53 S | 151 10 E |
| Sydney, Can. | 151 | 46 7N | 60 7W |
| Sydney, U.S.A. | 158 | 41 12N | 103 0W |
| Sydney Mines | 151 | 46 18N | 60 15W |
| Sydproven | 12 | 60 30N | 45 35W |
| Sydra, G. of = Surt | 61 | 31 40N | 18 30 E |

Syke Tambelan, Kepulauan


| Place | Page | Lat. | Long. |
|---|---|---|---|
| Syke | 48 | 52 55N | 8 50 E |
| Syktyvkar | 78 | 61 45N | 50 40 E |
| Sylacauga | 157 | 33 10N | 86 15W |
| Sylarna, Mt. | 72 | 63 2N | 12 11 E |
| Sylhet | 98 | 24 54N | 91 52 E |
| Sylt, I. | 48 | 54 50N | 8 20 E |
| Sylva, R. | 84 | 58 0N | 56 54 E |
| Sylvan Beach | 162 | 43 12N | 75 44W |
| Sylvan Lake | 152 | 52 20N | 114 10W |
| Sylvania | 157 | 32 45N | 81 37W |
| Sylvester | 157 | 31 31N | 83 50W |
| Sym | 76 | 60 20N | 87 50 E |
| Symington | 35 | 55 35N | 3 36W |
| Symón | 164 | 24 42N | 102 35W |
| Symonds Yat | 28 | 51 50N | 2 38W |
| Synnott Ra. | 136 | 16 30 S | 125 20 E |
| Syr Darya | 76 | 45 0N | 65 0 E |
| Syracuse, Kans., U.S.A. | 159 | 38 0N | 101 40W |
| Syracuse, N.Y., U.S.A. | 162 | 43 4N | 76 11W |
| Syrdarya | 85 | 40 50N | 68 40 E |
| Syria ■ | 92 | 35 0N | 38 0 E |
| Syriam | 98 | 16 44N | 96 19 E |
| Syrian Des. | 92 | 31 30N | 40 0 E |
| Sysert | 84 | 56 29N | 60 49 E |
| Syston | 28 | 52 42N | 1 5W |
| Syuldzhyukyor | 77 | 63 25N | 113 40 E |
| Syutkya, mt. | 67 | 41 50N | 24 16 E |
| Syzran | 81 | 53 12N | 48 30 E |
| Szabolcs-Szatmár □ | 53 | 48 2N | 21 45 E |
| Szamocin | 54 | 53 2N | 17 7 E |
| Szamotuły | 54 | 52 35N | 16 34 E |
| Szaraz, R. | 53 | 46 28N | 20 44 E |
| Szazhalombatta | 53 | 47 20N | 18 58 E |
| Szczara, R. | 53 | 53 15N | 25 10 E |
| Szczebrzeszyn | 54 | 50 42N | 22 59 E |
| Szczecin | 54 | 53 27N | 14 27 E |
| Szczecin □ | 54 | 53 25N | 14 32 E |
| Szczecinek | 54 | 53 43N | 16 41 E |
| Szczekocimy | 54 | 50 38N | 19 48 E |
| Szczrk | 53 | 49 42N | 19 1 E |
| Szczuczyn | 54 | 53 36N | 22 19 E |
| Szczytno | 54 | 53 33N | 21 0 E |
| Szechwan □ | 109 | 30 15N | 103 15 E |
| Szécsény | 53 | 48 7N | 19 30 E |
| Szeged | 53 | 46 16N | 20 10 E |
| Szeghalom | 53 | 47 1N | 21 10 E |
| Székesfehérvár | 53 | 47 15N | 18 25 E |
| Szekszárd | 53 | 46 22N | 18 42 E |
| Szendrö | 53 | 48 24N | 20 41 E |
| Szentendre | 53 | 47 39N | 19 4 E |
| Szentes | 53 | 46 39N | 20 21 E |
| Szentgotthárd | 53 | 46 58N | 16 19 E |
| Szentlörinc | 53 | 46 3N | 18 1 E |
| Szerencs | 53 | 48 10N | 21 12 E |
| Szeshui | 33 | 34 50N | 113 20 E |
| Szigetvár | 53 | 46 3N | 17 46 E |
| Szlichtyogowa | 54 | 51 42N | 16 15 E |
| Szob | 53 | 47 48N | 18 53 E |
| Szolnok | 53 | 47 10N | 20 15 E |
| Szolnok □ | 53 | 47 15N | 20 30 E |
| Szombathely | 53 | 47 14N | 16 38 E |
| Szprotawa | 54 | 51 33N | 15 35 E |
| Sztum | 54 | 53 55N | 19 1 E |
| Sztuto | 54 | 54 20N | 19 15 E |
| Sztutowo | 54 | 54 20N | 19 15 E |
| Szûrvas | 53 | 46 50N | 20 38 E |
| Szydłowiec | 54 | 51 15N | 20 51 E |
| Szypliszki | 54 | 54 17N | 23 2 E |


## T


| Place | Page | Lat. | Long. |
|---|---|---|---|
| 't Harde | 46 | 52 24N | 5 54 E |
| 't Zandt | 46 | 53 22N | 6 46 E |
| Ta-erh Po, L. | 106 | 43 15N | 116 35 E |
| Ta Khli Khok | 100 | 15 18N | 100 20 E |
| Ta Lai | 101 | 11 24N | 107 23 E |
| Taalintehdas | 74 | 60 2N | 22 30 E |
| Taan | 107 | 45 30N | 124 18 E |
| Taavetti | 75 | 60 56N | 27 32 E |
| Taba | 92 | 26 55N | 42 30 E |
| Tabacal | 172 | 23 15 S | 64 15W |
| Tabaco | 103 | 13 22N | 123 44 E |
| Tabagné | 120 | 7 59N | 3 4W |
| Tabar Is. | 135 | 2 50 S | 152 0 E |
| Tabarca, Isla de | 59 | 38 17N | 0 30W |
| Tabarka | 119 | 36 56N | 8 46 E |
| Tabarra | 59 | 38 37N | 1 44 E |
| Tabas, Khorasan, Iran | 93 | 33 35N | 56 55 E |
| Tabas, Khorasan, Iran | 93 | 32 48N | 60 12 E |
| Tabasará, Serranía de | 166 | 8 35N | 81 40W |
| Tabasco □ | 165 | 17 45N | 93 30W |
| Tabatinga | 174 | 4 11 S | 69 58W |
| Tabatinga, Serra da | 170 | 10 30 S | 44 0W |
| Tabayin | 98 | 22 42N | 95 20 E |
| Tabelbala, Kahal de | 118 | 28 47N | 2 0W |
| Taber | 152 | 49 47N | 112 8W |
| Taberg | 162 | 43 18N | 75 37W |
| Tabernas | 59 | 37 4N | 2 26W |
| Tabernas de Valldigna | 59 | 39 5N | 0 13W |
| Tabigha | 90 | 32 53N | 35 33 E |
| Tabira | 170 | 7 35 S | 37 33W |
| Tablas, I. | 103 | 12 25N | 122 2 E |
| Table B. | 151 | 53 40N | 56 25W |
| Table Mt. | 128 | 34 0 S | 18 22 E |
| Table Top, Mt. | 138 | 23 24 S | 147 11 E |
| Tableland | 136 | 17 16 S | 126 51 E |
| Tabletop, mt. | 137 | 22 32 S | 123 50 E |
| Tábor | 52 | 49 25N | 14 39 E |
| Tabor | 90 | 32 42N | 35 24 E |
| Tabora | 126 | 5 2 S | 32 57 E |
| Tabora □ | 126 | 5 0 S | 33 0 E |
| Tabory | 84 | 58 31N | 64 33 E |
| Tabou | 120 | 4 30N | 7 20W |
| Tabouda | 118 | 34 44N | 5 14W |
| Tabrīz | 92 | 38 7N | 46 20 E |
| Tabūk | 92 | 28 30N | 36 25 E |
| Täby | 72 | 59 29N | 18 4 E |
| Tacámbaro | 164 | 19 14N | 101 28W |
| Tacarigua, L. de | 174 | 11 3N | 68 25W |
| Tach'aitan | 105 | 37 50N | 95 18 E |
| T'ach'eng | 105 | 46 45N | 82 57 E |
| Tach'eng | 106 | 38 35N | 116 39 E |
| Tach'engtzu | 107 | 41 44N | 118 52 E |
| Tach'i | 109 | 24 51N | 121 14 E |
| Tachia | 109 | 24 25N | 120 28 E |
| Tachiai | 108 | 23 44N | 103 57 E |
| Tachibana-Wan | 110 | 32 45N | 130 7 E |
| Tachikawa | 111 | 35 42N | 139 25 E |
| Tach'in Ch'uan, R. | 108 | 31 57N | 102 11 E |
| Tach'ing Shan, mts. | 106 | 40 50N | 111 0 E |
| Tachira | 174 | 8 7N | 72 21W |
| Tachira □ | 174 | 8 7N | 72 15W |
| Tachov | 52 | 49 47N | 12 39 E |
| Tachu | 108 | 30 45N | 107 13 E |
| Tacina, R. | 65 | 39 5N | 16 51 E |
| Tacloban | 103 | 11 15N | 124 58 E |
| Tacna | 174 | 18 0 S | 70 20W |
| Tacoma | 160 | 47 15N | 122 30W |
| Tacuarembó | 173 | 31 45 S | 56 0W |
| Tacumshin L. | 39 | 52 12N | 6 28W |
| Tadcaster | 33 | 53 53N | 1 16W |
| Tademaït, Plateau du | 118 | 28 30N | 2 30 E |
| Tadent, O. | 119 | 22 30N | 7 0 E |
| Tadjerdjert, O. | 119 | 26 0N | 8 0W |
| Tadjerouna | 118 | 33 31N | 2 3 E |
| Tadjettaret, O. | 119 | 22 0N | 7 30W |
| Tadjmout, O. | 118 | 25 37N | 3 48 E |
| Tadjoura | 123 | 11 50N | 42 55 E |
| Tadjoura, Golfe de | 123 | 11 50N | 43 0 E |
| Tadley | 28 | 51 21N | 1 8W |
| Tadmor, N.Z. | 143 | 41 27 S | 172 45 E |
| Tadmor, Syria | 92 | 34 30N | 37 55 E |
| Tado | 174 | 5 16N | 76 32W |
| Tadotsu | 110 | 34 16N | 133 45 E |
| Tadoule L | 153 | 58 36N | 98 20W |
| Tadoussac | 151 | 48 11N | 69 42W |
| Tadzhik S.S.R. □ | 85 | 35 30N | 70 0 E |
| Taechŏnni | 107 | 36 21N | 126 36 E |
| Taegu | 107 | 35 50N | 128 37 E |
| Taegwandong | 107 | 40 13N | 125 12 E |
| Taejŏn | 107 | 36 20N | 127 28 E |
| Taerhhanmaoming-anlienhoch'i | 106 | 41 50N | 110 27 E |
| Taerhting | 105 | 37 15N | 92 36 E |
| Taf, R. | 31 | 51 55N | 4 36W |
| Tafalla | 58 | 42 30N | 1 41W |
| Tafang | 108 | 27 10N | 105 39 E |
| Tafar | 123 | 6 52N | 28 15 E |
| Tafas | 90 | 32 44N | 36 5 E |
| Tafassasset, O. | 119 | 23 0N | 9 11 E |
| Tafelbaai | 128 | 33 35 S | 18 25 E |
| Tafelney, C. | 118 | 31 3N | 9 51W |
| Tafermaar | 103 | 6 47 S | 134 10 E |
| Tafí Viejo | 172 | 26 43 S | 65 17W |
| Tafiré | 120 | 9 4N | 5 10W |
| Tafnidilt | 118 | 28 47N | 10 58W |
| Tafraout | 118 | 29 50N | 8 58W |
| Taft, Phil. | 103 | 11 57N | 125 30 E |
| Taft, Ala., U.S.A. | 163 | 35 10N | 119 28W |
| Taft, Tex., U.S.A. | 159 | 27 58N | 97 23W |
| Taga Dzong | 98 | 27 5N | 90 0 E |
| Taganrog | 83 | 47 12N | 38 50 E |
| Taganrogskiy Zaliv | 82 | 47 0N | 38 30 E |
| Tagant | 120 | 18 20N | 11 0W |
| Tagap Ga | 98 | 26 56N | 96 13 E |
| Tagbilaran | 103 | 9 39N | 123 51 E |
| Tage | 135 | 6 19 S | 143 20 E |
| Tággia | 62 | 43 52N | 7 50 E |
| Taghmon | 39 | 52 19N | 6 40W |
| Taghrīfat | 119 | 29 5N | 17 26 E |
| Taghzout | 118 | 33 30N | 4 49W |
| Tagish | 152 | 60 19N | 134 16W |
| Tagish L. | 147 | 60 10N | 134 20W |
| Tagliacozzo | 63 | 42 4N | 13 13 E |
| Tagliamento, R. | 63 | 45 38N | 13 5 E |
| Tàglio di Po | 63 | 45 0N | 12 12 E |
| Tagomago, Isla de | 59 | 39 2N | 1 39 E |
| Tagua, La | 174 | 0 3N | 74 40W |
| Taguatinga | 171 | 12 26 S | 46 26W |
| Tagula | 135 | 11 22 S | 153 15 E |
| Tagula I. | 135 | 11 30 S | 153 30 E |
| Tagum (Hijo) | 103 | 7 33N | 125 53 E |
| Tagus = Tajo, R. | 55 | 39 44N | 5 50W |
| Tahahbala, I. | 102 | 0 30 S | 98 30 E |
| Tahakopa | 143 | 46 30 S | 169 23 E |
| Tahala | 118 | 34 0N | 4 28W |
| Tahan, Gunong | 101 | 4 45N | 102 25 E |
| Tahara | 111 | 34 40N | 137 16 E |
| Tahat Mt. | 119 | 23 18N | 5 21 E |
| Tāherī | 93 | 27 43N | 52 20 E |
| Tahiti, I. | 131 | 17 37 S | 149 27W |
| Tahoe | 160 | 39 12N | 120 9W |
| Tahoe, L. | 160 | 39 0N | 120 9W |
| Tahora | 142 | 39 2 S | 174 49 E |
| Tahoua | 121 | 14 57N | 5 16 E |
| Tahsien | 108 | 31 17N | 107 30 E |
| Tahsin | 108 | 22 48N | 107 23 E |
| Tahsinganling Shanmo | 105 | 49 0N | 122 0 E |
| Tahsingkou | 107 | 43 23N | 129 39 E |
| Tahsintien | 107 | 37 37N | 120 50 E |
| Tahsüeh Shan, mts. | 108 | 31 15N | 101 20 E |
| Tahta | 122 | 26 44N | 31 32 E |
| Tahulandang, I. | 103 | 2 27N | 125 23 E |
| Tahuna | 103 | 3 45N | 125 30 E |
| Tahung Shan, mts. | 109 | 31 30N | 112 50 E |
| Tai | 108 | 30 41N | 103 29 E |
| Taï | 120 | 5 55N | 7 30W |
| T'ai Hu | 105 | 31 10N | 120 0 E |
| Tai Shan | 109 | 30 17N | 122 10 E |
| T'aian | 107 | 36 12N | 117 7 E |
| T'aichiang | 108 | 26 40N | 108 19 E |
| T'aichou | 109 | 32 22N | 119 45 E |
| T'aichou Liehtao | 109 | 28 30N | 121 53 E |
| T'aichung | 105 | 24 9N | 120 37 E |
| T'aichunghsien | 109 | 24 15N | 120 35 E |
| Taieri, R. | 143 | 46 3 S | 170 12 E |
| Taiga Madema | 119 | 23 46N | 15 25 E |
| T'aihang Shan, mts. | 106 | 35 40N | 113 20 E |
| Taihape | 142 | 39 41 S | 175 48 E |
| T'aiho, Anhwei, China | 109 | 33 10N | 115 36 E |
| T'aiho, Kiangsi, China | 109 | 26 50N | 114 53 E |
| T'aihsien | 109 | 32 17N | 120 10 E |
| T'aihsing | 109 | 32 10N | 120 4 E |
| Taihu | 109 | 30 30N | 116 25 E |
| T'aik'ang | 106 | 34 4N | 114 52 E |
| Taikkyi | 98 | 17 20N | 96 0 E |
| T'aiku | 106 | 37 23N | 112 34 E |
| Tailem Bend | 140 | 35 12 S | 139 29 E |
| Tailfingen | 49 | 48 15N | 9 1 E |
| Taïma | 92 | 27 35N | 38 45 E |
| Taimyr = Taymyr | 77 | 75 0N | 100 0 E |
| Taimyr, Oz. | 77 | 74 20N | 102 0 E |
| Tain | 37 | 57 49N | 4 4W |
| T'ainan | 109 | 23 0N | 120 10 E |
| T'ainanhsien | 109 | 23 21N | 120 17 E |
| Tainaron, Akra | 69 | 36 22N | 22 27 E |
| Tainggya | 98 | 17 49N | 94 29 E |
| T'aining | 109 | 26 55N | 117 12 E |
| Taintignies | 47 | 50 33N | 3 22 E |
| Taiobeiras | 171 | 15 49 S | 42 14W |
| T'aipei | 109 | 25 2N | 121 30 E |
| T'aip'ing | 109 | 30 18N | 118 6 E |
| Taiping | 101 | 4 51N | 100 44 E |
| Taipu | 170 | 5 37 S | 35 36W |
| T'aip'ussuchi | 106 | 41 55N | 115 23 E |
| Taisha | 110 | 35 24N | 132 40 E |
| T'aishan | 109 | 22 17N | 112 43 E |
| Taishun | 109 | 27 33N | 119 43 E |
| Taita □ | 126 | 4 0 S | 38 30 E |
| Taita Hills | 126 | 3 25 S | 38 15 E |
| Taitao, Pen. de | 176 | 46 30 S | 75 0W |
| T'aitung | 105 | 22 43N | 121 4 E |
| Taivalkoski | 74 | 65 33N | 28 12 E |
| Taiwan (Formosa) ■ | 109 | 23 30N | 121 0 E |
| Taiwara | 93 | 33 30N | 64 24 E |
| Taïyetos Óros | 69 | 37 0N | 22 23 E |
| Taiyiba, Israel | 90 | 32 36N | 35 27 E |
| Taiyiba, Jordan | 90 | 31 55N | 35 17 E |
| T'aiyüan | 106 | 37 55N | 112 40 E |
| Ta'izz | 91 | 13 43N | 44 7 E |
| Tajapuru, Furo do | 170 | 1 50 S | 50 25W |
| Tajarhī | 119 | 24 15N | 14 46 E |
| Tajicaringa | 164 | 23 15N | 104 44W |
| Tajima | 112 | 35 19N | 135 8 E |
| Tajimi | 111 | 35 19N | 137 8 E |
| Tajimi Gifu | 55 | 35 25N | 137 5 E |
| Tajitos | 164 | 30 58N | 112 18W |
| Tajo, R. | 57 | 40 35N | 1 52W |
| Tajumulco, Volcán de | 165 | 15 20N | 91 50W |
| Tājūrā | 119 | 32 51N | 13 27 E |
| Tak | 100 | 16 52N | 99 8 E |
| Takachiho | 110 | 32 42N | 131 18 E |
| Takahashi | 110 | 34 51N | 133 39 E |
| Takaka | 143 | 40 51 S | 172 50 E |
| Takamatsu | 110 | 34 20N | 134 5 E |
| Takanabe | 110 | 32 8N | 131 30 E |
| Takaoka | 111 | 36 40N | 137 0 E |
| Takapau | 142 | 40 2 S | 176 21 E |
| Takapuna | 142 | 36 47 S | 174 47 E |
| Takasago | 110 | 34 45N | 134 48 E |
| Takasaki | 111 | 36 20N | 139 0 E |
| Takase | 110 | 34 7N | 133 48 E |
| Takatsuki | 111 | 34 51N | 135 37 E |
| Takaungu | 126 | 3 38 S | 39 52 E |
| Takawa | 110 | 33 47N | 130 51 E |
| Takayama | 111 | 36 18N | 137 11 E |
| Takayama-Bonchi | 111 | 36 0N | 137 18 E |
| Takefu | 111 | 35 50N | 136 10 E |
| Takehara | 110 | 34 21N | 132 55 E |
| Takeley | 29 | 51 52N | 0 16 E |
| Takeo, Camb. | 101 | 10 59N | 104 47 E |
| Takeo, Japan | 110 | 33 12N | 130 1 E |
| Tåkern | 73 | 58 22N | 14 45 E |
| Takestan | 92 | 36 0N | 49 50 E |
| Taketa | 110 | 32 58N | 131 24 E |
| Takh | 95 | 33 6N | 77 32 E |
| Takhman | 101 | 11 29N | 104 57 E |
| Taki | 135 | 6 29 S | 155 52 E |
| Takingeun | 102 | 4 45N | 96 50 E |
| Takla L. | 152 | 55 15N | 125 45W |
| Takla Landing | 152 | 55 30N | 125 50W |
| Takla Makan | 105 | 39 0N | 83 0 E |
| Takoradi | 120 | 4 58N | 1 55W |
| Taku, China | 107 | 38 59N | 117 41 E |
| Taku, Japan | 110 | 33 18N | 130 3 E |
| Taku, R. | 152 | 58 30N | 133 50W |
| Takuan | 108 | 27 44N | 103 53 E |
| Takum | 121 | 7 18N | 9 36 E |
| Takuma | 110 | 34 13N | 133 40 E |
| Takushan | 107 | 39 55N | 123 30 E |
| Tal-y-llyn | 31 | 52 40N | 3 44W |
| Tal-y-sarn | 31 | 53 3N | 4 12W |
| Tala, Uruguay | 173 | 34 21 S | 55 46W |
| Tala, U.S.S.R. | 77 | 72 40N | 113 30 E |
| Talach'in | 106 | 36 42N | 104 54 E |
| Talagante | 172 | 33 40 S | 70 50W |
| Talaint | 118 | 29 37N | 9 45W |
| Talak | 121 | 18 0N | 5 0 E |
| Talamanca, Cordillera de | 166 | 9 20N | 83 20W |
| Talara | 174 | 4 30 S | 81 10 E |
| Talas | 85 | 42 45N | 72 0 E |
| Talas, R. | 85 | 44 0N | 70 20 E |
| Talasea | 135 | 5 20 S | 150 2 E |
| Talasskiy, Khrebet | 85 | 42 15N | 72 0 E |
| Talata Mafara | 121 | 12 38N | 6 4 E |
| Talaud, Kepulauan | 103 | 4 30N | 127 10 E |
| Talavera de la Reina | 56 | 39 55N | 4 46W |
| Talawana | 136 | 22 51 S | 121 9 E |
| Talawgyi | 98 | 25 4N | 97 19 E |
| Talayan | 103 | 6 52N | 124 24 E |
| Talbot, C. | 136 | 13 48 S | 126 43 E |
| Talbragar, R. | 141 | 32 5 S | 149 15 E |
| Talca | 172 | 35 20 S | 71 46W |
| Talca □ | 172 | 35 20 S | 71 46W |
| Talcahuano | 172 | 36 40 S | 73 10W |
| Talcher | 96 | 20 55N | 85 3 E |
| Talcho | 121 | 14 35N | 3 22 E |
| Taldom | 81 | 56 45N | 37 29 E |
| Taldy Kurgan | 76 | 45 10N | 78 45 E |
| Taleqan □ | 93 | 36 40N | 69 30 E |
| Talesh, Kūlhā-Ye | 92 | 39 0N | 48 30 E |
| Talfit | 90 | 32 5N | 35 17 E |
| Talga, R. | 136 | 21 2 S | 119 51 E |
| Talgar | 85 | 43 19N | 77 15 E |
| Talgar, Pic | 85 | 43 5N | 77 20 E |
| Talgarth | 31 | 51 59N | 3 15W |
| Talguharai | 122 | 18 19N | 35 56 E |
| Talguppa | 93 | 14 10N | 74 45 E |
| Tali, Shensi, China | 106 | 34 48N | 109 48 E |
| Tali, Yunnan, China | 108 | 25 45N | 100 5 E |
| Tali Post | 123 | 5 55N | 30 44 E |
| Taliabu, I. | 103 | 1 45 S | 125 0 E |
| Taliang Shan | 108 | 28 0N | 103 0 E |
| Talibong, Ko | 101 | 7 15N | 99 23 E |
| Talihina | 159 | 34 45N | 95 1W |
| Talikoti | 96 | 16 29N | 76 17 E |
| Talimardzhan | 85 | 38 23N | 65 37 E |
| Taling Ho, R. | 107 | 40 54N | 121 38 E |
| Taling Sung | 101 | 15 5N | 99 11 E |
| Talitsa | 84 | 57 0N | 63 43 E |
| Taliwang | 102 | 8 50 S | 116 55 E |
| Talkeetna | 147 | 62 20N | 150 0W |
| Talkeetna Mts. | 147 | 62 20N | 149 0W |
| Tall 'Asūr | 90 | 31 59N | 35 17 E |
| Talla | 122 | 28 5N | 30 43 E |
| Talladale | 36 | 57 41N | 5 20W |
| Talladega | 157 | 33 28N | 86 2W |
| Tallahassee | 157 | 30 25N | 84 15W |
| Tallangatta | 141 | 36 15 S | 147 10 E |
| Tallarook | 141 | 37 5 S | 145 6 E |
| Tallåsen | 72 | 61 52N | 16 2 E |
| Tallawang | 141 | 32 12 S | 149 28 E |
| Tällberg | 72 | 60 51N | 15 2 E |
| Tallebung | 141 | 32 42 S | 146 34 E |
| Tallering Pk | 137 | 28 6 S | 115 37 E |
| Tallinn (Reval) | 80 | 59 29N | 24 58 E |
| Tallow | 39 | 52 6N | 8 0W |
| Tallowbridge | 39 | 52 6N | 8 1W |
| Tallulah | 159 | 32 25N | 91 12W |
| Talluza | 90 | 32 17N | 35 18 E |
| Talmage | 153 | 49 46N | 103 40W |
| Talmest | 118 | 31 48N | 9 21W |
| Talmont | 44 | 46 27N | 1 37W |
| Talnoye | 82 | 48 57N | 30 35 E |
| Taloda | 96 | 21 34N | 74 19 E |
| Talodi | 123 | 10 35N | 30 22 E |
| Talou Shan, mts. | 108 | 28 20N | 107 10 E |
| Talovaya | 81 | 51 13N | 40 38 E |
| Talpa de Allende | 164 | 20 23N | 104 51W |
| Talsarnau | 31 | 52 54N | 4 4W |
| Talsinnt | 118 | 32 33N | 3 27W |
| Taltal | 172 | 25 23 S | 70 40W |
| Taltson L. | 153 | 61 30N | 110 15W |
| Taltson R. | 152 | 61 24N | 112 46W |
| Talwood | 139 | 28 29 S | 149 29 E |
| Talyawalka Cr. | 140 | 32 28 S | 142 22 E |
| Talybont | 31 | 52 29N | 3 59W |
| Tam Chau | 101 | 10 48N | 105 12 E |
| Tam Ky | 100 | 15 34N | 108 29 E |
| Tam Quan | 100 | 14 35N | 109 3 E |
| Tama | 158 | 41 56N | 92 37W |
| Tama Abu, Pegunungan | 102 | 3 10N | 115 0 E |
| Tamala | 137 | 26 35 S | 113 40 E |
| Tamalameque | 174 | 8 52N | 73 49W |
| Tamale | 121 | 9 22N | 0 50W |
| Taman | 82 | 45 14N | 36 41 E |
| Tamana | 110 | 32 58N | 130 32 E |
| Tamanar | 118 | 31 1N | 9 46W |
| Tamano | 110 | 34 35N | 133 59 E |
| Tamanrasset | 119 | 22 56N | 5 30 E |
| Tamanrasset, O. | 118 | 22 0N | 2 0 E |
| Tamanthi | 98 | 25 19N | 95 17 E |
| Tamaqua | 162 | 40 46N | 75 58W |
| Tamar, R. | 30 | 50 33N | 4 15W |
| Támara | 174 | 5 50N | 72 10W |
| Tamarang | 141 | 31 27 S | 150 5 E |
| Tamarite de Litera | 58 | 41 52N | 0 25 E |
| Tamashima | 110 | 34 32N | 133 40 E |
| Tamási | 53 | 46 40N | 18 18 E |
| Tamaské | 121 | 14 55N | 5 55 E |
| Tamatave | 129 | 18 10 S | 49 25 E |
| Tamatave □ | 129 | 18 0 S | 49 0 E |
| Tamaulipas □ | 165 | 24 0N | 99 0W |
| Tamaulipas, Sierra de | 165 | 23 30N | 98 20W |
| Tamazula | 164 | 24 55N | 106 58W |
| Tamazunchale | 165 | 21 16N | 98 47W |
| Tambacounda | 120 | 13 55N | 13 45W |
| Tambai | 123 | 16 32N | 37 13 E |
| Tambelan, Kepulauan | 102 | 1 0N | 107 30 E |

Tambellup Taunton


| | | | |
|---|---|---|---|
| Tambellup | 137 | 34 4S | 117 37E |
| Tambo | 138 | 24 54S | 146 14E |
| Tambo de Mora | 174 | 13 30S | 76 20W |
| Tambohorano | 129 | 17 30S | 43 58E |
| Tambora, G. | 102 | 8 12S | 118 5E |
| Tamboritha, Mt. | 141 | 37 31S | 146 51E |
| Tambov | 81 | 52 45N | 41 20E |
| Tambre, R. | 56 | 42 55N | 8 30W |
| Tambuku, G. | 103 | 7 8S | 113 40E |
| Tamburâ | 123 | 5 40N | 27 25E |
| Tamchaket | 120 | 17 25N | 10 40W |
| Tamchok Khambab (Brahmaputra) | 99 | 29 25N | 88 0E |
| Tamdybulak | 85 | 41 46N | 64 36E |
| Tame | 174 | 6 28N | 71 44W |
| Tame, R. | 28 | 52 43N | 1 45W |
| Tamega, R. | 56 | 41 12N | 8 5W |
| Tamelelt | 119 | 26 30N | 6 14E |
| Tamenglong | 98 | 25 0N | 93 35E |
| Tamerfors | 75 | 61 30N | 23 50E |
| Tamerlanovka | 85 | 42 36N | 69 17E |
| Tamerton Foliot | 30 | 50 25N | 4 10W |
| Tamerza | 119 | 34 23N | 7 58E |
| Tamgak, Mts. | 121 | 19 12N | 8 35E |
| Tamiahua, Laguna de | 165 | 21 30N | 97 30W |
| Tamil Nadu □ | 97 | 11 0N | 77 0E |
| Tamines | 47 | 50 26N | 4 36E |
| Taming | 106 | 36 20N | 115 10E |
| Tamins | 51 | 46 50N | 9 24E |
| Tamluk | 95 | 22 18N | 87 58E |
| Tammisaari (Ekenäs) | 75 | 60 0N | 23 26E |
| Tammun' | 90 | 32 18N | 35 23E |
| Tamnaren | 72 | 60 10N | 17 25E |
| Tamou | 121 | 12 45N | 2 11E |
| Tampa | 157 | 27 57N | 82 30W |
| Tampa B. | 157 | 27 40N | 82 40W |
| Tampere | 75 | 61 30N | 23 50E |
| Tampico | 165 | 22 20N | 97 50W |
| Tampin | 101 | 2 28N | 102 13E |
| Tamri | 118 | 30 49N | 9 50W |
| Tamrida = Hadibu | 91 | 12 35N | 54 2E |
| Tamsagbulag | 105 | 47 14N | 117 21E |
| Tamsagout | 118 | 24 5N | 6 35W |
| Tamsalu | 80 | 59 11N | 26 8E |
| Tamsweg | 52 | 47 7N | 13 49E |
| Tamu | 99 | 24 13N | 94 12E |
| Tamuja, R. | 57 | 39 33N | 6 8W |
| Tamworth, Austral. | 141 | 31 0S | 150 58E |
| Tamworth, U.K. | 28 | 52 38N | 1 41W |
| Tamyang | 107 | 35 19N | 126 59E |
| Tan An | 101 | 10 32N | 106 25E |
| Tana | 74 | 70 7N | 28 5E |
| Tana Fd. | 74 | 70 35N | 28 30E |
| Tana, L. | 123 | 13 5N | 37 30E |
| Tana, R., Kenya | 126 | 0 50S | 39 45E |
| Tana, R., Norway | 48 | 69 50N | 26 0E |
| Tanabe | 111 | 33 44N | 135 22E |
| Tanabi | 171 | 20 37S | 49 37W |
| Tanacross | 147 | 63 40N | 143 30W |
| Tanafjorden | 74 | 70 45N | 28 25E |
| Tanagro, R. | 65 | 40 35N | 15 25E |
| Tanahdjampea, I. | 103 | 7 10S | 120 35E |
| Tanahgrogot | 102 | 1 55S | 116 15E |
| Tanahmasa, I. | 102 | 0 5S | 98 29E |
| Tanahmerah | 103 | 6 0S | 140 7E |
| Tanami | 136 | 19 59S | 129 43E |
| Tanami Des. | 136 | 18 50S | 132 0E |
| Tanana | 147 | 65 10N | 152 15W |
| Tanana, R. | 147 | 64 25N | 145 30W |
| Tananarive | 129 | 18 55S | 47 31E |
| Tananarive □ | 129 | 19 0S | 47 0E |
| Tananarive = Antananarivo | 125 | 18 55S | 47 31E |
| Tananger | 71 | 58 57N | 5 37E |
| Tanant | 118 | 31 54N | 6 56W |
| Tánaro, R. | 62 | 44 9N | 7 50E |
| Tanaunelia | 64 | 40 42N | 9 45E |
| Tanba-Sanchi | 111 | 35 7N | 135 48E |
| Tanbar | 97 | 25 55S | 142 0E |
| Tancarville | 42 | 49 29N | 0 28E |
| Tanchai | 108 | 25 58N | 107 49E |
| T'anch'eng | 107 | 34 38N | 118 21E |
| Tanda, U.P., India | 95 | 26 33N | 82 35E |
| Tanda, U.P., India | 95 | 28 57N | 78 56E |
| Tanda, Ivory C. | 120 | 7 48N | 3 10W |
| Tandag | 103 | 9 4N | 126 9E |
| Tandala | 127 | 9 25S | 34 15E |
| Tândărei | 70 | 44 39N | 27 40E |
| Tandil | 172 | 37 15S | 59 6W |
| Tandjungpandan | 102 | 2 43S | 107 38E |
| Tandlianwald | 94 | 31 3N | 73 9E |
| Tando Adam | 94 | 25 45N | 68 40E |
| Tandou L. | 140 | 32 40S | 142 5E |
| Tandragee | 38 | 54 22N | 6 23W |
| Tandsbyn | 72 | 63 0N | 14 45W |
| Tandur | 96 | 19 11N | 79 30E |
| Tane-ga-Shima | 112 | 30 35N | 130 59E |
| Taneatua | 142 | 38 4S | 177 1E |
| Tanen Range | 101 | 19 40N | 99 0E |
| Tanen Tong Dan, Burma | 99 | 16 30N | 98 30E |
| Tanen Tong Dan, Thai. | 100 | 19 43N | 98 30E |
| Taneytown | 162 | 39 40N | 77 10W |
| Tanezrouft | 118 | 23 9N | 0 11E |
| Tanfeng | 106 | 33 45N | 110 18E |
| Tang | 38 | 53 31N | 7 49W |
| Tang, Koh | 101 | 10 16N | 103 7E |
| Tang Krasang | 101 | 12 34N | 105 3E |
| Tang La | 99 | 32 59N | 92 17E |
| Tang Pass | 99 | 32 59N | 92 17E |
| Tanga | 99 | 5 5S | 39 2E |
| Tanga □ | 126 | 5 20S | 38 0E |
| Tanga Is. | 135 | 3 20S | 153 15E |

| | | | |
|---|---|---|---|
| Tangail | 98 | 24 15N | 89 55E |
| Tanganyika, L. | 126 | 6 40S | 30 0E |
| T'angch'i | 109 | 29 3N | 119 24E |
| Tanger | 118 | 35 50N | 5 49W |
| Tangerang | 103 | 6 12S | 106 39E |
| Tangerhütte | 48 | 52 26N | 11 50E |
| Tangermünde | 48 | 52 32N | 11 57E |
| T'angho | 109 | 32 10N | 112 20E |
| Tangier | 162 | 37 49N | 75 59W |
| Tangier = Tanger | 118 | 35 50N | 5 49W |
| Tangier I. | 162 | 37 50N | 76 0W |
| Tangier Sd. | 162 | 38 3N | 75 5W |
| Tangkak | 101 | 2 18N | 102 34E |
| T'angku | 107 | 39 4N | 117 45E |
| T'angkula Shanmo | 98 | 33 0N | 92 0E |
| Tanglha Shan | 99 | 33 0N | 90 0E |
| Tangorin P.O. | 138 | 21 47S | 144 12E |
| Tangra Tso | 99 | 31 25N | 85 30E |
| Tangshan | 106 | 34 25N | 116 24E |
| T'angshan | 107 | 39 40N | 118 10E |
| T'angt'ang | 108 | 26 29N | 104 12E |
| T'angt'ou | 107 | 35 21N | 118 32E |
| Tangt'u | 109 | 31 34N | 118 29E |
| Tanguiéta | 121 | 10 40N | 1 21E |
| Tangyang, Chekiang, China | 109 | 29 17N | 120 14E |
| Tangyang, Hupeh, China | 109 | 30 50N | 111 45E |
| Tangyen Ho, R. | 108 | 28 55N | 108 36E |
| Tanimbar, Kepulauan | 103 | 7 30S | 131 30E |
| Taning | 106 | 36 32N | 110 47E |
| Taniyama | 110 | 31 31N | 130 31E |
| Tanjay | 103 | 9 30N | 123 5E |
| Tanjore = Thanjavur | 97 | 10 48N | 79 12E |
| Tanjung | 102 | 2 10S | 115 25E |
| Tanjung Malim | 101 | 3 42N | 101 31E |
| Tanjungbalai | 102 | 2 55N | 99 44E |
| Tanjungbatu | 102 | 2 23N | 118 3E |
| Tanjungkarang | 102 | 5 20S | 105 10E |
| Tanjungpinang | 102 | 1 5N | 104 30E |
| Tanjungpriok | 103 | 6 8S | 106 55E |
| Tanjungredeb | 102 | 2 9N | 117 29E |
| Tanjungselor | 102 | 2 55N | 117 25E |
| Tank | 94 | 32 14N | 70 25E |
| Tankan Shan | 109 | 22 3N | 114 16E |
| Tanleng | 108 | 30 2N | 103 33E |
| Tanndalen | 72 | 62 33N | 12 18E |
| Tannin | 150 | 49 40N | 91 0W |
| Tannis B. | 73 | 57 40N | 10 15E |
| Tano, R. | 120 | 6 0N | 2 30W |
| Tanoumrout | 119 | 23 2N | 5 31E |
| Tanout | 121 | 14 50N | 8 55E |
| Tanquinho | 171 | 12 42S | 39 43W |
| Tanshui | 109 | 25 10N | 121 28E |
| Tanta | 122 | 30 45N | 30 57E |
| Tantan | 118 | 28 29N | 11 1W |
| Tantoyuca | 165 | 21 21N | 98 10W |
| Tantung | 107 | 40 10N | 124 23E |
| Tantura = Dor | 90 | 32 37N | 34 55E |
| Tanuku | 96 | 16 45N | 81 44E |
| Tanum | 73 | 58 42N | 11 20E |
| Tanunda | 140 | 34 30S | 139 0E |
| Tanur | 97 | 11 1N | 75 46E |
| Tanus | 44 | 44 8N | 2 19E |
| Tanworth | 28 | 52 20N | 1 50W |
| Tanzania ■ | 126 | 6 40S | 34 0E |
| Tanzawa-Sanchi | 111 | 35 27N | 139 0E |
| Tanzilla, R. | 152 | 58 8N | 130 43W |
| T'aoan | 107 | 45 20N | 122 50E |
| Taoch'eng | 108 | 29 3N | 100 10E |
| Taoerh Ho | 107 | 45 42N | 124 5E |
| Taofu | 108 | 31 0N | 101 9E |
| Taohsien | 109 | 25 37N | 111 24E |
| T'aohua Tao | 109 | 29 48N | 122 17E |
| T'aolo | 106 | 38 45N | 106 40E |
| Taormina | 65 | 37 52N | 15 16E |
| Taos | 161 | 36 28N | 105 35W |
| Taoudenni | 118 | 22 40N | 3 55W |
| Taoudrart, Adrar | 118 | 24 25N | 2 24E |
| Taounate | 118 | 34 32N | 4 41W |
| Taourirt, Alg. | 118 | 26 37N | 0 8E |
| Taourirt, Moroc. | 118 | 34 20N | 2 47W |
| Taouz | 118 | 31 2N | 4 0W |
| T'aoyüan, China | 109 | 28 54N | 111 29E |
| T'aoyüan, Taiwan | 109 | 25 0N | 121 4E |
| Tapa | 80 | 59 15N | 26 0E |
| Tapa Shan | 108 | 31 45N | 109 30E |
| Tapachula | 165 | 14 54N | 92 17W |
| Tapah | 101 | 4 12N | 101 15E |
| Tapajós, R. | 175 | 4 30S | 56 10W |
| Tapaktuan | 103 | 3 30N | 97 10E |
| Tapanui | 143 | 45 56S | 169 18E |
| Tapauá | 174 | 5 40S | 64 20W |
| Tapauá, R. | 174 | 6 0S | 65 40W |
| Tapeta | 120 | 6 36N | 8 52W |
| Taphan Hin | 100 | 16 13N | 100 16E |
| Tapia | 56 | 43 34N | 6 56W |
| Tapieh Shan, mts. | 109 | 31 20N | 115 30E |
| T'ap'ingchen | 106 | 33 42N | 111 44E |
| Tapini | 135 | 8 19S | 147 0E |
| Tápiószele | 53 | 47 45N | 19 55E |
| Tapiraí | 171 | 19 52S | 46 1W |
| Tapirapé, R. | 170 | 10 41S | 50 38W |
| Tapirapecó, Serra | 174 | 1 10N | 65 0W |
| Taplan | 140 | 34 33S | 140 52E |
| Tapolca | 53 | 46 53N | 17 29E |
| Tappahannock | 162 | 37 56N | 76 50W |
| Tapsing | 99 | 30 22N | 96 25E |
| Tapti, R. | 96 | 21 25N | 75 0E |
| Tapu | 109 | 24 31N | 116 41E |
| Tapuaenuku, Mt. | 143 | 41 55S | 173 50E |
| Tapul Group, Is. | 103 | 5 35N | 120 50E |
| Tapun | 98 | 18 22N | 95 27E |

| | | | |
|---|---|---|---|
| Taquara | 173 | 29 36N | 50 46W |
| Taquari, R. | 173 | 18 10S | 56 0W |
| Taquaritinga | 171 | 21 24S | 48 30W |
| Tara, Austral. | 139 | 27 17S | 150 31E |
| Tara, Japan | 110 | 33 2N | 130 11E |
| Tara, U.S.S.R. | 76 | 56 55N | 74 30E |
| Tara, Zambia | 127 | 16 58S | 26 45E |
| Tara-Dake | 110 | 32 58N | 130 6E |
| Tara, R. | 66 | 43 10N | 19 20E |
| Tarabagatay, Khrebet | 77 | 48 0N | 83 0E |
| Tarābulus, Leb. | 92 | 34 31N | 33 52E |
| Tarābulus, Libya | 119 | 32 49N | 13 7E |
| Taradale | 142 | 39 33S | 176 53E |
| Tarahouahout | 119 | 22 47N | 5 59E |
| Tarakan | 102 | 3 20N | 117 35E |
| Tarakit, Mt. | 126 | 2 2N | 35 10E |
| Taralga | 141 | 34 26S | 149 52E |
| Taramakau, R. | 143 | 42 34S | 171 8E |
| Tarana | 141 | 33 31S | 149 52E |
| Taranagar | 94 | 28 43N | 75 9E |
| Taranaki □ | 142 | 39 5S | 174 51E |
| Tarancón | 58 | 40 1N | 3 1W |
| Taranga | 94 | 23 56N | 72 43E |
| Taranga Hill | 94 | 24 0N | 72 40E |
| Taransay, I. | 36 | 57 54N | 7 0W |
| Taransay, Sd. of | 36 | 57 52N | 7 0W |
| Táranto | 65 | 40 30N | 17 11E |
| Táranto, G. di | 65 | 40 0N | 17 15E |
| Tarapacá | 174 | 2 56S | 69 46W |
| Tarapacá □ | 172 | 20 45S | 69 30W |
| Tarare | 45 | 45 54N | 4 26E |
| Tararua Range | 142 | 40 45S | 175 25E |
| Tarascon, Ariège, France | 44 | 42 50N | 1 37E |
| Tarascon, Bouches-du-Rhône, France | 45 | 43 48N | 4 39E |
| Tarashcha | 82 | 49 30N | 30 31E |
| Tarat, Bj. | 119 | 26 4N | 9 7E |
| Tarauacá | 174 | 8 6S | 70 48W |
| Tarauacá, R. | 174 | 7 30S | 70 30W |
| Taravo, R. | 45 | 41 48N | 8 52E |
| Tarawera | 142 | 39 2S | 176 36E |
| Tarawera L. | 142 | 38 13S | 176 27E |
| Tarawera Mt. | 142 | 38 14S | 176 32E |
| Tarazat, Massif de | 119 | 20 2N | 8 30E |
| Tarazona | 58 | 41 55N | 1 43W |
| Tarazona de la Mancha | 59 | 39 16N | 1 55W |
| Tarbat Ness | 37 | 57 52N | 3 48W |
| Tarbela Dam | 94 | 34 0N | 72 52E |
| Tarbert, Ireland | 39 | 52 34N | 9 22W |
| Tarbert, Strathclyde, U.K. | 34 | 55 55N | 5 25W |
| Tarbert, W. Isles, U.K. | 36 | 57 54N | 6 49W |
| Tarbert, L. E. | 36 | 57 50N | 6 45W |
| Tarbert, L. W., Strathclyde, U.K. | 34 | 55 58N | 5 30W |
| Tarbert, L. W., W. Isles, U.K. | 36 | 57 55N | 6 56W |
| Tarbes | 44 | 43 15N | 0 3E |
| Tarbet, Highland, U.K. | 36 | 56 58N | 5 38W |
| Tarbet, Strathclyde, U.K. | 34 | 56 13N | 4 44W |
| Tarbolton | 34 | 55 30N | 4 30W |
| Tarboro | 157 | 35 55N | 77 3W |
| Tarbrax | 138 | 21 7S | 142 26E |
| Tarbū | 119 | 26 0N | 15 5E |
| Tarcento | 63 | 46 12N | 13 12E |
| Tarcoola | 139 | 30 44S | 134 36E |
| Tarcoon | 139 | 30 15S | 146 35E |
| Tarcău, Munţii | 70 | 46 39N | 26 7E |
| Tardets-Sorholus | 44 | 43 17N | 0 52W |
| Taree | 141 | 31 50S | 152 30E |
| Tarentaise | 45 | 45 30N | 6 35E |
| Tarf Shaqq al Abd | 122 | 26 50N | 36 6E |
| Tarfa, Wadi el | 122 | 28 16N | 31 15E |
| Tarfaya | 116 | 27 55N | 12 55W |
| Targon | 44 | 44 44N | 0 16W |
| Targuist | 118 | 34 59N | 4 14W |
| Tarhbalt | 118 | 30 48N | 5 10W |
| Tarhit | 118 | 30 58N | 2 0W |
| Tarhūnah | 119 | 32 15N | 13 28E |
| Tari | 135 | 5 54S | 142 59E |
| Tarib, Wadi | 122 | 18 30N | 43 23E |
| Táriba | 174 | 7 49N | 72 13W |
| Tarifa | 57 | 36 1N | 5 36W |
| Tarija | 172 | 21 30S | 64 40W |
| Tarija □ | 172 | 21 30S | 63 30W |
| Tarim, R. | 105 | 41 5N | 86 40E |
| Tarime □ | 126 | 1 15S | 34 0E |
| Taringo Downs | 141 | 32 13S | 145 33E |
| Taritoe, R. | 103 | 3 0S | 138 5E |
| Tarka, R. | 128 | 32 10S | 26 0E |
| Tarkastad | 128 | 32 0S | 26 16E |
| Tarkhankut, Mys | 82 | 45 25N | 32 30E |
| Tarko Sale | 76 | 64 55N | 77 50E |
| Tarkwa | 120 | 5 20N | 2 0W |
| Tarlac | 103 | 15 29N | 120 35E |
| Tarland | 37 | 57 8N | 2 51W |
| Tarleton | 32 | 53 41N | 2 50W |
| Tarlsland | 152 | 57 03N | 111 40W |
| Tarlton Downs | 138 | 22 40S | 136 45E |
| Tarm | 73 | 55 56N | 8 31E |
| Tarma | 174 | 11 25S | 75 45W |
| Tarn □ | 44 | 43 49N | 2 8E |
| Tarn-et-Garonne □ | 44 | 44 8N | 1 20E |
| Tarn, R. | 44 | 44 5N | 1 2E |
| Tärna | 74 | 65 45N | 15 10E |
| Tarna, R. | 53 | 48 0N | 20 5E |
| Tårnby | 73 | 55 37N | 12 36E |
| Tarnobrzeg □ | 54 | 50 40N | 22 0E |
| Tarnów | 54 | 50 3N | 21 0E |
| Tarnów □ | 54 | 50 0N | 21 0E |
| Tarnowskie Góry | 54 | 50 27N | 18 54E |

| | | | |
|---|---|---|---|
| Táro, R. | 62 | 44 37N | 9 58E |
| Tarong | 139 | 26 47S | 151 51E |
| Taroom | 139 | 25 36S | 149 48E |
| Taroudannt | 118 | 30 30N | 8 52W |
| Tarp | 48 | 54 40N | 9 25E |
| Tarpon Springs | 157 | 28 8N | 82 42W |
| Tarporley | 32 | 53 10N | 2 42W |
| Tarquinia | 63 | 42 15N | 11 45E |
| Tarqumiyah | 90 | 31 35N | 35 1E |
| Tarragona | 58 | 41 5N | 1 17E |
| Tarragona □ | 58 | 41 0N | 1 0E |
| Tarrasa | 58 | 41 26N | 2 1E |
| Tárrega | 58 | 41 39N | 1 9E |
| Tarrytown | 162 | 41 5N | 73 52W |
| Tarshiha = Me'ona | 90 | 33 1N | 35 15E |
| Tarso Emissi | 119 | 21 27N | 18 36E |
| Tarso Ovrari | 119 | 21 27N | 17 27E |
| Tarsus | 92 | 36 58N | 34 55E |
| Tartagal | 172 | 22 30S | 63 50W |
| Tartan, oilfield | 19 | 58 22N | 0 5E |
| Tartas | 44 | 43 50N | 0 49W |
| Tartna Point | 140 | 32 54S | 142 24E |
| Tartu | 80 | 58 25N | 26 58E |
| Tartus | 92 | 34 55N | 35 55E |
| Tarumirim | 171 | 19 16S | 41 59W |
| Tarumizu | 110 | 31 29N | 130 42E |
| Tarussa | 81 | 54 44N | 37 10E |
| Tarutao, Ko | 101 | 6 33N | 99 40E |
| Tarutung | 102 | 2 0N | 99 0E |
| Tarves | 37 | 57 22N | 2 13W |
| Tarvisio | 63 | 46 31N | 13 35E |
| Tarz Ulli | 119 | 25 46N | 9 44E |
| Tas-Buget | 85 | 44 46N | 65 33E |
| Tasahku | 98 | 27 33N | 97 52E |
| Tasâwah | 119 | 26 0N | 13 37E |
| Taschereau | 150 | 48 40N | 78 40W |
| Taseko, R. | 152 | 52 4N | 123 9W |
| Tasgaon | 96 | 17 2N | 74 39E |
| Ta'shan | 123 | 16 31N | 42 33E |
| Tashauz | 76 | 42 0N | 59 20E |
| Tashet'ai | 106 | 41 0N | 109 21E |
| Tashi Chho Dzong | 98 | 27 31N | 89 45E |
| Tashihch'iao (Yingk'ou) | 107 | 40 38N | 122 30E |
| T'ashihk'uerhkan | 85 | 37 47N | 75 14E |
| Tashkent | 85 | 41 20N | 69 10E |
| Tashkumyr | 85 | 41 40N | 72 10E |
| Tashkurghan | 93 | 36 45N | 67 40E |
| Tashtagol | 76 | 52 47N | 87 53E |
| Tasikmalaya | 103 | 7 18S | 108 12E |
| Tasjön | 74 | 64 15N | 15 45E |
| Taşköpru | 82 | 41 30N | 34 15E |
| Tasman Bay | 143 | 40 59S | 173 25E |
| Tasman Glacier | 143 | 43 45S | 170 20E |
| Tasman, Mt. | 143 | 43 34S | 170 12E |
| Tasman Mts. | 143 | 41 3S | 172 25E |
| Tasman Pen. | 138 | 43 10S | 148 0E |
| Tasman, R. | 143 | 43 48S | 170 8E |
| Tasman Sea | 142 | 36 0S | 160 0E |
| Tasmania, I., □ | 138 | 49 0S | 146 30E |
| Tassil Tin-Rerhoh | 118 | 20 5N | 3 55E |
| Tassili n-Ajjer | 119 | 25 47N | 8 1E |
| Tassili-Oua-Ahaggar | 119 | 20 41N | 5 30E |
| Tasty | 85 | 44 47N | 69 7E |
| Tasu Sd. | 152 | 52 47N | 132 2W |
| Tata, Hung. | 53 | 47 37N | 18 19E |
| Tata, Moroc. | 118 | 29 46N | 7 50W |
| Tatabánya | 53 | 47 32N | 18 25E |
| Tatar A.S.S.R. □ | 84 | 55 30N | 51 30E |
| Tatarsk | 76 | 55 20N | 75 50E |
| Tatarskiy Proliv | 77 | 54 0N | 141 0E |
| Tatebayashi | 111 | 36 15N | 139 32E |
| Tateshina-Yama | 111 | 36 8N | 138 11E |
| Tateyama | 111 | 35 0N | 139 50E |
| Tathlina L. | 152 | 60 33N | 117 39W |
| Tathra | 141 | 36 44S | 149 59E |
| Tat'ien, Fukien, China | 109 | 25 42N | 117 50E |
| Tat'ien, Szechwan, China | 108 | 26 18N | 101 45E |
| Tatinnai L. | 153 | 60 55N | 97 40W |
| Tatlayoka Lake | 152 | 51 35N | 124 24W |
| Tatnam, C. | 153 | 57 16N | 91 0W |
| Tato Ho, R. | 108 | 31 25N | 100 42E |
| Tatra = Tatry | 54 | 49 20N | 20 0E |
| Tatry | 54 | 49 20N | 20 0E |
| Tatsu | 108 | 29 40N | 105 45E |
| Tatsuno | 110 | 34 52N | 134 33E |
| Tatta | 94 | 24 42N | 67 55E |
| Tattenhall | 32 | 53 7N | 2 47W |
| Tatu Ho, R. | 108 | 29 35N | 103 47E |
| Tatuī | 173 | 23 25S | 48 0W |
| Tatum | 159 | 33 16N | 103 16W |
| Tat'ung, Anhwei, China | 109 | 30 48N | 117 44E |
| Tat'ung, Shansi, China | 106 | 40 9N | 113 19E |
| Tatura | 141 | 36 29S | 145 16E |
| Tatvan | 92 | 37 28N | 42 27E |
| Tauá | 170 | 6 1S | 40 26W |
| Taubaté | 173 | 23 5S | 45 30W |
| Tauberbischofsheim | 49 | 49 37N | 9 40E |
| Taucha | 48 | 51 22N | 12 31E |
| Tauern, mts. | 52 | 47 15N | 12 40E |
| Tauern-tunnel | 52 | 47 0N | 13 12E |
| Taufikia | 123 | 9 24N | 31 37E |
| Taumarunui | 142 | 38 53S | 175 15E |
| Taumaturgo | 174 | 9 0S | 73 50W |
| Taung | 128 | 27 33S | 24 47E |
| Taungdwingyi | 98 | 20 1N | 95 40E |
| Taunggyi | 98 | 20 50N | 97 0E |
| Taungtha | 98 | 20 45N | 94 50E |
| Taungup | 98 | 18 51N | 94 14E |
| Taungup Pass | 98 | 18 40N | 94 45E |
| Taungup Taunggya | 99 | 18 20N | 93 40E |
| Taunsa Barrage | 95 | 31 0N | 71 0E |
| Taunton, U.K. | 28 | 51 1N | 3 7W |

**Taunton** **Tetbury**


| | | | |
|---|---|---|---|
| Taunton, U.S.A. | 162 | 41 54N | 71 6W |
| Taunus | 49 | 50 15N | 8 20E |
| Taupo | 142 | 38 41S | 176 7E |
| Taupo, L. | 142 | 38 46S | 175 55E |
| Tauq | 92 | 35 12N | 44 29E |
| Taurage | 80 | 55 14N | 22 28E |
| Tauramena | 174 | 5 1N | 72 45W |
| Tauranga | 142 | 37 35S | 176 11E |
| Tauranga Harb. | 142 | 37 30S | 176 5E |
| Taureau, Lac | 150 | 46 50N | 73 40W |
| Tauri, R. | 135 | 8 8S | 146 8E |
| Taurianova | 65 | 38 22N | 16 1E |
| Taurus Mts. = Toros Dağlari | 92 | 37 0N | 35 0E |
| Táuste | 58 | 41 58N | 1 18W |
| Tauz | 83 | 41 0N | 45 40E |
| Tavani | 153 | 62 10N | 93 30W |
| Tavannes | 50 | 47 13N | 7 12E |
| Tavas | 92 | 37 35N | 29 8E |
| Tavda | 84 | 58 7N | 65 8E |
| Tavda, R. | 84 | 59 30N | 63 0E |
| Taverny | 43 | 49 2N | 2 13E |
| Taveta | 124 | 3 31N | 37 37E |
| Taviche | 165 | 16 38N | 96 32W |
| Tavignano, R. | 45 | 42 7N | 9 33E |
| Tavira | 57 | 37 8N | 7 40W |
| Tavistock | 30 | 50 33N | 4 9W |
| Tavolara, I. | 64 | 40 55N | 9 40E |
| Távora, R. | 56 | 41 0N | 7 30W |
| Tavoy | 101 | 14 7N | 98 18E |
| Tavoy, I. = Mali Kyun | 99 | 13 0N | 98 20E |
| Taw, R. | 30 | 50 58N | 3 58W |
| Tawang | 99 | 27 37N | 91 50E |
| Tawas City | 156 | 44 16N | 83 31W |
| Tawau | 102 | 4 20N | 117 55E |
| Tawngche | 98 | 26 34N | 95 38E |
| Tawnyinah | 38 | 53 55N | 8 45W |
| Tāworgha' | 119 | 32 1N | 15 2E |
| Taxila | 94 | 33 42N | 72 52E |
| Tay Bridge | 35 | 56 28N | 3 0W |
| Tay, Firth of | 35 | 56 25N | 3 8W |
| Tay, L., Austral. | 137 | 32 55S | 120 48E |
| Tay, L., U.K. | 35 | 56 30N | 4 10W |
| Tay Ninh | 101 | 11 20N | 106 5E |
| Tay, R. | 35 | 56 37N | 3 38W |
| Tay Strath | 37 | 56 38N | 3 40W |
| Tayabamba | 174 | 8 15S | 77 10W |
| Tayao | 108 | 25 41N | 101 18E |
| Tayaparva La | 95 | 31 35N | 83 20E |
| Tayeh | 109 | 30 5N | 114 57E |
| Taylor, Can. | 152 | 56 13N | 120 40W |
| Taylor, Alaska, U.S.A. | 147 | 65 40N | 164 50W |
| Taylor, Pa., U.S.A. | 162 | 41 23N | 75 43W |
| Taylor, Tex., U.S.A. | 159 | 30 30N | 97 30W |
| Taylor, Mt. | 143 | 43 30S | 171 20E |
| Taylor Mt. | 161 | 35 16N | 107 50W |
| Taylorville | 158 | 39 32N | 89 20W |
| Taymyr, Oz. | 77 | 74 50N | 102 0E |
| Taymyr, P-ov. | 77 | 75 0N | 100 0E |
| Taynuilt | 34 | 56 25N | 5 15W |
| Tayport | 34 | 56 27N | 2 52W |
| Tayr Zebna | 90 | 33 14N | 35 23E |
| Tayshet | 77 | 55 58N | 97 25E |
| Tayside □ | 35 | 56 25N | 3 30W |
| Taytay | 103 | 10 45N | 119 30E |
| Tayu | 109 | 25 38N | 114 9E |
| Tayülo | 105 | 29 13N | 98 13E |
| Tayung | 109 | 29 8N | 110 30E |
| Taz, R. | 76 | 65 40N | 82 0E |
| Taza | 118 | 34 10N | 4 0W |
| Taze | 98 | 22 57N | 95 24E |
| Tazenakht | 118 | 30 46N | 7 3W |
| Tazin L. | 153 | 59 44N | 108 42W |
| Tazin, R. | 153 | 60 26N | 110 45W |
| Tazoult | 119 | 35 29N | 6 11E |
| Tazovskiy | 76 | 67 30N | 78 30E |
| Tbilisi (Tiflis) | 83 | 41 50N | 44 50E |
| Tchad (Chad) ■ | 117 | 12 30N | 17 15E |
| Tchad, Lac | 117 | 13 30N | 14 30E |
| Tchaourou | 121 | 8 58N | 2 40E |
| Tchentlo L. | 152 | 55 15N | 125 0W |
| Tchibanga | 124 | 2 45S | 11 12E |
| Tchin Tabaraden | 121 | 15 58N | 5 50E |
| Tczew | 54 | 54 8N | 18 50E |
| Te Anau L. | 143 | 45 15S | 167 45E |
| Te Araroa | 142 | 37 39S | 178 25E |
| Te Aroha | 142 | 37 32S | 175 44E |
| Te Awamutu | 142 | 38 1S | 175 20E |
| Te Horo | 142 | 40 48S | 175 6E |
| Te Kaha | 142 | 37 44S | 177 44E |
| Te Karaka | 142 | 38 26S | 177 53E |
| Te Kauwhata | 142 | 37 25S | 175 9E |
| Te Kinga | 143 | 42 35S | 171 31E |
| Te Kopuru | 142 | 36 2S | 173 56E |
| Te Kuiti | 142 | 38 20S | 175 11E |
| Te Puke | 142 | 37 46S | 176 22E |
| Te Waewae B. | 143 | 46 13S | 167 33E |
| Tea Tree | 136 | 22 11S | 133 17E |
| Teaca | 70 | 46 55N | 24 30E |
| Teague | 159 | 31 40N | 96 20W |
| Tean | 109 | 29 21N | 115 42E |
| Teangue | 36 | 57 7N | 5 52W |
| Teano | 65 | 41 15N | 14 1E |
| Teapa | 165 | 17 35N | 92 56W |
| Teba | 57 | 36 59N | 4 55W |
| Tebay | 32 | 54 25N | 2 35W |
| Teberda | 83 | 43 30N | 43 54E |
| Tébessa | 119 | 35 22N | 8 8E |
| Tebicuary, R. | 172 | 26 36S | 58 16W |
| Tebing Tinggi | 102 | 3 38S | 102 1E |
| Tébourba | 119 | 36 49N | 9 51E |
| Téboursouk | 119 | 36 29N | 9 10E |
| Tebulos | 83 | 42 36N | 45 25E |
| Tecapa | 163 | 35 51N | 116 14W |
| Tecate | 164 | 32 34N | 116 38W |
| Techa, R. | 84 | 56 13N | 62 58E |
| Tech'ang | 108 | 27 22N | 102 10E |
| Techiang | 108 | 28 19N | 108 5E |
| Techiman | 120 | 7 35N | 1 58W |
| Tech'in | 108 | 28 30N | 98 52E |
| Tech'ing | 109 | 23 8N | 111 46E |
| Techirghiol | 70 | 44 4N | 28 32E |
| Techou | 106 | 37 19N | 116 19E |
| Tecomán | 164 | 18 55N | 103 53W |
| Tecoripa | 164 | 28 37N | 109 57W |
| Tecuci | 70 | 45 51N | 27 27E |
| Tecumseh | 156 | 42 1N | 83 59W |
| Tedavnet | 38 | 54 19N | 7 2W |
| Tedesa | 123 | 5 10N | 37 40E |
| Tedzhen | 76 | 37 23N | 60 31E |
| Tees B. | 72 | 54 37N | 1 10W |
| Tees, R. | 33 | 54 36N | 1 25W |
| Teesdale | 32 | 54 37N | 2 10W |
| Teesside | 33 | 54 37N | 1 13W |
| Tefé | 174 | 3 25S | 64 50W |
| Tegal | 103 | 6 52S | 109 8E |
| Tegelen | 47 | 51 20N | 6 9E |
| Teggiano | 65 | 40 24N | 15 32E |
| Teghra | 95 | 25 30N | 85 34E |
| Tegid, L. | 31 | 52 53N | 3 38W |
| Tegina | 121 | 10 5N | 6 11E |
| Tegucigalpa | 166 | 14 10N | 87 0W |
| Tehachapi | 163 | 35 11N | 118 29W |
| Tehachapi Mts. | 163 | 35 0N | 118 40W |
| Tehamiyam | 122 | 18 26N | 36 45E |
| Tehilla | 122 | 17 42N | 36 6E |
| Téhini | 120 | 9 39N | 3 32W |
| Tehrān | 93 | 35 44N | 51 30E |
| Tehrān □ | 93 | 35 0N | 49 30E |
| Tehsing | 109 | 28 54N | 117 34E |
| Tehua | 109 | 25 30N | 118 14E |
| Tehuacán | 165 | 18 20N | 97 30W |
| Tehuantepec | 165 | 16 10N | 95 19W |
| Tehuantepec, Golfo de | 165 | 15 50N | 95 0W |
| Tehuantepec, Istmo de | 165 | 17 0N | 94 30W |
| Tehui | 107 | 44 32N | 125 42E |
| Teich, Le | 44 | 44 38N | 0 59W |
| Teifi, R. | 31 | 52 4N | 4 14W |
| Teign, R. | 30 | 50 41N | 3 42W |
| Teignmouth | 30 | 50 33N | 3 30W |
| Teikovo | 81 | 56 55N | 40 30E |
| Teil, Le | 45 | 44 33N | 4 40E |
| Teilleul, Le | 42 | 48 32N | 0 53W |
| Teishyai | 80 | 55 59N | 22 14E |
| Teiuş | 70 | 46 12N | 23 40E |
| Teixeira | 170 | 7 13S | 37 15W |
| Teixeira de Sousa = Luau | 124 | 10 40S | 22 10E |
| Teixeira Pinto | 120 | 12 10N | 13 55E |
| Tejo, R. | 57 | 39 15N | 8 35W |
| Tejon Pass | 163 | 34 49N | 118 53W |
| Tejung | 108 | 28 46N | 99 19E |
| Tekamah | 158 | 41 48N | 96 14W |
| Tekapo, L. | 143 | 43 53S | 170 33E |
| Tekax | 165 | 20 20N | 89 30W |
| Tekeli | 85 | 44 50N | 79 0E |
| Tekeze, W. | 123 | 13 50N | 37 50E |
| Tekija | 66 | 44 42N | 22 26E |
| Tekirdağ | 92 | 40 58N | 27 30E |
| Tekkali | 96 | 18 43N | 84 24E |
| Teko | 108 | 31 49N | 98 40E |
| Tekoa | 160 | 47 19N | 117 4W |
| Tekoulât, O. | 118 | 22 30N | 2 20E |
| Tel Adashim | 90 | 32 39N | 35 17E |
| Tel Aviv-Yafo | 90 | 32 4N | 34 48E |
| Tel Hanan | 90 | 32 47N | 35 3E |
| Tel Hazor | 90 | 33 2N | 35 2E |
| Tel Lakhish | 90 | 31 34N | 34 51E |
| Tel Malhata | 90 | 31 13N | 35 2E |
| Tel Megiddo | 90 | 32 35N | 38 11E |
| Tel Mond | 90 | 32 15N | 34 56E |
| Tela | 166 | 15 40N | 87 28W |
| Télagh | 118 | 34 51N | 0 32W |
| Telanaipura = Jambi | 102 | 1 38S | 103 30E |
| Telavi | 83 | 42 0N | 45 30E |
| Telciu | 70 | 47 25N | 24 24E |
| Telefomin | 135 | 5 10S | 141 40E |
| Telega = Doftana | 70 | 45 17N | 25 45E |
| Telegraph Cr. | 152 | 58 0N | 131 10W |
| Telekhany | 80 | 52 30N | 25 46E |
| Telemark fylke □ | 71 | 59 25N | 8 30E |
| Telén | 172 | 36 15S | 65 31W |
| Teleneshty | 70 | 47 35N | 28 24E |
| Teleño | 56 | 42 23N | 6 22W |
| Teleorman □ | 70 | 44 0N | 25 0E |
| Teleorman, R. | 70 | 44 15N | 25 20E |
| Teles Pires (São Manuel), R. | 174 | 8 40S | 57 0W |
| Telescope Peak, Mt. | 163 | 36 6N | 117 7W |
| Teletaye | 121 | 16 31N | 1 30E |
| Telford | 28 | 52 42N | 2 31W |
| Telfs | 52 | 47 19N | 11 4E |
| Telgte | 48 | 51 59N | 7 46E |
| Telichie | 139 | 31 45S | 139 59E |
| Télimélé | 120 | 10 54N | 13 2W |
| Telkwa | 152 | 54 41N | 126 56W |
| Tell | 90 | 32 12N | 35 12E |
| Tell City | 156 | 38 0N | 86 44W |
| Teller | 147 | 65 12N | 166 24W |
| Tellicherry | 97 | 11 45N | 75 30E |
| Tellin | 47 | 50 5N | 5 13E |
| Telluride | 161 | 37 58N | 107 54W |
| Telok Anson | 101 | 4 3N | 101 0E |
| Teloloapán | 165 | 18 21N | 99 51W |
| Telom, R. | 101 | 4 20N | 101 46E |
| Telpos Iz. | 78 | 63 35N | 57 30E |
| Telsen | 176 | 42 30S | 66 50W |
| Teltow | 48 | 52 24N | 13 15E |
| Telukbetung | 102 | 5 29S | 105 17E |
| Telukbutun | 101 | 4 5N | 108 7E |
| Telukdalem | 102 | 0 45N | 97 50E |
| Tema | 121 | 5 41N | 0 0E |
| Temagami L. | 150 | 47 0N | 80 10W |
| Temanggung | 103 | 7 18S | 110 10E |
| Temapache | 165 | 21 4N | 97 38W |
| Temax | 165 | 21 10N | 88 50W |
| Tembe | 126 | 0 30S | 28 25E |
| Tembeling, R. | 101 | 4 20N | 102 23E |
| Tembleque | 58 | 39 41N | 3 30W |
| Temblor Ra, mts. | 163 | 35 30N | 120 0W |
| Tembuland □ | 129 | 31 35S | 28 0E |
| Teme, R. | 28 | 52 23N | 2 15W |
| Temecula | 163 | 33 26N | 117 6W |
| Temelelt | 118 | 31 50N | 7 32W |
| Temerloh | 101 | 3 27N | 102 25E |
| Temir Tau | 76 | 53 10N | 87 20E |
| Temirtau | 76 | 50 5N | 72 56E |
| Témiscaming | 150 | 46 44N | 79 5W |
| Temma | 138 | 41 12S | 144 42E |
| Temnikov | 81 | 54 40N | 43 11E |
| Temo, R. | 64 | 40 20N | 8 30E |
| Temora | 141 | 34 30S | 147 30E |
| Temosachic | 164 | 28 58N | 107 50W |
| Tempe, S. Afr. | 161 | 29 1S | 26 13E |
| Tempe, U.S.A. | 161 | 33 26N | 111 59W |
| Tempe Downs | 136 | 24 22S | 132 24E |
| Temperanceville | 162 | 37 54N | 75 33W |
| Tempestad | 174 | 1 20S | 74 56W |
| Tempino | 102 | 1 55S | 103 23E |
| Témpio Pausania | 64 | 40 53N | 9 6E |
| Temple | 159 | 31 5N | 97 28W |
| Temple B. | 138 | 12 15S | 143 3E |
| Temple Combe | 28 | 51 0N | 2 25W |
| Temple Ewell | 29 | 51 9N | 1 16W |
| Temple Sowerby | 30 | 54 38N | 2 33W |
| Templemore | 39 | 52 48N | 7 50W |
| Templenoe | 39 | 51 52N | 9 40W |
| Templeton, Austral. | 138 | 18 30S | 142 30E |
| Templeton, U.K. | 31 | 51 46N | 4 45W |
| Templeton, U.S.A. | 163 | 35 33N | 120 42W |
| Templeton, R. | 138 | 21 0S | 138 40E |
| Templeuve | 47 | 50 39N | 3 17E |
| Templin | 48 | 53 8N | 13 31E |
| Tempo | 38 | 54 23N | 7 28W |
| Tempoal | 165 | 21 31N | 98 23W |
| Temryuk | 82 | 45 15N | 37 11E |
| Temse | 47 | 51 7N | 4 13E |
| Temska, R. | 66 | 43 17N | 22 33E |
| Temuco | 176 | 38 50S | 72 50W |
| Temuka | 143 | 44 14S | 171 17E |
| Ten Boer | 46 | 53 16N | 6 42E |
| Tena | 174 | 0 59S | 77 49W |
| Tenabo | 165 | 20 2N | 90 12W |
| Tenaha | 159 | 31 57N | 94 15W |
| Tenali | 96 | 16 15N | 80 35E |
| Tenancingo | 165 | 19 0N | 99 33W |
| Tenango | 165 | 19 0N | 99 40W |
| Tenasserim | 100 | 12 6N | 99 3E |
| Tenasserim □ | 100 | 14 0N | 98 30E |
| Tenay | 45 | 45 55N | 5 30E |
| Tenbury | 28 | 52 18N | 2 35W |
| Tenby | 31 | 51 40N | 4 42W |
| Tenda | 45 | 44 5N | 7 34E |
| Tenda, Col de | 45 | 44 9N | 7 32E |
| Tendaho | 123 | 11 39N | 40 54E |
| Tende | 45 | 44 5N | 7 35E |
| Tendelti | 123 | 13 1N | 31 55E |
| Tendjedi, Adrar | 119 | 23 41N | 7 32E |
| Tendrara | 118 | 33 3N | 1 58W |
| Tendre, Mt. | 50 | 46 35N | 6 18E |
| Teneida | 122 | 25 30N | 29 19E |
| Ténéré | 119 | 23 2N | 16 0E |
| Tenerife, I. | 116 | 28 20N | 16 40W |
| Ténès | 118 | 36 31N | 1 14E |
| T'eng Ch'ung | 99 | 25 9N | 98 22E |
| Teng, R. | 101 | 20 30N | 98 10E |
| Tengah □ | 103 | 2 0S | 122 0E |
| Tengah Kepulauan | 102 | 7 5S | 118 15E |
| Tengchow = P'englai | 107 | 37 49N | 120 47E |
| Tengch'uan | 108 | 26 0N | 100 4E |
| Tengch'ung | 108 | 25 2N | 98 28E |
| Tengfeng | 106 | 34 27N | 113 2E |
| Tenggara □ | 103 | 3 0S | 122 0E |
| Tenggol, P. | 101 | 4 48N | 103 41E |
| T'enghsien, Honan, China | 109 | 32 41N | 112 5E |
| T'enghsien, Kwangsi Chuang, China | 109 | 23 23N | 110 54E |
| T'enghsien, Shantung, China | 105 | 35 8N | 117 9E |
| Tengiz, Ozero | 76 | 50 30N | 69 0E |
| Tengko | 99 | 32 30N | 98 0E |
| Tengk'o | 108 | 32 32N | 97 35E |
| Tengk'ou | 106 | 40 18N | 106 59E |
| Tenigerbad | 51 | 46 42N | 8 57E |
| Tenille | 157 | 32 58N | 82 50W |
| Tenindewa | 137 | 28 30S | 115 20E |
| Tenkasi | 97 | 8 55N | 77 20E |
| Tenke, Congo | 127 | 11 22S | 26 40E |
| Tenke, Zaïre | 127 | 10 32S | 26 7E |
| Tenkodogo | 121 | 12 0N | 0 10W |
| Tenna, R. | 63 | 43 12N | 13 43E |
| Tennant Creek | 136 | 19 30S | 134 0E |
| 'Tenneco', oilfield | 19 | 54 6N | 4 42E |
| Tennessee □ | 155 | 36 0N | 86 30W |
| Tenneville | 47 | 50 6N | 5 32E |
| Tennsift, Oued | 118 | 32 3N | 9 28W |
| Tenom | 102 | 5 4N | 115 38E |
| Tenosique | 165 | 17 30N | 91 24W |
| Tenri | 111 | 34 46N | 135 55E |
| Tenryū | 111 | 34 52N | 137 55E |
| Tent L. | 153 | 62 25N | 107 54W |
| Tenterden | 29 | 51 4N | 0 42E |
| Tenterfield | 139 | 29 0S | 152 0E |
| Teófilo Otôni | 171 | 17 50S | 41 30W |
| Tepa | 120 | 6 57N | 2 30W |
| Tepalcatepec, R. | 164 | 18 35N | 101 59W |
| Tepao | 108 | 23 21N | 106 33E |
| Tepehuanes | 164 | 25 21N | 105 44W |
| Tepetongo | 164 | 22 28N | 103 9W |
| Tepic | 164 | 21 30N | 104 54W |
| Tepi'ng | 107 | 37 28N | 116 67E |
| Teploklyuchenka | 85 | 42 30N | 78 30E |
| Tepoca, C. | 164 | 29 20N | 112 25W |
| Tequila | 164 | 20 54N | 103 47W |
| Ter Apel | 46 | 52 53N | 7 5E |
| Ter, R. | 58 | 42 0N | 2 30E |
| Téra | 121 | 14 0N | 0 57E |
| Tera, R. | 56 | 41 54N | 5 44W |
| Téramo | 63 | 42 40N | 13 40E |
| Terang | 140 | 38 15S | 142 55E |
| Terawhiti, C. | 142 | 41 16S | 174 38E |
| Terborg | 46 | 51 56N | 6 22E |
| Tercan | 92 | 39 50N | 40 30E |
| Terceira | 16 | 38 43N | 27 13W |
| Tercero, R. | 172 | 32 58S | 61 47W |
| Terdal | 96 | 16 33N | 75 9E |
| Terebovlya | 80 | 49 18N | 25 44E |
| Teregova | 70 | 45 10N | 22 16E |
| Terek-Say | 85 | 41 30N | 71 11E |
| Terembone Cr. | 139 | 30 25S | 148 50E |
| Terengganu □ | 101 | 4 55N | 103 0E |
| Tereshka, R. | 81 | 52 0N | 46 36E |
| Teresina | 170 | 5 2S | 42 45W |
| Terewah L. | 139 | 29 52S | 147 35E |
| Terezinha | 174 | 0 44N | 69 27W |
| Terges, R. | 57 | 37 49N | 7 41W |
| Tergnier | 43 | 49 40N | 3 17E |
| Terhazza | 118 | 23 45N | 4 59W |
| Terheijden | 47 | 51 38N | 4 45E |
| Teriang | 101 | 3 15N | 102 26E |
| Terkezi | 117 | 18 27N | 21 40E |
| Terlizzi | 65 | 41 8N | 16 32E |
| Termas de Chillan | 172 | 36 50S | 71 31W |
| Terme | 82 | 41 11N | 37 0E |
| Termez | 85 | 37 0N | 67 15E |
| Términi Imerese | 43 | 37 59N | 13 51E |
| Términos, Laguna de | 165 | 18 35N | 91 30W |
| Termoli | 63 | 42 0N | 15 0E |
| Termon | 38 | 55 3N | 7 50W |
| Termonfeckin | 38 | 53 47N | 6 15W |
| Tern, oilfield | 19 | 61 17N | 0 55E |
| Ternate | 103 | 0 45N | 127 25E |
| Terneuzen | 47 | 51 20N | 3 50E |
| Terney | 77 | 45 3N | 136 37E |
| Terni | 63 | 42 34N | 12 38E |
| Ternitz | 52 | 47 43N | 16 2E |
| Ternopol | 80 | 49 30N | 25 40E |
| Terowie, N.S.W., Austral. | 139 | 32 27S | 147 52E |
| Terowie, Vic., Austral. | 140 | 33 10S | 138 50E |
| Terra Bella | 163 | 35 58N | 119 3W |
| Terra Nova B. | 13 | 74 50S | 164 40E |
| Terrace | 152 | 54 30N | 128 35W |
| Terrace Bay | 150 | 48 47N | 87 10W |
| Terracina | 64 | 41 17N | 13 12E |
| Terralba | 64 | 39 42N | 8 38E |
| Terranuova | 63 | 43 38N | 11 35E |
| Terrasini Favarotta | 64 | 38 10N | 13 4E |
| Terrasson | 44 | 45 7N | 1 19E |
| Terrebonne B. | 159 | 29 15N | 90 28W |
| Terrecht | 118 | 20 10N | 0 10W |
| Terrell | 159 | 32 44N | 96 19W |
| Terrenceville | 151 | 47 40N | 54 44W |
| Terrick Terrick | 138 | 24 44S | 145 5E |
| Terry | 158 | 46 47N | 105 20W |
| Terryglass | 39 | 53 3N | 8 14W |
| Terryville | 162 | 41 41N | 73 1W |
| Terschelling, I. | 46 | 53 25N | 5 20E |
| Terskey Alatau, Khrebet | 85 | 41 50N | 77 0E |
| Terter, R. | 83 | 40 5N | 46 15E |
| Teruel | 58 | 40 22N | 1 8W |
| Teruel □ | 58 | 40 48N | 1 0W |
| Tervel | 67 | 43 45N | 27 28E |
| Tervola | 74 | 66 6N | 24 49E |
| Teryaweyna L. | 140 | 32 18S | 143 22E |
| Tešanj | 66 | 44 38N | 17 59E |
| Teseney | 123 | 15 5N | 36 42E |
| Tesha, R. | 81 | 55 32N | 43 0E |
| Teshio | 112 | 44 53N | 141 44E |
| Teshio-Gawa, R. | 112 | 44 53N | 141 45E |
| Tešica | 66 | 43 27N | 21 45E |
| Tesiyn Gol, R. | 105 | 50 28N | 93 4E |
| Teslin | 147 | 60 10N | 132 43W |
| Teslin L. | 152 | 60 15N | 132 57W |
| Teslin, R. | 152 | 61 34N | 134 35W |
| Teslió | 66 | 44 37N | 17 54E |
| Teso □ = Eastern □ | 126 | 1 50N | 33 45E |
| Tessalit | 121 | 20 12N | 1 0E |
| Tessaoua | 121 | 13 47N | 7 56E |
| Tessenderlo | 47 | 51 4N | 5 5E |
| Tessier | 153 | 51 48N | 107 26W |
| Tessin | 48 | 54 2N | 12 28E |
| Tessit | 121 | 15 13N | 0 18E |
| Test, R. | 28 | 51 7N | 1 30W |
| Testa del Gargano | 65 | 41 50N | 16 10E |
| Teste, La | 44 | 44 37N | 1 8W |
| Tét | 53 | 47 30N | 17 33E |
| Tetachuck L. | 152 | 53 18N | 125 55W |
| Tetas, Pta. | 172 | 23 31S | 70 38W |
| Tetbury | 28 | 51 37N | 2 9W |

Tete Tijibadok


Tete 127 16 13 S 33 33 E
Tete □ 127 15 15 S 32 40 E
Teterev, R. 80 50 30N 29 30 E
Teteringen 47 51 37N 4 49 E
Teterow 48 53 45N 12 34 E
Teteven 67 42 58N 24 17 E
Tethull, R. 152 60 35N 112 12W
Tetiyev 82 49 22N 29 38 E
Tetlin 147 63 14N 142 50W
Tetlin Junction 147 63 29N 142 55W
Tetney 33 53 30N 0 1W
Teton, R. 160 47 58N 111 0W
Tétouan 118 35 35N 5 21W
Tetovo 66 42 1N 21 2 E
Tettenhall 28 52 35N 2 7W
Tetuán = Tétouan 118 35 30N 5 25W
Tetyukhe 77 44 45N 135 40 E
Teuco, R. 172 25 30 S 60 25W
Teufen 51 47 24N 9 23 E
Teulada 64 38 59N 8 47 E
Teulon 153 50 23N 97 16W
Tevere, R. 63 42 30N 12 20 E
Teviot, R. 35 55 21N 2 51W
Teviotdale 35 55 25N 2 50W
Teviothead 35 55 19N 2 55W
Tewantin 139 26 27 S 153 3 E
Tewkesbury 28 51 59N 2 8W
Texada I. 152 49 40N 124 25W
Texarkana, Ark., U.S.A. 159 33 25N 94 0W
Texarkana, Tex., U.S.A. 159 33 25N 94 3W
Texas 139 28 49 S 151 15 E
Texas □ 159 31 40N 98 30W
Texas City 159 27 20N 95 20W
Texel, I. 46 53 5N 4 50 E
Texhoma 159 36 32N 101 47W
Texline 159 36 26N 103 0W
Texoma L. 159 34 0N 96 38W
Teyang 108 31 8N 104 24 E
Teykovo 81 56 55N 40 30 E
Teynham 29 51 19N 0 50 E
Teyr Zebna 90 33 14N 35 23 E
Teza, R. 81 56 41N 41 45 E
Tezin 94 34 24N 69 30 E
Teziutlán 165 19 50N 97 30W
Tezpur 98 26 40N 92 45 E
Tezzeron L. 152 54 43N 124 30W
Tha-anne, R. 153 60 31N 94 37W
Tha Deua, Laos 100 17 57N 102 38 E
Tha Deua, Laos 100 19 26N 101 50 E
Tha Nun 101 8 12N 98 17 E
Tha Pia 100 17 48N 100 32 E
Tha Rua 100 14 34N 100 44 E
Tha Sala 101 8 40N 99 56 E
Tha Song Yang 101 17 34N 97 55 E
Thaba Putsoa, mt. 129 29 45 S 28 0 E
Thabana Ntlenyana, Mt. 129 29 30 S 29 9 E
Thabazimbi 129 24 40 S 26 4 E
Thabeikkyin 98 22 53N 95 59 E
Thai Binh 100 20 27N 106 20 E
Thai Muang 101 8 24N 98 16 E
Thai Nguyen 100 21 35N 105 46 E
Thailand (Siam) ■ 100 16 0N 102 0 E
Thakhek 100 17 25N 104 45 E
Thakurgaon 98 26 2N 88 28 E
Thal 94 33 28N 70 33 E
Thal Desert 93 31 0N 71 30 E
Thala 119 35 35N 8 40 E
Thala La 99 28 25N 97 23 E
Thalabarivat 100 13 33N 105 57 E
Thalkirch 51 46 39N 9 17 E
Thallon 139 28 30 S 148 57 E
Thalwil 51 47 17N 8 35 E
Thame 29 51 44N 0 58W
Thame, R. 29 51 52N 0 47W
Thames 142 37 7 S 175 34 E
Thames, Firth of 142 37 0 S 175 25 E
Thames, R., Can. 150 42 20N 82 25W
Thames, R., N.Z. 142 37 32 S 175 45 E
Thames, R., U.K. 28 51 30N 0 35 E
Thames, R., U.S.A. 162 41 18N 72 9W
Thâmit, W. 119 30 51N 16 14 E
Than Uyen 100 22 0N 103 54 E
Thana 96 19 12N 72 59 E
Thanbyuzayat 98 15 58N 97 44 E
Thanesar 94 30 1N 76 52 E
Thanet, I. of 29 51 21N 1 20 E
Thang Binh 101 15 50N 108 20 E
Thangoo P.O. 136 18 10 S 122 22 E
Thangool 138 24 29 S 150 35 E
Thanh Hoa 100 19 48N 105 46 E
Thanh Hung 101 9 55N 105 43 E
Thanh Thuy 100 22 55N 104 51 E
Thanjavur (Tanjore) 97 10 48N 79 12 E
Thanlwin myit, R. 99 20 0N 98 0 E
Thann 43 47 48N 7 5 E
Thaon 43 48 15N 6 25 E
Thap Sakae 101 11 30N 99 37 E
Thap Than 100 15 27N 99 54 E
Thar (Great Indian) Desert 94 28 25N 72 0 E
Tharad 94 24 30N 71 30 E
Thargomindah 139 27 58 S 143 46 E
Tharrawaddy 98 17 38N 95 48 E
Tharrawaw 98 17 41N 95 28 E
Tharthār, Bahr ath 92 34 0N 43 0 E
Thasopoúla, I. 68 40 49N 24 45 E
Thásos 68 40 50N 24 50 E
Thásos, I. 68 40 40N 24 40 E
That Khe 100 22 16N 106 28 E
Thatcham 28 51 24N 1 17W
Thatcher, Ariz., U.S.A. 161 32 54N 109 46W
Thatcher, Colo., U.S.A. 161 37 38N 104 6W
Thaton 98 16 55N 97 22 E
Thau, Étang de 44 43 23N 3 36 E
Thaungdut 98 24 30N 94 40 E
Thaxted 29 51 57N 0 20 E
Thayer 159 36 34N 91 34W
Thayetmyo 98 19 20N 95 18 E
Thayngen 51 47 49N 8 43 E
Thazi 99 21 0N 96 5 E
The Alberga, R. 139 27 6 S 135 33 E
The Bight 167 24 19N 75 24W
The Corrong 139 36 0 S 139 30 E
The Dalles 160 45 40N 121 11W
The Diamantina 139 26 45 S 139 30 E
The English Company's Is. 138 11 50 S 136 32 E
The Entrance 141 33 21 S 151 30 E
The Four Archers 138 15 31 S 135 22 E
The Frome, R. 139 29 8 S 137 54 E
The Granites 136 20 35 S 130 21 E
The Great Divide 141 35 0 S 149 17 E
The Grenadines, Is. 167 12 30N 61 30W
The Hague (s'Gravenhage) 47 52 7N 7 14 E
The Hamilton, R. 139 26 40 S 135 19 E
The Johnston Lakes 137 32 25 S 120 30 E
The Lake 167 21 5N 73 34W
The Loup 38 54 42N 6 32W
The Macumba, R. 139 27 52 S 137 12 E
The Neales, R. 139 28 8 S 136 47 E
The Oaks 141 34 3 S 150 34 E
The Officer, R. 137 27 46 S 129 46 E
The Pas 153 53 45N 101 15W
The Range 127 19 2 S 31 2 E
The Rock 141 35 15 S 147 2 E
The Salt Lake 139 30 6 S 142 8 E
The Stevenson, R. 139 27 6 S 135 33 E
The Thumbs, Mts. 143 43 35 S 170 40 E
The Warburton, R. 139 28 4 S 137 28 E
Theale 28 51 26N 1 5W
Thebes 122 25 40N 32 35 E
Thedford 158 41 59N 100 31W
Theebine 139 25 57 S 152 34 E
Thekulthili L. 153 61 3N 110 0W
Thelma, oilfield 19 58 25N 1 18 E
Thelon, R. 153 62 35N 104 3W
Thénezay 42 46 44N 0 2W
Thenon 44 45 9N 1 4 E
Theodore 138 24 55 S 150 3 E
Thepha 101 6 52N 100 58 E
Thérain, R. 43 49 15N 2 27 E
Thermaïkos Kólpos 68 40 15N 22 45 E
Thermopílai P. 69 38 48N 22 45 E
Thermopolis 160 43 14N 108 10W
Thesprotía □ 68 39 27N 20 22 E
Thessalía □ 68 39 30N 22 0 E
Thessalon 150 46 20N 83 30W
Thessaloníki 68 40 38N 23 0 E
Thessaloníki □ 68 40 45N 23 0 E
Thessaly = Thessalía 68 39 30N 22 0 E
Thetford 29 52 25N 0 44 E
Thetford Mines 151 46 8N 71 18W
Theun, R. 100 18 19N 104 0 E
Theunissen 128 28 26 S 26 43 E
Theux 47 50 32N 5 49 E
Thevenard 139 32 9 S 133 38 E
Thiámis, R. 68 39 34N 20 18 E
Thiberville 42 49 8N 0 27 E
Thicket Portage 153 55 19N 97 42W
Thief River Falls 159 48 15N 96 10W
Thiel 120 14 55N 15 5W
Thiene 63 45 42N 11 29 E
Thierache 43 49 51N 3 45 E
Thiers 44 45 52N 3 33 E
Thies 120 14 50N 16 51W
Thiet 123 7 37N 28 49 E
Thika 126 1 1 S 37 5 E
Thika □ 126 1 1 S 37 5 E
Thille-Boubacar 120 16 31N 15 5W
Thillot, Le 43 47 53N 6 46 E
Thimphu (Tashi Chho Dzong) 98 27 31N 89 45 E
þingvallavatn 74 64 11N 21 9W
Thionville 43 49 20N 6 10 E
Thírá 69 36 23N 25 27 E
Thirasiá, I. 69 36 26N 25 21 E
Thirlmere, L. 32 54 32N 3 4W
Thirsk 33 54 15N 1 20W
Thisted 75 56 58N 8 40 E
Thistle I. 140 35 0 S 136 8 E
Thistle, oilfield 19 61 20N 1 35 E
Thitgy 98 18 15N 96 13 E
Thitpokpin 98 19 24N 96 1 E
Thiu Khao Phetchabun 101 16 20N 100 55 E
Thívai 69 38 19N 23 19 E
Thiviers 44 45 25N 0 54 E
Thizy 45 46 2N 4 18 E
þjorsa 74 63 47N 20 48W
Thlewiaza, R., Man., Can. 153 59 43N 100 5W
Thlewiaza, R., N.W.T., Can. 153 60 29N 94 40W
Thmar Puok 100 13 57N 103 4 E
Tho Vinh 100 19 16N 105 42 E
Thoa, R. 153 60 31N 109 47W
Thoen 100 17 36N 99 12 E
Thoeng 100 19 41N 100 12 E
Thoissey 45 46 12N 4 48 E
Tholdi 95 35 5N 76 6 E
Tholen 47 51 32N 4 13 E
Thomas, Okla., U.S.A. 159 35 48N 98 48W
Thomas, W. Va., U.S.A. 156 39 10N 79 30W
Thomas, L. 139 26 4 S 137 58 E
Thomas Street 38 53 27N 8 15W
Thomastown 39 52 32N 7 10W
Thomasville, Ala., U.S.A. 157 31 55N 87 42W
Thomasville, Fla., U.S.A. 157 30 50N 84 0W
Thomasville, N.C., U.S.A. 157 35 5N 80 4W
Thommen 47 50 14N 6 5 E
Thompson, Can. 153 55 45N 97 52W
Thompson, U.S.A. 162 41 52N 75 31W
Thompson Falls 160 47 37N 115 26W
Thompson Landing 153 62 56N 110 40W
Thompson, R., Can. 152 50 15N 121 24W
Thompson, R., U.S.A. 158 39 46N 93 37W
Thompsons 161 39 0N 109 50W
Thompsonville 162 42 0N 72 37W
Thomson, R. 138 25 11 S 142 53 E
Thomson's Falls = Nyahururu Falls 126 0 2N 36 27 E
Thon Buri 100 13 43N 100 29 E
Thonburi 101 13 50N 100 36 E
Thônes 45 45 54N 6 18 E
Thongwa 98 16 45N 96 33 E
Thonon-les-Bains 45 46 22N 6 29 E
Thonze 98 17 38N 95 47 E
Thorez 83 48 4N 38 34 E
þorlákshöfn 74 63 51N 21 22W
Thornaby on Tees 33 54 36N 1 19W
Thornborough 138 16 54 S 145 2 E
Thornbury, N.Z. 143 46 17 S 168 9 E
Thornbury, U.K. 28 51 36N 2 31W
Thorndon 29 52 16N 1 8 E
Thorne, U.K. 33 53 36N 0 56W
Thorne, U.S.A. 163 38 36N 118 34W
Thorne Glacier 13 87 30N 150 0 E
Thorney 29 52 37N 0 8W
Thornham 29 52 59N 0 35 E
Thornhill 35 55 15N 3 46W
Thornthwaite 32 54 36N 3 13W
Thornton-Beresfield 141 32 50 S 151 40 E
Thornton Celveleys 32 53 52N 3 1W
Thornton Dale 33 54 14N 0 41W
Thorpe 29 52 38N 1 20 E
Thorpe le Soken 29 51 50N 1 11 E
Thouarcé 43 47 17N 0 30W
Thouin, C. 136 20 20 S 118 10 E
Thousand Oakes 163 34 10N 118 50W
Thrace = Thráki 68 41 10N 25 30 E
Thráki 68 41 9N 25 30 E
Thrakikón Pélagos 68 40 30N 25 0 E
Thrapston 29 52 24N 0 32W
Three Bridges 29 51 7N 0 9W
Three Forks 160 45 5N 111 40W
Three Hills 152 51 43N 113 15W
Three Hummock I. 138 40 25 S 144 55 E
Three Kings Is. 142 34 10 S 172 10 E
Three Lakes 158 45 41N 89 10W
Three Pagodas P. 100 15 16N 98 23 E
Three Points, C. 120 4 42N 2 6W
Three Rivers, Austral. 137 25 10 S 119 5 E
Three Rivers, Calif., U.S.A. 163 36 26N 118 54W
Three Rivers, Tex., U.S.A. 159 28 30N 98 10W
Three Sisters, Mt. 160 44 10N 121 52W
Threlkeld 32 54 37N 3 2W
Threshfield 32 54 5N 2 2W
þ ó risvatn 74 64 50N 19 26W
Throssell, L. 137 27 27 S 124 16 E
Throssell Ra. 136 17 24 S 126 4 E
þ ó rshöfn 74 66 12N 15 20W
Thrumster 37 58 24N 3 8W
Thuan Moa 101 8 58N 105 30 E
Thubun Lakes 153 61 30N 112 0W
Thueyts 45 44 41N 4 9 E
Thuillies 47 50 18N 4 20 E
Thuin 47 50 20N 4 17 E
Thuir 44 42 38N 2 45 E
Thule 12 77 30N 69 0W
Thun 50 46 45N 7 38 E
Thundelarra 137 28 53 S 117 7 E
Thunder B. 156 45 0N 83 20W
Thunder Bay 150 48 20N 89 0W
Thunder River 152 52 13N 119 20W
Thundulda 137 32 15 S 126 3 E
Thunersee 50 46 43N 7 39 E
Thung Song 101 8 10N 99 40 E
Thunkar 98 27 55N 91 0 E
Thuong Tra 100 16 2N 107 42 E
Thur, R. 51 47 32N 9 10 E
Thurgau □ 51 47 34N 9 10 E
Thüringer Wald 48 50 35N 11 0 E
Thurlby 29 52 45N 0 21W
Thurles 39 52 40N 7 53W
Thurloo Downs 139 29 15 S 143 30 E
Thurmaston 28 52 40N 1 8W
Thurmont 162 39 37N 77 25W
Thurn P. 49 47 20N 12 15 E
Thursby 32 54 40N 3 3W
Thursday I. 138 10 30 S 142 3 E
Thurso, Can. 150 45 36N 75 15W
Thurso, U.K. 37 58 34N 3 31W
Thurso, R. 37 58 36N 3 30W
Thurston I. 13 72 0 S 100 0W
Thury-Harcourt 42 49 0N 0 30W
Thusis 51 46 42N 9 26 E
Thutade L. 152 57 0N 126 55W
Thuy, Le 100 17 14N 106 49 E
Thylungra 139 26 4 S 143 28 E
Thyolo 127 16 7 S 35 5 E
Thysville = Mbanza Ngungu 124 5 12 S 14 53 E
Ti-n-Amzi, O. 121 17 35N 4 20 E
Ti-n-Barraouene, O. 121 18 40N 4 5 E
Ti-n-Emensan 118 22 59N 4 45 E
Ti-n-Geloulet 118 25 58N 4 2 E
Ti-n-Medjerdam, O. 118 25 45N 1 30W
Ti-n-Tarabine, O. 119 21 37N 7 11 E
Ti-n-Zaouatène 118 48 55 S 77 9W
Tia 141 31 10 S 151 50 E
Tiahualilo 164 26 20N 103 30W
Tianguá 170 3 44 S 40 59W
Tiankoura 120 10 47N 3 17W
Tiaret (Tagdent) 118 35 28N 1 21 E
Tiarra 141 32 46 S 145 1 E
Tiassalé 120 5 58N 4 57W
Tibagi 173 24 30 S 50 24W
Tibagi, R. 173 22 47 S 51 1W
Tibari 123 5 2N 31 48 E
Tibati 121 6 22N 12 30 E
Tiber = Tevere, R. 63 42 30N 12 20 E
Tiber Res. 160 48 20N 111 15W
Tiberias 90 32 47N 35 32 E
Tiberias, L. = Kinneret, Yam 90 32 49N 35 36 E
Tibesti 119 21 0N 17 30 E
Tibet 99 32 30N 86 0 E
Tibet □ 105 32 30N 86 0 E
Tibiri 121 13 34N 7 4 E
Tibleş, mt. 70 47 32N 24 15 E
Tibleş, Mţii 70 47 41N 24 6 E
Tibnīn 90 33 12N 35 24 E
Tibooburra 139 29 26 S 142 1 E
Tibro 73 58 28N 14 10 E
Tibugá, Golfo de 174 5 45N 77 20W
Tiburón, I. 164 29 0N 112 30W
Ticehurst 29 51 2N 0 23 E
Tichit 120 18 35N 9 20W
Ticino □ 51 46 20N 8 45 E
Ticino, R. 62 45 23N 8 47 E
Tickhill 33 53 25N 1 8W
Ticonderoga 162 43 50N 73 28W
Ticul 165 20 20N 89 50W
Tidaholm 73 58 12N 13 55 E
Tiddim 98 23 20N 93 45 E
Tiderïdjaouine, Adrar 118 23 0N 2 15 E
Tideswell 33 53 17N 1 46W
Tidikelt 118 26 58N 1 30 E
Tidjikdja 120 18 4N 11 35W
Tidore 103 0 40N 127 25 E
Tidra, I. 120 19 45N 16 20W
Tiébélé 121 11 6N 0 59W
Tiébissou 120 7 9N 5 18W
Tiéboro 119 21 20N 17 7 E
Tiefencastel 51 46 40N 9 33 E
Tiego 120 12 6N 2 38 E
T'iehling 107 42 17N 123 50 E
Tiel 46 51 53N 5 26 E
Tielt 47 51 0N 3 20 E
Tien Shan 85 42 0N 80 0 E
Tien Yen 100 21 20N 107 24 E
T'ienchang 107 32 41N 118 59 E
T'ienchen 106 40 30N 114 6 E
Tiench'eng 109 21 31N 111 18 E
T'ienching 107 39 10N 117 15 E
T'ienchu 108 26 55N 109 12 E
T'ianch'üan 108 30 4N 102 50 E
T'ienchuangt'ai 107 40 49N 122 6 E
Tienen 47 50 48N 4 57 E
T'ienho 108 24 47N 108 42 E
T'ienhsi 108 24 26N 106 5 E
Tiénigbé 120 8 11N 5 43W
Tienkianghsien 69 30 25N 107 30 E
T'ienlin 108 24 19N 106 15 E
T'ienmen 109 30 37N 113 10 E
T'ieno 108 25 9N 106 57 E
Tienpai 109 21 30N 111 1 E
T'ienshui 105 34 35N 105 15 E
T'ient'ai 109 29 9N 121 2 E
Tientsin = T'ienching 105 39 10N 117 15 E
T'ientung 108 23 39N 107 8 E
T'ienyang 108 23 43N 106 44 E
Tierp 72 60 20N 17 30 E
Tierra Alta 174 8 11N 76 4W
Tierra Amarilla 172 27 28 S 70 18W
Tierra Colorada 165 17 10N 99 35W
Tierra de Barros 57 38 40N 6 30W
Tierra de Campos 56 42 10N 4 50W
Tierra del Fuego, I. Gr. de 176 54 0 S 69 0W
Tiétar, R. 56 39 55N 5 50W
Tieté, R. 171 20 40 S 51 35W
Tieyon 139 26 12 S 133 52 E
Tiffin 156 41 8N 83 10W
Tifi 123 6 12N 36 55 E
Tiflèt 118 33 54N 6 20W
Tiflis = Tbilisi 83 41 50N 44 50 E
Tifrah 90 31 19N 34 42 E
Tifton 157 31 28N 83 32W
Tifu 103 3 39 S 126 18 E
Tigalda I. 147 54 9N 165 0W
Tighnabruaich 34 55 55N 5 13W
Tigil 77 58 0N 158 10 E
Tignish 151 46 58N 64 2W
Tigre □ 123 13 35N 39 15 E
Tigre, R. 174 3 30 S 74 58W
Tigu 99 29 48N 91 38 E
Tiguentourine 119 28 8N 8 58 E
Tiguila 121 14 44N 1 50W
Tigveni 70 45 10N 24 31 E
Tigyaing 98 23 45N 96 10 E
Tīh, Gebel el 122 29 32N 33 26 E
Tihodaine, Dunes de 119 25 15N 7 15 E
Tījī 119 32 0N 11 18 E
Tijiamis 103 7 16 S 108 29 E
Tijibadok 103 6 53 S 106 47 E

Tijirit, O Tolox


Tijirit, O. 120 19 30N 6 15W
Tijuana 164 32 30N 117 3W
Tikal 166 17 2N 89 35W
Tikamgarh 95 24 44N 78 57 E
Tikan 138 5 58 S 149 2 E
Tikhoretsk 83 45 56N 40 5 E
Tikhvin 80 59 35N 33 30 E
Tikkadouine, Adrar 118 24 28N 1 30 E
Tiko 121 4 4N 9 20 E
Tikrit 92 34 35N 43 37 E
Tiksi 77 71 50N 129 0 E
Tilamuta 103 0 40N 122 15 E
Tilburg 47 51 31N 5 6 E
Tilbury, Can. 150 42 17N 84 23W
Tilbury, U.K. 29 51 27N 0 24 E
Tilcara 172 23 30 S 65 23W
Tilden 158 42 3N 97 45W
Tilemsès 121 15 37N 4 44 E
Tilemsi, Vallée du 121 17 42N 0 15 E
Tilghman 162 38 42N 76 20W
Tilhar 95 28 0N 79 45 E
Tilia, O. 118 27 32N 0 55 E
Tilichiki 77 61 0N 166 5 E
Tiligul, R. 82 47 35N 30 30 E
Tililane 118 27 49N 0 6W
Tilin 98 21 41N 94 6 E
Tilissos 69 38 15N 25 0 E
Till, R. 35 55 35N 2 3W
Tillabéri 121 14 7N 1 28 E
Tillamook 160 45 29N 123 55W
Tillberga 72 59 42N 16 39 E
Tilley 152 50 28N 111 38W
Tillia 121 16 8N 4 47 E
Tillicoultry 35 56 9N 3 44W
Tillsonburg 150 42 53N 80 44W
Tilmanstone 29 51 13N 1 18 E
Tilos, I. 69 36 27N 27 27 E
Tilpa 139 30 57 S 144 24 E
Tilrhemt 118 33 9N 3 22 E
Tilsit = Sovetsk 80 55 6N 21 50 E
Tilt, R. 37 56 50N 3 50W
Tilton 162 43 25N 71 36W
Timahoe 39 52 59N 7 12W
Timanskiy Kryazh 78 65 58N 50 5 E
Timaru 143 44 23 S 171 14 E
Timashevo 84 53 22N 51 9 E
Timashevsk 83 45 35N 39 0 E
Timau 126 0 4N 37 15 E
Timbákion 69 35 4N 24 45 E
Timbaúba 170 7 31 S 35 19W
Timbédra 120 16 17N 8 16W
Timber L. 158 45 29N 101 0W
Timber Mtn. 163 37 6N 116 28W
Timbio 174 2 20N 76 40W
Timbiqui 174 2 46N 77 42W
Timboon 140 38 30 S 142 58 E
Timbuktu =
Tombouctou 120 16 50N 3 0W
Timdjaouine 118 21 47N 4 30 E
Timétrine Montagnes 121 19 25N 1 0W
Timfi Óros 68 39 59N 20 45 E
Timfristós, Óros 69 38 57N 21 50 E
Timhadite 118 33 15N 5 4W
Timimoun 118 29 14N 0 16 E
Timimoun, Sebkha de 118 28 50N 0 46 E
Timiris, C. 120 19 15N 16 30W
Timiş □ 66 45 40N 21 30 E
Timiş, R. 70 45 30N 21 0 E
Timişoara 66 45 43N 21 15 E
Timmins 150 48 28N 81 25W
Timmoudi 118 29 20N 1 8W
Timok, R. 66 44 10N 22 40 E
Timoleague 39 51 40N 8 51W
Timolin 39 52 59N 6 49W
Timon 170 5 8 S 42 52W
Timor □ 103 8 0 S 126 30 E
Timor, I. 103 9 0 S 125 0 E
Timor Sea 136 10 0 S 127 0 E
Timur □ 103 9 0 S 125 0 E
Tin Alkoum 119 24 30N 10 17 E
Tin Gornai 121 16 38N 0 38W
Tin Mtn. 163 36 54N 117 28W
Tina, Khalîg el 122 31 20N 32 42 E
Tinaca Pt. 103 5 30N 125 25 E
Tinaco 174 9 42N 68 26W
Tinafak, O. 119 27 10N 7 0W
Tinahely 39 52 48N 6 28W
Tinambacan 103 12 5N 124 32 E
Tinapagee 139 29 25 S 144 15 E
Tinaquillo 174 9 55N 68 18W
Tinaroo Falls 138 17 5 S 145 4 E
Tinca 70 46 46N 21 58 E
Tinchebray 42 48 47N 0 45W
Tindivanam 97 12 15N 79 35 E
Tindouf 118 27 50N 8 4W
Tindzhe Dzong 95 28 20N 88 8 E
Tineo 56 43 21N 6 27W
Tinerhir 118 31 29N 5 31W
Tinfouchi 118 28 58N 5 54W
T'ing Chiang, R. 109 24 24N 116 35 E
Tingan 100 19 42N 110 18 E
Tingch'u, R. 108 28 20N 99 12 E
Tingewick 28 51 59N 1 4W
Tinggi, Pulau, Is. 101 2 18N 104 7 E
Tinghai 109 30 0N 122 10 E
Tinghsi 106 35 33N 104 32 E
Tinghsiang 106 38 32N 112 59 E
Tinghsien 106 38 30N 115 0 E
Tingkawk Sakun 98 26 4N 96 44 E
Tingk'ouchen 106 39 48N 106 36 E
Tinglev 73 54 57N 9 13 E
Tingnan 109 24 47N 115 2 E
Tingo Maria 174 9 10 S 76 0W
Tingpien 106 37 36N 107 38 E
Tingshan 109 31 16N 119 51 E
Tingsryd 73 56 31N 15 0 E
Tingt'ao 106 35 4N 115 34 E
Tingvalla 73 58 47N 12 2 E
Tingyüan 109 32 32N 117 41 E
Tinh Bien 101 10 36N 104 57 E
Tinharé, I. de 171 13 30 S 38 58W
Tinié 121 14 17N 1 30W
Tinioulig, Sebkra 118 22 30N 6 45W
Tinjoub 118 29 45N 5 40W
Tinkurrin 137 32 59 S 117 46 E
Tinnia 172 27 0 S 62 45W
Tinnoset 71 59 45N 9 3 E
Tinnsjø 71 59 55N 8 54 E
Tinogasta 172 28 0 S 67 40W
Tinos 69 37 33N 25 8 E
Tiñoso, C. 59 37 32N 1 6W
Tinsukia 98 27 29N 95 26 E
Tintagel 30 50 40N 4 45W
Tintagel Hd. 30 50 40N 4 46W
Tintern 31 51 42N 2 41W
Tintern Abbey 39 52 14N 6 50W
Tintigny 47 49 41N 5 31 E
Tintina 172 27 2 S 62 45W
Tintinara 140 35 48 S 140 2 E
Tinto, R. 57 37 30N 5 33W
Tinui 142 40 52 S 176 5 E
Tinwald 143 43 55 S 171 43 E
Tioga 162 41 54N 77 9W
Tioman, I. 101 2 50N 104 10 E
Tioman, Pulau, Is. 101 2 50N 104 10 E
Tionaga 150 48 0N 82 0W
Tione di Trento 62 46 3N 10 44 E
Tior 123 6 26N 31 11 E
Tioulilin 118 27 1N 0 2W
Tipongpani 99 27 20N 95 55 E
Tipperary 39 52 28N 8 10W
Tipperary □ 39 52 37N 7 55W
Tipton, U.K. 28 52 32N 2 4W
Tipton, Calif., U.S.A. 163 36 3N 119 19W
Tipton, Ind., U.S.A. 156 40 17N 86 30W
Tipton, Iowa, U.S.A. 158 41 45N 91 12W
Tiptonville 159 36 22N 89 30W
Tiptree 29 51 48N 0 46 E
Tiptur 97 13 15N 76 26 E
Tira 90 32 14N 34 56 E
Tiracambu, Serra do 170 3 15 S 46 30W
Tirahart, O. 118 23 55N 2 0W
Tiran 93 32 45N 51 0 E
Tirân 122 27 56N 34 35 E
Tirana 68 41 18N 19 49 E
Tirana-Durrësi □ 68 41 35N 20 0 E
Tirano 62 46 13N 10 11 E
Tirarer, Mont 121 19 35N 1 10W
Tiraspol 82 46 55N 29 35 E
Tirat Carmel 90 32 46N 34 58 E
Tirat Tsevi 90 32 26N 35 31 E
Tirat Yehuda 90 32 1N 34 56 E
Tiratimine 118 25 56N 3 37 E
Tirdout 121 16 7N 1 5W
Tire 92 38 5N 27 50 E
Tirebolu 92 40 58N 38 45 E
Tiree, I. 34 56 31N 6 55W
Tiree, Passage of 34 56 30N 6 30W
Tîrgovişte 70 44 55N 25 27 E
Tîrgu Frumos 70 47 12N 27 2 E
Tîrgu-Jiu 70 45 5N 23 19 E
Tîrgu Mureş 70 46 31N 24 38 E
Tîrgu Neamţ 70 47 12N 26 25 E
Tîrgu Ocna 70 46 16N 26 39 E
Tîrgu Secuiesc 70 46 0N 26 10 E
Tirich Mir Mt. 93 36 15N 71 35 E
Tiriola 65 38 57N 16 32 E
Tiririca, Serra da 171 17 6 S 47 6W
Tirlyanskiy 84 54 14N 58 35 E
Tirna, R. 96 18 5N 76 30 E
Tîrnava = Botoroaga 70 44 8N 25 32 E
Tîrnava Mare, R. 70 46 15N 24 30 E
Tîrnava Mica, R. 70 46 17N 24 30 E
Tirnavos 68 39 45N 22 18 E
Tîrnova 70 45 23N 22 1 E
Tîrnăveni 70 46 19N 24 13 E
Tirodi 96 21 35N 79 35 E
Tirol □ 52 47 3N 10 43 E
Tiros 171 19 0 S 45 58W
Tirschenreuth 49 49 51N 12 20 E
Tirso, L. 64 40 8N 8 56 E
Tirso, R. 64 40 33N 9 12 E
Tirstrup 73 56 18N 10 42 E
Tirua 142 38 25 S 174 40 E
Tiruchchirappalli 97 10 45N 78 45 E
Tiruchendur 97 8 30N 78 11 E
Tiruchengodu 97 11 23N 77 56 E
Tirumangalam 97 9 49N 77 58 E
Tirunelveli (Tinnevelly) 97 8 45N 77 45 E
Tirupati 97 13 45N 79 30 E
Tiruppattur 97 12 30N 78 30 E
Tiruppur 97 11 12N 77 22 E
Tiruturaipundi 97 10 32N 79 41 E
Tiruvadaimarudur 97 11 2N 79 27 E
Tiruvallar 97 13 9N 79 57 E
Tiruvannamalai 97 12 10N 79 12 E
Tiruvarur (Negapatam) 97 10 46N 79 38 E
Tiruvatipuram 97 12 39N 79 33 E
Tiruvottiyur 97 13 10N 80 22 E
Tisa, R. 66 45 30N 20 20 E
Tisdale 153 52 50N 104 0W
Tiseirhatène, Mares de 118 22 51N 9 30W
Tishomingo 159 34 14N 96 38W
Tisjön 72 60 56N 13 0 E
Tisnaren 72 58 58N 15 56 E
Tisno 63 44 45N 15 41 E
Tišnov 53 49 21N 16 25 E
Tisovec 53 48 41N 19 56 E
Tissemsilt 118 35 35N 1 50 E
Tissit, O. 119 27 28N 9 58W
Tissø 73 55 35N 11 18 E
Tista, R. 98 25 23N 89 43 E
Tisted 73 56 58N 8 40 E
Tisza, R. 53 47 38N 20 44 E
Tiszaföldvár 53 47 0N 20 14 E
Tiszafüred 53 47 38N 20 50 E
Tiszalök 53 48 0N 21 10 E
Tiszavasvári 53 47 58N 21 18 E
Tit, Alg. 118 27 0N 1 37 E
Tit, Alg. 119 23 0N 5 10 E
Tit-Ary 77 71 50N 126 30 E
Titaguas 58 39 53N 1 6W
Titahi Bay 142 41 6 S 174 50 E
Titai Damer 123 16 43N 37 25 E
Titchfield 28 50 51N 1 13W
Titel 66 45 29N 20 18 E
Tithwal 95 34 21N 73 50 E
Titicaca, L. 174 15 30 S 69 30W
Titilagarh 96 20 15N 83 5 E
Tititira Head 98 43 38 S 169 26 E
Titiwa 121 12 14N 12 53 E
Titlis 51 46 46N 8 27 E
Titograd 66 42 30N 19 19 E
Titov Veles 66 41 46N 21 47 E
Titova Korenica 63 44 45N 15 41 E
Titovo Uzice 66 43 55N 19 50 E
Titule 126 3 15N 25 31 E
Titumate 174 8 19N 77 5W
Titusville 156 41 35N 79 39W
Tiumpan Hd. 36 58 15N 6 10W
Tivaouane 120 14 56N 16 45W
Tivat 66 42 28N 18 43 E
Tiveden 73 58 50N 14 30 E
Tiverton 30 50 54N 3 30W
Tivoli 63 41 58N 12 45 E
Tiwi 93 22 45N 59 12 E
Tiyo 123 14 41N 40 57 E
Tizga 118 32 1N 5 9W
Tizi n'Isly 118 32 28N 5 47W
Tizi Ouzou 119 36 42N 4 3 E
Tizmín 165 21 0N 88 1W
Tiznados, R. 174 8 50N 67 50W
Tiznit 118 29 48N 9 45W
Tjalang 103 4 30N 95 43 E
Tjangkuang, Tg. 102 7 0 S 105 0 E
Tjareme, G. 103 6 55 S 108 27 E
Tjeggelvas 74 66 37N 17 45 E
Tjepu 103 7 12 S 111 31 E
Tjeukemeer 46 52 53N 5 48 E
Tjiandjur 103 6 51 S 107 7 E
Tjibatu 103 7 8 S 107 59 E
Tjikadjang 103 7 25 S 107 48 E
Tjimahi 103 6 53 S 107 33 E
Tjirebon = Cirebon 103 6 45 S 108 32 E
Tjöllong 71 59 6N 10 3 E
Tjöme 71 59 8N 10 26 E
Tjonger Kanaal 46 52 52N 6 52 E
Tjörn 73 58 0N 11 35 E
Tjörnes 74 66 12N 17 9W
Tjuls 73 57 30N 18 15 E
Tjurup 102 4 26 S 102 13 E
Tkibuli 83 42 26N 43 0 E
Tkvarcheli 83 42 47N 41 52 E
Tlacolula 165 16 57N 96 29W
Tlacotalpán 165 18 37N 95 40W
Tlaquepaque 164 20 39N 103 19W
Tlaxcala 165 19 20N 98 14W
Tlaxcala □ 165 19 30N 98 20W
Tlaxiaco 165 17 10N 97 40W
Tlell 152 53 34N 131 56W
Tlemcen 118 34 52N 1 15W
Tleta di Sidi Bouguedra 118 32 16N 8 58W
Tleta Sidi Bouguedra 118 32 16N 9 59W
Tlumach 80 48 46N 25 0 E
Tłuszcz 54 52 25N 21 25 E
Tlyarata 83 42 9N 46 26 E
Tmassah 119 26 19N 15 51 E
Tmisan 119 27 23N 13 30 E
To Bong 100 12 45N 109 16 E
T'o Chiang, R. 108 28 56N 105 33 E
To-Shima 111 34 31N 139 17 E
Toad, R. 152 59 25N 124 57W
Toay 172 36 50 S 64 30W
Toba 111 34 30N 136 45 E
Toba Kakar 94 31 30N 69 0 E
Toba, L. 102 2 40N 98 50 E
Toba Tek Singh 94 30 55N 72 25 E
Tobago, I. 167 11 10N 60 30W
Tobarra 59 38 35N 1 41W
Tobelo 103 1 25N 127 56 E
Tobercurry 38 54 3N 8 43W
Tobermore 38 54 49N 6 43W
Tobermorey 138 22 12 S 138 0 E
Tobermory, Can. 150 45 12N 81 40W
Tobermory, U.K. 34 56 37N 6 4W
Tobin, L. 136 21 45 S 125 49 E
Tobin L. 153 53 35N 103 30W
Toboali 102 3 0 S 106 25 E
Tobol 84 52 40N 62 39 E
Tobol, R. 84 58 10N 68 12 E
Toboli 103 0 38 S 120 12 E
Tobolsk 84 58 0N 68 10 E
Tobruk = Tubruq 117 32 7N 23 55 E
Tobyhanna 162 41 10N 75 15W
Tocantínia 170 9 33 S 48 22W
Tocantinópolis 170 6 20 S 47 25W
Tocantins, R. 170 14 30 S 49 0W
Tocca 157 34 6N 83 17W
Toce, R. 62 46 5N 8 29 E
Tochigi 111 36 25N 139 45 E
Tochigi-ken □ 111 36 45N 139 45 E
Tocina 57 37 37N 5 44W
Toconao 172 34 35N 83 19W
Toconhão, Serra do 171 14 30 S 47 46W
Tocópero 174 11 30N 69 16W
Tocopilla 172 22 5 S 70 10W
Tocumwal 141 35 45 S 145 31 E
Tocuyo, R. 174 10 50N 69 0W
Todd, R. 138 24 52 S 135 48 E
Toddington 29 51 57N 0 31W
Todeli 103 1 38 S 124 34 E
Todenyang 126 4 35N 35 56 E
Todi 63 42 47N 12 24 E
Tödi 51 46 48N 8 55 E
Todjo 103 1 20 S 121 15 E
Todmorden 32 53 43N 2 7W
Todos os Santos, Baía de 171 12 48 S 38 38W
Todos Santos 164 23 27N 110 13W
Todos Santos, Bahia de 164 31 48N 116 42W
Todtnau 49 47 50N 7 56 E
Toe Hd., Ireland 39 51 29N 9 13W
Toe Hd., U.K. 36 57 50N 7 10W
Toecé 121 11 50N 1 16W
Toetoes B. 143 46 42 S 168 41 E
Tofield 152 53 25N 112 40W
Tofino 152 49 11N 125 55W
Töfsingdalems National Park 72 62 15N 12 44 E
Tofta 73 57 11N 12 20 E
Toftlund 73 55 11N 9 2 E
Tōgane 111 35 33N 140 22 E
Togba 120 17 26N 10 25W
Toggenburg 51 47 16N 9 9 E
Togian, Kepulauan 103 0 20 S 121 50 E
Togliatti 81 53 37N 49 18 E
Togo ■ 121 6 15N 1 35 E
Toguzak, R. 84 54 3N 62 44 E
Tōhoku □ 112 39 50N 141 45 E
Toi 111 34 54N 134 47 E
Toinya 123 6 17N 29 46 E
Toiyabe Dome 163 38 51N 117 22W
Toiyabe, Ra. 163 39 10N 117 10W
Tōjō 110 34 53N 133 16 E
Tok, R. 84 52 46N 52 22 E
Tokaanu 142 38 58 S 175 46 E
Tokachi, R. 112 42 44N 143 42 E
Tokaj 53 48 8N 21 27 E
Tokala, G. 103 1 30 S 121 40 E
Tokanui 143 46 34 S 168 56 E
Tokarahi 143 44 56 S 170 39 E
Tokat 92 40 22N 36 35 E
Tŏkchŏn 107 39 45N 126 18 E
Tokelau Is. 130 9 0 S 172 0W
Toki 111 35 18N 137 8 E
Tokmak, Kirgizia, U.S.S.R. 84 42 55N 75 45 E
Tokmak, Ukraine, U.S.S.R. 82 47 16N 35 42 E
Toko Ra. 138 23 5 S 138 20 E
Tokomaru Bay 142 38 8 S 178 22 E
Tokombere 121 11 18N 3 30 E
Tókomlós 53 46 24N 20 45 E
Tokoname 111 34 53N 136 51 E
Tokong 101 5 27N 100 23 E
Tokoroa 142 38 20 S 175 50 E
Tokorozawa 111 35 47N 139 28 E
T'ok'ot'o 106 40 15N 111 12 E
Toktogul 85 41 50N 72 50 E
Tokuii 110 34 11N 131 42 E
Tokule 123 14 54N 38 26 E
Tokunoshima 112 27 56N 128 55 E
Tokushima 110 34 4N 134 34 E
Tokushima-ken □ 110 35 50N 134 30 E
Tokuyama 110 34 0N 131 50 E
Tōkyō 111 35 45N 139 45 E
Tōkyō-to □ 111 35 40N 139 30 E
Tōkyō-Wan 111 35 25N 139 47 E
Tolaerh 105 35 8N 81 33 E
Tolaga Bay 142 38 21 S 178 20 E
Tolageak 147 70 2N 162 50W
Tolbukhin 67 43 37N 27 49 E
Toledo, Spain 56 39 50N 4 2W
Toledo, Ohio, U.S.A. 156 41 37N 83 33W
Toledo, Oreg., U.S.A. 160 44 40N 123 59W
Toledo, Wash., U.S.A. 160 42 29N 122 58W
Toledo, Montes de 57 39 33N 4 20W
Tolentino 63 43 12N 13 17 E
Tolfino 152 49 6N 125 54W
Tolga, Alg. 119 34 46N 5 22 E
Tolga, Norway 71 62 26N 11 1 E
Tolima □ 174 3 45N 75 15W
Tolima, Vol. 174 4 40N 75 19W
Tolitoli 103 1 5N 120 50 E
Tolkamer 46 51 52N 6 6 E
Tolkmicko 54 54 19N 19 31 E
Tollarp 73 55 55N 13 58 E
Tollesbury 29 51 46N 0 51 E
Tolleson 161 33 29N 112 10W
Tollhouse 163 37 1N 119 24W
Tolmachevo 80 58 56N 29 57 E
Tolmezzo 63 46 23N 13 0 E
Tolmino 63 46 11N 13 45 E
Tolna 53 46 25N 18 48 E
Tolna □ 53 46 30N 18 30 E
Tolne 73 57 28N 10 20 E
Tolo 124 2 50 S 18 40 E
Tolo, Teluk 103 2 20 S 122 10 E
Tolokiwa I. 138 5 30 S 147 30 E
Tolon 121 9 26N 1 3W
Tolosa 58 43 8N 2 5W
Tolox 57 36 41N 4 54W

Tolsta Hd Tregnago


Tolsta Hd. 36 58 20N 6 10W
Toluca 165 19 20N 99 50W
Tolun 106 42 22N 116 30E
Tom Burke 129 23 5S 28 4E
Tomahawk 158 45 28N 89 40W
Tomakomai 112 42 38N 141 36E
Tomales 163 38 15N 122 53W
Tomales B. 163 38 15N 123 58W
Tomar 57 39 36N 8 25W
Tómaros Óros 68 39 29N 20 48E
Tomaszów Lubelski 54 50 29N 23 23E
Tomaszów Mazowiecki 54 51 30N 19 57E
Tomatin 37 57 20N 4 0W
Tomatlán 164 19 56N 105 15W
Tombé 123 5 53N 31 40E
Tombigbee, R. 157 32 0N 88 6W
Tombodor, Serra do 171 12 0S 41 30W
Tombouctou 120 16 50N 3 0W
Tombstone 161 31 40N 110 4W
Tomdoun 36 57 4N 5 2W
Tomé 172 36 36S 73 6W
Tomé-Açu 170 2 25S 48 9W
Tomelilla 73 55 33N 13 58E
Tomelloso 59 39 10N 3 2W
Tomingley 141 32 31S 148 16E
Tomini 103 0 30N 120 30E
Tomini, Teluk 103 0 10S 122 0E
Tominian 120 13 17N 4 35W
Tomiño 56 41 59N 8 46W
Tomintoul 37 57 15N 3 22W
Tomioka 111 36 15N 138 54E
Tomkinson Ranges 137 26 11S 129 5E
Tommot 77 58 50N 126 20E
Tomnavoulin 37 57 19N 3 18W
Tomnop Ta Suos 101 11 20N 104 15E
Tomo, Colomb. 174 2 38N 67 32W
Tomo, Japan 110 34 23N 133 23E
Tomobe 111 36 40N 140 41E
Toms Place 163 37 34N 118 41W
Toms River 162 39 59N 74 12W
Tomsk 76 56 30N 85 12E
Tomtabacken 73 57 30N 14 30E
Tonalá 165 16 8N 93 41W
Tonale, Passo del 62 46 15N 10 34E
Tonalea 161 36 17N 110 58W
Tonami 111 36 56N 136 58E
Tonantins 174 2 45S 67 45W
Tonasket 160 48 45N 119 30W
Tonawanda 156 43 0N 78 54W
Tonbridge 29 51 12N 0 18E
Tondano 103 1 35N 124 54E
Tondela 56 40 31N 8 5W
Tønder 73 54 58N 8 50E
Tondi 97 9 45N 79 4E
Tondi Kiwindi 121 14 28N 2 02E
Tondibi 121 16 39N 0 14W
Tone-Gawa, R. 111 35 44N 140 51E
Tone, R. 137 34 23S 116 25E
Tone R. 30 50 59N 3 15W
Tong 28 52 39N 2 18W
Tonga Is. ■ 130 20 0S 173 0W
Tonga Trench 143 18 0S 175 0W
Tongaat 129 29 33S 31 9E
Tongala 141 36 14S 144 56E
Tongaland 129 27 0S 32 0E
Tongareva I 143 9 0S 158 0W
Tongariro, mt. 142 39 7S 175 50E
Tongchŏnni 107 39 50N 127 25E
Tongeren 47 50 47N 5 28E
Tongio 141 37 14S 147 44E
Tongjosŏn Man 107 39 30N 128 0E
Tongking = Bac-Phan 101 21 30N 105 0E
Tongking, G. of 101 20 0N 108 0E
Tongnae 107 35 12N 129 5E
Tongobory 129 23 32S 44 20E
Tongoy 172 30 25S 71 40W
Tongres = Tongeren 47 50 47N 5 28E
Tongsa Dzong 98 27 31N 90 31E
Tongue 37 58 29N 4 25W
Tongue, Kyle of 37 58 30N 4 30W
Tongue, R. 160 48 30N 106 30W
Tongyang 107 39 9N 126 53E
Tonj 123 7 20N 28 44E
Tonk 94 26 6N 75 54E
Tonkawa 159 36 44N 67 22W
Tonkin = Bac-Phan 100 22 0N 105 0E
Tonkin, G. of 100 20 0N 108 0E
Tonlé Sap 100 13 0N 104 0E
Tonnay-Charente 44 45 56N 0 55W
Tonneins 44 44 24N 0 20E
Tonnerre 43 47 51N 3 59E
Tönning 48 54 18N 8 57E
Tonopah 163 38 4N 117 12W
Tonoshō 110 34 29N 134 11E
Tonosí 166 7 20N 80 20W
Tonsberg 71 59 19N 10 25E
Tonstad 71 58 40N 6 45E
Tonto Basin 61 33 58N 111 15W
Tonyrefail 31 51 35N 3 26W
Tonzang 98 23 36N 93 42E
Tonzi 98 24 39N 94 57E
Tooele 160 40 30N 112 20W
Toolonda 140 36 58S 141 5E
Toombeolo 38 53 26N 9 52W
Toomevara 39 52 50N 8 2W
Toompine 139 27 15S 144 19E
Toongi 141 32 28S 148 30E
Toonpan 138 19 28S 146 48E
Toora 141 38 39S 146 23E
Toora-Khem 77 52 28N 96 9E
Toormore 39 51 31N 9 41W
Toowoomba 139 27 32S 151 56E
Top 93 34 15N 68 35E
Top Ozero 78 65 35N 32 0E
Topalu 70 44 31N 28 3E
Topaz 163 38 41N 119 30W
Topeka 158 39 3N 95 40W
Topki 76 55 25N 85 20E
Topla, R. 53 49 0N 21 36E
Topley 152 54 32N 126 5W
Toplica, R. 66 43 15N 21 30E
Toplița 70 46 55N 25 27E
Topocalma, Pta. 172 34 10S 72 2W
Topock 161 34 46N 114 29W
Topola 66 44 17N 20 32E
Topol'čany 53 48 35N 18 12E
Topoli 83 47 59N 51 45E
Topolnitsa, R. 67 42 21N 24 0E
Topolobampo 164 25 40N 109 10W
Topolovgrad 67 42 5N 26 20E
TopolvǔT Mare 66 45 46N 21 41E
Toppenish 160 46 27N 120 16W
Topsham 30 50 40N 3 27W
Topusko 63 45 18N 15 59E
Toquima, Ra. 163 39 0N 117 0W
Tor Bay, Austral. 137 35 5S 117 50E
Tor Bay, U.K. 23 50 26N 3 31W
Tor Ness 37 58 47N 3 18W
Tor, oilfield 19 56 40N 3 35E
Torá 58 41 49N 1 25E
Tora Kit 123 11 2N 32 30E
Torata 174 17 3S 70 1W
Torbat-e Heydarīyeh 93 35 15N 59 12E
Torbat-e Jàm 93 35 8N 60 35E
Torbay, Can. 151 47 40N 52 42W
Torbay, U.K. 30 50 26N 3 31W
Torchin 80 50 45N 25 0E
Tordal 71 59 10N 8 45E
Tordesillas 56 41 30N 5 0W
Tordoya 56 43 6N 8 36W
Töre 74 65 55N 22 40E
Töreboda 73 58 41N 14 7E
Torfajökull 74 63 54N 19 0W
Torgau 48 51 32N 13 0E
Torgelow 48 53 40N 13 59E
Torhout 47 51 5N 3 7E
Tori 123 7 53N 33 35E
Torigni-sur-Vire 42 49 3N 0 58W
Torija 58 40 44N 3 2W
Torin 164 27 33N 110 5W
Toriñana, C. 56 43 3N 9 17W
Torino 62 45 4N 7 40E
Torit 123 4 20N 32 55E
Torkovichi 80 58 51N 30 30E
Tormac 66 45 30N 21 30E
Tormentine 151 46 6N 63 46W
Tormes, R. 56 41 7N 6 0W
Tornado Mt. 152 49 55N 114 40W
Tornby 73 57 32N 9 56E
Torne älv 74 65 50N 24 12E
Torneå = Tornio 74 65 50N 24 12E
Torness 37 57 18N 4 22W
Torneträsk 74 68 24N 19 15E
Tornio 74 65 50N 24 12E
Tornionjoki 74 65 50N 24 12E
Tornquist 172 38 0S 62 15W
Toro 56 41 35N 5 24W
Torö 73 58 48N 17 50E
Toro, Cerro del 172 29 0S 69 50W
Toro Pk. 163 33 34N 116 24W
Törökszentmjklés 53 47 11N 20 27E
Toronátos Kólpos 68 40 5N 23 30E
Toronto, Austral. 141 33 0S 151 30E
Toronto, Can. 150 43 39N 79 20W
Toronto, U.S.A. 156 40 27N 80 36W
Toronto, L. 164 27 40N 105 30W
Toropets 80 56 30N 31 40E
Tororo 126 0 45N 34 12E
Toros Dağlari 92 37 0N 35 0E
Torphins 37 57 7N 2 37W
Torpoint 30 50 23N 4 12W
Torpshammar 72 62 29N 16 20E
Torquay, Austral. 140 38 20S 144 19E
Torquay, Can. 153 49 9N 103 30W
Torquay, U.K. 30 50 27N 3 31W
Torquemada 56 42 2N 4 19W
Torralba de Calatrava 57 39 1N 3 44W
Torran Rocks 34 56 14N 6 24W
Torrance 163 33 50N 118 19W
Torrão 57 38 16N 8 11W
Torre Annunziata 64 40 45N 14 26E
Tôrre de Moncorvo 56 41 12N 7 8W
Torre del Greco 65 40 47N 14 22E
Torre del Mar 57 36 44N 4 6W
Torre-Pacheco 29 37 44N 0 57W
Torre Pellice 62 44 49N 7 13E
Torreblanca 58 40 14N 0 12E
Torrecampo 57 38 29N 4 41W
Torrecilla en Cameros 58 42 15N 2 38W
Torredembarra 58 41 9N 1 24W
Torredonjimeno 57 37 46N 3 57W
Torrejoncillo 56 39 54N 6 28W
Torrelaguna 58 40 50N 3 38W
Torrelavega 56 43 20N 4 5W
Torremaggiore 65 41 42N 15 17E
Torremolinos 57 36 38N 4 30W
Torrens Cr. 138 22 23S 145 9E
Torrens Creek 138 20 48S 145 3E
Torrens, L. 140 31 0S 137 50E
Torrente 59 39 27N 0 28W
Torrenueva 59 38 38N 3 22W
Torreón 164 25 33N 103 25W
Torreperogil 59 38 2N 3 17W
Torres, Mexico 164 28 46N 110 47W
Torres, Spain 56 41 6N 5 0W
Tôrres Novas 57 39 27N 8 33W
Torres Strait 135 9 50S 142 20E
Torres Vedras 57 39 5N 9 15W
Torrevieja 59 37 59N 0 42W
Torrey 161 38 12N 111 30W
Torridge, R. 30 50 51N 4 10W
Torridon 36 57 33N 5 34W
Torridon, L. 36 57 35N 5 50W
Torrijos 56 39 59N 4 18W
Törring 73 55 52N 9 29E
Torrington, Conn., U.S.A. 162 41 50N 73 9W
Torrington, Wyo., U.S.A. 158 42 5N 104 8W
Torroboll 37 58 0N 4 23W
Torroella de Montgri 58 42 2N 3 8E
Torrox 57 36 46N 3 57W
Torsås 73 56 24N 16 0E
Torsby 72 60 7N 13 0E
Torsjok 72 57 5N 34 55E
Torsö 73 58 48N 13 45E
Torthorwald 35 55 7N 3 30W
Tortola, I. 147 18 19N 65 0W
Tórtoles de Esgueva 56 41 49N 4 2W
Tortona 62 44 53N 8 54E
Tortoreto 63 42 50N 13 55E
Tortorici 65 38 2N 14 48E
Tortosa 58 40 49N 0 31E
Tortosa C. 58 40 41N 0 52E
Tortosendo 56 40 15N 7 31W
Tortue, I. de la 167 20 5N 72 57W
Tortuga, Isla la 167 11 8N 67 2W
Torud 93 35 25N 55 5E
Torugart, Pereval 85 40 32N 75 24E
Torun 54 53 0N 18 39E
Torup 73 56 57N 13 5E
Torvastad 71 59 23N 5 15E
Torver 32 54 20N 3 7W
Tory I. 38 55 17N 8 12W
Torysa, R. 53 48 50N 21 15E
Torzhok 80 57 5N 34 55E
Tosa 110 33 24N 133 23E
Tosa-shimizu 110 32 52N 132 58E
Tosa-Wan 110 33 15N 133 30E
Tosa-yamada 110 33 36N 133 38E
Toscaig 36 57 23N 5 49W
Toscana 62 43 30N 11 5E
Tosno 80 59 30N 30 58E
Töss, R. 51 47 32N 8 39E
Tossa 58 41 43N 2 56E
Tostado 172 29 15S 61 50W
Tostedt 48 53 17N 9 42E
Tosu 110 33 22N 130 31E
Toszek 54 50 27N 18 32E
Totak 71 59 40N 7 45E
Totana 59 37 45N 1 30W
Toten 71 60 37N 10 53E
Toteng 128 20 22S 22 58E
Tôtes 42 49 41N 1 3E
Totland 28 50 41N 1 32W
Totley 33 53 18N 1 32W
Totma 81 60 0N 42 40E
Totnes 30 50 26N 3 41W
Totonicapán 166 14 50N 91 20W
Totskoye 84 52 32N 52 45E
Tottenham 141 32 14S 147 21E
Totton 28 50 55N 1 29W
Tottori 110 35 30N 134 15E
Tottori-ken □ 110 35 30N 134 12E
Touamotou, Archipel des 131 17 0S 144 0W
Touat 118 27 30N 0 30E
Touba 120 8 15N 7 40W
Toubkal, Djebel 118 31 0N 8 0W
Toubouai, Îles 131 25 0S 150 0W
Toucy 43 47 44N 3 15E
Tougan 120 13 11N 2 58W
Touggourt 119 33 10N 6 0E
Tougué 120 11 25N 11 50W
Toukmatine 119 24 49N 7 11E
Toul 43 48 40N 5 53E
Toulepleu 120 6 32N 8 24W
Toulon 45 43 10N 5 55E
Toulouse 44 43 37N 1 27E
Toummo 119 22 45N 14 8E
Toummo Dhoba 119 22 30N 14 31E
Toumodi 120 6 32N 5 4W
Tounan 109 23 41N 120 28E
Tounassine, Hamada 118 28 48N 5 0W
Toungoo 98 19 0N 96 30E
Touques, R. 42 49 22N 0 8E
Touquet, Le 43 50 30N 1 36E
Tour-du-Pin, La 45 45 33N 5 27E
Touraine 42 47 20N 0 30E
Tourane = Da Nang 100 16 4N 108 13E
Tourcoing 43 50 42N 3 10E
Tourcoingbam 121 13 23N 1 33W
Tournai 47 50 35N 3 25E
Tournan-en-Brie 43 48 44N 2 46E
Tournay 44 43 13N 0 13E
Tournon 45 45 4N 4 50E
Tournon-St.-Martin 42 46 45N 0 58E
Tournus 45 46 35N 4 54E
Touros 170 5 12S 35 28W
Tours 42 47 22N 0 40E
Touside, Pic 119 21 1N 16 18E
T'outaokou 107 42 44N 129 12E
Touwsrivier 128 33 20S 20 0E
Tovar 174 8 20N 71 46W
Tovarkovskiy 81 53 40N 38 5E
Tovdal 71 58 47N 8 10E
Tovdalselva 71 58 20N 8 16E
Towamba 141 37 6S 149 43E
Towanda 162 41 46N 76 30W
Towcester 29 52 7N 0 56W
Tower 158 47 49N 92 17W
Towerhill Cr. 138 22 28S 144 35E
Town Yetholm 35 55 33N 2 19W
Towner 158 48 25N 100 26W
Townsend 160 46 25N 111 32W
Townshend, C. 133 22 18S 150 30E
Townshend, I. 138 22 16S 150 31E
Townsville 138 19 15S 146 45E
Towson 162 39 26N 76 34W
Toyah 159 31 20N 103 48W
Toyahvale 159 30 58N 103 45W
Toyama 111 36 40N 137 15E
Toyama-ken □ 111 36 45N 137 30E
Tōyō 110 33 26N 134 16E
Toyohashi 111 34 45N 137 25E
Toyokawa 111 34 48N 137 27E
Toyonaka 111 34 50N 135 28E
Toyooka 110 35 35N 134 55E
Toyota 111 35 3N 137 7E
Toyoura 110 34 6N 130 57E
Toytepa 85 41 3N 69 20E
Tozeur 119 33 56N 8 8E
Tra On 101 9 58N 105 55E
Trabancos, R. 56 41 0N 5 3E
Trabzon 92 41 0N 39 45E
Tracadie 151 47 30N 64 55W
Tracy, Calif., U.S.A. 163 37 46N 121 27W
Tracy, Minn., U.S.A. 158 44 12N 95 3W
Tradate 62 45 43N 8 54E
Trafalgar 141 38 14S 146 12E
Trafalgar, C. 57 36 10N 6 2W
Traghan 119 26 0N 14 30E
Traian 70 45 2N 28 15E
Trail 152 49 5N 117 40W
Trainor L. 152 60 24N 120 17W
Traipu 171 9 58S 37 1W
Tralee 39 52 16N 9 42W
Tralee B. 39 52 17N 9 55W
Tramelan 50 47 13N 7 7E
Tramore 39 52 10N 7 10W
Tramore B. 39 52 9N 7 10W
Tran Ninh, Cao Nguyen 100 19 30N 103 10E
Tranas 73 58 3N 14 59E
Tranås 73 55 37N 13 59E
Trancas 172 26 20S 65 20W
Tranche-sur-Mer, La 42 46 20N 1 27W
Trancoso 56 40 49N 7 21W
Tranebjerg 73 55 51N 10 36E
Tranemo 73 57 30N 13 20E
Tranent 35 55 57N 2 58W
Trang 101 7 33N 99 38E
Trangahy 129 19 7S 44 43E
Trangan, I. 103 6 40S 134 20E
Trangie 141 32 4S 148 0E
Trångsviken 72 63 19N 14 0E
Trani 65 41 17N 16 24E
Tranoroa 129 24 42S 45 4E
Tranquebar 97 11 1N 79 54E
Tranqueras 173 31 8S 56 0W
Trans Nzoia □ 126 1 0N 35 0E
Transcona 153 49 50N 97 0W
Transilvania 70 46 19N 25 0E
Transkei □ 129 32 15S 28 15E
Transtrand 72 61 6N 13 20E
Transvaal □ 128 25 0S 29 0E
Transylvania = Transilvania 70 46 19N 25 0E
Transylvanian Alps 70 45 30N 25 0E
Trápani 64 38 1N 12 30E
Trappe Peak, Mt. 160 45 56N 114 29W
Traqowel 140 35 50S 144 0E
Traralgon 141 38 12S 146 34E
Traryd 73 56 35N 13 45E
Trarza □ 120 17 30N 15 0W
Tras os Montes e Alto-Douro □ 55 41 25N 7 20W
Trasacco 63 41 58N 13 30E
Trasimeno, L. 63 43 10N 12 5E
Träslöv 73 57 8N 12 21E
Trat 101 12 14N 102 33E
Traun 52 48 14N 14 15E
Traun-see 49 47 48N 13 45E
Traunstein 49 47 52N 12 40E
Trävad 73 58 15N 13 5E
Traveller's L. 140 33 20S 142 0E
Travemünde 48 53 58N 10 52E
Travers, Mt. 143 42 1S 172 45E
Traverse City 156 44 45N 85 39W
Traverse I. 13 48 0S 28 0E
Travnik 66 44 17N 17 39E
Trawbreaga B. 38 55 20N 7 25W
Trawsfynydd 31 52 54N 3 55W
Trayning 137 31 7S 117 46E
Traynor 153 52 20N 108 32W
Trazo 56 43 0N 8 30W
Trbovlje 63 46 12N 15 5E
Trebbia, R. 62 44 52N 9 30E
Trebel, R. 48 54 0N 12 50E
Trebinje 66 42 44N 18 22E
Trebisacce 65 39 52N 16 32E
Trebišnica, R. 66 42 47N 18 8E
Trebišov 53 48 38N 21 41E
Trebizat 66 43 15N 17 30E
Třebon 52 48 59N 14 48E
Trebujena 57 36 52N 6 11W
Trecate 62 45 29N 8 42E
Tredegar 31 51 47N 3 16W
Trefeglwys 31 52 31N 3 31W
Trefriw 31 53 9N 3 50W
Tregaron 31 52 14N 3 56W
Trégastel-Plage 42 48 49N 3 31W
Tregnago 63 45 31N 11 10E

**Tregrasse Is** **Tullow**


Tregrasse Is. 138 17 41S 150 43E
Trèguier 42 48 47N 3 16W
Trégunc 42 47 51N 3 51W
Tregynon 31 52 32N 3 19W
Treharris 31 51 40N 3 17W
Treherne 153 49 38N 98 42W
Trèia 63 43 30N 13 20E
Treig, L. 37 56 48N 4 42W
Treignac 44 45 32N 1 48E
Treinta y Tres 173 33 10S 54 50W
Treis 49 50 9N 7 19E
Trekveid 128 30 35S 19 45E
Trelde Næs 73 55 38N 9 53E
Trelech 31 51 56N 4 28W
Trelew 176 43 10S 65 20W
Trélissac 44 45 11N 0 47E
Trelleborg 73 55 20N 13 10E
Trélon 43 50 5N 4 6E
Tremadoc 31 52 57N 4 9W
Tremadoc, Bay 31 52 51N 4 18W
Tremblade, La 44 45 46N 1 8W
Tremelo 47 51 0N 4 42E
Trementina 159 35 27N 105 30W
Tremiti, I. 63 42 8N 15 30E
Tremonton 160 41 45N 112 10W
Tremp 58 42 10N 0 52E
Trenary 156 46 12N 86 59W
Trenčin 53 48 52N 18 4E
Trenche, R. 150 47 46N 72 53W
Trenggalek 103 8 5S 111 44E
Trenque Lauquen 172 36 0S 62 45W
Trent, R. 33 53 33N 0 44W
Trentham 32 52 59N 2 12W
Trentino-Alto Adige □ 62 46 5N 11 0E
Trento 62 46 5N 11 8E
Trenton, Can. 150 44 10N 77 40W
Trenton, Mo., U.S.A. 158 40 5N 93 37W
Trenton, Nebr., U.S.A. 158 40 14N 101 4W
Trenton, N.J., U.S.A. 162 40 15N 74 41W
Trenton, Tenn., U.S.A. 159 35 58N 88 57W
Trepassey 151 46 43N 53 25W
Trèport, Le 42 50 3N 1 20E
Treptow 48 53 42N 13 15E
Trepuzzi 65 40 26N 18 4E
Tres Arroyos 172 38 20S 60 20W
Três Corações 173 21 30S 45 30W
Três Lagoas 171 20 50S 51 50W
Tres Marías, Is. 164 21 25N 106 28W
Três Marias, Reprêsa 171 18 12S 45 15W
Tres Montes, C. 176 47 0S 75 35W
Tres Pinos 163 36 48N 121 19W
Três Pontas 173 21 23S 45 29W
Tres Puentes 172 27 50S 70 15W
Três Puntas, C. 176 47 0S 66 0W
Tres Rios 173 22 20S 43 30W
Tres Valles 165 18 15N 96 8W
Tresco I. 30 49 57N 6 20W
Treshnish Is. 34 56 30N 6 25W
Treska, R. 66 41 45N 21 11E
Treskavika Planina 66 43 40N 18 20E
Trespaderne 58 42 47N 3 24W
Tretower 31 51 53N 3 11W
Trets 45 43 27N 5 41E
Treuchtlingen 49 48 58N 10 55E
Treuddyn 31 53 7N 3 8W
Treuenbrietzen 48 52 6N 12 51E
Treungen 75 59 1N 8 31E
Treviglio 62 45 31N 9 35E
Trevinca, Peña 56 42 15N 6 46W
Treviso 63 45 40N 12 15E
Trevose Hd. 30 50 33N 5 3W
Trévoux 45 45 57N 4 47E
Trgovište 66 42 20N 22 10E
Triabunna 138 42 30S 147 55E
Triánda 69 36 25N 28 10E
Triang 101 3 13N 102 27E
Triangle 162 38 33N 77 20W
Triaucourt-en-Argonne 43 48 59N 5 2E
Tribsees 48 54 4N 12 46E
Tribulation, C. 138 16 5S 145 29E
Tribune 158 38 30N 101 45W
Tricárico 65 40 37N 16 9E
Tricase 65 39 56N 18 20E
Trichinopoly = Tiruchchirappalli 97 10 45N 78 45E
Trichur 97 10 30N 76 18E
Trida 141 33 1S 145 1E
Trier 49 49 45N 6 37E
Trieste 63 45 39N 13 45E
Trieste, G. di 63 45 37N 13 40E
Triggiano 65 41 4N 16 58E
Triglav 63 46 30N 13 45E
Trigno, R. 63 41 55N 14 37E
Trigueros 57 37 24N 6 50W
Trikeri 69 39 6N 23 5E
Trikhonis, Límni 69 38 34N 21 30E
Tríkkala 68 39 34N 21 47E
Tríkkala □ 68 39 41N 21 30E
Trikora, G. 103 4 11S 138 0E
Trilj 63 43 38N 16 42E
Trillick 38 54 27N 7 30W
Trillo 58 40 42N 2 35W
Trim 38 53 34N 6 48W
Trimdon 33 54 43N 1 23W
Trimley 29 51 59N 1 19E
Trincomalee 97 8 38N 81 15E
Trindade 171 16 40S 49 30W
Trindade, I. 15 20 20S 29 50W
Trinidad, Boliv. 174 14 54S 64 50W
Trinidad, Colomb. 174 5 25N 71 40W
Trinidad, Cuba 166 21 40N 80 0W
Trinidad, Uruguay 172 33 30S 56 50W
Trinidad, U.S.A. 159 37 15N 104 30W
Trinidad & Tobago ■ 167 10 30N 61 20W
Trinidad, I., Argent. 176 39 10S 62 0W
Trinidad, I., S. Amer. 167 10 30N 61 15W
Trinidad, R. 165 17 49N 95 9W
Trinitápoli 65 41 22N 16 5E
Trinity, Can. 151 48 22N 53 29W
Trinity, U.S.A. 159 30 50N 95 20W
Trinity B., Austral. 133 16 30S 146 0E
Trinity B., Can. 151 48 20N 53 10W
Trinity Mts. 159 40 20N 118 50W
Trinity R. 159 30 30N 95 0W
Trino 62 45 10N 8 18E
Trion 157 34 35N 85 18W
Trionto C. 65 34 38N 16 47E
Triora 62 44 0N 7 46E
Tripoli = Tarabulus 92 34 31N 33 52E
Tripoli = Tarābulus 119 32 49N 13 7E
Trípolis 69 37 31N 22 25E
Tripp 158 43 16N 97 58W
Tripura □ 98 24 0N 92 0E
Trischen, I. 48 54 3N 8 32E
Tristan da Cunha, I. 15 37 6S 12 20W
Trivandrum 97 8 31N 77 0E
Trivento 65 41 48N 14 31E
Trnava 53 48 23N 17 35E
Trobriand Is. 135 8 30S 151 0E
Trochu 152 51 50N 113 13W
Trodely I. 150 52 15N 79 26W
Trogir 63 43 32N 16 15E
Troglav, mt. 63 43 56N 16 36E
Trögstad 71 59 37N 11 16E
Tróia 65 41 22N 15 19E
Troilus, L. 150 50 50N 74 35W
Troina 65 37 47N 14 34E
Trois Fourches, Cap des 118 35 26N 2 58W
Trois Pistoles 151 48 5N 69 10W
Trois-Riviéres 150 46 25N 72 40W
Troisvierges 47 50 8N 6 0E
Troitsk 84 54 10N 61 35E
Troitskiy 84 55 29N 37 18E
Troitsko-Pechorsk 78 62 40N 56 10E
Trölladyngja 74 64 54N 17 15W
Trolladyngja 74 64 49N 17 29W
Trollhättan 73 58 17N 12 20E
Trollheimen 71 62 46N 9 1E
Tromöy 71 58 28N 8 53E
Troms fylke □ 74 68 56N 19 0E
Tromsø 74 69 40N 18 56E
Trona 163 35 46N 117 23W
Tronador, Mt. 176 41 53S 71 0W
Tröndelag, N. □ 74 65 0N 12 0E
Tröndelag, S. □ 71 62 0N 10 0E
Trondheim 71 63 25N 10 25E
Trondheimsfjorden 74 63 35N 10 30E
Trönninge 73 56 38N 12 59E
Trönö 72 61 22N 16 54E
Tronto, R. 63 42 50N 13 46E
Troodos, mt. 128 34 58N 32 55E
Troon 34 55 33N 4 40W
Tropea 65 38 40N 15 53E
Tropic 161 37 44N 112 4W
Tropoja 68 42 23N 20 10E
Trossachs, The 34 56 14N 4 24W
Trostan Mt. 38 55 4N 6 10W
Trostberg 49 48 2N 12 33E
Trotternish, dist. 36 57 32N 6 15W
Troup 159 32 10N 95 3W
Troup Hd. 37 57 41N 2 18W
Trout L., N.W. Terr., Can. 152 60 40N 121 40W
Trout L., Ont., Can. 153 51 20N 93 15W
Trout Lake 150 46 10N 85 2W
Trout, R. 152 61 19N 119 51W
Trout River 151 49 29N 58 8W
Trout Run 162 41 23N 77 3W
Trouville 42 49 21N 0 5E
Trowbridge 28 51 18N 2 12W
Troy, Turkey 92 39 55N 26 20E
Troy, Alabama, U.S.A. 157 31 50N 85 58W
Troy, Kans., U.S.A. 158 39 47N 95 2W
Troy, Mo., U.S.A. 158 38 56N 90 59W
Troy, Montana, U.S.A. 160 48 30N 115 58W
Troy, N.Y., U.S.A. 162 42 45N 73 39W
Troy, Ohio, U.S.A. 156 40 0N 84 10W
Troy, Pa., U.S.A. 162 41 47N 76 47W
Troyan 67 42 57N 24 43E
Troyes 43 48 19N 4 3E
Trpanj 66 43 1N 17 15E
Trstena 53 49 21N 19 37E
Trstenik 66 43 36N 21 0E
Trubchevsk 80 52 33N 33 47E
Truc Giang 101 10 14N 106 22E
Trucial States = Utd. Arab Emirates 93 24 0N 54 30E
Truckee 160 39 20N 120 11W
Trujillo, Colomb. 174 4 10N 76 19W
Trujillo, Hond. 166 16 0N 86 0W
Trujillo, Peru 174 8 0S 79 0W
Trujillo, Spain 57 39 28N 5 55W
Trujillo, U.S.A. 159 35 34N 104 44W
Trujillo, Venez. 174 9 22N 70 26W
Truk Is. 131 7 25N 151 46E
Trull 28 50 58N 3 8W
Trumann 159 35 42N 90 32W
Trumansburg 162 42 33N 76 40W
Trumbull, Mt. 161 36 25N 113 32W
Trumpington 29 52 11N 0 6E
Trún 66 42 51N 22 38E
Trun, France 42 48 50N 0 2E
Trun, Switz. 51 46 45N 8 59E
Trundle 141 32 53S 147 42E
Trung-Phan, reg. 100 16 0N 108 0E
Truro, Austral. 140 34 24S 139 9E
Truro, Can. 151 45 21N 63 14E
Truro, U.K. 30 50 17N 5 2W
Trŭscŭu, Muntii 70 46 14N 23 14E
Truskmore, mt. 38 54 23N 8 20W
Truslove 137 33 20S 121 45E
Trustrup 73 56 20N 10 46E
Truth or Consequences 161 33 9N 107 16W
Trutnov 52 50 37N 15 54E
Truxton 162 42 45N 76 2W
Truyère, R. 44 44 38N 2 34E
Trwyn Cilan 31 52 47N 4 31W
Tryavna 67 42 54N 25 25E
Tryon 157 35 15N 82 16W
Trzciarka 54 53 3N 16 25E
Trzciel 54 52 23N 15 50E
Trzcinsko-Zdroj 54 52 58N 14 35E
Trzebiez 54 53 38N 14 31E
Trzebinia 54 50 11N 19 30E
Trzeblatów 54 54 3N 15 18E
Trzebnica 54 51 20N 17 1E
Trzemeszno 54 52 33N 17 48E
Tržič 63 46 22N 14 18E
Tsafriya 90 31 59N 34 51E
Tsaidam 105 37 0N 95 0E
Tsak'o 108 31 56N 99 35E
Tsamandás 68 39 46N 20 21E
Tsamkong = Chanchiang 109 21 15N 110 20E
Tsana Dzong 99 28 0N 91 55E
Tsanga 99 30 43N 100 32E
Ts'angchi 108 31 48N 105 57E
Ts'angchou 106 38 10N 116 50E
Tsangpo 99 29 40N 89 0E
Ts'angyüan 108 23 9N 99 15E
Ts'ao Ho, R. 107 40 32N 124 11E
Tsaochuang 107 34 30N 117 49E
Tsaochwang 174 35 11N 115 28E
Ts'aohsien 106 34 50N 115 31E
Tsaoyang 109 32 8N 112 42E
Tsaratanana 129 16 47S 47 39E
Tsaratanana, Mt. de 129 14 0S 49 0E
Tsarevo = Michurin 67 42 9N 27 51E
Tsaring Nor 99 34 40N 97 20E
Tsaritsáni 68 39 53N 15 14E
Tsau 128 20 8S 22 29E
Tsaukaib 128 26 37S 15 39E
Tsebrikovo 82 47 9N 30 10E
Ts'ehung 108 25 2N 105 47E
Tselinograd 76 51 10N 71 30E
Tsengch'eng 109 23 17N 113 49E
Ts'enkung 108 27 13N 108 45E
Tsetserleg 105 47 36N 101 32E
Tshabong 128 26 2S 22 29E
Tshane 125 24 5S 21 54E
Tshela 124 5 4S 13 0E
Tshesebe 129 20 43S 27 32E
Tshhinvali 83 42 14N 44 1E
Tshibeke 126 2 40S 28 35E
Tshibinda 126 2 23S 28 30E
Tshikapa 124 6 17S 21 0E
Tshilenge 126 6 12S 23 40E
Tshinsenda 127 12 15N 28 0E
Tshofa 124 5 8S 25 8E
Tshombe 129 25 18S 45 29E
Tshwane 128 22 24S 22 1E
Tsigara 128 20 22S 25 54E
Tsihombe 125 25 10S 45 41E
Tsilmamo 123 6 1N 35 10E
Tsimlyansk 83 47 45N 42 0E
Tsimlyanskoye Vdkhr. 83 48 0N 43 0E
Tsinan = Chinan 106 36 32N 117 0E
Tsineng 128 27 05S 23 05E
Tsinga, mt. 68 41 23N 24 44E
Tsinghai □ 105 36 0N 96 0E
Tsingtao = Ch'ingtao 107 36 5N 120 25E
Tsinjomitondraka 129 15 40S 47 8E
Tsiroanomandidy 129 18 46S 46 2E
Tsivilsk 81 55 50N 47 25E
Tsivory 129 24 4S 46 5E
Tskhinali 79 42 22N 43 52E
Tso Chiang, R. 108 22 52N 108 5E
Tso Morari, L. 95 32 50N 78 20E
Tsochou 108 22 36N 107 36E
Tsoch'üan 106 37 3N 113 27E
Tsodilo Hill 128 18 49S 21 43E
Tsogttsetsiy 106 43 43N 105 35E
Tsokung 108 29 55N 97 44E
Tsona Dzong 99 28 0N 91 55E
Tsoshui 106 33 40N 109 9E
Tsouhsien 106 35 24N 116 58E
Tsu 111 34 45N 136 25E
Tsu L. 152 60 40N 111 52W
Tsuchiura 111 36 12N 140 15E
Tsugaru-Kaikyō 112 41 35N 141 0E
Tsukumi 110 33 4N 131 52E
Tsukushi-Sanchi 110 33 25N 130 30E
Tsumeb 128 19 9S 17 44E
Tsumis 128 23 39S 17 29E
Tsuna 110 34 28N 134 56E
Ts'ungchiang 108 25 45N 108 54E
Tsunhua 107 40 12N 117 56E
Tsuni 108 27 43N 106 52E
Tsuno-Shima 110 34 21N 130 52E
Tsuru 111 35 31N 138 57E
Tsuruga 111 35 45N 136 2E
Tsuruga-Wan 111 35 50N 136 3E
Tsurugi 111 36 37N 136 37E
Tsurugi-San 110 33 51N 134 6E
Tsurumi-Saki 110 32 56N 132 5E
Tsuruoka 112 38 44N 139 50E
Tsurusaki 110 33 14N 131 41E
Tsushima 111 35 10N 136 43E
Tsushima, I. 110 34 20N 129 20E
Tsvetkovo 82 49 15N 31 33E
Tu, R. 98 22 50N 97 15E
Tua, R. 57 41 19N 7 15W
Tuai 143 38 47S 177 15E
Tuakau 142 37 16S 174 59E
Tual 103 5 30S 132 50E
Tuam 38 53 30N 8 50W
Tuamarina 143 41 25S 173 59E
Tuamgraney 39 52 54N 8 32W
Tuamotu Arch = Touamotou 131 17 0S 144 0W
Tuan 108 23 59N 108 3E
T'uanch'i 108 27 28N 107 7E
T'uanfeng 109 30 38N 114 52E
Tuao 103 17 47S 121 30E
Tuapse 83 44 5N 39 10E
Tuatapere 143 46 8S 167 41E
Tuath, Loch 34 56 30N 6 15W
Tuba City 161 36 8N 111 12W
Tubac 161 31 45N 111 2W
Tubai Is. = Toubouai, Îles 131 25 0S 150 0W
Tuban 102 6 57S 112 4E
Tubarão 173 28 30S 49 0W
Tubas 90 32 20N 35 22E
Tubau 102 3 10N 113 40E
Tubayq, Jabal at 122 29 30N 27 30E
Tubbergen 46 52 24N 6 48E
Tübingen 48 48 31N 9 4E
Tubize 47 50 42N 4 13E
Tubja, W. 122 25 27N 38 55E
Tubruq, (Tobruk) 117 32 7N 23 55E
Tubuai, Îles 131 25 0S 150 0W
Tuc Trung 101 11 1N 107 12E
Tucacas 174 10 48N 68 19W
Tucano 170 10 58S 38 48W
Tuch'ang 109 29 15N 116 13E
T'uch'ang 109 24 42N 121 25E
Tuchodi, R. 152 58 17N 123 42W
Tuchola 54 53 33N 17 52E
Tuchów 54 49 54N 21 1E
T'uch'üan 107 45 22N 121 41E
Tuckanarra 137 27 8S 118 1E
Tuckernuck I. 162 41 15N 70 17W
Tucson 161 32 14N 110 59W
Tucumán 172 26 50S 65 20W
Tucumán □ 172 26 48S 66 2W
Tucumcari 159 35 12N 103 45W
Tucupido 174 9 17N 65 47W
Tucupita 174 9 14N 62 3W
Tucuracas 174 11 45N 72 22W
Tucuruí 170 3 42S 49 27W
Tuczno 54 53 13N 16 10E
Tudela 58 42 4N 1 39W
Tudela de Duero 56 41 37N 4 39W
Tudor, Lac 151 55 50N 65 25W
Tudora 70 47 31N 26 45E
Tudweiliog 31 52 54N 4 37W
Tuella, R. 56 41 50N 7 10W
Tuen 139 28 33S 145 37E
Tueré, R. 170 2 48S 50 59W
Tufi 135 9 8S 149 19E
Tugidak I. 147 56 30N 154 40W
Tuguegarao 103 17 35N 121 42E
Tugur 77 53 50N 136 45E
Tugwa 128 17 27S 18 33E
Tukangbesi, Kepulauan 103 6 0S 124 0E
Tukarak I. 150 56 15N 78 45W
Tukobo 120 5 1N 2 47W
Tūkrah 119 32 30N 20 37E
Tuku, mt. 123 9 10N 36 43E
Tukums 80 57 2N 23 3E
Tukuyu 127 9 17S 33 35E
Tukzar 93 35 55N 66 25E
Tula, Hidalgo, Mexico 165 20 0N 99 20W
Tula, Tamaulipas, Mexico 165 23 0N 99 40W
Tula, Nigeria 121 9 51N 11 27E
Tula, U.S.S.R. 81 54 13N 37 32E
Tulak 93 33 55N 63 40E
Tulancingo 165 20 5N 98 22W
Tulanssu 105 36 52N 98 24E
Tulare 163 36 15N 119 26W
Tulare Basin 163 36 0N 119 48W
Tulare Lake 161 36 0N 119 53W
Tularosa 161 33 4N 106 1W
Tulbagh 128 33 16S 19 6E
Tulcán 174 0 48N 77 43W
Tulcea 70 45 13N 28 46E
Tulcea □ 70 45 0N 29 0E
Tulchin 82 48 41N 28 55E
Tuléar 129 23 21S 43 40E
Tuléar □ 129 21 0S 45 0E
Tulemalu L. 153 62 58N 99 25W
Tulgheş 70 4 58N 25 45E
Tuli, Indon. 103 1 24S 122 26E
Tuli, Rhod. 127 21 58S 29 13E
Tuliuchen 106 39 1N 116 54E
Tulkarm 90 32 19N 35 10E
Tulla, Ireland 39 52 53N 8 45W
Tulla, U.S.A. 159 34 35N 101 44W
Tulla, L. 34 56 33N 4 47W
Tullaghoge 38 54 36N 6 43W
Tullaghought 39 52 25N 7 22W
Tullahoma 157 35 23N 86 12W
Tullamore, Austral. 141 32 39S 147 36E
Tullamore, Ireland 39 53 17N 7 30W
Tullaroan 39 52 40N 7 27W
Tulle 44 45 16N 0 47E
Tullibigeal 141 33 25S 146 44E
Tullins 45 45 18N 5 29E
Tulln 52 48 20N 16 4E
Tullow 39 52 48N 6 45W

**Tullus** **Uddingston**


| | | | |
|---|---|---|---|
| Tullus | **123** | 11 7N | 24 40E |
| Tully, Austral. | **138** | 17 56S | 145 55E |
| Tully, Ireland | **38** | 53 44N | 8 9W |
| Tully, U.S.A. | **162** | 42 48N | 76 7W |
| Tully Cross | **38** | 53 35N | 9 59W |
| Tûlmaciu | **70** | 45 38N | 24 19E |
| Tulmaythah | **117** | 32 40N | 20 55E |
| Tulmur | **138** | 22 40S | 142 20E |
| Tulnici | **70** | 45 51N | 26 38E |
| Tulovo | **67** | 42 33N | 25 32E |
| Tulsa | **159** | 36 10N | 96 0W |
| Tulsequah | **152** | 58 39N | 133 35W |
| Tulsk | **38** | 53 47N | 8 15W |
| Tulu Milki | **123** | 9 55N | 38 14E |
| Tulu Welel, Mt. | **123** | 8 56N | 35 30E |
| Tulua | **174** | 4 6N | 76 11W |
| T'ulufan | **105** | 42 56N | 89 10E |
| Tulun | **77** | 54 40N | 100 10E |
| Tulungagung | **103** | 8 5S | 111 54E |
| Tum | **103** | 3 28S | 130 21E |
| Tuma | **81** | 55 10N | 40 30E |
| Tuma, R. | **166** | 13 18N | 84 50W |
| Tumaco | **174** | 1 50N | 78 45W |
| Tumatumari | **174** | 5 20N | 58 55W |
| Tumba | **72** | 59 12N | 17 48E |
| Tumba, L. | **124** | 0 50S | 18 0E |
| Tumbarumba | **141** | 35 44S | 148 0E |
| Tumbaya | **172** | 23 50S | 65 20W |
| Tumbes | **174** | 3 30S | 80 20W |
| Tumbwa | **127** | 11 25S | 27 15E |
| Tumby B. | **140** | 34 21S | 136 8E |
| T'umen | **107** | 42 55N | 129 50E |
| T'umen Kiang, R. | **107** | 42 18N | 130 41E |
| Tumeremo | **174** | 7 18N | 61 30W |
| Tumiritinga | **171** | 18 58S | 41 38W |
| Tumkur | **97** | 13 18N | 77 12E |
| Tumleberg | **73** | 58 16N | 12 52E |
| Tummel, L. | **37** | 56 43N | 3 55W |
| Tummel, R. | **37** | 56 42N | 4 5W |
| T'umot'eyuch'i | **106** | 40 42N | 111 8E |
| Tump | **93** | 26 7N | 62 16E |
| Tumpat | **101** | 6 11N | 102 10E |
| Tumsar | **96** | 21 26N | 79 45E |
| Tumu | **120** | 10 56N | 1 56W |
| Tumucumaque, Serra de | **175** | 2 0N | 55 0W |
| Tumut | **141** | 35 16S | 148 13E |
| Tumutuk | **84** | 55 1N | 53 19E |
| Tumwater | **160** | 47 0N | 122 58W |
| Tuna, Pta. | **147** | 17 59N | 65 53W |
| Tunas de Zaza | **166** | 21 39N | 79 34W |
| Tunbridge Wells | **29** | 51 7N | 0 16E |
| T'unch'i | **105** | 29 50N | 118 26E |
| Tuncurry | **141** | 32 9S | 152 29E |
| Tunduru | **127** | 11 0S | 37 25E |
| Tunduru □ | **127** | 11 5S | 37 22E |
| Tundzha, R. | **67** | 42 0N | 26 35E |
| Tune | **71** | 59 16N | 11 2E |
| Tung Chiang, R. | **109** | 22 55N | 113 35E |
| Tung-Pei | **77** | 44 0N | 126 0E |
| Tunga La | **99** | 29 0N | 94 14E |
| Tunga Pass | **98** | 29 0N | 94 14E |
| Tunga, R. | **97** | 13 42N | 75 20E |
| Tungabhadra Dam | **97** | 15 21N | 76 23E |
| Tungabhadra, R. | **97** | 15 30N | 77 0E |
| Tungachen | **106** | 36 15N | 165 12E |
| Tungan | **109** | 26 24N | 111 17E |
| T'ungan | **109** | 24 44N | 118 9E |
| T'ungcheng, Anhwei, China | **109** | 31 3N | 116 58E |
| T'ungcheng, Hupeh, China | **109** | 29 15N | 113 49E |
| Tungch'i | **108** | 28 43N | 106 42E |
| T'ungchiang, Heilungkiang, China | **105** | 47 40N | 132 30E |
| T'ungchiang, Szechwan, China | **108** | 31 56N | 107 15E |
| Tungchingch'eng | **107** | 44 9N | 129 7E |
| Tungchuan | **105** | 35 4N | 109 2E |
| T'ungch'uan | **106** | 35 95N | 109 5E |
| Tungch'uan | **108** | 26 9N | 103 7E |
| Tungfanghsien, (Paso) | **100** | 18 50N | 108 33E |
| Tungfeng | **107** | 42 40N | 125 34E |
| T'unghai | **108** | 24 8N | 102 43E |
| Tunghai Tao | **109** | 21 2N | 110 25E |
| Tunghsiang | **109** | 28 14N | 116 35E |
| T'unghsien | **105** | 39 45N | 116 43E |
| T'unghsin | **106** | 37 9N | 106 28E |
| T'unghua | **107** | 41 45N | 126 0E |
| Tungi | **98** | 23 53N | 90 24E |
| T'ungjen | **105** | 27 43N | 109 10E |
| Tungkan | **108** | 23 22N | 105 9E |
| Tungkou | **107** | 39 52N | 124 8E |
| Tungku | **108** | 31 52N | 100 14E |
| T'ungku | **109** | 28 32N | 114 23E |
| Tungkuan | **109** | 23 0N | 113 39E |
| T'ungkuan | **105** | 34 37N | 110 27E |
| Tungkuang | **106** | 37 53N | 116 32E |
| Tungla | **166** | 13 24N | 84 15W |
| Tunglan | **108** | 24 30N | 107 23E |
| T'ungliang | **108** | 29 52N | 106 2E |
| T'ungliao | **107** | 43 37N | 122 16E |
| Tungling | **109** | 31 0N | 117 54E |
| Tungliu | **109** | 30 13N | 116 55E |
| T'unglu | **109** | 29 49N | 119 40E |
| Tungnafellsjökull | **74** | 64 45N | 17 55W |
| T'ungnan | **108** | 30 14N | 105 48E |
| Tungning | **107** | 44 3N | 131 7E |
| T'ungpai | **109** | 32 22N | 113 24E |
| Tungp'ing | **106** | 35 55N | 116 18E |
| Tungpu | **99** | 31 42N | 98 19E |
| Tungshan | **109** | 23 40N | 117 31E |
| Tungshih | **109** | 24 12N | 120 43E |
| Tungsten, Can. | **152** | 61 57N | 128 16W |
| Tungsten, U.S.A. | **160** | 40 50N | 118 10W |
| Tungt'ai | **109** | 32 50N | 120 46E |
| T'ungtao | **108** | 26 21N | 109 36E |
| T'ungtien | **108** | 26 40N | 99 32E |
| Tungt'ing Hu | **109** | 29 18N | 112 45E |
| Tungtzu | **108** | 28 8N | 106 49E |
| Tunguchumuch'inch'i | **106** | 45 33N | 116 50E |
| Tunguska, Nizhmaya, R. | **77** | 64 0N | 95 0E |
| Tunguska, Podkammenaya, R. | **77** | 61 0N | 98 0E |
| T'ungwei | **106** | 35 18N | 105 10E |
| T'ungyü | **107** | 44 48N | 123 6E |
| Tunhua | **107** | 43 20N | 128 10E |
| Tunhuang | **105** | 40 10N | 94 50E |
| Tuni | **96** | 17 22N | 82 43E |
| Tunia | **174** | 2 41N | 76 31W |
| Tunica | **159** | 34 43N | 90 23W |
| Tunis | **119** | 36 50N | 10 11E |
| Tunis, Golfe de | **119** | 37 0N | 10 30E |
| Tunisia ■ | **119** | 33 30N | 9 10E |
| Tunja | **174** | 5 40N | 73 25W |
| Tunkhannock | **162** | 41 32N | 75 56W |
| T'unliu | **106** | 36 19N | 112 54E |
| Tunnsjøen | **74** | 64 45N | 13 25E |
| Tuno I. | **73** | 55 58N | 10 27E |
| T'unpuli Shan | **105** | 35 0N | 89 30E |
| Tunstall | **29** | 52 7N | 1 28E |
| Tuntatuliag | **147** | 60 20N | 162 45W |
| Tunungayualuk I. | **151** | 56 0N | 61 0W |
| Tunuyán | **172** | 33 55S | 69 0W |
| Tunuyán, R. | **172** | 33 33S | 67 30W |
| Tuolumne | **163** | 37 59N | 120 16W |
| Tuolumne, R. | **163** | 37 36N | 121 13W |
| Tuoy-Khaya | **77** | 62 32N | 111 18E |
| Tupã | **173** | 21 57S | 50 28W |
| Tupaciguara | **171** | 18 35S | 48 42W |
| Tuparro, R. | **174** | 5 0N | 68 40W |
| Tupelo | **157** | 34 15N | 88 42W |
| Tupik | **77** | 54 26N | 119 57E |
| Tupinambaranas, I. | **174** | 3 0S | 58 0W |
| Tupirama | **170** | 8 58S | 48 12W |
| Tupiratins | **170** | 8 23S | 48 8W |
| Tupiza | **172** | 21 30S | 65 40W |
| Tupman | **163** | 35 18N | 119 21W |
| Tupper | **152** | 55 32N | 120 1W |
| Tupper L. | **156** | 44 18N | 74 30W |
| Tupungato, Cerro | **172** | 33 15S | 69 50W |
| Tuque, La | **150** | 47 30N | 72 50W |
| Túquerres | **174** | 1 5N | 77 37W |
| Tur | **90** | 31 47N | 35 14E |
| Tura, India | **98** | 25 30N | 90 16E |
| Tura, U.S.S.R. | **77** | 64 20N | 99 30E |
| Tura, R. | **84** | 57 12N | 66 56E |
| Turaba, W. | **122** | 21 15N | 41 32E |
| Turagua, Serranía | **174** | 7 20N | 64 35W |
| Turaiyur | **97** | 11 9N | 78 38E |
| Turakina | **142** | 40 3S | 175 16E |
| Turakirae Hd. | **142** | 41 26S | 174 56E |
| Tūrān | **93** | 35 45N | 56 50E |
| Turan | **77** | 51 38N | 101 40E |
| Turbenthal | **51** | 47 27N | 8 51E |
| Tureburg | **72** | 59 30N | 17 58E |
| Turégano | **56** | 41 9N | 4 1W |
| Turek | **54** | 52 3N | 18 30E |
| Turen | **174** | 9 17N | 69 6W |
| Turfan Depression | **105** | 42 45N | 89 0E |
| Turgay | **84** | 49 38N | 63 30E |
| Turgay, R. | **84** | 48 1N | 62 45E |
| Tŭrgovishte | **67** | 43 17N | 26 38E |
| Turgutlu | **92** | 38 30N | 27 48E |
| Turhal | **82** | 40 24N | 36 19E |
| Turia, R. | **58** | 39 43N | 1 0W |
| TuriaçI | **170** | 1 40S | 45 28W |
| TuriaçI, R. | **170** | 3 0S | 46 0W |
| Turigshih | **100** | 18 42N | 109 27E |
| Turin = Torino | **62** | 45 3N | 7 40E |
| Turin Taber | **152** | 49 47N | 112 24W |
| Turinsk | **84** | 58 3N | 63 42E |
| Turkana □ | **126** | 3 0N | 35 30E |
| Turkana, L. | **80** | 4 10N | 32 10E |
| Turkestan | **76** | 43 10N | 68 10E |
| Turkestanskiy, Khrebet | **85** | 39 35N | 69 0E |
| Túrkeve | **53** | 47 6N | 20 44E |
| Turkey ■ | **92** | 39 0N | 36 0E |
| Turkey Creek P.O. | **136** | 17 2S | 128 12E |
| Turki | **81** | 52 0N | 43 15E |
| Turkmen S.S.R. □ | **85** | 39 0N | 59 0E |
| Turks Is. | **167** | 21 20N | 71 20W |
| Turks Island Passage | **167** | 21 30N | 71 20W |
| Turku (Åbo) | **75** | 60 30N | 22 19E |
| Turku-Pori □ | **75** | 60 27N | 22 15E |
| Turkwell, R. | **126** | 2 30N | 35 20E |
| Turlock | **163** | 37 30N | 120 55W |
| Turnagain, C. | **142** | 40 28S | 176 38E |
| Turnagain, R. | **152** | 59 12N | 127 35W |
| Turnberry, Can. | **153** | 53 25N | 101 45W |
| Turnberry, U.K. | **34** | 55 19N | 4 50W |
| Turneffe Is. | **165** | 17 20N | 87 50W |
| Turner | **160** | 48 52N | 108 25W |
| Turner Pt. | **138** | 11 47S | 133 32E |
| Turner River | **136** | 17 52S | 128 16E |
| Turner Valley | **152** | 50 40N | 114 17W |
| Turners Falls | **162** | 42 36N | 72 34W |
| Turnhout | **47** | 51 19N | 4 57E |
| Türnitz | **52** | 47 55N | 15 29E |
| Turnor L. | **153** | 56 35N | 108 35W |
| Turnov | **52** | 50 34N | 15 10E |
| Turnovo | **67** | 43 5N | 25 41E |
| Turnovo □ | **67** | 43 4N | 25 39E |
| Turnu Mǎgurele | **70** | 43 46N | 24 56E |
| Turnu Roşu Pasul | **70** | 45 33N | 24 17E |
| Turnu-Severin | **70** | 44 39N | 22 41E |
| Turö | **73** | 55 2N | 10 40E |
| Turon | **159** | 37 48N | 98 27W |
| Tuross Head | **141** | 36 3S | 150 8E |
| Turriff | **37** | 57 32N | 2 28W |
| Tursha | **81** | 56 50N | 47 45E |
| Tursi | **65** | 40 15N | 16 27E |
| Turtle Hd. I. | **138** | 10 50S | 142 37E |
| Turtle L., Can. | **153** | 53 36N | 108 38W |
| Turtle L., N.D., U.S.A. | **158** | 47 30N | 100 55W |
| Turtle L., Wis., U.S.A. | **158** | 45 22N | 92 10W |
| Turtleford | **153** | 53 23N | 108 57W |
| Turua | **142** | 37 14S | 175 35E |
| Turubah | **92** | 28 20N | 43 15E |
| Turukhansk | **77** | 65 50N | 87 50E |
| Turun ja Porin lääni □ | **75** | 60 27N | 22 15E |
| Turzovka | **53** | 49 25N | 18 41E |
| Tuscaloosa | **157** | 33 13N | 87 31W |
| Tuscánia | **63** | 42 25N | 11 53E |
| Tuscany = Toscana | **62** | 43 28N | 11 15E |
| Tuscola, Ill., U.S.A. | **156** | 39 48N | 88 15W |
| Tuscola, Tex., U.S.A. | **159** | 32 15N | 99 48W |
| Tuscumbia | **157** | 34 42N | 87 42W |
| Tushan | **106** | 25 50N | 107 33E |
| Tushino | **81** | 55 44N | 37 29E |
| Tuskar Rock | **39** | 52 12N | 6 10W |
| Tuskegee | **157** | 32 24N | 85 39W |
| Tůšnad | **70** | 47 30N | 22 33E |
| Tustna | **71** | 63 10N | 8 5E |
| Tuszyn | **54** | 51 36N | 19 33E |
| Tutaryd | **73** | 56 54N | 13 59E |
| Tutbury | **28** | 52 52N | 1 41W |
| Tutikorin | **97** | 8 50N | 78 12E |
| Tutin | **66** | 43 0N | 20 20E |
| Tutóia | **170** | 2 45S | 42 20W |
| Tutoko Mt. | **143** | 44 35S | 168 1E |
| Tutong | **102** | 4 47N | 114 34E |
| Tutova, R. | **70** | 46 20N | 27 30E |
| Tutrakan | **67** | 44 2N | 26 40E |
| Tutshi L. | **152** | 59 56N | 134 30W |
| Tuttlingen | **49** | 47 59N | 8 50E |
| Tutuaia | **103** | 8 25S | 127 15E |
| Tutye | **140** | 35 12S | 141 29E |
| Tuva, A.S.S.R. □ | **77** | 51 30N | 95 0E |
| Tuxford | **33** | 53 14N | 0 52W |
| Tuxpan | **165** | 20 50N | 97 30W |
| Tuxtla Gutiérrez | **165** | 16 50N | 93 10W |
| Tuy | **56** | 42 3N | 8 39W |
| Tuy An | **100** | 13 17N | 109 16E |
| Tuy Doc | **101** | 12 15N | 107 27E |
| Tuy Hoa | **100** | 13 5N | 109 17E |
| Tuy Phong | **101** | 11 14N | 108 43E |
| Tuya L. | **152** | 59 7N | 130 35W |
| Tuyen Hoa | **100** | 17 50N | 106 10E |
| Tuyen Quang | **100** | 21 50N | 105 10E |
| Tuymazy | **84** | 54 36N | 53 42E |
| Tuyun | **108** | 26 15N | 107 32E |
| Tuz Gölü | **92** | 38 45N | 33 30E |
| Tuz Khurmatli | **92** | 34 52N | 44 41E |
| Tuz Khurmatu | **92** | 34 50N | 44 45E |
| Tuzkan, Ozero | **85** | 40 35N | 67 28E |
| Tuzla | **66** | 44 34N | 18 41E |
| Tuzlov, R. | **83** | 47 28N | 39 45E |
| Tvååker | **73** | 57 4N | 12 25E |
| Tværsted | **73** | 57 36N | 10 12E |
| Tvarskog | **73** | 56 34N | 16 0E |
| Tved | **73** | 56 12N | 10 25E |
| Tvedestrand | **71** | 58 38N | 8 58E |
| Tveitsund | **71** | 59 2N | 8 31E |
| Tvelt | **71** | 60 30N | 7 11E |
| Tvyrditsa | **67** | 42 42N | 25 53E |
| Twain Harte | **163** | 38 2N | 120 14W |
| Twardogóra | **54** | 51 23N | 17 28E |
| Twatt | **37** | 59 6N | 3 15W |
| Tweed, R. | **35** | 55 42N | 2 10W |
| Tweede Exploërmond | **46** | 52 55N | 6 56E |
| Tweedmouth | **35** | 55 46N | 2 1W |
| Tweedshaws | **35** | 55 26N | 3 29W |
| Tweedsmuir Prov. Park | **152** | 52 55N | 126 20W |
| Twello | **46** | 52 14N | 6 6E |
| Twelve Pins | **38** | 53 32N | 9 50W |
| Twentynine Palms | **163** | 34 10N | 116 4W |
| Twillingate | **151** | 49 42N | 54 45W |
| Twin Bridges | **160** | 45 33N | 112 23W |
| Twin Falls | **160** | 42 30N | 114 30W |
| Twin Valley | **158** | 47 18N | 96 15W |
| Twinnge | **98** | 21 58N | 96 23E |
| Twisp | **160** | 48 21N | 120 5W |
| Twistringen | **48** | 52 48N | 8 38E |
| Two Harbors | **158** | 47 1N | 91 40W |
| Two Hills | **152** | 53 43N | 111 45W |
| Two Mile Borris | **39** | 52 41N | 7 43W |
| Two Rivers | **156** | 44 10N | 87 31W |
| Two Thumbs Ra. | **143** | 43 45S | 170 44E |
| Two Tree | **138** | 18 25S | 140 3E |
| Twofold B. | **141** | 37 8S | 149 59E |
| Twong | **123** | 5 18N | 28 29E |
| Twyford, Berks., U.K. | **29** | 51 29N | 0 51W |
| Twyford, Hants., U.K. | **28** | 51 1N | 1 19W |
| Ty | **73** | 56 27N | 8 32E |
| Tyborön | **73** | 56 42N | 8 12E |
| Tychy | **54** | 50 9N | 18 59E |
| Tyczyn | **54** | 49 58N | 22 2E |
| Tydd St. Mary | **29** | 52 45N | 0 9E |
| Tykocin | **54** | 53 13N | 22 46E |
| Tyldal | **71** | 62 8N | 10 48E |
| Tyldesley | **32** | 53 31N | 2 29W |
| Tyler, Minn., U.S.A. | **158** | 44 18N | 96 15W |
| Tyler, Tex., U.S.A. | **159** | 44 18N | 96 15W |
| Tylldal | **71** | 62 7N | 10 45E |
| Tylösand | **73** | 56 33N | 12 40E |
| Týn nad Vltavou | **52** | 49 13N | 14 26E |
| Tynagh | **39** | 53 10N | 8 22W |
| Tyndall, Mt. | **143** | 43 15S | 170 55E |
| Tyndinskiy | **77** | 55 10N | 124 43E |
| Tyndrum | **34** | 56 26N | 4 41W |
| Tyne & Wear □ | **35** | 54 55N | 1 35W |
| Tyne, R., Eng., U.K. | **35** | 54 58N | 1 28W |
| Tyne, R., Scot., U.K. | **35** | 55 58N | 2 45W |
| Tynemouth | **35** | 55 1N | 1 27W |
| Tynset | **71** | 62 17N | 10 47E |
| Tyre = Sūr | **90** | 33 19N | 35 16E |
| Tyrifjorden | **71** | 60 2N | 10 8E |
| Tyringe | **73** | 56 9N | 13 35E |
| Tyristrand | **71** | 60 5N | 10 5E |
| Tyrnyauz | **83** | 43 21N | 42 45E |
| Tyrol = Tirol | **52** | 46 50N | 11 20E |
| Tyrone □ | **38** | 54 40N | 7 15W |
| Tyrone, Co. | **38** | 54 40N | 7 15W |
| Tyrrell Arm | **153** | 62 27N | 97 30W |
| Tyrrell, L. | **140** | 35 20S | 142 50E |
| Tyrrell L. | **153** | 63 7N | 105 27W |
| Tyrrell, R. | **140** | 35 26S | 142 51E |
| Tyrrhenian Sea | **60** | 40 0N | 12 30E |
| Tysfjörden | **74** | 68 10N | 16 10E |
| Tysmenitsa | **80** | 48 58N | 24 50E |
| Tysnes | **71** | 60 1N | 5 30E |
| Tyssedal | **71** | 60 7N | 6 35E |
| Tystberga | **73** | 58 51N | 17 15E |
| Tyulgan | **84** | 52 22N | 56 12E |
| Tyumen | **84** | 57 0N | 65 18E |
| Tyumen-Aryk | **85** | 44 2N | 67 1E |
| Tyup | **85** | 42 45N | 78 20E |
| Tyvoll | **71** | 62 43N | 11 21E |
| Tywardreath | **30** | 50 21N | 4 40W |
| Tywi, R. | **31** | 51 48N | 4 20W |
| Tywyn | **31** | 52 36N | 4 5W |
| Tzaneen | **129** | 23 47S | 30 9E |
| Tzefa | **90** | 31 7N | 35 12E |
| Tzermiadhes Neapolis | **69** | 35 11N | 25 29E |
| Tzoumérka, Óros | **68** | 39 30N | 21 26E |
| Tzu Shui, R. | **109** | 29 2N | 112 55E |
| Tzuch'ang | **106** | 37 12N | 109 44E |
| Tzuch'eng | **107** | 36 39N | 117 56E |
| Tzuch'i | **109** | 27 42N | 116 58E |
| Tz'uch'i | **109** | 29 59N | 121 14E |
| Tzuchien | **99** | 27 43N | 98 34E |
| Tzuchin | **109** | 23 38N | 115 10E |
| Tzuchung | **108** | 29 49N | 104 55E |
| Tz'uhsien | **106** | 36 22N | 114 23E |
| Tzuhsing | **109** | 25 58N | 113 24E |
| Tzukuei | **105** | 31 0N | 110 38E |
| Tzukung | **108** | 29 20N | 104 50E |
| Tz'uli | **109** | 29 25N | 111 6E |
| Tzummarum | **46** | 53 14N | 5 32E |
| Tzupo | **105** | 36 49N | 118 5E |
| T'zuyang | **108** | 32 31N | 108 32E |
| Tzuyang | **108** | 30 7N | 104 39E |
| Tzuyün | **108** | 25 45N | 106 5E |


# U


| | | | |
|---|---|---|---|
| U Taphao | **100** | 12 35N | 101 0E |
| Uad Erni, O. | **118** | 26 30N | 9 30W |
| Uainambi | **174** | 1 43N | 69 51W |
| Uanda | **138** | 21 37S | 144 55E |
| Uarsciek | **91** | 2 28N | 45 55E |
| Uasadi-jidi, Sierra | **174** | 4 54N | 65 18W |
| Uasin □ | **126** | 0 30N | 35 20E |
| Uassem | **90** | 32 59N | 36 2E |
| Uato-Udo | **103** | 4 3S | 126 6E |
| Uatumã, R. | **174** | 1 30S | 59 25W |
| Uauá | **170** | 9 50S | 39 28W |
| Uaupés | **174** | 0 8S | 67 5W |
| Uaxactún | **166** | 17 25N | 89 29W |
| Ub | **66** | 44 28N | 20 6E |
| Ubá | **173** | 21 0S | 43 0W |
| Ubaitaba | **171** | 14 18S | 39 20W |
| Ubangi, R. = Oubangi | **124** | 1 0N | 17 50E |
| Ubaté | **174** | 5 19N | 73 49W |
| Ubauro | **94** | 28 15N | 69 45E |
| Ube | **110** | 33 56N | 131 15E |
| Ubeda | **59** | 38 3N | 3 23W |
| Uberaba | **171** | 19 50S | 47 55W |
| Uberlândia | **171** | 19 0S | 48 20W |
| Ubiaja | **121** | 6 41N | 6 22E |
| Ubolratna Phong, L. | **100** | 16 45N | 102 30E |
| Ubombo | **129** | 27 31S | 32 4E |
| Ubon Ratchathani | **100** | 15 15N | 104 50E |
| Ubondo | **126** | 0 55S | 25 42E |
| Ubort, R. | **80** | 51 45N | 28 30E |
| Ubrique | **57** | 36 41N | 5 27W |
| Ubundi | **126** | 0 22S | 25 30E |
| Ucayali, R. | **174** | 6 0S | 75 0W |
| Uccle | **47** | 50 48N | 4 22E |
| Uchaly | **84** | 54 19N | 59 27E |
| Uchi Lake | **153** | 51 10N | 92 40W |
| Uchiko | **110** | 33 33N | 132 39E |
| Uchiura-Wan | **112** | 42 25N | 140 40E |
| Uchte | **48** | 52 29N | 8 52E |
| Uchterek | **85** | 41 45N | 73 12E |
| Uckerath | **48** | 50 44N | 7 22E |
| Uckfield | **29** | 50 58N | 0 6E |
| Ucluelet | **152** | 48 57N | 125 32W |
| Ucolta | **107** | 32 56S | 138 59E |
| Ucuriş | **70** | 46 41N | 21 58E |
| Uda, R. | **77** | 54 42N | 135 14E |
| Udaipur | **94** | 24 36N | 73 44E |
| Udaipur Garhi | **95** | 27 0N | 86 35E |
| Udamalpet | **97** | 10 35N | 77 15E |
| Udbina | **63** | 44 31N | 15 47E |
| Uddeholm | **72** | 60 1N | 13 38E |
| Uddel | **46** | 52 15N | 5 48E |
| Uddevalla | **73** | 58 21N | 11 55E |
| Uddingston | **35** | 55 50N | 4 3W |

**Uddjaur** **Ust Kuyga**


Uddjaur 74 65 55N 17 50 E
Uden 47 51 40N 5 37 E
Udgir 96 18 25N 77 5 E
Udhampur 95 33 0N 75 5 E
Udi 121 6 23N 7 21 E
Udine 63 46 5N 13 10 E
Udine □ 63 46 3N 13 13 E
Udipi 97 13 25N 74 42 E
Udmurt, A.S.S.R. □ 84 57 30N 52 30 E
Udon Thani 100 17 29N 102 46 E
Udubo 121 11 52N 10 35 E
Udvoj Balken 67 42 50N 26 50 E
Udzungwa Range 127 11 15 S 35 10 E
Ueckermünde 48 53 45N 14 1 E
Ueda 111 36 24N 138 16 E
Uedineniya, Os. 12 78 0N 85 0 E
Uele, R. 124 3 50N 22 40 E
Uelen 77 66 10N 170 0W
Uelzen 48 53 0N 10 33 E
Ueno 111 34 53N 136 14 E
Uere, R. 124 3 45N 24 45 E
Uetendorf 50 46 47N 7 34 E
Ufa 84 54 45N 55 55 E
Ufa, R. 84 56 30N 58 10 E
Uffculme 30 50 45N 3 19W
Ufford 29 52 6N 1 22 E
Ugad R. 125 20 55 S 14 30 E
Ugalla, R. 126 6 0 S 32 0 E
Ugamas 128 28 0 S 19 41 E
Uganda ■ 126 2 0N 32 0 E
Ugborough 30 50 22N 3 53W
Ugchelen 46 52 11N 5 56 E
Ugento 65 39 55N 18 10 E
Ugep 121 5 53N 8 2 E
Ugie 129 31 10 S 28 13 E
Ugijar 59 36 58N 3 7W
Ugine 45 45 45N 6 25 E
Ugla 122 25 40N 37 42 E
Uglich 81 57 33N 38 13 E
Ugljane 63 43 35N 16 46 E
Ugra, R. 80 54 45N 35 30 E
Ugurchin 67 43 6N 24 26 E
Uh, R. 53 48 40N 22 0 E
Uherske Hradiště 53 49 4N 17 30 E
Uhersky Brod 53 49 1N 17 40 E
Uhrichsville 156 40 23N 81 22W
Uig, Lewis, U.K. 36 58 13N 7 1W
Uig, Skye, U.K. 36 57 35N 6 20W
Uinta Mts. 160 40 45N 110 30W
Uitenhage 128 33 40 S 25 28 E
Uitgeest 46 52 32N 4 43 E
Uithoorn 46 52 14N 4 50 E
Uithuizen 46 53 24N 6 41 E
Uitkerke 47 51 18N 3 9 E
Ujda = Oujda 118 34 45N 2 0W
Ujfehértó 53 47 49N 21 41 E
Ujh, R. 95 32 40N 75 30 E
Ujhani 95 28 0N 79 6 E
Uji 111 34 53N 135 48 E
Ujjain 94 23 9N 75 43 E
Ujpest 53 47 22N 19 6 E
Ujszász 53 47 19N 20 7 E
Ujung Pandang 103 5 10 S 119 20 E
Uka 77 57 50N 162 0 E
Ukara I. 126 1 44 S 33 0 E
Ukehe 121 6 40N 7 24 E
Ukerewe □ 126 2 0 S 32 30 E
Ukerewe Is. 126 2 0 S 33 0 E
Ukholovo 81 54 47N 40 30 E
Ukhrul 98 25 10N 94 25 E
Ukhta 78 63 55N 54 0 E
Ukiah 160 39 10N 123 9W
Ukki Fort 95 33 28N 76 54 E
Ukmerge 80 55 15N 24 45 E
Ukraine S.S.R. □ 82 48 0N 35 0 E
Uksyanskoye 84 55 57N 63 1 E
Ukwi 128 23 29 S 20 30 E
Ulaanbaatar 105 47 55N 106 53 E
Ulaangom 105 49 58N 92 2 E
Ulak I. 147 51 24N 178 58W
Ulamambri 141 31 19 S 149 23 E
Ulamba 127 9 3 S 23 38 E
Ulan Bator = Ulaanbaatar 105 47 55N 106 53 E
Ulan Ude 77 52 0N 107 30 E
Ulanbel 85 44 50N 71 7 E
Ulanga □ 127 8 40 S 36 50 E
Ulanów 54 50 30N 22 16 E
Ulaya, Morogoro, Tanz. 126 7 3 S 36 55 E
Ulaya, Shinyanga, Tanz. 126 4 25 S 33 30 E
Ulbster 37 58 21N 3 9W
Ulceby Cross 33 53 14N 0 6 E
Ulcinj 66 41 58N 19 10 E
Ulco 128 28 21 S 24 15 E
Ulefoss 71 59 17N 9 16 E
Ulëza 68 41 46N 19 57 E
Ulfborg 73 56 16N 8 20 E
Ulft 46 51 53N 6 23 E
Ulhasnagar 96 19 15N 73 10 E
Ulinda 141 31 35 S 149 30 E
Uljma 66 45 2N 21 10 E
Ulla, R. 56 42 45N 8 30W
Ulladulla 141 35 21 S 150 29 E
Ullånger 72 62 58N 18 16 E
Ullapool 36 57 54N 5 10W
Ullared 73 57 8N 12 42 E
Ulldecona 58 40 36N 0 20 E
Ullswater, L. 32 54 35N 2 52W
Ullvättern, L. 72 59 30N 14 21 E
Ulm 49 48 23N 10 0 E
Ulmarra 139 29 37 S 153 4 E
Ulmeni 70 45 4N 46 40 E
Ulricehamn 73 57 46N 13 26 E
Ulrum 46 53 22N 6 20 E
Ulsberg 71 62 45N 9 59 E
Ulsfeinvik 71 62 21N 5 53 E
Ulster □ 38 54 45N 6 30W
Ulster Canal 38 54 15N 7 0W
Ulstrem 67 42 1N 26 27 E
Ultima 140 35 22 S 143 18 E
Ulubaria 95 22 31N 88 4 E
Ulugh Muztagh 99 36 40N 87 30 E
Uluguru Mts. 126 7 15 S 37 30 E
Ulva, I. 34 56 30N 6 12W
Ulvenhout 47 51 33N 4 48 E
Ulverston 32 54 13N 3 7W
Ulverstone 138 41 11 S 146 11 E
Ulvik 71 60 35N 6 54 E
Ulvo 73 56 40N 14 37 E
Ulya 77 59 10N 142 0 E
Ulyanovsk 81 54 25N 48 25 E
Ulyasutay 105 47 45N 96 49 E
Ulysses 159 37 39N 101 25W
Ulzio 62 45 2N 6 49 E
Um Qeis 90 32 40N 35 41 E
Umag 63 45 26N 13 31 E
Umala 174 17 25 S 68 5W
Uman 82 48 40N 30 12 E
Umánaé 12 70 40N 52 10W
Umánaé Fjord 10 70 40N 52 0W
Umaria 99 23 35N 80 50 E
Umarkhed 96 19 37N 77 38 E
Umarkot 93 25 15N 69 40 E
Umatilla 160 45 58N 119 17W
Umba 78 66 50N 34 20 E
Umbertide 63 43 18N 12 20 E
Umboi I. 135 5 40 S 148 0 E
Umbrella Mts. 143 45 35 S 169 5 E
Umbria □ 63 42 53N 12 30 E
Ume, R. 74 64 45N 18 30 E
Umeå 74 63 45N 20 20 E
Umera 103 0 12 S 129 30 E
Umfuli, R. 127 17 50 S 29 40 E
Umgusa 127 19 29 S 27 52 E
Umi 110 33 34N 130 30 E
Umiat 147 69 25N 152 20W
Umka 66 44 40N 20 19 E
Umkomaas 129 30 13 S 30 48 E
Umm al Aranib 119 26 10N 14 54 E
Umm al Qaiwain 93 25 30N 55 35 E
Umm Arda 123 15 17N 32 31 E
Umm az Zamul 93 22 35N 55 18 E
Umm Bel 123 13 35N 28 0 E
Umm Digulgulaya 123 10 28N 24 58 E
Umm Dubban 123 15 23N 32 52 E
Umm el Fahm 90 32 31N 35 9 E
Umm Hagar 123 14 20N 36 41 E
Umm Koweika 123 13 10N 32 16 E
Umm Lajj 92 25 0N 37 23 E
Umm Merwa 122 18 4N 32 30 E
Umm Qurein 123 16 3N 28 49 E
Umm Rumah 122 25 50N 36 30 E
Umm Ruwaba 123 12 50N 31 10 E
Umm Said 93 25 0N 51 40 E
Umm Sidr 123 14 29N 25 10 E
Ummanz I. 48 54 29N 13 9 E
Umnak. 147 53 20N 168 20W
Umnak I. 147 53 0N 168 0W
Umniati, R. 127 18 0 S 29 0 E
Umpang 101 16 3N 98 54 E
Umpqua, R. 160 43 30N 123 30W
Umrer 96 20 51N 79 18 E
Umreth 94 22 41N 73 4 E
Umshandige Dam 127 20 10 S 30 40 E
Umtali 127 18 58 S 32 38 E
Umtata 129 31 36 S 28 49 E
Umuahia-Ibeku 121 5 33N 7 29 E
Umvukwe Ra.. 127 16 45 S 30 45 E
Umvuma 127 19 16 S 30 30 E
Umzimvubu, R. 129 31 38 S 29 33 E
Umzingwane, R. 127 21 30 S 29 30 E
Umzinto 129 30 15 S 30 45 E
Una 94 20 46N 71 8 E
Una, Mt. 143 42 13 S 172 36 E
Una, R. 63 44 50N 16 15 E
Unac, R. 63 44 42N 16 15 E
Unadilla 162 42 20N 75 17W
Unalanaska I. 147 54 0N 164 30W
Uncastillo 58 42 21N 1 8W
Uncia 174 18 25 S 66 40W
Uncompahgce Pk., Mt. 161 38 5N 107 32W
Unden 73 58 45N 14 25 E
Underbool 140 35 10 S 141 51 E
Undersaker 72 63 19N 13 21 E
Undersvik 72 61 36N 16 20 E
Undredal 71 60 57N 7 6 E
Unecha 80 52 50N 32 37 E
Ungarie 141 33 38 S 146 56 E
Ungarra 140 34 12 S 136 2 E
Ungava B. 149 59 30N 67 30W
Ungava Pen. 50 60 0N 75 0W
Ungeny 82 47 11N 27 51 E
Unggi 105 42 16N 130 28 E
Ungwatiri 123 16 52N 36 10 E
Uni 84 56 44N 51 47 E
União 170 4 50 S 37 50W
União da Vitória 173 26 5 S 51 0W
União dos Palamares 170 9 10 S 36 2W
Uniejów 54 51 59N 18 46 E
Unije, I. 63 44 40N 14 15 E
Unimak I. 147 54 30N 164 30W
Unimak Pass. 148 53 30N 165 15W
Union, Mo., U.S.A. 158 38 25N 91 0W
Union, S.C., U.S.A. 157 34 49N 81 39W
Union City, N.J., U.S.A. 162 40 47N 74 5W
Union City, Ohio, U.S.A. 156 40 11N 84 49W
Union City, Pa., U.S.A. 156 41 53N 79 50W
Union Gap 157 46 38N 120 29W
Unión, La, Chile 176 40 10 S 73 0W
Unión, La, Colomb. 174 1 35N 77 5W
Unión, La, El Sal. 165 13 20N 87 50W
Union, La 164 17 58N 101 49W
Unión, La, Spain 59 37 38N 0 53W
Unión, La, Venez. 174 7 28N 67 53W
Union, Mt. 161 34 34N 112 21W
Union of Soviet Soc. Rep. ■ 77 47 0N 100 0 E
Union Springs 157 32 9N 85 44W
Uniondale Road 128 33 39 S 23 7 E
Uniontown 156 39 54N 79 45W
Unirea 70 44 15N 27 35 E
United Arab Emirates ■ 93 23 50N 54 0 E
United Arab Republic ■ 113 27 5N 30 0 E
United Kingdom ■ 27 55 0N 3 0W
United States of America ■ 155 37 0N 96 0W
Unity 153 52 30N 109 5W
Unjha 94 23 46N 72 24 E
Unnao 95 26 35N 80 30 E
Uno, Ilha 120 11 15N 16 13W
Unshin, R. 38 54 8N 8 26W
Unst, I. 36 60 50N 0 55W
Unstrut, R. 48 51 16N 11 29 E
Unter-Engadin 51 46 48N 10 20 E
Unterägeri 51 47 8N 8 36 E
Unterkulm 50 47 18N 8 7 E
Unterseen 50 46 41N 7 50 E
Unterwalden nid dem Wald □ 51 46 50N 8 25 E
Unterwalden ob dem Wald □ 51 46 55N 8 15 E
Unterwaldner Alpen 51 46 55N 8 15 E
Unterwasser 51 46 32N 8 21 E
Unturán, Sierra de 174 1 35N 64 40W
Unuk, R. 152 56 5N 131 3W
Ünye 82 41 5N 37 15 E
Unzen-Dake 111 32 45N 130 17 E
Unzha 81 57 40N 44 8 E
Unzha, R. 81 58 0N 43 40 E
Uors 51 46 42N 9 12 E
Uozu 111 36 48N 137 24 E
Upa, R. 53 50 45N 16 15 E
Upal 123 6 56N 34 12 E
Upata 174 8 1N 62 24W
Upavon 28 51 17N 1 49W
Upemba, L. 127 8 30 S 26 20 E
Upernavik 12 72 49N 56 20W
Upington 128 28 25 S 21 15 E
Upleta 94 21 46N 70 16 E
Upolu Pt. 147 20 16N 155 52W
Upper Alkali Lake 160 41 47N 120 0W
Upper Arrow L. 152 50 30N 117 50W
Upper Austria = Oberösterreich 52 48 15N 14 10 E
Upper Chapel 31 52 3N 3 26W
Upper Foster L. 153 56 47N 105 20W
Upper Heyford 28 51 54N 1 16W
Upper Hutt 142 41 8 S 175 5 E
Upper Klamath L. 160 42 16N 121 55W
Upper L. Erne 38 54 14N 7 22W
Upper Lake 160 39 10N 122 55W
Upper Manilla 141 30 38 S 150 40 E
Upper Marlboro 162 38 49N 76 45W
Upper Musquodoboit 151 45 10N 62 58W
Upper Sandusky 156 40 50N 83 17W
Upper Volta ■ 120 12 0N 0 30W
Upperchurch 39 52 43N 8 2W
Upphärad 73 58 9N 12 19 E
Uppingham 29 52 36N 0 43W
Uppsala 72 59 53N 17 38 E
Uppsala län □ 72 60 0N 17 30 E
Upshi 95 33 48N 77 52 E
Upstart, C. 138 19 41 S 147 45 E
Upton, U.K. 32 53 14N 2 52W
Upton, U.S.A. 158 44 8N 104 35W
Upton-upon-Severn 28 52 4N 2 12W
Upwey 28 50 40N 2 29W
Ur 92 30 55N 46 25 E
Ura-Tyube 85 39 55N 69 1 E
Urabá, Golfo de 174 8 25N 76 53W
Uracará 174 2 20 S 57 50W
Urach 49 48 29N 9 25 E
Uraga-Suidō 111 35 13N 139 45 E
Urakawa 112 42 9N 142 47 E
Ural, Mt. 141 33 21 S 146 12 E
Ural Mts. = Uralskie Gory 78 60 0N 59 0 E
Ural, R. 84 49 0N 52 0W
Uralla 141 30 37 S 151 29 E
Uralsk 84 51 20N 51 20 E
Uralskie Gory 78 60 0N 59 0 E
Urambo 126 5 4 S 32 47 E
Urambo □ 126 5 0 S 32 0 E
Urana 141 35 15 S 146 21 E
Urandangi 138 21 32 S 138 14 E
Uranium City 153 59 34N 108 37W
Uraricaá, R. 174 3 20N 61 56W
Uravakonda 97 14 57N 77 12 E
Urawa 111 35 50N 139 40 E
Uray 76 60 5N 65 15 E
Urbana, Ill., U.S.A. 156 40 7N 88 12W
Urbana, Ohio, U.S.A. 156 40 9N 83 44W
Urbana, La 174 7 8N 66 56W
Urbánia 63 43 40N 12 31 E
Urbano Santos 170 3 12 S 43 23W
Urbel, R. 58 42 30N 3 49W
Urbino 63 43 43N 12 38 E
Urbión, Picos de 58 42 1N 2 52W
Urcos 174 13 30 S 71 30W
Urda, Spain 57 39 25N 3 43W
Urda, U.S.S.R. 83 48 52N 47 23 E
Urdinarrain 172 32 37 S 58 52W
Urdos 44 42 51N 0 35W
Urdzhar 76 47 5N 81 38 E
Ure, R. 33 54 20N 1 25W
Uren 81 57 35N 45 55 E
Ures 164 29 30N 110 30W
Ureshino 110 33 6N 129 59 E
Urfa 92 37 12N 38 50 E
Urfahr 52 48 19N 14 17 E
Urgench 76 41 40N 60 30 E
Urgun 93 32 55N 69 12 E
Urgut 85 39 23N 67 15 E
Uri 95 34 8N 74 2 E
Uri □ 51 46 43N 8 35 E
Uribante, R. 174 7 25N 71 50W
Uribe 174 3 13N 74 24W
Uribia 174 11 43N 72 16W
Urim 90 31 18N 34 32 E
Uriondo 172 21 41 S 64 41W
Urique 164 27 13N 107 55W
Urique, R. 164 26 29N 107 58W
Urirotstock 51 46 52N 8 32 E
Urk 46 52 39N 5 36 E
Urla 92 38 20N 26 55 E
Urlati 70 44 59N 26 15 E
Urlingford 39 52 43N 7 35W
Urmia, L. 92 37 30N 45 30 E
Urmia (Rezā'iyeh) 92 37 40N 45 0 E
Urmston 32 53 28N 2 22W
Urner Alpen 51 46 45N 8 45 E
Uroševac 66 42 23N 21 10 E
Urrao 174 6 20N 76 11W
Urshult 73 56 31N 14 50 E
Urso 123 9 35N 41 33 E
Ursus 54 52 21N 20 53 E
Uruaca 171 15 30 S 49 41W
Uruaçu 171 14 30 S 49 10W
Uruapán 164 19 30N 102 0W
Urubamba 174 13 5 S 72 10W
Urubamba, R. 174 11 0 S 73 0W
Uruçuca 171 14 35 S 39 16W
Uruçuí 170 7 20 S 44 28W
Uruçuí Prêto, R. 170 7 20 S 44 38W
Uruçui, Serra do 170 9 0 S 44 45W
Urucuia, R. 171 16 8 S 45 5W
Uruguai, R. 173 24 0 S 53 30W
Uruguaiana 172 29 50 S 57 0W
Uruguay ■ 172 32 30 S 55 30W
Uruguay, R. 172 28 0 S 56 0W
Urumchi = Wulumuchi 105 43 40N 87 50 E
Urup, I. 77 43 0N 151 0 E
Urup, R. 83 44 19N 41 30 E
Urutai 171 17 28 S 48 12W
Uruyén 174 5 41N 62 25W
Uruzgan □ 93 33 30N 66 0 E
Uryupinsk 81 50 45N 42 3 E
Urzhum 81 57 10N 49 56 E
Urziceni 70 44 46N 26 42 E
Usa 110 33 31N 131 21 E
Usa, R. 78 66 20N 56 0 E
Uşak 92 38 43N 29 28 E
Usakos 128 22 0 S 15 31 E
Usambara Mts. 126 4 50 S 38 20 E
Usedom 48 53 50N 13 55 E
Useko 124 5 8 S 32 24 E
Usfan 122 21 58N 39 27 E
Ush-Tobe 76 45 16N 78 0 E
Ushakova, O. 12 82 0N 80 0 E
Ushant = Ouessant, Île d' 42 48 25N 5 5W
Ushashi 126 1 59 S 33 57 E
Ushat 123 7 59N 29 28 E
Ushibuka 110 32 11N 130 1 E
Ushuaia 176 54 50 S 68 23W
Ushumun 77 52 47N 126 32 E
Usk 31 51 42N 2 53W
Usk, R. 31 51 37N 2 56W
Uskedal 71 59 56N 5 53 E
Üsküdar 92 41 0N 29 5 E
Uslar 48 51 39N 9 39 E
Usman 81 52 5N 39 48 E
Usoga □ 126 0 5N 33 30 E
Usoke 126 5 7 S 32 19 E
Usolye Sibirskoye 77 52 40N 103 40 E
Usoro 121 5 33N 6 11 E
Uspallata, P. de 172 32 30 S 69 28W
Uspenskiy 76 48 50N 72 55 E
Usquert 46 53 24N 6 36 E
Ussel 44 45 32N 2 18 E
Ussuriysk 77 43 40N 131 50 E
Ust 52 50 41N 14 2 E
Ust Aldan = Batamay 77 63 30N 129 15 E
Ust Amginskoye = Khandyga 77 62 30N 134 50 E
Ust-Bolsheretsk 77 52 40N 156 30 E
Ust Buzulukskaya 81 50 8N 42 11 E
Ust Doneckij 83 47 35N 40 55 E
Ust Donetskiy 83 47 35N 40 55 E
Ust Ilga 77 55 5N 104 55 E
Ust Ilimpeya = Yukti 77 63 20N 105 0 E
Ust-Ilimsk 77 58 3N 102 39 E
Ust Ishim 76 57 45N 71 10 E
Ust Kamchatsk 77 56 10N 162 0 E
Ust Kamenogorsk 76 50 0N 82 20 E
Ust Karenga 77 54 40N 116 45 E
Ust Khayryuzova 77 57 15N 156 55 E
Ust Kut 77 56 50N 105 10 E
Ust Kuyga 77 70 1N 135 36 E

Ust Labinsk Vatoloha, Mt


Ust Labinsk 83 45 15N 39 50 E
Ust Luga 80 59 35N 28 26 E
Ust Maya 77 60 30N 134 20 E
Ust Mil 77 59 50N 133 0 E
Ust Nera 77 64 35N 143 15 E
Ust Olenek 77 73 0N 120 10 E
Ust-Omchug 77 61 9N 149 38 E
Ust Port 76 70 0N 84 10 E
Ust Tsilma 78 65 25N 52 0 E
Ust-Tungir 77 55 25N 120 15 E
Ust Urt = Ustyurt 76 44 0N 55 0 E
Ust Usa 78 66 0N 56 30 E
Ust-Uyskoye 84 54 16N 63 54 E
Ust Vorkuta 76 67 7N 63 35 E
Ustaoset 71 60 30N 8 2 E
Ustaritz 44 43 24N 1 27W
Uste 81 59 35N 39 40 E
Uster 51 47 22N 8 43 E
Usti na Orlici 53 49 58N 16 38 E
Usti nad Labem 52 50 41N 14 3 E
Ustica, I. 64 38 42N 13 10 E
Ustka 54 54 35N 16 55 E
Ustron 54 49 45N 18 48 E
Ustrzyki Dolne 54 49 27N 22 40 E
Ustye 77 55 30N 97 30 E
Ustyurt, Plato 76 44 0N 55 0 E
Ustyuzhna 81 58 50N 36 32 E
Ušće 66 43 43N 20 39 E
Usuki 110 33 8N 131 49 E
Usulután 166 13 25N 88 28W
Usumacinta, R. 165 17 0N 91 0W
Usva 84 58 41N 57 37 E
Uta 66 45 24N 21 13 E
Utah □ 160 39 30N 111 30W
Utah, L. 160 40 10N 111 58W
Ute Cr. 159 36 5N 103 45W
Utena 80 55 27N 25 40 E
Ütersen 48 53 40N 9 40 E
Utete 124 8 0S 38 45 E
Uthai Thani 100 15 22N 100 3 E
Uthal 94 25 44N 66 40 E
Uthmaniyah 92 25 5N 49 6 E
Utiariti 174 13 0S 58 10W
Utica 162 43 5N 75 18W
Utiel 58 39 37N 1 11W
Utik L. 153 55 15N 96 0W
Utikuma L. 152 55 50N 115 30W
Utinga 171 12 6S 41 5W
Uto 110 32 41N 130 40 E
Utrecht, Neth. 46 52 3N 5 8 E
Utrecht, S. Afr. 129 27 38S 30 20 E
Utrecht □ 46 52 6N 5 7 E
Utrera 57 37 12N 5 48W
Utsjoki 74 69 51N 26 59 E
Utsunomiya 111 36 30N 139 50 E
Uttar Pradesh □ 95 27 0N 80 0 E
Uttaradit 100 17 36N 100 5 E
Uttersberg 72 59 45N 15 39 E
Uttersley 73 54 56N 11 11 E
Uttoxeter 32 52 53N 1 50W
Utva, R. 84 51 28N 52 40 E
Ütze 48 52 28N 10 11 E
Uudenmaan lääni □ 75 60 25N 25 0 E
Uusikaarlepyy 74 63 32N 22 31 E
Uusikaupunki 75 60 47N 21 25 E
Uva 84 56 59N 52 13 E
Uvac, R. 66 43 35N 19 40 E
Uvalde 159 29 15N 99 48W
Uvarovo 81 51 59N 42 14 E
Uvat 76 59 5N 68 50 E
Uvelskiy 84 54 26N 61 22 E
Uvinza 126 5 5S 30 24 E
Uvira 126 3 22S 29 3 E
Uvlova, R. 52 49 34N 13 20 E
Uvs Nuur, L. 105 50 20N 92 45 E
Uwa 110 33 22N 132 31 E
Uwainhid 92 24 50N 46 0 E
Uwajima 110 33 10N 132 35 E
Uxmal 165 20 22N 89 46W
Uyeasound 36 60 42N 0 55W
Uyo 121 5 1N 7 53 E
Uyu, R. 98 24 51N 94 57 E
Uyuk 85 43 36N 71 16 E
Uyuni 172 20 35S 66 55W
Uyuni, Salar de 172 20 10S 68 0W
Uzbekistan S.S.R. □ 85 40 5N 65 0 E
Uzen, Bol. 81 50 0N 49 30 E
Uzen, Mal. 81 50 0N 48 30 E
Uzerche 44 45 25N 1 35 E
Uzès 45 44 1N 4 26 E
Uzgen 85 40 46N 73 18 E
Uzh, R. 80 51 15N 29 45 E
Uzhgorod 80 48 36N 22 18 E
Uzlovaya 81 54 0N 38 5 E
Uzun-Agach 85 43 35N 76 20 E
Uzunköprü 67 41 16N 26 43 E
Uzure 126 4 40S 34 22 E
Uzwil 51 47 26N 9 9 E


# V


Vaal, R. 128 27 40S 25 30 E
Vaaldam 129 27 0S 28 14 E
Vaals 47 50 46N 6 1 E
Vaalwater 129 24 15S 28 8 E
Vaasa 74 63 16N 21 35 E
Vaasan lääni □ 74 63 2N 22 50 E
Vaassen 46 52 17N 5 58 E
Vabre 44 43 42N 2 24 E
Vác 53 47 49N 19 10 E
Vacaria 173 28 31S 50 52W
Vacaville 163 38 21N 122 0W
Vach, R. 76 60 56N 76 38 E
Vache, I.-à 167 18 2N 73 35W
Väddö 72 59 55N 18 50 E
Väderum 73 57 32N 16 11 E
Vadnagar 94 23 47N 72 40 E
Vado Ligure 62 44 16N 8 26 E
Vadodara 94 22 20N 73 10 E
Vadsø 74 70 3N 29 50 E
Vadstena 73 58 28N 14 54 E
Vaduz 51 47 8N 9 31 E
Vaerøy, Nordland Fylke, Norway 74 67 40N 12 40 E
Vaerøy, Sogn og Fjordane, Norway 71 61 17N 4 45 E
Vagney 43 48 1N 6 43 E
Vagnhärad 72 58 57N 17 33 E
Vagos 56 40 33N 8 42W
Vagsöy, I. 71 62 0N 5 0 E
Váh, R. 53 49 10N 18 20 E
Vaigach 76 70 10N 59 0 E
Vaigai, R. 97 9 47N 78 23 E
Vaiges 42 48 2N 0 30W
Vaihingen 49 48 44N 8 58 E
Vaihsel B. 13 75 0S 35 0W
Vaijapur 96 19 58N 74 45 E
Vaikam 97 9 45N 76 25 E
Vaila I. 36 60 12N 1 34W
Vailly Aisne 43 49 25N 3 30 E
Vaippar, R. 97 9 0N 78 25 E
Vaison 45 44 14N 5 4 E
Vajpur 96 21 24N 73 45 E
Vakarel 67 42 35N 23 40 E
Vakhsh, R. 85 37 6N 68 18 E
Vaksdal 71 60 29N 5 45 E
Vál 53 47 22N 18 40 E
Val d' Ajol, Le 43 47 55N 6 30 E
Val-de-Marne □ 43 48 45N 2 28 E
Val-d'Oise □ 43 49 5N 2 0 E
Val d'Or 150 48 7N 77 47W
Val Marie 153 49 15N 107 45W
Val-St.-Germain 47 48 34N 2 4 E
Valadares 56 41 5N 8 38W
Valahia 70 44 35N 25 0 E
Valais □ 50 46 12N 7 45 E
Valais, Alpes du 50 46 47N 7 30 E
Valandovo 66 41 19N 22 34 E
Valasské MeziríU5 53 49 29N 17 59 E
Valaxa, I. 69 38 50N 24 29 E
Valcheta 176 40 40S 66 20W
Valdagno 63 45 38N 11 18 E
Valdahon, Le 43 47 8N 6 20 E
Valday 80 57 58N 31 9 E
Valdayskaya Vozvyshennost 80 57 0N 33 40 E
Valdeazogues, R. 57 38 45N 4 55W
Valdemarsvik 73 58 14N 16 40 E
Valdepeñas, Ciudad Real, Spain 57 38 43N 3 25W
Valdepeñas, Jaén, Spain 57 37 33N 3 47W
Valderaduey, R. 56 42 30N 5 0W
Valderrobres 58 40 53N 0 9 E
Valdes Pen. 176 42 30S 63 45W
Valdez 147 61 14N 146 10W
Valdivia 176 39 50S 73 14W
Valdivia □ 176 40 0S 73 0W
Valdivia, La 172 34 43S 72 5W
Valdobbiádene 63 45 53N 12 0 E
Valdosta 157 30 50N 83 48W
Valdoviño 56 43 36N 8 8W
Valdres 71 60 55N 9 28 E
Vale, U.S.A. 160 44 0N 117 15W
Vale, U.S.S.R. 83 41 30N 42 58 E
Valea lui Mihai 70 47 32N 22 11 E
Valença, Brazil 171 13 20S 39 5W
Valença, Port. 56 42 1N 8 34W
Valença do Piauí 170 6 20S 41 45W
Valence 45 44 57N 4 54 E
Valence-d'Agen 44 44 8N 0 54 E
Valencia, Spain 59 39 27N 0 23W
Valencia, Venez. 174 10 11N 68 0W
Valencia □ 59 39 20N 0 40W
Valencia, Albufera de 59 39 20N 0 27W
Valencia de Alcántara 57 39 25N 7 14W
Valencia de Don Juan 56 42 17N 5 31W
Valencia des Ventoso 57 38 15N 6 29W
Valencia, G. de 59 39 30N 0 20 E
Valencia, L. de 167 10 13N 67 40W
Valenciennes 43 50 20N 3 34 E
Valensole 45 43 50N 5 59 E
Valentia Hr. 39 51 56N 10 17W
Valentia I. 39 51 54N 10 22W
Valentine, Nebr., U.S.A. 158 42 50N 100 35W
Valentine, Tex., U.S.A. 159 30 36N 104 28W
Valenton 160 48 45N 2 28 E
Valenza 62 45 2N 8 39 E
Våler 71 60 41N 11 50 E
Valera 174 9 19N 70 37W
Valguarnera Caropepe 65 37 30N 14 22 E
Valhall, oilfield 19 56 17N 3 25 E
Valier 160 48 15N 112 9W
Valinco, G. de 45 41 40N 8 52 E
Valjevo 66 44 18N 19 53 E
Valkeakoski 75 61 16N 24 2 E
Valkenburg 47 50 52N 5 50 E
Valkenswaard 47 51 21N 5 29 E
Vall de Uxó 58 40 49N 0 15W
Valla 72 59 2N 16 20 E
Valladolid, Mexico 165 20 30N 88 20W
Valladolid, Spain 56 41 38N 4 43W
Valladolid □ 56 41 38N 4 43W
Vallata 65 41 3N 15 16 E
Valldalssæter 71 59 56N 6 57 E
Valle 71 59 13N 7 33 E
Valle d'Aosta □ 62 45 45N 7 22 E
Valle de Arán 58 42 50N 0 55 E
Valle de Cabuérniga 56 43 14N 4 18W
Valle de la Pascua 174 9 13N 66 0W
Valle de Santiago 164 20 25N 101 15W
Valle de Zaragoza 164 27 28N 105 49W
Valle del Cauca □ 174 3 45N 76 30W
Valle Fértil, Sierra del 172 30 20S 68 0W
Valle Hermosa 165 25 35N 102 25 E
Valle Nacional 165 17 47N 96 19W
Vallecas 56 40 23N 3 41W
Valledupar 174 10 29N 73 15W
Vallejo 163 38 12N 122 15W
Vallenar 172 28 30S 70 50W
Valleraugue 44 44 6N 3 39 E
Vallet 42 47 10N 1 15W
Valletta 60 35 54N 14 30 E
Valley 31 53 17N 4 31W
Valley Center 163 33 13N 117 2W
Valley City 158 46 57N 98 0W
Valley Falls 160 42 33N 120 8W
Valley Okolona 159 34 0N 88 45W
Valley Springs 163 38 11N 120 50W
Valley View 162 40 39N 76 33W
Valleyfield 150 45 15N 74 8W
Valleyview 152 55 5N 117 17W
Valli di Comácchio 63 44 40N 12 15 E
Vallimanca, Arroyo 172 35 40S 59 10W
Vallo della Lucánia 65 40 14N 15 16 E
Vallon 45 44 25N 4 23 E
Vallorbe 50 46 42N 6 20 E
Valls 58 41 18N 1 15 E
Vallsta 72 61 31N 16 22 E
Valmaseda 58 43 11N 3 12W
Valmiera 80 57 37N 25 38 E
Valmont 42 49 45N 0 30 E
Valmontone 64 41 48N 12 55 E
Valmy 43 49 5N 4 45 E
Valnera, Mte. 58 43 9N 3 40W
Valognes 42 49 30N 1 28W
Valona (Vlora) 68 40 32N 19 28 E
Valongo 56 40 37N 8 27W
Valpaços 56 41 36N 7 17W
Valparaíso, Chile 172 33 2S 71 40W
Valparaíso, Mexico 164 22 50N 103 32W
Valparaiso 156 41 27N 87 2W
Valparaiso □ 172 33 2S 71 40W
Valpovo 66 45 39N 18 25 E
Valréas 45 44 24N 5 0 E
Vals 51 46 39N 10 11 E
Vals-les-Bains 45 44 42N 4 24 E
Vals, R. 128 27 28S 26 52 E
Vals, Tanjung 103 8 32S 137 32 E
Valsbaai 128 34 15S 18 40 E
Valskog 72 59 27N 15 57 E
Válta 68 40 3N 23 25 E
Valtellina 62 46 9N 10 2 E
Valverde del Camino 57 37 35N 6 47W
Valverde del Fresno 56 40 15N 6 51W
Valyiki 81 50 10N 38 5 E
Vama 70 47 34N 25 42 E
Vambarra Ra. 136 15 13S 130 24 E
Vamdrup 50 55 26N 9 10 E
Vammala 75 61 20N 22 55 E
Vámos 69 35 24N 24 13 E
Vamsadhara, R. 96 18 22N 84 15 E
Van 92 38 30N 43 20 E
Van Alstyne 159 33 25N 96 36W
Van Bruyssel 151 47 56N 72 9W
Van Buren, Can. 151 47 10N 67 55W
Van Buren, Ark., U.S.A. 159 35 28N 94 18W
Van Buren, Me., U.S.A. 157 47 10N 68 1W
Van Buren, Mo., U.S.A. 159 37 0N 91 0W
Van Canh 100 13 37N 109 0 E
Van der Kloof Dam 128 30 04S 24 40 E
Van Diemen, C., N.T., Austral. 136 11 9S 130 24 E
Van Diemen, C., Queens., Austral. 138 16 30S 139 46 E
Van Diemen G. 136 11 45S 131 50 E
Van Gölü 92 38 30N 43 0 E
Van Horn 161 31 3N 104 55W
Van Ninn 100 12 42N 109 14 E
Van Reenen P. 129 28 22S 29 27 E
Van Tassell 158 42 40N 104 3W
Van Tivu, I. 97 8 51N 78 15 E
Van Wert 156 40 52N 84 31W
Van Yen 100 21 4N 104 42 E
Vanavara 77 60 22N 102 16 E
Vancouver, Can. 152 49 20N 123 10W
Vancouver, U.S.A. 160 45 44N 122 41W
Vancouver, C. 137 35 2S 118 11 E
Vancouver I. 152 49 50N 126 0W
Vandalia, Ill., U.S.A. 158 38 57N 89 4W
Vandalia, Mo., U.S.A. 158 39 18N 91 30W
Vandeloos Bay 97 8 0N 81 45 E
Vandenburg 163 34 35N 120 44W
Vanderbijlpark 86 26 42S 27 54 E
Vanderhoof 152 54 0N 124 0W
Vanderlin I. 138 15 44S 137 2 E
Vandyke 138 24 10S 147 51 E
Vänern 73 58 47N 13 30 E
Vänersborg 73 58 26N 12 27 E
Vang Vieng 100 18 58N 102 32 E
Vanga 126 4 35S 39 12 E
Vangaindrano 129 23 21S 47 36 E
Vanguard 153 49 55N 107 20W
Vanier 150 45 27N 75 40W
Vanimo 135 2 42S 141 21 E
Vanivilasa Sagara 97 13 45N 76 30 E
Vaniyambadi 97 12 46N 78 44 E
Vankleek Hill 150 45 32N 75 40W
Vanna 74 70 6N 19 50 E
Vannas 74 63 58N 19 48 E
Vannes 42 47 40N 2 47W
Vanoise, Massif de la 45 45 25N 6 40 E
Vanrhynsdorp 128 31 36S 18 44 E
Vanrook 138 16 57S 141 57 E
Vans, Les 45 44 25N 4 7 E
Vansbro 72 60 32N 14 15 E
Vanse 71 58 6N 6 41 E
Vansittart B. 136 14 3S 126 17 E
Vanthli 94 21 28N 70 25 E
Vanua Levu, I. 130 16 33S 178 8 E
Vanwyksvlei 128 30 18S 21 49 E
Vanylven 71 62 5N 5 33 E
Vapnyarka 82 48 32N 28 45 E
Var □ 45 43 27N 6 18 E
Vara 73 58 16N 12 55 E
Varada, R. 97 14 46N 75 15 E
Varades 42 47 25N 1 1W
Varaita, R. 62 44 35N 7 15 E
Varaldsöy 71 60 6N 5 59 E
Varallo 62 45 50N 8 13 E
Varanasi (Benares) 95 25 22N 83 8 E
Varangerfjorden 74 70 3N 29 25 E
Varazdin 63 46 20N 16 20 E
Varazze 62 44 21N 8 36 E
Varberg 73 57 17N 12 20 E
Vardar, R. 66 41 25N 22 20 E
Varde 73 55 38N 8 29 E
Varde Å 73 55 35N 8 19 E
Vardø 74 70 23N 31 5 E
Varel 48 53 23N 8 9 E
Varella, Mui 100 12 54N 109 26 E
Varena 80 54 12N 24 30 E
Värendseke 73 57 4N 15 0 E
Varennes-sur-Allier 44 49 12N 5 0 E
Vareš 66 44 12N 18 23 E
Varese 62 45 49N 8 50 E
Varese Ligure 62 44 22N 9 33 E
Vårgårda 73 58 2N 12 49 E
Vargem Bonita 171 20 20S 46 22W
Vargem Grande 170 3 33S 43 56W
Varginha 173 21 33S 45 25W
Vargön 73 58 22N 12 20 E
Varhaug 71 58 37N 5 41 E
Varillas 172 24 0S 70 10W
Varing 73 58 30N 14 0 E
Värmdö, I. 72 59 18N 18 45 E
Värmeln 72 59 35N 13 0 E
Värmlands län □ 72 59 45N 13 20 E
Varmlandssaby 72 59 7N 14 15 E
Varna, Bulg. 67 43 13N 27 56 E
Varna, U.S.S.R. 84 53 24N 60 58 E
Varna, R. 96 17 13N 73 50 E
Varnamo 73 57 10N 14 3 E
Varnsdorf 52 49 56N 14 38 E
Värö 73 51 16N 12 15 E
Varpelev 73 55 22N 12 17 E
Värsjö 73 56 23N 13 27 E
Varsseveld 46 51 56N 6 29 E
Varteig 71 59 23N 11 12 E
Varto 92 39 10N 41 28 E
Vartofta 73 58 6N 13 40 E
Vartry Res. 39 53 3N 6 12W
Varvarin 66 43 43N 21 20 E
Varzaneh 93 32 25N 52 40 E
Várzea Alegre 170 6 47S 39 17W
Várzea da Palma 171 17 36S 44 44W
Varzi 62 44 50N 9 12 E
Varzo 62 46 12N 8 15 E
Varzy 43 47 22N 3 20 E
Vas □ 53 47 10N 16 55 E
Vasa 74 63 6N 21 38 E
Vasa Barris, R. 170 11 10S 37 10W
Vásárosnamény 53 48 9N 22 19 E
Väsby 73 56 13N 12 37 E
Vascão, R. 57 37 44N 8 15W
Vascongadas 58 42 50N 2 45W
Vaşcău 70 46 28N 22 30 E
Väse 72 59 23N 13 52 E
Vasht = Khāsh 93 28 20N 61 6 E
Vasii Levski 67 43 23N 25 26 E
Vasilevichi 80 52 15N 29 50 E
Vasilikón 69 38 25N 23 40 E
Vasilkov 80 50 7N 30 28 E
Vaslui 70 46 38N 27 42 E
Vaslui □ 71 46 30N 27 30 E
Väsman 72 60 9N 15 5 E
Vassa 74 63 6N 21 38 E
Vassar, Can. 153 49 10N 95 55W
Vassar, U.S.A. 156 43 23N 83 33W
Vast Silen, L. 72 59 15N 12 15 E
Västerås 72 59 37N 16 38 E
Västerbottens län □ 74 64 58N 18 0 E
Västerdalälven 72 60 30N 13 25 E
Västernorrlands län □ 72 63 30N 17 40 E
Västervik 73 57 43N 16 43 E
Västmanland □ 72 59 55N 16 30 E
Vasto 63 42 8N 14 40 E
Vasvár 53 47 3N 16 47 E
Vatan 43 47 4N 1 50 E
Vaternish Pt. 36 57 36N 6 40W
Vatersay, I. 36 56 55N 7 32W
Vathí 69 37 46N 27 1 E
Váthia 69 36 29N 22 29 E
Vatican City ■ 63 41 54N 12 27 E
Vatin 66 45 12N 21 20 E
Vatnajökull 74 64 30N 16 48W
Vatnås 71 59 58N 9 37 E
Vatne 71 62 33N 6 38 E
Vatneyri 74 65 35N 24 0W
Vatoloha, Mt. 129 17 52S 47 48 E

Vatomandry Vijayadurg


Vatomandry 129 19 20S 48 59E
Vatra-Dornei 70 47 22N 25 22E
Vats 71 59 29N 5 45E
Vättern, L. 73 58 25N 14 30E
Vättis 51 46 55N 9 27E
Vaucluse □ 45 44 3N 5 10E
Vaucouleurs 43 48 37N 5 40E
Vaud □ 50 46 35N 6 30E
Vaughan 161 34 37N 105 12W
Vaughn 160 47 37N 111 36W
Vaulruz 50 46 38N 7 0E
Vaupés □ 174 1 0N 71 0W
Vaupés, R. 174 1 0N 71 0W
Vauvert 45 43 42N 4 17E
Vauxhall 152 50 5N 112 9W
Vavincourt 43 48 49N 5 12E
Vavoua 120 7 23N 6 29W
Vaxholm 72 59 25N 18 20E
Växjö 73 56 52N 14 50E
Vaygach, Ostrov 76 70 0N 60 0E
Vaza Barris, R. 171 10 0S 37 30W
Veadeiros 171 14 7S 47 31W
Veagh L. 38 55 3N 7 57W
Vechta 48 52 47N 8 18E
Vechte, R. 46 52 34N 6 6E
Vecilla, La 56 42 51N 5 27W
Vecsés 53 47 26N 19 19E
Vedaraniam 97 10 25N 79 50E
Vedbæk 73 55 50N 12 33E
Veddige 73 57 17N 12 20E
Vedea, R. 70 44 0N 25 20E
Vedelgem 47 51 7N 3 10E
Vedia 172 34 30S 61 31W
Vedra, Isla del 59 38 52N 1 12E
Vedrin 47 50 30N 4 52E
Veendam 46 53 5N 6 52E
Veenendaal 46 52 2N 5 34E
Veenwouden 46 53 14N 6 0E
Veerle 47 51 4N 4 59E
Vefsna 74 65 48N 13 10E
Vega, Norway 74 65 40N 11 55E
Vega, U.S.A. 159 35 18N 102 26W
Vega Baja 147 18 27N 66 23W
Vega Fd. 74 65 37N 12 0E
Vega, I. 74 65 42N 11 50E
Vega, La 167 19 20N 70 30W
Vegadeo 56 43 27N 7 4W
Vegesack 48 53 10N 8 38E
Vegfjorden 74 65 37N 12 0E
Veggerby 73 56 54N 9 39E
Veggli 71 60 3N 9 9E
Veghel 47 51 37N 5 32E
Vegorritis, Limni 68 40 45N 21 45E
Vegreville 152 53 30N 112 5W
Vegusdal 71 58 32N 8 10E
Veii 63 42 0N 12 24E
Veinticino de Mayo 172 38 0S 67 40W
Veitch 140 34 39S 140 31E
Vejen 73 55 30N 9 9E
Vejer de la Frontera 57 36 15N 5 59W
Vejle 73 55 43N 9 30E
Vejle Amt □ 73 55 2N 11 22E
Vejle Fjord 73 55 40N 9 50E
Vejlo 73 55 10N 11 45E
Vela Luka 63 42 59N 16 44E
Velanai I. 97 9 45N 79 45E
Velarde 161 36 11N 106 1W
Velas, C. 166 10 21N 85 52W
Velasco 159 29 0N 95 20W
Velasco, Sierra de. 172 29 20S 67 10W
Velay, Mts. du 44 45 0N 3 40E
Velb 46 52 0N 5 59E
Velddrif 128 32 42S 18 11E
Velden 47 51 25N 6 10E
Veldhoven 47 51 24N 5 25E
Veldwezelt 47 50 52N 5 38E
Velebit Planina 63 44 50N 15 20E
Velebitski Kanal 63 44 45N 14 55E
Veleka, R. 67 42 4N 27 30E
Velenje 63 46 23N 15 8E
Velestínon 68 39 23N 22 43E
Vélez 174 6 1N 73 41W
Velez 66 43 19N 18 2E
Vélez Blanco 57 37 41N 2 5W
Vélez Málaga 57 36 48N 4 5W
Vélez Rubio 59 37 41N 2 5W
Velhas, R. 171 17 13S 44 49W
Velika 66 45 27N 17 40E
Velika Gorica 63 45 44N 16 5E
Velika Kapela 63 45 10N 15 5E
Velika Kladuša 63 45 11N 15 48E
Velika Morava, R. 66 44 30N 21 9E
Velika Plana 66 44 20N 21 1E
Velikaya, R. 80 56 40N 28 40E
Veliké Kapušany 53 48 34N 22 5E
Velike Lašče 63 45 49N 14 45E
Veliki Backa Kanal 68 45 45N 19 15E
Veliki Jastrebac 66 43 25N 21 30E
Veliki Ustyug 78 60 47N 46 20E
Velikiye Luki 80 56 25N 30 32E
Veliko Turnovo 67 43 5N 25 41E
Velikonda Range 97 14 45N 79 10E
Velikoye, Oz. 81 55 15N 40 0E
Velingrad 67 42 4N 23 58E
Velino, Mt. 63 42 10N 13 20E
Velizh 80 55 30N 31 11E
Velké Karlovice 53 49 20N 18 17E
Velke Mezirici 52 49 21N 16 1E
Velký ostrov Zitný 53 48 5N 17 20E
Vellar, R. 97 11 [illegible]N 79 36E
Velletri 64 41 43N 12 43E
Velling 73 56 2N 8 20E
Vellinge 73 55 29N 13 0E
Vellir 74 65 55N 18 28W
Vellore 97 12 57N 79 10E
Velsen-Noord 46 52 27N 4 40E
Velsk 78 61 10N 42 5E
Velten 48 52 40N 13 11E
Veluwe Meer 46 52 24N 5 44E
Velva 158 48 6N 100 56W
Velvendós 68 40 15N 22 6E
Vem 73 56 21N 8 21E
Vembanad Lake 97 9 36N 76 15E
Veme 71 60 14N 10 7E
Ven 73 55 55N 12 45E
Vena 73 57 31N 16 0E
Venado 164 22 50N 101 10W
Venado Tuerto 172 33 50S 62 0W
Venafro 65 41 28N 14 3E
Venarey-les-Laumes 43 47 32N 4 26E
Venaria 62 45 12N 7 39E
Venčane 66 44 24N 20 28E
Vence 45 43 43N 7 6E
Vendas Novas 57 38 39N 8 27W
Vendée 42 46 50N 1 35W
Vendée □ 44 46 40N 1 20W
Vendée, Collines de 42 46 35N 0 45W
Vendée, R. 42 46 30N 0 45W
Vendeuvre-sur-Barse 43 48 14N 4 28E
Vendôme 42 47 47N 1 3E
Vendrell 58 41 10N 1 30E
Vendsyssel 73 57 22N 10 0E
Veneta, Laguna 63 45 19N 12 13E
Venetie 147 67 0N 146 30W
Véneto □ 63 45 30N 12 0E
Venev 81 54 22N 38 17E
Venézia 63 45 27N 12 20E
Venézia, Golfo di 63 45 20N 13 0E
Venezuela ■ 174 8 0N 65 0W
Venezuela, Golfo de 174 11 30N 71 0W
Vengurla 97 15 53N 73 45E
Vengurla Rocks 97 15 50N 73 22E
Venice = Venézia 63 45 27N 12 20E
Vénissieux 45 45 43N 4 53E
Venjansjön 72 60 58N 14 2E
Venkatagiri 97 14 0N 79 35E
Venkatapuram 96 18 20N 80 30E
Venlo 47 51 22N 6 11E
Vennesla 71 58 15N 8 0E
Venø, Is. 73 56 33N 8 38E
Venraij 47 51 31N 6 0E
Venta de Cardeña 57 38 16N 4 20W
Venta de San Rafael 56 40 42N 4 12W
Venta, La 165 18 8N 94 3W
Ventana, Punta de la 164 24 4N 109 48W
Ventersburg 128 28 7S 27 9E
Ventimíglia 62 43 50N 7 39E
Ventnor 28 50 35N 1 12W
Ventotene, I. 64 40 48N 13 25E
Ventry 39 52 8N 10 21W
Ventspils 80 57 25N 21 32E
Ventuari, R. 174 5 20N 66 0W
Ventucopa 163 34 50N 119 29W
Ventura 163 34 16N 119 18W
Ventura, La 164 24 38N 100 54W
Venturosa, La 174 6 8N 68 48W
Venus B. 141 38 40S 145 42E
Veoy 71 62 45N 7 30E
Veoy Is. 71 62 45N 7 30E
Vera, Argent. 172 29 30S 60 20W
Vera, Spain 59 37 15N 1 15W
Veracruz 165 19 10N 96 10W
Veracruz □ 165 19 0N 96 15W
Veraval 94 20 53N 70 27E
Verbánia 62 45 50N 8 55E
Verbicaro 65 39 46N 15 54E
Verbier 50 46 6N 7 13E
Vercelli 62 45 19N 8 25E
Verdalsøra 74 63 48N 11 30E
Verde Grande, R. 171 16 13S 43 49W
Verde Pequeno, R. 171 14 48S 43 31W
Verde, R., Argent. 176 41 55S 66 0W
Verde, R., Goiás, Brazil 171 18 1S 50 14W
Verde, R., Goiás, Brazil 171 19 11S 50 44W
Verde, R., Chihuahua, Mexico 164 26 59N 107 58W
Verde, R., Oaxaca, Mexico 164 15 59N 97 50W
Verde, R., Veracruz, Mexico 165 21 10N 102 50W
Verde, R., Parag. 172 23 9S 57 37W
Verden 48 52 58N 9 18E
Verdhikoúsa 68 39 47N 21 59E
Verdigre 158 42 38N 98 0W
Verdon-sur-Mer, Le 44 45 33N 1 4W
Verdun 43 49 12N 5 24E
Verdun-sur-le Doubs 43 46 54N 5 0E
Vereeniging 129 26 38S 27 57E
Vérendrye, Parc Prov. de 150 47 20N 76 40W
Vereshchagino 84 58 5N 54 40E
Verga, C. 120 10 30N 14 10W
Vergara 58 43 9N 2 28W
Vergato 62 44 18N 11 8E
Vergemont 138 23 33S 143 1E
Vergemont Cr. 138 24 16S 143 16E
Vergt 44 45 2N 0 43E
Verín 56 41 57N 7 27W
Veriña 56 43 32N 5 43W
Verkhnedvinsk 80 55 45N 27 58E
Verkhneuralsk 84 53 53N 59 13E
Verkhniy-Avzyan 84 53 32N 57 33E
Verkhniy Baskunchak 83 48 5N 46 50E
Verkhniy Tagil 84 57 22N 59 56E
Verkhniy Ufaley 84 56 4N 60 14E
Verkhniye Kigi 84 55 25N 58 37E
Verkhnyaya Salda 84 58 2N 60 33E
Verkhoturye 84 58 52N 60 48E
Verkhovye 81 52 55N 37 15E
Verkhoyansk 77 67 50N 133 50E
Verkhoyanskiy Khrebet 77 66 0N 129 0E
Verlo 153 50 19N 108 35W
Verma 71 62 21N 8 3E
Vermenton 43 47 40N 3 42E
Vermilion 153 53 20N 110 50W
Vermilion, B. 159 29 45N 91 55W
Vermilion Bay 153 49 50N 93 20W
Vermilion Chutes 152 58 22N 114 51W
Vermilion, R., Alta., Can. 153 53 22N 110 51W
Vermilion, R., Qué., Can. 150 47 38N 72 56W
Vermillion 158 42 50N 96 56W
Vermont □ 156 43 40N 72 50W
Vern, oilfield 19 55 35N 4 45E
Vernal 160 40 28N 109 35W
Vernalis 163 37 36N 121 17W
Vernayez 50 46 8N 7 3E
Verner 150 46 25N 80 8W
Verneuil, Bois de 50 48 59N 1 59E
Verneuil-sur-Avre 42 48 45N 0 55E
Vernier 50 46 13N 6 5E
Vernon, Can. 152 50 20N 119 15W
Vernon, France 42 49 5N 1 30E
Vernon, U.S.A. 159 34 0N 99 15W
Vero Beach 157 27 39N 80 23W
Véroia 68 40 34N 22 18E
Verolanuova 62 45 20N 10 5E
Véroli 64 41 43N 13 24E
Verona 62 45 27N 11 0E
Veropol 77 66 0N 168 0E
Verrieres, Les 50 46 55N 6 28E
Versailles 43 48 48N 2 8E
Versoix 50 46 17N 6 10E
Vert, C. 120 14 45N 17 30W
Vertou 42 47 10N 1 28W
Vertus 43 48 54N 4 0E
Verulam 129 29 38S 31 2E
Verviers 47 50 37N 5 52E
Vervins 43 49 50N 3 53E
Verwood, Can. 153 49 30N 105 40W
Verwood, U.K. 28 50 53N 1 53W
Veryan 30 50 13N 4 56W
Veryan Bay 30 50 12N 4 51W
Verzej 63 46 34N 16 13E
Vesdre, R. 47 50 36N 6 0E
Veselí nad Luznici 52 49 12N 14 15E
Veselie 67 42 18N 27 38E
Veselovskoye Vdkhr. 83 47 0N 41 0E
Veselyy Res. 83 47 0N 41 0E
Veshenskaya 83 49 35N 41 44E
Vesle, R. 43 49 17N 3 50E
Veslyana, R. 84 60 20N 54 0E
Vesoul 43 60 40N 6 11E
Vessigebro 73 56 58N 12 40E
Vest-Agder fylke □ 71 58 30N 7 15E
Vest Fjorden 71 68 0N 15 0E
Vesta 166 9 43N 83 3W
Vestby 71 59 37N 10 45E
Vester Hassing 73 57 4N 10 8E
Vesterålen 74 68 45N 14 30E
Vestersche Veld 46 52 52N 6 9E
Vestfjorden 74 67 55N 14 0E
Vestfold fylke □ 71 59 15N 10 0E
Vestmannaeyjar 74 63 27N 20 15W
Vestmarka 71 59 56N 11 59E
Vestnes 71 62 39N 7 5E
Vestone 62 45 43N 10 25E
Vestsjaellands Amt □ 73 55 30N 11 20E
Vestspitsbergen 12 78 40N 17 0E
Vestvågøy 74 68 18N 13 50E
Vesuvio 65 40 50N 14 22E
Vesuvius, Mt. = Vesuvio 65 40 50N 14 22E
Veszprém 53 47 8N 17 57E
Veszprém □ 53 47 5N 17 55E
Vésztö 53 46 55N 21 16E
Vetapalam 97 15 47N 80 18E
Vetlanda 73 57 24N 15 3E
Vetluga 81 57 53N 45 45E
Vetluzhskiy 81 57 17N 45 12E
Vetovo 67 43 42N 26 16E
Vetralia 63 42 20N 12 2E
Vetren 67 42 15N 24 3E
Vettore, Mte. 63 44 38N 7 5E
Veurne 47 51 5N 2 40E
Vevey 50 46 28N 6 51E
Vévi 68 40 47N 21 38E
Veys 92 31 30N 49 0E
Vézelise 43 48 30N 6 5E
Vezhen, mt. 67 42 50N 24 20E
Vi Thanh 101 9 42N 105 26E
Viacha 174 16 30S 68 5W
Viadana 62 44 55N 10 30E
Viana, Brazil 170 3 0S 44 40W
Viana, Port. 55 38 20N 8 0W
Viana, Spain 58 42 31N 2 22W
Viana do Castelo 56 41 42N 8 50W
Vianden 47 49 56N 6 12E
Vianen 46 51 59N 5 5E
Vianna do Castelo □ 56 41 50N 8 30W
Vianópolis 171 16 40S 48 35W
Viar, R. 56 37 45N 5 54W
Viaréggio 62 43 52N 10 13E
Vibank 153 50 20N 103 56W
Vibey, R. 56 42 21N 7 15E
Vibo Valéntia 65 38 40N 16 5E
Viborg 73 56 27N 9 23E
Viborg Amt □ 73 56 30N 9 20E
Vic-en-Bigorre 44 43 24N 0 3E
Vic-Fezensac 44 43 45N 0 18E
Vic Fézensac 44 43 47N 0 19E
Vic-sur-Cère 44 44 59N 2 38E
Vic-sur-Seille 43 48 45N 6 33E
Vicarstown 39 53 5N 7 7W
Vicenza 63 45 32N 11 31E
Vich 58 41 58N 2 19E
Vichada □ 174 5 0N 69 30W
Vichuga 81 57 25N 41 55E
Vichy 44 46 9N 3 26E
Vickerstown 32 54 8N 3 17W
Vicksburg, Mich., U.S.A. 156 42 10N 85 30W
Vicksburg, Miss., U.S.A. 159 32 22N 90 56W
Vico, L. di 63 42 20N 12 10E
Viçosa, Min. Ger., Brazil 170 20 45S 42 53W
Viçosa, Pernambuco, Brazil 170 9 28S 36 14W
Viçosa do Ceará 170 3 34S 41 5W
Vicosoprano 51 46 22N 9 38E
Victor 158 38 43N 105 7W
Victor Emanuel Ra. 135 5 20S 142 15E
Victor Harbour 139 35 30S 138 37E
Victoria, Argent. 172 32 40S 60 10W
Victoria, Austral. 138 21 16S 149 3E
Victoria, Camer. 121 4 1N 9 10E
Victoria, Can. 152 48 30N 123 25W
Victoria, Chile 176 38 13S 72 20W
Victoria, Guin. 120 10 50N 14 32W
Victoria, H. K. 109 22 25N 114 15E
Victoria, Malay. 102 5 20N 115 20E
Victoria, Tex., U.S.A. 159 28 50N 97 0W
Victoria, Va., U.S.A. 158 38 52N 99 8W
Victoria □, Austral. 131 37 0S 144 0E
Victoria □, Rhod. 127 21 0S 31 30E
Victoria Beach 153 50 40N 96 35W
Victoria de las Tunas 166 20 58N 76 59W
Victoria Falls 127 17 58S 25 45E
Victoria, Grand L. 150 47 31N 77 30W
Victoria Harbour 150 44 45N 79 45W
Victoria I. 148 71 0N 111 0W
Victoria, L., N.S.W., Austral. 140 33 57S 141 15E
Victoria, L., Vic., Austral. 139 38 2S 147 34E
Victoria, L., E. Afr. 126 1 0S 33 0E
Victoria, La 174 10 14N 67 20W
Victoria Ld. 13 75 0S 160 0E
Victoria, Mt., Burma 98 21 15N 93 55E
Victoria, Mt., P.N.G. 135 8 55S 147 32E
Victoria Nile R. 126 2 25N 31 50E
Victoria, R. 136 15 10S 129 40E
Victoria R. Downs 136 16 25S 131 0E
Victoria Ra. 143 42 12S 172 7E
Victoria Res. 151 48 20N 57 27W
Victoria Taungdeik 99 21 15N 93 55E
Victoria West 128 31 25S 23 4E
Victoriaville 151 46 4N 71 56W
Victorica 172 36 20S 65 30W
Victorino 174 2 48N 67 50W
Victorville 163 34 32N 117 18W
Vicuña 172 30 0S 70 50W
Vicuña Mackenna 172 33 53S 64 25W
Vidalia 157 32 13N 82 25W
Vidauban 45 43 25N 6 27E
Videlv, R. 71 58 50N 8 32E
Vidigueira 57 38 12N 7 48W
Vidin 66 43 59N 22 28E
Vidio, Cabo 56 43 35N 6 14W
Vidisha (Bhilsa) 94 23 28N 77 53E
Vidöstern 73 57 5N 14 0E
Vidra 70 45 56N 26 55E
Viduša, mts. 66 42 55N 18 21E
Vidzy 80 54 40N 26 37E
Viedma 176 40 50S 63 0W
Viedma, L. 176 49 30S 72 30W
Vieira 56 41 38N 8 8W
Viejo Canal de Bahama 166 22 10N 77 30W
Viella 58 42 43N 0 44E
Vielsalm 47 50 17N 5 54E
Vien Pou Kha 101 20 45N 101 5E
Vienenburg 48 51 57N 10 35E
Vieng Pou Kha 100 20 41N 101 4E
Vienna, Illinois, U.S.A. 159 37 29N 88 54W
Vienna, Va., U.S.A. 162 38 54N 77 16W
Vienna = Wien 53 48 12N 16 22E
Vienne 45 45 31N 4 53E
Vienne □ 44 45 53N 0 42E
Vienne, R. 42 47 5N 0 30E
Vientiane 100 17 58N 102 36E
Vieques, I. 147 18 8N 65 25W
Vierlingsbeek 47 51 36N 6 1E
Viersen 48 51 15N 6 23E
Vierwaldstättersee 51 47 0N 8 30E
Vierzon 43 47 13N 2 5E
Vieux-Boucau-les-Bains 44 43 48N 1 23W
Vif 45 45 5N 5 41E
Vigan 103 17 35N 120 28E
Vigan, Le 44 44 0N 3 36E
Vigevano 62 45 18N 8 50E
Vigia 170 0 50S 48 5W
Vigía Chico 165 19 46N 87 35W
Vignacourt 43 50 1N 2 15E
Vignemale, Pic du 44 42 47N 0 10W
Vigneulles 43 48 59N 5 40E
Vignola 62 44 29N 11 0E
Vigo 56 42 12N 8 41W
Vigo, Ría de 56 42 15N 8 45W
Vihiers 42 47 10N 0 30W
Vijayadurg 96 16 30N 73 25E

Vijayawada (Bezwada) Voitsberg


Vijayawada (Bezwada) **96** 16 31N 80 39 E
Vijfhuizen **46** 52 22N 4 41 E
Vikedal **71** 59 30N 5 55 E
Viken, L. **73** 58 40N 10 2 E
Vikersund **71** 59 58N 10 2 E
Viking **152** 53 7N 111 50W
Viking, gasfield **19** 53 30N 2 20 E
Vikna **74** 64 52N 10 57 E
Vikramasingapuram **97** 8 40N 76 47 E
Viksjö **72** 62 45N 17 26 E
Vikulovo **76** 56 50N 70 40 E
Vila Alferes Chamusca **129** 24 27 S 33 0 E
Vila Arriaga **125** 14 35 S 13 30 E
Vila Bittencourt **174** 1 20 S 69 20W
Vila Cabral = Lichinga **127** 13 13 S 35 11 E
Vila Caldas Xavier **127** 14 28 S 33 0 E
Vila Coutinho **127** 14 37 S 34 19 E
Vila da Maganja **127** 17 18 S 37 30 E
Vila da Ponte **125** 14 35 S 16 40 E
Vila de Aljustrel **125** 13 30 S 19 45 E
Vila de João Belo = Xai-Xai **129** 25 6 S 33 31 E
Vila de Liquica **103** 8 40 S 125 20 E
Vila de Manica **125** 18 58 S 32 59 E
Vila de Rei **57** 39 41N 8 9W
Vila de Sena = Sena **127** 17 25 S 35 0 E
Vila do Bispo **57** 37 5N 8 53W
Vila do Conde **56** 41 21N 8 45W
Vila Fontes **125** 17 51 S 35 24 E
Vila Fontes Velha **127** 17 51 S 35 24 E
Vila Franca de Xira **57** 38 57N 8 59W
Vila Gamito **127** 14 12 S 33 0 E
Vila General Machado **125** 11 58 S 17 22 E
Vila Gomes da Costa **129** 24 20 S 33 37 E
Vila Henrique de Carvalho = Lunda **124** 9 40 S 20 12 E
Vila Junqueiro **127** 15 25 S 36 58 E
Vila Luiza **129** 25 45 S 32 35 E
Vila Luso = Moxico **125** 11 53 S 19 55 E
Vila Machado **127** 19 15 S 34 14 E
Vila Marechal Carmona = Uige **124** 7 30 S 14 40 E
Vila Mariano Machado **125** 13 3 S 14 35 E
Vila Moatize **127** 16 11 S 33 40 E
Vila Mouzinho **127** 14 48 S 34 25 E
Vila Murtinho **174** 10 20 S 65 20W
Vila Nova de Fozcôa **56** 41 5N 7 9W
Vila Nova de Ourém **57** 39 40N 8 35W
Vila Nova do Seles **125** 11 35 S 14 22 E
Vila Novo de Gaia **56** 41 4N 8 40W
Vila Paiva Couceiro **125** 14 37 S 14 40 E
Vila Paiva de Andrada **127** 18 37 S 34 2 E
Vila Pery = Chimoio **127** 19 4 S 33 30 E
Vila Pouca de Aguiar **56** 41 30N 7 38W
Vila Real **56** 41 17N 7 48W
Vila Real de Santo Antonio **57** 37 10N 7 28W
Vila Robert Williams **125** 12 46 S 15 30 E
Vila Salazar, Angola **124** 9 12 S 14 48 E
Vila Salazar, Indon. **103** 5 25 S 123 50 E
Vila Teixeira da Silva **125** 12 10 S 15 50 E
Vila Vasco da Gama **127** 14 54 S 32 14 E
Vila Velha **173** 20 20 S 40 17W
Vila Verissimo Sarmento **124** 8 15 S 20 50 E
Vila Viçosa **57** 38 45N 7 27W
Vilaboa **56** 42 21N 8 39W
Vilaine, R. **42** 47 35N 2 10W
Vilanculos **129** 22 1 S 35 17 E
Vilar Formosa **56** 40 38N 6 45W
Vilareal □ **56** 41 36N 7 35W
Vileyka **80** 54 30N 27 0 E
Vilhelmina **74** 64 35N 16 39 E
Vilhena **174** 12 30 S 60 0W
Viliga **77** 60 2N 156 56 E
Viliya, R. **80** 54 57N 24 35 E
Viljandi **80** 58 28N 25 30 E
Villa Abecia **172** 21 0 S 68 18W
Villa Ahumada **164** 30 30N 106 40W
Villa Ana **172** 28 28 S 59 40W
Villa Ángela **172** 27 34 S 60 45W
Villa Bella **174** 10 25 S 65 30W
Villa Bens (Tarfaya) **116** 27 55N 12 55W
Villa Cañas **172** 34 0 S 61 35W
Villa Cisneros = Dakhla **116** 23 50N 15 53W
Villa Colón **172** 31 38 S 68 20W
Villa Constitución **172** 33 15 S 60 20W
Villa de Cura **174** 10 2N 67 29W
Villa de María **172** 30 0 S 63 43W
Villa de Rosario **172** 24 30 S 57 35W
Villa Dolores **172** 31 58 S 65 15W
Villa Franca **172** 26 14 S 58 20W
Villa Frontera **164** 26 56N 101 27W
Villa Guillermina **172** 28 15 S 59 29W
Villa Hayes **172** 25 0 S 57 20W
Villa Iris **172** 38 12 S 63 12W
Villa Julia Molina **167** 19 5N 69 45W
Villa Madero **164** 24 28N 104 10W
Villa María **172** 32 20 S 63 10W
Villa Mazán **172** 28 40 S 66 30W
Villa Mentes **172** 21 10 S 63 30W
Villa Minozzo **62** 44 21N 10 30 E
Villa Montes **172** 21 10 S 63 30W
Villa Ocampo, Argent. **172** 28 30 S 59 20W
Villa Ocampo, Mexico **164** 26 29N 105 30W
Villa Ojo de Agua **172** 29 30 S 63 44W
Villa San Agustín **172** 30 35 S 67 30W
Villa San Giovanni **65** 38 13N 15 38 E
Villa San José **172** 32 12 S 58 15W
Villa San Martín **172** 28 9 S 64 9W
Villa Santina **63** 46 25N 12 55 E
Villa Unión **164** 23 12N 106 14W
Villablino **56** 42 57N 6 19W
Villabruzzi **91** 3 3N 45 18 E
Villacampo, Pantano de **56** 41 31N 6 0W
Villacañas **58** 39 38N 3 20W
Villacarlos **58** 39 53N 4 17 E
Villacarriedo **58** 43 14N 3 48W
Villacarrillo **59** 38 7N 3 3W
Villacastín **56** 40 46N 4 25W
Villach **52** 46 37N 13 51 E
Villaciaro **64** 39 27N 8 45 E
Villada **56** 42 15N 4 59W
Villadiego **56** 42 31N 4 1W
Villadossóla **62** 46 4N 8 16 E
Villafeliche **58** 41 10N 1 30W
Villafranca **58** 42 17N 1 46W
Villafranca de los Barros **57** 38 35N 6 18W
Villafranca de los Caballeros **59** 39 26N 3 21W
Villafranca del Bierzo **56** 42 38N 6 50W
Villafranca del Cid **58** 40 26N 0 16W
Villafranca del Panadés **58** 41 21N 1 40 E
Villafranca di Verona **62** 45 20N 10 51 E
Villagarcía de Arosa **56** 42 34N 8 46W
Villagrán **165** 24 29N 99 29W
Villaguay **172** 32 0 S 58 45W
Villaharta **57** 38 9N 4 54W
Villahermosa, Mexico **165** 17 45N 92 50W
Villahermosa, Spain **59** 38 46N 2 52W
Villaines-la-Juhel **42** 48 21N 0 20W
Villajoyosa **59** 38 30N 0 12W
Villalba **56** 40 36N 3 59W
Villalba de Guardo **56** 42 42N 4 49W
Villalón de Campos **56** 42 5N 5 4W
Villalpando **56** 41 51N 5 25W
Villaluenga **56** 40 2N 3 54W
Villamañ!n **56** 42 19N 5 35W
Villamartín **56** 36 52N 5 38W
Villamayor **58** 41 42N 0 43W
Villamblard **44** 45 2N 0 32 E
Villanova Monteleone **64** 40 30N 8 28 E
Villanueva, Colomb. **174** 10 37N 72 59W
Villanueva, U.S.A. **161** 35 16N 105 31W
Villanueva de Castellón **59** 39 5N 0 31W
Villanueva de Córdoba **57** 38 20N 4 38W
Villanueva de la Fuente **59** 38 42N 2 42W
Villanueva de la Serena **57** 38 59N 5 50W
Villanueva de la Sierra **56** 40 12N 6 24W
Villanueva de los Castillejos **57** 37 30N 7 15W
Villanueva del Arzobispo **59** 38 10N 3 0W
Villanueva del Duque **57** 38 20N 4 38W
Villanueva del Fresno **57** 38 23N 7 10W
Villanueva y Geltrú **58** 41 13N 1 40 E
Villaodrid **56** 43 20N 7 11W
Villaputzu **64** 39 28N 9 33 E
Villar del Arzobispo **58** 39 44N 0 50W
Villar del Rey **57** 39 7N 6 50W
Villarcayo **58** 42 56N 3 34W
Villard **45** 45 4N 5 33 E
Villard-Bonnot **45** 45 14N 5 53 E
Villard-de-Lans **45** 45 3N 5 33 E
Villarino de los Aires **56** 41 18N 6 23W
Villarosa **65** 37 36N 14 9 E
Villarramiel **56** 42 2N 4 55W
Villarreal **58** 39 55N 0 3W
Villarrica, Chile **176** 39 15 S 72 30W
Villarrica, Parag. **172** 25 40 S 56 30W
Villarrobledo **59** 39 18N 2 36W
Villarroya de la Sierra **58** 41 27N 1 46W
Villarrubia de los Ojos **59** 39 14N 3 36W
Villars **45** 46 0N 5 2 E
Villarta de San Juan **59** 39 15N 3 25W
Villasayas **58** 41 24N 2 39W
Villaseca de los Gamitos **56** 41 2N 6 7W
Villastar **58** 40 17N 1 9W
Villatobas **58** 39 54N 3 20W
Villavicencio, Argent. **172** 32 28 S 69 0W
Villavicencio, Colomb. **174** 4 9N 73 37W
Villaviciosa **56** 43 32N 5 27W
Villazón **172** 22 0 S 65 35W
Ville de Paris □ **43** 48 50N 2 20 E
Ville Marie **150** 47 20N 79 30W
Ville Platte **159** 30 45N 92 17W
Villedieu **42** 48 50N 1 12W
Villefort **44** 44 28N 3 56 E
Villefranche **43** 47 19N 146 0 E
Villefranche-de-Lauragais **44** 43 25N 1 44 E
Villefranche-de-Rouergue **44** 44 21N 2 2 E
Villefranche-du-Périgord **44** 44 38N 1 5 E
Villefranche-sur-Saône **45** 45 59N 4 43 E
Villel **58** 40 14N 1 12W
Villemaur **43** 48 14N 3 40 E
Villemur-sur-Tarn **44** 43 51N 1 31 E
Villena **59** 38 39N 0 52W
Villenauxe **43** 48 36N 3 30 E
Villenave **44** 44 46N 0 33W
Villeneuve, France **43** 48 42N 2 25 E
Villeneuve, Italy **62** 45 40N 7 10 E
Villeneuve, Switz. **50** 46 24N 6 56 E
Villeneuve-l'Archevèque **43** 48 14N 3 32 E
Villeneuve-lès-Avignon **45** 43 57N 4 49 E
Villeneuve-sur-Allier **44** 46 40N 3 13 E
Villeneuve-sur-Lot **44** 44 24N 0 42 E
Villeréal **44** 44 38N 0 45 E
Villers Bocage **42** 49 3N 0 40W
Villers Bretonneux **43** 49 50N 2 30 E
Villers-Cotterets **43** 49 15N 3 4 E
Villers-Farlay **47** 47 0N 5 45 E
Villers-le-Bouillet **47** 50 34N 5 15 E
Villers-le-Gambon **47** 50 11N 4 37 E
Villers-sur-Mer **42** 49 21N 0 2W
Villersexel **43** 47 33N 6 26 E
Villerslev **73** 56 49N 8 29 E
Villerupt **43** 49 28N 5 55 E
Villerville **42** 49 26N 0 5 E
Villiers **129** 27 2 S 28 36 E
Villingen = Schwenningen **49** 48 3N 8 29 E
Villisca **158** 40 55N 94 59W
Villupuram **97** 11 59N 79 31 E
Vilna **152** 54 7N 111 55W
Vilnius **80** 54 38N 25 25 E
Vils **52** 47 33N 10 37 E
Vilsbiburg **49** 48 27N 12 23 E
Vilslev **73** 55 24N 8 42 E
Vilusi **66** 42 44N 18 34 E
Vilvoorde **47** 50 56N 4 26 E
Vilyuy, R. **77** 63 58N 125 0 E
Vilyuysk **77** 63 40N 121 20 E
Vimercate **62** 45 38N 9 25 E
Vimiosa **56** 41 35N 6 13W
Vimmerby **73** 57 40N 15 55 E
Vimo **72** 60 50N 14 20 E
Vimoutiers **42** 48 57N 0 10 E
Vimperk **52** 49 3N 13 46 E
Viña del Mar **172** 33 0 S 71 30W
Vinaroz **58** 40 30N 0 27 E
Vincennes **156** 38 42N 87 29W
Vincent **163** 34 33N 118 11W
Vinchina **172** 28 45 S 68 15W
Vindel älv **74** 64 20N 19 20 E
Vindeln **74** 64 12N 19 43 E
Vinderup **73** 56 29N 8 45 E
Vindhya Ra. **94** 22 50N 77 0 E
Vinegar Hill **39** 52 30N 6 28W
Vineland **162** 39 30N 75 0W
Vinga **66** 46 0N 21 14 E
Vingnes **71** 61 7N 10 26 E
Vinh **100** 18 45N 105 38 E
Vinh Linh **100** 17 4N 107 2 E
Vinh Loi **101** 9 20N 104 45 E
Vinh Long **101** 10 16N 105 57 E
Vinh Yen **100** 21 21N 105 35 E
Vinhais **56** 41 50N 7 0W
Vinica **63** 45 28N 15 16 E
Vinita **159** 36 40N 95 12W
Vinkeveen **46** 52 13N 4 56 E
Vinkovci **66** 45 19N 18 48 E
Vinnitsa **82** 49 15N 28 30 E
Vinstra **71** 61 37N 9 44 E
Vinton, Iowa, U.S.A. **158** 42 8N 92 1W
Vinton, La., U.S.A. **159** 30 13N 93 35W
Vintu de Jos **70** 46 0N 23 30 E
Viöl **48** 54 32N 9 12 E
Violet Town **141** 36 38 S 145 42 E
Vipava **63** 45 51N 13 38 E
Vipiteno **63** 46 55N 11 25 E
Viqueque **103** 8 42 S 126 30 E
Vir **85** 37 45N 72 5 E
Vir, I. **63** 44 17N 15 3 E
Virac **103** 13 30N 124 20 E
Virachei **100** 13 59N 106 49 E
Virago Sd. **152** 54 0N 132 42W
Virajpet **97** 12 15N 75 50 E
Viramgam **94** 23 5N 72 0 E
Virarajendrapet (Virajpet) **97** 12 10N 75 50 E
Viravanallur **97** 8 40N 79 30 E
Virden **153** 49 50N 100 56W
Vire **42** 48 50N 0 53W
Virgem da Lapa **171** 16 49 S 42 21W
Vírgenes, C. **176** 52 19 S 68 21W
Virgin Gorda, I. **147** 18 45N 64 26W
Virgin Is. **147** 18 40N 64 30W
Virgin, R., Can. **153** 57 2N 108 17W
Virgin, R., U.S.A. **161** 36 50N 114 10W
Virginia, Ireland **38** 53 50N 7 5W
Virginia, S. Afr. **128** 28 8 S 26 55 E
Virginia, U.S.A. **158** 47 30N 92 32W
Virginia □ **156** 37 45N 78 0W
Virginia Beach **156** 36 54N 75 58W
Virginia City, Mont., U.S.A. **160** 45 25N 111 58W
Virginia City, Nev., U.S.A. **160** 39 19N 119 39W
Virginia Falls **152** 61 38N 125 42W
Virginiatown **150** 48 9N 79 36W
Virgins, C. **176** 52 10 S 68 30W
Virieu-le-Grand **45** 45 51N 5 39 E
Virje **66** 46 4N 16 59 E
Viroqua **158** 43 33N 90 57W
Virovitica **66** 45 51N 17 21 E
Virpaza, R. **66** 42 14N 19 6 E
Virserum **73** 57 20N 15 35 E
Virton **47** 49 35N 5 32 E
Virtsu **80** 58 32N 23 33 E
Virudhunagar **97** 9 30N 78 0 E
Vis **63** 43 0N 16 10 E
Vis, I. **63** 43 0N 16 10 E
Vis Kanal **63** 43 4N 16 5 E
Visalia **163** 36 25N 119 18W
Visayan Sea **103** 11 30N 123 30 E
Visby **73** 57 37N 18 18 E
Viscount Melville Sd. **12** 74 10N 108 0W
Visé **47** 50 44N 5 41 E
Višegrad **66** 43 47N 19 17 E
Viseu, Brazil **170** 1 10 S 46 20W
Viseu, Port. **56** 40 40N 7 55W
Vişeu **70** 47 45N 24 25 E
Viseu □ **56** 40 40N 7 55W
Vishakhapatnam **96** 17 45N 83 20 E
Vishera, R. **84** 59 55N 56 25 E
Vishnupur **95** 23 8N 87 20 E
Visikoi I. **13** 56 30 S 26 40 E
Visingsö **73** 58 2N 14 20 E
Viskafors **73** 57 37N 12 50 E
Vislanda **73** 56 46N 14 30 E
Vislinskil Zaliv (Zalew Wislany) **54** 54 20N 19 50 E
Visnagar **94** 23 45N 72 32 E
Višnja Gora **63** 45 58N 14 45 E
Viso del Marqués **59** 38 32N 3 34W
Viso, Mte. **62** 44 38N 7 5 E
Visoko **66** 43 58N 18 10 E
Visp **50** 46 17N 7 52 E
Vispa, R. **50** 46 9N 7 48 E
Visselhovde **48** 52 59N 9 36 E
Vissoie **50** 46 13N 7 36 E
Vista **163** 33 12N 117 14W
Vistonis, Limni **68** 41 0N 25 7 E
Vistula, R. = Wisła, R. **54** 53 38N 18 47 E
Vit, R. **67** 43 30N 24 30 E
Vitanje **63** 46 40N 15 18 E
Vitebsk **80** 55 10N 30 15 E
Viterbo **63** 42 25N 12 8 E
Viti Levu, I. **143** 17 30 S 177 30 E
Vitiaz Str. **135** 5 40 S 147 10 E
Vitigudino **56** 41 1N 6 35W
Vitim **77** 59 45N 112 25 E
Vitim, R. **77** 58 40N 112 50 E
Vitína **69** 37 40N 22 10 E
Vitina **66** 43 17N 17 29 E
Vitória **171** 20 20 S 40 22W
Vitoria **58** 42 50N 2 41W
Vitória da Conquista **171** 14 51 S 40 51W
Vitória de São Antão **170** 8 10 S 37 20W
Vitorino Friere **170** 4 4 S 45 10W
Vitré **42** 48 8N 1 12W
Vitry-le-François **43** 48 43N 4 33 E
Vitsi, Mt. **68** 40 40N 21 25 E
Vittangi **74** 67 41N 21 40 E
Vitteaux **43** 47 24N 4 30 E
Vittel **43** 48 12N 5 57 E
Vittória **65** 36 58N 14 30 E
Vittório Véneto **63** 45 59N 12 18 E
Vitu Is. **135** 4 50 S 149 25 E
Vivegnis **47** 50 42N 5 39 E
Viver **58** 39 55N 0 36W
Vivero **56** 43 39N 7 38W
Viviers **45** 44 30N 4 40 E
Vivonne, Austral. **140** 35 59 S 137 9 E
Vivonne, France **44** 46 36N 0 15 E
Vivonne B. **140** 35 59 S 137 9 E
Vivsta **72** 62 30N 17 18 E
Vizcaíno, Desierto de **164** 27 40N 113 50W
Vizcaíno, Sierra **164** 27 30N 114 0W
Vizcaya □ **58** 43 15N 2 45W
Vizianagaram **96** 18 6N 83 10 E
Vizille **45** 45 5N 5 46 E
Vizinada **63** 45 20N 13 46 E
Viziru **70** 45 0N 27 43 E
Vizovice **53** 49 12N 17 56 E
Vizzini **65** 37 9N 14 43 E
Vlaardingen **46** 51 55N 4 21 E
Vladicin Han **66** 42 42N 22 1 E
Vladimir **81** 56 0N 40 30 E
Vladimir Volynskiy **80** 50 50N 24 18 E
Vladimirci **66** 44 36N 19 45 E
Vladimirovac **66** 45 1N 20 53 E
Vladimirovka, U.S.S.R. **83** 44 37N 44 41 E
Vladimirovka, U.S.S.R. **83** 48 27N 46 5 E
Vladimirovo **67** 43 32N 23 22 E
Vladislavovka **82** 45 15N 35 15 E
Vladivostok **82** 43 10N 131 53 E
Vlamertinge **47** 50 51N 2 49 E
Vlaming Head **137** 21 48 S 114 5 E
Vlasenica **66** 44 11N 18 59 E
Vlasim **52** 49 40N 14 53 E
Vlasinsko Jezero **66** 42 44N 22 37 E
Vlašió, mt. **66** 44 19N 17 37 E
Vlasotinci **66** 42 59N 22 7 E
Vleuten **46** 52 6N 5 1 E
Vlieland, I. **46** 53 30N 4 55 E
Vliestroom **46** 53 19N 5 8 E
Vlijmen **47** 51 42N 5 14 E
Vlissingen **47** 51 26N 3 34 E
Vlora **68** 40 32N 19 28 E
Vlora □ **68** 40 12N 20 0 E
Vltava, R. **52** 49 35N 14 10 E
Vlůdeasa, mt. **70** 46 47N 22 50 E
Vo Dat **101** 11 9N 107 31 E
Vobarno **62** 45 38N 10 30 E
Vočin **66** 45 37N 17 33 E
Vodice **63** 43 47N 15 47 E
Vodnany **52** 49 9N 14 11 E
Vodnjan **63** 44 59N 13 52 E
Voe **36** 60 21N 1 15W
Voga **121** 6 23N 1 30 E
Vogelkop = Doberai, Jazirah **103** 1 25 S 133 0 E
Vogelsberg **48** 50 37N 9 30 E
Voghera **62** 44 59N 9 1 E
Vohémar **129** 13 25 S 50 0 E
Vohipeno **129** 22 22 S 47 51 E
Voi **126** 3 25 S 38 32 E
Void **43** 48 40N 5 36 E
Voil, L. **34** 56 20N 4 25W
Voineşti, Iaşi, Rumania **70** 47 5N 27 27 E
Voineşti, Ploeşti, Rumania **70** 45 5N 25 14 E
Voíotía □ **69** 38 20N 23 0 E
Voiron **45** 45 22N 5 35 E
Voiseys B. **151** 56 15N 61 50W
Voitsberg **52** 47 3N 15 9 E

Voiviis Limni, L
Walla Walla

Voiviis Limni, L. 68 39 30N 22 45 E
Vojens 73 55 16N 9 18 E
Vojmsjön 74 64 55N 16 40 E
Vojnió 63 45 19N 15 43 E
Vojvodina, Auton. Pokragina 66 45 20N 20 0 E
Vokhma 81 59 0N 46 45 E
Vokhma, R. 81 59 0N 46 44 E
Vokhtoga 81 58 46N 41 8 E
Volary 52 48 54N 13 52 E
Volborg 158 45 50N 105 44W
Volchansk 81 50 17N 36 58 E
Volchya, R. 82 48 0N 37 0 E
Volda 71 62 9N 6 5 E
Volendam 46 52 30N 5 4 E
Volga 81 57 58N 38 16 E
Volga Hts. = Privolzhskaya V.S. 79 51 0N 46 0 E
Volga, R. 83 52 20N 48 0 E
Volgodonsk 83 47 33N 42 5 E
Volgograd 83 48 40N 44 25 E
Volgogradskoye Vdkhr. 81 50 0N 45 20 E
Volgorechensk 81 57 28N 41 14 E
Volissós 69 38 29N 25 54 E
Volkerak 47 51 39N 4 18 E
Völkermarkt 52 46 39N 14 39 E
Volkhov 80 59 55N 32 15 E
Volkhov, R. 80 59 30N 32 0 E
Völklingen 49 49 15N 6 50 E
Volkovysk 80 53 9N 24 30 E
Volksrust 129 27 24 S 29 53 E
Vollenhove 46 52 40N 5 58 E
Volnovakha 82 47 35N 37 30 E
Volo 140 31 37 S 143 0 E
Volochayevka 77 48 40N 134 30 E
Volodary 81 56 12N 43 15 E
Vologda 81 59 25N 40 0 E
Volokolamsk 81 56 5N 36 0 E
Volokonovka 81 50 33N 37 58 E
Volontirovka 82 46 28N 29 28 E
Vólos 68 39 24N 22 59 E
Volosovo 80 59 27N 29 32 E
Volozhin 80 54 3N 26 30 E
Volsk 81 52 5N 47 28 E
Volstrup 73 57 19N 10 27 E
Volta, L. 121 7 30N 0 15 E
Volta, R. 121 8 0N 0 10W
Volta Redonda 173 22 31 S 44 5W
Voltaire, C. 136 14 16 S 125 35 E
Volterra 62 43 24N 10 50 E
Voltri 62 44 25N 8 43 E
Volturara Áppula 65 41 30N 15 2 E
Volturno, R. 65 41 18N 14 20 E
Volubilis 118 34 2N 5 33W
Vólvi, L. 68 40 40N 23 34 E
Volzhsk 81 55 57N 48 23 E
Volzhskiy 83 48 56N 44 46 E
Vondrozo 129 22 49 S 47 20 E
Vónitsa 69 38 53N 20 58 E
Voorburg 46 52 5N 4 24 E
Voorne Putten 46 51 52N 4 10 E
Voorst 46 52 10N 6 8 E
Voorthuizen 46 52 11N 5 36 E
Vopnafjörður 74 65 45N 14 40W
Vorarlberg □ 52 47 20N 10 0 E
Vóras Óros 68 40 57N 21 45 E
Vorbasse 73 55 39N 9 6 E
Vorden 46 52 6N 6 19 E
Vorderrheim, R. 51 46 49N 9 25 E
Vordingborg 73 55 0N 11 54 E
Voreppe 45 45 18N 5 39 E
Voríai Sporádhes 69 39 15N 23 30 E
Vórios Évvoïkós Kólpos 69 38 45N 23 15 E
Vorkuta 78 67 48N 64 20 E
Vorma 71 60 9N 11 27 E
Vorona, R. 81 52 0N 42 20 E
Voronezh, R.S.S.R., U.S.S.R. 81 51 40N 39 10 E
Voronezh, Ukraine, U.S.S.R. 80 51 47N 33 28 E
Voronezh, R. 81 52 30N 39 30 E
Vorontsovo-Aleksandrovskoïe = Zelenokumsk. 83 44 30N 44 1 E
Voroshilovgrad 83 48 38N 39 15 E
Voroshilovsk = Kommunarsk 83 48 3N 38 40 E
Vorovskoye 77 54 30N 155 50 E
Vorselaar 47 51 12N 4 46 E
Vorskla, R. 82 49 30N 34 31 E
Vorukh 85 39 52N 70 35 E
Vorupør 73 56 58N 8 22 E
Vosges 43 48 20N 7 10 E
Vosges □ 43 48 12N 6 20 E
Voskopoja 68 40 40N 20 33 E
Voskresensk 81 55 27N 38 31 E
Voskresenskoye 81 56 51N 45 30 E
Voss 71 60 38N 6 26 E
Vosselaar 47 51 19N 4 52 E
Vostok I. 131 10 5 S 152 23W
Vostotnyy Sayan 77 54 0N 96 0 E
Votice 52 49 38N 14 39 E
Votkinsk 84 57 0N 53 55 E
Votkinskoye Vdkhr. 78 57 30N 55 0 E
Vouga, R. 56 40 46N 8 10W
Voulte-sur-Rhône, La 45 44 48N 4 46 E
Vouvry 50 46 21N 6 21 E
Voúxa, Ákra 69 35 37N 20 32 E
Vouzela 56 40 43N 8 7W
Vouziers 43 49 22N 4 40 E
Voves 43 48 15N 1 38 E
Voxna 72 61 20N 15 30 E
Voy 37 59 1N 3 16W
Vozhe Oz. 78 60 45N 39 0 E
Vozhgaly 81 58 24N 50 1 E
Voznesensk 82 47 35N 31 15 E
Voznesenye 78 61 0N 35 45 E
Vráble 53 48 15N 18 16 E
Vrácevšnica 66 44 2N 20 34 E
Vrådal 71 59 20N 8 25 E
Vradiyevka 82 49 56N 30 38 E
Vraka 68 42 8N 19 28 E
Vrakhnéika 69 38 10N 21 40 E
Vrancea □ 70 45 50N 26 45 E
Vrancei, Munţi 70 46 0N 26 30 E
Vrangelja, Ostrov 77 71 0N 180 0 E
Vrangtjarn 72 62 14N 16 37 E
Vranica, mt. 66 43 59N 18 0 E
Vranje 66 42 34N 21 54 E
Vranjska Banja 66 42 34N 22 1 E
Vranov 53 48 53N 21 40 E
Vransko 63 46 17N 14 58 E
Vratsa 67 43 13N 23 30 E
Vratsa □ 67 43 30N 23 30 E
Vrbas 66 45 0N 17 27 E
Vrbas, R. 66 44 30N 17 10 E
Vrbnik 63 45 4N 14 32 E
Vrboviec 63 45 53N 16 28 E
Vrbovsko 63 45 24N 15 5 E
Vrchlabí 52 49 38N 15 37 E
Vrede 129 27 24 S 29 6 E
Vredefort 128 27 0 S 26 58 E
Vredenburg 128 32 51 S 18 0 E
Vredendal 128 31 41 S 18 35 E
Vreeswijk 46 52 1N 5 6 E
Vrena 73 58 54N 16 41 E
Vrgorac 66 43 12N 17 20 E
Vrhnika 63 45 58N 14 15 E
Vriddhachalam 97 11 30N 79 10 E
Vridi 120 5 15N 4 3W
Vridi Canal 120 5 15N 4 3W
Vries 46 53 5N 6 35 E
Vriezenveen 46 52 25N 6 38 E
Vrindaban 94 27 37N 77 40 E
Vrnograč 63 43 12N 17 20 E
Vrondádhes 69 38 25N 26 7 E
Vroomshoop 46 52 27N 6 34 E
Vrpolje 66 43 42N 16 1 E
Vršac 66 45 8N 21 18 E
Vršački Kanal 66 45 15N 21 0 E
Vrsheto 67 43 15N 23 23 E
Vryburg 128 26 55 S 24 45 E
Vryheid 129 27 54 S 30 47 E
Vsetín 53 49 20N 18 0 E
Vu Liet 100 18 43N 105 23 E
Vŭcha, R. 67 41 53N 24 26 E
Vučitrn 66 42 49N 20 59 E
Vught 47 51 38N 5 20 E
Vuka, R. 66 45 28N 18 30 E
Vukovar 66 45 21N 18 59 E
Vulcan, Can. 152 50 25N 113 15W
Vulcan, Rumania 70 45 23N 23 17 E
Vulcan, U.S.A. 156 45 46N 87 51W
Vŭlcani 66 46 0N 20 26 E
Vulcano, I. 65 38 25N 14 58 E
Vulchedrŭma 67 43 42N 23 16 E
Vulci 63 42 23N 11 37 E
Vŭleni 70 44 15N 24 45 E
Vulkaneshty 82 45 35N 28 30 E
Vunduzi, R. 127 18 0 S 33 45 E
Vung Tau 101 10 21N 107 4 E
Vûrbitsa 67 42 59N 26 40 E
Vutcani 70 46 26N 27 59 E
Vuyyuru 96 16 28N 80 50 E
Vvedenka 84 54 0N 63 53 E
Vyara 96 21 8N 73 28 E
Vyasniki 81 56 10N 42 10 E
Vyatka, R. 84 56 30N 51 0 E
Vyatskiye Polyany 84 56 5N 51 0 E
Vyazemskiy 77 47 32N 134 45 E
Vyazma 80 55 10N 34 15 E
Vyborg 78 60 43N 28 47 E
Vychegda R. 78 61 50N 52 30 E
Vychodné Beskydy 53 49 30N 22 0 E
Východočeský □ 52 50 20N 15 45 E
Východoslovenský □ 53 48 50N 21 0 E
Vyg-ozero 78 63 30N 34 0 E
Vyja, R. 81 41 53N 24 26 E
Vypin, I. 97 10 10N 76 15 E
Vyrnwy, L. 31 52 48N 3 30W
Vyrnwy, R. 31 52 43N 3 15W
Vyshniy Volochek 80 57 30N 34 30 E
Vyškov 53 49 17N 17 0 E
Vysoké Mýto 53 49 58N 16 23 E
Vysoké Tatry 53 49 30N 20 0 E
Vysokovsk 81 56 22N 36 30 E
Vysotsk 80 51 43N 36 32 E
Vyssi Brod 92 48 36N 14 20 E
Vytegra 52 61 15N 36 40 E

W

Wa 121 10 7N 2 25W
Waal, R. 46 51 59N 4 8 E
Waalwijk 47 51 42N 5 4 E
Waarschoot 47 51 10N 3 36 E
Waasmunster 47 51 6N 4 5 E
Wabag 135 5 32 S 143 53 E
Wabakimi L. 150 50 38N 89 45W
Wabana 151 47 40N 53 0W
Wabasca 152 55 57N 113 45W
Wabash 156 40 48N 85 46W
Wabash, R. 156 39 10N 87 30W
Wabawng 98 25 18N 97 46 E
Wabeno 156 45 25N 88 40W
Wabi Gestro, R. 123 6 0N 41 35 E
Wabi, R. 123 7 35N 40 5 E
Wabi Shaballe, R. 123 8 0N 40 45 E
Wabigoon, L. 153 49 44N 92 34W
Wabowden 153 54 55N 98 38W
Wabrzezno 54 53 16N 18 57 E
Wabuk Pt. 150 55 20N 85 5W
Wabush City 151 52 55N 66 52W
Wabuska 160 39 16N 119 13W
W.A.C. Bennett Dam 152 56 2N 122 6W
Wachapreague 162 37 36N 75 41W
Wachtebeke 47 51 11N 3 52 E
Waco 159 31 33N 97 5W
Waconichi, L. 150 50 8N 74 0W
Wad ar Rimsa 92 26 5N 41 30 E
Wad Ban Naqa 123 16 32N 33 9 E
Wad Banda 123 13 10N 27 50 E
Wad el Haddad 123 13 50N 33 30 E
Wad en Nau 123 14 10N 33 34 E
Wad Hamid 123 16 20N 32 45 E
Wâd Medanî 123 14 28N 33 30 E
Wad Thana 94 27 22N 66 23 E
Wadayama 110 35 19N 134 52 E
Waddān 119 29 9N 16 45 E
Waddān, Jabal 119 29 0N 16 15 E
Waddeneilanden 46 53 25N 5 10 E
Waddenzee 46 53 6N 5 10 E
Wadderin Hill 137 32 0 S 118 25 E
Waddesdon 29 51 50N 0 54W
Waddingham 33 53 28N 0 31W
Waddington 33 53 10N 0 31W
Waddington, Mt. 152 51 23N 125 15W
Waddinxveen 46 52 2N 4 40 E
Waddy Pt. 139 24 58 S 153 21 E
Wadebridge 30 50 31N 4 51W
Wadena, Can. 153 51 57N 103 38W
Wadena, U.S.A. 158 46 25N 95 2W
Wädenswil 51 47 14N 8 30 E
Wadesboro 157 35 2N 80 2W
Wadhams 152 51 30N 127 30W
Wadhurst 29 51 3N 0 21 E
Wadi 121 13 5N 11 40 E
Wādī ash Shāfi' 119 27 30N 15 0 E
Wādī Banī Walīd 119 31 49N 14 0 E
Wadi Gemâl 122 24 35N 35 10 E
Wadi Halfa 122 21 53N 31 19 E
Wadi Masila 91 16 30N 49 0 E
Wadi Sabha 92 23 50N 48 30 E
Wadlew 54 51 31N 19 23 E
Wadowice 54 49 52N 19 30 E
Wadsworth 160 39 44N 119 22W
Waegwan 107 35 59N 128 23 E
Waenfawr 31 53 7N 4 10W
Wafou Hu 109 32 19N 116 56 E
Wafra 92 28 33N 48 3 E
Wagenberg 47 51 40N 4 46 E
Wageningen 46 51 58N 5 40 E
Wager B. 149 65 26N 88 40W
Wager Bay 149 65 56N 90 49W
Wagga Wagga 141 35 7 S 147 24 E
Waghete 103 4 10 S 135 50 E
Wagin, Austral. 137 33 17 S 117 25 E
Wagin, Nigeria 137 12 42N 7 10 E
Wagon Mound 159 36 10N 105 0W
Wagoner 159 36 0N 95 20W
Wagrowiec 54 52 48N 17 19 E
Wah 94 33 45N 72 40 E
Wahai 103 2 48 S 129 35 E
Wahiawa 147 21 30N 158 2W
Wahnai 94 32 40N 65 50 E
Wahoo 158 41 15N 96 35W
Wahpeton 158 46 20N 96 35W
Wahratta 140 31 58 S 141 50 E
Wai 96 17 56N 73 57 E
Wai, Koh 101 9 55N 102 55 E
Waiai, R. 143 45 36 S 167 45 E
Waianae 147 21 25N 158 8W
Waiau 143 42 39 S 173 5 E
Waiau, R. 143 42 47 S 173 22 E
Waiawe Ganga 97 6 15N 81 0 E
Waibeem 103 0 30 S 132 50 E
Waiblingen 49 48 49N 9 20 E
Waidhofen, Niederösterreich, Austria 52 48 49N 15 17 E
Waidhofen, Niederösterreich, Austria 52 47 57N 14 46 E
Waigeo, I. 103 0 20 S 130 40 E
Waihao Downs 143 44 48 S 170 55 E
Waihao, R. 143 44 52 S 171 11 E
Waiheke Islands 142 36 48 S 175 6 E
Waihi 142 37 23 S 175 52 E
Waihola 143 46 1 S 170 8 E
Waihola L. 143 45 59 S 170 8 E
Waihou, R. 143 37 15 S 175 40 E
Waika 126 2 22 S 25 42 E
Waikabubak 103 9 45 S 119 25 E
Waikaka 143 45 55 S 169 1 E
Waikaoti 131 45 36 S 170 41 E
Waikare, L. 142 37 26 S 175 13 E
Waikaremoana 142 38 42 S 177 12 E
Waikaremoana L. 142 38 49 S 177 9 E
Waikari 143 42 58 S 172 41 E
Waikato, R. 142 37 23 S 174 43 E
Waikawa Harbour 143 46 39 S 169 9 E
Waikerie 140 34 9 S 140 0 E
Waikiekie 142 35 57 S 174 16 E
Waikokopu 142 39 3 S 177 52 E
Waikokopu Harb. 142 39 4 S 177 53 E
Waikouaiti 143 45 36 S 170 41 E
Wailuku 147 20 53N 156 26W
Waimakariri, R. 143 42 23 S 172 42 E
Waimangaroa 143 41 43 S 171 46 E
Waimanola 147 21 19N 157 43W
Waimarie 143 41 35 S 171 58 E
Waimarino 143 40 40 S 175 20 E
Waimate 143 44 53 S 171 3 E
Waimea 147 21 57N 159 39W
Waimea Plain 143 45 55 S 168 35 E
Waimes 47 50 25N 6 7 E
Wainfleet All Saints 33 53 7N 0 16 E
Wainganga, R. 96 21 0N 79 45 E
Waingapu 103 9 35 S 120 11 E
Waingmaw 98 25 21N 97 26 E
Wainiha 147 22 9N 159 34W
Wainuiomata 142 41 17 S 174 56 E
Wainwright, Can. 153 52 50N 110 50W
Wainwright, U.S.A. 147 70 39N 160 10W
Waiotapu 142 38 21 S 176 25 E
Waiouru 142 39 28 S 175 41 E
Waipahi 143 46 6 S 169 15 E
Waipahu 147 21 23N 158 1W
Waipapa Pt. 143 46 40 S 168 51 E
Waipara 143 43 3 S 172 46 E
Waipawa 142 39 56 S 176 38 E
Waipiro 142 38 2 S 176 22 E
Waipori 131 45 50 S 169 52 E
Waipu 142 35 59 S 174 29 E
Waipukurau 142 40 1 S 176 33 E
Wairakei 142 38 37 S 176 6 E
Wairarapa I. 142 41 14 S 175 15 E
Wairau, R. 143 41 32 S 174 7 E
Wairio 143 45 59 S 168 3 E
Wairoa 142 39 3 S 177 25 E
Wairoa, R. 142 36 5 S 173 59 E
Waitaki Plains 143 44 22 S 170 0 E
Waitaki, R. 143 44 23 S 169 55 E
Waitara 142 38 59 S 174 15 E
Waitchie 140 35 22 S 143 8 E
Waitoa 142 37 37 S 175 35 E
Waitotara 142 39 49 S 174 44 E
Waitsburg 160 46 15N 118 10W
Waiuku 142 37 15 S 174 45 E
Wajir 126 1 42N 40 20 E
Wajir □ 126 1 42N 40 20 E
Wakaia 143 45 44 S 168 51 E
Wakasa 110 35 20N 134 24 E
Wakasa-Wan 111 34 45N 135 30 E
Wakatipu, L. 143 45 5 S 168 33 E
Wakaw 153 52 39N 105 44W
Wakayama 111 34 15N 135 15 E
Wakayama-ken □ 111 33 50N 135 30 E
Wake 110 34 48N 134 8 E
Wake Forest 157 35 58N 78 30W
Wake I. 130 19 18N 166 36 E
Wakefield, N.Z. 143 41 24 S 173 5 E
Wakefield, U.K. 33 53 41N 1 31W
Wakefield, Mass., U.S.A. 162 42 30N 71 3W
Wakefield, Mich., U.S.A. 158 46 28N 89 53W
Wakema 98 16 40N 95 18 E
Wakhan □ 93 37 0N 73 0 E
Wakkanai 112 45 28N 141 35 E
Wakkerstroom 129 27 24 S 30 10 E
Wako 150 49 50N 91 22W
Wakool 140 35 28 S 144 23 E
Wakool, R. 140 35 5 S 143 33 E
Wakre 103 0 30 S 131 5 E
Waku 135 6 5 S 149 9 E
Wakuach L. 151 55 34N 67 32W
Walachia □ 70 44 40N 25 0 E
Walamba 127 13 30 S 28 42 E
Walberswick 29 52 18N 1 39 E
Wałbrzych 54 50 45N 16 18 E
Walbury Hill 28 51 22N 1 28W
Walcha 141 30 55 S 151 31 E
Walcha Road 141 30 55 S 151 24 E
Walcheren, I. 46 51 30N 3 35 E
Walcott 160 41 50N 106 55W
Walcz 54 53 17N 16 27 E
Wald 51 47 17N 8 56 E
Waldbröl 48 50 52N 7 36 E
Waldeck 48 51 12N 9 4 E
Walden, Colo., U.S.A. 160 40 47N 106 20W
Walden, N.Y., U.S.A. 162 41 32N 74 13W
Waldenburg 50 47 23N 7 45 E
Waldorf 162 38 37N 76 54W
Waldport 160 44 30N 124 2W
Waldron, Can. 153 50 53N 102 35W
Waldron, U.K. 29 50 56N 0 13 E
Waldron, U.S.A. 159 34 52N 94 4W
Waldshut 49 47 37N 8 12 E
Waldya 123 11 50N 39 34 E
Walebing 137 30 40 S 116 15 E
Walembele 120 10 30N 1 14W
Walensee 51 47 7N 9 13 E
Walenstadt 51 47 8N 9 19 E
Wales 147 65 38N 168 10W
Walewale 121 10 21N 0 50W
Walgett 133 30 0 S 148 5 E
Walhalla, Austral. 141 37 56 S 146 29 E
Walhalla, U.S.A. 153 48 55N 97 55W
Waliso 123 8 33N 38 1 E
Walkaway 137 28 59 S 114 48 E
Walker 158 47 4N 94 35W
Walker L., Man., Can. 153 54 42N 96 57W
Walker L., Qué., Can. 151 50 20N 67 11W
Walker L., U.S.A. 163 38 56N 118 46W
Walkerston 138 21 11 S 149 8 E
Wall 158 44 0N 102 14W
Walla Walla, Austral. 141 35 45 S 146 54 E
Walla Walla, U.S.A. 160 46 3N 118 25W

**Wallabadah** **Weaverham**

Wallabadah 138 17 57 S 142 15 E
Wallace, Idaho, U.S.A. 160 47 30N 116 0W
Wallace, N.C., U.S.A. 157 34 50N 77 59W
Wallace, Nebr., U.S.A. 158 40 51N 101 12W
Wallaceburg 150 42 40N 82 23W
Wallacetown 143 46 21 S 168 19 E
Wallachia = Valahia 70 44 35N 25 0 E
Wallal 139 26 32 S 146 7 E
Wallal Downs 136 19 47 S 120 40 E
Wallambin, L. 137 30 57 S 117 35 E
Wallaroo 140 33 56 S 137 39 E
Wallasey 32 53 26N 3 2W
Walldurn 49 49 34N 9 23 E
Wallerawang 141 33 25 S 150 4 E
Wallhallow 138 17 50 S 135 50 E
Wallingford 162 43 27N 72 50W
Wallis Arch. 142 13 20 S 176 20 E
Wallisellen 51 47 25N 8 36 E
Wallowa 160 45 40N 117 35W
Wallowa, Mts. 160 45 20N 117 30W
Walls 36 60 14N 1 32W
Wallsend, Austral. 141 32 55 S 151 40 E
Wallsend, U.K. 35 54 59N 1 30W
Wallula 160 46 3N 118 59W
Wallumbilla 139 26 33 S 149 9 E
Walmer, S. Afr. 128 33 57 S 25 35 E
Walmer, U.K. 29 51 12N 1 23 E
Walmsley, L. 153 63 25N 108 36W
Walney, Isle of 32 54 5N 3 15W
Walnut Ridge 159 36 7N 90 58W
Walpeup 140 35 10 S 142 2 E
Walpole 29 52 44N 0 13 E
Walsall 28 52 36N 1 59W
Walsenburg 159 37 42N 104 45W
Walsh, Austral. 138 16 40 S 144 0 E
Walsh, U.S.A. 159 37 28N 102 15W
Walsh, R. 138 16 31 S 143 42 E
Walshoutem 47 50 43N 5 4 E
Walsoken 29 52 41N 0 12 E
Walsrode 48 52 51N 9 37 E
Waltair 96 17 44N 83 23 E
Walterboro 157 32 53N 80 40W
Walters 159 34 25N 98 20W
Waltershausen 48 50 53N 10 33 E
Waltham, Can. 150 45 57N 76 57W
Waltham, U.K. 29 53 32N 0 6W
Waltham, U.S.A. 34 42 22N 71 12W
Waltham Abbey 29 51 40N 0 1 E
Waltham Forest 29 51 37N 0 2 E
Waltham on the Wolds 29 52 49N 0 48W
Waltman 160 43 8N 107 15W
Walton 162 42 12N 75 9W
Walton-le-Dale 32 53 45N 2 41W
Walton-on-the-Naze 29 51 52N 1 17 E
Walu 98 23 54N 96 57 E
Walvis Ridge 15 30 0 S 3 0 E
Walvisbaai 128 23 0 S 14 28 E
Walwa 141 35 59 S 147 44 E
Wamaza 126 4 12 S 27 2 E
Wamba, Kenya 126 0 58N 37 19 E
Wamba, Nigeria 126 8 58N 8 34 E
Wamba, Zaïre 121 2 10N 27 57 E
Wamego 158 39 14N 96 22W
Wamena 103 3 58 S 138 50 E
Wampo 99 31 30N 86 38 E
Wamsasi 103 3 27 S 126 7 E
Wan Hat 98 20 14N 97 53 E
Wan Kinghao 98 21 34N 98 17 E
Wan Lai-Kam 98 21 21N 98 22 E
Wan Tup 98 21 13N 98 42 E
Wana 94 32 20N 69 32 E
Wanaaring 139 29 38 S 144 0 E
Wanaka L. 143 44 33 S 169 7 E
Wanan 109 26 25N 114 50 E
Wanapiri 103 4 30 S 135 50 E
Wanapitei 150 46 30N 80 45W
Wanapitei L. 150 46 45N 80 40W
Wanaque 162 41 3N 74 17W
Wanbi 140 34 46 S 140 17 E
Wanborough 28 51 33N 1 40W
Wanch'eng 108 22 51N 107 25 E
Wanch'üan 106 35 26N 110 50 E
Wanch'uan 106 40 50N 114 56 E
Wandanian 141 35 6 S 150 30 E
Wanderer 127 19 36 S 30 1 E
Wandiwash 97 12 30N 79 30 E
Wandoan 139 26 5 S 149 55 E
Wandre 47 50 40N 5 39 E
Wandsworth 29 51 28N 0 15W
Wanfercée-Baulet 47 50 28N 4 35 E
Wanfuchuang 107 40 10N 122 34 E
Wang Kai (Ghâbat el Arab) 123 9 3N 29 23 E
Wang Noi 100 14 13N 100 44 E
Wang, R. 100 17 8N 99 2 E
Wang Saphung 100 17 18N 101 46 E
Wang Thong 100 16 50N 100 26 E
Wanga 126 2 58N 29 12 E
Wangal 103 6 8 S 134 9 E
Wanganella 141 35 6 S 144 49 E
Wanganui 142 39 35 S 175 3 E
Wanganui, R., N.I., N.Z. 142 39 25 S 175 4 E
Wanganui, R., S.I., N.Z. 143 43 3 S 170 26 E
Wangaratta 141 36 21 S 146 19 E
Wangchiang 109 30 7N 116 41 E
Wangch'ing 107 43 14N 129 38 E
Wangdu Phodrang 98 27 28N 89 54 E
Wangerooge I. 48 53 47N 7 52 E
Wangi 126 1 58 S 40 58 E
Wangiwangi, I. 103 5 22 S 123 37 E
Wangmo 108 25 14N 105 59 E
Wangts'ang 108 32 12N 106 21 E
Wangtu 106 38 42N 115 4 E
Wanhsien, Hopeh, China 106 38 49N 115 7 E
Wanhsien, Kansu, China 105 36 45N 107 24 E
Wankaner 94 22 42N 71 0 E
Wanki Nat. Park 128 19 0 S 26 30 E
Wankie 127 18 18 S 26 30 E
Wankie □ 127 18 18 S 26 30 E
Wanless 153 54 11N 101 21W
Wanna Lakes 137 28 30 S 128 27 E
Wannien 109 28 40N 116 55 E
Wanon Niwar 100 17 38N 103 46 E
Wanshengch'ang 108 28 58N 106 55 E
Wanssum 47 51 32N 6 5 E
Wanstead 143 40 8 S 176 30 E
Wantage 28 51 35N 1 25W
Wantsai 109 28 5N 114 22 E
Wanyin 98 20 23N 97 15 E
Wanyüan 108 32 4N 108 5 E
Wanzarīk 119 27 3N 13 30 E
Wanze 47 50 32N 5 13 E
Wapakoneta 156 40 35N 84 10W
Wapato 160 46 30N 120 25W
Wapawekka L. 153 54 55N 104 40W
Wapikopa L. 150 52 50N 88 10W
Wapiti, R. 152 55 5N 118 18W
Wappingers Fs. 162 41 35N 73 56W
Wapsipinican, R. 158 41 44N 90 19W
Warabi 111 35 49N 139 41 E
Warandab 91 7 20N 44 2 E
Warangal 96 17 58N 79 45 E
Waratah 138 41 30 S 145 30 E
Waratah B. 139 38 54 S 146 5 E
Warboys 29 52 25N 0 5W
Warburg 48 51 29N 9 10 E
Warburton 141 37 47 S 145 42 E
Warburton, R. 143 27 30 S 138 30 E
Warburton Ra. 137 25 55 S 126 28 E
Ward, Ireland 38 53 25N 6 19W
Ward, N.Z. 143 41 49 S 174 11 E
Ward Cove 152 55 25N 132 10W
Ward Hunt, C. 135 8 2 S 148 10 E
Ward Hunt Str. 135 9 30 S 150 0 E
Ward Mtn. 163 37 12N 118 54W
Ward, R. 139 26 32 S 146 6 E
Warden 129 27 50 S 29 0 E
Wardha 96 20 45N 78 39 E
Wardha, R. 93 19 57N 79 11 E
Wardington 28 52 8N 1 17W
Wardle 32 53 7N 2 35W
Wardlow 152 50 56N 111 31W
Wardoan 133 25 59 S 149 59 E
Wards River 141 32 11 S 151 56 E
Ward's Stone, mt. 32 54 2N 2 39W
Ware, Can. 152 57 26N 125 41W
Ware, U.K. 29 51 48N 0 2W
Ware, U.S.A. 162 42 16N 72 15W
Waregem 47 50 53N 3 27 E
Wareham, U.K. 28 50 41N 2 8W
Wareham, U.S.A. 162 41 45N 70 44W
Wareham, oilfield 19 50 40N 2 8W
Waremme 47 50 43N 5 15 E
Waren 48 53 30N 12 41 E
Warendorf 48 51 57N 8 0 E
Warialda 139 29 29 S 150 33 E
Wariap 103 1 30 S 134 5 E
Warin Chamrap 100 15 12N 104 53 E
Wark 35 55 5N 2 14W
Warkopi 103 1 12 S 134 9 E
Warkworth, N.Z. 142 36 24 S 174 41 E
Warkworth, U.K. 35 55 22N 1 38W
Warley 28 52 30N 2 0W
Warm Springs, Mont., U.S.A. 160 46 11N 112 56W
Warm Springs, Nev., U.S.A. 161 38 16N 116 32W
Warman 153 52 19N 106 30W
Warmbad, Namibia 128 19 14 S 13 51 E
Warmbad, Namibia 128 28 25 S 18 42 E
Warmbad, S. Afr. 129 24 51 S 28 19 E
Warmenhuizen 46 52 43N 4 44 E
Warmeriville 43 49 20N 4 13 E
Warminster 28 51 12N 2 11W
Warmond 46 52 12N 4 30 E
Warnambool Downs 138 22 48 S 142 52 E
Warnemünde 48 54 9N 12 5 E
Warner 152 49 17N 112 12W
Warner Range, Mts. 160 41 30 S 120 20W
Warner Robins 157 32 41N 83 36W
Warneton 47 50 45N 2 57 E
Warnow, R. 48 54 0N 12 9 E
Warnsveld 46 52 8N 6 14 E
Waroona 137 32 50 S 115 58 E
Warora 96 20 14N 79 1 E
Warracknabeal 140 36 9 S 142 26 E
Warragul 141 38 10 S 145 58 E
Warrawaqine 136 20 51 S 120 42 E
Warrayelu 123 10 40N 39 28 E
Warrego, R. 139 30 24 S 145 21 E
Warrego Ra. 138 25 15 S 146 0 E
Warren, Austral. 141 31 42 S 147 51 E
Warren, Ark., U.S.A. 159 33 35N 92 3W
Warren, Pa., U.S.A. 156 41 52N 79 10W
Warren, R.I., U.S.A. 156 41 43N 71 19W
Warrenpoint 38 54 7N 6 15W
Warrens Landing 153 53 40N 98 0W
Warrensburg 158 38 45N 93 45W
Warrenton, S. Afr. 128 28 9 S 24 47 E
Warrenton, U.S.A. 160 46 11N 123 59W
Warrenville 139 25 48 S 147 22 E
Warri 121 5 30N 5 41 E
Warrie 136 22 12 S 119 40 E
Warrina 136 28 12 S 135 50 E
Warrington, N.Z. 143 45 43 S 170 35 E
Warrington, U.K. 32 53 25N 2 38W
Warrington, U.S.A. 157 30 22N 87 16W
Warrnambool 140 38 25 S 142 30 E
Warroad 158 49 0N 95 20W
Warsaw 156 41 14N 85 50W
Warsaw = Warszawa 54 52 13N 21 0 E
Warsop 33 53 13N 1 9W
Warstein 48 51 26N 8 20 E
Warszawa 54 52 13N 21 0 E
Warszawa □ 54 52 30N 17 0 E
Warta 54 51 43N 18 38 E
Warta, R. 54 52 40N 16 10 E
Waru 103 3 30 S 130 36 E
Warud 96 21 30N 78 16 E
Warwick, Austral. 139 28 10 S 152 1 E
Warwick, U.K. 28 52 17N 1 36W
Warwick, N.Y., U.S.A. 162 41 16N 74 22W
Warwick, R.I., U.S.A. 162 41 43N 71 25W
Warwick □ 28 52 20N 1 30W
Wasa 152 49 45N 115 50W
Wasatch, Mt., Ra. 160 40 30N 111 15W
Wasbank 129 28 15 S 30 9 E
Wasbister 37 59 11N 3 2W
Wasco, Calif., U.S.A. 163 35 37N 119 16W
Wasco, Oreg., U.S.A. 160 45 45N 120 46W
Waseca 158 44 3N 93 31W
Wasekamio L. 153 56 45N 108 45W
Wash, The 33 52 58N 0 20W
Washburn, N.D., U.S.A. 158 47 23N 101 0W
Washburn, Wis., U.S.A. 158 46 38N 90 55W
Washford 28 51 9N 3 22W
Washington, U.K. 35 54 55N 1 30W
Washington, D.C., U.S.A. 162 38 52N 77 0W
Washington, Ga., U.S.A. 157 33 45N 82 45W
Washington, Ind., U.S.A. 156 38 40N 87 8W
Washington, Iowa, U.S.A. 158 41 20N 91 45W
Washington, Miss., U.S.A. 158 38 35N 91 20W
Washington, N.C., U.S.A. 157 35 35N 77 1W
Washington, N.J., U.S.A. 162 40 45N 74 59W
Washington, Ohio, U.S.A. 156 39 34N 83 26W
Washington, Pa., U.S.A. 156 40 10N 80 20W
Washington, Utah, U.S.A. 161 37 10N 113 30W
Washington □ 160 47 45N 120 30W
Washington Court House 156 39 34N 83 26W
Washington I., Pac. Oc. 131 4 43N 160 25W
Washington I., U.S.A. 156 45 24N 86 54W
Washington Mt. 156 44 15N 71 18W
Washir 93 32 15N 63 50 E
Wasian 103 1 47 S 133 19 E
Wasilków 54 53 12N 23 13 E
Wasior 103 2 43 S 134 30 E
Waskaiowaka, L. 153 56 33N 96 23W
Waskesiu Lake 153 53 55N 106 5W
Wasm 122 18 2N 41 32 E
Waspik 47 51 41N 4 57 E
Wassen 51 46 42N 8 36 E
Wassenaar 46 52 8N 4 24 E
Wasserburg 49 48 4N 12 15 E
Wassy 43 48 30N 4 58 E
Wast Water, L. 32 54 26N 3 18W
Waswanipi 150 49 40N 75 59W
Waswanipi, L. 150 49 35N 76 40W
Watangpone 103 4 29 S 120 25 E
Wataroa 143 43 18 S 170 24 E
Wataroa, R. 143 43 7 S 170 16 E
Watawaha, P. 103 6 30 S 122 20 E
Watchet 28 51 10N 3 20W
Water Park Pt. 138 22 56 S 150 47 E
Water Valley 159 34 9N 89 38W
Waterberg, Namibia 128 20 30 S 17 18 E
Waterberg, S. Afr. 129 24 14 S 28 0 E
Waterberg, mt. 128 20 26 S 17 13 E
Waterbury 162 41 32N 73 0W
Waterbury L. 153 58 10N 104 22W
Waterford, Ireland 39 52 16N 7 8W
Waterford, S. Afr. 128 33 6 S 25 0 E
Waterford, U.S.A. 163 37 38N 120 46W
Waterford □ 39 51 10N 7 40W
Waterford Harb. 39 52 10N 6 58W
Watergate Bay 30 50 26N 5 4W
Watergrasshill 39 52 1N 8 20W
Waterhen L., Man., Can. 153 52 10N 99 40W
Waterhen L., Sask., Can. 153 54 28N 108 25W
Wateringen 46 52 2N 4 16 E
Waterloo, Belg. 47 50 43N 4 25 E
Waterloo, Can. 150 43 30N 80 32W
Waterloo, S. Leone 120 8 26N 13 8W
Waterloo, U.K. 32 53 29N 3 2W
Waterloo, Ill., U.S.A. 158 38 22N 90 6W
Waterloo, Iowa, U.S.A. 158 42 27N 92 20W
Waterloo, N.Y., U.S.A. 162 42 54N 76 53W
Watermeal-Boitsford 47 50 48N 4 25 E
Watermeet 158 46 15N 89 12W
Waternish 36 57 32N 6 35W
Waterton Lakes Nat. Park 152 49 5N 114 15W
Watertown, Conn., U.S.A. 162 41 36N 73 7W
Watertown, N.Y., U.S.A. 162 43 58N 75 57W
Watertown, S.D., U.S.A. 158 44 57N 97 5W
Watertown, Wis., U.S.A. 158 43 15N 88 45W
Waterval-Boven 129 25 40 S 30 18 E
Waterville, Ireland 39 51 49N 10 10W
Waterville, Me., U.S.A. 151 44 35N 69 40W
Waterville, N.Y., U.S.A. 162 42 56N 75 23W
Waterville, Wash., U.S.A. 160 47 45N 120 1W
Watervliet, Belg. 47 51 17N 3 38 E
Watervliet, U.S.A. 162 42 46N 73 43W
Wates 103 7 53 S 110 6 E
Watford 29 51 38N 0 23W
Watford City 158 47 50N 103 23W
Wath 33 53 29N 1 20W
Wathaman, R. 153 57 16N 102 59W
Watheroo 137 30 15 S 116 0W
Watien 109 32 45N 112 30 E
Wat'ing 106 35 25N 106 46 E
Watkins Glen 162 42 25N 76 55W
Watlings I. 167 24 0N 74 35W
Watlington, Norfolk, U.K. 29 52 40N 0 24 E
Watlington, Oxford, U.K. 29 51 38N 1 0W
Watonga 159 35 51N 98 24W
Watou 47 50 51N 2 38 E
Watraba 139 31 58 S 133 13 E
Watrous, Can. 153 51 40N 105 25W
Watrous, U.S.A. 159 35 50N 104 55W
Watsa 126 3 4N 29 30 E
Watseka 156 40 45N 87 45W
Watson, Austral. 137 30 29 S 131 31 E
Watson, Can. 153 52 10N 104 30W
Watson Lake 147 60 6N 128 49W
Watsontown 162 41 5N 76 52W
Watsonville 163 36 55N 121 49W
Watten 37 21 1 S 144 3 E
Wattenwil 50 46 46N 7 30 E
Wattiwarriganna Cr. 139 28 57 S 136 10 E
Watton 29 52 35N 0 50 E
Wattwil 51 47 18N 9 6 E
Watubela, Kepulauan 103 4 28 S 131 54 E
Wau 135 7 21 S 146 47 E
Waubach 47 50 55N 6 3 E
Waubay 158 45 42N 97 17W
Waubra 140 37 21 S 143 39 E
Wauchope 141 31 28 S 152 45 E
Wauchula 157 27 35N 81 50W
Waugh 153 49 40N 95 20W
Waukegan 156 42 22N 87 54W
Waukesha 156 43 0N 88 15W
Waukon 158 43 14N 91 33W
Wauneta 158 40 27N 101 25W
Waupaca 158 44 22N 89 8W
Waupun 158 43 38N 88 44W
Waurika 159 34 12N 98 0W
Wausau 158 44 57N 89 40W
Wautoma 158 44 3N 89 20W
Wauwatosa 156 43 6N 87 59W
Wave Hill 136 17 32N 131 0 E
Waveney, R. 29 52 24N 1 20 E
Waver R. 32 54 50N 3 15W
Waverley 142 39 46 S 174 37 E
Waverly, Iowa, U.S.A. 158 42 40N 92 30W
Waverly, N.Y., U.S.A. 162 42 0N 76 33W
Wavre 47 50 43N 4 38 E
Wavreille 47 50 7N 5 15 E
Wâw 123 7 45N 28 1 E
Waw an Namus 119 24 24N 18 11 E
Wawa, Can. 150 47 59N 84 47W
Wawa, Nigeria 121 9 54N 4 27 E
Wawa, Sudan 122 20 30N 30 22 E
Wawanesa 153 49 36N 99 40W
Wawoi, R. 135 7 48 S 143 16 E
Wawona 163 37 32N 119 39W
Waxahachie 159 32 22N 96 53W
Waxweiler 49 50 6N 6 22 E
Way, L. 137 26 45 S 120 16 E
Wayabula Rau 103 2 29N 128 17 E
Wayatinah 138 42 19 S 146 27 E
Waycross 157 31 12N 82 25W
Wayi 123 5 8N 30 10 E
Wayne, Nebr., U.S.A. 158 42 16N 97 0W
Wayne, W. Va., U.S.A. 156 38 15N 82 27W
Waynesboro, Miss., U.S.A. 157 31 40N 88 39W
Waynesboro, Pa., U.S.A. 156 39 46N 77 32W
Waynesboro, Va., U.S.A. 156 38 4N 78 57W
Waynesburg 156 39 54N 80 12W
Waynesville 157 35 31N 83 0W
Waynoka 159 36 38N 98 53W
Waza 94 33 22N 69 22 E
Wāzin 119 31 58N 10 51 E
Wazirabad, Afghan. 93 36 44N 66 47 E
Wazirabad, Pak. 94 32 30N 74 8 E
We 102 6 3N 95 56 E
Weald, The 29 51 7N 0 9 E
Wear, R. 35 54 55N 1 22W
Weardale 32 54 44N 2 5W
Wearhead 32 54 45N 2 14W
Weatherford, Okla., U.S.A. 159 35 30N 98 45W
Weatherford, Tex., U.S.A. 159 32 45N 97 48W
Weaver, R. 32 53 17N 2 35W
Weaverham 32 53 15N 2 30W

Webb City Whitby


Webb City 159 37 9N 94 30W
Weber 142 40 24S 176 20E
Webera, Bale, Ethiopia 123 6 29N 40 33E
Webera, Shewa, Ethiopia 123 9 40N 39 0E
Webster, Mass., U.S.A. 162 42 4N 71 54W
Webster, S.D., U.S.A. 158 45 24N 97 33W
Webster, Wis., U.S.A. 158 45 53N 92 25W
Webster City 158 42 30N 93 50W
Webster Green 158 38 38N 90 20W
Webster Springs 156 38 30N 80 25W
Wecliniec 54 51 18N 15 10E
Weda 103 0 30N 127 50E
Weda, Teluk 103 0 30N 127 50E
Weddell I. 176 51 50S 61 0W
Weddell Sea 13 72 30S 40 0W
Wedderburn 140 36 20S 143 33E
Wedge I. 132 30 50S 115 11E
Wedgeport 151 43 44N 65 59W
Wedmore 28 51 14N 2 50W
Wednesbury 28 52 33N 2 1W
Wednesfield 28 52 36N 2 3W
Wedza 127 18 40S 31 33E
Wee Elwah 141 32 2S 145 14E
Wee Waa 139 30 11S 149 26E
Weed 160 41 29N 122 22W
Weedsport 162 43 3N 76 35W
Weemelah 139 29 2S 149 7E
Weenen 129 28 48S 30 7E
Weener 48 53 10N 7 23E
Weert 47 51 15N 5 43E
Weesen 51 47 7N 9 4E
Weesp 46 52 18N 5 2E
Weggis 51 47 2N 8 26E
Wegierska-Gorka 54 49 36N 19 7E
Wegorzewo 54 54 13N 21 43E
Wegroów 54 52 24N 22 0E
Wehl 46 51 58N 6 13E
Wei Ho, R., Honan, China 106 34 58N 113 32E
Wei Ho, R., Shensi, China 106 34 38N 110 20E
Wei-si 99 27 18N 99 18E
Weich'ang 107 41 56N 117 34E
Weichou Tao 108 21 3N 109 2E
Weich'uan 106 34 19N 114 0E
Weida 48 50 47N 12 3E
Weiden 49 49 40N 12 10E
Weifang 107 36 47N 119 10E
Weihai 107 37 30N 122 10E
Weihsi 108 27 18N 99 18E
Weihsin 108 27 48N 105 5E
Weilburg 48 50 28N 8 17E
Weilheim 49 47 50N 11 9E
Weimar 48 51 0N 11 20E
Weinan 106 34 30N 109 35E
Weinfelden 51 47 34N 9 6E
Weingarten 49 47 49N 9 39E
Weinheim 49 49 33N 8 40E
Weining 108 26 50N 104 19E
Weipa 138 12 24S 141 50E
Weir, R., Austral. 139 28 20S 149 50E
Weir, R., Can. 153 56 54N 93 21W
Weir River 153 56 49N 94 6W
Weisen 51 46 42N 9 43E
Weiser 160 44 10N 117 0W
Weishan, Shantung, China 107 34 49N 47 6E
Weishan, Yunnan, China 108 25 16N 100 21E
Weissenburg 49 49 2N 10 58E
Weissenfels 48 51 11N 11 58E
Weisshorn 50 46 7N 7 43E
Weissmies 50 46 8N 8 1E
Weisstannen 51 46 59N 9 22E
Weisswasser 48 51 30N 14 36E
Weiswampach 47 50 8N 6 5E
Wéitra 52 48 41N 14 54E
Weiyüan 106 35 6N 104 14E
Weiyuan 106 35 10N 104 20E
Weiz 52 47 13N 15 39E
Wejherowo 54 54 35N 18 12E
Wekusko 153 54 45N 99 45W
Wekusko L. 153 54 40N 99 50W
Welbourn Hill 139 27 21S 134 6E
Welby 153 50 33N 101 29W
Welch 156 37 29N 81 36W
Welcome 138 15 20S 144 40E
Weldon 35 55 16N 1 46W
Welega □ 123 9 25N 34 20E
Welford, Berks., U.K. 28 51 28N 1 24W
Welford, Northampton, U.K. 28 52 26N 1 5W
Welkenraedt 47 50 39N 5 58E
Welkite 123 8 15N 37 42E
Welkom 128 28 0S 26 50E
Welland 150 43 0N 79 10W
Welland, R. 29 52 43N 0 10W
Wellen 47 50 50N 5 21E
Wellesley Is. 138 17 20S 139 30E
Wellin 47 50 5N 5 6E
Wellingborough 29 52 18N 0 41W
Wellington, Austral. 141 32 35S 148 59E
Wellington, Can. 150 43 57N 77 20W
Wellington, N.Z. 142 41 19S 174 46E
Wellington, S. Afr. 128 33 38S 18 57E
Wellington, U.K. 28 50 58N 3 13W
Wellington, Col., U.S.A. 158 40 43N 105 0W
Wellington, Kans., U.S.A. 159 37 15N 97 25W
Wellington, Nev., U.S.A. 163 38 47N 119 28W
Wellington, Okla., U.S.A. 159 34 55N 100 13W
Wellington □ 143 40 8S 175 36E
Wellington Bridge 39 52 15N 6 45W
Wellington, I. 176 49 30S 75 0W
Wellington, L. 141 38 6S 147 20E
Wellington, Mt. 142 36 55S 174 52E
Wellington (Telford) 28 52 42N 2 31W
Wello, L. 137 26 43S 123 10E
Wellow 28 51 20N 2 22W
Wells, Norfolk, U.K. 29 52 57N 0 51E
Wells, Somerset, U.K. 28 51 12N 2 39W
Wells, Me., U.S.A. 162 43 18N 70 35W
Wells, Minn., U.S.A. 158 43 44N 93 45W
Wells, Nev., U.S.A. 160 41 8N 115 0W
Wells, N.Y., U.S.A. 162 43 24N 74 17W
Wells Gray Prov. Park 152 52 30N 120 15W
Wells L. 137 26 44S 123 15E
Wellsboro 156 41 46N 77 20W
Wellsford 142 36 16S 174 32E
Wellsville, Mo., U.S.A. 158 39 4N 91 30W
Wellsville, N.Y., U.S.A. 156 42 9N 77 53W
Wellsville, Ohio, U.S.A. 156 40 36N 80 40W
Wellsville, Utah, U.S.A. 160 41 35N 111 59W
Wellton 161 32 46N 114 6W
Welmel, W. 123 6 0N 40 20E
Welney 29 52 31N 0 15E
Welo □ 123 11 50N 39 48E
Wels 52 48 9N 14 1E
Welshpool 31 52 40N 3 9W
Welton 33 53 19N 0 29W
Welwel 91 7 5N 45 25E
Welwitschia 128 20 16S 14 59E
Welwyn 153 50 20N 101 30W
Welwyn Garden City 29 51 49N 0 11W
Wem 28 52 52N 2 45W
Wembere, R. 126 4 45S 34 0E
Wembury 30 50 19N 4 6W
Wemmel 47 50 55N 4 18E
Wemyss Bay 34 55 52N 4 54W
Wenatchee 160 47 30N 120 17W
Wench'ang 100 19 38N 110 42E
Wencheng 109 27 48N 120 5E
Wenchi 120 7 46N 2 8W
Wenchiang 108 30 43N 103 56E
Wenchou 109 28 1N 120 39E
Wench'uan 108 31 28N 103 35E
Wendell 160 42 50N 114 51W
Wendesi 103 2 30S 134 10E
Wendo 123 6 40N 38 27E
Wendover, U.K. 29 51 46N 0 45W
Wendover, U.S.A. 160 40 49N 114 1W
Wenduine 47 51 18N 3 5E
Wengan 108 27 0N 107 32E
Wengch'eng 109 24 22N 113 50E
Wenge 126 0 3N 24 0E
Wengen 50 46 37N 7 55E
Wengniut'ech'i 107 42 59N 118 48E
Wengpu 108 32 55N 98 30E
Wengyüan 109 24 21N 114 7E
Wenhsi 106 35 23N 111 8E
Wenhsiang 106 34 36N 110 34E
Wenhsien, Honan, China 106 34 56N 113 4E
Wenhsien, Kansu, China 106 58 0N 104 39E
Wenling 109 28 22N 121 18E
Wenlock 138 13 6S 142 58E
Wenlock Edge 23 52 30N 2 43W
Wenlock, R. 133 12 2S 141 55E
Wenshan 108 23 22N 104 13E
Wenshang 106 35 37N 116 33E
Wenshui, Kweichow, China 108 28 27N 106 31E
Wenshui, Shansi, China 106 37 25N 112 1E
Wensleydale 32 54 18N 2 0W
Wensu 105 41 15N 80 14E
Wenteng 107 37 10N 122 0E
Wentworth 140 34 2S 141 54E
Wentworth, Mt. 138 24 12S 147 1E
Wenut 103 3 11S 133 19E
Weobley 28 52 9N 2 52W
Weott 160 40 19N 123 56W
Wepener 128 29 42S 27 3E
Werbomont 47 50 23N 5 41E
Werda 128 25 24S 23 15E
Werdau 48 50 45N 12 20E
Werder, Ethiopia 91 6 58N 45 1E
Werder, Ger. 48 52 23N 12 56E
Werdohl 48 51 15N 7 47E
Weri 103 3 10S 132 30E
Werkendam 46 51 50N 4 53E
Werne 48 51 38N 7 38E
Wernigerode 48 51 49N 0 45E
Werribee 140 37 54S 144 40E
Werrimull 140 34 25S 141 38E
Werrington 30 50 31N 4 22W
Werris Creek 141 31 18S 150 38E
Wersar 103 1 30S 131 55E
Wertheim 49 49 44N 9 32E
Wervershoof 46 52 44N 5 10E
Wervik 47 50 47N 3 3E
Wesel 48 51 39N 6 34E
Weser, R. 48 53 33N 8 30E
Wesiri 103 7 30S 126 30E
Wesleyville 151 49 8N 53 36W
Wessel, C. 138 10 59S 136 46E
Wessel Is. 138 11 10S 136 45E
Wesselburen 48 54 11N 8 53E
Wessem 47 51 11N 5 49E
Wessington 158 44 30N 98 40W
Wessington Springs 158 44 10N 98 35W
West 159 31 50N 97 5W
West Auckland 33 54 38N 1 42W
West B. 151 45 53N 82 8W
West, B. 159 29 5N 89 27W
West Baines, R. 136 15 36S 129 58E
West Bend 156 43 25N 88 10W
West Bengal □ 95 25 0N 90 0E
West Branch 156 44 16N 84 13W
West Bridgford 33 52 56N 1 8W
West Bromwich 28 52 32N 2 1W
West Burra, I. 36 60 5N 1 21W
West Calder 35 55 51N 3 34W
West Canada Cr. 162 43 1N 74 58W
West Cape Howe 137 35 8S 117 36E
West Chester 162 39 58N 75 36W
West Coker 28 50 55N 2 40W
West Columbia 159 29 10N 95 38W
West Covina 163 34 4N 117 54W
West Derry 162 42 55N 71 19W
West Des Moines 158 41 30N 93 45W
West End 166 26 41N 78 58W
West Falkland Island 176 51 30S 60 0W
West Fen 33 53 5N 0 5W
West Frankfort 158 37 56N 89 0W
West Glamorgan □ 31 51 40N 3 55W
West Grinstead 29 50 58N 0 19W
West Haddon 28 52 21N 1 5W
West Harbour 131 45 51S 170 33E
West Hartford 162 41 45N 72 45W
West Haven 162 41 18N 72 57W
West Hazleton 162 40 58N 76 0W
West Helena 159 34 30N 90 40W
West Hurley 162 41 59N 74 7W
West Indies 158 15 0N 70 0W
West Kilbride 34 55 41N 4 50W
West Kirby 32 53 22N 3 11W
West Lavington 28 51 16N 1 59W
West Linton 35 55 45N 3 24W
West Looe 30 50 21N 4 29W
West Lulworth 28 50 37N 2 14W
West Lunga, R. 127 12 35S 24 45E
West Magpie R. 151 51 2N 64 42W
West Malling 29 51 16N 0 25E
West Memphis 159 35 5N 90 3W
West Meon 28 51 2N 1 3W
West Mersea 29 51 46N 0 55E
West Midlands □ 28 52 30N 1 55W
West Milton 162 41 1N 76 50W
West Monroe 159 32 32N 92 7W
West Nicholson 127 21 2S 29 20E
West Pakistan = Pakistan 93 27 0N 67 0W
West Palm Beach 157 26 44N 80 3W
West Paris 101 44 18N 70 30W
West Parley 28 50 46N 1 52W
West Plains 159 36 45N 91 50W
West Pt. 140 35 1S 135 56E
West Point, Can. 151 49 55N 64 30W
West Point, Jamaica 166 18 14N 78 30W
West Point, Ga., U.S.A. 157 32 54N 85 10W
West Point, Miss., U.S.A. 157 33 36N 88 38W
West Point, Nebr., U.S.A. 158 41 50N 96 43W
West Point, Va., U.S.A. 162 37 35N 76 47W
West Pokot □ 126 1 30N 35 40E
West, R. 162 42 52N 72 33W
West Rasen 33 53 23N 0 23W
West Reading 162 40 20N 75 57W
West Riding (□) 26 53 50N 1 30W
West Road R. 152 53 18N 122 53W
West Rutland 162 43 36N 73 3W
West Schelde = Westerschelde 47 51 23N 3 50E
West Sole, gasfield 19 53 40N 1 15E
West Spitsbergen 12 78 40N 17 0E
West Sussex □ 29 50 55N 0 30W
West-Terschelling 46 53 22N 5 13E
West Virginia □ 156 39 0N 18 0W
West-Vlaanderen □ 47 51 0N 3 0E
West Walker, R. 163 38 54N 119 9W
West Wittering 29 50 44N 0 53W
West Wyalong 141 33 56S 147 10E
West Yellowstone 160 44 47N 111 4W
West York 162 39 57N 76 46W
West Yorkshire □ 33 53 45N 1 40W
Westall 139 32 55S 134 4E
Westbank 152 49 50N 119 25W
Westbourne 29 50 53N 0 55W
Westbrook, Maine, U.S.A. 162 43 40N 70 22W
Westbrook, Tex., U.S.A. 159 32 25N 101 0W
Westbury, Austral. 138 41 30S 146 51E
Westbury, Salop, U.K. 28 52 40N 2 57W
Westbury, Wilts., U.K. 28 51 16N 2 11W
Westbury-on-Severn 28 51 49N 2 24W
Westby 158 48 52N 104 3W
Westend 163 35 42N 117 24W
Wester Ross, dist. 36 57 37N 5 0W
Westerbork 46 52 51N 6 37E
Westerham 29 51 16N 0 5E
Westerland 48 54 51N 8 20E
Western □, Kenya 126 0 30N 34 30E
Western □, Uganda 126 1 45N 31 30E
Western □, Zambia 127 13 15N 27 30E
Western Australia □ 137 25 0S 118 0E
Western Bay 151 46 50N 52 30W
Western Germany ■ 48 50 0N 8 0E
Western Ghats 97 15 30N 74 30E
Western Is. □ 36 57 40N 7 0W
Western River 140 35 42S 136 56E
Western Samoa ■ 130 14 0S 172 0W
Westernport 156 30 30N 79 5W
Westerschelde, R. 47 51 25N 4 0E
Westerstede 48 51 15N 7 55E
Westervoort 46 51 58N 5 59E
Westerwald, mts. 48 50 39N 8 0E
Westfield, U.K. 29 50 53N 0 30E
Westfield, U.S.A. 162 42 9N 72 49W
Westgat 47 51 39N 3 44E
Westhope 158 48 55N 101 0W
Westhoughton 32 53 34N 2 30W
Westkapelle, Belg. 47 51 19N 3 19E
Westkapelle, Neth. 47 51 31N 3 28E
Westland □ 143 43 33S 169 59E
Westland Bight 143 42 55S 170 5E
Westlock 152 54 9N 113 55W
Westmalle 47 51 18N 4 42E
Westmeath □ 38 53 30N 7 30W
Westmine 137 29 2S 116 8E
Westminster 162 39 34S 77 1W
Westmorland 161 33 2N 115 42W
Westmorland (□) 26 54 28N 2 40W
Weston, Malay. 102 5 10N 115 35E
Weston, U.K. 28 52 51N 2 2W
Weston, Oreg., U.S.A. 160 45 50N 118 30W
Weston, W. Va., U.S.A. 156 39 3N 80 29W
Weston I. 150 52 33N 79 36W
Weston-super-Mare 28 51 20N 2 59W
Westport, Ireland 38 53 44N 9 31W
Westport, N.Z. 143 41 46S 171 37E
Westport, U.S.A. 160 46 48N 124 4W
Westport B. 38 53 48N 9 38W
Westray 153 53 36N 101 24W
Westray Firth 37 59 15N 3 0W
Westray, I. 37 59 18N 3 0W
Westree 150 47 26N 81 34W
Westruther 35 55 45N 2 34W
Westview 152 49 50N 124 31W
Westville, Ill., U.S.A. 156 40 3N 87 36W
Westville, Okla., U.S.A. 159 36 0N 94 33W
Westward Ho 30 51 2N 4 16W
Westwood 160 40 26N 121 0W
Wetar, I. 103 7 30S 126 30E
Wetaskiwin 152 52 55N 113 24W
Wetherby 33 53 56N 1 23W
Wethersfield 162 41 43N 72 40W
Wetlet 98 21 13N 95 53E
Wettingen 51 47 28N 8 20E
Wetwang 33 54 2N 0 35W
Wetzikon 51 47 19N 8 48E
Wetzlar 48 50 33N 8 30E
Wevelgem 47 50 49N 3 12E
Wewak 135 3 38S 143 41E
Wewaka 159 35 10N 96 35W
Wexford 39 52 20N 6 28W
Wexford □ 39 52 20N 6 25W
Wexford Harb. 39 52 20N 6 25W
Wey, R. 29 51 19N 0 29W
Weybourne 29 52 57N 1 9E
Weybridge 29 51 22N 0 28W
Weyburn 153 49 40N 103 50W
Weyburn L. 152 63 0N 117 59W
Weyer 52 47 51N 14 40E
Weymouth, Can. 151 44 30N 66 1W
Weymouth, U.K. 28 50 36N 2 28W
Weymouth, U.S.A. 162 42 13N 70 47W
Weymouth, C. 133 12 37S 143 27E
Wezep 46 52 28N 6 0E
Whakamaru 142 38 23S 175 63E
Whakatane 142 37 57S 177 1E
Whale Cove 148 62 11N 92 36W
Whale Firth 36 60 40N 1 10W
Whale, R. 151 58 15N 67 40W
Whales 13 78 0S 165 0W
Whaley Bridge 32 53 20N 2 0W
Whalley 32 53 49N 2 25W
Whalsay, I. 36 60 22N 1 0W
Whalton 35 55 7N 1 46W
Whangamomona 142 39 8S 174 44E
Whangarei 142 35 43S 174 21E
Whangarei Harbour 142 35 45S 174 28E
Whangaroa 142 35 4S 173 46E
Whangumata 142 37 12S 175 53E
Whaplode 29 52 42N 0 3W
Wharanui 143 41 55S 174 6E
Wharfe, R. 33 53 55N 1 30W
Wharfedale 31 54 7N 2 4W
Wharton, N.J., U.S.A. 162 40 53N 74 36W
Wharton, Tex., U.S.A. 159 29 20N 96 6W
Whauphill 34 54 48N 4 31W
Whayjonta 139 29 40S 142 35E
Wheatland 158 42 4N 105 58W
Wheatley Hill 33 54 45N 1 23W
Wheaton, Md., U.S.A. 162 39 3N 77 3W
Wheaton, Minn., U.S.A. 158 45 50N 96 29W
Wheeler, Oreg., U.S.A. 160 45 45N 123 57W
Wheeler, Tex., U.S.A. 159 35 29N 100 15W
Wheeler Peak, Mt. 160 38 57N 114 15W
Wheeler, R. 153 57 34N 104 15W
Wheeler Ridge 163 35 0N 118 57W
Wheeling 156 40 2N 80 41W
Whichham 32 54 14N 3 22W
Whidbey I. 152 48 15N 122 40W
Whidbey Is. 136 34 30S 135 3E
Whiddy, I. 39 51 41N 9 30W
Whimple 30 50 46N 3 21W
Whipsnade 29 51 51N 0 32W
Whiskey Gap 152 49 0N 113 3W
Whiskey Jack L. 153 58 23N 101 55W
Whissendine 29 52 43N 0 46W
Whistleduck Cr. 138 20 15S 135 18E
Whistler 157 30 50N 88 10W
Whiston 32 53 25N 2 45W
Whitburn 35 55 52N 3 41W
Whitby 33 54 29N 0 37W

Whitchurch Winterberg


Whitchurch, U.K. 31 51 32N 3 15W
Whitchurch, Devon, U.K. 30 50 31N 4 7W
Whitchurch, Hants., U.K. 28 51 14N 1 20W
Whitchurch, Here., U.K. 28 51 51N 2 41W
Whitchurch, Salop, U.K. 32 52 58N 2 42W
Whitcombe, Mt. 131 43 12S 171 0E
Whitcombe, P. 131 43 12S 171 0E
White B. 151 50 0N 56 35W
White Bear Res. 151 48 10N 57 05W
White Bird 160 45 46N 116 21W
White Bridge 35 57 11N 4 32W
White Butte 156 46 23N 103 25W
White City 158 38 50N 96 45W
White Cliffs, Austral. 140 30 50S 143 10E
White Cliffs, N.Z. 143 43 26S 171 55E
White Deer 159 35 30N 101 8W
White Esk, R. 35 55 14N 3 11W
White Hall 158 39 25N 90 27W
White Haven 162 41 3N 75 47W
White Horse Hill 28 51 35N 1 35W
White I. 142 37 30S 177 13E
White L., Austral. 136 24 43S 121 44E
White L., U.S.A. 159 29 45N 92 30W
White Mts. 163 37 30N 118 15W
White Nile = Nîl el Abyad, Bahr 123 9 30N 31 40E
White Nile Dam 123 15 24N 32 30E
White Otter L. 150 49 5N 91 55W
White Pass 147 59 40N 135 3W
White Plains, Liberia 120 6 28N 10 40W
White Plains, U.S.A. 162 41 2N 73 44W
White, R., Ark., U.S.A. 159 36 28N 93 55W
White, R., Colo., U.S.A. 160 40 8N 108 52W
White, R., Ind., U.S.A. 156 39 25N 86 30W
White, R., S.D., U.S.A. 158 43 10N 102 52W
White River, Can. 150 48 35N 85 20W
White River, S. Afr. 129 25 20S 31 00E
White River, U.S.A. 158 43 48N 100 5W
White River Junc. 162 43 38N 72 20W
White Russia = Byelorussia, SSR 80 53 30N 27 0E
White Sea = Beloye More 78 66 30N 38 0E
White Sulphur Springs, Mont., U.S.A. 160 46 35N 111 0W
White Sulphur Springs, W. Va., U.S.A. 160 37 50N 80 16W
White Volta, R., (Volta Blanche) 121 10 0N 1 0W
White Well 137 31 25S 131 3E
Whiteadder Water, R. 35 55 47N 2 20W
Whitecourt 152 54 10N 115 45W
Whiteface 159 33 35N 102 40W
Whitefish 160 48 25N 114 22W
Whitefish L. 153 62 41N 106 48W
Whitefish Pt. 156 46 45N 85 0W
Whitegate, Clare, Ireland 39 52 58N 8 24W
Whitegate, Cork, Ireland 39 51 49N 8 15W
Whitegull, L. 151 55 27N 64 17W
Whitehall, Ireland 39 52 42N 7 2W
Whitehall, U.K. 37 59 9N 2 36W
Whitehall, Mich., U.S.A. 156 43 21N 86 20W
Whitehall, Mont., U.S.A. 160 45 52N 112 4W
Whitehall, N.Y., U.S.A. 162 43 32N 73 28W
Whitehall, Wis., U.S.A. 158 44 20N 91 19W
Whitehaven 32 54 33N 3 35W
Whitehead 38 54 45N 5 42W
Whitehorse 147 60 43N 135 3W
Whitehorse, Vale of 28 51 37N 1 30W
Whitekirk 35 56 2N 2 36W
Whiteman Ra. 135 5 55S 150 0E
Whitemark 138 40 7S 148 3E
Whitemouth 153 49 57N 95 58W
Whiten Hd. 37 58 34N 4 35W
Whitesail, L. 152 53 35N 127 45W
Whitesand B. 30 50 18N 4 20W
Whitesboro, N.Y., U.S.A. 162 43 8N 75 20W
Whitesboro, Tex., U.S.A. 159 33 40N 96 58W
Whiteshell Prov. Park 153 50 0N 95 40W
Whitetail 158 48 54N 105 15W
Whiteville 157 34 20N 78 40W
Whitewater 156 42 50N 88 45W
Whitewater Baldy, Mt. 161 33 20N 108 44W
Whitewater L. 150 50 50N 89 10W
Whitewood, Austral. 138 21 28S 143 30E
Whitewood, Can. 153 50 20N 102 20W
Whitfield 141 36 42S 146 24E
Whithorn 162 54 55N 4 25W
Whitianga 142 36 47S 175 41E
Whitland 31 51 49N 4 38W
Whitley Bay 35 55 4N 1 28W
Whitman 162 42 4N 70 55W
Whitmire 157 34 33N 81 40W
Whitney 150 45 31N 78 14W
Whitney, Mt. 163 36 35N 118 14W
Whitney Pt. 162 42 19N 75 59W
Whitstable 29 51 21N 1 2E
Whitsunday I. 138 20 15S 149 4E
Whittier 147 60 46N 148 49W
Whittington, Derby, U.K. 33 53 17N 1 26W
Whittington, Salop, U.K. 28 52 53N 3 0W
Whittle, C. 151 50 11N 60 8W
Whittlesea 141 37 27S 145 9E
Whittlesey 29 52 34N 0 8W
Whittlesford 29 52 6N 0 9E
Whitton 33 53 42N 0 39W
Whitwell, Derby, U.K. 33 53 16N 1 11W
Whitwell, Isle of Wight, U.K. 28 50 35N 1 19W
Whitwell, U.S.A. 157 35 15N 85 30W
Whitwick 28 52 45N 1 23W
Whitworth 32 53 40N 2 11W
Whixley 33 54 2N 1 19W
Wholdaia L. 153 60 43N 104 20W
Whyalla 140 33 2S 137 30E
Whyjonta 139 29 41S 142 28E
Whyte Yarcowie 107 33 13S 138 54E
Wiarton 150 44 50N 81 10W
Wiawso 120 6 10N 2 25W
Wiay I. 36 57 24N 7 12W
Wiazow 54 50 50N 17 10E
Wibaux 158 47 0N 104 13W
Wichian Buri 100 15 39N 101 7E
Wichita 159 37 40N 97 29W
Wichita Falls 159 33 57N 98 30W
Wick, Scot., U.K. 37 58 26N 3 5W
Wick, Wales, U.K. 31 51 24N 3 32W
Wick R. 37 58 28N 3 14W
Wickenburg 161 33 58N 112 45W
Wickepin 137 32 50S 117 30E
Wickett 159 31 37N 102 58W
Wickford 29 51 37N 0 31E
Wickham 28 50 54N 1 11W
Wickham, C. 138 39 35S 143 57E
Wickham Market 29 52 9N 1 21E
Wicklow 39 53 0N 6 2W
Wicklow □ 39 52 59N 6 25W
Wicklow Gap 39 53 3N 6 23W
Wicklow Hd. 39 52 59N 6 3W
Wicklow Mts. 39 53 0N 6 30W
Wickwar 28 51 35N 2 23W
Widawa 54 51 27N 18 51E
Widdrington 35 55 15N 1 35W
Wide B. 138 4 52S 152 0E
Wide Firth 37 59 2N 3 0W
Widecombe 30 50 34N 3 48W
Widemouth 30 50 45N 4 34W
Widgiemooltha 137 31 30S 121 34E
Widnes 32 53 22N 2 44W
Wiek 48 54 37N 13 17E
Wielbark 54 53 24N 20 55E
Wieleń 54 52 53N 16 9E
Wieliczka 54 50 0N 20 5E
Wielun 54 51 15N 18 40E
Wien 53 48 12N 16 22E
Wiener Neustadt 53 47 49N 16 16E
Wieprz, R., Koszalin, Poland 54 54 26N 16 35E
Wieprz, R., Lublin, Poland 54 51 15N 22 50E
Wierden 46 52 22N 6 35E
Wiers 47 50 30N 3 32E
Wieruszów 54 51 19N 18 9E
Wiesbaden 49 50 7N 8 17E
Wiesental 49 49 15N 8 30E
Wigan 32 53 33N 2 38W
Wiggins, Colo., U.S.A. 158 40 16N 104 3W
Wiggins, Miss., U.S.A. 159 30 53N 89 9W
Wight, I. of 28 50 40N 1 20W
Wigmore 28 52 19N 2 51W
Wigston 28 52 35N 1 6W
Wigton 32 54 50N 3 9W
Wigtown 34 54 52N 4 27W
Wigtown (□) 26 54 53N 4 45W
Wigtown B. 34 54 46N 4 15W
Wihéries 47 50 23N 3 45E
Wijangala 139 33 57S 148 59E
Wijchen 46 51 48N 5 44E
Wijhe 46 52 23N 6 8E
Wijk bij Duurstede 46 51 59N 5 21E
Wil 51 47 28N 9 3E
Wilamowice 53 49 55N 19 9E
Wilangee 140 31 28S 141 20E
Wilber 158 40 34N 96 59W
Wilburton 159 34 55N 95 15W
Wilcannia 140 31 30S 143 26E
Wildbad 49 48 44N 8 32E
Wildervank 46 53 5N 6 52E
Wildeshausen 48 52 54N 8 25E
Wildhorn 50 46 22N 7 21E
Wildon 52 46 52N 15 31E
Wildrose, Calif., U.S.A. 163 36 14N 117 11W
Wildrose, N. Dak., U.S.A. 158 48 36N 103 17W
Wildspitze 52 46 53N 10 53E
Wildstrubel 50 46 24N 7 32E
Wildwood 162 38 59N 74 46W
Wilgaroon 141 30 52S 145 42E
Wilhelm II Coast 13 67 0S 90 0E
Wilhelm Mt. 135 5 50S 145 1E
Wilhelm-Pieck-Stadt Guben 48 51 59N 14 48E
Wilhelmina Kanaal 47 51 36N 5 6E
Wilhelmina, Mt. 175 3 50N 56 30W
Wilhelmsburg, Austria 52 48 6N 15 36E
Wilhelmsburg, Ger. 48 53 28N 10 1E
Wilhelmshaven 48 53 30N 8 9E
Wilhelmstal 128 21 58S 16 21E
Wilkes-Barre 162 41 15N 75 52W
Wilkes Land 13 69 0S 120 0E
Wilkesboro 157 36 10N 81 9W
Wilkie 153 52 27N 108 42W
Wilkinson Lakes 137 29 40S 132 39E
Willamina 160 45 9N 123 32W
Willamulka 140 33 55S 137 52E
Willandra Billabong Creek 140 33 22S 145 52E
Willapa, B. 160 46 44N 124 0W
Willard, N. Mex., U.S.A. 161 34 35N 106 1W
Willard, N.Y., U.S.A. 162 42 40N 76 50W
Willard, Utah, U.S.A. 160 41 28N 112 1W
Willaumez Pen. 138 5 3S 150 3E
Willaura 140 37 31S 142 45E
Willberforce, C. 138 11 54S 136 35E
Willbriggie 141 34 28S 146 2E
Willcox 161 32 13N 109 53W
Willebroek 47 51 4N 4 22E
Willemstad 167 12 5N 69 0W
Willenhall 28 52 36N 2 3W
Willeroo 136 15 14S 131 37E
Willesborough 29 51 8N 0 55E
Willet 162 42 28N 75 55W
William Cr. 139 28 58S 136 22E
William, Mt. 140 37 17S 142 35E
William, R. 153 59 8N 109 19W
Williambury 137 23 45S 115 12E
Williams, Austral. 137 33 2S 116 52E
Williams, U.S.A. 161 35 16N 112 11W
Williams Lake 152 52 2N 122 10W
Williamsburg, Ky., U.S.A. 157 36 45N 84 10W
Williamsburg, Va., U.S.A. 162 37 17N 76 44W
Williamsburg, Va., U.S.A. 162 37 16N 79 43W
Williamson 156 37 46N 82 17W
Williamsport 162 41 18N 77 1W
Williamston 157 35 50N 77 5W
Williamstown, Austral. 141 37 51S 144 52E
Williamstown, Ireland 38 53 41N 8 34W
Williamstown, Mass., U.S.A. 162 42 43N 73 12W
Williamstown, N.Y., U.S.A. 162 43 25N 75 53W
Williamstown, N.Y., U.S.A. 162 43 25N 75 54W
Williamsville 159 37 0N 90 33W
Willimantic 162 41 45N 72 12W
Willingdon 29 50 47N 0 17E
Willis Group 138 16 18S 150 0E
Willisau 50 47 7N 8 0E
Williston, S. Afr. 128 31 20S 20 53E
Williston, Fla, U.S.A. 157 29 25N 82 28W
Williston, N.D., U.S.A. 158 48 10N 103 35W
Williston L. 152 56 0N 124 0W
Williton 28 51 9N 3 20W
Willits 160 39 28N 123 17W
Willmar 158 45 5N 95 0W
Willoughby 33 53 14N 0 12E
Willow Bunch 153 49 20N 105 35W
Willow L. 152 62 10N 119 8W
Willow Lake 158 44 40N 97 40W
Willow River 152 54 6N 122 28W
Willow Springs 159 37 0N 92 0W
Willow Tree 141 31 40S 150 45E
Willow Wall 107 41 30N 120 40E
Willowlake, R. 152 62 42N 123 8W
Willowmore 128 33 15S 23 30E
Willows, Austral. 138 23 45S 147 25E
Willows, U.S.A. 160 39 30N 122 10W
Wills Cr. 138 22 43S 140 2E
Wills, L. 136 21 25S 128 51E
Wills Pt. 159 32 42N 95 57W
Willunga 140 35 15S 138 30E
Wilmete 156 42 6N 87 44W
Wilmington, Austral. 140 32 39S 138 7E
Wilmington, U.K. 30 50 46N 3 8W
Wilmington, Del., U.S.A. 162 39 45N 75 32W
Wilmington, Ill., U.S.A. 156 41 19N 88 10W
Wilmington, N.C., U.S.A. 157 34 14N 77 54W
Wilmington, Ohio, U.S.A. 156 39 29N 83 46W
Wilmington, Vt., U.S.A. 162 42 52N 72 52W
Wilmslow 32 53 19N 2 14W
Wilnecote 28 52 36N 1 40W
Wilpena Cr. 140 31 25S 139 29E
Wilrijk 47 51 9N 4 22E
Wilsall 160 45 59N 110 4W
Wilson, U.S.A. 162 40 41N 75 15W
Wilson, N.C., U.S.A. 157 35 44N 77 54W
Wilson Bluff 137 31 41S 129 0E
Wilson Inlet 137 35 0S 117 20E
Wilson, Mt. 161 37 55N 105 3W
Wilson, R., Queens., Austral. 139 27 38S 141 24E
Wilson, R., W. Australia, Austral. 136 16 48S 128 16E
Wilson's Promontory 141 38 55S 146 25E
Wilster 48 53 55N 9 23E
Wilton, U.K. 28 51 5N 1 52W
Wilton, U.S.A. 158 47 12N 100 53W
Wilton, R. 138 14 45S 134 33E
Wiltshire □ 28 51 20N 2 0W
Wiltz 47 49 57N 5 55E
Wiluna 137 26 36S 120 14E
Wimblington 29 52 31N 0 5E
Wimborne Minster 28 50 48N 2 0W
Wimereux 43 50 45N 1 37E
Wimmera 133 36 30S 142 0E
Wimmera, R. 140 36 8S 141 56E
Winam G. 126 0 20S 34 15E
Winburg 128 28 30S 27 2E
Wincanton 28 51 3N 2 24W
Winchelsea, Austral. 140 38 10S 144 1E
Winchelsea, U.K. 29 50 55N 0 43E
Winchendon 162 42 40N 72 3W
Winchester, N.Z. 143 44 11S 171 17E
Winchester, U.K. 28 51 4N 1 19W
Winchester, Conn., U.S.A. 162 41 53N 73 9W
Winchester, Conn., U.S.A. 162 41 55N 73 8W
Winchester, Idaho, U.S.A. 160 46 11N 116 32W
Winchester, Ind., U.S.A. 156 40 10N 84 56W
Winchester, Ky., U.S.A. 156 38 0N 84 8W
Winchester, Mass., U.S.A. 162 42 28N 71 10W
Winchester, N.H., U.S.A. 162 42 47N 72 22W
Winchester, Tenn., U.S.A. 157 35 11N 86 8W
Winchester, Va., U.S.A. 156 39 14N 78 8W
Wind, R. 160 43 30N 109 30W
Wind River Range, Mts. 160 43 0N 109 30W
Windber 156 40 14N 78 50W
Winder 157 34 0N 83 40W
Windera 139 26 17S 151 51E
Windermere 32 54 24N 2 56W
Windermere, L. 32 54 20N 2 57W
Windfall 152 54 12N 116 13W
Windflower L. 152 62 52N 118 30W
Windhoek 128 22 35S 17 4E
Windischgarsten 52 47 42N 14 21E
Windmill Pt. 162 37 35N 76 17W
Windom 158 43 48N 95 3W
Windorah 138 25 24S 142 36E
Window Rock 161 35 47N 109 4W
Windrush, R. 28 51 48N 1 35W
Windsor, Austral. 141 33 37S 150 50E
Windsor, Newf., Can. 151 48 57N 55 40W
Windsor, N.S., Can. 151 44 59N 64 5W
Windsor, Ont., Can. 150 42 18N 83 82W
Windsor, N.Z. 143 44 59S 170 49E
Windsor, U.K. 29 51 28N 0 36W
Windsor, Col., U.S.A. 158 40 33N 104 55W
Windsor, Conn., U.S.A. 162 41 50N 72 40W
Windsor, Miss., U.S.A. 158 38 32N 93 31W
Windsor, N.Y., U.S.A. 162 42 5N 75 37W
Windsor, Vt., U.S.A. 162 43 30N 72 25W
Windsorton 128 28 16S 24 44E
Windward Is. 167 13 0N 63 0W
Windward Passage 167 20 0N 74 0W
Windy L. 153 60 20N 100 2W
Windygap 39 52 28N 7 24W
Windygates 35 56 12N 3 1W
Winefred L. 153 55 30N 110 30W
Winejok 123 9 1N 27 30E
Winfield 159 37 15N 97 0W
Wing 29 51 54N 0 41W
Wingate Mts. 136 14 25S 130 40E
Wingen 141 31 54S 150 54E
Wingene 47 51 3N 3 17E
Wingham, Austral. 141 31 48S 152 22E
Wingham, Can. 150 43 55N 81 20W
Wingham, U.K. 29 51 16N 1 12E
Winifred 160 47 30N 109 28W
Winisk 150 55 20N 85 15W
Winisk L. 150 52 55N 87 22W
Winisk, R. 150 55 17N 85 5W
Wink 159 31 49N 103 9W
Winkleigh 30 50 49N 3 57W
Winkler 153 49 15N 97 56W
Winklern 52 46 52N 12 52E
Winneba 121 5 25N 0 36W
Winnebago 158 43 43N 94 8W
Winnebago L. 156 44 0N 88 20W
Winnecke Cr. 136 18 35S 131 34E
Winnemucca 160 41 0N 117 45W
Winnemucca, L. 160 40 25N 119 21W
Winner 158 43 23N 99 52W
Winnetka 156 42 8N 87 46W
Winnett 160 47 2N 108 28W
Winnfield 159 31 57N 92 38W
Winnibigoshish L. 158 47 25N 94 12W
Winning Pool 136 23 9S 114 30E
Winnipeg 153 49 50N 97 9W
Winnipeg Beach 153 50 30N 96 58W
Winnipeg, L. 153 52 0N 97 0W
Winnipeg, R. 153 50 38N 96 19W
Winnipegosis 153 51 39N 99 55W
Winnipegosis L. 153 52 30N 100 0W
Winnipesaukee, L. 162 43 38N 71 21W
Winnisquam L. 162 43 33N 71 30W
Winnsboro, Lou, U.S.A. 159 32 10N 91 41W
Winnsboro, S.C., U.S.A. 157 34 23N 81 5W
Winnsboro, Tex., U.S.A. 158 32 56N 95 15W
Winokapau, L. 151 53 15N 62 50W
Winona, Miss., U.S.A. 159 33 30N 89 42W
Winona, Wis., U.S.A. 158 44 2N 91 45W
Winooski 156 44 31N 73 11W
Winschoten 46 53 9N 7 3E
Winsen 48 53 21N 10 11E
Winsford 32 53 12N 2 31W
Winslow, U.K. 29 51 57N 0 52W
Winslow, U.S.A. 161 35 2N 110 41W
Winstead 162 41 55N 73 5W
Winster 33 53 9N 1 42W
Winston-Salem 157 36 7N 80 15W
Winsum 46 53 20N 6 32E
Winter Garden 157 28 33N 81 35W
Winter Haven 157 28 0N 81 42W
Winter Park 157 28 34N 81 19W
Winterberg 48 51 12N 8 30E

Winterborne Abbas

Yaapeet


| | | | |
|---|---|---|---|
| Winterborne Abbas | 28 | 50 43N | 2 30W |
| Winters | 159 | 31 58N | 99 58W |
| Winterset | 158 | 41 18N | 94 0W |
| Winterswijk | 46 | 51 58N | 6 43E |
| Winterthur | 51 | 47 30N | 8 44E |
| Winterton, Humberside, U.K. | 33 | 53 39N | 0 37W |
| Winterton, Norfolk, U.K. | 29 | 52 43N | 1 43E |
| Winthrop, Minn., U.S.A. | 158 | 44 31N | 94 25W |
| Winthrop, Wash., U.S.A. | 160 | 48 27N | 120 6W |
| Winton, Austral. | 138 | 22 24S | 143 3E |
| Winton, N.Z. | 143 | 46 8S | 168 20E |
| Winton, U.S.A. | 157 | 36 25N | 76 58W |
| Wirksworth | 33 | 53 5N | 1 34W |
| Wirral | 23 | 53 25N | 3 0W |
| Wirraminna | 140 | 31 12S | 136 13E |
| Wirrulla | 139 | 32 24S | 134 31E |
| Wisbech | 29 | 52 39N | 0 10E |
| Wisborough Green | 29 | 51 2N | 0 30W |
| Wisconsin □ | 158 | 44 30N | 90 0W |
| Wisconsin Dells | 158 | 43 38N | 89 45W |
| Wisconsin, R. | 158 | 45 25N | 89 45W |
| Wisconsin Rapids | 158 | 44 25N | 89 50W |
| Wisdom | 147 | 45 36N | 113 1W |
| Wiserman | 147 | 67 25N | 150 15W |
| Wishaw | 35 | 55 46N | 3 55W |
| Wishek | 158 | 46 20N | 99 35W |
| Wiske, R. | 33 | 54 26N | 1 27W |
| Wisła | 53 | 49 38N | 18 53E |
| Wisła, R. | 54 | 53 38N | 18 47E |
| Wisłok, R. | 53 | 50 7N | 22 25E |
| Wisłoka, R. | 53 | 49 50N | 21 28E |
| Wismar | 48 | 53 53N | 11 23E |
| Wismar B. | 48 | 54 0N | 11 15E |
| Wisner | 158 | 42 0N | 96 46W |
| Wissant | 43 | 50 52N | 1 40E |
| Wissembourg | 43 | 48 57N | 7 57E |
| Wissenkerke | 47 | 51 35N | 3 45E |
| Wistoka, R. | 54 | 49 50N | 21 28E |
| Witbank | 129 | 25 51S | 29 14E |
| Witchita | 159 | 37 40N | 97 22W |
| Witchyburn | 37 | 57 37N | 2 37W |
| Witdraai | 128 | 26 58S | 20 48E |
| Witham | 29 | 51 48N | 0 39E |
| Witham, R. | 33 | 53 3N | 0 8W |
| Withern | 33 | 53 19N | 0 9E |
| Withernsea | 33 | 53 43N | 0 2W |
| Witkowo | 54 | 52 26N | 17 45E |
| Witley | 29 | 51 9N | 0 39W |
| Witmarsum | 46 | 53 6N | 5 28E |
| Witney | 28 | 51 47N | 1 29W |
| Witnossob, R. | 128 | 23 0S | 18 40E |
| Wittdün | 48 | 54 38N | 8 23E |
| Witten | 48 | 51 26N | 7 19E |
| Wittenberg | 48 | 51 51N | 12 39E |
| Wittenberge | 48 | 53 0N | 11 44E |
| Wittenburg | 48 | 53 30N | 11 4E |
| Wittenoom, W. Australia, Austral. | 132 | 22 15S | 118 20E |
| Wittenoom, W. Australia, Austral. | 136 | 18 34S | 128 51E |
| Wittersham | 29 | 51 1N | 0 42E |
| Wittingen | 48 | 52 43N | 10 43E |
| Wittlich | 49 | 50 0N | 6 54E |
| Wittmund | 48 | 53 39N | 7 35E |
| Wittow | 48 | 54 37N | 13 21E |
| Wittstock | 48 | 53 10N | 12 30E |
| Witzenhausen | 48 | 51 20N | 9 50E |
| Wiveliscombe | 28 | 51 2N | 3 20W |
| Wivenhoe | 29 | 51 51N | 0 59E |
| Wiyeb, W. | 123 | 7 15N | 40 15E |
| Wladyslawowo | 54 | 52 6N | 18 28E |
| Wlen | 160 | 51 0N | 15 39E |
| Wlingi | 103 | 8 5S | 112 25E |
| Włocławek | 54 | 52 40N | 19 3E |
| Włodawa | 54 | 51 33N | 23 31E |
| Włoszczowa | 54 | 50 50N | 19 55E |
| Woburn, U.K. | 29 | 51 59N | 0 37W |
| Woburn, U.S.A. | 162 | 42 31N | 71 7W |
| Woburn Sands | 29 | 51 1N | 0 38W |
| Wodonga | 141 | 36 5S | 146 50E |
| Wodzisław Sl. | 54 | 50 1N | 18 26E |
| Woerden | 46 | 52 5N | 4 54E |
| Woerht'ukou | 106 | 42 35N | 112 19E |
| Woerth | 43 | 48 57N | 7 45E |
| Woevre | 43 | 49 15N | 5 45E |
| Wognum | 46 | 52 40N | 5 1E |
| Wohlen | 51 | 47 21N | 8 17E |
| Wokam, I. | 103 | 5 45S | 134 28E |
| Wokha | 98 | 26 6N | 94 16E |
| Woking, Can. | 152 | 55 35N | 118 50W |
| Woking, U.K. | 29 | 51 18N | 0 33W |
| Wokingham | 29 | 51 25N | 0 50W |
| Wolbrom | 54 | 50 24N | 19 45E |
| Woldegk | 48 | 53 27N | 13 35E |
| Wolf Creek | 160 | 47 1N | 112 2W |
| Wolf L. | 152 | 60 24N | 133 42W |
| Wolf Point | 158 | 48 6N | 105 40W |
| Wolf, R. | 152 | 60 17N | 132 33W |
| Wolf Rock | 30 | 49 56N | 5 50W |
| Wolfe I. | 150 | 44 7N | 76 20W |
| Wolfeboro | 162 | 43 35N | 71 12W |
| Wolfenbüttel | 48 | 52 10N | 10 33E |
| Wolfenden | 152 | 52 0N | 119 25W |
| Wolfheze | 46 | 52 0N | 5 48E |
| Wolfram | 138 | 17 6S | 145 0E |
| Wolf's Castle | 31 | 51 53N | 4 57W |
| Wolfsberg | 52 | 46 50N | 14 52E |
| Wolfsburg | 48 | 52 27N | 10 49E |
| Wolgast | 48 | 54 3N | 13 46E |
| Wolhusen | 50 | 47 4N | 8 4E |
| Wolin | 54 | 53 40N | 14 37E |
| Wollaston, Islas | 176 | 55 40S | 67 30W |
| Wollaston L. | 153 | 58 7N | 103 10W |
| Wollaston Pen. | 148 | 69 30N | 115 0W |
| Wollogorang | 138 | 17 13S | 137 57E |
| Wollongong | 141 | 34 25S | 150 54E |
| Wolmaransstad | 128 | 27 12S | 26 13E |
| Wolmirstedt | 48 | 52 15N | 11 35E |
| Wołomin | 54 | 52 19N | 21 15E |
| Wołow | 54 | 51 20N | 16 38E |
| Wolseley, Austral. | 140 | 36 23S | 140 54E |
| Wolseley, Can. | 153 | 50 25N | 103 15W |
| Wolseley, S. Afr. | 128 | 33 26S | 19 7E |
| Wolsingham | 32 | 54 44N | 1 52W |
| Wolstenholme Sound | 12 | 74 30N | 75 0W |
| Wolsztyn | 54 | 52 8N | 16 5E |
| Wolvega | 46 | 52 52N | 6 0E |
| Wolverhampton | 28 | 52 35N | 2 6W |
| Wolverton | 29 | 52 3N | 0 48W |
| Wolviston | 33 | 54 39N | 1 25W |
| Wombera | 123 | 10 45N | 35 49E |
| Wombwell | 33 | 53 31N | 1 23W |
| Wommels | 46 | 53 6N | 5 36E |
| Wonarah P.O. | 138 | 19 55S | 136 20E |
| Wonboyn | 141 | 37 15S | 149 55E |
| Wonck | 47 | 50 46N | 5 38E |
| Wondai | 139 | 26 20S | 151 49E |
| Wondelgem | 47 | 51 5N | 3 44E |
| Wonder Gorge | 127 | 14 40S | 29 0E |
| Wongalarroo L. | 140 | 31 32S | 144 0E |
| Wongan | 137 | 30 51S | 116 37E |
| Wongan Hills | 137 | 30 53S | 116 42E |
| Wongawal | 137 | 25 5S | 121 55E |
| Wonosari | 103 | 7 38S | 110 36E |
| Wŏnsan | 107 | 39 11N | 127 27E |
| Wonston | 28 | 51 9N | 1 18W |
| Wonthaggi | 141 | 38 37S | 145 37E |
| Wonyulgunna Hill, Mt. | 137 | 24 52S | 119 44E |
| Woocalla | 140 | 31 42S | 137 12E |
| Wood Buffalo Nat. Park | 152 | 56 28N | 113 41W |
| Wood Green | 138 | 22 26S | 134 12E |
| Wood Is. | 136 | 16 24S | 123 19E |
| Wood L. | 153 | 55 17N | 103 17W |
| Wood Lake | 158 | 42 38N | 100 14W |
| Wood Mt. | 153 | 49 14N | 106 30W |
| Woodah I. | 138 | 13 27S | 136 10E |
| Woodanilling | 137 | 33 31S | 117 24E |
| Woodbine | 162 | 39 14N | 74 49W |
| Woodbourne | 162 | 41 46N | 74 35W |
| Woodbridge | 29 | 52 6N | 1 19E |
| Woodburn | 139 | 29 6S | 153 23E |
| Woodbury, U.K. | 30 | 50 40N | 3 24W |
| Woodbury, U.S.A. | 162 | 39 50N | 75 9W |
| Woodchopper | 147 | 65 25N | 143 30W |
| Wooden Bridge | 39 | 52 50N | 6 13W |
| Woodend | 140 | 37 20N | 144 33E |
| Woodford | 39 | 53 3N | 8 23W |
| Woodfords | 163 | 38 47N | 119 50W |
| Woodhall Spa. | 33 | 53 10N | 0 12W |
| Woodham Ferrers | 29 | 51 40N | 0 37E |
| Woodlake | 163 | 36 25N | 119 6W |
| Woodland | 160 | 38 40N | 121 50W |
| Woodlands | 137 | 24 46S | 118 8E |
| Woodlark I. | 135 | 9 10S | 152 50E |
| Woodley | 29 | 51 26N | 0 54W |
| Woodpecker | 152 | 53 30N | 122 40W |
| Woodplumpton | 32 | 53 47N | 2 46W |
| Woodridge | 153 | 49 20N | 96 9W |
| Woodroffe, Mt. | 137 | 26 20S | 131 45E |
| Woodruff, Ariz., U.S.A. | 161 | 34 51N | 110 1W |
| Woodruff, Utah, U.S.A. | 160 | 41 30N | 111 4W |
| Woods, L., Austral. | 138 | 17 50S | 133 30E |
| Woods, L., Can. | 151 | 54 30N | 65 13W |
| Woods, Lake of the | 153 | 49 30N | 94 30W |
| Woodside, S. Australia, Austral. | 140 | 34 58S | 138 52E |
| Woodside, Victoria, Austral. | 141 | 38 31S | 146 52E |
| Woodstock, N.S.W., Austral. | 141 | 33 45S | 148 53E |
| Woodstock, Queens., Austral. | 138 | 19 35S | 146 50E |
| Woodstock, W.A., Austral. | 136 | 21 41S | 118 57E |
| Woodstock, N.B., Can. | 151 | 46 11N | 67 37W |
| Woodstock, Ont., Can. | 150 | 43 10N | 80 45W |
| Woodstock, U.K. | 28 | 51 51N | 1 20W |
| Woodstock, Ill., U.S.A. | 158 | 42 17N | 88 30W |
| Woodstock, Vt., U.S.A. | 162 | 43 37N | 72 31W |
| Woodstown | 162 | 39 39N | 75 20W |
| Woodville, N.Z. | 142 | 40 20S | 175 53E |
| Woodville, U.S.A. | 159 | 30 45N | 94 25W |
| Woodward | 159 | 36 24N | 99 28W |
| Woodward, Mt. | 137 | 26 0S | 131 0E |
| Woody | 163 | 35 42N | 118 50W |
| Wookey | 28 | 51 13N | 2 41W |
| Wookey Hole | 28 | 51 13N | 2 41W |
| Wool | 28 | 50 41N | 2 13W |
| Woolacombe | 30 | 51 10N | 4 12W |
| Woolamai, C. | 141 | 38 30S | 145 23E |
| Wooler | 35 | 55 33N | 2 0W |
| Woolgangie | 137 | 31 12S | 120 35E |
| Woolyeenyer, Mt. | 137 | 32 16S | 121 47E |
| Woombye | 139 | 26 40S | 152 55E |
| Woomera | 140 | 31 11S | 136 47E |
| Woonona | 141 | 34 21S | 150 54E |
| Woonsocket | 162 | 42 0N | 71 30W |
| Woonsockett | 158 | 44 5N | 98 15W |
| Wooramel | 137 | 25 45S | 114 40E |
| Wooramel, R. | 137 | 25 30S | 114 30E |
| Wooroloo | 137 | 31 48S | 116 18E |
| Wooroorooka | 139 | 29 0S | 145 41E |
| Wooster | 156 | 40 38N | 81 55W |
| Wootton Bassett | 28 | 51 32N | 1 55W |
| Wootton Wawen | 28 | 52 16N | 1 47W |
| Worb | 50 | 46 56N | 7 33E |
| Worcester, S. Afr. | 125 | 33 39S | 19 27E |
| Worcester, U.K. | 28 | 52 12N | 2 12W |
| Worcester, Mass., U.S.A. | 162 | 42 14N | 71 49W |
| Worcester, N.Y., U.S.A. | 162 | 42 35N | 74 45W |
| Worcestershire (□) | 26 | 52 13N | 2 10W |
| Worfield | 28 | 52 34N | 2 22W |
| Wörgl | 52 | 47 29N | 12 3E |
| Worikambo | 121 | 10 43N | 0 11W |
| Workington | 32 | 54 39N | 3 34W |
| Worksop | 33 | 53 19N | 1 9W |
| Workum | 46 | 52 59N | 5 26E |
| Worland | 160 | 44 0N | 107 59W |
| Wormerveer | 46 | 52 30N | 4 46E |
| Wormhoudt | 43 | 50 52N | 2 28E |
| Wormit | 35 | 56 26N | 2 59W |
| Worms | 49 | 49 37N | 8 21E |
| Worms Head | 29 | 51 33N | 4 19W |
| Worplesdon | 29 | 51 16N | 0 36W |
| Worsley | 137 | 33 15S | 116 2E |
| Wortham, U.K. | 29 | 52 22N | 1 3E |
| Wortham, U.S.A. | 159 | 31 48N | 96 27W |
| Wörther See | 52 | 46 37N | 14 19E |
| Worthing | 29 | 50 49N | 0 21W |
| Worthington | 158 | 43 35N | 95 30W |
| Wosi | 103 | 0 15S | 128 0E |
| Wota (Shoa Ghimirra) | 123 | 7 4N | 35 51E |
| Wotton-under-Edge | 28 | 51 37N | 2 20W |
| Woubrugge | 46 | 52 10N | 4 39E |
| Woudenberg | 46 | 52 5N | 5 25E |
| Woudsend | 46 | 52 56N | 5 38E |
| Wour | 119 | 21 14N | 16 0E |
| Wouw | 47 | 51 31N | 4 23E |
| Wowoni, I. | 103 | 4 5S | 123 5E |
| Woy Woy | 141 | 33 30S | 151 19E |
| Wragby | 33 | 53 17N | 0 18W |
| Wrangell | 147 | 56 30N | 132 25W |
| Wrangell, I. | 152 | 56 20N | 132 10W |
| Wrangell Mts. | 147 | 61 40N | 143 30W |
| Wrangle | 33 | 53 3N | 0 9E |
| Wrath, C. | 36 | 58 38N | 5 0W |
| Wray | 158 | 40 8N | 102 18W |
| Wreck I. | 162 | 37 12N | 75 48W |
| Wrekin, The, Mt. | 28 | 52 41N | 2 35W |
| Wrens | 157 | 33 13N | 82 23W |
| Wrentham | 29 | 52 24N | 1 39E |
| Wrexham | 31 | 53 5N | 3 0W |
| Wriezen | 48 | 52 43N | 14 9E |
| Wright, Can. | 152 | 51 52N | 121 40W |
| Wright, Phil. | 103 | 11 42N | 125 2E |
| Wright, Mt. | 151 | 52 40N | 67 25W |
| Wrightlington | 28 | 51 18N | 2 16W |
| Wrightson, Mt. | 161 | 31 49N | 110 56W |
| Wrightsville | 162 | 40 2N | 76 32W |
| Wrightwood | 163 | 34 21N | 117 38W |
| Wrigley | 148 | 63 16N | 123 27W |
| Writtle | 29 | 51 44N | 0 27E |
| Wrocław | 54 | 51 5N | 17 5E |
| Wrocław □ | 54 | 51 0N | 17 0E |
| Wronki | 54 | 52 41N | 16 21E |
| Wrotham | 29 | 51 18N | 0 20E |
| Wroughton | 28 | 51 31N | 1 47W |
| Wroxham | 29 | 52 42N | 1 23E |
| Września | 54 | 52 21N | 17 36E |
| Wschowa | 54 | 51 48N | 16 20E |
| Wu Chiang, R. | 108 | 29 42N | 107 20E |
| Wu Shui, R. | 109 | 27 7N | 109 57E |
| Wuan | 106 | 36 45N | 114 2E |
| Wubin | 137 | 30 6S | 116 37E |
| Wuch'ang, Heilungkiang, China | 107 | 44 55N | 127 10E |
| Wuch'ang, Hupeh, China | 109 | 30 30N | 114 15E |
| Wuch'eng | 108 | 30 48N | 98 46E |
| Wuch'i | 108 | 31 28N | 109 36E |
| Wuchiang | 109 | 31 10N | 120 37E |
| Wuchih Shan, mts. | 100 | 18 45N | 109 45E |
| Wuch'ing | 107 | 39 25N | 117 7E |
| Wuchou | 105 | 23 33N | 111 18E |
| Wuch'uan, Inner Mong., China | 106 | 41 8N | 111 24E |
| Wuch'uan, Kwangsi-Chuang, China | 109 | 21 29N | 110 49E |
| Wuch'uan, Kweichow, China | 108 | 28 30N | 107 58E |
| Wuchung | 106 | 38 4N | 106 12E |
| Wufeng | 109 | 30 12N | 110 36E |
| Wuhan | 109 | 30 35N | 114 15E |
| Wuho | 107 | 33 9N | 117 53E |
| Wuhsi | 105 | 31 30N | 120 20E |
| Wuhsiang | 106 | 36 50N | 112 52E |
| Wuhsing | 109 | 30 49N | 120 5E |
| Wuhsüan | 108 | 23 36N | 109 39E |
| Wuhu | 105 | 31 18N | 118 20E |
| Wuhu (Wou-tou) | 109 | 31 21N | 118 30E |
| Wui, Anhwei, China | 109 | 28 53N | 119 48E |
| Wui, Hopeh, China | 106 | 37 49N | 115 54E |
| Wui Shan, mts. | 105 | 27 30N | 117 30E |
| Wukang | 109 | 26 50N | 110 15E |
| Wukari | 121 | 7 57N | 9 42E |
| Wulachieh | 107 | 44 5N | 126 27E |
| Wulanhaot'e | 105 | 46 5N | 122 5E |
| Wulanpulang | 106 | 41 8N | 110 56E |
| Wulehe | 121 | 3 42N | 0 0E |
| Wuliang Shan, mts. | 108 | 24 0N | 100 55E |
| Wuliaru, I. | 103 | 7 10S | 131 0E |
| Wulien | 107 | 35 45N | 119 12E |
| Wuluk'omushih Ling | 105 | 36 25N | 87 25E |
| Wulumuchi | 105 | 43 40N | 87 50E |
| Wulunku Ho, R. | 105 | 46 58N | 87 28E |
| Wum | 121 | 6 40N | 10 2E |
| Wuming | 108 | 23 11N | 108 12E |
| Wuneba | 123 | 4 49N | 30 22E |
| Wuning | 109 | 29 16N | 115 0E |
| Wunnummin L. | 150 | 52 55N | 89 10W |
| Wunsiedel | 49 | 50 2N | 12 0E |
| Wunstorf | 48 | 52 26N | 9 29E |
| Wuntho, Burma | 98 | 21 44N | 96 2E |
| Wuntho, Burma | 99 | 23 55N | 95 45E |
| Wupao | 106 | 37 35N | 110 45E |
| Wup'ing | 109 | 25 9N | 116 5E |
| Wuppertal, Ger. | 48 | 51 15N | 7 8E |
| Wuppertal, S. Afr. | 128 | 32 13S | 19 12E |
| Wurarga | 137 | 28 25S | 116 15E |
| Würenlingen | 51 | 47 32N | 8 16E |
| Wurung | 138 | 19 13S | 140 38E |
| Würzburg | 49 | 49 46N | 9 55E |
| Wurzen | 48 | 51 21N | 12 45E |
| Wushan, Kansu, China | 106 | 34 42N | 104 58E |
| Wushan, Szechwan, China | 108 | 31 3N | 109 57E |
| Wushench'i | 106 | 38 57N | 109 15E |
| Wustrow | 48 | 54 4N | 11 33E |
| Wusu | 105 | 44 27N | 84 37E |
| Wutai | 106 | 38 44N | 113 18E |
| Wuti | 107 | 37 46N | 117 39E |
| Wuting | 108 | 25 33N | 102 26E |
| Wuting = Huimin | 107 | 37 32N | 117 33E |
| Wuting Ho, R. | 106 | 37 8N | 110 25E |
| Wut'ungch'iao | 108 | 29 24N | 104 0E |
| Wutunghaolan | 107 | 42 49N | 120 11E |
| Wuustwezel | 47 | 51 23N | 4 36E |
| Wuwei, Anhwei, China | 109 | 31 22N | 117 55E |
| Wuwei, Kansu, China | 105 | 37 55N | 102 48E |
| Wuyang | 106 | 33 25N | 113 36E |
| Wuyo | 121 | 10 23N | 11 50E |
| Wuyüan, Inner Mong., China | 106 | 41 6N | 108 16E |
| Wuyüan, Kiangsi, China | 109 | 29 17N | 117 54E |
| Wuyün | 105 | 49 17N | 129 40E |
| Wyaaba Cr. | 138 | 16 27S | 141 35E |
| Wyalkatchem | 137 | 31 8S | 117 22E |
| Wyalong | 139 | 33 54S | 147 16E |
| Wyalusing | 162 | 41 40N | 76 16W |
| Wyandotte | 156 | 42 14N | 83 13W |
| Wyandra | 139 | 27 12S | 145 56E |
| Wyangala Res. | 141 | 33 54S | 149 0E |
| Wyara, L. | 139 | 28 42S | 144 14E |
| Wych Farm, oilfield | 19 | 50 38N | 2 2W |
| Wycheproof | 140 | 36 0N | 143 17E |
| Wye | 29 | 51 11N | 0 56E |
| Wye, R. | 28 | 52 0N | 2 36W |
| Wyemandoo, Mt. | 137 | 28 28S | 118 29E |
| Wyk | 48 | 54 41N | 8 33E |
| Wylfa Hd. | 31 | 53 25N | 4 28W |
| Wylye, R. | 28 | 51 8N | 1 53W |
| Wymondham, Leicester, U.K. | 29 | 52 45N | 0 42W |
| Wymondham, Norfolk, U.K. | 29 | 52 34N | 1 7E |
| Wymore | 158 | 40 10N | 97 8W |
| Wynberg | 128 | 34 2S | 18 28E |
| Wynbring | 139 | 30 33S | 133 32E |
| Wyndham, Austral. | 136 | 15 33S | 128 3E |
| Wyndham, N.Z. | 143 | 46 20S | 168 51E |
| Wynne | 159 | 35 15N | 90 50W |
| Wynnstay | 31 | 52 36N | 3 33W |
| Wynnum | 139 | 27 27S | 153 9E |
| Wynyard | 153 | 51 45N | 104 10W |
| Wyola, L. | 137 | 29 8S | 130 17E |
| Wyoming □ | 154 | 42 48N | 109 0W |
| Wyong | 141 | 33 14S | 151 24E |
| Wyre Forest | 28 | 52 24N | 2 24W |
| Wyre, I. | 37 | 59 7N | 2 58W |
| Wyre, R. | 37 | 53 52N | 2 57W |
| Wyrzysk | 54 | 53 10N | 17 17E |
| Wysoka | 54 | 53 13N | 17 2E |
| Wyszków | 54 | 52 36N | 21 25E |
| Wyszogród | 54 | 52 23N | 20 9E |
| Wytheville | 156 | 37 0N | 81 3W |


## X


| | | | |
|---|---|---|---|
| Xai-Xai | 129 | 25 6S | 33 31E |
| Xambioá | 170 | 6 25S | 48 40W |
| Xanten | 48 | 51 40N | 6 27E |
| Xanthi | 68 | 41 10N | 24 58E |
| Xanthi □ | 68 | 41 10N | 24 58E |
| Xapuri | 174 | 10 35S | 68 35W |
| Xau | 128 | 21 15S | 24 44E |
| Xavantina | 173 | 21 15S | 52 48W |
| Xenia | 156 | 39 42N | 83 57W |
| Xieng Khouang | 100 | 19 17N | 103 25E |
| Xilókastron | 69 | 38 4N | 22 43E |
| Xinavane | 129 | 25 2S | 32 47E |
| Xingu, R. | 175 | 2 25S | 52 35W |
| Xiniás, L. | 69 | 39 2N | 22 12E |
| Xique-Xique | 170 | 10 50S | 42 40W |
| Xuan Loc | 101 | 10 56N | 107 14E |
| Xuyen Moc | 101 | 10 34N | 107 25E |


## Y


| | | | |
|---|---|---|---|
| Ya 'Bud | 90 | 32 27N | 35 10E |
| Yaamba | 138 | 23 8S | 150 22E |
| Yaan | 108 | 30 0N | 102 59E |
| Yaapeet | 140 | 35 45S | 142 3E |

Yabassi Yorktown

Yabassi 121 4 30N 9 57 E
Yabba North 141 36 13 S 145 42 E
Yabelo 123 4 57N 38 8 E
Yablanitsa 67 43 2N 24 5 E
Yablonovyy Khrebet 77 53 0N 114 0 E
Yabrīn 92 23 7N 48 52 E
Yach'i 108 27 35N 106 40 E
Yachiang 108 30 4N 101 7 E
Yacuiba 172 22 0 S 63 25W
Yadgir 96 16 45N 77 5 E
Yadkin, R. 157 36 15N 81 0W
Yadrin 81 55 57N 46 6 E
Yaeyama-Shotō 112 24 25N 124 0 E
Yagaba 121 10 14N 1 20W
Yagoua 124 10 20N 14 58 E
Yagur 90 32 45N 35 4 E
Yaha 101 6 29N 101 8 E
Yahk 152 49 6N 116 10W
Yahuma 124 1 0N 22 5 E
Yaihsien 100 18 14N 109 29 E
Yaizu 111 34 52N 138 20 E
Yajua 121 11 27N 12 49 E
Yakage 110 34 37N 133 35 E
Yakataga 147 60 5N 142 32W
Yakiang 99 30 4N 101 15 E
Yakima 160 46 42N 120 30W
Yakima, R. 160 47 0N 120 30W
Yako 120 12 59N 2 15W
Yakoruda 67 42 1N 23 29 E
Yakshur Bodya 84 57 11N 53 7 E
Yaku-Jima 112 30 20N 130 30 E
Yakut A.S.S.R. □ 77 62 0N 130 0 E
Yakutat 147 59 50N 139 44W
Yakutsk 77 62 5N 129 40 E
Yala 101 6 33N 101 18 E
Yalabusha, R. 159 33 53N 89 50W
Yalbalgo 137 25 10 S 114 45 E
Yalboroo 138 20 50 S 148 40 E
Yalgoo 137 28 16 S 116 39 E
Yalikavak 69 37 6N 27 18 E
Yalinga 117 6 20N 23 10 E
Yalkubul, Punta 165 21 32N 88 37W
Y'allaq, G. 122 30 21N 33 31 E
Yalleroi 138 24 3 S 145 42 E
Yallourn 141 38 10 S 146 18 E
Yalpukh, Oz. 70 45 30N 28 41 E
Yalta 82 44 30N 34 10 E
Yalu Chiang, R. 107 39 45N 124 20 E
Yalung Chiang, R. 105 26 35N 101 45 E
Yalutorovsk 76 56 30N 65 40 E
Yam Kinneret 90 32 49N 35 36 E
Yamada 110 33 43N 130 49 E
Yamaga 110 33 1N 130 41 E
Yamagata 112 38 15N 140 15 E
Yamagata-ken □ 112 38 30N 140 0 E
Yamagawa 110 31 12N 130 39 E
Yamaguchi 110 34 10N 131 32 E
Yamaguchi-ken □ 110 34 20N 131 40 E
Yamal, Poluostrov 76 71 0N 70 0 E
Yamana 92 24 5N 47 30 E
Yamanaka 111 36 15N 136 22 E
Yamanashi-ken □ 111 35 40N 138 40 E
Yamankhalinka 83 47 43N 49 21 E
Yamantau 78 54 20N 57 40 E
Yamantau, Gora 84 54 15N 58 6 E
Yamato 111 35 27N 139 25 E
Yamatotakada 111 34 31N 135 45 E
Yamazaki 110 35 0N 134 32 E
Yamba, N.S.W., Austral. 139 29 26 S 153 23 E
Yamba, S. Australia, Austral. 140 34 10 S 140 52 E
Yambah 138 23 10 S 133 50 E
Yâmbiô 123 4 35N 28 16 E
Yambol 67 42 30N 26 36 E
Yamdena 103 7 45 S 131 20 E
Yame 110 33 13N 130 35 E
Yamethin 98 20 29N 96 18 E
Yamil 121 12 53N 8 4 E
Yamma-Yamma L. 139 26 16 S 141 20 E
Yampa, R. 160 40 37N 108 0W
Yampi Sd. 136 16 8 S 123 38 E
Yampol 82 48 15N 28 15 E
Yamrat 121 10 11N 9 55 E
Yamrukohal, Mt. 67 42 44N 24 52 E
Yamun 90 32 29N 35 14 E
Yamuna (Jumna), R. 94 27 0N 78 30 E
Yan 121 10 5N 12 11 E
Yan Oya 97 9 0N 81 10 E
Yana, R. 77 69 0N 134 0 E
Yanac 140 36 8 S 141 25 E
Yanagawa 110 33 10N 130 24 E
Yanahara 110 34 58N 134 2 E
Yanam 96 16 47N 82 15 E
Yanaul 84 56 25N 55 0 E
Yanbu 'al Bahr 92 24 0N 38 5 E
Yancannia 139 30 12 S 142 35 E
Yanchep 137 31 30 S 115 45 E
Yanco 141 34 38 S 146 27 E
Yanco Cr. 141 35 14 S 145 35 E
Yandabome 138 7 1 S 145 46 E
Yandal 137 27 35 S 121 10 E
Yandanooka 137 29 18 S 115 29 E
Yandaran 138 24 43 S 152 6 E
Yandil 137 26 20 S 119 50 E
Yandoon 98 17 0N 95 40 E
Yanfolila 120 11 11N 8 9W
Yangambi 126 0 47N 24 20 E
Yangch'angtzukou 106 41 31N 109 1 E
Yangch'eng 106 35 32N 112 26 E
Yangchiang 109 21 55N 111 55 E
Yangchiaoch'iao 109 29 45N 112 45 E
Yangchiapa 106 42 6N 113 46 E
Yangchou 109 32 24N 119 26 E
Yangchoyung Hu 105 29 0N 90 40 E
Yangch'ü = T'aiyüan 106 37 55N 112 40 E
Yangch'üan 106 37 54N 113 36 E
Yangch'un 109 22 10N 111 47 E
Yanghsien 106 33 20N 107 30 E
Yanghsin 109 29 53N 115 10 E
Yangi-Yer 76 40 17N 68 48 E
Yangibazar 85 41 40N 70 53 E
Yangikishlak 85 40 25N 67 10 E
Yangiyul 85 41 0N 69 3 E
Yangku 106 36 8N 115 48 E
Yangliuch'ing 107 39 11N 117 9 E
Yangp'i 108 25 40N 100 0 E
Yangp'ing 109 31 13N 111 33 E
Yangp'ingkuan 106 33 2N 105 56 E
Yangshan 109 24 28N 112 38 E
Yangshuo 109 24 45N 110 24 E
Yangtze (Ch'ang Chiang) 109 1 48N 121 53 E
Yangyang 107 38 4N 128 38 E
Yangyüan 106 40 5N 114 12 E
Yanhee Res. 101 17 30N 98 45 E
Yanko Cr. 139 35 17 S 145 15 E
Yankton 158 42 55N 97 25W
Yanna 139 26 58 S 146 0 E
Yanonge 126 0 35N 24 38 E
Yantabulla 139 29 21 S 145 0 E
Yantra, R. 67 43 35N 25 37 E
Yany Kurgan 85 43 55N 67 15 E
Yao, Chad 117 12 56N 17 33 E
Yao, Japan 111 34 32N 135 36 E
Yao Yai, Ko 101 8 0N 98 35 E
Yaoan 108 25 32N 101 12 E
Yaoundé 121 3 50N 11 35 E
Yaowan 107 34 10N 118 3 E
Yap Is. 103 9 30N 138 10 E
Yapen 103 1 50 S 136 0 E
Yapen, Selat 103 1 20 S 136 10 E
Yapo, R. 174 0 30 S 77 0W
Yappar, R. 138 18 22 S 141 16 E
Yaqui, R. 164 28 28N 109 30W
Yar 84 58 14N 52 5 E
Yar-Sale 76 66 50N 70 50 E
Yaracuy □ 174 10 20N 68 45W
Yaraka 138 24 53 S 144 3 E
Yaransk 81 57 13N 47 56 E
Yaratishky 80 54 3N 25 52 E
Yarcombe 30 50 51N 3 6W
Yarda 117 18 35N 19 0 E
Yardea P.O. 139 32 23 S 135 32 E
Yare, R. 29 52 36N 1 28 E
Yarensk 78 61 10N 49 8 E
Yarfa 122 24 40N 38 35 E
Yarí, R. 174 1 0N 73 40W
Yaringa North 137 25 53 S 114 30 E
Yaringa South 137 26 3 S 114 28 E
Yarkand = Soch'e 105 38 24N 77 20 E
Yarkhun, R. 95 36 30N 72 45 E
Yarm 33 54 31N 1 21W
Yarmouth, Can. 151 43 53N 65 45W
Yarmouth, U.K. 28 50 42N 1 29W
Yaroslavl 81 57 35N 39 55 E
Yarra Yarra Lakes 137 29 40 S 115 45 E
Yarraden 138 14 28 S 143 15 E
Yarraloola 136 21 33 S 115 52 E
Yarram 141 38 29 S 146 40 E
Yarraman 139 26 50 S 152 0 E
Yarraman Cr. 139 26 46 S 152 1 E
Yarranvale 139 26 50 S 145 20 E
Yarras 141 31 25 S 152 20 E
Yarrawonga 141 36 0 S 146 0 E
Yarrow 35 55 32N 3 0W
Yarrowee, R. 140 38 18 S 144 30 E
Yarto 140 35 28 S 142 16 E
Yartsevo 77 60 20N 90 0 E
Yarumal 174 6 58N 75 24W
Yaselda, R. 80 52 26N 25 30 E
Yashi 121 12 23N 7 54 E
Yashiro-Jima 110 33 55N 132 15 E
Yasin 95 36 24N 73 15 E
Yasinovataya 82 48 7N 37 57 E
Yasinski, L. 150 53 16N 77 35W
Yasnogorsk 81 54 32N 37 38 E
Yasothon 100 15 50N 104 10 E
Yass 141 34 49 S 148 54 E
Yasugi 110 35 26N 133 15 E
Yas'ur 90 32 54N 35 10 E
Yatagan 69 37 20N 28 10 E
Yate 28 51 32N 2 26W
Yates Center 159 37 53N 95 45W
Yates Pt. 143 44 29 S 167 49 E
Yathkyed L. 153 62 40N 98 0W
Yathong 141 32 37 S 145 33 E
Yatsuo 111 36 34N 137 8 E
Yatsushiro 110 32 30N 130 40 E
Yatsushiro-Kai 110 32 30N 130 25 E
Yatta 90 31 27N 35 6 E
Yatta Plat. 126 2 0 S 38 0 E
Yattah 90 31 27N 35 6 E
Yatton 28 51 23N 2 50W
Yauyos 174 12 10 S 75 50W
Yaval 96 21 10N 75 42 E
Yavan 85 38 19N 69 2 E
Yavari R. 174 4 50 S 72 0W
Yavorov 80 49 55N 23 20 E
Yawatahama 110 33 27N 132 24 E
Yawri B. 120 8 22N 13 0W
Yaxley 29 52 31N 0 14W
Yazagyo 98 23 30N 94 6 E
Yazd (Yezd) 93 31 55N 54 27 E
Yazdan 93 33 30N 60 50 E
Yazoo City 159 32 48N 90 28W
Yazoo, R. 159 32 35N 90 50W
Ybbs 52 48 12N 15 4 E
Yding Skovhøj 75 55 59N 9 46 E
Yea 141 37 14 S 145 26 E
Yealering 137 32 36 S 117 36 E
Yealmpton 30 50 21N 4 0W
Yearinan 141 31 10 S 149 11 E
Yebbi-Souma 119 21 7N 17 54 E
Yebbigué 119 22 30N 17 30 E
Yebel Jarris Tighzert, O. 118 28 10N 9 37W
Yebyu 99 14 15N 98 13 E
Yechŏn 107 36 39N 128 27 E
Yecla 59 38 35N 1 5W
Yécora 164 28 20N 108 58W
Yedashe 98 17 24N 95 50 E
Yeddou 118 28 5N 9 2W
Yeeda River 136 17 31 S 123 38 E
Yeelanna 139 34 9 S 135 45 E
Yefremov 81 53 15N 38 3 E
Yegorlyk, R. 83 46 15N 41 30 E
Yegorlykskaya 83 46 5N 40 35 E
Yegoryevsk 81 55 27N 38 55 E
Yegros 172 26 20 S 56 25W
Yehchih 108 27 39N 99 0 E
Yehsien 106 33 37N 113 20 E
Yehud 90 32 3N 34 53 E
Yehuda, Midbar 90 31 35N 34 57 E
Yei 123 4 3N 30 40 E
Yei, Nahr 123 5 50N 30 20 E
Yelan 81 50 55N 43 43 E
Yelan Kolenovski 81 51 16N 40 45 E
Yelandur 97 12 6N 77 0 E
Yelanskoye 77 61 25N 128 0 E
Yelarbon 139 28 33 S 150 49 E
Yelatma 81 55 0N 41 52 E
Yelets 81 52 40N 38 30 E
Yelimané 120 15 9N 22 49 E
Yell, I. 36 60 35N 1 5W
Yell Sd. 36 60 33N 1 15W
Yellamanchilli (Elamanchili) 96 17 26N 82 50 E
Yellow Sea 105 35 0N 123 0 E
Yellowdine 137 31 17 S 119 40 E
Yellowhead P. 152 52 53N 118 25W
Yellowknife 152 62 27N 114 21W
Yellowknife, R. 152 62 31N 114 19W
Yellowstone L. 160 44 30N 110 20W
Yellowstone National Park 160 44 35N 110 0W
Yellowstone, R. 158 46 35N 105 45W
Yelnya 80 54 35N 33 15 E
Yelsk 80 51 50N 29 3 E
Yelvertoft 138 20 13 S 138 53 E
Yelwa 122 10 49N 8 41 E
Yemanzhelinsk 84 54 58N 61 18 E
Yemen ■ 91 15 0N 44 0 E
Yemen, South ■ 74 15 0N 48 0 E
Yen Bai 100 21 42N 104 52 E
Yenakiyevo 82 48 15N 38 5 E
Yenan 106 36 42N 109 25 E
Yenangyaung 98 20 30N 95 0 E
Yenanma 98 19 46N 96 48 E
Yenchang 106 36 44N 110 2 E
Yench'eng, Honan, China 106 33 37N 114 0 E
Yench'eng, Kiangsu, China 107 33 24N 120 10 E
Yench'i 105 42 4N 86 34 E
Yenchi 107 42 53N 129 31 E
Yench'ih 106 37 47N 107 24 E
Yenchihsien 107 42 46N 129 24 E
Yenchin 108 28 4N 104 14 E
Yench'ing 106 40 28N 115 58 E
Yenching 108 29 7N 98 33 E
Yenchou 105 35 40N 116 50 E
Yench'uan 106 36 52N 110 11 E
Yenda 141 34 13 S 146 14 E
Yendéré 120 10 12N 4 59W
Yendi 121 9 29N 0 1W
Yenfeng 108 25 52N 101 5 E
Yenho 108 28 35N 108 28 E
Yenhsing 108 25 22N 101 44 E
Yenisaia 68 41 1N 24 57 E
Yenisey, R. 76 68 0N 86 30 E
Yeniseysk 77 58 39N 92 4 E
Yeniseyskiy Zaliv 76 72 20N 81 0 E
Yenne 45 45 43N 5 44 E
Yenotyevka 83 47 15N 47 0 E
Yenpien 108 26 54N 101 34 E
Yenshan, Hopeh, China 107 38 3N 117 12 E
Yenshan, Yunnan, China 108 23 40N 104 22 E
Yenshou 107 45 27N 128 19 E
Yent'ai 107 37 35N 121 25 E
Yent'ing 108 31 19N 105 20 E
Yenyüan 108 27 25N 101 33 E
Yenyuka 77 58 20N 121 30 E
Yeo, L. 137 28 0 S 124 30 E
Yeo, R. 28 51 1N 2 46W
Yeola 96 20 0N 74 30 E
Yeotmal 96 20 20N 78 15 E
Yeoval 141 32 41 S 148 39 E
Yeovil 28 50 57N 2 38W
Yepes 56 39 55N 3 39W
Yeppoon 138 23 5 S 150 47 E
Yeráki 69 37 0N 22 42 E
Yerbogachen 77 61 16N 108 0 E
Yerevan 83 40 10N 44 20 E
Yerilla 137 29 24 S 121 47 E
Yerington 163 38 59N 119 10W
Yerla, R. 96 17 35N 74 30 E
Yermakovo 77 52 35N 126 20 E
Yermo 163 34 58N 116 50W
Yermolayevo 78 52 58N 56 12 E
Yerofey Pavlovich 77 54 0N 122 0 E
Yerseke 47 51 29N 4 3 E
Yershov 81 51 15N 48 27 E
Yerūshalayim 90 31 47N 35 10 E
Yerville 42 49 40N 0 53 E
Yes Tor, Mt. 30 50 41N 3 59W
Yesagyo 98 21 38N 95 14 E
Yesan 107 36 41N 126 51 E
Yeşilirmak 82 41 0N 36 40 E
Yeso 159 34 29N 104 87W
Yessentuki 83 44 0N 42 45 E
Yeste 59 38 22N 2 19W
Yeu, I. d' 42 46 42N 2 20W
Yevlakh 83 40 39N 47 7 E
Yevpatoriya 82 45 15N 33 20 E
Yevstratovskiy 81 50 11N 39 2 E
Yeya, R. 83 46 40N 39 0 E
Yeysk Staro 82 46 40N 38 12 E
Yhati 172 25 45 S 56 35W
Yhú 173 25 0 S 56 0W
Yi, R. 172 33 7 S 57 8W
Yialí, I. 69 36 41N 27 11 E
Yiáltra 69 38 51N 22 59 E
Yianisádhes, I. 69 35 20N 26 10 E
Yiannitsa 68 40 46N 22 24 E
Yibal 91 22 10N 56 8 E
Yidhá 68 40 35N 22 53 E
Yinchiang 108 27 58N 108 20 E
Yinch'uan 105 38 30N 106 20 E
Yindarlgooda, L. 137 30 40 S 121 52 E
Ying Ho, R. 109 32 30N 116 32 E
Yingch'eng 109 30 55N 113 33 E
Yingchiang 108 24 48N 98 5 E
Yinghsien 106 39 36N 113 12 E
Yingk'ou 107 40 38N 122 30 E
Yingp'an, Chiang, G. 108 21 20N 109 30 E
Yingp'anshan 108 27 56N 105 34 E
Yingshan, Hupeh, China 109 31 37N 113 46 E
Yingshan, Hupeh, China 109 30 50N 115 45 E
Yingshan, Szechwan, China 108 31 6N 106 35 E
Yingshang 109 32 36N 116 16 E
Yingtan 105 28 12N 117 0 E
Yingte 109 24 10N 113 24 E
Yinkanie 140 34 22 S 140 17 E
Yinmabin 99 22 10N 94 55 E
Yinnietharra 137 24 39 S 116 12 E
Yioúra, I. 68 39 23N 24 10 E
Yipang 101 22 15N 101 26 E
Yirga Alem 124 6 34N 38 29 E
Yíthion 69 36 46N 22 34 E
Yizre'el 90 32 34N 35 19 E
Ylitornio 74 66 19N 23 39 E
Ylivieska 74 64 4N 24 28 E
Yngaren 73 58 50N 16 35 E
Ynykchanskiy 77 60 15N 137 43 E
Yoakum 159 29 20N 97 10W
Yobuko 110 33 32N 129 54 E
Yog Pt. 103 13 55N 124 20 E
Yogyakarta 103 7 49 S 110 22 E
Yoho Nat. Park 152 51 25N 116 30W
Yojoa, L. de 166 14 53N 88 0W
Yŏju 107 37 20N 127 35 E
Yokadouma 124 3 35N 14 50 E
Yōkaichi 111 35 6N 136 12 E
Yōkaichiba 111 35 42N 140 33 E
Yokkaichi 111 35 0N 136 30 E
Yoko 121 5 50N 12 20 E
Yokohama 111 35 27N 139 39 E
Yokosuka 111 35 20N 139 40 E
Yokote 112 39 20N 140 30 E
Yola 121 9 10N 12 29 E
Yolaina, Cordillera de 166 11 30N 84 0W
Yom Mae Nam 101 15 15N 100 20 E
Yonago 110 35 25N 133 19 E
Yŏnan 107 37 55N 126 11 E
Yonezawa 112 37 57N 140 4 E
Yong Peng 101 2 0N 103 3 E
Yong Sata 101 7 8N 99 41 E
Yongampo 107 39 56N 124 23 E
Yŏngchon 107 35 58N 128 56 E
Yŏngdŏk 107 36 24N 129 22 E
Yŏngdŭngpo 107 37 31N 126 54 E
Yŏnghŭng 107 39 31N 127 18 E
Yŏngju 107 36 50N 128 40 E
Yŏngwŏl 107 37 11N 128 28 E
Yonibana 120 8 30N 12 19W
Yonker 153 52 40N 109 40W
Yonkers 162 40 57N 73 51W
Yonne □ 43 47 50N 3 40 E
Yonne, R. 43 48 23N 2 58 E
Yonov 121 7 8N 8 42 E
Yoqueam 90 32 40N 35 6 E
York, Austral. 137 31 52 S 116 47 E
York, U.K. 33 53 58N 1 7W
York, Ala., U.S.A. 157 32 30N 88 18W
York, Nebr., U.S.A. 158 40 55N 97 35W
York, Pa., U.S.A. 162 39 57N 76 43W
York, C. 138 10 42 S 142 31 E
York Factory 153 57 0N 92 18W
York Haven 162 40 7N 76 46W
York, Kap 12 75 55N 66 25W
York, R. 162 37 15N 76 23W
York Sd. 136 14 50 S 125 5 E
York, Vale of 23 54 15N 1 25W
Yorke Pen. 140 34 50 S 137 40 E
Yorkshire Wolds 33 54 0N 0 30W
Yorkton 153 51 11N 102 28W
Yorktown, Tex., U.S.A. 159 29 0N 97 29W

**Yorktown** **Zell**


Yorktown, Va., U.S.A. **162** 37 14N 76 30W
Yornup **137** 34 2S 116 10E
Yoro **166** 15 9N 87 7W
Yosemite National Park **163** 38 0N 119 30W
Yosemite Village **163** 37 45N 119 35W
Yoshii **110** 33 16N 129 46E
Yoshimatsu **110** 32 0N 130 47E
Yoshkar Ola **81** 56 49N 47 10E
Yŏsu **107** 34 47N 127 45E
Youanmi **137** 28 37S 118 49E
Youbou **152** 48 53N 124 13W
Youghal **39** 51 58N 7 51W
Youghal B. **39** 51 55N 7 50W
Youkounkoun **120** 12 35N 13 11W
Young, Austral. **141** 34 19S 148 18E
Young, Can. **153** 51 47N 105 45W
Young, Uruguay **172** 32 44S 57 36W
Young, U.S.A. **161** 34 9N 110 56W
Young Ra. **143** 44 10S 169 30E
Younghusband, L. **140** 30 50S 136 5E
Younghusband Pen. **140** 36 0S 139 25E
Youngstown, Can. **153** 51 35N 111 10W
Youngstown, U.S.A. **156** 41 7N 80 41W
Youssoufia **118** 32 16N 8 31W
Yoweragabbie **137** 28 14S 117 39E
Yowrie **141** 36 17S 149 46E
Yoxall **28** 52 45N 1 49W
Yoxford **29** 52 16N 1 30E
Yozgat **92** 39 51N 34 47E
Ypané, R. **172** 23 29S 57 19W
Yport **42** 49 45N 0 15E
Ypres **47** 50 50N 2 52E
Ypsilanti **156** 42 18N 83 40W
Yreka **160** 41 44N 122 40W
Ysabel Chan. **135** 2 0S 150 0E
Ysbyty Ystwyth **31** 52 20N 3 50W
Ysleta **161** 31 45N 106 24W
Yssingeaux **45** 45 9N 4 8E
Ystad **73** 55 26N 13 50E
Ystalyfera **31** 51 46N 3 48W
Ystradgynlais **31** 51 47N 3 45W
Ystwyth, R. **31** 52 24N 4 2W
Ythan, R. **37** 57 26N 2 12W
Ytre Adal **71** 60 15N 10 14E
Ytterhogdal **72** 62 12N 14 56E
Ytyk-Kel **77** 62 20N 133 28E
Yü Chiang, R., China **105** 22 50N 108 6E
Yü Chiang, R., China **108** 22 50N 108 6E
Yu Shui, R. **108** 28 37N 110 23E
Yüan Chiang, R. **109** 29 0N 111 50E
Yüan Chiang, R (Hong.) **108** 29 12N 111 43E
Yüanan **109** 31 3N 111 34E
Yüanchiang, Hünan, China **109** 28 50N 112 23E
Yüanchiang, Yunnan, China **108** 23 40N 102 0E
Yüanch'ü **106** 35 18N 111 41E
Yüanli **109** 24 27N 120 39E
Yüanlin **109** 23 45N 120 30E
Yuanling **109** 28 30N 110 5E
Yüanmou **108** 25 42N 101 32E
Yuanyang **108** 23 10N 102 58E
Yüanyang **108** 35 3N 113 57E
Yuat, R. **135** 4 10S 143 52E
Yuba City **160** 39 12N 121 37W
Yūbari **112** 43 4N 141 59E
Yūbetsu **112** 43 13N 144 5E
Yucatán □ **165** 21 30N 86 30W
Yucatán Basin **14** 20 0N 84 0W
Yucatán Channel **166** 22 0N 86 30W
Yucca **161** 34 56N 114 6W
Yucca Valley **163** 34 8N 116 30W
Yücha **108** 26 55N 101 24E
Yucheng **106** 36 55N 116 40E
Yüch'i **108** 24 25N 102 35E
Yuch'i **109** 26 10N 118 11E
Yüchiang **109** 28 24N 116 53E
Yüch'ien **109** 30 12N 119 24E
Yüch'ing **108** 27 13N 107 54E
Yudino **76** 55 10N 67 55E
Yüehhsi, Anhwei, China **109** 30 54N 116 22E
Yüehhsi, Szechwan, China **108** 28 36N 102 35E
Yüehyang **109** 29 20N 113 7E
Yuendumu **136** 22 16S 131 49E
Yufu-Dake **110** 33 17N 131 33E
Yugoslavia ■ **66** 44 0N 20 0E
Yühsien **106** 34 10N 113 30E
Yuhsien, Hunan, China **109** 27 2N 113 20E
Yuhsien, Shansi, China **106** 38 5N 113 24E
Yühuan Tao, I. **109** 28 5N 121 15E
Yukan **109** 28 43N 116 35E
Yukhnov **80** 54 44N 35 15E
Yūki **111** 36 18N 139 53E
Yukon □ **147** 63 0N 135 0W
Yukon, R. **147** 65 30N 150 0W
Yukti **77** 63 20N 105 0E
Yukuhashi **110** 33 44N 130 59E
Yule, R. **136** 20 24S 118 12E
Yuli **122** 9 44N 10 12E
Yülin **100** 18 10N 109 31E
Yulin, Guangdong, China **109** 22 36N 110 7E
Yulin, Shensi, China **105** 38 15N 109 30E
Yuma, Ariz., U.S.A. **161** 32 45N 114 37W
Yuma, Colo., U.S.A. **158** 40 10N 102 43W
Yuma, B. de **167** 18 20N 68 35W
Yumali **140** 35 32S 139 45E
Yumbe **126** 3 28N 31 15E
Yumbi **126** 1 12S 26 15E
Yumbo **174** 3 35N 76 28W
Yümenhsien **105** 40 17N 97 12E
Yün Ho **107** 33 16N 118 45E
Yun Ho **109** 35 0N 117 0E
Yuna **137** 28 20S 115 0E
Yünan **109** 23 14N 111 31E
Yunaska I. **147** 52 40N 170 40W
Yünch'eng, Shansi, China **106** 35 1N 110 59E
Yünch'eng, Shantung, China **106** 35 35N 115 56E
Yunfou **109** 22 56N 112 2E
Yungan **109** 25 50N 117 25E
Yungas **174** 17 0S 66 0W
Yungay **172** 37 10S 72 5W
Yungch'eng **106** 33 56N 116 22E
Yungchi **106** 34 52N 110 26E
Yungch'ing **106** 39 19N 116 29E
Yungch'uan **108** 20 22N 105 52E
Yungch'un **109** 25 19N 118 17E
Yungfeng **109** 27 20N 115 27E
Yungfu **109** 24 59N 109 59E
Yungho **106** 36 44N 110 39E
Yunghsin **109** 16 55N 114 18E
Yunghsing **109** 26 8N 113 6E
Yunghsiu **109** 29 8N 115 42E
Yungjen **108** 26 4N 101 42E
Yungk'ang, Chekiang, China **109** 28 53N 120 2E
Yungk'ang, Kwangsi Chuang Aut. Region, China **108** 22 48N 107 51E
Yungnien **106** 36 49N 114 33E
Yungning, Kwangsi Chuang A. R., China **108** 22 45N 108 29E
Yungning, Ningsia Hui A. R., China **106** 38 18N 106 18E
Yungning, Yunnan, China **108** 27 50N 100 40E
Yungningchai **106** 36 35N 108 51E
Yungp'ing **108** 25 25N 99 36E
Yungshan **108** 28 11N 103 35E
Yungsheng **108** 26 42N 100 45E
Yungshun, Hunan, China **108** 29 3N 109 50E
Yungshun, Kwangsi Chuang, China **108** 22 48N 108 55E
Yungt'ai **109** 25 52N 118 55E
Yungteng **106** 36 44N 103 24E
Yungting **109** 24 49N 116 46E
Yunho = Lishui **109** 28 6N 119 34E
Yünhsi **109** 33 0N 110 22E
Yünhsiao **109** 24 1N 117 15E
Yünhsien, Hupeh, China **105** 32 50N 110 53E
Yünhsien, Yunnan, China **108** 24 25N 100 6E
Yünlin **109** 23 42N 120 31E
Yunling Shan, mts. **108** 28 30N 98 50E
Yunlung **99** 25 50N 99 25E
Yünmeng **109** 31 1N 113 39E
Yunnan □ **108** 25 0N 102 30E
Yunndaga **137** 29 45S 121 0E
Yunomae **110** 32 12N 130 59E
Yunotso **110** 35 5N 132 21E
Yunquera de Henares **58** 40 47N 3 11W
Yunta **140** 32 34S 139 36E
Yünyang **108** 30 55N 108 56E
Yüp'ing **108** 27 14N 108 54E
Yupyongdong **107** 41 49N 128 53E
Yur **77** 59 52N 137 49E
Yurga **76** 55 42N 84 51E
Yuria **84** 59 22N 54 10E
Yuribei **76** 71 20N 76 30E
Yurimaguas **174** 5 55S 76 0W
Yurya **81** 59 1N 49 13E
Yuryev Polskiy **81** 56 30N 59 47E
Yuryevets **81** 57 25N 43 2E
Yuryuzan **84** 54 27N 58 28E
Yuscarán **166** 13 58N 86 51W
Yusha, Jebel **90** 32 4N 35 41E
Yüshan **109** 28 40N 118 15E
Yüshanchen **108** 29 31N 108 25E
Yushe **106** 37 4N 112 58E
Yüshu **105** 33 1N 96 44E
Yushu **107** 44 46N 126 34E
Yüt'ai **106** 35 2N 116 40E
Yüt'ien **107** 39 53N 117 45E
Yütu **109** 26 0N 115 24E
Yütz'u **106** 37 42N 112 44E
Yüwang **106** 37 9N 106 28E
Yuyang **108** 28 44N 108 46E
Yüyang **109** 30 12N 119 56E
Yüyao **109** 30 3N 121 9E
Yüyao **109** 30 0N 121 20E
Yuyu **105** 40 20N 112 30E
Yuyü **106** 40 10N 112 25E
Yüyuan **109** 28 9N 121 11E
Yuzha **81** 56 40N 42 10E
Yuzhno-Sakhalinsk **77** 47 5N 142 5E
Yuzhno-Surkhanskoye Vodokhranilishehe **85** 37 53N 67 42E
Yuzhno-Uralsk **84** 54 26N 61 15E
Yuzhnyy Ural, mts. **84** 53 0N 58 0E
Yvelines □ **43** 48 40N 1 45E
Yverdon **50** 46 47N 6 39E
Yvetot **42** 49 37N 0 44E
Yvonand **50** 46 48N 6 44E


# Z


Za, O. **118** 34 5N 2 30W
Zaalayskiy Khrebet **85** 39 20N 73 0E
Zaamslag **47** 51 19N 3 55E
Zaan, R. **46** 52 25N 4 52E
Zaandam **47** 52 26N 4 49E
Zab, Monts du **119** 34 55N 5 0E
Zabalj, Yugo. **66** 45 21N 20 5E
Zabalj, Yugo. **66** 45 23N 20 5E
Zabari **66** 44 22N 21 15E
Zabarjad **122** 23 40N 36 12E
Zabaykalskiy **77** 49 40N 117 10E
Zabkowice Slaskie **54** 50 22N 19 17E
Zabljak **66** 42 19N 19 10E
Zabludow **54** 53 0N 23 19E
Zabno **54** 50 9N 20 53E
Zābol **93** 31 0N 61 25E
Zābolī **93** 27 10N 61 35E
Zabré **121** 11 12N 0 36W
Zabrze **54** 50 24N 18 50E
Zacapa **166** 14 59N 89 31W
Zacapu **164** 19 50N 101 43W
Zacatecas **164** 22 49N 102 34W
Zacatecas □ **164** 23 30N 103 0W
Zacatecolua **166** 13 29N 88 51W
Zacaultipán **165** 20 39N 98 36W
Zacoalco **164** 20 10N 103 40W
Zadar **63** 44 8N 15 8E
Zadawa **121** 11 33N 10 19E
Zadetkyi Kyun **101** 10 0N 98 25E
Zadonsk **81** 52 25N 38 56E
Zafed **90** 32 58N 35 29E
Zafora, I. **69** 36 5N 26 24E
Zafra **57** 38 26N 6 30W
Zagan **54** 51 39N 15 22E
Zagazig **122** 30 40N 31 12E
Zaghouan **119** 36 23N 10 10E
Zaglivérion **68** 40 36N 23 15E
Zaglou **118** 27 17N 0 3W
Zagnanado **121** 7 18N 2 28E
Zagorá **68** 39 27N 23 6E
Zagora **118** 30 14N 5 51W
Zagórów **54** 52 10N 17 54E
Zagorsk **81** 56 20N 38 10E
Zagórz **54** 49 30N 22 14E
Zagreb **63** 45 50N 16 0E
Zāgros, Kudha-ye **93** 33 45N 47 0E
Zagubica **66** 44 15N 21 47E
Zaguinaso **120** 10 1N 6 14W
Zāhedān **93** 29 30N 60 50E
Zahirabad **96** 17 43N 77 37E
Zahlah **92** 33 52N 35 50E
Zahna **48** 51 54N 12 47E
Zahrez Chergui **118** 35 0N 3 30E
Zahrez Rharbi **118** 34 50N 2 55E
Zailiyskiy Alatau, Khrebet **85** 43 5N 77 0E
Zainsk **84** 55 18N 52 4E
Zaïr **118** 29 47N 5 51W
Zaïre, R. **124** 1 30N 28 0E
Zaïre, Rep. of ■ **124** 3 0S 23 0E
Zaječar **66** 43 53N 22 18E
Zakamensk **77** 50 23N 103 17E
Zakariya **90** 31 43N 34 57E
Zakataly **83** 41 38N 46 35E
Zakavkazye **83** 42 0N 44 0E
Zakhu **92** 37 10N 42 50E
Zákinthos **69** 37 47N 20 54E
Zákinthos, I. **69** 37 45N 27 45E
Zakopane **54** 49 18N 19 57E
Zala □ **53** 46 42N 16 50E
Zala, R. **53** 46 53N 17 6E
Zalaegerszeg **53** 46 53N 16 47E
Zalakomár **53** 46 33N 17 10E
Zalalövö **53** 46 51N 16 35E
Zalamea de la Serena **57** 38 40N 5 38W
Zalamea la Real **57** 37 41N 6 38W
Zalau **121** 10 30N 8 58E
Zalazna **84** 58 39N 52 31E
Zalec **63** 46 16N 15 10E
Zaleshchiki **82** 48 45N 25 45E
Zalewo **54** 53 55N 19 41E
Zalingei **117** 13 5N 23 10E
Zaltan, Jabal **119** 28 46N 19 45E
Zaltbommel **46** 51 48N 5 15E
Zalǔ **121** 47 12N 23 5E
Zambeke **126** 2 8N 25 17E
Zambèze, R. **127** 18 46S 36 16E
Zambezi, R. **127** 18 46S 36 16E
Zambezia □ **127** 16 15S 37 30E
Zambia ■ **125** 15 0S 28 0E
Zamboanga **103** 6 59N 122 3E
Zambrano **174** 9 45N 74 49W
Zametchino **81** 53 30N 42 30E
Zamora, Mexico **164** 20 0N 102 21W
Zamora, Spain **56** 41 30N 5 45W
Zamora □ **56** 41 30N 5 46W
Zamość **54** 50 50N 23 22E
Zamuro, Sierra del **174** 4 0N 62 30W
Zamzam, W. **119** 31 0N 14 30E
Zan **121** 9 26N 0 17W
Zanaga **124** 2 48S 13 48E
Záncara, R. **58** 39 20N 3 0W
Zandvoort **46** 52 22N 4 32E
Zanesville **156** 39 56N 82 2W
Zangue, R. **127** 18 5S 35 10E
Zanjan **92** 36 40N 48 35E
Zannone, I. **64** 40 38N 13 2E
Zante = Zákinthos **69** 37 47N 20 54E
Zanthus **137** 31 2S 123 34E
Zanzibar **126** 6 12S 39 12E
Zanzibar I. **126** 6 12S 39 12E
Zanzūr **119** 32 55N 13 1E
Zaouatalaz **119** 24 57N 8 16E
Zaouiet El Kahla **119** 27 10N 6 40E
Zaouiet Reggane **118** 26 32N 0 3E
Zapadna Morava, R. **66** 43 50N 20 15E
Zapadnaya Dvina **80** 56 15N 32 3E
Západné Beskydy **54** 49 30N 19 0E
Zapadočesky □ **52** 49 35N 13 0E
Západoslovenský □ **53** 48 30N 17 30E
Zapala **176** 39 0S 70 5W
Zapaleri, Cerro **172** 22 49S 67 11W
Zapata **159** 26 56N 92 17W
Zapatón, R. **57** 39 0N 6 49W
Zaporozhye **82** 47 50N 35 10E
Zapponeta **65** 41 27N 15 57E
Zara **92** 39 58N 37 43E
Zaragoza, Colomb. **174** 7 30N 74 52W
Zaragoza, Coahuila, Mexico **164** 28 30N 101 0W
Zaragoza, Nuevo León, Mexico **165** 24 0N 99 36W
Zaragoza, Spain **58** 41 39N 0 53W
Zaragoza □ **58** 41 35N 1 0W
Zarand **93** 30 46N 56 34E
Zarasai **80** 55 40N 26 12E
Zarate **172** 34 7S 59 0W
Zaraysk **81** 54 48N 38 53E
Zaraza **174** 9 21N 65 19W
Zarembo I. **152** 56 20N 132 50W
Zari **73** 13 8N 12 37E
Zaria **121** 11 0N 7 40E
Zarisberge **128** 24 30S 16 15E
Zarki **54** 50 38N 19 21E
Zarnów **54** 51 16N 20 9E
Zarnuqa **90** 31 53N 34 47E
Zarów **54** 50 56N 16 29E
Zarqa, R. **90** 32 10N 35 37E
Zaruma **174** 3 40S 79 30W
Zary **54** 51 37N 15 10E
Zarza de Alange **57** 38 49N 6 13W
Zarza de Granadilla **56** 40 14N 6 3W
Zarza, La **57** 37 42N 6 51W
Zarzaïtine **119** 28 32N 9 5E
Zarzal **174** 4 24N 76 4W
Zarzis **119** 33 31N 11 2E
Zas **56** 43 4N 8 53W
Zashiversk **77** 67 25N 142 40E
Zaskar Mountains **95** 33 15N 77 30E
Zaskar, R. **95** 33 55N 77 2E
Zastron **128** 30 18S 27 7E
Zatec **52** 50 20N 13 32E
Zator **54** 49 59N 19 28E
Zavala **66** 42 50N 17 59E
Zavareh **93** 33 35N 52 28E
Zaventem **47** 50 53N 4 28E
Zavetnoye **83** 47 13N 43 50E
Zavidovići **66** 44 27N 18 13E
Zavitinsk **77** 50 10N 129 20E
Zavodoski, I. **13** 56 0S 27 45W
Zavolzhye **81** 56 37N 43 18E
Zawadzkie **54** 50 37N 18 28E
Zawidów **54** 51 1N 15 1E
Zawiercie **54** 50 30N 19 13E
Zâwyet Shammâs **122** 31 30N 26 37E
Zâwyet Um el Rakham **122** 31 18N 27 1E
Zâwyet Ungeila **122** 31 23N 26 42E
Zayandeh, R. **93** 32 35N 32 0E
Zayarsk **77** 56 20N 102 55E
Zaysan **76** 47 28N 84 52E
Zaysan, Oz. **76** 48 0N 83 0E
Zãzamt, W. **119** 30 29N 14 30E
Zazir, O. **119** 22 0N 5 40E
Zázrivá **53** 49 16N 19 7E
Zbarazh **80** 49 43N 25 44E
Zbaszyn **54** 52 14N 15 56E
Zbaszynek **54** 52 16N 15 51E
Zblewo **54** 53 56N 18 19E
Zdandijk **46** 52 82N 4 49E
Zdolbunov **80** 50 30N 26 15E
Zdrelo **66** 44 16N 21 28E
Zdunska Wola **54** 51 37N 18 59E
Zduny **54** 51 39N 17 21E
Zeballos **152** 49 59N 126 50W
Zebediela **129** 24 20S 29 17E
Zedelgem **47** 51 8N 3 8E
Zeebrugge **47** 51 19N 3 12E
Zeehan **138** 41 52S 145 25E
Zeeland **47** 51 41N 5 40E
Zeeland □ **47** 51 30N 3 50E
Ze'elim **90** 31 13N 34 32E
Zeelst **47** 51 25N 5 25E
Zeerust **128** 25 31S 26 4E
Zefat **90** 32 58N 35 29E
Zegdou **118** 29 51N 4 53W
Zege **123** 11 43N 37 18E
Zegelsem **47** 50 49N 3 43E
Zegoua **120** 10 32N 5 35W
Zehdenick **48** 52 59N 13 20E
Zeil, Mt. **136** 23 24S 132 23E
Zeila **91** 11 15N 43 30E
Zeist **46** 52 5N 5 15E
Zeita **90** 32 23N 35 2E
Zeitz **48** 51 3N 12 9E
Zele **47** 51 4N 4 2E
Zelendolsk **81** 55 55N 48 30E
Zelengora, mts. **66** 43 22N 18 30E
Zelenika **66** 42 27N 18 37E
Zelenogradsk **80** 54 53N 20 29E
Zelenokumsk **83** 44 30N 44 1E
Zelenovski **83** 48 6N 50 45E
Zelhem **47** 52 0N 6 21E
Zell **49** 47 42N 7 50E

|  | | | | |  | | | | |
|---|---|---|---|---|---|---|---|---|---|
| Zell am See | 52 | 47 19N | 12 47 E | | Zhuantobe | 85 | 43 43N | 78 18 E | |
| Zella Mehlis | 48 | 50 40N | 10 41 E | | Zhukovka | 80 | 53 35N | 33 50 E | |
| Zelouane | 86 | 35 1N | 2 58W | | Zhupanovo | 77 | 51 59N | 15 9 E | |
| Zelzate | 47 | 51 13N | 3 47 E | | Ziarat | 94 | 30 25N | 67 30 E | |
| Zémio | 126 | 5 2N | 25 5 E | | Zichem | 47 | 51 2N | 4 59 E | |
| Zemmora | 118 | 35 44N | 0 51 E | | Ziebice | 54 | 50 37N | 17 2 E | |
| Zemora, I. | 119 | 37 5N | 10 56 E | | Ziel, Mt. | 136 | 23 20 S | 132 30 E | |
| Zemoul, W. | 118 | 29 15N | 7 30W | | Zielona Góra | 54 | 51 57N | 15 31 E | |
| Zemst | 47 | 50 59N | 4 28 E | | Zielona Góra □ | 54 | 51 57N | 15 30 E | |
| Zemun | 66 | 44 51N | 20 25 E | | Zierikzee | 47 | 51 40N | 3 55 E | |
| Zenica | 66 | 44 10N | 17 57 E | | Ziesar | 48 | 52 16N | 12 19 E | |
| Zenina | 118 | 34 30N | 2 37 E | | Zifta | 122 | 30 43N | 31 14 E | |
| Zentsūji | 110 | 34 14N | 133 47 E | | Zigazinskiy | 84 | 53 50N | 57 20 E | |
| Zepce | 66 | 44 28N | 18 2 E | | Zigey | 117 | 14 50N | 15 50 E | |
| Zeravshan | 85 | 39 10N | 68 39 E | | Ziguinchor | 120 | 12 25N | 16 20W | |
| Zeravshan, R. | 85 | 39 32N | 63 45 E | | Zihuatanejo | 164 | 17 38N | 101 33W | |
| Zeravshanskiy, Khrebet | 85 | 39 20N | 69 0 E | | Zikhron Ya'Aqov | 90 | 32 34N | 34 56 E | |
| Zerbst | 48 | 51 59N | 12 8 E | | Zile | 92 | 40 15N | 36 0 E | |
| Zerhamra | 118 | 29 58N | 2 30W | | Zilfi | 92 | 26 12N | 44 52 E | |
| Zerków | 54 | 52 4N | 17 32 E | | Zilina | 53 | 49 12N | 18 42 E | |
| Zermatt | 50 | 46 2N | 7 46 E | | Zillah | 119 | 28 40N | 17 41 E | |
| Zernez | 51 | 46 42N | 10 7 E | | Zillertaler Alpen | 52 | 47 6N | 11 45 E | |
| Zernograd | 83 | 46 52N | 40 11 E | | Zima | 77 | 54 0N | 102 5 E | |
| Zeroud, O. | 119 | 35 30N | 9 30 E | | Zimane, Adrar in | 118 | 22 10N | 4 30 E | |
| Zerqani | 68 | 41 30N | 20 20 E | | Zimapán | 165 | 20 40N | 99 20W | |
| Zestafoni | 83 | 42 6N | 43 0 E | | Zimba | 127 | 17 20 S | 26 25 E | |
| Zetel | 48 | 53 33N | 7 57 E | | Zimbabwe Rhodesia ■ | 127 | 20 16 S | 31 0 E | |
| Zetland (□) | 26 | 60 30N | 0 15W | | Zimovniki | 83 | 47 10N | 42 25 E | |
| Zetten | 46 | 51 56N | 5 44 E | | Zinal | 50 | 46 8N | 7 38 E | |
| Zeulenroda | 48 | 50 39N | 12 0 E | | Zinder | 121 | 13 48N | 9 0 E | |
| Zeven | 48 | 53 17N | 9 19 E | | Zinga | 127 | 9 16 S | 38 41 E | |
| Zevenaar | 46 | 51 56N | 6 5 E | | Zingem | 47 | 50 54N | 3 40 E | |
| Zevenbergen | 47 | 51 38N | 4 37 E | | Zingst | 48 | 54 24N | 12 45 E | |
| Zévio | 62 | 45 23N | 11 10 E | | Zini, Yebel | 118 | 28 0N | 11 0W | |
| Zeya | 77 | 54 2N | 127 20 E | | Ziniaré | 121 | 12 44N | 1 10W | |
| Zeya, R. | 77 | 53 30N | 127 0 E | | Zinjibar | 91 | 13 5N | 46 0 E | |
| Zeyse | 123 | 5 44N | 37 23W | | Zinkgruvan | 73 | 58 50N | 15 6 E | |
| Zeytin | 92 | 37 53N | 36 53 E | | Zinnowitz | 48 | 54 5N | 13 54 E | |
| Zêzere, R. | 56 | 40 0N | 7 55W | | Zion Nat. Park | 161 | 37 25N | 112 50W | |
| Zgierz | 54 | 51 45N | 19 27 E | | Zipaquirá | 174 | 5 0N | 74 0W | |
| Zgorzelec | 54 | 51 10N | 15 0 E | | Zippori | 90 | 32 64N | 35 16 E | |
| Zhabinka | 80 | 52 13N | 24 2 E | | Zirc | 53 | 47 17N | 17 42 E | |
| Zhailma | 84 | 51 30N | 61 50 E | | Ziri | 63 | 47 17N | 11 14 E | |
| Zhalanash | 85 | 43 3N | 78 38 E | | Zirje, I. | 63 | 43 39N | 15 42 E | |
| Zhamensk | 80 | 54 37N | 21 17 E | | Zirl | 52 | 47 17N | 11 14 E | |
| Zhanadarya | 85 | 44 45N | 64 40 E | | Zisterdorf | 53 | 48 33N | 16 45 E | |
| Zhanatas | 76 | 43 11N | 81 18 E | | Zitácuaro | 164 | 19 20N | 100 30W | |
| Zharkol | 84 | 49 57N | 64 5 E | | Zitava, R. | 53 | 48 14N | 18 21 E | |
| Zharkovskiy | 80 | 55 56N | 32 19 E | | Zitiste | 66 | 45 30N | 2 32 E | |
| Zhashkov | 82 | 49 15N | 30 5 E | | Zitsa | 68 | 39 47N | 20 40 E | |
| Zhdanov | 82 | 47 5N | 37 31 E | | Zittau | 48 | 50 54N | 14 47 E | |
| Zheleznogorsk-Ilimskiy | 77 | 56 34N | 104 8 E | | Zitundo | 129 | 26 48 S | 32 47 E | |
| Zherdevka | 81 | 51 56N | 41 21 E | | Zivinice | 66 | 44 27N | 18 36 E | |
| Zhetykol, Ozero | 84 | 51 2N | 60 54 E | | Ziway, L. | 123 | 8 0N | 38 50 E | |
| Zhigansk | 77 | 66 35N | 124 10 E | | Ziz, Oued | 118 | 31 40N | 4 15W | |
| Zhigulevsk | 81 | 53 28N | 49 45 E | | Zizip | 92 | 37 5N | 37 50 E | |
| Zhirhovsk | 81 | 50 57N | 44 49 E | | Zlarin | 63 | 43 42N | 15 49 E | |
| Zhitomir | 80 | 50 20N | 28 40 E | | Zlatar | 63 | 46 5N | 16 3 E | |
| Zhizdra | 80 | 53 45N | 34 40 E | | Zlataritsa | 67 | 43 2N | 24 55 E | |
| Zhlobin | 80 | 52 55N | 30 0 E | | Zlatibor | 66 | 43 45N | 19 43 E | |
| Zhmerinka | 82 | 49 2N | 28 10 E | | Zlatista | 67 | 42 41N | 24 7 E | |
| Zhodino | 80 | 54 5N | 28 17 E | | Zlatna | 70 | 46 8N | 23 11 E | |
| Zhovtnevoye | 82 | 47 54N | 32 2 E | | Zlatograd | 67 | 41 22N | 25 7 E | |

|  | | | | |  | | | | |
|---|---|---|---|---|---|---|---|---|---|
| Zlatoust | 78 | 55 10N | 59 40 E | | Zuidbroek | 46 | 53 10N | 6 52 E | |
| Zletovo | 66 | 41 59N | 22 17 E | | Zuidelijk-Flevoland | 46 | 52 22N | 5 22 E | |
| Zlitan | 119 | 32 25N | 14 35 E | | Zuidlaarder meer | 46 | 53 8N | 6 42 E | |
| Złocieniec | 54 | 53 30N | 16 1 E | | Zuidland | 46 | 51 49N | 4 15 E | |
| Złoczew | 54 | 51 24N | 18 35 E | | Zuidlaren | 46 | 53 6N | 6 42 E | |
| Zlot | 66 | 44 1N | 22 0 E | | Zuidwolde | 46 | 52 40N | 6 26 E | |
| Złotoryja | 54 | 51 8N | 15 55 E | | Zújar | 59 | 37 34N | 2 50W | |
| Złotów | 54 | 53 22N | 17 2 E | | Zújar, Pantano del | 57 | 38 55N | 5 35W | |
| Złoty Stok | 54 | 50 27N | 16 53 E | | Zújar, R. | 59 | 38 30N | 5 30 E | |
| Zmeinogorsk | 76 | 51 10N | 82 13 E | | Zula | 123 | 15 17N | 39 40 E | |
| Zmigród | 54 | 51 28N | 16 53 E | | Zulia □ | 174 | 10 0N | 72 10W | |
| Zmiyev | 82 | 49 45N | 36 27 E | | Zülpich | 48 | 50 41N | 6 38 E | |
| Znamenka | 82 | 48 45N | 32 30 E | | Zululand | 129 | 43 19N | 2 15W | |
| Znin | 54 | 52 51N | 17 44 E | | Zumaya | 58 | 43 19N | 2 15W | |
| Znojmo | 52 | 48 50N | 16 2 E | | Zumbo | 127 | 15 35 S | 30 26 E | |
| Zoar | 128 | 33 30 S | 21 26 E | | Zummo | 121 | 9 51N | 12 59 E | |
| Zobia | 126 | 3 0N | 25 50 E | | Zumpango | 165 | 19 48N | 99 6W | |
| Zoetermeer | 46 | 52 3N | 4 30 E | | Zundert | 47 | 51 28N | 4 39 E | |
| Zofingen | 50 | 47 17N | 7 56 E | | Zungeru | 121 | 9 48N | 6 8 E | |
| Zogno | 62 | 45 49N | 9 41 E | | Zuni | 161 | 35 7N | 108 57W | |
| Zolder | 47 | 51 1N | 5 19 E | | Zupania | 66 | 45 4N | 18 43 E | |
| Zollikofen | 50 | 47 0N | 7 28 E | | Zur | 66 | 42 13N | 20 34 E | |
| Zollikon | 51 | 47 21N | 8 34 E | | Zura | 84 | 57 36N | 53 24 E | |
| Zolochev | 80 | 49 45N | 24 58 E | | Zūrandului | 70 | 46 14N | 22 7 E | |
| Zolotonosha | 82 | 49 45N | 32 5 E | | Zürich | 51 | 47 22N | 8 32 E | |
| Zomba | 127 | 15 30 S | 35 19 E | | Zürich □ | 51 | 47 26N | 8 40 E | |
| Zombi | 126 | 3 35N | 29 10 E | | Zürichsee | 51 | 47 18N | 8 40 E | |
| Zomergem | 47 | 51 7N | 3 33 E | | Zuromin | 54 | 53 4N | 19 57 E | |
| Zongo | 124 | 4 12N | 18 0 E | | Zuru | 121 | 11 27N | 5 4 E | |
| Zonguldak | 82 | 41 28N | 31 50 E | | Zurzach | 51 | 47 35N | 8 18 E | |
| Zonhoven | 47 | 50 59N | 5 23 E | | Zut, I. | 63 | 43 52N | 15 17 E | |
| Zorgo | 121 | 12 22N | 0 35W | | Zutendaal | 47 | 50 56N | 5 35 E | |
| Zorita | 57 | 39 17N | 5 39W | | Zutphen | 46 | 52 9N | 6 12 E | |
| Zorleni | 70 | 46 14N | 27 44 E | | Zuwárrah | 119 | 32 58N | 12 1 E | |
| Zornitsa | 67 | 42 23N | 26 58 E | | Zuyevka | 84 | 58 27N | 51 10 E | |
| Zorritos | 174 | 3 50 S | 80 40W | | Zuzemberk | 63 | 45 52N | 14 56 E | |
| Zory | 54 | 50 3N | 18 44 E | | Zvenigorodka | 82 | 49 4N | 30 56 E | |
| Zorzor | 120 | 7 46N | 9 28W | | Zverinogolovskoye | 84 | 55 0N | 62 30 E | |
| Zossen | 48 | 52 13N | 13 28 E | | Zvezdets | 67 | 42 6N | 27 26 E | |
| Zottegam | 47 | 50 52N | 3 48 E | | Zvolen | 53 | 48 33N | 19 10 E | |
| Zouar | 119 | 20 30N | 16 32 E | | Zvonce | 66 | 42 57N | 22 34 E | |
| Zouérabe | 116 | 22 35N | 12 30W | | Zvornik | 66 | 44 26N | 19 7 E | |
| Zousfana, O. | 118 | 31 51N | 1 30W | | Zwaag | 46 | 52 40N | 5 4 E | |
| Zoutkamp | 46 | 53 20N | 6 18 E | | Zwanenburg | 46 | 52 23N | 4 45 E | |
| Zqorzelec | 54 | 51 9N | 15 0 E | | Zwarte Meer | 46 | 52 38N | 5 57 E | |
| Zrenjanin | 66 | 45 22N | 20 23 E | | Zwarte Waler | 46 | 52 39N | 6 1 E | |
| Zuarungu | 121 | 10 49N | 0 52W | | Zwartemeer | 46 | 52 43N | 7 2 E | |
| Zuba | 121 | 9 11N | 7 12 E | | Zwartsluis | 46 | 52 39N | 6 4 E | |
| Zubair, Jazâir | 123 | 15 0N | 42 10 E | | Zwedru (Tchien) | 120 | 5 59N | 8 15W | |
| Zubia | 57 | 37 8N | 3 33W | | Zweibrücken | 49 | 49 15N | 7 20 E | |
| Zubtsov | 80 | 56 10N | 34 34 E | | Zwenkau | 48 | 51 13N | 12 19 E | |
| Zueitina | 119 | 30 58N | 20 7 E | | Zwetti | 52 | 48 35N | 15 9 E | |
| Zuénoula | 120 | 7 34N | 6 3W | | Zwickau | 48 | 50 43N | 12 30 E | |
| Zuera | 58 | 41 51N | 0 49W | | Zwijnaarde | 47 | 51 0N | 3 43 E | |
| Zug | 51 | 47 10N | 8 31 E | | Zwijndrecht, Belg. | 47 | 51 13N | 4 20 E | |
| Zug □ | 51 | 47 9N | 8 35 E | | Zwijndrecht, Neth. | 46 | 51 50N | 4 39 E | |
| Zugar | 123 | 14 0N | 42 40 E | | Zwolle | 46 | 52 31N | 6 6 E | |
| Zugdidi | 83 | 42 30N | 41 48 E | | Zymoelz, R. | 152 | 54 33N | 128 31W | |
| Zugersee | 51 | 47 7N | 8 35 E | | Zyrardów | 54 | 52 3N | 20 35 E | |
| Zugspitze | 49 | 47 25N | 10 59 E | | Zywiec | 54 | 44 42N | 19 12 E | |
| Zuid-Holland □ | 46 | 52 0N | 4 35 E | | | | | | |
| Zuid-horn | 46 | 53 15N | 6 23 E | | | | | | |
| Zuidbeveland | 47 | 51 30N | 3 50 E | | | | | | |

# Alternative Spellings

NOTE: The following list gives the principal places where new names or spellings (given first) have been adopted. Earlier forms still in use are cross referenced to the new form. Place names of which the national spelling varies considerably from the English form, e.g. Livorno – Leghorn, are also included.

Aachen, Aix la Chapelle
Aalst: Alost
Abercorn, see Mbala
Åbo, see Turku
Acre, see 'Akko
Adrianople, see Edirne
Affreville, see Khemis Miliana
Agram, see Zagreb
Agrigento: Girgenti
Ahvenanmaa: Åland Is.
Aix la Chapelle, see Aachen
Ain Mokra, see Berrahal
Ain Salah, see In Salah
Ain Touta: MacMahon
'Akko: Acre
Akmolinsk, see Tselinograd
Al Hoceima: Alhucemas, Villa Sanjurjo
Al Khalih: Hebron
Al Khums, see Homs
Al Lādhiqiyah: Latakia
Al Marj: Barce
Al Mawsil: Mosul
Al Mukha: Mocha
Al Qasabat: Cussabat
Al Quds: Jerusalem
Åland Is., see Ahvenanmaa
Alashantsoch'i: Payenhaot'e
Alba Iulia: Karlsburg
Albert, L., see Mobutu Sese Seko, L.
Albertville, see Kalemie
Alcazarquivir, see Ksar el Kebir
Aleppo, see Halab
Alexandretta, see İskenderun
Alexandria, see El Iskandariya
Alhucemas, see Al Hoceima
Allenstein, see Olsztyn
Amraoti: Amravati
An Geata Mór: Binghamstown
An Nhon: Binh Dinh
An Uaimh: Navan
Andulo, see Macedo da Cavaleiros
Ankara: Angora
Annaba: Bône
Annobón, see Pagalu
Antakya: Antioch
Anvers: Antwerp, Antwerpen
Apollonia, see Marsa Susa
Ar Riyād: Riyadh
Arabian Gulf, see Persian G.
Arkhangelsk: Archangel
Arlon: Aarlen
Artemovsk: Bakhmut
Athínai: Athens
Augusto Cardosa: Metangula
Aumale, see Sour el Ghozlane
Auschwitz, see Oswiecim

Bac Lieu, see Vinh Loi
Bagenalstown, see Muine Bheag
Bahia, see Salvador
Baile Átha Cliath: Dublin
Baile Deasmhumhna: Ballydesmond
Bakhmut, see Artemovsk
Bakwanga, see Mbuji-Mayi
Ballydesmond, see Baile Deasmhumhna
Baltiysk: Pillau
Banaras, see Varanasi
Banda Aceh: Kutaradja
Bandar Maharani, see Muar
Bandar Penggarem, see Batu Pahat
Bandundu: Banningville
Banghāzī: Benghazi
Bangladesh: East Pakistan
Banjul: Bathurst
Barce, see Al Marj
Baroda, see Vadodara
Basel: Basle
Basutoland, see Lesotho
Batavia, see Jakarta
Batu Pahat: Bandar Penggarem
Bayan Tumen, see Choybalsan
Béchar: Colomb-Béchar
Bechuanaland Prot. see Botswana
Bedeau, see Ras el Ma
Bejaïa: Bougie
Belém: Pará
Belgard, see Białogard
Belize: British Honduras
Belogorsk: Kuibyshevka Vostochnaya
Benares, see Varanasi
Benghazi: Banghāzī
Benin: Dahomey
Beograd: Belgrade
Berdyansk: Osipenko
Bern: Berne
Berrahal: Ain Mokra
Bezwada, see Vijayawada
Bharat: India

Bharuch: Broach
Bhavnagar: Bhaunagar
Bhilsa, see Vidisha
Białogard: Belgrad
Binghamstown, see An Geata Mór
Binh Dinh, see An Nhon
Bir Mogreïn: Fort Trinquet
Bitola: Monastir
Björneborg, see Pori
Bolzano: Bozen
Bône, see Annaba
Borgå, see Porvoo
Botswana: Bechuanaland Prot.
Bougie, see Bejaïa
Brahestad, see Raahe
Braniewo: Braunsberg
Bratislava: Pressburg
Braunsberg, see Braniewo
Breslau, see Wrocław
Bressanone: Brixen
Brest: Brest Litovsk
British Guiana, see Guyana
British Honduras, see Belize
Brixen, see Bressanone
Brno: Brünn
Broach, see Bharuch
Broken Hill, see Kabwe
Brugge: Bruges
Brunico: Bruneck
Brünn, see Brno
Brusa, see Bursa
Bruxelles: Brussel, Brussels
Bucureşti: Bucharest
Budweis: České Budějovice
Bujumbura: Usumbura
Bukavu: Costermansville
Bunclody: Newtownbarry
Bursa: Brusa

Ca Mau, see Quang Long
Caesarea, see Qesari
Cairo, see El Qàhira
Calicut: Kozhikode
Cambridge: Galt
Candia, see Iráklion
Canton, see Kuangchou
Caporetto, see Kobarid
Caribrod, see Dimitrovgrad
Carlsbad, see Karlovy Vary
Carmona: Uíge
Cattaro, see Kotor
Cawnpore, see Kanpur
Ceanannus Mór: Kells
Ceará, see Fortaleza
Celebes, see Sulawesi
Cerigo, see Kíthira
Cernauti, see Chernovtsy
České Budějovice: Budweis
Ceylon, see Sri Lanka
Chad: Tchad
Changan, see Hsian
Changchiak'ou: Kalgan
Charleville, see Rath Luirc
Chefoo, see Yent'ai
Cheju-do: Quelpart
Chemnitz, see Karl Marx Stadt
Chemulpho, see Inch'ŏn
Cheribon, see Cirebon
Chernovtsy: Cernauti, Czernowitz
Chernyakhovsk: Insterberg
Ch'ich'ihaerh: Lungkiang
Chihli: Po Hai
Chilin: Yungki
Chilumba: Deep Bay
Chilung: Keelung
Chios, see Khíos
Chipata: Fort Jameson
Chisinau, see Kishinev
Chistyakovo, see Thorez
Chitipa: Fort Hill
Chkalov, see Orenburg
Choybalsan: Bayan Tumen
Chongjin: Seishin
Chtimba: Florence Bay
Churchill, R.: Hamilton R.
Cieszyn: Teschen
Cirebon: Cheribon
Cluj: Klausenburg
Coatzacoalcos: Pto. Mexico
Cocanada, see Kakinada
Colomb-Béchar, see Béchar
Cologne: Köln
Congo (Kinshasa), see Zaïre
Conjeeveram, see Kanchipuram
Constance, see Konstanz
Constanţa: Küstenje
Constantinople, see İstanbul
Copenhagen, see København
Coquilhatville, see Mbandaka
Corfu, see Kérkira
Corunna, see La Coruña
Costermansville, see Bukavu

Courtrai, see Kortrijk
Craigavon: Lurgan and Portadown
Crete, see Kríti
Cuamba, see Novo Freixo
Cussabat, see Al Qasabat
Cyclades, see Kikládhes
Cyrene, see Shahhat
Czernowitz, see Chernovtsy

Dahomey, see Benin
Dairen, see Lüta
Damascus, see Dimashq
Damietta: Dumyât
Danzig, see Gdańsk
Daugavpils: Dvinsk
Deep Bay, see Chilumba
Deutsch Krone, see Wałcz
Dimashq: Damascus
Dimitrovgrad: Caribrod
Dimitrovo, see Pernik
Djerba: Houmt Souk
Djibouti: Fr. Terr. of the Afars & the Issas
Dnepropetrovsk: Yekaterinoslav
Dobrich, see Tolbukhin
Donetsk: Stalino
Dor: Tantura
Dorpat, see Tartu
Drissa, see Verchnedvinsk
Droichead Nua: Newbridge
Dublin, see Baile Átha Cliath
Dubrovnik: Ragusa
Dumyât: Damietta
Dunaújváros: Sztalinvaros
Dundo: Portugalia
Dunkerque: Dunquerque, Dunkirk
Durrësi: Durazzo
Dushanbe: Stalinbad
Dvinsk, see Daugavpils
Dzaudzhikau, see Ordzhonikidze

East Pakistan, see Bangladesh
Edirne: Adrianople
Edward, L., see Idi Amin Dada, L.
Eisenhüttenstadt: Stalinstadt, Furstenberg
El Asnam: Orléansville
El Bayadh: Géryville
El Eulma: St. Arnaud
El Harrach: Maison Carrée
El Iskandariya: Alexandria
El Jadida: Mazagan
El Kala: La Calle
El Qàhira: Cairo
El Suweis: Suez
Elblag: Elbing
Elizabethville, see Lubumbashi
Ellore: Eluru, Elluru
Escaut, see Schelde
Esfahān: Isfahan
Essaouira: Mogador
Evvoia: Euboea

Faizabad: Fyzabad
F'Dérik: Fort Gouraud
Fengtien, see Shenyang
Fernando Póo, see Macias Nguema Biyoga
Firenze: Florence
Fiume, see Rijeka
Flanders, see Vlaanderen
Florence Bay, see Chtimba
Florence, see Firenze
Flushing, see Vissingen
Formosa, see Taiwan
Fort de Polignac, see Illizi
Fort Flatters, see Zaouiet El-Kahla
Fort Gouraud, see F'Dérik
Fort Hall, see Muranga
Fort Jameson, see Chipata
Fort Lamy, see Ndjamena
Fort Rosebery, see Mansa
Fort Rousset, see Owando
Fort Rupert: Rupert House
Fort Hill, see Chitipa
Fort Manning, see Mchinji
Fort Trinquet, see Bir Mogreïn
Fortaleza: Ceará
Fredrikshald, see Halden
French Terr. of the Afars & the Issas:, see Djibouti
Fribourg: Freibourg
Frunze: Pishpek
Fuchou: Minhow
Fünfkirchen, see Pécs
Fyzabad, see Faizabad

Gagarin: Gzhatsk.
Gago Coutinho, see Lumbala
Gallipoli, see Gelibolu

Galt, see Cambridge
Gamlakarleby, see Kokkola
Gand, see Gent
Gävle: Gefle
Gdańsk: Danzig
Gelibolu: Gallipoli
Geneva (Lake), see Léman
Genève: Geneva (Town)
Genoa: Génova
Gent: Gand, Ghent
George River, see Port Nouveau-Québec
Géryville, see El Bayadh
Ghazaouet: Nemours
Ghent, see Gent
Girgenti, see Agrigento
Glatz, see Kłodzko
Gliwice: Gleiwitz
Glorenza: Glurns
Glubczyce: Leobschütz
Goleniów: Gollnow
Gorkiy: Nijni Novgorod
Gorodok, see Zakamensk
Göteborg: Gothenburg
Gottwaldov: Zlin
Great Whale River, see Poste de la Baleine
Grosswardein, see Oradea
Guardafui, C., see Ras Asir
Guinea-Bissau: Portuguese Guinea
Gunza: Porto Amboim
Guyana: British Guiana
Gzhatsk, see Gagarin

Haeju: Haiju
Haerhpin: Pinkiang
Hailaer: Hulun
Halab: Haleb, Aleppo
Halden: Fredrikshald
Haleb, see Halab
Halq el Qued: La Goulette
Hamadia: Victor Hugo
Hamilton R., see Churchill R.
Hämeenlinna: Tavastehus
Hannover: Hanover
Hebron, see Al Khalih
Heijo, see P'yŏngyang
Helsinki: Helsingfors
Hermannstadt, see Sibiu
Hirschberg, see Jelenia Góra
Hollandia, see Jayapura
Homs: Al Khums, Leptis Magna
Hot Springs, see Truth or Consequences
Hot'ien: Khotan
Houmt Souk, see Djerba
Hovd: Jargalant, Kobdo
Hsian: Changan
Hulun, see Hailaer

Iaşi: Jassy
Ibiza: Iviza
Idi Amin Dada, L.: Edward, L.
Ieper: Ypres
Ighil Izane: Relizane
Ilebo: Port Francqui
Illizi: Fort de Polignac
In Salah: Ain Salah
India: Bharat
Inoucdjouac: Port Harrison
Insterberg, see Chernyakhovsk
Iráklion: Candia
Iran: Persia
Isfahan, see Esfahān
İskenderun: Alexandretta
Isiro: Paulis
İstanbul: Constantinople
Ivano-Frankovsk: Stanislav
Iviza, see Ibiza
Izmir: Smyrna

Jabalpur: Jubbulpore
Jadotville, see Likasi
Jaffa, see Tel Aviv-Yafo
Jakarta: Batavia
Jambi: Telanaipura
Jamnagar: Navanagar
Jargalant, see Hovd
Jassy, see Iaşi
Javhlant, see Ulyasutay
Jayapura: Sukarnapura, Hollandia
Jelenia Góra: Hirschberg
Jelgava: Mitau
Jerusalem: Al Quds
Jesselton, see Kota Kinabalu
João Pessoa: Paraiba
Jubbulpore, see Jabalpur

Kabwe: Broken Hill
Kakinada: Cocanada
Kalamata: Kalámai
Kalemie: Albertville

Kalgan, see Changchiak'ou
Kalinin: Tver
Kaliningrad: Königsberg
Kananga: Luluabourg
Kanchipuram: Conjeeveram
Kanchow: Kanhsien
Kanpur: Cawnpore
Kaolan, see Lanchou
Karl Marx Stadt: Chemnitz
Karlovac: Karlstadt
Karlsburg, see Alba Iulia
Karlstadt, see Karlovac
Karlovy Vary: Carlsbad
Kaschau, see Košice
Kaskinen: Kaskö
Katowice: Stalinogrod
Kaunas: Kovno
Keelung, see Chilung
Keijo, see Sŏul
Kells, see Ceanannus Mór
Kendrapara: Kendlapara
Kenitra: Port Lyautey
Kérkira: Corfu
Khanh Hung: Soc Trang
Khemelnitski: Proskurov
Khemis Miliana: Affreville
Khíos: Chios
Khodzhent, see Leninabad
Khotan, see Hot'ien
Kikládhes: Cyclades
Kinshasa: Leopoldville
Kirov: Viatka, Vyatka
Kirovograd: Kirovo Yelisavetgrad, Zinovyevsk
Kisangani: Stanleyville
Kishinev: Chisinau
Kitakyūshū: Kokura, Moji, Tobata, Wakamatsu & Yawata
Kíthira: Cerigo
Klaipeda: Memel
Klausenburg, see Cluj
Kłodzko: Glatz
Kobarid: Caporetto
Kobdo, see Hovd
København: Copenhagen
Kokkola: Gamlakarleby
Kokura, see Kitakyūshū
Kolarovgrad, see Sumen
Kolchugino, see Leninsk Kuznetski
Köln, see Cologne
Kolobrzeg: Kolberg
Kommunarsk: Voroshilovsk, Stavropol
Königsberg, see Kaliningrad
Konstanz: Constance
Kortrijk: Courtrai
Košice: Kaschau
Koszalin: Köslin
Kota Kinabalu: Jesselton
Kotor: Cattaro
Kovna, see Kaunas
Kozhikode, see Calicut
Kraljevo: Rankovicevo
Krasnodar: Yekaterinodar
Kristiinankaupunki: Kristinestad
Kríti: Krete, Crete
Kropotkin: Romanovsk
Ksar Chellala: Reibell
Ksar el Kebir: Alcazarquivir
Kuangchou: Canton, Panyu
Kučově, see Qytet Stalin
Kuybyshev: Samara
Kuibyshevka Vostochnaya, see Belogorsk
K'unming: Yunnan
Küstenje, see Constanţa
Kutaraja, see Banda Aceh

La Calle, see El Kala
La Coruña: Corunna
La Goulette, see Halq el Qued
Laibach, see Ljubljana
Lanchou: Kaolan
Lappeenranta: Villmanstrand
Latakia, see Al Lādhiqiyah
Lauenburg, see Lebork
Lebork: Lauenburg
Leeu-Gamka: Fraserburg Road
Leghorn, see Livorno
Legnica: Liegnitz
Léman, Lake: Geneva, Lake
Lemberg, see Lvov
Leninabad: Khodzhent
Leninsk Kuznetski: Lenino, Kolchugino
Lensk: Mukhtuya
Leobschütz, see Glubczyce
Leopold II, L., see Mai-Ndombe, L.
Léopoldville, see Kinshasa
Leptis Magna, see Homs
Lesotho: Basutoland
Leuven: Louvain

# Geographical Terms

This is a list of some of the geographical words from foreign languages which are found in the place names on the maps and in the index. Each is followed by the language and the English meaning.

*Afr.* afrikaans
*Alb.* albanian
*Amh.* amharic
*Ar.* arabic
*Ber.* berber
*Bulg.* bulgarian
*Bur.* burmese

*Chin.* chinese
*Cz.* czechoslovakian
*Dan.* danish
*Dut.* dutch
*Fin.* finnish
*Flem.* flemish
*Fr.* french

*Gae.* gaelic
*Ger.* german
*Gr.* greek
*Heb.* hebrew
*Hin.* hindi
*I.-C.* indo-chinese
*Ice.* icelandic

*It.* italian
*Jap.* japanese
*Kor.* korean
*Lapp.* lappish
*Lith.* lithuanian
*Mal.* malay
*Mong.* mongolian

*Nor.* norwegian
*Pash.* pashto
*Pers.* persian
*Pol.* polish
*Port.* portuguese
*Rum.* rumanian
*Russ.* russian

*Ser.-Cr.* serbo-croat
*Siam.* siamese
*Sin.* sinhalese
*Som.* somali
*Span.* spanish
*Swed.* swedish
*Tib.* tibetan
*Turk.* turkish

**A.** (Ain) *Ar.* spring
–á *Ice.* river
a *Dan., Nor., Swed.* stream
–abad *Pers., Russ.* town
Abyad *Ar.* white
Ad. (Adrar) *Ar., Ber.* mountain
Ada, Adasi *Tur.* island
Addis *Amh.* new
Adrar *Ar., Ber.* mountain
Aïn *Ar.* spring
Äkra *Gr.* cape
Akrotíri *Gr.* cape
Alb *Ger.* mountains
Albufera *Span.* lagoon
–ålen *Nor.* islands
Alpen *Ger.* mountain pastures
Alpes *Fr.* mountains
Alpi *It.* mountains
Alto *Port.* high
–älv, –älven *Swed.* stream, river
Amt *Dan.* first-order administrative division
Appennino *It.* mountain range
Arch. (Archipiélago) *Span.* archipelago
Arcipélago *It.* archipelago
Arq. (Arquipélago) *Port.* archipelago
Arr. (Arroyo) *Span.* stream
–Ås, –åsen *Nor., Swed.* hill
Autonomna Oblast *Ser.-Cr.* autonomous region
Ayios *Gr.* island
Ayn *Ar.* well, waterhole

**B**(a). (Baía) *Port.* bay
B. (Baie) *Fr.* bay
B. (Bahía) *Span.* bay
B. (Ben) *Gae.* mountain
B. (Bir) *Ar.* well
B. (Bucht) *Ger.* bay
B. (Bugt.) *Dan.* bay
Baai, –baai *Afr.* bay
Bāb *Ar.* gate
Bäck, –bäcken *Swed.* stream
Back, backen, *Swed.* hill
Bad, –baden *Ger.* spa
Bādiya,–t *Ar.* desert
Baek *Dan.* stream
Baelt *Dan.* strait
Bahía *Span.* bay
Bahr *Ar.* sea, river
Bahra *Ar.* lake
Baía *Port.* bay
Baie *Fr.* bay
Bajo, –a, *Span.* lower
Bakke *Nor.* hill
Bala *Pers.* upper
Baltǎ *Rum.* marsh, lake
Banc *Fr.* bank
Bander *Ar., Mal.* port
Bandar *Pers.* bay
Banja *Ser.-Cr.* spa resort
Barat *Mal.* western
Barr. (Barrage) *Fr.* dam
Barracão *Port.* dam, waterfall
Bassin *Fr.* bay
Bayt *Heb.* house, village
Bazar *Hin.* market, bazaar
Be'er *Heb.* well
Beit *Heb.* village
Belo-, Belyy, Belaya,

Beloye, *Russ.* white
Ben *Gae.* mountain
Bender *Somal.* harbour
Berg,(e) –berg(e) *Afr.* mountain(s)
Berg, –berg *Ger.* mountain
–berg, –et *Nor., Swed.* hill, mountain, rock
Bet *Heb.* house, village
Bir, Bîr *Ar.* well
Birket *Ar.* lake, bay, marsh
Bj. (Bordj) *Ar.* port
–bjerg *Dan.* hill, point
Boca *Span.* river mouth
Bodden *Ger.* bay, inlet
Bogaz, Boğaz, –ı *Tur.* strait
Boka *Ser.-Cr.* gulf, inlet
Bol. (Bolshoi) *Russ.* great, large
Bordj *Ar.* fort
–borg *Dan., Nor., Swed.* castle, fort
–botn *Nor.* valley floor
bouche(s) *Fr.* mouth
Br. (Burnu) *Tur.* cape
Braţul *Rum.* distributary stream
–breen *Nor.* glacier
–bruck *Ger.* bridge
–brunn *Swed.* well, spring
Bucht *Ger.* bay
Bugt, –bugt *Dan.* bay
Buheirat *Ar.* lake
Bukit *Mal.* hill
Bukten *Swed.* bay
–bulag *Mong.* spring
Bûr *Ar.* port
Burg. *Ar.* fort
Burg, –burg *Ger.* castle
Burnu *Tur.* cape
Burun *Tur.* cape
Butt *Gae.* promontory
–by *Dan., Nor., Swed.* town
–byen *Nor., Swed.* town

**C.** (Cabo) *Port., Span.* headland, cape
C. (Cap) *Fr.* cape
C. (Capo) *It.* cape
Cabeza *Span.* peak, hill
Camp *Port., Span.* land, field
Campo *Span.* plain
Campos *Span.* upland
Can. (Canal) *Fr., Span.* canal
Canale *It.* canal
Canalul *Ser.-Cr.* canal
Cao Nguyên *Thai.* plateau, tableland
Cap *Fr.* cape
Capo *It.* cape
Cataracta *Sp.* cataract
Cauce *Span.* intermittent stream
Causse *Fr.* upland (limestone)
Cayi *Tur.* river
Cayo(s) *Span.* rock(s), islet(s)
Cerro *Span.* hill, peak
Ch. (Chaîne(s) ) *Fr.* mountain range(s)
Ch. (Chott) *Ar.* salt lake
Chaco *Span.* jungle
Chaîne(s) *Fr.* mountain range(s)
Chap. (Chapada) *Port.* hills, upland

Chapa *Span.* hills, upland
Chapada *Port.* hills, upland
Chaung *Bur.* stream, river
Chen *Chin.* market town
Ch'eng *Chin.* town
Chiang *Chin.* river
Ch'ih *Chin.* pool
Ch'ŏn *Kor.* river
–chŏsuji *Kor.* reservoir
Chott *Ar.* salt lake, swamp
Chou *Chin.* district
Chu *Tib.* river
Chung *Chin.* middle
Chute *Fr.* waterfall
Co. (Cerro) *Span.* hill, peak
Coch. (Cochilla) *Port.* hills
Col *Fr., It.* Pass
Colline(s) *Fr.* hill(s)
Conca *It.* plain, basin
Cord. (Cordillera) *Span.* mountain chain
Costa *It., Span.* coast
Côte *Fr.* coast, slope, hill
Cuchillas *Spain* hills
Cu-Lao *I.-C.* island

**D.** (Dolok) *Mal.* mountain
Dágh *Pers.* mountain
Dağ(ı) *Tur.* mountain(s)
Dağları *Tur.* mountain range
Dake *Jap.* mountain
–dal *Nor.* valley
–dal, –e *Dan., Nor.* valley
–dal, –en *Swed.* valley, stream
Dalay *Mong.* sea, large lake
–dalir *Ice.* valley
–dalur *Ice.* valley
–damm, –en *Swed.* lake
Danau *Mal.* lake
Dao *I.-O.* island
Dar *Ar.* region
Darya *Russ.* river
Daryācheh *Pers.* marshy lake, lake
Dasht *Pers.* desert, steppe
Daung *Bur.* mountain, hill
Dayr *Ar.* depression, hill
Debre *Amh.* hill
Deli *Ser.-Cr.* mountain(s)
Denizi *Tur.* sea
Dépt. (Département) *Fr.* first-order administrative division
Desierto *Span.* desert
Dhar *Ar.* region, mountain chain
Dj. (Djebel) *Ar.* mountain
Dō *Jap., Kor.* island
Dong *Kor.* village, town
Dong *Thai.* jungle region
–dorf *Ger.* village
–dorp *Afr.* village
–drif *Afr.* ford
–dybet *Dan.* marine channel
Dzong *Tib.* town, settlement

**E**il.-eiland(en) *Afr., Dut.* island(s)
–elv *Nor.* river
–'emeq *Heb.* plain, valley
'erg *Ar.* desert with dunes
Estrecho *Span.* strait
Estuario *Span.* estuary

Étang *Fr.* lagoon
–ey(jar) *Ice.* island(s)

**F.** (Fiume) *It.* river
F. Folyó *Hung.* river
Fd. (Fjord) *Nor.* Inlet of sea
–feld *Ger.* field
–fell *Ice.* mountain, hill
–feng *Chin.* mountain
Fiume *It.* river
Fj. (–fjell) *Nor.* mountain
–fjall *Ice.* mountain(s), hill(s)
–fjäll(et) *Swed.* hill(s), mountain(s), ridge
–fjällen *Swed.* mountains
–fjard(en) *Swed.* fjord, bay, lake
Fjeld *Dan.* mountain
–fjell *Nor.* mountain, rock
–fjord(en) *Nor.* inlet of sea
–fjorden *Dan.* bay, marine channel
–fjörður *Ice.* fjord
Fl. (Fleuve) *Fr.* river
Fl. (Fluss) *Ger.* river
–flói *Ice.* bay, marshy country
Fluss *Ger.* river
foce,–i *It.* mouth(s)
Folyó *Hung.* river
–fontein *Afr.* fountain, spring
–fors, –en, *Swed.* rapids, waterfall
Foss *Ice.*, *Nor.* waterfall
–furt *Ger.* ford
Fylke *Nor.* first-order administrative division

**G.** (Gebel) *Ar.* mountain
G. (Gebirge) *Ger.* hills, mountains
G. (Golfe) *Fr.* gulf
G. (Golfo) *It.* gulf
G. (Gora) *Bulg., Russ., Ser.-Cr.* mountain(s)
G. (Gunong) *Mal.* mountain
–gang *Kor.* river
Ganga *Hin., Sin.* river
–gat *Dan.* channel
–gau *Ger.* district
Gave *Fr.* stream
–gawa *Jap.* river
Geb. (Gebirge) *Ger.* hills, mountains
Gebel *Ar.* mountain
Geziret *Ar.* island
Ghat *Hin.* range of hills
Ghiol *Rum.* lake
Ghubbat *Ar.* bay, inlet
Gji *Alb.* bay
Gjol *Alb.* lagoon, lake
Gl. (Glava) *Ser.-Cr.* mountain, peak
Glen. *Gae.* valley
Gletscher *Ger.* glacier
Gobi *Mong.* desert
Gol *Mong.* river
Golfe *Fr.* gulf
Golfo *It., Span.* gulf
Gomba *Tib.* settlement
Gora *Bulg., Russ.*, *Ser.-Cr.* mountain(s)
Góry *Pol., Russ.* mountain
Gölü *Tur.* lake
–gorod *Russ.* small town
Grad *Bulg., Russ., Ser.-Cr.* town, city

Grada *Russ.* mountain range
Guba *Russ.* bay
–Guntō *Jap.* island group
Gunong *Mal.* mountain
Gurǎ *Rum.* passage

**H.** Hadabat *Ar.* plateau
–hafen *Ger.* harbour, port
Haff *Ger.* bay
Hai *Chin.* sea
Haihsia *Chin.* strait
–hale *Dan.* spit, peninsula
Hals *Dan., Nor.* peninsula, isthmus
Halvø *Dan.* peninsula
Halvøya *Nor.* peninsula
Hāmad, Hamada, Hammādah *Ar.* stony desert, plain
–hamn *Swed., Nor.* harbour, anchorage
Hāmūn *Ar.* plain
Hāmūn *Pers.* low-lying marshy area
–Hantō *Jap.* peninsula
Harju *Fin.* hill
Hassi *Ar.* well
–haug *Nor.* hill
Hav *Swed.* gulf
Havet *Nor.* sea
–havn *Dan., Nor.* harbour
Hegyseg *Hung.* forest
Heide *Ger.* heath
Hi. (hassi) *Ar.* well
Ho *Chin.* river
–hø *Nor.* peak
Hochland *Afr.* highland
Hoek, –hoek *Afr., Dut.* cape
Höfn *Ice.* harbour, port
–hög, –en, –högar, –högarna *Swed.* hill(s), peak, mountain
Höhe *Ger.* hills
Holm *Dan.* island
–holm, –holme, –holzen, *Swed.* island
Hon *I.-C.* island
Hora *Cz.* mountain
–horn *Nor.* peak
Hory *Cz.* mountain range, forest
–hoved *Dan.* point, headland, peninsula
Hráun *Ice.* lava
–hsi *Chin.* mountain, stream
–hsiang *Chin.* village
–hsien *Chin.* district
Hu *Chin.* lake
Huk *Dan., Ger.* point
Huken *Nor.* head

**I.** (Île) *Fr.* island
I. (Ilha) *Port.* island
I. (Insel) *Ger.* island
I. (Isla) *Span.* island
I. (Isola) *It.* island
Idehan *Ar., Ber.* sandy plain
Île(s) *Fr.* island(s)
Ilha *Port.* island
Insel(n) *Ger.* island(s)
Irmak *Tur.* river
Is. (Inseln) *Ger.* islands
Is. (Islas) *Span.* islands
Is. (Isola) *It.* island
Isola, –e *It.* island(s)
Istmo *Span.* isthmus

**J.** (Jabal) *Ar.* mountain
J. (Jazira) *Ar.* island
J. (Jebel) *Ar.* mountain
J. (Jezioro) *Pol.* lake
Jabal *Ar.* mountain, range
–jaur *Swed.* lake
–järvi *Fin.* lake, bay, pond
Jasovir *Bulg.* reservoir
Jazā'ir *Ar.* islands
Jazira *Ar.* island
Jazireh *Pers.* island
Jebel *Ar.* mountain
Jezero *Ser.-Cr.* lake
Jezioro *Pol.* lake
–Jima *Jap.* island
Jøkelen *Nor.* glacier
–joki *Fin.* stream
–jökull *Ice.* glacier
Jūras Līcis *Lat.* bay, gulf

**K.** (Kap) *Dan.* cape
K (Khalïg) *Ar.* gulf
K. (Kiang) *Chin.* river
K. (Kuala) *Mal.* confluence, estuary
Kaap *Afr.* cape
Kai *Jap.* sea
Kaikyō *Jap.* strait
Kamennyy *Russ.* stony
Kampong *Mal.* village
Kan. (Kanal) *Ser.-Cr.* channel, canal
Kanaal *Dut., Flem.* canal
Kanal *Dan.* channel, gulf
Kanal *Ger., Swed.* canal, stream
kanal *Ser.-Cr.* channel, canal
Kang *Kor.* river, bay
Kangri *Tib.* mountain glacier
Kap *Dan., Ger.* cape
Kapp *Nor.* cape
Kas *I.-C.* island
–kaupstaður *Ice.* market town
–kaupunki *Fin.* town
Kavïr *Pers.* salt desert
Kébir *Ar.* great
Kéfar *Heb.* village, hamlet
–ken *Jap.* first-order administrative division
Kep *Alb.* cape
Kepulauan *Mal.* archipelago
Ketjil *Mal.* lesser, little
Khalïg, Khalïj *Ar.* gulf
khamba, –ïdg *Tib.* source, spring
Khawr *Ar.* wadi
Khirbat *Ar.* ruins
Kho Khot *Thai.* isthmus
Khōr *Pers.* creek, estuary
Khrebet *Russ.* mountain range
Kiang *Chin.* river
–klint *Dan.* cliff
–Klintar *Swed.* hills
Kloof *Afr.* gorge
Knude *Dan.* point
Ko *Jap.* lake
Ko *Thai.* island
Kohi *Pash.* mountains
Kol *Russ.* lake
Kolymskoye *Russ.* mountain range
Kólpos *Gr., Tur.* gulf, bay
Kompong *Mal.* landing place
–kop *Afr.* hill

–köping *Swed.* market town
Körfezi *Tur.* gulf
Kosa *Russ.* spit
–koski *Fin.* cataract, rapids
–kraal *Afr.* native village
Krasnyy *Russ.* red
Kryash *Russ.* ridge, hills
Kuala *Mal.* confluence, estuary
kuan *Chin.* pass
Kuh –hha *Pers.* mountains
Kul *Russ.* lake
Kulle *Swed.* hill, shoal
Kum *Russ.* sandy desert
Kumpu *Fin.* hill
Kurgan *Russ.* mound
Kwe *Bur.* bay, gulf
Kyst *Dan.* coast
Kyun, –zu, –umya *Bur.* island(s)

**L.** (Lac) *Fr.* lake
L. (Lacul) *Rum.* lake
L. (Lago) *It., Span.* lake, lagoon
L. (Lagoa) *Port.* lagoon
L. (Límni) *Gr.* lake
L. (Loch) *Gae.* (lake, inlet)
L. (Lough) *Gae.* (lake, inlet)
La *Tib.* pass
La (Lagoa) *Port.* lagoon
–laagte *Afr.* watercourse
Läani *Fin.* first-order administrative division
Län *Swed.* first-order administrative division
Lac *Fr.* lake
Lacul *Rum.* lake, lagoon
Lago *It., Span.* lake, lagoon
Lagoa *Port.* lagoon
Laguna *It., Span.* lagoon, intermittent lake
Lagune *Fr.* lake
Lahti *Fin.* bay, gulf, cove
Lakhti *Russ.* bay, gulf
Lampi *Fin.* lake
Land *Ger.* first-order administrative division
–land *Dan.* region
–land *Afr., Nor.* land, province
Lido *It.* beach, shore
Liehtao *Chin.* islands
Lilla *Swed.* small
Límni *Gr.* lake
Ling *Chin.* mountain range, ice
Linna *Fin.* historical fort
Llano *Span.* prairie, plain
Loch *Gae.* (lake)
Lough *Gae.* (lake)
Lum *Alb.* river
Lund *Dan.* forest
–lund, –en *Swed.* wood(s)

**M.** (Maj, Mai) *Alb.* mountain, peak
M. (Mont) *Fr.* mountain peak
M. (Mys) *Russ.* cape
Madína(h) *Ar.* town, city
Madiq *Ar.* strait
Maj *Alb.* peak
Mäki *Fin.* hill, hillside
Mal *Alb.* mountain
Mal *Russ.* little, small
Mal/a, –i, –o *Ser.-Cr.* small, little
Man *Kor.* bay
Mar *Span.* lagoon, sea
Mare *Rum.* great
Marisma *Span.* marsh
–mark *Dan., Nor.* land
Marsá *Ar.* anchorage, bay, inlet
Masabb *Ar.* river mouth
Massif *Fr.* upland, plateau
Mato *Port.* forest
Mazar *Pers.* shrine, tomb
Meer *Afr., Dut., Ger.* lake sea

Mi., Mti. (Monti) *It.* mountains
Miao *Chin.* temple, shrine
Midbar *Heb.* wilderness
Mif. (Massif) *Fr.* upland, plateau
Misaki *Jap.* cape, point
–mo *Nor., Swed.* heath, island
–mon *Swed.* heath
Mong *Bur.* town
Mont *Fr.* hill, mountain
Montagna *It.* mountain
Montagne *Fr.* hill, mountain
Montaña *Span.* mountain
Monte *It., Port., Span.* mountain
Monti *It.* mountains
More *Russ.* sea
Mörön *Hung.* river
Mt. (Mont) *Fr.* mountain
Mt. (Monti) *It.* mountain
Mt. (Montaña) *Span.* mountain range
Mte. (Monte) *It., Port., Span.* mountain
Mţi. (Munţi) *Rum.* mountain
Mts. (Monts) *Fr.* mountains
Muang *Mal.* town
Mui *Ar., I.-C.* cape
Mull *Gae.* (promontory)
Mund, –mund *Afr.* mouth
Munkhafed *Ar.* depression
Munte *Rum.* mount
Munţi(i) *Rum.* mountain(s)
Muong *Mal.* village
Myit *Bur.* river
Myitwanya *Bur.* mouths of river
–mýri *Ice.* bog
Mys *Russ.* cape

**N.** (Nahal) *Heb.* river
Naes *Dan.* point, cape
Nafúd *Ar.* sandy desert
Nahal *Heb.* river
Nahr *Ar.* river, stream
Najd *Ar.* plateau, pass
Nakhon *Thai.* town
Nam *I.-C.* river
–nam *Kor.* south
–näs *Swed.* cape
–nes *Ice., Nor.* cape
Ness, –ness *Gae.* promontory, cape
Nez *Fr.* cape
–niemi *Fin.* cape, point, peninsula, island
Nizhne, –iy *Russ.* lower
Nizmennost *Russ.* plain, lowland
Nísos, Nísoi *Gr.* island(s)
Nor *Chin.* lake
Nor *Tib.* peak
Nos *Bulg., Russ.* cape, point
Nudo *Span.* mountain
Nuruu *Mong.* mountain range
Nuur *Mong.* lake

**O.** (Ostrov) *Russ.* island
O (Ouâdi, Oued) *Ar.* wadi
–ö *Swed.* island, peninsula, point
–öar, (–na) *Swed.* islands
Oblast *Russ.* administrative division
Öbor *Mong.* inner
Occidental *Fr., Span.* western
Odde *Dan., Nor.* point, peninsula, cape
Oji *Alb.* bay
Ojo *Span.* spring
Oki *Jap.* bay
–ön *Swed.* island peninsula
Ondör *Mong.* high, tall

–ör *Swed.* island, peninsula, point
Oraşul *Rum.* city
Ord *Gae.* point
Óri *Gr.* mountains
Oriental *Span.* eastern
Órmos *Gr.* bay
Óros *Gr.* mountain
Ort *Ger.* point, cape
Ostrov(a) *Russ.* island(s)
Otok(–i) *Ser.-Cr.* island(s)
Ouadi, –edi *Ar.* dry watercourse, wadi
Ouzan *Pers.* river
Ova (–si) *Tur.* plains, lowlands
–øy, (–a) *Nor.* island(s)
Oya *Hin.* point
Oya *Sin.* river
Oz. (Ozero, a) *Russ.* lake(s)

**P.** (Passo) *It.* pass
P. (Pasul) *Rum.* pass
P. (Pico) *Span.* peak
P. (Prokhod) *Bulg.* pass
–pää *Fin.* hill(s), mountain
Pahta *Lapp.* hill
Pampa, –s *Span.* plain(s) salt flat(s)
Pan. (Pantano) *Span.* Reservoir
Pantao *Chin.* peninsula
Parbat *Urdu* mountain
Pas *Fr.* gap
Paso *Span.* pass, marine channel
Pass *Ger.* pass
Passo *It.* pass
Pasul *Rum.* pass
Patam *Hin.* small village
Patna, –patnam *Hin.* small village
Pegunungan *Mal.* mountain, range
Pei, –pei *Chin.* north
Pélagos *Gr.* sea
Pen. (Península) *Span.* peninsula
Peña *Span.* rock, peak
Península *Span.* peninsula
Per. (Pereval) *Russ.* pass
Pertuis *Fr.* channel
Peski *Russ.* desert, sands
Phanom *I.-C., Thai.* mountain
Phnom *I.-C.* mountain
Phu *I.-C.* mountain
Pic *Fr.* peak
Pico(s) *Span.* peak(s)
Pik *Russ.* peak
Piz., pizzo *It.* peak
Pl. (Planina) *Ser.-Cr.* mountain, range
Plage *Fr.* beach
Plaine *Fr.* plain
Planalto *Span.* plateau
Planina *Bulg., Ser.-Cr.* mountain, range
Plat. (Plateau) *Fr.* level upland
Plato *Russ.* plateau
Playa *Span.* beach
P-ov. (Poluostrov) *Russ.* peninsula
Pointe *Fr.* point, cape
Pojezierze *Pol.* lakes plateau
Polder *Dut.* reclaimed farmland
–pólis *Gr.* city, town
Poluostrov *Russ.* peninsula
Połwysep *Pol.* peninsula
Pont *Fr.* bridge
Ponta *Port.* point, cape
Ponte *It.* bridge
Poort *Afr.* passage, gate
–poort *Dut.* port
Porta *Port.* pass
Porţil, –e *Rum.* gate
Portillo *Span.* pass
Porto *It.* port
Porto *Port., Span.* port

Pot. (Potámi, Potamós) *Gr.* river
Poulo *I.-C.* island
Pr. (Průsmyk) *Cz.* pass
Pradesh *Hin.* state
Presa *Span.* reservoir
Presqu'île *Fr.* peninsula
Prokhod *Bulg.* pass
Proliv *Russ.* strait
Prusmyk *Cz.* pass
Pso. (Passo) *It.* pass
Pta. (Ponta) *Port.* point, cape
Pta. (Punta) *It., Span.* point, cape, peak
Pte. (Pointe) *Fr.* point cape
Puerto *Span.* port, pass
Puig *Cat.* peak
Pulau *Mal.* island
Puna *Span.* desert plateau
Punta *It., Span.* point, peak
Puy *Fr.* hill

**Q**al'at *Ar.* fort
Qanal *Ar.* canal
Qasr *Ar.* fort
Qiryat *Heb.* town
Qolleh *Pers.* mountain

**R**amla *Ar.* sand
Rann *Hin.* swampy region
Rao *I.-C.* river
Ras *Amh.* cape, headland
Rãs *Ar.* cape, headland
Recife(s) *Port.* reef(s)
Reka *Bulg., Cz., Russ.* river
Repede *Rum.* rapids
Represa *Port.* dam
Reshteh *Pers.* mountain range
–Rettō *Jap.* group of islands
Ría *Span.* estuary, bay
Ribeirão *Port.* river
Rijeka *Ser.-Cr.* river
Rio *Port.* river
Río *Span.* river
Riv. (Riviera) *It.* coastal plain, coast, river
Rivier *Afr.* river
Riviera *It.* coast
Rivière *Fr.* river
Roche *Fr.* rock
Rog *Russ.* horn
–rück *Ger.* ridge
Rūd *Pers.* stream, river
Rudohorie *Cz.* ore mountains
Rzeka *Pol.* river

**S.** (Sungei) *Mal.* river
Sa. (Serra) *It., Port.* range of hills
Sa. (Sierra) *Span.* range of hills
–saari *Fin.* island
Sadd *Ar.* dam
Sagar, –ara *Hin., Urdu* lake
Saharã *Ar.* desert
Sahrâ *Ar.* desert
Sa'id *Ar.* highland
Sakar *Fin.* mountain
–Saki *Jap.* point
Sal. (Salar) *Span.* salt pan
Salina(s) *Span.* salt flat(s)
–salmi *Fin.* strait, sound, lake, channel
Saltsjöbad *Swed.* resort
Sammyaku *Jap.* mountain, range
Samut *Thai.* gulf
–San *Jap.* hill, mountain
Sap. (Sapadno) *Russ.* west
Sasso *It.* mountain
Se, Sé *I.-C.* river
Sebkha, –kra *Ar.* salt flats
See *Ger.* lake
–see *Ger.* sea
–şehir *Turk.* town
Selat *Mal.* strait
–selkä *Fin.* bay, lake, sound, ridge, hills

Selva *Span.* forest, wood
Seno *Span.* bay, sound
Serír *Ar.* desert of small stones
Serra *It., Port.* range of hills
Serranía *Span.* mountains
Sev. (Severo) *Russ.* north
–shahr *Pers.* city, town
Shan *Chin.* hills, mountains, pass
Shan-mo *Chin.* mountain range
Shatt *Ar.* river
–Shima *Jap.* island
Shimāli *Ar.* northern
–Shotō *Jap.* group of islands
Shuik'u *Chin.* reservoir
Sierra *Span.* hill, range
Sjö, sjön *Swed.* lake, bay, sea
Sjøen *Dan.* sea
Skär *Swed.* island, rock, cape
Skog *Nor.* forest
–skog, –skogen *Swed.* wood(s)
–skov *Dan.* forest
Slieve *Gae.* range of hills
–sø *Dan., Nor.* lake
Sør *Nor.* south, southern
Solonchak *Russ.* salt lake, marsh
Souk *Ar.* market
Spitze *Ger.* peak, mountain
–spruit *Afr.* stream
–stad *Afr., Nor., Swed.* town
–stadt *Ger.* town
Staður *Ice.* town
Stausee *Ger.* reservoir
Stenón *Gr.* strait, pass
Step *Russ.* plain
Str. (Stretto) *It.* strait
–strand *Dan., Nor.* beach
–strede *Nor.* straits
Strelka *Russ.* spit
–strete *Russ.* straits
Stretto *It.* strait
Stroedet *Dan.* strait
–ström, –strömmen *Swed.* stream(s)
–stroom *Afr.* large river
Suidō *Jap.* strait, channel
Sûn *Bur.* cape
Sund *Dan.* sound
–sund, –sundet *Swed.* sound, estuary, inlet
–sund(et) *Nor.* sound
Sungai, –ei *Mal.* river
Sungei *Mal.* river
Sur *Span.* south, southern
Sveti *Bulg.* pass
Syd *Dan., Swed.* south

**T**ai –tai *Chin.* tower
Tal *Mong.* plain, steppe
–tal *Ger.* valley
Tall *Ar.* hills, hummocks
Tandjung *Mal.* cape, headland
Tao *Chin.* island
Tassili *Ar.* rocky plateau
Tau *Russ.* mountain, range
Taung *Bur.* mountain, south
Taunggya *Bur.* pass
Télok *I.-C., Mal.* bay bight
Teluk *Mal.* bay, gulf
Tg. (Tandjung) *Mal.* cape, headland
–thal *Ger.* valley
Thok *Tib.* town
Tierra *Span.* land, country
–tind *Nor.* peak
Tjärn, –en, –et *Swed.* lake
Tong *Nor.* village, town
Tong *Bur., Thai.* mountain range
Tonle *I.-C.* large river, lake
–träsk *Swed.* bog, swamp
Tsangpo *Tib.* large river
Tso *Tib.* lake

Tsu *Jap.* entrance, bay
Tulur *Ar.* hill
T'un *Chin.* village
Tung *Chin.* east
Tunnel *Fr.* tunnel
Tunturi *Fin.* hill(s), mountain(s), ridge

**U**ad *Ar.* dry watercourse, wadi
Udjung *Mal.* cape
Udd, udde, udden *Swed.* point, peninsula
Uebi *Somal.* river
Us *Mong.* water
Ust *Russ.* river mouth
Uul *Mong., Russ.* mountain, range

**V.** (Volcán) *Span.* volcano
–vaara *Fin.* hill, mountain, ridge, peak
–våg *Nor.* bay
Val *Fr.,* it. valley
Valea *Rum.* valley
–vall, –vallen *Swed.* mountain
Valle *Span.* valley
Vallée *Fr.* valley
Valli *It.* lake, lagoon
Väst *Swed.* west
–vatn *Ice., Nor.* lake
Vatten *Swed.* lake
Vdkhr. (Vodokhranilishche) *Russ.* reservoir
–ved, –veden *Swed.* range, hills
Veld, –veld *Afr.* field
Velik/a, –e, –i, –o *Ser.Cr.* large
–vesi *Fin.* water, lake, bay sound, strait
Vest *Dan., Nor.* west
Vf. (vîrful) *Rum.* peak, mountain
–vidda *Nor.* plateau
Vig *Dan.* bay, inlet, cove, lagoon, lake, bight
–vik, –vika, –viken *Nor., Swed.* bay, cove, gulf, inlet, lake
Vila *Port.* small town
Villa *Span.* town
Ville *Fr.* town
Vinh *I.-C.* bay
Vîrful *Rum.* peak, mountain
–vlei *Afr.* pond, pool
Vodokhranilishche *Russ.* reservoir
Vol. (Volcán) *Span.* volcano, mountain
Vorota *Russ.* gate
Vostochnyy *Russ.* eastern
Vozyshennost *Russ.* heights, uplands
Vrata *Bulg.* gate, pass
Vrchovina *Cz.* mountainous country
Vrchy *Cz.* mountain range
Vung *I.-C.* gulf
–vuori *Fin.* mountain, hill

**W.** (Wâdi) *Ar.* dry watercourse
Wâhât *Ar.* oasis
Wald *Ger.* wood, forest
Wan *Chin., Jap.* bay
Webi *Amh.* river
Woestyn *Afr.* desert

**Y**am *Heb.* sea
Yang *Chin.* ocean
Yazovir *Bulg.* reservoir
Yoma *Bur.* mountain range
–yüan *Chin.* spring

–**Z**aki *Jap.* peninsula
Zalew *Pol.* lagoon, swamp
Zaliv *Russ.* bay
Zan *Jap.* mountain
Zatoka *Pol.* bay
Zee *Dut.* sea
Zemlya *Russ.* land, island(s)